# Contemporary Literary Criticism

# Contemporary Literary Criticism

Excerpts from Criticism of
the Works of Today's Novelists,
Poets, Playwrights, Short Story
Writers, Filmmakers, Screenwriters,
and Other Creative Writers

**Sharon R. Gunton**
**Editor**

Gale Research Company
Book Tower
Detroit, Michigan 48226

## STAFF

Sharon R. Gunton, *Editor*

Daniel G. Marowski, *Senior Assistant Editor*

Emily W. Barrett, Thomas Ligotti, Robyn V. Young, *Assistant Editors*

Phyllis Carmel Mendelson, *Contributing Editor*

Carolyn Bancroft, *Production Supervisor*
Lizbeth A. Purdy, *Production Coordinator*

Linda M. Pugliese, *Manuscript Coordinator*
Marie Lazzari, *Manuscript Assistant*

Robert J. Elster, *Research Coordinator*
Carol Angela Thomas, *Research Assistant*

Earlene Alber, Frank James Borovsky, Robert L. Brubaker, Ann K. Crowley,
Catherine E. Daligga, Lee Ferency, Kathleen Gensley, Denise Gottis, Jeanne A. Gough,
Serita Lanette Lockard, Brenda Marshall, Marie M. Mazur, Francine Melotti-Bacon,
Denise Michlewicz, Anna C. Wallbillich, Gloria A. Williams, *Editorial Assistants*

L. Elizabeth Hardin, *Permissions Supervisor*
Filomena Sgambati, *Assistant Permissions Coordinator*
Janice M. Mach, Mary P. McGrane, Patricia A. Seefelt, *Permissions Assistants*

Copyright © 1982 by Gale Research Company
Library of Congress Catalog Card Number 76-38938
ISBN 0-8103-0119-9
ISSN 0091-3421

# Contents

Preface  7            Appendix  479

Authors Forthcoming in *CLC*  9            Cumulative Index to Authors  489

Cumulative Index to Critics  497

*Filmmakers in this volume:*

Lindsay Anderson  1923-  ...............11

Michelangelo Antonioni  1912-  ...........19

John Cassavetes  1929-  ................44

René Chomette
   *see* René Clair

René Clair  1898-1981 .....................57

Brian De Palma  1940-  .................72

Vittorio De Sica  1902-1974 ..............84

Marguerite Duras  1914-  .................98

Rainer Werner Fassbinder  1946-  ........105

Bob Fosse  1925-  .....................121

Jean-Luc Godard  1930-  ...............128

John Huston  1906-  ...................157

Kon Ichikawa  1915-  ..................176

Buster Keaton  1895-1966................188

Joseph Francis Keaton
   *see* Buster Keaton

Fritz Lang  1890-1976 ....................200

Richard Lester  1932-  .................218

Laurence Olivier  1907-  ................234

Nagisa Oshima  1932-  .................245

Pier Paolo Pasolini  1922-1975 .............258

Sam Peckinpah  1925-  ..................272

Jean Renoir  1894-1979...................286

Carlos Saura  1932-  ....................313

Martin Scorsese  1942-  ................323

Joan Micklin Silver  1935-  .............341

Jerzy Skolimowski  1938-  ..............347

Yurek Skolimowski
   *see* Jerzy Skolimowski

Steven Spielberg  1947-  ................357

Jonas Sternberg
   *see* Josef von Sternberg

Josef von Sternberg  1894-1969 ............368

François Truffaut  1932-  ...............380

Melvin Van Peebles  1932-  .............409

Andy Warhol  1928-  ....................414

Peter Weir  1944-  .....................424

Orson Welles  1915-  ...................431

Billy Wilder  1906-  ....................455

Samuel Wilder
   *see* Billy Wilder

Frederick Wiseman  1930-  .............467

# Preface

As the film industry has grown, its influence has also expanded. Now considered a major art form, the film has become the subject of extensive scholarly criticism, much of it focused on the literary qualities of outstanding productions in the medium, rather than on technical or cinematographic aspects.

To make some of the most important comment more readily available, Volume 16 and Volume 20 of *Contemporary Literary Criticism* are devoted to evaluations of filmmakers whose works have already received much critical acclaim or seem destined to attain significance in the future. In keeping with the literary direction of the series, criticism has been selected which considers film in relation to its theme, formal style, characterization, and intent. Most of the filmmakers included have functioned as writers as well as directors; all of them are responsible for the distinctive styles of their productions.

For this volume, we have chosen criticism of artists such as Jean Renoir and Orson Welles because of the magnitude of their work and their influence on their successors. Others, like Bob Fosse and Steven Spielberg, have been chosen for coverage because of their limited, yet distinctive, contributions to the art.

This special volume of film criticism complements other volumes of *CLC* and follows the same format, with some slight variations. The list of filmmakers treated is international in scope and, as in the other *CLC* volumes, includes artists who are living now or have died after January 1, 1960. Since this volume of *CLC* is intended to provide a definitive overview of the careers of the filmmakers included, the editors have included approximately 40 filmmakers (compared to 150 authors in a standard *CLC*) in order to devote more attention to each filmmaker.

## New Features

In the publishing history of *CLC,* numerous changes have been made in the coverage and format of the series, often at the suggestion of users. The editors are always glad to consider further suggestions. The following are some recent changes.

Beginning with Volume 10, *CLC* contains an appendix which lists the sources from which material has been printed in that volume. It does not, however, list books or periodicals merely consulted during the preparation of the volume.

In the same volume, the critic's name is listed at the beginning of each selection. Beginning with Volume 19, unsigned criticism is preceded by the title of the journal or book in which it appeared.

Also beginning with Volume 19, in the text of each author entry, titles by that author are printed in boldface type. This allows the reader to ascertain without difficulty the works which are being discussed. In addition, the table of contents includes birth and, if applicable, death dates for each author.

## References and Notes

Page numbers appear after each fragment (unless the entire essay was contained on one page), and all credit lines include the complete essay title, volume, and issue number of all journal entries, inclusive pagination for all essays, and total pagination for all books. An asterisk following a credit line indicates that the essay or book contains information on more than one author.

Notes in many entries directing the user to consult *Contemporary Authors* for detailed biographical and bibliographical information refer to a series of biographical reference books published by the Gale Research Company since 1962, which now includes detailed biographical sketches of more than 65,000 authors who have lived since 1960, many of whose careers began during the post-World War II period, or earlier.

## Acknowledgments

The editors wish to thank the copyright holders of the excerpts included in this volume and the permission managers of many book and magazine publishing companies for assisting us in locating copyright holders. We extend our appreciation to the staffs of the Detroit Public Library, the libraries of the University of Michigan, and Wayne State University Library, especially Dr. Vern M. Pings, Director, Dr. Ruth J. Patrick, Assistant Director, Howard A. Sullivan, Assistant Director, and Hugh O'Connor, Interlibrary Loans of Wayne State University Library, for making their resources available to us. We are also grateful to Fred S. Stein for his assistance with copyright research and Louise Kertesz for her editorial assistance.

# Authors Forthcoming in *CLC*

With the publication of *Contemporary Literary Criticism,* Volume 12, the series expanded its scope to encompass songwriters, filmmakers, cartoonists, screenwriters, producers, and other creative writers whose work is often evaluated from a literary perspective. These writers take their place with the novelists, poets, dramatists, and short story writers who will continue to be the primary focus of *CLC.* Material in Volume 21 will be selected to be of special interest to young adult readers. Volume 22 will include criticism on a number of authors not previously listed, and will also feature criticism on newer works of authors included in earlier volumes.

## To Be Included in Volume 21

Lenny Bruce (American humorist)—Iconoclastic comedian who shocked and amused audiences of the 1950s and early 1960s with his irreverent social commentary

Jimmy Cliff (Jamaican songwriter)—First songwriter to popularize reggae music outside Jamaica, best known for his songs in the film *The Harder They Come*

Elvis Costello (British songwriter)—One of the most influential performers of the New Wave movement

Paula Danziger (American young adult novelist)—Author who bases such humorous novels as *The Cat Ate My Gymsuit* on her own experiences and those of her students

Roderick Haig-Brown (Canadian young adult and adult novelist, nonfiction writer, and poet)—Writer noted for his variety and sensitivity to Canadian nature, he has helped to define a Canadian literature for young people

Mollie Hunter (Scottish young adult novelist and playwright)—Award-winning author of fiction based on folklore and fantasy such as *The Kelpie's Pearls*

Janis Ian (American songwriter)—Writer of "Society's Child" at the age of sixteen, she has written consistently about the restrictions and problems imposed on young people by society

Albert Innaurato (American playwright and scriptwriter)—Author of the long-running Broadway hit *Gemini,* a play dealing with

an adolescent dilemma in a comic fashion

Waylon Jennings (American songwriter)—Songwriter whose pairing of traditional country themes with rock music has helped interest many young people in country music

Agnes Nixon (American television scriptwriter)—Creator of the ground-breaking series *All My Children;* she is often called "Queen of the Soaps"

Flannery O'Connor (American short story writer, novelist, and essayist)—One of the most important figures of the Southern Renascence whose works such as *Wise Blood* and *A Good Man Is Hard to Find* are characterized by acts of sudden, bizarre violence and peopled with grotesques

Philippa Pearce (British young adult novelist and short story writer)—Carnegie Medal winner and author of *Tom's Midnight Garden,* which is often called one of the most perfect books written for young people

Erich Maria Remarque (German novelist)—Author of *All Quiet on the Western Front,* an outstanding modern novel of war

Jerome Siegel and Joe Schuster (American cartoonists)—Creators of Superman, a comic book character who has influenced young adults for decades

Roger Zelazny (American novelist and short story writer)—Contemporary science fiction writer whose works emphasize disciplines such as psychology and linguistics rather than the hard sciences favored by earlier writers

## To Be Included in Volume 22

Sterling A. Brown (Black American poet)—Will feature criticism on *The Collected Poems*

Anthony Burgess (British novelist, translator,

and critic)—Will feature criticism on new novel, *Earthly Powers*

William S. Burroughs (American novelist)—Will

feature criticism on new novel, *Cities of the Red Night*

Günter Grass (German novelist)—Will feature criticism on new novel, *The Meeting at Telgte*

Eugène Ionesco (French playwright)

John Irving (American novelist)—Will feature criticism on new novel, *The Hotel New Hampshire*

Doris Lessing (British novelist and short story writer)—Will feature criticism on new novel, *The Syrian Experiments*

Dorothy Livesay (Canadian poet and critic)

Toni Morrison (Black American novelist and short story writer)—Will feature criticism on new novel, *Tar Baby*

Iris Murdoch (British novelist and playwright)—Will feature criticism on new novel, *Nuns and Soldiers*

Vladimir Nabokov (Russian-born American novelist)

Charles Simic (Yugoslavian-born poet)—Will feature criticism on new collection, *Classic Ballroom Dances*

D. M. Thomas (British novelist and poet)—will feature criticism on new novel, *The White Hotel*

Gore Vidal (American novelist and playwright)—Will feature criticism on new novel, *Creation*

P.G. Wodehouse (British short story writer and novelist)

# Lindsay Anderson

## 1923-

**Indian-born British director, film critic, and author.**

**Anderson is probably best known as a proponent of the British "Free Cinema" movement. Conceived at the National Film Theatre in 1956, this theory emphasized the artist's responsibility toward society and the individual. Anderson outlined the precepts of "Free Cinema" in his manifesto article, "Stand Up! Stand Up!" Britain's cinematic approach had formerly been literary; Anderson lashed out at critics and filmmakers and asked that they emphasize "the significance of the everyday" in their work. The tenets of "Free Cinema" are apparent in Anderson's documentary and feature work.**

**Anderson introduced subjectivity into contemporary British cinema with *This Sporting Life*. The film chronicles Frank Machin's fervent rebellion against a *nouveau riche* society. Like other Anderson characters, he attacks the petty standards that signify success.**

***If . . .* is Anderson's most controversial film. The film is a condemnation of the British public school system, but Anderson did not intend it to be a 1960s view of student unrest. *If . . .* studies the relationship between authority and the search for individualism and is viewed as his most successful juxtaposition of fantasy and reality.**

***O Lucky Man!* also fuses real and imaginary worlds, creating a dreamlike existence where disasters are reduced to media messages. This quality provides a less solid basis for his attack on the British public school system. Although the film is Anderson's broadest satire, it is considered to be his least successful.**

**Anderson's cinematic output is purposely limited due to his desire to portray his convictions through other art forms. Though the "Free Cinema" movement has faded, Anderson continues to create works for the theater which reflect the dreams of "everyman." According to Anderson, realism must be aesthetically pleasing as well as sociologically accurate. Anderson states that his aim is "not to interpret, nor to propagandize, but to create."**

### GAVIN LAMBERT

The first time [that one sees *O Dreamland*], it is like a blow in the face; the second, one approaches it with a kind of eager dread. For ten minutes it assaults eye and ear with a rough-edged but sharp-centred impression of this South Coast amusement park, in which the ugliness and degradation of most of the distractions offered are symbolised by the mocking mechanical laughter of a dummy sailor. There is a working model of the execution of the "atom spies", the Rosenbergs, which reconstructs the ritual for sixpence at the door. . . . [Whether] the rendezvous is with violent death or a smutty peepshow, with a fire-eater or a gambling machine, a listless caged animal or an old mug of tea, reactions appear the same. People stare. . . . Signs of real vitality are produced by greed. . . . (pp. 175-76)

Everything is ugly. A *papier-maché* facade with a swollen, grimacing gargoyle, an immense "artistic" statue representing a coyly nude pseudo-classical figure, a "Swiss beer garden" in which local music and yodelling emanate from twitching, squeaking puppets, the steaming, slippery, greasy trays of food labelled SAUSAGES and ONIONS in the Happy Family Restaurant; feet shuffle clumsily across ground fouled with all kinds of litter, buttocks encased in grey, shapeless material spread and crease over stools at counters; and all the time the sleek charabancs pour in. It is almost too much. The nightmare is redeemed by the point of view, which, for all the unsparing candid camerawork and the harsh, inelegant photography, is emphatically humane. Pity, sadness, even poetry is infused into this drearily tawdry, aimlessly hungry world. It is infused by imaginative comment . . . but even more by the director's absolute fidelity to his subject. . . .

All these people, one realises, are seeking something they will probably never find. The Rosenbergs die again and they bleakly, willingly stare—but there is nothing perverse about it, only a kind of uncertain passivity, an oppressive, sometimes intolerable sense of loss and deprivation. The pleasures are sad not because they are ugly but because there is nothing else. Where else should they go? At the end, the camera moves swiftly, vertiginously up to a panoramic view of Dreamland twinkling and blaring in the night—and it is like a plea for release. (p. 176)

*Gavin Lambert, "Free Cinema," in* Sight and Sound *(copyright © 1956 by The British Film Institute), Vol. 25, No. 4, Spring, 1956, pp. 173-77.\**

### JOHN BERGER

There is an indication of Anderson's attitude right at the beginning of *Every Day Except Christmas;* it is affectionately dedicated to several of the Covent Garden porters whose twelve hours of work from midnight to mid-day are the subject of the film. The key word is affectionately. Personally I would never have used such a word; for me it has too many avuncular, dutiful associations. But Anderson gives it new associations and justifies his use of it by the film that follows. He approaches his heroes (there are no villains) and so also makes us approach them, on a basis of natural equality. He neither idealises them— nor does he "study" them. . . . What he does is to muck in with them. . . . Having dissolved the problem of his relationship to his subject, and having decided to leave in abeyance the question of what the single purpose, the concluding argument of the film is going to be, he is intensely open-minded, open-eared, open-eyed to the ironies, the contrasts, the undertones, the warm, momentary, human revelations in the scenes through which he takes his cameraman. . . .

[The] imaginative connecting power of the [opening] sequence is remarkable. It connects numerous ideas. It suggests the middle class nature of the monarchy, the present "safeness" of English life, and in contrast to that, somewhere, a memory of what a London broadcast could mean to clandestine listeners during the war, the way those who work at night begin working rather silently, the apparent vulnerability of a sleeping city that leaves its lights on as a kind of bluff. Anderson does not of course expound these points. He simply acknowledges them as associations, as ingredients on different levels of the total meaning of the scene.

At the same time his attitude is never precious because he never allows himself to be led away from the popular basis of his theme—in this case the work and life of the porters. (p. 13)

In the film's treatment of this central theme, the strength and limits of Anderson's approach are most clearly revealed. . . . We are never told what the average wage of a porter is; we see none of the rackets that probably exist higher up the commercial scale of the trade; the important town-planning argument for moving the market out of the centre of the city is not touched upon. In the 'thirties all this would have been the stuff of documentary. But despite this I believe that Anderson is renewing the tradition he has inherited. I have listed what he does not give us. What he does give us are images, in the literal and poetic sense of the word. . . .

Such images have a culminating effect. They spring from, and provoke, a sustained sense of sympathy. Finally, one salutes the night porters, and one is made to feel indivisible from the daily life—gay, impressive, tragic and silly—around Wakefield. Whilst it is true that our problems today are not just simply the result of a world shortage of friendliness, it is becoming increasingly clear that in an age of official genocide humanism is a positive, even a subversive force. . . . But apart from this there are two other more specific reasons why Anderson's attitude is particularly relevant to our time. First. The squalor of our society today—as distinct from the 'thirties— is revealed more sharply in the values it breeds than in plain economic facts. And this demands a far more subtle approach from the social commentator. A man's hopes become more significant than his wage packet. Second. This is a period of scepticism. And in face of this an artist like Anderson demonstrates his commitment, not to a preconceived generalisation, but to the complicated reality of his subject matter. He produces images that are so vibrant that they persuade us to remember and create explanations *for ourselves*—and so to begin to abandon our scepticism. His films are like daylight after formalised dreams. They are full of people who are noisier than private thoughts, more intractable than all categories. (p. 14)

*John Berger, "Look at Britain!" in* Sight and Sound *(copyright © 1957 by The British Film Institute), Vol. 27, No. 1, Summer, 1957, pp. 12-14.*

**PETER BAKER**

[*This Sporting Life*] is more about life than sport, less about kitchen sinks than the people who live near them. It is also unique: which in Britain means it risks being misunderstood by the public, torn to shreds by the critics and ridiculed by the Wardour-street hucksters.

I had expected a simple film about simple people. What Anderson has done is to make as complicated a film as Welles' *Citizen Kane* about people as complicated as . . . you or me. It is the intensity of thought that has gone into *This Sporting Life* that compels attention and, finally, admiration. Whether in the final analysis it achieves communication, I am not so sure. . . .

Anderson's film is almost a perfect example of the British temperament to compromise. It has no excesses: its very balance of style and content is as disarming in its conventionality as Burton beer and Cheddar cheese. Yet the one provides as substantial a meal for the mind as the other does for the belly. In a period in world cinema when one can only be square like Hitchcock or Hawks provided the hep youngsters like Truffaut or Godard applaud you, when almost any experiment is praised by almost every critic just because it is an experiment, when even the Italian renaissance is in danger of losing communication with its audiences through sheer intellectualism, it is good to find a new director who believes that art of its very nature owes some allegiance to tradition. That the director should be Lindsay Anderson will surprise only those who have innocently misunderstood or wantonly misinterpreted his conception of 'commitment'. *This Sporting Life* takes a crisis in a man's life and makes of it the fulcrum of the whole film. . . .

The structure makes use of nearly every piece of cinema vocabulary since films learned to talk (indeed, some of the juxtaposition of images reminds one of Soviet or German cinema of the late 'teens and early 'twenties). There is never any sense of gimmickry or intellectual snobbism; instead a sense of honest craftsmanship applied to the problem of how best to project the story.

There are weaknesses. The characters and their dialogue smack of the real thing, but too often Anderson's direction of his actors betrays his long stint at the Royal Court. . . .

If I have over-praised *This Sporting Life* it is because I was expecting arrogance and saw compassion, expected Socialism and saw an apolitical humanity. It is a film to delight anyone who enjoys craftsmanship in the cinema; it is a film to make you think; and, I hope for a great mass audience, it is a film in the best sense, to entertain. . . .

If *This Sporting Life* fails to pay its way, there is no future for the British cinema.

*Peter Baker, "'This Sporting Life'" (© copyright Peter Baker 1963; reprinted with permission), in* Films and Filming, *Vol. 9, No. 6, March, 1963, p. 32.*

**ROBERT VAS**

[In *This Sporting Life*] Lindsay Anderson is the first to free himself from what seven years ago he was the first to aim at:

the direct attack, the deliberate harnessing of poetry to propaganda, which came then as a shot in the arm but which has gradually been left behind by the complexity of life itself, so that it now seems a constricting rather than a liberating attitude. Here Anderson demonstrates that his social consciousness is not, and never really was, a programme: it is the *sine qua non* of the existence of his world. He doesn't need to pull out and dwell on all those now fashionable aspects of English life—the North, the rainy Sunday, the tired face of the Establishment. His world simply exists within this context. Freed from the anxious guidance of a reporter/sociologist director, the characters are encouraged to discover their own feelings as they go along. . . . It is, simply and naturally, a film of the senses. (pp. 56-7)

[The] sudden, subjective glimpses at the beginning, counterpointed by the tough realism of the setting, stir up our interest in the character and encourage us to look out for his *interior* drama. Our continuity will obviously be a loose one, drawing the "molecules" of the hero's thoughts and emotions into a slowly thickening texture. Everything that happens is going to be seen from his point of view.

Just how consistently this interior quality is present throughout the film (although in different forms) emerges clearly from one scene—in fact the weakest in the entire work—when it is *not* present. This is the evening out at the restaurant, where Machin behaves as he never really would—at least, not at that stage of the story. . . . Here the subjective view is abandoned, and the film takes the standpoint of a detached onlooker. (p. 57)

At its best, however, the "portrait of a man" blends with the "story of a man": interior and at the same time narrative cinema. . . . We approach the story through the interior drama, and soon realise that in fact the interior drama *is* the story. The result is a thick texture, carrying the complexity of life itself, defying us to give a straight answer to the question of what the film is finally about.

We may approach *This Sporting Life* as a study in human behaviour or, as its creators prefer to call it, in temperament. . . . [Frank Machin's] is the typical fate of tragic heroes who strive to achieve something worthwhile but go about it the wrong way, and cannot help getting into a mess which they are then unable to explain. His real purpose is a frantic search for his own identity. His character may bear a literary, almost intellectual charge in its tragic emphasis, but his best means of expression are his bare fists.

The blow of the fist comes like a visual motif in this film . . . , in which emotions and behaviour find their expression in physical terms. (pp. 57-8)

The film-makers' aim was to avoid sociological generalisations, to present a character who is larger than life and for that reason better fitted to stand for a wider, more hazardous poetic truth. . . . Here everything takes a compressed and dramatically heightened form. The Machin actually visible on the screen will be much bigger than in the pages of [David Storey's book on which the film is based]; so his behaviour and Mrs. Hammond's reactions assume additional size, a further edge of intensity.

It is Mrs. Hammond's character (seen in contrast with his, and yet from his point of view) which fully brings out the scope of the film. Her strange and silently suffering nobility, her dignified misery, her full-time self-destruction, would make her a perfect Chekhovian character, if her suppression of self were not at the same time so perversely stupid and unnatural. (p. 58)

Although she becomes [Machin's] mistress she cannot let her feelings go along with it. By then we cannot even judge which does most harm: his aggressive demands or her unnatural renunciation of life. Instead of the best the relationship brings out the worst in both of them. The sense of approaching tragedy is heightened by his inability to put his feelings into words; by the fact that his only way of expression, the physical, is exactly the one by which he alienates her. The *huis clos* feeling of their inability to communicate brings with it the explosion: the violent, final break.

It is at this moment of his "tragic guilt" that the account of the relationship reverts to Frank's personal story, and the picture gains a frightening, almost abstract charge. . . . Here, living up to the size and power of its hero, *This Sporting Life* achieves that universality of tragedy which has so far eluded the new British directors. Here pain *is* called pain, and the feeling is one of liberation . . . (pp. 58-9)

[An earlier shot of Mrs. Hammond's profile summarizes the film-maker's attitudes; it is] a pathetic amalgam of the robust and tender, eruptive and suppressed, demanding and accepting—and out of these many contrasts emerges something of the duality of contemporary Britain, the mixture of aggression and withdrawal, anger and passivity. . . .

The main protest here is not, as one critic holds, a consciously social one: "gladiatorial slaves and suave, unscrupulous tycoons." It lies rather in the heat of the emotions, in an outcry against "not taking things too seriously," being ashamed to feel. To ask for "coolness" and "detachment" (as did another critic) from a film which intends to be and is "hot" seems a very English miscalculation. And through this heat is communicated, in the words of its author—"the whole tragedy of living, of being alive" today, in Britain, in the world. . . .

To reach this point, Lindsay Anderson had to get rid of a certain kind of facile romanticism which mingles with the genuinely humane in *Every Day Except Christmas*. He emerges as a talent with strong reserves, able to encompass the small psychological glimpses as well as the overall emotional sweep. . . .

All in all, it is not so much a *film d'auteur* as, rather, a film *with* an author. . . .

It is an exploratory work, and this involves numerous falterings, mistakes, impurities in style and content. But it is an arrival as much as a departure; a breakthrough perhaps to a more demanding audience, and more courage in production; a password to the unashamed expression of emotion. (p. 59)

*Robert Vas, "Arrival and Departure," in* Sight and Sound *(copyright © 1963 by The British Film Institute), Vol. 32, No. 2, Spring, 1963, pp. 56-9.*

**GAVIN MILLAR**

Lindsay Anderson thinks "*If* . . . is really a vision, something like the Writing on the Wall." We should therefore look for something prophetic, cryptic, poetic, transforming. Anderson and his skilful screenwriter David Sherwin have certainly written something on the wall, but a good deal of rubbing out's been going on and, in some really crucial places, parts of the wall seem to be missing.

No one in the cinema has ever done such an effective hatchet-job on the English Public School. In *If . . . . .* Anderson and Sherwin expose its horrors wittily and savagely: the brutality, the exploitation of slave labour, the tyranny of petty restrictions, the sexual confusion and hypocrisy, the interdependence of hierarchy and conformity. . . .

All this is well and carefully done. But there is more. The legacy of Kipling first of all. Anderson was born in India, of Scottish extraction. The legend of service with honour is for him a giant lie, since it is a life inevitably corrupted by the system of government it upholds. However benevolent it is, Anderson will have no time for paternalism. And Kipling would not recognise Mick, the hero of this new *If . . .* , as an Englishman at all. . . . So bitter is Anderson's vision that there is not one single member of the staff, no single senior prefect, who even remotely enjoys the comfort of a clear conscience. . . .

The sides, in other words, are pretty neatly drawn up. All the more reason then why we must look very hard at the credentials of our new leader. He 'knows what it's all about'. What what's all about? It's not the Jews this time, or the RC's, or the vegetarians, but it is a sort of conspiracy theory nonetheless. The 'it' is 'them' and they're against 'us'. But of course they are, and the justice of what Anderson's saying and the sincerity and passion with which he says it are truly painful. What's more, the tenacity of his stand against them over the years is truly admirable.

But it's a local justice, not an absolute one, and its applications must be constantly defined and made precise, otherwise all the passion and sincerity and tenacity in the world will only confuse his sympathisers and—more importantly—his work. 'It all', 'them' and 'us' are inadequate descriptions of the elements involved in the coming revolutionary struggle, and the film doesn't do enough to clarify them.

If there is going to be one then, by God, we need to know what it's going to be about. But that's just the trouble. (p. 42)

Why can one not hail this brave and unusual essay in personal cinema as a masterpiece? Why can't we read the writing on the wall? We said we might look, in a vision, for something poetic. Isn't this it?

Anderson has shown himself in all his work eager to break the narrow bounds of documentary realism. . . . At moments in *If . . .* this delicate skirmishing on the borders of realism is apt and tender, as when Bobby Phillips watches his hero Wallace exercising in the gym; or striking and uncanny, as when the housemaster's wife drifts naked through the deserted dorm, caressing towels and clothing. . . . But whether out of a need to suppress the tenderness, or an impatience to express the fury, these moments and this balance are lost in the headlong drive to the end.

If the account of the school's horrors scores by its patient accuracy, it does it no service now to explode these strict terms of reference. . . . *If . . .* is a film concerned with revolution, but about anger. And if we can't read the writing on the wall, perhaps it was because the hand shook a little. (p. 43)

*Gavin Millar, "Film Reviews: 'If . . .','' in* Sight and Sound *(copyright © 1969 by The British Film Institute), Vol. 38, No. 1, Winter, 1968-69, pp. 42-3.*

## JOHN SIMON

[*If . . .* is a] film of considerable distinction though missed excellence. . . . *If . . .* is much more effective while it chronicles the faintly surreal realities of English public-school life than when it enters the domain of the surreal whole hog. The story of three musketeers of nonconformity in a tradition-sodden English school functions admirably on the level of smug authoritarianism crossed by petty defiance; but the final holocaust would have required both more imaginative writing and, in the director, the unlikely combination of a Jean Vigo and a Luis Buñuel. (p. 109)

The infiltration of the surreal is not uncleverly managed. . . . [Strange] strands crop up in the fabric of things, but they are not shown as one person's vision, rather as a world slowly turning psychotic.

This may sound defensible, even challenging, on paper; on the screen, it comes out untidy, indeed pretentious. . . . As in *This Sporting Life,* one gets a feeling of richly sculptured individual scenes, but a deficient sense of the whole and somewhat nebulous continuity.

Still, David Sherwin's script has many racy moments, Lindsay Anderson's direction is always textured and full of gusto, and a cast of mingled newcomers and old-timers blends into a flawlessly incongruous cross section of bankrupt paideutics. The funny or cruel scenes work very handily; it is only the apocryphal and apocalyptic material that fails to persuade. Yet the film is never uninteresting, seldom unspirited, and there is some sort of intelligence even in its miscalculations. (p. 110)

*John Simon, "The Youth Film: 'If . . .'; 'Greetings'; 'Changes'; 'Three in the Attic'" (originally published as "Youth Kick," in* The New Leader, Vol. LII, No. 5, March 17, 1969), *in his* Movies into Film: Film Criticism 1967-1970 *(copyright © 1971 by John Simon; reprinted with permission of The Dial Press),* Dial, *1971, pp. 109-13.\**

## ALBERT JOHNSON

*If . . .* is one of the most extraordinary studies of adolescence and education in the history of motion pictures. . . . This film is both a commentary upon and indirect indictment of the traditions of private education in England. The elements of satire and anarchy, of poetic fantasy and melodrama, are allegorically mingled into something rare and timeless. Each of the film's eight episodes is a challenging immersion into that mysterious world of youth-in-formation, a milieu that piques the curiosity of older generations beyond measure. *If . . .* opens the doors to this private domain, explaining or intimating at will, with seeming indiscretion, the limitless angers, passions, and flights of imagination that youth encompasses. (p. 48)

*Albert Johnson, "Film Reviews: 'If . . .','' in* Film Quarterly *(copyright 1969 by The Regents of the University of California; reprinted by permission of the University of California Press), Vol. XXII, No. 4, Summer, 1969, pp. 48-52.*

## MICHAEL DEMPSEY

*If. . . .* is so full of patchy, obscure, muddled elements that we often cannot be sure if our view of the rebels matches Anderson's. The film reeks of material insufficiently absorbed and attitudes not fully formulated. Nevertheless, too much in the movie fails to jibe with the "revolution" that the twin media of reviews and publicity condition us to expect. The film questions and undermines the values and tactics of the rebels too thoroughly to function as a pamphlet, and this is fortunate. In the end, the interest complexity of *If*. . . . attacks society all the more trenchantly for being so impervious to change that it forces many would-be reformers to become as evil as it is. (p. 20)

*Michael Dempsey, "'If. . . .',"* in Film Heritage *(copyright 1969 by F. A. Macklin), Vol. 5, No. 1, Fall, 1969, pp. 13-20.*

## STEPHEN FARBER

[*If* . . .'s] first problem for an American audience is its provincial English public-school setting. Director Lindsay Anderson wants us to see the school as a microcosm of English society—an institution dominated by the same hypocritical religion, military brutality and upper class privilege that flourish even more viciously on the outside. But he lingers so long and so intensely on scenes that cannot be considered representative, that take place *only* in a boys' school . . . that the connections between school and society become more and more tenuous. The virtue of the film is its specificity. It would be easy to say that the school equals the System, but that is such a bland equation that it is quite unfair to the film's witty detail and rich texture. *If* . . . is good enough to resist generalization. Yet perhaps this strength does imply a certain limitation of the film. David Sherwin's dialogue is brilliant, particularly in its observant mimicry of various kinds of official rhetoric, but the film keeps threatening to fall into parody. Its satire is almost always exactly on target, and the targets are really too easy to hit. The film does an expert job of dissecting the particular institution that it examines, but it needs another dimension—either more compassion or more rage—if it is to strike us as a truly visionary portrait of the cracks in Western civilization.

What gives *If* . . . a contemporary twist and an immediate relevance—and what is probably most baffling to the expectant young audience—is its skeptical consideration of the student rebel. . . . The film's disparagement of student rebellion is not to be confused with backlash hysteria, for Anderson clearly puts the blame for the rebels' pettiness and destructiveness on the institution itself. . . . And the rebellion of the three crusaders reflects the ignorance and insularity of their school. Because they are so isolated from the breadth of life in the world outside, these kids have lost all sense of perspective, all sense of what *matters*. The film shrewdly recognizes that the viciousness of the crusaders is the most insidious legacy of a sterile liberal education at the service of a demoralized, reactionary society.

The trouble with student rebels is that they are *not* true revolutionaries; the boys in *If* . . . have no real link with more profoundly disenchanted groups in their world. . . . The boys are completely indiscriminate in the images of violence that they admire—the motorcyclist and the Establishment soldier excite them as much as the Negro rioter. Revolutionary figures quickly become pop heroes. (pp. 469-70)

What makes *If* . . . tricky to evaluate is its mixing of fantasy and reality, and its refusal to provide conventional movie hints that will enable us to tell the two apart. Anderson presents the boys' fantasies with a strange literalness. But I think he always keeps his distance. (p. 471)

There are a few moments in the film when Anderson needlessly changes point of view, suddenly presenting a fantasy of a minor character (the housemaster's wife, the much-desired "scum" Bobby Phillips). Those moments are clearly flaws, but I am more sympathetic to the confusing ease with which the film slips in and out of the crusaders' fantasies. Many films—from Busby Berkeley to Fellini—have included outright fantasy sequences, but *If* . . . deals with subtler distortions of reality, the way in which we make slight adjustments in our perceptions to satisfy our fantasy images of ourselves more resoundingly. (p. 472)

The degree of fantasy in the final scene may be unclear, but its skeptical attitude is perfectly clear and devastating.

But there is something unsatisfying about the conclusion. The assembly itself, like most of the film, is played for satiric laughs, and is undeniably hilarious, but it is hard to change mood once the scene shifts to the slaughter on the quad. . . . [The final shot of Mick is] an upsetting image, but really too strong for the film. Suddenly Anderson tries to frighten us; this image seems meant as an angry, prophetic, almost apocalyptic warning of the violence that awaits us on our once-placid playing fields. But the rest of the film is too cool and witty to suddenly scream of apocalypse. We may wish that the film had fury in addition to irony, but it never really is able to shock us, unsettle us, move us. *If* . . . is a fine, provoking intellectual critique of contemporary kinds of repression and rebellion, but it rarely provides an emotional experience. And one feverish concluding shot cannot supply a film with the passion that it has not previously been able to muster. (p. 473)

*Stephen Farber, "Before the Revolution,"* in The Hudson Review *(copyright © 1969 by The Hudson Review, Inc.; reprinted by permission), Vol. XXII, No. 3, Autumn, 1969, pp. 469-76.*

## ELIZABETH SUSSEX

Anderson's work is based on the assumption that 'art is real', and that cinematic art is 'poetry'. . . . What is meant by 'poetry' . . . is a fusion between style and content, between the thing said and the way of saying it, that makes the two inseparable and at the same time creates something new. His poetry begins with realism, with images drawn from the everyday, that are also so charged with the artist's particular vision that they acquire a deeper meaning, intensifying reality and becoming in themselves an experience. (p. 12)

But if Anderson always wanted art to show a belief in humanity, a mistake that people make is to regard this as a simple notion. On the contrary a belief in humanity, intelligently held, becomes increasingly complex the harder you look at humans. It was a belief in humanity that led Blake to write 'Cruelty has a human Heart,/And Jealousy a Human Face;/Terror the Human Form Divine,/And Secrecy the Human Dress.'

To take the comparison with Blake a little further: most of Anderson's criticism and early films are Songs of Innocence (*Thursday's Children*) and Experience (*O Dreamland*). As with Blake the two apparently irreconcilable opposites are first presented separately, and later welded together in a single vision of the world. (p. 14)

[*Thursday's Children*] is not about the nature of suffering. It is about the joy of discovery, the joy of being alive. (p. 21)

*Thursday's Children* shows emotion and discipline working in harmony—the ideal at the heart of Anderson's most personal films. The picture as a whole has the kind of order that could be this way and no other. And every physical detail, every cut and every close-up, consolidates this sense of rightness. . . . (pp. 22-3)

But *Every Day Except Christmas* is a youthful film: the last of Anderson's Songs of Innocence and the last film he was ever to make in quite this optimistic spirit of unqualified delight.

The film works in the first place because of Anderson's remarkable talent for making people interesting. (p. 34)

The porters in this film . . . belong to a different world from the people in *O Dreamland*. The fact that they might frequent a place like Dreamland in their spare time is irrelevant to what Anderson wants to tell us about them. *Every Day Except Christmas* is consistently idealistic. The more you analyse it, the more the detail adds up in this way. (p. 35)

In terms of toughness and maturity [*This Sporting Life*] takes a huge stride forward from *Every Day Except Christmas*. . . . *This Sporting Life* is the most passionate film that has ever emerged from a British studio. . . . (p. 48)

Everywhere in the film, a particularly vivid kind of authenticity can be taken for granted, and yet it was, and still is, a very rare quality. (p. 50)

[*If* . . .] could be interpreted as being about the way in which people blind themselves to reality, cut themselves off from emotion, refuse to see both life and death as they really are. The threshold between fantasy and reality in the film is then something that must vary according to how much reality the individual spectator can bear. And the film's supreme achievement is in enabling audiences to interpret it according to their own idea of what is real. (p. 83)

> *Elizabeth Sussex, in her* Lindsay Anderson *(© 1969 by Movie Magazine Limited; reprinted by permission of Movie), Frederick A. Praeger, Publishers, 1970, 96 p.*

### VINCENT CANBY

"O Lucky Man!" clearly has a number of things on its mind, but as a movie, it is a very mixed bag.

Because Mr. Anderson is much more bold and free as a director than [David] Sherwin is inventive as a social satirist, **"O Lucky Man!"** always promises to be much more stimulating and funny than it ever is. Staying with it through its almost three-hour running time becomes increasingly nerve-racking, like watching superimposed images that never synchronize. The result does not match the ambition of the intention. The wit is too small, too perfunctory, for the grand plan of the film and the quality of the production itself. . . .

The score exhibits real irony about the ghastly indecencies that Sherwin so ponderously tries to ridicule. In this day and age, for those of us who have grown up with the truly epic visions of film makers like Buñuel and Chaplin, it's hardly enough for a film to qualify as "serious" or "important" by pointing out to us the excesses of capitalism, the awesomeness of technology gone mad, or even that poor people can act like beasts, just like rich people.

A more disturbing proposition by far would be a film that might suggest that rampant capitalism and technological madness could

possibly succeed, by some terrible fluke, in fulfilling their promises. That is something that would force us to rethink the clichés we liberals live by. **"O Lucky Man!"** . . . is a kind of homage to those clichés.

> *Vincent Canby, "'O Lucky Man!'" in* The New York Times *(© 1973 by The New York Times Company; reprinted by permission), June 14, 1973 (and reprinted in* The New York Times Film Reviews: 1973-1974, *The New York Times Company & Arno Press, 1975, p. 66).*

### STANLEY KAUFFMANN

*O Lucky Man!* is so much the worst of [Anderson's three features] that it seems twisted by rancor—pickled in Anderson's bile because he wasn't called a genius for the first two. The film exudes conceit and pigheadedness, and is steeped in self-display and self-reference, a three-hour effort at self-canonization. . . .

There is no single moment that is not well directed, some moments much better than that. But what is supposed to be a work of radical daring, in method and matter, is only a laborious sophomoric dud. (p. 204)

When the film isn't being excruciatingly banal in its "exposure" of the ills of our time, it's being equally painful in its opposing glimpses of purity and the lost Eden. (p. 205)

The picture is apparently intended as a picaresque account of a hero protected by innocence, whose goodheartedness sees him through. (I would have thought it was his good looks that made the happy ending, but no matter.) This is all shattered by the blow that Anderson smites. (pp. 205-06)

The film could have ended an hour sooner or gone on three hours more: the plain truth is that Anderson [has] *absolutely nothing to say*—and I use the word "say" in its widest possible sense. . . .

Out of this mess of pretentiousness and egotism and aimless skill, what emerges finally? A great zero for this film and a hovering zero for Anderson's film future. (p. 206)

> *Stanley Kauffmann, "'O Lucky Man!'" (originally published in* The New Republic, *Vol. 168, No. 24, June 16, 1973), in his* Living Images: Film Comment and Criticism *(reprinted by permission of Brandt & Brandt Literary Agents, Inc.; copyright © 1970, 1971, 1972, 1973, 1974, 1975 by Stanley Kauffmann), Harper & Row, Publishers, 1975, pp. 204-07.*

### WILLIAM S. PECHTER

[If] *O Lucky Man!* is a celebration of success, it is of success in a bad world, a world in which, as the sophomoric cynicism of the song lyrics has it, "only wealth will buy you justice" and "Someone's got to win the human race/If it isn't you, then it has to be me." And, in being a kind of *apologia pro vita sua* for the director, it seems to me very much a work of bad faith and guilty conscience. To be sure, Anderson doesn't exempt himself from the film's indictment of the world's corruption: he in fact portrays himself much less indulgently than he does his hero, and without the defense of the hero's innocence. . . . And yet for all the self-criticism that the film implies, for all its bitter knowledge about the character of that establishment to which star and director have gained entry and the certainty that Anderson regards *O Lucky Man!* as a subversive work, it seems to me decidedly half-hearted and weighed down by a terrible complacency of spirit; for all the willfulness involved, there was something really more likable about the desire of *If* . . . to join the revolution than there is in this film's cynical seeing through the "opium" of such commitments. (p. 76)

William S. Pechter, "Politics on Film" (copyright © 1973 by William S. Pechter; reprinted by permission of the author), in Commentary, Vol. 56, No. 3, September, 1973, pp. 74-7.*

### COLIN L. WESTERBECK, JR.

So many things seem to me wrong about [the killing of the hapless spider at the end of *This Sporting Life*], it is hard to know where to begin to criticize—or better still, exorcise—such an image. On the simplest and most literal level, unless one is trying to document lapses of sanitation under the National Health, one doesn't find spiders in hospital rooms. The spider is out of place there. It doesn't belong. It's an intrusion, an imposition, an importation.

Perhaps a more serious breach of art, however, is the fact that this spider isn't even an accurate image for the dilemma in which Anderson's rugby player finds himself. Where is the capricious hand of fate that crushes him? It doesn't exist in the film Anderson made. . . . Frank is the victim of his own character, not of the gods or fate—a smalltime Macbeth or Lear, not Oedipus or Agamemnon. To dramatize his catastrophe with this crushed spider is to play him false.

Unfortunately, Anderson's . . . *O Lucky Man!* is an attempt to make a whole movie about that spider. (pp. 501-02)

In *This Sporting Life* the image of the spider was at least inappropriate. We had seen a pretty good film until we got to the spider, and if his sequence was disconcerting, we could just throw it out without having to throw out the rest of the film as well. When Anderson clouts Michael with the script [in *O Lucky Man!*], however, the gesture is all too apt. This is exactly what Anderson has been doing to his hero throughout *O Lucky Man!*—interfering with him, playing the hand of fate in his life. But I doubt that Anderson sees it that way. On the contrary, he seems to think of Michael as someone he has endowed with a quite independent life, a life that almost has some objective existence. The retroactive effect of putting the casting session at the end of the film is to suggest that everything which went before is not Anderson's fantasy at all. It is, rather, a set of real experiences that have led up to Anderson's fantasies and prepared Michael to enact them.

There is something not a little egomaniacal and selfish in this conceit. It makes the whole film seem the sort of mistake a man makes when he has told some fish story for so long that he has begun to believe it himself. . . .

Can Anderson really think that his making a film about the ills of the world will cure them, or at least compensate us who suffer them? O Lucky Man, to have such a gift to bestow. (p. 502)

Colin L. Westerbeck, Jr., "The Spider's Stratagem," in Commonweal (copyright © 1973 Commonweal Publishing Co., Inc.; reprinted by permission of Commonweal Publishing Co., Inc.), Vol. XCVIII, No. 21, September 21, 1973, pp. 501-02.

### JUDITH CRIST

Anderson has shown such sensitivity and perception in the filming of [*In Celebration*], in barely opening the sets but doing so with an intensity of atmosphere that is overwhelming, that the work offers the best of film and of filmed theater. . . .

This is the stuff of true drama, the little murders and petty mayhem of family dealings from memory and guilt and the weapons we dredge from past and present to use. Anderson and a superb cast have made it a harrowing and satisfying suspense drama. Each face becomes as familiar as the small talk; Storey's mastery of minor moments is underlined by the camera, which delineates the blood bonds that hold us all. (p. 77)

Judith Crist, "The Wisdom of the Aging," in New York Magazine (copyright © 1975 by News Group Publications, Inc.; reprinted with the permission of New York Magazine), Vol. 8, No. 11, March 17, 1975, pp. 76-7.*

### JOHN RUSSELL TAYLOR

It might be possible on the basis of *Wakefield Express* to imagine Anderson as a soft-hearted liberal, a sentimental kind of humanist who rather uncritically loves people, the quainter the better. But the humanity of *Thursday's Children* is something altogether tougher, harder won. . . . Though the information conveyed by the film is by no means uncomplicatedly optimistic—only a third of the children, we learn, can ever hope to achieve true speech—*Thursday's Children* comes across as a hymn to man's potential, a study not so much of suffering as of triumph over suffering. (p. 74)

If *Thursday's Children* showed a new tough-mindedness in Anderson's work, *O Dreamland* moved further into something very like savagery. . . . (p. 75)

[The] film could superficially be read as a denunciation of the exploitation of the working classes in a consumer society where rubbish such as we see for ourselves was all that was offered as cheap popular entertainment. But the film does not feel like that. Despite the opening shots of a chauffeur polishing a Bentley, it is hard to feel that the filmmaker's attitude toward the people he shows is entirely compassionate; often it is hard to see it as compassionate at all. . . . Humane, in a true, critical, unsentimental sense, the film may be, but anger replaces the conventional gesture of condescending sympathy. "Only connect" is the film's message, and anger at those who refuse even to try, who remain passively stuck in their tawdry amusement-park world, is the only humanly possible reaction. (pp. 76-7)

[*O Dreamland*] has the richness and complexity of a poem, and a highly personal poem at that, transcending its immediate occasion and its period through sheer force of the creator's conviction. And it does contain in microcosm much of the later Anderson—his humanity and his savagery, his pity and his anger, and the impossibility of pinning him down to any simple formula. *O Dreamland* is immediately recognizable as a work from the same hand as *If* . . . (p. 77)

*Every Day Except Christmas* is an extremely *soigné*, effective, romantic documentary of a rather old-fashioned kind. (p. 80)

[However, most] of *Every Day Except Christmas*, for all its technical skill, its cunning assemblage of vivid, vivifying detail, is just that little bit too bland and rosy to be altogether truc. It is rosy realism which does not quite come across as a genuine feeling. The act of selection and the nature of the selection are fair enough—obviously some sort of selection is inevitable and any selection must at least imply the criteria by which it is made—but I have the impression that the darker, tougher sides of Anderson's observation are being deliberately suppressed. . . . (pp. 80-1)

[*This Sporting Life*'s] most immediately striking quality is its unashamed emotionalism. Here is no stiff-upper-lip understatement of emotion; when the characters suppress or repress their emotions, it only produces an even more powerful charge of violence—every scene in the film is charged with the passion of what is not said and done, as well as what is. (p. 84)

[For] a film of such boldness in conception and complexity in execution the errors are amazingly few—the film remains true to David Storey's conception, but at the same time takes on the quality of an *auteur* work, the unmistakable expression of Lindsay Anderson's own tender, violent temperament in images of unshakable power. (pp. 88-9)

*The White Bus* is deliberately light and slight, but it is, beneath its deceptively whimsical exterior, already an exercise in the freer, even less realistic form of cinema Anderson was to move on to in *If* . . . Except that it does not seem as arid as calling it an exercise in anything might imply; fantasy and documentary reality meet, mingle, and are interfused inextricably in a film that moves with the unpredictable, unanalyzable certainty of a poem. Though not at all "poetic" in the vague, impressionist sense of the term—everything in it is absolutely sharp and precise—it yet uses the procedures of poetry to transfigure its prosaic materials into something rich and strange. (p. 90)

[*If* . . .] is an extraordinary film, a film that virtually defies ordinary verbal description because it works as only the cinema can, on the indistinct border between fantasy which has the solidity of tangible experience and reality which seems as remote and elusive as a dream. (p. 91)

The film is a rich, complex, obscure metaphor of the way we live now, the tone of the times. . . . With one small exception . . . there is nothing in the film that could not be real, and nothing that absolutely has to be. (p. 92)

*If* . . . carries even further the characteristic technique we have observed in *This Sporting Life* and *The White Bus* of creating strangeness, ambiguity, and magic by juxtaposing things in unexpected ways, so that all the pieces, each perfectly credible in itself, do not quite fit into an immediately credible whole. There is a disturbing sense of a gap in the system somewhere, which always keeps us on our toes, ready to use our intelligence as well as react through our instincts. (p. 94)

The inspiration of *If* . . . , as of much of Buñuel, is anarchic in the strict philosophical sense of the term—it confronts rival notions of reality, of responsibility, rather than merely opposing order with chaos. And in detail the film is richly, meaningfully contradictory. . . . Tradition is both loved and criticized: rebellion is romantic, backward-looking, and practically doomed. Anyone looking for a simple left-wing liberal tract,

condemning the public-school system, disapproving of violence, advocating sweet reasonableness as the best way toward making things "better," will find naught for his comfort in *If* . . . (p. 95)

[*O Lucky Man!* is obviously] a fable suggesting a journey from innocence to experience through a fantastic dream vision of modern Britain. . . . It is the sort of film which invites—indeed, compels—one to suspend intellectual judgment till one has seen it through, accepting each stage in Mick's journey as one would a dream of one's own, and wait for illumination to burst afterward. It works on this level only as a whole, and finally works on one as the slap does on Mick—it explodes into meaning all at once, in a nonrational way. As soon ask the significance of any particular detail in the film, like the gold suit or the suckling by the vicar's wife . . . as ask why *If* . . . goes from black-and-white to color and back again in the eccentric but completely unquestionable way it does. If you ask the question the film is failing in its effect on you—it should move, and move you, with the certainty of a sleepwalker. Lindsay Anderson's most extraordinary quality as a filmmaker—and in this he comes closest perhaps to Pasolini—is his ability to keep his instincts uncontaminated by his intellect, his intellect unmuddled by his instincts. His films are about ideas, but defy paraphrase. (pp. 98-9)

*John Russell Taylor, "Lindsay Anderson," in his* Directors and Directions: Cinema for the Seventies *(reprinted by permission of Hill & Wang, a division of Farrar, Straus & Giroux, Inc.; in Canada by A D Peters & Co Ltd; copyright © 1975 by John Russell Taylor), Hill & Wang, 1975, pp. 69-99.*

**GORDON GOW**

The social and the psychological elements of David Storey's *In Celebration* build rather slowly but nevertheless very strongly to an emotional peak which is tremendously moving. . . . The result is a love-hate drama, risking sentimentality in its determination to be honest, and succeeding in Lindsay Anderson's skilled marshalling of the . . . cast. . . . (p. 29)

Once, during the slow stuff early on, Anderson cuts well away to a short sequence when Colin picks up Andrew in his car on their way north, and this abrupt intrusion of familiar action-type cinema, as opposed to the cinema-of-words that prevails, is arguably a mistake. It increases my surprise at the omission of some short visual observations—a montage, maybe—of the actual celebratory dinner. . . . [Such] events, of course, are not anything more in themselves than circumstances which bring out the dramatic essence of the plays, and in the theatre we accept the convention that the occasions have gone by during the interval. But the film of *In Celebration,* when I saw it, had no interval. . . . Emotionally, for a British film, [the] overall effect is remarkably potent, and seamlessly joined to the social and psychological theses. (p. 30)

*Gordon Gow, "Reviews: 'In Celebration'" (© copyright Gordon Gow 1976; reprinted with permission), in* Films and Filming, *Vol. 22, No. 10, July, 1976, pp. 29-30.*

# Michelangelo Antonioni

## 1912-

**Italian film director, screenwriter, and film critic.**

**Antonioni is best described as a director who exposes the core of the human soul. His films depict human alienation and the destruction of established values.**

*Cronaca di un amore,* **Antonioni's first feature film, contains qualities characteristic of much of his later work: desolate landscapes, unresolved plot, and discontented, aimless characters. In** *Le amiche,* **based on a short story by Cesare Pavese, Antonioni focuses on male-female relationships, using sparse dialogue. This technique would later become an Antonioni trademark.**

*L'avventura* **brought Antonioni international renown. In the film, the plot remains unfulfilled, and Antonioni's use of such an unusual technique caused an uproar at the 1960 Cannes Film Festival.** *L'avventura* **is the first of three films to center on revealing aspects of relationships.** *La notte* **and** *L'eclisse* **also rely on elaborate detail to conceal the emptiness of affluent life.**

*Blow-Up* **portrays a male photograher caught up in the mod society of London in the mid-sixties. Based on a story by Julio Cortázar,** *Blow-Up* **relates an artist's struggle to reveal truth through rationalism. His next film,** *Zabriskie Point,* **was filmed in the United States and is generally viewed as an intense depiction of the futility of both idealism and materialism. In 1975, Antonioni directed** *The Passenger,* **a film which contains many characteristics of his earlier works. However, Antonioni's reliance on existential themes has prompted critics to compare the film to Camus's** *The Stranger.*

**Writing on** *Blow-Up,* **Max Kozloff has defined Antonioni's "repertoire of themes": "Without doubt, most of his earlier perceptions are present: of the insufficiency and transcience of human affection, of chilled eroticism, of the muteness of objects, of intermittent hysteria, and a sundered social fabric." (See also** *Contemporary Authors,* **Vols. 73-76.)**

### RICHARD ROUD

Unlike the first works of many directors (Bresson, for example), *Cronaca di un Amore* can be seen today not only as a fully realised work but also as a virtually complete definition of Antonioni's artistic personality and technique. Significantly, it ran counter to the neo-realist method then prevailing in Italy. (p. 8)

Antonioni is a man of the left and certain social preoccupations make themselves felt in this film. Guido's studies were interrupted by the war and he has since been forced to earn his living as a car salesman. When he suggests to Paola that she leave her husband, her ironic glance at his packet of Nazionali cigarettes is warning enough that she cannot accept a life without luxury. Throughout all Antonioni's work, one finds unsentimental illustrations of his belief that the emotions are often conditioned by social factors and tastes. At the end of *Le Amiche,* for example, Clelia refuses to marry the workman who loves her. She has made a life for herself in the *haute couture* world of Turin and is unwilling to slip back to the slums of her childhood; for she, like Claudia in *L'Avventura,* is really an outsider in the world of wealth.

Whenever Antonioni's social preoccupations gain the upper hand, however, his work seems to suffer. *I Vinti (The Vanquished),* for example, deals with delinquent youth in France, Italy and England. . . . [Beyond] a general suggestion that the adolescents have unsuitable home lives, there is no attempt to show *why* an Italian, for instance, has gone into the smuggling racket. If Antonioni had taken any one of the three episodes and allowed himself to develop it fully, then perhaps the film might have avoided the impression of a perfunctory enquiry. A generalised concern for social problems, however praiseworthy in the abstract, is not enough to make a convincing film. (p. 9)

In the words of Scott Fitzgerald, one of his favourite authors, Antonioni lives permanently in the world of three o'clock in the morning, the real dark night of the soul. It is a world of suicide and despair, a world in which passions are real but transient, in which guilt and remorse are permanent and inescapable and one is held to account as much for what one has allowed to happen as for what one has done: a world that is grey and cold, hard and spare, and where the sun rarely shines. *L'Avventura* marks a lightening of this outlook, and it remains to be seen whether *La Notte* will return to it. . . .

*Le Amiche* begins with an attempted suicide and finishes with an achieved one. Between these two acts is inscribed a world of boredom, the metaphysical boredom of the rich, who, their material problems solved, are faced with the futility of existence, the *"difficulté d'être."* In a sense *Le Amiche* can be seen as a first sketch for *L'Avventura.* The social surroundings are the same and the bored and restless Momina, whose only distraction is in her love affairs, is a draft for the Giulia of *L'Avventura.* (p. 10)

A view of life, a personality, are defined in the themes Antonioni chooses, but they find their complete expression in the form of his films. His preoccupation with the influence of environment (both social and physical) can be seen from his consistent and exclusive use of natural settings. His characters are always seen against a real background. Yet these natural locations have been chosen, with as much care as any studio set was ever designed, to express the mood of the film and the emotions of the characters. The desolate autumnal wastes of the Po Valley through which Aldo aimlessly circles in *Il Grido,* the oppressive presence of the horizon, the perspectives which open on to infinity, are the exact reflection of Aldo's state of soul; and, one might add, of Antonioni's. In his best films, one always feels that Antonioni's characters are expressions of himself. And this is what gives his work its unity. (pp. 10-11)

I cannot recall a single instance in which Antonioni uses a real close-up. He never isolates a character entirely from his surroundings. Rather, he prefers to use the two-shot combined with long takes . . . , action within the shot and a great many tracking and panning movements. . . . His camera constantly follows his people, literally tracking them down. . . . [He] makes much use of composition in depth, though the effect he most often achieves is not to link the two or three people in the frame but to separate them, to demonstrate the gulfs existing between them. For the same reason, in his two-shots, the actors seldom look directly at each other. This is especially true of *Il Grido,* in which the whole drama springs from Aldo's inability to communicate. Every shot is full of diagonal lines which never cross; every character has his own problems and is incapable of helping any of the others. Every man is an island.

In the same way that Antonioni uses composition in depth to isolate his characters from each other, so his use of real exteriors, two-shots, long takes and tracking movements dissociates his characters from their backgrounds. There is an essential dialectic at work here: people are seen against authentic backgrounds which relate directly to their states of mind and feeling, but at the same time they are necessarily alienated from their surroundings, apart, separate and alone. . . .

But there is another element at work in these films: an autonomous and non-functional use of camera movements to create spatial patterns which are satisfying in their own right. There is a scene in *Signora senza Camelie* which perhaps brings this out best. Clara has come home to find that her husband has taken an overdose of sleeping tablets. As she enters their living room, the camera describes a clockwise elliptical movement. This movement is answered by a corresponding counter-clockwise movement at the end of the sequence as we leave the house. No dramatic point has been made by these two movements: the effect is as gratuitous as when a theme is reversed in a fugue, and it is similarly divorced from any emotional significance. Or so it seems. I would say that Antonioni is the kind of artist who is incapable of doing anything clumsily. Beauty is for him an absolute necessity even in such relatively unimportant matters as getting a camera into a room and out again. He is proposing to us an additional, non-representational element for our pleasure: a formal choreography of movements which accompanies the film, providing a non-conceptual figure in the carpet, an experience in pure form. (p. 11)

*Richard Roud, ''Films,'' in* Sight and Sound *(copyright © 1961 by The British Film Institute), Vol. 30, No. 1, Winter, 1960-61, pp. 8-11.*

### IAN CAMERON

Structurally [*L'Avventura*] is remarkable for its almost complete lack of resolution—particularly in the case of Anna, who is, after all, one of the two leading characters in the first part of the film. Little explanation is given for her disappearance, and none at all of what she has done. . . .

We receive information as it is presented to the characters, in the wrong, or rather ''illogical,'' order. Example: we are not actually told until near the end of the film, when she mentions it to Patrizia, that Claudia comes from a poor family. In retrospect one can find sufficient evidence of her social position earlier in the film, but one only realizes its significance after one has been told—Antonioni relies heavily on the audience's power of recollection. (p. 3)

We are shown what the characters see and learn what they learn, but without identifying with them, so that our appreciation of their feelings must be primarily intellectual. We are therefore more conscious than the characters of the meaning of their behavior (as we would not be if we started identifying with them). This places us in a position to correlate our observations of all the characters and reach the general conclusions which Antonioni expects us to draw. (pp. 3, 5)

Why should we condemn [Anna's fiance, Sandro, for pursuing Claudia]? The expected answer is that standard woman's-pic gambit: ''If you don't just *know,* I can't tell you.'' With Antonioni, it's not moral unawareness that prevents him from judging Sandro: his output could be summed up as a critique of society by way of its moral precepts. The complex of reasons underlying the refusal to condemn Sandro is central to the whole of Antonioni's work.

In the first place, judgment implies the acceptance of standards. But what standards? ''We make do with obsolete moral standards, out-of-date myths, old conventions,'' said Antonioni. . . .

The rejection of ''obsolete'' moral standards could mean, as it does for [Roger] Vadim, the substitution of a personal code according to which actions are judged. But Antonioni does not propose a replacement and therefore refrains from judgments. ''I'm not a moralist,'' he insists (and one can only agree on the most superficial level). ''My film is neither a denunciation nor a sermon.''

He would not, I'm sure, allow that he had the right to condemn Sandro's actions, for the implication would be that he was in some way superior to Sandro, an ideal which would hardly appeal to Antonioni who has in his film totally abandoned the ''superannuated casuistry of positives and negatives,'' as Tommaso Chiaretti remarks in his introduction to the published script of *L'Avventura.* Thus ''there are no heroes in Antonioni's films, only protagonists.'' Being himself a product of the milieu which he depicts in his films, Antonioni does not believe that he is qualified to judge his characters. (p. 7)

Sandro's yen for Claudia derives partly from his insecurity: he needs comforting as well as the boost to his ego that would come from her seduction. He finds refuge from his troubles in his over-riding impulse—desire is only part of it—for Claudia. Now Antonioni sees this as a general condition: the world is sexually awry because men have found in a compulsive eroticism some diversion from their problems. ''Why do you think that eroticism has flooded into literature and entertainment? It is a symptom (perhaps the easiest one to perceive) of the emotional sickness of our time . . . man is uneasy . . . so he reacts, but he reacts badly, and is unhappy.''

Antonioni sets out to show us that the sexual urge that has taken hold of Sandro is not something particular and therefore significant only on a personal level. Throughout the film we are presented with sexual behavior that is silly, lewd, or grotesque. . . . [Sex] in Antonioni's eyes has degenerated from a joyful expression of emotion into a gloomy means of escape. . . .

In Antonioni's world, actions are often determined as much by the surroundings as by the people themselves—either in an immediate and physical way by the setting or by conditioning from the environment which tends to limit their choice. At times Claudia and particularly Sandro seem to be activated more by social and environmental forces than by their own decisions. Thus placed outside the area of individual moral judgments, their actions take on a wider significance. . . . Unlike some other directors who attempt to analyze behavior, Antonioni makes his characters retain a human unpredictability. They do not perform actions worked out to be consistent with a thesis. In fact this sort of unreasoned but not gratuitous action is of the greatest importance to Antonioni. ''I wanted to show that sentiments which convention and rhetoric have encouraged us to regard as having a kind of definite weight and absolute duration, can in fact be fragile, vulnerable, subject to change. Man deceives himself when he hasn't courage enough to allow for new dimensions in emotional matters—his loves, regrets, states of mind—just as he allows for them in the field of technology.'' (p. 8)

In *L'Avventura* there are two main elements which provide the environment for the action: the sexual looseness of the secondary characters, and the barrenness and/or solitude of the locations—the island, the deserted village, the train without passengers, and the hotel on the morning after the party. . . .

Throughout the film, the locations and even the climatic conditions play a crucial part in its development. Anna's home, which is glimpsed in the opening sequence, and Sandro's rather precious flat help to characterize them. In addition to its function as a symbol of barrenness, the island location allows us to see the characters separated from the milieu in which they are accustomed to operate. (p. 10)

[The ending of *L'Avventura* is hardly happy]—the fade-out music is discordant and behind [Claudia and Sandro] in the last shot are an expanse of blank wall and mountains covered in snow. But it is easier to find some optimism in it than in any of his other films except perhaps *La Notte*.

Claudia has lost a certain purity of purpose which made the love scenes lyrically exuberant. (In the published script there is a dialogue exchange with Patrizia on the yacht, suggesting that Claudia is a virgin.) At the end she is thrown for the first time into the sort of emotional turmoil which is a commonplace for the others. But having vastly more personality than they, she will recover. She will—as Antonioni has said—not leave Sandro. . . . They will stay together out of ''a mutual sense of pity''—and of shame which Claudia shares as she has contributed to his downfall by abandoning him to his friends. And perhaps with the help of Claudia, Sandro will somehow find the strength to give up his comfortably lucrative job and resume his vocation.

Sandro may not be any less weak than he was previously but at least he has found some feeling of responsibility for the way his actions affect others or, at any rate, Claudia. This has come out of his contact with her. Sandro's irresponsibility, his lapsed vocation and his unsatisfactory love affair at the beginning of the film are all bound up together and related to the weakness of his social environment. I agree with Chiaretti when he says in his introduction to the script, ''*L'Avventura* could not have taken place except in an anaemic milieu like that of the Italian bourgeoisie.''

This, I think, is the core of the film: on a general level, the connection between the condition of a society and its morality; individually the integration of sexual behavior with the rest of the personality—for instance, the relevance of Sandro's emotional life to his work. (p. 15)

[*Cronaca di un amore*] and *La Signora senza camelie* are much darker in feeling than *L'Avventura*—actions never have the hoped-for result, because of people's inability to realize how others—or even they themselves—will react. In every interview he gives, Antonioni talks about the fragility of emotions. The characters in the early films are totally unable to allow for emotional changes, and so all actions calculated to produce a particular result are doomed to failure. It was not until *L'Avventura* that Antonioni could see any way out of this gloomy situation.

The sensitivity to objects and locations that distinguished *L'Avventura* is already to be found in *Cronaca*. Antonioni has said, ''I have a great feeling for things, perhaps more than for people, although the latter interest me more.'' He is able to use his feeling for things to aid him in describing the action which is psychological rather than physical, internal rather than external. It is often not obvious from what the characters are doing, but must be suggested through the way they are shown. Antonioni had realized that the human face is a rather inexpressive object when isolated from its surroundings in a close-up. He used no big close-ups at all. Instead he paid particular attention to the relationship of the characters with their setting. The insolubility of Paola's problem in *Cronaca* is demonstrated through her unease in Guido's room, which, by the meanness of its furnishings, represents his social class and the level of poverty to which she would have to descend if she went away with him. (pp. 16-17)

*La Signora senza camelie* is complementary to *Cronaca* in form/ content. . . . *Cronaca* is almost an exposition of the Antonioni view of class barriers. Paola and Guido are separated because Paola has crossed the barrier into a higher class and cannot return, while Guido is finally unable to cross. *Signora* builds on the essentials that have been demonstrated in *Cronaca* to show the disastrous effects of the *status quo* on one character, Clara, who, having irrevocably left her original milieu, finds that she is unfitted for survival in the class to which she aspires. Through their form, both plot and treatment, the two films are founded on Antonioni's deeply held belief in the wrongness of a class-based society. He is out to make a fundamental critique of the system rather than to make a superficial attack on the resulting evils. (p. 20)

[*Le Amiche*] has elements of both the earlier and later films. It combines the pessimism of the early ones (Rosetta) with the glimmers of hope which appear later. It is more comprehensive than any of the others in treating the usual subject matter from three angles. Of the three stories, the only one which progresses smoothly is the one which obeys the corrupt conventions of the society in which it takes place. In Momina, we have the most complete expression of Antonioni's hate of the system.

The only leading character in his films who has successfully adjusted to the system, she is also the only one who is utterly detestable (to Clelia and the audience, though not perhaps to Antonioni). (p. 31)

*Le Amiche* is the transition film between the early and late periods in another way: in its structure. Through successive films up to *Il Grido,* there is a reduction in plot and its gradual replacement with a different sort of structure, which is common to the last three films. *Cronaca* is the only one which has a plot in which the external action can be summarized briefly. The minor characters always have a functional place in the plot. *Signora* reduces the neat dovetailing of plot. Instead the film follows a character through a progression of events which lead him or her to a different position at the end. Paola in *Cronaca* had not been changed at all by what happened to her in the film. *Le Amiche* has forsaken plot completely for an interlocking pattern of incidents which is so complex that it is impossible to pick out a story line. All the characters have a significance more important than their contribution to the action. Two, Cesare and Mariella, have no essential effect on what happens to Clelia or to Rosetta. This is a forerunner of the situation in *L'Avventura* where all the minor characters are significant as an environment for the main action, although they hardly take part in it.

With the plot construction has disappeared the irony which is something essentially derived from the plot. In its final appearance in *Le Amiche* it has become rather attenuated compared to the earlier films where it was the main theme. Consequently the feeling of futility has disappeared. Its presence in the early films reflected the mood of much of serious Italian cinema at the start of the 'fifties. With the removal of the one thing which linked him with his contemporaries, Antonioni parted company completely with the rest of the Italian cinema. (pp. 31-2)

The defects of *Il Grido (The Outcry)* get in its way very badly, especially on first viewing. Like *Signora* and *I Vinti* and even *La Notte,* it has a seriously flawed surface.

To begin with, Antonioni has gone outside his usual little world again, and failed again in making his characters convincing. In this he is an extremely limited director. It's said that he made a very thorough study of conditions in the Po Valley before starting on *Il Grido.* Certainly that's what it looks like: very accurate but external and lacking life, this in spite of the fact that he spent his childhood there. And if he aimed to deal with immediate social problems, he ended by making a film with slighter social implications than any of the others. . . .

*Il Grido* has an atmosphere which is pursued relentlessly and humorlessly throughout the film: it's not tragic, just ever so glum. And the glumness is reinforced by the surroundings—the Po Valley in winter, all bare and muddy. The sameness of the landscape throughout the film reflects the hero's inability to forget. "The completely open horizon counterpoints the psychology of the central character," as Antonioni has said. But after a couple of hours one finds oneself adding, "Who cares?" (p. 32)

The personal/political linkage which is intended between the destruction of Aldo and the destruction of Goriano's whole way of life seems terribly forced, partly perhaps because the film and its hero have become such a bore that we have lost sympathy. . . .

[There are two main reasons for the difference between *L'Avventura* and its predecessors:] one personal, one technical.

The personal reason is the appearance of hope in Antonioni's picture of the world. Although he had already lost the obsession with futility which pervades the early films, in *Il Grido* he is more consistently gloomy than in any of the others. At least Paola and Clara and Rosetta had some good times before things went wrong. In *Il Grido* these are all over before the picture starts. At the end of *L'Avventura* there is hope: that Claudia and Sandro will stay together, and that Sandro will, after his moment of truth, be able to work up the strength necessary to drop his degrading but lucrative work for Ettore and practice again as an architect. (p. 34)

*La Notte* is an attempt to go beyond what was achieved in *L'Avventura.* In fact, I don't think that anyone who hasn't seen *L'Avventura* has much chance of understanding it. . . .

[The first scene of *La Notte*] contains in outline most of the themes that are developed later in the film. The place of the artist in modern society. The crisis in Giovanni's career and in Lidia's marriage with him. The corruption of the benefits of life in a scientific age when they are placed at the service of a capitalist society. Champagne for the dying rich, beautiful nurses to keep up their morale. These images suggest a dying society and culture which are being kept alive artificially. (p. 35)

[The combination of bleakness and hope at the end of *La Notte*] is that of *L'Avventura.*

Although the couple have escaped from the corrupt milieu of the Gherardini house, the conclusion is a compromise. Lidia only lets Giovanni make love to her because she hasn't the will to resist: she can't see any other hope for them. But the fact that Giovanni makes love to her indicates a desire on his part to maintain their relationship. . . . In one way it is a more hopeful film than *L'Avventura* because it insists on the certainty of social as well as emotional change, and because this time the couple are helped by another character—Valentina. This is the first time in any Antonioni film that we are shown one person able to help others. In the earliest films, such attempts are automatically doomed. Here admittedly, she does not help them by a conscious action, but merely by her existence. Valentina herself is essentially a hopeful character—in spite of her unhappiness—as she is evidence that individuals can overcome the influences on them from a corrupt society. . . .

*L'Eclisse* can be viewed as the third part of a loosely connected trilogy on personal relationships in postwar society. It is concerned with the same themes as its two predecessors, but it is as a partial reversal of them that it is the completion of the trilogy. Not that it is the opposite of them in the way that *L'Avventura* is the opposite of *Il Grido.* There the contrast was between the leading characters: a simple man who could not lose the memory of his past life and a sophisticated man who finds it only too easy to forget. In *L'Eclisse* the social level and the problems of the characters are very similar to those in *L'Avventura* and *La Notte,* but their choices are the reverse. It is this opposition which links the film to its predecessors—just as *Il Grido* and *L'Avventura* are connected by the contrast between them. (p. 45)

In the previous two films, a large part was played by money as a corrupting force. Sandro in *L'Avventura* has abandoned his vocation for the easy money he can make by estimating for a successful architect, Ettore. Gherardini in *La Notte* is a man whose only noticeable characteristic is his wealth. A measure of Lidia's desperation at the end of that film is her comment that Gherardini's offer of a job for Giovanni is a good opportunity. Whatever salvation the two couples achieve in these films it is partly due to their final escapes from the world of Ettore and Gherardini.

This aspect appears more strongly in *L'Eclisse* where there is a direct conflict between feelings and money, without the complicating factor of artistic vocations. (p. 47)

The feeling of the final sequence, though, is much stronger than [a feeling of sadness that Piero and Vittoria are about to break up]. At a first viewing I was quite terrified by the ending of *L'Eclisse,* much more than by most things which are calculated to terrify. I think this comes from the coldness which builds up during the sequence as night falls. The feeling is one of solitude—even the shots of people are of people alone. Antonioni said that at the end of *L'Avventura* the protagonists had arrived at a mutual sense of pity. "What else is left if we do not at least succeed in achieving this?" Piero and Vittoria have failed to establish a relationship. Although they are fond of each other and physically attracted, their outlooks on life are so different that they cannot find any real understanding. And what is left? Solitude.

The other thing that makes this conclusion frightening is its lack of specificity. The shots could be of the evening after their last meeting in Ercoli's office, when they fail to turn up for their date, but it could equally be any other evening. We are invited to generalize, to conclude with Antonioni that solitude is man's usual state. Although the invitation has never been so clear as in the conclusion of *L'Eclisse,* we are expected to do so in all three films, to relate the actions not just to the characters themselves, but to put them in their social, political and temporal context. All the small external references in the films point the way to this—diverse examples: unemployment, a rock number, a revolutionary design of motor yacht (*L'Avventura*), socialism, the replanning of cities, industrial relations (*La Notte),* the Twist, the color problem, the bomb (*L'Eclisse).* Very closely tied to the time at which they were made, the films are in no way didactic, that is, they do not set out to make a comment, but only to present the director's view of the world.

This view is consistent throughout the last three pictures. The appearance of *L'Eclisse* would seem to make superfluous discussions of whether the ending of *La Notte* is more or less optimistic than the ending of *L'Avventura,* and indeed whether either is optimistic at all. We see from the contrasting example of Piero and Vittoria that although it is possible to generalize from the problems which face the characters in all the films, the resolutions are specific and depend on the individual psychology of each of the couples. The picture of life and personal relationships in the second half of the twentieth century is too complex to allow a glib summing-up of Antonioni's outlook. The meaning of over six hours of film can hardly be compressed into a few sentences of conclusion. But finally the value of Antonioni lies less in the generalities than in the observation and the manner of presenting behavior. His triumph is the maintenance of spontaneity in the face of the most intricate calculation in the *mise-en-scene.*

The form of the "trilogy" comes from the parallel between the first two films, particularly in their endings which are countered by *L'Eclisse.* The first two end at dawn with a renewal of a relationship which had been partly destroyed during the previous night. *L'Eclisse* starts at dawn with the breaking of a relationship: Vittoria leaves Riccardo's apartment alone, whereas the other couples escape together from the place where they have spent the night. The dawn symbolizes self-knowledge

and a fresh beginning. At the end of *L'Eclisse,* Piero remains in Ercoli's office which is an image of capitalism, like the hotel in *L'Avventura* and Gherardini's house in *La Notte.* Vittoria leaves alone again. Consistent with the symbolism of the previous films, *L'Eclisse* ends with the coming of night. The last sequence of Antonioni's trilogy of change centers on the image of progress which was already to be seen in the opening sequence of its first film: a building site. (pp. 54-5)

*Ian Cameron, "Michelangelo Antonioni: A Study by Ian Cameron," in* Film Quarterly *(copyright 1962 by The Regents of the University of California; reprinted by permission of the University of California Press), Vol. 16, No. 1, Fall, 1962, pp. 2-56.*

## PENELOPE HOUSTON

[*The Eclipse*] begins, as *L'Avventura* and *La Notte* ended, at dawn. Outside the window a water-tower looms like some futuristic mushroom; inside, a man sits rigid in a chair, inertia containing anger, while a girl restlessly circles the room. The affair is over; they have talked themselves to a standstill; and this time neither can pick up the shattered pieces. It is, unmistakably and in every detail, an Antonioni sequence. . . . Intellectually, one is aware of what Antonioni is doing and why he has chosen to do it in this dehumanising way. But at the same time, in its deliberate echoing of the more sombre moods of *La Notte,* the scene pushes style towards the thin edge of mannerism. . . .

Far from being a return journey over ground already covered, it takes Antonioni out into new areas, covers a wider range than perhaps any of his films since *Le Amiche* has attempted. The continuity is one of feeling, never of plot, and the second affair, which contains whatever of plot the film has to offer, only begins when the nature of the heroine has been fully exposed. . . .

[Changes] between script and screen show Antonioni refining down his conception, giving the film over during its making to a mood which is also an expression of his heroine. What Vittoria is looking for she hardly knows—and her refrain of "I don't know" becomes an accompaniment to both affairs. Her intellectual fiancé, Riccardo, has worn her out; her relationship with Piero . . . will founder on incompatibility. Piero is a new character for Antonioni, in that about him hang the clouds neither of failure nor of intellectual effort. (p. 90)

[It is the entry] into Piero's world . . . which gives *The Eclipse* its extra dimension. The two long stock exchange sequences are not merely brilliantly manoeuvred set-pieces, but confrontations for Vittoria. The Antonioni heroine runs the risk of seeming too self-absorbed, too solitary, too devitalised by her own sensitivity. Here, on the floor of the stock exchange, she encounters a world with other ideas of happiness than the song of the wind in the railings; and it is from her reaching out towards that harder world—towards what it has to offer of confidence, know-how, assertive vitality—that the film acquires its range of references. (pp. 90-1)

Here, more even than in *L'Avventura* or *La Notte,* Antonioni uses the books on people's tables, the paintings and photographs on their walls, not merely as short-cuts to describe character but as extensions of personality. This incessant concern with objects, with the furniture of living, the cathedral pillars of the stock exchange, the window flung open upon a water-tower or a church, is integral to his whole way of looking at life. People are not only what they are, but what they live with. Vittoria has escaped from her mother's home to her own flat in a suburb so aggressively modern that it looks like some ground plan for next year's Ideal Home Exhibition, and her new environment has become part of her.

People are so obsessed by the idea of gloom hanging like a thundercloud over Antonioni's films that they can contrive to make *all* his settings sound depressing. (One critic even described the building on the street corner as 'derelict', whereas it is quite clearly, and in the context inevitably, under construction.) For the director himself this is obviously a world in the process of being built; and there is no indication that he is less than fascinated by it, that he would contemplate with pleasure an existence stripped of plate-glass and concrete. The pull is never back from the "soulless" present towards a kindlier past, and Antonioni is the least nostalgic of filmmakers. Yet the fears that overshadow this world—in the newspaper headlines, in the Kenyan girl's forecast of African uprisings, in the mother's propitiatory offering of salt to the gods of the market—combine the elements of primitive threat and nuclear terror. The final sequence of *The Eclipse,* that much-discussed abstract succession of shots after the film's characters have left the screen, sums up these intimations of mortality. . . .

[In] this film, everything is a matter of context. It is the force of association which makes these images of a suburban street corner, on a summer evening, come as an echo from the end of the world; as it is the juxtaposition of the mechanics of the stock exchange with an alertness to the tiny details of personality which gives the scenes their density. A man who has suffered a crushing loss on the market sits at a café table in the sunshine gravely doodling flowers on a scrap of paper. Vittoria's mother, who has just made a neat profit, haggles over the price of a kilo of pears. A cheerful drunk, sauntering down a night street, is next seen as a dead hand behind the shattered windscreen of a waterlogged car. "There are days when a chair, a table, a book, a man seem much the same . . .'' Beneath the cool, clean physical landscape of the Roman suburb lies the disordered landscape of the emotions. Antonioni's style has always been founded on a juxtaposition of people and places. In *The Eclipse,* however, juxtaposition has become fusion: the two landscapes are made one, the visual imagery and the mental imagery effortlessly interlock. (p. 91)

*Penelope Houston, "Film Reviews: 'The Eclipse',"* in Sight and Sound *(copyright © 1963 by The British Film Institute), Vol. 32, No. 2, Spring, 1963, pp. 90-1.*

## PETER COWIE

One of the most fascinating aspects of *Cronaca di un amore* is its objective study of the clash of social standards. The glossy bars, the elegance of Paola's clothes, and the luxury of Fontana's home . . . are contrasted expertly with the dingy hotels where Paola and Guido (who has "degenerated" into a car salesman since their first affair) are compelled to meet. . . . The closing images of the film, as Paola stands weeping in a deserted street at night, her opulent evening dress splashed with mud, summarise this contrast. There is in Paola a fundamental fear of poverty and squalor. (pp. 9-10)

Technically, this first feature provides a foretaste of the methods Antonioni uses in his more mature work. Long takes & elaborate panning shots are prolific, and the scene on the bridge, when Paola and her lover nervously decide on the murder of Fontana, runs for almost four minutes. The tension and evasion

that are the film's overtones are subtly explored by Antonioni's groupings. For example, as the lovers wait for Fontana so that they can kill him, one sees Paola looking fixedly towards the lower right-hand corner of the frame, while Guido is viewed slightly from above with his back to Paola. The angle of the shot serves to lengthen the woman's stare and to stress the mental strain of the situation. (p. 10)

Apart from certain individual scenes, however, *Cronaca di un amore* remains very much an apprentice work, clearly indicative of the potentialities of its director (yet they were scarcely noticed at the time). Michel Mayoux' contemporary verdict [in *Cahiers du Cinéma*] has endured well: "Oscillating between the Latin worship of plastic beauty . . . and the search for a personal style *Cronaca di un amore,* an imperfect work on both levels, finds its equilibrium and its meaning in another dimension, that of an exasperated eroticism". . . . (p. 11)

Gradually Antonioni's *mise-en-scène* is becoming more precise and meaningful. He has devoted a great deal of attention [in *La signora senza, camelie*] to the physical background of the film (weak in *Le amiche* but impressive again in *Il grido*, and the cold wintry landscape impinges on the actions and attitudes of the characters themselves. The narrative flow is markedly smooth compared with the perfunctory episode in *L'amore in citta,* and the number of shots is exceedingly small compared with *I vinti.* As in *Cronaca di un amore*, the symbols of class distinction are legion—Clara's lavish fur coat, like the fur coverlet on her bed in the earlier film, the paintings in her room, the plethora of bouquets.

The more immediate background of the film is that of the Italian cinema. It is not a colourless, vaguely self-satisfied industry like the cinema shown in [Luchino] Visconti's *Bellissima,* but an industry that runs to aesthetic and commercial extremes. On the one one side there is the amoral, tawdry world of Cinécittà before it usurped Hollywood as the centre of world production, with its derelict sets, its sagging tents, its bedraggled, peeling buildings, and its miserable extras. On the other side there is the smart entourage of the international Festival with its attendant producers who have their tame intellectuals and a tight grip on their money. For Clara Manni, the distance between these groups is immense. Throughout the film one hears the expression *sbagliare* (to make a mistake), and it is symptomatic of Clara's inability to choose her own path in life. She is indeed a *Woman without a Destiny*—the title of one of her own films, ironically a commercial success. (pp. 14-15)

[*Le amiche*] provides a perfect bridge between Antonioni's early works and the trio of superb films that begins with *L'avventura* (*Il grido* seems almost out of place and but for its excellent craftsmanship might have been made after *Gente del Po*). The interest in the relationship of the social classes in Italy is still very much to the fore. The sophisticated but frivolous world of *le amiche* is accentuated by the presence of Clelia, who like Claudia in *L'avventura* is really an outsider. One of the ironies of the film is that her own class-consciousness ruins what promises to be the love affair of her life. Nobody, Antonioni seems to be saying, is free from class prejudice in modern society and in this respect this, with *La notte* and *Cronaca di un amore*, is one of his most Marxist films. The relentless quality of his scrutiny is stressed by the camera movements. In the earlier films, he tended to devote most of his attention to the composition of individual images. With *Le amiche,* however, he introduces his now familiar method of panning and tracking with the characters in order to catch their slightest reaction. (pp. 16-17)

One of the subtleties of *Le amiche* is that while the fracas in the fashion salon shows Momina as the one responsible for Rosetta's suicide, the implication that arises from Antonioni's handling of the script is that Lorenzo's weakness is to blame. The women are, as usual in Antonioni's work, superior creatures to the men—Nenè has more artistic talent than Lorenzo, Momina is more sophisticated than Cesare, her architect lover, and Clelia is more cultured than her Carlo.

Closely allied to this feeling of depression in Lorenzo is an air of alienation that pervades all the other characters. It is the harbinger of the hopeless encounters of *Il grido*. None of the women in *Le amiche* can communicate their feelings adequately; moreover, they are highly inhibited. Rosetta dies because she can convey her thoughts only to Clelia, and Clelia is an outsider. Even her happy conversation with Lorenzo by the river cannot explain articulately the motives for her first attempt at suicide. The chatter in the salon and in Momina's apartment is grotesquely superficial, like that at the party in *La notte*. Yet this frustration does not become unbearable, for Antonioni tempers it with elegance—the paintings of Lorenzo, the pottery of Nenè, the exquisite gowns of Clelia's collection, the melancholy beauty of the beach sequence. (pp. 17-18)

The technical link with Antonioni's later films lies in the power and economy of the imagery itself. The earlier films often shifted helplessly into long dialogue scenes when an emotional predicament had to be analysed. In *Le amiche*, words are used sparingly. Key scenes such as Rosetta's suicide and the famous party on the beach, are treated with the utmost economy. The girl's death is shown in two austere shots only—one from above, one from the river, of her body being recovered—immediately after her final break with Lorenzo in the deserted streets of Turin.

The merit of *Le amiche* is that it signifies Antonioni's break with conventions. Hitherto he has been a competent, meticulous illustrator of themes that might be found in the work of other Italian and French directors. But in *Le amiche* the plot is sacrificed to the style, a style that is not just formally attractive and supple, but one which respects the duration of real time on the screen and which attempts to catch the reflection of the characters' inner thoughts and feelings without forcing them to explain themselves to the audience through intellectual conversation. No episode is more symptomatic of this method than the excursion to the beach by Clelia and her companions. Separated from the luxurious surroundings to which they are accustomed, the characters become strangely deprived of their gloss; like the miserable layabouts in Fellini's *I vitelloni*, they are stirred by the solitude and coldness of the seashore to become aware of things they might otherwise ignore. Rosetta, for instance, is deeply hurt by a conversation she overhears in which Momina is implying that Lorenzo is returning to the arms of Nenè. . . . (pp. 18-19)

Yet *Le amiche* remains to some extent a flawed film, because in it Antonioni has tried to study no less than eight people in depth. . . . The diffuse nature of the plot prevents Antonioni from concentrating his attention on any one of the friends. He would be far more penetrating in his analysis of this society if he confined himself to one or two people. It is this major advance that Antonioni is to make in *L'avventura* and his subsequent films. . . .

Antonioni has always been a student of the couple; in *Il grido* he studies four such relationships and if the film is short of a masterpiece it is not due to the technique or the construction

but to the fact that two of these liaisons are fragmentary and without depth. The film is nonetheless given a hard spine, lacking in *Le amiche*, by the continuous presence of the man. (p. 19)

The form of *Il grido* is particularly interesting and, with its gloomy, picaresque background, not unlike Bergman's *Sawdust and Tinsel* (where for Albert, a life of resignation at the end is perhaps even more dreadful than the suicide of Aldo). It proceeds to trace the decline of a man, analysing his movements sympathetically but relentlessly. Fusco's piano refrain remains throughout indicative of this simple form as well as being the plaintive expression of a man in search of his own melancholy truth.

In the manner of many of Antonioni's men, Aldo is discontented. Each of the women he lives with offers him something, not without effort, not without tears. Yet he grows impatient with them all. Irma has evidently satisfied him for seven years and it is only when the crisis occurs at the start of the film that he perceives his ignorance of her real feelings. (p. 20)

The second woman in *Il grido*, Elvia . . . is more "respectable" than Irma, and more conventionally romantic. . . .

Elvia is the most attractive personality in the film and Antonioni obviously intends to show that she would make anyone but Aldo a perfect wife. She acts like an affectionate mother towards Rosina and is completely unaware that her sister's eyes have been on Aldo from the start—significantly she gives the ribbons Aldo buys for *her* in the "Miss Popularity" contest to her sister. Yet, like so many inhabitants of the Antonionian and Bergmanian worlds, she reveals her essential selfishness by complaining to Aldo that he had not bothered about her sufficiently during the years of their separation. (p. 21)

Alain Resnais has commented, "In Antonioni's *Il grido* where the main character ends by committing suicide, the very intensity of the suffering bears witness to the grandeur of Man". Aldo has emerged ultimately and paradoxically as a strong character, unwilling to compromise with his life. He has done better, Antonioni seems to be saying, in having sought and not found his "peace of mind" than he would have done had he abandoned the struggle earlier. . . .

Antonioni's technique is still not quite as masterly as it is in *L'avventura*. The misty atmosphere of the Pro Valley is certainly well grasped and Antonioni has himself remarked that "the empty landscape counterpoints the psychology of the leading character in the film". . . . (p. 23)

The symbolism is also somewhat pedestrian, particularly at the end, with Irma separated from Aldo by the familiar barred window and then by the wire fence surrounding the refinery. The demonstration by the townsfolk against the appropriation of land for a jet airbase seems incongruous, too, unless the bulldozers, poised to destroy the flimsy houses, symbolise the impending destruction of Aldo's life. More probably though, it represents a further attempt by Antonioni to stress the change in landscape and fashions. Similar allusions, though none so heavy handed, are scattered throughout the film. . . . All these incidents subtly suggest the vain struggles of the old to keep up with the new, just as Antonioni's films as a whole outline the failure of anachronistic morals and sentiments to keep pace with advances in other spheres of life. But in a sense they are reminiscent of the worse faults of *I vinti* and some of the documentaries, and it is only in *Le amiche*, *L'avventura* and subsequently that Antonioni has found a successful way of dovetailing his social comments into the fabric of the film. For all that, *Il grido* is an exceptionally good film, uncompromising in the formal rigour of its construction and astonishing in its grasp of a spiritual malaise. (pp. 23-4)

Certainly *L'avventura* is Antonioni's most important work, for prior to it he had been fumbling his way slowly but surely towards a mode of expression hitherto unknown in the cinema, and he has succeeded since in perfecting that expression at the same time as making it less exciting, less fresh. It is a film like [Resnais's] *Hiroshima Mon Amour* in which every shot is meticulously composed and designed to establish a mood, a mood of anticipation in which love can shrivel or grow. (pp. 24-5)

When [Claudia and Sandro] travel across Sicily, they are in search less of Anna than of themselves and of their emotions.

In all Antonioni's major works, such a crisis occurs at an early stage. . . . All these films, too, are about discovery—discovery of an emotional predicament that encircles the characters until they are stifled by it and have to do something hideous and drastic to escape. (pp. 25-6)

There remains the eternal question of why Claudia should be attracted by such a worthless character. Paradoxically, it is thus the weakness of Claudia rather than the weakness of Sandro that makes *L'avventura* such a fascinating film. (pp. 28-9)

Antonioni's primary contribution to the cinema has been his ability to convey thoughts without having recourse to unrealistic and verbose dialogue. "I think it is much more cinematic to try to grasp the thoughts of a character by showing their reactions such as they are, rather than conveying all that in a reply, having to resort practically to an explanation". . . . Yet the method has its limitations, for it exposes ruthlessly the vacuity of so many of the film's characters. Corrado and Giulia, Raimondo and Patrizia, Ettore and Anna's father, are no more than sketches of their types (the lecherous young artist is almost a caricature), who struggle pathetically to occupy the hours "between the last coffee and the first aperitif". (p. 32)

*La notte* is undoubtedly the most desolate of Antonioni's works to date. Visually it is incredibly satisfying; emotionally it is sterile but realistic. (p. 33)

All the characters (except for the brusque, mundane industrialist) are enmeshed by their own indolence. None of them is as immortal a creation as the Claudia of *L'avventura*. Only Tommaso, whose shadow falls across the entire film, seems to have been of real worth. Yet he too is exhausted, devoured by a physical malaise as Lidia and Giovanni are devoured by a spiritual one. "My life has been more shadow than substance" he admits in the hospital.

The importance of *La notte* lies not in its protagonists, but in the attitudes to modern life that it discloses. It shows the death of love with uncompromising rigour (although the melodramatics of *Cronaca di un amore* are no longer required by a director now so assured of his craft), and it hints strongly too that the *haute bourgeoisie* in Italy (as, presumably, elsewhere) is gradually apprehending its moral bankruptcy. The freedom from work leaves them with little to do except brood and erode emotionally. It is this disquieting situation that Antonioni crystallises in *La notte* with more insight than in *Le amiche* and with less sympathy than in *L'avventura*. (p. 39)

It was clear when *La notte* appeared that Antonioni's next film would be crucial in his progress. Many believed that he could produce nothing more than a repetition of the pitiless view of the world that dominated *La notte*. Yet *L'eclisse* signifies a remarkable development and extension of Antonioni's talent. The literary, elongated dialogue that threatens to paralyse so many of his earlier films has been replaced with an almost wholly successful language of images (significantly, the first and the last seven minutes of *L'eclisse* are practically bereft of conversation). (pp. 39-40)

[The montage at the end of *L'eclisse*] seems to epitomise the conclusions to be drawn from Antonioni's films as a whole. It suggests an anguished philosophy, one which was intolerable for a man like Pavese. Obviously Antonioni too would commit suicide if he really felt the sentiments he portrays. He is, rather, an objective observer, frighteningly certain of the future. Indeed, what hope is there in a world where love is so easily betrayed and principles so idly ignored? It is to the credit of *L'eclisse* that, although much of it borders on the abstract, such a conviction should pervade it so strongly. Metaphysically, the title obviously implies that as far as sentiments are concerned, our epoch corresponds to an eclipse. And, for Antonioni, the bourgeois that he shows to be so smug and the intellectuals that he shows to be so nihilistic are alike condemned.

Antonioni has pared his instruments down to a degree of sharpness and lucidity rarely found in the cinema. Often enough there are moments of superb composition that seem unnecessary to the film, but *L'eclisse* contains far less expendable material than any of its predecessors. . . . Never has he succeeded so well in delineating the uselessness and fragility of love in modern society. *L'avventura* may be more humane, more hopeful, more naturalistic, but *L'eclisse* is at once the most elegant and pitiless film Antonioni has made. (pp. 45-6)

It is obvious that for Antonioni, as for Bergman, the cinema is a vital means of expression. This accounts in some measure for the lack of compromise in even his humblest films, and for the absolute grasp of the nuances in his various characters. The feelings that disturb these characters are frequently more interesting than they are themselves. Thus Antonioni has brought to the screen the psychological approach normally reserved for the novel, and yet *L'eclisse* seems to hint more strongly than any of his other films that Antonioni is far from being a novelist *manqué* and is definitely willing, if a clash is inevitable, to sacrifice dialogue to imagery. (pp. 46-7)

This profound emphasis on characterisation is not the only revolutionary aspect of Antonioni's work. Someone called him "the eternal experimental director", and his attention to technique is meticulous.

But undoubtedly the distinctive flavour of Antonioni's films lies in their ruthless dissection of the characters' emotions, and their tacit ridicule of the pretensions of a moribund society. His opulent apartments, yachts and gardens are filled with a lugubrious air, and as Derek Hill has written [in *London Magazine*], "in all his films virtually every scene has the sad nostalgia of an act performed for the last time, as if the world had been condemned to die the next day". . . . The failure or lack of love is the common denominator to his films, and if he seems unduly preoccupied with eroticism it is because he shares the views of his compatriot and admirer Alberto Moravia, who has said, "My interest in sex depends on sex being a way of relating with reality. It is one of the main ways of getting into touch with another person, one of our best means of connection''. Morality has vanished from the world that Antonioni reveals. . . . In this respect Antonioni takes his position as a contemporary matriarch, for he is desperately concerned with the future as opposed to the fossilised past. (pp. 48-9)

> Peter Cowie, ''Michelangelo Antonioni,'' in his An-
> tonioni, Bergman, Resnais *(copyright © 1963 by Pe-
> ter Cowie), The Tantivy Press, London, 1963, Barnes
> & Co., Inc., New York, 1963, pp. 5-49.*

## GEOFFREY NOWELL-SMITH

Empiricism has always been the agnostic's epistemology, and Antonioni is a radical agnostic. In his films there is never any certainty, any definite or absolute truth. The meaning of single events is often ambiguous, and cumulatively these events add up to a picture of a world from which order, value and logic have disappeared. This should not be taken in too metaphysical a sense. The characters in Antonioni films do not go around, like the followers of Sartre or [Maurice] Merleau-Ponty, earnestly trying to put back the essences into existence. They are simply faced with the business of living in a world which offers of itself no certainty and no security, at least not in the immediate present. And when a character does seem to have assured himself somehow, through his job or through his relationship with another person, his security is probably (though not necessarily: again Antonioni is not Sartre) an illusion, for which he will have to pay before long.

This sense of fundamental insecurity which affects the more lucid of Antonioni's characters (the stupid ones are generally more or less immune, and probably happier as a result) is no doubt largely subjective. Their particular existentialist inferno is very much of their own making. But in a less acute form the same general malaise can be seen to affect the whole of society, and to be reflected in the physical environment which modern man has created for himself and in which he has chosen to live. The deserted village in *L'Avventura* is a perfect example. Visually it recalls instantly the vacant surfaces and deranged perspectives of [Giorgio de] Chirico's *Pittura metafisica,* and it means much the same thing. This civic townscape, devoid of citizens, dehumanised and absurd, in which two people come together and make love, acts in a sense as a symbol, or a parable, for the whole of modern life. Man, it seems to say, has built himself his own world, but he is incapable of living in it. He is excluded from his own creation, and his only refuge lies in fortuitous encounters with another being in the same predicament. In a word, he is ''alienated'' (p. 17)

The question is primarily one of emphasis. By insisting that each of his films begins with a story, particular people in a particular situation, Antonioni is asking the critic to look more at the particulars and less at the sublime but depressing generalities they supposedly reflect. The point is well taken. Except for *La Notte,* which still seems to me a deeply pessimistic film, and rather dogmatic in its pessimism into the bargain, none of Antonioni's work is ever so arid, or so alienating, as a conventional analysis of his ideas might suggest. In each of his films there is a positive pole and a negative, and a tension between them. The abstraction, the ''ideology'', lies mostly at the negative pole. The concrete and actual evidence, the life of the film, is more often positive—and more often neglected by criticism.

As with all Antonioni's later films, the story of *The Eclipse* [*L'Eclisse*] is cast in the form of a sort of spiritual journey towards, ideally, self-discovery and the discovery of the world. The discovery may not be consummated; indeed the journey may end, as with *Il Grido* and perhaps *La Notte,* only in destruction. (pp. 17-18)

In Antonioni's intention *The Eclipse* is a positive film, and if this comes across in effect it is because Vittoria herself is so positive. She is bright, she is honest, she is ravishingly beautiful, she is unquenchably alive, she is even (shock to the critics) happy, or capable of being so. She is also, sometimes, rather tiresome, but that is by the way. The important thing is that in a situation where at times everything seems to conspire to destroy her and all that she stands for, she survives—at least until the next round. The search will go on, and it will have been worth while.

To say that *The Eclipse* is a film about alienation, therefore, is largely to miss the point. The film is not about alienation, it is about Vittoria. If in the course of the film the spectator is moved to feel, or rather to think, that Vittoria is in fact alienated, that she has an alienated relationship with an alienated world, this is a different matter entirely. But even on this relatively concrete level the word remains a blanket concept, and a wide one, in danger of stifling whatever lies underneath. Throughout the trilogy, and even in the earlier films, there are sequences and shots which reflect a consistent view of the world and of the human situation from which alienation, or some related concept, could be isolated as a key factor. Such, for example, is the Stock Exchange sequence in *The Eclipse.* Vittoria here is seen as an outsider, a looker-in on a world which has a dynamic of its own, which she cannot share in or even understand. Watching the curious spectacle of finance in action she is both alienated from it and conscious of her alienation. But is it Vittoria here who is alienated, or is it not rather the Exchange and the whole financial game itself—alienated in that its players live in a neurotic world in which scraps of paper have taken the place of the sound material values they are supposed to represent? Either way there is a lack of essential *rapport.* As in the deserted village sequence, there is something about this world that refused to make sense. Both sequences function artistically by generating an impression of strangeness, lack of connection, and out of the strangeness comes the idea that the world is more than strange: estranged in fact—for which alienated is a synonym. (p. 18)

As should be clear from his films, Antonioni's main concern as an artist is with things and with people, with shapes, light and shade, social facts and human thoughts and emotions. He is not concerned, as far as I can see, with any apparatus of concepts and symbols. His films cannot be fitted easily into any pre-cast conceptual mould, and his way of expressing his ideas is generally speaking direct and literal, and does not require symbols or symbolic interpretations to achieve significance. Each action, each visual detail, has its place in a particular plot. The recurrence of some of these details and of certain themes may suggest that they are meant to have a general as well as a particular validity. This is only reasonable: Antonioni is a very consistent and consistently thoughtful director. But it is not possible to isolate details from their immediate context and attribute to them the value of universal symbols. (p. 19)

[Despite] the air of finality given to the images [at the end of *The Eclipse*], we don't really know that this is the end at all. It may not even be the end for Piero and Vittoria as a couple; it is certainly not the end of the world. As Antonioni himself has put it (I quote from memory), this is an eclipse not the millenium, and "up to now no eclipse has yet been definitive." One should not forget either that a highly selective and elliptical montage such as Antonioni uses in this sequence is one of the most subjective of all cinema techniques. Uniquely in this sequence he is offering a purely lyrical (and for that reason not literal, but not symbolic either) interpretation of the events shown. His camera here is the voice of a lyric poet who draws on real material but fuses it together in a purely imaginative way in order to envisage subjectively a purely imaginative possibility—that the light should have gone out on the love between Piero and Vittoria. The idea of indeterminacy, axiomatic in Antonioni's work, insists that we admit theoretically an alternative possibility, and that further events may yet falsify the picture we have built up of what is happening. At any instant we have only the moment to go on in provisionally interpreting the events, and at this moment it seems to be the end. It feels like the end, and that is what Antonioni is really trying to say.

This final sequence of *The Eclipse* is unique in Antonioni's work in that it does to a certain limited extent rely on symbols for effect, and in that he does seem for the first time to want to break away from the Flaubertian realism which is his normal vein into a more imaginative and lyrical style. This breakaway is in fact foreshadowed in parts of *La Notte,* in particular in the long, disturbing sequence of Lidia's solitary walk around Milan. But even in *The Eclipse,* except at the end, what I would call the Flaubertian note remains dominant—the note of the painstaking and accurate stylist, the careful investigator of behaviour and environment, the ruthless analyst of sentimental and intellectual failure, the essential realist. Antonioni's realism is not naturalism or *verismo.* It is too finely wrought, pared down too sharply to the essentials of what has to be said. It is also too interior, as much concerned to chart the movements of the mind, however objectively regarded, as it is to observe physical emotions and things. But—and this is why Antonioni, like Flaubert, remains basically a realist—movements below the surface are generally left to be deduced from surface reactions. They are not artificially exteriorised in terms of convenient symbols, as in expressionism, nor are they supposed to inhabit a metaphysical world of their own. (pp. 19-20)

In all Antonioni's films together (except perhaps *Cronaca di un Amore*) the expressionist details could probably be counted on the fingers of one hand, and even those few dismissed as irrelevant. . . .

When, for example, one has been up all night and is very tired, one's mode of perception (mine at least) is subtly altered; one is more susceptible to resonances in the physical properties of objects than under more normal conditions. It is this feeling that is communicated, very sharply, by the opening sequence of *The Eclipse,* not only in the tense exhaustion of the characters but in the oppressive presence of objects, in the buzzing of an electric fan that grates persistently on an already exposed aural nerve. The effect is both irritating and, to a spectator not yet attuned, unnatural; but perhaps for that very reason, all the more authentic and true.

Where in this oppressive physical and social environment do the characters find any escape? How can they break out of the labyrinth which nature and other men and their own sensibilities have built up around them? Properly speaking there is no escape, nor should there be. Man is doomed to living in the world—this is to say no more than that he is doomed to exist. But the situation is not hopeless. There are moments of happiness in the films, which come, when they come, from being at peace with the physical environment, or with others, not in withdrawing from them. Claudia in *L'Avventura,* on the yacht and then on the island, is cut off, mentally, from the other people there, and gives herself over to undiluted enjoyment of her physical surroundings, until with Anna's disappearance even these surroundings seem to turn against her and aggravate rather than alleviate her pain. In *The Eclipse* Vittoria's happiest moment is during that miraculous scene at Verona when her sudden contentment seems to be distilled out of the simple sights and sounds of the airport: sun, the wind in the grass, the drone of an aeroplane, a juke-box. At such moments other people are only a drag—and yet the need for them exists. The desire to get away from oneself, away from other people, and the satisfaction this gives, arise only from the practical necessity for most of the time of being aware of oneself and of forming casual or durable relationships with other people. And the relationships too can be a source of fulfilment. No single trite or abstract formulation can catch the living essence of Antonioni's version of the human comedy. (p. 20)

*Geoffrey Nowell-Smith, "Shape Around a Black Point," in* Sight and Sound *(copyright © 1964 by The British Film Institute), Vol. 33, No. 1, Winter, 1963-64, pp. 15-20.*

**JOHN RUSSELL TAYLOR**

In each of [Antonioni's early films *N. U. (Nettezza Urbana),* *L'Amorosa Menzogna,* and *Superstizione*] the accent is, far more than in most documentaries, placed fairly and squarely on the people: the street-sweeper, the hopefuls on the fringes of show-business, the camera-shy old men and women of Camarino weaving their spells. . . . And the thing which all these people have in common, as pictured by Antonioni, is their solitude: the sorcerers are as alone in the modern world as the forgotten fisherman of the Po: the 'performers' in the photo-romances are pathetic in their hopeless ambitions and set apart by the tawdry glamour which surrounds them in the eyes of their equally foolish and pathetic readers; even with the street-cleaners, who do a job of work just like anyone else and no doubt lead perfectly ordinary family lives, the emphasis is placed rather on their aspect as 'forgotten men', moving unnoticed about the city streets, doing the most squalid work for a populace which asks only to remain unconscious of their existence. To match this view of life the style of photography adopted is correspondingly bare and unadorned, avoiding strong contrasts and concentrating on the middle range of greys to evoke the misty banks of the Po, the cheerless Marshes, the empty streets of Rome at dawn and nightfall. Already, without being more than a little wise after the event, we can see the hand of the mature Antonioni at work in these small but very characteristic works. (pp. 55-6)

[In 1950] *Cronaca di un Amore* went into production, in the proper neo-realist manner, in the streets of Milan. But that is about all of neo-realism it had in it; otherwise, right from the first, Antonioni showed his independence of the style then dominant in the Italian cinema, and in which as a documentarist he had been nurtured. Most obviously, he forsook the working-class milieux which were almost a *sine qua non* of the neo-realist film, and turned his attention instead to the prosperous middle classes which had been more or less taboo as a subject of serious film-making in Italy since the dominance of the much-despised 'white telephone' school of the 1930s. They were, however, the class that Antonioni knew best, and in a way the film could be regarded as a logical extension of neo-realist principles to hitherto more or less unexplored territory. But in other respects the film deviated markedly from the neo-realist norm. It used professional actors, for one thing; its social criticism, if there at all, was present only very indirectly, by implication, the story concentrating with almost Racinian intensity and single-mindedness on the relationships of the three central characters, whose social situation is only a small, relatively insignificant element in the plot; and above all the film is made in a highly conscious, rigorously disciplined style about as far distant as can be imagined from neo-realism's preoccupation at the time with making feature films look as much as possible like newsreels. Even in this first full-length film it was clear at once that a major new talent had arrived, already mature and highly personal in his means of self-expression. (pp. 56-7)

The type of cinema which resulted from all this has been labelled 'anti-cinema', on the model of the 'anti-play' and the 'anti-novel'. And in a sense this is true; Antonioni's approach to film-making contradicts a lot which at the time of his appearance was taken as axiomatic. It is against the neo-realistic concept of cinema, certainly, but it is also against, for example, Eisenstein's earlier concept of a cinema built on dynamic montage (to which, despite a general unwillingness to practise it, cinema intellectuals continue to pay a sort of lip-service) and equally against his later concept based on histrionic performance. It is against, too, the concept of the cinema as a bag of tricks, most influentially put about by the cinema's arch-magician Orson Welles and seldom without powerful advocates, from Ingmar Bergman to Akira Kurosawa. Instead, what we are given is a quietist, interior cinema such as few have attempted in the past—most notably Carl Dreyer and Robert Bresson: it is a concept of cinema very similar to the concept of theatre put forward by [Maurice] Maeterlinck, who like Antonioni was not interested in external action but only in soul-states. (p. 57)

In the films which come after *Le Amiche* Antonioni progressively cuts down plot in the normal sense of the term to the absolute minimum represented by *L'Eclisse,* and as he does so the critic, deprived of any possible assistance from the films' literary values, is thrown back increasingly and (for most critics it seems) disconcertingly on his response to the films as cinema and his intuitive sympathy with Antonioni's approach and subject-matter.

I am not saying that this sort of sympathy is a *sine qua non* for appreciating Antonioni's later work (though there is no denying that with him as with any artist it helps), but simply that when the subject-matter is left, literarily speaking, so naked it becomes very easy for the viewer insensitive or hostile to Antonioni's strictly cinematic art to isolate the necessarily very thin plot-content (thin, again, in its purely literary aspect, what can be put down on paper) and then say: 'If that's all he's using this great battery of cinematic know-how to say, is it really worth the trouble?' The answer to that is that, if the solid literary values of a traditional 'well-written script' are what you are looking for in the cinema it is probably not worth the trouble: Antonioni's films (any of them, but particularly from *Le Amiche* on) are not for you. By the time we come to *Le Amiche* there is no doubt that Antonioni has passed decisively beyond the stage at which a writer-director's work can be compartmentalized: this much is scripting, and then the director sets out to realize on the screen what the writer has put on paper. Indeed, he had passed this stage already with

*Cronaca di un Amore,* but in *Le Amiche* the fact that he has done so becomes inescapable. From here on the scripts come to have virtually no meaning in themselves: though they have all been published it would be impossible to gain any adequate idea of the films from them; they are at best the scant *aide-mémoire* of someone who already has something very like the finished film complete in his mind before he starts work. (pp. 67-8)

In many ways Antonioni still remains one of the least predictable of the great figures in the modern cinema: a great innovator, not so much in the details of technique (bare compositions with solitary figures lost in great vistas of modern architecture and scenes between two characters who talk mainly with their backs to each other, to 'express alienation', were a fad of 1961-2, but that has little to do with real technical advances and their assimilation) as in his whole approach to story-continuity in the cinema, Antonioni has pursued a consistent and fairly solitary road. And yet the achievement of his films has been by no means consistent: he could not now, certainly, make a film as crude as the French and Italian episodes of *I Vinti,* but the peaks of *Le Amiche, L'Avventura* and *L'Eclisse* have alternated with the relative failures of *Il Grido* and *La Notte.* The distinction between triumph and disaster in his work seems to be more finely drawn than in the work of any other director of comparable stature, and every film he makes is liable to elicit in advance almost as much dread as eagerness from even his most fervent admirers—a feeling intensified by the knowledge that his years as the height of fashion are bound to be paid for in the not too distant future by a violent reaction against his work. (p. 81)

*John Russell Taylor, "Michelangelo Antonioni," in his* Cinema Eye, Cinema Ear: Some Key Film-Makers of the Sixties *(reprinted with the permission of Hill & Wang, a division of Farrar, Straus & Giroux, Inc.; in Canada by A D Peters & Co Ltd; copyright © 1964 by John Russell Taylor), Hill & Wang, 1964, pp. 52-81.*

## PENELOPE HOUSTON

[*The Red Desert*] is a romantic view, no doubt, of the industrial process. But it belongs to another order of romanticism from the Soviet-style worship of controlled power, or the cottage industry idealism which expresses itself in a loathing of the conveyor-belt and the factory. It is forms and colours, architectural firmness and clarity of line, which Antonioni emphasises: the object rather than its purpose. (p. 80)

Antonioni is employing colour as the major unsettling element in a total landscape of disturbing strangeness. It is a winter landscape, in which people look pinched and chilled, and the light in any case plays tricks with colour values. In the last sequence of *The Eclipse* Antonioni made the ordinary look remote and ominous. Here he takes a step back, as it were, towards the more alien surroundings of *L'Avventura* or *Il Grido,* where the characters not only felt lost, but *were* lost.

In this countryside around Ravenna, ships sail through the mist, as in the Norfolk Broads, so that they appear to have invaded the land. At the end of what critics seem to have agreed, on rather slender evidence, to describe as the "orgy sequence", the group of Sunday afternoon idlers precipitately abandon their harbour shack when a ship which has docked alongside hoists a yellow quarantine flag. Giuliana stares at her four friends, each standing isolated in the gathering fog, looking towards her, as stationary and remote as the group poised on the gravel walk of the formal garden in [Resnais's *Last Year at Marienbad*]. The faces are held in turn in a series of misty, questioning close-ups; then another shot of the group, still frozen in their attitudes; and then the fog comes between, blurring everything. This idea of actual fog becoming one with mental fog sounds elementary to the point of naïveté. But by taking the scene out of any realistic context, by giving the figures that formal remoteness, and by contriving to hint at a suspension of time, Antonioni makes the stylisation work as a powerful element in his sense of dislocation. Giuliana has gone beyond reason, and the film has followed her.

And this is how he handles colour, using it to dissolve order and confound expectation, to strike a series of dissonant chords or to construct a momentary visual harmony. (pp. 80-1)

It is overwhelming; it unbalances the film; it allows the aesthetic experience to get dangerously the upper hand. But if *The Red Desert* seems to me in the long run a magnificent failure (magnificent, that is, in its courage and its ambitions), this is not because there is too much landscape, but because Antonioni has peopled it too sparsely, and has put too much faith in his own truism: that the emotions are lingering behind the technological advances, and that we are bringing nineteenth century nervous systems into twentieth century situations. (p. 81)

In this world of walking wounded, the mind is the first casualty; and *The Red Desert* presents a study of a mind rocking on its foundations, shaken by fears as nameless and inexplicable as that cry out of the fog heard and forgotten during the arid Sunday roistering in the red-walled shack on the docks. But the dislocated mind cannot quite so automatically be related to the dislocated landscape, where the glittering radio towers and the man-made islands rise from the industrial sludge, and the birds no longer fly through the lethal fumes from the refineries.

In *The Eclipse* Antonioni held all the forces at his disposal in a fine, precarious equilibrium: characters and setting interlocked, as in the child's demonstration in *The Red Desert* that two drops of coloured liquid, coalescing on a microscope slide, add up to not two but one. This time, the effect ought to be similar, but the forces are pulling in different directions, and the centre fails to hold. Part of the problem, perhaps, arises from the central split in Antonioni's own mind: he senses the technological change as a vague threat, which he cannot pin down or isolate, and against which he can only utter the muffled warnings of a hesitant Cassandra. But he reacts positively and directly to the calm geometrical promise it holds out, and to its alien fascinations. . . .

Antonioni is a complex artist who can be extraordinarily naïve. He is also, and to his finger-tips, a film-maker, catching his dissolving world through images of space and light and time. *The Red Desert* is a film of unresolved tensions, of gaping fissures between what appears on the screen and the elusive mental image not of a brave but a timorous new world. But its power is in the act of seeing, in those haunting images of a desperate beauty, threatening or threatened. (p. 103)

> *Penelope Houston, '"The Red Desert": The Landscape of the Desert," in* Sight and Sound *(copyright © 1965 by The British Film Institute), Vol. 34, No. 2, Spring, 1965, pp. 80-1, 103.*

**RICHARD SCHICKEL**

[The scene where the young woman offers herself to the photographer in exchange for the film is the most important in-cident] in the long chain of circumstances out of which Michelangelo Antonioni has expertly fashioned the fuse that finally ignites his *Blow-Up,* which seems to me one of the finest, most intelligent, least hysterical expositions of the modern existential agony we have yet had on film. The most obvious of its many endlessly discussible implications—that we are so submerged in sensation and its pursuit that we cannot feel genuine emotion any more—is hardly novel. But the cool specificity of Antonioni's imagery (it always reminds me of Henri Cartier-Bresson's great still photography), his effortless, wonderfully intelligent control of his medium, the feeling he conveys of knowing precisely what he wants to say, and the sense that his perfection of style grows organically out of his awareness, not out of a desire to show off cinematic technique—these are indeed novelties in a day when febrile frenzy is often mistaken for mature motion picture art. (pp. 91-2)

But if the central symbolic mystery—like that of the disappearance of the girl in Antonioni's earlier *L'Avventura*—remains insoluble, the quality of daily life as it is experienced by his characters has that brilliant hard-edged clarity that we most often associate with the dream state. In particular, the contrast between the almost sexual passion the photographer works up when doing fashion work and the essentially trivial and vapid nature of his subject is a superbly realized comment on the values of our time, as well as a remarkably realistic study of the mood of such sessions and of a style of conducting them that is quite common. (pp. 92-3)

That [Antonioni] sees at the motivating center of our noisy desperation an existential mystery of the most profound sort—and has no pat answer for it either—is further evidence of the personal restraint, the lack of self-indulgence, the emotional control with which he—uniquely among the great new directors—tempers and informs all his excursions to the heart of our contemporary darkness. (p. 93)

> *Richard Schickel, "'Blow-Up'" (originally published in a slightly different form in* Life, *Vol. 62, No. 3, January 20, 1967), in his* Second Sight: Notes on Some Movies 1965-1970 *(copyright © 1972 by Richard Schickel; reprinted by permission of Simon & Schuster, a Division of Gulf & Western Corporation), Simon & Schuster, 1972, pp. 91-3.*

**PAULINE KAEL**

[What] would we think of a man who conducted a leisurely tour of "swinging" London, lingering along the flashiest routes and dawdling over a pot party and mini-orgy, while ponderously explaining that although the mod scene appears to be hip and sexy, it represents a condition of spiritual malaise in which people live only for the sensations of the moment? Is he a foolish old hypocrite or is he, despite his tiresome moralizing, a man who knows he's hooked?

It's obvious that there's a new kind of noninvolvement among youth, but we can't get at what that's all about by Antonioni's terms. He is apparently unable to respond to or to convey the new sense of community among youth, or the humor and fervor and astonishing speed in their rejections of older values; he sees only the emptiness of pop culture.

Those who enjoy seeing this turned-on city of youth, those who say of *Blow-Up* that it's the trip, it's where we are now in consciousness and that Antonioni is in it, part of it, ahead of it like Warhol, may have a better sense of what Antonioni is about than the laudatory critics. Despite Antonioni's negativism, the world he presents looks harmless, and for many in the audience, and not just the youthful ones, sex without "connecting" doesn't really seem so bad—naughty, maybe, but nice. Even the smoke at the pot party is enough to turn on some of the audience. And there's all that pretty color which delights the critics, though it undercuts their reasons for praising the movie because it's that bright, cleaned-up big-city color of I-have-seen-the-future-and-it's-fun. Antonioni, like his fashion-photographer hero, is more interested in getting pretty pictures than in what they mean. But for reasons I can't quite fathom, what is taken to be shallow in his hero is taken to be profound in him. Maybe it's because of the symbols: do pretty pictures plus symbols equal art? (p. 32)

The best part of *Blow-Up* is a well-conceived and ingeniously edited sequence in which the hero blows up a series of photographs and discovers that he has inadvertently photographed a murder. It's a good murder mystery sequence. But does it symbolize (as one reviewer says) "the futility of seeking the hidden meanings of life through purely technological means"? I thought the hero did rather well in uncovering the murder. But this kind of symbolic interpretation is not irrelevant to the appeal of the picture: Antonioni loads his atmosphere with so much confused symbolism and such a heavy sense of importance that the viewers use the movie as a Disposall for intellectual refuse. (p. 33)

Just as [Resnais's] *Marienbad* was said to be about "time" and/or "memory," *Blow-Up* is said (by Antonioni and the critics following his lead) to be about "illusion and reality." They seem to think they are really saying something, and something impressive at that, though the same thing can be said about almost any movie. In what sense is a movie "about" an abstract concept? Probably what Antonioni and the approving critics mean is that high fashion, mod celebrity, rock and roll, and drugs are part of a sterile or frenetic existence, and they take this to mean that the life represented in the film is not "real" but illusory. What seems to be implicit in the prattle about illusion and reality is the notion that the photographer's life is based on "illusion" and that when he discovers the murder, he is somehow face to face with "reality." Of course this notion that murder is more real than, say, driving in a Rolls-Royce convertible, is nonsensical (it's more shocking, though, and when combined with a Rolls-Royce it gives a movie a bit of box office—it's practical). They're not talking about a concept of reality but what used to be called "the real things in life," the solid values they approve of versus the "false values" of "the young people today."

Antonioni is the kind of thinker who can say that there are "no social or moral judgments in the picture": he is merely showing us the people who have discarded "all discipline," for whom freedom means "marijuana, sexual perversion, anything," and who live in "decadence without any visible future." I'd hate to be around when he's making judgments. Yet in some sense Antonioni is right: because he doesn't *connect* what he's showing to judgment. And that dislocation of sensibility is probably why kids don't notice the moralizing, why they say *Blow-Up* is hip.

The cultural ambience of a film like this becomes mixed with the experience of the film: one critic says Antonioni's "vision" is that "the further we draw away from reality, the closer we get to the truth," another that Antonioni means "we must learn to live with the invisible." All this can sound great to those who don't mind not knowing what it's about, for whom the ineffable seems most important. . . . *Blow-Up* is the perfect

movie for the kind of people who say, "now that films have become an art form . . ." and don't expect to understand art.

Because the hero is a *photographer* and the blow-up sequence tells a story in pictures, the movie is also said to be about Antonioni's view of himself as an artist (though even his worst enemies could hardly accuse him of "telling stories" in pictures). Possibly it is, but those who see *Blow-Up* as Antonioni's version of [Fellini's] *8*—as making a movie about making a movie—seem to value that much more than just making a movie, probably because it puts the film in a class with the self-conscious autobiographical material so many young novelists struggle with (the story that ends with their becoming writers . . .) and is thus easy to mistake for the highest point of the artistic process. (pp. 35-6)

When journalistic details are used symbolically—and that is how Antonioni uses "swinging" London—the artist does not create a frame of reference that gives meaning to the details; he simply exploits the ready-made symbolic meanings people attach to certain details and leaves us in a profound mess. (The middlebrow moralists think it's profound and the hippies enjoy the mess.) And when he tosses in a theatrical convention like a mimed tennis game without a ball—which connects with the journalistic data only in that it, too, is symbolic—he throws the movie game away. It becomes ah-sweet-mystery-of-life we-are-all-fools, which, pitched too high for human ears, might seem like great music beyond our grasp. (p. 37)

> *Pauline Kael, "Tourist in the City of Youth: 'Blow-Up'" (originally published as "Tourist in the City of Youth,"* in The New Republic, *Vol. 156, No. 6, February 11, 1967), in her* Kiss Kiss Bang Bang *(© 1967 by Pauline Kael; reprinted by permission of Little, Brown and Company in association with the Atlantic Monthly Press), Atlantic-Little, Brown, 1968, pp. 31-7.*

**MARSHA KINDER**

[In *L'Avventura, La Notte, L'Eclisse,* and *Il Deserto Rosso,* Antonioni] does not imply that the new world is totally negative, but recognises it has many important values—the power necessary for man to master his environment; an efficiency which may improve his lot by wiping out hunger, poverty and physical pain; and the creation of a pure, abstract beauty. Yet despite these values, he also suggests that this world poses a real threat because it implies the loss of other values—of long-term personal relationships, of the uniqueness of the individual. Thus, he presents us with a clash between two incompatible value systems, which is essentially a tragic view. . . .

Antonioni does not offer an easy answer to the problem of the conflict between the two value systems. He seems to accept the new world as inevitable although it means a sacrifice of important values from the past. The only hope seems to be understanding and a sympathetic acceptance of whatever human contact is possible. Understanding alone won't suffice— as Anna, Valentina and Guiliana demonstrate. Nor will an unthinking acceptance—as in the case of Sandro, Giovanni, Piero and Giuliana's husband. The most positive characters must achieve both, as Claudia and Vittoria ultimately do.

Although these four films focus on how changes in the modern world affect human relationships, they also imply that a similar change is taking place in art. For example, both central male characters in *L'Avventura* and *La Notte*—Sandro and Giovanni—are artists who sold out; and in both cases the loss in artistic power is linked to their failure in a love relationship. . . .

I think we can best examine the change in art and its relationship to the theme of emotional loss by focusing on *L'Avventura*. (p. 133)

[An] abstract, dehumanised quality comes out in the scene where Claudia visits the art gallery, while Anna and Sandro are making love. She is more intrigued and delighted by the reactions of the people than by the paintings, which have no relation to human beings. The lack of permanence is also suggested in the scene where they discover the ancient vase on the island. It has lasted for centuries, but as soon as someone from the modern world touches it, it is destroyed. There is also a suggestion that art has become a source of exploitation, a means to an end rather than an end in itself. For example, Goffredo uses his paintings merely to express his sexual desire and as a means of gratifying that desire by seducing his models. In their momentary passion he and Giulia knock over his easel and carelessly destroy the 'art'. Similarly, Gloria (the prostitute who takes Claudia's and Anna's place with Sandro) claims that she is a writer who communicates with the spirits of Tolstoi and Shakespeare. She reduces art to a cheap publicity trick and exploits it just as she exploits sex: she is a cheap substitute both for art and love. Thus, in this film Antonioni implies that art has undergone three main changes: it is no longer permanent, it is no longer related to human subjects or to the individual, and it has become a source of economic exploitation.

The implications of these changes are developed much further in *Blow-Up*. In this film contemporary art not only lacks permanence, but actually values the moment. This helps to explain why the central character is a photographer rather than an architect, for photography is concerned with capturing the moment. Moreover, contemporary art places a value on something in a particular context. One of the basic justifications of pop art, for example, is that it takes familiar objects and puts them into a new context that gives them a new value. In other words, the value lies not in the object itself, but in its relationship with a specific context. This notion is mocked in the scene where Thomas goes to hear the Yardbirds and gets away with part of the smashed guitar. The fragment, which was so highly valued in that particular situation, is merely a worthless piece of junk once he gets outside into a new context. . . .

Secondly, contemporary art not only is abstract and detached from human involvement, but it actually becomes a substitute for such involvements. This is brought out in the comic scene when shooting his model with his camera becomes a substitute for sexual intercourse. Although Thomas claims he would prefer to shoot pictures of real people rather than beautiful models, he shows no greater understanding of the human significance of these photographs. In fact, he uses exactly the same language to describe them that he uses for his fashion photos. . . .

Thirdly, the economic exploitation of art is practised not only by the amateur (like Goffredo) or the complete phoney (like Gloria), but by the most competent artists, which implies it has become an accepted part of contemporary art. The commercial photographer and the rock and roll star who are really 'good' are expected to succeed—to make money, to be well received. The stereotype of the artist is no longer an undiscovered genius starving in the garret. Artistic talent and success have become compatible and almost synonymous.

The expanded treatment of these changes leads to two other important implications about contemporary art. It implies that the creative process depends on accident and spontaneity and is really not carefully controlled. (p. 134)

Another characteristic of contemporary art is the confusion between the artist (the creator) and his instrument of creation. This is another example of ambiguity and is linked to the minimising of control that the artist has during the act of creation. This idea is suggested in the mob's reaction to the guitar, and also in the relationship between Thomas and his camera. At one point he contradicts himself by saying he 'saw' the murder, when what he really means is that his camera saw it.

I do not mean to imply that *Blow-Up* is solely about art, but rather that it is the main focus. As in the earlier films, there is a very strong relationship between art and life—and it is not at all clear which imitates which. . . .

Ambiguity is perhaps the most obvious quality in the film. We find it in the dress of the people on the street, which makes it very difficult to tell the boys from the girls. . . . And perhaps most obviously, in the neon sign over the park, which Antonioni had constructed to be intentionally ambiguous and which is only momentarily in focus. Thus, as in his earlier films, Antonioni is suggesting that there is a new style of behaviour which is in marked contrast to a more traditional body of values, but his emphasis is on the changes in art rather than in human relationships. (p. 135)

In *Blow-Up* there is a radical change in pace as compared with the earlier films. The only similarity is that it has an important expressive function in both. The pace in the earlier films is generally very slow, and this has the significant function of taking the emphasis away from the action and focusing it instead on the mood or inner feelings of the characters. . . . [Lidia in *La Notte* is typical of those characters that] are all looking for something that is missing, but they are not sure what it is or where to find it. The visual images are charged with emotional effects that take time to work on the viewer.

The most effective use of pacing in the four films occurs in *L'Eclisse,* where it is absolutely essential to the film's meaning. The centre of interest is the relationship between Vittoria and Piero, who represent two worlds that move at entirely different speeds; and this difference in pace helps to define each world and its values. . . . Their relationship is like an eclipse, which implies two things. First, an eclipse suggests a loss, or a dimming of power; and their relationship is certainly limited. Secondly, an eclipse also implies a temporary period when the paths of two heavenly bodies are in conjunction. This is exactly what human relationships have become—brief moments of togetherness between longer periods of emotional isolation, the temporary conjunction of two human bodies moving in different orbits at different speeds. The difference in pace is an indication that their relationship cannot last. (pp. 135-36)

The rapid pace of *Blow-Up* is well suited to a character who is constantly on the move and concerned with capturing the moment. The pace of the film helps to express Thomas's conception of art and experience. He constantly moves from one context to another and is incapable of focusing his attention on a subject for very long, and this is partially expressed by the rapid succession of visual images. (p. 136)

If we turn to the structure of *Blow-Up,* we find that it shares similarities with that of the earlier films, but they are used for different functions. The basic structure of all five films is a cyclical pattern comprised of episodes which contain a certain amount of repetition and leave a number of questions unanswered. One way of achieving the cyclical quality is by having every picture begin and end in the morning. In the earlier films the repetitious cycle implies the interchangeability of persons. . . . The absence of a conventional dramatic structure also helps to suggest that in these films action is not the main focus and that the central meaning must be found elsewhere.

This is not at all the case in *Blow-Up.* Here, the absence of a conventional dramatic plot and the unanswered questions help to reveal Thomas's fragmented view of experience, which is comprised of separate moments. No episode reaches a climax or resolution; no human relationship builds or develops. This structure also implies that Thomas doesn't really care about finding the answers. In *L'Avventura* Claudia at first thought she cared about what happened to Anna, then only pretended to care, and finally had to admit she really didn't and to accept what that implied. But in *Blow-Up* there is no pretence: motives, causes, people simply don't matter to Thomas. This lack of a conventional plot also helps to express Thomas's conception of art. If an artist assumes that accident and spontaneity play an important role in art and if he values ambiguity, then he is unlikely to have a tightly controlled plot with a resolution that neatly ties together all the loose ends; for such a structure implies that the artist has carefully planned out everything in advance. He avoids the conventional mystery plot.

Yet there is an irony in the structure of *Blow-Up.* Although on first view it seems to be episodic and rather random in order, a closer examination reveals that it does have a rather artificial order. Many of the encounters that Thomas has in the first half of the film (before he meets Jane) are repeated in reverse order in the second half, which makes a neat circular pattern after all. . . . The structure, then, is not haphazard, which implies a distance between Thomas's and Antonioni's view of art. I think this distinction can be clarified by a closer examination of the mime troupe, which frames the film.

The art of the mime troupe in the final scene suggests an important contrast with the other examples of art in the film. For one thing, it is not temporary; pantomime is a traditional art form linked to the past, and the imaginary tennis game is a sustained creation that does build. Secondly, it is an art which requires engagement—not only from the performers, but also from the audience looking on who contribute to the illusion. It also requires the involvement of the camera, which follows the path of the imaginary ball; and finally succeeds in winning the active participation of Thomas, who has been detached throughout the film. He actually retrieves the imaginary ball for them, and has to put down his camera to do it. This act recalls the first interaction between Thomas and the troupe in the opening scene when he contributes money to their cause. Thirdly, the artists in this instance are in control of what they are creating: the illusion of the spontaneous or accidental (that is, when the ball goes over the fence) is obviously controlled; there is no instrument (like a guitar or camera) other than the creators themselves; the ambiguity between illusion and reality is carefully controlled and is based upon a wilful act of imagination that is totally missing from Thomas's conception of art. This is the kind of art that is being replaced in the contemporary world, and its position at the end of the film helps to stress its significance.

I am suggesting, then, that Antonioni is critical of the style he employs in *Blow-Up.* It is not that the style is inherently 'bad', but that it can be used to imply a conception of experience that threatens to destroy values of the past. Yet he demonstrates that he can use it as effectively as his contemporaries. In this film he seems to allude to the styles of others, which was not characteristic of his earlier films—the fast pace of Lester, the Hitchcock-like treatment of the murder in the park, the mime troupe which seems to belong in a Fellini film, and even the allusiveness which is so characteristic of Godard. Yet he uses the allusions quite differently by making the borrowed elements peculiarly his own, by making them essential to the meaning of his own film, by putting them in a new context while still retaining and exploiting the context from which they are derived. This is the essence of artistic control, which is so antithetical to Thomas's conception. (pp. 136-37)

*Marsha Kinder, "Antonioni in Transit," in* Sight and Sound *(copyright © 1967 by The British Film Institute), Vol. 36, No. 3, Summer, 1967, pp. 132-37.*

**CHARLES THOMAS SAMUELS**

Like *L'Avventura, Blow-Up* concerns the search for something that is never found. As in *La Notte,* the peripatetic hero fails to accomplish anything. Like the other protagonists, the photographer is the embodiment of a role, although here he is so fully defined by his function that he is not even named. As in Antonioni's other films, the climax is reached when the protagonist comes to face his own impotence. . . .

The events in *Blow-Up* dramatize the same theme one finds in Antonioni's other films. The photographer, a creature of work and pleasure but of no inner force or loyalty, is unable to involve himself in life. He watches it, manipulates it; but, like all of Antonioni's male characters, he has no sense of life's purpose. Thus, when faced with a challenge, he cannot decisively act. Unable to transcend himself, except through ultimate confrontation with his soul, he represents modern paralysis. (p. 124)

[He] is part of his world. Hiding behind a tree, like the murderer, he shot with a camera what the latter shot with a gun; and he did not save the older man. He is blond, and so is the murderer. For all his aloof contempt, he is as frivolous as the mod clowns who frame his experience. In the last scene, when he hears their "tennis ball," he effectively actualizes the charade existence that they share in common. His final gesture of resignation—like Sandro's tears, Giovanni's loveless copulation, or Piero's and Vittoria's failure to meet—shows clearly that the photographer cannot change. (p. 126)

The modern world, however, seems bent on destroying its traditions. On the wall of the photographer's apartment, an old Roman tablet is overwhelmed by the hallucinatory violence of the modern painting at its side. More important, traditional human pursuits are being drained of their force. Politics is now playacting; a pacifist parade marches by with signs bearing inscriptions like "No," or "On. On. On." or "Go away." Pleasure is narcotizing, whether at the "pot" party or in the rock 'n roll club. Love is unabsorbing, as the photographer learns from his friend's marriage. Art has lost its validity. Murder is ignored.

These last implications are forcefully portrayed in the film's main scenes of human interaction. . . .

Through turning sparse, functional dialogue into a system of verbal echoes, Antonioni achieves the economy of tight verse. Yet he does not sacrifice naturalness. (p. 127)

[An example of Antonioni's economical use of dialogue to establish meaning occurs when the painter's wife] hears the photographer's confession of failure and declares her own. Bill's art is no alternative to the destruction symbolized by the murder; his art is another version of it. They can no more deal with their marriage than the photographer can deal with the crime. She can only slink away in compassion for their mutual impotence, leaving him to futile pursuit, marijuana, and his depressing moment of truth. . . .

The incredible greenness of a park that was the ironic setting for murder suggests another of Antonioni's means. When the photographer discovers the body's loss, he looks up at the tree, whose leaves now rattle angrily, and sees the leaves as black against a white sky. Like the sound analogies and the verbal cross-references, the color in **Blow-Up** aids comprehension. . . .

Colorful though it is, **Blow-Up** seems to be moving toward colorlessness, black and white—almost as if Antonioni were trying to make us face the skull beneath the painted flesh. (p. 128)

> *Charles Thomas Samuels, "The Blow-Up: Sorting Things Out," in* The American Scholar, *(copyright by the Estate of Charles Thomas Samuels; reprinted by permission), Vol. 37, No. 1, Winter, 1967-68, pp. 120-31.*

## ROBIN WOOD

In essential characteristics as in theme, **Il Deserto Rosso** belongs with its three immediate predecessors, in some respects carrying their tendencies to new extremes. Here for the first time the protagonist is overtly presented as neurotic, and therefore *explicitly* incapable of fulfilling her inner needs. At the same time, certain aspects of the film mark a new phase in Antonioni's development. In obvious ways he was breaking new ground, working in a milieu remote from the intellectual-socialite world of the preceding films, and shooting for the first time in colour. These factors may be partly responsible for the comparatively open and exploratory nature of **Il Deserto Rosso**. . . .

Like so much else in the film, [Corrado's] behaviour . . . is extremely ambiguous. Antonioni . . . sees him merely as 'taking advantage of [Giuliana] and of her state of mind' ('. . . it is her own world which betrays her . . .'); but it is at least as valid (and the two views, though seemingly contradictory, are not incompatible) to see his actions as motivated by an extreme protective tenderness which is as much concern for his own vulnerability as for hers. He is drawn to her because she expresses in an extreme form his own innermost tendencies; she represents for him also the *temptation* of defeat, as a means of evading the need to struggle. (p. 111)

Corrado's function in the film, then, is roughly analogous to that of Marion Crane in [Hitchcock's] *Psycho:* he represents a reflection, within a recognisable normality, of the central figure's psychotic traits. We find similar reflections in some of the minor characters. We recall, for example, that the workman whom Corrado and Giuliana visited at the radar installations had been in 'hospital' with her. We recall also the workman's wife who, in her husband's absence, expresses her opposition to his going to Patagonia. Her unnatural fear of being alone (even for a day, she says) relates clearly to Giuliana's alienation. We are to see Giuliana, then, not merely as a neurotic woman, but as an extreme extension of a general contemporary condition. Virtually the whole film is devoted to the detailed

study of her alienation which is offered as the study of the human predicament in an industrialised society. . . .

[When the hut interior is smashed for firewood it] is one of the moments in the film when Antonioni seems to be groping beyond any concern with the 'modern condition' as such towards more fundamental and permanent metaphysical issues, Giuliana's alienation making her hypersensitive to existence, to time and flux. Antonioni *thinks* here in the movement and rhythms of film as a great poet thinks in the movement and rhythms of verse, 'thinking' here being indistinguishable from feeling. (p. 112)

The use of effects or incidents whose interpretation is complex or very uncertain is one of the film's chief characteristics, and partly accounts for its unsettling quality. There is the mysterious scream, for instance (if that is what it is), heard while the party are in the hut. Giuliana and Linda hear it, and *we* hear it, though, at a first viewing, we are very unsure at the point where it is discussed whether we have or not—characteristically, we are put in the position of sharing Giuliana's uncertainty. . . . For Giuliana the mysterious cry becomes an expression of vulnerability and desolation, it insidiously suggests the vague, inexplicable 'something terrible about reality' that she talks of to Corrado later. (pp. 113-14)

The striking thing about Giuliana's escape world is that it is devoid not merely of industry but of human beings. The mysterious ship that 'braves the seas and storms of this world, and, who knows?, of other worlds' is utterly empty. It somehow fulfils a desire in Giuliana that makes possible a sense of universal harmony, so that '*Everything* was singing'; but it is a harmony that depends on the exclusion of humanity and all the complexities of human interchange. . . .

[Antonioni would like the viewer] to see **Il Deserto Rosso** as being about Giuliana's failure to adjust to the society in which she lives—unexceptionable in itself. . . . [However] the film precisely reverses its creator's expressed intentions. It is also, in its 'instinctive ambiguity', a far richer and more complex work than Antonioni's statements about it would lead one to expect. Apart from Giuliana and Corrado, the characters are all too peripheral for us to get to know very much about them; one gets the feeling that Antonioni is reluctant to examine them closely or in detail. Consequently, we never discover clearly just what their 'adjustment' entails: it seems to amount to little more than an ability to handle machinery and be impervious to noise. Beyond this, the chief characteristic the minor characters reveal is a singular ineffectuality in relationships, an inability, indeed, to form relationships on any but the most superficial level. (p. 115)

The scene of the abortive little would-be orgy in the hut reveals the film's true moral position unequivocally. The cheaply promiscuous pawing and sniggering talk of aphrodisiacs—pornography on the most infantile level—illustrates the trivialising of sex and of human relationships that marks the 'adjusted' characters (Corrado, initially at least, finds it distasteful). After it, Giuliana's straightforward request to her husband to make love comes across as representing a healthy normality, a desire for true intimacy and depth of relationship. Whatever Antonioni may say, it is Giuliana in whom all the film's true positive values are embodied. . . . In the world Antonioni creates in **Il Deserto Rosso** it is the neurotic and incapable woman who is closest to anything that could be defended as a tenable 'normality'. (pp. 116-18)

The ending of the film, where Giuliana tells Valerio that birds don't get killed flying through the poisonous yellow factory-smoke because they learn to *avoid* it, can scarcely be taken as a simple statement of the need to adjust. It is rather the summing-up of her final position of total defeat: she will henceforth try to get along, not by coming to terms with her abnormal condition or with her environment . . . , but simply by blocking them out—by systematically deadening her own responses. Unlike the birds, she can't fly away: she has to live among the objects and sights that are poisonous to her. We see her walking away against a background of factories and yellow containers that is again an out-of-focus blur. The very last shot of the film, which immediately follows, shows us the same factories in focus. The intention, presumably, was to convey to the spectator a sense of release not shared by the protagonist (like the last shot of *Psycho*). The effect is converted into one of bitter despair, by the loathing of industrialism on human grounds that the film has by now defined; this is scarcely mitigated by the feeling for the *aesthetic* beauty of factories. In the background rises the poisoned yellow smoke, and the sense of the parable is surely clear: to avoid it is to live a life of spiritual paralysis, to accept it is to die. (pp. 119-20)

In *Il Deserto Rosso* we never really accept industrialism as sufficient explanation of Giuliana's condition, and are left wondering whether she would be able to adjust to *any* milieu. Whereupon the whole ostensible subject of the film crumbles away, and we are left asking ourselves, '*Why* a neurotic for protagonist?'. (pp. 122-23)

The somewhat enervating effect of much of Antonioni's recent work seems to be intimately connected with the split between conscious and unconscious intentions. In *Il Deserto Rosso* the complex of tendencies analysable in the films from *L'Avventura* on reaches its culmination in some respects and begins to be transcended in others. Here the enervating effect of self-conscious insistence on style is offset by the constant fertility of invention and the readiness to leave things relatively open (in details if not in overall sense). . . . [To] center a statement about the contemporary condition on a highly, perhaps incurably neurotic woman who is unable even to begin coping with her situation, unable to draw upon any insight or awareness, and to reduce the other characters to ciphers, is again to make things too easy. What Penelope Houston called 'unresolved tensions' in the film amount to spiritual deadlock, and, given the director's ambivalent (or confused?) attitude to his subject-matter, Giuliana was perhaps the only kind of protagonist possible. One of the consequences is a singular lack of development within the film. The ending makes it clear that Giuliana hasn't made any significant progress, a point emphasized by the fact that she is dressed as she was at the beginning.

If not the greatest, *Blow Up* seems to me easily the most likeable of Antonioni's later films; and its freshness and vivacity make one look forward to his future work with an eagerness one would scarcely have anticipated in the days of *La Notte* and *L'Eclisse.*

*Il Deserto Rosso* marked a break with the past in comparatively peripheral ways; *Blow Up* makes the break more extreme and decisive. (pp. 123-25)

What one first notices about *Blow Up* is its tempo, its effect of spontaneity, its lack of mannerisms. Where *La Notte,* for example, seems much longer than it really is, *Blow Up* seems shorter. The preoccupation with beauty of style as an end in itself that characterized the preceding films is largely absent. The cleanness and directness of expression in *Blow Up* suggests a much more immediate (hence for Antonioni healthier, be-

cause less self-conscious) involvement with the subject matter. (p. 125)

The spirit of enquiry and exploration foreshadowed in certain aspects of the previous film is a much stronger determinant in *Blow Up,* and this is surely closely connected with the new hero-figure. Antonioni here sets out to examine how a man can try to live in the more 'advanced' environments of modern civilisation, instead of starting from the assumption that he can't. Or that, at least, is about half the truth. . . .

Antonioni's later films are built not so much on plots as on cumulative episodes, linked by a common theme or principle of composition. In *Blow Up* he uses a classic mystery-thriller plot, but uses it only as one element—albeit a central one—in the whole. The form of the film can be compared to a Theme-and-Variations, bearing in mind that all the best sets of variations are not merely strung together like beads, but have a cumulative effect. (p. 126)

Ambiguity, uncertainty, the blurring of distinctions, inform every episode in the film. Far from attempting a documentary examination of London, Antonioni selects only what is relevant to this central compositional principle, so that even the most incidental details fall naturally into place in the total picture. Nothing is definitively identifiable: outside the junkshop Thomas sees two feminine-looking men walking poodles, and shortly after, in the park, a masculine-looking woman in male uniform picking up litter with a pointed stick. Nothing is quite what it looks like: the façade of Thomas's house/studio seems to have no relation to the world behind it, the restaurant where he goes for lunch is indistinguishable from a private house. Objects are separated from their functions, or become wildly incongruous with the environments in which they are placed or the human behaviour around them. . . . No one has any sense of *positive* purpose: even the posters in the protest march with which Thomas, driving from the restaurant, gets tangentially involved, are exclusively negative. Most of them simply say 'NO'; some are upside down ('ON'), therefore meaningless or contradictory. Any doubts that Giuliana's vision of existence in *Il Deserto Rosso* was essentially shared by her creator should be decisively removed by *Blow Up,* which is singlemindedly concerned with life on quicksand. (pp. 126-28)

Relationships in the world of *Blow Up* are unstable, enigmatic or deceptive, [Patricia] lives with Thomas's artist friend yet seems on intimate terms with Thomas, who fondles her in front of her lover. When Thomas sees the artist making love to her, she is making no response whatever—she seems to be merely allowing him to use her to work himself off. The relationship gives her no sense of identity, or of belonging. The relationship between [Jane] and the man in the park is almost (but not quite) certainly not what it looks like. And what of her relationship with Thomas? When she finds she can't get the photos he has taken of her in any other way, she begins to take off her clothes. He stops her, and gives her a roll of film she thinks is the one she wants (it isn't); whereupon she *continues* her attempt to seduce him. So where does her interest in getting the film end and her interest in having Thomas make love to her begin? Clearly, there is no answer.

In a life of quicksands, purpose falters, deviates, collapses. (pp. 128-31)

One of the first things [Jane] says to Thomas in the park is 'No, we haven't met—you've never seen me.' The invitation to deliberate prevarication or suppression takes on far more sinister overtones as the film progresses. The main drift of

*Blow Up* seems to me very clear: we are shown a young man inhabiting a world in which everything combines to undermine the firmness of his hold on reality. The mystery surrounding the murder comes as a test: he is subjected to a *deliberate* undermining of his confidence in his own perceptions, and he crumbles. The cumulative effect of the episodes (or variations), both on Thomas and on the spectator, should also be clear, with various points quite unconnected with the mystery-thriller narrative (Thomas's failure to answer Ron's 'Free like him?'; his joining in the battle for the guitar) acting as landmarks in the protagonist's development. The murder is, nonetheless, at the core of the film. (p. 131)

Moral distinctions in the quicksand world of *Blow Up* are as blurred as any others, and definitions such as 'Good' and 'Wicked' cease to have validity or even meaning. Legal proceedings would categorize [Jane] very precisely as 'Murderer's Accomplice', while we see, with Thomas, an evidently very complicated and bewildered, and highly sensitive and vulnerable, human being.

The notorious episode with the teenage girls is relevant here. No one wants to admit to being shocked by it, but lots of people profess to be shocked that Antonioni should try so hard to shock us. Surely the shocking thing about the scene is that it isn't presented as shocking? In fact, it is very funny and charming. (p. 137)

What becomes of first importance to Thomas is not abstract justice but something very concrete and personal. With his hold on reality weakening, he must get a picture of the corpse; in other words, he must *know* that he has seen what he has seen. Alternatively (or, better still, as well) he must share his knowledge with another consciousness. The importance these aims assume is the index of the weakening of Thomas's own confidence. The drug orgy amid which he finds Ron and into which he himself (we presume) is finally drawn, is not a bit of cheap sensationalism nor a bit of spurious local colour in the 'Swinging London' scene. It is the logical culmination of a film, constructed like a poem of thematically related images, about the way in which perceptions can be tampered with, undermined, and finally broken down. Thomas emerges from it at dawn with his camera, but it is too late—the corpse, and with it Thomas's last chance to prove to himself the reality of what he has seen, has gone. (p. 138)

Although a slight figure (whose slightness accounts for that of the film of which he is the dominating consciousness), Thomas is a far more active and positive figure than most of Antonioni's male protagonists, and his defeat accordingly seems at first to carry that much more weight. At the same time his very activeness is to some extent at odds with the drift of the film as a whole: we are not at the end really convinced that so chirpy and resilient a man would be so decisively undermined by the experiences we are shown him undergoing. Isn't Antonioni manipulating the character against its nature, in order, once again, to bring the film round to a final and too easy defeat? There remains some conflict between the traditional plot-and-character narrative at the core of the film and the more typically Antonionian 'poetic' form of thematically related episodes and images. The latter is, as usual, contrived to express a predetermined defeat, and plot and character are forced to submit, even though they seem to want to develop more 'openly'. The artist's description in the film of how his paintings develop, spontaneously and subconsciously, so that it is only later, by finding a clue and following it, that he understands them, is probably intended as a 'testament' description of how Anto-

nioni makes his films, and one can see that their 'variation' form of related episodes supports this. But this doesn't really contradict the 'predetermined' effect of his films—predetermination can as easily work subconsciously as deliberately, *more* easily, perhaps, when it remains unchecked by fully conscious recognition. Antonioni has found a more 'open' hero, but he is still incapable of making a truly 'open' film—as one sees immediately if one sets *Blow Up* beside another film about contemporary bewilderment and confusion, Godard's *Une Femme Mariée*. . . .

Like *Il Deserto Rosso*, *Blow Up* tries to make a clear distinction between objective reality and its protagonist's failure to maintain his grasp of it. The last shots of the two films are closely parallel: Giuliana walks past out-of-focus factories and stockyards, which Antonioni slides *into* focus for us to contemplate as they really are; Thomas's confidence in his perceptions of reality have collapsed, but *we* are left to contemplate the real grass. Yet in both films the characters' breakdown carries weight disproportionate to the 'placing' of that breakdown: there remains grave doubt whether the encouragement to share the central figures' disturbed vision doesn't greatly outweigh any attempts to detach us from its distortions and limitations. During *Blow Up*'s final tennis-match, the camera-movements follow the imaginary ball's trajectory as to place the audience subjectively in the hallucinated position of Thomas and the mime group, just as in *Il Deserto Rosso,* through the use of soft-focus and colour distortions, the audience participates in Giuliana's alienation. This in itself can be readily enough defended as honesty on Antonioni's part—Giuliana and Thomas, if extreme cases, are to be taken as to some extent representative modern consciousnesses, not clearly distinguishable from ourselves and the director, and the films derive their force from this. It is less defensible when placed in the context of Antonioni's tendency to manipulate his films towards a pre-ordained defeat. The overall effect of Antonioni's films is still to limit rather than extend the spectator's sense of the possibilities of life. (pp. 138, 140)

> *Robin Wood, "Part II: Colour Films," in* Antonioni *by Ian Cameron and Robin Wood (© 1968 by Movie Magazine Limited; reprinted by permission of Movie), Frederick A. Praeger, Publishers, 1968, pp. 106-40.*

## STEPHEN HANDZO

*Zabriskie Point* is Antonioni's clearest statement on a world that has perhaps already ended without realizing it, leaving us all hanging on by flywheel effect waiting for the desensitized apocalypse (like the Nathanael West who haunted airports hoping for planes to crash only-they-never-crash). . . .

Thematically, *Zabriskie Point* is something of a step backwards for Antonioni. Whereas in *Red Desert* he seemed to be working toward a rapprochement of "science" and "feeling," he has opted here for a mindless hippie-New Left and anti-technology, anti-rational, anti-organizational expiation. . . . Perhaps Los Angeles convinced Antonioni that it was already too late and that blowing-it-all-up was the only way out. Or perhaps that is where Antonioni has been all along, simultaneously fascinated and repelled by modernity, doomed forever to mix Marcusean heavythink, Tom Wolfe switched-on sociology, and *Vogue* photography. (p. 15)

Having, perhaps, bored even himself with boring accounts of the bored Italian bourgeoisie, Antonioni now casts his lot with the Marcusean young who dare to paint obscenities on the impersonal walls of Late International Style campus architecture, urinate in corridors color-coordinated in Industrial Psychologist Modern, and copulate in computer centers. Indeed, what more apt locus than the American multiversity could Antonioni have chosen to illustrate the crises of post-industrial society?

*Zabriskie Point* finds America at an impasse, torn by the contradictory values of the [Mr. Allens] who want to erect houses on its mountaintops (mountains, erection, phallus, construction, achievement, aspiration, activity, accomplishment, ambition, houses, offices, institutions, masculinity, business, competition, acquisition, stability, machinations, technics, skyscrapers, guns) and the Darias who would rather make love in its valleys (valley, vagina, vulnerability, passivity, sensitivity, sensuality, fellatio, femininity, sharing, spontaneity, appreciation, indifference, improvisation, humanism, mobility, nature.) (p. 16)

Mark and Daria are implicated in [Allen's] world even though they may think it is a world they never made. They benefit from its technology—reverting to innocence and open spaces in a plane and car respectively—and from whence did they derive their own values if not from the mass higher education subsidized by the tax dollars of the [Allens]?

Ironically, if technology and nature are ever to be reconciled, it will be through the kind of balanced design suggested by [Allen's] houses, which, in fact, harmonize rather successfully with the landscape. Daria feels "at home" in the desert; [Allen] would make the desert a home. . . . For [Allen], instead of temporary escape and isolated forays of short-lived, self-serving gratification, the desert could be made to support an alternative life. The risk, of course, is that however fine the original plans, the infections of smog, neon, and billboards would inevitably follow, humans being as regrettably imperfect as they are. (But wouldn't the likes of Mark and Daria litter the sandscape with half-eaten tacos and used prophylactics, or paint peace symbols and clenched fists on the Grand Canyon?) (pp. 16-17)

In many ways, the United States stands poised at the juncture of critical decisions concerning its future, but Antonioni is an infirm counselor. His characteristic attitude is ambivalence. Antonioni knows history, he knows that any course of action has unforeseeable ramifications, that post-Freudian man is aware of his own neurotic motivations, that action itself is ambiguous. (pp. 17-18)

What American youth perhaps wanted *Zabriskie Point* to be was a scathing indictment of the status quo culminating in an affirmative, self-righteous, implied call-to-arms for a mass Woodstockian uprising. What it got was Mark and Daria: two-against-the-world who would much rather be making love in the desert if only the mean world would stop invading their lives. (p. 19)

Antonioni finds American youth achieving consciousness of its unique historical destiny as the American ethos has sunk to its nadir. (The conjunction of Mark and Daria, and their discovery of each other, takes place at the lowest point, geographically, in the United States.) Whether a new society can arise from the ashes of the old is dubious. (To continue exploration of Zabriskie's symbolic subtext: Daria is headed for Phoenix but never gets there; the mythic bird, Mark, is fatally wounded as he touches ground.) Antonioni may be able to see the forest of the tranquil future through the trees of the troubled present, but he also implies that even if the revolutionary youth culture succeeds, it will inherit a society that has spent its force. The Revolution may be inevitable, but is only slightly less obsolescent than the Establishment as the West dims to twilight. (pp. 19, 22)

[Audiences] come away from *Zabriskie Point* feeling that something is missing or that this is "not America." *Zabriskie Point* is America but it is also Antonioniland and which is paradoxically nowhere and anywhere that the West has loosed the ambiguous gift of technology, shattering and detribalizing traditional cultures into remnants devoid of content and leaving behind a broken landscape of jetports and rice paddies. (pp. 22-3)

Cinema is rife with Good-Bad movies; in *Zabriskie Point,* Antonioni may have created the first Brilliant-Godawful movie, simultaneously sophisticated, puerile, gratifying, maddening, elegantly simple and pretentiously naive. (p. 24)

> *Stephen Handzo, "Michelangelo in Disneyland," in*
> Film Heritage *(copyright 1970 by F. A. Macklin),*
> *Vol. 6, No. 1, Fall, 1970, pp. 7-24.*

**ROY HUSS**

Whether or not one agrees that *Blow-Up* deserves to be called a film classic is perhaps ultimately unimportant. What is clear is that it will continue to fascinate serious moviegoers. This is probably because it rests firmly on what I call the three keystones of film art—three ingredients that have been intrinsic to it from the beginning. These are the ease and gracefulness with which it treats the real world as malleable, while seeming to faithfully document it; the success with which it spatializes time and abstract thought; and the degree to which it is able to enlist the detached-but-involved interest of the eavesdropper and the voyeur. (pp. 2-3)

Antonioni has always avoided a self-conscious display of his mastery of the medium, but in *Blow-Up* he enters a new dimension. By transforming Cortázar's amateur photographer into a professional one, a would-be transcriber of life as well as an artificer of fashion, he makes the aesthetics of documentary filmmaking itself one of the key themes of the film. Whether the photographer's camera has created, distorted, or merely recorded reality becomes a question of technique as well as one of psychology and epistemology.

[The] second keystone of cinematic art [is] the way in which the film medium best reveals time and emotion through the dynamics of space-play. . . . [Drama] for the film medium meant movement—not movement bound by the exigencies of limited setting or by the range of gestures of performers, as in the theatre, but movement born of the constant shifting of spaces and planes, of light and shadow. When involving actors, a filmed sequence made the most dynamic use of space when the threat of a confrontation exploded into a frantic pursuit, as it did in the great locomotive chase in Keaton's *The General.* (p. 3)

In *Blow-Up,* as in [Resnais's *Last Year at Marienbad*] and [Bergman's] *The Seventh Seal,* we see it as a very cerebral, but nevertheless spatially oriented, kind of pursuit—a pursuit of a moment in time that epitomizes some crisis of identification or of self-awareness, and that takes us through endless corridors (*Marienbad*) or over medieval landscapes (*The Seventh Seal*). In *Blow-Up,* as in these other films, the search for self rightly takes the form of a physical quest, in which the protagonist moves successively through a park, in and out of a jungle of photographic equipment, among crowds of hostile and indifferent people. However, here too Antonioni enriches an artistic element by actually making it a subject for study: he not only dramatizes the photographer's quest by choreographing his position with relation to people, objects, and background, but he also allows him, as artist-creator, to "spatialize" dramas of his own. . . . (pp. 3-4)

The third keystone upon which film art makes a bid for our involvement—that of appealing to the voyeur and eavesdropper in all of us—also goes back to its origins, to the lure of the peep show. . . . Antonioni's camera allows us to witness an orgy and several abortive seductions, and, as one critic remarks, lasciviously watches with us from a low angle as the two teenagers, their behinds straining the material of their tight mini-skirts, climb the stairs to the photographer's studio. Yet as before, Antonioni carries his convention a step further: he not only makes us voyeurs but he also studies the act of voyeurism itself. (p. 4)

*Blow-Up* is Antonioni's contribution to the subject of the artist's involvement with his medium. In fact, in many ways, it is a filmmaker's film: Antonioni's fascination with the art and craft of still photography—a sister art to cinematography—shines through at every point. . . .

The filmmaker's involvement with his own craft is revealed in *Blow-Up* in one of the most spell-binding sequences of cinematic art—the one in which the photographer enlarges the series of photographs of the man and woman in the park. In a *tour de force* of artistic transcendence, Antonioni uses his own camera to compel the still-photographer to create a motion picture of the crime—a parallel to the photo-animation that occurs in the mind of the amateur photographer in Cortázar's story. . . . But it is only when Antonioni begins to pan his own camera over the series of photos—sometimes dollying in on one of them for a "close-up"; once following [the photographer] behind a translucent enlargement hanging on the drying-line for a "reverse angle shot" of the photographed park scene—that he begins to activate the series of stills into a kind of motion picture. By finally erasing the image of the photographer himself from the screen, Antonioni reveals even more decisively his directorial presence and control. (p. 5)

> *Roy Huss, in his introduction to* Focus on "Blow-Up," *edited by Roy Huss (© 1971 by Prentice-Hall, Inc.; reprinted by permission of Prentice-Hall, Inc., Englewood Cliffs, New Jersey), Prentice-Hall, 1971, pp. 1-6.*

### JOHN FRANCIS LANE

[Antonioni] doesn't try to push any political message [in *Chung Kwo*]—and indeed it seems a pity that in Shanghai for example we get a tourist view of the city looking much as one has always seen it, even if the Red Light district shines with a different kind of red today, rather than any glimpse into what happened during the Cultural Revolution. When a group of peasants take their 'elevenses' and sit round the table to discuss a point in Mao's Thought that has to do with their work, we are not told in the commentary what they are saying. But Antonioni leaves one to draw one's own conclusions: indeed, one can see from the faces that they are intensely concerned with what they are discussing and that it *is* important to them.

At other times, the Italian commentary . . . will intellectualise, as when during a visit to the Great Wall (a Sunday excursion

for the Chinese family) it quotes Brecht, reminding us that great monuments were not built 'by' emperors or kings but 'by' the slaves who often sacrificed their lives. Antonioni takes a political attitude more subtly in showing us the happiness on the faces of the Chinese people. . . .

[*Chung Kwo*] is a notable achievement as a documentary. But I suspect that it will be remembered not so much for what it shows us about China . . . , but for what it could represent as a personal experience to an artist such as Antonioni, finally exploring a country where there is no such thing as alienation, 'no sense of anxiety or haste,' as the commentary says in the opening sequence. (p. 87)

> *John Francis Lane, "Antonioni Discovers China," in* Sight and Sound *(copyright © 1973 by The British Film Institute), Vol. 42, No. 2, Spring, 1973, pp. 86-7.*

### ROY ARMES

*Chung Kuo,* in many ways a reaction to [the interiority of Antonioni's previous films], presents a surface view of people and settings. Aside from a couple of references to Marco Polo, there is no awareness of history and nowhere does Antonioni attempt any sort of analysis of, say, the meaning of the cultural revolution. We are left with the material gathered by the camera—bland figures in an unspectacular landscape. We see a society without hunger, cities without anxiety, people without poverty or pain. . . . [Antonioni] resists the idea of examining the inevitable cultural paradoxes—there are no clips from Sternberg movies of the 1930s to stress the incongruity of Mao's China and our imaginations, coloured by memories of Marlene Dietrich as Shanghai Lily. Antonioni presents his material in long, uninterrupted sequences without humorous or explanatory detail so that we are driven to reach our own conclusions about the significance of, say, these Chinese sipping tea or simply wandering around amid the relics of an imperial past. The tension comes from the relation of camera and subject. Though we never see Antonioni or his crew at work, the reactions of the Chinese make us continually aware of the camera. The citizens filmed in a Peking square stare back at Antonioni as intently as he examines them. The most remarkable sequence in the whole film comes when a visit is made to a town far off the beaten track which at first seems deserted (echoes of the abandoned village in *L'avventura*). When the inhabitants appear, drawn by the unaccustomed presence of Westerners, the unseen camera seems to hunt them down, so that they turn away and hide—out of fear? timidity? politeness? Following the same journey pattern as so many of Antonioni's films, *Chung Kuo* too comes back finally to what had been its starting point in Peking: the enigma of the Chinese people. (p. 122)

> *Roy Armes, "Red Deserts," in* London Magazine *(© London Magazine 1974), Vol. 13, No. 5, December, 1973-January, 1974, pp. 118, 120-22.*

### PAULINE KAEL

It was possible for people who got caught in the Mod alienation and the mystery of *Blow-Up* to ignore or misunderstand Antonioni's moralism. In *Zabriskie Point*, it saps his style. He has rigged an America that is *nothing but* a justification for violent destruction, and the only distraction—love in the desert sands—is inane. It is a very odd sensation to watch a message movie by a famous artist telling us what is wrong with America while showing us something both naïve and decrepit; if it weren't for this peculiar sense of dislocation and the embarrassment one feels for Antonioni, *Zabriskie Point* would be just one more "irreverent" pandering-to-youth movie, and (except photographically) worse than most.

But the dislocation is crucial: *Zabriskie Point* is a disaster, but, as one might guess, Antonioni does not make an ordinary sort of disaster. This is a huge, jerry-built, crumbling ruin of a movie. At the opening, he tries briefly to capture the ambience of revolutionary youth, but he soon returns to his own kind of apparently aimless scenes in his own kind of barren landscape. . . . It's as if he were baffled by America and it all got away from him, and so he, like other filmmakers, picked up the youth mythology so popular in the mass media; but he uses it as a rigid, schematic political point of view, and it doesn't fit his deliberately open-ended, sprawling style. (p. 114)

*Zabriskie Point* is pitched to youth—that is, to the interests and values of the rebellious sons and daughters of the professional and upper middle classes—the way the old Hollywood movies used to be pitched to lower-middle-class values. The good guys (youth) and the bad guys (older white Americans) are as stiffly stereotyped as in any third-rate melodrama, and the evil police have been cast from the same mold as the old Hollywood Nazis. Antonioni has dehumanized them, so that they can be hated as pigs, but since he has failed to humanize the youth, it's dummies against dummies. (pp. 114-15)

It's a dumb movie, unconsciously snobbish, as if America should be destroyed because of its vulgarity. We're embarrassed for Antonioni not because he insults America—everybody does that, and we're used to it—but because he insults our intelligence. (p. 116)

[He is] saying that America is nothing but garden furniture and books and the contents of our freezers—that we are a nation not of people but of objects. . . . *Are* we nothing but material objects, or is it that Antonioni can't connect with us and so, like his alienated protagonists in earlier films, turns us into objects? I think the deadness of *Zabriskie Point* comes from his own inability to respond to America and his falling back on treating everyone in it as an object in a demonstration. In the ending, when Antonioni makes extraordinarily pretty pictures of chaos, isn't he doing just what he attacked the "decadent," "irresponsible" photographer in *Blow-Up* for doing? (He used the title *Blow-Up* on the wrong movie.) I doubt if he's much interested in his theme of revolutionary action; I think it's the other way around—politics provides the excuse for photogenic explosions. (p. 117)

> Pauline Kael, "The Beauty of Destruction" (origi-
> nally published in a slightly different form in The
> New Yorker, Vol. XLVI, No. 1, February 21, 1970),
> in her Deeper into Movies (© 1970 by Pauline Kael;
> reprinted by permission of Little, Brown and Com-
> pany in association with the Atlantic Monthly Press),
> Atlantic-Little, Brown, 1973, pp. 113-19.*

## LEE ATWELL

Antonioni is certainly due recognition as a master film-maker, but in the case of *The Passenger,* it is misplaced and tends to ignore the weaknesses of a work that exhibits an uneasy blend of commercialism and art, ultimately satisfying the demands of neither. . . .

*The Passenger* nevertheless remains, if only in part, a meditative exercise that deliberately avoids the mechanics of suspense so masterfully deployed in *Blow Up.* [Claire] Peploe's original story, entitled *Fatal Exit*, resembles the early stories of Sartre and Camus that utilize melodramatic fiction to convey existential concepts. Its closest filmic counterpart is perhaps in Godard and Truffaut, who successfully infused their own personal visions and cinematic vitality into the thriller format with *A Bout de souffle* and *Tirez sur le pianiste*. Antonioni, on the other hand, has never demonstrated any genuine interest in this sort of material. Even in *Blow Up,* where the "who-done-it?" framework seems most relevant, our attention is constantly deflected toward the values implicit in the photographer's behavior and his problem of grasping an objective view of reality. Here, the conventional suspense elements are perfectly in accord with Antonioni's subject and method, but in *The Passenger* this is not always the case. . . .

Rather than produce a fast-paced thriller with existential undertones, Antonioni gives the story a languid, leisurely ambience, dwelling on existential motifs exteriorized through psychological behavior. Jack Nicholson's world-weary journalist is seen as symptomatic of the modern man who reaches a point of no return and "feels the need for a personal revolution." (p. 57)

When speaking of his character's need for a "personal revolution," Antonioni cannot, I think, be implying that he acts out of a change in political perspective. The film's evidence simply does not support this view. Locke does not assume Robertson's identity for any other reason than to escape his past, and in doing so he acts out of "bad faith," refusing to accept responsibility for the situation in which he finds himself. Furthermore, he acts out of ignorance of the dead man's existential situation. All this seems to complicate matters for the sake of narrative intrigue, but Antonioni seeks to put matters into perspective through the introduction of a young girl Locke meets casually in Barcelona. . . . Her main function . . . is that of a catalyst, a positive force moving David forward from the impasse in which he finds himself. (p. 59)

Antonioni has always stated that because of his intuitive, evolving conception of working, he is unable to understand a particular work fully until he has finished it. Here, discrepancies appear because he has begun with a *finished* story and rationalized himself into it rather than letting his expressive needs grow out of the material. Altering it to suit his own nature, he has succeeded in creating some memorable sequences that are in themselves noteworthy but do not contribute to the underlying conventions of the story in an effective manner. . . .

Beginning with *L'Eclisse,* Antonioni has exhibited a strong predilection for indirect, symbolic finales of a virtuoso order, and although experimental and poetic in structure, related directly to the theme or underlying premise of the film. This explains why the director imposes a similar ending on *The Passenger.* (p. 60)

If we compare this sequence with the mimed tennis game which concludes *Blow Up,* and so movingly suggests the photographer's impoverished values, or the apocalyptic fantasy of the heroine, expressing her ultimate disillusion with American capitalist society, in *Zabriskie Point,* the virtuosity of this extended take appears like "The Emperor's New Clothes." If we are to assume that the central character's death has any significance, why does Antonioni go to such pains to avoid it? Because he wants to create an aura of suspense—very much in the manner of Hitchcock in *Rope*—to enliven the final moments of a story, and a character, which do not particularly interest him. As a result, Locke's death does not acquire any existential meaning and the final shot suggesting the continuity of life is merely an added afterthought rather than a meaningful gesture. Its resignation is that of a master film poet who has just completed an assignment full of beautifully conceived moments that fail to cohere into a satisfying artistic whole. (p. 61)

*Lee Atwell, "'The Passenger'," in* Film Quarterly *(copyright 1975 by The Regents of the University of California; reprinted by permission of the University of California Press), Vol. XXVIII, No. 4, Summer, 1975, pp. 56-61.*

## JOHN SIMON

If vacuity had any weight, you could kill an ox by dropping on it Michelangelo Antonioni's latest film, *The Passenger*. Emptiness is everywhere: in landscapes and townscapes, churches and hotel rooms, and most of all in the script. Never was dialogue more portentously vacuous, plot more rudimentary yet preposterous, action more haphazard and spasmodic, characterization more tenuous and uninvolving, film making more devoid of all but postures and pretensions. In his great films (*L'Avventura, The Eclipse*), Antonioni managed to show real people gnawed on by aimlessness, boredom, self-hate, against backgrounds of gorgeous isolation or bustling indifference. They were people whose words and gestures we recognized, whose obsessions or despair we could understand, especially as they were surrounded by vistas or artifacts that objectified their malaise.

In *The Passenger,* however, everything must be taken on the say-so of the film makers, on the slender evidence of a pained expression or a painfully written line or two. (p. 16)

The symbolic superstructure had better rest on a little basic believability before reaching for the higher metaphysics; but *The Passenger* is using its pseudo-Hitchcockian framework without any of Hitchcock's ability to couch his machinations in ostensible reality. . . .

Motivation is as scant as probability. One quasi-stenographic scene is supposed to convey what went wrong between David and Rachel. . . . [Human] behavior is reduced to mere uncompelling idiograms. . . .

But there is another layer here, the Antonioni-autobiography layer, where the director unconvincingly superimposes his own problems on those of his characters. . . . Antonioni's self-pity preempts the chance of genuine pity evolving for the characters. . . .

But what about dialogue? When David first accosts The Girl at the Palacio Güell, here is their initial exchange: "I was trying to remember something." "Is it important?" "No—what is it, do you know? I came in by accident." "The man who built it was hit by a bus." "Who was he?" "Gaudí." "Was he crazy?" I cannot say whether the scenarist who has two people meet like this is crazy, but he might easily have suffered a concussion when hit by a bus. When the dialogue isn't being coyly lunatic, it is dismally platitudinous. . . .

And then there is the pretentiousness, as when The Girl walks up to the window of the ultimate hotel room. "What do you see?" David asks from the bed on which he sprawls. "A little boy and an old woman. They are having an argument about which way to go." A bit later he asks again: "What can you

see now?" "A man scratching his shoulder. A kid throwing stones. And dust." Compare this with John Peale Bishop's poem, *Perspectives Are Precipices*, from which it may derive, and you'll see the difference between genuine symbolism and mere attitudinizing. . . .

What, then, are the film's contributions? It plays around fairly effectively with video tape and the tape recorder, but this sort of thing was handled better in *Blow-Up* with still photography. The film's vistas are beautiful enough, as always in Antonioni, and are well chosen to evoke moods. But without any human beings we can feel for, these sights, including some interesting interiors, remain no more than the interior and exterior decorator's art. There are some bravura shots [especially the seven minute take at the end of the film.]. . .

Now [this take] is all very ingenious, involving a crane and a special camera that can dangle perfectly horizontally, and some fancy choreography. But what does it mean? That time passes and brings with it equally trivia and tragedy? That life tramples indiscriminately big and small events? But this could be done much better (as it was at the end of *The Eclipse*) if we were not obliged to wonder, "How in hell did he get that shot?" or to exclaim, "My, isn't that clever!" It is directing that calls attention to itself for its own sake, and, among other things, serves to obscure from us the killing and wrap it in adventitious mystery. The sequence, with all its cleverness, is ostentatious and obfuscatory. Technique is to be admired only when it submerges itself in dramatic necessity. (p. 20)

*John Simon, "Antonioni: 'The Passenger' Will Please Refrain . . ." (reprinted by permission of Wallace & Sheil Agency, Inc.; copyright © 1975 by John Simon), in* Esquire, *Vol. 84, No. 1, July, 1975, pp. 16, 20, 39.*

## GORDON GOW

*Zabriskie Point* is the most intricate of all [Antonioni's] films to date. If there is a political point to be dredged from the student phase at the beginning, it is incidental to the major theme of individuality at bay. Both Mark and Daria are opposed to the regimented society that hems them in. He lunges out against it with the clumsiness of the proverbial bull in a china shop, while she is comparatively adjusted and cool. . . .

[The] visual stress in the opening phase of the film, set in Los Angeles, implies a brain-washed society. And this is echoed in the ideas of Daria's current employer, the property developer Mr Allen. . . . What he had in mind is an environment for a mindless community, seemingly offered a carefree holiday-orientated existence, but in conditions so thoroughly preordained as to obliterate the need to think. (p. 33)

[Our] dislike of the conformity that Mr Allen represents, albeit with benignity, is channelled through our sympathy for Daria's calm and reasoning attitude to life. This girl is no sluggard. She isn't keen on work, yet she does it—'for the bread'—and if her emotional involvements are apt to be thin, we are shown in the key sequence at Death Valley that she can share with Mark an impulse which is both sexual and spiritual. Their time together on the sun-parched lake bed is indeed a time of love. And the most essential of the intermingled themes in *Zabriskie Point* is the importance of love, and the difficulty of sustaining it, within a conformist and materialistic society.

The film introduces tangential themes in the somewhat rambling style Antonioni favours. The first is sparked off by Mark's determination to assert his solidarity with the rebels but to do it in an individual way, which we have been given to understand is against the policy of the student group. (pp. 33-4)

If this first tangent underlines the prevalence of violence, and of a self-righteous readiness to retaliate, the second tangent suggests that a retreat which embodies an attempt at reform cannot be easy to attain. This we glean when Daria takes a little time out during her drive towards the Arizona house of Mr Allen, and goes to the small town called Ballister where she seeks but does not find James Patterson—a character destined never to be seen in the film. (p. 34)

[Patterson] might be taken as a wish-projection of Mark's unfocused quest. Here is a loner, wanting to be socially beneficial, doing something about it, and evidently putting up with the grumblings of the Ballister townsfolk who consider him a 'do gooder'—which in their book is an uncomplimentary term.

But of course Mark will never reach even this amount of fulfilment. His self-destruction is not a simple thing, not inevitable. He might have acquired with time the staying power of a James Patterson. But his youngish impulsive drive, and his entanglement of rebellion and a certain basic honesty that relates to moral convention, combine to bring about his death.

First, however, there is his love for Daria, fleeting and elegiac. This is the very core of the film. Their meeting is a *jeu d'esprit*, an exceptionally light conceit for Antonioni and one that works beautifully. It lifts the film out of reality and into an ambiance of discreet fantasy. (pp. 34-5)

In Death Valley they provide an affirmation of life. The dried-up lake bed, the fierce sun, the relentless dust—none of these can deter their mutual rejoicing. On the contrary, within that gently fantasised environment, the irritants of nature are transmuted into a vision of beauty.

Viewed now, retrospectively, as a testament to the hope that was implicit in flower power, the development of the *Zabriskie Point* 'love-in' assumes a sad irony. (p. 35)

Mark's flight out of Los Angeles, as well as having a realistic plot motivation, is symbolic of his discontent with earthly restraints: 'I needed,' he says, 'to get off the ground.' And no doubt it is for this same reason that he takes dangerously to the air again. . . . (pp. 35-6)

The difficulty confronting an individualist in modern society is a problem known to many of the male characters of Antonioni: not least of course to Locke . . . , assuming the identity of another man, in the latest Antonioni film *The Passenger*. But for Mark it culminates with a tragically abrupt punctuation mark, which Mark has virtually wished upon himself, but which nevertheless, we cannot help but feel, he could without too much effort have avoided. Maybe Daria thinks to herself during the closing sequence that she ought to have made a greater effort to help Mark. But her sexuality is of a casual nature in keeping with the wishful freedom of her era, and love is likewise transient. This element of dissatisfaction with herself is combined with a resentment of diehard established values, and of the increase of social conformity. Such is her state of mind as envisaged by Antonioni in his now famous explosion sequence. (pp. 36-7)

What reverberates and repeats for Daria is hatred. She wants a fate more violent than Mark's to overtake the signs of conformity that he resisted in his own insufficient way. Perhaps Daria's personal resistance will be stronger. Certainly the up-surge of music and the gold-flooded sky as she drives on again, to no known destination, would imply a measure of optimism. But what the entire explosion sequence also implies, with hindsight, is a division between the peaceful ethos of flower power, with which Daria has not been absolutely identified, and the more practical strain in this girl: a strain that might well turn into the abrasive demeanour that one finds among malcontents in these mid-1970s. Because the peaceful ways, being extreme, were impractical, they have given place here and there to a certain bitterness, not unrelated of course to the increase in crime and to the more heated conflict between individualism and technology.

*Zabriskie Point* has a significance that endures, gathering strength as the passing years help so heartlessly to reinforce its observations of life. (p. 37)

> Gordon Gow, "A Michelangelo Antonioni Film: 'Zabriskie Point'" (© copyright Gordon Gow 1975; reprinted with permission), in Films and Filming, Vol. 21, No. 10, July, 1975, pp. 33-7.

**BERNARD F. DICK**

Superficially, *The Passenger* is an assumed-identity film that observes the conventions of the genre as if they were rubrics for an ancient liturgy. The genre works according to a formula that admits of some variation depending on whether the masquerade is a comic ruse (Wilder's *The Major and the Minor* and *Some Like It Hot*), a means of saving face (Capra's *Lady for a Day*), or a matter of survival (Paul Henreid's *Dead Ringer*). In its more serious form, the assumed identity film has the following features: (1) the masquerade ends in failure, often in death; (2) the pretender becomes a fugitive from society, forsaking even his wife and friends; (3) if he takes on the identity of someone with underworld connections, he will run afoul of the syndicate because of his inability to deliver what it expects of him; (4) the pretender then becomes a man on the run, and his odyssey will, for the moment, transform the film into a road movie with its own conventions including the travelling companion with whom the fugitive has a short-lived but blissful affair, and the fortuitous event (e.g., car trouble) that brings the journey to a close; (5) the key figures in the deception assemble in the same place for the dénouement.

What distinguishes *The Passenger* from other films of this type is Antonioni's approach to the genre. In one sense, it is impossible to take the film literally because Jack Nicholson does not play both Locke and Robertson. . . . Clearly Robertson and Locke are twin aspects of the same person, like Elisabet and Alma in Bergman's *Persona*. Locke is theoretical man, an interviewer to whom Third World revolutionaries are material for a documentary; Robertson is practical man, a gunrunner to whom they are a source of income. (pp. 66-7)

Antonioni takes the conventions of the assumed identity film and pushes them to their epistemological and existential conclusions. Any serious film or work of literature that centers about masquerade, deception, or the discrepancy between illusion and reality ([Miguel Cervantes's *Don Quixote*, Luigi Pirandello's] *Six Characters in Search of an Author*, [Jean] Anouilh's *Traveller without Luggage*, [Jean] Genet's *The Balcony*) is, at least implicitly, epistemological. . . .

Furthermore, if a writer really intends to explore the consequences of exchanging one life or one mode of being for another, he will inevitably move into the realm of the existential.

Why would one man switch places with another unless his own life were purposeless, unless he wanted to *become* something and not merely *be?* It is the philosophical core of the film, along with the literary analogues it evokes, that makes *The Passenger* unique in its genre. (p. 67)

The same charge that has been levelled against Sartre has been levelled against Antonioni, namely that his works are static. This is hardly the occasion to place Sartre and Antonioni within the context of the static that extends all the way back to Aeschylus' *Prometheus Bound.* Still it should be noted that Antonioni expresses visually what Sartre expresses verbally: the state of being trapped in the glue of existence. When fluidity has congealed, when freedom has ossified, there can be no movement.

David Locke is a man whose freedom has ossified. He has no being-for-others, only being-for-itself, which is mere nothingness. He will remain in that state until he frees himself of David Locke and becomes David Robertson, who, despite his shady (or is it?) profession, was at least committed to something. . . .

It is impossible to watch the opening scenes of *The Passenger* without thinking of Camus' *The Stranger,* where the Algerian sun melts a freshly tarred road into a sheet of adhesive and dyes the golden sand red. It is an indifferent landscape, as unfeeling as Mersault, who responds to his mother's death, an Arab's murder, and his own execution with the same virile silence. . . .

While Locke is a kinsman of Mersault, he is the brother of Roquentin, the narrator of Sartre's *Nausea,* who finds recording his thoughts in a diary as agonizing as Locke finds interviewing uncommunicative subjects for a documentary. Both suffer from *mauvaise foi* (self-deception), for neither is free. Roquentin is a slave to his diary and the book he is writing about the Marquis de Robellon; Locke is trapped in a job that holds no more surprises and a marriage that has turned sour. Both are moral sleepwalkers, acted upon rather than acting, influenced not by freedom of choice but by the presence of objects. (p. 68)

Roquentin's past was his diary, Locke's is his documentary, which Antonioni intercuts with the force of a flashback, although within the context of the film it is being viewed by Mrs. Locke and television producer Martin Knight. We learn much about Locke from the documentary. While he had the interviewer's knack of asking the right questions, he received answers that were so politically cautious that they meant nothing. In one instance, a witch doctor, annoyed at Locke's perfectly appropriate question about the disparity between his education and his current profession, walks off camera. The documentary form restricts Locke to the role of dispassionate recorder, limiting him to a life of fact, not fancy. Clearly Locke wants not only to change lives but also to change films; as David Locke he is the faceless creator of a documentary, but as David Robertson he can be the star of a road flick or a cloak-and-dagger movie. . . .

*The Passenger* moves between the two poles of the absurd and the existential; between Camus' incongruous universe where Sisyphus pushes his rock up the hill, only to have it roll back down, and Sartre's where men must struggle to achieve an essence even if it means keeping a rendezvous with death. Because the existentialist is more aware of the incongruous than the rationalist, he can see as basic truths what a more parochial mind would see as paradoxes. To ask if Locke's parable is Antonioni's indictment of self-knowledge is to ask

if *The Stranger* is Camus' criticism of the absurd. Even Sartre did not know if Camus were writing for or against the absurd in the novel. Obviously he was doing both, for *The Stranger* shows the glory of absurd man in maintaining his stony silence even to the end and the tragedy of absurd man who never says all he might have said.

What we learn from the film is more important than what Locke learns. The spectator's knowledge is always greater than the protagonist's because the spectator can relate the protagonist's knowledge to something beyond fiction—to some school of philosophy or religious thought, even to the problem of evil. . . .

[In the final scene] of *The Passenger,* Antonioni combines the existential and the absurd into an aesthetic. It is no longer a question of what Locke knows or even what we know, but what the camera knows. (p. 71)

The camera is free, and we are also. But free for what? To speculate on what is happening (or has happened) in the hotel room? Ironically, the frustration of not being out in the square has changed to the frustration of being in the square when we would rather be back in the room. (p. 72)

This incredible sequence is Antonioni's answer to the question that haunted Roquentin: Can one ever record what he sees or experiences with total accuracy? Certainly not with words which make an adventure of the present an exploit of the past, but perhaps with the camera whose eye is more exact than man's. Yet Antonioni would deny this, for cinematic knowledge is also limited. Life conceals its secrets even from the scrutiny of the camera. In his folly, man thinks that the closer he gets to an object, the better he can discern its nature. Yet the closer he gets to the object, the more ambiguous it becomes. . . .

In *The Psychology of the Imagination,* Sartre writes: "There is accordingly something overflowing about the world of 'things.' There is always, at each moment, intimately more than we can see." Antonioni has respected the privacy of things and has not robbed existence of its mysteries. But he has taken life in all of its contingent sloppiness and by his genius stamped it with the seal of the necessary. Antonioni has also kept his appointment—with art. (p. 73)

*Bernard F. Dick, "'The Passenger' and Literary Existentialism," in* Literature/Film Quarterly *(© copyright 1977 Salisbury State College), Vol. 5, No. 1, Winter, 1977, pp. 66-74.*

**HARLAN KENNEDY**

[*Il Mistero di Oberwald*] begins like a horror extravaganza, with Gothic-lettered credits leaping out from a blood-red mountainscape. Soon Antonioni turns all the notorious vices of video—the soft definition, the shimmer of parallel lines, the tendency of colors to trail—into expressionist virtues. Cocteau's talky period piece [*L'Aigle a deux têtes,* on which the film is based], about a widowed queen . . . and the young rebel with whom she falls in love, becomes a playground for a ghostly, ectoplasmic dance. Antonioni washes color in and out to match mood or character, and he deploys video's supreme facility for trick photography to riveting trompe l'oeil effect. The result, instead of apologizing for video, exults in it, and some of the images—the blood-red prelude, a yellow cornfield as biliously beautiful as a van Gogh—remind one that Antonioni can be the cinema's boldest painter. (p. 18)

*Harlan Kennedy, "Venice: From 'Basta' to Bravo," in* American Film *(reprinted with permission from the January-February issue of* American Film *magazine; © 1981, The American Film Institute, J. F. Kennedy Center, Washington, DC 20566), Vol. VI, No. 4, January-February, 1981, pp. 18-21.\**

# John Cassavetes

## 1929-

**American director, actor, screenwriter, and producer.**

**Cassavetes dramatizes an intimate view of reality in sensitive, experimental films. While not always popular successes, they bear the mark of a director intensely involved with his material.**

**Cassavetes's outstanding acting ability led to a teaching position at an actors's workshop. The exercises he did with his students developed the style of his first film, *Shadows*. It brought Cassavetes recognition as a director, and was hailed as a breakthrough in underground film technique.**

**Under contract with Paramount, he produced two films, *Too Late Blues* and *A Child Is Waiting*, the latter completed by Stanley Kramer. Neither film was particularly well received, and Cassavetes opted for an independent filmmaking career. Both *Faces* and *Husbands*, his next films, focused on the unhappy, insular people of middle-class America. In *Faces*, Cassavetes analyzes "the millions of marriages that just sort of glide along." A biting study of communication breakdown, it was regarded as a highly personal depiction of marital strife. Continuing the theme of marital dissension, *A Woman Under the Influence* is seen by some critics to be strongly influenced by the writings of R. D. Laing. It seems to be the culmination of concepts hinted at in the two previous films.**

**Cassavetes's best work effectively studies the depths of emotion that people find inexpressible. However, in less successful films, such as *The Killing of a Chinese Bookie*, his techniques are considered merely actors's exercises rather than intimate, controlled directorial works. (See also *Contemporary Authors*, Vols. 85-88.)**

### ALBERT JOHNSON

American films have become so glossy in their technical mastery and box-office attitudes that one greets with surprise and a sort of awe an independent group of film artists, not particularly interested in financial gain, who have created a celluloid diamond of neorealism and called it *Shadows*.

It is, first of all, the best American film about racial relations yet made. Secondly, one hopes it heralds the beginning of a tradition of cinematic vitality and honesty dealing with the experiences of ordinary human beings in the United States. . . . [The] entire film is an improvisation on life and emotional disturbances among a certain milieu of city strugglers—un-

known singers, artists, dancers, and actors who comprise part of the so-called "bohemian" strata of society. Its theme is loneliness, the chief cause of frustration among the young, but strengthened by counter-themes of color prejudice, the lack of artistic values in this country, and the casual cheapening of ideals. (p. 32)

[In] *Shadows*, the imagery is the really eloquent force. Cassavetes aims for the unobtrusive observation of truth—the suddenly dramatic revelation of character in a commonplace environment. His insight into the complexities of white and Negro relationships in an urban environment, and his belief in capturing the looks, tones, and movements of people off-guard, brings him close to a kind of stylized documentary. (p. 33)

Despite the crudities of lens and the occasionally discordant soundtrack, . . . the truthfulness is inescapable, making *Shadows* a notably dynamic film gesture toward total reality. (p. 34)

*Albert Johnson, "'Shadows'," in* Film Quarterly *(copyright 1960 by The Regents of the University of California; reprinted by permission of the University of California Press), Vol. XIII, No. 3, Spring, 1960, pp. 32-4.*

### R. E. DURGNAT

[The characters in *Shadows*] are *shadows* because they are classless, rootless, virtually raceless, and hemmed in by an ideology of competitiveness which forces on the individual an individualism run mad and, faced with the "simple" things, can only despise or (which comes to the same thing) sentimentalise them.

The film is sometimes agonising (Lelia's disappointment after her first sexual experience: "I never knew love could be so awful!") but taken all in all its humour is too scathing, it has too much warmth, vitality and sense of friendship to be downbeat. On the contrary, its *frankness* has a truly liberating effect. . . .

For here is a film with neither false aesthetic "distance" nor a forced lyricism; no formal "style" is allowed to impose an unreal dignity or coldness on the characters; even the comic relief is derived, realistically, from the story's emotional situations and not derived from them. . . . The improvisational form frees the narrative from the conventional dramatic "emphases'' and the excessive psychological clarity of constructed plots. Its study of everyday conversation—the nuances, the sudden spurts and withdrawals of feeling—is as entertaining as it is full of insights.

*Shadows* isn't the first film to be improvised, it's not the first good film about contemporary youth, it's not the first good film about Negroes. But it is all these things with such *thoroughness* that its example is going to be very influential indeed. And it's chock full of truth. (p. 30)

*R. E. Durgnat, "New Films: "Shadows"' (© copyright R. E. Durgnat 1960; reprinted with permission), in* Films and Filming, *Vol. 7, No. 2, November, 1960, pp. 29-30.*

**RAYMOND DURGNAT**

[*Too Late Blues*] plunges us again into the harsh and blistering world of *Shadows*. (p. 29)

If the focus of *Shadows* was rootlessness that of *Too Late Blues* is cruelty. The characters constantly turn on each other with a nagging, ranging spite. (pp. 29-30)

The story is neatly constructed, the dialogue so sharp and biting as to be naturalistic rather than natural, the images are less blemished, gritty and eloquent than those of *Shadows*. Still, many scenes seem improvised, the compositions and staging informal, even haphazard. The film sweeps from a casually discursive style to banging emotional scenes which combine a convincing notation of detail with almost grossly effective situations . . . and reach a quite exceptional intensity. . . .

The film generally has many errors of continuity, tone, and nuance. Often the crescendo of feelings seem disrupted. . . . The network of friendships arising in the band as a *community*, and the *creative* theme, are assumed rather than explored. . . .

The band's final reconciliation . . . is phoney in conception and weakened by the director's attempt to restore authenticity by a laconic, sombre style. The "shaped" story and the discursive scenes sometimes gell dissatisfyingly. (p. 30)

*Too Late Blues* supplements, rather than repeating, *Shadows*, although I would like to see Cassavetes next time move further from his *Shadows* stamping ground of bars, parties, quick lays and slogging matches. I think he could learn something from the emotional subtlety of Chayefsky's underestimated *The Middle of the Night* and from Renoir's ability to combine improvisational freshness with a mellower variegation of moods. This film deserves very severe criticism by the highest standards, and one can't criticise away its power and drive. (pp. 30-1)

*Raymond Durgnat, "New Films: 'Too Late Blues'"(© copyright Raymond Durgnat 1961; reprinted with permission), in* Films and Filming, *Vol. 8, No. 3, December, 1961, pp. 29-31.*

**ALBERT JOHNSON**

It is . . . quite interesting to discover in John Cassavetes' new film, *Too Late Blues,* a truly challenging Hollywood film, giving an unusual interpretation of a group of white jazz musicians in Los Angeles. It is still not *the* jazz film for which we have all been waiting, but more than its predecessors it reveals with authenticity the awkward, nonintellectual passions and weaknesses of people who make a living out of playing jazz music. It explores character with [depth and sincerity],

and in the screenplay Cassavetes and his collaborator, Richard Carr, have managed to capture the argot—swift, hardboiled, and sometimes poetic—of music-making hipsters without a cause. It is a very strange and exciting film to come from a major Hollywood studio. (pp. 49-50)

[Despite] the early perplexities of the film (one is not really certain about Ghost's motivations or personality from the outset, yet this is deliberately part of the scriptwriters' intentions), *Too Late Blues* holds one with its contrasting atmospheres of footloose jazz characters. . . . (p. 50)

Cassavetes succeeds in presenting a moving love-story of life among the jazz people, full of crowded, interracial parties and artistic insecurity. Perhaps, too, here and there throughout the film, the director, seeking to uncover the hearts of his characters, has partially exposed their agonized souls. (p. 51)

*Albert Johnson, "Film Reviews: 'Too Late Blues'," in* Film Quarterly *(copyright 1962 by The Regents of the University of California; reprinted by permission of the University of California Press), Vol. XV, No. 2, Winter, 1961-62, pp. 49-51.*

**GORDON GOW**

Infinitely more calculated than *Shadows*, [*Faces*] still holds the feeling of spontaneity, of life going on unpredictably, movements unplanned, conversations disjointed and overlapping, remarks half-heard. . . .

The characters are 'types', well-heeled Americans for whom life has gone stale with the onset of middle-age. Indigenous, perhaps: yet universal in their emotions and frustrations. . . .

Long-winded the film may be (indeed *is*) but its truth is undeniable, even when it arrives at something akin to romanticism: a germ of hope to buffer the stark emptiness of the coda. [The suicide] sequence that inclines toward the romantic is still expressed in realistic terms, more stark than anything else in the movie. . . . (p. 35)

*Faces* is a work of great talent. Its flaw is merely the familiar one of the artist too close to his own work to judge best where a sequence might be curtailed to advantage: thus, in portraying boredom for example, Cassavetes is now and then in danger of being just a bit of a bore. A small flaw, in the circumstances. Preferable by far to the committee-planned movie that blinkers reality in its anxiety to hold our attention. One feels bound to note the flaw because it's there, but one forgives it wholeheartedly in a film which merges art and life to near-perfection, and which manages at one and the same time to be both critical and compassionate. (pp. 35-6)

*Gordon Gow, "'Faces'" (© copyright Gordon Gow 1968; reprinted with permission), in* Films and Filming, *Vol. 15, No. 3, December, 1968, pp. 35-6.*

**CLAIRE CLOUZOT**

In *Faces,* John Cassavetes stigmatizes the American middle-aged upper-middle-class couple: in the midst of the Youth Era, someone has touched the untouchable, the unfashionable, the unsellable. Until now the fatigued adults of *Faces* had served as background character parts, as caricatures to be made fun of. They were, to pronounce the horrible word, parents. But Cassavetes has brought these neglected elements of society into the limelight. . . . (p. 31)

What matters in *Faces* is gestures, looks, attitudes, and small reactions in the small events of life. Richard and Maria are not particularly attractive, not particularly outstanding, not particularly picturesque. They are well-to-do people with the right home, the right job, and the proper automatism of pouring themselves a drink every day at the same hour. . . .

Cassavetes treats them with no complacency, but with a balance of compassion and lucidity. This makes the film sometimes cruel, often moving. Cassavetes presents the people of *Faces* as neither good nor bad, but *the way they are,* showing their ridiculous, their silly, their pitiful sides. (p. 32)

If *Shadows* was an important landmark for the critics and the aesthetics of the American cinema, *Faces* is one for the American public. . . .

For the first time, a film seems to work not for escapist reasons but for reasons of therapy. Suddenly, to watch other couples work out their differences up there on the mirror of the screen where one's own reflections are caught seems to help. . . .

This aspect of collective exorcism in *Faces* is just one suggestion. But the effect of the film, the very combination of fiction and direct filming which makes people respond so readily to *Faces,* cannot be denied. . . . Without knowing anything of *cinéma-vérité,* they have assimilated its very principles via television watching. People are what they are on the tube: neither magnified, nor embellished, but small, pimplish, real. And so they are in *Faces.* (p. 34)

The goal of *Faces* was modest, and so is its bearing. Cassavetes's film works better as a description of a class than as a sociological explanation. The purpose of the film is neither to expose the reasons of people's behavior nor to offer formulas for their happiness but to use *cinéma* to show their *vérité.* For the first time, a film speaks to the American public of Americans, the "forgotten" ones who have committed no murders, achieved no sexual prowess, nor blown up or discovered a planet but who live, get married, settle, get bored, divorce, and die. (p. 35)

> Claire Clouzot, "Reviews: 'Faces'," in Film Quarterly *(copyright 1969 by The Regents of the University of California; reprinted by permission of the University of California Press), Vol. XXII, No. 3, Spring, 1969, pp. 31-5.*

### PAULINE KAEL

*Husbands,* directed by Cassavetes, extends the faults of his last film, *Faces;* one might even say that *Husbands* takes those faults into a new dimension. It is, as *Faces* was, semi-written by Cassavetes and semi-improvised by the actors. This time, the film is about three suburban husbands—Cassavetes (a dentist), Gazzara (a Peter Max sort of commercial artist), and Peter Falk (profession unspecified)—who go on a bender after attending the funeral of a fourth. . . . One assumes they are meant to be searching for themselves, their lost freedom, and their lost potentialities—and one can guess that Cassavetes believes that their boyishness is creative. But the boyishness he shows us isn't remotely creative; it's just infantile and offensive.

The three leads are like performers in a Norman Mailer movie, role-playing at being lowlifes. Despite the suburban-commuter roles they have chosen, they punch and poke each other like buffoonish hardhats. When one cries, "Harry, you're a phony," the riposte is "Nobody calls me a phony"—and this sort of exchange may be followed by gales of laughter. In fact, they act very much like Gazzara, Falk, and Cassavetes doing their buddy-buddy thing on the "Dick Cavett Show." They horse around, encouraging each other to come up with dialogue like "The man is right. When the man is right, he's right." Since their performances don't have enough range for a full-length film, they become monotonous; Cassavetes apparently deceives himself and others into taking this monotony for fidelity to life. He replaces the exhausted artifices of conventional movies with a new set of pseudo-realistic ones, which are mostly instantaneous clichés. As a writer-director, he's so dedicated to revealing the pain under the laughter he's a regular Pagliacci. To put it in the puerile terms in which it is conceived, Cassavetes thinks that in *Husbands* he has stripped people of their pretenses and laid bare their souls.

Cassavetes' method was originally, back in the *Shadows* days, to combine a group of actors' improvisations into a loose story; now he writes and stages sequences to look improvised. (pp. 222-23)

His approach to filmmaking is an actor's approach, and when it's effective it has certain resemblances to Harold Pinter's approach to theatre. The three men interacting onscreen are like the basic Pinter stage situation. We don't know anything about the supposed characters or their connections to the world—when they're throwing up their past lives we don't know what they're throwing up—but the actors have occasional intense and affecting moments, going through emotions that they set off in each other. We're glued to the acting in this movie, because that's really all there is, and maybe the best clue to the chaos of Cassavetes' method comes from the subsidiary players. The three leads are, after all, successful actors who have chosen to do what they're doing; they seem to be having a good time, and it's their psychodrama and their picture. (p. 223)

*Husbands* is a messy synthesis—a staged film with a documentary-style use of professional performers. We don't know what to react to: we can't sort out what we're meant to see from what we see. We know that the people around the table in the bar wouldn't sit there while these clowns bully them unless they were paid for it, but we also know that the sequence is supposed to reveal something that "ordinary" movies don't. But what does it reveal except the paralysis and humiliation of the bit players? . . . Cassavetes' camera style is to move in for the kill, like those TV newsmen who ask people in distress the questions that push them to break down while the camera moves in on the suffering eyes and choking mouth. In the past, Cassavetes has given some erratic evidence of being a compassionate director; I think he forfeits all claims to compassion in *Husbands.* A long closeup scene in a London gambling club in which an elderly woman is approached by Peter Falk and coyly propositions him is perhaps the most grotesquely insensitive movie sequence of the year. It's hideous not because this is truth that the spectator seeks to evade but because this is bad acting and a gross conception. It reveals nothing more than a sensitive director would reveal by a look or a gesture, and at a discreet distance. Since Cassavetes conveys no sense of illusion—since he's after the naked "reality"—we don't think about the role, we think about the actress, and we wonder if she could ever get enough money to compensate for what is being done to her. (p. 224)

> Pauline Kael, "Megalomaniacs" *(originally published in* The New Yorker, *Vol. XLVI, No. 46, January 2, 1971), in her* Deeper into Movies *(© 1971*

*by Pauline Kael; reprinted by permission of Little, Brown and Company in association with the Atlantic Monthly Press), Atlantic-Little, Brown, 1973, pp. 220-24.\**

## NIGEL ANDREWS

*Shadows, Faces, Husbands:* John Cassavetes' titles serve both to define and to impersonalise his films' subject area. The announced theme provides a broad orientation, but the audience is finally left to interpret the raw material—fragmented narrative, improvised dialogue and action, long sequences apparently incidental to the main characters—at will. Thus, *Husbands* . . . is both a 'universal' male's-eye-view of marital restlessness *and* a haphazard idiosyncratic 48 hours out of the lives of three fugitives from New York suburbia. The titles of Cassavetes' trilogy have become more tangible, as the focus shifts from the rootless youth of *Shadows* to the grounded suburbanites of *Faces* and *Husbands*. . . .

In *Faces,* Richard and Maria, having vainly sought alternatives to the marital impasse, ended up sitting on the stairs together, speechless and unloving. Belonging had become a kind of imprisonment. In *Husbands,* self-styled a comedy by Cassavetes, marriage is less of an impasse: Gus and Archie return home without regrets, albeit with the bribery of expensive presents, while Harry simply walks out on his wife. Male comradeship, that recurring American dream from Fenimore Cooper to Hemingway, is a revitalising interlude rather than a final escape route for the three.

Framed between a funeral and a return to suburbia, their 48 hours on the town becomes an attempt to extract life from a world that seems to be dying around them, choked by false or inhibited emotional response. The drunken sing-song in the bar seems at first too long a scene for its tenuous relevance, but in retrospect it is crucial. Where the forced solemnity of the funeral struck no responsive chord in Gus, Archie or Harry, the naïve sentimentality of 'Apple Blossom Time in Normandy' and 'Pack Up Your Troubles' becomes a vehicle for real feeling. . . .

When the quest for honesty takes them on a whirlwind trip to London, ambassadors of American bravado the the phlegmatic English, the film becomes a shade obvious. Cassavetes' upper-crust Londoners are caricatured . . . and one feels he is making use of a convenient but outworn formula, the Jamesian view of the American in Europe as brash innocent confronting old-world decadence. . . .

[It] is a measure of how richly *Husbands* is an advance on pure *cinéma vérité* that the main roles demand more than the rough authenticity of the nonprofessional: they need the professional's pinpoint accuracy and quick-change command of mood. Cassavetes' precarious position midway between Hollywood and the American underground is fully vindicated by a film that combines the best values of both worlds.

*Nigel Andrews, "Film Reviews: 'Husbands'," in* Sight and Sound *(copyright © 1971 by The British Film Institute), Vol. 40, No. 2, Spring, 1971, p. 106.*

## STANLEY KAUFFMANN

[*Minnie and Moskowitz*] is by far John Cassavetes' worst film, with none of the good touches of *Faces,* without even any of the pseudo inquiry of *Husbands*. Guess what the theme is. Two lonely people! Misfits! Who find each other!! Even Chayefsky gave up this facile honesty twenty years ago.

He's a Very Human car-park in New York. But not just a car-park, of course; he's really searching. He searches on out to L.A. where he meets this Very Human girl. She, too, is searching, can't communicate, is a sexual object to men who merely use her, and is battered by life but is still golden, deep down inside. (p. 24)

Cassavetes boasts that his film is an "upper." What's chiefly wrong with it is that you know from the beginning that it was made to *be* an upper. A down-beat ending would by no means be the only truthful one for the story, but from the start you know that every vicissitude in the film is designed to make the up-beat ending glow.

The camera style is Cassavetes' usual "spying," a method intended to make everything look like reality observed but that only emphasizes the presence of photography. (When will the "truthful-cinema" types learn that reality in films means working *for* the camera, not trying to pretend that it isn't there?) Cassavetes' script is analagous. It tries to sound improvised and perhaps is, in part, but its sweaty efforts to "disappear" only make it stick out—excursions, doodlings, and all. (p. 32)

*Stanley Kauffmann, "From a Star to a Czar" (reprinted by permission of Brandt & Brandt Literary Agents, Inc.; copyright © 1972 by Stanley Kauffmann), in* The New Republic, *Vol. 166, No. 4, January 22, 1972, pp. 24, 32-3.*

## RICHARD SCHICKEL

[*Faces*] is, I think, a great and courageous film in which Cassavetes has dared more than any American director in recent memory, and it is important to understand the nature of what he has done. (p. 217)

[Several] qualities have led to a few dissenting dismissals of *Faces* as "a home movie." But this charge confuses style with substance and misses entirely the compassionate intelligence which Cassavetes—who also wrote the script—brings to his subject. He has a shrewd and highly moral vision of the special quality of affluent middle-class life in America, *circa* now, baby. And for all the superficial looseness of the film, he never once loses track of his point. On the contrary, he keeps boring in on it from every possible angle.

Infidelity is really only a device to heighten Cassavetes's true subject, the banality of the way too many of us live. His couple . . . are battered by this banality, sick, sad and tired, searching unconsciously for warmer and more human lives. Unable to define or to express what they want, each of them stumbles into potentially melodramatic situations that end up near to tragedy but nearer still to comedy.

Herein lies part of the film's originality, for customarily in our movies and plays and books infidelity is played firmly within one mode or the other. In *Faces* our expectations are endlessly jostled, as are those of the main characters. (pp. 217-18)

As a writer, Cassavetes has an uncanny ear for the sounds, at once funny and terrifying, that we make to fill the silent spaces in existence. As a director, he has the courage to make a long film in just eight scenes, stretching our attention spans (attenuated by TV and the voguish quick-cut style) almost to the breaking point, holding us with lovingly wrought physical details and closely observed psychological nuances. (pp. 218-19)

Do not infer that this film is dreary or depressing, no matter how it may seem in outline. Cassavetes is one of those remarkable artists who have learned to dissect us without at the same time learning to despise us. Somehow, without resort to sentiment, special pleading or falsification, he makes us share the healthily curious, oddly loving spirit in which he approaches his subjects. That is the light that illumines a dark work and which, perversely, cheers us as we emerge from a film that is truly and deeply an experience. (p. 219)

*Richard Schickel, "'Faces'" (originally published in a slightly different form in* Life, *Vol. 66, No. 2, January 17, 1969), in his* Second Sight: Notes on Some Movies, 1965-1970 *(copyright © 1972 by, Richard Schickel; reprinted by permission of Simon & Schuster, a Division of Gulf & Western Corporation), Simon & Schuster, 1972, pp. 217-19.*

## RICHARD COMBS

*Minnie and Moskowitz* is a particularly frenetic switchback ride; a continual rebounding from Moskowitz' complaint (among many): 'It's mainly just being alone that irritates me,' to Minnie's multiple anxieties about involvement: 'Somebody light bores me, somebody heavy depresses me.' The journey turns up some rewarding perceptions, but is ultimately and unexpectedly disappointing, with the film attempting to combine wholehearted indulgence of its characters with some sly, philosophic definition, extracting from rambling duologues pointed turns of phrase placed in audible quotes (the director tempted to turn advocate and sum up for the jury), and allowing much obscure contrivance to loom behind moments that pretend to be unaffectedly true.

What has been most remarked and admired in Cassavetes' method is his incorporation of quasi-underground improvisation with conventional forms of story-telling. In a superficial way, *Minnie and Moskowitz* makes do with a minimum of structure, its story only existing very loosely to bring together the unlikeliest of lovers. . . .

Cassavetes undercuts some of the romantic ground of his own film-making past. Locking the central pair into a kind of two-person, peripatetic encounter group, *Minnie and Moskowitz* seems far removed from the belief, implicit in the restless explorations of the youths in *Shadows* and, to a diminishing extent, of their middle-aged successors in *Husbands,* that life's possibilities can still be surprised by lightning raids. When Moskowitz declares: 'All you have to do to have a good time is be yourself,' the optimism is qualified by a later confession: 'I'm having trouble feeling what is right. I just don't feel as much any more.' He is not alone in his dilemma, and the general solution is simply to maintain the verbal pressure until feeling is bulldozed back into being. (p. 116)

Minnie in fact emerges as the credible centre of the film . . . , combining hints of genuine romanticism, the compulsive behaviour which provokes Seymour into complaining about Minnie's lack of timing, and even such dangerously loaded revelatory tics as her constant donning and doffing of sunglasses. But Moskowitz is continually left out on the limb of the blatant contrivance that underlies such apparently 'improvisatory' scenes as his encounter with a loudly articulate hobo [and] the predictable bolstering of Jewish humour which is imported from time to time from his family background. . . . More than any other director, Cassavetes depends on a generous response to the reality of his people; and *Minnie and Moskowitz* is finally

a two-figure equation too unbalanced to be easily acceptable. (pp. 116-17)

*Richard Combs, "'Minnie and Moskowitz'," in* Sight and Sound *(copyright © 1973 by The British Film Institute), Vol. 42, No. 2, Spring, 1973, pp. 116-17.*

## PAULINE KAEL

The theories of R. D. Laing the poet of schizophrenic despair, have such theatrical flash that they must have hit John Cassavetes smack in the eye. His new film, *A Woman Under the Influence,* is the work of a disciple: it's a didactic illustration of Laing's vision of insanity, with . . . Mabel Longhetti [as] the scapegoat of a repressive society that defines itself as normal. The core of the film is a romanticized conception of insanity, allied with the ancient sentimental mythology of madness centering on the holy fool and with the mythology about why Christ was crucified. The picture is based on the idea that the crazy person is endowed with a clarity of vision that the warped society can't tolerate, and so is persecuted. (p. 392)

It's never suggested that there's something wrong with Mabel for not getting herself together. Others reduce her to pulp; she's not a participant in her own destruction. The romantic view of insanity is a perfect subject for Cassavetes to muck around with. Yet even in this season when victimization is the hottest thing in the movie market this scapegoat heroine doesn't do a damn thing for him. He's always on the verge of hitting the big time, but his writing and directing are grueling, and he swathes his popular ideas in so many wet blankets that he is taken seriously—and flops. In *Faces* and *Husbands* Cassavetes might almost have been working his way up to Laing; his people were already desolate, hanging on to marriages that made no sense to them because nothing else did, either. . . .

Mabel, however, is more (and less) than a character, since she's a totally sympathetic character: she's a symbolic victim, and a marriage victim especially. Cassavetes has hooked Laing on to his own specialty—the miseries of sexual union. (p. 394)

Like all Cassavetes' films, *A Woman Under the Influence* is a tribute to the depth of feelings that people can't express. As a filmmaker, he himself has a muffled quality: his scenes are often unshaped and so rudderless that the meanings don't emerge. This time, he abandons his handsome, grainy simulated-*cinéma-vérité* style. The shots are planned to make visual points that bear out the thesis (though there are also arbitrary, ornamental angles, and vistas that make a workingman's cramped house big as a palace). But once again he has made a murky, ragmop movie. Actually, he doesn't know how to dramatize, and one can try to make a virtue of this for only so long. When the actors in his films strike off each other, there are tentative, flickering moods that one doesn't get in other kinds of movies, but these godsends are widely spaced, and it's a desert in between. He still prolongs shots to the point of embarrassment (and beyond). He does it deliberately, all right, but to what purpose? Acute discomfort sets in, and though some in the audience will once again accept what is going on as raw, anguishing truth, most people will—rightly, I think—take their embarrassment as evidence of Cassavetes' self-righteous ineptitude.

His special talent—it links his work to Pinter's—is for showing intense suffering from nameless causes; Cassavetes and Pinter both give us an actor's view of human misery. It comes out as metaphysical realism: we see the tensions and the power plays but never know the why of anything. Laing provides Cassavetes with an answer. However, his taking over Laing's views has cost him something: he didn't have comic-strip villains—or villains at all—before he swallowed Laing. In his earlier films, he commiserated with those who couldn't make contact except by brutalizing each other. Their drunken hostilities and blighted, repetitious conversations weren't held against them; their insensitivities were proof of the emptiness they felt. He used to love violent characters and outbursts of rage. Now the actors, no longer given their heads, are merely figures in a diagram. (pp. 394-95)

Details that are meant to establish the pathological nature of the people around Mabel, and so show her isolation, become instead limp, false moments. We often can't tell whether the characters are meant to be unconscious of what they're doing or whether it's Cassavetes who's unconscious. Mabel's children keep murmuring that they love her, and there are no clues to how to decipher this refrain. Are the children coddling her—reversing roles and treating her like a child in need of reassurance? Or are they meant to be as unashamedly loving as she is? And what are we to make of Nick the pulper's constant assertions of love? The movie is entirely tendentious; it's all planned, yet it isn't thought out. I get the sense that Cassavetes has incorporated Laing, undigested, into his own morose view of the human condition, and that he somehow thinks that Nick and Mabel really love each other and that *A Woman Under the Influence* is a tragic love story. (p. 396)

> Pauline Kael, "Dames" (originally published in The New Yorker, *Vol. L. No. 43, December 9, 1974*), in her Reeling (copyright © 1974 by Pauline Kael; reprinted by permission of Little, Brown and Company in association with the Atlantic Monthly Press), Atlantic-Little, Brown, 1976, pp. 390-96.*

### STANLEY KAUFFMANN

The curse of filmmaking, as John Cassavetes shows us [in *A Woman under the Influence*], is that it's too easy. No, of course not the financing and so on, but the basic process of making a film. . . .

Cassavetes is enraptured. He puts his camera in real houses and he gives his actors things to say as lifelike as he can make them and he even puts some non-actors in the cast and he lets the camera run and run, lets the people improvise on their lines, and the camera keeps running and running and the people keep on doing and saying and quarreling and crying and making up, and after it's all done he takes the film out of the camera and shows it to us. For goodness' sake, there it is. What more can we want? . . .

This sentimentality about method is, unsurprisingly, joined to sentimentality about subject. His definition of truth is, apparently, anything that commercial films overlook or skimp. He certainly didn't invent this booby credo, but he bears the banner onward. . . .

You can read [the plot] any way you like. Some have said, quite erroneously, that it's an indictment of society. Is every spouse indictable if he/she is not clinically trained or completely self-negating? The husband here is shown to be a loving man with no more egotism than gives him the power to love. Some have said, also quite erroneously, that the film dramatizes R. D. Laing. But Laing doesn't stop at saying that madness is caused by society ("hell is other people" in Sartre's familiar phrase). Laing goes on to say that madness is the sanity of the

mad, a way of coping. This woman doesn't cope. She is wretched. She would clearly rather not be the way she is.

But, admittedly, the film isn't really "about" anything. . . . To me this film is utterly without interest or merit. It tries to establish its bona fides simply by existing: it's up there on the screen and is therefore to some degree incontrovertible. This might be argued for a documentary, where the film would be a medical record. Not here.

> Stanley Kauffmann, "Films: 'A Woman under the Influence'" (reprinted by permission of Brandt & Brandt Literary Agents, Inc.; copyright © 1974 by Stanley Kauffmann), in The New Republic, *Vol. 171, No. 26, December 28, 1974, p. 20.*

### WILLIAM S. PECHTER

It seems I waited too long to write my obligatory piece on "The Vanishing Heroine in American Movies," and events have now passed me by. . . .

Mabel Longhetti, in John Cassavetes's *A Woman Under the Influence,* is neither strong-willed nor independent, but she's assertive beyond ignoring and to the point of stridency. What she wants, or believes she wants, is just to be otherwise—not to break out of the housewifely mold, but to fit in—yet she can't. "Tell me what you want me to be. I can be any way you want me," she implores her lumpish, blue-collar husband, Nick, who only replies rather gallantly that he wants her to be just who she is. In some time less enlightened than our own, Mabel's words might be understood to stand in some straightforward relation to her feelings; now we have the perspective to see them as the symptom of a problem that she, pathetically, can't see for herself. This housewife isn't mad for failure to adjust to her role but because the role itself breeds madness. It's her very trying to live up to her husband's and society's expectations of her good behavior as a wife and mother that proves her undoing.

This, at any rate, is one interpretation of *A Woman Under the Influence* (though it's subject to others), and it's certainly the interpretation that's winning the movie its current acclaim. (p. 138)

[Though] this depiction of the anguish of being a wife and the oppressiveness of marriage is the work of a director whose previous films have depicted the pathos of being a husband and have celebrated marriage on impulse, it isn't really a case of Cassavetes's new film's exploiting feminist ideas in any opportunistic way. . . . (p. 139)

What's troubling about this isn't the overrating of the film itself so much as the number of people who are apparently able to see in Mabel's situation an expression of the general plight of women in our society. No doubt, there *are* women for whom marriage is a dungeon and who feel chained there by the social roles marriage entails. But is Mabel one of them? . . . Mabel's "madness" is . . . , in a Laingian sense, creative: a privileged state of heightened insight; and to emphasize her "normality" there's a family gathering on Mabel's release from hospitalization in which all assembled are seen to behave, in ways that are socially acceptable, quite as crazily as anything we've seen of Mabel. But that others may also be crazy in no way makes Mabel more sane.

There *is* an argument to be made against Mabel's commitment, though it's not, I think, the Laingian but the Thomas Szasz-civil-libertarian one: that others shouldn't have the power to institutionalize Mabel merely because her deviant behavior embarrasses or even distresses them. Yet Mabel's madness does bring her not insight but pain; her behavior produces effects and responses in others different from what she desires; it's dysfunctional. To see her hectoring passers-by in the street, in her little-girl's get-up of ankle-socks and barrette, is to know this, and to aestheticize or ideologize her pain by calling it creative is to turn a deaf ear to it, to practice a species of callousness. And if it seems to us, in our enlightenment, that the roles to which she aspires are in themselves discreditable ones, we nevertheless are, I think, as little entitled to deny those roles to her as we are to deny beneficiaries of the civil-rights movement their right to become American Legionnaires. (pp. 139-40)

Yet what is that identity of Mabel's with which those roles of wife and mother are supposed to conflict? For all that Cassavetes's films are reputed to be centered on people—rather than, say, technique—one looks in vain for an answer to this question. Where the character of Mabel ought to be is a blank space captioned "Victim"; despite her array of colorful eccentricities, she's as much a blank as the personalityless heroine of *The Stepford Wives* whose fear of being sapped of her personality we're supposed to share. As Mabel's chief victimizer, Nick has at least a few traits one can identify, though this doesn't mean one can reconcile the bluff but "supportive" Nick of the earlier parts . . . with the insensitive clod who consigns Mabel to shock treatment . . . ; he's simply a different character with the same name brought on to clinch the film's case. It's not that Nick develops; characters in Cassavetes's films don't develop; they shift and swerve into new directions. And Cassavetes's technique—for his films' prolix repetitiousness *is* a technique—is to make one lose track of what's gone before and accept the new character as a development of the old by dint of sheer reiterative insistence: to bludgeon one into forgetfulness. (pp. 140-41)

> *William S. Pechter, "Heroines & Their Hairdresser" (originally published in a different version in* Commentary, *Vol. 59, No. 5, May, 1975), in his* Movies plus One *(copyright © 1970, 1971, 1972, 1973, 1974, 1975, 1976, 1977, 1978, 1982 by William S. Pechter; reprinted by permission of Horizon Press Publishers), Horizon Press, 1982, pp. 138-48.**

## MARSHA KINDER and BEVERLE HOUSTON

*Woman Under the Influence* draws on all three traditional visions of female madness, combining elements of each with great subtlety and perceptiveness. From one perspective, Mabel is an Eve who is weak, passive, and childlike. Thus it is difficult for her to resist husband, parents, friends—all those who are trying to make her conform to their expectations. Yet her childlike nature has its positive side; she is vital and creative in contrast to the conventional adults who condemn her. . . . Although she is presented as having an artistic temperament, Mabel's creativity is restricted to the invention of games and she never considers other outlets for her talents. (p. 11)

Mabel's touch of Lilith resides in her repressed sexuality. Restless and lonesome for intimacy, she reaches out to a kind stranger in a bar though she really loves her husband. But his job and male friends keep him occupied and her needs are great. Even with her husband's friends, she makes innocent mistakes because she doesn't understand the limits set on physical affection. As a result of Mabel's nature, her husband suf-

fers: he is cuckholded; he is embarrassed in front of his friends, who think he is married to a crazy; he is nagged by his mother to keep his wife in line for the sake of the children.

At the same time, the film develops another perspective on the situation. Mabel is clearly victimized by the familiar authoritarian male triangle of husband, doctor, and father. Yet they are not melodramatic villains, perverts, or emotional zombies from the *Gaslight* tradition. Instead, they are kind and loving—more like the men in Renoir's films who commit acts of cruelty out of ignorance and clumsiness. The extreme realism of the film shows how a woman can be driven to "madness" under the most benign conditions. On the one hand, this underlines the fact that it is not her fault, yet at the same time it makes her situation more terrifying. (pp. 11-12)

Most interesting and frightening is her complex interaction with her husband, who undeniably loves her, but whose understanding and patience are extremely limited. Even worse for Mabel is the double bind he repeatedly creates for her. Sometimes, they are in cahoots, together against the world, and he reinforces her eccentricity. But when she goes "too far," he gets frightened and becomes the incarnation of conventional authority. This authority makes him so righteous that he will beat her up in front of the children to assure her proper behavior. He is frequently so confused that he doesn't know whether to kiss her or slug her. One of the most valuable dimensions of the film is the fluid, detailed development of their interchanges, showing how reality and her "madness" are a mutual creation.

From a broader perspective, the film also reveals how Mabel is "under the influence" of the entire social structure, which (in the Laingian sense) establishes the schizophrenogenic family context. Madness grows not out of the weakness of individuals, but out of the psychodynamics of the social group, with its double-bind situations, and its insistence on the need to control the self and others in order to maintain the norms. In this sense, the society creates madness by defining it. Mabel's eccentric behavior is defined as crazy and she is punished accordingly. In contrast, society is willing to tolerate the equally extreme behavior of the husband who bullies her and the doctor who chases her across the room and over the furniture in an attempt to control her. (p. 12)

*Woman Under the Influence*, with its penetrating realism, offers [great] insight into the fluid definitions of sanity and the ways in which ordinary social interaction can create madness. This understanding is totally communicated through particulars; the ideology and analysis are invisible. This strategy forces the audience to experience the pressures of the double-bind situation with Mabel and her family; we are drawn into the schizophrenogenic unit, which makes us terribly uncomfortable and anxious. The film has tremendous power to move and disturb us. Yet like the other "enlightened" films—[Bergman's] *Persona*, [Bresson's] *Une Femme Douce*, and [Antonioni's] *Red Desert*—and despite its brilliance and emotional power, *Woman Under the Influence* ends up showing the female as history has always wanted to see her—lovely, sensitive, and powerless—the inevitable victim. (pp. 12, 33)

> *Marsha Kinder and Beverle Houston, "Madwomen in the Movies: Women Under the Influence," in* Film Heritage *(copyright 1976 by F. A. Macklin), Vol. 11, No. 2, Winter, 1975-76, pp. 1-12, 33.**

## JONATHAN ROSENBAUM

Beginning with *Shadows,* the films of John Cassavetes have been at once limited and defined by their anti-intellectual form of humanism, an unconditional acceptance of the social norms of his characters that exalts emotion and intuition over analysis and, in narrative terms, looseness and approximation over precision. Used as an instrument for delivering a thesis (as in *Faces*) and/or allowing actors to indulge themselves in fun and games (as in *Husbands*), it is a style which characteristically operates like a bludgeon, obscuring at least as much as it illuminates while confidently hammering home its proud discoveries. But when it serves as a means for exploration, as in *Shadows* or *A Woman Under the Influence*—however halting or incomplete a method it may be for serving that function—it deserves to be treated with greater credence. Obviously this distinction fails to acknowledge the thematic continuity of Cassavetes' work: the fact, for instance, that *Too Late Blues, Faces* and *A Woman Under the Influence* all contain suicide attempts by women in the presence of men, or that male camaraderie and lack of communication between the sexes—treated successively in the first two sequences of *Shadows*—have remained constants in his work. But notwithstanding this consistency of preoccupations, his films vary considerably in the extent to which they allow all their characters to have their say, reaching one extreme in the multiple viewpoints represented in *Shadows* and quite another in the coarse misogyny comprising virtually the entire viewpoint of *Husbands. A Woman Under the Influence* occupies a certain middle ground between these poles: if its narrative structure is dictated almost entirely by the viewpoint of Nick—so much so that Mabel's six-month stay in hospital is neither depicted nor (improbably) marked by a single visit from her husband—her own grasp of her situation assumes an increasing importance in the latter section of the film after she returns; and her children assume a pivotal role in the final scene, readmitting her into the family with a directness and lack of self-consciousness that neither Nick nor any of the in-laws seem capable of articulating. The danger of Cassavetes' approach here and elsewhere is that of presenting an audience with a *tabula rasa,* in which one is invited to find one's own biases and assumptions confirmed: hence the unpersuasive feminist readings that have been given to his film, along with equally unconvincing responses which take a reverse tack—both positions reflecting nothing more than a spectator's personal identification with one character or another, which the film's method explicitly encourages. The notion that people's understandings run deeper than their ideologies is certainly a contestable one, yet it operates as a prerequisite for appreciating Cassavetes' work. . . . [In *A Woman Under the Influence*] this dubious notion is compulsively enacted through raw nerves made flesh, and powerfully embodied in a family's grappling efforts to achieve its own coherence. (pp. 12-13)

*Jonathan Rosenbaum, "Feature Films: 'A Woman Under the Influence',"* in Monthly Film Bulletin *(copyright © The British Film Institute, 1976), Vol. 43, No. 504, January, 1976, pp. 12-13.*

**JOHN SIMON**

The films of John Cassavetes are, by and large, sterile actors' exercises. They are not even for all kinds of actors, but mostly for the friends of Cassavetes and amateurs like his family or his wife's family. They are doggedly pretentious and often of enormous duration; unless you are an actor, or a friend or relative of the director, you should find them quintessentially trivial and boring. Cassavetes, who is quite a good actor but a bad director and worse writer, has insisted ever more emphatically over the years that his films are "scripted," though

they seem to be taped and transcribed improvisations, possibly re-enacted from such "scripts." At least I *hope* that this is how it is done; if Cassavetes is telling the truth, and he really writes this trash that postures as plot, characterization, and dialogue, he would be an even bigger simpleton than I take him to be. . . .

[Consider] *A Woman Under the Influence.* It did not begin to enlighten us about whether the woman was demented or unjustly viewed as such, whether her husband loved her or not, whether her family and her doctor treated her rightly or wrongly. It did not remotely come to grips with whether she had extramarital relations, whether her love for her children was genuine or some form of infantilism and hysteria, and whether anything was changed after her return from the asylum. Many feminists hailed the picture as a major plea in behalf of oppressed womanhood; yet it was by no means clear whether and by what the heroine was oppressed, and whether her abject stupidity, indeed near-idiocy, made her a representative specimen. . . .

In any case, *A Woman Under the Influence* struck me as muddleheaded, pretentious, and interminable, fooling some people because of its factitious social significance. *The Killing of a Chinese Bookie,* cut from the same burlap, makes two strategic errors: its subject cannot even lay claim to significant social comment, and it tries for something like a thriller plot, for which Cassavetes and his pals have no real affinity. On top of kids playing with typical improvisations and cameras, we get kids playing with guns—disastrously. (p. 65)

[When] not very bright or clever people try to convey to the movie audience that someone or something is supposed to be dumb, they sink to levels of stupidity and ineptitude that strike people of normal intelligence as positively feeble-minded.

So, for example, when Cosmo tells about two girls in Memphis who cut off a gopher's tail, ate it, and died of botulism, we wonder—there being no botulism outside of canned food—who is being inept: the character, the improvising actor, or the filmmaker. . . . Not only are ignorance and witlessness fulgurating in the movie, we do not even know whom to ascribe them to and how to evaluate them. (pp. 65-6)

[The] movie becomes ever more clumsy and incredible: not only do things become totally divorced from sense, but also the filmmaking cannot or will not make clear just what happens during various key scenes. We do not find out just when Cosmo gets shot, what kind of wound he incurs, and why it seems insignificant and staunched when that suits the filmmakers, and profusely bleeding and presumably fatal when that makes for a splashier effect.

Not even Cosmo is decently examined and comprehended by the Cassavetes method; the other characters, except for an occasional touch of (usually spurious) colorfulness, remain total ciphers. . . .

There is always the joker who says sneeringly, "Muddled, contradictory, stupidly bungling—that is just the way life is!" Maybe, but in that case give us *cinéma-vérité* rather than actors' improvisations posturing as life. If, on the other hand, you're trying to give us something more—art, perhaps—it is your obligation to probe a bit below the surface, to try at least to raise some questions worth the asking. Cassavetes offers up only a lot of extreme closeups and murky lighting—both literally and figuratively—and fails either to penetrate or to illuminate his subject. (p. 66)

*John Simon, "Technical Exercise, Exercise in Futility," in* New York *Magazine (copyright © 1976 by News Group Publications, Inc.; reprinted with the permission of* New York *Magazine), Vol. 9, No. 9, March 1, 1976, pp. 65-6.*

## JUDITH CRIST

*The Killing of a Chinese Bookie* is a mess, as sloppy in concept as it is in execution, as pointless in thesis as it is in concept. Ironically, it is as if an artsy-smartsy amateur had attempted a remake of one of those taut little low-budget crime thrillers in which Cassavetes established himself as an actor of noteworthy intensity in the Fifties. Though even an amateur would opt for a bit more credibility in plot, a bit more intelligence in the endless improvised chitchat, a bit more stability in the camerawork, a modicum of coherence in the characterizations. (p. 50)

All of this takes 135 minutes packed with inaction, much inane conversation in the strippers' dressing room, dreary glimpses of the dreary stage show, confusing encounters with strangers, pretentious references to death, and whiz-bang jokes like "Karl Marx said opium was the religion of the masses" and "Two girls ate a gopher tail and died of botulism." They have to be jokes—don't they? Actually, it's all a bad joke, on the faithful as well as on the unwary, with the ultimate gall being the claim in the film's promotion that its hero is "today's 'everyman' who will even murder to keep the pressure out of his life." Ho hum. (p. 51)

*Judith Crist, "To Each His Everyman," in* Saturday Review *(copyright © 1976 by* Saturday Review; *all rights reserved; reprinted by permission), Vol. 3, No. 13, April 3, 1976, pp. 50-1.\**

## ROBERT E. LAUDER

Even though his latest film, *The Killing of a Chinese Bookie,* is a disaster, John Cassavetes, among presently working American directors, comes closest to being a genius. . . .

Hopelessly in love with people, John Cassavetes is hung up on the mysterious meaning of man. Neither a lack of depth nor commercialism is evident in Cassavetes' work. . . .

More than any other contemporary director, Cassavetes can pack a scene with emotional content. Both *Husbands* and *A Woman Under the Influence* border on being great films because of Cassavetes' capacity for capturing the struggles and strains of everyday living, for photographing what someone has called "the texture of domestic dailiness." . . .

Operating out of a more profound vision of life than any of his contemporaries, Cassavetes is also a master technician. His film style has been accurately described as somewhere between Hollywood and *cinéma vérité.* Largely improvisational and intuitional, Cassavetes' camera sometimes without discrimination records the details of daily living. Often using a handheld camera focusing on his real-life relatives, Cassavetes produces films that are both brilliant and amateurish, compassionate and cluttered, mature and maddening. . . .

When he is at his best, Cassavetes can involve an audience in a scene and within seconds have its members identifying with wounded humanity projected on the screen. If a Cassavetes scene works, a viewer will have a difficult time distancing himself from Cassavetes' creatures. . . .

Cassavetes' persistent weakness is his lack of control. He often engages in cinematic overkill. His intuitions are good but his sense of timing is way off. Scenes from any of his last five films could be used as examples. A good illustration is the bar scene in *Husbands.* In an uncanny way, Cassavetes so captures the setting, the characters' conversation and the mood of the barroom that the viewer can almost taste the beer, smell the smoke and feel the loneliness. But Cassavetes stays too long and the scene eventually loses the necessary distance and perspective that art should have. (p. 427)

Absence of balance is one of the many things wrong with *Chinese Bookie.* The film is Cassavetes' most self-indulgent. In telling the story of Cosmo Vitelli, the owner of a strip joint who, because of gambling debts, is pressured into assassinating a powerful criminal, Cassavetes has made a film that is so erratically edited and so lacking in structure that he may be the only person who can make sense of the film. One wonders if parts of the film may be missing. The strongest positive element in *Chinese Bookie* is Cassavetes' affection for his characters: his love for them seems to illuminate their humanity for the viewer. In the seedy surroundings of a strip joint Cassavetes is able to see naked souls rather than naked bodies. With his camera Cassavetes strips away the pretense and bravura and unveils the beauty and lovableness of dreamers, even those whose dreams have dried up and died. (pp. 427-28)

*Robert E. Lauder, "The Genius of John Cassavetes," in* America *(© America Press, 1976; all rights reserved), Vol. 134, No. 19, May 15, 1976, pp. 427-28.*

## MARSHA KINDER

[*Opening Night*] is highly ambitious in its basic conception, yet terribly disappointing in its realization. This is particularly devastating since the main conflict in the film is between the writer's static vision recorded in the script and the players' improvisation embodied in a living performance. . . .

*Opening Night* immediately plunges us into a double reality of stage and screen and a double perspective on the performance. At first we identify with the actress [Gena Rowlands]: we share her nervous anticipation and see the audience from her point of view. But as soon as she begins to interact with Cassavetes [who portrays a photographer], we resume our more familiar role as audience and become involved with the film through exposure to the play. Thus we are forced to impose on ourselves the schizoid split between actor and viewer—the very process of doubling that will become so crucial for the central characters both in the play and in the film. (p. 50)

Contrasting sharply with the hot red carpet on which the couple restlessly pace back and forth and the emotional sparks ignited by their dynamic interaction, [the photographer's] powerful still photographs are static. They express the playwright's main theme of old age, which she forces her heroine and audience to accept; yet both Gena Rowlands as actress and John Cassavetes, in their double roles try to escape or transform the limits of this theme (both in style and content) through dynamic improvisation. This conflict is embodied in the dramatic punning on "stage." Rather than accept the rigid conventions of the traditional stage, or the definition of human life as a line drawn between fixed points that mark the boundaries between separate stages of development, Rowlands and Cassavetes stage a rebellion against such classifications by physically representing art and life as a constant stage of transformation and growth.

The polarity between youth and old age first comes to life as Gena and her seasoned collaborators leave the theater and are mobbed by young autograph hounds. Gena encounters an 18-year-old would-be actress, who reminds her of a younger version of herself. . . . We see Gena staring at the girl's blurred distorted image through the misted window as if she were looking at an old moving picture of herself. This powerful image simultaneously imprints Gena's consciousness and our own; again, we are forced into the same kind of schizoid split between viewer and actress that Gena experiences. When the young girl is struck down by a car a few moments later, Gena is the only one in the limousine who responds emotionally to the reality of what she has seen, insisting on stopping the car. In later sequences, she will make this experience the basis of a series of hallucinations, in which the girl represents her former self desperately struggling to stay alive. These psychotic episodes become her primary means of discovering an authentic way of playing the role of the aging heroine in *The Second Woman*. Although this sequence of events may represent a well-known interior approach to acting, the film never succeeds in convincing us that Gena's extreme psychic struggle is really essential or that it actually leads to the final improvisation where she spars—verbally, physically, and emotionally—with Cassavetes in order to give the play and its loser-heroine a dash of hope. (p. 51)

The seance is another form of theatrical performance or ritual that tries to externalize interior or nonphysical experience. Apparently, Cassavetes is using this scene to express the playwright's means of dealing with her emotions and her medium. Not surprisingly, Gena flees from the seance just as she tries to escape from the play, despite her promise to accept a starring role in both. Gena is committed only to her fluid, intuitive sense of emotional authenticity, which is always focused on the present moment and which is supposedly the basis of her greatness as an actress. Although this all sounds fine in theory and despite the high quality of the acting performances, the causal connection between theory and practice within the film is not really convincing. This is especially true in the seance, which is precisely the point at which the film starts to be disappointing, for we sense the action is highly contrived, not only by the playwright but also by Cassavetes the film-maker.

*Opening Night* is very ingenious and inventive in comparing the media of stage and screen and in playing with the multiple artistic and personal realities that they both draw upon. Where it goes astray is in developing Gena's descent into madness and alcoholism as a means of discovering an authentic way to reinterpret her theatrical role. Even if the film had succeeded in convincing us that this path was essential and that it actually led to the particular improvisation that follows, the weakness of that finale would still make us seriously question whether it was really worth all the *Sturm und Drang*. Gena's torment smacks more of gratuitous masochism, either pathetically chosen by the actress out of some misguided notion of the suffering artist or imposed on her by her tyrannical director. . . . (pp. 51-2)

Of course, they are both well aware of this pattern, which is the explicit subject of two improvisational scenes that are embarrassing to watch. . . . When she complains that it is humiliating, her director allows her to slap both him and John (who double for each other on many levels) before subjecting her to repetitions of the scene, which are perhaps intended to desensitize both the actress and the audience to humiliation in the service of art. We have seen similar scenes in *Faces* and *Woman Under the Influence* where they were far better motivated both psychologically and aesthetically and where they consequently had far greater emotional power. . . .

The extreme exaggeration [when Gena staggers drunkenly into the theater] makes both his motivation and her subsequent performance on stage totally unbelievable. The frank acknowledgment of Gena's masochism and her director's sadism within these two scenes explicitly identifies humiliation as the basic subject of the improvisations, yet it does not really lessen the gratuity or justify the pain.

I think my disappointment with *Opening Night* is intensified by the brilliance of the early sequences that open so many fascinating possibilities and by my extreme admiration for Cassavetes's earlier films. He is still one of the most talented, original directors who courageously succeeds in making personal films with great emotional resonance within or in spite of the Hollywood industry. (p. 52)

Marsha Kinder, "Reviews: 'Opening Night'," in Film Quarterly (copyright 1978 by The Regents of the University of California; reprinted by permission of the University of California Press), Vol. XXXI, No. 3, Spring, 1978, pp. 50-2.

**RICHARD COMBS**

[*Opening Night*] is in many ways the logical extension and distillation of John Cassavetes' treatment of the actor as prime subject and co-creator of his films: a play-within-a-film story that never bothers to make too close a distinction between actress Myrtle Gordon's working out of her problems with a distasteful role on stage and Gena Rowlands' own experimentation with the part of Myrtle. As usual with Cassavetes' films, there is a lack of self-consciousness about the layering of ironies on art imitating life, and vice versa. . . . Since film-making is treated not as a form that mediates in life, but as 'life' itself, both the on- and off-stage events become equally raw material, each a possible permutation of the other. (p. 192)

Unexpectedly, given its concern for such actorish tantrums, *Opening Night* remains probably Cassavetes' coolest film, mainly because the offstage relationships are never reduced, in the usual, psychologising style, to explanation for what is going on behind the footlights. . . . The fact that 'acting' and theatricality have formally been made the subject of the film is a subtle strengthening factor, if not distancing then at least providing a context for the kind of indulgence Cassavetes has always extended to his actors, and which in the past has often just spilled sloppily over the confines of plot and character. . . .

Ultimately, perhaps, the very formlessness which Cassavetes establishes as the first condition for working with his actors leads to a kind of collapse. Since *Opening Night* is not a meditation on another art form but an opportunity for its practitioners to work out their temperamental/creative problems, there is nothing left to contain the haphazard fooling around once the integrity of the play-within-the-film is destroyed altogether—as it is, gradually, by the performers making themselves comfortable with it or, in Myrtle's words, by their dumping it upside down to 'see if we can't find something human in it'. . . .

A paradoxical strength, revealed by both this film and *The Killing of a Chinese Bookie,* is Cassavetes' ability to slide in a conventionally dramatic situation, which anchors but does not confine his subsequent permutations and free associations. The gangland killing which the hero of *The Killing of a Chinese Bookie* is forced to carry out serves to identify the narrative, but it never really gains the expected purchase on either the characters or the atmosphere, which dreamily find more idiosyncratic routes out of the *film noir* situation. In *Opening Night,* everything flows from the powerful opening sequence. . . . [The girl who is killed] becomes for Myrtle an ever more substantial figment of her own youthful dreams, and finally a hostile inquisitor, invoking all the years of rapt sacrifice and renunciation of normal life spent in movies and theatres, and demanding now that Myrtle demonstrate in her own life how it was all justified. . . .

*Exorcist*-like overtones are hard to avoid as Myrtle's relationship with the wraith degenerates from the querulous to the messily violent. But what Cassavetes continually keeps in view is both the emotional validity of the hallucination and its function in Myrtle's own psychodrama. It becomes the means by which she expunges her feelings of bad faith towards her past—just as, through her struggle with the elderly playwright, she must overcome her ill-will towards her own future—before she can carry on with any self-respect in her present role. (p. 193)

*Richard Combs, "'Opening Night',"* in Sight and Sound *(copyright © 1978 by The British Film Institute), Vol. 47, No. 3, Summer, 1978, pp. 192-93.*

**JAMES MONACO**

[Acting], its art and craft, is the key to John Cassavetes's cinema. He started as an actor (he's a good one) and he still acts to make money to finance his own films. He seems to be more interested in the process of shooting a film than he is in the end result, and he designs his movies more often than not as attractive exercises for himself and his actor friends and relations. (p. 299)

Cassavetes's movies are family affairs; in fact they're like nothing so much as home movies, with all the problems and advantages thereof.

They go on too long, they're often too private and self-indulgent, they never seem to come to the point, they're loosely plotted—certainly leagues away from the intricately constructed Hollywood formula film—they don't seem to show much care for production values, and they tend to be repetitive. When Cassavetes finds an idea he likes, he'll run it into the ground. But they're also exhilaratingly verisimilitudinous—they're slices of life cut with precision enough for a biopsy; at their best they sing with pleasure in the craft of acting; and taken together they give us a rich portrait of contemporary sexual politics and its attendant anxieties that is unrivaled in the medium. They may be home movies, but these amateurs are professionals, workers who love their craft.

The result of this classically amateur provenance is that, as the critical cliché has it, people are either passionate devotees of John Cassavetes's movies, or they despise them. The key, I think, is how far you are willing to go to participate in this rather self-absorbed process. Cassavetes seems constitutionally incapable of playing to a broad audience. He makes movies for himself and his friends because that's all he knows how to do. . . . [Despite] all the aforementioned crotchety difficulties

one has with his movies, there is an essential humanism there that's undeniable. . . . [It's] available in any Cassavetes movie, for those who want to actively participate in the process. To do so, you have to give up a number of ideas about what a (commercial) movie should be—ideas about pace and construction and meaning—and learn to appreciate John's naturalistic rhythms.

Cassavetes's films may seem avant-garde: they are certainly the closest approach by commercial films to the so-called New American Cinema of personal art films. . . . But really, there isn't that much that's innovative about Cassavetes's cinema. (pp. 299-300)

[The] shape of Cassavetes's actor-centered moodpieces was foreshadowed on the stage as early as Chekhov, a playwright who was entirely dependent on the talents and techniques of his actors. . . . Like Cassavetes's films, Chekhov's plays are about rather sad people—losers, if you like—who don't ever seem to get anywhere, but who enthrall audiences with their inaction, their self-centeredness, and their cosmically funny failures. The creation of pure atmosphere—and a rather lackadaisically maudlin one at that—has been legitimate ever since. Not only is Cassavetes not an innovator, but he can trace his roots straight to one of the grandfathers of the modern theater!

Perhaps that's part of the problem. His films are highly theatrical. There isn't one of them that couldn't be converted easily into a stage play. They take place almost exclusively in interiors. (p. 300)

Clearly, Cassavetes's people aren't outdoor folk. They don't thrive in the sunshine. They're interior characters in both senses of the word, and that seems more a theatrical trait than a cinematic characteristic. The director further emphasizes this with a very insouciant, almost sloppy mise en scène. Everything is organized around the actor and his work. Closeups are preferred. Most scenes are shot in long takes. Cassavetes's technique is to load the camera with as much film as it can carry, then turn it on and let the actors do their stuff. If a scene works in one take, he's not going to shoot it over again to get reverse angles and master shots. If a character's out of the frame, so be it. It's the words and delivery that are most important. (p. 301)

He enjoys shooting in restaurants and bars because those are the locations where people have nothing much to do but talk, and talk is at the center of his world—a universe of discourse. In fact, a better theatrical referent than Chekhov might be Harold Pinter. Both the filmmaker and the playwright deal with characters who at first appear from a comic perspective only to reveal in sharp and often poignant outbursts the violence and frustration which always lies just beneath the surface. Both take particular pleasure in the colors of speech—both are erstwhile actors who are very aware just what a pleasure it is to deliver monologues with wit and style; fun for the actors, certainly, and perhaps also for audiences. Pinter is more elegantly fey; Cassavetes is certainly more naturalistic, less symbolic, and elusive: that's to his credit. Neither cares very much where the piece is going; they just want to catch these actor/characters in the act of being. Existential? Yes, I'm afraid so. Both are eventually limited by their commitment to an essentially pessimistic worldview. But while Pinter's people take it out on each other, tyrannize each other, and kill, Cassavetes's people seldom do. If they hurt one another, and they do, it's not out of viciousness, but because they can't help themselves, much less each other. (p. 302)

The year 1959 was truly a watershed in world cinema, and John Cassavetes's *Shadows* served as the representative milestone in this country. (p. 305)

*Shadows* succeeded because, almost naively, it broke all the narrative rules of commercial filmmaking. It was largely improvised by a cast of unknowns. . . . We have time to get to know these people, and if often it's too apparent that they are working at acting, there's something nevertheless charming and refreshing about this style. It's Brechtian, in a way, since it brashly admits its fiction. We know we're watching actors, not real people, and paradoxically that gives the film a riveting sense of reality. Jean-Luc Godard was doing something like this in France at the time. It's an attitude toward the underlying assumptions of filmmaking that's exceptionally modern. It's easy to understand why *Shadows* became a model for the new independent cinema (with which Cassavetes was never again associated): it strikes at the very foundations of the Hollywood dream movie. It's not entirely a conscious act of rebellion, but that makes it all the more likeable. (pp. 305-06)

Exactly what Cassavetes demands from an audience is more obvious in *Faces* than in any of his other films. These people don't work in screen time, they work in real time. Force them into screen time with its neatly edited ellipses and thoughtful connections, and they become characters; leave them in real time, rough, sometimes boring, with idiosyncratic rhythms, disconcerting jumps, and inactive holes, and they tend to remain people. The effect of watching people rather than characters on the screen is startling, and I think, worth the effort films like these require. (p. 308)

*A Woman Under the Influence* is rare in its understanding of the dehumanizing forces of working-class life as well as sexist marriage patterns, but inasmuch as the film has a political dimension—it makes it clear that this neurosis isn't arbitrary; there are "influences" at work—it stops far too short. (p. 310)

It became clear in Cassavetes's next two films after *A Woman Under the Influence* that he was locked in a bind of his own. No American writer/director knows more about the triangular relationship between character, acting, and reality. But finally, this isn't enough: the triangle becomes more and more constricting. (p. 311)

Like Ingmar Bergman, with whom he's often compared (*Opening Night* is certainly parallel with *Persona*, *A Woman Under the Influence* with *The Passion of Anna*, *Faces* with *Scenes from a Marriage*), Cassavetes eventually disappoints because he can't or won't extricate himself from this swampy delta of neurotic recrimination. He gives his actors enormous freedom, but he and his actors together team up to repress his characters. For people who go along with him, his films are emotionally draining experiences. But this isn't the only identifying characteristic of realism, as either style or attitude. People do learn to cope, sometimes even successfully; they don't always submit. Except for *Minnie and Moskowitz,* the most spirited of Cassavetes's movies, his characters are in search of a way to liberate themselves from their authors, both writer/director and actors. From *Faces* to *Opening Night,* Cassavetes operates as an artistic tyrant: characters, and fiction, don't have a chance against this champion of actors and of a very precise (and often precious), limited reality. Like Bergman's, Cassavetes's films are stuck in the existential fifties. They haven't learned the truth of the sixties, that it is at least possible to take action, that passive suffering isn't the only legitimate response to psychological binds. (pp. 311-12)

*James Monaco, "Who's Talking? Cassavetes, Altman, and Coppola," in his* American Film Now: The People, the Power, the Money, the Movies *(copyright © 1979 by James Monaco; reprinted by arrangement with The New American Library, Inc., New York), Oxford University Press, New York, 1979, pp. 295-348.**

**MORRIS DICKSTEIN**

Martin Scorsese's *Mean Streets* and even *Taxi Driver* used a good deal of loose, inconsequential action (or inaction) to work up a feeling of the New York streets. . . . When the action of these films finally blows, unravels, they're all the more effective for having seemed so plotless.

The lonely prophet of this kind of script and visual style—so carefully designed to look like cinéma vérité—was John Cassavetes. Particularly in films like *Faces* and *A Woman Under the Influence*, Cassavetes is a master of the hidden poetry of ungainly people, the heartrending psychopathology of everyday life. His roots are with the independent filmmakers of an earlier period, when all "technique" smacked of Hollywood slickness and artificiality, when a hand-held camera and grainy close-ups were emblems of authenticity. Yet Cassavetes surpasses the seventies directors who followed him in his ability to achieve genuinely moving moments, poignant epiphanies of individual lives. (p. 55)

*Morris Dickstein, "Summing Up the Seventies: Issues," in* American Film *(reprinted with permission from the December issue of* American Film *magazine; © 1979, The American Film Institute, J. F. Kennedy Center, Washington, DC 20566), Vol. V, No. 3, December, 1979, pp. 55-8.**

**BOB EDELMAN**

[*Gloria*] is typical of its director, John Cassavetes: sometimes irritating and confusing but always original and thought-provoking, with moments of undeniable brilliance. In a quick shot, or camera angle or movement, Cassavetes eloquently captures the anguish, fear, paranoia, intimacy and hope of his characters. . . . [When Gloria tugs at Phil, this simple gesture] hints at Gloria's basic humanity, and the potential of caring between two different human beings. Also, he effectively displays the reality behind the picture-postcard glitter of New York. . . .

But the film is also maddeningly illogical. Police inexplicably allow Gloria and Phil to leave the murder scene. Cabs appear out of nowhere when there is the need for a getaway car. Phil changes a $100 bill and travels alone to Pittsburgh, with no adults questioning his age.

*Gloria* may be irritating in its inconsistencies, but it is nonetheless exciting, like free form jazz. Cassavetes, not afraid to take chances as a director, has chosen not to direct "packages" and count his money. There is a special rawness to *Gloria,* that of a hungry novice.

*Bob Edelman, "'Gloria': A Review," in* Films in Review *(copyright © 1980 by the National Board of Review of Motion Pictures, Inc.), Vol. XXXI, No. 8, October, 1980, p. 475.*

**DAVID DENBY**

[The] subway-poster ads [for *Gloria*] with Gena Rowlands brandishing a snub-nosed .38, as if she were a taller, skirted version of George Raft, give a very accurate notion of the movie—a crime genre film with plenty of action and lots of moody underbelly-of-the-city flourishes. *Gloria* is a great deal of fun. It is also something of a stunt. There have been tough and even violent women in past American movies (Barbara Stanwyck, Ann Sheridan, et al.), but few women have killed quite so easily and with so little remorse as Rowlands's Gloria Swensen. *Gloria* is hardly a profound study in the psychology of violence, nor is it always credible; it's an exciting movie designed to evoke "Clint Eastwood, move over!" reactions from press and public. (p. 62)

[Gloria's shoot-out scene] is an example of what's best about *Gloria*. Working within genre conventions for the first time, Cassavetes has picked up his tempo while managing to avoid clichés. He brings his own, highly idiosyncratic melancholy to the portrait of New York—the inexpressibly sad apartments and streets of the city's mustier regions (the Grand Concourse, Riverside Drive), the background of generalized sordidness and paranoia, against which the occasional acts of kindness and courage stand out so surprisingly. Cassavetes stays off the beat: The mob rubout, for instance, is staged with complete matter-of-factness (the men report to work complaining of traffic jams), and Gloria, in her many acts of violence, strikes so directly and boldly that she half paralyzes her victims with surprise. Like the Western hero or some of the Lee Marvin characters, she is a woman motivated by a private sense of honor (as far as we know, she has no grudge against the mob). Her protection of the little boy is presented as a given element of her nature—a sort of natural female gallantry. . . .

[Unfortunately Phil has] been saddled with such irritating baby-macho lines as (to Gloria) "I'm the man! *I'm* the man!" (He sounds like a tiny Cassavetes blowhard—he'll grow up to be Ben Gazzara.) We never like this little pest, so Gloria's gradual warming toward him doesn't pull on our heartstrings as it's meant to. But *Gloria* is a fine action film, with a thrilling heroine, making her way like an enraged samurai through the dark and corrupt city. (p. 63)

*David Denby, "Movies: 'Gloria'," in* New York Magazine *(copyright © 1980 by News Group Publications, Inc.; reprinted with the permission of* New York *Magazine), Vol. 13, No. 40, October 13, 1980, pp. 62-3.*

# René Clair

## 1898-1981

(Born René Chomette) French director, critic, novelist, and actor.

Clair's films are deeply human, juxtaposing satire, comedy, sentiment, and fantasy. Throughout, his primary intent is to present the essential goodness of humanity. As Raymond Spottiswoode wrote in 1933, "[Clair] excels in the fluidity of his action and the fertility of his ideas. Even in his worst films an occasional shrewd observation reveals a sensitive mind, obscured sometimes by sentimentality and sometimes untrammelled and riotous."

Clair was a journalist before becoming an actor. Though he eventually tired of acting, Clair found filmmaking irresistible, and he left his job as a writer to assist director Jacques de Baroncelli. The experience Clair gained enabled him to make his first film, *Paris qui dort (The Crazy Ray)*. Its graceful energy is repeated in subsequent works which reveal his dedication to the surreal. The study of movement in *Paris qui dort* was considered impressive, and cubist painter Francis Picabia asked Clair to make a film to be shown between acts of a production by the Swedish Ballet. The resultant film, *Entr'acte*, displays Clair's fondness for sight gags and bourgeois satire, elements which distinguish much of his later work.

Clair loved silent cinema, considering it the pure cinema of images. He was so disturbed by the advent of sound in the late 1920s that he considered abandoning filmmaking. However, Clair soon learned to use sound as a complement to visual images. *Sous les toits de Paris (Under the Roofs of Paris)*, his first sound film, reflects a new thematic as well as technical aspect. Clair chose to concentrate on the working class while creating aural images rather than dialogue. *Le million* returns to Clair's interest in surrealism, and its juxtaposition of reality and fantasy met with universal acclaim. *À nous la liberté* studies the conflict between a man's soul and the increasing automation of society. When his next films were also poorly received and he was in need of financing, Clair moved to Britain.

*The Ghost Goes West*, his first British film, was successful, but Clair's light, sure touch was not in evidence in subsequent works, and he returned to France. During the production of a new film, World War II began, and Clair reluctantly moved his family to Hollywood. Clair's work in the United States is generally considered undistinguished, and most critics agree that the American context did not suit Clair, despite the technological advantages available in Hollywood.

Clair returned to France in 1946 and began to make more personal films. *Les belles-de-nuit* serves as a final return to his world of fantasy. Many consider it a rediscovery of the sentiments of his early films and, in some ways, a metaphoric film about film. In 1960, Clair became the first filmmaker to be elected to the Académie Française solely on the basis of his achievement in cinema. (See also *Contemporary Authors*, Vol. 103.)

### JEAN-GEORGE AURIOL

[At the head of the young French school of directors] there is without hesitation René Clair, whose first film, made in 1922, with unbelievably limited means, *Paris qui dort*, remains still the only French comic film that can be shown along with the old Max Linder films, which have almost all disappeared today. René Clair amazed all eyes with the film he made, on a scenario by Picabia, for a scene in the Swedish Ballet in 1922—I am speaking of *Entr'acte*. This short and admirable bit of mystification has such spontaneous movement and such real richness that it can be considered as a chef-d'oeuvre. Clair next sought to react against the theatrical cinema, so generally admired in France, through films that were full of movement and without literary pretensions. Then, after directing a number of films that were more to his taste, but sufficiently ordinary to obtain a financial success, he is now reduced to the point of taking refuge in facile, elegant plays, and transposing into the French style the marvelous buffoonery of Keaton or the easier passages in the admirable humor of Chaplin. (p. 260)

> Jean-George Auriol, "Whither the French Cinema" (translation revised by Maria McD. Jolas for this publication), translated by Maria McD. Jolas, in transition (copyright, 1929, by transition), No. 15, February, 1929, pp. 257-63.*

### ALEXANDER BAKSHY

[René Clair] enjoys the combined benefits of talent and good fortune. He has produced ["*Sous les Toits de Paris*,"] a picture that in many ways is a little masterpiece, and he has been lucky enough to be the first artist in a field that has been dominated by Hollywood robots. Indeed, so great is one's relief and delight at seeing a fresh mind, unencumbered with hollow conventions and equipped with taste, subtle wit, and imaginative insight, apply itself to fashioning a work of art that the shortcomings of the picture inevitably recede into the background. There I shall leave them for the moment, to stress the more important fact—the fascination and charm of René Clair's offspring.

The quality of the picture is revealed almost from its opening scenes. . . . The length of the [opening] song, the dulness of the music, and the solemnity of the singing would have been enough to condemn this scene for any Hollywood talkie. But here comes the miracle of art. By introducing a slight action, so slight that it is almost entirely confined to an exchange of glances between the peddler and a prowling pickpocket, the artist sets off the vital force. Instantly the characters become intensely alive, the singing acquires the quality of suspense, and the whole scene begins to sparkle with humor and to throb with the pulse of human life. By vivifying touches such as this, one scene after another is transformed into a palpitating reality. . . . [This] testifies to the freshness of approach and the sense of vital and significant detail with which René Clair treats the material of human life. His imaginative vision of this life is the source of the authentic Parisian atmosphere that distinguishes his picture, that makes it so stimulating in its sober earnestness.

But greatly as I admire this creative interpretation of the material of life and the flawless acting in which it is embodied, I am not prepared to regard **"Sous les Toits de Paris"** as an important advance in the solution of the problem of cinematic form in the talkies. René Clair undoubtedly achieves a fair measure of success in blending scenes with dialogue with scenes without dialogue. He succeeds, however, only by the extensive use of music, of which, as it happens, he has an abundant supply in his story and setting. But even he is occasionally obliged to resort to music as mere accompaniment, as in the old silent pictures; and this method, if applied to less musical stories, would be dodging the issue of cinematic dialogue. (pp. 25-6)

> Alexander Bakshy, "A Notable Achievement," in The Nation, *Vol. CXXXII, No. 3418, January 7, 1931, pp. 25-6.*

### NATIONAL BOARD OF REVIEW MAGAZINE

It may be that [*Sous Les Toits de Paris*] will not circulate widely through America because foreign tongues are not considered remunerative adjuncts to motion pictures except in localities where there is a definite audience of foreign extraction. It is a pity, for France has not sent us a more delightful movie than this one. As a matter of fact enjoying the picture depends very little on being able to understand French. . . . (p. 13)

Out of very slight material comes a gay and charming picture. Its atmosphere recalls the good old "Vie de Boheme," but there is a vast difference between the lightly loving Bohemians of Murger's day and the similar gentry with whom M. Clair has concerned himself. (pp. 13-14)

Sentiment has been saltily mixed with cheerful cynicism, and the rather commonplace tale of flirtation and light-hearted faithlessness never runs into danger of becoming tearful or tragic. . . .

What gives solidity and its greatest charm to all this is the background and atmosphere of Paris—the French Paris untouched by tourists and never seen in movies. . . .

But the enthusiastic analyst of the cinema will find a double pleasure in this picture through watching the way it has been

made. . . . Most of all he will perhaps be struck by the sparing but immensely suggestive employment of actual dialogue. There is hardly more speech than there used to be titles in the best of the silent films, and yet you are satisfied you have heard all that was worth hearing—certainly all that was necessary to hear. It is far more movie than talkie, which exercises the imagination and rests the ear. M. Clair has used the best of the new form without losing any of the good of the old. (p. 14)

> *"Exceptional Photoplays: 'Sous les toits de Paris',"* in National Board of Review Magazine *(copyright, 1931), Vol. VI, No. 2, February, 1931, pp. 13-14.*

### JAMES SHELLEY HAMILTON

[*Le Million*] is indescribably gay and amusing, done in a style that is partly French, but chiefly René Clair's own. . . . In *Le Million* he has gone in for fewer subtleties—just swift straight comedy that flirts with what is sometimes rather contemptuously called slap-stick. Through it all he has scattered some lively tunes that quicken the pace rather than halt it, and in his rapid stride he manages, lightly but pointedly, to have some fun with various things: with greed and infidelity, to name the more serious ones, with gangsters and gangster films, with football and collegiate films, and most gleefully of all with that solem-old institution, grand opera. . . .

If a funnier, more original and individual screen comedy is to be looked for to follow *Le Million,* there is no one in sight to expect it from but René Clair himself. (p. 14)

> *James Shelley Hamilton, "'Le Million',"* in National Board of Review Magazine, *Vol. VI, No. 6, June, 1931, pp. 13-14.*

### ALEXANDER BAKSHY

Rene Clair's **"Le Million"** . . . , like his earlier **"Sous les Toits de Paris,"** is one of those rare pictures that make you their willing captive immersed in their mood and letting yourself be carried away on the wings of their fancy. In **"Le Million"** the fancy is much more exuberant than it was in the other picture, but it enforces submission upon you just as effectively, so that like everybody else around you, you inevitably exclaim: "What charm! What invention! What fun!" This spontaneous reaction, confirmed by the laudations you hear on all sides, is sufficient proof of the unique qualities of the film. It is the work of an artist who sees beyond the obvious and who can view the comedy of life with a good-natured cynicism that proclaims its authentic "sophistication." From under this gentle leg-pulling there gradually emerges a fantastic world inhabited by not quite normal human beings who now and again burst into dancing and singing that reveals their hidden kinship with puppets. It is René Clair's great achievement as an artist that though his characters' behavior is at times so grotesquely fantastic, it never appears incongruous with their surroundings or inconsistent with their more normal actions. But the achievement is a tour de force that only disguises its fundamental weakness.

The problem that René Clair sets himself to solve in **"Le Million"** is the old one of screen musical comedy. It has repeatedly been proved that the forms of singing and dancing seen in stage musical comedy are intolerably false and incongruous when transferred to the screen. . . . Now René Clair attempts to justify musical comedy by means that are directly opposite to those of Hollywood. Instead of making singing and dancing more natural, more in accord with the daily life of his characters, he makes the daily life of his characters more un-natural, more in accord with stage singing and dancing. Thus the story of a lost lottery ticket becomes a series of madcap adventures in which the normal is hardly distinguishable from the eccentric. Clair's success in this daring experiment reveals the measure of his talent as an entirely convincing and vastly entertaining interpreter of human foibles. But his fantastic treatment is even more restricted in its application than the naturalistic one of Hollywood. Moreover, his approach to the problem of musical comedy is confined to the choice of subject, whereas the only way to solve the problem is to discover a cinematic form that would make dancing and singing spring as freely from the nature of the screen entertainment as they spring from the nature of the stage performance. (pp. 645-46)

*Alexander Bakshy, "Films: Fantasy All the Way," in* The Nation, *Vol. CXXXII, No. 3440, June 10, 1931, pp. 645-46.\**

## FRANCIS FERGUSSON

[If René Clair's] *Le Million* is better than most Hollywood comedies, it is because he is still supported by the Molière formula, which is far better theatre than our own funny-paper slapsticks. *Le Million* is the story of a young man who wins a lottery, and loses his winning ticket, which everyone in Paris then tries to steal. By chopping this film into a series of neatly built scenes; but putting it all in a snappy rhythm, like a quick march, and setting part of it to music; and by using his settings like the traditional French stage with three doors, out of which angry people are always popping, René Clair shows that he is simply transferring the old comedy to the screen. In this he is successful within the limitations of his scenario. It is a relief to meet unsentimental juveniles, treated as part of the whole satire. (p. 634)

*Francis Fergusson, "A Month of the Theatre," in* The Bookman, *New York, Vol. LXXIII, No. 6, August, 1931, pp. 632-34.\**

## C. A. LEJEUNE

[Clair's] films achieve a peculiarly happy combination of instinct and training that I have never quite seen paralleled in the cinema; you find it in his conversation too, and in his approach to a story, and in his attitude towards the accidents of life. He has an infectious, rather ingenuous sense of fun that leaps all the time to meet a comic conclusion already suggested by his practical experience of technique; he is at once spontaneous and considered, fantastic and yet curiously precise. The tradition of laughter which he has created for Europe is akin to, and yet distinct from, the laughter of American slapstick; it is based on an acceptance of the school of Sennett, but expressed in an individual and spirited personal idiom, a kind of passion for the camera's resources that leads him up the most varied and lovely avenues of discovery before he achieves his end.

The odd combination of the approach of Chaplin with the mentality of France which coloured *Sous les Toits de Paris* is typical, in a lesser measure, of all Clair's work; it has given humanity to his technique and grit to his fantasy. . . . But if Clair lacks that ultimate sense of frustration in Chaplin, he has a certain robustness of comedy, a certain mass consciousness,

that Chaplin definitely misses in his later work. . . . (pp. 162-63)

*Sous les Toits de Paris* was, in its time, a new break in sound-pictures; it did make a definite attempt towards the constructional and contrapuntal use of cut-in sound images. The few words in the film—used, like the dialogue in the German talkies, only at the apex of action—are not quite of the stuff of the direction, take their shape from a different tissue. They have not been chosen . . . for their direct and individual image. They are concessions to the machine, rather than an integral part of the machine's supply. Except in such a scene as the one in which they are cut off sharp by the closing of the café door—used in fact for their sound and not for their content—they add nothing to the value of the film. The true material of the sound *montage* is the music; the individual phrases of the theme song, the commentary of traffic, of street sounds, of accordion notes, which amplify without ever duplicating the content of a scene. (p. 164)

[*Le Million*] is the maturer bit of work, and relates the modern Clair to the director of *The Italian Straw Hat,* who was ready to turn every device of slapstick and timing, repetitive emphasis and caricature, to his comic purpose. In both these films—his best and dryest—Clair has been ruthless with tradition; he has tried to produce an effect of unreality by the unreal treatment of real things, and all his lighting and grouping, his architecture and photography, has been focussed to that single end. *Le Million* is the richer film of the two, simply by the addition of sound, rightly used and fully understood. (p. 165)

The comedy line of music runs alongside and explains the development of the plot; not only do the creditors, the police and the neighbours proclaim themselves in song, but a choir of unseen commentators reflects upon every action. . . . In this use of musical commentary, as well as in his free slapstick conception of movement, Clair shows himself again as closer to Sennett than to Chaplin; but the Frenchman has a wit and a judgment that makes his knockabout something more than just good movie; this comic parade of law and order, this burlesque of pomp and sentiment, this fooling and fighting, rushing and smashing, has a strongly marked logic of its own. (pp. 165-66)

*C. A. Lejeune, "René Clair," in her* Cinema (reprinted by the permission of the Estate of C. A. Lejeune), *Alexander Maclehose & Co., 1931, pp. 159-66.*

## FRANCIS BIRRELL

*A Nous La Liberté* is, as the title suggests, a pictorial discussion of the problem of liberty, in which the cameraman is aided by the disillusioned airs of Auric. Clair treats the modern world in terms of modern sensibility. A convict evidently lacks liberty. An employee in a Taylorised world is barely distinguishable from a convict. The owner of the factory is too busy to have a minute to himself, and if he buys a smart wife, he merely exists to decorate her dinner table. . . .

These ideas are, in a way, literary. But they are realised by visual means. *A Nous La Liberté* is not a talkie, but a sound-film, based on a definite rhythm. There is a little talking to help through the necessary plot, not to illustrate the theme. For Clair composes in sound-space. The film is perhaps a trifle long. I felt it might have been better had it been a quarter of an hour shorter. Still, it is extremely funny, immensely various, and intellectually sound. Clair is free to do what he wants, to choose his theme, to write his scenarios, to pick his musicians and his painters, to use what actors he likes, to get along without stars. He is, in fact, captain of his own quarter-deck, as practically no one is in the film-world. He is not handicapped before he starts with ready-made themes, bought by somebody else, from sloppy novels or worn-out comedies. He is allowed, in fact, to be a creator. Perhaps even more than for his actual productions Clair is important to us for having in his own art attained the liberty he predicates in his latest film, the liberty both to think and to design. It is not mere chance that his actors are announced on the screen in the order of their appearance. They are subordinated officially to the director. The hierarchy is observed. Yet, of course, Clair can make them act delightfully, and we all, too, are charmed to recognise several friends out of the *Million*. Yet the main attraction of *A Nous La Liberté* is the spectacle it offers of a subtle and completely untrammelled intelligence, working freely in its own material. (p. 230)

Francis Birrell, "Two Film Directors," in The New Statesman & Nation (© 1932 The Statesman & Nation Publishing Co. Ltd.), Vol. III, No. 52, February 20, 1932, pp. 230-31.*

### PHILIPPE SOUPAULT

[In order to judge fairly "A Nous la Liberté"] we must consider it from two different points of view. We must look at both its technique and its ideas. Technically this film is distinguished for its great freshness, novelty and interesting cinematic suggestions. On the other hand, the director might perhaps be reproached for having tied a string of gags together, which weakened the general effect and unity of his picture. However, the details have been carefully chosen, and the gags are rather ingenious. The most remarkable thing about the film is the way in which René Clair has employed the sound effects of the movietone. In the matter of sound there are possibilities shown here which forecast a completely new technique. Sound does not merely record the voices of human beings or the song of birds; it also serves to create an atmosphere.

From this point of view we can only praise René Clair for his "A Nous la Liberté." From the technical point of view this production will undoubtedly have a great influence on the future of the movietone. But if it is considered from another angle, we are forced to make a great many reservations. The scenario which René Clair has devised is highly ingenuous, *simpliste* and, we might even say, a little silly. (p. 74)

It is obvious that René Clair has not forgotten the lessons he learned from Charlie Chaplin, but he is not so great a poet as the director of "City Lights." His scenario seems at times to have been created for twelve-year-old children. In the end we are a little irritated by the constant reminders of prison life, by these elementary comparisons and phraseology. To tell the truth, René Clair believes the public to be more stupid than it really is. Besides, since the subject he attacked was the great one of human liberty and mechanization, he owed it to himself to treat it with the seriousness which such tormenting issues demand, and not by repeating the same old saws, not by tying together the same old commonplaces about love, work and liberty. (pp. 74-5)

Philippe Soupault, "'A nous la liberté'," in The New Republic, Vol. LXXI, No. 913, June 1, 1932, pp. 74-5.

### MARGARET MARSHALL

[With "A Nous la Liberté"] René Clair establishes himself as the most accomplished and intelligent exponent of the art of the cinema. This is not to say that he is unsurpassed in all aspects of film-making. The Russians provide richer photography; the Lubitsch "touch" has a human warmth that Clair lacks—and probably scorns. The interesting fact about M. Clair is that he has mastered his technique as a whole so thoroughly that he is now able to employ it freely in creating a style of his own. In his hands the film, about which so little in the way of definition or scope has been understood, much less formulated, emerges almost for the first time as a separate and fully developed form of artistic expression.

M. Clair made it clear in his first picture, "**Sous les Toits de Paris**," that the film as a form of art must not be confused with the necessarily static stage play. Motion, both obvious and subtle, is the distinctive element of the camera as a medium, and it is in terms of motion that M. Clair has worked out his motion-picture technique. (pp. 659-60)

"**Le Million**" was another experiment, this time in fantasy. Again, the effect of fantasy was achieved not through any trick of setting or photography but by the mobile use of the camera before referred to. The chase, which is equally suited to the mood of fantasy and the technique of the moving camera, played a large part in "**Le Million**." . . .

"**A Nous la Liberté**" combines the stylized realism of "**Sous les Toits**" and the fantasy of "**Le Million**." Implications as well as events are allowed to assume dramatic and convincing shape. From a realistic scene the spectator is led quite imperceptibly into the fantasy of implication until the two are inextricably fused. . . .

[Despite] the intellectual cast of the film, its characters are flesh and blood; its action is as fast and as funny, even aside from its implications, as Chaplin at his best. More deftly than ever M. Clair has created a film in terms of motion in which the expression of the eyes and the movements of the body play a great part. . . .

The technique of René Clair as displayed in "**A Nous la Liberté**" is much closer to the technique of music than of any other art. The picture has a theme, the theme of prison, which is first stated simply and then repeated throughout the picture with variations of rhythm and elaboration, rising to a climax in the scene . . . in which mille-francs notes, silk hats, and respectable gentlemen whirl within the prison-like walls of a great modern factory dedicated to mass production and profit. Throughout, also, there is a constant contrapuntal interplay of regimentation and human fallibility, efficiency and impulse. The winking of an eye, a fluttering handkerchief, a flower; any one of these can—and does in M. Clair's gay world—set a whole system at naught.

But just as surely and just as gaily the system sets at naught all human values. For M. Clair's irony is complete and impartial. The flowers and birds with which he elicits human longing are invariably paper flowers and music-box birds. Without a word he implies that the workers who own the factory which turns out phonographs and profits endlessly without their help may find dancing and fishing a little tiresome. Finally, at the end, he catches the former factory-owner, who is "free" once more to roam with his friend, looking wistfully after a passing limousine. Yet M. Clair is no cynic. Cynicism, like pessimism, presupposes the possibility of perfection. Because M. Clair entertains no such possibility, except perhaps in the field of art, his gaiety is pure, entirely devoid either of morals or malice. (p. 660)

*Margaret Marshall, "Films: The Art of René Clair,"
in* The Nation, *Vol. 134, No. 3492, June 8, 1932,
pp. 659-60.*

## CHARLES DAVY

In René Clair's *A Nous la Liberté* a comparison was suggested between life in prison and life in a mass-production gramophone factory. Clair, it was said, would have liked to press this comparison home, but his backers wanted light entertainment, not social pungency. Possibly, in directing *Le Dernier Milliardaire*, he was similarly handicapped, for whenever the stage is set for satire—and it often is—he is inclined to sheer off towards farcical fantasy. *Le Dernier Milliardaire* has many delightful moments, but it suffers badly from a curious incoherence, probably because the conventions of its artificial world are never clearly defined. . . .

There are a good many . . . touches of Clair's unexpected irony—so many, indeed, that one feels the picture ought to be more entertaining than it is. Its central weakness, I believe, is that the humour lacks perspective; there is no solid background to supply light and shade. Clair might have produced a magnificent satire on dictators and financiers, but he has chosen—or has been compelled—to deprive his characters of human reality, so that too often they seem to be displaying the arbitrary animation of marionettes.

*Charles Davy, "The Cinema: 'Le dernier milliardaire'," in* The Spectator *(© 1934 by* The Spectator;
*reprinted by permission of* The Spectator*), Vol. 153,
No. 5550, November 9, 1934, p. 714.*

## JAMES SHELLEY HAMILTON

Clair has somehow come to be looked on as a satirist, though he hasn't an atom of the passion and indignation that puts the force into all great satire. For the most part he has found his fellow men, particularly his countrymen, odd and amusing creatures, whose petty ways he enjoys making an amiable show of on the screen. If the people are simple and not too malicious (like many of his Parisian underworld characters and his vagabonds) he is apt to be kindly and rather gentle with them, though completely frank. With middle-class pretentiousness and arrogance his portraiture moves definitely toward caricature, with a sharp, witty edge. Hitherto he has kept his locale in France, and his plots generally farcical.

In *Le Dernier Milliardaire* he has gone outside of France, into a mythical kingdom called Casinario, and he has picked the butts of his fun-making from all over the world. . . . There is no one to feel tender about in this film—everyone is the comic victim of the love of money. . . . (p. 13)

Casinario is perhaps a miniature of a topsy-turvy world, trying to maintain its place in the universe by desperate efforts to keep whirling faster. It is dizzying and hilarious, with several of René Clair's favorite actors in it to provide a lot of fun. The moral—if by chance the young lovers who run away supply a moral—seems to be that if you can escape to a desert island you can be happy though naked—if you have a radio.

*Le Dernier Milliardaire* comes nearest of all Clair's films to showing where he stands as a social commentator. Human stupidity and selfishness and folly, with their resulting woes to the race, do not stir him to reform or revolution or even bitterness—he remains amused and, though intensely interested, detached. Perhaps he is convinced that there must be a different kind of human being before there can be a different kind of world. . . . (p. 14)

*James Shelley Hamilton, "Exceptional Photoplays:
'Le dernier milliardaire'," in* National Board of Review Magazine, *Vol. X, No. 9, December, 1935, pp. 13-14.*

## MAURICE BARDECHE and ROBERT BRASILLACH

It may be admitted that the first French talkie of any real importance, *Sous les Toits de Paris*, displayed faults inevitable at that period, for it made use of music and also of silence in rather haphazard fashion. The introduction of the street singer, who keeps the film perfectly static while he sings his lines, was almost obligatory at the time. . . . Every detail is based on real life, the most vulgar incidents of real life. But if we compare this realism with that of the settings in German pictures, we see that in them the realism was dignified by a loving care for lighting and by a prodigious use of the pictorial medium. Theirs was the realism of a painter; but René Clair's realism is, as before, that of the ballet. He puts his characters in fancy dress and provides them with the appropriate accessories, but at the same time he stylizes them, simplifies their outline, and leads them into that world which is peculiarly his. . . . [We] almost feel that it is life itself which has copied René Clair, for here we come up against a real artist with a quite special manner of perceiving the universe. (pp. 222-23)

Had Clair really been trying simply to tell us a story we should not come upon those sequences that drag, those moments when the plot refuses to develop. We are given a series of pictures rather than a true narrative, for just as in *Les Deux Timides*, where its technical discoveries were more important than the whole, so *Sous les Toits* introduces the ingenious *tours de force* to which Clair was to devote himself right up to the time of *Quatorze Juillet*. The quarrel between Albert and Pola in pitch darkness was a genuine invention in those early days: images and words no longer ran side by side but intersected one another in a sort of pattern. . . . The tendency indicated in *Les Deux Timides* is continued, for the ballet no longer takes first place—it becomes an accompaniment as in Greek tragedy, where one by one the principal characters detach themselves from the group and the chorus is reduced to the role of commentator. It remains, however, as witness to the drama; and René Clair was never to abandon these onlookers, among whom his films had found their original inspiration.

*Le Million* affords striking proof of this. . . . It is the gayest of Clair's pictures, rich in minor characters conceived without a trace of exaggeration and seeming, against those luminous backgrounds, as fresh and unruffled as dolls in a shop window. As in *Le Chapeau de Paille*, the whole composition moves forward with appropriate animation, and there is also a similar technical experimentation and a similar tendency to chop the thing up into distinct sequences. Here creative invention has functioned completely, and we are as infinitely far away from everyday life as *Entr'acte* was. . . . Even the characters have little real connection with the story; their movements inscribe a sort of cryptogram whose real meaning can be guessed if we hold the key to the cipher. . . . The madman in pants belongs to either film indifferently, and *Entr'acte* is clearly the key to all Clair's work.

Or rather it is the key to his technique, for the lovers from *Les Deux Timides* from now on will be constantly with us. . . . [In *Sous les Toits de Paris*] Clair has abandoned the open air of *Les Deux Timides* and has returned to the artifice of *Le Voyage Imaginaire,* inventing freely and creating a new form of poetry. . . . [The] spectator falls victim to the atmosphere of make-believe and garlands, utilized with unfaltering good taste and underlined with the most gracious and smiling irony.

The same gracious good nature suffuses the best part of *A Nous la Liberté,* unquestionably the most complete expression of Clair's genius, and which a number of cinema theaters consequently suppressed. . . . [The setting] is clearly an unreal and enchanted place, a playground for birds that have flown out of picture postcards and figures from a merry-go-round. One is reminded of "Alice in Wonderland," in which pretense and absurdity are presented with such naturalness, for this is the world on the other side of the mirror. Birds speak, flowers sing—but they are stuffed birds and celluloid flowers. Nowhere has the cinema brought us so perfectly created a world as in this imaginative and innocent dream inspired by some tune from a hand organ. (pp. 223-25)

*A Nous la Liberté* is rather imperfectly constructed, and it overstresses both the similarity between the factory and the prison as well as the numerous chases, but it is undoubtedly the film in which René Clair put most of himself. Memories of many celebrated pictures, such as [Chaplin's] *The Pilgrim, The Gold Rush,* and *City Lights,* are added to the creative qualities of *Le Million,* to themes repeated from *Entr'acte,* to atmosphere borrowed from *Les Deux Timides* or *Chapeau de Paille.* Yet Clair had never before penetrated so far into the world of pure imagination. By the time we reach the magnificent confusion of the end, he seems actually to have risen above his subject, his characters, his personal experiences, and even life itself. . . .

It is impossible not to like this ambitious and perhaps badly constructed film in which, twice over, Clair so fully expressed himself, both in delineating the sorrows of love amid the beauties of the make-believe landscapes, and in this game which has no other motive than play. (p. 226)

*Quatorze Juillet* is probably the most ambitious of any of Clair's ventures, only in this case instead of concerning himself with outward appearances he was concerned with inner content. . . . Even *Le Million* was a summing up of one particular cinematic method only; *Quatorze Juillet* sums up all the René Clair films.

It may well be that Clair will be compelled later on to abandon his most noticeable traits and much that lay at the roots both of his popularity and of his charm. But in this film it seems that he wanted to perfect a formula, to clear it of extraneous matter, to transmute it into classicism, and to avoid all else. With a severity which must surely have cost him a good deal, he avoided all obvious technical tricks and set himself none of those problems which formerly interested us so greatly. . . . This film is simple, almost unadorned. . . . (p. 227)

From the dance of inanimate objects to *Quatorze Juillet* is a long way, yet this development is a natural one. We have still not left the world of the dance. The love troubles of the earlier films are essentially choreographic, like those in so many folk dances. (p. 228)

René Clair does not need music. His characters are even ready to take their places in the dance, the prodigious concierge and the members of the provincial-Parisian family as well as the bistro owner, the taxi driver, the dance-hall managers, and cloakroom attendants. It almost gives one the impression that he is holding them back, forbidding them to dance in order not to break the spell of this pitiful tale where Annabella laughs through her tears.

After *Quatorze Juillet,* René Clair abandons Paris—Paris, the only thing in which he really believes. *Le Dernier Milliardaire* was quite a disappointment to his admirers, and with some reason. Just as after *Les Toits, Le Million* and *A Nous la Liberté* took refuge in an imaginary world, so after *Quatorze Juillet, Le Dernier Milliardaire* abandoned Paris for burlesque and satire. Unfortunately, principally because the actors are mediocre and theatrical, this ambitious farce hardly succeeds in making one laugh. The best things in it are again the dance figures and the two or three comedy inventions. . . . [It] seems to me that in *Le Dernier Milliardaire* there is a dryness and overintellectualization which already threatened the earlier films and *A Nous la Liberté.* There is nothing here about love, unless it is something ridiculous; nothing of that poignancy which formerly gave so much value to backgrounds and to ballets alike. Clair this time offered us a feast of nothing but intelligence and irony; his touch is recognizable but it sometimes grates a little. If the future brings him back to imaginary worlds and music, bittersweet romance, ballets of lovemaking, and anxious lovers we shall forgive him. It would be foolish to try to put limits on what he may do. (pp. 228-29)

*Maurice Bardeche and Robert Brasillach, "The Films of René Clair" (1935; originally published in their* The History of Motion Pictures, *edited and translated by Iris Barry, W. W. Norton & Company, Inc., 1938), in* The Emergence of Film Art: The Evolution and Development of the Motion Picture, as an Art, from 1900 to the Present, *edited by Lewis Jacobs, Hopkinson and Blake, Publishers, 1969, pp. 222-29.*

**MARK VAN DOREN**

"The Ghost Goes West" is more amusing and more imaginative than the average film of whatever provenance, and indeed the audience of which I was a part laughed loud and long. But that is perhaps the point. It laughed too loud and long, and laughed in the wrong places—provided there is any meaning in the reference one naturally makes to Clair's earlier work, where the finest kind of balance was maintained between the ridiculous and the delicate, between the false and the true, between exaggeration and exquisiteness. "Sous les Toits de Paris" maintained those balances so skilfully that it came as near to perfection as any conceivable film of its kind—and there has actually never been another of its kind, as there has never been a director like Clair at his best. At his best he played upon his audiences with a wonderfully sound and subtle touch, producing upon the human instrument a comic music not unlike that which Shakespeare produced through the older medium of words. But he has lost that touch, and he was losing it even before he left Paris, as "The Last Billionaire" ["Le Dernier Milliardaire"] made depressingly plain. Traces of it survive in "The Ghost Goes West"; the picture, as I have said, is better than the average, and for all I know it will be a success in the United States. But the vulgarity which once was Clair's most beautiful asset is now beyond his control, and therefore has lost its beauty. The touch is not positive any more. (p. 138)

The story is obviously a rich one for Clair's purposes, since it provides him ample opportunity for that careful prance along the wall between sentiment and satire which he has always delighted to take as his artist's risk. But he constantly slips. The battle is neither funny nor heroic, and if it tries to be both at the same time, as it probably does, it fails, becoming as it proceeds a rather embarrassing mess. The chorus of creditors in the castle is feeble and artificial. And the Florida business is handled with a barren vulgarity of which Hollywood comedy has rarely achieved the match. I am not referring, of course, to the vulgarity which Clair satirizes; I am referring to the vulgarity of his satire, which is mechanical and desperately uninspired. There is no lack of nice things here and there along the way, and there is always the reminder that this man once held a precious secret in his hands. But he has lost it, and I cannot believe that anything outside of himself is to blame. (p. 140)

> *Mark Van Doren, "Films: Rene Clair Goes West," in* The Nation, *Vol. 142, No. 3682, January 29, 1936, pp. 138, 140.*

### ROGER MANVELL

Clair has a happy time with [the delightful situation in ***The Italian Straw Hat***], which provides the motivation for his incredible collection of 1895 bourgeois characters. The realism of the film lies in the settings and in the formalities of the wedding, in all those things people do to make them seem important and dignified in their own eyes. . . .

As a piece of story telling the film moves slowly enough, but it contains so much carefully contrived humour and is so well acted . . . that it survives repeated viewings. (p. 220)

[All through the film episodes] are worked out with little need for captions or dialogue. That the film is both too slow and too long for popular entertainment I have no doubt, and the characters of the officer, the fainting wife and the bridegroom's sorrowful valet become repetitive and tedious. For it is the elderly folk who distinguish this film. They are comic types, no doubt, but wickedly apt and typical in their behaviour. The deceived husband, standing upright and indignant in a footbath, still wearing a frock-coat but without any trousers, is perhaps the funniest portrait of all. While searching the bridegroom's apartments for his lost wife he is the image of stupid suspicion, looking behind doors where the lovers had been hiding only after he has given them every chance to escape. It is characters like these which give the film its final right to survive as one of the richest and most meticulously made comedies of the silent period of film-making, almost in fact, without equal. . . . (p. 221)

> *Roger Manvell, "Revaluations—4," in* Sight and Sound *(copyright © 1950 by The British Film Institute), Vol. 19, No. 5, July, 1950, pp. 219-21.*

### GAVIN LAMBERT

*Les Belles-de-Nuit* contains elements of the earlier Clair, as there are constant elements in the work of any individual artist, but its material is entirely different. In *Sous les Toits* and the others, a formal pattern was imposed on simple everyday incidents; here, as in *La Beauté du Diable,* the material itself is deliberately formal, and if Clair returns directly to any personal source at all, it is, rather, to one of his first silent films, *Le Voyage Imaginaire.* But his art now is most nearly like that of an eighteenth century philosophical French *conte* (a period and a manner which he has always admired), and it gives the same kind of pleasure. The characters are not intimately but formally presented; the appeal is one of idea, of intellectual manœuvring and calculated fantastication. . . .

Reality and fantasy inter-act, the story moves constantly from one state to the other and back again, each scoring off the other as in a game of chess, and a nice eighteenth century kind of moral finally emerges to the effect that every age always thinks a preceding one was better. There is no attempt at making anything "convincing" on the realistic level; it is obviously improbable that the young man's dreams would be so continuous, so neatly inter-related, and so persistent in mood. . . . The tone of the film is light, detached, and civilised, and its humour varies from the charming aside of the serious-looking girl in the post-office who turns up in a dream sequence set two hundred years earlier still wearing her enormous horn-rimmed specs, to the brilliantly devised episode in which the hero dreams he is conducting his opera, the orchestra playing with road drills, hack saws, vacuum cleaners and other domestic implements. The skill with which Clair interleaves dream and reality is often prodigious; he plays a series of witty conjuring tricks on the cinema. Where *Les Belles-de-Nuit* is inferior to its eighteenth century models is in its element of repetitiousness. It hasn't the unflawed concentration so necessary to this kind of art, and the stylised settings could have contributed more positively and elegantly to the dreams; the final chase in reverse from the stone age—though it begins with a deliciously glimpsed monster—to the present also strikes too farcical a note. . . .

*Les Belles-de-Nuit* seems to me as a whole, in spite of imperfections, to consolidate the development of Clair. Like Chaplin he has had his uncertain period and emerged as personal and as alive as ever.

> *Gavin Lambert, "Film Reviews: 'Les belles-de-nuit,'" in* Sight and Sound *(copyright © 1953 by The British Film Institute), Vol. 23, No. 1, July-September, 1953, p. 33.*

### ALEXANDER SINGER

*Belles de la Nuit* is one of René Clair's dream-reality mixtures in which a young music teacher . . . struggles to become a successful composer, find true love, fend off the machine age, retain his sanity. All this with one foot in kaleidoscopic dreams and the other on a banana peel.

The belles of the title are four beautiful women [the music teacher] meets in his dreams. They belong to different periods in French history, the salient characteristics of which are broadly satirized. These lovelies, of course, are inspired versions of the women he knows in real life. . . .

Clair keeps his melange from flying apart by interweaving recurring elements. Each shift to an earlier period of French life is prefaced by an old gentleman denouncing the France of his old age and extolling the one of his youth—the French period Clair satirizes next. . . .

The music [the teacher] composes, which accompanies him in his dream voyages, is melodic and nostalgically romantic—the very antithesis of the cacophonies of contemporary life, which Clair satirizes most of all.

> *Alexander Singer, "Film Reviews: 'Belles de la nuit'," in* Films in Review *(copyright © 1954 by the National Board of Review of Motion Pictures, Inc.), Vol. V, No. 4, April, 1954, p. 191.*

## GAVIN LAMBERT

[Clair remarked that the dramatic problem of *Les Grandes Manoeuvres*] lies in its change of mood halfway through; what begins as a comedy of seduction ends as a tragedy of love. (p. 146)

Through Armand's discarded loves Clair introduces us to various conditions of life in the town, sketching in unwitting cuckolds, indignant fathers and jealous rivals with light, penetrating strokes. Up to the time that Armand and Marie-Louise realise they are in love, indeed, the development on both levels—their relationship, and the background of provincial busybodies, gossips and interested parties—is faultless. The sense of period is exact but unostentatious; using colour for the first time, Clair employs a discreet, tasteful palette that evokes *salon* painters of the era. . . . [The locales] are quietly, satisfyingly alive, and reflect Clair's half humorous, half nostalgic, severely affectionate attitude towards the period. . . . Clair knows exactly the level on which he is working. The gently stylised movements, the light and even rhythm, set his own personal tone of comedy.

Later developments, however, demand more than he seems prepared to give them. Certainly the film becomes more "serious"—in the sense that there is less comedy; but it fails to convey human passions suddenly taking over, or a game becoming earnest. . . . [The] drama itself never touches that intensity which would make the reversal, the twist, really telling. The tensions of love are not there, the inherent cruelty of the situation never materialises; the atmosphere becomes rather dry and laboured. . . . (pp. 146-47)

By this time the force of what might have been a finely bitter climax is dissipated, for Clair's self-imposed remoteness, his non-committal approach to the lovers, has reduced the human dimension of his material to a purely intellectual one—and the film is not brilliant enough on this level to survive. . . .

To place *Les Grandes Manoeuvres* in relation to Clair's recent work is not altogether simple. In some ways it seems his most ambitious postwar film, though all his films are more ambitious than they seem. That Clair has "lost something" since the days of his famous prewar films is now generally agreed; that he has also gained something has been less often remarked. The heart of the matter lies in a not always satisfactory balance-sheet. In turning increasingly to the comedy of ideas, of intellectual fantastication, he has sometimes sacrificed gaiety and vitality to an excessive dryness, and one guesses this to be due to a personal disillusion. Each of his postwar films has conveyed a kind of loss or discontent. *Le Silence est d'Or* seemed like a valedictory to a period of vanished happiness; *La Beauté du Diable* was at times grimly concerned with the evil potentialities of science, and Faust's visions in the mirror struck a new disturbing note in his work; *Les Belles-de-Nuit* was a dream fantasy based on the idea that each age is falsely nostalgic about the preceding one; now *Les Grandes Manoeuvres* offers a fable on the illusion of love. The failure of the second half of this film makes one wonder, really, what Clair believes in. Undoubtedly aware, in his own elegant phrase, of "the disadvantages of the human condition," he seems disinclined any longer to present in his work, any of the advantages. If the story of *Les Grandes Manoeuvres* is to have any final dramatic weight, the desirability of love must be made real; it is precisely at this point that Clair withdraws, that the film becomes only an exercise. If Clair will have nothing to do with illusion, he could, all the same, take more positive account of reality. (p. 147)

*Gavin Lambert, "Film Reviews: 'Les grandes manoeuvres'," in* Sight and Sound *(copyright © 1956 by The British Film Institute), Vol. 25, No. 3, Winter, 1955-56, pp. 146-47.*

## LOTTE H. EISNER

[Once more in *Les Grandes Manoeuvres*] Clair exploits his extraordinary gift for suggesting subtle comical traits with a skillful virtuosity that, by means of image itself, brings humorous innuendos to the surface—effects that were somewhat neglected in his previous sound films. Again he juggles with purely visual understatements, with ellipses derived from sheer optical transition, with fine contrasts, counterpoints born out of terse and rhythmical editing. Subsidiary characters are not relegated to the ranks of shadowy extras; minute touches reveal them directly. His work is thereby instilled with life and movement. *Les Grandes Manoeuvres* is a film of glances that pierce the facade of a materially fortified society—smug, static, sheltered. It creates before our eyes the image of the *Belle Epoque* where the gaily colored military uniform has as yet nothing to do with the tragic hopelessness of the "grey war of the trenches," and where there are no other conquests but the defenseless hearts of ladies of upright morals and outright consent in the insipid *dolce far niente* of peacetime garrisons. . . .

*Les Grandes Manoeuvres* is Clair's first color film; many have expected from him a rhythm of hues, a music of delicate nuances. . . . Although a director fond of imagery, René Clair still fumbles, gropes, lacking the courage to employ potent contrasts of color. Perhaps he will find that courage in his next film; here, he is taking the cautious steps of the beginner. . . .

Clair, it may be remarked, is more at ease in that comedy of chevalresque wagers, in the *qui pro quo* of the treacherous whim. When the lieutenant truly falls in love, when matters have to be taken in earnest, the director's verve is more controlled, the tone becomes dry. (p. 28)

It is then its visual qualities that give the greatest charm to a film which cannot be classed among Clair's best. It may be that the extreme conscientiousness and minute care that the French devote to the problems of color will seem exaggerated to the American reader. But it must be remembered that France is the native land of the impressionist movement in painting, where refinement in the use of hues and shades has been extraordinarily developed, not only among painters but also among the public. Mindful of generations of great painters behind them, the French film-makers undertake with enthusiasm and yet also with humility the task of defining, each in his own way, the elusive imponderables that arise whenever reality is to be expressed through art. (pp. 28-9)

*Lotte H. Eisner, "Critiques: 'Les grandes manoeuvres'," in* Film Culture *(copyright 1956 by Film Culture), Vol. 2, No. 1, 1956, pp. 27-9.*

## PETER JOHN DYER

René Clair is one of those few, very rare directors whose films gain by seeing twice and cannot be properly estimated until that second visit. His shaded, delicate style, with its thin but determinate narrative line, suggests more than it reveals. . . .

Clair's highly individual work has developed identifiably. He is never a stranger. His career has not taken sudden twists and *bouleversements*. *Porte des Lilas,* with its refusal to surprise or astonish, its parsimonious exteriors, its dislike of technical *bravura,* is a formula film—the Clair formula of classicism. . . .

This story has a charming and tentative beauty in its relationships, in its feeling for friendships and loyalties. The development is muted, refined, it has infinite discretion. Admittedly it drags a little in the middle and there is no particular sequence that stands out above any other. Whether one is content to be enveloped in such a restrained atmosphere of almost unbroken harmony is really a matter of personal taste. . . .

This film is conceived from literature and not from life. At the height of his powers, in the days of his young films, Clair was one of a group of intellectual directors whose work, however slight it seemed at first glance, displayed an unmistakable spirit of progress and positive purpose. *Porte des Lilas,* though neither too dry or over-intellectualised as Clair can be, nevertheless has a faded, out-of-touch air about it that succeeds in making a corner of Clair's beloved Paris look about as tactile as cloud-cuckoo-land.

There is no denying this film's sadness, which is an authentic sadness—nor is there any trace of bitterness. Classicism such as Clair's, however, can go beyond being a fool-proof formula, especially when it has served a director for over thirty years: it can become a mere formality, where deliberate lack of surprise no longer surprises, it even begins to tire.

Clair's favourite visual comedy situation is to build a kind of top-heavy house of cards, gently rock one foundation, and then watch the construction collapse in a concatenation of minor physical disasters. Remove one card from a film as flimsy as *Porte des Lilas,* and the structure would come down flat. René Clair can no longer sustain his ideas beyond a mood, and this mood is a shade too remote, too contented, for a man who made a film about a silent film director—and called it *Le Silence est d'Or*—every bit of ten years ago.

> *Peter John Dyer, "'Porte des lilas'" (© copyright Peter John Dyer 1957; reprinted with permission), in* Films and Filming, *Vol. 4, No. 3, December, 1957, p. 21.*

### LOUIS MARCORELLES

"Every man has a past. For every generation there are a few years to which it always returns to rediscover its own youth", wrote René Clair some years ago. The remark admirably sums up the spirit of his latest film, *Porte des Lilas* . . . and I should like to supplement it with this extract from an interview which took place during the production: ". . . the carefree atmosphere we once enjoyed no longer exists. I want to re-create it". . . . [The] marked, though respectful, reserve of the younger generation suggest both Clair's fidelity to his rose-coloured world, and his deliberate determination in some degree to close his eyes to the passage of time. (pp. 145-46)

In the 'thirties Clair resolved his situations in furious, crazy chases; in the 'forties, when he was working in America, he superseded physical movement by an almost metaphysical sense of the absurd which was often reminiscent of Camus. Today there is hardly a trace of the old chases and nonsense; the puppets have begun to suffer in earnest and have not the heart to play hide-and-seek like children.

But Clair, the tough director hostile to sentimentality in any form, will still not allow his characters to surrender completely to realism. Hence the curious mixture of tenderness and coldness which is so confusing for the spectator. From time to time, it seems, the man who creates the gay, tender and charming moments of the film falls victim to an irrepressible bitterness in his personality. You perceive an irony like Mérimée's, a cold uncompromising ferocity which flashes out at the only truly remarkable moment of the film—the scene where Maria explains to her great friend Juju . . . , in a corner of the covered gateway, that she is going to the dance hall with the gangster, and politely asks him to let her go. Here, in this brief scene between the heartless girl and her foolish lover, we see one direction in which the creativeness of the ageing René Clair might expand. But even in this incident, Juju, bloated and pitiful, an improbable lover, forestalls true satire by emphasising the incongruity of the situation.

As a whole the actors hesitate oddly between the realism of the characters they play and the unreality with which Clair has always cloaked types like the villains of *Sous les Toits de Paris* and *Le Million.* . . .

All of them—good or bad—share a common reluctance to face the test of experience. One can only guess at the depth of pessimism which is masked by Clair's determination to ignore the real weight of people and situations. Even the settings emphasise this sense of a deliberate search for unreality, an evasion of truth. Clair has reconstructed in the studio the same working-class Paris that we saw in *Sous Les Toits* a quarter of a century ago.

A creative artist has the right, like anyone else, to grow old; but the most recent films of Renoir or Chaplin or Clair are no less significant than the work they produced at the height of their powers. On the contrary, they reveal the great directors to themselves, throw new light on their past work, demand a revaluation of all they have achieved. Could the Clair figures which charmed us so much in the 'thirties have developed into anything other than these, their successors of the 'fifties? Clair has not, like Cocteau, the whim to assume the airs of an ageing coquette. Behind his images, at once too cold and too tender, you sense a man who understands real life, who has directly and brutally encountered a world which he no longer finds sympathetic. But he seems reluctant to come out and face reality, to touch humanity; the restraint in the expression dries up reality. Even so, and in spite of its limitations and the trail of nostalgic evasions, *Porte des Lilas* is still the author's most personal film since 1945, and we can at least begin to sense in it the dilemma of a creator imprisoned in his own legend and so far unable to come to terms with an age in which he feels himself a stranger. (p. 146)

> *Louis Marcorelles, "Film Reviews: 'Porte des lilas'," in* Sight and Sound *(copyright © 1958 by The British Film Institute), Vol. 27, No. 3, Winter, 1957-58, pp. 145-46.*

### BRENDA DAVIES

Even in his days as an innovator René Clair was firmly rooted in cinema tradition. It should come as no surprise therefore to find him making a thoroughly traditional French bucolic comedy. What is rather unexpected about *Tout l'Or du Monde* . . . is that its lineage appears to be from *Joffroi* through *Clochemerle* and the [Jacques] Tati films rather than through his own early work. It is positively earthy and almost totally lacking in the characteristic Clair element of fantasy. Nevertheless the theme and the gentle satire with which it is treated both have their relation to the earlier Clair, and he has retained all his ability to work up a series of gags on the slenderest of threads. (p. 145)

[The] film itself comes down firmly on the side of the simple life. Audience sympathy is enlisted unmistakably for 'Toine, the shy shepherd who is content to "spend his life among his apple trees," and the speculator is characterised or caricatured as a greedy heartless villain. . . .

But no one is really in any doubt where Clair stands in these matters. Like Renoir (*Le Déjeuner sur l'Herbe*) . . . , he is adding his vote for the old comfortable unhygienic past and against the brave new automatic age. It is a natural attitude for a man of his generation and it is expressed in this film with humour and charm. . . . [The] film has a leisurely tempo of its own and needs no artificial accelerator. Indeed Clair demonstrates his mastery of a witty visual shorthand time and time again. We see old Dumont hacking away at a hated hoarding on his land, we see the hoarding falling towards him—cut to a shot of the village belfry and the old man's demise is established. It is this kind of stylistic economy which gives the film a personal touch and a sharpness which is lacking in the screenplay. Without it, . . . the satire could have been too slack to stretch over ninety minutes. As it is the chuckles flow continuously, and if the targets are wide they are hit with a satisfying regularity. (p. 146)

*Brenda Davies, "Film Reviews: 'Tout l'or du monde'," in* Sight and Sound *(copyright © 1963 by The British Film Institute), Vol. 32, No. 3, Summer, 1963, pp. 145-46.*

### GORDON GOW

The light touch is something we experience all too rarely in films nowadays, and it takes a master like René Clair to remind us how satisfactory it can be. . . . [It] has been reported on the one hand that the story of *Tout l'Or du Monde* is based on fact and really happened in France not long ago, and on the other that Clair had had such a subject in mind way back in the early 1930s just after he finished *A nous la Liberté*. . . .

Working on the assumption that Clair has been cogitating all this since the early 1930s, one gathers that what held him up so long was a fear that the resultant film might prove a bit static; a fear that turns out to have been well founded. About halfway through, the plot of *Tout l'Or du Monde* very nearly grinds to a standstill, which is a pity, because it is here that Clair is getting in some deft jibes at the publicity game, and these in themselves are extremely funny.

Yet if the progression of the thing is awkward, that light touch I mentioned is a saving grace. . . .

[Where anything sentimental] encroaches, there are few to match Clair at the knack of keeping things in check. Where others pluck heartstrings, he applies the fingertips with a touch that provokes soft but unmistakable reverberations. (p. 24)

*Gordon Gow, "'All the Gold in the World'" (© copyright Gordon Gow 1963; reprinted with permission), in* Films and Filming, *Vol. 9, No. 10, July, 1963, pp. 24-5.*

### RAYMOND DURGNAT

*Les Fetes Galantes* is certainly pleasant to look at, as bright uniforms rush, in those smoothly counterpointed columns of Clair's farces, across battlefields, up and down corridors round trenches, in and out of a picturesque castle, in every possible direction and dimension.

Yet that's all the movie is—bright and pretty. What makes it so thin is not, as Clair possibly hoped, the intensity with which he suggests the unreality or reality. Its unreality, alas, is primarily that which arises when a dried-up creator has recourse to stereotypes of the least interesting sort, and manipulates them through the most obvious situations. The film is never real enough for its unreality to be interesting. The slapstick is both dogmatic and incessant. It's preoccupied with details and all too often childish. The real comparison is with the slapstick classic where Harold Lloyd waded through the middle of a Mexican revolution; Clair's film just hasn't the hectic strength, amounting to delirium, of the American film. The parading (but hungry) army's quickening pursuit of a hen is a textbook specimen of slapstick technique—and just about as funny as a textbook specimen. . . .

To the film's credit it never drags, it's an ok pastime if that's all you want. At least something sprightly is always happening. And after the slow temps-morts which have unfortunately become the characteristic rhythm of the '60s, its old-fashioned rapidity is a mellow pleasure.

*Raymond Durgnat, "Reviews: 'Les fetes galantes'" (© copyright Raymond Durgnat 1967; reprinted with permission), in* Films and Filming, *Vol. 13, No. 7, April, 1967, p. 10.*

### HARRIET R. POLT

[*Les Deux Timides*] is only 66 minutes long, but they're 66 minutes of delight. It's hard to describe how a film which has all the elements of slapstick and general mayhem (fire-crackers, fake bandits, wife-beating, two court trials, and so forth) can at the same time be so guileless and tender. This tenderness, an integral part of Clair's style, will be recognized by those familiar with *Le Million* and *A Nous La Liberté*. It also derives from the spirit of Max Linder (rather than of Chaplin). . . . The humor, at any rate, is uproarious, while devoid of that slightly sadistic turn inherent in so many comedies. . . .

But what remains most impressive about the film is Clair's camera and editing. His split screen sequences are enormously effective. (p. 19)

I know people who claim not to like silent films. *Les Deux Timides* should be the ideal vehicle for converting them. (p. 20)

*Harriet R. Polt, "'Les deux timides' ('Two Timid People')," in* Film Society Review, *May, 1967, pp. 19-20.*

### JILL FORBES

*Paris qui dort* reveals aspects of the director which tend to get buried in the genial exuberance of his more well-known sound movies. It is quite explicitly a film about film, about the joy and possibilities of handling a medium which still seems fresh. . . . Paris is the monuments of the Second Empire and the International Exhibitions celebrating the progress of technology—but also a city transformed by the magical properties of the camera lens. The Eiffel Tower in close-up, viewed section by section, ceases to be the symbol of thrusting commercialism and becomes a pattern of criss-cross lines, an inexhaustible adult playground. Material objects, like clocks in the street or a radio loudspeaker, are seen in unfamiliar perspectives, and so seem to take on an altogether new significance. But what really accounts for Clair's excitement is that these things can be presented in an added dimension, that of the flow of time. . . . The story itself is banal and of no interest whatsoever, though plot occasionally intrudes, as when Clair maintains a shot of his characters talking without explanatory titles or, towards the end, when his technical resources begin to dry up and the style of the film becomes anecdotal. . . . But it is the director's delight in the technical possibilities of the medium that carries this film: it is easy to see why Clair leaped into sound at the first possible opportunity, and it is understandable that after seeing *Paris qui dort* Dziga Vertov was in despair at having been pre-empted. (pp. 208-09)

> Jill Forbes, "'Paris qui dort' ('The Crazy Ray')," in Monthly Film Bulletin (copyright © The British Film Institute, 1975), Vol. 42, No. 500, September, 1975, pp. 208-09.

## LUCY FISCHER

For Clair the essence of the cinema was its relation to the marvelous—to dream, imagination, and fantasy. Cinema for Clair was fundamentally a poetic medium, liberated from the constraints of a mimetic relation to reality. For him the truly seminal cinematic tradition was that of Méliès and magic. . . .

Somehow for Clair this vision of the cinema was predicated on the notion of silence. Sound carried the weight of reality and would have the power to disturb the fragile poetic ambience central to the cinematic experience. . . . (p. 36)

For Clair the cinema was primarily a visual form and the adoption of speech brought with it the threat of enslaving visual material to verbal. (p. 37)

What is particularly exciting about [*Le Million, Sous les toits de Paris,* and *À nous la liberté*] is that they represent attempts at dealing with a virginal medium. The uses of sound had not yet been codified, and the works reflect an aural conception that is far more open and explorative than it would come to be in later years. . . .

[Clair's] explorations were all involved with subverting the illusion of realistic sound in order to liberate the medium and restore to it its poetic powers.

*Le Million* is a monumental effort in that direction; but in order to understand the manner in which it articulates Clair's theoretical project it is necessary to examine the kinds of sound techniques against which he was reacting.

The most problematical aspect of the sound film for Clair was dialogue. At times he based his opposition on the fear that dialogue would lead to theatricality and destroy the primacy of the visual material. But more profoundly, Clair saw speech as grounding the film in mundane reality, as having the power to break the spell of fantasy so crucial to the experience of cinema. (p. 38)

For Clair the cinema and music were seen as sharing a common and privileged relation to the abstract and the poetic. . . .

Clearly René Clair identified music with the poetic and the imaginative. He saw in music its spiritual and etymological relation to the Muse. And it is therefore understandable that in the face of the coming of sound he would have seized upon it as the aural element most relevant to his artistic preoccupations. If speech and natural sound had the capacity to constrain the poetic possibilities of the cinema, music surely had the power to liberate them.

Thus the coming of sound afforded René Clair the unique opportunity to literalize a metaphor that had been central to his theoretical conception of the cinema; and *Le Million* is a film that bears the mark of that process of translation. If the silent film, figuratively, aspired to music, the sound film, quite literally, would embrace it. (p. 39)

[It] is in the *style* of *Le Million* that the sense of poetic abstraction is achieved; and that style is highly dependent on Clair's use of music.

The most general way that music functions to undermine the illusion of reality in *Le Million* is by allowing Clair to avoid synchronous dialogue. Some dialogue of this kind does occur but it is rare. Rather, a variety of musical forms are utilized as "substitutions." Sometimes Clair employs the style of silent film and has his characters mime a situation while on the sound track music is played in rhythmic accompaniment. (pp. 40-1)

One never has the sense that the songs are coming from the *particular* characters depicted. Rather the sound is nonspecific and detached. The characters seem enveloped in a silence through which the sound track cannot pierce. This separation of sound and image is clearly deliberate and by refusing the illusion of synchronous sound, Clair seems to be emphasizing the status of the music as film *score*.

The chorus is also used in a more experimental fashion in *Le Million* as part of the overall strategy to avoid conventional dialogue. (p. 41)

[The] chorus functions to convey certain plot information without the necessity of employing dialogue. The particularly innovative quality of this technique is that Clair removes the chorus from the concrete space of the narrative and allows them to function in a psychological domain. The detached and immaterial quality of the chorus seems also to emphasize its existence on the sound track rather than its literal presence within the fiction of the film.

In addition to the manner in which each of these sound techniques in *Le Million* works individually to abstract the world of the narrative, there is a way that their combination produces a highly synthetic and disorienting stylistic hybrid. Thus the film continually vacillates between a variety of aural styles: synchronous dialogue, mismatched singing, on-screen chorus, offscreen chorus, and scored accompaniment to mimed gesture. In creating this stylistic collage Clair seems as well to be suggesting a variety of musical-theatrical forms. (p. 42)

[There] are times when the rhythmic quality associated with music in the film seems to "overflow" into such additional elements as gesture and speech and to inform them with a quasi-musical sense. (p. 43)

The use of machine sounds for rhythmic purposes within the song seems to be an example of the kind of interpretive transposition to which Clair alluded and his perceptive insight into the sound quality of cartoons seems somewhat illuminating in relation to the use of natural sounds in *Le Million*. (pp. 45-6)

Aside from employing "real" sounds for musical purposes, Clair enlists musical techniques for the representation of "real" sounds. (p. 46)

[By] far the most complex aspect of the use of music in *Le Million* is in its relation to the narrative line. . . . [From] the outset the narrative line of the film is directly identified with music. This technique simultaneously weakens the diegetic illusion as well as augments the sense of musical structure that permeates the film.

One of the basic strategies of *Le Million* involves using musical continuity as a means for establishing narrative continuity. (p. 47)

[The most inclusive and complex aspect of musical structure is] the manner in which the notion of musical form becomes the literal subject of the plot of the film. *Le Million* as we know, begins in Michel's loft and at first revolves around his apartment house and the surrounding courtyard. Soon, however, events begin to occur which connect the space of Michel's neighborhood to that of the Paris opera house. . . .

Although on the surface this seems merely a clever plot complication, closer examination reveals a more significant level of meaning. For after elaborating extensive musical strategies within the film and positing a highly abstract and synthetic narrative, when the action of *Le Million* spills onto the opera stage it seems less a mark of arbitrary plot development than of self-reflexivity. (p. 49)

What Clair achieves through the plot design of *Le Million* is really quite extraordinary. He develops an abstract, musically informed narrative and then moves it almost imperceptibly into the space of a musical event. Thus the opera sequence at the end of the film works retrospectively to illuminate the operetta structure that has been functioning throughout.

In *Le Million* René Clair not only elaborates the poetic possibilities of the musical sound film but situates within the work itself a literal reference to the formal model upon which it is based. (p. 50)

Lucy Fischer, *"René Clair, 'Le million', and the Coming of Sound,"* in Cinema Journal (© 1977, Society for Cinema Studies), Vol. XVI, No. 2, Spring, 1977, pp. 34-50.

### RICHARD COBB

Clair is *the* poet of the Paris night: a bluish sensuous night of dark velvet, carrying a whiff of powder and the promise of adventure, indeed, a perfectly convincing evocation of the Parisian night of the 1930s. . . .

[The] abiding attraction of René Clair is not merely a matter of nostalgia, though there must always be plenty of that, because he *is* a period piece. He evokes the easy, unsuspecting sociability of a city the inhabitants of which share a common slang and most basic assumptions, and enjoy a wide area of mutual encounter: the café, the street, the market, the staircase, the shop. No one is especially afraid of anyone else; and nearly all can converse in an imaginative and briefly expressed irreverence. The common ideology is scepticism, softened by friendship, understanding and habit. . . .

[In] Clair, there is nearly always more satisfaction in coming down than in going up. The room is only at the top physically and there is a sort of release in the gambler cleared out, in the cashier who has gone off with the cash, in the banker who has taken to the quays or the Halles, in the industrialist who has headed for the open road. The only allowable success is in love; and if you do win the lottery, you give it all away,

remembering all your friends and neighbours, organizing a splendid repast, champagne, *vins de choix,* in which all, even the *agent* and the *entrepreneur des pompes junèbres,* will readily join in.

Join in what? A celebration, even a way of life aimed at the satisfaction of simple enjoyment, conversation, food and drink, the spring, sunshine, and of course, the cadre, the *only* cadre for personal and collective fulfillment, PARIS. Clair's Paris no doubt sometimes *sent le carton-pâte,* quite a number of his streets look as if they had been put up in Epinay (they had), the roofs and shop-fronts especially often seem overdone. Yet they *are* recognizable. Of course Clair is an artist and an urban poet, of course his films are delightfully light-hearted fantasies. But there is much more to him than that. He is as convincing a witness of place and period as Carco or MacOrlan. But, surely, it will be objected, people cannot all have been so *nice*? Well, I think, on the whole, they *were.* . . .

Paris by night is no longer a reality lived by its inhabitants, no longer a place for the lonely, in which they may feel drawn by the inviting blaze of a café; it has been reduced to a jaded round of tourist night spots. . . . Paris has largely lost its human dimensions; René Clair's Paris really *did* exist; but it doesn't any more.

Richard Cobb, *"The Period Paris of René Clair,"* in The Times Literary Supplement (© *Times Newspapers Ltd. (London) 1977; reproduced from The Times Literary Supplement by permission),* No. 3921, May 6, 1977, p. 549.

### TOM MILNE

Although the balletic wit over which Clair's critics once went into ecstasies has been looking increasingly fragile for some years now, the charm is still undeniably there [in *Le Million*], though in moments rather than in overall conception. . . . [There] is no doubt that, historically, Clair must be credited with developing the musical style brought to perfection by [Rouben] Mamoulian in *Love Me Tonight*. But where Mamoulian's fantasy seemed to be liberated by the camera's musical role, with Clair the process is almost entirely mechanical. Shots are governed less by any musical rhythm (or indeed by any impulse or motivation in the characters) than by a mathematical process whereby a shot of someone running one way will be followed by someone running in another. . . .

Since the musical score is also remarkably uninspired, being largely a matter of choral chants designed to get assorted lines of crooks, creditors, police or revellers on the move again, the main impression produced by the film is of actions arbitrarily stimulated by galvanic shocks. Significantly, *Le Million* is at its best not in motion . . . , but in repose. . . . For the most part . . . the characters are simply puppets, delightful enough to spend a moment or two with . . . ; but when they run through the film flirting, rearing or quarrelling purely in response to plot stimuli in a hermetically sealed world, one's interest and sympathies tend to waste away for lack of oxygen. (pp. 246-47)

Tom Milne, *"Retrospective: 'Le million',"* in Monthly Film Bulletin (copyright © The British Film Institute, 1977), Vol. 44, No. 526, November, 1977, pp. 246-47.

**JOHN PYM**

The fragile but enduring beauty of *Sous les Toits de Paris* stems not so much from Lazare Meerson's gleaming designs, the virtuoso, scene-setting camera movements or the charming effervescence of its slight plot, as from Clair's tone: the gay urbanity with which his hero Albert, a man with a most precarious profession, accepts—with a mixture of regret and cheerfulness—the loss of Pola. Although Clair's escalating frivolity occasionally threatens to turn into self-indulgence . . . , the film's controlled and justly famous set-pieces remain as fresh, suffused with light and as gently amusing as they ever were. . . . Although Clair has been accused of an awkwardly mechanistic approach to comedy, too great a fondness for reversing tracking shots, for imposing a slightly barren symmetry on his films, it would be a dull person indeed who entirely failed to respond to the witty camera movement at the beginning of the film up and down the building in which Albert lodges: unoriginal though the device is, it still affords us the Chekovian feeling of passing a door, or in this case a series of windows, glimpsing human activity and gaining a momentary flash of other complete, if wholly fantastical lives. (pp. 247-48)

> *John Pym, "'Sous les toits de Paris'," in* Monthly Film Bulletin *(copyright © The British Film Institute, 1977), Vol. 44, No. 526, November, 1977, pp. 247-48.*

**CELIA McGERR**

*The Crazy Ray* [*Paris qui dort*] is a visual essay on [motion]. The film denies motion and obstructs it; it creates it where it didn't exist, and constantly juxtaposes the mobile to the immobile. His camera moves in and out of the tower, dances around it and glides up and down it—and in so doing endows this massively stationary object with lightness and mobility. Conversely, he takes human beings, twists them into shapes and poses, and has his camera record their immobility under the ray's force. . . . (p. 36)

*Entr'acte* is Clair's most delightfully obnoxious film, twenty minutes of cheerful audacity and high spirits. While revealing Clair's talent and virtuoso command of formal technique, it puts that technique to a nonsensical purpose. It is a plotless film, divisible into larger sections but devoid of any sort of narrative line. . . . In *Entr'acte*'s free-association surreality, one looks in vain for a sane, comforting image. It might seem therefore that this work is anomalous in Clair's career, but actually the film's good humor has much in common with what is to come in his later features. There can be little doubt, however, that in *Entr'acte* Clair has transformed reality more completely than in any of his other films. (p. 38)

But what is most important in the prophetic sense about the film is its technical expertise. The brilliance of Clair's montage and his manipulation of the viewer are the work of a young enthusiast experimenting and discovering as much as he possibly can. While Clair's approach will mellow and touch but occasionally this almost feverish pitch in his later work, the vitality and sense of total involvement will remain with him. In terms of technique, *Entr'acte* is full of cinematic tricks perfectly brought off. (p. 40)

[*Le voyage imaginaire*] is concerned with the importance of objects. Clair uses specific objects, not with the surrealistic purity of *Entr'acte*'s free association, however, but as a means of establishing motifs in the narrative—and especially as a basis for building extended sight gags. (p. 47)

[Fitted] into the course of Clair's career, *Le voyage* is an indispensable work despite its flaws. While it is still a fantasy, its fantastic elements are, in a sense, grounded in reality—as a dream is part of the real life of the dreamer. The fantasy has become subjective, psychologically motivated. What the film lacks, however, is strong linking among all its parts; the characters are too weak, the gags often gratuitous, and much of the dream just overwhelms the more simplistic sections. (p. 48)

The jump from the zealous but unpolished *Le voyage imaginaire* to the smoothly confident *An Italian Straw Hat* [*Un chapeau de paille d'Italie*] is a large one indeed. The [later] film doesn't suffer from the slowness of *Le voyage;* its structure is sound instead of shaky; its characters are full of life rather than uninspired. Yet, for all its problems, the earlier comedy possesses something one cannot find in *An Italian Straw Hat:* a glimmer of humanity. Brilliant in its satire as the later work is, an inventive transposition of a classic stage work to the mute screen, gay, clever, effervescent, it refers back to *Entr'acte* rather than forward in the promising direction pointed to by *Le voyage*. It is too often a cold exercise in satire, fun but curiously hollow. . . . (p. 59)

*Les deux timides* is one of the most visually ambitious—and successful—films of the silent era. It belongs to that period marked by a technical perfection which was not to be achieved again (on such a universal level) until well into the sound age. In *Les deux timides* Clair uses just about every unusual pictorial device extant in filmmaking: freeze frames, flashbacks, handheld shots, reverse motion, exceptionally soft-focused photography, split-screen—even small jump cuts. . . . Most importantly, however, all these devices are not employed gratuitously or self-consciously for effect. On the contrary, they blend so well into the plot of the film that they serve to draw the spectator further into the story, rather than simply evoke appreciative sighs at Clair's virtuosity. (p. 61)

The silent films of René Clair reveal a clear line of development from avant-garde aesthetics to optimistic human observation. For Clair, *le silence était d'or*, silent films were golden—pure cinema, the cinema of images. (p. 71)

[Clair's] first sound film, *Sous les toits de Paris* ( . . . *Under the Roofs of Paris*), continues his innovative quest, as he searches for ways of dealing artistically with sound. It is paradoxical, perhaps, but sound actually clarified Clair's filmic vision, for the themes he takes up in this film and the ones that follow are those which we have come to associate with him.

Four of the five films Clair directed between 1930 and 1934 (*Under the Roofs, Le million, À nous la liberté, Quatorze juillet*) deal for the most part with the working class, their loves and losses. Clair saw dialogue as an obstacle to be overcome by his performers, and for authenticity had them improvise their own words. Despite his preference for creating a little world of his own, Clair's characters in these films are realistically presented. (pp. 75-6)

Clair's best trick with sound is a simple gag he will repeat in *Le million* and *À nous la liberté*. We see an object, but the wrong sound appears to be issuing from it. In *Under the Roofs,* the morning after Albert and Pola have shared his apartment, his alarm goes off. As he reaches out sleepily to stop the bell, Clair inserts a close-up of Pola's shoe. Albert touches the shoe, thinking it is the clock, and the ringing suddenly stops. After the joke has been made, Clair cuts to Pola, who has really turned off the alarm clock. Albert never realizes the truth. In *Le million* Clair develops this device even further and in fact much of that film's humor is based on such asynchronous use of sound. (p. 82)

[There] are many forlorn moments in [*Under the Roofs*], the first of Clair's to suggest a topical relevance to his era. From *Les deux timides,* Clair always treats his characters with tenderness, but here that tenderness if often bittersweet, even pathetic. These are Depression characters in a depressed Paris. And it must be noted that Clair comes closer to Chaplinesque pathos in this movie (and in *À nous la liberté*) than he ever did before or ever will again. But the visual economy with which he presents the less gay events taking place under the Parisian rooftops only heightens their emotional appeal. Again, it is in use of objects that he achieves his most powerfully expressive moments. (p. 84)

At first glance, *Le million* seems to start up where *Under the Roofs of Paris* left off. But—a church bell playing a popular song? Men crawling over the tops of apartment houses in the middle of the night? A crowd of people singing and dancing for no apparent reason? This is not the world depicted in *Under the Roofs,* where behavior is essentially realistic. The delight of *Le million* is its melding of the real and the fantastic. Like much of *Le voyage imaginaire* and *Le fantôme du Moulin Rouge, Le million* is an excursion into surreality. Yet this time the bizarre activity cannot be "logically" accounted for, since it is justified neither by dream nor by science fiction; its surreality arises from the familiar behaving in a most unfamiliar way. It is the fullest example we have of the uniquely Clairian universe, and, ironically, it is sound which allows him to create its surrealism. (p. 89)

Seeing *Le million* today, fifty years after its release, one cannot help feeling exhilarated by the sheer audacity of it all. Like *Les deux timides,* the film glows with the excitement of technical experimentation: Clair and his band of technicians were dreaming up new filmmaking processes, trying to invent a new visual/sonic language to replace the old. Their achievement has a surprising confidence and impertinence that dare us to put aside expectation and immerse ourselves in magic created by striking juxtapositions of sound and image. (p. 91)

Part of the triumph of *Le million* is its making the audience stop questioning the reality of what it sees. We know something isn't quite right, but it's difficult to say just what is wrong. The gauze which drapes the settings doesn't alter the furnishings or distort them, . . . ; rather it enshrouds them with a kind of tangible haze that makes us squint a bit to distinguish them fully. Eventually the visual aspect of *Le million* becomes completely logical. (p. 98)

*À nous la liberté* was never intended as a social manifesto, and it is a mistake to ransack the film for a serious, cohesive political doctrine. There is none to be found. . . . What the film does concern itself with, as is obvious from its title, is personal freedom. Clair outlines a mythical society, closely resembling our own, in which freedom is a meaningless word; because of the stylization of decor and the generally nonrealistic approach, the issue is drained of any immediate topical relevance and becomes instead a kind of fable of modern times. (pp. 101-02)

The visual key to the film is the abundance of repeated patterns: prison bars; ceiling beams; staircases; chairs pushed against long tables; the constant flow of objects on conveyor belts and ever-changing digits on an office wall; row after row of personnel files; Louis's ubiquitous insignia. The decor epitomizes the rigor and lack of individuality of this society. (p. 108)

In *Quatorze juillet* the focus is on love, rather than the friendship glorified in *À nous la liberté.* The sequence of Jean's and Anna's discovery of their mutual love is the highlight of the film, a little masterpiece of mood, atmosphere, and emotional expression. . . . This sequence is a perfect example of Clair's uncanny ability to transform everyday reality into images so romantic they approach fantasy. (p. 113)

There is very little satire in [*Quatorze juillet*], but the small, mild amount of it is nicely handled. . . . But Clair does not dwell on satirical aspects. He prefers to concentrate on his characters.

And concentrate he does. No other film of his contains so many close shots. . . . Twenty-two years later in *Les grandes manoeuvres,* a similarly erotic film, the close up is a rarity, and the long shot is used almost exclusively in order to cut off the audience from the characters' emotions. In *Quatorze juillet,* on the other hand, he is always trying to draw us further in. (p. 115)

The mood of absurdity of *Le dernier milliardaire* is about as different as can be imagined from the gentle calm of *Quatorze juillet.* The characters are all more or less lunatic, the prevailing spirit completely anarchic. As with *Duck Soup,* there is never a serious moment, but unfortunately Clair can't pull off the satire and slapstick with the unflagging lightness of Leo McCarey's film. His main problem, as he realized much later, lies in the casting. . . . [Humor] rarely arises from the individual *personae* of the [supporting] actors, but rather from an occasional funny line or situation. The wit isn't fresh or appealing, but exasperating in a silly sort of way.

The satire lacks the delicacy of that in *An Italian Straw Hat,* and the political barbs are even less coherent and pointed than those in *À nous la liberté.* . . . It's as if Clair just didn't feel like thinking through his ideas, and all he gives us are surface gags strung together with determination but little wit or purpose. Its lack of sophistication is especially disheartening after the perspicacity of *Le million, À nous la liberté,* and *Quatorze juillet.* (pp. 118-20)

*Break the News* is without question Clair's weakest film. Every foot of it reflects his lack of interest in the project, and the film is so visually nondescript it looks as if it had been shot either in great haste or with stultifying lethargy. (p. 132)

This is Clair's most overplotted film, full of improbabilities. . . . The absurdities are not compensated for by intriguing direction. The camera set-ups are uninspired, the editing perfunctory for the most part. (p. 133)

[*The Flame of New Orleans* has a] light quality that marks a modest but welcome return to form after the plodding, mirthless *Break the News.* Like its predecessor, *Flame* is essentially a star vehicle, but one so finely worked, fitted so carefully to that star's *persona,* that one can hardly believe the two films were fashioned by the same hand. André Bazin finds *Monsieur Verdoux* to be about the myth of Chaplin: knowledge of that myth is almost a sine qua non for understanding and hence full enjoyment of that film. So it is with *Flame,* though to a lesser degree. Not really a parody of [Marlene] Dietrich, it does what *Ninotchka* did with [Greta] Garbo; it plays a little game of sorts with her image. (p. 139)

[Stylistic broadness] is typical of *I Married a Witch,* a film greatly dependent on smart dialogue and screwball-type comedy. Despite the many special effects and sight gags, the film generally lacks the poetic visual style and flair of the Parisian films or even *The Flame of New Orleans.* But there is a moment of Clair's unique poetry that comes as a graceful pause in the general mayhem. Word, movement, camera work, editing, and even the speed of the film itself are memorably combined at the film's seemingly tragic climax, the second death of Jennifer. (p. 145)

[*And Then There Were None*] is very much René Clair, despite his allegations to the contrary, for in the film's comic base we can closely link it to the rest of Clair's work. It is the Clairian version of Film Noir—a black comedy, not so very far removed from the macabre qualities of his very first films made some twenty years earlier. He replaced [Agatha] Christie's "little bluffs" with tricks and deceits of his own, creating another of those environments in which things are often not what they may seem to be. (p. 151)

*And Then There Were None* takes a prominent Clairian ideal— brotherhood—negates it at first, and then affirms it. Clair and [Dudley] Nichols created a screenplay in which the comforting sense of community found in *Under the Roofs of Paris* and *Quatorze juillet* becomes a nightmare of isolation. (p. 152)

As usual, Clair concentrates in a variety of ways on objects. But in the seriocomic context of his thriller, innocent objects take on a sinister significance, becoming potential murder weapons and instruments of terror. Huge close-ups and careful placement in the deep-focus *mise-en-scène* also endow traditional signifiers of murder—a poisoned glass, a carving knife, a noose —with Hitchcockian menace. (p. 156)

*Le silence est d'or* is brimful of tributes: to the Paris of Clair's youth (it takes place circa 1906); to the first filmmakers (it is the story of a director and his company); and to film itself, referred to as "the invention of the century: an hour of crazy laughter, an hour of oblivion." After Clair's five years out of France, *Le silence est d'or* seems like a little sigh of relief. (pp. 161-62)

*Le silence d'or* is not a film about how films are made, but an essay on art and love. Art never imitates life for René Clair: it transcends life and exalts living. It transforms the commonplace into the extraordinary, reality into surreality—but a magic, romantic surreality that is Clair's own. For the first time since Michel and Béatrice sat under a cardboard moon in *Le million,* sharing a bench and a love song, Clair has placed two very ordinary people in a hybrid world of the actual and the artificial. It is not the out-and-out fantasy of *I Married a Witch* or *The Ghost Goes West,* but a kind of living dream world, where the daily routine is infused with the poetry of the dream. Jacques is still Jacques, Madeleine is still Madeleine; they still live in Paris on a meager salary; but by offsetting their lives with their

art they become sublime creatures who evoke romance and wonderment in others. (p. 164)

*And Then There Were None* showed a René Clair who gave great attention to choreographed movement and camera work. *Le silence est d'or* is marked by similar care given to narrative structure. All of Clair's postwar films become increasingly self-conscious, occasionally at the expense of spontaneity. They are also more and more melancholy; both their construction and their new quality of sadness, Clair finds, are the result of his age. (p. 169)

*La beauté du diable* (1950) is his version of *Faust;* though still a comedy . . . it is the first, and perhaps only, Clair film made as if he were saying, "Now I am being serious." Another one of his movies unable to be screened for legal reasons (as of this writing), *La beauté du diable* appears to be even more carefully worked out than *Le silence est d'or.* Clair's initial idea for it involved a series of variations on the Faustian theme. After teaming on this ambitious project with writer Armand Salacrou he decided on a traditional narrative line, but the version they ultimately produced, after over a year's work, was a complete reworking of the legend. (p. 170)

It is disappointing that Clair appears to have overstepped himself with [*La beauté du diable*], yet as with all his carefully made movies, there is still a wealth of ideas. Much of the dialogue is bright and witty; the film itself is extremely well constructed, barring the precipitous finish. Clair's use of mirrors throughout *La beauté du diable* suggests the presence of one of his most inspired objects. Not only is Mephisto the image of Faust as an old man, and as such constantly reminds Faust of both his past and his future, but mirrors themselves are the vehicle which connects the present to the knowledge of the future. The scene of Faust's discovery of his fate is apparently the visual high point of the film. Sources indicate that Clair's technical invention in *La beauté* is varied and often dazzling. . . . (pp. 173-74)

*Les belles-de-nuit* is, in my opinion, Clair's late masterpiece, a film which completely reaffirms his love for and understanding of humanity, and his faith in the form of comedy. It is not a consistently joyous movie, for in it we find some of the lowest psychological lows in any of his films. Conversely, however, we are also shown the highest high. The film is thematically complex, yet its simple, farcical structure gives it a straightforward, unpretentious air. Clair has laid aside the aspirations of *La beauté du diable,* yet has fulfilled them in this work, perhaps without having really tried. (p. 177)

*Celia McGerr, in her* René Clair *(copyright © 1980 by Twayne Publishers, Inc.; reprinted with the permission of Twayne Publishers, a Division of G. K. Hall & Co., Boston), Twayne, 1980, 239 p.*

# Brian De Palma

## 1940-

American director and screenwriter.

De Palma's best-known films lie somewhere between the thriller and horror genres. The plots are often confusing and shrouded in mystery. Dreams and the supernatural are integral parts of many of De Palma's films, as are grisly, horrifying deaths and murders. Critics see De Palma as the most Hitchcockian of all current filmmakers.

De Palma's first films give little clue as to his future. *Greetings* and *Hi, Mom!* are youth-oriented films satirizing the beliefs and ideals of the older generation. When the films were first released, catch phrases such as "semi-underground" were used to describe them, contributing to their status as "cult" films.

*Phantom of the Paradise* is a pivotal film in De Palma's body of work. It contains much of the humorous satire of *Greetings* and *Hi, Mom!* More importantly, however, it includes many of the elements of thriller and horror films. A sense of uneasiness is created through the use of offbeat humor and special effects. These devices are repeated in De Palma's later films.

*Carrie* was De Palma's first great commercial success. The film combines terror, pathos, supernatural elements, and dark humor, and is suspenseful throughout. More than his earlier *Sisters* and *Obsession*, *Carrie* deals in what De Palma calls "surrealistic, erotic imagery." *The Fury* is so similar in theme to *Carrie* that many critics see it as a direct, albeit inferior, steal, and have viciously attacked De Palma for his lack of sustainable creativity.

*Dressed to Kill* is the most Hitchockian of De Palma's films. Its scenes of extreme violence and explicit sex have led some people to term the film pornographic. However, others see it as a modern-day extension of Hitchcock's films. De Palma himself refutes this, saying that "*Dressed to Kill* has more of a Buñuel feel to it."

*Blow Out* contains many of the same elements as his previous films. De Palma describes the work as a "detective thriller" about a film sound effects editor who witnesses a political assassination. Thus, despite his statements to the contrary, De Palma seems to be shaping a body of work which will likely continue to be compared with the films of Hitchcock. At the same time, however, many critics find the combinations of diverse elements in De Palma's films to be highly original and creative.

## VINCENT CANBY

"Murder à la Mod," the first feature to be released here by de Palma, is [an] ambitious and abrasive work. It opens with an unseen director screen testing girls for the lead in a nudie murder mystery, which without the nudie element, becomes the frame for the film itself.

It's as difficult to tell the difference between the reality and the illusion within the film as it is between the blood and catchup in the film-within-the-film.

"Murder à la Mod" has a mind and reality of its own. It's completely logical in its use of cinematic tricks—speeded-up action and slow motion, and slapstick humor that is not funny, juxtaposed with mayhem that is.

There is a limit as to just how far this sort of playfulness can be carried. In the context of most of today's moviemaking, however, it's fun to see directors who are willing to acknowledge the movie form, and who do not try to convince us that what we see on the screen is necessarily "real." When they don't try—curiously—we often do believe, which is what movies are all about.

*Vincent Canby, "Films for Film's Sake," in* The New York Times *(© 1968 by The New York Times Company; reprinted by permission), May 2, 1968, p. 57.**

## PAUL SCHRADER

"Greetings" [is] the funniest and most contemporary American comedy since [Kubrick's] "Dr. Strangelove." This comparative judgement is less indicative of the excellence of "Greetings," than it is of the general irrelevance of American comedies. "Greetings" isn't a very great film, but it certainly is a rarity. It shines out like a gas lantern in an amphitheater. . . .

When "Greetings" first flashes on the screen, the young viewer is taken back: they really are talking about things he cares about. American comedies—even the funny ones—are notoriously behind the times, but the so-called "youth films" are not only old-fashioned, but bland and glum. . . . As any hipster knows, there are some guys who can get away with saying "Hey man" and some who can't. Brian DePalma is one who can.

"Greetings" manages to include a satirical comment on just about every cause or fad that fills the youthful mind: the draft, computer dating, shoplifting, stag films, JFK's assassination, abstract sculpture, sex positions, Vietnam, high-culture movies, and peeping toms. In other words, everything that movies usually avoid.

DePalma blends the comic styles of Godard and The Committee. Like Godard, DePalma has the courage not to move the camera to let a scene play out its inherent humor. . . . Like The Committee "Greetings" has a cynical, no-bullshit sense of humor, like Godard it exhibits an artificial and ambiguous frame of reference, teasing the viewer with wry camera movements.

"Greetings," however, still retains the taint of a youth exploitation film. Unfortunately DePalma's excellent script and actors do not free him from more basic directional responsibilities. Although he doesn't have to intercut like a TV editor to rescue inept performances, he is obliged to organize his tour de forces. "Greetings" is essentially a picaresque, a collection of humorous anecdotes. He seems more interested in matching his last laugh, than building for a potentially greater and deeper form of humor. He doesn't have enough confidence in any plot line to follow it through. About thirty minutes into the film the director's hold on the audience breaks, and although the material is as funny as before, the audience is no longer knee-slapping. DePalma has failed to build a suspense and drama over a ninety-minute span. "Greetings" is like an anthology of brilliant high-school satires. This is what student films should look like. . . .

All in all, "Greetings" does have the most hilarious scenes on American screens in many years.

> *Paul Schrader, "Review: 'Greetings'" (reprinted by permission of the author), in* Cinema, *Vol. 5, No. 2, 1969, p. 45.*

### A. D. MALMFELT

*Greetings* is, quite simply, a fraud. For it pretends to be about the young and the hip, while actually being about what the middle-aged and the square consider the young and hip to be. Yet, oddly enough, even the film's detractors appear not actively to dislike it. The worst objections have been to the effect that the film is very crudely made but that it at least has its heart in the right place. . . . In point of fact, *Greetings* has its heart in the right place only on a commercial level. But even if one assumes that the makers of the film have not intentionally pandered to some public concept of what the youth of today is all about for the sake of their own financial gain, the kindest thing that can then be said is that they have failed not morally but intellectually. (pp. 37-8)

[There] is no evidence of a directorial personality at all, much less one capable of imposing on the film a world vision extending beyond the limitations of the script. . . . In their quest for the contemporary [the filmmakers] have paid close attention to the miscellaneous parts of their film but have given little evident thought to the whole, either as a structural work or as an expression of some rational point of view. Everything has been sacrificed to the twin goals of presenting an easily recognizable picture of youth and of provoking a few laughs. It seems not to have occurred to them that to be conceptually silly, thematically inconsistent and technically incompetent is not necessarily Where It's At. (p. 38)

The function of the film director is to direct the camera and the actors, in that order. Observed from this point of view, director de Palma is far more conspicuous by his absence than by his presence. His handling of actors is extremely tentative. It is as if he did not want to push anyone to work very hard, or simply wanted to get his scene shot and move on to the next location. Except when placed in a fixed position from which they do not move, the actors almost never relate to the camera. . . . There is only one fulfilled characterization in the entire film, and that a vignette. All this might be excusable for one reason or another, but what is not is that none of the actors have anything in common with which to relate—they are working in a vacuum. And it is one of the director's principal responsibilities to his actors to provide them with an atmosphere to which they can relate that can be transmitted to the camera.

But if de Palma's handling of actors is deficient in itself, it becomes absolutely Wellesian by comparison with his handling of the camera. The camera almost invariably is in the wrong place, most often unnecessarily far from the action. . . . One thing, however, must be mentioned in favor of de Palma's use of the camera: it was almost always pointed in the right direction. De Palma also edited, and it can be said that the director deserved the editor.

What is significant about *Greetings* is not the film in itself but the film in the context of the time in which it was released. It has, largely because of its content, come to represent something which it is not but which is so badly needed at this time that a counterfeit can pass for the real thing. We are in need of a young native cinema. . . . The reasons why *Greetings* has received all the attention it has are varied, but center around the fact that this need exists and there is little else available that can even partially fulfill it. *Greetings,* while being an almost complete cinematic failure, has become a sociological success by default. (pp. 39-40)

Probably the most irritating aspect of the film is that it deals with several of the most profoundly disturbing issues of our day and does not, except on an aesthetic level, give anyone a single uncomfortable moment. A comedy, especially a social comedy, is not obligated to be bland. Such a comedy, even if it be farcical rather than satirical, should be able to irritate and provoke. It is absurd to attempt to create a comedy solely on the basis of stimulating laughter. . . . What de Palma [has] done has been to take Vietnam, the draft, the Kennedy assassination, pornographic movies, computer dating and women and place them all on the same level to be played with equally and mildly. The film, like its male protagonists, has no toughness. . . .

Strangely enough, one of the disjointed parts of *Greetings* has some merit and is funny: the dialogue. Not all of it, not even most of it, but some of it. Like bright pools of water in a barren land, there are lines which stand out as being life-like and, at times, witty. (p. 41)

> *A. D. Malmfelt, "'Greetings'," in* Film Society Review, *Vol. 4, No. 8, April, 1969, pp. 37-41.*

### HOWARD THOMPSON

With an unconventional technique, including quick-cut editing and speeded-up locomotion reminiscent of the old silent comedies, plus an impromptu flavoring, ["**The Wedding Party**"] starts extremely skittishly, levels off appealing and comes in a neat winner.

The opening chapter, with a formidable old country house swarming with wedding relatives and guests, bounces along with an arch, peppery detachment that gets a bit wearing, along with a frisky musical score heralding the humor. Some viewers may wonder if the writer-director-producer team—Cynthia Munroe, Brian de Palma and Wilford Leach—hasn't simply aimed its camera helter-skelter and let fly. Not at all.

The picture often verges on slapstick, and once or twice plunges in headfirst. A wonderfully funny and brash chase scene toward the end, with the reluctant bridegroom pursued by two pals, is pure Mack Sennett. And some of the wedding participants and their monologues seem overly caricaturized. But at about midpoint the human element begins to shine through. . . .

Best of all is the exact middle sequence, when a hilarious premarriage banquet develops into a near-seduction scene upstairs between the tipsy bridegroom and the wallflower church organist, that can only be called endearing. The utterly natural flow and simplicity of this vignette, as sweet as it is comical, is the real pulse of the picture. . . .

As newcomers to the feature film field, the independent team of Miss Munroe, Mr. Leach and Mr. de Palma . . . are welcome. They have created something fresh and funny.

> *Howard Thompson, "'The Wedding Party',"' in* The New York Times *(© 1969 by The New York Times Company; reprinted by permission), April 10, 1969 (and reprinted in* The New York Times Film Reviews: 1969-1970, *The New York Times Company & Arno Press, 1971, p. 28).*

### ROGER GREENSPUN

Among contemporary urban-scene-movies . . . Brian De Palma's **"Hi, Mom!"** stands out for its wit, its ironic good humor, its multilevel sophistications, its technical ingenuity, its nervousness, and its very special ability to bring the sensibility of the suburbs to the sins of the inner city. With no recognizable landmark further north than Cooper Square, it nevertheless *feels* like Bronxville or the quieter stretches of the upper East Side.

Not that it aspires to quietness or that it even for a second eschews relevancy. . . .

**"Hi, Mom!"** turns approximately every other current social misery to a comedy that is sometimes quite elaborately successful and sometimes only well intentioned. As in De Palma's previous **"Greetings,"** the humor, at its best, is understated but highly structured—so that you have to work a bit for your laughs. But **"Hi, Mom!"** is much sharper, crueler, funnier. Although it scatters some shots (often in a kind of fast-motion photography that seems an addiction of De Palma's) it pulls enough together to suggest some major insights. . . .

But it is the minor insights that most happily remain: the white black-power activist . . . who for a second demurs before painting his body *entirely* black; the pornographic-movie impresario . . . who wants to make "the first children's exploitation film— nothing dirty, nothing smutty;" or the mere idea of the TV show that chronicles the opening night of "Be Black, Baby!" A production of National Intellectual Television, it is called "N.I.T. Journal," which, (to my mind), comes under the category of what oft was thought, but ne'er so well expressed.

> *Roger Greenspun, "'Hi, Mom!'" in* The New York Times *(© 1970 by The New York Times Company; reprinted by permission), April 28, 1970 (and reprinted in* The New York Times Film Reviews: 1969-1970, *The New York Times Company & Arno Press, 1971, p. 158).*

### JOHN SIMON

*Hi, Mom!* is, regrettably, an almost total waste of time. The filmmakers have run out of ideas: they either try to milk the same situations as [in *Greetings*] (making Peeping-Tom sex films), or if they come up with something new (militant Black Theater that humiliates and manhandles white liberal audiences), they stretch it out as desperately as beggars their last crust of bread.

There are even more basic problems. *Hi, Mom!* is clearly improvisatory cinema, an enterprise that requires true brilliance somewhere. It may be in the director (*e.g.*, Fellini, in some of his earlier films), or it may be in the performers. . . . Here, however, brilliance is not forthcoming. . . . And whereas *Greetings* had a unifying plot device—how to stay out of the Army—there is not such central motif here. . . . I could go on, but let me leave a stone or two unturned, in case you do want to see the film for the sake of your fond recollections of its predecessor. It needs to keep its few mild surprises undivulged. (p. 124)

> *John Simon, "The Youth Film: 'Hi, Mom!'; 'The Magic Garden of Stanley Sweetheart'" (originally published as "Youth Films: Onward and Downward," in* The New Leader, *Vol. LIII, No. 11, May 25, 1970), in his* Movies into Film: Film Criticism 1967-1970 *(copyright © 1971 by John Simon; reprinted with permission of The Dial Press), Dial, 1971, 124-26.*

### VINCENT CANBY

[De Palma] is a very funny filmmaker. He's most funny, so far, anyway, when he's most anarchic, and **"Get to Know Your Rabbit,"** though somewhat inhibited by conventional form, has enough hilarious loose ends and sidetracks to liberate the film from its form. . . .

Movies that promote the importance of non-conformity are almost always fraudulent or, what's worse, they're sentimental. . . . **"Get to Know Your Rabbit"** largely avoids those pitfalls, and with a great deal of comic exuberance. It also reinforces my expectation that De Palma will one day make a really fine American comedy.

> *Vincent Canby, "'Get to Know Your Rabbit',"' in* The New York Times *(© 1973 by The New York Times Company; reprinted by permission), September 21, 1973 (and reprinted in* The New York Times Film Reviews: 1973-1974, *The New York Times Company & Arno Press, 1975, p. 103).*

### VINCENT CANBY

[**"Sisters"**] is a good, substantial horror film with such a sense of humor that it never can quite achieve the solemnly repellent peaks of Roman Polanski's "Repulsion." Never, however, does it become the sort of Nancy Drew detective tale it otherwise resembles, at least in outline. . . .

Mr. De Palma, best known for his anarchic comedy . . . , reveals himself here to be a first-rate director of more or less conventional material that has associations not only with "Repulsion" but also with Hitchcock's "Psycho." The "Psycho" associations are unfortunate, since they tip one important plot point sooner than is absolutely necessary. . . .

An intelligent horror film is very rare these days. **"Sisters"** . . . is just the thing to see on one of those nights when you want to go to the movies for the old-fashioned fun of it.

> *Vincent Canby, "'Sisters'," in* The New York Times *(© 1973 by The New York Times Company; reprinted by permission), September 27, 1973 (and reprinted in* The New York Times Film Reviews: 1973-1974, *The New York Times Company & Arno Press, 1975, p. 106).*

### VINCENT CANBY

Brian De Palma's **"Phantom of the Paradise"** is a very busy movie.

Among other things it attempts to be a put-on of "Faust," "The Phantom of the Opera," "The Picture of Dorian Gray," rock music, the rock music industry, rock music movies and horror movies.

The problem is that since all of these things, with the possible exception of "Faust" (and I'm not really sure about "Faust"), already contain elements of self-parody, there isn't much that the outside parodist can do to make the parody seem funnier or more absurd than the originals already are. . . .

Compared with even the last of [De Palma's earlier films,] **"Phantom of the Paradise"** is an elaborate disaster, full of the kind of facetious humor you might find on bumper stickers and cocktail coasters.

The movie spends much too much time just laying out the plot, which is fatal to parody of any sort. It also becomes quite enchanted with its own special photographic effects, as well as with its bizarre sets, which, because there's very little of interest going on within them, become the mildly amusing surrogate subjects of the film.

Almost redeeming the movie is the rock score by [Paul] Williams, and the comic orchestrations that trace the evolution of rock from the duck-tailed, surfing nineteen-fifties and sixties to the seventies and the triumphant emergence of androgyny. The concert scenes—filled with pandemonium, blinking lights and extraordinary sounds—are well staged but hardly seem worth the terrific time and effort that must have been required. Almost any A.I.P. "Beach" picture or Vincent Price horror film, being the real thing, is funnier.

> *Vincent Canby, "'Phantom of the Paradise'," in* The New York Times *(© 1974 by The New York Times Company; reprinted by permission), November 2, 1974 (and reprinted in* The New York Times Film Reviews: 1973-1974, *The New York Times Company & Arno Press, 1975, p. 291).*

### PAULINE KAEL

Brian De Palma, the writer-director of **"Phantom of the Paradise,"** thrives on frowzy visual hyperbole. When he tries to set up a simple scene establishing that boy composer loves girl singer, he is a helpless amateur, but when he sets up a highly

stylized paranoid fantasy with gyrating figures on a stage and an audience that is having its limbs hacked off, you can practically hear him cackling with happiness, and the scene carries a jolt. De Palma, who can't tell a plain story, does something that a couple of generations of student and underground filmmakers have been trying to do and nobody else has ever brought off. He creates a new Guignol, in a modern idiom, out of the movie Guignol of the past. . . . [A] mixture of "The Phantom of the Opera" and "Faust" (via "The Devil and Daniel Webster") isn't enough for De Palma. He heaps on layers of rock satire, and parodies of "The Cabinet of Dr. Caligari," "The Hunchback of Notre Dame," "Psycho," and "The Picture of Dorian Gray"—and the impacted plots actually function for him. De Palma is drawn to rabid visual exaggeration and sophisticated, satirical low comedy. This slapstick expressionism is idiosyncratic in the extreme. It's De Palma's flukiness that makes **"Phantom"** so entertaining.

Though you may anticipate a plot turn, it's impossible to guess what the next scene will *look* like or what its rhythm will be. De Palma's timing is sometimes wantonly unpredictable and dampening, but mostly it has a lift to it. You practically get a kinetic charge from the breakneck wit he put into **"Phantom;"** it isn't just that the picture has vitality but that one can feel the tremendous kick the director got out of making it. And one can feel the love that went into the visual details of this production—the bird motifs, the shifting patterns of the interiors. De Palma's method is very theatrical, with each scene sharply divided from the next. . . . His technique is inspired amateurishness; his work resembles what hundreds of student filmmakers have done, but there's a level of personal obsession which makes the material his own. . . . De Palma loves the clichés for their shameless, rotten phoniness. The movies of the past haven't made him their innocent victim; rather, they have wised him up. He doesn't just reproduce grotesque old effects; his driving, redeeming sense of humor cuts through the crap in movies at the same time that it cuts through the crap in the rock world. Few directors work in such a screwily personal way, but that sense of humor of his is like a disinfectant.

De Palma is the only filmmaker to have come up from the underground and gone on for years working the same way with a larger budget. In 1963, I was on the jury at the Midwest Film Festival which gave a prize to **"Woton's Wake,"** a twenty-eight-minute film he made in 16-mm. when he was still a student. It had many of the same elements as **"Phantom"**—figures running from skyscrapers, parodies of early horror films. And it was funny in much the same corny, off-the-wall way. What it didn't have was rock. De Palma has done some bright, giddy work (as in the 1968 **"Greetings"**)—almost like a revue artist putting together a collection of skits. His intricate sequences are like Rube Goldberg infernal machines—they buzz along and blow up—but in the past he hasn't been able to shape a feature film and keep the whole thing buzzing until it explodes in the viewer's head. However, rock gives **"Phantom"** a unifying pulse, and De Palma uses the score . . . so that the satirical points, the story climaxes, and the musical numbers all peak together—and sizzle. (pp. 366-68)

De Palma, like most underground filmmakers, didn't start with conventional methods. And what he's trying to do is to deal with his experience of maniacal movies in terms derived from those movies. From the way his scenes plunge into vacuity whenever he tries to show ordinary human relations it's clear that his energy runs high only when he lets his carny spirit and his movie-fed imagination take over. . . . He's a movie freak with brains and talent. The faults and virtues are so similar in **"Woton's Wake"** and **"Phantom,"** . . . that it's evident that he hasn't learned commercial techniques. I doubt whether he'll ever be able to handle exposition or naturalistic scenes, and his dialogue is unsure and too casual, as if he were still a student filmmaker just playing around.

But this incompetence isn't necessarily crippling: it's in terms of the conventional standards of moviemaking that De Palma is an amateur. . . . When he sticks to what he can do, he's got a great style, but he can't do the routine scenes that establish character relations and give a movie "heart." He lurched his way through **"Sisters"** trying to get by with expositional stuff that went flat. In **"Phantom,"** the scenes in which Winslow shows his affection for Phoenix seems "obligatory," because they have no satiric edge; we don't care about them, because the director doesn't. A cutaway shot of Phoenix snickering when a male singer scrambles to stand up in his high platform shoes is worse than obligatory: it looks as if the director couldn't decide whether or not he was doing a put-on of klutzy techniques. It can't be simple boredom that blocks De Palma; probably most directors are bored by these scenes, yet they still manage to do what's needed. It must be that something in him (his wit?) fights the material. Maybe the answer isn't that he needs to learn the routine techniques for getting through the normal scenes but, rather, that he needs to let his own attitudes toward those scenes come out. He's being paralyzed by his own unexpressed feelings. **"Phantom,"** fortunately, has so much spirit that it buckjumps right past the dead spots, but it wouldn't be so blotchy if De Palma weren't a little nervous about the hot spiel in his blood. (pp. 368-69)

> *Pauline Kael, "Spieler" (originally published in* The New Yorker, *Vol. L, No. 38, November 11, 1974), in her* Reeling *(copyright © 1974 by Pauline Kael; reprinted by permission of Little, Brown and Company in association with the Atlantic Monthly Press), Atlantic-Little, Brown, 1976, pp. 366-71.\**

### RICHARD COMBS

Too broad in its effects and too bloated in style to cut very deeply as a parody of *The Phantom of the Opera*, Brian De Palma's [*Phantom of the Paradise*] is closer to the anything goes mode of a *Mad* magazine lampoon. De Palma's last feature to be released in this country, *Blood Sisters* [also released as *Sisters*], was a reasonably efficient pastiche/parody of Alfred Hitchcock; here he seems to have been infected with a large dose of [Ken] Russellmania, and while not up to the razzle-dazzle effects that the Master commands on a doubtlessly larger budget, *Phantom of the Paradise* nevertheless offers fair competition to and comes on much like *Tommy*. . . . Unfortunately, the mating of the [Phantom and Faust] legends proves simply to be the film's most spectacular coup, rather than the basis for any kind of comic reworking of either. The entertainment, in fact, develops into a loudly trumpeted advertisement for an ever-receding subject, and the packaging becomes increasingly desperate; like the noisily unimaginative messiah plot which overtakes *Tommy* once the hero has been projected through the looking glass into his true identity, *Phantom of the Paradise* winds itself by way of conclusion into an awful mélange of orgiastic pop concert and the vicarious, electronic excitement of a Kennedy-Oswald-*Manchurian Candidate* assassination attempt, televised coast-to-coast. . . . The presentation of Paul Williams' pastiche rock songs . . . redeems the

movie in patches, and in those songs where he picks up the Faustian elements of the plot, Williams treats them with greater wit and variety than De Palma manages in his overblown, comic-strip visuals. (p. 113)

> *Richard Combs, "'Phantom of the Paradise'," in* Monthly Film Bulletin *(copyright © The British Film Institute, 1975), Vol. 42, No. 496, May, 1975, pp. 112-13.*

### PENELOPE GILLIATT

Brian De Palma's **"Obsession"** is an *hommage* to Hitchcock's **"Vertigo."** . . . But it is intellectually muddleheaded in a way that Hitchcock's films never are. It is not up to the Master's insteps. There is a point at which *hommage* has an enfeebling trait of echolalia. (p. 61)

The plot proceeds, but it keeps faltering, because of De Palma's damaging affection for throwing the obvious into doubt. The screen gets the shimmers at key moments, which is a cheat. Are we watching a subjective expression of the hero's troubled state of mind? Or dreams? Or hallucinations? Story points keep being coated in Vaseline. . . .

Brian De Palma obviously has an idiosyncratic point of view and a load of monkey-on-a-stick energy, but he wrecks his talent again and again by mistaking the random for the free-wheeling. The confusion is typical of our times, and ruinous to this particular film: in making a thriller, exactitude counts. **"Obsession"** raises a good many questions that are never answered. It is also sometimes fogged enough to let a plot point rely on characters' witlessness, and such a reliance is not at all the same thing as dramatic irony. Dramatic irony rests on an audience's having fuller information than the characters, not on its being more clever. (p. 62)

> *Penelope Gilliatt, "Sweet Coz," in* The New Yorker *(© 1976 by The New Yorker Magazine, Inc.), Vol. LII, No. 24, August 2, 1976, pp. 61-2.\**

### JOHN SIMON

*Obsession* attitudinizes in three directions: toward the Hitchcockian thriller, toward the old-fashioned tearjerker, and toward the sophisticated European film, with cultural references strewn like bread crumbs along the way of Hansel and Gretel.

Such a mishmash could be endearing; as it happens, it is neither mish nor mash so much as mush. . . .

[Paul] Schrader and De Palma have loaded their penny dreadful with allusions high and low. There are overtones of *The Winter's Tale*, the Bluebeard story, *Rebecca*, and, of course, *Vertigo*. There are quotations from Dante's *Vita nuova*, likewise a tale of loving obsession. And there is more: The fresco with whose restoration Sandra assists is by Bernardo Daddi; it is a Virgin and Child, whose damaging has revealed an earlier work underneath—which one of them is to be sacrificed for the other? Why such fuss over a lesser master like Daddi, for whom Sandra and the restorers finally opt? Because Sandra's heart, however ironically and ferally, belongs to Daddy. And why the Virgin and Child? Because love between child and mother is what really motivates Sandra. And why is it the earlier work that is sacrificed? An anterior life must be abandoned both by Michael and Sandra for the sake of a *vita nuova*.

The movie is full of such otiose allusiveness and gamesmanship. Sandra's last name is Portinari—after Dante's Beatrice, of course. A minor character, said to be a bore, is called D'Annunzio after you know whom; another one is called Farber, although I can't say whether after [film critics] Manny or Stephen. The place where Michael doesn't quite dare accost Sandra is the Ponte Vecchio, where Beatrice withheld her greeting from Dante. Since a suitcase figures prominently in several Hitchcock films, photography, editing, and music combine to pump ominousness into the stairs of San Miniato, even though they have no dramatic function whatsoever. The first part of the film takes place in 1958—the date of *Vertigo*. The score was finished, just before he died, by Bernard Herrmann—the composer of *Vertigo*. And so on.

All this would be mere harmless minor nonsense if the plot as a whole weren't such a major piece of arrant absurdity. Sandra's behavior is *a priori* incredible, and it's only because we don't know till later who she is that we swallow the preposterousness that surrounds her. . . .

Countless details are fudged over in one way or another; if all else fails, there is always manic editing. Most incredible, though, is that the real villain should, with all his verve, choose so slow and risky a method of skullduggery as he does, and that the bright and decent Sandra should be so manipulable and obtuse. Toward the end, the behavior of all the characters becomes even less explicable, and the last slender links to sanity, indeed humanity, are frenetically severed.

De Palma's direction has its splashy slickness, but the people serve as mere props for the effects. The director was best at low-budget jobs like *Greetings* and *Hi, Mom;* considerably less good with medium-priced items such as *Sisters* and *Phantom of the Paradise;* and, if this is any indication, untrustworthy with bigger budgets. (p. 60)

John Simon, "Obsessions: On Land, Sea, and In Between," in New York Magazine (copyright © 1976 by News Group Publications, Inc.; reprinted with the permission of New York Magazine), Vol. 5, No. 33, August 16, 1976, pp. 60-1.*

## PAULINE KAEL

*Carrie* is a terrifyingly lyrical thriller. The director, Brian De Palma, has mastered a teasing style—a perverse mixture of comedy and horror and tension, like that of Hitchcock or Polanski, but with a lulling sensuousness. He builds our apprehensions languorously, softening us for the kill. You know you're being manipulated, but he works in such a literal way and with so much candor that you have the pleasure of observing how he affects your susceptibilities even while you're going into shock. Scary-and-funny must be the greatest combination for popular entertainment; anything-and-funny is, of course, great—even funny-and-funny. But we come out of a movie like *Carrie,* as we did out of [Steven Spielberg's] *Jaws,* laughing at our own childishness. (p. 208)

*Carrie* is a menstrual joke—a *film noir* in red. This picture has some of the psychic grip of [Martin Scorsese's] *Taxi Driver,* yet isn't frightening in the same way, because it's essentially a pretty piece of paste jewelry. *Carrie* looks like a piece of candy: when De Palma is most distinctive, his work calls up so many junky memories it's pure candied exploitation—a funny archetypal nightmare. De Palma uses tawdriness as a tuning fork. No one else has ever caught the thrill that teen-agers get from a dirty joke and sustained it for a whole picture.

There are no characters in *Carrie;* there are only schlock artifacts. The performers enlarge their roles with tinny mythic echoes; each is playing a whole cluster of remembered pop figures. (p. 209)

I don't think that before *Carrie* anyone had ever done a satiric homage to exploitation films. Who but De Palma would think of using old-movie trash, and even soft-core pornos, to provide "heart" for a thriller? The banal teen-age-movie meanness that the kids show toward Carrie gets the audience rooting for her, and it becomes the basis for her supernatural vengeance. This is the first time a De Palma picture has had heart—which may explain why De Palma, despite his originality, has never made it into the big winners' circle before. (p. 211)

After the rarefied phoniness of *Obsession,* De Palma has come back to his own exploitation themes in *Carrie;* the voyeur has got into the girls' locker room this time, bringing that romanticizing, hypnotic camera with him. De Palma was always a sexual wit; now he's a voluptuary wit. . . .

There are only a few places where the film seems to err in technique. The speeded-up sound when the high-school boys are trying on tuxedos is a dumb, toy effect. And at the prom, when Carrie sees red, the split-screen footage is really bad: the red tint darkens the image, and there's so much messy action going on in the split sections that the confusion cools us out. But the film is built like a little engine, and it gets to us.

For a sophisticated, absurdist intelligence like De Palma's, there's no way to use camera magic except as foolery. He's uncommitted to anything except successful manipulation; when his camera conveys the motion of dreams, it's a lovely trick. He can't treat a subject straight, but that's all right; neither could Hitchcock. If De Palma were an artist in another medium—say, fiction or poetry—he might be a satirist with a high reputation and a small following. Everything in his films is distanced by his persistent adolescent kinkiness; he's gleefully impersonal. Yet, working in movies, he's found his own route to a mass audience: his new trash heart is the ultimate De Palma joke. (p. 212)

Pauline Kael, "The Curse" (originally published in The New Yorker, Vol. LIII, No. 40, November 22, 1976), in her When the Lights Go Down (copyright © 1975, 1976, 1977, 1978, 1979, 1980 by Pauline Kael; reprinted by permission of Holt, Rinehart and Winston, Publishers), Holt, 1980, pp. 208-12.

## BARRIE PATTISON

[In **Obsession,**] De Palma has suppressed his own strong personal style . . . consciously manipulating [the familiar Hitchcockian] elements so that the suspense is maintained to the key decision and understanding of the final shot. It's a stylish and accomplished achievement. . . .

Along with Ted Flicker's work De Palma's *Greetings* and its quasi sequel *Hi Mom!* were the most accurate expression of the late sixties in America. . . . These films lead to the flamboyance of *Phantom of the Paradise* while the comparatively subdued *Get to Know Your Rabbit* or *Sisters* edge towards *Obsession.* . . .

One of the most entertaining films of the year, *Obsession* confirms De Palma and his collaborators as among the most talented of contemporary film makers.

*Barrie Pattison, "Films of the Month: 'Obsession',"
in* Film *(reprinted by permission of British Federation of Film Societies), No. 44, December, 1976,
p. 6.*

## ROYAL S. BROWN

De Palma sets us up with a cinematic technique in the same
way Hitchcock sets us up for the shower scene in *Psycho,* with
the rainstorm, the gothic setting, and the kinky motel manager
with his stuffed animals, all of which play on negative predispositions in the audience's minds. In both cases, the directors have shown an awareness that the deepest impression comes
not from the jolting, unprepared violence found in B-horror
flicks, but from modulated variations, as extreme as some may
be, which are all threads of a single fabric.

De Palma fits *Carrie*'s finale into the film very much the way
a composer would close a musical composition, by reusing a
"progression" that has been solidly established within the artistic structure. Each of the film's three climactic scenes—the
locker room sequence leading up to Carrie's first menstruation;
the sequence where Carrie and Tommy Ross are crowned queen
and king of the senior prom and then doused in pig's blood;
and the concluding sequence—are all shot in slow motion. So
by the time the third sequence of slow-motion lyricism begins,
the audience is well acquainted with the inevitable modulation
to blood, whether menstrual, pig, or, ultimately, the blood of
death. (pp. 54-5)

In spite of its fairly conventional story line, *The Wedding Party,*
with its jump cuts, its slow and fast motion, and its often
improvised acting, indicated a revolt against traditional American
cinematic continuity and acting styles. . . . *Murder à la Mod,*
filmed in 1966, was De Palma's first film to be commercially
released. Not only did the film provide the director with his
first suspense vehicle, it also gave him the opportunity to play
around with existing cinematic vocabulary. In addition to telling the murder story three times from three different points of
view, De Palma adapted his film style to suit each character.
He describes these styles as soap opera (for the girl who gets
killed); Hitchcock (for a male character involved in the action);
and, in an extension of what he had already done in *Woton's
Wake,* silent comedy (for a deaf-mute, horror-film actor). (pp.
55-6)

*Greetings,* after *Murder à la Mod,* was another game of three.
This time, however, the three principal characters are male
and reflect three pervasive concerns of the sixties: the Kennedy
assassination, the Vietnam War, and the sexual revolution (in
the form of pornography). Once again filled with New Wave
jump cuts and freeze frames, which De Palma had by this time
expertly integrated into his own style, *Greetings* evokes Godard
on a broad level. For while the movie makes us cringe at the
1960s' political and social absurdities by simply documenting
them, the counterculture lives led by the three protagonists are
seen as not much of an improvement on the "Great Society."
Like Godard, whose Maoists in the 1968 *La Chinoise* play
childish games in an apartment while they seek a way to destroy
bourgeois values, De Palma is not as interested in taking sides
as he is in entering into a dialectic exposing both, even if one
side is inevitably favored. (pp. 56-7)

In between *Hi, Mom!* and [*Get to Know Your Rabbit*], De Palma
did an experimental film entitled *Dionysus in '69.* Presented
completely in split screen, the film shows, on one side, the
Performance Group's adaptation of *The Bacchae* by Euripides

and, on the other side, the audience involvement in the play.
*Dionysus in '69* brought together two of the most important
sides of De Palma's creative vision: his documentary view of
reality as modified by the artistic and electronic documentation
of it; and his concern with myths that continually manifest
themselves. . . .

*Sisters* became not only De Palma's first straight suspense film
but also a tribute to Hitchcock. It abounds in allusions: the
voyeurism, the innocent bystander drawn into the arena of
crime, the red herrings, the chaotic violence with Freudian
overtones, and the macabre humor. (p. 57)

Between *Sisters* and *Obsession,* De Palma did a film, *Phantom
of the Paradise,* that in some ways seemed to hark back to his
earlier work. . . . *Phantom* is obsessed with the various aspects
of the seventies' pop culture, in particular its music . . . and
also its drugs, its freaks, its orgies, its marketing manipulations, its youth craze, and ultimately its death wish.

But it is precisely here that the film definitely belongs to what
we might term De Palma's second phase. For while his films
of the sixties often stress revolt as an attempt to reaffirm life,
*Phantom,* as well as his other films of the seventies, depicts
existence as an extended love affair with death. *Phantom* shows
this in a cynical, satirical, and often extremely frenetic fashion;
death is seen as a kind of monstrous spectacle that feeds on
youth. De Palma throws in the Faust legend and his version
of *The Picture of Dorian Gray* and blends them with a staple
of movie mythology, *The Phantom of the Opera.* The movie,
however, remains a strange mixture of nearly all the elements
of De Palma's cinematic vocabluary.

But *Carrie* successfully brings together all these elements. . . .
One thing that gives *Carrie* its particular depth is its human
dimension. The film is anything but a continuation of the voguish *Exorcist-Omen* type of demonry. . . . The telekinesis
element, for instance, is considerably played down, in contrast
to the Stephen King novel on which the film is based. (p. 58)

Another side of *Carrie*'s human dimension can be seen in the
director's refusal to indulge in melodramatic taking of sides.
This ability to embrace the good and bad of all his characters
stems directly from De Palma's own personality. . . .

*Carrie* represents the most profound—and distrubing—use De
Palma has yet made of mythic motives and structures. The
essence of myth is to move backward: The ending is known
from the start. In *Carrie,* the opening sequence immediately
establishes the basic opposition that will dominate the film.
Starting with a crane shot of a group of high school girls playing
volleyball in their gym suits, the camera slowly descends and
moves in on Carrie as she misses the shot that loses the game
for her side. She is brutally vilified by her classmates. Unable
to meet the demands of a highly competitive society, she is
established as an outsider, one of the most prevalent types in
both myth and fairy tales. And De Palma has accomplished
this exposition in an almost purely visual manner, using means
that belong entirely to film. Both camera angle and camera
movement become part of a symbolic language perfectly adapted
to both the story and the medium. (p. 59)

In true mythic fashion, the power that helps the heroine attain
an exalted position (even if it is only queen of the ball) comes
from outside the "normal" social order. Carrie's telekinesis
serves as a fairy godmother helping her overcome the evil
mother to go to the ball. But the fairy tale ends here, and more
serious myth takes over completely. Carrie must fall, even if

she takes a good portion of her tormentors with her. She is therefore destroyed, first by the society she has momentarily risen above; then by her mother, whose fanatical religious attitudes she has opposed to attain her moment of glory; and finally by the very force that helped her both in her rise and in her vengeance—the telekinesis turns in upon itself, consuming Carrie and the house she lived in. (p. 60)

The final victory is that of the nonsocial forces, the forces of the irrational, whether in dream or in their extreme form, death. In this sense, *Carrie* is a kind of reverse *Psycho*: Hitchcock gives us the zinger (the shower scene) toward the beginning and then spends the rest of the film unraveling the mystery of this illogical irruption of the irrational. De Palma, on the other hand, spends the entire first half of *Carrie* building up the suspense leading to the prom scene (the Hitchcockian bomb the audience knows will explode) and then creates a second movement of suspense as Carrie's mother waits, sacrificial knife in hand, for her daughter to bathe away the pig's blood. The shocker . . . comes at the very end, leaving the audience with absolutely no rational crutch to lean upon. (pp. 60-1)

In *Carrie,* De Palma also remains faithful to the 1960s' part of his creative personality, for the film shows an acute sensitivity to ambiguous American attitudes toward religion. Instead of pitting diabolical forces of evil against a religious-oriented good, *Carrie* sets up religious fanaticism, along with scapegoatism, as the primary negative force in the film.

The iconography of the fanaticism—the myriad candles, the grotesque crucifix—is strongly Catholic. But, theologically and from the character of Carrie's mother, the religion smacks of a certain brand of evangelical Protestantism, particularly in the anti-female attitude that has repressed Carrie. Woman caused the fall of man, dooming the race to mortality and the pain of childbearing; menstrual blood symbolizes both procreation and mortality. De Palma sums up the entire Eden myth: The title sequence . . . presents a group of nude girls romping, in slow motion, in the haze of locker room steam. A simple, lyrical flute theme—the same as heard at the end—plays on the sound track. This scene of innocence leads to the shower and Carrie's first menstruation, bringing us to a view of woman as evil.

*Carrie* manipulates the audience with narrative and structure, both of which must be equally stressed in effective myth. The film accomplishes the tour de force of giving the audience a story it can identify with while constantly using structure to remind the spectators that the story is limited by neither time, space, nor psychological motivation. (p. 61)

*Royal S. Brown, "Considering De Palma," in* American Film *(reprinted with permission from the July-August issue of* American Film *magazine;* © *1977, The American Film Institute, J. F. Kennedy Center, Washington, DC 20566), Vol. II, No. 9, July-August, 1977, pp. 54-61.*

### VINCENT CANBY

"The Fury" was directed by Brian De Palma in what appears to have been an all-out effort to transform the small-scale, Grand Guignol comedy of his "Carrie" into an international horror/spy/occult mind-blower of a movie. He didn't concentrate hard enough, though "The Fury" is bigger than "Carrie," more elaborate, much more expensive and far sillier. Let's face it—it's the De Palma "1900"—a movie that somehow got out of hand.

It's also, in fits and starts, the kind of mindless fun that only a horror movie that so seriously pretends to be about the mind can be. Mr. De Palma seems to have been less interested in the overall movie than in pulling off a couple of spectacular set-pieces, which he does. He leaves the rest of "The Fury" to take care of itself. . . .

The things that keep one sitting through "The Fury" when one's mind knows better are the occasional action sequences . . . and the special effects that finally bring the movie to an end that recalls [Antonioni's] "Zabriskie Point," on a more personal level.

*Vincent Canby, "Psyching a Spy," in* The New York Times *(© 1978 by The New York Times Company; reprinted by permission), March 15, 1978 (and reprinted in* The New York Times Film Reviews: 1977-1978, *The New York Times Company & Arno Press, 1979, p. 182).*

### PAULINE KAEL

There's an ecstatic element in Brian De Palma's new thriller *The Fury:* he seems to extend the effects he's playing with about as far as he can without losing control. This inferno comedy is perched right on the edge. It may be to De Palma what *The Wild Bunch* was to Peckinpah. You feel he never has to make another horror movie. To go on would mean trying to kill people in ever more photogenically horrific ways, and he's already got two killings in *The Fury* which go so far beyond anything in his last film, *Carrie,* that that now seems like child's play. There's a potency about the murders here— as if De Palma were competing with himself, saying "You thought *Carrie* was frightening? Look at this!" He's not a great storyteller; he's careless about giving the audience its bearings. But De Palma is one of the few directors in the sound era to make a horror film that is so visually compelling that a viewer seems to have entered a mythic night world. Inside that world, transfixed, we can hear the faint, distant sound of De Palma cackling with pleasure.

Most other directors save the lives of the kind, sympathetic characters; De Palma shatters any Pollyanna thoughts—any expectations that a person's goodness will protect him. He goes past Hitchcock's perversity into something gleefully kinky. In *Carrie,* he built a two-way tension between our hope that the friendless, withdrawn, telekinetic heroine would be able to sustain her Cinderella happiness at the school prom and our dread of what we feared was coming. De Palma builds up our identification with the very characters who will be destroyed, or become destroyers, and some people identified so strongly with Carrie that they couldn't laugh—they felt hurt and betrayed. *The Fury* doesn't have the beautiful simplicity of the Cinderella's-revenge plot of *Carrie,* and it doesn't involve us emotionally in such a basic way; it's a far more hallucinatory film. (p. 418)

This isn't going to be a gross horror film; it's visionary, science-fiction horror. De Palma is the reverse side of the coin from [Steven] Spielberg. [*Close Encounters of the Third Kind*] gives us the comedy of hope, *The Fury* the comedy of cruelly dashed hope. With Spielberg, what happens is so much better than you dared hope that you have to laugh; with De Palma, it's so much worse than you feared that you have to laugh. (pp. 419-20)

The violence is presented in such a stylized, aestheticized way that it transcends violence. . . . De Palma pans around the rooms and landscapes slowly—a Godardian ploy—to give us more and more to look at, and to key up our expectations. He doesn't quite make good on his promises: he doesn't provide the crucial actions—the payoffs—within the circling, enlarging movements. But the expansiveness is essential, because of the stodgy dialogue; he anticipates the boredom of the ear by providing excitement for the eye.

No other director shows such clear-cut development in technique from film to film. In camera terms, De Palma was learning fluid, romantic steps in *Obsession;* he started to move his own way in *Carrie*—swirling and figure skating, sensuously. You could still see the calculation. Now he has stopped worrying about the steps . . . What distinguishes De Palma's visual style is smoothness combined with a jazzy willingness to appear crazy or campy; it could be that he's developing one of the great film styles—a style in which he stretches out suspense while grinning his notorious alligator grin. He has such a grip on technique in *The Fury* that you get the sense of a director who cares about little else; there's a frightening total purity in his fixation on the humor of horror. It makes the film seem very peaceful, even as one's knees are shaking.

*The Fury* isn't tightly structured; there are rising and falling waves of suspense, and De Palma's visual rhythms outpace the story. . . . The visual poetry of *The Fury* is so strong that its narrative and verbal inadequacies *do not matter.* No Hitchcock thriller was ever so intense, went so far, or had so many "classic" sequences. (pp. 420-21)

> *Pauline Kael, "Shivers" (originally published in* The New Yorker, *Vol. LIV, No. 5, March 20, 1978), in her* When the Lights Go Down *(copyright © 1975, 1976, 1977, 1978, 1979, 1980 by Pauline Kael; reprinted by permission of Holt, Rinehart and Winston, Publishers), Holt, 1980, pp. 418-24.\**

## ANDREW SARRIS

[If] I were tempted to turn off my mind, it would be for something like Brian DePalma's latest exercise in torrential terror. By the end of *The Fury,* the bloody, extra-sensory carnage seems a bit much, but I must confess that the film as a whole tended to absorb me into its wild fancies. I *was* entertained. The movie *was* fun. Still, the spoilsport critic within this fun-loving fool is not entirely sure that *The Fury* deserves a clean bill of health as a coherent piece of work.

To the adolescent aggressiveness of *Carrie,* DePalma and his novelist-scenarist John Farris have added the political paranoia of the post-Watergate era in which the CIA can be accused of virtually anything.

DePalma and Farris have more than one surprise in store for us before the ultimate bloodbath. At first glance, the director seems shameless in filching Hitchcock's wrist-clutching climaxes from *Saboteur* and *To Catch a Thief,* and Antonioni's explosive catharsis from *Zabriskie Point,* but DePalma develops his own gruesome variations on these stylistic flourishes, and overall there is more bloodshed here than in any movie since Sam Peckinpah's *The Wild Bunch.* Indeed, the spilling of blood in *The Fury* comes close to being hard-core pornography for the medium in a way that supposedly real sex is not.

For a project so lurid, the acting is surprisingly thoughtful and solid. . . . *The Fury* is much heavier on grown-up guilt than *Carrie* was, and there is no easy indulgence of the audience's thirst for universal revenge. It remains to be seen whether the public will rally to a movie that wallows so deeply in its own weltschmerz.

> *Andrew Sarris, "Blowing the Mind Circuits" (reprinted by permission of* The Village Voice *and the author; copyright © The Village Voice, Inc., 1978), in* The Village Voice, *Vol. XXIII, No. 12, March 20, 1978, p. 39.\**

## VINCENT CANBY

Any movie that contains a doctor-nurse joke is all right by me. Brian De Palma's **"Home Movies"** contains not one but several doctor-nurse jokes or, even better, doctor-nurse sequences. . . .

**"Home Movies"** also contains jokes about innocent young men who are still virgins and virginal-looking young women who aren't, sexist jokes, jokes about marital infidelity and closet homosexuals, even movie jokes. They aren't all hilarious, but even the ones that aren't knee-slappers are friendly, if only for being well-meant. . . .

[**"Home Movies"**] is a movie that deals proudly in undergraduate humor. . . .

**"Home Movies"** is nothing if not casual in form. Sometimes it's a movie-within-a-movie and sometimes it's simply a movie, though it's always about Denis Byrd . . . , an earnest, shy young man who is described variously as "an extra in his own life," "a frozen frame in his own movie" and "forgotten in his own time." . . .

I'm not sure it's fair to put **"Home Movies"** into commercial release. . . . Order and consistency are not its strong points. However, in its antic, anarchic, ebullient way, it recalls the young Brian De Palma who, before winning commercial success with such suspense-horror films as **"Carrie"** and **"The Fury,"** delighted a small, fanatically loyal audience with his low-budget comedies, **"Hi, Mom"** and **"Greetings."** That's very nice, indeed.

> *Vincent Canby, "Screen: De Palma on Youth," in* The New York Times, *Section C (© 1980 by The New York Times Company; reprinted by permission), May 16, 1980, p. 13.*

## ROGER ANGELL

A fatal air of insideyness and glorified amateurism infects [**"Home Movies"**], which is a low comedy about sex, ugly parents, and filmmaking. Almost everyone in the picture is making a movie or is about to appear in one. . . . [The picture] sometimes appears to be part of film sequences being explicated to a class. . . . The youthfully experimental and extemporaneous circumstances under which **"Home Movies"** was to be made must have convinced someone (perhaps Mr. De Palma) that it would be appropriate to make it a farce—a very bad decision indeed, because convincingly zany, knockabout comedy is one of the most difficult of all forms, requiring a sharp script, first-class acting, and rigorous cutting and pacing. None of these are in evidence in this picture, which counts heavily on its self-congratulatory amateurism and gawky charm to carry it past a great many rough places. . . . **"Home Movies"** will probably cause many a giggle among the film cognoscenti in its audiences . . . , but I wonder how many of them will smile about it afterward, when they're alone. The movie is too small and messy to qualify as a disaster. (pp. 148-49)

Roger Angell, "A Quilt of Horsemen," *in* The New Yorker (© 1980 by The New Yorker Magazine, Inc.), Vol. LVI, No. 13, May 19, 1980, pp. 143-44, 147-49.*

**DAVID DENBY**

[*Dressed to Kill*] is the first great American movie of the eighties. Violent, erotic, and wickedly funny, *Dressed to Kill* is propelled forward by scenes so juicily sensational that they pass over into absurdity. De Palma releases terror in laughter: Even at his most outrageous, Hitchcock could not have been as entertaining as this.

For the easily frightened moviegoer, De Palma's flamboyance is reassuringly "cinematic": You can see that he's using film techniques and tricks to get at unconscious fears and to extend the lyrical possibilities of violence, and you admire his sadistic virtuosity even as he's manipulating you unconscionably. As in such past De Palma thrillers as *Sisters* and *Carrie,* he draws on preposterous, *National Enquirer* materials—a murderous transvestite in a blond fright wig—and yet his style has infinitely more authority than that of directors working in culturally respectable forms. Trash liberates his imagination and his lawless sense of play. . . .

Hitchcock remains the dominant influence . . . , but there's more than a touch of the greater master Buñuel in the subversive reality-or-fantasy games and in the way that De Palma sees women's sexual fantasies as both dangerous and funny. Of course, De Palma is no surrealist; he's a tabloid fatalist. . . .

De Palma may be the first director to use pornography as a way of dramatizing the unconscious. . . . De Palma has perfected a tactile, sensuous, smoothly gliding camera style that gives erotic tone to the simplest of expository scenes, yet he flirts more than once with actual pornography, putting us into a muzzy trance and then jerking us out of it with a derisive laugh. (p. 44)

De Palma is definitely a new kind of movie amoralist. He combines moods normally kept apart—frivolous joking and terror—and he's so single-minded in his pursuit of beautifully bloody thrills, and then in drawing the laughter out of them, that he can't be bothered with socially responsible statements or even with our feelings about his characters. A transvestite who wants a sex-change operation is an object of hilarity and menace for him—a figure out of a newspaper article, a figure to be *used*—and a nice woman looking for sex unwittingly becomes a victim. De Palma kills off Kate even though she certainly doesn't "deserve" it. . . . De Palma is mocking the hygienic, joy-of-sex attitudes of the young audience; he's saying that sex can be dangerous stuff. His jokes have a subversive edge.

De Palma is a sensational director in the root sense of the word—trusting the camera more than anything else, he heads straight for what's gorgeously lurid, for what appeals to the senses as pure excitement. People looking for fully rounded characters and moral accountability are always offended by his movies, and detective-story aficionados, who like an entirely consistent and plausible puzzle plot, will be annoyed by his cavalier attitude toward exposition. . . . [The second half of the movie] can be picked apart as wildly implausible. But that's really missing the point—it's like seeing a great opera and complaining that the plot isn't very satisfying. . . .

[De Palma's] mischief in this film comes within hailing distance of Buñuel's viciously gleeful irresponsibility in a masterpiece like *L'Age d'Or,* and he sends up Hitchcock more than once. He plays with the medium, with the audience, and with the masters who have formed him. (p. 45)

David Denby, "Deep Threat," *in* New York *Magazine (copyright © 1980 by News Group Publications, Inc.; reprinted with the permission of* New York *Magazine), Vol. 13, No. 29, July 28, 1980, pp. 44-5.*

**PAULINE KAEL**

In **"Dressed to Kill,"** everybody is spying on everybody else, or trying to. And the director, Brian De Palma, who also wrote the script, is the master spy. . . .

Over the years, De Palma has developed as an artist by moving further into his material, getting to deeper levels of erotic comedy and funnier levels of violation. If he has learned a great deal from Hitchcock (and Welles and Godard and Polanski and Scorsese and many others), he has altered its nature with a funky sensuousness that is all his own. The gliding, glazed-fruit cinematography is intoxicating but there's an underlay of dread, and there's something excessive in the music that's swooshing up your emotions. You know you're being toyed with. The apprehensive moods are stretched out voluptuously, satirically—De Palma primes you for what's going to happen and for a lot that doesn't happen. He sustains moods for so long that you feel emotionally encircled. He pulls you in and draws the wires taut or relaxes them; he practically controls your breathing. . . .

He knows where to put the camera and how to make every move count, and his timing is so great that when he wants you to feel something he gets you every time. His thriller technique, constantly refined, has become insidious, jewelled. It's hardly possible to find a point at which you could tear yourself away from this picture. (p. 68)

There's very little dialogue altogether in **"Dressed to Kill;"** what talk there is is casual, funny, and often good-naturedly off-color. Most of the film's humor, though, is visual, and it's not innocent at all. Visual humor is generally slapstick; this isn't. You could try to single out the gags that make **"Dressed to Kill"** visually funny, but describing the gags wouldn't convey its humor. What makes it funny is that it's permeated with the distilled essence of impure thoughts. De Palma has perfected a near-surreal poetic voyeurism—the stylized expression of a blissfully dirty mind. He doesn't use art for voyeuristic purposes; he uses voyeurism as a stratgey and a theme—to fuel his satiric art. He underlies the fact that voyeurism is integral to the nature of movies. . . . Throughout the film, De Palma plays with the visual theme of outside and inside voyeurism (the person peeking through windows is always much safer than the person who sneaks inside), and he also keeps dividing things in two—often the screen itself. (pp. 68-9)

De Palma's sense of humor makes him the least respectable of the front-rank American directors. He presents extreme fantasies and pulls the audience into them with such apparent ease that the pleasure of the suspense becomes aphrodisiacal. . . . Yet though he draws the audience in by the ironic use of sentimental conventions, when he explodes the tension (the shocks are delivered with surgical precision), those people in the audience who are most susceptible to romantic trickery sometimes feel hurt—betrayed—and can't understand why the rest of us are gasping and laughing. Life plays obscene jokes on soft, creamy-pink Kate Miller, who wants nothing more than to give and receive pleasure; just when she's happy and sated and feels grateful, she discovers something so humiliating that she gets the cold shakes. . . . Like Hitchcock, like Polanski, like Buñuel, De Palma has a prankish sense of horror. Most parodists of gothic tricks flatten them out (as in [Mel Brooks's] "High Anxiety"); De Palma's humor heightens them—he's probably the only American director who knows how to use jokiness to make horror more intense. Through visual storytelling, he can get at the currents of sexiness and fear and guilt that were the hidden strength of the great silent horror films, but he taps those currents for a different purpose. De Palma replays film history as farce. He has kept the dirty fun of a bad boy at the center of his art. It gives his work a lurid, explosive vitality. (p. 69)

There is a peculiarity about "**Dressed to Kill**": when the explanation comes, it's weightless. You've probably already figured out most of it anyway, and since everything else plays on several levels, this scene, which has only one, seems prosy and obligatory. You recognize how carefully the murder motive was prepared and how everything fits together, but the explanation has no tingle: you don't feel its connections with what makes the picture frightening. . . . Here De Palma sabotages the rational explanation, which goes rattling on. Then, at the end, he uses a ploy—a pause and then a starting up again—that resembles the endings of "**Carrie**" and "**The Fury**," but to get a different psychological effect. In those pictures, he jolted the audience out of the gothic atmosphere, and most of us left the theatre laughing. This time, the spell isn't broken and he doesn't fully resolve our fear. He's saying that even after horror has been explained, it stays with you—the nightmare never ends. (p. 71)

Pauline Kael, "Master Spy, Master Seducer," in The New Yorker (© 1980 by The New Yorker Magazine, Inc.), Vol. LVI, No. 24, August 4, 1980, pp. 68-71.

**ROBERT ASAHINA**

De Palma's latest effort, **Dressed to Kill,** borrows liberally from his previous films: the "surprise" ending, a shock that turns out to be merely a nightmare, recalls **Carrie;** the element of voyeurism derives from **Hi Mom!** and **Home Movies.** But these are nothing compared to what De Palma steals from Hitchcock. Adding a little nudity and sex, he makes off with more or less everything from *Psycho,* right down to the shower scene and the psychopathic killer who dresses in women's clothing.

What De Palma leaves behind is Hitchcock's cynical Catholicism. His point of view, as both a writer and a director, is simply amoral; he dispatches his characters in spectacularly gory fashion with no justification other than sheer delight in the kinetic possibilities of killing on screen. The violence in his movies—with the important exception of **Carrie**—is committed for esthetic reasons alone. . . . De Palma makes films that are meaninglessly violent. . . .

In **Dressed to Kill** the blood and gore seem to serve no purpose except to convey the filmmaker's contempt for his audience. The film's gruesome ending is purely gratuitous. Who is getting pleasure out of such violence? It can only be De Palma himself, smirking at his own manipulativeness. Audiences are not annoyed at such violence because it arouses feelings they are

afraid to deal with; they are disgusted that they have let their emotions be toyed with so cheaply.

The impression that De Palma is preoccupied with his own filmmaking is borne out as well by the hammy estheticism of **Dressed to Kill.** Split screens are used throughout the movie. Is this a device to indicate the killer's derangement, or just a cinematic indulgence? Probably the latter. . . .

[It] is the absence of any point to the sex or violence that makes **Dressed to Kill** truly offensive. (p. 27)

Robert Asahina, "Manipulating the Moviegoer," in The New Leader (© 1980 by the American Labor Conference on International Affairs, Inc.), Vol. LXIII, No. 15, August 11, 1980, pp. 26-7.*

**GEORGE MORRIS**

There is plenty of terror in **Dressed to Kill,** but the aesthetic distance that separates De Palma from Hitchcock can be measured by the absence of any emotion approaching pity. De Palma never tries to get inside Dr. Elliott, the would-be transsexual murderer. . . : he merely uses the characters as a catalyst for the succession of jolts that provide the film with its tenuous unity. The director has learned too well from Hitchcock how to manipulate the emotions of an audience, but whereas Hitchcock directed the means of the manipulation toward a larger end, De Palma is consumed by the methods alone. Hitchcock was always straining to perceive the nature of evil; De Palma, at least at this point in his career, seems more interested in exploiting its more sensational manifestations. (p. 54)

Despite, or perhaps because of, his slavish recapitulation of key sequences from Hitchcock, De Palma has never been able to transform the borrowings into anything more than inferior quotations from superior films. Unlike, say Claude Chabrol, De Palma lacks the searing vision that would assimilate Hitchcock's techniques into a coherent work of personal expression. **Dressed to Kill** lurches along from one set piece to another, but there is nothing but dead space in between.

De Palma is sloppy when it comes to the details and logic that might enable us to suspend our disbelief. . . . [Too] often De Palma's toying with fantasy and reality degenerates into simply lying to the audience. (pp. 54-5)

De Palma's defenders may counter by claiming that he is not trying to achieve the unity of character and theme or the degree of audience involvement that characterize Hitchcock's more classical works. But in order to challenge generic modes and conventions, one must first take them seriously, and it is on this level that De Palma fails more seriously. He ridicules everything about the material except the quality of its formal execution. And because of his derisory attitude, the style and tone never jell. The ostensibly lyrical tracking is clumsily executed; the split-screen devices become meaningless flourishes; the hyped-up editing generates more laughter than suspense. Moreover, he denies most of the central characters one single moment of grace. . . .

De Palma's contempt extends to those of us out there in the dark, who have paid our $5 to shriek at his clinically calculated gooses. The skill with which he can now operate the elements of filmmaking makes his methods even more insidious. . . . Of this, at least, De Palma can be sure: **Dressed to Kill** is the first great cockteasing film of the Eighties. (p. 55)

George Morris, "*Dressed to Kill and No Place to Go*" (*copyright © 1980 by George Morris; reprinted by permission of the author*), *in* Film Comment, *Vol. 16, No. 5, September-October, 1980, pp. 54-5.*

## PAULINE KAEL

**"Blow Out"** isn't a comedy or a film of the macabre; it involves the assassination of the most popular candidate for the Presidency, so it might be called a political thriller, but it isn't really a genre film. For the first time, De Palma goes inside his central character. . . . And he stays inside. He has become so proficient in the techniques of suspense that he can use what he knows more expressively. You don't see set pieces in **"Blow Out"**—it flows, and everything that seems to go right to your head. It's hallucinatory, and it has a dreamlike clarity and inevitability, but you'll never make the mistake of thinking that it's only a dream. (p. 74)

Jack is a man whose talents backfire. He thinks he can do more with technology than he can; he doesn't allow for the human weirdnesses that snarl things up. (p. 77)

At the end, Jack's feelings of grief and loss suggest that he has learned the limits of technology; it's like coming out of the cocoon of adolescence. **"Blow Out"** is the first movie in which De Palma has stripped away the cackle and the glee; this time he's not inviting you to laugh along with him. He's playing it straight, and asking you—trusting you—to respond.

In **"The Fury,"** he tried to draw you into the characters' emotions by a fantasy framework; in **"Blow Out,"** he locates the fantasy material inside the characters' heads. There was true vitality in the hyperbolic, teasing perversity of his previous movies, but this one is emotionally richer and more rounded. And his rhythms are more hypnotic than ever. It's easy to imagine De Palma standing very still and wielding a baton, because the images and sounds are orchestrated.

Seeing this film is like experiencing the body of De Palma's work and seeing it in a new way. Genre techniques are circuitry; in going beyond genre, De Palma is taking some terrifying first steps. He is investing his work with a different kind of meaning. His relation to the terror in **"Carrie"** or **"Dressed to Kill"** could be gleeful because it was Pop and he could ride it out; now he's in it. When we see Jack surrounded by all the machinery that he tries to control things with, De Palma seems to be giving it a last, long, wistful look. It's as if he'd finally understood what technique is for. This is the first film he has made about the things that really matter to him. **"Blow Out"**

begins with a joke; by the end, the joke has been turned inside out. In a way, the movie is about accomplishing the one task set for the sound-effects man at the start: he has found a better scream. It's a great movie. (pp. 77-8)

Pauline Kael, "*Portrait of the Artist As a Young Gadgeteer,*" *in* The New Yorker (*© 1981 by The New Yorker Magazine, Inc.*), *Vol. LVII, No. 23, July 27, 1981, pp. 74, 77-8.*

## MICHAEL SRAGOW

De Palma makes movies about divided personalities, characters uncertain of their social and psychological identities, torn between impulse and reason. He plays dark games with them among the land mines of our cities, where a rape, a race riot or a revolution could be just around the corner. His material is often Grand Guignol, but the intelligence behind it is as sophisticated as Edgar Allan Poe's.

A daring writer and director, De Palma attacks his controversial themes with new frankness and confidence in *Blow Out*. This powerful political thriller—raunchy, funny, yet poetic—is the most startlingly fresh film released so far this year. Its vision of a robotized United States, tranquilized by the media and caught up in the escapist politics of "patriotism," registers like a clarion call to the nation: get serious! . . .

It's unusual for political thrillers to carry a tragic sting, but in *Blow Out,* the characters' downfalls, particularly Jack's, are determined partly by their personalities. Jack is a victim of his media obsessions—a voyeur of his own life—trying to use technology to beat technology. As the movie progresses, his feelings of impotence tighten around him like a noose. . . . (p. 38)

*Blow Out* is a thrillingly complicated film, exact in its elusiveness. The random encounters between characters have been carefully planned; they show us how conspiracies derive from incompetence and accidents as well as deviousness and evil. The movie starts out like a game of "What's wrong with this picture?" and adds another game: "What's wrong with this sound?" Then it dares to ask the most puzzling question of all: "What's wrong with this country?" By using suspense techniques at full tilt, De Palma has managed to turn national torpor into an American moviemaking triumph. (p. 40)

Michael Sragow, "'*Blow Out': The Sounds of Violence,*" *in* Rolling Stone (*by Straight Arrow Publishers, Inc. © 1981; all rights reserved; reprinted by permission*), *Issue 351, September 3, 1981, pp. 38, 40.*

# Vittorio De Sica

## 1902-1974

Italian director, actor, and screenwriter.

De Sica is regarded as one of the most important directors to emerge with the movement known as neorealism. This style of filmmaking emphasizes the importance of social consciousness. Using nonprofessional actors, realistic settings or location filming, and grainy film stock, De Sica employed true-to-life "newsreel" footage to investigate characters that audiences find moving and compelling. With screenwriter Cesare Zavattini, De Sica created a body of work which was most critically successful in the late 1940s and early 1950s.

De Sica was a successful stage and film actor before becoming a director. Dissatisfaction with Carmine Gallone's direction in the film *Manon Lescaut* led De Sica to direction, and his first film as director was *Rose Scarlette* in 1940. His first important film is felt to be *I bambini ci guardano (The Children Are Watching Us)*, which portrays the breakup of a marriage through the eyes of a child. *Sciuscià (Shoeshine)* marked the beginning of the neorealistic movement. The film arouses the sympathies of the audience through its depiction of postwar Italy. De Sica's best-known works are *Ladri di biciclette (The Bicycle Thief)*, *Miracolo a Milano (Miracle in Milan)*, and *Umberto D.* All of these films include elements of neorealism, although *Miracle in Milan* also contains dream sequences and comedy. The relationship between the individual and his social status is the dominant theme of these three films, and *The Bicycle Thief* is regarded by many critics as the best film to come out of neorealism.

After *Umberto D.*, De Sica's artistic success began to decline. Even though *Il tetto (The Roof)* is viewed today as an engaging film, it was not successful upon release and marked De Sica's last effort in the neorealist style. De Sica made a great many films in the 1960s and early 1970s, but critics feel that these films are glossy and commercialized, and not nearly as significant as his earlier works. However, De Sica continued to act in many films and television series (which helped to finance his directorial efforts), and he enjoyed commercial success as the director of *Two Women, Marriage, Italian Style*, and *Garden of the Finzi-Continis*.

It is ironic that De Sica found his greatest commercial successes in films that are regarded as mere shadows of his neorealistic films. In fact, a few critics rate De Sica as a minor director on the basis of his later films and the lack of emotion in the directorial style of his early work. However, most feel that De Sica's and Zavattini's contributions to neo-realism are among the most successful and important innovations in film.

## LINDSAY ANDERSON

What is it about these Italian pictures which makes the impression they create so overwhelming? First, their tremendous actuality, second, their honesty, and third, their passionate pleading for what we have come to term the humane values. The uses of adversity are once again demonstrated: lack of money has made it necessary to shoot on real locations, against backgrounds which themselves forbid the phoney and the fake. But it is chiefly the impulse of generous and uncompromising emotion which gives to *Sciuscia*, as to the [Roberto] Rossellini films, a force unknown to the Warner heavy. . . . [The] setting of *Sciuscia* is contemporary, and . . . it has no respect for the old lies, the safe conventions. It is the story of two shoeshine boys loose in "liberated" Rome—Rome liberated not only from Fascism but also from order and security. It is the boys' highest ambition to own a horse of their own; in contriving to get hold of enough money, they become party, all but innocently, to a black market deal. They are caught by the police and, since they refuse to implicate their friends, sent to prison as juvenile delinquents.

The atmosphere of the exhausted, disintegrated city is superbly conveyed; the rough, newsreel quality of [the] photography, the sharp cutting, the abrupt naturalism of the acting persuade us that we are watching scenes as they actually take place, people as they actually are. This in itself is enough to make *Sciuscia* an exceptional film. But with the story's development it seems to attain another degree of excellence; the film acquires a real significance. The friendship of Giuseppe and Pasquale is an affair of innocence—the boys are never sentimentalised, but they are shown, for all their acuteness, as innocents, with innocent love, candour and trust. By contact with the world we see these qualities perverted and finally destroyed. . . . [When the boys are sent to prison] *Sciuscia* becomes a tragedy.

The prison scenes, persuasively detailed, are austere and horrifying; but the agony is never piled on—the director has rightly felt that the thing in itself is agonising enough. . . . The climax may be described as symbolic . . . , but it is the true kind of symbolism, implicit in the material, growing naturally out of what has gone before.

Comparison with the other Italian pictures is inevitable. *Sciuscia* is as good as either of the two Rossellini films [*Rome, Open City* and *Paisa*], perhaps better: it is tighter, firmer in structure, with no less honesty, but more courage. . . . Vittorio de Sica's direction is sensitive and straightforward, with some charmingly lyrical touches at the beginning, where they are not out of place. (pp. 38-9)

> *Lindsay Anderson, "Film Reviews: 'Sciuscia'" (reprinted by permission of the author), in* Sequence, *No. 4, Summer, 1948, pp. 38-9.*

## RICHARD WINNINGTON

*Bicycle Thieves* is a wholly satisfying film in that de Sica has so simplified and mastered the mechanics of the job that nothing stands between you and his intention. It can be likened to a painting that is formed in an intensity of concentration, and is as good as finished before it reaches the canvas. In fact, *Bicycle Thieves,* as a film properly should, relates to plastic and in no sense to dramatic or literary art. de Sica displays this with the opening compilation of visuals, which at once places his family in an environment of slow, sapping industrial poverty, where the bicycle and the bed linen represent the last claims of domestic pride, and where the pawnshop and the tenement fortune-teller batten on misery. It is, needless to say, a Rome the visitor sees though seldom penetrates, but where, before the war, he might have admired the triumphs of Mussolini's industrial architecture. (pp. 27-8)

[Although, by] some process of magnetism, de Sica has drawn from [the] boy an unparalleled child performance, it is the man who is his symbol of the human plight. He is the helpless individual, herded with, yet isolated from his fellows, who is caught in a situation. To de Sica and many Italians who have absorbed their Kafka and Sartre, this is the general theme of the century. It might be said to parallel the situation of Italy herself.

The story of that heartrending Sunday search after the stolen bicycle is now too familiar to bear retelling. Its simplicity, far from being evidence of slightness, is the outcome of a discipline that has rigorously set itself against any facile effects of "poetry", but has evolved a complex pattern of mood and incident. The ironies, humours, oddities and heartbreaks of this adventure in the modern jungle connect with the experience of any town-dweller who has been isolated at some time or times by misfortune, great or small, and finds his familiar world suddenly hostile and strange.

*Bicycle Thieves* is the true genre movie, and a superlative exercise in screen realism. . . .

de Sica's lifetime of experience in the theatre and cinema as a leading man and comedian . . . may account for his power to compel those flawless performances from his amateurs. But it is a painter's instinct . . . which enriches his films with such comprehensive detail. His detached compassion, his sense of irony, his tolerant understanding, are the fruits of long study of his fellow men in difficult times. Anger does not show in his films, and anger is a concomitant of hope. Yet I do not find the conclusion of *Bicycle Thieves* wholly pessimistic. Comradeship did to some extent sustain this man and doubtless, one feels, will do so again.

With *Bicycle Thieves,* de Sica considers he has sufficiently exploited "realism" for the moment. An artist who has found his true medium somewhat late in life, he possesses an unpredictable capacity for development. And in Cesare Zavattini he has found the scriptwriter who can play Prévert to his Carné. Their next film (the third of the trilogy which *Shoeshine* started), will essay a new form—"irrealism". (p. 28)

> *Richard Winnington, "Films of the Month: 'Bicycle Thieves'," in* Sight and Sound *(copyright © 1950 by The British Film Institute), Vol. 19, No. 1, March, 1950, pp. 26-8.*

## ROBERT F. HAWKINS

Vittorio De Sica's latest film, *Miracolo a Milano,* is far from the "world" which he and co-scripter Cesare Zavattini described in *The Bicycle Thief.* In *Miracolo* De Sica and Zavattini leave behind the simple, direct approach to human problems, and attempt the difficult trick of marrying realism to fantasy. They almost succeed. . . .

[This film], for better or for worse, swings heavily towards Zavattini's side. It is not De Sica's picture primarily, and when judgment is passed this proportion of paternity should be kept well in mind. (p. 26)

The authors intended *Miracolo a Milano* to be a fable told against a backdrop of the harsh realities of present-day Italian life. (p. 27)

What are De Sica and Zavattini trying to say?

Several themes seem to be combined. First, there is an exhortation to be simple in heart. Second, there is an assertion that the brotherhood of man, asked for in *The Bicycle Thief,* is able (by the aid of a miracle) to defeat power unjustly used. Third, the authors suggest that the good must seek peace and happiness elsewhere than in this world.

But De Sica and Zavattini commit a fundamental error when they try to apply to these moral problems their particular concepts of the poor. One of Zavattini's books is entitled *The Poor Are Crazy (I poveri sono matti).* And De Sica upheld a similar viewpoint while he was shooting *Miracolo.* "Beggars," he said to me, "are in their own way quite crazy and live in a poetic, completely happy, impractical world of their own. This is the world I want to convey in my film."

Such conceptions do not fuse well with realistic themes, and the beggars' "poetic" laziness (there is no indication, in the film, that any of them works or even desires a job) doesn't jibe with their often very real desires for jewels, houses, millions. The ensuing contradictions result in confusion and weakness all around.

For purposes of study, *Miracolo a Milano* divides handily into two very different halves. The first comes closest to De Sica's "world," and in it he dominated the material. The first half of *Miracolo* contains some of the finest things he has ever done. (pp. 27-8)

In the second half of *Miracolo* De Sica's warm humanity, with one notable exception (the scenes in which Toto and his girl express their love for each other with childish delight and innocence), is dominated by co-scripter Zavattini's cold intellectual gymnastics. With its many comic and satiric moments, the second half is undoubtedly more "entertaining," but shallower, and less successful. De Sica's careful, straight-from-the-heart character-sketching has given way to Zavattini's literary script and dialogue, and to the "miracles." The rapid-fire of Zavattini's intelligently amusing incidents makes one lose sight, temporarily, of the film's objectives, clearly and warmly felt in the first half. Zavattini's cleverness has éclat and humor, but does not survive second thought very well.

And one wishes that some of the film's symbols had been clearer. Particularly the dove. Why is it taken away from Toto, given back, taken away, and returned once more? Why are one's sympathies for the poor weakened by making them appear lazy and often selfish? Similarly, one wishes (as De Sica surely does) that the trick photography, so vital in providing an illusion of the blending of the real and the unreal, could have been less obviously mechanical. . . . Finally, one wishes that the proof of Toto's "goodness" emerged more from his actions than from Zavattini's dialogue. (pp. 28-9)

What remains to be said, then, of this rich, complex, controversial film? A safe, but also well-considered, appraisal would rate it higher than the elegant failure many have called it, lower than the great, complete motion picture others have deemed it. Undoubtedly, in spite of its defects, it touches greatness, and this alone places it well above the current world level. (p. 30)

*Robert F. Hawkins, "De Sica Dissected: His Humanism Succumbed to Zavattini's Devices," in* Films in Review *(copyright © 1951, copyright renewed © 1979, by the National Board of Review of Motion Pictures, Inc.), Vol. II, No. 5, May, 1951, pp. 26-30.*

**KAREL REISZ**

*Sciuscia, Bicycle Thieves, Miracle in Milan* and *Umberto D.* are political films in the sense that they deal with problems which are subject to legislation and political control; but they offer no solutions and propagate no specific programme. Zavattini has spoken of the new style as "a moral discovery, an appeal to order" and the films themselves bear out that the impulse behind them is primarily a moral one. What remains remarkable about them as a group is that their moral passion, which was born of the war and could find expression only after the release from fascism, has grown in intensity with every film. (pp. 87-8)

De Sica's extraordinary tact with people enables him to get performances that are always real and dignified. Whether they are more than this must depend on the players chosen and in *Umberto D.* they sometimes fall short. In the scenes demanding strong emotional reactions, de Sica's unadorned method of observation occasionally leaves the players, as it were, too much on their own in the centre of the screen.

The best scenes in *Umberto D.* . . . have a purity of effect which gives them, in context, a profound poetic intensity. Although the episodes mount, in a dramatic sense, slowly, there is behind them a kind of passionate identification with the characters' human predicament which creates an extraordinary concentration. De Sica has brought his subject to the screen with a directness which springs from an inner conviction and faith in his characters. It gives the film, in spite of faults in execution, the unmistakable authority and completeness of a masterpiece. (p. 88)

*Karel Reisz, "Film Reviews: 'Umberto D'," in* Sight and Sound *(copyright © 1953 by The British Film Institute), Vol. 23, No. 2, October-December, 1953, pp. 87-8.*

**GEORGE N. FENIN**

In my opinion, [*Umberto D.*] represents undoubtedly the apex of what can be considered the first phase of the Italian neorealism; it is also the closest and most precious attempt at "filmed life." . . .

In *Umberto D.* the symbiosis of Zavattini and De Sica has reached the most perfect fusion of style and message. The escapism of *Miracle in Milan,* the workman's tragedy in *Bicycle Thief* has risen to the pathos of loneliness in *Umberto D.* The film maintains the dignity of an art without compromise as it reflects the anguished conditions in post-war Italy. The pessimism is gradual. The squatters of *Miracle in Milan* do have hope and fly with their brooms to "where good morning really means good morning;" the unemployed Lamberto Meggiorani of *Bicycle Thief* is, on the other hand, shaken by despair; still, he is young and strong and his wife and son are symbols to justify his future renewal of a struggle for life.

But the pensioned civil servant of *Umberto D.* is alone, desperately alone. He is an old man whose mission in this life is finished. . . . But he is, above all, a human being, representing a category of the underprivileged, whose unjust treatment casts a terrible verdict of guilt upon an indifferent society, practising that egotism that Schopenhauer rightly defined as the "unmeasurable ruler of the world." And the passivity . . . of Umberto dramatizes authentically the tragedy of so many living corpses, crushed by a war which they did not want, sundered from a meaningful existence. Thus, the film provides the theme for a social document of unheard-of-honesty in its expression, blending the realism of the best of Balzac with the Dostoyevskyan conception of Evil as a supreme form of indifference, and sending forth a message of Tolstoyan charity and brotherhood towards all the Umberto D's who were once men, and who wait today, with resignation, for a cross on their graves. . . .

*Umberto D.* bitterly reflects upon our consciences the vision of the inexorable fate of man's condition. But the theme of old age, although essential, is integrated by the skillful and vigorous "encadrement" of a man within a particular time, in a specific society, whose actions are pitilessly vivisected. The problem acquires therefore much larger proportions, posing deeper questions about our contemporary society.

To quote Herman G. Weinberg: "Forget all the gaudy superlatives, long since tarnished with mis-use, and find new ones for *Umberto D.* Here is that rarest thing in films, a work of the most uncompromising honesty. This is, indeed, so rare as to make *Umberto D.* shine like the proverbial 'good deed in a naughty world'—the good deed in this case being a film of the purest luminosity." (p. 30)

*George N. Fenin, "'Umberto D.'," in* Film Culture *(copyright 1955 by* Film Culture*), Vol. 1, Nos. 5-6, Winter, 1955, pp. 30-1.*

**VERNON YOUNG**

[*Umberto D.*] may easily be construed as an artless and unbuttered slice of life, a testimony of "naturalism": ostensibly a method of expressing reality without inhibition, without overtones and as far as possible without style. Nothing could be further from the case. Like *Shoe Shine* or *Bicycle Thief,* and with justification even more subtle, De Sica's *Umberto D.*—a masterpiece of compassion . . .—might be termed *super*-naturalism if this compound had not been preempted for another kind of experience entirely. The fidelity of De Sica's attention to the plight of the man, Umberto, realistic in its living details, is enriched by a host of modulations working under and through the story line, so delicately registered as to be imperceptible save to that second awareness evoked from most spectators without their being able to define it. Cinematically created, these modulations are not arresting, since they accumulate from thematic relationships in the scenario. De Sica's use of the camera is clear-eyed, rather than ingenuous. As in his other naturalist films, his cinematographer [G. R. Aldo] . . . is not called upon to exhibit striking angles or movement: De Sica's compositions rarely startle one by their ingenuity. *What* he focuses on at a given point is more significant than the *way* he focuses. The way is never neglected, it simply isn't exploited; for it is to De Sica's purpose to move with un-elliptical life as closely as he dares without vitiating motion-picture technique altogether. To subordinate the essentially cinematic as he does is itself a technique of ineffable skill; and to efface his signature as a director from the style of a film argues a modest purity of aim.

In *Bicycle Thief,* De Sica developed the film's rhythm by a *pas de deux* of man and boy in their scouting expedition through the city, the boy nervously anxious to keep in time with his father's mood and intention. The adjustments of temper and of tempo, the resolution, the haste, anger and embarrassment, the flanking movements, the frustrations and periodic losses of direction: these constituted a form of situational ballet which gave the film its lyricism. There is no such springy movement in *Umberto D.*; the quality of its form is established otherwise.

The possessive theme is Time; its epiphanies are sounded in a scale of variations. (pp. 592-93)

Sound, which is time, is always extraneous to Umberto D. It impinges; it does not involve him. The clatter of social life is beyond the fringes of his consciousness; he hears it but it isn't speaking to him. (p. 594)

Visually the narration is equally cogent, taking in without appearing to emphasize the incongruities, the excrescences, the implacabilities of life at a level of civilization where the meretricious and the ugly are accepted or suffered, where in fact the vitality of a people cut off, by a superimposed culture, from its native modes, expresses itself by choice through a corrupt aesthetic. . . . There are some remarkable instances in this film of De Sica's sparing use of a background object as *direct* symbol. The old man's coat hanging lifelessly on a gigantic stand which looks like a monstrous underwater growth is analogous to the social situation in which man is an unbraced, drowning remnant in the ruins of a cheaply florid dream of empire—and when Umberto D. returns to his room the last time, a shot of the hallway gives prominence to a stuffed falcon among the bric-a-brac. The most impressive *vis-a-vis* is depicted in the painful scene of Umberto D.'s tentative rehearsal of begging. . . . An overpowering classical column, cracked at the base, is the backdrop for this joyless act.

De Sica's balance between the lifelike and the cinematic is tenuous; if he had actors less responsive to the naked untheatricality he is commonly after, his muted formalism might suffer from the risks he takes. . . . Few directors could manage, without losing their hold on the continuity, the beautiful cadence in this film where the coming of day is enacted through the actions of Maria as she gets out of bed. The scene is wordless, leisured and almost unbearably intimate. There is little in it that could not be performed on a stage, but in its brief duration and its breathing nearness, in the particular placing of the camera for each view of the pregnant girl struggling to experience joy which gives way to fear and then to a day-dream indifference, it is a marvel of movie timing and perspective.

Maria, while subordinate to Umberto D., is by an inspired implication complementary. Neglected youth and discarded old age. . . . In *Shoe Shine* the horse was a symbol, if you like, of the unattainable, a dream of power and freedom. The bicycle in *Bicycle Thief* was an occupational necessity which became a projection of the man's self-respect. Flick [Umberto's dog], neither ideal nor economic necessity, may be felt as representing the last thing a man will surrender: it is the love in the man, Umberto.

When De Sica and Cesare Zavattini . . . avoided the easier termination, of suicide accomplished, by ending the film on an inconclusive (which is not to say indecisive) note—Umberto D and the dog gamboling under the cedars—we can be sure they were saying very clearly: Life sometimes leaves you nothing but love, and in your deprivation and anguish you cannot bear to support even such a burden. But this is your only identity and until the day you die you must not put aside the little humanity left to you. . . . Umberto D. tries to entrust the dog to another; he tries to give it away; he tries to destroy it. In the end he is still, as our idiom says, "stuck with it". (pp. 594-96)

*Vernon Young, "'Umberto D.': Vittorio De Sica's 'Super'-Naturalism," in* The Hudson Review *(copyright © 1956 by The Hudson Review, Inc.; reprinted by permission), Vol. VIII, No. 4, Winter, 1956, pp. 592-96.*

## WINTHROP SARGEANT

[The] credit line "Directed by Vittorio De Sica" has so far been reserved almost entirely for the pictures, like **"Shoe-Shine,"** into which he has poured the enthusiasm and ingenuity of a fervent artist, in the belief that in them alone lies his chance for a distinguished place in the history of his craft. These films, so startlingly different from the ones that De Sica acts in for other producers, deal for the most part with serious subjects—notably, the subject of poverty, omnipresent in Italy—and they contrive to temper the uncompromising realism of documentaries with a compassionate humanity not often found in the output of the cinema industry. Probably not more than two of these films have been anything like financial successes, one reason being that most Italians, who willingly pay millions of lire to clap and bravo over the merest flick of De Sica the actor's eyebrow, thoroughly detest the most eloquent creations of De Sica the director. "Why do you have to show Italy in rags?" is typical of the criticisms he gets from his otherwise adoring fellow-countrymen. (p. 35)

The basis of the appeal that these De Sica-directed films have for an international audience is clear enough: They avoid the clichés of movie-making. In large measure, this is because their casts hardly ever include professional actors. . . . [They play their] roles not on studio sets but in actual alleys, run-down apartment houses, and similarly forlorn surroundings, while the restless eye of the camera lights on unforgettably realistic details—the litter in a slum-district gutter, a leaky faucet, flies buzzing around a sink, and everywhere the tide of grime that impoverished humanity battles against day in and day out—which give De Sica's pictures the immediacy and seriousness of life itself. Having cut through the artificialities of movie convention by presenting his audience with drab reality, De Sica proceeds to add the element that establishes him as an artist and a poet: the drama—often humorous as well as heartbreaking—of human dignity struggling and surviving amid this grinding squalor. In building up the drama, he shows a rare feeling for the awesome power of the small tragedies that plague the lives of the poor . . . and, as portrayed by his characters, tragedies of this kind assume heroic proportions. There is little doubt that he has a deep understanding of conflicts between pride and poverty, and he trains his camera on these conflicts, making them the principal theme of his films. (pp. 35-6)

*Winthrop Sargeant, "Bread, Love, and Neo-Realismo—1," in* The New Yorker *(© 1957 by The New Yorker Magazine, Inc.), Vol. XXXIII, No. 19, June 29, 1957, pp. 35-58.*

### ARLENE CROCE

*Il Tetto* (**The Roof**) is the latest result of the fruitful collaboration between Vittorio deSica and Cesare Zavattini. It is only four years old but, except for its smooth technical finish, it seems much older. The story of a young newly married couple who are forced by poverty and family circumstances to join a squatters' colony (similar to the one in *Miracle in Milan*) which exists on the edge of Rome, it is, perhaps, too obviously the sort of material which might be expected to engage the sympathies of deSica and Zavattini. (p. 49)

The curious failure of *Il Tetto* brings up once again the old fundamental distinction between art and life, if only because it is on a version of this distinction that Zavattini bases his artistic credo as a film-maker: "In most films, the adventures of two people looking for somewhere to live, for a house, would be shown externally in a few moments of action, but for us it could provide the scenario for a whole film, and we would explore all its echoes, all its implications." The actual facts of daily life become, then, not a premise for dramatic extension, but the drama itself. "All its echoes, all its implications" are therefore the perceptible social, economic, political, and moral reverberations which are revealed in the most ordinary acts of men and women. This philosophy of the film, which derives from an attitude toward life, Zavattini long ago christened neorealism. . . . As an example of neorealism, *Il Tetto* does not go the limit, and for Zavattini it may represent a certain concession to metaphor and to the tame world of fiction. But for deSica the descent from poetry to journalism proves almost fatal; he is unable to lift the level of *Il Tetto* above that of a human-interest editorial. (pp. 49-50)

*Il Tetto,* to be sure, has the most honorable intentions toward its subject. Like *The Bicycle Thief,* it sets out to show what can befall a man who must sweat for the bare rudiments of existence—a job, a roof over his head. But to say this about *The Bicycle Thief* is to evoke nothing of its essence, whereas all the pathos of *Il Tetto* is pretty much contained in just such a synoptic description. Generalizations about the lives of the poor, the afflicted, the dispossessed are bad because they risk nothing beyond a nominal identification and thereby lose all power to persuade. What binds us to the poor is not their poverty but their humanity. The principals of *Il Tetto* have no interior life. They "typify," we are made to feel, the lack of personal differentiation which some believe is true of the lower classes. But if it is true, it is surely as vicious a social condition

as the material poverty and not to be abstracted from that poverty as a sign of "simplicity" or "universality."

Universality, a sense of brotherhood, is what Zavattini naturally wants to convey. Any man, or—as he claims—Everyman, can be the hero of a Zavattini film. A puritanical distrust of "art," however, renders the hero faceless. It is the minor characters in this film who—briefly—live and, in one penetrating moment which deserves to stand beside the best of *Umberto D.,* deSica immortalizes a homely little maid who says she wants some perfume. But in the over-all quality of its encounter with life, *Il Tetto* seems like a cramped, compromised rehearsal for the big poetic liberation of the deSica classics. It fails, ultimately, because the two people it tells you it cares about remain merely a pair of pleasant-looking nonentities. Only art can tell us who they are. (p. 50)

*Arlene Croce, "Film Reviews: 'Il tetto'," in* Film Quarterly *(copyright 1959 by The Regents of the University of California; reprinted by permission of the University of California Press), Vol. XIII, No. 2, Winter, 1959, pp. 49-50.*

### GORDON GOW

Although Vittorio De Sica's *Il Tetto* comes late to Britain and belongs very firmly to the neo-realist tradition that one had been inclined to consider out-moded, there is an undeniable freshness about it which takes no heed of fashion, and its story of a young couple in Rome who seek a roof over their heads is as persuasive and heart-felt as anything De Sica has given us.

This is, of course, one of the films he really wanted to make, and the kind for which he labours cheerfully as an actor in other director's films, some of them quite trivial. *Il Tetto* involves, so we gather, not a personal financial risk but a true sense of dedication.

It could be said that Zavattini's script piles on the agony: not exaggerating, perhaps, but certainly making the utmost of the predicament in hand. Yet as the unhappy, impoverished pair try to reconcile themselves to life in a two-room apartment overflowing with relatives, as they search in vain for something, and as they make their desperate bid to assemble four brick walls on wasteland overnight before the police arrive at dawn to demolish such semi-illegal dwellings unless they are quite complete, the truth De Sica draws from every single actor in his cast is far stronger than the sentimentality of the tale he tells.

Not for the first time he plucks from poverty, and in one memorable passage when the newly-married couple have to bed down in a room already occupied by three other people, one of them a child, he evokes a compassion as real as anything he accomplished in *Bicycle Thieves* or *Umberto D.*

The total effect of *Il Tetto* never quite equals its distinguished predecessors, possibly because in this case the principals are so young and alight with love and energy that even in their gloomiest moments a glimmer of hope pervades them and we know, if they don't, that eventually things will go right enough. This is consoling but it diminishes tension, and not the least of De Sica's achievements is the way he manages to generate tension here when reason and familiarity work against it. . . .

Much of the credit for [the] performances belongs, no doubt, to De Sica's inspiration and control. Under his guidance the smallest supporting parts assume a wealth of subtle detail and even the background figures moving through the streets of Rome perform small and delicate manoeuvres that add verisimilitude to this sensitive fragment of life.

Quite possibly neo-realism has had its heyday, but it can still warm the heart when practised by a master.

> Gordon Gow, "'Il tetto'" (© copyright Gordon Gow 1960; reprinted with permission), in Films and Filming, Vol. 7, No. 1, October, 1960, p. 26.

## ERIC RHODE

The sentimentality which many critics have felt in **Bicycle Thieves** arises, I feel, from the unresolved contradictions set up by its two themes. Ostensibly a protest against degrading social and economic conditions, this theme is never more than a cover or excuse for the theme of solidarity against loneliness, in which De Sica and Zavattini are really involved emotionally. Their embarrassment at this confusion can best be seen at the climax of the film. This, oddly enough, is not the moment of degradation when the father is caught stealing the bicycle, but the moment when the father strikes his son, and then suspects the child has been drowned (symbolically suggesting that he has killed the son himself); and it is a crisis filmed in a nervous, tentative way—almost as if the editor had had to work with insufficient material.

The confusion here arises, I believe, because De Sica and Zavattini are unable to give their central theme a socially realistic significance and have had to tack it on to the bicycle story; which is in itself an excellent idea, but one too slight to bear the weight of much social comment. . . . In **Bicycle Thieves** [determinism] is used—unsuccessfully, I feel—to merge together the two themes.

The trick, though, which has I think most fuddled critics into thinking this is a film of protest is the repeated shift to the child at moments of crisis: we look at the world through his eyes. When the father is almost arrested, and the social significance of the film should be made clear, the camera cuts to the boy's face and one of the accusers says: "That was a fine thing to teach your son." By doing this, De Sica and Zavattini blur us into thinking that they are dealing with a social problem on an adult level: when all they are giving us, in fact, is a child's reaction to the situation. . . . So in this film the outlook of the father is, by implication, shown as identical with that of his son. One might see this as a point of some satirical force about a society which doesn't educate its members sufficiently for them to cope with complex moral problems; but I think not. The same trick is played in **I Bambini ci Guardano** (1943). Here the child's rejection of its mother in the last moments of the film is made to imply a serious moral criticism of the mother's behaviour which, if one tries to think about it as a possible adult judgment, is plainly silly.

Yet by giving us its glimpse of a child's vision, **Bicycle Thieves** remains permanently interesting. . . . [The] despair of a child confronted by an aggressive world and a problem too difficult for it to grasp is enacted with an almost Dickensian power.

What I find really strange about this film is that it has been taken as a work of protest. The contrary, I think, would be more true. As **Bicycle Thieves** develops, the feeling behind it becomes more and more conservative. . . . After the encounter with the thief, the suggestion that all men are evil becomes clearly explicit and darkens the final section of the film. The theme of solidarity, for instance, turns against itself; the crowd which protects the thief and almost lynches the father is similar to the crowd which denounces the father when he attempts to steal the bicycle; and, as he fails in this, the football crowd, which up to then had seemed desirable, howls bestially from a nearby stand. Even more horrible is the suggestion—I may be going too far in seeing this—that it's thanks to the father's scruples that he is slow in stealing the bicycle, and so is caught. The weeping of father and son, therefore, in the last moments of the film, is not at social injustice but at their realisation of fallen man, at the never ending corruption about them, at the corruption within themselves. Their only hope as they clasp hands is in the solidarity of family life; which seems to me a piteously inadequate hope in the face of such complete despair . . .

**Umberto D** is a later, and I think better, film. Though even here there is little sign of social protest, this is much more plausible since Umberto himself is a genteel old man. Yet it is interesting to note how, after the first reel, the problem of old age pensioners is quickly shelved, while the two metaphysical themes—of the nature of authenticity and man's loneliness in the face of death—become the film's main concern.

The handling of these two themes is finely done, with techniques similar to those in **Bicycle Thieves**. The identification of Umberto with his dog, for instance, is a far more effective device than the identification of father and son in the previous film. . . . Just as impressive are the long sequences of the old man shuffling around his room and of the servant girl wandering around her kitchen at dawn. With great economy, these scenes describe the moments when the old man and the girl are at their most authentic. . . . Unfortunately, these brilliant scenes emphasise the arbitrary quality of the social satire: the scenes in the hospital or with the exploiting landlady appear—from the realist point of view—contingent to the main themes. And the ending of the film on a note of weak uplift (in conflict with the pessimism of its inherent logic) suggests that yet again De Sica and Zavattini aren't really aware of what kind of film they are making.

Let me draw some conclusions from this. In their inability to synthesise their Augustinianism with the optimism of the neorealist movement; in their inability to think beyond the family unit to the problems of society (a failure prevalent in Italian films); and in their over-emphasis on the truth of a child's vision, De Sica and Zavattini resort, somewhat uncertainly, to Christian ideas. . . . I am suggesting that De Sica and Zavattini are using Christianity (perhaps sub-consciously) as an escape from facing up to social problems. This is a debatable point. What is less debatable is the effect of naturalism on their work. It is totally pernicious. For not only does it not help them to resolve the contradictions between their social and metaphysical themes, but it doesn't help them to confront the social conditions of their time. Perhaps the methods of realism might have taken them further; but that would have required a clearer idea of what realism is. (pp. 28-30)

> Eric Rhode, "Why Neo-Realism Failed," in Sight and Sound (copyright © 1961 by The British Film Institute), Vol. 30, No. 1, Winter, 1960-61, pp. 26-35.*

## PETER BAKER

Watching **Two Women** is like being at the burial of two friends. From neo-realism to neo-decadence, the Zavattini-De Sica life cycle has been spent. That is, providing De Sica wants us to take this work seriously and not, as has often had to be the case in the past, as one of his money-making chores with which to finance such works of distinguished genius as **Umberto-D.** The re-union with Za, the overall obsession with attacks of fascism and the church, the distinguished original of [an Alberto] Moravia novel . . . I can only believe it is intended as more than a routine chore.

What, then, has gone wrong?

The story line is simple and direct. . . . Superficially it is dreadful novelette; but Zavattini has pressed it to serve him almost as De Sade with *Justine,* as a skeleton on which to hang the philosophy of fatalism, that there is no escaping evil so the sensible person accepts it and compromises with it. If this is not what Za is trying to say, then I am wrong; the film is not to be taken seriously! . . .

De Sica directs with a glossy professionalism that has the hard-stare of Hollywood instead of the warm-heart of Rome. His locations are authentic enough, but failing to come to grips with his story and characters he goes all out to get the gaudy facade right, and leaves the heart empty. . . .

De Sica having failed to do a De Sade would nearly have done a De Mille (it has all the "humanised" sadism necessary!) had it not been for some of the individual scenes which lift the picture from the morass. The peasants' feast destroyed not by bombs but by doubts; the German officer arrogantly baiting the pathetically rich land-owner; or the momentary beauty of aircraft flares lighting the valley like a misdirected constellation. But I am saddened to see De Sica of all people falling for the trap, honestly believing he could compromise with popular "box-office". . . .

**Two Women** for me will mark the day when one of my idols finally . . . sold out.

*Peter Baker, "'Two Women'" (© copyright Peter Baker 1961; reprinted with permission), in* Films and Filming, *Vol. 7, No. 12, September, 1961, p. 27.*

## VERNON YOUNG

[In *La Ciociara (Two Women),* De Sica] is less than ever concerned directly with the fate of a single class; more than ever and with more driving force than ever before, concerned with the fate of people. As before, however, his generalization is absorbed in the particular through that reconciliation of intense compassion with scrupulous objectivity which is his personal genius—and the particular, in the person of Cisera, the widow from Ciociaria, cries aloud that in "one world" there is no place to hide. . . .

It's inseparable from the De Sica view that misery *must* love company, in order to purge and renew itself. Faced with a condition wherein the church stands stripped, our brothers-in-arms are rapists, the Communist at home is wide of the human mark, and dead cyclists rot in the postcard landscape, the surviving individual can only turn to something he can cherish—and may God help those who have nobody to help. (p. 15)

A De Sica film makes demands on one's talent for simplicity, since it deceptively appears to have no style; for style is the integration of an artist's temperament in the form of his art, and the De Sica film is one in which as far as possible the eye behind the camera betrays no consciousness of *itself.* Which is why De Sica baffles the aesthetic analyst: he directs one's own eye not toward art but toward life, thereby making pro-

nouncements on the art nearly superfluous. We know it *isn't* life we're watching, but the cinematic subtleties it's our function and pleasure to elucidate have been predigested in the *conception* of the film, leaving the critic little to say of specifically cinematic import until De Sica commits an error of judgment. This is an extremely rare occurrence and the fact that he makes some in *La Ciociara* is no relief to me; all but the terminating one are too trivial to be recorded, but that one is puzzling enough to be questioned aloud. As in most of De Sica's films, life comes to rest at a fateful moment which is not so much the end of the *movie* as the point at which De Sica discreetly takes his leave—on tiptoe, as it were—of the characters whom he has been accompanying, making no untoward cinematic flourish that will disturb their moment of truth. This time the effect is shattered, owing to the prolonged finality of the backtracking shot that frames Cisera with her daughter in her arms, announcing all too heavily, "closing tableau," a disappointingly sententious touch which might have been less damaging if the preceding content had not been so excruciatingly untheatrical.

De Sica's "life-like" purism commits him to an exacting degree of consistency. And commits him to what would be in anyone else an anxious degree of dependence on his actors. Perhaps the secret of his success in this direction is precisely that he never expresses anxiety, only confidence. (pp. 15-16)

*Vernon Young, "The Moral Cinema: Notes on Some Recent Films," in* Film Quarterly *(copyright 1961 by The Regents of the University of California; reprinted by permission of the University of California Press), Vol. XV, No. 1, Fall, 1961, pp. 14-21.*

## JOHN RUSSELL TAYLOR

If we would rush to see new films by [Federico] Fellini, [Luchino] Visconti and De Sica, should we not rush with even more enthusiasm to get the three for the price of one? Perhaps we might, but if we do we shall be disappointed [in *Boccaccio 70*]. The three stories have only the vague and hopeful connection with Boccaccio that they are all faintly saucy, one being comic, one fantastic would-be satirical, and one sentimental. None of the directors is anywhere near his best and De Sica, as a matter of fact, is (one hopes) absolutely at his worst. . . .

De Sica's episode, **The Raffle,** is an attempt to do Sophia Loren's pizza-seller bit from **L'Oro di Napoli** over again in colour and wide screen. . . . [De Sica is not much] of a comedy director; he can manage the light fantastic of **Miracle in Milan,** but the spirit of broad rustic farce eludes him, and a lot of frantic rushing round and face-making on the screen proves no substitute for real lightness of touch on the camera. (p. 91)

*John Russell Taylor, "Film Reviews: 'Boccaccio 70'," in* Sight and Sound *(copyright © 1963 by The British Film Institute), Vol. 32, No. 2, Spring, 1963, pp. 91-2.*

## JOHN FRANCIS LANE

[Carlo Ponti, the producer of **The Condemned of Altona,** should have realised that Vittorio De Sica was the wrong person to tackle *Les Sequestres D'Altona,* Jean-Paul Sartre's] penetrating play about the German problem. . . .

**Altona** is a typical example of how Rome is trying to copy the Hollywood formula, and is not getting away with it. De Sica and Zavattini are too sensitive and intelligent to be able to make films in [this] manner. . . . (p. 131)

De Sica, who nowadays seems to accept directorial assignments as casually as he once accepted acting roles in every other film, deserves most of the creative blame. After all, he is still one of the world's top ten living film-makers. In order to get *Altona* into movement, he and his director of photography, Roberto Gerardi, have captured some magnificent outdoor shots of Hamburg. By far the best thing in the film is the opening. . . .

And at the end of the film, in substitution for the brilliant confrontation between father and son which was the most important scene in the play, the two men drive down to the docks. They stop at a level-crossing and Franz smiles ironically as he sees a goods train with tanks and armoured cars pass by. From the top of a tower overlooking the whole Gerlach empire, Franz shouts the line about taking the responsibility of the century upon his shoulders. Then he and his father come crashing down to their death. In a brilliant last shot, we see the workmen running from all directions to inspect the two corpses which lie in the middle of the vast dock: for a few seconds there is a terrifying glimpse of the futility of man to do anything against the power and corruption of Capital. The 'message' which Zavattini probably wanted to convey is in these scenes; but the film has long since been submerged within the four walls of Franz's room, surrounded by the over-symbolic murals of Italy's leading social realist Renato Guttuso. This intellectual bogging down of what in the producers' minds was a commercial proposition wrecks the film: the product is in the end neither highbrow nor commercial. (p. 132)

> John Francis Lane, *"A Case of Artistic Inflation,"* in Sight and Sound *(copyright © 1963 by The British Film Institute), Vol. 32, No. 3, Summer, 1963, pp. 130-35.*

## GORDON GOW

Although De Sica's *Altona* is a muddled piece of film-making, lunging erratically from melodrama to neo-realism, it retains the dramatic onslaught of Sartre's play. Essentially, of course, it is a thing of theatre, too organised and extravagant at any rate to belong in De Sica's kind of cinema. But the problems that form its core are vital and thought-worthy, and the acting . . . is outstanding. (p. 21)

[The] direction is all over the place. De Sica is strong whenever he has an opportunity to expand into real exteriors: at the industrialist's shipyard there is some fine visual stuff high up amid the scaffolding, and there is a good bit when the recluse finally ventures out into the world and beholds the shocking sight of a Hamburg shop-window full of good food. But inside the house, where much of the time is spent, things are awkward. The discovery of the secret in the attic calls for a suspense prelude which De Sica soft-pedals lamentably, and there are far too many routine visuals everywhere but in the attic. There the walls provide their own nervy atmosphere, because they are covered with haunting sketches of nazi victims, and De Sica sets his actors off-centre against these walls with a melodramatic flourish that suits the occasion. A similar flourish was needed throughout the entire film, but it is attained only fitfully. . . .

It is an instinct for restraint that sets the film so often against the grain of theatre inherent in the writing. A smoother, franker approach would have been better, an acknowledgement that

events have been deliberately contrived to force an argument which digs deep into the intricacies of life. (p. 22)

> *Gordon Gow, "Reviews of New Films: 'The Condemned of Altona'" (© copyright Gordon Gow 1963; reprinted with permission), in* Films and Filming, *Vol. 9, No. 12, September, 1963, pp. 21-2.*

## GORDON HITCHENS

"We are showing three divergent views of Italy today, cutting across the entire social scale," explains De Sica of *Yesterday, Today and Tomorrow.* "Although different in time and place, the three episodes are bound together by universal qualities of humor, humanity and compassion and hopefully stand for modern society everywhere."

De Sica and his scenarists have fabricated a largely successful entertainment, but his statement about the film is pompous (so unlike De Sica). Humor he gives us, and I suppose, "humanity" (whatever that is); but of compassion there is not a trace, nor need there be for such a charming, light-hearted work; finally, the characters and situations appear, in many ways, uniquely Italian and seem not at all to "stand for modern society everywhere." De Sica is making an extravagant claim for what is simply a highly polished, slick, fast sex comedy. (p. 43)

> *Gordon Hitchens, "Film Reviews: 'Yesterday, Today and Tomorrow'," in* Film Comment *(copyright © 1964 by Lorien Productions, Inc.; all rights reserved), Vol. 3, No. 1, Winter, 1964, pp. 43-4.*

## DOUGLAS McVAY

It is true that Vittorio De Sica's work has deteriorated considerably in the past decade. But it is also, I would submit, still equally true that both the overall body of his films and his best pictures (*Bicycle Thieves, Miracolo a Milano, Umberto D,* and to a somewhat lesser extent *I Bambini Ci Guardano*), remain fully worthy of comparison with those of Antonioni, Visconti or Fellini. . . .

Made under Fascist rule, *I Bambini Ci Guardano* (1943) was regarded at the time of its issue as being sufficiently dangerous in its implied criticisms of contemporary Italian morals to be banned from showing outside Rome: and even today, the fame of De Sica's later pictures has overshadowed it. . . . [Within] this comparatively early work are already displayed the mature qualities of technical assurance and psychological penetration which were to produce the post-war masterpieces.

*I Bambini* . . . is domestic tragedy, as distinct from the economic tragedy of *Bicycle Thieves* or the human tragedy of *Umberto:* and it may be argued with a measure of truth that De Sica's genius loses something of its essential character when not directly involved with the stiffening hardships of Italian life which he was subsequently so unforgettably to depict.

There is, indeed, at moments in the film a certain unaccustomed romanticism of style: a preoccupation, for example, with opportunities for chiaroscuro and picture-postcard composition in the seaside scenes. From a purely literary and dramatic standpoint, also, the scriptwriters have run the risk, by making the personality of the lover in their eternal-triangle story superficially at any rate such an unpleasant one, of emphasizing here and there . . . the archetypally melodramatic associations of this theme. Yet the lover's function is, in the end, unimportant. He serves only to precipitate the family crisis: and in a way, perhaps, his apparent mediocrity only points the more the in-explicable motives of our sexual conduct, and the fact that, criticism of morals or no, this is fundamentally a story in which no-one is at heart to blame. . . . The husband must have given the wife *some* cause to leave him, be it merely that falling off in physical attraction. . . . But we can hardly feel he wronged her wittingly: certainly, from the man's subsequent attempt at reconciliation . . . , his forgiveness to the mother, and above all his abiding tenderness towards their child, De Sica gives us not to think so. Yet she, though she returns and once more tries her best, cannot resolve the unstated crisis, and leaves again. This time not even her love for her small son stays her.

This is the most poignant aspect of *I Bambini Ci Guardano.* The drama and conflict are, as I have indicated, shown el-liptically: because they are throughout observed by the uncom-prehending eyes of the person they predominantly affect—the person who, alone not adult and 'responsible,' has done no wrong and so must suffer most. . . .

But it is, by the very nature of the plot, in the sequences involving father and son that the bond of feeling is seen at its most intense. It is a different sort of bond from that of the father and son in *Bicycle Thieves,* because of the change in class *milieu,* and the shift of emotional stance. The characters here are of a more sensitive and refined temperament, and they are also much more acutely concerned in a mutual and em-barrassing situation: true, the loss of a mother and wife is not exactly a matter of financial life and death to them; but never-theless, a mother and wife is not a bicycle. (p. 12)

For once in a De Sica film there is no 'moral recompense', not even the austerely implied one of a *Bicycle Thieves* or a *Sciuscia.* The father, after committing his boy to the impersonal care of a seminary, commits suicide: and Prico, when his mother in repentance comes to visit him, turns his back on her, and in a lingering, hopeless final shot walks slowly away from her, out of the long room. . . .

*I bambini ci guardano:* the children are watching us. Through-out his film, often by means of the most imaginative combi-nations of images, De Sica stresses the significance of this title. (p. 13)

Beyond [the] subtleties of incidental observation, there is the attempt to interpret and visually recreate the understandings and misunderstandings, the dreams and fears and confusions of a four-year-old mind, which results in perhaps the film's most striking directorial triumph. (pp. 13-14)

*Sciuscia* contains some fine moments. The screenplay indicts not only the adult crooks who employ the boys, but also the mixture of bad living conditions and ineffectual 'good works' provided by the adult authorities for the young prisoners. It is a telling (if slightly obvious) touch to have the escape from gaol occur while priests are treating the inmates to a film show of 'News from the Free World.' This sequence, in which riot and fire break out in the darkened, crowded hall, is one of the picture's two set-pieces of action, an expertly constructed pat-tern of panicking, running figures and light and shade. The other set-piece is a fight between Pasquale and another boy in the prison shower-baths, the white settings and unclad bodies blending with the stiffly pumping arms of the combatants to create a strange stylisation. . . .

The film's closing images . . . possess genuine pain: as Pas-quale cradles Giuseppe's corpse in his arms and cries again and again, 'What have I done?,' the police silently look on;

but the horse symbol of the lost innocence and unfulfilled yearnings of all these boys, moves unknowingly away on the leafy bank, in a final sad juxtaposition of carefree life and tragic death.

Yet, despite its clear virtues, *Sciuscia* strikes me as having been over-praised. De Sica's technique here veers curiously from formalism (more consistently sophisticated and disci-plined than was the case in *I Bambini Ci Guardano,* where romantic glossiness was once or twice evident) to a naturalism rather rougher (and less satisfying) than in *Ladri di Biciclette* and *Umberto D.* The latter two pictures are conceived and executed in a kind of realism which, while ostensibly docu-mentary in its locations and plot, is actually highly calculated, both plastically and dramatically. The mood produced by this calculation is one of sustained, gradually increasing compas-sion, in situations, portrayals, visuals, music, sound effects and narrative rhythms.

In *Sciuscia,* calculation and compassion are only intermittent. At times, there is instead an emphasis on the noisy, defiant, irrepressible ebullience and toughness of the gangs of boys: an emphasis which, while no doubt more strictly truthful, is both less moving and less poetic than the approach of the later films. . . .

But with *Ladri di Biciclette* (1948) . . . De Sica directed the first of three consecutive films which arguably form his crown-ing achievements. (p. 14)

The father is driven by his hatred for the theft and his displaced position to attempt to get his own back on humanity by stealing another bike, and thus depriving a member of society which has deprived him. But there is to be no salvation. Where dis-honesty (in the person of the boy who stole his bike) succeeds in escaping detection, the victim himself—who is inherently honest—fails to escape when *he* endeavours to turn thief. He is caught in the act: but, to complete the cruel and pitiful irony, he is allowed to go free. There remains for him only the shame of the deed to torment his conscience: and the trembling, mute expression in the eyes of his small son to tear at his soul.

De Sica was not sure whether to have his hero tempted into stealing: but I feel that Antonio's trials might well have pro-voked him to such a step. No-one can fail to be moved by the awful torture with which this man in the concluding sequences is beset: and the drama's resolution, generally held to be in the same tradition of 'moral victory' as that of *Umberto D,* I don't find really so hopeful; the gesture of the child's hand gripping his father's doesn't seem quite to redeem it. But per-haps the less austere conception of the story, as compared to that of *Umberto,* doesn't call for such a final compensation. For Antonio and his family the pain, though not little, will end: Antonio, we feel, is young enough and strong enough to get another job; but Umberto is too old—his age, alas, is his tragedy.

*Bicycle Thieves* is not totally without faults. It has two plot contrivances: no sooner has the father at one point slapped his son, than he fears the boy may be drowned, thus engineering a conveniently swift *rapprochement;* and Antonio twice hap-pening to meet the thief is definitely excessive—notwithstand-ing any compensatory sense . . . that other people have troubles which may lead them to do wrong. . . . As for Antonio's final action, though, it is dramatically credible and morally tenable where those of Chaplin's Monsieur Verdoux (another victim of circumstances) aren't: simply due to the difference in degree, in scale, between the two sets of circumstances and actions.

The central situation of theft in *Bicycle Thieves* (like Umberto's being wholly without family to care for him) doesn't—as Antonio's wife herself says—happen every day. But it is an outcome of a far more widespread situation (poverty and lack of employment): just as Umberto's derives from the wholly universal one of old age's redundancy and *inner* loneliness.

Despite its minor limitations of theme and narrative structure, *Ladri di Biciclette* has the visual and verbal directness of a near-masterpiece. The script is tight as can be, unerring in the small things [as in the big]. . . . (pp. 14-15)

And De Sica proves worthy of it: not merely in his vivid capturing of locale and his economy of exposition, but in touches such as the bogus fortune-teller's surreptitious glance at her clients' money and her simulated disdain to receive it; in his handling of the central family group and above all of Maggiorani, whose consistently affecting performance may be exemplified by his first reaction of stupefied despair as he returns from his chase down the tunnel, and by his breakdown in the closing passages; and not least, in the film's intense feeling for atmosphere. . . .

*Miracolo a Milano* (1951) . . . stands quite apart from the rest of De Sica's *oeuvre* in being a thoroughgoing fantasy: yet it is my favourite amongst his films, and it may even be his finest achievement. . . .

One realises that *Miracolo* could have been a very different, more sober film had De Sica and Zavattini so intended. The position of the down-and-outs is fundamentally tragic: they are pitiable people, who huddle together, long for a place in the sun, sing their pleas for 'a hut and a bed,' stamp their feet, blow on their nails, still manage to laugh, and move as a crowd yet as a hopeful entity. . . . Given the opportunity to wish for anything they want, most of the characters request and receive material benefits: but two lovers (one black, one white) each secretly ask to change colour, so that they may marry without stigma; finishing up, poignantly, just as far apart as before. Thus De Sica and Zavattini with a concise eloquence and imaginatively poetic vision rare in the cinema's treatment of the racial problem, symbolise the fact we must all face: that prejudice is less easy to surmount than poverty. But the film's tragic aspects are only implicit in the exuberance of the general satire. Instead of showing the paupers rising to power, kicking out their dictators, then being kicked out themselves as new autocrats, Zavattini and De Sica have a happy ending. In the mood of fantasy, everyone flies off into 'a new life.' The situation is fairy-tale: the principle hopefully real. (p. 15)

I have nothing but praise . . . for De Sica's incisive use of the crowds, of noise and movement. . . . It is a tribute to De Sica that he so packs the screen with splendid compositions that nearly every shot is concentrated visual art: yet so precisely are these pictorial effects integrated into the texture of the action that afterwards few shots stand out in the mind; this is not a 'showy' film. (pp. 15-16)

All this might suggest that *Miracolo a Milano* is 'true-to-life,' and therefore admired in the same way as *Bicycle Thieves*. This is not so. *Miracolo* is a fantasy, and a parable: and it has been attacked on these very grounds. The fact is that an effort of sympathy has to be made by audiences who see this film: but the sympathy is aesthetic, not emotional. No-one can fail to be moved by the characters who inhabit De Sica's film, and by their environmental predicament: in speech, action, motive, they are all real people. . . . Where the effort of believing must come is as regards the things which happen to these real

people, because in this film, surrealism reacts on actuality: characters drawn true-to-life are involved in supernatural events.

In *Bicycle Thieves* this did not happen—which is why many people have called *Bicycle Thieves* genuine, and wholehearted, and great, and *Miracolo* superficial, tricksy, gimcrack. Their feeling has been that, with the fantasy of *Miracolo*, De Sica violated the great truthful spirit of documentary, of Italian neo-realism, which he began through *I Bambini* . . . , and carried on past *Sciuscia* and *Bicycle Thieves* to its culminating point in *Umberto D.*

This seems to me to be a most unperceptive view. Surely neo-realism, or film realism as a whole, is not a concept which depends entirely on mere technique. The grandeur of the Italian post-war movement lies in its feeling for reality in character, not for simply authenticity in incident. It is the feelings of the ordinary man which must be valid if neo-realism is to count, and not the things which happen to him. If the *characters* of *Bicycle Thieves* had been glibly novelettish, all the care lavished on details of *milieu* and plot would have gone for nothing. . . .

In *Miracolo a Milano,* the *characters* remain warm and believable, however fantastic the agencies at work upon them. Emotional sincerity is preserved. This, despite its trick camerawork and heavenly manifestations, is a picture which is truly representative of the best in neo-realism. It has all the realism that is necessary: reality of feeling. And indeed, though the film is almost all artistry, for me the purest art occurs in the fantasy episodes. . . .

What the story says, ultimately, is that God (here epitomised by the dove) will always be on the side of good (Toto), even when the flock (the down-and-outs) momentarily err. Moderation is the text preached: when the paupers become nouveau riche, show too much love for wealth and forget the humanity which caused its miraculous appearance, the dove is snatched back. Yet God does not desert His servant: and Toto (who, with Edwige, is alone immune to corruption) manages through his simple faith to make atonement for the surrender to temptation of his companions. They realise in the end that they need faith and courage to make their broomsticks fly: and though they will have to work hard in the 'better land' they go to, they will, inspired by Toto's example, triumph.

I do not think that a film more uncompromising in its depictions yet more optimistic in its conclusions has been made: and at every viewing, it evokes nothing but pity, and joy of heart. . . . As a result, the film now seems to me unflawed: and not only De Sica's probable masterpiece, but one of the two best Italian films I've seen. . . .

The film is a sustained exhibition of directorial wizardry: the three-dimensional, tactile creation of a physical environment is perhaps unequalled on the screen; and there is an utter unity of image and sound—especially music. . . . The touches of daringly overt yet successful symbolism are innumerable. . . .

And innumerable, too, are the flashes of visual and aural wit. . . . Yes, *Miracolo,* one feels more and more certain, marked the summit of De Sica's career. (p. 16)

·   ·   ·   ·   ·

Scripted by Zavattini alone, *Umberto D* (1952) maintained De Sica's high level. So complex is the picture that, at each viewing, I have felt its message to vary. At first sight, I took it to be that Umberto is prevented by his dog from suicide: that the animal, by shrinking from him as death approaches them, saves his master's life and renews his belief in the camaraderie of existence. The film, in fact, as it progressed, gradually mingled these two ideas (on the surface, despair; beneath, hope) to create an extraordinary dramatic concentration and subtlety. . . .

Yet after my most recent viewing, I believe that the heart of the film does lie in Zavattini's philosophy: but that this philosophy is less affirmative than stoical. Zavattini shows us other people who are no better off than Umberto, whose pride cannot tolerate Umberto's pride, who will not help him—because they cannot help themselves. The secret of the piece, in fact, lies not so much in its painful portrait of old age, poverty and loneliness, as in the sense it builds up that not only Umberto, but everyone around him, the whole city (country, world?), has its own struggle, its own troubles, its own hopes: and consequently that sympathy for any other individual is short. (p. 51)

De Sica's creative degeneration began . . . with the Italo-American, Selznick production *Stazione Termini* (*Indiscretion*), made in 1953. . . . Although Zavattini's basic plot-theme smacked unsatisfyingly of commercial romantic requirements, a director of De Sica's stature could hardly fail to elevate it to some extent above its mere amorisms. That the elevation is not great enough is due to De Sica's preoccupation with the complexities of background detail, minor characterisation, cutting and visual effect being offset partly by the fundamental, slightly novelettish narrative idea, but much more damagingly by the dialogue grafted on to this idea by Truman Capote. (pp. 51-2)

Visually, nonetheless, there is much to admire in *Stazione Termini:* the crowds in genuine De Sica tradition, full of strange characters colourfully introduced; the firm line and chiaroscuro of Aldo's camerawork; the roving images of platform and track, office and cafe, accentuating the immense, inhuman impersonality of the location. . . .

[In] *Il Tetto* (1956), one felt a falling-off from past summits. This story . . . , while directly in the line of De Sica's greatest work with Zavattini (for all its rather bizarre and local plot-theme), seemed to lack the intensity of treatment that marks his masterpieces: to remain a realistic, second-rate *Miracolo a Milano.*

One sequence, that early on where the couple can't make love in the communal sleeping quarters and have to go outside to do so, has the tenderness, sadness and poetry of this director at his best. . . . But the power is not sustained throughout, as it is in De Sica's finest achievements: and so by its makers' highest standards *Il Tetto* must be called a disappointment.

Nor nearly, however, so heavy a disappointment as its successor: *La Ciociara* (*Two Women*), made in 1960, and easily the least distinguished De Sica-Zavattini collaboration I have seen. Admittedly, in adapting Alberto Moravia's novel, scenarist and director were unwisely moving from their established sphere of peacetime back into the wartime territory of Rossellini. Yet even so, I am surprised that they could not have invested this territory with a greater illusion of reality. By comparison, *Il Tetto* seems almost a model of neo-realism. . . .

Some of the weaknesses of *La Ciociara,* such as the stock characters of the bespectacled idealist student and his counterpart the intellectual Nazi officer, are the fault of Moravia and Zavattini. But most of them, disturbingly, must be laid at De Sica's own door. Only at . . . brief moments . . . does the

director approach his former marvellously unaffected level of visual statement.

Elsewhere, his deployment of composition, incident and characterisation again and again lapses into banality. (p. 53)

[It's hard to understand why De Sica directed *The Condemned of Altona*.] But then De Sica's whole career in the past decade has become a puzzling let-down. The artist who once devoted himself so consistently and poetically to everyday people and situations has gradually turned to melodramatic events and grotesque characters. . . .

The first half of the narrative is decidedly wordy and stagey: and on celluloid, this staginess is in no way decreased by De Sica's handling. . . .

The second half slowly improves: an episode where Franz, the conscience-ridden ex-Nazi, breaks out of his self-imposed, fifteen-year imprisonment, and reels incredulously through rebuilt Hamburg, briefly revives memories of De Sica's old mastery of candid-camera reportage. . . . Yet the total impact remains distinctly remote. One is chilled by the grey, grim, cautionary tale: but no more. . . .

*Yesterday, Today and Tomorrow* is . . . a tolerable enough entertainment. Yet it still seems disappointingly flimsy by comparison with Vittorio De Sica's finest work. True, it is intended as little more than a romp. But when one looks at the director's latter-day serious films (*La Ciociara, The Condemned of Altona*), one can't help feeling that [De Sica, Italy's poet of postwar, has lost his sensitive technique] through endeavouring to return to the years of conflict. One can only hope that the future will prove this feeling to be wrong. Vittorio De Sica's yesterday was fruitful. His today is less so. What will be his tomorrow? (p. 54)

Douglas McVay, "Poet of Poverty, Part One: The Great Years," and "Poet of Poverty, Part Two: Umberto—and After" (© copyright Douglas McVay 1964; reprinted with permission), in Films and Filming, Vol. 11, Nos. 1 and 2, October and November, 1964, pp. 12-16, 51-4.

**GWENNETH BRITT**

According to Stanley Kauffmann, scriptwriter Cesare Zavattini and director Vittorio de Sica got their ideas for depicting contemporary youth in *A Young World* by visiting the Cinematheque Francaise in Paris and there looking at nouvelle vagueeries.

Critic Kauffmann regards as sad this stategem by which two sixty-four-year-olds hoped to disguise the second-hand quality of their projected truckle to the most numerous portion of today's movie-goers (the young).

I don't think it's any sadder than what de Sica and Zavattini have been doing throughout their entire collaboration, and in saying this I *do* include *Shoeshine, The Bicycle Thief, Miracle in Milan, Umberto D* and all their other films. Seen today, without the intellectual hoopla with which they were launched, and subsequently promoted in leftist-dominated film societies, all Zavattini-Sica films have the same basic faults as their latest, *A Young World,* does—i.e., a conscienceless use of hackneyed sentimentality peppered with slogans and "business" calculated to win friends in Left, Right and Center, the Church, and *every* minority. (p. 380)

[If] you'd *really* like to know the lengths to which Zavattini and de Sica go to recruit *any* organized group in support of their films, study the abortionists in *A Young World*. They are lesbians. Having lesbians be abortionists will amuse a certain sector of today's intelligentsia, but, lest the lesbian-international take offense, Z and de S top it by putting a copy of a well-known book on the desk of one of them so the audience will not write them off as *ignorant* abortionists.

The title of the book they selected gave me a laugh (de Sica deliberately let the camera go to it). It is [Marcel] Proust's *A la Recherche du Temps Perdu*. (p. 381)

> *Gwenneth Britt, "Film Reviews: 'A Young World',"*
> in Films in Review *(copyright © 1966 by the National Board of Review of Motion Pictures, Inc.), Vol. 17, No. 6, June-July, 1966, pp. 380-81.*

## MONIQUE FONG

It is important that the audience be taken unawares by *Shoe-Shine,* that it should experience fear and hope and be unable to guess the outcome of the story.

It is a story that unfolds before our eyes; the children caught in it do not realize what is happening to them. . . . [They] do not try to express themselves nor even to influence their own lives. It is their innocence, in fact, that creates the story and makes it great. (p. 17)

Since *Shoe-Shine* is neither an accusation nor a propaganda work, we are spared a "crucial point." The story simply proceeds, step by step, until there is nothing further to narrate. Great skill is shown in putting the single moral-bearing sentence of the story—"If these children have become what they are, it is because we have failed to keep them what they are supposed to be"—into the mouth of the corrupt lawyer, a man to whom lying is a profession and whom we saw, just a moment earlier, falsely accusing Pasquale in order to save his own client. (pp. 17-18)

In *Shoe-Shine* the concern is to create an atmosphere and to win the audience through conviction. (p. 18)

[Two] distinct worlds come face to face, the world of children and the world of grown-ups. If there were only the children's world, there would be no dramatic impact, no tragedy. But the picture deals with children who come into conflict with grown-ups, and with grown-ups who have just emerged from the shocking experience of the war and a profound political upheaval. In these two worlds the rules of the game are entirely different, and the conflict is born of the impossibility that one group will understand and adapt itself to the rules of the other. The two worlds do not interpenetrate. They exclude each other. (p. 19)

The great strength of Vittorio De Sica and his scenarists lies in not having taken sides with either of these two worlds. The children are not idealized, nor the grown-ups satirized. Both are shown as they are. Before these boys, who are cruel, shrewd, violent, and uncompromising, looms the world of grown-ups who have been rendered powerless and indifferent by time and events, by life, dissolute men who are too weak to stand up to anything. Such a man is the prison doctor. . . . It is the same with the other adult characters, some of whom are little more than silhouettes and yet remain unforgettable: . . . above all, the two priests who give the film showing. It is not without reason that the director has shown them terrified by the fire,

and their clamor for "light, light" is intentionally ironic. Through them, a whole religion is projected. It should not be forgotten that the jail is a reconstructed old convent, and the first shot we see of it a disused altar.

The children live, love, and die, but it is through the grown-ups that the dramatic conflict arises and is resolved. Grown-ups persuade Pasquale and Giuseppe to become thieves and black marketeers. Grown-ups arrest them and separate them, judge them and punish them. . . . It seems that Vittorio De Sica wanted to emphasize adult guilt. . . . (pp. 20-1)

*Shoe-Shine* makes an important dramatic contribution. For the first time, a film with a subject of this order has been made without becoming an accusation, a sermon, or a propaganda work. The result is that the audience is much more deeply stirred and more anxious to find a solution, although Vittorio De Sica did not even intend to indicate one. (p. 27)

> *Monique Fong, "'Shoe-Shine': A Student Film Analysis,"* in Hollywood Quarterly *(copyright, 1969, by The Regents of the University of California; reprinted by permission of the University of California Press), Vol. 4, No. 1, Fall, 1969, pp. 14-27.*

## VINCENT CANBY

["**The Garden of the Finzi Continis**"] is certainly the best film that Vittorio De Sica has made in years, but the shabby habits he acquired when directing such things as "**Sunflower**" and "**A Place for Lovers**" keep intruding upon this new, much more ambitious work to render it less affecting than it has every right to be.

Mr. De Sica's way with end-of-an-era romance is to shoot almost everything in soft focus, as if he didn't trust the validity of the emotions in what seems to be a perfectly decent screenplay. The film's mood of impending doom is not discovered by the viewer, but imposed on him, by a syrupy musical score and by a camera that keeps panning to and from the sky, and shots of the sun, seen through the same sort of treetops that hover over the actors in the world of Newport cigarettes.

This is particularly frustrating because it has the effect of constantly reducing and denying the complexities of the characters and the performances. . . .

["**The Garden of the Finzi Continis**"] is a very melancholy movie, but its sentiments are essentially those contained on Micol's 78 r.p.m. recording of Tommy Dorsey's "Getting Sentimental Over You." They are prettily expressed but not profoundly moving.

> *Vincent Canby, "Screen: 'Garden of the Finzi Continis',"* in The New York Times *(© 1971 by The New York Times Company; reprinted by permission), December 17, 1971 (and reprinted in* The New York Times Film Reviews: 1971-1972, *The New York Times Company & Arno Press, 1973, p. 189).*

## STANLEY KAUFFMANN

I love Vittorio De Sica's films of his best period, from the end of World War II to 1952, preeminently *The Bicycle Thief* and *Miracle in Milan*. . . . But I don't like *The Garden of the Finzi-Continis*. It attempts a serious theme and is neither good art nor good show biz. (pp. 95-6)

The subject of the Jews under Mussolini has never been the main matter of a film, as far as I know; it's an interesting idea and I wish the result had been better. The fundamental flaw is the script.

The story is about the love of a middle-class Jewish youth for the Finzi-Contini daughter and her inability to return anything but sisterly love. So the chief motions of the plot are utterly divorced from the theme. There are plenty of peripheral incidents that deal with growing Fascist oppression, but the plot is simply not an engine of the idea; it's only a time-filler, to plug the gap between the seeming safety of 1938 and the inevitabilities of 1943. The boy-girl story, as such, could have been between Catholics in Brazil.

De Sica has lavishly contributed shortcomings of his own. Nothing that can be sugared is left plain. The camera zooms as if this were the first time he had directed and he couldn't get over his delight with lenses. The colors are like endless boxes of candied fruit. The editing flutters with nervousness, and that weariest of pastoral shots, the camera looking upward as it moves along under trees, is used repeatedly. De Sica is weeping right along with his sad story, and his tears get very much in the way of ours. (p. 96)

> Stanley Kauffmann, "'The Garden of the Finzi-Continis'" (originally published in The New Republic, Vol. 166, No. 8, February 19, 1972), in his Living Images: Film Comment and Criticism (reprinted by permission of Brandt & Brandt Literary Agents, Inc.; copyright © 1970, 1971, 1972, 1973, 1974, 1975 by Stanley Kauffmann), Harper & Row, Publishers, 1975, pp. 95-6.

## STANLEY KAUFFMANN

The late Vittorio De Sica was a fine artist, a polished hack, and a flabby whore—not necessarily in that order. His film career, as director and actor, was neither a slide nor an ascent: it simply varied. From a beginning in flossy drivel during the early 1930s he moved to his best films between 1946 and 1952 (*The Bicycle Thief, Miracle in Milan, Umberto D.*) and moved from them to too wide a range of quality. Much of his subsequent directing was not even shown in this country. . . . He surfaced again as a fine director with *Two Women* in 1961, then in 1972 he made another serious attempt with *The Garden of the Finzi-Continis*—unsuccessful, I think. . . .

*A Brief Vacation* is billed as his last film. Last or not, it's very pleasant, not at his best level yet with a lot in it that shows the experience of a gifted man. . . .

*A Brief Vacation* states, strongly, some early De Sica-Zavattini social concerns, then softens them a bit, although the color photography . . . is much less soppy than in *Finzi-Continis*. . . .

The romance is the weakest part of the film, both because the role of the ailing mechanic is played by a man who is only a good-looking actor and because that whole narrative strand is handled with constraint and embarrassment. The gallery of women patients is rather obviously selected and balanced; it's not a Magic Mountain, only a modestly magic molehill. But the film is frequently touching because De Sica-Zavattini handle the young wife's home and working life with fidelity and utter understanding. . . .

> Stanley Kauffmann, "Films: 'A Brief Vacation'" (reprinted by permission of Brandt & Brandt Literary Agents, Inc.; copyright © 1975 by Stanley Kauffmann), in The New Republic, Vol. 172, No. 10, March 8, 1975, p. 22.

## COLIN L. WESTERBECK, JR.

When Vittorio De Sica died a few months ago, he had just released a last film which is remarkable because it could easily have been his first film. It has been a quarter of a century since De Sica did his classic work—*Shoeshine, The Bicycle Thief, Umberto D*—as part of the Neo-Realist movement in Italy. Yet this final film, *A Brief Vacation,* again renews and extends the vision that those Neo-Realist films established as De Sica's own. Whereas most of De Sica's earlier films deal with periods of extreme adversity in their characters' lives, this film is about a period of relative happiness. But this doesn't represent any basic change in De Sica's sentiments. His films have always suggested a sort of two-sidedness to human experience. Often in the earlier films, the only thing that mitigates for us the characters' suffering is the implication that life at its best is not really much different from what it is at its worst. *A Brief Vacation* may show us the other side of the picture, but it is the same picture De Sica had been painting since he began as a director. (p. 19)

The parallel construction that De Sica put on Clara's story binds her present happiness to her past unhappiness. It makes us see the two as inseparable. The one condition can never escape its association with the other. The parallel construction is also typical of the way De Sica always expressed this sense he had of life. In *Umberto D* there is a moment when Umberto looks out the window of the lodgings from which he is being evicted and contemplates suicide. The camera assumes a point-of-view shot, showing us the street as Umberto sees it, and then suddenly zooms down on the cobblestones below as if Umberto were jumping. But he hasn't jumped, and the next morning when he leaves, as he looks up at his room one last time from the street, the camera again assumes a point-of-view shot. Now the shot inverts what Umberto saw the night before and controverts the finality of what he felt. That matched pair of shots, like all the matched episodes in Clara's story, sustains a kind of momentum in life, a capacity for simple endurance, which seems for De Sica to transcend all other emotions.

All De Sica's great films have been stories of how people either exercise or acquire this capacity to endure, and the reason all his characters have needed such a capacity is that they have all been exiles in life, outsiders who had no choice except to endure hardship. Umberto turned out of his rooms, Antonio turned out of his job in *The Bicycle Thief,* the Finzi-Continis turned out of their garden, Clara turned out of the sanitarium: what they all share is the fate of being dispossessed, disenfranchised, cut off, stranded.

Clara is an outsider in both her own family and the sanitarium where she momentarily escapes from that family. At home, her husband, his brother and his mother all suck the life out of her by their loveless dependence. But at the sanitarium she is from the beginning just as much an outsider, for the whole premise of such a place is that one should want to leave it. All her friends want to do so, but she of course would like to stay. Precisely because of the happiness the sanitarium affords her, Clara is really alienated there as she was at home. The fact is that the only society into which Clara really fits, the only decent company for her to keep, is that of Umberto, Antonio and all the other extraordinary, lonely figures with whom De Sica peopled the screen. (pp. 19-20)

*Colin L. Westerbeck, Jr., "The Screen," in* Commonweal *(copyright © 1975 Commonweal Publishing Co., Inc.; reprinted by permission of Commonweal Publishing Co., Inc.),* Vol. CII, No. 1, March 28, 1975, pp. 19-20.

## TOM MILNE

Neo-realism lives again in an opening sequence [of *Una Breve Vacanza* (*A Brief Vacation*)] where De Sica and Zavattini perpetrate another of those familiarly strident tableaux in which an Italian family swap vociferous recriminations amid the squalor of a cramped and rancid apartment. 'Lives', however, is hardly the word for the larger-than-life melodramatics resuscitated here, and *Breve Vacanza* is as dead as a doornail from the word go. Arguably, this opening sequence might be marginally more affecting were it not subjected to the grotesque distortions of dubbing, but nothing could save the fiction that follows from looking like anything other than a masturbatory fantasy by courtesy of women's lib. Clara's translation from the stews and sweatshops of Milan to a never-never mountain sanatorium whose main preoccupation appears to be romance rather than health, is really just the old Hollywood myth of the ugly duckling who becomes beautiful simply by taking her glasses off told all over again; and the characters who surround our Cinderella, from Prince Charming to ogre husband by way of the respectfully worshipful doctor, are all culled from the stereotypes of women's magazines.

*Tom Milne, "'Una breve vacanza' ('A Brief Vacation')," in* Monthly Film Bulletin *(copyright © The British Film Institute, 1975),* Vol. 42, No. 496, May, 1975, p. 101.

## VINCENT CANBY

In common with many other great men, Vittorio de Sica . . . had a chronic weakness that was as disorienting to him as a whiff of booze can be to the alcoholic. Mr. De Sica, the social critic (**"The Bicycle Thief"**) with an immense talent for comedy as both an actor (**"It Started in Naples"**) and as a director (**"Marriage Italian-Style"**), was from time to time subject to fits of teary sentimentality that upset his balance and completely dissolved his judgment.

As a sentimentalist Mr. De Sica never went on a bender by himself. He surrounded himself with friends, as if the making of these ponderously romantic movies were really occasions of great conviviality. Perhaps they were, though it never shows in the completed pictures. . . .

That **"The Voyage,"** which Mr. De Sica made the year before he died, is only now reaching us is not difficult to understand. The film . . . has the manner of something out of sync with itself and the world around it. . . .

Nothing in the movie fits. The casting of two extremely English actors as Sicilian aristocrats need not have been ludicrous. . . . (p. 255)

The English-language screenplay . . . is chock full of the kind of lines you haven't heard since Andrew and Virginia Stone penned their screen version of "Song of Norway."

Some are funny . . . but most are simply out of touch with the feelings and emotions the movie should be dealing in. (p. 256)

*Vincent Canby, "From Pirundello Novel," in* The New York Times *(© 1978 by The New York Times Company; reprinted by permission), December 1, 1978 (and reprinted in* The New York Times Film Reviews: 1977-1978, *The New York Times Company & Arno Press, 1979, pp. 255-56).*

## TOM ALLEN

In some ways it is humiliating that De Sica should go out with such a whimper [with *The Voyage*]. His career, between the highlights of *Shoe Shine* and *Yesterday, Today and Tomorrow,* could be described as a march from the Paris theatre to Third Avenue in popularizing both neo-realism and the modern commercial Italian film; he was conqueror of the Bloomingdale's gold coast and standard bearer of the New York art house during its many crises of identity. But those days are gone forever, and *The Voyage,* a sedate jewel of a film, is one of De Sica's quietest, least compromising works. . . .

"The voyage" itself refers to Cesare and Adriana's journey for a cure, their first chance to discover themselves. It is an ominous time when World War I headlines are announcing the end of La Belle Epoch. From Sicilian villas through Neapolitan night spots and onto the grand hotels of the Venetian Canals, the voyage progresses through a stately historical panorama. De Sica's savoring en route of a [Georges] Melies film and the French Can Can reveal, somewhat, his cultural preoccupations in an otherwise uncommonly discreet film of thwarted emotions. Fortunately, the [film] is as ravishing as the opulent sets. In the De Sica legacy, perhaps this is the one film he conceived of as fit for mounting under a crystal jar. We are invited more to a formal *objet d'art,* a stereopticon of a passing age, than to a melodrama.

*Tom Allen, "De Sica's Last Voyage" (reprinted by permission of* The Village Voice *and the author; copyright © The Village Voice, Inc., 1978), in* The Village Voice, Vol. XXIII, No. 49, December 4, 1978, p. 57.

# Marguerite Duras

## 1914-

**French director, screenwriter, playwright, and author.**

**Duras began filmmaking after a successful career as a novelist and scriptwriter. Prior to making her own films, she was best known for her screenplay of Alain Resnais's *Hiroshima mon amour*. Duras's filmic technique is based on her literary style. Her films are characterized by long silences, dialogue which conveys inner emotions, and an abstract conception of time. Her abilities as a writer enable her to, in her own words, "understand the import, the power of a word."**

**Raised in Indochina, Duras emigrated to Paris at age seventeen, where she studied law and physical science. In 1941, she began writing novels, many of which have been filmed by other directors. Duras now prefers not to film her own literature, feeling that the audience is otherwise more concerned with the transition to the screen than with the film itself.**

***Détruire, dit-elle (Destroy, She Said)* established her reputation as an "anti-art" artist. In this film, Duras creates a world of interchangeable personalities and reduces life to a vacuum. The characters's blandness is intentional; Duras encourages the audience to interpret the film in a variety of ways. Like her other works, *India Song* is cold, austere, and ambiguously symbolic. Its plot is minimal, developing instead an interior conflict that is felt rather than seen.**

**Perhaps Duras's most controversial work is *Le camion (The Truck)*. While earlier works frustrate and alienate viewers because of their unusual structure, many critics feel that *Le camion* antagonizes the audience. Lacking a plot, the work is a description of a hypothetical film. When *Le camion* was shown at Cannes, the audience shouted insults which, several critics noted, was most likely the reaction Duras desired.**

**Duras's films are not intended as entertainment. They are meant to be mulled over scene by scene. While some critics admire her adeptness in transferring verbal narrative to the screen, others have labeled her work boring and pretentious. It is generally agreed, however, that the formal structure of her films makes initial enjoyment difficult, since her techniques are intentionally anti-cinematic. (See also *CLC*, Vols. 3, 6, 11, and *Contemporary Authors*, Vols. 25-28, rev. ed.)**

### ROGER GREENSPUN

I'm not sure that I can reasonably explain the pleasure I take in Marguerite Duras's **"Destroy, She Said,"** much of which I find unendurable, but an explanation on some level is worth trying. . . .

Although **"Destroy, She Said"** avoids most of the vulgar conventional ties to place and character, and although it says very little once that it does not also say twice, it gives the impression finally of precision, eloquence and considerable wit.

The setting . . . might do for a low-budget remake of [Resnais's] "Last Year at Marienbad.". . .

Thor and Stein are "about to become" writers, a professional status that the movie accepts without comment.

I find that I also accept a good deal, not only in the film's genuinely brilliant scenes (a phony card game in which Elisabeth is entrapped by the others; a superbly poised mirror scene in which Elisabeth and Alissa more or less exchange personalities), but in its many less than brilliantly stylized dialogues and indirect confrontations.

The movies made from Miss Duras's novels, even "Hiroshima, Mon Amour," have in large measure depended upon an evocation of mood, a sense of dense and strange beauty foreign to the lucidity and simplicity of her own directorial decisions. She apparently means her film to portend revolution, holocaust, and rebirth (thus, the film's title), but she maintains her own sense of order and decorum to the end.

Roger Greenspun, "'Destroy, She Said'," in The New York Times (© 1969 by The New York Times Company; reprinted by permission), September 26, 1969 (and reprinted in The New York Times Film Reviews: 1969-1970, The New York Times Company & Arno Press, 1971, p. 79.)

### JOHN SIMON

[Marguerite Duras's *Destroy, She Said* is an abomination.] Hitherto the author was content to write bad novels or bad scripts for other directors; here for the second time she combined writing and directing, and the result seems not so much bad doubled as bad cubed.

Two men and two women, in weirdly posed, arbitrary groupings, make endless, arcanely opaque statements past one another. It is supposed to take place in a hotel, but it is obviously someone's country house and backyard. You never see anyone else (though you hear the sounds of a ghost tennis game—*Son* of *Blow Up?*), except for the husband of one of the women who shows up at the end of the film to be pounced on by the other four; there is no action, minimal movement, and only that somnambulistic dialogue which, Mlle Duras proudly affirms, is interchangeable. In the end, there is the obligatory Bach fugue, by now indispensable to true avant-garde films, which is heard in a huge crescendo signifying, according to the author, the coming of the Revolution. It could as easily signify the rising birth rate or the devaluation of the franc. (pp. 386-87)

> *John Simon, "The Festival and Awards Game: Un-magnificent Seventh" (originally published as "Un-magnificent Seventh," in* The New Leader, *Vol. LII, No. 19, October 19, 1969), in his* Movies into Film: Film Criticism 1967-1970 *(copyright © 1971 by John Simon; reprinted with permission of The Dial Press), Dial, 1971, pp. 382-98.**

### JOHN RUSSELL TAYLOR

Like *scènes à faire* that should absolutely not be *faites*, there are inescapable questions which just should not be asked. With *Détruire, Dit-Elle* [*Destroy, She Said*], the fatal question is 'What's it all about?' It is reasonably easy to say what happens, up to a certain point. . . . In an extraordinary final scene [three characters] . . . plan a little visit, and listen to sounds and music, signalling the approach of some great, but welcome, perhaps even necessary, destructive force through the surrounding forest. Legitimate, obviously, to wonder who or what they are, what, if anything, they represent, what the forest, the famous view no one can ever find, the sounds in the final sequence, may signify. But fatal to expect any clear, unequivocal answer, and to make 'understanding' on this level a condition of accepting the film. It works—and powerfully, hauntingly—in quite another way: as a series of obscure rituals played out with the greatest seriousness by people who perhaps themselves do not even half grasp their significance, like the rather funny, rather sinister card game with no rules in which the three engage their victim (patient? initiate?). Very severely made, mostly in long-held, almost static shots, and impeccably acted, the film transfers to the screen with uncanny precision the special world of Marguerite Duras the writer: as in her novels, the outer form may be prose, but the inner life is pure poetry.

> *John Russell Taylor, "Festivals 69: London," in* Sight and Sound *(copyright © 1970 by The British Film Institute), Vol. 39, No. 1, Winter, 1969-70, p. 11.**

### VINCENT CANBY

Because Miss Duras writes so elliptically, there is no special sense that she has padded [the original play of **"La Musica"**] until the confrontation in the hotel lobby. At that point, however, one realizes that all that has gone before has been rather superior but ultimately superfluous vamping. . . . (p. 215)

**"La Musica"** is intellectually chic moviemaking of the sort that is quite entertaining while it is going on but practically ceases to exist, even as a memory, when it's over. (p. 216)

> *Vincent Canby, "'La Musica'," in* The New York Times *(© 1970 by The New York Times Company; reprinted by permission), September 15, 1970 (and reprinted in* The New York Times Film Reviews:

1969-1970, *The New York Times Company & Arno Press, 1971, pp. 215-16).*

### VINCENT CANBY

The most insidious thing about the nouveau movie, which is a polite way of describing Marguerite Duras's newest, most minimal film, **"Nathalie Granger,"** is that it traps you in its own time, unlike the nouveau roman, which can be skipped through or read at leisure in an afternoon or a year.

You can't skip through **"Nathalie Granger."** To see it you are forced to watch it for as long as it lasts, while, in turn, it watches its characters, rather as if the camera were a Siamese cat whose feelings had been hurt.

Without betraying the slightest interest, the camera records the physical appearance of two expressionless women [Isabelle and The Other Woman]. . . .

The camera paces through the house, looking into mirrors, down hallways, through windows. There is a report on the radio about a murder and a police manhunt. The telephone rings. Wrong number. "There is no telephone here, madame," [The Other Woman] says into the receiver. Funny? Not really. It's too pretty and solemn. A salesman calls. He tries desperately to sell a Vedetta Tambour 008 washing machine that comes in three colors. For a brief moment, the ghost of Pinter's wit walks over the grave of the film. [Isabelle] goes into the garden, again. [The Other Woman] falls asleep. A cat saunters through. The camera just stares. When a person or a cat leaves a room, Miss Duras seems to say, that room is empty. Such are the discoveries of **"Nathalie Granger,"** a dead-end movie that, I confidently hope, few of us are ready for.

> *Vincent Canby, "'Nathalie Granger'," in* The New York Times *(© 1972 by The New York Times Company; reprinted by permission), October 7, 1972 (and reprinted in* The New York Times Film Reviews: 1971-1972, *The New York Times Company & Arno Press, 1973, p. 313).*

### NORA SAYRE

Stiff as uncooked asparagus, the figures who stalk through Marguerite Duras's **"Woman of the Ganges"** don't have to act, since the movie is narrated in English by two invisible women with lush French accents. "Soch loff, soch dee-sire!" they repeat, as they warble away. . . .

[It] becomes quite difficult to tell who's alive or dead in this movie. (All of the performers behave like zombies, but some are probably supposed to be ghosts.) It's also very hard to know who did what to whom in the past.

Amid all the pacing through corridors, there's little spoken dialogue and barely any action. So it's an event when two characters bid each other good evening, when sand dribbles between someone's fingers, or when a muslin curtain stirs in the wind. There's some pretension to significant imagery here, but the result makes you want to yell or weep with boredom.

Meanwhile, the narrators sluggishly state their passion for one another—"You're so yonk, and I loff you ssso moch"—and some of the others say that they've lost their memories. Since Marguerite Duras neglected to give them any perceptible emotions the response seems healthy.

*Nora Sayre, " 'La femme du gange',," in* The New York Times *(© 1974 by The New York Times Company; reprinted by permission),* June 7, 1974 *(and reprinted in* The New York Times Film Reviews: 1973-1974, *The New York Times Company & Arno Press, 1975, p. 220).*

## MICHAEL TARANTINO

[*Woman of the Ganges*] is a deliberate journey through a self-endowed world, in which cinema itself, as a means of expression, is alternately questioned, denied, and finally affirmed. . . .

It is explanation itself which functions as the principal theme of *Woman of the Ganges*. The plot is ostensibly concerned with a group of people who have returned to a scene from their past. Entering into this void, they try to re-establish the relationships which had originally failed. What the film presents us with, however, is a series of "plot elements", as it attempts to re-create the past through the characters' present. . . .

Duras builds images of painful simplicity, which resemble paintings set into motion—but not emotionalized—in the far regions of the frame. Characters, in trying to re-create or re-evaluate the past, emerge as still-life objects. . . .

For its characters, the space of *Woman of the Ganges* is a utopian wasteland. It is a feeling more than an area, which Duras illuminates through a negation of cinema as a formal property. . . .

In this decidedly static atmosphere, the characters's movement is slow and deliberate. No one runs. No one yells. They are presented to us on the same plane as the revolving door, which leads into and out of the hotel standing at the center of the (non) narrative. The camera, in attempting to deal directly with time and space, ultimately gives the impression of flattening out the subjects through its gaze, and extending the objects from within by treating them "equally". . . .

*Woman of the Ganges* is a fascinating achievement whose success ultimately lies in the mind of the viewer—a mind which must be cleared of nodding affirmations or denials.

In *Pour Un Nouveau Roman*, Robbe-Grillet talks of the artist's need for the reader's co-operation—one which would be active, conscious, and creative. The reader must "invent" the work and the world in which it is situated. Duras extends this plea to the cinema. . . . The space is deep but the action is shallow. The viewer must fill in the blanks. We occupy the off-screen space.

*Michael Tarantino, "'Woman of the Ganges',," in* Take One *(copyright © 1974 by Unicorn Publishing Corp.), Vol. 4, No. 6, November 4, 1974, p. 28.*

## DEAN McWILLIAMS

Rather than attempting a detailed realistic evocation of a resort hotel such as those in Resnais' *Last Year at Marienbad* or Visconti's *Death in Venice*, Duras' setting is reduced to bare essentials [in *Destroy, She Said*]: a building with plain white interiors, a broad lawn surrounded by trees and a tennis court, no bell-boys, desk clerk or elaborate interiors or exteriors. . . . The building is obviously a private chateau rather than a hotel and the women wear black dresses despite the references to summer heat. The result is a disconcerting feeling of subtle disparity.

The concern for abstraction is also reflected in the emphasis on simplicity, order and balance in the composition of the shots. Figures are carefully posed within the frame, often at oblique angles to each other and to the camera, suggesting their inability to communicate. (p. 267)

The few references to specific times, either days or hours, which occur in [Duras'] novel have been removed from the film. The temporal experience of viewing the film is thus both more abstract and more durational: time does not mount or ascend towards any resolution or goal but merely accumulates oppressively. Duras has exploited the unprecedented control that a filmmaker can impose on the viewer's sense of *durée*. Unlike the reader of a novel who can read fast or slow, skip or reread pages or even put the book down and take a break, the filmgoer moves through the narrative at the exact pace determined by the film's editor. Add to this the camera's power of focussing our attention exclusively on one or more characters and we see how the film artist can merge the time experience of the viewer outside the narrative with that of the characters within the film. (p. 268)

*Dean McWilliams, "The Novelist as Filmmaker: Marguerite Duras' 'Destroy, She Said'," in* Literature/Film Quarterly *(© copyright 1975 Salisbury State College), Vol. III, No. 3, Summer, 1975, pp. 264-69.*

## MOLLY HASKELL

[In **"India Song,"** Marguerite Duras's] most perfectly realized film, the present is in a constant state of deliquescence. As in her previous films, the voices function as an echo chamber whereby the past is imprinted and repeated to infinity. . . .

The fact that it is possible to enjoy [the] characters, to come under the film's spell, and not see it as a parable about the imminent demise of the bourgeoisie is perhaps as much a function of Duras's ambivalence as the audience's, and a triumph of style and an instinctive woman's empathy over strict ideology. . . .

**"India Song"** is the most *feminine* film I have ever seen. This is not just in the obvious details of decor, the gauzy, languid atmosphere, the feeling for textures and color and romantic lighting, but in the overwhelming sensual importance granted such things in the way life-and-love is remembered, the crucial importance of setting, of mise-en-scene, in the female memory. As women look for "total" experiences, so experiences remembered become total, decor merges with the romantic songs and suicidal sadness of a living for love that is at once destitute, debilitating, and intense, There is in the whole a pervasive sensuality, a kind of active, or enveloping, passivity that is feminine in feeling, being at odds with the masculine need to "make something happen."

The techniques and concerns of Duras's previous films are fused into a rarefied work of lyricism, despair, and passion. . . .

What raises this Duras above the others for me is not a sudden quickening of narrative pace: it is fully as static as **"La Femme du Gange"** [**"Woman of the Ganges"**]. Silence remains the dominant figure of speech, emptiness the controlling figure of style, boredom the essential mood. Together they are the co-ordinates of a vacuum that, like the impinging revolution in **"Destroy She Said,"** threatens to envelop and silence forever this threadbare civilization. Yet how elegant are these last few threads, and how exquisitely, how seductively Duras has rendered them. . . . It is [an] eruption of passion along with the score . . . that gives **"India Song"** an emotional immediacy Duras's other films have lacked. However ironically the song (which would fall under Noel Coward's heading of 'cheap music') was intended, it imbues the film with a kind of primitive emotional hunger that is all the more moving for its austere setting.

I am sure that Duras's apologists will manage to defend the film on structural or political grounds that ignore (in embarrassment?) the emotional pull, and the importance of the stars themselves. But Duras is *not* an abstract avant-garde filmmaker, she falls somewhere between narrative and non-narrative film. . . . (p. 134)

> Molly Haskell, *"The Most Feminine Film I've Ever Seen"* (reprinted by permission of The Village Voice and the author; copyright © The Village Voice, Inc., 1975), in The Village Voice, Vol. XX, No. 42, October 20, 1975, pp. 136, 134.

## MICHAEL TARANTINO

*India Song* is a film which simultaneously represents a departure from, and a codification of, Marguerite Duras' oeuvre. The narration introduces characters who have appeared frequently in Duras' films and novels. . . . However, their position as protagonists is extremely tenuous. They do not develop in the traditional sense from work to work. Rather, they remain elusive, representing a constant flux of just "being". The acts they encompass pale in relationship to their reactions to same. . . .

The narrative employed in *India Song* is common to Duras' work. However, the manner in which the film unfolds stylistically represents a significant variation. The past is witnessed through the unfolding of the present. The narrative's structural foundations are re-examined from the advantageous position afforded by the present. There are no flashbacks. Time is not segmented. It is a continuum. A murder, a love affair, a suicide—each act is alluded to by the inquisitive off-screen voices. In *Nathalie Granger* and *La Femme du Gange* this technique functioned as a complement to the dialogue taking place between the characters on screen. *India Song* extends this formula one step further. . . .

*India Song* is a film of reverberations: the aural textures of the spoken word, the hypnotic strains of the period-inducing tango music, the blank stare of an actor, a river, a beggarwoman, India itself. To talk extensively of plot is to distort the central experience, which is somewhat akin to discovering the framework. Connotative in nature, it suggests the general through the specific. When Duras cuts from the mansion at the end of the film to a map of India, it is not merely an act of spatio-temporal disjunction or a facile attempt to link the sociological with the intimate. Like the movement of the camera, the advance from shot to shot is perfectly controlled. Logic permeates each and every emotion, defining it beyond the signification of the image.

The character of the beggarwoman presents an excellent example of how Duras pieces together a work—whether it be film or novel. First mentioned in the novel *The Vice-Consul,* this woman never appears on screen in *India Song*—yet she remains a central presence. Like the interweavings of the past, the fact that she is mentioned is enough to testify to her existence outside of the frame and to the social conditions beyond the enclosed space of the mansion. . . .

In writing dialogue for her novels, Duras calls attention to the silences existing in conversation. *Destroy, She Said* is a startling testament of unuttered phrases. In her films, this pre-occupation with silence takes on an added dimension. The author now has complete control over the length of the breaks, while the audience must "see" them in time. They confront the viewer and demand acknowledgment. (p. 42)

> Michael Tarantino, *"Review & Interview: 'India Song',"* in Take One (copyright © 1976 by Unicorn Publishing Corp.), Vol. 5, No. 4, October, 1976, pp. 42-3.

## RICHARD ROUD

The ostensible subject of **Le Camion** is a film-maker (played by Mme. Duras herself) going over the script of a film she wants to make with the other leading player. . . .

[The] device of discussing an unmade film is *only* a device; it is not the real subject of the film. True enough, for much of the time we do get Duras reading lines to [Gérard] Depardieu, and the actor asking questions about the characters each would be playing (this is a film in the conditional tense). Who would she be, asks Depardieu of the woman he, as truck-driver, would give a lift to. *Declassée,* says Duras; that's all one can say about her. But of course there is much more to be said, because this woman is a number of women. To begin with, she is the heroine of *Hiroshima, mon Amour* grown old. . . . Depardieu is made to suggest that the woman has perhaps escaped from a local lunatic asylum. Duras neither confirms nor denies the accusation. Perhaps she is on the way to the christening of her nephew Abraham, whose family lives in an impossible spot to which there is only one bus a day. She talks once or twice about her childhood—far, far away from France. 'There was a river.' The Mekong, perhaps? We are never told, but the woman could be the young heroine of [René Clément's] *Barrage contre le Pacifique,* she could also be Anne-Marie Stretter, Lol V. Stein. She is almost certainly the Asian beggar woman from *India Song*. But she is probably also Jewish.

In short, she is Marguerite Duras in all her fictional and non-fictional roles—all the women she was, all the women she imagined herself to be. And, like Duras, this woman is someone who has lost faith in politics, lost faith in the proletariat. . . .

[Much] of the action of the film is on the road; for the lorry itself, a magnificent five-axle, blue Fruehauf, is the third character of the film. Its movements through the countryside and the roundabouts are as rhythmical as what Penelope Gilliatt once called Duras' back-stitching dialogue. I must confess that I don't really know what back-stitching is, but it sounds right for Duras' style. And the truck goes in for some back-stitching too; its movements are all the more premonitory because we never see its driver, nor do we hear the sound of the engine. . . .

'So that's how it ends?' asks Depardieu. Yes, it's over. That is all we ever find out about the two people. The camera then moves forward towards the table where they are sitting and moves past them to a bright source of light: a white-curtained window with what seems to be some mystical light glowing from behind. Then the camera angle changes, and we see past the two actors and their table to an open window: her lips are moving, but the dialogue track has gone dead. All we hear (as we have heard at various moments throughout the film) is one of Beethoven's 'Diabelli Variations'. And then we see through an open window on to a terrace with a tall oak waving in the wind—and, next to it, a single klieg light. So that is what provided the 'mystical' brightness behind the curtain, one could say. Or, the light is there to show us that while pretending to talk about making a film, a film has actually been made: the one we have just seen. One could say both these things, and say them dismissively. But *Le Camion* is *not* an exercise *de style;* it is not just about a woman talking about making a film. Its real subject is Marguerite Duras in 1977, just as the real subject of *Providence*, David Mercer or not, is Alain Resnais in 1977.

Much as I liked *India Song*, I prefer *Le Camion*. *India Song* had many obvious attractions: its gorgeous interiors, its exoticism, its seductive tango music, its even more seductive Delphine Seyrig. *Le Camion* has nothing: nothing but Marguerite Duras and Gérard Depardieu; that room and that truck, that landscape and Beethoven. And with these meagre materials, Duras has made her most achieved film. It is also her shortest: one hour and eighteen minutes. But a film of this intensity, of this spareness, couldn't be borne for much longer. And also of this degree of pessimism: 'Let the world go to wrack and ruin,' says Duras the Woman. And yet, however pessimistic her intentions, the sheer nerve of a film like this, plus its physical beauty . . . , gave me a sense of exaltation that was anything but a 'downer'. (p. 145)

Richard Roud, "The Left Bank Revisited," in Sight and Sound (copyright © 1977 by The British Film Institute), Vol. 46, No. 3, Summer, 1977, pp. 143-45.*

### JOHN COLEMAN

I have slumped through *India Song* twice. It does not improve on closer acquaintance. To be fair to Mlle Duras, she is quotably her worst enemy: 'I make films to kill time. If I had the courage to do nothing, I'd do nothing . . . That's the most sincere thing I can say about my activities.' At this rare moment in time, reviewer and film-maker join hands. A more killing way with time—I talk about mine—it would be hard to conjure. Calcutta (maybe), 1937 (perhaps), a doomy love-affair (who knows?). That is the plot. But against whom is it engineered? . . . To relieve the visual tedium (it looks as if it were shot in an aquarium in need of dusting), many voices say hinting, dislocated things over. Leprosy, heat and famines recur verbally, as well as a really successful non-sequitur about an Indian female who spent ten years trekking to the Ganges, losing a dozen children en route. The happening can only be there to tickle the mind if you believe in nothing. I think Marguerite Duras thinks, when she does, that all art has to start from scratch. I refuse to allow that she has done anything important, significant or new: the tiny, residual impression left by *India Song* is of a sad, stale odour attempting to pass itself off as a fresh scent. This may be enough for habitués of the Portobello Road and other Flea Markets, who will find meaning in the fall of a stuffed sparrow: and buy the thing.

John Coleman, "Killing Time," in New Statesman (© 1977 The Statesman & Nation Publishing Co. Ltd.), Vol. 94, No. 2427, September 23, 1977, p. 421.*

### PAULINE KAEL

[The control in Duras's] new film, *Le Camion—The Truck*—suggests that she has become a master. But there's a joker in her mastery: though her moods and cadences, her rhythmic phrasing, with its emotional undertow, might seem ideally suited to the medium, they don't fulfill moviegoers' expectations. Conditioned from childhood, people go to the movies wanting the basic gratification of a story acted out. Many directors have tried to alter this conditioning, breaking away from the simplest narrative traditions, and they've failed to take the largest audience with them. Duras doesn't even get near the mass of moviegoers, though somehow—God knows how—she manages to make her own pictures, her own way. Hers is possibly the most sadomasochistic of all director relationships with the audience: she drives people out of the theatre, while, no doubt, scorning them for their childish obtuseness. At the same time, she must be suffering from her lack of popularity. Her battle with the audience reaches a new stage in *The Truck,* in which the split between her artistry and what the public wants is pointed up and turned against the audience. She brings if off, but she's doing herself in, too. And so it isn't a simple prank. (p. 292)

*The Truck* is a spiritual autobiography, a life's-journey, end-of-the-world road movie; it's a summing up, an endgame. The hitchhiker travels in a winter desert; she's from anywhere and going nowhere, in motion to stay alive. (pp. 292-93)

The film alternates between sequences in the room and sequences of the rolling truck, always at a distance. Each time she cuts to the outdoors, you're drawn into the hypnotic flow of the road imagery, and though you know perfectly well there will be nothing but the truck in the landscape, you half dream your way into a "real" movie. And each time you find yourself back with Duras, you're aware of being treated like a chump, your childishness exposed. (p. 293)

The audience reacts at first with highly vocal disbelief and then with outbursts of anger, and walkouts. Even those of us who are charmed by her harmonious, lulling use of the film medium and in awe of her composure as a performer are conscious that we have, buried under a few layers, the rebellious instincts that others are giving loud voice to. They're furious in a way they never are at a merely bad, boring movie, and this anger is perfectly understandable. But it's high comedy, too: their feelings have been violated by purely aesthetic means—an affront to their conditioning. (pp. 293-94)

*The Truck* is a class-act monkeyshine made with absolutely confident artistry. She knows how easy it would be to give people the simple pleasures that they want. Her pride in not making concessions is heroic; it shows in that gleam of placid perversity which makes her such a commanding camera presence.

She can take the insults without flinching because she's completely serious in the story of the despairing hitchhiker. In her method in *The Truck,* she's a minimalist, like Beckett, stripping her drama down to the bones of monodrama, and her subject is the same as his: going through the last meaningless rites. . . . [Her] spoken text is attitudinizing—desultory self-preoccupation, mystification. Not pinning anything down, she leaves everything floating allusively in midair. This is, God help us, a vice women artists have been particularly prone to. Who is this hitchhiker on the road of life? Ah, we are not to know. . . . The hitchhiker's declaration that she no longer believes in the possibility of political salvation is meant to have shock value; the world—i.e., Paris—is being told what Marguerite Duras's latest stand is. (p. 294)

There's something of the punitive disciplinarian in her conception of film art; **"The Truck"** is a position paper made into a movie. It's accessible, but it's accessible to a piece of yourself that you never think to take to the movies. Let's put it this way: if you were studying for a college exam and knocked off to go see **"The Truck,"** you wouldn't feel you were playing hooky. Duras makes us aware of our own mechanisms of response, and it's tonic and funny to feel the tensions she provokes. Her picture has been thought out with such supple discrimination between the values of sound and image that one could almost say it's *perfectly* made: an ornery, glimmering achievement. (p. 295)

> *Pauline Kael, "Contrasts" (originally published in* The New Yorker, *Vol. LIII, No. 32, September 26, 1977), in her* When the Lights Go Down *(copyright © 1975, 1976, 1977, 1978, 1979, 1980 by Pauline Kael; reprinted by permission of Holt, Rinehart and Winston, Publishers), Holt, 1980, pp. 291-98.\**

## JANET MASLIN

In **"The Truck,"** the director and novelist Marguerite Duras plays a woman whose lips curl into a joyless, knowing half-smile every time she makes mention of despair. Her film should appeal most strongly to those viewers who are similarly attuned to the romantic possibilities of gloom. However, even those who have little patience for Miss Duras's preciousness may find her work as haunting and determinedly self-possessed as it is quietly infuriating. . . .

**"The Truck"** is full of exasperatingly banal interchanges, which are in no way improved or illuminated by Miss Duras's admission of her character's banality. It is also rather coyly self-pitying, because Miss Duras and her character seem to overlap, and the character is at times made to seem pathetic.

But the scenes of the truck take on an eerie grandeur after a while, and Miss Duras's disdain for her audience's expectations becomes perversely transfixing. It's a pity that her script is not as stern and unrelenting as the film's visual style.

> *Janet Maslin, "Film Festival: 'The Truck' Talks and Talks but It Says Very Little," in* The New York Times *(© 1977 by The New York Times Company; reprinted by permission), September 27, 1977 (and reprinted in* The New York Times Film Reviews: 1977-1978, *The New York Times Company & Arno Press, 1979, p. 110).*

## TERRY CURTIS FOX

The last thing I felt like doing that Tuesday was see a film by Marguerite Duras. I'd been exhausted by festivaling all day. The rigors of *The Truck* were, I feared, more than I could take. By film's end, I found myself exhilarated, ready to dance, party, take the long walk home. Not that *The Truck* is any less rigorous than Duras's usual fare. Just that *The Truck* is such a joyous expression of rigor it leaves you energized, heady from the motion of the rolling beast. . . .

For all her devotion to cinema, Duras has always been a novelist who makes films. The closer she is to novelistic form, the more successful her films. *India Song,* in which images and dialogue have no inherent one-to-one relationship, works pre-

cisely as a cinematic novel, the dissociation serving the function of an omniscient narrator commenting through style on everything which is seen/heard. *The Truck* at once invites us to see the writer at work and to see this vision as an artistic device.

That device—the story that is not precisely the one of the film—works as narrative in almost pure form. We are, after all, being told a story. We are even given a chance to hear questions about why elements of the story are given and others left out. And, as we watch the truck on the road, we are offered the opportunity to envision the emotional landscape which caused the story to take place. None of this detracts from the story itself. It merely gives the tale added dimension, added weight.

Between Duras and Depardieu there is a perfect balance of intellect and intuition. She refines and he reacts. Together they force the narrative back to its emotional base. Through their dialogue, we understand that for Duras, the passion of intellect and the passion of love are interchangeable. It is an extraordinary conceit. More extraordinary still, she has made a film in which this conceit is so organically and voluptuously expressed.

> *Terry Curtis Fox, "Two for the Road" (reprinted by permission of* The Village Voice *and the author; copyright © The Village Voice, Inc., 1977), in* The Village Voice, *Vol. XXII, No. 42, October 17, 1977, p. 54.\**

## WILLIAM F. VAN WERT

Marguerite Duras has pioneered what she calls the "multiple work of art," a text which is simultaneously a novel, a play, a dance, a film, an opera. Duras has broken the "rules," the long-standing codes which separated the various art forms, in order to provide a bridge from one to the other. . . . Duras's sense of the multiple work of art stems from her growing disillusionment with writing and reading as obsolete forms. She writes, she says, from compulsion, maintaining a love-hate relationship with phrases, reading very little herself, acknowledging that others don't read anymore. The solution seems to be a mass art form, a form which blends into each medium, an answer to mass reproduction, a multiproductive text. That text often operates as a cross between ritual and play, between sleep-walking and future-fantasy, with an aesthetic that could appropriately be termed creative destruction. . . .

Her rejuvenating sense of the multiproductive text has been at the root of the apparently anti-cinematic narratives of her recent films. . . . Duras has refined her cinematic form, gradually eliminating concrete references for symbolic ones, restricting the camera's movement and the editor's arbitrary eclipse-cuts for long, repetitive takes and for fixed frames that are both boring and fascinating, flattened out and trance-inducing. Her narrative, then, operates within a neutralized comic strip and acting gives way to complex sound-image relationships: the "voices" are freed of their speakers, sometimes functioning as pure sounds. Bouncing off the figurative walls of the closed-room frame, sound and voice move in a dialectic between meditation and interview. . . .

Such formal concerns are usually associated with the most self-conscious of the experimental films in this country, not with commercially viable feature films. That Duras has incorporated this formalism successfully within a narrative tradition is largely a testament to the strength of feminist film criticism and Lacanian film criticism in France, both of which have championed

Duras's films in recent years. But what of the primary film viewing experience? Why are her films so difficult, so boring, yet so important and so rewarding? . . . [They] are a learning experience through confrontation, not through pleasure and identification. Duras is a committed artist who disdains works of art and who has minimal confidence in the impact of an art work upon an audience: thus, her formalism. And for someone who is a novelist with a poet's ear for music, she is incredibly silent. Unlike *Hiroshima mon amour* and [Henri Colpi's] *Une aussi longue absence,* Duras's own films contain no poetic camera movements nor do they fill up the static camera shots with interesting or beautiful spoken text. Her films have forced me to confront film as a potential *non-seeing* process, one in which split-screen is replaced by split sound tracks. And as her visual sense becomes more assured, more *pro forma* or perfunctory, Duras's experiments in sound become more audacious, more subtle and, yes, more formal. Her experiments in language have precisely to do with separating the visual track from the sound track and with breaking down the sound track into autonomous parts of music or spoken text—as audible statement, as memory recall, or simply as the whisperings of longing and desire. (pp. 22-3)

Duras's structure seems often to "deaden" what is visually present in the frame to evoke what is visually absent but present on the sound track. (p. 24)

[With the film frame of *India Song*] so compressed, with actors moving as though they were statues and reciting as though they were reading from an old hymnal, and with the proliferation of unidentified voices and the plethora of symbolic sounds on the sound track, the wonder is that Marguerite Duras has been able to continue making films and acquire any following at all. One thing is certain: her recent successes will not induce a lapse into formula. It seems a safe prediction that she will expand the possibilities of sound in film even further. (p. 29)

*William F. Van Wert, "The Cinema of Marguerite Duras: Sound and Voice in a Closed Room," in* Film Quarterly *(copyright 1979 by The Regents of the University of California; reprinted by permission of the University of California Press), Vol. XXXIII, No. 1, Fall, 1979, pp. 22-9.*

# Rainer Werner Fassbinder

## 1946-

German director, playwright, and actor.

Fassbinder is considered by many to be the leading director of the German New Wave, a movement marked by a radical break with Germany's past. He advocates rebellion against moral and social complacency; however, he also acknowledges that the rebel is doomed to failure. Instead of psychological character studies, Fassbinder creates fables that state their messages in bold, short strokes. His nihilistic view of Marxist society, along with his precarious balance between the very stylized and sharply realistic, have caused him critical difficulties.

Fassbinder's acting career started in Munich's "Action Theater," an avant-garde theatrical troupe. A year later, Fassbinder founded the Anti-Theater, intended as an alternative to the German theatrical standards he found boring and narrow. Sparse decor and uninflected performance characterize his first film, *Love Is Colder than Death*. This film also reflects his fascination with love's power. Fassbinder says, "Love is the best, most insidious, most effective instrument of social repression."

The theme of isolation also figures prominently in Fassbinder's work. Fassbinder admits he creates compulsively to avoid his own loneliness. His most autobiographical film, *Fox and His Friends*, tells the story of a homosexual befriended only for his momentary wealth and soon abandoned. Significantly, Fassbinder plays the lead character.

*The Bitter Tears of Petra von Kant* also intertwines love and politics. Like most of Fassbinder's characters, Petra is an outsider, a victim, and, ultimately, a loser. Other characters are not so much victims of love as of a complacent and monotonous society.

*The Marriage of Maria Braun* is Fassbinder's first international success. Maria is a victim of both love and society. As one of Fassbinder's strongest heroines, she battles oppression only to meet an ironic and violent death. Unexpected violence, such as Maria's death, appears frequently in Fassbinder's films as both a stylistic and thematic pivot.

Fassbinder acknowledges Hollywood director Douglas Sirk as his strongest influence. He shares Sirk's fondness for the melodramatic, using exaggerated camera angles and mirror techniques. But although Fassbinder creates extended melodramatic situations, his treatment is distant and deadpan. While some critics question the speed with which he makes films, most accept his use of a skeletal frame for his work. Some resent his films, labeling him overrated and undertalented. After over thirty films, Fassbinder remains a paradox: a pessimistic artist who enjoys Hollywood's most sentimental films, and a politically curious intellectual involved in changing the status quo while admitting the futility of his efforts. (See also *Contemporary Authors*, Vols. 93-96.)

## BRUCE BERMAN

[*The Merchant of the Four Seasons*] is a complex, depressingly moving tale that, when it is not steeped in the deliberateness of its development and representation of emotional and environmental vacuity, sheds much-needed light on the ill-effects of the petit-bourgeois mentality, in this case "mentality" as manifested by Hans Epp and his severely entrenched family. (p. 39)

In terms of method, *The Merchant of the Four Seasons,* which was made initially for German television, retains a washed-out colour and a starkness of imagery (omnipresent crosses, gilt-edged picture-frames on barren walls, etc.), that despite their obvious thematic contributions render the visual terrain not very screen-worthy on one level, although revealing and certainly relevant to the depiction of Fassbinder's vision of a perverted lower-middle class. Stylistically, Fassbinder's work here can be likened to Godard's favourable middle period. . . . The scene staged at the film's end where, almost predictably, Hans' funeral takes place on a brilliant spring morning with birds singing and sun glowing, struck me as particularly Godardian in its irony. We are reminded that Hans (as we are all to varying degrees), the victim of (political) circumstance and perhaps life itself, can only cease to be a failure when he ceases to be. (pp. 39-40)

Bruce Berman, "Reviews: 'The Merchant of the Four Seasons'," in Take One (copyright © 1972 by Unicorn Publishing Corp.), Vol. 4, No. 4, November-December, 1972, pp. 39-40.

## CHRISTIAN BRAAD THOMSEN

Fassbinder's debut-film, *Love is Colder than Death*, has often been compared with Jean-Luc Godard's first film, *Breathless*, because both films introduced an unusually explosive period of production, and because both reveal a very personal reaction to the influence of the American gangster-film. (p. 12)

[Fassbinder's] debut-film was redolent of [a] pictorial emptiness, a feeling that we are starting afresh from the absolute null-point, in an attempt to build something upon the smoking ruins at which Godard arrived and has bequeathed to his contemporaries. Fassbinder tells a gangster-story, but already in the first scene in his first film he demonstrates that his gangster-world is in reality a reflection of the bourgeois world, with which his gangsters only apparently break by their way of living, but from which they never ultimately can free themselves. . . . Fassbinder repeats this same, absolutely static image-conception in his second film, *Katzelmacher,* about a Greek immigrant worker whose arrival in a little German provincial town triggers the latent fascist tendencies of the inhabitants. The world of this little provincial town could be interchangeable with that of his gangster-film: it is nearly void of maturity and sentiment, and is wholly static. (pp. 12-13)

Fassbinder's subsequent films deepen and vary the central themes of his first two films: the boredom and emptiness which grope their way to violent expression. Throughout Fassbinder's films, frustrations are resolved by violent action. . . .

Fassbinder's first films will be remembered especially for their pictorial emptiness, for those endless static-camera sequences which purify situations of their "dramatic" content. Taking as his point of departure this emptiness, which is of an aesthetic and contextual nature, Fassbinder gradually discovers a succession of human feelings and social contexts which are more constructive. He additionally discovers a filmic language which slowly allows itself to be built up on the ruins left by Hollywood. (p. 13)

*Warning* lies mid-way in Fassbinder's work, and it is a turning-point. It is Fassbinder's most obviously autobiographical film, since it deals with the making of a film and gives a non-idealized portrait of Fassbinder and of his permanent crew of actors and co-workers. . . . *Warning* deals with the price they have to pay for functioning as a group, and with the tensions which, time and again, threaten to scatter them. . . . (pp. 13-14)

The director's dream of delegating the film's creation to all is just an excuse for his self-pitying plaint, that it is always *he* who has to do it all. In reality, none of the others gets an opportunity to participate in the decision-making process. . . . The film-crew's dreams, which might originally have been real and sympathetic, have become perverted, introverted and insincere. Their relation to each other and to film is incestuous, self-infecting and claustrophobic. . . .

*Warning* is a merciless, brutal and self-critical film, but behind the brutality is hidden—as always in Fassbinder's work—a great and slightly embarrassed tenderness for the characters he depicts. The film's characters seem to arrive at a temporary solution, when the actual filming gets under way, for this effort has, *quand même*, a kind of meaning. What destroys Fassbinder's characters in his earlier films is their disjunctive relation to their work, that is, to their own creative energies. . . .

The merciless self-criticism which Fassbinder indulges in in *Warning* is not feigned. Although the film deals with hollow phrases, it is not itself hollow. He takes its self-criticism seriously, and in his subsequent films he is finally prepared to address himself to a large audience without compromising. . . .

Besides being a tale of individual suffering, [*The Merchant of the Four Seasons*] is also a pointed unmasking of bourgeois family life, of the hypocrisy, ambitions, and essential coldness of the family's existence. It is Fassbinder's most apparently naturalistic film, while at the same time the naturalism swings over into a stylized pop-artish pathos of great originality and direct emotional appeal. . . .

At the same time he made this film about woman's repression of man, Fassbinder made *The Bitter Tears of Petra von Kant*. . . . These two films must be seen in context, because they demonstrate that Fassbinder is not dominated by the current trendy, over-simplifying and jargon-ridden evaluations of our society's social mechanisms. (p. 14)

[In *Petra von Kant*, the] dialogue has been brilliantly reduced to a maxim-like simplicity, without loss to its emotional complexity. The long, fixed camera-positions and precise picture composition chisel this love-story out in stone, but perhaps the most remarkable quality of the film is that it deals with some of the seemingly "eternal" questions, while at the same time Fassbinder demonstrates how the characters' understanding of love is intimately connected with their social rôles. This thorough-going insistence upon the connection between peoples' social existence and their emotional consciousness exemplifies Fassbinder's assertion that, "when society is changed, people's consciousness will also be changed." (p. 15)

In his treatment of the problems central to women's liberation, Fassbinder has continued to expand his criticism of the individualistic revolt which has characterized his work right from the first gangster-film. The individualistic revolt achieves nothing, or at the most it serves—by the fate it meets—to sketch a caricature of the individualistic society which the rebel attempts to defy. Fassbinder defined this with the utmost symbolic clarity in his American-South melodrama, *Whity*. . . .

Fassbinder's tv films are told with a charming, almost dreamlike optimism, but he never completely loses contact with the realities, and in the last of the films he clearly demarcates the limits of the spontaneous human solidarity with which he works. The upper limit is, in his eyes, the right of private ownership of the means of production. . . .

There is a conspicuous difference between Fassbinder's feature films and his television films. *Eight Hours Don't Make a Day* presents a much more optimistic side than his feature films. . . .

Fassbinder's experience in the medium of television seems also to have influenced the trend of his future production. . . . [The relationship of the two lonely creatures in *Fear Eats Up Souls*] provokes the latent fascist tendencies present in the pair's bourgeois environment. . . . Fassbinder allows love to win over the environment's pettiness and intolerance. This is in harmony with his experiences with television, and is an important element in Fassbinder's artistic programme, that one ought to make films which give people the courage to live their lives. But in spite of his declared good will, it's difficult to make films which end 100% happily, the way our world looks today. There lies a fruitful artistic tension for Fassbinder in the conflict between his own wish for things to be resolved as well as possible, and the limited possibilities for happy endings which our everyday life in the Western world provides. (p. 16)

*Christian Braad Thomsen, "Fassbinder's Holy Whores," in* Take One *(copyright © 1973 by Unicorn Publishing Corp.), Vol. 4, No. 6, July-August, 1973, pp. 12-16.*

**TONY RAYNS**

Like Rainer Werner Fassbinder's other recent imitations of life, *Fear Eats the Soul* [*Angst essen Seele auf*] achieves a remarkable balance between stylisation and realism. . . .

The movie is an expansion/revision of a story told by a minor character in Fassbinder's own *Der amerikanische Soldat* [*The American Soldier*] (1970), and also a remake/revision of Douglas Sirk's *All That Heaven Allows* (1955). Its plot is an extraordinary mesh of low-key melodrama and social criticism. . . .

*Angst essen Seele auf* begins like a fairy-tale: as in a dream, Emmi is lured into the Moroccan bar by the Arab music on its juke-box, and invited to dance for what is evidently the first time in many years. Stage by stage, everything that follows is hilariously—and agonisingly—predictable; Fassbinder plays on audience expectations so thoroughly that his exposition astonishes by its very exhaustiveness. The types of racial fear and prejudice are catalogued succinctly. . . .

Fassbinder circumscribes the movie's area of interest by fading out on anything irrelevant to his direct concerns (the first night that the couple share; their turning-point holiday). He films his active characters in neutral mid-shots, never lending disproportionate weight to one or another in the compositions, and the legions of anonymous onlookers who provide the movie's moral 'context' in static, posed tableaux. . . . The overall approach invites comparison with other European critiques of American genres . . . ; but Fassbinder is clearly as interested in vindicating Sirk as he is in using a rhetorical style to make his unequivocal statements on film. This 'politicised weepie' realises both aims with an assurance of a kind almost vanished from narrative cinema.

> *Tony Rayns, ''Film Reviews: 'Fear Eats the Soul','' in* Sight and Sound *(copyright © 1974 by The British Film Institute), Vol. 43, No. 4, Autumn, 1974, p. 245.*

**RICHARD COMBS**

On the face of it, the world of *Petra von Kant*—a supremely stylised region where the rules of play, in decor as in passion, are dictated by the high-fashion, high-camp predilections of its decadent queen—shares very little with the wry social comedy of *Fear Eats the Soul*. . . . But there is an odd complementary quality about the two films, the suggestion of a mirror reflection in the way the areas of stylisation are inverted, and a clearly continuing line in the way the form and mannerisms of Hollywood melodrama are worked into the texts. Where *Fear Eats the Soul* tells, broadly, a mundane tale of love crushed by social prejudice and repression, and lends to the affair between the ageing char and the hapless immigrant both a kind of dignity and a sense of the solid network of social interferences and cultural differences through the applied gravity of its style, *The Bitter Tears of Petra von Kant* is, initially, all style, the pleasure dome-apartment of the heroine a theatrical forum for her theorising on life and love, until the mundane matters of doubt, jealousy and betrayal gradually trickle in to give the lie to the whole baroque edifice. Both films are explicitly symbolic in structure. . . . [The] subject of the film might almost be the steady accumulation and then the gradual dismantling of Petra's style. . . . Fassbinder choreographs the comic-tragic course of Petra's *mauvaise foi* with a sureness only occasionally blemished by a dead moment or an awkward movement from his players, and achieves a greater self-suf-

ficiency of style than in *Fear Eats the Soul*. In this etiolated atmosphere, props and lighting assume a rich and perverse significance. . . . Hollywood idioms percolate the emotional tone of the film, not only in the Sternberg lighting but in Petra's early dictation of a letter to a designer called Mankiewicz (''Mankiewicz plus Brecht'' was the *Image et Son* tag for *Petra*), hinting at the similarly problematic aspects of love and commitment in *Letter to Three Wives*. And like the paintings scattered through *Fear Eats the Soul,* both identifying and satirising their milieux, a principal icon here is the enormous mural covering one wall, with its classical nudes in easy, bacchanalian love-play mockingly overlooking the attenuated games of Petra's ménage, but also collaborating with the androgynous (not to say drag) appearance of some of the players to soften the strictly lesbian outlines of the relationships and intimate some universal experiences of passion unrequited or simply too idiosyncratic to be long sustained. (p. 100)

> *Richard Combs, ''Feature Films: 'Die Bitteren Tränen der Petra von Kant' ('The Bitter Tears of Petra von Kant'),'' in* Monthly Film Bulletin *(copyright © The British Film Institute, 1975), Vol. 42, No. 496, May, 1975, pp. 99-100.*

**GEORGE LELLIS**

[*The Merchant of Four Seasons*'s] biggest *coup* is that our feelings for the man are never really for him personally—he is ugly and unsympathetic throughout. The film remains outside of him, something that gives us, in the final analysis, more of a portrait of the world that made him than one of the man himself. And it is a cold, unfeeling world. That Hans Epp is fundamentally unloved is established from the picture's first frame, when he comes home from the Foreign Legion and his mother tells him it's too bad all the *good* ones die in wars and those like him remain; but the rest of the work portrays a society in which all potentially meaningful things are ritualized into mechanism. . . . As an attack on society, *The Merchant of Four Seasons* is diffuse, to say the least, but it is in this diffusion that it achieves most of its power, and its ultimate, paradoxical lucidity.

One cannot look at the film without thinking of Brecht. Events in it are never quite believable as naturalism, and their blunt portrayal, particularly early in the work, mixed with the script's stilted, haltingly wordy dialogue, clearly suggest that distancing is its stylistic aim. . . . A story which some ten or twenty years ago would have been presented as a subjective, solipsistic study of a suicide here becomes a vision of German life which implies throughout that such an existence must change. The film calls out for a committed response not only because we know that Fassbinder is an engaged film-maker, but also because it allows us no other way to respond. *Merchant of Four Seasons* treats a psychological subject, but denies the audience all of its conventional psychological responses. (pp. 18-19)

*The Merchant of Four Seasons* is often a beautiful film to look at, but one never can (as with, let us say, Fellini or Antonioni or even Godard) separate its physical beauty from its moral message. (p. 19)

[*The Merchant of Four Seasons* works] on two levels, seeking to find the logic in emotions and the emotion in logic, the place of politics in the personality, the personal need for political change. (p. 20)

> *George Lellis, ''Retreat from Romanticism: Two Films from the Seventies,'' in* Film Quarterly *(copyright*

*1975 by The Regents of the University of California; reprinted by permission of the University of California Press), Vol. XXVIII, No. 4, Summer, 1975, pp. 16-20.\**

**TONY RAYNS**

The most striking difference between [*The Merchant of Four Seasons*] and earlier Fassbinder movies is the immense gain in simplicity and clarity, qualities about which there is nothing deceptive. As the chronicle of a man whose dreams and aspirations are systematically denied him by his petit bourgeois environment, *Merchant* could hardly be more straightforward: its linear narrative . . . is a step-by-loaded-step catalogue of the betrayals and humiliations that Hans suffers, while occasional fragmentary, dream-like flashbacks serve to expose the roots of his oppression. The other main change is the nature of the *mise en scène;* the Godardian unpredictability and genre permutations of the earlier films are replaced by a kind of hypernaturalism, still very stylised in its deployment of the actors and locations and in its use of dialogue, but absolutely keyed to mundane realities. . . . The fascinating tension between this wish for a 'transparency' of style and the formal innovations intrinsic to the process of realising it—a tension that later forms the very substance of movies like *Martha* and *Effi Briest*—is here kept very much in check. *Merchant* consequently achieves an extraordinary reading of 'ordinary' events, and does so with apparently effortless ease. . . . The film's theme is double-edged. The sympathetic portrayal of Hans' suffering is intensified by the character's own inarticulateness; Fassbinder takes pleasure in speaking 'for' a man incapable of doing so himself, just as Petra von Kant's theatrical outpourings of grief spell out emotional responses that are commonly repressed or understated. At the same time, though, Hans' eminently understandable withdrawal into resentful silence tends to redirect attention the more strongly on to the other characters, whose actions and attitudes caused his plight, and as it proceeds the film develops an extremely thorough-going critique of petit bourgeois society in terms much less equivocal than, say, Chabrol's. Fassbinder sharpens his critique by locating it historically. . . . [The] inexorable quality of the exposition is sometimes blackly humorous in the manner of later Fassbinder, without in any way compromising the director's commitment to his stance. . . . *Merchant of Four Seasons* stands up strongly as an all-but-exemplary product of Fassbinder's theory of political film. And although it evidences a much greater authorial control than many of its predecessors, a major factor contributing to its success is the admirably unified ensemble playing. (pp. 175-76)

*Tony Rayns, "Feature Films: 'Der Händler der vier Jahreszeiten' ('The Merchant of Four Seasons'),"* in Monthly Film Bulletin *(copyright © The British Film Institute, 1975), Vol. 42, No. 499, August, 1975, pp. 175-76.*

**JONATHAN ROSENBAUM**

[Fassbinder] has been devoted to social reform and the perpetuation (through updating) of the dominant codes of narrative cinema. Far from being "radical" or "subversive", as has often been claimed, his cinema is liberal in the best and most hallowed sense of the word. . . . In *Faustrecht der Freiheit* [*Fox*]—working with narrative elements traceable back to [Erich von] Stroheim and von Sternberg as well as Sirk—he is relating a fable of class exploitation within a homosexual milieu

that is rather obvious and predictable in overall design, but clever and nuanced in many of its individual details. The cultural snobbery of Eugen, his parents and his friends is underlined far past the point of necessity or plausibility (leading to a howler when his mother describes seeing the "Firebird Suite" at the opera), and some of the eventual cruelties of the clan similarly seem too clearly designed to ram home a thesis. But on the other hand, the actual movement of the money is delineated with refreshing sharpness. . . . Gullible from the word go and scarcely the master of a destiny that seems sealed before the end of the first reel (with the camera stationed at a low angle *before* he trips and falls near a lottery counter), Fox is a sentimental victim of no mean proportions, and Fassbinder's casting of himself in the part against type has the advantage of making the role somewhat more palatable: an unromantic hero if ever there was one . . . , he brings some rudimentary counterpoint to the fable through the sheer unwholesomeness of his appearance. . . . [The] sinister Max finally comes to seem a much closer surrogate for the writer-director than the figure of Fox himself.

*Jonathan Rosenbaum, "Feature Films: 'Faustrecht der Freiheit' ('Fox'),"* in Monthly Film Bulletin *(copyright © The British Film Institute, 1976), Vol. 43, No. 504, January, 1976, p. 6.*

**PENELOPE GILLIATT**

["**The Bitter Tears of Petra von Kant**"] is a lucid, beautiful work of innovation which hides its fondness for its characters under a cloak of august formalism. One remembers at the end that the dedication reads, "A case history of one who here became Marlene." Marlene is an apparently minor character who never speaks—of the six women in the film, she is the mute—but the story, in recall, is about the effect of its events on her sensibility. It is typical of the ricochet movement of Fassbinder's films that at the time we should regard her only as a witness. (p. 264)

There are fibre-glass figures and costume drawings everywhere in the working part of the room. We are watching a woman who is almost suffocated by stylishness, surrounded by copies of herself. Everything is ersatz. (p. 265)

Yet, all the time, this creation of perfect bones and mascara, seeking to control everything around her, has very little mastery, which is one of the abiding and passionate themes of Fassbinder's apparently unemotional works. The same idea runs through "**Fox and His Friends.**" . . . In all the sumptuous sophistication of both Petra's and Fox's experiences, there is much pain, much innocence. Just as Fox is robbed of his fortune by tutelage in good living, so Petra is tormented in her fortunate world of a room, furnished with a copy of a great painting and bald-headed, long-necked mannequins. (p. 266)

Fassbinder's films ache, in spite of their apparent formalism. On the face of it, "**Petra**" is a theatrical film. Six women, no men; five acts, separated by change of dress; no change of scenery, much change of mood. The set moves from bed to corridor to carpet. In one of the final episodes, when Petra is sprawled on the floor with the telephone, the pile carpet becomes a field of razed earth.

Fassbinder shoots in very long takes. The camera seldom moves. We become obsessed with the contradiction of composed and worldly faces uttering primitive anguish. . . . Everything is terse and minimal. Noun and verb. Fassbinder is concerned here with the sort of love that rests in contest. So his real heroine is not Petra, the victimizer turned victim, but her silent assistant, who has been tortured by the sight of sadistic love's punishments.

This is a political film, as Fassbinder's always are, as well as a sage film about love. Petra believes that what she has earned she can break. In her agony of longing for Karin, the lower-class model who has made a reputation out of working for her and then found it easy to leave her, she stamps on a tray laid with an expensive tea set. All fragments. But she is only breaking a talisman of her elegant ambitions: it is no triumph, because she is not destroying her passion for Karin. The passion is born of capitalism, Fassbinder implies, for Petra still truly believes that she paid for Karin by giving her the benefit of her greater talent and income, constituting a superiority of class in the tournament. The changeover of power is shown by Fassbinder with a curtness veiling sympathy. The dialogue is sharp in a stylized set of scenes. It is often the case that extreme stylization covers extreme pity. This is so of **"The Bitter Tears of Petra von Kant."** (pp. 267-68)

> *Penelope Gilliatt, "Exile" (originally published as "Fassbinder," in* The New Yorker, *Vol. LII, No. 17, June 14, 1976), in her* Three-Quarter Face: Reports & Reflections *(reprinted by permission of Coward, McCann & Geoghegan, Inc.; copyright © 1980 by Penelope Gilliatt), Coward, McCann & Geoghegan, 1980, pp. 235-82.\**

## STANLEY KAUFFMANN

[The] trouble with [*The Bitter Tears of Petra von Kant*] is that it equates methods with powers. One pitfall in latterday film-making is the gross overestimate of certain filmic procedures as symbology. Fassbinder thinks he can make a film of his stage play by thickly impasting some of those procedures. The confinement to one room, the slow-moving camera are assumed to create depth—partly on the ground that they contravene conventional commercial procedures. To this, Fassbinder adds some obviously arty Franco-German apparatus: the arbitrarily silent "slave," a lot of unclothed female dressmaker's dummies, a frontally naked male in a huge painting (the only male in the film). All this is facile, and it's distracting because its glibness diverts us to an awareness of Fassbinder's status-hunger. The film world still—*still,* after the best work of Antonioni and Bresson and Bergman and Ozu has shown us how cinema metaphors can be fulfilled—turns over on its back like a puppy when scratched if a director merely *employs* some cinematic imagery. It's like calling a poet fine merely because he employs figures of speech. Fassbinder is in control, intelligently, of what he's doing; but after all the controlling is done, he hasn't plumbed very far. (p. 28)

> *Stanley Kauffmann, "Sex and Murder" (reprinted by permission of Brandt & Brandt Literary Agents, Inc.; copyright © 1976 by Stanley Kauffmann), in* The New Republic, *Vol. 174, No. 28, July 17, 1976, pp. 28-9.\**

## PAUL THOMAS

Rainer Werner Fassbinder is a man who knows how to hate. More to the point—but very much connected with it—Fassbinder's films may have extended the language and method of film more than those of any young film-maker of his generation. (p. 2)

Melodramatic elements abound in Fassbinder's films. Why should Ali be stricken with the "immigrant's disease" at the end of *Fear Eats the Soul* just as Emmy so movingly forgives and accepts him? Why does *Wildwechsel* . . . need the *coup de grâce* of Hanni's being told by the gynecologist . . . that her baby was born dead and deformed? It's arguable that the remarkable thing is the extent to which Fassbinder gets away with hitting home in this fashion; but it would be hard to argue that Fassbinder is not laying it on too thickly when he has Hanni, the sexually precocious child, react to the news by playing hopscotch in the courtroom corridor. Fassbinder would presumably not deny that such moments in his films (and there is no shortage of them) are extreme: he simply would not admit this as *criticism*. (p. 5)

Fassbinder's program is not an easily inviting one. It asks us to rethink the relation between film and audience, to reconsider the ways in which film *can,* in fact, raise consciousness. Fassbinder has no time for Eisenstein; making the masses into an epic hero does not break with the epic-heroic mode, and by the same token devalues the individual qualities that go to make up mass action. But these individual qualities are very much Fassbinder's stock in trade. He is, in general, uninterested in the "great," the notable, the distinguished. . . . (pp. 6-7)

If there is a single spoken line in his films that sums up his animus against this society, it is in *Fox* when an upper-class character says, in passing, of a lower-class character, "People like that are too crude to be in despair." On the contrary, says Fassbinder, one cannot be "too crude" to have feelings, for there is nothing refined or exalted about feelings, but only about the way some people look at other people. (p. 7)

[*Why Does Herr R. Run Amok?*] is all too obviously a film in which every color, every shade, every tone, every filter is calculated with exquisite care to create, enhance, and sustain what becomes an unbearable paranoia, in which the sheer weight of the ordinary, the stream of meaningless verbiage, makes the eventual "senseless" murder something of a relief. *Herr R.* is a minor masterpiece because of the tension of the everyday it presents; it spins out this tension in a series of sequences in which screen time and elapsed time are one. At the same time, it's not at all sensational; the hysteria it expresses consists in the drabness and the stultifying boredom Fassbinder has the effrontery to present, flatly and directly. . . .

*Herr R.* stands out from Fassbinder's previous output by *not* being a succession of set-pieces, by not being punctuated by visual effects, but a film sustained and developed by carefully considered visual means. . . . Yet Fassbinder's evident desire to accentuate reality by means of an extreme presentation of its contours eventually seemed to him to be politically counter-productive. . . . (p. 10)

[*The Bitter Tears of Petra von Kant*] is self-consciously "artificial," the acting proto-artificial; it is very much a chamber-film, of people who choose to present to the world versions of themselves, a film of personas and personages. The sequences correspond to act divisions in a play, yet the film itself is not Fassbinder's most theatrical film at all; it deals with a woman who habitually puts herself in theatrical situations. (p. 13)

[In *Effi Briest*, Fassbinder's] anger at a society that would permit such muted atrocities is contained only by the requirements of a controlled form. The stylization of the film, as in *Petra von Kant,* mirrors the stylization of the characters, their emotional responses, and the stylization of the society they live in and make up. . . .

[The] film is spare, attenuated; there are short, truncated sequences, often ending in semi-stills of one of the characters; there are fades in and out of white; there are titles and voice-over narrations. Fassbinder, in an almost Bressonian manner, leaves out crucial scenes (Effi's marriage, the childbirth) because it is the *process,* the formality, the tight-lippedness of the characters that matter more than the incidents that express them. . . .

Fassbinder here, and in all his best films, is in full control of his faculties as a director, taking full cognizance of where his ideas about film direction may lead. All his films are memorable, in a distinct and unsettling way; shots and sequences have a luminosity and vividness, actors and personages a presence, that make an ineradicable impression. (p. 15)

Fassbinder is, above all else, a director of *impact;* in order not to be pushed under by the weight of an unbearable reality, he aims to strike back at this reality, and this defiance explains his anger and his furious productivity alike. (p. 16)

Fassbinder's films are very much the kind of films we cannot imagine being made by anyone else; he has attempted, and is still constantly attempting, to reconcile the way he stamps them with an approach which is distinctively his own with the demands of revolutionary art as he sees them. . . .

Fassbinder, instead of *having* a message, is concerned to *pitch* a message, to generate responses among his audience (and his actors), responses they can live out and act upon. If film cannot reflect reality in any simplistic sense, it *can* portray the inhuman consequences of the social mechanism. This means we must recognize that film is not a reflective device but a transformative agency. Fassbinder has thus been stubbornly working to liberate not only the heads of his audience but the politically committed cinema itself. (p. 17)

*Paul Thomas, "Fassbinder: The Poetry of the Inarticulate," in* Film Quarterly *(copyright 1977 by The Regents of the University of California; reprinted by permission of the University of California Press), Vol. XXX, No. 2, Winter, 1976-77, pp. 2-17.*

**THOMAS ELSAESSER**

At no point during his career has Fassbinder renounced the autobiographical element in his films. His self-criticism does not affect the material but rather the manner of its presentation. The central experience—one might go so far as to call it the trauma that motivates his productivity—is emotional exploitation. His films are fictionalised, dramatised, occasionally didactic versions of what it means to live within power structures and dependencies that are all but completely internalised, and as such apparently removed from any possibility of change or development.

Repetition, reiteration therefore has a particularly important function in his work, on the thematic as well as the formal level. The films reproduce human relations 'as they are', while constantly retracing the contours of a circularity in the utopian hope of finding a way out at the weakest point. . . . As far as the films are concerned, they attempt to prove, with varying degrees of conviction, that the personal predicament has a wider symptomatic significance. And if Fassbinder's cinema shows any kind of progression in this respect, it is not in the way that his characters perceive escapes from the sado-mas-

ochistic bind, but in the remarkable inventiveness he shows, his concrete penetration of a contemporary social reality when orchestrating the theme across different human situations. (pp. 25-6)

From the many emotional 'languages' that the commercial cinema has evolved, Fassbinder makes virtually no use of suspense, comedy or horror. His films have been described as sentimental, mawkish, moving between pathos and bathos, and it is true that he seems to concentrate rather exclusively on the varieties of pathos, understood as the emotional rhetoric of bourgeois tragedy and melodrama. The forms that this pathos takes, strident, with ironic overtones, or low-key, as in *Effi Briest,* might tempt one to think of it as personal, a kind of direct translation of what Fassbinder 'feels' about the world. On the other hand, it might well be a matter of translating his chosen theme: what romantic or domestic melodrama connotes in an unambiguous way is the presence of subjectivity in the discourse, a necessary precondition for an audience to feel affected by the victimisation in his films. However, the general basis on which this communication takes place—a certain diffuse emotionality, a mixture of nostalgia and regret, of operatic sentimentality and a somewhat cloying intensity—is not peculiar to Fassbinder. . . .

[The] problem as it emerges from the films, is how to articulate threatening and aggressive emotional states (moments of betrayal, deception, manipulation, emotional cruelty, but also equally 'aggressive' manifestations of unconditional love, self-sacrifice, exuberance) in aesthetic forms that make them tolerated, acceptable. Fassbinder has ventured out into regions of extremes, where the directness of the emotional assault has to be mediated, and the spectator's susceptibility managed, channelled via the mechanics of identification and distanciation. (p. 28)

Fassbinder is right; there is something masturbatory about [his early] films, even if the shoddiness of the decor and the tinsel glamour of the actresses manages to moralise the attitude of self-satisfaction into a critical stance. Not only is the recurring topos of inadequacy the explicit sign of that ambition to make a 'real' Hollywood movie, of which the film one is watching is the touching, pathetic, melancholy echo, but the discontinuity which inadequacy implies also places the king-size dreams of the characters—defiantly asserted against an unresponsive environment—as ambitions fated with ludicrous inevitability to fizzle out ignominiously. The films thus reflect a twofold frustration: an imagination at second-hand is further foiled at the level of performance, and Fassbinder shows himself a realist with critical intentions only insofar as these are documents, records of what one might call emotional starvation fantasies. . . .

The dialectics of escapism and realism, deeply embedded in the fabric of the American action film, are pulled apart by Fassbinder's gangster films. Voyeuristic projection is allowed to float dangerously out of its unconscious self-evidence (where an autonomous fictional spectacle normally keeps such impulses fixated), and emerges disjointedly as the unpleasant perception of the film as an artefact, or the exaggerated gesture of self-conscious make-believe: we begin to worry whether the actors themselves can keep up the pretence. This discrepancy, forced to the point of physical discomfort in films like *The American Soldier* and *Whity,* a discrepancy between awkwardness and beauty, lends itself to an ambiguous dialogue about the cinema itself, its manipulative images and its rhetoric of effect. But it also represents a provisional formulation of Fassbinder's moral theme, for he everywhere makes palpable—whether deliberately or by default—the sometimes terrifying and often grotesque distance between the subjective *mise en scène* of the characters and the objective *mise en scène* of the camera. . . . (p. 29)

What is ambiguous and at the same time attractive about Fassbinder's early protagonists is that the degradation of their imaginative-emotional language (their imitations of tough guy or femme fatale mannerisms) and the degradation of their moral and social environment (they are failures, marginals, 'small fry') seem to cancel each other out, to create a precarious, momentary dignity: the typical commitment of Fassbinder's humanism. (p. 30)

Fassbinder since [*The Merchant of Four Seasons*] has moved from an essentially self-conscious form of distanciation . . . to a more straightfaced psychological and emotional realism. (p. 31)

The typical situation in a Fassbinder film, where a mother/father, wife/husband or friend/colleague make demands on the hero/heroine that are sadistic, or betray, deceive or abandon him/her is dramatised in such a way that these dominating figures, from whom there is objectively or subjectively no escape, also have their reasons, are sometimes well-meaning or possess complex motives over not all of which they have control (*Merchant of Four Seasons, Wildwechsel, Fear Eats the Soul, Martha, Fear of Fear*). The hero, by contrast, is given a moral/emotional innocence that almost makes him the holy fool in a Dostoievskian world of universal prostitution. His simple-mindedness, his obstinacy in hanging on to simple truths and direct feelings become a form of higher wisdom, the gesture that unmasks the stupidity of self-interest, prejudice and oppression. Evil then appears depersonalised, as somehow inherent in the social system as a whole. What the films ultimately appeal to is solidarity between victims. (pp. 31-2)

Fassbinder's melodramas can and do make the very important distinctions between the different levels of individual motivation, between private morality and class morality, between human impulses and ideological impulses. It is by these disjunctions and discontinuities that Fassbinder develops his pathos, and through it he creates the vacuum in which social and psychological pressures become visible as they distort natural instincts and needs into manifestations of evil. But insofar as these pressures and forces cannot be named or analysed other than by pointing to their absence from the characters' consciousness, the purely inter-personal drama tends to imply that to understand is to forgive. . . .

[However, *Fox* and *Mother Küsters' Trip to Heaven*] seem to indicate that Fassbinder himself is having doubts: they show an even more definite parti-pris for the hero/heroine, and they are less scrupulous about balancing the other characters' points of view. The spectrum of identification becomes narrower, and with it perhaps more radical. The villains are more like villains, their portrayal is elliptical to the point of parody. For that reason, these films are less convincing aesthetically, even though the director's point of view becomes clearer. That a certain moral ambiguity should be directly proportional to aesthetic persuasiveness seems to suggest that the path between making committed, critical cinema and being 'popular' within a basically bourgeois art form is a narrow one. (p. 32)

Fassbinder's notion of realism is . . . remarkable not least for its frank admission of the habitual functions of escapist entertainment: encouraging daydreams, private fantasies, wish fulfilment . . . except that he talks about liberation and utopia rather than escape.

More important than whether the films actually permit an audience to dream their own better future is that Fassbinder, in his search for an unprovocative realism that makes audience identification possible, has discovered for the German cinema the importance of being artificial in order to appear realistic. . . .

Where the 'young' German film of the Sixties produced at best a flat, black-and-white naturalism, Fassbinder's carefully composed colour schemes, his selection of the typical detail available for an unobtrusive symbolism without being pressed into it, represent the kind of heightened realism that makes the traditionally closed world of the melodrama take on topicality, even where it wants to be existentially timeless. (p. 33)

His greatest talent as a story-teller lies perhaps in the way he can give his material the shape of an apparently inescapable, fatal logic. This logic may be false somewhere: it is after all the overwhelming chain of miseries, humiliations and defeats seen from the point of view of the eternal victim, in a world where even the oppressors are shown to be victims. It almost amounts to a form of apologetics for leaving things as they are. But what his critics have been quick to spot as a mystification, the endless litany of victimisation, accompanied by a lugubrious celebration of despair ('the gesture of impotence'), is in another sense the craftsman's delight in creating ever more perfectly constructed vicious circles. In this case, the films are autobiographical in a very straightforward manner: they translate into fictional terms and formal configurations the personal experience of film-making. . . . Fassbinder wants to articulate a message of utopian liberation while being himself in chains. The realism of such a cinema, and probably its radicalism, cannot be in its overt social criticism alone, important though this may be, but in the contradictions it sustains when expressing in formal terms the conditions of its existence. The films themselves offer no way out: the more Fassbinder courts his public by dramatising the agonies of social and emotional victims, the more his cinema is in danger of becoming formalistic, static inside his own perfected dramaturgy. So far he has treated his theme as a tragedy—which it is; to break the deadlock of too facile a pessimism and still make a cinema of enlightenment for a mass audience, he may have to see it also as a comedy. In the meantime, the fact that such a cinema continues to exist is Fassbinder's real achievement, and the implicit challenge that makes his work political. (pp. 35-6)

> *Thomas Elsaesser, "A Cinema of Vicious Circles"*
> *(copyright © Thomas Elsaesser), in* Fassbinder, *edited by Tony Rayns, British Film Institute, 1976, pp. 24-36.*

### VINCENT KLING

[Fassbinder's characters] start at a point of freedom from external constraints far beyond any [Sirk's] characters could have imagined, but they are every bit as miserable. They almost always have more than enough money to do whatever they want or to travel wherever they please; they often have jobs that they quite enjoy; they live in a society that does not care about their political convictions, religious beliefs or sexual orientations. Even so, they are no more free than the title character of *Effi Briest,* who is driven to her death by the strict codes of militaristic, imperialistic, censorious Prussian upper-class society at the end of the nineteenth century. Thinking about the implications of Fassbinder's work obliges us to become aware of how little times have changed, or at least of how relatively little what we call the times has to do with questions of human freedom. . . . Fassbinder's "liberated" people yearn to be normal and fully conventional, as they compulsively put aside their true individuality, which modern society would theoretically permit them to exercise, in favor of imitating some very restrictive pattern of deadly middle-class behavior learned early in life. More than ever, they assent to the very values and postulates from which they think they would like to break away.

Heads they lose, tails they lose: when Fassbinder's characters grasp the courage to assert their human freedom in an uncompromising way, they achieve neither happiness nor even reasonable contentment. However much external conditions appear to them as doors to freedom, the doors open only onto more insidious traps. On the other hand, as soon as the characters attempt a gradual or tactful method of getting what they want, they reveal their essential helplessness by giving way to pressures and adversities from their surroundings in a manner sufficiently out of proportion with the cause to expose some prior and long-standing weakness. (pp. 66-7)

In lieu of showing immediate outer causes of his characters' guilt and frustration, Fassbinder gives hints, but no more, that unresolved childhood conflicts may be at the roots of the disturbances. He does not develop the study of origins in any systematic way, probably because he is more interested in their effects than their causes, and when he gives them fleeting treatment, he often casts them in the form of tedious verbal motifs all the more convincing as illustrations of weakness for being lachrymose and sentimental. Fassbinder has a gift for showing the hypnotic power of self-pitying platitudes. (p. 68)

Fassbinder's visuals, decors and settings help reveal the absence of freedom, reinforcing the viewer's awareness that the characters are inexorably trapped. Effi Briest is constantly being seen through doorways, framed in the limits of domesticity; the camera rarely opens out to any appreciable distance when it is on her. Though sartorially apt for her time, the veils on her hats convey to the contemporary viewer a feeling of forced concealment. (p. 69)

For all the undeniable unity, coherence, and grasp of technique that Fassbinder demonstrates in his films, his artistry sometimes remains questionable in the viewer's mind. . . . [Admiring] critics are now discussing some aspects of Fassbinder's films as manifestations of great artistic control, as highly disciplined techniques for subtly creating alienation and distancing, when they may in fact be manifestations of mere impatient sloppiness. (p. 71)

Despite the number of films already to his credit, it is much too soon in the development of Fassbinder's craft to make a definite judgment about his technical ability. Surely it is not critically sound to begin with the assumption that everything about his work is outstanding and then justify as special inspirations moments that would be considered lapses in any other director. It may indeed be that Fassbinder is leaning very much toward structuralist method, attempting to make the medium part of the message by using technical discrepancies and incongruities for distancing and for *Verfremdung*, but no one has yet explained this in detail. . . . On the other hand, Fassbinder is clearly not a prisoner of his occasional slovenliness, or at least not inevitably so. (pp. 71-2)

His increasing popularity accords well with Fassbinder's self-portrait as the artless and naive filmmaker driven on by the confessional urge. What the self-portrait fails to include is any reference to a subtle and persistent technique of allusion, which reveals in Fassbinder and demands from his viewers a great deal of knowledge about literature and film.

If these allusions are missed, the theme is not lost. To the viewer who can catch some of them, however, Fassbinder seems either more or less of an artist (depending on the viewer's disposition) than he would seem without them—more because they raise the particular story line to a universal level by recalling other and similar fates, or less because they often appear to be short-cuts designed to avoid working out the story elements fully in their own terms. (p. 72)

> *Vincent Kling, "A Second Gold Age? West German Cinema and One of Its Directors," in* Chicago Review *(reprinted by permission of* Chicago Review; *copyright © 1977 by* Chicago Review*), Vol. 28, No. 3, Winter, 1977, pp. 59-74.*

### JOHN SIMON

[Fassbinder] turns out movies the way other people shed dandruff, and is generally considered the new Godard or, at the very least, the *Wunderkind* of the German cinema. The main influences on him would seem to be Brecht and Warhol, the unendurably static Jean-Marie Straub and the souped-up second-rate American action directors, which shows that, if nothing else, he is catholic to the point of self-contradiction. . . .

An aura of arrogance is everywhere, as if Fassbinder were saying, "I can slap movies together as fast and loose as I wish because I am a *Wunderkind*." The procedure, I am afraid, makes him into a bit of *Blunderkind*. He turns out, as I see it, two kinds of movies: bad ones and not-so-bad ones. [*Mother Küsters Goes to Heaven*] is one of the latter. . . .

It is a perfectly serviceable story, but Fassbinder develops it with his customary mixture of heavy underscoring and cavalier offhandedness. Occasionally there is some satiric bite, but more often the film contents itself with facile and predictable observations, which the director now shoots with greater assurance than before, but still without particular distinction. Here the ending happens to be happy; it could just as easily have been otherwise. (p. 70)

> *John Simon, "The Unimportance of Being Ernest," in* New York *Magazine (copyright © 1977 by News Group Publications, Inc.; reprinted with the permission of* New York *Magazine), Vol. 10, No. 11, March 14, 1977, pp. 69-70.\**

### PENELOPE GILLIATT

["**Mother Küsters Goes to Heaven**"] is like Brecht's plays and poems in declining open sensibility, but all the same its coinage is care for people, with a guttersnipe wit about the self-deceptions that slaughter intent. . . . The film has a melodramatic plot, but it is no melodrama. Any work of fiction is beyond melodrama when its logic is clear and large enough. The picture tells us that rhetoric is no escape; that a guru-disciple relationship between sexes or classes is damned; that primitivism of expression—losing one's mind, having a tantrum, using emotional bribery—makes savages of us all; that, since no film artist would hand you the keys to character, the only thing to watch is outward conduct. Mother Küsters does not, of course, go to heaven, as the title bitterly states. But she has made the best choice with her sausage and dumplings, and to have choice is, indeed, a sort of heaven on earth. The Communists were not the answer: they were hilariously hemmed in by their inherited classiness, and someone less lonely than Mother Küsters would have broken down their well-bred walls to find out what they really felt. The anarchist was not the answer, either: he seemed made for the oddly baleful fête champêtre of the magazine-office sit-in. And the pugnacious pregnancy of Mother Küsters' daughter-in-law was certainly not the answer: no new way of life was going to be born from that. The film, like Fassbinder's **"The Bitter Tears of Petra von Kant,"** has sins of hypocrisy on its mind: play-acted phone calls, plagiarized sensitivity. Fassbinder's style paradoxically makes an ideal of theatricality rather than of naturalism. In his attitude toward his characters, he is like a burglarious child shaking a piggy bank to get out the hoard: rattling them upside down and from side to side to try to get the truth out of them. (pp. 272-73)

*Penelope Gilliatt, "Exile" (originally published as "No Sadness that Art Cannot Quell," in* The New Yorker, *Vol. LIII, No. 6, March 28, 1977), in her* Three-Quarter Face: Reports & Reflections *(reprinted by permission of Coward, McCann & Geoghegan, Inc.; copyright © 1980 by Penelope Gilliatt), Coward, McCann & Geoghegan, 1980, pp. 235-82.\**

## VINCENT CANBY

[The characters in **"Katzelmacher"** are lower middle-class lay-abouts who] sit on—or lean against—the railing outside a Munich apartment house in various positions of boredom. They bicker. They brood. Mostly they just stare into space, lined up all in a row like the crows in Hitchcock's "The Birds." . . .

[The] characters, with the possible exception of Jorgos . . . , who never says much, are either slobs or dimwitted, and though they are totally self-absorbed and given to parroting clichés, they are sometimes capable of the unexpected gesture as when Marie decides to leave Erich for Jorgos. . . .

The static camera, the exaggerated mannerisms of the actors, the jump-cuts, the repeated themes and variations of scenes, all recall Godard, but the major influence on the film appears to be Mr. Fassbinder's early work in the theater.

The screenplay, in fact, is an adaptation of a Fassbinder play, but having seen the film twice I find it difficult to imagine it as anything except an extraordinarily stylish film. It's quite unlike anything else I've seen. . . .

**"Katzelmacher"** is scathing about the postwar German economic boom that has, of course, been so kind to the film maker himself. More importantly the film is an early glimpse of his dazzling talent. . . .

*Vincent Canby, "'Katzelmacher'," in* The New York Times *(© 1977 by The New York Times Company; reprinted by permission), June 4, 1977 (and reprinted in* The New York Times Film Reviews: 1977-1978, *The New York Times Company & Arno Press, 1979, p. 62).*

## VINCENT CANBY

Although **"Gods of the Plague"** is described as a sequel to **"Love Is Colder Than Death,"** . . . it makes an appropriate companion piece to **"The American Soldier,"** a comically dead-panned contemplation of American gangster films of the 30's

and 40's. Where **"The American Soldier"** comes close to parody, though, **"Gods of the Plague"** is absolutely straight, which is not to say that it's realistic or that its narrative is important for itself. . . .

**"Gods of the Plague"** is the quintessential American gangster film if the quintessential American gangster film had been adapted and updated to accommodate a bunch of small-time Munich hoods for whom the holdup of a rather ordinary suburban supermarket is "the big job." If **"The American Soldier"** is about movies, **"Gods of the Plague"** is one of the movies it's about. . . .

[Franz's] joylessness is profound, and it's consistent with his vision of a world in which everyone is an inmate.

The plot of **"Gods of the Plague"** is not quite as complex as that of [Howard Hawks's] "The Big Sleep," but it helps to have some program notes, because Mr. Fassbinder, aping Franz's taciturnity, doesn't waste time on explanations. . . .

It's a world of perpetual gray, of chance meetings, faithlessness, revenge, informers and crooked cops. People talk but they don't communicate. Someone says something and there's a 10-second delay before there's any response, as if the person spoken to felt that if he waited long enough there'd be no reason to answer. Everyone is mannered, even Franz's loony mom, who is not unlike the mom in **"The American Soldier."** Occasionally it recalls Jean-Luc Godard's "Breathless," but where Mr. Godard's characters have dreams, Mr. Fassbinder's have been sentenced to life imprisonment and know it.

**"Gods of the Plague"** is the work of a very young man who has just discovered the secret pleasures of angst. (p. 65)

*Vincent Canby, "'Gods of the Plague'," in* The New York Times *(© 1977 by The New York Times Company; reprinted by permission), June 11, 1977 (and reprinted in* The New York Times Film Reviews: 1977-1978, *The New York Times Company & Arno Press, 1979, pp. 64-5).*

## STANLEY KAUFFMANN

[*Effi Briest*] is beautiful. It renders [Theodor Fontane's] book as fully and texturally as could be possible in 140 minutes, and it's a work in and of itself, intrinsically cinematic. What's more, it shows that Fassbinder is probably going to keep astonishing us. . . .

*Effi Briest* doesn't have the tragic dimensions of *Madame Bovary* or of Kate Chopin's *The Awakening* because Effi is much more a victim than a rebel, but her extramarital affair is fated from the start and so is her sorry finish. . . .

The fadeouts all through the picture constitute a visual theme. Every fade is to white, not black—a "burn to white," as the trade more properly puts it. These fadeouts convey a feeling of the age's worship of purity. . . . (p. 20)

Throughout the film the register of emotion is cool. Feelings are perfectly credible, but always *portrayed* rather than meant to move us. Perhaps Fassbinder wanted to "contain" the story, to keep it from seeming too purply; and/or it may have been to convey, as with the dying duellist, a sense of acceptance, of actors-in-life playing the roles to which fate and society have assigned them. (pp. 20-1)

And Fassbinder's handling of the actors' movements, his compositions, support this tone. Although he never strains realism, we realize more and more clearly that the realism is being delicately abstracted. . . .

So far there is no definable Fassbinder directorial style in the films I've seen. On the other hand I can think of no other director who could have made two such good films as *Jail Bait* and *Effi Briest* in two such disparate styles. Unsympathetically, one can call him eclectic. For me, he shows prodigious range. (p. 21)

*Stanley Kauffmann, "'Effi Briest'" (reprinted by permission of Brandt & Brandt Literary Agents, Inc.; copyright © 1977 by Stanley Kauffmann), in The New Republic, Vol. 176, No. 26, June 25, 1977, pp. 20-1.*

## PENELOPE GILLIATT

As with most of Fassbinder's films, [in **"Effi Briest"** the concern] is in the sophistry of the powerful; it is kin to his **"Chinese Roulette,"** a mysterious comedy of calculated mannerisms. (p. 278)

Fassbinder thinks a great deal about oppressed groups, including women. **"Effi Briest"** is his masterpiece. . . . [His Effi] is the victim of an education that makes girls beguiling and frivolous objects, and so leads inevitably to a whim on the part of society to inhibit them with taboos. Effi is not only intimidated by the ghost but also fearful of committing crimes against bourgeois society, and terrorized by the possibility of appearing to the respectable to be a tart. . . . Life is lived by a system of fear and loneliness. God is not supposed to be a comfort, or society to provide companions. Effi is a naturally congenial and lively being, but Bismarck's Prussia blanches her spirit. Fassbinder's film has to do with the monstrous dictates of others about her life. (pp. 279-80)

**"Effi Briest"** is a vivid story of the dousing of a tonic personality by manners, misleading expectations, misled hopes. It is a fiercely philosophical picture. . . . This magnificent, inquiring film, though it is an epic in its way, is no spectacle; it is, above all, a spyglass on our consciousnesses. Effi Briest knows very well that she was a child and then a mother without ever being a woman. The bourgeoisie is sleepwalking, says the film, but its victims are only too alert. (p. 280)

*Penelope Gilliatt, "Exile" (originally published as "A German Masterpiece," in The New Yorker, Vol. LIII, No. 19, June 27, 1977), in her Three-Quarter Face: Reports & Reflections (reprinted by permission of Coward, McCann & Geoghegan, Inc.; copyright © 1980 by Penelope Gilliatt), Coward, McCann & Geoghegan, 1980, pp. 235-82.\**

## BARBARA LEAMING

In the past Fassbinder's films have often been concerned with isolated people—with the outsider. In *Fear of Fear,* once again the central figure is set apart—she is a woman whose world is largely a world of family, a family that perceives her not only as an outsider, an intruder, but more importantly as someone "abnormal." For them, there is no question of what it is which constitutes the norm, for her sister-in-law explicitly and flatly states, "We are normal." They are the ones certainly who hold power; they are then the ones who determine the norm. Yet it is not even this outsider status within her husband's family which seems to mark the critical point in Margot's passage towards madness. There is a far more crucial sense of

strangeness, of alienation, which she feels: her failure to identify with her own image. And it is this alienation from image—and hence from role—which provides the central structuring device of Fassbinder's film. . . . The apartment is filled with square and oval mirrors, waiting to catch her glance, waiting—if she were "normal"—to confirm her identity, to confirm her sense of self. But for Margot this face in the mirror remains "other," remains an image and nothing more. . . . For us, however, in the audience, the recognition of the image has quite different effects. Seeing the image as an image, we, in turn, see the figure reflected in the glass and on the screen itself as an image as well. It is never a "natural," unchangeable reality which we face in Fassbinder's film. Rather it is always an image made by someone, and hence is subject to change. . . .

The mirror is not, of course, the only device serving to call attention to the status of images as images in the film. Fassbinder has further developed one of his earlier devices of framing within the frame of the screen. The interior frame which limits the material we see calls attention to the ordering and shaping of what we see; it calls attention to the "work" in the production of an image which is never posited as "natural." . . .

Unlike the filmmakers of the transparent classical realist cinema, Fassbinder uses frames within the frames and other devices to make it difficult for us to see. For example, Margot's sister-in-law functions as a kind of voyeur, watching Margot's every move out of the house through a window. It is significant that this window, the emblem for realist art, is not able to give direct access to the sights she watches below, for her view is obscured by a leafy tree or a curtain. She, like us, must look through something. (p. 14)

What happens when Fassbinder reveals his filmic frame of reference so clearly in this film and in so many other of his works is a question of crucial importance. When an image with which we are already familiar appears in a new context, something happens to the content of that image—our attention is shifted away from the signified to the signifier. Suddenly style becomes visible as style. In terms of his manipulation of the sign system, Fassbinder's work is similar to that of certain Pop artists. . . . In Fassbinder's films, materials exist in a realm of similar simultaneity: signifier becomes signified, yet echos in our memory as signifier still. The sign as convention has been revealed, its "naturalness" called into question. As in Pop Art, style has become "subject matter." The political significance of Fassbinder's interest in style as subject matter ought perhaps to be clarified, for in no sense is this an outmoded art for art's sake, a precious formalism. Rather, Fassbinder reveals to us an art made by people, an image made by people, a world made by people, a world, an image which is changeable by people. He reveals or demands active rather than passive spectators. People who transform. People who change.

*Fear of Fear,* then, is the politicization of style. Stylistic politics. As Jorge Luis Borges has said, "Each writer *creates* his precursors." In *Fear of Fear,* Fassbinder creates his precursors and thereby creates a politics. (p. 15)

*Barbara Leaming, "Rainer Werner Fassbinder's 'Fear of Fear'," in Take One (copyright © 1977 by Unicorn Publishing Corp.), Vol. 5, No. 10, July-August, 1977, pp. 14-15.*

## JANET MASLIN

If you have any doubt that there's such a thing as being too prolific, by all means go see Rainer Werner Fassbinder's **"Sa-**

tan's Brew.'' Mr. Fassbinder attempting physical, almost slapstick comedy, is Mr. Fassbinder at his least funny or enlightening; and the film, a kind of ''Father Knows Best'' on acid, showcases most of the director's worst qualities without leaving room for his best. Made in Germany early last year, this is an ice-cold work, and a stubborn and difficult one. The meager rewards it delivers are no match for the enormous energy it demands. (pp. 90-1)

Mr. Fassbinder can be both ironic and provocative when, as in **''Mother Kusters Goes To Heaven,''** his only successful comedy, he gently contrasts people's manners with their desires. But in **''Satan's Brew''** his blunt directorial style merely exaggerates the coarseness of his characters, and his humor turns stolid and didactic. . . .

For all its brutishness, though, **''Satan's Brew''** is finally not vulgar enough. The film's premise calls for both precision and abandon and, while an exaggerated, reference-laden meticulousness is Mr. Fassbinder's specialty, he seems incapable of doing anything very freely. His characters follow their animal instincts, but they do so in such a careful way they might as well be trained seals. None of them flouts convention with the kind of spontaneity or enthusiasm that might have lent real wit to the film's bloodless, brittle scheme. (p. 91)

> Janet Maslin, ''Call in the Family,'' in The New York Times (© 1977 by The New York Times Company; reprinted by permission), August 10, 1977 (and reprinted in The New York Times Film Reviews: 1977-1978, The New York Times Company & Arno Press, 1979, pp. 90-1).

## PENELOPE GILLIATT

[''Satan's Brew''] is a deliberate slap in the face. . . . [Walter Kranz] operates from the same feckless, uninhibited, unscrupulous, and unpredictable position that Fassbinder does in hurling this movie at us. The film creates an irritable weather all its own. People behave like cross morons, pretend to less intelligence than they actually have, move with the gestures of wooden puppets on tangled strings. (p. 62)

Fassbinder has made this shock-the-middlebrow picture go at a rattling pace, piling on evil comic details to see how much we will take. . . . Fassbinder forever pits words against physical expressiveness in this film, and throws sense out of joint. . . . Fassbinder has given himself the license to go haywire, perhaps in the interests of testing our endurance while we are having a sadomasochistic charade thrown at us like so much mud. Spattered and spluttering, we must be prepared to roll with the punch. Exceptional talent—and Fassbinder appears to possess it—often has moments of running amok. Better to go too far than not to move; and there may even be a compassionate nut of truth about the fate of the underendowed buried somewhere in this gaudy piece of provocation. (pp. 62-3)

> Penelope Gilliatt, ''Japanese Friends, a German Agent Provocateur,'' in The New Yorker (© 1977 by The New Yorker Magazine, Inc.), Vol. LIII, No. 26, August 15, 1977, pp. 60-3.*

## ANDREW SARRIS

[*Satan's Brew*] strikes me as a minor setback in [Fassbinder's] career. While it does not make me reconsider my previous appraisals, it does suggest certain limitations to his talent. What

he has attempted on this occasion is a form of savage screwball comedy, which descends irrationally and intentionally into depravity and disgust. . . .

Fassbinder quotes Artaud as his guide, but one is reminded instead of the Cocteau of *Les Enfants Terribles* and the Chabrol-Gegauff of *Les Cousins*. Unfortunately, Fassbinder is unable to furnish any behavioral conviction to his players, and, as if to admit this deficiency, he allows his plot to fizzle out in a fit of Pirandellian playfulness. These are not real bullets, as it turns out; only the wife's death in the hospital is absolutely irrevocable.

Regrettably, Fassbinder displays no flair for farce, and he is never really overtly funny. Indeed, Fassbinder should never actively seek humor but allow it to lurk in the background of his dark lyricism. The best moments in *Satan's Brew* are characterized by either self-mocking sentimentality (with gliding camera movements to match) or hard-edged sexuality (in which exposure is indecorous, if not indecent, because of its casual integration with the dramatic action). Fassbinder's cynicism about power on all levels of human intercourse finds ample expression here, but this cynicism is more nakedly schematic than it ever has been before.

> Andrew Sarris, ''A Summer Spate of Sugar and Spite'' (reprinted by permission of The Village Voice and the author; copyright © The Village Voice, Inc., 1977), in The Village Voice, Vol. XXII, No. 35, August 29, 1977, p. 45.*

## TOM ALLEN

[Although *Why Does Herr R. Run Amok?*] was made for German television, it is not on a par even with the *Visions* series on American Public Broadcasting, which gives young playwrights and filmmakers a forum. Fassbinder's exercise is more the equivalent of a loft production or an unpublished novel in the trunk. As I see Fassbinder's career in a spotty perspective, the film predates even his first tentative sparring with the aesthetic options of cinema, his so-called Sirkian conversion. . . .

[The film is] a case history of banality with each entry contributing to the construct of a seemingly complacent architectural draftsman. The everyday abrasions from his wife, son, boss, and neighbors are within the general norm. Kurt Raab is a stereotypic middle-class clerk who would be as much at home in Manhattan and Tokyo as in Berlin; and I don't believe that it would be fair to Fassbinder in this particular film to read into Raab's regimented social life a metaphor for fascist programming in contemporary German society. Actually, Kurt could be my cousin in East Elmhurst. *Why Does Herr R. Run Amok?* is a composite of such noncompelling familiarity.

> Tom Allen, ''A Fassbinder from the Trunk'' (reprinted by permission of The Village Voice and the author; copyright © The Village Voice, Inc., 1977), in The Village Voice, Vol. XXII, No. 47, November 21, 1977, p. 43.

## ROBERT HATCH

*Why Does Herr R. Run Amok?* is a clinical exercise designed to test how long a man can be expected to endure an existence that is, without relief, stale, flat and unprofitable. Herr R. is boring; worse than that, he suffers the capacity to be bored. . . .

On occasion, Herr R. thrusts feebly against the bladder of narcotic misery within which he is suspended. . . . But there is no heat to sustain these sparks of animation; they expire in sighs and silences. And so one day, when a neighbor is running on about her discovery of the techniques and apparel of skiing, the almost repellently soft and undemanding Herr R. picks up a lethally heavy candlestick. The feeling one gets from this denouement can scarcely be called catharsis, because what leads up to it is too inert to be called tragedy; but most viewers, I think, will find it a relief. *Why Does Herr R. Run Amok?* is an exhausting movie. . . .

The overall effect is appalling—and is so intended; *Herr R.* is a completely successful work. It means to show what is really contained in the observation that most people lead lives of quiet desperation. I cannot honestly say that I pitied Herr R.; there is nothing within him solid enough to pity. But I believe in him as one of the "humours"; I have gone through days as savorless as his whole existence is shown to be. One leaves the Fassbinder-[Michael] Fengler demonstration in a mood to rejoice at being alive. And in retrospect I am impressed by the film—it is a tour de force of enervated horror.

> Robert Hatch, "Films: 'Why Does Herr R. Run Amok?'" in The Nation (copyright 1977 The Nation magazine, The Nation Associates, Inc.), Vol. 225, No. 19, December 3, 1977, p. 602.

### JILL FORBES

*Effi Briest* is a film of velleity and distance because it is a portrait of the artist much more than the portrayal of a society. Whatever the apparent moral differences between them, all characters share a simultaneous acceptance of a perfectly coherent system of values, and a knowledge that this system cannot account for all their desires and emotions—even von Instetten who fights a duel because he must, not because he needs to, while openly avowing his love for his wife. . . . What Fassbinder has filmed is the author at work rather than the work itself: using a rigid pattern of sequences introduced by titles which are quotations from [the book's author, Theodor] Fontane and ending on fades to white whose ultimate effect is hypnotic rather than tedious; composing frames within the laws of classical perspective; shooting through gauzes and nets and in mirrors; choosing black-and-white rather than colour, and eschewing most of the technical repertory except the focus pull. And yet the film is beautiful to look at rather than psychologically compelling or politically significant. . . . [Fassbinder] is not self-indulgent, but if he continues to hover, without settling, between the 'realist' and the 'aesthetic' modes there is no reason why *Effi Briest* should not continually be reproduced without adjustment—except, perhaps, that this is no longer the turn of the century. (p. 46)

> Jill Forbes, "Feature Films: 'Fontane Effi Briest' ('Effi Briest')," in Monthly Film Bulletin (copyright © The British Film Institute, 1978), Vol. 45, No. 530, March, 1978, pp. 45-6.

### JAN DAWSON

[Although the ingredients of Fassbinder's Sixties gangster films are still much in evidence,] *The American Soldier* comes closer than any of Fassbinder's previous films to articulate the method behind its own coherent madness and to spelling out the moral, or at any rate the moral philosophy, behind its characters'

seemingly amoral actions. . . . Although on the surface a long way from the Romantic tradition, Fassbinder's *American Soldier* in fact harks back to that tradition by depicting an inescapable link between love and death. Its moments of greatest tenderness and compassion all involve corpses. . . . It's as if the characters can only express the tenderness they feel when 'the other' has lost his potential to betray, manipulate or demand. . . . Fassbinder, as early as 1970, has transcended the conventions of [the B-melodrama and gangster] genres, extrapolating their theatrical emotions into a theatricality of style. The separate monologues, and the presence, not so much of an invisible fourth wall as of an invisible room-divider, belong to the conventions not of the screen but of the stage. . . . The characters in *The American Soldier* act out their frustrations in movie clichés, but their creator has already moved far beyond them, fusing an unmistakable personal style from the most disparate and unpromising sources.

> Jan Dawson, "Feature Films: 'Der Amerikanische Soldat' ('The American Soldier')," in Monthly Film Bulletin (copyright © The British Film Institute, 1978), Vol. 45, No. 533, June, 1978, p. 111.

### JAN DAWSON

More than any other of Fassbinder's early *films noirs*, *Gods of the Plague* is primarily a mood piece, its narrative impressionistically sketched and expressionistically recorded. Each scene achieves a near-absolute existential immediacy, and the causal connections between them, only thinly suggested (expository dialogue, even more than the film's other conversations, is minimal and monosyllabic), remain the subject of speculative reconstruction rather than of any self-evident logic. The relationships between the characters themselves similarly elude definition, projection, retrospection and permanence. . . . Though the country-outing sequence, with its freewheeling aerial shots of the car moving down empty lanes, and the absurd reunion punch-up which leaves the underworld underdogs piled up, winded and semi-conscious, on top of one another, recalls the *nouvelle vague* and some of the ephemeral joy of Godard's *bande à part*, the charm of Fassbinder's petty criminals is considerably less evident, largely because, despite certain marked moral delineations . . . , he deliberately refrains from personalising them. If Johanna and the policeman, both guilty of guile . . . , carry the weight of the film's moral opprobrium, its sympathies are less easy to pin down; or rather, they comprehensively embrace all the pain and compromise of all those characters merely trying to 'get by' in a society (glimpsed only in refractory images) which consistently frustrates their effort. . . . [If] the film's women betray the rules of love, friendship and the inexorable present tense, they are also capable of a truly Christian charity. Their relationship to larger-than-life Hollywood archetypes is defined, not just by the stark contrasts of Dietrich Lohmann's lighting, but by the framing and composition. What lifts the film above its variously signalled sources is the audacity with which Fassbinder combines a strictly behaviourist approach to his characters with an elaborately baroque visual style. The movie's many mirrors function, however, not just decoratively but also cruelly: a halfway house between dream and reality, they end by offering those who gaze into them, as into the great beyond, merely a different, usually a harsher view of the reality they yearn to escape. (pp. 113-14)

> Jan Dawson, "Feature Films: 'Götter der Pest' ('Gods of the Plague')," in Monthly Film Bulletin

*(copyright © The British Film Institute, 1978), Vol. 45, No. 533, June, 1978, pp. 113-14.*

## RICHARD COMBS

Since Fassbinder's message about oppression, and its social and emotional forms, was intended for a mass audience and not a coterie of cinephiles, his self-ordained task was to 'create' that audience by recreating the communal style of the greatest popular cinema in history. Although *Chinese Roulette* (1976) still relates to that tradition—it is a melodramatic chamber piece, in which the romantic triangles of four *haut bourgeois* characters tensely overlap—it pointedly introduces 'foreign' elements into Fassbinder's usual stock company of players, and its political references (the Nazi past, contemporary political terrorism) supply not so much a message as teasing clues to the games its people play.

[Both *Chinese Roulette* and *Despair* (1978)], in fact, are dominated by an intellectual, puzzle-making mood. But if the key to the acrostic in *Chinese Roulette* is Fassbinder's familiar disgust with bourgeois institutions, and in *Despair* his prescience of fascism in the identity crisis of poor, mad Hermann Hermann, the answers never satisfactorily account for the structures that contain them. This whiff of formalism might also have something to do in both cases with their peculiarly literary conceits. (pp. 258-59)

Artificiality, as a theme and a stylistic strategy, has been common to all Fassbinder's films in the 70s. The rhetoric of melodrama boosts the emotional content of his material, while it highlights by schematising all the social mechanisms of repression and control. *Chinese Roulette* . . . pushes such artificiality up a few stops, until it arrives at an hysterical intensity and formal extravagance not far removed from the horror movie. . . .

The customary implications of Fassbinder's bourgeois melodramas are at once intensified and abstracted by the horror movie milieu. A familiar kind of hyper-naturalism prevails in those scenes where characters and camera seem to be conducting a delirious dance of death—circling each other through the vistas of glass and coldly glittering bric-à-brac. But where this thoroughly excavated naturalism shades into a more menacingly opaque expressionism, Fassbinder slyly manages to generalise his disgust and his desire to *épater le bourgeoisie*. He might be jabbing at a state of mind that cannot be precisely located in present-day Germany, seeking broader metaphors behind his local targets, while turning inward (abandoning the communal mythology of his 70s films) for his ammunition. Private meanings appear to cluster about the film, and even the concrete political clues deepen rather than elucidate the air of mystery. . . .

Oddly enough, much of the black humour of *Chinese Roulette,* particularly its relish for casting a crippled child as its wicked master of ceremonies, might have been invented by Vladimir Nabokov. Exchanging references, as it were, Fassbinder's adaptation of *Despair* . . . occasionally sallies some of the horror imagery . . . more successfully incorporated in *Chinese Roulette.* If consistently carried through, however, such a style would not have been inappropriate to *Despair,* since it is part of Nabokov's riddling way with fiction to call for just those kinds of 'dramatic' effects that emphasise the author's presence. And if anything accounts for the failure of Fassbinder's version, for all the decorative brilliance with which he reproduces some of Nabokov's *trompe l'oeil* imagery, it is his inability to find any overall 'holding' metaphor for the novel's shifting levels of fantasy. (p. 259)

For a while, the film confidently operates in the same sardonic key as its source, piling on levels of unreality. . . . But it forever fixes Hermann in the same sharp, crystalline perspective as its splendidly artificial décor, never allowing one to relate to the other except in the ghostly, geometric patterns created by the ceaselessly roving camera, which might be looking (as in Fassbinder's more prosaic dramas) for the real toad at the centre of this baroquely unreal world. The objective view freezes to rather solemn, pedantic effect the subjective layers of the novel, which Nabokov steadily peeled away, disclosing in this act his true subject. Ironically, the cosmopolitan origins of *Despair* are belied by Fassbinder's determination to anchor it in local circumstances, and a parochial stylistic sophistication, while *Chinese Roulette* is freed from just such constraints by its rather Nabokovian playfulness and lack of formal inhibitions. (p. 260)

*Richard Combs, "'Chinese Roulette' and 'Despair',"* in Sight and Sound *(copyright © 1978 by The British Film Institute), Vol. 47, No. 4, Autumn, 1978, pp. 258-60.*

## JOHN L. FELL

*Despair* invents an act of demented disassociation with which the audience cannot itself become complicitly engaged because the narrative mode is not expressionistic. Instead, it is overlaid by self-reflexive irony upon irony. The book is written as a memoir-diary: "the lowest form of literature," its author says. Rereading, the writer discovers his fatal mistake in commission of the perfect crime.

Nabokov's plot intact, [Tom] Stoppard and Fassbinder have enlarged the döppelgänger motif (including plays on old movie scenes), politicized time and place, and exteriorized Hermann's aberrations by means of fantasized, conjectural intrusions.

Doubling, of course, here advances double narrative functions: the visual evidence of Hermann's disassociation during his lovemaking, shared by ourselves through either party's eyes, and the satirized Felix-double, authenticated by the protagonist alone. As a self-conscious design it is foregrounded during an episode when Ardalion, Lydia and Hermann attend a movie, a made-up American silent with funny German intertitles about twin brothers, one a murderer under siege from cops led by his brother. . . .

With Hermann viewing his own primal scene, the audience as concurrent witness, the film has thus far been operating already in a kind of quadroscopic realm of voyeuristic permutations. Henceforth, the reflexive nudge of movie-within-movie complicates matters yet again, however ironically, its intentions underlined by Hermann himself, who once pretends to be a film director needing a double for his new production; he is trying to persuade Felix to work for him.

Politics prove to be less skillfully insinuated. Where the novel was denuded of topicality but for its satiric Bolshevism, the film plants depression brownshirts, reparations, Versailles, and anti-Semitism with stolid good intention. The effect is rather as if Nabokov and Christopher Isherwood had been assigned by Alexander Korda to collaborate on a film biography of George Grosz, a venture that could have amused but would hardly have satisfied either. (p. 60)

The director's, writer's and actors' triumph in *Despair* has been to translate Nabokov's largely conversationless world into a glittering mire of snobbish puns and monologues. Who is audacious enough to conjecture how Nabokov might have viewed such extensions of himself? Apparently he did enjoy the ping pong game in Kubrick's *Lolita*. (p. 61)

*John L. Fell, "'Despair',"" in* Film Quarterly *(copyright 1979 by The Regents of the University of California; reprinted by permission of the University of California Press), Vol. XXXIII, No. 1, Fall, 1979, pp. 59-61.*

### JAN DAWSON

[*The Third Generation* is Fassbinder's] most violently outspoken film yet, and incidentally the first from Germany . . . to represent fictional terrorists on the screen. Expanding into a high-camp melodrama the idea of collective responsibility underlying his *Germany in Autumn* episode, Fassbinder disregards the politically rigidified idea of terrorists as either demons or martyrs, and instead locates the colourful members of his terrorist cell . . . at the centre of a complex, wheels-within-wheels social machine governed only by the laws of greed, profit, cross and double-cross. . . .

[In] Fassbinder's angry, and only superficially cynical, apocalyptic vision, there are no right or left, no good or bad guys. . . .

*The Third Generation* is not the first Fassbinder film to suggest a kinship between cops and outlaws (this motif ran through his earliest thrillers, as through many of the *films noirs* which inspired them). . . . But it is the first of his films to locate these twin themes unequivocally in contemporary society or to relate them to post-'68 developments there. If its characters still behave with theatrical, nay, Sirkian relish, the film's references are none the less more frequently drawn from actuality than from the movies. . . .

[The] spectator is overwhelmed by the *choice* of meanings offered by the film's multi-track sounds, by the impossibility of making any kind of coherent sense from the Babel of the new technology. The flickering screens in the corner of nearly every frame (images within images echoing the theme of wheels within wheels) connect and question both the medium of film and the ideology of surveillance. The watchers are watched and the biters bit. Nothing is sacred in a society which has substituted communications systems for forthright communication. Not even terrorism, the nation's sacred monster.

It is in this consequent spirit that Fassbinder dares to make fun of his misfit desperadoes, to show them squabbling over properties on the Monopoly board or over possible exotic aliases. In Germany at least, his irony has proved as unpopular as his adulation might have done. (p. 245)

*Jan Dawson, "The Sacred Terror," in* Sight and Sound *(copyright © 1979 by The British Film Institute), Vol. 48, No. 4, Autumn, 1979, pp. 242-45.**

### TOM NOONAN

[Only] someone like Fassbinder, a man who solemnly proclaimed a film with an all-woman cast "strictly autobiographical" could make *The Marriage of Maria Braun.*

Maria builds her life around her love for Hermann, in spite of their separation. Regardless of whether or not her love is "real,"

it is the passion that sustains her. It is also the carrot that Fassbinder dangles before Maria as he enmeshes her in a web of complications. As the reality of a reunion with her husband is repeatedly denied, Maria's love becomes an abstraction that retreats further and further into fantasy. (pp. 40-1)

Control is the key to Maria. She is always completely in command. But she can't have the one thing she wants more than anything else—her man. . . . [We feel a heart-rending sympathy for Maria]; she too has an ideal love that eludes her, always lying just out of reach, waiting to be realized. She is only believing in, and following, the rituals of her culture. And in the surrounding confusion, she clings even tighter. (p. 41)

*Maria Braun* is another one of Fassbinder's unrelenting schematics. There is still another protagonist burdened with, and bewildered by, a life whose day-to-day routines demand submission but make little sense. Fassbinder portrays victims. His characters may be vivacious in the beginning, but at the film's end they are enervated, passive, often dead. (p. 42)

Much of *Maria Braun* is familiar melodrama: there is the theme of unrequited love; the woman who gives her all for love; the slow ebbing away of her self that results; the baby, prophetically stillborn; the schemers and heart-breaking complications; and the final, tragic nobility of the heroine's emotions. But in *Maria Braun,* the sex roles and accompanying expectations are chaotic; sometimes they confirm our anticipations, other times deny them. . . .

This intricate blend of characters and their emotions creates, like most melodrama, a self-contained mini-world, complete with a moral viewpoint that we are urged to accept as basically correct. But for Fassbinder, this process has an added dimension—a conflict with other beliefs and preconceptions, about what is "male" and "female," and their relative merits. The tragedy he presents is Maria's loss of "femaleness"—sympathy, intuition, empathy, nurturant qualities—and its replacement by "maleness"—a tough, cynical competitiveness that leads to self-destruction. (p. 43)

Ethics, not esthetics, is Fassbinder's goal in grabbing our emotions while they're off-guard. The intensity he creates is thought-provoking, not sentimental. The world outside the frame of the film is what interests Fassbinder; metaphorically, *Maria Braun* tells the story of postwar Germany: success at a price— a loss of emotions, a coldness now considered to be characteristic of Germans. The theme is familiar. Fassbinder is intensely dissatisfied with the "miracles" of modern capitalism. His characters are casualties of the economic rationalism that pervades our thinking; Fassbinder sees it as a rigged game that degrades people and drives them apart. But even if it were fair, it would not be worth playing, he says, for we spiritually prostitute ourselves in the pursuit of a private materialism. . . .

Art, when it is good, is a process of personal transformation; the artist puts down more than he or she consciously, or rationally, knows. And this is the power of Fassbinder's films; they speak to the subconscious. The disturbing criticism present in *Maria Braun* has an effect on us because it is implanted at a deep level. By playing with genre preconceptions, Fassbinder establishes a broadly based connection with the audience. We don't really need to know where his material came from or what he is alluding to for his conversation to work, either; the morals of the old melodramas are reflected in our culture. Much of the beauty of *Maria Braun* is Fassbinder's ability to use past film conventions without becoming bound or limited by them; he can still articulate personal concerns. (p. 44)

Artists like Fassbinder continually challenge the way we look at things. He takes powerful and encompassing chunks of everyday life and carries on a dialogue that slowly grows, then dawns on you with a gasp, a quick catch of the breath. That Fassbinder works his art with ''popular'' forms can only be a further attestation to his acute perceptiveness and sensitivity. (p. 45)

Tom Noonan, '''The Marriage of Maria Braun','' in Film Quarterly (copyright 1980 by The Regents of the University of California; reprinted by permission of the University of California Press), Vol. XXXIII, No. 3, Spring, 1980, pp. 40-5.

### DAN ISAAC

*The Marriage of Maria Braun* must be recognized . . . as a powerful and mordant study of post-war Germany, a portrayal very much in the mood and style of Bertolt Brecht. Concerned with the ''economic miracle,'' as the Germans themselves like to call it, Fassbinder treats a subject that other German filmmakers have studiously avoided.

*''Eine schlechte Zeit für Gefuhle''*—''a bad time for feelings''—says one character early on, which pretty much sums up the pervasive mood of Fassbinder's icy approach to the miracle of German recovery. . . . But in *The Marriage of Maria Braun* Fassbinder has finally found the right subject; the result is a near masterpiece. The marriage referred to in the title is the marriage of modern Germany to economic recovery and the corporate values that accompany it. . . .

The finest touch to this *film noir* is something that goes on in the background and is left untranslated in the titles: a series of radio broadcasts punctuate particular scenes, commenting on and reflecting the political mood of the period. . . . In the last scene we hear the sports announcer hysteria of a soccer game between Germany and Hungary, the final sign of a descent into the sterile hell of an economic recovery that leaves Germany unredeemed—at least, in the gospel according to Fassbinder. (p. 46)

Dan Isaac, ''The Lincoln Center Film Festival,'' in Midstream (copyright © 1980 by The Theodor Herzl Foundation, Inc.), Vol. XXVI, No. 4, April, 1980, pp. 45-7.*

### ROBERT HATCH

The atmosphere of *In a Year of Thirteen Moons* is dark, claustrophobic, filmed in hot colors, often at bizarre, cubist angles and heavy with *Weltschmerz*. Time and again it pauses for long, philosophical contemplation of the distastefulness of being and the seduction of ending—maunderings of the sort I thought even the Germans had renounced in our time. . . .

Fassbinder mistrusts the social system as profoundly as he despairs of human relationships. He expresses this most explicitly through the history of Saitz, who had risen from black-market trickster to whoremaster to real estate millionaire and whom Elvira runs to earth in one of his vast but empty high-rises, locked in with a few henchmen and engaged in a childish parody of an old Jerry Lewis comedy he apparently keeps running endlessly on a TV set. This occupation I take to be a

warning to tycoons that the fate of Howard Hughes awaits them. . . .

*In a Year of Thirteen Moons* is appalling, a delirium of sensibility turned rancid. Most of us have, one time or another, felt abused, traduced, godforsaken; one develops a resistance. But for those who live under the sway of the moon—and Fassbinder clearly includes himself among them—resistance may be hard to sustain, and ceremonies must be evoked. This film, it could well be, is his way of defying his demon. Like Genet, I suspect, he creates out of the worst he can find in himself. (p. 797)

Robert Hatch, ''Films: 'In a Year of Thirteen Moons','' in The Nation (copyright 1980 The Nation magazine, The Nation Associates, Inc.), Vol. 230, No. 25, June 28, 1980, p. 797.

### RAYMOND DURGNAT

We're tempted to say that Fassbinder is a better playwright than film director. But we can't quite convince ourselves that he began with some acute sense of how human beings oppress and twist one another and themselves, and that he lost it on film through believing that Douglas Sirk . . . was a Marxist pioneer of alienation effect by exaggeration. We see these movies as soft-edge, soft-core, bourgeois self-criticism. . . .

On all his actors Fassbinder's carefully formalized visuals impose a strange style which certainly hits the jackpot of a fashionable aesthetic. Following an almost mechanical alternation of passion and blankness (limp deadpan, tears, limp deadpan), Fassbinder succeeds only too well in transforming illusionistic acting into a series of arbitrary signs half-disembedded from any illusionistic continuum. Presumably intended as an alienation effect, it prompts the reflection that if so much has to be added to the dramatic plane, then that dramatic plane simply excludes what ''illusionistic'' (well-constructed) screenplays include. (p. 66)

Although Fassbinder's brandished Marxism surrounds [*The Merchant of Four Seasons*] with a vaguely progressive aura, he's really as rear-guard, or ingrown, a figure as Herzog. His glitter-*kammerspiel* substitutes for psychology a portentous moralizing about egoism and power games. It adapts the autocritical bourgeois tradition . . . to a sense of chic physical oddity developed in various fields by Andy Warhol, Helmut Newton, and the Ugly Model Agency.

Possibly Fassbinder anticipates a perennial tendency in art, evident also in a chic-punk form: once venality and its charm are accepted, analysis has nothing to reveal, and irony replaces it. Whence the yin and yang in Germanic culture of the lyrical-transcendental, and of irony in the ''Berliner,'' or Brechtian, or Sternbergian mode. We're not objecting to this world-view, only asking for a solution to the spectator's boredom that non-development can reinforce. Given the Fassbinder conjunction of deadlock without surprise or suspense, his figures become icons of flatness and falseness, lacking irony and a sense of something living inside.

Fassbinder achieves his tone—somewhere in the vicinity of post-absurdism and magic realism—but his characters are clockwork oranges. . . . One admires Fassbinder's unusual freedom from class bias, and the evenness with which he promenades his vision through its projection onto all classes and conditions of men; but the equanimity and lucidity is foreshortened by something which freezes all these forms in their brittle perfection. The films have a shriveled consistency—like that of figures in a gay Marxist cuckoo clock. (p. 68)

*Raymond Durgnat, "From Caligari to 'Hitler'" (copyright © 1980 by Raymond Durgnat; reprinted by permission of the author), in* Film Comment, *Vol. 16, No. 4, July-August, 1980, pp. 59-70.* *

## VINCENT CANBY

There no longer can be any doubt about it: Rainer Werner Fassbinder is the most dazzling, talented, provocative, original, puzzling, prolific and exhilarating film maker of his generation. . . .

Mr. Fassbinder has demonstrated that he is quite capable of adapting his cinematic vision to fit the works of others . . . , but it's his original screenplays that give the true measure of this great, unpredictable talent. He makes movies the way other, lesser directors talk about them—easily, quickly and precisely. When he shoots a film, he is speculating about the subject as well as about the craft of film making, examining both as he goes along, freely, without being bound to arrive at some preset destination. His movies are the logbooks of an adventuring mind.

Some Fassbinder films are, of course, less successful than others, but that's beside the point. Each is a part of what can now be recognized as a single continuing work, and if one film ends in something of a muddle, there's always another coming along that may clear things up. A Fassbinder movie isn't necessarily an end in itself. It's a way of thinking.

Fassbinder films are so packed (visually and aurally) with information, references, asides, questions and unexpected connections (and, as a result so demanding) that most other contemporary movies look puny in comparison. Watching a good Fassbinder movie is like doing a double crostic after too many games of tick-tack-toe.

**"The Third Generation"** has you sitting on the edge of your seat even before you are sure what it's about. . . .

The film is about a cell of "third generation" terrorists, earnest, humorless, committed, largely middle-class boobs for whom terrorism has become a style of living without connections to political passions of any sort. . . .

It's not by chance that whenever we see the conspirators, either singly or in various combinations, we always see a television set flickering somewhere in the vicinity. What ideas they do possess have arrived predigested, second- or third-hand, and have more to do with fashion than with intellect. . . .

These people are mutations, distant spinoffs of the members of the notorious Bader-Meinhof gang. They are people for whom political commitment is a matter of secret passwords, disguises and assumed names. . . .

**"The Third Generation"** is one of the richest looking and sounding films I've ever experienced. . . . [Fassbinder] seems incapable of shooting a scene that isn't dense with detail, sometimes breathtakingly beautiful ones, which, in this case, serve to emphasize the deadly foolishness of the lives being lived in the foreground. . . .

**"The Third Generation"** is fascinating. It's also worrying. I keep wondering how long Mr. Fassbinder can continue this remarkable pace.

*Vincent Canby, "Film: Fassbinder on Terrorism," in* The New York Times, *Section C (© 1980 by The New York Times Company; reprinted by permission), September 9, 1980, p. 9.*

## RICHARD COMBS

The mood of *The Third Generation,* one might assume, is rampaging cynicism. The film looks in two directions, at the modern capitalist state of West Germany and at the terrorist radicals who bedevil it, and seems to pronounce a curse on both their houses. Such a feat is possible, however, not because the film is two-faced but because the situation it describes is so complex. . . .

In cut and dried terms, this is the message of Fassbinder's latest film. But it does not account for some of its most curious features, not least of which is that it is more emotionally than politically painful. Although some historical long view of the German experience is implied, the film actually works as a claustrophobically intense soap opera, a black farce of political mannerisms or, as an opening title puts it, "a comedy in six parts, about party games, full of suspense, excitement and logic, horror and madness. . ." . . .

It is no wonder, then, that the film seems such a riotous *kammerspiel,* since all the generations have been let loose in it. . . .

The film's action, too, is all in the family. The members of the cell are domestic monsters first and political actors second, and reserve their scorn for the new member who is still burdened with his suitcase of revolutionary theory. What the discussion of ideology boils down to in the end is the old Fassbinder problem of victimization: his peculiar sense of doom about personal and social relations in which everyone alternately plays out the roles of victim and victimizer. . . .

If the characters' personal situations are vicious circles, then their chances of changing anything politically are even more remote. It is a stagnation which one often feels has overwhelmed the film itself, although Fassbinder actively denies morbid introspection even as his characters sink into it. It is difficult in the end to reduce *The Third Generation* to a single message, simply because it squeezes in so much contradictory "communication." . . .

*Richard Combs, "Dilettantism and 'realpolitik'," in* The Times Literary Supplement (© Times Newspapers Ltd. (London) 1980; reproduced from The Times Literary Supplement *by permission), No. 4042, September 19, 1980, p. 1020.*

# Bob Fosse

## 1925-

**American director, choreographer, dancer, actor, and screenwriter.**

**The world Fosse creates is artificial and theatrical. His films are "musical dramas," musically-oriented films with sophisticated themes and stark realism.**

**Following a career as a dancer on Broadway, Fosse began to choreograph. The stage musicals he later directed developed his creativity in dance as well as his awareness of show business. These elements are reflected in his first film, *Sweet Charity,* which he had previously directed and choreographed on Broadway. Based on Fellini's *Nights of Cabiria, Sweet Charity* has received critical acclaim for Fosse's distinctive musical numbers. However, some critics feel that *Sweet Charity* is not indicative of his later style, believing that Fosse felt compelled to film a flamboyant production with an established star such as Shirley MacLaine. *Cabaret* is considered a landmark film: a movie with music rather than a movie musical. This film, based on Christopher Isherwood's *Berlin Stories,* provides musical entertainment while analyzing Nazi Germany. By focusing on the cabaret's stage to draw a sharp contrast between reality and fantasy, Fosse makes the nightclub a microcosm of life.**

**Fosse's autobiography, *All That Jazz,* has been likened to Fellini's *8½.* Fosse portrays himself as an obsessed, exhausted director who drives himself to death because of his desire to succeed. Although Fosse has been criticized for emphasizing the destructive side of show business, his view of the theater and his choreography are considered exciting and innovative.**

**Of his decision to create a dramatic musical form, Fosse says, "Today I get very antsy watching movies in which people are singing as they walk down the street. . . . You can do it on the stage. The theater has its own personality—it conveys a removed reality. The movies bring that closer."**

## TOM MILNE

[The trouble with *Sweet Charity* is that its star, Shirley MacLaine, is] required to dance—and in Bob Fosse country at that. . . .

[Choreographically] speaking the most exhilarating moments in the film are two numbers—'Hey, Big Spender' and the trio of eccentricities that make up 'Rich Man's Frug'—in which the star does not appear. Here, with his characteristically tight, neurotically precise and almost off-balance steps, where the dancers hug close together as though afraid to break the magic circuit, Bob Fosse is Bob Fosse as he is nowhere else in the film.

For, doubling as director, he pulls constantly against himself, undermining his own meticulous algebraics by inserting choppy efforts at *mise en scène* instead of choreographing his way out of difficulties. . . . Subsequently the direction settles down to become much less queasy, but there is still a plethora of irritatingly unnecessary dissolves, zooms, frozen shots and pretty montages, usually illustrating the extremes of happiness or despair that Charity has already expressed, or *should* express in dance.

All of which may make it sound as though *Sweet Charity* doesn't work at all. Contrariwise, it does, often magnificently. . . . [For] all his Lelouchian devotion to decorative bravura, Mr. Fosse is obviously very good with actors. . . .

[Charity herself] is irresistible, carrying the film over its stylistic flurries and only at the end falling into the kind of sentimental whimsy that dogged . . . Fellini's original. It is perhaps symptomatic of the film's indecision, however, as to what it should be doing and with whom, that emotionally her part is allowed to build to two dance numbers, one for each lover. . . .

[One hopes] that in his second film Bob Fosse will get a chance to create a musical with, by and for dancers. Meanwhile, *Sweet Charity* joins [Francis Ford Coppola's] *Finian's Rainbow* and [William Wyler's] *Funny Girl* in proving that there is still musical life in the old Hollywood dog. Who, watching the electrifying contortions of a row of pleading, hissing, finger-snapping taxi-dancers for the superbly weary, sleazy erotica of 'Hey, Big Spender', could doubt it?

*Tom Milne, "'Sweet Charity',"* in Sight and Sound *(copyright © 1969 by The British Film Institute), Vol. 38, No. 2, Spring, 1969, p. 98.*

## ROBIN BEAN

[*Sweet Charity*] is Bob Fosse's first film as a director, and the result is breathtaking. . . . [While] one would expect the staging of the musical numbers to be exceptional I wasn't prepared for the instinctive and sensitively imaginative way Fosse works with film as a visual medium. He shows more understanding of images and technique than any director of a musical before. (p. 39)

*Sweet Charity* represents the Hollywood musical at its very best, and is possibly the greatest one. Inventive, invigorating, fresh, never letting up for one moment, it makes [Robert Wise and Jerome Robbins's] *West Side Story* seem very unsatisfying in retrospect; though the latter had a brilliant score, visually it lacked the dynamic impact which Fosse achieves. For Fosse, *Sweet Charity* is a great achievement. . . . By the time the flower children arrive, the cinema is almost awash—and that is a remarkable thing these days. (p. 40)

> *Robin Bean, "'Sweet Charity'" (© copyright Robin Bean 1969; reprinted with permission), in* Films and Filming, *Vol. 15, No. 7, April, 1969, pp. 39-40.*

### ROGER GREENSPUN

"Cabaret" is not so much a movie musical as it is a movie with a lot of music in it. . . . Fosse's approach has been not to open up but rather to confine, on a small and well-defined stage, as much of "Cabaret" as means to be musical theater.

Thus the film has a musical part and a nonmusical part . . . , and if you add this to the juxtaposition of private lives and public history inherent in the scheme of the "Berlin Stories" [on which the film is based], you come up with a structure of extraordinary mechanical complexity. Since everything has to do with everything else and the Cabaret is always commenting on the life outside it, the film sometimes looks like an essay in significant cross-cutting, or associative montage. Occasionally this fails; more often it works.

Fosse makes mistakes, partly because his camera is a more potent instrument than he realizes, but he also makes discoveries—and "Cabaret" is one of those immensely gratifying imperfect works in which from beginning to end you can literally feel a movie coming to life.

The film gains a good deal from its willingness to isolate its musical stage—even to observe it from behind the heads of a shadowy audience in the foreground—so that every time we return to the girls and their leering master (by now, a superbly refined caricature) we return, as it were, to a sense of theater. And when at certain moments that theater is occupied only by Liza Minnelli, working in a space defined only by her gestures and a few colored lights, it becomes by the simplest means an evocation of both the power and fragility of movie performance so beautiful that I can think of nothing to do but give thanks.

> *Roger Greenspun, "'Cabaret'," in* The New York Times *(© 1972 by The New York Times Company; reprinted by permission), February 14, 1972 (and reprinted in* The New York Times Film Reviews: 1971-1972, *The New York Times Company & Arno Press, 1973, p. 222.*

### PAULINE KAEL

*Cabaret* is a great movie musical, made, miraculously, without compromises. It's miraculous because the material is hard and unsentimental, and until now there has never been a diamond-hard big American movie musical. . . . [It] is everything one hopes for and more; if it doesn't make money, it will still make movie history.

After *Cabaret*, it should be a while before performers once again climb hills singing or a chorus breaks into song on a hayride; it is not merely that *Cabaret* violates the wholesome approach of big musicals but that it violates the pseudo-naturalistic tradition—the "Oklahoma!"-"South Pacific"-"West Side Story" tradition, which requires that the songs appear to grow organically out of the story. (p. 409)

The usual movie approach to decadent periods of history is to condemn decadence while attempting to give us vicarious thrills. Here, in a prodigious balancing act, Bob Fosse . . . keeps this period—Berlin, 1931—at a cool distance. We see the decadence as garish and sleazy, and yet we see the animal energy in it, and the people driven to endure. The movie does not exploit decadence; rather, it gives it its due. . . . The movie is never cynical (it may be one of the least cynical big movies ever made); it is, on the contrary, so clear-eyed that it winks at nothing. Though it uses camp material, it carries camp to its ultimate vileness—in the m.c.'s mockery of all things human, including himself. . . . *Cabaret* does not merely suggest Egon Schiele's moribund, erotic figures and the rictus smiles and rotting flesh in the paintings and graphics of artists such as James Ensor and George Grosz but captures the same macabre spirit—and *sustains* it. What makes the art of such men powerful is that they help us recognize the sensual strength of decadence. When there is nothing to believe in but survival and pleasure, gaiety has a ghastly, desperate edge, but the way people still seek pleasure is testimony to something both base and fascinating. Everything seems to become sexualized. The grotesque amorality in *Cabaret* is frightening, not because it's weak but because it's intensely, obscenely alive.

The method of the movie is to embrace this life and to show us the appeal of its horror, and by this satiric embrace to put us at a distance. (pp. 409-11)

*Cabaret* is the only expensive American movie musical . . . that takes its form from political cabaret. The political satire here might be thought to have too easy and obvious a target, but, as it works out, the associations we have with this target— from art and literature and journalism—enable the satire to function at a higher level of ironic obscenity than would be possible with a more topical subject. And the picture goes way beyond topical satire into a satire of temptations. . . . Decadence comprises so much more than any specific satirical target that the movie's cold embrace of decadence is a richly suggestive form of satire. (pp. 412-13)

*Cabaret* demonstrates that when you revolt against the organic "Oklahoma!" conception of musicals you can create a new organic whole by style and imagination—if you have enough faith in the audience to do it right. (p. 413)

> *Pauline Kael, "Grinning" (originally published in* The New Yorker, *Vol. XLVII, No. 53, February 19, 1972), in her* Deeper into Movies *(copyright © 1972 by Pauline Kael; reprinted by permission of Little, Brown and Company in association with the Atlantic Monthly Press), Atlantic-Little, Brown, 1973, pp. 409-13.*

### STANLEY KAUFFMANN

[Fosse] has handled *Cabaret* like a smart Broadway musical director: always bright, always intent—not on authenticity but on keeping one step ahead of the audience's jadedness. He can do it. . . .

Unlike the Broadway version, the musical elements are split off from the rest: almost all the songs occur on the cabaret stage, the rest of the picture is "straight." I suppose this is in aid of realism, but it doesn't quite succeed. First, as usual in movie musicals, the numbers are much too lavish and complex for the theater in which they're supposed to be done. Second, Fosse is much more comfortable with the musical numbers than with "life." But one clever non-number is more than clever. A sequence in a country beer garden begins with a close-up of an appealing youth singing a pleasant *heimisch* song. Slowly the camera pulls back and reveals his Nazi armband. The refrain becomes fervent, the camera keeps pulling back, more and more people join with Nazi fervor, and what started out as schmaltz ends as scare. Overly neat, perhaps, but so is most symbolic action. (p. 98)

*Cabaret* is far better than most movie musicals; but Fosse's smartness, Minnelli's professional unhealth, and the scripts chrome-plated carpentry keep it from being as moving as it wanted to be. (p. 99)

> *Stanley Kauffmann, "'Cabaret'" (originally published in* The New Republic, *Vol. 166, No. 10, March 4, 1972), in his* Living Images: Film Comment and Criticism *(reprinted by permission of Brandt & Brandt Literary Agents, Inc.; copyright © 1970, 1971, 1972, 1973, 1974, 1975 by Stanley Kauffmann), Harper & Row, Publishers, 1975, pp. 97-9.*

### COLIN L. WESTERBECK, JR.

*Cabaret* is ultimately pretty weak schnapps. It takes the Berlin of the 1930's—the Berlin of George Grosz cartoons and Christopher Isherwood stories (on which the film was based . . .)— and turns it into a backdrop for a musical. . . . An audience today could get pimples from a story like Fritz' and Natalya's, so the sugar loaf has to be sourdoughed with Nazism the way it is in *Cabaret*—or leavened with a few pogroms the way it is in *Fiddler on the Roof*. The Czar and Hitler play approximately the same role in these musicals that leukemia plays in *Love Story*.

The film's heroine, Sally Bowles, is a lot like Fritz. She too is saved from herself by her own ineptness and endeared to us. She wants passionately to be a femme fatale, "a most strange and exceptional person," as she herself often puts it. But she is hopelessly miscast playing such a role in life. . . .

Fosse demonstrates in this film that he has now learned the tricks of the movie musical trade.

The choreography that looks best on a stage often looks chaotic in a movie. On a stage the dance gestures have to be extravagant and the acrobatics spectacular. But in a film such movement goes by in a blur, especially when the camera tries to get close enough to catch the expressions of the dancers as well. . . . It is the camera that moves boldly and dramatically here—that exerts itself and has to be choreographed. . . .

The restructuring Fosse has done seems to appeal to him because it allows cross-cutting between the numbers done on the cabaret stage and developments in the society outside—as if the former were a commentary on the latter as well as a part of it. The fact is that *Cabaret*'s wistful treatment of Germany during the rise of Nazism is only a part of our own society. *Cabaret* is only worth thinking about as a document of our times, not as a commentary on someone else's. As an interpretation of history, *Cabaret* is trivial the way that all musicals are.

> *Colin L. Westerbeck, Jr., "3.2 Schnapps," in* Commonweal *(copyright © 1972 Commonweal Publishing Co., Inc.; reprinted by permission of Commonweal Publishing Co., Inc.), Vol. XCVI, No. 7, April 21, 1972, p. 167.*

### DAVID BRUDNOY

*Cabaret* is superb drama enriched by music, *not* a "musical" padded with the usual tacked-on, hoked-up plot. While its story centers on an American showbiz-obsessed girl, her affair with a Cambridge graduate student, and their joint friendship with a wealthy German aristocrat, *Cabaret*'s theme is the gradual obliteration of freedom in Germany as the National Socialists rise from hooliganism to apparent idealism to—in the years after that covered by the film—supreme power. . . .

*Cabaret* never oversteps drama into bathos, never bludgeons its point, never obscures the simple love story with the political message. Instead, it merges the two with remarkable effectiveness. Its force and beauty everywhere apparent, *Cabaret* is exquisitely intelligent cinema, ranking with the finest movies made in recent years. (p. 476)

> *David Brudnoy, "Cabaret and Elsewhere," in* National Review *(© National Review, Inc., 1972; 150 East 35th St., New York, NY 10016), Vol. XXIV, No. 16, April 28, 1972, pp. 476-77.\**

### JOE BLADES

What one remembers from [*Cabaret*] are the visual elements:

(1) the touching moment in which Fritz hides his frayed cuffs from Natalia;

(2) Joel Grey's garish makeup and facial contortions;

(3) the Nazi beating intercut with the Swiss hand-clapping dance at the cabaret;

(4) the splattered body of a murder victim on the streets as Max's limousine passes;

(5) the ugly spectacle of the Kit Kat Klub—ladies wrestling in mud; the laughing crowd; the telephones on the tables; and most of all,

(6) the method by which the sweet-faced youth is revealed to be a Nazi brown shirt. (p. 237)

These images, largely the responsibility of photographer Geoffrey Unsworth—and the lingering ones far exceed the six listed above—become the visual equivalents of Isherwood's writing. On screen, lifted from the pages of *Goodbye to Berlin* are the drifters, the whores, the cabaret *artistes*, the S.A. men, and the society children. As flickering images on pieces of celluloid, they stand in their own right as powerful reminders of the *insouciance*, the decay, and the forced joyousness—in the midst of joylessness—of pre-Hitler Berlin. (p. 238)

> *Joe Blades, "The Evolution of 'Cabaret'," in* Literature/Film Quarterly *(© copyright 1973 Salisbury State College), Vol. 1, No. 3, July, 1973, pp. 226-38.*

### VINCENT CANBY

["**Lenny**"] looks to be about three-fourths dramatized biography and one-fourth recreated stage performances. . . .

This one-fourth of the film is so brilliant . . . that it helps cool one's impatience with the rest of the film, which is much more fancily edited and photographed but no more profound than those old movie biographies Jack L. Warner used to grind out about people like George Gershwin, Mark Twain and Dr. Ehrlich. In movies, now as then, genius is principally defined by the amount of time spent dealing with disappointment. . . .

However, **"Lenny"** is never very precise about what happened to Lenny or why. . . .

[The] interviews are full of phony, simulated cinéma vérité-type irrelevancies in speech and manner that you never for a minute believe, any more than you believe that Lenny was just a sweet brilliant fellow who had some hard luck.

The movie makes no point of Lenny's terrible childhood or his ambivalent feelings toward his father. . . .

Honey's affairs with other women, accepted and sometimes encouraged by Lenny, are touched upon so gently as to seem of little importance, as is Lenny's dependence on drugs. . . .

Mr. Fosse, the director of **"Cabaret,"** is also inhibited here. The production, photographed in glorious black-and-white, has a fine, seedy look but this, after all, is just more description. Was Lenny truly some kind of mad prophet or simply an accidental product of his times, which, though he died in 1966, were really the gung-ho nineteen-forties and the uptight fifties? It's to the film's credit that it raises this question, though it doesn't supply us with much information with which to answer it.

*Vincent Canby, "'Lenny',"* in The New York Times *(© 1974 by The New York Times Company; reprinted by permission), November 10, 1974 (and reprinted in* The New York Times Film Reviews: 1973-1974, The New York Times Company & Arno Press, 1975, *p. 296).*

### STANLEY KAUFFMANN

[In *Lenny* Fosse has moved] toward a directing style that would itself approximate the anarchic effect that Bruce used to have with his performances. Apparently Fosse has modeled his work on the arch-anarchist of our film era, Godard. . . . *Lenny* wants to be, in form and feeling, an anarchic "act" about a man who did anarchic "acts," and, in that form and feeling, it succeeds much more than in what is actually said and done. . . .

The film's troubles are in the script by Julian Barry, who wrote the poor play of the same name. But the troubles here are not exactly the same. The play was toothless and was festooned with arty touches. . . . The film script has none of that artiness and it does have some teeth: the trouble is that they are taken out, like dentures, and shown to us. For instance, during one performance, Bruce spots a black man in the audience and calls him "nigger"; then he spots others whom he identifies as "kike," "spick," "wop," etc. The real Bruce would have kept on using those terms without mitigation, possibly to make us see how close we all are to using them, even if we don't admit it, and anyway just to make us angry and to make us laugh at our embarrassment over our anger. But Barry's Bruce explains. He explains that he's repeating those terms in order to take the sting out of them, so that no little kid will ever be hurt by them again. (p. 18)

[There] are biographical gaps and distortions. . . . The wildness of Bruce's sex life is only sketched. . . . His discovery

of his "dirtiness" as performer, and his strength therein, is almost incidental. His decline into drugs is shown but not motivated or dramatized, as is his decline into legalistic boringness. . . . There are gaps in the script that are supposed to be filled in either by our knowledge of Bruce or of movies: either by facts or by the conventional strophes of disintegration in film heroes. (pp. 18, 33)

I hope that the film will serve one real purpose: I hope it will close the subject of Lenny Bruce. (p. 33)

*Stanley Kauffmann, "Films: 'Lenny'" (reprinted by permission of Brandt & Brandt Literary Agents, Inc.; copyright © 1974 by Stanley Kauffmann), in* The New Republic, *Vol. 171, No. 24, December 14, 1974, pp. 18, 33-4.*

### JOHN SIMON

[*Lenny*] is a mess—precisely because it is neither fact nor imaginative fiction. Fosse and Barry never figured out for themselves how this nothingy little comic grew into a heroic figure and, rightly or wrongly, a legend; they further becloud the issue with "arty" fragmentation and time shifts, so that past (the unknown, two-bit comedian), present (the phenomenally risen and fallen, one and only Lenny Bruce) and future (his mother, wife, and agent spinning out his myth in posthumous interviews with a heard but unseen journalist) are utterly scrambled, and we cannot even superficially follow the transitions, evolutionary and deteriorative, that marked the man's story.

The film makers were clearly hampered by the need to appease Bruce's widow and mother. But with a marvelous mother like the one on screen, no boy could have grown up troubled; and with a basically so loving husband-wife relationship, whence came the divorce, and all those marital and post-marital agonies? . . . The film's dishonesty is epitomized by the scene in which Bruce gets his wife to have sex with a lesbian as he watches and, eventually, joins in. The idea is to evoke moral deterioration, have a daring and salacious scene, and still not offend any moviegoers. . . .

The fragmented structure, furthermore, prevents us from seeing the Bruce routines whole; the best ones, indeed, are absent altogether. . . .

Most painful about this lackluster film are the bits of barbershop Freudianism in the posthumous interviews: "He had to prove it to himself."—"Insecurity?"—"Insecurity." (p. 44)

*John Simon, "Films: 'Lenny'" (reprinted by permission of Wallace & Sheil Agency, Inc.; copyright © 1975 by John Simon), in* Esquire, *Vol. LXXXIII, No. 2, February, 1975, p. 44.*

### CAROLINE LEWIS

Bob Fosse and Julian Barry are singularly unsuccessful at suggesting the complexity beneath the masks of [Lenny Bruce in *Lenny*]. Where the camp extravagance of *Cabaret* was a fitting metaphor for the theatricality that both masked and exaggerated the incipient frenzy of Nazi Germany, Fosse's staging of *Lenny* at all times serves to obscure his subject. Lenny's wife, mother and agent (themselves put across in unnuanced, stereotypic roles) are interviewed in the present, and at every point in Lenny's career Fosse cuts back for their view of events—a technique guaranteed to flatten out the film by showing the comedian who insisted on speaking for himself (down to the final, self-destructive obsessiveness with which he pored over and expounded on his trial transcripts) through the eyes of less articulate observers. . . . Although writer and director recognise that Bruce was obsessed with the tyranny of social stereotypes, they fail to convey his struggle to explode those stereotypes through a mastery of original juxtaposition, a painful self-analysis turned outwards upon an embarrassed, enraged and fascinated audience. By focusing on Bruce's use of four-letter words, and the fear this generated in the late Fifties and early Sixties, the film-makers obscure the fact that if Bruce were around today he would still be outrageous, because he would find ways to be uncomfortable with himself and his audience. . . . When the time comes for breakdown, with the half-clothed comedian wandering on to the stage and losing the thread of what he is saying in a fog of drugs and fatigue, Fosse's presentation is still too remote and unaccented for the moment to register as anything but another 'shtick'. The shuttered look of the film, its endless close-ups and staccato style, suggest a stage-play insufficiently adapted for the screen—or perhaps an extended metaphor to the effect that Lenny was always on as a performer, his life always a blend of the public and the private. A more constructive approach might have been to allow for a greater variety of public and private moments, to incorporate the sense that when Lenny made his appearances the stage was too small to hold him and that the boundaries between the self and the audience, the conventional and the obscene, were always being called into question. (p. 110)

> *Caroline Lewis, "'Lenny'," in* Monthly Film Bulletin *(copyright © The British Film Institute, 1975), Vol. 42, No. 496, May, 1975, pp. 109-10.*

### GORDON GOW

I suppose there must have been some occasion in the past when I was as emotionally affected by a film as I have been now by *Lenny*. But I cannot remember when. *Lenny*, I can say for sure, has moved me deeply. . . .

The film's structure is daringly reminiscent of [Orson Welles's] *Citizen Kane*. . . . Bob Fosse's direction, however, goes its own realistic way, inviting no comparison with Welles but maybe renewing appreciation of the [Peter] Bogdanovich influence through the decision to shoot in black-and-white. . . . For *Lenny* has leanings towards such organised effects are carefully restrained, and yet the pervading realism is allied quite often to stunning examples of composition and lighting, as when spotlights blaze towards the lens through the smoky dimness of a nightclub, throwing the foreground figure of Lenny into silhouette. . . .

If Lenny is presented contentiously as 'the conscience of America' he is also drawn in human terms, warts and all. His traces of exhibitionism are not denied, nor is his quest for [the] combination of emotive release and enriched experience. . . . Fosse is essentially a choreographer, which I mean, of course, as a compliment—a choreographer warm and true in spirit, whose conjurings of eloquent movement in total unison with the realistic vein make *Lenny* the best directed movie to come out of the United States in this decade. . . .

The valid truths of Lenny's creed are nowadays perhaps obvious, yet there are still enough diehards about to make them worth repeating. . . . (p. 38)

One might argue that Lenny's obsession with truth above all is too overbearing. . . .

His yearning for a recognition of 'what is' rather than the media concept of 'what should be' was perhaps the strongest validity in his ethos. And if he wasn't anywhere near the lifestyle of Francis of Assisi, he had nevertheless a dedication that I for one can only envy and look back upon with awe.

But certainly, with it, he had very human contradictions in his behaviour, and the film's acknowledgement of these will serve to indicate the peril of the hurdles which only a high measure of courage can surmount. Lenny had a lot of it: in the long run, not enough. People called him self-destructive, and some of them said it derisively, as though self-destructive acts were naughty deeds that their perpetrators could simply eschew with a snap of the fingers. If Fosse's *Lenny* can break that barrier down in just one mind, it will have proved its worth. That it exists at all is enough for me: I rate it high among the greatest movies of all time. (p. 39)

> *Gordon Gow, "Reviews: 'Lenny'" (© copyright Gordon Gow 1975; reprinted with permission), in* Films and Filming, *Vol. 21, No. 10, July, 1975, pp. 38-9.*

### FRED KAPLAN

[*Lenny* is] a travesty. The Lenny Bruce of this film is so prettified that he comes off as little more than a naughty David Steinberg. Hoffman plays him with that charming-cute Benjamin Braddock grin of his as if Bruce were just one of the boys. The Lenny Bruce of this film sermonizes after doing most of his bits on stage, so that in your heart you should know that he was a deep-humanist and loving-reformist. . . . It's this sort of sanctimoniousness, making Lenny Bruce out to be a goo-goo, that makes the film a runaway disaster.

What's missing from this portrait is the vibrance, the brilliantly zany improvisation, the wild pace, the jazz-like virtuosity in Bruce's performance, in his whole personality. (p. 40)

[The filmmakers are] so concerned with presenting Lenny Bruce as a Serious and Concerned Social Martyr that there's scarcely a knee-slapping laugh in the whole picture. There is also no historic or social context laid out, no ambience, and the whole spirit and meaning of Lenny Bruce is thereby grossly distorted. . . .

What *Lenny* misses, among other things, is the insanity, often the nihilism, at the very core of Bruce's routines, of his personality, of his contemporaries. . . .

But even if you want to look at Lenny Bruce as a serious saint and prophet, the film is still a failure because Bruce's most powerful social criticism is not included. . . . It's as if Bruce is To Be Dug solely for talking about cocksucking and transvestism before it was o.k. to do so. But since this aspect of his humor isn't particularly shocking anymore, and since Hoffman performs it too heavy-handedly, the power is gone. It seems gratuitous and not terribly imaginative.

In sum, what we have here is Bruce's *chutzpah* and lunacy mellowed and subdued to a hallowed (but hollow) solemnity, and his truly important social humor omitted entirely. In short, we end up with a *bland* Lenny Bruce.

But why not? For what Fosse & Barry present here is just another tedious Hollywood celeb-bio. Lenny Bruce is depicted as just a nice Jewish boy hoping for the bigtime in show-biz, but gets ruined by a *shiksa* stripper who turns him on to nasty drugs and, besides, nobody understands him, and so he dies a loner, and afterwards everybody exploits him. Including, the script fails to mention, the people who made this very cornball movie. (p. 41)

Fred Kaplan, "'Lenny'," in Cinéaste (copyright © 1975 by Gary Crowdus), Vol. VI, No. 4, 1975, pp. 40-1.

## DAVID DENBY

*All That Jazz,* an appalling work, is about an artist helplessly driving himself toward a heart attack. Gideon is the man who has the stuff, the divine fire, the man everyone loves and depends on. No one else counts. . . .

*All That Jazz* is a characteristic product of our confessional age. After the success of dance musicals like Michael Bennett's *A Chorus Line* and Fosse's *Dancin',* it was only a matter of time before the star choreographer-director stepped out in front of his performers and made his sufferings and triumphs the subject of the show. But *All That Jazz,* Fosse's summing up of life, love, and art, goes beyond mere self-celebration. Not since Chaplin (in *Limelight*) has anyone given way to the supreme foolishness of dramatizing his own death. The movie is a monstrous ego trip. . . . What's depressing about *All That Jazz* is the banality of Fosse's journey into his own life. To my ears Fosse's confession sounds like the familiar maudlin display of theater people when they try to tell "the truth" about themselves. . . .

Fosse flaunts his weaknesses and his sins as a way of picking up points for honesty. . . .

Yet apart from a most unpleasant megalomania, very little is actually revealed; Fosse's over-elaborate method prevents any real exposure. . . . [Clutter] spins through the movie . . . , producing a series of fragments, images, instant epiphanies, but nothing *sustained.* It's as if the film had been put together by an editing machine free-associating wildly on a psychoanalyst's couch. (p. 63)

We never do find out what women mean to Gideon, though we can see that they are all obsessed with him, young and old, starting with the mischievous nightclub strippers, recalled in flashback, who fondled the adolescent Gideon so eagerly that he went onstage to dance with a large stain on his pants. That stain spreads throughout the movie: *All That Jazz* is indeed an indiscretion, and not the youthful kind that you're happy to indulge. . . . We're meant to cluck our tongues over this womanizer Gideon, this bastard. But how silly, how vain! To agonize in public over your ruthless treatment of talented and beautiful women is a very luxurious form of self-criticism—it's more like boasting. In any case, hasn't it occurred to Fosse that his ex-lovers still speak well of him because they are dancers and need his friendship in order to work? Wandering around a hospital, Gideon sees an elderly woman in agony; he kisses her, tells her she's beautiful, and she attains peace, presumably ready to accept her own death. Fosse/Gideon is the Godhead, the show-biz genius-savior. No one even *dances* unless he's around to watch and approve. (pp. 63-4)

For a while, the framework of putting on a show gives Fosse's megalomania a plausible outlet. There's an exhilarating opening sequence, done without dialogue, in which Gideon selects a chorus line from a hundred or so dancers. As the chosen dancers mesh into a unit, the spins and leaps, highlighted and "rhymed" by the editing, snap into place like the parts of a beautifully calibrated machine. Here, as in *Cabaret,* Fosse doesn't shoot an overall pattern; he goes for the brilliant dance image, the sustained individual pose, and then throws a succession of such images and poses on the screen as if he were flipping through a deck of picture cards. . . . Predictably, the show's backers—Philistines all—shake their heads in dismay, convinced that the [erotic production] number is too raunchy for Broadway. But Fosse is being disingenuous here. . . . The sheer *ungraciousness* of this movie gets you down.

Once Gideon suffers his heart attack, *All That Jazz* becomes zany on a grotesque scale. . . . *All That Jazz* culminates in Gideon's death, which is presented as a huge nightclub number. . . . The number is a kind of awesome catastrophe, as tasteless and ugly as anything perpetrated by Ken Russell in his long career of gaudy excess. Fosse's wisdom comes down to this: Everything in life, including death—*especially* death—is just another routine, another number. Suspended between self-love and self-disgust, Fosse may actually believe this rancid nonsense, and some theater and movie people may find it profound—crazier movies than this one have been hailed as masterpieces. *All That Jazz* is so far removed from entertainment that a few solemn types may take it for a bold and courageous work of art. (pp. 64-5)

David Denby, "Broadway Melody of 1979," in New York Magazine (copyright © 1980 by News Group Publications, Inc.; reprinted with permission of New York Magazine), Vol. 13, No. 1, January 7, 1980, pp. 63-5.

## ROGER ANGELL

The folks over at *MAD* [*Magazine*] are going to have an easy time of it when they get around to putting out their version of **"All That Jazz,"** . . . which is based, we are given to understand, on Fosse's own life in the theatre. For one thing, the *MAD* artists and writers won't have to waste any time thinking up their customary funny, far-out version of the events up on the screen, because Bob Fosse and his associates, including the producer and co-author, the late Robert Alan Aurthur, have come up with a picture that defies further broadening: it is its own *MAD,* and the balloons in the strips can be filled in with dialogue right out of the picture. (pp. 69-70)

Come to think of it, and because the *MAD* artists like big, messy layouts, they should probably slap another figure right into the middle of [the] last two scenes—Warner Baxter, of course (little mustache, worn-out face, disarming smile), popping aspirins and smoking a million cigarettes and coughing his head off and saying almost exactly the same lines to Ruby Keeler and Ginger Rogers and the other brave, tired kids in the rehearsal scenes of the first big Warner Brothers backstage movie musical of them all, the 1933 hit "42nd Street." Two musicals for the price of one! . . .

Well, I guess the *MAD* artists are going to be pretty pooped themselves, because they'll certainly have to put in that mysterious female, swathed in yards of white tulle and swirling veils, called Angelique . . . , who seems to represent Ms. Death, and who will have to have a "Prop. F. Fellini, Roma" stamped on her rump . . . and familiar Fosse dance numbers—a blur of long legs and outthrust hips, tucked-in chins, hats cocked over eyes, snapping fingers, and sensuous kicks and pelvic twists and . . . Well, you'll get the idea when you see the magazine, or even the movie. (p. 70)

[A lot of moviegoers] are going to love the movie . . . because it's fun and because it's about *life* (*ta-dahh!*). It's hard to take exception to this notion, because this is a picture about show-biz people, who are theatrical by nature and must invent a drama for themselves every day. They call this life, but in this case I call it hokum—of a very high, rich order. Go ahead and enjoy it, but watch out for the old cholesterol. (p. 71)

*Roger Angell, "Heads and Hearts," in* The New Yorker *(© 1980 by The New Yorker Magazine, Inc.), Vol. LV, No. 47, January 7, 1980, pp. 68-71.*

### ANDREW SARRIS

To say that Fosse's *All That Jazz* has been influenced by Fellini's *8* is merely to sum up two decades of a chi-chi Broadway reverence for the European art film in contradistinction to Hollywood's "commercial product." . . .

The calculations and the imitations have worked to the extent that the film looks dazzling throughout, and several of the dance numbers are genuine show-stoppers. Yet there is something missing at the center of the film. Who exactly is [Gideon], and why should we care what happens to him? Fosse and Company tend to evade these questions as if they are not worth answering in an ambiguous and artsy European-type film. . . . Fortunately or unfortunately, *All That Jazz* is better danced, photographed, and edited than it is written. The dialogue never takes off on its own. At best, it just sits there without distracting from the visual and choreographic pyrotechnics. The besetting deficiency of *All That Jazz* is therefore not coldness, but vagueness. . . .

Still, the film remains fascinating as much because of, as in spite of its incongruities. The loveliest scene of all shows . . . Gideon . . . giving a private dance lesson to his daughter. . . . One waits in vain for the Gideon character to keep building from this exquisite communion of father and daughter, but, as always, we return to square one with an ostentatiously womanizing genius engaged in an overly ritualized form of self-destruction. Perhaps that is all that Fosse has learned from his undeniably hectic and exhilarating existence. It is not nearly enough for the demands of dramatic narrative on the screen.

The kinetic spectacle is something else again. *All That Jazz* should be savored as the first truly grown-up musical we have seen on the screen for some time, which only goes to prove that talent is the next best thing to genius. . . . I have always wondered why with his carefully cultivated womanizing image Fosse has taken such great pains to desex his female dancers. This studied androgyny may provide a key to a certain psychological desperation in the . . . Gideon character. The implied merger of the sexes in a rhythmic unity may suggest a desire to be alive all the time instead of only part of the time. It is only a hunch, but *All That Jazz* may just be Fosse's pantheistic yearnings coming out of the closet at long last. Non-mystical spectators may be less amused by Fosse's sneaky stabs at self-congratulation. I suppose it goes with the territory.

*Andrew Sarris, "Autobiographical Portraits as Reel Life" (reprinted by permission of* The Village Voice *and the author; copyright © News Group Publications, Inc., 1980), in* The Village Voice, *Vol. XXV, No. 1, January 7, 1980, p. 35.\**

### STANLEY KAUFFMANN

[*All That Jazz* is] disguised and altered autobiography. It's about Bob Fosse. . . .

The story of his life might be spectacular, but this is something else. Except for one brief flashback, it's a latter-day self-destructive agon. . . . (p. 24)

Even this material might have held better than it does, despite the theater's perennial belief that its smallest doings are of cosmic gravity, if several elements had been different. . . . [These include] the script. It may be substantially true, but it's trite, and about two-thirds of the way along, it slackens and sags. . . . The last third of the film, Scheider fantasizing in his hospital bed, is a drag, unrelieved by frenetic editing and splashiness. . . .

Everything the hero touches ultimately comes out Wonderful, no matter how worried others may be, including the re-editing of his film that he does casually between dance rehearsals. . . .

The first half hour or so, aside from the matters of private life, made me think that Fosse and friends were trying to preempt the film territory of *A Chorus Line*. . . . But the personal stuff soon overwhelms the professional stuff, and the personal stuff is bor-*ring*, as show biz puts it—even Fosse's hospital nightmares, which are done as big production numbers. I've rarely been so glad to see a protagonist die. My only fear was that there would be still another number in which he tip-tapped up to the pearly gates. (p. 25)

*Stanley Kauffmann, "Autobiographies" (reprinted by permission of Brandt & Brandt Literary Agents, Inc.; copyright © 1980 by Stanley Kauffmann), in* The New Republic, *Vol. 182, No. 4, January 26, 1980, pp. 24-5.\**

### ARTHUR SCHLESINGER, JR.

[*All That Jazz* is] an exquisitely conceived meditation on life and death. It is Felliniesque in a narrower sense too—in the flux and reflux of time, in the individuation of the supporting faces, in the imaginative audacity of the images. But Fellini's influence is creative, not constricting. *All That Jazz* remains entirely American and personal in its idiom and preoccupation. . . .

Scheider and Fosse marvelously evoke the whirl in which movies are made on stage and screen, the thousand things demanding immediate attention, the insistent beat of music in the background.

*Arthur Schlesinger, Jr., "Autobiography of Frenzy," in* Saturday Review *(copyright © 1980 by* Saturday Review; *all rights reserved; reprinted by permission), Vol. 7, No. 3, February 2, 1980, p. 28.\**

# Jean-Luc Godard

## 1930-

French director, screenwriter, actor, and critic.

Godard is one of the most important figures to emerge from the *nouvelle vague* (new wave): the auteurist school of film proposed by a group of critics intent upon being the complete creators of their films. Godard's style is regarded as abstract, dealing with the very nature and phenomenon of cinema. His desire to examine every aspect of the cinema has made him both controversial and misunderstood as well as lauded. Although not universally popular, he is unarguably one of the greatest influences on cinema since the 1960s.

Raised in Switzerland, Godard attended the Sorbonne, where his interest in cinema was nurtured. He first became involved with the cinema at the age of twenty, acting in films made by Jacques Rivette and Eric Rohmer. During the fifties Godard wrote film criticism for such journals as *La gazette du cinéma,* which he founded with Rivette and Rohmer, and *Les cahiers du cinéma.* He made his first short film in 1954 and continued making short, experimental films until 1959, when he directed his first feature-length film, *A bout de souffle* (*Breathless*).

Like the films that were to follow, *A bout de souffle* was low-budget, rapidly shot, and heavily improvised. It received critical acclaim and proved to be strongly reminiscent of the *film noir* genre, featuring aimless characters and a fascination with the gangster mode. Its freeform style forced the audience to follow the film's erratic leaps from point to point. In this and other early films, Godard's primary themes were already apparent, among them the idea that the sacrifice of personal dignity for materialistic purposes is prostitution. Godard's early films showed expansive knowledge and appreciation of American movies. His love of cinema and his complete understanding of cinematic art underlies his work. Although Godard is not technically innovative, he is highly regarded for his expert manipulation of the elements and theories of cinema.

Beginning with *La Chinoise,* Godard's films became more political. Yet, throughout, they are highly personal in style and theme. Most of Godard's work of the late 1960s was the result of his collaboration with Jean-Pierre Gorin in the Groupe Dziga Vertov. Along with Gorin, Godard worked on several projects, many of which were left unfinished. During their filming of *Tout va bien,* Godard was involved in a near-fatal motorcycle crash. Gorin undertook most of the filmmaking; as a result *Tout va bien* is not a definitive Godard work. From 1968 to 1980 Godard directed videotape films, experimental in nature and not widely distributed.

Of *Every Man for Himself,* his first commercial film since 1968, Godard says: "For the first time in twenty years, I have a feeling that rules have to be discovered; one should neither obey nor revolt automatically. It's better to discover what can be yours in the system and accept or change it. But work it and discover the unknown. Cinema is still an adventure for me." (See also *Contemporary Authors,* Vols. 93-96.)

## ARLENE CROCE

*Breathless* shows what the modern French version of [*la nouvelle vague*] really looks like, and the result is one of the most genuinely novel films of the lot. As parody, it is as subtly intellectual as [Robert Aldrich's] *Kiss Me Deadly* was exaggeratedly visceral; as improvisation, it is as unified and witty as [John Huston's] *Beat the Devil* was chaotic and arch; and as an example of new-wave camp, it is a beaut. . . .

The principle of novelty, in *Breathless,* lies in its acceptance of an exhausted genre—the Hollywood grade-B crime film—as a simulacrum of reality. Its plot is little more than that of the quickie digest: Footloose Killer on the Run Tangles with Double-dealing Broad as Cops Close In—Big Paris Manhunt. These mediocre clichés are played out in the deadpan style of an *actualité,* producing a dual impression of great moral wit and intense neurotic despair. The term "romantic nihilism" which critics have applied to many of the new-wave films and to *Breathless* in particular is apt enough. But the trouble with it is that it tends to make a generalizing cultural analysis of what are essentially cinematic fun and games. . . .

*Breathless* accomplishes much that is necessary for our present. Classic parallels are uncovered in the commonplace and are witty beyond any since Cocteau's own historic rummagings on behalf of another generation. (p. 54)

*Breathless* is a mannerist fantasy, cinematic jazz. Watching it, one can hardly avoid the feeling that Godard's intention, above all, was to produce slices of cinema—shots, figments, iconography—what the *Cahiers* critics talk about. His reality is always cinematized; the camera is always "there." . . . (pp. 54-5)

Action is all. This article of faith, central to the *film noir,* is what has always made the aesthetic truth of the *film noir* seem so shallow to American and British critics; the identification of personality and behavior is both absolute and rudimentary, unpardonably so. Hence, in **Breathless,** Michel's "Burglars burgle, lovers love, murderers murder . . . they can't help it" becomes an exact reflection of the crime movie's puerile fatalism.

But it would be a shame to depend exclusively on the words in this film, good as they are. **Breathless,** from beginning to end, is the total expression of its own meaning. If action is all, spontaneity, improvisation, is the only possible style. It is the style cultivated by Michel as an expression of impermissible masculine virtuosity. He at least is the hero of his own life, even if his life is a cheap film and, in the end, not worth living. **Breathless** sees an art form as a life-style and vice versa; quite logically, it ends with its hero's death. (p. 55)

Patricia, the American, irretrievably square, emotionally immobile, centerless, complacent, and uncomprehending, touches Michel, the Frenchman, at all those points where he is most vulnerable. She is the triumphant actual artifact of a culture of which he, in his delusion, is the copy, the dupe. He is the dynamo, she the void. Their long magnificently impromptu scene together in and out of bed inaugurates a dialectic of contemporary national manners that is almost Jamesian in its proportions. Their mutual assimilation of each other's backgrounds is as comically and painfully incomplete as it is conscientious. After she betrays—or, more accurately—disposes of him by calling the police, who shoot him down in the street, his bitter and just pronouncement upon her as a human being, "Tu es dégueulasse" ["You are disgusting"], is as far as the film goes. No one says, *"Tu es New York"; "Tu es Paris,"* although it is implied at every second. **Breathless** shows, with power, irony, and precision, what great cultural convulsions have taken place in our time. Again, as of old, the megalopolis frames the last spasm of the fleeing killer. Paris, beautiful, for centuries dedicated to an ease of individual enterprise, was created for deaths larger than this. (pp. 55-6)

> Arlene Croce, "Reviews of Films in General Release: 'Breathless'," in Film Quarterly (copyright 1961 by The Regents of the University of California; reprinted by permission of the University of California Press), Vol. XIV, No. 3, Spring, 1961, pp. 54-6.

## RAYMOND DURGNAT

No wonder Jean-Luc Godard called it *A Bout de Souffle (Breathless)*—the characters stop running only to start talking and their talking is a logorrhoea of caprice, probing and self-defence. Superficially it is a study of a lost generation; but generations are never lost without good reason, and the film is not an account of motives and causes (if it were it would be a criminological case-history) but a study in sensibility. Its nearest equivalent in English literature is Henry James to whose elephantine precision, hesitations and self-consciousness in the pursuit of obscure yet vaguely huge soul-states it approximates by the flippant paradox, the pun and the *non sequitur*. If Henry James in search of clarifications seems to pant like a bloodhound pursuing its own tail, the hero of *A Bout de Souffle* has abandoned the vicious circles of self-analysis for the shrug, the droop or jut of a fag, and the facetious grimace. . . .

What distinguishes *A Bout de Souffle* from a mere demonstration of falsity (which would be too easy to be interesting) is

that the inauthenticity is conscious, total and follows a sinewy discipline of its own. It is lived, not just brooded over. . . .

Michel is not serious about life and death, but he is very serious about moral commitment. . . .

This distinction, far from justifying his action, doesn't even palliate it; no amount of argument can make him seem, for a moment, a moral character. But no amount of censure, however deserved, can detract, for a moment, from his integrity towards his commitments. His irresponsibility is a search for freedom, not *from* himself, but *for* himself, and he envisages freedom in spiritual terms. . . .

The principal bond between Patricia and himself is non-sensual. There is something derisory about the quivering of the sheets under which they retire to make love. . . . Their mutual fascination is a cerebral passion; there are elements of the sex-war (she wants him to need her, he has slept with infinitely more women than she has men—in a visual parody of the scissors-cut-paper game) but the battle is fought out under cover of frivolity. He refuses to make like Romeo and she insists on going off for a business date. Her search for romance and his for loyalty-in-freedom chase each other with all the nostalgia of opposites—and complementaries.

Their informality on the bed conceals a profound alienation— is possible only because they touch at so few points. Just before they make love the radio announces "the synchronisation of our networks," which is only one way of putting it, but one feels their synchronisation is just that, i.e., a coast-to-coast hook-up of their nervous systems—not an integration, neither puts out roots into the other. In his quest for freedom he is never so foolish as to consign himself to the treadmill of deliberate self-contradiction, which may defend one from the danger of turning consistency into dogma but is more likely to give free play to one's feelings than to free one from them. Nonetheless his commitment, like her confusion, presupposes a detachment from his own emotions, which is why I call him inauthentic. He is a bore and a nuisance in that he is more concerned with being free than with being himself—he is all the more lordly for being unconcerned with his dignity, his soul, or any sort of hatred, but he is also a martyr and a bit of a nit. (p. 16)

> Raymond Durgnat, "Some Mad Love and the Sweet Life" (© copyright Raymond Durgnat 1962; reprinted with permission), in Films and Filming, Vol. 8, No. 6, March, 1962, pp. 16-18, 41.*

## TOM MILNE

I consider *Vivre sa Vie* [*My Life to Live*] to be not only Godard's most mature and most personal film, but also something of a masterpiece. The full range of the cinematic vocabulary which he spread out in his earlier films with the vivid and random excitement of a child learning to talk is here applied with a rigorous economy and exactness which show his complete and imaginative mastery of the medium, together with a new element of repose. . . .

[Like *A Bout de Souffle*, *Vivre sa Vie* has a thriller-novelette basis.] But where it is possible to appreciate *A Bout de Souffle* unexactly on a "B" film plane, as an excitingly told tale, I doubt whether anyone could, or would, sit through *Vivre sa Vie* on this level. Although the value and originality of *A Bout de Souffle* lies in its thick texture and its flashes below the surface, its real meat is the exterior story of a young man determined to fulfil the exhortation "live dangerously to the end." In *Vivre sa Vie,* on the other hand, this exterior is simply a shell to be peeled away; and the shell is necessary only in so far as it encloses what (for want of a better word) one might call the soul.

Hence the Brechtian structure of the film, which is divided into twelve distinct chapters, each preceded by a title summarising the characters and main action to follow. By this means attention is drawn away from the dramatic progress of Nana's story, and concentrated on her reaction to each event as it occurs. Godard has thus abandoned the fast and furious pace which is an integral feature of *A Bout de Souffle* and the "B" feature genre (and, incidentally, of *Une Femme est une Femme*), and in *Vivre sa Vie* the camera, often completely static, is allowed all the time it wants to capture a brief, revelatory moment; in fact, the camera is used, precisely and exactly, to isolate and examine each of these moments as it occurs. . . .

The motif of the film is stated in the first chapter, in Paul's story of the schoolgirl essay about the hen (*poule,* in French, is also the slang for prostitute): "The hen is an animal which is composed of an outside and an inside. If one takes away the outside, there is the inside . . . and when one takes away the inside, there is the soul." *Vivre sa Vie* sets out systematically to peel layer upon layer from a girl to see what lies beneath. (p. 12)

The film is constructed, in a sense, in three movements, starting from the exterior shell, and moving in to the long central documentary sequence on the facts and figures of prostitution, where Nana, as a prostitute, is shown to us reduced to the status of an object. And finally, the crucial last phase of the meetings with the young man with whom she falls in love, and with the philosopher who confirms her reawakening to the need to be something more than an object. At the same time, the film is built on three levels, and it only works properly if the three levels are seen together. Firstly, as a story about a woman who becomes a prostitute and is shot by gangsters. Secondly, as a total portrait of a woman. Thirdly, as a deeply personal statement by Godard himself. For Anna Karina, who plays Nana, is Godard's wife, and it is Godard's own voice which is dubbed on for the young man in the idyllic love scene of the last episode. It is therefore Godard himself who reads the Edgar Allan Poe story about the artist whose portrait of his wife became so perfect that, when it was completed, her life was transposed to the portrait, and she died.

Here we have an imaginative statement of Godard's conception of the film and also a pointer to the rôle of the last scene— the shooting of Nana—which has already been much criticised as "arbitrary", and a cheap thriller climax. On the story level, it *is* arbitrary. On the portrait level, it is less so, because Nana has been reduced to an object, and has just become aware of this when she dies. As the philosopher suggests in his conversation with her, "Speech means almost a resurrection in relation to life, in the sense that, when one speaks, one exists in another life from when one is silent." Nana, at the end of the film, has just "spoken about herself," and because she has been inextricably caught up in the life of silence (i.e. prostitution), that life must get rid of her. But it is on the Poe/Godard imaginative level that the ending is really essential. For if the film has completely and truthfully captured Nana's portrait, then her life will be transferred to the portrait, and she *must* die. (p. 50)

*Tom Milne, "Jean-Luc Godard and 'Vivre sa vie'," in Sight and Sound (copyright © 1963 by The British Film Institute), Vol. 32, No. 1, Winter, 1962-63, pp. 9-12, 50.*

## ISABEL QUIGLY

Jean-Luc Godard's *Le Petit Soldat,* which has been banned for three years as too topical, too controversial and in general too embarrassing for export, turns out to be an intense, unlikeable work, highly interesting, hugely depressing, and strangely 'clinging,' one of those films whose images hang about afterwards, hauntingly nasty and antiseptic, secretly full of meaning and of dire, alarming point. It is a film about politics in action that refuses to make political statements, and while one longs, can hardly fail, to take sides, to hate or approve *before* any action, even, Godard will not allow it. 'A plague on both your houses' is as far as he will go, and the result is not so much balanced as remote and sometimes meaningless. This effect of blurred outlines and non-commitment is enhanced by the fact that, in a film about a nationalistic war, all the fighters on either side seem (to a non-French or non-Algerian eye) racially indistinguishable.

Godard's tone is neutral; his style hygienic, as it were urban, and dateless, a strange style that moves with complete confidence between the functional (the sub-functional, in fact, clinical and white, with lighting like that of medical photographs or police documents) and the—apparently—spontaneous and decorative. . . .

What mainly limits [the story] is Godard's lack, not just of political interest or comment, but of political understanding, of any sort of historical background for his characters, who are seen (in spite of references to parents, and the war, and even a single touching moment in which the lack of 'good brave causes' is bewailed) to be moved by such a hotchpotch of trivial motives that they would hardly seem to stand up to the solid reality of torture. The script, Godard's own, so presumably very definitely intended, is the film's main weakness: without it one might accept even some visual absurdity—guns in broad daylight apparently unnoticed, ham-fisted assassination attempts that wouldn't fool the Keystone Cops. But its whimsicality and archness and its quite lurid 'highbrowness" (perpetual-student brand) obtrude at every turn. . . .

This still leaves a good deal. Faults, limitations, irritations still leave a film that seems to have been made by a man who hasn't thought but has *seen* his subject, has lived and seen life in terms of the cinema, with the strength (visual strength) and limitations that implies. His psychology is childish, his people are undeveloped, his ideas unformed. And the world he shows is cancerous; but it is recognisably, horribly, a small part of our own. (p. 13)

*Isabel Quigly, "Confused Alarums," in The Spectator (© 1963 by The Spectator; reprinted by permission of The Spectator), No. 7045, July 5, 1963, pp. 13, 15.*

## MICHAEL KUSTOW

[Godard loves] defiantly simple definitions. Let me try one: a Godard film is one in which several people play a game which ends in a death. Yes, but that's not enough: let's try something even simpler. The cinema is made of pictures on a strip of moving celluloid through which light passes. The existences of Godard's characters are unstable; just as precarious is the enterprise of making such a film. Godard makes us feel his awareness of the constant fragility of his fiction, the illusoriness of his medium.

His films have been compared with Pop Art, and they share its planned obsolescence. . . . Godard's films are as mutable as his characters' grasp on their own existence. To accuse him of flippancy, to claim (as John Coleman did recently) that his switching of tones is just a stylistic affectation, is like telling Picasso that a bicycle seat is a bicycle seat and not a bull's head.

*Bande à Part* gives us a chance to appreciate the way Godard turns inconsequence into art. . . . [The urban raggle-taggle of Balham] is invested by the narrator's voice with a lunar strangeness, being described with images drawn from the stars, the planets, the Dead Sea. The result is to theatricalise it, not by fantasticated photography but by the alliance of unemphatic images with a metaphoric text to produce a *dérèglement des sens.* (And doesn't Arthur claim that his surname is Rimbaud— 'comme mon père'?)

Within this enclosing stylisation, many sequences follow a pattern beginning in objective description and shifting into a theatrical key. (pp. 11-12)

Another way in which Godard wields his scalpel of artifice is by breaking illusion, as in the one minute's silence in the café sequence. Here we are made aware of the sound-track: what we took as a given fact of screen reality is suddenly shown as a technical device which can be shut off at will. We stare at the three characters who are now at a loose end, images on celluloid deprived of one of their senses. It is a shattering expression of a sense of impermanence, transience.

Shortly after this Arthur tells Odile what a good shield she'll make when the shooting starts. Then they get up to dance, in one of the film's most remarkable takes. They are doing a routine—something immensely theatrical. But they are doing it with intense self-absorption, with no concern at all for an audience. Dancing, Odile flowers. From a timid, fearful dormouse she becomes a tall woman, graceful and happy to be alive, moving her limbs and her breasts, answering the music. This kind of intersection of fragments—a cinematic trick, a foreboding of violence, a dance—is quintessential Godard. . . .

Out of this epiphany the narrator (who is Godard/The Cinema, aiding latecomers with a plot run-down, drawing a metaphor, pointing a legend, promising a future episode) plucks one of Godard's favourite themes. "Franz did not know whether the world was becoming a dream or a dream becoming the world." . . .

Godard's most flamboyant *coup de théâtre,* of course, is the shooting-bout between Arthur and his uncle. . . . [Arthur's] refusal at this point to die commonsensically, his triumph over his opponent, who succumbs to the normal laws of life and death, make us think about the power of art, of make-believe, over life. But these are not gratuitous reflections: they have been earned by the shifting, delicate rhythms of what has come before. . . .

[Odile is Arthur's] legacy to Franz, and we see them embark on a precarious last-reel happiness, aware of apartness, accepting it. This time it is the generous of spirit who come through: Godard has already let us see into their hearts by giving to them the only two monologues in the film. . . .

Both of these moments combine the two elements of Godard's style: dream and documentary. Franz's story tells of men's inability to distinguish between truth and fiction: but it is performed and photographed as objectively as a TV interview. Odile's song, a quaint rhymed ditty, is the natural expression of her new love for Arthur, and as such is shot in loving close-up. . . . But Godard cuts across this intimacy impassive mid-shots of a *clochard* and a man in bed, first alone, then with a woman. They are all asleep. We may be sure they are dreaming. In *Bande à Part,* Godard further perfects a cinema which leads us easily from our firm real-life world into the sea of dreams, which may be vulnerable in life but are necessary for living. His cinema does not offer lessons or solutions: it seems to come to him "as naturally as leaves to a tree." He is justified in ending the cheeky list of contributors on the credits with 'CINEMA: JEAN-LUC GODARD'. (p. 12)

*Michael Kustow, "'Bande à part'," in* Sight and Sound *(copyright © 1965 by The British Film Institute), Vol. 34, No. 1, Winter, 1964-65, pp. 11-12.*

**TOM MILNE**

Godard has always been two or three years ahead of his time. All the same, one wasn't quite prepared for the way everything else (from [Antonioni's] *The Red Desert* downwards) began to look rather old-fashioned and strained as soon as *Une Femme Mariée* [*The Married Woman*] appeared on the scene. Comparisons are impossible, of course: *The Red Desert* is in its own way just as remarkable a film. It is simply that Godard has realised—and found a technique for dealing with his realisation—that modern life is so complex, and human relationships so intangibly tangled, that fully rounded and polished artistic statements with all the ends tucked neatly out of sight are no longer possible. . . .

Godard's sub-title [**"Fragments of a Film Made in 1964"**] refers to the collage effect of the film, which moves freely between fragments—scenes, bits of scenes, bits of bits of scenes, a printed page, a word, half a word. But at the same time (one must never expect single strands from Godard), it is a film about fragmentation. The film opens with a disembodied hand sliding slowly forward across a white sheet; and it ends with the same hand (Charlotte's) slowly withdrawing, leaving blankness, nothing.

The scenes of love-making which open and close the film are composed entirely of human fragments—a hand, a leg, a head, a trunk. The effect is extraordinary, as though the world had split into separate pieces, separating people from one another. This feeling of dislocation is carried through the whole film. . . . (p. 107)

The anguish which runs through the film, implicitly in Charlotte's behaviour, explicitly in Godard's direction, comes from this separateness: Charlotte senses her solitude, senses the ultimate impossibility of human relations. Unlike Giuliana [in *The Red Desert*], it doesn't make her behave insanely, it just governs her life like an invisible hand pushing her relentlessly along. When she and Robert (her lover) part at the end, full of hopes and promises to return to each other and get married, Charlotte knows that it is all over, not so much because there is any reason for the affair to end, as because there seems to be no reason for it not to. It would be wrong to suggest that this feeling of almost cosmic disintegration dominates the film in any explicit sense. . . . Charlotte is living her life happily and unthinkingly in the present tense, with the menace no more than a background which one has got so used to that one no longer notices it: a radio blaring its grotesquely inflated list of road casualties to an empty room, a voice mentioning Auschwitz and evoking only puzzlement (''Auschwitz? . . . oh yes . . . thalidomide . . .''). (pp. 107, 109)

*Une Femme Mariée* operates on various levels, and works on all of them. At bottom, it is the eternal triangle, almost classically exposed. Charlotte has a lover, Robert; she has a husband, Pierre, with whom she still enjoys physical passion; she is pregnant, but doesn't know which of them is the father, and is afraid. But unlike Truffaut's *La Peau Douce,* which was a case history, Godard's hymn to *la peau douce* is a sociological document. Charlotte is not a woman, but Woman. What Godard is after in his portrait is that mysterious, anonymous being assailed on all sides by the shrill voices of advertisements, advising her to dress, paint and otherwise distort herself towards some nebulous ideal of sameness and sinfulness. . . .

*Une Femme Mariée* is a film of the outside, totally unconcerned with ethics or morals. . . .

[Charlotte is not soulless]; it is simply that in her life, and the routine which surrounds her, the outlets are blocked. Godard, in fact, makes it quite clear that, ultimately, Nana, Odile . . . and Charlotte are of the same species, though their particular contexts in life draw the soul from Nana, the emotion from Odile, and the body from Charlotte. But they converge at a point: ''on est coupable'' [''we are guilty'']. . . .

To describe the film in terms of concentration camps and dislocated, fragmented worlds, may make it sound portentous, which is the last thing of which *Une Femme Mariée* can be accused. In the first place, it is too sure-footedly relaxed to allow portentousness. In the second, it is consistently and caustically funny. (p. 109)

Charlotte's crack about spectators in the cinema [''I'm very comfortable like this. And anyway, it's the ideal position for the spectator in the cinema.''], delivered while hunched down comfortably in the front seat of Robert's car, almost disappearing from sight, is the metaphorical equivalent of Godard's easy, informal approach to filmmaking. A film is enjoyable to make, and made to be enjoyed. The surface texture of the film, already broken up by interviews, digressions, cut-ins of street signs, book titles and so forth, is also studded with puns and gags, both visual and verbal. . . .

With Godard an image can be, at one and the same time, a private joke, a public gag, a clue, an imaginative link, or a serious statement. When he uses the Hitchcock poster, for instance, it is a) a *hommage* to one of his favourite directors; b) a wry comment on the fact that Hitchcock is one of the few directors grand enough in France to warrant having his face on cinema posters; c) a legitimate means of underlining the minatory aspect of the film; and d) it serves as quotation marks to the thriller parody which runs through the film. . . . Fascination with the *vérité* of *cinéma* and the *cinéma* of *vérité* is one of the constants of Godard's work, and determines the rigorous yet tangential attitude of his camera, at one moment probing for the truth behind the façade, at the next leaping away to show that it is all façade anyway. . . .

*Une Femme Mariée* is focused steadily on three faces: the husband, grave and puzzled, haunted by memories of what Charlotte once was to him; the lover, serene and untroubled, content with her presence; and Charlotte, presenting the same candid, troubled gaze to both, uncertain as to the difference,

if any, in her feelings for them. Godard fixes these images on the screen and invites us to see what lies behind them; at the same time, by inviting his characters to step out of character (in the interviews, for instance), he invites us to take another look at the façade. We are reminded not only that this is ''truth twenty-four times a second,'' but that it is perhaps as true a truth as any. . . .

Parenthetically: this is Godard's most subtle ending to date. His love of flamboyantly theatrical dénouements is satisfied, but this time it happens at double remove: by proxy, as it were, and also off-stage. (p. 110)

The subtlety of the ending is matched by a new clarity and assurance throughout. The whole film is organised with astounding precision, so that its patchwork elements are like the spokes of a wheel, leading outwards from the hub and also providing support for the frame. The hub, of course, is Charlotte, while the frame is her circular voyage between husband and lover; and the whole superstructure of the film dovetails into an analysis of the cul-de-sac of her existence.

Charlotte is haunted by doubts as to whether her chance of true happiness lies with husband or lover: in his ruthless analysis, Godard demonstrates that there is no difference in kind, only in procedure. ''Love,'' says the song which Charlotte sings, ''is of infinite sadness. It vanishes like the day.'' (pp. 110-11)

Even if love is transient, however, it is of infinite tenderness, as the second verse of Charlotte's song affirms: ''Like the day, it returns.'' The corollary to the lover who grows like the husband, is the husband who becomes like the lover and so closes the vicious circle. . . .

Godard is the most open-ended of artists. He doesn't make problem pictures of the sort which deal with a controversial subject and come up with an answer. He assumes that the controversy is embedded in life, and maybe isn't even controversial. *Le Petit Soldat* refused to tackle the Algerian ''problem'', and yet, as Godard says, the film now stands as ''witness to an epoch'' and its complex moral repercussions. In *Une Femme Mariée,* Charlotte's questions to the doctor about contraception and sexual pleasure, and Robert's casual assertion of police corruption—both delivered as though the subjects were unexceptional and needed no apology or introduction— reveal far more about defensive attitudes, and also hurt more, than any amount of reasoned, documented attacks.

Nor does he start with an answer and work backwards in order to find the given data. . . . ''Intelligence,'' in Roger Leenhardt's definition, ''is to understand before asserting''; and what we are left with at the end of *Une Femme Mariée* is simply a closely and passionately documented question-mark. (p. 111)

Tom Milne, ''Jean-Luc Godard, ou la raison ardente,'' in Sight and Sound *(copyright © 1965 by The British Film Institute), Vol. 34, No. 3, Summer, 1965, pp. 106-11.*

**RICHARD ROUD**

Comic strips seem to represent many things for Godard: first, a source book for the contemporary collective subconscious; secondly, a dramatic framework derived from modern myth— in much the same way as Joyce used the Ulysses myth; thirdly, a reaction against the subtleties of the psychological novel;

finally the attraction of comic strip narrative with its sudden shifting of scene, its freedom of narration, its economy.

The plot of *Alphaville* is pure comic strip. . . . (p. 164)

Just like a [Roy] Lichtenstein painting ("Oh, Brad, (gulp) it should have been that way"), the dialogue often echoes the balloons: "Let this serve as a warning to all those who try to . . ." etc. Characterisation, too, has been reduced to a minimum. . . .

But *Alphaville* doesn't look like a comic strip, and this is where Godard diverges from the true pop artist, who has been defined as "a man who offers a coincidence of style and subject, one who represents mass-produced images and objects in a style which is also based upon the visual vocabulary of mass production." In other words, the pop artist not only likes the fact of his commonplace objects, but more important, exults in their commonplace look. Godard resembles much more pop fringe figures like Larry Rivers and [Robert] Rauschenberg who, although fascinated by pop imagery, translate it into a non-pop style.

The second time I saw *Alphaville,* it was precisely the great refinement and plastic beauty of its style that impressed me. Like the volume of [Paul] Eluard poems which the dying Henri Dickson . . . presses into Lemmy's hand, Alphaville is the Capital of Pain (*Capitale de la Douleur*), and the visual style of the film is painful, menacing, anxiety-ridden. (p. 165)

*Alphaville* is built visually on extreme contrasts. . . . Basically there is the contrast of the straight line and the circle. For Godard, the circle represents evil: a man must go straight ahead, says the condemned man on the diving-board. So everything in Alphaville that represents the tyranny of the computers is circular. Lemmy's hotel suite is built in circular form; the staircases in the government buildings are spiral; even the city itself is, like Paris, circular, and to get from one place to another one must take a circular route. The corridors may be straight, but one always ends up where one started. And of course the computers move in circles. Time, says Alpha 60, is an endless circle. Lemmy [Caution], however, maintains that all one has to do is to go straight ahead towards everything one loves, straight ahead: when one arrives at the goal, one realises that one has nevertheless looped the loop (*bouclé la boucle*).

The inhabitants of Alphaville even talk in circles. Whenever anyone says hello, the reply is invariable: "Very well, thank you, please." "You must never say *why;* only *because,*" admonishes Natacha. Death and life are inscribed in the same hopeless circle.

Contrast is also displayed in Godard's treatment of the sound. The main musical theme is . . . syrupy and romantic, but it never gets beyond the introductory cadence. And it is intercut with harsh discordant noises: the slamming of doors, the whirling of the computers, and worst of all, the electronic grating voice of Alpha 60, which is as unpleasant as it is indescribable. It would sound like a death-rattle were it not for the absolute evenness and soulless monotony of its delivery. Godard has always liked to flash brutally from a bright scene to a dark one, but this is carried to extreme proportions in *Alphaville,* where the greyness of the streets is continually contrasted with the blinding floodlights of the electronic nerve centres. Like so many lasers, they torture the brain, at the same time exercising a hypnotic fascination in their rhythmical flashing. (p. 166)

*Richard Roud, "Anguish: 'Alphaville'," in* Sight and Sound *(copyright © 1965 by The British Film Institute), Vol. 34, No. 4, Autumn, 1965, pp. 164-66.*

**JOHN BRAGIN**

The essence of Jean-Luc Godard's **La Femme Mariée** is the transmutation of the dramatic into the graphic. The comings and goings of the characters, and the development of the story, are presented in the matter-of-fact way which is characteristic of Godard, and whose episodic nature reached its height in his film *Vivre Sa Vie*. The graphic elements in Godard's films are by no means new, they can be found in all of his work. What is new is the consistent movement into the graphic from the dramatic which is used as the basis of expression in this film, and which was only found in kernels in his other works. . . . Two of the film's title cards read successively: IN BLACK, AND WHITE, and it is between two contrasting poles that Charlotte moves, first searching at one, and then along a line to the other. The points on this line occur as encounters, which are strung together on the thread of Charlotte's movements over a period of two days. These movements are presented in Godard's almost throwaway style, and simply constitute the links between the important encounters. . . . By tracing, in this way, a complete line of Charlotte's activities during this period of time, Godard allows himself to be able to stop at certain points of importance, and to raise these, by use of graphic means, to a higher pitch than the line itself. These points of absolute ideas and emotions, presented as black or white, are not value judgments as to the good of one or the evil of another. They are of relief, or contrast, not of morality. Godard is a moralist because of his insistence upon carrying the eventualities of any choice to their furthest point. He is not, though, a traditional moralist because he does not choose beforehand which given choice is good. For Charlotte, as for all of Godard's women, choices involve the decision to follow one set of absolutes, or another. (p. 42)

For Godard, any printing is grist for the mill. Sometimes he breaks up signs which exist in the environment of his characters, such as the camera panning across the sign at Orly Airport: PASSAGE CINEMA, breaking PASSAGE into PAS SAGE, "misbehaving": a reflection on the secret meeting of Robert and Charlotte. (p. 43)

The name EVE, found in the word RÊVES, "dreams," is like DANGER, creating a symmetry in that EVE is exactly composed of all the letters between the first and last letter of the word. Eve too is an absolute, the first woman, and like *The* Married Woman. (The French censors got the title changed to *Une Femme Mariée* [A Married Woman], though this is contrary to the whole method of the film.) Eve is also a figure in mythology, and corresponds to Charlotte's cloudy, dream-like vision of an ideal, an absolute to follow. Godard has always been concerned with mythopoeic, transcendent values in man, but always measured against his actual being. And the tragedy in his films is the constant failure of his characters to find, and measure up to, the ideals which they seek. Because of his sternness and his uncompromising position he often seems a misanthrope. . . .

[In *Contempt*], the dramatic presentations of "static essentials," especially in reference to the different interpretations of the Odyssey which come up in the film, are forerunners to the "static essentials" (the phrase is Pavese's) which are presented even more directly, especially in graphic form, in *La Femme Mariée*.

It is in the café sequence, when Charlotte overhears the conversation between the two girls, that the images, graphic and dramatic, and the sound track, dialogue, effects, and music, are intertwined with the most complexity. The girls' conversation is about the impending loss of virginity by the girl on frame right. Quite simply, she represents ignorance, and her friend represents knowledge. This situation is a microcosm of Godard's approach to the whole film. (p. 44)

[The] important points, ideas, and phrases . . . are printed in the center of the frame, an outline of the conversation, not a reproduction of it. In this abstraction from the dramatic situation we are shown the mechanics of the device, as well as the device itself. In this way we follow Godard's method of movement from the dramatic situation to the graphic representation of it. The bones of the method are laid bare by this very schematic presentation. This idea of the work itself evincing the process of its creation as an integral part of its form was born with the Action Painters, and is manifest in many fields of art. It is the illustration of the artist's confrontation of the material reality which he molds. It evokes a feeling of honesty in the texture and rawness of the materials which are not glossed over to hide their essential nature, simply to create a slick, and therefore lying, image. The constant references to film in Godard's works, the self-consciousness of each work, are there to keep the perspective that the work is subordinate to the creator.

We move completely into the graphic realm with the second part of this sequence. The magazine Charlotte is reading is full of stylized drawings which advertise women's undergarments, and photographs of the mid-sections of men showing form-fitting clothing. . . . Comparison with Pop Art here is perfectly valid, for much of Pop involves simplicity of pattern, and the use of contemporary, stylized images. In other words, for Godard, this sequence is handled in exactly the same way in which one would handle a standard dramatic sequence cut into a film—a sequence involving the real world of people and their environment. This bringing of the graphic or imagistic world to the same level as the real world is clinched by the final shot in this sequence. It is a still frame of the drawing of a woman, in the same style as many we have seen in the sequence. But all of a sudden we notice Charlotte's head enter at the bottom of frame right and move along the frame line. It is a billboard, and its huge existence as an object moves us from the more abstract drawings in the magazine, back to Charlotte's movements in the more traditional pre-Godard world of things and people. But, for Godard's woman who is alive today, it is the image-as-object she must contend with, just as she does with other objects and people in her world. (pp. 44-5)

Rhetoric, even formal rhetoric, ends and gives way to unity in the three love scenes which occur at the beginning, middle, and end of the film. The act of love becomes a ritual celebrating life. And all value judgments such as sacred, profane, and adulterous give way to the celebration of this rite. Dialogue is gone; the lovers speak in unison, and the immoral is not a violation of conventional moralities, but any act which paralyzes the consummation of this love. Selection and emphasis also reach their highest point during these sequences. Godard's compositions are based on the fragmentation of the lovers' bodies to create patterns which are so powerful just because they do not deal with whole forms. Given the familiarity of the human form, perhaps the *most* familiar of all forms to us,

Godard is able to fragment it, breaking it down to create new patterns because of the suggestibility inherent in not seeing the whole form. . . .

Three times we see the lips of a character repeating "je t'aime" over and over again, without actually hearing the words. This, like the fade-in and fade-out, slows the pace, emphasizing both the activity of love-making and the visual patterning. By forcing the spectator to read the lips of the character (and it is a simple enough phrase for this) Godard draws him into being one with the speaker, as the viewer himself repeats the phrase over and over, in his own mind. (p. 47)

[When the film ends, Charlotte and Robert's] affair ends, because there is no more reality to the situation after Robert leaves. There is nothing for Godard to photograph. Charlotte's indecision was grounded in Robert's presence as an alternative to her husband. Her husband and her lover were the points, or poles, between which she encountered the emotions and ideas which structure the film. The material reality was the cause of her frustration. Her final acceptance of the end of the situation frees her from the hell which she has been experiencing.

But this is by no means either fatalism or a final answer to her question. It is only the elimination of the tension: the elimination of the immediate need to find her definition. Robert will return, and if she has not forgotten him, the problem may arise again. Other situations may, in the future, confront her with the need to take up the search again. Just as this film is called *Fragments of a Film Shot in 1964,* so is the total film only a fragment of life: a technique which could be called one of emotional and intellectual collage. Unlike works of drama in the past, which were based on characters in situations which changed their whole lives, this film is only the presentation of a momentary conflict or tension. This conflict gives birth to many kinds of emotions, "static essentials," which Godard orders so that we may understand them more clearly. It is a disturbance that for the time it exists consumes the total energies of Charlotte. All the more, because the film exists so much in and for the moment in its use of things contemporary, it is incisive. An instantaneous plunge into the fabric of the life of a character that lingers in the mind as a reality which is immutable, and constantly re-echoes there long after the film has been seen. (pp. 47-8)

> *John Bragin, "Film Review: 'The Married Woman',"* in Film Quarterly *(copyright 1966 by The Regents of the University of California; reprinted by permission of the University of California Press), Vol. XIX, No. 4, Summer, 1966, pp. 42-8.*

**JOHN THOMAS**

Let me insist from the outset that *Alphaville* is a film about flickering lights, circular staircases, labyrinthine hallways, and Zippo lighters. That it's also a film about alienation, the dehumanization of man and all that other stuff serious movies are required to be about is undeniable; but in Godard's world this second set of themes carries no greater weight than the first, and neither can be said to constitute the "meaning" of the film. . . .

It's necessary to say all this because *Alphaville* is so clearly the ultimate Message Movie that one may fail to see that it is, equally, the ultimate Meaningless Movie. Godard creates his future society with its rigid logic out of a series of images joined with carefree illogic, sketches his computer with the technique of a [Jackson] Pollock. (p. 48)

Important as its intellectual content may be, I think the film's message is not its Message but the structure of its images. For the Message of *Alphaville* is negative, an attack on the over-organized, hyper-intellectual world of modern man. But the structure of its images—the seemingly erratic development of a number of gratuitous visual themes—is the very poetry that Godard, speaking through Lemmy Caution, offers as Alphaville's salvation. . . .

Chief among the images that create the texture of this film is a flashing light. . . . To try to establish any "meaning" for this symbol would, I think, be pointless. The flashing light is as characteristic of modern civilization as anything else you might name, and particularly appropriate to Alphaville, where direct sunlight is rarely seen. I cannot stress too much that what is important is that the image is *there*, and is its own justification.

This light is in fact the central visual theme of *Alphaville*. In the opening five minutes there is little else. . . .

These first few minutes are among the most gripping in the film, not because anything happens, but because these particular images have been arranged in this particular way. In this sequence the whole substance and strategy of *Alphaville* stand revealed. These patterns of flickering light *are* the movie; what else in it is of greater importance? (p. 49)

The film is basically psychological rather than political; it attacks not the superstate but the modern habit of judging experience through the intellect and at the expense of feeling. But what's interesting is the way Godard handles this material—putting it in comic-book or fairy-story form and eliminating the psychological subtleties that another director might have thought important. In a sense he is admitting that his story cannot be taken seriously because it's been done all too often. Inundated as we are with this sort of thing in serious movies and novels, it's almost impossible for an artist to deal with such themes without sliding into parody. Godard's strategy is to admit this, dip consciously into parody, and thereby disarm the viewer. This approach also seems necessary because Godard wants his protagonist to be a genuine Hero, but can find no Heroes in today's world. . . . Lemmy Caution occupies in France a role analogous to that of Batman here. He is as completely a man of the past as Alphaville is a city of the future, and he cannot exist in our world except as pasteboard. . . . As a man committed to the importance of memory and history he records with his camera each significant event in the present, preserving it so that it becomes an integral part of the continuity of life. This is exactly what the people of Alphaville cannot do. They see themselves as unique, alone in the universe, devoid both of history and potentiality. Because he is rooted firmly in the values of the past, Caution has the inner confidence that it takes to be a Hero, and Alphaville must fall inevitably before his attack.

Here is the weak spot in Godard's Message. He can offer as an alternative to Alphaville nothing more than a return to the values of the past. But Alpha 60 has its point to make, too. We do live today between Past and Future, cut off from our historical roots but as yet unable to formulate the new values that we need to sustain ourselves. (pp. 50-1)

It is the irony of *Alphaville* that, despite his worship of the past, Godard has created out of his imagery this poetry of the future. In a sense the film *Alphaville* offers us a surer way out of the city. . . .

This tension between two points of view—between, in essence, two Godards—is the most interesting aspect of the film. Godard's movies have always been interesting because Godard himself is interesting. . . .

*Alphaville* is both portrait and prescription. What Godard has given cannot yet be analyzed because we still have to find words that offer some emotional equivalent to his images. (p. 51)

*John Thomas, "Film Reviews: 'Alphaville',"* in Film Quarterly *(copyright 1966 by The Regents of the University of California; reprinted by permission of the University of California Press), Vol. XX, No. 1, Fall, 1966, pp. 48-51.*

**JOHN SIMON**

In the phrase "the new sensibility"—it may or may not have been coined by Susan Sontag—the operative word is, of course, *new,* not sensibility. (p. 272)

[The] concept of "the new sensibility" . . . is supposed to account for the revolution in the arts . . . ; and for a realm of film-making whose summit is Godard and bottom the "underground movies" or "New American Cinema," as, in its newly sensible way, it likes to call itself. These and many more the Pandora's box of contemporary pseudo-art has unleashed upon us: every kind of plague in fact, excepting only hope.

Who was the Pandora who actually opened the lid? As far as film is concerned, I would locate the moment of disaster—inasmuch as this can be done at all, and it can be done only approximately—in a seemingly innocent scene of Jean-Luc Godard's *Breathless*. . . . In this particular scene I'm talking of, the lovers have gone to the movies and are watching an American, or American-style, western, complete with thundering hooves and guns. But suddenly, we hear from the soundtrack two idiot voices reciting at each other Apollinaire's beautiful poem, "*Cors de chasse*." . . . What business have the characters in a vulgar American western reciting one of France's finest twentieth-century lyrics at each other—and antiphonally, at that, as though it were dialogue that they were improvising?

Godard was doing one of three things here. He may have been trying to make fun of Apollinaire's poem by introducing it into a ridiculous context, or he may have been hoping to elevate the western to the stature of genuine art. Most likely, though, he was merely tossing a poem he had just stumbled on into an antithetical environment to create a comic shock effect. But whatever the intention, the "sensibility" that will indulge in this kind of effect is unmistakable. It is cynical, pretentious, and disaffected. Cynical, because it is willing to make a value judgment in the most casual, indeed backhanded, way; pretentious, because it will allude without justification to something that is supposed to confer intellectual prestige on the film-maker himself; disaffected, because it does not care what the cost as long as it gets its kicks. . . . [*Breathless* leaves us] with something that strikes us as sensationalism and showing off.

It is in this direction that Godard has proceeded. One watched with horror the gratuitous but arrogant devices multiply, the idea being to jolt us, if possible continuously. . . . It is not a mere shock, a titillation, a disturbance or reversal of the established order. A surprise makes us expand and, perhaps, exclaim; a jolt makes us contract and, most likely, gasp. A surprise surpasses the expected, a jolt merely bypasses it. (pp. 272-74)

What are the Godardian devices? To list a few at random: in-jokes, usually verbal or visual references to New Wave films, often one's own; allowing actors to improvise at length while the camera holds their faces in a close-up; using stop-shots on the slightest excuse (usually while someone is photographing somebody) or on none; panning back and forth *ad nauseam* between the faces of two talkers, often with an object in between them; using a handheld camera on the least provocation. . . . (p. 274)

Devices such as these, and many kindred ones, are not necessarily bad—they may even be good—but when used promiscuously, repetitiously, excessively, with the notion that they are *ipso facto* good, they become distasteful and ultimately dull. Godard's "new" rapidly turns into something other, and less, than the traditional: it becomes instant antique. Why do these innovations age so swiftly? Because, having nothing but them to lean on, Godard has to work them into the ground; because behind the devices there is nothing. (p. 275)

A piece of film has happened, and that is supposed to be its justification. It is because it is; it is like this because it is like this.

Or in other words, has the emperor no clothes? How marvelous! Who wants clothes anyway? There is more enterprise in walking naked. Nudity is so much more daring and more real. Well, that may be so in the case of avowed nudity, in nudity for a purpose, say, to show off a glorious body. But Godard's films pretend to clothes, they pretend to be constructs, artifacts, demonstrations of human action; in fact, however, they are nothing: not even nudity, only skeletons, and even those artificial, made of cardboard. Consider the dialogue even: here are two passages from **Contempt.** "Why do you assume this thoughtful air?—Because I am thinking of something, would you believe it?—Of what?—Of an idea." And again: "Why don't you love me any more?—That's life.—Why do you despise me?—That I will never tell you, not even if I were on the point of death." How pretentiously pseudomeaningful these utterances are, yet even a slightly closer look reveals them to be trite and hollow. Nor will it do to say that in Godard the words are unimportant. In his films, as he himself has proclaimed, "you have to listen to the people talking." (pp. 275-76)

**The Married Woman,** such as it is, is Godard's best film since **Breathless,** and [the scene where two girls exchange dating and sex talk], with its schizoid editing and incompletely overheard conversation, works well enough. One gets the feeling that these girls dabbling in sex, the sleazy stuff in the magazines, and the heroine's adulterous, tergiversations are all somehow connected, and part of the moral *anomie* of our world. But we cannot "really see, really hear" more than a fragment of what is going on in that scene, which is probably what Godard intended and may be just right—only it remains unclear how this challenges us to overcome anything at all. In the "context of the film" the young woman's dilemma is seen as essentially pleasurable, and, except for a very few minor inconveniences, there is no evidence that her sexual ambidexterity is anything but a happy feast for her ego.

It will surely be objected that an artist is not obliged to take a stand, and that the mere presentation of existing problems is a sufficient task. True enough, provided that the presentation is incisive, suggestive, and provocative enough. But Godard's

way, even in this more successful film, is merely to sketch in the ambience: sex in the magazines, sex on the posters, sex in the chitchat at the next table—immature, exaggerated, un-evaluated sex. Very good; we get the point. But how does it affect the heroine; with what aspect of her personality, formed by what experiences, does it mesh? Exactly why can't she choose? What does the lover offer her that the husband does not, and vice versa? How does the society, if it is to blame, corrupt one in a profounder sense than by posters and periodicals? Godard does not really flesh out and develop the problem; he merely sketches in its context adroitly but without much urgency. And when the characters are to reveal themselves, he resorts to *cinéma-vérité* and has the actors (apparently) improvising at great, pretentious, vacuous, and boring length, while he holds their faces in assiduous frontal close-up. (Sometimes we are not far removed from the drivel of Andy Warhol.) Granted we do not look for answers from the artist, only for enlightenment on what the issues and possibilities are; but from Godard, we get either obfuscation or oversimplification.

Rather than inventiveness and multifariousness, I would call the hallmarks of Godard irresponsibility and overreliance on the accidental. The film-maker is running off after every whimsical, extraneous notion that occurs to his undisciplined mind, while being, at the same time, tied to the apron strings of chance, which, under the honorific "improvisation," is supposed to work wonders for him. I dare say one may call the mysterious process of creation with equal right by any name: inspiration, improvisation, or for all I care, indeterminacy principle. But there is a vast difference between the distances from the center artists allow their works to wander, between the widths to which authors open their arms to embrace the unforeseen. Godard's invention does not explore so much as it rambles; his camera does not merely welcome the occasional stroke of luck—rather, having had its lens cleaned with a lucky rabbit's foot, it assumes that whatever it stumbles on will perforce be genius. Unfortunately, where anything goes, almost nothing works. (pp. 284-85)

In the cinema, chance is improvisation, or shooting at random, which may pay off under certain circumstances. In **Masculine Feminine,** when the hero interviews a Miss Nineteen, a silly teen-age beauty contest-winner, the staggering ignorance and coy stupidity of the girl, and the pitiful way in which she tries to minimize and cope with them, constitute a genuine stroke of luck: an obtuseness and frivolity emerge that are almost the equal of any artist's conception of them. Even so it may be questioned whether such an obvious patch of *cinéma-vérité* blends smoothly enough with the palpably contrived elements of the plot. But in a film like **The Married Woman,** where a bunch of actors is asked to improvise on metaphysical subjects, or in **My Life to Live** [Vivre sa vie], where a third-rate philosopher and a tenth-rate actress are expected to produce an impromptu Platonic dialogue, the results are, as they might be presumed to be, paltry.

Of course, Godard's courting of chance takes on more basic forms than bits of interpolated *cinéma-vérité.* . . . [Chance] is definitive only to the uncritical mind that accepts whatever pops up; as Godard's Lemmy Caution says in **Alphaville,** "I believe in the immediate inspirations of my consciousness." (In Peter Whitehead's English translation of the screenplay, the French *conscience* is rendered as "conscience"—a possible meaning, but surely not the right one here.)

What are these "immediate inspirations" of Godard's? They are the wish fulfillments of a childish psyche, the dreams of glory we know from [William] Steig's cartoons, the games played with toy pistols and machine guns in backyards translated verbatim onto the screen, bang-bang by bang-bang, and ending with a whimper. (pp. 285-87)

[*Alphaville* is] the perfect masturbatory fantasy, in which a brutish hero, but one with intellectual pretensions, triumphs over all opposition, but opposition so bumbling that one finds oneself taking its side out of sheer compassion. In his *Studies in Words,* C. S. Lewis has warned us that "when we try to define the badness of a work, we usually end by calling it bad on the strength of characteristics which we can find also in good work." And he gives this among other caveats: "The novel before you is bad—a transparent compensatory fantasy projected by a poor, plain woman, erotically starving. Yes, but so is *Jane Eyre.*" Well, I think there is a very clear difference between *Alphaville* and *Jane Eyre.* It lies, above all, in the nature of the needs. Charlotte Brontë was starving for love, for bare, essential human love, the very minimum and, if you will, maximum to which a normal, passionate, sentient and intelligent human being is entitled to. Godard's need is to compensate, or overcompensate, for puerile, irresponsible, indeed criminal, appetites; moreover, so infantile is his craving for instant gratification that he does not even bother to present the other side of a question or to give us a sense of the difficulties that have to be overcome, or to examine how the physical and intellectual prowess of his alter ego is evolved. Such matters are brushed aside, and Lemmy Caution proceeds with unthinking brutality to triumph over almost completely supine villains. In the end, the opposition's evil takes on an arbitrary, sporadic character, whereas that of Godard's alter ego is deepseated, convincing, and the more appalling for not being recognized as such. (pp. 287-88)

The horrible misconception underlying Godard worship is the assumption that to take all the liberties and perform all the tricks of which no other art is capable makes a film automatically good. Actually it makes it only film; unless one is prepared to argue that film, just because it is not fiction, theatre, or basket weaving, is a marvel, one had better avoid this tack. (p. 290)

The key to Godard's "creation" is—I cannot reiterate it often enough—giving in to every impulse, responding to every stimulus, recording everything in sight. And this is the very thing that gets him friends and worshipers. In an age when indiscriminate thrill-seeking is the *summum bonum,* Godard epitomizes the common man with his even more common cravings. But ask yourself which great artist became great by reflecting faithfully the yearnings of the little man, and nothing much else? (p. 293)

There is, however, something even more dispiriting than man's lack of ethics, aesthetics, or thought that these films appeal to: his inability to see, his inability to use his senses, his stupidity. "*Etre sage, c'est voir, c'est vraiment voir*" ["Being wise is being able to really see"], says Godard's mouthpiece in *Masculine Feminine,* and it is at least a valid half-truth. Modern youth is losing its ability to see and hear, let alone taste, smell, and touch. The basic sound is the roar of the discothèque, the basic sight is the vacant stare of the doped-up, transistorized television watcher. Consequently, the only way to see is not to look out into the world, but in, into TV, movies, happenings, psychedelic projections. One sees only what the movie-maker, for example, shows one. A tree in nature is of no interest; but let there be a tree in a Godard movie, and our youth is ecstatic, "Look! A tree!" It begins to appear as if only Godard could

make a tree. Under the circumstances, because Godard puts so much brute sight and sound into his films, he gives the new blind, the new deaf their only seeing and hearing. And that, I submit, is truly dreadful. (pp. 295-96)

*John Simon, "Godard and the Godardians: A Study in the New Sensibility" (originally given as a lecture at Williams College), in his* Private Screenings *(reprinted by permission of Wallace & Sheil Agency, Inc.; copyright © 1967 by John Simon), The Macmillan Company, 1967, pp. 272-96.*

### ANDREW SARRIS

The increasing fragmentation of Godardian cinema seems to indicate a depletion of emotional energy. It is not so much that Godard is repeating his effects as that he is ritualizing them into frozen cerebral patterns. The rapport of fiction with reality so dear to Godard's film-making aesthetic has degenerated from exploration to exploitation. Whereas he once explored the continent of Karina's countenance, he is now content (in *Made in U.S.A.*) to exploit the mannerisms she has picked up along the way. Godard's spectacle is still dazzling to behold, but the images are devoid of feeling. The superficiality of his political rhetoric becomes offensive at that precise moment when his own personal suffering fades from the screen. . . . As Godard has become increasingly entangled with his heroes, their morbid destiny has seemed to dim his vision of the real world, or rather his dim smoke-glassed vision has made his characterizations more morbidly passive.

Congenital anti-Godardians miss the point entirely when they accuse Godard of insincerity or frivolity. (To charge that Godard lacks talent requires an intransigent illiteracy in the language of the medium.) At his most felicitous, Godard seeks to capture childhood and student feelings in the midst of the modern world. He fully understands the emotional truth of nostalgia as tranquility recollected in hysteria. (pp. 28-9)

Godard is still one of the most interesting and stimulating filmmakers in the world today, but he no longer possesses the moral or aesthetic authority to prescribe the future course of the cinema if indeed he ever did. . . . The cinema, as Godard once observed long ago, is everything. Eclecticism is no longer a mortal sin, and effectiveness is not necessarily a sign of surrender. Moviegoing is more fun today than it has ever been. The world and man and now are being discovered and rediscovered in a new burst of freedom and experiment. There are many false starts and harsh stops, but the vitality of the medium and the métier is undeniable. If Jean-Luc Godard wants to join in the fun, he is welcome, but if Saint Jean Godard prefers to convert his films into exercises in self-flagellation, he runs the risk of becoming a bore. (p. 30)

*Andrew Sarris, "Jean-Luc versus Saint Jean," in* Film Heritage *(copyright 1968 by F. A. Macklin), Vol. 3, No. 3, Spring, 1968, pp. 27-30.*

### PAULINE KAEL

Only the title of Jean-Luc Godard's new film is casual and innocent; *Weekend* is the most powerful mystical movie since [Bergman's] *The Seventh Seal* and [Ichikawa's] *Fires on the Plain* and passages of Kurosawa. We are hardly aware of the magnitude of the author-director's conception until after we are caught up in the comedy of horror, which keeps going further and becoming more nearly inescapable. . . . The danger for satirists (and perhaps especially for visionary satirists) is that they don't always trust their art. They don't know how brilliantly they're making their points; they become mad with impatience and disgust, and throw off their art as if it were a hindrance to direct communication, and they begin to preach. When Godard is viciously funny, he's on top of things, and he scores and scores, and illuminates as he scores. When he becomes didactic, we can see that he really doesn't know any more about what should be done than the rest of us. But then he goes beyond didacticism into areas where, though he is as confused and divided as we are, his fervor and rage are so imaginatively justified that they are truly apocalyptic. It is in the further reaches—in the appalling, ambivalent revolutionary vision—that *Weekend* is a great, original work.

*Weekend* begins with a callous disrespect for life which is just a slight stylization of civilized living now; it's as if the consumers of **The Married Woman** had become more adulterous, more nakedly mercenary, and touchier. The people in **Weekend** have weapons and use them at the slightest provocation, and it seems perfectly logical that they should get into their cars and bang into each other. . . . As long as Godard stays with cars as the symbol of bourgeois materialism, the movie is superbly controlled; the barbarousness of these bourgeois— their greed and the self-love they project onto their possessions—is exact and funny. But the movie goes much further— sometimes majestically, sometimes with brilliantly surreal details that suggest a closer affinity between Godard (who is of Swiss Protestant background) and Buñuel than might have been expected, sometimes with methods and ideas that miss, even though the intentions are interesting. The couple wreck their car, and as they wander the highways, lost among battered cars and bleeding dead, they have a series of picaresque adventures, encountering figures from literature and from films, until they meet a new race of hippie guerrillas—revolutionary cannibals raping and feeding on the bourgeoisie. It is both the next step and a new beginning.

The movie has extraordinary sections [such as the sequence of the wife's erotic confession]. (pp. 138-39)

But not all the big scenes work. There is respite in the story, a musicale sequence (which might be one of the cultural programs outlined in *La Chinoise*) in which a pianist plays Mozart in a farmyard while a few peasants and farm laborers listen or walk by. We are so alerted to the technical feat of this sequence . . . that the actions caught seem too mechanical. And the meaning of the sequence is too ideological and too ambiguous (like much of *Les Carabiniers*); Godard may possibly believe in that musicale—that is to say, Godard may believe that art must be taken to the peasants—but more likely he's satirizing the function and the place of art, of himself along with Mozart. This might be clearer if it were not for another, and worse, ideological sequence—a big symbolic garbage truck manned by a Negro and an Algerian, who empty the refuse of our civilization and make speeches directly at us. The more "direct" Godard is, the more fuzzy and obscure he is. Who can assimilate and evaluate this chunk of theory thrown at us in the middle of a movie? . . . Though the movie slackens during this agitprop, the horrors soon begin to rise again, and they get higher and higher. Some of this doesn't work, either: Godard has been showing us life going wild and depraved into nightmare, beyond totem and taboo, but his method has been comic and Brechtian. . . . Godard shoves at our unwilling eyes the throat-cutting of a pig and the decapitation of a goose. Now, when people are killed in a movie, even when the killing

is *not* stylized, it's generally O.K., because we know it's a fake, but when animals are slaughtered we are watching life being taken away. No doubt Godard intends this to shock us out of "aesthetic" responses, just as his agitprop preaching is intended to affect us directly, but I think he miscalculates. I look away from scenes like this, as I assume many others do. Is he forcing us to confront the knowledge that there are things we don't want to look at? But we knew that. Instead of drawing us into his conception, he throws us out of the movie. And, because we know how movies are made, we instinctively recognize that his method of jolting us is fraudulent; he, the movie director, has ordered that slaughter to get a reaction from us, and so we have a right to be angry with him. Whatever our civilization is responsible for, that sow up there is his, not ours. (pp. 140-41)

> *Pauline Kael, "Weekend in Hell" (originally published in* The New Yorker, *October 5, 1968), in her* Going Steady *(copyright © 1968 by Pauline Kael; reprinted by permission of Little, Brown and Company in association with the Atlantic Monthly Press), Atlantic-Little, Brown, 1970. pp. 138-44.*

**PAULINE KAEL**

*Masculine Feminine* is that rare movie achievement: a work of grace and beauty in a contemporary setting. Godard has liberated his feeling for modern youth from the American gangster-movie framework which limited his expressiveness and his relevance to the non-movie centered world. He has taken up the strands of what was most original in his best films—the life of the uncomprehending heroine, the blank-eyed career-happy little opportunist-betrayer from *Breathless,* and the hullygully, the dance of sexual isolation, from *Band of Outsiders* [*Bande à part*]. Using neither crime nor the romance of crime but a simple romance for a kind of interwoven story line, Godard has, at last, created the form he needed. It is a combination of essay, journalistic sketches, news and portraiture, love lyric and satire.

What fuses it? The line "This film could be called The Children of Marx and Coca-Cola." The theme is the fresh beauty of youth amidst the flimsiness of pop culture and pop politics. . . .

It is fused by the differing attitudes of the sexes to love and war even in this atmosphere of total and easy disbelief, of government policies accepted with the same contempt as TV commercials. The romance is punctuated with aimless acts of aggression and martyrdom: this is young love in a time of irreverence and hopelessness. These lovers and their friends, united by indifference and disdain toward the adult world, have a new kind of community in their shared disbelief. Politically they are anti-American enough to be American. (p. 127)

There are all sorts of episodes and details and jokes in the film that may be extraneous, but they seem to fit, to be part of the climate, the mood, the journalistic approach to this new breed between teen-agers and people. Even if you don't really like some pieces or can't understand why they're there, even if you think they're not well done . . . , they're not too jarring. The rhythms, and the general sense, and the emotion that builds up can carry you past what you don't understand: you don't need to understand every detail in order to experience the beauty of the work as it's going on. An Elizabethan love song is no less beautiful because we don't catch all the words; and when we look up the words, some of the meanings, the references, the idiom may still elude us. Perhaps the ache of painful, transient beauty is that we never can completely understand, and that, emotionally, we more than understand. *Masculine Feminine* has that ache, and its subject is a modern young lover's lament at the separateness of the sexes.

Godard has caught the girl now in demand (and in full supply) as no one else has. . . . The young girls in the movie are soulless—as pretty and lost and soulless as girls appear to a lover who can make physical contact and yet cannot make the full contact he longs for, the contact that would heal. The girl he loves sleeps with him and is forever lost to him. She is the ideal—the girl in the fashion magazines she buys.

Possibly what flawed the conception of Godard's *My Life to Live* was the notion of the prostitute giving her body but keeping her soul to herself, because there was no evidence of what she was said to be holding back. Now, in *Masculine Feminine,* Godard is no longer trying to tell just the girl's story but the story of how a lover may feel about his girl, and we can see that it's not because she's a prostitute that he gets the sense that she isn't giving everything but because she's a girl and (as the camera of *My Life to Live* revealed though it wasn't the story being told) a love object. A lover may penetrate her body but there is still an opaque, impenetrable surface that he can never get through. He can have her and have her and she is never his.

The attraction of this little singer is that she isn't known, can't be known, and worst of all, probably there's nothing to know (which is what we may have suspected in *My Life to Live*). The ache of love is reaching out to a blank, which in this case smiles back. This male view of the eternal feminine mystery is set in the childlike simplicity of modern relations: before they go out on their first date, the boy and girl discuss going to bed. Easy sex is like a new idiom, but their talk of the pill is not the same as having it, and the spectre of pregnancy hovers over them. The old sexual morality is gone, but the mysteries of love and isolation remain; availability cancels out the pleasurable torments of anticipation, but not the sadness afterward.

With the new breed, Godard is able to define the romantic problem precisely and essentially. This approachable girl who adores Pepsi—the French cousin of Jean Seberg in *Breathless*—is as mysterious as a princess seen from afar, *more* mysterious because the princess might change if we got close. (pp. 128-29)

In *Masculine Feminine* Godard asks questions of youth and sketches a portrait in a series of question-answer episodes that are the dramatic substance of the movie. The method was prefigured by the psychiatric interview in Truffaut's *The 400 Blows* (Léaud, now the questioning hero, was the child-hero who was quizzed), the celebrity interview in *Breathless,* and cinema vérité movies by Jean Rouch and Chris Marker. It is most like Chris Marker's rapturous inquiry of the young Japanese girl in *The Koumiko Mystery*. There are informal boy-to-boy conversations about women and politics; there is a phenomenal six-minute single-take parody-interview conducted by the hero with a Miss Nineteen, who might be talking while posing for the cover of *Glamour;* and there are two boy-girl sessions which define the contemporary meaning of masculine and feminine. These dialogues are dating talk as a form of preliminary sex play—verbal courtship rites. The boy thrusts with leading questions, the girl parries, backs away, touches her hair. Godard captures the awkwardnesses that reveal, the

pauses, the pretensions, the mannerisms—the rhythms of the dance—as no one has before. *Masculine Feminine* is the dance of the sexes drawing together and remaining separate. He gets the little things that people who have to follow scripts can't get: the differences in the way girls are with each other and with boys, and boys with each other and with girls. Not just what they do but how they smile or look away. (pp. 129-30)

We watch them telling lies and half truths to each other and we can't tell which are which. But, smiling in the darkness because we know we've all been there, we recognize the truth of Godard's art. He must have discovered his subject as he worked on it (as a man working on a big-budget movie with a fixed shooting schedule cannot). And because he did, we do, too. . . . [There's] life in *Masculine Feminine,* which shows the most dazzlingly inventive and audacious artist in movies today at a new peak. (p. 130)

> *Pauline Kael, "'Masculine Feminine'," in her* Kiss Kiss Bang Bang *(© 1968 by Pauline Kael; reprinted by permission of Little, Brown and Company in association with the Atlantic Monthly Press), Atlantic-Little, Brown, 1968, pp. 127-30.*

**STANLEY KAUFFMANN**

The story [of *Pierrot le Fou*] would be trite—a mod *Elvira Madigan*—if it asked for any attention as such. It would also be incredible. That [a] mousy little baby-sitter is also involved with killers and is undisturbed by a corpse in the next room on the night that she and her lover first go to bed—all this would be ludicrous if we were meant to take the narrative seriously. But in a frantic way Godard is deliberately fracturing story logic, using narrative only as a scaffolding for acrobatics, cinematic and metaphysical. The question is whether those acrobatics are consistently amusing and/or enlightening. I think not. (p. 139)

For me, the film is a function of three boredoms. (I exclude my own.) The hero is bored by his Parisian life, which precipitates the story. The girl is soon bored by the tranquil island where he takes her, which brings about their deaths. And, principally, Godard is very soon bored. I think that the whole film after they flee the girl's Paris apartment is a series of stratagems to keep Godard himself from falling asleep: improvisations, high-school philosophizing, grotesqueries, and supersanguinary violence. His quick mind seems to have flown ahead to his next film while he is faced with the need to finish this one. Boredom has been a (one may say) vital element in art from Gogol and Musset to Beckett and Ionesco, but in their cases, boredom has been the subject, not the artist's own reaction to the making of his art. (pp. 139-40)

Godard, a man of [large and desperate] hungers, keeps snatching at themes to nourish his interest. He has gobbled at blood (a midget with scissors in his neck in *Pierrot*), alienation, the Vietnam war, Maoism, fantasy youth revolt, real youth revolt. If anything ever gripped him profoundly, even if only for a couple of months, what a film we might get! (p. 140)

> *Stanley Kauffmann, "'Pierrot le Fou'" (originally published in* The New Republic, *Vol. 160, No. 8, February 22, 1969), in his* Figures of Light: Film Criticism and Comment *(copyright © 1967, 1968, 1969, 1970, 1971 by Stanley Kauffmann; reprinted by permission of Harper & Row, Publishers, Inc.), Harper, 1971, pp. 138-40.*

**JOHN WEIGHTMAN**

[*Le Gai Savoir*] is such a silly and pretentious film that one cannot help wondering what Jean-Luc Godard is now up to. The hand-outs say that it was begun as a documentary on education, commissioned by French television, but that it has so far been banned in France. I cannot understand why; the censors must be even more obtuse than one supposes if they fear that such a tedious work might arouse dangerous passions, apart from acute irritation with M. Godard himself. Perhaps, after all, they rejected it simply because it is bad. It is even a *tour de force* of badness. In purporting to deal with education, Godard manages to be more boring and irrelevant than the most boring Sorbonne professor. God knows, I have sat through some scores of dreary *discours en trois points,* but they had more to them than this vapid verbalisation, which can only be considered as a form of cinematographic suicide. (p. 56)

[*A bout de souffle, Pierrot le fou,* and *Bande à part* are] tragedies, because their heroes are trying to live against the grain and are doubly betrayed by society. In spite of their underlying sentimentality, which is rather naïve, they contain charmingly poetic passages: the love-making to the sound of *"Travailler en musique"* in *A bout de souffle;* the pastoral wanderings in *Pierrot le fou* and, best of all, the café dance sequence in *Bande à part.* The beauty of these episodes lies in the lyrical appreciation of life, even in extreme or hopeless situations. At its best, the cinema is even more effective than the novel in conveying those important but almost indefinable emotions that cling around the processes of living. In these films, as I remember them, Godard excels in rendering the raw, yet touching, unreliability of human relationships.

Something of this same quality is to be found in four other films: *Le Petit Soldat, Une Femme Mariée, Une Femme est une Femme* and *Masculin-Féminin* [*Masculine Feminine*]. All of these are rather scrappy, as if Godard hadn't quite made up his mind what themes he really wanted to deal with. . . . [*Une Femme Mariée* and *Masculin-Féminin*] were like notes for films that Godard was fumbling towards but had not quite bothered to make. He is implying in the first that the boredom of middle-class adultery is almost equivalent to the humdrum security of married life, and in the second that young people live together untidily, like kittens or puppies, without fully understanding themselves or each other. Well and good, but possibly he is misled by the immediate realism of the camera into thinking that any fragments of life can be juxtaposed, and that connections and conclusions can be as arbitrary as one likes. . . .

*Une Femme est une Femme* is easily the most successful work in this group, and perhaps the only endearing film that Godard has ever made. In spite of some uncertainties, this story of a striptease artist with domestic longings dodging between two men, one too reliable the other too unreliable, is very delicately carried out. . . .

*La Chinoise, Week-End, One plus One* and, now, *Le Gai Savoir* fall into a quite different category, since they show a direct preoccupation with social satire and political activity. (p. 57)

Coherence was certainly never Godard's strong suit and he now seems to have abandoned it altogether. *Week-End,* which contains some fine sequences, and in particular a splendid traffic jam, is not even comprehensible in parts, because the background music drowns out the voices. It appears to be an attack on the consumer society, which is seen as consisting of motor-cars, eroticism, and a denial of the imaginative fac-

ulty. . . . I suspect, from these films, that Godard is tempted by barbarism, violence, and destruction, more than he is repelled by materialism. And the temptation is a symptom which upsets his work, rather than an element which has been assimilated into it.

He is trying to be an overt critic of society, when his own sensibility is all at sixes and sevens. This means that he inflicts upon the spectator a lot of half-baked stuff which is neither enlightening politically nor adequate artistically. . . . [The] only tolerable section of *One plus One* is the documentary about a Rolling Stones recording session, with Mick Jagger repeatedly caterwauling an invocation to the Devil in the nocturnal gloom of a vast studio. This has a sort of decadent beauty, because the devil-worship is not without a grain of truth. But are the Rolling Stones a good thing, or a symbol of the cultural perversions of the consumer society? The film dwells on them with love, but how can one be both a Maoist and an admirer of the Rolling Stones? (p. 58)

More puzzling still than the incoherence is the fact that Godard has tended increasingly to replace images by words, while at the same time making the words more or less nonsensical. . . .

[In] spite of what he says, Godard has not evolved into intelligent commitment. He has just exchanged his romantic admiration of the outlaw for a muddled and uninteresting obsession with the concept of revolution, which he is handling about as badly as possible. He appears to have renounced the things he was gifted for and to be trying to do something for which he has no talent, and in a way that is not even suited to his medium. (p. 59)

*John Weightman, "Whatever Happened to Godard?" in* Encounter *(© 1969 by Encounter Ltd.), Vol. XXXIII, No. 3, September, 1969, pp. 56-9.*

**STANLEY KAUFFMANN**

[*Two or Three Things I Know about Her*] is more interesting than many other Godard films because, for one reason, it seems to have sustained the director's own interest. There is no feeling, as in *Pierrot le Fou,* that this very bright man has embarked on something to which he is committed long after his darting mind has really left it and that he has been forced to invent irreverences and interpolations to keep himself interested. For another reason, the film is devoid of the worst aspects of Youth Worship that sometimes taint his work; it is about people, some of whom are young. But the chief merit is that it develops its themes within itself, for the most part, not by imposition. The interplay between the facts of the changing city . . . and the changing lives of Paris is graphic. And when the heroine moves easily from action within a scene to speak to us directly about herself and her quandaries, which she does often, it creates two dualities of consciousness—hers about her life and her "acting" of it, ours about the film as fictional truth and about the making of that truth. There is a nice sense of metatheater, in Lionel Abel's term: of the heroine living her life and simultaneously seeing herself, as the protagonist of a drama she is watching. And all the while, a tightening circle of chromium-plated, electronic wolves is yapping at her heels.

But the impasted artistic and philosophical freight is once again tedious. The interviewing of characters by an unseen interviewer, which is supposed to break open film convention, is now a Godardian convention. The sound track, with Godard quoting away, has an air of dormitory discovery—a sophomore discovering, under the midnight lamp, what life and metaphor are All About. When we get a huge close-up of bubbles floating on the surface of coffee in a cup while Godard whispers about Being and Nothingness, it remains bubbles and quotations; there is no transformation into philosophical comment or Pongeist poem. (pp. 259-60)

[The] heroine is pleasant and composed. While the film stays with her, in her complications of self-knowledge, there is some sense of genuine phenomenological dilemma, some inquiry into the data of consciousness. When Godard sloshes *stuff* at us, belatedly discovered by him and untransmuted, we get a Child's Garden of Phenomenology. (p. 260)

> *Stanley Kauffmann, "'Two or Three Things I Know about Her'" (originally published in* The New Republic, *May 9, 1970), in his* Figures of Light: Film Criticism and Comment *(copyright © 1967, 1968, 1969, 1970, 1971 by Stanley Kauffmann; reprinted by permission of Harper & Row, Publishers, Inc.), Harper, 1971, pp. 258-60.*

**PENELOPE GILLIATT**

Godard's voice carries. He has finished two new films, **"See You at Mao"** and **"Pravda,"** each about an hour long, in a style going toward the most didactic and thorny destinations, yet he can't for the life of him suppress the force and grace of that singular delivery of his. Even these raw first works of a new stage that is now tough going seem likely in the end to reach the ears of people out of sympathy with his radical politics, not because of the yelling powers of polemics but because of the carrying powers of a poet's voice. Godard can make a silly film or an endearing one, but he can't make an ineloquent one. His path now goes away from narrative completely, and it isn't exactly a paved highway. (pp. 83-4)

The voice of the two films is political and speculative, raised to a pitch of slightly mysterious tension because of Godard's own urgencies. There is a faint trill in the air, the unmistakable upper harmonic of somebody at work on something original and hard to do. Godard is intent now on making "revolutionary films" in which everything will be concrete and nothing suave. . . . Godard now wants to make films that are as dogmatic as possible. He wants to strip them of the emotionalism that he obviously finds wheedling and mechanical in traditional movies, including his own early ones. He wants to pound people with language. Godard is the most literary of filmmakers, in a sense that is different from the usual one, with his way of plastering words even across images—on posters, in graffiti, on children's blackboards—as well as pouring them into the sound track by the bucketful. In these new movies, it is almost as if he wanted to attack people with so much repetition and so much claptrap that they will be whipped into hauling themselves, bleeding and half-concussed, across some threshold of boredom into another way of seeing things. And yet, in spite of his irate theories and his intentness on creating the texture of a gaudy, comfortless, grainless present where what is to come is somehow more palpable than what is current, he keeps arriving at moments of film that are agelessly composing.

Godard has always been obsessed with the energy that can be released by pitting opposites against each other: kindergarten colors, world-worn reflexes; pious mottoes, godless mishaps; computer voices, real blood; windbag commentaries, suffering people; clever creator, simple-minded creation. This, say his films as they perpetually tug apart in the middle, is what it's like to be living merrily when something is terribly wrong, to be in a jet filled with air-hostess smiles and the sound of the "Wedding March" on the Muzak system when no one in the plane can recover the feeling of what it was ever really like to grin and when no one there believes in marriage. Our jet—capitalism, industrialism, revisionism, the whole shooting match—is going nowhere, say the films, and some expert pilot had better hijack it.

In **"Mao"** and **"Pravda,"** Godard is pushing documentary to a place it has never been. The sound nearly always plays against the image. . . . Often the **"Pravda"** commentary goes into an extended pastiche of a conversation between Lenin and Rosa Luxemburg, deliberately unconvincing and batteringly trite: "That's what we've got to do, Rosa," says fake Lenin earnestly. "We've got to organize these causes and sounds along antirevisionist lines." Which practically makes you want to thump the screen with fury that such a bright filmmaker can talk such garbage to contrary-minded purpose—except that he then goes even further and becomes peculiarly soothing with his morganatic marriage of overbred sound and simple image by linking the high-flying talk to an inexplicable and beautiful shot of a red rose lying in a puddle. . . . The commentary will gabble through theories about production and wealth while there is a Gainsborough shot of people loading hay onto a cart. And always there is this Brechtian dislocation somewhere, reminding us that a movie is not real but only an aping of the real, and that while traditional filmmakers are concerned with the reflection of reality, Godard is concerned with the reality of the reflection. In both these films, it is clear that something slightly cracks Godard's heart—mad stranger though he will be in most people's experience of what is saddening—about the ebbing of a man's vital energy when he sells it to an unknown employer and when his capacity for work is a piece of merchandise up for bidding. . . . The commentary mutters, barely audible in the din, that what a car-factory worker produces for himself is not the thing he assembles but money. One grows fond of Godard's way of talking to himself about his political worries. It sounds very like him. A cracked whisper, urgent. Sometimes one that can hardly be made out. . . . **"Mao"** is quite a picture, tense and shapely, with Cruikshank's or Hogarth's attention to the bony English face, and torn apart aesthetically in order to reflect a struggle that Godard deeply minds about. The fight he sets up between words and images is a metaphor for political struggle and for our own sense of concrete reality, where there is always a disjuncture between what we say or think and what we experience. You are not a unity, say these films. You are trying to be a unity, but the fact is you are not. (pp. 84-7)

> *Penelope Gilliatt, "The Current Cinema: 'See You at Mao' and 'Pravda',"* in *The New Yorker (copyright © 1970 by The New Yorker Magazine, Inc.), Vol. XLVI, No. 15, May 30, 1970 (and reprinted in* Focus on Godard, *edited by Royal S. Brown, Prentice-Hall, Inc., 1972, pp. 83-7.*

**LEO HAMALIAN**

[Since] visual interruptions are slipped in much as the auditory interruptions are [in *Sympathy for the Devil* (*One Plus One*)], Godard may be suggesting that our inner, unconscious awareness is dominated by what we see and hear on the edges of our perception, almost subliminally or at least not with our full attention. What if our culture (depicted in the "outside" scenes) subjects us to pornography, propaganda, violence, and the cynical commercialism of television? The pornography, hinting at perversion, is associated with fascism in the film and the fascism with violence: as the customers in the porno shop leave, they first ritualistically slap the faces of two boys who sit helpless and hurt in a corner. The graffiti are forms of witty propaganda for radicalism: the black panthers toss guns to each other as though they were toys and at the end the revolutionaries are preparing for a shoot-out with the authorities. The radicals too are guilty of violence. Meanwhile, the Stones prepare, rehearse, re-work the music which gleefully, almost maliciously acknowledges the perpetual presence of Satan, of the demonic force that Godard seems to be saying can be used either to destroy or to create. (pp. 310-11)

[In the interview with Eve Paradise,] there is no sure way to know what Godard is implying, although the audience applauded the answers enthusiastically. The scene has a simple and innocent quality bordering on the idiotic. The girl is capable of saying nothing more than "yes" or "no" and the questions themselves are often absurd or have a fashionable, pop-art streak in them. "Eve" on the other hand is apparently trying to liberate herself from words, while the television interviewer uses them to obfuscate very often. But it is apparently Eve who trots around London painting words on walls. And Eve is inevitably associated with the virginal young women who are slaughtered by the word-spouting black revolutionaries. Everything is stood on its head. There is nothing that cannot have its reversal. The blacks given to violence shoot the girls, the white middle-class lapping it up in books abuse their boys. Against these scenes of outward violence of one kind or another, there is the "pure" world of the Stones' studio, where mind and heart fuse in the creation of something revolutionary that will give pleasure instead of inflicting pain.

Godard shows us a world outside the recording studio which is bleak and fragmented, the waste land of Eliot filtered through the sensibility of a French "painter in letters". It's not Kafkaesque because there is nothing hallucinatory about it—it's mundane and ordinary. The forces of liberation are not really liberating (pornography and repression are linked), and the paths of glory lead but to the grave. Television is Power and may invade Paradise if it wishes. "Advertising" is so much a poison in our bloodstreams that we must advertise even our politics and our most deeply-felt convictions, as though nothing any longer were private. The natural animal spirit of the Stones is overlaid with the voice spewing filth, as though the words might magically contaminate the music (if that hidden voice is the voice of the Devil, then the title has more than one meaning). At the end, the flags of anarchy are flying proudly over the carnage on the beach—and what is more, some film director is turning the revolution into a commercial success. Is this the part the film director will play in the revolution? Or is Godard indulging in brilliant self-parody? And those marvelous savage sounds created by the Stones—is this the culmination of two thousand years of Christianity, is this the final gift of our technology and science? (p. 312)

Godard is satirizing almost everything his camera touched upon, from the Black Power movement to the Stones themselves. Yet he has at the same time an affection and fondness for both, so that he appears to be espousing a revolutionary view and a counter-revolutionary view at the same time. . . .

[Is] Godard a revolutionist or not? will the darling of the New Left henceforth be regarded as a relapsed liberal? and is Godard moving away from political dogmatism, towards a purer form

of film purged of the propaganda he so openly has used in earlier films? I myself think so. I believe Godard is tired of violence. He is also tired of hypocrisy. He himself has described *Sympathy* as having two parallel themes: creation and destruction. It seems weighted on the side of the latter. It is almost as though Godard would annihilate the world his camera contemplates. It is a tribute to his genius that the film is somehow strengthened by that impulse, that he has not caught the disease he is documenting. The film is beautifully photographed and carefully composed, with the famous counterpuntal techniques of Godard brought out in dazzling design. It is a film worth waiting to see. (p. 313)

Leo Hamalian, "Waiting for Godard," in Journal of Popular Culture *(copyright © 1970 by Ray B. Browne), Vol. IV, No. 1, Summer, 1970, pp. 308-13.*

**JOAN MELLEN**

*Wind from the East,* one of the latest of Godard's revolutionary epics, fails miserably: first, aesthetically, because Godard cannot find a myth or a situation by which to bring to life its Maoist ideology, a problem he has failed to solve in many of his films. It is conceptually weak and inane as well, failing to make any coherent statement about revolutionary purpose, although the basis of Godard's technique in this film is the accumulation of statements. (p. 65)

Because he relinquishes the aesthetic potential of his medium with its capacity to move at will from one segment of time and place to another, Godard cannot convey the sense of historical struggle. But his choice of an unrelieved placard style, substituting statement for a nuanced development of dramatic conflict exposes as well disturbing features in Godard's new ideology. It is one thing to note that Godard's imagery of primitive idyll as the prelude to class struggle is painfully naive and inadequate given the highly complex social organization Godard hopes to change. But the methods Godard selects as the tools of social change—brutality, terrorism, coercion—are presumably the very abuses of human dignity he finds so appalling in bourgeois society. . . .

An anti-democratic, authoritarian tone pervades both the style of *Wind from the East* with its preaching narrators and its content as well. The very title gives Godard away. Refusing to use film for the purpose of persuasion, a motive shared by other politically conscious directors from Eisenstein to Rossellini, Godard is forced to demand acceptance for his ideas on the basis of an appeal to his current favorite authority, Mao Tse-Tung. Although the last part of the film raises substantive questions of interest to revolutionaries, Godard allows no debate—despite the fact that a dialectic of ideas could have added conflict and interest to a very static film. . . .

[The end of *Wind from the East* that calls for terrorism] substitutes the dubious heroics of a clandestine handful and is as elitist as it is self-defeating. Certainly it delays awareness for those not yet won to revolutionary consciousness. . . . His goal is the levelling of existing societies, confident in his self-delusion that a revolutionary, industrialized society will spring from the wreckage as from the forehead of Zeus. . . .

In its ultimate advocacy of terrorism and murder, Godard's infantile rantings turn out to be dangerous as well as poor filmmaking. For Godard's films may well appeal to those who like him believe that a revolution involves only the "right" views and a ready bomb. Because such a course can lead only to self-deception and defeat, **Wind from the East** militates against the very revolutionary aim Godard has so zealously and so recently discovered. Shrill, mindless slogan-mongering without argument or reason, combined with childish miming, is the last thing that the politically conscious worker, Godard's implicit hero, would find either appealing or convincing. On the contrary, he would more likely reject **Wind from the East** for its smug self-indulgence and its lack of any real connection with his life. He, as were we, will be bored. Those who accept Godard as a revolutionary will be inoculated against the revolution. (p. 67)

> Joan Mellen, "'Wind from the East'," in Film Comment (copyright © 1971 by Film Comment Publishing Corporation; all rights reserved), Vol. 7, No. 3, Fall, 1971, pp. 65-7.

**RICHARD SCHICKEL**

Godard's vision of [the young Maoists in **La Chinoise (The Chinese Girl)**] is persuasively realistic. And chilling.

And comic. What always saves Godard's work for me is his superb sense of irony. His sympathetic fascination with the outsiders who always people his films rarely deteriorates into sentimentality. Quite the contrary—they are absurd creatures. In **La Chinoise,** for instance, adolescent inattention and ineptitude keep undercutting everyone's revolutionary fervor, as do the sexual crosscurrents which keep swirling about. And when these humorless idealists move from talk to action, things fall still further apart. They carefully plan an assassination and, of course, gun down the wrong man, then must go back and get the right one. Their bungling perhaps reads as a comment on the futility of revolution, the fact that they go unpunished for their crimes a comment on the impotence and fatuity of the adult world that has driven them to this desperate expedient. Godard's attitude is summed up with admirable economy in the film's throwaway ending. . . . (pp. 172-73)

In outline, I am afraid the picture sounds simpler, more straightforward than it really is. Indeed, what I have set down is only my interpretation of Godard's intentions. He hates to cue audience response to scenes and characters, hates to be in the position of begging them for approval. Working in the most seductive of the arts, he has therefore developed a carefully unseductive style—distant, elliptical, severely objective in its visualizations, arhythmic in its editing method. . . . Which accounts for the sequence that has by now become his trademark—a long excruciating scene where his normally restless camera sits on its haunches and peers like an unblinking cat at some endless discussion (in **La Chinoise** it is between a girl and a philosopher) that anyone else would cut out of the script without bothering to shoot it at all.

He is, in short, all the things his detractors say he is—pretentious, sophomoric, self-indulgent. But he is also all the things his supporters claim he is—a director who succeeds in capturing and bringing back alive some of the shyest, most skittish social and psychological demons of our time. (p. 173)

> Richard Schickel, "'La Chinoise'" (originally published in a slightly different form in Life, Vol. 64, No. 15, April 12, 1968), in his Second Sight: Notes on Some Movies, 1965-1970 (copyright © 1972 by, Richard Schickel; reprinted by permission of Simon & Schuster, a Division of Gulf & Western Corporation), Simon & Schuster, 1972, pp. 171-74.

**PETER HARCOURT**

[The distinction of **À Bout de souffle**] lay in its ability to embody in the texture of the film itself the uncertainties and fragmentariness that form the basic ingredients of its view of life and the view of life of many Godard films to follow. **À Bout de souffle** abounds in *non-sequiturs* which become part of this meaninglessness. It also abounds in jump-cuts and restless tracking shots that deprive us of any sense of a logical transition from scene to scene as they deprive us as well of the sense of ever being still. Also in the movie as part of its gangster-film atmosphere, there is the feeling of persecution, a sense of the net closing in. The mechanics of the city seem to work against the protagonists. (pp. 215-16)

One of the most crucial elements that deepen Godard's fractured universe is his technique of allusion. The many allusions lend to all his films the irony of wit, yet sometimes with an indecipherable ambiguity. (p. 216)

It is important to insist upon the contribution that [the] texture of uncertainty in a Godard film makes towards the total impact it has upon us—towards its 'meaning', in fact—helping to underline as it does all the things we cannot know. For in a Godard film, even the most private allusions that are probably missed by us are cumulatively part of the feeling we get from him of a man terribly isolated and uncertain about his ability to make contact with more than a handful of people. . . . (p. 217)

[The] element of male persuasion, if fundamental to **Le Mépris** [**Contempt**], to **Pierrot le fou** and to **Masculin-Féminin,** the most romantic films that Godard has ever made, is there as well in different forms in **Le Petit Soldat, Vivre sa vie, Bande à part, Une Femme mariée,** and **Alphaville.** Basically, this element of persuasion would seem to be related to a belief in salvation through love—love always as defined, of course, by Godard's particular males.

This belief in love provides the shallow optimism of the endings of both **Bande à part** (playfully) and **Alphaville** (portentously, with all its Orphic references so out-of-key with Eddie Constantine's immobile face). But more frequently, more compellingly, this belief in love which is the prime motivation of so many of Godard's characters seems to be enmeshed within a context of violence from which it cannot escape. It is as if Godard presents his characters as inescapably addicted to it but recognizes that it will destroy them by the end. It is in essence a belief in *l'amour fou,* a love that is instantaneous and inexplicable and, one must deduce, primarily aesthetic, not based upon a recognition of the character or personality of the loved one at all. (pp. 220-21)

The love asserted by Michel in **À Bout de souffle,** by Bruno in **Le Petit Soldat,** by Ferdinand in **Pierrot le fou,** and by Paul in **Masculin-Féminin** is invariably of a very abstract kind. It scarcely takes account of the diversity and human complexity of the loved one at all. It fails to allow her to live her own life. (p. 221)

[The] heroic stance assumed by so many of Godard's characters alternates with a longing for escape from it, as Michel in **À Bout de souffle** longed to get away to Rome and Ferdinand in **Pierrot le fou** away to the Mediterranean. This longing for escape is also part of Godard's characters' longing for love. Love provides them with a temporary relief from their lonely sense of isolation and offers release from the heroic responsibilities of defining one's own character when all alone in the world. . . . Furthermore, it seems to take place in suspended time, in a kind of stasis. Whether within the extended bedroom scene in *À Bout de souffle,* the even more extended apartment scene in *Le Mépris,* or the Mediterranean idyll in *Pierrot le fou,* the scenes of love in a Godard film always take place in little recesses apart from the main flow of the film. And in both *Vivre sa vie* and *Une Femme mariée,* the supposedly most tender moments in the film are so abstract and stylized that they deprive us as viewers of any *feeling* of love at all. (p. 222)

The films of Jean-Luc Godard seem split between two basic impulses, impulses that are completely self-contradictory: to achieve permanence through the unquestionable authority of his art; and yet to insist that everything is flux, in motion, uncontrolled, that so much in life simply happens *par hasard.* So the characters themselves fluctuate between two opposing tendencies: from *Le Petit Soldat* to *Masculin-Féminin,* his protagonists long for the reality of meaningful action outside themselves and yet long to retreat into a world away from action, a world given up to the celebration of personal love. (pp. 232-33)

[The] twin poles are there, throughout Godard's films, often irreconcilably, generally self-destructively. They parallel and partially embody the classic alternatives between action and contemplation. At times, in interviews, Godard himself has seemed well aware of this. Yet there is a confusion about the intermixing and criss-crossing as it exists in the films, a confusion that suggests elements that Godard doesn't understand. (p. 233)

[The] conflict in Godard between love and politics is yet another manifestation of the split nature of his sensibility, of the conflict between the mind and the body, between the desire for thought and the need for action. . . . [These] twin desires are mutually self-destructive. It is as if Godard recognizes that individualism is no solution, as Paul's friend explained to him in *Masculin-Féminin,* whether the individualism of reflective thought or of romantic love. Yet Godard has been unable to find a full commitment elsewhere. So his work now flounders. He remains as prolific as ever, and as inventive; but both the scale of his work and the size of his audiences are trickling away. (pp. 246-47)

With the rejection of love and the suppression (still not complete) of his lyrical style, there has disappeared as well any sign of . . . reflective intelligence, any sense of the characters trying to follow Leenhardt's principle of thinking *before* they act.

The political activists in *La Chinoise, Weekend, One Plus One,* and *Le Vent d'Est* [*Wind from the East*] act as if without reflection. Their thinking is a mindless slogan-mongering, as if in the effort to hypnotize themselves into believing that such slogans are the only truth. They are often seen declaiming from books or repeating phrases conned by rote from an imperfect tape-recorder. Thus they have more in common with the mechanical voice of Alpha 60 than they have with the absurdly romantic assertions of the stolid Lemmy Caution. Godard's political activists are the direct descendants of his ape-like soldiers in *Les Carabiniers.* And what, we must ask, are the *political* implications of this?

Standing to one side of his major work in the early days, *Les Carabiniers* . . . now takes on a harsh prophetic quality. No one at that time would have seen in Godard's riflemen, if not the hope exactly, at least the only prospect for the future. The film was accepted by those who admired it as a grimly anti-war film, depicting with cool detachment the brutalizing processes of war and the futility of its ends. It seemed to me to

be a kind of cinematic Dada, its uncharacteristic detachment partly the proof of the immense creative flexibility of Godard, partly, I have always assumed, the result of the direct influence of Rossellini. Viewed in isolation, the film can still seem like this; but in the light of his later work, certain ambiguities become, lamentably, rather less ambiguous.

The mindless, sub-human characteristics of Godard's riflemen lead directly to the cannibals that end *Weekend,* devouring (so to speak) the very society that has nurtured them. Similarly, in *Les Carabiniers* the execution of the beautiful partisan, who, like the sailors in [Eisenstein's] *Potemkin,* calls out to her 'brothers' to save her from her fate, and who till the very end recites Mayakovsky, is simultaneously the execution of beauty and the extinction of poetry—the two qualities in which Godard, up until *Weekend,* has struggled to believe. With the extinction of these qualities, we have the extinction as well of the only humane values that have shone through the desperately uncertain world that Godard has created for us throughout his many, remarkable films, the only qualities (as Robin Wood has suggested) that might make a revolution actually worth fighting for.

What have we left? Clearly, *Alphaville.* But the destructive mechanics lie less in the computerized technology that threatens human individuality, banning words like tenderness, conscience, and love from human contemplation, than in the characters themselves—in their mechanical, slogan-bound, loveless response to the world that surrounds them and in their passive acceptance of the need for brutality. Furthermore, the magnificently executed farm-yard recital in *Weekend* gives us the sense of Western art in total decline, Mozart fumblingly played and passively observed by a scattering of inattentive spectators.

Godard's cinema has become increasingly a self-destructive cinema. In *À Bout de souffle,* the presence of the impersonal violence of the world outside was constantly threatening to engulf the characters and disrupt their little recesses of talk and love; but by *Deux ou Trois Choses que je sais d'elle* [*Two or Three Things I Know about Her*] . . . , these recesses have vanished. The violence of impersonal construction-noises almost totally overwhelms the soundtrack and obliterates the characters. The most human voice in the film is the voice of Godard, urgently whispering to us in his self-questioning way, wondering whether what he is showing us is what he ought to be showing us, wondering whether this tree or that is the right one to dwell upon. (pp. 247-49)

If throughout Godard's work there has been [a] sense of the harsh impersonal realities of the social/political world impinging upon the inner life of the individual, in films like *Le Gai Savoir, One Plus One,* and *Le Vent d'Est,* there is no longer any inner life to impinge upon. The riflemen have triumphed. The human world has been destroyed. Art and beauty and the painful uncertainties of human love are no more.

What might we take to be Godard's political position? He would seem to believe now in the validity of revolution, but perhaps not really. Perhaps not really, because he nowhere shows that he fully understands what the issues of a revolution actually are, what the outcome might entail. Politically, he is an old-fashioned, idealist Marxist, offering us the oversimplification of the workers against the bosses as the terms on which a revolution must be fought. This might have been valid for Cuba and China—essentially agricultural communities exploited by foreign owners. But for modern, industrialized Europe and America, these comforting over-simplifications no longer have the validity they might once have seemed to have. (p. 249)

Godard's professed espousal of revolution seems less the result of an informed interest in the issues in contemporary society than a last-ditch gesture of total despair in the face of the complete incomprehensibility of the universe as he himself has experienced it. Since he has cut himself off from an idealized belief in the validity of beauty, the truth of art, and the liberation from the self brought about by human love, Godard's interest in revolution would now seem to be accompanied by a loss of faith in the processes of life itself. To my mind, this represents a most reactionary attitude.

The attitude is reactionary because self-deceiving. Like Bergman at his most rhetorical, in films like *Hour of the Wolf* and *Shame*, Godard is confusing his own inner distress with political reality. He is attempting to project outwards his inner tensions and split response to the complexities of life on to the more public world of political struggles. In his earlier work, when the personal seemed paramount, this was fair enough. Certainly there *is* a relationship between the senselessly impersonal urbanized society and the difficulties we find in establishing the inner security of love; and certainly in the violence around us we can find to a degree an impersonal counterpart for the violence that we might at times feel within ourselves. But in understanding such a relationship, balance is everything. If we are ever to be successful in wringing some improvement out of the absurdities of this world, it will be necessary (so it seems to me) to separate our nervous and imaginative disorders from the more public issues that exist outside, interdependent though these two might be. (pp. 250-51)

Godard's work remains fascinating for us, even when tedious, even when perversely muddle-headed, because of the nature of the issues it confronts, issues central to the world we live in, to the future of the cinema, and to Godard himself. Every formal detail in his films and every statement that each of his characters makes raises questions of the most far-reaching kind—questions not only of artistic procedure but of philosophical implication and political applicability. In fact, it is this questioning, this restlessly uncertain quality of every word and every image, that makes his films seem so much of our times.

Godard may yet prove himself to be one of those artists—like van Gogh or Artaud—whose uncompromising artistic sensibility drives them into the state that we conventionally call madness and who thus destroy themselves by their own art. But by so rigorously confronting the issues that obsess him, issues simultaneously aesthetic and political, he is at the forefront of the heroes of our time. (pp. 253-54)

> Peter Harcourt, "Godard le fou: A Glimpse of the Struggle between Love and Politics in the Work of Jean-Luc Godard," in his Six European Directors: Essays on the Meaning of Film Style (copyright © Peter Harcourt, 1974; reprinted by permission of Penguin Books Ltd), Penguin Books, 1974, pp. 212-54.

## JEROME H. DELAMATER

Jean-Luc Godard's *Pierrot le Fou* is an intricate and complex film, rich in visual and verbal allusion to painting, literature, and other films. It moves with its two leading characters, Ferdinand and Marianne . . . , in a somewhat picaresque journey through a life of trying to escape from society, hypocrisy, and commercialism to a life of crime and violence, ultimately ar-

riving at death, perhaps the only true liberation. Godard's style, an introverted and self-consciously cinematic one, is so closely linked with his narrative and his thematic elements that the two are almost inseparable. *Pierrot le Fou* is a profound film that contrasts the humane and the inhumane in revelations of the best that man can accomplish versus the worst, which seems to be his more natural tendency.

Godard's use of color is the first noticeable attribute of the film. *Pierrot le Fou* is not simply a color film; instead, it uses color as part of the journey theme and as an emphasizing device. Colored filters, for instance, show mood and make distinctions, and a progression throughout the film from dark to light signifies the progression of Ferdinand and Marianne from society's strictures to death's liberation. Simply put, it is a film that could not have been photographed in black and white and still have retained its essence. (p. 5)

Godard's use of color is akin to his use of visual and verbal allusions to paintings and painters. The opening sequences of *Pierrot le Fou* are, in fact, covered by Jean-Paul Belmondo's voice-over reading about Velazquez from a book on art history. Considered in retrospect, it is an almost too obvious comment on the film itself. As the world of Velazquez was sad, so is the world of Ferdinand; the world of Ferdinand, like that of Velazquez, is inhabited by princesses, midgets, and clowns. (p. 6)

Other paintings by Picasso and Renoir as well as by Modigliani, Rouault, Rauschenberg, and others either decorate walls or are inserted at particular times throughout the film. Those painters whose work Godard shows in the film have, like Godard, defied tradition. They sought freedom in their art away from traditional restrictions just as Ferdinand is seeking freedom.

The literary references in *Pierrot le Fou* are also strong and important. . . . Art and literature seem to represent human values for Godard, and Ferdinand and Marianne emphasize this several times in discussions about the nature of novels and in quick replies about particular writers. As they are riding through Paris that first night, for example, Marianne comments that she wishes real life would have the clarity, logic, and formality of life in novels. (pp. 6-7)

In a way, *Pierrot le Fou* is a modern *Aucassin et Nicolette*. *Aucassin et Nicolette* is unique of its kind because it is written in alternating verse and prose; it is generally believed that when presented originally, the prose was recited by one performer and the verse sung by another. . . . *Aucassin et Nicolette* is a somewhat ironic tale, a mild parody of the *roman courtois;* likewise, *Pierrot* parodies not only the gangster movie but also the musical and in many ways the art of film in general.

Bernardin de Saint Pierre's *Paul et Virginie* and Daniel Defoe's *Robinson Crusoe* are closely linked with the period of isolation that Ferdinand and Marianne experience. . . . *Paul et Virginie* is not just a pastorale of two innocent young lovers living apart from society whose idyll is broken when society intrudes; it is also a novel of colors and painterly precise descriptions, much as *Pierrot* is a movie of colors and painterly precise photography. Ferdinand and Marianne gain almost as much freedom as possible through their Robinson Crusoe return to nature, yet their isolation becomes a decided limitation. They find, of course, that they cannot stay away from life; their retreat is like the world of Jules Verne novels, Marianne says, but they must return to their detective stories with cars and guns and nightclubs.

Perhaps the most fundamental references in *Pierrot le Fou,* however, are those to movies. Not only does Godard force on the viewer a self-conscious awareness that he is watching a film, but also throughout the film Godard makes his characters talk about movies. For Ferdinand, knowing movies is as important as knowing books; immediately after his lesson on the world of Velazquez, while talking about the maid's having gone to the movies, he equates seeing Nicholas Ray's *Johnny Guitar* with getting the right kind of education. . . . [If] *Johnny Guitar* does not fit into the genre of the Western, [and] it is its own genre, then *Pierrot* is the same kind of film. It does not fit neatly into the genre of the gangster film; it is its own multi-faceted genre film. Likewise, the reference to [Julien Duvivier's] *Pépé le Moko,* possibly the prototype of the French gangster-romance, shows an affinity with *Pierrot le Fou.*

Life as it is seen through film is special. No one is more aware of this than Godard, and in *Pierrot le Fou* he constantly reminds the audience that they are seeing a movie—not real life. The references are often subtle and exclusively cinematic, but occasionally they are overt, as well. Marianne, for instance, remembers an incident from a Laurel and Hardy movie to help them get away without paying for gas. Later, as they are planning to burn the Peugeot in order to give the impression that they have been killed in an accident, she tells Ferdinand to pull the car closer to the wreck; it must appear authentic since, after all, they are not in the movies. This type of reference draws attention to itself precisely because of its amusing irony: they *are* in the movies, and denying it emphasizes that fact.

Godard has always been inclined to use cinematic devices in an obvious way and to ignore what are generally considered to be "traditional" approaches to filmmaking. *Pierrot le Fou* is typical Godard in this respect. For example, during the sequence in which Ferdinand runs from the café through the streets and along the beach to the apartment house where the midget is holding Marianne prisoner, Godard ignores screen direction. . . . [The] problems of involvement and communication that lie at the heart of the film are united with the theme and the technique of *Pierrot le Fou.*

Ferdinand and Marianne are complex characters, individual and subtle. There is an attraction-repulsion between them that underlies their actions and is a result of their basic differences. Both are searching for freedom; they want to get away from their previous existences, but once they are away, they want to return to the activity they have left. (pp. 7-9)

Ferdinand is caught in [Marianne's] milieu. Ferdinand refers to [Jean Renoir's] *La Chienne* in which Michel Simon allows himself to be possessed by a girl; the same thing happens to Ferdinand. He is searching for freedom, and she becomes his mode of achieving it. In the process, however, she enslaves him just as his wife did before her.

Though they are not one-dimensional characters, Marianne and Ferdinand are, nonetheless, comic-strip characters. . . . Their various scenes almost seem inspired by incidents from the book of cartoons which they carry during the film: *La Bande des Pieds Nickele,* the comic strip of the (freely translated) loafers or ne'er-do-wells. Marianne and Ferdinand are loafers, seeking fulfillment wherever they can find it, by making up stories, by acting out guerrilla theater, and ultimately by killing.

Throughout *Pierrot le Fou* Ferdinand seems to be playing two roles. One is that of a naturally pensive and philosophical person who knows books and movies and painting and who keeps a diary; his name is Ferdinand. The other is a man of action who steals cars and runs throughout the country with a girl who inspires him to each new pursuit; his name is Pierrot. . . . Pierrot is, of course, one of the Italian art comedy clowns who are beset with problems of love. Though chiefly a comic figure, the original Pierrot is somewhat sad, as well, for he must work so hard to overcome the society which usually rejects him. In Godard's film Ferdinand gradually assumes more of the Pierrot qualities as the movie progresses. . . . Whereas Pierrot is the winner, if not the survivor, in the old plays, Ferdinand realizes that there are no winners. At the end of the film, as he paints his face blue, assuming the mask he has rejected all along, Ferdinand actually becomes Pierrot. The thinking man becomes the acting man and blows himself up.

As thinking man, Ferdinand writes a diary during the course of the picture, and the diary becomes an integral part of the visual aspect of *Pierrot le Fou.* Godard inserts pages from the diary, but individual words rather than complete sentences are often all that can be caught from the way they are photographed. It is through the diary, though, that Ferdinand reveals himself. He ruminates on the meanings of life and decides that those who lose in life are the real winners. He dissects Marianne's name and finds the French words for "sea," "soul," and "bitter." He philosophizes that once one has achieved what one wants in life, life still remains an unsolved mystery. This then is Ferdinand/Pierrot's story. He has run away from his wife and Paris; he has attempted to achieve communication and interaction; he has gained the solace of an isolated existence, but all to no avail. Life has still given him little satisfaction, and, significantly, the last word he enters in the diary is *mort.* (pp. 10-12)

*Pierrot le Fou* may be Godard's *Fleurs du Mal.* During his discussion with Samuel Fuller . . . , Ferdinand discovers the nature of cinema: it is like a battleground, full of love, hate, action, violence, and death—in a word, emotion. The description especially suits *Pierrot le Fou,* which, like Baudelaire's *Fleurs du Mal* (the title Fuller gives for his next movie is *Flowers of Evil*), suggests that beauty and corruption are of an inseparable nature. Like Baudelaire's poems as well, *Pierrot* is an imagistic movie, especially in its use of water. The sun and the sea together at the end represent the idea of eternity, for example. Life consists of paradoxes. Painting, literature, and film are among man's greatest achievements; war and murder and leading lives of quiet desperation are among his worst, yet the two are inseparable. Ferdinand cannot accept it anymore, and, accordingly, he destroys himself. (p. 12)

*Jerome H. Delamater, "Jean-Luc Godard's 'Pierrot le fou'," in* Film Heritage *(copyright 1975 by F. A. Macklin), Vol. 10, No. 3, Spring, 1975, pp. 5-12.*

**COLIN MacCABE**

In the programme notes to *Mahagonny,* the notes which Yves Montand refers to in *Tout va bien,* Brecht defines epic theatre in terms of a radical separation of its elements and distinguishes three such elements in the opera—the music, the text and the setting. In cinema, thanks to the work of Christian Metz, we can distinguish five different elements: the moving picture image, recorded phonetic sound, recorded musical sound, recorded noise and writing. Considered from the position suggested by the notes to *Mahagonny, Deux ou trois choses* can certainly be considered as an epic film, for its whole progress is a constant separation of its constitutive elements. Perhaps the element which is most obviously separated out in the film's progress is writing. So accustomed are we to a cinema which hides its writing away at the beginning or end of a film that it is with some shock that we discover it at all in Metz's classification, but such a cinema is directly challenged in *Deux ou trois choses* where it is impossible to ignore writing, as the book covers punctuate the action. This punctuation recalls Brecht's demand for a literalisation of the theatre; which literalisation was conceived exactly as the punctuation of representation with formulation, and this is exactly how the writing functions in *Deux ou trois choses*—constantly forcing us back to the problem of theoretically articulating the incidents which are represented on the screen. (p. 46)

*Tout va bien* attempts to demonstrate [matters of expression] horizontally, syntagmatically. It is the repetition of shots that reveals the mechanism to us. Thus as the strikers sit round discussing the significance of their actions the film gives us a montage of events—giving them their historical significance—and it is this montage which isolates the significant features of the occupation and articulates them in a way that makes clear their relationships. It is this learning which is the central point of the film—the education of the strikers, the education of [Jane] Fonda and Montand, the education of us in the cinema. We must learn to say 'I' historically—to understand that 'I' not as the punctual subject of a set of actions; eating, sleeping, going to the cinema but as the crystallisation of a set of differing social relationships. (p. 50)

[In] the question of film and politics, it is not politics *or* film but politics *and* film. Filmic questions are political questions and vice versa (one could recall emblematically that Eisenstein wanted to make a film of *Das Kapital*). I would like to demonstrate this position by taking the filmic weaknesses of *Deux ou trois choses* and analysing their political implications and to operate the reverse procedure with *Tout va bien*. . . . [A] purely formal separation would be dependent on the conception of a simple autonomous spectator sitting in the cinema and . . . thus to extract the spectator from any class position is always to confer a fundamental homogeneity whatever its apparent breaks. The separation in *Deux ou trois choses* does to a certain extent remain on this formal level. If we take for example the repeated chords of the Beethoven music we can grant that a formal split is achieved between image and soundtrack but it is doubtful if this separation involves any interruption which will enable the spectator to study a set of relationships there where there had been an identity. . . . [The] formal nature of the separation is exactly that which enables the spectator to remain untouched by it—to remain mixed in. *Deux ou trois choses* still offers an aesthetic position to the viewer from which the formal operations can still be read as the tics of an original genius. If we return to Brecht's strictures against the integrated work of art we can remember that Brecht insisted that the spectator must not become a passive (suffering) part of the total work. It is this passivity which is encouraged by the formal nature of *Deux ou trois choses* and which finds its reverberations at other levels within the film. (pp. 52-3)

In order to understand the position of the film it is necessary to consider the two monologues delivered by Juliette's son Christophe. When Christophe recounts his dream we find ourselves in that perfect world, the two twins, North Vietnam and South Vietnam, where the symbol is completely defined and exhausted by the thing symbolised—where words and things are completely co-extensive—in other words exactly in that world of pleasure and belief where there is no difference, no separation, no knowledge. That he is still in the plenitude of

the infant world (*infans* = unable to speak) is made clear by the question he next asks his mother 'Mummy what is language?' The next time we see him his discourse is no longer so transparent, we can hardly understand his essay on the theme 'There are both boys and girls at our new school this year, which means that our class is mixed. Is friendship between boys and girls possible and desirable, yes or no?' What is obvious, however, is that this lack of transparency has been brought on by the contact with difference—with the girls with whom he has started to go to school. The film places itself in much the same position as Christophe, hesitating between the comfortable world of belief and the difficult world of knowledge—hesitating in the moment of entering into language before the world of knowledge and desire it opens up—hesitating between the art cinema and the political cinema. (p. 53)

The political weakness of the film can finally be grasped through a consideration of its central gest—prostitution. The newspaper report is transformed from a shocking identity into a set of commonplace relationships determined above all by the need to consume. But it is simply as consumer—as passive—that the film attempts to grasp the social relations it investigates. Production is almost absent from the film and with it the contradiction which is immediately brought with production, with the class struggle. This emphasis on the passive consumer finds its counterpart in a residual humanism that informs the film. Talking about *Deux ou trois choses,* Godard constantly stressed prostitution as the typical state of our society. But exactly insofar as this view of prostitution as typical takes us away from the concrete conditions of the Paris suburbs, so it leads us towards a position in which all our individual souls are prostituted to the grand machine—rather than an understanding of the machine and its contradictions—rather than an understanding of our social relations. (p. 54)

The audience [of *Tout va bien*] is constantly reminded that it is the struggle that matters—all attempts at identification, as in the sequence at the end of the strike when we see Fonda and Montand working in the various positions of the workers, are beside the point, they are criticised in the film, because they leave us powerless. We must understand the struggle of forces and how it operates in our lives. . . . [If] we consider the lessons they learnt from the struggle we can pinpoint the political weaknesses of the film. In the supermarket Fonda poses the question as to where to begin, to which the answer is, everywhere at once. This answer is politically incorrect and is not in any sense criticised in the film. To start everywhere at once is to ignore the necessity of analysis and of conscious intervention in the social process—it is in fact to ignore politics in favour of morals. . . . Two basic social events are here taken as the gest, the identity to be resolved into relations: the first is the Communist Party's attack on the activities of Maoist groups at Flins in June 1968 and the second is the Communist Party's sale of their programme for popular unity—'changer de cap'—in supermarkets in France. What is less important, in this context, than the punctual correctness or incorrectness of the positions, is whether one can agree with the gestic analysis that this reveals, that of the Communist Party's identity with the bourgeoisie. In other words it is not whether one actually thinks the film is right to criticise either the French Communist Party's attack on the activities at Flins, or whether the Party was politically right to make the sale in the supermarket, but whether those events are typical, in the sense that they reveal a complete homogenisation between the Communist Party and the ruling bourgeois order. Given this attitude to the Communist Party it is not surprising that politics is abandoned because the political arena is understood as a homogeneous area completely given over to the bourgeoisie. But the abandonment has effects at the filmic level. Simply to take the most obvious point we can see in this film a relative suppression of writing, exactly that which in *Deux ou trois choses* is heterogeneity. The only titles are 'May 1968', 'May 1972' and 'Class Struggle', together with the moral at the end of the film, but that is in some sense isolated, outside. Otherwise any writing is given diegetic motivation within the film. This suppression of writing finds its echo in the first report that we hear Jane Fonda read, in which she declares that the written press is dead. To give up this weapon in the heterogeneisation of the cinema is to risk a lapse into a plenitude of the image—a fall into belief and away from knowledge. This fall can be specified in the different positions of the monologues in the three groups in the factories. While we are constantly made aware of the site of the discourse of the boss and the CGT delegate—are aware of it, that is, as a specific articulation—the *gauchistes* are presented to us as the voice outside difference—the pure presence of truth. . . . [The] specific site of the voice and its contradictions are lost as we hear the authentic voice of the working class. This lack of distance from the *gauchistes* is emphasised, at what I might call the theatrical, not the filmic level, by Frédéric's dress (the black sweater, the moustache), or by Georges, the old worker, that stereotype of the proletarian 'salt of the earth'.

This lack of distanciation, this suppression of writing, the abolition of politics and theory has political results, and predictable political results. The inability to find one full expressive discourse, to find the word which endures and marks a slice of history, the word which Fonda is looking for, entails, if you cannot find an expressive discourse, a fall back into the expressive moment at which one beats up a foreman—a policeman—or a supermarket. If we think again of those two first 'Today' sequences, they both carry images of 'correct' political action which are not placed in any contradiction with the soundtrack. The first involves the moment when the two youths running from a policeman suddenly realise they can beat him up, and the second is when the band of young people ransack a supermarket. Both these incidents reveal a profoundly reactionary political position—a position very close to a fascist idealisation of violence. When the two youths turn on the policeman it is divorced from any concrete political situation in which the policeman is being used as an arm of the state in a particular area of the class struggle, rather it is presented as the typical situation of the policeman against youth. It is exactly the typicality of the situation which depoliticises it. Similarly, the ransacking of the supermarket is divorced from any political position other than that if you force people into a confrontation with the police it will make them revolutionaries—in fact it will make them prisoners. (pp. 54-6)

The list of pronouns which ends *Tout va bien* are all interchangeable with a punctual 'I'—'Those who don't like it' are always caught in a set of specific relationships, they represent an objective political force towards which one must take a position. *Tout va bien* appeals to the Maoist slogan 'Count on one's own energies', a slogan which means 'Count on the political energies of the particular group you are in', but in the film it is given an individual meaning, we are individually obliged, says the film to learn to say 'I' historically. (pp. 56-7)

*Colin MacCabe, "The Politics of Separation," in* Screen (© *The Society for Education in Film and Television, 1976), Vol. 16, No. 4, Winter, 1975-76, pp. 46-61.*

**JAMES MONACO**

The idea of participation is integral to Godard's films: it confronts us on every level. To paraphrase *Le Gai Savoir*, these are not the films that *should* be made, but when those films *are* made they will have to follow some of the lines these films have laid down. The main focus of Godard's energies, ever since he started writing about film in 1952, has been towards an understanding of the phenomenon of film (and by extension other arts). . . . (p. 102)

[The phrase "The sign forces us to see an object through its significance"] will be Godard's motto as a filmmaker a decade later: it is typically hermetic, almost mystical; it is as ambiguous as a line of modern poetry, yet it urgently wants to state a basic axiom: that there is no way we can sense the objective world without first understanding how our systems of signs—our languages, both verbal and non-verbal—"signify," how they mean, and how they thereby change our perceptions. (p. 105)

What impresses us about Godard's films is their collage of cultural data and artifacts. Godard's characters—all of them, from Michel Poiccard and Patricia straight on through to "He" and "She" in *Tout va bien*—are afloat in a raging sea of images and sounds, metaphors and syllogisms, political half-truths and cultural clichés. And if there can be said to be one central action that unites and connects the various films, it is the battle to rescue life from abstraction, to return to the comfort of the concrete. (p. 109)

*A bout de souffle* is a montage of roles, images, models—vehicles for expression (and vehicles for transportation too—Patricia isn't the only "Belle Américaine" in the film; there are classic Cadillacs, Oldsmobiles, and Thunderbirds as well). But it is important to look also at the kind of stories being told. With Truffaut and Bogart Godard shares two characteristic themes: the isolation of the hero and the betrayal of women. He has taken the two to extremes. People in Godard's films seldom make any kind of human contact. . . . People in Godard's films (with very few exceptions) are paralyzed from the beginning. They may *talk* about love, about politics, but they seldom *make* either. At their best they reveal something of that terrifying internal battle between the paralysis of contemplation and the desire for action.

What is the cause of that paralysis? Godard will spend the next ten years working out answers to that question. *A bout de souffle* might be better translated "Out of Breath" than "Breathless." Godard is out of breath, beaten, at the beginning of his career. (p. 110)

[The main mood of *Une Femme est une femme*] is neither tragic nor comic; this is a love story, one of the few successful ones of the sixties. . . . It is the only one of Godard's thirty-six films that celebrates the life-force wholeheartedly, a song of innocence. (p. 117)

*Vivre sa vie* is more an essay than a play. . . . [It] is pervaded with a naturalistic sense of fate. As Truffaut described the film: "There is a girl, she is in a fixed situation, desperate straits, and from the beginning. At the end of the road lies death." There is no exit. (pp. 123-24)

*Vivre sa vie* may be esthetically distanced, it may be something of a factual essay on its subject, but it is this personal (and painful) atmosphere which makes it finally such an affecting film. . . . The films so often end with death, not only because that is still the most effective dramatic period, but also because an important facet of Godard's own romantic, existential cinematic personality is Keatsian, half in love with easeful death. Politics will bring him out of that bind, but politics are still a good distance off at the time of the ironically titled *Vivre sa vie*. If we are works of art, we may be eternal, but we are frozen in that eternal moment, as Pirandello pointed out. If we are commodities then we must eventually be disposed of. Obviously the search is, then, for a condition of existence beyond commodity, even beyond art. *Vivre sa vie*, combining fiction and reality, begins the search. (pp. 124-25)

The subject of *Les Carabiniers*—war—is the ultimate testing ground for theories of distancing and "unrealization": how else can the absurdity and absolutism of that phenomenon be treated? (p. 131)

For Godard, the necessary leverage is not memory, satire, or irony, but the language of film itself. The experience of war is one thing; the knowledge of it which we gain through film and literature is quite another. If we know, generally, the difference between "film" and "real life," we should be able to extrapolate from the filmic image some sense of the actuality. (pp. 131-32)

Michel-Ange and Ulysse live within this semiological world, not merely as objects of it; they share Godard's perplexity with the confusion of signs. They are enticed into the army with promises of plunder ("you can take anything you want, Hawaiian guitars, elephants . . ."), but it turns out there is no reality behind those words; they return to their wives, Vénus and Cléopâtre, at the end of the film with only a box of picture postcards. They have captured the images, not the objects. (p. 133)

Separating sign and object, signifier and signified, is thus clearly a political point. . . . The signifiers betray us: "anti-personnel bombs" are conceivable, shrapnel imbedded in a womb is not; "body counts" are acceptable, while the blood and guts of a single mutilated death are not. To be able to abstract is to be able to wage war and commit murder. The battle for Godard is to rescue life from abstraction. (pp. 133-34)

*La Femme mariée* is the midpoint of the road between *Vivre sa vie* and *2 ou 3 choses que je sais d'elle*. Between the former, a personal portrait of a prostitute, and the latter, a semiological essay on the metaphor of prostitution, we have *La Femme mariée*, in Godard's original title. . . . [The title was changed by the French censors] to *"Une" Femme mariée*, lest the unsuspecting viewer make the generalization from the definite article that Godard very much intended! . . . The film is obviously a portrait of its eponymous heroine, but it views its subject through a complex semantic screen. . . . It is the relationship between *a* married woman and *the* married woman that fascinates Godard; the connection between the specific and existential and its reflection in the general culture. (pp. 145-46)

[Now] for the first time, we approach the film as an essay rather than a fiction. It is the freedom of the form that makes *La Femme mariée* so direct, refreshing, and passionate. (p. 147)

[Both *Alphaville* and *Pierrot le fou*] are global, encompassing summations of his moral universe. Both are love stories; one ends in life and re-invention of love; the other ends in death and negation. Both are highly "poetic"—general, abstract, and moral, and as a consequence lyrical rather than exegetical narratives. (p. 155)

[In *Made in U.S.A.* we have Anna] Karina as Bogart, an essay on the "coca-colonization" of France, and an attempt to comment on the underside of French politics as seen through the Ben Barka affair. Yet these various motivations, in themselves, would not have resulted in the dark reconditeness of *Made in U.S.A.* if Godard had not also decided once again to film the "spaces between people." . . . [The] film concentrates on episodes and images which are often all but unintelligible. It is meant to follow directly in the tradition of [Howard Hawks's] *The Big Sleep*, whose incidents confused even Raymond Chandler. Chandler's world was dark, impenetrable, and paranoid, and the angst which pervaded it had first attracted the critics of the New Wave in the fifties; Godard is simply transferring the breakdown of logic and ethics which frightened Philip Marlowe from the Private Eye metaphor to a more specific mode. . . . [*Made in U.S.A.* is] a series of tentative statements whose provenance is the logic of structure, not the making of sense. (pp. 174-75)

*2 ou 3 choses* attempts to divine the particular in the general and the general in the particular by forcing a fusion of viewpoints: the "her" of the title refers not to Juliette or to Marina Vlady who plays her so much as to the city of Paris. Juliette does not personify the city, but the stories of the two, on separate, parallel levels, are congruent. (p. 178)

One might find it relatively easy to dismiss the sociology of *2 ou 3 choses* as fatuous or stillborn. But when we take into account Godard's own relationship with his materials, the film comes painfully alive. There is a passion here to make images, sounds, and words serve our understanding, and a knowledge of how they so often do not. (p. 179)

[The shot of the coffee cup] is the most personal—and most painful—moment in all of Godard. Poets sometimes speak this privately and directly to us; filmmakers seldom do. All the while, the eloquent, liquescent, shimmering black coffee swirls in the swollen cup. (p. 182)

Godard's pensive, restive, ineffable coffee cup does make it possible to "link up, to move from one subject to another." It is the bridge between poetics and politics. After telling us two or three things that he knows about her, Godard decides to listen more, to look around him more. He is finished with film as an end in itself. He moves on to film as a means to another, larger end, "a new world where people and things would find harmony among themselves." (p. 183)

Like *Masculin-féminin*, *La Chinoise* is about the culture of the generation that succeeded Godard's and focuses on a group. *Weekend*, like *Made in U.S.A.*, has fictional overtones and depends on a large measure of fantasy for its effect. As their English titles indicate, they are also both about the Americanization and embourgeoisement of French life. Finally, *Le Gai Savoir* might just as easily have been called *2 ou 3 choses que je sais d'elle*; both are profoundly personal and intensely epistemological. (p. 189)

[The nine films Godard completed between 1968 and 1973] came out of a matrix of contradictions, both political and esthetic, personal and public. The spirit of paradox which had motivated so many of Godard's earlier films was now expressed in political rather than philosophical language, but it is still in the struggles with those contradictions that we find the energy, wit, and feeling of Godard's art.

He wanted to make a new cinema which was political, concrete, active, and collective, but the evidence of the Dziga-Vertov period shows how very difficult this was. (p. 213)

[We] can see that Godard and his films during [the Dziga-Vertov] period clearly reflect one of the central contradictions of the politics of the left, especially as it was demonstrated in the sixties. Godard symbolizes the dilemma of the bourgeois intellectual revolutionary: thoroughly committed to radical politics, but prevented by his class and role from participating existentially in the struggle—the dilemma of the "unoppressed" white, male, middle-class, middle-aged professional. (p. 217)

Two basic esthetic-political problems dominated the films of the Dziga Vertov group. The first of these Godard phrased this way:

> The old principle says "go and fetch images and then try to edit them." The point we are at now is to *build* images—build images as simple as possible so that you can build your analysis.

This is the logical outgrowth, many times removed, of the ideas Godard first expressed in "Montage, mon beau souci." The second problem, a corollary in a way, was the "tyranny of image over sound." Images and sounds would now be "built" and opposed to each other in strictly dialectical fashion, for "realism does not consist in reproducing reality, but in showing things as they really are," and "photography is not a reflection of what is real but what is real in this reflection." It follows that the Dziga-Vertov films will shift the virtual focus from the "reality" in front of the camera (and "behind" the screen) to the "reality" of the screen's own surface. Image will be opposed to image, sound to sound, image to sound, and sound to image. . . .

The first step along the Dziga-Vertov road to correct ideas, *Un Film comme les autres (A Film Like Any Other)*, was a sublimely simple statement/illustration of these two basic concepts. . . . *Un Film comme les autres* is not at all like other films. (p. 221)

*One Plus One*, in contrast, is Godard's "last bourgeois film," in his own words, yet there are surprising echoes of the theory which underlay *Un Film comme les autres. One Plus One*, as its title announces, is a film of elementary arithmetic. The equation is not complete; the problem is left to be worked out. . . . (p. 222)

[*British Sounds* is] another blow for the equality of sound and image. Because its politics are more concrete than those of most of the other Dziga-Vertov films, and because Godard has achieved a delicate balance between the political material and the esthetic structure, *British Sounds* has a clarity and force that makes it considerably more effective politically. (pp. 224-25)

*Pravda* has an interesting and ingenious semiology, but bad politics. The title is ironic (the word means "truth," but it is also the name of the Russian newspaper, a clarion of "revisionism")—and it may possibly be itself a critique of the film. (p. 228)

In its failure, *Pravda*, points up the two parallel difficulties which haunt the Dziga Vertov group: first, their curious propensity for examining distant situations rather than the immediate realities of their comrades' lives and their own; and second, the tendency for baroque, dogmatic, effulgent ideology to cloud the images and sounds of "concrete analysis of concrete situations." The two failures are linked, for both make it possible for the Dziga-Vertov films to ignore people in order to celebrate the esthetics of dogma. In the battle between theory and practice, the former too often wins out. . . .

[*Vent d'est*] is probably the most complete and thorough of the Dziga-Vertov films. It takes the broad view and tries to summarize the contemporary Marxist political situation, the position of the militant filmmaker, and the relationship between the two. As a result, it is a dense and tricky film which, more than the others, requires that the viewer become deeply involved in the process of the film before it can be comprehended. (p. 230)

[*Tout va bien* is] a film that balances the microcosm of sexual politics against the more general politics of class struggle; a film that uses the conventional elements of fictional cinema in order to enlarge the Brechtian theory of *Lehrstücke;* a film that admits it's a film, but doesn't become paralyzed by that knowledge; a film about reality—the way things really are—but one which does not "reproduce reality." . . . (p. 240)

*Tout va bien* is the first love story of the *rapports de production,* the first comedy of disrealization. (pp. 244-45)

[The purpose of *Letter to Jane* is] the familiar litany of the Dziga Vertov group. . . . The dialogue between producer of cinema and consumer of cinema is essential; the aim is to break the barriers of communication and create an identity between them; that's the only way we can get at truth, existential truth. But the problem lies not only with languages that we recognize as languages (English, French) but also with languages that we do *not* recognize as languages (the language of the journalistic still photograph). (p. 246)

*Letter to Jane* has no answers; many of the intricate statements it makes about the semiology of the photograph (and related issues) can be contradicted, criticized. But the basic point remains: reality is not understood simply: it is, for us in the twentieth century, both reticulated and mediated: reticulated because linear causality is no longer sufficient; mediated because we comprehend it now not primarily through our own eyes and ears, but through technological media which change reality as they transmit it. (p. 250)

[Godard's fast-moving] nature is driven by a violent passion to comprehend, not merely how one thing connects with another, but how everything is part of everything else. This makes Godard's films difficult, sometimes inscrutable, often very private, but it also makes of him a poet of cinematic relativity. . . . He has felt and understood the unity of the culture that stretches from Bach to Batman, from Racine to the Rolling Stones, and he has drawn from his study several very real, hard, ineluctable truths:

> that this culture represses and constricts us as much as it expresses our fears and desires,
> that our cities are Alphavillean nightmares,
> that our culture turns women into objects of consumption and men into fearful, paralyzed dreamers, half in love with easeful death,
> that our machines of communication and transportation have overwhelmed us, so that it is they who can be said to "live," not us,
> that our social contract is ludicrously twisted.
>
>                                    (pp. 251-52)

Godard's art is *consciencieux,* a conflation of conscience and the consciousness of self, an intimate confluence of the personal and the moral, of method and sentiment. It leaves me breathless. (p. 252)

> James Monaco, "Godard," in his The New Wave: Truffaut, Godard, Chabrol, Rohmer, Rivette (copyright © 1976 by James Monaco; reprinted by permission of Oxford University Press, Inc.), Oxford University Press, New York, 1976, pp. 98-252.

### DENNIS GILES

*Weekend* is the last film of Godard's *contemplative* phase, a film which prepares the *break* of 1968. With *Deux ou trois choses* of the previous year, it is a *site* on which Godard discovers the economic structures which motivate human behavior. . . .

In *Weekend,* Godard reveals civil society in its most corrupt form from the viewpoint of an entomologist; in *Deux ou trois choses* he shows the subjective problems of an individual caught in the economic meshes of this "society of needs." Civil society . . . is characterized by an unreal split between political and economic society. The civil man (Corinne, Roland, Juliette) finds political matters external to his life. . . .

With Godard's 1968 *break,* this individual isolation disappears from his films. The personal interests of the disparate radicals in *Vladimir and Rosa* (1970) become united by the Chicago Trial into a community of emotion and purpose. In speaking of his break, Godard finds the same passage from the pursuit of personal needs to the realization that he need not film alone, that his cause is the cause of others, that he can break out of his selfish isolation by a communal act of filming. . . . (p. 170)

Godard makes the leap to the Marxism which was tempting him, yet outside him. No longer is there the question, "What am I; what am I to do?" for Godard or his characters. He now films the Marxist answer, "I am what *we* do." . . .

As Godard matures, his characters lose their individuality. One might say they lose their "character" and become "characteristic" of a group or class. Juliette in *Deux ou trois choses* is presented as representative of all bourgeois housewives who live in the suburban housing projects just as the apartment buildings shown become representative of all suburban housing developments. The characters who flaunt their individuality in small outrageous acts disappear from the films of Godard. . . .

In *Vladimir and Rosa,* as in *Pravda,* Godard plays an abstract character named Vladimir (Lenin) in order to explain Marxist theory and pose the problems of Marxist cinema. He is not playing the individual Lenin in any kind of historical re-creation but rather invoking the idea of Lenin as one who combined theoretical Marxism with revolutionary practice—a Lenin who realized Marxist ideas in physical reality—thus cueing us as to Godard's intention of actualizing Marx on film. (p. 171)

For Marx the class has a character, while the individual has no character independent of class. The individual is prevented from being an individual by the material relations which enslave him and alienate him from himself. His needs of subsistence and the menace of others have fused him to a class which *subsumes* him under itself and enslaves his mind through class-bound ideological formations. Under capitalism, the individual is "unreal" except as a class being.

So Godard's characters become "typical" representatives of a communal being they share with others. The individual no longer exists *as individual* beyond the time of *La chinoise.* There are no longer unique protagonists, no longer any "heroes"; according to "Father" Brecht, it is the masses who make history, not heroes.

It is not only Godard's characters but also the content of his images which lose particularity. The material reality within the frame becomes the most general, everyday reality. . . . Godard is not speaking of *a* man but of *man,* not of *a* city but *city,* etc. While [John] Ford loves to dwell on small activities like shaving, walking, eating, etc., he presents them both for their own sake and because they reveal individual character. Whereas Godard is no longer interested in the character of individuals and films the everyday not out of any special love or affection for it but because he speaks of *all* men who shave, walk, eat, etc., and must invoke the activities and the sites of these activities. (pp. 171-72)

Godard can say that film, as an ideological formation, is "not the reflections of reality, but the reality of the reflection"—a reflection, a *re*-presentation which *appears* real to consciousness, but is not reality itself. . . . For Godard, film is ideology, cannot be anything but ideology. His work in film is an ideological struggle in which he films against the current ideology of the bourgeoisie in order to reveal it *as* ideology, thus breaking its hold by showing men that their consciousness is a false consciousness. Since film is itself ideology and as such is a bourgeois representation of the world which shows an imaginary world, Godard films *against* the language of film. His struggle is an ideological one because ideology is the field of his action, i.e., he films against yet *within* an ideological problematic. (p. 173)

Godard must film *within* ideology to speak to an audience whose consciousness is ideologically determined. If he did not assume such an ideological base, no bourgeois would understand his speech. Yet the intention is to break the audience *out of* an ideological conception of life. Godard must film both within their language and against it. How does he achieve this contradictory task?

The film must be designed to break through ideology and produce and develop a new consciousness in the spectator so that he will criticize his ideological notions. In order to induce the spectator to self-criticism, one must make him see himself in the film, but not to the extent of total identification where he is swept along by the film and abandons himself to it. He must maintain a self *outside* the film to which he can apply the film, seeing its problematic as *his* problematic. In short, he must be able to *think while watching the film,* to criticize himself by considering the problem. This means that there must not be such a total emotional empathy with the people in the film that he cannot step outside it.

If the film starts with ideology in order to break out of it into "reality," the film must contradict itself, by the radical discovery of what is other than itself. That is, Godard, like Brecht before him, criticizes or exposes ideological themes through the discovery of non-ideological themes. The film goes outside itself, breaks with its own problematic, with the "givens" of existence in order to show that these familiar realities are unreal. (p. 174)

Godard and Brecht expose the lived, known reality by a shift of gears or rather a *shift of viewpoint* which distances the spectator from that reality he thinks he knows so well, a reality which he does *not* know because he is entangled in it, has never examined it from the outside. Godard thus shifts from a consciousness within ideology to the "astronomical" viewpoint of an anthropologist, sociologist, economist. . . . Unlike the films of Ford and Hawks, Godard's Marxist films reveal character *in order to change it* by exposing the falsehood of the original consciousness to another. It is the opinion of Marx, Brecht and Godard that a man must move out of the prevailing ideology in order to reach the consciousness that moves him to economic and political action which might change the world. Changing the world first implies a change from a static consciousness to an active one—from a consciousness immersed in the discovery of things as they are (pre-1968 Godard) to a consciousness which sees the world as crying out to be changed.

The bourgeois ideology sees the world as essentially *there, static, resistant to change*. Godard, in his "bourgeois" phase, demonstrates again and again that the world prevents the completion of meaningful acts, rendering them pathetic or ridiculous (*Pierrot*). . . .

But Marxist theory sees reality as process—as dialectic. The world changes through the working out of the contradictions of existence. . . .

The contradictions within the film lead to the spectator being in disharmony with the film, or, to be more specific, the spectator adopts the attitude toward the film that the film has toward itself—if the film is self-critical, the spectator is critical of the actions, words and characters in it. . . .

The dissociations, the contradictions within the film must be pointed out, heightened by the structure of the film itself. In particular, the "joints" must be illuminated in order that the spectator can clearly see the contradictions involved. (p. 175)

For a Marxist, the world is not only contradictory but also discontinuous. Times and spaces do not flow evenly, but develop unevenly. Godard's films have always assumed a special discontinuity. His locations remain unlinked on film; he shows no coherent geography. One could not translate the movements of Michel in *A bout de souffle* to a map of Paris. Occasionally one could trace a line, but huge gaps would appear in his itinerary. Godard's shots are not at all the consistent exploration of a continuous world outside the camera. One never quite knows where one is in relation to the previous shots. (pp. 176-77)

The Marxist film in the hands of Godard, on the contrary, presents itself as incomplete. Godard hopes to convert the spectator from his traditional role as spectator into an actor who finishes the film after experiencing it. As the ideological "reality" is revealed as ideological by the spectator, he criticizes his ideological world, seeing it as false. But ideally, the change in the spectator's consciousness leads him to act upon the newfound "false" world in which he lives, to transform it into a community. In *Vladimir and Rosa* Godard not only points out the inhuman social reality which underlies the political (ideological) trial of the Chicago Seven, but combines his analysis with exhortations of the revolutionary action, some of them quite specific actions. The film ends with Juliet Berto looking into the camera at the spectators, crying out that we are all prisoners, that we must seize our freedom. One cannot then say that *Vladimir and Rosa ends* when the theater lights go on—it is a film conceived and executed as open-ended, an unfinished act to be completed by the spectators become actors outside the theater. Such a film is an endless act. Through this *uncompleted cinema*, Godard hopes to achieve on film what [Louis] Althusser demands of theater: an art whose object is to destroy the consciousness the spectator brings to the theater,

to dissolve his pre-given, static and ideological consciousness of himself and his world. . . .

When Godard speaks [the] last words of the film *Deux ou trois choses*, he voices the necessity to set aside all previous cinema (including his own), to put all past "knowledge" behind him. To film on a *tabula rasa*—an empty blackboard where nothing is determined. At zero there are no laws, no previous habits of language. Film is pure possibility, yet to be constituted. The only reality is the knowledge that nothing is (yet) real. (p. 177)

To return to zero is to realize that civilization is only an arrangement of products for sale. That the economics of capitalism is the "real" city. That the buildings are only facades determined by and subordinate to economic relations. That the streets are the means to get from one product to another to another—avenues of purchase. That Hollywood (and the cinema it represents) is only a product among products.

To return to zero is to discover the unreality of all that which Godard has previously filmed. That he was deceived. That all he so rigorously analyzed was only appearance. (pp. 177-78)

To return to zero is for Godard to discover that the "reality" he films is only an ideological construct, that reality is not seen but thought by film, that reality is still to be constituted in the world. To return to zero as filmmaker and thinker is to realize that he, Godard, can only point toward a truth not yet realized, that the function of cinema is to incite men to realize reality by exposing the lie of that which poses as reality. To return to zero is to refute a bourgeois cinema which believed that the appearance was reality, unconscious of the fact that this "reality" was being constructed by the ideological nature of cinema itself. For Godard at zero, the truth of the image is no longer self-evident. In the bourgeois world, nothing *is* with any certainty. At zero, Godard films in the knowledge that no *thing* which exists in this unreal world is knowable as such, that apparent being is false, bourgeois, that knowledge is still to be constructed as the world is constructed, that he must build a world he knows to be real in order to guarantee the truth of his thoughts. (p. 178)

> *Dennis Giles, "Godard and Ideology," in* Film Reader *(copyright © 1977 The Silver Screen), No. 2, 1977, pp. 169-79.*

### TERRY CURTIS FOX

While his work still graces repertory houses and college classrooms, it is no longer the predominant oeuvre, the major topic of conversation it once was. The man who, in a typical mixture of ego, self-mockery, and dead accuracy, once signed himself JEAN-LUC CINEMA GODARD has disappeared. (p. 1)

Godard is not a case of a man who, like Hitchcock, was simply a generation ahead of his critics. Godard never imagined our dreams so much as we imagined his. There is a remarkable consistency to the man: He began life as a film critic, and, while at times we imagined him to be simply self-conscious, it is, in the most profound sense, a critic he has remained.

Godard has consistently turned his work against itself. His films examine themselves, thus necessarily shrinking in scope and appeal as every word, every movement is challenged and reconsidered. He has felt compelled to make the camera define things, to limit the scope of view. While he began praising a tradition of filmmaking in which depth of field was everything—in which the more you could see in a single shot, the more happy ambiguities could be found—Godard's radical departure turned out to be the one-shot-for-one-idea cinema. Balance *Married Woman* (1964) against *Comment Ca Va* and one notes not a similarity of style but of *intent*. They are both movies concerned with showing the viewer how society's means of communication influence personal behavior. In a world where there is too much to see, where ''information overload'' makes definitions seem impossible, Godard makes large pictures of small things.

But, after 1968, two things happened to Godard's work that make a major difference. Like the typewriters and industrial tools that, in *Comment Ca Va,* are pushed to the foreground to indicate the proletarian presence, the blackboard became the framework of the film. Instead of fragmentary narration, which retained character and, hence, emotion, Godard became obsessed with words themselves. . . .

As America moved right, Godard's continued leftism seemed a social indiscretion. People weren't supposed to be into that anymore; the last thing one wanted was a harangue, even if the harangue were also a means whereby thinking might be changed. European leftism, which stressed theory and perceived Communism as a conservative force, became increasingly foreign to American eyes. And then there was the Palestinian question. . . .

*Ici et Ailleurs* [the film he shot in a PLO camp] is a curious work, at once a defense of Palestinian terror and a renunciation by Godard of his romantic attachment to it. (Where did emotion go in Godard? Into these loving shots of training soldiers, that's where.) The film as it finally emerged is a realization that the difference between living in France and living in the Middle East makes it impossible for Godard to make an honest film. He wants, he says, to give back his images. But the people to whom those images belong are dead—killed, not by Israelis, but by other Arabs. . . .

Feeling for Palestinians is not limited to Godard. The problem with *Ici et Ailleurs* is not simply that, no matter what qualifiers are attached to the film, and no matter how incisive the cinematic arguments may be, the movie does contain those heroic images of soldiers, militaristic moments of ''moral cretinism'' (the term is Godard's, from *Les Carabiniers*) that cannot be denied. The attitude toward the Palestinians is simply not well thought out. As a cinematic thinker, as a linguistic investigator, Godard is without peer. Politically, he is not nearly as cogent. . . .

*Numero Deux* (1975) and *Comment Ca Va* (1976) are not the abandonment of politics and the return to narrative that some of Godard's erstwhile American followers keep praying for. Unlike [Bob] Dylan, Godard did not find God and reconsideration after his near-fatal 1971 traffic accident. . . . *Numero Deux* is the annunciation of yet another Godardian period, one in which the individual is once again emerging as an important factor within society's political structure. At the same time, *Numero Deux* is not the remake of *Breathless,* as it was originally described. . . .

Whenever these and other video Godard moments are described, the proviso ''they are not really films'' is almost always attached. Both *Numero Deux* and *Comment Ca Va* are ''really'' films. In fact, *Comment Ca Va,* which describes itself as a film ''between active and passive,'' is a movie between video and film. Godard essentially uses video for images of analysis. Technically restricted to simpler images than film stock, Godard uses videotape when he wishes to illustrate a point. Film images, even when shot in the simplest manner, continue to contain complexities that reveal an emotional content. *Numero Deux* and *Comment Ca Va* represent an attempt to create works of both analysis *and* emotion. . . .

Neither will make Godard popular again. But then that is not what either movie wishes to do. The disappearing Jean-Luc Godard has managed to create that form of cinema that is neither documentary nor fiction. In the past 10 years, Godard has gone from Dickens to Hegel. On top of CINEMA we must now superimpose DISCOURS. (p. 41)

Terry Curtis Fox, "Looking for Mr. Godard" (reprinted by permission of The Village Voice *and the author; copyright © The Village Voice, Inc., 1977), in The Village Voice, Vol. XXII, No. 44, October 31, 1977, pp. 1, 41.*

## ANDREW SARRIS

No Godard film since *Pierrot le fou* has excited me as much as *Sauve qui peut (La Vie)* [released in the United States as *Every Man for Himself*]. Though his feeling for narrative has still not progressed from A to B and his disdain for psychological consistency and sociological probability is as outrageously apparent as ever, his zest for cinema is undiminished. *Sauve qui peut* is perhaps more like a piece of music than a movie. Every image is suffused with such elegant and exquisite insights into what makes the medium interact with its material that the total effect is intoxicating. Godard once wrote that the late Nicholas Ray was *cinema*. Perhaps the same can be said of Godard today. I would not care to debate Godard's ''ideas'' or speculate on his knowledge of the world and its people, though he is undoubtedly wiser and more reflective than many of his detractors imagine, and no great art can reflect entirely the triumph of intuition over intellect.

Is Godard's cinema, then, great art? I would argue that it is, without challenging Wilfrid Sheed's gibe that Godard had the talent of a fifth-rate Albanian novelist. . . .

What is the film about? It is what Godard now feels after his 50th birthday from moment to moment. . . .

Godard reminds us again and again of many of his films, but he provides something new as well, a mellower tone and a genuinely funny wryness about his own grotesque contradictions. . . . I now identify with him more closely than at any time since *Une Femme est une femme* back in 1961. Somewhere on the screen he has captured the subtle reality of what it is to be a thinking, feeling being in these ridiculously convulsive times. I do not think that he has gone soft, but rather that he has gone deep. In the end, the Godard character may or may not be dying. A little joke prolongs the uncertainty. We pass some musicians, and somehow come through the other side from cinema to *verite*. Godard is an artist on film once more, and he makes his ''instant replays'' seem as apt and prophetic for the '80s as his jump-cuts proved to be in *Breathless* for the '60s. (p. 41)

Andrew Sarris, "Waiting for Godard, Resnais, and Fuller" (reprinted by permission of The Village Voice *and the author; copyright © News Group Publications, Inc., 1980), in The Village Voice, Vol. XXV, No. 22, June 2, 1980, pp. 41, 46.**

## ROBERT ASAHINA

Though I have some serious reservations about [*Every Man for Himself*] and the post-modern tradition it exemplifies, it is nonetheless an important work of art, a signal event in film history.

Godard's most impressive achievement is to refashion the formal tools of naturalism. Until now, the approach has been not to call attention to the medium but to focus attention on the development of plot and characters. He expands the mode by employing a whole range of cinematic devices—slow motion, freeze-frames, intertitles—that in the hands of lesser directors typically announce the triumph of empty form over trivial content.

I initially suspected that *Every Man for Himself* was also pretty inconsequential. We follow the meandering misadventures of a trio of seemingly negligible individuals without, at first, having a great deal of interest in their fates. . . .

As the film unfolds, instead of engaging our emotions, Godard overcomes our indifference by using his dazzling command of film syntax to provide startlingly naturalistic flashes of the complexities of their lives. For instance, at the end of the movie (it would be wrong to call it the climax of the skeinlike structure), Paul by chance spots his wife and daughter on the street and rushes toward them. Since a previous meeting had been unsatisfactory for all concerned, we expect that he will be angry or even violent. Our expectation is heightened because Godard turns the image of Paul's running into a slow blur just before he reaches the two. But it turns out that Paul is seeking reconciliation. When his ex-wife spurns him, he backs away apologetically, stepping off the curb, and is struck by a speeding automobile.

This epitomizes how the director manipulates the rhythm of a scene to allow meaning to emerge organically. The suspense and frustration find their perverse resolution in an accident, the perfect metaphor for the arbitrary yet meaningful flow of the characters' existences. Paul has about as much control over his wife and daughter, or himself, as he does over the car that hits him and sends him flying onto the pavement. (p. 19)

Despite its breathtaking facility, *Every Man for Himself* contains an irritating dose of the unlamented Godard of the late '60s. To begin with, there are his patented non sequiturs. A man compliments Denise for her "beautiful black hair" when it is obviously brown. Paul is distressed by the voice of an unseen opera singer he alone can hear, until it mysteriously ceases. . . .

Then there are the annoying puns and in-jokes. One of Isabelle's clients is Mr. Person, a rather crude moniker for an anonymous John. . . .

Present, too, are the pseudophilosophical musings that plague French films. "Life," Denise proclaims, is "a gesture made at a faster pace." . . .

Finally, and most annoyingly, Godard allows Paul to step out of character and comment on himself at the end of the film. Lying in the street after being hit by the car, he says, "I'm not dying—my life hasn't flashed in front of my eyes."

All of these irritating tics are, I suspect, the director's way of distancing himself and us from his characters. Godard is right to shun melodrama, to refuse to let the audience empathize or identify emotionally with his characters. But the detachment evident in these silly Godardisms is the cheapest of ironies. A director can only undercut his characters so many times without undermining the appeal of his entire enterprise.

Still, we should be grateful that Godard has rediscovered playfulness and abandoned the Marxism that, during the past decade, turned his films into strident sermons. . . .

From a formal point of view, *Every Man for Himself* represents the next logical step after the movies he made in the late '60s, so its appearance in 1980 suggests that the intervening decade was wasted. In fact, this film almost seems the precursor, rather than the successor, to the works of the German postmodernists who appeared during the '70s, particularly Peter Handke and Wim Wenders; it could have been the impressive original of which such films as *The Left-Handed Woman* and *The American Friend* were pale copies.

On the other hand, Godard has taken the postmodern esthetic further than the Germans have. Handke and especially Wenders are committed to a cinema where meaning is revealed through plot and characterization. The fragmented narrative form of their works is disturbing because it merely obscures the content, no matter how trivial. In *Every Man for Himself*, however, Godard has for the most part achieved that elusive unity of form and content that characterizes true and lasting art. (p. 20)

Robert Asahina, "Flashes of Life," in The New Leader (© 1980 by the American Labor Conference on International Affairs, Inc.), Vol. LXIII, No. 20, November 3, 1980, pp. 19-20.

**PAULINE KAEL**

**"Every Man for Himself"** has been widely hailed as a return to [Godard's] great, innovative work of the sixties. It's wonderful to feel the pull of Godard's images again, to feel the rhythmic assurance. There was a special, anarchic sensuousness in the hasty, jerky flow of a Godard film. And there still is. In **"Every Man for Himself,"** he demonstrates his nonchalant mastery; he can still impose his own way of seeing on you. But the movie may also make you feel empty. More than the fat has been burned out of **"Every Man for Himself":** the juice is gone, too.

The film is about money and people selling themselves—their minds or their bodies. . . . These characters (and the people around them) have lost hope, are without direction, and don't take pleasure in anything. Sex has become an aberrant, mechanical way to connect, and work yields no satisfaction. They go through the motions of living and searching, but they're dead—and they don't deserve to live. We might almost be back in the world of Antonioni, except that Godard has a gagster's temperament.

His philosophical shorthand jokes give the film a dry whimsicality. The camera may suddenly have a lapse of attention and wander off from the ineffectual principal characters (ineffectuality is a rule of life here) to follow the more entertaining movements of a passerby. Or Godard will toss a joke into the background of a scene: two young motorcyclists yell "Choose!" to the pretty girl with them; one of the men slaps her face, hard, and between slaps the battered girl refuses, crying, "Your turn to choose." . . . But Godard doesn't bring off his old tricks with the surreal snap they once had; he doesn't seem as sensitive as he once did—the shadings are coarser, heavier. Sometimes the jokes are like clever, dispirited imitations of Godard's wit. How can anything be really funny when the people on the screen are so drab, so emotionally atrophied? (p. 197)

**"Every Man for Himself"** lacks the friction that came from the multiple ideas and points of view in Godard's sixties films. He's still employing his provisional, trying-it-on style, but his thinking is absolutist, and the satirical bits have nothing to bounce off. It's all a statement of the same melancholy theme. Paul is corrupted, and so he mopes and displays malaise, like a mannequin. Godard's films were always full of mannequins—they acted out their dreams, strutting and posing and having a good time; they got so far into their dreams you couldn't tell if they were the real thing or not. You don't think at all about the limp, burnt-out Paul Godard. Who would want to know more about him? You can see what he is: he's the spirit of selling out. At the end, Paul Godard has been struck by a car; the driver speeds off, and though Paul's estranged wife and his daughter are among the onlookers, no one comes to his aid. He is left to die in the street, or perhaps to live—nobody bothers to find out. And this isn't a joke, it isn't irony—it's simply Godard (who was in a near-fatal accident some years ago) accusing us of deserting him. When he was making ascetic revolutionary tracts, audiences gave up on him, other filmmakers wearied of being denounced by him, and the press gradually lost interest in him. And so there we all are—the onlookers, who do nothing to help him. He's saying, "You're all hit-and-run drivers." His political extremism has been replaced by a broader extremism—total contempt, shaded by masochism. This film says that we don't care about him, nobody cares about anybody, and he has given up on us. It's Every Man for Himself.

One of the blessings of Godard's sixties films was the absence of psychology: the characters did what they did, and the films didn't ask why. Suddenly we're confronted with a Godard movie in which the hero is named Godard (and Paul, after Jean-Luc's father), and in which he is unwanted by the woman he wants, is suffering moral rot, and is left to die alone. It's a masochistic film about rejection: Godard can't think of any reason for these people *not* to reject his surrogate. (p. 198)

What made Godard's impulsive style so sharply exciting in the sixties was that his films were of the moment yet kept that moment fresh. He was the master of digressions that would spontaneously connect in a way that made you laugh while your head was spinning. . . . His way of incorporating the topical, the transient, and the accidental subverted your schoolbook ideas of drama, and he tweaked your empathic involvement with his characters by offhand changes of tone. . . . His films were more contemporary than anyone else's; they were full of the signs of the future which were all around us but which we hadn't quite become conscious of. . . . **"Every Man for Himself"** does have some of the flavor of here and now, but though the picture wanders all over the place, it never comes together; it has no center. If it were possible to have lyricism without emotion, that might describe the film's style. Godard shows no love for his characters and none for his principal actors. (p. 200)

This is the only time I have ever felt that the smattering of narrative in a Godard film wasn't enough; there's so little going on in **"Every Man for Himself"** that you want more drama. The movie features that old standby, the prostitute as metaphor. . . . Godard had already used up this prostitute metaphor. It was central in **"My Life to Live,"** and it was better there. . . . This time, he makes it more explicit and all-inclusive than ever before. He's saying "Everything is for sale." It's simplistic cynicism, like that of the barroom pundit who tells you, "Every man has his price." We are supposed to accept it as a basic truth of capitalist society that, like everyone else, Paul has sold himself and that this has infected his consciousness. He says, "I make movies to keep myself busy. If I had the strength, I'd do nothing." Who can believe that the actual Godard would rather do nothing? He doesn't make the movies of someone who'd rather do nothing. He wants to make movies, all right, but he also wants to get back at us. It's apparent from this film that he feels mistreated, neglected, and, as he said recently on a Dick Cavett show, "pushed away." (pp. 203-04)

The alienation in **"Every Man for Himself"** has a "commercial" aspect, which is new in Godard's work: almost all the audience laughter comes from sex jokes and the deadpan attitudes toward weird sex. . . . I got the feeling that Godard doesn't believe in anything anymore; he wants to make movies, but maybe he doesn't really believe in movies anymore, either. Maybe he has given up caring what they're about; it could be that the sex scenes are there to sell the picture—that self-contempt and contempt for the public have come into play, and that along with the experimenting he is doing some conscious whoring. (p. 205)

> Pauline Kael, "The Civilization of the Rump," in
> The New Yorker (© 1980 by The New Yorker Magazine, Inc.), Vol. LVI, No. 40, November 24, 1980,
> pp. 197-98, 200, 203-05.

## J. HOBERMAN

*Numero Deux* is a mirthless caricature of domesticity. In addition to some startlingly explicit sex scenes, the film is crammed with garrulous grandparents, battles over the TV set, family members retreating into the world of stereo headphones, curious children, and sullen marital disagreements. While *Two or Three Things* was sumptuously cinemascopic, the fact that everything here is shown on two small TV monitors contributes to the bleak sense of isolation and claustrophobia. Even the few exteriors appear to have been shot looking down from a window.

But none of this withstanding, *Numero Deux* is among the most visually compelling films Godard has ever made. He uses his video monitors to invent a dozen new ways of splitting the screen or layering the image. . . . Godard is a master of expressive cacophony. When he piles up his TV sets so that fractured movie trailers are blasting out on top of the nightly news, the film becomes exhilaratingly kinetic. . . .

Yet the film is bound to be misunderstood—for all his interest in realism, clinical sex, naked old people, Godard is hardly a naturalist. His notion of a human being is as stylized as Giacometti's, and about as cuddly. . . .

Like many Godard films, *Numero Deux* bogs down in the home stretch, then rallies for a poignant ending. The light shifts in his studio so that we see the exhausted filmmaker sitting and resting his head on the consoles. . . . The penultimate shot—a close-up of Godard's weary hands caressing the control board—may be the most movingly confessional image he's given us since *Pierrot le Fou*.

*Numero Deux* is undoubtedly too radical for some, and too dour for others. But compared to it, virtually every other movie in town is just a cavity on the screen.

*J. Hoberman, ''Godard's 'Numero deux,' or Three New Things We Know about Him'' (reprinted by permission of* The Village Voice *and the author; copyright © News Group Publications, Inc., 1981), in* The Village Voice, *Vol. XXVI, No. 25, July 17-23, 1981, p. 41.*

# John Huston

## 1906-

American director, screenwriter, author, and actor.

Huston's films are notable for their symbolism and strong plots. His heroes are often loners who struggle to achieve an unobtainable goal. Huston has worked on many different types of films, including westerns, mysteries, and documentaries. Some of his films have been poorly received, but most have been both popularly and critically successful.

Huston's early life was marked by a series of career changes. His education was sporadic because his father, actor Walter Huston, travelled extensively. The younger Huston left school to become a professional boxer, and in succeeding years acted in New York, joined the Mexican cavalry, worked as a reporter, then as a scriptwriter, studied art in Paris, and became editor of *Mid-Week Pictorial*. Huston's early screenplays, written for Gaumont-British in 1932, include *A House Divided* and *Murders in the Rue Morgue*.

Huston was hired by Warner Brothers as a screenwriter in 1938. After the success of his screenplay *The Amazing Dr. Clitterhouse*, Huston was promoted to director. His first directorial effort, an adaptation of Dashiell Hammett's novel *The Maltese Falcon*, was very successful, and established him as a gifted and important director. Huston's next films continued somewhat in the thriller style of his first film. During World War II, however, Huston made three documentaries for the army. *The Battle of San Pietro* and *Let There Be Light* are considered to be effective in depicting the physical and psychological traumas of World War II; in fact, *Let There Be Light* is so explicit that it was banned by the War Department and was not widely screened until late 1980.

Huston's most successful film, *The Treasure of the Sierra Madre*, was the first film he made after the war. The theme of struggle in the face of failure is portrayed with bitterness, and critics agree that Huston's characters and plot are among the most significant creations in film. *The Red Badge of Courage*, *The African Queen*, and *Moulin Rouge*, all made during the early 1950s, were also highly successful.

Huston fell into disfavor with critics later in the decade. Many critics feel that Huston's *Moby Dick* proves that Herman Melville's novel could not possibly be effective on film. Other films in the 1950s and early 1960s are considered slight and unworthy of his reputation. *Freud*, *Night of the Iguana*, and *The Bible* are memorable for his attempts at extending his filmic technique, but critical evaluation is lukewarm. *The Bible* is remembered particularly for Huston's portrayal of Noah. This was his first important acting role, and in the late 1960s and 1970s Huston's acting overshadowed many of his directorial efforts.

Huston's recent work has been marked by a calmer, more compromising outlook. *Fat City* and *The Life and Times of Judge Roy Bean* reveal Huston's cynicism at its peak, but the films are more philosophical than much of his earlier work. Similarly, *Wise Blood* shows Huston more as a man of thought than a man of action. Huston's directorial style in *Wise Blood* is reminiscent of his early work, and critics see the film as one of his most impressive creations.

Huston's films are not necessarily innovative. Many critics agree that Huston's most important asset is his ability to present his beliefs economically and clearly. Huston's recent films are technically very similar to his earliest work. They uphold Huston's filmic philosophy: "Everything must serve the idea. . . . The means used to convey the idea should be the simplest and the most direct and clear. . . . [It] seems to me that this is a universal principle of art. To say as much as possible with a minimum of means. And to be always clear about what you are trying to say." (See also *Contemporary Authors*, Vols. 73-76.)

## BOSLEY CROWTHER

["**The Maltese Falcon**"] turns out to be the best mystery thriller of the year, and young Mr. Huston gives promise of becoming one of the smartest directors in the field. . . .

[With "**The Maltese Falcon**," Mr. Huston gives] us again something of the old thrill we got from Alfred Hitchcock's brilliant melodramas or from "The Thin Man" before he died of hunger.

This is not to imply, however, that Mr. Huston has imitated any one. He has worked out his own style, which is brisk and supremely hardboiled. We didn't see the first "Falcon". . . . But we'll wager it wasn't half as tough nor half as flavored with idioms as is this present version. . . . For the trick which Mr. Huston has pulled is a combination of American ruggedness with the suavity of the English crime school—a blend of mind and muscle—plus a slight touch of pathos. . . .

It's the slickest exercise in celebration that has hit the screen in many months, and it is also one of the most compelling nervous-laughter provokers yet.

> *Bosley Crowther, "'The Maltese Falcon'," in* The New York Times *(© 1941 by The New York Times Company; reprinted by permission), October 4, 1941 (and reprinted in* The New York Times Film Reviews: 1939-1948, *The New York Times Company & Arno Press, 1970, p. 1813).*

## BOSLEY CROWTHER

"**In This Our Life**" is neither a pleasant nor edifying film: It is, again, one of those Snow-White-and Rose-Red sister yarns, in which the evil and mischievous sister . . . deserts her loving fiance and runs off with her good sister's spouse. Then, when she has driven the latter to suicide by her selfish and frivolous ways, she returns home and tries to lure her old flame away from her sister, with whom he has taken up. And finally she reaches rock bottom when she tries to escape a hit-run killing charge by brazenly alleging that the deed was done by a local Negro boy.

This last, as a matter of fact, is the one exceptional component of the film—this brief but frank allusion to racial discrimination. And it is presented in a realistic manner, uncommon to Hollywood, by the definition of the Negro as an educated and comprehending character. Otherwise the story is pretty much of a downhill run, with [the evil sister] going from bad to worse in her selfish pursuit of "happiness" and the good people growing better and more beatified in marked contrast.

The effectiveness of such a picture, in which a problem of personality forms the core, depends both upon the central character and upon the establishment of an atmosphere. Director John Huston, unfortunately, has not given this story sufficient distinction—such, for instance, as was given by William Wyler to "The Little Foxes." The telling of it is commonplace, the movement uncomfortably stiff.

> *Bosley Crowther, "'In This Our Life'," in* The New York Times *(© 1942 by The New York Times Company; reprinted by permission), May 9, 1942 (and reprinted in* The New York Times Film Reviews: 1939-1948, *The New York Times Company & Arno Press, 1970, p. 1864).*

## BOSLEY CROWTHER

["**San Pietro**"] is a grim pulse-pounding illustration of the cold, relentless violence of war. . . .

[It] is a fine piece of camera reporting and an eloquent document of the face of war. . . .

But it is also a splendid little drama of the human side of the Italian campaign, for it closes with some heart-stirring pictures of the people of the liberated town. And it relates these baffled, battered people to the soldiers who set their town free in tender and juxtaposed glimpses of their faces and the moves toward their new life. . . . In "**San Pietro**" there is war's harsh reality and there is the soothing aftermath of hope.

> *Bosley Crowther, "'San Pietro'," in* The New York Times *(© 1945 by The New York Times Company; reprinted by permission), July 12, 1945 (and reprinted in* The New York Times Film Reviews: 1939-

1948, *The New York Times Company & Arno Press, 1970, p. 2072).*

## JAMES AGEE

Several of the best people in Hollywood grew, noticeably, during their years away at war; the man who grew most impressively, I thought, as an artist, as a man, in intelligence, in intransigence, and in an ability to put through fine work against difficult odds, was John Huston, whose "**San Pietro**" and "**Let There Be Light**" were full of evidence of this many-sided growth. I therefore looked forward with the greatest eagerness to the work he would do after the war.

His first movie since the war has been a long time coming, but it was certainly worth waiting for. "**The Treasure of the Sierra Madre**" is Huston's adaptation of B. Traven's novel of the same title. It is not quite a completely satisfying picture, but on the strength of it I have no doubt at all that Huston, next only to Chaplin, is the most talented man working in American pictures, and that this is one of the movie talents in the world which is most excitingly capable of still further growth. "**The Treasure**" is one of very few movies made since 1927 which I am sure will stand up in the memory and esteem of qualified people alongside the best of the silent movies. And yet I doubt that many people will fully realize, right away, what a sensational achievement, or plexus of achievement, it is. You will seldom see a good artist insist less on his artistry; Huston merely tells his story so straight and so well that one tends to become absorbed purely in that; and the story itself— a beauty—is not a kind which most educated people value nearly enough, today.

This story and Huston's whole handling of it are about as near to folk art as a highly conscious artist can get; both also approach the global appeal, to the most and least sophisticated members of an audience, which the best poetic drama and nearly all the best movies have in common. Nominally an adventure story, this is really an exploration of character as revealed in vivid action; and character and action yield revelations of their own, political, metaphysical, moral, above all, poetic. . . . [The story demonstrates the development of the] characters in relation to hardship and hard work, to the deeply primitive world these modern primitives are set against, to the gold they find, and to each other. It is basically a tragic story and at times a sickeningly harsh one; most of it is told as cheerfully brutal sardonic comedy. . . . (p. 136)

[The story is rich] in themes, semi-symbols, possible implications, and potentialities as a movie. Huston's most wonderful single achievement is that he focuses all these elements as simply as rays in a burning glass: all you see, unless you look sharp, is a story told so truly and masterfully that I suspect the picture's best audience is the kind of men the picture is about, who will see it only by chance.

But this single achievement breaks down into many. I doubt we shall ever see a film more masculine in style; or a truer movie understanding of character and of men; or as good a job on bumming, a bum's life, a city as a bum sees it; or a more beautiful job on a city; or a finer portrait of Mexico and Mexicans (compare it with all the previous fancy-filter stuff for a definitive distinction between poetry and poeticism); or a crueler communication of absolute desolateness in nature and its effect on men (except perhaps in "Greed"); or a much more vivid communication of hardship, labor, and exhaustion (though I wish these had been brutally and meticulously presented rather than skilfully sketched); or more intelligent handling of amateurs and semi-professionals . . . ; or a finer selective eye for location or a richer understanding of how to use it; or scenes of violence or building toward violence more deeply authentic and communicative (above all in Huston's terrific use of listlessness). . . . This is one of the most visually alive and beautiful movies I have ever seen; there is a wonderful flow of fresh air, light, vigor, and liberty through every shot, and a fine athlete's litheness and absolute control and flexibility in every succession and series of shots. Huston shows that he is already capable of literally anything in movies except the profoundest kind of movie inventiveness, the most extreme kind of poetic concentration, artiness, soft or apathetic or sloppy or tasteless or excessive work, and rhetoric whether good or bad. His style is practically invisible as well as practically universal in its possible good uses; it is the most virile movie style I know of; and is the purest style in contemporary movies, here or abroad. (pp. 136-37)

There are a few weaknesses in the picture, most of which concern me so little I won't even bother to mention them. Traven's Teutonic or Melvillean excitability as a poet and metaphysician sometimes, I think, misleads him—and John Huston; magnificently as Walter Huston does it, and deeply as he anchors it in flesh and blood, the Vast Gale of Purifying Laughter with which he ends the picture strikes me as unreal, stuck-onto-the-character, close to arty; yet I feel tender toward this kind of cliché, if I'm right that it is one. . . . The only weakness which strikes me as fundamental, however, is deep in the story itself: it is the whole character of the man played by Bogart. This is, after all, about gold and its effects on those who seek it, and so it is also a fable about all human life in this world and about much of the essence of good and evil. Many of the possibilities implicit in this fable are finely worked out. But some of the most searching implications are missed. For the Bogart character is so fantastically undisciplined and troublesome that it is impossible to demonstrate or even to hint at the real depth of the problem, with him on hand. It is too easy to feel that if only a reasonably restrained and unsuspicious man were in his place, everything would be all right; we wouldn't even have wars. But virtually every human being carries sufficient of that character within him to cause a great deal of trouble, and the demonstration of that fact, and its effects, could have made a much greater tragi-comedy—much more difficult, I must admit, to dramatize. (p. 137)

It seems worth mentioning that the only thing which holds this movie short of unarguable greatness is the failure of the story to develop some of the most important potentialities of the theme. In other words, "Hollywood," for once, is accountable only for some minor flaws. (pp. 137-38)

> *James Agee, "Films," in* The Nation, *Vol. 166, No. 5, January 31, 1948, pp. 136-38.\**

### BOSLEY CROWTHER

In making this screen translation of an old Maxwell Anderson play ["**Key Largo**"] . . . Director John Huston has certainly done a great deal to tighten and speed a still overcrowded story of the forces of evil versus good. He has dropped out a lot of prior build-up, thrown away some complexities and avoided the final fatalism which Mr. Anderson always seems to indulge.

Now he has got a story of two strong men who come face to face in a hotel, shut down for the summer, on a sweaty Florida key. . . .

With remarkable filming and cutting, Mr. Huston had notably achieved a great deal of interest and tension in some rather static scenes—and scenes, too, that give the bald appearance of having been written for the stage. Though largely confined to a few rooms, he kept people on the move and has used an intrusive hurricane for some slam-bang melodramatic effects. . . .

But the script prepared by Mr. Huston and Richard Brooks was too full of words and highly cross-purposed implications to give the action full chance. Talk—endless talk—about courage and the way the world goes gums it up. And the simple fact is that much of it is pompous and remote. Also the presentation of old-time gangsterism in this light shows up its obsolescence.

> *Bosley Crowther, "'Key Largo'," in* The New York Times *(© 1948 by The New York Times Company; reprinted by permission), July 17, 1948 (and reprinted in* The New York Times Film Reviews: 1939-1948, *The New York Times Company & Arno Press, 1970, p. 2267).*

### MANNY FARBER

[John Huston] is a smooth blend of iconoclast and sheep. If you look closely at his films, what appears to be a familiar story, face, grouping of actors, or tempo has in each case an obscure, outrageous, double-crossing unfamiliarity that is the product of an Einstein-lubricated brain. . . . His films, which should be rich with this extraordinary experience are rich with cut-and-dried homilies; expecting a mobile and desperate style, you find stasis manipulated with the sure-handedness of a Raffles.

Though Huston deals with the gangster, detective, adventure thriller that the average fan knows like the palm of his hand, he is Message-Mad, and mixes a savage story with puddin'head righteousness. His characters are humorless and troubled and quite reasonably so, since Huston, like a Puritan judge, is forever calling on them to prove that they can soak up punishment, carry through harrowing tasks, withstand the ugliest taunts. Huston is a crazy man with death: he pockmarks a story with gratuitous deaths, fast deaths, and noisy ones, and in idle moments has his characters play parlor games with gats. Though his movies are persistently concerned with grim interpersonal relationships viewed from an ethic-happy plane, half of each audience takes them for comedies. The directing underlines a single vice or virtue of each character so that his one-track actions become either boring or funny; it expands and slows figures until they are like oxen driven with a big moralistic whip.

Money—its possession, influence, manufacture, lack—is a star performer in Huston's moral fables and gilds his technique; his irony toward and preoccupation with money indicate a director who is a little bitter at being so rich—the two brief appearances Huston makes in his own films are quite appropriately as a bank teller and a rich, absent-minded American handing out gold pieces to a recurring panhandler. . . .

His style is so tony it should embarrass his threadbare subjects. The texture of a Panama hat is emphasized to the point where you feel Huston is trying to stamp its price tag on your retina. He creates a splendiferous effect out of the tiniest details—each hair of an eyelid—and the tunnel dug in a week by six proletarian heroes is the size of the Holland Tunnel. (p. 642)

The arty, competent Huston would probably seem to an old rough-and-ready silent film director like a boy who graduated from Oxford at the age of eight, and painted the Sistine Chapel during his lunch hours. (p. 643)

Manny Farber, ''Films,'' in The Nation, Vol. 168, No. 23, June 4, 1949, pp. 642-43.

## JAMES AGEE

The first movie [John Huston] directed, *The Maltese Falcon,* is the best private-eye melodrama ever made. *San Pietro,* his microcosm of the meaning of war in terms of the fight for one hill town, is generally conceded to be the finest of war documentaries. *Treasure of Sierra Madre,* which he developed from B. Traven's sardonic adventure-fable about the corrosive effect of gold on character, is the clearest proof in perhaps twenty years that first-rate work can come out of the big commercial studios.

Most of the really good popular art produced anywhere comes from Hollywood, and much of it bears Huston's name. To put it conservatively, there is nobody under fifty at work in movies, here or abroad, who can excel Huston in talent, inventiveness, intransigence, achievement or promise. . . .

Risk, not to say recklessness, are virtual reflexes in him. Action, and the most vivid possible use of the immediate present, were his personal salvation; they have remained lifelong habits. Because action also is the natural language of the screen and the instant present is its tense, Huston is a born popular artist. In his life, his dealings and his work as an artist he operates largely by instinct, unencumbered by much reflectiveness or abstract thinking, or any serious self-doubt. (p. 35)

Each of Huston's pictures has a visual tone and style of its own, dictated to his camera by the story's essential content and spirit. In *Treasure* the camera is generally static and at a middle distance from the action . . . ; the composition is—superficially—informal, the light cruel and clean like noon sun on quartz and bone. Most of the action in *Key Largo* takes place inside a small Florida hotel. The problems are to convey heat, suspense, enclosedness, the illusion of some eighteen hours of continuous action in two hours' playing time, with only one time lapse. The lighting is stickily fungoid. The camera is sneakily 'personal'; working close and in almost continuous motion, it enlarges the ambiguous suspensefulness of almost every human move. In [*We Were Strangers*] the main pressures are inside a home and beneath it, where conspirators dig a tunnel. Here Huston's chief keys are lighting contrasts. Underground the players move in and out of shadow like trout; upstairs the light is mainly the luminous pallor of marble without sunlight: a cemetery, a bank interior, a great outdoor staircase.

Much that is best in Huston's work comes of his sense of what is natural to the eye and his delicate, simple feeling for space relationships: his camera huddles close to those who huddle to talk, leans back a proportionate distance, relaxing, if they talk casually. He loathes camera rhetoric and the shot-for-shot's-sake; but because he takes each moment catch-as-catch-can and is so deeply absorbed in doing the best possible thing with it he has made any number of unforgettable shots. He can make an unexpected close-up reverberate like a gong. (p. 37)

The most inventive director of his generation, Huston has done more to extend, invigorate and purify the essential idiom of American movies, the truly visual telling of stories than anyone

since the prime of D W Griffith. To date, however, his work as a whole is not on the level with the finest and most deeply imaginative work that has been done in movies—the work of Chaplin, Dovzhenko, Eisenstein, Griffith, the late Jean Vigo. For an artist of such conscience and caliber, his range is surprisingly narrow, both in subject matter and technique. In general he is leery of emotion of the 'feminine' aspects of art—and if he explored it with more assurance, with his taste and equipment, he might show himself to be a much more sensitive artist. With only one early exception, his moves have centered on men under pressure, have usually involved violence and have occasionally verged on a kind of romanticism about danger. Though he uses sound and dialogue more intelligently than most directors he has not shown much interest in exploring the tremendous possibilities of the former or in solving the crippling problems of the latter. While his cutting is astute, terse, thoroughly appropriate to his kind of work, yet compared with that of Eisenstein, who regarded cutting as the essence of the art of movies, it seems distinctly unadventurous. . . .

Conceivably Huston lacks that deepest kind of creative impulse and that intense self-critical skepticism without which the stature of great artist is rarely achieved. A brilliant adapter, he has yet to do a Huston 'original', barring the war documentaries. He is probably too much at the mercy of his immediate surroundings. When the surroundings are right for him there is no need to talk about mercy: during the war and just after he was as hard as a rock and made his three finest pictures in a row. Since then the pictures, for all their excellence, are, like the surroundings, relatively softened and blurred. (p. 38)

James Agee, ''Huston on the Analyst's Couch'' (© copyright James Agee Trust; reprinted with permission; originally published in Life, Vol. 29, No. 12, September 18, 1950), in Films and Filming, Vol. 9, No. 11, August, 1963, pp. 35-8.

## GAVIN LAMBERT

[In *The Asphalt Jungle,* as] in nearly all his previous films, Huston has selected a group of people whose conflicting motives and ambitions set the course of the story, and provide a dual tension, since their activities are usually illegal and the relations between them constantly changing. In *The Asphalt Jungle,* as in *The Maltese Falcon* and *Treasure of the Sierra Madre,* the people are brought together by common greed. But whether the motives are noble . . . or debased, Huston's attitude remains objective. His observation is sharp, and the characters here . . . are as brilliant as any he has presented. But a refusal to identify himself with any character, to show compassion, to leave the outside view, requires a complete power of analysis that the film does not wholly sustain. It falls short of a cruel, definitive picture of the squalor and corruption of a big city as well as of a humane one. The portrait of the hoodlum who at moments regrets his lost innocence is drawn with no more sympathy than the others, and yet it is on his fate that the film concludes, building up rather protractedly to his death in the fields. This final stroke is highly effective, but its emphasis also sums up the limited human approach.

The strong, confident style, the presentation of duplicity seasoned with irony, leaves one in no doubt of the force of personality behind *The Asphalt Jungle.* (pp. 287-88)

Gavin Lambert, ''Writer and Director: 'The Wooden Horse' and 'The Asphalt Jungle','' in Sight and Sound

*(copyright © 1950 by The British Film Institute), n.s.
Vol. 19, No. 7, November, 1950, pp. 286-88.\**

## BOSLEY CROWTHER

[Thanks to John Huston] **"The Red Badge of Courage"** has been transferred to the screen with almost literal fidelity. . . .

Don't expect too much from it in the way of emotional punch—at least, not as much as is compacted in [Stephen] Crane's thin little book. For, of course, Mr. Crane was conveying the re-actions of his hero to war in almost stream-of-consciousness descriptions, which is a technique that works best with words. . . .

[The] major achievement of this picture is the whole scene, it re-creates of a battlefield near the Rappahannock (Chancellorsville) from the soldier's point of view. . . . Mr. Huston, who made **"San Pietro,"** one of the great documentaries of World War II, can conceive a Civil War battle, and he has done so magnificently in this film.

Furthermore, he has got the sense of soldiers in that long-ago day and war—their looks, their attitudes, their idioms—as suggested in the writings of the times. . . .

Also, Mr. Huston has captured and etched vividly most of the major encounters of the hero that Mr. Crane described—the heartbreaking death of the Tall Soldier, the stunning blow on the head—all but the shocking discovery of the rotting corpse in the woods. . . .

But, in most respects, Mr. Huston has put **"The Red Badge of Courage"** on the screen, and that means a major achievement that should command admiration for years and years.

> *Bosley Crowther, "'The Red Badge of Courage',"
> in* The New York Times *(© 1951 by The New York
> Times Company; reprinted by permission), October
> 19, 1951 (and reprinted in* The New York Times
> Film Reviews: 1949-1958, *The New York Times
> Company & Arno Press, 1970, p. 2558).*

## GAVIN LAMBERT

[*We Were Strangers* is a] collective study of men in a crisis. (p. 82)

Huston has . . . conceived his film as a melodrama—which has earned him the disapproval of those who consider that melodrama should be reserved for "unimportant" subjects like *The Maltese Falcon,* and who feel that it vitiates anything more "serious". Nevertheless, there are many major dramatic and literary works highly seasoned with melodrama. . . . The flaws in *We Were Strangers* are in details of the treatment, not imposed by the choice of treatment itself. In some ways it is carefully stylised: in the striking camera-work by Russell Metty with its powerful groupings and broad contrasts; in the dialogue's consistent convention of broken accents and slightly formal, slightly unrealistic quality, most of the time highly effective and once or twice too declamatory (China's "There are no marble vaults for *our* dead . . ."). None of these conventions muffles or holds up the drama. Structurally it is a taut, exact, almost flawless piece of work. It lacks depth at times because of Huston's attitude to people; he concentrates his passion on physical tension and details, on exterior climaxes, and the rest he observes and records, excitingly but imperviously. Thus the comradeship of the men, whose theme

is so beautifully stated in a brief sequence at night when Guillarmo improvises a calypso on his guitar, is later assumed rather than conveyed—and the effect of their parting, after the plan has failed, loses some of its force. The same limitations of feeling are apparent in his handling of the love-affair, which is never false but remains undeveloped. (pp. 83-4)

*We Were Strangers,* its own remarkable qualities apart, marks an important point in Huston's work. In the past, he has always concentrated on a group of people with conflicting motives and actions, telling the story through them, never really taking sides with any character; and this has set him apart from other Hollywood directors. . . . *Key Largo* is unique for Huston in being a completely empty, synthetic work. It is academically interesting because Huston showed, for the first time, two characters of his own generation professing positive beliefs and some faith in human values: the soldier's widow and her dead husband's army friend, a cynic at first but regenerated at the close. They are as false as the others, but significant perhaps in the light of *We Were Strangers,* where the group of people is brought about for noble, unselfish reasons, motivated by common beliefs. Fenner already believes in the values to which Frank at the end of *Key Largo* was supposed to have been converted.

Huston, however, does not identify himself with Fenner, reserves his sympathy—he is too struck with the savage irony of the situation, the place of this desperate mission in the revolution as a whole. He has made a film about heroes, but it is not heroic; as an artist, he appears to appreciate intellectually the necessity of heroism, but to be more personally aware of the effectiveness of human weakness and viciousness; in some ways the portrait of Arliete, the police chief, is the most full-blooded in the picture. While Huston's sympathies are clear enough, he has held them back partially from the characters, and for this reason the personality behind the film remains at last elusive. (p. 85)

> *Gavin Lambert, "'We Were Strangers'" (reprinted
> by permission of Gavin Lambert), in* Shots in the
> Dark: A Collection of Reviewers' Opinions of Some
> of the Leading Films Released between January 1949
> and February 1951, *edited by Edgar Anstey & others,
> Allan Wingate (Publishers) Ltd, 1951, pp. 82-5.*

## BOSLEY CROWTHER

Whether C. S. Forester had his salty British tongue in his cheek when he wrote his extravagant story of romance and adventure, **"The African Queen,"** we wouldn't be able to tell you. But it is obvious—to us, at least—that Director John Huston was larking when he turned the novel into a film. . . .

[The movie] is a slick job of . . . hoodwinking with a thoroughly implausible romance, set in a frame of wild adventure that is as whopping as its tale of off-beat love. And the main tone and character of it are in the area of the well-disguised spoof.

This is not noted with disfavor. Considering the nature of the yarn, it is hard to conceive its presentation in any other way—that is in the realistic channels of the motion-picture screen. For Mr. Forester's fable of love suddenly taking bloom in the hearts of a lady missionary and a Cockney rumpot while they're trying to escape down a German East African river in a wheezy steam-launch during World War I is so personally preposterous and socially bizarre that it would take a lot of doing to be made convincing in the cold, clear light of day. In the brilliance of Technicolor and with adventure intruding at every turn, any attempt at serious portrayal would be not only incongruous but absurd.

And so Mr. Huston merits credit for putting this fantastic tale on a level of sly, polite kidding and generally keeping it there, while going about the happy business of engineering excitement and visual thrills. . . .

[Mr. Huston and his writer, James Agee,] have let the yarn slide onto the mud flats of heavy drama that Mr. Forester laid down, and while it is in that situation, they have let it become soggy in plot and mood. After running impossible rapids, eluding a German fort and keeping the romance skipping nimbly on the surface of sly absurdity, they have grounded their picture on a barrier of sudden solemnity and sanded it in with emotions that are neither buoyant nor credible. No wonder the fantastic climax that is abruptly and sentimentally contrived appears the most fulsome melodrama, unworthy of Mr. Huston and this film.

However, while it is skipping—and that is most of the time—there is rollicking fun and gentle humor in this outlandish **"African Queen."** There's nothing subtle or moralistic, mind you, outside of the jesting display that nature's most formidable creature is a serene and self-righteous dame.

> Bosley Crowther, "'The African Queen'," in The New York Times (© 1952 by The New York Times Company; reprinted by permission), February 21, 1952 (and reprinted in The New York Times Film Reviews: 1949-1958, The New York Times Company & Arno Press, 1970, p. 2591).

### GAVIN LAMBERT

Pierre la Mure did not claim that his *Moulin Rouge* was an accurate biography of Toulouse-Lautrec, but a dramatic evocation of the artist and his background; and since John Huston has based his film upon the book, one imagines his intention to have been the same. Obviously, then, one mustn't reproach it for factual errors and fictionalised episodes—though one may feel this kind of approach to be ultimately pointless . . . ; but one can, and must, complain that *Moulin Rouge* . . . adds up to an unacceptably glib and misleading portrait of a famous artist. (p. 194)

The concentration on visual effect suggests that Huston may have been more interested in his surface than his people. . . . On the surface, *Moulin Rouge* is far from tasteless, apart from one lapse into the "art-film," with quickly cut juxtapositions to give still pictures the illusion of movement. . . . It is strange that such a sharp division should exist between Huston's surface appreciation of his material, and the material itself; that he should have used its visual richness only to embellish a void of indifferent writing and construction, to say nothing of [amateurish] performances. . . . [The] sad fact remains that with all its careful, superior craftsmanship, *Moulin Rouge* does for an artist and his art little more than most concerto films have done for composers. (p. 195)

> Gavin Lambert, "'Moulin Rouge'," in Sight and Sound (copyright © 1953 by The British Film Institute), Vol. 22, No. 4, April-June, 1953, pp. 194-95.

### PETER BARNES

[*The Maltese Falcon* reveals John Huston's] style at its best—direct, analytic, and disciplined. This film succeeds brilliantly as a character thriller, but also, through its ruthless elimination of inessentials, gains an extra depth. All the characters are obsessed; their lives are devoted to one pursuit only, the acquisition of money (in the shape of the fabulous maltese falcon, "the stuff that dreams are made of"). *The Maltese Falcon* and, later, *The Treasure of Sierra Madre* show what film art can gain by a relentless concentration on two or three characters only: what might be called "observation in depth" rather than painting the usual broad but superficial canvas—"observation in breadth." For the art of the film loses much by its refusal to abstract or isolate a subject or to work within definite limits. (pp. 281-82)

[Huston's *The Treasure of Sierra Madre*] seems in retrospect his finest achievement. . . . [The] film has a rare power and depth. As in *The Maltese Falcon,* Huston is concerned with people whose lives are dominated by a ruthless desire for wealth. Though not very worthy members of society, they have, to start with, certain sparks of comradeship and kindliness. But hardship and loneliness individualize like acid, bringing to the surface all the suspicion and hatred in their characters. They begin by pooling the gold and end by fighting for their share.

By concentrating on the three men and not emphasizing the accurately realized background, *Sierra Madre* does achieve a certain universality. Bogart's desire for an eternal leisure relieved by wine and women and Tim Holt's adolescent dream of a peach farm reveal the petty vulgarities of a cheap civilization. This is a work of real integrity and power. Critics who complain of its detachment, and of Huston's artistic detachment in general, fail to see that detached artists are often more truly sensitive to the spirit of their time than the committed.

*We Were Strangers* . . . is important in that it raised the first serious doubts about Huston's talents. In all his previous work, he had dealt either with the American scene or with themes that touched America very closely. But with this story of Cuban revolutionaries who plan to overthrow a fascist government, he was treating a subject outside his usual scope. The film has numerous virtues, a bold dramatic style, a taut structure, dialogue of real force, and acting . . . of great subtlety and power. Many scenes are outstanding . . .—and all the action sequences are carried off with superb assurance and skill. But something is missing. This is not just a story of political murder: deeper issues are involved; moral problems have to be settled. In the assassination of the heads of the government, innocent people are to be sacrificed. The ethics of such a sacrifice are briefly discussed, but only briefly, as it is not the business of the film to deal with them. However, it is here that one can detect the fatal flaw. *We Were Strangers* would not have been a better film if Huston had included a fuller discussion of the moral problems involved. But a director must have an imaginative understanding of everything connected with the material he is working on; and if his material involves, as Huston's did, a sense of deep ethical issues, then the director's own awareness and understanding of these issues is relevant. He must convey the sense of them even if they are outside the scope of his film. Huston has failed to achieve this sense; there is a failure of intellect, a failure to be aware of the full power and complexity of his subject.

With *The Asphalt Jungle* . . . , he returned to the solid realities of the American scene for his subject; and the result is noticeably beneficial. Gone is the uncertainty, the fatal touch of fantasy which characterizes the former work; instead, there is a complete understanding of all the aspects of his material.

Only a minor film, *The Asphalt Jungle* has a solidness and completeness that *We Were Strangers* lacks.

Despite undeniable virtues, however, these two films disappointed. They did not fulfill the promise of *Sierra Madre,* but gave evidence of a talent marking time. (pp. 281-84)

[Huston's next three films were totally] unlike his previous work, both in style and content, they represent in their mediocrity, inherent vulgarity, and emptiness, the unexpected collapse of a unique talent. The first of these films, *The African Queen* . . . , is probably the best. . . . But the script lacks bite, and the direction is monotonous and ineffective. Gone is the hard confident style and acute approach to character; in its place is flabbiness and a curious air of unreality which have become the hallmark of Huston's later work.

No redeeming features cover the appalling vulgarity of *Moulin Rouge.* . . . Even granting that the film does not attempt to be an accurate biography of the artist, its glibness and superficiality are completely unacceptable. . . . But what really appalls is the lack of depth, the purely superficial treatment of Lautrec's life and times. This is in fact a "gimmick" film with the leading actor performing on his knees. The agony, the desperate loneliness of the creative artist, is never even remotely caught; and neither is the authentic period atmosphere despite all the cancan girls, hansom cabs, and bustles. One short dance sequence in Becker's *Casque D'or* is worth the whole of *Moulin Rouge.* Once again, Huston's lack of personal acquaintance with his material has betrayed him.

It was confidently expected that a return to the style of *The Maltese Falcon* would produce a film of some worth. But *Beat the Devil* proved to be completely empty and pointless. This satiric thriller about a gang of crooks on the track of a vast uranium deposit in Africa is neither mildly amusing nor remotely convincing. The plot does bear a vague resemblance to that of *The Maltese Falcon,* but Huston has adopted a fatally fatuous manner towards his subject. He no longer seems to believe in his films. . . . Except for some bizarre close-ups, this is two hours of unrelieved tedium. From *The Maltese Falcon* to *Beat the Devil,* the decline is complete. (pp. 284-85)

> Peter Barnes, "The Director on Horseback," *in* The Quarterly of Film, Radio, and Television *(copyright, 1955, by The Regents of the University of California; reprinted by permission of the University of California Press), Vol. X, No. 2, Winter, 1955, pp. 281-87.*

**TONY RICHARDSON**

[In *Moby Dick* John Huston] has been unable to make the book his own cinematically, and the final gesture the film makes is simply that Melville once wrote a "Great Book". . . .

As with [*The Red Badge of Courage*], Huston has seized on the heightened pressure of the book. But he has failed to comprehend the balance, the interior stresses by which it was produced. The spectacle he can certainly provide—the painted Queequeg, the weird Coleridgean calm, the whalebone leg of Ahab—but, because he has been unable to realise the context, the ordinary weary grind of life on the *Pequod*, the careful expertise of the whale hunts, these become just so many theatrical effects. Wherever the film touches on the pure routine (the melting down of the whale, for instance) it is, significantly, at its most perfunctory. The hunts themselves become in Hus-

ton's handling a wild, artificial threshing for exciting action sequences.

There could, of course, have been many valid ways of making this film. . . . But because his approach is finally external, Huston falls between all stools, grasping eclectically for the instant pay-off. The chapel scene . . . has something of the Visconti manner both in setting and technique; the departure of the *Pequod* suggests an unsuccessful attempt to be Ford. Only the opening—a solitary figure picking his way beside a mountain stream and turning into close-up for a forthright "Call me Ishmael"—has real boldness. For the rest, though the film is a physically battering experience (chases and storms are staged with the maximum sound and fury), there is little that convinces. (p. 151)

[*Moby Dick*] is a sad straying of the talent that once created *The Maltese Falcon* and *The Asphalt Jungle.* (p. 152)

> *Tony Richardson, "'Moby Dick',"* in Sight and Sound *(copyright © 1957 by The British Film Institute), Vol. 26, No. 3, Winter, 1956-57, pp. 151-52.*

**ARLENE CROCE**

*The Roots of Heaven* is about the hunting and killing of elephants. It remains for the *kitsch*-hounds to pick up the scent. . . .

On the face of it, *The Roots of Heaven* is promising Huston material. Like nearly every film he has ever made, it is concerned with a prodigious undertaking: sometimes it is the pursuit of wealth, sometimes it is an objective in war, or blowing up a ship or a politician, or killing a whale. Usually it involves a protracted physical, ordeal of utmost realism. . . . The trouble with *The Roots of Heaven,* and with the last half-dozen or so of Huston's efforts, is that the virtues of this approach exist quite independently of the film itself. A style of *modus operandi*, elaborate with suggestions of integrity, perfectionism, devotion and marvelous temperament . . . , has come to be substituted for quality as an accomplished fact in work done. Huston's true style has evolved as a sort of behind-the-scenes swagger, which finds an exact correlation in the increasingly improvised and decorative nature of his films. All the energies of production are spent upon surface; in effects of color, lighting, and framing . . . ; in an impressionistic gloss on costumes, scars, sweat, sand, and the precise entry of bullets into flesh. The appeal is to the eye, or as it were, to the eye-*cum*-guts.

Yet it is sad to find Huston's most reliable gift, his tremendous physical expertise, deserting him at this point. By which I mean not so much his technical command as his sense of muscular stress and excitement in his material, his ability to exert the pressure of the physical universe upon his actors, so that all curses of climate, weather, terrain, fortune, fatigue, and impossible odds become proofs of human endurance. (p. 43)

[In fact, his actors] are moving in a world of ideas, the issues are larger than any mere physical texture, or directorial talent for such, can serve. The great irony is that the "issues" are not so cinematically inexpressible as one would suppose from this film, with its hasty digest of plot developments and its numerous speeches uttered in the eyes-on-the-far-horizon style. (pp. 43-4)

*The Roots of Heaven* is no better and no worse than the conventional action film with pretensions. (p. 44)

*The Barbarian and the Geisha* finds the director on holiday in Japan, shooting from a script that contrives to blend "The

Cavalcade of America'' and ''My True Story.'' . . . ''I wanted to make a Japanese film,'' Huston is reported to have said. Whatever that may mean, the result is about as ''Japanese'' as *Sayonara*. It is a long drone of a film, logy with local glamour, unpleasantly jingoistic in tone. . . . It marks, perhaps, the nadir in Huston's absorption with appearances, and it is saddening to think that the director of *The Asphalt Jungle* . . . has gained professional freedom and international celebrity in order to become . . . yet another taskmaster who goes out in the midday sun. (p. 45)

Arlene Croce, ''Film Reviews: 'The Roots of Heaven' and 'The Barbarian and The Geisha','' in Film Quarterly *(copyright 1958 by The Regents of the University of California; reprinted by permission of the University of California Press), Vol. XII, No. 2, Winter, 1958, pp. 42-5.*

## EUGENE ARCHER

The Hemingway personality has become a familiar stereotype in contemporary folklore, but its influence on the American screen has not been readily apparent. Although the novelist's protagonists—disillusioned outcasts indulging in sensory sensations for the sake of experience—have emerged as prototypes for the characters who inhabit the specific genre of dimly-lit melodramas of the American underworld, the crucial elements of the Hemingway style are less frequently encountered in modern drama. The ruthless excision of non-essentials for the purpose of lucidity and unity, although Aristotleian in concept, imposes complex demands upon a medium which is primarily visual, while the insistence upon the principles of courage, pity and honour as the only extant values which cannot be wholly distorted by the process of living in the contemporary wasteland presents a difficult problem for an industry geared to more acceptable ethical standards. In a medium dedicated to the synonymous relationship of such terms as love and marriage, poverty and happiness, sex and sin, the emergence of a director with seriousness of purpose is in itself unusual. When, as in the case of John Huston, the principles include an insistence upon serious themes and an artistic method which emphasises functionality, the parallel with the Hemingway tradition is unavoidable.

Considered in the light of this analogy, the work of John Huston appears at a certain disadvantage. Interesting as his films are in terms of narrative content, the subjects lack the originality expected from the work of a creative artist. Huston's films are all adaptations of novels or plays, and although he writes most of his own scripts, the subjects can be considered only in regard to choice of material. . . . Huston's early work falls primarily into the categories of melodrama (*The Maltese Falcon*) and social comment (*The Treasure of the Sierra Madre*), or a combination of the two (*The Asphalt Jungle, We Were Strangers*). More recently, his selections have grown more varied, and shown a tendency toward art for its own sake—as in the comedy, *The African Queen,* the biography, *Moulin Rouge,* and the ambitious adaptations of classic novels, *The Red Badge of Courage* and *Moby Dick.* The diversity of this material is in itself suggestive of an unusual artistic temperament, but it is in his technique that Huston's personality most clearly emerges. The gradual sharpening of individual images, the intensive concentration on problems of composition, the precise gradation of sequences within a carefully organised pattern, the application of different editing devices to varied types of material, the rigid prohibition of excesses either in manner or in content, all suggest an endeavour to express his subject with Flaubert's *mot juste,* to communicate with his audience in the most exact and lucid terms. . . .

The melodramatic plot [of *The Maltese Falcon*], dealing with a weird assortment of conspirators searching for a valuable statuette and an unsentimental private detective determined to avenge his partner's murder, is both suspenseful and satirical, and the technique, while not adventurous, extends each ingredient to its fullest cinematic effect. . . .

*In This Our Life* (1942), in contrast, struggles for social comment. Ellen Glasgow's novel about a decaying Southern family dominated by a predatory younger daughter contains elements of insight into the influence of the outmoded social traditions of the modern Southern aristocracy, but in its cinematic adaptation the subtler implications of the theme are subordinate to a conventionally melodramatic plot. . . . The film's interest lies less in the central action than in the detailed implications of a changing social climate. (p. 13)

The comparative failure of *In This Our Life* prompted Huston to repeat the more successful formula of *The Maltese Falcon* in his third film, *Across the Pacific*. Using an inferior wartime espionage plot as subject, Huston concentrates on concealing the theme from the audience for the greater portion of the film. Huston's gift for atmospheric detail is again apparent in his handling of a ship's departure into a fog, when the montage of tightening ropes, the rumbling of engines, and the slow weaving motion past the docks builds the scene into a vivid experience. The regular spray of the sea waves on deck, the hypnotic revolutions of a ceiling fan, the heat-inducing tinkling of ice in a glass, all combine to convey a world of sensory sensations to the audience. The drama centres on the trio of actors who distinguished the earlier film. . . . The measured relationships between these characters dominate the film, and Huston amplifies them by bringing the camera close to the actors' faces, where a minute flicker of the eyelids or a twitch about the mouth gives a sudden intensity to the stresses of this unexpected intellectual conflict. After the long suspenseful development aboard ship, as the relationships are gradually clarified and brought toward a climax, the actual ending—a Japanese attempt to blow up the Panama Canal, foiled by the hero and heroine who abandon their interesting poses of blase cynicism—disappointingly reduces the film to a comic-strip level. Although the absurd conclusion spoils the final effect, it does not completely negate the skilfully manipulated tension of the earlier reels. The film emerges as a minor but workmanlike directorial exercise within a conventional suspense format. (pp. 13-14)

Using the terse style of his Hollywood films [in *Report from the Aleutians*], Huston obtained a great deal of difficult footage from one of the least known areas of the war, the Aleutian atoll where American forces launched attacks on Kiska and Attu. . . .

With emphasis on weather as an opposing force, the camera records the struggles of men to unload ships and transport equipment across areas impassable to vehicles. When the site is established, the film becomes impressionistic, with shots of clusters of tents on beds of ice, the smoke curling upward, then swept horizontal by the incessant wind, the bulldozers pushing through the slushy ice, the American Liberators departing from watery fields on missions toward the intensively guarded Kiska, the quiet, deadly effect of flak and anti-aircraft exploding in small black puffs from the ground below. This fragmentary film may be considered a prelude to Huston's second wartime documentary, *The Battle of San Pietro,* perhaps the finest film to come out of World War II. . . . Huston endeavours in this film to symbolise the nature of the war by illustrating a single battle against an impregnable position. In an unforgettable sequence, the American troops charge against enemy gunfire so intensive that it literally becomes a wall of fire. . . . The film ends when one peak is finally taken and the Germans withdraw. In its stark conclusion, the exhausted American soldiers enter the shattered town of San Pietro, as the Italian villagers emerge from their caves and holes, too numb from the war to greet its end with even a simulated joy. The effect is poignant and ironic, with none of the triumphant elation expected from a victory. This overwhelming anti-war motif is emphasised by the film's technique. The raw, grey photography captures the poverty and ugliness of the environment without neglecting the stark elemental beauty of the mountainside. The narration is sober and restrained, avoiding editorialising, but sincere in its admiration for the soldiers' courage and comprehensive in its portrait of military life and understanding of enlisted men's psychology. The film as a whole has a compelling sense of immediacy, with the Germans as a hidden enemy, formidable in the security of their positions. In its final effect, *The Battle of San Pietro* is as solemn a protest against warfare as the screen has ever depicted—a strange film to appear under War Department auspices in 1944.

As an example of documentary technique, this film was equalled only by Huston's last war film, *Let There Be Light,* a study of mental therapy in the Army rehabilitation programme for psychoneurotic veterans. Huston took his camera inside Army hospitals, and peered without self-consciousness at the actual faces of patients, recording true case histories of servicemen in a frank exposition of some of the war's effects. The film is at once compassionate and uncompromisingly candid in its approach to the subject, and is generally considered a masterpiece in the documentary field. . . .

Harsh, gripping and distinctively personal, [*The Treasure of Sierra Madre*] commanded respect for its large theme in spite of numerous minor defects, and amply fulfilled the promise of *The Maltese Falcon.* Although Huston's technique had not fully matured, *The Treasure of the Sierra Madre* remains an exciting film to watch. Huston's direction, clean and original, shows a youthful vigour and strength of purpose which his later, more accomplished works lack.

*Key Largo,* released the same year, was much less ambitious, but technically more glib. A diluted adaptation of Maxwell Anderson's poor verse play, the film reduces the outmoded fascism versus democracy theme to the level of a conventio_al gangster thriller with a climax borrowed from *To Have and Have Not.* As a directorial exercise, however, *Key Largo* is an interesting study in atmosphere and closeted character melodrama. . . . (p. 4)

As finally released, *The Red Badge of Courage* seemed erratically brilliant, containing one of the finest battle sequences ever filmed and many eloquent cinematic details, but with much of its effectiveness nullified by awkward continuity and an ill-advised narrator who sententiously informed the audience that, the novel being a literary classic, the film must in consequence be a classic as well. If *The Red Badge of Courage* fell short of its goal, *The African Queen,* also released in 1951, did not. The hilarious adventure of a dissipated tugboat captain and a passionate missionary, deriving its comedy from the rich and complex interplay of two of the screen's great comic char-

acterisations . . . , emerged as one of the most original films ever made, an authentic classic, and one of Huston's two best films. (pp. 14, 28)

*Beat the Devil* (1954), a satire of *The Maltese Falcon,* is parody within parody, a private joke, amusing to the initiated, incomprehensible to the uninformed. If the wit is introverted, the technique is haphazard, skirting the borderline of embarrassment veering toward the irrational, and trailing off into trivia. It is a film for connoisseurs, who treasure it highly—most highly, perhaps, because it is valueless for the layman. For Huston, *Beat the Devil* (which he wrote in collaboration, significantly, with Truman Capote) is an act of self-indulgence harmless in itself but disturbing in its implications. "Art for art's sake" is a respectable creed, but divorcement from one's audience in a medium as commercially oriented as the cinema must be considered a dangerous trend. Ths result of the tendency is apparent in *Moby Dick.* . . . [*Moby Dick*] is a technical masterpiece, impressive in conception, formidable in execution, and emotionless at the core, a film for critics rather than patrons, difficult not to admire, impossible to enjoy. . . .

[*The Roots of Heaven*] is relentlessly "modern," with a popular anti-war theme, African backgrounds shot on location, an international cast speaking in mixed and frequently unintelligible accents, an excessive running time, and a musical score by the fashionable Malcolm Arnold which strongly resembles his earlier composition for *The Bridge on the River Kwai.* The Cinemascope width is too obviously epic for such a film, and the neo-romantic script intersperses crude passages of character analysis ("I don't know why I'm telling you all this," the heroine murmurs to the hero) with large symbols which are a good deal too elliptically vague. In spite of such flaws as uneven acting and a diffusion of dramatic effects (for which Huston must share the blame with Darryl Zanuck, who chose the cast and did most of the editing), *The Roots of Heaven* emerges as an interesting, sometimes impressive film which holds out some hope for Huston's future. Still too objective in regard to association with his subjects, Huston remains willing to attempt major themes and to experiment with unusual material. The elephant-protector Morel . . . is a modern hero of some stature, and in his attention to this character Huston indicates his continued respect and admiration for the individualist who goes his own way, suing others only as practicable means towards his ends, and finds his ultimate rewards in his own integrity. (p. 28)

> Eugene Archer, "Taking Life Seriously" (© copyright Eugene Archer 1959; reprinted with permission), in Films and Filming, Vol. 5, No. 12, September, 1959, pp. 13-14, 28, 33.


## EUGENE ARCHER

In the first part of this monograph [see excerpt above] we considered the early Huston. In later years his work has become more introspective. He has increasingly focused his attention on a handful of characters in conflict with their environment . . . small people in a big world. . . .

In [the opening scene of *The Asphalt Jungle*] the film has captured the impression of the hunted desperation which pervades the underworld mentality, and conveyed a sympathy and comprehension toward certain elementary factors of criminal existence which suggest a point of view as decisive as that of the jungle it invades. The deterministic factors which may have contrived to produce this world are at once irrelevant. The area is shadowy and elusive, governed by animal law and jungle ethics, but at the moment of crisis, the only reality is tangible.

The first section of the film establishes this environment by introducing the men scheduled to participate in an elaborate criminal operation, and in this exposition the observation extends to some of the further boundaries of underworld activity. . . . At length [their] masks are pierced and the reasons for the twitches relentlessly exposed to reveal an assortment of human vices: alcohol, greed, lechery, self-pity, all examined with a dispassionate objectivity which accepts the human condition without apology or embarrassment.

The structure of *The Asphalt Jungle* is more complex than anything Huston had previously attempted, and it is expressed with an advanced technique commensurate with his material. An expert criminal arrives in the city to supervise a million dollar jewel robbery, and methodically arranges for the financing and execution of the plan and the ultimate disposition of the proceeds. The plan is organised along the lines of a business venture. . . .

[The] business analogy is maintained throughout the film. The protagonists conduct their affairs along lines rigidly determined by a profit-and-loss economy, with their negotiations assuming a heightened interest through an acute awareness of the high cost of failure. . . . The film records the minor struggles for success which are symptomatic of any semi-civilized society, but it constantly suggests that these men who attempt to function as best they can within their predestined framework are actually existing on the edge of extinction, and their lives are governed by acceptance of this decisive fact.

It is this underlying meaning which gives symbolic power to the film. The protagonists are not good men gone wrong, nor is the robbery a rational plan spoiled only by a careless mistake. These doomed protagonists cannot expect salvation and cannot hope to avoid the fate which has become the core of their existence. The robbery merely represents an endeavour to obtain the limited rewards which their situation offers. . . .

Huston's directorial method is elaborately designed to weave this material into a cohesive pattern. The action is edited sharply for tension, with the aid of many short scenes, incisive observation of detail, and rapid cuts for effect. By examining every aspect of a scene with objective clarity and rarely focusing on a detail which does not record some revelation of character in expression or gesture, however minute, Huston is able to decisively characterise each participant during the early development of the plot. (p. 9)

Harsh as this analytical approach to character appears, these figures, coldly studied at moments of weakness and duplicity, emerge as people far too truthful to be rejected or ignored. The essential humanity of the director's insight is most clearly felt when Huston momentarily abandons his doomed criminals to record the fallacy of the opposing point of view, the implacable determination of the judicially oriented citizen to enforce the law by wilful extermination of its infringers. This uncompromising moral condemnation by the professional lawmaker assumes ironic force to the observer not yet adjusted to the realisation that the criminal mentality is moulded by economic pressures very similar to his own. The conclusion underscores this meaning by bringing the action full circle. Accompanied by the pathetic girl who hopes to find regeneration in selfless devotion to another human being, the solitary Neanderthal figure of the opening, delirious and on the borderline of death, struggles to return to his point of origin, the green

Kentucky meadows which represent pre-natal innocence. The figure has made no bid for sympathy in the film, and makes none now: he is a ruthless gunman, large and brutal, not involved in the complexities of the plan, dominating the action by physical proportions rather than by heroic character. The nature of his final flight toward a non-existent ideal, returning beyond the concrete to die in the fields, suggests an attempt at tragedy which the film has not previously implied, and carries its meaning to a point beyond all previous deterministic investigations of the theme.

In the odyssey of *The African Queen,* man's indefatigable spirit proves triumphant over the forces of a hostile nature and the militant circumscription of twentieth century civilisation. If the approach is comic, the theme would do credit to Melville. Neither the tugboat, the African Queen, nor its crew seem qualified for adventure or high romance, but when the occasion arises they meet it with heroic dispatch. The drama is a testament to human endurance and natural instinct against the worst that man and nature can provide.

True comedy is always closely related to pain, as in the famous example of the man who steps on a banana peel. In *The African Queen,* one of the richest comedies ever made, the central situation is essentially tragic. Charlie Allnutt, the tugboat captain, and Rose, the prim missionary, are trapped by the Germans in British West Africa in World War I. . . . [Their] seemingly impossible, supremely arduous journey resembles the heroic efforts of other Huston protagonists—the miners' trek to the forbidden mountain in *The Treasure of the Sierra Madre,* the revolutionaries' tunnel in *We Were Strangers,* the soldier returning to his regiment in *The Red Badge of Courage,* the jewel thieves of *The Asphalt Jungle,* Ahab in *Moby Dick.* If the quest in this case is not tragic but comic, it is an achievement of treatment rather than material, a question of subtle exaggeration bringing elements of heroic tragedy to a point of sublime ridiculousness. The close relationship of comedy to tragedy is illustrated here at its furthest extreme. C. S. Forester's novel is generally considered a dramatic melodrama rather than a farce, and Huston's film, hilarious from its opening scene to its gloriously happy ending, was initially received by several critics as a serious dramatic adventure. (p. 10)

When the narrator of *Moby Dick* reads Melville's opening lines in measured tones, he evokes a mood of apprehension at once suggestive of a great work of art. Huston's obeisance to the author's "Call me Ishmael", plunging the narrative immediately into action without allowing time for a visual placement of mood, indicates the difficult quality of this adaptation. The film makes no allowance for the limited comprehension of its audience in its attempt to retain as much of the complexity of the novel as can be captured cinematically.

Huston has developed his adaptation according to a thoughtful structure, beginning with an artful exposition of paths of water leading to the sea which is wholly appropriate to Melville's metaphysical conception. Mysticism underlies the depiction of the three aspects of man in the key opening scenes: Coffin's tavern, where sailors boisterously dance to a sea chanty on a stormy night to express the joy of living in defiance to forbidding nature; Father Mapple's narration of the legend of Jonah, a pious reminder of man's inconsequence in a mystic universe; and the ship's departure, where active man abandons domestic ties, an eternal wanderer deliberately severing the emotional bonds of home and family which remain the motivating objects of his search. The first appearance of Ahab at sea fore-shadowed by the ghostly tapping of his footsteps on the deserted deck, introduces the book's great theme, ably expounded in Ahab's long and arresting conversation with Starbuck about the nature of infinity, and the exciting whaling sequence which follows amplifies the nature of the quest. Huston's method of editing and reshaping long sections of the book for cinematic continuity functions admirably until the actual search for Moby Dick begins. From the moment of the departure from fertile seas to approach the fatal area of encounter with the white whale, Huston elaborates each successive incident in Melville's concluding chapters. . . . Memorable though each incident is within its context, the accumulation of so much significant development conspires to defeat its purpose by over-extension of dramatic weight. When the climax comes, it is fine enough to sustain a lesser film, but it is unable to rise to quite the soaring grandeur necessary to complete this massive structure.

A failure of this nature seems typical of Huston, whose reticent objectivity is unsuited to the full-bodied statement which Melville requires. Huston's tendency to withdraw from overt comment is noticeable in earlier passages of the film. When Ishmael's journey to the sea seems built towards the logical culmination of crashing waves and a panoramic vista, Huston curiously substitutes a distant backdrop of an immobile coastline for an incomplete effect. Later, the fine episode of the ship's departure from Nantucket, brilliantly created by intercutting from seamen labouring in preparation for the voyage to the tragic faces of women watching silently from the shore, seems to lead naturally to some positive conclusion, whether grandiose (the ship as man's aspiration severing its inhibiting roots in search of greater destiny) or moving (the women in foreground representing conventional humanity watching the fragile craft vanish into the formidable infinity of sea and sky). The actual ending of the scene, a quiet distant shot of a toy ship slowly moving toward the mouth of the harbour, seems a deliberate avoidance of an essential large effect. The obvious justification for muting early climaxes in preparation for the finale is negated by the limitations of the proper conclusion, suggesting a crucial weakness in the director's temperament which renders him incapable of interpreting a theme of these proportions. (p. 25)

Huston has chosen three key passages from the novel for his text. Father Mapple's sermon articulates the conventional viewpoint of moral man, while Ahab, in long speeches to Starbuck, defines the nature of his defiance of the unwritten laws. For these expressions of the theme Huston abandons his usual flow of visual movement to focus directly on the speaker and thus actively force the observer's attention. The sermon emphasises man's humility before the will of God by recounting the parable of Jonah, who sought a land where God's hard law would not exist. As punishment for this transgression, God in the form of nature sends a tidal wave, and casts Jonah into the sea to be swallowed by a whale. Jonah's submission within the inferno takes the form of humble prayer, without request for deliverance—"I leave eternity to Thee." When Jonah is saved, he devotes the remainder of his life to preaching the doctrine of humility, with man at the mercy of an all-powerful Deity.

Ahab's search for the whale represents the opposite point of view. The whale may be defined as unknown nature wearing the mask of evil, and Ahab in his quest represents man searching for knowledge. The desire for vengeance against the mute beast which mutilated his body is merely an aspect of Ahab's deeper motivation, his proud refusal to accept the doctrine of the insignificance of man. . . .

The ethical problem posed by Ahab's obsession lies not within his right to pursue his goal, which must be considered heroic, but in his obligations to society. By taking the blind, unmotivated men of the Pequod with him on his quest, Ahab has overstepped the boundaries of morality and assumed identification with the evil which he seeks to conquer. It is this dilemma which defeats Starbuck, who fears the wrath of God; but he is prevented from murdering Ahab because such an act would in itself involve the assumption of decisive powers in defiance of the inevitable. In Ahab's final speech he suggests the weight of the responsibility which he has assumed by the act. Probing into the reasons for his pursuit of inevitable destruction, he challenges the crux of Starbuck's religious conviction. . . .

If *Moby Dick* does not capture the full force of Melville's pessimistic philosophy, it conveys more depth in these three speeches than any American film of recent years. Considerably more than a technical achievement, Huston's film is probably as distinguished an adaptation of a great novel as the contemporary screen is capable of producing.

In a discussion of his style, Huston once commented: "Maybe it's what Hemingway says about writing: 'You must write it as if you were there.' Maybe, I just try to to do it as if I were there."

A director's style cannot be adequately evaluated according to the standards applied to literary technique, due to the basic distinction between the processes of invention and interpretation. Working with other men's material imposes a limitation on the activity of a director which, considered from a literary standpoint, cannot be disregarded. Since Huston's cinematic works, both as writer and director, are all adaptations, he is necessarily required to operate within the range of the original subject matter, without undue imposition of his individual personality. A more subjective director might re-shape his material along personal lines, but Huston's basic approach to his work demands subordination to the requirements of his material. His adaptations, uniformly faithful to the original intentions of the authors, give little insight into Huston's temperament: the scripts are economical, sophisticated, carefully constructed, and invariably avoid personal statement. Factors of personality emerge only in choice of material indicating a preference for journalistic prose, protagonists whose weaknesses do not extend to softness and avoid self-pity, themes which express social or moral issues through violent action and ironic counterpoint. . . .

Huston's cinematic devices stem from a specific theory of film aesthetics. The screen is basically a conventional, not a realistic art, with physical qualities derived from human actions. . . .

Based on this principle, Huston's style is consciously derived from the nature of the subject, with its ultimate aim a simple expression of the meaning to be derived from that subject and communicated clearly to the observer. . . .

These cinematic devices, entirely justified by aesthetic theories, are limited only by the calculation by which they are applied to Huston's films. The cold precision of his application of technical methods to a dramatic medium remains Huston's one serious defect as an artist. Technical dexterity, while admirable as manner, can never be wholly satisfactory as a substitute for valid emotional drama, and Huston's apparent inability to engage himself subjectively with his material gives much of his work the character of chamber drama, artfully moulded and graphically observed, but essentially dispassionate. Nevertheless, the body of work which this objective manner has formulated has been constructed to withstand the closest scrutiny into form and content, and emerges as a considerable achievement by a responsible modern artist. (p. 34)

Eugene Archer, "Small People in a Big World" (© copyright Eugene Archer 1959; reprinted with permission), in Films and Filming, Vol. 6, No. 1, October, 1959, pp. 9-10, 25, 34.

## GORDON GOW

Right from the beginning, it's clear that **The Unforgiven** is a western in search of significance. The credit titles are backed up by a dust storm, a white moon in a blue-black sky, and a grim vision of cracked earth and cattle-skulls. The significance, once found, turns out to be familiar: this is a story of racial prejudice, deep-ingrained, acted out amid the also familiar tradition of the Western. The combination of familiarities is blended into a solemn-paced film that might occasionally give western addicts the fidgets, but compensates with spirited outbreaks of action and a fair share of visual poetry. (p. 21)

Gordon Gow, "New Films: 'The Unforgiven'" (© copyright Gordon Gow 1960; reprinted with permission), in Films and Filming, Vol. 6, No. 10, July, 1960, pp. 21-2.

## GERALD WEALES

Much was to be expected of **The Misfits**. With two men as talented as John Huston and Arthur Miller behind the cameras and two personalities as powerful as Clark Gable and Marilyn Monroe in front of them, the resulting film should have been a strong one. One might have expected it to be very good or very bad, but it was a surprise that it should have turned out so dull.

The original Miller story . . . out of which the book and movie grew is a reasonably effective moral tale that uses a pathetic roundup of wild horses as setting and device. The three men in the story—the aging Gay, the youthful Perce, the pilot Guido—are explicitly identified with the mustangs they capture. The men, like the horses, are misfits; none of them has a place in the world of job, home, and family. . . . The story suggests that the men, who have never been tamed to the routine world, have no more chance of survival than do the horses, which are destined to become dog food. Once, perhaps, the West was wide and rich enough for a man on a horse to be proud, wild, free; now the men can hang onto their independence only by destroying the symbol of it. (p. 46)

The greatest disappointment in the film is director John Huston; he is the one who should have made the camera do its work. The bringing down of the stallion is effective enough, the visual analogy that the story intended it to be, but for the most part the running of the horses and the rodeo are conventionally filmed. Huston never manages to make us see Reno or Guido's house as they should be seen, the first an image of the rootlessness of the characters, the second a symbol of conventional living abandoned and then reaccepted. . . . Through the film as a whole, it is almost as though Huston and Miller worked against one another: scene, dialogue, scene, dialogue—the film runs almost in labeled segments. But the scenes might have been shot by any Hollywood director, the dialogue written by any pseudo-serious script man.

Even with such exalted mustang hunters, the result is still dog food. (p. 47)

Gerald Weales, "The Tame and Wooly West," in The Reporter (© 1961 by The Reporter Magazine Co.), Vol. 24, No. 5, March 2, 1961, pp. 46-7.*

## RAYMOND DURGNAT

John Huston's career is curiously unequal. The life of Toulouse-Lautrec is viewed through the prism of Pierre La Mure's dim-witted tear-jerker, while **The Misfits** is eked out with bits of arty-craftiness like Marilyn Monroe embracing a tree trunk to show she loves life in all its forms. Often between the idea and the execution there interposes a kind of gangling, almost cynical nonchalance, at other times an almost naive solemnity. One feels John Huston is two people—the thoughtful, basically rather ascetic, middlebrow, and, far more interesting, the rugged extrovert for whom life is keenest during the brawl, the hunt, and the genial drinking-session. In Huston the two often seem to cancel out rather than link up—perhaps after all his best films are those where Bogart, saturnine, craven, vulnerable, establishes the emotional core which somehow seems to me to be lacking in **We Were Strangers** and **Moby Dick**. . . .

In its amiable way [the] least serious of all Huston's films [**The List of Adrian Messenger**] retains a rather cerebral flavour. . . .

[Whereas] **Beat the Devil** was so relaxed that it lost all its tensions and just fell apart, **Adrian Messenger** is firm, sharp and atmospheric, whether the scene is a seamy dockside murder or the panoply of a hunt in full cry. The bane of English detective films of the *Trent's Last Case* tradition are the stuffy countryhouse settings, the stiff-upper-lip characters, the interminable conversations. Huston takes all these elements and makes them thoroughly filmic. . . . (p. 25)

Huston's London, with its florid Italian organ-grinder churning out 'A wandering minstrel I', is [gloriously Edwardian]. . . . Huston is so charmed with the spirit and ceremonies of gentlemanly tally-ho that in the final sequence he comes within striking distance of doing for fox-hunting what Hemingway did for the bullfight. In fact Huston's country gentry ideally combine English politeness with American zest and remind us that Huston, like the regretted Jacques Becker, is, unconsciously perhaps, a moralist preoccupied with the question of what causes, manners and attitudes are worthy of the *real* gentleman, nature's. (p. 26)

Raymond Durgnat, "'The List of Adrian Messenger'" (© copyright Raymond Durgnat 1963; reprinted with permission), in Films and Filming, Vol. 9, No. 10, July, 1963, pp. 25-6.

## RICHARD WHITEHALL

[One] of the most fashionable blood-sports seems to be baiting John Huston. The fury of disciples suddenly recognising false idols is not a pretty one. . . . [Because] **Adrian Messenger** and **The Secret Passion** [released in the United States as **Freud**] are bad films . . . then it also follows that **The Maltese Falcon** must have been a bad film. This is one of the sillier aspects of the 'Cahiers' school of criticism, which has spread to its British and American hangers on. Well, **Maltese Falcon, Key Largo, Sierra Madre,** still look pretty good. Huston's decline seems to date from his decision to enter the characterless international cinema with **African Queen,** which still looks pretty bad.

His films, as his more vituperative critics now claim, may always have been static, but the eloquence of his groupings and the precision and control with which his tableaux melted into each other stamp his early Americana (with the exception of *Across the Pacific,* but including *In This Our Life*) with a very definite Huston style. What happened to the style is anyone's guess, it was intermittently visible in *The Unforgiven* (the man-hunt in the dust storm) and *The Misfits* (the mustang hunt) but in [*Adrian Messenger* and *The Secret Passion*] it has been reduced to self caricature. *Adrian Messenger* had to coast along on its gimmick, and . . . *The Secret Passion* is packed with bewigged and bewhiskered actors who seem, at any moment, about to peel off their make-up just to show the disguise is only skin-deep.

*The Secret Passion,* like *Moby Dick,* like *Moulin Rouge,* is not a film one can take very seriously . . . , it is the inevitable result of a director who has increasingly let the literary take precedence over the visual in his work. This one is full of literary devices, the sort of thing analysed and applauded in the stodgier books on film appreciation. . . . In action, these devices just look clumsy. . . .

[*The Secret Passion*] is twenty years out of date, a period piece in every sense of the word. The groupings are stiff, the compositions based on the careful arrangement of the players in static attitudes, like so many formal photographs from a family album. The style, indeed, seems to be less Huston than William Dieterle in his biographical period, for *The Secret Passion* looks and sounds exactly like a belated addition to the Warner wax-works (Louis Pasteur, Emile Zola, Juarez, Dr Erlich—the last two co-scripted by Huston) which had such unaccountable success in the late 'thirties.

Huston seems to have confused the dehumanisation of character with scientific detachment, just as his chilly studies in clinical analysis spill over into the antihumanist handling of the personal relationships. . . . Frigidity and lust are reduced to a passionless anonymity of emotion, and one remains unconvinced that a spirit of enquiry can exist in a dead world. Certainly the subject is full of dangers, which aren't always avoided (Freud's first encounter with the Oedipus complex and the following dream sequence is dramatised documentary at its most unconvincing, although there is one rather good, sustained, passage in which [Cecily Koertner] is twice taken through the details of her father's death until she is forced to admit that he died, not in a hospital, but in a brothel—'He died of lust!'). One would like to know how the film stands up against [G. W.] Pabst's essay into Freudian analysis, *Secrets of a Soul,* but it can't hold a candle to [Ingmar] Bergman's *Wild Strawberries,* which employs somewhat similar methods of character dissection. (p. 22)

[In *The Secret Passion* a] magnificent subject has been given the dimensions of a charade. (p. 23)

*Richard Whitehall, "'Freud—The Secret Passion'" (© copyright Richard Whitehall 1963; reprinted with permission), in* Films and Filming, *Vol. 10, No. 1, October, 1963, pp. 22-3.*

**STEPHEN TAYLOR**

Ideas interpreted on a scale different from the one in which they were conceived frequently accumulate new meaning along the way. Huston's rescaling—you might call it "cinematizing"—of [*The Night of the Iguana*] results in a reduction of meaning, yet sometimes the results are surprisingly beneficial. Listening to the protagonists reel off accounts of their spiritual difficulties and arrive verbosely at poetic solutions to them, it becomes patently clear that [Tennessee] Williams' thinking is no longer abreast of the times. . . . Williams has fallen behind, has been overtaken by America, and Huston's reinterpretation, whether by deliberate deflation or plain vulgarization, often acts to soften the blow.

Watching *The Night of the Iguana* as Huston's film rather than Williams' play—which is not quite impossible—other difficulties arise. Half the time the dialogue appears wholly unrelated to the action; one or the other is more often than not superfluous, and both together are excessive. It is like watching one ball game on television and listening to another on the radio: you need two minds to follow the action. Huston has simply failed to find the images necessary to maintain coherence. The talk and cinematography move at different speeds, and the effect can be dizzying. (pp. 51-2)

[Credibility] is the central problem of *The Night of the Iguana.* Its principal theme is the state of being at the end of one's tether, as frequent cuts to an iguana at the end of *its* tether repeatedly remind us. Whatever power the stage version had was mustered by dint of rhetoric, the gathering force of anguished oratory. But Huston, as good as he is with *mise-en-scène,* is most at home in films that are laconic, verbally thrifty. Consequently, for lack of imagery to support all the talk, the credibility of the action collapses. Williams' thunder erupts, has its moments, but ultimately disintegrates into the clatter of tin cans. What makes this all so unfortunate is that there is a lot of nascent good in the film, though in the end it has to be placed alongside the thousands of other movies which afford evidence that seeing is by no means believing. (p. 52)

*Stephen Taylor, "Film Reviews: 'The Night of the Iguana'," in* Film Quarterly *(copyright 1964 by The Regents of the University of California; reprinted by permission of the University of California Press), Vol. XVIII, No. 2, Winter, 1964, pp. 50-2.*

**ALLEN EYLES**

[In *The Maltese Falcon*] Huston displays a rare talent for the film medium is in his exact manipulation of his actors, cameraman, set designer, and others, to capture such a rich, near flawlessly correct mood, not just at moments and scenes but throughout the length of the film. It is an extremely powerful and richly suggestive work and has a rare solidity as a whole. It is a great film. (p. 49)

[Huston's hand is] obvious in his superb relating of actors to the camera, as in the way the latter closes in on Spade's bulk so that it cuts between Brigid and Cairo at their first meeting to suggest how he is in the middle, listening in to pick up what he can. There is the beautiful economy of the handling of Miles' death: a shot of a signpost, then of Miles Archer below it, his smile vanishing as a gun is brought up just inside the frame and fired at him; and lastly Miles' body tumbling down the slope behind the fence, the change in mood punched home by the score, changing from its earlier, vaguely unsettling, rather eerie quality. . . .

Huston particularly exploits contrasts of shape and size: Spade jammed between two large policemen questioning him; Spade seeming to tower over Cairo in a low-angled shot as he slowly advances, hands clasped to the back of his head, clearly about to regain the advantage from his gun-wielding visitor (whose body bounces as it falls after a delayed punch, making him seem even more helpless); or the emphasis on Greenstreet's girth by the low-placed camera shooting past it onto his face in conversation with Spade.

Continually the director enlarges our understanding of characters and makes us feel more forcefully the mood of a scene without carrying it too far so that his effects are ostentatious decoration. . . .

More than just a private-eye picture, this is a compelling study of human frailty. It is almost satirical (which is why it is so entertaining) but always truth-observing. Never ponderous, superbly balanced, it works as a whole and its magic can never be finally explained. (p. 50)

> *Allen Eyles, "'The Maltese Falcon'" (© copyright Allen Eyles 1964; reprinted with permission), in* Films and Filming, *Vol. 11, No. 2, November, 1964, pp. 45-50.*

### JOHN RUSSELL TAYLOR

The most consistent feature of John Huston's very diverse output is a certain brisk directness of style. He is not necessarily incapable of subtlety, but he prefers to state rather than to imply, to drive straight through the middle of a subject rather than circle it warily first. This means that his failures—like most of *The Bible*—are startlingly shameless and undisguised. But the manly, neck-or-nothing approach can also work astonishingly well with a lot of otherwise intractable material. We last saw it doing so in that weird hodge-podge *Casino Royale,* where only the Huston episode at the beginning made no attempt at subtlety and no bones about playing it up to the hilt as farce. This worked, while everyone else was much too clever by half. . . . [Right] at the other end of the dramatic scale, Huston's direct attack has paid off with an almost equally surprising success in his version of Carson McCullers' elusive novella *Reflections in a Golden Eye*. . . .

The story is one of those overheated essays in Southern Baroque. It all takes place on a military station in Georgia, and everybody in sight is very peculiar indeed. (p. 99)

The mind boggled, in prospect, at how on earth [these peculiarities] could turn out on screen. And would Huston, of all people, be the right director to put it there, supposing it could be done? In the event, he has carried it off simply by ignoring, or seeming to ignore, the difficulties altogether. Equipped with a script by Chapman Mortimer and Gladys Hill which follows the original with a remarkable degree of literal fidelity, Huston has done likewise. The more extraordinary inventions of the original are put straight on to the screen as though they are the most normal things in the world. Quite a lot of the film is funny, especially in the character of Leonora, the major's wife and virtually the only reasonably sane person around. . . . But the sort of unconscious absurdity which is always waiting on the side-lines to engulf the whole enterprise never in fact does so, simply because Huston acts throughout as though it is not there. (p. 100)

> *John Russell Taylor, "Film Reviews: 'Reflections in a Golden Eye',"* in Sight and Sound *(copyright © 1968 by The British Film Institute), Vol. 37, No. 2, Spring, 1968, pp. 99-100.*

### PAULINE KAEL

The worst problem of recent movie epics is that they usually start with an epic in another form and so the director must try to make a masterpiece to compete with an already existing one. This is enough to petrify most directors but it probably delights Huston. What more perverse challenge than to test himself against the Book? It's a flashy demonic gesture, like Nimrod shooting his arrow into God's heaven.

Huston shoots arrows all over the place [in *The Bible*]; he pushes himself too hard, he tries to do too many different things. The movie is episodic not merely because the original material is episodic but also because, like [D. W.] Griffith in *Intolerance,* he can find no way to rhythm together everything that he's trying to do. Yet the grandeur of this kind of crazy, sinfully extravagant movie-making is in trying to do too much. . . . Huston's triumph is that despite the insanity of the attempt and the grandiosity of the project, the technology doesn't dominate the material: when you respond to the beauty of such scenes in *The Bible* as the dispersal of the animals after the landing of the Ark, it is not merely the beauty of photography but the beauty of conception. (p. 132)

Huston retains that angry God, and Eve as the source of mischief, and phrases disquieting to modern ears, like "Fair are the angels of God." He hasn't taken the fashionable way out of trying to turn it all into charming metaphors and he hasn't "modernized" it into something comfortable and comforting. He doesn't, in the standard show business way, twist the story to make the hero sympathetic. (p. 133)

The movie may present a problem for religious people who have learned not to think of the Bible stories like this: it is commonly understood now that although the childish take the stories for truth, they are then educated to know that the stories are "metaphorical." The movie undercuts this liberal view by showing the power (and terror) of these cryptic, primitive tribal tales and fantasies of the origins of life on earth and why we are as we are. This God of wrath who frightens men to worship ain't no pretty metaphor.

One of the worst failures of the movie is, implicitly, a rather comic modern predicament. Huston obviously can't make anything acceptable out of the Bible's accounts of sinfulness and he falls back upon the silliest stereotypes of evil: the barbaric monsters who jeer at Noah's preparations for the Flood look like leftovers from a Steve Reeves Hercules epic, and the posing, prancing faggots of Sodom seem as negligible as in *La Dolce Vita.* God couldn't have had much sense of humor if He went to the trouble of destroying them. Even their worship of the Golden Calf seems like a nightclub act, absurd all right, but not nearly as horrible as the animal sacrifices that God accepts of Abel and orders of Abraham. It is a measure of the strength of Huston's vision that we are constantly shocked by the barbarism of this primitive religion with its self-serving myths; it is a measure of weakness that he goes along with its strange notions of evil without either making them believable or treating them as barbaric. Only in the rare moments when the Bible's ideas of wrong and our ideas of wrong coincide—as in Cain's murder of his brother—can Huston make sin convincing. (pp. 133-34)

Probably the most seriously flawed sequence is the Tower of Babel, and as it is one of the most brilliant conceptions in the work, it is difficult to know why it is so badly structured and edited. The ideas remain latent: we can see what was intended, but the sequence is over before the dramatic point has been developed. And in this sequence, as in several others, Huston seems unable to maneuver the groups of people in the fore-ground; this clumsiness of staging and the dubbing of many of the actors in minor roles produce occasional dead scenes and dead sounds. It would be better if the musical score *were* dead: it is obtrusively alive, and at war with the imagery. (p. 134)

> Pauline Kael, "Epics: 'The Bible', 'Hawaii', 'Dr. Zhivago'" (originally published in a different form as "Epics: 'The Bible' and 'Hawaii'," in The New Republic, *Vol. 155, No. 17, October 22, 1966), in her* Kiss Kiss Bang Bang *(© 1966 by Pauline Kael; reprinted by permission of Little, Brown and Company in association with the Atlantic Monthly Press), Atlantic-Little, Brown, 1968, pp. 131-37.**

## HANS KONINGSBERGER

Last October, in the oldest gothic abbey of Italy, Fossanova, John Huston completed filming *A Walk with Love and Death,* a novel of mine published in 1961. . . . I was present from the beginning and worked with the director, which is not stan-dard practice; and Huston is not a standard director. . . .

[It] was my good fortune as a writer that Huston is a man who believes in books. Real books are seldom seen circulating in the movie world; its dealings are with story *outlines,* as if what mattered in literature was really and only what the personages ended up doing to each other, and the rest just decoration—a parallel to saying, never mind whether this painting is a Ver-meer or a Picasso or a Smith; just tell me its subject.

Huston, then, wanted to film (as he has always done) a *novel:* not the movements of the people in a story but the idea of the book. . . .

Important to a writer were two qualities of Huston's. . . . The first one is his bitter aversion to shortcuts, clichés, mixed metaphors. No matter, for instance, how difficult it was to convey a passage of time, he would sooner work on it for a week than resort to the trees-in-leaf-and-then-bare type of film trick. (p. 2)

[This] leads me to a second quality of his working ways. His artistry, I think, is under perpetual observation of his almost purely mathematical concept of film-reality, vastly different for him from book-reality and real-reality. Thus I had to *explain* every word and every action to him in precise terms in order to get away with them; no vagueness was admitted. . . .

[His] analytical way of investigating a scene was the precise opposite of the writer's synthetical way. I looked at my char-acters from the inside out, saw them in a synthesis which was clear and natural, but in which I might very well be mistaken about one particular utterance or action. His was the analysis: he accepted the whole, but weighed each part, and if I could not convince him, not only of its naturalness but indeed of its unavoidable necessity, he wanted it rewritten, or at times re-wrote it himself. (p. 3)

> Hans Koningsberger, "From Book to Film—via John Huston," in Film Quarterly *(copyright 1969 by The Regents of the University of California; reprinted by permission of the University of California Press), Vol. XXII, No. 3, Spring, 1969, pp. 2-4.*

## JOHN RUSSELL TAYLOR

There are two films yoked together in *The Kremlin Letter* . . . : the film it was apparently meant to be, and the film it actually turns out to be. The situation is not extraordinary; what is extraordinary is that both are interesting, and both in their different ways equally characteristic of their creator. There is little doubt that the film John Huston set out to make may be read in the light of the little scene he gives himself near the beginning. He is the admiral called on to discharge Patrick O'Neal . . . from the U.S. Navy so that he can take his place in a complicated counter-espionage manoeuvre. . . . O'Neal is puzzled and unhappy; the admiral is coldly furious. He sees it, quite simply, as a dereliction of duty, a failure of loyalty and, worst of all, a wilful copping out of the group. O'Neal, as far as he is concerned, has chosen to put some sort of personal whim or maybe some private loyalty in front of his loyalty to the group of which he is a part. And that is unfor-givable.

It can hardly be accidental that this, on one level, is the theme of the film. . . . [The] whole latter part of the story may be seen as a re-examination of that subject which has so often come up in Huston's films—in *We Were Strangers, The Treas-ure of Sierra Madre, The Asphalt Jungle:* the perhaps arbitrary formation of a group to do something, idealistic or cynically commercial or downright criminal, anything which involves a group loyalty and eventually brings individual members of the team to a choice between the survival of the whole and the interests of the single member. And the answers are not always easy. . . .

But all this seems to be taking the film rather solemnly, and indeed it is. Even if Huston meant it to be about the group, loyalty and so on, it does not come out quite that way. Like a painting in which the painter has changed his mind about the design after the first sketch, *The Kremlin Letter* occasionally lets us glimpse an original intention showing through. But the final design is very different. The finished film bears about the same relationship to *We Were Strangers* that *Beat the Devil* does to *The Maltese Falcon:* mocking, fantasising, taking cool pleas-ure in sheer throwaway virtuosity. The plot is ridiculously complicated, with so many bluffs and counterbluffs that ob-viously nobody is expected to follow every last in and out. Instead it provides a perfectly sufficient excuse for a rich gallery of grotesques. . . .

No doubt, as serious people say, we should expect more of Huston. But even at his most casual, as in *Sinful Davy,* he does have the gift of making film-making look as though he enioys it, of being so prodigal of invention that it doesn't matter if we don't care for one or two of his ideas—he's got a million of them. *The Kremlin Letter* comes at you in a breathless rush, and carries you off on a switchback course of comedy, satire, irony and deeper meaning. Even if we forget the meaning and concentrate on the fun—as Huston himself has done for long stretches—the eventful trip through Hustonland should leave us with little cause for complaint.

> John Russell Taylor, "Film Reviews: 'The Kremlin Letter'," in Sight and Sound *(copyright © 1970 by The British Film Institute), Vol. 39, No. 4, Autumn, 1970, p. 220.*

## MICHAEL DEMPSEY

No historical data could explain the pervasive terror of that tiny fragment of the Hundred Years War that John Huston treats in his beautiful and under-rated *A Walk With Love and Death*. . . .

Huston starts with the ordinary reality of this war—the bewildering way that enemies and friends become interchangeable—and works towards more universal overtones of doom and fear. His style is simple and low-keyed, but there is never any question of linkage between his medieval world and the modern *zeitgeist*. The lovers reject participation in the skirmishes, and society (embryonic as it is) in turn rejects them. The movie spurns conventional characterization for atmosphere and then spurns the conventional atmospheric devices used most expertly and facilely in films like *Romeo and Juliet* and *Elvira Madigan*.

Huston, trying for epiphanies, shows his hand immediately. In the very first scene, Heron strides buoyantly towards us from the far side of a deserted field. The day is fragrant with breezes, leafy greenness, sunlight. "Spring came on forever," he narrates, trying to crystallize the moment for himself—a freshet of an awakening season which the earnest student and hopeful poet translates as best he can into words. He stops to drink at a brook. The camera tilts down upon a body drifting downstream. The intrusion without warning of death, the gentle directness of Huston's staging, his refusal to show the actual killing—these qualities form a precis of the film. His technique is unobtrusively, yet precisely, cinematic; Heron's words set the mood as much through their sound and rhythm as through their literary content. The whole thrust is towards such simplification. (pp. 14-15)

Huston refuses the noisy violence that is obligatory to most war movies. Dealing with a foetal society shattering and reshattering itself through its members' blood-lust, the director rigorously curbs the blood, keeping if offscreen, filming it in long shot, or using fast cuts. . . . As a result, death and destruction, like happiness and love, seem, in that peculiar and upsetting manner which the movie dwells on ceaselessly, to start and stop virtually simultaneously. But whereas the editing and the set-ups make love appear gossamer and evanescent and beautiful because it is so, these same devices make death a stealthy force soundlessly savaging its victims, arriving from nowhere with little or no warning, as though it were dreamed. Both love and death are brief; but love is brief because it cannot withstand the hammer blows which death smashes against it, while death is brief because its power is too strong for love to resist for long. It is characteristic that Huston returns for just a passing second to the white horse, formerly a harbinger of courage and joy, now a carcass hacked open by starving people for its meat. (pp. 16-17)

The last few minutes of the movie [where Claudia and Heron are alone in the monastery] deserve special notice. . . . What many other directors would have made a pond of tears, Huston makes a definitive image of unassuming bravery. This ending, worthy of what [Robert] Bresson gave us in *The Diary of a Country Priest, Mouchette,* and *Balthazar*, makes questions about the connection between us and the Middle Ages seem laughable. We are not so swamped with good movies that we can afford to neglect this flawed, lovely vision. (p. 18)

*Michael Dempsey, "'A Walk with Love and Death'," in* Film Heritage *(copyright 1971 by F. A. Macklin), Vol. 6, No. 2, Winter, 1970-71, pp. 14-18.*

### VERNON YOUNG

*Fat City* is a work of art. This is the movie John Huston had under his skin for years to justify all the premature applause. . . . Allowing for the dreary level of consciousness conveyed by characters who live in the basement of themselves, the film is as perfect as a film can be—. . . a kind of American *Lower Depths*, it takes place in a California town where sunshine is merely something that makes everyone in the film squint, so much of his time is spent in the gym, in the ring, in a bar, in an unmade bed. . . . The deadbeats and dumb hopefuls who comprise this lost colony are dupes of their own making; especially, one might add, they are victims of their total helplessness when groping for language. You feel that if they ever augmented their vocabulary with two fateful words, the increase could change their lives: they might just understand that they are trying to punch their way out of paper bags they have themselves inflated and climbed into. Reuben Lura, the fight manager, is the only articulate figure, and nobody listens to him. (pp. 172-73)

*Vernon Young, "Fat Shakespeare, Fat City, Lean Wilderness," in* The Hudson Review *(copyright © 1973 by The Hudson Review, Inc.; reprinted by permission), Vol. XXVI, No. 1, Spring, 1973, pp. 170-76.\**

### JAMES NAREMORE

[Huston made from *The Maltese Falcon*] one of the classics of dark cinema, a film important not only for its fidelity, but because it bears his own distinctive signature.

The very choice of *Falcon* was consistent with the personality Huston would convey in nearly all his subsequent work—perhaps *Falcon* even determined that personality to some degree. Notice how neatly it fits into the Huston canon; most of his good films—*Treasure of the Sierra Madre, Key Largo, We Were Strangers, The Asphalt Jungle, The Roots of Heaven, Beat the Devil, The Misfits, Fat City*—have depended on simple visual symbolism and sharp contrasts of character. They are all quasi-allegorical adventures about groups of exotic, eccentric people, and, as several commentators have observed, they usually end on a note of great, ironic failure. Even *The African Queen,* which isolates two completely different character types, is barely an exception to these rules; it merely has a smaller cast and a more optimistic comedy, an act of God intervening to save the protagonists. It would be a more typical film if it ended about fifteen minutes earlier, at the point where Bogart and Hepburn collapse with exhaustion as the camera rises above high grass to show the open sea only a few feet away. Ultimately, however, Huston is less interested in success or failure than in the moments of truth that an adventurous quest leads up to. As a result, the point in his version of *Falcon* is not the bird itself, nor the fact that it ends up being a phony. Huston wants to show the greed, the treachery, and sometimes the loyalty of his characters. The focus at the end of the picture is on Sam Spade's curious integrity, and on Sidney Greenstreet as he taps a bowler hat on his head and gaily wanders off in search of the real bird.

Huston's films have also shown his admiration for a male world, though he is sometimes more ambivalent towards that world than a director like Hawks. Raymond Durgnat has rightly pointed out that "*Treasure of Sierra Madre* and *The Misfits* are 'tragic critiques' of the Hawksian ideal, respecting it, fairly, but going beyond their tough conformism to a profounder humanism." . . . *Falcon* is hardly an example of profound humanism, but Huston does seem more conscious than Hammett of the male myth which underlies the novel. The film is more emphatic, more stylized than the book, and it shows us very clearly that the underworld characters are foils for Spade's masculinity. A single room tells us that Spade scorns luxury; he is not effeminate like Cairo and he has no soft belly like Gutman. This contrast is elaborated by other details: Spade does not need to carry a gun, but the "boy" Wilmur—whose very name sounds prissy—ludicrously brandishes two big forty-fives in a desperate and unsuccessful attempt to assert manhood. More important, Spade's professional ethics, his willingness to turn in a woman he loves out of loyalty to a dead partner he never liked much anyway, is at bottom a victory for the "male" ethic. It is true that in the past he cuckolded Archer (mostly, we suspect, at the insistence of Archer's wife), but his behavior as we actually see it is fundamentally different from Brigid O'Shaunnessy or Mrs. Archer. As in most private-eye stories, the women in Huston's film are fickle and dangerous killers, and they have to be rejected or sent off to prison at the end if the hero wishes to survive. *The Maltese Falcon* is one of the purest examples of this classic form; significantly, the one trustworthy female in the movie is Effie Perine, whom Spade treats like a little sister. She sits on his desk and rolls his cigarettes, and at one point he calls her a "good man."

But if *Falcon* is typical of Huston's themes, it is also the finest achievement of his visual style. In this respect we can see most clearly the difference between his work and Hammett's. Hammett's art is essentially straightforward and deadpan, but Huston, contrary to his reputation, is a highly energetic and expressive storyteller who likes to make comments through his images. (pp. 241-43)

In the good Huston films, nearly everything—the actor's movements, the camera set-ups, the editing—works to create a somewhat stylized quality. Huston's camera never retards or works against the power of a script by utterly meaningless bravura, and usually he generates such interest that we don't care to analyze his technique. But clearly he does not eschew rhetoric, and the effect he produces on the screen seldom looks truly spontaneous. . . . Actually, Huston is somewhat less rigid in his late films, such as *Freud,* where he lets the camera slide a little here and there to catch an actor who has strayed out of the frame. In a movie like *Falcon,* however, the actors are used like models—an unusual attribute, coming as it does from a director who has always been happy to let the characters find their own way.

I bring out these qualities of Huston's work not because they are defects but because they help define a temperament. L. B. Mayer believed that Huston was a realist because *The Asphalt Jungle* was filled with seamy detail and a morbid sense of humor. Actually, Huston's world is no more ultimately real than that of Hawks or Minnelli. His best films have had tough, even grimy settings, and he has always rigorously excluded Hollywood romance; but he cannot avoid what Agee called a "romanticism about danger," and he loves to point a moral. Chiefly with his camera style, he loads male adventure stories with allegorical significance, and many of his pictures, despite their superficial realism, are like existentialist morality plays. Even his filming of *Moby Dick* forsakes Melville's visionary manner and turns the novel into a typical Huston movie—a cautionary tale about a group of odd characters engaged in a quest. It is no surprise that the last line of *The Maltese Falcon,* Bogart's corny remark about the black bird ("the stuff that dreams are made of"), is Huston's invention. But the same quality of mind that put that blemish on the film is responsible for much of what is good about it, namely the sheer liveliness of the images, the way they give Hammett's fairly straight

crime novel the air of dark comedy. . . . [Against] this, and somehow enhancing it, is the overt drama of Huston's camera. The film is just stylized enough to present the private eye story as it has to be presented—as a male myth rather than as a slice of life; and Huston's wit is just sly enough to humanize the film without destroying the power of its melodrama. (pp. 248-49)

*James Naremore, "John Huston and 'The Maltese Falcon'," in* Literature/Film Quarterly *(© copyright 1973 Salisbury State College), Vol. 1, No. 3, July, 1973, pp. 239-49.*

## PENELOPE GILLIATT

The real puzzle about ["**The Mackintosh Man**"] is the fact that such a rock-hard, witty director wanted to make it. It has very little humor, apart from quixotries of speech habits; no drive of intellect; some dazed factual mistakes about England; and a lot of holes in the plot. It doesn't work as a parody of spy thrillers, or as a spy thriller in itself, or as the sort of sly joke that "**The List of Adrian Messenger**" was. Sometimes it has Huston's gaunt comprehension of heroism, but the mediocre Maurice Jarre music is a general measure of the film. Huston, of all directors, usually possesses force, but this movie is flabby. It has echo-chamber moments, like the telling of some story remembered from a long time ago, which is often a majestic thing, but not in thriller plots. Though there are interludes of sexual sophistication in the dialogue direction which remind you of Huston's career as a writer, and though lines show Huston's gift of containing as much movement in conversation as in physical action, these wonders of the dramatic art don't happen often. The film contains a fine chase between a car and a lorry; a touch of Huston's unimitative feeling for what is going on in the brain of a man; a slightly desperate attempt to update the story from a Cold War spy narrative to one about a Maoist; . . . a number of terrifically alarming nurses, maids, and women cocktail-party guests; an ambulance that is an excellent character; beats of pity for men with loyalties that are matted by their pasts. Not a great deal more, though. A matter of a strengthy man taking his ease, perhaps.

*Penelope Gilliatt, "The Current Cinema: 'The Mackintosh Man'," in* The New Yorker *(© 1973 by The New Yorker Magazine, Inc.), Vol. XLIX, No. 24, August 6, 1973, p. 71.*

## PAULINE KAEL

As a movie, this Empire gothic [*The Man Who Would Be King*] has elements of *Gunga Din* and of a cynical *Lost Horizon,* along with something that hasn't been a heroic attribute in other Empire-gothic movies: the desire to become the highest-ranking person that one can envision. The heroes are able to achieve their goal only because of the primitiveness of the people they conquer, and this is very likely the stumbling block that kept the movie from being financed for the twenty-odd years that Huston wanted to do it. Maybe he was able to, finally, on the assumption that enough time has passed for the heroes' attitude toward the native populations of India and Kafiristan—the benighted heathen—to seem quaint rather than racist. Huston's narrative is both an ironic parable about the motives and methods of imperialism and a series of gags about civilization and barbarism. (pp. 107-08)

The script, by Huston and Gladys Hill, is a fine piece of craftsmanship, with every detail in place, and with some of Kipling's devices carried further, so that the whole mad, jinxed adventure is tied together. But *The Man Who Would Be King* isn't rousing, and it isn't a comedy, either. It's a genre movie made with full awareness of the campy pit into which it will sink if the laconic distancing ever lapses. Huston has to hold down the very emotions that most spectacles aim for. . . . *The Man Who Would Be King* is in subdued reds and browns, and the persistent dusty earth tones underscore the transiency of the heroes' victory. There are no soaring emotions. Huston tells his whopper in a matter-of-fact tone, and he doesn't play up the cast of thousands or the possibilities of portentous spectacle in the bizarre stone "sacred city" of Alexander the Great, built on a mountain.

The director's love of the material is palpable; it makes one smile. Yet the most audacious parts of the film don't reach for that special clarity which makes action memorably poetic. . . . Huston's is a perverse form of noblesse oblige—he doesn't want to push anything. He won't punch up the moments that are right there waiting, even though we might have enjoyed basking in them, and getting a lift from them. He sets up the most elaborate, berserk fairy-tale scenes and then just sits back; he seems to be watching the events happen instead of shaping them. Huston has said that Danny and Peachy are destroyed because of *folie de grandeur,* and that's what he risks, too. I admire his pride; he treats the audience with a sophisticated respect that's rare in genre films, and this movie is the best sustained work he's done in years. . . . But Huston's courtliness has its weakness. No doubt he believes in telling the story as simply as possible, but what that means in practice is that he shoots the script. It's exemplary, and he's a good storyteller. But he's not such a great *movie* storyteller here. . . . And so the ironies in *The Man Who Would Be King* go by fast—when we want them to vibrate a little.

Huston's even-tempered narrative approach doesn't quite release all that we suspect he feels about the material. It may be that he's so far into the kind of thinking that this story represents that he doesn't take us in far enough. If he had regressed to an earlier stage of movie history and presented Kipling's jingoism with emotional force, the film might have been a controversial, inflammatory epic. If he had rekindled the magical appeal of that jingoism and made us understand our tragic vulnerability to it, it might have been a true modern epic. The way he's done it, the story works only on the level of a yarn. But it's a wonderful yarn. . . . Huston is cynical without a shade of contempt—that's why the film is likable. Yet when you play fascinated anthropologist, equally amused by the British and the natives, you may have licked the problem of how to do Kipling now without an outcry, but you're being false to why you wanted to film the story in the first place. (pp. 108-09)

The theme of *The Man Who Would Be King* gets at the essence of the attitudes underlying John Huston's work. Huston might be the man without illusions on a quest. Here, as in *The Maltese Falcon, The Asphalt Jungle, The Treasure of Sierra Madre,* his characters are after money. But when Danny and Peachy are battling mountain snowstorms, risking blindness and death to get to the backward country they mean to pillage, one knows that it isn't just for gold—it's because conquering and looting a country are the highest score they can imagine. And when they view Alexander the Great's treasure, the jewels and gold pieces seem a little ridiculous; the treasure will be scattered, like the gold dust in *The Treasure of Sierra Madre.* . . .

Huston finds a grisly humor in the self-deceptions of ruthless people chasing rainbows; that might almost be his comic notion of man's life on earth. He earns esteem by not sentimentalizing that quest. (Yet his inability to show affection for characters who live on different terms shows how much the rogues mean to him.) Huston isn't too comfortable about any direct show of emotion; he's in his element (and peerlessly) with men who are boyishly brusque, putting down their own tender feelings shamefacedly. (p. 110)

In the story [on which the film is based], Kipling was able to satirize his own gnomic vision of fraternity, and at times Huston and [co-screenwriter] Gladys Hill, ringing changes on the mystic-fraternity theme—"rejuvenating" it   might almost be borrowing from Edgar Rice Burroughs. Huston seems to be enjoying himself in this film in the way he hasn't for a long time. It communicates the feeling of a consummated dream. (p. 111)

*Pauline Kael, "Brotherhood Is Powerful" (originally published in* The New Yorker, *Vol. LI, No. 46, January 5, 1976), in her* When the Lights Go Down *(copyright © 1975, 1976, 1977, 1978, 1979, 1980 by Pauline Kael; reprinted by permission of Holt, Rinehart and Winston, Publishers), Holt, 1980, pp. 107-12.\**

**ANDREW SARRIS**

John Huston is clearly a survivor, and . . . *Wise Blood* provides ample evidence that he has outlasted every movie mogul who ever tried to sweeten the sourness and pessimism in Huston's personality. . . . Admirers of the late Flannery O'Connor may have strong reservations about Huston's direction and Benedict Fitzgerald's screenplay. Actually, Huston and Fitzgerald have softened the novel's unbearably bleak ending ever so slightly, but most of the pain and suffering and excruciating guilt have been retained.

I respect the film enormously, but I don't have the slightest desire ever to see it again. Yet I think every thoughtful person should see *Wise Blood* once if only to experience a profound and original depression. . . .

There are incongruities in the Southern milieu . . . , little vaguenesses and lacunae that occur in the transition between the controlled coherence of the printed page and the haphazard details of uncoordinated location shooting. Nonetheless, there is something so overwhelmingly un-compromising about *Wise Blood* as an American movie that it should be supported as a matter of course by anyone who has ever been the slightest bit condescending to the notion of "Hollywood." . . .

I am not sure that Flannery O'Connor's vivid gargoyles belong on a movie screen. When one actually sees them in the flesh they seem too desperately disconnected for the black humor of their colorful dialogue to redeem them. . . .

Still, *Wise Blood* never ceased to fascinate me simply because it is the project that John Huston chose to undertake in his old age. . . . As I plunged ever deeper into the abyss of alienation to the mournfully orchestrated melody of "The Tennessee Waltz," I felt oddly stirred by the feeling that Huston was celebrating his own survival in the endless swamp of his cynicism and despair. I shall never be all that wild about his total career, but I am prepared to concede at long last that I have grossly underestimated his resourcefulness as an artist.

*Andrew Sarris, "Of Blood and Thunder and Despair" (reprinted by permission of* The Village Voice *and the author; copyright © News Group Publications, Inc., 1980), Vol. XXV, No. 8, February 25, 1980, p. 34.*

## STANLEY KAUFFMANN

The look of [*Let There Be Light*] is unexceptional, as is the editing. The lighting is like that of every other wartime documentary; the editing is in shot and reverse shot for conversation, quick cross fades for time lapse, etc. The exceptional quality of the film is not cinematic: it's in the concern of the filmmaker and the nakedness of the subjects.

A group of combat soldiers arrives at a US army hospital suffering from various kinds of shell shock, as it used to be called. . . . Each one gets an interview with an army psychiatrist in which sodium amytol is injected or hypnosis is used to relieve stress and enable him to talk. Each one is "cured"— at least to the point where, six weeks later, they are all playing softball and then are discharged from the hospital. (p. 20)

The film is misleading. It says nothing about the possibility of recurrence in these men; and, worse, it says nothing about the sufferers with combat psychoneurosis who took longer to leave or who never got out of hospitals. . . . There is no instance in the film of a soldier who did not respond fairly quickly to treatment: and no hint that there were others in worse shape who could not have been discharged.

I don't impute craftiness to Huston—at the time of making the film, anyway. He took a giant first step, as large as he was presumably permitted at the time, maybe even a bit further. Milestones are honorable, essential: *Light* is a milestone. But— and it's not the first instance—suppression has helped its reputation. (pp. 20-1)

*Stanley Kauffmann, "Old But New, New But Old,"* in The New Republic *(reprinted by permission of* The New Republic; © *1981 The New Republic, Inc.), Vol. 184, No. 5, January 31, 1981, pp. 20-1.**

# Kon Ichikawa

## 1915-

**Japanese director, screenwriter, and cartoonist.**

**Ichikawa is one of Japan's best-known filmmakers. His films are highly regarded because of their beautiful color and architecture. The characters in his films often exhibit some sort of abnormal behavior; leading some critics to label his works "bizarre comedies." However, Ichikawa is very serious about his filmmaking, and uses comedy primarily as a means of social satire.**

**Ichikawa was a cartoonist before he began making films, and his first film, *A Girl at Dojo Temple* (1946), reflects his early career. The film, a puppet version of a Kabuki play, was banned because its script had not been submitted to authorities for approval. Undaunted, Ichikawa continued to make films, including *Pu-san (Mr. Poo)*, a satirical look at Japanese life, based on a popular cartoon character. In 1956, Ichikawa made *The Burmese Harp*, a war film which attracted international attention. Ichikawa's subsequent films have been fairly well received. Although *Kagi (Odd Obsession)* has been dismissed by some critics for its unrealistic plot and crude humor, and *Nobi (Fires on the Plain)* has been termed "physically repulsive" because of its scenes of violence and cannibalism, these films have found supporters who realize the importance of such unusual aspects to Ichikawa's themes.**

**Ichikawa's most important films are *Alone on the Pacific, An Actor's Revenge,* and *Tokyo Olympiad.* These films show man struggling not only with nature or with others, but with himself, in order to attain a goal. The importance of these films lies in the mixture of humor and pathos involved in the character's journey toward fulfillment of his personal goal. Just as important is Ichikawa's filmic technique. He records events as they happen, without editorializing or being subjective, and allows the struggle for victory to develop naturally into a significant climax. These films solidified Ichikawa's growing international reputation.**

**The wide range of subject matter in Ichikawa's films shows that he is as adept at handling "serious" topics as he is at satire. Ichikawa works with his wife, Natto Wada, on the scripts for most of his films, and he admits that her influence is the major reason that he has adapted many literary works for the screen. Ichikawa shows both the light and the dark sides of human nature, but viewers often find his films depressing. He admits that he would like to be more optimistic in his art, but he films what he sees: "I look around for some kind of humanism, but I never seem to find it."**

## ALASTAIR STEWART

What [*The Burmese Harp*] says is perhaps this: There are certain men who take it upon themselves to live unselfishly as far as they can, perhaps because it gives purpose to their actions. To do this takes internal and external courage. Contact with peaceful eternity follows the realization that all selfish endeavour achieves nothing. . . .

The harp is symbolic from the start. But at the start the symbolism is crude and sentimental. This is not only justifiable, but also right. For here, things are represented as they appear to the Universal Private. He reminisces. To him the harp represents brief rests and that incentive to continue, a more enduring peace. It represents the pains a clever friend will go to, to provide a little home comfort a long way from home. (p. 27)

*The Burmese Harp* works on three levels. The situation is seen from three points of view: that of the Universal Private (all the men of that and any other platoon), that of a captain, and that of a developing saint. The three are unified by the overlapping of experiences and characterization. The captain is halfway between plain man and saint. He is a gentleman warrior by vocation. He understands Mizushima, but is not himself of saintly calibre. The presentation of three points of view creates an illusion of three-dimensional reality. Mizushima's ascent in the hierarchy of understanding, from a plain man with a difference to a saint, is therefore convincing. The situation justifies the mystic conclusions he draws. The more so, because even his attitude is objectified. . . .

I was impressed by the film's dignity. The right image and true symbol are used almost unfailingly—the cracked earth for purgation; figures of contemplation and revelation; Mizushima's literally being inside Buddha; and still water for peaceful eternity. Though used in a modern story (where they are revitalised) they lose none of their traditional grace. The black and white photography is superb: sometimes histrionic but never melodramatic, as it might easily have been. Light and shade are used with admirable subtlety. The music reflects the mood of the images aptly, both where it is and where it isn't part of the action. The German hymn "O Haupt voll Blut and Wunden" is heard when Mizushima wakes in the cave. Acting is restrained, but never painfully so.

At a time when English-speaking artists are looking for a calculus in which to express themselves seriously . . . , *The Bur-*

*mese Harp* should be welcomed as a corrective. Perhaps we shall survive moribund conventions. (p. 28)

Alastair Stewart, "'The Burmese Harp'," in Film Journal (copyright by Melbourne University Film Society), No. 14, November, 1959, pp. 27-8.

## DONALD RICHIE

The visuals [in *Conflagration* (*Enjo,* 1958) are] superb. For practically the first time CinemaScope was here used intelligently and creatively; and the textures captured in black and white were—even for Japan—beyond compare. Particularly impressive was the use of architecture. Ichikawa . . . would situate their action at the far left, for example, balancing it with architectural detail which, as one scene followed the other, perfectly re-created the temple atmosphere. . . . [Such] set-ups served primarily to emphasise the meaning of the scene. Though aesthetically prodigal, the film never exploited aestheticism for its own sake.

Just as beautiful and just as disturbing was *The Key (Kagi,* 1959), at present tentatively titled *Obsession.* . . . If *Conflagration* equated beauty and love and sex with destruction, *The Key* equated sex with illness, sex with medicine, sex with death. The film . . . examines the sex life of a middle-aged Kyoto couple and parallels this with the premarital activities of their daughter and her young doctor fiancé.

But the picture, like the novel, is only superficially interested in who goes to bed with whom and sacrifices any melodramatic possibilities by making each member of the quartet perfectly aware of what the others are doing. (pp. 78-9)

Sex is almost palpable in the film. . . . [The] screen is cluttered with hypodermic needles, catheters, sex rejuvenation machines, unmade beds, loosely flung *yukata*—all filmed by [Kazuo] Miyagawa in some of the most magnificently muted colour ever to reach the screen. Sex becomes so sordid, and is presented with such near-claustrophobic intensity, that one longs for outdoor scenes, anything to get away from that dark and keyholed and magnificently photographed house. Yet this quality accounts for the power of this very powerful film: the spectator is made a *voyeur*.

More, he is made a participant. Although all the principals know at least as much as the spectator, nothing is ever discussed, nothing is brought into the open; rather, everything is hidden, secreted away. The film becomes remarkably suggestive as one double meaning follows another, until finally it verges on prurience. . .

Yet, despite all this, *The Key* is never meretricious. Unlike other Japanese efforts, titillation is not the ultimate intention. Ichikawa is telling us something unpleasant, certainly, but none the less true: a new interpretation of the love-death theme, in which some of the most sordid of human actions are captured by means of the sheerest visual beauty.

*Fires on the Plain (Nobi,* 1959) is taken from the war novel by Shohei O-oka and is frankly concerned with death and with that last refuge of desire, cannibalism. It, too, says much more than a mere précis of the story-line might indicate. Again the film contributes a studied and controlled visual style—fully half of the picture is without dialogue—which, like all strong styles, creates a world of its own, one which forces our sympathy and enmeshes our emotions. That we experience no revulsion—and the major theme of the last third of the film is

the eating of human flesh—is due entirely to the quality of the script . . . , to the director's honesty and to the at times appalling beauty of the images.

Few films have more lucidly reflected the daily horrors which make up the catastrophe of war. . . .

Although these three films are not without flaws (*Conflagration* has some awkward scenes; *The Key* has a ridiculous ending; *Fires on the Plain* is paced so slowly that many have found it dull), they do represent an entirely new direction for the Japanese film. More important, they are perfectly valid emotional experiences in their own right. They unmistakably establish the 44-year-old Kon Ichikawa as one of Japan's finest directors. (p. 79)

Donald Richie, "Japan: The Younger Talents," in Sight and Sound (copyright © 1960 by The British Film Institute) Vol. 29, No. 2, Spring, 1960, pp. 78-81.*

## COLIN YOUNG

The *comédie noire* may be going out of fashion. When [*Odd Obsession*] was shown at Cannes in 1960 only the Japanese visitors thought it funny, and their laughter was written off as being eccentric, or at best ill-mannered. Only later did the grudging admission appear that perhaps it was a comedy after all, of a very stylish sort, and the jury gave it a prize. Unfortunately . . . , American audiences are proving as dense as the fashionable group at Cannes. They simply do not know that, or when, they are to laugh. This is puzzling, because it is not only an exceedingly well-made film, but also vastly entertaining, in a grisly sort of way. (p. 53)

[*Odd Obsession*] is concerned to show but not to "deal in" the prurience of the old man who is a bit of a *voyeur*—even with his own wife (he takes pictures of her asleep in the nude). It does not try to encourage *voyeurism* in its audience.

Drama sometimes deals with special cases. This is a special case. The sensualities of its characters are shown blandly, with humor rather than with any pornographic intention. Of course these sensualities are bizarre and exist in a hot-house atmosphere where there seems none of our usual concern with scruple.

This leads to some extremely well-written scenes. . . . Ichikawa never plays for obvious laughs, and is apparently content to draw us into his characters so that we can discover this absurdity. . . .

[*Odd Obsession* is much less obvious than the novel on which it is based]. The film does not replace the literary device [of the diary] with a visual one; it uses its time to concentrate on the extremely bizarre situations which it develops. If it does this so subtly as to confuse, this is a pity, because it is finally as comedy that this film should be judged and enjoyed. (p. 54)

Colin Young, "Film Reviews in General Release: 'Odd Obsession'," in Film Quarterly (copyright 1962 by The Regents of the University of California; reprinted by permission of the University of California Press), Vol. 15, No. 2, Winter, 1961-62, pp. 53-4.

## RAYMOND DURGNAT

[In *Odd Obsession,* Ichikawa] attains the purity of style for which he strove. The domestic courtesies are observed. Voices are rarely raised. Dawn whitens beyond the bamboos. The photography, with its dull purples and mauves, has an elegiac warmth; and the characters' cold, bleak, sexual frustrations are gazed on with so detached and reticent an eye that before they can become contemptible they attract our compassion. Cynical as it is, the film has a certain reverence and humility before the mysteriousness of people's feelings.

Twice only does it offend Western sensibilities: once with—a classic clanger, this—a quick cut from the youngsters kissing, to railway goods-trucks' automatic couplings banging together, and on to piston-rods, whistles, the lot. The idea of mechanical callousness is conveyed so abruptly that the symbol seems merely humourless. The final double poisoning may offend our ideas of dramatic decorum—but, after all, if we really want to understand Japanese art, and the Japanese mind, we will have to sharply modify those ideas sooner or later anyway.

The smooth impassivity of the acting is quite eerie. Medical details—about blood pressure, cerebral hemiplegia—are stated with placid detail. . . . Typical of the film's quiet, cryptic poetry is a cut from a close-up of the daughter, with lipstick, to a close-up of her mother, whose face is made up like a Noh mask, pallid and grey. The film never seemed inspired, and those who are embarrassed by the subject matter are unlikely to get anything from it at all. Others will sense its solidity and tenderness, and respect an unusual, if minor, film. (p. 34)

> *Raymond Durgnat, "'Odd Obsession'" (© copyright Raymond Durgnat 1962; reprinted with permission), in* Films and Filming, *Vol. 8, No. 5, February, 1962, pp. 33-4.*

### JOHN GILLETT

In the case of Kon Ichikawa our knowledge is confined to four films: *The Burmese Harp, Conflagration, Odd Obsessions* and *Fires on the Plain,* only one of which suggests his former preoccupation with bizarre comedy; yet together they reveal a highly contemporary artist tormented by a particularly fiery private hell. Perhaps it is symptomatic that two of the films are concerned with war: as with other Japanese directors of his generation . . . , memories of the war and the shattering implications of the defeat were inevitably carried over into the post-war period. Certainly, *Fires on the Plain* . . . recalls the conflict with ferocious immediacy: no film has recorded the physical and mental degradation of an army in retreat with such obsessive zeal. And yet, as we follow the tubercular Private Tamura, an outcast from his unit, in his terrible journey across the Filippino plains, Ichikawa maintains such a rigour and discipline that the physical horrors appear inevitable and quite without gratuitous sensationalism. . . .

[Harsh] realism is reflected in the characterisation. No cheerful, comic soldiery here; the Japanese army is shown as sly, greedy, treacherous and uneasy about the consequences of surrender and defeat. This laying bare of a national psychosis stems, of course, from the original novel. . . . The adaptation, by Natto Wada (Ichikawa's wife) is extraordinarily faithful to the original except in one important respect—the ending—and it is here that the film seems to falter most. Ichikawa shows Tamura stumbling off across the plain in search of a place "where people live normal lives." As one is never sure if he survives or not, the effect is of a sudden snuffing out, a bleak end to a brutal story. But [the novel's] epilogue describes Tamura's experiences in a mental hospital, his meditations on the meaning of his experiences, his awareness of a God whom he be-

lieved guided him, and his moral victory in never knowingly eating human flesh. The omission of these final thoughts gives a clue to the film's limitations: by concentrating on so much of the book's surface detail, Ichikawa has blurred the strange poetic and spiritual implications of his hero's odyssey.

Curiously enough, this kind of mood was present in *The Burmese Harp.* There is one montage sequence in *Fires on the Plain,* showing Tamura moving through a field of corpses, which immediately recalls the earlier film, yet the feeling is not recaptured. This deliberate emotional detachment is part of Ichikawa's method, and in some ways his strength. When the young boy sets fire to the temple in *Conflagration* we understand his motives, although his innermost personal feelings are kept at a respectable distance. This kind of reticence is common to both Japanese film and literature, but in Ichikawa's case Western influences can also be found in both his style and visual methods. Yet, in *Fires on the Plain,* it seems to me that Ichikawa's attitude towards his hero's experiences is finally too literal and constricted. . . . Ichikawa has given us an authentic vision of hell in what is, by any standards, a remarkable film; nevertheless, it is a pity that he was not able to show his hero's catharsis on the other side of the inferno. (p. 91)

> *John Gillett, "Film Reviews: 'Fires on the Plain' and 'Odd Obsessions'," in* Sight and Sound *(copyright © 1962 by The British Film Institute), Vol. 31, No. 2, Spring, 1962, pp. 91-2.*

### BOSLEY CROWTHER

Never have I seen a more grisly and physically repulsive film than **"Fires on the Plain."** . . . So purposely putrid is it, so full of degradation and death as it recounts the harrowing experiences of a Japanese army straggler in Leyte toward the end of World War II, that I doubt if anyone can sit through it without becoming a little bit ill and losing appetite for the next meal. That's how horrible it is.

To note this is a tribute to its maker, for it is perfectly obvious to me that Kon Ichikawa, the director, intended it to be a brutally realistic contemplation of one aspect of war. Plainly he wanted the spectator not only to see but to feel the progressively worse degradation of a sick soldier cast off in an alien land, released from the discipline of a shattered unit, compelled to forage for himself, bereft of the power of decision, with only an animal instinct to survive.

And he has made these sensations so graphic, so shockingly vivid and real through the slow accumulation of details that are almost too hideous to describe, that when he finally drags his starving hero to a confrontation with the ultimate shame—that of eating the flesh of another human—one is actually almost numbed to that horror. . . .

Mr. Ichikawa's camera is relentless in revealing such things as wounds that ooze blood, piled-up dead bodies, teeth dropping from the hero's head because of malnutrition and a soldier killing a comrade to make a meal. . . .

But, with all the horror in it, there are snatches of poetry, too. Mr. Ichikawa is sensitive to the contrasting beauties of the natural scene. Shots of a church spire above treetops, of birds wheeling in the air, of two young lovers coming into a deserted village (to be shot in reckless terror by our man) stand in delicate juxtaposition to the details of abnormality. If you do go to see this picture, these touches will stun you, too.

Bosley Crowther, "Screen: A Look at the Horror of War," in The New York Times (© 1963 by The New York Times Company; reprinted by permission), September 25, 1963, p. 39.

## TOM MILNE

Kon Ichikawa's *Alone On the Pacific* starts out from what might be the heroic story of a Japanese boy's solo crossing of the Pacific in a small yacht, but as Ichikawa tells it, what emerges is not so much the heroism as the boy's pleasure in getting away from parents, friends, and the trappings of civilisation. . . .

Ichikawa uses his flashbacks beautifully to point his theme. Typical is the one in which the boy quarrels with his father (who wants him to go to university), and storms angrily out of the house; Ichikawa cuts to a tranquil long shot of the yacht becalmed in a sunny sea, before returning to the action on the yacht itself. At the same time, his cunning balance between comedy and drama makes the same point. Where most directors might have tended to establish the comedy first, just to make sure, before getting to the serious stuff (almost certainly falling into false heroics as a result), Ichikawa keeps his comedy mostly for the second half. (p. 10)

Unlike Ichikawa's other studies in obsession, in which one feels that the hero is progressing towards self-realisation at the centre of his obsession—the piles of unburied war dead in *The Burmese Harp*, the burning of the temple in *Conflagration*, the last refuge of cannibalism in *Fires On the Plain*—here one feels that the boy's progress is *away* from the San Francisco he so ardently desires to reach. For San Francisco, like Osaka, is a glare of headlights and traffic and hurrying people, and he doesn't even bother to look when he gets there. Even when he eventually wakens and has time to look around, Ichikawa somehow manages to suggest, it will still mean nothing to him compared with the pleasure of running before the wind on a blue sea, alone on the Pacific. (p. 11)

Tom Milne, "Inside and Outside," in Sight and Sound (copyright © 1965 by The British Film Institute), Vol. 34, No. 1, Winter, 1964-65, pp. 9-11.*

## WILLIAM JOHNSON

*Enjo* [is] a beautifully made and moving film. . . .

Its construction, far from being slack, is an intricate nest of flashbacks. . . . The procedure is not in the least original (there is an obvious and close parallel with [Welles's] *Citizen Kane*), but Ichikawa handles it so deftly that it seems neither artificial nor confusing, and in the end it proves to be justified.

Ichikawa tries a little too hard to squeeze significance out of the characters surrounding Goichi. Some of them are types (though not, to Western eyes, stereotypes), unchanging from scene to scene. . . .

Most of the flaws in the construction and characters of *Enjo* are neutralized by the film's sheer visual integrity. . . . The photography is designed not for virtuosity but for aptness. The compositions within the side Daieiscope format are balanced without seeming calculated. The lighting of the interiors is often low-key without melodramatically pitting pools of light against black shadows. With its directness and control, the visual treatment of *Enjo* reflects the obsessive integrity of Go-ichi himself—yet also, from time to time, it reveals Goichi's pent-up emotions through some breath-taking images. (p. 43)

The film's most unusual images are, not surprisingly, of fire. In the flashback of the father's funeral, his coffin is set on a pyre on a beach. There is a close-up of the coffin as its sides begin to burn; then, with a great crash, the lid bursts open and a huge flame roars up from inside—to Goichi, perhaps, his father's spirit; to the spectator, Goichi's grief. In any event, this searing image helps explain why Goichi decides in the end to set fire to the beloved temple, preferring to destroy it rather than see it desecrated by people to whom it means nothing. (pp. 43-4)

The fire is the supreme moment of eloquence for *Enjo*'s inarticulate hero. This scene points out, in retrospect, how far Ichikawa has made images speak on behalf of Goichi. With the spare, brooding interiors of the monastery and the gray, crowded streets of the nearby city, the calm clarity of the temple and the bright sunlight of the flashback memories, Ichikawa has opened window after window on Goichi's seemingly inaccessible soul. This is his great achievement—that he succeeds in making his neurotic Japanese Buddhist priest both familiar and fascinating. (p. 44)

William Johnson, "Film Reviews: 'Enjo'," in Film Quarterly (copyright 1965 by The Regents of the University of California; reprinted by permission of the University of California Press), Vol. 18, No. 3, Spring, 1965, pp. 42-4.

## CID CORMAN

[In *Tokyo Olympiad*] Ichikawa has made a document of such yielding warmth and variety, of "play" and candor, of "eye" rather than "I," of the heroic in defeat rather than triumph, and triumph shared, as to provide the documentary a new classic.

*Tokyo Olympiad* is a "classic" in at least three ways. First . . . a human document. Ichikawa has shots (and one feels the director behind the photography) of human faces that would satisfy and delight a Cartier-Bresson. The faces touch every continent, every age, and virtually the whole gamut of human emotion. . . .

Secondly, Ichikawa gives the event, the Olympics, more stature than, in fact, it has—by showing what is most human about it, constantly implying man's world. I doubt if *anyone* would otherwise have realized such meaning in such a spectacle. Where [Leni] Riefenstahl glories to the physical machine of man [in her *Olympiad*] Ichikawa lets the image tell the sense and senselessness of human effort. As Donald Richie has pointed out already—to his own surprise—the film is unbelievable funny. . . . Ichikawa *sees* the humor of the rhythms of the walking-race, the craziness of a cycling race whose crowded racers can see each other only contestantwise and not the magnificent countryside through which they hurry. Or the brilliant shot of the crowd *seen* through the blue of speeding cyclists. (p. 39)

Ichikawa needs almost no more wordage than an occasional actual interspersion from event—as simple and shocking as, say, the young blonde American girl in the opening parade turning to one of her colleagues behind and yelling "Shut up!" How much presence is charged in passing. Ichikawa's willingness to record human foibles and even uglinesses within champions is not aimed at "criticism," but at seeing honestly what an individual is, beyond the mass of participation. There are crowds, certainly, and one is never unaware of "numbers"—as in the striking cityscapes, but Ichikawa avoids generalization except through individual performance and instance.

And thirdly, *Tokyo Olympiad* is a classic, for it makes itself felt peculiarly and decisively *as* a film. For it is precisely as a cutting-room labor, as editing, that the film *works*. No doubt, Ichikawa-san had a clear broad sense of what he hoped to make of the mass of footage before he began—but in the very nature of the event, the material, he could not be sure of either conditions or the particular images that would occur. Some shots, telephoto, are incredible in their intimacy and frankness, revelation. And he does not fake his colors; darkness is darkness, dimness is dimness. One feels very little of the slick and much more feels care and thought at every point.

Ichikawa doesn't stick to actual chronology either, and he makes no effort at giving equal space to each event. Some events are represented by the quickest image notation, and some are more extended. This was to be expected—but the briefest image is suggestive and lovely and his longer passages justify themselves in terms of the whole. Often he picks up details one would not anticipate: the shoes, the headgear, the key-point of body-tension—whether the shotput pressed under the chin, the bent legs of a swimmer about to plunge, or a weightlifter's feet and torso and cry. He has an uncanny ear for the "right" sound. . . . He grasps eloquently the grace and proportion of the gymnast and blends the images of one performer and another until we feel there is only one contestant, ourselves. And all this is done so tacitly that one realizes a great deal almost without realizing it.

The marathon is used as the final focal sequence of the entire occasion, and justly so, for Ichikawa has tracked the spirit animating the Games into his vital simple single figure, and the face of Abebe Bikila, the Ethiopian runner, becomes a torch. But how unobtrusively Ichikawa has guided us to the event (one almost believes he *wrote* the sequence). For he has not only opened the film with the light being carried on foot, hand to hand, from Greece through Asia (shades of Aeschylus!), but he has focussed individually on one of the losing athletes from unknown Chad and has projected ably and gently the young man's pride, isolation, and aspirations, frustrated utterly despite intense effort. *But*—when Bikila wins the marathon one feels that the young man from Chad has had, in that event, his triumph—as we have had, too.

Such statements are at the heart of this film, and although Ichikawa has had inklings of such feelings in his work before, never have they been shown on so ample and exacting a scale. To have made this film, and one made so largely in the editing (although the photography is most distinguished), cannot have failed to enlarge the maker's capacity and should require of him new dimension to draw on for future work. And for others, too, I hope. So that what was the very epitome of the competitive becomes rather the epitome of human *relation*, of fellow-feeling—and not in any callow or shallow way, but in the fulness and take of event. (pp. 39-40)

*Cid Corman, "'Tokyo Olympiad'," in Film Comment (copyright © 1965 by Lorien Productions, Inc.; all rights reserved), Vol. 3, No. 3, Summer, 1965, pp. 38-40.*

### JOHN GILLETT

Near the beginning of Kon Ichikawa's film of the Tokyo Olympic Games [*Tokyo Olympiad 1964*], a great iron builder's weight is seen crashing into a half-demolished building as the Olympic Stadium begins to grow. The tone is set: this is to be a film about violent physical activity; though not quite a hymn to straining muscles and national pride. Sport for me, Ichikawa seems to say, comprises graceful bodies in motion plus a kind of bizarre unnaturalness almost akin to vaudeville and the circus. And it is to Ichikawa's credit that he manages to alternate these concepts without any obvious changing of gears, looking at the events with a hundred camera eyes which seem like one, and always seeking the involving, close-up view.

Such is the sustained beauty of the filming that it is tempting to stop and make a catalogue of exceptional moments, or relish the way Ichikawa has made the torch carrying sequence seem 'directed' as in a story film, culminating in the great shot of planes weaving the Olympic emblem in a sky spattered with pigeons and with the symbolic flame blazing in the foreground. His unit seemed to have everything, notably a marvellous range of telephoto lenses; but all the technical know-how and equipment in the world need a master to control them, and a close look at individual sequences shows that Ichikawa's genius lies in the strict selectivity of the material. . . . [True] to the great Japanese film tradition, Ichikawa is not afraid to take an event to pieces: thus, the women's hurdles are shown first at ordinary speed, then we flashback to the preparations and see the whole thing again in slow motion, shot from one set-up and silent except for a shattering percussive clap when a hurdle is knocked over.

Until we saw *Alone on the Pacific,* it was difficult to believe that Ichikawa's early career included satirical comedies and cartoons. Now, in the Olympics film, one somehow remembers Horie pottering about his little boat and coping as best he can. This is the same ironic, slightly lugubrious artist's eye which now watches the Russian weight throwers' rhythmic tics. . . . Each viewer will find his own favourite bits of humorous observation. . . .

[Leni Riefenstahl's *Olympiad*] packs a greater voltage of excitement which can still set an audience cheering; Ichikawa's is simply more human without being mawkish, not least in the final parade where the swaying mass of competitors merges imperceptibly into the throng of spectators and one feels there is perhaps one world after all. At [the Cannes Film Festival], Ichikawa ruefully reported the misgivings of the Japanese Olympics Committee, who would obviously have preferred a newsreel to an artist's personal view. "They even asked whether I could re-shoot some of it, but I was able to reply truthfully that circumstances prevented it." And how lucky for the cinema.

*John Gillett, "Film Reviews: 'Tokyo Olympiad 1964'," in Sight and Sound (copyright © 1965 by The British Film Institute), Vol. 34, No. 4, Autumn, 1965, p. 199.*

### JOHN COLEMAN

[Awkward], idiotic incidents are characteristic of the films of Kon Ichikawa [and] provide a sort of subliminal signature. They erupt in the tremendous decorum of Japanese manners, rather like small volcanoes, threatening stability, poise, elegance. Their effect is as strange and thunderous as more celebrated items (the cannibalism in *Fires on the Plain,* for instance), because they endanger a whole traditional code. . . . Ichikawa is too Japanese not to be preoccupied with the forms of his country, but a part of him appears to be concerned with sending them up. . . . [In the unpleasant film *Punishment Room*] Ichikawa looks as if he admires the causeless rebels. In a way, one can hardly blame him: their elders are so feeble and venal, and presumably that's his point.

The same film proffers a fine instance or two of Ichikawa's peculiar home-brew of comedy and tragedy. Rape conventionally offends, but the tough kid's arm shakes terribly as he pours out a drugged drink for his prey; and when he and his chum hump the girls back to a flat, the lift has broken down. Reluctantly one comes round to the Ichikawan view: one thing at a time. The preliminaries here *are* funny, even if the outcome is to be sordid. I haven't seen *Kagi* . . . since I rather dismissively reviewed it in these columns, but I suspect I'd find more in this 'essay in oriental damaroidery'—my former phrase—today. A more extended acquaintance with Ichikawa's films eases one into a firmer sense of Japan: he conveys more of that weird, polite, brutal, hierarchic society than the gentler Ozu or the Mizoguchi whose investment was so steadily in the past. . . .

What is hard to make out is how much one likes the films for themselves as art devotedly drawn from life, and how much one's interest is attached by the very strangeness of the manners and humours on display. Early Ichikawas like *Poo-San* (1955), based on a popular comic-strip character, and *A Billionaire* (1954) really move off in all directions, flailing generally at social disorders of the day. The 'timid, honest' hero of the second one could be a kind of Nipponese Eddie Bracken. . . .

If such fragmented tragi-comedies were truly representative of Ichikawa's body of work, then there would be no cause for an [Ichikawa film] season. But in 1954 he made *The Heart* as well. This is a patient exploration of a difficult situation: a husband with homosexual inclinations has married his wife mainly because the male friend he fancied was proposing to ask for her hand himself. The friend commits suicide: the husband lives down the years, a guilty recluse. A young student turns up, the husband takes to him as he had to his dead friend, it's to him that he entrusts his terrible secret before killing himself in turn. This sombre, devious stuff, drawn from a novel by Soseki Natsume, *sounds* more like book than film. What is so remarkable is the tact with which Ichikawa has transferred it to celluloid: he uses flashback effortlessly, his people's faces stand in for whole paragraphs, the technique—slow tracks, quick cuts—stays unobtrusive.

Sometimes, in fact, Ichikawa seems to be over-enamoured of technique. . . . In the cloying *Being Two Isn't Easy* (1962), a child's-eye view of the adult world, he allows himself a few moments of animation (a moon as banana and boat) which ring false in the context, much as his expressionist sets at the close of *The Men of Tohoku* do. It's the old trouble of effects drawing too much attention to themselves; the work they might be doing is supplanted by one's consciousness of them. I think the same criticism may fairly be levelled against the very beautiful *Bonchi* (1960). . . . Some of the charming compositions and overhead shots here . . . invite applause rather than involvement. It's as if Ichikawa, who is known to sketch out his incidents and angles pretty thoroughly before shooting begins, were determined to prove how lovely, even appealing, the worst meannesses and horrors can be. He has a point, but I find it hard to accommodate. *Fires on the Plain* disturbed me by going, as it were, aesthetic about degradation. Even *The Burmese Harp*, the magnificent film which first brought Ichikawa to world attention, has its posed and picturesque irrelevancies. . . .

[Yet Ichikawa] is far more than an illustrator, English-style. His range . . . is incredible: I don't see why he should resent being called eclectic. He emerges as a great, dark talent, capable of infusing an experience of childhood, a cold look at delinquency, a tale of old man's impotence, a study of matriarchy, a cartoon-strip chain of calamities, with his own unsettling brand of comic pessimism. He is probably Japan's severest clandestine critic.

*John Coleman, "Ichikawa," in* New Statesman *(© 1966 The Statesman & Nation Publishing Co. Ltd.), Vol. 72, No. 1848, August 12, 1966, p. 236.*

**TOM MILNE**

First impressions can be misleading, and there is something very wrong with the image of Kon Ichikawa arrived at mainly by way of *The Burmese Harp* [1956], *Conflagration* [1958] and *Fires on the Plain* [1959]—as a man obsessed by human suffering and expressing his pity through a series of long, slow, painful, humanistic affirmations. Ichikawa is obsessed by suffering all right, but he is not a humanist in any modern sense of the word. . . . [The] humanistic definition imposes much too narrow limits, and could only grapple with a film like *The Key* [1959] by sweeping its almost mockingly flippant final sequence tidily away under the carpet as "silly". . . .

[The Ichikawa hero] is essentially an outsider, a man struggling to escape from the world in which he lives, rather than to change it or even accept it as he finds it. He may seem to take the sins of the world on his shoulders, but less to atone for them than to protect himself. (p. 185)

[Ichikawa's work often recalls the relish for the horrors of physical decay which marked the Jacobean dramatists. In Ichikawa relish and pain] go hand in hand. It is a landscape of anarchism, dissolution and decay from which the heroes of *The Burmese Harp, Conflagration* and *Fires on the Plain* recoil in anguish, and which recurs throughout Ichikawa's work wherever his raw material is sympathetic (and sometimes where it is not). In these three films, Ichikawa's involvement with the anguish is too deep to allow him to draw back, to set his sense of the futility of his characters' struggles to escape their dilemma in a proper perspective; but in his more characteristic, and perhaps greater films—*The Key, The Revenge of Yukinojo,* and (in a slightly different way) *The Heart*—the anguish and the mockery are inextricably mingled. . . .

Even more than *The Key, The Revenge of Yukinojo* (1963) conjures up the aura of the Jacobeans, with a grisly revenge plot, comic sub-plot and ironic final twist which might have flowed entire from the pen of either [John] Webster or [Cyril] Tourneur. The actor Yukinojo, a female impersonator, is in a way the perfect Ichikawa hero. As a female impersonator . . . , he has withdrawn from his proper place in society; but when he is forced by convention to revenge his parents, who were driven to madness and ruin by a triumvirate of scheming businessmen when he was a mere child, he is called upon to reassume a place he can no longer fill. Ichikawa plays happily, and brilliantly, with the paradox of the twittering, trembling hero who suddenly sheds his disguise to close with his enemy, delicately and victoriously parrying the latter's sword-thrusts with a tiny dagger. . . .

Visually, the film is one of Ichikawa's most striking successes, obviously owing much to Kabuki, but also oddly reminiscent of modern-style Elizabethan staging in its use of bare stages, black drapes and simple structural shapes to allow the director to indulge his favourite composition of a single figure picked out against some architectural detail. Most of the extraordinarily effective exteriors look unashamedly stagey, perfectly calculated to evoke the sort of no-man's-land between two worlds in which the main action takes place. . . . (p. 186)

One would have thought that [*Bonchi* (1960), a] story of a young man oppressed by a society in which women wield the power and demand daughters, while he can only produce sons from a variety of wives and mistresses, would have appealed strongly to [Ichikawa]. Yet the film is lackadaisically done, with a stylish but flabby central stretch. The beginning is scathingly brilliant. . . . Though beautifully designed and constructed, the film as a whole somehow betrays a lack of involvement.

The same thing is true of *Her Brother* (1960) and *Punishment Room* (1956), the first a rather weepy tale of a spinsterish girl whose adored younger brother dies of tuberculosis, the second a cut-to-pattern addition to Japan's juvenile delinquency cycle. *Her Brother* is extremely good of its kind, *Punishment Room* is less so, though containing some brilliant sequences which lift it out of the rut. . . . In both cases Ichikawa contrives to turn the principal character into one of his typical outsiders: the girl in *Her Brother* being cut off from pursuing her own life and marrying by her singleminded devotion to her wayward brother, the young delinquent of *Punishment Room* by his anarchic refusal to admit that he belongs either to society or to its outlaws. By Ichikawa standards, however, they are undistinguished works, although here and there one does find welcome flashes of his avid mockery. . . .

Superficially, both [*Poo-San* (1953) and *A Billionaire* (1954)] bear out Ichikawa's early reputation as the Japanese Frank Capra. Their heroes are simple, honest, little men, and the timid tax-collector of *A Billionaire* even wages a single-handed war against tax evasion, pitting his naïve honesty against national cunning. The difference is that this humble tax-collector, and the ineffectual mathematics teacher of *Poo-San,* also live under the shadow of their dread of war. . . .

It is easy to trace a direct line of descent from *A Billionaire* and *Poo-San* to *The Key* and *The Revenge of Yukinojo.* The other, more lyrical, more "socially responsible" line descending from the trio of war films, seems to end up a curious byway with *Hakai (The Sin,* 1962). Here, Ichikawa delves into Hollywood problem picture territory with a story, set in 1904, of a pariah boy who is a member of Japan's outcast tribe, and whose tribulations are an exact replica of those experienced by the Negro who passes for white. . . . What makes the film so distinctive is Ichikawa's style, which lifts the film on to the same plane of brooding torment as Dostoievsky's novels. . . . (p. 188)

Ichikawa keeps so tight a grip on his narrative that it never sags until the boy reaches the point of no return, and must discover himself or be discovered. In a protractedly tearful sequence, he confesses before the assembled children in his class, and it isn't long before everybody in the room is weeping in an agony of pity, remorse and despair. Someone once remarked of Hemingway that, like all tough men, he leaned so far over back wards to avoid sentimentality that he fell head over heels right into it. Exactly the same is true of Ichikawa when he drops his guard of mockery to become completely solemn. . . .

Perhaps, though, it is simply a question of finding the right material; for his earlier *The Heart* (1955), another Dostoievsky

subject of brooding torment, manages very successfully to avoid the trap of sentimentality. This, reduced to its essentials, is simply the story of a man who, obsessed by a sense of guilt for the death of his closest friend, gradually withdraws further and further into himself until he finally commits suicide. . . . If the film were not set in the years just before the First World War, one would be tempted to suggest that there hangs over it that shadow of nuclear destruction which is never far from Ichikawa's work. As it is, all the various strands of the film lead to the same point—the extinction of life. . . . (p. 189)

*Tom Milne, "The Skill beneath the Skin," in* Sight and Sound *(copyright © 1966 by The British Film Institute), Vol 35, No. 4, Autumn, 1966, pp. 185-89.*

## PHILIP STRICK

The reconstruction of a single-handed voyage from Osaka to San Francisco . . . seems an unlikely choice for anything but a formal doumentary film. As one might expect, however, Ichikawa's *Alone on the Pacific* . . . makes a far richer meal of it than this. In his hands, the inevitable flashbacks to the early difficulties undergone on land by the would-be voyager, Horie, become as vital to the film's theme as is the struggle with the sea itself. The impersonal resistance of the Pacific, in fact, is shown to be a relatively manageable challenge. . . .

Ichikawa is concerned here, as usual, with the fine distinction between individualism and self-centredness. Without belittling his hero's achievement, he affectionately emphasises Horie's clumsy and boorish qualities. . . . (p. 145)

[Horie's] journey is across weaknesses and doubts—and at its close the voyager reclines exhausted in an upholstered armchair against a wall of blazing, clinical whiteness. Clear links, then, with for example *Fires on the Plain* and *An Actor's Revenge,* although neither the doomed, tottering soldier and his resistance to cannibalism, nor the sensitive Yuki and his tragic resignation to the need for murder, have the robust resilience of the introspective sailor who seems indestructible even when swamped by the fiercest of typhoons. Of all Ichikawa's self-questioning heroes, Horie always manages to look as if he'll produce the right answers somehow.

One need hardly mention that the film is, of course, beautifully made. What is particularly striking is the effortlessness of it all, the fluency with which Ichikawa describes each stage of the voyage. He films from all angles, including helicopter shots from above underwater shots from below, yet there is never a false note—not even in the cabin scenes which presumably were shot in a studio. For all the storm sequences, what is conveyed most strongly and typically by Yoshihiro Yamazaki's brilliant photography is a dream-like sense of peace, with the tiny boat coasting along in sunlight while its passenger fiddles with a kettle or hangs his washing out to dry. By comparison, the flashbacks have a visible gloom, filmed in the dark recesses of the father's factory of the claustrophobic shadows of the family home—although these are perhaps the scenes that Ichikawa handles best. . . . (pp. 145-46)

Ichikawa sets [his characters] out across his vast screen with unfaltering visual flair; in particular the scenes at the workshop, beginning with an oppressive overhead shot, show father and son drifting further and further apart until they are at opposite sides of the frame; while the arguments around the table at home are a lesson in what can be done with deep-focus staging.

If **Alone on the Pacific** makes no claim to be Ichikawa's greatest film, it remains a delightful demonstration of the director's extraordinary versatility. (p. 146)

> Philip Strick, "Film Reviews: 'Alone on the Pacific'," in Sight and Sound (copyright © 1967 by The British Film Institute), Vol. 36, No. 3, Summer, 1967, pp. 145-46.

## DAVID WILLIAMS

Despite its period setting **An Actor's Revenge (Yukinojo Henge)** seems to have been an exception to some [generalizations on Japanese cinema]. Even among the more sympathetic reviews in this country a predominant impression was one of remoteness. . . . The reluctance expressed by some people about taking the film on its own terms might almost have resulted from the conviction that the life of the sexually ambiguous actor in the early nineteenth century was a phenomenon of modern Japan—that familiarity was necessary for understanding. Whereas strangeness is part of what Ichikawa saw in it too, however local the history. If his treatment of this strange hero and his predicament is sympathetic, then that is the point. (p. 4)

Critics seemed to discuss the idiosyncratic visual style of the **Revenge** only as a curious decorative adjunct to the story, whereas I would rather say it is the key to the film and in a way part of its theme. . . . What is inescapable in the **Revenge** is its self-consciously spectacular appearance and structure full of tricks and jokes and all in stylishly rich and flamboyant colour. It is also under the kind of total control by the director one associates with an animated cartoon. (p. 5)

The thematic as distinct from stylistic importance of theatre is of course explicit, and deserves careful attention. The film presumably derived the idea of play upon play from the novel [on which it is based], or the book can have supplied very little. To begin with, the whole story of revenge, love and suicide is the kind of melodrama that was the staple of Kabuki. Then the structure of the film narrative isolates Yuki's plot as if in a play. The film opens with people discussing the new company arrived from Osaka. Then comes Yukinojo's first appearance, on stage as a woman, staggering pitifully through falling snow. As she falls we cease to hear the weird intonations of the Kabuki performer, and the sound-track refocuses on the actor's inner voice as he sees (and so do we in the inset) the murderers of his parents in the audience, and begins his plot. Throughout this sequence Ichikawa adjusts the relative 'reality' of the actor's two situations. If anything, the stage snow looks more like real snow at those moments when we are hearing from the actor's own inner self. We are surely to see Yuki's stage role here as related to his real one, but concentrating deceptively on his lonely suffering rather than on his unnerving capabilities as a righter of wrong. It is the kind of scene the Lady Namiji is to play for real later on. It ends with the entrance of an old man along the gangway that runs at stage level through the audience in Kabuki theatres. But as if to underline the real importance of what is passing on stage, Ichikawa here blots out from the picture the audience we should otherwise see. The great striped curtain is pulled across the stage, neatly filling the cinemascope screen to the sound of applause. (pp. 9-11)

Some problems in the film's style remain. Perhaps it is only the usual concession of period films to modernity that allows Namiji and Ohatsu a decidedly twentieth-century, even 'Hollywood-Japanese' look. More important is the music. To talk in terms of Japanese and Western here may be inappropriate since it is clear that what we think of as Western-style music is just as familiar to a Japanese. Having acknowledged this, there is no simpler way to describe the film's music than to say there are two or three kinds: some traditional-sounding Japanese (of the kind useful for underlining action); some, a kind of cool jazz gently backing the secret exploits of Yuki and the thieves; and some lush, sentimental, orchestral strings reserved for the scenes between Yuki and Namiji. It is the last kind that presents a difficulty. When Yuki is clearly putting on an act for the girl, the presence of that music is ironic. Later, when Yuki gives less away to the audience, it might be logical to suppose that the same music is meant to tell us he is still faking. But that seems over simple, especially since the music, however mushy, only derives a clear meaning from the context. We are left with the same love scene but without the explanation this time. The difficulties experienced by directors who want to control the amount and kind of music in their films are familiar, so that all this which looks so deliberate could be accidental after all, but if so it is out of character with the rest. (p. 13)

Critics' phrases such as 'The Skull Beneath the Skin' and 'cutting a little nearer the bone that one expects' look like responses to the layered world of the **Revenge** where games are played with expectations. But it seems ill-advised to abstract a 'meaning' where the form and very material of the film are so much involved. It is as much as anything a brilliant and funny entertainment. The relativity of the real and the staged, of actor and role, is expressive of the many uncertainties of sympathy and obligation, but that is not the only reason for its presence. The actor's dilemmas, although pointed up by his doubleness, are hardly simplified by it. One might say our interest is in watching a man coping with difficulties, some inside and some outside himself, which are reflected for us in the very presentation of the story. (pp. 14-15)

> David Williams, "'An Actor's Revenge'," in Screen (© The Society for Education in Film and Television 1970), Vol. 11, No. 2, March-April, 1970, pp. 3-15.

## TOM MILNE

With **The Wanderers** [**Matatabi**], happily, the evident need for an internationally saleable gimmick had led Ichikawa to a . . . congenial model in the Hong Kong kung-fu phenomenon, from which he borrows not the 'martial art' itself, but the blandly invincible hero and the nonstop string of gymnastically stylised fights. The notion of a battle in which hordes are formally defeated without a blow being noticeably struck obviously appeals to Ichikawa's sense of the absurd; and he battens gleefully on to the formula, with swords flashing and striking apparently of their own volition out of the darkness as in **An Actor's Revenge,** and punctuating shots of spurting blood now and again indicating that even games have their consequences. (pp. 55-6)

With its gradual revelation of formalities to be observed, and the minutely calculated variations in the levels of hospitality offered in different houses (as well as assorted social reactions from the guests), this whole opening segment is vintage Ichikawa. Then follows a rather statutory but pleasing flurry of action—one battle taking place in a closed room, another in a mist-swathed field at dawn—since the toseinin must fight for their host, if required, after accepting his hospitality: a curious mixture of hieratic Japanese gestures and Hong Kong knockabout, of comic-strip formality and bloody brutality in which, as the narrator observes, the main point is to cross swords rather than fight to the death, but in which deaths unfortunately will occur, incurring great expense since each side hires mercenaries in order to put up a more imposing front.

After this the plot catches up on Ichikawa, and the film plods rather laboriously through dull acres. . . . Gradually, however, one realises that the familiar Ichikawa trap is beginning to close, and the film gets on top of itself again with a quizzical questioning of social pressures. Motivated purely by his society's conception of duty into killing his father, the young hero finds himself outcast as a patricide; motivated purely by pity for the girl . . . , he takes her with him in his escape, and is forced to sell her into slavery in order to survive. Outlawed even by outlaws, morally cut off from his friends . . . , there is only one place left for him: on the rubbish dump. . . . (p. 56)

> Tom Milne, ''Film Reviews: 'The Wanderers','' in
> Sight and Sound (copyright © 1974 by The British
> Film Institute), Vol. 43, No. 1, Winter, 1973-74, pp.
> 55-6.

## WILLIAM JOHNSON

There is no obvious claim to depth or originality in Kon Ichikawa's 1973 film, *The Wanderers (Matatabi)*. Set in rural Japan in the turbulent years of the early nineteenth century, it draws on many elements of the samurai film. But its total effect is much more: comic, elegant, mordant, heartbreaking, breathtaking. It's easy to appreciate the technical mastery behind the film—an almost flawless sense of timing and imagery. It's less easy to see just how this criss-cross of moods attains such cumulative power. . . .

In a directorial career that spans more than a quarter of a century and some fifty films, Ichikawa has shifted unpredictably between stylization and naturalism and between gravity and offbeat humor, often incorporating both opposites in the same film. Unlike other well-known Japanese directors such as Ozu, Kurosawa, and even the much younger Oshima, Ichikawa cannot be associated with a single dominant tone. (p. 16)

Any simple curve in Ichikawa's development can be abstracted only from a zigzag of continual explorations. He has always been willing to take chances, to try out new mixtures of stylization and naturalism, of gravity and humor, in percentages that run almost the whole range from zero to one hundred.

There is also a less elusive continuity in Ichikawa's work. Nearly all of his films can be found to revolve around a recurring set of themes. . . . Many of Ichikawa's protagonists [are] innocents, little men, misfits, outsiders, chickens surrounded by foxes. Mr. Pu in *Pu-San* establishes the prototype. (pp. 17-18)

One reason for the richness of *The Wanderers* is that it centers around three different innocents. They are *toseinin*—peasant imitations of masterless samurai who wander from village to village, ready to work or fight for anyone who will give them food and lodging. Ichikawa does not try to make them superficially distinct from one another, like Lester's Musketeers; in fact, the three are physically quite similar to walk and talk in much the same way, so that their appearance quickly establishes them as an ''all for one'' trio. But Ichikawa soon draws out unmistakable differences. . . . The film gains considerable depth from this double image of the *toseinin*, as they respond

both corporately and individually to the turbulent events around them.

I may have given the impression thus far that Ichikawa's interest centers on rather freakish people in rather freakish circumstances. But most of his characters seem unusual only because they lack the veneer of sophistication with which most of us mask our naiveties and obsessions—and which Ichikawa removes in order to focus more clearly on human realities. At the same time he chooses circumstances that will throw light on *social* realities. If the foreground events sometimes look bizarre, it's because they stem from an all-too-familiar tension in the background.

This is the second element in Ichikawa's recurring set of themes: an environment which threatens his characters, buffets them, takes them by surprise. Most of Ichikawa's films are set amid the breakdown of some kind of moral, social, political, or cultural order. Beliefs, customs, and laws are called into question; they shift, collide, collapse. Sometimes the process may be muted and subtle, as in *Kagi,* which implies rather than underlines the breakdown of traditional family relationships. In other films collapse is explicit: *Fires on the Plain* hinges both on the defeat of militaristic Japan and on the breakdown of moral and human values among desperate survivors.

Ichikawa does not reduce his protagonists to passive figures in a panorama of collapse, any more than he reduces his filmic environment to a backcloth for larger-than-life characters; he fuses the two elements into a dynamic whole. In *The Wanderers* he does this with magisterial ease. Dispensing with ''establishing shots'' of the world his wanderers live in, he follows their adventures and misadventures in such a way that the larger picture steadily accumulates. I cannot recall seeing any other film which so brilliantly combines microcosm and macrocosm. (pp. 18-19)

[In *The Wanderers*], he gives an ironic, detached view of the foreground action. The fights, for example, are stylized, sometimes evoking a rhythmic dance, sometimes the flicker of an abstract film, but never settling into any formalist rigidity. This is the secret of Ichikawa's stylization: he takes it just far enough to achieve great visual clarity, to open up the viewer's eye and imagination.

Thus the story of *The Wanderers* emerges in brief, graphic, sometimes abrupt vignettes. At first the adventures of the *toseinin* are linear, and shared. . . . But [then the] simple plot breaks up into apparently unconnected subplots. (p. 19)

Ichikawa plays brilliantly with one of the stock elements of the Japanese period film . . . : the conflict between two different obligations, or between obligation and desire. Normally such a conflict would dominate the action; in *The Wanderers* it seems to drop out of nowhere, allowing Genta little time for prior soul-searching. . . . The real conflict that Genta faces goes beyond any obvious duties or desires and involves the whole meaning of his way of life. (pp. 19-20)

*The Wanderers* may sound like a gloomy film relieved only by the impersonality of Ichikawa's style. But this is doubly wrong. Much of the content is not gloomy at all, and the visual clarity of Ichikawa's style often intensifies the viewer's emotional response. There is considerable warmth in the relations of the major characters. The solidarity of the *toseinin*, however shaky, is real. . . .

Ichikawa focuses sharply on the satisfactions which remain amid all the instability: not only food and sex but also the pleasurable awareness of being alive, as reflected by shots of the *toseinin* walking against a backdrop of misty mounts, or through a forest flecked with snow, or past a tranquil pond with an expanding ring of ripples. Such scenes are commonplace in Japanese films . . . , but instead of lingering on them, Ichikawa summons them up briefly and dynamically, stressing the moment's joy without its melancholy.

Although *The Wanderers* contains hardly any camera movements and no flashy cutting . . . , it crackles throughout with dynamism which sets it quite apart. Sometimes the compositions are oblique offbeat: Ichikawa shows us only half the ripples in the pond, or sets up a fortune, chopping off a man's finger with the visual elegance of a jeweler cutting a precious stone. More often he gives an equivalent twist to the structure and rhythm of the film: he cuts in on some scenes in mid-action and pares away explanations so that the full grasp of a scene may be delayed; and he either omits linking scenes or reduces them to brief vignettes, letting the film skip elusively through time and space. While these devices never approach the point of obfuscation, they help keep the viewer slightly on edge and off balance and thus induce . . . alertness and concentration. . . .

Ichikawa's dynamism springs most of all from his mating of opposites (stylization and naturalism, humor and gravity) without upsetting the film's formal and emotional balance. Often in *The Wanderers* the opposites appear together, creating dense and vivid signs. . . . (p. 20)

In all of his films—and with dazzling success in *The Wanderers*—he sets out to bring the struggle of life into the sharpest possible focus. He embraces both the general and the particular, conjuring up formal elegance without betraying the sheer grittiness of the phenomenal world. He refuses to exaggerate either the good or the bad of mankind and of society; and he also refuses to imply that the bad is susceptible either to a panacea (the activist's temptation) or no cure at all (the escapist's). Yet he also triumphs over the occupational hazard of the moderate, who may end up defined only by the extremes he is trying to avoid. The most positive of moderates, Ichikawa works from the conviction that nothing is more important than to *see*. . . .

*The Wanderers* is a tour de force that looks simple. In it, the polar opposites that have marked all of Ichikawa's work meet in a consummate point of balance. In it, too, this sixty-year-old filmmaker has achieved a remarkable fusion of technical mastery and creative vigor. It is a film to be seen and vividly remembered by anyone who cares about the camera, people, society, or survival. (p. 21)

> *William Johnson, "Ichikawa and the Wanderers,"* in Film Comment (copyright © 1975 by The Film Society of Lincoln Center; all rights reserved), Vol. 11, No. 5, September-October, 1975, pp. 16-21.

**JOAN MELLEN**

After [Masaki Koboyashi's] *The Human Condition,* the two most important Japanese films about the Second World War were Kon Ichikawa's *The Harp of Burma* and *Fires on the Plain*. . . . In making two such different films on the same subject—the horrors of war experienced by besieged and abandoned Japanese soldiers—Ichikawa reveals his own lack of a consistent point of view or personal commitment. Ichikawa's anti-war films are the opposite of Kobayashi's, whose films may be more didactic but reveal a much more coherent and persuasive understanding of history.

Ichikawa's anti-war works are far less intellectually serious than *The Human Condition*. They take their coloration from the novels from which they are adapted and from the personalities of both Ichikawa and his screenwriter wife, Natto Wada. Ichikawa has always willfully insisted that the ideas expressed in his films are of no particular consequence. We are apt, therefore, to discover among his works, ostensibly dealing with the same subject, inconsistencies of philosophy. Ichikawa's uneasiness with value judgments has led to his fondness for making films about athletic events such as *Tokyo Olympiad* (1965), *Youth,* and a segment of the international production about the Munich Olympic games, *Visions of Eight* (1972). As Ichikawa says at the end of *Youth,* seemingly speaking of high-school baseball tournaments but actually revealing as well his aesthetic credo, "the thing is the game itself, not who wins." What his films "say" is of less concern to Ichikawa than the way it is said, a philosophy that has sometimes led him to make films, like *Youth* itself, magnificent in their technique, but shallow and devoid of any serious content. Thus we can find among Ichikawa's *oeuvre* the lyrical *Harp of Burma,* a sentimental if often beautiful whitewash of the Japanese presence in Southeast Asia, and the fiercely expressionistic *Fires on the Plain,* a film unrelenting in its criticism of the Japanese army and bitter in its denunciation of official imperviousness toward the sick and wounded during the last days of the war. (pp. 189-90)

In contrast to the paeans of Ozu are Kon Ichikawa's biting assessments of the Japanese family's suffocating, insidious emasculation of the individual. Of all Japanese directors, Ichikawa affects the most aesthetic distance from his subject matter. But much more than in anti-war films like *The Harp of Burma* or *Fires on the Plain* are the characters in Ichikawa's films about the Japanese family treated as though they were insects beneath a clinician's microscope. Ichikawa would anatomize that sanctified institution of the family as if, by observing its workings as he would the tentacles of an insect, he could free us all of its deadly grasp. In Ichikawa's bitter satires about the Japanese family there is rarely a character wholesome enough to be entrusted with the director's point of view. . . . Stifled by the family, Ichikawa's people fall into two categories; they are either weak and puerile or strong and domineering. Both types are treated as equally repulsive. For Ichikawa, in the best and most honest of his films, the Japanese family seems to possess a particular capacity to cultivate the most unsavory qualities of human nature. (p. 331)

[The] Japanese family is viewed by Ichikawa as a nurturer of madness and a cultivator of the dark places of the human soul. Repression—politely if inaccurately termed *enryo,* or "reserve," and justified by Japanese as permitting the emotional privacy of the other—also breeds its opposite, as Ichikawa well knows. The more circumscribed expected behavior becomes, the more likely it is to produce its opposite: actions violent, perverse, meaningless, and destructive, both of the self and of others. In the finest of Ichikawa's "home dramas" the family closes in unrelentingly on the individual. (p. 332)

In *Bonchi* Ichikawa focuses on a matriarchal family, through which he observes the absurdities of the family system in general. In particular, in *Bonchi* Ichikawa finds the Japanese family plagued by an egomaniacal drive, above all other considerations, to perpetuate itself. The leaders of this family, a grandmother and her daughter, a mother, demand of their one scion, who happens, unfortunately for him, to be a male, that as soon as he reaches manhood he marry and produce a daughter. This reversal of traditional expectations, in which sons are demanded with no less hysteria, allows Ichikawa with sly humor equally to satirize the absurdity of the patriarchy in Japan. In *Bonchi* a granddaughter must be produced so that power in the family can be continued through the female line. The husband of this daughter would be adopted into the family, the couple living within the matrilineal household. But Ichikawa's real point is that the institution of the family, whether dominated by men or women, places its own survival ahead of the needs and feelings of individuals. (p. 335)

In *Ten Dark Women* (*Kuroi Junin no Onna,* 1961) Ichikawa again attacks the myth of the supportive Japanese family, this time in a black comedy about a married man who has nine mistresses. The women eventually form an alliance against this weak man, who has proven to be so capable of using them all. They band together, plotting his murder, and gather at a party where his wife, in the presence of all, will shoot him. She, however, plans only to pretend to kill him so as to keep him exclusively for herself, a game to which he, knowing himself defeated, assents. Ichikawa and screenwriter Natto Wada thus satirize and condemn the unlimited prerogatives afforded the Japanese male. Part of their argument is that the Japanese man, having been emasculated precisely by his unlimited sexual license, is now unworthy of the privileges afforded him by male-chauvinist Japanese society. (p. 338)

In Ichikawa's films there is the pervasive sense that most things will remain forever unknowable, impenetrable to our inquiries. Particularly mystifying is the attraction between men and women. Ichikawa would no more think of asking why the ten women want this man than he would how the old grandmother in *Bonchi* became the kind of person who would be willing to go to any lengths of cruelty. And for Ichikawa, knowing the origins of our motives—even if we could—would not help us because we cannot change anyway. The miseries of the Japanese family appear to be so much more endemic in his films than in those of any other Japanese director because of Ichikawa's predilection to see both social life and human nature as immutable. Such a view allows him brilliantly to explore the perversities nurtured by obsessional personalities, like the daughter in *Younger Brother* or Mizoguchi in *Conflagration,* although it sometimes considerably weakens the range of his art.

Because Ichikawa is so skeptical about the viability of our holding for long any convictions at all, he refuses to confine himself exclusively to the role of opponent of the Japanese family system. Thus could the same director also make a semi-sentimental, pro-family film like *Being Two [Years Old] Isn't Easy* (*Watashi wa Nisai,* 1962). Ichikawa has termed this film his "hymn to life," created "in the hope of making a little imprint on my heart," indicating that, although it may contain some satiric elements, in this film he is also offering positive values in which he personally believes. The endorsement of the family in *Being Two Isn't Easy* reflects, Ichikawa says, his own point of view.

Actually, *Being Two Isn't Easy* is an uneven film reflecting an ambivalence within Ichikawa regarding the Japanese family. . . . The first part brilliantly and satirically exposes how children's personalities are distorted by parents' imposing on them their own needs, a theme perfectly in keeping with the entire Ichikawa canon. But instead of sustaining this point of view, in the second half of the film Ichikawa moves toward an endorsement of family life. By the end, Ichikawa is exalting

the sanctities inherent in the family through the love of the child for his now-dead grandmother, a love which is so elevated in this film that it allows the baby to form his first connection with the outside world and even, Ichikawa implies, makes it possible for him psychically to grow up to be a man. (pp. 338-40)

In *Being Two Isn't Easy* Ichikawa locates value in the natural processes of life and in the links of love between the generations. The family is revealed to provide life-giving, essential strengths in exchange for the freedoms it necessarily and inevitably extracts from us, freedoms we would have lost anyway through living in the world as it is. Not only is it unavoidable that we grow up within the nuclear family, but this institution allows us love and continuity available nowhere else.

We thus leave Ichikawa with the family intact. That, albeit with reservations, he returns to an institution he so bitterly satirized in films like *The Key, Bonchi* and *Younger Brother*—that he so contradicts himself—is not, however, an unusual quality in directors of his generation and older. These artists, while recognizing its abuses of the individual, have ultimately found it impossible to conceive of Japan without the family at its center. *Being Two Isn't Easy* brings Ichikawa close to the spirit of Ozu, who also approaches the family with a full understanding of how it limits us. The argument of this film, as of so many of Ozu's, is that the enrichment the family provides far outweighs any limitations it may impose. (p. 342)

*Joan Mellen, in her* The Waves at Genji's Door: Japan through Its Cinema *(copyright © 1976 by Joan Mellen; reprinted by permission of Pantheon Books, a Division of Random House, Inc.), Pantheon Books, 1976, 463 p.**

## TOM ALLEN

It is almost impossible to cite an American director who has aged as gracefully in his idiosyncrasies as Ichikawa over the last three decades. It is also difficult to name a local director who parallels his many permutations of style. Ichikawa's films slide between clinical realism and wry observation of human foibles. There is a chilling haughtiness in his work, yet sometimes he plays to the pit with a low buffoonery that is almost beyond the American sensibility. He is not a classicist so much as an eclectic who has adapted serious literature, popular best sellers, and original material to his own purposes. . . .

Ichikawa, in his 1958 *Conflagration,* predated the passionate atavism of *Equus,* yet he had the fine, discreet sense to stay close to the original author, Mishima. . . . Ichikawa did not employ realism to pierce the hidden mysteries of fanatic pathology. He knew the worth of stylization. . . .

*Mr. Pu,* adapted from a popular comic strip, is a revelation. It is a true celebration of losers in the dog-eat-dog world of post-War Japan. There is no obeisance to the sentimental redemption of a happy ending, Ichikawa trains a Hogarthian eye on hard times among the genteel poor; and if any director has ever been ebullient about the wolves shearing the meek of the world, it is he. . . .

While [*Conflagration* and *Mr. Pu*] evidence neither the arc of transcendency achieved by Ozu and Mizoguchi nor the heroic aspiration typical of Kurosawa, they surpass most of the comparable films of their time. Thematically, *Mr. Pu* is superior to anything in the American *Marty* school; and, stylistically,

***Conflagration*** is on par with Bergman's work in *Wild Strawberries*.

In Ichikawa's other films, however, such as ***An Actor's Revenge*** (1963) and ***I Am a Cat*** (1975), there are some disturbing signs of a falling off. With lesser material, he tends to stifle nuance and ambiguity through facile reaction shots, and he sometimes indulges in sensationalistic montage that has little to do with narrative or mood. Nevertheless, there is a direct link between ***Mr. Pu*** and ***I Am a Cat*** . . . through Ichikawa's uncanny identification with fumbling, ineffectual anti-heroes. But the residue of good will seems depreciated in the latter film. Still, I suspect that [Ichikawa's films will provide an] unsettling introduction to one of the world's most volatile film stylists.

*Tom Allen, ''Ichiban Ichikawa-San'' (reprinted by permission of* The Village Voice *and the author; copyright © The Village Voice, Inc., 1977), in* The Village Voice, *Vol. XXII, No. 50, December 12, 1977, p. 49.*

# Buster Keaton

## 1895-1966

(Born Joseph Francis Keaton) American director, actor, screenwriter, and producer.

Keaton's silent films are among the most important works in the development of American comedy. His films of the 1920s are now considered as impressive as those of Charlie Chaplin. Keaton's films are a mixture of comedy and pathos, with Buster playing a protagonist trying to extricate himself from dangerous situations. Stunts were filmed in long shot, so that their danger is fully apparent to the viewer. In front of the camera, Keaton had the ability to remain stoical and aloof through the most outrageous situations, a talent which won for him a large following in the 1920s.

Keaton began his theatrical career at an early age. He appeared in his parents's vaudeville routine, and was called "the human mop" because they threw him all over the stage. Keaton later claimed that this experience helped him perform the difficult stunts that he staged in his films. He worked in vaudeville until 1917, when he appeared in his first film, *The Butcher Boy,* with Fatty Arbuckle. Throughout the early and mid-twenties, Keaton made many popular shorts and features, including *Cops, The Three Ages,* and *Sherlock Jr.* At this time, Keaton had total artistic control over his films. However, by the time he made his best films, *The General* and *Steamboat Bill Jr.,* stifling restrictions had been put on his work, such as the hiring of co-directors and artistic supervisors. In 1928, when his contract was transferred from United Artists to MGM, Keaton became little more than a hired hand in the films in which he starred. His work deteriorated steadily, personal problems sapped his skills, and many people thought he was dead until the 1950s. At that time, Keaton began to appear once again in films, including Chaplin's *Limelight,* and critical reevaluations of his early work began to appear. Most of these were extremely favorable.

Keaton's most important physical asset was his face. Impassive, never smiling, "The Great Stone Face" seemed ready for any disaster. Critics today see Keaton as a solitary filmmaker, an artist who planned his films and routines very carefully (when he was allowed to). Admirers say that his films are beautiful as a result of creative and exciting photography. Many critics feel the scenes Keaton shot in the Northwest wilderness for some films (particularly *The General*) are still unsurpassed. Above all, Keaton created films in a slapstick style that audiences still find engaging today.

## R. E. SHERWOOD

In one of his earlier comedies, "The Paleface," Buster Keaton captured a quality of wistfulness that marked him as one apart from the ordinary run of movie gag-grabbers. It is this same quality that has made Chaplin great.

Keaton returns to the mood of "The Paleface" in "Go West"—a comedy which, when viewed analytically, is in fact a soul-stirring tragedy. It is the story of a boy, known on the program as "Friendless," who is kicked about from pillar to post—from New York, N.Y., to Needles, California—until he finally finds a startling treasure of human warmth and sympathy in the person of a brown-eyed cow. For this cow he conceives a devastating affection, and his loyal heart is shattered when an inexorable ranch-owner compels him to lead his bovine girl friend to the slaughterhouse.

A [James Matthew] Barrie, a [Ferenc] Molnar, or a [George Bernard] Shaw could not have conceived a romance like that. It is the utterly mad but oddly significant sort of story that could flourish only on the screen.

Buster Keaton plays it with his usual dead pan, and with occasional sidesteps into the realms of ridiculousness. In these moments he is terribly funny, but for the major part of the picture, he is inexpressibly sad.

Toward the end, a herd of cattle breaks loose in a city street—and here, unfortunately, Buster Keaton loses control. The cows refuse to do their bit toward the development of screen art, and the story ends lamely.

But "Go West" is a good picture—the best, I think, that Keaton has done since "Our Hospitality."

R. E. Sherwood, "The Silent Drama: 'Go West',"
in Life, Vol. 86, No. 2246, November 19, 1925, p. 26.

## JAMES AGEE

Keaton worked strictly for laughs, but his work came from so far inside a curious and original spirit that he achieved a great deal besides, especially in his feature-length comedies. (For plain hard laughter his 19 short comedies . . . were even better.) He was the only major comedian who kept sentiment almost entirely out of his work, and he brought pure physical comedy to its greatest heights. Beneath his lack of emotion he was also uninsistently sardonic; deep below that, giving a disturbing tension and grandeur to the foolishness, for those who sensed it, there was in his comedy a freezing whisper not of pathos but of melancholia. With the humor, the craftsmanship and the action there was often, besides, a fine, still and sometimes dreamlike beauty. Much of his Civil War picture *The General* is within hailing distance of Matthew Brady. And there is a ghostly, unforgettable moment in *The Navigator* when, on a deserted, softly rolling ship, all the pale doors along a deck swing open as one behind Keaton and, as one, slam shut, in a hair-raising illusion of noise. (p. 85)

> *James Agee, "Comedy's Greatest Era" (© copyright The James Agee Trust; reprinted by permission), in* Life, *Vol. 27, No. 10, September 5, 1949, pp. 70-82, 85-6, 88.**

## PENELOPE HOUSTON

The hero of *The General* is a little engine driver, turned down by the Confederate recruiting sergeants, dismissed as a coward by his girl, who, in pursuit of his stolen engine, penetrates the Unionist lines, spies on a military conference, rescues the girl, recovers the engine and steams back in triumph to the Confederate encampment. The exploits are preposterously heroic; their manner of execution is brisk but detached. Confronted with the outlandish or the alarming—the disappearance of his train, the discovery that in setting fire to the railway bridge he has placed himself on the wrong side of the blaze, or that, in his grand scheme to fire on the enemy train, he has directed the cannonball straight into the cab of his own engine—Keaton remains imperturbable. This, one feels, is how he expects things to behave; there is no need for undue alarm. It is out of this laconic, matter-of-fact acceptance, this obstinate persistence in effort, however misguided, this untroubled, dream-like logic, that Keaton builds his comedy technique. The film advances in a series of triumphs and setbacks, with each check stimulating him to fresh activity, fresh displays of ingenuity. The train puffs past first the retreating Confederate troops, then the advancing Yankees, while its driver, sublimely unaware, busily saws wood for the engine. It runs steadily towards an obstacle across the line while Keaton, spread-eagled against the front of the engine, comes as close to trepidation as we ever see him before he casually bounces the log out of the way with a neat jab from one he is already clasping. (p. 198)

With these simple resources—a railway line, a train to chase and one to be chased—the comedy follows a classically direct course, with scarcely a gag or a situation inserted for its own sake. It is only when the film leaves the trains behind, in the final battle scenes, the fooling with the sword that flies from its scabbard for the last time to impale an enemy sniper, that the effects seem rather too deliberately contrived, the situations a little too real to be altogether funny. In part this may be because the film, directed by Keaton in collaboration with Clyde Bruckman, conveys, unobtrusively, so exact and stylish a sense of its period. The comedian has strayed on to a real battlefield and, momentarily, the illusion cracks.

Human relationships, defying logic, breaking his solitary concentration of purpose, form the smallest part of any Keaton film. Here, his attitude towards the girl . . . characteristically combines protective affection with exasperation. When she arranges her well-intentioned booby-trap in the path of the enemy train or, under fire from their pursuers, snatches up a broom and begins sweeping out the engine cab, he finds her endearingly ridiculous. But for Keaton the real world is elsewhere.

Innocently and without bravado, Keaton has the measure of his surroundings. He does not, like Harold Lloyd, want to be admired or successful; he is not, like Harry Langdon, a child at large in a puzzling universe; he has not, like Chaplin, assumed the dreams and the sorrows of the world. But his enduring, unsentimental self-sufficiency has its own intimations of melancholy, in the contrast between his determination and his resources as he marches off down the line in pursuit of his runaway train and, always, in the sad, thoughtful eyes set in the pale poker face. Keaton is the most exact, the most mathematically precise, of comedians, yet as one laughs one wonders: the quintessential Buster Keaton seems always to retreat a little, behind the enigmatic, impassive mask of the comedian. (pp. 198-99)

> *Penelope Houston, "Film Reviews: 'The General'," in* Sight and Sound *(copyright © 1953 by The British Film Institute), Vol. 22, No. 4, April-June, 1953, pp. 198-99.*

## CHRISTOPHER BISHOP

Where the goals in Chaplin's films are social, physical, and explicit, those in Keaton's are metaphysical and implicit. Chaplin's art is rooted in a period which could believe in social solutions, while, for Keaton, there are no solutions—or rather, the solutions, like the problems, lie somewhere just outside the frameline, somewhere beyond the film's conclusion. His films, unlike Chaplin's, end happily, his ambitions and those of his girl meeting finally at one point. But these endings suggest a temporary adjustment of ultimate divergences; any solutions fate may provide for this man are essentially irrelevant. One critic has spoken of "the admirable play of horizontals and verticals" in his films; the fundamental disparity between Keaton's line and that of the other characters is final and immutable. Keaton is willing to join in the game, a game not entirely innocent, in which the stakes may be life and death—but it is not his game, and one senses that, for him, all has already been lost.

Keaton moves in a windless vacuum of his own, his directions suggesting the trajectory of a bullet moving through a wind tunnel, buffeted by whirlwinds of ceaseless violence. His lack of engagement extends to his audiences as well, from whom he has always seemed separated as if by a glass and soundproof wall. His lack of emotional response, his endlessly rigid and inflexible behavior imply a previous hurt which even he cannot remember, but which controls his every movement. The dignity and silence of Keaton's suffering speak, as do Garbo's, of an immensity of early sorrow which cannot be put into words. There is in his films always something withheld, a little turned away from the audience, the nature of which is open to conjecture. It is this quality of reserve which in the end makes his performances so powerful. (p. 14)

> *Christopher Bishop, "The Great Stone Face," in* Film Quarterly *(copyright 1958 by The Regents of the University of California; reprinted by permission of the University of California Press), Vol. XII, No. 1, Fall, 1958, pp. 10-15.*

## PAUL ROTHA

Keaton at his best as in *The General, College,* and the first two reels of *Spite Marriage,* has real merit. His humour is dry, exceptionally well constructed and almost entirely mechanical in execution. He has set himself the task of an assumed personality, which succeeds in becoming comic by its very sameness. He relies, also, on the old method of repetition, which when enhanced by his own inscrutable individuality becomes incredibly funny. His comedies show an extensive knowledge of the contrast of shapes and sizes and an extremely pleasing sense of the ludicrous. Keaton has, above all, the great asset of being funny in himself. He looks odd, does extraordinary things and employs uproariously funny situations with considerable skill. The Keaton films are usually very well photographed, with a minimum of detail and a maximum of effect. It would be ungrateful, perhaps, to suggest that he tries to take from Chaplin that which is essentially Chaplin's, but nevertheless Keaton has learnt from the great actor and would probably be the first to admit it. (p. 214)

*Paul Rotha, "The American Film (concluded)," in his* The Film Till Now: A Survey of World Cinema *(© Paul Rotha 1949, 1951, 1960, 1963), revised edition, Vision Press Limited, 1963, pp. 189-216.\**

## J.-P. LEBEL

Keaton's profoundly visual kind of comedy depends on his skill in directing which permits him to use space itself as an element in his gags. And thus by using different shots of a railway track describing a hairpin bend on a steep slope together with shots of a locomotive prankishly advancing and retreating, Keaton can gallop through woods, tumble down the slope and scale rocks (*The General*). Ultimately this turns into a sort of abstract locomotive ballet. Using an ingenious system of deceptively crossing railway tracks (one of the two, no longer in use, is suspended in the air), Keaton then superposes two trains going at top speed, one forward, the other (his, the General) backward, and after having led us to believe the two will inevitably crash, he isolates one train perched on its track in a ridiculous, grotesque position, as the other, roaring forward, disappears.

Keaton makes the Northerners who pursue him look ridiculous, and uses scenic elements to jeer at them: by his retreat which suddenly reveals how to avoid a crash as well as the grotesque position in which the Northerners now find themselves, he makes them look ridiculous; by placing his train directly beneath their shelf, out of their reach, he seems to be there deliberately to jeer at them.

The mad humour of this scene rests on a genuine visual pun, the result of mathematically precise direction. (p. 51)

Keaton is never so great as when he manages to organise (to seize simply) the countryside into his overall design, giving, in a flashing surge of beauty, his personal vibration to the secret modulation of its lines, to its concrete harmony—as when he gallops indefatigably through the antediluvian country of *Seven Chances*, or that shot from *Battling Butler* in which, in a kind of immense and muddy lunar circus, one sees Keaton's small but steady silhouette reduced to two legs at the ends of which two enormous muddy masses—his feet—run towards a horizon far in the distance out of sight.

These images give birth to both laughter and overwhelming beauty, each of which nourishes the other. These images are the affirmation of this body which imposes itself on the world and fits so perfectly into space. Keaton runs to embrace this world which belongs to him and to which he belongs; it is

because his is a match for the unleashed elements in *Steamboat Bill Junior,* for example, that he succeeds in taming them. (p. 56)

But none of these marvellous images, these moments of beauty which spring at us in forests, city streets and rocky amphitheatres are the results of any systematic search for "beautiful shots". Keaton is not of those who confuse directing with pretty images.

There is no fancy-work, nothing designed "to impress" in his films. He is not one of those who, contemptuous of the comic cinema, feels obliged to give it a bit of dignity, to make of it an "art film" by using remarkable photographic effects and adding brilliant supporting players. Buster Keaton's cinema is elegant; but it is never precious. The beauty of his films is, like all real beauty, involuntary but necessary; for the perfect geometry and the visual supremacy inherent in all of Keaton's images are functional. They are the inevitable product of Keaton's intensity (which they resolve) and the world around him. And Keaton's directing is the directing of his behaviour in the world; it is the literal *positioning* of his action. With nothing extraneous added, Keaton's *positioning* enables him to "accomplish" his action and give it its form.

Though Keaton's work abounds in touches of genius which can often be related to that category known as "brilliant directorial finds", he never introduces anything extraneous for its own sake; everything relates to, and helps to further, the story-action. (pp. 57-8)

When, in *Steamboat Bill Junior,* by a simultaneous rotation in opposite directions of two barber chairs by two young barbers, Keaton finds himself face to face with the girl with whom he falls immediately in love, what we have is not merely a simple directing trick, but rather a veritable *presentation through positioning,* the visual equivalent of love at first sight.

The way Keaton perceives a scene through "a frame of a folded arm," and the way the trainer's body hides Keaton until the former steps aside to reveal him (*Battling Butler*) are absolutely functional and necessary visions, being the physical and spatial expression of a moment in Keaton's life, the translation in physical terms of a moral relationship. (pp. 58-9)

But there is no need to look for exceptional moments to praise Keaton's consummate directorial artistry; every example we have given of Keaton's "perfect geometry", of his sense of linear organisation and of the way his body fits so perfectly in space is ample proof that Keaton's direction is above all the *positioning in a setting* of a body *in action,* and is evidence of the geometrical precision and the expressive richness of this positioning. (p. 60)

[The difference between Chaplin and Keaton is profound.] Chaplin seldom comes to grips with nature because his comedy is the comedy of a socially-determined being whose acts find fulfilment in a social milieu. Keaton is a more elemental comic, which is to say that his acts find their fulfilment in a more natural (in the literal sense of the word) environment; his relations with the world itself are more direct; if he is a "man of the world", that is because his conflict is usually the conflict of man versus object, not man versus man, and his object is often, in this sense, the whole world itself. Keaton thus needs nature. (p. 61)

Keaton's directing is nothing more than a positioning, with no flourishes, with no "extraordinary angles", of the extraordinary being he incarnates. Keaton, like Chaplin, "considers himself the centre of the action.'' It is their action that is different, and that takes different forms, and there's the precise difference between them.

Chaplin is mainly *demonstration*. He is above all the *subversive manifestation* of himself. His body is principally the sign of his exuberant presence, with all that that implies. His principal task is therefore to present this sign, to show that it exists. For which reason the camera is almost always focused directly on Chaplin and only occasionally moves back to ''take in a wider arabesque.''

Keaton is essentially *action*—action upon which his behaviour, his fitting into space and his adjustment to it, depends; the result of this action is seen in relation to its setting. Keaton exists above all in his acts, acts which, like for Chaplin, reveal his character, of course, but which implicate at one and the same time both him and the setting in which his acts take place. And that is why almost all his scenes are shot with the camera taking in a wider area. (p. 62)

A film like *The Three Ages* . . . , which parodies [Griffith's] *Intolerance,* is very well constructed, but lacks the rigour of the latter. For in all three of the ages, what happens depends on what Keaton does, and on the genetic impetus of the action he represents.

The liveliness of every one of Keaton's films is due to what he does and how he reacts to things. There is no foreign interference. Scenes might follow one another in any order whatsoever; Keaton is the constant, the strong thread tying them together, and that thread is never broken.

Most striking about Keaton is precisely the fact that many of his films *are* so well constructed. There is a kind of symmetry in the structure, usually a result of *turnabouts*. . . .

[The *turnabout*] is the principal *form* of the relation uniting Keaton to the situations in which he finds himself. Keaton's scenario symmetry is therefore not imposed arbitrarily from without; it is, on the contrary, the natural expression and development of his activity as expressed in the gag. And if this symmetry seems to reflect his taste for geometry, well, a love for geometry is one of Keaton's basic characteristics and it is geometrically that he confronts and controls the world. (p. 69)

The symmetry of the construction [of *The General*] not only allows Keaton to display an unflagging inventiveness, but is also based uniquely on his actions. The logic of his behaviour and his perseverance in what he is doing are responsible for the film's structural equilibrium. And we are once again witness to the functional use that Keaton the creator puts to what in others might appear to be artifice.

*College* is probably the only film in which this symmetry is a bit overstressed. The film itself is a *tour de force* which concludes at the end a gag begun at the beginning, as Keaton succeeds in accomplishing all that he originally failed at. And thus two series of gags form one sole gag, stretched out in the middle and enclosing the middle between the premises and the conclusion. The turnabout—original failure becoming final victory—which serves as the film's spring, is perfectly justified, since everything Keaton does in the film comes as the result of his determination to succeed in what he failed at. The film's symmetrical construction is therefore admirable; it is not imposed on Keaton from without, but, on the contrary, emanates directly from him.

At the beginning of *College,* unfortunately, Keaton the director decided to spice things and thereby introduced an artificial symmetry. And every time that Keaton the actor appears to compete in an athletic event, Keaton the director feels it necessary to show us *systematically* the normal way to throw a javelin, run a race, pole-vault, etc. This symmetry, showing the exercise as it should be done and then showing it as catastrophically performed by Keaton, inasmuch as it is not the natural outgrowth of Keaton's inner behaviour, seems contrived; this would be relatively unimportant if it did not serve to deprive the gags that follow of their comical efficacity. And so, in every pause between the model performance of the feat and Keaton's taking the stage, one seems to feel the director whisper, as P. Demun remarked, ''Watch out! You're now going to see something you don't expect.'' By taking away the element of surprise, the gag falls flat. And falls all the flatter because as a rule Keaton's impenetrability, which always leaves the spectator wondering what he'll do next, is usually one of the surest laugh factors.

But this slight disappointment at the beginning is amply compensated for by our laughter at the end, when the indomitable Keaton throws weights, leaps hedges and pole-vaults superbly, gloriously triumphing over everything that stymied him earlier on. This time the symmetry is perfect in the comic situation.

The scenario is therefore for Keaton a kind of positioning of himself. Instead of imposing on himself the iron collar of formal dramatic construction, he lets the action grow freely out of himself.

Both in his scenarios and his direction Keaton strives to keep all jarring elements (dramatic twists, gimmicky angles or erudite centrings) from getting between, on the one hand, his actions and attitudes towards things, and, on the other, the spectator. His art is one that ever seeks the greatest simplicity, which is to say that he does not explicitly pose himself problems of expression, but that he is spontaneously creative. One must nevertheless lose sight of the important role played by composition in his films, composition taking the form of ''geometrisation'' both as concerns the individual and the film in its entirety, in its construction. It is this acute sense of composition which, in the long run, is responsible for the simplicity and the limpidity of the positioning of Keaton in cinematic space and time. (pp. 70, 73-4)

[Keaton] gives us the example of a director's style of absolute simplicity which is, however, perfectly original and perfectly necessary.

It is the luminous simplicity of his *mise-en-scène* that makes Keaton modern, that puts him in a class with Griffith as one of the greatest artists the cinema has known. (pp. 74-5)

Keaton's direction distinguishes itself by rejecting most of that which is said to be the stuff of direction.

But let us not be deluded into believing that this ''simple'' direction is insignificant. As we have already seen, its very limpidity presupposes consummate artistry and, consequently, great expressive richness. His contempt for all that is traditionally called aesthetic enables Keaton to define an aesthetic.

Indeed, if Keaton seems to comply with Lenin's dictum that ''ethics are the aesthetics of the future'', the ethics that emerge from his films are nothing other than his activity in the world. There is no doubt that Keaton is a film-maker; he is also a total creator, the only difference between him and his illustrious *confrères* being that while they have a ''world vision'', he has a "world action". His expressive perfection therefore consists first of all in putting forth this "world action." (p. 75)

But this "world action"—the direction of which requires a tremendous physical discipline, a keen visual eye, a sense of choreography and an ability to dominate cinematic space by making the body and its very admirable movements fit into space perfectly—this "world action" is not gratuitous; it is not a game; it is full of ethical meaning. (pp. 75-6)

All action, inasmuch as it brings about results and reflects a certain way of viewing things, is based on reason and has itself a certain meaning; this meaning is expressed in the *form* that the action takes; and because an action does not proclaim its intentions it does not mean that they are not inherent in the action. And that is what Buster Keaton's attitude in the world implies—that attitude which, in the comic film, takes the form of the gag. . . . (p. 76)

Apart from the habitual turnabouts in Keaton's films, we have [in *Convict 13*] a perfect example of his "amorality". Keaton spares no one. Neither the prisoners nor the executioner are particularly praiseworthy. But Keaton raises no moral question, puts his actions to the service of no established code of conduct: he acts. And all that matters is his action and its efficacity. There is no explanation as to why he is going to be hung, no question of justice or injustice. All we have is the *fact;* and the fact is that he is going to be hung.

His problem is how to get out of an unpleasant situation. He gets out of it. He takes advantage of the mutiny to join forces with the ruling forces: the cops. He becomes a cop. He does not choose to become a cop (the film is not a defence of cops). It's just that the best way to avoid being executed is to become the executioner, the cop. Everything depends on the uniform you wear.

Nor is it a matter of putting *moral relativity* in perspective, of the uniform you wear making you black or white. . . .

Keaton makes no attempt to "explain things"; he merely takes the most efficacious role in regard to the given situation. And thus he gives us an example of the American form of the "survival of the fittest", of the American success-mystique. In the struggle for success anything goes; but above all, Keaton's amorality shows superficial morality up for what it is, the mere outer forms of morality with the deeper meanings lost. By posing himself no moral questions in a world that calls itself moral, his amoral success makes this pseudo-morality absurd. For, if he doesn't inform us why he is going to be hung (no moral cause) he nevertheless does show us that a man is going to be hung (implication: morality) and, consequently, by turning the mechanisms of this hanging into an opportunity for genuine opportunism (and doing so brilliantly) he also makes mincemeat of the presumed moral foundations of these actions.

It is therefore uniquely in terms of his action that Keaton resolves upon a course to be taken; and if this action implies moral judgment or enlightenment, such is uniquely with respect to the conditions which permit its effectiveness.

Keaton's amorality, similarly applied, can be found in *Cops*.

His amorality lies in the fact that he *accepts everything* without any preconceived ideas. There's no denying that he lights his cigarette with an anarchist's bomb; nor does he divert the bomb from its original target since he, in turn, throws it back into the midst of the crowd of cops. By doing so he sparks their anger; they, of course, blindly consider him to be an anarchist,

whereas he is entirely oblivious to moral problems and, in short, couldn't care less.

Keaton is not a cop hater; but—comically and normally—cops represent blind repression, and Keaton cannot help being aware of that. If there seems to be a latent value judgment made in regard to the police in his films, this is all due solely to "realism". (pp. 82-4)

If the study of certain "values" inherent in Keaton's work has given us some information on what gives his behaviour coherence, on his "world action", it is clear that no study can explain this world action to us, nor give us the key to it.

Indeed, Keaton's "amorality", his "horror of the mechanised world", his particular conception of love, his open attitude towards the world, his "poetic use of things" for example—none of these things can give a meaning to his work for the simple reason that it is not these things *which make him act.* They are rather the conditions of his action—or what results from it—not the basis for this action. (pp. 101-02)

It is therefore clear that the significance of Keaton's "world action" can only be found in this action itself. (p. 102)

Keaton's action manifests itself in the use of objects. We are using object here in the fullest sense of the word; the object may be a situation that Keaton must master, the situation itself being the relation between several objects (as was the case in the final gag in *The General*). In every situation the problem presents itself to Keaton in the form of a good distribution and a proper organisation of things in space.

In this sense human beings may well be considered objects against which he must position himself and which he must put in order.

In the handling of objects Keaton displays his talents for organisation, geometrization, adjustment, and physical and poetic mastery of things; in a word, all that constitutes his manner of adjusting to the world, his manner of being, his "world action".

The form that this handling takes is the gag. If Keaton's most important dealings are with real objects (mechanical or other), and if these objects are to constitute the principle subject of this study, let us nevertheless not forget that the Keaton gag can very well be expressed in the form of a confrontation with nature resolved in his perfect positioning in space. In such cases laughter is derived from the organisation of spatial lines and of Keaton's body in the spatial framework. In that respect, the largest "object" Keaton uses in his gags is the world itself.

As a comic personality Keaton inevitably uses objects curiously; his reaction to a situation is never an ordinary one. He handles objects either positively or negatively. For Keaton every problem is posed in terms of success and failure. He is constantly seeking the form which will lead him to success (or to failure); i.e. the form which will put his way of adjustment in concrete form: which will lead to his integration or his non-integration. (pp. 103-04)

Let us be clear; we have no intention of making a god or "superman" a sort of "victory machine" of Keaton; he is not infallible. We have never meant to imply that he is the absolute master of all, and particularly of the universe. It is his form that matters when he deals with the world, and if he and his form triumph *most of the time* (not always and not systematically) that is because he never gives in and never gives up. . . .

Most of Keaton's films are built along the following lines: Keaton is determined to accomplish something—usually for a woman: either he must "win" her by being glorious, he must overcome her father's resistance, or he must save her from various dangers. At the start things go badly for him, but at the end, "in a final sprint of gags" he turns the tide. . . . (p. 134)

Note that if Keaton's qualities are responsible for bringing gags to successful conclusions, the gags themselves are not conceived to bring out these qualities; on the contrary, Keaton's qualities appear as such precisely because Keaton can bring the gags to successful conclusions. But make no mistake: Keaton's qualities, personality and moral force are nothing other than his actions.

Note, too, that in most [cases] the successful conclusion is due to perfect positioning, thus perfect directing; all of which proves once again that Keaton's directorial genius stems from his ability to position himself and his action.

The point is not that this "dialectical" gag form is the only kind of gag form Keaton uses, but that it is the most perfect form, gathering as it does all the different aspects of his adjustment to the world, and showing them with the greatest comic intensity. (p. 135)

[By] *seeking to perfect the burlesque gag, Keaton discovers the driving form of his adjustment to the world,* of his "world action"—nor is this because he wants to reveal "exemplary qualities", to give a certain meaning to his world action, or to deliver any message.

The meaning of the gag structure only comes later; not Keaton's to worry about it. *Keaton's "world action" is not the fruit of ethical reflection but of comic practice.* By merely trying to bring laughter, he creates new forms.

It is *our* duty to find the meaning of these forms; because they do have an objective meaning doesn't necessarily mean their creator was aware of it. (pp. 135-36)

> *J.-P. Lebel, in his* Buster Keaton, *translated by P. D. Stovin (translation © 1967 by The Tantivy Press; originally published as* Buster Keaton, *Editions Universitaires, 1964), Tantivy Press, 1967, 179 p.*

**PENELOPE HOUSTON**

*The Boat* has all the resilience, pig-headedness, and strangeness of the best Keaton films. It ends perfectly; but if it were to go on one has no doubt that this extraordinary family (wife and children behave like extensions of Keaton himself) would next be found setting up some ultra-ingenious desert island shack. The survival power of the Keaton character is never seriously in question. But the element of melancholy . . . still bites. Keaton's humour is seldom destructive except at his own expense; and the collapse of the house at the beginning of *The Boat* seems to me one of the most strangely and sorrowfully and totally comic moments in cinema.

By now, the principles of Keaton films were set—of Keaton, that is, looked on as director rather than performer. There are obvious rules of construction, like the slow starts and all-out finishes. But I would suggest three basic elements of Keaton comedy, all in evidence in *The Boat.* First, there is the concern with plot, adventure, real hazards. I find the storm sequence reminiscent, of all unlikely things, of the hurricane in [Ichikawa's] *Alone on the Pacific,* a comparison one could never

begin to make if Buster were just a booby adrift in a studio mock-up boat. Second, there is the sense of place. In *The Boat* this is no more than the modest little harbour whose yachts and boat-houses can be seen in the background of the launching sequence. But if this scene were staged in a studio tank, it could become just a pretty gag. Here it acquires the utter lunacy of some freakish happening in real life.

In other films, background takes on more value: the dusty, countrified streets of small towns, the Model Ts racing down country lanes, the railroad always somewhere near the centre of town. . . . Even in the two-reelers, Keaton was clearly prepared to go to great trouble for the sake of a single shot: there's an extraordinary one, for instance, in *The Paleface,* which finds him on horseback in the middle of a great misty landscape of oil derricks, like something out of [Antonioni's] *The Red Desert.* But more significant than this is the sense of a world beyond the comedy: the river settlement of *Steamboat Bill,* the orchard alongside the millionaire's ornate encampment in *Battling Butler. Steamboat Bill* contains a shot which seems quintessential Keaton. He is standing in the foreground, gazing mournfully out at us; behind him, unobserved, the heroine has crept up and is dithering about whether to attract his attention. She is on the right of the frame; backwards to the left stretches the riverside path, with people wandering about. The moment is caught and framed by the unconcerned presence of other people.

The third obvious Keaton principle is his fondness for keeping as much of the action as possible within a shot. It started, presumably, with a natural pride in letting the audience see that those leaps and falls and glissades of movement were all his own work. There could be no cutting, because to cut into the action would suggest a cheated effect. In *College,* when he's pretending to be no athlete, he runs towards the camera down a line of hurdles, knocking down every one; in *Steamboat Bill* he stands stock still while the falling house collapses around him; in *Seven Chances* he dances about the screen, slipping and dodging under a rain of falling boulders. He was prepared to risk his neck for an effect which might last twenty seconds on the screen. The camera had to get far enough back to take it all in, to exploit a connoisseur's satisfaction in the number of ways of staging a fall. And so he hit on the technique which happens to be most in line with modern, or at least 1960s, aesthetics. (p. 65)

Though no one could call Keaton a theoretician of comedy, every published interview suggests that he had a total grasp of what he wanted to do, how an effect would come across, and what he expected from his co-directors. In his performances, he liked to build pyramids of action. He falls off a roof; gets caught up on a projecting pole; is catapulted off that into a room; slides along the floor; snatches at what turns out to be a fireman's pole; slithers down that to ground level, and is at once off again. Here each cut flicks the action forward, so that the whole lunatic route from top to bottom of the building is as neat as an equation. But effects like this are perhaps less characteristic than the moments when the camera simply pauses, at a distance, waiting for Buster to emerge head first from a window or dash down a street.

What distinguishes his feature films qualitatively from each other is partly the sheer flow of comic invention (inexhaustible in *Seven Chances,* decidedly sparse in *Battling Butler*), and partly the extent to which he managed fully to realise a character. *The Three Ages,* for instance, is so limited by its parody form that it virtually breaks down into three interlocked two-reelers. Marvellous jokes—the first sight of Wallace Beery riding the mastodon, answered by Buster in his sea captain attitude on the back of a brontosaurus; the golf swing with the stone age club; his consternation when surrounded by those Thurberesque neanderthal women. But this is basic Buster; not much more. (pp. 65-6)

For variations in Keaton comedy, however, the three films I'm inclined to look at . . . are *Seven Chances, Go West* and *Steamboat Bill Jr.* Here character really comes into its own; and a different character each time, even though all three films end identically with Buster coming out on top after his three most extravagant action sequences. (p. 66)

[The] more one sees of the great comedies, the more one realises how essentially Keaton needed the freedom not to create gags, but to create worlds. The wistful cow-puncher, mounting his horse by rope-ladder; the college boy doing an immense run-up to the high jump, only to have the bar topple off as he gets there; the snappish young businessman snatching back his tip from the hatcheck girl; the running figure on top of the train, all owe part of their comic truth to their settings. (p. 67)

Penelope Houston, *"The Great Blank Page," in* Sight and Sound *(copyright © 1968 by The British Film Institute), Vol. 37, No. 2, Spring, 1968, pp. 63-7.*

## STANLEY KAUFFMANN

Keaton has never been forgotten, but he has been comparatively neglected. That comparison is, obviously, with Chaplin. Now some points seem clear. As performer, Keaton is certainly Chaplin's equal. As director, he is Chaplin's superior, more flexible in his camera movement, more sensitive to pictorial quality as such. As producer of whole, organic works, he is not quite as good as Chaplin. As manager of his career, he is not remotely in Chaplin's league. Chaplin had great business and promotive sense; Keaton had practically none. (p. 20)

Artistically, there are close similarities and wide differences between them. Both understood the body as the source of comic life, both had incredible control of their bodies—an identification of physicality with comic performance that may never be seen on stage or film again. . . . Both understood that mere physical miracle was eventually sterile, that it had to be used in support of a character, a basically fixed character, as in the ancient tradition of clowning. In Chaplin's earliest shorts, one can see him moving toward the Tramp. In *Coney Island,* where Keaton supports Fatty Arbuckle, one can see him moving toward *his* character. (And, incidentally, disproving the myth that he never smiled.) Both pantomime artists dreaded the coming of sound, and neither was at his best in speaking roles. (p. 21)

The differences between them are also interesting. In a primary but not exclusive sense, Chaplin is balletic, Keaton acrobatic. It would not be Chaplin's best style to do the skip across a table, over a man's shoulders, and the dive headfirst out a transom that Keaton does in *The Goat.* Keaton would not have done the globe dance in *The Great Dictator.* Intrinsic to Chaplin's silent films is an unheard music, to Keaton's the unheard sound of daily life. Chaplin's recurrent images are the theater and the road, Keaton's are boats (*Balloonatics, The Navigator, Steamboat Bill Jr.*) and trains (*Our Hospitality, Go West, The General*). Many of Chaplin's long films have better structures than Keaton's: Chaplin would never have let a film run ten minutes or more, as does *Our Hospitality,* before we get the

first hint that it's a comedy. Most of Keaton's pictures are more obviously carpentered together than most of Chaplin's; they build toward a big climax, but they also deliberately delay it, filling in with comic figurations. Most Chaplin films are works of genius. Most Keaton films are vehicles for a genius. (pp. 21-2)

Stanley Kauffmann, *"Buster Keaton Festival" (originally published in* The New Republic, *Vol. 163, No. 17, October 24, 1970), in his* Living Images: Film Comment and Criticism *(reprinted by permission of Brandt & Brandt Literary Agents, Inc.; copyright © 1970, 1971, 1972, 1973, 1974, 1975 by Stanley Kauffmann),* Harper & Row, Publishers, 1975, pp. 19-22.

## GERALD MAST

[Only] Buster Keaton could rival Chaplin in his insight into human relationships, into the conflict between the individual man and the immense social machinery that surrounds him; only Keaton could rival Chaplin in making his insight both funny and serious at the same time. On the one hand, the Keaton canon as a whole is thinner, less consistent than the Chaplin canon; the character he fashioned—with his deadpan, blank reaction to the chaos that inevitably and inadvertently blooms around him—lacks the range, the compassionate yearnings, the pitiable disappointments of Chaplin's tramp. On the other hand, Keaton made a single film, *The General,* that is possibly more even, more unified, and more complex in both conception and execution than any individual Chaplin film. (p. 152)

Chaplin and Keaton are the two poles of silent comics. Chaplin's great strength is his development of character and the exhausting of a particular comic and social situation; Keaton's strength is the tightness of his narrative structures and his contrast between the numbers one and infinity. Chaplin is sentimental; his gentle, smiling women become idols to be revered. Keaton is not sentimental; he stuffs his females into bags and hauls them around like sacks of potatoes; he satirizes their finicky incompetence and even raises his fist to the silly lady in *The General* who feeds their racing locomotive only the teensiest shavings of wood. It was especially appropriate and touching to see the two opposites, Chaplin and Keaton, united in *Limelight* (1952), both playing great clowns who were losing their audiences and their touch. (p. 153)

The great question *The General* poses in the course of its narrative is how to perform heroic action in a universe that is not heroic. Buster, with his typical dead-pan expression, merely tries to go about his business while the world around him goes mad. A metaphor for the feeling of the whole film is the shot in which Buster is so busy chopping wood to feed his engine that he fails to notice that the train is racing past row after row of blue uniforms marching in the opposite direction. Johnny Gray has inadvertently propelled himself behind the enemy's lines. Johnny Gray simply wants to run his train; unfortunately, the Union Army wants to steal the train and use it to destroy his fellow Confederates. In the course of merely trying to save the train, Johnny rescues his lady love and accidentally wins a terrific victory for the South.

That heroism occurs as an accident in *The General* is at the center of its moral thrust. It is an accident that the cannon, aimed squarely at Johnny, does not go off until the train rounds a curve, discharging its huge ball at the enemy instead of at the protagonist. It is an accident that Buster's train comes to a rail switch just in time to detour the pursuing Union train. . . . [Heroism] and successful military strategy are accidental in *The General*. . . . Buster's character exposes the folly of the accidents of heroism. For how less heroic, how less aspiring, less grand can a man be than little Buster? Buster merely uses his shrewd common sense against impossible odds, and he is lucky to get away with it. (pp. 156-57)

Such antiheroism is common to all the Keaton films; he is always the sensible little guy who inadvertently runs up against senseless objects that dwarf him. The thing that distinguishes *The General* is that the senseless object, the huge infernal machine of this film, is war. Men themselves have been transformed into a machine (an army), and the business of this machine is murder and destruction. This antiheroic comic epic must necessarily become an antiwar story, too, for the military heroism *The General* consistently debunks is the Circe that turns men into murdering and destructive swine. Buster never is hypnotized, and his film makes sure we keep our eyes open, too. (pp. 158-59)

The film is as shrewd, as caustic, as hard-edged as Johnny Gray himself. His girl, a typical figure of sentiment and romance . . . , is degraded into an incompetent and feeble representative of romantic notions; Johnny Gray ultimately must fight her as well as the pursuing army. There is no place in the world of *The General* for sentiment, for the same reason that there is no place for heroism. Romance and heroism are twins, and *The General* wages war on both. Unlike the Chaplin films, there are no flowers, no roses, in *The General*. As soon as you admit a rose, you must also admit a gun to fight for it.

True, the character Buster plays, Johnny Gray, is a southerner, a seemingly romantic choice. But Buster chose to play a rebel because the South lost the war, because the South was romantically blind about fighting the war, and because the South, like Buster, was the little-guy underdog. Though Johnny plays a southerner, the film is impartial; ultimately Johnny must sneak his train (even its name is a military one) past both the Union and the Confederate lines. Despite the film's comic conclusion and inventive gags, *The General,* with its mixture of burlesque and grimness (many men die in this film), is the spiritual ancestor of that recent mixture of laughs and war horrors, [Kubrick's] *Doctor Strangelove.* (p. 160)

> *Gerald Mast, "Movie Czars and Movie Stars," in his* A Short History of the Movies *(© 1971; reprinted by permission of the publisher, The Bobbs-Merrill Company, Inc.), Bobbs-Merrill—Pegasus, 1971, pp. 120-60.\**

## NORMAN SILVERSTEIN

The year 1922 has been celebrated for the appearance of [Eliot's] *The Waste Land* and [Joyce's] *Ulysses*. It was also the year *The Reader's Digest* began publication. Buster Keaton's **"Cops"** (1922), I would maintain, is a great work of art, belonging with Eliot's poem and Joyce's novel rather than with the trivial works with which it has been associated because its discourse has depended on gags. (p. 269)

Keaton's gags are more philosophical than slapstick in that they test the nature of reality. In **"Cops,"** objects prove to have a side so hidden as to allow indeterminacy to reign in our perception of the received world. . . .

If things have a hidden side, people also are capable of conscious and unconscious duplicities; they too are "indeterminate." (p. 271)

For Keaton's hero in **"Cops,"** the resistance of phenomena to certainty, the duplicity of people and things, and the failure of epistemological systems to establish roads to knowledge—all these compel him to abandon the world.

In **"Cops,"** Keaton tries to remove man from objects, whether natural or contrived, so that man will be isolated from deep meanings and, though locked into his separateness from people and things, be free. His method involves using gags for an assault on the logic that sustains our world. His discovery of the indeterminacy of the things of the world is no less remarkable than Eliot's or Joyce's. . . . (p. 272)

Obviously Keaton operates against the sentimental pattern— the normative realistic discourse—of the Horatio Alger rags-to-riches myth which has usually been conveyed in melodramatic or comic form. . . . Keaton differs from ordinary practitioners by using the gag, which is neither dramatic nor comic, to interrupt continually the story of a poor protagonist's progress in search of material success and love. (p. 274)

> *Norman Silverstein, in his introduction to "Buster Keaton's Gags," by Sylvain du Pasquier, edited and translated by Norman Silverstein, in* Journal of Modern Literature *(© Temple University 1973), Vol. 3, No. 2, April, 1973, pp. 269-75.*

## PENELOPE GILLIATT

Keaton's character in **"Sherlock Jr."** is very much Buster's. Sherlock is cultivated, well dressed, virtuous, and fortunate. He is the forerunner of the well-heeled central figure of **"Battling Butler"** (1926), of the posh college son of the old captain in **"Steamboat Bill, Jr."** (1928), and, most of all, of Rollo Treadway, the augustly decorous hero of **"The Navigator"** (1924, but later than **"Sherlock Jr.").** In the beginning of his dream, The Boy is constantly buffeted by the alien film's overcutting by what Keaton once called to me "the homeless camera." (Like Renoir, among most other great directors, Keaton detested restless editing, and chose that audiences be able to watch in their own time what he was doing.) No sooner does Sherlock jump off a rock into water than it turns out to be snow. No sooner is he on a mountain than he finds himself on flat earth again, between two alarmingly interested lions. Aesthetically, the film plays a subtle and entrancing trick. The movie that the dozy, wistful projectionist is watching is "real," or else his dream of walking into it would not be "unreal;" therefore, the idea that cinema is an illusion is illusory. Sherlock as a figment of film dream can still be harmed by the legerdemain of moviemaking. **"Sherlock Jr."** transports us because of its gaiety, and also because it understands the truths about the universe which lie in pretense and magic. (p. 48)

> *Penelope Gilliatt, "Farce, Comedy, and a Sag in the Male Loner's Facelift," in* The New Yorker *(© 1975 by The New Yorker Magazine, Inc.), Vol. LI, No. 28, September 1, 1975, pp. 46-8.\**

## E. RUBINSTEIN

Keaton's addiction to his scrupulously well-made plots grew out of his awareness that the most astonishing comic invention demands the most conventional of dramatic contexts. But as this awareness apparently intensified over the years, it also began to threaten to limit his work. In *Seven Chances* (1925) and *Battling Butler* (1926) the plot exacts too much of our attention, repeatedly subduing Buster to its complex needs, cheating us of occasions to watch the Keaton body at work. (p. 244)

In *The General* (1926) Keaton has conquered the problem with a success no one could have anticipated. Here the plot attains a Euclidean harmony of shape even as it forces its protagonist again and again to explore the very limits of his own physical resourcefulness; the tension between the demands of the action and the possibilities of the actor is flawlessly maintained over eight reels. So it is, perhaps, that the succeeding film, *College* (1927), is the most nearly episodic of the major Keaton features. Perfection of form, attained in *The General*, no longer seems a challenge. Yes, even in *College* the familiar narrative framework is present: the given situation demands a hero but instead gets a Buster; a Buster under pressure finally explodes into a hero unparalleled and so settles the situation. But the narrative framework is present as if only to permit discrete and self-contained illustrations of Keaton's bodily pyrotechnics, and the nature of these illustrations is fixed more nearly by the range of extracurricular activities college students may most likely pursue (athletics, part-time jobs) than by any internal demands of narrative sequence: whether a soda-jerk sequence will precede or follow this or that demonstration of virtuoso athletic incompetence is now determined mainly by Keaton's sense of how best to space his laughs.

[*Steamboat Bill, Jr.*] offers neither the narrative tautness of *The General* nor the comfortable narrative looseness of *College;* it is the work of a maker of comedies once again at peace with his chosen conventions. *Because* the protagonist is Buster, his father, seeing the long-absent son of his dreams return from the East in the person of an effete runt, will instantly withdraw his love. His girl will turn out to be the daughter of his father's rival steamboat operator. His home town on the Mississippi will prove a place where all his New England college refinements will seem a nasty joke either on his relations or on himself. And then, the pattern of ruination being as ineluctably logical in *Steamboat Bill* as in *King Lear,* his home town will be physically destroyed by a terrible storm. Since, however, he inhabits a world without reason, he will manage to rescue from the subsequent flood everyone who counts in the plot. Father and child, swain and beloved, even sworn business enemies will be momentarily reconciled. In the last shot, capitalising on this instant of harmony, he will salvage a preacher floating past in order to have the hard-won peace certified by a marriage ceremony. So it is, so precisely, we feel, it must be, in a Keaton movie. One reward of *Steamboat Bill* is an entirely satisfactory sense of the sheer inevitability of its events.

If [Mack] Sennett liberated comedy from the fixed arena of the stage, Keaton, more than anyone else, took it upon himself to explore the implications of what Sennett had done, using the film frame to show what it must mean to operate in a world where danger lies not only within the frame but without, the world any single frame excludes but does not deny. The cyclone sequence of *Steamboat Bill* completes Keaton's explorations. (pp. 244-45)

From the beginning Keaton understood the range of comic possibilities of cinematic silence. Sometimes the joke is on Buster: a door unexpectedly slams shut, Buster jumps, we laugh—and we laugh all the harder when Buster is alone on the screen and it therefore appears to us that Buster alone in the universe has heard the frightening sound. At other times

Keaton's emphasis is different. We laugh in *The General* when a weirdly beautiful monomaniac chops wood atop a train even as an enemy army, moving implacably to the right of the frame as the train moves implacably to the left, silently engulfs him. But here the joke turns on us. Though we offer excuses different from Buster's—he was (we guess) distracted by the roar of his engine and his own intentness on the job before him, while we were distracted by the silence of Keaton's medium—we have in a sense participated in his error: at best we may have heard a piano in a movie theatre playing martial music, but like Buster himself we have surely failed to hear an army. . . .

Though there seems little truth to the easy assumption that the imagery of the great films of the 1920s is the function of their want of words . . . , with Keaton silence and expressiveness of image do seem part of a single ontological condition. We can't know how Keaton's visual style would have been affected by sound had he enjoyed in the 1930s the freedom that was his a decade before. But we can see that *Steamboat Bill,* again like *The Cameraman,* displays a mastery of *mise-en-cadre* which no other comedies have equalled. (p. 245)

*E. Rubinstein, "Observations on Keaton's 'Steamboat Bill Jr.',"* in Sight and Sound (copyright © 1975 by The British Film Institute), Vol. 44, No. 4, Autumn, 1975, pp. 244-47.

**ANDREW SARRIS**

One of Buster Keaton's inimitable images is worth a thousand words of explicatory prose. . . . This kind of hyperbolic heraldry gets me into trouble with people like Walter Kerr, who chides me . . . for describing Buster Keaton as "cerebral." I stand by my opinions, however, as I would much prefer to have people see Keaton's movies than sob over his memory. . . . But if any group can be credited with saving Keaton, it is that body of European intellectuals and academics who steadfastly regarded Keaton as an immortal artist rather than as a dated comic. And if Keaton has become, like Chaplin, a figure of speech in the discussion of cinematic style, it is because his films have been studied as high art, and not merely enjoyed as escapist entertainment.

Also, I don't believe the "fun" argument is as strong a motivation for looking at silent movies as is the "art" argument. For anything old to be appreciated in our Now-oriented culture, it must be certified as spinach rather than as ice cream. We are still more puritanical than we care to admit, and we have never treated comic talent with the awe and respect it deserved. In any event, Keaton was always a very special case in that he often became so preoccupied with the peculiar implications of his visual and kinetic ideas that he lost sight of his audience and even his characters. Hence, he was never the most efficient laugh machine in Hollywood. Chaplin, Laurel and Hardy, and Lloyd easily surpass him on that score. Where Keaton excels is in the dreamlike gravity and grace with which he transforms the unimpeachably material world into the purest fantasy. Funny? Not really. Certainly, not entirely. Beautiful, rigorous, resourceful, inventive, creative, evocative, expressive.

But don't take my word for it. . . . Try to forget all your preconceptions about Keaton and silent comedy. You will be startled and disconcerted by elements of the romantic, the adventurous, and the heroic in the Keaton characterizations. Forget even about the tell-tale porkpie hat. It wasn't glued to his head as the derby was to Chaplin's. . . . I envy people who have not yet seen Keaton's legacy.

*Andrew Sarris, "Revivals: Buster Keaton Festival" (reprinted by permission of* The Village Voice *and the author; copyright © The Village Voice, Inc., 1976), in* The Village Voice, *Vol. XXI, No. 4, January 26, 1976, p. 117.*

**PAUL WARSHOW**

[When Fleming's *Gone With the Wind* was re-released in 1967, the distributors tried to "modernize" the film.]

An analogous thing has been done recently to Buster Keaton's silent comedy feature, *The General*. . . . And here the changes are even more serious, not least because *The General,* unlike *Gone With the Wind,* is a masterpiece by one of the great film-makers (perhaps the greatest film-maker of the silent era).

The distributors have made basically two kinds of change: one, the less serious, in the visuals; the other, far more serious, because fundamental, in the sound track. Both seem to have been carried out, at least in part, in the futile and misguided attempt to "modernize" the film, to make it seem less like a silent and a product of its period.

Let us deal first with the less serious change: the changing of the intertitles to subtitles superimposed over the images—and, in at least one case, the complete elimination of the text of an intertitle. The worst thing about the change is that the subtitles keep one from giving one's full attention to the images (this is of course also true with subtitles in foreign sound films, but there it is the lesser of two evils). Moreover, aesthetically speaking, most of the intertitles probably *should* be separate: at least those that contain, not a functional bit of dialogue, but a fairly independent joke (and aesthetically "impure" as written jokes are in a silent film, with Keaton these jokes are usually funny or charming). The change might—wrongly, I think— seem justified because, in eliminating the intertitles, it eliminates an annoyance presented by the intertitles in almost all silent films: they slow the film down inordinately because they are up there excruciatingly long (I can usually read them three times). But the solution is not subtitles: the solution is to shorten the length of time the intertitles are on the screen, leaving them up only as long as it takes everyone but cretins and illiterates to read them. (p. 39)

But the really terrible change is in the sound track: in the addition, along with the music, of realistic, quasi-synchronous sound. While Johnny is trying to escape silently with Annabelle from the Union headquarters, a window falls down on his hands: this print supplies the realistic sound of the window falling and landing. A group of soldiers takes aim, smoke rises from their guns, enemies fall dead: this print supplies the sound, as realistic as in any sound film, of the guns going off (indeed most of the realistic sound in this print is the sound of gunfire).

On the face of it this change offers us More, but in fact it gives us immeasurably Less, because it temporarily destroys the film at its roots—as it would with any silent comedy. For the absence of realistic sound is silent comedy's defining element, its very foundation. To add realistic sound is to destroy this foundation and throw off the delicate balance between stylization and realism that enables the comedy to work. . . . Although most of the audience will not be conscious of the process itself, at the point in *The General* when realistic sound comes in, it is as though a cloud has appeared and darkened the world of film. The stylized fantasy-world of silent comedy is temporarily gone and has been replaced by a much more realistic world: suddenly the pain is "real" pain, the deaths are "real"

deaths; it is no longer the world Keaton gave us, it is no longer funny.

It must be admitted that the people who added the realistic sound to this print have exercised a certain amount of restraint. They have not inserted realistic sound in all the places they could have, only in some, so the comic world is destroyed only in patches, temporarily. The musical score, on the whole, is appropriate and, as musical accompaniment generally does, helps push the film in the direction of greater stylization, both when the music is the sole accompaniment and when it is joined by the realistic sound (which pushes the film in the opposite direction: toward realism). The film is still funny. It is simply less funny, funny less often, than it was. But this restraint hardly makes the additions that *have* been made less objectionable. And in one way this piecemeal destruction is even worse, in that it's more insidious. If the violation were total, many more people would be aware of it. This way they are likely to conclude that Keaton is less funny than he's cracked up to be—or than they remembered. (pp. 39-40)

*Paul Warshow, "More Is Less: Comedy and Sound," in* Film Quarterly (copyright 1977 by The Regents of the University of California; reprinted by permission of the University of California Press), *Vol. XXXI, No. 1, Fall, 1977, pp. 38-45.**

**GARRETT STEWART**

Buster Keaton wrote, starred in, and directed movies when the movies were still in awe of themselves and their very gift for movement. Keaton's kinesis happened also to coincide with the crisis of mimesis in other narrative forms, the growing doubt about story's responsibility toward that "real" world which cinema had so recently learned to simulate and resee. The art of duplication had turned dubious. In the process it had also turned in on itself to discover why. Perhaps the most analytically disposed of all the silent film-makers outside the Russian school, certainly among American directors, Buster Keaton was quick to avail himself of film's position at the fountainhead of modernism. As the period's greatest exegete, Hugh Kenner, points out, the epoch of literary modernism was still in the process of arriving when film emerged as a narrative art, and movies could therefore readily indulge themselves in modernism's reflexive vantage: "Keaton's great creative period was 1921-1927, the age of *Ulysses* and 'The Hollow Men.' In being his own subject he was equally Joyce's and Eliot's contemporary." Indeed, some of Keaton's finest films "might almost be subtitled portraits of the artist as a young man, with a complexity of symbolic displacement hardly to be matched by the auto-inspection of earlier craftsmen." These movies are also portraits of their art form as a young medium. Near in time to the genesis of their form, Keaton's films frequently convert that proximity into subject by foregrounding in the narrative a fascination with their own origins, wittily intent to differentiate the screen image from its predecessors in drama, plastic art, still photography, even mirror reflection. This explains the critical truism that Keaton is a "film-maker's film-maker," his a "pure cinema"; yet while obsessing over their own formal properties, Keaton's films are often guided by self-interrogation toward a larger question about the relation of art to technology, dream to machine. (pp. 348-49)

[Cinematic self-definition is] richly explicit and extensive in Keaton's minor masterpiece of 1924, *Sherlock Jr.* . . . When its hero jumps before our incredulous eyes through a two-dimensional nickelodeon screen into the inner sanctum of cinematic space, we are spectacularly taken aback by Keaton's epistemological modernity and critical wit. In a single leap of reflexive faith, his film enters upon, and its hero with it, an inquest into its own constitution and—because it is all a dream—into the vexed connection between cinematic art and the unconscious. (p. 349)

Theatrical rather than sculptural precursors, however, are . . . invoked in *Sherlock Jr.* It is historically as well as theoretically fitting that the screen through which Keaton makes his inconceivable dive into the inverted looking-glass space of film should be bordered by folds of drapery, the exaggerated bulk of pillars and proscenium arch, and of course the orchestral chasm of a theatrical auditorium turned movie palace. A vaudeville stage comedian who discovered his true acrobatic and visual genius with the coming of film was in a perfect position to celebrate the newfound freedom of *projected* drama as part of the weave and texture of his dramatic narratives. The decor of this crucial theatrical set for *Sherlock Jr.* thus visualizes before us in architectural hybrid the line of succession from staged to filmed comedy, layer upon flanking layer back toward the screen's *tabula rasa,* revealed behind the parted stage curtain just before the start of "Hearts and Pearls." Of course all we have to do is imagine ourselves half a century before the proliferation of the urban triplex theaters with their stacked or staggered, featureless spaces and their functionless floor-to-ceiling drapes, slit conveniently down the middle; imagine ourselves as the original audience of Keaton's movie, probably watching it just past a former vaudeville stage's pit, proscenium, and looped velvet curtains—and we catch at once the planned match of concentricity. Keaton gave his original spectators the nearest equivalent he could devise of the Elizabethan play-within-the-play and its theatrical progeny, and gave it with the same twin intent behind the Renaissance model: to comment on theater as art and, or so as, to probe more knowingly, through the theatricalization of motive, the minds of dramatic characters. (pp. 350-51)

If *Sherlock Jr.* is, as critical consensus has it, an "essay" as much as a story . . . , then its thesis as well as its plot derives from [the] melding in Keaton's imagination of comparative aesthetics—screen as against stage art, for instance—with a complementary sense of film's abiding bond to dream. (pp. 351-52)

[*Sherlock Jr.* is so deeply rooted in] technological self-acknowledgement, as linked to the engineering of our dreams, that it has its protagonist investigate screen space by plunging into it, as if, like Alice's looking-glass, the screen suddenly went "all soft like gauze." The impossible leads us to posit the primal, to know whereof we see. Inside a movie whose mechanical origins are taken at first for granted, we journey, by a demented leap through the impenetrable, birthward toward an exhaustive encounter with film's generative logic, first things first. Within a manufactured film "reality" our hero moves from *homo fictus* to the even more disorienting status of *homo incisus,* cut or edited man. He takes leave of both his senses and his tenses by a lunge into a spliced reality where time and space are relative. Though before we took cuts for granted, unconsciously providing them with their sequential mortar, now we see editing for the arbitrary phenomenon it is at base. As one locale shoves another from the screen, Buster is here, now there, subject to the bludgeoning illogicality of that very principle of cutting, constructive disjunction, upon which all film narrative is founded.

But one fact needs to be repeated about this dizzying but definitive initiation into screen space, a fact which Keaton stresses

with consummate economy: Buster must first fall asleep to make this possible. It is all a dream, sprung from the very springs of the "dream machine." (p. 352)

Only with the frames of *Sherlock Jr.* and "Hearts and Pearls" thus locked into identity are we ready for Buster's admission to the rigidly delimited premises of the film within, the first interior he will see as a bona fide "insider." The only film that now exists visibly for us, and that therefore exists at all as perceptual narrative, is the one Buster has invaded. We have surrendered in a slow inward tracking shot our ironic distance from the hero's confounding initiation, and are prepared to credit him as a screen image. Crucially, he has been able to enter the illusory deeps of the screen, not *in propria persona* as Buster but only *en role* as his fantasized self, the celebrated detective knocking at what we take to be the same door earlier closed to him. But then this is, of course, how all of us enter the fictive confines of film, not as ourselves but by matching our lives and fantasies with the larger-than-life images before us, as Buster had earlier superimposed his own friends and foes, from the safe vantage of the projection room, upon the human images of "Hearts and Pearls." If we were ever able, in our own clothes, at our own human scale, to enter the infinitely deceptive vertical flatland of a movie universe, we might suffer just as summarily from its alien logic and unearthly laws. Instead we must keep the dream objectified as art, and Buster's miraculous ability to do otherwise, even for a furious few moments, is a comic aberration meant to expose as incredible its own foolhardy illusion.

It is important to note too, that Buster is *twice* repulsed by the screen world before gaining entry, in ways which emphasize his dual unsuitedness, first heroic and then ontological, to its sphere of action. To start with he is booted out into the orchestra pit by the villain of "Hearts and Pearls," who is also, by superimposition after the first scene, the former villain of his real-life misadventures, and upon attempted reentry he finds himself violently at variance with the nature of screen space. The parable is double. Still as Buster, he has no more chance of victory over a disreputable nemesis in a fiction than in life. And still a living man, with weight and girth, he has no credentials for the insatiable engulfments of time and terrain which are the stuff of film narrative. Even when his twin initiation is over, first by physical humiliation and then by a bout of mechanical editing that schools him even more gruelingly in screen rules, he must still pay the price of selfhood to purchase the sureties of fiction, must die or dissolve from man into manufactured role in order ultimately to ford the torrent of discrete scenes here used to flood the unbridgeable crevasse dividing life from the lifelike, the world from its virtual presence in a cinematic apparition. (pp. 356-57)

Not for nothing—but rather to induce this next-to-nothing, the cinematic phantom—does Buster go to sleep leaning on an idle second projector in the booth, while the first one spins away at its business of transmitting "Hearts and Pearls." . . . The machine upon which Buster rests and soon sleeps, as upon an upright electronic pillow, projects not a coherent manufactured narrative but instead the imposition of his own unconscious fantasies upon the preternaturally receptive plot of the film actually being shown to the theater audience. The second unlit projector therefore becomes the true dream machine, and out of the seething unconscious of its dozing operator is raised from latency the most eloquent "symbolic displacement" . . . in all of Keaton's cinematic artistry. The emergent Buster Jr. is a supple and transparent celluloid automaton, an ocular robot from the unconscious who will soon be cavorting with Olympian assurance through the gnarled garden of machines and mechanized obstacles that await him within the screen's purely visual universe. By analogy with the term "android," we might call this mechanical counterfeit a "celluloid," a specter visibly punned into presence not just as an arbitrarily twinned shape but as a symbol of any actor's summons to being as a screen image. Cinema as dream projection and cinema as mechanical product meet, as nowhere so clearly before or since, in a human icon compact of both unconscious cause and technological effect.

Objectified and sent forth into his own dream, an incomparable physical actor has removed himself one step from his medium to meditate on his very status as a filmic mirage. We are about to go through the cinema's looking-glass, that is, with the only creature, a secondhand entity mechanically devised, who is properly constituted to inhabit (speaking in a metaphor to which I am now ready to be bound) its framed space, a creature mysteriously "there" but depthless, like a mere, sheer mirror image. Our realization that persons and objects on screen are simply flat pretenses of depth, however, does not always supervene in the act of viewing. Buster Jr., before becoming Sherlock Jr., is delivered into this world by a process of what we might call reverse superimposition, and is, like all screen images though more candidly, as thin as the celluloid through which light projects him. Before reaching the screen he is what all film figures are while still in the projection booth, no more substantial than the film that holds and discloses them. But even here, though inescapably transparent, the illusion of Buster Jr. lulls us into a sense of a certain roundedness, however innocent his image may be of density or specific gravity. When we stare ourselves into fictive acquiescence in a theater, if we do not go so far as to posit hypnotically a stagelike presence for our heroes and heroines, what I think we feel about the impossibility of stepping through the screen frame into the movie is not so much that the screen would stop us, as that once through it there would be nothing there to inhabit or accost but unbodied illuminations.

And so the viewing imagination is gripped by perhaps the ultimate illusory myth of cinematic manifestation: that screen people are closer to sculptures in light than to a veneer of reflection. We know we cannot touch them, yet when Buster does so it causes more of a rent in our aesthetic common sense than a tear in the white sheet of screen, which is not intuited by us in the midst of our voyeurism as an opaque scrim so much as a bordering and a threshold. Just as idiom has us looking not *on* a mirror, or *at* it, but *in* or *into* it—as if it were a reflecting pool with depth as well as surface, where our watery doubles float or sink away—the subtlest illusion of movie space is that the screen is a frame, not a plane, past which is recess and perspective, though nothing quite palpable within. When Sherlock in costume spruces up before and then steps through that huge assumed mirror, the allegory of his access to even deeper reaches of the fictional world is staged to perfection precisely because he does not break a giant pane

of glass to effect the joke. A shape of light, he steps through to a world that is all cast shadows upon a background of brightness, however three-dimensional these shapes conspire to appear.

This, then, is what is also confessed in the projection booth beyond the obvious visual coding of the dream self breaking free. In that masterfully layered statement, image over and above image over and above star and director both, we see Keaton the conceptual artist and self-consciously speculative moviemaker, represented by proxy as Buster the projectionist and purveyor of comic film, generate by a second mirage of creative technology Buster the protean mechanical presence, Keaton the celluloid image. This subsidiary creature is soon, of course, to undergo a second metamorphosis into character, and by becoming Sherlock Jr. to begin acting out the fantasies of his controlling twin as if they were his own, those subjective dreams of superhuman prowess released like himself into the paradoxical objectivity of screen life. Alice, back from her second wonderland on the other side of the mirror, was onto something at the end. And if the Red King was her fantasist all along, not she his, then he offers us a paradigm of the quintessential film director, dreaming before our eyes, with improbable presumption and authority, the dreams of others and our own. (pp. 363-65)

When the groundbreaking Keaton movies of the early twenties and such later Chaplin classics as *City Lights* (1931) and *Modern Times* (1936) managed to lift their heads above the immediate turmoil of comic narrative to consider their own innate automatism, overt self-consciousness was born. These lithe and wily films of the silent era come down to us not just as modern artifacts but as modernist documents, self-contemplative and anything but naïve about their birthright in an age of industrial extremity. They are comedies of mechanization that know how cinema itself emerged as an emancipating new engine tooled to restore us to ourselves, our image and our dreams. Cinema is thus acknowledged in many of its own early products, and never more brilliantly than in *Sherlock Jr.*, as an unprecedented *ars ex machina*, expanding the freehold of dream either by exiling all harsh or inhospitable technologies or, in its early slapstick plots, foiling them face-on with the more flexible inventiveness of soul and body. The success of the cliché "dream machine" was clinched from the date of coinage by its oxymoronic tenor, for it catches that subsuming paradox of all cinematic art. Mechanical counterfeit had gone deeper than ever dreamed, to dream itself. Though no one has yet invented a cybernetic device to simulate the functions of the unconscious mind, long before any computer started thinking cinema had offered us a machine that not only reproduced the surface of our lives but—just at a time when human history most direly desired such an escape clause—a machine that could also, and without threat to the spirit's autonomy, do our dreaming for us if we so chose. (pp. 366-67)

*Garrett Stewart, "Keaton through the Looking-Glass," in* The Georgia Review *(copyright, 1979, by the University of Georgia), Vol. XXXIII, No. 2, Summer, 1979, pp. 348-67.*

# Fritz Lang

## 1890-1976

Austrian-born director, screenwriter, producer, and actor.

Lang's work is among the most influential in cinema. His silent films are monuments of narrative technique and architectural brilliance, while his later films explore the psychology of human desire and motivation. Lang concentrated on movement in his films. Yet he explored the theme of human beings in relation to society in depth, creating works (particularly *M* and *Fury*) which have become classic pieces of cinema.

Lang's first screenplays were filmed by Joe May, and Lang acted in some of them. His first directorial effort, *Halbblut* (*The Half-Breed*), was not a great success, but it was soon followed by two successes, *Die Spinnen* (*The Spiders*) and *Der müde Tod* (*Destiny*). The first film in which Lang revealed his social and political concerns was *Dr Mabuse der Spieler* (*Dr. Mabuse the Gambler*). The film was coscripted by Thea von Harbou, who later became Lang's wife, and who worked with Lang on all of his films until 1932.

Lang's next important film, *Die Nibelungen*, combines a medieval poem and Norse tale. In contrast, *Metropolis*, which followed, is a futuristic look at contemporary social systems that is among Lang's more influential films. *M* was Lang's first sound film, and his use of the new medium heightens the tension required for his depiction of a psychopathic child killer. Lang's last German film, *The Testament of Dr. Mabuse*, a sequel to his earlier film, contains such serious anti-Nazi overtones that it was banned by the government.

However, based on the appeal of his other films, Lang was asked to be the head of the Nazi film industry. Instead, Lang left Thea von Harbou, a member of the Communist party, and fled to France, where he made *Liliom* in 1935. Lang then settled in the United States. The psychological themes Lang had begun to develop in his last German films are examined fully in *Fury*, his first American film, and in later films, including *You Only Live Once*, *Scarlet Street* (a remake of Jean Renoir's *La chienne*), and *The Big Heat*.

Lang showed his versatility by making a number of successful Westerns, including *The Return of Frank James* and *Rancho Notorious*. His work also includes a war story, *An American Guerrilla in the Philippines*, and a political thriller, *Hangmen Also Die!*, written with Bertolt Brecht. In 1959 Lang returned to Germany to make *The Tiger of Eschnapur* and *Das indische Grabmal* (*The Indian Tomb*), which were condensed ("mutilated," according to Lang) into one film, entitled *Journey to the Lost City* in the United States and *Tiger of Bengal* in Britain. Lang's last film was *Die tausend Augen des Dr Mabuse* (*The Thousand Eyes of Dr. Mabuse*), in which a Mabuse-like criminal is at work in a sophisticated modern environment.

Lang was generally most interested in what action he could depict on screen, yet his films are felt to be consistently intriguing in plot, characterization, and the theme of the individual attempting to come to grips with society, law, and crime. Some critics feel that his German films are his best, citing their swift narrative and sweeping visuals. Others believe that his American films, with their stronger focus on plot and psychological drama, are more important. (See also *Contemporary Authors*, Vols. 77-80; obituary, Vols. 69-72.)

## BERTRAM HIGGINS

Anyone who is indifferent or hostile to the Cinema should make a point of seeing *Destiny*. . . . [It is a very remarkable German production that is] bound, sooner or later, to effect radical changes in the standards of film-making. . . .

[It] is necessary to give as much publicity as possible to the new forms of psychological fantasy of which *Destiny*, for all its faults, is such an admirable example. (p. 284)

The narrative loses most of its attractiveness in [a] condensed synopsis; one has to see the film to realize how beautifully it has been treated by Fritz Lang, the scenario-writer and producer. . . . There are two strange blemishes in the technique of the production: the lines dividing the real from the symbolical story are not preserved with sufficient distinctness; and even if we allow for recent changes in the metaphysical conception of Time, "The stories of the three lights" are full of disturbing contradictions. But there can be no question that, despite its constructional faults, and the inadequacy of the subtitles in translation, *Destiny* is one of the most original and impressive films that have ever been made. (pp. 284-85)

> Bertram Higgins, "The Cinema: 'Destiny' at the Polytechnic Hall," in The Spectator (© 1924 by The Spectator; reprinted by permission of The Spectator), Vol. 132, No. 4991, February 23, 1924, pp. 284-85.

## IRIS BARRY

The producer [of *The Niebelungs*], Fritz Lang, already famous in this country as the begetter of *Destiny* and *Sumurun*, was once a painter, which probably explains why, in utilizing, not the opera-glass but the field-glass method, he has seemed to insist, quite rightly, that the visual beauty of a film is just as important as its dramatic economy and effectiveness. Actually he has completely subdued the dramatic element to the visual one. The human beings in this epic of Siegfried remain legendary characters: these kings and queens in their bleak inaccessible castles on mountain-tops behave with the passionlessness and dignity of actors in a pageant. Architecture and trees, dragons, dwarfs and the elementals in the heavy mist-shrouded forests are the real protagonists, and the emotional situations in the tangled and sinister love-affairs of Siegfried and his brother-in-law Gunther are keyed down to give them their proper value in the producer's conception. . . . The camera's divorce from reality . . . is one of the most effective achievements of moving photography: no real white dove, no real ravens even photographed with the subtlest lighting and distortion could equal the intensity and meaning of those formal bird-shapes in the Dream. The use of tone, of sharp black and clear white and clean silver, here and throughout, is very accomplished and lovely. . . .

The major fault of *The Niebelungs* . . . , however, is the horrible sub-titling. One hears that the German titles were simple and direct, as they ought to be, but the English captions, if one can call them English, are a horrible medley of mock-Saxon, inverted phrase and sheer nonsense. . . .

The need of constant experiments to discover the methods of story-telling best adapted to the many types of films, to fix the dramatic conventions of cinematography, has been recognized. Too little attention has been given up to the present to the fact that, besides telling a story well, a film should also be agreeable to look at, a harmonious succession of pictorial compositions. *The Niebelungs* is a very important picture indeed, because though not wholly successful it brings to the notice of the public, and, one hopes to the notice of the producers, this crying necessity for conscious pictorial as well as dramatic organization.

*Iris Barry, "The Cinema: 'The Niebelungs'," in* The Spectator *(© 1924 by* The Spectator; *reprinted by permission of* The Spectator*), Vol. 132, No. 5007, June 14, 1924, p. 955.*

**EVELYN GERSTEIN**

["**Metropolis**"], for all its thesis and its subtitular dialectic . . . , is much more akin to the romantic vagaries of "**Siegfried**" than to the realities of [F. W. Murnau's] "**The Last Laugh**." For Fritz Lang, who directed both "**Siegfried**" and "**Metropolis**," is not a cinema radical. . . . [He] thinks in terms of sheer visual beauty, composition, and group rhythms rather than of dynamics. He is still of the theater of [Max] Reinhardt in the fluency of his groups and the rhythmic progression of his pageant. . . . "**Metropolis**" lacks cinematic subtlety. It is only in the "shots" of machinery in motion and in the surge of the revolutionists that it is dynamic. The camera is too often immobile, the technique that of the stylized theater.

Yet here for the first time the chill mechanized world of the future . . . has been given reality. Here is the city, that tormented circus of buildings which touch the sky, of tunnels that disrupt the places under the earth. Through the air man has hurled his obstructions, his bridges and traffic ways. Yet only the machines seem real; gigantic purring gods grinding down life. Machines, machines, machines, sliding through the earth,

challenging the cosmos, pounding out human resistance as they set the awful tempo of life.

There is no loveliness here, except in the gardens of the rich, high above the levels of the city, where space and light are not mortified for efficiency. Below the surface of the earth the workers and their children crawl through a timed eternity, strapped to the dynamos like so many numbered robots. There is no rest, no beauty, no life below the gardens of the higher levels. Man is inanimate. Life is metronomic. It is only the machines that are alive. (pp. 323-24)

As Lang has directed it, "**Metropolis**" is more stylized fantasy than realism. Even in the torrentous revolt of the workers as they pour through the machine-rooms, alive, demoniacal, there is an air of unreality. This is not revolution as the Russians stage it. It has neither taste nor smell. Yet it is magnificent. Even the most careless groupings are beautifully composed. Lang is too much the artist to deny the imagination. . . .

"**Metropolis**" is utterly devoid of humor. Thea von Harbou, its author, wrote it originally as a novel and then adapted it to the screen. Only her concept of Metropolis itself is intellectual. The rest is sentimental symbolism. There is no individualization within the type. Her persons are puppets. There is the Capitalist, his Son, Mary the spiritual leader of the workers, et al. The Son is the eternal mediator who, with the help of the woman Mary, although only after a revolution intervenes, brings "brains" and "brawn" together for the final fade-out.

Perhaps it is because of its original form that "**Metropolis**" lacks concision. One of the most interesting episodes of the entire film is that in which the inventor transmits the shape and likeness of Mary to the woman of his creation by encircling bands of electricity, yet it is only partially developed. The robotess, or creature of human invention, breeds revolution and is stoned by the mob, but the formula which gave her life is never mentioned again. The inventor is himself hurled from the cathedral roof by the blond and shining John, the hero; but what of the formula?

It is Metropolis itself, the city of domed basements and curving machine-rooms, of massed buildings that conceal the sky, of aeroplanes that ply their corner-to-corner traffic, of trains that seem to shoot into unmeasured and untracked space, that makes Fritz Lang's film so significant. (p. 324)

*Evelyn Gerstein, "Moving Pictures: 'Metropolis'," in* The Nation, *Vol. 124, No. 3220, March 23, 1927, pp. 323-24.*

**IRIS BARRY**

If "**Metropolis**" fails to be quite a great film, the fault lies, not with its brilliant German producers, nor with its subject matter, nor with the actual treatment of this picture-parable of life next century. It fails because the cinema as yet fails to be quite adequate as a means of expression.

Here on the screen is a concrete picture of a great city of the future. . . . The imagination of Fritz Lang, the director, and of the studio-architects and designers who have brought this vision to "life" proved adequate enough here. The film shows us the making of an artificial human being: shows us television. We can accept these miracles. . . .

But I fear that the intelligent part of the audiences that see "**Metropolis**" will find it very difficult to admire the peacock-strewn pleasure gardens of the future, in which the free and gilded inhabitants of the skyscrapers of the future disport them-selves, heedless of the tragic workmen deep below. It is sad, too, to find that men of the future dress just as hideously as do those of to-day. But the costume is not very convincing, anyhow, in "Metropolis": and though part of the film is con-ceived in an expressionist mood, and part of it quite natural-istically, some of it is mere picture-postcard. The expressionist parts are far and away the best, and the workmen turn out better than their masters.

The weaknesses of the cinema are most apparent in the story. It is pure melodrama . . . , and frankly treated as such. So grandiose a theme as that which "Metropolis" attempts to develop demanded, of course, something on the epic scale. . . .

Yet "Metropolis" is by far the most nearly adult picture we have seen. There are moments when it touches real greatness: in its handling of crowds, not for the sake only of the spectacle, but for what emotion the movement of the crowd can express. Its architecture is beautiful, its pictorial composition frequently superb.

> *Iris Barry, "The Cinema: 'Metropolis'," in* The Spectator *(© 1927 by The Spectator; reprinted by permission of* The Spectator*), Vol. 138, No. 5152, March 26, 1927, p. 540.*

### WILLIAM HUNTER

[What] is this "bigness of outlook" that distinguishes *Me-tropolis*? The architectural sets and the photography are ex-tremely competent craftsmanship. After that, what? It is a vision of the future. . . . The idea of the machine city of the future, of robots, etc., is the common property of all up-to-date journalists. No one in the cinema to-day could conceive and transmit the future as it will probably be. A subject which occupies some of the best minds of Europe, which has such unplumbed depths, and which is certainly too dark and complex for such a glib and facile solution as *Metropolis* offers, is unlikely to be translated into terms of images. It is necessary to drug one's sensibilities, to stop asking oneself the many awkward questions that occur as the film unfolds, in order to be able to accept such grossness as the pathetic reconciliation of father and son, or the cheap contrast of Capital and Labour supplied by the Garden of Pleasure and the underground city. *Metropolis* came from a paper-covered thriller which can be purchased in translation in any Woolworth's store. I doubt whether even the critics who praise "the bigness of outlook and power of broad visualisation" of the film would be able to stomach the book. What makes the film interesting while its literary counterpart is unbearable are the technical qualities, the brilliance of the camera-work and the mass architecture. But excellence of production does not transmute a fundamen-tally worthless theme into a work of art, nor ever will do. (pp. 24-5)

> *William Hunter, "The Achievement of the Cinema," in his* Scrutiny of Cinema, *Wishart & Co, 1932, pp. 22-49.**

### WILLIAM TROY

["M"] is based on the crimes and the final apprehension by the police of the famous child murderer of Düsseldorf. Cer-tainly no subject could be more inherently horrible, more dan-gerously open to a facile sensationalism of treatment. Yet such are the tact and the genius with which Fritz Lang has handled it that the result is something at once more significant than either the horror story, pure and simple . . . , or the so-called psychological "document" of the type which Germany has sent us so often in the past. The result is, in fact, a film which answers to most of the demands of classical tragedy. In the first place, Lang has concentrated his interest not on the cir-cumstances but on the social and human consequences of the crimes. We are shown a whole city thrown into panic by what is for every class the least pardonable of all acts of vio-lence. . . . [This] provides a formal suspense more sustained than would any playing on the usual modes of physical horror. It also provides a certain nervous relief. The horror, as is proper and necessary in the films, is conveyed by implication rather than representation. It is implied through a very few miracu-lously appropriate symbols—a child's toy balloon caught in a telegraph wire or a child's ball rolling to a stop from the scene of the crime. Bloodlust is identified with the strain of Grieg which the criminal whistles whenever the passion is upon him. The whole pattern—lust, the victim, and the circumstances—is symbolized in the frame of glittering knives in which the criminal, staring in a shop window, sees the image of his latest victim reflected. Because these symbols are one and all visual or aural, peculiar to the talking screen, they serve to make "M" of the very highest technical interest. But they are not enough to explain why it may also be considered a great trag-edy. . . . The modern psychopath . . . attains to the dignity of the tragic hero. It does not matter that the forces are no longer on the outside. They are perhaps the more ruthless for being inside him. The *moirae* may be given different names by the doctors, the judges, and the audience, but they have lost none of their ancient inevitability.

The last thing that may be said about "M," therefore, is that it confirms our belief in the continued vitality of the tragic emotion. Few other attempts to substitute for the old gods, fates, or destiny a modern fatalism of psychological mecha-nisms have been so successful. . . . It may be that Fritz Lang and Peter Lorre [who played the child murderer] are better artists in their fields than most of those who have sought to revive tragedy in our time. Or it may be—and "M" gives strength to the supposition—that the cinema is able to supply a language for modern tragic experience that is at once fresher, more various, and more poetic than the flat statement of nat-uralistic drama. (pp. 454-55)

> *William Troy, "Tragedy and the Screen," in* The Nation, *Vol. 136, No. 353, April 19, 1933, pp. 454-55.*

### SIEGFRIED KRACAUER

Owing to its two parts, [*Dr. Mabuse the Gambler*] is of an extraordinary length—a dollar-dreadful rather than a penny-dreadful. Trash need not be untrue to life; on the contrary, life may culminate in heaps of trash, such as no writer could ever amass. However, instead of making *Dr. Mabuse* reflect familiar surroundings, Lang frequently stages the action in settings of pronounced artificiality. Now the scene is an expressionist club-room with painted shadows on the wall, now a dark back street through which Cesare might have slipped with Jane in his arms. Other decorative forms help these expressionist ones to mark the whole as an emotional vision. *Dr. Mabuse* belongs in the *Caligari* sphere. . . . It is by no means a documentary film, but it is a document of its time.

The world it pictures has fallen prey to lawlessness and de-pravity. A night-club dancer performs in a décor composed of outright sex symbols. Orgies are an institution, homosexuals and prostitute children are everyday characters. The anarchy smoldering in this world manifests itself clearly in the admirably handled episode of the police attack against Mabuse's house—an episode which through its imagery intentionally recalls the tumultuous postwar months with their street fights between Spartacus and the Noske troops. Circular ornaments emerge prominently time and again. Both the tricky floor in a new gambling club and the chain of hands formed during a spiritualist séance are shown from above to impress their circular appearance upon the spectator. Here, as in the case of *Caligari,* the circle denotes a state of chaos. (pp. 82-3)

The film succeeds in making of Mabuse an omnipresent threat which cannot be localized, and thus reflects society under a tyrannical regime—that kind of society in which one fears everybody because anybody may be the tyrant's ear or arm.

Throughout the film Mabuse is stigmatized as a man of genius who has become Public Enemy No. 1. . . . [In the end,] Mabuse is wrecked; but social depravity continues, and other Mabuses may follow. Here as well as in *Caligari* not the slightest allusion to true freedom interferes with the persistent alternative of tyranny or chaos.

*Dr. Mabuse* adds to *Caligari* only in one respect: it attempts to show how closely tyranny and chaos are interrelated. . . . [Chaos] breeds tyrants like Mabuse who, for their part, capitalize on chaos. (pp. 83-4)

[The plot of *Destiny*] forces one point strongly upon the audience: that, however arbitrary they seem, the actions of tyrants are realizations of Fate. The agent of Fate supports tyranny not only in all three episodes but also in the story proper. The death he inflicts upon the young lover appears so senseless that it is as if some unscrupulous tyrant had pulled the strings. . . . [No] paradoxical meaning can be read into the shocking actions of Fate in *Destiny*. The film ends with the girl's self-renunciation accompanied by a caption that emphasizes its religious significance: "He who loses his life gains it." . . .

The long-lived power of *Destiny*'s imagery is the more amazing as all had to be done with the immovable, hand-cranked camera, and night shots were still impossible. These pictorial visions are so precise that they sometimes evoke the illusion of being intrinsically real. (p. 90)

In *Destiny* Fate manifests itself through the actions of tyrants; in [*Die Nibelungen*], through the anarchical outbursts of ungovernable instincts and passions. To mark as fateful the doom these impulses bring about, the story closely interlinks causes and effects. From the moment when the dying dragon with a movement of his tail makes the ominous leaf drop on Siegfried's back down to the moment of Attila's self-chosen death, nothing seems left to mere chance. An inherent necessity predetermines the disastrous sequence of love, hatred, jealousy and thirst for revenge. (p. 93)

This Fate-conditioned story materializes through scenes which seem to be staged after decorative paintings of a bygone period. . . . It is amazing that despite their too pronounced beauty and their somewhat outmoded taste—a taste already outmoded in 1924—these pictures are still effective. The constructional austerity they breathe may account for it. Lang knew why . . . he relied upon the spell of such decorative compositions: they symbolize Fate. The compulsion Fate exerts is aesthetically mirrored by the rigorous incorporation of all structural elements into a framework of lucid forms.

There are many elaborate scenic details. . . . But far from pretending to self-sufficiency, each of these details assumes its specific function only within the composition as a whole. To heighten the impression of pictorial unity, extensive use is made of simple, large and solemn architectural structures dominating the scene. (pp. 93-4)

*Nibelungen* unfolds in lingering scenes that have all the qualities of stills. Their slow procession, which characterizes the mythic realm as a static one, is calculated to draw attention to the action proper. This intrinsic action does not coincide with the succession of treacheries and murders, but is to be found in the development of smoldering instincts and imperceptibly growing passions. It is an all but vegetative process through which Fate realizes itself. (p. 95)

Outstanding instances of grand-style manner were the three films Fritz Lang produced during the stabilized period. They dealt with thrilling adventures and technical fantasies symptomatic of the then current machine cult. The first of them was *Metropolis.* . . . (p. 149)

[What is important in *Metropolis*] is not so much the plot as the preponderance of surface features in its development. In the brilliant laboratory episode, the creation of a robot is detailed with a technical exactitude that is not at all required to further the action. The office of the big boss, the vision of the Tower of Babel, the machinery and the arrangement of the masses: all illustrate Lang's penchant for pompous ornamentation. In *Nibelungen,* his decorative style was rich in meaning; in *Metropolis,* the decorative not only appears as an end in itself, but even belies certain points made through the plot. It makes sense that, on their way to and from the machines, the workers form ornamental groups; but it is nonsensical to force them into such groups while they are listening to a comforting speech from the girl Maria during their leisure time. In his exclusive concern with ornamentation, Lang goes so far as to compose decorative patterns from the masses who are desperately trying to escape the inundation of the lower city. Cinematically an incomparable achievement, this inundation sequence is humanly a shocking failure. . . . (pp. 149-50)

Lang's subsequent film, the mystery thriller *Spione* (*The Spy,* 1928), shared two traits with his *Dr. Mabuse.* It featured a master spy who, like Mabuse, led several different lives: besides the spy, he was also the president of a bank and a music-hall clown. And exactly like *Dr. Mabuse,* this new film refrained from conferring moral superiority upon the representatives of the law. Espionage and counterespionage were on the same level—two gangs fighting each other in a chaotic world. Yet there was one important difference: while Dr. Mabuse had incarnated the tyrant who takes advantage of the chaos around him, the master spy indulged in the spy business for the sole purpose, it seemed, of spying. He was a formalized Mabuse devoted to meaningless activities. By emphasizing this figure, the film reflected the neutrality prevalent during that period—a neutrality which also manifested itself in the absence of any distinction between legal and illegal pursuits and in a prodigal abundance of disguises. No character was what he appeared to be. This constant change of identities was appropriate to denote a state of mind in which the paralysis of the self interfered with any attempt at self-identification. As if to fill the void, Lang piled up sensations which conveyed no meaning. His imaginative virtuosity in shaping them reached its climax with a train wreck in a tunnel. Since it proved impossible to stage the catastrophe in life-size proportions, he gave the impression of it through confused mental images of the persons involved in this shock situation.

*The Spy* would have been a true forerunner of the Hitchcock thrillers if Lang had not fashioned it after the pompous manner of *Metropolis,* so that empty sensations took on the air of substantial revelations. Virtuosity alienated from content posed as art. (p. 150)

In his third film, *Die Frau im Mond* (*The Girl in the Moon,* 1929), Lang imagined a rocket projectile carrying passengers to the moon. The cosmic enterprise was staged with a surprising veracity of vision; the plot was pitiable for its emotional shortcomings. These were so obvious that they discredited many an illusion Lang tried to create by showy virtuosity. (p. 151)

[*M* was Lang's] first important film after the pretentious duds he had made during the stabilized period. *M* again reaches the level of his earlier films, *Destiny* and *Nibelungen,* and moreover surpasses them in virtuosity. To increase the film's documentary value, pictorial reports on current police procedures are inserted in such a skillful way that they appear to be part of the action. Ingenious cutting interweaves the milieus of the police and the underworld: while the gang leaders discuss their plans, police experts, too, sit in conference, and these two meetings are paralleled by constant shifts of scene which hinge on subtle association. The comic touch inherent in the cooperation between the lawless and the law materializes on various occasions. Witnesses refuse to agree upon the simplest facts; innocent citizens indict each other fiercely. Set against these gay interludes, the episodes concentrating upon the murders seem even more horrifying.

Lang's imaginative use of sound to intensify dread and terror is unparalleled in the history of the talkies. Elsie's mother, after having waited for hours, steps out of her flat and desperately shouts the child's name. While her "Elsie!" sounds, the following pictures pass across the screen: the empty stairwell . . . ; the empty attic; Elsie's unused plate on the kitchen table; a remote patch of grass with her ball lying on it; a balloon catching in telegraph wires—the very balloon which the murderer had bought from the blind beggar to win her confidence. Like a pedal point, the cry "Elsie!" underlies these otherwise unconnected shots, fusing them into a sinister narrative. (pp. 219-20)

The film's true center is the murderer himself. [He is] a somewhat infantile petty bourgeois who eats apples on the street and could not possibly be suspected of killing a fly. His landlady, when questioned by the police, describes this tenant of hers as a quiet and proper person. He is fat and looks effeminate rather than resolute. A brilliant pictorial device serves to characterize his morbid propensities. On three different occasions, scores of inanimate objects . . . surround the murderer; they seem on the point of engulfing him. Standing before a cutlery shop, he is photographed in such a way that his face appears within a rhomboid reflection of sparkling knives. . . . Sitting on a café terrace behind an ivy-covered trellis, with only his cheeks gleaming through the foliage, he suggests a beast of prey lurking in the jungle. Finally, trapped in the lumber room, he is hardly distinguishable from the tangled debris in which he tries to evade his captors. Since in many German films the predominance of mute objects symbolizes the ascendancy of irrational powers, these three shots can be assumed to define the murderer as a prisoner of uncontrollable instincts. Evil urges overwhelm him in exactly the same manner in which multiple objects close in on his screen image. (pp. 220-21)

In its exploration of this character, who is not so much a retrogressive rebel as a product of retrogression, *M* confirms the moral of [Josef von Sternberg's] *The Blue Angel:* that in the wake of retrogression terrible outbursts of sadism are inevitable. Both films bear upon the psychological situation of those crucial years and both anticipate what was to happen on a large scale unless people could free themselves from the specters pursuing them. The pattern had not yet become set. In the street scenes of *M,* such familiar symbols as the rotating spiral in an optician's shop and the policeman guiding a child across the street are resuscitated. The combination of these motifs with that of a puppet incessantly hopping up and down reveals the film's wavering between the notions of anarchy and authority. (p. 222)

[*The Last Will of Dr. Mabuse*] is inferior to *M.* In it, Lang accumulates mere thrills, elaborating upon them zealously. Whenever Baum feels swayed by Mabuse, the latter's ghostly apparition emerges with clocklike punctuality. Since repetitious shock effects tend to neutralize each other, the result is monotony rather than an increase of suspense. Nevertheless the film includes . . . brilliant episodes which testify to Lang's "uncanny genius for invoking terror out of the simplest things." (p. 249)

*Siegfried Kracauer, in his* From Caligari to Hitler: A Psychological History of the German Film *(copyright 1947 © 1975 by Princeton University Press; reprinted by permission of Princeton University Press), Princeton University Press, 1947, 361 p.**

**ROGER MANVELL**

Looking at *Siegfried* in 1950, a quarter of a century after it was made, one is aware of the outstandingly good and bad elements in it after as little as twenty minutes' screening. . . . The so-called "expressionist" style in German silent cinema, which encouraged directors and designers to stylise both décor and acting, rapidly passed out of fashion. *Siegfried* seems farther away from present day film-making than the silent films of [D. W.] Griffith or [Sergei] Eisenstein because of this excessive stylisation.

First of all the action of Lang's film is taken at a pace which is much too slow for the modern viewer, so that in almost every shot one accepts the implications of the scene long before the actors complete it. Every emotion is registered with emphatic gestures and facial expression in the manner common to the films of the period, except in the work of a few of the more exceptional players in Griffith's films. The characters are, of course, larger and psychologically simpler than life in their legendary setting, so that some heroic magnification is correct. . . . (pp. 84-5)

Human characterisation, however, was not Lang's main consideration. He wanted to create a legendary atmosphere, and to create it by pictorial means. It was more important for him that Kriemhild should sit a still and statuesque figure in the archway of a window than that she should show the nervous impulses of a woman waiting for a likely prince. Siegfried and his warrior kings observe strict formation in the Burgundian court and processions and church services alike are seen to be perfect in their pictorial symmetry. If this exact symmetry oppresses you, then the architecture of *Siegfried* with its vast, spacious walls, its balance of curved masses with angular masses, its geometrically patterned floors and its long flights of steps will soon become a visual bore. But if you like symmetry, then you will find (for a time, at least) a nobility and grandeur in these palaces and courts, and in the costumes with their equally symmetrical designs from the Reinhardt theatre.

The most impressive and beautiful scenes in the film are those in the forests, the misty glades and the caverns through which Siegfried has to travel before he reaches the Kingdom of Burgundy. After many viewings spread over nearly twenty years I still find the sequence of Siegfried's approach to the dragon through the high trees one of the most beautiful in the silent cinema, and the dragon himself . . . the most impressive of all the screen's giant monsters. The descent into the cave holding the Rhine treasure hoard is a wonderful studio spectacle, and the shot of the slowly petrifying dwarfs is completely convincing. One's memory of this long film returns in the end to these scenes, or to those of the ride of Siegfried on his horse led by Alberic through the mists, and his death at the end of the film in the little artificial glade.

The rest of the film is best projected at sound speed. This substantially quickens the intolerably slow pace of the action in the midst of architectural sets which appear increasingly cold and dead as the film develops. (p. 85)

*Roger Manvell, "Revaluations—I: 'Siegfried' 1922-1924," in* Sight and Sound *(copyright © 1950 by The British Film Institute), Vol. 19, No. 2, April, 1950, pp. 83-5.*

## LINDSAY ANDERSON

It seems a long time since Fritz Lang gave us a good film: in fact, the sense of strain and stylistic pretentiousness in his recent work—when it has not been mere commercial hokum—had almost made one abandon hope. This makes it the more unfortunate that his latest film [*The Big Heat*] should have passed almost unnoticed. For it is an extremely good thriller, distinguished by precisely those virtues which Lang's pictures have in the past few years so painfully lacked: tautness and speed; modesty of intention; intelligent, craftsman-like writing. Above all, it is directed with a dramatic incisiveness, a sharp-edged observation that keeps the pitch of interest and excitement continuously high. . . .

*The Big Heat* is one of those enjoyable films which make no great claims for themselves, yet which so balance style and intention . . . that they are finally more satisfying than many more ambitious works. The film lacks the density of [Huston's] *Maltese Falcon;* one or two of its elements are over-conventional; Lang's viewpoint remains exterior. All the same, it creates its world, and proves that, when his interest is engaged, this director still has at his control the technique of a master.

*Lindsay Anderson, "Film Reviews: 'The Big Heat'," in* Sight and Sound *(copyright © 1954 by The British Film Institute), Vol. 24, No. 1, July-September, 1954, p. 36.*

## LINDSAY ANDERSON

*Human Desire* is an odd film, more persuasively transplanted than Lang's previous attempt at a Zola-Renoir story (*Scarlet Street*), even if ultimately the proper conclusions of the story are shirked.

The American railroad setting is quite acceptable . . . ; and some of the script changes are even welcome. In relieving the engine-driving hero of his congenital sadistic mania, Alfred

Hayes has given the story a sharper focus. The design is now clearer and simpler: the seduction and destruction of the honest driver, *homme moyen sensuel,* by the feline tramp who has become the unwilling accomplice of her husband in the murder of her wealthy lover. There is something old-fashioned in the situation, but it remains a valid one, and one senses its appeal to Lang's harsh, Germanic temperament.

This harshness is apparent in the film. There is a welcome lack of gloss about it. The little town at the end of the line is a grey place. And the relationships, for at least the first half of the story, have an interestingly European quality to them—a complication of motive and reaction that seems strange in a Hollywood film of today. . . .

Inevitably, pressures of commercialism and production codes being what they are, the film collapses. Returning from the midnight sortie in which he has pursued the drunken husband across the railway yard, with intent to kill, the lover has to confess: "*I couldn't do it. . . .*" The actor can't believe it; we can't believe it; and Lang hardly tries to convince us. The good parts of the film are good enough to make one regret its final disintegration.

*Lindsay Anderson, "Film Reviews: 'Human Desire'," in* Sight and Sound *(copyright © 1955 by The British Film Institute), Vol. 24, No. 4, Spring, 1955, p. 198.*

## GAVIN LAMBERT

[One can see] that Lang's career in the classic German cinema, embracing as it did most of its tendencies, serves in itself as a kind of allegory. In a variety of stylistic disguises the same obsessions appear and recur—in the *Nibelungen* saga, which added to expressionism an architectural solidity and massive fresco-like sweep, fatality of legend; in the contemporary melodramas, *The Spiders,* the two *Mabuse* films, *The Spy,* fatality of power and violence; in *M,* fatality of the sadistic inner self; in the early scripts for Joe May and Otto Rippert (*Plague in Florence, Woman with the Orchid*) and in *The Half-Caste* and *The Master of Love,* fatality of sexual domination; in *Metropolis,* fatality of the machine future. Lang had studied painting and architecture before coming to the cinema, and it is in his legendary and spectacle films, naturally, that a sensuous plastic quality is uppermost, but the images in his melodramas were no less assiduously composed. As in *Siegfried* he discovered the expressiveness of architectural form, so in *The Spy* and *Doctor Mabuse* he discovered the expressiveness of light and, of course, darkness. In these films he effectively created a language of screen melodrama as well as many of its myths. (pp. 16-17)

Behind the two *Mabuse* films, *The Spiders* and *The Spy* is the . . . idea of demonic, almost abstract, power-organisation determined purposelessly to overthrow human society by acts of outrage and violence. . . . Finally, in *M,* the horrific life-and-death struggle is embodied in a single character, the child-murderer wretchedly trying to escape from his impulses and hallucinations.

These films are not only Lang's most original and lasting achievements of his German period, but remain the most haunting melodramas of the cinema. Their most obviously chilling feature is the suggestion of a cosmic terror at work behind society, a senselessly destructive presence capable at any moment of manifesting itself with an unspeakable outrage. (p. 17)

There is no moral force in [*The Spiders* and *The Testament of Dr. Mabuse*], only fascination and horror. In dramatic terms Lang made the menace of power vividly suggestive and disturbing . . . , but without pity for its victims or indignation against their aggressors. Less completely ruthless, in fact, the films would have been less startling as melodrama. It is only in *M*, when Lang concentrates on the individual so brilliantly portrayed by Peter Lorre, that a kind of steely intellectual compassion is evoked, through the actor's subtle facial play and his last grovelling confession of helplessness. But even here, perhaps, one is struck more by the fatality of instinct than the particular human predicament. From the beginning Lang's method was to abstract, to make "absolute." It was a method that, though he modified its expressionist tendencies, he preserved in America; it is apparent in *Fury*, in *You Only Live Once*, in *Woman in the Window* and *Scarlet Street;* and, under the surface of something as characteristically American as *The Big Heat*, it is still there.

The trilogy of *Fury, You Only Live Once* and *You and Me* stands in a rather ambiguous relation to the American social cinema of the 30's. In one sense (disappointing though the third film is) they remain its most daringly conceived contribution; in another, they scarcely belong to it at all. The difference lies deeper than in the extreme harshness of temperament in the first two films; it is in what the films are *about*. *Fury* is not . . . *about* a lynching, but an almost abstract study of mob hysteria; this hysteria has a number of results, of which the attempted lynching is one and the ferocious destructive bitterness it arouses in the victim . . . is another. *You Only Live Once* and *You and Me* are not *about* the difficulties of ex-convicts going straight in American society—but, again, dramatic abstracts of society's indifference to the outcast, whom it creates, punishes and then forces back into crime so as to feel justified after all. (pp. 17-18)

*You Only Live Once* is an extremely sombre melodrama in which the indictment of society, though less direct [than in *Fury*], is equally bitter, and the outcome is wholly despairing. While Joe Wilson is presumably reconciled, and society will presumably allow him and Catherine to work in the same town in future, Eddie Taylor and his wife Joan are killed at the end of their desperate flight from the forces of order. This change of emphasis is implicit from the beginning. . . . This time society is accused by the spectacle of his confusion and desperation. It is guilty of no concerted vicious outburst, but a blind multiplicity of indifference and hard-heartedness that amounts, the film suggests, to an act of betrayal. (p. 20)

[The events of the film] sound unacceptably fabricated. Yet it is this arbitrariness that gives to the film its curious and memorable force. Critics at the time reproached Lang with sacrificing valid social comment to melodrama; but they misunderstood, I believe, his purpose. From the opening scene of Eddie's release—asked if he'll go straight, *"I will, if they'll let me,"* he replies—a world of inexorable foreboding and melancholy is created, a world of terrible *angst* in which guilt and innocence, calculation and fate, are confused. The imagery is continuously dark and concentrated. . . . The images evoke that feeling of anonymous terror preceding an act of atrocity that shivered through the melodramas of the 20's. . . . (pp. 20-1)

Here, as the exposition gives way to action . . . the reference to the world of *Doctor Mabuse* seems explicit; and from this moment the drama of *You Only Live Once* stays in a kind of doomed imaginary country of night, rain, penumbral mist and darkness. (p. 21)

In *You Only Live Once* even more than in *Fury*, Lang's preoccupation with the values of "classic tragedy" and "prearranged fate" . . . seems especially meaningful.

In *You and Me* the method breaks down because the scheme itself is not valid. . . . Unlike the two preceding films, the central motivation is psychological, proceeding from the relationship between Joe and Helen; Joe reverts to crime not on account of social pressures but of his discovery of Helen's past, just as her attempt to deceive him springs from fear of losing his love. One can argue that society is responsible because it made the law that criminals on parole may not marry, but to elevate this to a tragic "injustice" is fairly absurd. The central relationship . . . fails to convince. . . . [The] falsity seems to come from the fact that the light intimate tone adopted for these passages is not suited to Lang. Aware of this, perhaps, he also places undue emphasis on stylistic trappings. The film opens with a montage sequence set to a Kurt Weill ballad—*"You cannot get something for nothing, only a chump would try it"*—which sets a note of wry sympathy for the poor and underprivileged in a heartless world, but has little to do with the story itself. . . . As an experiment it is not very successful either, for the images are mainly no more than literal illustrations to the words; and the two other semi-expressionist sequences with music by Weill . . . are hardly more integrated into the general texture of the film. The dance-hall song has some point, as its tale of parted underworld lovers conjures up a series of images in Helen's mind. The style, however—bizarre dockland cafés with a sailor bearing a parrot on his shoulder, a hammock in which giant starfish recline, flamingo statues and a clientèle straight from [Pabst's] *Dreigroschenoper*—is hardly appropriate to working class life in America.

These setpieces, and the generally over-emphatic visual style . . . also deflect from what should have been the film's true purpose: the penetration of American life on a more personal, intimate level than Lang was, perhaps, equipped yet to achieve. The abstractions now exist in a vacuum. As the introductory sequence vaguely reproaches society, so the prison-evocation relates back to *You Only Live Once;* but in fact society . . . is positive. . . . (pp. 21, 55)

.   .   .   .   .

[Since *You and Me*], Lang has been more prolific but, with a few exceptions, less personal in his work. He has never attempted anything as ambitious, as broadly conceived, as his films of the '30s, and even the most interesting of his later ones remain minor in comparison. All the same, the output as a whole is far from negligible; and a work as recent as *The Big Heat* (1953) has shown that his talent, if seriously engaged, has not been exhausted by the whole Hollywood experience. (p. 92)

[*The Return of Frank James* and *Western Union*] have conventional scripts and . . . rather indifferent playing. They lack dramatic tension, they are diffusely narrated, and in spite of the admirable period reconstruction of Richard Day's sets, they fail to create a living atmosphere. The clear air and the sweeping landscapes of the West seemed to stimulate Lang only as a painter, for it is in their markedly tasteful and exploratory use of Technicolor that the main interest of both films lies. The landscapes are soft and luminous, they have a rich, idyllic glow; and there are some night scenes . . . that have seldom been equalled for their delicate, subtle shading. Yet one doesn't feel that colour holds much dramatic meaning for Lang; it seems mainly a decorative adjunct. . . . The feeling in these films is remote and external, and though they contain some traditional prairie comedy with experienced players . . . , there is something academic, laborious, about it. (pp. 92-3)

Lang was, however, commercially re-established; and he was now able to make an anti-Nazi subject—not one, as it turned out, but three in succession. *Man Hunt* (1941), *Hangmen Also Die* (1942) and *The Ministry of Fear* (1943) represent a curious sideline in his work. The first and third, set mainly in London, are really stories that Hitchcock should have made, depending for effect on ingenuity in plotting physical tension and excitement, in developing their intrigues and chases against naturalistic backgrounds. But this is not Lang's method. For thrillers, the films are wrongly paced—too applied, too expository—and their (mainly nocturnal) London backgrounds are as weirdly synthetic as Pabst's in *Dreigroschenoper* . . . . Overladen with suggestions of vague terror and menace in everything—a tree or a clock, even, seems macabre, a phenomenon or object of intrinsic ill-will—these films dissipate their real source of tension, the game of hunter and hunted.

Only *Hangmen Also Die,* written in collaboration with Berthold Brecht . . . , has real authority and power. Its plot is not always plausibly contrived, and it suffers from disunity in casting . . . ; but its characterisation of the Nazis is highly original— these frightening but ironically observed members of a terrorgroup remind one of Lang's German melodramas. . . . *Hangmen Also Die* seems more penetrating now than any other American film about Europe under the Nazis. Once again, though, it is interesting to note the dramatic force with which criminals are characterised, the lack of real individual power in the "other side." . . .

*Woman in the Window* (1944), *Scarlet Street* (1945) and *The Secret Beyond the Door* (1947) were made under conditions of relative independence and form a kind of trilogy. The first two have strong qualities, and possess what Lang's intermediate work lacked—a consistent, self-created world; and yet, apart from the fact that their scope is deliberately limited, there is something a little arid in their brilliance. Purposeful, imaginative, scrupulously executed, they voluntarily withdraw from the contemporary world.

All three revive some earlier themes: *Woman in the Window* and *Scarlet Street* the *femme fatale* and her trapped, insignificant victim, *The Secret Beyond the Door* the extravagant, tormented psychopath. The first two bear unmistakable imprints of the harsh schematic method and preoccupation with fatality in their opening scenes, but *Woman in the Window* is as a whole the most satisfactory. It has a strong melodramatic situation. . . . (p. 93)

[The film's adventure is] described with an assiduous deliberation that gives it an almost dreamlike quality. Everything *seems* real—yet, surely, it cannot be. But the sleeper is not to wake, and nightmarish sequels . . . arrive with the same inexorable, ominously charged momentum. It is only with the entrance of the blackmailer . . . that this momentum begins to slacken; the sense of accumulating fatality is not matched by a gathering intensity of rhythm, the inevitable begins to hover on the edge of the obvious. Yet perhaps this was Lang's intention; for, knowing the trap is bound to close, one is still fascinated to learn exactly how, and when. . . .

But the ending, which reveals the whole adventure to have been indeed a dream, is surely indefensible. Lang himself has tried to justify it: *"If I had continued the story to its logical conclusion, a man would have been caught and executed for committing a murder because he was one moment off guard . . . I rejected this logical ending because it seemed to me a defeatist ending, a tragedy for nothing brought about by an implacable Fate—a negative ending to a problem which is not universal, a futile dreariness which an audience would reject."* This seems, really, a confession that the story itself, if real, is pointless; in which case, why make it at all? From another point of view, turning "reality" at its harshest moment into a dream is itself defeatist and negative. The film's "logical ending" is, in fact, the moment when the desperate professor takes the poison, unaware that his blackmailer has just been killed in a gunfight with the police and that he has nothing more to fear. (p. 94)

One doesn't know whether, in the last eight years, Lang has found difficulty in obtaining congenial subjects, or whether the conventionality of much of his output has reflected an inner lassitude. The films have ranged from workmanlike commerce (*I Shall Return, The Blue Gardenia*), to another exercise in the *Man Hunt-Ministry of Fear* style (*Cloak and Dagger*), to rather sterile artiness (*House by the River, Rancho Notorious*). They show an almost complete indifference to contemporary reality, and their characterisation is mainly thin and perfunctory. Occasionally, as in *Cloak and Dagger,* a spy thriller with extremely unorthodox European settings, there are moments of characteristic bravura; but they exist in a vacuum, which the fact that the hunted formula this time is an atomic one does nothing to break.

The most revealing film of this period, *Clash by Night* (1952), . . . suggests an acquaintance with American life that stopped about 1937. It is in fact an adaptation . . . of an early play by Clifford Odets, and no effort is made to freshen its idiom or outlook. . . . Some tarnished dialogue strikes a wry, rueful note that seems almost self-parody now. . . .

A film like this seems to mirror, if not a retreat, a self-imposed distance from contemporary reality; and, remembering the formal, enclosed worlds of *Woman in the Window* and *Scarlet Street,* one guesses that the general movement of the American cinema since the end of the war towards naturalism has not been congenial to Lang. With *The Big Heat* (1953), however, he found a subject—a small town dominated by a racketeer, and a young detective's determination to break his tyranny— in which he could combine American "realism" and the more abstract, symbolic menace of his most characteristic melodrama. The result is a minor but frequently brilliant film that stands comparison with his best work. . . .

In its greater variety of human comment, and its more intimate observation of character, *The Big Heat* marks a development in Lang's work. The policeman's coldblooded, grasping widow, his anxious, fading mistress, the cruel sensual Vince . . . and his frivolous, childish girl-friend Debby—these are unusually rounded portraits, presented more acutely and vividly for themselves than is usual with Lang; and, at the centre, is the impressive, restrained figure of Bannion the detective. . . . This characterisation has a suggestion of moral force and human fervour that the enemies of Mabuse and Haighi never possessed. Bannion, like Eddie Taylor in *You Only Live Once,* is one of Lang's few personal heroes.

The texture of the film is richer and more concentrated than in any of his work since the '30s, and its tension slackens only in the last twenty minutes. . . . (p. 96)

*The Big Heat* is a resolutely interior film, distinguished from most contemporary American melodrama by its relatively formal approach to settings, its indifference to documentation. The world of shadows persists, and their force reminds one of Lotte Eisner's remark that the shadow, in Lang's films, is always an image of destiny. . . .

When Lang first came to America, he found [new forms by which to express new experiences, new visions], and contact with a new reality produced *Fury* and *You Only Live Once*. These films sprang from actual situations, but Lang treated them as manifestations of a more general one—as, again, the basic material of *The Big Heat* resembles that of a score of American thrillers, but a personal imagination transforms it and relates it to the artist's own created world. But, between *You Only Live Once* and *The Big Heat*, Lang's imaginative vision has seemed frequently under-nourished; neither *Woman in the Window* nor *Scarlet Street* enlarges the experiences communicated by his best work: they are, rather, skilful minor variations on it. What they lack is a true *raison d'être*. Neither the professor nor the cashier is organically related to the society in which he lives; but Lang is not the kind of director to make the interior dramas of personal life real in themselves—abstracted, poverty, sexual desire, loneliness, cease to become powerful motivating factors and are merely conditions of life coldly taken for granted in view of what is to come.

In Lang's best films, society is always composed of victims and aggressors. For his characters really to live, he needs to place or ensnare them on one side or the other. The same struggles, marked by violence of an ingenuity and refinement that reveals a uniquely sinister imagination, are fought over and over again. Nor are they, necessarily, ennobling, for the director's impassivity precludes a tragic feeling. The violence, as such, is untouched by pity or anger; it admits only an intellectual horror.

The world of Fritz Lang is remarkable for its absence of beauty. . . . And Fritz Lang's America is not essentially different from Fritz Lang's Germany (or Fritz Lang's London); it is less openly macabre, its crime and terror exist on a comparatively realistic level, but both countries are really another country, a haunted place in which the same dramas constantly recur. The shadow of outrage lies across *Fury, You Only Live Once, Scarlet Street, The Big Heat,* as it does across *Doctor Mabuse* and *M*, and the obsessed little New York cashier is trying, like the child-murderer of Dusseldorff, to escape "the man behind you." . . .

A part of Lang's peculiar talent is that the surface world of his films—urban, nocturnal, the cities and machines that men have constructed, hardly ever the natural, the untouched world—is rich in symbols of evil prescience. . . . The destiny which advances, it need hardly be said, is not beautiful or pleasant; it is organised terror or the breakout of the "Caligari within."

It is this persistent imaginative projection of an anxiety neurosis that gives Lang's films their unique power; as works of art they are restricted by the fact that their ultimate gesture is too passive, too unmoved, but they discover, and convey, a new *frisson*. In the shadow of its premonition, human relations break down, guilt and violence are at large, and though for the first time in *The Big Heat* the ending shows a crusader still going about his business—Bannion is called out on a new job —one feels little doubt that he will soon be up against a situation equally ominous. (p. 97)

    *Gavin Lambert, "Fritz Lang's America: Part One"*
    *and "Fritz Lang's America: Part Two," in* Sight and
Sound *(copyright © 1955 by The British Film Institute), Vol. 25, Nos. 1 and 2, Summer and Autumn, 1955, pp. 15-21, 55; 92-7.*

## FRANÇOIS TRUFFAUT

Fritz Lang seems to be constantly settling his accounts with society. His main characters are always outsiders, marginal people. The hero of *M* was portrayed as a victim. In 1933, Lang had to get out of Germany quickly in the face of Nazism. From then on, all of his work, even the Westerns and the thrillers, will reflect this violent break and very soon afterward we see the theme of revenge grafted on to the experiences of persecution. Several of Lang's Hollywood films are painted on this canvas: a man becomes involved in a struggle that is larger than any one person; perhaps he is a policeman, a scientist, a soldier, a resister. Then someone close to him, a woman or a child he loves, dies and the conflict becomes his individual fight, he is personally affected; the larger cause moves into the background and what takes its place is personal vengeance. . . .

Lang is obsessed with lynching, gun-to-the-head justice, and good conscience. His pessimism seems to grow with each film, and in recent years his work has become the bitterest in the history of film. That's why his latest films have failed commercially. First there was the hero-victim, subsequently the hero-avenger. Now there is only the man who is marked by sin. There are no longer any likable characters in his recent movies such as *While the City Sleeps* or *Beyond a Reasonable Doubt*. They are all schemers, opportunists, evil. Life is like a ride on a roller coaster. (p. 65)

Lang takes larger-than-life stories and improves on them, not by making them psychologically subtle, or more believable, but by bending them to his own obsessions. Lang expresses himself with great freedom. I know more about Lang, what he is and how he thinks, after seeing *While the City Sleeps,* a film he made to order, than I know about René Clément after watching *Gervaise.* . . . (p. 66)

There is only one word to describe Lang's style: inexorable. Each shot, each maneuver of the camera, each frame, each movement of an actor is a decision and is inimitable. (p. 67)

*You Only Live Once* should be seen often, and Lang's later films should be thought about in light of it. The man was not only a genius, he was also the most isolated and the least understood of contemporary filmmakers. (p. 68)

    *François Truffaut, "Fritz Lang in America" (1958), in his* The Films in My Life, *translated by Leonard Mayhew (copyright © 1975 by, Flammarion; translation copyright © 1978 by, Simon and Schuster; reprinted by permission of Simon and Schuster, a Division of Gulf & Western Corporation; originally published as* Les films de ma vie, *Flammarion, 1975), Simon and Schuster, 1978, pp. 64-8.*

## JOHN RUSSELL TAYLOR

The first thing to strike the casual observer about Fritz Lang's recent films is his apparent interest in returning to his own sources and going over his own past. His latest film, *The Thousand Eyes of Dr. Mabuse,* takes up a line previously represented in his work by *The Testament of Dr. Mabuse* in 1933 and *Doctor Mabuse the Gambler,* one of his earliest works . . . dating right back to 1922. (p. 43)

Certain themes run inescapably through his career from the beginning right up to date, and of them all that represented by Dr. Mabuse, which reaches its apotheosis and logical conclusion in the latest episode, is the most persistent and pervasive. It can be traced back, in a rudimentary state, to one of Lang's very earliest films, *Die Spinnen* (1919), a series meant to be in four parts, though only two were actually made, about an organisation of international criminals bent on world domination with the aid of the lost treasure of the Incas. Here everything stays unmistakably on the level of popular adventure; but the fantasy of criminals conquering the world, common enough at the time, provided a germ which—fertilised perhaps by Lang's temporary contact with the mad Dr. Caligari and his strange power over men—was to blossom some three years later into *Dr. Mabuse der Spieler.* (p. 44)

[By] the time we come to *Spione* (1928), the next film to take up the theme, Lang has clearly begun to see the place of the master mind in a rather different light. Where Dr. Mabuse originally had clearcut and relatively "normal" criminal aims which he was the better able to pursue because of the chaotic state of the world, Haighi, the criminal genius of *Spione*, seems to have no aim beyond the general disruption of society. Living, like Mabuse but more explicitly than Mabuse, in and on the confusions of the postwar world, he heads an international spy ring which appears to exist just for its own sake and to function in a void—no particular cause, even self-interest as it is usually understood, seems to motivate their actions. Mabuse's skill as a master of disguise is here permitted to a number of characters, with a consequent further blurring of distinctions. Nobody is ever quite what he seems, and the sheet-anchor of normality is absent. This time we have moved right into the world of crime, and when spies fight spies without our ever clearly knowing what, if anything, either side is meant to represent, it is not always easy to make out where, even in the most conventional terms, our sympathy should lie. Dramatic conflict proper tends to be replaced by the mechanical thrills of a series of brilliant technical set-pieces. . . .

If it seemed an incidental, almost accidental, characteristic of Haighi that as a crook he was strangely disinterested, involved in crime mainly for its own sake, with Mabuse in *Das Testament* this very lack of normal motivation is erected into a principle of life. The only aim of chaos is chaos, of destruction destruction. Lang in fact regarded, and regards, this film as a deliberate reflection, albeit oblique and distorted, on the Nazi party and its ethos, putting many of the Nazi slogans about the prime need for total destruction before a new world could be built into the mouth of the mad doctor, and permitting him, further, to will deliberately and explicitly what the Nazis willed only by implication: a new world of crime and disorder in which civilisation would be destroyed and mankind return to the condition of animals. . . .

[In his films of the next ten years] the processes set in motion in Lang's mind by the rise of Nazism seem to be working themselves out, and although *Hangmen Also Die* has wonderful sequences, . . . they are not for the most part conceived on anything like the same level of imaginative intensity as their German predecessors. Instead, with the tide turning against Hitler and the urgency of that particular crisis daily diminishing, Lang chose to turn, virtually for the first time, to the superwoman as a substitute for the superman, the *femme fatale* who achieves by sheer sexual allure very much what the Dr. Mabuses achieve by the exercise of intellect and will power. (p. 45)

Since those days, the raw plot material of Lang's American films has been very much in the normal run of the American cinema, with occasional hints of favoured themes—*femmes fatales* in *Moonfleet* or *Human Desire,* glimmerings of satanic intellect from the publisher in *While the City Sleeps* or the hero-villain of *Beyond a Reasonable Doubt,* varying degrees of mental derangement . . . But the real culmination of Lang's "thought" on the subject of the superman has been reserved for his return to the German cinema; until, in fact, *The Thousand Eyes of Dr. Mabuse.* There are a number of overt references back to the earlier works in the cycle: from the first are borrowed the clairvoyant side of Mabuse's interests and his mastery of disguise, from the second come his strictly non-commercial aims in crime and the doubts they cause among members of his gang, as well as the idea of Mabuse's influence persisting after death through his writings and personality. . . . But in one particular the film pushes the reasoning of the earlier works even further, to its logical conclusion: while Mabuse in *Das Testament* merely seeks to reduce human civilisation to primal anarchy, the later Dr. Mabuse plots for no less than to gain control of the major atomic factories in the world. And why? What good will it do him? None, he admits in the key scene of the film, except to give him the ultimate pleasure of putting his finger on the button and returning the whole world to the scattered atoms from which it was made. Destruction for its own sake can go no further.

Even though this steady, logical progression from *Die Spinnen* to *The Thousand Eyes of Dr. Mabuse* does exist, and provides one thread of continuity running through Lang's work, it is finally only one of several, and by no means the most important. To concentrate upon it without qualification would suggest that Lang is a "philosophical" director. . . . But this, really, he is not: he makes films with ideas rather than films of ideas. As he remarked recently, "I live through my eyes," and in the end it is his power to embody his ideas visually which accounts for the lasting effect of his films. The main conflict in them is not primarily on the intellectual level, between good and bad, order and disorder, but on the intuitive, between darkness and light. (pp. 45-6)

*John Russell Taylor, "The Nine Lives of Dr. Mabuse," in* Sight and Sound *(copyright © 1962 by The British Film Institute), Vol. 31, No. 1, Winter, 1961-62, pp. 43-6.*

**JOHN GILLETT**

*Tigress of Bengal* is an incoherent amalgam of portions of [*The Tiger of Eschnapur* and *The Indian Tomb*], weighed down by childish American dialogue and out-of-synch dubbing. Yet enough remains to prove their unmistakable authorship. To find their origins we have to go back over forty years, to a scenario written by Lang and Thea von Harbou for the silent version directed by Joe May, for whom Lang was then working. And one has only to look at Lang's own *Die Spinnen* of 1919 (and, to a lesser extent, *Destiny* and *Kriemhild's Revenge*) to find the connection. Lang has always had an affection for schoolboy hokum, the super serial of adventure and intrigue set in some never-never land of the imagination, and the two Indian films belong defiantly to this enjoyable if outdated tradition.

The pleasure to be derived from the films does not lie in the story—they are films for the eye, not the brain, and there's no need to be snooty about them on this account. The "mysterious *mise-en-scène''* so beloved by French critics becomes their justification. Shot partially on location in India, with studio work in Germany, they again display Lang's feeling for architectural values (this time in colour) and elaborately worked-out action sequences. Here are all the trappings of the adventure serial: mysterious palaces inhabited by evil princes and lovely dancers; corridors which lead nowhere; underground passages (some of them straight out of *Die Spinnen*) which lead only to the tiger pit or a secret prison for lepers. Through it all, Lang's camera tracks and prowls, always settling for the most revealing set-up and producing beautiful images from dappled sunlight, gleaming costumes and heavily decorated interiors. Even in this truncated version, his personality continually imposes itself through a characteristic camera movement, a grouping, or the way a scene is put together. Lang's return to Germany was probably a painful as well as a nostalgic experience. Yet there is something enjoyable in finding a director returning to the themes he first explored nearly half-a-century ago, and relishing their absurdities with a good deal of the old glee.

> John Gillett, "Film Clips: 'Tigress of Bengal'," in Sight and Sound *(copyright © 1962 by The British Film Institute), Vol. 31, No. 3, Summer, 1962, p. 147.*

### LOTTE H. EISNER

These days many passages in *Metropolis* seem old-fashioned and even vaguely ridiculous, especially those in which the *Kolossal* is overlarded with sentiment. Lang had not yet attained the simplicity of *M,* in which reality is made to resound quite naturally with overtones of the weird. . . .

The deliberate symmetry of *Siegfried* conveys a slow, inexorable rhythm like that of the destiny brooding over the epic. But in the crowd scenes in *Metropolis* the rhythm becomes dynamic. In addition to having an observant mind, Lang has the gift of assimilating in a very personal manner what he has seen. (p. 223)

To describe the mass of inhabitants in the underground town in *Metropolis* Lang used Expressionistic stylization to great effect: impersonal, hunched, servile, spiritless, slavish beings dressed in costumes of no known historical period. The stylization is extreme during the change of shift when the two columns meet, marching with rhythmic, jerky steps, and when the solid block of workers is heaped into the lifts, heads bowed, completely lacking individual existence. (p. 225)

Apart from these machine-men, Lang seeks more and more to make his groups of extras fall into a geometrical pattern. In *Siegfried* the human body was often used as a scenic element. But in *Metropolis* it becomes a basic factor of the architecture itself, immobilized with other bodies into triangles, ellipses or semicircles.

Yet in spite of this geometrical stylization, the last vestige of the Expressionist aesthetic, Lang never becomes trite. Even when his crowd is 'architecturalized' it remains alive. . . . (p. 229)

The scenes set in the immense office, with a few actors lost in the vastness, are less forceful than those with the crowds of workers. The mawkish garden where the children of the rich are sent out to play and the Nazi-style sports stadium in which these gilded youths are trained in athletics, together with the pleasure-house ruled by the bogus Maria, all contrast with the gauntness of the underground town. (p. 232)

In *Metropolis,* as in all his films, Lang handles lighting admirably: the futuristic city appears as a superb pyramidal accumulation of shimmering sky-scrapers. By means of trick shots and hyper-elaborate lighting, illuminated windows and stretches of dark wall stand out like the white and black squares of a chess-board; the light seems to explode, spreading a luminous mist, falling as iridescent rain. (p. 233)

On the rare occasions when Lang relaxes his hold on the lighting effects, we suddenly notice that the machines have practically no *raison d'être:* they do no more than compose a kind of moving background, an accompaniment, a sort of noises-off; in the noisy visual orchestration of *Metropolis*—a silent film—we can almost hear them, like the factory whistle. (p. 235)

In *Die Spinnen* Lang reveals another aspect of his genius. This unfinished serial—only two episodes were filmed—has a profusion of varied incidents which overflow their framework, complicating the action; these colourful, multiple adventures, overlapping or interlinked, now defy all understanding. In the existing copy, the titles judged necessary for it to be understood at the time are unreadable, which does not make matters easier.

It is surprising that a young director in his third film . . . should show such mastery in directing certain sequences. The scenes actually filmed in a train without back-projection, the chases in which every detail of suspense is calculated and placed with the logic and precision we admire in his later works, the atmosphere created by skilful lighting and sets—all these proofs of Lang's talent are already there to be seen for those who can *see.* (p. 237)

The secret trapdoors, the complicated lifts guarded by a Chinaman with a cutlass, the ground caving in, the terrifying underground chambers in which sinister gentlemen in top hats hold secret meetings, the armour-plated vaults, the sliding partitions, the cellars filled with poison gas—all these accessories, of course, Lang drew from the common stock of the suspense film.

Lang succeeds in using them to good effect, and since nothing goes to waste in this 'conscious and conscientious' director, for whom 'all films, whatever they be, demand much care and reflection' he was to use them again in his later films.

Thus the mirror in *Die Spinnen* which 'televises' scenes before the beautiful vamp Lio Shah anticipates the multiple television screens in *Die Tausend Augen des Dr Mabuse* (*The 1000 Eyes of Dr Mabuse,* 1960). There is also a parallel in *Metropolis* when the master learns about the riot from his foreman, whom he can see and talk to through a sort of television screen in his study. (pp. 238-39)

Lang uses his wealth of contemporary settings [in *Dr Mabuse der Spieler*] quite differently from the settings of *Die Spinnen:* they heighten and also explain the atmosphere, practically joining in the action; they are much more than a background. But this setting, despite certain features which recall Expressionism, especially in the tavern sequences, was not created in that style, the only suggestions of which come from occasional harsh lighting effects. (pp. 240-41)

As had already happened in *Destiny,* the settings create the atmosphere, heighten it, and make the spell-binding chiaroscuro of the *Stimmung* pulse with life. . . . Here and there the *objets d'art* shine out insistently, Expressionistically, as if they are infused with an insidious latent life. An enormous, primitive, fluorescent statue catches the eye, the crystal of a chandelier sparkles, an immense mask seems to split the screen.

All these precious objects are no longer elements of the setting, as they were in *Die Spinnen,* and even less the ornamental arabesques on a kind of back-cloth. Their luminous presence makes the silence more and more oppressive, and they are as it were the hieroglyphs of an ineffable solitude and despair. (pp. 241-42)

Lang is concerned with every detail. . . . And his precision, his taste for detail and his desire for rigorous authenticity are apparent from the very first sequences. An example is the attack on the man bearing the contract in the train. On three occasions three characters consult their watches in three different places. Step by step, with a meticulous inventiveness, the intrigue moves remorselessly forward, and the editing emphasizes the quasi-simultaneity of the events. If an audience these days can sit through the four hours of *Mabuse* without tiring . . . it is thanks to the precision of the editing. (p. 245)

After the first *Mabuse* a film like *Spione* (*Spies*) is disappointing. It lacks the rigour one admires so much in the two episodes of *Mabuse.* The fault may be Lang's for having tried to introduce too many small traits of character. More plausibly, it may be attributed to Thea von Harbou and her taste for pompous melodrama. Thea von Harbou always dwells excessively on the feelings and reactions of her characters. The action gets clogged, and Lang's vigorous editing suffers accordingly. (p. 246)

The influence of Thea von Harbou is obvious in *Die Frau im Mond.* In the vast expanses of white sand in the lunar landscapes the falsity of the turgid sentiments is especially jarring: the grandiosity of the fantasy often becomes plain bathos. From one end of this sentimental piece to the other, Fritz Lang's genius only comes through in the rocket-launching scenes, which are exact in their prediction of the future. Good examples are the scenes before the take-off, where the newsreel tone is even more convincing than the science-fiction inventions. (p. 249)

> *Lotte H. Eisner, in her* The Haunted Screen: Expressionism in the German Cinema and the Influence of Max Reinhardt, *translated by Roger Greaves (translation copyright © 1969 by Thames & Hudson; reprinted by permission of the University of California Press; originally published as* L'ecran démoniaque, *revised edition, Le Terrain Vague, 1965), University of California Press, 1969, 360 p.\**

## ROGER GREENSPUN

[Even] if Fritz Lang's *The 1,000 Eyes of Dr. Mabuse* were no better than some of the enjoyable post-Lang *Mabuse* sequels, one would have had to like it. In fact, *The 1,000 Eyes* is a superb film, dense, complex, exuberant, mysterious, fully worthy of its premiere setting, and deserving much more than the ignorant indifference that met its arrival. (p. 54)

All the world of *The 1,000 Eyes of Dr. Mabuse* is cursed. In part, by a continuation of the old curse that was not really broken in 1945; in part, by a universal resignation, a willingness merely to look at so many scenes of disorder caused by the faceless terror. The ultimate shock is that the faceless terror is as cursed as everybody else, with nothing really to do in his underground room except look at the imminence of his own destruction and then go up into the sunlight and, after routine dodges, suffer it. For all he has made happen, and for all his technical expertise and ingeniousness, Mabuse has failed radically in perceiving any message beyond the medium. Half blind, half invisible, he doesn't sense that there are other relations possible that depend upon not merely settling for a sophisticated point of view.

The act of seeing in the later films of Fritz Lang—an act that includes the bemused gaze of a middle-aged man caught by the portrait of a beautiful woman in an art gallery window (*The Woman in the Window,* 1944), or the intent squint of a hunter centering his human prey in the sights of a powerful rifle (*Man Hunt,* 1941)—involves for the protagonist a decision not merely to look but rather to enter into the scene his imaginative concentration has in part called into being. Such a decision is a submission to fate, which is also a submission to willful desire and an invitation to act. At the very least, it is a way of getting into trouble. But since trouble is the nature of our lives, and since our century has shown wonderful ingenuity in surpassing the wildest fantasies of Lang's evil geniuses, getting into trouble has at least a certain relevance to living to recommend it. Mistaken in our impulses and acts, misled by our desires and our fears, we seem to have lost our way in a maze. But Lang's camera needs only the slightest movement—a short, straight track—to reveal that we are actually caught in a web, a universal conspiracy precisely directed toward insane ends. Uncertainty is what we know of our environment, and in assurance there is neither comfort nor even truth. The night and fog that envelop so many of Lang's films had probably better not lift. The better way is not out into the daylight, out inward into that deeper darkness where Travers, as if by an intensity of voyeurism, wills his way through to his love, enters the realm of her magic sleep and, by blindly joining for a while in the rhythms of her dreaming, finds through dreaming a way to life. (pp. 56-7)

*The 1,000 Eyes* compares very favorably with at least one of the earlier Mabuse films. *The Testament* has its own stories, but over the years Lang seems to have refined his style and deepened his understanding of what his master criminal is up to. . . .

*The Testament of Dr. Mabuse* uncovers schemes; *The 1,000 Eyes* senses connections. The traps that abound in the earlier film are most often the products of architecture, city planning, industrial design. The traps that lie hidden in the later film are usually revealed only to exceptional perception—nothing is there unless you are alert and suspicious enough to see it. Mabuse's underground room in *The Testament* is an empty sound chamber with real brick walls; the trapped young lovers have to blast a hole to escape from it. The underground room in *The 1,000 Eyes* is a real nerve-center with a sham exterior. The young lovers whom Mabuse leaves there to die escape easily enough through an opened door, and nothing really is caught except in shifting images on television screens. Plan has become process, and everything, even the end of the world, is relative. (p. 57)

> *Roger Greenspun, "Roger Greenspun on 'The 1,000 Eyes of Dr. Mabuse',"* in Film Comment (*copyright © 1973 by Film Comment Publishing Corporation; all rights reserved), Vol. 9, No. 2, March-April, 1973, pp. 54-7.*

## ALFRED APPEL, JR.

The dream stylization of *The Woman in the Window* is in part achieved by its use of fated or fateful coincidences. In our dreams and nightmares, a single face may appear and reappear in different guises. . . . Lang effects his Gothicism . . . subtly, utilizing a straw hat. The boater was a common enough sight in the Forties, but, save for the three important characters who wear them, *The Woman in the Window* offers a sea of fedoras. (p. 14)

The motif of the straw hat telescopes the dreamer's anxiety, his justifiable paranoia. From [Professor Wanley's] point of view, the straw hat suggests that he is being pursued by the serial selves of a single, protean nemesis. The "coincidence" of the hat, no coincidence at all, helps to define the coordinates of the labyrinth from which [Wanley] seems unable to escape. Darkened rooms, corridors, car interiors, and the menacing walls of a once-benign street all contribute to his sense of entrapment. . . .

At least one critic has complained that the setting of *The Woman in the Window* is unrealistic, too barren, the victim of its low budget. . . . The rain-washed studio streets of *The Woman in the Window*, a *noir* convention, are expressive enough, and one shouldn't complain that they are empty; our dreams are also low-budget productions, peopled in a very selective fashion. If the buildings in these nocturnal scenes are too clearly sets, can it not be argued that this contributes positively to the stylized, dreamlike ambience? *Dr. Caligari*, another mental set, is even less "realistic" than *The Woman in the Window*, whose stark façades, the result of design or expediency, also bring to mind the unadorned and disquieting architectural caprices in the paintings of de Chirico. . . .

*The Woman in the Window,* as its title suggests, is a compendium of glassy surfaces, of ad hoc mirrors and unreliable reflectors—so many traps in the labyrinth. The dream itself, featuring the professor's alter ego, is a kind of fun-house mirror, if only because it recasts the club's doorman and hatcheck clerk as the blackmailer and Mazard (as we discover when the dream is over). [The woman], however, has no "real life" equivalent, and her illusory nature is literally communicated through mirrors or windows which belie their everyday optical functions. . . .

The death of Mazard seems authentic enough, but again mirrors serve as metaphor. As in *Scarlet Street* and *The Big Heat,* the killing is reflected in a mirror, a modest infinite regress; and the multiple images of the two accomplices establish the circumscribing nature of the crime, its infinite range of consequences. [The woman and Wanley] are each contained by a mirror of their own, doubling the spatial tension in the room and accentuating the psychic distance which separates these two strangers. (p. 15)

"*Only* a dream," grumble critics and viewers, as though dreams were meaningless constructs. . . . According to [the D.A.], "It's too late for us," and Wanley's dream attests to that truth, which he must live with if not accept. Unlike Wanley, most of us censor our worst nightmares or refuse to consider their implications. The pathos of *The Woman in the Window* is predicated on the definitive self-knowledge supplied by Wanley's nightmare. Viewed as the logical culmination of a myriad of effects, as the exit from the labyrinth, the dream-ending should seem considerably less blatant.

If Orson Welles is the baroque master of *film noir,* then Fritz Lang is its classicist, an economical and precise craftsman whose carefully controlled effects are all the more powerful for the compression of their means. *The Woman in the Window,* with its running time of ninety-nine minutes, could be profitably studied by those contemporary directors of thrillers who usually need two hours to tell their stories. (p. 16)

*Alfred Appel, Jr., "Fritz Lang's American Nightmare," in* Film Comment *(copyright © 1974 by The Film Society of Lincoln Center; all rights reserved), Vol. 10, No. 6, November-December, 1974, pp. 12-17.*

## DAVID L. OVERBEY

The figure of the *femme fatale,* appearing as early as *Die Spinnen,* turns up again and again as a constant motif in [Lang's] work; thus the career girl [as portrayed in his unfilmed scenario *Death of a Career Girl*] is less an outgrowth of [a] chance encounter at Cannes than of previous portraits of women. Kriemhild, one of the earlier versions, also pursued a goal to its logical, destructive end, shedding all human emotions save that of revenge (a form, after all, of ambition), leaving more than one dead man behind her, and finally destroying herself in the process. Indeed, Kriemhild is perhaps Lang's most deadly, self-deadening and archetypally powerful female figure. She too rejects maternal feelings and romantic love; to remain indifferent to Etzel the Hun required, after all, such icy determination as even the career girl might be incapable of achieving. The most immediate antecedent of the career girl is Marion Menil in *Die tausend Augen des Dr. Mabuse.* Using her sexual powers to attempt a takeover of Henry Travers' financial empire, Marion has, however, been hypnotised into working for Dr. Jordan. The spell is broken ultimately by her human emotion, which allows her to save both Travers and herself, thus escaping the fate of Kriemhild and the career girl. Such salvation is more typical of Lang's women, as can be seen in Sonja (*Spione*), Mae Doyle (*Clash by Night*) and Debby Marsh (*The Big Heat*).

The career girl, indeed, resembles Dr. Jordan or even Mabuse himself, on a smaller scale. She even uses many of the same electronic devices as Jordan in the last Mabuse film. . . . [The] secret recordings in *Career Girl* closely parallel those in *Tausend Augen,* and are negatively related to the positive values of respect, trust and the right of individual privacy. Denying love, the career girl inhabits a world in which personal advantage is taken whenever and however possible, with no thought to the rights of others to speak openly and without fear of reprisal on any level. What the career girl does, of course, is to incorporate on the personal and business planes those techniques which Lang had ascribed earlier to Mabuse. From the animated dreams in *Die Nibelungen* (telling the truth), to the newsreels in *Fury* (telling an ambiguous truth), to the portrait of Kitty March in *Scarlet Street* (mocking the truth), to the television images of *Die tausend Augen des Dr. Mabuse* and the eavesdropping career girl (recording the truth for evil ends), one can follow the progress of the perversion of the image in the modern world as sadly but accurately observed by Fritz Lang. In *Career Girl,* it is even more horrifying because the corruption is no longer that of a master criminal working on a grandly mad scale, but of a private citizen, a zombie-like version of each of us, spying on her fellows for personal gain, at once both symptom and cause of her agonising death-in-life. (pp. 241-42)

Had [*Death of a Career Girl*] been made, Lang would have returned full circle, back to *Der Müde Tod,* but with a startling difference. In that film, arguably the most personal of the director's European work, the figure of Death seeks to demonstrate that he is stronger than love. The final point of the film, of course, is quite the opposite, for the two lovers eventually triumph (a motif echoed later by Eddy and Joan in *You*

*Only Live Once*) by being joined together in a life beyond death. Forty-four years later, Lang found himself reversing that motif exactly. If death were exhausted then, it is love which is exhausted in *Death of a Career Girl*. It is perfect Langian irony that two deaths should equal a 'happy ending', and that an ending with the protagonist alive, beautiful and 'successful' should be the saddest in any of his work. (p. 243)

> David L. Overbey, "Fritz Lang's Career Girl," in Sight and Sound (copyright © 1975 by The British Film Institute), Vol. 44, No. 4, Autumn, 1975, pp. 240-43.

### LOTTE H. EISNER

Lang's films are characterised by their peculiar mixture of realism and fantasy. . . . Even during his German period, in which so many critics find evidence of Expressionist influence—for instance the three-dimensional effects achieved in *Metropolis* or *M* by means of lighting—the films demonstrate Lang's mastery in combining documentary structures and adventure fantasy.

Again and again Lang declares that every film must evolve its own style according to the subject matter. Yet in every film we encounter the characteristic Lang elements—not only in *Metropolis* where the documentary element is projected into the future, or in *Destiny* where the fantastic elements dominate the realistic. . . . Lang's films, like those of every great cinema creator, reveal a profound underlying unity. (pp. 140-41)

[Lang believes that] character determines human fate: character is the demon of man. All Lang's American films will demonstrate this belief, with their recurrent questions: Where does guilt begin? What is innocence? What is good and what is evil? (p. 148)

The subjects of Lang's films are very varied—often he accepted subjects that were offered him. . . . Yet there are always inner connections: whether in the preliminary preparation or the studio work, they were turned into Lang subjects.

One means by which this was achieved was his characteristic stress on detail. The accumulation of detail, the power of the camera to isolate it at once gives him his spontaneity and his realism. . . . In his American films detail is no longer symbol as in his German period. In *Fury* symbols may still be important . . . and even in *You Only Live Once* there is the frog image; yet their significance is deeper. (p. 369)

It is an academic question . . . whether Lang's German films or his American period are to be valued more highly. . . .

American films were made in a different time and a different environment. There is doubtless, a profound difference in perspective, but there is also a firm continuity of vision. Lang, of course, matured as a natural process of aging common to all men, and the change in environment of course played a part in this maturation. The first films, then, are not exactly the same as the later films, but the same man made them all; both periods are always related in essentials (*Big Heat,* for example, can be taken to correspond to *M* in many ways). (p. 380)

> Lotte H. Eisner, in her Fritz Lang, edited by David Robinson, translated by Gertrud Mander (translation copyright © Martin Secker & Warburg Limited 1976; reprinted by permission of Oxford University Press, Inc.; in Canada by Secker & Warburg Limited), Secker & Warburg, 1976 (and reprinted by Oxford University Press, New York, 1977), 416 p.

### DAVID THOMSON

In Lang's films, interiors are atmospheric geometry before they are a home for anyone. [Late] in *Ministry of Fear,* [Stephen Neale] and the girl come to an apartment which they realise is an unoccupied trap—but it is only as unowned as every other interior in the movie. The precious home in *The Big Heat*—though shaken by the bomb outside—is as neutral as an advertisement living room. Joan Bennett's rooms in *Woman in the Window* and *Scarlet Street* are dens from schoolboy dreams. *Rancho Notorious* is found in the cardboard Rockies. The hotel in *The 1000 Eyes of Dr. Mabuse* is a laboratory rat community, and *Metropolis* is a lonely child's model of the world.

This is a cinema in which we are always conscious of art direction, and thus of the fabricated and organised spectacle. Where does Lang trust nature or reality, save in the unavoidable seashore of *Moonfleet,* some obligatory Western landscape in the early 40s, and the uncharacteristic *Clash by Night*? That is a woman's picture more typical of producer Jerry Wald. But it has a 'documentary' section on fishing—essentially redundant—put together from footage Lang shot while waiting for filming to begin. Otherwise, Lang's exteriors are meticulous studio mock-ups, and this artifice saps all the vitality of nature. (p. 116)

Action never falters in Lang; it is his language, just as his emphasis comes in acceleration. This was always apparent in his work, and no silent director made such restless films. *Dr. Mabuse, the Gambler,* from 1922, has such a teeming profusion of incident that its 3 hours pass like an express. Time's speed is referred to throughout *The Ministry of Fear*. . . .

The wonder [of *The Ministry of Fear* is that Lang] could compress so much into 85 minutes and make a work more lucid than [Graham Greene's] novel. He never relents from the exposition of significant action through space, shape and light: a designed image taut with irrational anxiety. If only to illustrate the order and consistency of his direction, notice the use of doorways and entrances in *The Ministry of Fear*. . . . They connect spatial areas, serve as metaphors for progress and ordeal, and comprise a visual pattern that nearly rhymes as the film progresses, so that the crazy adventure seems more than ever ordained. (p. 117)

All his life, I think, Lang was misunderstood or treated too lightly. So long-lived, he could not be avoided in film histories, or denied the stature that we give to heroic survival. His German period was more 'respectable' for many people. It was filled with classics; and Lang was safer than, say, Leni Riefenstahl, because of his decision to leave Germany. Yet the sureness in their films is very similar. Lang had no equal at studio film-making, and he showed how stifling a form that could be. His brilliance was so cold that it was hard to touch, let alone analyse. . . . I do not question Lang's own liberalism. But I do believe he made authoritarian films, so expressive that we should beware of the cinema. (p. 118)

> David Thomson, "Lang's Ministry," in Sight and Sound (copyright © 1977 by The British Film Institute), Vol. 46, No. 2, Spring, 1977, pp. 114-18.

### GEORGE WILSON

*You Only Live Once* is one of Fritz Lang's most widely admired American films and is thought to be among the finest of the 'social consciousness' films of the 1930s. The movie is praised for its technical excellence, its richness of visual texture and its generally moving depiction of the story's star-crossed lovers. These judgments are absolutely correct as far as they go; and yet, I believe, they do not begin to go far enough. In particular, *You Only Live Once* exhibits a kind of structural and stylistic complexity which carries it into areas of concern that the usual remarks fail entirely to reflect. . . . The thematic concerns of the film and the methods by which they are expressed are of very considerable interest on their own. Moreover, understood in the context of the subtle framework that organises its significance, certain segments and aspects of the movie which have seemed flawed or worse appear in a new and more satisfactory light—the ending, for example, which is commonly thought to be a disastrously maudlin lapse.

Considered from a historical perspective, I know of no American film from the period, with the possible exception of von Sternberg's last two films with Dietrich, which exhibits the same consistently high level of cinematic complexity and sophistication. (p. 221)

[*You Only Live Once*] seems obsessed with facets of perception and blindness. Through the visuals and the dialogue we are repeatedly introduced to questions concerning sight and the failure to see, pictures and picturing and the various senses of the word 'vision'. . . .

A striking and peculiar aspect of the film is the way in which it signals the possibility of manipulating our perception of its action. At several points, in several ways, the audience is led into making a mistake of perceptual judgment after which a wider context is revealed in terms of which the judgment is shown for the mistake it is. (p. 222)

*You Only Live Once* is structured by an interlocking network of characters and events which express, with significant variations, the nature of this failure and its human consequences. Most striking, perhaps, is the way in which the audience is deeply implicated in these concerns. The movie explores with elaborate care the ways in which film may complicate and enhance our difficulties in seeing the world accurately by leading perception astray with methods of its own. . . .

[The] movie systematically depicts a hierarchy of human relationships: the relationships of love, marriage and family; the relationship of a person to important sub-groups within society and his or her relationship to the social order and to the state. And all these relationships are portrayed as being perpetually threatened by the failure of people within these actual or potential ties to see and understand the others in a full and satisfactory way. Lang's vision here seems to be one of despair. The sighted blind will find themselves a human situation only by chance if, indeed, they find themselves a place at all. . . . *You Only Live Once* has a kind of complexity and a kind of greatness that we may, not surprisingly, fail to see. (p. 226)

*George Wilson, "'You Only Live Once': The Doubled Feature," in* Sight and Sound *(copyright © 1977 by The British Film Institute), Vol. 46, No. 4, Autumn, 1977, pp. 221-26.*

## ROBERT A. ARMOUR

Lang's films reflect the struggle within his people as they respond to the pushes and shoves from the dual sides of their character. In medieval morality plays the struggle would have been represented by good and bad angels whispering into the ear of the character trying to resolve his dilemma, and frequently Lang is able to find a similar material representation of the struggle.

Many of Lang's chief characters are people driven by some inner conflict of the sort symbolized by Jekyll and Hyde. Kriemhild, in Lang's version of *The Nibelungenlied,* is, at the opening of the film, a lovely woman; but after the murder of her husband, her loveliness is destroyed by her desire for revenge. . . . In *Fury* Joe Wheeler is also consumed by the desire for revenge. . . . And Dave Bannion in *The Big Heat* is also driven by revenge. (pp. 27-8)

It should be clear that Lang's films do not exclusively dwell on these interior struggles, for such is not always the substance of exciting film entertainment. These interior struggles are triggered and symbolized by external struggles that bring visual excitement and suspense to the screen. The personal, inner struggles in Lang's films are the elements that give psychological realism to his characters, but the external struggles between the central characters and the forces that try to dominate them are the elements that motivate and give meaning to the inner struggles. . . .

In a sense the dark [inner] struggle becomes a classic encounter between good and evil. The character struggles with a human desire—revenge, illicit love, power—on one hand and the dictates of his conscience on the other. There is pressure to be evil, but there is also pressure to be good. (p. 28)

[Classical] fate may be the controlling factor in a number of Lang's early films . . . ; but as Lang learned more about psychology and societal influences, he began to create characters who struggle not against the classical Fate, but against some modern representation of it. This is not the Greek or Roman version of fate, but a newer version that is the result of the influences of determinism. . . . The struggle of man against some supernatural force, as in *Siegfried,* has become the struggle of man against some aspect of society, as in *The Big Heat.* In both cases the forces are gigantic and man seems small and puny beside them, but the struggle itself is important to Lang. (pp. 30-1)

Regardless, however, of the nature of the fate or the size of the group representing that fate, the struggle that really counts for Lang is the interior struggle that takes place inside the hero as a result of the external struggle. Fate, no matter what its manifestation, is not the central issue with most of Lang's characters; the struggle with themselves is more important as the exterior opponents are replaced by man's inner self. The exterior struggles are important and interesting, especially in Lang's films that comment on social issues and war, but these struggles achieve thematic significance through the inner struggles they trigger. (pp. 32-3)

Lang has a reputation as a director who makes excessive use of violence, but such criticism fails to take into account his own understanding of the art of the cinema. Lang's films do seem violent, but not in the vein of the blood and gore that so characterizes the films of latter-day filmmakers, such as Sam Peckinpah. Lang made the violence a part of the theme of the dark struggle. . . . Fear, pain, and violence—the three are united as the central device for depicting the struggles. In the tradition of the classical Greek theater, the violence is rarely seen. . . . The violence is more suggested than shown. Lang knew that it could be more effective on the viewer done that way; he leaves it to us to imagine the horror of the violence. Through our imaginations we become his collaborators in the creation of horror. (pp. 35-6)

Sometimes the hallucinations in Lang's films are inspired by guilt. A character undergoing psychological stress caused by guilt for actions he has performed may hallucinate and have visions that reflect the guilt. These are the strangest of the hallucinations used by Lang; those inspired by dreams or illness are easily accepted by the audience because many people have experienced strange visions while asleep or ill. But the hallucinations which reveal guilt are different. They may occur to a Lang character while he is walking down the street or driving his car. (pp. 37-8)

The use of hallucination is especially appropriate for a director who works with man's inner struggles. The hallucination depicts well what is happening in a man's mind and reflects the stress caused by the struggle.

Since the struggles of Lang's films are characterized by Jekyll-Hyde exchanges of personality, it is natural that on some occasions there will be confusion of character. In a psychological drama when one side of the person's character is exchanged for another, there may not be an accompanying physical change to symbolize the inner change, as there was in the original Jekyll-Hyde myth. In other words, the character may change, but another person looking at the changed person may not be able to discern the change simply from the character's physical appearance. (pp. 38-9)

[Lang's] films are dotted by easily recognized archetypes, characters and experiences that are representatives of the perceptions we hold in common and express through our dreams and art forms. These archetypes in Lang's films become central to the conflicts that make up the struggles. . . . Lang frequently calls upon the archetype of the superman, a character that is often responsible for the conflict in his films. Supermen, such as Dr. Mabuse or Haighi in *Spies,* are actually the source of conflict in their films, the characters who force others to confront evil and to experience the struggle. As the source of conflict, the superman is actively involved in it and represents one side of the struggle. On the other hand, the seductress, another of Lang's archetypes, is frequently the cause of the conflict and struggle in his films, but usually not as directly involved as a participant as is the superman. . . . The struggle belongs to the men, not to the women who were partly to blame for it. Similarly in Lang's films the virgin is usually not directly involved in the struggle, but she is supportive of her man whose struggle concerns her. (p. 42)

Lang also involves his characters in retellings of well-known myths that tend to heighten the struggles and make them more universal. He uses the myths of the Tower of Babel and the Garden of Eden in *Metropolis* and the story of the Nibelungen treasure in the Nibelungen Saga. Some myths he uses without naming, such as the Flood and Holocaust in *Metropolis* and Beauty and the Beast in *The Big Heat.* These myths are statements of conflict, and their narratives describe the struggles that are familiar to most men, at least in their subconscious form. . . .

I believe it fair to judge Lang a flawed genius. He made films of great power and substance, films that leave an impact on the viewers. His films challenge the viewers' intellects and remain visually appealing. But often his taste or working conditions let him down and permitted him to strain an image or oversentimentalize an idea. These flaws stand out from his strengths like a weed among roses, detracting from the flowers but at the same time heightening their beauty through contrast.

The flaws in Lang's films are important because they cause strange reactions in contemporary audiences. Viewers today

laugh where Lang did not intend a laugh . . . or challenge the premise when Lang wanted understanding (the heart uniting the brains and the hands at the end of *Metropolis*). Lang sometimes permits his sentimentality and ideology to intrude upon his plots, forcing awkward moments, such as the conclusions of *Metropolis* and *You Only Live Once.* Rarely are such moments totally wrong. The idea may well be justified by the actions which lead up to the moment; it is usually the presentation of the idea in an overdone image—such as the flag waving at the end of *American Guerrilla*—that is flawed. (p. 169)

Lang, like Aeschylus and Shakespeare, was expert at creating the atmosphere of tragedy. He knew how to find the right visuals to establish a tone of horror that anticipated violence and the dark struggle. . . .

In a similar manner Lang knew the technique for developing suspense. Through the careful control of pace, selected editing, and misdirection, Lang was able to create anticipation of action. (p. 170)

[Perhaps] most important of Lang's attributes is the worthiness of the theme that dominated his films. The dark struggles within and among his characters become statements of the dark side of our own personalities. Lang depicted struggles that represented the everyday struggles of each of us—struggles with jealousy, hate, revenge, and political and criminal tyranny. He understood how each of us is driven and confused by these conflicts. In the final analysis Fritz Lang was a first-rate entertainer who never allowed us to lose sight of his message. The dark struggle is a worthy theme, a theme that gives meaning to the visual images that dominate the films of Fritz Lang. (p. 171)

> *Robert A. Armour, in his* Fritz Lang *(copyright © 1978 by Twayne Publishers, Inc.; reprinted with the permission of Twayne Publishers, a Division of G. K. Hall & Co., Boston), Twayne, 1978, 199 p.*

**DON WILLIS**

The earliest examples we have of Lang's work, *The Golden Sea* and *The Diamond Ship*—completed parts one and two of a projected four-part "series" called *The Spiders* (1919)—are in some ways representative of much of that work. Serial-like, they feature the most rudimentary of "thrills"—actors menaced by rooms filling up with water or the walls of a room coming together—and have, to put it mildly, no character, story, or thematic interest. Pre-art, they qualify at best as slow, dull camp. The second part is perhaps even more slowly paced than the first, and duller. . . . "Action," in both parts, usually means that (a) something is about to happen, and (b) something has happened, but (c) thanks to the awkward staging and editing you can't quite be sure what or how.

Lang's *Destiny* (1921), a three-story film with a linking narrative, has some stunning sets and effects, but the first two stories are dramatically nil. The third story, an Oriental fantasy-comedy, is slight but amusing, and the framing story, in which Death comes between two lovers, has occasional force. As with other silent German Langs like *Siegfried*—the first part of *Die Nibelungen* (1924)—*Metropolis* (1926), *Spies* (1928), and *Woman in the Moon* (1928), the pictorial overwhelms the dramatic. The above-cited films tend to make better stills than films. (p. 3)

Structurally, *Metropolis* is not just crude. It's downright brazen in its crudeness. You begin to wonder if this incredible series of narrative coincidences might not be part of some arcane aesthetic tactic. But it finally seems closer to simple didacticism than to aesthetics—*Metropolis,* or A Portrait of Freder's Consciousness Rising in His Time.

*Metropolis,* with its mixture of spectacle and camp, is a gigantic, grotesque curiosity. . . . Freder and Maria are simply bad ideas, but that robot is not quite as easily dismissed from the mind. . . .

[In *Woman in the Window*] Lang's vaunted "determinism" begins to look more like tired writing or heavy-handed irony— a mechanical "Well, wouldn't you know it?" as the "last thing you'd expect to happen" invariably does happen in his American films. . . . Sentimental optimism: the pardon arrives in the nick of time. Sentimental pessimism: the pardon arrives a moment too late. Lang's American films are sentimentally ironic situation dramas. (p. 5)

Lang's conception of Fate in his American films might best be described as Sternberg without wit. *You Only Live Once* and *Woman in the Window* are, in significant ways, near-opposites of a film like *The Blue Angel* (1930), in which the hero Professor Rath becomes tragicomically enmeshed in the gears of a mechanism which *he* set in motion. The Sternberg picture— stingingly comic—has none of the phony somberness of *You Only Live Once,* whose fugitives are "innocents" abroad in a mean, nasty world which is (carefully) peopled with insensitive, uncaring employers and officials. The tone of the Lang film is whining, self-pitying. Poor little Eddie and Joan can't escape "the stain of the world," to quote one character. The script constitutes a too-easy absolution of individual responsibility. Glumly, it proposes that it's *others* who set the gears in motion. (pp. 5-6)

[*Scarlet Street* (1945)] is plot-constricted too, but it's a solidly constructed melodrama—one of Lang's few good American films. . . . Johnny and Kitty are two of the very few characters in Lang's American films to have a life apart from the demands of a plot. His hearty low humor and lusty self-appreciation, and her languourousness—she *oozes* in and out of beds, sofas and his arms—provide a type of human spectacle which Lang usually had no time to appreciate in his films. Their pet exclamations . . . are emblematic of their absolute willfulness, their impatience with objects—like other people—foreign to their universe.

*Hangmen Also Die!* (1943), from a story by "Bert Brecht" and Fritz Lang (as the screen credits list them), is one of Lang's most uneven films. The "inspirational" scenes of Czech resistance to the Nazi occupation in World War II are the worst. . . . The second half of the movie—the frame-up of an informer—is standard Lang thriller stuff, both clever and contrived, over-elaborate yet sometimes exciting. It's indicative of the film's general unevenness that one of the most devastating bits—a man's bowler hat rocking back and forth until it stops, as he dies offscreen—is preceded by the awkwardly staged, fast-motion smothering of the same man. (pp. 6-7)

*Cloak and Dagger* (1946), yet another of Lang's World War II dramas, is flimsy taken either as a suspenser or as a character study. The lighting . . . is evocative Warners "noir," but the treatment of the subject—OSS operations inside wartime Germany—is strictly Hollywooden. . . . The characters' emotional-fireworks displays are unearned, gratuitous—as in *Ministry of Fear* the past remains sealed off from the present. Lang has to content his artistic self with shooting the main characters

in mirrors, a reflex gesture left over from *M* and *Woman in the Window*. (pp. 7-8)

The *Blue Gardenia* is smooth and bland—a plot, with no overtones, undertones, or point—Hitchcock's *Blackmail* . . . with nothing on it. . . . The film has a "B"-mentality script, a "B" look, "B" acting, a budding "B" romance . . . , and a laughably hasty "B" wrapup. *Beyond a Reasonable Doubt* (1956) is all plot too, with no humor, characters, or life to distract the viewer from the course of that plot—the Lang express makes few stops. The film exists solely for its twist ending. . . . Lang's *Human Desire* (1954) is a dully written and acted remake of Renoir's 1938 *La Bête Humaine,* and *Moonfleet* (1955), a routine costumer, has a little of everything—action, suspense, comedy, horror . . .—but not much of anything in the way of narrative interest—which is not quite the same thing as plot. . . .

Why was Lang so often cast in the role of hack, peddling plots? Was he typed for thrillers—Hitchcock, Jr.? Or did his semi-adolescent fascination with the intricacies of pulp crime stories simply happen to mesh with the demands of a plot-centered American film industry? Whatever the explanation for this casting, his professional quandary was unfortunate, because the presence in Lang's films of such startling characters as Johnny and Kitty in *Scarlet Street,* the Gestapo people in *Hangmen Also Die!* and Ryan's character in *Clash by Night* suggests that he had a darker talent, one that too often went untapped or under-exercised, in both his German and his American films. Thrillers may too often have been an "escape" for him as well as for his audience. (p. 8)

*Fury* attempts to situate its lynch-mob story within the story of a "typical American couple." . . . The larger story does not survive the inevitable, and perhaps necessary, compression and the schematic plot, in which elements like peanuts, a torn coat, and [the] misspelling of the word "memento" turn up with too-handy regularity. However, the mob sequences themselves, and the scenes of the newsreels singling out members of that mob—and isolating their awful exultation—still carry a surprising impact. . . . [The] best sequences in *Fury* portray a frightening "right" or "good" run wild—small town citizens burning a jail that houses a supposed kidnapper; later the victim of this assault . . . wreaking legal revenge on them. Lang gets the viewer rooting *for* and *against* the "good guy" . . . at the same time. One becomes caught between exultation and horror, as the punishment—the act of revenge—takes on the configuration of the crime. Only then does Lang appear to be exploring the implications of the action and violence in his films, the implications of his fascination with violent crime. . . . Only then does he seem to illuminate both the subjective attraction and the objective ugliness of violence. (p. 9)

Lang made two camp versions of the *M-Fury-The Big Heat* syndrome—*Rancho Notorious* (1952) and *Secret beyond the Door* . . . (1948)—which are far from good but also far from dull. The more celebrated of the two, *Rancho Notorious*— weakest of Lang's revenge sagas—is striking, garish, fast moving, always faintly ridiculous, and sometimes—as with "The Ballad of Chuck-a-Luck" . . .—wholly ridiculous. . . .

[*Secret beyond the Door* . . .] is certainly not "only melodrama," a charge that may apply to four out of five Lang films, but not to this one. It's closer to something like camp horror-romance-psychological drama. It switches gears with hilarious abruptness. . . . The pulpy, stream-of-consciousness narration . . . is an unintentional joy in itself, and the movie's big surprise and shock scenes are more comic than horrific. Only spoilsports will object that this is Lang making a joke of *M*.

The emotional "fury" of Lang's *Fury* and *The Big Heat* seems to have had its source in the second half of Lang's silent version of *Die Nibelungen—Kriemhild's Revenge* (1924). The first half, *Siegfried,* is like a static prologue, but *Kriemhild's Revenge* is powerful and, finally, even disturbing. The implacability of character suggested by the cry, in *M,* of "The only thing that will stop you is death!" also informs the action of *Kriemhild's Revenge,* in which (unlike *Metropolis*) differences between the principals—Kriemhild, Hagen, Attila—are not subject to arbitration. Justified revenge becomes slaughter as Kriemhild's foes fall, and "right" becomes indistinguishable from "wrong."

But this theme of implacability finds what may be its most moving expression in Lang in, surprisingly—since it is so little shown or seen—. . . *Liliom* (1934), . . . perhaps his finest film. . . . The rhetorical power of the last 15 minutes of *M* becomes the sustained comic-dramatic power of *Liliom,* in which the protagonist's compulsion is not only named but analyzed. Becker's cry of "I can't help it!", vividly visualized in the newsreel freezes on the mob members in *Fury,* Lang first caught on a film-within-a-film in *Liliom:* the heavenly officials weighing the evidence for and against Liliom . . . run him a scene from his life—during an argument, he slaps his girl, Julie

. . .—pinpointing for him and them his responsibility for his actions. (p. 10)

The film-within-a-film in *Liliom* is neither condemnation nor exoneration of Liliom. It's only a description of someone both controlling and controlled by his actions, accountable yet helpless. In the film, Liliom is shuttled back and forth between heaven and earth, purgatory and hell, in a very determined celestial attempt to find just the right place for him. The problem is that from one angle, he's guilty; from another, innocent. He is punished, repentant, yet incorrigible; nearly damned by his misdeeds, finally saved by his almost-good-deeds.

The legacy of Lang the artist is mostly one of parts of films—parts of *Scarlet Street, Testament of Dr. Mabuse, Fury, M, Hangmen Also Die!,* and *The Big Heat.* But it's also the whole of *Kriemhild's Revenge* and, perhaps above all, *Liliom,* the two decided exceptions to the rule of Lang the melodramatist, the Lang shallowly fascinated by crime and violence and psychopathology. Only in *Kriemhild's Revenge* and *Liliom* does that fascination become the *subject* of the film, and the impersonal become personal. (p. 11)

*Don Willis, "Fritz Lang: Only Melodrama," in* Film Quarterly *(copyright 1980 by The Regents of the University of California; reprinted by permission of the University of California Press), Vol. XXXIII, No. 2, Winter, 1979-80, pp. 2-11.*

# Richard Lester

## 1932-

**American director and television producer.**

**Lester's style often recalls the old days of slapstick and silent films. His most successful films combine a frenetic pace with visual gags.**

**Lester left for Europe at the age of twenty-two. While there, he wrote a musical and took it to England in hopes of selling it. His visit was timely, coinciding with the debut of commercial television. Lester not only sold the musical, but found a job as a television director. With Peter Sellers and Spike Milligan, Lester wrote for *The Goon Show,* an improvisational comedy series. The collaboration of Lester, Sellers, and Milligan led to a short film, *The Running, Jumping, and Standing Still Film.* This rough, virtually unedited film was an outgrowth of *The Goon Show.***

**Beginning in 1963, Lester made two films with the Beatles, *A Hard Day's Night* and *Help!* Here the surrealistic comedy of *The Goon Show* is combined with the Beatles's own unique brand of humor. However, a few critics contended that Lester indulged in visual tricks excessively.**

**Lester's style has varied from film to film. While *How I Won the War* is filled with black humor; *Robin and Marian* is a sentimental romance. *Petulia* is an incisive satire; *Juggernaut* is a suspenseful adventure film. In the words of Richard T. Jameson, the best of Lester's films have made "eloquence of frenzy." As Jameson writes: "From the snowfields of 'Ticket to Ride' in *Help!* to the out-of-focus shimmers of light and color framing the microcosmic *Juggernaut,* the extreme busyness of his films and frames has always been deployed against nothingness."**

## JOHN SEELYE

[The] three motifs introduced during the early moments of [*A Hard Day's Night*]—running (flight), antagonism towards the establishment (order), and subsequent mayhem (misrule)—are extended by variation throughout the remainder of the action. The unifying tension is that which exists between the harried manager of the troupe . . . and his obstreperous charges, a good-natured badinage which has, as always in such cases, an underlying darkness. The Manager wants them to "behave," to "shape up," to "stop clowning around." They, on the other hand, seek to escape his supervision and to disobey his orders. One is invariably reminded of a group of school boys on an outing in the charge of a bullying but ineffectual master. (p. 53)

*Hard Day's Night* is different from the usual pap. For one thing, it is technically exciting—in both senses of the words. The camera is very much alive: it runs, it jumps, it seldom is caught standing still. Unlike the bland flatness of the Elvis movies (which are reminiscent of the old *SatEvePost* illustrations), the image on the screen has depth. Gilbert Taylor, the cameraman, takes his techniques as he finds them, and he finds them everywhere. Much of the acting is apparently designed to suggest improvisation, and the camera assists this by a pseudo-documentary awkwardness. As in a documentary, the camera is insistently *there,* probing, pointing, pursuing, predicating. There are, as well, suggestions of nouvelle vague: the sequences in which the Beatles jape and juggle are presented in such a way as to remind one of the filmic high jinks in recent French movies. (pp. 53-4)

> John Seelye, "'A Hard Day's Night'," in Film Quarterly (copyright 1964 by The Regents of the University of California; reprinted by permission of the University of California Press), Vol. XVIII, No. 1, Fall, 1964, pp. 51-4.

## GEOFFREY NOWELL-SMITH

[*A Hard Day's Night*] is a shining illustration of the often untenable maxim about the whole being greater than the sum of its parts. In the first place the Beatles themselves collectively, as a group and governing ungrammatically the singular verb, is (or are) clearly much more than simple Paul, John, George and Ringo. The same principle holds good for the film, which, broken down into its individual components, is pretty poor and insipid stuff. It is not in the conventional sense well written, having no construction to speak of and dialogues which no American director of musicals would look at and which are for the most part a lot less lively than the Beatles' own spontaneous repartee. It can hardly be called well directed, unless you believe that the rapid gyrations of a hand-held camera are intrinsically more exciting or cinematic than more usual methods, which is patently not true. (p. 196)

And yet it works. And it works, or so it seems to me, on a level at which most British films, particularly the bigger and more pretentious, don't manage to get going at all. . . . *A Hard Day's Night,* though not exactly a *film d'auteur,* is in all other respects exactly the opposite. It is utterly slapdash, but it is consistent with itself. It works as a whole. It is coherent and has a sense of direction to it and a point.

The key to it lies in the personality, or non-personality, of the protagonists. They are not simply romantic idols, nor are they exactly comedians. They exist to a certain degree as individuals, but even more they function as a group. What they are presumably like as people in real life is not quite the same as the public image they cannot help projecting to the fans. At the same time the romantic group image is not totally synthetic. It has grown up much more naturally and spontaneously than is usual on the pop scene.

It is greatly to the credit of the makers of *A Hard Day's Night* (producer Walter Shenson; director Richard Lester) that they have realised all this, and built their film entirely around this situation. . . . The effect is consistently harmless and agreeable, and in all fairness one could hardly ask more than that. . . .

*A Hard Day's Night* does provoke one or two further critical reflections. It is an unstable compound, which does indeed hold together, but precariously. There is a lot of British B-Picture badness about it which could and should have been eliminated. All the more so in that in its more inspired moments it strikes and nearly manages to exploit a vein of humour and occasionally pathos which is pure gold. The knockabout scenes in the field between rehearsals and the episode of Ringo on the loose with nowhere to go are in the classic tradition of screen comedy, and because they are so good only emphasise the mediocrity of much of the rest. This mediocrity in fact is in the formula, which is designed to protect the protagonists against themselves and against the consequences of being either too funny or too sad too long.

Equally mediocre are the scenes of the concert towards the end. Whether through cowardice or plain clumsiness these scenes have been totally emasculated. They are "distanced" sufficiently by intercutting shots of audience reaction and TV line-up and mixing to prevent the Beatles coming through direct as they would in the flesh. At the same time the distancing produces none of the devastating debunking effect of the candid camera in [Wolf Koenig and Roman Kroiter's] *Lonely Boy*. The television studio atmosphere is misjudged entirely, and the rapid pans across the audience capture none of the frenzy and hysteria which the Canadians extracted from a few well chosen close-ups. But teenage hysteria is not a pretty thing to look at, or even to think about, and the makers of *A Hard Day's Night* wanted a pretty film at all costs. In this they have succeeded, but at a price of honesty and with a wastage of talent which makes one wonder just how far it was all worth while. (p. 197)

*Geoffrey Nowell-Smith, "'A Hard Day's Night'," in* Sight and Sound *(copyright © 1964 by The British Film Institute), Vol. 33, No. 4, Autumn, 1964, pp. 196-97.*

## RAYMOND DURGNAT

[*The Knack* is] crazy, but not twee, since the whimsy has a good sound emotional springboard, in all the embarrassments and yearnings that beset teenagers in their efforts to reach one another. It's a very frank film, and it translates into modern terms the sexual grotesquerie that was part of the charm of the dear old Crazy Gang—as when the hero, clambering over some park railings to save the heroine from a fate worse than death,

gets his fly-buttons hooked on the spikes, and hangs there immobilised. The film has a demented ubiquity of sexual innuendo: Tolen, offering to play Nancy some records, promises, 'You'll like Theolonius—he's deep—he's satisfying—', and Tom worries Colin by commenting, on the subject of elephant's trunks, that 'any limb that isn't in constant use atrophies and drops off'. . . .

The erotomaniac humour is nicely counterpointed by a volley of anarchist-spirited jokes, with a double-bedstead weaving in and out of the traffic like a Kon-Tiki raft, and a real little classic gag about a kindly old gentleman gallantly helping pregnant [Nancy] across the road. . . .

The weak point of *The Knack* is, precisely, a tendency to lose a scene's point in a fandango of gags. At times, certainly, it captures [the atmosphere of Ann Jellicoe's play, on which the film is based,] very well. . . . But the film's so funny that, as a whole, it dissipates the play's emotional voltage, its anxious strain and violence, all the eerier for being located in the style.

*Raymond Durgnat, "'The Knack'" (© copyright by Raymond Durgnat 1965; reprinted with permission), in* Films and Filming, *Vol. 11, No. 10, July, 1965, p. 25.*

## JOHN SEELYE

There is, I would say, very little of the censor laws' "redeeming social significance" [in *Help!*]. Unlike *Hard Day's Night,* which by means of a picaresque structure ran through a series of wonderful satiric sketches, *Help!* is a hapless farce from beginning to end, with many a limp-wristed flap at expected targets: mad science, Scotland Yard, James Bond movies. Even Terry Southern gets a fingery flutter. But there is no point, no bite, no edge. It's cotton candy, and in wide-screen Technicolor. From the few side remarks that I caught—and the Liverpuddlian accents *still* muffle a lot of meaning—the thing may be one huge in-joke, hinging on the farcical plot in which a fat caliph tries to recover a mystical ring now being worn by the unknowing Ringo. (pp. 57-8)

In all truth, however, there is little cause for complaint. The film was made for Beatle fans, like all the rest of the paraphernalia of magazines, wigs, photographs, posters. We can rejoice that it never stoops to the Elvis-epicac level, that it *is* sumptuous, expensive, unsparing in color, sound, and all the sensuous elements available to the modern film-maker. There is no feeling of vulgar waste, moreover—except as a monument or a circus involves a certain amount of conspicuous redundance—no sense of film-flam. You go and you have a good time, without feeling that you are being pandered to. Still, the first Beatle film was made for the same audience, and it somehow transcended its own purpose. (p. 58)

*John Seelye, "'Help!'" in* Film Quarterly *(copyright 1965 by The Regents of the University of California; reprinted by permission of the University of California Press), Vol. XIX, No. 1, Fall, 1965, pp. 57-8.*

## PHILIP FRENCH

The eleven minutes of *The Running, Jumping and Standing Still Film* immediately established [Richard Lester's] rapport with Goonery, [the British comedy school of the 1950's]. With it Lester found a visual style that was absent from earlier Goon films . . . and present only intermittently in the television Goon programs which he directed. . . . There is the use of silent film techniques, the camera trickery, the Sisyphian surrealism of scrubbing the grass, the brutal slapstick of the hand luring the simpleton across the field only to sock him for his pains, the comic chauvinism of the Union Jack-bedecked kite being prepared for spaceflight, and the nostalgic sepia tone print of the film itself. All these elements together with the mood of tough yet relaxed inconsequentiality, the pursuit of logic beyond the bounds of sanity, the rather disturbing national ambivalence . . . were to reappear later. (p. 369)

[With *It's Trad Dad!,* Lester] seized the opportunity to make one of the most extraordinarily inventive movies of the last ten years which is not only highly amusing but gently satirized its own convention as well. Using a *Hellzapoppin*-type narrator who talks to the actors and assists in furthering the action, the film opens with the statement that the place in which the story is set must remain nameless—and there, sure enough, is the "You are now entering" sign on the outskirts of the town with the name missing. (p. 370)

*It's Trad Dad!* is a slight film, basically dead at the center. Yet looking back on it, one is astonished that the almost prodigal comic and visual imagination behind its direction should have gone largely unnoticed. . . .

[Although] Lester turned in a competent job [with *Mouse on the Moon*] one could sense that he was little engaged by the standard British comedy leads at his service, or the whimsical celebration of pseudo-Ealing tweeness that the tedious script made inescapable. (p. 371)

[Lester] is trying to reveal, to present, not to state, though in the process he doesn't so much pressure reality as kick it around. In a recent radio interview . . . , Lester said: "In making films, the Eisenstein syndrome isn't in it. It's just a matter of communication. If you want to show exuberance or show emotions in a raw state to an audience just go out and do it, and use any device that you know—whether it be borrowed or new. I mean we're all terribly eclectic anyway in film making because there are all those films that one has seen and loved and you must profit by these and use them to create your own vocabulary."

This attitude derives in part from Lester's experience in TV, and he has made it clear that he is not working for posterity: "I don't really have any desire for any of my films to go into time capsules. And I expect *A Hard Day's Night,* which I haven't seen for a year, to be absolutely dreadful now. Because it was of that period, of the pop explosion." (pp. 372-73)

Lester's pictures are of their moment—as it says on the wall outside Tolen's bedroom in *The Knack,* "There is no tomorrow. Then how about this afternoon?" His style is not consciously elaborated. His films are made with a free-wheeling exuberance; always a good deal of room is left for improvisation, though rarely in the dialogue. Which is to say that the improvisation tends in the direction of communication between the performers (or director) and the audience through action, rather than between characters themselves in terms of deepening understanding. Indeed, one feels that Lester has a fear of anything that might slow down the impetus of his action. There is a risk here that all comedy directors should be aware of and that Lester has yet properly to face. There are just too many jokes in his pictures. He doesn't seem to know how *not* to get a laugh or even to appreciate that it might sometimes be a good thing not to. (p. 373)

[If] Lester seems insufficiently sure of himself to slow down the pace, that he always feels it's necessary to keep piling on the gags, there is at least one quite conscious motivation behind the complexity of his technique. "Audiences," he says apropos of the door-battering sequence, "seem to be able to grasp such an extraordinary amount in any given frame of a film, that I'm sort of trying to find the upper limit of it." (p. 375)

[*Help!* and *The Knack*] take him on from *A Hard Day's Night* along parallel tracks. Thematically all three are related; they are about the revolution of youth against crusty middle-age and they are a celebration of this revolt. Lester explains that these attitudes spring from the material rather than being the expression of a personal program: "I prefer the social attitudes of the young people to the disapproval of their parents. . . . If you deal with a subject, you have to take sides somewhere so I've chosen the side which I have most sympathy for and therefore I suppose it could be called anarchy because it's a youth revolution. But it isn't a conscious attitude—it's not anarchy in its political sense."

This is a central issue in *A Hard Day's Night* inasmuch as it is about the Beatles themselves as a social phenomenon. Its expression is direct, and generally amiable, though sometimes it can be brutally crude as in the confrontation with the military gentleman in the railway carriage. In *Help!* it is largely peripheral (though it is reflected in the Beatles' own speech) for essentially *Help!* is a formal exercise.

*The Knack* is immediately concerned with this revolution as was the original play, but there's no reason to believe that Lester has any serious ideas about society or any compelling interest in social problems. (p. 376)

The charge made against a good deal of *The Knack* is that it is gratuitous; and one must concede that there is some truth in this argument. Nevertheless it is possible to relate most of what happens thematically to a total concept and an overall spirit. As a continuous exercise in a type of surreal logic it holds together very well—from the monks in the bus through the egg breaking like a bomb and returning into its shell to the Albert Hall Reunion. These fragments and incidents are part of an experience of a city at the time the picture was made, part of a film which sets out to present the relationship of these four people within their rapidly changing environment. . . . (pp. 377-78)

To see nothing but frenzy in *Help!* is to miss the point entirely, and to misunderstand the nature of a film which, though slighter than *The Knack* in the sense of "content," is Lester's most ambitious undertaking. In fact to see frenzy as the picture's principal note, is to misread an extremely cool, self-conscious movie. Its flaws, such as they are, are largely attributable to the height of the ambition rather than to any inherent weakness in the conception.

Lester himself, in a characteristically self-mocking way, has provided the best description of *Help!:* "I said in a more fatuous moment recently that it's Wilkie Collins' *The Moonstone* drawn by Jasper Johns."

It is a paradoxical movie—its innovatory character lies precisely in its apparent lack of originality, its depth in the consistency of its two-dimensionality, its informality in its deliberately mannered style. (p. 378)

The principal influence, the controlling idea, is the adventure strip cartoon of the Superman-Batman genre, some examples of which are arranged on the music rest of the organ in the

Beatles' apartment, the suggestion being that they are to be played as music. This conditions the narrative style: the pace, the range of color, the dialogue and the use of captions which are often placed in the corner of the screen as in a comic square. This is the chosen film-form and adhered to throughout, not used merely as a point of departure. One example of its use is in the hollowed-out numbers which introduce the five rapid assaults on Ringo in the early part of the film.

Subsidiary visual techniques include the devices of color and design of Sunday supplement photographers and commercial artists; Lester employs these openly and ironically. And, of course, and inevitably, surrealism.

From the cinema comes the idea of the total chase picture, both serious and slapstick, of which this is the extreme form. The allusions to other pictures are endless and, such being the way of Lester, immensely affectionate. (pp. 378-79)

Thirdly, there is an exploitation of the role that Indians play and have played in British culture. . . . This once totally serious attraction-repulsion relationship with the exotic, terrifying East is now bound up with two modern factors: "the comic oriental" and end-of-Empire nostalgia, both staple features of Goonery. (p. 379)

Finally there is the contemporary British scene—the Beatles themselves, older, more individualized now, more assured, *sui generis* yet representative of a new and puzzling generation; the Establishment, symbolized by Scotland Yard, Buckingham Palace, the West End jeweler, the army, fundamentally unchanged but attempting to use the Beatles, simultaneously patronizing and identifying with them; the New Men. . . . It is the highly stylized treatment of all these figures that gives them a validity and vitality lacking in their more realistic counterparts in *A Hard Day's Night.* (pp. 379-80)

[No] longing for the simple life is remotely implied [in *Help!*]; what is seen is the contradictory demands that are made on public figures. There is however more than a hint of nostalgia for a time when comics could be taken seriously (which is to say on their own terms) just as the whole film recognizes the passing of a simple age in which one could get an unaffected frisson from stories of oriental menace.

Lester rarely milks a single gag. His technique in *Help!* is more the building of a comic house of cards concluding with the addition of a perilous joker, which he leaves miraculously tottering as he passes on to the next exercise. . . . *Help!* also suggests a rotating kaleidoscope—a constant change of symmetrical figures produced by a realignment of the same disparate elements, with a few new ones thrown in. It is Lester's own feeling for the material and his sense of cinematic rhythm that produce the symmetry.

For what Lester seems able to do is to bring together diverse strands of contemporary life, of the very moment he makes his picture, transmute (but not dilute) them, and present them in such a way that the result is immediately acceptable to a wide-ranging international public. What in effect he has is the genius of the greatest popular entertainers. He involves his audience, often without them knowing it, in the consideration of problems and the acceptance of experiences that in other circumstances they might well reject. (p. 381)

> *Philip French, "Richard Lester" (reprinted by permission of the author; originally published in* Movie, *Autumn, 1965), in* The Emergence of Film Art: The Evolution and Development of the Motion Picture

As an Art, from 1900 to the Present, *edited by Lewis Jacobs, Hopkinson and Blake, Publishers, 1969, pp. 368-81.*

## PETER HARCOURT

[In] *Help!,* the most wonderful transformations of reality occur.

Richard Lester's style is one of endless enterprise, of an apparently inexhaustible zaniness that can become wearying by the end. Well-trained in the techniques of his trade by making advertising films, he clearly takes pleasure in all the tricks of focus and exposure, in the strange effects a camera can achieve; and in *Help!* he has responded with great freshness to the possibilities of colour. Throughout the film, especially during the songs, he has striven to create a visual quality that is as thoughtless and carefree as the singing itself. Everything is light-hearted, everything is played for laughs. . . . [In] the most inventive sequence of the film, the one shot in the Alps, while we listen to their "She's got a Ticket to Ride" number, we watch bizarre images of them clowning about in the snow, all dressed in black, sometimes perched upon a grand piano isolated in the wilderness with a surrealist absurdity, sometimes skiing and tumbling about with the kind of quick-cutting and trick effects that we associate with the Keystone Cops. But these visual gags, successful though they are, are really imposed upon the music. The kids of all ages throughout the world do not *laugh* when they are listening to the Beatles. These fans are more moved than that.

For there is about the Beatles a kind of purity of appeal, a winning simplicity of manner, that is in the long run oddly served by all these antics on the screen. It is a characteristic of the film . . . that it never slows down. It never allows any one image more than a few seconds on the screen. Even the Beatles themselves are not allowed to exist as individuals. Gone is the attempt, granted at least to Ringo in *A Hard Day's Night,* to permit some sense of their individual personalities to emerge. The camera cuts back and forth from one Beatle to the next as if to guarantee them their collective anonymity. . . .

What is the effect of all this endless running and jumping, this refusal to stand still? Up to a point, it seems an attempt to render in visual terms some of the energy of the Beatles' music; but beyond that point, it would seem to betray a fear that we might perhaps get to know what they are like in some detrimental way, that they might make some kind of appeal different from the interminable androgynous charm which now seems to have been such a large part of their success. For like the characters in *The Knack,* the Beatles inhabit that no-man's-land of adolescent get-with-it-ness, that formerly awkward age which exists between sexual awareness and sexual experience, but which can now seem such a ball if we bring to it the right kind of style and a determination not-to-be-square. . . .

[Beneath] all the assertive gaiety of this enterprising film, there is a sadness—a sadness that is the result of a lack of trust in how the Beatles really are, and in their ability to create their own effect instead of having everything contrived for them by the techniques of the film. Again like *The Knack,* like the too-clever advertisement that finally undermines the product it is trying to sell, the film seems to be nudging us too hard, to be urging us too insistently to get-with-it at all costs, to be crazy, cool, superficial and detached. . . . It is both the excitement and achievement, if at the same time the present limitation of Richard Lester, that he, although American, has so successfully understood this new British modishness and has transferred its surface qualities with such inventiveness to the screen. (p. 200)

*Peter Harcourt, "'Help!'" in* Sight and Sound *(copyright © 1965 by The British Film Institute), Vol. 34, No. 4, Autumn, 1965, pp. 199-200.*

## ALFRED R. SUGG

[The] fact that no one has taken Mr. Lester to task for creating a fiction-nonfiction . . . indicates that the film—unlike literature—is a basically ambivalent art.

Once the fiction-nonfiction phrase has been uttered with respect to the Beatles films, however, we must admit that that is precisely their peculiar strength, illustrated perhaps best by the brilliant opening shots of *Help!* where we see the Beatles (in black and white) documentarily photographed exactly like the Tommy Dorsey orchestra used to be photographed in order to drive the customers out to buy popcorn. No sooner have we adjusted to this thing—image relation with the world, however, than the "screen" is suddenly struck by *colored* darts. The black-and-white shots of the Beatles were not documentary at all, but a film within a film. The darts did not come from the back of theatre, but from the fiction, where the Beatles' images also have a fictional role (i.e., that of dartboard!). But the cry of Help! which this role surely elicits (they are constantly bombarded) never eclipses its relevance to their reality outside the fiction. Just as with *A Hard Day's Night,* we feel that the whole structure of *Help!* is an expression of the performers' painful positions in the real world, where they are chased, stared at, and bombarded by us, the fans. (p. 8)

[The Beatles as entertainers are relatively unimportant to the value of the film as film. A contrast in the cinematic styles of the two films will clarify this.] In the first, the song sequences—set pieces in a kind of tongue-in-cheek documentary design—are fictionally anchored to the images on the screen. That is, the reality that the record company was in touch with pervades the fiction itself. These sequences are not without cinematic flavor nor imaginative design—i.e., the girls climbing the wire-mesh dividers in the baggage compartment, with its perhaps obvious but nonetheless effective reference to the age-old question as to which side of the zoo-fence the monkeys are on; the studio shots with all the blank sterility of the homosexual producer and the fiercely unsexual orgy of the mechanically screaming girls in the audience—but their documentary orientation is most negatively realized in the "rehearsal break" shots where the camera swings freely, soaringly, breathtakingly up into the air and lyrically watches the boys scamper like goony gazelles across the geometrically patterned landscape. This freedom from the real world the Beatles live in, is exactly the landscape for their second film, which loses literary-fictional strength just where it gains cinematically. And in regard to their songs, the images are never "freer," never more cut off from reality than when they are singing. If it can be said that no film exploits its medium properly unless the sound track is disjoined from the visual track, *Help!* earns its right to not only its tremendous popular success but to its not always open-armed critical acclaim as well. In *Help!,* one feels that the director is fully aware of and determined to enjoy the kind of freedom that is mostly exploited in the medium of words but which is a very real dimension of the film medium as well. Significantly, in the second film, while the Beatles seem *always* to be singing, they are rarely seen singing as such. Rather than the creation of a fictional-real context, that the

camera photographs and that includes the occasion for singing, the singing affords the occasion for the thrillingly cinematic compositions of visual images both in frame and in sequence. Cut from their documentary moorings just because of the reality of their subject, the images dart and linger; the perspective dances its own kind of frug; the cutting has its own kind of go-go beat.

The matter of rhythm suggests another way to differentiate between the two films and at the same time to further our understanding of their filmic merits. In the first, the "script" was loaded with the sort of joke that perfectly expresses the Beatles' kind of cool: namely, quick and understated. (What do you call that haircut, someone asks one of them, to pick only the most famous example out of a veritable host. "Arthur," the Beatle mumbles as the cut is made. I've seen the film twice and I still haven't really heard the answer though I think I have identified the frames where it must occur.) The cutting is as quick as the wit, but, significantly for the purpose at hand, right with it, reinforcing it by repeating it. In *Help!,* however, the same Beatles rhythm, the same dryness, the same quickness, the same straightfacedness is effected without any tie to the Beatles *themselves* at all. Let me mention one example at some length. . . . (pp. 10-11)

Mr. Lester, seeing one supposes the resemblance between the shape of the wide screen and the shape of the slit through which people inside tanks look at the world outside of tanks, contrives a shot of a Beatle (Paul?) looking out of such a slit, his famous face clipped and pruned by the intransigent apperture. He further contrives to place the tiny oblong (with cropped face) in the very middle of the monstrous oblong of a screen that is otherwise blacked out by the tank and by which nothing short of Flanders Fields could conceivably be cropped. The result is visually stunning, cinematically funny, and editorially significant. But it is over before, really, the audience has had half a chance to see what was done. And the rhythm of the joke (*in* to be sure, but no less brilliant for that) is moreover exactly the rhythm of the Beatles' delivery: a lightning-fast, deadpan aside, without buildup or aftertaste, hurried for the most part to make room for the next. Nor is the director far behind. Immediately after the tank-slit shot, he cuts in a standard shot of a huge cannon about to go off. Faces grimace; muscles tense; fingers, if I'm not mistaken, plug up the ears of everyone around the gun. The cannon fires, terrifically. When the smoke clears, however, we see not devastation but one of the canoneers removing a speck from his eye. And we're off to another set-up! The cannon-speck sequence is a reduplication of the oblong-screen sequence, and, moreover, it has the effect of the haircut question-answer bit. (p. 12)

By choosing the "very real" Beatles as subject, Mr. Lester was free (and became freer) to combine his pictures into autonomous cinematic tropes without losing touch with reality. What they are (the Beatles) stimulated the rhythms and patterns of the film as film, which is the only artistically satisfactory way of saying in film what they are. To state the same point another way, let me say that even those other films that effectively involve themselves with cinematic language (Mr. Lester's own *The Knack,* for example) pale in comparison to the Beatles films because they invariably deal with a fiction instead of a fact. In this regard, the "languages" seem unable to fuse, but rather tend to rob each other by their assertions of themselves. (p. 13)

*Alfred R. Sugg, "The Beatles and Film Art," in* Film Heritage *(copyright 1966 by F. A. Macklin), Vol. 1, No. 4, Summer, 1966, pp. 3-13.*

## JULES FEIFFER

[In *A Funny Thing Happened on the Way to the Forum*] Richard Lester has painted on film a manic montage of vaudeville turns, girlie-book jokes, movie bits and gag cartoons that congeal, magically, into art. . . . With Designer Tony Walton he has built an ancient Rome noble only in its houses of debauchery and steeped everywhere else in a middle-class decay that could easily make it a First Century Watts. Within this he manages, quite improbably, to expand space to the point of infinity and suffuse it with the light of a Steinberg cartoon.

*Forum* on stage was a raucous, rakish, baggy-toga burlesque, set slightly off-balance by its star, Zero Mostel, whose talent gave it an unneeded class, and, again off-balance, by a score with more wit and urbanity than audiences, under the circumstances, were prepared to listen to. Delightful though it was, the show was not of one piece and never really up to the not terribly well-matched styles of Mostel and Composer-Lyricist Sondheim. What was needed to meld all elements together was the sharp identity Lester brings to all his work, so that on film the show becomes not the mixed bag it was on stage, but a further sighting into the prankish environs of Richard Lester, as fixed an orbit, in its way, as the worlds of Welles and Fellini. (p. 10)

Jules Feiffer, "A Manic Montage of Raucous Rome," in Life *(courtesy of* Life Magazine; © *1966 Time Inc.; reprinted with permission), Vol. 61, No. 20, November 11, 1966, pp. 10, 16.*

## PENELOPE HOUSTON

[On the one hand, Lester's film *A Funny Thing Happened on the Way to the Forum* has] the framework of [Bert] Shevelove and [Larry] Gelbart's Broadway hit, its slow fuse Jewish-American humour, its carefully set up jokes about dithering middle-aged men and bullying wives let loose in Brooklyn-on-Tiber. This humour takes time: above all, time for the actors to build contact with the audience. On the other hand, there is Richard Lester's style, glancing, cool, nerveless, and dependent on perpetual motion. Lester seems to circle the comedy, jabbing, weaving, feinting, hardly landing a solid punch.

What works with the Beatles, in fact, won't do when the actors are a generation older, and physically more resistant to the whole idea of being stood on their heads. . . . Style, as the film progresses, becomes more and more like conscientiously strenuous decoration, an effort to manufacture exuberance. Why take a shot upside-down; or flick through half-a-dozen of the briefest, most eye-straining glimpses of the characters; or turn a song into a display exercise for the camera, shuffling through locations as though they were playing cards? The only answer would seem to be, why not. . . .

Too much of the [film] is either frantically diversified action (a chariot-chase, for instance, which gathers speed without comic momentum), or an effort to lift the text almost bodily across the footlights. . . . And the film slips away down the gap between two entertainment formulas.

Penelope Houston, "'A Funny Thing Happened on the Way to the Forum'," in Sight and Sound *(copyright © 1967 by The British Film Institute), Vol. 36, No. 1, Winter, 1966-67, p. 47.*

## MARSHA KINDER

*The Knack* makes a serious satirical statement about certain middle-class attitudes which have found new expression in youthful approaches to sex. Tolen's knack with women is acquired by adapting to sex a number of traditional middle-class attitudes toward work and material success. He sees girls as fancy gadgets to be manipulated, as interchangeable objects who look and act alike. In order to manipulate them successfully, one must acquire the knack. The only halfway human relationships established are not between manipulator and object, but between those who have the knack and those who are trying to get it; and such relationships are essentially competitive.

The knack is compared with two kinds of activity, both competitive. First, the knack is portrayed as a marketable skill in a commercial society. . . . This analogy is dramatized when Nancy goes to buy a dress. The salesman uses his sexual line to sell dresses; it is almost impossible to distinguish between the commercial and sexual pitch. . . .

Just as the salesman has a stock speech that he repeats to all customers, so the women consumers also have a stock response. When Nancy goes from door-to-door crying "rape," one woman replies with "not today," a typical stock response to salesmen. (p. 30)

In the hilarious scene where Colin ineffectually tries to use a hammer, nails and screws to bar his front door, the knack is related to the Protestant work ethic and the glorification of the task well done. This comparison is emphasized by the titles, which seem to come from a workman's manual. Colin's ineffectuality is contrasted with Tolen's proficiency in driving a motorcycle full of gadgets, and a motorboat—both symbols of masculine power and energy—and in knowing exactly how to clean a window (his description sounds like a TV commercial for a window cleaner).

The contrast between Tolen and Colin is even more significant when the knack is compared to an athletic skill. The film develops an important contrast between competitive sports and playful games. The knack is an athletic skill requiring lots of practice and keen competitiveness. Making love to a girl is like running a mile; you try to perfect your technique so that you can break a new time record. In such a sport, you are competing—not with the girl, who is merely the track—but with the other runners. (pp. 30-1)

But sports are not only a competitive battle, they are also games, hence playful and fun; this is Colin's attitude. In the scene where Colin, Tom and Nancy ride the bed across London, they turn an arduous physical task into a delightful, fantastic game. The game is not competitive; its goals are neither efficiency nor achievement, but fun. . . . It is completely antithetical to Tolen's kind of life games.

One of the best scenes is the lion taming in Tom's room, for here Lester is in tight control of the tonal components. This is the only scene in which we see clearly the juxtaposition of the two kinds of games. . . . We anticipate having another amused response as in the earlier fantasy sequences, but then something unexpected happens. We don't see fun, but cruelty. . . . Tolen breaks through [Nancy's] initial reserve, and then callously turns her over to Colin. The tone has gradually moved from light playfulness to dark cruelty.

But at the very point when the tone becomes most ominous Lester brilliantly steers it back to lightness. Colin, of course, is unable to take over. While Tolen had tried to conquer and subdue Nancy's will and individuality, to turn her into a tame, domesticated creature like the rest of his women, Colin instinctively transforms the game into playful fun. . . . This contrast between two kinds of game is like the contrast between Colin's bed ride through London and Tolen's bed gymnastics through lines of inter-changeable women. Lester has sharpened the distinction by juxtaposition. (pp. 31-2)

As soon as [Nancy] refuses to play the role [Tolen assigns her when they are in the park together]—a passive object being acted upon—he loses control and power; or more precisely, the knack no longer works.

When Nancy regains consciousness, she immediately begins a new game. She realizes that Tolen has lost control and that she can impose her fantasy—that the rape has occurred—on the others. But she also realizes that she would rather play the game with Colin, because she can actually learn more from him. Thus they share the mutually attractive fantasy that Colin has raped her, and this fantasy becomes the basis for a human relationship that recognizes the individuality of both. . . . [By condemning Nancy and Colin's sexual relation], Tolen joins the chorus of adult voices who have been condemning youth throughout the film—voices with which he has always been in essential agreement.

Probably the reason why most critics emphasize the energy and spontaneity of *The Knack* is that these are unquestionably dominant qualities in Lester's style. But it should also be noted that such spontaneity and energy is incompatible with the kind of conformity and monotony implicit in Tolen's attitude toward sex. The opening fantasy sequence implies that Tolen has the potential to perform the same sexual act repeatedly with an endless line of identical girls. This achievement may require an extraordinary amount of energy, but it is performed in a repetitious, monotonous way without much room for imagination or spontaneity.

Lester seems to be using techniques associated with commercial art, which he simultaneously parodies and transforms into a source of value. To give one example, many shots give the impression of magazine layouts, particularly in the fantasy sequences. . . . Where, then, do we get the sense of spontaneity? Magazine layouts usually convey exactly the opposite impression—one of carefully controlled design. Lester's spontaneity apparently arises from the differences in the kind of fantasy being portrayed. Unlike the monotony of Tolen's fantasy, with its unvarying line of look-alike mannequins, in the bed riding fantasy we have a number of variations on the same theme—what you can make out of a bed. . . . This fantasy is markedly different from the other because it is not based solely on quantitative exaggeration; the variation it implies is also qualitative.

Thus Lester transforms commercial magazine layout technique into a vehicle for demonstrating a variety of imaginative solutions to an artistic problem. Any discussion of *The Knack* should report its energy and spontaneity, but not at the expense of its other important distinction as serious and significant satire. (pp. 32-4)

*Marsha Kinder, "'The Knack . . . and How to Get It'," in* Film Society Review, *March, 1967, pp. 30-4.*

**RICHARD CORLISS**

*How I Won the War* is, at its best, a stinging study of war's corruption, a stringent depicting of war's large lies—strata-

gems, if you like—and small ones. . . . *How I Won the War* shows the moral side [of war]. And it is . . . a brave film. . . .

Lester could have been braver—if he had made a film condemning the American position in Vietnam, for example (*War* does contain one gratuitous reference to the current police action), or the Israeli military mystique in the Middle Eastern War—but we are not asking the man to slit his cinematic wrists as a gesture of protest. If he has not gone far enough in satirizing war, he has at least gone further than any other commercial film-maker. . . . (p. 35)

Lester's choice of World War II, a conflict that can be justified as an act of self-defense against National Socialism, forces him into the position which he accepts gladly—that all war is (his term) obscene. This raises the standard question: if Country A marches on Country B with the objective of demolishing or appropriating B, isn't B required to bear arms in an attempt to save the lives of its people? Lester dodges this question. He simply says that, once involved in a war, everyone is tainted—a general philosophy a lot less radical than the sum of its brutal parts. In his death speech, the soldier played by John Lennon says, "I fought this war for three reasons. The first one got me in. I don't remember what it was now." Neither, it seems, does Lester. But if he had investigated that first reason—self-defense, national sovereignty, or abduction of the king's wife—and found in it a point weak enough to be satirized, he would have made a more honest film and, incidentally, solved one of the unsolvable problems.

*How I Won the War* is also diluted by having to aim the same satirical spear at two targets, war and war films. Since the latter is a much broader target and thus easier to hit, the film is most successful when describing the usual war-movie types: the blustering sergeant, the cowardly volunteer, the pompous general, the nice-guy Nazi. The difference in Lester's approach is that none are meant to be either funny or blameless. When the German officer who captures Goodbody, and who is the only man in the film with whom he can speak, casually remarks that he has killed "quite a few" Jews, Goodbody cannot feel morally superior simply because the mass murders for which he is responsible were carried out without regard to race, color, or creed. . . . Lester has said, and the film bears it out, that he wanted to evoke, not our sense of humor, but our sense of horror. And this he does, for example, when an officer tries to convince us and himself that "it's very important to raise a laugh on the battlefield." It will be difficult for anyone moved by this scene to laugh on a battlefield again.

The film has been accused of being so involved with technique that it stifles any emotional response. It is true that Lester never lets us forget (in the manner of Bergman's *Persona*) that we are watching a film: as the camera closes in on a hysterical soldier, the sergeant says to us, "Go away. Haven't you seen enough?" . . . The message may be muddled, but *How I Won the War* is more than a message; it is a film, and one of the few anti-war films that transcend the sentimental. (pp. 35-6)

*Richard Corliss, "Film Reviews: 'How I Won the War'," in* Film Quarterly *(copyright 1968 by The Regents of the University of California; reprinted by permission of the University of California Press), Vol. XXI, No. 2, Winter, 1967-68, pp. 35-6.*

**STANLEY KAUFFMANN**

[The least of Lester's early films] had scintillating moments, and the best of them are fireworks displays that spell out some secrets of our times. [*How I Won the War*] is Lester at his very best. (p. 30)

[The] script, filigreed with good wiry dialogue, serves as a fine trampoline for Lester. These are numerous "plants" of material—visual and verbal—to which later reference is made, too neatly modulated to be called running gags. There is a barrage of parodic transformations. For instance, a blimpish colonel gives the lieutenant a gung-ho speech in a dugout. When the camera pulls back at the end of his exhortation, the dugout—suddenly—is on a stage, and the curtain descends as the colonel finishes roundly. (Lester does not leave it there. The audience in that theater is sparse and the applause is slack.) A number of incidents are swiftly replayed in different settings, as in a spoof of *Marienbad*. The music yawns scoffingly: whenever we cut back to these bedraggled desert rats, we get a swell of grandiose Oriental goo on the soundtrack in *Lawrence of Arabia* style. And we are continually reminded that the whole thing is a film. (p. 31)

With the light-fingered help of his editor, John Victor Smith, Lester caroms the film off a series of colored bubble gum pictures of WW II battles—cheap unreal icons of events that Lester makes more truly unreal. Yes, the film tells us that war is hell and that the most hellish thing about it is that fundamentally men love it. But Lester is telling it all from a particular point of view. When Lester's film is not (occasionally) straining to be funny, it is *genuinely* not funny—the kind of comedy at which one does not laugh, comedy that seems to take place in a cavern of ice where all the laughter has already been laughed, has been caught and frozen in glittering, frightening stalactites.

This is because Lester's film speaks from the very center of the Age of the Put-on. This is the heart of the sixties speaking about Dunkirk, Alamein, the murder of the Jews. No German officer would actually have said what Lester's German says about murdering Jews. (He is quite unperturbed—neither triumphant nor vicious nor tormented.) This film is the Mod generation's view of the war and of our mourning for it—a view of history not as tragedy but as stupidity. To them, we of an older generation who are still involved with such matters as this century's evil and guilt are simply entangled, in another way, in the same stupidity. And stupidity is funny; but this stupidity was so huge that it is deeper than ha-ha funny. The film's viewpoint is morally shocking, in the most serious sense, and is seriously debatable; but it is neither immoral nor amoral, and it is brilliantly, scathingly put. (p. 33)

*Stanley Kauffmann, "'Closely Watched Trains'; 'How I Won the War'" (originally published in* New American Review, *January, 1968), in his* Figures of Light: Film Criticism and Comment *(copyright © 1967, 1968, 1969, 1970, 1971 by Stanley Kauffmann; reprinted by permission of Harper & Row, Publishers, Inc.), Harper, 1971, pp. 29-34.\**

### STEPHEN FARBER

It is impossible to talk about what *Petulia* means without talking about how it is structured and composed; form, for once, is truly indistinguishable from content. (p. 67)

Larry Marcus's script and Lester's direction of *Petulia* constantly play against sentimentality. . . . The love scenes between Archie and Petulia are all joyless—an abortive tryst at a remote-controlled motel, where registration, room location, even sexual stimulation are done by machine; a jaunt through a tomblike supermarket late at night; an awkward, fumblingly lustful embrace in Archie's car. Even Petulia and Archie's night together is austerely filmed. . . . Lester has never dealt convincingly with love (he has usually not even tried), but here he turns that weakness into strength: his peculiarly unromantic temperament transforms what might have been mawkish material into a bitter but compassionate drama of human isolation. (pp. 67-8)

The melancholy in all of [Archie's and Petulia's] encounters makes the futility of their relationship clear enough, but the structure of the scenes is, again, even more telling. Lester and Marcus shatter time in fascinating ways. . . . [The] intercutting of one character's present with another character's past—I can't think of any clear precedent in other films—gives us exactly the feeling that Lester must have wanted to convey, the sense of two lives being lived simultaneously, intersecting but essentially, perpetually disjointed. There is no way that Archie can *ever* reach Petulia's past, no way for him to know the experiences that have made her what she is. Time past and time present do not meet; they are like two parallel lines, fragments from different lives. A simple intercutting of the *present* experiences of both characters would not so poignantly render their separateness. (p. 68)

Lester uses detail effectively to reinforce the feelings of isolation, incongruity, melancholy that define the relationship of Petulia and Archie. His camera often settles for a moment on what seems a gratuitous face or group—laundresses working silently in the basement of the Fairmont Hotel, a clown selling balloons outside a supermarket, a Negro sitting alone in the furnace room of a hospital, gardeners spraying plants in front of Petulia's mansion, actors filming a commercial in Muir Woods, a group of nuns in the Japanese gardens or priests on the tour boat to Alcatraz. But this pageant has relevance; Lester is persistently calling our attention to the faces of strangers, faces from lives we will never know or understand, but that we glimpse and puzzle over for a moment as they pass us. Similarly, Archie's television runs on and on in the background of scenes, with messages from Vietnam, but Archie does not really know how to listen. Any of these things might upset his complacency if he looked hard enough; but other lives only rarely break through the barriers we have unconsciously built around ourselves. (p. 69)

*Petulia* is annoying from time to time. Lester cannot resist playing, throwing in coy comic bits that destroy the mood he has worked to achieve. Some of the straight satiric "business"—the mechanical furnishings of the motel, several hypocritical hippies, an unfeeling chorus of bystanders around Petulia's ambulance . . . , the stilted conversation of Petulia's inhuman father-in-law—is cold, obvious, predictable. The film's opening—fast cutting back and forth between crippled rich folks being wheeled into the Fairmont's basement and a screaming rock band upstairs—is about as ugly and unpromising as that of any film this year. . . . In other words, the people who made this film have made mistakes. But even the mistakes are interesting and discussible. Every moment in the film is alert, intelligent, has a reason for being there. That is a rare enough quality in American films. The compassion and ability to sustain dramatic scenes that reveal a new maturity in Lester's talent are added pleasures. (p. 70)

*Stephen Farber, "'Petulia'," in* Film Quarterly *(copyright 1968 by The Regents of the University of California; reprinted by permission of the University of California Press), Vol. XXII, No. 1, Fall, 1968, pp. 67-70.*

## PAULINE KAEL

There is a sequence of a girl dancing in *A Funny Thing Happened on the Way to the Forum* but the director, Richard Lester, breaks it up so much with camera and editing that we can't see the dance, only flashes of parts of her body, and we can't even tell if the girl *can* dance because the movement is almost totally supplied by *his* means. This technique is a good one for concealing the ineptitude of performers, but Lester's short-term camera magic keeps cutting into and away from the co-medians . . . , who never get a chance to develop a routine or to bring off a number. What are we being distracted from? . . .

[Seeing] the result, we get the sense that Lester thinks it would be too banal just to let us see a dance or a pair of comedians singing a duet. Yet if they're good, they're a lot less banal than camera movement designed to cover emptiness. We go to see great clowns precisely for the way they move, for the grace and lightness of their style. The marvel of buriesque is that those lewd men become beautiful: their timing and skill transform the lowest forms of comedy. When Lester supplies the rhythms for them by film editing he takes away the one great asset of burlesque: that triumph of style which converts leering into art. He takes away their beauty and they become ugly and gross; he turns artists back into mugging low comics. (He also uses the women execrably: they are blank-faced bodies or witless viragos.) (p. 138)

It's difficult to make dance and song "work" on screen, and it's understandable that a talented, inventive director should fall back upon what looks so "cinematic"—the nervous camera, the restless splicing, the succession of "visual" jokes. But the sight gags of television commercials have a purpose: they are there to sell something and they make their point and they're over. In *Forum* as in *The Knack,* when Lester strings these gags together, they're just pointless agitation—just "clever" and "imaginative." He proceeds by fits and starts and leaves jokes suspended in mid-air: it's as if he'd forgotten what it's all for. And for an audience the experience becomes one of impatience and irritation—like coitus interruptus going on forever. (p. 139)

Pauline Kael, "'A Funny Thing Happened on the Way to the Forum'," in her Kiss Kiss Bang Bang (© 1968 by Pauline Kael; reprinted by permission of Little, Brown and Company in association with the Atlantic Monthly Press), Atlantic-Little, Brown, 1968, pp. 138-39.

## MICHAEL DEMPSEY

Working with a brashly theatrical script (the John Antrobus-Spike Milligan play), Lester predictably opens [*The Bed Sitting Room*] up by spreading the scenes across a vast landscape. But he also insists on the play's theatricality and tries for a visual style that will combine both approaches. (p. 33)

[Lester] succeeds where he failed in *How I Won the War.* The earlier movie also featured caricatures going through hopefully surrealistic routines, but the director failed to stylize the lo-cations. Thus, the actions and the dialogues . . . took place against quite ordinary backgrounds. The clash wrecked the movie, made it both unfunny and uninvolving. In *The Bed Sitting Room,* whose dialogue and acting are far superior, Les-ter provides settings congruent with his caricatures. Thus, even when they go astray, the actors never look like your lead-brained neighbors shooting 8mm monkeyshines on their front lawn. This fusion of styles is highly unstable. (pp. 33-4)

This method, which provides no "real" people with whom we can "identify," makes for a "cold" film. Though artists and critics . . . are strenuously questioning the concepts of char-acterization and feeling in literature, film audiences still seem to want the most naive kind of "warmth," an emotional bath in which they can splash around. But Lester avoids emotion-alism. He has enough sense to cool off an overheated subject and present it with perspective. But his direction does more than subvert movie routines by eliminating easy climaxes. Be-cause he so consistently resists tugging at heartstrings, he can achieve momentary epiphanies that infuse the movie with the sweetness of sudden recollection, brief beauties that we barely grasp before they vanish. One of these moments is just a shot of a tossed stone splashing into a polluted lake. The film's wandering family rests beside the fetid water; the splash crys-tallizes the scene into a passing suggestion of the family's lost serenity. Two others interrupt hectic banter on a subway where they live for a while: the husband, locked off the train, glaring fearfully through the window; the wife, chopping up a Hershey bar and jabbering mindlessly, suddenly worrying about being left alone. In such moments, by revealing for just an instant fears his people dare not yield to and old joys they dare not dwell upon, Lester gives the movie extra resonance. (p. 34)

[In this film], Lester reiterates his attack from *How I Won the War* on the conventions of war films. Such genre movies, even when explicitly antiwar, have usually failed because (as many have noted) audiences ignored the message and lapped up the thrills. These thrills have been not just gung-ho heroics but also such things as piled corpses, mangled civilians, starving children, emaciated remnants of death camps, blasted cities—all intended to make us cry, with Lester's mad movie-maker, "Oh, the horror, the horror," while enjoying the pleasure of being shocked and the greater pleasure of feeling either helpless or vengeful, but in either case, impotent. If we see no actual war in *The Bed Sitting Room,* it is because we have had it, and rightly so, with the horrors of movie-wars, whether documen-tary or fictional. At a time when war flares all over the globe, Lester calls for an end to using their atrocities and pain as visual propaganda against war and for a humanitarianism that the most bellicose hawks and vicious rednecks can and do profess without altering their policies in the slightest.

But, during the final sequences, it begins to seem that we may, after all, behold horror. Ominous clouds gather, the characters grow apprehensive, the end appears imminent. Yet Lester ends the film quite inconclusively. . . . The mixed feelings of the scene are stirring. Lester wants to express hope in a renewal of life, and consequently he now fills the screen with his bright-est, most sensuous colors. Yet he cannot repress despair. The authoritarians are benevolent and funny, yet perhaps they will prove all the worse for that. The resurgence of the now men-tionable bomb darkens the mood. Yet the geniality and lilt in both the colors and the voices are particularly unexpected after the brittleness, polemics, harsh editing, and cynicism of recent Lester movies. Here we sense him drawing upon the gaiety that flickered in *Petulia* and may have seemed purely a Beatle trait in his two films with them. *The Bed Sitting Room,* a far less frenetic film than any of these, extends the range of his expressiveness. (pp. 34-5)

Michael Dempsey, "War As Movie Theater—Two Films," in Film Quarterly (copyright 1972 by The Regents of the University of California; reprinted by *permission of the University of California Press), Vol. XXV, No. 2, Winter, 1971-72, pp. 33-6.**

## RICHARD SCHICKEL

*Petulia* is a terrific movie, at once a sad and savage comment on the ways we waste our time, our money and ourselves in upper-middle-class America. It is a subject much trifled with in movies these days, but rarely—if ever—has it been tackled with the ferocious and ultimately purifying energy displayed in this highly moral, yet unmoralistic, film.

Its strength stems from two sources, the passionate intensity with which director Richard Lester fastens his camera's eye on the inanimate artifacts of our consumer culture and the complex, highly charged (but subtly controlled) style—rather like a mosaic set in very rapid motion—with which he presents his vision of a world where the thing is king, an absolute sovereign holding all of us in thrall. . . . ["The visible hieroglyphs of the unseen world" are] the true subject of *Petulia*. A fully mechanized motel, a parody of a *Playboy* bachelor's pad, an inhumanly efficient hospital (a sort of medical factory)—what these hieroglyphs tell us about the true quality of our unseen world, the doomed hopes for ease and grace they contain! In a sense Lester is practicing in art what we all attempt in daily life—reading character by studying a man's possessions, which in the day of standardized people is a very useful gift. And from the place his characters choose to eat lunch, from the show flickering on an unwatched TV set in the corner, from the stuff they give their kids, we learn who his people are, what they really want, in a way that almost makes dialogue superfluous.

As for the style, it is the now conventionalized and commercialized one based on the quick cut and the deliberate jumbling of time sequence, which is no longer worth discussing, let alone deploring, since it is *the* style of the sixties. The point is that Lester uses it with superb natural ease. Too often in American films this technique is regarded as no more than an opportunity to show off, an extra added attraction tacked on for no discernible good reason. Here this style, which emphasizes the fact that movies are themselves a mechanically based art, works brilliantly; style and substance are organically, inextricably related, working like a reciprocating engine to drive home Lester's point. (pp. 187-88)

For the length of the movie [the characters] twist and turn, attempting to elude the destinies their natures and the distorted values of their time, place and class impose upon them, but for all their venturings, both comic and grisly, they remain in the end pretty much as we found them, screwed-up prisoners of a screwed-up world.

This is, I think, a measure of the film's honesty, but there are others. Petulia and friend are nice enough to identify with, but they are not, finally, so charming or delightful that you feel like indulging them to excess. Each has a hard core of selfishness and foolishness that cannot be washed out; they contain within themselves the very qualities against which they are in rebellion—how could they not, since they, too, are the creatures of their era? Their tragedy is that, unlike the majority of their fellow sufferers, they are aware of what's happening to them. . . . They know, they know—and still they can't quite make it to decency and repose.

It is gut-grinding to watch them try, even when they make you laugh. And laugh you do, in rueful self-recognition, for Lester,

his leading actors and screenwriter Lawrence B. Marcus are confident and mordant throwaway ironists.

Still, the triumph rightly belongs to Lester. . . . [He] has at last controlled his enormous gift for movie making and placed it in the service of a brilliantly conceived, carefully aimed, splendidly detailed satire. He demands much of the audience, a toughness, a stern ability to put down the desire—always present at the movies—for the happy-ending cop-out. On the other hand, he gives much—a rich, terrible examination of the contemporary social and psychological malaise. (pp. 188-89)

*Richard Schickel, "Petulia" (originally published in a slightly different form in* Life, *Vol. 64, No. 22, May 31, 1968), in his* Second Sight; Notes on Some Movies, 1965-1970 *(copyright © 1972 by, Richard Schickel; reprinted by permission of Simon & Schuster, a Division of Gulf & Western Corporation), Simon & Schuster, 1972, pp. 187-90.*

## DAVID L. OVERBEY

[*The Three Musketeers*] is well within the tradition of . . . the swashbuckling sub-genre. Although there is none of the fragmented narration through the editing which one usually associates with Lester . . . , the fragmentation through anarchic humour of a serious world view remains part of the Lester method. There is a constant rush of jokes on every level, from the traditional slapstick surrounding insanely furious sequences of swordplay to near-whispered comic comment by a set of court dwarves. Characters are conceived in comically larger than life, so that the usually romantic Constance . . . is here beautiful but clumsy—falling down stairs, walking into walls, or catching her foot in a pail of water while being embraced by D'Artagnan. . . . Most of the comedy works well. When it doesn't, we are faced with a problem in the modern cinema which must have given Lester, too, more than a few moments of puzzlement as he worked with the material. . . .

A work like *The Three Musketeers* has at least two facets, one romantically 'serious' and the other rather fantastic adventure. Certainly, as previous versions have indicated, the latter aspect is open to comedy (perhaps necessarily so), whereas the more 'serious' aspects of plot—those concerning Milady de Winter and the Queen's diamonds—are more problematical. One does not, of course, expect a historical political treatise on the period of Louis XIII and Richelieu. Dumas was not Aldous Huxley, and *The Three Musketeers* is not *Grey Eminence*. . . . Still, for the suspense and a rather romantic suspension of disbelief to work, one must take the same romantic intrigue as a necessary given, if only to provide a foundation for the comedy. To undercut the courtly romance is to take the chance that the entire structure will collapse. . . .

[Lester] chose to treat the entire tale as comic, undercutting even the English lord's platonic love for the Queen. The dialogue for the most part remains true to the romantic myth. . . . But a consciously absurd visual image, like the secret shrine which the Duke has built in homage to his 'divinity', the Queen, makes it nearly impossible to care finally if the Queen's reputation and Peace in the World are ever saved. Even Richelieu, for all the oddly out-of-tune stolidity with which he is played by Charlton Heston, seems to be surrounded at the Bastille by henchmen and torturers who are comically incompetent rather than sinister.

Yet, all of this being duly noted, what might seem to be a disastrous conception of the material works rather well as entertainment. If we must give up our legitimate concern for the Queen, if the King-Richelieu-Milady axis cannot be taken as a serious threat to anyone, if even Constance and D'Artagnan are more lustily anxious than romantic, we are still carried along by the film's furious pace, and what is taken away is at least partially returned to us by some audaciously fresh comedy. If one gag does not come off, there is another following fast on its heels which does. The film is also often stunning to watch. Even if Lester is, indeed, having a bit of fun with the excesses of [Ken] Russell, the huge sets and pretty costumes are none the less sensuously appealing. Probably because of the emphasis on editing in his previous films, Lester's compositional abilities have been unjustly overlooked. If his frames were, before, composed to fit into a jigsaw arrangement, they are now composed carefully for their own sake. For whatever reasons of necessity or choice, the unfragmented narrative approach works with the material here. . . . (p. 117)

*David L. Overbey, "'The Three Musketeers'," in* Sight and Sound *(copyright © 1974 by The British Film Institute), Vol. 43, No. 2, Spring, 1974, pp. 116-17.*

## STANLEY KAUFFMANN

*The Three Musketeers* is full of action, dash, and slapstick, and it depressed me very much. This is Richard Lester's first picture since *The Bed Sitting Room* (1969), a picture that showed a sad lapse in Lester's judgment of scripts though not in his unique and wonderful filmic style. *The Three Musketeers* has a sounder script, but it shows an absolute abandonment of the style that made Lester Lester. Such films as *A Hard Day's Night* and *The Knack* and *How I Won the War* overflow with imaginative pyrotechnics that manage to be brilliant and helpful at the same time. *The Three Musketeers* overflows with nothing but what must in Lester's case be called conventional ebullience. It tries to render the Dumas novel as action comedy and, if memory is serving, it takes that vein somewhat further than the Doublas Fairbanks version did. Here it's not only D'Artagnan who is a somewhat overheroic hero; virtually all the other characters except Richelieu are used for laughs, one way or another. But none of it is Lester comedy, cinematic eruption. Almost all of it is script-y, devised, derivative—and harmful to Dumas. (pp. 274-75)

The script, by George Macdonald Fraser, is a sequence of stunts and set pieces, rather than a strong sequential narrative. D'Artagnan and his three friends are stripped of character and become interchangeable brawlers—so Dumas is robbed of his nice touches of sentiment. And the conclusion is just a limp pageant. . . .

It's one dragged-out forced laugh. No sweep, no romance, no convincing chivalric tradition to mock. And, worst of all, no Lester. Not the Lester who has been missing for too long. (p. 275)

*Stanley Kauffmann, "'The Three Musketeers'" (originally published in* The New Republic, *Vol. 170, No. 17, April 27, 1974), in his* Living Images: Film Comment and Criticism *(reprinted by permission of Brandt & Brandt Literary Agents, Inc.; copyright © 1970, 1971, 1972, 1973, 1974, 1975 by Stanley Kauffmann),* Harper & Row, Publishers, 1975, pp. 274-75.*

## JAMES MONACO

Seen today, [Lester's] little *jeu d'esprit* [*The Running, Jumping, and Standing-Still Film*] is reminiscent of nothing so much as Georges Méliès, Mack Sennett, and early American comedy; and it foreshadows in Lester's work that important strain of Goon Show humor which he will later apply to topics of Universal Significance. (p. 26)

[*A Hard Day's Night*] is a critical essay on the subject of Beatlemania and media manipulation and, at the same time, the most successful hype in the history of the Beatle myth. This is characteristic, really, of nearly all Lester's films: that they analyze what they are doing at the same time that they do it. And, as always, the form that Lester chooses is equally important here: a quasidocumentary about the group and about the people in it, and about the fierce pressures of media adulation: the crowding, the hysteria, the hotel-room claustrophobia, the lock-step schedule, and most important, the psychological tension which operates on four human beings as they become transformed into archetypes and debased into stereotypes. . . .

The "media-ization" of the Sixties turned public images into social metaphors more vital than the private personalities of the people who bore those images—and that's what Lester did with the Beatles in *A Hard Day's Night*. He also made an entertaining movie, full of high spirits and good music. . . .

While the Beatles continued to maintain the fiction that they were playing themselves, Lester was forced to construct some sort of characters *around* them [for his film *Help!*]. His only real choice was to amplify and extend the images of *A Hard Day's Night;* but this time the film participates in the process of the media-ization of the Beatles without criticizing it. The resulting caricatures were to haunt the Beatles for years, so it is no surprise to find they "felt like guest stars in their own film." What it lacks in understanding, *Help!* tries to make up for with flash and filigree. This is the first film in which Lester allows full reign to the Surrealist-Farce style he had developed in his television work. Indeed, only *Help!* and *The Bed-Sitting Room* really fit the received opinion about Richard Lester, the demonic stylist.

*The Knack . . . and How to Get It* (to give it its full title) was made after the first Beatles film and before the second in a period of furious activity for Lester. The three films taken together are something of an accidental trilogy about the very special situation of being young in the Sixties. "If you want to be pompous about it," says Lester, "in the Beatles pictures were four young people who could communicate without speech because they had a sort of inner language, and *The Knack* was about four people who spoke endlessly to each other without any communication at all." The fascination with language, which is clearly evident in *The Knack* for the first time, will become one of Lester's strongest and most rewarding preoccupations.

*The Knack* is a superbly complex film, resplendent with dense verbal and visual imagery. Lester already had a reputation for being a filmmaker of extraordinary visual power. The scenic complexity of his films was sometimes condemned as merely decorative, or "busy." But *The Knack* certainly proves that Lester is no decorator: the richness of detail in each shot contributes immensely to the power of the film, and the point. The soundtrack of the film is equally dense and meaningful; it very nearly stands on its own as a work of art. . . .

*The Knack* is nominally about the classic problems involved in coming of age sexually, but Lester and [screenwriter Charles] Wood have added to the play a background landscape that displays with considerable understanding the generational tensions which were so characteristic of life in the Sixties. The old-people's chorus that comments ironically throughout the film is one aspect of that landscape; the house that Nancy, Tolen, Colin, and Tom are so intimately involved with is another—possibly more important. It is a carefully preserved relic of art deco and the Thirties and, if Tom wants to paint over everything white, Lester certainly doesn't. The young people have moved into an old house, but the old house is not an object of nostalgic humor for the film—rather it is treated with a good deal of respect. The result of all this is a resonant relationship between the foursome and their environment that helps give *The Knack* its surprising depth. Like its characters, *The Knack* is a youthful work that improves with age. (p. 29)

*Petulia* is an unusual film for Lester: a dense melodrama in an expanse of satire and farce and, more important, his only film with specifically American themes and settings. . . .

The film is awash in images of death and decay, even as it ends with a birth. Only Archie's (and Lester's) irony and anger offer an alternative to this dark road; the film is otherwise uncompromising. David Danner . . . is a true Mad Ave sex symbol: beautiful and impotent. Petulia Danner, the "archkook," wears her cutesy mask even in the delivery room and avoids commitment by false challenges. Warren, Archie's ex-wife's new beau, is a "wonderful human being" in his own right. . . . Mr. Danner evokes ghostly (and, on Lester's part, quite conscious) shadows of Kane thirty years earlier. And Archie, at the center, is a soap-opera doctor, even if he has a slightly better grip on his reality than the others. This is a civilization so dominated by media images that television sets are as important in hospital rooms as beds—so necessary in fact that the shells must be there even if the guts aren't. (p. 30)

But *Petulia* is a film of desperate characters who, however, are treated with considerable compassion. . . . It is, after all, Archie's anger that is the central emotion of the film, the warp of its fabric; and the significance of this emotional orientation can't be overestimated. This anger is the heart of *Petulia* and, in opposition with the paralysis which grips its characters, informs the film's structural and moral tensions. The result is something other than a sour portrait of a City of Night. . . . It would be easy to castigate these people; Lester's achievement is that he maintains sympathy with them, and suggests—between the frames of supercilious satire and formalist legerdemain—a quiet rage against the dying of the light.

Running on, murmuring continuously in the background of the film like an atonal refrain, is Vietnam—the central fact of our existence in the Sixties. The foreground is dominated by sexual politics—the central fact of our existence in the Seventies. The film details various subtle, gnawing pressures of contemporary sexual politics; and (an even greater achievement) it avoids the crude heroines-and-villains stereotypes, balancing the conflicting peccadilloes of its men and women so finely that we can easily comprehend how both sexes are caught in sexist conventions, how both men and women are paralyzed by the roles their media culture has forced upon them. And this in a film made seven years ago, during the wave of Bondian *machismo*! Lester's homecoming film gives us the America of the Sixties as few of us understood it at the time, but as it really was. (pp. 30-1)

*The Bed-Sitting Room* is his most mannered film, but there are some good reasons for its relatively cold and intellectual mode. Once again, Lester has set up a particularly intricate aesthetic problem—and then solved it with intricate care. How do you handle the Bomb on film? . . . Lester's solution is not the most successful (Stanley Kubrick's *Dr. Strangelove* is more humanely comical and less coldly farcical, and therefore more effective), but *The Bed-Sitting Room* does explore with Lester's usual thorough intelligence some important rhetorical methods.

Based on the stageplay by John Antrobus and Spike Milligan (with a screenplay again by Charles Wood), the film bears some strong likenesses to the tragi-farce's of Beckett (especially *Endgame* and *Happy Days*). But it's wrong to make too much of this similarity—Milligan's and Lester's experience with the [television] Goon Show seems a much more appropriate source. That style is a good one, since Lester thought of the whole "Bomb question" as rather an exercise in nostalgia. The bomb was something of a "period piece": "Lost in the shuffle of Vietnam, Civil Rights, like Aldermaston, something of the past it seems to me," he said, "it goes with *Jailhouse Rock* and Elvis Presley—in fact before *Jailhouse Rock;* "the 'Blue Suede Shoes' period of Elvis Presley."

Maybe Goonish farce is the only fitting mode for such a subject. But there is something too precise, too well-figured, about *The Bed-Sitting Room*. If there is a flaw that threads itself through Lester's work, it is most evident here: an icy, mannered show of intelligence that makes his films sometimes more thought-about than felt. . . .

If the film is not puppy-dog warm, it's still full of wit; if it demands a lot from its audience, it nevertheless more than repays attention. It shows us an absurd world whose universal dream of easeful death would be nearly perfect if it were not for the almost equally absurd—but irrepressible—life force that insists on bubbling up, even as Western civilization settles comfortably in the void like a pig squatting in a mud puddle. All of Lester's films have roots in this precious acquaintance with the life force, but *The Bed-Sitting Room* is the clearest statement of his view of the conflict. It gives us the best advice: Keep moving! . . .

It is [a] dotty, attic, quizzical sense of humor which has always been Lester's basic strength. It depends not so much on contrived comedy (although Lester can set up a joke as well as anyone making films today) as on a pervasive attitude toward reality which is both genuinely affectionate and quietly subversive. The fondness Lester feels for the objects of his wit never obscures his satirist's moral anger at the surrounding illogic and inhumanity. (p. 31)

> James Monaco, *"Some Late Clues to the Lester Direction: A New Look at the Director," in* Film Comment *(copyright © 1974 by The Film Society of Lincoln Center; all rights reserved), Vol. 10, No. 3, May-June, 1974, pp. 25-31.*

**PAULINE KAEL**

[*Juggernaut* is fast], crackerjack entertainment, with the cool, bitchy wit and the outrageously handsome action sequences of some of the best of the Bond pictures. It's surprisingly crisp fun, considering that it was directed by that most misanthropic of talented directors, Richard Lester. Though he eliminates practically every trace of human warmth, he manages to supply the characters with enough blackhearted existential bravado to keep the film sociable. Anybody who makes a picture like this one has to be a bit of a bastard, but Lester demonstrates what a sophisticated director with flair can do on a routine big-action project. (p. 347)

Lester lets you know right from the start that if the genre is basically the same as that of *The Poseidon Adventure* the tone certainly won't be. . . . He doesn't go in for scenes of panic or screaming hysteria; instead, he has the ship's social director . . . constantly rebuffed in his attempts to cheer people up. Where the usual disaster film gives us pathos, Lester gives us slapstick. The movie is a commentary on other directors' groveling for audience response.

Those not used to Richard Lester's neo-Noël Coward mixture of cynicism, angst, and anti-establishment sentimentality (is there anybody more British than an American convert?) may at first be thrown. He's a compulsive gagster, but the jokes are throwaway-fast and tinged with contempt. He uses famous actors, but he uses them like bit players—like props, almost. (pp. 347-48)

Lester likes to turn heroism into a joke, but in *Juggernaut* the derring-do isn't cancelled out, as it was in *The Three Musketeers*—quite the reverse. The cynical, dangling gags that counterpoint the gallantry make it more gallant. The picture has a structural flaw: it reaches its visual climax early, with the arrival of the dismantling team, who parachute down into giant storm waves and then fight their way up rope ladders to board the ship. The subsequent action sequences can't compete with the violent beauty of that arrival, and the actual dismantling of the bombs is too much like the prolonged safecracking scenes of heist pictures, though Lester and his cinematographer, Gerry Fisher, work microscopically close and achieve some almost abstract aesthetic effects. (p. 348)

> *Pauline Kael, "Stuck in the Fun" (originally published in* The New Yorker, *Vol. L, No. 33, October 7, 1974), in her* Reeling *(copyright © 1974 by Pauline Kael; reprinted by permission of Little, Brown and Company in association with the Atlantic Monthly Press), Atlantic-Little, Brown, 1976, pp. 342-49.\**

**PENELOPE GILLIATT**

The extension [of **"The Three Musketeers"** into **"The Four Musketeers"**] exists for a reason that is perfectly in keeping with the cheerful chaos of the work as a whole: meaning to shoot one film, . . . Lester simply shot enough footage for two films and decided to cut the thing down the middle with a headsman's axe. . . . (p. 79)

As one result of the Siamese-twin operation on the film, we get a rapid blast of the-plot-so-far delivered to us like grapeshot at the beginning of Part II. No one is likely to make head or tail of it, but then no one is likely to care, either. I daresay that if Dumas were alive he would turn in his grave, . . . but I don't suppose Lester's audiences, rapt in the high-speed bawdry of his film, are going to give the relatively staid original author much of a thought. There isn't the time; there isn't the sobriety. A spirit of unstoppable slapstick reigns over the picture, and cohesiveness is nowhere. Things go by fits and starts: giggling fits, false starts. The pratfall is king, and his queen is a particular kind of schoolboy pleasure in anachronism in which antique speech is always taking rude turns and, you feel, having the reviving effect on bored children of gazing out of the classroom window on a hot day when a master is droning on about the unchristianity of cruel wars' being fought between

fellow-Christians. This is the thesis of the picture, if rampage can be said to have a thesis. (pp. 79-80)

[The] fragmentariness of the film is sometimes destructive of humor. It gives the jokes the nature of children's repartee: they are appealingly experimental, with a brave spirit of try-anything-once, but they are in danger of falling flat because the hilariously reckless narrative method builds up no credit system. Richard Lester's unique fractured style, which in his **"Petulia"** was a moving expression of the distress of urban people whose love for one another seemed so fragile that it was likely to splinter in their hands and cause them to bleed to death, is put here to much less reflective use. But the rowdy funniness of the film works with its own pop splendor. (p. 81)

> *Penelope Gilliatt, "Passion," in* The New Yorker *(© 1975 by The New Yorker Magazine, Inc.), Vol. LI, No. 6, March 31, 1975, pp. 76-81.\**

**JOHN SIMON**

Intelligent reinterpretation is one thing; sensationalistic or smartass revisionism, quite another. [In *Robin and Marian*] we take Robin Hood, his merry men, and Maid Marian, but show them as middle-aged folk in an autumnal mood, at the end of their chivalric tether. We connect the story even more tightly than usual with Richard the Lionhearted by having Robin and Little John fight under him in the Third Crusade, and making the film begin at Châluz, where Richard meets his end. . . .

That is revisionism for you! Knighthood, so far from being in flower, is mostly weeds and nettles, and even they are going to seed. Sir Walter Scott's hero-king has become a moody tyrant, and when legend is not countered with wanton deflation, facts are chosen for their somberness. . . .

What's wrong with revisionism having a field day? A little of it, on acceptable historical premises, is perfectly welcome. . . . But I find this systematic debunking quite cheap: what yields a shoddier, more facile effect than standing tradition on its head? It is not all that different from painting a mustache on the Mona Lisa. (p. 81)

Heroes haven't gone at all. It is only paltry sentimentalists like [screenwriter James] Goldman—and perhaps Lester, under his superficial toughness—that consider heroes a wonderful, lost breed; in fact, they exist as much, or as little, as they ever did, even if they no longer wield broadswords or longbows for the delectation of backward children in adults' clothing. Do not misunderstand me: the historical work—film, novel, whatever—that honestly tries to understand the age it deals with, and does not use it as a fancy-dress ball for jaded modern sensibilities or an easy way of capitalizing on anticlimaxes—and then, introducing a grand, old-fashioned climax after all, a lopsided *liebestod*, no less—is fine. But trying to have it every which way is, to me, contemptible. . . .

Lester's direction is equally divided. There is quite a bit of the Lester of *The Three Musketeers* and even the four Beatles here—debunking with wisecracks and sight gags; but there is also the Lester of *Petulia* and *Juggernaut* who, under a hard-boiled façade, slips in some hoary, sentimental heartbreak. I can see possible good in both approaches, but I object to their clumsy and meretricious miscegenation. (p. 82)

> *John Simon, "Robin Hood and His Merry Menopause," in* New York *Magazine (copyright © 1976 by News Group Publications, Inc.; reprinted with*

the permission of New York Magazine), Vol. 9, No. 13, March 29, 1976, pp. 81-2.*

## JUDITH CRIST

[*Robin and Marian* provides] a worldly, wise, and witty response to our eternal wonderment about *how* our heroes lived ever after, happily or not. . . .

[It is] a story as satisfying as any that came before, and far, far richer in nuance, detail, and pertinence, thanks to two masters of the genre—screenwriter James Goldman . . . and director Richard Lester. . . . Both know the blend of anachronism and actuality that puts vitality into the past and resurrects the figures in long-ago landscapes; both sense the starkness of the realism underlying the romantic adventure, the frailty of heroes who have human instincts, the fullness of living that obliterates our historic awareness of the transience of life. . . .

[It] is a legend in itself, of heroes who grow old in flesh but not in spirit, who can still have a glory day. Lions in autumn—with all its crispness and glow. (p. 44)

Judith Crist, "Sherwood Ever After," in Saturday Review (copyright © 1976 by Saturday Review; all rights reserved; reprinted by permission), Vol. 3, No. 14, April 17, 1976, pp. 44, 47.*

## JOHN SIMON

Richard Lester is a competent farce director, whether he is directing farce or anything else. Yet [*The Ritz*] falls, unfarcically, flat. . . .

[Farce], especially the kind that depends on a multiplicity of doors flying open and shut as ill-assorted people rush through them toward outrageous consequences, needs . . . stage space to play with. The buzzing human insects must describe bizarre trajectories, inscribe absurd patterns in their boxlike space, to illustrate the whims of that waggish demiurge variously identified as author, director, or life. Take away the spatial antics of farce, its solid geometry, and you're left with a flimsy contrivance.

Which does not mean that the filmmakers cannot refeel and rethink the farce in terms of the new dimensions and perimeters. . . . [But] Lester did not muster that camera energy that distinguishes even his lesser efforts. It may also be that Hollywood did not want to rub the noses of the provinces in all that pederasty with which the public bath, where the action takes place, is awash. Certainly some of the more "daring" lines of the play are not in the movie.

The best thing is an opening closeup of an egg yolk slithering through an hourglass. I have no idea whether this is an old Italian custom at death vigils, a proleptic reference to what the film will wind up with all over its face, or a piece of pure surrealism like Dali's melting watches. Whatever it is, it grabbed my amused attention. The rest of *The Ritz* is no yolk. (p. 50)

John Simon, "Flattening the Ritz, Flattering the Duke," in New York Magazine (copyright © 1976 by News Group Publications, Inc.; reprinted with the permission of New York Magazine), Vol. 9, No. 35, August 30, 1976, pp. 50-2.*

## JAY COCKS

Antic, frantic, mechanical but amusing anyhow, *The Ritz* is of particular interest because it is the first major movie about homosexuality that does not give a thought to redeeming social value. There is not a trace of seriousness in *The Ritz.* In both the traditional and contemporary meanings of the word, it is a gay movie. (p. 72)

Richard Lester, who seems to work almost as fast as Googie Gomez talks . . . keeps the proceedings right on his customary sardonic course. Lester obeys the first law of this kind of farce, bestowing his sidelong misanthropy equally on straight characters and gays. (p. 73)

Jay Cocks, "Bubble Bath," in Time (copyright 1976 Time Inc.; all rights reserved; reprinted by permission), Vol. 108, No. 9, August 30, 1976, pp. 72-3.

## STANLEY KAUFFMANN

As far as theme is concerned, [*Butch and Sundance: The Early Days*] might as well be called *The Deer Hunter: The Early Days*. Once more we plunge into the primal American myth of male friendship: why this friendship and its adventures are the best things in life; how women are meant to watch and wait and understand, with a brave grave sigh, that men must be off on their manly doings. The fact that the doings in the case of *B and S* are outlawry—theft, violence, and, eventually, murder—matters little under the grand rubric of light-hearted, essentially boyish male palship.

What a bore it is, that idea, that American idea. . . . But because it *is* part of our heritage, sometimes it can be exploited affectingly: with limited charm, as in the first *B and S* (1969) or by direct visceral grapple, as in Peckinpah's *The Wild Bunch*. When the charm is merely laborious, as in the new *B and S,* or when the visceral appeal falls very short, as it does here, the result is tedious—even repellent. . . .

[It's] really Part One, as its subtitle tells us. It spends its time trying to plant antecedents for the earlier [George Roy Hill film, *Butch Cassidy and the Sundance Kid*]—a jump into a river, a train robbery—and it has no shape. It's just a series of adventures, which could have been shorter or longer, and none of the adventures is amusing or exciting or moving. . . .

[Richard Lester] once made his own pictures, marvelously. . . . Now he makes other people's. One of the tenets of auteur criticism is that the tension between a director and the studio system is fruitful. Even theoretically, that could have been true only for a director born into the system, not one who once had freedom and lost it. Lester these days is like Samson in Gaza. (p. 26)

Stanley Kauffmann, "Outlaws and Inlaws" (reprinted by permission of Brandt & Brandt Literary Agents, Inc.; copyright © 1979 by Stanley Kauffmann), in The New Republic, Vol. 180, No. 25, June 23, 1979, pp. 26-7.*

## ANDREW SARRIS

The good news is that *Butch and Sundance: The Early Days* can stand on its own four feet without making us sob longingly for the original. Lester has achieved a cooler and more distant tone for the material than did the redhot Hill before him. . . . *Butch and Sundance: The Early Days* is worth a look simply for its wit, humor, and expertise. It is such a relief to see a clever movie for a change that the absence of emotional explosions may not seem like such a dreadful handicap. A respected colleague sitting next to me at the screening complained that Lester had indulged in much ado about nothing. I can understand this reaction. Lester has often been too ornate for his own good, and there have been more than a few occasions when he has cultivated visual beauty for its own sake. . . .

The point is that if audiences seek rollicking fun in **Butch and Sundance: The Early Days** they will be disappointed, but if they are content with a stylish proto-buddy-buddy entertainment rendered with a muted pathos and longing they will almost be enchanted. I say "almost" because there remains something tentative and undefined in the nature of the adventure. One is never sure what is at stake in the entwined destinies of the two characters. Do they really long for a normal life, or are they already lusting for legendary status? Perhaps there have been too many movies on the subject of the Old West being swept away by Modern Times, and Lester . . . and company have expended all their energy simply to avoid the most flagrant cliches and the corniest regrets. The ending, as is so often the case nowadays, is particularly noncommittal as it witnesses a successful train robbery with bemused detachment and a grace more physical than spiritual. . . . [Yet] I must admit that by its very nature this movie, for all its elegance, doesn't really go anywhere.

> *Andrew Sarris, "Western Gibes, Wimbledon Lobs" (reprinted by permission of* The Village Voice *and the author; copyright © News Group Publications, Inc., 1979), in* The Village Voice, *Vol. XXIV, No. 25, June 18, 1979, p. 57.\**

## ANDREW SARRIS

Against the background of a return to flag-waving patriotism, demonically derisive movies like Richard Lester's **Cuba** . . . seem suddenly anachronistic in the very casualness of their anti-American assumptions. . . . Americans are not merely ugly, but grotesquely hideous. Certainly, [Lester did not] set out to make any overt political statements, to win over any hearts and minds, as it were. **Cuba,** though shot in Spain, treats Castro's triumphant entrance into Havana in 1959 as if it were the Second Coming of Christ, or, at the very least, the ideological equivalent of Lenin's arrival at the Finland Station. Lester and his scenarist, Charles Wood, are not "selling" Castro to the non-Marxist infidels. They are commemorating his historically "inevitable" victory in the context of the slightly comical spectacle of greed and venality in the last days of the Batista regime. . . .

[If] the chaos of Cuba is in the background of the film, the romance of *Casablanca* is clearly in the foreground, and it is in its foreground that **Cuba** fails most dismally. . . . By the time we get the final shootout between the Castro and Batista forces, Lester has completely lost control of the movements of his characters on his historical chessboard, and the picture as a whole joins that fascinating and proliferating category assigned for the Ambitious Failure. . . .

The Americans in **Cuba** are inelegant to a fault (Lester's most likely). By contrast, the most corrupt of the Batista Cubans is endowed with style and savvy. Ironically, however, **Cuba** will probably never be shown to Cuban audiences because of what can be interpreted by the authorities as a puzzling frivolity about a "serious" subject. For their part, American audiences will be put off less by the film's political "line" than by its

strange mix of moods, none of which seem to deliver what they promise. Up to now I have tended to give Lester the benefit of the doubt whenever I could. On the surface **Juggernaut** may have seemed a bit threadbare as a disaster film, and **Robin and Marian** a bit tired as a period romance, but I felt an oddly throbbing though dissonant passion underneath. Lester's art has never been full-bodied or wholehearted. His films are all a bit askew, the laughs flattened out, the tears congealed. What I do respect in Lester and in *Cuba* is a feeling for complexity in the narrative structure. In an age dominated by neo-formulaic filmmaking, Lester's loose ends and dangling characters seem stylistically heroic. . . . I cannot buy the canonization of Castro at this time. It seems to me that Lester and Wood, like too many warriors of the left, have not yet traversed the remarkably short distance between the Finland Station and the Gulag Archipelago. It is not a question of shifting to the right, but of scrutinizing more closely a neo-Stalinist certitude in the treatment of historical and political subjects.

> *Andrew Sarris, "History As Farce" (reprinted by permission of* The Village Voice *and the author; copyright © News Group Publications, Inc., 1979), in* The Village Voice, *Vol. XXIV, No. 52, December 24, 1979, p. 49.\**

## ANDREW SARRIS

The switch of directors from Richard Donner to Richard Lester [during production of the Superman movies] may have involved more than window dressing and contractual squabbles, but it is difficult from this corner to sort out the Donner footage from the Lester footage and assign responsibility and meaning for each. . . .

Still, I suspect that the switch from Donner to Lester has resulted in a perceptible shift from the rollicking adventurousness of *Superman I* with its intimations of a happily unfurrowed brow, to a mood of pessimism and disenchantment in **Superman II.** Again, I got the feeling of decline and fall from the very first shot of the skyline around the Daily Planet. The screen seemed comparatively gray and somber, and then the next scene seemed equally gray and somber, and so on and so forth. *Superman I* seemed in retrospect glossier, shinier, livelier. The change may not be due just to Lester's dark, uneasy fragmented view of human existence, but also to an inevitable evolution of the screen Superman. In his first incarnation, he was superior in strength to everyone he encountered on earth. In **Superman II** he is pitted against superfiends from his own planet, and the contest hangs in the balance almost to the end.

> *Andrew Sarris, "Surprise! Two Super Films" (reprinted by permission of* The Village Voice *and the author; copyright © News Group Publications, Inc., 1981), in* The Village Voice, *Vol. XXVI, No. 24, June 10-16, 1981, p. 51. \**

## DAVID DENBY

The original *Superman*, directed by Richard Donner, was one of the most disjointed, stylistically mixed-up movies ever made. The mystico-sublime rubbed elbows with low farce and pop irony, and everything gave way to disaster-movie squareness in the end. But now all is well. Richard Lester, of Beatles-movie fame, took over the direction of **Superman II,** and Lester has brought unity and a high style to the material. The fantasy and playfulness that Lester has always striven for fall to him easily this time, and without the nagging, jumpy irritability that turned so many of his other movies sour. (pp. 49-50)

***Superman II*** is still a pop daydream, but it has its roots in common feelings . . . , and the emotion enlarges the fantasy, takes the pre-packaged gleam off it. (p. 50)

*David Denby, "The Decline and Fall of Mel Brooks," in* New York *Magazine (copyright © 1981 by News Group Publications, Inc.; reprinted with the permission of* New York *Magazine), Vol. 14, No. 25, June 22, 1981, pp. 48-50.\**

# (Baron) Laurence Olivier

## 1907-

**British director, actor and producer.**

**Olivier has directed several successful adaptations of Shakespearean plays, although he is probably best known for his role as protagonist in these films. Though Olivier takes liberties with plot and characterization, most critics feel that his alterations lend new depth to Shakespeare's work.**

**Olivier's theatrical career began at the age of eleven with a role in *Julius Caesar*. Though versatile in any form of drama, Olivier developed a special affinity for Shakespeare. Fillipo del Guidice, an Italian film director, offered Olivier the opportunity to create his own cinematic versions of Shakespeare's plays. Olivier was reluctant, believing that these works were suitable only for the stage. However, he decided that "something had to be done to give the plays a reality that was acceptable to the new audience without outraging the reality of Shakespeare." Critics generally agree that Olivier succeeded admirably in his versions of *Henry V, Hamlet,* and *Richard III*. While using innovative techniques, he retained the eloquence of Shakespeare's works.**

**Olivier next directed the film adaptation of Terence Rattigan's play *The Sleeping Prince*. Entitled *The Prince and the Showgirl*, the film has a light romantic content which contrasts strongly with his previous work. However, some critics found it relying too heavily on conventions of the stage.**

**In making *The Three Sisters* for the American Film Theatre, Olivier chose not to alter Chekhov's work as he had Shakespeare's. He attempted to preserve the play exactly as written, without incorporating any stylistic innovations. Many critics were disappointed in Olivier's film, which lacked his usual originality of translation from stage to screen.**

**Olivier's distinctions have not been limited to artistic endeavors. He was knighted in 1947 and in 1970 was created baron.**

### BOSLEY CROWTHER

["**Henry V**" is] a stunningly brilliant and intriguing screen spectacle, rich in theatrical invention, in heroic imagery and also gracefully regardful of the conventions of the Elizabethan stage. . . .

Certainly the story in this chronicle could not have lured Mr. Olivier too much, nor could the chance to explore a complex character have been the bait to draw him on. For the reasons for Henry's expedition against France, as laid down in the play, are neither flattering to him nor to his churchly counselors. The Bishops conspire to urge Henry to carry his claims against France in order to distract the Commons from confiscating their lands; and Henry apparently falls for it, out of sheer royal vanity and greed. His invasion of France is quite clearly a war of aggrandizement, and his nature appears slightly naive when he argues the justice of his cause.

But that, of course, is Shakespeare; and Mr. Olivier and his editor, Reginald Beck, have not attempted to change it. They have simply cut large chunks out of the play, especially the plot of the traitors, to get at the action and the meat. Thus reduced of excessive conversations (though it might have been trimmed even more), they have mounted the play with faithful service to the spirit and the word. That service is as truly magnificent as any ever given to a Shakespearian script. . . . (p. 2122)

The tumult of the armorers' preparations, the stretch of bowmen and the clash of steel-casqued knights is vividly recreated. Not since "The Birth of a Nation" do we recall a more thrilling and eerie charge of horsemen than the charge of the knights in "Henry V." . . .

Mr. Olivier has leaned perhaps too heavily toward the comic characters in the play—at least, for American audiences, which will find the dialects a little hard to get. The scenes with the Welsh and Irish captains are too parochial for our taste. And certainly the writing-in completely of the Falstaff deathbed scene, with the echoing voice of Harry carrying over from "Henry IV, Part Two," is obviously non-essential and just a bit grotesque.

However, in all other matters—in the use of music, in the brilliance of costumes . . . , in toning the whole film to the senses—Mr. Olivier has done a tasteful job. Thanks to him and to all those who helped him, we have a glowing "touch of Harry in the night." (p. 2123)

*Bosley Crowther, "At the Stanley: 'Henry V'," in* The New York Times *(© 1946 by The New York Times Company; reprinted by permission), June 18, 1946 (and reprinted in* The New York Times Film Reviews: 1939-1948, The New York Times Company & Arno Press, 1970, pp. 2122-23).*

### JAMES AGEE

*Henry V* was all simple, engaging action, and Olivier gave it a clarion confidence and sweetness. *Hamlet* is action in near-paralysis, a play of subtle and ambiguous thought and of even subtler emotions. Olivier's main concern has been to keep these subtleties in focus, to eliminate everything that might possibly distract from the power and meaning of the language. He has stripped the play and his production to the essentials. In the process, he has also stripped away a few of the essentials. But on the whole, this is a sternly beautiful job, densely and delicately worked. (p. 389)

There is little novel interpretation of character: even that might distract from the great language, or distort it. There is no clear placement in time, no outside world except blind sky, faint landscapes, ruminant surf, a lyrical brook. . . . The production is as austere, and as grimly concentrated, as *Henry V* was profuse and ingratiating. Only the wild, heartfelt, munificent language is left at liberty.

Olivier was determined to make the play clear in every line and every word—even to those who know nothing of Shakespeare. For the most part, he manages to elucidate even the trickiest turns of idiom by pantomime or a pure gift for thought transference. But wherever it has seemed necessary, old words have been changed for new. (pp. 389-90)

In the process of cutting a 4-hour play to 2 hours' playing time, the editing has also been very drastic in places. . . . Olivier and his co-editor, Alan Dent, have gone out of their way to save a small jewel ("The bird of dawning singeth all night long"). But now and then, apparently for the sake of pace, they needlessly throw something overboard.

Olivier and Dent are neither vandals, boobs nor megalomaniacs. They knew what they were doing. They felt, mostly with very good reason, that they had to do it. Mostly as a result of cutting, their *Hamlet* loses much of the depth and complexity which it might have had. *Hamlet* is a sublime tragedy, but it is also the most delightful and dangerous of tragicomedies. Some of the tragicomedy remains and is the best thing in the film. But some of the best went out with Rosencrantz and Guildenstern.

Unluckiest of all, the audience is allowed to know less than it might about the Prince himself (nobody can ever know enough about him). It sees too little of his dreadful uncertainty, his numbed amazement over his own drifting, his agonized self-vilification. It understands too little of him as "passion's slave." (pp. 390-91)

But within his chosen limits, Olivier and his associates have done excellently—from grandiose poetic conceptions (e.g., the frightfully amplified heartbeats which introduce the Ghost) to clever little captures of mood (e.g., the cold, discreet clapping of gloved hands which applaud the half-drunken King). (p. 391)

A man who can do what Laurence Olivier is doing for Shakespeare—and for those who treasure or will yet learn to treasure Shakespeare—is certainly among the more valuable men of his time. In the strict sense, his films are not creative works of cinematic art: the essential art of moving pictures is as overwhelmingly visual as the essential art of his visually charming pictures is verbal. But Olivier's films set up an equilateral triangle between the screen, the stage and literature. And between the screen, the stage and literature they establish an interplay, a shimmering splendor, of the disciplined vitality which is art. (p. 396)

> *James Agee, "Time: Olivier's 'Hamlet'" (copyright 1948 by the James Agee Trust; copyright renewed © 1975 Time Incorporated; all rights reserved; re-printed by permission), in* Time, *Vol. LI, No. 26, June 28, 1948 (and reprinted in his* Agee on Film, *Vol. 1, Grosset & Dunlap, 1969, pp. 333-402).*

**ARTHUR VESSELO**

Olivier's *Hamlet* calls for the fullest critical consideration. It is elaborate, skilful and, in patches, excellent; but it is also in patches tedious, and its methods raise the whole question of how best Shakespeare can be translated into film terms, if the thing is to be done at all. There are only two basic approaches in the adaptation of a stage-play to the screen: the one is to concentrate above all on the *film* and to chop and change, to add and subtract, as the nature of the film medium demands; the other is to concentrate first and foremost on faithfulness to the original, and to let accepted film methods go hang wherever they interfere with this aim. In the case of Shakespeare, there is no doubt whatever which course must be followed, if only because of the outcry which a film-maker would have to face if he dared to tamper to any extent with a Shakespeare play (as witness the arguments even over the excisions, made obviously with the greatest care, that were necessary to bring "Hamlet" down to a possible screen running-time); but it seems that Olivier has still thought that he might be able, by some ingenious tricks of technique, to get the best of both worlds.

This is presumably the explanation of the long and tiring moving shots through the castle of Elsinore; of the exaggerations of physical action, here and there, where attention should on the contrary be focused almost entirely on the words; of the unsuccessful fantastications over the ghost; of the superfluous passages of visual illustration, showing the death of Hamlet's father, Hamlet fighting the pirates, Ophelia floating down the stream, and so forth; and of a variety of other pieces of business and of background stylization which, with the best of intentions, do not come off.

The treatment of the soliloquies is in its own way characteristic: Olivier has had the idea of converting them to a naturalistic mode by having them delivered as "spoken thought" while the actor puckers his brow but does not move his lips. This is most effectively done up to a point, but whether it could have been continued throughout must remain uncertain, for it is interrupted after a while by straight soliloquy, and the alternation of methods from then on destroys both consistency and illusion. The whole thing is over-conscious, like so much else, and one feels that straight soliloquy right through would have been a vast improvement. (pp. 99-100)

The one exceptional point where Shakespeare really leaves room for spectacular by-play on a major scale is, of course, the duel scene, and full advantage has been taken of it.

There is a place for filmed versions of Shakespeare plays, and perhaps an important one. But the importance lies in the power of the screen to transmit Shakespeare to a wide audience, not in the power of Shakespeare's producers to embellish the film medium. (p. 100)

> *Arthur Vesselo, "British Films of the Quarter," in* Sight and Sound *(copyright © 1948 by The British Film Institute), Vol. 17, No. 66, Summer, 1948, pp. 99-100.\**

**PARKER TYLER**

Let me not seem to underrate the superior intelligence that has gone into many phases of [Olivier's] filmic *Hamlet;* it is not an outrage on taste and achieves a few illuminated moments. But I take it as a bad movie simply because it is far more conscious of being *traditional cinema* than of being *traditional theatre*. . . . . . (p. 528)

The way in which this **Hamlet** best succeeds is, alas! that of a certain approved film-pattern: the action in relation to the camera movement is always tactful, *physically* appropriate; one never quite meets a boring staticity of image. When the movie ended, my own chief impression was, however, not of the drama itself, the strange humanity and poetic elevation, the simple depth of spirit in the work; it was merely that Hamlet's story *took place,* that Shakespeare's Denmark held a special castle, with such long halls and lofty ceilings, certain winding stairs, shadowy nooks, and stately columns. Thus I had seen an invention of archaeological documentation, and little more to add to my experience of the play. It was the same with **Henry V,** but there at least the spirit of archaeology and history obviously applied. If it be thought that Olivier achieved this effect in **Hamlet** only by the way, Olivier's own testimony may be cited aside from the fact that Hamlet's personal exit on his bier is turned into a prolonged ritual march as his corpse is borne up a continuous flight of stairs past the principal back-grounds of the previous action. Olivier has displaced the internal view of *Hamlet* as an individual's drama into an external view of it as the Tragedy of Elsinore. (pp. 528-29)

The whole *interpretive* problem of the chief role is that Hamlet should somehow be a lucid positive, not an opaque negative. Olivier's strategy was to pretend to honor the traditional "mystery" of Hamlet's hesitation while he patently accepted the quasi-scientific Oedipal interpretation, as more than one touch of stage-business indicates. A very unfortunate piece of business was the carnal and gratuitous device by which we are informed that the play's incestuous motivation does not exclude the relation between Laertes and Ophelia. By accepting the two most obvious "interpretations" of Hamlet's character, Olivier utterly relieved himself of the obligation of a personal interpretation; thus, he has operated more as director than actor and composed a "filmic essay" on Everybody's "Hamlet." . . . (p. 529)

I suppose one should praise the diction, which on the basis of clarity and dignity leaves almost nothing to be desired. Olivier's outstanding technical feat is the arrangement of dialogue with filmic movement; it has been neatly done, but meanwhile, if the film has gained, the poetry—quite apart from the actual cuts—has suffered. I submit that Shakespeare's rhetoric, so vaulting and various, does not synthesize well with film movement; it is too psychologically and metaphorically "cinematic" on its own ground. This is vividly brought out in the "To be or not to be" soliloquy, when the camera approaches Olivier's head from behind till we can almost count the blond hairs; we then virtually pass inside it to see Hamlet's "thoughts." Technically the device must have had a certain demand, but all it amounts to in effect is an optical version of that "sea of troubles" adequately characterized by the lines themselves, and as if this were not a little too much, we are also shown the actual sea turning over angrily at the foot of the cliff beneath Hamlet.

The device of *narratage* has become increasingly familiar in contemporary movies. It is, of course, only the familiar fictional device of the indirect narrative transposed to filmic terms; that is, the voice of a narrator, precisely, *supplements* rather than *renders* the film story. . . . Now, in the scene of the soliloquy just referred to, what did Shakespeare's lines amount to but "narratage," or verbal commentary on Hamlet's mood

as pictorially rendered? *Should the lines have been entirely omitted,* Hamlet's mood would have been adequately rendered insofar as we would have known his state of tumultuously anxious brooding. Therefore I submit that Olivier reduced the lines here to a sheer pleonasm; either *verse* or *visual imagery* was redundant. (pp. 529-30)

[Shakespeare's tragedy] suffers from its "modernization" by film. *Hamlet* is an historic tragedy in the psychological sense as much as in any other. Insofar as Hamlet himself is a "modern" character, his play is not *tragedy* but *ironic comedy* in the way that Shakespeare pointed up with such ingenuity; indeed, his guilt-complex, as it hovered on the verge of consciousness, almost averted the conventional revenge-tragedy that finally takes place. Paradoxically, Olivier's best scene is the one where Hamlet baits the meddling Polonius. If the motif of conscious mockery and an irony beyond tragedy, so richly hinted by Shakespeare himself, had been developed into a character conception and systematically carried through, Sir Laurence's film might have been quite a different story. (p. 530)

    *Parker Tyler, "'Hamlet' and Documentary," in* The
Kenyon Review *(copyright 1949; copyright renewed
© 1977, by Kenyon College), Vol. XI, No. 3, Summer, 1949, pp. 527-32.*

**HENRY RAYNOR**

In making **Hamlet,** Olivier emphasised the fact that his film was an "Essay" in interpretation, and in doing so did much to disarm criticism. (p. 10)

Olivier's description of his own **Hamlet** makes it possible to be more lenient than we might otherwise have been to the oddities of Alan Dent's revised script. Olivier has plucked, it seems, the heart out of Hamlet's mystery. . . . "This," Olivier said of his film by way of introduction, "is the tragedy of a man who could not make up his mind." There is sufficient tradition, theatrical as well as scholarly, behind this to make it irrelevant to suggest that the play contains subtleties hardly explained by such a simplification. Olivier has given us one possible explanation, and his film had the distinct merit of being shaped from the original to carry home that interpretation. But other mysteries remain: Hamlet's treatment of Ophelia? Let her seem quite palpably to be the decoy, and that becomes credible without making any suggestion that the hero is at that stage not only foul-minded but also pathologically suspicious. But why is Ophelia treated with such absolute brutality? It might at least have been made to appear that they were, before calamity overtook the Prince, genuinely and innocently in love. (pp. 10-11)

Olivier's essay in interpretation was a painful simplification, then, to anyone who finds the character of Hamlet credible as Shakespeare left it: "credible" does not mean "consistent," for the Hamlet of Shakespeare, driven by events and by his own imagination to the very rim of sanity, is not, and surely could not be, consistent. Nevertheless, the film script, with its occasional modernisation and its insistence on one possible interpretation, is by no means the worst acting edition that has been carved out of the play. (p. 11)

**Hamlet** had its unfortunate aspects: an Ophelia frankly discordant, a jettisoning of the flash and outbreak of the Prince's wit in favour of a rougher, more boisterous humour in the scene with Osric, and Olivier's unfortunate inadvertent impression of age. The acting was unequal and much of the poetry thrown away; the production style, with its conscientious attempt to be "cinematic"—deep focus photography, elaborate camera movement—sometimes muffled the drama of the narrative itself. Olivier's own speaking reduced everything to intense intimacy; one seemed at moments to be actually aware of his thinking, but by denying poetry he denied both the depth and the loftiness of Hamlet.

*Henry V* was an easier task. Either Henry was a precisian, legalistic and intelligent, with the orator's gift of rising to the occasion, edged into war by an Archbishop whose political schemes he unwittingly served, or he was a born and heaven-sent leader, vigorous, decisive, eloquent and dynamic; the text allows either interpretation, and Olivier chose the traditionally heroic. The transposition of speech and scene did not over-simplify or falsify the text, the brightness and fantasy of setting were a delight to the eye, unmarred by the half-realism of *Hamlet.* There were some jarring notes, like the misplaced humour of the Council scene and the Archbishop's tedious analysis of Salic Law; where Shakespeare is dull, it is better to cut ruthlessly than to play as comedy a scene with definite but outdated serious point.

Both *Henry V* and *Hamlet* had seriously conceived styles as *films,* unlike the Shakespeare adaptations of the '30's. The charge of the French knights in *Henry V* was unoriginal to those who had seen [Eisenstein's] *Alexander Nevsky,* but it created the right excitement and was edited with a real sense of rhythm. The film as a whole sustained a visual flow and pace, though one cannot help feeling its progress from the Elizabethan Theatre to the actualities of the Agincourt campaign and back again, was ultimately a highbrow mistake, a confusion of conventions. *Hamlet,* the bigger problem, contained bigger failures; it is difficult to imagine why exactly Hamlet's body had to be carried to the top of the Castle Keep for Horatio's explanatory public meeting, and doubly difficult to understand the absolute panic at the end of the Play Scene; the Ghost, challenging as it does a director's imagination, failed visually and aurally. On the other hand, Olivier genuinely explored the relationship of speech to spectacle in his treatment of "To be or not to be" by using the image of actual waves and their sound to suggest the "sea of troubles" in Hamlet's mind; the camera caught the tension of his first meeting with the Ghost, and that scene and the duel achieved an exciting rhythm. (pp. 11-12)

> Henry Raynor, "Shakespeare Filmed," in Sight and Sound (copyright © 1952 by The British Film Institute), Vol. 22, No. 1, July-September, 1952, pp. 10-15.*

### DEREK PROUSE

A shot of the crown of England, held high, opens Laurence Olivier's adaptation of Shakespeare's *Richard III* . . . ; a close-up of the new king, Edward IV, tense, almost incredulous, and then the crown descends with ambiguous firmness upon his head. . . . The mood has been instantly and excitingly set, in a brilliant expansion of the play—for this opening scene is actually the last scene of *Henry VI,* Part Three, and it also makes a highly effective prologue to the introduction of Gloucester that follows. A Gloucester not exaggeratedly repellent, who will assume his full depravity through subtler means than greasepaint as the action unfolds; his first soliloquy (shot with remarkable agility in a single take) blocks in with irresistible authority the character's general outlines—the rasp-

ing staccato voice with its hint of hysteria ready to burst through the sarcastic arrogant inflections, the deadly seriousness behind the levity betraying a powerful maladjustment. (p. 144)

In the film, Gloucester's influence is never absent; whether gaudily parading his deformity or slinking like a black spider round a pillar, he relentlessly disseminates his bile. Erupting on a council of nobles his nimble wit and apparent playfulness foxes and disquiets, but when the mask is dropped the private dangerous face beneath can shock and chill. . . . The cinematic conception of the whole play marks a resounding advance over the laboured *Hamlet*; character and direction are informed with a thrilling intelligence and grasp, invention is always neat and genuinely constructive to mood and situation.

In the second hour one's interest in the complicated intrigue is less consistent; one regrets the meandering structure of the play rather than the handling of the film. Judicious pruning has done its best to thin the treacherous jungle, to emphasise the main line of the action, but there lacks a compelling dramatic balance—evil holds all the cards and we can only wait for ambition to o'erleap itself. Richard's coronation, however, becomes a moment of sardonic triumph. Love and kingship have both been realised, yet resist enjoyment; only from a more and more monstrous flouting of morality can any satisfaction be wrested. (pp. 144-45)

*Richard III* is not only a very worthy and remarkable achievement but a strong contender for the best Shakespearean film yet made. (p. 145)

> Derek Prouse, "Film Reviews: 'Richard III'," in Sight and Sound (copyright © 1956 by The British Film Institute), Vol. 25, No. 3, Winter, 1955-56, pp. 144-45.

### JAMES E. PHILLIPS

[The film version of *Richard III*] simplifies and clarifies the basic political situation on which the entire plot action depends. Shakespeare's original relied on an Elizabethan audience's general knowledge of the Wars of the Roses, which were then no more remote than the Civil War is to present day American audiences, for an understanding of the intricate dynastic tangle in which Richard was involved. . . . By judicious cutting and rearrangement of Shakespearean material, supplemented by equally judicious borrowings from the Henry VI trilogy, Sir Laurence's adaptation deftly sketches the outlines of the family brawl that constitutes the action of the play. (pp. 399-400)

[However] are there points in the original play which the screen adaptation has missed that are more truly deserving of praise? The answer to such a question, of course, assumes that the measure of any production of a Shakespearean play must be the full intent and scope of the dramatist's conception as revealed in the accepted text of his play. . . .

In terms of its debilitating effect on the full dramatic and poetic richness of the original play, perhaps the cutting of old Queen Margaret, much remarked upon by reviewers of the film, best illustrates one of those elements in Shakespeare's drama deserving of praise that the film adaptation has sacrificed for reasons of its own. Probably no reader of Shakespeare would deny that Margaret needs some cutting down. (p. 401)

The effect of her absence is strikingly pointed up in the film version of the play. There, Richard himself emerges as an arch-villain operating against a group of victims who are at worst gullible, and at best innocent, bewildered sheep who suddenly discover a fox in the fold. (pp. 401-02)

Audiences familiar with the *Henry VI* trilogy, as the first audiences of *Richard III* probably were, would not have needed Margaret's reminders of the utter corruption of both these houses as much as we might today. They would have had clearly in mind not only the brutal acts of Edward, Richard, and Clarence against Margaret's family, but also the equally brutal acts of Margaret herself. . . . (p. 402)

Nevertheless, Shakespeare saw fit to introduce Margaret into the final play of his tetralogy as a reminder of this background of universal corruption. Modern audiences can be grateful that he did so. The "I told you so" tenor of her tirades keeps the whole cast of characters in proper perspective. . . . Without Margaret, the film version accordingly deprives the portrait of Richard of some of its original subtlety and shading. And without her, the play loses much of the somber tone of inevitability that is usually considered one of the chief "points deserving of praise" in the original.

Another praiseworthy point in the play that is deleted from the film is of quite different order. . . . This is the scene in which Clarence pleads futilely with the assassins sent by Richard to murder him. Granted the episode is of little relevance to the progress of the plot and the development of the title character, it is still one of the most dazzling bits of theater and poetry in the Shakespeare canon. (pp. 402-03)

In the film version of Richard's wooing of Anne, however, one can see most clearly, perhaps, the results—for better and for worse—of sacrificing subtle dramatic values in order to obtain simplified theatrical effects. Judging from reactions of undergraduate students and others not intimately familiar with the play itself, I am not convinced that Sir Laurence's simplified version is completely effective even at that. (p. 404)

The breakdown [of Anne], as Shakespeare portrays it, now begins to move rapidly. Richard plays his trump card—omitted in the film—when he appeals to her sense of Christian duty by vowing that he will shed "repentant tears" for his murder of her husband and her father-in-law, and she responds that "it joys me too, To see you are become so penitent." In the context of the long scene, her remark is credible enough at this point. More important, it is the line that reveals the fundamental difference in treatment of the scene between the play and the film. Sir Laurence realized quite rightly, as a reviewer in a national magazine has pointed out, that sheer sexual appeal was the actual basis of Richard's incredible triumph over Anne. But Shakespeare's original goes beyond this bald fact by showing that only when sexual desire can be made acceptable to the participant in terms of a moral or religious rationalization does it become convincing in terms of recognizable patterns of human behavior. Sir Laurence went directly and vividly to the heart of the matter, but, in so doing, he has sacrificed something of Shakespeare's more extended and more credible analysis of the complex relationship between Richard and Anne.

For these dramatic values thus cast aside in the interests of clarity of outline and vividness of theater, Sir Laurence's adaptation has substituted elements of varying effectiveness. The introduction of Edward IV's mistress, Jane Shore, is a visual delight, but her silent, leering presence confuses readers of the play who cannot immediately place her, baffles non-readers of the play throughout, and in the final analysis adds very little that is dramatically relevant to the play as a whole. The battle scenes at the end are an attempt at theatrical spectacle so con-

fusing to critics and audiences alike that further comment here is probably unnecessary. On the credit side, however, the film version has reduced the long scene between Richard and his young nephews in a way that has distilled the essence of the dramatic values inherent in the episode as Shakespeare wrote it. (pp. 404-05)

In the final analysis, however, it is our understanding of Richard himself that must be the test of the screenplay in relation to Shakespeare's original conception. Sir Laurence's portrayal of the character is little short of brilliant in conveying the "alacrity of spirit" that Richard himself confesses he had once possessed but lost by the end of the play. The film makes vivid and convincing this high-pitched exhilaration of Richard's demonstration to himself that he could win a woman and a crown. It reveals admirably his hypnotic cunning, his intellectual agility, and his delight in any and all manifestations of his amoral personal power. But the film falls short of Shakespeare in failing to make convincing, on the one hand, the physiological basis of Richard's psychological warp; and on the other hand, the psychological disintegration that was both cause and effect of his downfall from power. (p. 406)

More damaging to a full realization of the character depicted by Shakespeare, however, is Sir Laurence's failure to establish clearly, either through dialogue or visualization, Richard's self-confessed loss of the "alacrity of spirit" that had carried him so far. Shakespeare depicted this thoroughly human breakdown of the central character mainly in Richard's soliloquy following the appearance of the ghosts of his victims on the night before the battle of Bosworth Field. A modern audience might well do without the ghosts themselves and their repetitious reminders that the life of a political tyrant does not pay. But the soliloquy that Richard delivers upon awaking after this dream is not only a revealing but also a deeply moving expression by a man whose brilliant self-confidence has at last and inevitably been broken. It is his final realization that "There is no creature loves me, And if I die no soul shall pity me" that makes Richard one of Shakespeare's great human creations. In the film, a confusing battle scene and the symbolic rolling of a crown are not adequate substitutes for this fact of lonely human tragedy that is truly most deserving of praise. (pp. 406-07)

*James E. Phillips, "'Richard III', Two Views: Some Glories and Some Discontents,"* in The Quarterly of Film, Radio, and Television *(copyright, 1956, by The Regents of the University of California; reprinted by permission of the University of California Press), Vol. X, No. 4, Summer, 1956, pp. 399-407.*

**PHILIP T. HARTUNG**

Marilyn Monroe and Laurence Olivier evidently thought Terence Rattigan's play, "The Sleeping Prince," worthy of their talents as producers. But Rattigan's thin little comedy, about an American chorus girl who stirs an aging and stodgy Carpathian grand duke into action, although a great hit in London, created little interest in New York. The movie, with a script written by Rattigan, does afford the two leads plenty of opportunity to display their individual abilities and they make the most of them. **"The Prince and the Showgirl,"** as the film is called, is still pretty slight; and even under Laurence Olivier's capable direction, the jokes and situations strain to be naughty and funny. As a Technicolor reproduction of 1911 London, the film is pleasant, especially when it moves out of the Belgrave Square living room of the Prince. . . . But the audience is always ahead of this meager plot about the chorus girl who expected gypsy violins when she was sent to entertain this visiting grand duke and who got instead a somewhat stuffy prince. (p. 303)

Philip T. Hartung, "Boys into Men—and Other Fables," in Commonweal (copyright © 1957 Commonweal Publishing Co., Inc.; reprinted by permission of Commonweal Publishing Co., Inc.), Vol. LXVI, No. 12, June 21, 1957, pp. 303-04.*

## PENELOPE HOUSTON

In directing his first non-Shakespearean film [*The Prince and the Showgirl*], Laurence Olivier has kept mainly to a stage tempo. Lines are theatrically pointed, pauses held, the pace is muted. This method throws the performances into high relief, and it is inevitably for its playing, its much-publicised union of talents, that the film will be seen. Olivier himself repeats his stage performance, an accomplished exercise in building a sizeable pile of bricks without a great deal of straw. . . .

Mildly entertaining, *The Prince and the Showgirl* remains in essence what it initially seemed in the stage production—lemonade in a champagne bottle. (p. 41)

Penelope Houston, "'The Prince and the Showgirl'," in Sight and Sound (copyright © 1957 by The British Film Institute), Vol. 27, No. 1, Summer, 1957, pp. 40-1.

## RUPERT BUTLER

The coupling of Laurence Olivier and Marilyn Monroe in *The Prince and the Showgirl* represents one of the shrewdest gimmicks in show-business; the film was guaranteed maximum curiosity value before one foot of it was shot. I found the combination of these two stars irresistible and salute a brave attempt to inject Ruritanian dash into the rather dreary provincialism of so much British Cinema. (p. 21)

One has become accustomed over the years to a certain amount of filmed theatre but there comes a time when stage conventions prove altogether too much for a predominantly visual medium. Characters' entrances and exits, perfectly natural in a theatre, can appear on the screen as patently artificial manoeuvres and key passages of dialogue cannot be satisfactorily split merely by a sharp shift of camera, or change of locale. The script's restless darting from embassy drawing-room to embassy staircase, to embassy entrance and back, eventually become a trifle monotonous. (pp. 21-2)

Rupert Butler, "New Films: 'The Prince and the Showgirl'," in Film (reprinted by permission of British Federation of Film Societies), No. 10, July, 1957, pp. 21-2.

## CONSTANCE A. BROWN

*Richard III* in particular offers as much as can reasonably be expected of a film. In Olivier's hands, one of Shakespeare's better plays (certainly not one of his best) is transformed into an intricate, subtle, coolly ironic plunge into one of those recesses of human nature that are generally avoided through the same fastidious impulses that make the manufacture of sewer covers a profitable business. In its rather stylized way, *Richard* is an extraordinarily honest film, and requires proportional honesty from anyone who hopes to assess it cor-

rectly—which may partly account for the fact that so far no one has bothered. . . .

Olivier's alterations of *Richard III* are so numerous that it would be virtually impossible (and pointless) to enumerate them all. It is in the major changes, in any case, that the interest lies, and they are fairly easily accounted for. The pattern of Olivier's major alterations suggests the operation of two basic principles which work together almost inextricably, the first being one of economy and cinematic expediency. . . .

The second principle is an interpretive one, involving judgment as to the relative importance of various parts of the play, and right at the heart of it is the removal of Queen Margaret. (p. 23)

As in Olivier's earlier films, the form in *Richard* is achieved through a complex imagistic structure with one dominant parabolic formal device. In *Henry V,* the device is the Globe Theater, which begins and ends the film. . . . *Henry V* is often criticized for beginning on the stage, which is attributed to Olivier's fancied theatrical orientation—but actually it works, and works brilliantly. The device which began as a textual expedient provided the film with a framework for the kind of tight structure Olivier compulsively seeks, and turned what might have been only another stagey film into a dynamic essay on the power of the camera as an extension of the imagination. . . .

In the case of *Richard III,* the central device of coherence is the crown.

The crown imagery is built around three coronations, a structure facilitated by the incorporation of the coronation of Edward IV from *Henry VI, Part 3* (the play immediately preceding *Richard* in Shakespeare's history cycle) into Olivier's film script. Olivier added the coronation partly to elucidate for modern audiences Shakespeare's version of the political situation existing in England before Richard achieved the crown, but its formal function is also evident. . . .

The parabolic curve from legitimate king to tyrant to legitimate king is clearly defined through the use of crown images. The crown motif is hurled at the audience immediately. (p. 24)

The film is concerned, then, with the nature of kingship and tyranny, which sets Olivier's *Richard* at some distance from the play. Although Shakespeare's play, to a degree, shares this concern, the primary focus is on plot and character per se. . . . Had Olivier tried to adapt *Richard III* simply by snipping out some of its less inspired passages, he would have accomplished little. Instead, by giving predominance to a theme obscured in the play, he has given his film a significance that the play does not have. Olivier's film, like the play, is a portrait of an individual tyrant. Unlike the play, Olivier's film surpasses melodrama to become a portrait of tyranny.

That Olivier's film is concerned with tyranny is obvious; exactly what it has to say about tyranny is more difficult to define. There are elements of *Richard* (besides the crown motif) which suggest that the film takes the orthodox libertarian line on tyranny—that tyranny is an immoral infraction of human freedom, and that, inevitably, human dignity will assert itself and the tyrant will be overthrown. One of these is the consistent use of Richard's shadow, and those of his conspirators, to trace and comment on the development of Richard's plot. . . . Richard's shadow plays freely through the film like a familiar demon, assuming different aspects as the action progresses. (p. 25)

Reinforcing Olivier's use of shadows is his persistent weaving of religious references into the fabric of his film. Generally, religious episodes and symbols are placed in ironic juxtaposition to Richard's acts—thus, by implication, condemning Richard's conduct as immoral. In Olivier's film script, the text of the play is augmented with religious chants which serve as an ironic comment on the action. . . .

Conventional religious symbols, like the chants, are employed by Olivier to suggest Richard's satanic aspect. Clarence and Hastings are both sacrificed to Richard's ambition, so both are associated with saintly images. While Clarence tells Brackenbury of his nightmares, he wanders to the recessed window of his cell. . . . The parallel of Clarence's position to that of the crucified Christ on the facing wall is unmistakable.

Hastings is likewise associated with religious images. When he is betrayed at the tower, he sits alone at the end of a long table, the rest of the coronation committee having removed themselves to a safe distance at the far end. . . .

Olivier employs the same technique to make another kind of comment on tyranny. Richard is not only placed in opposition to religion, but his subordination of religion, his exploitation of religion to achieve his own ends, is made clear in the film through the interaction of Richard and religious trappings. (p. 26)

The film places heavy emphasis on the scene at the castle. As in the play, the entire sequence is built around the basic discrepancy between the reluctance of the assembled citizens to accept Richard and the favorable attitude which Richard's henchmen try to instill by pretending that it already exists. . . . At the point when the action reaches its climax, the film reaches an imagistic climax. Richard throws back his head, savoring his power. The camera cuts to the madly swinging bell, then dissolves to the bells of Richard's coronation.

Certainly Richard's descent of the bell rope is a concrete representation of his intense lust to put his new power into immediate force, but it is much more than that. The essence of Richard's tyranny, and the tyranny of every man who ever mobilized religion to gain his own ends or had an insane lust to see someone on his knee, are packed into a single visual image.

Still another aspect of Olivier's interpretation of *Richard III* which tends to support the notion that the film is an anti-tyranny apologue is the way Olivier has chosen to represent Richard's psychological make-up. He does indeed, as he has said, play Richard as a paranoiac—an interpretation which the play invites. Some of Richard's waspish diatribes take on a new significance when they are viewed as being partly inspired by self-indulgent delusions of persecution. . . . Richard is portrayed as a special kind of paranoiac—one whose resentment finds its supreme expression (and its chief compensatory device) in sadistic aggression and a lust for power that is quite literal and physical as well as figurative and psychological.

The progress of Richard's logic in his first speech suggests that his quest for power is a substitute for normal sexual activity. . . . The particular form which Richard's quest for power takes is suggested in a few lines from *Henry VI, Part 3*:

> And I, like one lost in a thorny wood,
> That rends the thorns and is rent with the thorns,
> Seeking a way and yet straying from the way;
> . . . Torment myself to catch the English crown,
> And from that torment I will free myself,
> Or hew my way out with a bloody axe.

The passage certainly exhibits a curious selectivity. Thorns are a common symbol of sterility. They were used as such by Christ in the parable of the sower, and the next line, "Seeking a way and yet straying from the way," seems to be an ironic reinforcement of the Biblical echo. The entire figure used in the passage has strong sado-masochistic implications, and the last lines do somewhat more than imply. That Olivier went out of his way to incorporate these lines into both his stage and screen performances, along with the passage referring to bribery of nature, on the ground that they "helped to explain Gloucester's character" should come as no surprise.

Olivier seems to have been thoroughly aware of this implicit aspect of Richard's character, and he has incorporated ample suggestions of sadism and power as a sexual object into his film. Richard's relationship to his throne is one way Olivier chooses to represent Richard's concept of power. . . . When Richard possesses the throne he possesses it in the fullest sense of the word—and the throne admits of no rivals.

Richard's sadism is more readily apparent. From the beginning he has a marked penchant for kicking doors (Brackenbury's and Anne's), human beings (a guard in the Abbey), and, presumably, whatever else may lie within range. . . . The closeness of the camera to the throne and the suddenness of the cut contribute to a subjective impression of violence and emphasize the narrowness with which the scepter misses smashing Buckingham's hand, which he pulls off the throne just in time.

The violent use of the scepter, with its implication of abuse of power, is repeated when Buckingham persists in his petitioning. (pp. 26-8)

Olivier has become noted for sensational and violent death scenes in Shakespeare, and he is sometimes inclined to recall an element of his interpretation which he wants to stress at this point in his performance as a device of emphasis. In *Richard III,* several of the film's major motifs recur in the death scene. The soldiers cluster around Richard to kill him, pull off his armor and stab him. . . .

The hilt of the sword, of course, provides the last ironic contrast of religion and Richard. The physical horror of his death, which is historically accurate, following More's version rather than Shakespeare's, forms a powerful comment on the fate of tyrants. The difficulty of killing him also bears implications about the nature of tyranny. (p. 28)

All of these elements of Olivier's interpretation—the crown imagery, the shadow, the use of religious reference, the portrayal of Richard's psychology—constitute a strong temptation to conclude that Olivier's film is an anti-tyranny moral fable. But *Richard* is designed to squeeze somewhat more meaning than this out of the concept of a tyrant, an undertaking which necessarily involves, in the interest of telling the truth, a certain amount of willful failure to assume any moral position whatsoever.

If *Richard III* were a moral fable, it would be natural to expect that some attractive alternative to Richard's tyranny would be presented in the film. However, this is clearly not the case. (pp. 28-9)

Olivier's film reflects the play's inherent absence of any satisfactory alternative to Richard in Edward's court. To visualize the corruption of the court Olivier added Mistress Shore, who is only alluded to in the play, to the cast of his film. She is always present in the court, ministering to the king or hovering in the background, and on the whole she is mute. . . .

Edward's inadequacy as a king, like Richard's tyranny, is elucidated through religious reference. After Edward has signed Clarence's death warrant, he exits leaning on the arm of Mistress Shore. . . . In addition to religious chants, religious symbols are used to stress Edward's corruption. During the scene in which Edward tries to reconcile the factious nobles, he lies in bed clutching a rosary. . . .

The established Church, which serves in Olivier's film partly as a contrast to Richard's villainy, fares no better as an alternative to Richard than Edward and his partisans (the second brother, Clarence, is not particularly promising as royal timber either, for he lacks the restrained unscrupulousness that characterizes Shakespeare's successful kings). In fact, the Church is subjected to a certain amount of oblique satire. (p. 29)

In Olivier's film, the conduct of the clergy is clearly presented as conforming to the general moral laxity which characterizes Edward's court. The two monks in the throne room may exchange scandalized glances, but they shrug and fold their arms. (pp. 29-30)

Perhaps it is possible to contend that Richmond is the alternative to Richard, but the film does not particularly support this hypothesis. There is even less of Richmond in the film than in the play, and what there is of him is not overwhelmingly appealing. He has a certain forthright manliness which is attractive enough—but it is hard to be persuaded on the basis of forthright manliness that there is anything appealing about him. He is too perfect a heroic figure to be believably human. . . . He cannot even be credited for defeating Richard. It takes Richard to do that. Richmond has all the compelling properties of a vacuum.

It is in Richard alone that the power of the play, and, even more so, of Olivier's film lies. Buckingham is the craftsman, the technician, the super-subtle instrument, Richard the master designer and driving force. He is utterly unscrupulous (which in itself is attractive enough—for the human fascination with powerful men can hardly be denied), but there is a great deal more to him than that. . . .

The essential ambivalence of Olivier's film is most evident in his portrayal of Richard. There are, as might be expected, two extreme ways to play Richard. At one pole he can be underplayed, so that he resembles Iago—sinister and clever, but about as amusing as a vial of undiluted sulphuric acid. At the other pole, he can be overplayed to the point where he becomes a lovable buffoon with an unfortunate tendency towards homicide. Olivier's interpretation lies somewhere between the two extremes. . . .

The Richard of the first part of the film limps up to the camera as soon as he is left alone with it. . . . It was the first time a cinematic character addressed himself to the audience so directly and personally, much less invited them to participate in a conspiracy. It is a delightfully brazen sort of behavior, characteristic of the audacity people admire in powerful men. (p. 30)

In addition to his comic bent for self-congratulation and his rhetorical dexterity, Olivier's Richard has certain idiosyncracies of behavior which are innocuous and rather charming. He tackles his projects with a hand-rubbing enthusiasm which almost belies their sinister nature. At times he is disarmingly absentminded. He stops on the brink of confusing the king's revocation of Clarence's death warrant with the warrant itself. . . . He is a Duke of Very Little Elegance. The kisses he bestows are sometimes conspicuously audible. . . .

Of course, Olivier's Richard is unmistakably deadly. The impression is reinforced from the beginning by his high-pitched, brittle precision of speech and his curious, reptilian appearance—hard, thin lips and an incessant, lizard-like blink. (p. 31)

Once Richard is exposed as a threat to the audience, he might be expected to lose his appeal entirely. Instead, after the scene at Baynard's Castle, he begins to take on some of the stature of a tragic hero, so that the basis for sympathy shifts markedly but is nevertheless retained. . . . It is the familiar pattern of the tragic hero committing a decisive act which sets him irrevocably on a path of self-destruction.

Richard retains his ferocity and personal force, even when the consequences of his acts begin to close in on him. . . . Olivier has omitted from his film the patently tragic "recognition" scene. . . . Richard's horror is conveyed effectively enough, however, for the speech is replaced in the film by a grisly howl that brings Richard's attendant running.

Richard also shares the tragic hero's ultimate comprehension and acceptance of his fate. The lines which convey Richard's attempts to maintain a semblance of confidence once he reaches the battlefield are delivered with a forced jauntiness that betrays his underlying despair. (pp. 31-2)

Thus Richard remains the powerful figure of Olivier's film. A delicate ironic balance is maintained between condemning Richard as a tyrant and loving him for it, which reflects the ambivalence of the human attitude toward tyrants and, by extension, the intrinsic ambivalence of tyrants themselves. Perhaps Olivier's surest asset as a director is this ironic poise, this wry detachment, this "curious, amoral strength." . . . (p. 32)

*Constance A. Brown, "Olivier's 'Richard III'—A Re-evaluation," in* Film Quarterly *(copyright 1967 by The Regents of the University of California; reprinted by permission of the University of California Press), Vol. XX, No. 4, Summer, 1967, pp. 23-32.*

**JUDITH CRIST**

Once again we are faced with a neither-film-nor-play production [*Three Sisters*], but it is, in Moura Budberg's liberal but satisfying translation and under Olivier's semicinematic direction, one at very least to fascinate devotees of the play. . . .

Through several performances, in Geoffrey Unsworth's luscious cinematography (and I mean the adjective in praise of the uncluttered and naturally generated glow his work achieves), and in the pacing there is somehow a sensuality and a sexuality underlying the work that I had not hitherto felt. This gives it an immediacy and a throb of life that avoid the by-now strictly-from-satire "I vunt to go to Moscow" stiltedness the play achieves. . . . Primarily, one senses it in . . . Masha, a woman of wit and intelligence rather than of vapors, vibrant in her temper and explosive in her emotions. And she is counterpointed beautifully by . . . Vershinin, who makes the caress of a glove lascivious and a simple pause epitomize erotica. (p. 79)

*Judith Crist, "Epitaph for a Small Loser," in* New York *Magazine (copyright © 1974 by News Group Publications, Inc.; reprinted with the permission of* New York *Magazine), Vol. 7, No. 10, March, 1974, pp. 77-9.*

**FOSTER HIRSCH**

In making *Hamlet* (in 1947), Olivier was concerned, as he had been with *Henry V,* about avoiding the static quality of filmed theater. Without sacrificing the integrity of the play, he wanted to give visual fluency to theatrical material. *Hamlet,* of course, is radically different from *Henry V,* and in moving from the extroverted spectacle of the chronicle play to Shakespeare's most introverted chamber drama, Olivier altered his style severely: the dark, moody, claustrophobic atmosphere of this second adaptation provides a striking contrast to the bright holiday tones of *Henry.* (p. 79)

Set in cavernous, sparsely furnished rooms in which the vast space is fragmented by arches, stairways, platforms, and columns, the film creates a deliberately closed environment. The dark, mostly bare rooms, and the vast, empty spaces are meant to be projections of Hamlet's tormented consciousness. In a muted way, therefore, the film's method is expressionist, its dark exterior world correlating to Hamlet's inner doubts, uncertainties, irresolutions. (p. 80)

The cold, bare, gloomy castle, though, and the stark black-and-white photography, with its sharp contrasts between light and shadow, have a strong visual impact. More conventional in its design than the earlier film, *Hamlet* still makes a bold visual impression. In terms of its decor and its chiaroscuro, the film is blatantly theatrical, but, as in *Henry,* Olivier's use of space is wonderfully fluid, open-ended. His camera work, even more than in the earlier film, is aggressively mobile. The movement of the camera enlarges the frame in which the drama is enacted, converting the closed space of the theater into filmic openness and endlessness. (pp. 80-1)

The almost constantly traveling camera provides continuity of place and action, thereby erasing the sharp divisions between act and scene that are part of Shakespeare's narrative construction. Olivier preserves spatial and temporal integrity by combining the moving camera with long takes. . . .

In his handling of time and place, then, Olivier stresses continuity rather than separation. The film has a self-consciously fluent and graceful movement, a sense of wholeness rather than fragmentation: individual scenes have a minimum of editing, and scenes are combined into sequences by the roving camera rather than by cuts. As a result, the film has a liquid, flowing quality which contributes substantially to the dreamlike ambiance, the lyrical haze in which the action seems to be suspended. (p. 81)

*Mise-en-scène* in *Hamlet* . . . becomes an integral expression of theme. Within the same shot, characters are often separated from each other by vast spaces; the use of deep focus allows us to see characters in the rear of the frame, at the end of long corridors or across large rooms, and the physical separation, realistically rendered, is emblematic of the emotional distance or the distrust between characters. The kind of separation between characters, made possible through deep focus, serves throughout as a visual signal of Hamlet's estrangement from everyone else. (pp. 81-2)

This method of separation within the frame is particularly forceful in dramatizing the growing alienation between Hamlet and Ophelia. The image of a shrunken Ophelia, framed by pillars in the rear of the screen as Hamlet, in the foreground, rants at her, boldly underlines their ruptured relationship. . . .

Olivier's methods, like those of Orson Welles, are both realistic (deep focus, the long take) and expressionistic (chiaroscuro,

setting as emanations of character). At times, Olivier uses devices that are meant to extend the sense of reality in which the action takes place; at other points, his approach is intentionally stylized and abstract.

One of his techniques for giving the play realistic touches are the glimpses of the "real" world beyond the castle. In several scenes, in the depth of the frame, there are views of hills and trees that look like the natural world as it appears in the backgrounds of Renaissance portraits. (p. 82)

Olivier's attempts to enclose the action by references to nature are more successfully managed in his use of the sound of breaking waves as aural punctuation throughout the scenes on the ramparts. Here, without disruption or strain, the inclusion of an aspect of the real world expands the sense of space in which the drama is played, opens it up to reality.

Typical of his methods, though, Olivier mixes natural sound in the scenes on the ramparts with the expressionistic sound of an ominous echoing heartbeat that is used whenever the Ghost appears. (p. 83)

One of Olivier's most controversial decisions was to preface the film with a speech from the play that suggests that Hamlet's problems are attributable to one flaw:

> So, oft if chances in particular men,
> That for some vicious mole of nature in them,
> By the o'er growth of some complexion,
> Oft breaking down the pales and forts of reason,
> Or by some habit that too much o'er-leavens
> The form of plausive manners, that these men,
> Carrying, I say, the stamp of one defect,
> Their virtues else, be they as pure as grace,
> Shall in the general censure take corruption
> From that particular fault.

The words appear on the screen as Olivier speaks them. After the speech, Olivier adds: "This is the story of a man who could not make up his mind." Olivier has often used the "one defect" theory in developing his characterizations for Shakespeare's tragic heroes. . . . His emphasis of the "one defect" theory in his prologue to *Hamlet,* however, is misleading, as his interpretation of the role is more complex than the simplistic "this is the story of a man who could not make up his mind" would indicate. (p. 88)

Both an ironic observer and a man of action, Olivier's Hamlet is, by fits and starts, embittered, overwrought, speculative, rash, impassioned, withdrawn; like any decent Hamlet, he is a network of contradictions. (p. 89)

Borrowing ideas, then, from many different approaches to the role, Olivier's Hamlet is many things at once. The actor is careful, however, not to emphasize the rigorous, extroverted, soldierly qualities of the character that would be the easiest for him to play, and he works instead at underlining the meditative qualities, the brooding introspection. He stresses Hamlet's negative traits, his unfitness for heroic action. He is consciously playing against type, making sure that he does not duplicate his performance as Henry V. The result is that the performance, appropriately, is riddled with ambiguity: Is this Hamlet capable of action? Is he really mad or is he only pretending to be?

Inevitably, however, his explosions are more vivid than the passages of philosophical introspection. (pp. 89-90)

The dense, interior Hamlet, scorched by self-doubt and existential despair, is intelligent but less effective. The voiceover technique used for the soliloquies prevents the actor from establishing direct communication with the audience. (p. 90)

As the director, Olivier took care not to present the play simply as a showcase for a star Hamlet. His performance is not an egocentric display of virtuosity or a blazing rendition of the beleaguered prince. It is, in fact, the least technical and least dazzling of his four major Shakespearean roles on film. . . . The character's interiority does not come easily to him, and Hamlet's tragic strain is simply more difficult for the actor to reach than the rich comic possibilities of Richard, the rhetorical flourishes of Henry, or the melodramatic excesses of Othello. (p. 91)

Within its inevitable limits—Olivier, after all, claimed that this was only a "study" in *Hamlet,* a sketch of the original—the adaptation is a major achievement, providing further demonstration that films can indeed accommodate Shakespeare. (p. 92)

[*Richard III*] is made with wonderful assurance. (p. 97)

As in [*Henry V*], the recurrent tableau effects, the sharp colors and symmetrical compositions, are based on Book of Hours illustrations; the historical drama unfolds before us like a series of pages from an illuminated medieval manuscript. The sets aren't as abstract as those in *Henry,* however, and the film adopts a predominantly uniform style rather than the multilayered textures used for the earlier work. Castle interiors and the streets of London, though, have the pastel hues of a children's coloring book, and the few landscapes offer a purely decorative and emblematic treatment of physical reality. (pp. 97-8)

Of his three Shakespearean films, in fact, Olivier's *Richard* has the loosest integration between form and content. Shakespeare's melodramatic history play might well have looked less like *Henry V* and more like *Hamlet.* The film's bold colors are pleasing, but how appropriate are they for the story of Richard Crookback's rise and fall? There seems no particular thematic rationale for Richard to hobble through such airy, fanciful settings. . . .

As in his two earlier films, Olivier's use of space within the abstract settings is entirely cinematic. Olivier continues here his employment of realist film techniques such as the depth of focus and the long take first fully articulated in *Hamlet.* Scene after scene is composed in eloquent, deep focus, with background details used to comment pertinently on foreground action. (p. 98)

Far more than in *Hamlet,* Olivier here respects the integrity and wholeness of soliloquies and set speeches. In the earlier film, the longer speeches were often presented in a fragmented style, with heavy editing to divide the attention of the audience between the speaker and his environment or his listeners. In *Richard III,* all of the big speeches are filmed in uninterrupted takes so that the actors have the chance to build and shape their delivery without interference from the editor. . . .

As in *Hamlet,* there are of course scenes in which Olivier departs from the realist methods of deep focus and the long take to use a more hectic and formative approach. This more fragmented style is used for passages of particular theatrical impact. . . .

As in both *Henry V* and *Hamlet,* Olivier is once again concerned about providing smooth transitions between scenes, about giving the heavily edited and condensed material a sense of continuity and flow. (p. 99)

In a further (and similarly strained) effort to underline thematic connections, Olivier uses two visual leitmotifs, the crown and Richard's shadow. The film begins with a shot of the crown; the scene of Richard's coronation opens with a low-angle shot of a crown that seems suspended in mid-air; at the end of the battle sequence, the crown is trampled under the hooves of horses. (pp. 99-100)

[Olivier] has simplified the structure of Shakespeare's bulky, unevenly balanced play, cutting its choral interludes and its often-wooden rhetorical embellishments and reducing the women's roles in order to concentrate on the main political intrigue of Richard's rise and fall and on his own incomparably witty, incisive, vaudevillian performance.

Unlike his earlier adaptations, Olivier here uses the film as a frame for his virtuoso impersonation of Shakespeare's demonic and captivating antihero. (pp. 101, 103)

Broad and theatrical as it is . . . , the performance has been scaled down for the camera. Using close-ups to establish intimacy with the audience, Olivier takes us into his confidence in a way that would not be available to a stage Richard. He establishes the direct contact with the audience that he so scrupulously avoided as Hamlet; he violates film convention by looking right at the camera, challenging us not to believe him. . . . Throughout the film, he uses asides to the camera as a means of continuing the dialogue he has set up with us. The soliloquies, for the most part, are delivered quietly, with a subtle play of features that wouldn't register on stage: Olivier uses close-ups to show us how Richard thinks.

Richard is an expert dissembler, and it is this aspect of the role that Olivier savors. He plays him as a great comedian, slyly winking at us as he tricks unknowing characters. Early in the film, his courtship of Lady Anne demonstrates Richard's relish for putting on a good show. He plays the wooing scene with calculated impudence, with delight in Richard's persuasive skills; and as he sets out to conquer the lady, whose husband he has killed, Olivier adds a quality that he alone among the great classical actors of his generation is capable of: he makes the hunchback sexy. (pp. 103-04)

Olivier underlines the character's mordant wit, emphasizing the discrepancy between what Richard says and what he means, particularly in the scenes where he dissembles before the court as he tries to pass himself off as a retiring person of low ambition who is unskilled with words and unpracticed in political double-dealing. Olivier pitches the ironies directly to us, in order to enlist our sympathy in his pursuits. (p. 105)

In the play's final movement, which swiftly charts the haunted king's downfall, Olivier explores the melancholy and doubt that gnaw at the once-confident, once-ebullient Machiavel. Olivier deepens the characterization by removing Richard's mask and allowing us to see the possessed monarch as a pitiful, burnt-out case. . . .

Olivier, then, despite the darker shadings near the end of the film, plays Richard as a buoyant and richly comic figure. Richard, after all, is not a tragic hero; he is the master of the revels in a rousing, popular, violent melodrama. To sustain the melodramatic flavor of the material, Olivier sees to it that the film has no noble characters. . . . The court consists of oily, self-serving politicians, wily double-dealers, or weak, vacillating, easily controlled characters like Edward's wife, Elizabeth. There is no honor here, with Richard and most of his adversaries a collection of ignoble politicians. (p. 106)

Olivier does a great deal of acting in [*The Prince and the Showgirl*], but, as both director and costar, he gallantly hands the film to his leading lady, allowing her many special moments that turn *The Prince and the Showgirl* into something of an homage to Marilyn Monroe. The film is punctuated with little set pieces that display Monroe's particular gifts as a light co-medienne and as a sentimental actress. While the Regent is jabbering on the phone, preoccupied with affairs of state and with court intrigue, and thoroughly insensitive to the girl's presence, the camera lingers on Monroe as she helps herself to hors d'oeuvres and reacts, a little drunkenly, to the prince's tactless comments about Americans. The scene is beautifully timed, and Olivier discovers an easy, sly sense of humor in his costar. In the coronation scene, the camera focuses on Monroe as she reacts to the splendor of the royal ceremony; the scene is a showcase for the childlike innocence and trem-bling vulnerability that Marilyn's audience always responded to. Olivier provides Monroe with a magnificent exit: the camera remains in place as Marilyn leaves the royal apartments; at the end of her long walk through the ornate rooms, she nods to the liveried footman just before she passes out of view, into the outside world, and that small, marvelously apt gesture perfectly summarizes the character's charm and dignity.

The wallbound material doesn't have the opportunity for spec-tacle, for movement, and for changes of scene that the Shake-spearean plays afforded, and Olivier's direction (wisely, under the circumstances) is less inventive than in any of his earlier projects. He treats the text as a duet for two accomplished light comedians, concentrating on matters of acting, on timing, nu-ance, gesture, rather than on visual adornment. Olivier uses unobtrusive camera movement and editing and minimal changes of scene to give some fluidity to the circumscribed mate-rial. . . . The scene at [the showgirl's] boardinghouse of her frantic preparations for her evening with the regent is also a delightful embellishment of the play's single drawing-room set; but later interpolations are less successful. The scenes at the coronation and the ball are filmed in a skimpy way that suggests a modest budget. The royal procession through the streets and in Westminster Abbey seems posed; the sense of space is cramped. It looks as if Olivier is faking it, and the entire sequence, while it breaks up the single-set confinement, has a theatrical rendering of physical reality that is jarring. Olivier works best in the interior scenes, where he can focus on acting, rather than in the big crowd scenes, where his direction is surprisingly stilted. When it strays from the story's theatrical confinement, when it ventures out into the "real" world, the picture is suspended uncomfortably in an undefined space be-tween theatrical convention and cinematic realism. (pp. 116-17)

Olivier's direction [of *Three Sisters*] contains genuine attempts to move the material gracefully from behind the proscenium, but nonetheless this is by far his least cinematic work. . . . *Three Sisters* concerns a group of characters who feel they have wasted their lives. . . . There are no heroes or villains in Chek-hov, though, since the playwright views his characters with an objectivity that confers humanity on all of them.

Olivier begins the film with a stunning shot of Chekhov's heroines glimpsed in silhouette behind a shimmering, scrimlike partition. The camera tracks in step with the sisters as they move sedately in single file through the vast empty space of their provincial house. The compositional quality of the open-ing announces Olivier's dependence on theater—the characters' ritualistic movement, the artificial backlighting that frames them, the unoccupied space, are means equally available to the stage director. . . . Olivier has excluded the world of physical real-ity, choosing instead to enclose the characters in theatrical settings that are both two- and three-dimensional. Weather, natural light, realistic sense of space, naturalistic decor—these are rigorously omitted from the film's spare design.

Olivier tiptoes in hushed tones through a play that he has called "the most beautiful in the world," and as a result his direction is more solemn and stately than it was for his Shakespearean adaptations. Olivier is not intimidated by Shakespeare; on the evidence of this film, he *is* afraid of Chekhov. His approach is too muted and remote, and his direction lacks the energy that propelled the Shakespearean films.

Chekhov presents his characters as they function in society—their private dramas of unrequited love, of regret for missed or wasted opportunities, are enacted in public, on lawns, in living rooms, where there is a continual coming and going of people. . . . [*Three Sisters*] is written for the unbroken, un-fragmented movement of actors on a stage. Realizing this, Olivier uses the camera as little and as quietly as possible; he tries . . . to include many group shots, and to depend on neutral medium shots that do not divide the audience's attention from the group interrelationships. Olivier uses close-ups sparingly, for emphasis. Despite his comparative discretion, however, the Act I dinner party, for instance, is not nearly so effective on film as it is on stage; the sense of ensemble movement and of simultaneous activity, which often has an exhilarating spon-taneity and lifelikeness in the theater, is missing here. The flow of life, so essential to Chekhov's mood and rhythm, is dissi-pated by Olivier's too-careful arrangement of actors for the camera.

Chekhov balances the tone and mood of his four acts; the scenes are arranged in complementary pairs, so that the high spirits of the Act I party are followed by the gloomy, isolated con-versations of Act II; the excitement instigated by the offstage fire in Act III is balanced by the somber leavetakings in Act IV. Olivier's direction is dark and heavy from the beginning, however; there is a stern, elegiac reading of the play that misses some of the humor. . . . The film's stately pace is unbroken except for superfluous interjections of a fire truck hurtling through a city street and an impressionistic dream sequence of two of the sisters wandering around a fogbound Moscow that they will never reach. Both these naive attempts to expand the material betray the film's otherwise deliberately confined at-mosphere. These two brief intrusions are failures of judgment unprecedented in Olivier's film-directing. (pp. 120-21, 123)

The film has a staid drawing-room atmosphere that belies Chek-hov's palpitating, reverberent subtext. (p. 123)

Olivier's film has a beautifully muted color scheme—rich browns and velvets, weighty dark tones for the interiors, with sharply contrasted lighting, and a gray, Corotlike, autumnal atmo-sphere for the last-act farewells in the garden. The film is intelligent, (too) dignified, and never fully moving. Even more than *The Prince and the Showgirl*, it looks like a filmed play rather than a full-fledged movie. (pp. 123-24)

*Foster Hirsch, in his* Laurence Olivier *(copyright © 1979 by G. K. Hall & Co.; reprinted with the per-mission of Twayne Publishers, A Division of G. K. Hall & Co., Boston), Twayne, 1979, 190 p.*

# Nagisa Oshima

## 1932-

Japanese director and screenwriter.

Oshima's films deal with the post-war experience and subsequent disorientation of Japanese society. He questions Japan's moral code and believes human sexuality to be a release of tension within a repressive environment. Oshima also centers on the criminal act, the nature of such an action, and the actual event. By doing so, he provides an objective, unemotional analysis of sensational aspects of contemporary behavior, often focusing on the difficulties of youth in Japan.

In 1962, Oshima formed his own production company, Sozosha, but because of his earlier commercial failures, it took four years to attain financial backing for his first independent feature. The Sozosha films are critical treatments of Japan's bourgeois society. *Diary of a Shinjuku Thief* and *Death by Hanging* commence with actual incidents and deal with controversial topics, challenging the conception of truth. By interpreting events in different ways, Oshima accentuates the fallibility of moral assumption.

*Death by Hanging,* considered Oshima's first major personal statement, depicts a Korean who survives his execution but cannot recall the crime for which he was convicted. Its distancing effects owe much to Brecht and Kabuki theater. The same theatricality is evident in *Diary of a Shinjuku Thief,* a tale of student unrest. Once again, several viewpoints are presented simultaneously, and Oshima stresses the importance of a fantasy life as a means of attaining a new level of being. Older people are treated unfavorably because of their unwillingness to be imaginative.

*Boy* uses a more conventional approach. Despite the family's unusual occupation—staging accidents to claim insurance money—they are traditionally Japanese in their attitudes. Though *Boy*'s subject matter is poignant, the film is not sentimental. The violent outcome of their existence is shown as an inherent result of Japanese lifestyles. When a real accident abruptly ends their career, the young boy is damaged irreparably. Significantly, an orphan played the boy and, after the film's completion, chose not to be adopted because of his disenchantment with the Japanese family system. Oshima says of the film, "The plight of the child is the plight of us all."

Oshima's most controversial film, *In the Realm of the Senses,* appeared briefly at the New York Film Festival before the U.S. Customs Service confiscated it because of its graphic sexual content. The tale of a consuming passion ending in murder, the film glorifies the sensuality of Old Japan. Like earlier films, it deals with an actual event and its consequences. More importantly, however, *In the Realm of the Senses* raises questions about the nature of obscenity. Oshima felt the film could be defined as either erotic or pornographic, but added that he sees nothing wrong with pornography: sex is a fundamental activity in which human beings participate. Although not overtly political, some critics see the sexual obsession of the protagonists as an attempt to transcend their political milieu.

Oshima was awarded the prize as best director at the Cannes Film Festival for *Empire of Passion.* Nevertheless, the film met with a tepid reception among critics. Considered a companion piece to *In the Realm of the Senses,* it intertwines love and death to create a statement about societal dictates. Oshima says of these doomed heroes what is true for all his characters: "In their reluctance to rebel there dwells a curious strength."

## JOHN SIMON

*Boy* is a film that tries to use Western avant-garde modes of obliquity in telling a rather humdrum tale of petty larceny in contemporary Japan. Unfortunately, the director, Nagisa Oshima, has nothing much to say about his characters. The film tells of a partly disabled war veteran who teaches his wife and young son how to pretend they have been hit by passing cars and collect hefty sums for not going to the police. Though there are vague attempts at examining how these activities affect the psyches involved, and their relation to one another, the film stays close to the surface, and the surface is far from interesting.

Nevertheless, one scene remains visually haunting: two small boys squatting in front of a snowman in an otherwise empty, flat, snowy landscape. The color film's way of rendering this essentially monochromatic subject matter, combined with the starkness of the wide-screen composition, makes for an impact comparable to that of certain modern paintings where the figure is pushed as far as it will go toward abstraction. But this is insufficient to redeem a hollow film. (p. 389)

*John Simon, "The Festival and Awards Game: Unmagnificent Seventh" (originally published as "More Moans for the Festival," in* The New Leader, *Vol. LII, No. 20, October 27, 1969), in his* Movies into Film: Film Criticism 1967-1970 *(copyright © 1971* *by John Simon; reprinted with permission of The Dial Press), Dial, 1971, pp. 382-98.\**

## DONALD RICHIE

A short while ago a young Korean student murdered and raped two Japanese girls. Director Oshima has returned to the case [in *Koshikei (Death by Hanging)*] and questioned not the guilt of the student but the justification of capital punishment and the whole problem of discrimination against the Koreans in Japan. He does not do so directly, however. Instead, he has chosen a Brechtian form. The young Korean, though hanged, refuses to die and so the police officers must act out his crime in order to convince him of his guilt. In so doing one of the officers inadvertently murders a girl. The ironies of the picture multiply—law is impossible without crime, for example—and the film ends with the unassailable logic of the young Korean's observation upon being warmly assured that it is indeed very bad to kill, that "then it is bad to kill me." The second half of *Koshikei* is somewhat loose and more than a little indulgent, but the general structure and the first half are remarkably incisive.

*Donald Richie, "'Koshikei' ('Death by Hanging'),"* in International Film Guide 1969, *edited by Peter Cowie (copyright © 1968 by The Tantivy Press), Tantivy Press, 1969, p. 113.*

## PHILIP STRICK

[*Boy*] displays its credits against the blackened sun of the Japanese flag. The symbol, recurring throughout the film, is intended as an ironic reminder of militant nationalism, the dominant mood (as Oshima sees it) of the society within which his little band of criminals makes its gestures of revolt. In addition, the flag stands for the paternalistic structure of the Japanese way of life, a structure both constricting and emasculatory which has already received a thorough trouncing in two other recent Oshima works, *Death by Hanging* and *Diary of a Shinjuku Thief.* In both these predecessors, youthful offenders against the established order struggle to reconcile their social transgressions with what they are conscious to be their moral ones—only to reach the conclusion that the values of the older generation are neither valid nor relevant to their own problems. . . .

[For the family of *Boy*], the flag is neither provider nor protector; rather, they are its victims—and in turn the boy is victim of his parents, whose exploitation of his body as a sacrificial offering to one car accident after another . . . is stoically accepted by him as their right. . . .

[The ten-year-old in *Boy*] could have been given the full sentimental treatment. Like the arrogantly vulnerable miscreants of *Shinjuku Thief,* however, he is contemplated by Oshima with a gaze that is almost cold. All the heart-rending sequences are there that one would expect, but their emotive qualities are carefully muted. . . .

Again like the preceding films, *Boy* spirals from the apparently rational to the fragmentation of crisis point—in this case the real accident unwittingly caused by the family—after which the central character can at last begin to think clearly, unaffected by the pressures which have previously confused him. (p. 162)

Since the basic narrative of *Boy* is of its own nature multifaceted, Oshima has confined his style to the most direct observation, with none of the extraordinary theatrical complications of his other works. . . . Yet the film has its undercurrents—the persistent links with rain and snow, the periodic return to the sea, the vital function of meal-times in the development of the family relationships, and of course the regular punctuating scene of a car halting abruptly as a small body bounces from it, an apocalyptic metaphor in which truth and deception are in disturbing contradiction.

Oshima has said that he made the film as a prayer for all human beings who find it necessary to live in this way, and that for him the group in *Boy* have come to represent a holy family. While the divinity of their journey may be open to question, their martyrdom, as befits a prayer, is celebrated with dignity, poetry, and a crystalline precision. (pp. 162-63)

*Philip Strick, "Film Reviews: 'Boy',"* in Sight and Sound *(copyright © 1970 by The British Film Institute), Vol. 39, No. 3, Summer, 1970, pp. 162-63.*

## MARGARET TARRATT

[In *The Boy,* traffic] is used to express a sense of social isolation and indeed, alienation. . . . The family forms a tight unit held together by mutual need against the rest of society. But within that unit there is continual antagonism both silent and violent. . . . Oshima has suggested that the father, who uses his war experiences as an excuse for his conduct, is an archetypal Japanese patriarch. In his authoritarian role, an analogy may be drawn between the Emperor rulers of Japan who have dominated the country for two thousand years. Such analogies, however, are remote from the fabric of the film. . . .

[The] movement between colour and monochrome together with the often unlinked scenes suggests that we are inhabiting the boy's private dream world. Rejecting the example of human beings, the boy's heroes are the men from outer space whom he believes to be strong, self-sufficient but beneficent. (p. 43)

The boy's long speech in the snow, the placing of his watch and the dead girl's boot on the snowman and his angry destruction of it, seem to overweigh the film with cumbersome symbolism—even if we realise that the placing of objects on a snowman is a Japanese custom. . . . The film is at its most impressive when symbolic overtones are absent, in the trivial details of everyday life permeated with a gnawing melancholy—a chilly tone which holds the attention. It is a film constructed in a minor key in which the big scenes are something of a fiasco. (pp. 43, 46)

*Margaret Tarratt, "Film Guide: 'The Boy'" (© copyright Margaret Tarratt 1970; reprinted with permission),* in Films and Filming, *Vol. 16, No. 11, August, 1970, pp. 43, 46.*

## GORDON GOW

[In *Diary of a Shinjuku Thief,* hands] are torn from the face of a clock. Time and customs are wishfully brought to a standstill while the revolutionary spirit of the world is concentrated into one uptight predicament in modern Japan. . . . The trouble with [the main characters] is that neither of them has much luck in the matter of obtaining orgasm, especially not together, and their conscientious and troubled search for a solution to this problem is intended by the film's director, Nagisa Oshima, to symbolise the need for a Japan to explode its social inhibitions and become a free new world. It is as well to be informed of this, because one could so easily run away with the thought that the film is all about sex and that political comment is peripheral. As a matter of fact, it seems to me to turn out like that anyway, however intensely one tries to see it in allegorical terms. It's as erotic as can be. They talk about sex, and they enact what they talk about, and anybody who can keep his mind on a political plane while all this is happening ought to stand for parliament at the next election or go and see a psychiatrist. (pp. 51, 55)

The style of the film is erratic; and technically there are signs of what I take to be economic stress, as for example in a crowded little room where a number of men talk about their sexual experiences, sometimes in shots of reasonable clarity, but often in an inconsistent haze. . . . It's a mélange of a film, and it doesn't work in my opinion; but one could never call it uninteresting. (p. 55)

> *Gordon Gow, "Reviews: 'Diary of a Shinjuku Thief'"
> (© copyright Gordon Gow 1970; reprinted with permission), in* Films and Filming, *Vol. 17, No. 2, November, 1970, pp. 51, 55.*

## IAN CAMERON

[The] departures from the rules of the genre in *Naked Youth* and *The Sun's Burial* were evidence that Oshima was more than just an accomplished *metteur-en-scène*. The violence was too extreme and distasteful to fit the accepted patterns of entertaining rough-stuff. (pp. 63-4)

*The Sun's Burial* also contains some noticeable departures from the idea of the good story well told—climactic moments of violence are shown in alienating long shots and there's a conspicuous lack of economy in the handling, with a multitude of individually motivated characters all playing a part in the complex thematic sub-structure. Neither *The Sun's Burial* nor *Naked Youth* fits into the established emotional modes of crime movies, whether optimistic or pessimistic. Virtue is certainly not triumphant—the good guys don't beat the bad guys, because Oshima does not work in those terms and there are no firm candidates for the position of good guy. But equally these films reject the patterns of romantic pessimism: we aren't offered the moving spectacle of the doomed but sympathetic criminal. . . . Although the pessimism of *The Sun's Burial* is as extreme as you will see on the screen, we are not invited to indulge in it as an emotional experience. Emotionally, these films have a drained quality which, excluding much identification, invites a more intellectual response. (pp. 64-5)

Many of the themes and approaches that appear in the later films are already discernible in *The Sun's Burial*. Not surprisingly, the shadow of the Second World War hangs over the whole film. (p. 65)

It is difficult to find any signs of hope in *The Sun's Burial*. The partial destruction of the slum by fire at the end of the film might be hopeful but for the fact that the heroine's father has contributed a hand grenade to the conflagration and an old man surveys the wreckage, commenting that it looks just like it did at the end of the war. The most positive quality in the film is the heroine's vitality, her ability to survive. . . . (p. 66)

The roots of [Japan's internal conflict] appear in *The Catch* through its concentration on the youths and children. At various moments of violence, Oshima dwells on the presence of children, stressing the effects which both the specific events and the general situation must have on them and hence on the future—or, from our viewpoint, the present. . . . The film . . . uses the children to throw into contrast the behaviour of the adults. (pp. 66-7)

[Part of the film concerns the] ignominious process of adjusting to the unappetising facts or rather of adjusting the facts to get off the hook and avoid any guilt or responsibility. In microcosm we are observing the Japanese nation coming to terms—false ones—with its militarist record, war-time atrocities and eventual defeat, thus achieving a spurious peace of mind. (p. 67)

*The Catch* is based on two contradictory movements in the plot. The villagers resolve events to their own satisfaction, building up a network of pretences that things haven't happened or that they have happened differently: a movement towards reassuring fiction. But the negro also acts as a catalyst in revealing hidden facts and stripping away the layers of hypocrisy and pretence: a movement toward truth. But as we learn more of the truth and the villagers become more enmeshed in their protective fiction, a third movement cuts across the other two and provides a point of identification for the audience. The younger participants do not share their elders' attitudes, but are exposed to the resulting actions, and even try to stop them. (p. 68)

In style, *The Catch* belongs very much with the early films: it is unorthodox but not particularly striking. . . .

Oshima's recent films offer more obvious evidence of ambition than the sex and violence movies or than *The Catch,* where the meaning resides in the subtle interaction of plot elements. Two of the newer films display the accepted post-Godardian apparatus of titles and obvious unreality, though these are used in a completely individual way. In *Death by Hanging,* the use of titles smacks less of Godard than of Brecht; the titles are simple announcements of what is about to happen. And, unlike Godard, Oshima has no doctrinaire objections to using the conventional means of the cinema when they suit his purpose. . . .

The later films show just how personal Oshima's early Shochiku films were—one can discern, if not a typical Oshima hero, at least a typical situation for an Oshima hero, that of a criminal (even *The Catch* can be said to centre on a criminal act). The concern with criminals in the Shochiku films is not just the result of having to work within a genre but more that the genre happened to be well fitted for expressing Oshima's concerns. The background to Oshima's films is of the malaises of post-war Japanese society. . . . (p. 69)

Although social problems are behind Oshima's films, there is a complete absence of [De Sica's] facile *Bicycle Thieves* cause-and-effect explanations of the protagonists' criminality. A distrust of cause-and-effect explanations is characteristic of Oshima, and their dangers are almost a theme of *The Catch*. Oshima's technique is to suggest connections and parallels rather than to present explanations. (p. 70)

[In *Death by Hanging*], more than in any other Oshima film I have seen, it is fair to talk of argument rather than of plot. *Death by Hanging* takes to an extreme a tendency which was already evident within the more realistic conventions of *The Catch*, which derives its form much less from the complications of the plot than from the thematic argument which underlies it at every point. *Death by Hanging* begins on the level of reality with the documentary reconstruction of an execution, moves to fiction with the failure of the execution and then progresses to a series of stages of fantasies within the basic fiction. But the fantasies are the means which Oshima uses to reach the truth which may lay behind the facts. (pp. 73-4)

If R's final gesture is a little too close to the sort of resolution favoured by the cinematic expressions of liberal idealism, the rest of [*Death by Hanging*] is extremely sophisticated in argument and dense in texture. . . .

Oshima's technique of suggesting connections is taken to its extreme in the series of parallels which make up the structure of *Diary of a Shinjuku Thief,* the most complex and ambitious of his films. . . . It might be described as a set of variations on the themes of renewal (or revolution) and imagination (or vision). It is a film in which every component has resonances which relate to every other component, though none of these relationships has the simplicity of an equation. (p. 80)

The parallel between Kara Juro's theatre and student riots works in two ways: if the theatre is revolutionary, the riot is as much a performance as Kara Juro's play. This implication is just as acceptable in the context of the film. Indeed, the idea of performing or acting is so crucial to [*Diary of a Shinjuku Thief*] that the more one sees it, the more most of the other themes seem to be subordinate to or derived from the idea of acting. It is also a theme that runs through Oshima's work. . . . (p. 81)

Kara Juro's role covers the whole of the film's range of reality and fiction (and contrarily in the conventionally fiction sequences he appears as himself), right through to the ritual artificiality of his ghost play. . . . The theme of the continual renewal of ideas, of the necessity for successive revolutions rather than for Revolution, is very important to Oshima; he sees revolution not as a once-and-for-all process but as the victory of new ideas over stale, static ones—in time the revolutionary vision will itself become static and need to be overthrown by further revolution. (p. 84)

The feeling of [Umeko's scene in the book store] is that each of [the well-known] revolutionaries, whatever else he may have done, has left some useful legacy of ideas. It is the temporal counterpart of the noises of protest which accompany some of the time checks and weather reports from around the world which indicate the spatial spread of revolution. (p. 88)

The whole image of the bookshop implies an irony in that this wealth of explosive revolutionary material is controlled by a non-revolutionary and is very much part of a conventional capitalist system. (pp. 90-1)

After the strident complexities of *Death by Hanging* and *Diary of a Shinjuku Thief, Boy* might seem like a complete change of approach, but its preoccupations are exactly those of the earlier movies. The subjects are again people who live outside society and whose actions contravene the law. But where the previous films described have looked at their relationship to others, *Boy* stresses their isolation. (p. 92)

Where the earlier films dealt with people very much as representatives of ideas, *Boy* deals with them primarily as characters. We watch the boy being forced back into his fantasies by the social isolation which results from the fact that they have to keep travelling. We see the growth of a relationship between the boy and his stepmother which is born of their complicity in doing jobs together. (p. 93)

[The accident] sequence could fit quite acceptably into a naturalistic chain of events—in a film which concerns fantasy and reality it could be expected to belong incontrovertibly to the reality. The way it is handled, however, serves to make its reality problematical without definitely labelling it as fantasy. It is in monochrome although colour is usual in the film, but then this is true of the whole sequence including the argument which precedes the accident; Oshima has said that he sees no great difference between using colour and using monochrome and feels free to use either without it expressing any particular formal or logical intention. . . . Both the accident and the ambulances arriving and departing are almost soundless—the combination of the almost suppressed soundtrack and the monochrome image produces a dream-like quality. The accident itself is almost bloodless, although at least the boy thinks that one or both of the people have been killed. Oshima's past record in this line does not point to him as a man likely just to gloss over the carnage which attends fatal motor accidents. Either the boy is wrong and the people have survived or his imagination does not extend to such physical details or, again, he may somehow have suppressed these in his memory—though at this stage in the film, the sequence is implicitly in the present tense rather than the remembered past. Finally, there is the single boot left behind after the ambulances have driven off, a detail which seems in the context to belong with the fantasy elements. . . .

The device, which appears in *Diary of a Shinjuku Thief,* of characters acting out their fantasies or desires in a more or less ritual form is used in *Boy* within a much more naturalistic framework. (p. 95)

*Boy* is in many ways the reverse of *Diary of a Shinjuku Thief:* most obviously, it does not have the violent shifts in style from sequence to sequence and the fragmentation which characterises its predecessor. *Shinjuku Thief* was a film about the power of imagination or fantasy and its various levels of reality and fantasy are quite clearly differentiated. *Boy,* on the other hand, deals with the failure of retreat into the world of fantasy to provide a satisfactory escape from the unpleasantness of the real world. Here the ability to differentiate between reality and fantasy is lost and, through the style of the film, this loss is shared by the audience. . . .

Within the strangeness of the forms he adopts and in spite of certain comprehension problems which are inevitable for a western audience, Oshima is the least inscrutable of all Japanese directors. This is not to deny that his films are extremely demanding of their audiences, but to say that they are susceptible to (and indeed reward) perfectly conventional analysis. They do not, like some Japanese films, invite us to treat them as exotic art objects surrounded with an aura of mystery. (p. 98)

> Ian Cameron, "Nagisa Oshima," in Second Wave, edited by Ian Cameron & others (© 1970 by Movie Magazine Limited; reprinted by permission of Movie), Frederick A. Praeger, Publishers, 1970, pp. 63-98.

**DAVID WILSON**

[*Death by Hanging*] is not so much based on facts as structured round them; a documentary fact merely provides the thematic framework around which Oshima builds a complex interplay between reality and appearance. . . .

[What we watch in *Death by Hanging*] is a masquerade, a formal demonstration of what Oshima has called 'the continual reciprocity between reality and fiction.' The idea is central to each of the three recent Oshima films we have seen. It is the basis of *Boy,* where the family's existence depends on an act of deception; and of course it recurs throughout *Diary of a Shinjuku Thief,* with its convoluted variations on the theme of performance. The disappearing body at the end of *Death by Hanging* is much more than the formalistic convenience it seems at first; with its repeated juxtaposition of real and apparent contradictions, the whole film has prepared us for this final *coup de théâtre.*

For a start, the film is based on a non-event: R is not hanged. . . . The cause and effect synthesis is thus immediately demolished, to be replaced by a series of circular antitheses. . . . The antitheses proliferate, and Oshima assembles them with an intellectual rigour the more remarkable because their interior logic is as unassailable as the prison doctor's whimsical idea that they are all ultimately murderers, since the execution of R involves them in an endless retributory spiral. . . . (p. 104)

Like the boy in *Boy,* R confronts reality only after he has first created and then destroyed a fantasy. Imagination continually alters our idea of reality; or in other words, the conflict between the State and the individual can be resolved not by a single revolutionary act (like the book-stealing in *Shinjuku Thief*) but by a continuing revolutionary process—and so can never be resolved. R lets himself be hanged again for his crime only when he is certain of his innocence; the relationship between the State and the individual depends on that kind of contradiction.

R's crime is personal and only implicitly political (and of course sexual; the idea of sex as a symbolic act is as important here as it is in *Shinjuku Thief*), but the Korean girl he accepts as his sister interprets it as an explicit political act—an act of retribution by the Korean minority in Japan for their years of repression by the Japanese. . . .

As we have come to expect of Oshima's films, *Death by Hanging* repeatedly turns arguments on their head. And in doing so it throws up a challenge (developed further in *Shinjuku Thief*) to the very nature of our conception of what is truth and what merely fiction. Not least in the final acknowledgment of the presence of an audience, which prompts a question about the reality of film *qua* film that only a close analysis of its elaboration in *Shinjuku Thief* could begin to answer. (p. 105)

> *David Wilson, "Film Reviews: 'Death by Hanging',"* in Sight and Sound *(copyright © 1971 by The British Film Institute), Vol. 40, No. 2, Spring, 1971, pp. 104-05.*

### PETER COWIE

Oshima's [*The Man Who Left His Will on Film* and *The Ceremony*] represent the two directions of his thinking. *The Man Who Left His Will on Film* is totally absorbed in the student struggle for power in the Tokyo of the late Sixties, and its style is correspondingly harsh and febrile, like *Shinjuku Thief. The Ceremony,* however, has the formal appeal of emotions recollected, sifted, assessed. . . .

*The Man Who Left His Will on Film* is in black-and-white, and shot mostly with a hand-held camera. *The Ceremony* is in scope and colour, its starched gatherings recalling Ozu. Yet both films are obsessed with suicide. . . . In the earlier work, Oshima is using film as a weapon, creating a powerful dialectic in the conversations between Motoki and his girl friend Yasuko until the truth . . . seems impossible to disentangle from illusion. In *The Ceremony,* Oshima emphasises the artificial atmosphere of much Japanese ceremonial, which allows the inhibited national spirit to accept militarism and xenophobia—feelings that in daily life would be rejected.

"For me," says Oshima, "The question of how to die in the Seventies is an answer to the question of how to live." With these two films, he shows himself to be the first director who can reflect the contemporary mood of protest while understanding the legacy of the past.

> *Peter Cowie, "'The Man Who Left His Will on Film' and 'The Ceremony',"* in International Film Guide 1972, *edited by Peter Cowie (copyright © 1971 by The Tantivy Press), Tantivy Press, 1972, p. 184.*

### JUDITH CRIST

[*The Ceremony*] is strictly for cineastes who can justify all sorts of incoherencies and inanities in the name of cult. This endless melodrama is, despite an interesting scene or two, strictly from the schmaltz-soap had-I-but-known school, and if its saga of the Sakurada family, recalled by a grandson who winds up its sole survivor, is a parable of Japanese history from 1946 to the present, it is a convoluted and tedious one. (p. 75)

> *Judith Crist, "Roadside Refreshment,"* in New York Magazine *(copyright © 1974 by News Group Publications, Inc.; reprinted with the permission of* New York Magazine*), Vol. 7, No. 6, February 11, 1974, pp. 74-5.**

### VINCENT CANBY

[For about one-third of its running time] **"Death by Hanging"** is a surprisingly uproarious contemplation of the moral issues involved in capital punishment. The prison officials, prosecutors, chaplain and witnesses argue back and forth and pick at each other with a Lewis Carroll sort of purposeful, cross illogic. . . .

As long as **"Death by Hanging"** sticks to capital punishment, it is, in its absurd way, provocative and entertaining. But the film's interests keep widening, its methods become increasingly, arbitrarily Godardian (read Brechtian), until it reaches a point of total confusion. . . .

Kafka, Freud and some other weighty presences are evoked by Mr. Oshima as straight editorializing, through Godardian monologues. One of R's problems is that he loved his sister, which doesn't seem to have a great deal to do with legalized murder and capital punishment.

Some of it is funny. More of it is tedious, and a lot of it curiously old-fashioned, even though it reminds us of the great Godard films of the mid-nineteen-sixties. Extreme movie styles date more quickly than hemlines.

> *Vincent Canby, "Oshima Work Brings Memory of Godard,"* in The New York Times *(© 1974 by The New York Times Company; reprinted by permission), February 15, 1974 (and reprinted in* The New York Times Film Reviews: 1973-1974, *The New York Times Company & Arno Press, 1975, p. 176).*

### RUTH McCORMICK

If we accept T. W. Adorno's assertion that the only choice open to a politically committed artist at this stage in history is to create a negative art, then Nagisa Oshima's *The Ceremony* must be considered a profoundly revolutionary work. Using as his metaphor a large, bourgeois family, Oshima seeks to analyze the nature of authoritarianism. On one level, the film can be seen as a study of this authoritarianism as manifest in the traditional Japanese family and, on another, as an exploration of the totality of postwar Japanese experience during the years 1946 to 1971.

One of the key aspects of traditional Japanese society is the fetishization of ritual; there is a set 'way' in which certain things are done, according to time-honored custom. Another is paternalism, which extends from veneration of the Emperor as father-figure to the whole nation to the recognition of the absolute supremacy of the senior male in the family. A third element is a spirit of resignation, an attitude of "it can't be helped", which lies at the root of the Japanese preoccupation with suicide and death.

It is with the above that *The Ceremony* is concerned, and with the fact that they can exist side by side with the vigorous pragmatism and commercial mindedness of the 'new' Japan. The film works on a psychological level by showing the contradiction between the highly formalized rituals in which the Sakurada family participates and the explosive encounters between family members—a dialectic of repression and rebellion. On the historical level, individuals in the family are analogous to various classes and character types in Japanese society and the interaction between them can be paralleled by political developments within the country. (p. 21)

If we look at *The Ceremony* from a purely aesthetic standpoint, it is a stately, beautiful, strangely entertaining prophecy of doom. (p. 25)

On the surface, *The Ceremony* seems to offer no escape for Masuo, the rebels in the Sakurada family, the Japanese, or, implicitly, any of us, from impotence in the face of the status quo. The only discordant note in what might otherwise be compared to a Greek tragedy is Masuo himself. He is an infuriating character, a real 'loser,' . . . a self-pitying bundle of 'ifs,' a totally negative creature. But he is the key to the film for the simple reason that he can remember and can use his imagination.

The readiness to die that is so much part of the traditional Japanese mentality is not just a religious phenomenon or the result of internalized aggression. The death wish is also the negation of the tension which is life. Like Eros, the life instinct, the death instinct seeks gratification and thereby the end of desire. This double-edged desire is consummated by Masuo's father, Setsuko, Terumichi and Ritsuko, in their ability to make love and to die. Tadashi, samurai who fetishizes death, also realizes his desire, failed as it is. What none of the aforementioned characters realize is their desire to become self-determining subjects of their own lives. They must die in order to escape the family.

Only Grandfather and Masuo, his legitimate though unlikely heir, do not 'die' in the sense that the others do. Grandfather's relationships with women are in the realm of domination, not Eros; as ruler, his desires are reality. Masuo, on the other hand, is totally impotent. His memories represent his totality in its unfolding moments, a history of unrealized desire, both sexual and political. But only he can dream and it is in fantasy that things are seen not as they are in the present but as they *could* be. (pp. 25-6)

Masuo's infatuation with baseball, rather than with Grandfather's business, makes him analogous to the artist, the vi-

sionary, the revolutionary. His powerlessness and inability to become a subject make him the ally of all the oppressed. In his quest for the maternal and his rejection of the 'practically useful,' Masuo can negate things as they are. His vision at the end of the film, after he has thoroughly exhausted the possibilities of past and present, is of himself as pitcher in a game with Terumichi as catcher, Ritsuko at bat, Tadashi as shortstop, under the happy supervision of Setsuko. His dream is an expression of his desire for rational action, sexual fulfillment, mutual understanding, and maternal warmth, a desire for solidarity with those he loves against the impossibilities of the existing order. A dream of the future is an essential element of hope, and rational theory, mediated by aesthetic imagination, can lead, perhaps, to a real revolutionary praxis. . . .

Never didactic or moralistic, Oshima doesn't preach. Glib slogans, rhetorical optimism and exhortations to victory are not for him. He presents us with seemingly insoluble problems and invites us to solve them. If his films are difficult making a revolution is more so. He flatly refuses to offer us any consolation that might reconcile us to the present, and attacks the dominant ideology to the point where it appears totally naked, stripped of all its false promises. It is in this absolute refusal to celebrate the status quo—or to give up hope that we can free ourselves from it—that his importance as a political artist lies. (p. 26)

*Ruth McCormick, "Ritual, the Family and the State: A Critique of Nagisa Oshima's 'The Ceremony'," in* Cinéaste *(copyright © 1974 by Gary Crowdus), Vol. VI, No. 2, 1974, pp. 21-6.*

**LAWRENCE VAN GELDER**

[The voice-over commentary on **"Diary of a Yunbogi Boy"**] smacks of an inept pastiche of the late Jimmy Cannon. . . .

**"Diary of a Yunbogi Boy"** seeks to stroke the fires of rebellion with the lump in the throat that presumably arises in the presence of what is intended to be a touching study of an impoverished Korean boy.

With all its drawbacks, looking at [Godard's] "Letter to Jane" after watching **"Diary of a Yunbogi Boy"** is almost like standing in the presence of a Rembrandt after being exposed to one of those hollow-eyed Keane paintings.

*Lawrence Van Gelder, "Comment on Stills," in* The New York Times *(© 1974 by The New York Times Company; reprinted by permission), April 12, 1974 (and reprinted in* The New York Times Film Reviews: 1973-1974, *The New York Times Company & Arno Press, 1975, p. 158).*

**CLAIRE JOHNSTON**

[Oshima] is perhaps the film-maker most actively concerned with the political and social implications of [the] upheaval in Japanese life during the last twenty years or so; all his films centre on the experience of young people and their inability to come to terms with the prevailing values of society. Oshima's characters live out the tensions that exist not only in Japanese society, but in all capitalist societies, which makes him one of the most important directors to have emerged in the past decade. . . .

[All Oshima's early work] falls within the teenage gangster *genre*, well-fitted for expressing his central preoccupations. In fact, all his films revolve around either a criminal way of life or a criminal act of some kind; for Oshima, crime expresses a working through of a profound and disquieting social disorganisation. . . .

[Oshima's early films] have a documentary conception, most of them being based on fact, and there is an attempt to distance the audience from any identification with the protagonists. . . . If *The Sun's Burial* conveys the hopelessness and terror arising from the dislocation in Japanese life, *The Catch* goes one step farther to explore the traditional Japanese community and its implicit value system, laying bare Japanese responsibility for the war. Oshima sees Japanese nationalism as irredeemable. The "otherness" of the Black is only an extreme case; the community is shown to have contempt and hatred for any outsider. . . . (p. 183)

*The Catch* represents Oshima's most angry and outspoken rejection of traditional values. The film suggests that the solution lies in achieving a completely new mode of being, and Oshima sees the only real hope for this resting with the young. Throughout the film, he places great emphasis on the children of the community and shows how they witnessed the entire proceedings. In the last image of the film a young boy moves away from the communal fire and builds a small fire of his own, a gesture of defiance that also hints at the possibility of change and renewal. (p. 184)

All Oshima's later films make use of illusion and fantasy as the means for exploring his interests in greater depth. . . . *Death by Hanging* starts with a painstaking account of execution by hanging in the manner of the conventional anti-capital punishment film, the story being inspired by an actual murder case. . . . By using a variety of interpretations of events that in themselves exist on entirely different levels of reality, Oshima succeeds in bringing into question the moral assumptions on which the execution is based. The representatives of Japanese bureaucracy such as the education officer, the priest and the doctor, are depicted as being trapped in their own specialist mentality and devoid of any social responsibility.

Oshima sees the Korean as a victim of Japanese imperialism who exists entirely in a world of fantasy; characteristically he chooses to be hanged at the end. In its alienation techniques, *Death by Hanging* owes much to *kabuki* theatre and to Brecht. . . . (pp. 184-85)

[In *Diary of a Shinjuku Thief*], as in *Death by Hanging,* Oshima does not set out simply to put forward one single viewpoint. What does emerge is the stress on the importance of the fantasy life to break through to a new mode of being. Oshima sees the failure of the older generation as being essentially a failure of imagination. (p. 186)

The formal eclecticism of Oshima's recent films, *The Ceremony* and *Dear Summer Sister,* demonstrate clearly the extent to which he has sought to reject the traditions of the Japanese cinema. The highly formalised, basically theatrical conception of *The Ceremony* contrasts sharply with the deliberately crude, home-movie quality of *Dear Summer Sister,* yet both films deal with a theme that has dominated Oshima's work over the last few years—the idea of what is Japan and what it means to be Japanese. (p. 187)

[Oshima's films] mark the arrival of a genuinely revolutionary cinema in Japan, a cinema that embodies the collective fantasies of postwar Japanese society. Oshima has stated that the realisation of unconscious desire is a necessary condition for revolutionary change. In founding his notion of cinema on the levels of the unconscious, the ideological and the formal itself, Oshima has gone a considerable way towards founding a revolutionary cinema for his country. (p. 188)

Claire Johnston, ''Nagisa Oshima,'' in Fifty Major Film-Makers, *edited by Peter Cowie (© 1975 by Peter Cowie), A. S. Barnes & Co., Inc., 1975, pp. 183-88.*

**STEPHEN HEATH**

[*Dear Summer Sister*] seems far from distanciation, seems to rely on identification, seems to aspire to a straightforward continuity (conventional—'academic'—editing), seems to have a simple narrative thread, and so on. Yet the film is also, and this is part of its interest, against these things insofar as it takes them as the point of the demonstration politically of the contradictions of a particular social reality. (p. 43)

*Dear Summer Sister* itself turns on history lessons—the reality of Japan in its development as 'world power'—and a history lesson, that of Sunaoko, the little sister who arrives in Okinawa to find her brother and who ends on the beach ('Miss Prosecutor') by demanding ('for my education, tell me') to know the truth. Lesson and truth, however, are not simple: at every step there are contradictions and the film 'blocks together' in a multiple heterogeneity. . . . The political comment—on Japanese war crimes and the continuing power of those responsible, on Japanese imperialism, on the exploitation of Okinawa—is clear and then at the same time difficult; the summer holiday—the strange language, the songs, the visit to the monument (with a shaky hand-held 'holiday movie' passage), the drive through the streets (Sunaoko questioning her father, the Judge, about the brothels)—and the summer visitors are constantly reinscribed politically but that political reinscription is then again constantly re-reinscribed, thought back into the family, into individual relations. The question of the film is 'what is it to be Japanese today?', and that question is *historical,* and that history includes the inscription of the subject, includes desire, sexuality, but politically. (pp. 43-4)

Stephen Heath, ''From Brecht to Film: Theses, Problems,'' in Screen (© The Society for Education in Film and Television 1976), Vol. 16, No. 4, Winter, 1975-76, pp. 34-45.*

**TONY RAYNS**

None of Oshima's films looks or behaves much like any of the others, and *In the Realm of the Senses* establishes yet another new tonality in his work. . . . At first, it is as if Oshima were endorsing his characters' rhapsodic isolation by enshrining it in a form that permits no other frame of reference. A vein of fatalism in the plotting reinforces this impression, giving the film the air of a self-fulfilling prophecy: Kichi's willing surrender to death is anticipated in two earlier couplings in which he thinks his partner has died, and several prominent appearances of knives and razors prefigure the climactic act of castration.

In fact, of course, Oshima challenges this complacency as surely as he challenged the supposed naturalism of *Boy.* The obvious authenticity of the lovemaking is offset by the unreality of Sada's insatiable demands and Kichi's hypervirility. (p. 37)

Locating the action of *In the Realm of the Senses* in 1936 determines the meaning of a number of incidental details, from the fact that the children harassing a tramp in the opening scenes are clutching miniature national flags to the presence of a squad of armed troops who briefly block Kichi's view as he waits for Sada; but it also makes the total absence of socio-political ideas from the film very striking. As Oshima has already demonstrated often (in the closing shot of *Death by Hanging*, for instance), absence can be as significant as presence.

However provocative such undercurrents may be—and it is clearly not accidental that Oshima should have made an ostensibly apolitical film at a time when Japanese political activists have lapsed into almost complete passivity—the film's primary force remains its exceptionally bold analysis of the implications of true sexual passion. . . . [Oshima] is interested in Sada and Kichi's sexuality precisely because it reflects the mainstream of the Japanese erotic tradition. . . . Much in the film—from the use of traditional music throughout to Sada's geisha trick of "laying" an egg from her vagina—evidences the acutely Japanese self-consciousness that makes Oshima's earlier work so troubled, and troubling. (p. 38)

> *Tony Rayns, "Tony Rayns on 'In the Realm of the Senses','" in* Film Comment *(copyright © 1976 by The Film Society of Lincoln Center; all rights reserved), Vol. 12, No. 5, September-October, 1976, pp. 37-8.*

## STEPHEN HEATH

The *intensity* of Oshima's work lies in a 'going beyond' of content that constantly breaks available articulations of 'form' and 'content' and poses the film in the hollow of those breaks. The films have an immediate presence of narrative articulation but that presence in each case presents the absence of another film the discourse of which, punctuating this film and its space, finds its determinations, its contradictions, its negativity. Split *in* the narrativisation, the films are thus out of true with—out of 'the truth' of—any single address: the subject divided in complexes of representation and their contradictory relations. (p. 109)

The work of Oshima is political and obliquely political, a return of the one on the other through questions posed to meanings, images, fictions of unity, the questions of subject relations and transformations. (p. 110)

> *Stephen Heath, "Narrative Space," in* Screen *(© The Society for Education in Film and Television 1976), Vol. 17, No. 3, Autumn, 1976, pp. 68-112.\**

## RUTH McCORMICK

In [*In the Realm of the Senses*], we witness a relationship between two people, who neither put on an exhibitionistic show for us, nor make us feel embarrassed that we may be spying on them. This, to my mind, is a major breakthrough in the depiction of eroticism in film. There is no fetishism of parts of the body; the sex scenes between the two, photographed from every conceivable angle, are never voyeuristic, and neither partner is objectified by the camera. In each scene, Oshima creates a total gestalt; the shots, mostly long and static, are composed so as to place the two protagonists at the center of simple, stunning settings, realistic without ever ceding to the peurile naturalism of most porno films. . . .

Some women have complained that the film's depiction of female sexuality—in that Sada is almost constantly the aggressor, the lover, whereas Kichi remains for the most part the passive recipient of her attentions—is a male fantasy. Now, while I doubt most men would object to receiving a certain amount of such attention, this is not the point. In the first place, in the context of the story, both as told in court by the real Sada and in Oshima's retelling, Sada was, in fact, the more aggressive. After all, it was indeed Kichi whose desire it was to receive death at the height of pleasure, while Sada chose to survive and, in fact, to continue her life of pleasure after four years of incarceration. Secondly, in most hardcore porno, it is the woman who is represented as the object of male lust, as the passive recipient of whatever the men choose to do to her or tell her to do. Sada's enthusiasm, her general control of the situation, could also be seen as a female fantasy. . . .

Kichi does indeed desire death, but not pain. When he finally asks Sada to kill him, he does so in a roundabout way (she had previously come *close* to strangling him to increase his pleasure at the moment of orgasm), saying, "If you start, don't stop. It hurts too much afterwards." Kichi sees death as a form of transcendence—the only one possible as a higher stage of the total sexual gratification he has already experienced. (p. 33)

Is *In the Realm of the Senses* political? In its almost total avoidance of the public sphere, what is its view of the world? Neither of the characters ever mentions the Emperor, the military, Manchuria, or in fact anything that does not relate directly to their intimate personal lives. How unlike most Japanese of their time they must have been! The point is made very clearly in one brief sequence, in which Kichi, strolling along the street on his way to meet Sada, totally ignores a battalion of marching soldiers, while other members of the populace greet them with cheers and waving flags. . . . The flags and uniforms have no relevance for Kichi; his erotic impulses remain totally unsublimated and so his death instinct is never channeled, as was the case with most Japanese men of the period, into any desire to kill, to conquer, to be a hero.

It could be argued, perhaps, that people like Sada and Kichi, so removed from the mainstream of society, are far from being revolutionaries. Perhaps, but they are certainly not potential counter-revolutionaries! Their self-involvement, their quest for gratification, childlike in many ways, becomes a moment of negation of the prevailing proto-fascist order. (pp. 33-4)

The aesthetic of *Senses* is deliberately and pervasively Japanese, 'purified' as it were, of Western influences. The photography is dark and, at the same time, luminous; this is a world of tatami, shuji and futons, of samisen and koto music. In the same sense, one could say that the pornography of the film is purified of any hint of the exhibitionism, objectification of 'work ethic' of its Western counterparts.

It is the interludes between Sada and Kichi's erotic bouts that hold the film together and give it its unique narrative texture, and these almost all feature either the elderly or children. . . .

The sequences involving the old people serve, as it were, as intimations of mortality, both presaging Kichi's death, and as reminders to the audience that they, too, will one day be old, and that sexuality exists as long as there is life—Eros always ends in Thanatos. If we are tempted to laugh at the sexuality of the old . . . , the only way we will escape the same situation is through the dubious good fortune, as with Kichi, of an early death. By the same token, the children serve, as they have before with Oshima, to represent life and renewal. . . . It would seem that in [the] last fantasy of Sada, that Kichi, as precious as he is to her, represents a death, while the little girl, an image perhaps of Sada herself, is life. She chooses life. In the dream, in the *promesse de bonheur* of childhood and play, lies the possibility of a liberating reality.

Herein lies the politics of Oshima's least 'political' film. At once the fulfillment of his wish to break the taboos set up by puritanical bourgeois civilization to ensure its own survival through sexual repression and the ideology of the family, it is, dialectically, a celebration of the life force and, in a period of political inactivity, when the forces of reaction seem to have won another temporary victory in our world, a glimpse of utopia. (p. 34)

> *Ruth McCormick, "'In the Realm of the Senses',"*
> *in* Cinéaste *(copyright © 1977 by Gary Crowdus),*
> *Vol. VII, No. 4, Winter, 1976-77, pp. 32-4.*

### MICHAEL SILVERMAN

[Ostensibly, *L'Empire des Sens (In the Realm of the Senses)*] can be seen as a fuck film; indeed, it is so explicit that it may never be shown in "respectable" art houses or at festivals subject to discreet censorship. Its spectacle inheres in the unremitting display of sexuality, so that an occasional exterior shot seems a lapse in concentration. . . . The lovers' pact is the unqualified prolongation of desire; and whereas in a romantic film . . . we understand that desire may be kept alive as memory which nourishes one partner after the other's death, here a lapse into sleep or a soft penis signal a point of absolute termination. Oshima's persistent narrowing denies any romantic or metaphysical gesture the opportunity of replacing the physical fact.

In part this critique of romantic desire and its replacement by the strictly sexual is marked by a restriction and isolation from any social network which might impinge upon sexual activity, making complicated demands. Thus, the woman's objection to the man's wife may be seen as a mark of traditional jealousy, but also as a wish to deny the husband a context apart from the absolutely sexual. (p. 58)

The film rigorously exposes the aim of possession: a placing of the other within a heavily restricted system of exchange, a construction of the object of desire as an enacting substitute for the fears of the self's own death. . . . Finally, the object of desire must die in order to insure the permanence of desire. This death is endlessly repeatable, constantly re-enforceable, and desire remains as a constantly affirmed element of the symbolic. . . .

In *L'Empire des Sens* the man's passivity renders him mysterious. As the object of desire he suggests depth of feeling which the woman, in the grip of obsession, cannot reach. At first his growing passivity seems intended to parallel the behavior prescribed for the traditional gentle lover of pillow books and poems; finally, though, he seems intent on preserving a mystery. (p. 60)

The severing of the penis and testicles after death . . . is an admission of desire's end, as well as a fetishizing of that desire's sign. Since the act is seen as pathetically insufficient, the mystery of desire has been preserved through death. We may suspect that the literal nature of possession in this instance permits the re-integration of the symbolic. . . . We may wish to say that desire for the possession of images cannot surely involve such extremity. . . . Still, we may be drawn by this film to put into question such problems as the preservation in wish form of a sexual and scopophilic imaginary, the role played by death in the economy of desire and the residence of the code of possession within various mental and social activities, including watching and talking about this extremely desirable film. (p. 61)

> *Michael Silverman, "Reviews: 'L'empire des sens',"*
> *in* Film Quarterly *(copyright 1977 by The Regents of the University of California; reprinted by permission of the University of California Press), Vol. XXX, No. 2, Winter, 1976-77, pp. 58-61.*

### JOAN MELLEN

[Oshima's *Boy*] is one of the bitterest satires ever to be made on the Japanese family. . . . Oshima argues, not that he is realistically representing a typical Japanese household, but that the entire situation symbolizes the essence of family life in Japan. The power relationships between parents and children, exaggerated through the outrageous fraud, are nevertheless meant to suggest those beneath the surface of all Japanese families. (p. 353)

The psychology of the typical young Japanese . . . is characterized by frustration and repression of one's deepest longings. Oshima's boy hero experiences each day a total violation of his personal integrity. He hates the cheating and fraud he is forced to perpetrate. But, recognizing the power of the family over his life, he says nothing. Pathetically, he is also intensely loyal to his parents. At first this may seem unrealistic, given their vicious exploitation of him. But they are all that he knows. . . . Oshima's choice of a ten-year-old was well calculated. By the age of ten the boy has already learned the extent to which he must conform; he has absorbed the rules of what it means to belong to a Japanese family. Yet he is young enough still to long for self-definition.

Oshima's use of atonal music creates a sense of discordance, another facet of this film's subtle departure from realistic naturalism. The music denotes a universe where natural order has been distorted. (p. 355)

In the character of the father Oshima offers not psychological realism but the spirit of the Japanese patriarch. In most households the sadism would not, of course, be so overt, but for Oshima it would be no less real. Behind the patriarch's authority Oshima finds the destruction of the young, inevitable in the family at this stage of Japan's social development.

The boy's psyche becomes so damaged that he begins to welcome the pain that comes to him from the accidents. So perverse has been his life experience that only suffering assures him of his normality, and indeed that he exists at all: "Even an ordinary child can say it hurts when it really hurts." Only pain allows him to feel like an ordinary child; the perverse has become the normal. In this scene the boy lies in a fetal position, highlighting the motif of his desire to return to the womb and so end his suffering. It involves a death wish as well, for if he ceased to exist, his suffering would thereby also end.

Oshima insistently rejects the sentimental approach to such subject matter adopted by his predecessors in the Japanese film. For us to weep for this boy would permit an easy catharsis. It would allow the audience relief without accepting the necessity of remedy. . . . The strongest comment Oshima will make is dispassionately to reveal that such abuse exists.

The airplane trip to Hokkaido the family takes near the end indicates that the fantasy life of the boy has all but encompassed his consciousness. He explains to his little brother, and seems almost to believe it, that the clouds are "monsters out of which men from outer space will appear." More than ever he reveals his need to be rescued. (p. 357)

With nowhere left for them to flee, and decreasing opportunities to ply their "trade," the violence within the family becomes more extreme. Oshima records the man striking his wife, her blood spurting onto the snow, in black-and-white rather than color. As with sentimentality, he renounces spectacle, which he sees as antithetical to the ability of film as a medium to confront us with the truth. . . . [In] a clever use of irony, Oshima has the baby, unnoticed, step accidentally in front of a car which cannot stop on the ice. The meaning of their staged accidents is expressed in the family's actually becoming the victims themselves of a real accident, although only the boy is humane enough to face its consequences.

The car slams into a telephone pole, killing the driver, a young woman. For this real accident and death, however, only our boy, and not his parents, assumes responsibility, as if at an unconscious level he believes that his having tortured drivers with fake accidents and unreal wounds has brought down upon him, with this death, a just retribution. What he feels as he flings himself angrily on his father, the real culprit, is an acute sense of responsibility for the suffering of others, which his own pain has taught him in spite of the amorality of the environment provided by his family. The red boot in the snow, now photographed in color, reiterates the colors of the Japanese flag, red sun on white. For Oshima this symbol returns guilt and responsibility to where they finally belong, not solely to the man, part victim and part victimizer, but once more to the State and its institutions.

Oshima takes measure of the psychic damage done to this boy in the last moments of the film. . . . It is in this final response of the boy that Oshima pleads for the valuable humanity being trampled and ignored in today's Japan. The slowness of Oshima's last fade informs us of the permanence of the boy's memory of this gratuitous death. His sense of himself as a murderer, irrational though it may be, is the only legacy for the future bequeathed him by his now dissolved family. (p. 358)

The most uncompromising critic among Japanese directors of his nation's structures, Oshima remains obsessed by Japan and the Japanese, in himself and in those around him. The heightened emotion in his films comes not from any climactic dramatic developments in the action but from the director's continuous, silent lament over the default of a corrupt nation he yet loves. The tone of his films, particularly of *The Ceremony,* is as strikingly ambivalent as that of the American novelist William Faulkner toward the benighted denizens of Yoknapatawpha County, Mississippi. . . .

Masuo, says Oshima, running an allegorical second story-line alongside that of his characters, represents all young Japanese forced after the War to submit to the institutions of the old Japan rapidly undergoing resurrection. Masuo, as a child, is already a participant in the first ceremony of the film, funeral rites for his dead father. The boy's hand is guided by his grandfather's in making the offering, a magnificent allegorical expression of the reconstituted old *zaibatsu,* or ruling class, appropriating the energies of all young Japanese almost at the moment the War ended. . . .

Oshima sees distorted sexuality as the inevitable consequence of political and social repression. The seductive aunt, Setsuko,

insisting on washing the eleven-year-old Masuo, has herself been seduced and sullied by the grandfather. Oshima makes it clear that she never washes her own daughter, Ritsuko, so feelingly. Setsuko finds an unnatural outlet for her thwarted sexual energies among her young nephews, for her opportunities for relationships with eligible men are as negligible as those of women under feudalism. (p. 361)

Before the character for "The End" appears, Oshima allows the screen to go black, offering no image. Any hope for a different, freer Japan has been lost. Moral defeat, like a dark cloud, has finally consumed those who saw the need for change. *The Ceremony* . . . chronicles the moral consequences of a neo-feudal epoch of prosperity following the early postwar period. And it is finally only Oshima who has placed the story of the Japanese family in its appropriate historical context. (p. 366)

[For Oshima, if the student revolts in *Diary of a Shinjuku Burglar*] accomplish only for a moment a demystification of Japan's "cherry blossom" identity, they have achieved something positive. Birdey and Umeko are not yet sexually free, just as Japan has not yet been liberated from her past. In how the two are inextricably connected lies the logic of *Diary of a Shinjuku Burglar.* But the film remains a minor work because the allegory is so much more interesting than its surface action.

Oshima also portrays the lost youths of the student movement in *The Man Who Left His Will on Film.* Self-referential in style, its circular plot at once suggesting inhibition that can find no release, the "story" is that of a student filmmaker who films his own suicide and then kills himself at the end of the film by jumping from a building. Oshima's only apparent "contribution" lies in the shot of the boy's actual death. . . . The effect is as if Oshima were offering us so authentic a work that it was actually entrusted to him by his own central character.

Any causal explanations for the death, however, as in Godard, must be provided through active participation by the audience itself in piecing together the boy's footage, which is randomly projected. Oshima leaves the chronology of events in as subtly elaborate a disarray as Alain Resnais did his in *Last Year at Marienbad.* He demands of his Japanese audience that it confront what has befallen the restless youths of the New Left, who have moved without purpose or direction through the new Japan despite the fury of their political protests. (pp. 368-69)

At the end of *The Man Who Left His Will on Film* a hand grabs the camera from the dead boy. Another man is about to assume the task of filming the meaning of his life. Just as the demonstrations at the end of *Diary of a Shinjuku Burglar* did not mean that the revolution was at hand, this film equally suggests the need for a permanent, ongoing struggle in which the first step must be attainment of greater self-knowledge on the part of these students. The man who picks up the camera and would take the hero's place may not end his life in an ineffectual suicide. His quest for truth may not fill him with the hopelessness experienced by Motoki, Oshima's hero. The camera's new owner may in fact see the revolution through to a further stage.

Oshima leaves us with a cacophony of images, debates, dreams, and fantasies. They reveal the trauma of the young in Japan, desperately opposed to the policies of an authoritarian state, yet incapable of creating a meaningful political opposition with which ordinary Japanese could identify. For such a bewildered generation, who have turned to tormenting each other, suicide becomes a ready option. Even the landscape of the revolution now seems uncertain, whether it will occur on the quiet middle-class streets photographed by Motoki, or amid violent demonstrations, as his radical friends would have us believe. Chronology has been so reversed as to make it impossible for us to reconstruct the action in a linear manner because any single solution to Japan's problems does not seem ready to hand. Like the deserted highway on which Motoki's girlfriend is raped and beaten, Japan has become a no-man's land. Everyone has been cast forth in isolation and without solace, with even the would-be revolutionaries sufficiently diverted to believe that their enemies are each other rather than the all-powerful State. (pp. 369-70)

> *Joan Mellen, "The Structures of Oshima," in her* The Waves at Genji's Door: Japan through Its Cinema *(copyright © 1976 by Joan Mellen; reprinted by permission of Pantheon Books, a Division of Random House, Inc.), Pantheon Books, 1976, pp. 353-72.*

## STANLEY KAUFFMANN

[The intent of *In the Realm of the Senses*], as the title indicates, is to submerge us in a sea of sensuality. Two professionals of sex are surprised, after their extensive experience, by the intensity of their response to each other. They move, almost transcendentally, to the utmost limits of physical experience, until he wants to die, in the literal as well as Elizabethan meaning, and she seals off their union at its height, so to speak, by severing his penis (with his dreamy consent). . . .

[The] idea of the film exists in one place, figuratively, the film in another, and there is a great gap between. First, it's full of heavy symbolism. Example: when the man first meets the woman, she is quarreling with another woman and has a knife in her hand; he laughs and says she should have something else in her hand. Second, the color photography is of the most blatantly Beautiful kind—dime-store shades of red and gold, unsubtle contrasts—and the compositions could not be more corny. . . . Third, because of our constant awareness of various contrivances, we never do sink into the sea: we watch. And merely to watch a series of sexual encounters in an allegedly serious film soon gets as dull as watching such encounters in unpretentious porn.

Far from being any kind of love story, as the two characters claim, and as some outside the picture have claimed, *Realm* registers only as the record of physiological coincidence: a woman of insatiable appetite meets a man of indefatigable potency. The fancy décor, the geisha trimmings, the cinematic attitudinizing don't elevate it beyond a demonstration of stamina that finally reaches the pathological.

And that last prolonged moment of amputation is unwatchable. . . . *Realm* has been only in the realm of the clinical for some time before the finish, varnished with the glibly poetical. So here the amputation is not only sickening, it's sententious! . . .

*Realm* is *at best* a sentimentally fallacious film, an Oriental *Elvira Madigan* undressed, exalted for some by its closeups of screwing. (p. 26)

> *Stanley Kauffmann, "Senses and Nonsenses" (reprinted by permission of Brandt & Brandt Literary Agents, Inc.; copyright © 1977 by Stanley Kauffmann), in* The New Republic, *Vol. 177, No. 27, July 2, 1977, pp. 26-7.\**

## JOAN MELLEN

[At the heart of Nagisa Oshima's **"In the Realm of the Senses"**] lie impulses quite foreign both to the Western approach to sexuality and to pornography. . . . [He] is here evoking an uninhibited, joyous sensuality which is said to have flourished in 10th-century Japan as an intrinsic part of an aristocratic culture in which people dedicated themselves to the appreciation of lovemaking, free of inhibition or anxiety; it was a mood reinvoked for the last time in the flurry of pleasure-seeking just prior to the opening of Japan to the West. . . .

Oshima's Sada and Kichizo [are] survivors of a world of sexual refinement long since lost by the 1930's—the period in which **"In the Realm of the Senses"** is set. Sada and Kichizo pursue the pleasure that was possible in that ancient and more beautiful Japan, heroically unwilling to allow themselves to be repressed by the culture of their own time, one in which Japan has already invaded Manchuria. Oshima suggests that sex in this old Japan was pure, divorced from psychopathology and Oedipal burdens, transcending social class. The body was as important as the spirit. He defies the premise at the heart of [Bertolucci's] "Last Tango in Paris" (to which **"In the Realm of the Senses"** has been mistakenly compared) that we bring all that we are and have been to the act of love. In Oshima's vision, equality is at the heart of Japanese sensuality.

Sada begins as a maid in the brothel run by Kichizo and his wife. . . . Later she becomes the dominant partner [in their sexual encounters]. . . . Social position is of no relevance to the relationship between lovers.

Kichizo first approaches Sada holding a sprig of cherry blossoms, Oshima's signal that we are exploring a last flowering of authentic Japanese culture in which sensuality was sufficient unto itself, sex neither mystical nor dirty. The Japanese, says Oshima, were once capable of love without shame. As opposed to the natural Japan of the past, the modern world in which Sada and Kichizo are called "perverts" because they never cease making love is ruled by militarists; the year is 1936, that of the famous aborted Officers' Coup which finally strengthened the army's stranglehold over the country. This fascism of the 30's Oshima depicts in terms of a denial of the senses. . . .

In its uniquely Japanese approach to love, **"In the Realm of the Senses"** utterly transcends Western pornography, even though we are witnesses to the sexual act. . . . [The] love scenes focus on the sexual ecstasy of the *woman*, the pleasure in which she is an active participant rather than a victim. The male feels no need to exhibit excesses of masculinity in violence. The eroticism is based not on the woman's being humiliated or overwhelmed, but upon mutual abandon. . . .

With reverence, Oshima invokes the Sada who in real life became a national figure precisely because she recreated that old Japan in which nothing about the body was felt to be disgusting and in which man and woman could alternately be givers and receivers of pleasure. In defiance of any pornographic impulse, the camera focuses on their faces or on their full figures, refusing to allow the viewer to play the role of salacious voyeur. Vicarious pleasure would indeed be perverse; such satisfaction can be ours only if we become as uninhibited as are Sada and Kichizo themselves. . . .

The ending, in which Sada strangles and then dismembers Kichizo, is disturbing, but no evocation of de Sade is intended, Sada's name notwithstanding. Oshima imitates the rupture of conventional vision practiced by Bunuel, who, in the opening shot of 'Un Chien Andalou,'' slit open an eyeball with a razor. But Kichizo's death is freely chosen as a gift to his lover, that she may "be happy strangling me." . . . Violence has been only one element of a love affair which has also included playfulness, patient good will and joy, and Sada emasculates Kichizo with a carving knife not out of anger or hatred, but to unite herself with a lover now immune to suffering. . . .

Sada and Kichizo are liberated, holy and sanctified, from a Japan which can no longer understand them, free from a tradition which associates sex with shame. In Sada, the sensuality of the old Japan lives on, as the real-life Sada devoted herself to further pursuits of pleasure after her four-year jail sentence expired.

Like the Japanese audience for whom Oshima has made his film, so remote are we from undiluted sensuality that much of **"In the Realm of the Senses"** becomes almost intolerable to watch. But, at its best it presents a striking picture of that bygone era of Japanese culture in which pornography was inconceivable and sensuality flourished, immune to any sense of sin or shame or guilt.

> *Joan Mellen, ''Is 'Senses' in the Realm of Pornography?'' in* The New York Times *(© 1977 by The New York Times Company; reprinted by permission), July 31, 1977 (and reprinted in* The New York Times Film Reviews: 1977-1978, *The New York Times Company & Arno Press, 1979, p. 84).*

### JOHN SIMON

[Too much of a muchness is one of the problems] with *In the Realm of the Senses,* although that is only one trouble with Nagisa Oshima's dreadful movie. . . .

[Oshima] has tried to tell a story about a man and a woman who love each other with such an insane passion that, as it becomes ever more fanatical and all-consuming, nothing will satisfy it except death. Well, why not? Such tales have been a staple of literature since narration began. . . . But Oshima set out to do something more difficult: to concentrate almost entirely on the two lovers, show their passion in constant close-up, as it were, and deal with the matter realistically, head on. A gallant conception, but one for which he is quite the wrong man, having neither the artistry nor the psychological insight. (p. 53)

It will not do, I think, to talk of cultural differences and the inscrutable East. . . . Nor will I be swayed by the contention that Oshima looks at passion dispassionately, and so deliberately keeps the temperature level down. In the first place, any number of needlessly graphic details leave little doubt about Oshima's pornographic intentions; in the second, what would be the point of making a film about passion in which one set out *not* to convey what passion is like? As soon make a film about beauty in which all the sights are ugly.

Rather, judging by several other films of his as well, Oshima strikes me as a profoundly untalented director who can even take such fascinating material as that which went into his movie *Boy* and come up with only one or two scenes that have any life in them. . . .

[An] able director would have understood that the film, for aesthetic as well as psychological reasons, cannot be all sex scenes, many of them involving group sex or exhibitionistic copulations before various observers, unless there were other things revealed to us about the principals as well. But no such information is forthcoming, and we might as well be expected to care about the obsessions of cockroaches. . . .

You might hope for some humor to relieve the aridity, or even to provide some ironic commentary. Well, the most Oshima can muster is Kichizo's comment after Sada eats some of his pubic hair, ''Careful, you'll grow a beard.'' . . .

If indeed this were a story about passion that could find its fullest expression only in death—as it is being touted—then, surely, some kind of joint *Liebestod* would be in order at the end. Instead, we get, in hideous detail, Sada's [act of murder and castration]. . . . Clearly there is vindictiveness and perversion at work here rather than romantic heightening.

It is typical of Oshima's feeble imagination that he ends his film here, where he ought to have started it. For if anything could have been interesting, it would have been the trial: What the woman said, why they acquitted her, how she became a national heroine, and how, if at all, she made good on ''the two of us forever.'' Instead, we get this inept attempt at pornography that would justify its failure at eroticism by calling itself art. (p. 54)

> *John Simon, ''Eye Poppers,'' in* New York *Magazine (copyright © 1977 by News Group Publications, Inc.; reprinted with the permission of* New York *Magazine), Vol. 10, No. 32, August 8, 1977, pp. 53-4.\**

### PETER COWIE

The disdainful reviews meted out to [*Ai no borei* (*Empire of Passion*)] are surely related to the film's gravity of expression, by comparison with the sex and violence of *Ai no corrida* [*In the Realm of the Senses*]. Oshima has moved further back in time (the earlier film took place in the Thirties) to a Nineteenth-century setting. . . . But the dictates of Japanese formalism where period works are concerned have not inhibited Oshima's sense of outrage. There is a fury that burns like a bright diamond at the heart of *Ai no borei,* and Seki and Toyoji live passionately to their last gasp. As Oshima says, in their reluctance to rebel, there dwells a curious strength.

These lovers are unhinged by the ghost of the man they have conspired to kill, and Oshima [creates] an oneiric atmosphere, in which dream and actuality merge. He introduces an element of surrealism by forcing one to watch the murdered man's body tumble in slow-motion into a gigantic pit, engulfing the camera. Death and sexual ecstasy are intertwined. (pp. 218-19)

In the final analysis, the ghost story is only an idiom for Oshima. His prevailing interest is in the impossibility of free love in a social grid. Seki may be sufficiently swept away by passion to acquiesce in the murder of her husband, but as his ghost assails her, and she shelters behind a bank of protective fires, she exclaims to Toyoji that she wants to live ''like a couple.'' . . . Guilt is ranged against desire, death against life. The lovers in *Ai no borei* . . . perish at the hands of a community that is insignificant beside their rage for experience. (p. 219)

> *Peter Cowie, '''Ai no borei' ('Empire of Passion'),'' in* International Film Guide 1979, *edited by Peter Cowie (copyright © 1978 by Thomas Yoseloff Ltd.), The Tantivy Press, 1979, pp. 218-19.*

### J. HOBERMAN

Nagisa Oshima's *Empire of Passion* is being promoted as the companion piece to his 1976 cause celebre, *In the Realm of the Senses*. . . . [They] both grimly depict the wages of sex as death. But whereas the marathon claustro-carnality of the earlier film made it a monumental, half-cracked tour-de-force—the *La Region Central* of hardcore porn—*Empire of Passion* is a banal, meandering will-o'-the-wisp. . . .

*Empire of Passion* begins promisingly but, like an unwelcome guest, grows simultaneously shriller and more sluggish as it edges towards the door. Oshima makes elaborate use of the changing seasons; there are a half dozen striking shots (mostly taken from the bottom of the well where the unquiet corpse has been pitched); but the bottom line is a botched James M. Cain plot with a less-than-eerie overlay. *The Rickshaw Man Always Rings Twice*, one colleague called it. Would that twice were all it was.

> *J. Hoberman, "Sympathy for the Devil" (reprinted by permission of* The Village Voice *and the author; copyright © News Group Publications, Inc., 1980), in* The Village Voice, *Vol. XXV, No. 50, December 17, 1980, p. 82.\**

### ROBERT HATCH

Nagisa Oshima's *Empire of Passion* is a tale of sexual abandon, murder and retribution, set in a nineteenth-century Japanese village and filmed with a regard for the beauty of the seasons, of the rural structures and furnishings, and the persons of the main characters that place it at some esthetic remove from ordinary life. One views it as though turning the pages in a volume of splendid lithographs recording the stages of a distant tragedy. It is a ghost story, but haunting also in the larger sense that one succumbs to its influence as to the misty fragments of a dream. . . .

It is, you see, one of the oldest of stories, and Oshima does not embellish it with novelties. He relies on its capacity to arouse horror and pity whenever it is told with conviction, and devotes himself to invoking the tyranny of passion in surroundings of serene loveliness. Japanese conventions for the expression of high emotion can seem extravagant, hence shallow, to Western eyes. It is a measure of Oshima's sympathy for his couple, and distress over their intemperance, that their behavior, though clearly foreign to our manners, does not seem false. We accord them the same bittersweet grief that we feel for our own legendary lovers. (pp. 716-17)

> *Robert Hatch, "Films: 'Empire of Passion'," in* The Nation *(copyright 1980* The Nation *magazine, The Nation Associates, Inc.), Vol. 231, No. 22, December 27, 1980, pp. 716-17.*

# Pier Paolo Pasolini

## 1922-1975

Italian director, screenwriter, author, and actor.

Pasolini's films seek to combine his Marxist sensibilities with a deep, non-denominational spirituality. They are considered highly controversial, anti-Catholic, and autobiographical. Decrying social injustice, Pasolini attacks the capitalist concept of man as a merchandiser marketing his fellow man.

After a successful career in literature, Pasolini turned to cinema as a new means of expression. *Accattone,* his first film, expresses the theme of man's exploitation of women for personal gain. Like Pasolini's other heroes, Accattone has no immediate goal besides survival. *Accattone* is considered a graceful transition from literature to film, and has received praise more for its vibrant spirit and authenticity than its technical prowess.

Pasolini gained international acclaim with *The Gospel According to Saint Matthew.* All formalities previously peculiar to "Bible movies" disappeared: Pasolini instead chose a neo-realistic filming style that proves to be well suited to the film's quiet Renaissance spirit. While fascinated with the myth of Jesus, Pasolini hoped to probe beyond historic aspects in search of a simple, unadorned reality reflecting God's love.

In *Edipo Re (Oedipus Rex)* and *Medea,* Pasolini juxtaposed pagan mythology with contemporary philosophy. *Oedipus Rex* is his most personal film: Pasolini considered it the symbolic key to his own life. Like Oedipus, Pasolini saw himself as "one who lives his life as the prey of life and his own emotions." These films met with popular critical reception, in contrast with *Porcine (Pigsty)* and *Teorema.*

Both *Pigsty* and *Teorema* provide more contemporary views of society. They also introduce several characters, as opposed to the solitary perspective of earlier films. Here Pasolini's preoccupation with the failings of bourgeois society is acknowledged: these films are his most powerful social protests. While these are his first attempts to depict an actual cinematic reality, it is philosophical rather than naturalistic. Although *Teorema* won the International Catholic Film Office Award, it was later banned by the Vatican.

The trilogy of *The Decameron, The Canterbury Tales,* and *The Arabian Nights* signifies Pasolini's penchant for storytelling. Their reception was controversial due to their graphic content; however, many find their medieval bawdiness witty and refreshing. Pasolini considered them a final attack on Western European decadence and an accurate portrait of medieval life. Most critics find the trilogy visually lush but thematically empty.

Pasolini's last film, *Salo: 120 Days of Sodom,* culminated a controversial career. Based on the Marquis de Sade's novel *120 Days of Sodom, Salo* is a fierce depiction of Fascist Italy as well as a final, pained allegory of exploitative humanity. *Salo* was banned in Italy before appearing in the United States, but it is considered particularly noteworthy for its contrast between indecent subject and formalized style. While some critics find *Salo* perceptive and insightful, others have accused Pasolini of self-indulgence. Elliot Stein says, "It has as much to tell about what human beings are capable of as *Anna Karenina* . . . but Sade tells us more than we want to hear, and Pasolini shows us more than we want to see."

Pasolini considered *Salo* to be a film about the sadism of modern humanity. He felt that sexual sadism was a metaphor for class struggle and power politics. Shortly after the completion of the film, Pasolini was murdered. Of his own life he had said "I love life with such violence and intensity that no good can come of it. How it will end I don't know. . . ." (See also *Contemporary Authors,* obituary, Vols. 61-64.)

## ROBIN BEAN

The world of the Roman pimps and petty thieves has been well explored by Pasolini in his scripts for [Mauro Bolognini's] *La Notte Brava* and [Franco Rossi's] *Mort di un Amico.* For his first film as a director [*Accattone*] he returns to the same theme, because, as he wrote . . . not so long ago, 'I don't want to explore new ground in my themes but simply to express my ideas with a new technique'.

The question in my mind is, should an artist confine himself to one problem and if so can he really express his ideas in a fresh way taking into consideration the ever changing social structure?

The Pasolini characters and their motivations differ little from those of the two previous films, and the failing of both is again repeated here. Each is a sharp penetration into the Roman slums as they exist (or existed?) but never once is an attempt made to say why an audience should be concerned. The value of life is practically ignored, his characters stand for everything that is against society. Pasolini is content to blame everything on poverty and lack of education, but he does not show why we should care. All one can conclude from his work is that these people would be worthless *even* if they had the chance to improve themselves. . . .

The new technique that Pasolini thinks he has discovered has been used many times before. His stylised images and symbolism are too obvious. Why have Accattone and the girl he wants to save from the streets play out a scene neatly framed against a church? Why make Accattone a minor poet when he has little comprehension of life? . . .

[Franco] Citti's natural responsive performance is the highlight of the film, even though the character has nothing to recommend it. His world has no logic, but unfortunately the film hasn't any either.

*Robin Bean, "'Accattone'" (© copyright Robin Bean 1962; reprinted with permission), in* Films and Filming, *Vol. 8, No. 12, September, 1962, p. 33.*

## GEOFFREY NOWELL-SMITH

[*Accattone*] is a film about the rejects of society, in the active and passive senses of the phrase; about those whom society has rejected and those who have rejected society, or have never belonged or never wanted to belong. In this category is included, at least for the purposes of the film, almost the entire population of Pigneto, the Roman suburb which Pasolini used as a location for the shooting of *Accattone:* casual labourers, the unemployed, complete down-and-outs—the *morti da fame*—thieves, petty crooks, ponces and tarts. It is a tough world, with its own special rules for survival. . . .

[There] are films about the underworld, dozens of them, but there is no great mythology comparable to that of the gangster film of the American Thirties; nor has there been any attempt to look at this world realistically, in the way neo-realism looked at the organized working class. It is an absurd story of wasted material, material for myth as well as for a revolutionary social critique, in which Pasolini, by writing scripts to be realised in a perverted and insipid way by Bolognini and others, has passively acquiesced, and for which he is, in part at least, personally responsible. Now with *Accattone,* directed by Pasolini himself, suddenly it is all there, the social conflicts, the sexual tensions, the authentic violence and the curious but logical morality of the anti-society; not only the reality, but in the person of the central character, Accattone . . . , the makings of the great myth. This is not to say that *Accattone* is a particularly good film. . . . It is at times melodramatic; the camerawork is heavy, groping and obtrusive. But at least it is authentic and alive—not dead material animated by a master of marionettes, but alive from the bottom with the life of the subject. . . .

[One] should give Pasolini the credit for an attempt, obviously deliberate even if not entirely successful, to translate an original approach to his material into cinematic terms. If *Accattone* does not look like early Rossellini it is because Pasolini had, thank God, no intention of making it look like early Rossellini.

The real subject of *Accattone* is not the underworld as such, but Accattone himself and his relationships with the world. . . . (p. 193)

The whole substance of the film is in these relationships—and in the more sinister Mafia-like system which underlies them—and the film works outward from Accattone, across his contacts with the others, in ever-increasing ramifications towards a picture of the underworld itself, seen as a complex of material relationships between individuals and impersonal forces. But the outer rings of the circle, which in fact, according to Pasolini's Marxist outlook, condition whatever happens at the centre, are too distant and unfocused to play a vital part in the construction of the film. Even the physical background, the landscape of decrepit shacks, slum apartments and wastelands, is hardly more than sketched in. Only the people matter, and their concrete situations from one moment to the next. . . . Unfortunately the camera style, which reflects the preoccupation with the central character, moving outwards towards the group, picking up faces and cross-cutting between the characters, is often too heavy-handed, too self-conscious and deliberate, underlining the obvious and reducing each event to the status of a "point to be made". The natural and essential fluidity of the script is broken, and the film divided into a series of set-pieces.

The best scenes are those in which one is least conscious of the camera. . . . The big, staged scenes, like the beating up of Maddalena by a gang of Neapolitans with an account to settle, are less effective, and it is here that Pasolini's inexperience begins to drag and one starts to make nasty remarks about literary men playing at cinema (Pasolini is certainly a better novelist than director). But it appears that he has now decided to devote himself seriously to film-making. His next film could be very good indeed. (pp. 193-94)

*Geoffrey Nowell-Smith, "'Accattone'," in* Sight and Sound *(copyright © 1962 by The British Film Institute), Vol. 31, No. 4, Autumn, 1962, pp. 193-94.*

## ROBIN BEAN

[*Mamma Roma*] is one of the most vicious indictments of the complete insensitivity of human society as a corporate body to concern itself in a personal way with that element of society they regard as worthless because it has no money, little education, virtually no prospects. . . .

As a director, as a creator of expression in film, [Pasolini's] work in *Accattone* left me cold; and in that respect the same nearly happened with *Mamma Roma*—that conscious striving for effect, cynicism and bludgeoning 'truth' (ie pretentiousness). But here his theme, characters and ideas are so strong that it really doesn't matter. (p. 27)

As a director Pasolini creates an unstable balance of effect; the unconscious personal mannerisms are quietly observed, but his juxtaposing of images, particularly in his onslaught on the church and religious belief, are sometimes ineffectual in their crudity. But here, as opposed to *Accattone,* he does succeed in conveying that there are moments of poetic beauty even in poverty surroundings, that there is a tragic irony in the structure of society: the poor sometimes achieve the happiness that affluence fails to bring to others. It also has a wider view of humanity than his previous film, establishing that even if society is a savage machine, there is still a personal responsibility to improve: 'What one is, is one's own fault' says Mamma. Maybe in Pasolini, the cinema will find it's own Dostoievski: Poverty is a social disease which society regards as enigma; crime is met with harsh reprisal regardless of circumstances. (p. 28)

*Robin Bean, "Reviews of New Films: 'Mamma Roma'" (© copyright Robin Bean 1964; reprinted with permission), in* Films and Filming, *Vol. 10, No. 6, March, 1964, pp. 27-8.*

### PETER JOHN DYER

It is easy enough to pick holes in **Mamma Roma** as a cry of social protest. The plot, on the face of it, is mawkish. . . . The development is arbitrary, with Mamma Roma drunkenly confiding instalments of her past to a string of grinning men who loom conveniently in and out of the darkness as she roams the neon-lit highway. . . . And yet **Mamma Roma** expresses exactly and unsparingly what its writer-director, Pier Paolo Pasolini, feels: complete subjective identification with the latent fatalism of his characters. . . . I happen to find all this extraordinarily moving for the reason that such melodramatic situations are, for all that, elementally true. Pasolini's evasion of conventional realism strikes me as being deliberately used to underline a similar evasion on the part of his characters; just as his unintegrated camera style mirrors their underlying states of mind, all opportunism and casual brutality.

In its rhetorical way the film is a good deal more powerful and assured than **Accattone.** There is a gaunt, prophetic splendour about those recurring shots of wasteland dotted with ruined, twisted pinnacles of stone and brick. . . . Several of [Mamma and Ettore's] scenes together—dancing the tango; trying out a new motor-bike—have a curious cut-off quality which appears not only to circumscribe them but to divorce Pasolini himself from society. Artistically such uncompromising isolation can either make or yet undo him. So far, at any rate, it has been his proudest decoration.

> *Peter John Dyer, "In Brief: 'Mamma Roma',"* in
> Sight and Sound *(copyright © 1964 by The British Film Institute), Vol. 33, No. 2, Spring, 1964, p. 97.*

### STANLEY KAUFFMANN

Pasolini, the atheistic Communist, [has] beaten his opponents by making the best film about Jesus in cinema history. He has not given us a Marxist or merely humane Jesus; [**The Gospel According to St. Matthew**] is Matthew's Jesus. It might have been expected that Pasolini would act on Rousseau's advice: "Get rid of the miracles, and the whole world will fall at the feet of Jesus Christ." This film does not "get rid" of the miracles. Pasolini has woven them, seamlessly, into his earthy film. That is one of his triumphs. . . .

His film about Jesus has in a sense a spiritual connection with [**Accattone** and **Mamma Roma**] through his conviction (more Christian than Communist) that, if one believes certain basic principles, then no one—*not anyone at all*—may be rejected or despised. . . .

The film looks like a quasi documentary; none of the actors wears make-up, the lighting is often blunt, the film sometimes grainy. . . .

The artistic sources of Pasolini's film are clear. First, he is following in the tradition of all those painters of the Renaissance and after to whom the Gospel story was an event of their own lives and who used their family and friends and countryside to certify this fact. Second, he is continuing the Italian film tradition of neo-realism, extending it for the first time (so far as I know) into the historical—to cut through the religiosity of previous film treatments of the story and to emphasize Jesus as Man—the Incarnation.

The paradoxical result is that Pasolini's frank, vernacular texture achieves the religious spirit. (p. 33)

Unlike any other picture on the subject that I know, this film by the Communist Pasolini was made for only one reason: love of Jesus. The effect of this utterly simple truth is overwhelming. It informs every moment of the picture and makes it, even when it is flawed or slow, an extraordinary experience. . . .

Yet, despite the abundance of beauties, the film is slow and undramatic—as any film about Jesus must be. First, there is the stumbling-block of the sermons and lessons. What is a camera to do with them? . . .

Second, there is the matter of basic drama. . . . Each spectator brings with him some sort of attitude towards Jesus, of whatever shade of belief, but he also brings expectations of the film-form as such. A film that is faithful to the story may satisfy his religious sense if he has any, as Passion Plays have done for centuries; but it cannot satisfy his unconscious or conscious artistic expectations.

That fact will not, of course, stop future film-makers from attempting the subject again and again. At least Pasolini's work, faults and all, will serve as a standard of honesty in motive and simplicity in art. (p. 34)

> *Stanley Kauffmann, "Pasolini's Passion" (reprinted by permission of Brandt & Brandt Literary Agents, Inc.; copyright © 1966 by Stanley Kauffmann),* in
> The New Republic, *Vol. 154, No. 13, March 26, 1966, pp. 33-4.*

### PATRICK MacFADDEN

The genre [of **Uccelacci e uccellini (The Hawks and the Sparrows)**] is the picaresque. And very much the moral-pointing literary picaresque of Eulenspiegel or Simplicius Simplicissimus. This, Pasolini states quite openly, is the Journey of Life. The three parts into which the film is divided mark the stages of awareness of the human intellect. The parable is further underpinned by drawing on the fable tradition of La Fontaine. Father and son on their dusty journey play out the business of living; their attempts to come to terms with social reality are either equivocal or outright failures. But at the end of the film, they have, hopefully, learned about their condition. The road is ended but the journey is just beginning; for Pasolini the marxist, freedom is the knowledge of necessity. And **Uccelacci e uccellini** is his latest gloss on that text. (pp. 28-9)

In terms of technique, it makes for unstylish cinema as well as suffering from the occasional longueur. But its best moments contain rare and beautiful things: the newsreels of Togliatti's funeral, for example, are deeply moving. And Toto's snow-wreathed monk, waiting for the sparrows while winter turns to spring, has both the immediacy and the distancing quality of great art. All in all, a troubled, restless, important film. (p. 29)

> *Patrick MacFadden, "Uccelacci e uccellini,"* in
> Take One *(copyright © 1966 by Unicorn Publishing Corp.), Vol. 1, No. 1, September-October, 1966, pp. 28-9.*

### MARC GERVAIS

[**Edipo Re (Oedipus Rex)** is a series of events], one following upon the other, unprepared, unexploited for their story values, in many ways even unexplained, but merely allowed to explode before us in their beauty, their mystery, their terror. And this is the magic of Pasolini's cinema, a cinema of frontal assault.

We are not asked to believe a story, we are simply buffeted by emotion. But not only by emotion, for in a Pasolini film ideas and reactions are clearly spelled out for us, and there's always question of a certain aesthetic and intellectual distance. Our reaction is one of enthralment, but of insight as well. Intellect and emotions are appealed to directly and personally, and we feel involved at the most profound level.

For Pasolini structures his film so as to capture man in those moments and situations completely beyond pretence and convention. *Edipo Re* is the Sophoclean tragedy stripped down to the elemental and the primitive. It is man and the desert and the scorching sun, man naked before his own fear and bewilderment, his lust, his meanness, his strength, his need, his love and compassion, man working out his own destiny, a free being, and yet very much at the mercy of a higher destiny, of mysterious powers beyond his control.

With a whirling, prowling camera that blinks at the sun and gasps and breathes almost in unison with Oedipus, Pasolini (true to his principles *re* the poetic cinema) invests his film with a wild, tormented, baroque quality. . . . Pasolini allows each moment all the time required to achieve full poetic and dramatic impact. No fancy jump cuts à la Godard, not that kind of distantiation. The realism is only a launching site, as it were, for Pasolini's soaring poetic assault. (p. 4)

Paradoxically enough, it is in this search for the primitive and the elemental that Pasolini courts the modern sensibility. The modern reflectors, the contemporary currents that have shaped his thinking, *his* sensibility, are ever present. The ambivalence of Oedipus (and of Pasolini) in the way they relate to the various events—horror, yet fascination, repulsion hand in hand with attraction—reflect the complexity of experience we are so aware of. Pasolini, too, makes sure that the film will be situated unmistakably in a Freudian context from the prologue on. And one could interpret much of the film, especially its epilogue, along the Marxist lines one expects in Pasolini's cinema. But it is in that search for the authentic experience, for brute reality, that the work is thoroughly contemporary in spirit. . . . In *Edipo Re,* Pasolini has created a truly personal work informed by his own sensibility, his convictions, his ambivalent attitudes, his doubts. But more, the film is universal man's cry of pain and bewilderment before the mystery of life.

Masterpiece? Probably not, for *Edipo Re* is anything but unflawed as a work of art. Some of the scenes, as I have indicated, verge on the falsely theatrical; and the strain in styles between the realistic and the baroque has bothered a number of critics. Now and again one feels that in his search for the visually poetic, Pasolini has allowed the picturesque and the liturgical to linger overlong. And it is quite possible that the high-pitched ranting and screaming, the violence and the blood-bath, ultimately work against the film. But this is one film, it seems to me, that should be judged by the magnitude of its achieved ambitions rather than on more or less incidental failures. . . .

Where *Edipo Re* was a series of events exploding in sound and fury (as they say), stretched out along a man's journey to his destiny, *Teorema* contains its passion, its torment and anguish, behind a façade of fashionable calm and elegance: a cool, gem-like creation, clear, mathematical, precise. The pace is slow and controlled, the camera in repose as it captures elegantly framed images of crystalline beauty. Once again, to be sure, we are pulled in by the film's intense beauty and passion. But true to his aesthetic, Pasolini achieves a certain distantiation by making his presence overwhelmingly felt as he moves his characters in preordained fashion, figures in some strange liturgy, working out his intellectualised pattern in a structure whose outline is deliberately open, visible. . . .

But for all its aesthetic quality, *Teorema* risks being one of those films doomed to be swallowed up in the controversy it engenders. It has become the focal point of larger issues and considerations beyond the aesthetic, issues very difficult to avoid; and as such, one feels obliged to touch upon them.

There is [the] accusation of obscenity, for example. . . .

Is the film really obscene, even when judged from the strictly moralistic point of view? . . . Pasolini himself has pointed out something essential: by the discretion and restraint exercised in his handling of the sexual encounters, and by their systematic reduction to the level of a certain *disincarnation,* these encounters take on the quality of symbols, part of a poetic language—and anything but peep-show material. (p. 5)

*Teorema,* to be sure, is shot through with paradox. It has already been noted that the precise, mathematical coolness of the film nevertheless burns with an intensity of emotion. But the paradox goes beyond that: the intellectual clarity and mastery evidenced in the film's structure ultimately open out on an ambiguity that remains, to a great extent, unresolved. . . .

*Teorema,* in its very structure, can be seen as an exercise in cutting through the superficialities of life in order to arrive at some fundamental realities. Or, in terms of what happens in the film, the *before* (superficiality) and the *after* (reality), balanced on a certain catalytic experience. . . .

*Teorema* [is], in spite of its clarity and precision, difficult to pin down intellectually, and impossible to reduce to any 'system'. For here is a film that has been explained as the expression of "la difficulté d'être d'un homosexuel," and as a thoroughly Freudian adventure—and yet it opens out on to metaphysical and sociological vistas well beyond the Freudian frame of relevance. It is also seen as a "Marxist condemnation of the spirit-stultifying aspects of bourgeois society," and it is certainly that, too. But it soars into areas which transcend the strictly materialistic horizons of orthodox Marxism. And as for the religious interpretation, well, it can always be pointed out that elements in the film may be seen as a bitter and painful reduction of religion to the level of futility and madness. . . . *Teorema* is a fascinating and compelling work of art, with a power to charm and captivate; but one of those films, too, with a terrible power to challenge. Forcing us into a direct confrontation with the deepest problems of human existence, Pasolini leaves us suspended, as it were, on the ultimate mystery. Using the Freudian and Marxist insights that have played so dominant a role in fashioning our contemporary way of structuring reality, he cuts through the spiritual death man is threatened with by that consumer society whose be-all and end-all is physical commodities. He shows us man bereft of all but the essentials, faced with his ultimate exigencies, his infinite thirst for something else. But just as man in life, when faced with its overpowering mystery, has an open option—he may (as Pasolini sees it) find his ultimate meaning in the religious solution, in the transcendent, or he may withdraw into the anguished conviction of the basic absurdity of everything, or even into madness or despair—so in *Teorema* the openness of the option is respected. Ambivalence, perhaps; but the final word is mystery. (p. 6)

*Marc Gervais, "Pier-Paolo Pasolini: Contestatore," in* Sight and Sound *(copyright © 1969 by The*

British Film Institute), Vol. 38, No. 1, Winter, 1968-69, pp. 2-7.

## VINCENT CANBY

["*Teorema*"] is the kind of movie that should be seen at least twice, but I'm afraid that a lot of people will have difficulty sitting through it even once. . . .

"*Teorema*" (theorem) is a parable, a movie of realistic images photographed and arranged with a mathematical precision that drains them of comforting emotional meaning. . . .

"*Teorema*" is a cranky and difficult film made fascinating by the fact that Pasolini has quite consciously risked [a calamitous response from his audience]. . . .

"*Teorema*" is not my favorite kind of film. It is open to too many whimsical interpretations grounded in Pasolini's acknowledged Marxism and atheism, which, like Bunuel's anticlericism, serve so well to affirm what he denies. Pasolini has stated that the young man is not meant to represent Jesus in a Second Coming. Rather, he says, the young man is god, any god, but the fact remains that he is God in a Roman Catholic land. . . .

Pasolini doesn't load this film with little calculated messages of purple prose. . . . Even though Pasolini is a talented novelist and poet, the film is almost completely visual. The actors don't act, but simply exist to be photographed. The movie itself is the message, a series of cool, beautiful, often enigmatic scenes that flow one into another with the rhythm of blank verse.

This rhythm—one of the legacies of the silent film, especially of silent film comedy—[is hard] . . . to accept. The seductions are ticked off one after the other with absolutely no thought of emotional continuity. So are the individual defeats, which are punctuated by recurring shots of a desolate, volcanic landscape swept by sulphurous mists. . . .

"*Teorema*" is a religious film, but I think it would take a very hip Jesuit to convert it into a testament to contemporary Roman Catholic dogma.

*Vincent Canby, "'Teorema' in Premiere at the Coronet," in* The New York Times *(© 1969 by The New York Times Company; reprinted by permission), April 22, 1969 (and reprinted in* The New York Times Film Reviews: 1969-1970, *The New York Times Company & Arno Press, 1971, p. 32).*

## JOHN SIMON

If Pier Paolo Pasolini's *Teorema* is not the worst film ever made, you can't blame it for not trying. . . .

[Do] not for a moment assume that the story proceeds by any sort of narrative logic. It jumps around in fragmented Godardian non sequiturs that arise from nowhere and trail off into nothing. At the slightest sign of a little consecutive action, Pasolini whisks us off to some unrelated nonincident, or to that wilderness with cloud shadows scurrying across it and another unrelated biblical quotation streaking across the soundtrack. (p. 146)

Nor are you to think that there is anything like meaningful dialogue in *Teorema*. The advertisements proudly proclaim that though there are only 923 words in the film (it is not clear whether that includes duplicates), it says everything. There is

no doubt that it says everything; unfortunately, however, without saying *something*. Pasolini has declared that the film is largely about the "cage of words" in which we are all cooped up, from which the Stranger, who represents (you have guessed it!) the Divine, extricates us. Yet since there is almost no talk, and what there is comes mostly after the visitation, it would seem that, if cage there be, it is the Stranger who tosses us into it. But, then, a cage of 923 words spread over an hour and a half has bars far enough apart for an elephant to walk through.

What of the visual elements? The color cinematography is handsome to look at, but what is *it* looking at? (pp. 146-47)

Behavior here is a series of poses. The daughter vacuously holds out her photograph album to the Stranger and says nothing, perhaps by way of preparation for catatonia. The Stranger and the son look through a book of reproductions of the paintings of Francis Bacon: Rimbaud, Bacon—we see what kind of sexuality the divinity likes in an artist. There are, in fact, a great many male crotch shots in the film, almost as if it were told from the point of view of a homosexual worm. (p. 147)

*Teorema* is totally vapid as film, yet might it not be valid as a parable? Frankly, I can't see how this God (Pasolini has also said—what hasn't he said?— that the Stranger is not Christ, but "the terrible God of Creation") reaches those five people: though the mystics have put erotic tropes to good use, I cannot take this by-the-numbers intercourse seriously even as a metaphor. And why do the five react as they do? What is the meaning of their reactions? Why should the buggered son become an action painter *ipso facto*, and the humped daughter a catatonic? Why not the reverse? Why should the mother become a whore and the servant a saint? Social class can't be the answer; the father, too, is rich, and he gives away his earthly goods to become an eremite. Why shouldn't the mother become a painter? She painted her face heavily enough. Why don't they all become pizza vendors, or clowns in a traveling circus, or a rock group called God's Very Own or The Grateful Had?

[The Stranger's] appearance suggests, if anything, a Caravaggio angel. The angel as sexually ambiguous—asexual, bisexual, androgynous—has fascinated pederastic painters and writers. . . . It may even be that *Teorema* is a conscious or unconscious homosexual pun. (p. 148)

It used to be a favorite subject of Scholastic disputation whether God, being omnipotent as well as immortal, could destroy himself. That question, at least, has been answered: by making a film like *Teorema*—easily. (p. 149)

*John Simon, "Sex: 'Teorema'" (originally published as "Metaphoric Sex, Symbolic Circus," in* The New Leader, *Vol. LII, No. 10, May 26, 1969), in his* Movies into Film: Film Criticism 1967-1970 *(copyright © 1971 by John Simon; reprinted with permission of The Dial Press), Dial, 1971, pp. 146-49.*

## SUSAN MACDONALD

Pasolini always remains detached from his characters. He is not interested in interpreting behaviour. He describes what he sees. His objectivity is alarmingly emotive, particularly when he contrasts a tragedy with the surrounding scenery. (p. 22)

Pasolini's reality is not naturalistic. It is, he says, philosophical and sacral. He tries to enlarge the reality he represents by dubbing his characters, preferably with a different voice, to make them more mysterious, larger than life. (p. 24)

His cinematic style underlines his sense of pastiche, being a combination of several styles, principally Mizoguchi, Chaplin and Dreyer. He sees these directors as 'epic-mythic': they see things from a point of view that is absolute, essential and, in a way, sacral. This is the same way in which Pasolini sees things. . . . (pp. 24-5)

Christ dies violently on the cross at the end of *Il vangelo secondo Matteo (The Gospel according to Saint Matthew,* 1964), screaming and accompanied by cut-in shots of tumbling buildings. Like Pasolini's other heroes he is a rebel. His Lenin-like figure, neurotic and fanatic, moves among the peasantry, a passionate revolutionary, threatening and cajoling, a man with a mission who has 'come not to bring peace but a sword'. There is little, or nothing, of the gentle divine in Pasolini's Christ. . . . He is a homosexual Christ, needing the adoration of his disciples, but isolated and able to give little affection in return. He is a Christ who spurns his mother with the words: 'Who is a mother, who are brethren to me?' but who suffers from his own act of rejection as he strides away in tears. Pasolini's Christ is both Marxist and religious. . . . (pp. 25-6)

With *Edipo Re (Oedipus Rex,* 1967) Pasolini reaches the peak of his autobiographical rebellion. He consciously reconstructs the origins of his Oedipus complex, exploring his relationships with the father he hated and the mother he adored. (p. 28)

[In *Oedipus*] Pasolini is crudely emphasizing the super-ego represented by the father repressing the child. But if Pasolini's ideas on psycho-analytic theory are naïve, he is here artistically effective and convincing, more so than in the rest of the film. When Pasolini abruptly cuts from the modern father clutching the baby's ankles in a fit of hate to the baby bound by wrists and ankles being carried across a Moroccan desert, the connections seem too tenuous. Pasolini is attempting to move from his own Oedipal situation into a generalized concept of the Oedipus complex, based on the myth of Oedipus. He has said that the basic operation in the film is to reproject psychoanalysis onto the myth. But it doesn't work on this level. (pp. 28-9)

*Oedipus Rex* is a patchy film, moments of violence and power are spoilt by naïvety and overstatement, and, for Pasolini, parts are surprisingly insensitive. (p. 30)

Throughout his work Pasolini is searching for a way of life that is both Marxist and embraces his feelings about religion. Often the two are confused. He originally intended Marxism as the unifying theme in his work. (p. 32)

[A] search for 'truth' is more plausible as the unity that permeates Pasolini's work. It is a truth that can be summed up in the Socratic 'Know thyself.' (p. 33)

*Susan Macdonald, "Pasolini: Rebellion, Art and a New Society," in* Screen *(© The Society for Education in Film and Television 1969), Vol. 10, No. 3, May-June, 1969, pp. 19-34.*

**PETER WHITEHEAD**

The equation [of *Theorem (Teorema)*] is simple. There is a family as perfect in form as one of Plato's proofs . . . father, mother, son, daughter, maid. The family institution, self-contained in its house, its home, is the private body politic in which the individuals should—so we have been educated to believe—derive the security they need to free themselves from their mythological beings—free as individuals, whenever necessary, to transcend the confines of the family, to become good social people, fearlessly taking their place in the more harrowing politics of the institutions of the world. Their guest, a beautiful, quiet young man, arrives and, quite passively, is used by each of them to sublimate their unconscious, repressed needs. He is the catalyst they use to confront in themselves that 'self' which has been denied fulfilment by their family social situation. For a brief moment, each one is gathered into the artifice of eternity . . . they experience fulfilment of their *entire* beings. . . .

The lack of any sense of meaning, religious or otherwise, is compensated for, in each of them, by perilous, private crusades . . . each must seek the existential solution to his own spiritual needs. The common denominator of the theorem is the desert, the void . . . and each member of the splintered group fulfils his private suffering. . . .

The only theorems ever evolved to explain the tragic insult that we resemble mere animals, fornicating and doing dirty things at night in bed for years and years and years, goddammit, were evolved by two sets of people . . . those who admitted to emotions as they are, the artists, and those admitted to them, by default as it were, in negative . . . the Church. (p. 38)

If you go deep enough into the myths and taboos of any individual mind, you go through all time and reach the equations of mystery and fear that will never, never be solved. We shall always be individuals, yet we shall always need to build institutions to protect us from our Godless solitude. Clearly the present solution, for the privileged few, who we see here in this film, or for the under-privileged many who have politics as their religion, is not the right one. So deeply moving and pessimistic is this film, showing as it does that we project our inner need of God only so briefly on to the world, having so little faith to keep it alive, for such a short time. I can only speculate that the Catholics who voted Pasolini his well-deserved prize (it deserves all the prizes) must have said, 'If this won't drive them in, then nothing will.' Nothing . . . will. (p. 39)

*Peter Whitehead, "'Theorem'" (© copyright Peter Whitehead 1969; reprinted with permission), in* Films and Filming, *Vol. 15, No. 9, June, 1969, pp. 38-9.*

**PETER WHITEHEAD**

There are only two reasons for taking a myth and re-working it. Either because a variation on it will communicate a new depth of understanding about that particular myth . . . or simply because myths are 'true'. They tend to be true in a way that we still do not understand. They work! But Pasolini seems to have done neither with [*Oedipus Rex*]—except to take the story and set it in Arabia and drag his hero through a series of parodies of Japanese samurai movies. This is Accatone telling a camp joke to the blokes back at the ghetto, about how the other half lives . . . (pp. 39-40)

Pasolini missed a chance that could have led to a whole new interpretation of the myth. Sophocles never explains why poor old Laius had to get killed by his son; it was not merely for being jealous of his arrival and taking his place in his wife's affections. What had he done? We know what Oedipus did. Oedipus was destroyed because he could not accept the horror of having killed his father, etcetera . . . (I think if Pasolini wanted to really bring the myth up to date, he ought to have set it in Puerto Rica and have Oedipus proud as hell that he bumped his impotent father off, and tickled pink that this female he just can't for the love of him stop . . . something so archetypal about her bone structure! His only problem on discovering it was his Mother would be to know if he can still claim benefit for her as his 'wife'. His eyes are wide open.) . . .

The tragedy seems to be that the more we 'evolve', the more we fall away from resolving the deepest taboos with which we mystify ourselves, and as society becomes so complex and so utterly dedicated to the present, the secrets of the past—scarred across more than just our dreams—will be abandoned as redundant. . . .

I'd like to think that Pasolini is suggesting something like this, the relevance still, of our ignorance of our compulsions, our taboos, our fears, our emotions (dirty word), by re-making *Oedipus Rex* and setting it with prologue and epilogue in present day time. But there is little sign of any real existentialist rethinking of the myth. It is more of an Italianising of it. . . .

The landscapes are beautiful, the buildings like a dream we would have liked to think Kafka had about Castles, the costumes are weird, surprising, fun, and some of the set pieces are fascinating. But the whole film is lost, its purpose somewhere else . . . it is slow, and never for a second moving, never really surprising once you've said—ah, Arabia!—and intellectually boring. Methinks he doth protest too much. It is a travelogue. And a pity. (p. 40)

> *Peter Whitehead, "'Oedipus Rex'" (© copyright Peter Whitehead 1969; reprinted with permission), in* Films and Filming, *Vol. 15, No. 9, June, 1969, pp. 39-40.*

### CALVIN GREEN

[*Pigpen*] abounds in symbols so extravagant and so abstruse that they continually appear to be shifting ground and flouting interpretation. No doubt, a number of interpretations are intended, and there is also no doubt that they are meant to be on several different "levels." Considering the incessant affectations of the film, interpretation seems hardly worth the effort. . . .

[However, a] viewer cannot help but be impressed by a sense of Pasolini's acuteness and the ambitions of his analyses. He sees European civilization as having learned little from the worst catastrophe it ever experienced. Instead of evolving to a higher plane of social development (Pasolini is a Communist), men cynically repeat themselves or rationalize their impotence. The moral vacuum created by this purgatory is Pasolini's justification for wrath. (p. 4)

In the film's modern drama all the characters are too facile and in the medieval, too alien. . . . The medieval story never clarifies the identity of the cannibals nor their awesome attraction and frightening repulsion engendered in the viewer. If Pasolini is accusing, we are all implicated, but the artist is too involved in the film's metaphorical devices to keep the accusatory finger from falling limp. The viewer is left puzzled rather than excited and concerned.

Since Pasolini is quite sincere about what he does, it cannot be smugness or charlatanism that leads to the obscurity of his allegories. Originally a poet and novelist, Pasolini's most re-

cent films bear the marks of literary formalism. It is not explicit talkiness that makes for a literary film, but a stylistic and structural preconception that does not really trust the inherent quality of the image itself to convey meaning. (pp. 4-5)

In *Pigpen*'s medieval story the camera tracks up and down and angles in from distant shots, possibly implying dramatic involvement ironic to the barren background. In the modern narrative, the images are presented with formal balance—a central figure with equal weight on either side—as in a Renaissance painting. In both cases, the style is intellectually absorbing but does nothing to elucidate the overall theme of the film. (p. 5)

> *Calvin Green, "L'homme politique: Man and the Revolution at the N.Y. Film Festival," in* Cinéaste *(copyright © 1969 by Gary Crowdus), Vol. III, No. 2, Fall, 1969, pp. 2-5, 36.\**

### PHILIP STRICK

With the conclusion of *Theorem*, Pasolini left us in the company of today's bourgeois *paterfamilias,* stripped of all save his despairing confusion, wandering distractedly across the acid volcanic wastes that had been glimpsed previously throughout the film like almost subliminal reminders of his cryptozoic ancestry. As if resuming the tale, *Pigsty* [or *Pigpen*] . . . begins in the same setting, with an identical outcast struggling across the lifeless ash-dunes; the pangs assailing him now, however, are no longer those of conscience or doubt but simply those of an excruciating hunger. Pasolini gives us no time to consider this apparent simplification before he has once again broadened the metaphor alarmingly by cutting in the first glimpses of the parallel story of which the film is composed. In direct balance to *Theorem* . . . , *Pigsty* punctuates the primitive with the ornate; although this time the two separate narratives are of roughly equal length, if not of equivalent complexity. . . .

*Pigsty* continues to chart the course of Pasolini's detachment from the ideology of his *Accattone* days. . . .

*Pigsty,* like *Theorem,* draws both comfort and despair from the gratified hungers of humanity, blames no one for their actions or their inactions, and ultimately adopts a fatalistic standpoint (the connection with *Edipo Re* is hinted enigmatically by the cannibal's final words) which concludes that other forces than man's are behind all that he attempts to do. (p. 99)

The wilful interlocking of two utterly different narratives has its own strange ambiguity. It can be argued that the exercise is meaningless, yet the results never are. The contrasts and clashes between [Willard Maas's] *Orgia* and *Porcile* set up disturbing, often indefinable echoes. . . . Since we know far more about the porcophile Julian than we do about the cannibal, the relationship between them is difficult to determine—particularly as the former is hardly as anti-social as the latter. But relationship there undoubtedly is, in their passion, in their detachment, and finally in their deaths.

Originally, Pasolini had planned that Julian would be visited by the ghost of Spinoza, assuring him that his love for the pigs is equivalent to a belief in God; this splendidly ambivalent interpolation is gone, but the sense of the self-destructive nature of any dedication remains, the theological aspects being brought out more by the cannibal's ceremonial disposal of heads in the marvellously gaping mouth of the volcano and his condemnation at the hands of some dishevelled clerics than by Julian's more amiable martyrdom. (pp. 99-100)

If one can conclude anything from the film, it is that Pasolini has transcended the efforts of any of his contemporaries to define the Italian dilemma in both poetic and cinematic terms. (p. 100)

> *Philip Strick, "Film Reviews: 'Pigsty'," in* Sight and Sound *(copyright © 1970 by The British Film Institute), Vol. 39, No. 2, Spring, 1970, pp. 99-100.*

## ROY ARMES

Pasolini is no austere modernist carving out a resolutely independent style but an artist whose principal stylistic device is pastiche. His films, like those of Jean-Luc Godard, are thus extremely heterogeneous and rely on the force of his personal involvement for their effective coherence. Despite the referential quality of his imagery and music, Pasolini's works bear the stamp of their author. (p. 55)

The basic polarity which gives tension to Pasolini's style and which, on the crudest level, can be expressed as the attempt to reconcile Freud and Marx, is very apparent if one compares . . . *Theorem* and *Oedipus Rex.* It is even more clearly expressed in *Pigsty,* which combines two episodes, the one modern and satiric, the other mythic and orgiastic. (pp. 55-6)

The Freudian element in Pasolini is most obvious in his own Oedipal situation, quite explicitly expressed in his version of the Sophoclean tragedy but implicit in much else, from *Mamma Roma* to *The Gospel According to St. Matthew*. . . . Pasolini does not concern himself with dogmas and heresy or formulate a critique of the Christian ethic. Rather he adopts a much less sophisticated attitude and expresses a deep sense of awe at reality, most clearly expressed in the Colchis sequences of *Medea*. . . .

The mythic stories of man's attempts to come to terms with his own religious sense and complicated sexuality have certain qualities that set them apart from the rest of Pasolini's work, in the kinds of emphasis they receive if not in the actual content. . . . One striking aspect of *The Gospel, Oedipus Rex* and the 'Orgy' episode of *Pigsty* is the combination of narrative simplicity and total ambiguity of meaning. . . . The films show men of enormous personal authority, but leave in doubt the divine nature of Christ, the moral implications of Oedipus's acts and the impulses behind Pierre Clémenti's acts of savagery, and this genuine mystery adds to the film's religious quality. As if to compensate for the simplicity and violence of the action, these works are given the most striking imagery to be found in Pasolini. . . . The ease with which Pasolini can find, in the Mediterranean, analogies for these primitive societies, makes clear that the modern predicament is not simply that of coming to terms with an urban environment. It is also that of mastering the basic and irrational forces within all of us. . . . (p. 56)

Pasolini's concern with Marxism has much the same origins as his Freudian obsession. In a very real sense it is part of his revolt against the values of his father who was both a Fascist and a petit-bourgeois. . . . [Pasolini's] first films, like his early novels, show the impact of the Roman slums and their inhabitants upon his artistic sensibilities. A film like *Accattone* self-consciously idealises the Roman thieves, whores and lay-abouts, but despite the novelty of its tone it lacks the originality of Pasolini's mature style. Because of Pasolini's inadequate technical command the various elements do not totally blend

and for much of the time one is confronted with a run-down version of the neo-realist approach. (pp. 56-7)

[In *Theorem* and half of *Pigsty*], Pasolini has confronted the problems of bourgeois society which are more closely linked to his own deepest preoccupations. Here he has evolved a style that is in marked contrast to his studies of Freudian myth. In this urban environment Pasolini presents stories built around elements of irony and parallelism. Unconcerned with mere reportage of social behaviour, he presents satiric portraits of middle-class families which disintegrate under the impact of self-realisation. . . .

For Pasolini the essential difference between cinema and literature is that the language of film lacks metaphor, it expresses reality with reality. Pasolini has . . . a reverential approach to reality itself as it is experienced, but his awareness of the qualities of film as language make him very distrustful of naturalism as a form of expression. He rigorously avoids the mere imitation of life. He likes using, in neo-realist fashion, non-actors chosen because of the appropriateness of their faces and figures. But he does not use them naturally: he poses them in positions taken from Piero della Francesca and dubs them with actors' voices. For him the only means which allows the cinema to compensate for the lack of metaphor (and hence, at a certain level, of poetry itself) is the notion of analogy. . . . Pasolini is concerned to rediscover the mythical element of reality. He does not demystify Christ—i.e., show him to be simply a man—he gives us, in *The Gospel,* Christ *and* two thousand years of Christian legend and art. Similarly, he does not unravel Greek legend in terms of modern psychology: he gives us in *Oedipus Rex* the mystery of Sophocles plus the ambiguities of Freud *and* his own personal involvement. (p. 57)

> *Roy Armes, "Pasolini" (© copyright Roy Armes 1971; reprinted with permission), in* Films and Filming, *Vol. 17, No. 9, June, 1971, pp. 55-8.*

## VINCENT CANBY

Pier Paolo Pasolini's very free, very barbaric **"Medea,"** which is less an adaptation of the Euripides play than an interpretation of it, is not completely successful, but it is . . . full of eccentric imagination and real passion. . . .

If your priorities are such, Pasolini's **"Medea"** can be an excellent argument for the kind of literal movie made by [Michael] Cacoyannis. . . .

**"Medea"** is something else entirely. Pasolini has the monumental and marvelous presumption to put himself ahead of Euripides (who was not, after all, a moviemaker), in an attempt to translate into film terms the sense of a prehistoric time, place and intelligence in which all myths and rituals were real experiences. . . .

Pasolini's Medea is no longer a rather ill-tempered woman spurned, an early Women's Liberationist, a mother guilty of the sort of murders that were . . . appalling to the ancient Greeks. . . .

In Pasolini's conception, Medea is a primeval soul who erupts almost spontaneously when transplanted into a civilization ruled by order. And this, I think, is where the film goes awry.

There is no real conflict between Pasolini's conception and Euripides's. Pasolini's supplements the other's, but because nothing in Pasolini's imagery in the scenes in Corinth is equal to the passion of the original text, or to Pasolini's own scenes early in the film, the movie seems to go thin and absurdly melodramatic. . . .

**"Medea"** is uneven, but I admire the reckless courage of its conception, even when it goes wrong. When it is right, as in the poetic and funny prologue, delivered by the centaur . . . , and in its eerie evocation of Medea's world, which (according to Pasolini) is our subconscious world, it is superb.

> *Vincent Canby, "Callas Stars in 'Medea'," in* The New York Times *(© 1971 by The New York Times Company; reprinted by permission), October 29, 1971 (and reprinted in* The New York Times Film Reviews: 1971-1972, The New York Times Company & Arno Press, 1973, p. 163).*

### ALEXANDER STUART

If you found that by the end of nearly two hours of **The Decameron** you'd had enough medieval bawdiness for quite some time, then be warned: miss out on **The Canterbury Tales**. It's not just that Pasolini's latest feature . . . is concerned with roughly the same themes and similar characters, but it lacks any indication of his very considerable talent. (p. 46)

Pasolini would seem to have selected the tales he uses . . . with a view merely to creating as bawdy a picture as possible of the chosen period. His underlying theme of the rise and development of the middle class might have been far more acceptable had it not necessitated such tampering with Chaucer's poetry. Apart from this concentration upon a particular social stratum, there is little unity and the links between tales are extremely weak. . . .

**The Canterbury Tales** is lengthy and tedious. . . . [One] feels cheated when such an exercise in medieval mediocrity is served up by a director capable of a master work of the force of **The Gospel According To St Matthew**. (p. 47)

> *Alexander Stuart, "Reviews: 'The Canterbury Tales'" (© copyright Alexander Stuart 1973; reprinted with permission), in* Films and Filming, *Vol. 19, No. 9, June, 1973, pp. 46-7.*

### JOHN COLEMAN

Pasolini's **The Canterbury Tales** is the first film to come my way in which the protagonist is the Fart. And even that has every aural sign of being dubbed in. . . . Chaucer was not above specific gags about breaking wind, bums, queynts and the normal processes of mankind. Pasolini, however, has somehow ended up below them during this lamentable excursion. You could say he turns up rumps. I have nothing against the male posterior, either figuratively or literally, but this disconnected succession of visual flashes, with the stress on buggery and women present, one feels, on sufferance, is of unmanageable vulgarity. . . . Words do not fail me about this pitiful travesty: contempt cuts them short.

> *John Coleman, "Jackal and Hide," in* New Statesman *(© 1973 The Statesman & Nation Publishing Co. Ltd.), Vol. 85, No. 2204, June 15, 1973, p. 901.*

### NIGEL GEARING

**Medea** is something of a relief in that it asserts an ideological dimension whose willed abandonment has rendered the trilogy a charming exercise in *fausse naïveté*. In this five-year-old

work, Pasolini is still conceding a social dimension to his elected myths: not, in this instance, an imaginative world "earthy, frolicsome, crowded with people and full of light" (his description of **Decameron**) but a stark confrontation between cultures sacred and profane, agrarian and bourgeois, 'epical-religious' and 'Western-pragmatic'. . . . On a formal level, Pasolini is refining a style evident in much of his previous work, but especially in **Oedipus**. Slow pans across palace walls and expectant lines of men; the blank, immobile scrutiny of an unchanging scene; set-ups which enclose the same piece of reality in two successively closer shots. The allegorical complexities of **Theorem** and **Pigsty** are eschewed, as are the evasive simplifications of the films to follow; balanced between them, **Medea** indeed effects Pasolini's intended "blend . . . of a philosophical reflection and a love intrigue"—a work which, like its heroine . . . , can be said to face in two directions at once but draws its major strength from past achievements.

> *Nigel Gearing, "Feature Films: 'Medea'," in* Monthly Film Bulletin *(copyright © The British Film Institute, 1975), Vol. 42, No. 497, June, 1975, p. 142.*

### DEREK ELLEY

The butchery [of the first twenty minutes of **Medea**] provides a neat excuse for Medea's later actions: infanticide is shown to be merely her innate (socially acceptable) function as a Colcian priestess resurfacing many years later for more personal reasons. Within Pasolini's intensely schematic telling, this works quite well; likewise his use of non-professionals, their natural gaucherie complementing his liking for static groups of people arranged like icon-portraits in passageways and arches. What, in his recent trilogy, has degenerated into untidiness, in **Medea** is still valid because of a rigid, completely unself-indulgent *mise-en-scène*. . . .

[It is Maria Callas's] physical presence which propels the rest of the film—a film badly in need of propelling to prevent it going into reverse. In retrospect one can see **Medea** as the last in a long line of films which became increasingly sparer and more static; what Pasolini has now lost in self-control he has gained in pace. **Medea** (1970) is beautiful to watch, baffling to follow, and interesting to analyse on paper. As a piece of filmmaking, presumably aimed at attracting audiences, it is unnecessarily slow, emotionally sterile, and extremely boring.

> *Derek Elley, "Reviews: 'Medea'" (© copyright Derek Elley 1975; reprinted with permission), in* Films and Filming, *Vol. 21, No. 10, July, 1975, p. 45.*

### JOHN RUSSELL TAYLOR

[**Il Vangelo Secondo Matteo** is the most serious, sober, and] deeply reverent film about Christ the cinema has given us. And yet, in a way, these are negative qualities: their presence does not necessarily mean that the director has come to terms with the central problems of his subject. It is not frivolous to say that the story has no suspense (everyone knows how it turns out); this is a problem in any dramatic representation of the life of Christ—the more so since it is all too easy to rely exclusively on the emotions that inevitably color it in the spectators' minds, instead of trying to make some positive contribution. It would not be fair to say that Pasolini has done this, but the film sometimes looks perilously like it. . . . The film is at times pictorially beautiful, and the nonprofessional players act with striking restraint: it is all quite distinguished, in a wan sort of way, but also, truth to tell, more than a little dull.

At least so it seems to me, though for many it is one of Pasolini's finest achievements. (p. 50)

*Oedipus* has a splendid opening sequence in pre-war Italy, which implies a whole Oedipal situation. But the body of the film, set in primitive Morocco and following Sophocles fairly closely, comes over as much more decked out than felt: one chafes at Pasolini's insistence on telling the story as though we had never heard it before, instead of taking some knowledge of it for granted and going on from there. (p. 55)

It is difficult to feel that in *Edipo Re*—except in the prologue and the brief coda that shows Oedipus walking through the streets of modern Bologna—Pasolini has done much more than take the myth, and Sophocles' telling of it, for granted, instead of rethinking it or reexperiencing it. And, given this feeling, the unlikely trappings he has found for the Sophoclean past seem far more arbitrary and dandyish than integral to his conception of the story. . . . The force of the intellectual notion— insisting on the universality of the myth by situating it outside history, beyond any specific cultural framework—can be appreciated intellectually, but it is not sufficiently felt, and the film remains, the prologue and coda apart, a clever but empty exercise in style.

[Not so the] contrasting (yet also closely related) . . . *Teorema*. This I believe to be Pasolini's masterpiece, the single work that triumphantly brings together all his talents at their highest, all his preoccupations at their most intense. . . . *Teorema* is the sort of film that makes one think what a nuisance it is that, in the cause of intellectually respectable criticism, one must pretend to be interested in what films *mean*. That is not true, of course: part of the fascination of this extraordinary, intricate, and teasing film is to work out exactly what Pasolini thinks he means by it. But the first thing that strikes one is its mastery as a piece of storytelling, the way it keeps its audience agog to know what will happen next. It is far and away Pasolini's most entertaining film to date. (pp. 56-7)

*Teorema* shows a new and complete mastery of means on Pasolini's part. The style is pure, simple, and direct, in Pasolini's familiar "reverential" manner. There are no fireworks, and sometimes, as in the episode of the maid's levitation, or in her eventual self-sacrificial act of burying herself alive, the effect is deliberately analogous to that of primitive painting, the filmmaker withdrawing into an apparent naïve literalness that leaves us to supply our own comment, should we feel any comment is necessary. . . . *Teorema* is Pasolini's first dramatic foray into the middle classes—something he had always avoided before, because of his ingrained dislike of the bourgeois and his unwillingness to spend any time with them, even on the set of a film. But the bourgeois background is simplified and stylized, with no attempt at realistic detailing: their world is hermetically sealed off from the world around them. (p. 59)

Visually [*Porcile (Pigpen)*] is of extraordinary splendor; it is beautifully photographed in color which makes the most of the alternation between the bare volcanic uplands of the first story (like the wasteland in which the father in *Teorema* ends his journey) and the glittering baroque palace where the family in the second story lives. The slow revelations of horror and bestiality in both are impeccably filmed and synchronized. And the structure of the film as a whole is built with the inevitability of a piece of great music, a pattern that is completed with perfect emotional logic by the last "say nothing" gesture of

the winning industrialist when he has satisfied himself that the aberrant son has been consumed, hair and hide, down to the last button.

The internal logic and emotional coherence of the film are so perfect that the last thing one wants to do is to look for meanings, to search for symbols and equivalences that, put together, could provide a clear, noncinematic statement on the human condition. (pp. 60-1)

If we really must find a formula for interpreting the film, the most useful is to see it in terms of an argument for the necessity of extreme solutions, of following through one's own logic to the end without flinching. The bandit is reduced to a state where the only way he can survive is to prey on his fellows, so why not follow this through to the extreme of actually eating them, and if he does, why should he be superstitiously ashamed? The industrialist's son lives in a world of human pigs—his parents are frequently compared to pigs, and the world around him is represented as a pigsty—so why shouldn't he follow this through to the extreme of literally living like a pig? In both cases, the central characters achieve a heroic integrity that the others lack: they are the only ones who manage really to live, by piercing through the outworn conventions and subterfuges of a society ripe for destruction. (pp. 61-2)

But then the great advantage of the film is that we do not have to label it, and probably do not want to label it. As private myth made public, it is sublimely self-sufficient, and stands alongside *Teorema* as one of Pasolini's most magisterial cinematic statements. . . . (p. 62)

In *Il Decamerone* [*The Decameron*] the air of joyful relaxation and good humor is complete: it is the loosest, most warmly human of all Pasolini's films, and also, obviously, the most commercial, a consideration which may or may not be coincidental. (p. 64)

[While] the interest of *Il Decamerone* at least is not negligible, it is hardly surprising if we choose to continue thinking of Pasolini as the fascinating combination of intellect and instinct revealed in *Teorema* and *Porcile*, the ingenious recreator of ancient myth in *Edipo Re* and *Medea*, the discoverer of the mystical in the heart of the ordinary in *Accattone*, and the whimsical fabulist of *Uccellacci e Uccellini*. If his later films are far less distinguished, that can hardly be more than a temporary accident of fate and film politics, bound sooner or later to be put unerringly right with a new masterpiece from one of the most extraordinary filmmakers in the world today. (pp. 67-8)

*John Russell Taylor, "Pier Paolo Pasolini," in his* Directors and Directions: Cinema for the Seventies *(reprinted by permission of Hill & Wang, a division of Farrar, Straus & Giroux, Inc.; in Canada by A D Peters & Co Ltd; copyright © 1975 by John Russell Taylor),* Hill & Wang, 1975, pp. 44-68.

**NATHANIEL TEICH**

Pasolini's *Medea* exemplifies how an artist uses a discernible conceptual structure as the formative and organizing principle of his work. For Pasolini, this conceptual structure is a non-dogmatic Marxist mode of analysis of individuals in society and cultures in history. (p. 54)

Free from a dependence on dialogue and verbal imagery, Pasolini presents a larger mythic world in a way that film does best: by portraying powerful visual imagery in action. (pp. 54-5)

In the film as a whole, Pasolini presents not only a psychological/personal drama but also a cultural/historical drama concerning the way culture operates and influences individual consciousness and behavior. He is interested not just, as the playwrights have been, in revelation of character by dramatizing Jason and Medea in conflict, but in illustrating the growth of consciousness in both characters in the context of formative cultural influences. . . .

Within the larger mythic world of his film, Pasolini successfully presents the two major kinds of myth: what is mythopoeic the genuine ritual and sacramentalism which are expressions of the primal mode of consciousness that sees everything in the world as sacred; and what is mythological—the organized, unified artistic construct produced by the literary or aesthetic consciousness. While the film as a whole, of course, belongs to the second species of myth, Pasolini's triumph is the cinematic immediacy of his epic mythology which represents how primal mythopoeic consciousness operates. The directly presentational medium of film is precisely suited to represent this non-rhetorical and pre-analytical view of the universe. (p. 55)

What Pasolini shows us is the primal consciousness of the universe, which Medea embodies, and which does not see things symbolically or metaphorically as mere analogies, but sees things sacramentally as identities and integrated wholes in which a living spirit is unified with the thing. (p. 56)

Pasolini emphasizes how the contrasts and conflicts between "primitive" Colchis and "rationally advanced" Greece affect Medea and Jason. This emphasis is particularly evident from comparisons with the notable prior dramatizations of the myth. While Euripides' prototype play, to which Pasolini acknowledges his debt, involves the issue of cultural conflict to some extent, almost all of the playwrights who follow are primarily concerned with character study. Pasolini's thematic emphasis is not simply attributable to the greater visual capabilities of film. Rather he uses these capabilities to make the specific content of his interpretation of the myth visible. The specific content of his interpretation is the product of a conceptual structure which organizes and unifies the specific form of the film. (pp. 56-7)

According to Pasolini's Marxist-humanism evident in the conceptual structure of his film, an individual's perceptions and values, as well as social structures and activities, are determined by the particular modes of consciousness and states of social organization in a given historical situation. As this principle applies to art, the work of art reflects the artist's particular consciousness which has been determined by his historical/cultural situation. Therefore, the specific content of Pasolini's interpretation of the Medea story is produced by the very same process of culturally determined conceptual structures that his film enacts as the myth of that process. (p. 61)

Pasolini presents a myth of what happens in Western culture and individual consciousness. At certain points in the historical cycles of self-consciousness as well as social organization, human existence must follow the inevitable route from the consecrated to the desecrated. But this need not be a myth of no hope. If we recognize the historical process as cycles of dialectical conflict and change, we see Pasolini's film as the opportunity to experience and understand a story about this process in the past.

Thus his **Medea** shows where he is in the contemporary situation, and perhaps where we are. As at the end of **The Hawks and the Sparrows** (although a more whimsical and didactic film), Pasolini cannot say *what* the content of the new synthesis is to be; he simply maintains, according to his Marxist humanism, that there *will be* that new synthesis. Thus in **Medea** he provides for us the secular ritual, the aesthetic and intellectual experience, the myth and the images to move to a higher state of awareness and organization, where we may strive for a new synthesis of consciousness and culture. (p. 62)

> *Nathaniel Teich, "Myth into Film: Pasolini's 'Medea' and its Dramatic Heritage," in* Western Humanities Review *(copyright, 1976, University of Utah), Vol. XXIV, No. 1, Winter, 1976, pp. 53-62.*

## ROBIN WOOD

[**Salo: 120 Days of Sodom**] is perhaps the most appalling fictional film I have ever seen (and I want the adjective to retain its ambiguity). I shall doubtless be haunted by it for a long time, but I'm not convinced that the haunting will be very profitable. It is a very difficult film to cope with, because it plays so disturbingly on the most dangerous ambivalences. The torments Dante imagined for sinners in the name of religion, the overtly erotic cruelties of de Sade, Nazi atrocities, and the ambiguously liberating/obsessive fantasies of Pasolini himself, all merge here until they become inextricable. One can perceive two clear, conscious strategies at work in the film, which constitute an effort towards purity of impulse: the attempt to distinguish cleanly between sexual acts based on mutual response and those based on power and degradation; and the struggle for a rigorous stylistic distancing of the whole catalogue of abominations the film comprises, Pasolini eschewing his habitual spontaneity for the deliberate execution of a carefully pre-planned scenario.

Yet the film's very obsessiveness undermines the attempted objectification: one quickly senses that it was Pasolini's own nightmares that he was striving to objectify, and the distinction between a film about obscenity and an obscene film becomes blurred. The division of the characters into ugly Fascist-bourgeois parent-figures and beautiful, young, innocent victims seems simplistic and sentimental, and the victims' almost total lack of protest at the atrocities inflicted on them seems to extend the sadism of their oppressors to a sadism of the film.

> *Robin Wood, "Notorious and Notable," in* The Times Educational Supplement *(© Times Newspapers Ltd. (London) 1976; reproduced from* The Times Educational Supplement *by permission), No. 3211, December 17, 1976, p. 18.*

## DAVID G. BEVAN

The film of **The Decameron** is not a fusion of Pasolini and Boccaccio, nor does it necessarily reflect Pasolini's view of Boccaccio; it merely reveals Pasolini's own imaginary experience derived from a particular reading. It is Pasolini who is the sole creator of his film. (p. 24)

The treatment of the subject-matter in the film attests both a desire to offer an authentic picture of man in the Middle Ages and, further, to delineate what is elementary and continuing in Man on an a-temporal level, beyond any specific historical figuration. . . .

For Pasolini the consciousness that formulated *The Decameron* was inseparable from the one which composed *De genealogia deorum gentilium,* that huge repository of Greek and Roman mythology which is one of the monuments of early classical scholarship. It is, therefore, not surprising that in his wish to re-discover the vitality of the Middle Ages Pasolini found it necessary to strip his written source of all of its rhetorical trappings, artifices of plot, and recitative structure. Couched in elegant, refined, bourgeois language, Boccaccio's *Decameron* seemed to raise an inadmissible screen between the addressee and the original experience. Pasolini renounced the approach of the lettered author that was Boccaccio's and substituted a candour and a naiveté which were for him much closer to the predominant spirit of mediaeval man. Beyond the sophisticated narratives of an a-typical educated scholar, Pasolini sought to touch the human pulse. (p. 26)

Early in the film a bustling, noisy, street-scene shows a wandering bard relating verbatim a tale from Boccaccio's *Decameron.* This delightful ploy enables Pasolini to insist within a single sequence on the gulf between the polished literary version and the brutally immediate cinematographic. Moreover, the book has become, significantly, a subordinate element in the primary phenomenon of the film. This hierarchy is further emphasised when, on several occasions later in the film, Pasolini himself appears as Giotto. The painter's brief appearance in Boccaccio's work is amplified on the screen to the point where Giotto, working on his religious fresco, comes to symbolise *the* creator-artist, comes to symbolise Pasolini himself since the latter is the creator-artist of the film. Nor is it only the palpable physical identity of both, which Pasolini's features suggest, that is noteworthy, but also the subject-matter of their respective creations. . . .

The conclusion would seem to be that the artist's task—be it Giotto or Pasolini—is to distil from man's experience that which is enduring and fundamental, and to give it expression. (p. 27)

It has been claimed that Pasolini introduces gratuitously his very personal idiosyncracies into his films and that, in these cases, he is guilty of a falsification and an individualisation of the original experience. However, all of the aspects commonly mentioned in this respect—misogyny, anticlericalism and homosexuality—figure already in Boccaccio, and any additional emphasis that there may seem to be is often due to the irreducibly concrete nature of film itself. . . .

Pasolini preserves in most respects the image of the Middle Ages that is contained in Boccaccio, but . . . divests it of the deceptive discretion of presentation. (p. 28)

> *David G. Bevan, "Pasolini and Boccaccio," in* Literature/Film Quarterly *(© copyright 1977 Salisbury State College), Vol. 5, No. 1, Winter, 1977, pp. 23- 9.*

### ROBERT J. WHITE

Where Sophocles has succeeded in making his *Oedipus Rex* topical and relevant, Pasolini has aimed at making his *Edipo Re* strange and indefinite, outside any specific set of cultural references. In Pasolini, the mythic is equated with the unfamiliar; the universal, with the particularly grotesque. (p. 32)

Pasolini's view of myth as an a-historical, symbolic reality . . . influences his conception of Oedipus. He seems to ascribe the intellectuality of Sophocles' Oedipus less to Oedipus the

mythic archetype than to the critical spirit and scientific outlook of fifth century Athens, to the outstanding achievements of a generation of sophists, scientists, and philosophers, that is, to a precise moment in history. Consequently he has deliberately and, one might say, perversely chosen to create a non-intellectual Oedipus. (p. 34)

[Pasolini, a Marxist], sees the emergence of the petit bourgeoisie with its attendant moral code as being a decidedly historical and temporal phenomenon. He maintains that in place of the soul, which is a transcendental reality, it has substituted conscience, which is at best a shadowy social convention. And so, in order to capture the mythicness of Oedipus, Pasolini attempts to reconstruct a pre-bourgeois mentality where conformity in conduct to a prescribed moral standard is not taken for granted. He has tried to place Oedipus in a more mythic, subproletarian world completely stripped of any traces of bourgeois morality. . . . Finally, by exploiting the spatio-temporal freedom of film, Pasolini is able to introduce into *Edipo Re* scenes and images that seem designed to speak directly to his audience's unconscious, to penetrate the labyrinthine recesses of their collective selves. (p. 35)

Pasolini's *Edipo Re* is, then, an attempt to inhabit the realms of myth and dream. Pasolini has worked through the medium of film, believing as he does that images are closer to myth than words. Whereas Sophocles took the myth of Oedipus and clothed it in history in order to interpret the times, Pasolini has taken the myth and stripped it of history in order to enter more fully into the myth. Taken together, the two approaches bear eloquent testimony to the Protean nature of myth. (p. 36)

> *Robert J. White, "Myth and Mise-en-Scène: Pasolini's 'Edipo Re'," in* Literature/Film Quarterly *(© copyright 1977 Salisbury State College), Vol. 5, No. 1, Winter, 1977, pp. 30-7.*

### DEREK ELLEY

[*Salò*] joins the list of little-seen but much-written-about *oeuvres de scandale* which fuel the fires of the censorship debate. This is perhaps the greatest pity, since the film is one of those works which is undoubtedly more horrifying in print than it is on screen. A mere catalogue of its more scandalous moments gives a totally false impression of its overall qualities, and, particularly in the case of *Salò,* those moments are far from being the *sine qua non* of its existence. Much of the content may be obsessive and much of it indecipherable to a reasonably balanced mentality, but its construction is far from haphazard and its logic, on its own terms, perfectly coherent. That logic is summarised early on by one of the Fascist overseers: 'All things are good when carried to excess.' And Pasolini invites the viewer into a downward spiral of humiliation and degradation pursued to the ultimate extreme of eventual death. . . .

[The] film is consistently pleasing to the eye, and Pasolini's *mise-en-scène,* visually discreet, mostly reliant on the long shot, and replete with controlled, geometric set-ups, is about as lip-smacking as a desiccated prune. A general heartlessness, a total unconcern for the individual, pervades the picture; this is not new in Pasolini, but some human concern would have given his scenario some justification. . . . Pasolini's grafting of Fascism on De Sade's theories is gratuitous at the least, but such deliberate provocation by the film-maker is rapidly neutralised by the steer monotony and obsessiveness of the argument. The film's thesis is made clear in the opening reel, and the remainder of the time is merely spent in demonstration and elaboration rather than development. . . . Pasolini was always a highly literary film-maker—and, for me, a writer and theoretician rather than a natural *cinéaste*—but in *Salò* even the literary artist plays second fiddle to private obsessions. The latent (and sometimes not so latent) homosexuality in his *oeuvre* here devours reason; the coprophilia and proctophilia is gloried in *per se*. No amount of wordy intellectualising can obscure the barrenness of *Salò*. In sum it is as pointless a waste of film stock as anything in the *Confessions* series.

> Derek Elley, "Reviews: Pasolini's 'Salo: 120 Days of Sodom'" (© copyright Derek Elley 1977; reprinted with permission), in Films and Filming, Vol. 24, No. 1, October, 1977, p. 31.

### ROBERT ASAHINA

[While] relatively modest· in depicting more or less conventional (oral and anal) sexual acts, *Salò* is painfully explicit in areas previously unexplored on American screens—specifically, urination, defecation and sexual torture. That New York audiences can calmly tolerate Pasolini's cinematic excess offers compelling testimony about a liberal society's power to accommodate (or inability to resist) the most extreme repudiations of its own underlying values, like decency. . . .

[This] kind of tolerance undermines the film's *raison d'être*. When Sade's notions lose their power to shock, or are no longer taken seriously, they also lose their political and moral significance. . . .

I cannot help concluding that Pasolini was less interested in the overall point of his adaptation (if there was any) than in its obscene details. But I do not think the reason for this is, as he suggests, that before Pasolini's death in 1975 . . . , his homosexuality and radical politics were warped by alienation into an impotent rage against society. I would look, instead, to the tension in *Salò* between Sade's material and Pasolini's technique, between the disgusting content and the stern formalism of its expression. Pasolini's sensibility, I believe, became its own primary object; and this estheticism was evidence of self-indulgence rather than estrangement. . . .

With such an inhuman detachment from inhumanly indecent acts, what *Salò* exhibits most is an extreme preciosity. Pasolini is simply too "elegant" to hate—or, in fact, to manifest feeling of any kind. . . .

*Salò*, in short, really has very little intelligent to say about either sex or politics. (p. 24)

> Robert Asahina, "A Weak Italian Trio," in The New Leader (© 1977 by the American Labor Conference on International Affairs, Inc.), Vol. LX, No. 23, November 21, 1977, pp. 24-6.*

### TOM ALLEN

[*The Arabian Nights* fails] to resolve the immense contradictions already bequeathed by the director. Why did one of the world's least popularist, most problematic filmmakers expend so much energy visualizing the enduring, seminal folklore of several cultures? Again we are regaled with an ambitious production that gorges the eyes with a sumptuous diorama beautifully filmed in exotic locales, but whenever we get in close, the mind is stupefied by wooden amateurs sleepwalking through a simplistic dress pageant. The arrogant whimsy of Pasolini, obvious in his bold strokes, never led him to master the simple

basis of film grammar so that as far as dramatic involvement is concerned, the film is frequently a bore.

Fortunately, *The Arabian Nights* does have elements that play to Pasolini's strengths. These are ancient tales that are based on piquant twists of fate, ritualistic trials of will, and erotic flourishes rather than on the emerging bourgeois psychology of Boccaccio and Chaucer in which even the bawdy episodes are pinned to latent character insights. Without Scherezade or Ali Baba or Sinbad, there is still ample opportunity in the volumes of Arabic lore for Pasolini's strange, documentary-based poeticism to flourish. For those who can hurdle the plodding foreground, *The Arabian Nights* is revealed as considerably more than a curiosity though considerably less than a masterwork.

> Tom Allen, "A Date Which Will Live in Fantasy" (reprinted by permission of The Village Voice and the author; copyright © News Group Publications, Inc., 1980), in The Village Voice, Vol. XXV, No. 31, July 30, 1980, p. 40.*

### J. HOBERMAN

More than a curiosity, but less than a fully realized work, Pier Paolo Pasolini's feature-length *Notes for an African Orestes* is an intriguing item that's almost invariably omitted from the late director's filmography. It shouldn't be. While *Orestes* has a general interest for anyone curious as to how a director's mind works, it is key to an understanding of the particular Freudian-Marxist-Christian world-view that was Pasolini's.

Having recently completed versions of *Oedipus* and *Medea* Pasolini planned to film his *Oresteia* in the third world. Aeschylus's myth of the first human tribunal—with its climactic transformation of the archaic Furies into the civilizing Eumenides—had, Pasolini thought, a special relevance to the situation of underdeveloped societies in the throes of modernization. . . .

Many of Pasolini's ideas are truly inspired. He uses a wounded lioness to represent the Furies and interpolates grisly newsreels of the Biafran war as Cassandra's vision. Other ploys are blithely goofy—half the film is accompanied by the Slavic anthems of the Red Army Chorus. Although disarmingly casual, *Orestes* is far from unstructured. Parts are extensively edited and Pasolini even roughs out a few scenes. . . .

Mixed in with the African film are Rome-shot sequences in which Gato Barbieri rehearses the film's score, and others wherein Pasolini interrogates a classroom of African students. His questions are leading ones: What do they think of his idea? Do they identify with Orestes? . . . These scenes are crucial, because they crystallize the film's problem. For all of Pasolini's progressive views, there's a subtly patronizing aspect to his project. Did he give it up when he realized that the end result of the "epic folk drama" he planned might have been something akin to a leftist's *Porgy and Bess*?

Actually, the essay form that *Orestes* takes suited Pasolini far better than his overblown glosses on Chaucer or *The Arabian Nights*. Like the Godard films of the late '60s, *Orestes* is a movie that requires an active viewer. The deconstructed narrative demands that you put Pasolini's film together in your head. (p. 40)

> J. Hoberman, "Unfree Radicals" (reprinted by permission of The Village Voice and the author; copyright © News Group Publications, Inc., 1980), in

*The Village Voice, Vol. XXVI, No. 1, December 31, 1980, pp. 40-1.*

### STEPHEN SNYDER

While, in life, [Pasolini's] hunger for the "rough trade" of the Roman slums ended in a violent death, in film, his metaphor of life-as-ingestion ("devour") assumed the monstrous proportions of a last supper of feces. . . . The compelling salience of the supper image in its stubborn and variegated reincarnations would suggest it commanded a station of prominence in the imagination of the filmmaker. . . . [The] dining metaphor does recur in Pasolini's work in a number of contexts, as an expression of spiritual hunger (*The Gospel According to Matthew*), as an act of assimilation or communion (*The Hawks and the Sparrows*, 1966), as a direct expression of the bodily hunger of poverty (*La Ricotta*), or as a natural metaphor of the animality of consumerism (*Salo, Pigsty*). (p. 19)

The filmic metamorphosis of his gastric metaphor captures the process by which his movies seem to grow out of each other, in the manner of a cocoon opening onto larger, more colorful creatures, each united by a common genetic inheritance, yet infused with novelty and uniqueness. One finds in his films a biological evolution, the later works still enlarging upon the territory opened in the earlier ones.

The sorting out of all the genetic strands involved is hopelessly complicated by Pasolini's insatiable eye and creative energies which sought to ingest all matters of life that came their way. (p. 20)

[His] spiritual sensibility cannot be stressed enough. It precedes and encapsulates his Marxist affinities with the result that his films cannot be approached with the simpleminded assumption that they are, or should be, political statements meant to illustrate Marxist ideology. In most cases, the political dimensions of the films are submerged in the dramatic heart of the narrative. What Pasolini takes from Marx is his criticism of capitalist mentality, specifically its reduction of man to a product, a piece of merchandise. He shares with him, also, the sense that the degree of freedom in a society is largely a measure of the freedom of its women. Thus, there is a strong sense throughout the canon of Pasolini's films that the exploitation of man by man inherent in capitalist economics (at least for Pasolini) begins with the exploitation of women by men. The relationship of prostitute to pimp becomes a defining model of sexual relationships generally. (p. 22)

With *The Gospel According to Matthew*, it becomes clear that Pasolini's natural commitment as an artist is less to intellectual abstractions via ideology than to the incarnate spirituality of life itself. . . . In one sense, Pasolini's achievement in this film is the release of the individual's capacity for a spiritual vision (neither institutionalized nor Platonic) from within himself, by which he keeps faith with the life of this world rather than striving to break from it. (p. 25)

The spiritual element liberated in *The Gospel According to Matthew* is not necessarily that of fundamentalist Christianity which perceives man only as a fallen creature in an arena of toil, whose salvation lies in detaching himself from earth to fly to an abode in the sky. Because he is both God and man, Pasolini's Christ is an affirmation of the director's own commitment to life and, hence, to the concrete world. . . .

What Pasolini proclaims is that the world itself, despite its surplus of misery and toil, is a spiritual event, and the capacity to perceive this transposes that world in a new light. . . .

[Reality] in Pasolini's vision is a holistic event—a unified process in which the distinctions between spirit and flesh, or the denial of either, emerge as symptoms of a withered imagination, a contraction of psychic life, a fragmentation in the soul which manifests itself as a desire to retreat from a confrontation with the total mystery of existence. Dualisms become symptomatic of a disease which wishes to control reality by narrowing its dimensions to manageable units. This disease constitutes the actual "fall of man" in Pasolini's works, the progenitor of the conditions of human misery.

Holistic consciousness is thus probably the most inclusive concept one may apply to Pasolini's work as a means of appreciating its opulence. In some manner the events and images which preside over his work—eating, sexual integration, seeing—receive special ordination from his sense of the crucial nature of holism in human development. (p. 26)

[Ultimately] for Pasolini, the cinema is an act of love which confirms man's creative spirit to be not only a part of life, but the power within life, a measure of his capacity to love. (p. 29)

*Stephen Snyder, in his* Pier Paolo Pasolini *(copyright © 1980 by G. K. Hall & Co.; reprinted with the permission of Twayne Publishers, a Division of G. K. Hall & Co., Boston), Twayne, 1980, 199 p.*

# (David) Sam(uel) Peckinpah

## 1925-

**American director, screenwriter, and actor.**

**Peckinpah is regarded by some as the most innovative director of Westerns since John Ford. His films are noted for seemingly gratuitous bloodshed, often filmed in slow motion. This is balanced by Peckinpah's strong personal vision: his work is often concerned with the plight of the loner and the instinct for survival. His best films are honest, lyrical evocations of the Western myth at odds with the aging of the hero and the progress of technology.**

**Peckinpah first gained prominence in the fifties as a television writer and director. Among other series, he worked on *Gunsmoke*, *The Rifleman*, and *The Westerner*. His first films, *The Deadly Companions* and *Ride the High Country* (also known as *Guns in the Afternoon*), were released in 1961 and created excitement in the film industry because of their strong moralizing and beautiful cinematography. These films helped Peckinpah gain the director's position for *Major Dundee*, which was substantially cut and re-edited by the producers.**

**Studio interference has played a major part in Peckinpah's career. *Ride the High Country* was released as a second feature for drive-in fare despite the fine reviews it received. Peckinpah tried to have his name removed from the credits of *Major Dundee* because of the studio's editing. Norman Jewison replaced him as director of *The Cincinnati Kid* after a few days of shooting because of disagreements between Peckinpah and the producers. These difficulties have continued in some of Peckinpah's more recent films, most notably *Pat Garrett and Billy the Kid*. Problems such as these forced Peckinpah to abandon filmmaking in the mid-sixties and to write and direct for television.**

**Peckinpah returned to films in 1969 with *The Wild Bunch*. The film has generated a great deal of controversy because of its graphic violence, but many critics believe that the violence expresses a moral viewpoint that audiences have misunderstood. These critics feel that Peckinpah *wants* his audience to become nauseated by human brutality and the consequences of uncontrollable rage. Despite this defense, Peckinpah's later films have come under heavy criticism. Films such as *Straw Dogs, The Getaway, Pat Garrett and Billy the Kid*, and *The Killer Elite* all contain murder and gunplay, and it is widely felt that the violence in these films is not as integral to their themes and plots as it is to *The Wild Bunch*.**

**Peckinpah's most recent films have not been well received. Although critics praise the filmmaking mastery still evident in** the visual splendor of *Bring Me the Head of Alfredo Garcia, Cross of Iron, The Killer Elite*, **and** *Convoy*, **the consensus is that style overcomes substance in these films. According to Stanley Kauffmann, "Peckinpah knows everything about filmmaking—past the point where it is knowledge. But his recent work is like hearing a virtuoso pianist at practice, doing double octaves and runs and trills. Dazzling, but where's the music?"**

### EUGENE ARCHER

William Faulkner made macabre comedy from the situation of a wagon transporting a coffin across miles of arduous terrain. **"The Deadly Companions"** . . . covers the same ground as "As I Lay Dying" and manages to make the plot look almost routine. . . .

The burden of this [film's] tasteless plot is partly relieved by scenic color photography and a capable cast. . . .

Their resourceful efforts would be more effective if the drama, as directed by Sam Peckinpah, did not move at the pace of a hearse.

> Eugene Archer, "The Screen: 'Deadly Companions'," in The New York Times (© 1962 by The New York Times Company; reprinted by permission), April 12, 1962, p. 41.

### DuPRE JONES

From [an] unlikely source comes an almost perfectly realised little film called *Guns in the Afternoon* [released in the United States as *Ride the High Country*] . . . , directed by Sam Peckinpah. . . . Sentimental moviegoers . . . are going to get quite a lot more than they bargained for: a movie full of intelligence, quiet charm, and thorough understanding of its materials. . . .

[What is so attractive about the film] is the intelligent way in which the direction and dialogue handle and exploit [the] nostalgia, developing it into a touching and significant tribute to the best elements of the Western myth. . . .

With this film Peckinpah displays not mere competence, but imagination and promise. Under his direction, [the lead actors] play with extraordinary ease and charm; his heavies—simultaneously funny and menacing—achieve the chilly balance which Ford tries for and often misses. . . . And certain individual touches are magnificent: a moronic gunman, frustrated at missing his human quarry, begins firing in wild fury at a flock of chickens.

DuPre Jones, "Film Reviews: 'The Man Who Shot Liberty Valance' and 'Guns in the Afternoon'," in Sight and Sound (copyright © 1962 by The British Film Institute), Vol. 31, No. 3, Summer 1962, p. 146.*

## TOM MILNE

[The last quarter of **Major Dundee**] may be cut to ribbons, but the first ninety minutes are magnificient.

The theme takes up and elaborates the conflict of **Guns in the Afternoon,** where two old comrades find themselves in a situation which revives and tests old loyalties. . . .

Despite the cuts which thin out the final stages of the story, . . . the film is a fascinating study in the swing of a pendulum. For all his air of authority and decision, everything Dundee touches goes subtly wrong. . . . As Dundee sinks lower and lower into self-distrust, so Tyreen rises; not because of a change of character—he remains perfectly consistent from his first sullen arrogance in prison to the final absurd gallantry of his single-handed charge against a French cavalry troop—but because he gains a kind of moral ascendancy. . . .

This theme is developed with a sweeping subtlety—broad strokes concealing the delicacy underneath—which recalls Ford at his best. Visually the film is magnificent, and its parched landscapes of dry brush and crumbling villages, its sculptural compositions, and proud cavalry movements across river and plain. Scene after scene might have come straight out of *Wagonmaster* or *My Darling Clementine,* but linking them all is a touch of the bizarre which is specifically Peckinpah's. . . .

At the same time there is a relaxed control, an unerring eye for juxtapositions, which reminds one that Peckinpah is one of those rare directors with an ability to keep his action racing swiftly, and yet leave one with the impression that there is all the time in the world for pleasurable contemplation. (p. 144)

Tom Milne, "Film Reviews: 'Major Dundee' and 'Invitation to a Gunfighter'," in Sight and Sound (copyright © 1965 by The British Film Institute), Vol. 34, No. 3, Summer, 1965, pp. 144-45.*

## PAUL SCHRADER

"**The Wild Bunch** is simply," says director Sam Peckinpah, "what happens when killers go to Mexico." And in the beleaguered career of Sam Peckinpah Mexico has become increasingly the place to go. It is a land perhaps more savage, simple, or desolate, but definitely more expressive. Sam Peckinpah's Mexico is a spiritual country similar to Ernest Hemingway's Spain, John London's Alaska, and Robert Louis Stevenson's South Seas. It is a place where you go "to get yourself straightened out." (p. 19)

Peckinpah carefully manages his violence [in **The Wild Bunch**], bargaining between the violence the audience wants and the violence he is prepared to give. Peckinpah uses violence the way every dramatist has, to make the plot turn. Then he applies vicarious violence to the plot mechanism. We don't really care whether it's logical if so-and-so is killed; we need more blood to satiate our appetite. . . . At the final level, the most difficult, Peckinpah goes beyond vicariousness to superfluity. We no longer want the violence, but it's still coming. Violence then

can either become gratuitous or transcend itself. Peckinpah enjoys walking the thin line between destructive and constructive violence. . . .

Robert Warshow wrote that the Western was popular because it created a milieu in which violence was acceptable. After years of simplistic Westerns, Peckinpah wants to more precisely define that milieu. Violence, Peckinpah seems to say, is acceptable and edifiable primarily for the spectator. It may also be edifiable for the participant, but only to the extent that it is suicidal. Like the Western code, it succeeds most when it is self-destructive. To be of any value violence must move from vicariousness to artifice. The spectator must be left "disinterested" in the Arnoldian sense, evaluating what he had previously reveled in.

In the post-slaughter epilogue of **The Wild Bunch** Peckinpah rubs the spectator's nose in the killing he had so recently enjoyed. New killers arrive to replace the old. A way of life has died, but the dying continues. . . .

The film is not about an antiquated Western code, but about Westerners bereft of the code. The Bunch are not Westerners who kill, but are killers in the West. **Ride the High Country** gave a perspective on why the code was valuable; **The Wild Bunch** gives a perspective on the age that could believe the Western code was valuable. . . .

In **The Wild Bunch** Peckinpah comes to terms with the most violent aspects of his personality. A long-time acquaintance of Peckinpah recently said of him, "I think he is the best director in America, but I also think he is a fascist." He was using the term "fascist" personally rather than politically. Peckinpah has a violent, domineering streak. There is in Peckinpah the belief that the ultimate test of manhood is the supression of others. . . .

The fascist edge of Peckinpah's personality does not make him particularly unique. It is a trait he shares with directors like Don Seigel, Howard Hawks, Samuel Fuller, Anthony Mann and all the rest of us who have always wanted to believe that those horseriding killers were really making the West safe for the women-folk. What makes Peckinpah unique is his ability to come face to face with the fascist quality of his personality, American films, and America, and turn it into art. . . .

In **The Wild Bunch** Sam Peckinpah stares into the heart of his own fascism. What had been formerly protected by the code is laid bare. The Western genre is ideally suited to such an examination; Jean-Luc Godard has noted that the Western is the only surviving popular fascist art form. In the past the Western had been able to perpetuate the myth of its own altruism, but, for Peckinpah, that myth had died its honorable death in **High Country**. The Westerners of **The Wild Bunch** have lost their code—only the fascism remains. The power of **The Wild Bunch** lies in the fact that this fascism is not peculiar to Peckinpah, but is American at heart. The America which created the Western . . . is the America Peckinpah determined to evaluate in his own life.

Like America's former macho-in-residence, Ernest Hemingway, Sam Peckinpah fights his private battles in public, both in life and art, but unlike Hemingway Peckinpah comes increasingly to terms with his own persona as he ages. As Hemingway approached death he relied increasingly on his code; as Peckinpah grows older he progressively discards his prefering to confront death head-on. **The Wild Bunch** is *The Old Man and the Sea* without a boat, a great fish or a native boy.

The great anguish of *The Wild Bunch* is the anguish of a fascist personality coming to terms with itself: recognizing its love of domination and killing, and attempting to evaluate it. (p. 22)

*The Wild Bunch* is a powerful film because it comes from the gut of America, and from a man who is trying to get America out of his gut. The trauma of expatriotism is a common theme in American art, but nowhere is the pain quite so evident as in the life of Sam Peckinpah. *The Wild Bunch* is the agony of a Westerner who stayed too long, and it is the agony of America. (p. 25)

*Paul Schrader, ''Sam Peckinpah Going to Mexico''
(reprinted by permission of the author), in* Cinema,
*Vol. 5, No. 3, 1969, pp. 18-25.*

**JOHN SIMON**

[*The Wild Bunch* is] an important bad film, avoidable by people who want genuine art, but recommended to all those interested in the faltering steps by which the American cinema might titubate into maturity.

There is no doubt that Peckinpah has a nice sense of time and place; that his locations and groupings, as well as the faces and peripheral activites that fill a shot have the right look and feel about them. But he is much less sure about the staging of the main action in a scene, except where seedy debauchery or sudden flare-ups of violence are concerned. (p. 173)

Despite an inventive twist or two, the plot settles all too comfortably into the usual western groove with all the beloved mythic commonplaces. But there are differences. The world of Peckinpah and his co-scenarist Walon Green is predominantly evil; there are no really good people anywhere, only the less bad and the much worse ones. (pp. 173-74)

Women are represented as particularly untrustworthy, and, next to women, children. Throughout the film we see kids enjoying the bloodshed and brutality around them and, whenever possible, joining in the fun, if only by torturing animals. . . . [It] may be the example of the adults that is to blame, but corrupt they are, and this is something new in a western. Except for Angel's concern for his villagers (he sacrifices his share of the loot for them), and the dignity of some of these folk, there are no unalloyed positive values in the film—even the gang's solidarity is labile and continually threatened from within. But Pike is idealized, and here the film goes soft. (p. 174)

The film has a good many . . . oversimplifications, exaggerations, or platitudes along its lengthy way. But then, again, there are powerful images: an ugly, mannish Mexican woman in Mapache's camp, who sits in full military gear suckling an infant; chickens scurrying underfoot and underhoof at the damnedest times; Pike trying to mount his horse and falling off because an old leg wound acts up as his men make sarcastic remarks; and, immediately afterward, Pike getting into the saddle and riding defiantly ahead. (pp. 174-75)

*The Wild Bunch* revels in bloodletting; not since baroque poetry and mannerist painting have there been such human fountains, blood spurting from them in manifold jets. . . . The result is, first, that a great deal of horror sneaks in subliminally, making it more bearable but still present; secondly, that much of the dying takes on a balletic quality which, again, makes it easier on the eye, though ultimately more appalling. Indeed, there is too much gore in the film.

The objection requires reflecting upon. Can one remonstrate with the frequency of refrains in a ballad? Can one cavil at the number of holes in travertine? The gore is of the essence. But cannot the essence be defective? By the use of slow motion, Peckinpah makes these deaths look rather like the similarly decelerated performances of shot putters or high jumpers in [Leni] Riefenstahl's and [Kon] Ichikawa's great films of the Berlin and Tokyo Olympiads.

The man whose face is suddenly bathed in crimson perspiration and who sinuously gravitates to the dust is a twin of the pole vaulter who has just cleared or not cleared an improbably high crossbar. The gun arcing away from him is the now useless pole, and he the winning or defeated athlete-hero hitting the sandlot. Win or lose is unimportant, what matters is the nobility of the sport. But killing and dying for sport should not look Olympic or Olympian: the gods who kill us for their sport should not get off the hook so cheaply.

But was it not so in Homer? Doesn't the *Iliad* chronicle, catalogue, itemize, deaths and the details of dying? True, but those are for us the least worthy parts of the poem—and hasn't the epic as a genre bit the dust precisely because it depended overmuch on war and violence and unlikely derring-do? Is not the epic as such an infantile form of art in both senses: a primitive art form and one appealing to puerile minds? The film, to the extent that it wants to achieve maturity, must outgrow the western. (pp. 175-76)

*John Simon, ''The New Violence: 'The Wild Bunch'''
(originally published as ''Violent Idyls,'' in* The New
Leader, *Vol. LII, No. 15, August 18, 1969), in his*
Movies into Film: Film Criticism 1967-1970 *(copyright © 1971 by John Simon; reprinted with permission of The Dial Press), Dial, 1971, pp. 173-76.*

**STEPHEN FARBER**

*Ride the High Country* was a sensitive, modest film, but Peckinpah has aimed much higher this time. *The Wild Bunch* is not a minor film; it's a sprawling, spectacular, ambitious, wilfully controversial picture, an assault on [an] audience's senses and emotions, an aggressive bid for the spotlight. Fortunately, the film deserves the spotlight. Its first impression is literally overpowering; *The Wild Bunch* is much more dazzling than *Ride the High Country,* but it loses some of the reflective qualities that made Peckinpah's early film so quietly memorable. There were stark images of violence in *Ride the High Country* too, but violence is the subject and the controlling passing of *The Wild Bunch.* Let me say right away that the violence does not offend me, even though this is the goriest film I have ever seen. But the gore is not gratuitous; the film is intelligent about the significance of violence in America, and in addition, the images of violence are quite simply beautiful. (p. 2)

I do object to some of the film's equivocations, and its tendency to sacrifice characterization to action and spectacle. The individual characters are just distinct enough to be believable, but none of them are really very interesting. The only way to accept the characters at all is to see them as one conglomerate character, the Wild Bunch. Peckinpah is interested in these men as a *group,* and he uses them to epitomize a major generic character, the Outlaw. But even granting this, the film, particularly on a second viewing, seems flat and underwritten.

The characters in *The Wild Bunch* are not complex, though the film's attitudes toward what they represent, toward violence, and toward the Western myth in general, are very complex;

but complexity is very close to confusion, and the film often seems out of control. . . . But I respect even the film's confusions, for they always seem to grow out of Peckinpah's most profound doubts and uncertainties, a very rich, intense self-questioning; they never seem concessions to the audience.

One first notices these confusions in the visual style of the film. The material is straightforward and conventional in many ways, and there are several elegant panoramic shots that are a staple of Westerns; but there are also some very contemporary tricks of film-making—slow motion, subliminal cutting—that testify to Peckinpah's dissatisfaction with the Western form, his desire to break it open and reconceive it. The sophistication of his technique does not always match the simplicity of the plotting and characterizations, and audiences encouraged by Peckinpah's mastery of the medium to expect a more subtle film are probably bewildered by the crude humor and old-fashioned melodrama of many scenes. The middle sections particularly lack dimension—effectively photographed but protracted, essentially hollow action scenes. And even the technique can turn surprisingly old-fashioned as in . . . the sentimental superimposition of the laughing faces of the Bunch over the final scene. (pp. 2-3)

*The Wild Bunch* has been compared to *Bonnie and Clyde* because of its sympathy for the outlaw and its mockery of all forms of "law and order"—whether the temperance union and railroad men in South Texas, Pershing's incompetent army along the border, or the coldblooded *federales* fighting Villa's revolutionaries in Mexico. But in one respect the film is sharper and more honest than *Bonnie and Clyde*—it does not flinch from showing the brutality of its heroes. . . . *The Wild Bunch* is more hardheaded because it admits the heroes' attraction to violence. We can't delude ourselves that the Bunch are innocent; they're clearly depraved and vicious—savages who love the thrill of slaughter.

And yet they do retain our sympathy. Perhaps one reason is that in a world where the "respectable" people seem equally sadistic, where indeed violence seems the primary fact of human nature . . . , the qualities of candor and resilience that distinguish the Bunch seem especially precious. . . . They are outsiders, failures, with nowhere to turn and no place to go, but they have not been defeated. They have the strength to endure. (p. 3)

During [the] last twenty minutes of his film Peckinpah so disturbs our emotions that we are literally drained by the conclusion. Just as we are convinced of the meaninglessness of the Bunch's life and death, Peckinpah once again twists our response and forces us to pay a final tribute to their irreverence and their resilience. It may be because of the tremendous complexity of the film's evaluation of the Bunch that many critics have been so outraged. What *is* Peckinpah trying to say? If he means to repel us by the life of violence, why that strangely sentimental finale? And if he means the film as a celebration of the outlaw, why must he so immerse us in the outlaw's brutality? There are no easy interpretations of *The Wild Bunch*. Peckinpah is feeling out his own responses to his characters' way of life, and he is asking us to struggle with him to make sense of the experiences on the screen. For all of its technical assurance, this is an unfinished, open-ended film, a tentative exploration of a peculiar, vanishing way of life, rather than a clearly formulated thesis film. Peckinpah has not resolved his own feelings about the masculine code of honor of the Westerner or about the violence of the outlaw, and *The Wild Bunch* reflects his confusions. We rightly demand more clarity from

an artist, but at the same time, the genuinely agonized temper of *The Wild Bunch* makes it a searching, unsettling film. (p. 5)

Peckinpah clearly means to say that violence is an inherent part of human nature, but it is interesting that the faces of the children almost always contain expressions of innocence and wonder that are not quite accounted for by the philosophical statement about their intuitive cruelty. . . . [The] faces of the children are still unformed, open to possibilities, and it is that sense of possibility that makes us dream. Children may be instinctively violent, but the freshness of their faces teases us to believe that they are capable of *something more* than violence. It is this something more that Peckinpah searches for in the Wild Bunch too—call it an inchoate sense of honor or loyalty or commitment—and just as often as he is wryly skeptical about the Bunch, he asks us to believe that they are redeemable. The children in the film embody innocence and evil, beauty and corruption, gentleness and brutality, and the film as a whole wavers between a harsh, very contemporary cynicism and an older, mellower belief in grand human possibilities that has always been the most sentimental affirmation of the Western. Traditional Westerns wallowed in this sentimentality and became rosy parables of virtue triumphant, while some very recent Westerns have gone to the other extreme and opted for a cynical stance that is often just as hysterical and glib. It is Peckinpah's effort to play these two attitudes against each other that makes his Westerns seem so rich; his mixture of realism and romanticism (a mixture that was already recognizable, on a much smaller scale, in *Ride the High Country*), even if not yet quite rationally proportioned, illuminates the Western myths so that they seem relevant, not remote. (pp. 5-6)

Peckinpah is an instinctive director, not an intellectual one, and his instinct for cinema is unquestionably masterful. But I would say that if he is to continue to grow as an artist, he needs to strive for more intellectual clarity; he needs to order and question his hidden assumptions even more ruthlessly, so that he can go on testing himself instead of simply repeating and reworking the themes of *The Wild Bunch*. I hope that his next film is not a Western. (p. 6)

*Stephen Farber, "Peckinpah's Return," in* Film Quarterly *(copyright 1969 by The Regents of the University of California; reprinted by permission of the University of California Press), Vol. XXIII, No. 1, Fall, 1969, pp. 2-11.*

## KENNETH R. BROWN

After viewing *Ride the High Country*, Jean Renoir remarked that "Mr. Peckinpah knows much about the music of the soul." But this could have been said even more accurately about *The Ballad of Cable Hogue*, because "the music of the soul" is really what it's all about. What Sam Peckinpah tried to do in this film was illuminate the essence, the *soul* of his characters—not through the realistic rendering of character and event, but by "objectifying" their various states of inner reality. This is indicated not merely by Peckinpah's "artifice," . . . but by the film's entire *style* and *content*, which are more closely unified than in almost any movie one could mention. . . .

It's as if Peckinpah turned his characters—indeed, the universe—inside-out, in order to expose the reality more fully. In this respect the film is reminiscent of *The Winter's Tale*, in which Shakespeare seems to have burned his own tragedies inside-out . . . in order to discover how Nature really functions. (p. 1)

It becomes obvious to anyone toward the end of *The Ballad of Cable Hogue* that it is not supposed to be a "realistic" movie . . . , yet the fact of the matter is that one ought to notice it from the very beginning. One of the most striking moments in the film occurs during the titles, when Hogue has spent his fourth day in the desert and is lying in the sand begging God to send him some water. Suddenly there is an overhead shot that seems to come from a great distance above Hogue, showing him lying amidst a whirlwind of sand, helpless, looking very much like an insect, completely at the mercy of Nature. Obviously, this is a God's-eye view of Man. God sees Hogue, has heard his plea, and He answers—and a moment later Hogue finds mud on his shoe. After this remarkable scene, it is difficult to understand how anyone could possibly expect that he is going to see a "realistic" film. Or even a comedy.

Although it lasts hardly more than a second and could be missed with the blink of an eye, this important scene not only sets up Peckinpah's approach to his material but also opens up one of the film's fundamental themes. . . . [It] illustrates the Biblical precept quoted in all of the film's advertising, and which is repeated numerous times during the course of the movie: "The Lord giveth, and the Lord taketh away." The point is not merely that an individual's life is sacred and that no one has the right to deprive him of it, but that ultimately it is suicidal even to try, because finally the victimizer becomes his own victim—he dehumanizes himself precisely to the extent that he dehumanizes the people around him. Peckinpah dealt with this same theme in *The Wild Bunch,* which illustrated the futility and madness of violence as it culminated in the suicidal and apocalyptic massacre at the film's end. But in that film he was investigating primarily the *consequences* of dehumanization; he watched his characters from the outside, remaining at a distance from them as they acted out the final scenes of their inevitable destruction. In *The Ballad of Cable Hogue,* however, the attempt is to expose his characters' interior. Peckinpah turns Hogue inside-out, "objectifies" his inner reality, while showing him in the process of destroying himself as he dehumanizes the people around him. If the emphasis in *The Wild Bunch* was on the consequences of man's dehumanization, in *Cable Hogue* it is on the causes of man's self-destructiveness—among which is the fact that he treats the people around him as objects, rather than as human beings.

Everything in *The Ballad of Cable Hogue* is represented as an object, because that's the way most of the characters see each other, and the way they see the world. (pp. 2-4)

The irony of Hogue's death represents the culmination of Peckinpah's attempt to turn his characters inside-out and expose the reality that lies within. When finally exposed, Hogue's soul—his essence—is revealed to be nothing more than an object. He has become dehumanized to the same extent that he dehumanized others: he is deprived of water and left in the desert to die—and when he discovers the only water for forty miles around, he sells it, and kills the first person who refuses to pay. Ownership and possession, and the way they deprive people of their humanity, are finally the subjects of *Cable Hogue.* Subtly, quietly, they work their will upon the selfish mind and destroy the individual's sense of what life is about—the honest and open communication among people. . . . *The Ballad of Cable Hogue* is about human objects struggling to become human beings. . . . In a very real sense, *The Ballad of Cable Hogue* is a vision of that Faulknerian nightmare of a

nation destroying itself through its inability to sever the umbilical to its past. A suicidal clinging to the petty hatreds and desires for revenge against those who have denied us our humanity—while losing the love and joy of living that alone makes survival in the desert worthwhile. (p. 30)

*Kenneth R. Brown, "Reality Inside-Out: 'The Ballad of Cable Hogue',"* in Film Heritage *(copyright 1970 by F. A. Macklin), Vol. 6, No. 1, Fall, 1970, pp. 1-6, 30.*

**VINCENT CANBY**

Peckinpah's funny and elegiac new film, **"Junior Bonner,"** . . . continues Peckinpah's preoccupation with what might be called reluctant past-primeness, that quality of being about to find oneself over-the-hill (and not liking it a bit). . . .

["**Junior Bonner"**] is Peckinpah in the benignly comic mood that, I suspect, is much more the natural fashion of this fine director than is the gross, intellectualized mayhem of his recent **"Straw Dogs."** **"Junior Bonner"** is about a man at a critical point in his life—will Junior be able successfully to ride a mean old black bull named Sunshine? Yet there is something as essentially comic as serious about the nature of the challenges Junior faces. . . .

The thing that distinguishes **"Junior Bonner,"** however, is not necessarily its broad streak of romanticism, but its affection for all of the Bonners. . . .

The movie seems to amble through its narrative with no great purpose until a moment, towards the end, when all of the Bonners—father, mother, sons, daughter-in-law and grandchildren—find themselves holding an odd reunion in an extremely crowded barroom. Like a lot of families, the Bonners love one another, and find it completely impossible to live together. The scene's climax: an uproarious barroom brawl in which absolutely no one is hurt. . . .

**"Junior Bonner,"** which looks like a rodeo film and sounds like a rodeo film, is a superior family comedy in disguise.

*Vincent Canby, "'Junior Bonner',"* in The New York Times *(© 1972 by The New York Times Company; reprinted by permission), August 3, 1972 (and reprinted in* The New York Times Film Reviews: 1971-1972, *The New York Times Company & Arno Press, 1973, p. 292).*

**VINCENT CANBY**

[There] are films that are simply lost in confusion—aimless enterprises that run on and on, sometimes with the sort of dazed looks you might expect, but often with expressions of deceptively intense purpose.

The last pretty well describes Sam Peckinpah's new film, **"The Getaway."** . . . More or less.

That qualification is necessary because if you take the characters at face value—which is what one usually does in this kind of film—then certain key decisions they make reflect on their sanity, which is otherwise unquestioned. From where any critic sits, it's impossible to tell whether this confusion is the result of the writing, the direction or the editing. . . .

For all his reputation as a director of action and violence . . . , Peckinpah is most effective and most eloquent when dealing with themes of love and loss, which are as apparent in the super-bloody **"The Wild Bunch"** as in the quieter **"The Ballad of Cable Hogue"** and this year's ruefully comic **"Junior Bonner."** The action and the violence of **"The Getaway"** are supported by no particular themes whatsoever. The movie just unravels.

Vincent Canby, "'The Getaway'," in The New York Times (© 1972 by The New York Times Company; reprinted by permission), December 20, 1972 (and reprinted in The New York Times Film Reviews: 1971-1972, The New York Times Company & Arno Press, 1973, p. 349).

## NIGEL ANDREWS

One of the ideas Peckinpah constantly illustrates in his films is that a moral code produced by one age or society is not necessarily valid in another. Thus the morality of a conventionally 'good' character—Steve Judd, let us say, in *Guns in the Afternoon*—may be implicitly criticised by Peckinpah as impractical in a contemporary context, derived as it is from old, received ethics rather than created out of the individual's own experience in his own age. Morality, Peckinpah suggests, should not be dependent on tradition, *or* on legislation, *or* on political or social ideologies. Once morality is made the province of a collective decision, or of a collective acquiescence in a pre-existing set of beliefs, the way has been opened for the suppression of individual choice.

The synthesis of individualism and survival, therefore, in Peckinpah's recent protagonists is not necessarily a moral fall from grace. Rather, it indicates the capacity of the characters, while remaining true to a central core of values, to adjust their life styles in order to maintain their equilibrium in an uncertain and treacherous age. This concept of 'equilibrium' I intend to discuss later in terms of Peckinpah's style, since most of the director's cinematic trademarks—slow motion, accelerated cutting, flashbacks and flashes forward—are placed in the films to create a deliberate and disorienting conflict of style with the orthodox narrative movement elsewhere; to violate 'normal' time and set up a new, catalysing tension between equilibrium and disorder. It's perhaps no accident that Junior Bonner, the quintessential Peckinpah hero, is a rodeo rider, a man whose way of life involves maintaining his balance on a belligerent and rebellious animal.

Peckinpah's films are concerned with exposing the fallibility of collective morality and with testing the reality and strength of an individual's moral decisions by placing him in a crisis situation. . . . Moral decisions taken *in extremis* are authentic and revealing precisely because they are spontaneous. Since such extreme situations tend to precipitate violence, Peckinpah's films have attracted constant public and critical indignation about their tendency to 'glorify' or 'dwell on' violence. This is an issue which has so monopolised critical concern that it is worth making two points. First, violence occurs in the films because it is a 'fact of life' and because a man's confrontation with violence provides the extreme test of his moral and physical courage. Second, violence is depicted realistically and vividly—'dwelt on', if one likes—because at this crisis point equilibrium must be *felt* to be threatened or momentarily lost, a feeling which the balletic or ritualised violence of the conventional Western never effectively creates. (p. 70)

*Cable Hogue* is a kind of blueprint for the two films that follow it, outlining in picaresque, schematic, and self-consciously comic form themes that the later films embody in a more coherent and powerful narrative structure. Thus, though dramatically it is the weakest of the films, it has the virtue presenting its themes within a clear-cut, readily accessible iconography. Cable's self-discovery 'out of nothing' is realised metaphorically in his discovery of water in the desert. . . .

Hogue's peculiar strength, that uncommon loyalty to self common to all Peckinpah's recent protagonists, renders his survival impossible in an age which sees humanity's unresisting surrender to the machine. By the end of the film, Hildy is travelling about in a car, Joshua on a motorcycle; but Hogue dies after being run over by the first automobile he sees. In Peckinpah's films life evolves repeatedly into this antithesis: man must preserve his independence but he must also stay alive, and the films are about the conflict between, or the hopeful reconciliation of these two imperatives. . . .

'Straw dogs' were used as substitute victims in ancient sacrificial ceremonies. The assumption of most reviewers was, accordingly, that the 'straw dogs' [of Peckinpah's film by the same name] were David and his wife Amy, victims of some gratuitous sacrificial impulse on the part of the villagers. But who is the 'Sage' if not David—the one character in the film whose pursuit of learning and belief in the supremacy of reason over blind force (he does not *initiate* a single violent act in the film) distinguishes him from those around him; as does, more concretely, his status as a foreigner in a close-knit village community? . . .

Like Cable Hogue, . . . David finds moral strength 'where it isn't'—that is, in no externally identifiable creed or ruling passion, but in himself, his reason—and the blackboard on which David works out his mathematical problems duly becomes the house's one untouchable icon. (p. 71)

Throughout the film David's unfamiliarity with violence, and with the instruments of violence, is stressed: it is Amy, for example, who imports the man-trap into the house, while David's inexpert handling of a gun is demonstrated in two sequences. The point is that David *does* adapt, that he is prepared to come to terms with violence, not only by using his gun and his impromptu weapons in the critical defence of his home, but also, on a deeper level, by recognising the violence in his own nature. (pp. 71-2)

Junior Bonner is the quintessential Peckinpah hero, owing all his strength to himself, none of it to the physical shelter of a home or the emotional shelter of personal relationships or public applause. He is an isolated figure, occupying his watchful place on the perimeter of the action—he takes no part in either the street carnival or the saloon brawl—and finding an emotional kinship only with those whose life styles, similarly fluid and unattached, celebrate a kind of continuous present . . . rather than a defeatist submission to the past . . . , or the sacrifice of the present moment to the future result inherent in his brother Curly's pursuit of material success or the fleeting rewards of competitive victory. . . .

Like David, Junior reconciles the ideals of survival and individualism. More than David, perhaps, he has learned to understand and confront their destructive counterparts in the modern world, violence and impersonality. (p. 73)

The problem of *The Getaway* lies in determining exactly where Peckinpah has located 'individualism', that stabilising loyalty to a chosen code of action which characterised David and Junior. Right from the beginning, Doc McCoy seems a character drawn against the grain of Peckinpah's previous heroes.

To begin with, he is first seen in captivity, having served five years of a ten-year sentence for armed robbery. Then, almost his first words in the film are 'Tell him I'm for sale.' . . . Not much later, Doc infringes another item in the Peckinpah concept of individualism—he initiates violence. . . . Since it's hard to look on Doc as a character whose way of life is endorsed by Peckinpah as were those of his predecessors, one begins to speculate that, Peckinpah having placed his story within a moral landscape markedly more vicious and impersonal than either [*Straw Dogs* or *Junior Bonner*] . . . , the emphasis has to be on survival, the fight for personal freedom overriding any concessions to a more generous or creative morality.

In many respects, *The Getaway* seems designed as the cynical obverse side of *Junior Bonner*. (pp. 73-4)

In one respect, Doc McCoy *is* in the tradition of past Peckinpah heroes. He is . . . one of 'the elect'. 'Special' is a recurring concept in the film. . . . Maybe, in a world where the luxury criteria of good and evil are being squeezed out by the more elemental criteria of life and death, captivity and freedom, the strength, expertise and courage of the Peckinpah hero must be harnessed to the pure struggle for survival. Maybe *The Getaway*'s chillingly simple moral is contained in Rudy's gunpoint threat to the kidnapped hotel-keeper: 'You've got two choices. You can live or you can die.' . . .

Peckinpah's experiments with cinematic time comprise one of the most interesting developments of his recent work. They seem to me to divide broadly into two categories: the interweaving of past and present events into a sequence designed to convey the idea of a continuous, unchanging way of life (the lyrical elisions of time in *Cable Hogue,* the credit sequences of *Junior Bonner* and *The Getaway*); and, in contrast, the accelerated editing of a single sequence in which simultaneous but geographically separate events are intercut. The latter technique, used extensively in *Straw Dogs,* is designed not to harmonise but to disrupt ideas of time, to suggest the slide into chaos threatening the equilibrium on which individual choice and action must be founded. . . .

['Equilibrium'] is a key idea in Peckinpah, the foundation for the qualities of control and rationality that characterise the protagonists of Peckinpah's last four films. . . .

'Assuming equilibrium' reads the inscription on David's blackboard prefacing his latest equation. That is precisely what David does assume; in the course of the film, however, every kind of equilibrium is threatened. . . .

The Peckinpah hero is distinguished by his ability to 'stand up', to maintain equilibrium, to remain loyal before all else to his own survival and individuality. This is not, as detractors of Peckinpah would have us believe, a latter-day Nietzschean moral system, predicating a hero of superior intelligence who ruthlessly overrides those weaker or less resourceful than himself. The point about David and Junior Bonner is that they do not impose their individuality on others, their beliefs, their values, their wants; they do not, on the one hand, initiate aggression, nor on the other, do they neglect their loyalty to those whose interests are linked to theirs and whose survival is precious to them. (p. 74)

*Nigel Andrews, "Sam Peckinpah: The Survivor and the Individual," in* Sight and Sound *(copyright © 1973 by The British Film Institute), Vol. 42, No. 2, Spring, 1973, pp. 69-74.*

## JON LANDAU

Sam Peckinpah thinks the Old West offered men the last unambiguous set of values and is fascinated by attempts to hold fast to them in a world where they no longer mean anything. In his disjointed, confused and generally inept *Pat Garrett and Billy the Kid,* he makes just two choices available to a pair of old friends: go down before the encroaching new order, or go to work for it at the cost of those unambiguous values. He sympathizes with Pat Garrett's instinct for survival in throwing in with the government, becoming a sheriff, and hunting down Billy the Kid; he admires Billy's refusal to run to Mexico and abandon his only true identity, that of an outlaw, but he believes in the inevitable spiritual death of the former and physical death of the latter. . . .

Peckinpah is interested only in the reverberations of the past: He disdains the details of storytelling, characterization and acting style. He photographs every frame in a luscious way that cries out for consideration as visual mythology, but his inattention to anything that might make it such leaves his movie looking more like a lavish, coffee-table edition of a Classics Illustrated comic book.

He has occasionally tried to expand the parameters of his point of view through the folktale style of *The Ballad of Cable Hogue* and *Junior Bonner,* but his excesses in this genre are just as great as in his macho tributes to men of action. His idea of humor is a small piece of slapstick followed by loud guffaw, while wit is completely alien to the man.

Peckinpah has accumulated sympathy even from viewers who think, as I do, that his films are heavy-handed, clumsy and unstimulating. There is no question that he has often been the victim of studio mistreatment. . . .

[The core of the drama in *Pat Garrett and Billy the Kid* lies in Billy's] unexplained refusal to heed Garrett's . . . warning to go to Mexico, rather than force his old friend to hunt him down. . . . Garrett, the realist, and Billy, the romantic, act out the predictable scenario, minus the tragic overtones that would have made the film comprehensible, if not original. The only thing unpredictable is the endless digressions, the constant additions and subtractions . . . of people whose purpose in the film we discover only moments before their name is called up younder, if at all. . . .

Apparently the deeper overtones of Garrett and the Kid's conflict didn't interest the director, who preferred to keep their problems and identities isolated and concentrated instead on the schematic progression to the inevitable shooting of the Kid. (p. 74)

In *Pat Garrett and Billy the Kid,* we never do know what Garrett wants and by the film's end his life appears to be a series of banal and automatic responses to banal and inevitable crises. Perhaps that automatic quality was supposed to be the source of the film's larger implications, with Peckinpah trying to suggest more by *not* explaining Garrett's character than he could have otherwise. If so, it just doesn't work. Neither does this very bad movie. (p. 75)

*Jon Landau, "Roundin' Up the Hot New Westerns," in* Rolling Stone *(by Straight Arrow Publishers, Inc. © 1973; all rights reserved; reprinted by permission), Issue 138, July 5, 1973, pp. 74-5.\**

## PETER BISKIND

It has been clear for some time to all but the most dogged of cultists that Sam Peckinpah's reputation, based on the undeniable merits of *Ride the High Country, Major Dundee,* and *The Wild Bunch,* but inflated beyond all recognition by his *auteurist* admirers, had to be scaled down in the light of his last four films. From *Ballad of Cable Hogue* to *The Getaway,* from bad to worse, Peckinpah's talent seemed to have faltered, to have wandered from the material that engaged it most centrally, into a marsh of mushy masculine sentimentality. *Pat Garrett and Billy the Kid* changes all that. It is a brilliant and perverse film. Part of its brilliance lies in its very perversity: its lack of plot; its collection of aimless, static scenes; its mumbled, whimsical, raunchy dialogue; its refusal to be coherent or conside. The remainder lies in the world of loss and limitation it evokes.

The landscape of *Pat Garrett and Billy the Kid* is familiar. It is one of male friendship and conflict, of casual and sudden violence, of slow motion shoot-outs, of children cavorting on the hangman's scaffold. Most familiar is the story itself, the story of the West growing old, of the passing of the western hero, a story that Peckinpah has told many times. It boils down to an exchange between Garrett and Billy. Garrett says, "The West is growing old, and I want to grow old with it." Billy replies, "Times change, not me." . . .

The structure of each of Peckinpah's westerns is defined by two men, brothers or close friends, whose differing responses to the closing of the frontier lead to a conflict which gives form to the moral dimensions of the films. (p. 1)

Pat Garrett is a pragmatist who bows to the inevitability of change and uses the tools that are his—his speed with a gun, his familiarity with the ways of outlaws—to gain employment and to survive, while his former friends, relics of a passing era, are rendered obsolete by the big ranchers who moved in behind them. If he is redeemed, he is redeemed by his awareness of his own equivocal situation. (p. 2)

The difference between the conclusion of *The Wild Bunch* and the conclusion of *Pat Garrett and Billy the Kid* is an index of the sense of pessimism and resignation that informs the latter. Pat Garrett is not redeemed but destroyed by the successful conclusion of his appointed task.

Billy the Kid, on the other hand, in rejecting Garrett's course, becomes the embodiment of values that are now obsolete. Not a hero in the old tradition of Gary Cooper and John Wayne, men of firm purpose animated by a high moral code, he is . . . a softer character, plump rather than lean, of some moral ambiguity. . . . The primary value to which he subscribes, and which distinguishes him from Pat Garrett, is loyalty to friends.

With regard to the story-line, then, this film differs only in detail and circumstance from Peckinpah's other westerns. What gives *Pat Garrett and Billy the Kid* its peculiar flavor is the elegiac tone of the film, the lamentation for a lost world, for a fugitive innocence and beauty. The characters are dominated by the past, by memory and recollection. We have stumbled in on the last act of a melancholy drama that is largely over. Everything of importance has already occurred. We view only the inevitable dénouement operating through passive characters who walk through their parts as if asleep. They are in the grip of an ineluctable necessity which they make only half-hearted efforts to elude. The characters, like the man deputized by Garrett in the barber shop, are at the mercy of fate, of predetermined roles, of formulaic codes of behavior that have ceased to have any real claim on them, but which nevertheless refuse to relinquish them. (pp. 3-4)

This overwhelming sense of external fate distinguishes *Pat Garrett and Billy the Kid* from Peckinpah's other films, which portray men as freely willing agents, fully responsible for their actions. Peckinpah's characters are complex beings, frequently overwhelmed by the savage self-destructive impulses that inhabit the self. In *Pat Garrett and Billy the Kid,* on the other hand, the autonomy of the characters is diminished, is subordinated to larger movements over which they seem to have little control. Interest shifts from interior conflicts, or even from conflicts between characters, to the relation of the characters to the vast historical and economic changes that are transforming the land. (pp. 4-5)

Peckinpah's heroes, at once the agents and victims of the "civilizing" process, the rationalization of western society, rebel against its consequences but enjoy no historical alternatives. They must resist or surrender. Either way, they are doomed. If Billy survives, he survives only as legend, in the eyes and hearts of the fascinated spectators who watch with frozen, fixed gazes as the grim drama is played out before them. (pp. 7-8)

*Pat Garrett and Billy the Kid* is an extraordinary achievement and reestablishes Peckinpah's claim on our interest. (p. 8)

> *Peter Biskind, "'Pat Garrett and Billy the Kid'," in*
> Film Heritage *(copyright 1974 by F. A. Macklin),*
> *Vol. 9, No. 2, Winter, 1973-74, pp. 1-8.*

## MARK CRISPIN MILLER

*Bring Me the Head of Alfredo Garcia* is at once the subtlest and strangest of Sam Peckinpah's films. It is what we must call his "most mature," because it presents what he sees less compromisingly than ever before, and because he relies on his last spectacular abilities to deliver its tremendous impact. It is not anywhere near as bloody as his most commercial pictures, yet it has died a swift and violent death [at the hands of the critics]. . . .

*Bring Me the Head of Alfredo Garcia* subsumes the director's dilemma into wider, more important conflicts, the ones dramatized in earlier films but with an unprecedented directness. Rather than rub the audience's collective nose in spectacular gore, Peckinpah has used the powers of his craft to make this film deliberately unprepossessing, but without, even here, abandoning the context of heroism that he knows so well.

It seems necessary to point out . . . that Peckinpah understands every aspect of heroism: its rarity, its loneliness, its tenuousness, its superficial attractiveness, the ease with which it's commonly misinterpreted or overlooked or mistaken for something else. He knows the difference between heroism and mere heroics, and he knows that his audience is generally not sensitive to this difference. . . . His is a complex, highly moral intelligence. (p. 2)

Not once since the too quiet release of *Ride the High Country* has a Peckinpah film repeated so even a moral and dramatic balance. Goodness and the good things of life have diminished, not in importance, but in accessibility; the bad things have proliferated, the destructive impulse burgeoning everywhere. Peckinpah's films still imply what is worthwhile, what must be preserved, even if what we see much more vividly than goodness is the multifarious complex of hateful urges which menaces that goodness. (p. 3)

The "outdated code" of "all the simple virtues that have become clichés," which Peckinpah might call the code of true manliness, comprises only a part of what he believes in. There is a complementary code of "feminine" values, virtues exemplified and propagated by women. . . . The feminine quality animates the furtive good of Peckinpah's world, and it is no less threatened than the old code of authentic manhood. (p. 4)

The knightly code and its complementary idyll of domesticity combine into a set of values that is not easily categorized. It contains something of the solid belief in family and place that informs such films as John Ford's *My Darling Clementine* and *The Searchers,* but celebrates sexual union and freedom in a way that the conventional Western never has. Yet it is defensive and fatalistic because it is predicated on the assumption that whoever adheres to its tenets will not survive. We might say, in this sense, that Sam Peckinpah suggests Ford in a black mood, reading a lot of Blake. (pp. 4-5)

[Peckinpah] thinks of himself as a story-teller first and foremost, and even his bitterest detractors would have to admit that his narratives . . . move quickly and grippingly, that his protagonists are complex, credible, unusual people, that he has a sophisticated sense of irony and always demonstrates masterful facility with all the elements of crisis. But beyond this, Peckinpah understands the large persuasiveness of his medium, and so is adept at grappling with the largely anachronistic issue of heroism. He can establish a heroic context, and make us uneasy by introducing into it a heroism that fails or is misplaced, or that is not real heroism but a mere series of postures. . . . Peckinpah intensifies our yearning to sympathize by establishing a glorious frame, a heroic context with those outlines we are familiar because we are familiar with the genre. (p. 5)

Peckinpah knows how to toy with all the assumptions and expectations that cinema has instilled within us, and he does this so unostentatiously that we can mistake his subtleties for excess, his ironic deflations and amplifications of types and clichés for a lack of artistic control. Often this distortion of convention goes unnoticed or is condemned for being improbable, when its improbability is intentional. . . . We expect [Spielberg's] *The Sugarland Express* and [Altman's] *Thieves Like Us* to end as they do. Therefore Peckinpah makes *The Getaway* end differently, but the getaway itself is so unlikely that it's almost sinister, as if its excessive cheeriness suggests what would really happen to such "outlaws" in the real world, much less what should happen to generic convention. And if we consider Peckinpah's cynicism, we must allow for the possibility that the ending of *The Getaway* might be intended to disappoint the demon within, whose demands for generic propriety are not altogether ingenuous.

It is this cynicism that lies behind Peckinpah's highly stylized . . . treatment of violence. His obsessive rendering of violence into gross lethargic ballet heightens our vicarious experience of it, makes it less of a kick and more of an indulgence, wherein the reluctant eye will linger and thereby learn. [As Peckinpah has said:] "Most people don't even know what a bullet hole in a human body looks like. I want them to see what it looks like. . . ." (pp. 5-6)

People will turn away and assume that Peckinpah's presentation implies celebration, or at least endorsement, and that the brutal approval of an audience applauding massacre accords perfectly with the director's intentions. Many critics, who ought to know better, make these fallacious assumptions. Their condemnation may be silly, but it is not Peckinpah's responsibility to lash out at this silliness. What he must do, intent as he is on edifying his viewers, is find a less blatant method of attack.

With *Alfredo Garcia* Peckinpah demonstrates his discovery of such a method: manipulation of sympathies, assumptions, and expectations, but manipulation that does not reduce characters to devices. . . . In his latest film Peckinpah sustains the possibility of heroism by presenting a perversion of it. He expands, intensifies, we might say "bloats" the figments of cinematic convention, not in the direction of camp or caricature, but naturalistically, making irresistibly believable and arresting the types and reactions we have come complacently to look for and accept. He translates back into ungainliness what Hollywood has portrayed romantically, but without any correlative diminution of vividness. Never before has he used his familiarity with audience response to such great effect, nor has he ever presented with such tenderness the things in which he so desperately believes. (p. 6)

*Mark Crispin Miller, "In Defense of Sam Peckinpah," in* Film Quarterly *(copyright 1975 by The Regents of the University of California; reprinted by permission of the University of California Press), Vol. XXVIII, No. 3, Spring, 1975, pp. 2-17.*

### ARTHUR G. PETTIT

If Peckinpah's sinister outlook is not confined to his Westerns, nevertheless his mordant philosophy has darkened the Western as no one else's has. His violent characters are compelling contributions to the genre. They are also nagging reminders of the pitfalls as well as the profits awaiting those who try to stand the traditional Western on its head. There is a strong current of ambivalence running through Peckinpah's work, a feeling that he remains trapped in his own uncertainties about the exact properties and consequences of the New West he has created. For all the blood, dirt and obscenity that mark Peckinpah's films, his Westerns contain large doses of romanticism mixed with the realism. By self-admission he is both drawn to and repelled by the American West, whether old or new.

Peckinpah's split-level approach to the West is rooted in doubts about what the Old West was really like, and what the New West is supposed to be like. More than any of his competitors, he sees the West as a vast theatre of metaphorical possibilities centered about the theme of Changing Times, with outmoded men walking a thin line between past and present, the old and the new. . . . Few film-makers have so densely peopled their work with characters who are emotionally or physically crippled. Peckinpah's West is a catalogue of washed-out male eccentrics stretching out beyond their reach, desperate men struggling to achieve mastery over self-annihilating impulses and forces outside their control. In all Peckinpah Westerns the message is the same: the frontier is vanishing, the land is being bulldozed beyond recognition, the West is closing in on itself, progress is snuffing out the old ways. Horses, six-guns and open spaces are giving way to cars, machine-guns and mobile homes. . . . The breathtakingly lovely hues of sun-drenched landscape clash harshly with the stink of urban decay, the numerous artifacts of destruction—scorpions, ants, vultures, bulldozers—offset by the wild beauty of the few ungutted spots of the West. (pp. 106-07)

No longer the spearhead of Manifest Destiny, the modern West has become the retreat for ritual, its urban landscape strewn with visual motifs advertising Peckinpah's disaffection with citified life: dark glasses (anonymity), mod-cowboy outfits (drugstore degradation of the old West), transistor radios (instant electronic entertainment), booster parades (collective celebrations of euphoria). The cinematic result is at once stunning realism and paralyzing chaos, a hodgepodge of colliding images of alienation and reverence, anger and affection—the theme of superannuation anchored in the need for Peckinpah's aging heroes to resolve their dilemma in haste, before time runs out. (pp. 107-08)

While trying to cope with a West gone mad and rotten beyond repair, Peckinpah pines for a West that never was, but should have been. While trying to rid his films of the message-mongering self-righteousness and one-dimensional hero-villain structure of the oldtime Western, he has moved both closer and farther from reality, unwittingly giving rise to a new set of legendary trappings of his own making. Foremost among these is Peckinpah's replacement of the saintly cowboy and the all-good badman as embarrassing aberrations with the supposedly all-bad badman as a hero in his own right. . . . Whatever its origins, the immediate significance of the removal of the all-good badman and the rise of the all-bad badman is the elimination of any need to explain how or why badmen went bad in the first place. Their present behavior is our only guide to their past. (p. 109)

Peckinpah's distinction in this field is that he can get away with it more successfully than most of his imitators, in part because he is a good artist often enough to appease the critics and a bad artist often enough to satisfy the public craving for blood and sex. Yet the tiresomely repetitious quality of his films since *The Wild Bunch,* reaching a new low in *Bring Me the Head of Alfredo Garcia,* opens the suspicion that Peckinpah may be joining lesser film-makers in turning out modish criminals who whore and slaughter with little moderation or mercy precisely because that is what is expected of him. . . . [However], we find on closer inspection that Peckinpah's badmen are not really that bad. Clearly warped, they are still far from the assortment of gargoyles that clutter the "gothic" films adapted from the works of Tennessee Williams, William Faulkner or Carson McCullers. Peckinpah keeps insisting that his badmen are not heroes, but either he deceives the public or himself. Heroes, after all, are men or women with whom we identify because we see ourselves in them, or more likely because we wish we did. In either case Peckinpah's badmen qualify as heroes; heroes of a peculiar stripe to be sure, peeled of the cumbersome layers of goodness that suffocated their forebears, but heroes nonetheless. (pp. 110-11)

Whether we like it or not, violence is central to most of Peckinpah's films. It is the source of their symmetry and moral complexity. There is a sense of tragic inevitability about Peckinpah's violence, a sense of the failure of men to own up to their beastly instincts until it is too late, until life or choice are eliminated through the neutralizing device of violence. The great power of Peckinpah's "dirty Westerns" flows from the merciless and unrelenting attack on the full spectrum of our senses. In viewing them we are forced to experience the most painful confusion of feelings, alternately uplifted and downgraded, exalted and violated. If the dialectics of tragedy through violence are not wholly realized in Peckinpah's better Westerns, especially *The Wild Bunch;* if we do not emerge from the blood-letting having experienced revulsion, powerlessness and shame, it may not be Peckinpah's fault. (p. 122)

> *Arthur G. Pettit, "Nightmare and Nostalgia: The Cinema West of Sam Peckinpah," in* Western Humanities Review *(copyright, 1975, University of Utah), Vol. XXIX, No. 2, Spring, 1975, pp. 105-22.*

**PAULINE KAEL**

Sam Peckinpah is a great "personal" filmmaker; he's an artist who can work as an artist only on his own terms. When he does a job for hire, he must transform the script and make it his own or it turns into convictionless self-parody (like *The Getaway*). Peckinpah likes to say that he's a good whore who goes where he's kicked. The truth is he's a very bad whore: he can't turn out a routine piece of craftsmanship—he can't use his skills to improve somebody else's conception. That's why he has always had trouble. And trouble, plus that most difficult to define of all gifts—a film sense—is the basis of his legend.

Most movie directors have short wings; few of them are driven to realize their own vision. But Peckinpah's vision has become so scabrous, theatrical, and obsessive that it is now controlling him. His new film, *The Killer Elite,* is set so far inside his fantasy-morality world that it goes beyond personal filmmaking into private filmmaking. The story, which is about killers employed by a company with C.I.A. connections, is used as a mere framework for a compressed, almost abstract fantasy on the subject of selling yourself yet trying to hang on to a piece of yourself. Peckinpah turned fifty while he was preparing this picture, and, what with booze, illness, and a mean, self-destructive streak, in recent years he has looked as if his body were giving out. This picture is about survival.

There are so many elisions in *The Killer Elite* that it hardly exists on a narrative level, but its poetic vision is all of a piece. Unlike Peckinpah's earlier, spacious movies, . . . this film is intensely, claustrophobically exciting, with combat scenes of martial-arts teams photographed in slow motion and then edited in such brief cuts that the fighting is nightmarishly concentrated—almost subliminal. . . . [The] film is airless—an involuted, corkscrew vision of a tight, modern world. . . . [The] film isn't about C.I.A.-sponsored assassinations—it's about the blood of a poet. (pp. 112-13)

Peckinpah has been simplifying and falsifying his own terrors as an artist by putting them into melodramatic formulas. He's a major artist who has worked so long in penny-dreadful forms that when he is finally in a position where he's famous enough to fight for his freedom—and maybe win—he can't free himself from the fear of working outside those forms, or from the festering desire for revenge. He is the killer-élite hero . . . in this hallucinatory thriller, in which the hirelings turn against their employers. (p. 115)

There's no way to make sense of what has been going on in Peckinpah's recent films if one looks only at their surface stories. Whether consciously or, as I think, part unconsciously, he's been destroying the surface content. In this new film, there aren't any of the ordinary kinds of introductions to the characters, and the events aren't prepared for. . . . Peckinpah can explain this disintegration to himself in terms of how contemptible the material actually is—the fragmented story indicates how he feels about what the bosses buy and what they degrade him with. He agrees to do these properties, to be "a good whore," and then he can't help turning them into revenge fantasies. His whole way of making movies has become a revenge fantasy: he screws the bosses, he screws the picture, he screws himself.

The physical rehabilitation of the hero in *The Killer Elite* . . . is an almost childishly transparent disguise for Peckinpah's own determination to show Hollywood that he's not dead yet—that, despite the tabloid views of him, frail and falling-down drunk, he's got the will to make great movies. He's trying to pick up the pieces of his career. Amazingly, Peckinpah does rehabilitate himself; his technique here is dazzling. In the moments just before violence explodes, Peckinpah's work is at its most subtly theatrical: he savors the feeling of power as he ticks off the seconds before the suppressed rage will take form. When it does, it's often voluptuously horrifying (and that is what has given Peckinpah a dubious reputation—what has made him Bloody Sam), but this time it isn't gory and yet it's more daring than ever. He has never before made the violence itself so surreally, fluidly abstract; several sequences are edited with a magical speed—a new refinement. (pp. 115-16)

No one is Peckinpah's master as a director of individual sequences; no one else gets such beauty out of movement and hard grain and silence. He doesn't do the expected, and so, scene by scene, he creates his own actor-director's suspense. The images in *The Killer Elite* are charged, and you have the feeling that not one is wasted. What they all add up to is something else—but one could say the same of [Pound's] *The Pisan Cantos.* Peckinpah has become so nihilistic that filmmaking itself seems to be the only thing he believes in. He's crowing in *The Killer Elite,* saying, "No matter what you do to me, look at the way I can make a movie." The bedevilled bastard's got a right to crow. (p. 119)

*Pauline Kael, "Notes on the Nihilist Poetry of Sam Peckinpah" (originally published in* The New Yorker, *Vol. LI, No. 47, January 12, 1976), in her* When the Lights Go Down *(copyright © 1975, 1976, 1977, 1978, 1979, 1980 by Pauline Kael; reprinted by permission of Holt, Rinehart and Winston, Publishers), Holt, 1980, pp. 112-19.*

### W. S. Di PIERO

*Cross of Iron* is a polemic against war, more specifically against war-as-necessity, and it tries to define the role of male virtue in such vicious circumstances. Honor is always defined by circumstance. The huge irony upon which the film turns, however, is that while men may excel in combat, their personal excellence never justifies the context. Here, as in *Ride the High Country* and *The Ballad of Cable Hogue,* Peckinpah is openly curious about the stern wisdom that underpins male vanity. (p. 7)

*Cross of Iron* is no closet drama. Peckinpah avoids the convenient black comedy and intellectual pieties of a [Lina] Wertmüller. The film is punctuated, often unexpectedly, with images of ruined anonymous bodies, humans made meat by the indifferent mechanics of war, a profanation of old values of human dignity. His critics notwithstanding, I don't think Peckinpah is interested in kineticism for its own sake. The violence in this film at every point serves his argument against the moral indifference of war. The polemic is relentless. . . .

Peckinpah also returns to an old obsession: the legacies of violence passed on from father to son. . . . [He] knows that we are bound to pass on to our children not only our animal instincts but also our monstrous inclination towards atrocity. . . . *Cross of Iron* is cogent and powerful, and its unembarrassed rawness persuades where the over-educated black humor of other war films fails. Peckinpah offers no consolation, no phony grace, no pious equivocation. One of his distinctions is that he is an intelligent film artist whose films are seldom polluted by artiness. (p. 8)

*W. S. Di Piero, "Sam Peckinpah's 'Cross of Iron'," in* Take One *(copyright © 1977 by Unicorn Publishing Corp.), Vol. 5, No. 8, March, 1977, pp. 7-8.*

### ANDREW SARRIS

Sam Peckinpah's *Convoy* is not merely a bad movie but a terrible movie. Anyone can make a bad movie—only a misguided talent can manage to be terrible. And there is visible talent, even in *Convoy*—particularly when men and machines are set into motion and smashed with an exquisite exuberance, as if visible matter were being transported to a realm beyond good and evil for the eternal edification of the naked eye.

But, then, the cardboard characterizations and comic-strip contrivances bring *Convoy* back down to earth with all the other infantile junk flicks of the late '70s. There is now no doubt that its director is scrambling for survival, taking whatever the traffic will bear. Never before has a Peckinpah film been so devoid of death and pain and even stress. . . .

[Never before] has Peckinpah seemed so nakedly Russian as a visual rhetorician. This is where the controversy may arise. Even his erstwhile admirers may be forced to admit that *Convoy* is lacking in content above the moronic level. But the "look" and "rhythm" of the film are something else again. Are we back in the magically auteurist regions of Raoul Walsh and Samuel Fuller, regions in which visual forms allegedly transcended genre conventions? I think not. The films of Walsh and Fuller and all the other controversial "action" or "genre" directors stand or fall on the integration of style and subject matter. The rationale for Peckinpah was quite different. His critical myth was that of the rebel who undertook genre assignments only to subvert them. From his earliest writing-directing jobs on *Gunsmoke, The Westerner,* and *The Rifleman,* one sensed an irony and a portentousness that seemed to denote a deep-seated disgruntlement with the false fictions of an era and an area Peckinpah deemed his own domain. His roots were in the West, and he felt it was his job to set the record straight—or at least make it more believable—for the more civilized sensibilities back East. . . .

[In 1962] Peckinpah's second film—*Ride the High Country*—was released to general indifference in the United States but wild enthusiasm in England and France. Word of European reaction filtered back to the States, and Peckinpah became an instant cult figure. I still consider *Ride the High Country* his supreme masterpiece, and never more so than in the context of *Convoy.* . . .

From *Major Dundee* on I never felt that Peckinpah was an artist with a compulsion to tell stories but rather an artist for whom stories were merely a pretext for the creation of images. Hence, the excessive use of slow motion tends to delay the narrative, as if Peckinpah would never be really content until he could stop the motion altogether, so his composition could be frozen with all its beauty intact, forever secure from the narrative's process of decomposition. Even his Russian-montage mannerisms advance the dramatic action less often than they restate it. . . .

In the '70s Peckinpah's career has zigzagged from the self-conscious pacifism of *The Ballad of Cable Hogue,* to the vicious violence of *Straw Dogs,* to the relatively conventional caper mechanics of *The Getaway* to the bloody rock-audience-oriented balladry of *Pat Garrett and Billy the Kid,* to the trashy-mystic-Mexican-modern nihilism of *Bring Me the Head of Al-*

*fredo Garcia,* to the martial-arts megalomania—with C.I.A. trappings—of *The Killer Elite,* to the simpleminded worship of the Wehrmacht in *Cross of Iron* down to the pits with *Convoy.*

It would seem that Peckinpah can no longer bend the medium to his will but can only embellish the banalities of the current market. One of his problems is that no one makes Westerns anymore, and, that, therefore, the Western is not a genre he can subvert, since it is extinct anyway. The *frisson* of auto cars invading the frontier landscape (in *The Wild Bunch* and *The Ballad of Cable Hogue*) is no longer available to him as an artistic strategy. Hence, he has attempted in *Convoy* to transform the truckers into the chivalric cowboy of old. At one point he photographs the trucks lining up side by side like a cavalry formation about to charge the enemy. But the transposed effect does not pack any emotional wallop. . . . There is not enough distance between them and us for Peckinpah to wax romantic over their mythical exploits. And they certainly do not qualify as spokesmen for our dissent and disillusion. By trying to turn one more pressure group in our midst into a noble order of heroes, Peckinpah sinks to the grotesque of Russ Meyer. . . . As it turns out, Peckinpah needed the Western for his art to flourish more than the Western ever needed him.

*Andrew Sarris, "Convoyeur" (reprinted by permission of* The Village Voice *and the author; copyright © The Village Voice, Inc., 1978), in* The Village Voice, *Vol. XXIII, No. 29, July 17, 1978, p. 39.*

## PAUL SEYDOR

[The true theme Peckinpah discovered in *The Deadly Companions*] has little to do with any ironic treatment of the western as a genre. The true theme is so central to much of his own work, to a good many westerns (*Stagecoach* is a classic expression of it), and to a sizable chunk of American literature (*Adventures of Huckleberry Finn* and "The Bear" are two outstanding examples) that he couldn't help feeling the shocks of recognition. That theme is a trek into the wilderness where, away from society, a person may be reborn or in some sense reconstituted, often through an ordeal of physical crisis or a trial of violence. Much of this journey finds Yellowleg and Kit tearing at each other with a savagery that is partly mirrored, partly exacerbated by the savagery of the landscape. "You don't know me well enough to hate me!" Yellowleg shouts. Yet Kit knows him clearly enough. He teamed up with Billy and Turk to rob the bank, so he finds himself in a doubly ironic position. He accidentally shoots the child while attempting to halt a crime he himself was planning to commit. The polarities in his psychological makeup are thus externalized in those with whom he associates and in what he does—the "accidental" killing revealing more truth about him than any of his good intentions does. The journey through the wilderness is necessary so that he can reveal to Kit those aspects of his character that she doesn't know (and, by extension, that he himself doesn't know either). His moral awakening at the climax is thus as much a revelation to himself as it is to Kit. (p. 21)

Peckinpah once declared, "I have never made a 'Western.' I have made a lot of films about men on horseback." The remark isn't pretentious or facetious, nor is the distinction it implies factitious. It is, rather, central to an understanding of his work, which is not that of a director who makes genre pictures but that of an artist who *uses* aspects of genre to make personal films. For all practical purposes, *Ride the High Country* is the real artistic beginning of his career, as it heralds his emanci-

pation from the western even as it demonstrates how thoroughly he had absorbed and mastered it, and marks his first command over the polarized structural motifs that inform this and all his subsequent films. These motifs are most evident in the pair of old westerners whose divergent paths late in their careers constitute the primary story. The love story, which as a convention is as common to the western as to, say, comic opera, is secondary, but Peckinpah makes its incorporation organic by using the education of the victimized Elsa and the ambivalent Heck as a way of focusing and thus giving dramatic urgency to the issues at stake in the main conflict between Steve and Gil. The basic issue of that conflict is, appropriately enough in view of a lot of the talk in the script, a biblical question: what does it profit a man to gain the world if he lose his soul? Peckinpah doesn't ask the question abstractly. He gives it a flesh-and-blood reality by telling the story of a man who has grown old and nearly been forgotten and by shaping it as a journey that goes from the low country (the town) through a pastoral wilderness (the farm and the trail) to a primitive frontier mining town far back in the mountains. The journey describes a kind of passage—moral, ecological, mythical—that cuts back through time or, rather, that relocates time along a continuum that is spatial rather than temporal. The story is so securely grounded in this geographic setting that the thematic argument can be followed simply by observing how the values change as the landscape the characters pass through changes and by observing how they look and act in one setting as against how they look and act in another. (pp. 32-3)

*Ride the High Country* has often been mistakenly viewed as an allegory about moral inflexibility versus moral relativism, but that misses the point of the farewell scene. . . . What is revealed is not only Steve's great generosity and capacity for forgiveness; what is revealed is that however severely he may have judged Gil, however harshly he may have treated him, Steve never ceased to believe that Gil was a good man. This is the source of the tremendous power the last scene exerts upon us and explains why Peckinpah grants Steve entry into his house justified. The film is not an allegory about legal jurisprudence; it is a beautifully felt story about salvation through friendship, Steve's purity consisting, in the final analysis, not in the rigidness of his devotion to legal principle but in the steadfastness of his faith in Gil. (p. 38)

There are two especially problematic aspects to a film that fails as *Major Dundee* fails, one for the artists involved and one for critics. . . . [In] the traditional arts when an artwork fails we can be pretty sure it is the *artist's* failure. But when a film fails, whose failure is it? If the failure is in part the filmmaker's, then how can one criticize without at the same time sounding as if one is tacitly endorsing the studio's despicable practice of mutilating films? All of these problems come to the fore with *Major Dundee* because the studio did mutilate it, because what is left is not necessarily in the form the director imagined it to be, and finally because it must be admitted that the picture has substantial problems apart from anything the studio did to it.

Asked once if "they" had cut a lot of *Major Dundee,* Peckinpah answered, "Yes, they cut a lot of it. They left out what it's about." Trying to figure what it's about is not the easiest job in the world because, with all due allowances made for the pressures under which Peckinpah worked and the interferences with which he had to contend, the film, both in conception and execution, remains the most confused of all his films. Much of the confusion stems from flaws in the basic structure . . .

and from certain intractable elements in the raw materials. . . . (pp. 53-4)

[Some] of the objections that have frequently been raised against Peckinpah and his films suggest a widespread misconception about the kind of artist he is and the kind of films he makes, and seem to be based on a critical fallacy. That fallacy consists in drawing a one-to-one relationship between the ideas that characters express and the artist's personal beliefs—as if an artwork were nothing more than a veiled sermon or confession. . . . [Peckinpah] literally has no ideas but in things, which is not the same as saying that he has no ideas or that his ideas are puerile. It is rather to say that his imagination is such that it cannot coalesce except upon substance, whether that substance be character, event, story, detail, convention, structure, or so on. Peckinpah has frequently been called a visual poet, and what this means is that his mind is such that its terms are the terms of metaphor, simile, image, and symbol. . . . This is why Peckinpah has so frequently been drawn to the western . . . because everything was there waiting for him: a repository of plots, characters, icons, conventions, settings, and themes— in short, a whole language of myth, symbol, and metaphor waiting to be exploited and capable of freeing his imagination for exclusive concentration on its most important task: giving form to its dictates.

In the case of Peckinpah's imagination, the paramount dictate originates in his discomfiture with all certainties and absolutes and finds expression in [polarized structural motifs] . . . and in the antitheses, ironies, and ambivalences which mark his films and make them studies in ambiguity. . . . (pp. 102-03)

[What] is so morally beautiful about *The Wild Bunch* is inseparable from what is so aesthetically beautiful about it; both are a function of the same imaginative impartiality which is so involved with and committed to its artistic materials that it cannot help granting even the vilest characters a full measure of the rich, pulsating vitality that animates every frame of the film and that leaves us with the unmistakable sense that each character, no matter how minor, exists in the fullness of his particular being. The extent to which this applies to all of Peckinpah's best films forces us to reevaluate the whole question of his so-called mindlessness and anti-intellectualism. . . . Sam Peckinpah is a first-rate storyteller and a great filmmaker. Is it necessary that our appreciation of his artistry have as corollaries attempts to make him into a second-rate thinker and a third-rate philosopher, especially when it is so plainly obvious that he is intellectual enough about what matters to him, which is manifestly and by his own admission making storytelling films?

With its story of men as deadly companions, unified through fighting and eventually through an ideal of personal loyalty, *The Wild Bunch* takes up where aspects of *Ride the High Country, Major Dundee,* and the aborted script for *Villa Rides* left off. . . . (p. 104)

[None] of Peckinpah's films is elaborately plotted. What he seems to need is a basic dramatic structure, the simpler the better, for the complexity comes from the richness and variety of texture, the elaboration from the way he dramatizes character and visualizes incident and event. The story he told [in *The Wild Bunch*] is a beauty, and it brought together the requisite ingredients—outlaw men living beyond their time, bargaining for freedom, compromising for gold, engaged in exploits that seem already the stuff of romance and legend, all set within a historical framework of violent social and political upheaval—

for him to make the story support the fullest, richest, and most comprehensive vision of life he has given us before or since. Although he said he wasn't deliberately trying to make an epic, *The Wild Bunch* became, and remains, his epic all the same. (p. 107)

In general, Peckinpah may be said to have two basic styles: one, seen primarily in his western films, that is open, somewhat lyrical, and expansive; the other, seen primarily in his films with contemporary settings, that is darker, tenser, and rather more jagged in its editing. However, there are elements of both styles in all of his films; and it can be seen that the contemporary-settings style is not so much an antithesis as an extension of the western-settings style. When the setting gets more contemporary and space is at a greater premium, then the sense of being quite literally crowded intensifies, the flow of images is more punctuated by competing images, the glimpses of open space are more sporadic, and the expansions into lyricism— exemplified chiefly in the slow-motion intercuts, the deep-focus shot, or an image held for a long time—are of far briefer duration. Similarly, the camera moves closer to the action (in a crowded setting even it has less space in which to maneuver), and as a consequence it sees less at any given moment, so the cutaways multiply. In *The Wild Bunch* the two styles are synthesized, because its setting is both savage and civilized, primitive and sophisticated, the most transitional of all his settings. His combination of deep focus, telephoto lenses, slow motion, and fast cutting is ideal for weaving the thick, pulsating, protean textures of life he is after and for expressing the psychological effects of living in a world of such density. (p. 131)

In *The Wild Bunch* Peckinpah made a tragedy, but at the last moment he carried the structure toward the comic; in [*The Ballad of Cable Hogue*], by contrast, he has made a comedy, but at the very end he deflects the structure toward the tragic. The terms are being employed here in their technical, that is, structural, sense; but much of the excitement and pleasure of these two films derives from the tension between mood and structure, the variations that Peckinpah is playing upon familiar patterns of drama, and the extremes to which he pushes and then transforms them. (p. 175)

[The] western film and the theme of anachronistic men have become virtually synonymous with one another in Peckinpah's career. . . . [*Pat Garrett and Billy the Kid*] is not centrally about men who have lived beyond their time. With its interlocking themes of casual violence and environmental determinism, it is as close as Peckinpah has come to making a film that is an explicit criticism of frontier life, of those "good" old days to which his characters often nostalgically refer. (p. 183)

If there is one thing that *Pat Garrett and Billy the Kid* is not, it is *another* of anything. Set three decades before *The Wild Bunch* and two decades before *Ride the High Country,* the film deposits us into just precisely the time to which the protagonists of those earlier films refer when they are speaking lyrically of the ways things used to be. Yet once back there, we find not a simpler, nobler way of life, but a grosser, dirtier, more violent and shabby one, where, ironically, the people are talking about the better times that existed even *farther* back in the past. Short of blasting his audience in its collective face with the point, Peckinpah could scarcely have been more explicit in demonstrating that the "glory" of the "Old West" exists not in fact but in fancy, specifically in the characters' memories. This was always more or less implicit in the earlier films. In *The Wild Bunch,* for example, the flashbacks—which show us Pike deserting a friend, leaving behind a member of the Bunch, and through carelessness allowing the woman he loves to be killed—serve only to give the lie to Pike's sentimental talk about the old days. By the same token, in *Pat Garrett* what the characters reminisce about contrasts markedly with the mood and manner in which the reminiscence is recalled. . . . Nearly every time a character recalls something from the past, what it concerns is some violent incident, some death, some killing. . . . (pp. 215-16)

Peckinpah's western films have always . . . been more about "today" than about yesterday. . . . Peckinpah resurrects an old, essentially antique mode of heroism that originates in the epic in order to indicate something of what he feels has both gone out of and is needed to withstand contemporary life. At the same time, [Peckinpah realizes] that a fixation on the past *qua* past is often nothing more than sentimentality and even primitivism, that the hard facts of the past are scarcely less grim than those of the present, and that the actual past does not always offer the most admirable models for emulation; and so [he refers to a mythic past and directs his vision toward a future he hopes] will be possible. (p. 270)

[The] idea of transcendence, a theme of Peckinpah's that has not received much attention, is never far from his concerns, and nowhere does he give it greater or more powerful expression than at the ends of his films: the mountains that, as they witness and ratify the death of Steve Judd, seem to absorb his very spirit and being; the release of the Wild Bunch into folklore, legend, and ultimately myth; the moving of Cable into the whole torrent of the years, his joining the souls that pass and never stop. Nor is the idea of transcendence limited to its metaphysical aspect. At least as often it takes the form of facing and then freeing oneself from the prison of the past, as Pike does, or simply of going beyond the limitations of any moment in life by staying in motion, acquiring more experience, literally more of life itself, so that the old habit or habit of thought can be broken in the collision of self and society. And the great archetype that we so often find at the center of American art and expression, the archetype that Emerson imagined as the single man planted indomitably against the huge world, has several times been visualized by Peckinpah in compositions and stagings, but nowhere so purely, so profoundly, or so essentially as in the scene that concludes with what may yet come to be regarded as the single most beautiful image in any of his films: Pike on his horse riding away from us into a limitless expanse of sand, sky, and sunlight—an image of the frontier and of our relationship to it that, in its richness of implication, suggestion, and significance, can stand with Fitzgerald's evocation of that new world which put us face to face for the last time in history with something commensurate to our capacity for wonder. (p. 271)

*Paul Seydor, in his* Peckinpah: The Western Films *(© 1980 by the Board of Trustees of the University of Illinois; reprinted by permission of the author and the University of Illinois Press), University of Illinois Press, 1980, 301 p.*

# Jean Renoir

## 1894-1979

French director, screenwriter, actor, and author.

Renoir is considered by many to be the cinema's most important French filmmaker. Best known for his poetic films of prewar France, Renoir is a predecessor of both the *nouvelle vague* and neorealism; his work reflects a painterly tradition of naturalism inherited from his father, impressionist artist Auguste Renoir. His films are expressions of humanism, passion, and friendship.

Renoir first turned to filmmaking as a means of photographing his wife, Catherine Hessling. His initial silent films served primarily as vehicles for her and contained avant-garde cinematic techniques. *Nana*, based on Emile Zola's novel, exemplifies Zola's naturalism. Despite the technical aptitude of his early work, Renoir's first films were unsuccessful, and he was forced to make low-budget films which are not considered indicative of his talent. He ended the silent era as an actor.

Sound proved a great asset to Renoir's quest for an accurate naturalism, and he convinced a studio to allow him to make a feature-length sound film, *La chienne*. Despite the studio's objection to the story of a prostitute, the solemn tone of the film served ultimately as a precursor to the *film noir* genre. Renoir began moving away from the structures of naturalism while working closely with actor-producer Michel Simon, and in the 1930s Renoir commenced his most prolific period.

*La grande illusion* (*The Grand Illusion*), Renoir's best-known film, was created as a denunciation of war and a plea for French nationalism. Considered the culmination of his films of the 1930s, *La grande illusion* reflects Renoir's belief that men are separated less by nation than by culture, race, or class. Renoir's message proved universal, and the film met with unanimous acclaim.

*La règle du jeu* (*The Rules of the Game*), made as Europe was about to go to war, was, in Renoir's words, "an exact description of the bourgeois of our time." Renoir intended the film as a bittersweet satire of war and camaraderie; however, it enraged the public and was later banned as "demoralizing." Renoir felt that audiences so despised the film because they recognized themselves in the characters. It is only in recent years that *La règle du jeu* has been accorded critical acclaim.

The violent reaction to *La règle du jeu* deeply upset Renoir, and he chose to relocate in Italy, where he worked with Luchino Visconti. However, when Italy declared war against France, Renoir opted for voluntary exile in the United States,

where he accepted a directorial position with Twentieth Century-Fox. His American films are generally considered more mannered than his earlier work, despite their variety of genres. However, depictions of the American South in *Swamp Water* and *The Southerner* show Renoir to be surprisingly adept at probing the essence of rural life. Nevertheless, the studio system proved stifling to Renoir, and he decided to work elsewhere.

In 1950 Renoir made his first color film, *The River*. Filmed in India, *The River* pays homage to Auguste Renoir through a newfound interest in pictorial motif, and the film opened to great acclaim. After the success of *The River*, Renoir was reinstated in the critical world as an eminent filmmaker, and he returned to France.

The films Renoir made upon his return reflect a continuing belief in the universality of humankind, though they are not considered as great as his earlier works. Such films as *Le testament du Dr. Cordelier* use techniques formerly reserved for television, and correspond technically with the work of Truffaut and Godard. Renoir's last film, *Le petit théâtre de Jean Renoir* (*The Little Theatre of Jean Renoir*), provides his final, amused look at the world. It is blatantly "puppet theater," simple in conception, and most consider it Renoir's means of reverting to the most basic elements of cinema. The film sums up Renoir's entire career, for it encompasses the themes he had long embraced: our relationship to our environment, our neighbors, and ourselves. (See also *Contemporary Authors*, obituary, Vols. 85-88.)

### JAMES SHELLEY HAMILTON

Changing a novel into a motion picture—really changing it from the medium of words into the medium of the camera—is a thorough-going process that is not often attempted except in the case of insignificant stories that do not matter to anyone. . . . A film has to be "like the book" in all the respects that made the book popular, or it's a disappointment to the large audience for whom it was made. . . .

*Madame Bovary* is successful [because it so thoroughly satisfies so many people who were fond of the book]. The film as shown here suffers somewhat from attempts to bring it down to the length considered acceptable to American audiences. . . .

Far more important is the fact that the film is Flaubert's novel, given beautiful and vivid form for the eye to see. This visual form is completely French, in the original, by which I do not mean that the dialogue is French—though it is—but that the shapes of landscape and town and people you see on the screen are saturated with an untranslatable atmosphere, as if the air itself had a language not spoken anywhere else. (p. 6)

Its truth was what made Flaubert's novel a classic, and the faithful way that truth has been put on the screen is what makes this film good. An American must bring to it some understanding of national differences—perhaps most important of all, to get the completest pleasure out of the film, he must appreciate the difference between French acting and what is called acting here. Our players—no matter how delightful—are for the most part merely themselves, moving about in parts that suit their personalities. The French actors act. To what they are they add a fine touch of theatricality (when it is not the real thing it is merely artificial) which heightens their performance into something more than what they merely are, and creates that thing more real than reality which is art. (p. 7)

> *James Shelley-Hamilton, "'Madame Bovary'," in* National Board of Review Magazine, *Vol. IX, No. 9, December, 1934, pp. 6-7.*

### FRANK S. NUGENT

Surprisingly enough, in these combustible times, the French have produced a war film under the title **"Grand Illusion."** . . . [It] serves to warn the British that they no longer have a monopoly upon that valuable dramatic device known as understatement. Jean Renoir, the film's author and director, has chosen consistently to underplay his hand. Time after time he permits his drama to inch up to the brink of melodrama: one waits for the explosion and the tumult. Time after time he resists the temptation and lets the picture go its calmer course.

For a war film it is astonishingly lacking in hullabaloo. There may have been four shots fired, but there are no screaming shells, no brave speeches, no gallant toasts to the fallen. War is the grand illusion and Renoir proceeds with his disillusioning task by studying it, not in the front line, but in the prison camps, where captors and captives alike are condemned to the dry rot of inaction. War is not reality; prison camp is. Only the real may survive it. . . .

[It] becomes a story of escape, a metaphysical escape on de Boeldieu's part, a tremendously exciting flesh and bone escape on the part of Marechal and Rosenthal. Renoir's narrative links the two adventures for a while, but ultimately resolves itself into a saga of flight. As an afterthought, but a brilliantly executed one, he aids a romance as one of his French fugitives finds shelter in the home of a young German widow. The story ends sharply, with no attempt to weave its threads together. It is probably the way such a story would have ended in life.

> *Frank S. Nugent, "A War Film without War Is 'Grand Illusion', the New French Drama Showing at the Filmarte," in* The New York Times (© 1938 by The New York Times Company; reprinted by permission), *September 13, 1938, p. 28.*

### THE NEW YORK TIMES

Exactly what Jean Renoir had in mind when he wrote, performed in and directed **"The Rules of the Game"** . . . is any-body's guess. This is the same M. Renoir, if you please, who gave us those notable imports, **"Grand Illusion"** and **"The Human Beast,"** not to mention **"The Southerner,"** from Hollywood. The new arrival, however, is really one for the buzzards.

Here we have a baffling mixture of stale sophistication, coy symbolism and galloping slapstick that almost defies analysis. The distributors claim that the picture, made shortly before the war, was banned by the Occupation on grounds of immorality. Rest assured it wasn't immortality. And there's nothing particularly sizzling in this account of some addle-headed lounge lizards tangling up their amours on a week-end house party in the country.

One minute they're making sleek Noel Coward talk about art and free love, the next they're behaving like a Li'l Abner family reunion, chasing each other from pantry to boudoir to the din of wrecked furniture, yelling and random gunfire. One carefully picturesque sequence, a rabbit hunt, may or may not be fraught with Renoir meaning, but the grand finale, in which everybody down to the cook joins in a hysterical conquest race, would shame the Keystone cops. . . .

The picture ends abruptly with an unaccountable murder, whereupon one of the philanderers murmurs that the victim didn't learn the rules of the game. If the game is supposed to be life, love or hide-and-seek, which makes more sense, it's M. Renoir's own secret. At any rate, the master has dealt his admirers a pointless, thudding punch below the belt.

> *H.H.T., "Four Films Bow Over Week-end," in* The New York Times (© 1950 by The New York Times Company; reprinted by permission), *April 10, 1950, p. 15.* *

### THOMAS T. FOOSE

[*The River*] is a wonderful film of great visual beauty.

*The River* is not a documentary. It does not deal with India's social conditions. It is not a large-scale, dynamic film like Renoir's *The Grand Illusion*. It is, instead, lyrical: a delicate idyll of the few months in which an adolescent English girl, living in India, passes from childhood and begins to be adult. This was the theme of Rumer Godden's novel. This is the theme of the film. India, in both, is colorful background.

But how hauntingly colorful! India's natural coloring and her beautiful ceremonials, are practically *painted* with the camera, in sequences that could not have been better composed by Jean Renoir's father. Indian melodies on the sound-track reenforce the visual lovelinesses. (p. 43)

The script maintains the Indian and British aspects of the story in an even balance. But the glimpses of India are so beautiful that the Indian aspects dominate one's memories. (p. 44)

*The River* is the kind of motion picture that proves the movies are an art. (p. 46)

> *Thomas T. Foose, "Film Reviews: 'The River'," in* Films in Review (copyright © 1951, copyright renewed © 1979, by the National Board of Review of Motion Pictures, Inc.), *Vol. II, No. 8, October, 1951, pp. 43-6.*

## GAVIN LAMBERT

[*The River*] makes it clear that we should accept Renoir for what he is—an imperfectionist, with talent great enough to contain the kind of faults that few directors today would dare to commit. . . .

[*The River*] shows Renoir's talent in full flower, the film of a humanist and a poet, and in its tender intuition, affectionate understanding, follows the line of his most memorable work. As in his best American films he absorbed and reflected a new locale, so here—with more leisure, more freedom—he creates, with evident fascination, an Indian background. . . .

The slightness of the story is filled out by the richness of the background, and a constant series of events, some everyday, some important. . . . (p. 123)

It is, deliberately, a westerner's view. Renoir communicates landscapes and customs as a charmed outsider, and reinforces this impression by using the English girl as narrator. . . . Against this background Renoir sets the leisure and the quietness of the English household—as the old waltzes the children play on their gramophone are contrasted with the village music. The drama of the whole film is, in a sense, as alien to its background as the waltz to the Indian music: a nostalgic, retrospective sketch of childhood and adolescence, stemming from a novel that is, basically, of today's ever so sensitive female school, but given a purity of feeling by Renoir's own personality. Its core, perhaps, is contained in the speech of the half-caste girl's white father, when he hears of the little boy's death and muses on the innocence and simplicity of childhood, finding a beauty, even a satisfaction, in the death itself. Both the half-caste girl and her father are new characters, not in the original novel, and they strengthen the central situation.

Not all of this, it must be said, is satisfactorily done. Renoir has made little attempt to shape his material. The film starts confusingly, overburdened by narration, slow to establish any direction or purpose. Its episodes are often carelessly linked together, scenes end with disconcerting abruptness, and one or two sequences—notably the children's party—undoubtedly suffer from untidy direction. (pp. 123-24)

The imperfections are undeniable, and at times really distracting; yet there is something marvellous about a film that can hold and entrance one in spite of them. . . .

Memorable alone in a contemporary film, *The River* does not contain one disagreeable character. Instead, one is aware of the sympathy, the wisdom and understanding of a remarkable artist who loves human beings. (p. 124)

> Gavin Lambert, "Reviews: 'The River'," in Sight and Sound (copyright © 1952 by The British Film Institute), Vol. 21, No. 3, January-March, 1952, pp. 123-24.

## LAURO VENTURI

Renoir is not a studio hack who turns into images whatever script a producer hands him. . . . Renoir is a seeker who is not complacent about past achievements, but who regards each new film as a challenge, as an opportunity to make actors project the way Jean Renoir thinks human beings ought to be, in atmospheres congenial to Renoir—i.e., those in which reality and dreams intermingle.

This last is the key to all his films. (p. 140)

In *Les Bas Fonds* (1936), in which Renoir's favorite themes are played in the keys of despair and "realism" then fashionable, there is the character of an actor, who, caught in the conflict of dream with reality, recited a few lines of Shakespeare and then hanged himself. I don't recall whether the actor's suicide had a dramatic purpose, but obviously that character bothered Renoir, for it now reappears in and furnishes the theme for *The Golden Coach,* which is not played in the key of despair, but in a style that has also been bothering Renoir for twenty years—*marivaudage.* . . .

For some incomprehensible reason Renoir has made [the story] as difficult as possible for the public to understand. A vague symbolism flits around throughout the film. . . . There is also directing as clever, tight, and smooth as any Renoir has ever done. (p. 141)

Vivaldi's music fits *The Golden Coach* like a glove, and it is interesting to note that it rarely stops, and reinforces, by this continuity, the feeling of *opera bouffe* more than of *commedia dell' arte.*

Angels may be holding up our earth but Renoir didn't show them to us in *The Golden Coach.* (p. 142)

> Lauro Venturi, "Film Reviews: 'The Golden Coach'," in Films in Review (copyright © 1954 by the National Board of Review of Motion Pictures, Inc.), Vol. V, No. 3, March, 1954, pp. 140-42.

## TONY RICHARDSON

A film with as many defects as *The Golden Coach* needs some extraordinary compensation. Its construction is lopsided; its narrative confused; its presentation is careless and often undramatic; its dialogue is frequently banal; and the acting in it ranges, with one exception, from the inadequate to the atrocious. Its compensation is not that it is utterly personal but that the creative personality revealed by the film, for all its flaws, is so utterly charming. (p. 198)

"Where does the theatre end and life begin?" is the question behind the whole film. It is characteristic, too, of Renoir, that when, as here, and even more frequently in *The River,* he reduces an idea to which he has responded with all the richness of his sensibility to a line of dialogue, it sounds at once portentous and trite.

If this wider, almost visionary, reference is the very fabric of the film, it is not allowed to obscure our delight in the texture of the fabric itself. Visually the film . . . is breath-taking. Its beauty lies, unusually, in colour rather than the compositional values. (p. 199)

> Tony Richardson, "Film Reviews: 'The Golden Coach'," in Sight and Sound (copyright © 1954 by The British Film Institute), Vol. 23, No. 4, April-June, 1954, pp. 198-99.

## CATHERINE de la ROCHE

[*French Cancan,* the] story of some legendary show people and of the great show they put on, has been well told, but the overwhelming impression left by this picture is of a perfect, an enchanted evocation of the very spirit of showmanship. In *La Grande Illusion* and *La Règle du Jeu,* in *The Southerner* and *The River,* Jean Renoir, magnificently at his best, developed large themes. With *French Cancan* he has renewed his style, creating a masterpiece on a light theme, in which his wise and humorous perception is combined with new brilliance and charm. A charm that is very personal, for the inspiration of this film seems to be the fascinating charm for *him* of show folk and their world. And how marvellously he has caught it! . . .

[In *French Cancan*,] Jean Renoir has achieved a wonderful blend of stylisation and reality, of poetic expression and robust showmanship. . . . Unlike *Le Carosse d'Or,* in which Jean Renoir had already presented a larger-than-life story of show people, but without achieving unity of style, this film is of a piece. It repays study, as much for the original use of each of the cinema's component elements—acting, colour, sound, design—as for the success with which these and the stylistic variations have been integrated. Above all, it is a picture to see, without a critic's notebook, as a rare pleasure.

> Catherine de la Roche, "Film Reviews: 'French Cancan','' in Sight and Sound *(copyright © 1955 by The British Film Institute), Vol. 25, No. 2, Autumn, 1955, p. 85.*

## PETER BRINSON

A tapestry is usually a series of scenes linked together by similarity of theme, nothing more. Renoir calls **French Can-Can** a tapestry. It flows . . . with stately inevitability from one composition to the next. (p. 18)

It might have been a noble story with the Moulin Rouge in the rôle of the Great Ideal. Renoir prefers the truth. Danglard [the central character], training and moulding his discoveries till they are stars, seducing them and moving on to his next conquest, is not a likeable figure. The Montmartre society in which he moves is unattractive, even a little sordid, however cleverly it is framed in the colour compositions of Renoir, Michel Kelber and Max Douy. Thus the film captures the authentic atmosphere of the period.

The trouble is that a film, presented as a series of pictures, tends to lack continuity and climax. It comes to you like snatches of song on the wind—with bits missing. I do not find here the air of a combined painting and novel which one expects a good film director to suggest, especially Renoir. The flow of a novel and the penetration of the novelist into the souls of his characters, these are missing. It is an unexpected weakness for Renoir is a brilliant director of people. (pp. 18-19)

He loves his characters even though he criticises them. His portrait of life is as gay, optimistic and authentic as the Can-Can which concludes the film and the world of show business to which the film is dedicated. (p. 19)

> Peter Brinson, "New Film: 'French Can-Can'" *(© copyright Peter Brinson 1955; reprinted with permission), in* Films and Filming, *Vol. 2, No. 1, October, 1955, pp. 18-19.*

## JAMES KERANS

Above all, in *La Grande Illusion,* we find lucidity and innocence. We find these qualities everywhere in Renoir, but never under such stress, for here they are not only signs of a style, but maneuvers in a gathering war. Are they the right maneuvers? We are bound to ask the question, regardless of our aesthetics, because we are being asked to agree and to act, as well as to admire. . . . [La Grande Illusion] is a persuasion:

it tries to turn us away from Z and toward A, and from this turning proceed the real excitement, tact, and beauty it offers.

Certain difficulties always latent in pacifist persuasion appear in acute form in *La Grande Illusion.* There can be none of the familiar coercions based upon organized honor or dogma—these are irrecoverably the property of the militant man. . . . I suppose one of the reasons *La Grande Illusion* is not always consciously and immediately recognizable as a pacifist film is that it avoids . . . noise and as a result actually *works* as one. (pp. 10-11)

One view of the film finds it a demonstration of the essential sympathy which binds men and which is perverted by the unnatural conditions of war into complementary killing and sacrifice. The affection and respect between de Boeldieu and von Rauffenstein cannot prevent one's killing the other, once they are factors in the war equation. Captor and captive are alike unwilling, war finds its metaphor in a crumbling fortress in which the elite of a culture die or kill by rules which misuse their capacities for loyalty and love. The solution is escape. . . .

I find this reading insufficient in that it does not follow the film carefully enough to distinguish one kind of fraternity from another, one kind of escape or eloquence from another. It is all too easy to enter upon the exquisite pain and traditional nobility which dictate our response to the Boeldieu-Rauffenstein drama. Few films, if any, can execute as beautifully as this one does the ready oratory of heroic resignation. . . . [Nothing] better shows the seriousness and integrity of Renoir's film than the risk it takes in refusing to "combat" the glorifications of heroic suicide with irrelevant seductions to pacifist survival. (p. 11)

The essential action of *La Grande Illusion,* that which organizes nearly all its material, is a dialectic, as we would expect in a persuasive strategy. The tendencies involved are hard to name, because they attach to a tremendous amount of detail, from rudimentary psychological gesture to the complexities of national honor. One tendency I call ceremony; the other, instinct. Under ceremony I range the impulse toward rules and order, reserve, sacrifice, honor, suicide, brotherhood by exclusion; under instinct: relaxation, conviviality, drift, disorganized emotion, survival, brotherhood by inclusion. Presumably, any person includes both tendencies, and a possible problem-play approach to the material would be to have a hero confronted with a series of choices which lead him one way or the other. The trouble with this approach is that it forces upon the deciding character a form of consciousness and clarity, of reflection, which both simplifies his character and eliminates alternatives to his choices. Renoir's solution is the "double" —a dialectical resource most familiar to us from the nineteenth-century novel (*La Grande Illusion* is very like *War and Peace* in many respects). From the moment they set out together on the aerial mission which opens the film, Maréchal and de Boeldieu are linked by common circumstances, and from this community proceeds the dialectic which says that they move toward opposite poles. They are further linked by the ironies involved in their "escapes," each of which is dependent upon the other. The irony of de Boeldieu's escape through honorable death is obvious; as for Maréchal—can one really escape at the expense of accepting (to say nothing of forgetting) another man's life? Escape to what? (p. 12)

Throughout the film white-glove militarism is given plenty of literal play and symbolic weight. . . . [In] their last conversation Maréchal and Boeldieu are talking about the fundamental differences between them, and the background business to the scene is Boeldieu's washing a pair of white gloves so that his large gesture shall be in high parade style; and the hand with which Rauffenstein shoots Boeldieu and closes so tenderly his dead eyes also wears a white glove. In the film these details do not seem like trifles embarrassingly inflated into opportunistic symbols; rather they are, as in music, passages through the major key in the midst of a series of modulations. In themselves and in their variants they speak everywhere for the ritualized distrust of and withdrawal from whatever puts a smudge on the immaculate glove, photograph, or honor of the career officer. (pp. 12-13)

More interesting than [Rauffenstein's and Rosenthal's] personal differences are the clusters of ideas which gather around them. Each is representative of a brotherhood, an international elite. Rauffenstein is the spokesman for the European corps of military aristocracy left over from the French Revolution, Rosenthal for the international fraternity (French jargon for Jewry) of the chosen people. The one is jealous, exclusive, moribund, and in the process of being dispossessed; the other aspires to belong anywhere and everywhere . . . , is ingratiating, flourishing, and assuming the places—in one sense, at least—of the first.

Renoir redeems this banal motif by the quality of the association between Rosenthal and Maréchal. . . . Maréchal is an "authentic" Frenchman, and he does cross over into the land of understanding in a gesture of hope—not unmixed with irony, as we have seen, but still hope, and even encouragement. But what of Rosenthal? We have been carefully told that his Frenchness, like the food which reaches him in prison, is by special favor, whatever may be his legal status. And yet it is Rosenthal who has the map of how to get to Switzerland. . . . The point would seem to be that it is the mark of the authentic Frenchman (or German, etc.) that he will put humanity—not some "other" nation, but humanity as detached as possible from specific national loyalties—before Frenchness. . . . (p. 14)

If we accept the polarity of ceremony and instinct as the scene, so to speak, of the action, we can see how much of the film is devoted to establishing the scene and the place of the various figures within it. But we have not said much about the action itself. In its simplest form, *La Grande Illusion* is the story of an escape from prison. With certain scenic and narrative embellishments the prison develops metaphorical qualities. . . . To escape from it, if you really have been in it, in the psychological sense, you must leave behind that part of you which is identified with it, and in doing so you sacrifice part of yourself. It is in this way, I think, that we are to understand the "sacrifice" of Boeldieu. . . . This is not precisely a man executing an assignment; rather, a man putting his life into practice. Fundamentally there is nothing accidental in his death, any more than there is any real military exigency behind Rauffenstein's plea—"[Stop or] I'll have to shoot you." The death of one and dereliction of the other are built into their morale, and the fortress prison is the scenic metaphor of their destiny. Boeldieu is sacrificed, but not so much by himself as by the moral imagination that created him.

The escape is a confusion of trials, sufferings, anger, insults, and affection for Maréchal and Rosenthal, whose uninhibited releasings of emotion vividly contrast with the polite, unchanging (and fatal) relations of their opposites. The German farm to which they finally win is the metaphorical opposite to Wintersborn. . . . It is only when the time has come to leave for the Swiss border that we realize with Maréchal the profundity and impossibility of the peace he has been offered, and, beyond him, its place in the dialectical action of the film. In this anonymous, irretrievable life we are given the terms of the pacifist's peace, not that we may have them, but that we may know them. (pp. 15-16)

Trying, as [Renoir] is, to state a truth about human possibility in terms which would be betrayed by dramatic intensity, he finds in the camera's steady revelations a wonderful resource. Perhaps the finest example is the series of compositions at the farm. After the claustrophobic density of the Wintersborn walls, and the perilous implications of its windows; after the bleak, shapeless exposures of the flight through the mountains, the shelter and freedom of the domestic life, multiplied with one invention after another of door and window composition, is transposed almost into that other dimension "where ask is have, where seek is find, where knock is open wide." (p. 17)

*James Kerans, "Classics Revisited: 'La Grande Illusion'," in* Film Quarterly *(copyright 1960 by The Regents of the University of California; reprinted by permission of the University of California Press), Vol. XIV, No. 2, Winter, 1960, pp. 10-17.*

## GIDEON BACHMANN

For those who see in the 1863 Manet painting, from which the title [of *Le Déjeuner sur l'Herbe*] is derived, the essence of natural peace, it may seem sacrilegious to have the two so closely associated, but it seems to me that this is a limited view of Manet. (pp. 40-1)

Renoir has some basic beliefs about life which he applies in his film work, of course, but first and foremost he avows "I am not consistent." And then, "Man changes with the outside world" and "Art should be practiced in connection with human reality." Also that "to be a great artist you must first of all be a child" and that nature becomes that which the artist sees. . . . Yes, this *is* a child's film—the film of a true artist, and the film of a man.

*Le Déjeuner sur l'Herbe* involves figures symbolizing (perhaps!) various aspects of all men. . . . Cleverly, his framework ("story") is derived from what could pass as our everyday life, and Renoir plays Oriental storyteller in involving us through our own apertures. What finally "occurs" is as unimportant as continuity, theme, montage, focus, and all the other rigidities of movie-making. At the same time the film is abstract, in the sense that a painting is an abstraction of nature, and it is unmatched in some areas: color, frame compositions, stylized acting . . . , and above all in feeling, in that overriding emotional quality which only the really great films have: in conveying the presence of its making. . . .

*Le Déjeuner sur l'Herbe* is a unique film—a seemingly effortless pleasantry, impressionistic and yet surreal, full of the unexpected as life is, almost facile in impact but lasting in the perturbations it causes. It is in the true sense a demanding film, but it demands nothing of us save to be ourselves. (p. 41)

*Gideon Bachmann, "Film Reviews: 'Le Déjeuner sur l'Herbe'," in* Film Quarterly *(copyright 1960 by The Regents of the University of California; reprinted by permission of the University of California Press), Vol. XIV, No. 2, Winter, 1960, pp. 40-1.*

## RICHARD WHITEHALL

Disjointed, lyrical, uneven, beautiful, [*Le Déjeuner sur l'herbe*] is magnificently in love with life, with nature. The warm, sunlit landscapes of Provence bring out in full the list enhancing qualities of his art. . . .

This passionate and poetic fable-fantasy, as luminous as a story by La Fontaine, is set in a not-too-distant future when Europe is united, and science is (almost) in control. It departs enough from realism to introduce Pan, thinly disguised as a goat herd yet, through the solidity of its detail and the authenticity of its background the film is firmly anchored in reality. The clue has been given, as always, by Renoir himself. "I distrust modern realism. It seems to me under the pretext of showing reality the realists stick to one side of reality—the dark side. The truth is that only a poetic interpretation of reality can lead an audience to discover the truth."

Very much a film d'auteur, there is a core of deep seriousness; the submersion of the individual in a technological and scientific society. . . .

There are no great set pieces, the whole production has an air of happy improvisation and complete spontaneity despite its careful pre-planning. There are numerous faults; the scales are weighted too heavily against the scientific view, which is hardly stated at all; the scenes preceding and following the main credit titles are suprisingly clumsy; several sequences, notably a Bacchic dance and a supernatural summer storm are too strenuously gay.

Against these flaws must be set the gaiety, the sheer exhilaration of this free expression of a fully integrated personality, to whom life and art are one and indivisible. . . .

*Le Dejeuner sur l'herbe* may not be a masterpiece, but I have a feeling that in 20 years time, when currently popular perversities are crumbling in their cans, this film with its haunting generosity of spirit will still be splendidly alive.

> Richard Whitehall, "New Films: 'Le dejeuner sur l'herbe'" (© copyright Richard Whitehall 1960; reprinted with permission), in Films and Filming, Vol. 6, No. 9, June, 1960, p. 23.

## PETER JOHN DYER

*La Fille de l'Eau* [is] an almost involuntary expression of several themes destined to preoccupy Renoir throughout his career. . . . Despite the coy story-titles, Renoir manages to lend the opening scenes considerable authenticity and persuasion, both in his economical portraits of the Raynal family—upstanding, college-boy son, rigidly puritanical mother, anonymous, bourgeois father preoccupied with his new car—and of the village itself, with its big house and courtyard, the surrounding farmland, the trees, rain-clouds, bridle-path, canal and barge. The film was shot on location, and in its feeling for café interiors, wooded exteriors, poachers, tramps, gipsies, rabbits and horses, cows lazing in the running water, one discovers exactly the same river-of-life metaphor which pulsates through *Boudu, Partie de Campagne, Swamp Water, The Southerner, The River* and *Déjeuner sur l'herbe*. (pp. 131-32)

Though the hero is rather a dull stick, or tends to become so in a trilby, there is no real suggestion of parody. The class theme, again a familiar one in Renoir's films, is played straight, almost portentously. . . . Behind the recurring image of the rich man patronising the poor . . . can be detected sometimes

cutting irony, sometimes an almost defiant nostalgia, but never less than a generous, wholehearted response to people, whether of the old social order, the new or the one in decline. (p. 132)

*Monsieur Lange* is the first film to marshal Renoir's strengths and weaknesses, often side by side, for inspection. The brilliantly oblique sequence of Lange and the prostitute, for instance, is quickly followed by one of those flat-footed and old-fashioned scenes of sexual menace for which Renoir has retained a surprising taste, with practically no variations, ever since *La Fille de l'Eau:* the villain advances, leering, the helpless little victim retreats, cowering, the camera tracks in like a dentist's drill on a molar, the music rises to a crescendo. . . .

Renoir's major films, especially his later ones, have often tended to seem a perverse tangle of compensations. Again and again, one finds passages of charm or delicacy threatened by others of portentous melodrama. . . . (p. 134)

> Peter John Dyer, "Renoir and Realism," in Sight and Sound (copyright © 1960 by The British Film Institute), Vol. 29, No. 3, Summer, 1960, pp. 130-35, 154.

## RAYMOND DURGNAT

Erotism in Renoir's work is linked so intimately with every aspect of life that it is impossible to separate them; every Renoir film is a hymn to fertility, to the great god Pan. But I think we can find a clue to [the criticism of scientific values made by Renoir in *Le Testament du Dr. Cordelier* and *Le Dejeuner sur l'Herbe*] in his *Boudu sauve des Eaux* (1932). . . .

[Boudu's] will and intellect alike are quite unequal to coping with the simplest table-manners; it is his nature to be free not just from conventions and daily routine but from all such trivialities as moral obligation and logical thought. He isn't very malicious and he's hardly altruistic, although the waywardness of his impulses often leads him into actions which might be classified as one or the other. . . .

This is "Hallelujah, I'm a bum!" acquiring a spiritual as well as an economic meaning; the old rapscallion has nothing whatsoever in common with Hamm and Clov or the tramps who glumly squat in Beckettland waiting for God(ot) and so prove that they are only Trappist monks in a fit of constipation. Boudu's rude erotism is only one of the strings to his bow; and the sexual conveniences of matrimony tempt him only briefly. He stands for himself now, for freedom from himself (suicide) if he feels like it. (p. 13)

But in *Le Testament du Dr. Cordelier* there is no incarnation of the life-force and the scientist who has dedicated himself to the joyless pursuit of objectivity punishes himself far more terribly. . . . Cordelier (the name means "monk") is a cold, austere individual. . . . (pp. 13-14)

Cordelier's thin, pliant lips, his taut, fastidious expression in which wrinkles show like cracks in bone-china, are set in the mask of unrelenting moral finesse, even highly repressed homosexuality. His theories are the only part of him that live. His dedication is negative. His instincts are immolated in intellectual pursuits. His tragic flaw is not that he sacrifices "all" to truth, but that he is frightened of ridicule. His integrity re-emerges in the intellectual sphere; he *risks* ridicule by asking Severin, a rival scientist, to counter-check his theories. . . .

[Opale] has no "normal" instincts—he is not "nature uninhibited by morality"—he is, specifically, as inhibited as Cordelier, whose repression results not from morality but from fear. . . .

[Far from opposing each other,] the two facets of the one personality are accomplices. Each transformation requires an increasing effort of the will, from Opale as from Cordelier, and gradually Cordelier finds he prefers being Opale to being himself; sadism is more fun than intellectual integrity. But although Cordelier's intellectual integrity defeats itself (by leading him to become Opale) it is, in itself, a virtue—and Cordelier is contrasted with the rival scientist, Severin, and his own lawyer, Maitre Joli. Whereas Cordelier's environment is bourgeois, Severin "lives" in a smartly clinical world of glass-topped desks and modern sculpture. . . .

Joli, Cordelier's—and Opale's—lawyer leads a pedantic and well-meaning existence. He is as superficial about the subtleties of the heart as any moral law is bound to be. . . . The moral is not, as some people seem to suspect, "intellectual integrity, scientific truth, must destroy itself because it leads to bringing out the worst in people". Quite the reverse; Opale is a result of Cordelier's frustrated love, and Severin's combination of moral indifference and dogmatic rationalism must bear a share of the guilt. . . .

The fact that Renoir's hero [in *Le Dejeuner sur l'Herbe*] shakes hands with a priest, and listens with sympathy to his complaint that he hasn't enough money to mend his church's leaking roof, outraged Renoir's natural sympathisers, left-wing anti-clericals; but since the scientist's belief in the supernatural finds its climax in the consultation of an oracular goat, one suspects that Renoir's point is that the priest is more human than the scientist because he has his lunacy, (i.e., the guts to be subjective).

Although the conception of Opale, the seduction scenes, and the whole middle section of *Le Dejeuner sur l'Herbe* should reassure the meanest doubter that Renoir is still *our* Renoir, we may regret that Renoir has devoted so much footage to a suffocating evocation of intellectual sterility, rather than a Renoir film. . . .

I think Renoir wants the spectator to sacrifice his aesthetic dignity, to join in, just as the scientist joins in the ludicrous, undignified behaviour as the wind disrupts the picnic. (p. 14)

> *Raymond Durgnat, "Another Word For It" (© copyright Raymond Durgnat 1962; reprinted with permission), in* Films and Filming, *Vol. 8, No. 7, April, 1962, pp. 13-15, 38-41.\**

**TOM MILNE**

[*Le Caporal Epinglé*], Renoir's *Grande Illusion* of World War Two, is the wickedly and tenderly witty chronicle of a prisoner-of-war's persistent attempts to escape from a German prison camp after the fall of France in 1940, against odds as unbendingly hostile as any Buster Keaton ever had to face. . . . Every foot of the film is shot through with the endearing stamp of Renoir's personality, just as irreverent as the *nouvelle vague*, and a good deal more loving.

This is a very funny film, but also a very moving one, in which Renoir catwalks the tragi-comic line with delicate balance. The opening sequence, after establishing shots of the aerial bombardment of France and the signing of the armistice, beautifully sets the tone. . . .

Comparison with *La Grande Illusion* is perhaps inevitable. Apart from the escape theme, the two films share many common elements: the idyll with a German girl, the comradeship of the prison, the fear that this comradeship will not persist outside, the final flight across open fields and the encounter with a peasant woman; even the theatrical reference (the camp concert in *La Grande Illusion* is paralleled in Ballochet's escape, while the female disguises of the concert find their echo in the prisoner disguised as a woman whom the corporal meets on his third escape. But as Renoir himself has pointed out, his preoccupations have changed. *La Grande Illusion* was "the problem of men of sharply differing social backgrounds, education and character when forced together in war . . . *Le Caporal Epinglé,* on the other hand, is a picture of the solidarity that binds men flung into the melting pot of despair, facing a situation together."

Moreover, instead of that gently upbeat talk of returning to fight again of the earlier film, at the end of *Le Caporal Epinglé* the corporal and his doggily faithful friend, Pater, stand together on one of the Paris bridges, looking down the river; Pater is timid, hesitant, until his face lights up with joy when the corporal gently insists, "But we *will* meet again, Pater." Here escape is an interior necessity, a thing complete in itself when fully shared. (p. 92)

[*Le Caporal Epinglé*] gives a strong impression of sun and light, open air, streets and fields, showing the prisoners arriving at a camp in the pouring rain and mud of an open field, gratefully drying themselves in the sun the following morning, working on a farm or among the trees of a forest, marching along the open roads, even sensuously experiencing a visit to a dentist's waiting-room. To Renoir, the physical world is one of man's greatest blessings (c.f. his work, *passim*, particularly *Boudu, Madame Bovary, Les Bas Fonds, La Règle du Jeu, Le Déjeuner sur l'Herbe*), and this film constantly hammers home that war and imprisonment mean the withdrawal from man of his privilege to enjoy this world, and his own humanity, in freedom. "I love a man who refuses to be enslaved," says the gentle German girl to the corporal, and this, at its simplest level, sums up the film. (p. 93)

> *Tom Milne, "Film Reviews: 'Le Caporal Epinglé'," in* Sight and Sound *(copyright © 1962 by The British Film Institute), Vol. 31, No. 4, Autumn, 1962, pp. 92-3.*

**PETER HARCOURT**

[Renoir] has succeeded in providing us with some of the warmest, most tender moments in the cinema. . . . [However], what aspects of life must Renoir exclude from his films to enable him to maintain this open and generous acceptance of all his characters? How does he deal with violence, for instance? and how does he handle the potentially destructive aspects of physical love? To understand all is to forgive all. To what extent, then, is it Renoir's understanding that brings about his constant readiness to forgive? (pp. 56-7)

Renoir manages to send us away from the cinema after what is thematically a grim story of destructive passion and of mistaken justice [*La Chienne*] with the feeling that, essentially, there has been no harm done. If only one can stand back in the margins of life (the ending seems to say) then all texts can be seen as equally curious and equally insignificant. And although the film is unrolled with a charm that attempts to preclude such an analysis, nevertheless beneath the charm, the moral seems to be there (p. 57)

*Boudu* is essentially a morality play which, like the end of *La Chienne,* is a celebration of total disengagement and of the essential innocence of the physically uninhibited spontaneous life. . . .

[The] real interest lies in the idealization of Boudu's mindless disengagement and in the symptomatic appearance of, first, the satyr and then the goat. For the cult of Pan in Renoir is central to his response to life (as apparently it was to his father's as well); and although the effect here or in the antic romp in *Une Partie de Campagne* is very different from *Le Déjeuner sur l'Herbe,* nevertheless it can be seen not only as the desire to reject the more inhibiting aspects of our formal civilization but, especially in *Déjeuner,* of all thought as well. In fact, in *Le Déjeuner sur l'Herbe* (1959), it is as if Renoir, in the face of the TV/scientific world, like Boudu, simply wants to be able to ignore it or banish it all with a magical pagan charm. . . .

Along with the joyous and nearly perfect *Une Partie de Campagne,* in *La Marseillaise, La Grande Illusion,* and in *La Règle du Jeu,* there is an involved seriousness and breadth of interest that seem to be struggling against Renoir's habitual urge to oversimplify and retreat. Yet even in these films a dominant quality is nostalgia. (p. 58)

Like *La Grande Illusion,* [*Le Caporal Epinglé*] deals, warmly and compassionately, with prisoners of war. The film is in essence a celebration of friendship between men who in civilian life might have very little in common. At the same time, there is a kind of moral disengagement from his material that seems particularly calculated to avoid pain. . . . (p. 59)

With *Le Caporal Epinglé,* as with so much of Renoir's previous work, it seems a lack of generosity . . . to complain. When what is offered is such a warm and pleasing experience, even the confusions seem part of the quality of the man. If, throughout all his films, we feel a worrying disengagement, the tendency to oversimplify in the interests of charm, equally we can respond to the uniqueness of his characters, allowing ourselves to be refreshed by the very beauty of those falsifications which, we realize, Renoir is offering us as proof of his own faith in life. (p. 60)

*Peter Harcourt, "Cinema: Jean Renoir," in* London Magazine *(© London Magazine 1962), Vol. 2, No. 9, December, 1962, pp. 56-60.*

## LOUISE CORBIN

[*Le Caporal Epinglé*] is not one of [Renoir's] best, and I was unable to work up any interest in his mishmash about French prisoners of the Germans during the last war. The prisoners themselves are dull dogs, and the things Renoir put them through often make no sense, and are a bore when they do.

In addition to directing, Renoir collaborated, with Guy Le Franc, on the script and dialogue. I am afraid Renoir is no longer capable of saying anything that isn't "safe." And "safe" remarks in the jumble-jungle that is French intellectual life today are even more platitudinous than "safe" remarks were in the days of the Third Republic. (pp. 114-15)

The stalag incidents in which Renoir involves them are old-hat, and it is saddening to notice how often Renoir resorts to excretory humor, and to the French equivalent of 4-letter Anglo-Saxon words, to "liven things up."

Something of Renoir's current mental confusion was revealed when he was asked to compare *Le Caporal Epinglé* to *La Grande Illusion.* "The whole point of the earlier picture," he is quoted as having said, "was to show that among individuals of a similar social background there exists an affinity that transcends national sentiments—even in wartime. This new story is about the solidarity between men facing a common ordeal. To the men of *La Grande Illusion* the invasion did not mean the end of their way of life—they were rooted on solid ground. Today's people move through quicksand, in a world that is in transition. Our illusions are gone, and, this being so, it is obviously impossible to make the same picture."

Quite a paragraph. Read it carefully and you will discover that denizens of the Left and of the Right, as well as those of the Center, can each find in it confirmation of their preconceptions. (p. 115)

*Louise Corbin, "Film Reviews: 'Le caporal epinglé'," in* Films in Review *(copyright © 1963 by the National Board of Review of Motion Pictures, Inc.), Vol. XIV, No. 2, February, 1963, pp. 114-15.*

## TOM MILNE

Renoir is the most unruffled of directors. . . . [The] rich dynamism of films like *Le Carrosse d'Or* and *Le Caporal Epinglé* is effortless and invisible. They are beautiful, but there is no sense of formal composition; they are full of movement, yet the camera, almost invariably upright, moves only when it must; they are extremely complex, yet seem to be built up at random. (p. 71)

The essence of Renoir is his three-dimensional view of things, hinted at as early as *La Chienne* in the puppet prologue which announces that what follows is neither tragedy nor comedy, but simply a story of ordinary people "comme vous, comme moi." . . . For Renoir, understanding is more important than approbation or condemnation, and the tiniest of details may be of vital importance. When Legrand murders Lulu in *La Chienne,* for example, it is ostensibly her mocking laughter when he tries to persuade her to come back to him that drives him to it. But as viewed by Renoir, there is something else: some trick of light from the window, falling on Lulu's hair as she lies in bed with the white fur of her peignoir framing her face, and making her more radiantly desirable than ever before. To Legrand's fury at her deception and cruel mockery, is added an extraordinary poignancy of loss, which makes the murder something more than a simple *crime passionel* of revenge. . . .

Renoir was intermittently attempting to create a three-dimensional effect on the screen, to suggest that people exist *in* a milieu rather than against a setting. With *Boudu Sauvé des Eaux,* he took a step forward by capturing and contrasting two different milieux to create the impression that his anarchistic tramp was a wild faun trapped in the strange, closed world of rooms, corridors, furniture and courtyards. . . . In both cases it is the three-dimensional effect which counts—the feeling that one can smell the grass or touch the leaves on the trees, and the feeling that one knows the exact geography of the Lestingois apartment and all its contents. . . .

[*Madame Bovary*] is a remarkable tribute to the way Renoir *encompasses* Flaubert's description of the Normandy countryside and Emma's boredom and despair. There are obvious gaps, of course. . . . Nevertheless, the whole feeling and meaning of the novel is intact. And Renoir's power of evocation is such that one can almost fill in the gaps oneself. (p. 72)

Throughout the film, Renoir gives firm substance to [the] contrast between reality and fantasy. Because of her impossible romantic demands, Emma's love affairs are doomed to failure: taking place as they do on the margins of the context of reality in which she lives, their only permanence is in her mind. (pp. 73-4)

It is in this film, even more than *Boudu Sauvé des Eaux,* that one becomes aware of Renoir's uncanny ability to give objects an almost animate existence. Sunlight, trees, grass, dusty roads, carriages, animals—all stand out in sharp relief, irradiating the action with their presence. . . .

It was also in this film that Renoir seems to have fully realised the power of a firmly anchored, almost stationary camera. Over and over again, without loss of movement but with immeasurable gain in depth, he shoots a sequence from a fixed standpoint, waiting for an action to resolve itself round the camera. (p. 74)

*Madame Bovary* is a singularly beautiful film, and it illustrates Renoir's belief that pictorial values are not a matter of composition *à la* Eisenstein, but of making the audience sharply aware of the special quality of each individual element in a scene. Although *Madame Bovary* is, in fact, deliberately composed in the sense that its characters are viewed carefully and precisely in their milieu, what gives it its special power, as Bazin remarked of Renoir in general, is "la qualité de son regard''—his unerring instinct for light, shade and textures. This, together with his careful juxtapositions and systematic use of composition in depth, is basically the technique which underlies all Renoir's later works, and which, with the rough edges smoothed away by familiarity, permit his warmly loving, *complete* view of humanity. (p. 75)

> Tom Milne, *"Love in Three Dimensions," in* Sight and Sound *(copyright © 1965 by The British Film Institute), Vol. 34, No. 2, Spring, 1965, pp. 71-5.*

**PETER COWIE**

The narrative pace of *The Crime of Monsieur Lange* is so fast, and the changes of scene so frequent, that one almost overlooks the brilliance of Renoir's sets and of the minor characters that make up the background to the film. The bustling activity in Valentine's laundry, and the somewhat lazier activity in Batala's printing room, are utterly genuine, and the realism of the party held to celebrate the 'Arizona Jim' film contract is breathtaking. . . .

But the film hinges on the relationship between Batala and Lange, and Renoir explores this on a very deep level. Batala becomes a Mephistopheles, and Lange sells him the copyright to his stories as Faust would sell his soul. . . .

*The Crime of Monsieur Lange* is more than a murder story, it is an attack on the church (people believe in Batala's appearance as a priest and are purblind to his shark-like smile), on patronage, on class prejudice and even on the cantankerous type of military hero. . . . *The Crime of Monsieur Lange* is a masterpiece of the French cinema, a beautifully constructed work that yet suggests that air of spontaneous creation that is part of Renoir's greatness.

> Peter Cowie, *"Reviews: 'The Crime of Monsieur Lange'''* (© copyright Peter Cowie 1965; reprinted

*with permission), in* Films and Filming, *Vol. 11, No. 10, July, 1965, p. 32.*

**JACQUES JOLY**

[*Rules of the Game*] is original precisely for the connection it makes between a traditional theatrical structure and a new content, and for the way it articulates their relation. For *Rules of the Game* is the one film in a thousand where the study of a given milieu is inseparable from a particular dramatic scheme: in it, artistic reflection is on a par with historical analysis.

Renoir's project was clear: to perform the "autopsy" of the bourgeoisie in crisis, to record the proof positive of a class overwhelmed by the events in Europe. . . . Renoir's film was intended, in his own words, as "an exact description of the bourgeois of the time." Directly, then, *Rules of the Game* is given as a totality; each of its characters becomes part of a whole and thereby acquires his significance. Thus, the secondary figures in the film form a survey of the bourgeois society of the time: through M. and Mme. de la Bruyère, the aristocrats of La Colinière are connected with the new industrialists from Turcoing; the homosexual, the South American diplomat, the retired general give us a rapid view of a certain society. . . . One thing is striking in Renoir's description: the allusive character of the references to contemporary history, together with the schematization of the secondary characters, who recall the puppet-figures of conventional social criticism. . . . Renoir's intention is, then, not to analyze the society of the time objectively, from outside, but to put together stroke by stroke—by reducing each character to his essential significance within the whole—an image of the bourgeois class which is capable of revealing its contradictions.

Locating his film in a History, Renoir at the same time proceeds to define the essential characteristics of that History: the world of *Rules of the Game* is a world of falsehood. . . . The theme of the film is that of a collective lie. . . . Individual duplicity here symbolizes the elevation of the lie to the status of an institution. Sincerity is impossible; it would challenge the foundations of an order. In the scene of the evening party at the château, Renoir casts over this world a shadow of what awaits it. (pp. 2-3)

This world, which is pushing France to catastrophe, still holds together only because it has turned in upon itself; it endures only on its own momentum. The structure of Renoir's film was thus dictated by its intentions. Renoir had to find a dramatic scheme that would serve at once as the symbol of this closed universe and the translation of its desire for diversion. He found it in a parallel development of the plot, at the level of the masters and at that of the servants. . . . The film is a game that ends in death, just as the bourgeoisie of France was playing with what was to be the ruin of the country. We now understand why the social and historical references remain allusive in character: Renoir enters into the game of the propertied class in order to expose its contradictions *from within. Rules of the Game* is above all a "critical" film, which recomposes a class reality using a dramatic scheme capable of appealing to the viewer's intelligence. (p. 3)

In *Rules of the Game,* each character is in strict solidarity with the class he belongs to. What is more, each social category contains in its margins a certain number of satellites—declassed individuals or parasites—opposed to those individuals who are perfectly integrated in the system. . . . Renoir shows us a closed world where each group is totally alienated from the one next above it. (p. 4)

The lesson of the film will be that one doesn't gain entry to a class if one is outside it. Jurieu's death, the departure of Octave and the dismissal of Marceau are necessary, from the moment they set eyes on what is beyond their reach. The film is a closed circuit; no real story appears in it, because it is really the film of a non-story. The more the plot unfolds, the closer we come to the starting point—a characteristic regression in a film in which rigid class structure permits no narrative development outside its closed system. The principal characters in *Rules of the Game* therefore cannot be human and are entitled to a personal story only *up to a certain point*. Not the least of the film's merits is this balance between individual elements and class traits in La Chesnaye or Christine, this way of dialectically constructing a character at once as a type and as an individual.

The Marquis de La Chesnaye is presented from the first as a psychological case. . . . The Semitic origins of this character, the sense that they constitute a social blemish, account in part for the sensitivity of the Marquis, which culminates with the presentation of the music-box to his guests, and in the scene in which he dismisses Marceau and Schumacher. Similarly, Christine de La Chesnaye is distant kin to the countess in *The Marriage of Figaro*. She is a stranger to the world to which she belongs at once by birth and by her Austrian origin, and has remained nostalgic for her "bohemian" childhood. The character of Christine perhaps recalls certain stage heroines from the 1930's, for example Anouilh's "wild woman." Renoir's skill consists in interesting the viewer in his characters, appealing to sentiment if need be, without ever abolishing a critical distance, a parallel reflection which gives the work its sense. We are introduced into this bourgeois world in order that we may discover its vanity and falsehood. . . . La Chesnaye and Christine may be human, but they are no less bound to their class interest. Their humanity has been merely apparent; it has never endangered their class logic.

Thus, Renoir lends his bourgeois protagonists an individual story only to dissolve it in the collective analysis of a class. In a certain sense, Christine and La Chesnaye have no right to a story; their adventure can unfold only in a false temporality, outside of real history. *Rules of the Game* is a "game of love and history" in which the former term is gradually engulfed by the latter—a privileged moment of diversion outside of a history which is soon to destroy it. . . . *Rules of the Game* is, then, not the story of a few characters, but more profoundly, through their lack of a story, the story of a class in crisis. At the end of the film, La Chesnaye and Christine have taken their proper place in their world in spite of their individual characteristics. *Rules of the Game* is the story of a class which discovers its solidarity.

Of course, this story Renoir tells us is not the "real" story of the French ruling class. As in *Grand Illusion* and *La Marseillaise*, Renoir's viewpoint remains that of a moralist. Where one might have expected an analysis of the reasons (and, no doubt, the limits) of the confused French reaction to Hitler, Renoir gives us only a portrait of this confusion. Besides, the characters in *Rules of the Game* are never presented as representative of the ruling class. They simply belong to the propertied class. . . . The film should be considered in its true dimension: the critique of certain more or less hypocritical values which have been swept away by the war. The crisis Renoir depicts is, then, a crisis of moral values, which does not prejudge the real destiny of the French bourgeoisie during and after the war. (pp. 4-5)

Renoir has discovered, beneath a complex of moral values endangered by the war, the profound cohesion of a class for which "appearance" is founded in a "reality," which continues to live (and perhaps to threaten) beneath the apparent crisis of moral values which concealed it. Here we reach the threshold which Renoir, for obvious reasons, could not dare to cross. Nevertheless, Renoir's film is not solely that trial of a closed world, that autopsy of a class in crisis which we mentioned at the outset: the bourgeois rules obeyed by the guests at La Colinière are not depicted as a vain and hollow style of life. Renoir has made us sensitive to the latest violence contained in this social structure, at both the individual and collective level. . . . But Renoir's film is not limited to satirically exposing the apparent "polish" of a social category which has sought to impose its own order; it also translates, into direct language, the potential for violence belonging to a class threatened in its very existence. . . . Ultimately, Renoir's lesson is that deep beneath the ridiculous surface of bourgeois properties lies a logic, a vital necessity. (p. 6)

[One] can consider *Rules of the Game* as the last part of a trilogy begun by *Grand Illusion and La Marseillaise*. Each of these films is closely connected with its contemporary historical problems; together they constitute, beyond the diversity of themes and times, a reflection upon the continuity of a history, which illuminates, and is illuminated by, the atmosphere of 1935-39. In *Grand Illusion,* Renoir, faced with the menace of Nazism, affirms his faith in certain human values, which become so many calls to reason addressed to the German people. The end of the film calls for a collaboration of all classes and all nations to safeguard peace. . . . *Grand Illusion* and *La Marseillaise* thus participate, to different extents, in a political optimism whose idealistic character history would soon expose. . . . It is therefore not surprising that the positive perspective, the optimistic vision of the first two films gave way, in the third, to an internal critique of the class in power: without abandoning the moralist viewpoint of his first two films, Renoir now analyzed the bankruptcy of certain moral values, the "lie" of a world gasping for breath. (pp. 6-7)

In *Rules of the Game,* artistic reflection and critical satire are combined: the study of past art is particularly appropriate to the description of a world incapable of reflecting upon present history. Art then takes constant refuge in a complex of rules inherited from the past, and recollects its former grandeur. The character of Octave "polarizes" the elements of this reflection, and at the same time poses the problem of the artist in society, and perhaps even (in terms less immediate but still present in the film) the problem of the relationship of the creator to his work. (p. 7)

Octave's character is thus enriched with a freedom of expression, including even redundancy and exaggeration, which belongs to him alone, whereas the other characters in the film remain the tributaries, even in expressing their personal feelings, of a certain "language" appropriate to their social position. The conventions which determine their physical and verbal expression objectively reveal their social conditioning, and prepare the conclusion of the film. (pp. 7-8)

Octave is merely an idealist, who wrongly insists on seeing the bourgeois around him as individuals. The film's job will be to force him to see the true face of his "friends" and the limits of his own freedom. . . .

[Octave] represents everything that Jean Renoir, as an artist, has avoided becoming: a man of the ruling class, the clown who, beneath a satiric exterior, remains in fact the lackey of capitalism. Here, Octave's role in the structure of the film takes on another meaning. Octave, we thought, brought an individual story into the game as long as he seemed to be leading it; now that story proves a lie, and turns against the two pariahs. His "story" betrays in fact the pseudo-artist's nostalgia for creation: he "stages scenes" in life to make up for those he cannot realize as a creator. Through the character of Octave, Renoir in a sense exercises the temptation to let the man precede the artist; the true freedom of Renoir consists in the distance he constantly adopts toward the established order, in order to criticize it or, at the very least, to satirize it. (p. 8)

By focusing the problems of the creative artist in the character of Octave, and by deciding to play the film's essential part himself, Renoir attempts to find the cinematic equivalent of those types of fictional narrative in which the problem of the creator is closely bound to the ideological content and the formal elements of the work: the viewer is invited to the performance of a work (the "game") whose author (Octave) is himself challenged by the director, who constantly establishes a distance between the film as spectacle and the film as reflection. (pp. 8-9)

> *Jacques Joly, in his essay in* La Nouvelle Critique *(copyright 1965 by La Nouvelle Critique), No. 168, July-August, 1965 (translated by Randall Conrad and reprinted as "Between Theatre and Life: Jean Renoir and 'Rules of the Game'," in* Film Quarterly, *Vol. XXI, No. 2, Winter, 1967-68, pp. 2-9).*

## PETER COWIE

[*Boudu sauvé des eaux*] is a devastating indictment of crass, middle-class values and conformism, an exercise of which Buñuel would have been proud. . . .

[Boudu] is viewed with immense sympathy by Renoir: he is nowhere near as dastardly as Batala in *Le Crime de Monsieur Lange* he is merely striking out against convention and putting bourgeois vanities to flight. . . .

*Boudu sauvé des eaux* is a hymn to Eros, filled with the exuberance that Renoir and Truffaut alone in the French cinema appear capable of creating. Like Catherine in *Jules et Jim*, *Boudu* is "une force de la nature", cataclysmic in his effect on the merely bookish, on those ignorant of the vibrancy of life itself.

> *Peter Cowie, "'Boudu'" (© copyright Peter Cowie 1965; reprinted with permission), in* Films and Filming, *Vol. 12, No. 2, November, 1965, p. 32.*

## PAULINE KAEL

[*Boudu Saved from Drowning (Boudu Sauvé des Eaux)*] is a more leisurely film than we are used to now, not that it is long, or slow, but that the camera isn't in a rush, the action isn't overemphatic, shots linger on the screen for an extra split second—we have time to look at them, to take them in. Renoir is an unobtrusive, unselfconscious storyteller: he doesn't "make points," he doesn't rub our noses in "meaning." He seems to find his story as he tells it; sometimes the improvisation falters, the movie gets a little untidy. He is not a director to force things; he leaves a lot of open spaces. This isn't a failure of dramatic technique: it's an indication of that movie-making

sixth sense that separates a director like Renoir from a buttoned-up-tight gentleman-hack like Peter Glenville or a genius-hustler like Sidney Lumet. Glenville suffocates a movie; Lumet keeps giving it charges to bring it to life. *Boudu* is a simple shaggy-man story told in an *open* way, and it is the openness to the beauty of landscape and weather and to the varieties of human folly which is Renoir's artistry. He lets a movie breathe. . . .

Boudu, bearded and long-haired like a premature Hell's Angel, is a dropout who just wants to be left alone. And this may help to explain why the movie wasn't imported earlier: he doesn't want romance or a job or a place in society (like the forlorn little hero of *A Nous La Liberté*), he isn't one of the deserving poor. There's no "redeeming" political message in *Boudu* and no fancy Shavian double-talk either.

Boudu is the underside of middle-class life, what's given up for respectability. We agree to be clean and orderly and responsible, but there is something satisfying about his *refusal*. There's a kind of inevitability—like someone acting out our dream—about the way he spills wine on the table, leaves the water running in the sink, wipes his shoes on the bedspread. There's some disorderly malice in him. He's like a bad pet that can't be trained: he makes messes. If Boudu's character were reformed, that would be defeat. (p. 141)

Renoir's camera reveals the actors as if they were there naturally or inadvertently—not arranged for a shot but found by the camera on the streets, in the shop, on the banks of the Seine. The camera doesn't overdramatize their presence, it just—rather reticently—picks them up, and occasionally lets them disappear from the frame, to be picked up again at a later point in their lives.

Despite the problems of sound recording in 1931, Renoir went out of the studio, and so *Boudu* provides not only a fresh encounter with the movie past but also a photographic record of an earlier France, which moved in a different rhythm, and because of the photographic equipment and style of the period, in a softly different light. The shop fronts look like Atget; the houses might have modeled for Bonnard. It is a nostalgic work, not in the deliberate, embarrassing way we have become inured to, but in spite of itself—through the accidents of distribution. [It was not released in the United States until 1967.] And because Renoir is free of the public-courting sentimentality of most movie directors, our nostalgia is—well—clean. (p. 142)

> *Pauline Kael, "A Shaggy-Man Story: 'Boudu Saved from Drowning'" (originally published as "A Shaggy-Man Story," in* The New Republic, *Vol. 156, No. 15, April 15, 1967), in her* Kiss Kiss Bang Bang *(© 1967 by Pauline Kael; reprinted by permission of Little, Brown and Company in association with the Atlantic Monthly Press), Atlantic-Little, Brown, 1968, pp. 140-42.*

## BRENDA DAVIES

[*La Marseillaise*] is an optimistic film, full of hope and the joy of creation. It glows with summer sunshine as the amateur soldiers tramp the long leafy road from Marseilles to Paris, arguing, laughing and occasionally bursting into that stirring song of theirs. But it is not all revolutionary fervour and high spirits. Renoir is very conscious that the trivialities of daily life do not disappear under the stress of cataclysmic events. . . .

For Renoir there are no villains—only stupidity and misunderstanding. There are chilling moments though, when the tragedy waiting in the wings is allowed to throw its long shadow. . . .

Technically Renoir is unobtrusive as always. It is all very simply done—or so it seems—and he handles great crowds with the same ease that he brings to intimate scenes, always choosing the most direct way of expressing his ideas without any loss of depth or subtlety. (p. 41)

In any Renoir work it is the people one remembers best, but *La Marseillaise,* with its balance between historical perspective and human values, has a sweep and a fervour that both includes and transcends the protagonists. It has nothing to do with patriotism and is as stirring to Anglo-Saxon blood as it is to the French. (p. 42)

Brenda Davies, "'La Marseillaise'," in Sight and Sound (copyright © 1968 by The British Film Institute), Vol. 37, No. 1, Winter, 1967-68, pp. 41-2.

## DANIEL MILLAR

Renoir's post-American films, from 1950 onwards, present genuine difficulties, though of a peculiar kind, just because they do not seem difficult or obscure at all. They appear to be, if anything, too easy—light, comic and sometimes farcical in spirit, colourful (only two of the seven films are in black and white) and almost self-indulgently sensuous, 'commercial' rather than 'art' films. . . .

[However,] the peculiar quality of the later films, their combination of a high degree of abstraction with a strongly sensuous realisation, was already latent in the pre-war films; and . . . Renoir's diversified output has a resonant inner unity. (p. 136)

The moral seriousness and social commitments of the pre-war films are transformed in the late films into moral schemas, set against romanticised but not sentimentalised social backgrounds. . . . Renoir's full-blooded humanism, while not inhibiting anger and a clear-eyed knowledge of moral failings, has largely precluded any metaphysical concept of evil, and virtually all traces have gone by the Fifties. The unity beneath diversity, traditionally expressed by the magic number three (with mystical overtones added by Christianity, though not particularly relevant for Renoir), is the philosophical principle backing this apparently technical pattern.

The triple schema naturally takes a variety of forms. It may involve the rejection of all three (*The Golden Coach,* 1952), choice by the spectator rather than by a major character (*Le Caporal Epinglé,* 1962), or even the splitting of one character into two roles (Nénette in *Le Déjeuner sur l'Herbe,* 1959). But treble choices are so persistent in the late phase as to alert us to their significant though occasional appearances in the Thirties films as well. (pp. 136-37)

[The] thematic parallels of *Le Crime de M. Lange* with *The Golden Coach* and *French Cancan* turn out to be less important than the structural parallels. A similar conclusion, more surprisingly, emerges from a comparison between *La Grande Illusion* (1937) and *Le Caporal Epinglé.* Both are set in prisoner-of-war camps, both concentrate mainly on three men and their shifting relationships but add a woman at a late stage to pair with the central man, both demand that the spectator himself—not the woman—compare and judge the attitudes and actions of the three men.

Once past these formal affinities, the differences assert control. In *La Grande Illusion* the main characters are laden with social

and political distinctions and with representative significance, though this enriches rather than diminishes their human personalities. . . . (p. 137)

*La Grande Illusion* is a film of ideas, though the ideas are given a local habitation and a name. *Le Caporal Epinglé* virtually escapes from ideas altogether; and yet it is paradoxically also more abstract, hardly at all concerned with divisions—even the French prisoners and their German captors are almost indistinguishable—and focused entirely on the notion and mechanics of escape, which had been almost incidental in *La Grande Illusion.* Only in their theoretical and practical attitudes to escape do the Caporal, Pater and Ballochet define themselves. The Caporal, who needs no name, is 'épinglé', pinned down, unfree; his motive, almost an instinct, is to free himself. His attitude is totally simple—no past, no future. Ballochet's attitude is clouded by past boredom, by opportunism, by cowardice and inertia, by false heroics—and so he dies. Pater's attitude is also clouded, less seriously, by resentment of the past, fear of the future, and dependence on the Caporal—but he reconciles these and succeeds. (pp. 137-38)

[The] new elements in Renoir's post-American films are (a) visual richness, as distinct from the earlier alert visual responsiveness (b) moral schemas, as distinct from the former multiple relationships establishing a social world. These could be interpreted as decline or a new richness. (p. 161)

Daniel Millar, "The Autumn of Jean Renoir," in Sight and Sound (copyright © 1968 by The British Film Institute), Vol. 37, No. 3, Summer, 1968, pp. 136-41, 161.

## JOHN BRAGIN

[The opening action of *La Marseillaise*] sets defining boundaries for the film, creates the tone of . . . revolution-as-theater, and allows Renoir to break from both the conventions of war and revolution films and the strictures of this particular story line. (p. 36)

A situation which recurs in many films of Renoir is the encounter and mutual understanding between figures from widely disparate classes or ways of life. The aristocratic commander of the Marseille forts, who walks onto the scene just as the main fort is successfully occupied, meets and comes to respect a leader of what he had formerly regarded as the common rabble of France: another Renoir touch. . . . The main tension—and intention—of Renoir in *La Marseillaise* seems to be the intermingling of . . . two theaters of action. He doesn't exploit crowd scenes or city and country panoramas, but implies the expanse of the spectacle through scenes such as the one on the battlements. In *La Regle du Jeu* he is even more successful, conveying the malaise of an entire civilization through the reverberations generated by the encounter of a relatively small group of people at an isolated chateau.

One method of accomplishing this is Renoir's extremely fluid camera, more fluid than in any other film of his I've seen. The feeling that things and people just happen to be there when the camera passes gives universal import to the glimpses of word, gesture, and character that the viewer catches with the tracking camera. The camera movement is a thread. . . . (pp. 36-7)

It is impossible to imagine Jean Renoir handling [the slaughter at the palace] in any other way than as theater on a grand scale, for it is not the momentary swings of the historical pendulum which interest him. The French Revolution, the First World

War, the eve of World War II, all interest him as situations within which man plays variations on the rending and reconnection of spiritual fraternity. In his latest films he does not so much abandon the scene of temporal strife as rise above it. From the solidity of the world, like the 'flesh and blood' Michelangelo pietà in St. Peter's, to art as the celebration of the grace of the spirit like Michelangelo's last work, the Rondanini pietà in Milan, *La Marseillaise* is the link between the engaged, often-turbulent Renoir of the thirties and the taut, detached philosopher-artist Renoir of the fifties. (p. 39)

*John Bragin, "The Revolutionary Theater: 'La marseillaise',' in* Film Society Review, *Vol. 4, No. 4, December, 1968, pp. 34-9.*

## WILLIAM S. PECHTER

The notion that Renoir's films are somehow formally lax has sprung in part from their structural looseness, a looseness, one should add, that now seems an inseparable part of their self-renewing freshness and modernity. . . . As early as in *Boudu Saved from Drowning* one is aware of the sustained development of a style in which the classical criteria of visual composition within a frame are abandoned in an attempt to open up the frame to depth of field and to peripheral fluidity—and a style in which the momentum of the films derives not from a pulse created in the editing but from the realization of those possibilities for expressive movement to be found in the imaginative transformation into movement of their subjects. Already in *Boudu Saved from Drowning* one sees a film that in great measure takes its movement from the kinetic thrust of its protagonist. . . . (pp. 198-99)

Unlike those of Dreyer or Eisenstein, Renoir's films rarely yield a composed still, yet if Renoir's films reject the ideal of compositional equilibrium—their movement perpetually spilling over the frame—it remains to be said that in their lavish attention to texture, light, and color they are works that must be described, above all, as painterly. . . . (pp. 199-200)

Bound up with [a] misconstruction of Renoir's films as engaging a world more "real" than that of, say, Eisenstein's (when what one actually means is that the world of Renoir's films is a more profusely imagined one) is that of Renoir's democratic style by which one's eye is given the freedom to see as one chooses. (pp. 201-02)

The marriage of Boudu's kind of freedom with society is impossible from the start; society can only aspire to some modified version of his model, and he only wander uninvolvedly at society's fringes, drifting affectlessly from dog to a jump in the river to passing entanglements to a jump back in the river to another dog (or goat) and on and on. To us, he may seem somewhat sad in his freedom, though there is not the slightest hint of sentimentality in the film (the sentimentality of the final shot having a quite different object) to support one's thinking that he finds himself so. Yet, sad or not, his freedom cannot fail to awaken in us the recognition of our lack of it. He offers us a vision of radical freedom, of a kind of freedom attainable only outside society. It is a vision that does not reappear in Renoir's work until *The Testament of Dr. Cordelier,* where it has become the inspiration for the Mr. Hyde liberated by Dr. Jekyll, but it remains a vision that haunts his work, forever hovering about the edges. What now comes to occupy that work's center is another but related vision: that of what freedom can be *within* society. (pp. 207-08)

If one may call the vision of Boudu's freedom precivilized, then the world into which one is plunged with *The Elusive Corporal* [*Le Caporal Epinglé*] reveals itself immediately as civilized in the extreme. (p. 208)

*The Elusive Corporal* in its entirety seems thematically to evoke the main body of Renoir's work in films. For a number of critics, the comparison with *Grand Illusion* has been to the later film's disadvantage, revealing a retreat from the political commitment the earlier film seemed to represent. It is true that the Germans in *The Elusive Corporal* are not seen, according to the conventions of World War II dramatizations, as bestial, or the camp as monstrous, but it's important to remember that the camp isn't a concentration camp and the conditions are not meant to be unbearable. The film *is* a call to resistance, but it's not so much Nazism or even suffering as it is the very condition of enslavement that the corporal stubbornly resists. And, increasingly, the prison camp comes to be seen as a figurative extension of the imprisonments of the world outside. . . . Yet, for all this, the possibility of individual freedom remains alive. . . . It finds its embodiment, above all, in the elusive corporal, who, though realized in his individual particularity . . . , remains nevertheless, without psychology or biography, an almost pure expression of the will to freedom. (pp. 212-13)

In Renoir's vision, the impulse toward freedom seems always to lead away from community, and, to the degree that Renoir's personality (which does, after all, enter *artistically* into his work) tends toward a gregarious pleasure in fellowship, this vision of freedom is always of something purchased at a heavy price. Of course, the vision of the individual in conflict with society has become a familiar enough one in art since the romantic movement, but it is Renoir's ability to imagine the claims of both poles that distinguishes his work and gives it its breadth and its fervor. . . . The corporal's almost tropistic movement toward freedom is heroic, but to the extent that it is also a movement away from other men, from the fraternal bond of the men in prison, it seems also to represent some sort of failure (albeit not the corporal's alone): a failure to realize or imagine a relationship among men within society in which individual freedom might flourish.

Perhaps Renoir's most positive image of a socialized freedom, a freedom in society, is that of the publishing cooperative in *The Crime of Monsieur Lange,* which requires the malicious intervention of Batala to jeopardize it, yet the cooperative is so essentially a community of fantasists as hardly to suggest possibilities available in any world but its own, its fragile existence sustained chiefly by the breath of fantasy of the film itself. And *The Crime of Monsieur Lange* ends, as recurringly do the other films, on images of escape. Out of the contrary movements toward freedom and society, Renoir has created [his greatest works] . . . ; and it is the failure to reconcile the two movements that has given his work, despite its immense gaiety, that sadness and ambiguity that characteristically underlie it. The corporal *must* escape, his doing so is his assertion of his humanity, yet, as he leaves Pater and the fraternity of the camp behind, an aspect of his humanity remains unrealized; he remains both elusive and pinned down. For one not only escapes from something but also to something else. And, though he is both beautiful and noble in its performance, the highest act of which the corporal is capable is escape from imprisonment. Like Boudu, he can only escape, and, reimprisoned, escape again. (pp. 213-14)

*William S. Pechter, "Radical Freedom: Aspects of Jean Renoir" (1969), in his* Twenty-Four Times a

Second: Films and Film-Makers *(copyright © 1960, 1961, 1962, 1963, 1965, 1968, 1969, 1970, 1971 by William S. Pechter; reprinted by permission of the author),* Harper & Row, Publishers, Inc., 1971, pp. 195-214.

### SUZANNE BUDGEN

[*La Règle du Jeu*] is based on the idea of man as a social being, to whom conventions are both irksome and necessary. Polite exchanges will embody our thought only up to a point; in the end the feelings will not be contained within these bounds and it is a matter of chance, or fate, whether the irruption of passion will end well or badly. The social conventions are not free or generous enough to allow for the full extension of a normal feeling person, so that, at any moment, bursts of emotion may occur. Society itself channels these to some extent in occasions of organized license, but not everyone is amenable to the dictates of society, and occasionally passion breaks loose and proves destructive.

The shoot is such an occasion; it is a crucial sequence, and is, in a sense, the key image of the film. . . . The shoot is also later seen to have prefigured the death of André. . . . We see very little of André's death, but the man is invested with the pathos of the repeated deaths that we have been shown during the shoot, and especially with a sense of the vulnerability of the last small creature to be killed, whose death-throes we are shown in all their quivering helplessness.

But the shoot is not just an image of death; visually it is spacious and splendid, with a sense of a particular place, and climate, and season, and, because it takes place in the domain of Schumacher and under his control, it allows full scope to his stern efficiency, while his grim hardness is thrown into relief by the softness of his victims. (pp. 5-6)

The social function of the shoot is shown as providing a context in which civilized people can give vent to a savage cruelty which is normally concealed. (p. 6)

The arrival of André opens the film; his death virtually closes it. . . . He is the irrational, the random, element, descending into an ordered, if far from ideal, situation, which he disrupts, and which destroys him. He is assisted in his enterprise by Octave who, though a familiar of all the other characters, and at ease in their world, is nevertheless not civilized as they are, not formal in his address nor ordered in his movements. . . . Between them, André and Octave are a threat to order, and the film demonstrates the power of society to destroy anything which threatens it. The conventions are not adequate to contain a full life but they make misfortune bearable and prevent disaster from destroying the social fabric; they do this by being selective and ruthless.

In the early part of the film relations are formal; indeed one of the many pleasures that it affords lies in the elegance of the scenes in the La Chesnayes' Paris house and of those in which the house-party at La Colinière is gradually assembled. Renoir puts us in presence of a group of people who speak with the readiness and ease of long acquaintance and who give to the spaces in which they move a sense of habitation and familiarity. In this film Renoir gives us language as an expression of social function (as distinct from position) as well as of temperament. Octave's mumbling, formless and casual, is related to his lack of defined social function, while Robert's easy stylishness is related to his wealth and rank, his pleasures and duties. (pp. 6-8)

The freedom of communication which obtains above stairs is not repeated below. Among the servants we see a formal hierarchy which has no equivalent above. . . . Life below stairs is altogether more rigid and less complex; the chef, judging his employers with what at first appears to be an egalitarian freedom, shows by those very judgements the limitations of his station in life. (p. 8)

[Significantly,] it is on the level of amorous intrigue that servants and masters are equated, though they do not actually intermix. In hot pursuit of Marceau, Schumacher disregards the rules which confine him to the corridors of the house, and chases through the halls and drawing-rooms, in among the guests and in and out of the concert room. However, because his idiom is different from theirs, the guests do not recognize what is going on and take his desperate rage as all part of the show. (p. 9)

A large part of the film is taken up with the concert. Fancy dress affords a temporary release from one's own personality and from rigidly precise rules of conduct. It allows one to try out other ways of being and behaving, and there is a generally accepted feeling that exchanges effected when the parties are disguised are no more binding than shipboard acquaintance— in both instances people are isolated from their normal lives. (p. 10)

The opening of the concert makes clear the shedding of personality that is involved. Robert and his guests, in their own persons so assured and easy, are here awkward, confused, and uncertain. Principally, of course, this is a demonstration of their amateurishness and gives the occasion an authentic sense of reality, but dramatically it does show a change of personal style which opens the way to the farcical manoeuvres which follow. (pp. 10-11)

The concert enshrines one of the most persistent images of the film, and this in its final and most elaborate form. . . . The effect of [Robert's musical toys] is partly to introduce a note of baroque fantasy into the urbanity and ordered luxury of Robert's household, but its principal function is to suggest the whole nature of automata, and, without any comparison being overtly drawn, to equate by association the actions and 'voices' of the various figures, governed as they are by rules not of their own making, with the lives of the people around them, they too acting in accordance with rules which they have not designed and which they have no power to alter. The automata also, by contrast, make the formal company seem free and human and natural. (p. 11)

[When] the 'masterpiece' goes out of control, . . . the harrowing noise that it makes, contrasted with the bland complacency of the figures, presents a spectacle of discord putting on an appearance of harmony that illustrates the essential nature of the confusion around it. It assaults our senses and establishes for a moment a predominance that annihilates the human scene. (p. 12)

Renoir's film gives us a picture of society as man organized for survival. He shows us a form of social life which was already disappearing, and the final shot, of the stone balustrade with only the shadows of the guest passing along it, followed by a totally black screen, is a poignant, and indeed, in its narrower implications, a prophetic comment, but it is, too, an image of melancholy commiseration with the human lot. It is a recognition that the most desperate strivings, as well as the keenest pleasures, have an end, and it is, as it were, a salute to the validity of what has gone before, as if, in the face of that end, one way of making life bearable is as decent as another. It suggests that the rules, in creating an order, if an artificial and limiting one, are making possible at least a degree of communication and reciprocal understanding, and a degree of pleasure if not of happiness. And, as we learn from Lisette's injunction to Jackie to be brave, because she is an educated young woman and knows how to behave, they also provide a structure of support which, while having no power to alter feelings themselves, nevertheless provide a pattern of behaviour by which one is held, as in a splint, until the feelings become more directly bearable.

The film recognizes the fact that conventions and courtesies make life into an ordered experience which can be compared to a game, together with the recognition that the pieces of the game are people, and that the moves and gambits are a means, often the only means, by which desperate feelings can find expression. It reflects an acceptance of this situation qualified by the need to make the nature of it known. (pp. 12-13)

*Suzanne Budgen, "'La règle du jeu'," in* Screen (© *The Society for Education in Film and Television 1970), Vol. 11, No. 1, January-February, 1970, pp. 3-13.*

## MARVIN ZEMAN

*The Little Theatre of Jean Renoir* is an old man's film: Renoir is using the film to express his view of life from the vantage point of seventy-six years, which differs sharply from that of the thirties, his days of youth. In **"Le Roi d'Yvetot"** Duvallier insists upon the veterinarian, his wife's lover, staying in his household. This is quite different from what Renoir's characters did previously in similar situations. . . .

In his early years, Renoir, at most, pointed out the problems of society; in this film he gives a solution. But Renoir does point out that this solution is usually arrived at only with the experience of age. Renoir manifests this by contrasting Duvallier's behavior with that of his young maid. . . .

It is interesting to compare Renoir's use of the Anderson story in **"La Dernier Reveillon"** to what he did with it in its predecessor, *La Petite Marchande d'Allumettes*. That film was made in 1928 when Renoir was young, and it has a young man's theme. Now, in his old age, Renoir is concerned with age, and the theme is changed accordingly. First, the young match girl is replaced by the two aging tramps. Second, and most important, Renoir changes the girl's dream. (p. 52)

Renoir seems to have attained the state of what the Japanese call *mono no aware*. According to Donald Richie this is "an elegiac emotion which occurs when we realize that the beauties and pleasures of our life will pass and fade and when we agree that, since this is the way it must be, it is therefore fitting that they do." . . . Renoir transmits this serenity partly through the simple settings and his unobtrusive camera. Whatever camera movement there is, is quite unnoticeable, and there are no camera tricks at all. . . .

This is also an old man's film in the sense that Renoir's oeuvre is so rich that he can "borrow" from and refer to his past films in a very natural and subtle way. (p. 53)

[All] in all, the film is charming (not in a cloying way) and enjoyable. If it is not one of Renoir's best films, it is very close, despite the limitations of the episode form. (p. 54)

*Marvin Zeman, "Reviews: 'The Little Theatre of Jean Renoir'," in* Film Quarterly *(copyright 1971 by The Regents of the University of California; reprinted by permission of the University of California Press), Vol. XXIV, No. 3, Spring, 1971, pp. 51-4.*

## STANLEY KAUFFMANN

[When *La Grande Illusion* was made,] the film was a warning of the futility of war in the face of growing wars, an anatomy of the upheaval of 1914-1918 to show contemporaries how grim machineries had once been set in motion. Today its pacifist intent, as such, seems somewhat less salient (though no less moving) because so many more human beings know how futile war is and know, too, that no film can abolish it. Today the film seems a hard perception of inevitabilities, not glibly cynical but, in the largest classical sense, pessimistic: a film that no longer asks for action but that *accompanies* us, noting our best, prepared for our worst. Since this state of mind, this undepressed pessimism, is today widespread, this film continues to speak, out of the change it incorporates, to changing man.

Yet—in a wonderful and important way—*La Grande Illusion* is a period piece, and Renoir was the ideal maker for it. (p. 307)

The movement of the film is . . . toward freedom; but that freedom implies return to other "prisons," of renewed military service or other straitenings of society. The officers' characters are unashamedly selected for contrast and symbolism—beginning with the fact that they are officers, not ordinary soldiers; but they are so well written, and played, that any suspicion of artifice is swept off by reality. (p. 309)

[We] have in [the] barracks a model of European society, with all major strands represented except the peasant/worker—who was excluded arbitrarily because this is an officers' camp. We know, as we watch, that we are being shown a model, but it is made with such fine observation and dexterity that it acquires size. (p. 311)

Enriching, supporting, fulfilling [the story] is Renoir's direction—his sheerly cinematic imagination. His skill with actors shines from every scene (he has been an actor himself), but two qualities of his filmic style are especially important: his use of a moving camera and his deep-focus composition. (p. 314)

Today the Big Illusion of the title includes at least three aspects: the illusion that war accomplishes anything of permanence; the illusion that, even without war, men will be brothers; and the illusion that truth can ever be anything more than a very necessary illusion. Yet the presentation of all these illusions is here in the hands of a man committed to love.

Inevitably, then, *La Grande Illusion* deals with transition, from a society committed to the idea of progress and perfectibility to an era in which men think less of perfection and more of achieving some proportion of good. The old world changes before our eyes. The aristocrats see that their ethos—the best of it along with the middling and worst—is dying. The bourgeoisie discover that the reliance by which their fathers lived—reliance on a society that, generation after generation, would respond predictably to ambition and application—is being changed in this cataclysmic war. (pp. 315-16)

*Stanley Kauffmann, "'Le Grande Illusion'" (originally published in* Horizon, *Vol. XIV, No. 3, Summer, 1972), in his* Living Images: Film Comment and Criticism *(reprinted by permission of Brandt &*

*Brandt Literary Agents, Inc.; copyright © 1970, 1971, 1972, 1973, 1974, 1975 by Stanley Kauffmann), Harper & Row, Publishers, 1975, pp. 307-16.*

## LEO BRAUDY

Renoir makes his world energetic and compelling through the complexity and irony with which he treats even his most cherished themes. His films do not come to a stop in the sense of the self-enclosed great work; they have a richness that eludes total schematization, a constant edge of self-awareness that never yields to either formal pomposities or fashionable fragmentation. Renoir has said that every director struggles between interior reality, the reality of the constructed world of the studio, and exterior reality, the reality of the world of nature. But his point is not the final commitment to one or the other, but the dynamics of the struggle itself. . . . The greatness of his films more often lies in their inconclusiveness, their openness, and their rich tentativeness than in any absolute formulation of the truths of nature or the truths of theater, the claims of the individual or the claims of society. (p. 16)

Renoir's films are not categorical and theoretical, but capacious and ironic. They present a rich critical problem, because nothing is ever single-valued in Renoir's world, no character can be easily made hero or villain, no set of ideas has automatic consent. Within the borders of his artistic vision and the continuity of his career, many of his basic interests remain the same: nature, the theater, society, the place of the hero. But the expression of these themes changes throughout the years, as the external pressure of new projects, new ideas, and new events works its way on him. (p. 18)

[The two basic elements in Renoir's films are] nature and theater, which, as Roger Greenspun has pointed out, come into the Renoir world with Renoir's two first films as a director: the canal and countryside of *La Fille de l'Eau* (1924) and the theater and artifice of *Nana* (1926). (p. 19)

[He] has absorbed the great themes and methods of art since the Renaissance and puts his own stamp upon them, not by catalogue and allusion but by spirit and understanding. Renoir's films realize the highest nature of art, in their capacity to assimilate, to criticize, to reconcile, and create anew within the confines of his capacious imagination. (p. 23)

From the very first film of his career Jean Renoir seems to have a complex awareness of the possible ambiguities of "naturalist freedom." He can appreciate the realistic detail that explodes artificial limits and punctures myths and fantasies. But he also appreciates the kind of realism that affirms new myths. (p. 30)

The use of the dream is one way in which Renoir, in his films principally set in nature, can relate to a natural world deeper than the world of lush descriptive detail. *La Fille de l'Eau* also embodies an awareness that appears in Renoir's films, especially those of the 1940s: violence and sexuality is as natural as lyricism and love. Nature can be a place of benevolent expansiveness or malevolent confinement. The canal itself is an image of limits, the barge forever in its one channel. (p. 31)

Renoir always uses his rivers as they suit his different ends in a particular film, without accepting any one-sided interpretation of the river as a benevolent image of all nature and man's absolute need to submit to its flow. (p. 32)

Renoir's camera is far from invisible. It is a kind of poaching camera, making its own paths through the world of his films. The early French films broke out into nature but preserved the woodenness of composition by frame, whatever the subject. Renoir's camera, on the other hand, can move into and out of a scene, exploring beyond the surface and withdrawing to show that there is more world than the frame can momentarily delimit. Like all great artists, Renoir will use conventions, but with artistic self-consciousness. (p. 44)

Nature in art can have both optimistic and pessimistic connotations, for there is a rainy naturalism as well as a sunny naturalism, a naturalism of urban melancholy to balance rural exuberance, a naturalism of fate to counteract the naturalism of freedom. The literary naturalism with which Renoir grew up is quite different from the luxuriant pictorial naturalism with which he is often associated, and his films exploit both varieties. (p. 50)

The dark side of naturalism is Renoir's true heritage—from Zola. His first three full-length sound films—*La Chienne* (1931), *La Nuit du Carrefour* (1932), and *Bondu Sauvé des Eaux* (1932)—are explorations of precisely this negative side of nature, which confines rather than liberates the human spirit. (p. 51)

Renoir's use of nature in his films . . . cannot be totally separated from his development of other, even antinatural, elements in his method and interests. The many variables involved in a particular film might be ordered and properly subordinated by someone interested in a clear schema. But what is more fascinating is the way these themes meld, change, and emerge reformed. Nature means certain things to Renoir, both as theme and setting. . . . He never makes the kind of commitment to its purity, innocence, and necessity to the film that the early French film directors or his own naturalistically oriented critics would want him to. Already in his first film, *La Fille de l'Eau*, he can juxtapose and try to integrate the demands of natural setting and semi-surrealist dream. The darker films of the 1930s, with their interest in the social world, then turn the simple hues of pastoral nature into the darker tones of natural passion. (pp. 62-3)

Renoir's use of theater goes beyond the artifice that every art possesses. In almost all of Renoir's films, even in those most committed to the image and method of nature, there is a conscious evocation of the theatrical and the stylized, all the way from simple inclusion of theatrical props and methods to the most elaborate exploration of the Elizabethan metaphor of the world as stage. Throughout Renoir's films there is a flirtation between naturalism and illusion. . . . Instead of being hermetically sealed within films, Renoir explores the possibilities of film by tracing that strange aesthetic frontier where the arts mingle, his sight basically unclouded by any artistic theory that equates artifice with constriction and nature with freedom. (pp. 69-70)

Renoir implies in fact that film is the proper place to explore such differences between source and treatment because film is potentially suprageneric, a commodious form within which to include and learn from the other arts. His interest in the theater goes beyond mere formal considerations to a world where form and content are inseparable. . . . Theater then becomes for Renoir a constantly renewing concern that has repercussions in visual technique, narrative structure, delineation of character, and dominant themes. (pp. 71-2)

In the films of the 1920s theater could be interpreted as an archaic mode of artistic representation, whose only continuing life could be in its allusive use in the cinema. In the Renoir films of the later 1930s, to which *La Chienne* and *Bovary* form a transition, the enclosed world of theater has become a model of the society to which nature must give way. The opening to the possibility of relations with others in a society is expressed through the image of theater. (pp. 84-5)

In direct analogy to . . . scenes of social occasion are those scenes in Renoir's films of the 1930s in which the theater becomes a microcosm within the larger world of the entire picture: the prison camp theatricals in *La Grande Illusion,* the shadow play in *La Marseillaise,* and the weekend theatricals in *La Règle du Jeu.* (p. 86)

The twin worlds of nature and theater, as they exist on both thematic, imagistic, and structural levels in Renoir's films, are brought together and reconciled by Renoir's fascination with society, its possibilities and its failings. . . . Society is the standard against which films of nature, like, for example, *Swamp Water,* or films of theater, like *Le Carrosse d'Or,* measure themselves. Society offers a thematic context within which the rival claims of natural exuberance and formal structure may be brought together, and their excesses controlled. (p. 104)

Renoir's interest in the social theme goes beyond [a] mere mirroring to present a recreation of society, sometimes better than the society of the audience, like the commune in *Lange;* sometimes more fallible, like the tenement in *Les Bas-Fonds;* and sometimes involving a grimmer truth, like the country house La Colinière of *La Règle du Jeu.* (p. 107)

With Renoir's sound films comes a greater awareness of the pressure of society upon the world of the film. Perhaps the movement from the image alone to sound plus image is responsible for Renoir's greater sensitivity. But a more apparent parallel to the new interest is Renoir's changed attitude toward the uses of theater. Because theater so obviously invokes the special social occasion, it can serve as a convenient shorthand for society itself. (p. 110)

In the films of the 1950s Renoir develops the possibility that movies can invite the isolated national viewer into a new community of internationality in art, not necessarily better morally or socially, but more whole and more benevolent. (p. 128)

The concentration on the hero and the society against or within which he defines himself is . . . basically a development of Renoir's sound films. . . . As if to compensate for that technical separation of the camera from the character, Renoir's sound films focus more and more on the dynamics of the relation of a character to his milieu. As our apprehension of cinematic character moves from the external to the internal, so the character itself is placed within a social milieu, and defined by its own circumstances and the many connections it has with the world around it. . . . Gradually through these films the shape of Renoir's typical hero takes form, varying as Renoir's own views of the different forces creating his character vary. The individual in many of these films tries to bring his natural energy into the structures of society. Theater may order and protect this energy against society's potential violence, but by the end of the 1930s such protection is futile, and society becomes a crowded monster swallowing up a fragile and crumbling inner world. What refuge there is from such pessimism about society centers on the hero. (pp. 167-68)

Two possibilities for heroism present themselves in the films of the 1930s: heroics to help society, and heroics that exist in spite of society. Renoir's central characters in these films have

a sense of their own separateness that none of the characters of his silent films possess. (p. 168)

In the films of the 1950s Renoir explores with great richness a kind of heroism hinted at only fleetingly in the films of the 1930s and 1940s. This is the heroism of perception, understood specifically as an aesthetic perception and creativity that can restore a society as well as understand it. . . . Religion appears fleetingly in the later films of Renoir. . . . Yet religion represents merely a more traditional order that purports to reconcile nature and society in much the same way that the theatrical and aesthetic vision of life does. . . . But despite the possibility that is never far from any art form, Renoir does not assert that the Director is God. It is God's order rather than God's authority or judgment that he seeks. (pp. 180-81)

*Leo Braudy, in his* Jean Renoir: The World of his Films *(copyright © 1971, 1972 by Leo Braudy; reprinted by permission of Doubleday & Company, Inc.),* Doubleday, 1972, 286 p.

## STANLEY KAUFFMANN

[*Le Petit Théâtre de Jean Renoir*] is something of a bundle of reminiscences. . . . The old-fashioned feeling of the picture comes less from the absence of modern editing and camera dynamics than from deliberate return to passé points of view: the fairy-tale artifice of the first episode with obviously false snowflakes; the comic cinematic discomfort of large operatic gesture in the second episode. . . .

This reminiscent atmosphere in *Le Petit Théâtre* promotes a feeling of ease. It's a film made by a man who knows why he has chosen as he has and how to fulfill his choices. The picture feels almost as if it had been made before, as if it were a three-part play in a repertory and these actors were coming out to give yet another performance for a director whom they know well. Part of this feeling comes from the fact that some of them do know Renoir well, part from the fact that the picture belongs to a familiar Renoir vein, and part from the fact that, without any conscious fervent adherence to principle, Renoir now can't help making films like Renoir—stylistically more so than ever, one might say. . . .

The trouble with this ease of fabrication is that now we see it as fabrication of another sort. The film's first episode deals with two deaths, the second with two deaths, the third with humiliation swallowed, and all this is treated as material for a gently smiling work of life-accepting warmth. I don't argue that death and discomfort must necessarily be grim, but I get the feeling that Renoir in this vein could make a film in a cancer ward with one wistful tear and a Gallic shrug at the end.

*Stanley Kauffmann, " 'Le petit théâtre de Jean Renoir' " (reprinted by permission of Brandt & Brandt Literary Agents, Inc.; copyright © 1974 by Stanley Kauffmann), in* The New Republic, *Vol. 170, No. 21, May 25, 1974, p. 22.*

## GRAHAM PETRIE

It is easy enough to recognize the visual beauty of [*The Golden Coach*] and especially of the colors, and to acknowledge the thematic links with other Renoir works—the nature-artifice conflict, the erection and dismantling of class barriers—but apart from these the film seems to offer little more than a somewhat obvious reworking of the question posed so bluntly by Camilla: "Where does the theater end and life begin?"

Renoir might in fact have done better to eliminate this line, which hardens the ambiguous and subtle structure of the film into rather too crude a formula. . . . [He] uses the ability of the cinema to make a series of artificially staged events *look* real to conduct an investigation (in this case relatively light-hearted) into concepts of reality and artifice, the relationship between life and art and life and theater. (pp. 40-1)

[By] taking us through two layers of artifice into something that finally appears to be "real," Renoir has merely strengthened our awareness of the artificiality and arbitrariness of what the screen will present to use. He has also confirmed our own status as audience, and we soon discover that we are watching another audience. . . . (p. 41)

Costumes, masks, disguises, roles, the division into actors and performers, all serve to make the central conflict between the natural and the artificial, the spontaneous and the theatrical, much less straightforward than it has appeared to many critics. One is forced to conclude from *The Golden Coach* . . . that it is impossible to make any rigid separation between them. (p. 42)

Graham Petrie, "Theater Film Life," *in* Film Comment *(copyright © 1974 by The Film Society of Lincoln Center; all rights reserved), Vol. 10, No. 3, May-June, 1974, pp. 38-43.*

## ROGER GREENSPUN

[*The Lower Depths (Les Bas-Fonds), The Diary of a Chambermaid,* and *Picnic on the Grass*] possess an incredible richness of idea and imagination, partly because of their strangeness. If Renoir's art were wholly a function of its thematic complexity . . . I'd have to put them among the glories of his career. But I am not persuaded that such complexity is always greatness, though it is a great boon to essay writers, or that there is so much foolishness in the vulgar common view that celebrates Renoir the populist realist or the nature-loving son of his famous father. That view isn't false; it is merely incomplete. (p. 22)

Renoir's realism follows several different lines. Some of it belongs to the classic realist preoccupations of, say, *The Southerner* or *Toni.* But more of it seems to grow out of an appreciation of the kind of "realism" your parents had in mind when they'd tell you to be realistic and maybe forget the nonsense you picked up at the movies. . . . (pp. 22-3)

But by the time of *Picnic on the Grass,* natural realism is being regularly subject to the apocalyptic rigors of a supernatural magic. (p. 23)

Everybody in *The Lower Depths* has a special point of view. For the Baron, life is a dream—of repeatedly changing his clothes. For the flop house landlord Kostilev . . . , half sniveling piety and half harsh brutality, it is a peak up to heaven and a hard cold stare down to the ground. For the flop house whore, it is romantic love. But for Kostilev's young wife it is only sex and money. For Pepel it is an inherited occupation (burglary), until it changes temporarily to murder, when he leads his comrades in the slaughter of the evil Kostilev, and then to the undefined realm of potentiality that is the particular value of a life on the road.

But the defined realms that precede the ending are of a fascinating sort. (p. 24)

The *Lower Depths* world isn't continuous. It is stratified, sharply delimited between foreground and background. . . .

This isn't great or even very good filmmaking. . . . But it is Renoir feeling out a territory that will become increasingly important in his movies: a humanized segment of nature ordered in degrees of wildness. . . .

You can find it everywhere in *Diary of a Chambermaid.* . . . The film has won a certain notoriety from the fact that all this outdoors is so palpably indoors. . . . *Diary* seemed to signal a theatrical Renoir—not simply a Renoir attracted to the metaphor of theatre (true of every film at least from *Nana,* 1926, on)—but a Renoir for whom the open exploitation of theatrical artifice in setting and performance could open a whole new kind of vitality. . . .

*Diary of a Chambermaid* is a film shot through with death, even more than *Grand Illusion,* and you can never tell in Renoir when any cliché may open into mysterious depths. . . .

By the kind of paradox that informs each of these Renoir movies, *Diary of a Chambermaid*—Hollywood sound stage, aquarium light and all—is virtually a study in the meaning of "ground," or earth, where things are hidden and from which they are able to grow. (p. 25)

*Picnic on the Grass* comes as close as any of the movies to satisfying the chip-off-the-Impressionist-painter's-block view of Renoir. . . . Pretty clearly Renoir is creating a "Renoir," one of his few, and for that reason among others *Picnic* belongs among the most consciously artificial of his works. It is also among the most ingeniously intellectual, and if a mechanical awkwardness attends all its lyrical tribute to ripeness and the powers of generation, that is perhaps because the grass is teeming with notions about where we are going and where we are. (pp. 25-6)

Like most pastorals, the subject of *Picnic on the Grass* is really political; a struggle between sane politics and crazy, between man and test tube, between sex and sterility, appetite and abstinence. Like most recreations of nature, the film's interest really is in artifice. And perhaps like most celebrations of leisure, its ideal really is work. . . . Like pornography, it is voyeuristic, obsessed, not too concerned with the larger humanity of its human beings. It leaves that concern to its intellectual sub-structure, which is almost endless in its ramifications. (p. 26)

*Rules of the Game* is rational comedy turned sour. *Picnic on the Grass* is romantic comedy turned to ecstasy. Among the major Renoir films it stands alone in proposing a happy ending based on social involvement rather than withdrawal or escape. And among the films we are examining, it is the only one to look forward to a just society without first killing some repressive power that inhibits it. It doesn't need death. Revolution has become evolution—a shift in terms not atypical of Renoir, for whom, it turns out, they apparently mean the same thing.

Clearly, both *Diary of a Chambermaid* and *Picnic on the Grass* redefine the concerns of *Rules of the Game,* a film that remains seminal not so much because it is the best, but because it is the best defined of Renoir's studies of house and garden, servants and masters, mixed alliances, interior and exterior space. . . .

Renoir is the most consistent of filmmakers, not in producing a steady succession of masterpieces, but in continually developing, re-examining, rediscovering the same basic materials. . . . In *Rules of the Game,* it is a place for irresolution, disguise, and secret assignation. In *Picnic on the Grass,* it is a genuine mystery, opening the way to a real change of heart and mind. In *Lower Depths,* it is the bottom, from which one or two can rise again. But in *Diary of a Chambermaid* it is a surface layer, covering buried treasures, buried bodies, and some seeds of a new life. . . .

As [Renoir's later films] leave behind the concerns of social politics they become more profoundly political. Striving for a degree of improvisatory freedom, they often seem more calculated. Depth of field gives way to an over-seeing fluidity, and the great houses lose their potency as architectural metaphors. . . .

In some ways the late movies gain through their preoccupations; in other ways they lose. The later Renoir is perhaps more valuable to think about; the earlier Renoir is more fun to see. (p. 27)

*Roger Greenspun, "House and Garden: Three Films by Jean Renoir," in* Film Comment *(copyright © 1974 by The Film Society of Lincoln Center; all rights reserved), Vol. 10, No. 4, July-August, 1974, pp. 22-7.*

## JONATHAN ROSENBAUM

Neither a major nor a minor work in the Renoir canon, *Toni* demands to be regarded more as an adventure of the director in contact with his material than as an integral and 'finished' composition. If the symmetrical framing device of the train arriving with fresh immigrants at the beginning and end of the film appears somewhat forced in relation to the whole, this is likely because Renoir began with notions of a social thesis and a Zola-derived sense of fatality from which his better instincts subsequently deviated. And it is the instinctual rather than the conceptual side of *Toni* that renders it a living work forty years after it was made. . . . Over and around the largely melodramatic plot is draped an expansive mood of leisurely improvisation, like an ill-fitting but comfortable suit of clothes, often permitting the accidental and random to take precedence over the deliberate, the individual detail over the general design. . . . [The] muddy fadeouts and slightly bumpy pans are all part of the film's charm and integrity. They are intimately related to what makes the film historically important: the choice of milieu and exclusively natural rural locations, the use of unknown actors and local non-professionals, and the risks and beauties of direct sound within this rough-and-ready context. . . . [An] occasional choppiness in the narrative as it carries us over three years tends to make the pleasures of the film more localised than continuous, but at the same time there is an effective play of 'internal rhymes' that strives to bridge the gaps. . . . Such details help to override the awkwardness and sense of strain that crops up from time to time in some of the performances. . . . Yet even these lapses often serve the positive function of bringing us closer to the people in the film, if not the characters. What one ultimately carries away from *Toni,* in fact, is a memory of felt presences rather than incarnations. (p. 237)

*Jonathan Rosenbaum, "'Toni'," in* Monthly Film Bulletin *(copyright © The British Film Institute, 1974), Vol. 41, No. 489, October, 1974, pp. 236-37.*

## RAYMOND DURGNAT

So far as the relationship between camera and action is concerned, [*Swamp Water*] marks a striking transfiguration of style. One might plausibly attribute it to Renoir's versatility (adapting his style to his material) or his prudence (adapting his style to the Hollywood consensus), or his responsiveness to actors (allowing the Hollywood actors to key the film's tone and tempo), or even the influence of producer, photographer, editor and studio, or to all these factors together. Its individuality lies in its sense of people handing things to one another, rather than confronting one another. . . .

In certain aspects, *Swamp Water* compromises between a Western and *Toni*. It resembles the former in that violence is consistent and integral rather than spasmodic and, as it were, incidental. Yet the integration of violence and communal emotion is simpler than in the tortuous constructions of William Faulkner. (p. 228)

Certainly the film accepts several ingredients from the American regional drama, including its violence, and the Manicheanism which is a product of its Puritanism. But the modification of material by style, or rather of genre by detail of content, may, in practice, as in *Les Bas-Fonds,* have an opposite effect. Renoir moves us directly from Ben in the swamp calling Trouble, to Ben back by his home still calling Trouble. Yet it leaves us in the middle of two uncompleted notions; it takes time for the second milieu to assert itself in our mind after the conspicuous action; it has an effect of *hanging over,* of incompletion, of sad human discouragement, rather than of a hard conflict. It is *indefinite.* We live in a world of confusion, of constant worry, of everyday desertions. (pp. 229-30)

The fascination of *Swamp Water* is precisely the homely and realistic *perspective* which it brings to the pioneer myth. (p. 230)

Renoir's achievement is the film's retention of ordinary human relationships; of people as mixtures of toughness and weakness, of good and bad. (p. 233)

[In *The Southerner,*] Renoir returns to regional, rural America, for what, with *The River,* is his only film to celebrate family virtues—although it significantly extends them. (p. 245)

Social consciousness in the overt sense seems absent. Renoir has acquiesced in the usual mythic apparatus of economic individualism, good neighbourliness, pioneer puritanism and a timely appeal to the Deity. Even if one accepts this political structure, an important distinction remains; nothing in the film allows them to be taken for granted, or assumes that they exist on tap, which is when they become mythical in the cheap sense. Almost every scene suggests an ingrained reluctance to give, an indifference like callousness, as the social norm. Devers is not a scapegoat for society but a representative of it. Although he has survived as an individualistic economic unit, he has become stunted as a man. The eventual reconciliation of the men is the result of a dishonest deal and it is not allowed to obliterate our sense of the hard-hearted hermit he has been for so many years and which essentially he is still. The happy end is not proposed as compensation for a wretched life, in the way which comes so easily to heirs of the puritan notion of salvation as a total redemption outside time. (pp. 245-46)

[The] film is non-committal: co-operation never quite becomes a Co-operative, and God may or may not exist to answer. But about the radical necessity for human solidarity for subsistence (on Sam's side), a minimally decent humanity (on everyone else's) and any social satisfaction (on Devers') the film is not equivocal. (p. 247)

Renoir's films will endure as testimonies to a unique—because historically unique—juncture of sensibilities: his, his actors', his collaborators', his times'. They are unrepeatable, neither replacing, nor being replaceable by, the most authentic and sensitive of those movies which resemble them, but corroborating them, communicating with them. (p. 395)

Perhaps the least reassuring part of Renoir's vision is that, despite a lack of emphasis on malice, it pivots on disorder: rape, murder, and revolution. . . . If Renoir's vision often entails a tragic or a stoic view of life, yet curiously eludes our usual classification of tragedy, it isn't because optimism, sensationalism or sentimentality dilute it. It is because that very sense of "orderly" accumulation which is characteristic of conventional tragedy is shaken by his sense of a "transformability" of ego, and of certain "absurdist" conjunctions. (p. 398)

Morally, Renoir's films can be grouped as "contradictory" pairs. *Nana*'s theme is its heroine's chastening, *Charleston* is her triumph. *Marquitta* is contradicted by *La Petite Marchande d'Allumettes*. In *La Chienne* the bourgeois is humiliated; in *La Nuit du Carrefour* he is vindicated. *Les Bas-Fonds* emphasises despair and evasion, *La Marseillaise* despair and revolution. A trio is formed by *The Golden Coach, French CanCan* and *Eléna et les Hommes*. Show-business is sad because a concomitant of stardom is the renunciation of life; show-business is happy because it's an apotheosis of life; politics is only a very dangerous form of show-business.

The "incoherence" of Renoir's moral code isn't a philosophical defect; it indicates an acceptance of the arbitrary which idealistic rationalists vainly strive to schematize away. Since guilt and injustice are inevitable, and self-centredness, even without malice, which also exists, is cruel, the best one can be is generous, resilient and stoic. (p. 400)

Renoir's mixture of vitalism and acquiescence betray a tribal temperament which has neither been uprooted nor crushed by the arid alienation of our era. Thus the *commedia,* the classical, the baroque and the fauve shade gradually into one another, the first and the last joining in the image of the pantomime bear to complete the circle: clown-actor-man-and-beast. One might define Renoir's art as a classicism which is sufficiently realistic to grant that its formality is a continuously shifting balance of impulses. Or as a realism sufficiently sophisticated to grant that masks, games, dreams and polite hypocrises are not only an evasion of life, but that part of it which we create. Or as a romanticism which accepts and understands that the truth of a feeling lies not primarily in a first fine careless rapture which time or compromise dilute and debase, but equally in a certain contemplation, dissimulation, detachment, and even convention, provided that withdrawal, whether weak or ironic, leaves one as generous towards others as towards oneself and as astringent towards oneself as towards others. For life is a continuing dance, not one simple saving or damning leap. (p. 403)

*Raymond Durgnat, in his* Jean Renoir *(copyright © 1974 by the Regents of the University of California; reprinted by permission of the University of California Press), University of California Press, 1974, 429 p.*

**PETER HARCOURT**

Along with those of Vigo, the films of Jean Renoir are the most tentative in the history of the cinema. They work by

indirection, implying qualities and attitudes that are rarely stated directly. Occasionally, something like a choric comment by one of his characters gives us a clue to Renoir's own atitude, a clue that we might be tempted to relate to something similar said by another character in a different film. For Renoir's films add up to one immensely rich and varied single work. Renoir himself is obviously conscious of this continuity. (p. 68)

More so than with any other film-maker, each individual film by Jean Renoir gains depth and lucidity when placed in the context of his complete works, when illuminated by the recurring motifs and structural characteristics of his other achievements. (p. 69)

Passion, Friendship, Nature—these three words might serve as focal points around which we could group the films of Jean Renoir; although finally we would have to add Art as well, to give *The Golden Coach* the centrality it deserves. (p. 73)

If *La Chienne* were better known, its extraordinary qualities might be better understood. The film is distinguished not only for its artistic qualities, but also for its qualities of moral complexity—one might even want to say of moral confusion—qualities that relate this early film to [Renoir's novel] *The Notebooks of Captain Georges*. As in the novel, there is in *La Chienne* the sense that Renoir may not himself be fully aware of the moral implications of the characters he has created. If its plot is taken from the novel by G. de la Fourchardière, the implications of its atmosphere seem very much to belong to Jean Renoir. (p. 74)

Magnificent as *La Chienne* is in the execution of its central scenes and modern as it seems today in the psychological alienation depicted in its central character, the film troubles me slightly in a way similar to *The Notebooks of Captain Georges* as I get the sense that Renoir himself may not fully recognize the implications of what he is doing. The ending seems too easy. We can see how it relates to Renoir's philosophy of acceptance, to his desire to be at one with all things. Encouraged by his father, Renoir wants to be able to accept all people and all actions simply for what they are, as part of Nature's richness and variety. A beautiful view of life, so compelling a part of Auguste's sensual world, but often less compelling in Jean's as he lived in more troubled times.

Inescapably a part of such a philosophy of acceptance is an amoral fatalism that leads to passivity when faced with situations that call for decision. In his biography of his father [*Renoir, My Father*], Renoir quotes with full approval Auguste's theory of a cork floating down a river. 'You swing the tiller over to the right or left from time to time but always in the direction of the current.' You cannot stand against the march of events, this parable seems to say. Again, there is a beauty and a wisdom in such a view of life, difficult to challenge in the gentleness of its implications; and for Renoir *père,* the philosophy seemed to lend clarity to his life. For Renoir *fils,* however, its acceptance posed a moral dilemma that he was never satisfactorily to resolve. In his most complex films—supremely in *La Règle du jeu*—the dilemma creates a tension and an urgency that are obviously a result of Renoir's attempt to sort these matters out. (pp. 78-9)

*La Chienne* gives us the sense of a man consistently trapped by the life that he leads. His job is dull and routine and his wife is a shrew. He escapes from this bourgeois tedium by retreat into fantasy—initially the fantasy of his painting, then the fantasy of his passion for Lulu. There is a certain unreality about both these retreats. While his art is meaningful as an escape for him, there is no sense that he values it with his mind, that he recognizes its worth. He is a genuine primitive, if you like, in the manner of Grandma Moses or Le Douanier Rousseau; but even Rousseau came to know something of the value of his work and to feel himself the equal of Picasso. The salient point for Renoir in Legrand's attitude to his own work is the total absence of intellectual interest in his own ability. Renoir shows no desire to relate Legrand's artistic gifts to any decision-making powers of his mind.

This, of course, relates to Renoir's view of art as inherited from his father, his view of the artistic activity as being *solely* a matter of intuition and feeling, but also to his fondness for the idea of the artist as craftsman, not as a specialist or professional in his own field. (p. 81)

If we think about it and try to understand it, *La Chienne* really presents us with a complex experience. It takes us through a most destructive and self-destructive series of situations, apparently endorsing a totally pessimistic fatalism, yet strives to leave us with the feeling of the warmth of whimsy and with a philosophical detachment at the end—or something like it; for it is difficult to describe the mood of [the] final shot. It is largely a matter of tone, difficult to interpret even in literature but particularly elusive in the movies. . . . [The] film leaves us with the feeling of many issues left unclear—in one way, a formal failure, one might say, a failure of the intelligence fully to shape and clarify its material; yet in another, part of the perennial interest in the film, one of the reasons it still seems so modern today.

Although a much more structured film, *Le Crime de Monsieur Lange* deals with some of the same ideas in a somewhat similar way. It again touches upon the theme of art and again presents the artist as a naïve primitive, essentially a fantasist. (pp. 82-3)

The 'passion' in *Monsieur Lange* is the passion of evil, evil lust and greed as embodied in Batala. It has also in this film clear political implications. Batala is the capitalist exploiter who cheats and lies and so keeps the people down. In fact, in any *book* on Renoir, *Lange* should occupy a prominent part. It is the one film that links Renoir most clearly with his colleagues of the thirties. It is in a sense the most *intelligent* film he ever made, formally the most intricate, the most clearly thought out. It is certainly the most symmetrical. With the printing press on one side of the courtyard, turning white paper black, and the laundry on the other, turning 'black' sheets white, it is very much one of the courtyard films of the time. . . . In this sense, important though it is, it is in these ways uncharacteristic. One detects the influence of Prévert and perhaps others actively involved with the Popular Front. But while the film lends itself to explanations in terms of the political ideology of the time, it is still very much a film by Renoir and still very much presents his personal moral universe, revolving round his great sense of uncertainty when faced with the need to act.

The positive values in the film are chiefly those of friendship, here given political meaning by the Popular Front atmosphere in which the film was made. The negative values, primarily embodied in Batala, are those of lust and greed. The art, such as it is, while initially a product of fantasy, is dependent upon the approval of the Co-op for its worldly success. Lange's art needs the atmosphere of approval and friendship in order to survive. The evil Batala, it appears, is capable of destroying all this. (pp. 84-5)

With the moral pattern of *La Chienne* and *Le Crime de Monsieur Lange* in mind, some of the confusions within the many-faceted achievement of *La Règle du jeu* begin to come clear. It is perhaps wrong to describe the film as formless, as I have done, for, in its way, it is indeed a highly structured and delicately nuanced work. But its form is not that of the well-made plot or swiftly-told story. . . . Part of the richness of this particular film is the result of a quite unusual number of traditions being drawn upon and referred to, traditions of French farce and social satire, which are themselves being qualified and refined. Thus, even more than *Monsieur Lange,* the film lends itself to a variety of interpretations and invites as many social and political explanations as it reveals characteristics of the mind of Jean Renoir. Yet the personal themes are there as well, even if in a subterranean way; and the moral ambiguity of the film is made yet more elusive by the ambiguity of our response to the figure of Octave, played in the film by Renoir himself.

In *La Règle du jeu* the passion theme is embodied partly in Jurieu, the ace aviator who is a fool on the ground, but chiefly by Schumacher, the gamekeeper. Schumacher is an outsider in every way. An Alsatian by birth, Germanic in manner when compared with this very French world, he longs to return to Strasbourg where men are men and poachers are shot. He wants to take his French wife, Lisette, away from this frivolous philandering world, while she on the other hand has no desire to leave *le service de Madame*. For those that accept the Rules of the Game, this life of idle pleasure does provide a little world that, in the film, groups itself around the Marquis and his mechanical toys (*his* kind of mechanical art, I suppose). Although a servant, Lisette is very much a part of this world and values it far more than she could her life with her husband away from the securities of this society. She is one of the insiders that honour the rules.

There are many outsiders, however, as well. In fact, it is one of the feats of this extraordinary film that, while presenting us with a highly conventionalized and artificial world, Renoir makes us feel that most of the people are outsiders in some way. The Marquis himself is a Jew. The Marquise, Christine, is an Austrian, somewhat ill at ease within the more sophisticated assumptions of her adopted society. Octave is a mysterious figure, most ambiguously defined. But he is very much a hanger-on, a kind of go-between, meddling about in the lives of other people. (pp. 85-7)

Throughout the film, Octave [has been uttering] characteristically choric comments like 'Everyone has his reasons' and wishing he could hide his head in the sand and not have to decide what is right and wrong. It is difficult not to see in these comments the personal endorsement of Renoir himself, perhaps struggling to come to grips with the moral implications of the approaching war. In any case, his final unexplained disappearance feels in the film like an act of self-banishment, almost of self-destruction. It is just one of the characteristics that gives this extraordinary film a personal charge that makes it difficult to interpret tidily in any social or political way; although obviously, as with *Lange* before it and before that with *Toni,* the social and political references are also very much there. (p. 89)

[Renoir's] longing for a simpler kind of universe, a universe where one can feel at ease with Nature and with one's friends, where one can simply *live* a child-like existence without the need for moral decision—this longing is less a theme in Renoir's films than an aspect of their atmosphere, a moral quality that is part of the mood they create. (pp. 89-90)

[The motif of longing contributes greatly to the human quality of Renoir's films], to their immense compassion for all living things. It also accounts for their formal imperfections, the sense that most of Renoir's films can give us that the potential power of individual moments is often greater than the clarity of the whole. (p. 90)

[All of Renoir's films] catch more than just a little bit of the truth of the particular time and place in which they were made, of the social and political upheavals of his day. If they also catch more than a little bit of the confusion that Renoir himself must have been experiencing at the time, this, too, becomes a part of their richness, a part of their feeling of sincerity. (p. 91)

The qualities that most endure, that are most worth living for in the world of Jean Renoir, would seem to be the qualities of simple friendship. This, his films imply, constitutes the natural order of things. With characteristic paradox, there are no films more dedicated to this ideal than his two war films, *La Grande Illusion* and *Le Caporal épinglé*. (pp. 92-3)

Certainly, *La Grande Illusion* is a magnificent film. If we are concerned with formal perfection, along with *Monsieur Lange* it is the most completely successful film in the Renoir canon. It is the most successfully balanced between the prison sequences of confinement and the farm sequences of liberation. Even the setting of the First World War seems now sufficiently distant in time for Renoir's characteristically gentle treatment of the war to work successfully and not to offend. Quite different from *La Règle du jeu* in this, *La Grande Illusion* has virtually no moments of intense personal feeling that exist, so to speak, to one side of the plot. Yet to my mind these characteristic moments are so much a part of the manner of Renoir that I have always felt in *La Grande Illusion* an element of thinness, as if everything is too neatly resolved by the end.

With *Le Caporal épinglé,* however, the situation is different. . . . [It] seems to me to provide, in its quiet, episodic way, a summing up of the main moral themes in Renoir. Beneath its grey surface are the characteristic concerns with friendship versus action, with the need to take a stand in this difficult world even at the risk of destroying yourself, or at least of alienating yourself from your friends. We must act, this film seems to say, even though we cannot discover the reasons for action. It is in this way one of the most personal films that Renoir has ever made. (pp. 93-4)

[Everywhere] in Renoir, in films as different in story-line as *Madame Bovary* and *La Règle du jeu,* there is a strong feeling for *la grisaille* of a wintry landscape, for the present bleakness of a countryside *potentially* green and alive. Nowhere more so than in *Le Caporal épinglé*. The film begins with Nazi planes dropping bombs—destructive newsreel footage that Renoir employs most skilfully to punctuate this film—and then with Nature dropping rain. Not a productive, fertilizing rain, but the depressive, wintry rain of a world that has lost its sun. (pp. 94-5)

The central problem within *Le Caporal épinglé* seems less the concern with the freedom and confinement than the search for a basis for constructive action, action which in turn might set a man free. The Corporal, nameless throughout the film, is the least personalized character that Renoir has ever created. In the penultimate sequence, when he explains that he has a family waiting for him at home, that there is a *domestic* reason for his continual efforts to escape from the camps, we might be

tempted *not* to believe him. For we really know nothing about him at all. (p. 95)

*Le Caporal épinglé* is a more personal statement by Jean Renoir than has generally been recognized. In his apparent impersonality, it is almost as if the Corporal *stands* for some obscure principle of action which Renoir now recognizes but cannot really personalize in a conventional way. The Corporal *must* go on escaping. Simply that. We never really know why. Of course, we may *think* we know, because we *think* we know about the war. Our common sense makes us assume that the Corporal has patriotic motives, that he shares our assumed ideals about truth and freedom and all the other abstractions that govern our thinking in times of war. Perhaps he does. But nowhere *in the film itself* does Renoir make this clear. It is as if Renoir has come to realize that in such a situation, one *must* take a stand, one *must* attempt to swim against the current, although Renoir himself cannot really explain why. (p. 96)

[Like] the ending of so many Renoir films, like *La Chienne, Le Crime de Monsieur Lange, Les Bas Fonds,* even like *La Grande Illusion* with Maréchal and Rosenthal becoming tiny specks in the snow, we have a shot of the Corporal walking away from us up the street. A river whistle hoots on the misty-grey morning as the Corporal, all alone, walks away to an unspecified future, away from his friend, to see we don't know whom. Again, our assumptions about the Resistance and other historical matters might allow us to *assume* that we know what he and Pater have been talking about. But Renoir keeps it unclear in the film itself. We do not *really know* what is happening at the end, *where* the Corporal is going to, *what* he is going to do. Characteristically, within an atmosphere of considerable warmth—the warmth of Pater's friendship—while we *see* that the Corporal is free, there is the feeling not of celebration but of forlornness at the end.

If children habitually fall from heaven to end the majority of Fellini's films on a note of hope, Renoir repeatedly gives us the feeling of his characters walking into a world without a future, a world where one must indeed feel *mal à l'aise*. Along with the habitual greyness, this recurring note of melancholy provides the dialectic tug necessary to counterbalance Renoir's irrepressible need to believe in the essential goodness of existence, the beauty of nature and the reassurances of friendship. The greatness of Renoir's films and their astonishing modernity lie in this ability to contain their own confusion, to find a form that, while apparently saying one thing, encourages us to feel another. (p. 100)

[Whatever] the simplistic implications of Renoir *the man's* view of life as he describes it to us, his films create for us an experience of uncertainty and confusion that enables us to realize that, no matter how attractive his philosophy might appear as he inherited it from his father, the violence and uncertainties of the modern world made it impossible for Renoir *the artist* fully to believe it himself. (p. 101)

> *Peter Harcourt, "A Flight from Passion: Images of Uncertainty in the Work of Jean Renoir," in his* Six European Directors: Essays on the Meaning of Film Style *(copyright © Peter Harcourt, 1974; reprinted by permission of Penguin Books Ltd), Penguin Books, 1974, pp. 68-101.*

### JOHN SIMON

[*La Chienne*] is quite a technical achievement. At a time when sound was in its puling infancy, there are atmospheric existential noises; when lenses were primitive, there is considerable deep focus; when equipment was heavy, there is much effective camera movement. And there is more: a story in which conventional concepts of good and evil are treated with a flexibility bordering on iconoclasm—which was most innovative of all. . . .

*La Chienne* is far from a great film. Based on an insignificant novel, it has a rather preposterous plot; its characters are, for the most part, either too stupid to follow up on options that any fool would grab at, or, like the hero's wife, so simplistically exaggerated as to lose all humanity. Even key details are unconvincing. . . .

*La Chienne* is fascinating, though, for a variety of nonartistic reasons. First, as a lesson in how unseriously cinema was taken not so long ago. . . . The mist that enshrouds ancient literature still envelops the films of the thirties.

Then there are the curious anecdotes and legends that surround this movie. We have it on Renoir's word that Simon, Marèse, and Flamant lived in real life a tragic triangle not unlike the one they enacted on screen. Yet another example, you might say, of life imitating art—or, in this case, pseudo-art. . . .

*La Chienne* gathers pretentious critical exegeses as an old hull does barnacles.

*John Simon, "Bitchcraft," in* New York *Magazine (copyright © 1976 by News Group Publications, Inc.; reprinted with permission of* New York *Magazine), Vol. 9, No. 20, May 17, 1976, p. 70.*

### PHILLIPE R. PEREBINOSSOFF

In *The Rules of the Game,* made in 1939, Renoir uses amateur theatricals to suggest the breakdown of the aristocracy and in *Grand Illusion,* finished in 1937, the theatricals in which soldiers dress in drag reflect the imbalances in society during wartime. (p. 50)

It is Robert de la Chesnaye in *The Rules of the Game* who suggests a celebration to honor the aviator Andre Jurieu, the hero of the moment. . . . Having "fun" is a duty which he takes seriously.

Theatricality is a very important part of la Chesnaye's life. His attempt to preserve his way of life is closely linked with the theater. . . . La Chesnaye protects himself from changes in the outside world by involving himself in theatrical amusements, long regarded as a suitable pastime for members of the aristocracy. La Chesnaye's theatrical soiree is very important to him; he greatly enjoys dressing up and he welcomes the task of directing or controlling an evening's entertainment. (pp. 50-1)

The theatrical party la Chesnaye organizes is one of the key events in the film. Everything comes to a head: the intrigues of the masters, as well as the intrigues of the servants who imitate their masters. The party sequence is not extraneous to the lives of the participants. The theatrical ball is clearly intended to represent the life style of the aristocracy, and the sequence makes its comment from within. . . . The party sequence is successful because it is in keeping with the life style and personalities of the participants and because it allows for the resolution of the events that have been developing throughout the film. (p. 51)

[The] theatrical party in *The Rules of the Game* is not superimposed; it is a natural outcome of the developments within

the movie. La Chesnaye's life is symbolized by the mechanical toys he avidly collects—his Romantic Negress, his motheaten warbler, his calliope—and by his consuming passion for theatricals. It is definitively in keeping with his character for him to organize the theatricals which serve as a culmination for the events in the film. (p. 52)

The costumes the principals wear for the theatrical evening, which are removed from their roles in life, help contribute to the loss of self which Christine and the others experience during the festivities. As a Tyrolean girl, Christine is completely out of step with Parisian society. In costume, she asks for passion and immediate action, not rules. Genevieve is a gypsy, Octave a bear. Their costumes directly relate to the loss of self each one of them undergoes. In costume, Christine finds it difficult to maintain her role as the wife of Robert de la Chesnaye. Genevieve can cease to be la Chesnaye's well-mannered mistress; as a gypsy she can get as drunk as she wants. (pp. 52-3)

The theatricals which represent la Chesnaye's way of life precipitate chaos. The amusements of his own society betray him. They propagate the decay of the society from within. The theatricals, the wearing of costumes, and the adoption of roles appropriate to members of the lower classes lead to an outbreak of violence which almost destroys the aristocratic society. In spite of the internal decay, la Chesnaye is able to survive, at least temporarily, by acting to preserve the facade of the old order in the face of a hostile, changing world.

As in *The Rules of the Game,* costumes in *Grand Illusion* serve to establish the kind of role confusion which can lead to an upheaval in the normal social order. Private entertainments which include men in drag conventionally precede a reversal of events which closely parallels the sexual turnabout. (pp. 53-4)

Moreover, the bonds which are formed in the film are all short lasting. . . . The bonds formed during wartime, Renoir seems to be saying, are artificial ones, and believing that it might be otherwise is part of the illusion of war. The so-called camaraderie formed during the theatricals is temporary at best.

In both *The Rules of the Game* and *Grand Illusion,* the theatrical interludes serve an integral function in developing each film's theme. The theatricals are not superimposed onto the films to allow the filmmaker to draw facile associations. Nor do the theatrical interludes exist in isolation within the confines of "the cinema." The theatricals do not appear out of place, as if somebody had temporarily forgotten what medium was being employed. Rather, the use of established theatrical conventions becomes an intimate part of two fully realized works of art. (p. 55)

*Phillipe R. Perebinossoff, "Theatricals in Jean Renoir's 'The Rules of the Game' and 'Grand Illusion'," in* Literature/Film Quarterly *(© copyright 1977 Salisbury State College), Vol. 5, No. 1, Winter, 1977, pp. 50-6.*

### ANDREW SARRIS

Renoir's career was a river of personal expression. The waters may have varied in turbulence and depth, but the flow of his personality was consistently directed to its final outlet in the sea of life. If the much abused term "humanism" could have been applied to Renoir's art and to no one else's, it might have provided an accurate definition for his work as a whole. In

Renoir's films, man's natural surroundings are almost always prominently featured, and it is this emphasis on man in his natural environment photographed by an unblinking camera that is the true precursor of neorealism. As Murnau represented the formal antithesis to Eisenstein's montage principles, Renoir represented the thematic alternative to Eisenstein's dialectics. . . .

Renoir's stylistic personality can be expressed at times by no more than a beat's hesitation in the rhythm of the players' movements. In one sequence of *La Regle du Jeu,* Renoir gallops up the stairs, stops in hoplike uncertainty when his name is called by a coquettish maid, and then, with marvelous post-reflex continuity, resumes his bearish shambling to the heroine's boudoir. If one could describe the musical grace note of that momentary suspension—and it is difficult to do—one could begin to understand the full range of Renoir's creative interpretation of human behavior. It might help if we thought of Renoir's cinema as a long dance, with Renoir himself as a dancing bear, that is, as both a performer and a creator of a social ritual. Film by film, from the '20s into the '70s, Renoir displayed the interdependence of art and nature, theatre and cinema, politics and ethics, people and things—and all on the screen at the same time.

> *Andrew Sarris, ''Jean Renoir: The Grand Illusionist'' (reprinted by permission of* The Village Voice *and the author; copyright © The Village Voice, Inc., 1979), in* The Village Voice, *Vol. XXIV, No. 9, February 26, 1979, p. 41.*

## ELIZABETH GROTTLE STREBEL

Renoir's receptivity to the French Left and active involvement with it played a critical role in shaping his artistic vision at a time when he was consciously evolving his own cinematic language. . . . *Le Crime de M. Lange* (1935) and *La Marseillaise* (1937) can both be seen as major artistic expressions of Popular Front consciousness. (p. 36)

In *Toni* we are dealing exclusively with a rural milieu, characterised by its initial appearance of openness, with an emphasis on exteriors captured in long shots with a wide angle lens. But in *Toni* we find a nature that is pressing in, confining, like the massive rock surfaces of the quarry which dwarf the workers and threaten to crush them. The narrative is centred on the fatalistic ebb and flow of passion and overt social comment is oblique, occurring as a sort of parenthesis round the film, with the migrant workers returning year after year to a fated existence. (p. 37)

With *Le Crime de M. Lange,* we turn from man and nature and forces seemingly beyond his control to man and society, where he is given the possibility of seizing control of his existence. Ostensibly, everything about the film is more closed. First of all, we are dealing mainly with interiors. The narrative centres on an enclosed circular courtyard, and the film keeps returning to the courtyard as a focal point. . . . Yet within the courtyard setting, as we shall see, there is a greater openness, a sense of overcoming limitations, the potential for breaking with prescribed patterns, leading to an openendedness at the end of *Lange* which is quite the reversal of *Toni.* Circularity here then is used to signify solidarity and organic binding.

*Le Crime de M. Lange* is the Popular Front film *par excellence,* full of the exuberance, optimism and confidence in the ability to transform social conditions which characterised that movement. . . .

The image of the working class in *Lange* is certainly romanticised and poeticised, particularly in [screenwriter Jacques] Prévert's dialogue. But then was not perhaps the Popular Front view of the working class also highly romanticised? In *Lange* there is no question of dealing with an industrialised proletariat. . . .

A somewhat more obscure reference to the Popular Front is the tearing down of the billboard which covers up the only window in Charles' room. Fresh air, health, housing, the general quality of the working man's living and working milieu, were to become central preoccupations of the Popular Front. . . .

Another way in which Renoir reflected Popular Front attitudes was in his approach to women. His focus here is on working-class women, but with subtle psycho-sociological distinctions. There is the classic tart that has appeared before in Renoir's films. . . . But there is also the working-class woman Valentine, resourceful, independent, mature, an active seductress, clearly a woman with a 'past' yet refusing to be exploited, who has no illusions about everlasting love with Lange. (p. 38)

[The] real power of *Lange* is an expression of Popular Front consciousness derives not so much from what is said as from how it is said, in other words from Renoir's special use of the cinematic language. And in this film we are dealing with two completely different models of structural organisation, in terms both of the *mise en scène* and of montage. (pp. 38-9)

[In] the final analysis, the most striking aspect of the film is the concordance between its manifest (thematic) content and latent (cinematographic) content, which makes its message particularly powerful. Indeed, it is the dramatic contrast of the two structural models that gives the thematic conflict its poignancy. (p. 40)

> *Elizabeth Grottle Strebel, ''Renoir and the Popular Front,'' in* Sight and Sound *(copyright © 1980 by The British Film Institute), Vol. 49, No. 1, Winter, 1979-80, pp. 36-41.*

## ALEXANDER SESONSKE

*La Petite Marchande d'allumettes* represents the first full flowering of a tendency that runs through Renoir's films from 1924 to 1970, a tendency to create an atmosphere of strangeness and unreality, to evoke the quality the French call *féerique.* Only this one among Renoir's films has that quality throughout; more often, it emerges within a prevailing naturalism to lend a sense of enchantment to a scene. (p. 43)

*La Petite Marchande d'allumettes* remains at least a lovely fantasy, constructed with delicacy and visual imagination, very nearly maintaining its fairy-tale atmosphere unbroken throughout. (p. 49)

*On purge bébé* is Renoir's film that comes closest to being a photographed play. . . . Lines are often spoken with great relish and dramatic flair; we notice the cleverness of a line or the way it is delivered more than its role in the dramatic situation or the interactions it furthers. This dialogue does, of course, characterize; almost all that we know about the characters we learn from what they say and the way they say it. But these characters have no depth. They have life but no lives. (p. 87)

No mere description of the plot of *La Nuit du carrefour* could capture the character of the film. Its hero is a detective; its genre, ostensibly that of the *film policier,* usually relies heavily on plot for its effect and treats each incident so as to maximize suspense. Yet in *La Nuit du carrefour* the working-out of the plot, the solution of the crime, seems almost incidental; rather than foster suspense, Renoir allows Maigret to discover the secrets of the garage before we are even sure there is need to be suspicious. An enumeration of the violent deeds committed makes *La Nuit du carrefour* sound like an action-packed adventure story; but the film feels languorous rather than violent. (p. 104)

We begin with a murder; at film's end we know, more or less, who committed what crimes. But we hardly feel that all of the confusion has been dispelled, all of the questions answered. Jean Renoir did not see his task as one of undoing and clarifying the mystery, but, rather, one of expressing it, of giving the mystery palpable form. (pp. 106-07)

[The] verbal content of the dialogue turns out not to be very significant; it reveals itself as a conventional element of the ordinary *film policier* and loses much of its point in a film whose aim is to express the mystery. (p. 111)

*La Chienne, La Nuit du carrefour,* and *Boudu sauvé des eaux* form a sort of exploratory trilogy within Renoir's work, an introduction to the possibilities of cinema with sound. Together they constitute a remarkably original group within the realm of French cinema in the early thirties. They are original not only in their independence of the trends and fashions of the day and their development of a style very different from those that were dominant in films of that time, but also in their freedom in almost every domain of cinematic form, their rejection of cliché and easy manipulation of audience emotion, the cool unsentimental objectivity with which they observe their very human characters, whose lives are firmly located within a precisely perceived milieu. (p. 137)

*Madame Bovary* is the most somber of all Renoir's films of the thirties. It is not visually gray, as *The Elusive Corporal* will be, but its emotional tone is overwhelmingly dark. . . . (p. 149)

In *Madame Bovary* the classical tendencies are stressed, the romantic ones suppressed, creating the most formal of all Renoir films, the most controlled, the least overflowing with movement and life. (p. 162)

What distinguishes *Toni* from earlier Renoir works is not so much the solidity and vividness of the background, but its persistence as the center of the film; the shift from seeing the group of immigrants arrive to observing the life of one individual among them seems not to take us away from this supporting context but deeper into it. The principal characters do not emerge from the setting but remain wholly within it. But above all, Renoir maintains the social milieu as the real object of his lens through much of *Toni* by allowing the dialogue to carry the development of the narrative while the images reveal the daily life of the community. (p. 169)

In *Madame Bovary* Renoir's classical style had placed the action at a distance. In *Toni,* by embedding the narrative so deeply in the social and physical setting, he draws us into the world of the film. Yet the emphasis on milieu rather than dramatic action lends a sort of impersonality to the narrative, reinforced by enclosing the action within shots of the arrival of a trainload of immigrants—as if it were not the individuality but the universality of these few humans that was being shown. (p. 171)

*Toni* does bear the stamp of neorealism and, ten years before the liberation of Rome, pointed toward a new cinema. The essence of neorealism is a convincing air of truthfulness at two quite different levels: the truth of the look of a certain environment at a particular time and the truth of a condition of life. (p. 172)

From *Toni* to *The Rules of the Game,* every film allows male companionship a significant role, both in the social setting and the narrative, with this camaraderie becoming the central relationship in several films, relegating male-female associations to a secondary place. From this expansion of the social context, these films gain a greater fullness of life; they delve more deeply into a larger range of characters than do the bourgeois films. (p. 176)

In contrast to the bourgeois films, neither duplicity, contempt, nor malice, nor great romantic dreams abound in *Toni*. They are not wholly absent, but seem incidental rather than the very stuff of life. Instead, sympathy, a sort of gentleness, an intuitive understanding of each other and a great tolerance and willingness to accept what befalls them characterize Toni and Fernand, the major figures among the men at Marie's. (p. 177)

Renoir's deep attachments have always been to people rather than ideologies; significant changes in his work have been influenced by particular persons or specific events rather than by adherence to a political party or program. . . .

Renoir stubbornly refused to be wholly political. Even when most engaged, the focus of his films remains on character rather than polemic or political action. His sympathies are usually apparent; yet even those characters who represent the political views he most opposed are viewed with warmth, as well as a detachment that renders political orientation as one aspect of a human life; Renoir does not cast his human figures in the reductive mold of politics. This helps his films of this time survive their period with almost undiminished impact; one need never have heard of the Popular Front to find *Le Crime de M. Lange* an absorbing and wholly comprehensible film. (p. 187)

The visual focus of *Le Crime de M. Lange* is not a person but a place, the courtyard with its surrounding complex of laundry, print-shop, and conciergerie. The life of the film flows through the court; the lives of the characters meet and mingle there. Rather than the isolation of each character within his own illusion, a sense of community and camaraderie pervades this film, with Lange's illusion becoming a reality for the court. (p. 191)

[In Guy de Maupassant's story *Une Partie de campagne*] the natural setting exists only as background, and a narrator's often condescending voice places every event at a distance. The events are the same in [Renoir's film based on the story], but Renoir has replaced cold observation with a celebration of nature, and the distant impersonal voice with an affectionate eye. As always, literary material has been a source for ideas, not a model to be scrupulously followed. But here the mere passage of time may have been instrumental to the change. Maupassant, writing a contemporary tale, could view with a cynical gaze the follies of his world; we, from our lives set in the murderous twentieth century, see 1860 as a more tranquil era when time moved at a gentler pace and the sweetness of life could be tasted in simple days marked by simple joys.

How much of the charm of Renoir's film lies in the way it evokes this feeling! And how much of the feeling depends upon nature having been brought into the foreground of the tale! (pp. 237-38)

With all their captivating shimmer of indefinite forms, almost every impressionistic image of *Une Partie de campagne* affirms that Jean Renoir's deepest pictorial debt to his father is compositional; repeatedly, the crossed diagonals of composition create a dynamic tension and movement within soft-textured images of verdure and gently undulant water reflecting bright sky. Thus Jean Renoir carries to the level of sheer form the theme of vibrant and powerful forces underlying nature's summer skin.

And thus the impressionistic moments may mislead us—if we are to be more than impressionistic in our account. For, important as they are in establishing the tone, the atmosphere, the appearance of the world of the film, they convey only a part of its reality. (p. 239)

If "impressionism" implies a concern only with ephemeral appearance, the mere capture of a transient moment in all its transience, then Renoir as film-maker and *Une Partie de campagne* as film are more than impressionistic. The transient moments occur, right enough, more feelingly perceived than by any other director of the thirties, but Renoir seldom reveals mere transience. Rather, almost every such fleeting impression in a Renoir film either appears as a contrast illuminating some intransient, intransigent reality of character or soon acquires depth through our growing awareness of its role in shaping these very human lives. . . .

Yet in this film the surfaces so catch our eye, surfaces of both nature and character, that we may easily fail to see anything else at all. (p. 240)

[The] image of calm liquid beauty with which *Une Partie de campagne* ends does not merely mock the self-pitying sentimentality of Henri and Henriette. Though ironic and unhappy, the ending is not hopeless, as it is not hopeful—life and the river persist; one may stagnate or move with the flow and be renewed. (p. 256)

[Once] we cease looking for Gorky, *Les Bas Fonds* reveals itself as a Renoir film. The unevenness remains, but now may be felt as Gorky impeding the development of a Renoir theme, rather than as Renoir betraying Gorky. For almost all of Renoir's departures from [Gorky's play *The Lower Depths*] bring *Les Bas Fonds* closer to the preceding Renoir films. The central theme of two lives coming together, then parting, echoes *Boudu*, where, too, circumstances bring one character to give up his form of life and come to share a very different life with another. . . . (p. 260)

[The] success of *La Grande Illusion*, like the failure of a *La Règle du jeu*, two years later, seems detached from at least some of its intentions, and due perhaps more to its hopeful tone, the depth of human sympathy expressed, and the quality of its performances than to any general acceptance or even recognition of a pacifist theme. For, like every other Renoir film, it fits only awkwardly the categories it tempts us to assign. A war film, as the *New York Times* reviewer called it? An escape story? A pacifist film? Yes—and no.

The war lurks there somewhere, of course; almost every frame acknowledges its existence. And yet . . . no trenches, no mud, no exploding shells. Idle heroes and no villains—especially no villains. . . . The protagonists, who begin as combatants, are reduced—or elevated—to being mere men. Still, on another, deeper plane the film reverses this movement; the war grows ever closer until the final scene thrusts it to the foreground again, calling the whole hopeful development of the film into question.

This physical distance from battle deprives Renoir's pacifism of its clichés. Many antiwar films make their plea by providing a surfeit of the horrors of war; Renoir's does not. Nor does he win our allegiance to peace with thrilling combat scenes. As James Kerans has said [see excerpt above], he does not fight the war for peace. Rather, he provides some glimpses of brave and honorable men—citizens, soldiers—interacting within the vague ambiance of the conflict, leaving us to find and feel in this display of life the futility and wastefulness of war. (pp. 287-88)

In its use of language *La Grande Illusion* may still remain unique, being not merely a multilingual film, but one in which language becomes a major dimension of subject matter. Beyond being a mere element in Renoir's search for truth, his insistence that each character speak his own tongue proves essential to a central theme: the role of language in human affairs. (pp. 319-20)

Among the facts that most interest Renoir is that love can transcend the barriers of language. And repeatedly, late in the film, he employs the most divisive aspects of language—the fact that different languages *are* different and mutually unintelligible, and the fact that a common language may be used to create barriers rather than destroy them—to express the closest ties developed in the film. (pp. 320-21)

The first image of *La Grande Illusion* is of a phonograph record, the last, of a field buried in snow. Tone changes from black to white; perspective, from close-up to extreme long shot; movement, from a spinning in place to the slow forward progress of two men moving together. These changes might be seen as symbolic of the distance covered in the film, in the life of its hero, in the world portrayed. And the greatest illusion may be that it cannot be, that we must forever spin in place, that this is merely a hopeful dream from a world long dead. (p. 322)

*La Marseillaise* is a film of ideas, with a continuity of ideas more than of actions, and each early scene both shows developing events and reveals the currents of thought which swept France toward the First Republic. (p. 326)

The opening scene of *La Marseillaise* reflects Renoir's approach to history—authentic and revealing in its details, reticent in its statement, refusing to reproduce that which we most expect. (p. 327)

*La Marseillaise* is the noisiest of Renoir films, full of crowd and battle noises, with a greater density and volume of sound and much more external music than any other Renoir film of the period. . . . [The] rich pattern of sound in *La Marseillaise* contains a collage of French accents, including even the German of Alsace, with this variety of voices then forming a kind of commentary on the diversity of peoples who joined to make the Revolution. The identification of the transitional drumbeat as the sound of the revolutionary army approaching Valmy then completes this pattern of sounds which are both internal and external, both elements within the overlapping worlds of French history and *La Marseillaise* and a commentary on their events. (pp. 349-50)

In its dark tone, its pessimistic mood, its air of fatality, *La Bête humaine* differs from every other Renoir film of the thirties. . . . [The] darkness of *La Bête humaine* may reflect Renoir's reaction to the debacle of European politics. (pp. 354-55)

In the environment and activities of the railroad, Renoir found a world of work and achievement that transcended the narrow circle of the doomed, a sort of second foreground for the film in which a sane and hopeful worker's milieu provides a contrast to the madness that overwhelms the central characters. (p. 356)

*La Bête humaine* became the occasion for another polar swing in Renoir's work—not only from light to dark, complex to simple, but more importantly from a film of ideas to a film of action. In both *La Grande Illusion* and *La Marseillaise* articulate characters discuss their situation rationally, see themselves with some objectivity, and act in ways that reflect the ideas they hold. In contrast, *La Bête humaine* becomes in Renoir's hands a film without ideas, where the actions have no rational basis but simply surge forth from some dark interior well. . . . Renoir's *La Bête humaine* is a tragedy, not an exposé. (p. 357)

Some critics see *La Règle du jeu* as part of a trilogy with *La Marseillaise* and *La Grande Illusion*. If so, then *La Règle du jeu* too is an historical film, though set in the present, being the final strand of a thread perceived in French history from 1789 to 1939. The thread is the relation of classes, and the substance of the trilogy is the transformation of the French middle class from revolutionaries to parasites. (p. 388)

[The] uniqueness of his films had always lain in their interplay of form and character, in the vitality of the characters these forms revealed, and in the critical light these creations cast upon our troubled world. In these works he had repeatedly used accidental conjunctions as occasions for the exercise of choice, converting dramatic contrivance into the most convincing characterization. Now, in the most complex work he had yet devised, he sought to express the state of mind of 1939 in a clockwork comic structure with cogs of character and chance. (p. 408)

Of the eight major characters in *La Règle du jeu,* six are absent from the final ceremony. Those present, Robert and Schumacher, are performers, not observers, of the rite whose function does not serve their double set of dancers but the class that assimilates them all, the masters by membership, the servants by adherence. The deed is done, the marauders repelled, Christine returned to the fold; the rite confirms the rule that rules them all, the sacrifice of reality to appearance, and thus reaffirms the rightness of their lives.

If "reality" is real, then appearance must accommodate it, else it will not present itself as appearance but as fantasy. The tales we tell, the games we play, if they will convince us, must take up those shreds of reality we can't avoid. The game of love and death disguises them to conform to the image that the world, and we, mistake for self. (pp. 410-12)

An inability to perceive the dissonance of one's own actions is pervasive in *La Règle du jeu* and in the world it portrays—if we acknowledge the volcano, we might stop dancing. (p. 425)

In almost every respect, the style of *La Règle du jeu* is simply a perfection and extension of that which Renoir had been developing since *Tire au flanc*. (p. 438)

*Alexander Sesonske, in his* Jean Renoir: The French Films, 1924-1939 *(copyright © 1980 by the President and Fellows of Harvard College; excerpted by permission), Cambridge, Mass.: Harvard University Press, 1980, 463 p.*

# Carlos Saura

## 1932-

**Spanish director and screenwriter.**

**Saura belongs to the generation that grew up under Franco, and the theme of the Spanish Civil War plays a major part in his work. While his early films use allegory as a means of masking political criticism, Saura's more recent work analyzes the psychological effects of a repressive society.**

**As a film student in Madrid, Saura resented pressure to create heavy-handed religious dramas. Instead, he opted to make a neorealistic film. *Los Golfos* features a young amateur cast, and its youthful focus helped Saura escape the political commentary of the censors. While Saura was eager to depict the evils of Franco's regime as accurately as possible, he could not be explicit. The necessity to alter the truth creatively stimulated moral commitment as well as artistic inventiveness. In *La Caza,* a hunting party serves as an analogy for war. However, because of heavy symbolism, Saura's early films are considered too allegorical and ponderous to enjoy.**

**In his next films, Saura often reverted from past to future to show various stages of character development. *The Garden of Delights* relies heavily on fantasy as well. Its use of grotesque imagery and surrealistic symbolism have led to comparisons with Buñuel. *La Prima Angélica* (*Cousin Angélica*), the first Spanish film to view the war from a loser's vantage point, indicates Saura's interest in the emotional intensity of children. To Saura, childhood is not a time of happiness, but an intensely frightening period. This same emphasis is found in *Cría Cuervos,* which underplays social forces and concentrates more on children's emotional perceptions.**

**Some critics feel the political urgency pulsating through Saura's earlier works has disappeared since Franco's death. Saura says he made political films as a moral obligation, but prefers now to concentrate on psychological studies.**

### FILM JOURNAL

The style of *Los Golfos* is one of a deceptively simple realism. The background is authentic. The industrial and slum areas of Madrid, market places, dance halls, and river banks are areas frequented by the group of boys who form the subject of this film. The camera acts as an observer, conversations are clipped as if overheard, incident follows incident in the apparently formless fashion of real life. Here the intention is to present a certain point of view which will assume the validity of the subject matter itself. It is an artistic method which succeeds because the director creates characters rather than sociological concepts. . . .

[The theme of *Los Golfos*] is the ultimate innocence of the delinquents. Their determination to raise enough money to launch Juan as a bullfighter has the selfish single-mindedness of the child. Their innocence springs from their lack of a realistic contact with society. No private existence can last for long if cut off from society as a whole. Outside realities intrude, usually accompanied by disaster. In *Los Golfos,* reality takes the form of failure and ignominy. The film's ending, which is totally crushing, is delineated with the realism already noted, a realism which now emerges in its true form as drama. The grubby bull-ring, the jeering spectators, Juan's humiliating attempts to kill the bull, are the tragic details of an uncompromising reality.

Luis Buñuel may be a more famous director and *Los Olvidados* a more notable film. But in *Los Golfos* the young Spanish director Carlos Saura avoids the more experienced artist's clinical coldness and covert sensationalism. He has succeeded in making that rare thing, a good film about juvenile delinquency, the result of an unsentimental realism and an honest humanitarianism.

> J. S., "Melbourne Film Festival, 1961: 'Los Golfos'," in Film Journal (copyright by Melbourne University Film Society), No. 18, October, 1961, p. 19.

### ROBIN BEAN

*Los Golfos* [which criticizes Spain's social structure] was obviously subjected to several cuts before being allowed out of Spain, and for this reason is difficult to judge as a complete work. . . .

Saura handles his subject in a harsh but not unsympathetic way. He avoids most of the pitfalls into which most Western directors fall when dealing with delinquents who find robbery an attractive substitute for work. But his film does have two major failings: he gives little insight into the characters of the boys and the motivating circumstances which have led to their present existence (here again this may be due to censorship ties); and he lets his camera roam excessively in street and market sequences. But for all its shortcomings *Los Golfos* has the imprint of a director who has a natural flair for cinematic invention. Saura's use of background noise for dramatic effect is at times ingenious, and his pictorial images have a compelling effect. His comments, if at times cynical (it is the most likeable of the five who becomes the victim of mob vengeance), make their point.

It demands attention and a good deal of thought, in spite of the mutilation to which it has been subjected.

*Robin Bean, "'The Hooligans'" (© copyright Robin Bean 1961; reprinted with permission), in* Films and Filming, *Vol. 8, No. 3, December, 1961, p. 31.*

### BOSLEY CROWTHER

Carlos Saura's penetrating and increasingly violent **"The Hunt"** . . . should give the New York cinema intelligentsia a new regard for filmmaking in Spain.

What is surprising about it is that it cloaks in its lean and cruel account of quarreling and ultimate murdering among four men on a routine rabbit hunt a cynical innuendo of what has happened to some middle-aged men of the generation that fought for Franco in the Spanish Civil War. . . .

To be sure, the average outsider might not immediately perceive in the seemingly nondescript environment and the accumulating details of the hunt all the subtle hints and signals that colloquially identify these men as veteran Falangists and their background as the civil war.

But any Spaniard familiar with his nation's history and geography should recognize the dry and barren region in which these sportsmen arrive in a jeep for a few days of rabbit-shooting as an area southwest of Madrid where some of the bitterest battles of the civil war were fought.

Any Spaniard should catch in a twinkling the significance in the fact that one of the men is nursing (or favoring) an old wound, that another is carrying a pistol of the type that the Germans used in the civil war and yet another is revealed as having good connections with the Government. These men are Franco veterans—all except the youngest in the group, who is evidently the son of a veteran—and they are stricken with morbidity.

This is the daring implication that Mr. Saura has to make: That men who have enjoyed some successes, have evidently lived comfortably (able to indulge themselves in hunting) are now bitter, degenerate and cruel, suspicious and distrustful of one another, avid to shoot and kill—or, as in the case of one of them, to withdraw in a mood of jealousy and hate.

Mr. Saura imparts his drama—his allegory, as it were, of war and of men fighting against their brothers—in some horrifyingly realistic scenes of men handling guns, shooting rabbits as the terrified creatures scurry up the hills, baking in the sun, grimly quarreling and finally blasting away at one another in frenzied duels. Tension grows, violence trembles and finally disaster bursts.

**"The Hunt"** is a powerful picture. . . .

*Bosley Crowther, "Film Festival: 'The Hunt'," in* The New York Times *(© 1966 by The New York Times Company; reprinted by permission), September 20, 1966, p. 39.*

### HENRY HART

[*The Hunt*] is an immature, and unbelievable, film. . . .

[It] is a jumble of veiled political allegories inappropriately spiced with the sort of perverted symbols Bunuel exploits. . . .

The three men are characterized too synthetically for such triangular carnage to be credible. No, it won't make you believe what happens in Mr. Saura's film to say, "But fascism *is* self-destructive". If so it cannot be demonstrated in the amateurish way childish symbols are here bumbled about.

Saura's imitations of Bunuel in *The Hunt* would be laughable were their visual content not so psychopathic—a skinned animal carcass is hacked apart; a sand crab is squashed; a ferret bites a rabbit's eye, and later, when it is shot, as is the rabbit, the camera dawdles over the quivers of their death throes. Also, a man is shot in the face, and, as blood covers everything but one eye, he guns down the "friend" who shot him. There are other pathic odds-&-ends, including a skeleton in a cave, the significance of which is unclear.

So is *The Hunt*.

*Henry Hart, "Film Reviews: 'The Hunt'," in* Films in Review *(copyright © 1967 by the National Board of Review of Motion Pictures, Inc.), Vol. XVIII, No. 6, June-July, 1967, p. 369.*

### ROGER GREENSPUN

The pleasantest surprise of the current New York Film Festival may well be Carlos Saura's **"The Garden of Delights."** . . .

Recent (i.e. 1930's) Spanish politics are by no means absent from **"The Garden of Delights,"** but now they are made explicit and they become dramatically useful to the Pirandellian permutations of a brilliantly playful and wonderfully funny comic invention. . . .

The crucial moments [involving the paralyzed Antonio's attempts to remember the number of his Swiss bank account] are so ludicrously, so elaborately miscalculated . . . that they would drive the soundest mind to amnesia. But Antonio makes some progress. . . .

I have my doubts about the machine shop and about much of the movie-mechanical whimsey in **"The Garden of Delights,"** but not about its fantastic sense of character situation. For the best dramatic moments are those that Antonio begins spinning out of his own head—wickedly erotic, or simply wicked—that constitute a totally private, perfectly obsessive world.

*Roger Greenspun, "'The Garden of Delights'," in* The New York Times *(© 1970 by The New York Times Company; reprinted by permission), September 19, 1970 (and reprinted in* The New York Times Film Reviews: 1969-1970, *The New York Times Company & Arno Press, 1971, p. 218).*

### JOAN MELLEN

Saura deals with the configuration of the fascist personality only in the abstract, and this is the central weakness of his imaginative use of the surreal in depicting how living in fascist Spain immobilizes and laments the sensibility [in *The Garden of Delights*]. . . .

In the last scene of *Garden of Delights* Saura, abandoning even the very thin veneer of realism with which he has cloaked his allegory, has all of his characters moving in wheelchairs, not only the still paralyzed Antonio. Staring immobile into space, they cannot look at or see each other: each selfishly pursues his own ends. With Antonio at the center, an image of the failed hope for Spain's future, they pass like marionettes before the camera. Fascism has dehumanized and devitalized them, left them shells of human beings, deadened all capacity of each to feel for the other, just as none of his family felt sympathetically toward Antonio's accident.

Saura's central metaphor is that of the absence of self-knowledge, the paralysis of individuals who have been destroyed by fascism. (p. 11)

> *Joan Mellen, "Fascism in the Contemporary Film," in* Film Quarterly *(copyright 1971 by The Regents of the University of California; reprinted by permission of the University of California Press), Vol. XXIV, No. 4, Summer, 1971, pp. 2-19.\**

### ROGER GREENSPUN

[Carlos Saura's **"Honeycomb"** is] the latest and the least of those movies that mean to unlock the secrets of middle-class matrimony by means of a willful indulgence in everyday unreality. Such films . . . seem invariably to follow a process of elegant dissolution—never inelegant dissolution—until all is laid bare in the destructive psychodrama of life. But in **"Honeycomb"** nothing is laid bare except the dullest of make-believe constructions covering for the lack of insight that would be necessary to sustain the most ordinary unhappy domestic drama.

Mr. Saura, normally a director of forceful personality, whether you like him or not . . . , hardly exists except at the very beginning and end of the movie. And if there is any reason for **"Honeycomb,"** it is to display the talents of what is virtually two-person cast. . . .

> *Roger Greenspun, "'Honeycomb'," in* The New York Times *(© 1972 by The New York Times Company; reprinted by permission), November 23, 1972 (and reprinted in* The New York Times Film Reviews: 1971-1972, *The New York Times Company & Arno Press, 1973, p. 337).*

### ROGER MORTIMORE

[*La Prima Angélica*] is an attempt to explain the significance of the Civil War to a generation, specifically the generation too young to have fought in it. Saura has claimed that his film is the first to be made about the Civil War from the point of view of the side which lost. Luis, the central character, lost the war as a child because it traumatized him, and the film demonstrates that thirty years later the wounds remain. The crippling effects of the traditional combination of church and family are seen here against the background of the national trauma of civil war. The film is notably critical of the church: its characters include a thuggish priest, a vindictive nun with stigmata and a priest expatiating on the dimensions of Eternity to a group of cowering boys, a scene which recalls a well-known passage in *A Portrait of the Artist as a Young Man.* For Stephen Dedalus, Ireland was 'the old sow that eats her farrow'; and so, for Saura, is Spain. Stephen Dedalus escapes but Luis does not, cannot. . . .

Saura's use of the same actors either as themselves when young or taking different roles thirty years earlier emphasises—like

the furniture shrouded in plastic sheets in the room where Luis stayed as a boy and where he stays again at his now elderly aunt's insistence—that despite the prosperity nothing has changed. Franco's victory merely destroyed the hopes aroused by the Second Republic.

In opposition to the conformity and sterility and bullying implicit in an acceptance of Franco's regime, implicit in the character of Anselmo, Saura places haunting moments. . . .

What is curious about *La Prima Angélica* is the complete absence of dramatic tension. The film is an assembly of montages . . . which cohere in the mind later, rather than in the moment of seeing the film. . . .

Saura always risks being praised for what he says rather than for how he says it. He admits that all his films are polemical, which means that criticism of them can always be dismissed as being right wing, as of course it usually is; but this situation tends to immunise him from self-criticism as well. Fortunately, *La Prima Angélica* is heartening in that its realism suggests that Saura has moved away from the aridity of *La Madriguera* [*Honeycomb*] (1969) and the artificiality of *Ana y los Lobos* [*Ana and the Wolves*] (1972). (p. 201)

> *Roger Mortimore, "Spain: Out of the Past," in* Sight and Sound *(copyright © 1974 by The British Film Institute), Vol. 43, No. 4, Autumn, 1974, pp. 199-202.\**

### SYLVIA MILLAR

Although Carlos Saura has frequently been accused of 'borrowing' from Luis Buñuel, and although he clearly pays homage to his friend and mentor in *La Caza* [*The Hunt*], the film does not set out to be a serious imitation. Saura's images on the whole are not surreal but grow organically out of the characters and landscape; this is no journey into the dreamworld of the subconscious but a finely worked psychological thriller which, without strain, can be taken as a pessimistic parable about Spanish society. . . . The paucity of action generates an atmosphere of listlessness and ennui: seemingly trapped by the heat and idleness of this endless day, the men are provoked into unaccustomed introspection. The telescopic sight on Luis' rifle is a sign of his ability to see further into moral realities although, too weak to face up to them, he finds oblivion in his brandy flask. . . . José's guilty obsession with death, indicated by the skeleton of a colleague who committed suicide, is a spectral reminder of the war and a self-inflicted reproach. His maudlin confidences are repellent to Paco, as is Juan's servility and dependence, against which Paco's killing of the ferret is a futile protest. . . . In this kind of merciless detail, Saura browses over the morbid weaknesses of his characters, immobilised by the self-indulgence and brutality of their class. Their only escape is through mutual destruction. The youth Enrique escapes Nemesis; and his fleeting relationship with the adolescent peasant girl Carmen might be taken as a forlorn hope for the future of democracy in Spain. (pp. 235-36)

> *Sylvia Millar, "Feature Films: 'La caza' ('The Hunt')," in* Monthly Film Bulletin *(copyright © The British Film Institute, 1975), Vol. 42, No. 502, November, 1975, pp. 235-36.*

### DEREK ELLEY

Saura's films are explicitly concerned with the problems of Spanish society, a society (as he sees it) which is not yet free of the guilt of the Civil War. This *eminence grise* colours all his works, in varying degrees; even in such an allegorical piece as *La caza* its influence can be felt. Much of Saura's output I find mannered and unapproachable . . . ; there is no doubting, however, his technical ability or deep-seated conviction. . . .

Superficial resemblances to [John] Boorman's *Deliverance* (1972) should not be allowed to diminish the stature of Saura's achievement. His mixed quartet undergoes little physical hardship, and there are no visual thrills to rivet the audience to its seats. Saura's film is considerably more claustrophobic: the nerve-ends are stifled rather than rubbed raw. From the opening credits, unwound over footage of caged ferrets, it is clear that we are in allegorical territory. (p. 33)

The early scenes of re-acquaintance and preparation are handled with a fine sense of atmosphere, and only the dialogue is over-obvious. . . . At all times one is aware that Enrique is a voice apart from the rest of the group, unhampered by past prejudices or memories. His rejection of much that the other three hold dear is a straightforward metaphor for the generation gap, yet his presence is dramatically required to act as a soundingboard for the older men's prejudices. Saura builds the suspense with great assurance. . . . The dialogue is direct and pithy, with extremes of friendliness and anger encompassed in the space of a few sentences. . . . And though one must utterly condemn the explicitness of [the hunting] scenes (rabbits mercilessly shot for real), the tension of the lead-up, with the men spread over the plain to the accompaniment of timpani and snare-drum, is undeniably powerful. . . . [Saura's] talent for the right image at the right time is always in evidence, and in view of the fact that his metaphors for the men's bottled violence is elsewhere so discreet, it is all the more disgraceful that he saw fit to murder wildlife just for the sake of greater reality.

The climax, when it does come, is sudden and unexpected—dog finally eating dog in out-and-out bloody hate. The theatricalism of the outburst is hardly noticed, so brief are the images, and a shot of one of the victims twitching foetus-like in the dust is a grim comment on the main characters. Saura's targets are often rather facile, and his use of the War as a unifying symbol for the men rather vague, but as pure cinema *La caza* grips from the first to the very last frame. (p. 34)

*Derek Elley, "Reviews: 'La caza'" (© copyright Derek Elley 1976; reprinted with permission), in* Films and Filming, *Vol. 22, No. 4, January, 1976, pp. 33-4.*

### VINCENT CANBY

["**Cousin Angélica**"] is a voyage into the past quite unlike any other I've ever seen in a movie, both because Spain's recent history is so particular and because of Mr. Saura's way of always dealing with memory so that it becomes an extension of the immediate present.

"**Cousin Angélica**" is not simply about Luis's childhood before and during the civil war. It's about Luis's recollections of his childhood as he renews contacts with his family. . . .

Mr. Saura doesn't use conventional flashbacks, which are as isolated from time and feeling as postcard pictures are removed from a tourist's actual experiences. . . .

En route once again to his relatives, the tearful Luis is comforted by his mother and father. There is nothing exceptional about this scene except that when we see the middle-age, car-

digan-wearing Luis being soothed by parents younger than he is we are suddenly presented not only with a memory of the past but with everything that's accrued in the intervening years—with fear, anger and humiliation, but, also with the sense of loss that has haunted his maturity. . . .

[Spain] is the real subject of the film, and at the time it was released there—1974—"Cousin Angélica" caused quite a stir with its references to the war, Spanish Catholicism and the possible nobility of at least some members of the Republican cause. Even if it's difficult for someone not familiar with the subtleties of Spanish life to get all of these references, the movie is extraordinarily compelling, an invitation into a world until recently closed, but whose vitality has remained undiminished. (p. 52)

*Vincent Canby, "Poignant Middle Age," in* The New York Times (© *1977 by The New York Times Company; reprinted by permission), May 13, 1977 (and reprinted in* The New York Times Film Reviews: 1977-1978, *The New York Times Company & Arno Press, 1979, pp. 51-2).*

### VINCENT CANBY

Childhood can be a most terrifying time. One must constantly observe the proscriptions of a primitive system of cause and effect that can be questioned only by the reckless or the ignorant. Squash a spider and it will rain. Step on a crack, break your mother's back. Sleep in the light of a new moon and you may never wake up. There is power in the knowledge of these things, as well as awful responsibility. One must be vigilant. One has to be alert for signs.

Such a child is Ana . . . , the 9-year-old heroine of Carlos Saura's beautifully acted, haunting Spanish movie, "**Cria!**" about a childhood so packed with trauma that one can scarcely believe that this acutely sensitive child will ever grow up to be [a] apparently composed, articulate woman. . . . (pp. 53-4)

"**Cria!**" is more ambitious [than "**Cousin Angelica**"] but, without the focal point of a strongly defined present, it lacks the cumulative impact of the earlier movie.

Its dreamlike reality is fragile. As it cuts among three time periods—Ana at 9, Ana a few years earlier at the time of the death of her mother . . . , and snippets of the grown-up Ana—one begins to wonder whether the movie is much more than an outline for another movie. One wants more than mood and memory, though that may be asking for more than Mr. Saura ever intended. . . .

The childhood that Mr. Saura imposes on Ana is enough to have crushed even someone who's gone through a successful Freudian analysis, much less someone of Ana's age and temperament. She watches her mother die—painfully—of cancer and blames her philandering father. . . .

It's one thing, I suspect, for a child like Ana to fantasize about murder and even to accept responsibility for a murder obtained through charms or prayers, but it's quite another kind of drama when you have a little girl running around and believing that she's knocking off people with poison. Mr. Saura stacks the cards against Ana. Unlike her two sisters, she has an uncanny knack for walking into rooms at the wrong time. She's more than vigilant. She's emotionally accident-prone.

Though "**Cria!**" seems arbitrarily and artificially structured, individual sequences are remarkably fine—Ana's attempts to make contact with her mute, paralyzed grandmother, her longing memories of her mother's combing her hair, her matter-of-fact questioning of the maid about what a woman's breasts look like, and a scene in which Ana and her two sisters become giddy and dance rock to a rock recording.

"**Cria!**" is a movie of marvelous moments. . . . (p. 54)

> *Vincent Canby, "'Growing Pains'," in* The New York Times *(© 1977 by The New York Times Company; reprinted by permission), May 19, 1977 (and reprinted in* The New York Times Film Reviews: 1977-1978, *The New York Times Company & Arno Press, 1979, pp. 53-4).*

## PENELOPE GILLIATT

A man of early middle age touches a bald place on his head for a moment. In another film, it might be that he was thinking of his looks. In Carlos Saura's wonderful Spanish picture "**Cousin Angelica**" . . . , the movement is one of trying to correct the blurring of time and history. . . .

When the hero, called Luis Cano, touches his head, he is trying to retrieve something lost. The idea of having the same actor play both the boy and the man tells us what we all know: that everyone is every age at the same time, eight and forty-eight and eighty, merely embossed in a slowly changing carcass. The film tells us, too, that people have faulty memories. In the present of the film, Luis is trying to put things in order. . . . Time passes after all. A boy grows into a man, a generation grows into aeons of men. Luis, this boy, this man, is concerned to make memory concrete, not diffuse; he has the mind of a mathematician, the doubts of a scholar. . . .

One's own mind goes back with the hero's to school as he remembers "how difficult it was to write a page without making a blot" before the days of ball-points. "It took all the pains in the world."

All the pains in the world are in this film. . . .

The film is a sanctified fancy about memory, a recovery from sourness. (p. 109)

> *Penelope Gilliatt, "In Passage," in* The New Yorker *(© 1977 by The New Yorker Magazine, Inc.), Vol. LIII, No. 14, May 23, 1977, pp. 109-11.**

## STANLEY KAUFFMANN

[What I've seen of Saura's work]—*The Hunt* and *The Garden of Delights*—has been rather onerous: gravy-rich photography and ponderous symbolism, like the worst Czech and Polish and Latin-American films. A Spanish moralist without Buñuel's humor makes for a long evening.

Much brighter news from Saura with . . . *Cousin Angelica*. . . .

[The] casting mixture is slightly confusing at first, but it's quickly sorted out, and its various points—of psychic implication and inheritance—are neatly made. (p. 26)

Saura handles the interplay of time with mostly extraordinary skill. The whole picture is directed with an ease that comes from no compulsion to prove anything, which was not true of

the earlier Saura that I saw. There are now sharp edges of humor. . . .

For a foreigner the picture's chief appeal is two kinds of travelogue: physical and psychological. The former, purely of landscape, should not be underrated. . . . The latter, from Spain, is still a relative novelty in the US. After every war come the questions about what the other side was *really* like. . . . Here, on a small scale, Saura gives us some idea of what a bourgeois Spanish family, very Catholic of course, thought of the war; how they lived; and how by indirection, it affected the way they live now.

But, interesting though it is, that's all the film does. The two time strands are juxtaposed and that's it. As for the protagonist himself, nothing happens. He arrives and he departs. He is just a mechanism. If the film was not to move toward some conclusion in him, then it needed a great deal more intrinsic weight as it went along. Aside from the travelogue rewards (which obviously don't apply in Spain), there are only the familiar tugs of time gone irretrievably by. The picture doesn't finish, it just ends. It's very much worth seeing, but it's not finally satisfying. (p. 27)

> *Stanley Kauffmann, "Old Wars" (reprinted by permission of Brandt & Brandt Literary Agents, Inc.; copyright © 1977 by Stanley Kauffmann), in* The New Republic, *Vol. 176, No. 22, May 28, 1977, pp. 26-7.**

## ROBERT HATCH

[*Cria* and *Cousin Angélica*] complement, in a way strengthen, each other; their methods are comparable, and they suggest what it is about life that seems to haunt Mr. Saura.

I say "seems," because it is presumptuous to generalize about the preoccupations of a man of Saura's sensibility on the basis of two works. But, speaking tentatively, what moves him are the passions and terror, the courage and ignorant audacity of childhood that go unremarked by the presiding adults whose catch-all admonitions are "mind your manners" and "run off now and play." His way of dealing with this material is to employ parallel time tracks, so smoothly interfaced that one must be alert to recognize from moment to moment which segment of experience is dominant. To say that Saura employs flashbacks would not at all convey the effect, which is to persuade the viewer that past and present are a single web. . . .

*Cria* is the story of a small girl who, for a period of several years up to the age of 9, becomes involved in adult affairs she only fractionally understands, but which she feels obligated to manipulate according to her view of what the situations require. . . .

Saura burdens her with a succession of misadventures that may strike some viewers as straining plausibility in the cause of a thesis. Ana cannot walk through a door or run an errand without stumbling on an "unsuitable" scene. . . .

But the film covers several years, perhaps a third of Ana's life up to then. It is a long time for a little girl to play avenging angel—not in fantasy, as any child may in an unhappy hour but, as she thinks, in reality. The implied happy ending did not reassure me; I wanted to know what those peculiarly unlucky years had done to Ana, whether she had mastered them or been scarred. However, Saura is not telling a story in the common sense; he is evoking the trancelike state of a child cruelly misused on the assumption that a barrier protects the young from adult predicaments. *Cria* is a nightmare from which at the end Ana awakens into the at least temporary relief of being really a child. (p. 698)

*Cousin Angélica,* operating from the present and with an adult at the focus, is a more "real," though no less subjective, work and here the old scars are evident enough. (pp. 698, 700)

[These two pictures] are not concerned with politics in any direct way, but neither are they works that would have been let out of Spain while Franco lived. It is not just that Saura allies himself implicitly with the Republicans; it is also that he detests the arrogant power of Spanish Catholicism to hold the bourgeoisie in a bondage of claustrophobic superstition. The atmosphere of both pictures is affluent and airless; the people appear to be strong and variously intelligent and well-intentioned, but too tightly clothed, confined by the authority of convention closely allied to class. Compared to similarly situated French or Italians, these Spaniards seem dominated—and by pressures that Franco certainly imposed but did not himself create. Again, it is rash to generalize from two films, but one does not get from Saura the impression that the collapse of a political tyranny will in itself set his countrymen free. Like the tormented protagonists of his splendid pictures, they will be required to come to terms with an ancient Spanish childhood. (p. 700)

> *Robert Hatch, "Films: 'Cria' and 'Cousin Angélica'," in* The Nation *(copyright 1977 The Nation magazine, The Nation Associates, Inc.), Vol. 224, No. 22, June 4, 1977, pp. 698, 700.*

## RICHARD SCHICKEL

[Both *Cria!* and *Cousin Angélica*] are about childhood and both of them are by the man who is, next to Buñuel, the most distinguished Spanish director. But that is where their similarity ends. *Cria!* is a dark and melodramatic comedy, highly original in plot, about how a child misperceives her actions and their consequences in the adult world. *Cousin Angélica,* though more stylistically unconventional, is a rather ordinary story about an adult attempting to refine and correct the memories of childhood. *Cria!* is an almost entirely successful work, while the other, earlier film must be regarded as an honorable failure. . . .

[*Cria!*] is at its best exploring the confusions that attend the preadolescent years. At that stage, kids have a way of being half-right about how the world works and a sunny, misplaced confidence that they have the whole thing taped. Naturally, they get tripped up a lot, but they get used to it and go bouncing off to school (as Ana does) without moral qualms or regrets. It is this ability to be both right and wrong about even such matters as death that Saura has caught in this deft and strangely touching film.

*Cousin Angélica,* by contrast, offers a routine story. . . . This muted film seems to mean more to its creator than he can communicate to an audience. Clearly the work of a careful and caring artist, *Cousin Angélica* fails to make manifest the emotions that inspired it and so fails to move the strangers before whom Saura has placed this otherwise well-wrought gift.

> *Richard Schickel, "Two Childhoods by Saura," in* Time *(copyright 1977 Time Inc.; all rights reserved; reprinted by permission), Vol. 109, No. 22, June 6, 1977, p. 76.*

## JOHN SIMON

Saura is concerned [in *Cría*] with apprehending the continuity between the past and the present, and, if possible, finding a resolution for Spain's political tragedy, the civil war that must have been terrible even for a five-year-old, and whose consequences manifestly haunt him still. (p. 72)

As a result [of Spanish censorship], one must read a Saura film to some extent as a coded document; the hateful father figure, for example, that figures in several of [his] movies is, surely, a symbol also of the Generalissimo and the conditions he imposed; the sundered and emotionally riven families must also be viewed as symbolizing a country rent apart. *Cría,* like other Saura films, has too much mood in it and too little event, but it is hard to tell whether the cause is a lack of things to say or a lack of freedom in which to say them. . .

Saura leaps freely back and forth between periods and places—or, more precisely, Anas—and the dreamlikeness is intensified by the fact that real events and others merely remembered or imagined are shot in the same way and intertwined. It may all be less of an artistic gain than an aestheticizing game.

Saura does not distinguish clearly between a nicely observed atmosphere with fine textural details and all-important plot elements, of which, in any case, there are too few. . . . So cavalier is the author-director about plot that a whole conversation between the child and the maid Rosa, a fat earth mother, is based on Ana's having been the third girl child born to her disgusted father—when all along it is quite obvious that Ana is in fact the second of three daughters. And though the film tries, with commendable restraint and control, to tell the entire story from the child's point of view, Ana simply does not see enough, and the verbal and visual languages of the film remain undernourished. (p. 73)

> *John Simon, "Star Dust," in* New York Magazine *(copyright © 1977 by News Group Publications, Inc.; reprinted with the permission of* New York Magazine*), Vol. 10, No. 25, June 20, 1977, pp. 72-3.**

## ANDREW SARRIS

[For a decade I have been looking at Saura films] and have found less and less to write about them. Some—*Garden of Delights, The Hunt*—are more ambitious than others, but all seem more intricate, more convoluted, and more fragmented than they have to be. Many of Saura's films . . . I have found particularly problematical because of their incessant juggling of fantasy and reality. From time to time I have been made aware that Saura is exploring the Spanish soul through the Franco years and beyond, but the director's symbolism tends to be guarded, mysterious, cabalistic, as if he dare not be too explicit. Similarly, his probes into repressed, twisted, often downright demented sexuality tend to be expressed with much too much facile trickery. In all these years I have come to respect Saura's intentions without enjoying his effects, or even being especially edified by them. He seems always to make omelets with the eggshells inside. . . .

[However, to watch the] three tots dance to pop records and mimic the grown-ups [in *Cria!*] is to see childhood at long last as a jungle of wild feelings in which death itself is stared at without flinching. Saura deserves full credit for the behavioral beauties of *Cria!,* even amid the conceptual confusion of old. . . . It is one of the most exhilarating entertainments of the year.

Andrew Sarris, "Random Notes on Rossellini and Other Current Concerns" (reprinted by permission of The Village Voice and the author; copyright © The Village Voice, Inc., 1977), in The Village Voice, Vol. XXII, No. 25, June 20, 1977, p. 43.*

## WILL AITKEN

I think I'd be willing to settle for a lot less from Carlos Saura and . . . *Cria Cuervos.* . . .

[The film's] two levels, the first presented head-on from Ana's viewpoint and the second apparent only from the gradual accretion of seemingly inconsequential detail, are enough for any film to handle. Saura specializes in a kind of allegorical realism, judging from some of his earlier work, particularly *The Hunt* (1966) and *The Garden of Delights* (1970). But Saura, trying to live up to critical claims that he is Bunuel's heir, has contrived to load his film down with trimmings it doesn't really need.

Saura is Bunuel's equal in his fluid transitions from reality to fantasy. . . .

Saura has real problems, though, trying to be a surrealist, and his *hommages* to other directors frequently add resonance in the wrong direction. The surrealist touches in *Cria Cuervos*—ominous things in the fridge, a perpetually mute and smiling grandmother in her wheelchair—come through to us as third-hand. Bunuel via Polanski: they lack the disorientingly vivid immediacy of Bunuel; they're studied, too predictable. (p. 13)

Saura gets into trouble when he goes for the macabre-funny touches, for at the same time he can't resist rubbing in the pathos inherent in the very notion of an eight-year-old orphan. In addition to a prosaically wicked guardian and the grinning grandmother, there's also Ana's pet guinea pig that we know at first glance—despite its apparent plump healthiness—is not long for Saura's world.

A similar failing in tone arises from the direction of Ana Torrent herself. We're too much aware of her wistful waif's face and enormous haunted child-actor's eyes. There are too many scenes where we sense Saura's manipulation instead of Ana's emotions. . . .

The best film allegories—and one thinks immediately of Renoir's *La règle du jeu*—are either the ones that don't allow an imbalance between the human and the emblem or those that play such an imbalance for all it's worth, as with Bunuel's *L'Age d'Or.*

Saura doesn't appear confident enough for either approach yet; more academic than instinctive, he seems awed by his title of heir apparent and by the other predecessors he continually alludes to. . . .

*Cria Cuervos* allows its audience no final catharsis. There's no release from Ana's mourning, Saura says, because there is no release from Spain's past. I would be tempted to agree with Saura's verdict (just as I'm tempted to agree to the enduring dismalness of Ana's existence because it reinforces my belief that there's no such thing as a happy childhood) except for the fact that I seem to catch glimpses of him enjoying the bleakness of it all. (p. 14)

Will Aitken, "Carlos Saura's 'Cria cuervos'," in Take One (copyright © 1977 by Unicorn Publishing Corp.), Vol. 5, No. 10, July-August, 1977, pp. 13-14.

## VERNON YOUNG

[A] gratuitously baffling chronology is provided by *Elisa, Vida Mia,* of Carlos Saura. If finally incomprehensible, . . . the whole *is* more agreeable than the sum of its parts. . . . Saura does have a certain respect for his milieu and, as we have seen before, an obsessively trenchant gift for recalling the woes and hungers of childhood and their traumatic reappearance in maturity. I think he has exploited this yield to its limits—in *The Garden of Delights, La Prima Angelica, Cria Cuervos*—and now repeats himself, precariously (like Resnais, Fellini or Bergman), the more so when he resorts to involutions of narrative that alienate one's attention when he might better be securing it. This film *appears* to resume the prolonged visit of young Elisa . . . to her self-exiled but doting father . . . , living in isolation somewhere on the Castilian plains—while writing a book! (is this a trend or merely a coincidence?), during which period she deceives and undeceives herself about her rupturing marriage and her past relationship to her father. *But does she?* For, after the halfway mark, notably, it is quite impossible to know (I challenge anyone!) *who* is experiencing *what* at a given moment—including inserts of ghoulish murder and incestuous embrace—how many roles [Elisa] is assuming (a further amplification of Saura's strategy in *Cria Cuervos*) or if, indeed, at least half the scenario is not a hallucination produced by her father's notes-towards-a-fiction. For my refusal to leave the cinema betimes, outcast by Saura's aggressively devised problems of continuity, [Elisa and her father] were largely responsible. Except for moments when uncharitably molested by their director, they engaged me with their gentility and their genuine air of troubled kinship. To have become as indifferent, as Saura has, to our grasp of what he has to say about characters whom he seems to have created with some affection is grotesque in a decisively negative reading of the term.

I suspect that he is divided between his native cast of temperament and a diehard international fashion: compulsively to interrupt logical sequence, even when the scenario as first conceived carries no such justification. (p. 332)

Vernon Young, "The Grotesque in Some Recent Films," in The Hudson Review (copyright © 1978 by The Hudson Review, Inc.; reprinted by permission), Vol. XXXI, No. 2, Summer, 1978, pp. 329-36.*

## TIM PULLEINE

[*Cria Cuervos*] is nothing if not fragmentary and allusive in venturing on to the fraught terrain of childhood sensibility.

The jumble of family snapshots accompanying the opening titles functions as a correlative for Saura's mosaic approach as well as introducing a key visual theme. . . .

The linking of imagination and memory is the movie's stock-in-trade to the extent of permeating its structure. For while the action has a contemporary setting, it is in effect taking place in the past tense, since the narrative is punctuated by episodes in which a grown-up Ana comments directly to camera about her childhood (not, she says emphatically, a paradise of innocence) from a vantage point some twenty years in the future—a time which for the audience can exist only in the imagination. . . . [The device of using the same actress to play Ana's mother and Ana as an adult] admits alternative interpretations: on the one hand, Ana has ultimately 'become' the figure around whom her childhood fantasy of reassurance has been woven; on the other, Ana's childhood comforter is a materialisation of her own older self. But the alternatives are not mutually exclusive, and it is at their intersection that the movie can be said to be taking place.

Such a notion achieves witty expression in the sequence in which Ana and her sisters are driven by Paulina to visit the country home of Amelia . . . and her husband, the sequence in which Ana's mother makes her most sustained imaginary appearance. Saura precedes this with the adult Ana's recollection of the event, so that when he cuts from her to a forward travelling shot from behind the car, our impression is of a journey into the past, even though the child we see is in fact being taken forward into a novel experience. The visual resonance is amplified both by the fact that Ana is staring back the way she has come and by her being viewed from behind the glass of the rear window, as if in a time capsule.

The two-way pull exerted here rhymes with that created earlier, when Ana is seen playing in the rambling garden with her siblings, and is suddenly transported to the roof above to gaze down on the scene and to feel herself flying above it; the disequilibrium in the images offers its own comment on the impossibility of a distanced view of the self. The matter-of-fact strangeness of that episode serves to recall that, while *Cria Cuervos* may seem to owe a debt to Resnais, Saura is also in some measure a disciple of his compatriot Buñuel. . . .

Ana's preoccupation with death fuses the film's personal and political levels, since it marks her as both the inheritor of an outmoded class and the potential agent of its destruction. Whether Ana's belief in the lethal properties of her tin of supposed poison is justified we never know—since Paulina emerges unharmed near the movie's end from an application of the powder, it may be that Ana's father actually died from other causes. What counts is her implicit trust in it and the communication of a perception of death which goes beyond that entailed in the burial of a pet guinea-pig. . . .

[Humour] is by no means absent from the film—consider the nursery theatricals, with the diminutive Maite cheerfully resigned to the supernumerary role of maid while her sisters lay claim to the leads. . . . It is true, though, that towards the end Saura allows the grip to slacken, and Paulina's burgeoning love affair with a brother officer of Ana's father is introduced to arbitrary and confusing effect.

The ending, however, is wholly effective. . . . On the sound-track a pop song blares out (possibly in homage to [Buñuel's] *Viridiana*, which also concluded by sending its heroine out into the world to a pop accompaniment). The effect is satisfyingly ambiguous, as the music simultaneously speaks for the anodyne of admass existence and refers us back to the images of Ana solitarily listening to her gramophone in the family home with its imprisoning memories.

*Tim Pulleine, "Film Reviews: 'Cria cuervos'," in* Sight and Sound *(copyright © 1978 by The British Film Institute), Vol. 47, No. 4, Autumn, 1978, p. 260.*

## CESAR SANTOS FONTENLA

If, in a way, *Cría cuervos* was the culmination of the line taken by Saura in *Peppermint frappé*, and *Elisa, vida mía* constituted a kind of questioning on the author's part of his own work and personality, *Los ojos vendados* indicates a new point of departure. Saura, still true to himself but having exorcised his ghosts, freed from the need to resort to a symbolism

that to some seemed excessively obvious and to others unduly cryptic, confronts in a spirit of inquiry the problems of post-Franco Spain through characters who throw themselves desperately into the search for their own identity. Torture, "white terrorism," the struggle to find a reason for living—or dying—and to pass from the condition of spectator to that of participant are, among others, the themes Saura lays on the table, in a game at once relentless and tender, in which "theatre" in its strictest sense and the "theatre" in which the characters indulge when they lie to themselves and to others, is a decisive factor. . . .

[Between the] beginning and end there is a story of love and re-encounter with an "ego" that is multiple and assumed in different degrees. There is also a great deal of autobiography, self-criticism and self-quotation, all done with clarity. A personal and a political film, *Los ojos vendados* is perhaps the first work in which Saura looks firmly not at the past, nor even the present, but at the future, a future which is of today, tomorrow and the day after tomorrow.

*Cesar Santos Fontenla, "'Los ojos vendados' ('Blindfold')," in* International Film Guide 1979, *edited by Peter Cowie (copyright © 1978 by Thomas Yoseloff Ltd.), The Tantivy Press, 1979, p. 294.*

## MARSHA KINDER

[In contrast to Saura's early] operatic films with their dramatic sweep of violent deeds and historical events, Saura's later works are more interior and subtle. They focus more narrowly on an individual within the close confines of a bourgeois family and stress the mental life of a particular consciousness—memories, dreams and fantasies—rather than external events. (pp. 16-17)

Saura's primary focus is the crippling influence of social and political forces on individuals, particularly during childhood, which is revealed through a return to the past or a reunion with family. . . . Saura's films achieve extraordinary subtlety in their psychological realism. He makes unusual demands on his actors, whose facial expressions and physical gestures must simultaneously convey both the masks required by the society and the underlying passions and ambivalences. Saura's films are masterpieces of repression in which the subtext is developed, not with the surreal wit or grotesquery of a Buñuel, but with the emotional intensity and psychological astuteness of a Bergman. As in Bergman's canon, Saura's films are woven together by recurring names, faces, characters, and situations that suggest a tapestry of recurring dreams. (p. 17)

Of all Saura's works, *The Garden of Delights* is the closest to Buñuel in its use of surreal symbolism; it depicts the discreet horrors of the bourgeoisie living under Franco repression. In tracing the mutual destructiveness of a powerful industrialist and his family of decadent pleasure-seekers, the film also evokes the grotesqueries of the Bosch painting . . . from which it derives its title. . . .

[One of the assumptions] that is powerfully demonstrated in Saura's *Garden of Delights* is that by fully probing the fantasies of individuals, it is possible to perceive an entire culture and to demystify political dynamics. . . . By choosing [a brain-damaged] character to control the film's point of view, Saura makes the gap between inner life and outward behavior essential to the plot and dramatizes quite literally the crippling influence of Spanish society on an individual consciousness. The film suggests that this destructive influence has been operating, not just in the accident, but all of Antonio's life. The accident merely confirms what was already true—his emotional, mental, and spiritual deterioration. (p. 18)

Saura is masterful in controlling the modulation of tone between the bitter satire, which is sometimes comic or absurd, and the psychological reality of the emotional pain. For example, in the sequence where Antonio's neglected wife tries to re-enact their first love scene in a boat on an idyllic lake, the replay almost turns into a parody of *An American Tragedy;* yet, the yearnings of this woman are still poignant, and the economic basis of the rejection is still underscored.

The film implies that all members of the family and of the society have suffered the same psychic damage as Antonio. This symbolic point is rendered concretely in the final powerful fantasy where each member of the family is isolated in a wheel chair, rolling across an elegant lawn like crippled performers in a perverted minuet.

In *Cousin Angelica* there is a shift from blatant symbolism to a more subtle personal expression; the crippling of consciousness is neither so literal nor so melodramatic, and the boundaries between inner life and outer events are more obscure. (p. 19)

Like other artists who dramatize the development of consciousness (Bergman, James, Proust), Saura bases his creation on germinal sensory images. This process is explicitly described in one scene where Luis remarks, "One day Proust dipped a madeleine in his tea and his mouth was full of the smell of his grandmother's garden." This associative process of drawing a story out of rich, concrete images controls both Saura's creative method and the film's narrative structure. . . .

The film is controlled by [the idea that you cannot see yourself as a child], for the adult Luis appears in all of his childhood memories; we never see him as a child. . . . After a while, we actually see the child *in Luis,* regardless of his external setting. We gradually understand that although Luis has come to bury his past, it is much more alive for him than the present and that his inner life is much more engaging than external events. This helps us to understand why he rejects Angelica as a woman and is much more attracted to her nine-year-old daughter. While he claims that being single means he is "free but alone," we see that he is actually bound to the ghosts from his past.

Yet like Saura, Luis is free to alter his memories, sometimes casting them with characters from his immediate environment. . . . Sometimes Luis's distortions are humorous—as when he pictures Angelica's father with his arm in a cast; although his uncle claims to have been wounded by shrapnel, it looks more like his arm was paralyzed in a fascist salute. Saura suggests that not only is our present determined by our past, but our past is reshaped by the present. The mediator is the individual consciousness.

The film opens with a powerful germinal image. As we hear choir boys singing, we see white mist drifting through a church schoolroom, which is illuminated by strange overexposed lighting; the camera slowly glides through wreckage, observing signs of violence from some unknown disaster. We do not yet know what happened, nor do we recognize the mode of reality—present event, nightmare, or memory. Yet the image immediately engages our attention and opens the door to Luis's consciousness. (p. 20)

Later in the film, when we return to this image, we realize it was a childhood memory of a traumatic incident in which Luis's school was bombed. In order to understand its full impact, we must learn what other memories it is associated with in Luis's mind. . . . The association between religion, death, and guilt is also strong in the memory of a theatrical performance of Christ's crucifixion. . . . All of [Luis's] memories reveal that, like the War, the Catholic Church effectively cripples the young with guilt and fear, inhibiting their enjoyment of sensual pleasures and stifling any rebellious political consciousness.

The other primary source of imprinting in Luis's childhood is art. While in many of his memories it is controlled by the Church (e.g., the religious pageant is evoked by music, the nightmare by the religious painting), the secular art is also powerful. . . . (pp. 20-1)

Reversing the central premise of *Cousin Angelica, Cría Cuervos* raises the question of what happens when you *can* see yourself as a child. An old Spanish proverb warns, "Raise ravens and they'll peck out your eyes."

This film presents the best portrayal of a child I have ever seen. . . . The intensity of Ana's passions is made so credible that, without any melodrama, we can accept a nine-year-old contemplating suicide and poisoning one of her family elders. . . . The child's perception of adult realities (e.g., her father's sexual adventures, which lead to his fatal heart attack, and his mistreatment of her mother, which is partly responsible for her death) is so convincing because, without fully comprehending all of the events, she intuits the emotional reality. Through her eyes, we are able to see the adults with a double perspective that may also partially reflect the adult Ana's consciousness. . . . As Ana's ancient grandmother sits in her wheelchair—paralyzed, mute, and expressionless—staring at yellowed photographs and listening to old phonograph records, we realize that her mind is totally absorbed in the past and that for her the present is dead. The young Ana feels great pity for this old woman, whom she would like to put out of her misery; as an adult, Ana will identify with this total immersion in memories. The grandmother evokes a remembrance of things past—not only of a Spain before Franco, but also of Antonio in Saura's own *Garden of Delights.*

Despite this intense inner life, on the surface Ana appears to be a "normal" nine-year-old, particularly when she and her older sister dance to pop records and dress up like women. In these scenes, Saura carefully avoids cuteness and sentimentality; he uses these potential clichés to enlarge the range of Ana's fantasy life. . . . Though the repressive Francoist society is still portrayed as shaping the individual consciousness of the protagonist—particularly through the self-centered domination of a militaristic father and the oppressive atmosphere of a rich, conservative family controlled by restrictive social and religious conventions—the social forces are further in the background than in previous Saura films. (pp. 23-4)

*Marsha Kinder, "Carlos Saura: The Political Development of Individual Consciousness," in* Film Quarterly *(copyright 1979 by The Regents of the University of California; reprinted by permission of the University of California Press), Vol. XXXII, No. 3, Spring, 1979, pp. 14-25.*

**TOM ALLEN**

Saura is one of those tightly controlled, long-distance filmmakers . . . who, rather than exploding into Felliniesque self-apotheosis, tends to implode within personal themes and a signatory style. Saura's *Garden of Delights* and *Cousin Angelica* . . . seethed in their contemporary portraits of familial disintegration and bitter memories of past repressions.

A funny thing, however, has happened to Saura on the way to the '80s. The director's latest films reveal a desperate, unconscious need for Franco and the good old bad days of repression that had added an urgency and subtextual sting to his films. Without a relevant nemesis, *Mama Turns 100* emerges as a lightweight parody of *Garden of Delights* (and, by implication, of Saura himself) and *Blindfolded* [*Los ojos vendados*] evolves as a stylish romance that fails in its secondary purpose as a political thesis because it lacks a credible right-wing villain. In Saura's new films, the Spain of a benign restored monarchy and chidings from Amnesty International seem colorless compared to the jackboots of the *Caudillo*. Without contextual bitterness, Saura's archetypal devices of memory connections and multiple identities seem robbed of their synapses, certainly of the subliminal resonances that simmered beneath his haunted, complex imagery. In *Mama Turns 100,* the nude scenes with a liberated, pot-smoking young woman have also led to a corresponding decline in the director's steamy eroticism. In Saura's latter-day career, the new freedom in Spain has exacted a bewildering, paradoxical cost.

*Tom Allen, "New Signals from Saura and Sirk" (reprinted by permission of* The Village Voice *and the author; copyright © News Group Publications, Inc., 1980), in* The Village Voice, *Vol. XXV, No. 3, January 21, 1980, p. 54.**

# Martin Scorsese

## 1942-

American director, screenwriter, and actor.

Scorsese's work is considered among the most impressive of the young filmmakers who emerged in the seventies. His bleak, unrelenting vision of life, death, and the struggle for redemption has gained for him a large following. Scorsese's films are personal pieces through which the audience sees the importance on the filmmaker of his Catholic upbringing and his young life in the "Little Italy" area of Manhattan.

At one time, Scorsese considered preparing for the priesthood. Instead, he enrolled at New York University and began making short films. Among these films is *The Big Shave*, which attracted the attention of a sponsor in Europe. Scorsese then directed commercials for English television, and in 1969 returned to the United States to work as an editor on *Woodstock*. During this period Scorsese also completed his first feature, *Who's That Knocking at My Door?*, which contains many elements found in his recent work, including Catholic iconography, conflicts between male protagonists, and the determined, self-destructive young hero.

Scorsese's first critical success was *Mean Streets*, which sets the tone for much of his future work. Perhaps Scorsese's most personal endeavor, the film is full of manic energy, conflict, tension, and street life, and the sympathetic, misguided characters seek redemption in a world in which they are already doomed. These same themes are handled with even less optimism in *Taxi Driver*, Scorsese's most highly regarded film. *Taxi Driver* advances the notion that purgation is possible only through death, and the violence of the street-wise hero, Travis Bickle, is felt to be among the most obsessional and disturbing depictions ever put on film.

Scorsese has complemented his true-to-life fiction by filming documentaries. *Italianamerican* is a thoughtful, loving portrait of Scorsese's parents, who discuss how they have been influenced by their Italian immigrant parents. Similarly, in *The Last Waltz*, Scorsese intercuts footage of The Band's last concert with interviews concerning the group's sixteen years on the road. In both of these films, while Scorsese recreates a time that seems more innocent, more romantic, he dulls the mythical gloss and shows the difficulties encountered by each group of people.

*New York, New York* is an attempt to recreate the musicals of the 1940s. It is soft, romantic, and encompasses a vast stage. In comparison, *Raging Bull* is a biography of boxer Jake La Motta which portrays the violent world of boxing as being indistinct from La Motta's view of society. *Raging Bull* is hard and constricted, and the camerawork is similar to that in *Mean Streets*—jarring and bouncy, with the camera seemingly becoming one of the fighters in the ring. The violence, language, and La Motta's attempts to redeem himself also echo Scorsese's earlier work. Although some critics have complained that Scorsese has dealt with these themes too often in his films, most agree that the unexorcised demon within Scorsese has allowed him to create films which are engrossing and meaningful to filmmaker and audience alike.

### VINCENT CANBY

J. R., the troubled hero of Martin Scorsese's first feature film, **"Who's That Knocking at My Door?"**, is the sort of young man who, in a total confusion of values, can one minute offer to "forgive" the girl he loves for having been forcibly raped, and the next minute accuse her of being a whore. Puritan Roman Catholicism, the kind that bedeviled Stephen Dedalus and Studs Lonigan, is alive and ill and in the movies. . . .

[Scorsese] has composed a fluid, technically proficient movie, more intense and sincere than most commercial releases.

It is apparent that the Italian-American milieu is a first-hand experience, but the vision Scorsese has made from it is detailed in the kind of self-limiting drama and dialogue that Paddy Cheyefsky abandoned some time ago, and in images that look very much like film school poetry. . . . I must say that I like Scorsese's enthusiasm even while wincing at some of the results. . . . (p. 71)

Scorsese is effective in isolating the moments of "Marty"-like boredom that J. R. accepts as concomitants to life. . . . However, the director . . . hasn't succeeded in making a drama that is really much more aware than the characters themselves. The result is a movie that is as precise—and as small—as a contact print. (pp. 71-2)

*Vincent Canby, "Scorsese's 'Who's That Knocking at My Door'," in* The New York Times *(© 1969 by The New York Times Company; reprinted by permission), September 9, 1969 (and reprinted in* The New York Times Film Reviews: 1969-1970, *The New York Times Company & Arno Press, 1971, pp. 71-2).*

**GEORGE LELLIS**

[*Who's That Knocking at My Door?* explores] the hermetic environments of working-class post-immigrant American society.... *Knocking*'s Italian-America [is a social structure] in which the isolation of imported nationalism and Roman Catholicism collides with dreary urban or industrial town living to produce characters somewhat dislocated in time and place. [The film doesn't seem] quite up to date.... A world where guys still wear white shirts and grey suits to a party ... becomes a world stable enough so that plot premises like ... *Knocking*'s Italo-Catholic obsessions with virgin brides become acceptable because no alternative forms of behavior are even suggested. If the results are somewhat synthetic and theatrical, they also have an admirable austerity and containment lacking in the wilder, so-called swinging movies so currently prevalent.

Synthetic and theatrical, too, are much of the [picture's] acting and dialogue. Lines seem lifted off the typewritten script-page and thrust into the mouths of the actors in desperate attempts to sound realistic. But all of the false starts, digressions, sputterings and silences of real conversation, while continually aped, become, in the attempt, all the more conspicuously affected and artificial under the camera-eye's glare.... Scorsese may not approve of his characters, or even like them, and he may handle them awkwardly at times, but at least he respects their humanity, which puts him far closer to early De Sica, or, more recently, Olmi, than any of Hollywood's aborted attempts of the fifties... *Who's That Knocking at My Door?* [is] ultimately most reminiscent of the old, somewhat over-written, T.V. "Playhouse 90" genre. It is as if that very genre which spawned Sidney Lumet and John Frankenheimer and so many others who were later to develop far more complex styles in film were now being nostalgically called-upon by young filmmakers working in a style which, with i·s small frame, formal black and white, and comparatively low depth of field, is oddly similar to the old television image.

*George Lellis, "'Who's That Knocking at My Door?'" in* Take One *(copyright © 1969 by Unicorn Publishing Corp.), Vol. 2, No. 4, December 30, 1969, p. 20.*

**HOWARD THOMPSON**

Watching **"Street Scenes 1970"** was a tingling, often riveting experience. This documentary was put together from footage taken during the turbulent demonstrations on Wall Street last May and in other parts of town and finally in Washington at the antiwar rally....

As a fast-flying, naturally piecemeal assemblage of tense events, often exploding violently and shot through with marvelously revealing human vignettes and testimonies, the final picture, supervised by Martin Scorsese, is admirable on two counts, especially.

One is the frightening vitality of actuality as recorded on raw film, especially in the churning chaos of the earlier Wall Street portion. The other is the balanced, accumulative tone of utterances, from all sides, directed at the candid camera.

Original though it may be, the final chapter, when the young moviemakers sprawl around a Washington hotel room and take personal political inventory, is entirely redundant....

Obviously, Mr. Scorsese and his team care deeply about vital issues. In their picture, so do many others.

*Howard Thompson, "'Street Scenes 1970'," in* The New York Times *(© 1970 by The New York Times Company; reprinted by permission), September 15, 1970 (and reprinted in* The New York Times Film Reviews: 1969-1970, *The New York Times Company & Arno Press, 1971, p. 215).*

**JON LANDAU**

*Mean Streets,* the most original American movie of the year, doesn't just explode—it erupts with volcanic force. It is a shocking, jolting, even pulverizing view of "Desolation Row," the claustrophobic, small-time petty Mafia world that is Martin Scorsese's vision of New York's Little Italy. In this semi-feudal empire, the random and the ritual, sacred and profane, and sane and insane are in perpetual conflict—and Scorsese shows us the turmoil bubbling beneath the society's surfaces just as he knows it, without a trace of Hollywood glamorizing, demystifying Italian criminal life even as he personalizes it....

Scorsese integrates realism, stylized elements, symbolism, surrealism and other nonlinear modes of exposition as part of a continuing struggle to relate method to meaning.

The film is suffused with an extraordinary realism. Scorsese's camera moves around like a tiger on the prowl, hand-held and lurking in forbidden places one moment, stationary, coolly observing the unexpected in the next. The often improvised, largely comic, always overlapping dialogue provides a perfect aural equivalent, while the acting virtually leaps off the screen....

Nearly every location contributes to the film's claustrophobic atmosphere. Scorsese shot the movie during the San Gennaro Festival so that the streets are crawling with people, imprisoning each character on his native turf. The incessant music ...—rock in the bars and cars, Italian standards in the restaurants, street music as part of the festival—provides a continual and numbing din that generates its own form of claustrophobia.

The stylization naturally spills forth into a network of symbols that some may find heavy-handed but which I found exhilarating because each is distilled from the natural objects and appearances of the community. Scorsese brazenly contrasts church icons with street icons: the cross versus the gun, the sensuous surface of a church statue versus the sensuous surface of a black bar dancer bathed in rhinestones; Giovanni's pictures of the Kennedys and Mussolini resting alongside one of the Pope....

Scorsese's most difficult task was to find a way of representing Charlie's inner conflicts. He finally hit upon a combination of voice-over monologues and elaborate fire symbolism....

If fire is one side of Scorsese's explosive visuals, his physical and verbal depictions of violence provide another. The random fighting in *Mean Streets* breaks out without warning or explanation. We either learn the reason for it after the fact or not at all. And in almost every case Scorsese extends the action beyond existing conventions, so that he not only generates shock but anxiety....

Scorsese uses each technique to depict both the dynamics of community life and Charlie's isolation from them. During a dance to "Pledging My Love" (the ultimate rock & roll death song) he stays on Charlie's enigmatic face for as long as he stays on the fighting, until we can no longer avoid his sense of loneliness, confusion, guilt and pain. He is trapped by the camera as surely as he is by the streets. . . .

*Mean Streets* is autobiographical without being sentimental or cynical. It penetrates so deeply into a particular way of life that it may alienate those for whom it is impossible to make the basic connections. But Scorsese has refused any compromises. He offers no explicit explanations, leaves the loose ends untied, and refuses to kill Charlie off at the end (it would have been too easy), so that we leave the theater not with a sense of catharsis, but with an unbearable anxiety about what can possibly become of him.

[If Scorsese had less faith in his audience he] . . . might have risked breaking up the realism of the soundtrack to offer a definitive clue to *Mean Streets'* meaning, by copping a line from Dylan's best music, ". . . to live outside the law you must be honest." To which [he] could have added, "It's all right Ma, it's life and life only." For if *Mean Streets,* a brilliant title, for a brilliant film, by a brilliant artist, *means* anything at all, it is most certainly that—and it is more than enough.

> Jon Landau, "Films: 'Mean Streets'," in Rolling Stone *(by Straight Arrow Publishers, Inc. © 1973; all rights reserved; reprinted by permission), Issue 147, November 8, 1973, p. 80.*

## STANLEY KAUFFMANN

Martin Scorsese grew up in New York's Little Italy and has made a film about his home neighborhood. This personal impulse, which would not exactly be hot news in any other art, is so unusual in American film that it has already knocked some people sideways. . . . [Scorsese] has made a previous feature set in lower Manhattan, *Who's That Knocking at My Door?* His new picture *Mean Streets* is very much better—more intense, better integrated. Nevertheless its intensity is often theatrical in the wrong way, it's both lumpy and discursive, and it ends up as only a fairly bright promissory note. (p. 229)

I think we're supposed to feel that the plot is not the point, that the film exists for its milieu and texture, but it doesn't come out that way. So much of the script gets mired in the tropes of gangster melodrama that plottiness intrudes; and, conversely, some scenes limp, so the very plottiness is bilked. As for texture the editing is jumpy and irresolute. . . . The color is garish and flashy in barroom scenes, in the esthetic fallacy of trying to look like what it's about, but abandoning this idea elsewhere. . . . Scorsese simply hasn't found the objective correlative in his . . . method. . . . (pp. 229-30)

The incompleteness of every inner motion affects the film as a whole. When it's over we want to know what it was about. To tell us what life is like today in Little Italy? A twenty-minute documentary could have made the (implicit) point that these former slums have changed inwardly, if not outwardly, into middle-class centers. And is this all there is to life in Little Italy? Is he telling us that everyone there is like this, that there is no escape? If so, just to name one instance, how did Scorsese come out of it? The film gives us no hint. (p. 230)

> Stanley Kauffmann, "Mean Streets" (originally published in The New Republic, *Vol. 169, No. 17, October 27, 1973), in his* Living Images: Film Comment and Criticism *(reprinted by permission of Brandt & Brandt Literary Agents, Inc.; copyright © 1970, 1971, 1972, 1973, 1974, 1975 by Stanley Kauffmann), Harper & Row, Publishers, 1975, pp. 229-31.*

## DAVID DENBY

[*Mean Streets* is certainly] a 'little' New York film . . . , with no stars and not much variety or glamour in the settings—in some respects the movie is the culmination of the lonely-streets-and-sullen-bedrooms style of student films produced in the last decade. . . . But emotionally, *Mean Streets* is grandiose and amazingly intense—'operatic' . . . in the manner of mid-Visconti, yet peculiarly American in its speed, energy, obscenity and humour. And Scorsese is no sweet little talent, but a large, dangerous and deeply flawed talent. . . .

As Scorsese introduces his people in short, character-revealing vignettes, for one dismaying moment you might think he was making a conventional 'wacky' caper picture about bumblers who want to be gangsters, or possibly an American *Big Deal on Madonna Street*. But it turns out that he doesn't need satire to ingratiate his characters with the audience; Scorsese, who grew up in Little Italy and obviously knows the scene, discovers the humour in the life itself and in the characters' naturally obscene idiom. And because he doesn't see these bums as 'little' people, but rather as very familiar friends who got bogged down, his film has none of the patronising, sentimental tone of bourgeois American movies about the working class (e.g. *Marty*). Pursuing his friends relentlessly in and out of bars, bedrooms and restaurants, up and down streets, stairways and hallways, he creates a life of crazy restlessness that we soon realise is totally satisfying to the characters, even though it's oppressively enclosed, barely touching on the world outside. . . .

Scorsese and his co-screenwriter Mardik Martin are weak on narrative construction, but they have a preternatural instinct for the psychology of dependent relationships. For once, the male friendship theme is developed with enough psychological richness to explain the emotions it generates; this time no one will suspect something embarrassing has been left out. . . . (p. 48)

As [the four main characters] bounce off one another—enraged, derisive, hilarious, sentimental—it becomes clear that their energy has no goal or purpose, certainly not love or career or even style. . . . Scorsese is celebrating emotional verve as a moral quality in itself, and this is something new in American movies and takes some getting used to. . . . The punks of *Mean Streets* . . . will never shape up; if they survive, they'll simply become *ageing* punks. . . . Scorsese's *Mean Streets* is remarkable, I think, for its moral realism—realism without cynicism. (p. 49)

[Scorsese's] film is bursting with noise, colour, movement, and the mood is consciously over-ripe—what shall we call the style, operatic naturalism? His characters don't perceive the city as dull and grey; yes, the neighbourhood may be crummy, but up on the roofs the ever-astonishing skyscrapers of New York twinkle on all sides, incredibly beautiful and powerful at night, and the local bars, admittedly lousy and stale, give off a satisfying glow. The film opens during the Feast of San Gennaro, a yearly outdoor confluence of grease, fragrance and overpowering crowds. Scorsese's point, I think, is that Little Italy has this suffocating, sweetness-of-hell atmosphere all the time. . . . Scorsese, while never suggesting that the city is a benign place, punctures the liberal view of the city as an unrelieved nightmare for poor ethnic groups. His city is hypnotic, irresistible, and for us to pretend that some people aren't drawn to the rottenness is sheer cant. (pp. 49-50)

Scorsese counts on our familiarity with improvisation and our approval of it as a method, and I feel he uses it better than anyone in American movies so far. . . .

[He] stays back from his people, letting them move around in their own space, which he respects, allowing them to draw strength from the streets, the music, their friends; and since these working-class characters don't repress much to begin with, there's no need for laceration or emotional striptease. Thus Scorsese's improvisation becomes a fast, explosively funny way of extending the actors' expressiveness. The near-musical texture of obscenity, for instance, would be impossible without improvisation; no one could possibly get down on paper the lunatic obsessiveness of the swearing, with its infinite variety of meanings conveyed through minute variations in rhythm and inflection. The mood of the dialogue is almost ecstatically high-pitched; Scorsese uses improvisation to make his people sound as free as possible. . . . But when he has an actor who can't pull it off he's in trouble. . . .

Scorsese is already a master of film texture and expressive atmosphere and directing actors, but as I said earlier, his narrative sense is weak. Once he sets up his relationships and moods, he's incapable of developing them. The endless quarrels and fist-fights don't lead anywhere; the Charlie-Johnny Boy dependency doesn't accumulate new meanings as the movie goes on, it's simply stated over and over with increasing vehemence. For a while, in the middle, you don't think the story is ever going to move forward again, and a terrible depression sets in; afterwards it seems as though the middle sequences could be shifted around without damage and some of them dropped altogether. The tension never sags, but since the actors rather than the narrative supply all the urgency, we get tired of being worked up emotionally only to learn what we already know. It's as if we were starting at the beginning each time, as if Scorsese didn't trust the audience to absorb or learn anything; he wants to recapitulate the movie in every scene, like a mad composer who can't relinquish a good melody.

We come out grateful for this experience but also feeling a bit mauled. Don't Italian-Americans ever communicate without slapping and shoving and brawling? Aren't there any quieter forms of intensity? Scorsese knows how to reach an audience in the gut, but some of his demands are obtuse. . . .

[His mistakes] are so forgivable because they emerge out of the same violent sincerity that makes the film exciting: Scorsese's impulse to express all he feels about life in every scene . . . and thus to wrench the audience upwards into a state of consciousness with one prolonged and devastating gesture, infinitely hurting and infinitely tender. *Mean Streets* comes close enough to this feverish ideal to warrant our love and much of our respect. (p. 50)

> David Denby, "'Mean Streets': The Sweetness of Hell," in Sight and Sound (copyright © 1974 by The British Film Institute), Vol. 43, No. 1, Winter, 1973-74, pp. 48-50.

**WILLIAM JOHNSON**

My expectations of [*Alice Doesn't Live Here Any More*] were based mainly on Scorsese's previous feature, *Mean Streets*. Though "widely acclaimed," as the ads say, this left me cold. Oh yes, I admired the efficiency of its making. Dark, glinting interiors, edgy dialogue, strategic bursts of action, long takes with the camera immobile or slowly prowling like a hit man

waiting to strike—sure, Scorsese knew what he wanted to put on the screen and how to get it there. You can see this ability taking shape in his short student films: the satirical *It's Not Just You, Murray* skips nimbly through space and time while the simple joke of *The Big Shave* comes out in a linear crescendo. Scorsese is not only efficient but versatile, matching different means to different ends. But what was the end in *Mean Streets*?

It seemed to be little more than high-class melodrama—a display of hyped-up situations and attitudes. (pp. 55-6)

Scorsese told interviewers that the film distilled youthful memories of New York City's Little Italy—it really was like that, he said, referring to the general atmosphere of the film rather than to specific events. If so, I could give *Mean Streets* the benefit of the doubt and assume a cultural gap due to my own English background.

But with Scorsese's short documentary on his parents, *Italian-american* . . . , the presumed cultural gap failed to show. The film was accessible and enjoyable. Of course, it gives an objectified view of the New York Italian experience, quite unlike the subjective dramatization of *Mean Streets*. All the same, the parents' speech and gestures embody the culture that is being discussed and, having a spontaneity that goes beyond any of the improvisation in *Mean Streets,* plays an important part in shaping the film as a whole. In short, Scorsese's directorial hand rests on this film much more lightly than on *Mean Streets*. So the cultural gap is probably not at issue, and my case against the melodrama of *Mean Streets* must remain open. . . .

Now comes *Alice,* which marks a big break with Scorsese's recent film-making. . . . With the leap from studio-made thirties to real seventies Scorsese is symbolically detaching himself from his own remembered past. He is turning from New York City to the desert states; from an exclusive and specific Italian milieu to a generalized Anglo-Saxon Protestantism . . . ; and from a predominantly male view of the world to the experience of a woman. (p. 56)

Scorsese spent a long time with Ellen Burstyn and writer Robert Getchell in working out the final details of Alice's character and experiences. In addition to its obvious advantages, this kind of collaboration involves risks—a possible loss of focus, a compromise rather than a reinforcement of creative ideas. Such weaknesses do seem to emerge toward the end of the film. David remains a curiously thin character: the viewer learns very little about his outlook on life, or for that matter his *way* of life (his ranching appears to be only a hobby). Yet he marks the culmination of Alice's odyssey: when last seen, she has given up another slice of her independence for this indefinite man. This editing looks like a retreat from sharper alternatives.

In other words, after trying to find fault with *Alice* for being too neat, I'm now suggesting that it isn't quite neat enough. But here, too, a shift of angle is possible. This isn't meant to be a conventional happy ending, with Alice finally in the arms of Mr. Right. It may be just a tentative halt in her odyssey. David remains "thin" because Alice herself doesn't know him yet, though she likes him well enough to find out more. . . .

The last scene of the film includes more than Alice, David, and the Monterey Motel. Taken with a telephoto lens, it also brings a distant mountain looming over the casual activities of the street—a confrontation of the permanent and the transient, of solidity and disorder, of Alice's dream and the reality she is learning to cope with. (p. 58)

Like the opening leap from past to present, this final image can also be applied to the film itself. The vigor of *Alice* arises in large part from a similar confrontation—between the elements loosely described . . . as "too neat" and "not neat enough." I am referring here not to the simple oppositions between studio and location, planning and improvisation (since *Mean Streets,* which incorporated all of these, lacked the particular quality of *Alice*), but to a flexibility or unexpectedness in the matching of form and content. . . . It is the continual shifting of modality between the schematic and the diffuse which stimulates the viewer to adjust his/her mental focus, and thus discover fresh implications in Alice's odyssey. (pp. 58-9)

> *William Johnson, "'Alice Doesn't Live Here Any More',"* in Film Quarterly *(copyright 1975 by The Regents of the University of California; reprinted by permission of the University of California Press), Vol. 28, No. 3, Spring, 1975, pp. 55-9.*

## STEPHEN FARBER

*Alice Doesn't Live Here Any More* is a [slick] Hollywood comedy, taken from [an] artificial, highly structured script by Robert Getchell. However, since it was directed by Martin Scorsese, the talented dynamo who made *Mean Streets,* the film has a raw energy that shatters some of the script's contrivances. . . . Alice Graham is a survivor, a woman with an enterprising spirit and a resilient sense of humor. (p. 415)

[But] *Alice Doesn't Live Here Any More* cannot be taken very seriously as a study of a contemporary woman. . . . [The] heroine's limited potential radically limits the scope of the film. At first Alice seems determined to make it on her own, but in the end, after a few crummy jobs as a barroom singer and waitress, she decides to settle down with Kris Kristofferson, a tranquil, warm-hearted Arizona rancher. Although she plans to continue with her singing career, she gives up her dream of returning to Monterey, the town where she started out as a singer. Some women have criticized the ending as a copout, but that misses the point; the whole movie is a copout because Alice's career ambitions are so unrealistic to begin with. She has no real singing talent; her obsession with singing springs from a childhood infatuation with Alice Faye, and she refuses to grow up.

The film might have been more interesting if Alice had come to realize the absurdity of her singing career, and then readjusted her aspirations and set out to find a career that would make use of her real strengths. But the film poses only two alternatives for Alice—pursuing a hopeless singing career, or settling down with a good man. The choice is an artificial one, unfairly restricted. The last shot is pure Hollywood schmaltz: As Alice tells her son that they will not be moving to Monterey, they pass a bar called "Monterey"; her dream is closer to home than she knew. The movie begins with a parody of *The Wizard of Oz,* but ends by reaffirming the same cloying message; Alice is like a grown-up Dorothy discovering that the land of Oz is right in her own back yard. The film-makers are patting Alice on the head and telling her not to expect too much; their condescension insults women with more complicated aspiration. (pp. 415-16)

> *Stephen Farber, "The Hausfrau, the Ugly Duckling, and the Funny Lady,"* in The Hudson Review *(copy-right © 1975 by The Hudson Review, Inc.; reprinted by permission), Vol. XXVIII, No. 3, Autumn, 1975, pp. 413-20.\**

## JULIAN C. RICE

[*Taxi Driver*] is, in part, a film about films. But it is unusual in being expressive of, and simultaneously about, a particular kind of film, which might be called "the pornography of violence." Through the windshield of Travis Bickle's cab, the audience sees the repeated image of movie marquees. Through most of the film, these marquees advertise erotic films, displaying titles like "Swedish Marriage Manual" or "Anita Nymphet." But after the film's bloody catharsis, and subsequent apotheosis of Travis, as a vigilante hero, the surrealistic street scene behind the closing credits reveals marquees, which contain the following camera-selected fragments, "Charles Bronson," "Mafia," "Blood," and "Killer." Although the cathartic scene of *Taxi Driver* includes the bloody killing of a "mafioso," the effect of the film is far different from that of other vigilante films, such as the Bronson vehicle, *Death Wish.* Scorsese [and coscreenwriter Paul Schrader] . . . present a protagonist with whom the audience will initially identify, but from whom they will unexpectedly be jolted into alienation. The alienation effect differentiates the film from the Violence genre, upon which it comments, and is achieved through the metamorphosis of Travis from a figure of naturalistic film fantasy to a horrifyingly familiar image of media "reality." After his brief incarnation as a political assassin, Travis returns in the final scene to the conventional hero image, which the audience is unexpectedly and uncomfortably forced to reject.

In this alternation between fantasy, truth, and fantasy, the film makes certain "connections," (one of its recurrent terms) between subjective aspects of contemporary culture and specific events of recent history. The overt externalizing of fantasy differentiates a psychotic person from a normal person. (pp. 109-10)

In *Taxi Driver,* however, the hero is only "partly fiction." . . . When Travis crosses the line from fiction to truth, he also traverses the line from hero to villain. Early in the film Travis has an innocent twelve-year old boy look, as he observes Manhattan corruption through his cab windshield. When Travis courts Betsy, this boyish sweetness blends with the manly toughness of the conventional, "realistic," film hero. (p. 110)

But at a political rally for a Presidential candidate, Travis appears with a literally new face. After seeing the cab door open, the camera follows the recognizable blue jeaned legs of the hero for a few steps before it stops. The camera then moves slowly upward to the familiar marine jacket with the "We are the People" button, before it dramatically reveals Travis transformed into a sort of Charles Manson-Mr. Hyde, complete with Mohawk haircut and uncharacteristic sunglasses. When Travis moves through the crowd toward the senator, the audience is in a familiar visual territory, but not one they are accustomed to seeing on a large screen. The grin on Travis's face comes from television or magazine images, rather than cinematic convention, especially in its resemblance to the halloween mask expression of [George] Wallace-assailant, Arthur Bremer. (p. 111)

In *Taxi Driver,* the usual Manichean pitting of good guy against bad guy is replaced by a quasi-religious sense of the inadequacy of all moral definition. We do not know how to receive Travis at the end of the film. The protagonists of most popular violent films resemble the vigilante hero that the newspapers have made of Travis. Moral definition is provided by the media. The television and movie screens have replaced the church in satisfying our simultaneous needs for limitless transcendence and secure moral definition. *Taxi Driver* breaks through these moral limits, and their reinforcing aesthetic convention by allowing Travis to assume, simultaneously, the roles of the conventional hero and the ultimate modern villain; in Travis, the cowboy and the terrorist are cubistically fused.

A sense of surrealistic fantasy and moral indefiniteness is communicated in the continual movement of the New York street scenes. There is a basic "disparity" between the symbolic atmosphere of these scenes and the naturalistic tone of the scenes, which include dialogue. This disparity helps to create the alienation effect which differentiates *Taxi Driver* from the genre films it obliquely reflects. . . . The film is a fantasy looking-glass, which most of us will not go through. But it is about a man who begins as a viewer of life, through the "screen" of his cab window, and who then goes through the looking glass to become an "actor" in a personal fantasy, where he paradoxically achieves that more vital reality, which the film "viewer" theoretically craves. Before the actual film begins in the cab dispatcher's office, the last scene on the titles discloses a reddish, surrealistic scene of endless lines of traffic and pedestrians, an overwhelming, anonymous monotony, which the color scheme identifies as a hell, containing sufferers groaning for redemption. (pp. 113-14)

The various fantasies are expressed against a New York background, which virtually necessitates escapism, in an atmosphere of imminent apocalypse, like the Los Angeles of [John Schlesinger's] *Day of the Locust*. Rushing columns of pedestrians and automobile traffic become oppressively repetitious. Certain images accentuate this effect: rain and wet streets, the motion of windshield wipers, the clicking of the taxi meter, the dancing of red, green, and blue lights on the cab windshield. The sameness, the nightmarish blending of colors and forms, stimulates a yearning for transcendental singularity and order. (p. 116)

Travis's vague physical ailments are never defined, and his spiritual malaise is not realistically motivated. As far as we know, Travis is simply unable to accept the lesser satisfactions that might be available to him. His refusal to accept the imperfections of life-as-it-is, expresses a universal and timeless discontent. (p. 117)

Redemption from [the] "mass" becomes Travis's obsession. When he cannot redeem himself, through Betsy as his savior, Travis attempts to integrate the redeemer into himself by saving the twelve-year old prostitute, Iris, from "the life." . . . Travis wishes to redeem his humanity from the mechanization that civilized life imposes. Iris represents, to Travis, the complete identification of a person with his job, to which Wizard had earlier referred, "a man takes a job . . . that job becomes what he is." She is no more than a depersonalized sexual machine, just as the driver is only an extension of his taxi. In fastening on the pimps, Travis has found a symbolic target for his rage against the restrictions on individual development, which civilization requires. Everyone in the film, except Travis, is a recognizable urban "type." The temporary selection of Senator Palantine as a target, helps to suggest that Travis's rage represents the eternal attack on civilization by its discontents, the individual striving for completion, against the conformity-requiring authority of the superego. The word, "palatine," means

"chief minister of the empire." Travis is angry at the depersonalizing quality of civilization itself.

The hero, who is almost martyred for us in *Taxi Driver,* is a scapegoat for our own rage, and the film suggests that our real-life criminals serve much the same purpose. (pp. 118-19)

Travis hears the unconsciously hypocritical Senator tell a TV interviewer that he wants to "let the *people* rule," that the *people* are already "beginning to rule" and that this grass roots emergence "will rise to an unprecedented swell." Travis's aspiration to individual "rule" will also reach an unprecedented swell, to be released in the orgasmic shootout with the enslaving forces, who possess Iris. Although Travis's violence is a result of sexual repression, this sexual deprivation is a metaphor for a spiritual deprivation in modern life, which intensifies the pressure for transcendental "rule." Even if their physical needs are satisfied, the people can never quite "rule," because of reduced individual expression, in an increasingly complex civilization. And the more structured a civilization becomes, the greater will be the risk of apocalyptic violence, under the appropriate name of "liberation." Travis's past as a Vietnam combat veteran has an obvious thematic correspondence to his crusade to liberate Iris, who makes it very clear that she does not want to be liberated. During their breakfast together, Iris says that her Pimp, Sport . . . may have a few faults, but he has never beaten her, and she is quite happy in "the life." Travis cannot accept this; he tells her what a girl-her-age *should* be doing and is adamant in refusing to see Sport as anything less than the worst "sucking scum." This corresponds to America's refusal to see that a different style of living, or system of government, is not necessarily evil, and that the people who live under this system do not necessarily feel oppressed. But the film suggests that Americans, who "feel" oppressed, simply by living in a populous, mechanically structured civilization, are likely to be stirred by the cause of "freedom," although the freedom they crave is psychological or even spiritual, rather than social and political.

At the end of the climactic shootout, the palpitating music, the overhead view of the sprawled bodies in Iris's slowly revolving room, the statue-like stance of the policemen with guns drawn, and the gradual descent down the apartment stairway transforms the dominant naturalistic tone of the film into an unexpectedly complete surrealism. The emphasis on the amount of blood glistening on the walls, accompanied by the music, and the slow motion camera movement, makes the blood symbolic. A purifying "liberation" has occurred. (pp. 119-20)

*Julian C. Rice, "Transcendental Pornography and 'Taxi Driver'," in* Journal of Popular Film *(copyright © 1976 by Michael T. Marsden and John G. Nachbar), Vol. V, No. 2, 1976, pp. 109-23.*

**ROBERT E. LAUDER**

Martin Scorsese's *Taxi Driver* has to be one of the most disturbing films ever made. Working with the metaphor of the city as sewer, Scorsese catches the sin-stained sensations of New York's teeming streets, where prostitutes, pimps and pushers parade under the scrutiny of Travis Bickle, the cruising cab driver who is a kind of contemporary Quixote. For Travis . . . , the city is a pile of filth that someone ought to clean up. . . .

Make no mistake about it: . . . the extraordinary talent of Scorsese is evident again and again. In the past critics have wondered if the young director's gifts were limited; even though his *Mean Streets* (1973) was widely acclaimed, this depiction of young hoodlums in Little Italy was similar in locale and characterization to Scorsese's earlier *Who's That Knocking at My Door?* But then the critical reception accorded *Alice Doesn't Live Here Anymore* (1974) confirmed that Scorsese could handle a wider world. His flexible talent is most evident if one contrasts *Taxi Driver* with the best film he has yet made, *Italianamerican.* That the same man could have made both films is amazing. In *Taxi Driver* the sophisticated use of lighting, color, camera angle and editing make the city streets so real that a viewer can feel fear even before violence occurs; in the documentary *Italianamerican,* Scorsese tenderly turns his camera on his own parents for 45 minutes and allows them to talk to and about one another, their family, their neighborhood, and Mrs. Scorsese's homemade meatball sauce. Though initially I found them hilarious, by the end of *Italianamerican* I had fallen in love with Scorsese's parents—and the magical talent of their 33-year-old son did it all.

Building to the climactic bloodbath, the vision of evil in *Taxi Driver* is almost overwhelming. (p. 467)

Scorsese's treatment of the material allows us to attribute the film's vision of evil to him as well. *Taxi Driver*'s fetid world is a Sartrian hell from which there is no exit. And, as with Sartre's play, this film overstates its case—the total absence of good mars the depiction of evil. . . .

Travis emerges as a contemporary redeemer, a modern mad messiah. Schrader and Scorsese seem to be saying that the contemporary city is so fouled up that the only Christ it deserves is a psychopath.

Its epilogue makes *Taxi Driver* a flawed film. . . .

The epilogue doesn't work on two levels: as a realistic ending to a story and as a thematic underlining of a vision of contemporary life. The epilogue doesn't work at the end of a supposedly realistic narrative because we are asked to believe too much. (p. 468)

The epilogue fails thematically because Schrader and Scorsese—by making Travis a contemporary savior—engage in cinematic overkill. Moreover, by depicting the pervasiveness of evil as it does, the epilogue weakens the film's earlier images of evil.

To put the problem another way, if everything is evil, then nothing is evil. Complete absence of good makes the depiction of the bad unreal. With his exceptional talent Scorsese can jolt us, scare us, depress us: but he can't convince us. (p. 469)

> Robert E. Lauder, "Hell on Wheels," in The Christian Century (copyright 1976 Christian Century Foundation; reprinted by permission from the May 12, 1976 issue of The Christian Century), Vol. 93, No. 17, May 12, 1976, pp. 467-69.

## GEORGE MORRIS

*Taxi Driver* is a remarkable achievement, a crazy, excessive, erratic masterpiece, but a masterpiece just the same. Scorsese has always interested me as a director, but he has also always annoyed me with his seeming inability to impose a cohesive structure upon his films. One of his chief weaknesses has been his tendency to play too many scenes at fever pitch. The absence of variation in the tone of *Mean Streets* and particularly *Alice Doesn't Live Here Anymore* irrevocably undercut the genuine climaxes of both films. In *Taxi Driver,* confronted with

volatile material which would readily lend itself to a similar treatment, Scorsese has wisely chosen the opposite tactic. He builds the film slowly, quietly, creating a mood of anxiety and imminent violence so that when the explosions finally occur within Travis Bickle's twisted psyche, the effect is all the more harrowing.

A positive side effect of this increased sense of formal structure is the marvelous way Scorsese continually surprises us throughout the film. Just when we feel certain the movie is going to go one way, he pulls the ground from under our feet and aims the material in another direction. . . .

With *Taxi Driver,* a thematic consistency becomes clear throughout Scorsese's work. The contradictions in Travis Bickle between a Puritan ethic and the need to find an outlet for his inarticulate rage and repression haunt [Charlie] in *Mean Streets* and the headstrong [Alice] in *Alice Doesn't Live Here Anymore.* The resolution of these contradictions that Travis settles upon gives this film its profoundly disturbing edge. There are all sorts of social and religious implications hovering around the edges of [the] script (lots of Bressonian overtones for instance), but the most unnerving one is the realization that there is a bit of Travis Bickle in all of us, a realization that is heightened by the subjective style of the film. This is what ultimately lifts *Taxi Driver* to a scale approaching modern tragedy. The pity and terror with which we view Travis' deterioration and the pathetic irony of his redemption reflect back upon ourselves, haunting the memory long after the last image has faded from the screen. (p. 66)

> George Morris, "The Fever Breaks," in Take One (copyright © 1976 by Unicorn Publishing Corp.), Vol. 5, No. 2, May 21, 1976, pp. 65-6.

## VERNON YOUNG

[Calculated] evasion is typical not only of [*Alice Doesn't Live Here Any More*], but of a disconcerting number of American items in which an alleged social inquest is taking place with sub-social witnesses whom we're supposed to take on trust as reliable emblems of the human lot. Alice is a boring nobody trying to become a boring somebody, with a minimum of qualifications for being anybody, a peculiar addiction to putrid language and, as extra baggage, [a] monstrous little hostage. . . .

What in the name of God constitutes a viable problem in this bogus history? A suburban housewife, unexpectedly widowed at a ripe age, discovers—or in fact does not discover—that she's insufficiently equipped to be anything more useful than a waitress, while clinging to the illusion that she's a talented singer because once in her salad days she placed in an amateur contest. So a waitress she becomes and this is supposed to pass as a spectacle of human waste or of the Female Search for Identity—yet all we're viewing is a dislocated mediocrity with a false notion of her own value and a knack for getting sympathy by weeping into her cocktail when she has "walked her feet off all afternoon" . . . and the crummy world hasn't given her instantly a crummy, well-paid job. (p. 260)

> Vernon Young, "Nobody Lives Here Any More," in The Hudson Review (copyright © 1976 by The Hudson Review, Inc.; reprinted by permission), Vol. XXIX, No. 2, Summer, 1976, pp. 259-64.*

## RICHARD COMBS

The opening shot of *Taxi Driver* plays probably the most seductive of trumps in the recent craze for power totems that has overtaken the American screen. . . . Out of a cloud of steam gushing over a New York street, a yellow cab floats majestically, mysteriously forward, its foreboding trajectory paced to the growling thunder of [the] score, its surface awash with abstract patterns of neon light. The powerful physicality of the image, and the state of extreme dislocation which it conveys, are the key to a kind of muscle-flexing sense of paradox on many levels: the film is about the soul sickness of urban alienation, played out . . . as a series of extrovert power plays involving American myths of gunmanship and Ideal Womanhood; its mood is one of determinist doom, feverishly embraced . . . ; and, following from this, its method is to construct a series of steel traps for its hero, all of which have firmly shut before the film is half over, though Scorsese's grandstanding style and Schrader's Bressonian pretensions continue to push for moments of religious transcendence. What is locked tightest into the contradiction, and most disturbingly into the film, is a confusion between objective and subjective viewpoints. . . . [A] strong streak of misogyny and racist sentiment (women are principally identified by Travis with betrayal; blacks with the irredeemable otherness and corruption of the city) often seems to be floating through the film, unattached to the protagonist. In one sequence, however, the two viewpoints are neatly crystallised as subjective effect flows from objective (not to say ironically distanced) scene-setting. Immediately after he makes his stormy break with Betsy, Travis is seen stopping with a passenger at an address, where the latter (played by Scorsese himself) proceeds to rant about his wife and the black man she is with in an upstairs window, insisting that Travis look, while the camera almost reluctantly pans up the building until it locks on to the window where the two icons of the hero's paranoid imaginings are shadowily visible. But for the most part, the subjective portions of the film remain pyrotechnical effects, Scorsese playing true to the purgatory of his character's mind by painting New York as a garish, otherworldly landscape, while objectively little is said about Travis' mental state. . . . One can sense Scorsese trying to forge a connection between . . . disparate episodes, to create a context like the vicious circles of family, religion and criminal code in *Mean Streets,* or the emotional entanglements of *Alice* which would sustain his characters. But Travis remains a rather desperately willed figure, and various iconography (the candles that blaze devotionally in Iris' room during her first conversation with Travis), parallels (between Betsy and Iris), and continuities (the Bressonian play with hands) stay persistently on the surface. Most crippling is the ending, in which the macho movie cliché of the heroine who returns to the hero once his capacity for purgative violence has been revealed is crossed with the film's vaguest gesture of empathy with Travis. Now at peace with his most destructive instincts, he simply disappears into another hallucinogenic light and colour painting of the New York streets. (p. 201)

Richard Combs, "'Taxi Driver'," in Monthly Film Bulletin (copyright © The British Film Institute, 1976), Vol. 43, No. 512, September, 1976, pp. 200-01.

## TOM MILNE

Scorsese's first feature was premiered at the Chicago Film Festival in 1967 under the title of *I Call First*. To increase the film's chances of distribution, Scorsese was persuaded to shoot a nude fantasy scene, and with this sequence added, *I Call First* was released and the title later changed to *Who's That Knocking at My Door*. Although at first glance this added sequence seems to dovetail quite neatly into the film, it is in fact almost disastrously disruptive for two reasons. First, it suggests that J. R.'s problem is that he wants to screw girls but can't because of his Catholic brainwashing, whereas Scorsese is really making a subtler point about the broads that can be screwed and the virgins that can be married. Now coming immediately after the nude sequence's interpolated implications of erotic frustration, the marvellously tender and absurd scene where J. R. toils upward through a pale and wintry forest, finally to stand like Cortez on the crest of the hill discovering undreamed-of vistas of unspoiled nature beyond, has acquired Freudian connotations which obscure the original point: tender in his aspiration, absurd in his magniloquent naiveté, it is an exact parallel to the doomed ingenuousness of his confident quest for an ideal purity. Secondly, by adding pointless complication, this interpolation of an undoubted fantasy in a film which is already playing tentatively with time and memory, raises totally unnecessary doubts and hesitations as one watches the film. . . . In point of fact, *Who's That Knocking at My Door* is a disarmingly straightforward film: a rough draft for *Mean Streets* in which Scorsese spells out his guidelines, his symbols and his meanings without ever quite welding them into an imaginative whole. . . . The main problem with the film, despite its frequent brilliance (Scorsese's talent is abundantly in evidence already) is that it really has two heroes—incipient hoodlum and aspiring saint. Not until *Mean Street* . . . was Scorsese able to bring the two together in the image of a man thirsting for purity as he burned in hell.

Tom Milne, "'Who's That Knocking at My Door'," in Monthly Film Bulletin (copyright © The British Film Institute, 1976), Vol. 43, No. 512, September, 1976, p. 203.

## VINCENT CANBY

[There are ritualized conceits in ] **"New York, New York,"** Martin Scorsese's elaborate, ponderous salute to Hollywood movies of the 1940's and early 50's in the form of a backstage musical of the period. (p. 70)

The big-band sounds are right, as are the sets and costumes and especially the movie conventions. **"New York, New York"** knowingly embraces a narrative line as formal and strict in its way as the shape of a sonnet. Even the sets are meant to look like back-lot sets, not the real world. . . .

Yet, after one has appreciated the scholarship for about an hour or so . . . one begins to wonder what Mr. Scorsese and his writers are up to. **"New York, New York"** is not a "parody," but the original genre is really not interesting enough to have had all of this attention to detail spent on it. It's not that the movie runs out of steam long before it has gone on for two hours and 33 minutes, but that we have figured it out and become increasingly dumbfounded. Why should a man of Mr. Scorsese's talent . . . be giving us what amounts to no more than a film buff's essay on a pop-film form that was never, at any point in film history, of the first freshness?

Even more disturbing is the movie's lack of feeling for the genuine feelings that those old movies were meant to inspire. . . .

"New York, New York" is not a disaster of the order of Peter Bogdanovich's "At Long Last Love." . . . Yet, **"New York, New York"** is a somehow more painful movie, being nervy and smug. (p. 71)

*Vincent Canby, "Nostalgic Doings," in* The New York Times *(© 1977 by The New York Times Company; reprinted by permission), June 23, 1977 (and reprinted in* The New York Times Film Reviews: 1977-1978, *The New York Times Company & Arno Press, 1979, pp. 70-1).*

## TOM MILNE

*New York, New York* looks at first glance like a tolerably successful pastiche, full of wayward longueurs that perversely assert themselves as being among its major pleasures. On reflection, one realises that Scorsese has simply inverted the basic premises of the musical, a move that requires a certain adjustment in the spectator. The protracted opening sequence (after a brief evocation of the V-J Day celebrations in Times Square), for instance, is entirely concerned with Jimmy Doyle's tortuously ingenious attempts, after seeing his pick-up routine rejected by two other girls, to deny Francine the privilege of saying no. Linguistically and dramatically speaking, it should outstay its welcome; but the peculiar pleasure of the sequence is that, being structured musically in a sort of rondo form (theme, variation, return), it assumes the role that would normally be played by a ballad in stating the hero's initial attraction to . . . the heroine. . . . Several other dramatic (i.e. non-musical) scenes emerge, in an analogous sense, as musical numbers, formally choreographed rather than dramatically staged. . . . In consciously quoting the Hollywood musical, these scenes have a little fun with its clichés: in making his last-minute dash for the train, Jimmy leaves it a little too late, and is last seen on the platform, forlornly trying to hold back the already departing train; and when he knocks up the J.P., he inadvertently breaks a pane of glass in the door, starting the proceedings off on a distinctly ominous note. The effect, rather than comic, is strangely moving; as though these hapless misquotations acknowledged that a whole world of simplicity and security could never be recaptured. Contrariwise, the musical numbers in the film are used to carry its entire burden of plot, characterisation and conflict. Almost invariably seen fragmented in rehearsal, or as snatches of performance staged without the usual production values or choreographic embellishments . . . , they are neither elaborate enough nor inventive enough to claim status as 'numbers'; their function is rather to elucidate the character tensions between the protagonists . . . , and to chart their inevitable progress to marital breakdown. Struggling, typically of a Scorsese hero, to escape a private hell, Jimmy Doyle is also typically unable to articulate the resentments he is only obscurely aware of and which thereby reinforce the vicious circle in which he is trapped: it is the music they want to make and the music they have to make which defines the exact nature of the rift between Jimmy and Francine. It is unfortunate that, in perhaps the one real weakness of the film, this dramatic role played by the music is undercut by the fact that the jazz (or bebop) Jimmy plays by choice is louder but otherwise only barely distinguishable from the sweeter swing he despises. On the other hand, this lapse may possibly be intentional, since the film is on the one hand about little romantic heartbreaks rather than grand tragic passions, and on the other about artistic trends that find their fulfilment in success rather than about creative discoveries that endure. The final reconciliation, at all events, is effected with

magnificent appropriateness through the final "New York, New York" number. . . . [It] not only brings the hitherto disparate musical and dramatic elements together for the first time, it not only rings out as the "major chord" Jimmy talks about (a reconciliation in which the important things in life assume their proper order and relation to each other), it also brings a new note to the film: the unmistakable, triumphant call of the Broadway musical which might be said (trend-wise, at least) to have driven, with *Oklahoma!*, one of the first nails into the coffin of the Big Band sound. (p. 195)

*Tom Milne, "'New York, New York',"* in Monthly Film Bulletin *(copyright © The British Film Institute, 1977), Vol. 44, No. 524, September, 1977, pp. 194-95.*

## RICHARD COMBS

If there is one central paradox to Martin Scorsese's movies, it must be their knack for harnessing a single-minded intensity of purpose to an instinct for charging off in a variety of directions. Such contradictory energy is also what makes his protagonists run; and on his home ground, in a Little Italy suffused with the pain of ruling passions running up blind alleys in *Mean Streets,* Scorsese is the peerless spokesman for a world where hell-raising is the only escape from some hell-bent obsession of temperament or ambition.

But, as indicated by the hesitant sketch of *Who's That Knocking at My Door* and the sterile steel trap of *Taxi Driver*—the before and after of *Mean Streets*—Scorsese may be a director with only one 'personal' movie to make and, on the other hand, too much talent and too little control to play the Hollywood genre game. . . .

With *New York, New York* . . . Scorsese has, if anything, taken on a slice of Hollywood—the showbiz musical—even more insulated by tradition and upholstery, and has turned out a craftier pastiche and something quite brilliant in the way of recreation. . . . Scorsese has made over a Hollywood staple in a wholly original way, not so much adapting the musical as invading it like some long-abandoned relic, turning many of its salient features inside out and generally confounding audience expectations with every second scene.

In story and character, *New York, New York* is an efficient blend of old-style Hollywood and street-smart Scorsese. . . .

Situated in fantasy, Jimmy Doyle . . . becomes uniquely blessed among Scorsese heroes—he is allowed to achieve his ambition, the fulfilment of what he calls the 'major chord', when you have everything in life that you want. But Scorsese plays the figure not as fantasy but as a character streaked by the same self-destructive fanaticism, unwavering drive and crippling ambivalence as any of his street punks on the make—and compresses the psychology of the character not into the predictable narrative of breakdown and break-up, but most tightly into the scenes where one most expects relaxation, i.e. the musical numbers. There is, for the first two-thirds of the film, very little sense of 'performance' about these numbers and considerable emphasis on the emotional tensions they submerge, diffuse or expose. . . .

It is the narrative sections between [the] numbers, handled somewhat elliptically and often as simple montage, that now have the quality of interludes, of 'shticks' for playing out variations on themes established elsewhere. . . .

In similar spirit, the pastiches of other musicals never acquire their expected weight, but serve simply to indicate where Scorsese has situated his film in relation to the musical tradition. If the overall theme has to do with the disappearance of the Big Band sound of the 40s and the emergence of 50s 'bebop', then Scorsese seems to be indicating that even more, for the 70s, the musicals of the 40s and 50s are gone beyond recall. (p. 252)

With its finale, *New York, New York* comes slam up to date, in spirit at least, when the quality of performance comes flooding back in Francine's rendition of the title number, and the film gives birth, as it were, to the style of grandstanding, biographical, star-is-made musical. . . . The passing of the old-fashioned, communal, let's-put-on-a-show type of musical . . . in favour of such individualistic celebrations is most cynically indicated, perhaps, in a remark by Jimmy, when he returns to playing in Harlem jazz clubs and is asked why he had slipped from sight for so long, and he replies that he had just been playing with bad musicians.

Scorsese delivers all this, both celebration and critique, in fine, airy style—his camera frequently serving the function of the bouncing ball that used to appear with on-screen song lyrics, indicating exactly where the emphasis should go. Crane shots float breezily above the big bands performing at the opening victory ball, while the scattered, broken scenes of Jimmy and Francine in rehearsal and on stage are filmed with a close-up intensity. Most rewardingly, the film seems to have effected a kind of opening-out—allowing Scorsese to tackle 'given' material more experimentally than in, and to pursue characteristic extremes of emotion without the over determined mechanisms of *Taxi Driver*. (pp. 252-53)

> Richard Combs, "Film Reviews: 'New York, New York'," in Sight and Sound *(copyright © 1977 by The British Film Institute), Vol. 46, No. 4, Autumn, 1977, pp. 252-53.*

## RICHARD COMBS

[Given *The Last Waltz*'s] title and subject, and Scorsese's tendency to work in an apocalyptic register, an air of *Götterdämmerung* hangs over *The Last Waltz*. This is the end of an era in popular music, one apostrophised finally by [Robbie] Robertson when he marvels that he and The Band have spent sixteen years on the road, quails before the prospect of pushing their luck any further, and then enumerates the performers, from Hank Williams through Janis Joplin to Elvis Presley, who have given their lives to the tradition. But more than this, the film is a collage of two decades of beginnings and endings, a two-hour whistle stop tour across the map of pop music, its sense of the history of its subject peculiarly internalised so that, in Scorsese's words, 'there's connective sense, but not really in terms of one thing leading to another; it makes spiritual sense.'

Such a notion of order, of course, is largely a matter of imposing private meanings on the public event. And this is the paradox on which *The Last Waltz* turns, in more than one direction. The emotional significance of the music for Scorsese, the selection of numbers he has made from the seven-hour concert featuring not only The Band but a galaxy of guests, the progression through the varieties of country, blues and rock'n'roll music, establish this as one of his most personal films. Consequently—yet unexpectedly, given the *cinéma vérité* tradition of concert films from [Michael Wadleigh's]

*Woodstock* through [D. A. Pennebaker's] *Monterey Pop* to its most consciously meditated and manipulated form in [Albert and David Maysles's] *Gimme Shelter*—the style he has chosen seems almost deliberately to remove the concert from the public domain and treat it as original feature material. . . .

In addition, three numbers were recorded after the event inside a studio. The florid camera movement bestowed on 'Evangeline' serves to underline its more lyrical quality and also perhaps its folk pedigree in the descent of rock music. The concluding number, 'The Last Waltz', a tribute to The Band, caps the rococo setting of the Winterland with further artifice as the camera, in one long caressing movement, pulls away from the group on their darkened sound stage and retreats down a lane of lights. . . .

Further distinguishing it from other film testaments to the rock culture of the 60s and early 70s, *The Last Waltz* has little room for its audience, except as a dimly perceived, surging mass in one or two shots. Scorsese's picture of a generation and its changes is concentrated entirely on the style of its performers, and in this respect is the most powerful, musically intense of all the concert record films. That the developments related in the course of *The Last Waltz*—cued by some intercut discussions between Scorsese and the members of The Band—all seem to occur at flashpoints of personal, musical and political history, fully expressed only in the exploding performances on stage, is, finally, both its strength and its weakness. The snatches of reminiscence from The Band. . . . At other times, a little augmentation might have prevented the historical moments being might have prevented the historical moments being swamped by their emotional associations: 'on the road' in itself is such a culturally specific concept that it seems rather skimped here in The Band's brief anecdotes about their hard first eight years and the presence of Lawrence Ferlinghetti reading a parody version of the Lord's Prayer.

But at its best the style of *The Last Waltz,* at once kaleidoscopic and concentrated, discursive and fixated, distils more about its subject and its times (and about its maker and his obsessions) than the impressionism of *cinéma vérité*. Before the credits, the film opens on an isolated sequence of a group of individuals playing pool: the game, says one, is called cut-throat, and the object is to keep your balls on the table while knocking everyone else's off. And this odd recall of the setting, ambience and social mechanisms of *Mean Streets* is later obliquely 'placed' by one of the concert guests who reads what she calls a one-line poem from the 50s, 'Get your cut throat off my knife.' When Scorsese cuts from Muddy Waters and the blues song 'Mannish Boy' to a sleek performance from Eric Clapton, the connection is pointed by a previous discussion with Levon Helm, who talks of the area around Memphis as the home of country, blues and blue grass performers, and in reply to the question, 'What's killed them?' says 'Rock 'n' roll'. . . .

[It] is only towards the end, when The Band becomes once more a backing group for Bob Dylan—who is summoned, like some demon presence, by a camera panning down from the lights and decorations on to a huge close-up of his illuminated hat—that one has a proper sense of the film (so smooth yet electrifyingly integrated is Scorsese's coverage) as the record of a live event. For the first time, the on-stage hesitations and consultations between numbers are included before the climactic, communal rendition of 'I Shall Be Released' and Robertson's final, voice-over observations on the road. The real ending, however, seems to have come a little before, in a conversation recorded between Scorsese and The Band in their retreat, an ex-bordello called The Shangri-la. Here, amid a decor congruent both with the decadent trimmings of the Winterland and an archetypal Scorsese setting, the director obtains an answer, if not to his first question then to the one that might have followed it, when one of the group sums up what he is doing now 'The Last Waltz' is over: 'Just making music, man, trying to stay busy.'

Richard Combs, "'The Last Waltz'," *in* Sight and Sound *(copyright © 1978 by The British Film Institute), Vol. 47, No. 2, Spring, 1978, p. 125.*

## J. HOBERMAN

[*Italianamerican*] is funny and touching. It's richer than a less personal documentary would have been, supplementing well [Scorsese's] hallucinated depiction of the mean streets outside.

In a sense, *Italianamerican* . . . is a home movie in reverse, with the grown child turning the camera on parents or parental figures. But Scorsese is fortunate: his progenitors are a delight. Prompted by his jumpy, occasionally bemused, presence at the edge of the frame, they recount their own parents' tales of the old country, show Instamatics . . . made during a trip back there, and detail their childhoods on the mythic Lower East Side. . . .

The film is interspersed with family photographs and street footage of 50 or 60 years ago, but an equally evocative visual element is the living room where most of the interview takes place. . . .

Scorsese intercuts this "only in America" setting with his mother's running commentary on her special sauce as she prepares it in the kitchen. For the most part, the elder Scorseses' enjoyment of the limelight is equaled by their son's pride in being able to give it to them. Through editing or will power, he's able to keep the conversation from focusing on their prize joint creation—himself. . . .

Although the pleasure that the family takes in each other's company is truly infectious, Scorsese ends the film on a slightly darker note. As the crew starts breaking down the lights, Mrs. Scorsese expresses a (how long suppressed?) desire to start vacuuming and get her apartment back in order. "Is he still taking this?" she asks in mock annoyance with a gesture toward the camera. "I'll murder you, you won't get out of this house alive!" It's a thought one suspects that also may have crossed Scorsese's mind while growing up there.

J. Hoberman, "There's No Place Like Home Movies" *(reprinted by permission of* The Village Voice *and the author; copyright © The Village Voice, Inc., 1978), in* The Village Voice, *Vol. XXIII, No. 17, April 24, 1978, p. 48.**

## TERRY CURTIS FOX

*The Last Waltz* was not just work; it was a special kind of anchor. [Marty Scorsese's] love affair with rock and roll, his commitment to music as a form, is at least as deep and abiding as his love and commitment to film. He has always *used* music in his films, knowing just what the kid would listen to in *Alice Doesn't Live Here Anymore,* manipulating the track of *Taxi Driver* with disc-jockey ease. The cultural conflict in *Mean Streets* is most directly expressed as a war between two styles of music, Italian and rock. . . .

*The Last Waltz* was conceived as "an opera." . . . If Scorsese's fiction films have musical structure, then *The Last Waltz,* with its meticulous script and preplanned camera angles, was constructed in the same manner as his narratives.

Unlike most rock-concert pictures, *The Last Waltz* is an extremely formal film. Coming off *New York, New York,* Marty shot the movie with the same dark, totally interior look. This is a movie in which daylight is never seen, in which the world is totally artificial, limited to stages and studios. . . .

The result is a movie that is about music and musicians, about living the life of rock and roll. In addition to the concert footage, Marty interspersed three studio-shot numbers, which gave him a chance to practice his pyrotechnics, as well as his own interviews with members of the Band, which give the film its rough balance. (p. 41)

Marty, who may be right when he calls himself "the world's worst interviewer," functions best as a documentarian when dealing with subjects he knows intimately.

It is not just that Scorsese knew where his cameras could go but he was not embarrassed to let unkind moments intrude upon the general celebration. . . . At the same time, while this is ostensibly a film about the Band, Scorsese's editing makes no bones about how much a Dylan event it becomes the moment the singer walks on stage. Everything else disappears behind his presence, and Scorsese, despite his friendships and commitments, does nothing to hide or minimalize this effect. It is not merely the best rock-concert movie ever made; it is as intensely personal as anything Scorsese has done.

Late in the film's editing, . . . Scorsese placed the footage of the Band's last song—. . . "Don't Do It"—at the beginning of the film. The concert thus becomes a flashback, while the interviews and studio shots are a meditation on the half-life of collective efforts and the weariness 16 years of road life can bring. Marty says the entire movie is about "Stage Fright," but a more appropriate metaphor is suggested when the Band, obviously stoned, attempts "Give Me That Old Time Religion." The improvised version is at once completely a Band song in its modalities, harmonics, and instrumental breaks, and a lethargic failure, falling apart before anyone can finish. "It's not like it used to be," someone says, and that seems to be the point of the film. Having become the Band, the members are, at the point of breaking apart, undefined by their success. They are no longer able to produce the work that sustained them. (p. 43)

Terry Curtis Fox, "Martin Scorsese's Elegy for a Big-Time Band" *(reprinted by permission of* The Village Voice *and the author; copyright © The Village Voice, Inc., 1978), in* The Village Voice, *Vol. XXIII, No. 22, May 29, 1978, pp. 41, 43.*

## JAMES MONACO

None of the new filmmakers has created as strong a public persona as Martin Scorsese. Hunted, haunted, asthmatic, diminutive, darkly bearded, a victim of religious nightmares, a mass of raging anxieties, Scorsese as we know him from interviews and photographs makes Paul Schrader, his only rival in film-noir paranoia, look by comparison like a happily adjusted Midwestern businessman. In fact, Scorsese's real success is to have made films at all. Each new project brings with it a baggage of stories about the director's agonies. The movies—

even the ones with relatively pleasant atmospheres—seem rooted in this pain.

Perhaps this suffering need not be in vain: within Scorsese there may lie an Italian-American Bergman waiting for the right moment to show himself. Bergman himself made a dozen unremarkable films before he found the necessary key of objectivity to turn his own nightmares into art. Scorsese may, too. He's already shown evidence that he can in *Who's That Knocking at My Door?* and *Mean Streets*. But right now, he remains the most brilliant of the New Hollywood's disappointments, seemingly torn between two recurrent, obsessive dreams: his own childhood in New York's Little Italy, whose basic components were a malevolent Church and a (to him) frightening ethic of machismo, and the opiates that Hollywood offered as an alternative to that disturbing reality. When he sticks to the earlier set of compulsions, he produces brilliant, if slightly muddled, images of a complex reality. When he shifts to the later set, as he seems increasingly to feel it necessary to do, the results are at best disappointing. (pp. 150-51)

When it was released, *Alice Doesn't Live Here Anymore* was hailed as a feminist classic by a number of major critics. . . . This film about women was designed to be very far removed from the macho world of *Mean Streets*. Its failure is that it really isn't. It's a hip Doris Day film. In fact, Alice actually has less freedom, fewer opportunities, and a markedly weaker character than her professional-virgin predecessor had in the fifties. She makes no conscious decision to hit the road, she's forced into it when her husband dies. . . . [The director and screenwriter] never allow her any success on the road. They do let her have a few interesting friendships with women, which form the heart of the film, but it's inevitable that she will sink back down into a complacent marriage before the film ends. The most dramatic sequences involve the macho character of Ben . . . , not the women's relationships. Alice is after all a klutz. It's rather charming in an old-fashioned way that she actually thinks to have a career of her own, such as it is, and it's interesting that she has a buddy-buddy relationship with her son, but after all she's really a dependent woman.

The filmmakers seem to think that they actually made a feminist film. They may have started out to do so. But *Alice* is more regressively chauvinist than a Russ Meyer softcore B simply because it pretends to be something it's not. (pp. 155-56)

*Taxi Driver* (1976) fails in similar ways. It was considered, like *Alice,* a great gamble. . . . Within the cramped Hollywood context of the seventies, perhaps it was. But it turned out to be an even greater critical and financial success than *Alice*. (p. 157)

*Taxi Driver* is a perfect match of the paranoid talents of writer Paul Schrader and director Scorsese. . . . It's an attempt to make a late-forties film noir more than twenty-five years later. At least on the film-buff level, it succeeds in recapturing that atmosphere. . . . Once again, Scorsese gets great performances from his cast. . . . He knows this mood, and has practiced with it in *Mean Streets,* so he's able to bathe the film in an effective wash of red and black fear.

The problem, and it is insurmountable, is that it is not 1948 anymore. It hasn't been for quite a while. So what's a film noir doing at a time like this? Mainly turning back the clock politically and artistically. . . . Scorsese's naked city is almost a joke: at best it's quaint. . . . Travis Bickle is certainly a magnificent construction within the crooked context of the film,

but Scorsese and Schrader don't give us a point of view from which to get a handle on him. (pp. 157-58)

[Despite] the inherent interest in *The Last Waltz*—the music, the memories of the sixties . . .—and despite the admirable technical quality, there's a certain pretension to the film we wish weren't there. Scorsese himself does *not* come across as a star and his interview questions are rather beside the point; the studio numbers are superfluous, they break the rhythm of the concert. Once again, Scorsese's reach has exceeded his grasp, but only by a thin margin this time. Boiled down to pure concert performance, *The Last Waltz* would be a perfectly cut gem of a film.

There's no doubt Martin Scorsese is an exceptionally interesting and imaginative director, but for more than five years now he's been setting self-destructive traps for himself, then stepping smartly right into them. He's capable of a great deal more, one surmises. In 1974 he shot a forty-eight-minute essay . . . called *Italianamerican*. Basically a documentary visit with his parents, it had many of the qualities missing from the feature films he has made since *Mean Streets*. The people weren't characters, they were people. The film wasn't a self-conscious parody of movies dead and gone, but honest and straightforward. Scorsese spoke for himself rather than hiding behind the pretentiously anxious film-noir mask. *Italianamerican* was relaxed, broadly humorous, not excessively ambitious, direct.

Marty should return to his roots and come home. (p. 161)

*James Monaco, "The Whiz Kids," in his* American Film Now: The People, the Power, the Money, the Movies *(copyright © 1979 by James Monaco; reprinted by arrangement with The New American Library, Inc., New York), Oxford University Press, New York, 1979, pp. 139-84.*\*

**FRANK DEFORD**

The violence in *Raging Bull* is ghastly and overdone. A nose crunches, broken for us to hear close up; copious amounts of blood gush out of orifices and gashes, drenching the ringside swells. To what purpose? There are, it seems to me, three possible motives for such displays of brutality. First, the obvious one: to exploit the worst in boxing and in us. Second, the reverse: to expose this barbaric exercise, drum up the reformers and hasten its abolition from the 20th century. Or third: as a dramatic device to inform us about the characters.

Alas, in *Raging Bull,* the spectacle of exaggerated violence is put to no use whatsoever. It is introduced in the same way the director of a skin flick every so often tosses in another bedroom adventure just because it's a skin flick. To me, that is asexual, just as *Raging Bull* is, ultimately, a-athletic, and amoral as well. This is the story of a boxer, Jake LaMotta—but what is he to boxing or boxing to him? About all the film tells us about LaMotta the middleweight is that, given his druthers, he would rather not give up sex and food before a fight. LaMotta might just as well be a bus driver.

As a man, he is revealed as scum. . . . But then, none of the characters around him possesses redeeming qualities, either. As a consequence, nothing changes and the film—like a lopsided fight—could be stopped at any point without altering the outcome.

Yet what an extraordinary piece of work is *Raging Bull*. Has any movie ever so utterly lacked soul and yet been so rewarding? The texture of the script . . . is never creased. The language is so uncannily correct that no matter how filthy the dialogue, it's never profane in spirit. . . .

Why Scorsese wanted to saddle himself with a film portraying a despicable human is all the more baffling because the director's other instincts are so correct. Scorsese's touches are everywhere. What this man does with kitchens! There was an America that existed in kitchens, that dealt with life from out of kitchens. Scorsese has that down pat, and he doesn't need authentic costumes and oldies-but-goodies playing in the background to pull it off. He also has grasped the precise pecking order of that world: how people confronted one another, how they talked, when they backed off, where they stood.

It is no mean accomplishment to capture interrelationships of a lost subculture, but unfortunately, Jake the person never gets off the dime. So while Scorsese's film is an achievement, it could've been much more. Understand, *Raging Bull* doesn't lose. It just never gets the shot it deserves at the champeenship. It remains a glorious contender.

> Frank Deford, "Raging Bull': Almost a Champeen,"
> in Sports Illustrated (© 1980 Time Inc.), Vol. 53,
> No. 23, December 1, 1980, p. 87.

### STANLEY KAUFFMANN

Seeing Martin Scorsese's [*Raging Bull*] is like visiting a human zoo. That's certainly not to say that it's dull: good zoos are not dull. But the life we watch is stripped to elemental drives, with just enough décor of complexity—especially the heraldry of Catholicism—to underscore how elemental it basically is.

Scorsese specializes in the primitive aspects of urban life, with an emphasis on the colors and conflicts of Italian-Americans. American films have developed a latter-day line in this vein. . . . Most Italian-Americans may very understandably be tired of this canted concentration on gutter and crime, but they had better brace themselves: because here it is again and—which may irritate them further—done better than ever, done excellently. Scorsese has filmed the life of the boxer Jake La Motta, his rises and falls and eventual retirement, and this time Scorsese's work is purged of heavy symbolism, of film-school display, of facile portent. His directing is imaginative but controlled; egregious mannerisms have coalesced and evolved into a strong style. Some of *Raging Bull* is shocking, but all of it is irresistible. (p. 26)

[Most] cheering is Scorsese's growth. Little Italy, the ceaseless conflict between the support and the restrictions of Catholicism, the alliances and counteralliances of family and of the Mafia are still his home ground. He tells us in the sequence under the opening credits that he is dealing with provenance and struggle: while La Motta—in slow motion—prances around a ring in a robe, warming up, the sound-track lays on the "Intermezzo" from *Cavalleria Rusticana*. It's a splendid *fixing* of the film.

Contradictorily Scorsese has both purged and complicated his filmmaking. *Taxi Driver* was better made than *Mean Streets* . . . and *Raging Bull* is a huge leap. He is still avid to move film all the time, eager to energize his screen, but instead of his former frantic cutting from long shots to closeups and back, with some reverse shots thrown in, he now more subtly cuts to shots in which the camera is already moving forward slowly. In the fight sequences, he sometimes creates the effect of putting the camera in a glove, inside a battered head, and he always keeps prime the feeling of complete physical collision. . . .

He has solved the visual problem of showing many fights; sometimes he varies with slow motion, sometimes with a series of stills, sometimes with isolated successive frames like the ones of astronauts on the moon. Never does he let us anticipate wearily that there are more fights to come; he never lets the matter get near tedium, and he never uses trickery that distracts. These sequences are legitimate and interesting variations, like a good composer's variations on a theme.

There are some bumps in the story line, and they may be connected with Scorsese's filmmaking process rather than the script. . . . Scorsese fell so in love with the making of this film, I think, with the actual shooting of scenes and sequences . . . that he found himself with more of a jigsaw to assemble in the editing room than do most directors. What holds this picture together more than its story line is its stylistic consistency, and style here means more than cinematic syntax, it means fire and personality. . . .

[One] laurel that must rest on Scorsese's head alone is praise for the acting—that is, for the casting and for the guidance of the actors. Many scenes are played in a very low key, not as patent Paul-Muni preparations for outbursts but to draw us into privacies, to take us beneath the skin. . . .

Some verses from John IX, 24-26, are appended at the end, but I don't grasp their relevance. More, I think it may be misguided to try to crystallize what the film is "about." Attempts have already been made to explain La Motta's character as reactive to the Italian-American atmosphere, but the script wouldn't have to be much different fundamentally if the protagonist were a black or an Irish Catholic or a Jew. La Motta is to be taken as given, a chunk of temperament like a character in a medieval morality play.

Finally *Raging Bull* is "about" what we see and hear, elevating its rather familiar materials, through conviction and the gush of life. After the socio-psychological explanations have limped on, this film, like some . . . good art works, is finally "about" the fact that it incontrovertibly exists and, by existing, moves us.

> Stanley Kauffmann, "Look Back in Anger" (re-
> printed by permission of Brandt & Brandt Literary
> Agents, Inc.; copyright © 1980 by Stanley Kauff-
> mann), in The New Republic, Vol. 183, No. 23,
> December 6, 1980, pp. 26-7.

### PAULINE KAEL

At first, we may think that we're going to find out what makes Jake La Motta's life special and why ["**Raging Bull**" has been] made about him. But as the picture dives in and out of La Motta's life, with a few minutes of each of his big fights . . . , it becomes clear that Scorsese isn't concerned with how La Motta got where he did, or what, specifically, happened to him. Scorsese gives us exact details of the Bronx Italian neighborhoods of the forties—everything is sharp, realistic, lived-in. But he doesn't give us specific insights into La Motta. . . .

"**Raging Bull**" isn't a biographical film about a fighter's rise and fall; it's a biography of the genre of prizefight films. Scorsese loves the visual effects and the powerful melodramatic moments of movies such as [Renée Daalder's] "Body and Soul," [Robert Wise's] "The Set-Up," and [Rouben Mamoulian's] "Golden Boy." He makes this movie out of remembered high points, leaping from one to another. . . .

Scorsese appears to be trying to purify the characters of forties movies to universalize them. Vickie is an icon—a big, lacquered virgin-doll of the forties. . . . Sitting at the edge of a swimming pool, . . . Vickie is a *Life* cover girl of the war years. (p. 217)

Scorsese is also trying to purify forties style by using the conventions in new ways. If you look at forties movies now, the clichés . . . may seem like fun, and it's easy to see why Scorsese is drawn to them. But when he reproduces them, he reproduces the mechanical quality they once had, and the fun goes out of them. The cardinal rule of forties-studio style was that the scenes had to be shaped to pay off. Scorsese isn't interested in payoffs; it's something else—a modernist effect that's like a gray-out. . . . Scorsese's continuity with forties movies is in the texture—the studio artificiality that he makes sensuous, thick, viscous; there are layers of rage and animosity in almost every sequence.

"**Raging Bull**" isn't just a biography of a genre; it's also about movies and about violence, it's about gritty visual rhythm, . . . it's about the two "Godfather" pictures. . . . (p. 219)

The picture seems to be saying that in order to become champ, Jake La Motta had to be mean, obsessive, crazy. But you can't be sure, and the way the story is told Jake's life pattern doesn't make much sense. (p. 220)

At the end, before going onstage for his public reading, Jake recites [Marlon] Brando's back-of-the-taxi speech from "On the Waterfront" while looking in his dressing-room mirror. Scorsese is trying to outdo everything great, even the scene of [Travis] talking to himself in the mirror in "**Taxi Driver**." What does it mean to have La Motta deliver this lament that he could have been a contender instead of a bum when it's perfectly clear that La Motta is both a champ *and* a bum? . . . The whole picture has been made looking in a mirror, self-consciously. It takes a while to grasp that La Motta is being used as *the* fighter, a representative tormented man in a killer's body. . . . It's all metaphors: the animal man attempting to escape his destiny. When Jake, in jail on a morals charge, bangs his head and his fists against the stone walls of his cell and, sobbing in frustration, cries out, "Why? Why? Why? It's so f--king stupid! I'm not an animal!," it's the ultimate metaphor for the whole film.

The tragedy in Scorsese's struggles with the material in both "**New York, New York**" and "**Raging Bull**" is that he *is* a great director when he doesn't press so hard at it, when he doesn't suffer so much. He's got moviemaking and the Church mixed up together; he's trying to be the saint of cinema. And he turns Jake's life into a ritual of suffering. (pp. 220-22)

Scorsese likes movies that aren't covered in sentimental frosting—that put the surliness and killing and meanness right up front. But "**Raging Bull**" has the air of saying something important. . . . By making a movie that is *all* guilty pleasures, he has forged a new sentimentality. "**Raging Bull**" is about a character he loves too much; it's about everything he loves too much. It's the kind of movie that many men must fantasize about: their macho worst-dream movie.

Scorsese is saying that he accepts totally, that he makes no moral judgment. . . . Scorsese doesn't care about the rhythm and balance of fighters' bodies. There's no dancing for these fighters, and very little boxing. What Scorsese concentrates on is punishment given and received. He turns the lowdown effects he likes into highbrow flash reeking of religious symbolism.

You're aware of the camera positions and of the images held for admiration; you're conscious of the pop and hiss of the newsmen's cameras and the amplified sound of the blows—the sound of pain. Scorsese wants his B-movie seaminess and spiritual meaning, too. He wants a disreputable, low-life protagonist; then he suggests that this man is close to God, because he is God's animal.

By removing the specifics or blurring them, Scorsese doesn't produce universals—he produces banality. What we get is full of capitals: A Man Fights, A Man Loses Everything, A Man Bangs His Head Against the Wall. Scorsese is putting his unmediated obsessions on the screen, trying to turn raw, pulp power into art by removing it from the particulars of observation and narrative. He loses the low-life entertainment values of prizefight films; he aestheticizes pulp and kills it. "**Raging Bull**" is tabloid grand opera. (pp. 222, 225)

*Pauline Kael, "Religious Pulp, or the Incredible Hulk," in* The New Yorker *(© 1980 by The New Yorker Magazine, Inc.), Vol. LVI, No. 42, December 8, 1980, pp. 217-18, 220, 222, 225.*

### ROBERT PHILLIP KOLKER

[Scorsese] does not create narratives that are easily assimilable. The formal structure of his work is never completely at the service of the viewer or of the story it is creating. There is an unashamed self-consciousness in his work and a sense of kinetic energy that sometimes threatens to overtake both viewer and story, but always provides a commentary upon the viewer's experience and prevents him or her from easily slipping into a series of narrative events. (pp. 207-08)

Scorsese is interested in the psychological manifestations of individuals who are representative either of a class or of a certain ideological grouping; he is concerned with their relationships to each other or to an antagonistic environment. Scorsese's films involve antagonism and struggle, and constant movement, even if that movement is within a tightly circumscribed area that has no exit. . . . [There] is no triumph for his characters. With the notable exception of *Alice Doesn't Live Here Anymore* all of his characters lose to their isolation or their antagonism. . . . [His] work shows a degree of stylization which eschews, for the most part, the sixties conventions of realism, defined primarily by location shooting and natural acting styles. In *New York, New York* he moves indoors entirely, depending on studio sets to achieve an expressive artificiality. But even in the preceding films, where locations are used, there is a sense that the place inhabited by the characters is structured by their perceptions and by the way we see and understand their perceptions. (p. 208)

[Scorsese's *mise-en-scène*] is never accommodating; his characters do not have homes that reflect comfort or security. The places they inhabit are places of transition, of momentary situation. . . . The Manhattan of *Taxi Driver,* the Little Italy of *Mean Streets,* even the Southwest of *Alice* are perfectly recognizable, almost too much so. The *mise-en-scène* of *Mean Streets* and *Taxi Driver* represent more than New York, a place of tough people, crowded streets, fights and whores. They represent, to borrow a notion of Roland Barthes', a New York-*ness,* a shared image of New York which has little to do with the city itself, but rather expresses what everyone, including many who live there, have decided New York should look like. At the same time . . . the New York of *Mean Streets* and *Taxi Driver* is reflective of the energy of the characters, in the former, and of the anomie of Travis Bickle, in the latter, and these qualities are communicated to us by means of the ways we are made to see the *mise-en-scène*. Our own perceptions and preconceptions merge with the filmmaker's within the narrative and are then filtered through a third point of view, that of the character or characters created by the narrative, resulting in a rather complex perspective.

The complexity is heightened by the fact that, up until *New York, New York*, and beginning again in *The Last Waltz*, Scorsese's films create a tension between two opposing cinematic forms: the documentary and the fictional. The documentary aspect offers the possibility of a seemingly objective observation of characters, places, and events; the other demands a subjectivity of point of view which in Scorsese's work is so severe that the world becomes expressionistic, a reflection of a particular state of mind. Scorsese is close to Godard in understanding the arbitrary nature of these conventions, and he freely mixes them. There is the sense in most of his work of capturing a "reality" of places and events that might exist even without his presence. Until *Taxi Driver*, he employs the hand-held camera and the rapid, oblique editing which have become associated with a "documentary" and improvisational style. His actors (particularly Robert De Niro and Harvey Keitel) create their characters with an off-handedness and an immediacy that gives the impression of unpremeditated existence. . . . When these qualities are interwoven with the subjective impressions of the world communicated to us by the ways the characters see their environment and themselves, and when Scorsese modifies the location shooting we have come to take for granted in contemporary film with artificial sets and stylized lighting, a complex perceptual structure is created that demands careful examination.

Scorsese started his commercial career with a film strongly influenced by the New Wave. *Who's That Knocking at My Door?*—a finger exercise for *Mean Streets*—is inscribed in the hand-held, jumpcut, non-transitional style that many filmmakers took from the surface of the French films of the early sixties. Its *mise-en-scène* is partly neo-realist, partly documentary, mixed with the subjectivity of perception and allusiveness that marks [Godard's] *Breathless* and [Truffaut's] *The Four Hundred Blows*. *Who's That Knocking?* is an "experimental" film in all senses: formally, it begins trying out the camera strategies, the restless, foreboding movement, that will become one of Scorsese's major formal devices. Contextually, it prepares the way for *Mean Streets*, J. R. . . . being an early version of Charlie in the later film—more of an oppressed Catholic than his later incarnation, less rooted in his environment, standing over and against New York rather than being enclosed within it as Charlie is. (pp. 209-11)

*Boxcar Bertha*, a film totally different from *Who's That Knocking?* and *Mean Streets*, still sets itself up as a link between them, if only by smoothing out the stylistic quirks apparent in the former and preparing for the consistent and assured approach of the latter. A violent film, situated in the seventies, late—*Bonnie and Clyde* mode of period evocation, it is a short, direct narrative which does little more than prepare for an enormous shoot-out at the end. . . . What Scorsese adds to the film is a further indication of his talent with the moving camera. . . . *Boxcar Bertha* is an important work not so much *by* Scorsese as *for* him; it permits him to work within the basic patterns of early-seventies film, its violence and its urgency, and to understand how those patterns can be worked together with the looser, more self-conscious and subjective elements of *Who's That Knocking?*

The integration occurs in *Mean Streets*, a film which can be seen as a "documentary" in the form of a carefully structured narrative fiction of four young men growing up on the fringes of society in New York's Little Italy, or as a subjective fiction of incomplete lives and sporadic violence in the form of a documentary of four young men in New York's Little Italy. . . . Scorsese investigates the almost incoherent street ramblings of disenfranchised men whose lives are defined by disorder, threatened by their own impulses, and, though confined by narrow geographical boundaries, paradoxically liberated by the turmoil of the bars, tenements, and streets that make up their confines. (pp. 211-13)

[None] of the characters in the film, with the possible exception of Tony, the barkeeper, has the center or sense of direction that we have come to expect from characters in conventional film fictions, and it is the purpose of the film to observe them in their randomness and as part of an unpredictable flow of events. When we see Charlie on the streets, no matter how central he may be to the narrative moment, he is composed in the frame as one figure among many, standing off-center, next to a building, other people moving by him. . . . Little violences, sporadic shootings, and fistfights punctuate the film as if they were parts of ongoing events, or as if they were moving toward some greater violence, which in fact they do. The end of the film is an explosion of gunfire and blood. (pp. 213-14)

It is difficult to accept or to understand a film that does not have emotional turmoil as its subject but merely as a referent, and chooses instead to make its own action its subject. *Mean Streets* is not about what motivates Charlie and Johnny Boy, not about what they think and feel (although these are present), but about how they see, how Charlie perceives his world and Johnny Boy reacts to it. In none of his films will Scorsese opt for the psychological realism of explained actions, defined motivations, or identifiable characters. . . . The world they inhabit is violent in the extreme, but it is a violence that is created by the characters' very attempts to make peace with it. From the point of view of the characters in *Mean Streets*, their world is perfectly ordinary, and Scorsese reflects this through the documentary nature of many of the images. But at the same time, we perceive a heightened sense of reality, a stylized, expressive presence most evident in the bar sequences, in the restless, moving camera, in the fragmentary, off-center editing.

Vitality and tension are apparent not only in the images, but in the dialogue . . . as well. Everyone in *Mean Streets* is a compulsive talker . . . , using words as an extension of themselves, a sign of their vitality. Their language is rooted in New York working-class usage, profoundly obscene and charged with movement. (pp. 217-18)

Scorsese, his co-writer [Mardik Martin], and his actors take the forms of the everyday language of a particular ethnic group, concentrate it and make it artificial, the artificiality creating the effect of the overheard and the immediate. The language of *Mean Streets* becomes a means of self- and group-definition, speaking of an unrooted life yet at the same time attempting to root that life in a community of shared rhythms and expressions. (p. 221)

*Mean Streets* does not, finally, define itself as any one thing. Although it depicts the activities of a group of disenfranchised urban ethnics, it does not attempt to comment on a social and economic class. A film about volatile emotions, it seems uninterested in analyzing emotions or baring souls. Although it deals with gangsters, it does not reflect upon or examine the generic tensions of the gangster film. . . . What it does reflect is Scorsese's (and hopefully our) delight in the film's capacity to capture a moment of communication, of interaction, and out of a series of such moments to fashion a sense of place and movement, energy and violence. It reflects Scorsese's growing control of point of view, his ability to shift from objective to subjective observation, often intermingling the two, until, in *Taxi Driver,* it is difficult to tell them apart. (pp. 221-22)

*Taxi Driver* is the inverted extension of *Mean Streets.* Where that film examines a small, isolated urban sub-community, *Taxi Driver* focuses on one isolated urban sub-individual. Where *Mean Streets* presents its characters in tenuous control of their environment, at home in their surroundings, *Taxi Driver* presents its character trapped by it, swallowed and imprisoned. More accurately, the objective-subjective points of view of *Mean Streets* that allow us to look both at and with the characters is replaced by a subjective point of view that forces us continually to see as the character sees, creating a *mise-en-scène* that expresses, above all, the obsessive vision of a madman. Finally, where *Mean Streets* celebrates urban life in its violence and its community . . . , *Taxi Driver* rigorously structures a path to violence that is separate from community, separate from the exigencies of any "normal" life, separate from any rational comprehension, but only the explosion of an individual attempting to escape from a self-made prison, an individual who, in his madness, attempts to act the role of a movie hero.

One further connection exists between the two films. *Mean Streets* is a diffuse *film noir.* Its dark, enclosed, violent urban world recalls many of the *noir* conventions. But, despite its violent end, it escapes the total bleakness of *noir* precisely because of its sense of community. Even though its characters *are* trapped, they do not evidence the loneliness, dread, and anxiety manifested in *film noir.* Again, despite the cruelty that ends the film, the bulk of it emphasizes a friendship—albeit unstable—among its characters. *Taxi Driver,* however, renders the conventions of *film noir* in an immediate, frightening manner. Its central character lives completely enclosed in a city of dreadful night; he is so removed and alone that everything he sees becomes a reflection of his own distorted perceptions. Travis Bickle . . . is the last *noir* man in the ultimate *noir* world: closed and dark, a paranoid universe of perversion, obsession, and violence. In the creation of this world, Scorsese goes to the roots of *film noir,* to certain tenets of German Expressionism that call for "a selective and creative distortion" of the world by means of which the creator of a work can represent "the complexity of the psyche" through a visual style that exposes the "object's internal life, the expression of its 'soul.'" Scorsese does want to "expose" the inner life of his character, but not to explain it. The internal life of Travis Bickle remains an enigma throughout the film. It cannot be explained, even through the most dreadful violence, and a major concern of the film is to frustrate our attempts at understanding that mind. But Scorsese is very interested in communicating to us the way a world looks as it is perceived by such a mind, and he uses "a selective and creative distortion" of perception in extraordinary ways. (pp. 223-24)

*Taxi Driver* is aware of its own formal identity. . . . The film defines its central character not in terms of social problems nor by any *a priori* ideas of noble suffering and transcendent madness, but by the ways we see the character and the way he sees himself and his surroundings. He is the climactic *noir*

figure, much more isolated and very much madder than his forebears. No cause is given for him, no understanding allowed; he stands formed by his own loneliness and trapped by his own isolation, his actions and reactions explicable only through those actions and reactions. (p. 227)

[There is] no analysis of, nor reasons given for, his behavior—none, at least, that make a great deal of rational sense. He can, perhaps, be viewed as a radically alienated urban castoff, a mutant produced by the incalculable dehumanization of our postindustrial society. . . . But the film withholds any political, social, or even psychological analysis. . . . However, after saying this, I must point out that the film does not neglect an analysis of the cultural aberrations that afflict Travis, and ourselves. Scorsese quietly, even hilariously, suggests one possible motivation for, or result of, Travis's psychosis. The more deeply he withdraws, the more he comes to believe in the American movie myths of purity and heroism, love and selflessness, and to actuate them as the grotesque parodies of human behavior they are. Travis Bickle is the legitimate child of John Wayne and Norman Bates: pure, self-righteous, violent ego and grinning, homicidal lunatic; each the obverse of the other; each equally dangerous. Together they create a persona so out of touch with ordinary human experience that the world he inhabits and perceives becomes an expressionist *noir* nightmare: an airless and dark trap that its inhabitant escapes only by drawing everything into it with him. The final irony occurs when Travis's act of slaughter, which he believes is an act of liberation and purification, is taken as such by everyone else, and we discover that we have been trapped by the same aberrations as he, that the double perspective we are offered by the film fuses, and we momentarily accept the lunatic as hero. (pp. 235-36)

[Consideration of] Travis's killing of the robber in the delicatessen and the manic preparations and rituals he puts himself through, should make the [violence at the end of the film] less surprising and perhaps less gratuitous than it first appears. Unfortunately, no matter how much is revealed by such analysis, it remains an excrescence, a moment of grotesque excess in an otherwise controlled work. It damages the film, permitting it to be rejected as only one more entry in the list of violent exploitations rampant in the mid-seventies. But even so damaged, the film is less cynical than many of its relatives, and no matter how much it may pander to the lowest expectations of an audience, it also holds back, tricks those expectations, and, save for those few minutes in which control is lost, remains a coherent, subtle work. (p. 245)

*Alice Doesn't Live Here Anymore,* which precedes *Taxi Driver,* is a film so completely its opposite that it might be by another hand. And although it has great formal energy, it is more important for its subject than its execution.

*Alice* is a film of light, concerned with realizing personal energies and impressing those energies onto the world in a non-destructive way. It is one of the rare films of the late sixties and early seventies that offers a notion of optimism, "a small step forward," as Diane Jacobs says [in her *Hollywood Renaissance*], out of the hatred and murder, passivity and manipulation that have informed most of our recent films. But it remains only a step, and we seem more likely to retreat from it—as does Scorsese—than to follow it through. In the context of Scorsese's work, *Alice* stands apart, almost as a dialectic to the dark violence of *Mean Streets* and *Taxi Driver,* almost offering the possibility that the violence can be contained and subdued. The violent character of . . . Ben is seen in the film partially as an intrusion, partially as a mode of behavior that exists and must be attended to. It is not allowed, as is similar behavior in the other films, to encompass and diminish everything else. But it does exist, and there is a sense of brooding and nervousness in the camera movements throughout the film that seems to portend something other than what these movements are covering and that relates the film to the essential concerns of Scorsese's other works: threat always exists; energies are always ready to be expended. Here the threats are overcome and the energies directed joyfully. (p. 251)

It is rare that a film, particularly when it takes the form of a journey, a road movie, leaves both us and its characters alone, without indicating momentous events and major change. Except for the event that sets Alice out (which is underplayed) and the violence of Ben (which Scorsese cannot avoid), *Alice* is content to observe possibilities of change and freedom, however limited, without forcing its characters to pay a price. No one dies (with the exception of Alice's husband), no one gets emotionally or physically hurt or scarred. . . . Coming, as it does, between *Mean Streets,* in which the community is dark and volatile, finally destructive, and *Taxi Driver,* where there is no community and the isolated man explodes into madness, *Alice* indicates that the dialectic is not dead and that American film could, conceivably, survive with its characters talking to each other, listening, and responding. It stands, with all its flaws, as an important entry into that recent group of American films that attempts to come to terms with women in a way other than the conventional modes of melodrama. (pp. 259-60)

*New York, New York* contains no location shots. With the help of production designer Boris Leven and cinematographer Laszlo Kovacs, Scorsese builds an artificial world. The result is odd, and I am not certain that what we perceive is what was intended. The opening titles of the film, the painted city skyline, immediately refer us to a pastel evocation of the forties and early-fifties studio musical. But as the film proceeds, this intended evocation begins to disappear and be replaced by a consciousness of the *methods* of evocation. The forties interiors and the strange, almost abstract suggestiveness of the exteriors develop their own attraction; the control of the *mise-en-scène* seems to become more important than why that control is being exercised, so that form threatens to refer only to itself. The viewer becomes aware not of *why* the studio sets are there (to evoke the atmosphere of the studio musical), only that they *are* there. Not that they are not fascinating in themselves. . . . But they are only fascinating as aspects of design. And they are inconsistent. Most of the interiors, with the exception of an oddly lit motel room and a nightclub lit entirely in red neon, are conventionally "real." They look like interiors evocative of the forties, whereas the exteriors evoke not a time but the idea of studio sets.

Scorsese has confused two levels of realism: illusionary realism, in which the cinematic space and its articulations create the illusion of a "real world," and a realism of form, in which the cinematic space points to its own existence, prevents the viewer from passing through the form into an illusion of reality, and uses that obstacle to create other levels of awareness. . . . If Scorsese was consciously attempting to correct the phenomenon of "evocation" films that followed upon [Arthur Penn's] *Bonnie and Clyde* in the late sixties and early seventies by demonstrating that the evocation of the past in film is only the evocation of the ways film evokes the past, the inconsistency of exterior artificiality and interior "realism" compromises his attempt.

There is also an extraordinary mixture of genres in the film. It is primarily a romantic musical in the post-*Cabaret* style, in which the musical numbers occur as part of the narrative, as an actual stage performance—or, in one sequence, a film performance—rather than expanding out of the narrative and into another spatial plane. . . . But here again Scorsese denies the tradition he apparently wants to celebrate, mixing a reflexivity that forces us to view the film as a self-conscious recreation not of a period but of a film of a period with a realism of quite recent origin. A film like Bob Fosse's *Cabaret* . . . attempts to turn the musical into a "realistic" genre, a melodrama with music. *New York, New York* continues that attempt, but at the same time undoes it by attempting to evoke older musicals that had no pretense to that kind of realism and flaunting the unreality of its appearance. If that were not complicated enough, exteriors are so lit and photographed as to appear similar to the *mise-en-scène* of *Taxi Driver,* so that a claustrophobic, barren, and occasionally foreboding effect is achieved that saturates the film with the aura of *film noir.* This in itself is not novel. . . . But it is not clear what the darkness of *New York, New York* is reflecting, since the temporal overlays are so uncertain. The occasional despair about "putting on the show" or about personal and financial security that manifested itself in some thirties musicals grew out of the Depression, the time in which the films were made and the time they reflected. *New York, New York* made in the seventies, is about the forties, and it is difficult to determine whether the *noir* elements of the film are merely part of the evocation of the forties *noir* style, an experiment in genre-mixing, or an attempt to create a setting for a romance that has its dark and anxiety-ridden moments. (pp. 261-63)

In his approach to the inarticulateness of the characters and to the somberness of their situation and surroundings, Scorsese avoids some of the glibness (but also the brightness) of *Alice Doesn't Live Here Anymore* and replaces its nervous energy with a slow, sometimes ponderous rhythm of emotional liberation emerging with considerable pain and uncertainty. But like *Alice,* this film does its best to avoid the melodrama and sentiment inherent in its subject, denying the emotional glut that might easily have been built up. Those sequences in which Francine begins to move on her own and in which Jimmy's separation from her is made complete are among the best indicators of Scorsese's control over the narrative movement. (p. 265)

It is difficult for American film to create a narrative that speaks to the immediate realities of people who do not and never will experience overwhelming insights and emotions, and to speak to these realities in a form that makes us understand them in a full social and political context. Cinema *can* do it: the films of Godard and Rohmer, of Alain Tanner and Rainer Werner Fassbinder prove that the cinematic imagination is more than able to work within valid emotional limits and a clear understanding of how people function in a world without heroism and emotional sacrifice. This is, of course, not within the American film tradition, and we must be content to observe and comment upon those films that at least question the tradition and offer other possibilities. Scorsese is rather unique among recent filmmakers in his ability to cover a full range of narrative possibilities, imitating, questioning, mocking them, sometimes all at the same time. If *New York, New York* fails to cohere because it attempts to do too much, its failure points to an ever greater success: the success of an active imagination, constantly probing and questioning, demanding that the forms of its art reveal and account for themselves. (pp. 268-69)

*Robert Phillip Kolker, "Expressions of the Streets: Martin Scorsese," in his* A Cinema of Loneliness: Penn, Kubrick, Coppola, Scorsese, Altman *(copyright © 1980 by Oxford University Press, Inc.; reprinted by permission), Oxford University Press, New York, 1980, pp. 206-69.*

## MICHAEL POWELL

Not since the beginnings of [Akira] Kurosawa have we seen such nervous authority. From [Martin Scorsese's] earliest films he started a dialogue with the audience compelling them to take part. Together with Robert De Niro he has invented a new film language. (p. 1)

[Scorsese and De Niro] are using a film language that dares the audience to stay ahead of them. It's the greatest compliment a filmmaker can pay to his audience; and we appreciate it. Half the time we yawn our heads off, as the film director underlines some point we found out for ourselves ten minutes ago. Scorsese-De Niro is a different ball game. Visual and verbal points are made with rapier-like touches. A word creates an image, an image begets a sequence, a one-line joke ends it, a reaction is long in coming and then explodes with unexpected violence, emotions are concealed, nothing is predictable, a sudden word, a face caught at the moment of truth, bring tears to our eyes. This is the world of Martin Scorsese. (pp. 1, 3)

I have heard people whine about the violence in **Mean Streets**, the violence in **Taxi Driver**. Scorsese is an artist. Pick up a copy of *The Disasters of War*. See that naked, maimed figure of a man, impaled on a stake? See those tumbled women, raped and murdered? See that priest hanged from a tree? Do you think that Goya was trying to get a cheap thrill out of these horrors? No more is Martin Scorsese. He has an eye that misses nothing, that looks on beauty and terror with the same dispassionate eye, with the same love and compassion. He cannot tell anything but the truth.

I wish we had a dozen more Scorseses. But it is not likely to happen. If we get one in every decade we'll be lucky. I'll settle for that. (p. 3)

*Michael Powell, in his introduction to* Martin Scorsese: The First Decade *by Mary Pat Kelly (copyright © 1980 by Mary Pat Kelly), Redgrave Publishing Company, 1980, pp. 1, 3.*

# Joan Micklin Silver

## 1935-

**American director and screenwriter.**

**Silver is one of the very few women whose films are independently produced. Her works are personal period pieces in which she attempts to recreate the feel of the times. Wit and the touching portrayal of human relationships add to the realism of her films.**

**Silver's first work, *The Immigrant Experience: The Long, Long Journey*, is a short film dealing with the arrival of Polish immigrants in America near the turn of the century. Silver expands this theme in *Hester Street*, her first feature film. In this work, a Russian Jewish family comes to America, much as in *The Immigrant Experience*, but Silver broadens her characters, and the themes associated with immigration provide a touching narrative.**

**Silver's next film, *Between the Lines*, deals with underground newspaper reporters who learn to face the loss of their idealism. Set in the 1960s, the film attempts to be both poignant and humorous—a remembrance of lost radicalism. Silver's most recent film, *Head over Heels*, is an adaptation of Ann Beattie's novel *Chilly Scenes of Winter*. Like *Between the Lines*, it treats the sixties and the need for individualism in the face of increasing pressures to conform.**

**In all of Silver's films, true humanity is the most prevalent theme; human interaction and the need to cope with problems exemplify this humanity.**

## JULIE SEMKOW

For all of us who are second- or third-generation children of immigrants, the narration from the beginning of [the exceptionally beautiful *The Immigrant Experience*] strikes deeply in our hearts. Indeed, most of the sequences from this true story are direct visual enactments of tales we've all heard, of the long, long journey our grandparents made.

Filmed on location in Greenwich Village and Ellis Island, the drama follows the arrival of 12-year-old Janek from Poland. (p. 45)

*The Immigrant Experience* has been sensitively and beautifully filmed. The actors are attractive and in many instances actually are Polish or of Polish origin. The young man who plays the youthful Janek is particularly engaging, as is the teacher whose role demands that she be severe and, paradoxically, tender. It is a film for all age groups and audiences, to afford understanding of the elements which influenced the development of diversity in the national character, and to re-create the conditions and emotions shared by immigrants of many origins, the heritage of most Americans. (p. 46)

*Julie Semkow, "'The Immigrant Experience: The Long, Long Journey',"* in Film Library Quarterly (© copyright, Film Library Information Council, 1973), Vol. 6, No. 4, Fall, 1973, pp. 44-6.

## STANLEY KAUFFMANN

Joan Micklin Silver made [*Hester Street*] with a script she adapted from a story by Abraham Cahan. It is utterly sincere and utterly abysmal. It's shot in poorly lighted black and white, the sound track is so flat it sounds as if it had been steamrollered, the camera use and editing would do little credit to a second-year film student, and the cast . . . is notable only for its memory of acting clichés. . . .

*Hester Street* looks like one of those Films from Great Literature made for educational film catalogues, and is not even a very good example of that questionable genre.

Considerable advance fuss has been made about Silver because she has bucked the System to make and to release her film. That's important, truly worth celebration. But to let the congratulations spill over on to the film that resulted from her independence would be ludicrous. (p. 21)

*Stanley Kauffmann, "Women at Work" (reprinted by permission of Brandt & Brandt Literary Agents, Inc.; copyright © 1975 by Stanley Kauffmann), in* The New Republic, Vol. 173, No. 16, October 18, 1975, pp. 20-1.*

## JILL FORBES

The great American melting pot shows a low profile in *Hester Street*. The time-honoured themes—progress, assimilation, education—are deployed with taste, discretion and, above all, humour. This is Joan Micklin Silver's first film, made in black-and-white, with a self-effacing camera, not a zoom, hardly a close-up. It is a quasi-documentary style which allows her actors to slip with ease from English to subtitled Yiddish and exploit the comic vein with a minimum of fuss in such devastating aphorisms as Mrs. Kavarsky's "You can't piss up my back and make me think it's rain''. The ironic symmetries of the fable and the comedy of the situations make the film thoroughly entertaining and belie any ethnographic intent. Yet *Hester Street* is a document in another sense. The portrait of an emerging community is shown as much through objects as through characters. . . . [Because] *Hester Street* is filmed without foreground or background, without height or depth, it succeeds both as infectious comedy and as a sensitive account of immigrant aspirations. Holding firmly to the middle ground, it entirely avoids parody or fetishism: American myths are rarely enacted so subtly or so sympathetically. (p. 262)

*Jill Forbes, " 'Hester Street',*" *in* Monthly Film Bulletin *(copyright © The British Film Institute, 1975), Vol. 42, No. 503, December, 1975, pp. 261-62.*

### GEOFF BROWN

[*Hester Street*] takes the bull by the horns, dealing solely . . . with life on New York's Lower East Side in 1896.

Its proportions and virtues are modest: it offers no labyrinthine saga of rags to riches to rags, no outsize characters flaunting their ethnic identity like a flag, no lashings of local colour. The narrative is dangerously slender, propelling a handful of ordinary characters along a well signposted road. . . . The plot . . . serves as a compact primer in the Americanisation of the immigrant Jew, stressing the impossibility of maintaining sacred habits and taboos in 'educated' New York.

The movie . . . has the qualities of a primer—stressing the same points repeatedly, presenting scenes crisply with few directorial distractions. Certainly, its perspective is limited. . . . Yet *Hester Street* covers its chosen ground with great skill and sensitivity.

*Geoff Brown, " 'Hester Street',*" *in* Sight and Sound *(copyright © 1976 by The British Film Institute), Vol. 45, No. 1, Winter, 1975-76, p. 58.*

### LAURENCE GREEN

[The astonishing *Hester Street*] by independent film maker Joan Micklin Silver is a deeply personal work, based on her own family's ethnic experiences as first generation settlers in New York. But the film derives its real strength from its deliberate understatement—nothing is forced or artificial—and the feeling of total involvement with characters and situations.

Pathos and humour are carefully balanced. . . .

Officialdom is gently ridiculed while at the same time showing the impracticality of formal procedure when dealing with individuals. . . .

The period atmosphere is so scrupulously accurate—from the bearded machinists wearing skull caps, sitting sewing at small tables in the garment factory, to the bustling market atmosphere of this tightly packed ghetto street flanked by tenements and lined with stalls, where the range of activity taking place varies from selling second-hand clothing to plucking chickens—that it has the effect of an animated family album.

The authenticity is further heightened by the use of black-and-white photography and by having half the dialogue spoken in Yiddish and sub-titled in English so that the film captures the true flavour of well researched documentary. (p. 34)

In short, then, this is a simple, glowing, beautifully observed film, totally devoid of sentimentality which must rank as a minor classic. (p. 35)

*Laurence Green, " 'Hester Street' " (© copyright Laurence Green 1976; reprinted with permission), in* Films and Filming, *Vol. 22, No. 4, January, 1976, pp. 34-5.*

### SONYA MICHEL

*Hester Street* is the film adaptation of *Yekl, A Tale of the Ghetto,* a story Abraham Cahan wrote in 1896 about Jewish immigrants from Eastern Europe. While remaining generally faithful to Cahan's original story, the film director, Joan Macklin Silver, adds dimension to it. She brings the period (the 1890's, when Jewish immigration was at its height) alive in colorful, richly detailed settings, and establishes a complex social context for the story, taking up where Cahan left off. (p. 142)

In general, Silver's casting seems to be something of a capitulation to American tastes. In the original story, the immigrants really do look different from the rest of the population. But Silver's Mrs. Kavarsky is far more attractive than the slovenly, "scraggy little woman" with warts on her face and her hair in disarray, whom Cahan describes, and her Mamie is also less Semitic-looking than Cahan's character. Thus the film imagery tends to undercut the anguish and self-hatred Jewish women felt (and which they frequently expressed in immigrant literature) when they realized they would never be considered beautiful by Anglo-Saxon standards.

For the most part, however, Silver's script differs in only a few minor details from the original story line. Her main modifications have been in terms of emphasis, most of them revealing strong feminist underpinnings. She shows clearly that a strong network of both emotional and practical support existed among the women of the ghetto. While there is evidence for this in Cahan's story, Silver's directing, through the work of the actresses in the film, tends to bring it into sharper focus. . . .

Silver eliminates [the] less-than-positive aspects of the female network by toning down Mrs. Kavarsky's impatience, and by omitting Fanny's betrayal altogether. At the same time, her directing underscores a sense of female solidarity. In the divorce scene, for instance, Silver has the rabbi's wife treat Jake coldly, even rudely, while she is kindly and solicitous toward Gitl. After the divorce, the rebbitsin and Mrs. Kavarsky triumphantly discuss Gitl's good fortune in getting rid of Jake and winning the honorable Bernstein.

Silver's Gitl also has more strength as an individual than Cahan's character does. (p. 144)

Silver's feminism may have pushed her in the direction of idealizing some of the female characters, but the spectre of Mamie, who has few compunctions about taking Jake from Gitl, counterbalances this tendency in the film as a whole. Too, Silver is actually more generous toward Jake than Cahan was. In both versions, he is shallow, selfish, and irresponsible, but Silver's directing imbues him with warmth (except, of course, toward Gitl), charm, and an engaging *joie de vivre*. Watching him stroll down Hester Street, we cannot help feeling some of the excitement and hope that filled many immigrants during their early years in the land where the streets were, mythically, paved with gold. Silver has not created an artificial scheme in which all men are bad, and all women good, but a realistic set of characters, some mixed, some neutral.

Silver understands, as Cahan did, that cultural differences affected men as well as women. (pp. 144-45)

In Cahan's version, Jake's devotion to his son is intermittent and somewhat opportunistic. Silver, however, presents their relationship in a more positive light, conveying the sense that Jake's feelings are sincere. In one of the most charming scenes in the film, Jake takes Yossele out for his first tour of the ghetto streets. Silver directs this sequence from the boy's point of view, giving us glimpses of the things he would be most likely to notice—the games and stunts of other children, the tempting treats offered by pushcart peddlers, and the effusive greetings of his father's friends. Jake is obviously proud of his son, yet his pride seems to be linked with a collective ghetto feeling that children represent the hope of the future, and therefore deserve special treatment.

Except for a few moments of impatience, the screen relationship between father and son is tender and whimsical. Unlike Cahan's Jake, this father treats his son not as an object, but as another person with feelings of his own. Although such behavior is atypical for Jake, Silver implies that he can make an exception for his son. . . . She seems to be using these scenes to suggest an alternative form of childrearing—of raising sons—which would break down the transmission and perpetuation of macho values from father to son. (p. 145)

Historians and sociologists often present a somewhat bland picture of immigration and assimilation, implying that the experience was unmitigatedly good for the Jews. To be sure, they escaped the persecution and restrictions of the Pale, but they did not enter a nation of unlimited opportunity. Full participation in American society bore a cultural pricetag. Accounts like *Yekl* and *Hester Street* reveal some of the tensions and conflict that actually underlay the acculturation of East European Jews. Silver is to be congratulated not only for bringing Cahan's story, with its hidden wealth of history, to public attention, but also for enhancing its fundamental truths with her own cinematic intelligence and sound insights. (p. 146)

> *Sonya Michel, "'Yekl' and 'Hester Street': Was Assimilation Really Good for the Jews?" in* Literature/Film Quarterly *(© copyright 1977 Salisbury State College), Vol. 5, No. 2, Spring, 1977, pp. 142-46.*

## JOHN SIMON

[*Between the Lines*] is meant to be a tale of deradicalization, of how a group of bright, undisciplined but idealistic kids who during the sixties put out a paper with some genuine bite to it . . . decline into slackness, indifference, jadedness, selling out. To make any sense, the action should be situated some eight years back, which is where, as I understand, the original scenario placed it. Updated to 1977, the movie taunts us with an unfillable lacuna: What kept these kids going till this day? Why is dissolution setting in now? Why haven't they already gotten over and beyond their disenchantment?

The film records, with however questionable accuracy, a particular moment of time, and misplaces it; we feel that the kids might just as well be bemoaning the death of Pancho Villa. More troublesome yet is that we are not given a sense of anyone's former power. . . . We do not experience these young people's talents; we do not believe that they were ever dangerous. Or are they phonies whom the picture is mocking?

Which brings us to the biggest difficulty with the film: the lack of a point of view. This was one of the troubles of *Hester Street,* too, where it was impossible to tell what value was to be placed on maintaining traditional Jewishness, and what value on Americanization. Are we to feel a sense of genuine loss in *Between the Lines,* or are we meant to laugh at these kids? Both, apparently, but, like double stops on the violin, *both* is too tall an order for a beginner—especially one who, like Mrs. Silver, exhibits no particular talent for her medium. The director makes the further mistake of not showing any ordinary things happening to her characters: Everything is a bit too cute, clever, perilous, or bizarre. We begin to think that the glorious times are *now,* not then.

Even so, the film does mark some advances over *Hester Street:* Its look is undistinguished rather than amateurish. . . . There are even a few quite arresting scenes, including one with a conceptual artist on the rampage, but the approach, for the most part, is distinctly schematic. Note, for instance, how the big party scene is handled, with pedestrian cutting back and forth between the various principals and the orgiastic dancers and band. And the characters never diverge much from type: the scrounging, lecherous, con artist of a rock critic; the hard-hitting but self-protective editor; the pompous square of a business manager; the two-faced, feelingless tycoon; the gallant shrimp of a cub reporter; the dedicated secretary-receptionist, who is the unwobbling pivot of the whole operation; and so forth. It is not that such people do not exist, but that the film does not sufficiently individualize any one of them. (pp. 75-6)

> *John Simon, "Belated Juvenilia," in* New York Magazine *(copyright © 1977 by News Group Publications, Inc.; reprinted with the permission of* New York Magazine*), Vol. 10, No. 18, May 2, 1977, pp. 74-6.\**

## CLARK WHELTON

Although *Between the Lines* is loaded down with silly dialogue, a poorly developed plot line, and fatuous characters who deserve everything negative that happens to them, the film somehow ends up as a convincing demonstration of why "underground" publications can't—or won't—defend themselves against overground money. Silver shows amateur journalists in a state of mutually destructive hostility. The moral is clear: People who are too disorganized to handle personal problems and hangups haven't got a prayer against a highly organized invader armed with dollars. . . .

*Between the Lines* never really deals with the complex relations between management and labor in the world of underground journalism, although it does point out that the "outsider" qualities which attract writers to underground papers almost guarantee that they will be unable to organize against a takeover attempt by the straight press. The *Mainline* succumbs with hardly a whimper. The editor, who early in the film roughs up a puny advertising manager in a dispute over space, cravenly caves in to the first order of the new owner and fires a "troublemaking" writer. No one seems very upset by any of this. Not even the writer. A receptionist resigns, but *Between the Lines* seems to imply that underground journalists don't care who owns the press.

But of course they do.

> *Clark Whelton, "Getting Bought: Notes from Overground" (reprinted by permission of* The Village

Voice *and the author; copyright © The Village Voice, Inc., 1977), in* The Village Voice, *Vol. XXII, No. 18, May 2, 1977, p. 51.*

**ANDREW SARRIS**

*Between the Lines* is more interesting for what it is than for what it is about, which is to say that it is a pleasant showcase for half a dozen talented performers rather than an overwhelming overview of the underground press or a compelling study of '70s disenchantment in '60s radicals.

In his interestingly reminiscent piece [see excerpt above], my esteemed colleague Clark Whelton indicated that he found the characters odious, but the point of the picture convincing. My reaction is exactly the opposite. I like most of the major characters, but they never seem to get anywhere. Perhaps, *that* is the point of the picture. . . .

At the very least, *Between the Lines* avoids the pompous self-righteousness of some of its severer critics. No one walks into a room to proclaim: "You are all a lost generation." The movie is too modest for such megalomania. What we have instead are useful insights into the subtle conflicts between the suppressed vanity of writers and their supposed public-spiritedness.

There is an attempt to grapple also with the volatile interplay of careerism and carnality between the sexes. . . .

[Six] moderately complex characters are three or four more than most current movies can reasonably claim, and I think that Joan Micklin Silver should get much of the credit for the growing gallery of glowing performances she has gathered in *Hester Street, Bernice Bobs Her Hair,* and *Between the Lines.* If there is something lacking in her work up till now it is the sense of a transcendent style capable of engulfing her very meticulous mise-en-scène in a torrent of personal expression. Thus far she has tended to see her subjects from the outside. One wonders if she will ever get far enough inside to be capable of a passionate folly. It may be that she will evolve ultimately into a polished objet d'art director on the order of [William] Wyler, [Louis] Malle, [Sidney] Lumet. If so, it would be pure sexism to argue that women directors must veer away from careful calculation toward fire and music. Nice, fun movies like *Between the Lines* are never in such oversupply that we can sneer at their not making the theatre rumble with revolutionary vibes.

*Andrew Sarris, "Two Cheers for a Nice Movie" (reprinted by permission of* The Village Voice *and the author; copyright © The Village Voice, Inc., 1977), in* The Village Voice, *Vol. XXII, No. 19, May 9, 1977, p. 47.*

**ELIZABETH STONE**

Invariably, in Silver's films, there's a scene in which a woman eyes herself in a mirror as she tries on a new image that she hopes (or fears) will become her identity. "The relationship between a person's past and present," says Silver, "is an ongoing concern, though it's not so much that I even knew that until I looked at my films with hindsight."

Though Silver is a serious filmmaker, she is not somber. The theme of change, lightheartedly treated, . . . runs through **"Bernice Bobs Her Hair"**—which Silver adapted (from the F. Scott Fitzgerald story) and directed for the PBS series "The

American Short Story." Bernice . . . finds that her small-town values and her tendency to cite the older generation as authorities make her fairly unpopular with her cousin Marjorie and Marjorie's Ivy-League circle of friends. Bernice submits to instruction: she changes her image, changes her conversational banter, and even bobs her hair on Marjorie's dare. But the film ends with Bernice's triumph. She snips off the sleeping Marjorie's braid and heads back home, suitcase in hand, in the middle of the night.

Though Bernice is of the 1920s and Gitl [of *Hester Street*] of the 1900s, their predicament touches us. Silver, who calls herself "a research nut," has an adroit eye for environmental detail, using that detail to evoke the spirit of an age—as background rather than foreground, as essence rather than actuality. The distinction has implications: as a people without a lengthy history, and no evolved mythology, we are willing to use our national past not only historically, but emblematically—one or another decade becomes, by tacit consent, a Golden Age, a Silent Age, an Age of Excess. The question isn't whether we should or shouldn't do this. The point is that we *do*, particularly if we haven't ourselves lived through that age. (pp. 31-2)

While using an age for its Image worked in **"Hester Street"** and **"Bernice,"** it doesn't work in **"Between the Lines,"** particularly because here Silver seems willing to make the sixties responsible for her characters' present state. But people are psychological beings as well as sociological beings: they have blocks, defenses, breakthroughs, inertias, pains and problems that have at least as much to do with their private selves as with their social selves. Silver, in making an era responsible for a condition, bypasses a more introspective—and necessary—probing. That her characters do this would be fine if *she* did not share their viewpoint.

Consequently, we are left with too many questions—which Silver seems not to perceive as questions. (p. 32)

The climactic moment is the purchase of *The Mainline* by a publishing mogul. We know it's meant to be a requiem for the age, that we're supposed to feel bad. But we don't. We haven't been given sufficient reason to. If anything, it seems as if the *Mainline* staff has, like Ulysses's companions, finally been freed from a Circean enchantment. One wonders what they'll do now, how they'll cope or grow or fall. But since those aren't the questions the film intends to raise, they're not the questions it answers.

Despite its flaws, **"Between the Lines"** offers some vital characterizations. . . . Joan Micklin Silver has always been able to create rounded female characters, though her male characters have emerged more as types than as people; in Max, however, she creates a three-dimensional male as well. (pp. 32, 34)

*Elizabeth Stone, "Joan Micklin Silver: Box Office but No Bankroll," in* Ms. *(© 1977 Ms. Magazine Corp.), Vol. VI, No. 2, August, 1977, pp. 31-2, 34.*

**NICOLAUS MILLS**

Joan Micklin Silver's *Between the Lines* is far more than a 1970s gang-spirit picture. A worthy successor to her *Hester Street,* it is the best film we have had so far on what happened to the college radicals of the 1960s. . . .

What makes *Between the Lines* so telling and unexpected is [a] kind of neat generational contrast [that] is precisely what Silver and screenwriter Fred Barron . . . allow for and then destroy by carefully avoiding a morality play in which the tough business world administers a dose of reality to the radical young. The real focus of *Between the Lines* rests not with the struggle between '70s money men and '60s print men but with the internal dissolution of a once-innovative paper. . . .

It is [the] state of restless ambivalence on the part of the *Mainline* staff that is grist for the pervasive humor of *Between the Lines,* and what follows for most of the picture is a series of encounters that are a combination of hip bedroom farce and comedy of manners. Silver is willing to keep her camera in place for long periods of time, and the result is a series of hilarious sequences. . . . (p. 453)

[The] comedy of *Between the Lines* maintains its edge because without recourse to preachment or ideology it fixes on the disparity between the lives of the *Mainline* staff in the '70s and the political turmoil that brought them together. Time and again we hear those on the paper refer back to the golden '60s . . . and the more they reminisce, the more apparent it becomes that their real tie to the '60s has been a loose one. (pp. 453-54)

What gives *Between the Lines* its richness is that it keeps this total picture in focus. It won't, as do so many attacks on the '60s, dismiss the wit and energy of the decade. Yet in scene after scene it makes clear that ten years later, when the wit and energy of the decade are all that its middle-class "radicals" retain, there was something fundamentally wrong—and certainly politically parasitic—in the lives they led. To pursue this kind of thinking at a time when so many retrospective studies of the '60s try to define its end in terms of a single event . . . is no mean accomplishment. A few novelists—notably Ann Beattie in *Chilly Scenes in Winter*, Eleanor Bergstein in *Advancing Paul Newman*, Lisa Alther in *Kin-Flicks*—have tried something similar, but Silver in a movie produced without a star and on a modest budget has gone further than they, and in addition opened up the biggest question of all for the generation of reporters and writers who came of age in the '60s—where next? (p. 454)

> *Nicolaus Mills, "Looking Back to the Sixties," in*
> Dissent *(© 1977 by Dissent Publishing Corporation),*
> *Vol. 24, No. 4, Fall, 1977, pp. 453-54.*

### JOHN A. GUTOWSKI

[*The Immigrant Experience: The Long, Long Journey*] has two goals. The first is to dramatize a slice of American immigration history as reflected in the experiences of a Polish peasant family upon their 1907 arrival to the New World. The second is to provoke discussion of success and self-fulfillment in relation to the American Dream. Though cut ethnographically thin, the film achieves its first goal in evocative dramatic scenes that powerfully convey the ordeal of assimilation throughout most of the footage. To accommodate the second goal the film requires two awkward devices: a narrational voice-over and a final contemporary scene, both of which express the American Dream but weaken the dramatic impact of the predominant, illustrative historical sequences. (pp. 257-58)

*The Long, Long Journey* interprets the immigrant experience according to the same vision of suffering, disorganization, alienation, and conflict that Oscar Handlin details in *The Uprooted*. . . . The film's ultimate debt to *Polish Peasant in Europe and America,* Handlin's chief data source, is brought to mind in a sequence where Janek and his sister write to brother

Wojtech back in Poland and follow Thomas and Znaniecki's classic formulation of the immigrant letter. Like its historiographic antecedents, the film emphasizes the pathology of the immigrant experience without much consideration of the social and cultural mechanisms that maintain ethnic identity, solidarity, and stability. Although the film places its family in Greenpoint, a well-known historically significant Polish community, there is no indication that the family is part of a Polish community, Polish neighborhood or any ethnic companionate network. Though the family is characteristically Roman Catholic, their religiosity amply illustrated, they have no connection with a Polish parish. Nor does Janek attend a parochial school; instead, he goes to a public school where he has no Polish counterparts. The priest who appears in the prescribed matchmaker role acts as agent of the Church rather than the neighborhood parish. Although removal of the family from ethnic-community contexts facilitates both the theme of alienation and a conception of ethnicity centered in the family, these occur at the expense of ethnographic fidelity.

Both the narration and the concluding scene force an otherwise penetrating drama into the fragile mold of an American success story that seems discontinuous with the drama itself. As we see him in 1907, Janek is an intelligent, aggressive, and ambitious youth, not unlike the hero of Horatio Alger who informs the American success ethos. As we hear and see him fifty-two years later, Janek has not advanced beyond the social and economic status of his father. According to the film's own linguistic yardstick for measuring successful Americanization—Janek the protagonist's own goal—Janek the narrator has actually regressed, since he cannot produce the dental phonemes that he had mastered fifty-two years earlier. Janek's pride in his meager acquisitions, his family stability, and his potentially upwardly mobile descendants may reflect the aspiration and destiny of the working-class immigrant. If so, this unexplained confusion of success with satisfaction becomes a mere afterthought, unrelated to the preceding drama.

Despite its flaws and shortcomings, *The Long, Long Journey* is a very good film, the best of those that deal with Polish-Americans. It has excellent acting, beautiful photography, and a compelling story. Its use of subtitles effectively renders its extensive Polish dialogue. The Polish folk melody employed as a recurrent theme song sadly and hauntingly intensifies the emotional charge in several key scenes. (pp. 258-59)

> *John A. Gutowski, "Folk Cultural Films: 'The Immigrant Experience: The Long, Long Journey'," in*
> Journal of American Folklore *(copyright © 1979 by the American Folklore Society; reproduced by permission), Vol. 92, No. 364, April-June, 1979, pp. 257-59.*

### DAVID DENBY

The romance at the center of Joan Micklin Silver's *Head Over Heels* is . . . rather murky, and that's a disaster for this very small movie, which gives little evidence of wanting to do anything more than tell us some intimate truths about its leading characters. . . .

Joan Micklin Silver, who wrote the screenplay as well as directed, has been faithful to the bleak mood of Ann Beattie's novel [*Chilly Scenes of Winter*], a book nearly punitive in its insistence that life is joyless, harsh, mediocre. The young people in this movie—the generation of the seventies—have been stripped of cultural identity, anger, rebellious instincts. These enervated children of the middle class lack the energy of the urban poor—not even pop culture speaks to them. Yet the grayness, the vacuumy deadness of both book and movie, seems to strike some people as the truth about life. My own feeling is that the acceptance of mediocrity as "the truth" gives way, much too easily, to a peculiarly despairing kind of sentimentality. In the Beattie-Silver view, which, despite the fancy bleakness, is not very different from the underlying message of soap opera, we are all saved if we have "someone to love." (p. 85)

Silver might have redeemed the dismalness of Beattie's themes if she had a richer sense of film texture or some sort of visual flair. She controls actors well, wringing a few laughs out of the general depressiveness, but she allows only one thing to happen at a time, one point to be made—and then she moves on. What I want is a little more life going on around the characters, a feeling of place, a little play and observation and color—something besides that quietly desperate man chasing that cipher of a girl. (pp. 85-6)

> *David Denby, "Love in a Cold Climate," in* New York *Magazine (copyright © 1979 by News Group Publications, Inc.; reprinted with the permission of* New York *Magazine), Vol. 12, No. 43, November 5, 1979, pp. 85-6.\**

## ROBERT ASAHINA

[*Head Over Heels*] has a great deal of charm and truth in its characterizations.

This is especially surprising because the novel is so excruciatingly dull and lifeless. (p. 23)

[Joan Micklin Silver] has given form to the very raw material of [Ann Beattie's] novel and pruned the weedy expanses of meaningless dialogue. . . .

Silver's direction is not as successful as her writing. She has studded the movie with annoying tics that she seems to have picked up from Woody Allen. Chief among these is her having Heard address the camera, a device that quickly becomes as tiresome as the *Annie Hall*-like fantasy sequences that she has also used. (As a result, *Head Over Heels* has been unjustly and unfavorably compared to *Annie Hall,* a much inferior film.) . . .

On the other hand, Silver has elicited very convincing performances from the supporting players. . . . (p. 24)

> *Robert Asahina, "Love Crazed," in* The New Leader *(© 1979 by the American Labor Conference on In-ternational Affairs, Inc.), Vol. LXII, No. 22, November 19, 1979, pp. 23-4.\**

## RENATA ADLER

"**Head Over Heels,**" based on a fine novel by Ann Beattie, wastes its first half hour. Then it lives up for a while to its aspirations, before disintegrating toward its close. . . . Charles' love is meant to be absolute, single-minded, of the sort that occupies consciousness totally. It never rings altogether true. In the year of pining, although he parks outside her house and makes scale models of it, although he never repairs the eyeglasses he broke the night she left him, although he talks constantly about her, in narration and in interior monologue (an unnecessary device, and one that almost never works in film), he neither gains nor loses weight, he manages to take his baths and go to work, he never has that desperate, ravaged look—or, on the other hand, any sign of a driving, overwrought ambition that might account for his surviving the year at all. (p. 172)

An early, considerable problem is the Laura character: another waif. Her eyes fill with tears a lot, and she laughs from time to time, but she is brittle, glacial, charmless. She talks too loud. She's finding herself. She says things like "I don't deserve to be happy." She demands to be taken to a pornographic film and, leaning forward in her seat, blows bubbles with her bubble gum. Whatever that's meant to be—charm, waifness, whimsy, characterization—it's awful. The relentless childlike quality of this person becomes repellent—not just because she's actually left a small child at home (which makes the underlying story a bit as though Joanie Caucus had become the object of a "Blue Angel" obsession) but because the childlikeness itself is mannered, artificial. . . .

The period when the film does pick up begins with the appearance of its first authentic adult, Laura's husband (Mark Metcalf), a salesman of A-frame houses, who is written and acted very well. One starts to trust the story—and then stays with it for a time. The intensity of love which has been its theme has occurred, after all, somewhere in most lives; audiences can draw upon their own sense of it. When the couple becomes uninteresting again, it is possible just to leave the film in spirit—or read into it a story that it does not really tell. At one point, near the end, there is a scene that's inexplicably moving. [Charles], eyes filled with tears, stands still and says, "It's over." It isn't. But somehow, when spoken by a character standing, near tears, alone, "It's over" is always a very moving line. (p. 174)

> *Renata Adler, "Waifness," in* The New Yorker *(© 1979 by The New Yorker Magazine, Inc.), Vol. LV, No. 41, November 26, 1979, pp. 171-72, 174.\**

# Jerzy Skolimowski

## 1938-

(Also Yurek Skolimowski) Polish director, screenwriter, and actor.

Skolimowski's early films established him as the spokesman of Poland's troubled youth. In these films, Skolimowski wished to show "that Polishness of what happens on our streets." While his later films are less insular, they maintain his quirkish humor and fascination with life's outsiders. His style is often considered Godardian; he disdains conventional narrative and studies youth's uncompromising moods.

While studying at Łódź, Skolimowski collaborated on scripts with Roman Polanski and Andrzej Wajda. *Rysopis (Identification Marks: None)* is his first feature. Skolimowski plays the introspective student who serves as the filmmaker's alter ego. It is a film of indecision: a tale of a quest that ends without resolution.

Due to censoring problems, Skolimowski's *Hands Up!* may never be released on either side of the Iron Curtain. According to Skolimowski, the title refers to his generation in Poland—the generation that has thrown up their hands in helplessness.

*Le Départ* is the first of Skolimowski's foreign language movies. Here he develops an interest in surrealistic comedy and abandons the introspection characterizing his Polish work. Two British films, *Deep End* and *The Adventures of Gerard*, demonstrate his capability within different genres: one is a psychological study, the other an historical parody. Despite his lack of familiarity with the English language, *Deep End*, in particular, is considered one of his finest films. An adaptation of Vladimir Nabokov's *King, Queen, Knave* proved less successful, and Skolimowski considers it the low point of his career.

In 1978, Skolimowski adapted Robert Graves's story *The Shout*, a British tale of primitive terror. Most critics consider *The Shout* to be his most successful synthesis of image, sound, and content. It also proved his most lucrative work.

Skolimowski now considers Poland a retreat rather than a work base, and does not limit himself geographically. Earlier prominent themes of alienation and the difficulties of youth have been replaced by an interest in visual imagery and surrealistic content. While some critics dislike his symbolism, claiming that it leads nowhere, others admire his inventiveness.

## AXEL MADSEN

Jerzy Skolimowski's **"Le Départ"** is the best the "new cinema" has come up with thus far. . . . It is the kind of film that makes one forget tedious hours of watching tedious miles of young filmmakers' attempts; the kind of film that in one blow justifies it all. . . .

**"Le Départ"** is modern cinema—digested and carried forward. Skolimowski accomplishes the feat of playing on what is evident and what is arbitrary in cinema, moving his audience forward with shots that begin as one thing and reveal quite another, with attitudes and lines of dialogue that question themselves, the film, and us. . . . Skolimowski is modern in the most post-McLuhan sense of modernity—everything can be true. Certainties and conditioned reflexes turn into question marks and puns, our points of reference are ridiculed. . . . The shocks and visual inventions are never gratuitous, really, and Skolimowski even brings home his message—that car hunger is often a youth's sublimation for sexual repressions—without crude Freudianisms. At the end, when we expect the traditional hotel room bedscene, Skolimowski surprises us a last time with a tender, "white" ending that is totally in character. . . .

**"Le Départ"** is totally incredible from beginning to end, but Skolimowski's amazing knowledge of what cinematic cement is made of hooks us from credit crawl to fadeout in a highwire act the likes of which we haven't seen in years. This continuity of the improbable is filmmaking at its newest. Skolimowski is a man to behold.

> Axel Madsen, "Reviews: 'Le Départ' ('The Start'),"
> in Cinema (© Spectator International, Inc.), Vol. 3,
> No. 6, Winter, 1967, p. 49.

## HOWARD THOMPSON

There have been stronger and bolder festival entries than Jerzy Skolimowski's **"Le Départ,"** but none more disarming. By any standards, festival or otherwise, this free-wheeling, inventive comedy of a youth obsessed with fast autos has been put together with fresh, deceptive simplicity that makes it a joy to watch . . .

["**Le Départ**"] is a small, clear-cut gem—a beautifully disciplined, imaginative exercise in moviecraft—that is snugly suited to its modest cast and proportions. . . .

The fade-out, after a lovely, flowing scene in a hotel bedroom, seems as right as the rest of **"Le Départ."** Right and real, funny and haunting.

> *Howard Thompson, "Jerzy Skolimowski's Comedy Focuses on Youth and Cars," in* The New York Times *(© 1967 by The New York Times Company; reprinted by permission), September 23, 1967, p. 20.*

## VINCENT CANBY

Mr. Skolimowski's **"Barrier"** is a bright, sardonic fantasy that is not only much more indigenously Polish than **"Le Départ,"** but, like Godard's work, is also a provocative personal statement that conforms to no predigested ideologies. Reffish and irreverent, **"Barrier"** has the exuberance of a youthful work, executed with technical facility and control more often associated with the work of an old pro than with that of a youngster.

It is not a particularly easy film. However, its bizarre juxtaposition of commonplace and fantastic incidents to give them surreal importance is so much a part of the film's point of view that seldom do its obscurities seem annoyingly arbitrary. Quite simply, it's fun to watch.

Spiritually, **"Barrier"** is a continuation of **"Identification Marks: None"** and **"Walkover,"** Mr. Skolimowski's tales of alienated youth in a socialist society. . . .

[**"Barrier"**] is a work of original cinema composition that also has certain timely political and social interest.

> *Vincent Canby, "Skolimowski's 'Barrier'," in* The New York Times *(© 1967 by The New York Times Company; reprinted by permission), September 27, 1967, p. 39.*

## KRZYSZTOF-TEODOR TOEPLITZ

[***Rysopis (Identification Marks: None)***] is a surprise. The fact that it was made out of pieces of film that normally are thrown into the trash basket after the professor has seen them shows that Skolimowski did not enter [film] school in order to learn something, but in order to realize a prepared plan and show his maturity. But what is even more important, Skolimowski for the first time presented in *Rysopis* an almost complete repertory of his way of thinking as well as his repertory of possibilities.

The title of the film suggests an explanation of its content. These are indeed the identification marks of the author: his autoportrait, a description of his daily life, of his love complications, a collection of casual reflections woven by student Leszczyc about himself. Leszczyc was played by Skolimowski himself, and he used the name also in his next film *Walkover.* It seems to be for Skolimowski a cryptonym used in his autobiography. Because *Identification Marks* indeed *is* his autobiography. . . . [In] a situation when all ideals, programs, and theses fail, documents become significantly meaningful—documents on human philosophies, reactions, impulses—even those that cannot be explained rationally.

Simultaneously, in *Identification Marks*, and more so in Skolimowski's next film *Walkover,* a second aspect came up: attempts to discipline these observations and confessions in the confines of social reality—which could be influences from the Czechoslovak film. (p. 30)

Skolimowski maintains in his public statements that he is under the influence of the Czechoslovak film. . . . [It] constitutes a confession of an almost complete change in orientation. Such a declaration could never have been made, for example, by [Andrzej] Wajda or [Wojciech] Has. Does it find a justification in the films of Skolimowski?

His heroes—the one from *Identification Marks* as well as those from *Walkover* or *The Barrier*—are undoubtedly blood-brothers of their contemporaries from Western films. But they live differently, and face different problems. All of Skolimowski's films are involved with the moment of choice and decision. . . .

[In] Skolimowski's later films the same question arises: to accept or not to accept a society with all its rules and demands. However, the question is not posed in an abstract society—but in an actual Polish reality. The director does not hasten to give an answer. His fullest expression is given in *The Barrier.* The dominating factor of this film is the fierce polemic with the older generation. The vision of this generation is contained in two images in the film: the anonymous mass of people absurdly stamping in one place, and the mighty choir in ridiculous newspaper-hats, singing an inarticulate, pathetic song. This is how Skolimowski sees the same people whom, not so long ago, Wajda portrayed in the harrowing light of burning barricades. What is he saying? Up to now not much: a feeling of his own individuality, expressed best in a lyrical love, and also his attempts to find a new moral scale. The hero from *The Barrier,* like the hero from *Identification Marks* and *Walkover,* will return to the school he ran away from, and will become a doctor. But what kind of a doctor? . . .

Skolimowski's creativity testifies to the intricate ways in which the face of the new generation of filmmakers is being formed—ways that lead from "sensitivity" to attempts at independent thinking. (p. 31)

> *Krzysztof-Teodor Toeplitz, "Jerzy Skolimowski: Portrait of a Debutant Director," in* Film Quarterly *(copyright 1967 by The Regents of the University of California; reprinted by permission of the University of California Press), Vol. XXI, No. 1, Fall, 1967, pp. 25-31.*

## PHILIP STRICK

It begins like nothing so much as a [Jean] Gabin picture, with meaty jazz score and stolen car hurtling at us through the night. And very rarely during the frolics that follow does *Le Départ* give any reminder that its inventive, lively, and sometimes rather glib young director is, in fact, Polish. Had this been his first film . . . , Skolimowski's nationality would have been largely irrelevant; but the trio of films he has so far made in Poland act as an inevitable reference point, particularly as in shedding his country he also seems to have cast off both the anger and the armoury that made his previous work bristle with such satisfying complexity. As *Le Départ* romps from one piece of slapstick to the next one begins to wonder uneasily if *Barrier,* allegiances to Godard and Fellini and all, was not—as it seemed to be—a daring rejection of contemporary Polish nostalgia, but actually a step backwards into the comparative security of already well-tried themes.

In retrospect, *Walkover* certainly seems to have been less fraught than *Barrier* with the same hangovers that obsessed [Andrzej] Munk and Wajda; while *Rysopis,* raw, introvert, and raggedly uncommunicative, begins to look remarkably like the most original of the three. The hero of **Barrier** may sit apart from the chaotic unanimity of the dance-hall where meaningless applause (fingers on glass) greets the pointless act (a man revolving on an overhead fan), just as medals used to be awarded for wartime heroism. Yet he, too, strives for a deed worth the doing, and his slide down the ski-slope on a smouldering suitcase, sabre in hand, blood-donation poster on head, takes him and us straight back to the brutal eradication of Polish hopes as described in [Wajda's] *Ashes and Diamonds* or *Lotna.* The war is over—but at least it *was* a war and at least it meant action, direction and purpose. And these are qualities which Skolimowski's characters, wandering like lost souls, have never previously been able to find.

With *Le Départ,* however, the insane glory has undergone a radical change. Jean-Pierre Léaud could only be French, and neutral buildings, glassy modern showrooms, and anonymous open roads are his battleground. He does have an obsession, but it is clearly defined, unlike the *malaise* of his predecessors, and it is centred not upon nationalist desperation but upon capitalist luxury—the need to obtain a Porsche long enough for him to take part in a motor rally. (p. 12)

Opting out in favour of the happy ending is of course one of the most ancient of tales, and Skolimowski's claims for the supremacy of sex are unlikely to surprise any but the most ardent of motor-rally fans, even if they come as a shock to his own hero. What does surprise is that the Polish rebel should reach so tame a conclusion. . . . Léaud puts all the vehemence and aggression of a freedom-fighter into his hunt for a vehicle, and to this extent is clearly linked with the belligerent Skolimowski image; at the same time, that image has softened so considerably that his frantic violence seems merely a combination of excess enthusiasm and ludicrously anti-social eccentricity. In a Polish environment it might have worked; in a curiously non-specific Belgian one it just comes out as cute.

Skolimowski's comedy, then, is not so much a departure as a modification. Apart from such tiny relics of Polanski-style humour as the trampish sausage-vendor, his Polishness has become submerged in a welter of international influences, including Wilder, Lester and [Milos] Forman, and while there is plenty of glossy self-indulgence (like the persistent close-ups of the bikini fashion parade), there is nothing really to equal the ski-run sequence in **Barrier,** the superb long-distance ten-minute take in **Walkover,** or that startling shot in **Rysopis** which takes us all the way down a flight of stairs. Dominating everything in **Le Départ,** of course, is the Godard touch. . . . (pp. 12, 49)

Fortunately, the film nevertheless gets along very nicely as sheer farce in its own right. . . . Skolimowski's visual flair, although muted, occasionally produces some spectacular shooting, especially of Porsches at high speed, and his taste for symbolism (wigs, mirrors, projected images, recurrent references to things Indian) has clearly not yet abandoned him. But if **Le Départ** adds anything to what we already knew about Skolimowski, it proves mainly that he is currently more inspired in his bitterness than in his jokes. (p. 49)

*Philip Strick, "London Festival, 1967: 'Le départ',"* in Sight and Sound *(copyright © 1968 by The British Film Institute), Vol. 37, No. 1, Winter, 1967-68, pp. 12, 49.*

**ROGER GREENSPUN**

Skolimowski stars himself in **"Identification Marks: None"** as a 24-year-old draft dodger who one day accepts the call and enters military service. . . .

Unfortunately, although everything that happens to him means to be of great significance, none becomes suggestive enough to arouse interest.

Not that the film doesn't try. Skolimowski strains for effects, for improbable shooting angles, for elaborate and fortuitous silhouettes and reflections—to such a degree that he would seem determined to find a visual formula for everything and everybody in his movie.

His use of subjective camera, sometimes in vast bravura passages requiring extended movement, works to depress both cinematic and dramatic excitement. In such passages we know that it is always a machine and never the eye that sees and that elicits the imitation of response.

*Roger Greenspun, "Poland's 'Identification Marks: None' Returns,"* in The New York Times *(© 1969 by The New York Times Company; reprinted by permission), December 3, 1969 (and reprinted in* The New York Times Film Reviews: 1969-1970, *The New York Times Company & Arno Press, 1971, p. 101).*

**JAN DAWSON**

Skolimowski's previous films all maintained a brittle tension between romanticism and cynicism, principally through the person of a questing, usually adolescent, hero unable—despite a succession of experiences revealing both the egotism and the utter separateness of other people—to suppress his expectation of a better world. They were at once a celebration of youthful energy and of a more mature disenchantment, alternately detached and wryly compassionate, with the director controlling the ebb and flow of audience sympathies as if the better to convince us of the absurdity of sharing his affection for his unreliable characters.

To this extent his hilarious **Deep End** runs true to form, while being—superficially—the most superficial of Skolimowski's films to date. (p. 16)

The ending is thematically consistent with Skolimowski's pervasive view of a greedy society in which people use and discard other people like objects and sex is equated with materialism. . . . Yet it is unsatisfying, not just because of its crude shock tactics but also because it echoes two of the film's clumsiest moments: a fantasy insert in which Mike holds Susan naked under the water, and a longer sequence in which he floats on top of a cardboard poster of a stripper who resembles her. These scenes seem intended to provide a single image of adolescent frustration, and their weakness lies in their explicitness, while Skolimowski's strength lies elsewhere: in ambiguous metaphors rather than precise similes, in mobile rather than static images, in surreal inconsequential details. . . . As long as it cuts rapidly from scene to scene **Deep End** sustains its momentum; but it is knocked off balance each time Skolimowski attempts to round off a sequence with a wilfully significant image.

Yet between these heavy parentheses the film contains so much that is dazzlingly brilliant that it seems uncharitable to dwell on them. It is a kaleidoscope of primary colours, used to tip both characters and settings into the realm of caricature, but also used for the sheer visual pleasure they offer, as Skolimowski seems self-parodyingly to acknowledge when . . . a roller-wielding hand appears in the background and proceeds to cover a wall with red paint. (pp. 16-17)

The many sudden, unexplained shifts of purpose and attitude show Skolimowski at his distinctive best. . . . [Yet] despite the verbal and visual fireworks, the film's mixture of slapstick, caricature and grim moral comment does not always coalesce; with a pop score by Cat Stevens and a frenetically running hero, it seems intermittently to be exploiting the swinging genre on which it so caustically comments. Like the best baroque, it is memorable for a wealth of details and its depiction of a turbulent world in a state of perpetual motion; but being the best baroque, it fits uneasily into a linear structure with a beginning, middle and end, to say nothing of a moral. (p. 17)

*Jan Dawson, "London Festival: Jerzy Skolimowski/ 'Deep End'," in* Sight and Sound *(copyright © 1971 by The British Film Institute), Vol. 40, No. 1, Winter, 1970-71, pp. 16-17.*

### NIGEL ANDREWS

Skolimowski's bewildering *The Adventures of Gerard* was kept in cold storage for months before its appearance. One sees the problem. The film is too naive to be Art and too sophisticated to be Entertainment. It also looks as if Skolimowski made it up as he went along, not so improbably in the light of some of his own confessions ('Laziness lies behind everything I have done'). *Gerard* in fact is the sort of film that only an established director would be allowed to get away with. . . .

The result is a sort of cross between [Sergei Bondarchuk's] *Waterloo* and [Richard Lester's] *The Running, Jumping and Standing Still Film*. . . . Like Lester, however, who seems stylistically the nearest point of reference, Skolimowski aspires to complete visual anarchy ('a world gone topsy-turvy . . .' narrates Gerard's voice early on, and the camera gyrates to turn Napoleon's army upside down), breaking formal barriers to achieve a fluid comic style. The story is rightly skeletal. . . .

The plot is simply on hand to plant signposts when the anarchy flags. Despite some witty dialogue and good set-up gags, the film's impetus is neither verbal nor histrionic but derives from a frenzied extension/burlesque of cinematic idiom. The cerebral, straight-to-camera soliloquy, Godard-style, is transformed into Gerard's perpetual braggadocio, directed unembarrassed and full-volume at the audience. Skolimowski peppers the action with accelerated film (and sound) and the occasional hiccoughed insert. . . .

If the film threatens at times to degenerate into a parade of conjuring tricks, it is redeemed partly by the air of baroque, Munchhausen-like fantasy that pervades Gerard's adventures, rich in such casually surrealist details as General Millefleur's accident-prone human dining-table; partly by the fact that Gerard is a genuine Skolimowski hero, quirky and single-minded in his pursuit of self-fulfilment, a Napoleonic counterpart of Marc in *Le Départ*. For all its chaotic surface, *Gerard* carries a distinctive signature.

*Nigel Andrews, "Film Reviews: 'The Adventures of Gerard'," in* Sight and Sound *(copyright © 1971 by The British Film Institute), Vol. 40, No. 1, Winter, 1970-71, p. 51.*

### MICHAEL WALKER

Although *Rysopis* clearly shows the amateur / clandestine nature of its creation, it provides an outline of Skolimowski's preoccupations; now it seems like a rough draft for the mature works which followed. (p. 35)

[If the plot] provides the general scheme of the film, its development derives from a movement within this scheme: that of the hero towards a moment of decision about his life. . . . As [Andrzej] moves from encounter to encounter, the familiar pattern of the journey-movie emerges, but the journey also has something of the form of a search: this progression has since become central to Skolimowski's films. In fact, in *Rysopis* the search aspect is weaker than in the subsequent films: Andrzej never really convinces us he is very likely to stay. But essentially the form is present. Here, as in the other films, the various stages of the journey/search are determined more by impulse than by careful consideration of the possibilities, but this seems to be Skolimowski's nature. All his heroes seem to live impulsively, reacting spontaneously to events as they present themselves, and his films have a corresponding vitality and freshness. In this respect *Rysopis* suffers to an extent from its long period of creation, and its vitality is occasionally naively self-advertising . . . but it has something of the restless energy conveyed so strongly in *Walkover* and *Le Départ*.

In presenting a picture of contemporary Poland, *Rysopis* is, inevitably, more loosely organised and episodic than the later works. It does however convey a sense of city life going on in the background to the film. The locations—Andrzej's attic, the coffee-bar, the shops, the wood yard next to the University—are palpably real. . . . Also pertinent is the chilling vision of the organs of the 'system': the draftboard; the veterinary clinic; the University. . . . Above all, however, in *Rysopis* one remembers the first, dawn exterior; the image of the shadows of the road workers, huge and immobile on a wall, set in contrast with the drunken trio on their way home, squabbling ineffectually with a passer-by. Particularly when one recalls the penchant of the Soviet cinema for uplifting climaxes at dawn, it strikes one as a brilliant opening comment on communist Poland. (pp. 36-8)

[*Walkover*] from the personal point of view can perhaps best be seen as a projection by Skolimowski to the age at which a boxer becomes concerned that he is no longer young. At the back of his mind one feels that there must have been the thought, that had he not entered films, the problem could have been a particularly personal one.

In contrast to the amateurish appearance of some of the techniques in *Rysopis, Walkover* strikes one throughout as a highly assured and professional work. It is an intensely physical film, giving an impression of *mise-en-scène*, driven by a powerful dynamo. . . . Skolimowski carves cleanly and coolly from the reality of contemporary Poland. The energy of the hero is translated into the energy of the *mise-en-scène*, but no emotional transfer occurs. . . . [Behind] the fast tracks and sudden zooms of the camera in *Walkover* there remains a total objectivity of viewpoint. Indeed, despite the profusion of detail in *Walkover*, one would say that Skolimowski's concern was with lucidity, and the identical sudden crane which greets both his knockout in the ring and the final announcement of him as a winner underlines the ambiguity of his approach. (pp. 39-40)

By making the time continuous within each sequence, Skolimowski integrates each of these movements with the disparate elements which form the background to the journey. Thus, whilst the camera is at the service of the protagonists, it never ceases to relate them to their environment. *Walkover* expresses at the same time the internal rhythms of the life of its hero, and the *melée* of impressions which comprise Skolimowski's vision of his country. (pp. 40-1)

*Walkover* introduces the theme of the 'personal struggle' into Skolimowski's work, just as *Rysopis* introduced that of the 'personal journey'. In his two minute recording for Teresa (which she never hears) Andrzej says that he will show her that it is necessary to fight for no matter what until one's last breath. He is not speaking simply as a boxer. Although he fights because boxing is his obsession, because in the ring he is searching for 'the last moment of happiness', equally it is to assert his identity, to prove himself *as an individual*. It is for much the same reasons that the hero of *Barrier* gives up his medical course, or Marc in *Le Départ* feels that he has to win the motor rally: both are struggling against conforming. . . . The final image of *Walkover* is . . . one of defeat. . . . (pp. 42-3)

It does however seem a less pessimistic ending than that of *Rysopis:* Andrzej does at least go down fighting. . . . This is his moment of decision in the film, a much more positive decision than that in *Rysopis,* and it leads, quite unexpectedly, to the result which provides the title of the film: Wielgosz has not turned up and Andrzej is given a walkover. The title is however ironic. . . .

In *Walkover* the background emphasis is on the new Poland which is displacing the old: most of the film takes place on the site of a large new industrial development. The choice of such a site has a specific political significance: the development is an example of the sort of heavy industry which the U.S.S.R. insists upon in her satellites for her own benefit, rather than permitting these countries to develop the light industries which would improve *their* standard of living. The choice thus underlines the powerful and repressive Soviet heritage, which the Poles, in common with their East European neighbours, have been unable to break free from. On the site, however, Skolimowski takes great delight in showing the individual Polish quirks which keep surfacing. (p. 43)

Teresa seems to represent the personal side of the heavy Soviet heritage. . . . [Skolimowski] has said of Teresa: 'She is a former Stalinist who has learned by heart what she should think and she recites it.' (p. 44)

The cross is a dominant image from Teresa's past which . . . , at her moment of distress, suddenly looms up before her—like a long forgotten (repressed?) memory. Even though we are not able to be precise about the spirit in which Skolimowski intended the manifestation, we can recognise its validity as a poetic device, resurrecting the spectre of Teresa's religious past. It is not irrelevant that Andrzej's 'mental image' when he is knocked out by Maniek is of Elzbieta Czyzewska, a vivid memory from *his* past: the cross appears before Teresa at a similar moment of stress (and, in fact, at a similar 'moment of truth'). Lest all this sound a little portentous however, I should add that whatever Skolimowski intended the cross to mean to Teresa, there certainly seems to be a dark humour behind this introduction of it in such a bizarre manner. (pp. 44-5)

Skolimowski's vision of religion in Poland takes the form of a society frozen in the past, with no contact with the outside world. (p. 46)

That this charge arises only obliquely is typical of Skolimowski's method. *Walkover* is a film in which many facets emerge only on repeated viewings. Even with these viewings,

however, elements remain obscure. One suspects that some are simply too indigenous to be grasped by outsiders, but there are others where one has an idea of what Skolimowski is saying, but it seems to be very deviously expressed. . . .

Particularly richly developed in the film, however, is the weaving of past and present. In the characters of his protagonists as well as the character of his country Skolimowski emphasises how, although the new has displaced the old, the heritage of the old lingers on, constantly surfacing and affecting the new. He does this whilst remaining rigorously in the present tense, and with only the minimal disturbance to the narrative flow of the film, so that we have to be constantly alert to the background references which he introduces. (p. 47)

Even more than *Walkover, Barrier* strikes one by its visual brilliance. Skolimowski has changed emphasis here, subordinating the surface verisimilitude so fundamental to his previous works to create a *mise-en-scène* with an unreal, almost surrealist/dreamlike atmosphere. There are even sequences which one would describe as 'pure fantasy'; however, lest this be thought of as departing too far from the path of realism, I should emphasise that not only were the stylistic innovations of *Barrier* all implicit in *Walkover,* but also that *Barrier* contains a portrait of contemporary Poland which is no less vivid *or* valid than that in *Walkover.* . . . Whereas in *Walkover* the 'poetic touches' were intermittent, in *Barrier* they inform the whole conception of the movie: its images, rhythm, development. Sequences of 'pure fantasy' are blended with stylised visualisations of reality, creating a richly poetic (*and* homogenous) texture.

In justifying the particular form of this stylisation—the 'dreamlike atmosphere' of the film—two points can be made:

1) It enables Skolimowski to pare away extraneous detail until he arrives at a condensed image which conveys immediately all that he requires. . . . [The] bleak décor of the pensioners' home in *Barrier* crystallises in one image Skolimowski's vision of a comfortless, cellular world, sealed off from all life outside. . . . [The] sequence has an almost nightmarish quality. . . . The fantasy sequences showing the people running in a continuous circle, circumscribed by a hall of mirrors, have a similar quality: everyone going through the same mindless routine without a flicker of dissent. This is how Skolimowski sees Polish society: with the lives of the people depersonalised and regimented to an extent which *is* nightmarish.

2) It emphasises the somnambulistic quality of the journey of the student. Having given up his medical course (his one *active* gesture of protest, though it derives more from frustration) he sets out seemingly without the remotest idea of what he is going to do. (pp. 48-9)

Why the student's journey should be so somnambulistic can I think be seen if we consider his role as a representative Skolimowski hero. It is first of all significant that Skolimowski himself does not play the role. . . . Remembering that Skolimowski was seven when the war finished, we could say that, just as the hero of *Walkover* was effectively a projection forward by the director, so the hero of *Barrier* is a similar projection back. However the student seems to have little in common with the Skolimowski in Andrzej Leszczyc. His dreamy passivity contrasts quite strongly with Andrzej's energetic questioning and he has a childlike naivety and simplicity of response which mark him as someone who is temperamentally altogether different. Certainly he starts out in a determined fashion, but his protest evaporates rapidly once he is on his own. It becomes clear that when the charlady in the restaurant gets up and sings the Skolimowski poem (an electrifying moment), the poem refers to *him:* his protest (that he is too young to celebrate with the war veterans) having become no more than a 'straightening of the tie'. And just as he is a dead loss as a revolutionary, so his attempt to 'start a new life' gets nowhere. He is, simply, a dreamer.

However, Skolimowski proves to have a great affection for his dreamy hero. He introduces him to the heroine in a spirit of romanticism quite alien to his previous works, and the film acquires a strong positive centre in their growing feeling for one another: she awakens the student from his dreamy state and gives a sense of purpose to his journey. . . . [For] the first time Skolimowski has presented us with a heroine who is pretty, charming and, above all, warm and responsive. . . .

The title of the film, we are assured, refers specifically to the barrier between generations. . . . When the student visits his father in the pensioners' home we can see how little communication there is between them. . . . Yet the non-communication is not just between father and son: the student is an outsider it seems simply because of his age. . . . [It] is in the restaurant scene that the theme finds its fullest expression. (pp. 49-50)

Although we should not perhaps take the student's bitterness as the last word on the veterans (it derives to a large extent from his own feeling of exclusion), there *is* a barrier simply because his father's generation is still so preoccupied with the war. . . . The war has created another barrier: between the men who can celebrate its heroic camaraderie and the women who (no matter for what reason) are left cold by it. . . .

Earlier the girl's attitude to her parents' generation had been more regretful than bitter, as we see from her attitude to the magazine vendor in the restaurant. . . . In the film, the vendor becomes her symbolic father: it is she who tries to make him aware of his potential: 'Why stoop to this in the prime of life?' But her concern is in vain. By converting the magazines into the paper hat form shown him by the student, the vendor has a sell-out. (p. 51)

Skolimowski's awareness of mortality under the pressures of contemporary living is quite striking. *Rysopis* and *Walkover* both contain road accidents, and *Barrier* and *Le Départ* each contain a heart-attack in a public place. Only in *Barrier* however is the heart-attack followed through to its bitter conclusion. Before the girl and the student can reach the ambulance taking the vendor, it moves away: an example of 'the image of separation' which occurs again and again in Skolimowski; here indicating the emphasis placed by the system on efficient despatch rather than human solicitude. . . .

The sudden collapse of the magazine vendor after his success could be seen as a dire warning of what might happen to the student: both are seeking to start a new life. But the former's failure serves more to underline the difference between the generations; the student clearly is more resilient (surviving the slide down the ski slope on his case!). Both attempts to start anew are in fact variations on a basic theme of the movie: that of rebirth, or resurrection. The setting of the film during the Easter period, with the strong emphasis on the ambient religious atmosphere, provides the background to the theme. Most of the people are celebrating Christ's resurrection, but for some there is the dream of a personal 'rebirth'; of starting a new life. . . .

The new life that the student *says* he wants for himself in the opening sequence shows absolutely no signs of ever happening. One might think that this is because he is so vague, but in fact the development of the film is towards his *enlightenment*, and consequent rejection of the property-owning ethos. (p. 52)

After the richness and complexity of *Walkover* and *Barrier, Le Départ* seems something of a disappointment, though by no means a failure. Primarily it lacks the density of these works, Skolimowski not surprisingly does not have as much to say about Belgium as Poland. . . .

Nevertheless, if *Le Départ* seems lightweight Skolimowski, it is nonetheless his film. The hero, Marc . . . is in the tradition of the dissatisfied Skolimowski heroes: a young hairdresser who dreams of becoming a famous rally driver. (p. 56)

[*Hands Up!*] is a continuation of the other Polish films. The 'hero' is a thirty-five year old doctor who graduated ten years ago: the crucial ten years referred to at the beginning of *Barrier*. There the student says 'I'm sparing myself ten years surrender of ambition and ideals'; of the hero of *Hands Up!* Skolimowski says 'He has lost all the ideals he had when he was a young student. His life consists of all the unimportant things surrounding him, and which he constantly replaces to achieve a kind of variation. He gets new cars, new houses, new wives. He is obsessed by owning things . . .' He also says 'It is my best and most mature film, and it is not funny at all.' . . .

[If] Polanski came to bear testament to our quirks and neuroses, Skolimowski one hopes will lead us to a heightened awareness of our inner drives and impulses. (pp. 61-2)

*Michael Walker, ''Jerzy Skolimowski,'' in* Second Wave, *edited by Ian Cameron & others (© 1970 by Movie Magazine Limited; reprinted by permission of* Movie*), Frederick A. Praeger, Publishers, 1970, pp. 34-62.*

**GORDON GOW**

[The films made by Jerzy Skolimowski] have indicated that he learned quite young how to study his fellow humans with a shrewd balance of objectivity and compassion. The process continues in *Deep End*. . . . Its internationalism, in the important sense, resides in the universality of the theme: the pitfalls of adolescence.

As Skolimowski himself grows older (he will never see 30 again, so they say), his central figures become increasingly younger, as if he were tracing life's enigma to its source. (p. 90)

The greater part of the film is played for humour, and the interesting thing is that this is never too extreme (as it was, I thought, in sections of *Le Départ*). It is difficult to tell whether Skolimowski was trying sometimes to mock the traditional British reserve: if so, he has seen it very quaintly and with a certain validity. . . .

The film has resolved itself into a heightened impression of the adolescent state, when life is moving far too fast and there seems to be no chance of stopping it. (p. 92)

*Gordon Gow, ''Reviews: 'Deep End''' (© copyright Gordon Gow 1971; reprinted with permission), in* Films and Filming, *Vol. 17, No. 8, May, 1971, pp. 90, 92.*

## ROGER GREENSPUN

The bath in **"Deep End"** is not so much a place for getting clean as a place for indulging fantasies, generally sexual, and Skolimowski, who drops symbols the way detective writers drop clues, is not about to ignore any of its possibilities. All through the film, the peeling blues and greens on the walls are being painted over with hot colors, mostly red, to match the growth of passion and to set things up for the climax, in which the décor is at least as important as the action—and indeed is inseparable from it. . . .

Like Truffaut's Antoine Doinel, to whom he owes a good deal, [Mike] muddles through. But unlike Antoine, what he muddles through to has only a nightmare relation to the cultural mainstream and the affectionate light of common day.

Although it has a strong and good story, **"Deep End"** is put together out of individual, usually comic routines. Many of these don't work, but many more work very well.

> Roger Greenspun, "*Skolimowski Director of Paris's Feature*," in The New York Times (© 1971 by The New York Times Company; reprinted by permission), August 11, 1971 (and reprinted in The New York Times Film Reviews: 1971-1972, The New York Times Company & Arno Press, 1973, p. 115).

## RICHARD COMBS

Skolimowski's erratic, piecemeal, yet distinctly Nabokovian adaptation of **King, Queen, Knave** seems subsequently to have been abandoned to its own hermetic limbo; one of those freakishly unreal landscapes that Skolimowski has scattered across the continent. . . .

Skolimowski thus adds his own twist to Nabokov's explanation of how, in dealing with German characters in a German setting, his ignorance of all things German 'answered my dream of pure invention'; and the film slyly demonstrates that the Nabokovian mechanics are still in good working order, though in the hands of a new engineer. (p. 53)

Centred vaguely on the efforts of the mad inventor commissioned by Dreyer to develop mechanical mannequins out of his bizarre discovery of a perfect rubber substitute for skin, Nabokov's ironic manipulations of his characters emphasised how, in their respective dreams and schemes, they reduced each other to dummies, playing-cards, inanimate articles, and worse. More eccentric in his stylisation, Skolimowski achieves the same effect with fizzing changes of mood, suggesting instead of teasing layers of dream fitful explosions of obsession. . . .

Skolimowski undoubtedly loses out to Nabokov at the periphery, where such incidental characters in the novel as the old landlord Enricht occasionally shuffle centre stage and seem about to take over the whole fiction ('For he knew perfectly well—had known for the last eight years at least—that the whole world was but a trick of his'). The sideline figures of the film—like the old man who stumbles by with a cross, temporarily barring Frank's way to another battering tryst—become just so many impedimenta, part of the bizarrely jangled soundtrack accompaniment to the obliviously comic *danse macabre* of the principal clowns. (p. 54)

> Richard Combs, "'*King, Queen, Knave*'," in Sight and Sound (copyright © 1974 by The British Film Institute), Vol. 43, No. 1, Winter, 1973-74, pp. 53-4.

## PETER COWIE

*Rysopis* ends as it began—in a void. It is a film with a question mark in every sentence, and the idea of the quest is given physical expression by Skolimowski's skilful subjective camerawork, leading his audience down staircases, through gigantic scrapyards, and along crowded streets that heighten the feeling of dislocation.

*Rysopis* may owe something to Godard in terms of technique and incident . . . ; but it is both too dour and too bitter to be French, and Skolimowski's own performance in the role of Andrzej carefully avoids magniloquent gestures and makes no appeal to sentimentality.

In *Walkover,* the personality of Andrzej is more clearly defined. The intelligent, rather sad face tucked truculently into the shoulders; a listener more than a talker; a disconsolate, reflective fighter. (p. 234)

*Barrier* is an obtuse fantasy that questions contemporary Polish society, championing the young student outsider at the expense of the generation that fed him and fought in the ruins of Warsaw during the Second World War. Everything in the film is related in symbolic terms. Sombre, menacing scenes tip over into comedy at their last gasp. . . . *Barrier* is like a piece of *avant-garde* animation where one has time only to respond to the welter of images, and not to reason out their larger meaning. It is as seductive as it is unpredictable, and if some sequences are intolerably pretentious (old Resistance fighters jostling together in a night-club, wearing paper hats for Stupidity), there are other moments of quiet, almost entranced reflection. (p. 235)

[*Le départ*] reveals a hitherto untapped vein of surrealist humour in Skolimowski. This film spurns the dictates of conventional narrative and screen logic. It is essentially a few random reflections on a theme—a young man's frustrated desire to participate in big-time motor racing that gradually comes to be identified with his sexual inhibitions. . . . Like Skolimowski's direction, Marc's compulsive behaviour not only ridicules each *cliché,* but endows it with fresh currency, even though his approach to life springs from conventional impulses (smoking to suggest maturity, abandoning a stolen car because a pet poodle appears on the back seat). His cheekiness is infectious, and provides a mordant contrast with the universal happiness preached by posters in the street; and his response to violence, like Paul's in [Godard's] *Masculin-Féminin,* reveals more curiosity than cynicism. (p. 236)

[*Hands Up!*], with Skolimowski again playing the leading role, forms a trilogy with *Rysopis* and *Walkover.* . . . It has the contours of a dream, as five doctors, now in their forties, meet on the anniversary of their qualification. . . . The extra-ordinary climax shows everyone struggling to escape from the railway coach which . . . has become, by a weird association of ideas, a replica of the wagons in which their older brothers and their fathers were sent to the gas chamber. Fear is the dominant characteristic of *Hands Up!*—fear of losing position, patronage, and privilege in a society that Skolimowski would appear to regard as being not much better than the one his elders struggled to replace after the war. (pp. 236-37)

With an even younger protagonist than Marc in *Le départ,* **Deep End** catches the mysterious awakening of adolescence, when fantasies are nourished by a frustration that only the experience of adult life can interpret. . . . One can almost smell the chlorine and sense the shabbiness of the dressing rooms. There are surrealistic touches typical of Skolimowski: as Susan skirmishes with the cashier, a man's hand and a brush move into sight at the end of the corridor, painting the green walls an unexpected and faintly alarming red—a foretaste of the tragic finale to the film. . . .

*Deep End* exerts a powerful spell and although it was shot in Germany and recorded in English, it is at no point banal or stilted. Skolimowski's understanding of human psychology, and of the bizarre currents of desire that course below the surface—at the "deep end"—of the mind, is uncanny. This film offers the conclusive proof that Skolimowski's is not just a quirkish Polish talent, but an arresting vision that can be transmitted to any locale and any period. (p. 238)

> *Peter Cowie, "Jerzy Skolimowski," in* Fifty Major Film-Makers, *edited by Peter Cowie (© 1975 by Peter Cowie), A. S. Barnes & Co., Inc., 1975, pp. 234-38.*

### JOHN COLEMAN

When it arrives—and, by some minor miracle of audiophonics, it does—the throaty clamour indicated by the title of Jerzy Skolimowski's latest excursion into English-speaking cinema is unlike most promises: quite up to expectations, one hell of a howl. Thus giving away the biggest, single effect in *The Shout,* I have made a choice which clearly reflects on the film as a whole: as a whole, it is a hole. Taken at what remove I know not . . . from a source of general repute, it comes out as about the craziest cinematic structure in a fair while. Skolimowski—too long absent from our screens—is an expatriate Pole of enormous talent, mostly leaning into the surreal. Whether he has genius is something else and this self-inflating doubt seems to beset even his better movies. One thinks especially of the anglicised side of his career and, accordingly, of *Deep End,* where he gave us a sly, merry and murky tale of kinds of life blossoming around a public baths in some echoing appearance of an East End, tiled and chlorinated remnant of Victoriana. . . . It was us rinsed into freshness, as well as a terminal bloodiness.

*The Shout* lies closer to Altman. . . . [It] is not only lethal but apparently aphrodisiac: see [Susannah] York's shameless behaviour. Much more amusement, in the indecipherable event, is provided by a very in-and-out context or set of flashes-forward. . . . Flames, and a screaming Francis Bacon-derived yowl (previously salted in), conclude the revel. A quantity of the detail is extremely attractive and special. (pp. 751-52)

> *John Coleman, "Crying Out Loud," in* New Statesman *(© 1978 The Statesman & Nation Publishing Co. Ltd.), Vol. 95, No. 2463, June 2, 1978, pp. 751-52.\**

### ANDREW SARRIS

[*The Shout*] reminded me more of early [Joseph Losey-Harold Pinter] than of the Skolimowski responsible for *Bariera* [*Barrier*] and *Deep End*. Most people seemed to like this menacing work more than I did. It may be that I am getting tired of malignant horror films and the easy way in which they exploit our rampant paranoia. The use of noise rather than blood to generate fear and loathing is somewhat imaginative in terms of this particular genre. But ultimately I was put off by Skolimowski's Caligariesque fudging on the facts of the plot. Did the [Alan] Bates character learn to render his death-dealing shout from the Australian aborigines? Did the story of the film really happen? Or is it a tale full of sound and fury, signifying

nothing? In the modern cinema one hesitates to ask these questions for fear of offending the sacred artist. (p. 40)

> *Andrew Sarris, "Catch as Catch Cannes: The Moles and the Moths" (reprinted by permission of* The Village Voice *and the author; copyright © The Village Voice, Inc., 1978), in* The Village Voice, *Vol. XXIII, No. 24, June 12, 1978, pp. 39-40.\**

### TOM ALLEN

I am more ready to accept Skolimowski as a bonafide stylist in the school of mechanico-yet-rapturous absurdism, which tended to self-destruct at the turn of the decade, than as an artist. And I'll settle for *King, Queen, Knave* as a molehill of dreck. . . .

For the first and perhaps purest example of a spoof that works, I would have to recommend Skolimowski's *The Adventures of Gerard.* It has the good sense to steer a delightful ninny of a hero across the massive canvas of Napoleon's campaign against Wellington in Spain. Invention is never allowed to flag, yet it remains chilly and stylistically distanced at the core. . . .

Combining touches of black humor and a handsome production on the throwaway epic scale that makes Bondarchuk's *Waterloo* look drab and ponderous, *The Aventures of Gerard* is an affectionate valentine to gallant foolhardiness. . . .

Nabokov's *King, Queen, Knave* is a jagged triangle: a haberdashery-tycoon husband preoccupied with inventing motorized mannequins; a neglected wife who initiates a young relative into sex and homicide; and the young target of her wiles tempted with pleasures and power beyond the ken of his humble origins. Skolimowski's treatment achieves only a clinically kinky and cliched burlesque rather than a vigorously erotic slapstick of manners. The film's final metaphor of the King transforming his Queen into an assembly-line window mannequin is an accurate reflection of the human level on which all the characters are treated. I fear the tendency to mannequinize his characters is also the central flaw of all of Skolimowski's films this past decade.

> *Tom Allen, "Old Stylists Never Die" (reprinted by permission of* The Village Voice *and the author; copyright © The Village Voice, Inc., 1978), in* The Village Voice, *Vol. XXIII, No. 50, December 11, 1978, p. 59.\**

### WILLIAM JOHNSON

*The Shout* was not the most inventive, the most beautiful or the most crisply made entry in the last New York Film Festival, but I found it by far the most engrossing. This surprised me, since in the two of Skolimowski's previous films that I'd seen (*Bariera,* made in his native Poland, and *Le Départ,* made in Belgium) he had relied on the sixties theme of dissatisfied youth, dressing it up with some neat but obvious visual gimmickry. With *The Shout,* the theme has gone but gimmicks recur. . . . [Since] Skolimowski is working here in yet another foreign language, amid the temptation to shift his energies from unfamiliar words to familiar images, he may be praised for showing visual restraint. But negative virtues cannot account for the strong positive impression made by this film.

The search for an explanation led me much further than I expected. (p. 53)

[Both Robert Graves's story, on which the film is based,] and Skolimowski's film can be enjoyed simply as skillful pieces of naturalistic fantasy. The only element that does not work in the film so well as in the story is Anthony's discovery of the soul-stones: since their nature, in the absence of Graves's description, is not easily grasped, they throw a gratuitously bizarre light on C's story and his mental condition. On the other hand, the cricket setting works much better in the film, where even the briefest cutback presents the viewer with the full ironic contrast between the game code that more or less unites the players and the urgent private codes that compel some of them to run amuck. (p. 54)

The film stresses certain elements in Graves which seem to invite a psychoanalytic interpretation, notably Charles's desire for Rachel and his antipathy to Anthony.

If *The Shout* yielded nothing more than secondhand Freud it would hardly be an engrossing film. In any case, Graves would rather see goddesses than complexes at work on the human psyche: in his introduction to *The Greek Myths* he tosses a few barbs at both Freud and Jung and insists on the historical origins of mythology in the shift from matriarchal to patriarchal society. Skolimowski, in self-exile from socialist Poland, is even more likely to view conflicts in political rather than psycho-analytical terms.

Sure enough, the film lends itself readily to interpretation as a parable about Marxist revolution—a double parable, in fact. If C's story is taken at face value, Anthony embodies the evils of the bourgeoisie. . . . Charles, by contrast, has broken with his bourgeois background (having spent years among victims of colonialist repression) and spurns its blandishments; he is a revolutionary prepared to use violence. . . .

If C's story is taken as self-serving propaganda, the same basic events appear in a different light. Charles's characterization of Anthony becomes problematic, and so does his claim to have broken with bourgeois culture. . . .

Like the Freudian interpretation, this parable is at most a tributary to the film's current of meaning. It goes further, but not far enough to explain why the film is engrossing: though it offers two alternative views of events instead of just one, it places them in a static context. Both the Freudian and the political interpretations overlook a brief but crucial element in the film: the dynamic role played by Rachel.

While she figures as little more than a pawn (or the stake) in the contest between Charles and Anthony, Rachel dominates the opening and closing scenes—to far-reaching effect. . . . [The] outer frame not only leaves the truth of C's story up in the air but it also raises uncertainties *outside* the conflict between Anthony and Charles. (p. 55)

[The] dramatic structure of *The Shout* coincides not only with elemental human patterns (the circle, the group of three) but also with the phenomenological division of film imagery; the intensity of these combined forces sparks a connection between the specific encounter of Anthony and Charles and a general field of human conflict.

Though this may seem ambitious enough, it still does not account for the full fascination of *The Shout*. As the title might suggest, the use of sound also plays an important role—and it is one that does *not* repeat the pattern of the imagery. In theory, the sound track could also be divided into three phenomenological levels: unorganized sound (noise), a steady frequency or set of frequencies (single tone or tonal complex) and a modulated sequence (speech, music). (p. 57)

The oddest way in which the sound track brackets Charles and Anthony together is in making them both seem equally real and unreal. In C's story, by far the longest of the film's three segments, Skolimowski uses a full range of naturalistic sound effects and speech to create a circumstantial background of reality. (In films with visions, dreams, hallucinations and the like, the image may remain normal but the sound track invariably cues the shift of mode by means of echoes, amplifications, distortions, or unexpected silence.) The other two segments, of course, throw doubt on the reality of C's story, but they do not disprove it; most significantly, Anthony never says a word that would reveal his "true" manner of speech. As a result, the Charles and Anthony of C's story come to share a dual nature: they are individual men *and* two sides of Charles at one and the same time.

Seen—or rather, heard—in this way, the film suggests that the Anthony and Charles of C's story might have been able to find a *modus vivendi*, combining their opposed forces instead of directing them against each other. Rachel in the outer frame may be regretful or angry not simply at Charles's death but at the lost opportunity. (pp. 58-9)

Is it a serious film that was intended to carry the weight of interpretation I have loaded onto it? Or is it an entertaining commercial film that plays, like Anthony, with serious-looking (and-sounding) elements? Or is it a serendipitous mixture of the two?

I opt for the last. The film's casting, setting and photography, and its touches of sex, satire and exoticism mark the distance that Skolimowski went to meet commercial requirements, while the skillful adaptation of Graves, the balance of sympathy between Charles and Anthony, and the obscure ending reveal a strong undertow of noncommercial intent. . . .

It may also be luck that the fabric of the sound film—three phenomenological levels of imagery intersected by indeterminate contexts of sound—matches the dramatic cross-currents of *The Shout;* but if so, it is luck of a different kind, a resource that the maker of any complex narrative film must be able to tap. . . . [The] maker of a film like *The Shout* has somehow to organize all the multifarious interactions of image, sound and content that baffle conscious preprogramming. Whatever the resource behind that "somehow," Skolimowski has at last tapped it. (p. 59)

*William Johnson, "Reviews: 'The Shout'," in* Film Quarterly *(copyright 1979 by The Regents of the University of California; reprinted by permission of the University of California Press), Vol. XXXIII, No. 1, Fall, 1979, pp. 53-9.*

## SHEILA BENSON

*The Shout* is a film of magic, terror and sensuality; it seduces you through your eyes and ears while keeping your mind spinning with the strands of its intricate story.

Skolimowski is deft in handling these multi-level fragments which mix present and future, and at suspicion, suggestion and innuendo. He carries a mood from one scene to the next with textures, with sound and with fragments of dialogue. (p. 25)

How do you convincingly create a sound which kills people at close range, knocks birds from the sky and topples grazing sheep? The sound which bursts from Bates—who crouches, head bent to his shoe-tops, gathering force before delivering it—is a roar, a rumble, a blast of air. It encompasses nature and electronics. It is indeed stunning.

A warning: One element in the story is not—to put it kindly—absolutely crystalline in the film.

*The Shout* is haunting enough that this difficulty doesn't damage it, but it seems to confuse audiences mightily. A fascinating work with a dream cast playing to perfection, it should provoke impassioned after-movie discussion. (p. 26)

*Sheila Benson, "A Stunning Roar that Kills," in* Pacific Sun *(Copyright ©1980 Pacific Sun Publishing Co., Inc.), Year 18, No. 22 , May 30-June 5, 1980, pp. 25-6.*

# Steven Spielberg

## 1947-

**American director, screenwriter, and producer.**

**Spielberg is one of the most successful of the many young directors who emerged in the seventies. Spectacle is perhaps the most prominent element in his films: the shark in *Jaws*, the alien spaceship in *Close Encounters of the Third Kind*. In these films, Spielberg creates the terror of the unknown to bring about a catharsis in his audience.**

**Spielberg began making short films while in high school. He spent three months at Universal Studios in 1967, sneaking past the guard each day to watch directors work in television. Spielberg's short film *Amblin'* won a number of awards and helped him become a television director. He directed episodes of six different programs, including *Night Gallery, The Psychiatrists*, and *Columbo*, and also directed three made-for-TV movies. The first of these movies, *Duel*, has been widely acclaimed as one of the best movies television has ever produced.**

**Spielberg's first feature, *The Sugarland Express*, contains a number of the best elements of *Duel*, including a choreographed car chase, but critics are divided as to the film's artistic merit. Spielberg himself has said, "If I had it to do all over again I'd make *Sugarland Express* in a completely different fashion." Spielberg was totally unprepared for the huge commercial success of his next film, *Jaws*. The movie combines humor, violence, contemporary problems, and horror, and the end result is an engrossing story that has received much critical acclaim. *Close Encounters of the Third Kind* received as much publicity for its special effects as for Spielberg's directorial prowess and screenwriting talents, and it is generally believed to be his best work to date.**

**Although Spielberg's directorial abilities seem to get lost among the special effects in his films, he still feels that his films are personal statements. As Spielberg has said: "A lot of my films are question-answer pictures leading up to an inevitable conclusion that the audience is waiting for, and hopefully they won't be disappointed." (See also *Contemporary Authors*, Vols. 77-80.)**

### TOM MILNE

With almost insolent ease, *Duel* . . . displays the philosopher's stone which the Existentialists sought so persistently and often so portentously: the perfect *acte gratuit*, complete, unaccount-able and self-sufficient. Steven Spielberg . . . sets the scene brilliantly from the outset. . . .

The glory of Richard Matheson's script is that there are no motivations, no explanations, simply the archetypal rivalry of the road carried to *reductio ad absurdum* heights. At first there are moments of unease—the commercial traveller's name, after all, is Mann—in the telephone call to his wife which suggests a background of marital stress, in the rather coy insistence . . . with which his efforts to put a face to his rival are frustrated. But all these hints of allegory (man's inability to cope with machine-age pressures) are held firmly in check, giving just a touch of abstract meaning to the unseen lorrydriver, just a touch of social fallibility to the ineffectual salesman, and leaving the way free for a simple mortal combat between hunter and hunted in which one can, if one likes, see the huge, lumbering lorry as the dragon, and the glitteringly fragile Plymouth sedan as the prancing, pitifully vulnerable knight in armour.

Adhering strictly to these limits and only once leaving the road . . . Spielberg and Matheson screw the tension almost to breaking point with a series of cunningly contrived incidents which simultaneously reveal the full extent of the lorry-driver's murderous intent and turn the timid salesman into an animal fighting desperately for his life. . . . Like Clouzot's *Wages of Fear*, *Duel* may be a once-only film, an exercise in tension which never seems quite so rewarding the second time round; but like *Wages of Fear* and unlike *Les Diaboliques*, it is a film built on legitimate suspense rather than sham trickery.

*Tom Milne, "'Duel'," in* Sight and Sound *(copyright © 1973 by The British Film Institute), Vol. 42, No. 1, Winter, 1972-73, p. 50.*

### PAULINE KAEL

"The Sugarland Express" is like some of the entertaining studio-factory films of the past (it's as commercial and shallow and impersonal), yet it has so much eagerness and flash and talent that it just about transforms its scrubby ingredients. . . . [Steven Spielberg] isn't saying anything special in "**The Sugarland Express**," but he has a knack for bringing out young actors, and a sense of composition and movement that almost any director might envy. Composition seems to come naturally to him . . . ; Spielberg uses his gift in a very free-and-easy, American way—for humor, and for a physical response to action. He could be that rarity among directors, a born entertainer—perhaps a new generation's Howard Hawks. In terms of the pleasure that technical assurance gives an audience, this film is one of the most phenomenal début films in the history of movies. If there is such a thing as a movie sense—and I think there is . . .—Spielberg really has it. But he may be so full of it that he doesn't have much else. There's no sign of the emergence of a new film artist (such as Martin Scorsese) in **"The Sugarland Express,"** but it marks the début of a new-style, new-generation Hollywood hand. (p. 300)

**"The Sugarland Express"** is mostly about cars; Spielberg is a choreographic virtuoso with cars. He patterns them; he makes them dance and crash and bounce back. He handles enormous configurations of vehicles; sometimes they move so sweetly you think he must be wooing them. These sequences are as unforced and effortless-looking as if the cars themselves—mesmerized—had just waltzed into their idiot formations. . . . [The] cars shimmer in the hot sunlight; in the dark, the red lights of the police cars are like eerie night-blooming flowers. The cars have tiffs, wrangle, get confused. And so do the people, who are also erratic and—in certain lights—eerily beautiful. . . . These huffy characters, riled up and yelling at each other, are in the combustible comedy style of Preston Sturges. . . . This movie enjoys orneriness and collision courses; as the Sturges movies did; it sees the characters' fitful, moody nuttiness as the American's inalienable right to make a fool of himself. It merges Sturges' love of comic confusion with the action world of cars to create a jamboree. (pp. 300-01)

You get the feeling that the director grew up with TV and wheels . . . and that he has a new temperament. Maybe Spielberg loves action and comedy and speed so much that he really doesn't care if a movie has anything else in it. But he doesn't copy old stuff. He isn't deep, but he isn't derivative, either. (p. 302)

Spielberg savors film, and you respond to that. **"The Sugarland Express"** has life to it. Not the kind of life that informs a young film like [Scorsese's] "Mean Streets" . . .—but the vitality that a director with great instincts can bring to commercial entertainment. (p. 303)

> *Pauline Kael, "Sugarland and Badlands" (originally published in* The New Yorker, *Vol. 50, No. 4, March 18, 1974), in her* Reeling *(copyright © 1974 by Pauline Kael; reprinted by permission of Little, Brown and Company in association with the Atlantic Monthly Press), Altantic-Little, Brown, 1976, pp. 300-06.**

### STEPHEN FARBER

**"The Sugarland Express"** is a prime example of the new-style factory movie: slick, cynical, mechanical, empty. Spielberg and his young writers, Hall Barwood and Matthew Robbins, have been weaned on old Hollywood movies, and they want to recreate the schlock that once mesmerized the masses. They have good memories, and a shrewd commercial instinct that the industry often confuses with talent.

Although **"The Sugarland Express"** is based on a real incident that happened in Texas in 1969, it seems perfectly synthetic—pure Hollywood—from first frame to last. (p. 203)

Everything is underlined; Spielberg sacrifices narrative logic and character consistency for quick thrills and easy laughs. He has a very crude sense of humor, indicated by his obsession with toilet jokes, and an irrepressible maudlin streak. Early on

Spielberg lingers over a shot of the couple's baby playing with a dog, and after the final tragedy, he moves in for a close-up as a police car drives over a discarded teddy bear. It's depressing to see a young director who is already so shameless.

This kind of movie is like a shifty campaign speech designed to please every segment of the public. Young moviegoers can weep for Lou Jean and Clovis as rebels against the system, cut down by the authorities because they love their baby. At the same time, Spielberg cunningly softens his portrait of the police so as not to alienate the Law and Order crowd. . . . **"The Sugarland Express"** is a "social statement" whose only commitment is to the box office. (pp. 203-04)

Toward the end the movie turns into another tired celebration of male camaraderie. Clovis and patrolman Slide . . . are striking up a beautiful friendship that the dumb bitch-wife destroys. In its misogyny **"The Sugarland Express"** echoes a whole series of popular American movies, but this is one element in the film that may not have been consciously calculated to sell. The amusing thing is that even these filmmakers' unconscious prejudices are not their own; their souls belong to Hollywood.

Spielberg is admittedly a skillful (if vulgar) technician, and he understands how to engineer car chases and crashes; but he doesn't have an original idea or the slightest feeling for people. A good way to test a young director is to look at his handling of actors; Spielberg fails that test miserably. Under his direction even the nonprofessionals act like Hollywood hams. . . . (p. 204)

> *Stephen Farber, "Something Sour," in* The New York Times *(© 1974 by The New York Times Company; reprinted by permission), April 28, 1974 (and reprinted in* The New York Times Film Reviews: 1973-1974, *The New York Times Company & Arno Press, 1975, pp. 203-04).*

### TOM MILNE

After *Duel*, Steven Spielberg's dazzling way with the cars in *The Sugarland Express* was almost a foregone conclusion: stately processions snaking through the countryside in the wake of the fugitives, multi-coloured roof-lights forming intriguing patterns in the night, pursuers retarded by the telephoto lens looming menacingly out of the heat-haze at the crest of a hill. But where *Duel* was motivated by a strange inner compulsion, *The Sugarland Express* seems peculiarly contrived, with a script (albeit based on fact) so self-consciously tailored to the 'road film' formula that from the very outset the illusory Eldorado of Sugarland becomes a dismayingly obvious metaphor for the bitter-sweetness of the odyssey we are invited to watch. . . . All too early on . . . the whole thing is revealed to be a storm in a teacup, and one watches with mounting disbelief as both police and public go through their extraordinary gyrations: it may have happened this way in real life, but in the film the fugitives are so unequivocally presented as poor, harmless innocents that the veritable army of police cars absurdly queueing up to be in at the kill looks very much as though both they and the film were taking a sledgehammer to crack a nut. Paradoxically, therefore, the film is at its best not on the road (despite the striking car imagery) but in the lay-bys: the moments of repose when the forced relationship between the couple and their hostage begins to evolve into something more than mere friendship. In themselves, though observed with fresh, delicate humour, the episodes which mark the stages in the relationship are not particularly original . . . . [There is] a sense of deprivation, a feeling that the staid young patrolman has never before encountered such freedom and fantasy, while the young couple have never experienced such stability as he represents. Never overtly stated, the point reverberates through the film. . . .

Tom Milne, " 'The Sugarland Express'," *in* Monthy Film Bulletin *(copyright © The British Film Institute, 1974), Vol. 41, No. 486, July, 1974, p. 158.*

### COLIN L. WESTERBECK, JR.

With a shark for a villain, Peter Benchley could hardly have missed making *Jaws* a best seller, nor is director Steven Spielberg likely to miss with his film adaptation. Benchley and Spielberg's only problem was that a shark is almost too good a villain. What way could they find to oppose such unadulterated power? Put up against the Muhammad Ali of sharkdom, the whole human race looks like a Joe Bugner.

The trouble is that where a shark is simple by nature, man is various. Where a shark is unmistakable and purposeful, man is ambiguous and self-contradictory. Accordingly, both the novel and the film try to cover the board by putting three very different men up against the shark, leaving us to amuse ourselves guessing which one really has what it takes to kill the best. This puts the movie, as an entertainment, roughly on a par with a quiz show—*What's My Line?* perhaps, or *To Tell the Truth.* (p. 210)

Although the final showdown with the shark provides the story's most incredible episode, it is also, in a sense, its moment of greatest realism. That is to say, Benchley probably came closest to truth here when he imagined that the one thing man has which is equal to a shark's is just instinct for survival, the taste for a desperate combat. It is this, rather than cunning, experience, or knowledge, that finally kills the shark. . . .

As to *who* kills the shark. . . . Well, it doesn't really matter which of three men does it. The fact is that the movie begins to blur the distinctions between them almost as soon as they are introduced. . . . Somewhere between the talk about eating dinner in the one scene and the talk of being eaten for dinner in the other, we come to realize that the three men in this movie are in fact all the same man.

Who is it that kills the shark, you may still be asking. Why, it's Peter Benchley, of course. The whole point of a novel like *Jaws* is to indulge in a little fantasy, so Benchley has paid himself the dividend of a three-for-one split of his personality. . . .

If we get to know Peter Benchley better than we ever really wanted to, that is not so disappointing as the fact that, at least in the movie, we also get to know the shark rather better than we cared to. Early in the film he remains an implied presence only. . . .

[The] further along the film goes, the more the shark, as it were, surfaces. When he is killed in the end it is in part because he has literally become a fish out of water, and for the same reason our psychological need as an audience to see him killed has pretty much abated by then. The fact that Spielberg was capable of doing acceptably realistic mock-ups of the shark for the closing scenes was not really a sufficient reason to do them. Rubber dummy, you're the one. The shark is far more frightening when he is still swimming unseen down in our subconscious. (p. 211)

Colin L. Westerbeck, Jr., "Gums," *in* Commonweal *(copyright © 1975 Commonweal Publishing Co., Inc.; reprinted by permission of Commonweal Publishing Co., Inc.), Vol. 102, No. 7, June 20, 1975, pp. 210-11.*

### JAMES MONACO

*Jaws'* singular financial performance is ultimately a matter of the craft of the film-makers involved. Not the art, the craft. *Jaws* is an extraordinarily well made entertainment. . . . There isn't an ounce of dead wood in it; it is the sum total of thousands of 'effects' (special and otherwise) tested and tuned to produce the desired response in the audience. *Jaws* is a landmark of modern cinematic engineering.

It is, therefore, something like the ultimate Hollywood movie. Not only does it represent the tradition of film as entertainment product (as opposed to film as personal statement), but it is also, like many memorable Hollywood entertainments of the past, an example of 'film as a contact sport.' Watching it one is aware that, as Howard Hawks once said in another context, 'that stuff's good, and that stuff's hard to do.' It doesn't matter with it *means;* in this kind of film-making the relevant question is, does it work? *Jaws* works. (p. 56)

James Monaco, " 'Jaws'," *in* Sight and Sound *(copyright © 1976 by The British Film Institute), Vol. 45, No. 1, Winter, 1975-76, pp. 56-7.*

### GORDON GOW

The right things certainly happen in *Jaws*. At given moments, the images before us lead to *frissons* of dread anticipation. The pulses pound. Excitement escalates. And by climax time, when it is impossible to disbelieve that one of the leading actors, screaming and vomiting blood, is actually being swallowed alive by a gigantic shark in an unnerving series of gulps, we are watching movie magic of the highest order. Trickery has mastered the illusion of truth.

The film is a condensation of Peter Benchley's novel, which deals not only in the suspense value of abrupt lethal sorties by a great white shark among the swimmers at a Long Island resort, but also in the attempts of local plenipotentiaries to hush up the danger so that the town will not suffer economically by a decrease in the number of its summertime tourists, on whom its very existence depends. The film brushes rather briskly across this ethical problem; it also makes a sprightly change in the ending, and totally eschews the sex quota that gave the book a certain amusing affinity to *Peyton Place*. What remains is a superior essay in horror.

Characters are simplified. . . . [Mostly] the humans are ciphers. The shark, on the other hand, is a wow.

Affectionately known during production as 'Bruce', the huge mechanical fish is in line of descent from Kong. But unlike the king of cinema monsters, this one has no truck with fantasy. Its titillation and terror reside in its utter realism. . . .

What Spielberg is doing in *Jaws,* though, is hardly to be esteemed to the same extent as his work on *The Sugerland Express* where he was able to bring unusual human endeavour to the forefront, giving characterisation equal consequence with the filmic exuberance of his 'road' show. The present exercise is a consolidation of received ideas from the history of suspense and horror films. It is none too original, yet exceedingly neat. (p. 30)

Gordon Gow, "'Jaws'" (© copyright Gordon Gow 1976; reprinted with permission, in Films and Filming, Vol. 22, No. 4, January, 1976, pp. 30-1.

## PAULINE KAEL

*Close Encounters of the Third Kind* is the most innocent of all technological-marvel movies, and one of the most satisfying. This film has retained some of the wonder and bafflement we feel when we first go into a planetarium: we ooh and aah at the vastness, and at the beauty of the mystery. The film doesn't overawe us, though, because it has a child's playfulness and love of surprises. . . . [The intelligent creatures in the machines from outer space] are benevolent. They want to get to know us. This vision would be *too* warm and soul-satisfying if it weren't for the writer-director Steven Spielberg's skeptical, let's-try-it-on spirit. He's an entertainer—a magician in the age of movies. Is Spielberg an artist? Not exactly—or not yet. He's a prodigy—a flimflam wizard-technician. The immense charm of *Close Encounters* comes from the fact that [this is a young man's movie] . . . and there's not a sour thought in it. (p. 348)

*Close Encounters* is a vindication of village crazies. Those people always give you the feeling they know something you don't, and in this scientific fairy tale it turns out they do. God is up there in a crystal-chandelier spaceship, and He likes us. The stoned, the gullible, the half-mad, and just plain folks are His chosen people. . . . Very few movies have ever hit upon this combination of fantasy and amusement—*The Wizard of Oz,* perhaps, in a plainer, down-home way.

*Close Encounters,* too, is a kids' movie in the best sense. You can feel the pleasure the young director took in making it. With his gift for investing machines with personality, Spielberg is the right director for science fantasy. He made a malevolent character of a truck in *Duel* his famous made-for-TV movie. In his first theatrical feature, *The Sugarland Express,* he had cars dancing, feuding, bonding. In his second film, *Jaws,* he turned a computer-operated shark into a personal enemy. And now he's got his biggest mechanical toys: the mother ship and the flying-saucer herald angels—whirring through the skies, flashing their lights. . . . *Jaws* was a nightmare movie; this is a dream. (pp. 349-50)

With a vast, clear sky full of stars, and a sense of imminence—much of the movie feels like being inside the dome of an enchanted cathedral waiting for the Arrival—terse, swift, heightened dialogue is called for. Instead, we hear casual, ordinary-man language, and, although it has an original, colloquial snap, Spielberg just doesn't have the feeling for words which he has for images. And he doesn't create the central characters . . . or develop them, in a *writer's* way; he's thinking about how to get them into the positions he wants them in for his visual plan. (p. 351)

Steven Spielberg is probably the most gifted American director who's dedicated to sheer entertainment. He may have different aims from the aims of people we call artists, but he has integrity: it centers on his means. His expressive drive is to tell a story in shots that are live and hopping, and his grasp of graphic dynamics may be as strong as that of anyone working in movies now. The spatial relationships inside the frame here owe little to the stage, or even to painting; Spielberg succeeds in making the compositions so startlingly immediate that they give off an

electric charge. He puts us right in the middle of the action, yet there's enough aesthetic distance—he doesn't assault us. Though the perspectives don't appear forced or unnatural, they're often slightly tilted, with people moving rapidly in or out of the frame, rarely intersecting the center and never occupying it. By designing the images in advance, Spielberg is able to cut without any confusion. Nobody cuts faster on shots full of activity than he does, yet it's never just for the sake of variety: it's what the movie is about that generates the images and the cutting pattern, and there's a constant pickup in excitement from shot to shot—a ziggety forward motion. (pp. 351-52)

*Close Encounters* shows an excess of kindness—an inability (or, perhaps, unwillingness) to perceive the streak of cowardice and ignorance and confusion in the actions of the authorities who balk the efforts of the visionaries to reach their goal. Having devised a plot in which the government systematically covers up information about U.F.O. sightings, Spielberg is much too casual about how this is done and imprecise about why. He has a paranoid plot, but he hasn't dramatized the enemy. . . . Impersonality doesn't enrage Spielberg, because he hasn't got at the personality hidden in it. Stock villainy isn't what's needed—something deeper is. He had similar trouble with the corrupt local merchants and politicians in *Jaws;* their corruption was tired, ritualized—it was necessary for the plot, that was all. In *Close Encounters,* there is nothing behind what the military men do except bureaucratic indifference. But that means they don't know what they're doing—and to be so totally blind is tragic, crazy emptiness. Spielberg has a genuine affection for harmless aberrants, but he doesn't fathom the dangerous aberrance of authority—particularly an authority that in its own eyes is being complete reasonable. (p. 352)

Spielberg may be the only director with technical virtuosity ever to make a transcendently sweet movie. *Close Encounters* is almost the oppose of *Star Wars,* in which a whole planet was blown up and nobody batted an eye. It seems almost inconceivable, but nobody gets hurt in this movie. . . . The film is like *Oklahoma!* in space, with jokes; it's spiritual cotton candy and it goes down easy. (p. 353)

Pauline Kael, "The Greening of the Solar System" (originally published in The New Yorker, Vol. LIII, No. 41, November 28, 1977), in her When the Lights Go Down (copyright © 1975, 1976, 1977, 1978, 1979, 1980 by Pauline Kael; reprinted by permission of Holt, Rinehart and Winston, Publishers), Holt, 1980, pp. 348-54.

## STANLEY KAUFFMANN

I was not aching to see *Close Encounters,* especially since I had disliked the previous work of its director, Steven Spielberg. His first feature, *The Sugarland Express,* had seemed facile, fake-honest naturalism. His second, *Jaws,* was made for one purpose, to scare, and flopped with me because it was so clumsily done. I was utterly unprepared for this third kind of close encounter with Spielberg. I was particularly unprepared for the last 40 minutes of this 135-minute film, in which two things happen. First, and less important, the SF film reaches its pinnacle to date. Second, the movement of SF as vicarious religion and the movement of (what I've called) the Film Generation meet, unify, and blaze.

The script, written by Spielberg, is not much. It's like a 19th-century opera libretto: it serves as an armature, with some passable and some feeble devices, on which to string a progressive series of splendors that are part of, yet distinct from, the story. . . . (p. 20)

The long, last, thrilling scene overpowers us because, given any reasonable chance to be overpowered by it, we *want* to be overpowered by it. The film does everything in idea and execution to make it possible. Outer-space creatures, if they ever come, may in fact prove to be malevolent, or stupider than we are. Those possibilities are not part of the faith. We need them to be benevolent and brighter, and that's what *Close Encounters* gives us. . . .

If Spielberg is what's called a post-literate, he has the strengths as well as the defects of post-literacy. The modern self that he represents may be straitened, even narcotized, as against the historical self of Western tradition, but that self, forlorn religiously, distraught politically, finds its consoling expression in the size and shaking powers of the finale of this film. That finale doesn't bring us salvation—there is no hint of what will come out of the encounter—it brings us companionship. We are not alone. That belief seems potent in itself, if not all that one could possibly want, and the film makes the belief believable. . . .

One of the chief attractions of the film form for the Film Generation is, I think, that an art dependent on technology seems the most fitting means of expression for an age dominated by technology. The finale of *Close Encounters* is a dazzling epiphany of that idea. The technology of the film makes the faith tenable, but the technology itself becomes indistinguishable from what it is conveying. Prayers are being answered by the act of answering. It's not a case of the medium being the message; the medium is a function of the recipient, the audience, through its delegates, Spielberg and company. (p. 21)

> *Stanley Kauffmann, "Epiphany" (reprinted by permission of Brandt & Brandt Literary Agents, Inc.; copyright © 1977 by Stanley Kauffmann), in* The New Republic, *Vol. 177, No. 24, December 10, 1977, pp. 20-2.*

### JOHN SIMON

If there is such a thing as a zap-and-zowie school of filmmaking, Steven Spielberg is its prime example. . . .

From the very beginning, Spielberg's speciality was shock. Sex not at all, violence to some extent, and plan shock above all. . . . While grandly orchestrating cars and helicopters, Spielberg left the human elements of [*The Sugarland Express*] on a level that was both primitive and factitious. About *Jaws* one can say at least that however worthless the scenes on land were, those on or in the water were gripping.

*Close Encounters* is science fiction, a genre that shows signs of becoming a favorite form of cinematic escapism for reasons that are not far to hand. . . . [Machines], gimmickry, and special effects obviate the need for such more complex human elements as characterization and dialogue, and make things easier for the new breed of illiterates both behind the cameras and in front of the screen. . . . (p. 7)

[I could tell you the plot or list the absurdities]—which, in this case, comes to be same thing—but why betray the few feeble surprises the movie holds? Let me stress merely that it is not so much a matter of a number of holes in the story, as of a story—and this may be a first—being built entirely out of holes.

A friend and I counted, in a matter of minutes, some thirty or forty of them. . . .

Under the many layers of contradiction, however, we come to the bedrock of solid nonsense. Thus, for instance, the visitors, despite their superior intelligence, are unable to crack the Earthlings' language. . . . The whole business of taking people from earth to the visitors' domain—either for thirty years, as in the case of the wartime aviators . . . or else for a few days, as in the case of Barry Guiler—is never made remotely clear; but, then, what is?. . .

In Spielberg's lopsided world, people and their relationships do not begin to make sense. . . . [People] have been turned into objects, while objects are accorded maximal importance. The movements of machines and gizmos of every kind are made volatile and manic: they zoom at us with exaggerated suddenness and fury. Almost every scene is treated as if it were a climax. . . . Only with extreme reluctance does the director-screenwriter accord us a few scenes of relative quietude; before we know it, all zap and zowie breaks loose again.

This is not to say that Spielberg isn't capable of shooting certain climactic scenes with genuine ability; but after all those bogus climaxes, all that fake excitement, the real thing begins to look specious and worse yet, anticlimactic. . . .

To clarify everything and make things cohere would have required, as Spielberg remarked in a press conference, a four-hour movie instead of the present one, slightly over half that length. Yet four hours of sense would go by faster and more pleasantly than two of nonsense. Moreover, I doubt whether anyone who could make a shorter period this nonsensical could have made much more sense at any length. Spielberg which in German means toy mountain—may indeed have made the most monumental molehill in movie history, conveniently cone-shaped to serve as a dunce's cap for an extremely swelled head. (p. 8)

> *John Simon, "Film Reviews: 'Close Encounters of the Third Kind'," in* Take One *(copyright © 1978 by Unicorn Publishing Corp.), Vol. 6, No. 2, January, 1978, pp. 7-8.*

### GARRETT STEWART

Without the steely perfection or visual profundity of [Stanley] Kubrick's *2001*, Spielberg's rousing entertainment [*Close Encounters of the Third Kind*] is easily the next most impressive venture in the film art of science fiction. Kubrick was out for apocalypse, Spielberg only for epiphany. Yet more is revealed than the cosmic visitation, for even more obviously than in Kubrick's masterpiece, *Close Encounters* offers a multiple comment on the genre in which Spielberg is working, the gifts he brings to it and their imaginative nurture in other genres, other film and fictional outlets for the imagination. The most resolutely popular of the successful young directors has given us the apotheosis of his own devoted audience, his Everyman, with the ordinary middle-American men and women whom we see struggling to shape the form of their destiny and that of their planet emerging as the director's personal stand-ins. . . .

Almost a decade after *2001*, Spielberg's film continues to acknowledge the ways science fiction taps directly the springs of cinema: technological kinesis, simulated environments, imaginary vistas made visible. With its brilliant flooding and blacklighting, especially in the blanching inferno of cosmic irradiation at the end, Spielberg's movie also draws self-evidently upon the *sine qua non* of film imagery. The movie at its transfiguring extravagant climax is a 'film-within-the-film' in nothing so much as its spectacular lambency. The aliens announce themselves in light; all but invisible in the brilliance of their own aura, like seraphic presences, they are also what Stanley Kauffmann calls all film images: figures of light. Light plus sound to be exact: their double ambience, their medium. To the tune of a strange encoded melody, the aliens seem to come singing 'Fiat lux', summoning revelation from both the night sky and the darkened screen that projects it, each a visionary's *tabula rasa*. . . .

[Spielberg] has braved the revolutionary effect of incorporating his score, as film structuralists would say, into the 'diegesis', the credited universe of the film's fictional present. Everyone in Spielberg's movie-within-the-movie listens for a good while, spellbound, to the movie's own staccato soundtrack, for it is by these celestial grace notes turned cinematic accompaniment that they have tracked their vision to the dazzling rendezvous. . . .

[But just] when the film spreads its wings to their full metaphysical reach, it is somehow most flawed and poorly thought out. Blandly disbelieving or later woodenly wonderstruck, Spielberg's poorly cast scientists, astronauts and politicians manage to dehumanise the intoxicating spectacle of the finish. Not caring to make his minor bureaucrats and army personnel a palpable threat, Spielberg has left them with nothing much to be or to do, and their flatness is one of those strategic miscalculations or missed chances that flow directly from the film's intent. . . . Spielberg lets the dialogue get short-changed. Principals excepted, the die is cast with indifferently selected bit players, and the cast dies left and right, especially when plot thickens and interest thins towards the climax, with no lines worth breathing life into and only the tenuous ozone of bedazzlement to inhale. (p. 168)

[Except for François Truffaut], Spielberg has . . . little interest in casting other members of the experimental team. . . . [And the] insistence on translating Truffaut's speeches throughout the film, an idea obviously dear to Spielberg in its hints of universality and achieved communication, inevitably serves to distract and decelerate the plot at eventful turns.

Other minor annoyances and questions proliferate in a film which too often seems stitched together of loopholes and loose ends. Why are the few dozen scientists convened to hear recordings of the mysterious five-tone chant taped by Lacombe's team in India huddled together in the front rows of an enormous indoor stadium? And why are they suddenly reading their sign-language charts with small flashlights in the gradually darkened auditorium, when there is no footage being screened, only a tape played? Is it the theatrical nature of the experience, with Truffaut spotlit on stage, that Spielberg wants to insinuate along the way as he moves towards the flamboyant staging of his overtly theatrical climax? Is it worth it? . . .

The sum impression of Spielberg's grand finale, subtracted from unquestionably by such defects, nevertheless tallies powerfully with his overarching themes. The climactic shots that work, that work wonders, are those in which we look on starry-eyed along with the scientists, the camera's frame filled to distraction with alighted marvels. But when we merely watch the spectators watching, the awe is oversold and devalued. . . .

Spielberg's optimism requires reaction shots, on our behalf, from his gathered faithful. Yet because wondrous events cannot be just told, but must be unfolded before our eyes, a sublimity

visibly pondered by others must run the risk of blunting to redundancy our own encounters. Spielberg's slackened inventiveness fails his climax at its very heart, for it should not be about incredible splendours so much as about their cleansing reception. Though no such lapses in dialogue or logistics can defuse the impact of the special effects . . . , Spielberg's genuine gusto and originality have been expended earlier, with those thematic preparations for the climax which seem tacitly to call up the history of fantasy film, including of course science fiction, as the theoretical meeting ground of cinematic technology and dream mechanisms. A meeting ground and also a proving ground for such interaction. (p. 169)

The shapes of American junk food provide the analogies closest to hand for the cosmic vehicles when they first appear to Roy, just as the term 'flying saucer' is of course also derived from such a reductive domestication of the unknown. Later the trucks carrying scientists to Devil's Tower are camouflaged with familiar advertising logos. In its easy humour about pop-culture commercialism, the movie often looks like a detoxified *Zabriskie Point*, or like slices of American life cut with the reverse side of Robert Altman's knife. And even the affectionate sarcasm vanishes for Spielberg's entirely unambivalent interest in one kind of consumer item—children's toys.

The expectant clash of cymbals with which a toy monkey at his bedside awakens Barry Guiler is surely, as *Newsweek* saw, an allusion to Kubrick's apes at the initial moment of ennobling contact in *2001*. Perhaps the most inspired single idea in *Close Encounters* is that toys should first intuit such encounters, the mechanical instruments of a child's objectified fantasy life responding promptly to the influx of cosmic energy around the bed of a sleeping child, as if . . . they were the child's dreams incarnate. The second toy we see is a mechanical Frankenstein who blushes red when his pants fall to his knees—the most famous of the screen's mechanically devised humanoids caught in a particularly humanising moment. Later, Barry's delightedly lisped sense that the alien machines are only outsized 'toys' in a 'train', come down to 'play' with him, reminds us of what we know to be true about their mechanical simulation by electronic miniatures on screen. Spielberg is thematically tooling up for his climax, when the director becomes a conceptual engineer for one of the most complicated twinkling erector sets ever devised. . . .

[In one scene Spielberg concentrates] on the debate over whether the children can see the rest of a four-hour TV movie. Roy says he promised only that they could watch 'five commandments', and this mumbled joke, plus our single peek at the screen, lets us know that the marathon film in question is Cecil B. DeMille's epic of revelation, *The Ten Commandments*. What we see briefly on the screen is probably the most renowned special effect in film history before *2001*, Moses' parting of the Red Sea. Spielberg has such Biblical parallels much in mind, along with the cinema history of their presentation. Not only does his own triumphant epiphany occur on a mountain top, but it comes after an ominous rending of the heavens derived from DeMille's own battery of effects. (p. 173)

*Close Encounters of the Third Kind* is a film precisely about film's power to envision *ex nihilo* what it cannot express or otherwise convey. This is the subject of its subtext, ramified with the outlines of film history and media advance cleverly in mind. On any cinema screen and all the more so with the increased sophistication of film technology, two-dimensional space opens upon an illusory flickering depth into which our eyes lead our imaginations. Yet there is often an imaginatively self-evident though invisible fourth dimension to contend with, a reflexive mirror intersecting the three other planes of film space, reflecting back on itself and back in time, toward the cinema's mechanical springs in technical invention and its psychological fountainhead in dreams projected as moving shapes.

What Spielberg has sensed at once so largely and so delicately is that science fiction, by the direct exploitation of this twin cinematic genesis in mechanics and fantasy, by its immediate confession of the dual modality implied by the phrase 'dream machine', is disposed more than other genres to manifest this fourth dimension of cinematic self-awareness. Implicitly a vindication of fantasy film, of cartoons, of all filmic devices and formulas by which reality gets idealised and remodelled, and by taking all along, and especially at the end, the measure of itself as film feat, Spielberg's new popular monument explores its generic identity both grandly and gaily. It negotiates as so many important films do, by a self-mirroring in the admitted dimension of their own fictionality, a clarifying confrontation with its own essential nature: that closest encounter of the fourth kind. (p. 174)

> *Garrett Stewart, "Close Encounters of the Fourth Kind," in* Sight and Sound *(copyright © 1978 by The British Film Institute), Vol. 47, No. 3, Summer, 1978, pp. 167-74.*

## JANE E. CAPUTI

[*Jaws*] is the ritual retelling of an essential patriarchal myth—male vanquishment of the female symbolized as a sea monster, dragon, serpent, vampire, etc.—administering a necessary fix to a society hooked on and by male control. The purpose of *Jaws* and other myths of its genre is to instill dread and loathing for the female and usually culminate in her annihilation. (p. 305)

The great white shark in *Jaws,* . . . actually represents the primordial female and her most dreaded aspects. (pp. 307-08)

When *Jaws* hit the international market the French translated its title as "Les Dents de la Mer," (The Teeth of the Sea), a fact which can easily lead us, not only to the idea of castration, but to the consideration of two related themes—the mythological motif of the *vagina dentata* (the toothed, i.e. castrating vagina) and male obsessive fear of abortion. (p. 312)

[It] is the *vagina dentata* itself which rips across the screen as the bloody, gnashing mouth of the shark. one scene from the film men peer into the mouth of a safely dead shark and quip, "Deep throat." As most are aware, fellatio was the subject of a widely viewed pornographic film of that name. Here man's deep-rooted fear of the castration implications of that act surfaces. . . . With the sea symbolically evoking the uterus and the shark's teeth the ferocious mouth of that womb, *Jaws* emerges as a full-blown male nightmare, not only of castration, but of *abortion*. For what is abortion but the action which most typifies a "Terrible Mother," a "destructive and deathly womb." (pp. 313-14)

There is no place this terror is clearer than in *Jaws*. The action takes place mainly in the ocean, the primal womb and source of life, but this is a uterus full of blood, gore, danger and death. There are scenes of dismembered limbs, legs falling off into the deep, etc. All of the victims of the shark, except one, are male—usually swimming or floating peacefully unaware when attacked.

Significant to this aspect is the strong emphasis the film deliberately places on boy children, closer to the fetal stage and more vulnerable to the mother, encouraging fetal feelings among the viewers. Again and again little boys are the focus of peril. . . .

There is not only a boyish slant to the victims of the shark, its two surviving killers are also markedly and stupidly puerile. One is terrified of the water and looks like he is perpetually in danger of wetting his pants. The other sticks his tongue out and makes lots of faces behind the back of Big Daddy Quint. Brody and Hooper join a long line of distinguished boy killers for youth is one of the more prominent characteristics of monster-slayers. (p. 315)

The association between the shark and the birthing Terrible Mother was suggested quite early in the film. When a shark is caught and displayed as the killer, Hooper remains unconvinced. To be sure, he proposes, they must cut open the dead shark to see if the *little boy is inside of it*. He subsequently performs a post-mortem caesarean section (amid much grunting and letting of waters) while Brody watches in revulsion. Later, the final scene in *Jaws* is clearly the representation of an initiatory ritual of matricidal rebirth. Confrontation with marine monsters . . . is the typical ordeal of initiation. Immersion in the waters (sacramentalized as baptism) is the classic symbol of rebirth. The sea monster successfully torn apart (and Daddy rid of in the bargain) the two boys, now men, emerge from the waters to paddle fearlessly for shore. (p. 317)

[In his *Film, Cinema, Movie: A Theory of Experience*, Gerald Mast remarks that in some films: "We film spectators are not only voyeurs; we also experience a kind of rape."] *Jaws* sets up its viewers for [two experiences of rape—the rapist's and the one who is raped]. Men can gloat over the rape/defeat of the primordial female, women are invited to internalize this defeat. Yet, there is still another rape in *Jaws*—as a matter of fact the film opens with one.

A group of teenagers sit around a campfire smoking and drinking. One boy keeps giving a girl the eye. She gets up and begins to run toward the beach. He gives chase, continually calling to her to "Slow down. Wait. I'm coming." As she throws off some of her clothes he adds, "I'm definitely coming." Reaching the water naked, the girl enters for a swim. By this point the boy has reached the beach and lies down on the sand. The girl calls out, telling him to take a swim too, but he refuses. Suddenly the shark attacks, whirling the girl on a labyrinthine circle of death through the water. She screams for what seems to be an eternity. Some of her words, though very scrambled, can be made out. She is yelling, "It hurts, it hurts." At this precise moment the camera cuts to the boy, stretched out on the beach and intoning, "I'm coming, I'm coming." No doubt he was. (pp. 317-18)

One can protest that the boy did not touch the girl, that it was indisputably the shark who killed her. Yes, but this is not supposed to be enacted and perceived as a "normal" rape scene. Rather, it is a carefully constructed from of subliminal cinematic rape, with the visual images leading to one interpretation, but the sound and succession of events suggesting another. . . .

[This] was the only female whom the shark ever attacked; every other victim, anyone who was even actively threatened by the shark, was male. . . . If the subliminal message is that the girl has been raped and murdered, then the shark is clearly the archetypal, revenging guardian spirit who throughout the rest of the film, with deliberate vengeance, attacks only males. (p. 319)

The purpose of *Jaws* is to instill relentless terror. Though the movie ends, its message is set for eternal mental replay. Yet all those who reeled and wondered under the ferocious assault of patriarchal myth in *Jaws* should remember that this great white shark, as well as whales, dragons, serpents, and sea monsters all represent the untamed female, the Mother, the *vagina dentata*, the Lesbian, the White Goddess, Tiamat, the wild, the unconscious. (p. 323)

> Jane E. Caputi, "'Jaws' as Patriarchal Myth," in Journal of Popular Film *(copyright © 1978 by Michael T. Marsden and John G. Nachbar), Vol. VI, No. 4, 1978, pp. 305-26.*

**B. H. FAIRCHILD, JR.**

Almost everyone both in and out of [*Close Encounters of the Third Kind*] seems . . . to be waiting for some kind of miraculous salvation, an escape, an awakening, from the bad dream of social stagnation and middle-class malaise which the first half of Spielberg's movie so emphatically reminds us of. And we would probably all arise and go now . . . were it not for the film's sustained promise that soon, suspensefully soon, our questions will be answered, our emptiness will be filled, that Something Out There will take us away from all this. And what will it be? UFO's? No, *Close Encounters* seems to me to be about UFO's only in the way that *King Kong* is about apes. Religion, then? Ideology? Science? No, it isn't science, says the movie's Major Walton. It is, replies Lacombe . . . , "an event sociologique." (p. 342)

*Close Encounters* is *about* a sociological rather than a scientific event, but the film is also a sociological event in itself. We, the audience, become the sociological content of the film. We swarm to the theater to witness a close encounter for the same reasons that Spielberg's characters rush to Devil's Tower. (p. 343)

[The] contrast between the two kinds of space, closed and open, is important to the film because it develops another landscape: the technological. Moving from the closed, limited spaces of the beginning—the world of small rooms, small yards, fences, the shoulders of a narrow highway—to the vastness of the Wyoming countryside and, of course, the eternal depths of the night sky, we move between two different technological realms. Indeed, in getting from one to the other, [Roy] Neary repeatedly has to overcome spatial limitations: crowds, roads, fences, barricades, and finally, forced enclosure. He moves from the small, cramped world of low technology (the kind he knows too well) to the outer or open-space world of high technology (whose envisioned possibilities rescue him from the lower realm).

High technology as it is seen in the baroque ballet of lights and sound at the film's climax might be described as aesthetic (if machines can be beautiful), coherent (meaningful, significant), and creative (opening up new dimensions). Low technology by contrast is non-aesthetic (synthetic ugliness), incoherent (chaotic, trivial), and productive (consumptive rather than creative). . . . Most of the time, these two levels, high and low, are distinct—violently so, in fact. The UFO's arrive to the din and howl of common mechanisms: Toys (musical monkeys, cars, record players) as well as the machinery of domestic life (stoves, refrigerators, vacuum cleaners, telephones). Usually the contrast is established through juxtapo-

sition: the immediate shift, for instance, from the dazzling spacecraft to the domestic disorder of Roy's home, particularly the television room filled with a chaos of technological junk. It is this oppression of *things* in *rooms* that provides a prelude to the central scene (or sociological event) of the film: the vision-crazed Neary's decision to turn his world (his house, his possessions) *inside out*. (pp. 344-45)

The two technologies may, then, exist at opposite ends of the spectrum, but they are nevertheless rooted in the same reality. They are, as the child tells us in a vision of innocence, "Toys!" As these "toys" emerge, lights flashing, from the cloud-embroiled heavens, we realize that they are indeed only toys in comparison with what they suggest: the vast unknown and unknowable, prophesied but certainly not limited by the high-technology aesthetics of other-worldly shapes, lights, and sounds. What transpires wondrously through the film is in fact sociological (and technological); what is suggested, on the other hand, is theological.

There was a time when these two areas—science-knowledge and God-knowledge—were connected, and the connection was the myth of the music of the spheres: the belief that astronomical and heavenly perfection was manifested in musical harmony inaudible to man in his fallen state. . . . Spielberg provides a kind of parody of this myth in the symphonic sequence following the landing of the largest spacecraft. Having finally deciphered the five-tone sequence transmitted in alien radio waves, the investigative team gradually enters into tonal interplay with the aliens, increasing the tempo until in a bursting crescendo the two, earthlings and celestial visitors, are communicating mystically in a kind of atonal fugue, a music of the spheres. It is music as language, and what could be more appropriate for man in the moment of transcendence, making the Promethean leap upward, to what?—if not God, then gods, or god-like gestures from the unknowable Beyond. (pp. 345-47)

[There] are three spatial dimensions in *Close Encounters:* not just outer space, or suburban space, but also inner space—mystical and theological consciousness. The face of this consciousness is appropriately innocent, and in this way the film is distinctly Romantic: each vision of the Beyond is a vision of innocence. Repeatedly, the screen is filled with the face of the beautiful child with the soft, blue light playing across it, and his beatific smile and joyous attraction to the creature that has entered his home are pure, spiritual ecstasy. . . . Throughout the film, adult faces become children's faces: Neary gazing upward, the expectant crowd at the highway, the policemen, and especially the investigative team at the landing. The organist stares open-mouthed at the celestial spectacle, and the light reveals his eerily childlike expression. Wonder and awe are everywhere. As the mothership looms over the mountain, first one voice and then another exclaims, "Oh, my God," beneath the empyreal vibrations of the soundtrack.

This is the point for which Neary was apparently destined. It is not God, but it is a version of the transcendental god in nature—in theological terms, the simple recognition that there is More, that the natural and mundane are not closed but open-ended and extend ultimately perhaps into the supernatural. It is mysticism of a kind that traditionally seems to lurk in the corners of science fiction. And this is Roy's salvation from the meaningless and insignificant. (pp. 347-48)

But this is not serious theology, or serious science, for that matter. It is cinema, and the brilliantly orchestrated close encounter is as much a film as the one in which it occurs. This is, I think, the point of having Truffaut as Lacombe. Truffaut is a director whose films often deal with children and innocence. And Lacombe is also a director (of the UFO investigative forces) who literally directs the filming of the UFO landing. The lines of cameras swivel and whirr as Lacombe conducts the organist and beckons to the film crew. The music swells, the lights dance, and Roy Neary walks bedazzled into the glowing maw of the unknown. It is not science. It is not religion. It is an *event sociologique*. And as I scan the Roy Nearies of the audience who have gathered to witness it, I realize that it is also Hollywood, an event cinematic, with all of the old thrill and magic and mystery. (p. 349)

> *B. H. Fairchild, Jr., "An Event Sociologique: 'Close Encounters'," in* Journal of Popular Film *(copyright © 1978 by Michael T. Marsden and John G. Nachbar), Vol. VI, No. 4, 1978, pp. 342-49.*

## JEROME KLINKOWITZ

Notice how [the film version of *Close Encounters of the Third Kind*] virtually stops once the giant mother ship arrives—half the shots are of people just standing there and staring. Their sense of wonder is what the movie is all about. The need, the anticipation, the whole sense of irresistible movement toward some goal is resolved when the mother ship looms into view. After that, the movie continues for another forty minutes, simply as a big clump of indulgence—like driving an hour to get a six-scoop ice cream sundae, then taking almost as much time to eat the thing. Little Barry Guiler first describes the spacecraft as "ice cream"; so does Roy Neary. Apparently audiences feel the same way.

*Close Encounters* in book form is more ice cream—packed tighter and flavored more sharply to compensate for the lack of cinematic effects. But there's more to reading the book than getting another scoop on the sundae. Certain themes are more apparent, and Spielberg is able to make a deeper and more complex statement. Reading his novel makes you want to see the film again, a new wrinkle in the economics of book-and-movie tie-ins. . . .

But there remain large elements of this novel which are pre-cinematic. This fact is most apparent in the realm of "special effects." At times Spielberg's language tries to create such effects, as when the space creature "flows" instead of walks. But often his descriptions are more suggestive than the effects themselves. . . .

Reading about these actions, rather than just seeing them, brings up considerations of motive and design; less random, the spectacle is that much less exciting. And somehow the words don't quite make it. . . .

Thankfully, Spielberg's novel capitalizes on the essentially middle class nature of his story, and this new fascination (only dimly present in the movie) makes up for what we lose in special effects. If the characters are so awestruck by their close encounters of the first, second, and third kinds, if they are so rooted in wonder that they must pursue these visions to the earth's end and then just stand and stare, it is because their own daily lives are so much like the opposite. . . .

The pity is that the fantasy is constructed almost completely within middle class terms. . . . The space ships are visualized as Detroit dream machines. And, at one point, Neary sees some technicians as looking like "a cooking-foil commercial." The

mother ship, the grand finale which is meant to knock us off our feet, looks like nothing more than "an oil refinery at night.". . .

Finally, death is what *Close Encounters* is about: death as a form of astronautics, the one solid hope beyond this dismal world. As he prepares to leave the planet, an official tells Neary he will now be considered legally dead. He agrees happily. The novel ends, like the movie, with the mother ship's departure, described here as "a brilliant, multicolored stairway up to the heavens," another movie set from countless middle class fantasies. The movie's last forty minutes, the book's closing chapters, have stood absolutely still because both have entered a state of death. . . .

By itself, this death-wish theme is the loveliest part of both book and film. But in its novelized form, Spielberg stresses that this heavenly vision is homemade, built of the stuff our imaginations keep telling us to flee. The dimensions of our prison, then, are all the more small, for our fantasies are made out of the very same stuff. (p. 78)

> *Jerome Klinkowitz, "Renewed Encounters," in* The North American Review *(reprinted by permission from* The North American Review; *copyright © 1978 by the University of Northern Iowa), Vol. 263, No. 3, Fall, 1978, pp. 77-9.\**

## JAMES MONACO

[*Sugarland Express* was meant to take advantage of Spielberg's] demonstrated strengths as a director of chase/road movies. It remains one of the most interesting of the genre. . . . Structurally, the chase is not only more exciting than most, but humorous as well. In all, quite an achievement. Since it leaves itself more time to deal with character, and since its people are complex, interesting, and rooted in reality, *Sugarland Express* is arguably a more interesting film than either of the two blockbusters that succeeded it. The chase draws us in, but it's the notoriety of the couple that is the real subject of the film, and that is a more interesting theme than either *Jaws* or *Close Encounters* has. (pp. 174-75)

[*Jaws* and *Close Encounters*] are surprisingly similar. Both present simple suspense stories with linear plots and make them exciting and absorbing through a continual, incessant panoply of cinematic effects. They are just the sort of films we should expect from a young man who has achieved breathless mastery of the medium. Not that character and human relationships aren't as freshly realized as they are in *Sugarland Express* . . . , but there's so little time to develop character in the two blockbusters that he only has space to sketch them in. Both films depend on machines more than human beings for their ultimate effect. (pp. 175-76)

To their credit, the special-effects staff of Universal . . . managed to jiggle a satisfactory performance out of Bruce [the mechanical shark in *Jaws*]. But it was minimal at best. Spielberg saved the day by devising a series of much less complicated, more purely cinematic effects that make *Jaws* the most cleanly efficient and thoroughly effective entertainment machine of the decade. (p. 176)

If *Jaws* is a lovely machine, *Close Encounters of the Third Kind* is a spacey tour de force. The tension between the characters and the machine of plot and effect was very much on Spielberg's mind. He says he finally wrote the film himself because he couldn't convince anyone else to do both the personal story of Roy Neary . . . and the larger narrative of the first meeting between humans and extraterrestrials. He wanted a balance between the macrocosm and the microcosm.

As it happened, the film that was shot concentrates strongly on the human stories that would have been minor subplots in most other versions of this archetypal SF plot. . . . Spielberg makes it especially difficult for us to follow the big story. In order to redirect our attention to the little stories, he has to contrive a very rickety MacGuffin (like the motivating red herrings by that name that power Hitchcock's films). The plot is shot through with false leads, gaping holes, and circuitious side trails. . . But it doesn't seem to matter. . . . (pp. 177-78)

Spielberg is saving the actual encounter for the climax. No film, in fact, has been more obviously designed to foster a sequel. it stops where we would expect it to begin. For most of the time, he wants to concentrate on Neary's obsession, and see how he can handle it on film. To keep us properly tense, he punctuates this modest enterprise with a string of devices almost as long as *Jaws*'s: the moving objects . . . the bright lights, the strange sunburns a few perfunctory chases, occasional shots of the ships (but not *the* ship!), a few quotes from *North by Northwest,* and most amusingly the lovely little scene in which Jillian tries to keep The Force out of her house. . . .

People who take science fiction seriously are even angrier with this film that they are with *Star Wars.* It assiduously avoids all of the issues that should adhere to the basic plot. Spielberg has stolen the subject matter and carefully left the theme behind. He keeps us entertained with some nice effects while he goes about the business of playing with his own mountain: the character of obsession. Then he brings in a little lukewarm apocalyptic quasi-religious ecstasy at the end to let us feel we've completed the experience and drawn the moral. (p. 178)

> James Monaco, "The Whiz Kids," in his American Film Now: The People, the Power, the Money, the Movies (copyright © 1979 by James Monaco; reprinted by arrangement with The New American Library, Inc., New York), Oxford University Press, New York, 1979, pp. 139-84.*

## DAVID DENBY

[*1941*] is an overblown repetitive, cartoon-style satire that runs into the ground a good hour before it ends. Yet there are things to be prized in it. . . . Set in Los Angeles the week after the Japanese bombed Pearl Harbor, *1941* jumps back and forth among a dozen or so parallel stories, all of them illustrating the confusion, incompetence, and nutty panic of a people expecting Japanese invasion at any moment. The movie is fun because Spielberg takes a fondly appreciative attitude toward the innocent righteousness of the time. He's made an homage to the gung-ho silliness of old war movies, a celebration of the Betty Grable-Betty Hutton period of American pop culture. In this movie, America is still a very young country—foolish, violent, casually destructive, but not venal. That we joke about a moment of national crisis shows we are still young—and sane. . . .

*1941* looks like a series of crazily animated Norman Rockwell paintings. The California settings, bathed in golden light, gleam with health, and Spielberg fills the screen with odd, jumpy movement. . . . The movie is full of projectiles, many of them fired off in the wrong direction. Spielberg has a talent for creating adolescent jerkiness: There's a muscular grace in his

scenes of excess. . . . When one of the G.I.'s, hot for a blonde, goes out of control, he practically becomes a rapist, yet Spielberg uses him as a projectile too—pure energy—and transforms his rampage into a scene out of a Gene Kelly film, with athletic flips, tumbles, spills, brawls, and so on. Shouldn't Spielberg direct a musical next time out? (p. 65)

> David Denby, "Broadway Melody of 1979," in New York Magazine (copyright © 1980 by News Group Publications, Inc.; reprinted with the permission of New York Magazine), Vol. 13, No. 1, January 7, 1980, pp. 63-5.

## ROBERT ASAHINA

*Jaws* and *Close Encounters of the Third Kind* having been very well received by critics and mass audiences, [Spielberg] decided his latest feature, *1941,* would be something entirely different—a comedy (the previous films were only unintentionally funny). So, keeping Stanley Kramer's *It's a Mad, Mad, Mad, Mad World* in mind, he began with a script . . . about the pandemonium in Los Angeles during the week after Pearl Harbor. Unfortunately, the director never asked himself whether the paranoid superpatriotism of that era actually was humorous. Was the xenophobia that led to the forced "relocation" and imprisonment of thousands of native Americans of Japanese descent really funny?

Of course, Spielberg's idea was to make a free-for-all comic fantasy, not a political satire. . . . [Thus] *1941* became another big-budget spectacular, laden with expensive special effects, explosions, crashes, mindless destruction, and crowd scenes. It also turned into a colossal bore, totally lacking in good belly laughs, or even mild chuckles.

The paucity of Spielberg's . . . comic imagination is apparent from the number of gags lifted from other movies. . . .

Incredibly, he has even stolen from his own films. Like *Jaws, 1941* begins with a girl . . . shedding her clothes as she runs along a beach; once again, an underwater menace—this time a Japanese submarine, instead of a shark—interrupts her skinny-dipping. It is beyond me why the director thinks it funny to lampoon his own work.

Equally mystifying is why he should try to emulate Kramer, although the two share an inability to construct a joke. In *1941,* Spielberg spends a lot of time on Hollis Wood's capture by and subsequent escape from the Japanese sub, but there is no payoff—we never learn what happens to him. Other gags simply aren't set up properly. . . .

Spielberg, once praised for his Hitchcockesque manipulativeness, is living proof that two hit movies are enough to guarantee that some studio will give you $26 million to fall flat on your face. (p. 22)

> Robert Asahina, "No Laughing Matters," in The New Leader (© 1980 by the American Labor Conference on International Affairs, Inc.), Vol. LXIII, No. 1, January 14, 1980, pp. 22-4.

## PAULINE KAEL

I wish that Steven Spielberg had trusted his first instincts and left **"Close Encounters of the Third Kind"** as it was. In his new, reëdited version, "The Special Edition," he has made some trims, put in some outtakes, and shot a few new bits. But if you saw it before and loved it, you may be bothered all the way through—not just because you miss some of the scenes that he has taken out (you miss even what you didn't think was great) but because the slightly different outtakes that Spielberg has substituted for the shots you remember keep jarring you. You can see why most of these outtakes weren't used originally, and some of them have the wrong lighting for where they've been inserted. (pp. 80-1)

It's true that the action is swifter and more streamlined, but I didn't mind the diversionary scenes of the original; they had their own scruffy charm, and part of what we love in fairy tales is their eccentricity. It's also more clear now from the beginning that Roy has become alienated from his family; his character is easier to understand, and there's more preparation for his leaving. Despite these changes, the structure, which was clumsy, is still clumsy—but does that really matter much in this huge toy of a movie?

The only really serious flaw in "Close Encounters" is one that can't be changed by cosmetic editing: in a picture with such a childlike vision, it seems wrong—unjust—that the cranks, the misfit dreamers, and the crazies who received the signals and fought their way to the mountain are not allowed to board the craft. . . .

"Close Encounters of the Third Kind" is one of the most euphoric comedy fantasies ever made. It will probably be a wonderful movie in any version, but I hope that this "Special Edition" will not replace the original—that the original will also be available to audiences. I want to be able to hear the true believer . . . tell people that he has seen Bigfoot as well as flying saucers. It may not seem like a big loss, but when you remember something in a movie with pleasure and it's gone, you feel as if your memories had been mugged. (p. 81)

> *Pauline Kael, "Who and Who," in* The New Yorker *(© 1980 by The New Yorker Magazine, Inc.), Vol. LVI, No. 28, September 1, 1980, pp. 74-6, 79-81.\**

### STANLEY KAUFFMANN

Steven Spielberg, the writer and director [of *Close Encounters of the Third Kind*] has re-edited some bits of the original, put in some footage that was omitted first time, and shot some new footage. . . .

It's a mistake. The second encounter isn't as good as the first. One special power of *Close Encounters,* I thought . . . was that it exemplified a Dionysian attribute of film: the exaltation available through film's technology and, therefore, repeatable—at will, more or less. Spielberg has interfered with its "immutability," which was probably a mistake in any event and is doubly so because he hasn't improved the picture. . . .

The worst alteration is that we now follow [Roy] into the strangers' spaceship at the end and get a look at its immense interior. Nothing that Spielberg could show us could match what he had made us imagine. Seeing is believing less. . . .

I don't get the idea behind these alterations, unless it's to make the film more of a one-on-one affair between one family's upset and international complications. Nothing is gained, something is lost—except for the good Gobi sequence. This "special edition" ought to be withdrawn. The third encounter should be, more or less, the first. (p. 24)

> *Stanley Kauffmann, "Late Summer Round-up," in* The New Republic *(reprinted by permission of* The New Republic; © *1980 The New Republic, Inc.), Vol. 183, Nos. 10-11, September 6-13, 1980, pp. 24-5.\**

### DAVID DENBY

Synthesizing [*Raiders of the Lost Ark*] out of trashy pop elements—occult and religous mumbo jumbo, cursed tombs, buried temples, cardboard Nazis—[Spielberg] has produced a work that is like a thirties serial, only grander, funnier, and blessedly free of interruptions. . . .

In pop filmmaking, neither death nor history ever matters. Only thrills matter, and, trying for bigger and bigger thrills, Spielberg has done something almost offensive. He's thrown in the kind of inspirational religioso stuff that used to be such an embarrassment in biblical spectaculars—sudden shafts of light and silvery specters flying about and forming themselves into death's heads. When Cecil B. DeMille produced effects like these in *The Ten Commandments,* they may have looked trashy, but they weren't cynically intended, and they suited the hammily reverent tone of the rest of the movie. *Raiders,* on the other hand, hasn't the slightest trace of a religious impulse. None of the characters is motivated by religous belief, and the spirit of the movie is farcical and mock-heroic. Thus when Spielberg opens the Ark, and the clouds race upward into the vortex and all that, the effect is both overblown and creepy. How can he expect us to be awed by a religious spectacle that is totally without feeling? (p. 68)

There are no real people in the work of Lucas and Spielberg, and that may be the main reason I always feel a little unsatisfied—as if my responses had been hollowed out—when their movies are over. They are both superb craftsmen, but neither shows much sign of developing into an artist, or even wanting to. But perhaps that doesn't matter very much. In a highly commercial way, these two have restored to American movies the kind of adolescent ecstasy that has been lost since the silents and the serials. Perhaps we should be grateful for the fun and look for art somewhere else. (p. 70)

> *David Denby, "Movie of Champions," in* New York Magazine *(copyright © 1981 by News Group Publications, Inc.; reprinted with the permission of* New York *Magazine), Vol. 14, No. 24, June 15, 1981, pp. 68, 70-1.\**

# Josef von Sternberg

## 1894-1969

(Born Jonas Sternberg) Austrian-born American director and actor.

Sternberg is best known for his series of erotic films featuring Marlene Dietrich as the definitive *femme fatale*. Ultimately, her exotic character consumed him, and his last films served only as a vehicle for her. Sternberg reveled in artificial atmosphere; he is considered a fine pictorial craftsman and his imagery supersedes plot.

Sternberg's career commenced as a film patcher in Hollywood. Later positions as an editor and writer led to his first feature film, *The Salvation Hunters,* which he wrote, produced, and directed. Reflecting a sensitive brand of realism and an emphasis upon sordid atmosphere, it displays the formal pictorial style that was to become Sternberg's trademark. His next projects proved abortive, and his lack of popular success made him an "untouchable." However, his work as an assistant director was so successful that his studio invited him to direct *Underworld.* In this film, Sternberg combined eroticism with an interest in exotic locales, elements also found in the films which followed. *The Docks of New York* is considered Sternberg's greatest silent film, similar in feeling to *The Salvation Hunters.*

*The Blue Angel* became the turning point of his career. Based on Heinrich Mann's novel, *Professor Unrath,* it tells the story of a professor led astray by a heartless music-hall girl. Most importantly, though, it introduced Sternberg's new star, Marlene Dietrich, with whom he developed a Pygmalion-Galatea relationship. She provided his films with a sensual languor that, complemented by Sternberg's taste for the exotic, displayed woman as the sexual arbiter. At the same time she became an obsession for Sternberg. Abandoning the everyday themes which had dominated his previous work, Sternberg depicts a *femme fatale* using men as helpless puppets. *The Blue Angel* acts as much more than an elegant vehicle for women's guiles, however; it criticizes social conditions in Germany and displays some of the most original sets ever produced up to that time.

*Morocco* and *Shanghai Express* are beautiful celebrations of romance which express the belief that sentimental attachment will be the victor over reason. *The Scarlet Empress* and *The Devil Is a Woman* were unsuccessful commercially and mark the end of Sternberg's relationship with Dietrich. Audiences tired of his highly stylized work and superficial characters. However, some feel that his sentimental romanticism is mis-

understood and regard him as one of cinema's greatest stylists, combining elements of formal cinema with nineteenth-century decadence. (See also *Contemporary Authors,* Vols. 81-84.)

NATIONAL BOARD OF REVIEW MAGAZINE

*Underworld* is just about the best underworld picture that has come along. Melodrama it is, but melodrama that is human, that keeps its actors people while unraveling a plot developed through the interplay of human temperaments, passions, feelings. Cinematically it is modern, in the stride of the art. Imaginatively it is frequently of the first rank, a finely visualized selection of touches that reveal not only the fabric of the characters but as well the predicament of their lives, intensified as they are by the decent instincts that urge them upward despite the dragging impulses that are the result of their conditioning in society's darker strata. . . . [It] brings a director, Josef Von Sternberg, very definitely into his own as among the real creators for the screen, thus fulfilling a prophesy more than hinted by *The Salvation Hunters.* . . .

[*Underworld*] is that rare thing on the screen, a film wrought on the iron of truth, on a framework of understanding visualized in telling, conclusive movement that is the target reached by all good art, and seldom reached, at least so unerringly, in motion pictures. And for its moral values . . . , they are coursing in the very veins of the story picture; fortunately, neither skin deep nor washed on with a smirk. It is the story picture of a man coming from darkness into light, surrendering at the last gasp the kingdom of his world to gain the kingdom of himself. As the film travels, we watch the coarse clay refining in a fierce burning. It is a parable of the primitive child-man attaining the civilized state, facing the moral problem, perceiving it, finally redeeming himself and the others of his tribe. The purely sentimental is untouched by the film. "Bull" Weed is set down for what he is, and his personal story is ended as it inevitably must end—at the hands of himself as much as at the hands of the law. (p. 10)

The pattern of action, cinematically concentrated at point after point, blots out such minor weaknesses as occur, even the old stuff such as the police chase in automobiles. When it weaves around the figure of "Bull", it is often superb. . . . *Underworld* opens with beautiful economy and swiftness, plays with its camera-work around each situation until it is complete, and brings them to a focus in a perfect ending.

*Underworld* is a film of integrity on the part of director, scenario writer, actors and cameraman, done with back-bone, which is to say, strength and grit. Best of all, at least for those looking for cinema growth on our native screen, it is a film made in America, with an actor and a director who need take off their hats to none. (p. 11)

> *"Exceptional Photoplays: 'Underworld',"* in National Board of Review Magazine *(copyright, 1927), Vol. II, No. 8, August, 1927, pp. 10-11.*

## NATIONAL BOARD OF REVIEW MAGAZINE

A story of mother love would, at first sight, seem strange material for Joseph von Sternberg's directorial genius. The director of **The Salvation Hunters, Underworld** and **The Last Command** has a record of achievement which would hardly qualify him to glorify motherhood in the exaggerated, hysterical manner which has been so much the mode on the screen. . . .

So it was at least to be expected that von Sternberg would treat the motherhood theme with a difference, would divorce it from the obvious and perhaps even point it up with a touch of irony.

These expectations **The Case of Lena Smith** largely fulfills. (p. 11)

[The plot] is not altogether proof against criticism. The concealment of the marriage until almost the end, does seem a little tricky though it is effective in confounding our moral snooper. Also, parts of the court proceedings seem somewhat arbitrary. On the one hand it is news to us that a woman in Lena's position would have been deprived of the custody of her child simply because it was illegitimate, and on the other hand it would have been immediately restored to her after she waved her marriage certificate. Nor is the conviction on the contempt charge convincing. . . .

Von Sternberg directs with his usual insight and his feeling for the scene, giving, in particular, a believable picture of Vienna. But sometimes he hurdles over difficulties somewhat too airily missing thereby the dramatic strengthening of his story by showing obstacles convincingly overcome. It is dangerous practice to confront a character with an insurmountable will and then to show him suddenly on the other side of the wall. We refer particularly to Lena's all too easy kidnapping of her son. She walks into a children's home in which there are apparently no locks, no night watchmen and no nurses on duty. But again this is a minor flaw in an otherwise exceptional picture, possibly a privilege of mother love seeking its own. (p. 12)

> *"Exceptional Photoplays: 'The Case of Lena Smith',"* in National Board of Review Magazine *(copyright, 1929), Vol. IV, No. 2, February, 1929, pp. 11-12.*

## NATIONAL BOARD OF REVIEW MAGAZINE

[In **Morocco**] like all motion pictures of the front rank, the material is that of the screen alone, the narrative thread an exceedingly simple one. It amounts to the way it is embroidered. And here the result is [a cinematic pattern that is] brilliant, profuse, subtle, and at almost every turn inventive.

*Morocco* sets its sound in the background. Its speech is purely that of pictures, except where the pictures can be told more effectively by sound. (pp. 4-5)

[When] a character speaks it is merely in substantiation of the thing the action has made you see and know. The artist gives his engagement supper to his friends. All is sumptuous, splendid, covered with light, gaiety and tender feeling. The tragic past of his fiancee is gone. Then the drums of the returning Legionnaires are faintly heard. You get the sensation of the stirring city in the warm night outside. . . . One could go on finding in this film a text book and finding in the firm and sinewy grasp of its director the resolve to bring the motion picture, with the new powers that science has given it, back to its own. . . .

As a study of the attraction that a man and woman of a certain type may have for one another—that can tear a woman from whatever of safety and pleasure her existence holds—**Morocco** is not unsubtle in its psychological reading. And this it is, perhaps, that leaves us feeling that we have seen something true if strange. (p. 5)

> *"Exceptional Photoplays: 'Morocco',"* in National Board of Review Magazine *(copyright, 1930), Vol. V, No. 9, November, 1930, pp. 4-5.*

## NATIONAL BOARD OF REVIEW MAGAZINE

**The Blue Angel** is surely one of the outstanding pictures of this season's screen offerings. Strictly speaking this is a foreign picture. For it was made in Berlin. But it is a foreign picture with English speech, occasional German interpolations being used for the sake of atmosphere and realism. . . .

[Again] we have a story of the disintegration of a fine character to the point of complete degradation with a tragic flash of his former self at the end which heightens the dramatic contrast. And again the emphasis is upon character delineation rather than upon action. . . . (p. 9)

**The Blue Angel** is notable from the directing angle on account of von Sternberg's clever combination of talking and silent film technique. He uses dialogue sparingly and climactically and employs long sequences of purely cinematic story telling. In other words, he allows the camera to tell the story whenever possible rather than letting the actor tell it vocally. (p. 10)

Occasionally Mr. von Sternberg's directorial style leads him into slow tempo as if building up for a dramatic suspense which never quite comes off. This is all the more noticeable in a picture which has a minimum of action and a surplusage of characterization and atmosphere. (p. 12)

> *"Exceptional Photoplays: 'The Blue Angel',"* in National Board of Review Magazine *(copyright, 1931), Vol. VI, No. 1, January, 1931, pp. 9-12.*

### JOHN ALFRED THOMAS

*Dishonored* is likely to seem a fabric of "hokum," especially when it is taken so seriously by its director. Each episode is protracted with fond care, the story moves slowly and ponderously, and the result naturally seems long drawn out. Furthermore, the picture concentrates on [Marlene Dietrich] and a mood, and what faults it has can be attributed mainly to the reverence in which Mr. Josef von Sternberg holds his own story, his own actress and his own mood.

To see only these defects, though, is to overlook much of positive value, much of promise, in *Dishonored.* (p. 12)

[Von Sternberg's] use of dialogue and sound is almost always an integral use and . . . it reinforces considerably the emotional and dramatic content of the picture. The fact remains that, despite its faults, the von Sternberg technique is one of the few intelligent approaches to the problem of uniting sound and speech with the motion picture. (p. 13)

[In this story], von Sternberg has written neither well nor wisely. The best thing that can be said for his story is that it presents a uniquely subtle sort of love, and presents it quietly. . . . Where others skulk in shadows von Sternberg revels in them and the scenes at a piano and in dark cells are memorable compositions. The camerawork is remarkable for its beauty and its ability to convey a mood.

The most obvious use of sound in the film is that of making a piano almost one of the protagonists. It is used to project the emotion of the person playing, usually the star, and in one sequence it makes a transfer by which you understand that the code message, written in music, spells the death of the enemy, a sequence ending in the sound of war. (pp. 13-14)

There are other points of interest, like the reticent handling by which sound indicates a picture to you without the redundancy of showing the image also, but they are likely to be overlooked because of the weaknesses of story, structure, attitude and sense of drag which tend to obscure them. **Dishonored** is not a first-rate picture, but it is an intelligent and possibly even important picture, produced by one who has the makings of a completely first-rate director. . . . (p. 14)

> *John Alfred Thomas, "Exceptional Photoplays: 'Dishonored'," in* National Board of Review Magazine, *Vol. VI, No. 4, April, 1931, pp. 12-14.*

### MARGARET MARSHALL

The direction and the photography, both sound and silent, of **"Shanghai Express"** . . . are of such excellence that only a first-rate story could match them. Unfortunately, the plot is hackneyed and intricate; what is more serious, it seems to be a superimposed mechanism rather than an organic part of the production. . . . The device of numberless swift kaleidoscopic shots is, of course, not new. But the vibrancy and freshness of treatment must be credited to the direction of Josef von Sternberg. It is he who makes the illusion of a train traveling through strange, war-ridden China [convincingly real]. . . . The characterizations are real, too, especially the lesser ones, which belong rather to the setting than to the story. It is only in so far as these very real characters are forced to take part in an unlikely plot that the illusion fades. (pp. 267-68)

> *Margaret Marshall, "A Chinese Episode," in* The Nation, *Vol. 134, No. 3478, March 2, 1932, pp. 267-68.*

### ARGUS

Director Josef von Sternberg has long been famous for the mannered pretentiousness of his photophays, but never has his weakness for ostentation reached the extremes to be found in *The Scarlet Empress*. . . .

Mr. von Sternberg has concentrated on the wild pageantry and the grim ferocity of the period, and, with his gift for atmospheric settings, pictorial effects, and visual suggestion, it seemed, at the outset of the film, that he was destined to vanquish his rivals.

It is not long, however, before the director's passion for lavish ostentation overreaches itself. Mr. von Sternberg's brooding preoccupation with the mood and color of a story, rather than with the story itself, frequently has made for a distinguished and original cinematic style, but here he carries the trait to such excesses that the picture comes to seem a particularly cruel burlesque of Sternberg methods.

> *Argus, "On the Current Screen: 'The Scarlet Empress'," in* Literary Digest, *Vol. 118, No. 13, September 29, 1934, p. 29.*

### WILLIAM TROY

The imagination can become a horrible thing indeed when it is given as much scope and freedom as Von Sternberg apparently enjoyed while making his version of the Catharine the Great legend ["**The Scarlet Empress**"]. Or perhaps one had better say that when, as happens every so often, Hollywood decides to make a mistake, it is able, because of the vastness of its resources of every kind, to make a truly colossal mistake. . . . Josef Von Sternberg now shows us just what can be hatched when an overcharged imagination is set loose upon an eighteenth-century Muscovite background. One had always recognized that the Russia to which Catharine came as a bright and ambitious young bride must have been far from a pleasant and civilized sort of place. But in "**The Scarlet Empress**" one is transported to such a nightmarish realm as never existed outside the less plausible tales of Hoffmann and Poe. Evidently Von Sternberg has read or been told that the Moscow palaces of Catharine's time retained many crude Tartar influences in their architecture and furnishings. This seed of archaeological discovery blossoms immediately in the directorial fancy into the most original grotesqueries of every description. . . . [The] lighting, or rather the absence of lighting, in the picture is alone sufficient to create the feeling of the sinister and the unhealthy, the uneasy conviction that what one is witnessing can only be the product of an elephantiasis of the imagination. . . .

> *William Troy, "Russia à la Mode," in* The Nation, *Vol. 139, No. 3613, October 3, 1934, p. 392.*

### SIEGFRIED KRACAUER

[*The Blue Angel*'s international success] can be traced to two major reasons, the first of which was decidedly Marlene Dietrich. Her Lola Lola was a new incarnation of sex. This petty bourgeois Berlin tart, with her provocative legs and easy manners, showed an impassivity which incited one to grope for the secret behind her callous egoism and cool insolence. . . . The other reason for the film's success was its outright sadism. The masses are irresistibly attracted by the spectacle of torture and humiliation, and Sternberg deepened this sadistic tendency by making Lola Lola destroy not only [the professor] himself but his entire environment. A running motif in the film is the old church-clock which chimes a popular German tune devoted to the praise of loyalty and honesty (*Üb' immer Treu und Redlichkeit* . . .)—a tune expressive of [the professor's] inherited beliefs. In the concluding passage, immediately after Lola Lola's song has faded away, this tune is heard for the last time as the camera shows the dead [professor]. Lola Lola has killed him, and in addition her song has defeated the chimes.

Besides being a sex story or a study in sadism, Sternberg's film vigorously resumes postwar traditions, marking the definite end of the paralysis. *The Blue Angel* can be considered a variation on Karl Grune's *The Street*. Like the philistine from the plush parlor, [the] professor is representative of the middle class; like the philistine, he rebels against the conventions by exchanging school for The Blue Angel, counterpart of the street; and exactly like the philistine, this would-be rebel again submits—not, it is true, to the old middle-class standards, but to powers far worse than those from which he escaped. It is significant that he increasingly appears to be the victim of the manager rather than Lola Lola's personal slave. Love has gone, indiscriminate surrender remains. . . . *The Blue Angel* poses anew the problem of German immaturity and moreover elaborates its consequences as manifested in the conduct of the boys and artists, who like the professor are middle-class offspring. Their sadistic cruelty results from the very immaturity which forces their victim into submission. It is as if the film implied a warning, for these screen figures anticipate what will happen in real life a few years later. The boys are born Hitler youths, and the cockcrowing device is a modest contribution to a group of similar, if more ingenious, contrivances much used in Nazi concentration camps.

Two characters stand off from these events: the clown of the artists' company, a mute figure constantly observing his temporary colleague, and the school beadle who is present at the professor's death. . . . He does not talk either. These two witness, but do not participate. Whatever they may feel, they refrain from interference. Their silent resignation foreshadows the passivity of many people under totalitarian rule. (pp. 216-18)

> *Siegfried Kracauer, "Murderer Among Us," in his* From Caligari to Hitler: A Psychological History of the German Film *(copyright 1947 © 1975 by Princeton University Press; reprinted by permission of Princeton University Press), Princeton University Press, 1947, pp. 215-22.**

## CURTIS HARRINGTON

[Do Josef von Sternberg's] films have any importance, other, let us say, than that of having brought to the screen the redoubtable filmic personality of Marlene Dietrich? The answer, which, I feel, is most definitely in the affirmative, lies in the perceiving of certain cinematic tendencies and ideas which are gradually gaining momentum in the commercial cinema of Europe and in the experimental cinema of the United States. (p. 405)

[In *The Salvation Hunters* (1924)], we can see the beginnings of a formal method of film construction and, more specially, the positive statement of an artist confident of the inner strength of the individual.

Placing his characters in the most disheartening of environments, where one would expect to find a story illustrating some fault with the social structure capable of producing such conditions, we find instead this slum-district background employed symbolically as a visual portrayal of inner ugliness, an ugliness with which the individual is confronted to conquer by himself, within himself. External reality here was primarily used to illustrate an inner conflict, although the story accepted on its immediate level, not on its symbolical one, produced exactly the same cumulative effect; the story could be understood on either level, depending, somewhat, on the spectator's preference or depth of perception. (pp. 406-07)

Today von Sternberg claims that it was his sole sincere work, and that all of his subsequent films were merely "arrogant gestures." . . .

Its creator presents the one film to us as a work of art, the others as commercial efforts, of little value. But then he makes one more statement which qualifies this: he adds that the only other film that came near in its realization to his aims was *The Devil Is a Woman*. . . .

The content of [*The Salvation Hunters* and *The Devil Is a Woman*] varies so that they might have been made by two different men, with widely divergent views of life and the world. But we can discover the explanation for this seeming discrepancy within the director's creative method; the formal structure of these two films, although they differ (for one is necessarily a work of greater maturity, if not of greater freshness), displays evidence of a control which von Sternberg lacked in many of his other films, and both are, for the most part, successful examples of his method. (p. 407)

Perhaps to ease his mind von Sternberg searched for, and soon found, a common denominator of content which appeared in both his sincere attempt, *The Salvation Hunters,* and his later, first outspokenly commercial film, *Underworld* [1927]. With this discovery in mind, the compromise did not seem, perhaps, so difficult. The common denominator was sex. Von Sternberg possessed a strong erotic sensibility, a feeling for women which he could get over on film, and he began to use this ability as a basis on which he could reconcile his aims with those of an essentially commercial industry. (p. 408)

[*The Case of Lena Smith* (1929)] was an important film, both in its formal development and in its story values. The theme of the film was antimilitaristic; it portrayed the self-righteous Viennese ruling class before World War I, the Prussian mind with its misdirected efforts toward discipline, and the general corruption bred by such thinking. . . . [It] was his only true attempt at a social theme.

Pictorially, there were the beginnings of many abstract devices which he was to exploit much further in later films. For the first time he painted a set completely white, so that the light and dark of a scene might be controlled entirely with the illumination. In this way the use of carefully directed spots and concealed lights behind furniture could give each camera view a richly varied chiaroscuro. He also used actors in silhouette in the foreground of various scenes. . . . (pp. 408-09)

In Heinrich Mann's novel *Professor Unrath* [which became *The Blue Angel* (1930)], von Sternberg found the sort of setting and characters he could most successfully adapt to his manner of filming and still make a commercial success. . . .

The settings constructed for *The Blue Angel* were perhaps the most significant single element in the film. At no moment were they actually realistic, but instead were imaginative *extensions* of reality. (p. 409)

Historically *The Blue Angel* has already assumed an important position, because it was one of the first sound films to display the immense creative potentialities of joining sound and image. At a time when most films were stilted and overfilled with dialogue, *The Blue Angel* came as a fresh, reassuring example of what could be accomplished with the new medium. . . .

In *Morocco* [1930] von Sternberg developed the formal, structural qualities of the film beyond any previous effort. The story itself was exceedingly simple, romantic; looked at objectively and as a reflection of reality, it bordered on the ridiculous. However, it was not von Sternberg's intention to produce a film of reflected reality, but rather to evoke cinematically an exotic locale peopled with extraordinary characters. In this he succeeded admirably. (p. 410)

An important factor in *Morocco* was the complete absence of background music. Only natural sounds and music where it would naturally occur, as in the two café sequences, were used. Seen today, at a time when background music is so often used as a crutch to sustain the emotional flow and meaning of a scene, it is remarkable to observe how von Sternberg's control over the formal devices of his medium made it possible for him to develop and sustain each scene by employing only sound effects and a minimum of dialogue. This absence of background music gave the film a sharp, immediate quality seldom found in films today. . . . (pp. 410-11)

Within the series of Dietrich-von Sternberg films culminating in 1935 with *The Devil Is a Woman,* there may be traced the development of his exotic-erotic theme material and formal style into a highly unique film complex. In *Dishonored* (1931) the story motivation became incongruous when the director stressed the abstract pictorial development of the theme. In *Shanghai Express* (1932) von Sternberg evoked the atmosphere of a revolutionary China with a minimum of means, and, more markedly than ever before, "directed" the action and speech patterns of his actors to fit in with the tempo and rhythmic development of the film as a whole. In *Blonde Venus* (1932), a story property which von Sternberg directed against his will, a banal piece of maudlin claptrap was so embellished by sheer directorial style as to become an unusual and provocative film. . . .

The most outstanding aspect of *Blonde Venus* was that it created a von Sternbergian America, a portrait of the United States as extraordinary as Kafka's. Here he was not concerned with reproducing the actual environment or atmosphere of the country (the story covered a wide territory), but instead attempted an imaginative projection of the thematic material at his disposal, that is, The South, A Flophouse, A Night Club, A Cheap Café, A Chemist's Apartment, etc. In this lies largely the film's uniqueness, for it seems actually a story told out of space and time. (p. 411)

As if he had decided henceforth to realize his cinematic theories with a more uncompromising attitude than ever before, von Sternberg produced in *The Scarlet Empress* (1934) a film that was in most respects a decided advance, aesthetically, over any previous effort. The story, in a literary sense, was almost entirely dispensed with, and there emerged a film developed solely from a visual point of view. The little dialogue was mostly an embellishment; it was not *necessary* to an understanding of the continuity. . . .

The implications of meaning which von Sternberg put into *The Scarlet Empress* were almost entirely erotic. . . . We saw the development of Catherine from a wide-eyed, innocent young girl into a shrewd and calculating woman through von Sternberg's eyes, and he illumined this character development with his very special sensibility.

The theme of the Fatal Woman, as exemplified in the literature of latter nineteenth-century romanticism, a theme which had run through almost all of his former films, became fully crystallized in von Sternberg's next and final film made with Dietrich, *The Devil Is a Woman* (1935). (p. 412)

In its total realization *The Devil Is a Woman* was von Sternberg's most successful film aesthetically since his first independent effort, *The Salvation Hunters,* made exactly ten years earlier. In this new film he crystallized all the tendencies that had been present ever increasingly in his immediately preceding films: elements used to create a unique, exotic, visually rich environment in which erotic adventures might take place, the whole being inspired by the Fatal Woman with the enigmatic smile, Marlene Dietrich. . . .

The continuity, narrated for the most part by one of the central characters, allowed von Sternberg to dispense with any attempt to tell his story with dialogue during the central action of the film; he developed each sequence as a purely visual statement, one of the few really successful attempts at flashback narrative. (p. 413)

[Von Sternberg] achieved his greatest success when he discovered his sexual ideal, Marlene Dietrich, and her films at first achieved an immense popularity. But as he developed and refined his exotic-erotic creations they became increasingly unhuman; audiences rebelled against the stylization, the unreal settings, the fabulous mythological creature that Dietrich became. . . .

The fact that *The Shanghai Gesture* [1941] was based on the old stage hit of the 'twenties . . . prevented the film from becoming either good drama or interesting cinema. Nevertheless von Sternberg succeeded surprisingly well in imbuing individual episodes with a considerable amount of purely cinematic movement; the whole, however, suffered from too much dialogue. (p. 414)

For the first time von Sternberg developed a male character similar to his female sensualists [in *The Shanghai Gesture*]. As in *Shanghai Express,* all the characters were sharply etched in a slightly stylized manner. The curious blend of the naturalistic and the unnatural in the performances of his actors made it seem at times that the performers were attempting to caricature the parts assigned to them; the balance is, in any case, a difficult one between the real as we expect it to be and the creative *abstraction* attempted by von Sternberg. (pp. 414-15)

*Curtis Harrington, "The Dangerous Compromise,"* in Hollywood Quarterly *(copyright, 1948, copyright renewed © 1976, by The Regents of the University of California; reprinted by permission of the University of California Press), Vol. III, No. 4, Summer, 1948, pp. 405-15.*

### GEOFFREY WAGNER

[The] personal theme of *The Blue Angel* foreshadows an impending social disaster. Sadism was about to be unleashed in mass form in Germany and the film is, of course, a study of the spiritual torture and humiliation of a small-town man with whom everyone can readily identify himself. (p. 49)

[From the outset], the professor is haunted by the figure of the clown in the background, for he, the man of ideals, is himself a clown in the world of *The Blue Angel.* Thus at the beginning, when the professor first enters, the cabaret is shown as chaotic, almost surrealistic, with its whirling clouds, miasmic veils, and shifting backdrops; at the end, when he is part of it, it is steady, and brutal in its clarity. Everything connected with the professor suggests this interpretation—his favorite pupil called Angst, the mitigation of his masculine nose blowing after meeting Lola Lola, the very nickname Unrath (or excrement), which was later given to the Jews.

Sex and sadism, individual and social, are the main themes of *The Blue Angel.* . . . The dead bird which, in almost the first words of the film, the professor is told will never sing again, is nevertheless singing again in Lola Lola's boudoir, and sings in the last shot of all in the person of Lola Lola herself. Then for an instant the twelve apostles, in agonized poses of broken stone, file around the great Hamburg church clock, and finally Marlene herself sings the lines which sum up the film—when a man burns in lust, who can find him salvation? (pp. 50-1)

But sexual tension carries its corollaries of nostalgia and despair. Ecstasy, by its very nature, cannot endure. Slowly, in contrast to the cabaret scenes, the camera travels back down the empty classroom when [the professor] is about to leave it for good. In this last lingering embrace, as it were, the scene tenderly dramatizes the protagonist's loneliness and nostalgia for his past life which, banal though it was, had the irrecoverable gift of innocence. Lola herself, in the final analysis, is not wholly evil; as the mad professor grips her by the throat she asks him what he wants of her. (p. 51)

Nevertheless, it can be said that the whole of the dramatic construction of *The Blue Angel,* like its photographic composition, is centered on the sex of Lola Lola. All the scenes, the very intrigue of the film itself, radiate from this, have this as their focal point. Thus there is maintained a natural and harmonious thematic balance which makes the presentation logical and inevitable, and infinitely more gripping than the hypocritical eroticism of later Hollywood productions by the same director. Von Sternberg created his atmosphere with an almost suffocating eroticism of costume to offset cabaret scenes which are, contrary to general opinion, apt to be highly antierotic on the screen; sexiness frequently wages war with eroticism. (pp. 51-2)

> *Geoffrey Wagner, "'The Blue Angel': A Reconsideration," in* The Quarterly of Film, Radio, and Television *(copyright, 1951, copyright renewed © 1979, by The Regents of the University of California; reprinted by permission of the University of California Press), Vol. VI, No. 1, Fall, 1951, pp. 48-53.*

**TONY RICHARDSON**

Inevitably, one approached a work so obviously personal [as *The Saga of Anatahan*] with certain associations and expectations. The subject itself seemed to give ideal scope for certain aspects of von Sternberg's past work: his eroticism, his sensationalism, his decorative flair. Part of the fascination of the film is that it satisfies none of these expectations—so much so, in fact, that it has an almost unconscious "alienation" effect. . . . Von Sternberg deliberately eschews violence, and most of the murders take place off screen; only in one set—a charming hut entirely hung with variously shaped shells—is there evidence of his mannered, personal use of décor. Instead, von Sternberg has attempted to treat the story of Anatahan as an epic of heroism and endurance. He has succeeded only in presenting a lame, shambling chronicle. . . . [The] events seem arbitrary and meaningless. There is no sense that time and isolation develop the characters in any way, enlarge or narrow their visions. In the same way, von Sternberg has failed convincingly to create the locale itself: the island remains a series of unrelated sets. (p. 34)

The failure, though, lies deeper. Von Sternberg has taken no consistent attitude to his material. At times, the film seems to be presenting a heroic picture of resistance and loyalty in the teeth of isolation; at others, merely a piece of detached observation on the effect of isolation on the sexual habits of those concerned—so detached that it might be dealing with some species of curious insects. This impression is heightened by the weirdly gnomic dispassion of the observations and the metaphors in the commentary. . . . [The] Japanese are extraordinarily potent [in their performances], physically and emotionally, and their impact is considerable enough to keep one's attention over stretches of the film. The very sketchiness of the characterisation capitalises on their raw, alien energy, so that they appear not so much the recognisable human beings of [Kurosawa's] *Rashomon,* but vivid *ubermarionettes* projected from the mind of the garrulous old *régisseur,* giving force and life to his shallow conceptions.

It is difficult to find much else to praise in the film, with its slow, wandering rhythm, its haphazard construction. Perhaps the kindliest thing that can be said about this "tribute to the Japanese people and their art" is that it is, as they say, a collector's piece. (p. 35)

> *Tony Richardson, "Film Reviews: 'The Saga of Anatahan'," in* Sight and Sound *(copyright © 1954 by The British Film Institute), Vol. 24, No. 1, July-September, 1954, pp. 34-5.*

**JACK SMITH**

Von Sternberg's movies had to have plots even tho they already had them inherent in the images. What he did was make movies naturally—he lived in a visual world. The explanations plots he made up out of some logic having nothing to do with the visuals of his films. The explanations were his bragging, his genius pose,—the bad stories of his movies. Having nothing to do with what he did, (& did well) the *visuals* of his films. . . .

I don't think V. S. knew that words were in his way, but he felt it—neglected them, let them be corny & ridiculous, let them run to travesty—and he invested his images with all the care he rightfully denied the words. And he achieved the richest, most alive, most right images of the world's cinema. . . . (p. 4)

His expression was of the erotic realm—the neurotic gothic deviated sex-colored world and it was a turning inside out of himself and magnificent. You had to use your eyes to know this tho because the sound track babbled inanities—it alleged Dietrich was an honest jewel thief, noble floosie, fallen woman etc. to cover up the visuals. In the visuals she was none of those. She was V. S. himself. . . . The plot [of *The Devil is a Woman*] piles up situation after situation—but needlessly—Sternberg graphically illustrates this by using a tired actor giving a bad performance. If his hero is a phoney for the purposes of the story, V. S. casts an actory actor in the part & leads him into hammy performance. Which comes to the acting in V. S. films. He got his effect directly through the eye. If the woman is deceptive he would *not* get Dietrich to give a great (in other words the convention of good acting wherein maximum craft conveys truthfulness) perf. of a woman conning. . . . For he was concerned with personal, intuitive, emotional values—values he found within himself—not in a script. With people as their unique selves, not chessmen in a script.

Possibly he might have been afraid of reaction if it were known that this visual fantasy world was really his own mind. He might have deliberately obscured, distracted attention from the shock that might have occurred if his creation had been understood through the eye. To close the ears would have thrown the viewer into an undersea, under-conscious, world where the realities were very different from what the script purported. He needn't have worried. As it was no one had that ability to see. He was misunderstood and well understood. Well understood in that his covert world disturbed; misunderstood in that no one knew why or appreciated the wonder of being disturbed. (pp. 4-5)

> *Jack Smith, "Belated Appreciation of V. S.," in* Film Culture *(copyright 1964 by Film Culture), No. 31, Winter, 1963-64, pp. 4-5.*

## JOHN GILLETT

[Ostensibly **The Scarlet Empress**] is about the marriage of the young and innocent Sophia Frederica to the mad Grand Duke Peter of Russia, and the insurrection which resulted in her becoming the new Empress Catherine. Looking at it today, one is continually puzzled (and delighted) by Sternberg's ambivalent attitudes towards the material. Surely nobody could have doubted that he was sending it up ("those ideas are old-fashioned—this is the eighteenth century" proclaims the ardent, black-wigged Count Alexei to the pouting young Catherine). Yet Sternberg's insolent wit was the last thing commented on at the time. Strange, too, how these comic anachronisms are made to alternate with set-pieces played solely for their dramatic or exotic appeal; all dialogue ceases and Sternberg constructs a sequence "painted with light" which fully confirms his reputation as one of the cinema's great visual stylists. . . .

Sternberg is supposed to have thought of the Empress as a fishwife, but it is all too raucous and calculated for comfort. The film's portrait of a harsh, hypocritical Court looks artlessly naive by comparison with the cynical inventions of [Erich von] Stroheim or [Ernst] Lubitsch. They may not have had all the experience of middle European high life that they claimed, yet they had a more genuine and ingrained sophistication which protected them against some of the traps Sternberg falls into.

Neither of these directors, however, could have surpassed **The Scarlet Empress**'s grand finale, with its clamour of trumpets and bells (in an enthusiastic flurry of Sternberg's favourite lap-dissolves), Dietrich stomping about the palace in a hussar's outfit and *The Ride of the Valkyries* on the soundtrack. Here, in the film's most strikingly assembled sequence, mad Peter is quickly despatched behind a huge black cross, the horsemen charge up the stairs and into the throne-room, and Sternberg's camera wings up to a final exultant close-up of Catherine, now looking as pop-eyed as the Grand Duke himself. After this, it would be churlish to ask for more.

> *John Gillett, "'The Scarlet Empress'," in* Sight and Sound *(copyright © 1965 by The British Film Institute), Vol. 34, No. 2, Spring, 1965, p. 96.*

## HERMAN G. WEINBERG

There are no scabrous passages ever in Sternberg, not because he is a moralist—although he is that, in its most salutary sense, without any *a priori* moral judgments, like a psychologist or psychoanalyst—but because it would be a waste of film foot-

age, every foot of which is precious to a director with so much to say, with so many comments to make. His characters hardly ever even kiss and on the rare occasions when they do it is usually hidden behind a fan, a cloak, a back, or in a half-light. He has better ways of indicating romantic feeling or, when he wants to, purely sexual ones, by innuendo in his incisive dialogue and telling imagery. So sure is he of what he is doing that he doesn't need to pander to his audiences. His is a cinematic language of the utmost circumspection. (p. 103)

Let us consider [a] criticism leveled against Sternberg in the past—his "mannerisms," i.e., his cinema calligraphy. Now, mannerism is a way of doing things and that is what style is. And if that style is different from the usual way of doing things it becomes a "mannerism." . . . Sternberg without his "mannerisms" would not be Sternberg. . . . (p. 104)

Sternberg's "mannerisms" do not exist in a vacuum and alone anymore than his art does. It is part of the whole clamorous and exultant world wherever interesting people are to be found in and out of the arts, in science and sociology too, wherever dedicated men and women with a salutary purpose are even "going against the grain" to accomplish their work.

Seen today, Sternberg's films remind us of all this, they are a reminder of the richness that has all but disappeared from the screens of the world, and of how beautiful it was to see the continuity of an intensely personal style maintained from film to film in a medium so frequently composed of anonymous works. (pp. 106-07)

By richness I don't just mean striking pictorial composition but something even better—an attitude. At the end of a Sternberg film you know the director's attitude on a hundred things or more. Most modern films have no more attitude than a picture calendar (with someone's advertisement). They are impersonal works, carrying no personal statement. The picture is one thing—its director another; there is not necessarily any bond between them. That's never so in the work of a true artist. He makes a personal statement by everything, even the slightest and most casual thing, he does. Nothing happens by chance in such films—and that is their worth because everything in them has been inserted because it has value. This makes a rich film. It is also possible to become so mesmerized by the witchery of a Sternberg film that only when it is over (I'm thinking particularly of **The Docks of New York**) do you realize it has been a silent film. This also makes a rich film. (p. 107)

We could sum up his work by saying that the iridescent flame of his technique, unique in the cinema, has been put to the service of what the Slavs call *zoll* and the Germans, *Weltschmerz*, that world pain, that life-hurt, for it is a sad, guilty world, and his sad, misanthropic films reflect this. . . . There are few resolutions in his films, although there is sometimes a gallant sort of hope. Shall we say something before concluding about the man behind the artist? His fastidiousness, his intransigence, his implacability where his art is concerned? But that brings us to the artist again. Let us just say that those who truly know him would agree that the frost of knighthood is in his manner, this mandarin among Hollywood directors. There is a considerable name in the history of the cinema—Josef von Sternberg—and he has earned it. (p. 110)

> *Herman G. Weinberg, in his* Josef von Sternberg: A Critical Study, *translated by Herman G. Weinberg (originally published as* Josef von Sternberg, *Editions Seghers, 1966), Arno Press, 1978, 254 p.*

## BOSLEY CROWTHER

[*The Blue Angel* is important because it so presciently shows the immaturity and sadism of the German middle class.] In its singular contemplation of the sudden disintegration of a pillar of bourgeois society under the quick, corrosive influence of a strong application of gutter sex, it starkly reveals the imperfection and fraudulence of the façade of middle-class decency and discipline that its ponderous hero represents. It sourly suggests the soggy culture out of which Nazism oozed. And in the sadistic frenzy of the schoolboys to torment and destroy their hated teacher after they have witnessed his weakness for the cabaret girl, we may spot the incipient viciousness of later Hitler Youth.

But I find *The Blue Angel* most engrossing because of the opening it makes upon the whole darksome, subterranean area of psychoneurotic sex. Where the custom in silent pictures was simply to treat the primal urge as a powerful but usually unholy and sinful appetite that overwhelms men *and* women by its sheer physical rush and urgency, the revelation in this picture is a sickly image of sex as a passion mixed up with deep obsessions to dominate and get revenge. And where the evil of it in the silents was mainly its immorality, the evil of it in *The Blue Angel* is its corruption into a social disease that infects the aggressions of people and causes them to act in debased and vicious ways. (pp. 71-2)

It is notable that Sternberg does not give us any scenes of Rath and Lola making love, none of the sort of erotic acrobatics that have shown up in later sex-charged films. This is tremendously important, for it is all too suggestively implied in the few shots he shows of the teacher fumbling clumsily and grossly with the slut that any sex act between them would be disgustingly callow and crude, totally without pleasure for either of them. This leads us back to the premise that it is sex in its more neurotic form that is the essence of this picture. (pp. 75-6)

> *Bosley Crowther, "'The Blue Angel'," in his* The Great Films: Fifty Golden Years of Motion Pictures *(copyright © 1967 by Bosley Crowther), G. P. Putnam's Sons, 1967, pp. 71-6.*

## JOHN BAXTER

It is only in the light of Sternberg's private life that the world of his films is illuminated; a world where fathers, if they appear at all, are self-interested and remote, mothers raucous harridans or dowagers of reptilian *hauteur,* children savages with the instincts of the jungle, men cowering victims who both fear and welcome the lash of contempt that their women, alone in his films retaining their individuality, can wield. . . .

If Sternberg's character is complex, his work is infinitely more so. He broke new ground in cinematography, and had enormous influence on cinema design and acting. Yet he invented nothing. . . .

But even if his sources are observable, it is clear that in arranging the material he borrowed Sternberg was motivated by a strongly personal and original style. (p. 14)

Sternberg's alternative to the Hollywood style of film-making was a synthetic language of personal statement. Story was unimportant, elapsed time insignificant; most of his films leap years in the telling, charting an emotional relationship or moral decline without respect for chronology. Imitating *Kammerspiel,* he used lighting, *décor* and minutely observed gestures

to entice from nature and the human face their hidden "spiritual power," and his development became a search for new elements that would allow him to distil in greater purity this inner essence. (p. 16)

No words can convey the atmosphere of a Sternberg film, so personal are his associations. That all his films were in some sense autobiographical cannot be doubted, but reminiscence was a passport into new worlds of artistic experiment. Contrary to popular opinion at the time, Sternberg's style was always the servant to his subject, though by choosing to examine the minute variations of emotional experience he laid himself open to charges of triviality. Certainly his work is trivial in plot. . . . But all his films explore perceptively some mood or emotional state, chart the development of an attitude, analyse the delicate evolutions of a relationship in ascendancy or decline. They have a psychological power that transcends simple plot. Under his scrutiny a reality emerges that is at once obvious and infinitely complex in its implications, the world of human emotion, of love and its dark concomitant, the desire to destroy. (p. 22)

> *John Baxter, in his* The Cinema of Josef von Sternberg *(copyright © 1971 by John Baxter), A. S. Barnes & Co., 1971, 192 p.*

## JOYCE RHEUBAN

Between the lines of [Sternberg's autobiography, *Fun in a Chinese Laundry,*] and behind the images of the films, one may detect the constant contention of discipline versus indulgence; intellect versus faith or the inexplicable; civilisation versus the savage or exotic; and the tendency to conceal versus the tendency to reveal. Finally, there is the role of Sternberg as artist: 'scientist' versus 'vamp'. These roles are paralleled in the projections of himself in his characters, generally as man versus woman. Within Sternberg the artist and the man, the two sides seem to vie for ascendancy. In the films, these contradictory personal proclivities are externalised, personified to fight it out on the screen; and the conflict is expressed in erotic terms. . . .

Sternberg's work displays obsessively this tension between his volatile 'dark forces' and the imposition of rational control. He exhibits his fascination with the contention of reason versus emotion by working out the dynamic possibilities of their co-existence, both dramatically through his characters and visually in his treatment of the images. Confronting his preoccupation with emotion, Sternberg is threatened with the danger to his objective control and the possibilty that, as artist, he may not be able to deal effectively with anything else. . . .

Dramatically, Sternberg conceals through ambiguity. He often purposely refuses to develop elements of characterisation, motivation or situation. Dialogue, particularly in the films starring Dietrich, is conspicuously evasive, and delivery often stylised to a flat monotone. . . .

Another way to hide one's feelings is to laugh at them. Sternberg's sardonic sense of humour is ruthlessly unsparing. The resounding outburst of the impressionable young lieutenant who refuses to order the execution of Dietrich as a traitor in *Dishonoured* is merely an elaborate build-up for the punch line. As Dietrich stands before the wavering firing squad, she takes the opportunity to adjust her nylons and touch up her lipstick while the lieutenant's idealistic monologue is heard offscreen. . . .

Sternberg conceals visually by means of intricate, diverting compositions of light and shadow, pattern and texture. He often literally 'veils' his images. He uses various textural and compositional elements and combinations of these elements placed before the camera—veils, streamers, nets, rain, smoke, glass, light and shadow. . . .

What seems to have attracted Sternberg so irresistibly to his 'dark forces' is their mystery. It is interesting to note that ambiguity and abstraction are the means he uses to disguise his fascination with them. The dramatic and visual style he employs to conceal that with which he is impelled to deal actually results in an effect of emotionalisation. Indeed, he refers to his visual technique as an 'emotionalisation of space'. The very air is a conductor of the emotional charge. (p. 35)

In the erotic relationships in the films between man and woman, Sternberg dramatically externalises that tension within himself between reason and emotion. The leading characters generally correspond to the two sides of this dichotomy—that is, 'scientist' and 'vamp'. Both characters are Sternberg nevertheless. It is therefore understandable that their relationships are always, at one point or another, relationships of conflict.

'Scientist' is a general term which refers in this context to the character who subscribes to some sort of discipline. This character, usually the leading man, metaphorically represents the tendency in Sternberg towards reason, control, intellect and civilisation. Most of Sternberg's male characters do subscribe to some discipline, formal or informal. . . .

Woman in Sternberg's films may be seen as the metaphorical externalisation of his 'dark forces'—those unruly tendencies that reside beneath a civilised surface. This woman is therefore essentially a being of charming beauty and irresistible mystery who can never be fully comprehended by the intellect. She is also potentially dangerous, because her powers are ungoverned and ungovernable by rational control. Sternberg fashions her as a stimulus to man's primitive desires and animal impulses and, at the same time, the very incarnation of those desires and impulses—elemental, pagan, exotic. (p. 37)

Sternberg's own version of the prototype movie vamp is, however, not so much the broadly characterised temptress who sets out to lure, seduce, humiliate and eventually destroy a man just for the fun and profit of it. She is rather the more passive, but highly persuasive, stimulus for the male character to destroy himself. Her irresistible attraction depends as much on the man's particular vulnerability as on her specific charms. This is why most of Sternberg's 'heroes' are of a common type. Because of their inhibitions or previous self-denial, they are all the more susceptible to seduction, and often beyond that to hopeless, irrational obsession. Man, the 'scientist', is minus; Woman, the 'vamp' is plus. Opposites attract.

It is of interest to observe the fatalistic way in which characters of such different ways of life and temperament inevitably gravitate towards one another in Sternberg's films. Since both characters personify aspects of a single personality (Sternberg's), their attraction to each other over vast and small expanses of space and time might be interpreted metaphorically as Sternberg's 'split personality' seeking completion. . . .

The blood relationship of Sternberg's 'vamp' to her prototype, dangerous by nature and evil as a matter of course, may be seen in his oblique and tenuous images of woman as, variously, black widow spider, black cat, or the ultimate *femme fatale*—

Death herself. Sternberg's dangerous women are most often dressed, seductively but ominously, in black. . . .

The inevitable connection of beauty with danger in Sternberg's Woman leads unavoidably to the motifs (again paradoxical) of love and hate and love and death. The love/hate motif is expressed primarily in the man's self-destructive response of intensified attraction as the 'vamp' becomes more dangerous, more powerful and sadistic. (p. 38)

Extraordinary as Sternberg's 'vamp' is, his female characterisation transcends this superficial classification. She becomes a sort of Superwoman, incredibly potent in the combination of feminine beauty and charm with the strength of a man. Sternberg's 'Lesbian accents', including Dietrich's frequent adoption of masculine attire and mannerisms, in addition to enhancing her aura of ambiguity, may also be explained as a suggestion of her omni-sexuality. . . .

The woman is generally at least an equal match for the man in the conflict at hand between reason and emotion. The characters often set out at the beginning of a film as in a contest, by shaking hands or sizing each other up with a glance. Often this Superwoman is stronger than the man, since she has access to additional weapons. . . .

For this extraordinary woman, sexual power is translated into military and political power. The motif of love and war in Sternberg's films relates of course to that of love and hate and love and death. . . .

The cinematic evolution of Sternberg's Woman and her relationships with the male characters may serve . . . as an index to the condition of his own psychological and artistic relationship to the tendencies the characters embody. A particularly convenient case study in an assessment of this evolution is that of Marlene Dietrich. (p. 39)

As the tension between reason and emotion seems to have increased while working with Dietrich, so does the correlative tension between revealing and concealing. Sternberg seems to reinforce his defences in the last films with Dietrich by 'completely subjecting' his 'bird of paradise' to his camouflaging stylisation of visual treatment, dramatic ambiguity and absurd, self-mocking humour. . . .

New and unconventional approaches and techniques are to be found in all Sternberg's previous and subsequent surviving films, but *The Scarlet Empress* and [*The Devil Is a Woman*] are relentlessly executed in modernist terms; according to an aesthetic strategy which functions as a direct expression of the artist's consciousness.

It is easy to imagine how anarchic these two films must have seemed at the time of their realisation (as they still are). Sternberg had conceived a most original stylistic strategy to accommodate that inner tension between revealing and concealing his peculiar preoccupations. These films represent the hyperbolic extensions of this strategy—one characterised by ambiguity, dramatic and visual abstraction and dehierarchisation, an indiscriminate mixture of genres, and black and absurdist humour.

In the essentially 'vamp' formula plot and characterisations of *Anatahan,* Sternberg's last film, may be seen yet another restatement of the same preoccupations. His purported aim is an 'experiment . . . to alert all of us . . . to the necessity of reinvestigating our emotions and the reliability of our controls.' However, his warning in *Anatahan* is relatively free of the diverting stylisation of concealment typical of previous films. Sternberg's 'didactic' intentions *are* better served in *Anatahan*—a film without the customary elliptical traps, cryptic ambiguities and mysterious charm of the enigmatic. *Anatahan* represents the work of a Sternberg relieved of the heightened tension of having to contend (in his own inimitable and captivating fashion) with his infatuation with Dietrich as a dangerously 'too perfect' medium for the expression of a subjective obsession. The labyrinthine abysses of the often outrageous, always beautiful style in which Sternberg's intellectual discipline demanded he dress his emotional indulgence, most dynamically expressed in the series of films with Dietrich, are more intriguing and exciting. In their extraordinarily direct communication of this quintessential quality of tension, these films best express the sensibility and personality of Josef von Sternberg. There are few subjects more intriguing and exciting than Sternberg himself. (p. 40)

> Joyce Rheuban, "Josef von Sternberg: The Scientist and the Vamp," in Sight and Sound (copyright © 1973 by The British Film Institute), Vol. 42, No. 1, Winter, 1972-73, pp. 34-40.

## TOM MILNE

*Thunderbolt* looks very much like an attempt to repeat the highly successful formula of *Underworld.* But where the earlier film had a triangle situation as three-dimensional as a pyramid based in the curious sort of love affair between the brutish Bull Weed and the gentle, courteously ironic Rolls-Royce . . . , *Thunderbolt* operates from a much simpler, more Hollywooden premise which leaves no place for the ambivalent moralities of Sternberg's world. . . . Clearly conscious of [a] shallowness in the characterisation, Sternberg tries to compensate by elaborating a cat (the mysterious lure of the underworld) and a dog (tranquil domesticity) as symbols of the emotional dilemma: a symbolism which eventually identifies Thunderbolt with the dog (dumb devotion), and would have been more effective, as well as more in keeping with twilight Sternbergian ethics, had Ritzy the cat been allowed to retain a hint of feline equivocation. Although it looks terrific, shot with all Sternberg's usual loving care for half-lights and shadows, this first half of the film seems to catch him in an uneasy attempt to reduce his vision to a 'reality' commensurate with the simplified characterisation. The visit to the Black Cat Club, for instance, never quite takes off into the dream-like fantasy of the gangster's ball in *Underworld,* despite its striking visual play with the predominantly Negro staff and customers against the glittering silvery-white decor, because Sternberg is evidently forcing himself to impose a note of vulgarity in order to contrast unfavourably with the later (and sadly mawkish) scenes of domestic bliss in the Moran home. . . . Sternberg's intermittent earlier experiments with sound . . . come into their own [in the scene of the wedding ceremony in the jail]: a single set, purely imaginative in quality, which allows the rivals to glare at each other from their cages set opposite each other across a narrow passageway (with the bars making caressing patterns of menace); allows for adjoining cells so that the voices-off of other prisoners add contrapuntally to the silent dialogue between the two men staring at each other (a fine moment when another prisoner asks Thunderbolt to describe the new inmate he cannot see, and Thunderbolt launches into a scathing pen portrait of a seducer); and above all, allows for the musical commentary, also mostly off, first by a prisoner singing spirituals, then by a harmony quartet, and finally by a prison

concert orchestra, which traces the progress of the emotional duel being played out. With this rigid formalism, Sternberg recaptures his emotional exactness (i.e. ambivalence). . . . *Thunderbolt* may be minor Sternberg, but no Sternberg film is less than essential viewing. (pp. 187-88)

> Tom Milne, "Retrospective: 'Thunderbolt'," in Monthly Film Bulletin (copyright © The British Film Institute, 1974), Vol. 41, No. 487, August, 1974, pp. 187-88.

## JOHN TIBBETTS

Never has Josef von Sternberg made the surfaces of reality seem so fragile and the shapes of illusion so tangible as in *The Last Command* (1928). He deliberately creates not one but several worlds and then dissolves the barriers between them. A carefully constructed film with meticulous attention to techniques, detail, and symbol—the whole nevertheless emerges not firm and clear, but vague and half-seen. This is a remarkable kind of alchemy . . . ; moreover, it is exemplary of his ability to shape, reshape, and destroy his worlds so that they are continually shifting and becoming; it is the essentially modern device of clarity seeking ambiguity, rather than the other way around. (p. 68)

The narrative structure is at least tri-level. I say "at least" because nothing is quite as it seems. There is a modern story of the making of a film about the Russian Revolution; there is a flashback to revolutionary Russia of 1917; and there is the Hollywood film itself which concerns that revolution. This last combines elements of the first two levels. It provides a fusion of them and extension of their meaning.

I have stressed the fusion of the three narrative levels. The connecting links among them are of three kinds: (1) similar characters and plot elements, (2) similar cinematic techniques, (3) leitmotif devices. (p. 69)

Similar cinematic techniques also unite the three levels. The whole of *The Last Command,* except a handful of exterior scenes, is a studio product. The flashback is treated in Sternberg's best studio style; and the "film" is shot in a studio. Just before the cameras turn for the "film," Sternberg takes great pains to show the apparatus of a Hollywood studio in action. Sternberg's preoccupation with studio shooting is well-known. It enabled him to have complete and dictatorial control over acting, camera movement, and lighting. It represents his own "command" over the entirety of *The Last Command.* . . .

The lighting is never flat: it is always low-key with much of the frame lost in inky darkness, allowing for select points of emphasis. When Sergius walks down the hallway of his cheap hotel to answer the casting office's call for an extra part (the call itself being another kind of command), he seems to materialize from the shadows. The effect is of transitoriness, as if he is only half real. . . .

[Cinematic] techniques aid the repetition of plot elements in the third level of narrative, the "film," effecting the final fusion of past and present, illusion and reality. What had been a bare set in the middle of a studio becomes, under the lights and wind machines, the stuff of the flashback. (p. 70)

Leitmotif devices also unite the three narrative levels. In the opening shots of the modern story Leo Andreyev, the Hollywood director/ex-revolutionary, has his cigarette lit by a dozen outstretched matches. This little tableau has an almost religious configuration. It is repeated many times in both the modern and flashback stories; mute obsequiousness and fawning homage move from one echelon of power to another, all the while gracefully balanced upon the tip of a slender cigarette. . . . Also there is Sergius' aide who, after gloating over his downfall, after wearing Sergius' coat and smoking his cigarettes, is shot to death in a brawl. The cigarette falls from his lips, a symbol of departed grace and power. Sternberg's achievement with this leitmotif device is twofold: he uses it extensively in the various narrative levels of **Command** as a linking device; and he invests it with comments on the cyclical destruction inherent in power structures. Perhaps it is fair to say that Sternberg knew quite a bit about the power of authority and the pitfalls that inevitably accompanied it. (p. 71)

[Reality] (the flashback and the modern story) is linked by style and content to the "film" being shot in the Hollywood studio. Great pains have been taken to show the artificialness of that "film," so we must accept the implications of this fusion, i.e., the irony of the general's ideals and authority as delineated by a camera and spotlight. Sergius is in command again—but of a Hollywood set. And Leo Andreyev, ex-revolutionary, embittered, is now a purveyor of Hollywood illusions. At the end Leo kneels in tribute to Sergius' artificial rebirth, to the man he fought against during the Revolution. By this time the validity and strength of these men's ideals have been ripped apart. The worlds of the flashback and the modern story collide; the barriers between them dissolve when the ghost images of the flashback populate the movie set—and this should be emphasized—*off* the set and behind the cameraman, illustrating the complete collapse of boundaries setting off the illusory from reality. . . .

The system of power structures and merging realities in **The Last Command** is really that of Sternberg himself. His ego was always the strongest push behind any of his films. His style here is particularly well-equipped to observe the oscillating series of authority shifts behind the merging worlds in his film. Judgments made on men like Leo and Sergius should be applied to Sternberg as well, who personifies a combination of the two—general and film maker. The arrogance of these three people builds structures subject to collapse: world succeeds upon world, revolution upon revolution throughout the entirety of **The Last Command.** (p. 72)

The merging boundaries of the worlds in this film are . . . quite in keeping with the building and tearing down of sets for the film making process. The almost militaristic power structures Sternberg delineated in the film are those of Hollywood itself. Still, the art of film making often reflects a shifting, elusive authority which evokes the question, "Who's in charge here?" There are many answers in **The Last Command,** all of them proving ephemeral. But doubtless Sternberg knew all the time. (p. 73)

> *John Tibbetts, "Sternberg and 'The Last Command',"* in Cinema Journal *(© 1976, Society for Cinema Studies), Vol. XV, No. 2, Spring, 1976, pp. 68-73.*

### DON WILLIS

A Sternberg film is built on paradox and dichotomy, its essence fixed not by one particular image that can be isolated, but by a particular pair of images, or series of images or motifs. . . .

[The Shanghai Gesture] is a Sternberg image set without a film: namely, a virtuoso crane into the depths of a gambling pit near the beginning and a complementary crane out again at the end, echoed by more clipped tracks into the gamblers themselves. As an evocation of a human vortex of feeling and chance, this is as electric and concise a 'fix' on the Sternberg theme as there is. (p. 106)

The whole structure and design of **The Blue Angel**—classroom/cabaret, professor/clown, students/audience—is symmetrical. . . . Lola, Kiepert, the clown with the frozen mock-empathetic expression and Rath's students are less characters than parts of a psychic-aesthetic whole, a completion of Rath, one summoning up the other, their insolence predicated on Rath's authoritarianism. His use of his handkerchief forms an absurd part of his regimen; Lola's panties, which he picks up in its place and with which he absently wipes his forehead, are merely an extension of that absurdity. **The Blue Angel** is a serio-comic vision of the world as fun-house-mirror image of personal sexual paranoia, a witty and sad confirmation of one's worst nightmares. (pp. 106-07)

The world of **The Devil is a Woman** is created in the image of Concha Perez, or in the reverse-image of Don Pasqual's stolidity. The script, essentially, is one scene replayed over and over—Concha teasing, tempting, then deserting him. The film is comically static, the point being in the repetition of the situation, not its dramatic development. Concha's capriciousness is invariably outrageous, and only nuances of her expression and movement distinguish one outrage from the next. . . .

This derisive imagery pervades Sternberg's films, giving them a look and feel unlike any others. It is less symbolism than visual inflection. . . . Only in a Sternberg film could you find so bizarre a romantic overture as Oland and Dietrich rudely blowing noise-makers at each other. . . . [Such] derisive sounds and images function as a putting in place of individual passions, a puncturing of any sense of the self as supreme. They effectively undermine sexual and romantic complacency. . . .

The meaning of [Dishonoured] may seem at first to lie somewhere between the snort of amused contempt with which von Seyffertitz dismisses the dancing dolls and his gallant salute of Dietrich's body; but the Dietrich-doll analogy bristles with all sorts of implications, not the least intriguing of which is that von Sternberg intends von Seyffertitz' salute to be taken ironically, not sentimentally. He is in fact the one who has enlisted Dietrich's services as a spy; thus he is also in effect the person, or agency, responsible for her execution. And so it is that, near-surrealistically, the film connects his casual flicking of the plastic dolls in one scene with the grotesque backward snap of Dietrich's body in another. It is as if, out of time, he had taken her life with a single gesture of the hand. His final salute of her body, then, is the equivalent of the ironic applause for Rath at the end of **The Blue Angel.** (p. 107)

[Two actions] are the key to **Dishonoured:** agent X-27 committing treason by allowing her lover and opposite number to escape; and the young lieutenant in charge of the firing squad suddenly refusing, on behalf of love and women, to give the order to have her shot. They're parallel actions in that both put sentiment before duty, but while the first is clearly romantic the second is, for want of an even remotely satisfactory word, lunatic-romantic. . . .

The unprepared viewer's first response is, necessarily, incredulity. If the sequence can be said to constitute an anti-war statement, it is only as, say, the Marx Brothers' *Duck Soup* constitutes an anti-war statement—that is, God knows how but somehow, in some odd corner of the viewer's violated mind. With its half-comic, half-horrific flurry of images, it reads, not necessarily in order, something like, love is sublime, love is ridiculous, love is sublime. It is unclear what exactly is undercutting what. The graphic death of X-27 seems to render the lieutenant's impassioned words just so much air, and in one sense it does: they are seen to have no practical effect. X-27 dies. But the lieutenant's outlandishly incongruous paean to love has an odd, lingering resonance. It is as if X-27's grand romantic gesture, refracted through the lieutenant's crazy-romantic gesture, had been broken down, analysed and found to be an act of insolence or presumption (or, in her country's terms, treason) implying, as in *The Blue Angel,* death. . . .

In a narrative which seems to be perfectly split into two sections—'innocence' and 'experience'—there is one constant in *Scarlet Empress:* Sternberg's occasional use of veils and netting to diffuse Catherine's emotions. For instance, in perhaps the key sequence of the first half, her wedding to Peter, Catherine is buried in the oppressive decor. Her presence behind her veil is signalled only by her quickened breath, which rhythmically stirs the candle flame before her face. Again, early in the second half of the film, after the birth of her baby (father uncertain), Catherine's face is seen as a blank, lost in the netting of her bed, as she cheerlessly dangles and then drops a diamond pendant given her for the occasion.

In the first image, Catherine's emotion is obviously great, but it is irrelevant to the proceedings. The innocent, passionate Catherine is lost both in the kinetic movement of the sequence upwards, which culminates in a shot of the Empress Elizabeth, the source of power, and in the general movement of the film upwards, to the climactic shot of the Empress Catherine at the top of the palace throne room.

The later image of the veiled, impassive Catherine is perhaps even more emotionally charged, but the source of emotion is indeterminate—the source seems roughly to be the entire first half of the film filtered through, simply, the image of the twisting pendant and Catherine's eyelids, which flicker in apparent indifference. . . .

*Anatahan* concludes with a coda which operates on a similar emotional principle. In it the 'queen bee' Keiko . . . , or her spirit, again faces her 'drones', or their spirits, the men she gave life if not love to on the island. As each man steps forwards out of the shadows, she seems to recall him, and speechlessly looks down and away from him. Both she and the men are virtually expressionless—no exchange of looks could 'say' what they might want to say to each other, as nothing in Catherine's face could adequately express her emotions at the moment when she receives the pendant. Yet the emotional content of the film as a whole seems refracted in only the slight, suggestive movement of Keiko's eyes. That content isn't quite love, pity, sorrow or understanding, but something inexpressible, as is the image of Catherine in the bed. (p. 108)

[Von Sternberg's] films, finally, are less about passion than about passion's context—the sand and wind, the goats and Amy's scarf at the end of *Morocco;* the noise-makers in *Dishonoured* and popping balloons in *The Devil is a Woman;* the crowds at the station at the end of *Shanghai Express* and outside the temple in [the uncompleted] *I, Claudius;* the wedding ceremony in *Scarlet Empress;* the quiet, extended scene of Lola heating an iron in *The Blue Angel* after Rath stalks out angrily vowing never to return. (In a minute or so he returns, subdued.) The point of the dissolve superimposing Lily and Captain Harvey over the crowd at the end of *Shanghai Express* seems not just that they lose themselves in it. The dissolve affirms both their disregard of the crowd and the physical fact of the crowd—it doesn't just go away. Love is not a transforming power in Sternberg's films: that's the real message of the lieutenant's harangue in *Dishonoured.* Love is its own end. (p. 109)

*Don Willis, "Sternberg: The Context of Passion,"* in Sight and Sound *(copyright © 1978 by The British Film Institute), Vol. 47, No. 2, Spring, 1978, pp. 104-09.*

# François Truffaut

## 1932-

French director, scriptwriter, critic, and actor.

Truffaut is both the formulator and one of the most skilled practitioners of the auteur theory of filmmaking which holds that the film's director should be the commanding presence in the work, responsible for script as well as direction. His best work combines an affectionate acceptance of life's consequences with an objectivity that precludes sentimentality. This recognition imbues his films with their characteristic bittersweet quality.

Truffaut's childhood was unhappy, like that of his alter ego, Antoine Doinel, in *The 400 Blows*. Neglected by his parents, Truffaut often skipped school and sought refuge in the cinema. The love of film he developed led Truffaut into an important friendship with André Bazin, an influential critic who became a father-figure to Truffaut. Bazin helped Truffaut when the army arrested him for desertion; as well, Bazin's journal, *Les Cahiers du Cinéma* published Truffaut's auteur manifesto, "Une certain tendance du cinéma français." This essay attacked France's postwar films, claiming they abused the rights of cinema by giving the public "its habitual dose of smut, nonconformity, and facile audacity." In their place, Truffaut proposed a "cinéma des auteurs," praising directors who write and invent what they shoot. The article became a hallmark for the young critic as well as the fledgling magazine. Not surprisingly, this theory encouraged many young critics to make their own films, resulting in the *nouvelle vague* (new wave). Among these directors, most notable are Jean-Luc Godard, Eric Rohmer, Claude Chabrol, Alain Resnais, and Truffaut.

Truffaut's directorial opportunity came with his marriage to Madeleine Morgenstern, whose wealthy father provided one-third of the cost of production for *The 400 Blows*. Intensely autobiographical, the film tells the story of a young Parisian boy who is mistreated and ignored by his family and society in general. The film won for Truffaut the 1959 Cannes Film Festival award for best director. Doinel emerged in later films as he grew older: the character's obsession with women and literature is intended to correspond with Truffaut's overwhelming love of film.

Truffaut's recent films are less autobiographical, although in *Day for Night*, Truffaut played himself as a director. Other films, such as *Small Change*, reflect his love for children. Although Truffaut borrows strongly from Renoir and Hitchcock, his themes and moral stance remain unique, providing a melancholic insight into human complexity. (See also *Contemporary Authors*, Vols. 81-84.)

## WILLIAM BERNHARDT

For some little time now we have been hearing and reading about the crop of rising young French directors but we have had little opportunity to see their work at firsthand. Signs of a change are in view with the arrival of François Truffaut's *Les Mistons* [*The Mischief Makers*]. . . .

Based on a story by Maurice Pons, *Les Mistons* . . . recalls the activities of five young French boys on the threshold of adolescence as they move through a summer in which the magic circle of childhood is broken and they stumble hesitantly, unsurely, into the mysterious world of puberty. Baffled by a change they do not yet fully comprehend, the boys release their bewilderment over an awakening sensuality on a pair of young lovers, Gerard and Bernadette . . . , spying upon and tormenting the pair, . . . and releasing their ambivalent emotions by projecting their unfulfilled lusts onto the ripe young body of Bernadette, who in their eyes becomes something of a goddess—mysterious, desirable, unobtainable, a legend.

All of this is revealed through a combination of visuals and commentary, both of which weave a spell of poetic sensuality combined with a nostalgic tenderness for the lost innocence of childhood. The summer becomes something of a ritualistic *rite de passage*. In the words of the commentary, the boys discover themselves but lose themselves; they discover a new kind of love but lose the old kind. No longer children, not yet adults, they have been touched by the age-old serpent, who has revealed to them "the fate and the privilege of the flesh." The ritual, mythic element is stressed by the commentary (references to serpents, gods and goddesses, nymphs and satyrs; the description of the tennis game between the lovers as a rite, a ceremony of desire) and by the use of slow motion to heighten certain actions. . . . (p. 52)

The world of the lovers is in its own way as full of ritual as that of the boys, with its bicycles and athletics, its love play and nuzzlings, but here again there is a certain loss of innocence through an awareness of the cruelty of life and love (the pair watch in fascination and disgust a praying mantis devour its mate) and the capriciousness of fate (Gerard is killed on a mountain-climbing expedition, leaving Bernadette to walk alone through the autumn days like a tragic young goddess in black).

Truffaut has told his story with economy and precision, infusing it with humor, tenderness, and a poetic beauty. . . . With his shots of girls walking, of girls riding on bicycles with skirts flying, and by keeping the camera close to Bernadette's body in the tennis game, he has evoked the proper air of sensuality. He has been completely successful in setting the tone desired and in the creation of mood in this "remembrance of things past." His film has more truth and life in its twenty-seven minutes than many films have in three or four times its length. (pp. 52-3)

*William Bernhardt, "Film Reviews: 'Les Mistons'," in* Film Quarterly *(copyright 1959 by The Regents of the University of California; reprinted by permission of the University of California Press), Vol. XIII, No. 1, Fall, 1959, pp. 52-3.*

## ARLENE CROCE

[*The 400 Blows* is a sad, bitter] story of a child's gradual disaffection from society. The child is tough, imaginative, exuberant; the society is dull, timid, corrupt. But the film's point of view isn't sentimental. . . . *The 400 Blows* does not exist on a plane of fantasy; its premises are not allegorical. It is about the suffering an average young schoolboy must endure if he has the bad luck to be considered a criminal by both his family and the state in what we can only take to be present-day Paris. Given the actualities of this situation, and a manifest talent for observation, Truffaut's approach may seem to American audiences strangely stoical. He seems to be able to accept bad luck in good grace and still move us to moral indignation.

Truffaut is not, in the political sense, engaged. He protests in terms of the transcendent values; he protests the inhumanity of man. The underlying sadness of his film is the sadness of the universal estrangement. . . . In *The 400 Blows,* "new wave" technique serves to unite poetry and journalism in the powerful idiom of a particular environment—an environment, moreover, that has long supplied certain historical privileges for what an aesthetic need can make of them. . . . *The 400 Blows* is a film about freedom. It could, I think, convey this idea to an audience of deaf illiterates in any part of the world, because its construction is very nearly as absolutely visual as that of a silent film. (pp. 35-6)

Where there is poetry in Truffaut's method, it is often graced with the kind of ambiguity cherished among the "new wave" directors. The ambiguity derives from a deliberate withholding of explicit comment, as in the interview scene—from the apparent determination of the director to express no opinions. Revelation is a matter of the direct perception of what people say and do, and what is revealed to you is your own feeling about the words and deeds of others. . . . The grown-up characters in the film may appear to us monsters of hypocrisy, but is it more correct to say that they control the world than to say that they are controlled by it? (p. 37)

In its retention of life's ambiguity, the "new wave" technique makes unique demands on the spectator. The novelty of it is the way it can open up a film in the mind of the audience, creating an experience which is insistently problematical. . . . [Even when Truffaut] seems to be putting things squarely up to you, as in the intense and disarming intimacy of the psychiatrist's interview, ambiguous sensations are evident, and there is a suspicion that, in some of the things he says, the boy may be lying. . . . The important thing, however, is that

at this moment, and at the end, you are no longer looking at the film—the film is looking at you. (pp. 37-8)

*Arlene Croce, "Film Reviews: 'Les quatre cents coups'," in* Film Quarterly *(copyright 1960 by The Regents of the University of California; reprinted by permission of the University of California Press), Vol. XIII, No. 3, Spring, 1960, pp. 35-8.*

## ERIC RHODE

That there's a Chaplinesque pathos about François Truffaut's *Les Quatre Cents Coups* [*400 Blows*] . . . isn't surprising; for like Chaplin's tramp, Antoine Doinel, the protagonist of this film, tries to live a way of life that quickly brings him into conflict with society. Antoine presents positives similar to Chaplin: he's a bit of a dandy, full of tricks and affection, with a lovely appreciation of life, and yet a sense of its absurdity also. But for him, the conflict with society is more than a matter of pathos; for Antoine is only twelve-and-a-half years old, and his history presents in an extreme form that most tragic experience of adolescence, the loss of spontaneity. (p. 89)

This is a deeply ironical film. For instance, Antoine's downfall is precipitated by his admiration for Balzac, one of the most eminent critics of society, and confirmed when he tries to return a stolen typewriter; and this irony takes on an increasing resonance because Antoine doesn't realise the ambiguity of social morality. (pp. 89-90)

Truffaut has said of his film that it should be judged not by its technical perfections but by its sincerity; but of course a man's sincerity can only be judged by his technique. It is in fact through the success of his technique that Truffaut catches so much of life's richness. . . . [With Truffaut] art conceals art; sequences are neither broken down and manipulated into aesthetic effect, nor is their moral complexity tampered with. The control of the film lies rather in the playing of complete sequences one against the other, like tesserae in a mosaic. For instance, before the tense scene in which Antoine is caught returning the typewriter, we are shown actuality shots of children absorbed in a Punch and Judy show, their faces gleaming with excitement. The point is clear—Antoine is a child like them—yet it doesn't hinder our involvement in the action. Here, as in life, we only realise the complexity of an event after we have lived through it. . . .

Truffaut's most impressive accomplishment is to catch the improvised quality of life; and this, one suspects, is why he is so much at home with children. . . . [It is through] Truffaut's lightness of touch and zest for life, and through [actor Jean-Pierre] Léaud's realisation of Antoine's stoicism and almost cockney resilience, that this film never becomes portentous or depressing. It is, truly, a film that speaks up for life. (p. 90)

*Eric Rhode, "Film Reviews: 'Les quatre cents coups'," in* Sight and Sound *(copyright © 1960 by The British Film Institute), Vol. 29, No. 2, Spring, 1960, pp. 89-90.*

## PIERRE KAS

[*Shoot the Piano Player*] demonstrates very strikingly the ascendancy of subject matter over the unraveling of plot. I certainly could not recount the story in a sentence, but it is very clear that François Truffaut has filmed timidity as it has never been done before. (p. 54)

Behind the façade of imposed events, everything in *Piano Player* happens as if the expression of personality had become more perceptible to the viewer; as if, within the framework of an externally imposed detective story plot, the individuality of the characters became therefore all the more apparent.

But no doubt it's a great betrayal of the film to wander in the meandering ways of a changing logic, when the first, the most durable, and the most persistent impression the film gives is one of charm. . . . *Shoot the Piano Player* has more charm than any film I've seen for years. But, do I mean that therefore it's impossible to guess the reasons why?

One is obviously the freedom of narrative. That's a paradox for a story with a detective plot. Ten examples of admirable American detective films can be cited where the iron rule of plot gives birth to a conception of the *useful*. Everything is sacrificed to effectiveness. Most French films that aspire to this genre are caricatures of the method. In *Shoot the Piano Player* it seems to me that plot, without disappearing, passes into the background to the profit of the characters and their relationships with each other. (p. 55)

I wonder if, in fact, I believe that Truffaut's secret is that he loves not only his characters but also the actors who incarnate his characters. (p. 56)

I thought at first that the essence of the film was the tone, until the moment when I said to myself that it was like the effect of the sleep-producing virtue of opium, or phlogiston. There is no tone in itself, apart from a certain vision of things. A catastrophic or aggressive vision of human relations could not be asserted on the basis of a charming tone. First the bitterness, the suffering before the atrocity of conversations, then the entertainment, the taste for the baroque, the restrained compassion, the taste for wandering, the taking of one's time—all finally characterize *Shoot the Piano Player*. Charm and kindness are finally what I believe to be the qualities of its author. (p. 57)

*Pierre Kas, "L'âme du canon," in* Cahiers du Cinema *(copyright © 1961 by Les Editions de l'Etoile; reprinted by permission of Les Editions de l'Etoile), No. 115, January, 1961 (translated by Leo Braudy and Tom Leitch and reprinted as a chapter in* Focus on "Shoot the Piano Player," *edited by Leo Braudy, Prentice-Hall, Inc., 1972, pp. 54-7).*

## RAYMOND DURGNAT

*Tirez Sur Le Pianiste* [*Shoot the Piano Player*] is less a parody than a new mutation of the "film noir". The toughs are absurd rather than frightening, the hero lays the lovelies because he's weak, ineffectual, shy and resigned. This "Romantic" hero, cursed by his own fine sensitivity, is by recent conventions not just an anti-hero, like *The Wild One*, but an anti-anti-hero—a soundly paradoxical basis for the film's extraordinary charm.

The story, by Truffaut out of David (*Dark Passage*) Goodis, recalls James M. Cain's *Serenade* in its baroque juxtaposition of fine art and skullduggery. . . .

In line with the admirable anti-psychologising trend of the French Cinema, Truffaut's film is festooned with mysterious, seemingly arbitrary details of setting and style, and its plot may seem a chain of contrived coincidences and unmotivated decisions. But the "new superficiality" in films (*and* novels *and* the theatre), the creative use of reticence, ambiguity and monotony, the stress on "style" and "spatial relationships,"

far from involving a rejection of "human values" is a salutary renunciation of theories of literature as systematic character-analysis. . . .

Twice Truffaut's hero does precisely what he has just decided not to do; he deserts his remorseful wife without a word, and leaves Lena for his brothers. The film is full of visual details, of stray lines of dialogue, which mean—something, but what? (p. 29)

Truffaut's eclecticism makes him the Cinema's key stylist, for he yokes the "drab," deadpan, realistic-enigmatic style of Ophuls-Bresson-Resnais with the newer "realistic expressionism" . . . effective enough to take patent artificiality in its stride. . . .

[*Tirez sur le pianiste*] doesn't quite come off. It's something to do with the thugs being too numerous, perfunctory and absurd and with Truffaut deliberately mocking everything that could as easily be menacing and nightmarish.

The "gesture-atmosphere" of Charlie recalls Truffaut himself—don't shoot the pianist if instead of a masterpiece he's half-amused, half-rediscovered himself with an intriguing, constantly brilliant, and exceptionally *pleasurable* film. (p. 30)

*Raymond Durgnat, "'Shoot the Pianist'" (© copyright Raymond Durgnat 1961; reprinted with permission), in* Films and Filming, *Vol. 7, No. 5, February, 1961, pp. 29-30.*

## RICHARD ROUD

[*Jules et Jim*] is very much a conscious attempt on Truffaut's part to make a synthesis of his first two films: to combine the "big" subject with obvious human significance of *Les Quatre Cents Coups* with what he calls the "plastic enterprise" of *Shoot the Pianist*. . . .

Friendship, Truffaut seems to be saying, is rarer and more precious than love. Or perhaps he is also saying that friendship, not being as natural or as innate as sex relationships, must always be destroyed by the forces of nature re-asserting themselves—just as in Goethe's *Elective Affinities*, to which several references are made in the film, the wilderness is always waiting to destory the carefully nurtured garden.

*Shoot the Pianist* moved back and forth between comedy and tragedy with intoxicating brio. In *Jules et Jim* both elements are constantly present, one within the other, as in a chemical suspension. Although the film begins gaily enough, one soon realises that, under the gaiety, tragedy is already present. And even at the end, terrifying though it is, one feels that life is nevertheless re-asserting itself. This precarious balance, this refusal of the genres, is of course very reminiscent of Jean Renoir; and indeed Renoir's influence can be felt throughout the film, in its treatment of character, direction of actors, and feeling for landscape. (p. 142)

What belongs undeniably and unmistakably to Truffaut is the film's sense of movement. . . . [His technique] is even more brilliant than in *Shoot the Pianist;* and as someone pointed out the other day, technique, after all, comes from the Greek word for art—*techne*. There will be those who will regret the simplicity of *Les Quatre Cents Coups,* and there will be those (myself included) who still have a sneaking nostalgia for the anarchy of *Shoot the Pianist*. But no one, I think, will have any more doubts about Truffaut's stature: he is right up there with the great directors (make your own list) of our time. (p. 143)

*Richard Roud, "Film Reviews: 'Jules et Jim'," in* Sight and Sound *(copyright © 1962 by The British Film Institute), Vol. 31, No. 3, Summer, 1962, pp. 142-43.*

## PAULINE KAEL

[*Shoot the Piano Player*] busts out all over—and that's what's wonderful about it. The film is comedy, pathos, tragedy all scrambled up—much I think as most of us really experience them (surely all our lives are filled with comic horrors) but not as we have been led to expect them in films. (p. 210)

*Shoot the Piano Player* is both nihilistic in attitude and, at the same time, in its wit and good spirits, totally involved in life and fun. Whatever Truffaut touches, seems to leap to life—even a gangster thriller is transformed by the wonder of the human comedy. A *comedy* about melancholia, about the hopelessness of life can only give the lie to the theme; for as long as we can joke, life is not hopeless, we can enjoy it. In Truffaut's style there is so much pleasure in life that the wry, lonely little piano player, the sardonic little man who shrugs off experience, is himself a beautiful character. This beauty is a tribute to human experience, even if the man is so hurt and defeated that he can only negate experience. (p. 211)

The subject matter of *Shoot the Piano Player* . . . seems small and unimportant compared to the big themes of so many films, but it only *seems* small: it is an effort to deal with contemporary experience in terms drawn out of that experience. (p. 212)

[The] piano player is intensely human and sympathetic, a character who empathizes with others, and with whom, we as audience, empathize; but he does not want to accept the responsibilities of his humanity—he asks only to be left alone. And because he refuses voluntary involvement, he is at the mercy of accidental forces. He is, finally, man trying to preserve his little bit of humanity in a chaotic world—it is not merely a world he never made but a world he would much rather forget about. But schizophrenia cannot be willed and so long as he is sane, he is only partly successful: crazy accidents happen—and sometimes he must deal with them. That is to say, no matter how far he retreats from life, he is not completely safe. And Truffaut himself is so completely engaged in life that he pleads for the piano player's right to be left alone, to live in his withdrawn state, *to be out of it.* Truffaut's plea is, of course, "Don't shoot the piano player." (p. 216)

*Pauline Kael, "Broadcasts and Reviews, 1961-63: 'Shoot the Piano Player'" (originally published as "'Shoot the Piano Player'," in* Film Culture, *No. 27, Winter, 1962-63), in her* I Lost It at the Movies *(copyright © 1965 by Pauline Kael; reprinted by permission of Little, Brown and Company in association with the Atlantic Monthly Press), Atlantic-Little, Brown, 1965, pp. 210-16.*

## GILLES JACOB

[*La Peau Douce*] is a trap: there have been plenty of films about adultery, but few have ventured to take the mechanism so methodically to pieces. . . .

Through his use of disconnection (light switches, camera shutters, gear-changes), Truffaut demonstrates the fragility of love; his world is one of objects and skins, of fleeting glances and fleeting contacts, as though love, in the steely world in which we live, were no more than two skins touching in a universe where things and people are sealed away from each other in impenetrable envelopes.

There is still much of the old Truffaut in *La Peau Douce* in the quotations from Renoir, from himself, and the *Tirez*-style baroque couplets, but a new, mature Truffaut is revealed. To the qualities which we already know, his freshness, charm, delicacy and reserve, a new deliberation has been added. . . .

The weaknesses are self-evident. There is a certain lack of conviction in the background details of an intellectual who directs an avant-garde review from an attic but lives the private life of a big businessman; and rather than the final shooting *à la* Godard, I would have preferred an ending which left Lachenay abandoned by both women. But these faults are small. . . . After the glittering lightning flashes of *Jules et Jim,* Truffaut has here made, in a film about adultery, his first adult film.

*Gilles Jacob, "Film Reviews: 'La peau douce'," in* Sight and Sound *(copyright © 1964 by The British Film Institute), Vol. 33, No. 4, Autumn, 1964, p. 194.*

## JAY COCKS

[*The Bride Wore Black*] is a good exercise, a faithful tribute and, unhappily, not a very good Truffaut film.

For anyone else, any Hollywood hack turning his hand to elegant suspense, this would be an enjoyable romp through fairly familiar territory: mysterious woman . . . sets out to avenge the murder of her husband. But Truffaut either does not understand or is not comfortable with the psychological and dramatic tensions implicit in such a story. . . .

It is perhaps unfair to belabor Truffaut for making a straight suspense film, but the real trouble is that there isn't any suspense and the comedy isn't funny. This just isn't Truffaut territory. . . . Julie in *Bride* is a slightly overweight middle-aged babe with venom in her veins. There is no love in her, and, we feel, none in Truffaut for her. She is a vehicle for a technical exercise. . . .

[In *Bride,* Truffaut] has perhaps done his homework too well. He has absorbed not only Hitchcock's technique (which, by the way, he duplicates rather poorly), but also Hitchcock's contempt for his characters. It does not suit him.

*Jay Cocks, "Take One Reviews: 'The Bride Wore Black'," in* Take One *(copyright © 1968 by Unicorn Publishing Corp.), Vol. I, No. 11, May-June, 1968, p. 24.*

## ANDREW SARRIS

François Truffaut's *The Bride Wore Black* has been reviewed as if it were a filmed sequel to Truffaut's book on Alfred Hitchcock. But it isn't. Whereas Hitchcock is basically a genre director, Truffaut's temperament is closer to the sprawling humanism of Renoir. Of course, no director can memorize the life's work of another director without picking up a few tricks and ideas along the way. . . . [The] mere fact that *The Bride Wore Black* is a violent melodrama with a soupçon of suspense is sufficient grounds for most critics to tag Truffaut with a Hitchcock label. However, even Renoir is not entirely a stranger to violent melodrama. The murders in *La Chienne, La Bête Humaine, The Crime of Monsieur Lange,* and *The Rules of the Game* are as memorable as any in the history of the cinema. But these murders do not make Renoir a genre director. Renoir's feeling for life flows over the violence like an inexhaustible torrent of tenderness. Whereas Renoir proudly sacrifices form (and art) for truth, Hitchcock salvages truth from an art that rigorously obeys the rules of the game. Truffaut breaks the rules of the genre without abandoning the genre, and thus teeters precariously between Hitchcock and Renoir without committing himself entirely to either.

Truffaut begins *The Bride Wore Black* by plunging into the action before its premises have been established. Thus the heroine has committed two murders and is well on her way to her third before the audience is informed of her motive. Truffaut's storytelling is consequently anti-Hitchcockian in that it sacrifices suspense for mystification. Once the audience is implicated in the lyricism of [Julie's] murderousness, it is too late to measure her motivation. *The Bride Wore Black* succeeds therefore as a *fait accompli.* Truffaut manages even to get away with a big hole in the plot. We are told that the heroine is tracking down five men who were involved in the prankishly accidental murder of her husband as he was descending the steps of the church with his bride on his arm, an overwhelmingly Orphic piece of sexual imagery reminiscent of a similar incident in Sam Fuller's *Forty Guns.* . . . But we are never told how the bride learned the identities of her bridegroom's murderers. By simply showing us the murderers, Truffaut discharges his obligations to the genre. If he had wanted us to think more seriously about the premise of the plot, he would have told us much sooner. (pp. 380-81)

*The Bride Wore Black* derives its dramatic power from the irony of an illusion. The bride of vengeful death enters the life of five men as a temptress. She is unreal, unconvincing, and discouragingly uncooperative, but it doesn't matter. Her victims will grasp at any straw that promises even a moment of pleasure. . . . If [Julie's] character were at all real, it would be impossible to forgive her for her mercilessness to this particularly pathetic child of woman. But because of the displaced sensibility of the film, the men are too real for the genre, and [Julie] too fantastic.

Thus a second film emerges over the smudged design of the first, a film more interesting than the first because it is closer to Truffaut's true feelings. This second film concerns the obsession of men with the ever-receding realities of women. What Truffaut has taken from William Irish's action novel is the urgency of a melodramatic situation, the urgency without which Truffaut's feelings would spill out over the edges of his frames until more of him would be offscreen than on. What Truffaut has taken from Hitchcock is an adroitness in balancing abruptness of action with a drifting for meaning, so that every characterization can be enriched with an intimation of inevitability. The difference between Truffaut and Hitchcock is the difference between a life style and a dream world. Truffaut's males are derived from the director's sense of reality void of melodrama. If Hitchcock and Irish had not intervened, Truffaut's lecherous males would talk on night after night about all the women they'd laid and about all the women they wanted to lay until even their lechery would disintegrate in the lassitude of an uneventful life. By contrast, Hitchcock's characters are designed expressly for their genre functions in the sense that they correspond to conflicting impulses in the director's personality. Hitchcock is what he is, and Renoir is what he is,

but Truffaut is still suspended between an art of meaningful forms and a world of changing appearances. Still, *The Bride Wore Black* is a film of undeniable if uncertain beauty by virtue of its director's critical intelligence in an era of mindless lyricism. (pp. 381-82)

*Andrew Sarris, "The New Wave," in* The Village Voice *(reprinted by permission of* The Village Voice; *copyright © by the Village Voice, Inc., 1968), Vol. 8, No. 45, August 22, 1968 (and reprinted in his* Confessions of a Cultist: On the Cinema, 1955-1969, *Hill & Wang, 1969, pp. 300-90).\**

**PAULINE KAEL**

François Truffaut's *Fahrenheit 451* isn't a very good movie but the idea—which is rather dumb but in a way brilliant—has an almost irresistible appeal: people want to see it and then want to talk about how it should have been worked out. *Fahrenheit 451* is more interesting in the talking-over afterward than in the seeing. (p. 146)

Of course, a gimmicky approach to the emptiness of life without books cannot convey what books mean or what they're *for:* homage to literature and wisdom cannot be paid through a trick shortcut to profundity; the skimpy science-fiction script cannot create characters or observation that would make us understand imaginatively what book deprivation might be like. (p. 147)

For American art-house audiences who are both more liberal and more bookish than the larger public, book burning is a just-about-perfect gimmick. Yet even at the science-fiction horror-story level, this movie fails—partly, I think, because Truffaut is too much of an artist to exploit the vulgar possibilities in the material. He doesn't give us pace and suspense and pious sentiments followed by noisy climaxes; he is too tasteful to do what a hack director might have done. One can visualize the scene when the hero, [Montag], reads his first book, *David Copperfield,* as it might have been done at Warners or MGM in the thirties, how his face would light up and change with the exaltation of the experience—the triumph of man's liberation from darkness. Well, ludicrous as it would have been, it might have been better than what Truffaut does with it— which is nothing. Truffaut is so cautious not to be obvious, the scene isn't dramatized at all, and so we're left to figure out for ourselves that [Montag] must have enjoyed the reading experience because he goes on with it. (p. 148)

If the reply is that in this movie the books represent the life that is not in the people, then surely it is even more necessary to see that the book people have life. Shouldn't they speak differently from the others, shouldn't they take more pleasure in language? Couldn't they give themselves away by the words they use—the love of the richness of words? It's all very well for the director not to want to be obvious, but then he'd better be subtle. He can't just abdicate as if he thought it would be too vulgar to push things one way or another. Criticism, in this case, turns into rewriting the movie: we can generally see what was intended but we have to supply so much of the meaning and connections for ourselves that it's no wonder that when it's over we start talking about how we would have done it. (p. 149)

Truffaut *wanted* to make *Fahrenheit 451:* why then, even allowing for the hurdles of language and technology, isn't it more imaginatively thought out, felt, why are the ideas dull, the characters bland, the situations (like the hero breaking into the chief's office) flat and clumsy? Why is the whole production so unformed?

I would offer the guess that it's because Truffaut, in his adulation of Alfred Hitchcock, has betrayed his own talent—his gift for expressing the richness of life which could make him the natural heir of the greatest French director of them all, Jean Renoir. Instead, he is a bastard pretender to the commercial throne of Hitchcock—and his warmth and sensibility will destroy his chances of sitting on it. (Roman Polanski and dozens of others will get there before him.) Truffaut can't use Hitchcock's techniques because they were devised for something tightly controlled and limited and because they are based on coercing the audiences' responses (and, of course, making them enjoy it). Hitchcock is a master of a very small domain: even his amusing perversities are only two- or three-dimensional. Truffaut has it in him not to create small artificial worlds around gimmicky plots, but to open up the big world, and to be loose and generous and free and easy with it. (p. 150)

> Pauline Kael, ''The Living Library: 'Fahrenheit 451''' (originally published in a slightly different form as ''The Living Library,'' in The New Republic, Vol. 155, No. 26, December 24, 1966), in her Kiss Kiss Bang Bang (© 1966 by Pauline Kael; reprinted by permission of Little, Brown and Company in association with the Atlantic Monthly Press), Atlantic-Little, Brown, 1968, pp. 146-50.

## PAULINE KAEL

Truffaut's new film, *Stolen Kisses,* is charming, certainly, and likable, but it's too likable, too *easily* likable. . . . *Stolen Kisses* isn't rigorous, and without rigor the tenderness is a little flabby. . . . When I saw Antoine in *The 400 Blows,* I thought he was basically a healthy and resilient child who wasn't too badly off—not as badly off as the picture made him out to be. But I didn't think Truffaut saw it that way, and the frozen frame at the end, with Antoine looking at the sea, suggested that his future was hopeless. Now Truffaut has made him so healthy that I can't believe that that sensitive boy could have become so *trivially* healthy. The child's desperation has disappeared, and the adult world is now a collection of harmless eccentrics, some of them unfortunate but most of them—well, lovable. Truffaut has turned Antoine into the sad sack who wins. (pp. 273-74)

The New Wave showed that it was easier to make films than the older generation had indicated, but there is a danger in this easiness which *Stolen Kisses* makes apparent: the possibility of losing the sense of illusion. This movie is so lightly done that the improvisatory style undercuts not merely the believability of the characters and incidents but the very beauty and mystery of movie art itself. The throwaway quality—the ease with which the story seems to make itself up as it goes along—is meant to be the picture's charm, and to some degree it is, but when we can see how it is all done, we may also lose interest. (p. 274)

Truffaut's aim has become, it appears, purely to please. Perhaps this is what Truffaut has really learned from Hitchcock. In his book on Hitchcock, whenever Hitchcock explains how something was calculated to tease and please the audience, Truffaut interprets the explanation as if this were the meaning of art. It can, however, be the meaning of commerce, and of emptiness. . . . Truffaut doesn't bother to create even the central character; he uses Léaud as he used Jeanne Moreau in *The Bride Wore Black*—for what the actor already is. In *Stolen*

*Kisses* Truffaut seems to start with the assumption that we already love his little Antoine and will find his ineptness and incompetence adorable. But I liked Antoine for his strength, and that is gone. . . . [The] idea of *Stolen Kisses* is an anti-passionate, anti-serious twentieth-century *éducation sentimentale.* . . . But it's a careless and, oh, so forgettable movie—almost a disposable movie. Truffaut himself appears to be such a small talent in *Stolen Kisses* that it may seem like overreacting even to put it down because it's so inoffensive in every way except in being so inoffensive. (pp. 275-76)

> Pauline Kael, ''The Small Winner'' (originally published in The New Yorker, Vol. LXV, No. 3, March 8, 1969), in her Going Steady (copyright © 1969 by Pauline Kael; reprinted by permission of Little, Brown and Company in association with the Atlantic Monthly Press), Atlantic-Little, Brown, 1970, pp. 273-77.*

## JOHN SIMON

*Stolen Kisses* is once more that special Truffaut blend of sentimentality and screwiness, of an alert eye, a spunky technique, and a respect for the zaniness of life. But this loose sequence of adventures and misadventures befalling Antoine Doinel (the child hero of *The 400 Blows* and youth hero of Truffaut's episode in *Love at Twenty*) upon his dishonorable discharge from military service . . . is too aimless, casual, slight. One wonders why film exhausts its major talents so quickly.

The answer is, more than anything else, quick imitation. If a writer evolves a new technique, it takes a relatively long time for it to become understood, accepted, and emulated. Film, however, displays its novelties perspicuously, palpably, immediately—there are no serious problems of translation, dissemination, interpretation, and film is mass-produced and mass-consumed everywhere. (pp. 184-85)

Truffaut's misfortune is to be so engagingly, seductively, accessibly filmic that his imitators have exhausted him before his time. But in addition, I dare say, there is a lack of substance in his vision.

*Stolen Kisses* opens and closes with a charming Charles Trenet song, sung by Trenet himself on the sound track, ''*Que devient-il de tout cela?*'' . . . ''What has become of all that?'' is indeed the prevailing mood of the film as young Antoine Doinel fluctuates between a sophisticated older woman and an only slightly less sophisticated *gamine* (not to mention an occasional prostitute), and goes from job to outlandish job. The tone is one of youthful turbulence and pathos recollected in wistfully smiling tranquillity, and Truffaut is a master of bittersweet buffoonery. . . . (p. 185)

But also at work is a very contemporary absurdist touch. Antoine, shaving before his mirror, suddenly begins to intone, over and over, three names, each for something like a minute. First it is that of the older woman (she is married to the man for whom he works as a business spy, and seems unattainable), then that of the young girl (she seems to have lost all interest in him), and lastly his own. It is a litany of despair, and a magic incantation, and a scientific attempt at dissecting a precious name. As Antoine, with suitable grimaces, rings ever more frantic changes on, tries to wrest ever more essential meaning from the three names, a bizarre spell emanates from the screen. Is this poetry or absurdity—the folly of youth attempting to find the true pitch of reality, or the existential anguish of mortal man trying to grasp the fleeting identity of the beloved and the self? . . .

Truffaut's tone is both modern and reminiscent, both sweet and acerbic. It is like a poem by Jacques Prévert, or an old photograph of a first love whom the change of fashions has made slightly ridiculous-looking. It's likable all right, this *Baisers volés,* yet from someone whose first films were so innovative, so individual and challenging, we want more. (p. 186)

John Simon, *"Declines and Pratfalls of Major Directors: 'Stolen Kisses'"* (originally published as *"Progress and Regression,"* in The New Leader, *Vol. LII, No. 6, March 31, 1969), in his* Movies into Film: Film Criticism 1967-1970 *(copyright © 1971 by John Simon; reprinted with permission of The Dial Press), Dial, 1971, pp. 184-88.*

### STANLEY KAUFFMANN

[Cuteness] is part of [Truffaut's] film-making psyche these days (all those cozy "inside" references in *The Bride Wore Black* and *Mississippi Mermaid*), and it is one of the reasons why *The Wild Child,* which is generally interesting, is not as good as it might have been. The visual aim of the film is not to look like 1798, but to look like an old film, a cute objective rather than an artistic one: the many uses of the iris, the tone of the black and white which is almost like 1920s sepia, the management of the crowd scenes like those in old operettas, all these are consciously quaint devices.

The best element is the straightforward narrative, which is truly simple, not quaintly so. (pp. 15-16)

The film's viewpoints are mixed—sometimes objective, sometimes the boy's or the doctor's—and this mixture doesn't help a cumulative sense of the unhusking of a human soul. . . .

Yet the picture has a certain deep-seated effect. I was bored through some of the middle because I knew, as anyone would, that we were going through a *gradus ad Parnassum,* that the original notion of idiocy was going to be disproved, that the savage boy was going to be transformed—to some degree, anyway—by civilized kindness and knowledge. Or else why would the picture have been made? Still there is a power in this old idea, partly because it flatters us. What a wonderful bunch we are, we civilized fellows, and how touching it is to see a forest creature being elevated to our midst. The figure of the boy is only occasionally pathetic, yet there is a tribal, almost smug pleasure in watching the doctor's gradual success with him. (p. 16)

*The Wild Child* has had an ecstatic critical reception. No surprise. When a sophisticated artist chooses an unadorned parabolic story and treats it in a consciously unadorned manner, it's a safe bet that the result will be hailed as profound simplicity, no matter how banal it may be. This film is neither a banal disaster nor a symbolic triumph. But it couldn't miss. (p. 17)

Stanley Kauffmann, *"'The Wild Child'"* (originally published in The New Republic, *Vol. 163, No. 14, October 3, 1970), in his* Living Images: Film Comment and Criticism *(reprinted by permission of Brandt & Brandt Literary Agents, Inc.; copyright © 1970, 1971, 1972, 1973, 1974, 1975 by Stanley Kauffmann),* Harper & Row, Publishers, 1975, pp. 15-17.*

### GRAHAM PETRIE

The sensitive viewer of a Truffaut film will find himself making constant and subtle re-adjustments of his standard assumptions and preconceptions; he will emerge with a new awareness of the incongruous rhythms of life, of the inextricable mingling of beauty and sadness in everyday experience, but he will feel that he has discovered these for himself. Exactly because he *does* feel this, however, he may give the film-maker less credit than he deserves for the subtlety and intelligence with which he has brought about these re-adjustments. The style may seem so unobtrusive or "natural," the people so real, the behaviour so spontaneous, the final response so instinctive, that the viewer may feel less that he has been brought *to* this new stage of sensitivity than that Truffaut has merely brought it *out of* him. Though this may be partially correct, and it is a major element of Truffaut's genius that he is able to re-awaken in us the capacities for joy and tenderness which contemporary life forces us ruthlessly to submerge, it is far from the whole story. (pp. 12-13)

Each of Truffaut's films attempts to solve a different stylistic problem in a different way. The rhythm and movement of the film are shaped by what Truffaut wishes to do with this particular material rather than by the desire to impose a recognisable visual or intellectual pattern on it. There is the sense therefore of a film finding its own way, fulfilling its own needs, triumphantly achieving its own potential. Yet at the same time there is nothing haphazard or totally arbitrary; what Truffaut aims at is neither the disruption of form nor the imposition of his own personal formal structure, but the creation of a new kind of form in which each object (and each person) is free to satisfy the requirements of its own nature. . . . By upsetting our traditional habits and assumptions he in fact gives us freedom—the freedom to escape from the visual specialisation, the limitation of emotional response to a few habitual, acceptable patterns, which the complexity of our environment constantly forces on us and which most of us unthinkingly accept. In everyday life we tend to see and feel only as much as allows us to find our way without difficulty (and without thinking) through the narrow segment of potential experience we have carved out for ourselves. We thus *recognise* and accept people and things around us rather than *seeing* or investigating them. Truffaut, to put it simply, helps us to become aware of all that we have left out. (pp. 31-2)

In the films dealing with Antoine Doinel, Truffaut's *alter ego,* there is much less virtuosity of style and the camera often seems content to record rather than to create. This is natural enough, given Truffaut's readiness to let each film take on the shape and pattern best suited to it. . . . In each of [the Antoine Doinel films] the focus is on fairly ordinary, normal people, on situations, settings and incidents such as everyone has experienced at one time or another. There is not then the kind of barrier presented by the circumstances of the other films: a *ménage à trois* centreing round a woman determined to ignore all conventional moral and social standards; an ex-concert pianist who feels himself responsible for his wife's suicide and determines to cut himself off from all emotional involvement as a result; a woman who sets out ruthlessly and coldly to murder five men. In these films the stylistic disorientation is essential if the audience is to be led to abandon moral and social preconceptions and to understand and sympathise with these people. The freedom we gain from responding to new visual rhythms and associations carries over into our assessment of human behaviour; we are open to a much wider range of experience than before and less inclined to judge on the basis of socially-conditioned reflexes and automatic assumptions. Aesthetic and emotional sensitivity merge with moral and intellectual flexibility.

In *Les 400 Coups* and *Baisers Volés* there is not the same need to bring the viewer into contact with behaviour and feelings which may at first be strange or alien to him. Young love, family quarrels, friendship, injustice, betrayal, happiness, misunderstandings, persecution, loneliness, tenderness—all these are elements of everyday experience, and instantly recognisable as such. Truffaut does not have to *create* recognition of our affinity with the characters of these films, as he has to with Charlie or Julie Kohler. The focus therefore is on *showing* us the characters, on letting them reveal themselves through their speech, behaviour, gestures, clothes, the settings they live in and move through, the relationships they enter into. Yet this is done with such care, such attention to detail, such respect and love for human beings, that we emerge from the film with much deeper insight and receptivity to the vast potential of human experience. Simply by showing us so much and so fully, Truffaut again takes us away from the narrow track of daily living, shows us how much we leave out, makes us aware of and newly sensitive to the radiant happiness, the inevitable sadness and frustration, the unnecessary misery of the world around us. He increases our capacity for joy, he gives each individual his full worth and value as a human being, and he shows us the cruel and stupid and thoughtless ways in which we destroy both joy and human dignity. (pp. 36, 38-9)

*Fahrenheit 451* is Truffaut's only attempt to date to make a "closed" film, one that takes us into a alien visual, intellectual or moral world and forces us to accept the conditions of this world for as long as the film may last. The difference between this particular film, however, and any film by Godard, Bresson or Bergman is that in the work of these directors the process is a continually enlightening one. . . .

Truffaut's better and more typical films do not so much offer us a different world which then conditions our relationship to the world of ordinary life; rather they make it possible for us to experience *more fully* the world of everyday experience. The style of Bresson or Godard forces us to experience the world as these men see it; they may lay bare relationships and patterns which we were not previously sensitive to, or did not even realise existed, but we are not allowed to *choose* these patterns—they are exposed to us and we can accept them or reject them. Truffaut's style upsets our characteristic patterns of emotional or moral response but, having done so, leaves us with the freedom and flexibility to select new patterns from the infinite number now opened up to us. (p. 62)

In a world where adaptability, flexibility, openness and responsiveness to the full potential of actual experience, and the ability to step out of dead and stereotyped patterns of feeling and thinking are essential for survival, Truffaut is one of the most necessary artists we have. (p. 64)

The importance placed on music in Truffaut's films makes it inevitable that the orchestration of natural sounds should play a comparatively minor role. In films where music is sparse or non-existent a director can obtain immensely subtle effects from the sound of bird-song, the scrape of footsteps on gravel, the creak of a door opening or shutting, or the rustle of wind through grass and leaves. . . . Natural sounds are used for thematic effect chiefly in *Les 400 Coups* and *La Peau Douce:* in the former the harsh, grating noises of daily activity in the school room are echoed in both jail and reformatory, creating an atmosphere of aural bleakness from which Antoine seldom escapes (even the revolving drum at the fairground produces a mechanical, monotonous, inhuman sound), and in the latter the abrupt, peremptory sound of buzzers, doors clicking open and shut, cases being thrown into cars and luggage racks, gear changes, jet planes, incessant traffic all help to create the impersonal fragmented environment of the film.

A more important effect is that created simply by tone of voice, vocal emphasis or monotony and pace of speech in many of the films. [In *Jules et Jim,* the] underlying tensions of the marriage between Jules and Catherine are forced to the surface, not by explicit dialogue, analysis or action, but by Catherine responding to Jules's harmless remark about Jim's fondness for German beer by a breathlessly passionate outpouring of the varieties and names of as many French wines as she can think of, unmistakably aligning herself with her countryman against Jules, who has suddenly become an intruder and a foreigner. (pp. 128-29)

It is only in *Fahrenheit 451* that Truffaut abandons [a] concern with "useless" dialogue, with allowing characters either to reveal themselves unconsciously through their everyday speech habits or to make a conscious or semi-conscious attempt to impose their idealised self-image on others. There are few of the asides, the casual remarks, the spontaneous interludes that give depth and authenticity to the other films. . . . (p. 139)

The atmosphere of Truffaut's films is rarely explicitly dreamlike (exceptions are parts of *Jules et Jim* and *La Mariée Etait en Noir* [*The Bride Wore Black*]), but the process which takes place in them is similar to that of the dream. In dreams we find our own natures and those of other people changed, we find ourselves doing things we would seldom "dream of" in waking life. Our personalities undergo subtle shifts, as do those of people we encounter, resulting in a mixture of familiarity and strangeness, often bringing to light aspects of character and behaviour more true and reliable than those of conscious assessments. In Truffaut's films style, setting, rhythm and music carry out the function of dream displacement and conventional responses are given no chance to take over; the world we experience is basically familiar but presented in a way which removes false recognition and security, the standardised, unthinking assumptions of everyday life. People and actions are recognisable, yet set in combinations and associations which expose us to new experiences and demand fresh responses. The result is to make us return to the world outside the cinema with the kind of insight into ourselves and other human beings that we could gain from dreams if pressures from within and outside ourselves did not quickly combine to make us forget or reject the dream-knowledge. . . . The cinema of Truffaut . . . is not one of wish-fulfilment; problems are not solved with the ease of dreams and the claims of reality are not set aside for ever. The characters of the films may share the dream-freedom of the audience to some extent, but this freedom is always brought into conflict with the limitations of everyday reality, and the exhilaration of their experience is mingled with sadness. We as audience do not escape or avoid problems while, or after, watching the films; rather we are given totally new ways of looking at and coming to terms with them. Truffaut gives us a world very like our own world and people with our own weaknesses, desires, obsessions, failures and minor achievements, but he makes us see that world, and hence ourselves, as though for the first time, with the clarity, insight and unpredictability of a dream. (pp. 146-47)

[Truffaut] lets us see others as we would see them if we overcame the preconceptions that govern our conscious lives. He reveals to us "anti-social" or "immoral" behaviour which suddenly becomes familiar and understandable because of its appeal to our own submerged and subconscious impulses, the needs and desires we suppress in order to get along without too much difficulty in daily life. The films are "natural," not just because they reproduce the surface of the reality around us, but because they appeal to our most truly natural instincts and longings and fears. . . .

The central figures in most of the films are those whom we tend to place in conventional categories, either in an attempt to avoid responsibility for understanding and helping them, or through fear of recognising our own fundamental affinity with them. (p. 148)

In most of Truffaut's films the effect of the style and the presentation of characters is to create in us an openness and responsiveness to the variety of life and experience available beyond the limits we choose for ourselves or allow to be set for us. We are brought to recognise our own affinity with characters we would normally see as having little relationship with ourselves, or made to see the inadequacies of conventional modes of existence when these are placed in conjunction with characters who try to go beyond them. At the same time Truffaut doesn't provide us with easy answers by simply reversing the conventional injunctions ("conform!", "work!", "earn money!", "get married!") and assuming that if we do none of these things then somehow everything will be very much better. There is a constant tension between the inhibiting, restrictive moral, social and economic world that is everyday life, and the dream world of freedom where responsibilities and confinements can be ignored. The impulse of the films is towards the dream, and one result of them is to make us aware of the limitations and to respond towards them in a new way. (p.169)

Although loneliness and loss are central factors in the world Truffaut creates, the films themselves are never depressing. He is well aware that most people live in worlds of their own, choosing to hold on to what is familiar and safe, however unsatisfactory, rather than taking the risk of losing this in an attempt to find something better. Some are forced into this through their own weakness or personal deficiencies that they are unable to overcome; others could perhaps break out but are too cowardly or inert to make the attempt. Truffaut himself refuses to make generalisations or categories in order to define people; he insists on humanising each individual to show both his affinities with others (and with ourselves) and the uniqueness which makes every person matter to himself and which makes the waste and hurt involved in each particular life even more telling. (pp. 177-78)

Society is seen as basically repressive, offering little satisfaction in terms of work or social achievement, for these quickly become dead routines and even writers succumb to habit and inertia. . . . Fulfilment has to be sought outside society, in personal relationships; although these offer real joy and satisfaction they inevitably come into conflict with social requirements and are either destroyed or muted. Yet while the joy lasts Truffaut conveys it with a zest and gaiety which no other film-maker has surpassed. . . . (p. 178)

Genuine friendship is rare and difficult and tends to be destroyed or interfered with by social pressures or sexual distractions. But where it exists and while it lasts Truffaut handles it with unaffected ease and naturalness. (p. 179)

Sexual relationships are more pervasive and more complex. Truffaut's men tend to be shy and passive, allowing the women to take the initiative and to dominate. The women have vitality, energy, a desire for new experiences which the men usually lack, harassed as they are by a sense of inadequacy and the routines and pressures of daily existence, and possessing often a fundamental gentleness denied the more ruthless females. Whereas the men find it difficult to disengage themselves sufficiently from the complexities of social existence and from the roles which they are constantly assuming to cope with these, the women have fewer ties and inhibitions and seem able to devote themselves more wholeheartedly to the pursuit of sensual or emotional satisfaction. (p. 180)

Although a consistent pattern emerges of the woman initiating and guiding love affairs, there is no sense that this makes them necessarily unsatisfactory while they last—though the passive and often helpless role of the man is one major reason for the ultimate breakdown which all the affairs, except that of Antoine and Christine, undergo. The characters rarely seem to be able to strike the right balance between submission and control, just as they can neither live completely unaffected by social requirements nor adapt to them. (p. 186)

Truffaut manages to make both commonplace and extraordinary love affairs take on something of the wonder and freshness of those of adolescence. (p. 187)

Behind this concept of adolescence is the traditional contrast of the innocence of childhood and the experience of the adult, except that, like Blake, Truffaut is never sentimental about children and is prepared to make innocence a quality of all who are "childlike," whatever age they may be. . . . (p. 188)

The attraction of freedom, of escape from the restrictions and confinements of society accounts for much of the joy and spontaneity of Truffaut's films, and in their style and movement, the people and events they create, their freshness and vitality, they convey themselves the "intoxication" which he associates with adolescence. Yet he is also well aware of the inadequacy and futility of attempting to lead a life of perpetual childhood, and of inner and outer needs for stability and commitment. But we give up too much in settling simply for these and making them the be-all and end-all of life and in attempting to disown the adolescent impulses as "childish" or "immature." If we forget them or surrender them completely, the result is to submerge ourselves in routine, sterility, indifference, cynicism, fear of change or novelty or new experiences. (p. 197)

One of Truffaut's greatest strengths as a director is his ability to reveal the limitations and confinements of daily experience in a way which makes us newly aware of and responsive to them. The limitations may be those of personality, habit, routine, stereotyped responses and gestures, the inadequacy of speech, the confinements of place, the needs and demands of other people, the nature and requirements of society and the unconscious adoption of social assumptions as our own and therefore "natural" or "instinctive"—but they are all ways in which our potential for developing as free and complete individuals can be restricted. Against these Truffaut sets up the attraction of the dream, not as a means of escape, but as a way of recovering spontaneity and imagination—qualities linked essentially to childhood and forgotten or discarded in the "realistic" acceptance of maturity. (p. 199)

Perhaps the most difficult element of Truffaut's films to convey is the blend of sadness and gaiety in all of them. The subjects and characters involve frustration, failure, loneliness and death, and yet the ultimate effect of the films is to make us feel happy—not "feeling good" in the sense that the film-maker has either solved all our problems for us or allowed us to pretend that there aren't really any problems after all, and not suffused in a warm glow of complacency and self-satisfied condescension—but *happy* in a way in which few of us have the chance or allow ourselves to be in ordinary life. . . . The films are firmly rooted in the world we all move in and seem to obey its laws, yet the result is to make us profoundly dissatisfied with that world and what we have made out of it. Truffaut's realism is essential for the humanising effect which his films have: we are brought into close emotional involvement with the characters and cannot escape recognising, for good or ill, our own affinity with them, while the style and framework of the films, by releasing us from conventional and stereotyped reactions leads to a freedom normally beyond our grasp, an awareness of and a desire to take in the dimensions of life which we normally ignore. (p. 200)

> *Graham Petrie, in his* The Cinema of François Truffaut *(copyright © 1970 Graham Petrie), A. S. Barnes & Co., 1970, 240 p.*

## DAVID WILSON

Truffaut has always been fascinated by innocence. And by children. . . . [In *L'Enfant Sauvage* (*The Wild Child*)] we have the archetypal innocent, and the systematic corruption of innocence: animal nature—in the shape of a wolf boy—tamed and 'civilised' by rational society, in the person of a well-meaning doctor and according to the notions of the time. It is the back-to-nature fantasy in reverse; a detailed, almost clinical examination of the process by which impulse is subdued by education. . . .

[The] film is sober, unemotional, pared down to essentials.

Style, in fact, is appropriately matched to content, here perhaps more rigorously than in any of Truffaut's previous films. . . .

[*L'Enfant Sauvage* is] as much a study of mentor as of pupil, for beneath that austere, seemingly impassive exterior there is a thirst for knowledge which not even the discouragement of failure can quench. . . . [One] gradually realises that the film is very much a reflection of its maker, as 'autobiographical' a work as *Les Quartre Cents Coups*. . . .

As an eighteenth-century rationalist Itard is naturally concerned to test his pupil's moral sense; but with Truffaut playing him it's impossible to resist the irony of his pleasure at awakening a sense of justice in the boy. Or indeed to wonder how far one could take a post-Freudian analysis of the housekeeper's role as surrogate mother. It would no doubt be possible to erect a structuralist framework around the film; the dualities (animal-human, reason-impulse, signs and meanings, words and objects) are there for the taking. Simpler, though, to observe what Truffaut means us to observe, in particular the obvious parallel with his first film. As Antoine Doinel was caged—literally as well as figuratively—by the environment which failed to respond to his need for affection, so here the wild boy is forcibly incarcerated in the name of a kind of freedom. Truffaut makes the point by juxtaposing the disorder of nature with the ordered geometry of civilisation: the emphasis on windows and walls as a recurring image, freedom or imprisonment depending on which way you're looking at them. . . .

[The end of the film] seems at first sight to offer a pessimistic gloss on the antithesis Truffaut has proposed. . . . In fact, Truffaut is unequivocal about whether the boy would have been happier left in the forest. The lessons will continue, Itard says, as the boy shuffles off to bed.

> *David Wilson, "Film Reviews: 'L'enfant sauvage',"* in Sight and Sound *(copyright © 1971 by The British Film Institute), Vol. 40, No. 1, Winter, 1970-71, p. 46.*

## STANLEY KAUFFMANN

[*Bed and Board* completes Truffaut's] life story disguised as Antoine Doinel. The first installment was *The 400 Blows,* then there was an episode in the anthology picture, *Love at Twenty,* then the pleasant *Stolen Kisses.* But there was a great discrepancy between the first Antoine and the hero of that last film, and it's no easier to believe in the wholeness of the character now that the story is concluded. . . .

Style is what is being hailed in *Bed and Board,* but charm is what is being merchandised, as calculatedly as in any France-for-export film of the 1930s. . . .

But for all the incessantly pumped *bonhomie,* the picture sags, with no such nice touches as the shoe-shop encounter of the lovelorn stranger in *Stolen Kisses.* If a fiction artist uses autobiography and it doesn't nourish his work, he *is* in trouble. Truffaut badly needs something in his life to fertilize his art, or he will indeed become—as I was worrying some time ago—a mere talented filmer of concocted scripts. Which is what he seems to want. (p. 40)

> *Stanley Kauffmann, "'Bed and Board'" (originally published in* The New Republic, *Vol. 164, No. 7, February 13, 1971), in his* Living Images: Film Comment and Criticism *(reprinted by permission of Brandt & Brandt Literary Agents, Inc.; copyright © 1970, 1971, 1972, 1973, 1974, 1975 by Stanley Kauffmann),* Harper & Row, Publishers, *1975, pp. 38-41.*

## DAVID BORDWELL

A photograph "directed" by Francois Truffaut in a recent *Esquire* [August, 1970] shows him reclining jauntily on a chair, his back turned to us while he puffs on an enormous cigar; his face is ingeniously reflected toward us in the open French window. The shot and the accompanying article seem to confirm what many have been suspecting for a long time. The cigar, the cutely oblique point-of-view, the claim that he makes films for the man in the street—isn't this all the outcome of Truffaut's whoring after false gods, and one portly god in particular? Pauline Kael, with typical nuance, concluded long ago that Truffaut is "a bastard pretender to the commercial throne of Hitchcock" [see excerpt above].

It is a tempting charge. After all, didn't the great trilogy and half of *The Soft Skin* [*La peau douce*] recall the work of the grand old man of French cinema, Jean Renoir? How could Truffaut go from such lyricism to the theatrics of *Fahrenheit 451, The Bride Wore Black, Stolen Kisses,* and *Mississippi Mermaid*? The Hitchcock in-jokes, Bernard Herrmann's scores, and the pulp-novel plots do suggest that he has degenerated from Renoir to Hitchcock—or, some would say, from Hyperion to a satyr.

The view seems to me unjust because, after all, we typed Truffaut too early in his career. . . . We were taken with his Renoirian delight in spontaneous digression, his celebration of life's looseness. We forgot that such artistic latitude can be as harmful as complete confinement. Renoir, who had always recognized the need for rigor in even the most seemingly casual style, concentrated his plots either spatially (as in *La grande illusion*) or formally (as in *La regle du jeu*) and turned later to theatricality because it offered challenging restrictions. "There's really no freedom without discipline," Renoir has said, "because without it one falls back on the disciplines one constructs for oneself, and they are really formidable. It's much better if the restraints are imposed from outside."

This remark pinpoints Truffaut's dilemma. After three very free films, he had to choose between inventing his own form (or anti-form, *á la* Godard) and following Renoir's lead in seeking a discipline that was not intolerably confining. He chose the latter, and, being of a different generation than Renoir, he turned not to the theater but to film genres. Thus the new direction in Truffaut's work springs from a subjection of his lyrical impulses to the pressures of a new form—or, more precisely, a new formula.

Enter Alfred Hitchcock. . . . Whereas Renoir's is the cinema of liberty, equality, and fraternity, Hitchcock probes a world of guilt, betrayal, and malignant coincidence. Renoir celebrates joy and love; Hitchcock excels in depicting fear, suspicion, and jealousy. . . .

Truffaut, whose temperament followed the Renoirian lines of autobiography, improvisation, and formal looseness, found the objectivity and concentration of Hitchcock an attractive restraint. (p. 18)

[Truffaut's introduction to his book *Hitchcock*] shows he understands Hitchcock's techniques—the "MacGuffin", the importance of timing and coincidence, the injection of uncertainty and suspicion into the most innocuous scenes, the use of glance to control point-of-view, and the strategy of putting a commercial gloss on a formally daring film. Not surprisingly these techniques of suspense, surprise, and subjectivity provide the formal discipline for Truffaut's next four films. Yet he doesn't use these devices mechanically. Rather, he opens them up, analyzes them, warms them—Renoirianizes them, we might say. The later films become essays toward a comfortable form, and in one for certain (*Stolen Kisses*) and perhaps in another (*Mississippi Mermaid*), we find a successful fusion of Renoirian lyricism and Hitchcockian intrigue.

Truffaut has always made his protagonists outsiders ("My characters are on the edge of society"), and in this his latest films are no different. . . . Crime forces [his] characters into flight; like the protagonists of *The 39 Steps, North by Northwest,* and *Strangers on a Train,* most of Truffaut's recent heroes are forced to become fugitives.

Once displaced from society, the characters must seek happiness on their own. . . . As in Hitchcock, changes of setting suggest changes in character: Montag moves from the city to nature, from the firehouse to the wintry landscape; [Mahé] begins at his sultry plantation and ends in a snowbound hut. But Truffaut's preference for ending his plots in pastoral settings, quite uncharacteristic of Hitchcock, is a reminder of his Renoirian affinities.

It is these affinities which counterbalance any tendency toward intrigue pure and simple. Truffaut's Renoirian impulses move him toward a more centrifugal, inclusive form. While Hitchcock's deterministic plots move toward a parable-like strictness, Truffaut (like Renoir) welcomes digressions that give us fitful glimpses of a wider context. The private griefs of Truffaut's protagonists are illuminated by the casual intrusions of strangers that remind us that beyond the individual, life flows

on. . . . Hence the tension which dominates Truffaut's latest films. The intrigue formula demands that every character be essential, that every detail advance the suspense. But the opposite tendency toward haphazard inclusiveness strains such an introverted form: strangers wander in, gratuitous details intrude, suggesting the casual irrelevancies that permeate everyday life. (p. 19)

Truffaut's journal of *Fahrenheit 451* . . . offers the clearest record of his attempt to give depth and humanity to a pure genre-picture. Realizing that science-fiction tends toward gimmickry, he worked against the grain, introducing archaicisms— old-fashioned telephones, dresses, houses, utensils—which he called "anti-gadgetry." . . . Throughout production, Truffaut recognized all the compromises inherent in the film—the simple-minded story, the stiff characters, the whiff of Stanley Kramer. He took a very *auteurist* gamble, hoping to transcend a formula by the force of his temperament: "When one is navigating in the waters of science-fiction, one is sacrificing verisimilitude and psychology, which is not a serious matter if one makes up in plausibility and lyrical feeling what one loses by being out of tune with reality."

How does this lyricization overhaul the apparatus of intrigue? *Fahrenheit 451* begins with the classic suspense-device of cinema: cross-cutting. Firemen slide down the pole and leap aboard the truck; a young man, gnawing an apple, gets a phone call warning him to flee; cut back to the firemen. But once they arrive, the plot doesn't follow the young man, as we might expect. He simply escapes and is quickly forgotten in the firemen's swift and expert search for books. "Why will they do it?" clucks the Captain. "Sheer perversity." The victim's fear, the methodical search, the surprising hiding places, the authorities' petulance—all gain an impetus from the suspense. The cross-cutting has caught our interest and channeled it to the real subject of the film.

This principle of deflected suspense rules Truffaut's subsequent films. He repeatedly builds our expectations by mystery and tension, only to divert our interest from plot to character. . . . Truffaut capitalizes on melodrama's ability to seize our attention and emotions, but then mildly mocks it by having his characters respond not as figures in an intrigue but as people in life.

Truffaut deflates Hitchcockian surprise as skilfully as he deflates suspense. . . . Only *The Bride Wore Black*, Truffaut's most Hitchcockian film, plays up its surprises to the very end. For this reason, one may admit that it is Truffaut's coldest film: for once he reduces his characters almost totally to their plot functions.

For Hitchcock, suspense and surprise follow from a rigorous use of cinematic point-of-view. . . . In Hitchcock, subjectivity is usually gained by confining a scene to only what one character sees or knows, thus ominously restricting the audience's knowledge as well. . . . Suspense derives from the audience's sharing the character's ignorance; surprise derives from a sudden shift from subjectivity to objectivity. (pp. 19-20)

Both on paper and on film, Truffaut has paid tribute to the power of Hitchcock's point-of-view technique. . . . [As] early as 1962 he noted: "The cinema becomes subjective when the actor's gaze meets that of the audience. And if the audience feels the need to identify (even in a film where the director has no such intention), it automatically does so with the face whose gaze it meets most frequently." (pp. 20-1)

There is a sense that Truffaut has tried to carry this technique into his recent films. An occasional subjective angle—with Montag watching the Captain punishing students, with Clarisse when she revisits the school—add a certain uneasiness to *Fahrenheit 451,* and *The Bride Wore Black* judiciously alternates our identification with the bride with an ironic omniscience. . . . But in these films, Truffaut has not followed Hitchcock's lead in dissecting the moral implications of point-of-view; it would seem to be the one technique Truffaut borrowed uncritically. In *Stolen Kisses,* though, he does analyze point-of-view, and so creates his richest blending of autobiography and detachment, spontaneity and discipline, lyricism and intrigue. . . . *Stolen Kisses* may not be his best film, but it is his most profound exploration of the tension between his Renoirian temperament and a Hitchcockian form.

These two imposing gods hover over the very first shots, indeed the very title, of *Stolen Kisses.* The long-shots of Paris and the recurrent *tricouleur* suggest Renoir reborn in the sixties. But then a pan and zoom to a window (echoing *Psycho*'s opening) take us to Antoine in a jail cell: the hint of crime and the question of spying will thread the film *à la* Hitchcock. If the ensuing story seems as relaxed as Renoir, it is because the lives of others casually intrude at the most unexpected moments; but the plot also moves into Hitchcockian regions of crime, secrecy, and voyeurism.

Still, Truffaut is more than the sum of Renoir and Hitchcock. The shut-down Cinémathèque, the atmosphere of Paris during the student strike, the references to *La Chinoise* and *Mississippi Mermaid,* and the reappearance of Antoine's idol Balzac are figures in a familiar and unique landscape. The film's theme—the relationship between love and work in the modern world—is also a characteristic Truffaut one, which is enriched by the homage he pays his French and American mentors.

The characters of *Stolen Kisses* see sex and love from the standpoint of their professions. . . . From the start . . . man and woman are both seen as rapacious and chilly, viewing sex as business-as-usual. (p. 21)

At first this theme is traced with methodical Hitchcockery. The vehicle is Antoine's stint as a detective; the method, surveillance; the motif, doors and windows. A private detective pries into the (primarily sexual) secrets of the populace; his role of curious but anonymous observer epitomizes the detached voyeurism of both the individual in modern society and us in the audience. . . . Like the prostitute's the detective's business is sex, but for him it is impersonal voyeurism.

Truffaut's visual style corroborates the surveillance theme. We watch people at a distance and through windows and glass doors; we see a mirror distort M. Tabard; we glimpse scenes played in doorways; we have doors banged shut in our faces; and we even view some scenes through Antoine's eyes. Truffaut has thoroughly absorbed what he needs of Hitchcock's idiosyncratic point-of-view techniques. *Stolen Kisses,* stylistically glosses *Notorious, Rear Window,* and *Psycho;* like them, it is a moral condemnation of voyeurism.

When Antoine joins the Blady Agency, the catalogue of work-misshapen loves swells; some entries are pathetic, others comic. (pp. 21-2)

The Tabard case is the central example of the film. "Everybody hates me," M. Tabard announces, and unwittingly demonstrates why. . . . Tabard lives for his business and ignores human warmth, while Antoine, incompetent at every job he

tries, lives for love. Small wonder, then, that he is dazzled by Madame Tabard. . . . But the moment Antoine sees her, he forgets his jobs: his ecstatic report to the Agency abandons professional objectivity for spontaneous poetry. . . .

As Truffaut's film deviates from the rigor of Hitchcockian formula, Antoine's infatuation moves him away from the discipline of surveillance and toward the intimacy of love. At the shaving mirror, Antoine tries to learn English. Later, when he hypnotically chants his name and the names of Madame Tabard and Christine into the same mirror, his monologue becomes a Gertrude-Steinian panegyric, a celebration of the happy cohesion of rhythms and accents. The comic narcissism of the scene aptly evokes the self-absorption of adolescent love. . . .

The affair moves toward an investigative complexity that satirizes the detached surveillance of the detective's role: the female agent shadowing Madame Tabard watches her visit to Antoine's rooming-house. . . . Because of his choice of love over work, Antoine has fallen into the intrigue; no longer the outside observer, now an observed participant. (p. 22)

Throughout the film, Christine's student activities have been her excuse for avoiding Antoine: she has escaped from love into her "job." But a shot of her at the table, facing away from the television image of student demonstrations, implies that she has repudiated her previous behavior. She yanks out a TV tube and calls Antoine, who is now a repairman. When he arrives, work becomes a pretext for love. The camera tracks over the parts-strewn floor (Antoine is in the wrong business again) to the ticking meter, tiptoes up the stairs, and peeps into—the wrong bedroom. The camera shamefacedly doubles back and discovers the couple in the parents' bed. These hand-held shots, a lyrical joke on Hitchcockian point-of-view, undermine the premise of the detective business and our involvement in the intrigue as cinematically as Antoine's behavior does dramatically. (pp. 22-3)

The climactic scene, as in most Truffaut films, takes place in nature (or as near it as Paris will permit). Antoine and Christine are sitting on a park bench when the man who has been shadowing her draws near. In a film so full of snooping, we have assumed him to be another detective. A shot taken from behind the lovers places them visually in the front row of the theatre, watching the man as we have been watching them. "I know all about life," the stranger says. "I know that everybody betrays everybody. I've no work, I've no obligation to anyone." He announces his perpetual love of Christine, and as he moves off he adds with a smile: "I am very happy." Truffaut will not let us savor Antoine's happiness without reminding us of the others—those who trail life, watching from a distance. Antoine was very nearly doing it himself, and he may be again; love isn't certain, even when divorced from work. Truffaut has invoked Hitchcockian intrigue only to dispel it, violating melodramatic formula by the force of his Renoirian sensitivity to joy and melancholy. . . .

*Stolen Kisses* and *Mississippi Mermaid* seem to me to represent a deepening and enrichment of Truffaut's synthesis of Renoir and Hitchcock. While *Fahrenheit 451* and *The Bride Wore Black,* full of undigested Hitchcock, are Truffaut's only in small touches, lyrical cadenzas, the more recent films subsume the intrigue elements—detection, voyeurism, the chase—to more personally expressive ends. . . . [*Mermaid*] marks a new maturity in Truffaut's handling of adult situations. His characters are no longer children (*The 400 Blows*), adolescents (*Stolen Kisses*), or adults who behave like adolescents (*Jules and Jim*). . . .

It is significant, then, that children, previously so central to Truffaut's vision, are of peripheral importance in his last four films. Is it too much to suggest that *L'Enfant Sauvage* marks Truffaut's return to the emotional impulse of *The 400 Blows* but with a new compassion for the adult? (He has remarked that he erred in making Antoine's mother too nasty; now he himself is playing the guardian-role.) Perhaps passing through a Hitchcock phase matured his sensibility, made him more aware of the sinister complexity of human nature. In any event, those who groan at Truffaut's pretentious photograph and charge him with Hitchcockian cynicism could not be more wrong. His last two films verify the sincerity of the impulse that led him to preface *Mississippi Mermaid* with the words: ''This film is dedicated to Jean Renoir.'' (p. 23)

> David Bordwell, ''Francois Truffaut: A Man Can Serve Two Masters,'' in Film Comment *(copyright © 1971 by Film Comment Publishing Corporation; all rights reserved), Vol. 7, No. 1, Spring, 1971, pp. 18-23.*

## JAN DAWSON

Where *Baisers Volés* was essentially a celebration of capriciousness—of ephemeral relationships between unique but emphatically temporary beings repeatedly sidetracked by life's infinite chances—*Bed and Board* . . . , the last of Truffaut's films in the Antoine Doinel cycle, is ultimately an apology for staying in the same place. Which may perhaps explain its air of rather laboured humour and intermittently forced charm. . . .

In the long run, people are shown to be not so much uniquely interesting as equally limited. . . . The sad thing is that, along with the character he has nursed and created, Truffaut too seems to be running out of energetic improvisation and to have discovered the meaning of boredom.

On one level, *Domicile Conjugal* [*Bed and Board*] is an elaboration of the anecdote from the opening sequence of *Tirez sur le Pianiste,* of the man who fell in love with his wife two years after he married her; and a feeling that Truffaut is dotting the i's on his old ideas rather than developing new ones hovers uneasily throughout the film, which all too frequently does no more than make explicit elements which were already *dramatically* evident in *Baisers Volés*. . . . The analytic Antoine, aspiring novelist and autobiographer, combines uneasily with the Antoine of childish impulses and enthusiasms, engrossed in his successive employments as carnation-dyer and manipulator of model boats. Truffaut appears to have equal difficulty in bringing his nostalgically reconstructed character into the estate of manhood and into thoroughly modern times. . . .

Where the film really comes to grief is in its attempts to satirise the stresses and strains of life in the Seventies with techniques and attitudes imperfectly borrowed from Jean Renoir. . . .

Where the film works best (and that is very well indeed) is when Truffaut, without looking directly over his shoulder, is developing one of his favourite themes: the uses and abuses of language. Antoine's disenchantment with the exotic Kyoko is economically charted through a series of enforcedly rather silent meals in which his fascination with all her Oriental ritual is seen to turn, first to discomfort and then to anger. Exoticism proves a shortlived substitute for wordplay, and after spending a good many evenings cross-legged on the floor and trying to overcome his embarrassment at Kyoko sending him flowers or offering to commit suicide with him, Antoine is soon reaching for the telephone to communicate in his native French with his unexotic wife, ready to agree with the secretary who has confided in him that she'd marry a lamp-post if only it could make conversation.

But though Antoine springs from time to time into gratuitous life (announcing that Mother's Day is a Nazi invention, dubbing his wife's asymmetrical breasts Laurel and Hardy, celebrating her pregnancy with a 'Childbirth without Pain' record, and destroying buckets of carnations in his search for the 'Absolute Red'), *Domicile Conjugal* on the whole seems more concerned with continuity and tidying up loose ends than with the sheer inconsequential vitality of its characters. (p. 225)

> Jan Dawson, '''Bed and Board','' in Sight and Sound *(copyright © 1971 by The British Film Institute), Vol. 40, No. 4, Autumn, 1971, pp. 225-26.*

## PAULINE KAEL

Truffaut has written, ''Once a picture is finished, I realize it is sadder than I meant it to be,'' but with *Two English Girls* he must have had the realization while he was shooting the picture, because he keeps trying to cover up the sadness with pat bits of gentleness and charm—his stock-in-trade. Yet what is intended to be light lacks the requisite gaiety; everything is muted, almost repressed. (p. 18)

The movie of *Jules and Jim* was about wrecked lives, too, but wildly wrecked and so intensely full of life that the movie had an intoxication all its own. Here, despite the links to that earlier film and occasional references to it, the exhilarating spirit has flickered out, and we can't be sure how much of the change is intentional, how much uncontrollable. The movie meanders, following the characters' endless arrivals and departures and changes of mind. They seem to waste away, pointlessly. When the older sister is dying of consumption and, seeing herself as Emily Brontë's heroine, says she has earth in her mouth, she might be describing the taste of the movie itself. What makes us feel so uneasy about it is not that it's morbid but that it's shallowly morbid, as if Truffaut couldn't enter all the way into the emotions of the characters. (p. 19)

Truffaut's most engaging quality—his tender, easy acceptance of life—defeats him here. The [Henri-Pierre Roché story from which the film was adapted] is about cross-cultural misunderstandings: the Frenchman's attitudes toward love are different from those of the English sisters—the older, Anne, an emerging independent bohemian, and the younger, Muriel, a rigidly high-principled puritan. Truffaut knows how to make French innocence witty, but he draws a blank on English innocence. The sisters are not mysterious, as his French heroines often are; they're merely incomprehensible. They emerge as dull rather than as English; one suspects that Truffaut may not see that there is a difference. . . . The atmosphere isn't dreamlike, but it's unreal; the passions that drive the girls seem no bigger than pimples. It isn't apparent what Claude's appeal is to the girls or what the girls mean to him, or why, fifteen years after his night with Muriel, he is still thinking of her; as he wanders among the embracing statues in the gardens of the Musée Rodin, he hears an English child being called Muriel and asks himself if she is his Muriel's daughter. We're conscious that the moment is meant to be Proustian, but ''meant to be'' is all it is. In *Jules and Jim,* each moment was seized (and we felt its essence); here the moments slide by, out of Truffaut's grasp and beyond ours. . . . I wish he had not fitted out *Two English Girls* with a fortune-teller whose prophecy is fulfilled. When he ends the movie on that fortune-teller's face, resorting to fate as if in apology for his own failure, we are left trying to sort out the feelings that he couldn't. It's an incredibly sad movie—bewilderingly sad. (pp. 20-1)

> Pauline Kael, "Dusty Pink" (originally published in The New Yorker, October 14, 1972), in her Reeling (copyright © 1972 by Pauline Kael; reprinted by permission of Little, Brown and Company in association with the Atlantic Monthly Press), Atlantic-Little, Brown, 1976, pp. 15-21.*

## RICHARD COMBS

Rather like the sudden revelation of a maliciously grinning face, finally visible through the detail of a drawing, François Truffaut's *A Gorgeous Bird Like Me* . . . ends on an unexpectedly sardonic joke. . . . The ending hints at a pattern to the contest of styles between Stanislas and Camille—parodics of reason and instinct, with the bias towards an anti-intellectual buffoonery in the cardboard caricature of the sociologist. But the rest of the film is too busy with repetitive and faintly parasitic gags to make much of the competition, and the pattern is meaninglessly scrambled by some casual dislocations. . . .

In place of the moral righteousness of the heroine of *The Bride Wore Black, A Gorgeous Bird Like Me* celebrates Camille's singleminded pursuit of a good time. Where Stanislas fails to see the wood for the trees, his own confusion of motives for the case history he finds in Camille, the film takes Camille's adventures at a joyous gallop which asserts the whimsical 'truth' of her own openly self-centred scheming. . . .

Truffaut clearly relishes the way Camille triumphs, a somewhat different goddess, over all the bric-à-brac and ephemera which elsewhere creates such confusion in his characters' lives. In the comic context of *A Gorgeous Bird Like Me,* a good deal of the savour is lost simply because this *femme* comes over as much less *fatale* than may have been intended.

In appearance little more than an interim film, *A Gorgeous Bird Like Me* relates loosely to—and halfheartedly parodies—Truffaut's comedy of the capriciousness of life in the Doinel saga as well as the serious themes of *L'Enfant Sauvage* and *The Bride Wore Black*. . . . But *A Gorgeous Bird Like Me* fails to turn the collision of expectations to comic effect, and the trajectory of Camille's career becomes increasingly directionless as the eccentrics she encounters *en route* turn unfailingly into belaboured stereotypes, and the film huffs and puffs from one frenetic incident to the next. Sadly its mock-comic ballad of freedom and imprisonment cracks under the strain.

> Richard Combs, "'A Gorgeous Bird Like Me'," in Sight and Sound (copyright © 1973 by The British Film Institute), Vol. 42, No. 4, Autumn, 1973, p. 235.

## VINCENT CANBY

One of the propelling impulses still is the need to make ordered and comprehensible a world that is disordered and incomprehensible. It's not the only impulse but it is an important one, and it has always seemed to me that one of the most moving aspects of the work of any artist is this ability to continue to function when, deep down, he must suspect an ultimate futility.

This suspicion is apparent throughout the best work of François Truffaut. . . . It's not the final disposition of things that is important, Truffaut's films keep saying, but the adventures and

the risks en route, the mad and often doomed challenges that are accepted in living. . . .

[*Day for Night*] is Truffaut's love letter to people who, for one reason or another, choose to live their lives halfway between reality and illusion. It's the highly comic and affecting chronicle of the members of a movie crew who gather at the Victorine Studios in Nice to make what looks to be (at least, from the bits we see of it) a sudsy romantic melodrama about a young wife who falls tragically in love with her father-in-law.

On its surface, *Day for Night* is a very inside movie, decorated with references to dozens of movies and moviemakers, packed with behind-the-scenes information about how movies are made. . . . (p. 1)

In *Day for Night,* Truffaut is emulating two earlier artists he admires a great deal, Balzac and Hawks, each of whom in his own way was fascinated by the details of a profession which, in turn, could express the essence of a character. If *Day for Night* were simply about how movies are made, however, it would be no more than a pleasantly frivolous film, charming in its details, perhaps, but as easily forgotten as a successful soufflé. It is, I think, a great deal more than that, since this profession, which Truffaut happens to know best, also happens to be an almost perfect metaphor for life as Truffaut seems to see it in his films.

Beautifully expressing one of the essential thoughts of the film is a line spoken by Severine . . . , a once-popular Hollywood actress who has returned to Europe to live and to play roles like that of the middle-aged mother in "*Meet Pamela,*" which is the title of the film-within-the-film. After a party celebrating her last day of shooting, Severine says of moviemaking: "As soon as we grasp things, they're gone." . . .

For all of its inside details, *Day for Night* seems to me to be less about moviemaking than about a way of facing the conundrum of human existence. A candle may turn out to be fake, life-long friendships may simply be temporary alliances, and what seems to be love may only be infatuation or simply a cheering gift, a one-night stand. Art may be actual experience, ransacked and reformed. This awareness, however, need not diminish the quality of the experience or art. It can, in fact, enhance it. To deprecate it is to deprecate the grand possibilities of life itself. (p. 31)

> Vincent Canby, "Night or Day, Truffaut's the One," in The New York Times, Section II (© 1973 by The New York Times Company; reprinted by permission), October 8, 1973, pp. 1, 31.

## BARBARA COFFEY

The films created by Francois Truffaut can be appreciated on many levels. As an *auteur,* he has complete aesthetic control over every aspect of his works, providing his audience with deliberate avenues that they can explore in order to comprehend more fully the complex characters, their situations, and the main themes. Acutely aware of the other arts, he recurrently makes references to literature, music, and art in his films— not only to provide suitable reinforcements of the *mise en scène* but, more importantly, to function as symbols which, in turn, extend the meaning of the cinema into an all-inclusive art. The question of mixed genres has dual implications: it suggests, first, that one must be *aware* of these references as narrative elements and secondly, that one must *know* about the works and their creators so that their underlying meaning can be interpreted as they appear in the context of the film. . . . Clearly, Truffaut has a natural tendency to mix genres for greater expressive effects, a tendency not limited to the films I want to discuss—*Jules et Jim* (1961) and *Deux Anglaises (et le Continent)* [*Two English Girls*] (1971). In these films, both of them based on novels by Henri-Pierre Roché, however, Truffaut's symbolic and narrative use of the arts of painting and sculpture is particularly revealing.

The two films are intimately connected with the art world and artists on a narrative level: Jules and Jim are young bohemians in the Paris of 1912, they become obsessed with the smile of an ancient statue, Jim gives a Picasso as a present; in *Two English Girls,* Anne is an emerging sculpturess and Claude, at one point, writes about art. Thus artistic concerns are essential to the very story and setting, but, let me add, they have a much more specific function than mere period decor. The significance of Truffaut's selection of art works becomes apparent when one realizes that it is deliberate, often centering on a theme or, as in *Jules and Jim,* related in a definite progression. In both films the works of one particular artist are stressed; for *Jules and Jim* it is Picasso and for *Two English Girls* it is Rodin.

The most important painting for Truffaut's earlier film is the first to appear, while Thérèse does her steam-engine act in Jules's bedroom. It is an early work of Picasso's called *The Embrace* (1900), painted during the young artist's first trip to Paris when he, like Jules, was discovering the city. The painting appears a second time at the chalet in Germany, again associated with Jules's bedroom. The first reference seems to be a visualization of the attitude that Jules is taking towards life and love, one that is synonymous with the direct, bold handling of forms. Both Jules and Picasso, at the early stages of their lives, were searching for a style of living (or painting) in a modern age. When one considers that the subjects seem to be a workman and a prostitute, the dream takes on a negative connotation. If Jules's desire was to possess a woman (indeed, the man in *The Embrace* is so distorted that he envelopes his companion), then the tone is ironic since Catherine would never be caught and trapped like an insect. When the painting appears at the chalet, amid the insect drawings, it is an incongruity along with the hourglass. The two seem to serve as reminders of his carefree youth when Jules was in greater control of his life and still retained his dreams.

*The Embrace,* in addition to deepening our awareness of Jules, also foreshadows one of the main themes of the film which is revealed especially in the last stanza of Catherine's song, "Le Tourbillon":

> On a continué à tourner
> Tous les deux enlacés
> Tous les deux enlacés.
> (And we whirl through life this way
> Embracing till this day,
> Embracing till this day.)

"Le Tourbillon" functions as an aural symbol of the theme of intertwined lives in much the same way that *The Embrace* works visually. Truffaut follows the lives of the principal characters as they are inevitably drawn into and out of various relationships. (pp. 1-2)

Another painting, also by Picasso, which sheds light on Truffaut's view of human relationships, is *The Acrobat's Family* (1905). This painting depicts a young acrobat, his wife holding an infant, and an ape observing intently. The inclusion of the ape is somewhat disconcerting but, in a way, it reflects the situation of the characters. The painting is shown as Jim is leaving Gilberte's bedroom and an immediate interpretation could be that Gilberte desires to settle down and assume the role of wife and mother, a situation that Jim regards as too conventional. The family group is yet another type of human relationship which will be transformed when the main characters are joined at the chalet. In a wider view the painting is even more significant since Truffaut seems to be telling us that what may appear at first to be abnormal, can be considered the norm when regarded in the proper context. In this case, the ape is not really out of place because the group is in a circus environment. We are being warned against judging the characters by our standards which clearly don't fit the context and instead we are urged to come to terms with them on their own ground. (pp. 3-4)

Jules and Jim were first entranced by Catherine's spell when they saw the crudely sculpted woman's face photographed by Albert. Later the two even made a pilgrimage to the location described in the film as an Adriatic island. They were so fascinated by her tranquil smile that they immediately decided to follow it if they ever found it. In Henri-Pierre Roché's novel, the smile is characterized even more fully as "a floating presence, powerful, youthful, thirsty for kisses and perhaps for blood." This rather ominous tone foreshadows both the positive and negative aspects of Catherine's personality. It is curious that Truffaut shifted the location of the statue from the Greek island of the novel to one in the Adriatic. He even changed the type of statue. Roché's version was a group containing a goddess, bearing "the archaic smile," as she was being abducted by a hero. This smile was characteristic of preclassical Greek sculpture of the sixth century B.C. Truffaut's intentions do not seem at all arbitrary when one considers that his aim was probably to lend an air of timelessness and nonspecificity so that the audience could more readily identify with the total submission of Jules and Jim. It was not only Catherine herself that was so captivating, but the embodiment in her of the vision of the absolute woman who could be all things to all men. Archaic Greek statuary is not at all spiritual or insubstantial; rather, it is oddly earthbound by the stiff, little smile worn by both males and females. The statue used by Truffaut has the quality of indistinctness—the eyes are closed and the head tilts up to face the sun. The high stone base seems to dehumanize the head that is attached to it. The woman of the Adriatic is much more like Catherine, the force of nature, [as depicted in the film], than a goddess being abducted by a hero. The situation in the film is, in fact, reversed. It is Catherine who is in total control up to the very end and neither Jules nor Jim has any particularly heroic qualities. Their humanness in succumbing to the power of Catherine's presence is perfectly substantiated by Truffaut's use of sculpture.

Art works can function explicitly as part of plot, in which case greater attention is called to them, as in the scene when Jim brings Picasso's *Little Girl with a Dog* (1905) to present to Jules and Catherine. This gouache/pastel is a study for a much larger work—*The Family of the Saltimbanques* (1905), in which the little girl carries a basket of flowers. The theme of *saltimbanques* (circus people) seems significant in that they were not part of the mainstream of society but existed apart, as entertainers and wanderers. . . . The poet Rainer Maria Rilke, in conjunction with this painting, asked:

> But tell me, who are they, these acrobats, even
> a little more fleeting than we ourselves—so

urgently, ever since childhood wrung by an (oh
for the sake of whom?) never-contented will?

Rilke seems to capture exactly what Truffaut is trying to convey
about the main characters. They are driven by forces that we
may have difficulty understanding, but Truffaut is eager to
awaken our minds to the possibilities that the human experience
can encompass. The painting is fairly well known; thus it is
not inconceivable that one would draw the connection between
the *Little Girl* and the odd assortment of her family group
(which includes a beautiful woman who sits alone on one side
of the canvas). The girl functions in isolation and exile; since
the painting is again shown at the chalet this idea could parallel
the situation of Catherine, Jim, and Jules. Their estrangement
from society is symbolized by the chalet in the country where
the trio seem to create their own rules to live by. The image
of the child is essential in many Truffaut films, including *Two
English Girls*. In the case of *Jules and Jim,* this work by Picasso
could also represent Sabine, who serves not only as the daughter of Jules and Catherine but seems, moreover, to signify some
other aspect of Catherine's personality—the part that requires
and demands attention from men. This idea is demonstrated
by the fact that Sabine is alternately fussed over by Jules and
Jim.

The vision of life for the principals is one of freedom from
responsibility, especially for Catherine, and many times it is
not only childlike but childish. . . . Picasso's *Little Girl* fits
into Truffaut's overall scheme that encourages us not to judge
these characters according to our standards. Jules and Jim opposed materialism and conventions and, of course, Catherine
adhered to her own unique code. But during the time at the
chalet and the ensuing disintegration of their lives, we must,
more than ever, avoid passing judgment.

The stylistic progression of Picasso's art is also manipulated
by Truffaut to correspond to the changes in the situations of
the characters. A cubist painting (c. 1913-1920) is shown over
Jim's bed at the chalet in Germany when the family group is
radically distorted into a *ménage à trois*. Picasso was departing decisively from reality by breaking up objects, then
reassembling them to create anew. The aim of cubism "was
to realise new combinations of known forms"—a process not
unlike the rearrangement of relationships instigated by Catherine's desire "to construct something better, refusing hypocrisy and resignation." Picasso's creation of analytical and synthetic cubism also parallels a growing complexity in the lives
of the trio. It is interesting to note that the work of Picasso's
collaborator, Georges Braque, was often indistinguishable from
his own. The two artists worked so closely during the formative
years of cubism, 1908-1913, that Picasso often referred to
Braque as his "wife." Braque once stated, "Picasso is Spanish
and I am French, as everyone knows, that means a lot of
differences, but during those years the differences did not count."
It seems clear that Truffaut was conscious of the parallel between the Picasso/Braque friendship and that of Jules and Jim.
The parallel relationships thus underline subtly the very fact
of a close friendship which, in the case of Jules and Jim, is
an enduring relationship, in spite of the element of inconstancy
represented by Catherine.

The last painting that appears in the film, *Mother and Child*
(c. 1921), is a work of Picasso's neoclassical style, in which
the artist returned to the human figure but rendered it as a
heavy form with monumental character. It is shown in Catherine's bedroom at the mill when Jim visits her. The subject
matter is analogous to the conversation in which he discusses

his decision to marry Gilberte and have children. Like Picasso
who reverted to classicism (*i.e.*, tradition), Jim has decided to
adopt a more conventional life-style. Seen from a wider viewpoint, the painting symbolizes the search of both the artist and
the characters in *Jules and Jim* for different or better ways of
either painting or living. One of the main reasons for using the
works of Picasso is that Truffaut wants to demonstrate concretely that the search is continuous and it is, in fact, the very
reason for existence.

A major artist serves a similar function for Truffaut's *Two
English Girls;* in this case, it is Auguste Rodin—a bold innovator in late nineteenth-century sculpture who was often
involved in controversy due to his uncompromising expression.
Official art, with its academic rules and prescribed subject
matter, did not suit Rodin's personal vision. He once said that
"forms are not fixed, but they are always in a state of changing
into others; being is a part of becoming, and it is the function
of art to find coherent meaning in that flux." One would almost
think, after viewing *Jules and Jim* and *Two English Girls,* that
Truffaut had stated this. It seems to signal another connection
between art and film and thus to explain why Truffaut looks
upon art as a symbolic device for the cinema. In the case of
*Two English Girls*, the theme of human relationships and how
they change is central. As in *Jules and Jim,* the three main
characters (two females and one male) are drawn into and out
of various combinations throughout the film. (pp. 4-8)

Rodin's monument to Honoré de Balzac is mentioned and
shown twice in the film: it seems to be a pivotal work. This
reference recalls Truffaut's *The 400 Blows,* in which Antoine
Doinel . . . reads (and plagiarizes) Balzac. The youngster sets
up a memorial complete with burning candle and a photograph
of the author (the same one that Rodin based his statue upon).
Clearly, then, Balzac has a personal meaning for Truffaut and
Antoine (the director's alter ego) in that he, too, suffered an
unhappy childhood and was sent to boarding school. But, more
importantly, it seems that Balzac's exhaustive study of French
society, contained in *La Comédie humaine,* serves as a model
of sorts for Truffaut in its examination of the diverse aspects
of the human condition. Balzac had a great meaning for Rodin,
as well; it took seven years for him to finish his monument to
the author and then it was rejected by an official committee.
The sculptor did not create a conventional portrait, but rather
an expression of Balzac's "relentless labor . . . his ceaseless
struggle . . . and magnificent courage." In the epilogue to *Two
English Girls,* Claude notes that the work was finally acknowledged as a masterpiece. Even the most radical creation would
be accepted after a period of time, as Rodin himself predicted.
The idea of change with time, and being as part of becoming,
seems to interest Truffaut, as it did Rodin, as a symbolic device
that expresses the illusion of life in such a limited medium as
a ninety-minute film.

There are even more art works in *Two English Girls,* but they
are not related as directly to each other nor are most of them
well-known works as in Truffaut's earlier film. At the seaside
home of the Brown family, which Anne invites Claude to visit,
there is a noticeable predominance of paintings and drawings
of females (in fact, this is true for the film as a whole), as if
to reinforce the idea that Claude is continually being manipulated by women who seem to wield the greater power in the
relationships. Indeed, Claude is usually associated with children, as in the prologue when, wearing a white suit (symbolizing his innocence, or more probably his weakness), he falls
from a high swing and lies injured as his mother and a group

of younger children surround him. There is a neoclassical painting in his bedroom when he stays with Mr. Flint, a neighbor of the Browns, which shows two young women on one side and a man with a child on the other. Also in the Brown home are two rather telling depictions of women which emphasize the contrast between the two English sisters with whom Claude has become involved. In the dining room (where both the audience and Claude first see Muriel) there is a sketch of a Dickensian woman with a large, shroud-like hat that seems to embody in her the image of a prim Sunday-school teacher. The other work is a circular drawing of a pre-Raphaelite beauty with long, flowing hair (situated between the door and an open window) which corresponds more closely to Anne, the bohemian sculptress. Thus, the choice of art works again deepens our knowledge of individuals.

Truffaut makes a direct reference to *Jules and Jim* at the point in the film when Claude is in a gallery choosing paintings for an exhibit of modern art. Picasso's *The Embrace* is a rather startling inclusion. In this case, I believe, he is referring to this work as a reminder of the theme of intertwined—*enlacés*—lives. In *Two English Girls*, as in *Jules and Jim,* people are inevitably drawn and bound together until there is a shift and then the process begins anew. It is a series of cycles which Truffaut explores visually in his two films with symbols and camera motion. (pp. 8-9)

Interestingly enough, not only does the inclusion of paintings function symbolically, but also their obvious exclusion. At one point when Diurka, Anne's other lover, is with her in the studio, Claude is shown climbing the stairs and it is apparent that some paintings have been removed from the walls since whiter rectangular areas are visible. It is as if Truffaut were trying to convey to the audience Claude's uncertainty and hesitation at that moment by omitting any visual clues.

The *auteur* as manipulator is not bound to accuracy of dating in the works he includes since they function primarily as symbols, not period decor. The gallery scene with Picasso's painting of 1900 seems to take place a few years prior to the turn of the century. In *Jules and Jim,* although Picasso's paintings are in relative chronological order according to his stylistic example, the first three paintings shown are dated 1900, 1905, and 1905 but the action is taking place between 1912 and 1914; the neoclassical work of 1921 is shown in 1933. Thus, Truffaut exercises total control and suits the analogy of Picasso's progress to his theme of the transiency of human relationships and emotions and the need for this change as part of the process of being.

Truffaut's use of artistic references requires that the audience come to his films with a certain amount of intellectual baggage. By being constantly aware of details one can attain enlightening shades and depths of meaning. Conversely, by considering the over-all view, one can see that the reliance on one particular artist throughout each film serves to unify the total experience. This device is used in much the same way as the narrator, that is, to assist the audience in perceiving and interpreting the themes and ideas which are expressed in a somewhat episodic form that includes extended periods of time. (pp. 9-10)

In the epilogue to *Two English Girls,* Claude, as a middle-aged man, is outside in the garden of the Musée Rodin observing the various pieces and groups of sculpture—the *Balzac, The Kiss, The Thinker*—and watching some young schoolgirls running about. With these works the director seems to be visually summing up the main themes of the film as well as his own

personal outlook. The mass of unfinished, roughhewn rock that the lovers in *The Kiss* (1896-98) are attached to, becomes "symbolic of their earthbound passion." The characters in the film are all very human and subject to the forces of passion. Anne, who is associated with Rodin, embodies the typical view of women held by this artist and described as "women who are not toys but full participating partners . . . yet amid this sweep of desire there are currents of questioning and gestures of restraint." When Claude and Muriel finally consummate their love, the setting is Calais—a reference to one of Rodin's most powerful groups, *The Burghers of Calais.* This work (also glimpsed in the epilogue) depicts a group of citizens who, during the Hundred Years' War, offered themselves as hostages to the English king in order to save the city. The idea of love (either for a city or between two people) is intermingled with sacrifice and sadness in a bittersweet combination. Claude and Muriel, his true love, are together after seven years of waiting, yet they must part again. . . . It would seem that Truffaut's view of the experience of love was not unlike that of Rodin, who visualized it in a different medium.

This director also sympathizes with Rodin's vision of humanity. *The Thinker* was part of the unfinished scheme for *The Gates of Hell* (1881 until the sculptor's death in 1917); he was placed at the top so that he would be in a position to contemplate the horror below (which included *Paolo and Francesco,* the doomed lovers from Dante's *Inferno*). *The Thinker* is included in the epilogue to *Two English Girls* as yet another statement on the inevitability of human entanglements and the sometimes tragic consequences that are part of the cycle of life. With the reference to this statue, we are reminded of our role as observers who must absorb the actions and hopefully learn from them. The final scene shows Claude, surrounded by a band of young girls, pass through the doors of the *musée.* Truffaut again symbolizes the never-ending cycles of life visually as Claude resumes his position among children, recalling the opening episode. In *Jules and Jim,* through the use of Picasso's paintings and the final scene at the crematorium, we are made aware of a progression of life, with continual experimentations, to its conclusion. (pp. 10-11)

> Barbara Coffey, "Art and Film in François Truffaut's 'Jules and Jim' and 'Two English Girls'," in Film Heritage (copyright 1974 by F. A. Macklin), Vol. 9, No. 3, Spring, 1974, pp. 1-11.

**STEPHEN FARBER**

*Day for Night* is conceived as a loving satire on the peculiar obsessions of movie people. Truffaut captures the vanity of actors; when asked to discuss the film they are shooting, each actor describes his own character as the protagonist. *Day for Night* also contains some tart observations on the single-mindedness of the director, Ferrand (played by Truffaut himself), who is immersed in the shadow world of movies. (p. 253)

[Although] it pokes fun at the egotism of actors, the film is really a love letter to a group of fabulous monsters. The clear-eyed but affectionate attitude toward actors helps to explain Truffaut's superb work with actors throughout his career. Similarly, Truffaut mocks the romanticism of movies (including his own earlier movies) without destroying all our illusions. (p. 254)

Setting out to deglamorize movies by exposing all the tricks, hard work and crazy accidents that contribute to the manufacture of illusions, *Day for Night* ends, ironically, as an inescapably romantic tribute to the filmmaking process. It captures the exhilaration of the work, and the happy feeling of improvisation on a set dominated by affection rather than envy. . . . In any hour Ferrand is confronted with half a dozen crises; he must choose the right gun for his hero, coax a recalcitrant cat into a scene, and decide how to rewrite the script for an unexpectedly pregnant actress or readjust the shooting schedule to stay within the budget. Each problem solved is a minor triumph. Few films have ever dealt so convincingly with people at work.

For Truffaut the work itself is obviously as meaningful as the results. In *Day for Night* he celebrates the *process* of transforming experience through art. (p. 255)

Truffaut deliberately stretches the truth to present the ideal working situation that he imagines: The filmmaking company is a genuine community; for a short period personal problems are forgotten, and everyone is caught up in the spirit of sacrifice. When the film is completed and the group finally disperses, it is a strangely melancholy conclusion. For an instant the process of filmmaking seems emblematic of all experience—rich and full of meaning for concentrated periods, but fragile and evanescent; everything vanishes just at the moment of deepest satisfaction. *Day for Night* is a lovely evocation of the world of filmmaking, but it is more than an insider's movie; it expresses Truffaut's humanism—his belief in communities built on mutual regard—and the same gently melancholy vision that informs all of his movies. Truffaut's sense of proportion is exquisite. He never tries to inflate the slight story, but his precision gives the comedy resonance. Taken on its own terms, this is just about a perfect movie. (p. 256)

> *Stephen Farber, "Movie Crazy," in* The Hudson Review *(copyright © 1974 by The Hudson Review, Inc.; reprinted by permission), Vol. XXVII, No. 2, Summer, 1974, pp. 252-58.\**

## DON ALLEN

Truffaut's films are always about himself; to a greater or lesser extent, less obviously in some films than in others, but nevertheless always. They are also always about love, again with a similar caveat. These elements are of course not mutually exclusive, but are combined in different ways from film to film. The typical Truffaut hero contains many of Truffaut's own personal characteristics *and* is involved in some sort of 'love' relationship. These two recurring preoccupations are announced in Truffaut's first film, *Les Mistons,* and have been taken up repeatedly throughout his work.

The two major themes may be variously subdivided. For example, the importance of friendship, especially male friendship; the role of women—dream goddesses, mother figures or whores; the intoxication with cinema and especially with the American B-film, to which many innuendoes and jokes refer; the fascination with language, as an instrument of or aid to communication.

The view of life which seems to me to emerge from the films (almost, one feels, without Truffaut being aware of it) is one of profound pessimism. Take, for instance, the ambiguity of his stance in connection with *L'Enfant Sauvage.* His apparent approval of the partially successful attempt to civilize the wild child, and his total endorsement in interviews of the desirability of the experiment, are out of harmony with the reaction of many spectators, who would question both the aims and meth-

ods of an experiment based on the assumption that a being forcibly indoctrinated by nineteenth-century pedagogy was likely to be happier than a 'savage' in his natural state. Truffaut seems not to have considered this alternative view.

In other films Truffaut is aware of the atmosphere of despair and makes conscious efforts to avert it by deliberately lightening the tone. The interpolation of very funny comic banter from the two ludicrous heavies in *Tirez sur le Pianiste* into a melodramatic love story involving two deaths—one caused by them—is the most disturbing example of this mixing of tones. Here the film works, probably because of the bitter-sweet juxtaposition; though this does not prevent the overriding melancholy from seeping through.

Pessimism about the human condition is a factor in most of Truffaut's films. 'L'amour fou', absolute and unconditional, is not this earth (Fabienne Tabard and also the 'man in the mac' in *Baisers Volés,* and Louis' feelings for Marion in *La Sirène du Mississippi*). The compromises which are possible may be encompassed within the frustrating limitations of marriage (notably in *La Peau Douce, Fahrenheit 451* and *Domicile Conjugal*), or in the couple relationship outside marriage (*La Peau Douce, Antoine et Colette, Baisers Volés,* etc.), or in the magnificent failure of the threesome in *Jules et Jim* and *Les Deux Anglaises et le Continent.* In more than half of the films, death comes to at least one of the lovers; in most of them, one character is left alone at the end. The celebrated 'opening endings' are perhaps less open than they seem—Truffaut is reluctant to emphasize the potentially tragic isolation of the individual survivors, or the potential boredom of the couples. (pp. 8-9)

At the moment Truffaut is a relatively unfashionable source of study. His limitations are so apparent; his interest in developing new cinematic techniques is virtually non-existent; he is content mainly to use existing procedures for his own purposes. With rare exceptions his films are 'well made' and tell a story. His emphasis tends to be on narrative and character study. . . . Many of Truffaut's adaptations from existing sources have a pronounced 'literary' flavour, far removed from the chimerical 'visual purity' demanded by some critics. There is a marked absence of actuality in his films. . . . There is almost no evidence of any serious political awareness in his films, and only limited, and purely marginal, social comment. Many contemporary critics dismiss him as a bourgeois anachronism who has been left behind by the currents of his time.

There is an element of truth in these criticisms; sufficient, it seems to me, to make it clear that Truffaut is not a major artist with an all-embracing, cosmic vision of the human condition, nor one who will exercise a revolutionary influence upon our times or even upon the cinema. Yet Truffaut is important almost *because* of his limitations and the small scale on which he works. . . . He will allow no criticism of the subject-matter of his films and fiercely asserts his right to film only what interests him passionately, subjects in which he has immersed himself for months or even years before shooting begins. Hence the immensely personal, bitter-sweet, nostalgic tone of much of his work. Truffaut's canvas may be that of a miniaturist, but within his chosen range he is a master. (pp. 9-10)

> *Don Allen, in his* François Truffaut *(copyright © 1974 by Don Allen), Martin Secker & Warburg Limited, 1974, 176 p.*

## MOLLY HASKELL

["The Story of Adele H."] is the recreation of a passion, but the passion entertained by this particular woman in love . . .

is seen not as desire or ecstasy, or with even a glimpse of mutuality, but as a dark and one-sided obsession, a pursuit remorselessly undertaken, with the female stalking the male, almost literally, to the ends of the earth. . . . Truffaut asks us to understand Adele's situation without identifying directly. This approach seems more logical in a Brechtian parable like [Schloendorff and von Trotta's] "The Lost Honor of Katharine Blum" than in a love story, which is what makes the Truffaut film so fascinating, but ultimately more as a tribute to an experience than as an experience itself. . . .

A French audience, for whom Leopoldine is a familiar name and the figure of Hugo is almost as oppressive as it is for Adele, would see that Adele's journey to the "new" world, in search of a "new" name, is also the search of a woman— a woman emblematic in the extreme of a woman's inherited disadvantages—for something else: for an identity apart from her father. The irony is that her failure to secure this adoptive identity becomes her "success," as she devotes herself to the passion that is her true identity. And thus does Truffaut, in rendering explicit the insight that has lain beneath the surface of many a "woman's film" . . . make the "woman's film" to end all "women's films." . . .

[A dark and terrifying side of love] becomes the exclusive tonality in **"The Story of Adele II."** . . . [In] intellectualizing the etiology of an obsession, Truffaut has made palatable to critics a theme that would otherwise be regarded as soap opera, but he has altered the premise in the process.

For instance, Adele's British officer . . . is a negligible figure—a handsome wastrel unable to cope with a passion he senses is not real love but rather a complexly motivated obsession which is an end in itself. . . .

By beginning with this assumption, by opening in darkness and doom of an obsession analytically understood and predictable, the Truffaut film becomes a meditation on the "woman's film" rather than a direct experience, and skirts the depths and heights of the great tragedies of obsession. (p. 144)

Truffaut understands, as Ophuls understood in "Madame De" and Hitchcock in "Vertigo" (with the interesting difference that the male obsession is fixated on the idealized *image* of a woman while the woman's is in the emotion itself), that such an obsession is not only magnificent but terrible, not only sublime, but selfish and cruel. But it was Hitchcock and Ophuls who gave us, in the most deeply sympathetic "rejected lovers" ever created on the screen . . . the true measure of this cruelty. This is what makes these films, for me, the greatest ever made, their sense of the wholeness that is forfeited or lost by the mad and by those who would defy society and live at its edge. They see, with ambivalence, the wholeness that is left behind, but they also see, with ambivalence, the obsession to which art and love and madness can lead. Loss and gain, the components of paradox, are simultaneously present in the vertiginous daring of their style, whereas Truffaut's "safe" devotion to the truth has the effect of constantly justifying Adele's actions, redeeming them with gravity, without ever plunging her into the abyss of romantic folly and cruelty that might, paradoxically, have given her the dimensions of greatness. (p. 145)

*Molly Haskell, "'The Story of Adele H.' Is a Tribute to an Experience" (reprinted by permission of* The Village Voice *and the author; copyright © The Village Voice, Inc., 1975), in* The Village Voice, *Vol. XX, No. 43, October 27, 1975, pp. 144-45.*

## GILLIAN PARKER KLEIN

It would be possible to approach *L'Histoire d'Adèle H.* as a continuation of its *auteur*'s concerns: the obsessions and limitations of romantic love; the search for identity; the attempt to transform life into art; or perhaps it should be seen as a rather somber *Day for Night,* playing against artistic conventions and deliberately confusing the illusion and reality of film. What I would like to suggest here is that Adèle Hugo's life is to be seen as epitomizing aspects of women's situation in general; that Truffaut is critically examining the destructive effect of the dominating images and personae of her period on a woman. . . .

If the film remains to an extent within the romantic conventions it is questioning, it is because they are being questioned, not dismissed, and thus their power as well as their inadequacy has to be recognized. The color, for example, is deep and brilliant, with darkness illuminated by tawny lamplight or the isolated highlight of a pale face, following the paintings of the time. The audience is moved by intense, iconic images—Adèle in rags is not a realistically grubby bundle, but a stark and dramatic figure. At the same time, the film does not aim to arouse straightforward emotions, and the powerful images or impassioned utterance is qualified by its context, kept at a certain distance. (p. 44)

At the beginning of *Adèle H.* we are told that the story we are about to see is true, but, as in other film of Truffaut, the voice-over speaks in a rapid, objective tone that suggests irony. Here it is a form of dramatic irony which emerges as this real life duly follows the plotted course of a nineteenth-century fictional character, who exists only to act out the conventions and thematic concerns of the author's age. . . .

The film's perspective (achieved by alternating involvement and distance) maintains the contradictions implied by the theme: Adèle is heroine and victim, noble and pathetic. The real dynamic of Adèle's odyssey is not Pinson but her own revolt, and the film respects her courage and tenacity. . . . (p. 45)

The film places her life in its historical context, in the age of revolution, revolt from slavery and counter-oppression. This moves Adèle to claim her freedom while at the same time denying her any means of achieving it, any dignified place in the "new world": in this way Adèle's life is emblematic of the ensuing historical period for women.

The form that Adèle's revolt takes—the love quest—is seen critically as a paradox. She rebels from one ruler to place herself under another, asserting the right to reject the name Hugo in order to take the name Pinson. . . . She is clearly "acting" playing a part written for her by the times, but this does not lessen the destructive effect.

Adèle is performing during these meetings with her lover, as her gestures, language, facial expressions and dramatic shifts of mood become at times almost theatrical; the performance is itself a comment on the love ideal. Truffaut uses other means to work against the surface meaning of the story: by conspicuous repetition, for example, certain scenes come to stand as comments upon the action. . . . [One such] scene is Adèle's dream about the drowning of her sister, Leopoldine. . . . The powerful multiple images, urgent commentary and rising music make this the most dramatic scene in the film. It is also central to the work's meaning in several ways. The drowning of Leopoldine and her husband, who had chosen to die in perfect union with his bride, was an enactment in reality of a central Romantic symbol: the transcendent marriage of two souls. Their

*Liebestod* transformed their lives, at the climax, into a work of art. . . . Only that which has been first realized in art can have a real existence, and so Adèle transforms herself into a heroine, her life into a hectic novella. But the drowning scene is above all an image of forcible annihilation—stifled constricted death. It is a precise representation of Adèle's lot as she pursues her life-as-art. The central paradox is that the more perfectly she succeeds in becoming the ideal, the literary heroine of the man's world, the more she is alienated from herself, loses the very identity she was struggling to assert. (pp. 45-6)

She is the embodiment of the male artist's fantasy, his creature. . . . Like Catherine, who becomes the "queen" of Jules and Jim because her smile is like that of an ancient statue, epitomizing female beauty and mystery, Adèle is the artist's image of "La Femme" for the age. And as Catherine changes her personality and clothing with the decades, Adèle slides from one Romantic role to another in quest of a realized self, but always caught within the artistic ideals of the day. . . .

But the female personae of the age, more victims than masters of fate (even as the drowning scene suggests), more often have possession of Adèle: the woman fatally controlled by love yet denied her soul's completion in the other; the girl ruined and abandoned; the vagabond mad woman surrounded by barking dogs. . . .

The film deliberately evokes the Gothic novel, as the traditional artistic form which for centuries has expressed women's sense of being isolated and controlled, physically and spiritually, by outside forces. (p. 47)

The [final] images of Adèle are intense and moving, paradoxically presenting her as a Romantic heroine: one long powerful sequence shows her uncompromising figure, clad in a flowing black cloak, striding alone through a succession of mazelike alleyways, silhouetted in this moral landscape by brilliant white light against pastel walls. She walks heedlessly past Pinson, whom she no longer even recognizes, elevated by contrast to his petty concern about scandal. The film both exposes and confirms Romantic conventions.

The brief final monochrome section of the film takes us, in a distanced, newsreel manner, up to Adèle's death 40 years later in 1915. The ending explicitly maintains the contradictions unresolved. Adèle is returned to France by the old ex-slave woman, to whom the name of Hugo means liberator, and is shut up in an asylum near Paris. Victor Hugo, once the radical exile, is honored by the new French government. He dies and is transformed into the great image of a national hero, given a state funeral and installed in the Panthéon for the greater glory of France. Adèle remains locked up, gardening and playing the piano. The daughters of the bourgeois revolution are to remain unliberated. And the Romantic principles which fired the revolution turn into their opposite, and, like the image of Hugo himself, become supports for the new establishment. The dying words of Hugo, "I see a black light," sum up the film's view of the paradoxical movement he stood for. As at the beginning, Adèle's life is placed within a wider context of contradictions.

The final shot in the concluding section achieves another reversal. The dry narrative and documentary-like footage give way to a lyrical, even exultant, moment repeated from earlier in the film. Adèle, in her black cloak, stands on rocks pounded by the ocean, speaking words taken from her journal: "That a girl shall walk over the sea to the new world to join her lover, this I shall accomplish!"

The point seems not to deny the contradictions—the words, while having symbolic power, do recall the Pinson affair; the shot does co-exist with the preceding ironic newsreel section—but rather, while acknowledging the conflict, the moment celebrates Adèle's revolt, and affirms a remaining core of value in the Romantic quest. (pp. 48-9)

*Gillian Parker Klein, "Reviews: 'L'histoire d'Adele H.'," in* Film Quarterly *(copyright 1976 by The Regents of the University of California; reprinted by permission of the University of California Press), Vol. XXIX, No. 3, Spring, 1976, pp. 43-9.*

## JAMES MONACO

[*Les Quatre Cents Coups,* **"Antoine et Colette"** from *L'Amour à Vingt ans* (*Love at Twenty*), *Baisers volés,* and *Domicile conjugal*] together form a remarkable work: an extended portrait of the *éducation sentimentale* of a young man portrayed by an actor who is growing, physically as well as emotionally and intellectually, during the course of twelve years of intermittent shooting. . . . As the series progressed, Léaud became a significant collaborator, and the ultimate portrait we have of Antoine Doinel may owe as much to Léaud [who played Doinel in the films] as to its ostensible model, Truffaut. (pp. 17, 19)

[There] is the sense that Antoine shares with Truffaut and Léaud the belief that the reality of art is somehow more valid, more enticing than the reality of the street. From Antoine's first adoring obsession with Balzac to his symbolic infatuation with Kyoko in *Domicile conjugal,* literary reality always takes precedence. (p. 19)

The series begins with two relatively straightforward realistic films—*Les Quatre Cents Coups* and **"Antoine et Colette"**; but by the time of *Baisers volés* there is a significant dimension of irony in each of Truffaut's films which must be taken into account when we decide how we should approach them. That irony is objective and material; in otherwords, it provides the films with a strict esthetic distance, one which is conveyed through the *material* nature—the objects of the film, its shots and cutting—rather than through strict narrative devices. This distancing irony is more important to a study of Truffaut's genre films, for it is those complex and subtle movies that depend most significantly on our understanding of that irony for their full effect, but it is worth noting here as well, since ignorance of this distancing effect makes both *Baisers volés* and *Domicile conjugal* seem much hollower and more facile than they actually are. In fact, nearly all of Truffaut's films operate on two parallel levels of meaning: there is the obvious *narrative* level—the characters, the story line, the atmosphere—but there is also a very real, if much less easily discerned, *material* level, congruent with the narrative but separate and distinct, which is concerned with purely cinematic esthetic matters. The dialectic between the narrative and material natures of Truffaut's films creates this subtle irony. (pp. 19-20)

[The material irony is clear] in *Domicile conjugal.* Besides the weight of the references to Truffaut's own previous films, the last chapter of the Doinel saga is redolent with allusions and evocations. The Renoiresque courtyard which now fairly limits Antoine's world becomes quite suffocating, until we realize that the thick layering of art is essential to the idea of the film. It is Antoine's novel, he explains, which has come between him and Christine: art is now antithetical to life. Though the weight of the references and allusions is heavy upon us, it is not precious, as it first seems, but necessary. What started in *Les Quatre Cents Coups* as the jeu d'esprit of a young filmmaker delirious with film history and his ardor for it became during the twelve years that followed a method. (p. 20)

The vitality of Truffaut's cinema is somehow more apparent in the Doinel films than in the genre films which were interspersed with them throughout the sixties. They are more straightforward than those complicated essays in cinematic modes of discourse and more concrete. What Truffaut loves best about cinema is its ability to capture the poetry of *la vie quotidienne;* he allows himself free reign in this respect in the Doinel films. . . .

Antoine steals a photo of Harriet Andersson from a theatre display case.

Ferrand dreams *he* steals glossies of Orson Welles.

Antoine teaches Christine to butter biscottes without breaking them.

Antoine has a date with a very tall girl. (*Formidable!*)

Kids take a penmanship lesson, ripping out failed pages one after the other. (p. 21)

None of the Doinel films tell a complete story (not even the last); each is a framework for the mosaic. As the Doinel story progresses, so does the complexity of the mosaic. (p. 22)

Both the mosaic technique and the dimension of ironic commentary have a common source, which they share with nearly all the innovative methods and techniques the *Cahiers* critics developed: Bazinian realism. Like Godard's "return to zero," Rohmer's para-literary essays, and Rivette's "stretched time," Truffaut's mosaics and material irony are motivated by a deep-rooted desire to increase the quotient of honesty and clarity in film and thereby decrease the distance between author and observer. . . . Antoine Doinel's *éducation sentimentale* is not only a matter of learning how to hold a woman or a job; it is also an investigation of the function of art. . . . From the point of view of Truffaut and Léaud the film buffs, the phantoms of the cinémathèque, the answer is obviously—and unhappily—yes. (pp. 22-3)

More evident (and more engaging) in the Doinel cycle is the continuous search for the answer to Alphonse's second question in *La Nuit américaine:* "Are women magic?" Actually, the question is rhetorical. We never doubt for a moment that Léaud's Doinel believes that women are the quintessence of magic. Throughout the cycle his attachment to jobs is perfunctory, even as the jobs themselves are only sources of comedic material. . . . He is at once aggressive and passive; he throws himself into situations involving women, but he often seems paralyzed once the relationship has been initiated. (p. 23)

[The] Antoine Doinel cycle is expressed in a whole set of passive-aggressive oppositions: men versus women, adults versus children, films versus life. These form the coordinate structure. . . .

Doinel in Truffaut's original conception had been much quieter and more secretive than the character who eventually emerged. Like Doinel, Truffaut explains, "Jean-Pierre was an anti-social loner and on the brink of rebellion; however, he was a more wholesome adolescent and quite often he was downright cocky." It was this tension between the reclusive, objective, flat portrait that Truffaut had conceived and the cocky, vivid, and somehow

aggressive personality of Léaud that gave resonance and dimension to the image of Doinel, not only in *Les Quatre Cents Coups* but also in the films that followed, which were much more evidently collaborative efforts. (p. 24)

The specificity which Léaud brought to the film is closely united, however, with an opposite, general relevance which was very much Truffaut's intention and which is equally important to the success of the film. Truffaut has described more than once the clinical syndrome that he felt was the basis of *Les Quatre Cents Coups:*

> I made my film on this crisis that specialists call by the nice name of "juvenile identity crisis," which shows up in the form of four precise disturbances: the onset of puberty, an emotional weaning on the part of the parents, a desire for independence, and an inferiority complex. Each one of these four factors leads to revolt and the discovery that a certain sort of injustice exists. . . .

Once Antoine passes that crisis, his personality and that of the films become much calmer; there is a definite difference of tone between *Les Quatre Cents Coups* and "**Antoine et Colette**," which succinctly provides the necessary bridge between childhood and adulthood. The anguish of the first film has faded, and Antoine finds himself in a period of relative hope. (p. 25)

*Baisers volés* is also situated in the period of relative calm between crises. (In a way, "**Antoine et Colette**" is a sketch for the film which succeeds it.) . . . *Baisers volés* is charming, humorous, cleanly executed, and generally affirmative; consequently it has been very popular. (p. 26)

[It] is a carpe diem piece about that last moment of the passage from youth to adulthood before responsibilities become unavoidable.

Thus the dramatic focus of the film does not rest with Antoine Doinel, although he remains the emotional focus and the organizing principle, but rather with the gallery of misused, abused, and ragged men with whom Antoine comes into fleeting contact: Georges Tabard, the magician's friend, Monsieur Henri, Julien, the deceived husband, Christine's pursuer, and—not least—Colette's tired husband Albert. Nearly all have been hurt by their relationships with women, and their lives are warnings to Antoine, who is still innocent. . . .

When Henri dies offscreen, in the midst of the life of the office, Antoine searches out a prostitute. Only after he understands the connection between love and death do things work out all right with Christine. The film is a set of variations on this theme. Only a few of them involve Antoine directly; for most of them he is an observer. The process that began with Antoine's ambiguous freedom at the end of *Les Quatre Cents Coups* ends with *Baisers volés:* he has satisfied his desire for independence; his successes with Fabienne Tabard and then with Christine have marked his new maturity; the discovery that a certain sort of injustice exists has been made. And he has started to learn how to cope with it. (p. 27)

*Domicile conjugal* is a necessary sequel to *Baisers volés*. The desperate knowledge that women are not magic must be assimilated. The narrative of the first years of Antoine and Christine's marriage is the story of Antoine's grudging acceptance of that fact. . . . Doinel is a considerably less attractive character in this last film than he has been heretofore. The charm of youth has faded, and he is ill-equipped to be a functioning adult. . . . In the previous films, Doinel could lose, but he could never be beaten. Now, reality threatens. Like all Truffaut's men, now that he is of age, Antoine is movingly vulnerable, open and wounded.

Our main sense of him in *Domicile conjugal,* as in *Les Quatre Cents Coups,* is deeply colored by his isolation. The film is a collection of lonely images of Antoine. . . . (p. 29)

In *Domicile conjugal* for the first time in the Doinel cycle we can see clearly that the provenance of a Truffaut film is political. A marriage is the smallest political unit, and domestic politics provide a microcosm for us. (pp. 29-30)

[An] unavoidable aspect of *Domicile conjugal,* as the title suggests sarcastically, is Christine's clear independence. Antoine may have dreams of becoming a novelist, but Christine has already had some success as a violinist. She brings in at least as much money as he does, and is never seen at housewifely chores. She has the baby independently of her husband, and she doesn't turn into a domesticated mother. When her husband leaves her, she raises the child, does her work, and finds time for a social life. She knows a good deal more about their situation than he does. (p. 31)

*Baisers volés* began with Antoine getting laid for his army buddies (and for us) and ended with him getting married (for us); *Domicile conjugal* completes the circle; its next scene shows Antoine at a bordello in the Place Pigalle. There is one more point to be made and the tall prostitute he chooses will make it. She has specific political opinions and voices them: "Some administration! The minute I saw what they looked like on TV, I knew we'd had it. Aren't you interested in politics?" she asks. It's a question which by now we'd all like to ask Doinel (and Truffaut). He fashions an answer, and Marie continues: ". . . remember: 'if you don't follow politics, politics will get you in the end!'" The scene is a grace note, not very important except to remind us that Truffaut is aware of the political implications of the film. It is a signal in the foreground that we should take a closer look at the background of the film. The narrative of *Domicile conjugal* might seem to avoid political questions, but the material of the film is strongly evocative.

Renoir comes to mind. Just as the bonhomie of the courtyard life is getting to be a bit much, one remembers the courtyard from *Le Crime de M. Lange* and the people who lived and worked together in and around it with such good spirits. . . . What Renoir was after in that film, and what Truffaut is intent upon in *Domicile conjugal,* is the delineation of an ideal community. Renoir was much more specific: *Lange* goes to considerable lengths to describe the benefits of cooperative organization and its ramifications. But Truffaut has only to allude to the Renoir film in order to convey much of the same information.

Like *Baisers volés, Domicile conjugal* contains a gallery of characters, each of whom reinforces its philosophical aura. But whereas in the earlier film those characters were isolated from each other—separate and alone, if parallel—in the last film of the cycle they have come together, with the courtyard as their focus. (pp. 31-2)

This adopted family of the courtyard provides a matrix for the developing relationship of Antoine and Christine. As Antoine himself has explained, for him the family is the main attraction of bourgeois life. Truffaut elaborates: "Antoine proceeds in life like an orphan and looks for foster families, but once he

has found them, he tends to run away, for he remains by nature an escapist." He has, remember, chosen the profession of novelist, which implies a strict isolation: it is not a communal art, and therefore serves to counterpoint both the domestic politics of Antoine and Christine and the larger politics of the courtyard.

Although we know there are other reasons, Antoine explains to Christine that it's the novel that has separated them:

> It's all I can think right now. That's why I'm so fouled up. But I'm sure that once it's done, we'll get along better.
>
> (pp. 32-3)

There is a devious logic at work here, and it points up the ironic dilemma of Truffaut's world: for him, films may very well be more important than people, but people are undeniably the most important element of films. In his own work, the focus shifts continually back and forth between characters on the one hand and the film medium itself on the other. The result is a richly allusive but quietly subtle conflation of art and reality. For example, images of separation, visual tropes which summarize Truffaut's own feelings about the human condition, punctuate most of his films.

Jules, Jim, and Catherine look out of separate windows of their shared villa, united and alone;

an airshaft separates Antoine and Christine in *Domicile conjugal;*

Antoine often calls to Colette from his window across the street in "Antoine et Colette," while at the concerts they attend they are separated by rows of seats. (p. 33)

[The] elusive tone which characterizes Truffaut's films and which is one of their most intriguing qualities is further complicated by the fact that we must "read" not only the content of a Truffaut shot but also its structure in order to get a complete sense of his meaning, for the two are often dialectically opposed. (p. 34)

It has always seemed significant to me that the first two Doinel films were widescreen, while the last two are regular width. Doinel's story may be seen as a rite of passage from the freedom of the widescreen to the limitations and compromises of the classic aspect ratio. Likewise, Truffaut forced upon himself the limitations of the more "mature" aspect ratio, almost as a test of faith.

The sum effect of Truffaut's idiom may lead us to expect a more precise, cooler, and more objective cinema than we actually get. The concrete mosaic and the combination of widescreen, realtime editing, and the considered pan may not be the most effective language for the romantic lyric essays that the latter Doinel films first appear to be. But in fact it is through the control of his idiom that Truffaut overcomes the pontential excesses of his sentiments. It is the dialectic between what he says and how he says it that allows him to make a private film about film language at the same time as he makes a public film about the loves and labors of Antoine Doinel. (p. 36)

*James Monaco, "Truffaut: The Antoine Doinel Cycle," in his* The New Wave: Truffaut, Godard, Chabrol, Rohmer, Rivette *(copyright © 1976 by James Monaco; reprinted by permission of Oxford University Press, Inc.), Oxford University Press, New York, 1976, pp. 13-37.*

**ALLEN THIHER**

[In *The 400 Blows,* the] presence of a camera aimlessly set in motion, breaking self-consciously with the canons of traditional filmic representation and setting forth a world that has no rapport with the film music, seems to confirm immediately our assertion that the absurd informs Truffaut's early work in its most basic formal aspects. It is, of course, at the most primary level of mimesis that these absurdist configurations are most evident, since Truffaut's representation of episodic experience is grounded in plots that are essentially discontinuous series of non-causally related events that reflect the radical, if often incoherent freedom that Truffaut's characters enjoy. (p. 184)

Whatever may be the autobiographical element in Truffaut's portrayal of Antoine's being branded as a delinquent, it is clear that his manner of depicting how the boy stumbles into crime and incarceration is grounded both in an absurdist sense of fortuitous being and an existentialist view of the radical responsibility that is the converse side of freedom. (p. 185)

[It] is the structure of freedom itself that somehow seems deficient. The boy is free to choose his acts, but these acts can turn against him and ultimately destroy his freedom. There is, then, more than a little romantic fatalism in this rather nihilistic vision of freedom. This paradox is, however, one of the defining features of this kind of existential nihilism, according to which freedom appears inevitably to turn against itself in self-destruction.

This nihilism seems to lie behind the film's final spree, Antoine's escape from the observation center. . . . The child's flight is a desperate, but gratuitous act that leads him to the sea, to the vast, mythic expanse that he had never seen before. In its limitlessness the sea appears to be the antithesis of all the constraints—school, family and prison—that had limited the boy's freedom. But in itself the sea is also a limit to the boy's flight, an absurd barrier not unlike the wall in Sartre's short story of the same name. It is an absurd presence marking the limits of freedom. . . .

[The] final image perhaps connotes death, the final absurd limit of all freedom. In this respect we again see another aspect of the fatalism that decrees that the boy's acts can only generate an ever increasing crescendo of catastrophes whose logical conclusion could be his death. When one turns to *Shoot the Piano Player* and *Jules and Jim* death is, in fact, the explicit limit that terminates each film. (p. 186)

In *Shoot the Piano Player* the absurdist configuration that gives rise to narrative ruptures also lies behind the gags and parodistic devices that constantly rupture the film's tonality. . . . (p. 187)

In Truffaut's absurdist world characters are governed only by the dictates of ironic self-consciousness, and thus his fleeing character can, in the most improbable manner, run into a street light, knock himself down, get up, and then begin a long conversation with a passing stranger who explains how he found marital happiness. Then the character resumes his flight with all the speed he can muster. This break with the codes of psychological verisimilitude and of standard narration signifies, from the film's outset, that we must read the film in terms of new codes predicated on those absurdist configurations that set the limits for representation at the end of the fifties. . . .

[*Shoot the Piano Player*] is a film that constantly tests the conventions of representation and their adequacy for representing what we might call conventional life.

The film begins and ends with the image of Charlie Kohler seated at his piano as he grinds out popular tunes for the motley crowd that gathers to dance in this down-and-out bar. The film thus fails to go beyond its opening situation, which is another way of designating a kind of absurd stasis in that the film cannot progress beyond this circular movement. (p. 188)

It is [a] mixing of conventions and resulting multi-leveled parody that has undoubtedly been responsible for the rather hostile reception that was once given to *Shoot the Piano Player.* The mixture of lyricism and parody, of gags and tragic seriousness, must be envisaged as another form of representation that signifies the absurd, the loss of certainty, the sense of discontinuity that underlie Truffaut's early work. . . .

The absurdist configurations that lie behind the shaping of episodic experience and the parodistic devices in Truffaut's early work also seem to determine his choice of themes. In this respect we can consider a privileged theme in [*The 400 Blows, Shoot the Piano Player,* and *Jules and Jim*] for an understanding of how the absurd orders the representation of character: throughout these films the theme of the characters' identity appears to be a key motif. It is a theme to which all the others are related and from which the other themes derive their full significance. Antoine's freedom, for example, derives in one sense from his identity as a legitimized bastard. (p. 189)

The bastard's accidental presence in the world is . . . a metaphor for man's presence, though the child can enjoy this gratuitous existence as a form of play until he must pass into the world of adults, and assume their identity. . . . [The] child's changing his identity ultimately gives expression to Truffaut's fatalism, for the child's attempt to be an adult can only result in a form of fall—the fall into adulthood—that leads to dereliction and abandonment.

In *Shoot the Piano Player* Truffaut pursues this vision of absurd dereliction even further in his portrait of Charlie/Edouard, the piano player whose two names point to the discontinuous identity he lives as he seeks to deny the past. Charlie today, Edouard yesterday, he seeks to live the present as a rupture that refuses any existential weight to that catastrophic past in which he sought his identity as a public image. In this sense Charlie has chosen to be the existentialist bastard who refuses all familial and hereditary links, though the film demonstrates, from beginning to end, the impossibility of escaping those ties. (pp. 189-90)

In the existentialist's world of gratuitous presence we can thus see that the converse side to one's radical freedom is the way in which one must exist for others. There is a public dimension of identity over which one has no control insofar as it is determined by the other. The absurdist man is therefore free to choose any identity, and yet tied paradoxically to a being-for-others, an identity he cannot choose and cannot even really know.

Charlie/Edouard's dereliction thus turns on his impossible impasse: as Charlie he attempts to deny his being-for-others and, as Edouard, he tried to exist only as a being-for-others. The first is, as the film demonstrates by the way the family clings to him and by the way others impose identities on him, a hopeless task, whereas to seek to exist only for others is a catastrophically inauthentic mode of being. (p. 190)

The final result of this profusion of identities and the mishaps that result from them is that the piano player withdraws from the world, determined to have no being-for-others, desiring to commit no act other than that most derisive non-act of beating on his tinny piano. (p. 191)

The antithesis to this kind of immobile presence, lived as a refusal of one's being-for-others, is of course to be found in the way Catherine seeks, in *Jules and Jim,* to renew her existence and invent new values at every moment. The absurdist configuration underlying this attempt at permanent creation is again that of rupture and discontinuity, as we clearly see when Catherine, dressing in a manner that recalls the boy in Chaplin's *The Kid,* can seemingly change even her sex at will. The question of Catherine's identity determines, in fact, the way Truffaut constructs his representational space throughout the film, for it is she who defines the limits within which the others attempt to find their own roles. . . .

Catherine's leaping into the Seine is a gratuitous act by which she shows that no label can be imposed upon her, no simplistic formula can give a résumé of her being. Like the water into which she leaps she sees herself as one and yet ever different. (p. 192)

In his third film, then, Truffaut seems to present a rather direct critique of the absurdist view of identity. The quest for total inventiveness, denying any continuity in time, only results in a disparate series of gestures and disconnected rituals until finally Catherine has no identity except that of an aging woman who has accumulated a repertoire of roles that are no longer adequate or even amusing.

The gratuitousness of man's presence in the world and the discontinuity of identity that underlie these films' vision give rise in turn to another essential motif. This is the motif of play, for it can be maintained that all of Truffaut's characters are essentially players and that the space of representation here is a ludic or play space. . . . [Absurd] man is almost obliged to be a player, for not only does play endow his being with at least a temporary justification, but, in a second and related sense, the disparate identities that he chooses to embody condemn him to be nothing more than a player, or an actor whose identity is nothing more than a series of roles.

In *The 400 Blows* periods of play alternate regularly with periods of constraint and confinement. Constraint takes place in those enclosed spaces such as the schoolroom, the dank apartment, the wire cage, or the observation center, that are so many emblems of societal efforts to repress the child's desire. They are also so many emblems of absurd enclosure that stands in opposition to the child's freedom, to his play instincts, to his sprees. . . . In *Shoot the Piano Player* Truffaut next portrays an adult player's failure to play in any authentic fashion. It hardly seems an accident, moreover, that Charlie/Edouard tries to define himself by playing the piano. As Edouard he attempts to use his playing to give himself a public role, whereas, as Charlie, he uses it as a defense against the world, as a way of isolating and protecting himself. But in both cases it is noteworthy that Truffaut frames all shots of the piano player playing so that the piano is a barrier between the player and the world. Charlie's use of the piano in this respect is fairly obvious, but there is little difference when we see Edouard at the piano. The piano, in one shot hemmed in between large columns, gives the impression of creating a kind of cell in which Edouard is locked. The piano player has thus perverted play, and what should be a form of affirmation in an absurd world becomes instead the walls of a prison house in which the self dies. (pp. 193-94)

It is in *Jules and Jim,* however, that Truffaut has developed his most complex testing of the notions of play in a world without constraint that seemingly allows the invention of any game one is audacious enough to contrive. (p. 194)

In the second half of the film Jim's decision to come to Germany to visit Jules and Catherine opens up a new period of play, for Jim comes to see if he, too, should marry, or in other words, give up the bohemian rules of the game that do not allow him to live with his mistress Gilberte (though he spends each night with her). Jim finds that he is still magnetically attracted to Catherine. Since Jules, in a gesture of near monastic renunciation, has given up all hope of making Catherine happy, the trio tries to find a *modus vivendi* through play, through inventing new rituals that will allow them to come to terms with their desire with self-given rules. . . .

When Jim leaves the play space, he is forced to confront choices, to commit himself to acts that have consequences that play acts seemingly do not. Or, more precisely, Jim's flaw is that he can neither commit himself to the given rules for societal games or accept the games that Catherine proposes. . . .

The stakes of the game this time are a child, for it is apparently only by Catherine's conceiving that a play equilibrium can be established in Jim's favor—for Jules has already shown his capacity for paternity. Yet, one also feels that the child would be a symbol of the plenitude that their game playing has not achieved. (p. 195)

[It] is important to stress how *Jules and Jim,* in differing in one important respect from *The 400 Blows* and *Shoot the Piano Player,* points beyond the New Wave towards such works as *Wild Child, Two English Girls* and *The Story of Adele H.* This difference is, in the simplest terms, that *Jules and Jim* is an historical film. *The 400 Blows* and *Shoot the Piano Player,* like most New Wave works, set forth experiential situations that are contemporary with the aesthetic axioms—and the absurdist configuration—that inform them. They are, moreover, works that are, in an existential sense, to be experienced as a radically present world: open, unordered, and gratuitous in its lack of determination. In *Jules and Jim,* on the other hand, the film's experiential space is self-consciously given as a world past, and we are thus invited to make use of our knowledge of that past in experiencing the film. . . . To view experience with its historical dimension is to view it, potentially at least, in terms of a rational ordering, and one might well maintain that the sharpness of Truffaut's attitudes towards absurdist notions is heightened by his historical sense in *Jules and Jim.* (p. 196)

It is with this historical dimension in mind that we can clearly see that in *Jules and Jim* Truffaut sets Goethe against Picasso, or an understanding of the limits of human possibilities against a belief in man's capacity to displace the values of the past—or, to return to the historical analogy, against the absurdist notion that man's radical freedom reduces the past to nothingness. But the only real survivor in any of these three films is Jules, and it is perhaps most significant that it should be the only father in the film, the only man to assure continuity, who can walk away from the crematorium. Moreover, he is the German whose renunciation, as Nietzsche said in thinking about Goethe, is perhaps to be seen as the only way to triumph over the absurd. In this case the final image of Jules walking through the cemetery is, then, as much Truffaut's way of presenting an image of the death of modernist and absurdist hubris as it is an image of dereliction and isolation. (p. 197)

Allen Thiher, *"The Existential Play in Truffaut's Early Films,"* in Literature/Film Quarterly *(© copyright*

*1977 Salisbury State College), Vol. V, No. 3, Summer, 1977, pp. 183-97.*

## VERINA GLAESSNER

*Small Change* ends up strangely formal and opaque, and not a little patronising. Patrick's segment of the film is reasonably successful simply because it is the most developed and allows Truffaut to rework a familiar theme with some deftness. Overall, the incidents seem at once too arbitrary and too trite. . . . If *The 400 Blows* and *Les Mistons* were disquieting precisely because they took their protagonists as allies, and through them allowed the audience to question social assumptions, here the story of the child martyr Julien Leclou is used simply to confirm the complacent view of 'middle France' presented elsewhere in the film. In fact, it is arguably not so much childish resilience that is being celebrated but a certain milieu as seen through a childhood documented from birth to puberty. . . . What sets *Small Change* apart from Truffaut's other films about children is not simply that the director has become, as he has admitted, more 'resigned' in his treatment of his adult characters, but that he has become more distant from the children. And distance tends to lend not so much an enchantment as a self-consciousness that expresses itself in a sentimental and nostalgic view of childhood. Hence the moments of saccharin cuteness that puncture the rather fragile charm the film periodically musters. (pp. 163-64)

*Verina Glaessner, "Feature Films: 'L'argent de poche' ('Small Change')," in* Monthly Film Bulletin *(copyright © The British Film Institute, 1977), Vol. 44, No. 523, August, 1977, pp. 163-64.*

## DEREK ELLEY

*L'argent de poche* [*Small Change*] may have a story-line which harks back to *Les quatre cents coups,* but in spirit it is an entirely new work. It is, in fact, the world of that earlier film (or at least, the classroom and escapade passages, rather than the darker borstal section) seen through the rose-tinted filter of the later Doinel films; the result, expressed in a freer form than any other of his works, has an infectious warmth which must be experienced rather than written about. . . .

The film celebrates not popular myths like the 'innocence' of children or childhood, or even the joy of schooldays, but the resilience of the human spirit, both child and adult.

*Derek Elley, "Reviews: 'Small Change'" (© copyright Derek Elley 1977; reprinted with permission), in* Films and Filming, *Vol. 24, No. 1, October, 1977, p. 34.*

## ANDREW SARRIS

There is a bite and a force to [*The Man Who Loved Women,* a] saga of a French provincial sad-faced skirt-chaser that places Truffaut for the moment halfway between the realms of Renoir and Bunuel. It may be that Truffaut is finally getting old enough to make the confessional mode of filmmaking pay off in emotional resonance. Here he has seemed to get deeper into his psyche than usual without at the same time seeming to repeat himself stylistically. One recognizes the Truffaut trademarks: the undigestedly literary form of narration, the privileged moments of fresh-air documentary, the construction of characters through

maxims and meditations, the jolting awareness of the artist's arbitrary control over his material. . . .

The darker aspects of the subject are emphasized by framing the narrative with the funeral of the protagonist. . . . Here was no man's man, but a woman's man, not a Don Juan or a Lothario necessarily, but a veritable worshipper of the idea of woman. He never wanted anyone to be hurt in the process of his practicing his religion, but he inflicted and suffered considerable pain all the same. There is, of course, much humor in the situation, but Truffaut never forces it into facetiousness. The funeral is always in the background, and with it the shifting of the point of view back and forth from beyond the grave so that the personality of Truffaut himself comes into play. . . .

Overall, the picture has a harsh look which contrasts sharply with Bunuel's sardonic glossiness of recent years. I said at the outset that Truffaut was halfway to Bunuel, but that is about as far as he can ever get. Truffaut has always been fascinated by and appreciative of obsessional cinema, but he has always been too intelligent to succumb himself. Even his most lyrical films are discreetly distanced from their subjects, less cold than cool, less hot than warm. From the beginning of his career to the present, Truffaut has served not so much as the poet of madness as the poet of sanity.

*Andrew Sarris, "Foreign Films for Grownups" (reprinted by permission of* The Village Voice *and the author; copyright © The Village Voice, Inc., 1977), in* The Village Voice, *Vol. XXII, No. 40, October 3, 1977, p. 44.*\*

## PAULINE KAEL

François Truffaut's *The Man Who Loved Women* begins with the arrival of the mourners at Bertrand's funeral. . . . When, in flashback, we see Bertrand . . . , the dedicated skirt-chaser whose lovemaking these women are honoring by their presence, it's a letdown. He's dead even when he's supposed to be alive. . . . Bertrand is like an elderly, dried-up pederast. There are, of course, joyless compulsive chasers, but Bertrand's chasing isn't intended to be joyless. Although his obsession may look to be about as exciting as building a two-foot replica of the Pentagon with toothpicks, he's meant to be irresistibly charming.

Bertrand's plight might have been a subject for one of Sacha Guitry's light farces—the absurd story of a roué who carries to extremes the proclivities that other men can keep in balance. And the movie has the structure of a boulevard farce. But it doesn't have a comic spirit. In its gross flippancy, it resembles *Such a Gorgeous Kid Like Me*—it may be even worse, because of the mixture of evasiveness and obviousness. . . . Bertrand's chance encounter with Vera . . . , whom he loved years before, and whose leaving him is supposed to indicate why he can't have an ongoing relationship, is so cryptically weighted with pauses, gulps, and shining eyes, and is so fundamentally uncommunicative, that it ranks with the flattest moments in all of Truffaut. (pp. 354-55)

If Bertrand were a highly respected, honored man—a man with children and friends, possibly a man with a deep commitment to his work (an artist, perhaps?)—and if he were split between other drives or goals and this, to him, shameful, somewhat incomprehensible compulsion, then there'd be a comic horror in his plight. Truffaut, however, doesn't set Bertrand's chasing in conflict with other aspects of his character; he isolates it. Bertrand is such a loner that he doesn't even hang out with men to talk about women. And what pleasure can he get? The women are so willing and compliant he can't get anything resembling the thrill of conquest. There isn't as much as a whiff of gunpowder from the sexual war. The film has a frosty, tony-swinger mentality: nobody's hurt, nobody pays. Can a man race from one affair to another the way Bertrand does without disrupting the women's lives, and without their interfering in his? Bertrand's existence is so smooth he seems programmed rather than sex-crazed; the film has the pacing of an industrial movie—one task after another. (pp. 355-56)

> *Pauline Kael, "The Unjoy of Sex" (originally published in* The New Yorker, *Vol. LII, No. 42, December 5, 1977), in her* When the Lights Go Down *(copyright © 1975, 1976, 1977, 1978, 1979, 1980 by Pauline Kael; reprinted by permission of Holt, Rinehart and Winston, Publishers), Holt, 1980, pp. 354-58.\**

## JOHN SIMON

François Truffaut has had a career not untypical of some of our most gifted filmmakers: a brilliant start followed by considerable floundering. No cinematic *oeuvre* could have begun more felicitously than his, with that remarkable trio of films, *The 400 Blows, Shoot the Piano Player,* and *Jules and Jim.* These pictures combined vitality with poignancy; they were informed by a nervous rhythm that could nevertheless linger over lyrical incidents, and a hard-bitten humor one could almost as easily cry as laugh at. Each of these films, for all the director's very pronounced personality, retained its own particular flavor: there were no repetitions, no transposable parts.

But already with his fourth feature, *The Tender Skin,* Truffaut was in trouble, and though there were many good sequences in *Stolen Kisses* and *The Wild Child,* and some good ideas unsteadily blinking in *The Story of Adèle H.,* there were other movies with little to recommend them. The main problem seems to be a certain sentimentality, an ingratiating bittersweetness that apportions the bitter and the sweet with almost culinary calculation. The sentimentality is not quite your standard sort, with things gallantly muddling through to a comforting conclusion; but failure and sadness have a way of becoming badges of achievement, permitting their bearers access to a world of bizarre, melancholy grace—perhaps free admission to the Cinémathèque Française.

No previous film of Truffaut's, however . . . can surpass *The Man Who Loved Women* in non-risktaking triviality. (p. 38)

[The] film begins with Bertrand's funeral, and also ends with it, as seen from the point of view of Geneviève, his literary editor and most enlightened girlfriend. For Bertrand is . . . the author of an amorous autobiography entitled *The Man Who Loved Women,* and the film moves along three planes: the plane of events, that of recording them in a book, and that of memory being transformed by art. But compared to what a Pirandello—to say nothing of a Proust—could do with this sort of material, Truffaut remains a piker; let us say an engineer of mechanical fluidity. At best he becomes impish, as when the same actress plays Bertrand's mother and the prostitute who initiates the hero as a boy, but even this conceit remains undeveloped.

On however many planes, though, the film is basically a retelling of the Don Juan story, and the artist who broaches one of our great myths or legends is duly bound to enrich it with his personal vision and interpretation. Truffaut, however, not only adds nothing to it, but actually detracts from the great tale by trivializing it. . . .

If there is any genuine feeling in this movie, it is less for women than for literature. . . . What [Truffaut] is still splendid at is pacing, and the film moves forward with the springiness of a stalking feline. This time, unfortunately, not a leopard, only a domestic tabby, bringing home a rather measly mouse. (p. 40)

> *John Simon, "The Engineer of Fluid Mechanics" (© John Simon, 1978; reprinted by permission of the author), in* National Review, *Vol. XXX, No. 1, January 6, 1978, pp. 38-40.*

## RICHARD ROUD

[It] is not surprising that, omnivorous reader that he is, Truffaut has now (after Chabrol, it must be said) discovered Henry James. What *is* surprising at first glance is that he should choose *The Altar of the Dead.* At first glance only, for has he not always been obsessed with . . . obsessions of every kind? The obsession of Adèle H. with her wayward lover, the obsession of Julie with revenge in *The Bride Wore Black,* the obsession of [Louis] with [Marion] in *Mississippi Mermaid.* The obsession of Julien Davenne in *La Chambre Verte,* however, is with death. . . .

As befits its subject matter, *La Chambre Verte* has quite a different look from Truffaut's other films. The tones are sombre, it is always raining, and the cemetery, dank and overgrown, is shot in an absolutely English shade of green. The esteem Truffaut has always expressed for Bresson is more visible than usual, especially in his own performance. It is a real performance—not like the one he gave in *Close Encounters*—but it is a very distanced and distancing one. He speaks abruptly, almost telegraphically. He (and the other characters) are often seen through panes of glass or in mirrors. Distance, again, in the chapel scene, where the wrought-iron grill separates the actors from the camera—and from us.

But there are other elements in the film that could only come from Truffaut—even though he says that he is unable to explain them. He has given Julien an elderly housekeeper who is the guardian of a deaf-mute little boy, and the scenes between Julien and the child are not unlike certain sequences in *L'Enfant Sauvage.* What the little boy has to do with the rest of the film is not clear: Truffaut, when asked, could only reply that he felt the child had to be there for 'reasons of balance'. I suppose what he means is that the presence of a young child, unthinkable in the James story, is an element which, to use Lindsay Anderson's timeworn phrase, 'speaks up for life'. But, and this is characteristic of Truffaut's fundamental honesty, he can speak up only with the greatest difficulty; supplementing sign language with a series of strangulated syllables. . . .

Truffaut's film is not really about death. Rather it is about death-in-life, about love and death, with love as the only 'answer' to death. Death conceived of as selfishness, the refusal ever to let go of what once belonged to one; the refusal to accept love and friendship unless the lover or friend is safely dead—and therefore totally manageable. Just as Julien can never forgive the wrong done him by his ex-friend, so that the betrayal has permanently embittered him, made him into what James called a 'spectator of life'; and spectators can never participate actively with the players in the game of life. . . .

Truffaut, with a leg up from Henry James, has surpassed everything he has done until now. And that one need no longer have apprehensions for his future; the man who made *La Chambre Verte* is never likely to fall back again to the level of *Domicile Conjugal.* (p. 166)

Richard Roud, "Turning Points: Ruiz/Truffaut," in Sight and Sound *(copyright © 1978 by The British Film Institute), Vol. 47, No. 3, Summer, 1978, pp. 163-66.*

## ANDREW SARRIS

Over the years Doinel has drifted away from both Truffaut and Leaud, and now [in *Love on the Run*] he seems less a coherent character than a construct around which episodes involving memory and desire can be enacted. Doinel has finally written a novel, which, though not a big seller, has won him a minor literary prize. He is still hanging by his fingernails to residence in an increasingly upper-class Paris, but neither Truffaut nor Doinel seem to notice the changing atmosphere around them. Truffaut has never tried to pass himself off as a social seismograph, and Doinel, like Truffaut, is too much a self-made man and an autodidact to indulge in the romantic fantasies of the university-bred left. . . .

His life is beginning to form a recognizable pattern, and it is too far removed from the pathological design of *The Man Who Loved Women.* Doinel, like Truffaut, also is obsessed with literature and death. Gradually Doinel's past begins to engulf his present and enshroud his future. . . . Truffaut's narrative instinct is at its most desperately unconvincing as it tries to fill in the years of [Colette's] married life since the very brief street encounter in *Stolen Kisses* in which she confronted Doinel with her husband and baby. . . . Colette is meant to represent the kind of self-possessed woman Doinel/Truffaut can confront on a basis of fraternity and equality. Hence, it is interesting that she seems overly contrived as a character. . . .

*Love on the Run* fails . . . to regenerate the Doinel character, and the more Truffaut flashes back to previous incarnations the gloomier the whole enterprise seems. Yet I wouldn't have missed *Love on the Run.* For the first time in the history of the cinema we have witnessed the Proustian spectacle of an actor/character flashing back to his lost glory and vitality. Truffaut has gone far beyond Doinel, and has never come close to acknowledging this fact, not even in *Day for Night,* in which he assumes a paternal relationship to Leaud divested of Doinel. Truffaut has not yet made his *Annie Hall.* (p. 47)

Andrew Sarris, "Three Accents on Love" (reprinted by permission of The Village Voice *and the author; copyright © News Group Publications, Inc., 1979), in* The Village Voice, *Vol. XXIV, No. 15, April 9, 1979, pp. 47, 78.*

## ANDREW SARRIS

[*The Green Room*] suggests the gradual evolution of Truffaut from seemingly the merriest of the old nouvelle vague directors to seemingly the most morbid of them all. The Pirandellian tensions between Truffaut the director and Truffaut the actor is exploited here to project a very personal contemplation of death. . . . The privileged cinematic moments in *The Green Room* have to do with Truffaut's candle-lit ceremonies dedicated to the dead in his own real and vicarious life. The love of the dead comes naturally to the lovers of old movies. Indeed,

the dead of the screen are venerated because they can no longer desecrate their images with the indiscretions of their errant flesh and life-sustaining foibles. Truffaut has been simply more candid than most of his colleagues in confessing that he has lived most of his life in a misty dream.

Andrew Sarris, "The Provincial Critic and the Venetian Blind" (reprinted by permission of The Village Voice *and the author; copyright © News Group Publications, Inc., 1979), in* The Village Voice, *Vol. XXIV, No. 38, September 17, 1979, p. 49.*

## JULIAN JEBB

With the important exception of *Stolen Kisses,* [*Love on the Run,* the Saga of Antoine Doinel's] love life through three and a half films is, to me, the least appealing of Francois Truffaut's glorious output. . . . The director loses some of his magic when faced with his alter ego. . . .

[*Love on the Run*] has individual scenes which no other director in the history of the cinema could achieve with such elegant, heart-stopping, comic authority. . . .

For all the tenderness and objectivity which Truffaut allows his hero, Doinel remains little more than a posturing, skirt-chasing, pretentious man—a nightmare Parisian whose arrogance is coated in self-pity. Nor, curiously, does he show any of the conventionally neurotic signs of a child who has suffered in the way we saw in *Les Quatre Cents Coups.* His only insecurity seems to be the highly conventional one of possessing a well developed libido. . . . The girls in the new movie are as terrific as ever. . . . One does pause to wonder quite how Antoine Doinel manages to gather such a gallery of lovelies round him, for his sex appeal isn't all that apparent. . . .

The themes are more easily identified. Doinel is maturing emotionally; we are to believe that perhaps the final winning of Sabine indicates that he will settle down. The flight is meant to be over. . . .

There is an atmosphere of delighted generosity which is wholly, mysteriously free of sentimentality and which could only be produced by this director. Truffaut may be full of invention and ideas, but he knows first things first—he understands love of any kind.

Julian Jebb, "Film Reviews: 'Love on the Run'," in Sight and Sound *(copyright © 1980 by The British Film Institute), Vol. 49, No. 1, Winter, 1979-80, p. 55.*

## ADELINE R. TINTNER

[By Truffaut's creative re-doing of Henry James's story "Altars of the Dead" into *La Chambre verte* (*The Green Room*)] he has offered what James himself considered the ideal form of criticism: "to criticise is to appreciate, to appropriate, to take intellectual possession, to establish in fine a relation with the criticised thing and make it one's own." (p. 78)

"The Altar of the Dead" is the only serious fictional attempt by James to present his idea of an afterlife which he thought of as an extension of the lives of the dead through relations with the living, depending for its force on the consciousness of the remembering person. (p. 79)

[A] view of the immortality of the soul is beautifully conveyed to us by Truffaut's variation that gives a dazzling reality to the

American writer's notion of the only kind of immortality possible—our conscious attempt to keep "them" within a continuing relation with us.

Truffaut does this by a blending of James's views with his own predispositions. By building up the character of the woman in the story as young and in contact with people, he makes the tensions between the necrophiliac hero and the healthy life-oriented heroine more dramatic. (pp. 79-80)

One of Truffaut's major changes was to alter the time and the setting to motivate his hero and to rationalize his almost psychotic fixation by invoking the horrors of war. . . . The additional alterations in the names of the characters and the introduction of a housekeeper, her young ward and the auction house scene are devices to enrich the visual field and to dramatize the story through episodic variety by using recognizable icons from Truffaut's films. (p. 80)

Truffaut has made very effective the chapel scene which in James's story had been but part of a church in a London suburb, for the filmmaker has put it directly in the cemetery so the characters move in it as if it were their total world. As night is their time, as candle light their illumination, so the city of the dead is their landscape. . . . [In] spite of close adherence to James's main thrust, Truffaut has converted a story, usually thought to be lugubrious and generally unpleasant to read, into a film of interesting liveliness. He has made certain changes which bring into visual focus the largely introspective consciousness of James's main character which relies chiefly on language and metaphor for its expression.

The title, *La Chambre verte,* **"The Green Room,"** is taken from the color of Cecilia's room which she has made into her kind of shrine, filled with portraits of her former lover. The nameless woman's room in "The Altar of the Dead" has "dark red walls" which give it "the flush of life." The change to green might be the kind of change that Truffaut recorded in the film made just before this one, **"The Man Who Loved Women,"** where the little girl's red dress is changed to blue after the novelist converts his experience into a work of art. It might also reflect the feeling that green was a color more consistent with Cecilia's "flush of life" than "dark red" and more indicative of healthy growth.

But the fact that the green room creates the title of the film gives it an importance beyond these two possibilities. [The title] invokes the green room in the Comédie Française, the salon in which the actors of the company act as hosts, rather than as performers, for distinguished spectators. It is also consistent with Truffaut's obvious immersion in James's fiction that he is probably remembering a crucial scene in *The Tragic Muse,* James's great novel of the theatre, actors and artists, which takes place in that famous green room—the "spacious saloon, covered with pictures and relics and draped in official green velvet . . . among portraits and scrolls, the records of a splendid history." Cecilia's room, too, is both a salon and a shrine, a place filled with mementoes of her lover, the chief actor in her life. It also fits in with Truffaut's interest in shrines and altars in *The 400 Blows* and *The Story of Adèle H.*

By making his hero restore a "dead" building, right within the precincts of the cemetery, the city of the dead becomes the important landscape of the film. He makes a ruin come to life, which is a preparation for making his dead friends come to life through flame. By multiplying the candles in the small chapel and creating a mass of light in the city of the dead, night is made into day. (pp. 81-2)

More important than the minor changes are the similarities and sympathies between the two creators. James and Truffaut, passionately devoted to their craft, had the same early immersion in literary models, having both reaped the advantage of irregular schooling, which permitted full-time devotion to intensive reading. (p. 82)

The success of Truffaut's version of the James story is not merely a happy accident, for it depends on his concept of author-director. By being personally responsible for all the aspects of a film, Truffaut makes the analogy between himself and James—"the filmmaker/author writes with his camera as a writer writes with his pen"—a reality. (p. 83)

*Adeline R. Tintner, "Truffaut's 'La chambre verte': Homage to Henry James," in* Literature/Film Quarterly (©copyright 1980 Salisbury State College), Vol. 8, No. 2, 1980, pp. 78-83.

### ANDREW SARRIS

I sincerely believe that *The Last Metro* must be seen by anyone seriously interested in the cinema. One may not be exactly enchanted by Truffaut's canny blend of history and romance in this tale of a theatre troupe's trials and tribulations in '40s German-occupied Paris. But who knows? . . .

*The Last Metro* reflects a certain degree of nostalgia for a period and a genre in which the moral commitments of characters could be taken for granted. What disturbs me the most about *The Last Metro* is that the uneasy mixture of fact and fantasy is never adequately articulated into a coherent whole. Truffaut is trying to establish connections between theatre and politics, between personal relationships and political involvements, between the idealism of the few and the pragmatism of the many. (p. 47)

Truffaut's characters in *The Last Metro* are not, by and large, obsessed ideologues. Even the members of the Resistance among them seem to be driven more by theatrical narcissism than philosophical conviction. . . . Truffaut maintains a discreet distance from the feelings of his characters so as to give them the necessary space in which to act with a degree of self-awareness. Yet if the politics remain muffled and subterranean, both literally and figuratively, the theatrics never take off to the loftier realms of [Carné's] *Les Enfants du Paradis* or [Renoir's] *Golden Coach.* The actual play in production within *The Last Metro* looks and sounds like a McGuffin for the sexual triangle lurking in the wings of the political melodrama. Again, Truffaut's "touches" invoke memories of '40s French icons like Louis Jouvet, Jean Cocteau, Jean Marais, and Robert Bresson as they interacted with ordinary Parisians in the audience. Truffaut is suggesting that there was nothing wrong with Parisians flocking to theatres for entertainment during the grim days of the Occupation, and there was nothing wrong with the people who supplied that entertainment. Even during the Holocaust.

Ay, there's the rub. Truffaut himself has gone into extensive rhetorical detail on the absurdities and cruelties of anti-Semitism and homophobia. Most of this rhetoric is hurled at the film's arch-villain, a French critic-collaborationist named Daxial, . . . reportedly based on a real person of the time. The Daxial character strikes me as too convenient a diabolical device to concentrate all the poisons of an era into one thoroughly discredited personality. Daxial makes it much too easy for a self-congratulatory euphoria to settle over an audience.

I do not want to be too hard on *The Last Metro*. That it will be one of the better films of 1981 goes almost without saying. Truffaut executes some very graceful maneuvers with Catherine Deneuve in terms of the overall mythology of movies, and it is often a pleasure to watch his critical intelligence at work on the problem of shifting moods. What I find lacking is an inner logic to the movie. Suspended in a limbo between Renoir and Lubitsch, *The Last Metro* seems unable to resolve itself in terms of either historical complexity or dramatic consistency. Hence, when he makes his last joke on the uneasy co-existence of cinema, theatre, and real life, a potentially rich laughter is congealed into a frozen smile of acquiescence with the director's stylistic intentions, though not with his emotional results. (p. 54)

*Andrew Sarris, "Who Is to Judge Truffaut?" (reprinted by permission of* The Village Voice *and the author; copyright © News Group Publications, Inc., 1981), in* The Village Voice, *Vol. XXVI, No. 7, February 11-17, 1981, pp. 47, 54.*

## ROBERT HATCH

[Truffaut's] films have a clarity and ease achieved only with a technique so mastered that it has become subconscious; it accommodates without strain the astonishing range of his interests. Truffaut is serious about his art, indeed a perfectionist, but he strikes no postures. . . .

[In *The Last Metro*] Truffaut has put together a convincing vision of how the Parisians reacted toward their oppressors and toward the French jackals who ran with that pack. . . .

That vision was composed of both hatred and fear, but felt and expressed, he persuades us, primarily as disgust and contempt. Everyone in the film adjusts to the situation—the huge, seemingly bland Bernard least of all. (p. 284)

Collaboration was for years thereafter, and perhaps still is, a painful and confused issue with the French. That is so, if I understand Truffaut correctly, because everyone was a collaborator in some degree. To survive was to collaborate; even sharing the boulevards with the Nazis was a kind of collaboration—you could, in pure theory, push them into the gutter. But there was collaboration from necessity and collaboration for profit, acquiescence with dignity and craven acquiescence. No director, except perhaps Marcel Ophuls in *The Sorrow and the Pity*, has drawn this distinction with the understanding and sympathy of Truffaut in *The Last Metro*. Moreover, by setting his story in the ambiguous world of the theater, Truffaut italicizes the ambiguity of life in that time. . . .

For that reason among others, and though it deals with dark matters, *The Last Metro* effervesces; it gleams with a determination not only to live but to enjoy life. (p. 285)

*Robert Hatch, "Films: 'The Last Metro'," in* The Nation *(copyright 1981 The Nation magazine, The Nation Associates, Inc.), Vol. 232, No. 9, March 7, 1981, pp. 284-85.*

# Melvin Van Peebles

## 1932-

Black American director, novelist, playwright, actor, and composer.

Van Peebles is one of the first American-born blacks to direct feature films. His work expresses the view of the repressed black who tries to overcome the restrictions placed upon him in a society dominated by whites. Therefore, fear, violence, and outrage are prominent in his work.

Van Peebles graduated from Ohio Wesleyan University with a degree in English literature. He began his career by making short films, hoping that they would arouse the interest of Hollywood producers. Instead, a major studio offered him a position as an elevator operator and parking-lot attendant. Van Peebles then went to Europe, and took a job editing the French edition of *Mad* magazine. He also toured in Brendan Behan's *The Hostage* with the Dutch National Theater. While in France, Van Peebles discovered that he could obtain a director's card if he wanted to adapt his own French writings. He then began to write novels and short stories in self-taught French. One of his works, *The Story of a Three Day Pass*, became the subject of his first feature film. Despite mixed reviews, the film attracted a great deal of attention in Hollywood, and Van Peebles quickly found himself in demand.

The first film Van Peebles made in the United States was *Watermelon Man*, a "black" comedy about a white bigot who turns black overnight. Critics were kind neither to Van Peebles nor to the film, and once again he found himself unwanted in Hollywood. No major studio would finance his next film, so he used his own money and loans from friends, and employed nonunion crews to make *Sweet Sweetback's Baadasssss Song*. Van Peebles had to promote the film himself. Despite what appeared to be insurmountable obstacles, *Sweet Sweetback* became a huge box-office success and was a top money-making film for a time. The film is an angry, profane picture of black repression and is one of the few films in which "the black man [wins] in the end." Despite Van Peebles's statement, the film is seen by many to be a one-sided, negative portrayal of both blacks and whites.

Critics find fault with Van Peebles for his amateurish directorial techniques and his lack of creativity in depicting characters and situations. However, Van Peebles has been praised for bringing realistic themes to his films. *Sweet Sweetback's Baadasssss Song* is certainly a revolutionary film in every sense, and Van Peebles's willingness to be direct and unrelenting has earned a cult following for his work. (See also *CLC*, Vol. 2, and *Contemporary Authors*, Vols. 85-88.)

## PENELOPE GILLIATT

I've tried hard to find something admirable or engaging about "The Story of a Three Day Pass," but I can't make it. I don't see why the fact that the film was directed by a Negro—Melvin Van Peebles—and was achieved in a bad, hard time should inhibit anyone from saying that it is a craven and unfelt picture. You could call it "unpretentious," but that would be a coverup, for the truth is that you pine for the film to be a little immodest and quit licking your boots. The story is very simple, and it could be fine. An American Negro soldier with three days' leave has an affair with a French girl—in France, tactfully—which ends in idly dealt-out perfidies and retaliations by the whites around him. If the film had mustered any natural effrontery about telling what happens, or any regard for its characters, that in itself would have been exhilarating, and the picture might have seemed true and grievous. The trouble is that the hero . . . has been given a fatally winsome and wet personality. He apologizes all the time for being a Negro. . . . [The] film wants to make its general point about the suspiciousness that whites have bred—though it doesn't possess the gumption to raise womanish moaning to the level of rage.

[The coyness of the girl] is enough to drive you up the wall. She stands bemused at the window in her nightdress, and looks throbbingly at things, and smells the air, and wishes that moments could last forever. But for all her enveloping wooziness she is also startlingly bigoted for a character who is supposed to be French. When her lover comes near her, she has an immediate fantasy of him as one of a band of cannibalistic savages in leopard skins. France has many right-wing problems, but this unfortunate hallucination is not one of them. The affair that the film depicts is very, very retarded, like some halcyon bunk-up between Christopher Robin and Winnie-the-Pooh. This is obviously because the picture is terrified that it is handling dynamite. If only it had hung on to the fact that it is supposedly handling people. . . . It's true that [the couple] are hampered by having no language in common, apart from entirely suitable kindergarten talk. She speaks to him in pidgin French and he speaks to her in pidgin West Indian English, and then each translates for the other, thus surreally supplying the other's instant subtitles and making the film marketable all over the place. I kept being reminded of the generally excruciating experience of watching ballet try to present a sexual narrative. The two depleted creatures here mime and swoon and posture, and seem like no human beings on earth. . . . Every frame and word of the picture expresses something affected and heedless of character. . . . [How] much better things would be if the movie could have found the courage to be grown-up. (p. 78)

> Penelope Gilliatt, "Telling It Like It Isn't," in The New Yorker (© 1968 by The New Yorker Magazine, Inc.), Vol. 64, No. 22, July 20, 1968, pp. 78-80.*

### HOLLIS ALPERT

If anyone wants proof of the total, blind, unmitigated insufferableness of the American film industry, merely reflect on the fact that not one feature film has ever been directed by a Negro. This came forcibly to my attention with *The Story of a Three Day Pass*, a *French* film directed by an American Negro, Melvin Van Peebles. And I wouldn't be making the comment now if I hadn't found the film so pleasantly and sincerely made, so filled with delightful touches of humor, and for a first effort, so surprisingly adept technically. . . . [It] is enriched by Van Peebles with insight and human detail.

It has some weak points, too; they come from a tendency to caricature and stereotype. The soldier's company commander is too patently a prejudiced idiot, and Van Peebles takes the opportunity to pillory a group of traveling Negro gospel-singing ladies who behave like a DAR bunch on a socially minded outing. Much, much better is his handling of [the hero]. . . . Just as good is . . . the Parisian who responds to the boy's need for a companion.

> Hollis Alpert, "The Van Peebles Story," in Saturday Review (copyright © 1968 by Saturday Review; all rights reserved; reprinted by permission), Vol. 51, No. 31, August 3, 1968, p. 35.

### STANLEY KAUFFMANN

*The Story of a Three Day Pass* is unredeemedly painful. . . . As Van Peebles is a Negro and as this may be the first fiction feature directed by a Negro, the event is a social milestone. It is nothing else. . . .

The story is triteness trying to be daring. . . . Its racial irony is muddy. . . .

Even this feeble script might have been given some appeal if Van Peebles had cinema imagination and an understanding of acting. He has neither. His attempts at lyric lift (in the love episodes) are lame, his attempts at cinema imagination (the soldier envisioning himself differently in a mirror, the girl seeing him as an African native) would be thought dubious in a first-year film student. . . .

If the film were an ambitious, gifted failure, there might at least be a case to be made for it on paper. But the racial comments are stale and childish, and the only quality that Van Peebles shows as filmmaker is his stamina in getting the film made at all. (p. 23)

> Stanley Kauffmann, "Hit and Myth" (reprinted by permission of Brandt & Brandt Literary Agents, Inc.; copyright © 1968 by Stanley Kauffmann), in The New Republic, Vol. 159, No. 6, August 10, 1968, pp. 14, 23.*

### CHARLES D. PEAVY

[Van Peebles's] short films, such as *Sunlight* and *Three Pickup Men for Herrick,* are rather mediocre productions. . . . [*Sunlight* illustrates] the tragedy of a black man who steals in an attempt to get enough money to marry the woman he loves. He is caught and imprisoned. Years later he is released from prison and returns in time to be the silent and unobserved witness at his daughter's wedding. The surprise ending and a rather nice score played by a group of San Francisco musicians do not offset the unexceptional photography and the wooden acting, although there are some notable shots achieved during the chase scene.

*Three Pickup Men for Herrick* is a well-conceived, if clumsily photographed, drama about the anxiety and suspense undergone by a group of men who stand at a 'pickup spot,' waiting for a white contractor to select some of them for a construction job. The opening scene, in which one of the workers walks to the 'pickup spot,' is almost interminable but there are a few good moments as the camera studies the face of the contractor as *he* studies the faces of the men, trying to determine by their expressions who would be best for the job, then shifts to the faces of the men as they strain to assume the attitudes they think are expected by the contractor. There is a genuine poignancy in the closing shot, which shows the two men who have not been selected walking away, hands in pockets, and looking strangely like baffled children. (p. 2)

The main concern of *Three Day Pass* is with attitudes toward miscegenation. For instance, every time the couple makes love each has his own private, racially-oriented fantasy. Turner imagines himself as a French *grand seigneur* of the eighteenth century, making love to his white chatelaine in a Provencal chateau, while Miriam imagines herself pursued by savage warriors in a jungle, who capture and threaten to ravish her. . . . The theme of *Three Day Pass* dates back to the sort of integrationist-assimilationist protest literature that is now eschewed by the adherents of the Black Arts Movement. . . . Perhaps this dated aspect of Van Peebles' film may be explained by the expatriate nature of his career, which would quite naturally separate him from the newest developments in American black nationalism. (p. 3)

> Charles D. Peavy, "An Afro-American in Paris: The Films of Melvin Van Peebles," in Cinéaste (copyright © 1969 by Gary Crowdus), Vol. III, No. 1, Summer, 1969, pp. 2-3.

### JOSEPH MORGENSTERN

"Watermelon Man" is an extension, right to the breaking point and then beyond, of that "Finian's Rainbow" gag about the bigoted Southern senator who magically turns black. . . . When things go badly, it's usually because director Melvin Van Peebles and writer Herman Raucher are horrendously clumsy craftsmen, and their failures are enough to make flesh of any color creep.

The script describes [the] predicament as one big off-color joke, which is accurate enough, and runs out of ideas as soon as the joke has been set forth. Unless, that is, your idea of an idea is extremely undemanding. . . . Early on, when [the hero] is chasing a yellow commuter bus to the accompaniment of silent-comedy music, the director seems to be setting a specific, parodic style. He also uses gospel music effectively in a shower-bath scene as [the hero] prays for divine enwhitenment. All too quickly, however, Van Peebles loses track of his initial impulses and his style becomes merely old-fashioned: Dagwood and Blondie Meet the Black Revolution.

Van Peebles is in a difficult spot as an inexperienced director who's been pressed into service by an industry that has suddenly decided, after decades of racism in its ranks, that it needs black directors. He can't sustain a sequence. Many of his shots don't match, and he's committed to a conventional technique in which they should. There's no way of knowing from this movie whether Van Peebles will grow, whether he'll get further chances to grow. . . .

Van Peebles goes back to the '30s as if he'd invented them for a symbolic montage in which [the hero] walks and walks and walks toward a bar in a black neighborhood and becomes blacker and more militant with each stride. That's the apparent point of the montage, at any rate. It's charmingly badly done, and if I sound condescending toward Van Peebles I guess I am.

> *Joseph Morgenstern, "Off-Color Joke," in* Newsweek *(copyright 1970, by Newsweek, Inc.; all rights reserved; reprinted by permission), Vol. LXXV, No. 21, May 25, 1970, p. 102.*

## JACOB BRACKMAN

There's a *white* suburban family in Columbia's **Watermelon Man**—. . . with a daddy, mommy, and spoiled, oblivious little girl and boy—and one morning the daddy, a bigoted insurance salesman, wakes up black. . . . Lots of funny stuff follows; a long elaboration on the joke of his newly acquired blackness. . . . **Watermelon Man** was directed by a black, and is therefore chock-full of classic grits-'n'-chitlins gags. All very breezy—set them up, punch them home.

Then, slowly, the comedy turns dark. For a bit, it seems the initial joke is simply being extended. . . . But then his wife leaves him, taking his kids. His boss encourages him to turn his talents for persuasion to exploiting poor blacks; a sort of underwriting for which he has no stomach. Finally, without home, family, friends, he hangs around sleazy black bars dreaming of his white life. In the final image, he's in a cellar training for street warfare with militant brothers. He rehearses the calisthenics of guerrilla combat—in African gown, and brandishing a spear—his face contorted in wounded rage. (pp. 68, 70)

[Beneath] the running gag of **Watermelon Man** lies the understanding that it's too awful to think about much—unless you're black, in which case you think about it the whole time. (p. 70)

> *Jacob Brackman, "Films: 'Watermelon Man'" (copyright © 1970, Esquire Publishing Inc.; used by courtesy of the magazine), in* Esquire, *Vol. 74, No. 4, October, 1970, pp. 68, 70.*

## ROGER GREENSPUN

I think that Melvin Van Peebles has the talent, the intelligence and even the instincts of a good filmmaker—despite a growing body of evidence to the contrary. The latest exhibit, **"Sweet Sweetback's Baadasssss Song,"** [is] Van Peebles's third and worst feature. . . .

[Ideas] have saved Van Peebles several times when weak performances or no money or merely deadheaded directing have gotten in the way of realization. But in this movie the failure

is so very nearly total that the ideas all turn into clichés and positively collaborate in taking things down. . . .

[The subject] is Sweetback's flight to the border, and his adventures during flight; and at one level of artiness or another, it is almost all predictable formula material.

The film is being presented as searing racial indictment—which may be a reasonable enterprise, but I don't think it is Van Peebles's enterprise, even when he tries to make it so. He is, from everything I have seen, better at exploring relations and sophistications than he is at proclaiming separations and simplicities—and his man on the lam, whatever he stands for, comes to look like nothing much more than an academic exercise in advanced cinematography, characterized by double exposure, multiple screen and minimal feeling. . . .

[The] moments which I really sense Van Peebles as a valuable presence are few and fleeting. But there are such moments . . . that show the director at work in the kind of moviemaking I hope he'll some day complete.

> *Roger Greenspun, "Van Peebles Returns in 'Sweet Sweetback',"" in* The New York Times *(© 1971 by The New York Times Company; reprinted by permission), April 24, 1971 (and reprinted in* The New York Times Film Reviews: 1971-1972, *The New York Times Company & Arno Press, 1973, p. 54).*

## CLAYTON RILEY

[The] Brother is in town with a flick called **"Sweet Sweetback's Baadasssss Song,"** and let me tell you: Van Peebles is absolutely *outside*. I mean, the cat is wonderfully crazy, you know. And Bearing Witness to his film is like staring at a Black key sliding through the cosmos, turning sturdy locks and letting out weird human figurines to scatter among us. Spilling psycho conversations in our ears. Through the lens of the Van Peebles camera comes a very basic Black America, unadorned by faith, and seething with an eternal violence.

It is a terrifying vision, the Blood's nightmare journey through Watts, and it is a vision Black people alone will really understand in all of its profane and abrasive substance.

The film is an outrage. Designed to blow minds. A disgraceful and blasphemous parade of brilliantly precise stereotypical Blacks and Whites, all drawn extravagantly and with impossible dimensions, all haunting our memory of what is true. . . .

Technically, the film dazzles, is a rough diamond glittering an inquisitive light upon a people and what is, in fact, their own business. Van Peebles employs the camera like a surgeon slicing away fat and other body tissues, always probing toward real or imagined diseases. Sealed into nearly every frame of **"Sweet Sweetback's Baadasssss Song"** is a desperate level of energy, a frenetic, often dizzying romp through a portion of the Republic, encountering or passing by its disgraceful streets, the crumbling houses in which live its pimps, whores, its witless members of the law enforcement world, its thieves and assassins who all, ultimately, are the Republic's victims.

Certainly the film is objectionable. Van Peebles can zoom in as smoothly, as gracefully, and as precisely on the Brothers who are into revolution as he can put a candid lens on Brothers who are into cocaine. And, seemingly, with the same intense concern. . . .

An immediate response to what Melvin Van Peebles has done could be seen at the screening of the film I attended. Shock.

Disgust. Towering rages everywhere. . . . And the outraged have a solid point, there is little positive Black imagery in **"Sweet Sweetback."** There is only the truth as Van Peebles has experienced it. But in spite of the absence of positive portraits, there are no inaccuracies, just exaggerations, larger-than-life scale models of Black folks caught in a life that should not—but *does* exist.

What consistently captures the attention here is the madness of Van Peebles as an artist, his existence in a private universe made public for a short time. Because to see his film . . . is to know the Brother possesses [a] kind of singular sense of purpose. . . .

Van Peebles utilizes [a] kind of functional insanity. With a nonprofessional cast, he charts a course through cinematic waters no one else has even put a toe in, makes visual revolutionaries of us all, lets us see a sector of ourselves we wish, perhaps, he had left alone. . . .

Van Peebles' gifts are plentiful and rich. Acting, unfortunately, is not one of these. . . . His direction of other actors, particularly the Whites in **"Sweet Sweetback,"** is incomplete; they are rendered poorly, become sketches instead of portraits and bring death on several of the more important scenes. (The police chief in action is pure cardboard, as are several other non-Black roles.) . . .

The survival of the Sweetbacks of the world, their ability to maintain their lives, is possibly America's most significant current event. All those welfare spooks are surviving, along with the Vietcong and so many other well-endowed outlaws.

> Clayton Riley, *"What Makes Sweetback Run?"* in The New York Times (© *1971 by The New York Times Company; reprinted by permission), May 9, 1971 (and reprinted in* The New York Times Film Reviews: 1971-1972, *The New York Times Company & Arno Press, 1973, p. 62).*

## PAUL D. ZIMMERMAN

Van Peebles dedicates [**"Sweet Sweetback's Baadasssss Song"**] "to all the brothers and sisters who've had enough of the Man" and, indeed, his story is a celebration of that moment when the black man breaks with society and struggles to survive. (p. 116)

There are flaws in Van Peebles's bleak vision. Bitterness has pushed him to paint all policemen as sadists, beating anyone black, carelessly killing suspects in their search for Sweetback, deliberately detonating their pistols next to the club owner's ears to deafen him. His attitude toward his hero is unsure. (Does he accept the stereotype of black man as sexual athlete or does he use it ironically?)

But his documentary style, despite its inclusion of arty split-screen effects, superimpositions and negative color, draws a harrowing portrait of black city life. Van Peebles creates an effective street collage of religious signs, voodoo storefronts, drab poolrooms, backyard garbage dumps and middle-aged black faces, their heavy eyes drained of hope and dulled with drink, their features worn by endless bouts with a dead-end world.

Van Peebles resists the temptation to preach except through the lyrics of his soul songs. . . .

Van Peebles's vision is unsparing. . . . [The] episode in the nightclub, as Sweetback, dressed in drag, makes love to a black woman amid the chuckling applause of a predominantly white audience, is one of the most effective metaphors of black degradation ever filmed. These moments represent personal cinema at its best—one man, telling it like he sees it, his dream of liberation unadulterated by studio pressures or commercial considerations. (p. 118)

> Paul D. Zimmerman, *"Stud on the Run," in* Newsweek *(copyright 1971, by Newsweek, Inc.; all rights reserved; reprinted by permission), Vol. 72, No. 19, May 10, 1971, pp. 116, 118.*

## PENELOPE GILLIATT

Alas! I mean, hurrah! there exists a furiously tasteless picture called **"Sweet Sweetback's Baadasssss Song."** It was made by a black man for blacks, and it is turning into a phenomenon of the industry. . . . **"Sweetback"** is a terrific fable. It is also a boot in the face for the wishes of moderates, black and white, who are likely to come away reeling. . . .

**"Sweetback"** is presumably the first of a line of films. The next ones will get gentler, with luck, and better characterized, and signed with a clearer authorship than this, but they can never be anything like "Guess Who's Coming to Dinner," or lose the tongue they have found here, which is a shock in the cinema. It is a language of energy, stamina, cheek, fury, blue jokes, clan loyalty, swagger, and a murderous skepticism. The film's whole style of overstatement is grating, and is meant to be. The film wasn't made for the approval of aesthetes. . . . **"Sweetback"** is bent on going too far. That is the film's great sense of the popular, maybe. . . .

[This] film holds out the image of a black frontier hero who survives every wound from whites and police, who holds enthralled any girl he wants, who makes peeping white cops nervous because a white woman wants him at an orgy, and who has more humor and self-command than anyone else around. The white authority figures in this film are a crumbling lot, amateurishly played, by a trick of casting that is certainly on purpose. The fable is a dream of weak cops and of power-driven white sensualists who have travelled beyond enjoyment. The blacks are funny, rude, unforgivable, with mouths forever closed against the other side, and equipped with blond wigs and drag wedding dresses that allow them to suggest a sarcastic hint of changing race or sex for the pleasure of a teased, yearning nobility. . . . [**"Sweetback"**] is fiercely on the side of a minority, and it takes the shape of a fable. The film sets a tone that is bound to be followed and that will later, to judge by the past, grow fonder of its characters. This angry start is impossible, haughty, not likable, but sometimes rather admirable in its context. (p. 68)

> Penelope Gilliatt, *"Sweetback," in* The New Yorker (© *1971 by The New Yorker Magazine, Inc.), Vol. 67, No. 18, June 19, 1971, pp. 68-9.\**

## JAMES MONACO

*Watermelon Man* was based on a gimmick: a bigoted white insurance salesman wakes up one morning to discover he's turned Black. Van Peebles's direction was lackluster. The film is by turns dull and annoying. One has the sense that . . . [Van Peebles was not] particularly happy bringing this fantasy to life. But as a "career move," *Watermelon Man* was smart. (p. 200)

*Sweet Sweetback* is not an easy film to admire: it's violent, even sadistic, obscene, frenzied, painful. Critics who disliked the film condemned it for trading on a classic Black stereotype, the buck. On the surface, the film has all the most extreme elements of the most cynical Blaxploitation ripoffs. But Van Peebles, I think, is using these elements, commenting upon them.

The images of the film fall quite neatly into three classic categories, elemental actions that triangulate (and strangulate) ghetto life in the U.S.:

● People run. ("Keep this Nigger boy running," said the note in *Invisible Man.*)

● People stomp and kick and shoot and cut.

● People fuck. (They don't "make love," they don't "have sex." This is pure badass fucking.)

The narrative is linear, and boring as such. Sweetback . . . , who works in a brothel when the film begins, is finally moved to action, stomps a couple of cops unconscious, then begins running. He runs for the rest of the film. The movie reaches a high pitch almost before the credits begin and it stays there until shortly before the end. Even the gut-wrenching violence becomes boring; it is a commonplace of the world the film delineates.

The pain with which Van Peebles washes the screen is meant to be transmuted into anger by audiences, and then into political action. The film is dedicated to "All the Brothers and Sisters who have had enough of The Man." Does it succeed in this militant aim? Does any film? At the end, as Sweetback finally escapes to Mexico, leaving the carcasses of the hounds sent to rip him to shreds floating bloodily in the Rio Grande, we cheer, we are relieved. Then a set of titles appears on the screen:

*"Watch Out. A Baadasssss Nigger is coming back to collect some dues."* But it's hard to believe. Sweetback's unitary drama is so existentially rooted that it is difficult to see how his anger can work politically.

It probably can't. (Historically, it didn't.) But the film succeeds as a *cri de coeur,* an announcement that Black militancy has reached your neighborhood movie screen and that things will never be the same. Sweetback himself is a role model, one of the first. Sweetback teaches the lesson of survival. We might ask that he be more intellectually analytical. (pp. 200-01)

*Sweetback* is a morality tale of sorts: an image to be examined and discussed. Such a hymn of pain had no antecedents in Black film when Van Peebles made *Sweet Sweetback,* but it certainly could look to forerunners in the novel, most notably [Richard Wright's] *Native Son* and [Ralph Ellison's] *Invisible Man.* Like Ellison's ephemeral hero, Sweetback embarks upon an odyssey of terror and confusion, consciously learning the lessons intuited in childhood. It leads him underground—literally—into the sewers which were the refuge for Invisible Man. In theme, Sweetback is even closer to *Native Son.* The film clangs with anger and rage. . . .

*Sweet Sweetback's Baadasssss Song* thus situates itself squarely in a long and important tradition in Black American narrative art. The Sweetback character has been mimicked and repeated a number of times since, but never with such purity of purpose and such élan. Van Peebles bent the medium of film to his will. No one else has bent it so far or so well since. (p. 202)

*James Monaco, "The Black Film (and the Black Image)," in his* American Film Now: The People, the Power, the Money, the Movies *(copyright © 1979 James Monaco; reprinted by arrangement with The New American Library, Inc., New York), Oxford University Press, New York, 1979, pp. 185-214.**

# Andy Warhol

## 1928-

American director, artist, and author.

Warhol's controversial work stems from his conviction that he is empty and what he creates is meaningless. Critics seem to interpret his films for him, since they lack any composition or traditional qualities of beauty. His films appear to be mass-produced; Warhol's studio is, in fact, named the Factory because of its high production rate. While his early films were silent, overly long, and inert, later works included characters and minor activity. These films featured Warhol's "super-stars": a group of minimally-talented people instructed only to "act normally." Warhol felt the presence of these "stars" far outshone their performances, that people are more interesting than stories. Though many find him a forerunner of minimalist cinematic expression and graphic screen sexuality, Warhol sees the camera only as a recorder of reality, not as an artistic tool.

Warhol studied art at Carnegie Institute of Technology, then worked as a commercial designer in New York. Warhol's early work popularized the reproduction of everyday objects, reflecting his preference for recreation over creation. In 1964, Warhol began making films because "Movies are easier to do than pictures. All you have to do is turn on the camera." Early films such as *Sleep* and *Empire* survey a motionless object for an extended period. Warhol stated that he "wanted the Empire State Building to be a star."

The films of 1964-65, such as *My Hustler* and *Vinyl*, further demonstrate Warhol's belief that everyone is a star. Consequently the quality of the film mattered little. Warhol, in fact, has often incorporated purposely anticinematic techniques, allowing the camera to wander and refusing to edit the film. Warhol also allows his team to collaborate as much or as little as they wish. Regardless of a film's critical reception, Warhol takes little credit for the finished result.

Warhol had his first commercial hit with *Chelsea Girls*. Many critics find its disjointed structure and disdain for cinematic technique an overbearing put-on. Devotees of underground movies, however, have applauded Warhol's use of twin screens as well as both black and white and color film. Warhol attributed this twin usage to the fact that he "finally had enough money for color film."

*Lonesome Cowboys* involves more plot and was shot on location. While action is more extensive in this film, characters are no deeper than before. *Blue Movie* follows a couple around an apartment and plays the passive observer as they talk, make love, shower, and eat. Warhol feels his greatest contribution to cinema has been in the area of sexual permissiveness on screen; since *Blue Movie* is a film of a real rather than enacted encounters, its documentary-like depiction of sex is noteworthy.

In 1968, a member of Warhol's Factory attempted to murder him. Though he survived, his creative output lessened, and successive films have been credited solely to his collaborator, Paul Morrissey. Warhol is the embodiment of his "nothing" philosophy. While others find artistic merit in his work, Warhol terms it "turning on a camera and letting people talk." When asked what the purpose of his films is, Warhol replied, "To take up time." (See also *Contemporary Authors*, Vols. 89-92.)

## HENRY GELDZAHLER

Andy Warhol's films conceal their art exactly as his paintings do. The apparently sloppy and unedited is fascinating. What holds his work together in both media is the absolute control Andy Warhol has over his own sensibility—a sensibility as sweet and tough, as childish and commercial, as innocent and chic, as anything in our culture. Andy Warhol's eight hour *Sleep* movie must be infuriating to the impatient or the nervous or to those so busy they cannot allow the eye and the mind to adjust to a quieter, flowing sense of time. What appears boring is the elimination of incident, accident, story, sound and the moving camera. . . . The slightest variation becomes an event, something on which we can focus our attention. As less and less happens on the screen, we become satisfied with almost nothing and find the slightest shift in the body of the sleeper or the least movement of the camera interesting enough. The movie is not so much about sleep as it is about our capacity to see possibilities of an aspect of film carried to its logical conclusion *reductio ad absurdum* to some, indicating a new awareness to others. Andy Warhol wants to keep his editing to an absolute minimum and allow the camera and the subject to do the work. This of course cannot deny the special qualities of his personality; for it is Andy Warhol that holds the camera and it is through his eyes that we see the scene. . . . Andy Warhol's film, in which we are constantly aware of the filmic process, sometimes even seeing the frames that end the reels, frames that any sophisticated movie maker would edit out, makes us aware of exactly the limitations and qualities of film itself. A more incident-filled story would draw our attention from the fact that we are seeing a film. *Sleep,* one of Andy Warhol's first movies, is an indication of what he will soon be able to do: make content-less movies that are exactly filmed still-lifes with the minimum of motion necessary to retain the interested attention of the unprejudiced viewer.

> *Henry Geldzahler, "Some Notes on 'Sleep'," in* Film Culture *(copyright 1964 by* Film Culture), *No. 32, Spring, 1964, p. 13.*

## JONAS MEKAS

[The work of Andy Warhol] is the last word in the Direct Cinema. It is hard to imagine anything more pure, less staged, and less directed than Andy Warhol's **"Eat," "Empire," "Sleep," "Haircut,"** movies. I think that Andy Warhol is the most revolutionary of all film-makers working today. He is opening to film-makers a completely new and inexhaustible field of cinema reality. It is not a prediction but a certainty that soon we are going to see dozens of **"Eat," "Haircut,"** or **"Street"** movies done by different film-makers and there will be good and bad and mediocre **"Eat"** movies, and very good **"Eat"** movies, and someone will make a masterpiece **"Eat"** movie. What to some still looks an actionless nonsense, with the shift of our consciousness which is taking place will become an endless variety and an endless excitement of seeing similar subjects or the same subject done differently by different artists. Instead of asking for Elephant Size Excitement we'll be able to find aesthetic enjoyment in the subtle play of nuances.

There is something religious about this. . . . There is something very humble and happy about a man (or a movie) who is content with eating an apple. It is a cinema that reveals the emergence of meditation and happiness in man. Eat your apple, enjoy your apple, it says. Where are you running, away from yourself, to what excitement? If all people could sit and watch the Empire State Building for eight hours and meditate upon it, there would be no more wars, no hate, no terror—there would be a happiness regained upon earth.

> *Jonas Mekas, "Movie Journal" (reprinted by permission of* The Village Voice *and the author; copyright © The Village Voice, Inc., 1964), in* The Village Voice, *Vol. IX, No. 43, August 13, 1964, p. 13.*

## GREGORY BATTCOCK

The presentation of the material in *Blow Job* is, once again, "anthological"—a mirror image, so to speak, which presents demands on our attention that are entirely without regard for that image's relation to the dialectic of the story. One of these demands arises through the use of the actor. . . .

The lengthy (35 minute) blow job is accented by the paucity of expression demonstrated by the beautifully inept actor. Like the protagonist of other Warhol films, he is left to his own devices and since he is obviously either incapable of or uninterested in coping with the situation he finds himself in a fairly ludicrous position. In this sense the actor becomes an element or tool used in such a way never before considered in the film. This is another example of Warhol's formidable ability to extend and redefine reality—a preoccupation intrinsic to art. (p. 20)

Sex isn't plainly illustrated. Neither are sexual parts, acts or movements. Except for a bit of leather jacket which occasionally appears on the screen, the actor is as without identity as is the act. It is neither a homosexual nor heterosexual incident but rather personal, human and catholic. . . .

The length of the film—of the blow job—is exaggerated probably to clarify the artist's dedication to the time element, as time is possibly the one most important element distinguishing the film medium from the other fine arts. And, if in most films, events are telescoped so that lengthy acts often appear much shorter on the screen, in a Warhol film they often appear longer, in their transition from actuality to the reality of the medium. . . .

If the medium and message are to be considered as one, the films of Andy Warhol are the best illustration of the concept popularized by Marshall McLuhan that the medium is the message. The deliberate recognition of the message = medium idea may partially explain why it is hardly necessary to see a Warhol film. There is little to see that can't be adequately described. (p. 21)

> *Gregory Battcock, "Notes on 'Blow Job': A Film by Andy Warhol," in* Film Culture *(copyright 1965 by* Film Culture), *No. 37, Summer, 1965, pp. 20-1.*

## GREGORY BATTCOCK

*Screen Test* is a transitional work both in technique and content. . . . Yet the "still image" device is still retained in *Screen Test.* (By "still image" I refer to Warhol's technique of reducing the action on the screen to small variations of posture on the part of the single image—variations that are further limited by Warhol's refusal to move the camera.) (p. 62)

The burden of the film rests squarely on the audience. The audience, never catered to, is abused, exposed and ridiculed. It is, at the same time, very much considered. The film represents certainly an extension of the new realism to such a degree that complacency which indeed goes hand in hand with much which is supposed to be avant-garde is notably absent. . . . If *Sleep* or *Empire* were films to turn on to, *Screen Test* is actively interesting because the viewer is forced into an immediate and not altogether unfamiliar involvement. (pp. 62-3)

In presenting these disturbing challenges to the nature of the medium, Warhol hinders understanding and sympathy by his choice of vehicle. However, sexual dualism represented on the screen can be taken as further proof of Warhol's intent to unmask the sexual fraud of the contemporary cinema. . . .

The films of Warhol represent a coherent series of attacks on the restrictions and hypocracies of the media. *Sleep* makes use of the reduction concept: *Couch* and *Henry Geldzahler* play with suspense and anticipation: *Blowjob* an essay in humanism: *Screen Test* deals with the actor and the audience: *Horse* the sadomasochism underlying the good guy versus bad guy facade of the Western: and *The Life Of Juanita Castro* representing in its scope and pattern, the epic.

In this procession of films, there is no pause for reflection and little self-indulgent repetition. If, by now, the earlier works are of the classical avantgarde, the newer ones continue to present the challenge, uncertainty and polemic which is art. (p. 63)

*Gregory Battcock, "Notes on 'Screen Test': A Film by Andy Warhol," in* Film Culture *(copyright 1965 by Film Culture), No. 38, Fall, 1965, pp. 62-3.*

## PARKER TYLER

A part of Warhol's negotiable charm as a modern entertainer is his work as applied art-naiveté. There is something both perverse and violent about pasting the camera eye on a limited field of vision, with limited action inside it, and asking the spectator to paste his eye over that, and just wait. The ensuing charm, I should say, is more than a trifle masochistic. But take the contrary view. A high pulse exists in the modern temper (I mean everybody's temper) for elective affinity with occupations that dissociate themselves from the ugly spectacle of war, and lesser lethal agents, as forms of cutthroat competition. The very peacefulness of just watching a man eat a mushroom (even though, as if on purpose, he takes forty-five minutes to bite, masticate, and swallow it all) has its exclusive charm: an exclusive charm that makes it easy for the watcher to feel both chic and restful. The idea of peace, I mean, is directly related to the ultra-passivity of the pre-conditioned, relaxing filmgoer. (p. 29)

The living organic world we see in *Sleep, Eat, Haircut,* and *Kiss* has a visually implosive force whose burden we must bear or else heave off. Warhol's point is exactly that what we see should reveal nothing new in proportion to the quantity of time required to watch it; indeed, his object might be to portray a deliberate "vicious circle": a closed process with no progress whatever, only an "endless" self-engrossment.

Inevitably, all mental interest and visual attention are governed by an economy that establishes a self-sustaining rhythm. . . .

The later Warhol films suggest that he divined in the physical accumulation of screen time a potential hypnotic effect on watchers which nothing else but drugs could guarantee. I think that his primitive films can be called experiments in dragtime which logically predicated an innoculation of the unwinding reel with drugtime. (p. 30)

For all that suspense or expectation is involved, *Haircut* or *Eat* might be totally outside time in a vacuum like that of far space. When, for example, we are asked by *Empire* to watch a famous landmark ("the world's tallest") standing quite motionless, with the camera equally unmoving, while the sun is allowed to take all of eight hours to go down and come up, we are being asked to submit ourselves to an endurance test; that is, to the opposite of an entertainment form . . . unless (which is, I think, the point) it should occur to us that this quantitative time, spreading out its minutes in a morgue, is merely the abstract proposition for a much more entertaining, specifically psychedelic, time. The latter provides a dramatically decisive change not in the object, but in the one viewing it. *Drugtime is the other pole of dragtime.* . . .

Narcotizing is very close to Narcissizing. The only distinction is that with drugs, the gazer's own image is not the object of fascination; rather it is the image of the world transmuted by a chemical change in the gazer's perceptive faculties. . . . Warhol's *Vinyl,* his first film with "progressive" social action, came along as a documentation of people in the mixed throes of narcotizing and narcissizing; also for the first time, there were credits for the title, the idea-man and the leads; otherwise, as usual, the film was titleless. . . . We are witnessing a snail-paced fantasy in which familiar homosexual sadism, enhanced

by drugtime, is putting on some kind of an act. Warhol still holds up a still, small mirror to nature, but now nature, by all the signs, is narcotized narcissism. (p. 87)

At best, *The Chelsea Girls* provides some scenes that, properly trimmed, would look like respectable *Cinema Verite.* But that is the limit of Warhol's homage to the film art, with the sole exception of a color sequence where his sliding Velvet Underground lights project the interior of an addict's trance. This sequence has quality but within the context of *The Chelsea Girls* it is only another form of Olympian self-documentation. . . .

Warhol's invasion of hallucination as promoted by drugs poses a procedural dilemma for his future film making. The formal restrictions super-exploited by his primitive style (the dragtime) imply an almost puritanical detachment from life: reality's fabulous deadpan dream. Now he has chosen to grapple with that peculiar collective secession from normally rational society that implements drugs to achieve its isolation. . . .

[The] primitive Warhol films might function as dialectic antitheses, demonstrating how what is excruciatingly tiresome and commonplace cries out for the right conversion-formula in the witness—not the intermediate witness, the camera, but the final witness, the audience. Warhol may have moved in some mysterious way his wonders to perform—those wonders so filmic and yet not filmic! (p. 88)

*Parker Tyler, "Dragtime and Drugtime: Or, Film à la Warhol" (copyright © 1967, by Evergreen Review, Inc.; reprinted by permission of the Estate of the author), in* Evergreen Review, *Vol. 11, No. 46, April, 1967, pp. 28-31, 87-8.*

## JAY WILSON

**"The Chelsea Girls,"** Warhol's most ambitious film to date, has been labeled "an odyssey of the new generation", "a voyage to the Hell of drop-outs and junkies". The theme, it would seem, is the searching trip; the chief symbol, that old haunt of artists, the Chelsea Hotel. . . . The agglomeration of scenes, in forty-five minute spurts projected two at a time on a split screen, hardly suggests any unified theme—of consecutive movement, ideas, or even locale. . . . You are faced not with obscurity but a more mysterious effect—mundane clarity. You expect the artistic film to speak a figurative language when its language is in fact simply literal.

The literal in **"The Chelsea Girls"** happens to be highly contrived. What the males and females say and do happens, for the most part, to be interesting. Several speakers in the accumulated reels begin their monologues: "What should I say?" This is less a ploy of amateur acting than actual self-consciousness, and Warhol has what seems to be remarkable good luck in recording a variety of awkward but fascinating poses. . . .

Andy Warhol's camera observes. Once selected, his subjects move and sometimes speak before the observing camera, but they never essentially change. This is not to say that the subjects are viewed as insects, pinned down by a cold eye, and finally squashed by a blackout. They are provoked, if only by being observed, to express some image of themselves; and in so doing they reveal both a pose and something of its antecedent. With utter candor they admit the put-on. Yet in all of Warhol's films I have seen, people remain subjects. . . . These people share a literalness of being, the quality we noticed in its primitive form in the Campbell's soup can, upon which Warhol conferred artistic immortality, thereby acquiring the reputation of crank. To study a person or an object for its literalness is acutely honest. Why then in these films does it seem a fraud?

We are accustomed to search for moral content in art. Rightly so, if we include the progressive revelation of truth as a moral objective of art. . . . All things call out their being to us. This is the truth to which art directs us and which, in the process of time, is gradually revealed by art. This view of art, it seems to me, provides an idiom congenial to the films of Warhol, films which, as things, strike most spectators as too crude to be art, too static to be life. (p. 6)

One major problem is that this film so relentlessly satirizes the audience. The film says: Did you come for pornography? Then you will be teased and finally bored. Did you come for photography? Then you will probably leave with a headache. Did you come for psychology? Then you will get contradictions, maybe utter incoherence. I have not seen that Andy Warhol has ever made any promises about his films, he has never ridden on any new wave. But don't we sometimes admire, even love, the person who we feel is making no effort at all to please us? . . .

Warhol's subjects, suddenly in front of the camera, simply endure its scrutiny as best they can. Often, understandably, the result is discomfiting for both subject and spectator. By the mere fact of duration Warhol's world becomes mundane. . . .

Yet **"The Chelsea Girls"**, like the rest of the Warhol films, is finally oppressive. No amount of interpretation, nor even the plentiful humor of the dialogues, can dispel the dry taste of its literalness. The whole movement of underground films now surfacing seems to be groaning under the onus of carrying a message without flagrantly moralizing. The flood of home-made *films poétiques* has by no means reached its crest. But the wave of Warhol's films contributes nothing to it. His films achieve exceptional mediocrity by exhibiting certain unvarnished truths which can neither purge nor please. Good art cannot long remain merely chic. Warhol's art evokes what James called "the ache of the actual", the sensation that being itself can be stripped down no farther than a literal pose. (p. 7)

*Jay Wilson, "Andy Warhol Literally," in* The Yale Literary Magazine *(copyright © by the Yale Literary Society 1967; reprinted by permission of* The Yale Literary Magazine*), Vol. CXXXV, No. 5, May, 1967, pp. 6-7.*

## HOWARD THOMPSON

[In this month's Andy Warhol picture, a stringy-haired blonde drawls,] "Are you as bored as I am?" Baby, we were stultified.

Undaunted devotees of underground cinema shouldn't be disappointed in "****" That's what it is called—or, rather Mr. Warhol, whose films have long since risen above, or beyond, mere title credits, calls it. Maybe it's just as well. . . .

The question, as with any Warhol film is why?

Mr. Warhol has superimposed three images on the screen, along with several soundtracks. Whether talking to themselves, one another or the camera, or wallowing around in frenzied deshabille or blinking in heavy-lidded stupor, they're truly a sight, for those who can take them, or [even] hear them. The subjects range from sex to hitchhiking to sex to Elsa Maxwell

to sex to Ronald Reagan to sex, while the soundtrack beep-beeps and moans with a kind of stringy, electronic music. It ends up on the seashore with a cavorting round-up of mangy looking beach sprites. . . .

Three-on-one imagery—and what images—may be revolutionary for Mr. Warhol, but it comes to nothing more than the tried and true process of montage, as old and familiar as the hills.

*Howard Thompson, "'****'," in* The New York Times *(© 1967 by The New York Times Company; reprinted by permission), December 17, 1967 (and reprinted in* The New York Times Film Reviews: 1959-1968, *The New York Times Company & Arno Press, 1970, p. 3719).*

## ANDREW M. LUGG

[Warhol's] early "epic" films are similar in many respects to the paintings. There is not much difference between a man sleeping—*Sleep* (1964) and a corpse. Neither even requires much manipulation to translate it into an artifact. In *Sleep*, which is more of a record than anything else, the "cinema" element is almost irrelevant. It simply provides an environment for the event.

*Empire* came shortly after *Sleep*. Differing from the earlier film, it is not completely descriptive. The daytime sequence is hurried along, compressed, to give the main focus of the record, the coming of night, more emphasis. Here, Warhol shows that he is willing to interfere with the natural order of things. Whereas in the paintings he seemingly strived to present the total event, in *Empire* he selected, albeit "marginally", parts of the event for display. This interference might be dismissed as trivial if it were not for the earlier work. *Empire* points to future developments. During the switch, [from painting to film-making], two new elements crop up in Warhol's work. Instead of beginning with the ikon, the well-known, and proceeding to the ordinary, he started with the unknown and built this into an ikon, a symbol, which later may be identified with the notion of a "superstar." That is, he no longer showed how a single possibility produces many alternatives, but how, starting from a many-faceted situation, a single "point" event can be refined. (pp. 12-13)

Second, and this is not unrelated to the first point, Warhol makes us aware of his own point of view. You do not have to know much about film-making to know exactly where the camera was placed.

What do these two elements signify? If editing is defined as the cutting away of parts of the whole, then Warhol was no longer an editor; he had become an assembler. Perhaps this is the fundamental difference between sub-division and gathering. . . .

In *The Life of Juanita Castro* (1965), Warhol shows us a "family portrait" of the Castro family. As usual in Warhol's films of this "era", the camera is stationary throughout the full 70 minutes and the actors perform within this portrait space. A few months later, *Vinyl* was made, but this time the camera is moved considerably between the two reels. Now, it would not be true to say that this film marks the point at which Warhol starts to move around. Even before *The Life of Juanita Castro*, he had finished *Camp*, a film resplendent with bad camera work. Nevertheless, *Vinyl* is the first indication that his "portraits" are to become more mobile; that direct representation will give away to a "theatre" with a variable point of view; that artificially imposed by the milieu, by the actors. Instead of staying on the outside, Warhol attempts to take the outside and put it on the inside or to take the inside and put it on the outside.

*Sleep* and *Empire* are films made with one eye shut. In this respect, they are like the **"110 Coca Cola Bottles."** Since [then], his development has been in terms of moving nearer (*My Hustler*—the zoom), moving across (*The Chelsea Girls*—the pan), moving around (*Bike Boy*—editing). **\*\*\*\*** is the work of a mobile film-maker, with both eyes open. Gradually, a complex cinematic rhetoric is being put together. Each film relates to the previous one, yet each film extends the previously laid down vocabulary.

As for the switch: it is the product of a peculiar sensibility. Frustrated by editing, Warhol made the choice to construct "mystery" from surfaces rather than to pare away the mystery to reveal the surface. But, in spite of all this, a concern for the things themselves and for an objective representation of these, untouched by personal fancy, still remains. (p. 13)

> *Andrew M. Lugg, "On Andy Warhol," in* Cinéaste *(copyright © 1968 by Gary Crowdus), Vol. I, No. 3, Winter, 1967-68, pp. 9-13.*

### PAMELA CRAWFORD

More than a randomly artistic, at times unconsciously brilliant and beautiful exposé of perversion and display of underground pop, hip and drug culture, Andy Warhol's *Chelsea Girls* is a violent reflection of 'our times', a roundabout comment on middle class society. Rather than a documentary on the times, it is a document of the times, hence, more real; the film had little or no inherent thoughtfulness, but it is thought-provoking, thus, of more critical value than a traditionally formulated statement. . . .

The continuous thread woven through Warhol's erratic and crude embroidery is the same as Ingmar Bergman's: suffering and guilt. . . .

*Chelsea Girls* has been deemed 'anti-film' and 'unartistic', without 'form' and 'dramatic content.' Quite the contrary. Not only does Warhol conform to two of [John] Grierson's rules for good documentary:

> (1) It must master its material *on the spot* and come in intimacy to ordering it.

> (2) It must follow Flaherty in his distinction between description and drama. (You photograph the *natural* but by juxtaposition of detail create an interpretation of it).

. . . but he is also an innovator in a newly-innovated movement —Camp. . . . (p. 20)

Firstly, Warhol masters his material and comes to intimacy with it by maintaining a congruity between his 'tools' and 'materials.' His nauseous, drugged, hysterical and lax technique is not out of text with his subject matter. . . .

Since Camp stresses form to the exclusion of content, Warhol created the form and conflict (dramatic content) of a male and female homosexual duel for attention, thereby relieving the need for any sort of plot or gesture from the artist. . . .

Some more concrete examples of dramatic content: the fag tirade of the Pope against the married chick obviously held the attention and caused reactions in the audience with whom I saw the film, as did the masochistic dyke scenes . . . the violent episodes. It seemed that the bawdier and more physical the action was, the more the audience stirred, was impressed. This is telling of two things: (a) that Shakespeare's 'groundling', who we all study and snigger condescendingly at, is not so far removed from us, and (b) the total spontaneity of the improvisations was effective. That is, one forgot momentarily the social and moral stigmas of the 'actors' . . . they became more universal in the sheer exhibition and display of their passions, perverted or not. . . .

One of the most impressive and ironic elements of the film was the great beauty of some of the characters and individual shots. Some unintentional movements of the camera often produced quite artistic compositions and patterns on the screen, especially those in color. The theme of finding beauty in randomly exposing and touching reality to media, or splattering media helter-skelter is indicative of abstract expressionism. . . .

If nothing else, we must laud Warhol for perpetuating the traditional American phenomenon: the successful rebel. He has the guts (if not the aplomb of a public spectacle) to disagree with and deviate from conventions, thumb his nose at and cajole the masses and elite minorities in the New York and American art 'scene', and make a minor fortune, establish a major infamy, doing it. (p. 21)

> *Pamela Crawford, "Andy Warhol's 'Chelsea Girls'," in* Cinéaste *(copyright © 1968 by Gary Crowdus), Vol. I, No. 3, Winter, 1967-68, pp. 20-1.*

### ERNEST CALLENBACH

Watching *The Chelsea Girls* is like listening in on a very long phone conversation. It's mildly titillating—you keep wondering whether something isn't bound to happen, and when you're ready to give up, the scene and characters change so you begin wondering all over again. It's also dubious—as if the people talking know you're listening, and are thus putting on a somewhat special show for your benefit. The movie exploits the voyeuristic element inherent in all cinema, and like Warhol's *Sleep* and *Empire* it is probably a healthy slap in the face with the dead herring of photographic "realism"; but it shrinks from going the whole way into a genuinely candid, totally eavesdropping form—the ultimate documentary solution toward which we seem to be lurching. Several of the characters, despite their incessant role-playing, are interesting, and you wish Warhol had taken the trouble (or had the talent?) to show them in depth—which we know is possible, since many *cinéma-vérité* films have done it with less outré people. But the best place to see *The Chelsea Girls* would really be on your TV set (if Warhol's friends were only permitted on the family medium) so you could talk, smoke, drink, doze, shoot, or whatever, and take them at their own pace. Warhol has kindly provided a second screen image, to which you can let your attention wander when the main image gets too lackadaisical, but even that cool gesture isn't enough to chill the medium below tepid.

> *Ernest Callenbach, "Short Notices: 'The Chelsea Girls'," in* Film Quarterly *(copyright 1968 by The Regents of the University of California; reprinted by*

*permission of the University of California Press),
Vol. XXI, No. 2, Winter, 1967-68, p. 60.*

## BRENDAN GILL

The speed and ease of [Warhol's] movie-making are based on the theory that nothing that an artist produces in the course of his work can fairly be called a mistake; everything he has done being of value *because* he has done it, all accidents are equally benign, and to have second thoughts about them, much less to consider "correcting" them, would be not only a waste of talent, time, and money but also a rude betrayal of the original inspiration. This appealingly circular theory has permitted Warhol to accumulate a very large number of movies in a very brief period of time; I have seen some of most of them and most of some of them, if not all of any of them, and I find that they run together in memory without boundaries—a vast human comedy that, in its serene mindlessness, resembles a mountain of sludge oozing slowly, relentlessly forth over the face of the earth and threatening to immortalize us all and engulf us all.

It is a comedy not to be judged by ordinary standards, since on Warhol's terms to be boring is every bit as interesting as to be interesting, and I perceive that I run the risk of seeming to praise Warhol when I say that I find his latest sampling of news from nowhere—a movie entitled "****" in apparent homage to the *News'* well-known system of rating movies— much less entertaining than its immediate predecessor, **"The Nude Restaurant."**. . . The characters in "****" are conventionally indistinguishable natives of the unconventional Warhol country; they sing and take drugs and make love and dance on the beach and sleep and eat and scratch and talk and talk and *talk,* and are as nearly all of one scruffy, tiresome family as so many Forsytes. At its opening, "****" is reported to have run for twenty-five hours; it has since been cut to two hours, and it is no doubt a triumphant vindication of Warhol's principles that the cutting away of over ninety per cent of his movie is undetectable.

*Brendan Gill, "The Accumulator," in* The New Yorker *(© 1968 by The New Yorker Magazine, Inc.), Vol. XLIII, No. 46, January 6, 1968, p. 74.**

## CLAIRE CLOUZOT

What is enjoyable in Warhol, as usual, is the mixture of humor (conscious or unconscious?) and perversion. Hence the best moments [in *I, A Man*] are the staircase misunderstanding between Baker and a Mao-capped girl who resists his pressing advances, the close-ups of four feet playing with each other under a bed where Baker and girl two are trying out new amorous techniques, or the scene where Baker weighs the breasts of a girl as if they were apples. Because of the number of seduction scenes one man performs with changing female partners, the female species is reduced to an object to be moulded without conviction. Warhol achieves the negation of femininity through the epidermic game of ambivalence—in which he is unbeatable. The final session of the film between a rather unattractive guilt-ridden married woman and the obsessive Baker is an unexpected study of the psychology of a frustrated women which goes a bit deeper than the rest of the film. . . .

Technically, *I, A Man* is Warhol's best film to date with an almost consistently focused photography and an interesting attempt at doing the editing inside the camera. (p. 59)

*Claire Clouzot, "Short Notices: 'I, a Man'," in* Film Quarterly *(copyright 1968 by The Regents of the University of California; reprinted by permission of the University of California Press), Vol. XXI, No. 4, Summer, 1968, p. 59.*

## DAVID DENBY

The dramatic action of [*Viva and Louis,* also known as ***Blue Movie*** and ***Fuck***] consists of the two characters struggling to find enough to say and do to fill up the time it takes for the film to pass through the camera. (p. 42)

Several shots have been lyrically "composed" in silhouette, and something approaching a rhythm, or at least a punctuation, has been established by alternating long static takes in the classic manner and machine-gun clusters of frames. . . . The scene in which Viva and Louis screw (from start to finish) has been deliberately overexposed, and the unfiltered daylight floods in on the sheets, the air, and the interlocked bodies, changing them all into a heavenly pale blue—copulating cherubs, lit by Hallmark cards. (pp. 42-3)

Warhol has produced a scene of sexual intercourse that is [totally] cold. . . . Of course love or feeling of any kind is Warhol's greatest enemy, and by no stretch of anyone's imagination could Louis and Viva's making it together be called the result of passion. (How could Warhol's people experience "passion"? They do maintain a certain disinterested tenderness for each other, though.) It's plain old screwing, and a pretty lowkey performance all around. Norman Mailer has expressed his uneasiness about actors actually fornicating on camera, on the grounds that such deep personal engagement, dedicated to creating art, would tend to debase personal engagement and the sexual act itself. I think I understand what he means, but the problem just doesn't arise here. The act is technically complete, but not much happens; there's no intimacy, no lust, no climax, and no satisfaction. The act hasn't been debased because it hasn't been fully represented; and it probably can't be fully represented, thank heaven, because the presence of the camera destroys nearly everything that makes sex a different experience than eating or taking a bath. . . .

Is it pornographic, then? Yes, by most legal definitions. But subjectively, it's not pornographic. It's lewd, and rather cold, and quite dull, but it has nothing of the solemn, impacted, fantasy quality of movie pornography. . . .

We may live our lives in constant reference to movie stars and talk about them in the most familiar terms. But as long as they are actors, as long as they are playing roles and trying to create illusions of some sort, there is a measure of respect, of reserve, and *distance* in our relations with them. In Warhol's documentaries, however, the people are always playing themselves, and because of this and what they do (taking off all their clothes), the saving distance is annihilated, we are brought disastrously close, and we can only respond with the full cruelty of personal evaluation. We judge their intelligence, their imagination, their sexuality, their nakedness, and so on. (p. 43)

Warhol's output is of no value, but great interest. This paradox might be resolved by reminding the reader of Warhol's dubious relation to an important aspect of modern culture. An earlier generation of dadaist creators announced its blasphemies and negation in a series of furious manifestos. Warhol publishes no manifestos. In fact, he doesn't think of his output as a negation at all: he's just doing what he knows best and what comes easiest. He's not reacting against anything. (p. 44)

David Denby, "Reviews: 'Viva and Louis', "in Film Quarterly (copyright 1969 by The Regents of the University of California; reprinted by permission of the University of California Press), Vol. XXIII, No. 1, Fall, 1969, pp. 41-4.

## MICHAEL GOODWIN

A delightful blasphemy, [*Imitation of Christ*] actually looks more like **Bike Boy** than **Lonesome Cowboys;** basically, it's just a series of encounters between Patrick/Jesus/Warhol and everybody else. Endless rap, much of it funny, and more in-references than the human mind can stand. Warhol's directorial hand is stronger here than in previous films—and a lot of the time he seems to be feeding lines to the actors. Certainly, Bridget's speech about her son ("They tell me he's a genius. If that's genius, I want no part of it!") sounds too much like Mrs. Warhol to be an accident.

As usual, Warhol's illusion/reality games are right on. The tension that he sets up between his people-as-people and the fantasies they enact is stunning; the only unfailing reality is the film running through the camera. Warhol's instinctive understanding of just how far he can manipulate the situation in front of the camera without turning it into a hollywood movie is beautiful. Seems like he's been picking up on Godard while everybody was busy noticing how much Godard was picking up on *him.*

Thinking back to Warhol's early Edison-experiments, it seems clear that he's been into *film* all along. Not movies, not cinema—just film.

Michael Goodwin, "Berkel-Eye," in Take One (copyright © 1970 by Unicorn Publishing Corp.), Vol. 2, No. 5, May 10, 1970, p. 28.

## PETER BUCKLEY

[*My Hustler*] really is just a home movie made by a few people who know a bit about cameras and a bit about their subject, and like any homegrown product, it has its ups and downs.

On the up side is much of the chat, which in its bitchy way is quite funny, observant, and full of the hollow ring of truth. The camera work for the most part is annoyingly perfect. . . . (pp. 72, 74)

But the downer, and it is a major one, is the basic premise that these shallow, one-dimensional people are worth examining at all. They, and their situation, like their existence, are not really worth a second look, let alone seventy minutes of film. Unless of course one is making a little home movie to pass the time, to experiment and to have a bit of a giggle—which is the summation of *My Hustler.*

One would be a fool to dismiss the work of Andy Warhol—his importance and his impact are beyond question—but one would be equally foolhardy to take him *that* seriously. Regardless of his value as an artist, and his film work is merely an extension of that art, he refuses to be taken seriously, yet anyone interested in the cinema should get to see *My Hustler.* (p. 74)

Peter Buckley, "Reviews: 'My Hustler'" (© copyright Peter Buckley 1971; reprinted with permission), in Films and Filming, Vol. 17, No. 9, June, 1971, pp. 72, 74.

## RICHARD SCHICKEL

[Ernie Kovacs's comment, "Show me a cowboy who rides sidesaddle, and I'll show you a gay ranchero"], which I heard the late great comedian throw away one time, is as accurate a summary of Andy Warhol's new movie, **Lonesome Cowboys,** as one can make. But the point of one of his films is never to be found in its content, but simply in its existence, whether it happens to be twenty-four hours long, as one of them is, or twenty-four minutes, as one of them might perfectly well be. None of the matters usually brought up when we talk about films—story, style, technique—has any relevance to his work. Indeed, I have no hesitancy in admitting that I left **Cowboys** ten minutes before it was over, on the grounds that since it had no beginning and no middle it probably didn't have an ending either. It seemed to me at least as important to get to my lunch appointment on time as it did to hang around and see whether Viva, his current superstar, got debagged one more time. (p. 229)

To be sure, **Cowboys** was shot in thirty-five millimeter (a first for him) and had an unprecedented four-day shooting schedule, but he remains firmly rooted, technically and aesthetically, to a point in film history around 1904-1905, when the first American story films were being shot. Like the primitives, all he does is borrow a real setting, place amateur actors in front of it, and instruct them to improvise dialogue and action based on a rough outline. A genius can stretch this technique to masterwork lengths (e.g., [D. W.] Griffith's *The Birth of a Nation),* but Warhol cannot or will not. . . .

[His] works in all media are repetitions of a single simple juxtaposition. . . . Warhol's virtue, if he may be said to have one, is that in his essential stupidity he makes the contrast between the [mindlessly banal and the haphazardly corrupt] very stark, stripping away the platitudes and hypocrisies with which we customarily attempt to unify these contradictory elements. (p. 230)

[Let] me be very clear. I don't think Warhol or **Lonesome Cowboys** is any good. I don't even think he is an artist, avant-garde or conventional. He is just very, very important—too important to go on mindlessly denigrating or trying to ignore as if he were just a fad like hula hoops. He may, like them, quietly disappear. But like his soup cans he is endlessly replicable in this culture of ours. (p. 232)

Richard Schickel, "'Lonesome Cowboys'" (originally published in a slightly different form in Life, Vol. 66, No. 23, June 13, 1969), in his Second Sight: Notes on Some Movies, 1965-1970 (copyright © 1972 by, Richard Schickel; reprinted by permission of Simon & Schuster, a Division of Gulf & Western Corporation), Simon & Schuster, 1972, pp. 229-32.

## STEPHEN KOCH

Warhol was a central protagonist in a social drama that tried to make the 1960's look like another Age of Innocence. A childlike, gum-chewing naïveté inflects his visions of electric chairs and the ripped bloody bodies dangling from car wrecks; it merges with the pornographic lusting in so many of his films to touch them with an almost sweet aesthetic anodyne. Like that of the classic *décadent,* his aesthetics is the narcotic to a sense of damnation; unlike that of the *décadent,* his aesthetics is that not of a rarified connoisseur but displays the chintzy joys of American naïveté. (pp. 11-12)

The hinge of redemption is death. And so is Warhol's central theme finally death. He is an artist whose glamour is rooted in despair, meditating on the flesh, the murderous passage of time, the obliteration of the self, the unworkability of ordinary living. As against them, he proposes the momentary glow of a presence, an image—anyone's, if only they can leap out of the fade-out of inexistence into the presence of the star. (p. 12)

Speaking very roughly, Warhol's early films belong in the stream of nonnarrative, "poetic" *avant-garde* cinema, a very vital branch of modernism linked historically to Duchamp, Cocteau, and Buñuel, and that transplant of modernist thinking to the American sensibility that has been most conspicuous here in painting. But parallel to the rise of post-war abstraction in painting was the emergence of the American film *avant-garde*. Warhol inherited both aspects of this parallel development. (p. 19)

Warhol is a sweet, silent, pathologically mild-mannered man with intuitive genius for stepping into the mainstream of philosophy, art, aesthetic history, and the sociology of both the media and the image in our time and simply standing there, as if he were in a chic living room at their exact point of convergence. Most writers agree that his gift is not fundamentally plastic but theatrical. . . . But almost nobody notices that Warhol's art has a remarkable relevance to certain traditions about art and the artist that have dominated important aspects of Western cultural life at least since Baudelaire, or that Warhol's style speaks to and through those traditions with an ultranaïve and often staggering economy of means. (pp. 21-2)

Here, I think, is the center of Warhol's power as an artist: The obsession of this profoundly withdrawn man—this profoundly withdrawn star—with human presence, which he invariably renders as a cool, velvety, immediate *absence*. That is his paradox, why he is the phantom of the media, why he is the tycoon of passivity, why the gaze of his vision as an artist operates the way it does. Presence: It is, of course, elusive, particularly because grasping it means a close examination of our own perceptions as we look. (pp. 29-30)

Warhol *is* a way of looking at the world, and all his work in whatever medium manifests that way. It is a style that renders the presence of the real absent, a prettification that is also a metaphysical transformation that both creates and springs from an alternate consciousness, an alternate world, an alternate sexuality, an alternate art, and an alternate film. (p. 30)

The most powerful of the silent Warhol films are dominated by [a] voyeuristic aesthetic, but their immediate look modulates considerably from case to case. In *Sleep,* the languid, immobile frame changes from one sleek pictorial voluptuity to another; from the image of the breathing abdomen, to a long shot of the nearly nude body (shot from the knee at an angle just high enough to reveal the sleeper's entire body stretching back into space), to a close-up of the sleeper's expressionless face—frontally, in profile—and then back again, the pattern recapitulated. But, in *Kiss,* almost every shot is framed in exactly the same way: It is the standard close-up of the kiss and fade-out. (p. 44)

[*Blow-Job*] is a piece of pornographic wit. *Kiss* and its fascination rest on a paradox of proximity and distance. The same paradox is at work in *Blow-Job,* but that paradoxical space of the close-up (in real life the space of the kiss, itself) is compounded by the fact that the film's real action is taking pace very much out of frame. Seeing *Kiss,* the audience witnesses

a nearness and distance impossible in life. In *Blow-Job,* that space is further displaced into an imagined focus of interest, twenty inches below the frame, which the face actually on the screen never for a moment lets us forget. Perversely obdurate, the frame absolutely refuses to move toward the midriff, insists upon itself in a thirty-five minute close-up that must be the apotheosis of the "re-action shot," never to be surpassed. But that same insistence, with equally obdurate perversity, diverts attention Elsewhere, lower down, towards the Great Unseen. . . . (p. 48)

In *Blow-Job,* the fellated penis in the focus of attention; it's excluded from the frame. In erotic and artistic terms, this exclusion marks the difference between Warhol and Morrissey as film-makers. Warhol is uninterested in a spectacle that gives quite that much: That perversity, if such it can be called, is perhaps what saves him from the risk he takes in every major work he has ever produced, which is to be a mere decorator. One senses the power of that refusal, and it becomes the theme of his art.

Warhol is a man who, for all his intelligence, does not really understand people very well: Personhood is a mystery to him. His works gain their power from proposing the structure of that mystery. His voyeuristic obsession with the portrait is the arena in which this aspect of his art is most obvious. On the other hand, he is deeply engaged in the impersonality of a pornographic experience of the Other: The alternate dimension of Warhol's mystified experience of the Person is a violent anonymity. (p. 50)

[In *Haircut* , as] in all the films, the spectator's gaze is kept extremely close to complete stillness (there are, however, as in the early films, some very slight, and very slow, movements of the camera, though almost exclusively as zooms). But, in *Haircut,* that stillness is not entirely unbroken; it is, in fact, invited, is even *directed,* to move. For the first time in Warhol films within the silent style, a visual *event* occurs (for example, the near vanishing of the cowboy into the darkness of the end of the loft); for the first time, attention is not held in focus on a single and singular visual phenomenon, with its small changes. It is forced to notice things and disregard others, however momentarily; one finds that one must choose where attention will be given. (p. 55)

*Haircut* is about holding still: It is about a cinematic paradox of movement and stillness, borrowed, among other things, from the aesthetic of the painted portrait and transposed to film. . . . Linich holds still to have his hair cut, to have his picture taken, to have a movie made about him. A movie about the stillness and motion of the eye itself. *Because,* as [Ronald] Tavel put it, *what Warhol was trying to move toward in the films was a stillness.* Here we must pause, for if this stillness is indeed Warhol's theme, its strange meaning is not yet clear. (pp. 57-8)

*Empire* is so stupendously perverse it is almost awesome. Utterly disregarding any possible source of visual interest for the audience, it follows a cinematic witticism to the bottom of the night, subsuming the greatest and most hilariously debased of all monuments to Warhols' beloved Art Deco into a work of absolute vacuity. (p. 60)

Yet *Empire* retains a spooky staying power as a *locus classicus* not of the screen but of the mind. . . . In *Empire,* the knot between the conceptual and the concrete is conceived in its simplest terms, literalized, and simply untied. It is one of Warhol's most striking techniques: The dissolution of central

imaginative and metaphoric tropes that dominates the art literalized and thereby dissolved. (pp. 60-1)

[Warhol's talking films] make the question of authorship an
intriguing and baffling little matter. They have a uniform style,
the true Warhol style. They are about his relationship to time,
his displaced experience of the camera, his remote fascinations.
(p. 65)

For all its fistfights, arm-twisting, groveling, whining, sneer-
ing, for all its he-men pilloried and tortured, *Vinyl* is silly with
a look of farcical cornball amateurism. The actors—very visibly reading their lines from idiot sheets out of frame—are
hardly able to get the words right, let alone believe what they
are being made to say. The film is laughably self-indulgent
with its subject. Obsession and disaffection, cliché and confusion, the monstrous and the ridiculous skitter all over the
screen like the peal of a long, embarrassed giggle.

And yet, there is something deadly serious about it all. (p. 70)

[*Vinyl* is] little more than a series of cinematic tableaux, a set
of sexualized poses. The screen is drenched with theatricalized
sex, sex that flexes its muscles, fills its chest, grimaces, and
then (naturally) *holds still*. The movement of the film through
the projector is an insistent reminder of the possibility of movement film itself promises, but that possibility is very much at
odds with a posturing immobility—a sexual immobility—that
is in fact what the film is about, both formally and in its content.
(p. 73)

Within the realm of its formal structure, the stillness in *Vinyl*
has the same motive as does bondage in ethics. *It is a consequence of guilt*.

That is the secret fascination of *Vinyl* and its language, the
reason for its place among the most interesting films made
within the celebrated vocabulary of sadomasochism. Warhol's
filmic language in *Vinyl* involves itself in the horrors that underlie the 1960's frenzied grace and frozen hysteria. And, as
in all of Warhol's best films, the effects seem to be located at
an extraordinary cinematic distance from our perceptions. (pp.
73-4)

If *Vinyl* is intended as entertainment, it must be judged a failure.
It is, as so often happens with Warhol's films, not a self-
contained spectacle but a work that creates a situation for its
spectator, playing with his perceptions, his indifference and
his fascinations, his curiosity and his anger. . . . The distancing effect of *Vinyl,* the yanking but limp-wristed alienations it
induces, function to destroy the prospect of a familiar, immediate gratification—narrative and sexual pleasure—in favor
of another, more remote and less familiar experience. (p. 74)

[*Hedy*] is one again dominated by a certain pictorialism, but
here the camera moves, following its characters through sin-
uous, undefined corridors of space, seeming to make the quad-
rilateral hall of the Factory a twisting shadowy region of distraction and confusion. (p. 75)

When the camera is indeed so kind as to have a look at Hedy
and her problems, we are invariably in an amorphous, faintly
expressionistic, theatrical and dreamlike space. But, when the
camera looks away, in order to zero in on a scab of paint or
a pillar or the battered wood of the floor, we are abruptly
returned to the concrete, to real space and real time, bereft of
its theatrics by a simple flick of the cameraman's wrist.

The inattentive camera is one of Warhol's most pronounced
stylistic habits. That camera *will not* give the spectacle before

it its full concern. One senses the constant tug of its refusal to
submit to the domination of the scene and its idea, its interest;
that camera is like a restless child who keeps looking away,
staring around the room, not giving in to that dominating experience that is everyone else's concern. (p. 77)

[*My Hustler*] is a film without mystery—without filmic mystery
and with few psychological mysteries, either. It seemed to be
more like a "real" movie. . . . If not precisely entertaining,
*My Hustler* was at least very interesting on some very simple
level. There were real people up there, there was a situation
on the screen, the situation was being consecutively played
out. It had human interest—is there another kind?—and just a
bit more as a result of its subject. (p. 82)

This is one of the first Warholvian works—certainly the first
discussed here—in which the work's fundamental qualities as
film don't happen to be particularly interesting. . . .

[It] is not the filming that can hold attention: It is the movements
of those bodies, filled with the clichéd tics of the national
vocabulary of masculine body language—so familiarly paro-
died everywhere that they have become absurd; we Americans
have caught on to at least that much. Yet they are also informed
with something that is almost primordial; a complex interchange, probing the realities of the body's space and its meanings. . . . (p. 84)

*The Chelsea Girls* is not a narrative work, but it does move
through time in the rhythm of narrative. It does develop, in a
strictly structural sense, toward a finality, as opposed to a mere
termination. But it is a finality that functions only by virtue of
bringing the eye to rest. Indeed, it does even better than that. . . .
(p. 90)

*The Chelsea Girls* seems almost an act of aggression, though
it must be called aggression of a very special kind. A cliché
leaps to mind: The film is mind-blowing, an inept cliché that
has leapt into a good many people's minds. The work overloads
the circuit of perception. Some may find it a little explosive
and shocking, there is a great deal of sadomasochism in it, and
a great many needles shooting methadrine. And, for its pleasures, the film may seem to fellate consciousness in a con-
tactless voluptuity. Fine, but I dislike the cliché. I feel a certain
contempt for it. We should prize our minds more highly, and
*The Chelsea Girls* seems to me, on the contrary, mind-defin-
ing. . . . Its special characteristic is to flirt with the idea of
entirely abandoning any aesthetic, stretching itself across the
realm of disorientation while at the same time quietly announcing its coherence. (p. 91)

*The Chelsea Girls* is haunted, dominated, by the problem of
authenticity.

It is sensed through an extraordinarily delicate, though usually
comic, exploration of its actors' presences, as their eroticism
is sensed through those presences. Everybody has surely guessed
that, within the psychological structure of *The Chelsea Girls'*
aesthetic, there is an important link between the whole operation of the film and the exclusively homosexual, sadomasochistic sexuality that pervades it. . . . But the film is also an
anthology of variations on an almost cautionary style of personal presence, something that *has* its own little drama, its
own story. (p. 94)

[In] the works immediately following *The Chelsea Girls* something absolutely grotesque happened to Warhol's two finest
gifts: his visual intelligence and his taste. It was simply this:
Degradation. *The Loves of Ondine, Nude Restaurant,* and, to

a lesser degree, *Lonesome Cowboys* are degraded and degrading works. Even one who prides himself on strong nerves must recoil from them. (p. 100)

[*Nude Restaurant*] is not so repellent a failure as *Loves of Ondine,* though, unlike that movie, which has at least some amusing moments before the catastrophe, I cannot think of a single inch of footage in *Nude Restaurant* that seems to me worth looking at. Watching it is rather like being present at the most boring party of one's entire life. Looking at all those bodies and g-strings, a wave of murderous indifference passes over the mind and clamps itself down, never to move until the last dull frame has been run through the projector. One thinks, pathetically, there is a book to write, surely there is something here. Did he perhaps imagine he was doing or saying something about pornography? One is too bored even to speculate. (p. 103)

[*Lonesome Cowboys*] is a bad film, even an abominably bad film. It is sloppily made. It does not do what it wants to do. It is very boring. But, even though it is bad, it is among the most critically interesting of Warhol's bad films, because it is a pivotal work in his career both as a film-maker and as a public personality. It is the last film he completed before being shot, the last properly attributed to him rather than Paul Morrissey, the last he directed entirely on his own. And, in that sense, it is very suggestive, particularly about the relation between the master and his pupil. (p. 105)

*Lonesome Cowboys* is definitely Warhol's own. He wanted to make a Western about sex, and, however deep his interest in that idea this very gifted man had no gift for dealing with it. (pp. 105-06)

Quite apart from the vision of human relations so arbitrarily sprung in the opening of *Lonesome Cowboys,* Warhol's idea had opened up to him a cinematic concept that, if used, might have made the film a really interesting work. He might have been able to refract the present and the real through the Western myth of an idylic past. Warhol had placed himself squarely in that cinematic situation to which Jean-Luc Godard refers when he speaks of documentary becoming fiction and fiction becoming documentary. (p. 107)

There are no crises in *Lonesome Cowboys,* because there is no critical consciousness. One senses that Warhol does not know what to do with his double vision of the world and the flesh, and that, even if he knew, he wouldn't or couldn't do it. Only a critical consciousness could undertake such a task—and Warhol has, from the beginning, pitched his very being on the complete refusal to assume critical consciousness. *He is a man to whom the world happens.* (p. 108)

*Stephen Koch, in his* Stargazer: Andy Warhol's World and His Films *(copyright © 1973 by Stephen Koch; reprinted by permission of Holt, Rinehart and Winston), Frederick A. Praeger, Publishers, 1973, 155 p.*

## JOHN RUSSELL TAYLOR

The essence of Warhol's art—and by extension that of the Factory he heads—is the straight look at things as they are, and acceptance of appearances as an important part, perhaps the most important part, of the truth. It is the same whether the object is a Campbell's Soup can or the Empire State Building or some people just living, just talking, just being in front of the camera. And if what people are is what they appear to be, what they appear to be is very importantly what they think they are, what they want to be thought. . . .

We all define ourselves to some extent according to our own fantasies: the only difference with Warhol's drag ladies is that the discrepancy between the fantasy and the visible reality is likely to be more evident. . . . The point about *My Hustler* or *Bike Boy* or *The Chelsea Girls,* is that everything is taken on trust, everything is right there in front of the camera. Inevitably some of the people are more interesting than others, but we decide this fairly and squarely on the evidence; there is no snide angling from behind the camera. The Warhol films play scrupulously fair with their characters; the films do not build myths, they merely record them. They are documentaries, but documentaries of the human spirit, of subjective rather than objective reality. (p. 137)

[Whatever] else may be said about the Warhol *équipe,* they are sublimely unpatronizing. They accept their "stars" absolutely on their own terms; the stars are whatever they want to be, whatever they think they are, and that is that. They are not representative of anything but themselves. And after all, why should they be? One could no doubt make out a case for seeing most of the Warhol films as parts of a large-scale survey of a certain homosexual/transvestite/drug scene is the margins of the New York art world, but it seems unlikely that there is anything systematic about it, or any intention to generalize, even about such a relatively small segment of the population. Empathy rather than abstraction and comment seems to be the aim. (pp. 138-39)

Warhol and his group believe that the increasing emphasis on the film director as superstar . . . is putting film theory and, worse, the film itself off on quite the wrong road. Directors, says Paul Morrissey, are all very well in their place, along with hairdressers, camera operators, dialogue coaches, and such, but finally what counts, what has always counted, is the person up there on the screen, the star in front of the camera rather than the exhibitionist itching to get out from behind it. (p. 139)

Logically, therefore, Warhol's own cinema should not be a director's cinema at all. And in some very important senses it is not. . . . Just as with his graphics he has frequently said that the cult of personality has nothing to do with it—anyone in the Factory could turn out "Warhol" graphics just as well as he, without his ever seeing what they are doing, much less laying hand to it himself—so "Warhol" movies can be made, and have been made, perfectly well when the master himself is nowhere near; "Warhol" is much more of a brand name than an artist's signature. . . . [It] does seem that the main element which can be identified as Andy Warhol's personal contribution is, paradoxically, the idea of impersonality. (pp. 139-40)

*John Russell Taylor, "Andy Warhol/Paul Morrissey," in his* Directors and Directions: Cinema for the Seventies *(reprinted by permission of Hill & Wang, a division of Farrar, Straus & Giroux, Inc.; in Canada by A D Peters & Co Ltd; copyright © 1975 by John Russell Taylor), Hill & Wang, 1975, pp. 136-64.*

# Peter Weir

## 1944-

**Australian director, screenwriter, and actor.**

**Weir's films convey his perception of the mystical in everyday events. A successful director emerging from Australia's recent New Wave, he juxtaposes the beautiful and the bizarre, creating a calm exterior that masks the unknown.**

**Weir made several short films before obtaining a directorial position at Film Australia. His first full-length film, *Three To Go,* won the Grand Prix of Australia and was nationally televised. In 1971, Weir won another Grand Prix for *Homesdale.* After making several documentaries, Weir directed his first feature, *The Cars that Ate Paris.* The film combines a variety of genres to provide social commentary on the modern automotive fetish. Though a dismal commercial failure, critics received it favorably.**

***Picnic at Hanging Rock* is considered one of Australia's finest films. Its ethereal visual quality belies the ominous subject matter. *Picnic at Hanging Rock* suggests that we live placidly on the edge of hellish disturbing forces beyond our control. Since the supernatural conquers, the film seems to justify a fear of the unknown.**

***The Last Wave* uses water imagery to depict unknown powers. Because of this film's link with aboriginal beliefs, it is a more mystic, brooding work than *Picnic at Hanging Rock.* Some critics, however, feel that Weir concerned himself more with establishing a darkly ominous tone than with narrative development. *The Plumber,* too, has a primitive influence similar to *The Last Wave,* but presents evil in the form of a young "bogeyman." Its form of black comedy is strongly reminiscent of the plays of Harold Pinter.**

**Weir says he does not set out to depict the supernatural deliberately. However, the pervasive image of unseen powers in his films echoes Edgar Allan Poe's words stated at the beginning of *Picnic at Hanging Rock:* "What we are and what we seem are but a dream, a dream within a dream."**

### ED PELTIER

Music and poetry are the arts most difficult to transfer to cinema. Peter Weir, an imaginative Australian writer-director, has accomplished this most successfully in the film *Incredible Floridas.* It derives its title from a line in a poem by Arthur Rimbaud: "I've struck, I tell you, incredible floridas" [the Spanish word for "full of flowers, choice or select"].

The film is built around the musical homage paid the 19th century French poet by 41-year-old Richard Meale, a leader in contemporary music in Australia. In his own words Meale reveals his early interest in Rimbaud's poetry, his fascination with the poet, and his many attempts over a period of years to put his feeling for Rimbaud into music.

Through uncluttered cinematic devices and with this music as background, the viewer becomes intimately acquainted with both Meale the composer, and Rimbaud the poet, in a linkage though 100 years apart in time, of these two creative minds. . . .

There will be viewers of this film who will be made curious about Rimbaud; others will be stimulated to greater knowledge of Meale and to developments in the musical life of Australia of which a glimpse is given here. . . .

The narration is well paced, its delivery readily understandable. Together, the director and the cameraman have captured the brooding, haunting quality of both Meale's music and Rimbaud's poetry to an extent rarely developed in a film on the two arts.

Ed Peltier, "'Incredible Floridas'," in Film News (© Rohama Lee, d/b/a/Film News Company), Vol. 31, No. 2, April-May, 1974, p. 33.

### PHILIP STRICK

Like all the best fantasies, [*The Cars that Ate Paris*] illuminates the truth with its headlights; the film's title in fact works as a metaphor, and Paris could as well be London, New York, or actually Paris. The erosion of humanity by malevolent technological influences is actually more cliché than truth, perhaps, and the peculiarly immediate effect of the car on the personality has been lovingly revealed by the cinema many times . . . , but *The Cars that Ate Paris* is closer to [Kurosawa's] *Dodes'ka-den* than to [Lazlo Benedek's] *The Wild One,* closer to Arrabal and Ballard than to Asimov. Which is not to say that the film is always certain of its destination; Australian domestic comedies, remorselessly twanging on the same threadbare lines of humour, have left their mark, and the Royal Portrait still hangs behind the mayoral desk. . . . But, as with that other masterpiece of anarchy, [George Romero's] *Night of the Living Dead,* the suspension of conventional dramatic laws adds a curious potency to the thrust of the film, and we find ourselves in an uneasy and uncharted territory where logic has taken a blind turning and there is no escape route. (p. 102)

*Philip Strick, "'The Cars that Ate Paris',"* in Monthly Film Bulletin *(copyright © The British Film Institute, 1975), Vol. 42, No. 496, May, 1975, pp. 101-02.*

## GEOFF BROWN

[In *The Cars That Ate Paris*] the dying town is in the clichéd position of living off the refuse of a materialistic society—symbolised in this instance by the automobile (the accidents are planned, the cars and victims then looted). But the obviousness of its theme has little adverse effect on the success of *The Cars That Ate Paris* . . . , a grotesque and engaging horror-comedy. . . .

[Weir's] directorial manner is cool and collected enough for the depicted events to seem startlingly matter-of-fact. The Mayor is the most fully developed character in the bizarre drama. . . .

In the hallowed horror movie tradition, Arthur [the hero] is about to tell the vicar his fears when his potential ally meets a nasty death off-screen—'accidentally', the town decides. Now the movie's pace tightens and the eccentricities loom larger. . . . [The Pioneer's Ball is] a marvellously funny sequence, and any participant in village fêtes or church socials will recognise the seeds of truth: the lady pianist mechanically pounds out jolly tunes; the Mayor half-heartedly leads the dancing; everyone's 'fancy dress' seems desperate. However, their costumes are nothing compared with those of the hospital patients, who make a triumphant entrance with cereal packets on their heads or cardboard boxes round their waists. . . .

True, the movie has its faults: the pacing is often sluggish (particularly in the opening stages), the structuring of the story is haphazard, and most of the performances could be sharpened with benefit. But after the boorish and boring adventures of Alvin Purple and Barry McKenzie, it's refreshing and encouraging to find an Australian film which never wallows in its country's inglorious *mores* but uses them tactfully to further an intriguing and compelling narrative of its own.

*Geoff Brown, "Film Reviews: 'The Cars that Ate Paris',"* in Sight and Sound *(copyright © 1975 by The British Film Institute), Vol. 44, No. 3, Summer, 1975, p. 192.*

## RICHARD COMBS

After his stylistic fumbling with the interesting fantasy material of *The Cars That Ate Paris,* Peter Weir seems to be on surer ground with *Picnic at Hanging Rock*—a pure 'atmosphere' piece, with all manner of submerged dreads and longings collecting thickly in the air of a Victorian summer. The consummate and consistent lushness of the film in this respect, however, could be seen as a kind of displacement; the uncertainty in the style of *Cars* has become the subject of *Picnic,* and what one might identify as the Weir method—working round his subject, following various tangents but never quite clinching the heart of the matter—finds its perfect complement here, not only in the unsolved mystery at the centre of the plot, but in the repressions and evasions of the Victorian setting. . . . The trouble with the film begins in the early stages with its tendency to emphasise the psychosexual inevitability of the three girls' ultimate communion with (and absorption by) the spirit of the Rock—"Everything begins and ends at exactly the right place

and time''—and continues in the latter stages with its compulsion to 'legitimise' this mystery without a solution by setting off a series of mini-mysteries concerning all the other characters. . . . The film's clumsiness in this respect is compounded by the one scene in which it attempts to crystallise its sense of the adventure on the Rock as a sexual odyssey: when Irma enters the school gym to confront her fellow pupils for the first time since her return, clad in a bright red dress, the hushed company of girls suddenly breaks out into hysterical screaming as they demand to know what happened and what Irma saw. A much more interesting project than *The Cars That Ate Paris, Picnic at Hanging Rock* for a while suggests that it has the measure of its ambitions; what finally irritates is not that it poses a riddle without an answer, but that in posing it the film seems to be overtaken by an attack of the stutters. (pp. 196-97)

*Richard Combs, "'Picnic at Hanging Rock',"* in Monthly Film Bulletin *(copyright © The British Film Institute, 1976), Vol. 43, No. 512, September, 1976, pp. 196-97.*

## TOM MILNE

Weir caps [the] opening movement of [*Picnic at Hanging Rock*] with an absolutely superb shot. As four girls set off to explore the Rock itself . . . , he cuts to a high-angle shot down on the rest of the party frozen in exquisitely elegant yet shamelessly carnal attitudes of post-prandial satiation. Like a painting by Auguste Renoir of the *bon bourgeois* at play, it evokes that magical moment when nature somehow contrives to unloose the bonds of convention. The theme, unfortunately, is not always allowed to speak for itself in this way. Perhaps because Joan Lindsay's novel never provides any explanation for the disappearance of the three girls—so maintaining the illusion of being a speculation on a real-life incident that a myth seems to have grown up that the novel was based on a genuine *fait-divers*—Weir seems to feel obliged to compensate not merely by elaborating hints, but by over-stressing those hints. . . .

[Just] before meeting her doom, one of the girls looks down at her fellow-pupils far below and begins to analyse the insignificance of human existence as though suddenly invaded by the spirit of Darwin. Gradually all the portents, swelled by slow-motion and symbolic swans, accumulate a weight the film cannot bear, and it slides inevitably into woolly melodrama. . . .

A pity, because when the film works, it works beautifully, as in the superb sequence, effortlessly welding space, time and setting into an indivisible whole where the girls drift past another picnicking party, an elderly English couple whose very proper nephew . . . steals away for a flirtation across the class boundaries with native manners . . . before being drawn into equally tantalising uncharted territory as he watches one of the passing girls delicately raise her skirt to cross a stream. His subsequent involvement to the point of obsession with the mystery—beautifully adumbrated by a cut, as he is questioned by a policeman about his feelings during the brief moment when he saw the girls passing, to a tranquil, shimmering sheet of water (he is now, in fact, brooding alone at a lakeside garden party)—is one of the unquestionable successes of the film, clear, pure and uncontaminated by the overstatement running riot elsewhere. As with his first feature, *The Cars That Ate Paris,* all the very talented Peter Weir needs is a little discipline, either self- or other-imposed.

Tom Milne, "'Picnic at Hanging Rock'," in *Sight and Sound* (copyright © 1976 by The British Film Institute), Vol. 45, No. 4, Autumn, 1976, p. 257.

## ED ROGINSKI

[The artificiality and repressiveness of Appleyard College are uncomfortably recognizable in *Picnic at Hanging Rock*.] The opening sequence of St. Valentine's morning is characterized by the excitement of the girls' exchange of greetings among themselves and their teachers. It closes, however, with the haunting image of one of the girls imprisoning a rose in a flower-press. What had been a delicate, vital blossom becomes a beautiful, dead icon.

The pressing of the rose emblematically depicts the emotional ambiance of the school. The symbol of eternal love is closed in the airless device just as the affection between Miranda and Sara . . . , an orphan and the school's youngest boarder, is enclosed in a social context which makes it inverted and incapable of further growth. While Miranda ambivalently warns Sara that she must learn to love others, she simultaneously extends the hope that Sara will one day visit Miranda's family. The ambiguity of the girls' relationship is a touchstone for the emotional bonding of the inhabitants of Appleyard.

Appleyard is a hot-house Eden. Its blossoms would not survive in natural settings, and Miranda at least seems hesitantly aware of their fragility. The film is threaded with various kinds of incipiently lesbian relationships. (p. 22)

Much of the film rests on a polarity between the conscious and the unconscious; light and dark, exposed and hidden. The very mode of celebrating Valentine's Day is significant. The pagan, Roman celebration honoring Juno, patroness of women, and Pan, the god of nature, has been transformed by Christianity into a martyr's feast-day. Pagan rituals have been abandoned, except for the exchange of love tokens. The ancient celebration of womanhood and nature has been suppressed, but nonetheless lies waiting beneath centuries of repression—waiting to surface again. (pp. 22-3)

The journey from Appleyard to Hanging Rock is a movement out of civilization in more than one sense. . . . The world [the girls from Appleyard] enter is timeless, and the portrayal of it is achieved by a display of filmmaking virtuosity that is overwhelming in its grace and terrible beauty. . . .

All [photographic] devices serve to reinforce the everpresent movement of the girls from the world of reality into the world of myth.

Mlle. de Poitiers speaks for the viewer when she voices her admiration for the beauty of youth, and her awe of the Hanging Rock. Miss McCraw, on the other hand, is irritated by human company and preoccupied by the Rock solely as physical object. She explains to the company that Hanging Rock is a result of "lava, forced up from deep down below, where it has lain for a million years." The response from one of the students, "Just think, a million years . . . waiting just for us," is indicative of both the self-centeredness of childish thinking, and the process of acculturation which has taught her that humanity is the center of the universe. There is, of course, an ironic truth lying much deeper than she realizes in her words; her own notion of their truth is woefully unrealized, however.

How untrue her notion is becomes apparent only gradually as the film, and the picnic, evolve. The first hints of it come from the soundtrack. . . .

But the eeriness of the sound track is compelling not only for what is heard, but also for what is not heard. . . . Except for the occasional buzz of insects, or the rustle of leaves by animals, an ominous silence prevails. Its effect is to impart a strange quality, bordering on the horrific, to the superficially familiar, natural setting. It is also strikingly kinaesthetic: the heat and the languor it produces come not only from watching the sun-drenched images on the screen, but also from the impending weight of the near-silence. Above all, there is a continuous and growing apprehension produced by the absence of sound.

The visual impact of the Hanging Rock itself conveys an overwhelming sense of animism that is the hallmark of this film. The Rock, an urcathedral complete with gargoyle-like figures embedded in its heights, creates the film's most disturbing reactions. (p. 23)

What happens on Hanging Rock is the enigma at the center of the film. It is the question asked by everyone—character and viewer alike. No explicit answers, apart from the unfolding of the film, and our experience of it, are given; implicit ones are. . . .

The questions, "How?" and "Why?" are the axes on which the remainder of the film spins.

A closer look at the ascent of the Rock, and at the Rock itself, is helpful. As the four girls climb, Marion, the intellectual among the group, notices the people below. They include not only the other members of the Appleyard party, but another separate group of holiday-makers. . . . They are the representatives of the larger world of which Appleyard is but a corner. It is a world of flux, less isolated and less insular than Appleyard, and consequently less secure in its perceptions of both the larger natural order and the parochial, social order of things. . . .

Marion, however, achieves a far wider vision. In reflecting on the people below, she comments that "a surprising number of human beings are without purpose, though it is probable that they are performing some function unknown to themselves." In this observation is a key to at least one perception of the meaning of the Rock, and the events of Valentine's Day, 1900. Marion implies that the human activity below, as seen from the heights of the Rock, is meaningless except within the context of some grander design. It is as if she is speaking for the forces which have caused the eruption of the Rock itself. Such forces might speak of human activity in the same terms the girls themselves apply to the group below: "Like a lot of ants . . . ." The analogy to the instinctual world of ants raises the question of whether human beings also function by merely fulfilling the designs of forces larger and more powerful than themselves.

Miranda, as usual, provides an answer of sorts: "Everything begins and ends at exactly the right time and place." She, like her namesake in *The Tempest*, has discovered a brave, new world. She and the others scale the Rock and transcend the limits of their civilized lives. They literally are lost on the Rock. Metaphorically, they are exploring the hidden depths of an instinctual world—a world of sensuality and passion. The ascent of the Rock functions as a primitive rite of passage for the young women, and the vehicle of this experience seems to be an acceptance of their existence as sexual beings.

For Hanging Rock is not only a temple-like edifice, but also an emblem of human sexuality. The topmost peaks are phallic; the caves and narrow passages below are vaginal in structure and contour. . . . [The] eye of the camera, hidden in the Rock, is our own. . . . *We* are buried in the Rock. Or our instinctual selves are—a truth that is discovered in the film by at least two survivors of the experience who live to tell the tale. (p. 24)

The scars on [the brows of Michael and Irma] mark them for the audience as having been singled out, or made different by some ineffable experience. Like Cain, they are marked as outsiders and are condemned to live differently from their peers. . . .

The Irma who re-enters the lives of her schoolmates is not the Irma they have known. She is no longer a child, but a woman, swathed in a red traveling ensemble; her appearance causes an outbreak of mass hysteria among the girls. . . .

The disappearance of the women on the Rock, and the reappearance of the survivors, Irma and Michael, cause hysterical reactions among others as well. Mrs. Appleyard's disintegration is the most visibly dramatic. . . . As her drinking increases, the sadism which has been swimming in her blood surfaces and seeks as its main prey the young Sara Waybourne. (p. 25)

How, and why, remain unanswered questions [when Sara is found dead]. As Mr. Whitehead has explained in an earlier sequence to Tom, the college handyman, "Some questions got answers and some haven't." It is a fitting epitaph for Sara, and an equally fitting epigraph for the entire film.

The close of the film, then, provides no factual answers, only more questions. But then, questions are the essence of this film. The viewer is left with the sensation of having encountered a visual representation of several human beings' involvement with an almost "motiveless malignancy." At least that is one perspective. For there is little doubt that the film is terrifyingly effective as a foray into the supernatural. But like all great horror films, it succeeds in making the psychological realities one cannot see even more fearful than those events outwardly depicted on the screen.

Another perspective requires that one view the events of the Picnic at Hanging Rock as taking place in a realm that is limited neither by the natural nor the supernatural—the realm of art. The film works best when seen in terms of visual metaphor. In the party of schoolgirls who picnic at the Rock, there are several who never return to Appleyard. They transcend its limits and free themselves from the conventions of a narrow and repressive world. By doing so they are absorbed into a world that is more mysterious, more powerful, and ultimately more disturbing than that which we are comfortable.

The impact of the film lies in just that ability to make its audiences uncomfortable. . . . [In] its suggestion that there is far more to our lives than the tiny framework within which we allow ourselves to interpret so-called reality, it is totally unsettling. (pp. 25-6)

*Ed Roginski, "Reviews: 'Picnic at Hanging Rock'," in* Film Quarterly *(copyright 1977 by The Regents of the University of California; reprinted by permission of the University of California Press), Vol. XXXII, No. 4, Summer, 1977, pp. 22-6.*

**RICHARD COMBS**

[Weir's] films—lush, beckoning fantasies, promising exotic vistas from strange new lands—have a seductiveness befitting an emergent cinema. Unfortunately, Weir's deftness with 'atmosphere' seems to have been developing at the expense of any narrative or thematic sense. The tantalising promise of *Picnic at Hanging Rock* was that the lush, repressed romanticism of its Victorian girls' school setting might have become its subject—implying that it was the secretiveness and fearfulness of this culture that had generated the unsolved mystery of the plot. But unwilling or unable to make more of this, Weir used his lyricism largely to fill in holes in the story: creating minor mysteries about incidental characters and generally wrapping events in mystical cotton wool. Such, more or less, is what has also happened to *The Last Wave*. . . . (pp. 121-22)

It is a film of disparate elements, which take a long time to slide into focus. The first half hour of so is the kind of allusive, foreboding scene-setting which is Weir's specialty: in a desert township, a sudden rainstorm and then huge chunks of ice come crashing out of a cloudless sky; in Sydney, freak weather conditions make the rush-hour traffic even more trying for lawyer David Burton. . . . David begins to suffer from recurrent nightmares of a dark, indistinct figure, approaching him through watery hallucinations. . . .

David is called in by a friend in a legal aid office to help in [a murder trial of aborigine youths] and discovers that one of the boys, Chris Lee . . . , is the figure of his dreams. Although the youths are unwilling to talk, David becomes obsessed with the idea that the crime is related to some ancient tribal secret (and to the increasingly strange weather). His efforts to press Chris on this point lead to the film's third and most mystical level: David is himself a throwback to an ancient spirit race who, in aboriginal lore, were the first inhabitants of Australia; his dreams represent some stirring of that previous life, connecting him both with the aborigines' secret and the prophecy of cleansing holocaust which that race left behind.

But long before the film has clinched this final revelation, a double awkwardness has set in, on both narrative and thematic grounds. The mechanics of the murder investigation and the subsequent trial seem, for one, an irrelevant construction, a rather clumsy device for bringing David and the aborigines together. Related to this are the sporadic attempts to motivate the hero, or at least to lend him the complexity which will support his later prophetic role. Such exposition tends to jut self-consciously from the film. . . . Once having detached them from an overweeningly colourful background, Weir has never been able to shape or define his characters with much confidence.

But if the film proceeds by fits and starts in this respect, at the deeper level it fails to jell at all. . . . In the jostle of his plot . . . , Weir never really establishes the validity or even the full significance of [the aboriginal] elements, allowing them to be undercut by the cruder cliffhanging devices: the escalating dream sequences and the final flurry of action in the underground temple of David's forebears.

In particular, the invocation of some weighty tribal 'secret' being guarded by the young aborigines, buttressed for a while in the script by a running argument as to whether city aborigines have any tribal ties, becomes an elaborate red herring. . . . In the end, the local inflections of *The Last Wave* float by on the general banality of its holocaust and hocus-pocus model. (p. 122)

*Richard Combs, "Film Reviews: 'The Last Wave',"
in* Sight and Sound *(copyright © 1978 by The British
Film Institute), Vol. 47, No. 2, Spring, 1978, pp.
121-22.*

## GORDON GOW

From the very outset of [*The Last Wave*, an] intelligently imaginative film, Peter Weir creates an eerie sense of nature gone awry. . . .

Supernatural forces are evidently at work. But their ways are subtle, for Weir is broaching again the gossamer mysticism he explored so superbly in his film of the Joan Lindsay novel *Picnic at Hanging Rock.* Neither an incomplete fragment of history nor a period atmosphere are to be conjured up this time, and the current film, while hardly reaching the quality of that last one, is probably the more arduous feat: an essay on atavism set in a wholly naturalistic present, against which the strong impressions of unknown influences are thrown into startling relief. (p. 34)

[The] supernatural hints are very suavely integrated. There is, for example, a clever little scene in a pub where naturalism extends to an overlay of dialogue and the chatter of a radio commentary, an everyday feeling upon which a *frisson* of something 'other' impinges when into the bar-room walks the aboriginal David [who] has hitherto [been] seen only as a dream figure. From such gentle fusions of the tangible and the uncertain, Weir expands occasionally into elaborate effects which (until the very last touch) are beautifully judged: the realism of croaking frogs on a rainy night, gathering a certain menace in close shots, blends moodily into another of the visions that might or might not be in David's dreams—Weir's special accomplishment here is to have us doubt whether what we see is dream or not, until the moment he is ready to enlighten us. . . .

Weir, putting another essay in eeriness on top of *The Cars That Ate Paris* and *Picnic at Hanging Rock,* sets himself a difficult course, and pursues it with admirable assurance. (p. 35)

*Gordon Gow, "The Last Wave"* (© copyright Gordon Gow 1978; reprinted with permission), in* Films and Filming, *Vol. 24, No. 7, April, 1978, pp. 34-5.*

## TIM PULLEINE

Early passages of Peter Weir's [*The Last Wave*] suggest that he has successfully married the vigour of his first film, *The Cars That Ate Paris,* to the plastic and enigmatic qualities of its successor, *Picnic at Hanging Rock.* . . . [The] episodes of Billy Corman's death and Burton's subsequent involvement in the legal proceedings are economically dovetailed into the narrative, with Weir integrating the various strands of the plot through the persisting water imagery—the sprinkler playing on Burton's lawn as he discusses his nightmare with his stepfather, the dripping tap in the mortuary where Corman's body is examined. All the more disappointing, then, that Burton's attempts to elucidate the increasingly bizarre situation in which he finds himself fail to exert sufficient grip on any of the available levels, and the movie quickly slackens. . . . Nor does the film manage more than a superficial commentary on the situation of its Aborigines, perhaps because Chris and Charlie are presented only as totemistic presences. . . . The concluding sequences do regain momentum—editing and settings combine to impart a sense of desperation to the subterranean voyage of

discovery—but their effect remains superficial, and the tidal wave registers not as the inexorable working-out of a fatal design but as just a gimmick to provide a shock ending. (pp. 66-7)

*Tim Pulleine, "'The Last Wave',"* in* Monthly Film Bulletin *(copyright © The British Film Institute, 1978), Vol. 45, No. 531, April, 1978, pp. 66-7.*

## VINCENT CANBY

["**The Last Wave**"] begins so brilliantly and with such promise that it's no real surprise that the closer it gets to its apocalypse, the less effective it becomes. The film's payoff is decidedly small, recalling nothing more esoteric than the discovery of the elephants' graveyard in one of the early Tarzan movies. Yet until we arrive at this breathless anticlimax, "**The Last Wave**" is a movingly moody shock-film, composed entirely of the kind of variations on mundane behavior and events that are most scary and disorienting because they so closely parallel the normal. . . .

Though the inspiration of Mr. Weir and his associates runs out before the end, "**The Last Wave**" is an impressive work. . . . He's a man whose ability to find the eerie in the commonplace might please Hitchcock.

*Vincent Canby, "Mysticism Down Under," in* The New York Times *(© 1978 by The New York Times Company; reprinted by permission), December 19, 1978 (and reprinted in* The New York Times Film Reviews: 1977-1978, *The New York Times Company & Arno Press, 1979, p. 263).*

## DAN YAKIR

Peter Weir's *The Last Wave* is an ambitiously conceived and dramatically executed film that combines a variety of genres—the psychological thriller, the courtroom drama, the disaster film, and the supernatural mystery—into a unique cinematic achievement. Its profound social and political implications are as unsettling as its buildup of suspense is subtle. With its linear narrative and direct, matter-of-fact tone, *The Last Wave* is a striking portrayal of the inner hysteria of a man and his world-order gone awry. . . .

[The] thunderstorm shatters the ordered complacency enjoyed by lawyer David Burton . . . and by the white society to which he belongs. In its apocalyptic culmination, the last wave of the storm is destined to destroy the civilization that all but annihilated the continent's aborigines. . . .

Burton loses his foothold on "reality" only to discover that it has a different level, looser in definition and related closely to the world of dreams. After losing the case, Burton's dreams materialize. Dream and reality become one.

The visual leitmotiv in the film is water—the mysterious overflowing of a bathtub, a drizzling faucet amidst the storm, a leaking car radio, and a lawn sprinkler that reminds even on a sunny day that the storm is never far away. But it is really the clash between dichotomous worlds that dominates the film: that of "civilized" society where the coziness and warmth of the home are often a smokescreen for a suffocating insularity, and the sacred aboriginal sites, which offer vast, open spaces suggesting a freer spirituality.

Weir's style is economical: the recurring shot of the dark Sydney skyline dominated by an omnipresent rainbow, and that of the calm ocean with a sickly halo of light curbing its horizon, are as chilling as they are lyrical.

Dan Yakir, "Apocalypse, Now" (reprinted by permission of The Village Voice and the author; copyright © The Village Voice, Inc., 1978), in The Village Voice, Vol. XXIII, No. 52, December 25, 1978, p. 48.

## PAULINE KAEL

Weir's occultism isn't even faintly erotic, and except for the first sequence **The Last Wave** is over-deliberate; the camera movements are ominous as if by habit.

Visually, the film is active until the first shot of [David Burton], a Sydney corporation lawyer. Every time he appears, the camera seems to hold on him—and the film croaks out. (p. 533)

Weir provides apparitions holding sacred stones, frog noises in the night, shadows in slow motion, and the kind of haunted-house acting that many of us have a certain affection for—the actors' sense of hopelessness is so disarming as they deliver a line and then try to find a suitable expression to go with it. But **The Last Wave,** which at its best recalls [Jacques Tourneur's] *I Walked with a Zombie,* is hokum without the fun of hokum. Despite all its scare-movie apparatus, the film fairly aches to be called profound. . . . This infernally sluggish movie is about the white man's burden of alienation. . . .

The maudlin hysteria in the film links it to some of the Hollywood movies of the late-sixties-early-seventies period. . . . It's the kill-us-because-we-deserve-to-die syndrome. Instead of seeing the victims of expansionist drives and colonial policies—the aborigines or blacks or Indians—as people whose rights were violated and must be restored as quickly as possible, these movies romanticize the victims. They are seen in terms of what whites are supposed to have repressed. (p. 534)

It's implicit in **The Last Wave** that the crime against the aborigines is what alienated the whites from their dreams, and that because of this crime a Biblical flood is coming—punishment and purification. It doesn't seem to matter that the flood will flush away the aborigines as well. This film is so infatuated with white guilt that the aborigines are created in our lost self-image. (pp. 534-35)

Weir doesn't develop any characters, so if all the people are to be killed the viewer has no particular cause for regret. Or even for much interest, because the film has worn us out with all its forebodings. Weir has reversed the techniques needed for audience involvement. Instead of starting with the ordinary, getting us to care about the characters, and building to a hallucinatory climax, he uses his dislocating tricks right at the start, and keeps using them in the Sydney streets and rooms. Nobody in the lawyer's home can pick up a toothpick without the scene's being invested with dread. But when Weir gets to the mystic big number—the journey to the "sacred place," where the lawyer reënacts the whites' primal crime against the aborigines—he might be shooting a documentary of everyday events. He's prosaic just when he needs to be imaginative to pull the movie together. (pp. 535-36)

Pauline Kael, "Doused" (originally published in The New Yorker, Vol. LIV, No. 49, January 22, 1979), in her When the Lights Go Down (copyright © 1975, 1976, 1977, 1978, 1979, 1980 by Pauline Kael; reprinted by permission of Holt, Rinehart and Winston, Publishers), Holt, 1980, pp. 533-36.

## VERNON YOUNG

**Picnic At Hanging Rock** is the second and the best of three films made by Peter Weir and the masterpiece to date of Australian independent filmmaking. To call it a masterpiece in the context of our current critical and advertising vocabulary is to court skepticism; the term is usually reserved for something weighty and pragmatic, believed to point a moral with social resonance. **Picnic** is frankly a diaphanous horror story. . . . (p. 416)

Weir's movie is permeated with suppressed eroticism that never crudely surfaces. By lyric touches and the art of indirection he conveys the somewhat smelly radiance that emanates from the girlish admixture of innocent crush and diffused smut which constitutes the eternal milieu of adolescents segregated from the other sex. The spoken language is refreshingly articulate—indeed, it is *language*—and every color composition exhales a natural or contrived beauty. Lovely girls, lovely analogies: swans, flowers, young trees reflected in darkening waters. I was reminded of Elie Faure's inspired image when describing the phenomenon of Watteau's art under the regime of Louis XIV: "a profound sigh of nature delivered from a corset of iron. . . ."

Having in mind . . . **Picnic at Hanging Rock,** I realize that the older I get in the service of the perishable art, the more I am convinced that if a film is not poetry, it is nothing much. (p. 417)

Vernon Young, "Film Chronicle: Trash and Poetry," in The Hudson Review (copyright © 1979 by The Hudson Review, Inc.; reprinted by permission), Vol. XXXII, No. 3, Autumn, 1979, pp. 411-17.*

## MARSHA KINDER

[**The Plumber** is] a 76-minute Pinteresque black comedy, which at times is hysterically funny and at other times emotionally disturbing. . . .

**The Plumber** is in some ways a more perfectly realized work than Weir's earlier, more ambitious films. . . . The brilliance of the film lies in taking [a] stock situation from domestic comedy, which would be farcical in the context of an *I Love Lucy* show, and transforming it into a desperate struggle for sanity and survival. (p. 17)

[The] ambiguity in the story greatly enriches its meaning. [Weir] consciously cultivates the reading of [Jill and Max's encounter] on many different levels—not merely as a sexual struggle between a swaggering macho bully and a timid, uptight woman, but also as a class struggle between the underprivileged working class and the snobbish, educated bourgeoisie; between the instinctive world of sexuality, improvisation, and charm and the academic world of reason, science and law; between the sixties counter culture that spawned underground rock stars and rebels and the seventies establishment that pursues world progress and personal advancement. (p. 18)

[The] movie suggests that both characters are victims of the class system and the established society. Despite her privileged status as a graduate student, Jill's role as a woman and as a housewife renders her powerless and vulnerable to male manipulation, not only from the obnoxious plumber [Max], but also from her husband [Brian] who assumes his career is far more important than her mental health. The only way that she can persuade anyone that the plumber is endangering her life is to prove that he poses a threat to private property—by accusing him of stealing money and the expensive watch that her husband gave her. Although Max is clearly innocent of these crimes, ironically he is guilty of far more dangerous attacks on her sanity. But these violations are not defined as crimes by the society. In order to survive the threat he poses, she herself has to commit a crime. That is the only way she can win the attention, sympathy and support of her husband, the university, and the law.

In some ways the confrontation between Jill and Max is analogous to the encounter between the lawyer and the aboriginal shaman in *The Last Wave.* Both plots involve a clash between two cultures. In *The Plumber* this connection is underscored by an inset story told by Jill to her husband very early in the film. . . . Intrigued with the story, Brian advises Jill to include it in her thesis—it would make the book more appealing to a wider audience. One can't help take this remark self-reflexively as a statement about Weir's own narrative strategy; but he chooses not to dramatize the event in a flashback and keeps his camera restricted to the university complex. Yet at certain moments throughout the film, the camera dwells on a photograph of [the shaman from Jill's story] and Jill intermittently plays musical tapes from his culture. These visual and audio cues lead us to see this earlier encounter as the "germinal seed" that controls Jill's reactions to the plumber and to reinterpret her interaction with Max in this ethnographic context. In both cases, Jill is confronting a powerful male who imposes his psychic reality and forces her into a passivity that threatens her identity; in both cases, she intuitively discovers a way to humiliate and defeat the man within his own male-dominated cultural context. (pp. 18-19)

There is a chain of scatalogical associations between . . . Max's low prestige job as a plumber (which directly involved him with the apparatus by which civilized man disguises his most humiliating biological function), and the sewer works in *The Last Wave,* which is chosen as sacred grounds by the aborigines because they know it's the only wasteland that western civi-

lization will avoid at all costs. As Rabelais and Swift have so powerfully proved, scatalogical imagery, particularly when humorous, can be extremely subversive. This subversive potential is fully realized in the most hilarious sequence of *The Plumber.* In the midst of her plumbing battles, Jill is manipulated by her husband into cooking a curry dinner for two of his distinguished academic visitors. . . . The civilized ritual of the dinner party is suddenly transformed back into the basic biological process [when the Indian uses the bathroom] which, as Buñuel so wittily reminded us in *Phantom of Liberty,* has two ends. Once he enters the john, the visitor is confronted with a comical labyrinth of pipes. . . . Instead of ruining the evening, this comical accident actually deflates the pomposity of the social rituals and humanizes hosts and guests. It works in everyone's favor—cinching Brian's invitation to Geneva, making Jill's bogeyman look benign, and dispelling the audience's nervous tension with laughter. Even the disturbing story of the shaman's humiliation now seems comical from this farcical perspective. . . . But just at the point when the Cowpers and we in the audience become too smug, the nightmare recurs with a vengeance. . . . This time the humiliating disaster is not pure farce. (pp. 19-20)

In *The Plumber* one area of stylistic richness is the music, which helps to control the skillful modulation of tones and which also underscores the conflict between the two central characters. The opponents each have a musical track which they use to project their personality and dominate the apartment space. . . .

Although *The Plumber* is much less ambitious than [Weir's] other works, it nevertheless proves that he is capable of working very effectively with a wide range of tones and it continues to fulfill his promise. (p. 20)

*Marsha Kinder, "Reviews: 'The Plumber'," in* Film Quarterly *(copyright 1980 by The Regents of the University of California; reprinted by permission of the University of California Press), Vol. XXXIII, No. 4, Summer, 1980, pp. 17-21.*

# (George) Orson Welles

## 1915-

American director, actor, screenwriter, producer, and novelist.

Welles is considered to be one of the most influential craftsmen of the cinema. His lighting techniques and long-focus shots have often been copied but rarely duplicated. All of Welles's films, beginning with the classic *Citizen Kane*, deal with the same basic themes: the fixity of human existence and the futile attempt to regain lost youth and innocence. The importance of Welles's films lies in his ability to portray these themes through a wide variety of characters.

Welles demonstrated his extraordinary gifts when he was a child. At the age of three, Welles was reading Shakespeare; by the age of ten, Welles had mastered Shakespeare's works. Welles acted in and directed eight plays a year while in high school. He lied his way onto the professional stage in Dublin at sixteen and from there developed a reputation as a fine leading actor and director. Welles's directorial efforts for the Federal Theatre Project have become legend—an all-black production of *Macbeth*, a bare-stage *Doctor Faustus*, and a modern-dress *Julius Caesar* exemplified his innovativeness. Welles was already a veteran radio actor when, on October 30, 1938, he narrated H. G. Wells's *The War of the Worlds*. The program was presented as a series of newscasts and was narrated with such realism that America was swept into panic. People fled their homes and caused massive traffic jams because they believed a Martian invasion was really taking place.

As a result of his growing notoriety, Welles was signed to a Hollywood film contract. "I didn't want money; I wanted authority," Welles has said of the contract, and the fact that a novice had received total directorial and editorial authority over his films immediately alienated him from Hollywood's elite. After two aborted projects, Welles completed *Citizen Kane*, a film which many critics feel he has never equalled. This highly-renowned work proved troublesome, for *Citizen Kane* is a thinly-disguised caricature of William Randolph Hearst, who tried to have the film either altered or suppressed. He was unsuccessful, but Hollywood's animosity toward Welles continued to grow because Welles's lifestyle and filmic subjects and techniques did not conform to the Hollywood idea of normality.

Because *Citizen Kane* was not an immediate box-office success, Welles's studio, RKO, decided to recut his next film, *The Magnificent Ambersons*. This became the first of many difficulties in the completion of Welles's films. He directed the first

scenes of *Journey into Fear* but was soon taken off the film, and his directorial work went uncredited. His next project, a four-part film entitled *It's All True*, was never completed, although critics who have seen brief clips of the film feel that it could have been among Welles's best work. *The Stranger* and *The Lady from Shanghai* were received indifferently, although the latter film is seen in retrospect as one of Welles's more important films.

Welles's subsequent work has received wildly contradictory criticism. For example, some critics believe that *The Trial* incorporates almost nothing of Kafka's novel into the film, while others feel that the theme of the novel is clearly stated in the film and is at the heart of Welles's artistic philosophy. *Macbeth* and *Othello* were poorly received upon their release, but recent criticism has been more favorable. *Mr. Arkadin* (*Confidential Report*), based on a novel by Welles, is seen either as an unimportant film or as an autobiographical work similar to *Citizen Kane*. However, most critics agree that *Touch of Evil* is a superior thriller with subtle yet significant directorial touches, and *Chimes at Midnight* (*Falstaff*) is believed to be Welles's best work since *The Magnificent Ambersons*. Nevertheless, Welles's successes have been produced with much difficulty, and he has acted in second-rate films, television programs, and commercials in order to finance his own work.

Some of Welles's films have been made under very unusual conditions. *Othello* took four years and three Desdemonas to complete. Other long-standing projects, including the films *Don Quixote* and *The Other Side of the Wind*, have never been completed despite being filmed over a number of years. Despite these setbacks and the condemnation of some critics, a new Welles project is always greeted with great anticipation. Even *The Immortal Story*, a short film originally made for television, and *F for Fake* display Welles's artistic ingenuity. Critics and other directors express admiration for Welles's innovative directorial techniques. The deeply human themes of his films, and his memorable portrayal of characters such as Kane, Macbeth, Othello, and Falstaff are ample evidence that, despite his erratic career, Welles is one of the true artists of the cinema. At their best, his works have been patterned after his conviction that "A film is a ribbon of dreams." (See also *Contemporary Authors*, Vols. 93-96.)

## HERMINE RICH ISAACS

[*Citizen Kane* is] an exciting work, vital and imaginative, full of the unbridled energy which Orson Welles brings to every new medium he invades. As in all Mr. Welles' ventures, it is free of the bonds of precedent, but there is always a compensating sense of what is appropriate to the medium. It is another success in this year's stream of successful 'one-man pictures'. And just as Orson Welles, producer and director, deserves credit for the excellence of *Citizen Kane,* Orson Welles, co-author . . . , and Orson Welles, actor, must be held responsible for the fact that it falls short of greatness. (p. 427)

It is the same familiar tale from every angle, this story of a shallow and arrogant newspaper owner and man of wealth, whose craze for power and the admiration of the world leads him into headstrong and unscrupulous dealings with everyone about him; until at last he has lost all his friends, even the second wife whom he loved in his way, and retires to die in lonely splendor among his fabulous objets d'art, in his castle on a man-made hill.

It is also, when it has all been told, the picture of a man who is really not worth depicting, and here is the film's weakness. *Citizen Kane* depends for its importance on implications which are external to the movie itself. It acquires a sort of reflected significance from the fact that it might be about a living man of whom we all know, a man who not only loves power but has it, who wields a sinister influence on millions of people through the medium of his newspapers and his money. In the picture this sway over the multitude is hinted at but never demonstrated; and yet it is only this power which lends the man stature enough to make him a vital subject. Without his power he is an unpleasant rich man, nothing more. (p. 428)

*Citizen Kane* is a motion picture to be seen, a photoplay that is more than photographed actors. It is Mr. Welles' first picture and not a perfect one, but it is rich in film ideas, and abundant in opportunity for everyone associated with it. . . . And above all, *Citizen Kane* has the kind of artistic unity which is rare in Hollywood's customary large-scale collaborations. (p. 432)

> *Hermine Rich Isaacs, "'Citizen Kane' and One-Man Pictures in General," in* Theatre Arts, *Vol. XXV, No. 6, June, 1941, pp. 427-34.*

## OTIS FERGUSON

"Citizen Kane" in its story uses the cut-back method—which is convenient but has its drawbacks in the constant interruption of a steady line. . . . For dramatic action, it shows its one big character in four main situations, supplemented by newsreel interludes here and there. This makes a pretty weak structure dramatically, so it has to be surrounded with a great deal of stationary talk, as Kane is described, analyzed, asked about, remembered, talked into existence and practically out of it. . . . The mood is established or heightened by an occasional symbol: the sled and the falling-snow toy, the curtain-warning light on the stage, the bird screaming in escape, etc. Symbols are a dime a dozen and justify their use in the result achieved. I thought the fading light filament and dying sound track at the end of the singer's career very effective; also the opening and close on the iron fence around the castle. The smoke rising to heaven at the end was trite to start with and dragged out absurdly.

As you can see, there is nothing startling in these component parts. The outstanding technical effect in the picture is in the conception of settings and the use of the camera. . . .

The camera here loves deep perspectives, long rooms, rooms seen through doors and giving onto rooms through other doors, rooms lengthened out by low ceilings or made immense by high-angle shots where the ceiling seems to be the sky. Figures are widely spaced down this perspective, moving far off at will, yet kept in focus. The camera loves partial lighting or under lighting, with faces or figures blacked out, features emphasized or thrown into shadow, with one point of high light in an area of gloom or foreground figures black against brightness, with the key shifting according to mood, with every scene modeled for special effects with light batteries of varying function and power, gobos, barndoors, screens, what not. (p. 369)

Sometimes all this is fine and really does the job it is put to. Along with the wide action range, it is a relief from too much closeness and light, an effect of stretching. But at other times it appears just willful dabbling: figures are in the dark for no reason—reading without the light to see, for example; or they are kept in darkness right among other clearly lighted figures. . . .

In the cutting there are several things noticeable. One is the long easy sweep you can get when a scene of action is covered in one long-range set-up. Another lies partly in the method of treatment and partly in lack of care, and that is the time-and-place confusion which arises when you go smack from the first two-thirds of a sentence to the last third of the same sentence, spoken elsewhere years later. This is done time and again and you might call it jump-cutting or you might call it the old shell game as far as the audience is concerned.

Another thing about the cutting that goes altogether to the fault of direction is the monotony and amateurism of handling simple dialogue. Over and over there are the two faces talking, talk, talk, talk, then close-up of the right speaker asking, then close-up of left speaker answering, then back to two. Outside of getting your name in large letters, being a director consists exactly in knowing how to break this up, to keep interest shifting, to stress the *reaction* to a line more sharply than the face saying it. This is what gives a picture life, and it isn't done by camera ructions, however clever.

Orson Welles was naturally entranced with the marvelous things the moving camera could do for him; and while much has resulted from this preoccupation, I think his neglect of what the camera could do *to* him is the main reason why the picture somehow leaves you cold even while your mouth is still open at its excitements. There may have been the heart and belief to put into it, but there wasn't the time to learn how this might be done, or much regard for any such humdrum skill. (p. 370)

As for the contributing departments in "Citizen Kane," Bernard Herrman's music is an active aid; the sets are made right, both for the fantastic and for use or living; it is an all-round class-A production. But the most effective things in it are the creation of Orson Welles's drawing board, not only in whole story ideas but in plausible and adult dialogue (witty, sardonic, knowledgeable), the impression of life as it actually goes on in the big world, the ready dramatic vigor. . . .

This stuff is fine theatre, technically or any other way, and along with them the film is exciting for the recklessness of its independence, even if it seems to have little to be free *for.* There is surely nothing against it as a dramatic venture that it is no advance in screen technique at all, but a retrogression. The movies could use Orson Welles. But so could Orson Welles use the movies, that is, if he wants to make pictures. Hollywood is a great field for fanfare, but it is also a field in which even Genius has to do it the hard way; and "Citizen Kane" rather makes me doubt that Orson Welles really wants to make pictures. (p. 371)

*Otis Ferguson, "From 'Hudson's Bay' to the Legion of Decency: Welles and His Wonders: II (originally published as "Welles and His Wonders: II," in* The New Republic, *Vol. 104, No. 24, June 16, 1941), in* The Film Criticism of Otis Ferguson, *edited by Robert Wilson (© 1971 by Temple University), Temple University Press, 1971, pp. 369-71.*

## ROGER MANVELL

**The Stranger,** to which the critics looked forward because Orson Welles once directed two remarkable films, is no successor to those earlier achievements, though it contains many technical points of presentation which remind one of them. **The Stranger** is good, but not excellent, thriller entertainment, in the same class as **Journey into Fear**. . . . The earlier scenes are beautifully done: the small-town setting is alive and vivid, and the character of the shop-keeper who works a "self-serve" store is himself the best piece of cinema in the film. **The Stranger** is full of fine touches of melodrama . . . , but in the end we come back to the many, almost choric, scenes in the shop which fix the film's terrors into a frame of reality that sharply sets them off. This is the technical trick of Hitchcock which used to work so well during his period of British melodramas. For all his extravagance, Hitchcock knew where to stop straining our credulity. **The Stranger** soon outpaced mine.

*Roger Manvell, "The Quarter's Film: Orson Welles," in* Sight and Sound *(copyright © 1946 by The British Film Institute), Vol. 15, No. 59, Autumn, 1946, p. 98.*

## PHILIP HOPE-WALLACE

The look of [*Macbeth*], which is after all the most important part of a film, is seldom felicitous. Macbeth's castle has even less geography than Hamlet's film Elsinore; it looks all too often like a rain-soaked scenic railway at a fun fair, a castle hewn from papier mâché rocks, but Welles is not the first producer of the play to have difficulty with the period. A vague impression of Wagnerian timelessness sits on the costumes. Few of the voices have an American tinge and it would not matter if they had; a sort of plausible Scots burr is generally aimed at.

What of the text there is remains unaltered, for the greater part, and it is spoken slowly, not to say funereally, either as dialogue or as soliloquy, dubbed over anguished, tight-lipped close-ups of the "speaker"; this can be effective, as it has been in Olivier's Shakespeare films, but meets with the usual difficulty: *i.e.* that we are forced to look, to watch, when all we ought, or need, to do is to listen. In other words where Shakespeare uses his unmatched power of evoking the mood, the thought, the scene *by word alone*, the camera feels itself to be a shy and otiose interloper. . . . Welles, fine film maker, is not unaware of the camera's power to add a visual counterpoint undreamt by Shakespeare. (pp. 22-3)

[Parts] of the great poetic drama come over well. . . . In such episodes we have an earnest of what Welles was trying for and in part has succeeded in doing. On the other hand, imagination is checked where we are shown too literally what in the play is only brought to us as a frightening rumour. . . . The appalling difficulties of trying to recreate a masterpiece of one

sort of medium . . . in terms of another, so utterly different, have not been ignored or solved. Those who are interested in the problem will find much to discuss; and those who come ignorant of Shakespeare to the cinema will probably receive an impression of portentous dismay, which is, after all, something. The attempt should not be written off as a failure, though one cannot help thinking that a more powerful effect might have been achieved if the film, properly, had been silent; simply a series of blood-curdling illustrations to a series of anonymous declamations from the sound track. (p. 23)

*Philip Hope-Wallace, "'Macbeth'," in* Sight and Sound *(copyright © 1951 by The British Film Institute), Vol. 21, No. 1, August-September, 1951, pp. 22-3.*

## TONY RICHARDSON

Welles breaks all the rules and cracks like a plant out-growing its pot the very capacity of the category we have established. For of all the *metteurs en scène* he is the most gifted and the most startling. Like many of the others he came from the theatre. . . . Now, with all the resources of the cinema at his disposal, it was to be expected that he would be even more potent. Seen for the first time, **Citizen Kane** is just that. The punches are so quick and deadly that his problem becomes not so much one of keeping our attention as of getting us to recover fast enough to take more punishment. Every trick, every effect known to the expert illusionist and master shock-tactician is deployed, down to the screech of the cockatoo. Viewing the film again, one sees not so much this naïve desire to shock and stun but the prodigious, squandering invention.

As serious drama the films mean nothing; the conception and development of the characters is on a magazine journalistic level. But this doesn't matter: when one has said it, one has said nothing about the films themselves. They are not so much dramas as gossip; rich, exhilarating, fabulous gossip about the times and the places and the people Welles has known. Certainly Welles has no moments of great penetration or insight, but as a presentation of the externals, the public personalities of men, their fights, their defeats, their celebrations, his films have never been surpassed. Welles scatters his fine images like an Eastern prince his jewels, and he can range from a splendid, sonorous catalogue of the properties, the castles, the swimming pools, the statues, the zoos, to scenes of . . . subtlety and complexity. . . . Above all it is the prodigality of energy, the sheer splendid life and go of it all, that makes his films so invigorating. Anyone who has created the dazzlingly lovely party sequence in **The Magnificent Ambersons,** or the entrancing sledge ride in the snow, has raised talent to a pitch where it is indistinguishable from genius. (p. 109)

*Tony Richardson, "The metteur en scene," in* Sight and Sound *(copyright © 1954 by The British Film Institute), Vol. 24, No. 2, October-December, 1954, pp. 62-6, 120.\**

## ROBERT DOWNING

Orson Welles' **Othello** is as moody, flamboyant and full of contradictions as its producer-adapter-director-star. Nevertheless, and notwithstanding many imperfections, Welles' **Othello** is a worthy attempt to bring Shakespeare to the screen.

The text has been industriously deleted and re-arranged. . . . But in certain passages Welles cut too deeply.

Emilia's character . . . is not properly established, and her relationship with Iago is not made clear until quite late. Cutting harms Desdemona's part. . . . While it is not necessary to feel "sympathy" for the Moor, one might understand him better in this film had Welles relied more on Shakespeare's lines than on brooding, wide-eyed, close-ups of himself. Welles is too detached, cold-blooded, and *watchful* in his portrayal. His reading of the closing speech, however, is masterly. (p. 341)

*Othello*'s photography is varied indeed. Many scenes are brilliantly composed, lighted and photographed; others are pale, trembling, and even out of focus. Good use is made of Venetian architecture. The music of Francesco Lavagnino and Alberto Barberis also helps to evoke the medieval spirit, though the recording is ragged. The dubbing is execrable, and lip synchronization is almost never achieved.

*Othello* is stamped with Orson Welles' amazing insight and gross negligence. But it is not a film that will be forgotten. Should Welles become able to discipline his genius, and should he have access to enough money to give his talents free play, he might yet provide the screen with its best Shakespeare. (pp. 341-42)

Robert Downing, "Film Reviews: 'Othello'," in Films in Review *(copyright © 1955 by the National Board of Review of Motion Pictures, Inc.), Vol. VI, No. 7, August-September, 1955, pp. 341-43.*

## PENELOPE HOUSTON

Orson Welles casts such a gigantic shadow that it becomes difficult to realise that in fact only six films (five if one chooses to discount the equivocal *Journey into Fear*) stand between the dazzling pyrotechnics of *Citizen Kane* and the choked and spluttering deadwood bonfire that is *Confidential Report*. . . . Fuelled with reminiscences of *Kane*—the fascination with the mystery and the apparatus of power, the involved flashback structure—and stoked up with bits from [Carol Reed's] *The Third Man*, from the spectacular seediness of the world of Harry Lime, this is a grandiose and ornate melodramatic construction. But beneath the baroque extravagance of its style, and the characteristic romantic retreat from reality into another Xanadu, the film crumbles emptily away. With *Kane*, Welles' especial genius was to persuade us that he was telling the story in the only way possible. Here, one early develops the uneasy conviction that the film-maker is saying nothing in particular, for all that he is undeniably saying it at the top of his voice. (pp. 86-7)

Welles, inevitably, embroiders this with all the hocus-pocus of the practised illusionist. The elaborate maze of flashbacks; the tilted camera and the extravagant camera angles; the huge and shadowy sets, transforming the castle in Spain into an ogre's gothic palace; the broken sentences, the overlapping dialogue, the sudden jagged burst of sound at a party, are all by now familiar elements in the Wellesian sleight of hand. . . . Where the material is second-hand, though, all this obsessive technical display can merely expend itself purposelessly, and the story disintegrates under it.

As *Lady From Shanghai* (a more substantial and entertaining film than this) has already sufficiently demonstrated, Welles' attitude to melodrama is fundamentally at the opposite extreme from that of Hitchcock. Where Hitchcock turns the commonplace upside down, allowing charwomen to carry revolvers and commercial travellers to dismember their wives, Welles appears to be drawn to melodrama by the opportunities it affords for eccentric and romantic characterisation. . . . That he does not himself make a great deal of Arkadin is perhaps inherent in the conception of the character; conscientiously a man of mystery, Arkadin remains for most of the film a formidable shadow, a man figuratively, if not after his first appearance actually, behind a mask. That, ultimately, is rather the impression that these restless and baffling melodramatics give one of Welles himself. The talent itself is still one immensely to be reckoned with; it remains for the heavyweight director again to take on something his own size. (p. 87)

Penelope Houston, "'Confidential Report'," in Sight and Sound *(copyright © 1955 by The British Film Institute), Vol. 25, No. 2, Autumn, 1955, pp. 86-7.*

## ERIC BENTLEY

[We get from Orson Welles] pathetically puerile entertainments: the movie *Macbeth* with Scotch accents affected by assorted amateurs from Utah. . . . And now *Othello,* a film bad from every point of view and for every public. It is, technically, gauche, the dialogue being all too obviously dubbed. It lacks popular appeal, as the story is neither simply nor skilfully told. To connoisseurs of Shakespeare, it can only be torture. And to the dwindling number of Welles admirers, the unhappy few among whom I count myself, it is one more disappointment. One is tempted to say that, while Shakespeare turned a sensational tale into high tragedy, Orson Welles has turned the tragedy back into a sensational tale. But this is to flatter Mr. Welles, who shows no sense of narrative, that is, of the procession of incidents, but only an interest in the incidents themselves—no, not even that, but only an interest in separate moments within the incidents, and this just for the opportunity they offer for effects, visual and auditory. Many of these effects are superb. Who but Welles would have given the curtain rings such a strident sound? Who but he would have set the opening of the temptation scene . . . to the clump of the actors' shoes on stone? If there were a real mind in charge of the production as a whole, Orson Welles would be the greatest assistant director of all time. (pp. 21-2)

[The] whole film is a precise example of formalistic decadence. Very much an Art Film, *Othello* is a rag-bag of the ideas of yesterday's avant-garde. . . . Even a Wellesite like myself, interested in each image as it impinges on the retina, sadly realizes at the close that the images add up to nothing. (p. 22)

Eric Bentley, "Theatre: 'Othello'," in The New Republic *(reprinted by permission of* The New Republic; *© 1955 The New Republic, Inc.), Vol. 133, No. 14, October 3, 1955, pp. 21-2.*

## DAVID ROBINSON

Any schoolboy Shakespearean or home movie-maker can fault this *Othello* . . . in a dozen ways. Its narrative goes by such fits and starts that it is often hard to follow the story. The cutting of the text seems often merely perverse: key scenes are excised and minor ones inflated disproportionately. Identifications and explanations are forgotten; raw edges abound. The poetry of this most poetic play seems deliberately obscured, while the rough post-synching and the variable quality of the sound make the clearest voices at times unintelligible.

It is so easy to see these things. It is too easy to rejoice in our own fine discrimination in catching so considerable an artist as Welles tripping, to dismiss the film so hastily that we overlook the splendours of an exciting, frustrating interpretation of the tragedy.

It is frustrating because we see by flashes just how marvellous it might all have been. . . . Constantly the visual and physical disposition of the characters reflects and emphasises their intellectual placing in the drama. The technique of the bed-time quarrel in *The Magnificent Ambersons,* for example, is perfectly suited to the counter-questions and cross-purposes of the last scene of *Othello.*

Visually the film is superb. . . . Only rarely the search for the picturesque gets out of hand, as it does, for instance, in the absurd Harry Lime chase of Roderigo and Cassio through the sewers.

The severe abridgement of the play destroys the fine narrative of the original, and—perversely as it seems—several of the finest, and dramatically most important, scenes are omitted. . . . The effect of this version is to throw into strong relief the two main figures, to concentrate on Othello and Iago almost to the exclusion of the other characters. Welles' own Othello is magnificent in the grandeur and simplicity with which it is conceived. . . . It is his magnificent simplicity, his freedom from any intellectual subtleties which gives complete conviction to his gullibility and complete tragic pathos to his fearful anger and murderous crime.

Iago, on the other hand, has been refined into a figure of impenetrable mystery. (p. 196)

Welles brings to *Othello* all his own rich visual invention and his fertile intelligence—unrestrained by too nice formalities of taste—to suggest, even in flashes, the rich potential of the cinema for interpreting the great tragedies. This flawed and faulty film is infinitely more vital, stirring, invigorating, than half-a-dozen more reverent, pedantically impeccable attempts. (p. 197)

> David Robinson, "'Othello'," in Sight and Sound (copyright © 1956 by The British Film Institute), Vol. 25, No. 4, Spring, 1956, pp. 196-97.

## PENELOPE HOUSTON

[*Touch of Evil*] might suggest that an instinct for grandiose melodrama is proving the most durable element in Orson Welles' still formidable talent. After the perversely extravagant crooks' tour of *Confidential Report,* this film represents a kind of marking time, evidence that Welles remains fascinated by power and its corruption, by the fatal flaw in the strong man . . . ; and evidence that he can still deal the technical cards out of the pack with a cardsharper's eye to subterfuge. . . . In essence, [the story] is not very complicated; as told by Welles, it becomes a jungle of confused motivations, nightmarish betrayals and discoveries. All the stylistic equipment—heavy shadows, suggestions of menace lurking just beyond camera range, tilted angles and half-heard dialogue—is called into play to convey the landscape of corruption. The opening, with a bomb planted in a car and the camera tracking its slow progress through a border town, immediately grips. The last scenes, shot among murky canals and crumbling oil derricks, with the hero scrambling after his victim to take down a confession on a tape-recorder, is a fine bravura exercise. But much of the rest is Welles at his most perversely obscure. (pp. 251-52)

Melodrama can survive without explanations; and in watching this shadowy, twisted thriller one may reflect not that the talent responsible for *Citizen Kane* is being wasted, but that Welles, after all, never managed really to explain Kane. . . .

[Whatever] the vicissitudes through which the film has passed since leaving his hands, it still carries one of the cinema's unmistakable signatures. No-one else, surely, could have made this thriller—though there may be moments when one feels that no-one else would have wanted to. (p. 252)

> Penelope Houston, "'Touch of Evil'," in Sight and Sound (copyright © 1958 by The British Film Institute), Vol. 27, No. 5, Summer, 1958, pp. 251-52.

## ANDRÉ BAZIN

There is little doubt that even if he had directed only *Citizen Kane* and *The Magnificent Ambersons,* Welles would have a major position in the history of the cinema. It is not to diminish the importance of his later films if I assert that, at least on a formal level, the essence of what Welles brought to the cinema is already present in his first two films.

Analysis and reflection reveal, above all, a stylistic unity. Within the context of Welles' filmography, these two works constitute a vast aesthetic land mass whose geology and relief justify simultaneous study.

Let us take up their orientation first. *Kane* and *Ambersons* together form what might be called the social realist cycle, to distinguish it both from the Shakespearean cycle composed by *Macbeth* and *Othello* and from the "ethical entertainments" comprising *The Lady from Shanghai* and *Mr. Arkadin.* "Entertainment" should not be understood here in a pejorative or even a restrictive sense. But it is obvious that these two latter films imposed an overall sense of amused contrivance on their thriller conventions. In other words, the seriousness of the message filters through the apparent futility of the game.

*Kane* and *Ambersons,* on the other hand, are the cinematic equivalents of realistic novels in the tradition of, say, Balzac. On one level they appear to be powerful, critical testimonies on American society.

But one must pass beyond this first level of significance, where one soon reaches, beneath these social deposits, the crystalline mass of moral significance. From this point of view, Welles' *oeuvre* is one of the least debatable in the history of the cinema, and takes its place beside the great spiritual landscapes created by Stroheim, Chaplin, Eisenstein, Renoir, Flaherty, Rossellini. . . . [One] of the major themes of Welles' imagination as it is revealed in a very special way in his first two films [is] the obsession with or, if one prefers, nostalgia for childhood. (pp. 64-5)

If one had any doubts, on the evidence of [*Citizen Kane*], about the obsession with childhood in Welles' work, *The Magnificent Ambersons* would provide a decisive confirmation. . . . Welles succeeded in infecting the principal character . . . with the same obsession as Kane. Not that George Minafer is in any way a duplicate of Kane. The social context, the historical moment, the biographical conditions in which the Amber[son] heir evolves, give his personal drama a completely di[fferent] character. But his tyrannical attachment to his mothe[r and] opposition to Eugene Morgan—the industrialist w[ho] and who represents both economic and social c[...]

similar egotistic "fixation" on the universe of his child-hood. . . . (p. 66)

[The] profound authenticity of the theme of childhood in *Citizen Kane* and *The Magnificent Ambersons* is revealed more per-suasively by the introduction in the story or *mise en scène* of significant and visibly unpremeditated details, which have im-posed themselves on the author's imagination by their affective power alone. For instance, the repeated use of snow, charac-teristic of childhood fantasies. . . . Nostalgia for snow is con-nected to our earliest games (to which should doubtless be added the specific symbolism of snow, whose threatened white-ness, auguring the mire to come, is particularly suited to the guilty innocence of childhood). . . . Indirectly linked to the theme of childhood by way of egotism and the need for social approval is Kane's taste for statues, through which he is ob-viously pursuing the impossible project of becoming a statue himself.

Once again, this interpretation, which we might call existential, does not pretend in any way to exhaust the meanings of Welles' first two films, whose labyrinths could be traced by other threads. What matters is that one should be no less sure of meeting the Minotaur there. Welles' *oeuvre* is a haunted one—that is all that it was necessary to demonstrate.

But more than the intellectual and moral message—which will become more precise and perhaps richer later on, in the sub-sequent films—it is their formal brilliance, their overwhelming originality of expression, to which *Citizen Kane* and *The Mag-nificent Ambersons* owe their historical importance and the de-cisive influence they have had on cinema all over the world. We can analyze the technique of the *mise en scène* in either film, for despite considerable variations between their styles, the essential aspects of their means of expression are the same. (pp. 66-8)

It is plausible, for example, to suppose that Welles, as a man of the theatre, constructs his *mise en scène* on the basis of the actor. One may imagine that the intuition of the sequence shot, this new unit in film semantics and syntax, grew out of the vision of a director accustomed to placing the actor within the décor, who experienced traditional editing no longer as a fluency or language but as a loss of efficacy, a mutilation of the spec-tacular possibilities of the image. For Welles, each scene to be played forms a complete unit in time and space. The acting loses its meaning, is deprived of its dramatic blood like a severed limb, if it ceases to maintain a living and responsive connection with the other characters and the décor. Further-more, the scene charges itself like an electrical condenser as it progresses and must be kept carefully insulated against all parasitic contacts until a sufficient dramatic voltage has been reached, which produces the spark that all the action has been directed toward. Take, for instance, Welles' favorite scene in *The Magnificent Ambersons:* the one in the kitchen between Fanny and George and Jack. . . . Wasn't [Welles] skill-ful [the] intolerable tension, created [be]tween the real feelings of the [and] behavior? Fanny's pain and [l]ike an awaited storm, but one [whose] violence one could not [ca]mera movement, or a close-up [dis]tion, would have broken this [and] participate intimately in the [ ] play at each moment on the [ ] and construct the action not [relat]ions between the characters

and their surroundings, but on the physical perception of these relations as dramatic forces, to make us present at their evo-lution right up to the moment when the entire scene explodes beneath this accumulated pressure, it was essential for the bor-ders of the screen to be able to reveal the scene's totality. (pp. 68, 72-3)

But the clarity of the scene in depth was not enough for Welles' theatrical approach; he also needed a "lateral" depth of focus. This is why Gregg Toland used very wide-angle lenses, bring-ing the angle of the shot close to that of the eye's normal vision. . . . Wide-angle lenses . . . have the effect of distorting perspective appreciably. They give the impression of a stretch-ing of length, which accentuates the deep focus even more. I won't risk the hypothesis that Welles planned this effect; but in any case he has turned it to his advantage. The stretching of the image in depth, combined with the nearly constant use of low angles, produces throughout the film an impression of tension and conflict, as if the image might be torn apart. No one can deny that there is a convincing affinity between this physical aspect of the image and the metaphysical drama of the story. As for the ceilings, especially in *Ambersons,* they help situate the characters in a closed universe, crushed on all sides by the décor. . . . The persistence of the low angle in *Citizen Kane* means . . . that we quickly cease to have a clear awareness of technique even while we continue to submit to its mastery. . . . [It is] likely that the method corresponds to a precise aesthetic intention: to impose a particular vision of drama on us—a vision that could be called infernal, since the gaze upward seems to come out of the earth, while the ceilings, forbidding any escape within the décor, complete the fatality of this curse. Kane's lust for power crushes us, but is itself crushed by the décor. Through the camera, we are capable in a way of perceiving Kane's failure at the same time we ex-perience his power. (pp. 74-5)

[The] value of deep focus, so passionately contested by some, probably lay for Welles in a certain way of placing the décor and characters. But it involves many consequences in addition to the construction of ceilings and a denser style of acting. To begin with, its technical demands make shot transitions more difficult. In any case, Welles was not the sort of man to stop at such a difficulty, even though the decision to have the whole scene played in the camera's distinct field of vision was con-tradictory to the classical practice of shot transitions. Better still, Welles quite often reinforces the maintenance of this dramatic unity by refusing to use camera movements that would in fact reestablish, by the succession of new framings, a hy-pothetical breakdown into shots. (pp. 76-7)

[Let] us examine a typical Welles scene: Susan's attempted suicide in *Citizen Kane*. The screen opens on Susan's bedroom seen from behind the night table. In close-up, wedged against the camera, is an enormous glass, taking up almost a quarter of the image, along with a little spoon and an open medicine bottle. The glass almost entirely conceals Susan's bed, enclosed in a shadowy zone from which only a faint sound of labored breathing escapes, like that of a drugged sleeper. The bedroom is empty; far away in the background of this private desert is the door, rendered even more distant by the lens' false per-spectives, and, *behind* the door, a knocking. Without having seen anything but a glass and heard two noises, on two different sound planes, we have immediately grasped the situation: Su-san has locked herself in her room to try to kill herself; Kane is trying to get in. The scene's dramatic structure is basically founded on the distinction between the two sound planes: close up, Susan's breathing, and from behind the door, her husband's knocking. A tension is established between these two poles, which are kept at a distance from each other by the deep focus. Now the knocks become louder; Kane is trying to force the door with his shoulder; he succeeds. We see him appear, tiny, framed in the doorway, and then rush toward us. The spark has been ignited between the two dramatic poles of the image. The scene is over. (pp. 77-8)

It is evident that the classical sequence composed of a series of shots, analyzing the action according to the way the director wants us to see it, is resolved here into only one shot. So that Welles' *découpage* in deep focus ultimately tends to absorb the concept of "shots" in a *découpage* unit which might be called the sequence shot.

Naturally, this revolution in the conventions of *découpage* is of interest less in itself than for its implications. To simplify, let us say that this synthetic language is more realistic than traditional analytical *découpage*. More realistic and at the same time more intellectual, for in a way it forces the spectator to participate in the meaning of the film by distinguishing the implicit relations, which the *découpage* no longer displays on the screen like the pieces of a dismantled engine. Obliged to exercise his liberty and his intelligence, the spectator perceives the ontological ambivalence of reality directly, in the very structure of its appearances. (pp. 78, 80)

Contrary to what one might believe at first, "*découpage* in depth" is more charged with meaning than analytical *découpage*. It is no less abstract than the other, but the additional abstraction which it integrates into the narrative comes precisely from a surplus of realism. A realism that is in a certain sense ontological, restoring to the object and the décor their existential density, the weight of their presence; a dramatic realism which refuses to separate the actor from the décor, the foreground from the background; a psychological realism which brings the spectator back to the real conditions of perception, a perception which is never completely determined a priori. In opposition to this "realistic" *mise en scène*, proceeding by "sequence shots" seized by the camera as blocks of reality, Welles frequently uses an abstract metaphorical or symbolic montage to encapsulate lengthy sections of the plot (the evolution of the relationship between Kane and his first wife; Susan's career as a singer). But this very old procedure, which the silent cinema abused, finds a new meaning here, in precise contrast to the extreme realism of the scenes in which events are respected integrally. Instead of a crossbred *découpage*, in which the concrete event is partially dissolved into abstraction by shot transitions, we have two essentially different narrative modalities. One can see this quite clearly when, after the series of superimpositions encapsulating three years of torture for Susan and ending on a light going out, the screen thrusts us brutally into the drama of Susan's attempted suicide. (pp. 80-1)

All great cinematic works doubtless reflect, more or less explicitly, the moral vision, the spiritual tendencies of their author. Sartre wrote in reference to Faulkner and Dos Passos that every novelistic technique necessarily relates back to a metaphysics. If there *was* a metaphysics, the old form of *découpage* couldn't contribute to its expression: the world of Ford and Capra can be defined on the basis of their scripts, their themes, the dramatic effects they have sought, the choice of scenes. It is not to be found in the *découpage* as such. With Orson Welles, on the contrary, the *découpage* in depth becomes a technique which constitutes the meaning of the story. It isn't

merely a way of placing the camera, sets and actors [*mettre en scène*]; it places the very nature of the story in question. With this technique, the cinema strays a little further from the theatre, becomes less a spectacle than a narrative.

Indeed, as in the novel, it isn't only the dialogue, the descriptive clarity, the behavior of the characters, but the style imparted to the language which creates meaning.

Far from being—as some persist in saying, assuming inattentiveness in the spectator—a return to the "static shot" employed in the early days of cinema by [Georges] Méliès, [Ferdinand] Zecca and [Louis] Feuillade, or else some rediscovery of filmed theatre, Welles' sequence shot is a decisive stage in the evolution of film language, which after having passed through the montage of the silent period and the *découpage* of the talkies, is now tending to revert to the static shot, but by a dialectical progress which incorporates all the discoveries of *découpage* into the realism of the sequence shot. Of course, Welles is not the only promoter of this evolution, to which Wyler's work also gives testimony. Renoir, for example, in all his French productions, did not cease to work in the same direction. But Welles has brought to it a powerful and original contribution which, like it or not, has shaken the edifices of cinematic tradition. (pp. 81-2)

*André Bazin, in his* Orson Welles: A Critical View, *translated by Jonathan Rosenbaum (translation copyright © 1978 by Harper & Row, Publishers, Inc.; reprinted by permission of Harper & Row, Publishers, Inc.; originally published in 1958), Harper, 1978, 138 p.*

## GORDON HITCHENS

Of course, even bad Welles is absorbing cinema; but how can one so praise a filmmaker without sounding condescending? The point is that [in *Mr. Arkadin*] Welles has a film that holds one's interest continually and yet is disappointing and embarrassing. This film is all technique and bravura and theatricality, but is utterly lacking in significance. It is a kind of decadence, with over-decorated sets, over-busy camera, over-characterized characters from Welles' grab-bag of international types. Because this is a "personal" film, so called, we expect a chaste and trembling virgin, but instead we find the mechanical passion and tired tricks of the over-rouged street-walker.

Welles has written here a vehicle for himself. . . . Such a voice needs a masterful writer of the epic stamp—Shakespeare, Marlowe, or Melville. . . . Such talent, and so little substance— small wonder that we are embarrassed.

Welles has here the undeveloped modicum of a major film. He is fascinated by the financial world's equivalent of himself—the lone, cold-hearted, versatile, and manipulative titan bursting with energy. The trouble is that Welles cannot organize his intuition into a coherent comment. His Tamburlaine of high finance is never seen in relationship to his wealth. . . . In the same way, we are told that Arkadin is a formidable sensualist, but we don't witness anything on the screen that would yield this extra dimension to the man's character. . . . This film, like others from Welles, is strangely asexual and, indeed, anti-sexual. The protagonist in these works is invariably isolated from even basic, elemental sexual contacts.

A further word about the story situation: the starting point of the film is "character," particularly the parable of the scorpion and the frog. Dialogue is unrelieved irony. There is no genuine menace, only off-screen maneuverings to which on-screen characters react. The film's central anecdote is leavened with humor, but the predominant tone is serious . . . and rather trivial. (pp. 36-7)

Welles' fundamental mistake in this film—and it may be the mistake that explains his entire career—has to do with Arkadin's supposed "tragic dignity", to use Welles' term. . . . Tragedy is a word much maligned in our time of a democratic application of its meaning to every pathetic situation that occurs in life. . . . Tragedy has to do with much more than "character", frogs, and scorpions. Tragedy has to do with wasted goodness and a strong character actuated by selfless, noble impulses identified with his own image. A tragic character is concerned with ultimate law informing us of Man, not simply of men as commonly individualized (in this case by Welles' Hallowe'en disguise). Tragic grandeur is awesome and mighty. Such figures are not private integers having no relation to their society, but rather are deliberate testers and discoverers of life's necessities. Such men are committed, perhaps irrationally, to some ethical standard outside of themselves, and this commitment presupposes a degree of optimism, an impulse toward perfectibility. In the Who's Who of tragedy—Ahab, Lear, Oedipus, et al—it is worse than pretentious to include the name of Arkadin. If film is content to be regarded as merely a secondary art, then let us be satisfied with such melodramas as this, all atmosphere and pulpy philosophy; but if film would aspire to the stature of dramatic literature, then let it enlarge our awareness through work that achieves true tragic dignity. (p. 37)

*Gordon Hitchens, "The Scorpion and the Frog: Part Two," in* Film Comment *(copyright © 1962 by Lorien Productions, Inc.; all rights reserved), Vol. 1, No. 1, 1962, pp. 36-7.*

## PARKER TYLER

Simply what he *is* and *has been* makes Welles the quintessential type of Big Experimental Cult hero—always achieving failure yet bringing it off brilliantly, decking it with eloquence and a certain magnificence; fusing in each film the vices and the virtues appropriate to them. Welles is the eternal Infant Prodigy, and as such wins the indulgence of adult critics and the fervid sympathy of the younger generation, which sees in him a mirror of its own budding aspirations and adventurous near-successes. . . . Welles does "big things" with fabulous ease and against manifest odds. Careful assessment of the actual results displays, along with the marred success, needless audacity and impertinent novelties. He puts on an intellectual circus even when engaged cinematically with Shakespeare. He proceeded to speak *Macbeth* with a Scottish brogue which ultimately was dropped; also, desiring to place the play in its "native" barbarous milieu, alien to the refined court verse, he put certain lines of Shakespeare's into a ridiculous light by timing them with lusty bits of staging. . . . [For Welles], the costume extravagance of the film, like the boisterous irony shed on its language, was a quality of arbitrary wit: a playfulness out of keeping with the solemn intentions of the original dramatic work. . . .

Another Shakespeare play, *Othello,* offers an even better example of Welles at work. Here, chiefly by tracking and a dolly that seemed to be over-oiled, the action is considerably augmented and "cinematized," so that the tragic effects, especially at the end, are turned into giddy *bravura.* (p. 33)

*All* Welles's heroes are "big doers" who crumble; *magnificos* who are crushed by secret starvation of personal desires or a cancerous guilt. Fair, hale, noble, with a beard (as in *Othello*) or middle-aged, ignoble and ugly (as in the police chief in *Touch of Evil*), Welles as actor-director shows high human ambition in the grip of an obscure corrosion. The inquisitive reporter bent on searching out the magnate Kane's secret, the adventurer hired by Arkadin (another kingpin of wealth) to discover his own past, bear the same relation to the Wellesian type as Iago does to Othello: he is the chosen nemesis. The hero of *Citizen Kane,* despite all appearances, had been doomed to unhappiness; the reporter's quest simply reveals the technical origin of this unhappiness: a mechanism that has done its work. Welles's hireling hero is the *other self,* enlisted precisely to be the means of revelation to himself and the audience. (p. 34)

Welles, more than any one person in the world at this moment, is a cult incarnate—whether we approach his example from the side of the Little or the Big Experimentalists. He may never do a complete and untarnished work of film art, at once deep in theme and adequate in execution. Yet as a tireless infant Hercules, he has shaken the film firmament, and may (bearded or unbearded) do so again. (p. 35)

*Parker Tyler, "Orson Welles and the Big Experimental Film Cult," in* Film Culture *(copyright 1963 by* Film Culture*), No. 29, Summer, 1963, pp. 30-5.*

## ERNEST CALLENBACH

Rare is the critic who can manage to look at a film like [*The Trial*] except through a kind of screen set up by the original work. No amount of consciousness about problems of adaptation, and all that, can gainsay this tendency—only ignorance is a real safeguard. Luckily, however, I have not read Kafka's novel for many years. Consequently, looking at Welles' *Trial,* I find it an interesting film, rather than a disappointing derivative. It is, of course, in many ways not only unKafka-like but positively anti-Kafka. (p. 40)

The film is an attempt to create a nightmare world, rather like that of *1984.* It is vaguely European in decor, with a melange of nineteenth-century monumentalism, now decayed, and some twentieth-century counterparts which at first seem to give the film an unfortunate dislocation; gradually one realizes that this *is* the landscape of a totalitarian nightmare. Though a few elements are discordant because of an unduly specific modernity . . . , it mixes the antique and modern in everything. Some of the settings might have been chosen with an eye to those ghastly Piranesi drawings of dungeons: but the ancient, crumbling buildings are inhabited by men who have erected, or perhaps only seized from prior uses, temporary partitions, makeshifts. It is, we soon learn, a world of sudden violence, avid sexuality, and inexplicable happenings generally. (pp. 40-1)

There is of course no love in this universe. . . . It is a world of bursts of ferocity, of murderous hates, mysterious beatings: a world of mutually brutalized slaves. . . . [It] systematically makes it hard to distinguish reality from fantasy. There is terrible power afoot, but vague and ill-limited. Side by side with the obscure politics and its sudden brutality exists a sullen and avid sexuality. (pp. 41-2)

*The Trial* abounds in comic scenes, and would be obviously quite a cut-up movie if audiences did not come prepared for High Culture—prepared, that is, for polite despair. What they find is K and Lena distractedly cuddling on an ocean of bureaucratic records, the grotesque ''Uncle Max,'' Bloch's derrière sticking up absurdly as he kisses Hassler's hand, etc. It is *not* a downbeat film, of course, but nobody can believe this because of the book. . . .

*The Trial* also abounds with virtuoso visuals, most of them stunningly successful; this is a movie in unabashed high style, with none of your realistic widescreen coolness. . . .

Welles, as usual, plays a demonic man of power (he appears first wreathed in steam, like something from the underworld) and his magnificent voice manages to give an electric tension between its sonorous, sensible sound and the outrageousness of what it says. Once Welles is on the screen, the powers of darkness become compelling and one has a vision of the film that might have been—

Even the present one, however, is surely a remarkable work. (p. 42)

> *Ernest Callenbach, ''Film Reviews: 'The Trial','' in* Film Quarterly *(copyright 1963 by The Regents of the University of California; reprinted by permission of the University of California Press), Vol. XVI, No. 4, Summer, 1963, pp. 40-3.*

## ROBERT HATCH

The most disconcerting thing about Orson Welles's screen version of *The Trial* is that in retrospect it doesn't seem to matter. At the moment, it is entertaining; at times its ingenuity and insight are admirable; it commits (except for a grotesquely inappropriate final shot) no factual offense against Kafka's novel. Yet a few days after I had seen it, it had slipped off my mind and left the book just as it was.

The same thing, I find, can be said of the pictures Welles made of *Macbeth* and *Othello*. They had great cinematic vigor, they were clearly intended as shocks to entrenched attitudes toward both the plays themselves and the suitability of the screen for the transmission of Shakespeare. But whereas I have had to work at erasing Olivier's movie-Hamlet from memory, Welles's Macbeth and Othello have obligingly bleached away. (p. 85)

[*The Trial*] goes astray because Welles is a romantic—and, I think, an optimist. . . . Kafka's story of a man who is the law's victim because he is the utterly lawful man becomes the tale of a student rebel, the sort of young man who looks as though he couldn't care less about the law and its institutions. In the book the law devours its most ardent disciple; in the picture the totalitarian police pick up a potential dissident (and quite properly, given the viewpoint). That is an idea for a picture, but it is not Kafka's idea. Nor did Kafka have it in mind to warn his public against the imminence of atomic war—he was dealing with a horror of the soul. The mushroom cloud at the end of the film is another example of the boy scout in Welles; he has never been able to pass a soapbox without jumping up for a brief exhortation. (p. 91)

> *Robert Hatch, ''Adult Prodigy,'' in* Horizon *(© 1963 American Heritage Publishing Company, Inc.; reprinted by permission), Vol. V, No. 6, July, 1963, pp. 85-91.*

## GORDON GOW

Well disposed as I am toward the Orson Welles *Macbeth* and *Othello,* I feel bound to call his *Chimes at Midnight* the most mature of his Shakespearean excursions, and to hope at the same time that my use of the word 'mature' will not be taken amiss. This film is not only cinematic but also profound. . . .

[Chiefly] it is Welles as *cinéaste*, rather than just actor, that the film places in a true perspective. At the time of *Citizen Kane* I was sure, and then over the years I doubted slightly, but now I am certain again that no greater man of the cinema has ever lived. *Chimes at Midnight* is a masterpiece. . . .

If the compositions are less extravagant than is the norm in a Welles film, they are never less than pertinent, and among them there is a striking one that sets Henry IV and Hal in a great shaft of light from a window of the castle, when, seen from a distance, enclosed by the austere stone walls, the image suggests the isolation of kingship more eloquently than words . . . even Shakespeare's. . . .

[The] battle that is waged when the rebels take arms against the crown brings a stronger complexity with it. Boldly, Welles has combined a richness of low comedy with the stark and inhuman aspect of war. . . . Encompassing the realistic and the absurd, and relating the one to the other, Welles has also maintained the essential sadness of an elegy . . . a lament for pleasure that cannot continue.

> *Gordon Gow, '''Chimes at Midnight''' (©copyright Gordon Gow 1967; reprinted with permission),* Films and Filming, *Vol. 13, No. 8, May, 1967, p. 25.*

## WILLIAM JOHNSON

Judged by first—even second or third—impressions, Welles's films are a triumph of show over substance. His most memorable images seem like elephantine labors to bring forth mouse-size ideas.

His films bulge with preposterously vast spaces: the echoing halls of Kane's Xanadu; the rambling castles of Macbeth, Othello, and Arkadin; the vertiginous offices of *The Trial;* the cathedral-like palace and tavern of *Falstaff*.

His camera moves with a swagger, craning down through the skylight of El Rancho in *Kane* and up over the bomb-carrying car in *Touch of Evil*. When the camera is still, the composition may cry out for attention with anything from multiple reflections . . . to a flurry of silhouettes. . . . (p. 13)

Of course, showmanship can be sublime, and even the harshest critics of Welles's films have some kind words for *Citizen Kane*. . . . Many of the stylistic effects that Welles used with such apparent ease in *Kane* have become common screen currency only during the last ten years—wide-angle perspective, unusually long takes, abrupt cuts, intricate leaps in time, terse vignettes, heightened natural sound, and so on. Though precedents can be found for each of these devices, Welles was the first director to develop them into a full-blown style. With the exception of some typical forties process shots, the whole of *Kane* looks and sounds almost as modern today as it did in 1941. . . .

Moreover, Welles's protean style clearly reflects the character of Kane—himself a kind of Barnum who conceals his private self behind a dazzling set of public images. It's possible for a critic to see no deeper into *Kane* than this and still give the film high marks for matching style and content.

Judged by these standards, Welles's other films are inferior. Neither their stylistic inventiveness nor their matching of style and content stands out so obviously as *Kane*'s. After a brilliant start, Welles's directing career seems to decline into potboilers . . . , distortions of literary originals . . . and a rehash of *Kane*—*Arkadin*—which demonstrates only too clearly the coarsening of his showmanship. . . .

But it's difficult to maintain a balanced view of Welles's strengths and weaknesses. While his detractors see little but empty showiness, anyone who likes most of his work runs the risk of slipping to the opposite extreme. With a filmmaker as vigorous and idiosyncratic as Welles, it's temptingly easy to find some justification for nearly everything he does. *Arkadin* is based on an exciting and fruitful idea; some of the sequences in the film are excellent; many others are exciting or fascinating—and so I could go on, justifying the film piece by piece to the conclusion that it is all good. But here I'd be falling into the same trap as those who deny the originality of *Kane* because (for example) Renoir had previously used deep focus. It's the total effect that counts, and just as the total effect of Welles's deep focus is quite different from Renoir's, and much more far-reaching, so the total effect of *Arkadin* falls far short of its piecemeal felicities.

Similarly, Welles's films *are* showy, but this is only one side of them. The other, quieter side gives a far better clue to what his films are all about. (p. 14)

One of Welles's films—*Magnificent Ambersons*—is nearly all stillness, or only the most leisurely of movements. Its tempo is set by the horse and buggy typical of the age that is ending when the film's action takes place. . . .

The elegiac mood of *Ambersons* sets it apart from the rest of Welles's films, but its theme recurs in all of them, sometimes burrowing deep beneath the surface, sometimes coming out into the open as in the Bernstein reminiscence. This theme can be summed up as loss of innocence. (p. 15)

Welles does not, of course, thrust a symbol at us and leave it at that. He has designed [*Citizen Kane*] so as to bring Kane's predicament to life before our eyes; and he does this largely by giving an almost tangible presence to the passing of time. This might be called a 3-D film, with time instead of spatial depth as the salient third dimension. . . . In the film's present tense, there is the reporter's vain search for the meaning of Rosebud, which mirrors the aged Kane's own yearning for his lost innocence. Concurrently, the flashbacks into Kane's past follow him step by step as he loses that innocence. These alternating images of past and present fuse together stereoscopically into a powerful, poignant vision of Kane's loss.

Welles's other films present variations of this basic theme. Whereas *Kane* states it comprehensively, spanning almost a lifetime of change, several of the other films focus on particular stages: on the initial innocence of Mike in *Lady from Shanghai* and of Joseph K in *The Trial;* on the moment of loss for Macbeth and Othello; on a time long after the loss for Arkadin and for Hank Quinlan in *Touch of Evil.* In the other three films the theme is not tied so closely to a single character: in *The Stranger,* Nazi-in-hiding Franz Kindler threatens the innocent coziness of a New England village; in *Falstaff,* as in *Ambersons,* the loss of innocence lies in the transition between two historical ages. (pp. 15-16)

In all of his films Welles uses [the] contrast between movement and stillness to embody the fragility of life, to compress the change of a lifetime or even of an age into a few vivid moments. Sometimes he reverses his usual method of injecting stillness

into movement. The calm flow of events in *Ambersons,* for example, is broken by the lively sleigh-riding sequence, its liveliness sharpened by the brightness of the snow and the airy rapidity of Bernard Herrmann's music. The sudden release of movement gives a physical reality to the passing of time.

*Falstaff* is one gigantic contrast of this kind. Its opening and closing scenes form a reflective prologue and epilogue that stand apart from the main action. The epilogue is straightforward: it shows Falstaff's bulky coffin being trundled slowly off into the distance. The prologue is more unusual. To create it, Welles has sliced half a dozen lines out of the middle of the scene in which Shallow summons potential recruits for Falstaff. . . . In these few lines Falstaff and Shallow reminisce about their youth. "We have heard the chimes at midnight, Master Shallow." "That we have, that we have. . . . Jesus, the days that we have seen!" Singled out in this way, the brief exchange carries a more powerful charge of nostalgia than in the scene as Shakespeare wrote it; and since the main action of the film is appended to the prologue like a huge flashback, this nostalgia affects everything that follows. (p. 16)

Welles's ability to bring out the unexpected in things usually taken for granted is at work throughout his best films. The most obvious example is found in the opposition between old and new in *Ambersons*. George, who stands for the innocent age that is dying, is the film's most objectionable character; Gene Morgan, who is helping create the age of noise and crowds and air pollution, is its most likable.

Characters like Kane and Quinlan gain depth from similar contradictions. Here, though, Welles avoids not only the obvious cliché of making them out-and-out monsters but the less obvious cliché of making them sympathetic monsters. They do not arouse any set pattern of responses. (p. 17)

Perhaps the most subtly unexpected relationships in any of Welles's films are found in *Falstaff*. As portrayed by Shakespeare, Falstaff is not only lazy, gluttonous, cowardly, lecherous, dishonest and the rest but also a great innocent. He is devoid of malice or calculation; no matter what is done to him, he remains open and trusting. . . .

Welles magnifies this innocence both by uniting the Falstaff scenes from several plays and by establishing the strong mood of nostalgia discussed earlier. But—and this is the unexpected stroke—he does not do this at Hal's expense. Even in the two parts of *Henry IV* as Shakespeare wrote them—and as they are usually produced on stage—it is hard not to take a dislike to Hal for his callousness and calculation. But Welles makes it as difficult as he can for the audience to take sides between Hal and Falstaff—or rather, to take one side and stick to it throughout. (p. 18)

The struggle between tradition and progress, old and new, order and disorder is one of the most powerful forces behind Welles's work. It is reflected in his American background and his love of Europe, and in his film-making that embraces both Shakespeare and modern American thrillers. . . .

The entire shaping of each film from *Kane* through *Falstaff* shows a desire to burst out of commonly accepted limitations. Welles is not content with a single viewpoint—in *Kane* there are at least seven different ones. . . . He is not content with the straightforward flow of time—four of his films (*Kane, Othello, Arkadin, Falstaff*) begin with the end of the action before leaping to the beginning, and *Kane* continues leaping throughout; *Ambersons* frequently skips across the years with the most laconic of vignettes. In *Touch of Evil* and *The Trial* the leaps are not so much in time as in space.

The same drive makes itself felt in almost every aspect of Welles's style. It is found not only in the contrast between successive scenes—from stillness to movement, as described earlier, or from silence to noise, darkness to light, and so on— but also within individual scenes, many of which contain visual extremes or discords that threaten to burst the frame. . . .

Welles's persistent attempts to harness opposites and contradictions generate a tremendous potential energy in his films. Usually this energy is released little by little, like a controlled nuclear reaction, maintaining a steady urgency that compels attention. But even his most controlled films are often on the verge of exploding. The three Shakespeare films, for example, suffer in varying degrees from inconsistency of acting styles and accents. . . .

The two biggest casualties of Welles's explosive pressure are *Arkadin* and *The Trial*. *Arkadin* is like a grenade that flies apart chiefly along its groovings: each episode holds together fairly well, but fails to connect with the others. *The Trial* is more like the nuclear explosion with which it ends: nearly everything in it disintegrates. (p. 19)

To explain the failure of *The Trial* it's easy to fall back on the accusation of size and showiness. It's easy to argue that Welles's style is too florid for Kafka, who relied on restraint to convey the bizarre misadventures of Joseph K. But these criticisms are irrelevant because they can be leveled at Welles's other films which do not fall to pieces.

Consider *Othello*, which has just as many reasons as *The Trial* for disintegrating. Much of the film leaps from place to place with no regard for topographical continuity: any attempt to visualize the interior layout of Othello's castle is quite pointless. As with *The Trial*, Welles in adapting the original shifts some scenes and alters others. . . . He breaks up the rhythms of Shakespeare's play, sometimes accelerating, sometimes almost halting the action. The settings and the cast are multinational. Most disruptive of all, his work on the film continued on and off for a period of three years.

Yet the film translates Shakespeare into screen terms with a superb coherence. (p. 20)

The binding force in *Othello* and in most of Welles's other films is his use of symbolism. Even the most explicit of Welles's symbols do not exist in isolation: they are rooted deep in the action of the film and share the same degree of reality.

Rosebud, for example, appears at first to be a pat and superficial symbol. As with all mysteries, its revelation is something of a letdown: the sled is "only" a symbol of Kane's childhood. But the symbolism is not confined to the object itself. In fact, the adult Kane is never seen looking at it—the word Rosebud is triggered by the sight of Susan's paperweight. But here again the symbolism goes beyond the object. The paperweight is not merely an artificial snow scene recalling a real one but a snow scene encapsulated and unattainable, like Kane's lost innocence. Moreover, when the paperweight appears in close-up Welles highlights it so that it takes on a glowing halation— very much like the glare of the stage lights when Susan makes her operatic debut. Kane drives Susan to her vocal disaster not just to show his power but because, his own desire being unattainable, he wants hers to come true. Susan fails—the ironic floodlight flickers out as her voice trails away—and she is able to come to terms with reality. But the glow of Kane's

desire continues to the end: the paperweight falls and smashes only after his death. . . .

It is the interlinking of symbols beneath the surface of *Kane* that accumulates the power of the final scenes.

This symbolism underlying conspicuous symbols can be found in nearly all of Welles's films. Anyone who's seen *The Lady from Shanghai* will remember the squid that pulses up and down in the aquarium as Mike and Elsa kiss. In isolation this might be an overemphatic comment on Elsa's predatory nature, but it works because Welles has imbued the whole film with visual and verbal imagery of the sea. The Lady herself comes from one seaport and has settled in another (San Francisco), and many scenes take place on or by the water. The squid is one of several images involving dangers that lurk beneath the surface, just as dangers lurk behind Elsa's alluring exterior: there are shots of a water snake and an alligator, and Mike relates a parable about sharks that destroy one another. Even the hall of mirrors connects with the pelagic imagery: the multiple reflections are like waves receding row after row, and when the mirrors are smashed Mike can finally step out onto terra firma, ignoring Elsa's last siren call. It is this cumulative imagery that helps place *The Lady from Shanghai* above other superior thrillers. . . . (p. 21)

Elsewhere the symbolism may be too rigid for the theme, or the theme too weak for the symbolism. *Macbeth* is conceived in terms of darkness, which is appropriate enough, but the darkness hardly varies: the film consists of one low-key scene after another. There is no vivid impression of Macbeth sinking from innocence into evil and despair as there is of Othello sinking from innocence into anguish. In *The Stranger* Welles does oppose darkness with light, as the film alternates between the shadowy belfry where Frank Kindler tinkers with the church clock and the whiteness of the New England colonial buildings. But here the situation is too static: the Nazi war criminal pretending to be a good small-town citizen is unchangingly evil all along.

*Arkadin* fails because its symbolism doesn't counteract but reinforces the centrifugal pressures. In order to suggest the multiple layers of Arkadin's personality, Welles locates the film in different elements—land, sea, air—and in different climates, from the sunny Mediterranean to wintry Germany. But the symbolism lacks a second layer of its own that would bind this geographic diversity together.

As to *The Trial*, it has no underlying symbolism whatsoever— all its symbolism is on the surface. The trouble is not so much that Welles departs from the book but that he does not depart far enough. . . . In adapting the book for the screen Welles had two choices: to tone down Kafka's incidents until they could plausibly fit the everyday settings of a real city, or to amplify Kafka's settings until they fitted the bizarre incidents. The latter choice, arguably the more faithful, was the one Welles made; and he amplifies the style along with the settings.

In making this choice, however, Welles cut himself off from a prime source of strength. *The Trial* is the only one of his films that is not rooted in reality. The best films are worlds of their own that touch common experience at enough points to be accepted as reflections of the real world. It is this basis of reality that sustains Welles's underlying symbolism, which is nearly always elemental in nature—images of air, water, snow, fire, light, darkness.

*The Trial* is not one world but a succession of different worlds. Many of the scenes are so dissimilar in location, tempo, and atmosphere that is is hardly possible to imagine them coexisting on any plane of reality. Weather, the progression of night and day, natural processes of all kinds are almost completely eliminated. There is nothing for any elemental symbolism to get a grip on.

It may be argued that *The Trial* is not meant to be coherent like Welles's other films for the simple reason that it is portraying an incoherent world—that by basing the style of this film on loose ends and nonsequiturs, Welles conveys the sharpest possible sense of the menacing absurdity of modern life. . . . Luckily Welles has provided his own standard of comparison in *Touch of Evil,* which portrays the incoherence of modern life with a remarkable coherence of style and symbolism.

This is a film of darkness. It begins and ends in the night, and there are many other nocturnal or twilit scenes in between. But it is not a monotonously dark film like *Macbeth.* The night is punctuated throughout with lights that make the darkness more menacing, from the glare of the exploding car to the pulsing of neon signs.

It is in this mechanical pulsing rather than in the light and darkness themselves that the underlying symbolism is to be found. *Touch of Evil* is geared to the automatic machinery of our time. (pp. 22-3)

Though Quinlan is the only character who has succumbed to the temptation of being a machine, nearly everyone in [*Touch of Evil*] is under pressure to do so. Action, dialogue, camera movement, and editing conspire to keep the film rolling onward with machine-like relentlessness. Characters are caught up in this tremendous momentum in much the same way that Joseph K is caught up in the legal labyrinth of *The Trial:* the important difference is that the momentum of *Touch of Evil* is not conveyed indirectly through fantasy but as a direct, tangible force. . . .

I don't want to overpraise *Touch of Evil.* For all its richness it remains a thriller with a Hollywood hero. But it does succeed superbly where *The Trial* fails—in revealing a nightmare world behind everyday reality.

Moreover, in *Touch of Evil* Welles is once again several years ahead of his time. It is only in the sixties that film-makers have really assimilated the effects of post-World War II technological development on everyday life. Before then technology was usually featured either as mere decor or . . . as the antithesis to a quiet upper-income semi-rural existence. Welles makes it an integral part of life, and though he also uses it to symbolize the temptation of evil he certainly does not present it as the cause. . . .

In every one of his films Welles has taken some kind of risk. He has always been willing to pit his recurring theme of lost innocence and his elemental symbolism against the explosive diversity of his other resources. His films depend for their success on a fine balance of all kinds of opposites—sophistication and simplicity, realism and expressionism, introversion and extroversion, clarity and confusion. And yet with each film, he has rejected the cautiousness and calculation that could assure him of balance at the expense of richness and resonance. He himself has never lost all of the innocence with which he first tackled *Kane.* (p. 24)

*William Johnson, "Orson Welles: Of Time and Loss,"* in Film Quarterly (copyright 1967 by The Regents of the University of California; reprinted by permission of the University of California Press), Vol. XXI, No. 1, Fall, 1967, pp. 13-24.

## TOM MILNE

Time past and past glories: it almost sums up Welles, from the splendour of the Ambersons to the chimes at midnight tolling the death of Merrie England, by way of the touch of evil which once was truth—and it recurs again in *The Immortal Story* [adapted from a story by Karen Blixen, written under the pseudonym of Isak Dinesen]. The original creators, I do not forget, are Franz Kafka, William Shakespeare and Karen Blixen; but the magnificence as film (of the last two, at least) belongs to the mind, the mise en scène, and above all the *presence* of Welles.

Not that *The Immortal Story*—for all its air of fairytale and its setting in a Chinese Xanadu—is so much about time past or time regained as about time created. . . .

The beauty of Karen Blixen's original story is that it fuses perfectly at all levels, opening out layer after layer into, precisely, a story of immortality, of how time past, present and future, fiction and reality, can be re-shaped to create a new time and a new legend. The beauty of Welles's adaptation, despite the slenderest of means . . . and barely adequate colour and lighting effects . . . , is that it manages to encompass, even add to, the delicate tracery of the original. Not merely the visual allusions—the cell-like room in which the clerk secretes himself "with the certainty that here no one could possibly follow or disturb him"—but the curious sense of timelessness which springs from the fact that Mr. Clay, in trying to bring the world of imagination under control, merely succeeds in lending wings to whatever facts he already possesses. (p. 31)

*Tom Milne, "1968 London Festival: 'The Immortal Story',"* in Sight and Sound (copyright © 1969 by The British Film Institute), Vol. 38, No. 1, Winter, 1968-69, pp. 31-2.

## WILLIAM JOHNSON

If [*The Immortal Story*] were signed by an unknown name like Orson Baddeleys instead of Orson Welles, I might (though I hope I wouldn't) credit its faults to the director and its virtues to chance and Isak Dinesen. . . .

Welles's adaptation [of Dinesen's story] is in places oddly careless. (p. 44)

[The] discrepancies blur the impact of the story as Dinesen wrote it, and if Welles's intention was simply to translate the story into cinematic terms he did not achieve a brilliant success. But was that his intention? . . .

[Right] from the beginning of *The Immortal Story* I found it casting a spell which its weaknesses failed to break.

The clue to the nature of this spell is in the screen figure of Clay. This is not one of the restless, ironic monsters of past Welles films—a Kane, Arkadin, or Quinlan. In every scene except one Clay remains immobile, rooted in his chair, speaking slowly and without a spark of humor. (p. 45)

It's dangerously easy to read nonexistent symbolism into films, but I think it's reasonable to see Clay, the would-be shaper of reality, as a reflection of Welles the film-maker. Reality asserts itself more strongly in films than in any other artistic medium, and it can frustrate even the most skilled of directors who struggle to shape it to their vision. . . . In fact, reality asserts itself so strongly in films that audiences customarily identify actors with the characters they play. Even people who think carefully about films often refer to the actor instead of the character, if only because the actor's screen presence is so much more memorable than the character's name. Thus to most viewers, with or without symbolism, Welles *is* Clay.

There is nothing in the film to show that Welles is conscious of this equivalence: he does not openly dramatize the film-maker's predicament as Bergman does, say, in *The Magician*. But the fact that Clay suggests this predicament no doubt attracted Welles to Dinesen's story in the first place, and it certainly accounts for the film's curious fascination.

Seen in this light, the film is no longer a somewhat clumsily faithful version of the original story. It is telling a subtly different story of its own. In transforming Dinesen's prose into images and sounds, Welles gives resonance to everything that hints at the impermanence of life.

Dinesen begins her story with a series of expository paragraphs; Welles draws on these for his narration but at the same time presents quick-cut scenes of Clay riding through the seaport in his carriage and of other merchants commenting on him as he passes. . . . Dinesen devotes two pages to describing Virginie's reactions when she enters Clay's house, which had been her father's before Clay drove him to ruin, but Welles is content with one vivid scene: Virginie looking at herself in the mirror and whispering, "The last time I looked in this I was a little girl." Welles's choice of incidental music . . . also amplifies the film's sense of time passing.

This is a recurring theme in Welles's films, but once again he creates new variations on it. In transferring Dinesen's four main characters to the screen, Welles focuses sharply on the different ways they respond to the impermanence of life. (pp. 45-6)

It is the real-life counterpart of this creative fury in Welles himself that makes the film so arresting. In *The Immortal Story* Welles does what he wants to do and what he knows how to do—light up a new facet of the theme of life's impermanence and man's struggle against it. The film is neither a flawless gem nor a flawed masterpiece, but it is memorable and alive. (p. 46)

*William Johnson, "Reviews: 'The Immortal Story',"* in Film Quarterly *(copyright 1969 by The Regents of the University of California; reprinted by permission of the University of California Press), Vol. XXIII, No. 1, Fall, 1969, pp. 44-7.*

**CHARLES HIGHAM**

[Welles's] personality as an artist is on the scale of a Hugo, a Balzac: he is expansive, grand, capricious, sometimes gross in his style; maddeningly prone to dissipate his energies; baroque and Gothic by turns; romantic, journalistic, slapdash, and brilliant. *Citizen Kane* remains his masterpiece, as the world has said; but many who thought his a tragedy without a third act, a story of a genius burned out, have been proven wrong. In *Chimes at Midnight*—that tender elegy to the vanished past of England, echoing in its mood the lovely valedictory of *The Magnificent Ambersons* for the vanished past of America—and more recently in *The Immortal Story*—a reflection on the tragedy of old age—the most durable aspect of this prismatic artist was shown at its best: a contemplative aspect, a calm, autumnal

quietness in contrast with the sounding brass of so much of *Kane, The Lady from Shanghai,* and *Touch of Evil.*

Welles's films often display a reckless sophomoric humor. . . . Humor of a gently destructive, playful, sometimes shoddy kind has flashed through film after film, like the sound of Welles himself laughing in great arched caves.

An inflated display of visual and aural effects often works through the sheer accumulation of grotesque detail: in many of Welles's works we have the sensation of rushing in a ghost train through a plaster fun-fair labyrinth, surrounded by screaming and clutching bone figures. We are like Michael, the sailor in *Lady from Shanghai,* sent hurtling through the mouths of gross distorted papier-mâché figures to arrive at the shocked contemplation of our own face in multiple in a bizarre hall of mirrors.

Most of Welles's images and sounds reflect the destructive element of the grotesque. The smashing, rending, tearing sounds on his tracks, and the trick he has of closing in on a face to show its blotched, spotted, moral and physical decay, reflect an obsession with violence and barbarism. In his films the faces of the aged are observed with a horror at corruption: they have no beauty, none of that fine, pure line which time brings to some faces. (p. 1)

Yet through the humor and the mad imagery, through the stillness or the hurdy-gurdy din of the master's films, one unmistakable thread may be traced: his passionate, magnificent love of life and of human beings. There isn't a single vicious streak in his work: even Bannister, the spidery evil lawyer of *Lady from Shanghai,* is judged with strict fairness. Welles's warmth and radiant kindness, his sheer generosity, suffuse every frame of his films. His message is clear, and is greeted with enthusiasm by the young even today, in the age of Godard and Antonioni: the corrupt destroy themselves, and riches and power utterly corrupt. (p. 2)

Welles's drawing of character has the bold strokes of a caricaturist. His method with actors is reflected in their mannered, edgy playing; he drives them on and on, bullying, coaxing, wheedling as theatrically as any stage producer in a thirties Hollywood musical. His own performances . . . are vivid sketches of personalities ideally suited to the cinema. Welles's chief weakness as an actor is that he plays almost every part at the same volume—fortissimo—just as his chief weakness as an artist is that in his vision a single lamp blazes with the dramatic intensity of a Turner sunset.

Technically, Welles's films have a remarkable sophistication. In *Kane* his style was at its most dynamic: the boldness of the compositions and the daring use of light and shadow were designed to hypnotize the audience. . . . (pp. 2-3)

Aurally, the American films are as exciting as they are visually captivating. The tracks leap and fizz like loose electric wires, full of screams, shouts, hisses, and explosions of music, designed by a man in love with sound. (p. 3)

Outside America Welles has not been able to control the aural aspects of his work. His habit of using his own voice to double for others' is a maddening one, learned in the cheeseparing days of radio. He cannot face dubbing and looping sessions, and even dodged much of the all-important post-recording that followed the disastrous completion of *Macbeth.* It is a wild impatience that has crippled him here; but he is also victim of a mystifying deafness to the way an audience *hears* a film. He evidently is indifferent to the way the sound track affects others when it is recorded. Perhaps the chief reason for his failure with the masses is that he has never quite calculated how an audience *sees* a picture—seeing it only, as it were, with his inner eye. Similarly, he evidently hears the sound track with his *inner* ear. It is a particular aspect of his genius that in such matters he is often closed off from the feelings of others. . . .

Welles's greatness has chiefly been thought to lie in his technical innovations or renovations, his experiments with lighting, cutting, and sound. But his true art was in breaking through the Hollywood conventions that shut out the truth about Americans or turned the authentic dramas of everyday life into comic strips of violence informed by cheap sociology. In breaking those barriers, he showed that the cinema could explore life as ruthlessly as the novel or the theater. If Welles's desire for truthfulness destroyed him, he will leave the truth as his monument.

And his films are not merely truthful. . . . Welles's are beautiful: the best of them are delectable artifacts. Their richness of visual texture remains unequaled in the cinema. . . . (p. 4)

[Welles's films crystallize his] half-adoring, half-repelled observation of the American reality: outwardly lavish and well upholstered, inwardly rotted by sickness, an inescapable moral cancer. His deeply sophisticated humor, so seldom commented on, is even more penetrating than Von Sternberg's. At heart, he is a cynic slightly blunted by geniality; if people are brutal, he enjoys it. But not coldly, gloatingly, like Hitchcock or Wilder. He savors evil with the relish of a man in love with life, in love with all its manifestations. (p. 5)

*The Magnificent Ambersons* is a film that shows the radical changing of an order, and the conflict of materialism with the romanticism of those still enmeshed in the past. It represents, too, a central conflict in Welles himself: between nostalgia and thrusting ambition, between mild inertia and a desire for action, between a love of the past and a hunger for the excitements of the future. On the one hand he is drawn to the youth and beauty and vigor of the young people in the story, yet on the other he is attracted to the fading older figures pushed aside by the thrust of commerce. Yet the conflict is not dialectically iron-cast; the situation contains an irony. The Amberson house is not really beautiful despite Welles's affectionate treatment of it. The tragedy of the Ambersons was not merely that they were blind to "progress," but that what they clung to was in itself the product of an earlier materialism, as insubstantial as a dream.

What prevents the film from working quite satisfactorily as a work of social comment is Welles's ambiguous response to the material. Tarkington suggested the irony of the Ambersons' predicament more firmly; the local people's regard for the magnificence of the Amberson household was meant to be a trifle absurd, since its grandeur was an expression of vulgarity. Welles, by falling in love with the house, makes the story more tragic, but he removes an important element from it. He mirrors the novel's surface, though, with extraordinary fidelity, capturing to perfection its elegiac tone, mirroring its sober North American poetry in a style less baroque than *Kane*'s. (p. 54)

There are curious lapses in this lovely elegiac work: in the early passages illustrating in montage the passing of the years before George Minafer's birth, we see George himself fully grown, in a boat with his mother, who looks no younger than she does in the main body of the film. [Fanny Minafer] is seen among the Greek chorus townspeople, commenting on the Minafers' behavior—an astonishingly slipshod touch. . . . These lapses illustrate the essentially private nature of Welles's art, and his . . . contempt for the audience, which, he feels sure, will not even notice these peculiarities.

Moreover, the film is full of unexplained introductions of characters, so that the audience is never informed about the precise relationship between the Minafers and the Ambersons, whether Jack is Fanny's brother, and how Major Amberson is related to them. Welles's obliviousness to the audience's needs has never been more clearly evidenced than by this film, his most withdrawn hermetic work; and the recutting of the last part was not merely due to the need for a shorter film but to the studio's desire for clarification.

It is, too, a fragmentary work, and the fragmentary nature of it does not entirely stem from its re-editing. Welles himself lays claim to the first three reels as they stand, and these, too, have a fragmentary character. The reason for this lies in the very heart of Welles's nature as an artist. His secrecy, his recessiveness behind the braggadocio, and his emotional detachment, his inability to move into an audience's mind and hold it, are here clearly shown. Audiences failed to respond to the film because it has no clear emotional binding thread. . . . There is no single character to identify with; the development of the characters we have instead is shown in hectic glimpses; we cannot love what we cannot fully understand; and as the audience sees these creatures fade and die and face their ruin, it is intrigued but not moved. For those who understand Welles's nature, for intellectuals not dominated by a need to identify at a cinema performance, the film works beautifully; for the common run of people, it works far less well. (pp. 56-7)

*Journey into Fear* is a film of a peculiar cramped tightness, so crammed with action and conversation that no one viewing can permit a full journey through its labyrinth. We find here the characteristic comedy which often seems to be carried into Welles's films . . . , and we also find a sharp vividness of visual observation. There may be discrepancies of continuity and character, odd shifts of tone that don't work. But the success of the film, though flawed, is real: it may be crude and unsure, but it creates a world of its own. (p. 82)

[The] film's most impressive, as well as its most famous, sequence is the ending on the balcony of the hotel at Batum. As the rain streams blindingly down the killer's glasses, as the figures edge past flapping awnings, as the crowd below is seen emphasized by the rain at an astonishing vertical angle, the film's virtuosity is at its most extraordinary. We have been released from the sweltering labyrinth of the ship to air and rain and light-slashed darkness, but we are still trapped in a nightmare, the murderous intensity of an evil dream. (p. 83)

The theme of *The Lady from Shanghai* links directly with Welles's other important themes: the misery of the rich, and the survival of the innocent. Just as Kane died imbedded in his own selfishness, alone in his dead castle, just as the Ambersons faded away in proud shadows, their great mansion an obscure boardinghouse in the midst of an industrial city which has greedily absorbed it, so the creatures of *The Lady from Shanghai* rot from within. Just as Kane's image is reflected in an eternity of mirrors at Xanadu, so Elsa Bannister and her husband, gorgon and evil mate, face a hall of mirrors before they die, seeing their truth reflected over and over again. (pp. 113-14)

Welles's intention [in *The Trial*] was to create a composite world, a microcosm of the totalitarian society. His own designs would probably have achieved this. But the converted station and the Zagreb locations had the effect of diffusing his vision. Their resplendent baroque quality, in the context, worked against his own concept: that human lives can be as ugly and cramped as those of insects.

Kafka's novel, icily gray, claustrophobically compressed, is a parable of the human condition. . . . Welles reworks the story in the terms of his own vision, letting us see the dangers of the great anonymous powers which hang threateningly over us, finishing his film meaningfully on a shot of a mushroom cloud. . . . In *The Trial* his admonition is that we must fight for our own identity before it is swallowed up in the giant international/totalitarian urban state we have created for ourselves.

It is a major theme, but it is, alas, delivered to us in a hoarse, exhausted whisper. The film's technical shortcomings, especially its appalling sound track, marred by wretched dubbing, and the second-rate playing of its cast . . . are not its most important defects. (pp. 160-61)

Welles acidly intended us to see [that] power can also be invisible and all-pervading, that the vast machinery of world politics can crush a man like an insect.

He simply fluffs the film, and the reason lies, I think, in the very privacy of his vision, his muffled remoteness from the public. In most of his films this is counterbalanced by the other side of his genius: the promoter's punch and drive that can deliver even the most obscure artistic point with brilliant energy. In *The Trial,* however, he has withdrawn completely from us, so that we have to peer into his world through the narrowest of apertures. It might be argued that, in the context, this very narrowness is appropriate. But it is one thing to portray narrowness, and another to convey it narrowly.

There are certain artists . . . who can speak in a whisper yet, by the perfect enunciation of every syllable, make us understand an argument. The Welles of *The Trial* is not in that category. When he whispers, the details are slurred. Here, his visual ideas are not clearly conveyed in the physical presentation of the work. The photography, which should be subtly gray, is merely flat and textureless, wearing out the eye and numbing the brain. The sound track, which should be furtively resonant and subdued, is characteristically scrambled, a mess of inchoate sounds.

The result is, for me, an agonizing experience; there is no film I have seen which for me as totally defies the eye and mind. After seven viewings, I have continued to have the feeling of struggling through wads of cotton wool to reach the interior of the work; what follows is a record of what I have seen; it cannot convey the sense of concern at Welles's recessiveness that I have experienced on each occasion. For me, *The Trial* is a dead thing, like some tablet found among the dust of forgotten men, speaking a language that has much to say to us, but whose words have largely been rubbed away. (pp. 161-62)

[I admire] *Chimes at Midnight* for its qualities of warmth and simplicity—qualities that survive its sometimes flawed technique. Why, then, does the film leave one with a feeling of inadequacy, a sense that something is missing? Chiefly, I think, because . . . it lacks the dynamism, the energy, the daemonic power that have marked Welles at his greatest. It falls short of being a masterpiece—though not far short—because of that failure of the energy which has so often marked Welles's career as an artist. There are not merely evidences here of exhaustion, but of an impatience with detail and finalization that, combined

with Welles's tragic perennial lack of funds, have left the work just short of the triumph it should have been. (p. 177)

*The Immortal Story* does not break any new ground technically —some critics have found it dull and unenterprising—yet its very lack of mannered camera angles and elaborate compositions is the film's most attractive feature. Welles's style is pared here to a romantic essence, stripped of all needless decoration.

If *The Fountain of Youth* excites with its verve and inventiveness, *The Immortal Story* moves us more deeply, for here we are made aware of how much of the elegiac flavor of *Ambersons* has survived. Cool and poised as the exquisite Satie piano works which run through it like a refreshing stream, *The Immortal Story* points to the late reflowering of this incomparable artist. (p. 188)

> *Charles Higham, in his* The Films of Orson Welles *(copyright © 1970 by The Regents of the University of California; reprinted by permission of the University of California Press), University of California Press, 1970, 210 p.*

### DAVID BORDWELL

The best way to understand *Citizen Kane* is to stop worshiping it as a triumph of technique. Too many people have pretended that Orson Welles was the first to use deep-focus, long takes, films-within-films, sound montage, and even ceilings on sets. . . . *Kane* is a masterpiece not because of its tours de force, brilliant as they are, but because of the way those tours de force are controlled for larger artistic ends. The glitter of the film's style reflects a dark and serious theme; *Kane*'s vision is as rich as its virtuosity.

The breadth of that vision remains as impressive today as thirty years ago. *Citizen Kane* straddles great opposites. It is at once a triumph of social comment and a landmark in cinematic surrealism. It treats subjects like love, power, class, money, friendship, and honesty with the seriousness of a European film; yet it never topples into pretentiousness, is at every instant as zestful, intelligent, and entertaining as the finest Hollywood pictures. It is both a pointed comedy of manners and a tragedy on a Renaissance scale. It has a Flaubertian finesse of detail and an Elizabethan grandeur of design. Extroverted and introspective, exuberant and solemn, *Kane* has become an archetypal film as boldly as Kane's career makes him an archetypal figure. . . .

In its own way, *Citizen Kane* . . . recapitulates and extends film tradition. On a primary level, it makes sophisticated allusions to several genres: the detective thriller, the romance, the musical, the horror fantasy, the hard-boiled newspaper film, the big-business story, the newsreel, and the social-comment film. But *Kane* is more than an anthology. Testing the Lumière-Méliès tension, Welles, like Eisenstein, gives the cinema a new contemplative density by structuring his material on the nature of consciousness. What Eisenstein does between individual shots, Welles does in the film's total organization. *Kane*'s great achievement, then, is not its stylistic heel-clicking, but its rich fusion of an objective realism of texture with a subjective realism of structure. Welles opens a new area to the cinema because, like Eisenstein, he not only shows what we see, but he symbolizes the way we see it.

*Kane* explores the nature of consciousness chiefly by presenting various points of view on a shifting, multiplaned world. . . .

The film expresses an ambiguous reality through formal devices that stress both the objectivity of fact and the subjectivity of point of view. It is because the best contemporary cinema has turned to the exploration of such a reality that *Kane* is, in a sense, the first modern American film. (p. 39)

David Bordwell, "'Citizen Kane'," in Film Comment (copyright © 1971 by Film Comment Publishing Corporation; all rights reserved), Vol. 7, No. 2, Summer, 1971, pp. 38-47.

**STEPHEN FARBER**

Although *The Magnificent Ambersons* was not the last film Welles made in America, he never again took on such large, quintessentially *American* themes as he did in his first two films. *The Magnificent Ambersons* deals with the price of technological "progress"—the contamination of the city and the influence of the automobile on modern American life, an extraordinary subject for a 1942 movie. . . .

The attempt is impressive, but the film has never struck me as an entirely satisfactory study of the emergent nightmare city of the twentieth century. The dying aristocratic world of the Ambersons is drawn with great affection and complexity, but the urban industrial world that will take its place is only a shadow; the contrast of nineteenth and twentieth century is asserted rather than explored dramatically. . . . [Welles' original version of the film] included many more scenes about the city rising around the Ambersons, scenes that might have effectively corroborated Eugene's bleak prophecy. The one scene that remains—George's last walk home through the altered, disfigured city near the end of the film—is brilliant, an example of Welles' astonishing resourcefulness and economy; thanks to the lucid, carefully-chosen images and the evocative narration, in just a few seconds we think we've seen more of the expanding city than we actually have. Outside of this scene, however, the swelling city is an offscreen character, and it needs to be a stronger *presence* in the film for the erosion of the Amberson style to be fully comprehensible.

Even Welles' original version may have been slightly out of balance in this regard. . . . [Judging] from Welles' other work, he seems to be more attracted to the past than to the future. His characters inhabit great cavernous houses cut off from the world, castles that easily turn into mausoleums; those magnificent, magical houses represent Welles' intoxication with imaginatively created, self-enclosed private worlds where one can retreat from the chaotic pressures of the present. . . .

The tranquillity savored in Welles' films is not, admittedly, the first thing one notices in watching them. The other side of his work, especially pronounced in the first two films, is the youthful energy of his style. Just as one is immediately struck by the tremendous *élan* of the *March of Time* parody or the newspaper party in *Citizen Kane,* the sequence in *The Magnificent Ambersons* that is most dazzling on first viewing is the hilarious, breathtaking scene of the automobile ride in the snow— the staccato rhythm provided by the overlapping dialogue gives the film a burst of exhilaration. It is the one moment in the film when the nineteenth and twentieth centuries seem to come together, and when Welles acknowledges his attraction to the machine, and to the speed and volatility of modern life. . . .

In *The Magnificent Ambersons* the Welles hero is split in two— the arrogant, domineering, but childish man of leisure, George Amberson Minafer . . . , and the gentle, self-effacing entre-preneur, Eugene Morgan. . . . It's an interesting concept, but *too* neat a paradox, too schematic. If Welles had played Eugene Morgan, the film might have developed a richer kind of tension. (p. 49)

Many of Welles' films are set in the past, but *The Magnificent Ambersons* is a different kind of journey backward in time— a journey back to childhood, a study of the claustrophobic intensity of family life. The film is full of painful family separations; the central one, as in *Citizen Kane,* is the separation of mother and son. *The Magnificent Ambersons* has the power of a dream formed in boyhood, a spell that can never be broken. Welles pays attention to the perversions of feeling within the suffocating cocoon of the family mansion. . . .

Welles follows Tarkington closely in all of this, but he sometimes extends the novel's implications. The most obvious variation is in the characterization of Fanny, [who becomes] one of the first truly *modern* characters in American films, an archetype for all those hysterically repressed, neurasthenic spinster heroines of the next decades. This characterization is not conceived in conventional, realistic terms. There's no apparent logic to many of Fanny's outbursts—they surprise us and make us uncomfortable. Even *within* a scene, her quicksilver shifts of emotion are startling and alarming. . . .

Though Welles never appears in *The Magnificent Ambersons,* his presence as narrator is crucial to the conception of the film. *The Magnificent Ambersons* contains the most beautiful, pertinent use of narration I have seen in movies. The narration is not used simply to provide information; it adds to the sensuous atmosphere of the film. The language itself, eloquently spoken by Welles, has a rich, lyrical quality that seems to belong to the aristocratic past; its literary cadences are part of the vanished courtly style that the film mourns. But in an even more important sense, the narration calls attention to the nostalgia that is the film's *subject* as well as its dominant mood. We are constantly aware of a voice reflecting on the past, wistfully invoking its mysteries. From the very start the hushed but intense tone of Welles' narration suggests the recreation of a child's fairy tale. The storyteller, the dreamer who calls up the past for us, haunted by the world he brings to life, becomes a character we want to evaluate along with the others. . . .

It's too simple, then, to say that *The Magnificent Ambersons* is no more than a film of nostalgic reverence, but there is no denying the melancholy intensity with which the film dwells on the Ambersons' decline. . . . One cannot account for the film's distinctive qualities by saying that Welles was simply being faithful to his source, what is inescapable in watching the film is the graceful, persuasive feeling he has for the material. This film contains some of the strongest, most haunting and desolate images in all of Welles' work. The same mournful sense of loss and regret in much later films like *Falstaff* and *The Immortal Story* seems easier to understand. . . .

[Among] great films, *The Magnificent Ambersons* is the one you remember for the sad, lush, seductive poetry of death. (p. 50)

Stephen Farber, "'The Magnificent Ambersons'," in Film Comment (copyright © 1971 by Film Comment Publishing Corporation; all rights reserved), Vol. 7, No. 2, Summer, 1971, pp. 49-50.

**CHARLES SILVER**

It's not very hard to find things wrong with *The Immortal Story.* . . . The sound, at least in the English-language version is rather bad. The lighting, sets, props and makeup have a decided air of cheapness and haste, reflecting the fact that this was, after all, only a television production. The continuity and editing tend toward a certain sloppiness, and the acting and *mise-en-scène* appear stolid, completely antithetical to the wild Welles we have known. Even more damning, perhaps, is the virtually total subservience to the narrative structure and dialogue of Baroness Blixen's fable. Unlike *Citizen Kane, The Magnificent Ambersons, The Lady from Shanghai, Touch of Evil* and even *Falstaff*, the points here seem to be made verbally rather than visually and, superficially at least, they appear to be those of Miss Dinesen, not those of Mr. Welles.

But most of what is important about *The Immortal Story*—or, for that matter, about the vast majority of other films—is the extent to which the director makes the film an expression of self. In this endeavor, despite all the aforementioned obstacles, Orson Welles succeeds in quite a lovely manner. Careful analysis of the *mise-en-scène* of *The Immortal Story* reveals it to be one of the most poignantly personal works in all cinema.

As in so many earlier Welles movies, the filmmaker assumes the role of narrator. In no previous film, however, has Welles' conception of himself been so crucial to the essence of the work. He is no mere interlocutor here, for he is telling a story about the telling of a story—a story about a fat old man who tells a story—a story, in fact, about Orson Welles. (p. 54)

The Wellesian hero, from Kane to Falstaff, is almost inevitably vanquished by his illusions. Mr. Clay, who has spent his whole life avoiding them, is finally killed in the attempt to transform illusion into reality. Clay does not succeed, for the sailor tells Levinsky that he will not repeat the story, thus frustrating the old man's design. In this, Welles suggests an admission of failure on his own part, a sense of defeat about his lifelong struggle to transcend his mortality through his skill at lying. Welles' lies—those cinematic "ribbons of dreams," as he calls them—are to him what Clay's million dollars are to the old merchant: "my brain and my heart; it is my life." Whereas Charles Foster Kane three decades ago could make choices, Mr. Clay moves ineluctably toward defeat and death. His very name implies mortality. (p. 55)

> Charles Silver, "'The Immortal Story'," in Film Comment *(copyright © 1971 by Film Comment Publishing Corporation; all rights reserved), Vol. 7, No. 2, Summer, 1971, pp. 54-5.*

**JOSEPH McBRIDE**

Welles' film audience is missing a revealing experience in not being able to see [his made-for-television film] *The Fountain of Youth*. Its mixture of bold theatrical stylisation, puckish humour and bardic intimacy draws on a side of Welles, the 'radio side', which seldom pokes through the intricate architectonics of his feature film work. *The Immortal Story* is told with a fabulist's simplicity, but it is still a story film conceived for the large screen, with all the pretence of showing real people involved in a real drama. *The Fountain of Youth* is more a chamber play than a drama. (p. 40)

But in *The Fountain of Youth* form follows function, for the theme of the piece is narcissism. . . . None of [Welles'] films has ever made such extensive use of mirrors, for instance, and the sheer physical data of the characters' faces and bodies . . . speak volumes. In fact, it is problematic who should be considered the protagonist of the tale: Caroline, who has Humphrey

in her spell, or Welles himself, who has both of them in *his* spell. (pp. 40-1)

The early sequences are suffused with that off-handed indulgence toward human weakness which Welles often uses to implicate the audience in the characters' dilemma. The prologue of *The Magnificent Ambersons,* for instance, presents the family's snobbery as charming and captivating. . . . The nostalgia Welles shares with his characters is a melancholic glance back at a time of moral innocence. He lets us indulge in the pleasures of irresponsibility before we have to face its consequences. In *The Fountain of Youth,* as in *Ambersons,* he dwells on the romantic quaintness of vanished artifacts and customs to keep us aware of their evanescence. . . .

Befitting the medieval (or is it futuristic?) nature of Humphrey's experiments, his laboratory is an eerily unreal chamber with outsize jars and bottles looming behind him like the odd shapes moving behind Welles in the studio/laboratory he inhabits. To clinch the connection, the director has placed one incongruous object in the laboratory—a bulky old-fashioned radio with a giant shell for a speaker. Like other Wellesian Faust figures (Bannister in *The Lady from Shanghai,* Arkadin, Quinlan in *Touch of Evil,* Clay in *The Immortal Story*), Humphrey tests his powers by constructing a fable with living characters. Removed, by his romanticism, from the world of ordinary people, he tries to twist reality to fit the shape of his own ego. The irony in *The Fountain of Youth* is that the man who pulls the strings is also attached to an invisible set of strings. . . .

Caroline is the *reductio ad absurdum* of romance, all surface and show. Humphrey doesn't want her for herself, but for what she represents. She is a token of everything missing in his life, beginning with sex, which is nothing if not a struggle to escape into a timeless state of perfect irresponsibility. The rub is, of course, that the moment of happiness disappears as soon as consciousness returns to savour it. In Welles' fundamentally romantic viewpoint, women stand for everything a man strives after but cannot possess. Since women symbolise everything which is greater than man, they are also the source of his destruction. They are beyond reason, beyond morality, beyond responsibility.

The last section of *The Fountain of Youth* is given over to a series of expressionistically lit, ballet-like gestures in which the two youths act out the consequences of Humphrey's narcissism while he, with scientific detachment, disappears from view. Welles fades in on the vial shining unnaturally out of the darkness, harsh electronic sounds hovering in the air. A hand comes out of the void to put the vial on a mantel, and the light rises to reveal both Caroline and Alan gazing into a mirror—the lens of the camera. The effect is profoundly disturbing, for we are watching them but they are watching *us.* (p. 41)

> Joseph McBride, "First Person Singular," in Sight and Sound *(copyright © 1972 by The British Film Institute), Vol. 41, No. 1, Winter, 1971-72, pp. 40-1.*

**ROGER MANVELL**

Welles's approach to *Macbeth* was bound to be unusual. First of all, he imposed upon it a theme which has no parallel in the text, and announced it himself at the beginning of the film. . . . The words were spoken over shots of the witches seen amid a swirl of mists at work over their cauldron, shaping the clay image of a baby, which was to be a symbol used throughout the film. *Macbeth*, Welles said, was a story which involves 'plotting against Christian law and order'; the hostile forces were 'agents of chaos, priests of hell and magic' making use of 'ambitious men' to achieve their dark and primal purpose. In order to provide a Christian symbol in the film he created a new character, a priest, to whom he gave lines taken over from other, suppressed characters. Welles cut the play extensively . . . ; he rearranged scenes; he even introduced lines from other plays.

The result is a Wellesian superstructure imposed upon the play, which is then bent to conform to this new thematic device; visually, it is often striking and splendid. But the verse is for the most part badly spoken, even by Welles himself. The original track of 1948 sounded, in his view, too American; later . . . he re-recorded two-thirds of the track in order to give the speech a more Scottish flavour. The result is that the sound is uneven in quality and often scarcely intelligible. . . . (p. 56)

Welles has described this elaborate re-visualization of the play as a 'violently sketched charcoal drawing of a great play'. He wanted it to be a 'Stonehenge-powerful, unrelieved tragedy'. It was to this end, therefore, that the sets created an artificial world of caves, rock-enclosed areas like the core of an extinct volcano, catacombs and cells with fiercely barbed window frames; it is a world of moving mist and falling water; swine wallow in mud at the castle entrance. Shots are distorted in mirrors to reflect the bent mind of Macbeth. The costumes are part Asiatic, part barbaric, made up alike of skins, cloth and metallic armour. Special effects are used to make the scenes of witchcraft macabre and unearthly. (p. 59)

Like *Macbeth*, *Othello* has a magnificent visual flair, stemming this time not from studio sets but from a brilliant use of the locations. Welles imposed no new or artificial interpretation on the play, as he had done so disastrously in the case of *Macbeth;* rather, he widened its environment by using Italian and Moroccan backgrounds. (p. 61)

It is unfortunate that once again the sound recording is so ill-balanced that the speech is often barely intelligible. The characterization, however, is better balanced than in *Macbeth*. . . . (p. 62)

Welles cut deep into the text of the play, isolating the dialogue and speeches he needed in order to carry the action forward, transposing when he felt the urge. A brilliant touch of improvisation, celebrated by now, was the resetting of the scene in which Roderigo . . . is himself murdered by Iago; Welles decided to film this in a Turkish bath because the costumes for Cassio and Roderigo were not available at the times of shooting. The result is one of the most effective scenes in the film, with Roderigo stabbed by Iago as he hides under the slatted boards in the Turkish bath, surrounded by clouds of steam.

However, the large number of strikingly lit architectural shots coming in quick succession on the screen makes the film restless, and to this extent more difficult to enter into. Satiety sets in; so much photographic beauty becomes a drug. The characters move rapidly, and the camera is tilted upwards to the point of obsession in order to achieve [a] kind of strictly formal beauty. . . . The film is at its best when this restlessness is broken and a certain degree of concentration is allowed. . . . Some of the later interchanges between Iago and Othello are fragmented into a series of emphatically tilted portraits, which

drain the drama from the speech, which is in any case under-emphasized, and so transform the scenes into a photographic exhibition. A similar beauty destroys, not enhances, the intensity of the later scenes between Othello and Desdemona, which are posed in a succession of beautiful architectural interiors. The music, too, though often apt, is sometimes used in such a way as to prove a further distraction, disintegrating the dramatic effect. (pp. 62-3)

[*Chimes at Midnight*] is a deeply moving film, in which Falstaff, the central figure, has an essential goodness, even a greatness, about him, which Prince Hal, finally dedicating himself to the formal duties of monarchy and the establishment of power, can no longer permit himself to recognize or even tolerate. Falstaff bears none of the marks of respectability, and Hal breaks his heart by publicly rejecting him. (p. 64)

From the start of the film certain photographic devices become marked. Shooting from a low angle is constant throughout the film; it emphasizes the power struggle between the King—an aloof, isolated figure, his throne set high on a great rostrum, in contrast to the restless, gyrating nobility. Falstaff's vast belly is emphasized by similar, up-tilted shots. (pp. 65-6)

The scenes of battle are finely staged, rather in the manner of Eisenstein in miniature. There are smoke and sunlight, tall lances against the sky, banners and small, decorative tents, galloping horsemen. . . . Hand-held, swiftly panning cameras, and many un-tilted shots emphasize the bloody violence of mediaeval warfare; some shots are speeded up, and the sequence ends with scenes of innumerable corpses scattered in the mud. (pp. 68-9)

*Chimes at Midnight* is one of Orson Welles's finest films, and one of the most successful screen adaptations from Shakespeare so far made. The much-criticized earlier adaptations of *Macbeth* and *Othello* have the great virtue that they are not reverential or academic exercises—in their best sequences they are pungent, lively, imaginative extensions of the tragedies, flights of fancy too often held back by technical shortcomings, obscurities in the story continuity and incessant over-indulgence in purely visual beauty. But the Shakespearean screen would be much the poorer without these earlier experiments, while *Chimes at Midnight* is nearly, if not quite, a masterpiece. (p. 70)

Roger Manvell, "*Shakespeare by Orson Welles*," in his Shakespeare and the Film *(copyright © 1971 by Roger Manvell; reprinted by permission of Holt, Rinehart and Winston; in Canada by J M Dent & Sons Ltd), J M Dent & Sons Ltd, 1971, pp. 55-71.*

### WILLIAM S. PECHTER

[Though] I expected *The Trial* to be bad, I went to it truly hoping for the best. And, in fact, though I expected it to be bad, bad as a mannerist painting can be bad, bad, for instance, as Welles's *Othello* is bad, I had not been expecting the worst; I had not expected that it might be boring. Orson Welles boring! And boring to stupefaction. (p. 162)

It is possible, perhaps, to dismiss *Citizen Kane* as little more than a bag of tricks, good tricks but tricks nonetheless; yet, although much of that film's excitement does derive from the sheer exuberance and audacity—real audacity—of its exploration of the medium's techniques, to regard the work as only this is, I think, considerably to underestimate it. But one may concede the case of *Citizen Kane,* and still there is *The Mag-*

*nificent Ambersons,* a less perfect work, perhaps; also, I think, a finer one. Beginning with its apparently random and casual collection of nostalgic images of bygone styles in clothes and motorcars, like so many snapshots from a family album, the film quietly deepens and extends itself into an almost achingly sorrowful picture of a vanished style of life, and of irrecoverable loss, and, in so doing, manages to achieve what *Citizen Kane,* in all its brilliant eclecticism, never does: a unified style of its own. And it is style as practiced by a film-maker capable of raising style to the level at which it becomes indistinguishable from genius.

But it is style—as, in Welles's work, it was never again to be—pressed wholly into the service of meaning. Nothing is gratuitous; from the sleigh ride through an impossibly soft and radiant snowscape—the snow as surreal as that which floats through Kane's crystal globe, the sleigh itself thereafter to give way to fuming, sputtering automobiles—to the "last of the great, long-remembered dances" at the Amberson mansion, all of the film's imagery is darkened and complicated by a sense, an almost tragic sense, of the impermanence of all that appears solid and substantial and of the evanescence of all that is beautiful. Like *Citizen Kane, The Magnificent Ambersons* is about a man's fall, but it is also about the fall of a house and a society. The film's narrative remains faithful to that of the Booth Tarkington novel from which it was adapted, but what Welles brings to that narrative, not in the novel, above all, is mystery. It is a quality that arises, in part, from the difference between the grayish naturalism of the novel and the rich chiaroscuro of the film. But the film's imagery itself seems, finally, to arise from the apprehension of some deeper kind of mystery: that mystery inherent in the way men come to be as they are and in the way all power declines and dies. (pp. 166-67)

If I appear to dwell on Welles's two earliest films, it is because, for all the attention that has been paid to them as works of technical brilliance yet remain insufficiently appreciated as works of art: that, and the fact that, among Welles's subsequent films, there is little else to dwell on. *Citizen Kane* is not a profound work, but, aside from that, it is almost everything else one might wish a first work to be: unmistakably individual, exploratory, exuberant, charged with an excitement undiminished after twenty years; and *The Magnificent Ambersons* is, I think, one of the most mysteriously beautiful films ever made. (pp. 168-69)

*Journey into Fear,* despite the fact that the credit for its direction is not given to Welles, is everywhere stamped with the mark of his individuality, as are the two other melodramas that sporadically succeeded it, *The Stranger* and *The Lady from Shanghai.* All are witty, exciting, above all enormously entertaining; and, if their brilliance seems to reside largely on their surface, where else should brilliance be? They are melodramas; only their enthusiasts have pretended they are more. . . . Then, in 1948, Welles made his first film of Shakespeare, *Macbeth,* with himself in the leading role. As a production of the play the film can be easily dismissed, with its drastic textual rearrangement and, but for Welles and Dan O'Herlihy, generally impoverished acting; it is also by far the most interesting film made of Shakespeare to pursue the idea that an adaptation of a play into film requires as radical and complete a transformation of the original materials as does the adaptation of a play into opera. . . . Welles's preoccupation in *Macbeth* is clearly with inventing a line of visual imagery raised to the level of the language, even if, in the accomplishment, what more often resulted was a reduction of the language to the level

of the visual imagery; one would really have to be, at the least, a Verdi wholly to succeed in what Welles was attempting, and Welles is not this. Still, though the achievement of Welles's film is decidedly not that of Shakespeare's *Macbeth,* the film does manage to achieve a striking, genuinely barbaric splendor of its own. And, despite the film's many failures, if one considers the respectfully dull ways that *Macbeth* has been done badly on our stages, one might be less inclined to undervalue that achievement. (pp. 169-70)

[The] special badness of Welles's *Othello,* with all its fussy inflation of eye-catching details, is of a kind to make the freewheeling carelessness of his *Macbeth* seem positively invigorating by comparison. It is the details, in fact, that take over this *Othello,* crowding out character, crowding out action, almost, but not quite, crowding out everything that is the play. All is sacrificed to the *mise en scène,* but it is a *mise en scène* now become an orgy of tilted camera angles, intricate composition, and florid chiaroscuro. Concern is now exclusively for effects, and not effects directed toward the end of any total meaning but rather isolated effects, singular flashes of brilliance (and some, admittedly, brilliant), indulged in only for themselves. Each scene is invested with an impact out of all proportion to its meaning or its relevance to context; each scene played and shot as though it were climactic. Gone is the marvelous rhythmic continuity of *Citizen Kane:* given way to a monotonous fluidity (almost every transition is a quick dissolve) as discrete, supercharged images flow one into the other. There is a word for Welles's film of *Othello.* It suffers not from lack of talent: rather, from a conspicuous waste of it. All has grown overripe; the individual cells have developed at the expense of the organism as a whole. The word is decadent.

And it is that word which best characterizes all of Welles's films since. There is little to choose from between *Mr. Arkadin* . . . and *Touch of Evil;* of the two, I tend to prefer the former, which seems to me more willing to accept itself at its own level of preposterousness, rather than go rummaging about among half-baked profundities. But, whatever one's preference, such distinctions as may be drawn between the two are fine, and *Touch of Evil* is, I think, profoundly bad. . . . The film is melodrama again, as was *Mr. Arkadin,* but, whereas Welles was once able to use his camera ingeniously to enhance such material, here the camera, with few exceptions, just gets in the way, intruding on the action, complicating it unnecessarily, further cluttering a film already, in its narrative, prodigally cluttered, and generally providing graphic evidence of what kind of artistic disaster may occur when a medium whose propensity is to reveal is taken in the hands of a director whose proclivity is to obscure. *Touch of Evil* probably contains more irrelevant movement per frame than anything else yet committed to film, movement finally signifying nothing so much as Welles's radical failure as a director. . . . Among more zealous lovers of cinema, *Touch of Evil* has attained something of the status of Welles's masterpiece; and for those, not necessarily cinema enthusiasts, who just relish the spectacle of a prodigious talent recklessly exploring all possible ways to squander and parody itself, *Touch of Evil* is, indeed, highly recommended. I found it deeply depressing.

Still, bad as *Othello* and *Mr. Arkadin* and *Touch of Evil* are, they manage to remain enjoyable on some level, however disturbing in their implications: *Othello* is an exercise in the rococo; *Mr. Arkadin* as nonsense; *Touch of Evil* as camp. . . . Bad as they are, they aren't boring. . . . [If] the essential difference between Welles's *Macbeth* and his *Othello* is that of using the medium to serve the play and using the play to serve the medium, what we have in *The Trial* is a case of there being no play, only medium. Even *Touch of Evil,* largely, I would guess, thanks to what is left of the thriller from which it was derived, has its characters and plot, threadbare and tattered as they may respectively be. To some extent, simply because *Othello is* a play, because it exists in its language and its action (not to mention, that is, its greatness), there is enough inherent strength in what remains from the play in Welles's *Othello* to survive even so bad a production of it as his—and it would be difficult to imagine one worse. But take away Kafka's style and his tone, and what have you? Take away the logic and order of Joseph K.'s nightmare, and what is there left? What Welles gives us is a succession of disjointed grotesqueries, each exploited for its own grotesqueness to the end of being picturesque. (pp. 171-73)

*The Trial,* boredom and all, is, finally, not without meaning, though not so much one it contains as one that contains it. In an idiom that appears to be narrative or dramatic, Welles has actually given us an instance of pure *mise en scène, mise en scène* freed of all necessity, concerned solely with independent visual effects. Perhaps a director of greater genius than Welles could to this and make it continuously interesting; but I doubt it. . . . Were *The Trial* visually beautiful to see, there would be no boredom, but the fact is that, for all the attention lavished on the refinement of the film's surface, that surface is one of an almost unrelieved ugliness; to John Grierson's famous dictum—when a director dies, he becomes a photographer—one feels compelled, on such evidence as *The Trial,* to add the corollary that, when the photographer is a dead director, he will be a bad photographer. . . . For anyone familiar with Orson Welles's talents at their peak, even more shocking than how bad *The Trial* is, is how bad it looks: it looks like the dregs of Cinema 16. (pp. 173-74)

*William S. Pechter, "Trials" (originally published in a different version in* Sight and Sound, *Vol. 33, No. 1, Winter, 1963-64), in his* Twenty-Four Times a Second: Films and Film-makers *(copyright © 1960, 1961, 1962, 1963, 1965, 1968, 1969, 1970, 1971 by William S. Pechter; reprinted by permission of the author), Harper & Row, Publishers, Inc., 1971, pp. 162-74.*

**JOSEPH McBRIDE**

It is clear that Welles's films are not moralistic in the sense that Howard Hawks's are, for example—as fables of exemplary behaviour; and just as clearly, they are not anarchistic and behaviouristic like Jean Renoir's. In a Welles film there is, for the most part, an extreme dissonance between the characters' actions and emotions and the underlying moral framework.

Welles will be as chivalrous to his characters as Renoir, but he will not allow the characters' actions to determine the form of the film. Instead, he will go so far as to construct a geometrical pattern of counterpoints and visual ironies, in *Kane,* to bind his hero into a system which makes him seem, from our contemplative vantage point, almost powerless. Or, in *The Magnificent Ambersons* and most of his later films, he will use a godlike narrator to detach us from the struggles of the hero; in most of his films he distorts chronological structure, beginning the film with scenes which depict or imply the hero's destruction, thus placing his subsequent actions in an ironic parenthesis. His opening scenes often contain a poetic or literal 'synopsis' of the story which is to follow. *Kane* has its news-

reel, *The Ambersons* its quasi-documentary on the town, *Macbeth* the witches' convocation, *Othello* its funeral procession and caging of Iago, *The Trial* its parable of the law, *Chimes at Midnight* the conversation between the two old men, Falstaff and Shallow, recounting their lives. These overviews serve a function similar in some ways to that of the chorus in a Greek tragedy: acquainting us with the broad outlines of the myth so that we will be aware of the consequences inherent in the hero's actions *as* he carries them out, and placing us in an exalted moral position which enables us to maintain a concurrent emotional sympathy and ideological detachment.

We should not suppose, however, that Welles is a determinist. . . . Welles is a deeply rhetorical artist, but an ironist, not a propagandist. In *The Trial,* for example, he seems to be making the best possible case for the worst character he can imagine as still capable of heroism  Kane is most charming at his most morally odious moments—starting a war, harassing innocent citizens with captivating arrogance—and most pathetic in his moments of tenderness. We can see that power, intellect, and charm come so easily to Welles himself that he tends to view them less as virtues than as moral temptations, but there is an even more sinister cast to this duplicity. Beyond masking an inability to lead a simple, stable emotional life, power and its attendant anxieties tend to plague the Welles hero past the point of futile compensation into the realm of gratuitous brutality. And with this comes a horrible sense of guilt—not the sentimental regret for being less than perfect, but the knowledge that emotional vulnerability has been the excuse for endlessly enlarging malignity, an obsession which thrusts its cause deeper and deeper into the subconscious and necessitates a greater and greater hypocrisy.

The creation of myth is not only a means by which the Welles hero conceals his moral weakness from himself and others; it is also the creation of a more easily manageable rationale for his actions. . . . The same pattern is repeated, with an increasingly melancholic self-awareness, for all of Welles's heroes, until in *Chimes at Midnight* the mask of deception becomes painfully candid. Falstaff is not only the hero of the tragedy; he seems to incorporate within himself the soul of the tragedian as well. He is a liar who expects no one to believe his lies, and so exaggerates them to the point of absurdity. The lies are no longer lies but a desperate confession.

And if *The Immortal Story* seems both the most intimately personal and the most theatrical work of Welles's career, the paradox is inevitable. Welles is the most theatrical of film directors, even more so than Cukor, Ophüls, or Bergman. His dual presence as both author and hero is all but essential to his work. *The Trial* suffers because of an excessive and stifling distance between Welles and his hero; Welles appears in the film as the hero's nemesis, and the moral rhetoric involved almost swamps any possibility of sympathy with the hero. In *The Magnificent Ambersons,* his only feature film in which he does not appear, the hero closely resembles Welles, and the metamorphosis is immeasurably smoother. (pp. 9-12)

Throughout his films, the moral presence of Welles makes itself felt through the eye of the camera. In a Welles film the camera is a character. . . . In *Kane* the camera shadows the reporter, whose face we never see. The intricate camera movements and 'long takes' characteristic of Welles help to immerse us in the maze-like ironies of his scenes. The camera is the audience, and the longer it moves without the distancing device of a cut, the more we are made aware of its (our) shifting relationship to the characters. Welles comments: 'I believe, thinking about my films, that they are based not so much on pursuit as on a search. If we are looking for something, the labyrinth is the most favourable location for the search. I do not know why, but my films are all for the most part a physical search.' Perhaps because they are also a moral search, an inquiry by the audience into the truth about the legendary hero. (p. 12)

Welles tends to prolong the tension among the characters and camera as long as possible, to approximate the intimacy of a theatrical experience. The long take, like the deep-focus photography of which Welles is fond, helps persuade us of the dramatic reality of the scene—a necessary counterpoint to the moral distancing—and in respecting the integrity of time and space, it asserts the moral unity of what is shown. Though the event, for example the long uninterrupted snow scene in *Kane* or the tortuous interogation scenes in *Touch of Evil,* may be highly dialectical in emotions and ideas, the integrality of the *mise-en-scène* functions as a metaphor for the inevitability of the actions' coincidence. The camera creates a moral labyrinth in which the characters must struggle, ironically unaware of the depth of their dilemma. An excellent example is the long dolly shot in *The Ambersons* moving along with George and Lucy as they argue in their carriage. We see the characters' feelings ('identify' with them), but the ceaseless variation of the distance between the camera and the carriage also distances us from them. This distortion, a contrapuntal actor-camera movement, a montage *within* the shot, helps to explain the mixture of compassion and irony omnipresent in Welles's films. If Welles is to be defined at all . . . , it will have to be in terms of his contradictions. . . . From *Citizen Kane,* an examination into legend which finds the possibility of definition illusory, to *Chimes at Midnight* and *The Immortal Story,* which turn the idea of legend into a monstrous, melancholy *jeu d'esprit,* Welles has been enchanting us with the spectacle of a magnificent being exalting and deriding himself in a single stroke. In a world from which dinosaurs and emperors have vanished, a world for ever growing smaller, Orson Welles survives to share with us his boundless delight in being himself. (pp. 12-13)

> *Joseph McBride, in his* Orson Welles *(copyright © Joseph McBride 1972), Secker and Warburg, 1972, 192 p.*

## MICHAEL MULLIN

[In *Macbeth,* Welles adopted] an expressionistic or subjective mode in which the consciousness of the hero colors the world which we see around him. If one is able to overlook glaring errors in execution, there is a good deal to be learned from watching what Welles has done. Consider, for example, the way in which his camera treats Macbeth. Many of the shots are from waist level, looking up, so that Welles's face seems to tower over the viewer, and, when his hand is extended, it looms grotesquely large as it nears the camera. Many of his lines are spoken as the camera looks elsewhere. . . . The mind of the speaker, the world around him, and the world we see are all one. That world is like none known on our earth, a castle which is a labyrinth of caves, their walls oozing with watery slime, while outside lies a barren wasteland. . . . The primitive era suggested by the costumes and by Welles's dirge-like prologue looks back to a time when mankind was emerging from the dark mists of devil worship. . . . Tricks of lighting . . . , visual shocks in the cutting and montage, and images of a voodoo doll being formed and then broken as Macbeth

traces his fall—all these combine to shape the world in which Macbeth finds himself cabin'd, cribb'd and confin'd.

In this warped, surreal world, Macbeth's visions are not hallucinations, but clairvoyance, a second sight truer than mere physical sight. And thus, his perceptions of the otherworld are validated by the technique of the film—as, conversely, they are invalidated by a realistic technique. In this world too, images and objects have powers which go beyond their literal meaning. At times they set an emotional tone. Usually it is fear—the fear of things unseen in the mist, of entrapment in the caves of Dunsinane, and of the dizzying vertigo induced by strange camera angles, movement, and montage. At other times, they go beyond the emotional to take on conceptual meanings, becoming emblems with abstract significance. On the simplest level, each side in the conflict between good and evil has its emblem; opposed to the Cross is the spiky emblem of the Witches: a thin Y formed by two spines sticking out from a long, thin pole. . . . Despite Christian symbols—even some bits in Latin from the baptismal rites—we never see anything like the world of justice and heroism which Shakespeare embodies in Duncan and his court, later in Malcolm and the English court. Nor does Welles endow his Lady Macbeth with the force of character which in part must keep us in sympathy with Macbeth as a man misled. Nor, despite the business of the voodoo doll, do Welles's Witches help expose Macbeth's better nature because there is no goodness in him for them to overcome. Welles's Macbeth is a vicious monster from the outset, a grotesque mutation adapted to an unnatural world. Even the great soliloquies of despair, meant to pull us back into sympathy with Macbeth in the final act, ring hollow because there has been nothing good—no honor, love, obedience, nor troops of friends—for this Macbeth to lose. In short, by allowing Macbeth's nightmare vision to control his setting and his cinematic technique, Welles kept much of the play's eerie atmosphere, but almost wholly lost the sense of good and evil warring within a man's soul. (pp. 337-38)

> *Michael Mullin, "'Macbeth' on Film," in* Literature/ Film Quarterly *(© copyright 1973 Salisbury State College), Vol. 1, No. 4, Fall, 1973, pp. 332-42.\**

## PETER COWIE

Welles did not *invent* any new cinematic processes: he fused the experience of three decades into one gigantic work that proclaimed with tremendous power just how effective a medium the cinema could be. He assimilated the styles and subtleties the cinema had evolved, often unwittingly, since Griffith. For practically every technical device in *Citizen Kane* there is a precedent; but there is no precedent for *Citizen Kane,* the film. (pp. 18-19)

Welles's vision is expressed not so much in Fordian terms as in the style of the German directors of the Twenties. The relaxed *bonhomie* of Ford's world eludes him, except in parts of *The Stranger* and *Chimes at Midnight*. But Welles uses architecture with much [strength]. . . . The castle wreathed with clouds at the start of *Citizen Kane* and *Macbeth* is remote, haunting, and Wagnerian in its suggestion of power. Arkadin's turreted headquarters in Spain, the clock tower that looms over *The Stranger,* or the Gothic mass of Henry IV's Windsor in *Chimes at Midnight,* are metaphors for vaulting oppression, all viewed from low camera set-ups to emphasise their physical weight. (p. 19)

One either loves or hates [Welles's] characters. At best they are like the figures of Dostoievsky, demented and impelled by some hidden Protean force; at worst they are like many Dickensian characters, thrust in briefly, overdrawn to the point of farce, pathetic in their contortions and glib statements. Yet all of them are eminently human. Nearly all of them are endowed with humorous qualities that lighten for an instant their brooding, menacing surroundings. Welles's world is divided into predators and victims or, to use Arkadin's metaphor, into scorpions and frogs. . . . None of [his] characters obeys a moral code. They are not . . . confounded by any deep-rooted ethic. They hammer out among themselves a rough code of justice: he that resorts to violence shall perish violently. They all regard themselves as above the law. . . . They are wanderers . . . in search of their own identity and are obsessed by this task even if, as in the case of Kane, it is done for them by someone else.

The leading figures in Welles's films are brought to their knees by a single fatal flaw, as in classical or Shakespearian tragedy; they are nearly all Manichean, unscrupulous, and damned; yet they are all capable of arousing one's sympathies. (pp. 20-1)

[Throughout] Welles's *oeuvre*, there is a marked absence of colourless figures. He is never one for half measures. . . . Equally, no action is left incomplete, no spring of tragedy unwound. Power is established only to be destroyed; the more massive the power, the more reverberating its fall. The poignancy of the situation is heightened because these characters always realise their plight in a moment of agonising and unexpected truth in the film—when Quinlan talks finally to Tanya, when Major Amberson speaks after Isabel's death, when Arkadin bellows in impotent rage for a seat on the plane that is bearing Van Stratten away to his beloved daughter. The act of destruction is repeatedly symbolised in an image of the Fall— the fall of Elsa and Arthur Bannister among the mirrors, the fall of Arkadin's plane, the fall of Quinlan into the filthy river, the fall of Franz Kindler from the clock tower, the fall of the shell from Clay's lifeless fingers. Death is everywhere in Welles's films, sometimes at the outset (the death-throes of Kane, the suicide of Arkadin, the funeral rites of Othello, the successful assassination of Linnekar on the Mexican border) and sometimes at the end, "all passion spent" (Macbeth, Quinlan, Joseph K, the Bannisters, Falstaff, Clay). (pp. 21-2)

The heroes of Welles's world are human in several respects, as one has seen, but one of the principles that seems to underlie these films is that material ambition will always override human relationships. . . . Perhaps the most embittered ending to a love affair in Welles's work is when Elsa, in **The Lady from Shanghai**, is abandoned by Michael O'Hara and sobs out after him, "Give my love to the sunrise!" This sentence is as revealing a comment as any on the blighted aims and lives of so many Wellesian protagonists. (p. 22)

*Peter Cowie, in his* A Ribbon of Dreams: The Cinema of Orson Welles *(© 1973 by Peter Cowie), revised edition, A. S. Barnes and Company, 1973, 262 p.*

### GORDON GOW

Elaborate in style and provocative in essence, **Touch of Evil** affirms the Orson Welles flair, which many have imitated but hardly any have equalled. As *auteur* and actor he dominates this film, matching his own richly eccentric characterisation of Hank Quinlan to a bold display of enthusiasm for the conjuring tricks of cinema. . . .

Because it was ten years since Welles had directed a film in his native America, **Touch of Evil** (1958) was a defiant comeback. Having been ahead of his time before, he seemed resolved to maintain the pace, even though Hollywood had progressed a tolerable way along the ambitious paths he indicated in his challenge of the 1940s: **Citizen Kane, The Magnificent Ambersons, The Stranger, The Lady from Shanghai**. If these were deemed idiosyncratic, **Touch of Evil** would be more so. (p. 28)

There is decidedly a moral core to **Touch of Evil,** couched within a first-rate thriller. The opening take, a virtuoso exercise lasting three minutes and ten seconds, is a complex piece of choreography for actors and camera in unison. It starts with a close view of a time bomb placed in a car that is about to be driven across the border. Deep focus is maintained as the camera pulls back and begins its *enchaînement*. The flow of movement is so seemingly natural and yet so deftly planned and executed that one might stop the projection at any point in the course of those three minutes and ten seconds and find that the composition within the frame is admirable. Tension seethes, because we know the explosion of the car is imminent. Simultaneously the unkempt look of the town is established, and at the same time attention is drawn to a pair of honeymooners, Mike and Susan Vargas . . . , as they walk along the street in a mutual absorption strong enough to obliterate for them the murk of their surroundings. (pp. 28-9)

[The] film's dialogue, most of it written by Welles, is surprisingly unexciting in itself, seldom more than utilitarian. The major effects are visual: it is through the eye that Welles compels us especially to ponder the implications of Quinlan's behaviour. (p. 30)

Of course **Touch of Evil** is a flamboyant film. Yet one cannot term it a show-off affair, for it is much too good for that. Crammed it may be with physically taxing feats . . . , and it might be said that such nods to the filmically knowledgeable are inserted simply for their own sake—but even if they are, the Welles enthusiast must warm to them. . . .

Perhaps, after many a look at this remarkable film, one can just about see how it would have boiled down to something quite commonplace in the hands of a hack. As it stands, though, **Touch of Evil** gives substance to the theory that even a meagre tale can be turned into magnificent cinema when it is directed by a master. (p. 32)

*Gordon Gow, "Cult Movies: 'Touch of Evil'" (©copyright Gordon Gow 1976; reprinted with permission), in* Films and Filming, *Vol. 22, No. 11, August, 1976, pp. 28-32.*

### JOHN COLEMAN

[Along] comes Orson Welles, with his finest sherry-selling voice, and he messes about arrogantly with the medium and one somehow doesn't mind. This is partly, of course, because he has taken fake, deception, fraud or what you will as his brief. Like a crooked advocate, he pretends to delve into serious matters (the nature of illusion, the assassination of honesty) while roguishly having himself a high time. **F for Fake** is mainly a very successful commercial for Welles. I'll buy. . . .

[The film] is a small triumph of editing, as well as a running commentary on film legerdemain. Welles, mostly in his stage conjuror's outfit of black hat and cape, converts a key into coins and back again at the outset for a kid, later plays games with a body suspended in air, as if his largest offer is to be trick-sorcery, before and amid settling down to unsettling us via an editola and the liberal use of rich brown voice-over. He delivers an early warning that he'll be honest for an hour: and the weakest segment of this fantastic compilation is, in fact, when he overruns this—with some matter of a gorgeous, recurrent Yugoslav chick called Oja Kodar whom Picasso is supposed to have painted 24 times . . . : all lies, obviously, but unfortunately spelt out as such, spoiling what pleasure might have emerged from our recognition of the imposition.

Fun comes in marginalia, which might comfortably have been the final title for [the] film. . . . It is agreeable to witness this master, happily not past, of chicanery in such high spirits.

*John Coleman, "All's Welles," in* New Statesman *(©1976 The Statesman & Nation Publishing Co. Ltd.), Vol. 92, No. 2383, November 19, 1976, p. 724.*

## RICHARD COMBS

Although it scarcely looks comparable to anything else in his career, [*F for Fake,* a] Quixotic essay in fictional documentary—conjured, it seems, out of nothing more substantial than an extraordinary dexterity at the editing table—may be Welles' most concerted, complete and certainly his wittiest attempt to exorcise the ghosts of Kane, Rosebud and his own 'failed' genius. A personal meditation on the art of fakery, and the fakery in art, *F for Fake* switches subjects and styles even faster than its ubiquitous presenter/narrator/director switches hats. But what unites the presences of master art forger Elmyr de Hory, biographer and tyro faker Clifford Irving, and Hungarian actress Oja Kodar—as well as a host of more putative personages, such as Picasso and Oja's own master forger grandfather—is the domineering absence of Welles, since what his film proposes is that fiction-making in any form is a lie and a puzzle and a constantly repeated disappearing act for its creator. . . . *F for Fake,* thus, is a puzzle fiendishly constructed to frustrate any single attempt to unlock it, or even to identify one ultimate and all-determining creator for the myriad of pieces that have gone into its making—despite the very recognisable flourishes with which Welles wraps himself in the cloak of his own montage, even doodling a signature at one point on the screen of a movieola. . . . [It] is hard to avoid the conclusion that Welles has created a maze in which his own commentators might lose themselves. *F for Fake* is truly a 'centreless labyrinth', in which the alleged credit-hogger, accused of doing down Herman Mankewicz to claim *Citizen Kane* as totally his own creation, parodies the very notion of 'pure' creativity and autonomous (and attributable) authorship. The ribbing of the experts continues, even in those sections which seem like the most reliable autobiography. . . . "The fake is as old as the Eden tree", intones Welles; and clearly, in answer to the critics who have deduced the dissipation of his own genius from the undisguised element of sham in his work, he holds up men like de Hory and Irving as his ideal of the creator—jesters at the court of art, who have demonstrated that the practitioners are not entirely their own men, nor are their works definitively tested by the names attached to them. . . . "We are going to die", he apostrophises before Chartres; and at the end, more playfully and pertinently, while performing a bit of levitation and quoting Picasso to the effect that, "Art is a lie, a lie that makes us realise the truth", he defines how little that truth has to do with the things we think of as 'real'. "Reality—it's the toothbrush waiting for you in a glass at home . . . a bus ticket . . . and the grave".

*Richard Combs, "'Verités et Mensonges' ('F for Fake')," in* Monthly Film Bulletin *(copyright © The British Film Institute, 1977), Vol. 44, No. 516, January, 1977, p. 12.*

## JORGE LUIS BORGES

[*Citizen Kane*] has at least two arguments. The first, of an almost banal imbecility, wants to bribe the applause of the very unobservant. It can be formulated in this way: a vain millionaire accumulates statues, orchards, palaces, swimming pools, diamonds, cars, libraries, men and women. Like an earlier collector (whose observations are traditionally attributed to the Holy Ghost), he discovers that these miscellanies and plethoras are vanity of vanities and that all is vanity. At the moment of his death, he yearns for one single thing in the universe: a fittingly humble sled he played with as a child! The second argument is far superior. It links Koheleth to the memory of another nihilist: Franz Kafka. The theme (at once metaphysical and detective-fictional, at once psychological and allegorical) is the investigation of the secret soul of a man through the works he has made, the words he has spoken, the many destinies he has smashed. . . . Overwhelmingly, infinitely, Orson Welles shows fragments of the life of the man, Charles Foster Kane, and invites us to combine them and to reconstruct them. The film teems with the forms of multiplicity, of incongruity: the first scenes record the treasures accumulated by Kane; in one of the last scenes, a poor woman, gaudy and suffering, plays with an enormous jigsaw puzzle on the floor of a palace that is also a museum. At the end, we understand that the fragments are not governed by a secret unity: the detested Charles Foster Kane is a simulacrum, a chaos of appearances. . . . In one of Chesterton's stories—"The Head of Caesar," I think—the hero observes that nothing is so frightening as a labyrinth without a center. This film is precisely that labyrinth.

We all know that a party, a palace, a great undertaking, a lunch for writers and journalists, an atmosphere of frank and spontaneous friendship are essentially horrible. *Citizen Kane* is the first film that shows these things with some awareness of this truth. (pp. 12-13)

*Jorge Luis Borges, "An Overwhelming Film," in* October *(copyright © 1980 by the Institute for Architecture and Urban Studies and the Massachusetts Institute of Technology), No. 15, Winter, 1980, pp. 12-13.*

## STANLEY KAUFFMANN

[In the restored version] Welles's *Macbeth* is now a bold, exciting, innovative film.

It is not Shakespeare's *Macbeth*. I'm not going to reopen the old critical hassle of whether or not there is an ideal *Macbeth* . . . ; I simply tell again the beads of my Shakespeare-on-film rosary: no film of a Shakespeare play can be that play. . . .

But Welles knew all this. . . . [It's] no surprise that his *Macbeth* has often been called expressionist. But in aesthetic terms, the most striking aspect of this restored film is Welles's apparently quite conscious attempt to fuse a third form out of theater and film. (p. 24)

[Most] of the standard objections to this film seem to me to miss the point. It's been dubbed the "papier-mâché" *Macbeth* because of its sets, it's been castigated for its obvious studio lighting. These strictures, and more, grow out of the belief that film automatically equals realism; and they grow out of hunger for the same kinds of cinematic virtuosity that Welles had shown in *Citizen Kane* and *The Magnificent Ambersons,* a poetic realism so prodigally inventive that it's almost as if he was making the first films ever and the world was lucky that the terrain was being discovered by a young man with genius.

In *Macbeth* he is moving past realism. . . . The film settings are meant to look like settings, the way they would in a symbolic stage production. The lighting and photography are meant to evoke the atmosphere of the theater. . . . The lighting of *Macbeth,* in most shots, surrounds the subjects with the magic air that surrounds theater actors in nonrealistic stage lighting, that strange feeling of the consecration of space. In *Macbeth* there is very little sense that Welles is trying to show that film can take things from the theater and do them better; he is taking from the theater *and* film and trying to do something else, to blend them, to give us a theater experience through film and vice versa, and therefore something different from a usual theater or film experience. (pp. 24-5)

With this general look of things, Welles has also worked for flowing motion. Whenever possible, a scene is led by the camera and the actors' movement into the next scene. . . . It's easy to say that Welles was going after the fluency of the Elizabethan stage, the speed that was such a big part of Granville Barker's theory of Shakespeare production, but doing it on film is more daring than on stage. On film it doesn't obey its medium, it challenges. It underscores artifice, rather than intensifying film realism. . . .

In his union of theater and film—neither filmed play nor stagy film but an aesthetic union—Welles is using ideas as revolutionary as those in *Kane,* though surely they have had much less influence. . . . The difference here from the theater is in the greater immediacy of that internal reality—a face, or some faces, sometimes as the whole of what we see; the voice-over soliloquies drifting up from inside; the almost palpable increase in envelopment by inner states. (p. 25)

*Stanley Kauffmann, "Restored and Revisited" (reprinted by permission of Brandt & Brandt Literary Agents, Inc.; copyright © 1980 by Stanley Kauffmann), in* The New Republic, *Vol. 183, No. 4, July 26, 1980, pp. 24-5.*

# Billy Wilder

## 1906-

(Born Samuel Wilder) Austrian-born American director and screenwriter.

Wilder is known primarily for comedies which display a dark side of humor and human nature. Wilder's filmmaking philosophy emphasizes the importance of the script, and his narrative skill is more evident than his visual talent. For this reason, Wilder is often overlooked by critics who think his biting satire overly clever and patently "Hollywood."

Wilder worked in Austria as a sports reporter before moving to Berlin. His journalistic love of detail is evident in his films. In 1929, Wilder was hired as a scriptwriter for the film *Menschen am Sonntag* and continued to write in Germany until Hitler came into power. In 1933, Wilder moved to Paris, where he wrote and co-directed *Mauvaise Graine*. The sale of another script financed Wilder's move to Paramount Studios in Hollywood.

While at Paramount, Wilder wrote with Charles Brackett. Under the tutelage of director Ernst Lubitsch, they cowrote elegant, sophisticated comedies. These operettas, as they were known, are noted for their witty double entendres and their use of masquerade and deception. Wilder's first solo project, *The Major and the Minor*, continued in the Lubitsch vein. In his next films, Wilder developed an increasingly black form of comedy. *Lost Weekend* and *Double Indemnity* both display tendencies of the *film noir* genre; they also graphically depict depraved aspects of human character. However, critics feel that his cynicism is often superficial, and that Wilder accepts Hollywood's need for a happy ending.

*Sunset Boulevard* marked the end of Hollywood's "golden age" as well as Wilder's collaboration with Charles Brackett. The film itself is a tale of endings. The lives *Sunset Boulevard* depicts do not merely end—they disintegrate. Wilder's choice of faded film stars to play roles reflecting their lives and the film's unabashed candor in dissecting their failings result in a work considered by many to be a definitive study of Hollywood.

Wilder's talent for farce is best displayed in *Some Like It Hot*. A fast-paced tale of men masquerading as women to avoid a gangland execution, *Some Like it Hot* is considered a tribute to human naivete. It is in this film that Wilder most clearly demonstrates his ability to direct actors. By casting Marilyn Monroe as a beautiful loser, he created a surprisingly insightful portrait of an otherwise stereotypical sex doll.

It appears that Wilder's traditional directorial style is not suited to Hollywood's new trends. His reputation as a filmmaker of overriding cynicism has limited his appeal: however, his gift for satire remains undisputed. (See also *Contemporary Authors*, Vols. 89-92.)

## BOSLEY CROWTHER

Nobody thinks much of it when little girls use mama's clothes to play dress-up. But when a full-grown young lady dons a kid's clothes to play a little girl, it makes a delightful idea for a very cunning film. At least, it has in the case of . . . "**The Major and the Minor**."(p. 1889)

"**The Major and the Minor**" is really just a cute twist on the mistaken-identity gag. . . .

But it takes more than a twist to make a picture, and that's where the Messrs. Wilder and Brackett have come in—by writing a script which effervesces with neat situations and bright lines. . . . [There] comes a time when certain facts must be imparted to young girls. The opportunity the authors have provided [Major Kirby] to convey this knowledge, via moths, is one of the priceless moments in the film. The gentlemen have written—and Mr. Wilder has directed—a bountiful comedy-romance. (p. 1890)

> *Bosley Crowther, "'The Major and the Minor,' a Charming Comedy-Romance, with Ginger Rogers and Ray Milland, at the Paramount," in* The New York Times *(© 1942 by The New York Times Company; reprinted by permission), September 17, 1942 (and reprinted in* The New York Times Film Reviews: 1939-1948, *The New York Times Company & Arno Press, 1970, pp. 1889-90).*

## BOSLEY CROWTHER

Charles Brackett and Billy Wilder have been happily disinclined to wax morose about the problems presented by occupation—and by "fraternization," specifically. Rather these two bright filmmakers have been wryly disposed to smile upon the conflicts in self and national interests which proximities inevitably provoke. And in . . . "**A Foreign Affair**," they have turned out a dandy entertainment which has some shrewd and realistic things to say. . . .

[Their] interest is in how human beings behave when confronted by other human beings—especially those of the opposite sex. And their logical conclusion is that, granted attractions back and forth, most people—despite regulations and even differences in language and politics—are likely to do toward one another that which comes naturally. . . .

Of course, they have made these observations in a spirit of fun and romance. And the shame of the captain's indiscretion is honorably white-washed in the end. But there is bite, nonetheless, in the comment which the whole picture has to make upon the irony of big state restrictions on the level of individual give-and-take.

Under less clever presentation this sort of traffic with big stuff in the current events department might be offensive to reason and taste. But as handled by the Messrs. Brackett and Wilder . . . it has wit, worldliness and charm. It also has serious implications, via some actuality scenes in bombed Berlin, of the wretched and terrifying problem of repairing the ravages of war.

> Bosley Crowther, "'A Foreign Affair'," in The New York Times (© 1948 by The New York Times Company; reprinted by permission), July 1, 1948 (and reprinted in The New York Times Film Reviews: 1939-1948, The New York Times Company & Arno Press, 1970, p. 2264).

**JAMES AGEE**

Charles Brackett and Billy Wilder have a long and honorable record in bucking tradition, breaking rules, and taking risks, according to their lights, and limits. Nobody thought they could get away with *Double Indemnity,* but they did; nobody thought they could get away with *The Lost Weekend,* but they did; apparently nobody thought they could get away with *Sunset Boulevard,* but they did; and now, one gathers, the industry is proud of them. There are plenty of good reasons why *Sunset Boulevard* (a beautiful title) is, I think, their best movie yet. It is Hollywood craftsmanship at its smartest and at just about its best, and it is hard to find better craftsmanship than that, at this time, in any art or country.

It is also, in terms of movie tradition, a very courageous picture. . . . "Unhappy endings" are not so rare, by now, but it is rare to find one as skilful, spectacular and appropriate as this one. Besides all that, *Sunset Boulevard* is much the most ambitious movie about Hollywood ever done, and is the best of several good ones into the bargain.

It is unlikely that any living men know Hollywood better than Brackett and Wilder; most of their portrait is brilliantly witty and evocative, and much of it is also very sharp. It seems to me, however, that this is essentially a picture-maker's picture. . . . I suspect that its main weakness as popular art lies not so much in unconventionalities of story or character, as in its coldness. And if it falls short of greatness—and in my opinion it does—I suspect that coldness, again, is mainly responsible. (pp. 411-12)

There is no use pretending to discuss all the virtues, or even all the limitations, of this picture: it is one of those rare movies which are so full of exactness, cleverness, mastery, pleasure, and arguable and unarguable choice and judgment, that they can be talked about, almost shot for shot and line for line for hours on end. The people of the present and their world are handled with a grimly controlled, mock-easy exactness which

seems about as good as a certain kind of modified movie naturalism can get; this exactness is also imposed on the obsoletes and their world, but within that exactness they are treated always, with fine imaginativeness and eloquence, as heroic grotesques. (p. 413)

Movies about Hollywood have always been better than novels about Hollywood . . . because they are made by people who know the world and the medium they are talking about instead of by people who don't, and who have dropped in only to visit, hack or, in their opinion, slum. But almost inevitably, the view from inside is also limited. The manner of telling the story is apt to be gimmicky or too full of mere "effectiveness" because that is apt to become a habit with nearly anyone who works in movies for long. . . . It seems to me that the makers of *Sunset Boulevard* are at times too gimmicky, contriving, and "effective"; on self criticism I am confused, as perhaps they are. (p. 414)

Brackett and Wilder apparently have little if any gift for working from inside, but they are first rate observers, and their films are full of that kind of life. It is true, I think, that they fail to make much of the powerful tragic possibilities which are inherent in their story; they don't even explore much of the deep anguish and pathos which are still more richly inherent, though they often reveal it, quickly and brilliantly. But this does not seem to me a shameful kind of failure, if indeed it is proper to call it a failure at all: they are simply not the men for such a job, nor was this the kind of job they were trying to do. But they are beautifully equipped to do the cold, exact, adroit, sardonic job they have done; and artists who, consciously or unconsciously, learn to be true to their limitations as well as to their gifts, deserve a kind of gratitude and respect they much too seldom get. (p. 415)

> James Agee, "Miscellaneous" (originally published as "Films of the Month: 'Sunset Boulevard'," in Sight and Sound, Vol. 19, No. 7, November, 1950), in his Agee on Film, Vol. 1 (copyright 1958 The James Agee Trust; reprinted by permission), McDowell, Oblensky, 1958, pp. 403-15.*

**PENELOPE HOUSTON**

In *Sunset Boulevard* the Brackett-Wilder team took an outsize, legendary character, examined her coldly and ironically—but did not destroy her legendary quality. Billy Wilder, now on his own, does rather the same, in a very different setting, in the hard and brilliant *Ace in the Hole.* . . .

The technique, in contrast to the leisurely, personal style of *Sunset Boulevard,* is one of impersonal, direct observation. . . . Wilder isolates individuals not in distracting asides from the main theme, but to provide an added, sharpened comment on the mass. . . .

The relative failure of the ending is an illustration of Wilder's limitations. His is a talent which one respects rather than likes. This is not the result of his choice of subject, nor of his occasional tendency to vulgarity (*A Foreign Affair*) or to sensationalism for its own sake (*The Lost Weekend*); it is because he seems to lack the powers of analysis which his cold, observant style demands. It is the technique of a reporter, brilliantly conveying the immediate impact of a character or situation, less successful in developing it. A more human director, or a more skilful analyst, could have made more out of [Chuck] Tatum's clash of conscience; Wilder is content to report it, as he reported Norma Desmond's tragedy, and Tatum is credible as a character in the sense that Norma Desmond is credible—a gigantic figure who catches the imagination, so that one accepts him at his own valuation. But as writer . . . and director Wilder has developed an exact, sardonic, objective style whose technical assurance carries him over passages where the quality of thought is unduly superficial. In *Ace in the Hole,* style and purpose achieve for the most part a fusion more impressive even than in *Sunset Boulevard,* and the result is perhaps his most remarkable film.

> Penelope Houston, "Films of the Month: 'Ace in the Hole'," in Sight and Sound (copyright © 1951 by The British Film Institute), Vol. 20, No. 2, June, 1951, p. 45.

## BOSLEY CROWTHER

A crackerjack movie entertainment has been made from **"Stalag 17"**. . . . [It is] a humorous, suspenseful, disturbing and rousing pastime. . . .

[This] film shows much more than the rompings of playful fellows that the ads might let you believe. . . . And the intensity of these rompings, which represent the normal spirits and grim despairs of healthy young men without incentives and without feminine companions, gives vitality to the film.

But the taut fascination of the offering is not in the comedy and the japes; it is in the unending conflicts among a campful of volatile men. (p. 2707)

[There] emerges something in this film that considerably underscores the drama. It is a cynical sort of display of effectiveness in a group dilemma of a selfish philosophy and approach. It isn't pretty, but it is realistic—another comment on the shabbiness of war. . . .

["Stalag 17"] is certainly one of this year's most smashing films. (p. 2708)

> Bosley Crowther, "'Stalag 17'," in The New York Times (© 1953 by The New York Times Company; reprinted by permission), July 2, 1953 (and reprinted in The New York Times Film Reviews: 1949-1958, The New York Times Company & Arno Press, 1970, pp. 2707-08).

## HENRY HART

No one should expect anyone so cynical as Billy Wilder to tell a simple Cinderella story straight, and he has not done so in *Sabrina.* . . .

*Sabrina* has everything light entertainment requires: a pleasant story gently mocking of the rich, whose customs and appurtenances are put opulently on view; bright dialogue: a cast of popular and competent actors: directorial savvy and chi-chi. There isn't much in *Sabrina* that is related to reality, but there are occasional bits of social satire, and one line of realistic dialogue satirizing the Cinderella theme itself: "Nobody poor has ever been called democratic for marrying somebody rich."

As for Billy Wilder, there is considerable evidence in *Sabrina* that when he is not hard boiled he is hard put to it. He resorts to farce a little oftener than skill requires: borrows from other directors a little too brazenly . . . ; and in his satire does not always distinguish between the truly powerful and the merely rich. (p. 361)

> Henry Hart, "Film Reviews: 'Sabrina'," in Films in Review (copyright © 1954 by the National Board of Review of Motion Pictures, Inc.), Vol. V, No. 7, August-September, 1954, pp. 361-62.

## GEORGE N. FENIN

*The Seven Year Itch* is another step down in the career of [Billy Wilder]. (p. 22)

[The Broadway play] was a simple, sometimes funny comedy enriched by nuances and subtle insights into the American "psychological" approach to the battle of sexes.

The screen version cannot advertise the same quality. . . . [Marilyn Monroe] was apparently forbidden to make the slightest attempt at acting: she has been built into the film as a symbol of sex, in a definite geometry of solids, the display reaching a paroxysm that leads us to suspect a streak of sadistic satire in Wilder's direction. Thus one follows the buildup with a great deal of curiosity, because it may be logically anticipating an unpredictable climax with an equally unpredictable creative contribution by the director. But after such a titillating game of senses,—which soon degenerates into rather cheap effects,—everything collapses. . . . The triumph of the pharisaic hypocrisy of the Production Code is total. No adultery, no danger of sudden repentance, for the camera focuses on our man in the street, destination family. Thus in the name of the Victorian values that still oppress our society, the incredible massacre of the story is carried out, the buildup wasted, and the audiences given a finale which does not carry any logical conclusion to the rather clearly expressed sexual appetites of the hero. (pp. 22-3)

[It] is proper to assume that Mr. Wilder could have found ways and means to respect the consistency of the story and satisfy the censors as well. (p. 23)

> George N. Fenin, "A Victorian Film," in Film Culture (copyright 1955 by Film Culture), Vol. 1, No. 4, Summer, 1955, pp. 22-3.

## FRANÇOIS TRUFFAUT

The metaphor is exaggerated. It doesn't take seven minutes to realize that *The Seven Year Itch* is beyond smut and licentiousness and that it takes us past the limits of evil to a kind of worn-down regret, good humor, and kindness. (p. 159)

The most important character in the play, the focus of all attention, is the man who is deliberately ordinary, somewhat less average both physically and intellectually, so as to ensure the identification of the male audience and the greater enjoyment—sadistic, "superior," maybe envious—of the women. In the film, the center of interest shifts to the heroine, for the excellent reason that when she is on screen there is nowhere to look but at her body, from head to toe, with a thousand stops along the way. Her body draws us up from our seats to the screen as a magnet attracts a scrap of metal.

On screen, there is no chance to reflect. Hips, nape, knees, ears, elbows, lips, palms of the hand, profiles win out over tracking shots, framing, sustained panoramas, dissolves. All this, it must be admitted, doesn't happen without a deliberate, measured, finally very effective vulgarity. Billy Wilder, the libidinous old fox, moves along with such incessant suggestiveness that, ten minutes into the film, we aren't sure what are the original or literal meanings of faucet, Frigidaire, under, above, soap, perfume, panties, breeze, and Rachmaninoff.

If we admire, rather than grow annoyed, it is because the film's verve and inventiveness, its cavalier vigor and naughtiness demand complicity. (pp. 159-60)

*François Truffaut, "Billy Wilder: 'The Seven Year Itch'" (1956), in his* The Films in My Life, *translated by Leonard Mayhew (copyright © 1975 by, Flammarion; translation copyright © 1978 by, Simon and Schuster; reprinted by permission of Simon and Schuster, a Division of Gulf & Western Corporation; originally published as* Les films de ma vie, *Flammarion, 1975), Simon and Schuster, 1978, pp. 159-61.*

### HENRY HART

[*The Spirit of St. Louis* is] good, albeit not great. . . .

No script, however ingenious, could by itself have made a film so good as this. Accomplished direction was also required, and that Mr. Wilder has abundantly supplied. . . .

On the morning of the take-off a small mirror is needed so Lindbergh can read a compass affixed over his head. One of the hundreds of spectators who have waited all night in the rain, a quite plain girl, offers her pocket mirror, and is allowed through the police lines. (p. 126)

Wilder cuts to this girl's face several times during Lindbergh's actual take-off to reemphasize that everywhere, in the most obscure lives, the young man about to risk his life had quickened good will, awe and love.

The dramatics of the take-off consisted in making the audience wonder whether Lindbergh could get a plane so heavily laden with gasoline off the ground, and, if he did, whether he would clear some telephone wires and roofs. Wilder cut from the sloshy runway to the trembling plane, back to the mirror girl, then *to the goggles* on Stewart's craning head. This last surprised the mind and pushed it from rationality into the imbalance of suspense. (pp. 126-27)

The flight itself is dramatized by accentuating the dangers from ice, compass failure, gasoline shortage, and fatigue. It surprised me that Lindbergh's poetical and philosophical reveries and insights while in flight were not well utilized. They are well stated in his book. A few were suggested, but so gauchely they came off as mediocre filler. (p. 127)

As in all major cinematic efforts, there are important flaws. First, vulgarity. The pre-flight Lindbergh is portrayed as a shrewd bumpkin instead of as one of the initiated, i.e., one of that elect company of human beings who have *volitionally* risked death *for a purpose*. More inexcusable were such boo-boisie bits as the suspender salesman and the balloon blisters on the tires of the disintegrating crate flown into Brooks Field. . . .

The worst flaw was Percy Waxman's score. It should have consisted of variations on old American themes. Instead, it was unmelodic blah alien to Lindbergh and the things that made his solo flight across the Atlantic possible. . . .

All these strictures are for the record.

Let none of them deter you from seeing *The Spirit of St. Louis.* Its achievements overshadow its imperfections, and make it not only a good picture but an inspiring one. (p. 128)

*Henry Hart, "Film Reviews: 'The Spirit of St. Louis'," in* Films in Review *(copyright © 1957 by the National Board of Review of Motion Pictures, Inc.), Vol. VIII, No. 3, March, 1957, pp. 126-28.*

### JOHN GILLETT

[The technical problems of *The Spirit of St. Louis* are] managed with all the professionalism and flair that Hollywood can muster for such occasions.

The presentation of the story itself, by Wilder and his co-scriptwriter Wendell Mayes, is less happily organised, however. Lindbergh is not only the central figure throughout, but during the latter half the narrative is, of necessity, restricted to one man, a plane and the limitless ocean below. Such a situation might provide a director of [Robert] Bresson's sensibilities with the opportunity for an analysis of the flyer's sense of isolation, his particular tensions. Rejecting the obvious austerities of such an approach, Wilder has adopted a direct, extroverted style which avoids false melodramatics and, without any deep exploration of character, stresses his hero's idealism and strength of will. Although the general pattern of Lindbergh's original is followed, with its often lively flashbacks into his past life, an element of vulgarisation has also been imposed on an essentially sober account. Some spurious, rough-and-ready "comic" interpolations, notably a semi-slapstick anecdote involving an Army airfield and an irate officer, disastrously dissipate the tensions of the flight itself; also the characterisation of the jolly and (to non-Catholic eyes) slightly repugnant little priest, and Lindbergh's whimsical conversations with a fly in the cockpit of *The Spirit,* seem alien to the flyer's personality. . . .

Wilder's handling is seen at its most positive . . . when dealing with the strictly factual aspects of what remains an unusually compelling adventure story. This terse, sharply documented style is most evident in the scenes showing the take-off from Roosevelt Field: the final preparations, the uncertain farewells before the plan taxis out into the mud and mist, strikingly evoke the "feel" of a great adventure. . . .

The qualified achievement of the film seems, in a way, to reflect the uneasiness currently felt by American film-makers over their audiences' willingness to accept the bare truth of a story. Apparently Lindbergh's flight is now only distantly remembered by younger members of the jet age public; and this fact may have influenced the decision to include those elements of supposedly "popular" appeal which periodically disfigure the narrative. Lindbergh's own account undoubtedly tells us more about the man himself than does this adaptation, which also misses the feeling of mystical exultation experienced by many flyers and perhaps most eloquently expressed in the writings of Antoine de Saint-Exupéry. Despite his considerable talents, Wilder would seem temperamentally ill-suited to an exploration of this level of experience. In *Spirit of St. Louis,* though, the director often seems closer to his subject than for some time, and for all its equivocations the film emerges as a genuine tribute to a dedicated man. (p. 39)

*John Gillett, "Film Reviews: 'The Spirit of St. Louis'," in* Sight and Sound *(copyright © 1957 by The British Film Institute), Vol. 27, No. 1, Summer, 1957, pp. 38-9.*

### GEORGE N. FENIN

After the whitewashed film version of *The Seven Year Itch* and the uninspired *Spirit of St. Louis,* Billy Wilder is now experimenting in the sophisticated and whimsical realm of Continental comedy [in *Love in the Afternoon*]. This is the story of an aged American *viveur* who becomes involved in a series of afternoon sexual affairs with the daughter of a private detective in Paris. It is not particularly "explosive," to be sure, but at times the director manages to sketch an interestingly sarcastic portrait of a lonely man—a man who slavishly indulges in fine foods and wines, in the jaded atmosphere of the Grand Hotel, in languid lights and soft music, and a man who is capable of celebrating his bedroom exploits with the smoothest of ease. He is presented as an appendix of the Golden Era of the past century.

The sardonic vein that is carefully built up to portray this study of a useless man is, unfortunately, completely spoiled by a ludicrous finale—another typical example of the Production Code's *Diktat*. . . . The climax of the story, and of the film, would have been much more coherent and honest had the two lovers merely separated as good friends, retaining, at most, a nostalgic remembrance of their love rites and experiences together.

Instead, a sanctimonious solution is shoved down the throats of the ever patient audiences. . . .

[Wilder] has still not been able to overcome what might be called a characteristically morbid love for cruelty in the introspective depiction of his characters, nor does he carry his conclusions to a legitimate and logical end.

With closer adherence to his principles and much less conformity to the Production Code, Wilder could give us some interesting films.

> *George N. Fenin, "'Love in the Afternoon'," in* Film Culture *(copyright 1957 by* Film Culture*), Vol. III, No. 4, November, 1957, p. 18.*

## PETER JOHN DYER

[*Some Like It Hot*] will not appeal to those who find female impersonation unamusing in any circumstances; and certainly, since it also contains two painfully accurate re-creations of gangland slaughter, its opportunities for offence are considerable. In fact the gangster sequences are the least successful part of the film. There is too much random detail and intramural humour . . . and the whole could be cut by at least one bloodbath. The horrifying Al Capone reunion dinner, for instance, is effectively staged . . . , but it is an unrelated *tour de force;* its sole purpose, to conclude the "drag" act necessitated in the first place by an involuntary witnessing of the St. Valentine's Day massacre, could have been more simply served.

Although the comedy never quite shakes off this basic confusion in styles, it comes to life from the start. . . .

Almost every character has a touch of consulting room fantasy. . . .

Obviously the day is that much nearer when Billy Wilder must film Hirschfeld's *Anomalies and Perversions* as a musical. So long as it casts Jack Lemmon as an Oedipus complex, there should be no grounds for complaint.

> *Peter John Dyer, "Billy Wilder's 'Some Like It Hot'," in* Sight and Sound *(copyright © 1959 by The British Film Institute), Vol. 28, Nos. 3-4, Summer-Autumn, 1959, p. 173.*

## HENRY HART

[*One, Two, Three*] is 1961's best comedy. Which is a rather sad fact, for Wilder comedy is socially disintegrative. It amuses, but it devitalizes, and we are less, not more, after it's over. However, while it's unreeling it's engrossing.

Au fond, or au naturel, Wilder is a bird of passage, a luftmensch, an intellectual vagabond. He bites the back, not the hand, that feeds him. Not only is nothing sacred to him, but nothing is ever on the level, and his wit consists in tilting truth until even the staidest mind is unsteady. To what end? Nothing, really, except a sort of verbal revenge of the "out" upon the "in".

Wilder burlesques *everybody*—the Coca-Cola tycoon . . . ; the South; nubile fillies from the South; Coca-Cola's go-getting sales director in Berlin; West Germans and East Germans; ex-Nazis and Prussian aristocrats; German Communists and Russian Communists; communism and capitalism; marriage and infidelity; and innumerable other aspects of contemporary life, sacred and profane. (p. 37)

It's the rapid-fire of gags . . . which really keeps this film moving. And breathless pace is all important, for, had the audience ever been given time for thought, the whole thing would have fallen apart. The gags are almost all grade-A. . . .

Billy Wilder is one of those ex-Viennese who believe things are hopeless but not serious. In fact, this ancient wheeze is actually one of the gags in this film.

*One, Two, Three* is amusing throughout all of its 108 minutes. But not vitalizing. Quite, in fact, the reverse. (p. 38)

> *Henry Hart, "Film Reviews: 'One, Two, Three'," in* Films in Review *(copyright © 1962 by the National Board of Review of Motion Pictures, Inc.), Vol. XIII, No. 1, January, 1962, pp. 37-8.*

## PAULINE KAEL

*One, Two, Three* is overwrought, tasteless, and offensive—a comedy that pulls out laughs the way a catheter draws urine. . . . [It] was actually shot in Berlin and Munich (where the Brandenberg Gate was reconstructed), but the real location is the locker-room where tired salesmen swap the latest variants of stale old jokes. . . . If you find these jokes fresh and funny, then by all means rush to see *One, Two, Three*, which will keep shouting them at you for two hours. It's like you-know-what hitting the fan. (p. 63)

In Hollywood it is now common to hear Billy Wilder called the world's greatest movie director. This judgment tells us a lot about Hollywood: Wilder hits his effects hard and sure; he's a clever, lively director whose work lacks feeling or passion or grace or beauty or elegance. His eye is on the dollar, or rather on success, on the entertainment values that bring in dollars. But he has never before, except perhaps in a different way in *Ace in the Hole*, exhibited such a brazen contempt for people. (p. 64)

Perhaps a diabolic satire *could* be written on the theme of Coca-Cola haves and have-nots, but Wilder's comedy isn't black and there are no disjunctions: his method is as mercenary as the characters. . . . There is one nice touch—an old man singing "Yes, We Have No Bananas" in German, and there's also the dance of a behind on a table that's quite a "set piece." But even the portrait of Khrushchev slipping from its frame, revealing Stalin's picture behind it, was a reprise of a dimly remembered gag. And the three Commissars whom Wilder revived from his earlier script for *Ninotchka* have become coarsened with the years—another indication of the changing climate of Hollywood. They were grotesquely pathetic and sentimental in 1939; now they are even more grotesquely crude than the Cagney character.

This being the age of the big production and the big promotion, there is a tie-in with Coca-Cola which provides truck-banners, super-market ads, contests, and window displays. Who is laughing at whom? The target has been incorporated in the profits of the joke. Perhaps Wilder (who owns 90 per cent of the picture) is closer to his Coca-Colonizer than one might have expected. Is this dollar diplomacy?

I felt that we in the audience were all being manipulated in some shameful way, and that whenever this feeling might become conscious and begin to dry up the laughs, Wilder showed his manipulative skills by throwing in little sops to sentiment—even more ugly in their way than the "wisecracks." Arlene Francis has said of her role, "My character is a warm, sensible woman who has a good marriage." That's better satirical dialogue than anything I heard in *One, Two, Three*—a movie that shovels on the wit. (pp. 64-5)

> *Pauline Kael, "'One, Two, Three'," in* Film Quarterly *(copyright 1962 by The Regents of the University of California; reprinted by permission of the University of California Press), Vol. XV, No. 3, Spring, 1962, pp. 62-5.*

## JOHN SIMON

Billy Wilder's films are belt-and-suspender films: they combine the jaunty, *sportif* appearance of the belt-wearer with the comfortable, homespun look of the suspender-wearer. I wish I could report that the results are foolproof and unimpeachable. Actually, they fall between two wears. . . .

[It] is time to realize that though Wilder has made some extremely skillful, effective, and, in part, even penetrating films, he has never done anything first-rate. One reason for this is, probably, insufficient artistic imagination; another, certainly, is excessive caution. (p. 23)

Wilder's formula is films that are vulgar enough to appeal to the typical movie audiences, yet spiked with just enough cynicism, naughtiness, tough wisecracking, and *double-entendres* to make the *avant-garde* moviegoer detect "meanings within meanings," an action that takes place "on several levels," and a Wilder who is really "laughing at the whole thing"—or whatever phrases are currently fashionable among avant-garde viewers. In other words, Wilder's films combine solid suspenders with sophisticated belts. (p. 24)

It is, I suppose, a truism to say that a serious, indeed tragic, problem is reduced to slapstick [in *A Foreign Affair*]. But the particular meretriciousness lies in the glib purveying of something to everybody. The unthinking spectator sees (a) a funny little German and his even funnier little son being neatly put in their places by a clever captain from Iowa, and (b) a hilarious mess on pompous papa's back, perpetrated while he was busily cleaning up another one. The "sophisticated" viewer, on the other hand, sees a worthless opportunist (American) sitting in judgment over worthless opportunists (German), and prescribing a cure about which he himself must be secretly snickering with his ex-Nazi concubine. Superficially, Wilder has pleased everybody. . . . (pp. 24-5)

[The reprehensible thing] is the moral equivocation, here as almost everywhere else, in Wilder's work. The forces of ostensible right and demonstrable wrong are shown to be equally out for the main chance, though the former, to be sure, outwit the latter. . . . If Mr. Wilder were honest, he would have to take one of three positions: he could commit himself to dissatisfaction with one way of life and approval of another, and be a moralist; he could come out against humanity in general with a curse on all our houses, and be a satirist; or he could stay away from enormous, shattering problems, and be an entertainer and escapist. Instead, he wants to be jolly, informative, and misanthropic all at once; he is offering us a product that is to be simultaneously a sneezing powder, an encyclopedia, and an atom bomb. . . . In my eyes, he is . . . a filmmaker with false or no morality. (p. 25)

Wilder's provinces are plot and dialogue; characterization, other than the skimpiest surface variety, is beyond him. He does not . . . get inside a character; still less can he make real the feelings of one character for another, except by using a conventional notation closer to stenography than to depth psychology. And so we find, even in Wilder's best films, characters depending on the whims of the plot, dictated, in turn, by what the public demands, or by what Wilder thinks it demands. . . . In *Double Indemnity* the unscrupulous, peroxided Cleopatra, who has used the corrupt hero as she has used or killed all men, has a sudden change—or birth—of heart, drops the gun with which she has already wounded him, and is herself killed by him. . . .

Is this fatal inconsistency of character merely an obeisance to the box office, or something more than that? Partly, doubtless, just that. (p. 28)

Yet there is more to it: Mr. Wilder is also a cynic. At the end of *Stalag 17*, an honest but stupid tough guy says admiringly of the opportunist turned hero: "What do you know? The crud did it!" In Wilder's films the cruds almost invariably end up doing the grand thing. . . . Mr. Wilder tells us we are all fools and rogues. That is cynical. He sugarcoats this with laughs and miraculous conversions in which he himself does not believe. That is more cynical yet. But we happily swallow his insults, which makes us fools; and he cashes in on them, which makes him a successful rogue. All fools and rogues: Q. E. D. But whereas cynicism undisguised is a bitter pill that has curative value, cynicism cynically sugarcoated, and so thickly as to nullify the medication, has no therapeutic, moral, or artistic validity. So that the point, ultimately, isn't how much cynicism Mr. Wilder brings to his artistry, but how little art he brings to his cynicism. (p. 29)

> *John Simon, "Something for Everybody" (originally published as "Belt and Suspenders: The Art of Billy Wilder," in* Theatre Arts, *Vol. XLVI, No. 7, July, 1962), in his* Acid Test *(copyright © 1963 by John Simon; reprinted with permission of Stein and Day Publishers), Stein and Day, 1963, pp. 22-9.*

## ELIZABETH SUSSEX

Set mainly in a bawdy-house that is never in the least bawdy, Billy Wilder's *Irma La Douce* is the kind of fantasy much favoured by Hollywood—a sex comedy from which sex has been carefully eradicated. Enticed into the cinema by the promise of untold orgies, audiences are sent away reassured that even wildly successful prostitutes have no sex life to speak of, and that the habitués of the Rue Casanova are perhaps a little more colourful but scarcely less wholesome than themselves. Now that so many continental directors are presenting a different, and more accurate, picture of prostitution, one can hardly blame Wilder for trying to suspend disbelief, and even disappointment, by laying on the charm with a trowel. The trouble is that in doing so, he has thrown sophistication overboard in what should have been an ultra-sophisticated film.

Treated simply as a piece of inverted romanticism, the story of Irma . . . , queen of the tarts, being wooed and won by Nestor . . . , the most honest man who ever came her way, is certainly amusing, but not amusing enough to hold the screen successfully for 141 minutes. . . . Instead of the sort of explosively uninhibited satire of the whole upside-down Hollywood code that Wilder is surely sharp enough to have made, *Irma La Douce* is, in fact, a fairly routine frolic. On this level, it has much of the best that Hollywood can give. . . .

Wilder's direction is distinguished not so much for what it does for the film as a whole, as for what it can pack into a single frame. Nestor's fight with Irma's former protector, Hippolyte the Ox, and a champagne-swilling party scene, in which Irma dances on a table top, are handled with splendid panache. This is, in fact, the right way to make a musical, and, on the stage, *Irma La Douce* was a musical. Under the circumstances it seems a pity that someone thought fit to change all that.

> Elizabeth Sussex, "'Irma La Douce'," in Sight and Sound *(copyright © 1964 by The British Film Institute), Vol. 33, No. 2, Spring, 1964, p. 98.*

## ANDREW SARRIS

The trouble with Billy Wilder in **"Kiss Me Stupid"** is that while he doesn't really believe in morality, he doesn't really enjoy immorality, and so we get another exercise in joyless jejune cynicism a la **"Irma la Douce."** Wilder's forte has never been visual style, but the studio decor in and around Climax, Nevada, sets a new low in drabness and dreariness rendered in all the penny-pinching, two-toned dustiness of black and white photography, that most realistic of all cliches. Wilder and I.A.L. Diamond milk Climax for all its galactic and climactic worth and throw in some clever topical gags about the Sinatra fils kidnapping and that little old winemaker me, but someone forgot to write in plausible situations for the pratfalls. That is to say, the dialogue is all there, good, bad, and mostly indifferent, but the scenario is missing, and even the dirtiest denouement in the world cannot obscure a series of false premises. . . .

Of course, no one who is condemned by the Legion of Decency can be all bad, but I wish Wilder hadn't tried to weasel out of his condemnation by posing as a starry-eyed idealist of the nouvelle vague at war with entrenched morality. Wilder has always been a clever entertainer with just enough nastiness in his personality to avoid the anonymity of studio production. Only Wilder would be vicious enough to staff the supposedly bawdy Belly-Button drive-in cafe with fat, old, and ugly waitresses, their navels bared. Left to his own dubious devices, Wilder operates on so many different levels of calculating cruelty that one wishes he were less free for the sake of his undeniable talent.

> Andrew Sarris, "Films: 'Kiss Me Stupid'" (reprinted by permission of The Village Voice *and the author; copyright © The Village Voice, Inc., 1965), in* The Village Voice, *Vol. X, No. 13, January 14, 1965, p. 14.*

## STEPHEN FARBER

*The Fortune Cookie* is almost the only recent American comedy that's about some recognizable contemporary menaces—insurance frauds, shyster lawyers, prying detectives, the American eagerness to confuse money and love. It also is in black and white and actually looks *cheap,* though it aims at big commercial success. This would be about enough to make it a movie worth seeing, but it also has some good writing and two shrewd performances. . . . Billy Wilder's satires, like *The Apartment,* usually look more cynical than they are; in this one the main problem is that [Willie], though his lines are indeed sour, is simply too much fun to watch, too charming a caricature to have much edge.

> Stephen Farber, "Entertainments: 'The Fortune Cookie'," in Film Quarterly *(copyright 1967 by The Regents of the University of California; reprinted by permission of the University of California Press), Vol. XX, No. 3, Spring, 1967, p. 61.*

## JOHN RUSSELL TAYLOR

Why *Meet Whiplash Willie*? What's wrong with *The Fortune Cookie* [the film's U.S. title] for a title? At least it has the virtue of sounding like a comedy, which Billy Wilder's new film is, rather than a B-Western, which it emphatically isn't. The new title does not even have the advantage over the original in mere intelligibility: before going to the cinema I knew what a fortune cookie was, but I needed the film to explain to me all about whiplash lawyers and their way of life. . . .

But then Wilder is never all that easy. With the gleeful vulgarity of *Stalag 17* or *Kiss Me Stupid* we all know where we are, even if it is somewhere that the more delicate of us may not choose to be. But as a rule he chooses not to isolate his wilful bad taste. Instead, he pushes drama further than anyone else would (in Hollywood, anyway) towards raving melodrama. . . . The treatment is tonic, but like many of the most effective tonics, it can leave a nasty taste in the mouth. And so it is with *Meet Whiplash Willie,* another of Wilder's sweet-sour cocktails. If it were just ruthless comedy everything would be quite straightforward. So it would if the story were treated instead as a drama of conscience leading to a sentimental conclusion. But Wilder being Wilder, it is both at the same time, and that is where the trouble comes in. (p. 147)

[The] ultimate trouble with the film is that it obstinately remains two films, and Jack Lemmon's film cannot indefinitely play feed to Walter Matthau's. There are inklings from quite early on that things will turn soft in the end, that the good, decent guy in Harry will win out, that he will see through his calculating wife and realise that his friendship with good, warmhearted, coloured Boom-Boom Jackson, the footballer who first knocked him for six, is tied up with his integrity as a human being and worth making sacrifices for. Inklings, but we may choose to ignore them, and Wilder at least lets us; they are there, but they are not forced under our noses.

For most of the way the comedy is hard, clear and ruthless, with a lot of funny lines and a bright, efficient surface—even to the appearance of modish chapter headings for the main phases of the action. And the end, when it comes, is quite quickly over, with Willie still unrepentant, figuring out how to sue his triumphant opponents for invasion of privacy. Not, in the last analysis, quite one of Wilder's best, but from the comedy-starved Hollywood of today, more than enough to be going on with. (p. 148)

*John Russell Taylor, "'Meet Whiplash Willie'," in Sight and Sound (copyright © 1967 by The British Film Institute), Vol. 36, No. 3, Summer, 1967, pp. 147-48.*

## BOSLEY CROWTHER

It is surprising how loath film-makers have been to make films about themselves, or about the magic medium of illusion they transmit to the world. As egotistical and narcissistic as most film artists are—including the writers and directors, who are the crucial creators, of course—they have seldom dared turn their cameras on their own involuted lives or explore the cultural importance and impermanence of most of the work they do. For that reason, *Sunset Boulevard* . . . was not only rare as an invasion of a ticklish subject when it came along, but it was—and still is—the most arresting and subtly philosophical film about Hollywood that there has been. (p. 198)

*Sunset Boulevard* takes a long look at the past of this mesmeric medium and makes the sardonic discovery that most of its yield is vaporous and vain, that the seeming triumphant creations accomplished in one age will be, with but few exceptions, crumbling celluloid in the next. It offers the sobering implication that the major output of movies is myth, momentary excitements and exaltations that are as evanescent as dreams. . . .

Norma Desmond, one of the great, glamourous stars of silent films who now dwells in a musty mansion set back from Sunset Boulevard, where she has been in archaeological seclusion for a couple of decades when the story begins, represents more than the delusions of grandeur of one old star. She represents the ostentation and arrogance of a whole generation of film-makers which has passed—a generation that produced a glittering output of gaudy trumperies and vast vulgarities, yet whose craftsmen assumed the postures and played the roles of great creators of Art.

She is further a haunting reminder of the massive mythology of silent-screen gods and goddesses whose well-advertised images drew millions of devoted worshipers into darkened temples all over the world. She is altogether a living relic of a tempo and taste that are dead. (p. 199)

[It] is notable that it is not a touching picture. As loaded as it is with what might be easy inducements to tearful nostalgia, it is brutal and unrelenting in its exposure of the haughty vanity and selfishness of Norma, who is wholly without true sentiment. (p. 200)

[There is something sad about the final scene]. But I find this calculated scene more a pointedly ironic comment upon the phoniness of much that is in films. Like everything else in the picture, it is a shrewd reflection of the basically evanescent creation of Hollywood. (p. 201)

*Bosley Crowther, "'Sunset Boulevard'," in his The Great Films: Fifty Golden Years of Motion Pictures (copyright © 1967 by Bosley Crowther), G. P. Putnam's Sons, 1967, pp. 198-201.*

## JOSEPH McBRIDE and MICHAEL WILMINGTON

Wilder's forte is the great American congame. In practically all of his movies (original stories and adaptations alike) the plot revolves around some sort of swindle. (p. 2)

In Wilder's view, sex and money are inextricably linked. His characters use sex to obtain cash and position and involve themselves in frauds to get sex. Sometimes, however, greed and lechery conflict, and the whole scheme blows up. . . . This kind of mordancy is often charming but sometimes, in more serious situations, makes Wilder's attitude seem repulsively petty. . . . Wilder uses the sex-greed conflict as a comment on human frailty; nature won't even let people be *evil*, just weak. Only in a few cases is he entirely sympathetic to their swindles—at the very lowest level, where they do little harm, or when the characters are actually trapped in a situation which has robbed them of choice. . . . Wilder simultaneously indulges in an irresponsible delight in the intricacies of deception and a curious moral sense which almost always leads him to condemn his characters for their weakness.

And it is perhaps too simple to suggest that Wilder's central characters are all con-men; usually there is an unholy alliance of sorts involving an innocent and a corrupt partner. (p. 3)

In general, Wilder's point of view is that of an innocent fascinated by the world's corruption and attempting, with some success and a great deal of comic tension, to join in on it. But the innocence is his ideal, and he ultimately returns to it . . . or else works out an appropriate retribution, frequently death, for his most absorbingly repellent characters. Wilder's material is almost always serious, and his approach almost always farcical and ironic. . . . In Wilder we can see perhaps one of the most interesting examples of a conflict between box-office values and uncompromising intentions. He works hard to come up with genuinely happy endings for most of his films, feeling that the audience deserves "a little bonus at the end because they sat still for what we had to tell." He is making exactly the films he wants to make, but there is a continual tension between his darker fascinations and his sense of audience communication—which probably accounts for his curious charm. . . . Wilder's humor, like all great comedy, springs from threatening situations. "Good taste" is a joke to him, because he plunges the audience into the sordid and the unbearable.

A secondary but pervasive Wilder "touch" is his cynical-romantic use of movie legends. Like Lenny Bruce and Terry Southern, Wilder likes to graft show-business argot and mannerisms onto the outside world. In almost every one of his films, there is a playful recalling of the movie past, often re-enacted by one of the original participants. In a way, Wilder is a quintessential fan. . . . In "exposing" faded glamour even while succumbing to its seductiveness, Wilder is again supplying the metaphor of the con-game. (p. 4)

Wilder's conception of life as a game, with the swifties on one side and the law on the other, may also account for his fondness for sports. He often names his characters after athletes, especially after college football players. A football game is the perfect stylization of the con-game; it is played out in the open, enforced rigorously by uniformed officials, it is action through grace and strategy—but the underbelly is gambling and commercialism. . . . His twin ideals seem to be the innocent whore and the innocent athlete, livers of a life at once instinctual and encircled with corruption, an irony which he, the clever pimp, can enjoy. (pp. 4-5)

Pimp and whore work out their balancing act between innocence and evil with two other typical characters in attendance—the policeman, instrument of society, and the morally vacuous "observer." The pattern varies considerably from film to film, however; sometimes both are present, sometimes they are combined into one unnerving character. . . . The observer is the voice of conscience, a more wrenching but less urgent character than the voice of authority. . . . This figure is often emotionally involved with the pimp, either by protecting him or by reproving him. And in rejecting the representative of normality (who can often be seen as a father-figure), the pimp is risking total alienation; to return from the abyss, he must domesticate his whore, or abandon her. Vice is fun, says Wilder, but you'll always get caught. . . . [*Some Like It Hot*, the] gayest of Wilder's comedies, his most highpowered piece of gag creation, hovers constantly on the edge of the macabre. The first things we see are a hearse, a gun battle, and a raid on a speakeasy fronting as a funeral parlor. . . . The psychotic intensity of the backdrop throws the boisterous vulgarity of the blue humor into a kind of limbo between innocence and depravity. The movie's ostentatious artificiality—the outrageous coincidences that keep the plot moving, the filthy stream of *double-entendre,* the many obvious grabs from old movies—all this seals us off from the desolation lurking in the wings. Seesawing between nightmare and farce, Wilder keeps a heady jump or two ahead of any kind of reality. (p. 5)

Wilder's flippancy toward plot and characterization in *Some Like It Hot,* droll as it is, only underscores the fact that he shares what Leslie Fiedler diagnosed as the shortcomings of many American story-tellers: a proclivity for edgy sex and violence and an inability to deal maturely with love and death. (pp. 6-7)

Wilder's exposition of the events [in *Ace in the Hole*] is not merely clever, it is a shrewd commentary on human nature. . . . The narrative has the purity of a mathematical formula, abetted by the almost documentary veracity of the physical details and the characters' behavior. (p. 7)

Perhaps the difficulty with some of Wilder's films is not "sentimentality" but a moralism which tends to overstate its case. . . . Wilder skimps seriously on the "innocent" in *Ace in the Hole,* a young reporter fresh out of journalism school who is corrupted by Tatum's brash sophistication. The ease in the boy's change from an idealist to Tatum's hanger-on implies that he was shallow from the beginning. Which is the point, of course, but it does indicate a limitation in Wilder's perspective. What would he have done with a strong idealist? . . .

Though Wilder shows an admirable tenacity in pursuing his premise, he builds his case in a way that [Erich von] Stroheim or [Ernst] Lubitsch, true cynics, would not. There is little sense in Wilder of human potentiality—as there is in Stroheim's McTeague and Trina in *Greed*—only a sense of more or less acquiescence to the rottenness of life. . . . *Ace in the Hole* appalls but fails to move—*Greed* is profoundly moving—and remains a moral "demonstration." On that level it can be faulted for not opening itself to all the possibilities of human response. (p. 8)

*Ace in the Hole,* for all its power, suggests that Wilder's talents are better attuned to the purely ridiculous than to the appallingly ridiculous. But what gives his comedy the urgency of a judgment on life is the blackness at the core of his heart. (p. 9)

*Joseph McBride and Michael Wilmington, "The Private Life of Billy Wilder," in* Film Quarterly *(copyright 1970 by The Regents of the University of California; reprinted by permission of the University of California Press), Vol. XXIII, No. 4, Summer, 1970, pp. 2-9.*

## JOSEPH McBRIDE and MICHAEL WILMINGTON

*Sherlock Holmes* is another example of Wilder's penchant for digging beneath the surface of famous personalities and professions to expose the painful contradictions between the image and the actuality. . . . Wilder and his coscenarist I.A.L. Diamond take a more serious attitude toward Holmes's weaknesses than his creator does, making him a more vulnerable and human figure. He operates beyond the law, like most of Wilder's central characters, but the fact that he is also a servant of the law makes his fallibility more poignant. Holmes's attraction to crime is not, as in the stories, the fascination exerted by imperfection on a superhuman "deductive machine," but, characteristically for Wilder, a man's dalliance with his own self-destructive impulses.

The classical detective story, the "whodunnit," is a highly moralistic genre which insists upon a totally rational moral system and an ambiguous approach to character. . . . To Wilder, a moralist *malgre lui,* the detective story's fascination with hidden vice implicates even the detective himself. His films almost invariably revolve around a con-game, as seen from the viewpoint of the swindler; but there, as in his adaptation of Agatha Christie's *Witness for the Prosecution,* the central character is a man of the law who is swindled into joining forces with a criminal. His Holmes is a jaded romantic, a reformed *roué* who exposes himself to criminals in order to exorcise the possibility of further corruption. (pp. 46-7)

In making Holmes more human, Wilder and Diamond have, curiously, neglected to adequately dramatize his legendary deductive genius. This would at first seem a serious weakness. . . . Reading the script, we might think that Holmes is merely a pathetic *schlemiel*—he is hoodwinked by a lady spy into betraying the most delicate secrets of the British government to the Germans—but Wilder's direction of his actor keeps us alert to the delicate vacillations of passion which are leading Holmes's intellect off its course. (p. 47)

The idealization of innocence which has always gone hand-in-hand with Wilder's skepticism has often led him to be as misogynistic as Doyle's Holmes, but here. . . . he treats the woman who deceived Holmes as a tragic dupe like Holmes himself. . . . She seems at first to fit into the Wilder gallery of scheming whores, with Holmes cast as the customary Wilder dupe. . . . But it is the *amateur* whore . . . who reaps Wilder's scorn. He respects professionals because they do not attempt to conceal their corruption; and we respect Frau von Hoffmannstahl even though she is deceiving Holmes, because she is not deceiving us. It is surely no accident, too, that she is a *German* spy, the tool of forces which Wilder has always confronted with thinly concealed outrage. There is an astonishingly callous touch toward the end of the film when Holmes and Mycroft destroy her fellow spies without the merest flicker of compunction. When Holmes learns of her death, at the very end, we finally realize the depth of his commitment to her: the man who cannot face the death of his desires retires once more to privacy and takes refuge in cocaine. Wilder has rarely equalled the intensity of this moment. (p. 48)

*Joseph McBride and Michael Wilmington, "The Private Life of Sherlock Holmes'," in* Film Quarterly *(copyright 1971 by The Regents of the University of California; reprinted by permission of the University of California Press), Vol. XXIV, No. 3, Spring, 1971, pp. 45-8.*

**STEPHEN FARBER**

Wilder's work, like the work of most of his contemporaries, is compromised; in his case, though, the compromises have been condemned with unusual severity. The common critical view of Wilder—much too simple a view, I believe—is that he is a cynic who repeatedly tempers the harshness of his vision in deference to the box office. (p. 9)

Wilder's tendency to caricature is one way of diluting the acid. But even at its most frivolous, this caricature cannot help exposing Wilder's misanthropic temperament. In **The Seven Year Itch,** a comic strip psychiatrist arrives early for an appointment and explains impassively, "My 3:00 patient jumped out of the window during his session, and I've been 15 minutes ahead of schedule ever since." Only a cynic could toss off a joke like that with such casual good humor, but in this case the character is so broadly overplayed that we don't have to take the satire on psychoanalysis *seriously*. . . . In dealing with Wilder, it is important to distinguish between such abrasive, disturbing black satire and more comfortable sick jokes—gag lines that *reveal* a cynical frame of mind without effectively or intelligently satirizing anything.

Wilder's eleventh hour conversions are even more troublesome compromises. In **Double Indemnity** the ruthless, scheming heroine shoots the hero once, and then drops her gun, for the first time in her life halted by a genuine pang of love. (pp. 9-10)

Certainly such conversions are possible. But Wilder is rarely successful at dramatizing them. His commitment seems to be to the cynical attitude expressed through the first three-fourths of these films, the morally uplifting conclusions are played, almost invariably, without conviction. . . . The more one considers Wilder's films, the more apparent it becomes that the confusions and contradictions in his work are not always simple compromises, and they are motivated by something more than a worship of the box office. Wilder's sensibility is far more complex than most people have been willing to grant. For a famous cynic he has surprisingly ambivalent feelings about innocence and corruption. . . .

Wilder is not ordinarily committed to message moviemaking: he wants to reveal the rottenness hidden beneath the placid surface of contemporary society, but he is clearly tantalized by the rottenness if it is on a daring enough scale. (p. 10)

[Wilder has a] disenchanted vision of today's world, dominated by Americans with "kissing sweet" toothpaste grins, who haven't the slightest shred of culture or refinement of elegance. But another director would be more bitter about that recognition. Wilder cannot suppress a sneaking sense of wonder at [Marilyn] Monroe's blissful obliviousness to the possibility of a more graceful way of life. (p. 11)

Wilder does not believe that innocence can survive unscathed. He does not believe that faith and trust are a reasonable basis for human relationships. His films chronicle the corruption of innocents, the fall from purity. But considering Wilder's reputation as a cynic, we would expect more ruthless mockery of the innocents. Instead they are treated with affection, even admiration. (p. 12)

The clearest indication of Wilder's conflicting feelings about innocence is the nature of love in his films. There are *never*, in Wilder, two completely innocent lovers. . . .

The innocents in Wilder's films are never attracted to other innocents, always to people who have been married or have had eventful sexual pasts; surely this is Wilder's comment on the impossibility of innocence's survival and the irresistible pull of corruption. But there is a pull in the other direction too—the most worldly characters hanker for the virgins. (p. 15)

[It] is striking how often Wilder's films actually deal with a relationship of young man or woman and aged lover. (pp. 15-16)

But even where the relationsip are between two people of the same age, they are relationships between playboys, prostitutes, promiscuous (or married) men or women on the one hand, and characters, who are relatively innocent or unattached; in Freudian terms, such a relationship is always a euphemism for an oedipal relationship. . . .

It is impossible to ignore how often Wilder deals with secretly oedipal relationships, and it may not be surprising that homosexuality plays a furtive role in a number of his films. Psychoanalysis argues that when the only heterosexual relationship desired is incestuous, the whole idea of heterosexuality becomes threatening. There is a distrust of love, often of women in Wilder's films that leads to a withdrawal into idealized homoerotic experiences. (p. 16)

Wilder's characters are denied the standard Hollywood version of love. In his films other motives stir the characters with a force love cannot begin to match [alcoholism, greed, power, fame, family reputation]. These are the motives that stimulate people into action. . . . (p. 17)

Wilder's faith is in dishonesty; he believes in the exuberance to be found in choosing your role and playing it to perfection. . . .

It would not be quite accurate . . . to call Wilder's style realistic. There is almost always a touch of flamboyance in the filmic details. . . .

It is Wilder's delight in the outrageous that is the most distinguishing visual characteristic of his films. In spite of Wilder's cynicism, there is a rather astonishing exuberance in the imagery of his films, an exuberance in the power of art that his films so often celebrate. (p. 20)

*Stephen Farber, "The Films of Billy Wilder," in* Film Comment *(copyright © 1971 by Film Comment Publishing Corporation; all rights reserved), Vol. 7, No. 4, Winter, 1971-72, pp. 8-22.*

**JOSEPH McBRIDE**

In his new movie, *Avanti!*, Billy Wilder is still trying hard to become Ernst Lubitsch. The strain shows, some of the romanticism is forced and mechanical, but there is much of which the Master might approve. . . .

In the last few years, as the porno revolution and advancing age have deprived Wilder of his old ability (and desire) to scandalize, he has relaxed considerably in his handling of sex. *The Private Life of Sherlock Homes,* and now *Avanti!* find him in a mellowing, more gracious mood; he is less defensive in his treatment of love, less cynical in his attitude toward women, and less inclined to find sport in sexual cruelty. (p. 1)

The dialogue is largely concerned with unseen events (details of the accident, the old couple's affair, complications with the funeral arrangements), and while this is partly attributable to the source being a stage play (by Samuel Taylor), it also adds to the pervasive feeling of nostalgia, the sense of the past being richer and more alive than the present. . . .

In keeping with the theme, Wilder's visual style is sedately elegant, comfortably old-fashioned in its use of unobtrusive cutting, smooth camera movements, graceful choreographic emphasis. A precise, economical style but in no way a dull one. . . . (p. 2)

Although *Avanti!* is a twist on the earlier Wilder-[Jack] Lemmon romantic plot, this time having the man cruelly denying the woman's feelings, it is more of a complication than a simple inversion. . . .

The nude swim, which takes its place among Wilder's classic exercises in bad taste, is the decisive blow to Wendell's stodgy dignity, although it takes him a while to realize it. It is characteristic of Wilder's approach to romanticism that he makes the swim so ridiculous, despite its almost religious significance to Pamela and its considerable erotic possibilities. (p. 8)

*Avanti!* is far from being Wilder's best film—it's not as consistently witty and inventive as *Kiss Me, Stupid* or *Some Like It Hot*—but if audiences and critics allow him to continue in the Lubitschian vein, he may reward us for our patience. (p. 9)

> *Joseph McBride, "The Importance of Being Ernst,"* in Film Heritage *(copyright 1973 by F. A. Macklin), Vol. 8, No. 4, Summer, 1973, pp. 1-9.*

## STEPHEN FARBER

[Wilder's] films have always exposed the deceptions of love; there are shadings in his romantic scenes. Still, *Avanti!* is, for him, an uncommonly tender and affectionate film. Although the central character is very sharply drawn, and although many incidental jokes—an Italian giving the Fascist salute to a visiting American statesman, a tracking shot past a group of nuns lined up to see *Love Story*—reveal his old acid touch, this film is less cruel than almost anything Wilder has done. It makes some nervous concessions to the audience, as Wilder's films usually have; a few inappropriately crude farcical scenes are signs of insecurity. . . . Gradually, however, Wilder finds his tone, and the movie takes hold. It is actually not so uncharacteristic as it first seems; it is a less troubled variation on the serious themes that have concerned Wilder throughout his career. (pp. 50-1)

*Avanti!* is somewhat reminiscent of *A Foreign Affair,* in which a prim American Congresswoman discovers the decadence of postwar Berlin. But in that film Wilder compromised his harsh portrait of American self-righteousness; *Avanti!,* by contrast, is one of his most straightforward anti-American satires. . . .

In contrast to the brutal, hard-driving American tourists, the Europeans are cultivated, romantic, indolent, tender, passionate. Wilder mocks the excesses of the Italians—particularly in the hilarious portrait of a conniving hotel valet and his murderous Sicilian girlfriend; but he obviously prefers the craziness of the Europeans to the ruthless efficiency of the Americans. . . .

Besides, the film absorbs us in the rich, languorous atmosphere of an exquisite European resort. Wilder is not known for his visual compositions, and *Avanti!,* like most of his movies, takes place inside, skimping on the glorious scenery. But his film is masterfully made. . . . *Avanti!* is a celebration of holiday, and it is one of those films that stimulates wanderlust: even the corridors of this hotel—blue, white and gold—are flooded with the sunlight of dream vacations. The film is something more than an escapist fantasy; it is *about* the importance of

escape from the sterile, single-minded American workaday world—a tribute to the lazy, romantic holiday spirit that industrious Americans find immoral. (p. 51)

The great advantage of *Avanti!* is that it has a point of view. As a *writer*-director Wilder can bring much more even to a relatively light movie; his obsessions enrich and transform any project he beomes involved in. . . . In *Avanti!* the elegant style grows from assurance and control; the film has an underlying seriousness that enables us to relax without abdicating intelligence. It is a very charming, alert, and human comedy. (p. 52)

> *Stephen Farber, "Two Old Men's Movies,"* in Film Quarterly *(copyright 1973 by The Regents of the University of California; reprinted by permission of the University of California Press,) Vol. XXVI, No. 4, Summer, 1973, pp. 49-52.*\*

## STANLEY KAUFFMANN

"Nobody's perfect." Possibly that is the most famous last line of any American film. Well, nobody, nothing, *is* perfect—perhaps; but the picture that closes with that line [*Some Like It Hot*] is almost the exception to the rule. It may be somewhat ungrateful to call a very funny film a masterpiece; it sounds like an attempt to take it out of human circulation. Still Billy Wilder has brought it on himself. What is worse, I have to insist that this unfailingly delightful farce is a triple milestone.

It is significant three ways in American film history. It is the best film (so far) by the last European director to flourish in this country. It is the best film of the last great sex star created by Hollywood. It is the last of the carefree American comedies that sprang up when sound came in, bloomed through the thirties, and had a revival after World War II. (p. 324-25)

The dialogue is not a collection of gags but a temperamental use of language: that is, vernacular is filtered through a chuckling temperament, diction is selected and arranged so that, while the characters speak always as themselves, the lines support and further the tone and action of the whole. . . .

In addition, there is a deft, knitted use of ideas. Themes are stated that are played back at odd angles. When the "girls" report for their jobs, the suspicious leader asks them their musical backgrounds and they say they studied at the Sheboygan Conservatory, which awes the others. Later, when Sugar is trying to impress Joe-as-millionaire, she tells *him* that she studied at Sheboygan. (p. 327)

Structurally, the script obeys and profits by two traditional formal injunctions. First, it conforms to Hebbel's all-inclusive dictum on the secret of dramatic style: "To present the necessary in the form of the accidental." Second, more specific to farce, it begins with a ridiculous but engaging premise (Wilder's "nugget"), then builds on this improbable premise with rigid logic. (pp. 327-28)

Farce, like melodrama, needs monochrome characters who will react predictably in given situations. *Some Like It Hot* has a well-blended spectrum of characters: the classic pair of youths, one aggressive and scheming, the other meek and wistful; the tough lady bandleader with the chromium smile; the near-sighted manager; the urbane, murdering Spats. With the exception of Joe . . . , none of them alters through the film, and almost none of them has, or is meant to have, depth. The exception is Sugar Kane. . . . (p. 328)

It would be foolish to burden *Some Like It Hot* with undue praise. I am interested in due praise. The beauty—no less a word will do—of a fine farce like this has little to do with the elements of high comedy: character dissection, moral reproof, social comment. There is no valid social comment in this picture; the gang wars, Sugar's millionaire-hunting, Osgood's profligate philandering, were chosen only as props, the way a juggler chooses ninepins instead of hats. (p. 331)

Watching it is like watching good trapezists. They, too, start from a ridiculous premise: what sane person would hang from bars in midair? Once there, they proceed with absolute logic. Farce gives us the thrill of danger (when Joe forgets to take off his bandstand earrings, racing to a date as the millionaire) and the thrill of split-second neatness (when he whisks them off just in time). Basically, that is the greatest joke of all: absolute order has been imposed on the chaos of life. Farce, as an artistic form, is identical with that order . We know that life, on either side of these two hours, is chaotic: there is pleasure here in seeing how neatly things fit together for people we like.

Possibly, to come at last to the third significance of *Some Like It Hot,* that is why it is the last really good farce produced in this country to date. There have been new imitations of old farces, there have been new farces, all inferior; they lack any real commitment to the sheer fun of design, to the ideal of a finely tuned comic machine that has no purpose other than fun. (pp. 331-32)

This film will make people laugh as long as future societies bear any perceptible relation to our own; and will make people laugh the second, third, sixth time they see it. If that isn't immortality, it's close enough. Nobody's perfect. (p. 332)

*Stanley Kauffmann, "'Some Like It Hot'" (originally published in a slightly different form as "Billy Wilder's 'Some Like It Hot'," in* Horizon, *Vol. XV, No. 1, Winter, 1973), in his* Living Images: Film Comment and Criticism *(reprinted by permission of Brandt & Brandt Literary Agents, Inc.; copyright © 1970, 1971, 1972, 1973, 1974, 1975 by Stanley Kauffmann),* Harper & Row, Publishers, *1975, pp. 324-32.*

### GEORGE MORRIS

As moving as much of it is, *Fedora* is a problematic film. I wish Wilder had given the thwarted romance between Barry and Fedora the same intensity he brings to the similar relationship between Sherlock Holmes and his German Spy. I also wish he had devoted less time to the unraveling of the surface mystery. . . .

And yet. And yet. *Fedora* is an elegant reminder of a formal perfection that has all but vanished from contemporary film-making. When Wilder's camera tracks past a luxurious ball-room of waltzing dancers, the exhilaration and beauty of the scene are tempered somewhat by the cranes and booms we see filming it. Even in this movie within a movie, the time for this kind of grandeur has almost gone. . . .

Like the three movies which precede it, *Fedora* is a film of memory. But this time, we must remember, too. No other Wilder film depends so much on associations from his other movies. In this respect, *Fedora* may prove unsatisfying for those who do not love and appreciate Billy Wilder's films. But those of us who do, it is a worthy addition to the work of one of the supreme artists of the American cinema. (p. 39)

*George Morris, "The Private Films of Billy Wilder" (copyright © 1979 by George Morris; reprinted by permission of the author), in* Film Comment, *Vol. 15, No. 1, January-February, 1979, pp. 34-9.*

### ANDREW SARRIS

From the first strains of Miklos Rozsa's vintage '40s score [in *Fedora*] we are transported to a timeless realm in which nothing has really changed. The cold cruelty of the blue Mediterranean forms an aptly Wilderean backdrop for a crazy yarn about a star who has apparently defeated time. . . .

Wilder may have outsmarted himself by his morbidly convoluted method of telling the story of Fedora by beginning after we have seen Marthe Keller run down by a train, thus setting into motion Detweiler's reminiscence about the "late" Fedora he had known. Long before the plot winds down, several of the characters find themselves wandering interminably around Fedora's coffin as they wait for the last of the needlessly explanatory flashbacks to run their course. Long before *noir* was a critical catch-word, Wilder's characters seemed to walk on the dark side of the street out of a natural predilection for peril. Even Wilder's comedies—*The Apartment, Sabrina, Avanti!,* most notably—have been shadowed by death and self-destruction. But in *Fedora* the cinema itself ends up in a coffin of Wilder's own design. And one can hardly expect 1979 screening audiences to join Wilder at the wake. *Fedora,* like D. W. Griffith's *The Stuggle,* Charles Chaplin's *Limelight,* Jean Renoir's *Picnic on the Grass,* Josef von Sternberg's *Ana-Ta-Han,* Carl Dreyer's *Gertrud,* Orson Welles's *Falstaff,* and John Ford's *Seven Women,* can be understood and appreciated only in the context of an entire career as a testament of twilight. . . . *Fedora* is far from the height of fashion. . . . I only hope that Wilder's career has not been reduced to retrospectives, and that he is allowed to come snapping back with the wit and verve of which he is still capable as the last surviving heir of Ernst Lubitsch.

*Andrew Sarris, "Some Like It Not" (reprinted by permission of* The Village Voice *and the author; copyright © News Group Publications, Inc., 1979), in* The Village Voice, *Vol. XXIV, No. 15, April 16, 1979, p. 41.*

# Frederick Wiseman

## 1930-

**American documentary filmmaker.**

**Wiseman is best known for his documentaries on institutions, such as prisons and hospitals, which expose, in his words, "the complex ambiguous feature of human helplessness." He intends to examine social and cultural values using an objective style which allows viewers to draw their own conclusions.**

**Wiseman is a follower of the *cinéma vérité* school. *Cinéma vérité* is a filming method employing hand-held cameras and live sound, but it also reflects a filmmaker's attitude toward the world he films. Wiseman's style follows in the tradition of the Drew Associates, the first contemporary American filmmakers to develop a style utilizing uncontrolled, spontaneous shooting while dealing aesthetically with their topic.**

**Wiseman had no film experience prior to making documentaries. He was an urban planner and a lawyer before producing *The Cool World*, directed by Shirley Clarke, in 1963. While a law professor at Boston College, Wiseman frequently took his students on field trips to Bridgewater State Hospital for the Criminally Insane, where he filmed *Titicut Follies*. This experience helped develop Wiseman's interest in the documentary as a form of exposition. *Titicut Follies* is perhaps the most controversial film Wiseman has made. It provoked the ire of Massachusetts legislators, who banned it in the state. As in most of his films, Wiseman does not use voice-over narration to explain any situations to the audience, feeling that "it would provide a false security for the viewer." Later films examine the welfare system and the police (*Law and Order*) and high school life (*High School*). *Hospital* again explores social issues within an institution, while *Essene* examines a monastery in relation to the changing mores of the outside world.**

**Though critics generally admire Wiseman's work, the subjects themselves do not always agree with Wiseman's treatment of them, accusing him of creating misleading cinema. While Wiseman feels that his audience can be credited with the intelligence to make its own decisions, opponents attack him as unwilling to take a stand. Though viewed by some as a muckraker, Wiseman does not consider himself a crusader, stating that he is merely "trying to see if you can pick up reflections of the larger issues of society in the institutions."**

## ROBERT HATCH

As far as content is concerned, Mr. Wiseman is relentlessly explicit [in *Titicut Follies*]. His documentation amply confirms what one had suspected—that Bridgewater, and presumably dozens of institutions like it across the country, are Gothic anachronisms. . . . The resemblance [to an old-fashioned zoo] is heightened by the life of the place: the inmates spend a large part of their time naked in the airless warmth and the large, slow-moving guards treat them with the indulgent informality of keepers for their charges. However, I can't recall ever seeing a zoo custodian bait the animals, as some of the guards ride their prisoners. . . .

The film makes clear—what we already know—that institutions like Bridgewater are ill-equipped and understaffed (except for the guards, who seem to congregate like elephants in the cramped alleys). Recreation is almost nonexistent (a bare exercise ground where monomaniacs harangue their fellows, a birthday party, a tense little woman trying to get men in their 50s and 60s to play a game suitable for 5 year olds). It is shameful, but that it is a snake pit, I'm not prepared to say. That is a matter of context, and *Titicut Follies* offers no more context than the typical TV network one-hour "controversy." I feel expected to express outrage, and am willing to do so—something is obviously very wrong. But before I begin yelling I need to know the quality of the iniquity and the identity of the villains.

Robert Hatch, "Films: 'Titicut Follies'," in The Nation (copyright 1967 The Nation Associates, Inc.), Vol. 205, No. 14, October 30, 1967, p. 446.

## ROBERT COLES

Ironically [*Titicut Follies*] is so effective because it is not another *Snake Pit*, another brutal and unrelenting exposé of life behind the closed doors of a mental hospital. Yes, there are some scandalous and disgusting moments, but by and large they are not those that offer us the standard "backward" scene, with its shrieks and groans and hilarious desolation or grim excitement. I have seen much worse in other state hospitals that Massachusetts maintains.

Something else is at work to give this film its power, and to unsettle its critics, many of whom are objecting to the nudity allowed or demanding to know why the faces of inmates are used, in clear violation of the right to privacy. . . . If Frederick Wiseman has offended the sensibilities of his fellow citizens he has done it I believe by making them nervous about far more than nudity (in this day of bikinis and miniskirts) or the individual's right to privacy (in this day of wire-tapping, of cleverly manipulative advertising, of espionage that has been into so many things that any number of people can reasonably doubt whose purposes they have served and with whose money).

After a showing of *Titicut Follies* the mind does not dwell on the hospital's ancient and even laughable physical plant, or its pitiable social atmosphere. What sticks, what really hurts is the sight of human life made cheap and betrayed. . . . But much more significantly, we see the "professionals," the doctors and workers who hold the fort in the Bridgewaters of this nation, and they are all over. (pp. 29-30)

*Titicut Follies* is a brilliant work of art, and as such it will not go unnoticed, despite the opposition to it. We are asked not to be outraged at others—a cheap and easily spent kind of emotion—but to look at ourselves, the rich and strong ones whose agents hurt the weak and maimed in the name of— what? Our freedom. Our security. Our civilization. Were men's "rights" violated, or do places like Bridgewater strip men of everything, their "rights," their dignity, their humanity? Does a man like Frederick Wiseman have the obligation to say, tell or show what he saw, or is the state entitled to *its* privacy? . . . All the while our Bridgewater State hospitals still stand; and the human beings in them bother us only rarely, when a film like this one comes along. . . . (p. 30)

> *Robert Coles, "Stripped Bare at the Follies" (reprinted by permission of the author), in* The New Republic, *Vol. 158, No. 3, January 20, 1968, pp. 18, 28-30.*

## NANCY ELLEN DOWD

The editing patterns in *Titicut Follies* are the unheralded and monstrous discoveries in the small of the mind. Two men become one, and two unrelated incidents form one episode as the intricately structured and highly organized madness reveals itself to an initiate. Perceptions and time are constantly regrouping—yet not in order that they should become credible or recognizable or even be given a name—simply changing. The film seems to have been cut as the hospital was perceived and the editing is touching and personal. . . .

[The] words in *Titicut Follies* almost never advance a story or even refer to some uncompleted action or to anything we ever expect to see again; when they do, (the TV screen and the suicide remark), they are underplayed, almost inaudible. The warden who jabbers on endlessly about Eddie Mitchell having been gassed is part of an open-ended scene which is never completed. We never see or hear anything about Eddie Mitchell again.

[There] is comparatively little dialogue in the film. Speech is most often in the form of a litany . . . , hypnotic, and like most speech not really saying anything. There are no hackneyed exposition techniques in *Titicut Follies*. (p. 30)

[Speech] is rarely directed at anyone. People are usually talking to themselves. There is still competition with background noise, and several people are often talking at once. There is also a lot of singing in the film—yet, unlike opera, unrelated to any action or plot. Performances abound. (pp. 30-1)

[*Titicut Follies*] has no conventional hierarchy of character importance necessitating that one of the principals be on screen at all times for a reason—a reason the audience can guess and

incorporate into a theme; nor is there a self-conscious departure-from-conventions attitude.

Moreover, the film is not sensationalist . . . ; nor does it try to make a succinct statement about mental hospitals. The film reveals. To its credit, *Titicut Follies* defies interpretation. (p. 31)

> *Nancy Ellen Dowd, "Popular Conventions," in* Film Quarterly *(copyright 1969 by The Regents of the University of California; reprinted by permission of the University of California Press), Vol. 22, No. 3, Spring, 1969, pp. 26-31.**

## JOSEPH FEATHERSTONE

Frederick Wiseman's remarkable documentary film, *High School*, is worth seeing. For it shows that our most serious educational problems aren't only in slum schools. What people think of as the good schools are failing their children, too. . . .

[Wiseman] sets out to portray a reputable high school, not a blackboard jungle. *High School* suggests no remedies. In words alone, its message can be reduced to a string of cliches: the schools are authoritarian, repressive, and so on. On film—on this film, anyway—the cliches take on density and complexity, carrying us beyond slogans into artistic truth. Scene after scene builds to a powerful cumulative effect—not of anger, but of immense sadness and futility: this is how we live. *High School* is an essay on emptiness.

Though far from sympathetic, the camera eye is not cruel. The teachers seem decent and well-meaning. What they say doesn't matter much. What counts are the numbing lessons the whole institution is teaching its students about themselves and life. (p. 28)

All hopes and dreams are dented, those of parents as well as students. I felt tugged in different directions watching an interview between some parents and a counsellor. The regal father is ambitious for his daughter, perhaps too ambitious. . . . [Why], one wonders, is the message at Northeast [High School] so insistent, and why is there so much bitter joy in the work of denial? At last the father imagines possibilities for the girl: the school is quick to snuff out visions. In another scene, I had the same torn feelings about the school's protection of students. A college counsellor tells a girl she can apply to all her dream colleges, but that she should have a college of last resort, "if none of your dreams came true." Again, sensible advice. But in Northeast, this begins to sound suspicious. Too many people are insisting on defeat. . . .

The school asks little from the students, as teachers keep saying. Order is the main thing, and most students seem to find it easy to pay homage to order. In a few scenes students are openly insulted. A girl has it explained to her how wearing a short dress to the prom is an insult to the school. She must learn to abide by the standards of the majority. (The majority is constantly invoked.) "I think it's nice to be individualistic, but there are certain places to be individualistic," the teacher says. Under pressure, near tears, the girl recants: "I didn't mean to be individualistic." (p. 29)

The camera lingers questioningly on the faces of the kids, but the faces are mysterious, and you have no way of fathoming what they make of this—some decent teaching about something interesting, for a change. Deliberately, Frederick Wiseman confines himself all through the film to what the school elicits from the students. We have no way of knowing what they feel about the school. It is entirely possible that they are as complacent about it as the staff, even though it obviously bores them. Maybe, after all, they learned the main lesson: don't expect much. . . .

**High School** should be seen for its own extraordinary merits. But it will surely become a weapon in the war of styles of life and classes now dividing America. Many will insist that the reason Northeast is such a mournful place is that it institutionalizes the attitudes of a repressed lower-middle class. There is room for this view. But it's incomplete. (p. 30)

> *Joseph Featherstone, "Documentary: 'High School'"*
> *(reprinted by permission of the author; © 1969 The*
> *New Republic, Inc.), in* The New Republic, *Vol. 160,*
> *No. 25, June 21, 1969, pp. 28-30.*

### PAUL BRADLOW

[Wiseman's] technique [in *Titicut Follies*] is that of the avant-garde direct cinema. *Homo homini lupus*—man is a wolf to man. The text could have many names, but for the moment let me choose the cleanest: "How Not to Run a Mental Hospital." . . .

From the very beginning, the camera is handled as a surgical instrument, a slashing knife, to jolt us from our complacency and indifference to ourselves. The blade of morality, with its fine point of compassion and biting edge of righteous indignation, cuts deeply. One feels, amidst the crude hilarity of the patients' chorus that introduces the film, a haunting sense of inner turmoil. . . .

The film's faults have perhaps been minimized by defenders and exaggerated by detractors; but its essential dramatic power is documented by the violent passions it has aroused on all sides. The soundtrack is harsh and fuzzy at times, but, curiously, this grating stridency only adds to the total impact. (p. 60)

*Titicut Follies* represents an honorable attempt in the vigorous stream of contemporary political tradition—an attempt to pass over the heads of the established delegates and bring the case to the people. (p. 61)

> *Paul Bradlow, "Two . . . but Not of a Kind: A Comparison of Two Controversial Documentaries about*
> *Mental Illness, 'Warrendale' and 'Titicut Follies',"*
> *in* Film Comment *(copyright © 1969 by Film Comment Publishing Corporation; all rights reserved),*
> *Vol. 5, No. 3, Fall, 1969, pp. 60-1.**

### PAULINE KAEL

**High School** is so familiar and so extraordinarily evocative that a feeling of empathy with the students floods over us. How did we live through it? How did we keep any spirit? When you see a kid trying to make a phone call and being interrupted with "Do you have a pass to use the phone?" it all floods back—the low ceilings and pale-green walls of the basement where the lockers were, the constant defensiveness, that sense of always being in danger of breaking some pointless, petty rule. When since that time has one ever needed a pass to make a phone call? This movie takes one back to where, one discovers, time has stood still. (p. 21)

**High School** seems an obvious kind of film to make, but as far as I know no one before has gone into an ordinary, middle-class, "good" (most of the students go to college) high school with a camera and looked around to see what it's like. . . .

This movie shows competent teachers and teachers who are trying their best but not one teacher who really makes contact in the way that means a difference in your life. The students are as apathetic toward the young English teacher playing and analyzing a Simon & Garfunkel record as toward the English teacher reciting "Casey at the Bat," and, even granted that as poetry there might not be much to choose between them—and perhaps Casey has the edge—still, one might think the students would, just as a *courtesy*, respond to the young teacher's attempt, the way one always gave the ingénue in the stock company a special round of applause. . . . The teachers come off much worse than the police do in *Law and Order. High School* is a revelation because now that we see school from the outside, the teachers seem to give themselves away every time they open their mouths—and to be *unaware* of it. (pp. 22-3)

[The final scene is] a great scene—a consummation of the educational process we've been watching: They are successful at turning out bodies to do a job. Yet it's also painfully clear that the school must have given [the] soldier more kindness and affection than he'd ever had before. There must be other students who respond to the genuine benevolence behind the cant and who are grateful to those who labor to turn them into men. For those students, this schooling in conformity is successful.

Wiseman extends our understanding of our common life the way novelists used to—a way largely abandoned by the modern novel and left to the journalists but not often picked up by them. What he's doing is so simple and so basic that it's like a rediscovery of what we knew, or should know. We often want more information about the people and their predicaments than he gives, but this is perhaps less a criticism of Wiseman's method than it is a testimonial to his success in making us care about his subjects. With fictional movies using so little of our shared experience, and with the big TV news "specials" increasingly using that idiot "McLuhanite" fragmentation technique that scrambles all experience—as if the deliberate purpose were to make us indifferent to the life around us—it's a good sign when a movie sends us out wanting to know more and feeling that there is more to know. (p. 24)

> *Pauline Kael, "High School and Other Forms of*
> *Madness" (originally published as "The Current*
> *Cinema: 'High School'," in* The New Yorker, *Vol.*
> *XLV, No. 35, October 18, 1969), in her* Deeper into
> Movies *(© 1969 by Pauline Kael; reprinted by permission of Little, Brown and Company in association*
> *with the Atlantic Monthly Press), Atlantic-Little,*
> *Brown, 1973, pp. 19-26.**

### PAULINE KAEL

[*Hospital*] was made at Metropolitan Hospital in New York, but although the hospital conditions are not pretty, it is not an exposé of man's inhumanity to man. The revelation of *Hospital* is the many surprising forms of man's humanity to man. . . . It is a melting-pot hospital, and the film demonstrates that the melting-pot dream has to some degree been fulfilled. There are so many human gestures within the misery, such as the solemn "Thank you"'s of aged poor patients for whom speech is no longer easy. The general decency of the staff toward the patients may shake cynics. . . . Their occasional crudeness, even roughness, seems to be part of a recognition of the facts of life for the poor in a big city. Only rarely (as with a doctor treating a student on a bad trip) does one have any doubt that they're people of good will doing their damnedest. (p. 101)

At the beginning, *Hospital* seems almost a random view, but as the scenes and details begin to accumulate, the vision takes hold. By the end, we are so thoroughly involved—in a way I think we rarely are in conventional, guided documentary—that tears well up, because we simply have no other means of responding to the intensity of this plain view of the ordinary activities in Metropolitan Hospital. The habitual cant and concealments of most documentaries seem, by contrast, chintzy and puritanical and fundamentally insulting. Movies that spare our feelings assume that there are things we are ashamed to look at. *Hospital* doesn't spare our feelings, and—I don't know exactly how or why—it seems to clean away the shame. We've gone through the barriers of middle-class good taste, and it's better on the other side. (p. 102)

> *Pauline Kael, "The Man Who Loved War" (originally published as "The Current Cinema: 'Hospital'," in* The New Yorker, *Vol. XLV, No. 50, January 31, 1970), in her* Deeper into Movies *(© 1970 by Pauline Kael; reprinted by permission of Little, Brown and Company in association with the Atlantic Monthly Press), Atlantic-Little, Brown, 1973, pp. 97-102.**

## RICHARD SCHICKEL

[The city] is full of poor people and old people, lunatics and junkies, and [a hospital] is one of the places where they make the transition—inevitable for those who exist on life's margin—from sociological statistics to medical ones. Some do so in agony, some in shame, many in bewilderment. But perhaps the most remarkable thing about them is how often they manage to clothe these conditions in dignity, in honorable resistance to fate. . . .

That is the theme of the film [*Hospital*]. The people of *Hospital* can administer an emetic to a young art student poisoned by a bad mescaline pill. . . . But they cannot cure his sickness with life. . . . The people of *Hospital* are in no position to practice preventive medicine on an entire society.

The chief characteristic of all of Wiseman's films—and the source of their tremendous emotional impact—is his instinctive sympathy for people who must confront the specific, human effects of vast, impersonal social forces. Armed only with professional skills, some common sense and some common decency, they become, as we see them through his eyes, impressive human beings. . . .

Wiseman's camera seems to miss nothing, but his tact is unique among the cinéma vérité people. One never feels the voyeur, no matter how intimate or revealing the scene he asks us to observe. Nor does one feel he is trying to impose upon his material some facile reforming zeal. He sees his difficult task in deliberately simple terms. He wants merely to show us the day-to-day quality of our society's institutions, thereby letting us render our own judgments of their quality.

It is tempting to come to a cheerful conclusion about *Hospital* ("As long as these good people are willing to undertake this good work, we have nothing to worry about"), but that is too easy. Wiseman is a gentle humanist, but he employs his humanism ironically to illuminate the gap between intentions and the job at hand. Inspiring as the staff of *Hospital* is, it is clearly

overmatched. The whole force of the film derives from this terrible, beautifully understated fact.

> *Richard Schickel, "Where Misery Must Be Confronted," in* Life *(courtesy of* Life *Magazine; © 1970 Time Inc.; reprinted with permission), Vol. 68, No. 4, February 6, 1970, p. 9.*

## STEPHEN MAMBER

*High School,* in addition to its other considerable merits, should lay to rest once and for all [the] mystique of "interesting personalities" in direct-cinema films. . . .

Frederick Wiseman's films are about indispensable institutions in conflict with the people they are supposed to be serving. . . . Each of his films has an episodic structure, a lack of emphasis on individual personalities, and a general diffidence about verbal information. What matters in a Wiseman film is not necessarily what people say to each other, but the tone in which they are speaking and the degree of emotion behind their words. Attitudes rather than factual information are the substantive content of his films. (p. 49)

[*High School*] is a series of interactions between students and their parents, teachers, and administrators. It's not a general study of educational methods or the attitudes of today's youth. We never see students at football games, dances, or even talking to each other beyond earshot of their elders. *High School* is a film of frustrating confrontations. . . . On the surface, the film might be seen as little more than a single-minded condemnation of secondary education in America. As a film-making objective this could have been sufficient, but the film would then be easy prey to the customary criticisms of bias, selectivity, and over-simplification. If *High School* were attempting to do no more than that, these objections might have at least partial validity. But through deliberate choices of content and structure, Wiseman suggests that his target is bigger and his attitudes more complex. The ability of *High School* to transcend its visible subject matter is the measure of its considerable power as a film experience. (pp. 49-50)

The idea of training (or indoctrinating) students to fit into the orderly processes of society might not be all that *High School* is about, but it is at least the guiding principle behind its structure. The film is concerned with the attitudes which the high school hopes to foster in its students and the all-pervasiveness of its philosophy, beyond classroom learning into matters of sexual relationships, competitiveness, dress habits, social graces, and roles within the family. . . .

The film has the remarkable quality of appearing to be a series of random occurrences. There is no specified time sequence to the film. Individual episodes never last more than three or four minutes (and frequently are much shorter), and if people appear in more than one sequence it seems to happen more by accident than by dramatic necessity. But unmistakable patterns emerge. First, we begin to notice how rarely we hear kids talking. The students are forced to be listeners, and what they are told starts sounding pretty much the same. . . . Along with the verbal barrage comes the variety of subservient, competitive roles which the students are forced to enact. (p. 50)

Although this sounds as if Wiseman has fashioned a sober polemic out of his material, his visual style and sense of drama are full of a purposeful black comedy which often makes us gasp, first in surprise, and then in recognition. . . . *High School* is a marvel of visual expressiveness, a display of a fully engaged sensibility adding a quiet commentary all its own. . . . Wiseman's almost freakish sense of humor, allowing us to laugh at boredom and repression, keeps *High School* from being a chamber of horrors like *Titicut Follies*. (pp. 50-1)

If there are villains in *High School* (or in any of Wiseman's films), they exist outside the film's milieu—in a general attitude in America which imposes a rigid, traditional philosophy on the administrators of its institutions. . . . *High School* can't be placed within the "cinema of personalities." Its effectiveness stems from the interchangeability of individuals enacting their specific social roles, from ritual processes enforced by organizational relationships.

*High School* takes special risks because it deals with a subject that we all know about. Wiseman has not shown us people or situations which are by themselves particularly interesting or that we couldn't know about in any other way. He surmounts this problem by seeing the logical connections within his material and vesting his film with the mathematical elegance of a neatly executed proof. The fragmented, highly selective structure of the film is a result of his sensing the parts of the high school experience which are relevant to his argument, and his willingness to sacrifice dramatic continuity for a unity which isn't apparent until the film's conclusion. Wiseman does not so much give us facts to consider as recall an atmosphere we might not have been in a position to evaluate at the time we were living within it. *High School* does more than imply that this kind of educational system leads to willing soldiers and spacemen. It leaves us doubting seriously whether America has the capability for altering its institutions to suit the shifting expectations and needs of those who are supposed to benefit by them. . . .

By showing attitudes within the high school rather than processes of learning and by avoiding the limitations of specificity that concentrating on certain individuals would have led to, Wiseman has adroitly left the task of what to make of all this to his audience. . . . Like other good *cinéma-vérité* film-makers, he doesn't stumble upon "great material"—he challenges us by a personal vision of the way we live. (p. 51)

> Stephen Mamber, "Reviews: 'High School'," in Film Quarterly (copyright 1970 by The Regents of the University of California; reprinted by permission of the University of California Press), Vol. XXIII, No. 3, Spring, 1970, pp. 48-51.

### DONALD E. McWILLIAMS

[To say] that a Wiseman film is about the institution or is primarily about the institution is to be superficial and ignore the complexity of his films. There are many levels at which his work can be examined. This arises in good part out of the non-narrative structure of his films, which makes his films both more complex and open to many interpretations. Repeated viewing of his films underlines the importance of structure. To take *Law and Order* as a case in point, one is aware that time is passing, but it is not chronological. The film does not seem to have any beginning and development to a climax. Yet the film has unity. Throughout the film, there are recurrences of voices on police radios and discussions between two policemen in parked patrol cars. The structure of the film becomes circular, a series of overlapping circles. One is drawn into the circles of experience and there seems to be no escape from the problems that occur within these circles. Nor, because of the juxtaposition of incidents and behavior that Wiseman places

within those circles, is it easy to arrive at any black-and-white conclusions about the police or even the lawbreakers. One becomes aware that only a superficial level is the film about the institution. There is violence throughout *Law and Order,* but it is not large-scale. Two policemen discuss a riot, but we see no riot. Wiseman ignores the sensational and concentrates on the everyday—husband-wife quarrels, lost juveniles, car-stealing, prostitution, drunkenness. Whilst there is physical violence in the film, it is between individuals. In fact, for me, the most lasting impression is the verbal violence, both deliberate and thoughtless. Whilst some film-makers film riots, Wiseman concentrates on person-to-person relationships; for the riot is a symptom of the malaise. It is only by zeroing in on the individual that there is any hope of understanding the causes. *Law and Order* at the deepest level is not about police at all, but about individuals, what they do and say to each other and the ambiguity of behavior. . . . (p. 23)

> Donald E. McWilliams, "Frederick Wiseman," in Film Quarterly (copyright 1970 by The Regents of the University of California; reprinted by permission of the University of California Press), Vol. XXIV, No. 1, Fall, 1970, pp. 17-26.

### E. MICHAEL DESILETS

*Titicut Follies* is a very important film because its impact touches areas of law regarding private rights and public rights, and the final legal fate of the film will be of extreme importance, as a step forward or backward, to the future of documentary film-making. (p. 30)

The film is not as exciting or lurid as I had been led to believe, nor is it especially dramatic. Its main force must lie in the viewer's awareness that he is watching real people in an institution that exists as fact. This is not *Marat/Sade*. This is the reality of the Massachusetts Correctional Institution at Bridgewater—at least as much of that reality as Wiseman chooses to let us see. . . . Wiseman is not guilty of "comment without correction," and if the institutions are the "real villains" of his films, that villainy and any resultant institutional guilt must be shared by real people at some point. In *Hospital* we watch a drug-taking young man fill the screen with vomit. We seem to watch vomit for a long time and can easily conclude that Wiseman is critical of the social conditions (people) that lead to this young man's misfortune. The scene is certainly not a negative comment about the hospital as an institution. Perhaps Wiseman overextends his effect—and it is an effect since it comes to us via his own editing of the film—because as Andrew Sarris remarked in a recent lecture, he confuses the cathartic with the emetic. But the point is that Wiseman is not merely "the fly on the wall," but has an opinion to share with his audience. No viewer is totally free to devise his own opinion. (pp. 30-1)

I do not think [*Titicut Follies*] is as exploitative as has been charged by many. Wiseman's intensification of Bridgewater's reality is not at all heavy handed when one considers the innate shock value of the subject matter, which includes happily sadistic hospital personnel; infirm, naked, and virtually mindless alcoholics; mild-mannered men who rape their own daughters, and so on. . . . Many of the conversations we hear in the film center on the Viet Nam war, politics, religion—whatever men anywhere talk about. These discussions are bizarrely contrasted by the surrealistic haranguing of one inmate who can say no more than three or four coherent words in a row before his speech degenerates into gibberish. In a fiction film this man would almost necessarily have to "represent" something. In *Titicut Follies* he is mostly a question mark. We wonder what makes him that way. (p. 31)

E. Michael Desilets, "Fred Wiseman: 'Titicut' Revisited," in Film Library Quarterly (© copyright, Film Library Information Council, 1971), Vol. 4, No. 2, Spring, 1971, pp. 29-33.

## EDGAR Z. FRIEDENBERG

The delayed development of hostile reactions by the subjects of Wiseman's films is one of the more revealing social responses his work evokes. *Titicut Follies* is, indeed, a disturbing document, but not for quite the reasons I, or presumably Bridgewater's directors, had expected. . . .

Having gone to see *Titicut Follies* expecting to be shocked by the exotic horrors of the snake pit, I emerged with a much sadder sense that what I had seen differed only in degree from everyday life. These patients were afflicted, certainly, but the nature of their disorder was clear enough, very common in America, and serious indeed. They suffered from disastrously low status compounded by poverty, which had drastically lowered their resistance to incarceration. . . .

[*Titicut Follies*] suggests that the hospital's social function may be useless and occasionally monstrous. The film shows quite clearly that the primary consequence of defining, and confining, the patients as criminally insane is to justify keeping the hospital running; the question of improving its services hardly arises.

What causes the authorities who first approve to later repudiate Wiseman's films and what shocks them into hostility is the tendency of his work to reveal that the institutions scrutinized are not merely defective but often superfluous: self-serving and self-perpetuating. The original conception of the medieval Ship of Fools showed the passengers as starving at a table laden with food. Each had strapped to his arm a spoon so long that he could feed his neighbor, though not himself—but this he would not do. The picture of society that builds up through Wiseman's work is just the converse, and surely no less fiendish. It appears to consist of interlocking sets of social institutions, seldom useful in themselves, which provide roles for their members and sustain one another through a system of cross-referrals which serve to validate the *raisons d'être* of all, using the clients who are supposed to benefit from their services as expendable counters in their own games.

The idea that official institutions exist to exploit more than to serve their clients is both valid and well-suited to the temper of our times. It is central to much of Wiseman's work and helps account for its power. When this implication is weak or absent, his films take on a different and, I think, less distinctive tone. *Hospital,* for example, is a study of an institution physically hardly more adequate than Bridgewater: a large general hospital perpetually inundated with the victims of urban violence and decay. But the impression it conveys is not merely of squalor but of continuous, grinding, backbreaking resourcefulness under impossible conditions. Its patients are real clients, their needs are desperate, and, somehow, they are seen, however fleetingly, as human beings; and their medical emergencies, at least, are dealt with. The result, however, is a film with very little irony; the viewer gets a justified feeling of *déjà vu,* since great urban hospitals and their dedicated, overworked staffs have long been a staple of commercial TV. . . .

[*Law and Order*] suffers to a lesser degree from the same difficulty as *Hospital.* The police as a social institution are ambiguous. (p. 20)

[Highly] essential service makes up a lot of the Kansas City policemen's job, but Wiseman's film suggests that they do it pretty badly. . . .

But whether they like it or not the Kansas City police, like the doctors in *Hospital,* though in a lesser degree, are involved with and sometimes useful and responsive to the community that supports them and, hence, not quite as effectively revealed by Wiseman's apparently artless dissection. His masterworks deal with two institutions that are remarkably similar in their values, their dependence on legal coercion to provide themselves with a clientele, and their centrality to American life. . . .

The two institutions, of course, are the high school and the military. Frederick Wiseman's *High School* is, with the possible exception of James Herndon's books (which are about junior high schools anyway), the most expressive and revealing document portraying these institutions—what happens in them, what they are really like, how parents as well as students respond to them, what the values reflected in their practices and conveyed through the experience of attending them must be. Much of what is shown in *High School* would be familiar to any serious critical observer of secondary schooling in North America. But there are two special insights it affords—one by its content and one by the response it evokes from teachers and prospective teachers—that were new to me, though they should not have been, and therefore seem worth reporting.

The first of these is the extremely hostile and degrading form of male chauvinism that pervades the high school and is taken for granted there. . . .

The jokes [during the sex education talk] have a clearly didactic function: to teach that any real feeling in connection with sexual relationships would be a serious offense against accepted practice. . . . The degradation of the girl's role in *High School* is pervasive, suffocating—and official.

The other unexpected insight *High School* provides comes from the fact that audiences of teachers and prospective teachers generally approve of it. They usually compare Northeast High favorably with the schools they went to or teach in: What's wrong with it? . . .

[Many] teachers view this film with delighted recognition when it is shown to them. The high school is the very heart of America, and Wiseman has captured its strength and rhythm perfectly. And in doing so he has provided an almost equally perfect projective device for its viewers. (p. 21)

The films have a point of view, sometimes revealed directly in the frequent close-up shots of the cruel mouths of the pushier and more manipulative characters or in Wiseman's sensitivity to and conception of what is significant. He seems never to overlook the swift, darting glances by which petty bureaucrats reveal status anxieties when their real audience is different from their ostensible one. . . .

Except for occasional visiting relatives, and a Louisville whore who is discussed but not depicted, there are no women in *Basic Training* to be degraded. But what it shows about these young soldiers certainly tells us what the institutions of American society make of sex, and what this costs. . . . *Basic Training,* though it has a cast of hundreds of young athletes, must be one of the least sexually arousing films ever made. . . .

For a central function of Basic Training is to alienate young men from access to their own feelings and values, and to destroy their capacity for spontaneous perception and response. Its effectiveness has been demonstrated at Song My and elsewhere, and Wiseman shows just how it is done and how the process looks, in the gracelessness of the soldiers' movements and the tuneless songs—''Mr. Nixon drop the bomb;/I don't want to go to Nam!''—they sing under orders. Even a sadist would get no satisfaction here; there is plenty of verbal humiliation but nothing as human as a beating or a fight. One of the ironies underscored in the film is the fact that though soldiers are taught to shriek mechanically as they lunge at bayonet targets, they are sent to disciplinary barracks for exhaustive punishment if they get into personal fistfights. As in *Dr. Strangelove,* no fighting is allowed in the War Room. . . .

[This] set of films is in itself enough to record and fully document the process of depersonalization in American institutions, and to show that this process is essential to the stable functioning of American society. The process seems essentially unrelieved. In these films freaks don't make it, as they occasionally do in real life—though not, as a rule, when that life is lived within one of those institutions. . . . Yet Wiseman's films do give strong grounds for hope, by their very existence and character. They could only have been made in a deeply polarized society, swept by confused alarms of struggle and flight, and one whose armies, God knows, are ignorant enough. The outcome of the struggle is therefore still in doubt to some degree. (p. 22)

> *Edgar Z. Friedenberg, ''Ship of Fools,'' in* The New York Review of Books *(reprinted with permission from* The New York Review of Books; *copyright © 1971 Nyrev, Inc.), Vol. XVIII, No. 6, October 21, 1971, pp. 19-22.*

### PATRICK SULLIVAN

[*Essene*] pays its attention to an Anglican religious community which on the surface has little or no connection to the urgent social and economic problems of [Wiseman's] previous films. A monastery in a rural setting—what could constitute a more radical departure from the concerns of those earlier visions of institutional inhumanity? In *Essene* we watch instead the rituals, routines, exchanges among a group of men committed to a life which secludes them from the deterioration of cities, the profanities of schooling, the anxieties and paralysis of so many institutional roles. . . .

With *Essene* Wiseman focuses our attention on the quite specific collisions between a quite limited number of individuals. The examination of social issues in this film is not accumulated through quick-cut series of collage sequences of particulars so much as it is achieved through the close-quartered, representative drama of reconciling self-discovery and contentment with social responsibility and cooperativeness. . . . As *Essene* disengages us from the visual immediacy of a more familiar world, we come into the presence of a more freshly dramatic situation than any of [Wiseman's] other films provided. . . .

There is strong emotion, but muted and ritualized by both the place and the persons. The group is a collection, the film makes us feel, of individuals struggling quietly to create community. The spoken word appears an awkward and weak vehicle. (p. 55)

[*Essene*] portrays a small society at work redefining itself both in the light of its particular members but also in light of larger cultural forces it both moves toward and with. The abbot is

trying to steer a middle course between firm rejection and overeager acceptance of the new spirit (he is clearly troubled by many of its psychological and social consequences).

Looked at as a whole, the film sympathetically directs our attention first to the absence of shared experiences and directions in the community and then gives us several opportunities to witness modes of defining and arbitrating the conflicts. As the film builds to its complex conclusion, the question of leadership burns incandescently. The abbot has led in the past through a mild but skilled consensus-building, carefully avoiding outright exclusions of anyone and therefore vulnerable to the consequences or an uneasy truce. As the film develops, that uneasy truce shows clear signs of no longer serving its limited purpose. . . .

Can the group generate a collective strength insuring cooperativeness and tolerance? Can the past traditions accommodate themselves to a consciousness so group-oriented that the contemplative ideals are not hopelessly compromised? Can an ages-old theological symbol-system fulfill the demands for personal therapy placed on it by these new group dynamics?

Such questions emerge organically from *Essene,* and they are scarcely so private to the world of an Anglican monastery somewhere in the midwest that they don't deserve our secular and even ''anti-denominational'' attention. Wiseman has shown in his accustomed documentary style—heavy on representative situations and encounters, a patient watching and listening for accumulated meanings—that any group which has accepted the necessity of reconstitution in today's culture is battling with basic problems of social philosophy and practice. . . . *Essene* is a film with a special resonance which may make it Wiseman's most important to date. (p. 57)

> *Patrick Sullivan, ''Reviews: 'Essene','' in* Film Quarterly *(copyright 1973 by The Regents of the University of California; reprinted by permission of the University of California Press), Vol. XXVII, No. 1, Fall, 1973, pp. 55-7.*

### STEPHEN MAMBER

While [*Basic Training*] is open to individual analysis apart from the director's other work, a more sophisticated argument can be developed in terms of Wiseman's selection of material with clear affinities to concerns in his other films. The most certain connections in this case are between *Basic Training* and *High School,* although I think a more complex web of connections between all the films could be explored (dealing with, for instance, such things as the function of the church services in both *Basic Training* and *Hospital*). Wiseman is not only sensitive to the similarities between institutions, but also to the neat matrix of inverse influences—the ways institutions take on the functions and appearances of each other. In *High School* Wiseman repeatedly points up militaristic aspects of the high-school experience; in *Basic Training* he emphasizes the high-schoollike aspects of the training process. . . . [They] come to be seen as two steps in much broader processes of molding and regulation of citizens in nonvoluntary situations. (pp. 12-13)

[Wiseman] prefers to seek out defining moments, situations which either reveal institutional philosophy or those which (by their possibly seeming out of place) make possible the kind of institutional crossconnections we are talking about. Basic training is, after all, a kind of educational process, and perhaps a more efficient, concentrated learning experience than the high-school years. The film is full of assembly lectures, not the doctors' sex talks in *High School* but now indoctrination lessons about Why We Are In Vietnam and the importance of the "winning tradition" in the Army. Where *High School*'s teachers drilled bored students on literature, *Basic Training*'s instructors "teach" about rifles, bayonets, land mines, and the like, to a far more rapt audience. . . . [The] accumulation of evidence is too strong to avoid the military-high-school connections.

A possible argument against Wiseman's films might use the above case to assert that this is the kind of thing Wiseman *shouldn't* be doing imposing an implicit, external point of view on his material. . . .

[Wiseman's films] through their deliberate avoidance of extended personality orientation (there is never anyone to identify with) and their lack of linearly plotted story, together with the thrust of Wiseman's broad cultural concerns beyond the questions of individual institutions, are clearly trying to focus audience attention upon large social questions. One never feels that, say, "this is exactly what Northeast High School must be like." Instead, I think one feels something like "I think I see what Wiseman is trying to say about high schools, and about their function in American life." The two responses are quite different.

Given the strong formative tendencies in Wiseman's work, what then is the importance of his working in undirected situations without narration? . . . [In Wiseman's case,] narrations could easily tend to simplify response. It is not just that narration is usually superfluous, but that the situations themselves can be so full of possible meanings that narration simply intrudes. The more important concern of noninterference during filming is crucial, for while we know that Wiseman is stating his case through editing (and to some extent through camera framing), it is essential that we not feel that what he films is false, in the sense that he has not set anything up or instructed people what to say or do. The reasons for audience faith at this level are complex, but the important point is that Wiseman's films are constructed from discrete units of observed life. . . . Wiseman has very broad interests . . . that do not necessitate direct intrusions upon events being filmed. (p. 13)

> *Stephen Mamber, "Cinéma Vérité and Social Concerns," in* Film Comment *(copyright © 1973 by Film Comment Publishing Corporation; all rights reserved), Vol. 9, No. 6, November-December, 1973, pp. 9-15.*

### JANE LARKIN CRAIN

[The] first thing to be remarked of [Wiseman's] movies is that they possess, for the most part, a style and verve that put *Dragnet* and *Emergency!* to shame. Where they do not, where the air of pointlessness and tedium we normally associate with institutional life takes over, it is in the case of institutions whose very reason to exist is saturated with ambiguity.

The most extreme instance of this sort of tedium arises in *Essene,* Wiseman's study of monastic life, in which a great deal of the monks' time seems given over to trying to figure out just what the meaning and justification of monastic life are in the first place. The insecurity and confusion of the monks in *Essene* are no doubt rooted in the misgivings and anxieties of the modern Church itself, in the retreat from formalism that, at least on the evidence of this film, has led only to an aimless experimentalism. (p. 71)

[In] view of widespread charges that the judicial system in general has become paralyzed by the cumbersomeness of its own machinery, by overcrowding, and by inadequate staffing, what is most arresting in *Juvenile Court* is not the expected resultant air of intractability and frustration but its very opposite: the sense, strongly held by the participants themselves and communicated very forcefully to the viewer, that many problems, the majority in fact, can be resolved satisfactorily— that is, with attentiveness to the special needs of each individual case—and that the framework of the institution itself can accommodate a complex burden of responsibility. (pp. 72-3)

A great deal of what goes on in the juvenile court, Wiseman's film suggests, depends for its ultimate social efficacy on the extent to which any individual's capacity for rational behavior can be relied on, and not even the most sophisticated knowledge can gauge this with consistent or infallible accuracy, let alone insure it.

Although Wiseman has said that his films are meant to reflect his own responses to his subjects, his narrative "voice" is remarkably unobtrusive, as his critics universally affirm. Indeed, one of the major achievements of his work is that we feel we are watching people engrossed in the business of their own lives, and largely indifferent to the presence of an outside observer. . . .

Just as, however, we might respond with acute embarrassment or estrangement in witnessing, say, other people's marital quarrels, there are a number of moments in Wiseman's work in which the very immediacy of the proceedings leaves the feeling that it would have been the better part of good taste, to say nothing of compassion, to avert our eyes, until the trouble eased. When, for example, an elderly man in *Hospital* is being questioned about a possible urinary disturbance, and is clearly mortified to the point of tears, it is difficult to see how spectatorship, so patently intrusive here, is justified. (p. 74)

*Basic Training* is in many ways the most satisfying of the movies simply because it tells a story that has a beginning, a middle, and an end. In addition, the clear-cut authority structure of the army helps to lend a sense of order to this film about army life; the movies about institutions that are themselves in disarray tend sometimes to be too faithful a mirror of their subjects. . . .

At a time when so much of fiction is trying to persuade us that ordinary experience lacks essential order and stature, Wiseman has come along to document the richness and continuity of that experience. While our final impressions of the institutions themselves may be somewhat fragmentary—Wiseman's adherence to an interior perspective takes its inevitable toll in the films' general lack of clear focus or sharp edges—we are left feeling that we really know the people who run them. (p. 75)

> *Jane Larkin Crain, "TV Vérité," in* Commentary *(reprinted by permission; all rights reserved), Vol. 56, No. 6, December, 1973, pp. 70-5.*

### MARGARET TARRATT

For *Juvenile Court* [Wiseman] spent over a month in the Juvenile Court of Memphis and Shelby County, Tenn and shot 62 hours of film, four per cent of which is used here. There is no narrative overtly manipulating the audience's responses and despite the choice involved in the shooting and editing of the material, a film of this length which does not incorporate an analytical structure may well serve to reinforce the prejudices and attitudes which the audience already brings to it. It is not possible to assess the extent of the effect on those filmed. . . . No-one ever speaks directly to the camera and the film functions as an outsider's exploration of an institution. (p. 43)

The film opens and closes with an exterior shot of the Court House. Otherwise the camera never moves from the confines of the building. In terms of the predicaments of the offenders or victims, the court, as observed by Wiseman, exists in a vacuum, clinical, bureaucratic, and ultimately irrelevant to those forces and conditions which have brought such institutions into existence. The tongue-tied child swathed in a fantastic turban of white bandages unable to relate the story of how his uncle poured hot grease on him, the hysterical seventeen-year-old who cannot believe that a casual escapade has become classified as armed robbery, the groups of expressionless boys being drilled in the cathartic rituals of PT all crystallise this problem in dramatic terms. (p. 44)

> *Margaret Tarratt, "Juvenile Court" (© copyright Margaret Tarratt 1974; reprinted with permission), in* Films and Filming, *Vol. 20, No. 11, August, 1974, pp. 43-4.*

### CHUCK KRAEMER

The style [of **"Primate"**] is typical of a Wiseman film: leisurely, flat, unnarrated, often repetitive, utterly free of polemic. But the subject matter is intensely emotional. Not only is it grisly, with enough vivesection, exotic behavior modification, implantations, vomiting and probing to turn the strongest stomach, but also profound in the questions it raises about science, compassion and the eternal tension between the rational and spiritual sides of man's nature.

Wiseman raises these questions simply by observing scientists as closely as scientists observe primates. In the process, he exposes their callousness, their obsessiveness, the little games they play with one another and with their funding foundations, and, most revealingly, their peculiarly narrow view of life in general. (pp. 1, 31)

To Wiseman's credit, the film does not exploit the lovableness of the animals. **"Primate"** is never sentimental. Although the animals appear pitiful, the point of the film is not just to protest cruelty. Wiseman is asking, subtly and usually through dark humor, "Is this *necessary*?" When the benefits to mankind are so far off, and when more urgent problems confront us daily, *must we know this*? . . . In our passion to know more and more about less and less, are we losing perspective?

Wiseman implies we are.

In **"Primate,"** as in earlier Wiseman films, the institution, the method and the bureaucracy are all shown to smother the original humanistic purpose. . . .

The "de-animalization" of the monkey becomes a metaphor for the subtler kind of de-humanization afflicting our social institutions generally—emergency room, classroom, courtroom, monastery, barracks. And, as **"Primate"** so vividly demonstrates, it permeates even the realm of "pure" science, with animals the inanimate means to dubious ends. (p. 31)

> *Chuck Kraemer, "Fred Wiseman's 'Primate' Makes Monkeys of Scientists," in* The New York Times, *Section 2 (© 1974 by The New York Times Company; reprinted by permission), December 1, 1974, pp. 1, 31.*

### RICHARD SCHICKEL

[*Primate*] is perhaps Wiseman's most important work. It differs from its predecessors in that his camera discovers no saving human grace among the employees of the Yerkes Primate Research Center in Atlanta. What he gives us—unfairly, according to Yerkes people—is a dismaying study of what he obviously believes to be idiot savants. Wiseman sees men and women apparently devoting their lives to tormenting our closest neighbors on the evolutionary scale, apes and monkeys, for reasons he considers inadequate.

In the first, often hilarious section, they are cast as voyeurs, peering coolly into cages, stop watches and check lists at the ready, to study the sexual behavior of their victims. "Did you record that interaction?" one of them inquires in the ineffable jargon of his craft, as male gorilla approaches female. The analogy between ape and human behavior in this realm is dubious at best, the more so when the subjects are "interacting" not in their natural state but in prison. This portion of *Primate* makes the Yerkes crowd look like fugitives from a Woody Allen movie.

Thereafter, however, the film turns almost unbearably dark in tone. . . .

*Primate* is a tough film, and like almost all of Wiseman's previous work, it is raising outraged howls from its subjects. As usual, these take the form of demands for a narration that would "explain" what they think they are doing. But Wiseman believes that showing unpremeditated behavior (plus the subjects' own dialogue) tells more about the human reality of an institution than after-the-fact rationalizations of that behavior. He does not pretend to be an objective reporter. *Primate* is obviously one man's honest, if controversial view of an institution. Nevertheless, this assault on scientism and social scientism, the unquestioning belief that "pure" research must—perhaps because people insist on calling it pure—be valuable for its own sake, raises an issue of extraordinary urgency. More than that, and more than any of the Yerkes experiments, it also raises questions about the nature of man and suggests disturbing answers.

> *Richard Schickel, "Viewpoints, Shooting the Institution: 'Primate'," in* Time *(copyright 1974 Time Inc.; all rights reserved; reprinted by permission), Vol. 104, No. 24, December 9, 1974, p. 95.*

### KARL E. MEYER

At its best, [*Welfare*] is very good indeed, if one can use the word *good* about a film whose subject is appalling and depressing. Shot in black and white at a New York welfare center, the documentary confronts us with the quotidian miseries of the poor as they are shuffled through the corridors of the welfare bureaucracy. We are in effect at the elbow of the bureaucrat as we hear tales from purgatory told by the often subliterate applicants for welfare money. We are in the world of the misfit and the mendacious, of the addict and the whore, of the crippled and the partly insane, and of the normally invisible poor.

It is strong stuff, unflinchingly presented. Without a word of narration, it makes dismayingly clear how our present welfare system degrades both the supplicant and the donor. . . .

Wiseman's *cinéma verité* technique is here wholly suited to his subject, the hidden cameras cunningly eavesdropping on people who only occasionally—with a flicker of the eye—show any awareness of the intruding lens. . . .

The film's pace has the deliberation of a *danse macabre*. . . .

It is overwhelmingly clear, from the film, that the welfare system brings out the worst in all who are implicated in it. . . . A monotonous refrain in the documentary is the bureaucratic jargon of buck-passing, the clients being described as "conversion cases" or "referrals." By indirection, and without a word of commentary, Wiseman has made his case. With more weight than a bale of editorials and articles, *Welfare* argues powerfully for a fresh approach to the problem of poverty— and for a new look at the idea of a guaranteed annual income.

If *Welfare* has a blemish, it is that the case is overargued. By training, Wiseman is a lawyer, the calling most given to repetition. As in his other films, such as *Hospital* (1970) and *High School* (1968), Wiseman tends to amass rather than distill his material, a bit like an attorney reluctant to let a single witness escape from the stand. It can be argued that *Welfare* would have twice the impact if it were half as long. Yet the offense is excusable.

> Karl E. Meyer, "Report from Purgatory," in Saturday Review (copyright © 1975 by Saturday Review; all rights reserved; reprinted by permission), Vol. 2, No. 26, September 20, 1975, p. 52.

### JAMES WOLCOTT

To reverse the Faulknerian rhetoric, the people in ["**Welfare**"] (as in "**High School,**" "**Juvenile Court,**" and "**Titicut Follies**") don't prevail but endure—barely. Anger hangs in the air and not all of the anger belongs to the welfare petitioners. . . . It is Wiseman's most tendentious film, hard-bearing and bitter-edged, and those who expect comprehensiveness or balanced-scale fairness are going to be infuriated.

And they'll have a good case, for Wiseman makes no attempt to show the Other Side (e.g., welfare chiselers, or people who escape from poverty because of welfare assistance); he's interested only in the victims . . . that Wiseman is unfair to the welfare system is like complaining that Charles Dickens was unfair to prisons in "Little Dorrit." No, what goes wrong in "**Welfare**" is that the documentary approach no longer seems expressive enough to convey Wiseman's social vision.

Technically, however, this latest work is his best: unpretentiously photographed . . . , crisply edited, and recorded with a clarity which captures every vocal inflection. Wiseman's great gift as a filmmaker is his patience—he lets a scene go on and on to the edge of boredom, and then over into revelation. There are three such scenes in "**Welfare.**" . . . These are among Wiseman's greatest moments because they reveal the poignancy of people losing their dignity, their bearings, their *lives* under a firmament of fluorescent lights.

But the worst scenes . . . well, by now it's banal to invoke Heisenberg's Principle of Uncertainty. When discreet the movie is superb but at the end, when Wiseman tries for dramatic thunder, he allows people to stridently perform for the lens. A destitute man wanders into an administrator's office and begins laying on his troubles, pouring out his soul. It's soon obvious that he's addressing his misery to the wrong supervisor and finally the supervisor asks, "Why are you telling *me* all

this?" And, of course, the unspoken answer is: That's where the camera is. The scene falsifies even more as the man slumps in a chair and begins talking, trying to strike a bargain with God, even mentioning that he's waiting for Godot—it's awful. The guy seems to have wandered in from the set of a Cassavetes film. . . .

"**Welfare**" represents a culmination of Wiseman's social vision since "**Titicut Follies,**" a despairing vision which holds that the white walls of prisons and hospitals and schools can hide the suffering of millions, but can't contain it. As quickly as it is mopped up, more blood is spilled. Yet "**Welfare**" is also a compromise; I think Wiseman has greater designs. For what Wiseman needs to give us is not just the prison but the streets and alleys which lead to the prison. Lionel Trilling has written that the prison isn't merely a symbol, "its connection with the will is real, it is the practical instrument for the negation of man's will which the will of society has contrived." Wiseman has graphically shown us the negation (particularly in "**High School**") and the histrionic moments in "**Welfare**" intimate that he's anxious to go beyond it. He's a lawyer, and I think he's ready to aim higher with his indictments.

> James Wolcott, "'Welfare' Must Be Seen" (reprinted by permission of The Village Voice and the author; copyright © The Village Voice, Inc., 1975), in The Village Voice, Vol. XX, No. 39, September 29, 1975, p. 126.

### STEPHEN MAMBER

Frederick Wiseman's extraordinary new film *Meat* is and is not about slaughterhouses. From the first shots of cows on an open range there is no doubt blood will flow, yet by the time the actual slaughtering arrives, it has already taken its place within a more involved process. . . . This isn't just meat, it's the meat industry—mechanized, scientific, diversified.

The connection between the packing house workers and the animals they're doing in is not pressed too hard, but the similarities of their plight is interesting. (p. 21)

A nightmare vision, *Meat* is one of Wiseman's studies (like *High School* and *Basic Training*) of things going far too well. Scant pretense remains of even the slightest variation from absolute institutional control. Life and death, food and work, are governed according to projected weekly kill figures. Labor reorganizations seek maximum efficiency. We feel ourselves grasping for trivial indications of humanity. A worker glancing hesitantly over his shoulder at a televised football game while he separates internal organs practically becomes a rebel against the system. We root for a temporarily errant sheep. Such moments are rare.

Inevitably, given Wiseman's predilection for images of captivity, the specter of concentration camps hangs heavy over *Meat*. . . . If *Primate* was an image of misdirected science in the name of unspecified progress, then *Meat* advances imaginatively Arendtian possibilities. There's nothing necessarily evil about the present activities of this institution; the evil lies in potential. One feels that workers could come to their positions some morning and find the company had expanded into new territory.

Wiseman's films used to have plenty of scenes clearly establishing institutional similarities, but of late the sense of connection has become more abstract, more pure. (pp. 21-2)

In *Essene, Primate, Welfare* and especially in *Meat,* the level of argument shifts. . . . In these later films, Wiseman does not appear so much to hold up the institutional mirror in order to reflect specific social problems, as to seek out institutional situations which are themselves representations of broader levels of ideas within American culture. Consequently, the episodes in the films are much longer and self-revelatory, not just pieces in larger puzzles. . . .

Wiseman's response to direct experience is to seek to record it in instances of deepest ambiguity and with the greatest range of possibilities.

In *Meat,* we could get by simply attending to the intricacies of the meat packing process. . . . But more interesting, because we find them in such an unexpected location, are Wiseman's dramatic aspirations, the comedy and the out-of-kilter imagery.

*Meat,* believe it or not, is a hysterically funny film. . . .

Because there is no narration in *Meat* and scarcely a story, except for following the slaughtering process, some may feel deceived by Wiseman's avoidance of a clearly stated social problem. Yet the surface simplicity of *Meat* should be taken as a challenge. We must see these events through fresh eyes, as if one really had a chance to improve them. (p. 22)

> Stephen Mamber, "One Man's Meat: Frederick Wiseman's New Film," in The New Republic *(reprinted by permission of* The New Republic; © *1976 The New Republic, Inc.), Vol. 175, No. 23, December 4, 1976, pp. 21-2.*

## SHEPHERD BLISS

[Watching *Canal Zone*] must be disturbing for people who know little of the Zone. I can testify that it is also an intense experience for an old-line Zonian. . . . Much of Wiseman's film confirms and illuminates my memories. . . .

I recall the Panama of my childhood as a spontaneous outburst of lush vegetation, sleek black panthers, huge boa constrictors, Latin hospitality, panoramas charged with such vivid hues that surely any filmmaker would want to capture them in gorgeous tropical color. Not Wiseman. He photographed the Zone, more appropriately, in black and white. (p. 286)

As an exposé of the US imperial presence in Panama, *Canal Zone* is effective. As a prescription for action or an "organizing tool," it is not. It depicts what has happened to the colonizers in the Zone as a tragedy, but it offers no solutions and seems even to be saying that no solution exists. . . .

Not by accident, death is ever-present in *Canal Zone.* Cemeteries, funerals and memorial services recur again and again; "they have not died in vain" is a frequent affirmation. The film even ends in a graveyard. What is dying, Wiseman seems to be saying, is a culture, a world-view, "the American way of life"—it has flourished for a while in alien soil but its roots are withering now. In the film's final moments, for those with good ears, the faint sounds of Spanish can be heard. The "problem" of Panama will be solved as the Panamanians speak their will in concert. (p. 287)

> Shepherd Bliss, "'Canal Zone': An American Way of Death," in Christianity and Crisis *(copyright © 1977 Christianity and Crisis, Inc.), Vol. 37, No. 19, November 28, 1977, pp. 286-87.*

## LOUISE SWEET

[*Canal Zone* is] a deliberate summation of Wiseman's previous work. . . . Its slow pace encourages the audience to consider Wiseman's long-standing preoccupation with the way institutions preserve order by demanding individual obedience. (p. 59)

Respectful of ambiguities, Wiseman brings a compassionate as well as a critical eye to the Canal Zone. Drawn to society's victims, he focuses on a wide range of flotsam and jetsam. . . . (pp. 59-60)

Wiseman ably demonstrates the complex system of values and symbols which wed self to community. The unexamined but much felt ideology is emphasised [in the portrayal of speakers] at public functions. . . . To dismiss or ridicule the rhetoric of these speakers is to miss the wider context of which Wiseman is acutely aware. . . . Wiseman's gift is to reveal the connection between general language and specific sympathetic responses—the process of 'socialisation' which explains how people can be united by an abstract idea, a sense of community which helps sustain them in times of personal crisis and here during the larger trauma of a transfer of power.

Wiseman is particularly adept at showing how language can reveal what it is intended to conceal. . . . [In] a memorable scene, a ham operator makes contact with a stranger 3,000 miles away. . . . Wiseman shows him sitting alone with his equipment, talking in a matter-of-fact way about loneliness. His position becomes indicative of a kind of abandonment which faces everyone at moments when decisions are out of their hands, and Wiseman clearly intends that this sequence should be integrated with more fundamental questions of decision-making.

By revealing how individuals are not entirely contained by the rules and laws of institutions, Wiseman repeatedly returns the audience to the gap between individual and institutional requirements, the point where socialisation remains incomplete. The audience is invited to reinterpret events in terms of its own experience. *Canal Zone* generates questions and leaves the attentive, uncynical viewer, like the participants, profoundly disquieted. (p. 60)

> Louise Sweet, "'Canal Zone'," in Sight and Sound *(copyright © 1978 by The British Film Institute), Vol. 47, No. 1, Winter, 1977-78, pp. 59-60.*

## MARY FRAZER

[All Frederick Wiseman's films] have had as their subject a particular aspect of American society: an organization, a profession or an occupation. *Model* observes the world of fashion in all aspects—agencies, photographers, commercials, techniques. Here as elsewhere Wiseman aims not to present a point of view but to show his subject as it is (or as it appears to be). . . .

This absence of a point of view makes the film more, not less, interesting: we have all the fascination of looking into another world and none of the annoyance of being told what to think about it. Nevertheless an attitude emerges; one in which, somewhat surprisingly, everybody involved comes out quite well. The models and photographers are highly professional and treat each other with respect and patience.

If Wiseman's aim is to render the camera as much like the human eye as possible . . . , his camera, like the eye, is not merely passive. It has the power to focus on something particular, to observe it and to be the means of our intelligence about it. And perhaps because how close film can come to the "truth" has always been one of Wiseman's concerns, **Model** is as much about methods of photography and filming which are, in varying degrees, in contrast to his own, as it is about the world of models.

> *Mary Frazer, "Ways of Seeing," in* The Times Literary Supplement *(© Times Newspapers Ltd. (London) 1981; reproduced from* The Times Literary Supplement *by permission), No. 4069, March 27, 1981, p. 349.*

# Appendix

THE EXCERPTS IN CLC, VOLUME 20, WERE REPRINTED FROM THE FOLLOWING PERIODICALS:

America
American Film
The American Scholar
The Bookman (New York)
Chicago Review
The Christian Century
Christianity and Crisis
Cinéaste
Cinema
Cinema Journal
Commentary
Commonweal
Dissent
Encounter
Esquire
Evergreen Review
Film
Film Comment
Film Culture
Film Heritage
Film Journal
Film Library Quarterly
Film News
Film Quarterly
Film Reader
Film Society Review
Films and Filming

Films in Review
The Georgia Review
Hollywood Quarterly
Horizon
The Hudson Review
Journal of American Folklore
Journal of Modern Literature
Journal of Popular Culture
Journal of Popular Film
The Kenyon Review
Life
Literary Digest
Literature/Film Quarterly
London Magazine
Midstream
Monthly Film Bulletin
Movie
Ms.
The Nation
National Board of Review
   Magazine
National Review
New American Review
The New Leader
The New Republic
New Statesman
The New Statesman & Nation

New York Magazine
The New York Review of Books
The New York Times
The New Yorker
Newsweek
The North American Review
October
Pacific Sun
The Quarterly of Film, Radio, and
   Television
The Reporter
Rolling Stone
Saturday Review
Screen
Sequence
Sight and Sound
The Spectator
Sports Illustrated
Take One
Theatre Arts
Time
The Times Educational Supplement
The Times Literary Supplement
transition
The Village Voice
Western Humanities Review
The Yale Literary Magazine

**THE EXCERPTS IN CLC, VOLUME 20, WERE REPRINTED FROM THE FOLLOWING BOOKS:**

*Agee, James*. Agee on Film, Vol. 1. *Grosset & Dunlap, 1969.*

*Allen, Don*. François Truffaut. *Martin Secker & Warburg Limited, 1974.*

*Anstey, Edgar, ed*. Shots in the Dark: A Collection of Reviewers' Opinions of Some of the Leading Films Released between January 1949 and February 1951. *Allen Wingate Ltd, 1951.*

*Armour, Robert A*. Fritz Lang. *Twayne, 1978.*

*Bardeche, Maurice, and Brasillach, Robert*. The History of Motion Pictures. *Edited and translated by Iris Barry. W. W. Norton & Company, Inc., 1938.*

*Baxter, John*. The Cinema of Josef von Sternberg. *A. S. Barnes & Co., 1971.*

*Bazin, André*. Orson Welles: A Critical View. *Translated by Jonathan Rosenbaum. Harper, 1978.*

*Braudy, Leo*. Jean Renoir: The World of His Films. *Doubleday, 1972.*

*Braudy, Leo, ed*. Focus on "Shoot the Piano Player." *Prentice-Hall, Inc., 1972.*

*Cameron, Ian, and Wood, Robin*. Antonioni. *Frederick A. Praeger, Publishers, 1968.*

*Cameron, Ian, & others, eds*. Second Wave. *Frederick A. Praeger, Publishers, 1970.*

*Cowie, Peter*. Antonioni, Bergman, Resnais. *The Tantivy Press, 1963, Barnes & Co., Inc., 1963.*

*Cowie, Peter*. A Ribbon of Dreams: The Cinema of Orson Welles. *Rev. ed. A. S. Barnes and Company, 1973.*

*Cowie, Peter, ed*. International Film Guide 1969. *Tantivy Press, 1969.*

*Cowie, Peter, ed*. International Film Guide 1972. *Tantivy Press, 1972.*

*Cowie, Peter, ed*. Fifty Major Film-Makers. *A. S. Barnes & Co., Inc., 1975.*

*Cowie, Peter, ed*. International Film Guide 1979. *Tantivy Press, 1979.*

*Crowther, Bosley*. The Great Films: Fifty Golden Years of Motion Pictures. *G. P. Putnam's Sons, 1967.*

*Durgnat, Raymond*. Jean Renoir. *University of California Press, 1974.*

*Eisner, Lotte H*. The Haunted Screen: Expressionism in the German Cinema and the Influence of Max Reinhardt. *Translated by Roger Greaves. University of California Press, 1969.*

*Eisner, Lotte H*. Fritz Lang. *Edited by David Robinson. Translated by Gertrud Mander. Secker & Warburg, 1976, Oxford University Press, 1977.*

*Elsaesser, Thomas*. Fassbinder. *Edited by Tony Rayns. British Film Institute, 1976.*

*Ferguson, Otis*. The Film Criticism of Otis Ferguson. *Edited by Robert Wilson. Temple University Press, 1971.*

*Gilliatt, Penelope*. Three-Quarter Face: Reports & Reflections. *Coward, McCann & Geoghegan, 1980.*

*Harcourt, Peter*. Six European Directors: Essays on the Meaning of Film Style. *Penguin Books, 1974.*

*Higham, Charles*. The Films of Orson Welles. *University of California Press, 1970.*

*Hirsch, Foster*. Laurence Olivier. *Twayne, 1979.*

*Hunter, William*. Scrutiny of Cinema. *Wishart & Co, 1932.*

*Huss, Roy, ed.* Focus on "Blow Up." *Prentice-Hall, 1971.*

*Jacobs, Lewis, ed.* The Emergence of Film Art: The Evolution and Development of the Motion Picture As an Art, from 1900 to the Present. *Hopkinson and Blake, Publishers, 1969.*

*Kael, Pauline.* I Lost It at the Movies. *Atlantic-Little, Brown, 1965.*

*Kael, Pauline.* Kiss Kiss Bang Bang. *Atlantic-Little, Brown, 1968.*

*Kael, Pauline.* Going Steady. *Atlantic-Little, Brown, 1970.*

*Kael, Pauline.* Deeper into Movies. *Atlantic-Little, Brown, 1973.*

*Kael, Pauline.* Reeling. *Atlantic-Little, Brown, 1976.*

*Kael, Pauline.* When the Lights Go Down. *Holt, Rinehart and Winston, 1980.*

*Kauffmann, Stanley.* Figures of Light: Film Criticism and Comment. *Harper & Row, 1971.*

*Kauffmann, Stanley.* Living Images: Film Comment and Criticism. *Harper & Row, 1975.*

*Kelly, Mary Pat.* Martin Scorsese: The First Decade. *Redgrave Publishing Company, 1980.*

*Koch, Stephen.* Stargazer: Andy Warhol's World and His Films. *Frederick A. Praeger, Publishers, 1973.*

*Kolker, Robert Phillip.* A Cinema of Loneliness: Penn, Kubrick, Coppola, Scorsese, Altman. *Oxford University Press, 1980.*

*Kracauer, Siegfried.* From Caligari to Hitler: A Psychological History of the German Film. *Princeton University Press, 1947.*

*Lebel, J.-P.* Buster Keaton. *Translated by P. D. Stovin. Tantivy Press, 1967.*

*Lejeune, C. A.* Cinema. *Alexander Maclehose & Co., 1931.*

*Manvell, Roger.* Shakespeare and the Film. *J M Dent & Sons, Ltd, 1971.*

*Mast, Gerald.* A Short History of the Movies. *Bobbs-Merrill-Pegasus, 1971.*

*McBride, Joseph.* Orson Welles. *Secker and Warburg, 1972.*

*McGerr, Celia.* René Clair. *Twayne, 1980.*

*Mellen, Joan.* The Waves at Genji's Door: Japan through Its Cinema. *Pantheon Books, 1976.*

*Monaco, James.* The New Wave: Truffaut, Godard, Chabrol, Rohmer, Rivette. *Oxford University Press, 1976.*

*Monaco, James.* American Film Now: The People, the Power, the Money, the Movies. *Oxford University Press, 1979.*

The New York Times Film Reviews. *10 vols. The New York Times Company and Arno Press, 1970-79.*

*Pechter, William S.* Twenty-Four Times a Second: Films and Film-makers. *Harper & Row, Publishers, Inc., 1971.*

*Pechter, William S.* Movies Plus One. *Horizon Press, 1982.*

*Petrie, Graham.* The Cinema of François Truffaut. *A. S. Barnes & Co., 1970.*

*Rotha, Paul.* The Film till Now: A Survey of World Cinema. *Rev. ed. Vision Press Limited, 1963.*

*Sarris, Andrew.* Confessions of a Cultist: On the Cinema, 1955-1969. *Hill & Wang, 1969.*

*Schickel, Richard.* Second Sight: Notes on Some Movies, 1965-1970. *Simon & Schuster, 1972.*

*Sesonske, Alexander*. Jean Renoir: The French Films, 1924-1939. *Harvard University Press, 1980.*

*Seydor, Paul*. Peckinpah: The Western Films. *University of Illinois Press, 1980.*

*Simon, John*. Acid Test. *Stein and Day, 1963.*

*Simon, John*. Private Screenings. *Macmillan, 1967.*

*Simon, John*. Movies into Film: Film Criticism 1967-1970. *Dial, 1971.*

*Snyder, Stephen*. Pier Paolo Pasolini. *Twayne, 1980.*

*Sussex, Elizabeth*. Lindsay Anderson. *Frederick A. Praeger, Publishers, 1970.*

*Taylor, John Russell*. Cinema Eye, Cinema Ear: Some Key Film-Makers of the Sixties. *Hill & Wang, 1964.*

*Taylor, John Russell*. Directors and Directions: Cinema for the Seventies. *Hill & Wang, 1975.*

*Truffaut, François*. The Films in My Life. *Translated by Leonard Mayhew. Simon and Schuster, 1978.*

*Weinberg, Herman G*. Josef von Sternberg: A Critical Study. *Translated by Herman G. Weinberg. Arno Press, 1978.*

# Cumulative Index to Authors

A., Dr.
See Silverstein, Alvin **17**
Abe, Kōbō **8**
Abell, Kjeld **15**
Abrahams, Peter **4**
Abse, Dannie **7**
Achebe, Chinua **1, 3, 5, 7, 11**
Acorn, Milton **15**
Adamov, Arthur **4**
Adams, Alice **6, 13**
Adams, Richard **4, 5, 18**
Adamson, Joy **17**
Adler, Renata **8**
Agnon, S(hmuel) Y(osef) **4, 8, 14**
Ai **4, 14**
Aiken, Conrad **1, 3, 5, 10**
Akhmatova, Anna **11**
Albee, Edward **1, 2, 3, 5, 9, 11, 13**
Alberti, Rafael **7**
Aldiss, Brian **5, 14**
Aleixandre, Vicente **9**
Alepoudelis, Odysseus
See Elytis, Odysseus **15**
Algren, Nelson **4, 10**
Allen, Woody **16**
Allingham, Margery **19**
Almedingen, E. M. **12**
Alonso, Dámaso **14**
Alta **19**
Alther, Lisa **7**
Altman, Robert **16**
Alvarez, A(lfred) **5, 13**
Amado, Jorge **13**
Ambler, Eric **4, 6, 9**
Amichai, Yehuda **9**
Amis, Kingsley **1, 2, 3, 5, 8, 13**
Amis, Martin **4, 9**

Ammons, A(rchie) R(andolph) **2, 3, 5, 8, 9**
Anderson, Jon **9**
Anderson, Lindsay **20**
Anderson, Poul **15**
Anderson, Roberta Joan
See Mitchell, Joni **12**
Andrade, Carlos Drummond de **18**
Andrews, Cecily Fairfield
See West, Rebecca **7, 9**
Andrić, Ivo **8**
Angelou, Maya **12**
Anouilh, Jean **1, 3, 8, 13**
Anthony, Florence
See Ai **4, 14**
Antoninus, Brother
See Everson, William **1, 5, 14**
Antonioni, Michelangelo **20**
Antschel, Paul
See Celan, Paul **10, 19**
Apple, Max **9**
Aquin, Hubert **15**
Aragon, Louis **3**
Archer, Jules **12**
Arden, John **6, 13, 15**
Arguedas, José María **10, 18**
Armah, Ayi Kwei **5**
Armatrading, Joan **17**
Arnow, Harriette **2, 7, 18**
Arp, Jean **5**
Arrabal, Fernando **2, 9, 18**
Arthur, Ruth M(abel) **12**
Arundel, Honor **17**
Ashbery, John **2, 3, 4, 6, 9, 13, 15**
Ashton-Warner, Sylvia **19**
Asimov, Isaac **1, 3, 9, 19**
Asturias, Miguel Ángel **3, 8, 13**

Atwood, Margaret **2, 3, 4, 8, 13, 15**
Auchincloss, Louis **4, 6, 9, 18**
Auden, W(ystan) H(ugh) **1, 2, 3, 4, 6, 9, 11, 14**
Avison, Margaret **2, 4**
Ayckbourn, Alan **5, 8, 18**
Aymé, Marcel **11**
Ayrton, Michael **7**
Azorín **11**
Bacchelli, Riccardo **19**
Bach, Richard **14**
Bagryana, Elisaveta **10**
Bainbridge, Beryl **4, 5, 8, 10, 14, 18**
Baker, Elliott **8**
Baldwin, James **1, 2, 3, 4, 5, 8, 13, 15, 17**
Ballard, J(ames) G(raham) **3, 6, 14**
Bambara, Toni Cade **19**
Baraka, Imamu Amiri **2, 3, 5, 10, 14**
See also Jones, (Everett) LeRoi **1**
Barfoot, Joan **18**
Barker, George **8**
Barnes, Djuna **3, 4, 8, 11**
Barnes, Peter **5**
Barondess, Sue Kaufman
See Kaufman, Sue **3, 8**
Barth, John **1, 2, 3, 5, 7, 9, 10, 14**
Barthelme, Donald **1, 2, 3, 5, 6, 8, 13**
Bassani, Giorgio **9**
Baumbach, Jonathan **6**
Baxter, James K. **14**
Beagle, Peter S(oyer) **7**
Beattie, Ann **8, 13, 18**

Beauvoir, Simone de **1, 2, 4, 8, 14**
Becker, Jurek **7, 19**
Beckett, Samuel **1, 2, 3, 4, 6, 9, 10, 11, 14, 18**
Beecher, John **6**
Behan, Brendan **1, 8, 11, 15**
Belcheva, Elisaveta
See Bagryana, Elisaveta **10**
Bell, Marvin **8**
Bellow, Saul **1, 2, 3, 6, 8, 10, 13, 15**
Belser, Reimond Karel Maria de
See Ruyslinck, Ward **14**
Benary-Isbert, Margot **12**
Benchley, Peter **4, 8**
Benedikt, Michael **4, 14**
Bennett, Hal **5**
Benson, Sally **17**
Berger, John **2, 19**
Berger, Melvin **12**
Berger, Thomas **3, 5, 8, 11, 18**
Bergman, Ingmar **16**
Bergstein, Eleanor **4**
Bernhard, Thomas **3**
Berrigan, Daniel J. **4**
Berry, Chuck **17**
Berry, Wendell **4, 6, 8**
Berryman, John **1, 2, 3, 4 6, 8, 10, 13**
Bertolucci, Bernardo **16**
Betjeman, John **2, 6, 10**
Betts, Doris **3, 6**
Bienek, Horst **7, 11**
Bioy Casares, Adolfo **4, 8, 13**
Birney, (Alfred) Earle **1, 4, 6, 11**
Bishop, Elizabeth **1, 4, 9, 13, 15**
Bishop, John **10**
Bissett, Bill **18**

Blackburn, Paul  9
Blackmur, R(ichard) P(almer)  2
Blackwood, Caroline  6, 9
Blais, Marie-Claire  2, 4, 6, 13
Blake, Nicholas
    See Day Lewis, C(ecil)  1, 6,
    10
Blatty, William Peter  2
Blish, James  14
Blixen, Karen
    See Dinesen, Isak  10
Blume, Judy  12
Blunden, Edmund  2
Bly, Robert  1, 2, 5, 10, 15
Bogan, Louise  4
Bogard, Dirk  19
Böll, Heinrich  2, 3, 6, 9, 11, 15
Bolt, Robert  14
Bond, Edward  4, 6, 13
Bonham, Frank  12
Bonnefoy, Yves  9, 15
Bontemps, Arna  1, 18
Booth, Martin  13
Borges, Jorge Luis  1, 2, 3, 4, 6,
    8, 9, 10, 13, 19
Bourjaily, Vance  8
Bowen, Elizabeth  1, 3, 6, 11, 15
Bowering, George  15
Bowers, Edgar  9
Bowie, David  17
Bowles, Jane  3
Bowles, Paul  1, 2, 19
Boyle, Kay  1, 5, 19
Boyle, Patrick  19
Bradbury, Ray  1, 3, 10, 15
Bragg, Melvyn  10
Braine, John  1, 3
Brand, Millen  7
Brathwaite, Edward  11
Brautigan, Richard  1, 3, 5, 9, 12
Brennan, Maeve  5
Breslin, Jimmy  4
Bresson, Robert  16
Breton, André  2, 9, 15
Brink, André  18
Brodsky, Joseph  4, 6, 13
Brodsky, Michael  19
Bromell, Henry  5
Broner, E(sther)
    M(asserman)  19
Bronk, William  10
Brooks, Gwendolyn  1, 2, 4, 5,
    15
Brooks, Mel  12
Brophy, Brigid  6, 11
Brosman, Catharine Savage  9
Broughton, T(homas) Alan  19
Broumas, Olga  10
Brown, Dee  18
Brown, George Mackay  5
Brown, Rita Mae  18
Brown, Sterling  1
Browning, Tod  16
Brunner, John  8, 10
Buchheim, Lothar-Günther  6
Buck, Pearl S(ydenstricker)  7,
    11, 18
Buckler, Ernest  13
Buckley, William F(rank), Jr.  7,
    18
Buechner, (Carl) Frederick  2, 4,
    6, 9
Buell, John  10

Buero Vallejo, Antonio  15
Bukowski, Charles  2, 5, 9
Bullins, Ed  1, 5, 7
Bunting, Basil  10
Buñuel, Luis  16
Burgess, Anthony  1, 2, 4, 5, 8,
    10, 13, 15
Burke, Kenneth  2
Burnshaw, Stanley  3, 13
Burr, Anne  6
Burroughs, William S(eward)  1,
    2, 5, 15
Busch, Frederick  7, 10, 18
Butor, Michel  1, 3, 8, 11, 15
Byatt, A(ntonia) S(usan)  19
Byrne, John Keyes
    See Leonard, Hugh  19
Cabrera Infante, G(uillermo)  5
Cain, James M(allahan)  3, 11
Caldwell, Erskine  1, 8, 14
Caldwell, Taylor  2
Calisher, Hortense  2, 4, 8
Callaghan, Morley  3, 14
Calvino, Italo  5, 8, 11
Camus, Albert  1, 2, 4, 9, 11, 14
Canby, Vincent  13
Canetti, Elias  3, 14
Capote, Truman  1, 3, 8, 13, 19
Capra, Frank  16
Carey, Ernestine Gilbreth  17
Carpentier, Alejo  8, 11
Carr, John Dickson  3
Carrier, Roch  13
Carroll, Paul Vincent  10
Carruth, Hayden  4, 7, 10, 18
Carter, Angela  5
Casares, Adolfo Bioy
    See Bioy Casares, Adolfo  4,
    8, 13
Casey, John
    See O'Casey, Sean  1, 5, 9,
    11, 15
Casey, Michael  2
Casey, Warren
    See Jacobs, Jim and Warren
    Casey  12
Cassavetes, John  20
Cassill, R(onald) V(erlin)  4
Cassity, (Allen) Turner  6
Castaneda, Carlos  12
Causley, Charles  7
Cavanna, Betty  12
Cayrol, Jean  11
Cela, Camilo José  4, 13
Celan, Paul  10, 19
Céline, Louis-Ferdinand  1, 3,
    4, 7, 9, 15
Cendrars, Blaise  18
Césaire, Aim'aae  19
Chabrol, Claude  16
Challans, Mary
    See Renault, Mary  3, 11, 17
Chaplin, Charles  16
Char, René  9, 11, 14
Charyn, Jerome  5, 8, 18
Chase, Mary Ellen  2
Cheever, John  3, 7, 8, 11, 15
Cheever, Susan  18
Child, Philip  19
Childress, Alice  12, 15
Chitty, Sir Thomas Willes
    See Hinde, Thomas  6, 11

Chomette, René
    See Clair, René  20
Christie, Agatha  1, 6, 8, 12
Ciardi, John  10
Cimino, Michael  16
Clair, René  20
Clark, Eleanor  5, 19
Clark, Mavis Thorpe  12
Clarke, Arthur C(harles)  1, 4,
    13, 18
Clarke, Austin  6, 9
Clarke, Austin C(hesterfield)  8
Clarke, Shirley  16
Clavell, James  6
Clifton, Lucille  19
Coburn, D(onald) L(ee)  10
Cocteau, Jean  1, 8, 15, 16
Cohen, Arthur A(llen)  7
Cohen, Leonard  3
Cohen, Matt  19
Colwin, Laurie  5, 13
Comfort, Alex(ander)  7
Compton-Burnett, Ivy  1, 3, 10,
    15
Condon, Richard  4, 6, 8, 10
Connell, Evan S(helby), Jr.  4, 6
Connelly, Marc(us)  7
Cook, Robin  14
Coover, Robert  3, 7, 15
Coppola, Francis Ford  16
Corcoran, Barbara  17
Corman, Cid (Sidney Corman)  9
Cormier, Robert  12
Cornwell, David
    See Le Carré, John  3, 5, 9,
    15
Corso, (Nunzio) Gregory  1, 11
Cortázar, Julio  2, 3, 5, 10, 13,
    15
Ćosić, Dobrica  14
Coward, Noel  1, 9
Cox, William Trevor
    See Trevor, William  7, 9, 14
Cozzens, James Gould  1, 4, 11
Craven, Margaret  17
Crayencour, Marguerite de
    See Yourcenar, Marguerite  19
Creasey, John  11
Creeley, Robert  1, 2, 4, 8, 11,
    15
Crews, Harry  6
Crichton, (John) Michael  2, 6
Crumb, Robert  17
Cummings, E(dward) E(stlin)  1,
    3, 8, 12, 15
Cunningham, J(ames)
    V(incent)  3
Cunningham, Julia  12
Dąbrowska, Maria  15
Dahl, Roald  1, 6, 18
Dahlberg, Edward  1, 7, 14
Daly, Maureen  17
Dannay, Frederick
    See Queen, Ellery  3, 11
Daryush, Elizabeth  6, 19
Davenport, Guy, Jr.  6, 14
Davidson, Donald  2, 13, 19
Davidson, Sara  9
Davie, Donald  5, 8, 10
Davies, (William) Robertson  2,
    7, 13
Davison, Frank Dalby  15
Dawson, Fielding  6

Day Lewis, C(ecil)  1, 6, 10
De Hartog, Jan  19
Deighton, Len  4, 7
Delany, Samuel R.  8, 14
De la Roche, Mazo  14
Delbanco, Nicholas  6, 13
Delibes, Miguel  8, 18
DeLillo, Don  8, 10, 13
Dennis, Nigel  8
De Palma, Brian  20
Deren, Maya  16
Desai, Anita  19
De Sica, Vittorio  20
Destouches, Louis-Ferdinand
    See Céline, Louis-
    Ferdinand  1, 3, 4, 7, 9, 15
Deutsch, Babette  18
De Vries, Peter  1, 2, 3, 7, 10
Dick, Philip K(indred)  10
Dickey, James  1, 2, 4, 7, 10, 15
Dickey, William  3
Dickinson, Peter  12
Didion, Joan  1, 3, 8, 14
Dillard, Annie  9
Dillard, R(ichard) H(enry)
    W(ilde)  5
Dillon, Eilís  17
Dinesen, Isak  10
Disch, Thomas M(ichael)  7
Dixon, Paige
    See Corcoran, Barbara  17
Doctorow, E(dgar)
    L(aurence)  6, 11, 15, 18
Donleavy, J(ames) P(atrick)  1,
    4, 6, 10
Donoso, José  4, 8, 11
Doolittle, Hilda
    See H(ilda) D(oolittle)  3, 8,
    14
Dorn, Ed(ward)  10, 18
Dos Passos, John  1, 4, 8, 11, 15
Drabble, Margaret  2, 3, 5, 8, 10
Drexler, Rosalyn  2, 6
Dreyer, Carl Theodor  16
Drummond de Andrade, Carlos
    See Andrade, Carlos
    Drummond de  18
Duberman, Martin  8
Du Bois, W(illiam) E(dward)
    B(urghardt)  1, 2, 13
Dubus, Andre  13
Dudek, Louis  11, 19
Dugan, Alan  2, 6
Duhamel, Georges  8
Duke, Raoul
    See Thompson, Hunter
    S(tockton)  9, 17
Dumas, Henry  6
Du Maurier, Daphne  6, 11
Duncan, Robert  1, 2, 4, 7, 15
Dunn, Douglas  6
Duras, Marguerite  3, 6, 11, 20
Durrell, Lawrence  1, 4, 6, 8, 13
Dürrenmatt, Friedrich  1, 4, 8,
    11, 15
Dylan, Bob  3, 4, 6, 12
Eastlake, William  8
Eberhart, Richard  3, 11, 19
Eckert, Allan W.  17
Edson, Russell  13
Ehrenbourg, Ilya
    See Ehrenburg, Ilya  18
Ehrenburg, Ilya  18

Eich, Günter  **15**
Eigner, Larry (Laurence
　Eigner)  **9**
Eiseley, Loren  **7**
Ekwensi, Cyprian  **4**
Eliade, Mircea  **19**
Eliot, T(homas) S(tearns)  **1, 2,
　3, 6, 9, 10, 13, 15**
Elkin, Stanley  **4, 6, 9, 14**
Elliott, George P(aul)  **2**
Ellis, A. E.  **7**
Ellison, Harlan  **1, 13**
Ellison, Ralph  **1, 3, 11**
Elman, Richard  **19**
Elytis, Odysseus  **15**
Emecheta, (Florence Onye)
　Buchi  **14**
Empson, William  **3, 8, 19**
Endo, Shusaku  **7, 14, 19**
Enright, D(ennis) J(oseph)  **4, 8**
Ephron, Nora  **17**
Epstein, Daniel Mark  **7**
Epstein, Jacob  **19**
Erenburg, Ilya
　See Ehrenburg, Ilya  **18**
Eshleman, Clayton  **7**
Espriu, Salvador  **9**
Evarts, Esther
　See Benson, Sally  **17**
Everson, William  **1, 5, 14**
Evtushenko, Evgeni
　See Yevtushenko, Yevgeny  **1,
　3, 13**
Ewart, Gavin  **13**
Exley, Frederick  **6, 11**
Fair, Ronald L.  **18**
Fallaci, Oriana  **11**
Farigoule, Louis
　See Romains, Jules  **7**
Fariña, Richard  **9**
Farley, Walter  **17**
Farmer, Philip José  **1, 19**
Farrell, J(ames) G(ordon)  **6**
Farrell, James T(homas)  **1, 4, 8,
　11**
Fassbinder, Rainer Werner  **20**
Faulkner, William  **1, 3, 6, 8, 9,
　11, 14, 18**
Fauset, Jessie Redmon  **19**
Faust, Irvin  **8**
Federman, Raymond  **6**
Feiffer, Jules  **2, 8**
Feldman, Irving  **7**
Fellini, Federico  **16**
Felsen, Gregor
　See Felsen, Henry Gregor  **17**
Felsen, Henry Gregor  **17**
Ferber, Edna  **18**
Ferguson, Helen
　See Kavan, Anna  **5, 13**
Ferlinghetti, Lawrence  **2, 6, 10**
Fiedler, Leslie A(aron)  **4, 13**
Finch, Robert  **18**
Fisher, Vardis  **7**
Fitzgerald, Penelope  **19**
FitzGerald, Robert D(avid)  **19**
Fleming, Ian  **3**
Follett, Ken(neth)  **18**
Forbes, Esther  **12**
Ford, John  **16**
Forrest, Leon  **4**
Forster, E(dward) M(organ)  **1,
　2, 3, 4, 9, 10, 13, 15**

Forsyth, Frederick  **2, 5**
Fosse, Bob  **20**
Fournier, Pierre
　See Gascar, Pierre  **11**
Fowles, John  **1, 2, 3, 4, 6, 9,
　10, 15**
Fox, Paula  **2, 8**
Frame, Janet  **2, 3, 6**
Francis, Dick  **2**
Francis, Robert  **15**
Fraser, George MacDonald  **7**
Frayn, Michael  **3, 7**
French, Marilyn  **10, 18**
Friedman, B(ernard) H(arper)  **7**
Friedman, Bruce Jay  **3, 5**
Friel, Brian  **5**
Friis-Baastad, Babbis  **12**
Frisch, Max  **3, 9, 14, 18**
Frost, Robert  **1, 3, 4, 9, 10, 13,
　15**
Fry, Christopher  **2, 10, 14**
Fuchs, Daniel  **8**
Fuentes, Carlos  **3, 8, 10, 13**
Fugard, Athol  **5, 9, 14**
Fuller, Roy  **4**
Gadda, Carlo Emilio  **11**
Gaddis, William  **1, 3, 6, 8, 10,
　19**
Gaines, Ernest J.  **3, 11, 18**
Gallagher, Tess  **18**
Gallant, Mavis  **7, 18**
Gallant, Roy A(rthur)  **17**
Gallico, Paul  **2**
García Márquez, Gabriel  **2, 3,
　8, 10, 15**
Gardner, John  **2, 3, 5, 7, 8, 10,
　18**
Garfield, Leon  **12**
Garner, Alan  **17**
Garner, Hugh  **13**
Garnett, David  **3**
Garrett, George  **3, 11**
Garrigue, Jean  **2, 8**
Gascar, Pierre  **11**
Gass, William H(oward)  **1, 2, 8,
　11, 15**
Gelber, Jack  **1, 6, 14**
Gellhorn, Martha  **14**
Genet, Jean  **1, 2, 5, 10, 14**
Gerhardi, William
　See Gerhardie, William  **5**
Gerhardie, William  **5**
Gessner, Friedrike Victoria
　See Adamson, Joy  **17**
Ghelderode, Michel de  **6, 11**
Gilbreth, Ernestine
　See Carey, Ernestine
　Gilbreth  **17**
Gilbreth, Frank B., Jr.  **17**
Gilliatt, Penelope  **2, 10, 13**
Gilroy, Frank D(aniel)  **2**
Ginsberg, Allen  **1, 2, 3, 4, 6, 13**
Ginzburg, Natalia  **5, 11**
Giono, Jean  **4, 11**
Giovanni, Nikki  **2, 4, 19**
Giovene, Andrea  **7**
Gironella, José María  **11**
Glanville, Brian  **6**
Glassco, John  **9**
Glissant, Édouard  **10**
Glück, Louise  **7**
Godard, Jean-Luc  **20**
Godwin, Gail  **5, 8**

Gold, Herbert  **4, 7, 14**
Goldbarth, Albert  **5**
Golding, William  **1, 2, 3, 8, 10,
　17**
Goldman, William  **1**
Gombrowicz, Witold  **4, 7, 11**
Gómez, de la Serna, Ramón  **9**
Goodman, Paul  **1, 2, 4, 7**
Gordimer, Nadine  **3, 5, 7, 10,
　18**
Gordon, Caroline  **6, 13**
Gordon, Mary  **13**
Gordone, Charles  **1, 4**
Gorenko, Anna Andreyevna
　See Akhmatova, Anna  **11**
Gotlieb, Phyllis  **18**
Gould, Lois  **4, 10**
Goyen, (Charles) William  **5, 8,
　14**
Goytisolo, Juan  **5, 10**
Gracq, Julien  **11**
Grade, Chaim  **10**
Grass, Günter  **1, 2, 4, 6, 11, 15**
Grau, Shirley Ann  **4, 9**
Graves, Robert  **1, 2, 6, 11**
Gray, Simon  **9, 14**
Green, Hannah  **3**
　See also Greenberg, Joanne  **7**
Green, Henry  **2, 13**
Green, Julien  **3, 11**
Greenberg, Joanne  **7**
　See also Green, Hannah  **3**
Greene, Gael  **8**
Greene, Graham  **1, 3, 6, 9, 14,
　18**
Gregor, Arthur  **9**
Grieve, C(hristopher) M(urray)
　See MacDiarmid, Hugh  **2, 4,
　11, 19**
Griffiths, Trevor  **13**
Grigson, Geoffrey  **7**
Grumbach, Doris  **13**
Guare, John  **8, 14**
Guest, Judith  **8**
Guillén, Jorge  **11**
Gunn, Bill  **5**
Gunn, Thom(son)  **3, 6, 18**
H(ilda) D(oolittle)  **3, 8, 14**
Haavikko, Paavo  **18**
Hacker, Marilyn  **5, 9**
Hailey, Arthur  **5**
Haley, Alex  **8, 12**
Hall, Donald  **1, 13**
Halpern, Daniel  **14**
Hamburger, Michael  **5, 14**
Hamill, Pete  **10**
Hamilton, Edmond  **1**
Hamilton, Gail
　See Corcoran, Barbara  **17**
Hammett, (Samuel) Dashiell  **3,
　5, 10, 19**
Hamner, Earl, Jr.  **12**
Hampton, Christopher  **4**
Handke, Peter  **5, 8, 10, 15**
Hanley, James  **3, 5, 8, 13**
Hansberry, Lorraine  **17**
Hanson, Kenneth O.  **13**
Hardwick, Elizabeth  **13**
Harper, Michael S(teven)  **7**
Harris, Christie  **12**
Harris, John (Wyndham Parkes
　Lucas) Beynon
　See Wyndham, John  **19**

Harris, MacDonald  **9**
Harris, Mark  **19**
Harrison, Jim  **6, 14**
Hartley, L(eslie) P(oles)  **2**
Hass, Robert  **18**
Hawkes, John  **1, 2, 3, 4, 7, 9,
　14, 15**
Hayden, Robert  **5, 9, 14**
Hazzard, Shirley  **18**
Heaney, Seamus  **5, 7, 14**
Hébert, Anne  **4, 13**
Hecht, Anthony  **8, 13, 19**
Hecht, Ben  **8**
Heifner, Jack  **11**
Heiney, Donald
　See Harris, MacDonald  **9**
Heinlein, Robert A(nson)  **1, 3,
　8, 14**
Heller, Joseph  **1, 3, 5, 8, 11**
Hellman, Lillian  **2, 4, 8, 14, 18**
Helprin, Mark  **7, 10**
Hemingway, Ernest  **1, 3, 6, 8,
　10, 13, 19**
Heppenstall, (John) Rayner  **10**
Herbert, Frank  **12**
Herbert, Zbigniew  **9**
Herlihy, James Leo  **6**
Herriot, James  **12**
Hersey, John  **1, 2, 7, 9**
Herzog, Werner  **16**
Hesse, Hermann  **1, 2, 3, 6, 11,
　17**
Heyen, William  **13, 18**
Hibbert, Eleanor  **7**
Higgins, George V(incent)  **4, 7,
　10, 18**
Highsmith, (Mary) Patricia  **2, 4,
　14**
Highwater, Jamake  **12**
Hill, Geoffrey  **5, 8, 18**
Hill, Susan B.  **4**
Hilliard, Noel  **15**
Himes, Chester  **2, 4, 7, 18**
Hinde, Thomas  **6, 11**
Hine, (William) Daryl  **15**
Hiraoka, Kimitake
　See Mishima, Yukio  **2, 4, 6,
　9**
Hitchcock, Alfred  **16**
Hoban, Russell C(onwell)  **7**
Hobson, Laura Z(ametkin)  **7**
Hochhuth, Rolf  **4, 11, 18**
Hochman, Sandra  **3, 8**
Hocking, Mary  **13**
Hoffman, Daniel  **6, 13**
Hoffman, Stanley  **5**
Holden, Ursula  **18**
Hollander, John  **2, 5, 8, 14**
Holt, Victoria
　See Hibbert, Eleanor  **7**
Holub, Miroslav  **4**
Hood, Hugh  **15**
Hope, A(lec) D(erwent)  **3**
Hopkins, John  **4**
Horgan, Paul  **9**
Horwitz, Julius  **14**
Household, Geoffrey  **11**
Howard, Elizabeth Jane  **7**
Howard, Maureen  **5, 14**
Howard, Richard  **7, 10**
Howes, Barbara  **15**
Hrabal, Bohumil  **13**

Hughes, (James) Langston **1, 5, 10, 15**
Hughes, Richard **1, 11**
Hughes, Ted **2, 4, 9, 14**
Hugo, Richard F(ranklin) **6, 18**
Hunt, E(verette) Howard **3**
Hunter, Evan **11**
Hurston, Zora Neale **7**
Huston, John **20**
Huxley, Aldous **1, 3, 4, 5, 8, 11, 18**
Ichikawa, Kon **20**
Ignatow, David **4, 7, 14**
Inge, William **1, 8, 19**
Innes, Michael
   See Stewart, J(ohn) I(nnes) M(ackintosh) **7, 14**
Ionesco, Eugène **1, 4, 6, 9, 11, 15**
Irving, John **13**
Isherwood, Christopher **1, 9, 11, 14**
Ivask, Ivar **14**
Jackson, Jesse **12**
Jackson, Laura Riding
   See Riding, Laura **3, 7**
Jackson, Shirley **11**
Jacobs, Jim **12**
Jacobson, Dan **4, 14**
Jagger, Mick **17**
James, P. D. **18**
Jarrell, Randall **1, 2, 6, 9, 13**
Jeffers, Robinson **2, 3, 11, 15**
Jennings, Elizabeth **5, 14**
Jhabvala, Ruth Prawer **4, 8**
Jiles, Paulette **13**
Johnson, B(ryan) S(tanley) **6, 9**
Johnson, Charles **7**
Johnson, Diane **5, 13**
Johnson, Eyvind **14**
Johnson, Marguerita
   See Angelou, Maya **12**
Johnson, Pamela Hansford **1, 7**
Johnson, Uwe **5, 10, 15**
Johnston, Jennifer **7**
Jones, D(ouglas) G(ordon) **10**
Jones, David **2, 4, 7, 13**
Jones, David
   See Bowie, David **17**
Jones, Gayl **6, 9**
Jones, James **1, 3, 10**
Jones, (Everett) LeRoi **1**
   See also Baraka, Imamu Amiri **2, 3, 5, 10, 14**
Jones, Madison **4**
Jones, Mervyn **10**
Jones, Preston **10**
Jones, Robert F(rancis) **7**
Jong, Erica **4, 6, 8, 18**
Jordan, June **5, 11**
Josipovici, G(abriel) **6**
Just, Ward **4**
Justice, Donald **6, 19**
Kallman, Chester **2**
Kaminsky, Melvin
   See Brooks, Mel **12**
Kane, Paul
   See Paul Simon **17**
Kaniuk, Yoram **19**
Kantor, MacKinlay **7**
Karapánou, Margaríta **13**
Kaufman, Sue **3, 8**
Kavan, Anna **5, 13**

Kawabata, Yasunari **2, 5, 9, 18**
Kazan, Elia **6, 16**
Keaton, Buster **20**
Keaton, Joseph Francis
   See Keaton, Buster **20**
Kellogg, Marjorie **2**
Kemal, Yashar **14**
Kemelman, Harry **2**
Keneally, Thomas **5, 8, 10, 14, 19**
Kennedy, Joseph Charles
   See Kennedy, X. J. **8**
Kennedy, William **6**
Kennedy, X. J. **8**
Kerouac, Jack **1, 2, 3, 5, 14**
Kerr, M. E. **12**
Kerrigan, (Thomas) Anthony **4, 6**
Kesey, Ken **1, 3, 6, 11**
Kessler, Jascha **4**
Kettelkamp, Larry **12**
Kherdian, David **6, 9**
Killens, John Oliver **10**
King, Francis **8**
King, Stephen **12**
Kingman, Lee **17**
Kingston, Maxine Hong **12, 19**
Kinnell, Galway **1, 2, 3, 5, 13**
Kinsella, Thomas **4, 19**
Kirkup, James **1**
Kirkwood, James **9**
Kizer, Carolyn **15**
Klein, A(braham) M(oses) **19**
Knebel, Fletcher **14**
Knowles, John **1, 4, 10**
Koch, Kenneth **5, 8**
Koestler, Arthur **1, 3, 6, 8, 15**
Kohout, Pavel **13**
Konrád, György **4, 10**
Konwicki, Tadeusz **8**
Kopit, Arthur **1, 18**
Kops, Bernard **4**
Kosinski, Jerzy **1, 2, 3, 6, 10, 15**
Kotlowitz, Robert **4**
Kotzwinkle, William **5, 14**
Kozol, Jonathan **17**
Krleža, Miroslav **8**
Kroetsch, Robert **5**
Krotkov, Yuri **19**
Krumgold, Joseph **12**
Kubrick, Stanley **16**
Kumin, Maxine **5, 13**
Kundera, Milan **4, 9, 19**
Kunitz, Stanley J(asspon) **6, 11, 14**
Kunze, Reiner **10**
Kurosawa, Akira **16**
Kuzma, Greg **7**
Lagerkvist, Pär **7, 10, 13**
La Guma, Alex(ander) **19**
Lamming, George **2, 4**
Landolfi, Tommaso **11**
Lang, Fritz **20**
Larkin, Philip **3, 5, 8, 9, 13, 18**
Latham, Jean Lee **12**
Lathen, Emma **2**
Lattimore, Richmond **3**
Laurence, (Jean) Margaret **3, 6, 13**
Lavin, Mary **4, 18**
Laye, Camara **4**
Layton, Irving **2, 15**

Lear, Norman **12**
Lebowitz, Fran **11**
Le Carré, John **3, 5, 9, 15**
Lee, Don L. **2**
   See also Madhubuti, Haki R. **6**
Lee, Harper **12**
Lee, Manfred B(ennington)
   See Queen, Ellery **3, 11**
Lee, Stan **17**
Leet, Judith **11**
Leffland, Ella **19**
Léger, Alexis Saint-Léger
   See Perse, St.-John **4, 11**
LeGuin, Ursula K(roeber) **8, 13**
Lehmann, Rosamond **5**
Lelchuk, Alan **5**
Lem, Stanislaw **8, 15**
L'Engle, Madeleine **12**
Lengyel, József **7**
Lennon, John **12**
Leonard, Hugh **19**
Lerman, Eleanor **9**
Lessing, Doris **1, 2, 3, 6, 10, 15**
Lester, Richard **20**
Levertov, Denise **1, 2, 3, 5, 8, 15**
Levin, Ira **3, 6**
Levin, Meyer **7**
Levine, Philip **2, 4, 5, 9, 14**
Levitin, Sonia **17**
Lewis, C(ecil) Day
   See Day Lewis, C(ecil) **1, 6, 10**
Lewis, C(live) S(taples) **1, 3, 6, 14**
Lezama Lima, José **4, 10**
Li Fei-kan
   See Pa Chin **18**
Lieber, Joel **6**
Lieber, Stanley
   See Lee, Stan **17**
Lieberman, Laurence **4**
Lima, José Lezama
   See Lezama Lima, José **4, 10**
Lind, Jakov **1, 2, 4**
Livesay, Dorothy **4, 15**
Llewellyn, Richard **7**
Llosa, Mario Vargas
   See Vargas Llosa, Mario **3, 6, 9, 10, 15**
Lloyd, Richard Llewellyn
   See Llewellyn, Richard **7**
Logan, John **5**
Lorde, Audre **18**
Lowell, Robert **1, 2, 3, 4, 5, 8, 9, 11, 15**
Lucas, George **16**
Lucas, Victoria
   See Plath, Sylvia **1, 2, 3, 5, 9, 11, 14, 17**
Lurie, Alison **4, 5, 18**
Luzi, Mario **13**
MacBeth, George **2, 5, 9**
MacDiarmid, Hugh **2, 4, 11, 19**
Macdonald, Cynthia **13, 19**
MacDonald, John D(ann) **3**
Macdonald, Ross **1, 2, 3, 14**
MacEwen, Gwendolyn **13**
MacInnes, Colin **4**
Mackenzie, Compton **18**
MacLean, Alistair **3, 13**
MacLeish, Archibald **3, 8, 14**

MacLennan, (John) Hugh **2, 14**
MacNeice, Louis **1, 4, 10**
Macpherson, Jay **14**
Madden, David **5, 15**
Madhubuti, Haki R. **6**
   See also Lee, Don L. **2**
Mailer, Norman **1, 2, 3, 4, 5, 8, 11, 14**
Major, Clarence **3, 19**
Malamud, Bernard **1, 2, 3, 5, 8, 9, 11, 18**
Mallet-Joris, Françoise **11**
Maloff, Saul **5**
Malraux, (Georges-) André **1, 4, 9, 13, 15**
Malzberg, Barry N. **7**
Mamet, David **9, 15**
Mamoulian, Rouben **16**
Manning, Olivia **5, 19**
Mano, D. Keith **2, 10**
Marcel, Gabriel **15**
Markandaya, Kamala (Purnalya) **8**
Markfield, Wallace **8**
Markham, Robert
   See Amis, Kingsley **1, 2, 3, 5, 8, 13**
Marley, Bob **17**
Marquand, John P(hillips) **2, 10**
Márquez, Gabriel García
   See García Márquez, Gabriel **2, 3, 8, 10, 15**
Marsh, (Edith) Ngaio **7**
Marshall, Garry **17**
Martinson, Harry **14**
Masefield, John **11**
Mathews, Harry **6**
Matthias, John **9**
Matthiessen, Peter **5, 7, 11**
Matute, Ana María **11**
Maugham, W(illiam) Somerset **1, 11, 15**
Mauriac, Claude **9**
Mauriac, François **4, 9**
Maxwell, William **19**
May, Elaine **16**
Mayne, William **12**
Maysles, Albert and David Maysles **16**
Maysles, David
   See Maysles, Albert and David Maysles **16**
McBain, Ed
   See Hunter, Evan **11**
McCaffrey, Anne **17**
McCarthy, Cormac **4**
McCarthy, Mary **1, 3, 5, 14**
McCartney, Paul
   See Lennon, John and Paul McCartney **12**
McClure, Michael **6, 10**
McCourt, James **5**
McCullers, (Lula) Carson **1, 4, 10, 12**
McElroy, Joseph **5**
McEwan, Ian **13**
McGahern, John **5, 9**
McGinley, Phyllis **14**
McGivern, Maureen Daly
   See Daly, Maureen **17**
McGuane, Thomas **3, 7, 18**
McHale, Tom **3, 5**
McIntyre, Vonda N(eel) **18**

McKuen, Rod  **1, 3**
McMurtry, Larry  **2, 3, 7, 11**
McNally, Terrence  **4, 7**
McPherson, James Alan  **19**
Meaker, Marijane
  See Kerr, M. E.  **12**
Medoff, Mark  **6**
Megged, Aharon  **9**
Mercer, David  **5**
Meredith, William  **4, 13**
Merrill, James  **2, 3, 6, 8, 13, 18**
Merton, Thomas  **1, 3, 11**
Merwin, W(illiam) S(tanley)  **1, 2, 3, 5, 8, 13, 18**
Mewshaw, Michael  **9**
Michaels, Leonard  **6**
Michaux, Henri  **8, 19**
Michener, James A(lbert)  **1, 5, 11**
Middleton, Christopher  **13**
Middleton, Stanley  **7**
Miguéis, José Rodrigues  **10**
Miles, Josephine  **1, 2, 14**
Millar, Kenneth
  See Macdonald, Ross  **1, 2, 3, 14**
Miller, Arthur  **1, 2, 6, 10, 15**
Miller, Henry  **1, 2, 4, 9, 14**
Miller, Jason  **2**
Miller, Walter M., Jr.  **4**
Miłosz, Czesław  **5, 11**
Mishima, Yukio  **2, 4, 6, 9**
Mitchell, Joni  **12**
Modiano, Patrick  **18**
Mohr, Nicholasa  **12**
Mojtabai, A(nn) G(race)  **5, 9, 15**
Momaday, N(avarre) Scott  **2, 19**
Montague, John  **13**
Montale, Eugenio  **7, 9, 18**
Montgomery, Marion  **7**
Montherlant, Henri de  **8, 19**
Moorcock, Michael  **5**
Moore, Brian  **1, 3, 5, 7, 8, 19**
Moore, Marianne  **1, 2, 4, 8, 10, 13, 19**
Morante, Elsa  **8**
Moravia, Alberto  **2, 7, 11, 18**
Morgan, Berry  **6**
Morgan, Robin  **2**
Morris, Steveland Judkins
  See Wonder, Stevie  **12**
Morris, Wright  **1, 3, 7, 18**
Morrison, Jim  **17**
Morrison, Toni  **4, 10**
Mortimer, Penelope  **5**
Moss, Howard  **7, 14**
Motley, Willard  **18**
Mott, Michael  **15**
Mrożek, Sławomir  **3, 13**
Mueller, Lisel  **13**
Mull, Martin  **17**
Munro, Alice  **6, 10, 19**
Murdoch, (Jean) Iris  **1, 2, 3, 4, 6, 8, 11, 15**
Musgrave, Susan  **13**
Nabokov, Vladimir  **1, 2, 3, 6, 8, 11, 15**
Nagy, László  **7**
Naipaul, V(idiadhar) S(urajprasad)  **4, 7, 9, 13, 18**
Narayan, R(asipuram) K(rishnaswami)  **7**

Nelson, Willie  **17**
Nemerov, Howard  **2, 6, 9**
Neruda, Pablo  **1, 2, 5, 7, 9**
Neufeld, John  **17**
Neville, Emily Cheney  **12**
Newby, P(ercy) H(oward)  **2, 13**
Newlove, Donald  **6**
Newlove, John  **14**
Newman, Charles  **2, 8**
Newman, Edwin  **14**
Ngugi, James  **3, 7**
  See also Wa Thiong'o, Ngugi  **13**
Nichol, B. P.  **18**
Nichols, Peter  **5**
Niedecker, Lorine  **10**
Nin, Anaïs  **1, 4, 8, 11, 14**
Nissenson, Hugh  **4, 9**
Niven, Larry  **8**
Norris, Leslie  **14**
Norton, Alice Mary
  See Norton, Andre  **12**
Norton, Andre  **12**
Nossack, Hans Erich  **6**
Nova, Craig  **7**
Nowlan, Alden  **15**
Nye, Robert  **13**
Nyro, Laura  **17**
Oates, Joyce Carol  **1, 2, 3, 6, 9, 11, 15, 19**
O'Brien, Darcy  **11**
O'Brien, Edna  **3, 5, 8, 13**
O'Brien, Flann  **1, 4, 5, 7, 10**
O'Brien, Richard  **17**
O'Brien, Tim  **7, 19**
O'Casey, Sean  **1, 5, 9, 11, 15**
Ochs, Phil  **17**
O'Connor, Edwin  **14**
O'Connor, (Mary) Flannery  **1, 2, 3, 6, 10, 13, 15**
O'Connor, Frank  **14**
Odets, Clifford  **2**
O'Donovan, Michael
  See O'Connor, Frank  **14**
Ōe, Kenzaburō  **10**
O'Faolain, Julia  **6, 19**
O'Faoláin, Seán  **1, 7, 14**
O'Flaherty, Liam  **5**
O'Hara, Frank  **2, 5, 13**
O'Hara, John  **1, 2, 3, 6, 11**
Olesha, Yuri  **8**
Oliver, Mary  **19**
Olivier, (Baron) Laurence  **20**
Olsen, Tillie  **4, 13**
Olson, Charles  **1, 2, 5, 6, 9, 11**
Ondaatje, (Philip) Michael  **14**
Onetti, Juan Carlos  **7, 10**
O'Nolan, Brian
  See O'Brien, Flann  **1, 4, 5, 7, 10**
O Nuallain, Brian
  See O'Brien, Flann  **1, 4, 5, 7, 10**
Oppen, George  **7, 13**
Orton, Joe  **4, 13**
Osborne, John  **1, 2, 5, 11**
Oshima, Nagisa  **20**
Otero, Blas de  **11**
Owens, Rochelle  **8**
Owl, Sebastian
  See Thompson, Hunter S(tockton)  **9, 17**
Oz, Amos  **5, 8, 11**

Ozick, Cynthia  **3, 7**
Ozu, Yasujiro  **16**
Pa Chin  **18**
Pack, Robert  **13**
Page, Jimmy  **12**
Page, P(atricia) K(athleen)  **7, 18**
Palazzeschi, Aldo  **11**
Paley, Grace  **4, 6**
Parker, Dorothy  **15**
Parks, Gordon  **1, 16**
Parra, Nicanor  **2**
Pasolini, Pier Paolo  **20**
Pasternak, Boris  **7, 10, 18**
Patchen, Kenneth  **1, 2, 18**
Paterson, Katherine  **12**
Paton, Alan  **4, 10**
Paz, Octavio  **3, 4, 6, 10, 19**
Peake, Mervyn  **7**
Peck, John  **3**
Peck, Robert Newton  **17**
Peckinpah, (David) Sam(uel)  **20**
Percy, Walker  **2, 3, 6, 8, 14, 18**
Perelman, S(idney) J(oseph)  **3, 5, 9, 15**
Perse, St.-John  **4, 11**
Peters, Robert L(ouis)  **7**
Petrakis, Harry Mark  **3**
Petry, Ann  **1, 7, 18**
Phillips, Jayne Anne  **15**
Piccolo, Lucio  **13**
Piercy, Marge  **3, 6, 14, 18**
Pincherle, Alberto
  See Moravia, Alberto  **2, 7, 11, 18**
Piñero, Miguel  **4**
Pinget, Robert  **7, 13**
Pinsky, Robert  **9, 19**
Pinter, Harold  **1, 3, 6, 9, 11, 15**
Pirsig, Robert M(aynard)  **4, 6**
Plaidy, Jean
  See Hibbert, Eleanor  **7**
Plant, Robert
  See Page, Jimmy and Robert Plant  **12**
Plante, David  **7**
Plath, Sylvia  **1, 2, 3, 5, 9, 11, 14, 17**
Plomer, William  **4, 8**
Pohl, Frederik  **18**
Poirier, Louis
  See Gracq, Julien  **11**
Polanski, Roman  **16**
Pomerance, Bernard  **13**
Ponge, Francis  **6, 18**
Poole, Josephine  **17**
Popa, Vasko  **19**
Porter, Katherine Anne  **1, 3, 7, 10, 13, 15**
Porter, Peter  **5, 13**
Potok, Chaim  **2, 7, 14**
Pound, Ezra  **1, 2, 3, 4, 5, 7, 10, 13, 18**
Powell, Anthony  **1, 3, 7, 9, 10**
Powers, J(ames) F(arl)  **1, 4, 8**
Pownall, David  **10**
Powys, John Cowper  **7, 9, 15**
Pratt, E(dwin) J(ohn)  **19**
Preussler, Otfried  **17**
Prévert, Jacques  **15**
Price, (Edward) Reynolds  **3, 6, 13**
Price, Richard  **6, 12**

Priestley, J(ohn) B(oynton)  **2, 5, 9**
Pritchett, V(ictor) S(awden)  **5, 13, 15**
Prokosch, Frederic  **4**
Puig, Manuel  **3, 5, 10**
Purdy, A(lfred) W(ellington)  **3, 6, 14**
Purdy, James  **2, 4, 10**
Puzo, Mario  **1, 2, 6**
Pym, Barbara  **13, 19**
Pynchon, Thomas  **2, 3, 6, 9, 11, 18**
Quasimodo, Salvatore  **10**
Queen, Ellery  **3, 11**
Queneau, Raymond  **2, 5, 10**
Quin, Ann  **6**
Quoirez, Françoise
  See Sagan, Françoise  **3, 6, 9, 17**
Rabe, David  **4, 8**
Rado, James  **17**
Radomski, James
  See Rado, James  **17**
Radvanyi, Netty Reiling
  See Seghers, Anna  **7**
Ragni, Gerome  **17**
Raine, Kathleen  **7**
Rand, Ayn  **3**
Randall, Dudley  **1**
Ransom, John Crowe  **2, 4, 5, 11**
Raphael, Frederic  **2, 14**
Rattigan, Terence  **7**
Raven, Simon  **14**
Ray, Satyajit  **16**
Read, Herbert  **4**
Read, Piers Paul  **4, 10**
Reaney, James  **13**
Rechy, John  **1, 7, 14, 18**
Redgrove, Peter  **6**
Reed, Ishmael  **2, 3, 5, 6, 13**
Renault, Mary  **3, 11, 17**
Renoir, Jean  **20**
Resnais, Alain  **16**
Rexroth, Kenneth  **1, 2, 6, 11**
Reyes y Basoalto, Ricardo Eliecer Neftali
  See Neruda, Pablo  **1, 2, 5, 7, 9**
Reynolds, Jonathan  **6**
Reznikoff, Charles  **9**
Rhys, Jean  **2, 4, 6, 14, 19**
Ribeiro, João Ubaldo  **10**
Ribman, Ronald  **7**
Rice, Elmer  **7**
Rich, Adrienne  **3, 6, 7, 11, 18**
Richard, Keith  **17**
Richards, I(vor) A(rmstrong)  **14**
Richards, Keith
  See Richard, Keith  **17**
Richler, Mordecai  **3, 5, 9, 13, 18**
Riding, Laura  **3, 7**
Riefenstahl, Leni  **16**
Ritsos, Yannis  **6, 13**
Rivers, Conrad Kent  **1**
Robbe-Grillet, Alain  **1, 2, 4, 6, 8, 10, 14**
Robbins, Harold  **5**
Robbins, Tom  **9**
Roberts, Kate  **15**
Roberts, Keith  **14**
Robinson, Jill  **10**

AUTHOR INDEX

Roddenberry, Gene  17
Rodgers, Mary  12
Rodgers, W(illiam) R(obert)  7
Rodríguez, Claudio  10
Roethke, Theodore  1, 3, 8, 11, 19
Rogers, Sam
See Shepard, Sam  4, 6, 17
Rogin, Gilbert  18
Rohmer, Eric  16
Roiphe, Anne  3, 9
Romains, Jules  7
Rosenblatt, Joe  15
Ross, (James) Sinclair  13
Rossner, Judith  6, 9
Roth, Henry  2, 6, 11
Roth, Philip  1, 2, 3, 4, 6, 9, 15
Rothenberg, Jerome  6
Rovit, Earl  7
Roy, Gabrielle  10, 14
Rózewicz, Tadeusz  9
Ruark, Gibbons  3
Rubens, Bernice  19
Rudkin, David  14
Rudnik, Raphael  7
Ruiz, José Martínez
See Azorín  11
Rukeyser, Muriel  6, 10, 15
Rulfo, Juan  8
Rushforth, Peter  19
Russ, Joanna  15
Russell, Ken  16
Ruyslinck, Ward  14
Ryan, Cornelius  7
Ryga, George  14
Sábato, Ernesto  10
Sachs, Nelly  14
Sackler, Howard  14
Sadoff, Ira  9
Safire, William  10
Sagan, Françoise  3, 6, 9, 17
Sainte-Marie, Buffy  17
Salama, Hannu  18
Salamanca, J(ack) R(ichard)  4, 15
Salinger, J(erome) D(avid)  1, 3, 8, 12
Salter, James  7
Samarakis, Antonis  5
Sanchez, Sonia  5
Sandburg, Carl  1, 4, 10, 15
Saner, Reg(inald)  9
Sansom, William  2, 6
Sarduy, Severo  6
Saroyan, William  1, 8, 10
Sarraute, Nathalie  1, 2, 4, 8, 10
Sarton, (Eleanor) May  4, 14
Sartre, Jean-Paul  1, 4, 7, 9, 13, 18
Saura, Carlos  20
Sauser-Hall, Frédéric-Louis
See Cendrars, Blaise  18
Sayles, John  7, 10, 14
Schaeffer, Susan Fromberg  6, 11
Schevill, James  7
Schisgal, Murray  6
Schorer, Mark  9
Schulberg, Budd  7
Schulz, Charles M(onroe)  12
Schuyler, James  5
Schwartz, Delmore  2, 4, 10
Schwarz-Bart, André  2, 4

Schwarz-Bart, Simone  7
Sciascia, Leonardo  8, 9
Scorsese, Martin  20
Scott, Paul  9
Seelye, John  7
Seferiades, Giorgos Stylianou
See Seferis, George  5, 11
Seferis, George  5, 11
Segal, Erich  3, 10
Seghers, Anna  7
Seidel, Frederick  18
Selby, Hubert, Jr.  1, 2, 4, 8
Sender, Ramón  8
Settle, Mary lee  19
Sexton, Anne  2, 4, 6, 8, 10, 15
Shaara, Michael  15
Shaffer, Anthony  19
Shaffer, Peter  5, 14, 18
Shalamov, Varlam  18
Shamlu, Ahmad  10
Shange, Ntozake  8
Shapiro, Karl  4, 8, 15
Shaw, Irwin  7
Shaw, Robert  5
Sheed, Wilfrid  2, 4, 10
Shepard, Sam  4, 6, 17
Sherman, Martin  19
Sherwin, Judith Johnson  7, 15
Sholokhov, Mikhail  7, 15
Shulman, Alix Kates  2, 10
Shuttle, Penelope  7
Sigal, Clancy  7
Silkin, Jon  2, 6
Sillanpää, Frans Eemil  19
Sillitoe, Alan  1, 3, 6, 10, 19
Silone, Ignazio  4
Silver, Joan Micklin  20
Silverberg, Robert  7
Silverstein, Alvin  17
Silverstein, Virginia
B(arbara)  17
Simak, Clifford D(onald)  1
Simenon, Georges  1, 2, 3, 8, 18
Simic, Charles  6, 9
Simon, Claude  4, 9, 15
Simon, (Marvin) Neil  6, 11
Simon, Paul  17
Simpson, Louis  4, 7, 9
Sinclair, Andrew  2, 14
Sinclair, Upton  1, 11, 15
Singer, Isaac Bashevis  1, 3, 6, 9, 11, 15
Singh, Khushwant  11
Sinyavsky, Andrei  8
Sissman, L(ouis) E(dward)  9, 18
Sisson, C(harles) H(ubert)  8
Sitwell, Edith  2, 9
Sjöwall, Maj
See Wahlöö, Per  7
Skelton, Robin  13
Skolimowski, Jerzy  20
Skolimowski, Yurek
See Skolimowski, Jerzy  20
Škvorecký, Josef  15
Slade, Bernard  11
Slavitt, David  5, 14
Slessor, Kenneth  14
Smith, A(rthur) J(ames)
M(arshall)  15
Smith, Betty  19
Smith, Florence Margaret
See Smith, Stevie  3, 8
Smith, Patti  12

Smith, Sara Mahala Redway
See Benson, Sally  17
Smith, Stevie  3, 8
Smith, William Jay  6
Snodgrass, W(illiam)
D(eWitt)  2, 6, 10, 18
Snow, C(harles) P(ercy)  1, 4, 6, 9, 13, 19
Snyder, Gary  1, 2, 5, 9
Snyder, Zilpha Keatley  17
Sokolov, Raymond  7
Solwoska, Mara
See French, Marilyn  10
Solzhenitsyn, Aleksandr
I(sayevich)  1, 2, 4, 7, 9, 10, 18
Sontag, Susan  1, 2, 10, 13
Sorrentino, Gilbert  3, 7, 14
Souster, (Holmes) Raymond  5, 14
Southern, Terry  7
Soyinka, Wole  3, 5, 14
Spacks, Barry  14
Spark, Muriel  2, 3, 5, 8, 13, 18
Spender, Stephen  1, 2, 5, 10
Spicer, Jack  8, 18
Spielberg, Peter  6
Spielberg, Steven  20
Spillane, Mickey  3, 13
Spivack, Kathleen  6
Springsteen, Bruce  17
Stafford, Jean  4, 7, 19
Stafford, William  4, 7
Stanton, Maura  9
Stead, Christina  2, 5, 8
Stegner, Wallace  9
Steinbeck, John  1, 5, 9, 13
Stern, Richard G(ustave)  4
Sternberg, Jonas
See Sternberg, Josef von  20
Sternberg, Josef von  20
Stevenson, Anne  7
Stewart, J(ohn) I(nnes)
M(ackintosh)  7, 14
Stewart, Mary  7
Stolz, Mary  12
Stone, Irving  7
Stone, Robert  5
Stoppard, Tom  1, 3, 4, 5, 8, 15
Storey, David  2, 4, 5, 8
Storm, Hyemeyohsts  3
Stout, Rex  3
Strand, Mark  6, 18
Stuart, (Hilton) Jesse  1, 8, 11, 14
Styron, William  1, 3, 5, 11, 15
Sukenick, Ronald  3, 4, 6
Suknaski, Andrew  19
Summers, Hollis  10
Susann, Jacqueline  3
Sutton, Henry
See Slavitt, David  5, 14
Swados, Elizabeth  12
Swados, Harvey  5
Swenson, May  4, 14
Symons, Julian  2, 14
Tabori, George  19
Tanizaki, Jun'ichiro  8, 14
Tate, (John Orley) Allen  2, 4, 6, 9, 11, 14
Tate, James  2, 6
Tavel, Ronald  6
Taylor, Eleanor Ross  5

Taylor, Elizabeth  2, 4
Taylor, Peter  1, 4, 18
Taylor, Robert Lewis  14
Tennant, Emma  13
Terry, Megan  19
Tertz, Abram
See Sinyavsky, Andrei  8
Theroux, Alexander  2
Theroux, Paul  5, 8, 11, 15
Thiele, Colin  17
Thomas, Audrey  7, 13
Thomas, D(onald) M(ichael)  13
Thomas, John Peter
See Thomas, Piri  17
Thomas, Piri  17
Thomas, R(onald) S(tuart)  6, 13
Thompson, Hunter S(tockton)  9, 17
Thurber, James  5, 11
Tindall, Gillian  7
Tolkien, J(ohn) R(onald)
R(euel)  1, 2, 3, 8, 12
Tomlin, Lily  17
Tomlin, Mary Jean
See Tomlin, Lily  17
Tomlinson, (Alfred) Charles  2, 4, 6, 13
Toole, John Kennedy  19
Toomer, Jean  1, 4, 13
Tournier, Michel  6
Townshend, Peter  17
Traven, B.  8, 11
Trevor, William  7, 9, 14
Trilling, Lionel  9, 11
Trudeau, Garry  12
Truffaut, François  20
Trumbo, Dalton  19
Tryon, Thomas  3, 11
Tunis, John R.  12
Turco, Lewis  11
Tutuola, Amos  5, 14
Tyler, Anne  7, 11, 18
Ungaretti, Giuseppe  7, 11, 15
Updike, John  1, 2, 3, 5, 7, 9, 13, 15
Uris, Leon  7
Ustinov, Peter  1
Vaculík, Ludvík  7
Van den Bogaerdes, Derek Niven
See Bogarde, Dirk  19
Van der Post, Laurens  5
Van Doren, Mark  6, 10
Van Duyn, Mona  3, 7
Van Itallie, Jean-Claude  3
Van Peebles, Melvin  2, 20
Van Vogt, A(lfred) E(lton)  1
Varda, Agnès  16
Vargas Llosa, Mario  3, 6, 9, 10, 15
Vassilikos, Vassilis  4, 8
Vicker, Angus
See Felsen, Henry Gregor  17
Vidal, Gore  2, 4, 6, 8, 10
Viereck, Peter  4
Visconti, Luchino  16
Vittorini, Elio  6, 9, 14
Voinovich, Vladimir  10
Vonnegut, Kurt, Jr.  1, 2, 3, 4, 5, 8, 12
Von Sternberg, Josef
See Sternberg, Josef von
Voznesensky, Andrei  1, 15
Wagman, Fredrica  7

Wagoner, David  **3, 5, 15**
Wahlöö, Per  **7**
Wain, John  **2, 11, 15**
Wajda, Andrzej  **16**
Wakefield, Dan  **7**
Wakoski, Diane  **2, 4, 7, 9, 11**
Walcott, Derek  **2, 4, 9, 14**
Waldman, Anne  **7**
Walker, Alice  **5, 6, 9, 19**
Walker, David Harry  **14**
Walker, Joseph A.  **19**
Walker, Margaret  **1, 6**
Walker, Ted  **13**
Wallace, Irving  **7, 13**
Wallant, Edward Lewis  **5, 10**
Wambaugh, Joseph  **3, 18**
Ward, Douglas Turner  **19**
Warhol, Andy  **20**
Warner, Francis  **14**
Warner, Sylvia Townsend  **7, 19**
Warren, Robert Penn  **1, 4, 6, 8, 10, 13, 18**
Wa Thiong'o, Ngugi  **13**
  See also Ngugi, James  **3, 7**
Waugh, Auberon  **7**
Waugh, Evelyn  **1, 3, 8, 13, 19**
Waugh, Harriet  **6**
Webb, Charles  **7**
Webb, Phyllis  **18**
Weber, Lenora Mattingly  **12**
Weidman, Jerome  **7**
Weir, Peter  **20**
Weiss, Peter  **3, 15**
Weiss, Theodore  **3, 8, 14**

Welch, James  **6, 14**
Weldon, Fay  **6, 9, 11, 19**
Weller, Michael  **10**
Welles, (George) Orson  **20**
Wells, Rosemary  **12**
Welty, Eudora  **1, 2, 5, 14**
Wertmüller, Lina  **16**
Wescott, Glenway  **13**
Wesker, Arnold  **3, 5**
Wesley, Richard  **7**
West, Jessamyn  **7, 17**
West, Morris L(anglo)  **6**
West, Paul  **7, 14**
West, Rebecca  **7, 9**
Westall, Robert  **17**
Westlake, Donald E(dwin)  **7**
Whalen, Philip  **6**
Wharton, William  **18**
Wheelock, John Hall  **14**
White, E(lwyn) B(rooks)  **10**
White, Patrick  **3, 4, 5, 7, 9, 18**
Whitehead, E. A.  **5**
Whittemore, (Edward) Reed  **4**
Wicker, Tom  **7**
Wideman, J(ohn) E(dgar)  **5**
Wiebe, Rudy  **6, 11, 14**
Wieners, John  **7**
Wiesel, Elie(zer)  **3, 5, 11**
Wight, James Alfred
  See Herriot, James  **12**
Wilbur, Richard  **3, 6, 9, 14**
Wild, Peter  **14**
Wilder, Billy  **20**

Wilder, Samuel
  See Wilder, Billy  **20**
Wilder, Thornton  **1, 5, 6, 10, 15**
Wilhelm, Kate  **7**
Willard, Nancy  **7**
Williams, (George) Emlyn  **15**
Williams, John A(lfred)  **5, 13**
Williams, Jonathan  **13**
Williams, Tennessee  **1, 2, 5, 7, 8, 11, 15, 19**
Williams, Thomas  **14**
Williams, William Carlos  **1, 2, 5, 9, 13**
Willingham, Calder  **5**
Wilson, Angus  **2, 3, 5**
Wilson, Brian  **12**
Wilson, Colin  **3, 14**
Wilson, Edmund  **1, 2, 3, 8**
Wilson, Ethel Davis  **13**
Wilson, John Anthony Burgess
  See Burgess, Anthony  **1, 2, 4, 5, 8, 10, 13, 15**
Wilson, Lanford  **7, 14**
Wilson, Robert  **7, 9**
Winters, Yvor  **4, 8**
Wiseman, Frederick  **20**
Wodehouse, P(elham) G(renville)  **1, 2, 5, 10**
Woiwode, Larry  **6, 10**
Wolf, Christa  **14**
Wolfe, Tom  **1, 2, 9, 15**
Wolitzer, Hilma  **17**
Wonder, Stevie  **12**
Wong, Jade Snow  **17**

Woods, Helen Ferguson
  See Kavan, Anna  **5, 13**
Wouk, Herman  **1, 9**
Wright, Charles  **6, 13**
Wright, James  **3, 5, 10**
Wright, Judith  **11**
Wright, Richard  **1, 3, 4, 9, 14**
Wright, Richard B(ruce)  **6**
Wurlitzer, Rudolph  **2, 4, 15**
Wyndham, John  **19**
Yanovsky, Vassily S(emenovich)  **2, 18**
Yates, Richard  **7, 8**
Yehoshua, Abraham B.  **13**
Yerby, Frank G(arvin)  **1, 7**
Yevtushenko, Yevgeny  **1, 3, 13**
Yglesias, Helen  **7**
Yorke, Henry Vincent
  See Green, Henry  **2, 13**
Young, Al  **19**
Young, Andrew  **5**
Young, Neil  **17**
Yourcenar, Marguerite  **19**
Yurick, Sol  **6**
Zappa, Frank  **17**
Zaturenska, Marya  **6, 11**
Zimmerman, Robert
  See Dylan, Bob  **12**
Zindel, Paul  **6**
Zinoviev, Alexander  **19**
Zuckmayer, Carl  **18**
Zukofsky, Louis  **1, 2, 4, 7, 11, 18**

AUTHOR INDEX

# Cumulative Index to Critics

**Aaron, Daniel**
Thornton Wilder **15**:575

**Aaron, Jules**
Jack Heifner **11**:264

**Abbey, Edward**
Robert M. Pirsig **6**:421

**Abbott, John Lawrence**
Isaac Bashevis Singer **9**:487
Sylvia Townsend Warner **7**:512

**Abeel, Erica**
Pamela Hansford Johnson **7**:185

**Abel, Elizabeth**
Jean Rhys **14**:448

**Abel, Lionel**
Samuel Beckett **2**:45
Jack Gelber **6**:196
Jean Genet **2**:157
Yoram Kaniuk **19**:238

**Abernethy, Peter L.**
Thomas Pynchon **3**:410

**Abicht, Ludo**
Jan de Hartog **19**:133

**Ableman, Paul**
Brian Aldiss **14**:14
Jurek Becker **19**:36
William Golding **17**:179
Mary Gordon **13**:250
Mervyn Jones **10**:295
Mary Renault **17**:402
Andrew Sinclair **14**:489

**Abley, Mark**
Agnès Varda **16**:560

**Abrahams, William**
Elizabeth Bowen **6**:95
Hortense Calisher **2**:97
Herbert Gold **4**:193
Joyce Carol Oates **2**:315
Harold Pinter **9**:418
V. S. Pritchett **5**:352

**Abramson, Doris E.**
Alice Childress **12**:105

**Abramson, Jane**
Peter Dickinson **12**:172
Christie Harris **12**:268
Rosemary Wells **12**:638

**Acheson, James**
William Golding **17**:177

**Ackroyd, Peter**
Brian Aldiss **5**:16
Martin Amis **4**:19
Miguel Ángel Asturias **8**:27
Louis Auchincloss **6**:15
W. H. Auden **9**:56
Beryl Bainbridge **8**:36
James Baldwin **5**:43
John Barth **5**:51
Donald Barthelme **3**:44
Samuel Beckett **4**:52
John Berryman **3**:72
Richard Brautigan **5**:72
Charles Bukowski **5**:80
Anthony Burgess **5**:87
William S. Burroughs **5**:92
Italo Calvino **5**:100; **8**:132
Richard Condon **6**:115
Roald Dahl **6**:122
Ed Dorn **10**:155
Margaret Drabble **8**:183
Douglas Dunn **6**:148

Bruce Jay Friedman **5**:127
John Gardner **7**:116
Günter Grass **4**:207
MacDonald Harris **9**:261
Joseph Heller **5**:179
Mark Helprin **10**:261
Russell C. Hoban **7**:160
Elizabeth Jane Howard **7**:164
B. S. Johnson **6**:264
Pamela Hansford Johnson **7**:184
G. Josipovici **6**:270
Thomas Keneally **10**:298
Jack Kerouac **5**:215
Francis King **8**:321
Jerzy Kosinski **10**:308
Doris Lessing **6**:300
Alison Lurie **4**:305
Thomas McGuane **7**:212
Stanley Middleton **7**:220
Michael Moorcock **5**:294
Penelope Mortimer **5**:298
Iris Murdoch **4**:368
Vladimir Nabokov **6**:358
V. S. Naipaul **7**:252
Joyce Carol Oates **6**:368
Tillie Olsen **13**:432
Grace Paley **6**:393
Frederik Pohl **18**:411
Davi Pownall **10**:418, 419
J. B. Priestley **9**:441
V. S. Pritchett **5**:352
Thomas Pynchon **3**:419
Frederic Raphael **14**:437
Simon Raven **14**:442
Peter Redgrove **6**:446
Keith Roberts **14**:463
Judith Rossner **9**:458
May Sarton **4**:472
David Slavitt **5**:392

Wole Soyinka **5**:398
David Storey **4**:529
Paul Theroux **5**:428
Thomas Tryon **11**:548
John Updike **7**:488; **9**:540
Gore Vidal **8**:525
Harriet Waugh **6**:559
Jerome Weidman **7**:518
Arnold Wesker **5**:483
Patrick White **4**:587

**Adamowski, T. H.**
Simone de Beauvoir **4**:47

**Adams, Alice**
Lisa Alther **7**:14

**Adams, George R.**
Lorraine Hansberry **17**:190
Ann Petry **18**:403

**Adams, Jacqueline**
Al Young **19**:479

**Adams, James Truslow**
Esther Forbes **12**:206

**Adams, John**
Roy A. Gallant **17**:131

**Adams, Laura**
Norman Mailer **11**:340

**Adams, Leonie**
John Crowe Ransom **4**:428

**Adams, M. Ian**
Juan Carlos Onetti **10**:376

**Adams, Percy**
James Dickey **7**:81

**Adams, Phoebe-Lou**
Richard Adams **18**:2
Joy Adamson **17**:3
Beryl Bainbridge **5**:40
Ann Beattie **18**:38
André Brink **18**:68
Robert Cormier **12**:133
Margaret Craven **17**:80
Roald Dahl **18**:109
John Fowles **15**:234
Dashiell Hammett **5**:161
James Herriot **12**:282
George V. Higgins **18**:234
Jamake Highwater **12**:285
Bohumil Hrabal **13**:290
P. D. James **18**:275
David Jones **7**:189
Jerzy Kosinski **6**:285
William Kotzwinkle **14**:311
Harper Lee **12**:341
Yukio Mishima **9**:385
N. Scott Momaday **19**:317
Berry Morgan **6**:340
Joyce Carol Oates **6**:374
Tillie Olsen **13**:433
Sylvia Plath **17**:352
Reynolds Price **6**:426
Jean Rhys **19**:394
João Ubaldo Ribeiro **10**:436
Philip Roth **15**:452
Françoise Sagan **17**:419
Khushwant Singh **11**:504
Jean Stafford **19**:431
Christina Stead **8**:500
Joseph Wambaugh **18**:532

**Adams, Richard**
Robert Newton Peck **17**:338

**Adams, Robert M.**
Adolfo Bioy Casares **13**:87
Eleanor Clark **19**:105
Edward Dahlberg **7**:63
Peter Matthiessen **11**:361
Mary McCarthy **14**:362
Alberto Moravia **18**:348
Robert M. Pirsig **4**:404
Severo Sarduy **6**:485
Mary Lee Settle **19**:409

**Adams, Robert Martin**
John Barth **10**:24
Samuel Beckett **14**:74
Jorge Luis Borges **10**:66
Richard Brautigan **12**:61
Anthony Burgess **10**:90
Lawrence Durrell **13**:185
T. S. Eliot **10**:171
William Faulkner **11**:201
Carlo Emilio Gadda **11**:215
William H. Gass **2**:154
José Lezama Lima **10**:321
Vladimir Nabokov **11**:393
Flann O'Brien **10**:363
Thomas Pynchon **11**:453
Alain Robbe-Grillet **10**:437
J.R.R. Tolkien **12**:586
Angus Wilson **2**:472

**Adams, Robin**
Frank Herbert **12**:279

**Adams, S. J.**
Ezra Pound **13**:453

**Adcock, Fleur**
John Berryman **13**:83
Robert Lowell **11**:331
Peter Porter **13**:453

**Adelman, Clifford**
John Berryman **3**:71

**Adelman, George**
Frank B. Gilbreth, Jr. and
Ernestine Gilbreth Carey
**17**:156

**Adkins, Laurence**
Eilís Dillon **17**:96

**Adler, Dick**
Ross Macdonald **1**:185

**Adler, Renata**
Mel Brooks **12**:75
Francis Ford Coppola **16**:232
Joan Micklin Silver **20**:346

**Adler, Thomas P.**
Edward Albee **11**:13
Harold Pinter **15**:424
Sam Shepard **17**:446

**Agar, John**
Jonathan Baumbach **6**:32
Laurie Colwin **5**:107

**Agee, James**
Frank Capra **16**:156
Charles Chaplin **16**:193
Maya Deren **16**:251
Carl Theodor Dreyer **16**:256
Alfred Hitchcock **16**:339, 342
John Huston **20**:158, 160
Buster Keaton **20**:188
Laurence Olivier **20**:234
Billy Wilder **20**:456

**Agena, Kathleen**
Charles Wright **13**:613

**Aggeler, Geoffrey**
Anthony Burgess **2**:86; **5**:85;
**13**:123

**Agius, Ambrose, O.S.B.**
Edward Dahlberg **7**:64

**Ahearn, Kerry**
Wallace Stegner **9**:509

**Ahokas, Jaakko A.**
Paavo Haavikko **18**:206
Frans Eemil Sillanpää **19**:418

**Ahrold, Robbin**
Kurt Vonnegut, Jr. **3**:501

**Aiken, Conrad**
William Faulkner **8**:206
St.-John Perse **11**:433
Karl Shapiro **15**:475

**Aiken, David**
Flannery O'Connor **10**:365

**Aiken, William**
David Kherdian **6**:281

**Aitken, Will**
Carlos Saura **20**:319

**Alazraki, Jaime**
Jorge Luis Borges **19**:45
Pablo Neruda **2**:309; **7**:261

**Albers, Randall**
Ai **14**:8

**Albert, Walter**
Blaise Cendrars **18**:90

**Albertson, Chris**
Laura Nyro **17**:313
Stevie Wonder **12**:662

**Aldan, Daisy**
Phyllis Gotlieb **18**:193

**Alderson, Brian W.**
Leon Garfied **12**:226
William Mayne **12**:395, 401

**Alderson, S. William**
Andre Norton **12**:464, 466, 470

**Alderson, Sue Ann**
Muriel Rukeyser **10**:442

**Alderson, Valerie**
E. M. Almedingen **12**:6

**Aldiss, Brian**
J. G. Ballard **3**:33
Frank Herbert **12**:272

**Aldrich, Nelson**
Piri Thomas **17**:497

**Aldridge, John W.**
James Baldwin **4**:42
Donald Barthelme **2**:39
Saul Bellow **2**:49, 50
Louis-Ferdinand Céline **7**:47
John Cheever **3**:105
John Dos Passos **4**:131
James T. Farrell **4**:157
William Faulkner **3**:150
William Gaddis **3**:177; **6**:193
Joseph Heller **5**:177
Ernest Hemingway **3**:231, 233
James Jones **3**:261
Jerzy Kosinski **2**:231
Alison Lurie **5**:260
Norman Mailer **1**:193; **2**:258
Mary McCarthy **3**:327, 328
Wright Morris **3**:342; **18**:352
John O'Hara **2**:323
Katherine Anne Porter **3**:392
Philip Roth **4**:459
Alan Sillitoe **3**:447
William Styron **3**:472
John Updike **2**:439
Robert Penn Warren **1**:356
Eudora Welty **2**:461
Colin Wilson **3**:536
Edmund Wilson **2**:474
P. G. Wodehouse **2**:478

**Aldridge, Judith**
Ruth M. Arthur **12**:27
Honor Arundel **17**:14, 15, 18

**Alegria, Fernando**
Jorge Luis Borges **2**:71

**Aletti, Vince**
Laura Nyro **17**:312
Stevie Wonder **12**:656, 660

**Alexander, Edward**
Isaac Bashevis Singer **11**:503

**Alexander, John R.**
Robinson Jeffers **2**:215

**Alexander, Michael**
Donald Davie **5**:113
Ezra Pound **7**:336

**Alexander, William**
Carl Sandburg **4**:463

**Alexandrova, Vera**
Mikhail Sholokhov **7**:420

**Algren, Nelson**
Clancy Sigal **7**:424

**Ali, Tariq**
Jules Archer **12**:19

**Allen, Bob**
Willie Nelson **17**:305

**Allen, Bruce**
Richard Adams **5**:6
Julio Cortázar **5**:110
Stanley Elkin **6**:168
John Gardner **8**:236
Mary Gordon **13**:250
Thomas Keneally **5**:212
Kenneth Koch **5**:219
Peter Matthiessen **7**:211
Wright Morris **18**:354
Iris Murdoch **6**:347
Joyce Carol Oates **6**:369
Manuel Puig **5**:355
John Sayles **10**:460
Isaac Bashevis Singer **6**:509
Paul West **7**:524
Patrick White **5**:485

**Allen, Carol J.**
Susan Fromberg Schaeffer
**11**:491

**Allen, Dexter**
Mary Lee Settle **19**:408

**Allen, Dick**
Margaret Atwood **2**:20
Wendell Berry **6**:61
Hayden Carruth **7**:40
Paul Goodman **2**:169
Thom Gunn **6**:221
Richard F. Hugo **6**:245
Philip Levine **2**:244
Lisel Mueller **13**:400
George Oppen **7**:281
Judith Johnson Sherwin **7**:414

**Allen, Don**
François Truffaut **20**:397

**Allen, Gay Wilson**
Carl Sandburg **10**:447

**Allen, Henry**
Robert M. Pirsig **4**:403

**Allen, John A.**
Eudora Welty **14**:564

**Allen, John Alexander**
Daniel Hoffman **13**:288

**Allen, L. David**
Arthur C. Clarke **18**:106

**Allen, Louis**
Shusaku Endo **14**:161

**Allen, Merritt P.**
Walter Farley **17**:116
Andre Norton **12**:455

**Allen, Patricia H.**
Zilpha Keatley Snyder 17:469

**Allen, Tom**
Vittorio De Sica 20:97
Rainer Werner Fassbinder 20:115
Kon Ichikawa 20:186
Yasujiro Ozu 16:450
Pier Paolo Pasolini 20:270
Carlos Saura 20:321
Jerzy Skolimowski 20:354

**Allen, Tom, S. C.**
Mel Brooks 12:81

**Allen, Walter**
A. Alvarez 5:17
Kingsley Amis 1:5
Riccardo Bacchelli 19:31
Saul Bellow 1:30
Elizabeth Bowen 1:40
Paul Bowles 1:41
Truman Capote 1:55
Ivy Compton-Burnett 1:61
James Gould Cozzens 1:66
Edward Dahlberg 1:71
John Dos Passos 1:79; 8:181
Lawrence Durrell 1:85
James T. Farrell 1:98; 8:205
William Faulkner 1:101
E. M. Forster 1:104
John Fowles 4:170
William Golding 1:120
Henry Green 2:178
Graham Greene 1:132
L. P. Hartley 2:181
Ernest Hemingway 1:142
Richard Hughes 1:149
Aldous Huxley 1:150
Christopher Isherwood 1:155
Pamela Hansford Johnson 1:160
Doris Lessing 1:173
Richard Llewellyn 7:206
Bernard Malamud 1:197
Olivia Manning 19:300
John P. Marquand 2:271
Carson McCullers 1:208
Henry Miller 1:221
Wright Morris 1:231
Iris Murdoch 1:234
P. H. Newby 2:310
Flannery O'Connor 1:255
John O'Hara 1:260
William Plomer 4:406
Anthony Powell 1:277
Henry Roth 2:377; 11:487
J. D. Salinger 1:298
William Sansom 2:383
C. P. Snow 1:316
John Steinbeck 1:325
William Styron 1:330
Allen Tate 2:427
Robert Penn Warren 1:355
Evelyn Waugh 1:358
Glenway Wescott 13:592
Rebecca West 7:525
Angus Wilson 2:471

**Allen, Ward**
Donald Davidson 2:112

**Allen, Woody**
S. J. Perelman 15:419

**Allott, Miriam**
Graham Greene 18:193

**Allsop, Kenneth**
J. P. Donleavy 6:139
Thomas Hinde 6:238

**Alm, Richard S.**
Betty Cavanna 12:99
Maureen Daly 17:89
Mary Stolz 12:548

**Almansi, Guido**
Alan Ayckbourn 18:27
Mario Luzi 13:354

**Alonso, J. M.**
Rafael Alberti 7:11
Jorge Luis Borges 9:117

**Alpert, Hollis**
Vincent Canby 13:131
Daniel Fuchs 8:220
William Kotzwinkle 14:311
Olivia Manning 19:300
Budd Schulberg 7:402
Melvin Van Peebles 20:410

**Altbach, Philip G.**
Jonathan Kozol 17:252

**Alter, Robert**
S. Y. Agnon 4:11
Yehuda Amichai 9:23
John Barth 9:71
Donald Barthelme 8:49
Saul Bellow 3:48, 49
Jorge Luis Borges 2:76; 6:94
Leslie A. Fiedler 13:212
John Hollander 8:298
Jerzy Kosinski 2:232
Norman Mailer 3:312; 11:342
Bernard Malamud 3:30, 321
Claude Mauriac 9:366
Elsa Morante 8:402
Alberto Moravia 18:346
Vladimir Nabokov 2:302; 8:414
Hugh Nissenson 4:380
Flann O'Brien 7:269
Manuel Puig 10:420
Thomas Pynchon 9:443
Raymond Queneau 10:429
Alain Robbe-Grillet 6:468
Earl Rovit 7:383
André Schwarz-Bart 4:480
Isaac Bashevis Singer 11:501; 15:507
J.I.M. Stewart 7:465
William Styron 15:527
John Updike 2:444
Kurt Vonnegut, Jr. 8:531
Elie Wiesel 3:526
Abraham B. Yehoshua 13:618

**Alterman, Loraine**
Jesse Jackson 12:291

**Altieri, Charles**
Robert Creeley 2:107
Robert Duncan 15:191
Robert Lowell 15:345

**Altman, Billy**
Peter Townshend 17:537, 539
Brian Wilson 12:652

**Alvarez, A.**
John Berryman 2:58; 3:65
Albert Camus 4:89
William Empson 19:154
E. M. Forster 1:109
Dashiell Hammett 3:218
Zbigniew Herbert 9:271
MiroslavHolub 4:233
Dan Jacobson 14:289
Philip Larkin 3:275
Robert Lowell 3:300
Hugh MacDiarmid 4:309
Norman Mailer 3:312
Sylvia Plath 2:335; 3:388
Jean Rhys 4:445
Jean-Paul Sartre 4:475
Edith Sitwell 9:493
Aleksandr I. Solzhenitsyn 7:436
Patrick White 3:521
Elie Wiesel 3:527
Yvor Winters 4:589

**Alvia, Sister**
Robert Newton Peck 17:339

**Amacher, Richard E.**
Edward Albee 1:5

**Amado, Jorge**
João Ubaldo Ribeiro 10:436

**Amanuddin, Syed**
James Welch 14:559

**Amberg, George**
Jean Cocteau 16:229

**Ambrose, Stephen E.**
Cornelius Ryan 7:385

**Ambrosetti, Ronald**
Eric Ambler 9:20

**Ames, Alfred C.**
Joy Adamson 17:5

**Ames, Evelyn**
J. B. Priestley 5:351

**Ames, Katrine**
Gordon Parks 16:460

**Amiel, Barbara**
Margaret Atwood 15:37
Chaim Potok 14:429
A. W. Purdy 14:435

**Amis, Kingsley**
Ray Bradbury 10:68
Arthur C. Clarke 13:155
Ivy Compton-Burnett 1:60
Ilya Ehrenburg 18:132
Leslie A. Fiedler 4:159
Christopher Isherwood 14:278
Philip Roth 1:293
Arnold Wesker 3:517

**Amis, Martin**
J. G. Ballard 6:27
Peter De Vries 7:77
Bruce Jay Friedman 5:127
Ernest J. Gaines 3:179
John Hawkes 7:141
Philip Larkin 13:337
Iris Murdoch 4:367
Vladimir Nabokov 8:412
Roman Polanski 16:472
Philip Roth 6:475

Fay Weldon 11:565

**Ammons, A. R.**
Mark Strand 18:514

**Amory, Cleveland**
Rod McKuen 1:210

**Amprimoz, Alexandre**
Joe Rosenblatt 15:448

**Amy, Jenny L.**
Robert Newton Peck 17:343

**Anderson, David**
Albert Camus 4:89, 90
William Golding 3:197, 198
Jean-Paul Sartre 4:477

**Anderson, David C.**
L. E. Sissman 9:491

**Anderson, Elliott**
Vladimir Nabokov 3:354

**Anderson, George**
Piri Thomas 17:499

**Anderson, H. T.**
Herbert Gold 14:208
Erich Segal 10:467

**Anderson, Isaac**
Agatha Christie 12:114
Joseph Krumgold 12:316

**Anderson, Jack**
Philip Levine 4:286
George MacBeth 2:252

**Anderson, Jervis**
James Baldwin 8:41

**Anderson, Joseph L.**
Akira Kurosawa 16:396

**Anderson, Lindsay**
Luis Buñuel 16:129
Vittorio De Sica 20:84
John Ford 16:305, 306
Elia Kazan 16:362
Fritz Lang 20:205
Yasujiro Ozu 16:447

**Anderson, Michael**
Edward Bond 6:85
Tennessee Williams 11:577

**Anderson, Patrick**
Ward Just 4:266

**Anderson, Poul**
Poul Anderson 15:14

**Anderson, Quentin**
Vladimir Nabokov 3:351

**Anderson, Reed**
Juan Goytisolo 10:244

**André, Michael**
Robert Creeley 2:107

**Andrews, Nigel**
John Cassavetes 20:47
Sam Peckinpah 20:277
Jerzy Skolimowski 20:350

**Andrews, Peter**
Michael Crichton 6:119
Ken Follett 18:157
Arthur Hailey 5:157
Irving Stone 7:471

CRITIC INDEX

**Andrews, Sheryl B.**
Barbara Corcoran 17:70
Andre Norton 12:460

**Angell, Roger**
Brian De Palma 20:80
Bob Fosse 20:126
Gene Roddenberry 17:413
Lina Wertmüller 16:600

**Angogo, R.**
Chinua Achebe 11:2

**Annan, Gabriele**
Simone de Beauvoir 4:47
Heinrich Böll 9:111
Anita Desai 19:133
Iris Murdoch 11:388
Jean Rhys 19:391
Sylvia Townsend Warner
19:459

**Annan, Noel**
E. M. Forster 4:166

**Anselm, Felix**
Hermann Hesse 17:194

**Ansorge, Peter**
Trevor Griffiths 13:256
Sam Shepard 6:495

**Appel, Alfred, Jr.**
Fritz Lang 20:211
Vladimir Nabokov 1:240; 2:300

**Apple, Max**
John Gardner 10:222

**Aptheker, Herbert**
W.E.B. Du Bois 13:180

**Araújo, Virginia de**
Carlos Drummond de Andrade
18:4

**Arbuthnot, May Hill**
Frank Bonham 12:53
Julia W. Cunningham 12:164
Maureen Daly 17:91
Jesse Jackson 12:290
Joseph Krumgold 12:320, 321
Madeleine L'Engle 12:350
Emily Cheney Neville 12:452
Alvin Silverstein and Virginia
B. Silverstein 17:455
Mary Stolz 12:553
Jade Snow Wong 17:566

**Archer, Eugene**
Ingmar Bergman 16:46
Bernardo Bertolucci 16:83
Federico Fellini 16:271
John Huston 20:164, 165
Sam Peckinpah 20:272

**Archer, Marguerite**
Jean Anouilh 13:18

**Arendt, Hannah**
W. H. Auden 6:21

**Argus**
Josef von Sternberg 20:370

**Aristarco, Guido**
Satyajit Ray 16:474

**Arland, Marcel**
Francoise Sagan 17:416

**Arlen, Michael J.**
Alex Haley 12:254

**Armes, Roy**
Michelangelo Antonioni 20:38
Robert Bresson 16:114
Claude Chabrol 16:170
Jean Cocteau 16:228
Federico Fellini 16:284
Pier Paolo Pasolini 20:265
Alain Resnais 16:505
Alain Robbe-Grillet 4:449
Agnès Varda 16:556

**Armour, Robert A.**
Fritz Lang 20:214

**Armstrong, Marion**
Fletcher Knebel 14:308

**Armstrong, William A.**
Sean O'Casey 1:252; 9:407

**Arnason, David**
Amos Tutuola 14:540

**Arnez, Nancy L.**
Alex Haley 12:250

**Arnheim, Rudolf**
Maya Deren 16:253

**Arnold, A. James**
Aimé Césaire 19:99

**Arnold, Armin**
Friedrich Dürrenmatt 15:193

**Arnold, Gary**
Woody, Allen 16:4

**Arnold, Marilyn**
John Gardner 18:177

**Arnolt, Vicki**
Hermann Hesse 17:215

**Aronowitz, Alfred G.**
John Lennon and Paul
McCartney 12:364
Peter Townshend 17:526

**Aronson, James**
Donald Barthelme 1:18
Saul Bellow 1:33
James Dickey 1:73
John Fowles 1:109
John Knowles 1:169
John Updike 1:345
Eudora Welty 1:363

**Aros, Andrew**
Christopher Fry 14:189

**Arpin, Gary Q.**
John Berryman 10:48

**Arthos, John**
E. E. Cummings 12:146

**Arthur, George W.**
Judy Blume 12:47
Robert Crumb 17:85

**Arvedson, Peter**
Roy A. Gallant 17:131

**Asahina, Robert**
Woody Allen 16:12
Mel Brooks 12:80
Brian De Palma 20:82
Jean-Luc Godard 20:153
Werner Herzog 16:334

Pier Paolo Pasolini 20:270
Eric Rohmer 16:538
Joan Micklin Silver 20:346
Steven Spielberg 20:366

**Ascherson, Neal**
Beryl Bainbridge 14:38
Rolf Hochhuth 18:256
György Konrád 10:304
Tadeusz Konwicki 8:327
Milan Kundera 4:278
Tadeusz Rózewicz 9:465
Yevgeny Yevtushenko 1:382

**Asein, Samuel Omo**
Alex La Guma 19:276

**Ashbery, John**
A. R. Ammons 2:13
Elizabeth Bishop 9:89

**Ashlin, John**
William Mayne 12:390

**Ashton, Dore**
Octavio Paz 10:392

**Ashton, Thomas L.**
C. P. Snow 4:504

**Asimov, Isaac**
Roy A. Gallant 17:127, 128

**Asinof, Eliot**
Pete Hamill 10:251

**Aspel, Alexander**
Ivar Ivask 14:286

**Aspler, Tony**
William F. Buckley, Jr. 7:36
William Gaddis 8:226
Josef Škvorecký 15:510

**Astrachan, Anthony**
Vladimir Voinovich 10:509

**Atchity, Kenneth John**
Jorge Luis Borges 2:71
James Jones 3:261
Robert Penn Warren 4:581

**Athanason, Arthur N.**
Pavel Kohout 13:326

**Atheling, William, Jr.**
Isaac Asimov 3:17
Arthur C. Clarke 1:58
Harlan Ellison 1:93
Robert A. Heinlein 1:139;
3:227

**Atherton, J. S.**
Anaïs Nin 11:398

**Atherton, Stan**
Margaret Laurence 6:290

**Atkins, Anselm**
Robert Bolt 14:90

**Atkins, John**
L. P. Hartley 2:182

**Atkinson, Brooks**
Sally Benson 17:49
Lorraine Hansberry 17:182
Elmer Rice 7:361

**Atkinson, Michael**
Robert Bly 10:58

**Atlas, Jacoba**
Mel Brooks 12:78
Joni Mitchell 12:436

**Atlas, James**
Samuel Beckett 6:37
Marie-Claire Blais 6:82
J. V. Cunningham 3:122
Alan Dugan 6:144
Paul Goodman 4:198
Mark Harris 19:206
Randall Jarrell 6:261
Galway Kinnell 5:217
W. S. Merwin 5:287
John O'Hara 6:386
Kenneth Rexroth 6:451
Laura Riding 7:375
Delmore Schwartz 4:478
L. E. Sissman 9:490
James Tate 2:431

**Atwell, Lee**
Michelangelo Antonioni 20:39

**Atwood, Margaret**
Ann Beattie 18:38
Marie-Claire Blais 6:80
E. L. Doctorow 18:126
Susan B. Hill 4:227
Erica Jong 6:267
A. G. Mojtabai 5:293
Tillie Olsen 13:432
Marge Piercy 14:420
Sylvia Plath 11:451
A. W. Purdy 14:430
James Reaney 13:472
Adrienne Rich 3:429; 11:478
Audrey Thomas 7:472

**Auchincloss, Eve**
Mavis Gallant 18:171
R. K. Narayan 7:257
Gilbert Rogin 18:457

**Auchincloss, Louis**
Katherine Anne Porter 7:316

**Aucouturier, Michel**
Aleksandr I. Solzhenitsyn 7:432

**Auden, W. H.**
Joseph Brodsky 4:77
Loren Eiseley 7:90
Christopher Isherwood 14:281
Chester Kallman 2:221
J.R.R. Tolkien 1:336; 12:564
Andrei Voznesensky 1:349

**Auriol, Jean-George**
René Clair 20:57

**Auster, Paul**
John Ashbery 6:14
John Hollander 8:300
Laura Riding 7:375
Giuseppe Ungaretti 7:484

**Avant, John Alfred**
Eleanor Bergstein 4:55
Gail Godwin 5:142
Gayl Jones 6:266
José Lezama Lima 4:291
Carson McCullers 12:427
Joyce Carol Oates 6:371, 373
Tillie Olsen 4:386
Patrick White 5:486

**Averill, Deborah**
Frank O'Connor **14**:395

**Avery, Evelyn Gross**
Richard Wright **14**:597

**Axelrod, George**
Gore Vidal **4**:556

**Axelrod, Rise B.**
Anne Sexton **15**:471

**Axelrod, Steven**
Robert Lowell **2**:249

**Axelrod, Steven Gould**
Saul Bellow **6**:60

**Axhelm, Peter M.**
Saul Bellow **13**:66
William Golding **10**:232

**Axthelm, Pete**
Gilbert Rogin **18**:457

**Ayd, Joseph D., S.J.**
Louis Auchincloss **18**:26

**Ayer, A. J.**
Albert Camus **9**:152

**Ayling, Ronald**
Sean O'Casey **11**:409; **15**:405

**Ayo, Nicholas**
Edward Lewis Wallant **10**:515

**Ayre, John**
Austin C. Clarke **8**:143
Mavis Gallant **7**:110
V. S. Naipaul **13**:407
Mordecai Richler **5**:378

**Baar, Ron**
Ezra Pound **1**:276

**Babbitt, Natalie**
William Mayne **12**:395
Katherine Paterson **12**:403, 486
Robert Westall **17**:559

**Babenko, Vickie A.**
Yevgeny Yevtushenko **13**:620

**Bachman, Charles R.**
Sam Shepard **17**:442

**Bachmann, Gideon**
Shirley Clarke **16**:215
Federico Fellini **16**:283
Jean Renoir **20**:290
Luchino Visconti **16**:572

**Backscheider, Nick**
John Updike **5**:452

**Backscheider, Paula**
John Updike **5**:452

**Bacon, Martha**
Walter Farley **17**:118

**Bacon, Terry R.**
Robert Creeley **11**:137

**Baer, Barbara L.**
Harriette Arnow **7**:16
Christina Stead **5**:403

**Bailey, Anthony**
James Baldwin **17**:38

**Bailey, Bruce**
George Ryga **14**:474

**Bailey, James**
Andrei Voznesensky **15**:553

**Bailey, Nancy I.**
Roch Carrier **13**:142

**Bailey, O. L.**
Eric Ambler **6**:2
Dick Francis **2**:142
George V. Higgins **4**:223
Maj Sjöwall **7**:501
Mickey Spillane **3**:469
Per Wahlöö **7**:501

**Bailey, Paul**
James Baldwin **15**:43
Gabriel García Márquez **3**:180
Nadine Gordimer **10**:239
P. D. James **18**:274
Yasunari Kawabata **2**:223
Brian Moore **3**:341
Alberto Moravia **11**:384
James Purdy **2**:351
Philip Roth **3**:437
Muriel Spark **5**:400
David Storey **2**:426
Paul Theroux **11**:531
Gore Vidal **6**:550
Tennessee Williams **7**:544

**Bailey, Peter**
Nikki Giovanni **2**:165
Melvin Van Peebles **2**:447

**Bair, Deirdre**
Samuel Beckett **6**:43

**Baird, James**
Djuna Barnes **8**:49

**Baker, A. T.**
A. R. Ammons **5**:30

**Baker, Carlos**
Truman Capote **19**:79
Ernest Hemingway **6**:234
Jessamyn West **17**:546

**Baker, Charles A.**
Robert Altman **16**:25

**Baker, Donald W.**
Edward Dahlberg **7**:63

**Baker, Houston A., Jr.**
James Baldwin **1**:16
Arna Bontemps **1**:37
Gwendolyn Brooks **15**:92
Sterling Brown **1**:47
W.E.B. Du Bois **1**:80
Ralph Ellison **1**:95; **3**:145
Leon Forrest **4**:163
Langston Hughes **1**:149
LeRoi Jones **1**:163
Ann Petry **1**:266
Ishmael Reed **2**:369; **6**:449
Jean Toomer **1**:341
Richard Wright **1**:380

**Baker, Howard**
Caroline Gordon **6**:206
Katherine Anne Porter **1**:273

**Baker, James R.**
William Golding **3**:200; **17**:169, 175

**Baker, Nina Brown**
Madeleine L'Engle **12**:344

**Baker, Peter**
Lindsay Anderson **20**:12
Vittorio De Sica **20**:89

**Baker, Roger**
Poul Anderson **15**:11
Beryl Bainbridge **4**:39
James Blish **14**:83
John Buell **10**:81
Paula Fox **8**:217
Janet Frame **3**:164
John Hawkes **1**:139
Jerzy Kosinski **1**:172
Alistair MacLean **13**:359
Larry McMurtry **3**:333
Harold Robbins **5**:378
Herman Wouk **9**:580
Rudolph Wurlitzer **2**:483
Helen Yglesias **7**:558

**Baker, Ruth**
Frank B. Gilbreth, Jr. and Ernestine Gilbreth Carey **17**:152

**Baker, William**
William Carlos Williams **13**:606

**Baker, William E.**
Jacques Prévert **15**:437

**Bakerman, Jane S.**
May Sarton **14**:481

**Bakker, J.**
William Gaddis **19**:189

**Bakshy, Alexander**
Frank Capra **16**:153
Charles Chaplin **16**:188
René Clair **20**:57, 58
Rouben Mamoulian **16**:418, 419

**Balakian, Anna**
André Breton **9**:132; **15**:90
René Char **9**:164

**Baldanza, Frank**
Alberto Moravia **2**:293
Iris Murdoch **1**:235
James Purdy **2**:350; **4**:424; **10**:421

**Baldeshwiler, Eileen**
Flannery O'Connor **1**:255

**Balducci, Carolyn**
M. E. Kerr **12**:297

**Baldwin, James**
Alex Haley **8**:259
Norman Mailer **8**:364

**Bales, Kent**
Richard Brautigan **5**:71

**Ballard, J. G.**
Philip K. Dick **10**:138
Harlan Ellison **13**:203
Frederik Pohl **18**:410
Robert Silverberg **7**:425

**Balliett, Whitney**
James Baldwin **17**:44
Ann Beattie **18**:40
Richard Condon **4**:105
Clancy Sigal **7**:424

**Ballif, Gene**
Jorge Luis Borges **6**:87
Vladimir Nabokov **6**:351
Sylvia Plath **11**:449
Alain Robbe-Grillet **6**:464
Nathalie Sarraute **8**:469

**Ballstadt, Carl**
Earle Birney **6**:78

**Balm, Trixie A.**
David Bowie **17**:63

**Bambara, Toni Cade**
Gwendolyn Brooks **2**:81

**Band, Arnold J.**
S. Y. Agnon **14**:2

**Bander, Edward J.**
Jules Archer **12**:16

**Bandler, Michael J.**
Chaim Potok **14**:430
Elie Wiesel **11**:570

**Bangs, Lester**
Chuck Berry **17**:51
David Bowie **17**:63
Mick Jagger and Keith Richard **17**:225, 226, 236
John Lennon and Paul McCartney **12**:381
Bob Marley **17**:270, 271
Joni Mitchell **12**:437
Jim Morrison **17**:289, 290, 292
Jimmy Page and Robert Plant **12**:474, 476
Bruce Springsteen **17**:481
Lily Tomlin **17**:523
Peter Townshend **17**:536
Frank Zappa **17**:586, 587, 591

**Banks, Joyce**
Ruth M. Arthur **12**:28

**Banks, R. Jeff**
Mickey Spillane **13**:527

**Banks, Russell**
Joyce Carol Oates **19**:355

**Bannerman, David**
Allan W. Eckert **17**:104

**Banning, Charles Leslie**
William Gaddis **10**:210

**Barber, Michael**
Simon Raven **14**:443
Gore Vidal **4**:557

**Barber, Raymond W.**
Jean Lee Latham **12**:324

**Barbera, Jack Vincent**
John Berryman **8**:88

**Barbour, Douglas**
Matt Cohen **19**:111
Louis Dudek **11**:160
Gwendolyn MacEwan **13**:358
B. P. Nichol **18**:368
Michael Ondaatje **14**:407

Joe Rosenblatt **15**:446
Rudy Wiebe **6**:566

**Barbour, Joan**
Anne McCaffrey **17**:282

**Barclay, Pat**
Robertson Davies **7**:72

**Bardeche, Maurice**
René Clair **20**:61

**Bargad, Warren**
Amos Oz **8**:436
Abraham B. Yehoshua **13**:617

**Bargainnier, E. F.**
Agatha Christie **12**:126

**Barge, Laura**
Samuel Beckett **10**:34; **11**:39

**Barghoorn, Frederick C.**
Aleksandr I. Solzhenitsyn **4**:508

**Barker, A. L.**
Edna O'Brien **5**:311

**Barker, Frank Granville**
Margaret Drabble **10**:163
J. B. Priestley **9**:442

**Barker, George**
Brian Aldiss **5**:14

**Barksdale, Richard K.**
Gwendolyn Brooks **5**:75
Langston Hughes **15**:294

**Barnard, Caroline King**
Sylvia Plath **17**:361

**Barnes, Clive**
John Bishop **10**:54
Alice Childress **12**:104, 105
Lawrence Ferlinghetti **2**:134
Jack Gelber **14**:193
Simon Gray **9**:240
Lorraine Hansberry **17**:191
Jack Heifner **11**:264
Arthur Kopit **1**:170
Richard O'Brien **17**:322
Gerome Ragni and James Rado
    **17**:378, 380, 383, 386, 387
Anthony Shaffer **19**:413
Sam Shepard **17**:436, 437, 438,
    441
Tom Stoppard **1**:328
Elizabeth Swados **12**:556
Lily Tomlin **17**:517
Michael Weller **10**:525
Lanford Wilson **7**:547

**Barnes, Harper**
James Tate **2**:431

**Barnes, Julian**
Richard Brautigan **5**:72; **9**:124
Vincent Canby **13**:131
Agatha Christie **12**:120
James Clavell **6**:114
Len Deighton **7**:76
B. S. Johnson **6**:264
Pamela Hansford Johnson **7**:184
G. Josipovici **6**:270
Richard Llewellyn **7**:207
Alistair MacLean **13**:359
Vladimir Nabokov **6**:359
Joyce Carol Oates **9**:402

Richard Price **12**:490

**Barnes, Peter**
John Huston **20**:162

**Barnes, Regina**
James T. Farrell **4**:158
Geoffrey Household **11**:277

**Barnouw, Dagmar**
Elias Canetti **14**:120
Doris Lessing **6**:295

**Barnstone, William**
Jorge Luis Borges **6**:93

**Barnstone, Willis**
Jorge Luis Borges **9**:120

**Baro, Gene**
Carolyn Kizer **15**:308
Henri de Montherlant **19**:324
Auberon Waugh **7**:512

**Barolini, Helen**
Lucio Piccolo **13**:441

**Baron, Alexander**
Bernard Malamud **2**:268

**Barr, Alan P.**
Akira Kurosawa **16**:405

**Barr, Donald**
Mary Renault **17**:392
George Tabori **19**:435

**Barrenechea, Ana María**
Jorge Luis Borges **1**:38

**Barrett, Gerald**
Jerzy Kosinski **10**:305

**Barrett, William**
Samuel Beckett **2**:48
Albert Camus **2**:99
Arthur C. Clarke **4**:105
William Faulkner **3**:154
William Golding **17**:168
Ernest Hemingway **3**:238
Hermann Hesse **2**:191
Fletcher Knebel **14**:308
Alain Robbe-Grillet **2**:377
Françoise Sagan **17**:423
Leon Uris **7**:491

**Barrow, Craig Wallace**
Madeleine L'Engle **12**:351

**Barrow, Geoffrey R.**
Blas de Otero **11**:425

**Barry, Iris**
Fritz Lang **20**:200, 201

**Barry, John Brooks**
T. S. Eliot **6**:165

**Barry, Kevin**
John Berryman **6**:65

**Barsam, Richard Meran**
Leni Riefenstahl **16**:522

**Barthelme, Donald**
Werner Herzog **16**:334

**Barthes, Roland**
Raymond Queneau **5**:357

**Bartholomay, Julia A.**
Howard Nemerov **6**:360

**Bartholomew, David**
Larry McMurtry **11**:371
Lina Wertmüller **16**:597

**Bartkowech, R.**
Alain Robbe-Grillet **14**:462

**Barzun, Jaques**
Lionel Trilling **11**:539

**Bassoff, Bruce**
William H. Gass **8**:244

**Batchelor, John Calvin**
Ann Beattie **18**:39
William Golding **17**:179
Mark Helprin **10**:262
Joyce Carol Oates **19**:355
Walker Percy **18**:400
Peter Rushforth **19**:407

**Batchelor, R.**
André Malraux **9**:353

**Bates, Evaline**
Ezra Pound **3**:397

**Bates, Gladys Graham**
Sally Benson **17**:48

**Bates, Graham**
Pär Lagerkvist **7**:198

**Bates, Lewis**
E. M. Almedingen **12**:2

**Bateson, F. W.**
W. H. Auden **6**:24
John Gardner **2**:151

**Bati, Anwer**
Ken Russell **16**:551

**Battcock, Gregory**
Andy Warhol **20**:415

**Bauer, Arnold**
Carl Zuckmayer **18**:555

**Bauer, William**
John Buell **10**:82

**Bauke, J. P.**
Jakov Lind **4**:292

**Baum, Alwin L.**
Alain Robbe-Grillet **14**:458

**Baum, Betty**
Robert Westall **17**:556

**Baumann, Michael L.**
B. Traven **8**:520; **11**:535, 537

**Baumbach, Elinor**
Sylvia Ashton-Warner **19**:22

**Baumbach, Jonathan**
Robert Bresson **16**:117
Truman Capote **8**:132
Ralph Ellison **1**:95
John Hawkes **4**:212
Stanley Kubrick **16**:377
Norman Mailer **4**:318
Bernard Malamud **1**:197, 199
Mary McCarthy **5**:275
Wright Morris **1**:232
Flannery O'Connor **1**:256
Grace Paley **6**:393
J. D. Salinger **1**:299
William Styron **1**:330

**Peter Taylor 1**:333
Edward Lewis Wallant **10**:511
Robert Penn Warren **1**:355

**Baumgarten, Murray**
Jorge Luis Borges **19**:52

**Baxter, Charles**
J. R. Salamanca **15**:464

**Baxter, John**
John Ford **16**:312
Josef von Sternberg **20**:375

**Baxter, Ralph C.**
Allan W. Eckert **17**:104

**Bayley, John**
Anna Akhmatova **11**:9
W. H. Auden **2**:27, 28
Anthony Burgess **4**:85
D. J. Enright **8**:203
Robert Lowell **4**:296
Amos Oz **11**:428
Vasko Popa **19**:375
Anthony Powell **10**:417
Varlam Shalamov **18**:479
Aleksandr I. Solzhenitsyn
    **4**:511; **7**:444; **10**:479; **18**:499
Alexander Zinoviev **19**:486

**Bazarov, Konstantin**
Ivo Andrić **8**:20
Heinrich Böll **3**:76
James A. Michener **1**:214
Aleksandr I. Solzhenitsyn
    **2**:411; **10**:483

**Bazelon, David T.**
Dashiell Hammett **19**:193

**Bazin, André**
Robert Bresson **16**:111
Luis Buñuel **16**:131
Charles Chaplin **16**:200
Orson Welles **20**:435

**Bazzdlo, Gretchen**
Lee Kingman **17**:246

**Beacham, Walton**
Erskine Caldwell **8**:124
Paul West **14**:568

**Beagle, Peter S.**
J.R.R. Tolkien **12**:567

**Bean, Robin**
Bob Fosse **20**:121
Pier Paolo Pasolini **20**:258, 259
Carlos Saura **20**:313

**Beards, Virginia K.**
Margaret Drabble **3**:128

**Beatie, Bruce A.**
J.R.R. Tolkien **3**:477

**Beattie, Munro**
Daryl Hine **15**:282
Irving Layton **15**:323
Dorothy Livesay **15**:341
A.J.M. Smith **15**:516

**Beatty, Jack**
Ann Beattie **18**:39
George V. Higgins **18**:235
William Maxwell **19**:308
Alice Munro **19**:346
V. S. Naipaul **18**:362

CRITIC INDEX

Paul Theroux 15:534

**Beatty, Jerome, Jr.**
Larry Kettelkamp 12:305

**Beatty, Richmond C.**
Donald Davidson 13:166

**Beauchamp, Gorman**
E. M. Forster 10:183

**Beauchamp, William**
Elizabeth Taylor 4:541

**Beaufort, John**
Martin Sherman 19:416
Elizabeth Swados 12:560
Tennessee Williams 19:473

**Beauman, Sally**
Julia O'Faolain 19:359

**Beauvoir, Simone de**
Henri de Montherlant 19:322

**Beaver, Harold**
William S. Burroughs 15:112
Allen Ginsburg 13:241
Joyce Carol Oates 11:404

**Bechtel, Louise S.**
Margot Benary-Isbert 12:31, 32
Walter Farley 17:117
Henry Gregor Felsen 17:121, 122
Mary Stolz 12:546
John R. Tunis 12:596
Lenora Mattingly Weber 12:632

**Beck, Marilyn**
Rod McKuen 1:210

**Beck, Richard**
Frans Eemil Sillanpää 19:417

**Beck, Warren**
William Faulkner 11:197; 14:171

**Becker, George J.**
John Dos Passos 15:183
Upton Sinclair 15:500

**Becker, Lucille Frackman**
Louis Aragon 3:14
Michel Butor 11:80
Henri de Montherlant 19:325
Georges Simenon 2:398, 399; 8:488; 18:481

**Becker, May Lamberton**
Betty Cavanna 12:97, 98
Maureen Daly 17:88
Walter Farley 17:115
Henry Gregor Felsen 17:119
Esther Forbes 12:207
Jesse Jackson 12:289
John R. Tunis 12:594, 595
Lenora Mattingly Weber 12:631, 632

**Beckett, Samuel**
Sean O'Casey 11:405

**Beckham, Barry**
Piri Thomas 17:499

**Bedford, William**
Robert Lowell 15:342
Eugenio Montale 18:342

**Bedient, Calvin**
A. R. Ammons 8:13
John Ashbery 15:29
W. H. Auden 2:27
Samuel Beckett 1:24
Leonard Cohen 3:110
Edward Dahlberg 7:67
Donald Davie 10:120
Richard Eberhart 11:178
T. S. Eliot 13:196
Louise Glück 7:119
John Hawkes 4:215
Anthony Hecht 19:209
Joseph Heller 5:178
Geoffrey Hill 5:184
Daniel Hoffman 6:243
Ted Hughes 2:202; 4:235
David Ignatow 7:182
Donald Justice 19:236
Thomas Kinsella 4:271; 19:256
Philip Larkin 5:228
Robert Lowell 3:303
George MacBeth 5:264
James Merrill 8:381
Joyce Carol Oates 2:314; 3:362
Octavio Paz 4:398
Sylvia Plath 14:426
Jon Silkin 6:498
Mark Strand 18:520
R. S. Thomas 6:532
Charles Tomlinson 4:545, 547
Mona Van Duy 7:499
Robert Penn Warren 10:523; 18:534, 538
John Hall Wheelock 14:571
Richard Wilbur 9:568
James Wright 5:520

**Beer, Patricia**
W. H. Auden 6:19
Beryl Bainbridge 18:33
Christopher Fry 14:188
Seamus Heaney 14:241
Eleanor Hibbert 7:156
Lisel Mueller 13:400
Alice Munro 10:357
Peter Redgrove 6:447

**Beerman, Hans**
Hermann Hesse 17:199

**Beesley, Paddy**
Horst Bienek 11:48

**Begley, John**
Oriana Fallaci 11:191

**Behar, Jack**
T. S. Eliot 13:198

**Beichman, Arnold**
Arthur Koestler 1:170
Anthony Powell 3:400

**Beja, Morris**
Lawrence Durrell 4:145
William Faulkner 3:153
Nathalie Sarraute 4:466

**Belgion, Montgomery**
André Malraux 4:334

**Belitt, Ben**
Jorge Luis Borges 2:75
Robert Lowell 4:297
Pablo Neruda 1:247

**Belkind, Allen**
Ishmael Reed 13:480

**Bell, Anthea**
Otfried Preussler 17:377

**Bell, Bernard**
William Styron 3:473

**Bell, Bernard W.**
Jean Toomer 4:550

**Bell, David**
Joyce Carol Oates 19:356

**Bell, Gene H.**
Jorge Luis Borges 9:118
Alejo Carpentier 8:135
Vladimir Nabokov 6:360

**Bell, Ian F. A.**
Ezra Pound 10:404

**Bell, Lisle**
Frank B. Gilbreth, Jr. and Ernestine Gilbreth Carey 17:152

**Bell, Millicent**
Margaret Atwood 2:19
Peter De Vries 2:113
Eugenio Montale 7:231
John O'Hara 2:325

**Bell, Pearl K.**
Martin Amis 4:20
John Ashbery 6:12
Beryl Bainbridge 4:39
James Baldwin 4:40; 15:42
Ann Beattie 18:40
Saul Bellow 8:70
Marie-Claire Blais 6:81
Louise Bogan 4:69
William F. Buckley, Jr. 7:35
John Cheever 15:130
Eleanor Clark 5:106
Arthur A. Cohen 7:51
Len Deighton 7:76
William Faulkner 6:177
Paula Fox 2:140
Nadine Gordimer 5:146
Juan Goytisolo 5:149
Günter Grass 4:206
Graham Greene 3:214
Joseph Heller 5:180
George V. Higgins 7:157
Maureen Howard 5:189
John Irving 13:293
Ruth Prawer Jhabvala 8:311
Charles Johnson 7:183
Diane Johnson 5:199
Uwe Johnson 10:284
James Jones 10:291
Milan Kundera 4:277; 19:270
Philip Larkin 13:337
John Le Carré 5:232
Alison Lurie 4:307
Bernard Malamud 18:321
Peter Matthiessen 5:275
Mary McCarthy 14:360
John McGahern 5:281
A. G. Mojtabai 9:385
V. S. Naipaul 7:254
Amos Oz 5:335
Cynthia Ozick 7:288
Walker Percy 8:438
Marge Piercy 18:409

Anthony Powell 3:403
J. F. Powers 8:447
Ishmael Reed 6:448
Adrienne Rich 6:459
Jill Robinson 10:439
Philip Roth 15:455
J. R. Salamanca 15:463
Anne Sexton 6:494
Alix Kates Shulman 10:475
Stephen Spender 5:402
Mario Vargas Llosa 6:546
Patrick White 3:523

**Bell, Robert**
Honor Arundel 17:12
Robert Cormier 12:137
Eilís Dillon 17:95, 96
Madeleine L'Engle 12:350
William Mayne 12:390, 399
Robert Westall 17:555, 557

**Bell, Vereen M.**
E. M. Forster 1:107
Ted Hughes 9:281
Richard F. Hugo 18:260

**Bellamy, Joe David**
Donald Barthelme 13:60
Sam Shepard 4:490
Kurt Vonnegut, Jr. 4:564

**Bellman, Samuel Irving**
Saul Bellow 8:81
Jorge Luis Borges 6:91
Jerome Charyn 5:103
Leonard Cohen 3:109
Stanley Elkin 6:169
William Faulkner 3:152
Leslie A. Fiedler 4:160, 161
Bruce Jay Friedman 3:165
William H. Gass 15:258
Ernest Hemingway 3:234
Yoram Kaniuk 19:239
Jack Kerouac 3:263, 264
Meyer Levin 7:205
Bernard Malamud 1:197; 3:320, 325
Saul Maloff 5:271
Wallace Markfield 8:380
James A. Michener 5:288
Harry Mark Petrakis 3:382
Philip Roth 3:435
John Updike 3:487
Elie Wiesel 5:490

**Bellow, Saul**
Camilo José Cela 13:144
Ilya Ehrenburg 18:131

**Bellows, Silence Buck**
Frank B. Gilbreth, Jr. and Ernestine Gilbreth Carey 17:155
Zilpha Keatley Snyder 17:471

**Bell-Villada, Gene H.**
Gabriel García Márquez 15:254

**Beloff, Max**
Paul Scott 9:477

**Beloof, Robert**
Stanley J. Kunitz 6:285
Marianne Moore 4:360

**Belton, John**
Claude Chabrol 16:177

**CRITIC INDEX**

**Benchley, Nathaniel**
Robert Newton Peck 17:337

**Bendau, Clifford P.**
Colin Wilson 14:585

**Bender, Marylin**
Alix Kates Shulman 2:395

**Bender, Rose S.**
Babbis Friis-Baastad 12:214

**Bendiner, Elmer**
Piri Thomas 17:498

**Bendow, Burton**
Grace Paley 4:393

**Benedikt, Michael**
David Ignatow 14:276
Galway Kinnell 2:230
Richard Wilbur 3:532

**Benestad, Janet P.**
M. E. Kerr 12:300

**Benét, William Rose**
Agatha Christie 12:111
Robert Francis 15:235

**Benham, G. F.**
Friedrich Dürrenmatt 11:174

**Benjamin, Cynthia**
Madeleine L'Engle 12:351

**Benn, M. B.**
Michael Hamburger 14:234

**Bennett, Joseph**
Anthony Hecht 8:266

**Bennett, Spencer C.**
John Lennon and Paul
McCartney 12:365

**Bennett, Virginia**
Truman Capote 19:80

**Benson, Gerard**
Leon Garfield 12:229

**Benson, Jackson J.**
Ernest Hemingway 6:232
John Steinbeck 9:517

**Benson, Mary**
Athol Fugard 14:189

**Benson, Sheila**
Jerzy Skolimowski 20:355

**Benstock, Bernard**
William Gaddis 3:177
Flann O'Brien 7:270
Sean O'Casey 5:317

**Benston, Alice N.**
W. S. Merwin 2:276

**Bentley, Allen**
Morris L. West 6:564

**Bentley, Eric**
Sally Benson 17:50
Truman Capote 19:81
Charles Chaplin 16:205
Robert Penn Warren 8:536
Orson Welles 20:434
Herman Wouk 9:579

**Bentley, Joseph**
Aldous Huxley 1:152

**Bentley, Phyllis**
Pearl S. Buck 11:69

**Benton, Michael**
Alan Garner 17:146

**Berendt, John**
Phil Ochs 17:333

**Berets, Ralph**
Saul Bellow 15:47
John Fowles 3:163

**Berger, Arthur Asa**
Robert Crumb 17:85
Stan Lee 17:257
Charles M. Schulz 12:529

**Berger, Charles**
Olga Broumas 10:77
James Merrill 18:331
Frederick Seidel 18:474

**Berger, Harold L.**
Frank Herbert 12:278

**Berger, John**
Lindsay Anderson 20:11

**Bergin, Thomas G.**
Aldo Palazzeschi 11:432
Lucio Piccolo 13:440
Salvatore Quasimodo 10:429

**Bergman, Andrew**
Frank Capra 16:159
Isaac Bashevis Singer 11:499

**Bergman, Andrew C. J.**
Peter Benchley 4:53
Guy Davenport, Jr. 6:124

**Bergmann, Linda Shell**
Ishmael Reed 13:479
Ronald Sukenick 4:531

**Bergonzi, Bernard**
Kingsley Amis 2:6, 9
W. H. Auden 6:22
John Barth 3:39
Paul Bowles 2:79
Anthony Burgess 2:85
Donald Davie 10:123
Nigel Dennis 8:173
Ilya Ehrenburg 18:135
Richard Fariña 9:195
John Fowles 2:138
Paula Fox 2:139
B. S. Johnson 6:262
Doris Lessing 3:283
William Maxwell 19:307
Iris Murdoch 2:297
Flann O'Brien 4:383
Anthony Powell 3:400
Thomas Pynchon 3:408
Alain Robbe-Grillet 4:447
Andrew Sinclair 2:401
C. P. Snow 4:501; 13:508
Evelyn Waugh 1:357; 3:510
Angus Wilson 2:473

**Berkson, Bill**
Frank O'Hara 2:320
Jerome Rothenberg 6:477

**Berkvist, Margaret**
Babbis Friis-Baastad 12:213

**Berkvist, Robert**
Allan W. Eckert 17:105
Earl Hamner, Jr. 12:258
Andre Norton 12:456, 457
Mary Rodgers 12:493

**Berlin, Isaiah**
Aldous Huxley 3:254

**Berlin, Normand**
Roman Polanski 16:469

**Berman, Bruce**
Rainer Werner Fassbinder
20:105

**Berman, Michael**
Milan Kundera 19:267

**Berman, Neil**
Robert Coover 15:143

**Berman, Paul**
Isaac Bashevis Singer 11:501

**Berman, Ronald**
William F. Buckley, Jr. 18:81

**Berman, Susan K.**
Fredrica Wagman 7:500

**Bermel, Albert**
Ed Bullins 1:47
Jean Genet 10:227
Christopher Hampton 4:211
Megan Terry 19:439

**Bermel, Joyce**
Hilma Wolitzer 17:562

**Bernays, Anne**
Alice Adams 6:1
Adrienne Rich 11:474

**Berner, Robert L.**
André Brink 18:68
Alan Paton 10:388

**Bernetta (Quinn), Sister Mary,
O.S.F.**
Allen Tate 4:539
See also Quinn, Sister Mary
Bernetta, O.S.F.

**Bernhardt, William**
François Truffaut 20:380

**Bernikow, Louise**
A. S. Byatt 19:77
Muriel Rukeyser 6:479

**Berns, Walter**
Daniel J. Berrigan 4:57

**Bernstein, Burton**
George P. Elliott 2:131

**Berrigan, Daniel**
Horst Bienek 7:28
Thomas Merton 11:373

**Berry, Mabel**
Maureen Daly 17:91

**Berry, Wendell**
Hayden Carruth 4:94

**Berryman, John**
Saul Bellow 10:37
T. S. Eliot 13:197
Ernest Hemingway 10:270
Randall Jarrell 13:299
Ezra Pound 13:460

**Bersani, Leo**
Julio Cortázar 2:104
Jean Genet 2:158
Norman Mailer 8:364
Henri de Montherlant 19:328
Alain Robbe-Grillet 1:288
Robert Wilson 7:551

**Berthoff, Warner**
Alex Haley 12:245
Norman Mailer 3:313
Iris Murdoch 3:345
Vladimir Nabokov 3:352
Muriel Spark 3:464
Edmund Wilson 2:475; 3:538

**Bespaloff, Rachel**
Albert Camus 9:139

**Bessai, Diane**
Austin C. Clarke 8:142

**Besser, Gretchen R.**
Julien Green 3:205

**Bessie, Alvah**
Norman Mailer 3:319

**Bester, Alfred**
Isaac Asimov 3:16
Robert A. Heinlein 3:227

**Bester, John**
Kenzaburō Ōe 10:372

**Beston, John B.**
Patrick White 18:544

**Bethell, Nicholas**
Aleksandr I. Solzhenitsyn 7:441

**Betsky, Celia B.**
A. Alvarez 5:19
Max Apple 9:32
Harriette Arnow 7:15
Don DeLillo 10:135
Margaret Drabble 2:119
John Hawkes 4:217
Doris Lessing 10:315
Iris Murdoch 4:370
Tim O'Brien 19:358
Marge Piercy 14:419

**Bettelheim, Bruno**
Lina Wertmüller 16:599

**Bevan, A. R.**
Mordecai Richler 5:377

**Bevan, David G.**
Pier Paolo Pasolini 20:268

**Bevan, Jack**
Arthur Gregor 9:253

**Bevington, Helen**
Louis Simpson 4:500

**Bewick, Elizabeth**
Josephine Poole 17:371

**Bewley, Marius**
A. R. Ammons 2:11
John Berryman 2:56
C. Day Lewis 6:128
Thomas Kinsella 4:270
Hugh MacDiarmid 2:253
Sylvia Plath 2:335
Herbert Read 4:440
Charles Tomlinson 2:436

**Bezanker, Abraham**
Saul Bellow 1:32
Isaac Bashevis Singer 3:454

**Bianco, David**
James Purdy 10:426

**Biasin, Gian-Paolo**
Carlo Emilio Gadda 11:211
Leonardo Sciascia 8:473

**Bick, Janice**
Christie Harris 12:269

**Bickerton, Dorothy**
Melvin Berger 12:41

**Bidart, Frank**
Robert Lowell 9:336

**Bien, Peter**
Yannis Ritsos 6:462

**Bienstock, Beverly Gray**
John Barth 3:41

**Bier, Jesse**
James Thurber 5:434

**Bierhaus, E. G., Jr.**
John Osborne 11:423

**Bigger, Charles P.**
Walker Percy 8:440

**Bigsby, C.W.E.**
Edward Albee 9:6, 9; 13:4
James Baldwin 13:51; 17:33
Imamu Amiri Baraka 14:43
Lorraine Hansberry 17:185
Arthur Miller 10:342
Willard Motley 18:357

**Bilan, R. P.**
Rudy Wiebe 14:574

**Billman, Carol W.**
Arthur Kopit 18:290

**Binding, Paul**
Jurek Becker 19:36
Rolf Hochhuth 18:256
Brian Moore 19:334

**Binham, Philip**
Paavo Haavikko 18:207, 208
Hannu Salama 18:460

**Binns, Ronald**
John Fowles 4:171

**Binyon, T. J.**
Eric Ambler 9:21
Peter Dickinson 12:175, 176

**Birbalsingh, F. M.**
Mordecai Richler 13:485

**Bird, Christopher**
Colin Wilson 14:584

**Birkerts, Sven**
Blaise Cendrars 18:97

**Birmingham, Mary Louise**
Jesse Jackson 12:289

**Birnbaum, Larry**
Frank Zappa 17:595

**Birnbaum, Milton**
Aldous Huxley 3:255; 4:239

**Birney, Earle**
A.J.M. Smith 15:513

**Birrell, Francis**
René Clair 20:59
Rouben Mamoulian 16:420

**Birstein, Ann**
Iris Murdoch 4:370
Sylvia Plath 17:352

**Bishop, Christopher**
Buster Keaton 20:189

**Bishop, Claire Huchet**
Joseph Krumgold 12:316

**Bishop, Elizabeth**
Flannery O'Connor 15:408

**Bishop, Ferman**
Allen Tate 2:428

**Bishop, John Peale**
E. E. Cummings 12:142

**Bishop, Lloyd**
Henri Michaux 8:390

**Bishop, Tom**
Jean Cocteau 8:145
Julio Cortázar 2:103
Raymond Queneau 5:359
Claude Simon 9:482

**Biskind, Peter**
Elia Kazan 16:371
Sam Peckinpah 20:278
Lina Wertmüller 16:588

**Bissell, Claude T.**
Hugh Garner 13:234

**Bissett, Donald J.**
Colin Thiele 17:493

**Black, Campbell**
Mary Renault 17:400
Isaac Bashevis Singer 6:507

**Black, Cyril E.**
André Malraux 1:203

**Blackburn, Sara**
R. V. Cassill 4:95
Peter Dickinson 12:169
Rosalyn Drexler 2:120
Jim Harrison 6:225
Maxine Hong Kingston 12:313
Alan Lelchuk 5:244
David Madden 5:266
Michael McClure 6:316
Toni Morrison 4:365
Marge Piercy 3:384
Alix Kates Shulman 2:395
Gillian Tindall 7:473
David Wagoner 5:474
Fay Weldon 6:562

**Blackburn, Thomas**
Sylvia Plath 17:344

**Blackburn, Tom**
Kingsley Amis 2:6

**Blackman, Ruth**
Sylvia Ashton-Warner 19:20

**Blackmur, R(ichard) P.**
E. E. Cummings 8:154; 12:140
Archibald MacLeish 14:336
Marianne Moore 13:393
John Crowe Ransom 5:363
Allen Tate 4:536

**Blackwood, Caroline**
Ingmar Bergman 16:49

**Blades, Joe**
Bob Fosse 20:123

**Blaha, Franz G.**
J. P. Donleavy 4:125

**Blair, Karin**
Gene Roddenberry 17:408, 411

**Blais, Marie-Claire**
Elizabeth Bishop 13:88

**Blake, George**
John Cowper Powys 9:439

**Blake, Nicholas**
Margery Allingham 19:12
Agatha Christie 12:113

**Blake, Patricia**
Aleksandr I. Solzhenitsyn
1:319; 7:439
Andrei Voznesensky 1:349

**Blake, Percival**
Leonardo Sciascia 8:474

**Blake, Richard A.**
Norman Lear 12:331
George Lucas 16:411

**Blakeston, Oswell**
Michael Ayrton 7:19
Gabriel García Márquez 3:180
Paul Theroux 15:535
P. G. Wodehouse 2:480

**Blamires, David**
David Jones 2:216, 217; 4:260;
13:308

**Blanford, S. L.**
Honor Arundel 17:13

**Blaser, Robin**
Jack Spicer 18:506

**Blassingame, Wyatt**
Harriette Arnow 7:15

**Blaydes, Sophia B.**
Simon Gray 9:242

**Blazek, Douglas**
Robert Creeley 2:107
W. S. Merwin 5:286
Diane Wakoski 4:573

**Bleikasten, André**
Flannery O'Connor 10:366

**Blindheim, Joan Tindale**
John Arden 13:26

**Blish, James**
Poul Anderson 15:11
John Brunner 10:77

**Blishen, Edward**
Alan Garner 17:150
William Mayne 12:391, 394

**Bliss, Shepherd**
Frederick Wiseman 20:477

**Bliven, Naomi**
Louis-Ferdinand Céline 4:103
Agatha Christie 12:125
Andrea Giovene 7:117
Eugène Ionesco 6:257
Anthony Powell 7:343
Emlyn Williams 15:578

**Bloch, Adèle**
Michel Butor 8:120
Pär Lagerkvist 7:200

**Blodgett, E. D.**
D. G. Jones 10:285
Sylvia Plath 3:388

**Blodgett, Harriet**
V. S. Naipaul 4:375

**Blomster, W. V.**
Christa Wolf 14:594

**Błonski, Jan**
Czesław Miłosz 11:377

**Bloom, Harold**
A. R. Ammons 5:25; 8:14; 9:26
John Ashbery 4:23; 9:41; 13:30;
15:26, 33
W. H. Auden 6:16
Saul Bellow 6:50
Jorge Luis Borges 6:87
James Dickey 10:141
Allen Ginsberg 6:199
Anthony Hecht 13:269
Daryl Hine 15:282
John Hollander 8:301, 302;
14:264
Philip Levine 9:332
Robert Lowell 8:355
Archibald MacLeish 8:363
James Merrill 8:388
Howard Moss 7:249; 14:375
Robert Pack 13:439
W. D. Snodgrass 10:478
Mark Strand 18:517
Robert Penn Warren 8:539;
18:535
Charles Wright 13:614

**Bloom, J. Don**
Alvin Silverstein and Virginia
B. Silverstein 17:454

**Bloom, Robert**
W. H. Auden 1:10; 11:13

**Blotner, Joseph L.**
J. D. Salinger 1:295

**Blow, Simon**
Julia O'Faolain 19:360
Sylvia Plath 11:451
Isaac Bashevis Singer 6:510

**Blue, Adrianne**
Buchi Emecheta 14:160

**Bluefarb, Sam**
Leslie A. Fiedler 13:213
Bernard Malamud 1:196; 9:350
John Steinbeck 5:407
Richard Wright 3:546

**Bluestein, Gene**
Bob Dylan 12:189
Richard Fariña 9:195

CRITIC INDEX

**Bluestone, George**
Nelson Algren 10:5

**Blum, David**
Peter Handke 15:268

**Blum, Morgan**
Peter Taylor 18:522

**Blumenberg, Richard M.**
Alain Resnais 16:510

**Blumenfeld, Yorick**
John Berger 19:37
Yevgeny Yevtushenko 1:382

**Blundell, Jane Boyarin**
Maya Angelou 12:14

**Bly, Robert**
A. R. Ammons 5:28
Carlos Castaneda 12:94
David Ignatow 14:274
Robert Lowell 4:297
Francis Ponge 18:419

**Blythe, Ronald**
William Golding 17:178
Erica Jong 6:267
Alice Munro 6:341
Joyce Carol Oates 6:368
Jean Rhys 19:391
David Storey 8:506

**Boak, Denis**
André Malraux 4:330

**Boardman, Gwenn R.**
Yasunari Kawabata 2:222
Yukio Mishima 2:286

**Boatwright, James**
Paul Horgan 9:278
James McCourt 5:278
Gore Vidal 6:549
Robert Penn Warren 1:356

**Boatwright, John**
Walker Percy 8:438

**Boatwright, Taliaferro**
Emily Cheney Neville 12:450

**Bobbie, Walter**
Stephen King 12:309

**Bobbitt, Joan**
James Dickey 15:173

**Bochner, Jay**
Blaise Cendrars 18:93

**Bodart, Joni**
Frank Herbert 12:272
Rosemary Wells 12:638

**Bode, Carl**
Katherine Anne Porter 7:318

**Bodo, Maureen**
Gore Vidal 10:504

**Boe, Eugene**
Christina Stead 2:421

**Boeth, Richard**
John O'Hara 2:324

**Bogan, Louise**
W. H. Auden 1:9
Richard Eberhart 19:140
Barbara Howes 15:289
Marianne Moore 13:396; 19:338
W. R. Rodgers 7:377

Muriel Rukeyser 15:456
Frederick Seidel 18:474

**Bogart, Gary**
Robert Newton Peck 17:340

**Bogdanovich, Peter**
Alfred Hitchcock 16:343

**Bohn, Chris**
Bob Marley 17:272

**Bohner, Charles H.**
Robert Penn Warren 1:354

**Bok, Sissela**
Vladimir Nabokov 1:245

**Boland, John**
Brian Aldiss 5:15
John Dickson Carr 3:101
Richard Condon 4:106
Harry Kemelman 2:225
Michael Moorcock 5:293

**Bold, Alan**
Robert Graves 1:130

**Boles, Paul Darcy**
Truman Capote 19:81

**Bolger, Eugenie**
Hortense Calisher 8:125
José Donoso 4:130

**Bollard, Margaret Lloyd**
William Carlos Williams 9:571

**Bolling, Douglass**
E. M. Forster 9:206
Doris Lessing 3:290
Clarence Major 19:296
Rudolph Wurlitzer 4:598; 15:588
Al Young 19:478

**Bolton, Richard R.**
Herman Wouk 9:580

**Bond, Kirk**
Carl Theodor Dreyer 16:260

**Bondy, François**
Günter Grass 2:173

**Bone, Robert A.**
James Baldwin 1:15; 17:29
Arna Bontemps 1:37
W.E.B. Du Bois 1:80
Ralph Ellison 1:95; 3:142
Jessie Redmon Fauset 19:170
Langston Hughes 1:147
Zora Neale Hurston 7:171
Willard Motley 18:357
Ann Petry 1:266
Jean Toomer 1:341
Richard Wright 1:378
Frank G. Yerby 1:381

**Bongiorno, Robert**
Carlo Emilio Gadda 11:209

**Boni, John**
Kurt Vonnegut, Jr. 5:465

**Boniol, John Dawson, Jr.**
Melvin Berger 12:40, 41

**Bontemps, Arna**
Ann Petry 18:403
Jean Toomer 13:551

**Booth, Martin**
Ted Hughes 14:272
John Matthias 9:361
Gilbert Sorrentino 14:500

**Booth, Philip**
Hayden Carruth 18:87
Richard Eberhart 11:176; 19:140
Randall Jarrell 1:159
Maxine Kumin 13:327
Mary Oliver 19:361
Louis Simpson 7:426

**Booth, Wayne C.**
Hunter S. Thompson 17:507

**Borden, Diane M.**
Ingmar Bergman 16:78

**Bordwell, David**
Charles Chaplin 16:199
François Truffaut 20:389
Orson Welles 20:445

**Borg, Mary**
Françoise Sagan 17:426

**Borges, Jorge Luis**
Adolfo Bioy Casares 4:63
Orson Welles 20:453

**Boring, Phyllis Zatlin**
Miguel Delibes 18:117

**Borinsky, Alicia**
Manuel Puig 5:355

**Borkat, Robert F. Sarfatt**
Robert Frost 9:222

**Boroff, David A.**
John A. Williams 13:598

**Borroff, Marie**
John Hollander 2:197
Denise Levertov 2:243
William Meredith 4:348
James Merrill 2:274

**Borrus, Bruce J.**
Saul Bellow 15:57

**Bosley, Keith**
Eugenio Montale 7:229

**Bosmajian, Hamida**
Louis-Ferdinand Céline 3:103

**Boston, Howard**
Eilís Dillon 17:93, 94
Jean Lee Latham 12:323

**Bosworth, David**
Kurt Vonnegut, Jr. 12:629

**Boucher, Anthony**
Margery Allingham 19:13
Agatha Christie 12:115, 116, 117
John Creasey 11:134
C. Day Lewis 6:128
Jan de Hartog 19:131
Eilís Dillon 17:95
Patricia Highsmith 2:193
P. D. James 18:272
Harry Kemelman 2:225
Mary Lee Settle 19:409
Anthony Shaffer 19:413
Mary Stewart 7:467

Julian Symons 2:426; 14:523

**Bouise, Oscar A.**
Allan W. Eckert 17:103
Eleanor Hibbert 7:155
Per Wahlöö 7:501

**Boulby, Mark**
Hermann Hesse 11:272; 17:207

**Boulton, James T.**
Harold Pinter 6:406

**Bouraoui, H. A.**
Nathalie Sarraute 2:385

**Bourdillon, Jennifer**
Otfried Preussler 17:374

**Bourjaily, Vance**
Kay Boyle 19:66
Roald Dahl 18:109
Jim Harrison 14:235
Philip Roth 9:460
John Sayles 14:483
George Tabori 19:436

**Bourne, Mike**
Jimmy Page and Robert Plant 12:476
Frank Zappa 17:588

**Bourneuf, Roland**
Hubert Aquin 15:17

**Boutelle, Ann E.**
Hugh MacDiarmid 2:253

**Boutrous, Lawrence K.**
John Hawkes 3:223

**Bowe, Clotilde Soave**
Natalia Ginzburg 11:228

**Bowen, Barbara C.**
P. G. Wodehouse 10:538

**Bowen, Elizabeth**
Henri de Montherlant 19:322

**Bowen, John**
Arthur Kopit 1:171

**Bowen, Roger**
Philip Larkin 18:297

**Bowering, George**
Milton Acorn 15:9
Margaret Atwood 2:19
Margaret Avison 2:29
Earle Birney 4:64
D. G. Jones 10:288
Margaret Laurence 3:278
Denise Levertov 15:336
Gwendolyn MacEwan 13:357
John Newlove 14:377
A. W. Purdy 6:428
Mordecai Richler 5:374
Audrey Thomas 7:472; 13:538

**Bowering, Peter**
Aldous Huxley 4:237

**Bowers, A. Joan**
Gore Vidal 8:526

**Bowers, Marvin**
L. E. Sissman 9:491

**Bowie, Malcolm**
Yves Bonnefoy 9:114

**Bowles, Gloria**
Diane Wakoski 7:505

**Bowles, Jerry G.**
Craig Nova 7:267

**Bowra, C. M.**
Rafael Alberti 7:7

**Boyce, Burke**
Esther Forbes 12:205

**Boyd, Blanche M.**
Renata Adler 8:5

**Boyd, Celia**
Honor Arundel 17:16

**Boyd, John D.**
Theodore Roethke 11:483

**Boyd, Robert**
James Purdy 2:350

**Boyd, William**
Gabriel García Márquez 15:252
Penelope Gilliatt 13:238

**Boyers, Robert**
Saul Bellow 3:57
Ingmar Bergman 16:79
Alan Dugan 6:143
Witold Gombrowicz 7:125; 11:241
Robinson Jeffers 2:214; 3:258
Arthur Koestler 6:281
Robert Lowell 8:349; 9:336
Sylvia Plath 11:447
Adrienne Rich 7:364
Theodore Roethke 8:457
W. D. Snodgrass 2:406
Gary Snyder 2:406
Richard Wilbur 6:569

**Boyle, Kay**
James Baldwin 1:15
Tom Wicker 7:534

**Boyle, Ted E.**
Kingsley Amis 2:6
Brendan Behan 1:26

**Boylston, Helen Dore**
Betty Cavanna 12:97
Henry Gregor Felsen 17:120
Lee Kingman 17:243

**Bozek, Phillip**
Hugh MacDiarmid 19:285

**Bracher, Frederick**
John Cheever 15:127
James Gould Cozzens 11:127

**Brackman, Jacob**
Robert Crumb 17:84
Melvin Van Peebles 20:411

**Bradbrook, M. C.**
T. S. Eliot 1:91; 2:130

**Bradbury, Malcolm**
J. G. Ballard 14:40
A. S. Byatt 19:75
Ivy Compton-Burnett 10:109
John Dos Passos 8:181
E. M. Forster 4:167; 10:180
John Fowles 3:162; 4:172
William Gaddis 8:227

Thomas Hinde 6:240
Aldous Huxley 4:244
Michael Mott 15:379
Iris Murdoch 4:367; 11:388
John O'Hara 11:413
C. P. Snow 4:505
Gilbert Sorrentino 14:501
Muriel Spark 2:418
Lionel Trilling 9:531
Evelyn Waugh 8:543
Angus Wilson 5:513

**Bradbury, Maureen**
Phyllis Gotlieb 18:193

**Bradbury, Ray**
Ray Bradbury 15:86

**Bradford, Melvin E.**
Donald Davidson 2:111, 112; 13:167
William Faulkner 1:102; 3:155; 18:149
Walker Percy 3:381
Allen Tate 2:429

**Bradford, Richard**
M. E. Kerr 12:300
James Kirkwood 9:319

**Bradford, Tom**
Ray Bradbury 10:69

**Bradley, Sculley**
Robert Frost 3:169

**Bradlow, Paul**
Frederick Wiseman 20:469

**Brady, Ann P.**
T. S. Eliot 15:213

**Brady, Charles A.**
David Kherdian 6:281
C. S. Lewis 14:322

**Brady, Patrick**
Albert Camus 9:147

**Brady, Veronica**
Thomas Keneally 19:245

**Bragg, Melvyn**
Kingsley Amis 13:14
William F. Buckley, Jr. 18:82
E. M. Forster 2:136

**Bragg, Pamela**
Frank Bonham 12:52

**Bragin, John**
Jean-Luc Godard 20:133
Jean Renoir 20:297

**Braine, John**
Richard Llewellyn 7:207
Fay Weldon 9:559

**Brander, Laurence**
E. M. Forster 15:224
Aldous Huxley 18:269

**Brandriff, Welles T.**
William Styron 11:514

**Brandt, G. W.**
John Arden 13:23

**Brasillach, Robert**
René Clair 20:61

**Brater, Enoch**
Samuel Beckett 6:42; 9:81; 14:78; 18:51

**Braudy, Leo**
John Berger 2:54
Thomas Berger 3:63
Bernardo Bertolucci 16:90
Richard Condon 4:107
Alfred Hitchcock 16:347
Norman Mailer 1:193; 8:368
Jean Renoir 20:301

**Braudy, Susan**
Nora Ephron 17:112

**Braun, Devra**
Lillian Hellman 18:225

**Braun, Eric**
Elaine May 16:433

**Braun, Julie**
Philip Roth 4:453

**Braver-Mann, Barnet G.**
Charles Chaplin 16:188

**Braybrooke, Neville**
Graham Greene 1:130
François Mauriac 4:337

**Brazier, Chris**
Mick Jagger and Keith Richard 17:239
Bruce Springsteen 17:482

**Brée, Germaine**
Louis Aragon 3:12
Marcel Aymé 11:21
Samuel Beckett 10:27
Stanley Burnshaw 13:128
Albert Camus 1:54; 11:93
Louis-Ferdinand Céline 1:57
Jean Cocteau 1:59
Georges Duhamel 8:186
Jean Giono 4:183
Julien Green 3:203
André Malraux 1:202
François Mauriac 4:337
Raymond Queneau 2:359
Jules Romains 7:381
Jean-Paul Sartre 1:306; 7:397

**Breit, Harvey**
James Baldwin 2:31

**Breitrose, Henry**
Shirley Clarke 16:215

**Brendon, Piers**
Donald Barthelme 5:53
Rosalyn Drexler 2:119
Daphne du Maurier 6:146
Robert Penn Warren 4:582

**Brennan, Anthony S.**
Samuel Beckett 14:80

**Breslin, James E.**
T. S. Eliot 6:166

**Breslin, Jimmy**
Gore Vidal 8:525

**Breslin, John B.**
C. S. Lewis 6:308
Phyllis McGinley 14:368
Tom McHale 5:281
Wilfrid Sheed 10:474
Susan Sontag 13:516

**Breslin, Patrick**
Miguel Ángel Asturias 8:25
Paul Theroux 15:534

**Breslin, Paul**
Geoffrey Hill 18:239

**Bresnick, Paul**
James Purdy 10:425

**Breton, André**
Luis Buñuel 16:152

**Brew, Claude C.**
Tommaso Landolfi 11:321

**Brewster, Ben**
Yasujiro Ozu 16:455

**Brewster, Dorothy**
Doris Lessing 1:173

**Brickell, Herschel**
Harriette Arnow 7:15

**Bricker, Karin K.**
Mavis Thorpe Clark 12:131

**Brickner, Richard P.**
Anthony Burgess 2:86
Jerome Charyn 8:136
Frederick Exley 11:186
Frederick Forsyth 2:137
Herbert Gold 7:120
William Kotzwinkle 14:309
Cormac McCarthy 4:341
Vladimir Nabokov 3:355
Harry Mark Petrakis 3:383
Muriel Spark 3:465
Richard B. Wright 6:581

**Bridges, Les**
Mickey Spillane 3:469

**Bridges, Linda**
Donald Barthelme 5:55
Alistair MacLean 13:359
Georges Simenon 8:487

**Brien, Alan**
Kingsley Amis 2:6
Alan Ayckbourn 8:34
Trevor Griffiths 13:255
John Osborne 5:333
Harold Pinter 6:418
Wole Soyinka 14:505
Tennessee Williams 8:547

**Brien, Dolores Elise**
Robert Duncan 15:188

**Brigg, Peter**
Arthur C. Clarke 13:148

**Briggs, Julia**
Leon Garfield 12:234

**Brignano, Russell Carl**
Richard Wright 4:594

**Brinnin, John Malcolm**
John Ashbery 6:12
Allen Ginsberg 6:201
Galway Kinnell 1:168
William Meredith 13:372
Sylvia Plath 1:269
William Jay Smith 6:512

**Brinson, Peter**
Jean Renoir 20:289

**Bristol, Horace**
Pearl S. Buck **7**:33

**Britt, Gwenneth**
Vittorio De Sica **20**:94

**Brivic, Sheldon**
Richard Wright **9**:585

**Brockway, James**
Beryl Bainbridge **10**:16
Angela Carter **5**:102
J. P. Donleavy **4**:126
Mavis Gallant **7**:111
Penelope Gilliatt **10**:230
Julien Green **3**:205
Susan B. Hill **4**:228
Ursula Holden **18**:257
Frederic Raphael **14**:438
Piers Paul Read **10**:435
Muriel Spark **5**:399; **8**:495
Emma Tennant **13**:537

**Broderick, Dorothy M.**
Jesse Jackson **12**:655

**Brodin, Dorothy**
Marcel Aymé **11**:22

**Brodsky, Arnold**
Stevie Wonder **12**:655

**Brodsky, Joseph**
Czesław Miłosz **11**:376
Eugenio Montale **9**:388

**Brody, Patricia Ann**
Joan Armatrading **17**:9

**Brogan, Hugh**
Mervyn Peake **7**:301

**Bromberg, Pam**
Lillian Hellman **18**:229

**Brombert, Victor**
St.-John Perse **4**:398

**Bromwich, David**
Conrad Aiken **5**:10
A. R. Ammons **9**:2
John Ashbery **15**:34
Hayden Carruth **10**:100
Robert Frost **9**:266
John Hawkes **4**:216
John Hollander **5**:187
Richard Howard **7**:167
Thomas Kinsella **19**:253
Doris Lessing **3**:288
Jay Macpherson **14**:346
Penelope Mortimer **5**:299
Michael Mott **15**:380
Iris Murdoch **3**:348; **6**:347
Howard Nemerov **9**:394
Robert Pinsky **9**:416
Eric Rohmer **16**:532
Anne Sexton **10**:467
Charles Simic **9**:479
Stevie Smith **8**:492
Muriel Spark **3**:465
Paul Theroux **5**:427
Robert Penn Warren **13**:572
Elie Wiesel **3**:528
Charles Wright **13**:615

**Broner, E. M.**
Maxine Hong Kingston **19**:250

**Bronowski, J.**
Kathleen Raine **7**:352

**Bronson, A. A.**
Joe Rosenblatt **15**:448

**Brooke, Jocelyn**
Elizabeth Bowen **1**:39

**Brooke, Nicholas**
Anne Stevenson **7**:462

**Brooke-Rose, Christine**
Ezra Pound **7**:328

**Brookner, Anita**
Ursula Holden **18**:259
Fay Weldon **19**:469

**Brooks, Anne**
Maureen Daly **17**:87
Mary Stolz **12**:548

**Brooks, Cleanth**
William Empson **19**:152
William Faulkner **18**:148
Randall Jarrell **1**:159
Marianne Moore **10**:347
Walker Percy **6**:399
Allen Tate **4**:539; **11**:522

**Brooks, Ellen W.**
Doris Lessing **3**:284

**Brooks, Peter**
Alain Robbe-Grillet **1**:287

**Brooks, Rick**
Andre Norton **12**:467

**Brooks, Thomas R.**
Muriel Spark **18**:506

**Brooks, Van Wyck**
Upton Sinclair **15**:497

**Broome, Peter**
Robert Pinget **7**:306

**Brophy, Brigid**
Kingsley Amis **2**:5
Simone de Beauvoir **2**:42
Hortense Calisher **2**:95
Ivy Compton-Burnett **3**:111
William Faulkner **1**:102
Jean Genet **2**:157
Shirley Hazzard **18**:213
Patricia Highsmith **2**:192
W. Somerset Maugham **1**:204
Henry Miller **2**:281
Françoise Sagan **3**:443; **6**:482
Georges Simenon **2**:397
Elizabeth Taylor **2**:432
Evelyn Waugh **3**:509

**Brophy, James D.**
W. H. Auden **11**:15

**Brose, Margaret**
Giuseppe Ungaretti **11**:558;
    **15**:538

**Brosman, Catharine Savage**
Jean-Paul Sartre **13**:503

**Brothers, Barbara**
Elizabeth Bowen **15**:79

**Broughton, Glenda**
Hilma Wolitzer **17**:563

**Broughton, Panthea Reid**
William Faulkner **6**:175
Carson McCullers **4**:345

**Brown, Alan**
Ernest Hemingway **19**:217

**Brown, Ashley**
Caroline Gordon **6**:204, 206;
    **13**:241
Allen Tate **2**:428

**Brown, Calvin S.**
Conrad Aiken **3**:4
William Faulkner **18**:149

**Brown, Clarence**
Jorge Luis Borges **19**:48
Czeslaw Milosz **5**:292
Vladimir Nabokov **1**:242

**Brown, Constance A.**
Laurence Olivier **20**:239

**Brown, Cynthia**
Barbara Corcoran **17**:75

**Brown, Deming**
Alexander Zinoviev **19**:487

**Brown, E. K.**
Louis Dudek **19**:136
E. J. Pratt **19**:382

**Brown, Edward J.**
Ilya Ehrenburg **18**:136

**Brown, F. J.**
Arthur Koestler **3**:271
Alberto Moravia **2**:293
Mario Puzo **1**:282
Muriel Spark **2**:417

**Brown, Frederick**
Louis Aragon **3**:13
Jean Cocteau **1**:60

**Brown, Geoff**
Woody Allen **16**:8
Satyajit Ray **16**:495
Joan Micklin Silver **20**:342
Peter Weir **20**:425
Brian Wilson **12**:648

**Brown, Harry**
Hollis Summers **10**:494

**Brown, Ivor**
J. B. Priestley **2**:346

**Brown, John L.**
Marguerite Yourcenar **19**:484

**Brown, John Russell**
John Arden **6**:8
John Osborne **5**:332
Harold Pinter **6**:408, 413
Arnold Wesker **5**:482

**Brown, Kenneth R.**
Sam Peckinpah **20**:275

**Brown, Lloyd W.**
Imamu Amiri Baraka **3**:35
Langston Hughes **10**:281

**Brown, Margaret Warren**
Jean Lee Latham **12**:323

**Brown, Merle E.**
Kenneth Burke **2**:88
Geoffrey Hill **18**:236
Philip Larkin **18**:295

**Brown, Ralph Adams**
Henry Gregor Felsen **17**:121
Andre Norton **12**:455
John R. Tunis **12**:595

**Brown, Richard**
John Kennedy Toole **19**:443

**Brown, Robert**
Stanley Elkin **14**:157

**Brown, Robert McAfee**
Elie Wiesel **5**:493

**Brown, Rosellen**
Margaret Atwood **8**:28; **15**:39
Marilyn French **18**:158
Tim O'Brien **7**:272
May Sarton **4**:471
Judith Johnson Sherwin **7**:414
Diane Wakoski **4**:572

**Brown, Royal S.**
Brian De Palma **20**:78

**Brown, Russell M.**
Robert Kroetsch **5**:221

**Brown, Ruth Leslie**
John Gardner **2**:151
Gilbert Rogin **18**:457

**Brown, Steve**
Arthur C. Clarke **18**:107

**Brown, T.**
Louis MacNeice **10**:323

**Brown, Terence**
Kingsley Amis **2**:6

**Brown, William P.**
John Brunner **10**:78

**Browne, Ray B.**
Irving Wallace **13**:569

**Browne, Robert M.**
J. D. Salinger **12**:511

**Browning, Dominique**
Susan Cheever **18**:101

**Browning, Preston M., Jr.**
Flannery O'Connor **3**:367

**Brownjohn, Alan**
Dannie Abse **7**:1
Elizabeth Daryush **19**:120
Donald Davie **5**:115
C. Day Lewis **6**:128
Geoffrey Grigson **7**:136
Thom Gunn **18**:199
Seamus Heaney **7**:148
Hermann Hesse **17**:215
Geoffrey Hill **18**:239
Elizabeth Jennings **14**:292
Thomas Kinsella **4**:270
Philip Larkin **5**:226
George MacBeth **9**:340
Leslie Norris **14**:388
Kenneth Patchen **18**:393
Anthony Powell **7**:341
Alan Sillitoe **19**:420
Louis Simpson **7**:428
D. M. Thomas **13**:541
Ted Walker **13**:567

**Brownjohn, Elizabeth**
Philip Larkin **5**:227

**Broyard, Anatole**
Saul Bellow **2**:52
William F. Buckley, Jr. **18**:83
Frederick Busch **18**:84
Peter Dickinson **12**:176
José Donoso **8**:179
Nora Ephron **17**:111
Jules Feiffer **8**:217
Ken Follett **18**:156
Penelope Gilliatt **10**:229
Herbert Gold **14**:208
Günter Grass **2**:172
Lillian Hellman **18**:227
Yoram Kaniuk **19**:239
Jerzy Kosinski **10**:307
Bernard Malamud **2**:266
A. G. Mojtabai **15**:378
Wright Morris **18**:353
Edna O'Brien **13**:415
Michael Ondaatje **14**:410
Marge Piercy **14**:420
V. S. Pritchett **15**:442
Jean Rhys **19**:393
Philip Roth **3**:436
Françoise Sagan **9**:468; **17**:427
Nathalie Sarraute **8**:473
Mark Schorer **9**:473
Georges Simenon **8**:488
Peter Taylor **18**:527
Anne Tyler **11**:553
John Updike **2**:440; **9**:539; **15**:545
Hilma Wolitzer **17**:563

**Bruccoli, Matthew J.**
James Gould Cozzens **11**:131
John O'Hara **3**:370

**Brudnoy, David**
James Baldwin **2**:33
Robin Cook **14**:131
Bob Fosse **20**:123

**Bruell, Edwin**
Harper Lee **12**:342

**Brukenfeld, Dick**
Joyce Carol Oates **3**:364

**Brumberg, Abraham**
Aleksandr I. Solzhenitsyn **4**:514; **18**:498

**Brummell, O. B.**
Bob Dylan **12**:183

**Brunette, Peter**
Archibald MacLeish **14**:338

**Bruning, Peter**
Ward Ruyslinck **14**:472

**Brustein, Robert**
Edward Albee **3**:6, 7
Jean Anouilh **1**:6
James Baldwin **4**:40; **17**:28
Brendan Behan **1**:26
Robert Bolt **14**:88
Federico Fellini **16**:278
Jack Gelber **1**:114
Jean Genet **1**:115
Joseph Heller **3**:228
Rolf Hochhuth **4**:230
William Inge **1**:153
Eugène Ionesco **1**:154
Arthur Kopit **18**:287
Stanley Kubrick **16**:378

Arthur Miller **6**:330
John Osborne **5**:332
Harold Pinter **1**:266; **3**:385, 386; **15**:426
Gerome Ragni and James Rado **17**:379
Ronald Ribman **7**:357
Jean-Paul Sartre **4**:476
Murray Schisgal **6**:489
Peter Shaffer **5**:386
Sam Shepard **17**:442
Martin Sherman **19**:416
Tom Stoppard **3**:470; **15**:524
Ronald Tavel **6**:529
Jean-Claude Van Itallie **3**:492
Gore Vidal **4**:552, 553
Peter Weiss **3**:514
Arnold Wesker **5**:482
Tennessee Williams **19**:470

**Bruun, Geoffrey**
Marguerite Yourcenar **19**:480

**Bryan, C.D.B.**
Julio Cortázar **2**:103
Craig Nova **7**:267

**Bryant, J. A., Jr.**
Allen Tate **14**:530
Eudora Welty **1**:361; **5**:480

**Bryant, Jerry H.**
James Baldwin **8**:41
John Barth **2**:36
Saul Bellow **2**:52
William S. Burroughs **2**:91
Ronald L. Fair **18**:140
Ernest J. Gaines **18**:165
Nikki Giovanni **19**:191
Joseph Heller **3**:228
James Jones **3**:261
Norman Mailer **2**:260
Bernard Malamud **2**:266
Carson McCullers **4**:344
Toni Morrison **4**:366
Flannery O'Connor **2**:317
Walker Percy **2**:333
Thomas Pynchon **2**:353
Ayn Rand **3**:423
John Updike **2**:441
Kurt Vonnegut, Jr. **2**:452
John A. Williams **5**:497

**Bryant, Nelson**
James Herriot **12**:282

**Bryant, Rene Kuhn**
Thomas Berger **8**:83
Heinrich Böll **6**:84
John Fowles **6**:187
Paula Fox **8**:219
John Hersey **7**:154
Doris Lessing **10**:316
James A. Michener **5**:291

**Bryden, Ronald**
Peter Barnes **5**:49
Doris Lessing **6**:299
Peter Nichols **5**:306
Françoise Sagan **17**:421
David Storey **4**:529
Paul West **7**:525

**Buache, Freddy**
Luis Buñuel **16**:138

**Buchanan, Cynthia**
Norman Mailer **2**:263

**Buchen, Irving H.**
Carson McCullers **10**:334

**Buchsbaum, Betty**
David Kherdian **6**:280

**Buck, Philo M., Jr.**
Jules Romains **7**:378

**Buck, Richard M.**
Andre Norton **12**:457

**Buckle, Richard**
John Betjeman **2**:60

**Buckler, Ernest**
Hugh Hood **15**:283

**Buckler, Robert**
Elia Kazan **6**:274
Thomas Williams **14**:582

**Buckley, Kathryn**
Joan Barfoot **18**:36

**Buckley, Peter**
Lily Tomlin **17**:522
Andy Warhol **20**:420

**Buckley, Priscilla L.**
Eric Ambler **6**:4

**Buckley, Tom**
Michael Cimino **16**:212
Irving Wallace **13**:570

**Buckley, Vincent**
T. S. Eliot **3**:138

**Buckley, Virginia**
Katherine Paterson **12**:487

**Buckley, William F., Jr.**
William F. Buckley, Jr. **7**:35
Lillian Hellman **14**:257
Gerome Ragni and James Rado **17**:381
Aleksandr I. Solzhenitsyn **4**:511
Hunter S. Thompson **17**:513
Garry Trudeau **12**:590
Tom Wolfe **2**:481

**Buckmaster, Henrietta**
Maxine Hong Kingston **19**:250
Barbara Pym **19**:387

**Bucknall, Barbara J.**
Ursula K. LeGuin **13**:349

**Budgen, Suzanne**
Jean Renoir **20**:299

**Budrys, Algis**
Frederik Pohl **18**:412
Keith Roberts **14**:464

**Buechner, Frederick**
Annie Dillard **9**:178

**Buell, Ellen Lewis**
E. M. Almedingen **12**:3
Margot Benary-Isbert **12**:31
Betty Cavanna **12**:97, 98
Maureen Daly **17**:90
Walter Farley **17**:115
Henry Gregor Felsen **17**:120, 122
Esther Forbes **12**:207

Lee Kingman **17**:243
Joseph Krumgold **12**:317
Jean Lee Latham **12**:32
Madeleine L'Engle **12**:345
William Mayne **12**:389
Andre Norton **12**:456
Otfried Preussler **17**:374
Mary Stolz **12**:545, 546, 547, 548, 549, 550, 551, 552
John R. Tunis **12**:593, 594, 595, 596
Lenora Mattingly Weber **12**:631

**Buell, Frederick**
A. R. Ammons **8**:17

**Buffington, Robert**
Frederick Busch **18**:85
Donald Davidson **2**:112
John Crowe Ransom **4**:430, 437

**Bufithis, Philip H.**
Norman Mailer **11**:342

**Bufkin, E. C.**
Iris Murdoch **2**:297
P. H. Newby **2**:310

**Buitenhuis, Peter**
Harry Mathews **6**:314
William Trevor **7**:475

**Bullins, Ed**
Alice Childress **12**:106

**Bulman, Learned T.**
Henry Gregor Felsen **17**:122
Jean Lee Latham **12**:323, 325
Andre Norton **12**:456

**Bumpus, Jerry**
Mario Vargas Llosa **15**:552

**Bunnell, Sterling**
Michael McClure **6**:321

**Bunting, Basil**
Hugh MacDiarmid **4**:313

**Burbank, Rex**
Thornton Wilder **1**:364

**Burch, Noel**
Alain Resnais **16**:496

**Burg, Victor**
Richard Elman **19**:150

**Burger, Marjorie**
Walter Farley **17**:116, 117

**Burgess, Anthony**
Kingsley Amis **1**:6; **2**:8
James Baldwin **1**:16
Samuel Beckett **1**:23; **3**:44
Saul Bellow **1**:31
Elizabeth Bowen **1**:40; **3**:82
Bridgid Brophy **6**:99
William S. Burroughs **1**:48
Albert Camus **1**:54
Louis-Ferdinand Céline **7**:46
Agatha Christie **1**:58
Ivy Compton-Burnett **1**:62
Don DeLillo **13**:178
E. L. Doctorow **18**:125
Lawrence Durrell **1**:87
T. S. Eliot **3**:139
E. M. Forster **1**:107

Carlos Fuentes **13**:231
Jean Genet **1**:115
Penelope Gilliatt **2**:160
William Golding **1**:121
Günter Grass **1**:125; **11**:251
Henry Green **2**:178
Graham Greene **3**:207
Joseph Heller **1**:140
Ernest Hemingway **1**:143;
  **3**:234
Aldous Huxley **1**:151
Christopher Isherwood **1**:156
Pamela Hansford Johnson **1**:160
Erica Jong **18**:278
Arthur Koestler **1**:169; **3**:270
John le Carré **9**:326
Colin MacInnes **4**:314
Norman Mailer **1**:190
Bernard Malamud **1**:199; **3**:322
Olivia Manning **19**:301
Mary McCarthy **1**:206
Henry Miller **1**:224
Iris Murdoch **1**:235
Vladimir Nabokov **1**:244; **3**:352
Flann O'Brien **1**:252
Lucio Piccolo **13**:440
Reynolds Price **13**:464
J. B. Priestley **2**:347
Alain Robbe-Grillet **1**:288
J. D. Salinger **1**:299
William Sansom **2**:383
Alan Sillitoe **1**:307
C. P. Snow **1**:317
Muriel Spark **2**:416
Paul Theroux **11**:528
John Wain **2**:458
Evelyn Waugh **1**:359; **3**:510
Angus Wilson **2**:472
Edmund Wilson **3**:538

**Burgess, Charles E.**
William Inge **8**:308

**Burgess, Jackson**
Robert Altman **16**:22
Stanley Kubrick **16**:380

**Burgess, John**
Satyajit Ray **16**:476

**Burhans, Clinton S., Jr.**
Joseph Heller **3**:230
Ernest Hemingway **8**:283
Kurt Vonnegut, Jr. **8**:530

**Burke, Frank**
Federico Fellini **16**:298

**Burke, Jeffrey**
Thomas Keneally **19**:248
Alberto Moravia **18**:349
Jayne Anne Phillips **15**:420
Richard Price **12**:492

**Burke, Kenneth**
Theodore Roethke **11**:479
Glenway Wescott **13**:590

**Burke, William M.**
John A. Williams **5**:497

**Burkom, Selma R.**
Doris Lessing **1**:174

**Burnett, Constance Buil**
Frank B. Gilbreth, Jr. and
  Ernestine Gilbreth Carey
  **17**:153

**Burnett, Michael**
James Thurber **5**:440

**Burnham, David**
Emlyn Williams **15**:577

**Burns, Alan**
Ann Quin **6**:442
C. P. Snow **1**:317

**Burns, Gerald**
W. H. Auden **4**:33
John Berryman **6**:62, 63
Austin Clarke **9**:169
Seamus Heaney **7**:147
Donald Justice **19**:236
Robert Lowell **5**:256
Frank O'Hara **5**:324
Charles Olson **5**:328
Ezra Pound **5**:348
Gary Snyder **5**:393
William Stafford **4**:520
Diane Wakoski **11**:564

**Burns, J.**
Noel Hilliard **15**:280

**Burns, Landon C., Jr.**
Mary Renault **17**:395

**Burns, Martin**
Kurt Vonnegut, Jr. **12**:608

**Burns, Mary M.**
Alice Childress **12**:107
Barbara Corcoran **17**:77
Peter Dickinson **12**:171
Jamake Highwater **12**:287
M. E. Kerr **12**:297, 298
Lee Kingman **17**:247
Jean Lee Latham **12**:325
Anne McCaffrey **17**:282
Nicholasa Mohr **12**:445
Andre Norton **12**:471
Robert Newton Peck **17**:340,
  342

**Burns, Stuart L.**
Jean Stafford **4**:517

**Burns, Wayne**
Alex Comfort **7**:52,53

**Burnshaw, Stanley**
James Dickey **10**:141

**Burroughs, Franklin G.**
William Faulkner **3**:157

**Burrow, J. W.**
Aldous Huxley **3**:254
J.R.R. Tolkien **3**:482

**Burroway, Janet**
James Leo Herlihy **6**:235
Mary Hocking **13**:284

**Burt, Struthers**
Kay Boyle **19**:62

**Burton, Dwight L.**
Betty Cavanna **12**:99
Maureen Daly **17**:88

**Burton, Thomas**
Alfred Hitchcock **16**:338

**Busch, Frederick**
J. G. Farrell **6**:173
John Hawkes **7**:140
Alice Munro **10**:356
Paul West **7**:523

**Bush, Roland E.**
Ishmael Reed **3**:424

**Busi, Frederick**
Alain Resnais **16**:513

**Butkiss, John F.**
Lee Kingman **17**:246

**Butler, Colin**
Hermann Hesse **17**:214

**Butler, Florence W.**
Henry Gregor Felsen **17**:120

**Butler, Geoff**
Rolf Hochhuth **18**:256

**Butler, Michael**
Heinrich Böll **11**:58

**Butler, Rupert**
Laurence Olivier **20**:239

**Butler, William Vivian**
John Creasey **11**:135

**Butscher, Edward**
John Berryman **3**:67
Shusaku Endo **14**:162
John Gardner **3**:185
Jerzy Kosinski **6**:282
John Sayles **14**:483
James Wright **5**:519
Rudolph Wurlitzer **4**:598

**Butt, John**
Carlos Fuentes **10**:208

**Butterick, George**
Ed Dorn **18**:129

**Butwin, Joseph**
Richard Brautigan **12**:62

**Byatt, A. S.**
Penelope Fitzgerald **19**:174
Diane Johnson **13**:305
Amos Oz **11**:429
V. S. Pritchett **15**:440
C. P. Snow **13**:514

**Byer, Kathryn Stripling**
Carolyn Kizer **15**:309

**Byers, Margaret**
Elizabeth Jennings **5**:197

**Byers, Nancy**
Jean Lee Latham **12**:324

**Byrd, James W.**
Willard Motley **18**:357

**Byrd, Max**
Jorge Luis Borges **6**:93
Peter DeVries **10**:136

**Byrd, Scott**
John Barth **1**:17

**Byrom, Thomas**
Frank O'Hara **13**:423

**Byron, Stuart**
Woody Allen **16**:12

**Cadogan, Mary**
William Mayne **12**:404

**Cahill, Daniel J.**
E. L. Doctorow **18**:121
Jerzy Kosinski **2**:232

**Cain, Joan**
Camilo José Cela **13**:147

**Čalas, Nicholas**
André Breton **9**:125

**Calder, Angus**
T. S. Eliot **2**:128
Alex La Guma **19**:273

**Calder, Robert L.**
W. Somerset Maugham **15**:369

**Caldwell, Joan**
Margaret Laurence **13**:344
Audrey Thomas **7**:472

**Caldwell, Stephen**
D. Keith Mano **2**:270

**Calisher, Hortense**
Yukio Mishima **2**:289
Vladimir Nabokov **1**:246
Christina Stead **5**:403

**Callaghan, Linda Ward**
Gene Roddenberry **17**:414

**Callahan, John**
Michael S. Harper **7**:138

**Callahan, John F.**
Alice Walker **5**:476

**Callahan, Patrick J.**
C. S. Lewis **3**:297
George MacBeth **2**:251
Alan Sillitoe **1**:308
Stephen Spender **2**:420

**Callan, Edward**
W. H. Auden **1**:9, 11; **14**:30
Alan Paton **4**:395

**Callan, Richard J.**
José Donoso **11**:147
Octavio Paz **19**:364

**Callenbach, Ernest**
Ingmar Bergman **16**:60
Charles Chaplin **16**:198
Shirley Clarke **16**:218
John Ford **16**:309
Alfred Hitchcock **16**:342, 344
Elia Kazan **16**:367
Satyajit Ray **16**:482
Andy Warhol **20**:418
Orson Welles **20**:438

**Callendar, Newgate**
Eric Ambler **4**:18
Isaac Asimov **9**:49
William Peter Blatty **2**:64
William F. Buckley, Jr. **18**:81,
  83
Robert Cormier **12**:136
John Creasey **11**:135
Peter Dickinson **12**:170, 171,
  177
Evan Hunter **11**:279, 280
P. D. James **18**:272
James Jones **3**:262
Harry Kemelman **2**:225
Emma Lathen **2**:236
Ross Macdonald **14**:336
Ellery Queen **11**:458
Georges Simenon **2**:399
Mickey Spillane **3**:469
J.I.M. Stewart **14**:512

Vassilis Vassilikos 8:524
Donald E. Westlake 7:528, 529

**Callow, Philip**
Andrew Sinclair 2:400

**Cambon, Glauco**
Michael Hamburger 14:234
Robert Lowell 8:348
Eugenio Montale 7:224
Giuseppe Ungaretti 7:482;
11:555; 15:536
Elio Vittorini 14:543

**Cameron, Ann**
Tom Robbins 9:454

**Cameron, Barry**
A. W. Purdy 14:432

**Cameron, Eleanor**
Julia W. Cunningham 12:164
Leon Garfield 12:226
Alan Garner 17:138
Joseph Krumgold 12:320
William Mayne 12:393
Emily Cheney Neville 12:452

**Cameron, Elspeth**
Margaret Atwood 13:4

**Cameron, Ian**
Michelangelo Antonioni 20:20
Nagisa Oshima 20:247

**Cameron, Julia**
Judith Rossner 6:469

**Camp, Richard**
Leon Garfield 12:221

**Campbell, Barbara**
Henry Gregor Felsen 17:124

**Campbell, Gregg M.**
Bob Dylan 6:157

**Campbell, Josie P.**
E. L. Doctorow 18:123

**Campbell, Patty**
Stan Lee 17:262

**Canary, Robert H.**
Robert Graves 11:256

**Canby, Henry Seidel**
Pearl S. Buck 18:75

**Canby, Vincent**
Lindsay Anderson 20:16
Shirley Clarke 16:218
Brian De Palma 20:72, 74, 75,
79, 80
Vittorio De Sica 20:95, 97
Marguerite Duras 20:99
Rainer Werner Fassbinder
20:113, 120
Federico Fellini 16:290
Bob Fosse 20:123
Alfred Hitchcock 16:359
Nagisa Oshima 20:249
Pier Paolo Pasolini 20:262, 265
Sam Peckinpah 20:276
Carlos Saura 20:316
Martin Scorsese 20:323, 330
Jerzy Skolimowski 20:348
François Truffaut 20:393
Peter Weir 20:428

**Cannella, Anthony R.**
Richard Condon 10:111

**Cannon, JoAnn**
Italo Calvino 11:92

**Cansler, Ronald Lee**
Robert A. Heinlein 3:227

**Cantarella, Helene**
Jules Archer 12:15

**Cantor, Peter**
Frederic Raphael 2:367

**Cantwell, Mary**
Alan Sillitoe 19:421

**Cantwell, Robert**
Erskine Caldwell 14:94
Upton Sinclair 15:498

**Capers, Charlotte**
Mary Lee Settle 19:409

**Capey, A. C.**
William Golding 17:177

**Capitanchik, Maurice**
E. M. Forster 2:135
Yukio Mishima 6:338

**Caplan, Brina**
John Gardner 18:176
Lillian Hellman 18:226

**Caplan, Lincoln**
Frederick Buechner 6:103

**Caplan, Ralph**
Kingsley Amis 1:6

**Capouya, Emile**
Albert Camus 2:98
Camilo José Cela 13:145
Robert Coover 7:57
Paul Goodman 7:129
James Leo Herlihy 6:234
Ignazio Silone 4:493
Aleksandr I. Solzhenitsyn 1:320
Dalton Trumbo 19:445

**Capp, Al**
Charles Chaplin 16:194
Mary McCarthy 5:276

**Capps, Benjamin**
Christie Harris 12:262

**Caprio, Betsy**
Gene Roddenberry 17:411

**Caputi, Jane E.**
Steven Spielberg 20:363

**Caputo, Philip**
Thomas McGuane 18:322

**Caputo-Mayr, Maria Luise**
Peter Handke 8:261

**Caram, Richard**
Anne Stevenson 7:463

**Cardinal, Roger**
André Breton 15:86

**Cardullo, Robert J.**
Robert Altman 16:37

**Carduner, Art**
Ingmar Bergman 16:69

**Carew, Jan**
John Irving 13:292
George Lamming 2:235

**Carey, John**
Richard Bach 14:35
Lawrence Durrell 4:147
Richard Eberhart 3:135
William Empson 8:201
D. J. Enright 4:155
Doris Lessing 6:292
John Updike 7:489

**Carey, Julian C.**
Langston Hughes 10:278

**Cargill, Oscar**
Pearl S. Buck 7:32

**Cargin, Peter**
Michael Cimino 16:208

**Carleton, Joyce**
Patrick Modiano 18:338

**Carleton, Phillips D.**
Frans Eemil Sillanpää 19:417

**Carlsen, G. Robert**
Frank Herbert 12:273

**Carlson, Dale**
M. E. Kerr 12:296
Rosemary Wells 12:638

**Carmody, Rev. Francis R., S.J.**
Roy A. Gallant 17:129

**Carne-Ross, D. S.**
John Gardner 3:185
Eugenio Montale 7:222

**Carpenter, Bogdana**
Zbigniew Herbert 9:274

**Carpenter, Frederic I.**
William Everson 14:163
Robinson Jeffers 2:212; 11:311;
15:300
Carson McCullers 12:417
Jessamyn West 17:547

**Carpenter, John R.**
Zbigniew Herbert 9:274
Greg Kuzma 7:196
John Logan 5:255
James Schevill 7:401
Gary Snyder 2:407
Diane Wakoski 2:459
Peter Wild 14:581
Charles Wright 6:580

**Carpenter, Richard C.**
Kay Boyle 19:63, 64

**Carpio, Virginia**
Andre Norton 12:464

**Carr, John**
George Garrett 3:190

**Carr, Patrick**
Peter Townshend 17:540
Neil Young 17:580

**Carr, Roy**
John Lennon and Paul
McCartney 12:379

**Carroll, David**
Chinua Achebe 1:1
Jean Cayrol 11:107

**Carroll, Paul**
John Ashbery 2:16
Robert Creeley 2:106
James Dickey 2:116
Allen Ginsberg 2:163
Frank O'Hara 2:321
W. D. Snodgrass 2:405
Philip Whalen 6:565

**Carruth, Hayden**
Ai 14:9
A. R. Ammons 9:30
W. H. Auden 1:11
John Berryman 2:56
Earle Birney 6:75
Robert Bly 15:68
Edward Brathwaite 11:67
Charles Bukowski 5:80
Cid Corman 9:170
Robert Creeley 8:153
J. V. Cunningham 3:121
Babette Deutsch 18:119
Annie Dillard 9:177
Robert Duncan 2:122
Loren Eiseley 7:91
Clayton Eshleman 7:97, 98
Robert Frost 10:198
Tess Gallagher 18:169
Jean Garrigue 8:239
Arthur Gregor 9:251
H. D. 8:256
Marilyn Hacker 9:257
Jim Harrison 14:235
William Heyen 18:230
John Hollander 8:301
Richard Howard 7:166
David Ignatow 7:174, 175,
177; 14:275
June Jordan 11:312
Denise Levertov 8:346
Philip Levine 2:244
Audre Lorde 18:309
Robert Lowell 4:299; 9:338
Archibald MacLeish 14:337
W. S. Merwin 8:390
Josephine Miles 2:278
Howard Nemerov 2:306
Charles Olson 9:412
Robert Pinsky 9:417
J. F. Powers 1:280
Kenneth Rexroth 2:370
Reg Saner 9:468
Anne Sexton 2:390; 4:484
Judith Johnson Sherwin 15:480
W. D. Snodgrass 18:492
Gilbert Sorrentino 7:448
Raymond Souster 14:502
David Wagoner 15:559
Diane Wakoski 2:459; 4:574
Theodore Weiss 8:545
Louis Zukofsky 2:487

**Carson, Katharine W.**
Claude Simon 9:485

**Carson, Neil**
George Ryga 14:472, 473

**Carson, Tom**
Paul Simon 17:467
Brian Wilson 12:653
Neil Young 17:582
Frank Zappa 17:594

**Carter, Albert Howard, III**
Italo Calvino 8:126
Thomas McGuane 7:213

**Carter, Angela**
Thomas Keneally 5:210

**Carter, Anne**
Eilís Dillon 17:100
Josephine Poole 17:373

**Carter, Lin**
J.R.R. Tolkien 1:339

**Carter, Paul**
Eugenio Montale 9:387

**Carter, Robert A.**
Arthur Gregor 9:253

**Carter, Steven R.**
Isaac Asimov 19:28
Julian Symons 14:523

**Carver, Ann Cathey**
Lucille Clifton 19:109

**Cary, Joseph**
Eugenio Montale 7:223; 9:386
Giuseppe Ungaretti 7:482
Louis Zukofsky 18:558

**Casari, Laura E.**
Adrienne Rich 11:479

**Casebeer, Edwin F.**
Hermann Hesse 3:245

**Caserio, Robert L.**
Gilbert Sorrentino 7:449

**Casey, Carol K.**
Eleanor Hibbert 7:156

**Casey, Jane Barnes**
Peter Taylor 18:527

**Casey, John**
T. Alan Broughton 19:73

**Cashin, Edward J.**
Walker Percy 14:411

**Caspary, Sister Anita Marie**
François Mauriac 4:337, 338

**Casper, Leonard**
Flannery O'Connor 6:375

**Cassidy, T. E.**
Jessamyn West 17:545

**Cassill, R. V.**
Mavis Gallant 7:110
Thomas Hinde 6:241
James Alan McPherson 19:309
Irwin Shaw 7:413
Wilfrid Sheed 2:393
Christina Stead 2:422
Thomas Williams 14:581

**Casson, Lionel**
Mary Renault 17:399

**Castor, Gladys Crofoot**
Betty Cavanna 12:98

**Catania, Susan**
Alvin Silverstein and Virginia
B. Silverstein 17:452

**Catanoy, Nicholas**
Mircea Eliade 19:147, 148

**Catinella, Joseph**
Christopher Isherwood 1:157
Joel Lieber 6:311
Bernard Malamud 1:201

**Causey, James Y.**
Camilo José Cela 4:95

**Caute, David**
Jean Genet 5:137
Lionel Trilling 9:531

**Cavan, Romilly**
Derek Walcott 4:574

**Caviglia, John**
José Donoso 11:149

**Cavitch, David**
William Stafford 4:521

**Cawelti, John G.**
Dashiell Hammett 19:195
Mario Puzo 6:430
Mickey Spillane 3:468

**Caws, Mary Ann**
André Breton 2:81; 9:125
Yves Bonnefoy 9:113
Blaise Cendrars 18:92

**Cecchetti, Giovanni**
Eugenio Montale 7:221

**Cecil, David**
Aldous Huxley 3:252

**Cerf, Bennett**
John O'Hara 2:324

**Cevasco, G. A.**
Pearl S. Buck 18:77

**Chabot, C. Barry**
Frederick Exley 11:187

**Chabrol, Claude**
Alfred Hitchcock 16:357

**Chace, William M.**
Ezra Pound 4:415

**Chaillet, Ned**
Athol Fugard 9:232
Hugh Leonard 19:281

**Chamberlain, Ethel L.**
E. M. Almedingen 12:8

**Chamberlain, John**
James Gould Cozzens 11:131
Mary McCarthy 3:326

**Chamberlin, J. E.**
Margaret Atwood 8:28
George MacBeth 5:265
W. S. Merwin 3:338
Charles Tomlinson 4:547;
6:535, 536
David Wagoner 5:475

**Chambers, Aidan**
Alan Garner 17:145, 147
William Mayne 12:404
Robert Westall 17:555

**Chambers, Colin**
Peter Shaffer 18:477

**Chambers, D.D.C.**
Matt Cohen 19:111

**Chambers, Robert D.**
Ernest Buckler 13:120
Sinclair Ross 13:492

**Chambers, Ross**
Samuel Beckett 9:77

**Chametzky, Jules**
Edward Dahlberg 14:134
Isaac Bashevis Singer 1:313

**Champagne, Roland A.**
Marguerite Duras 11:167

**Chang, Charity**
Barbara Corcoran 17:74

**Changas, Estelle**
Elia Kazan 16:368

**Chankin, Donald O.**
B. Traven 8:517

**Chapin, Katherine Garrison**
Allen Tate 4:536

**Chaplin, William H.**
John Logan 5:253

**Chapman, Raymond**
Graham Greene 1:133

**Chapman, Robert**
Anthony Burgess 4:83
Ivy Compton-Burnett 3:112

**Chappell, Fred**
George Garrett 3:191
Richard Yates 7:554

**Chappetta, Robert**
Bernardo Bertolucci 16:88
Roman Polanski 16:466

**Charnes, Ruth**
M. E. Kerr 12:303

**Charters, Ann**
Charles Olson 5:326

**Charters, Samuel**
Robert Creeley 4:117
Robert Duncan 4:142
Larry Eigner 9:180
William Everson 5:121
Lawrence Ferlinghetti 6:182
Allen Ginsberg 4:181
Charles Olson 5:329
Gary Snyder 5:393
Jack Spicer 8:497

**Charyn, Jerome**
Kōbō Abe 8:1
Martin Amis 9:26
T. Alan Broughton 19:72
R.H.W. Dillard 5:116
Elizabeth Jane Howard 7:165
Margaríta Karapánou 13:314
William Kotzwinkle 14:311
Richard Price 12:492
James Purdy 10:424
Judith Rossner 9:457
Joseph Wambaugh 18:533
Jerome Weidman 7:518
Kate Wilhelm 7:538

**Chase, Richard**
Saul Bellow 1:27

**Chasin, Helen**
Alan Dugan 6:144
May Sarton 4:472

**Chassler, Philip I.**
Meyer Levin 7:205

**Chatfield, Jack**
William F. Buckley, Jr. 18:83

**Chatham, Margaret L.**
Roy A. Gallant 17:133

**Chazen, Leonard**
Anthony Powell 3:402

**Cheatwood, Kiarri T-H**
Ayi Kwei Armah 5:32

**Cheever, John**
Saul Bellow 10:43

**Chelton, Mary K.**
Anne McCaffrey 17:281

**Cheney, Brainard**
Donald Davidson 2:112
Flannery O'Connor 1:254

**Chernaik, Judith**
Beryl Bainbridge 14:39

**Cherry, Kelly**
John Betjeman 10:53

**Cherry, Kenneth**
Vladimir Nabokov 8:413

**Cheshire, Ardner R., Jr.**
William Styron 11:518

**Chesnick, Eugene**
John Cheever 7:48
Nadine Gordimer 7:133
Michael Mewshaw 9:376

**Chester, Alfred**
Terry Southern 7:454

**Cheuse, Alan**
Alejo Carpentier 11:100
Carlos Fuentes 13:231
John Gardner 5:132
Jerzy Kosinski 15:317
André Schwarz-Bart 4:480
B. Traven 11:534

**Chevigny, Bell Gale**
Toni Cade Bambara 19:32
Julio Cortázar 15:148
Tillie Olsen 4:387

**Chiari, Joseph**
Jean Anouilh 8:23
Jean Cocteau 8:144

**Childs, E. Ira**
Peter Townshend 17:534

**Chomsky, Noam**
Saul Bellow 8:81

**Christ, Ronald**
Jorge Luis Borges 2:70, 73;
4:75
José Donoso 8:178
Gabriel García Márquez 3:179
Pablo Neruda 5:301; 7:260
Octavio Paz 3:375; 4:397;
6:398
Manuel Puig 5:354
Mario Vargas Llosa 9:542

**Christensen, Paul**
Ed Dorn 18:128

**Christgau, Georgia**
Joan Armatrading **17**:8
Bob Marley **17**:273

**Christgau, Robert**
Chuck Berry **17**:54
Richard Brautigan **9**:124
Mick Jagger and Keith Richard **17**:225, 237
John Lennon and Paul McCartney **12**:358
Patti Smith **12**:539
Peter Townshend **17**:525
Stevie Wonder **12**:658, 659

**Christie, Ian Leslie**
Ken Russell **16**:541

**Chrzanowski, Joseph**
Jorge Luis Borges **19**:49

**Churchill, David**
Peter Dickinson **12**:175

**Churchill, R. C.**
John Cowper Powys **15**:433
P. G. Wodehouse **10**:537

**Churchill, Winston**
Charles Chaplin **16**:189

**Ciardi, John**
Robert Frost **13**:223
Stanley Kunitz **14**:312
Richard Wilbur **14**:576
William Carlos Williams **13**:602

**Cifelli, Edward**
John Ciardi **10**:106

**Ciplijauskaité, Biruté**
Gabriel García Márquez **3**:182

**Cismaru, Alfred**
Simone de Beauvoir **2**:43
Albert Camus **11**:95
Aimé Césaire **19**:96
Marguerite Duras **6**:149; **11**:164
Eugène Ionesco **9**:289
Robert Pinget **13**:442

**Cixous, Helen**
Severo Sarduy **6**:485

**Claire, Thomas**
Albert Camus **9**:150

**Claire, William F.**
Stanley Kunitz **11**:319
Sylvia Plath **17**:347
Allen Tate **9**:521
Mark Van Doren **6**:541

**Clancy, Cathy**
Piri Thomas **17**:502

**Clancy, William P.**
Carson McCullers **12**:413
Brian Moore **7**:235

**Clapp, Susannah**
Caroline Blackwood **9**:101
Penelope Fitzgerald **19**:172
Ursula Holden **18**:257
Margaríta Karapánou **13**:315
Seán O'Faoláin **7**:274
George MacBeth **9**:340
David Plante **7**:308
Barbara Pym **19**:386

Hilma Wolitzer **17**:562

**Clare, Anthony**
Susan Sontag **13**:518

**Clarens, Carlos**
Eric Rohmer **16**:530, 531

**Clareson, Thomas D.**
James Blish **14**:83

**Clark, Gerry**
Bernice Rubens **19**:405

**Clark, John R.**
Doris Betts **6**:69
Alan Sillitoe **1**:308

**Clarke, Gerald**
Gore Vidal **2**:449
P. G. Wodehouse **2**:480

**Clarke, Henry Leland**
Melvin Berger **12**:38

**Clarke, Jane H.**
Jesse Jackson **12**:289

**Clarke, Kenneth**
Jesse Stuart **14**:516

**Clarke, Loretta**
Paul Zindel **6**:587

**Claudel, Alice Moser**
David Kherdian **9**:317

**Clausen, Christopher**
T. S. Eliot **10**:171

**Clayton, John**
Richard Brautigan **12**:63

**Clayton, John Jacob**
Saul Bellow **6**:50

**Clements, Bruce**
Robert Cormier **12**:137

**Clements, Robert J.**
Pablo Neruda **2**:308
Irving Stone **7**:469
Vassilis Vassilikos **4**:551

**Clemons, Walter**
Lisa Alther **7**:12
James Baldwin **5**:43
Saul Bellow **6**:55
Peter Benchley **8**:82
G. Cabrera Infante **5**:96
E. L. Doctorow **6**:133
Nora Ephron **17**:113
J. G. Farrell **6**:173
Joseph Heller **5**:176, 182
George V. Higgins **7**:158
Maureen Howard **5**:189
Erica Jong **4**:263
Milan Kundera **4**:276
Doris Lessing **6**:302
Alison Lurie **4**:305
Ross Macdonald **1**:185
James McCourt **5**:278
Carson McCullers **1**:210
Vladimir Nabokov **6**:354
Donald Newlove **6**:364
Joyce Carol Oates **2**:316; **3**:363
Flannery O'Connor **2**:317
Grace Paley **4**:391
Robert M. Pirsig **4**:403
Manuel Puig **5**:354

Adrienne Rich **6**:458
Isaac Bashevis Singer **3**:456
Raymond Sokolov **7**:430
Tom Wicker **7**:534
Richard B. Wright **6**:582

**Clever, Glenn**
E. J. Pratt **19**:383

**Clifford, Gay**
Staley Middleton **7**:221
Bernice Rubens **19**:403

**Clifford, Paula M.**
Claude Simon **9**:485

**Clifford, William**
Walter Farley **17**:116

**Clinton, Craig**
John Arden **15**:24

**Clinton, Farley**
William Safire **10**:447

**Cloonan, William**
André Malraux **13**:368

**Cloutier, Pierre**
Hugh Hood **15**:285

**Clouzot, Claire**
John Cassavetes **20**:45
Andy Warhol **20**:419

**Clucas, Humphrey**
Philip Larkin **5**:227

**Clum, John M.**
Peter Shaffer **14**:487

**Clurman, Harold**
Edward Albee **2**:2; **5**:14
Jean Anouilh **3**:12
Fernando Arrabal **2**:15; **9**:41
Alan Ayckbourn **5**:37; **8**:35; **18**:30
Samuel Beckett **2**:47; **6**:33
Ed Bullins **1**:47; **5**:83
Alice Childress **12**:106
D. L. Coburn **10**:108
E. E. Cummings **8**:160
Brian Friel **5**:129
Jean Genet **2**:158
Trevor Griffiths **13**:256
John Guare **14**:220
Bill Gunn **5**:153
Christopher Hampton **4**:211, 212
Lorraine Hansberry **17**:190
Lillian Hellman **18**:226
Rolf Hochhuth **4**:230
William Inge **8**:308
Eugène Ionesco **4**:250
Preston Jones **10**:296
Arthur Kopit **18**:287, 291
David Mamet **15**:355, 356
Terrence McNally **4**:347; **7**:217, 218
Mark Medoff **6**:322
Arthur Miller **1**:218; **6**:335
Jason Miller **2**:284
Sławomir Mrożek **13**:399
Clifford Odets **3**:320
John Osborne **5**:330
Miguel Piñero **4**:402
Harold Pinter **6**:405, 410, 415, 419; **15**:426

David Rabe **4**:426; **8**:450, 451
Terence Rattigan **7**:355
Eric Rohmer **16**:537
Anthony Shaffer **19**:413
Peter Shaffer **5**:388
Sam Shepard **6**:496, 497; **17**:437, 442
Neil Simon **11**:496
Bernard Slade **11**:508
John Steinbeck **5**:408
Tom Stoppard **1**:327; **4**:526; **5**:411; **8**:501; **15**:521
David Storey **5**:417; **8**:505
Elizabeth Swados **12**:557
George Tabori **19**:437
Megan Terry **19**:438
Gore Vidal **2**:450
Joseph A. Walker **19**:454, 455
Richard Wesley **7**:519
Thornton Wilder **6**:573
Tennesse Williams **2**:465; **5**:500, 504; **7**:545
Lanford Wilson **7**:549; **14**:592

**Clute, John**
Samuel R. Delany **14**:147

**Cluysenaar, Anne**
László Nagy **7**:251
Jon Silkin **6**:498

**Coale, Samuel**
Jerzy Kosinski **3**:273; **6**:284
Alain Robbe-Grillet **6**:468

**Coates, John**
Patrick White **18**:545

**Coates, Ken**
Aleksandr I. Solzhenitsyn **18**:500

**Cobb, Jane**
Betty Cavanna **12**:97
Henry Gregor Felsen **17**:120
Frank B. Gilbreth, Jr. and Ernestine Gilbreth Carey **17**:154, 155
Lee Kingman **17**:243
Mary Stolz **12**:547

**Cobb, Richard**
René Clair **20**:68

**Cocks, Geoffrey**
Thomas Pynchon **18**:437

**Cocks, Jay**
Mel Brooks **12**:77
Michael Cimino **16**:208
Werner Herzog **16**:326
Richard Lester **20**:231
Gordon Parks **16**:460
Harold Pinter **3**:388
Bruce Springsteen **17**:480
François Truffaut **20**:383
Frank Zappa **17**:587

**Cocks, John C., Jr.**
Federico Fellini **16**:274

**Cockshott, Gerald**
John Ford **16**:307

**Coe, Richard L.**
Lily Tomlin **17**:521

**CRITIC INDEX**

**Coe, Richard N.**
Jean Genet **1**:117
Eugène Ionesco **6**:251

**Coelho, Joaquim-Francisco**
Carlos Drummond de Andrade
**18**:4

**Coffey, Barbara**
François Truffaut **20**:393

**Coffey, Warren**
Kurt Vonnegut, Jr. **3**:494

**Cogell, Elizabeth Cummins**
Ursula K. LeGuin **13**:348

**Cogley, John**
Dan Wakefield **7**:502

**Cogswell, Fred**
Earle Birney **1**:34
Phyllis Gotlieb **18**:191
Joe Rosenblatt **15**:446

**Cohen, Arthur A.**
Joseph Brodsky **4**:77
Cynthia Ozick **3**:372
Marguerite Yourcenar **19**:483

**Cohen, Dean**
J. P. Donleavy **1**:76

**Cohen, Debra Rae**
Anne McCaffrey **17**:283

**Cohen, George**
Robin Cook **14**:131

**Cohen, Henry**
Aimé Césaire **19**:96

**Cohen, J. M.**
Yevgeny Yevtushenko **13**:619

**Cohen, Larry**
Jules Feiffer **2**:133

**Cohen, Mitch**
Brian Wilson **12**:652
Neil Young **17**:578

**Cohen, Mitchell S.**
Elaine May **16**:433

**Cohen, Nathan**
Mordecai Richler **5**:371

**Cohen, Stephen F.**
Aleksandr I. Solzhenitsyn
**18**:497

**Cohn, Dorrit**
Alain Robbe-Grillet **1**:289

**Cohn, Ellen**
Lily Tomlin **17**:517

**Cohn, Jeanette**
Hilma Wolitzer **17**:564

**Cohn, Nik**
Mick Jagger and Keith Richard
**17**:234
Paul Simon **17**:465
Bruce Springsteen **17**:480

**Cohn, Ruby**
Edward Albee **1**:4; **2**:4
Fernando Arrabal **18**:20
James Baldwin **2**:32
Imamu Amiri Baraka **2**:35
Djuna Barnes **4**:43

John Dos Passos **4**:133
Lawrence Ferlinghetti **2**:134
John Hawkes **4**:215
Robinson Jeffers **11**:310
Kenneth Koch **5**:219
Robert Lowell **11**:324
Arthur Miller **2**:279
Harold Pinter **6**:405
Kenneth Rexroth **11**:472
Thornton Wilder **15**:569
Tennessee Williams **2**:465

**Cohn-Sfetcu, Ofelia**
Hubert Aquin **15**:15

**Colby, Rob**
Olga Broumas **10**:76

**Colby, Thomas E.**
Hermann Hesse **17**:206

**Coldwell, Joan**
Marie-Claire Blais **13**:96

**Cole, Barry**
Ann Quin **6**:442

**Cole, Laurence**
Jean Rhys **2**:372

**Cole, Sheila R.**
Julia W. Cunningham **12**:166

**Cole, Terry M.**
Sonia Levitin **17**:263

**Cole, William**
Charles Causley **7**:42
Alex Comfort **7**:54
Richard Condon **10**:111
Louis Simpson **7**:429
R. S. Thomas **6**:531

**Coleby, John**
E. L. Doctorow **15**:180
Robert Nye **13**:413
David Rudkin **14**:471
George Tabori **19**:438
Francis Warner **14**:553

**Colegate, Isabel**
Susan B. Hill **4**:227
Joyce Carol Oates **6**:369

**Coleman, Alexander**
Alejo Carpentier **11**:99
José Donoso **11**:145
Pablo Neruda **2**:309
Nicanor Parra **2**:331
Marguerite Yourcenar **19**:484

**Coleman, Sister Anne Gertrude**
Paul Vincent Carroll **10**:95

**Coleman, John**
Robert Altman **16**:44
Mel Brooks **12**:79
Marguerite Duras **20**:102
Kon Ichikawa **20**:180
Elia Kazan **16**:367
Jack Kerouac **2**:227
Pier Paolo Pasolini **20**:266
Simon Raven **14**:439
Satyajit Ray **16**:487
Jerzy Skolimowski **20**:354
Leon Uris **7**:490
Orson Welles **20**:452

**Coleman, Ray**
Joan Armatrading **17**:8
Bob Marley **17**:268, 269

**Coles, Robert**
Shirley Ann Grau **4**:208
Kenneth Koch **8**:324
Jonathan Kozol **17**:249
Cormac McCarthy **4**:343
Tillie Olsen **13**:432
Walker Percy **14**:415
Muriel Rukeyser **10**:442
William Stafford **7**:461
William Styron **1**:331
Frederick Wiseman **20**:467
James Wright **3**:544

**Collier, Carmen P.**
Pearl S. Buck **7**:32

**Collier, Christopher**
Esther Forbes **12**:212

**Collier, Eugenia**
James Baldwin **2**:33
Melvin Van Peebles **2**:447

**Collier, Michael**
Delmore Schwartz **10**:463

**Collier, Peter**
Earl Rovit **7**:383

**Collings, Rex**
Wole Soyinka **5**:397

**Collins, Anne**
Stephen King **12**:311

**Collins, Harold R.**
Amos Tutuola **5**:443

**Collins, J. A.**
Christopher Fry **14**:185

**Collins, Michael**
Tom Wolfe **15**:584

**Collins, Ralph L.**
Elmer Rice **7**:360

**Collins, Robert G.**
George Lucas **16**:412

**Colmer, John**
Shirley Hazzard **18**:215

**Colombo, John Robert**
B. P. Nichol **18**:366

**Columba, Sister Mary, P.B.V.M.**
Rosemary Wells **12**:638

**Combs, Richard**
Woody Allen **16**:4
Robert Altman **16**:24
John Cassavetes **20**:48, 53
Claude Chabrol **16**:182
Brian De Palma **20**:76
Rainer Werner Fassbinder
**20**:107, 117, 120
Werner Herzog **16**:322, 323,
333
Elaine May **16**:431
Gordon Parks **16**:459
Martin Scorsese **20**:330, 331,
332
Jerzy Skolimowski **20**:353
François Truffaut **20**:393
Peter Weir **20**:425, 427

Orson Welles **20**:453

**Commager, Henry Steele**
Esther Forbes **12**:209
MacKinlay Kantor **7**:194

**Compton, D. G.**
Samuel Beckett **3**:47
Frederick Buechner **2**:84
John Gardner **2**:151
Bernard Kops **4**:274
Vladimir Nabokov **6**:352
Frederic Prokosch **4**:422

**Compton-Burnett, Ivy**
Ivy Compton-Burnett **15**:139

**Conarroe, Joel**
John Berryman **8**.91, **13**.76
Richard Howard **7**:167
Howard Nemerov **2**:307
Anne Sexton **2**:391
W. D. Snodgrass **2**:405

**Condini, Nereo**
Eugenio Montale **7**:230
Octavio Paz **19**:368
Isaac Bashevis Singer **6**:511
Tom Wolfe **9**:579

**Condon, Richard**
John le Carré **15**:324

**Conley, Timothy K.**
William Faulkner **9**:200

**Conn, Stewart**
Anne Stevenson **7**:463

**Connell, Evan S., Jr.**
Simone de Beauvoir **2**:43
James Dickey **2**:116
Gilbert Rogin **18**:459
Wilfrid Sheed **2**:392

**Connelly, Kenneth**
John Berryman **1**:34

**Connelly, Robert**
Luchino Visconti **16**:565

**Conner, John W.**
E. M. Almedingen **12**:5
Honor Arundel **17**:15, 16
Judy Blume **12**:44
Frank Bonham **12**:53
Nikki Giovanni **4**:189
Jesse Jackson **12**:290
Madeleine L'Engle **12**:348,
349, 350
John Neufeld **17**:309
Lenora Mattingly Weber **12**:635

**Connolly, Cyril**
Ernest Hemingway **6**:225
Louis MacNeice **4**:315
Ezra Pound **4**:408, 414

**Conquest, Robert**
Ezra Pound **7**:334
Aleksandr I. Solzhenitsyn
**2**:413; **4**:513

**Conrad, Randall**
Luis Buñuel **16**:145

**Conron, Brandon**
Alice Munro **19**:343

**Conroy, Jack**
Charles Bukowski **2**:84

**Consiglio, Alberto**
Rouben Mamoulian **16**:421

**Contoski, Victor**
Robert Duncan **2**:123
David Ignatow **7**:175
David Kherdian **6**:281
W. S. Merwin **18**:334
Czesław Miłosz **11**:376
Marge Piercy **6**:403; **18**:405
Charles Simic **9**:480

**Conway, John D.**
Paul Vincent Carroll **10**:98

**Coogan, Tim Pat**
Brian Moore **19**:332

**Cook, Albert**
Djuna Barnes **4**:43
André Malraux **4**:327

**Cook, Bruce**
Kingsley Amis **8**:11
James Baldwin **3**:32; **17**:39
Heinrich Böll **6**:84
William S. Burroughs **1**:49
Evan S. Connell, Jr. **4**:109
Gregory Corso **1**:64
Robert Duncan **1**:83
Allen Ginsberg **1**:118
Lillian Hellman **8**:281
Marjorie Kellogg **2**:224
Thomas Keneally **5**:211
Jack Kerouac **1**:166
Jerzy Kosinski **1**:171
Ross Macdonald **2**:256
Norman Mailer **1**:193
Brian Moore **7**:235
Charles Olson **1**:263
Ezra Pound **1**:276
Budd Schulberg **7**:403
Irwin Shaw **7**:413
Georges Simenon **2**:399
Gary Snyder **1**:318
Dalton Trumbo **19**:446, 448
Arnold Wesker **5**:484
William Carlos Williams **1**:372

**Cook, Carole**
V. S. Pritchett **15**:443
Eudora Welty **14**:565

**Cook, David**
Roald Dahl **18**:108
Camara Laye **4**:283

**Cook, Martha E.**
Donald Davidson **19**:128

**Cook, Reginald L.**
Robert Frost **1**:111

**Cook, Richard M.**
Carson McCullers **12**:429

**Cook, Roderick**
Harry Mathews **6**:314
Berry Morgan **6**:340

**Cook, Stanley**
William Golding **17**:173

**Cooke, Judy**
Peter Rushforth **19**:406

**Cooke, Michael G.**
Ronald L. Fair **18**:141
Alex Haley **12**:246, 252
Gayl Jones **9**:308
Margaríta Karapánou **13**:314
George Lamming **4**:279
Michael Mott **15**:381
Joyce Carol Oates **9**:403
Jean Rhys **4**:445
William Styron **1**:331
John Updike **2**:443
Alice Walker **9**:558
Robert Penn Warren **4**:581

**Cookson, William**
David Jones **4**:260
Hugh MacDiarmid **4**:310

**Cooley, Peter**
Daniel Halpern **14**:231
Daniel Hoffman **13**:286
Ted Hughes **2**:201
David Ignatow **14**:275
Peter Wild **14**:581

**Coombs, Orde**
James Baldwin **8**:40

**Coon, Caroline**
Joan Armatrading **17**:8

**Cooper, Arthur**
Richard Adams **5**:5
Richard Condon **6**:115
Michael Crichton **2**:109
J. P. Donleavy **6**:142
Ward Just **4**:266
John le Carré **3**:281
James A. Michener **5**:290
Wright Morris **7**:245
Gordon Parks **16**:459
Ishmael Reed **6**:450
Philip Roth **2**:378
Irwin Shaw **7**:414
David Storey **5**:417
Gore Vidal **6**:549
Fay Weldon **6**:563

**Cooper, Jane**
Muriel Rukeyser **15**:456

**Cooper, Nina**
Gabriel Marcel **15**:362

**Cooper, Philip**
Robert Lowell **4**:300

**Cooper, Susan**
Colin Thiele **17**:494, 495

**Cooper, William**
C. P. Snow **19**:427

**Cooperman, Stanley**
W. S. Merwin **1**:212
Philip Roth **3**:438
Marguerite yourcenar **19**:481

**Coover, Robert**
José Donoso **4**:127
Carlos Fuentes **8**:224
Gabriel García Márquez **15**:253

**Copland, R. A.**
Noel Hilliard **15**:279

**Coppage, Noel**
David Bowie **17**:66
Mick Jagger and Keith Richard **17**:233
Joni Mitchell **12**:439
Willie Nelson **17**:304
Laura Nyro **17**:314
Phil Ochs **17**:334
Buffy Sainte-Marie **17**:431
Neil Young **17**:583

**Corbin, Louise**
Jean Renoir **20**:293

**Cordesse, Gérard**
William S. Burroughs **15**:110

**Core, George**
Edna O'Brien **8**:429
Seán O'Faoláin **7**:273
John Crowe Ransom **2**:364; **5**:366
Jean Rhys **14**:447
William Styron **1**:331
Allen Tate **4**:537
William Trevor **9**:529

**Corke, Hilary**
John Cheever **3**:106

**Corliss, Richard**
Ingmar Bergman **16**:58
Richard Lester **20**:224
Garry Marshall **17**:277

**Corman, Cid**
Kon Ichikawa **20**:179
George Oppen **13**:433

**Corn, Alfred**
Elizabeth Bowen **15**:78
John Hollander **8**:302
Eugenio Montale **18**:339
Boris Pasternak **7**:300
Reg Saner **9**:469
L. E. Sissman **18**:489

**Cornwell, Ethel F.**
Samuel Beckett **3**:45
Nathalie Sarraute **8**:471

**Corodimas, Peter**
Ira Levin **6**:305
Françoise Sagan **17**:425

**Corr, Patricia**
Evelyn Waugh **1**:356

**Corrigan, Mary Ann**
Tennessee Williams **11**:571, 575

**Corrigan, Matthew**
Charles Olson **5**:328

**Corrigan, Robert W.**
Edward Albee **5**:11
John Arden **6**:9
Saul Bellow **6**:51
Robert Bolt **14**:89
Friedrich Dürrenmatt **8**:196
Michel de Ghelderode **6**:197
Arthur Miller **1**:218
John Osborne **5**:332
Harold Pinter **6**:417
Thornton Wilder **5**:494

**Corrigan, Sylvia Robinson**
Sylvia Plath **17**:350

**Corrington, John William**
James Dickey **1**:73
Marion Montgomery **7**:233

**Cort, David**
Jules Archer **12**:16

**Cortázar, Julio**
Jorge Luis Borges **8**:102

**Cortínez, Carlos**
Octavio Paz **10**:393

**Corwin, Phillip**
Kay Boyle **5**:67

**Cosgrave, Mary Silva**
Maya Angelou **12**:13

**Cosgrave, Patrick**
Kingsley Amis **3**:8
Robert Lowell **4**:300
Georges Simenon **3**:452
Julian Symons **14**:523

**Cosman, Max**
Sylvia Ashton-Warner **19**:21

**Cott, Jonathan**
Bob Dylan **6**:156
Mick Jagger and Keith Richard **17**:234
John Lennon and Paul McCartney **12**:356
Jim Morrison **17**:287
Patti Smith **12**:542

**Cotter, James Finn**
Robert Bly **10**:62
William Everson **14**:167
Nikki Giovanni **19**:192
Thom Gunn **18**:204
Robert Pinsky **19**:371
May Sarton **14**:482
Barry Spacks **14**:511
Mark Van Doren **6**:542
David Wagoner **15**:559
John Hall Wheelock **14**:571

**Cottrell, Robert D.**
Simone de Beauvoir **8**:58

**Coughlan, Margaret N.**
E. M. Almedingen **12**:4

**Covatta, Anthony**
Elio Vittorini **6**:551

**Coveney, Michael**
Athol Fugard **5**:130
Sam Shepard **6**:496

**Cowan, Louise**
Caroline Gordon **13**:243
John Crowe Ransom **5**:363
Allen Tate **2**:431
Robert Penn Warren **6**:555

**Cowan, Michael**
Norman Mailer **8**:371

**Cowie, Peter**
Michelangelo Antonioni **20**:24
Ingmar Bergman **16**:50, 65
Nagisa Oshima **20**:249, 256
Satyajit Ray **16**:480
Jean Renoir **20**:294, 296
Eric Rohmer **16**:531
Jerzy Skolimowski **20**:353
Orson Welles **20**:451

**Cowley, Malcolm**
  Conrad Aiken 10:3
  Pearl S. Buck 7:31; 11:71
  Erskine Caldwell 14:93
  E. E. Cummings 3:118
  John Dos Passos 4:135
  William Faulkner 8:210
  Robert Frost 4:173
  Ernest Hemingway 13:270; 19:212
  Doris Lessing 6:303
  John O'Hara 2:325
  Ezra Pound 4:407
  Upton Sinclair 15:500
  James Thurber 5:430

**Cox, C. B.**
  James Baldwin 17:27
  William Golding 17:163

**Cox, David**
  Wilfrid Sheed 4:489

**Cox, Kenneth**
  Hugh MacDiarmid 4:311
  Ezra Pound 4:413
  C. H. Sisson 8:490
  Louis Zukofsky 7:562; 11:582

**Coxe, Louis**
  David Jones 2:217
  Anne Sexton 2:391

**Coyne, John R., Jr.**
  Frederick Forsyth 5:125
  Dick Francis 2:142
  E. Howard Hunt 3:251
  Ward Just 4:266
  Donald E. Westlake 7:528
  Tom Wolfe 2:481

**Coyne, Patricia S.**
  Kingsley Amis 3:10
  Erica Jong 4:265
  Joyce Carol Oates 9:402
  Wilfrid Sheed 2:395
  Morris L. West 6:564

**Crabtree, Paul**
  Louis Auchincloss 18:27

**Craft, Robert**
  Aldous Huxley 5:193

**Craft, Wallace**
  Eugenio Montale 7:230

**Crago, Hugh**
  Andre Norton 12:460
  J.R.R. Tolkien 12:573

**Craib, Roderick**
  Bernard Malamud 3:322

**Craig, George**
  Michel Butor 15:115

**Craig, Patricia**
  Beryl Bainbridge 18:33
  Joan Barfoot 18:36
  William Mayne 12:404
  Edna O'Brien 8:429
  Julia O'Faolain 19:360
  Katherine Paterson 12:485
  Frederic Raphael 14:438
  Fay Weldon 19:468

**Craig, Randall**
  Jean Genet 2:160
  Bernard Pomerance 13:444
  Robert Shaw 5:390
  Sam Shepard 4:489
  E. A. Whitehead 5:489

**Crain, Jane Larkin**
  Alice Adams 13:1
  Caroline Blackwood 9:101
  André Brink 18:66
  E. M. Broner 19:72
  William F. Buckley, Jr. 18:81
  Sara Davidson 9:175
  Lawrence Durrell 6:153
  Bruce Jay Friedman 5:126
  John Gardner 5:134
  Gail Godwin 8:248
  Shirley Ann Grau 9:240
  Milan Kundera 4:276
  Alan Lelchuk 5:244
  Doris Lessing 6:299
  Grace Paley 4:394
  Walker Percy 6:401
  Kathleen Raine 7:353
  C. P. Snow 6:518
  Muriel Spark 5:398
  Mario Vargas Llosa 6:545
  Gore Vidal 4:555
  David Wagoner 5:474
  Frederick Wiseman 20:474
  Sol Yurick 6:583

**Crane, Peggy**
  Joy Adamson 17:6
  Jean Rhys 14:446

**Crankshaw, Edward**
  Yuri Krotkov 19:264
  Aleksandr I. Solzhenitsyn 1:319

**Cranston, Mechthild**
  René Char 14:126

**Crawford, Pamela**
  Andy Warhol 20:418

**Creagh, Patrick**
  Giuseppe Ungaretti 7:484

**Creeley, Robert**
  Robert Duncan 4:141
  William Everson 5:121
  Robert Graves 6:210
  Charles Olson 5:326
  Ezra Pound 3:395
  William Stafford 4:519
  William Carlos Williams 5:507
  Louis Zukofsky 4:599; 18:559

**Creighton, Joanne V.**
  Joyce Carol Oates 19:348

**Creighton, Luella**
  Dalton Trumbo 19:444

**Crews, Frederick C.**
  E. M. Forster 13:219
  Shirley Ann Grau 4:207
  Philip Roth 2:379

**Crews, Harry**
  Elliott Baker 8:39

**Crichton, Michael**
  Frederick Forsyth 2:136
  Kurt Vonnegut, Jr. 3:495

**Crick, Francis**
  Michael McClure 6:319

**Crick, Joyce**
  Michael Hamburger 5:159

**Crider, Bill**
  Stephen King 12:310

**Crinklaw, Don**
  John Gardner 3:186

**Crinkley, Richmond**
  Edward Albee 2:3

**Crisp, Quentin**
  Graham Greene 18:198

**Crist, Judith**
  Lindsay Anderson 20:17
  Mel Brooks 12:81
  John Cassavetes 20:52
  Julia W. Cunningham 12:163
  Harry Kemelman 2:225
  Richard Lester 20:231
  Laurence Olivier 20:241
  Nagisa Oshima 20:249
  Satyajit Ray 16:488
  Alain Resnais 16:514
  Ken Russell 16:547

**Croce, Arlene**
  Ingmar Bergman 16:47
  Shirley Clarke 16:217
  Vittorio De Sica 20:88
  Jean-Luc Godard 20:128
  John Huston 20:163
  Stanley Kubrick 16:377
  Satyajit Ray 16:475
  François Truffaut 20:381

**Croft, Julian**
  Robert D. FitzGerald 19:182

**Croft, L. B.**
  Yevgeny Yevtushenko 13:620

**Cromelin, Richard**
  David Bowie 17:58

**Crompton, D. W.**
  William Golding 17:171

**Cross, Michael S.**
  Frank Herbert 12:279

**Cross, Richard K.**
  Richard Eberhart 19:143

**Crouch, Marcus**
  Ruth M. Arthur 12:28
  Margot Benary-Isbert 12:34
  Peter Dickinson 12:175
  Leon Garfield 12:228
  Alan Garner 17:144
  Andre Norton 12:464

**Crouch, Stanley**
  James Baldwin 17:42
  Ishmael Reed 13:480

**Crow, John**
  Harlan Ellison 13:203

**Crowder, Richard H.**
  Carl Sandburg 1:300; 15:467

**Crowe, Linda**
  Honor Arundel 17:13

**Crowson, Lydia**
  Jean Cocteau 8:148

**Crowther, Bosley**
  Jean Cocteau 16:222, 223, 227
  Carl Theodor Dreyer 16:256
  Federico Fellini 16:270
  John Ford 16:305, 309
  John Huston 20:157, 158, 159, 161
  Kon Ichikawa 20:178
  Elia Kazan 16:360, 363
  Norman Lear 12:326
  Laurence Olivier 20:234
  Alain Resnais 16:498
  Carlos Saura 20:314
  Josef von Sternberg 20:375
  Agnès Varda 16:554
  Andrzej Wajda 16:577
  Jessamyn West 17:548
  Billy Wilder 20:455, 457, 462

**Crozier, Andrew**
  Ed Dorn 18:128

**Crump, G. B.**
  Tom Stoppard 15:519

**Cruse, Harold W.**
  W.E.B. Du Bois 2:120

**Cruttwell, Patrick**
  Sylvia Ashton-Warner 19:23
  Adolfo Bioy Casares 4:63
  Jerzy Kosinski 3:274
  Iris Murdoch 2:296
  Patrick White 7:529

**Cuddon, J. A.**
  Peter De Vries 2:114
  James Purdy 4:423
  Frederic Raphael 2:367
  Claude Simon 4:497

**Culbertson, Diana**
  Alberto Moravia 7:243

**Cullen, Elinor S.**
  Ruth M. Arthur 12:26

**Culler, Jonathan**
  Walker Percy 8:439

**Culpan, Norman**
  Andre Norton 12:470, 471

**Cumare, Rosa**
  Flann O'Brien 5:317

**Cumming, Joseph B., Jr.**
  Richard O'Brien 17:325

**Cunliffe, Marcus**
  Irving Stone 7:469

**Cunliffe, W. Gordon**
  Heinrich Böll 11:57
  Günter Grass 1:126
  Uwe Johnson 10:283

**Cunningham, Laura**
  Richard Price 6:427

**Cunningham, Valentine**
  Louis Auchincloss 6:15
  John Barth 5:51
  Donald Barthelme 3:43
  Richard Brautigan 12:70
  Pearl S. Buck 18:80
  Alejo Carpentier 8:134

Margaret Craven **17**:79
Len Deighton **4**:119
Don DeLillo **13**:179
Ilya Ehrenburg **18**:137
Buchi Emecheta **14**:159
Shusaku Endo **7**:96; **14**:161
Penelope Fitzgerald **19**:172
Frederick Forsyth **5**:125
Mervyn Jones **10**:295
Anna Kavan **5**:206
William Kotzwinkle **5**:220
Mary Lavin **4**:282
Colin MacInnes **4**:314
Stanley Middleton **7**:220
Yukio Mishima **4**:358
Vladimir Nabokov **3**:355
Hans Erich Nossack **6**:364
David Plante **7**:307
Bernice Rubens **19**:404
Ward Ruyslinck **14**:471
Françoise Sagan **9**:468
William Sansom **6**:484
Emma Tennant **13**:536
Paul Theroux **8**:513
Gillian Tindall **7**:474
Ludvík Vaculík **7**:495
Harriet Waugh **6**:559
Arnold Wesker **5**:483
Patrick White **4**:587

**Cuppy, Will**
Agatha Christie **12**:112, 113

**Curran, Thomas M.**
Shusaku Endo **19**:161

**Current-Garcia, Eugene**
George Seferis **11**:494

**Currie, William**
Kōbō Abe **8**:2

**Curtis, Anthony**
Alan Ayckbourn **18**:30
W. Somerset Maugham **15**:365
J. B. Priestley **5**:351

**Curtis, C. Michael**
Sara Davidson **9**:175
Annie Dillard **9**:179

**Curtis, Jerry L.**
Jean Genet **10**:224

**Curtis, Penelope**
Katherine Paterson **12**:485

**Curtis, Simon**
Donald Davie **5**:113
Seamus Heaney **7**:151

**Curtius, E. R.**
William Goyen **14**:209

**Cuscuna, Michael**
Jim Morrison **17**:289

**Cushman, Jerome**
Jascha Kessler **4**:270

**Cushman, Kathleen**
Kurt Vonnegut, Jr. **12**:610

**Cushman, Keith**
Marilyn French **18**:157
Mark Schorer **9**:474

**Cutler, Bruce**
Louis Simpson **7**:428

**Cutter, William**
S. Y. Agnon **4**:15

**Cutts, John**
Frank Capra **16**:157
Carl Theodor Dreyer **16**:258
Lorraine Hansberry **17**:184

**Cyclops**
Garry Marshall **17**:275

**Czajkowska, Magdalena**
Tadeusz Rózewicz **9**:463

**Dabney, Lewis H.**
William Faulkner **6**:174

**Dacey, Philip**
Arthur Gregor **9**:255

**Daemmrich, Horst S.**
Eugène Ionesco **11**:289

**Dahlie, Hallvard**
Brian Moore **1**:225; **7**:237
Alice Munro **10**:357

**Daiches, David**
W. H. Auden **1**:8
Saul Bellow **3**:55
Elizabeth Bowen **1**:39
Ivy Compton-Burnett **1**:60
Elizabeth Daryush **19**:119
C. Day Lewis **1**:72
T. S. Eliot **1**:89
William Empson **3**:147
Christopher Fry **2**:143
Robert Graves **1**:126
Henry Green **2**:178
Aldous Huxley **1**:149
Hugh MacDiarmid **2**:252
Louis MacNeice **1**:186
Bernard Malamud **3**:323
Henry Roth **6**:473
Edith Sitwell **2**:403
Stephen Spender **1**:322
Evelyn Waugh **1**:356

**Daiker, Donald A.**
Hugh Nissenson **4**:381

**Dale, Peter**
John Berryman **2**:58
Basil Bunting **10**:84
Stanley Burnshaw **13**:128,129

**Daley, Robert**
Mark Harris **19**:200
John R. Tunis **12**:597

**Dalgleish, Alice**
Madeleine L'Engle **12**:346, 347

**Dallas, Karl**
Joni Mitchell **12**:435
Jim Morrison **17**:287
Phil Ochs **17**:330
Frank Zappa **17**:593

**Dalton, David**
Mick Jagger and Keith Richard **17**:239
Jim Morrison **17**:292
Paul Simon **17**:466

**Dalton, Elizabeth**
E. M. Broner **19**:71
Vladimir Nabokov **1**:245
John Updike **1**:344

**Daltry, Patrice M.**
Lee Kingman **17**:245

**Daly, Maureen**
Mary Stolz **12**:551

**Dame, Enid**
Chaim Potok **7**:322

**Dana, Robert**
Yukio Mishima **2**:286

**Dangerfield, George**
Rayner Heppenstall **10**:272
Compton Mackenzie **18**:313
Carson McCullers **12**:410

**Daniel, John**
Ann Quin **6**:441
Isaac Bashevis Singer **6**:507

**Daniel, Lorne**
Andrew Suknaski **19**:432

**Daniel, Robert D.**
Walker Percy **14**:414

**Daniel, Robert W.**
W. D. Snodgrass **10**:478

**Daniels, Robert V.**
Larry Woiwode **10**:540

**Danielson, J. David**
Simone Schwarz-Bart **7**:404

**Danischewsky, Nina**
Ruth M. Arthur **12**:26
Peter Dickinson **12**:167

**Danner, G. Richard**
Eugène Ionesco **15**:298

**D'Arazien, Steven**
Hunter S. Thompson **9**:528

**Dardess, George**
Jack Kerouac **5**:213

**Darling, Frances C.**
Henry Gregor Felsen **17**:120

**Darrach, Brad**
George V. Higgins **4**:224
Joyce Carol Oates **2**:313
Ezra Pound **7**:336
Irving Stone **7**:471

**Das Gupta, Chidananda**
Satyajit Ray **16**:481

**Datchery, Dick**
Agatha Christie **12**:120

**Dauenhauer, Richard**
Paavo Haavikko **18**:206

**Dault, Gary Michael**
Joe Rosenblatt **15**:447, 448

**Dauster, Frank**
Gabriel García Márquez **3**:182

**Davenport, Basil**
Daphne du Maurier **11**:162
Carson McCullers **12**:409

**Davenport, G.**
J.R.R. Tolkien **3**:482

**Davenport, Gary**
Sean O'Faoláin **14**:406

**Davenport, Gary T.**
E. M. Almedingen **12**:4
Matt Cohen **19**:113
Seán O'Faoláin **7**:275

**Davenport, Guy**
E. M. Almedingen **12**:4
Michael Ayrton **7**:17
Beryl Bainbridge **8**:36
Thomas Berger **8**:82
Wendell Berry **8**:85
Richard Brautigan **12**:58
Frederick Buechner **2**:82
Paul Celan **10**:101
Louis-Ferdinand Céline **3**:104
Evan S. Connell, Jr. **4**:110
Joan Didion **1**:75
J. P. Donleavy **4**:124
Donald Hall **13**:260
Miroslav Holub **4**:233
Michael Mott **15**:379
Charles Olson **6**:388; **9**:412
Nicanor Parra **2**:331
Chaim Potok **2**:338
James Purdy **2**:350
J.I.M. Stewart **7**:466
Harriet Waugh **6**:560
Eudora Welty **14**:564
Richard Wilbur **6**:569
Louis Zukofsky **2**:487; **4**:599; **7**:560

**Davey, Frank**
Bill Bissett **18**:58
E. J. Pratt **19**:380
Joe Rosenblatt **15**:446

**David, Jack**
B. P. Nichol **18**:369

**Davidon, Ann Morrissett**
Simone de Beauvoir **8**:57
Grace Paley **4**:391
Gore Vidal **4**:557

**Davidson, Michael**
Jack Spicer **18**:509

**Davidson, Peter**
Sylvia Plath **17**:346

**Davidson, Richard B.**
Christie Harris **12**:266

**Davie, Donald**
A. R. Ammons **5**:30
John Berryman **8**:87
Austin Clarke **6**:112
Elizabeth Daryush **19**:120
T. S. Eliot **15**:210
Thom Gunn **18**:202
Michael Hamburger **5**:159
Anthony Hecht **8**:267
John Hollander **8**:299
Galway Kinnell **5**:217
John Peck **3**:377
Ezra Pound **13**:456
Andrew Sinclair **14**:488
Paul Theroux **11**:529
J.R.R. Tolkien **12**:572

**Davies, Brenda**
René Clair **20**:65
Jean Renoir **20**:296

**Davies, Brian**
Robert Bresson **16**:103
Claude Chabrol **16**:168

CRITIC INDEX

**Davies, R. R.**
Joanne Greenberg 7:135
Diane Johnson 5:198
William Sansom 6:482

**Davies, Russell**
Richard Condon 8:150
Joan Didion 8:177
Michael Hamburger 14:234
Thomas Hinde 11:273
Francis King 8:321
S. J. Perelman 15:418
Kate Roberts 15:445
Josef Škvorecký 15:511
C. P. Snow 19:429
William Trevor 9:528

**Davis, Arthur P.**
Arna Bontemps 18:64
Ann Petry 18:404

**Davis, Charles T.**
Robert Hayden 5:68

**Davis, Cheri Colby**
W. S. Merwin 13:383; 18:332

**Davis, Deborah**
Julio Cortázar 5:109

**Davis, Fath**
Toni Morrison 4:366

**Davis, George**
George Lamming 2:235
Clarence Major 3:320

**Davis, Hope Hale**
John Cheever 8:140
Oriana Fallaci 11:190

**Davis, L. J.**
Richard Brautigan 12:71
Richard Condon 4:106
Peter De Vries 7:78
Stanley Elkin 4:153
Leon Forrest 4:163
Lois Gould 4:200
Hannah Green 3:202
John Hersey 2:188
Stanley Hoffman 5:184
James Jones 10:291
William Kennedy 6:274
Ira Levin 6:307
John O'Hara 2:324
J. F. Powers 8:448
Philip Roth 2:379
Françoise Sagan 6:481
Ronald Sukenick 4:531
J.R.R. Tolkien 8:516
Vassilis Vassilikos 8:524
Richard B. Wright 6:582

**Davis, Lavinia**
Margot Benary-Isbert 12:31
Maureen Daly 17:90

**Davis, M. E.**
José María Arguedas 10:10

**Davis, Mary Gould**
Betty Cavanna 12:98
Esther Forbes 12:207
John R. Tunis 12:595, 596

**Davis, Ossie**
Lorraine Hansberry 17:184

**Davis, Paxton**
Eric Ambler 9:18
George Garrett 3:189

**Davis, Richard**
Woody Allen 16:2
Claude Chabrol 16:169
Ken Russell 16:541

**Davis, Richard A.**
Sam Shepard 17:439

**Davis, Rick**
Richard Brautigan 9:125
Richard Condon 10:111

**Davis, Robert Gorham**
Saul Bellow 2:49
Paul Bowles 19:57
John Dos Passos 1:78
William Styron 3:472

**Davis, Robert Murray**
Evelyn Waugh 1:359

**Davis, Stephen**
Bob Marley 17:267
Jimmy Page and Robert Plant
12:480
Brian Wilson 12:645

**Davis, William V.**
Robert Bly 15:63, 67

**Davison, Peter**
Robert Creeley 8:151
Robert Frost 4:175
Tess Gallagher 18:169
Doris Grumbach 13:257
Robert Hass 18:209
John Hollander 8:298
Galway Kinnell 2:229
Denise Levertov 8:345
Sylvia Plath 2:337
Anne Sexton 8:482
William Stafford 7:460

**Davy, Charles**
René Clair 20:61
Rouben Mamoulian 16:422

**Davy, John**
Arthur Koestler 1:169

**Dawson, Dorotha**
Walter Farley 17:115

**Dawson, Helen**
David Storey 4:529

**Dawson, Jan**
Robert Altman 16:20, 21
Rainer Werner Fassbinder
20:116, 118
Werner Herzog 16:328
Roman Polanski 16:470
Jerzy Skolimowski 20:349
François Truffaut 20:392
Andrzej Wajda 16:583

**Dawson, Rosemary**
Betty Smith 19:422

**Day, A. Grove**
James A. Michener 1:214

**Day, Doris M.**
Peter Shaffer 14:487

**Day, Douglas**
Robert Graves 1:127

**Day, James M.**
Paul Horgan 9:278

**Daymond, Douglas M.**
Mazo de la Roche 14:150

**Dean, Joan F.**
Peter Shaffer 18:475

**Deane, Seamus**
Seamus Heaney 7:150
Thomas Kinsella 19:253

**Debicki, Andrew P.**
Dámaso Alonso 14:15
Claudio Rodríguez 10:439

**De Bolt, Joe**
John Brunner 8:110

**Debrix, Jean R.**
Jean Cocteau 16:223

**DeBuys, William**
Paul Horgan 9:279

**Decancq, Roland**
Lawrence Durrell 8:191

**De Charmant, Elizabeth**
Giorgio Bassani 9:74

**Deck, John**
Harry Crews 6:17
Henry Dumas 6:145
J. G. Farrell 6:173
Michael Moorcock 5:294
John Seelye 7:406

**Dector, Midge**
Leon Uris 7:491

**Deedy, John**
J. P. Donleavy 4:123
Nora Ephron 17:114
Upton Sinclair 11:498

**Deemer, Charles**
Renata Adler 8:7
James Baldwin 17:38
John Cheever 3:108
Peter Handke 5:165
Bernard Malamud 3:324

**Deen, Rosemary F.**
Randall Jarrell 6:259
Galway Kinnell 3:268

**Deer, Harriet**
Stanley Kubrick 16:387

**Deer, Irving**
Stanley Kubrick 16:387

**De Feo, Ronald**
Martin Amis 4:21
Beryl Bainbridge 8:37
Thomas Bernhard 3:65
William S. Burroughs 2:93
José Donoso 4:128
Frederick Exley 11:187
William Gaddis 6:195
Gabriel García Márquez
2:149; 10:216
John Gardner 5:131, 134
Graham Greene 6:219
John Hawkes 1:138
Richard Hughes 11:278
Dan Jacobson 4:255
Jerzy Kosinski 1:172

Iris Murdoch 6:345
Howard Nemerov 6:360
Sylvia Plath 1:270
Anthony Powell 3:404
James Salter 7:388
Gilbert Sorrentino 3:461
William Trevor 7:477
John Updike 5:460
Angus Wilson 5:514

**Deford, Frank**
Martin Scorsese 20:334

**Degenfelder, E. Pauline**
Larry McMurtry 7:213

**Degnan, James P.**
Kingsley Amis 2:10
Roald Dahl 1:71
Wilfrid Sheed 2:394

**Degnan, James P., Jr.**
Betty Smith 19:424

**Deitz, Paula**
Frederick Busch 18:84

**De Jonge, Alex**
Frederik Pohl 18:413
Aleksandr I. Solzhenitsyn 9:506

**Dekker, George**
Donald Davie 8:166

**Dekle, Bernard**
Saul Bellow 1:32
E. E. Cummings 1:69
John Dos Passos 1:80
William Faulkner 1:102
Robert Frost 1:111
Langston Hughes 1:148
John P. Marquand 2:271
Arthur Miller 1:219
John O'Hara 1:262
J. D. Salinger 1:300
Upton Sinclair 11:498
Thornton Wilder 1:366
Tennessee Williams 1:369
William Carlos Williams 1:371

**Delahanty, Thornton**
Rouben Mamoulian 16:419

**Delamater, Jerome H.**
Jean-Luc Godard 20:145

**Delaney, Marshall**
See Fulford, Robert

**Delany, Paul**
A. Alvarez 5:19
Margaret Atwood 4:24
John Berger 19:39

**De la Roche, Catherine**
Jean Renoir 20:288

**Delattre, Genevieve**
Françoise Mallet-Joris 11:355

**De Laurentis, Teresa**
Italo Calvino 8:127

**De Laurot, Edouard**
Federico Fellini 16:270

**Delbanco, Nicholas**
Frederick Busch 10:93
Graham Greene 9:251
Doris Grumbach 13:257

**Deligiorgis, Stavros**
David Kherdian 9:318

**Della Fazia, Alba**
Jean Anouilh 1:7

**Delong-Tonelli, Beverly J.**
Fernando Arrabal 9:36

**Del Rey, Lester**
Frederik Pohl 18:412

**De Luca, Geraldine**
J. D. Salinger 12:517

**DeMara, Nicholas A.**
Italo Calvino 11:87

**Demarest, Michael**
Michael Crichton 6:119

**DeMaria, Robert**
Diane Wakoski 2:459

**Dembo, L. S.**
Charles Olson 2:327
George Oppen 7:283
Louis Zukofsky 2:488

**Demetz, Peter**
Rolf Hochhuth 18:250

**De Mille, Richard**
Carlos Castaneda 12:95

**Demorest, Stephen**
Neil Young 17:579

**Demos, E. Virginia**
Larry Kettelkamp 12:307

**DeMott, Benjamin**
Margaret Atwood 2:20
James Baldwin 2:32
John Barth 14:58
Jorge Luis Borges 2:70
Anthony Burgess 13:126
Vincent Canby 13:132
Truman Capote 19:84
Eleanor Clark 19:107
Robert Coover 15:142
E. L. Doctorow 18:124
T. S. Eliot 2:127
Russell C. Hoban 7:162
Doris Lessing 2:240
Mary McCarthy 14:357
Henry Miller 2:283
Philip Roth 9:462
Josef Skvorecký 15:512
William Styron 15:526
William Trevor 14:537
John Updike 5:459
Kurt Vonnegut, Jr. 2:453
John Wain 15:562
Derek Walcott 14:550
Patrick White 18:547

**DeMott, Robert**
Mary Oliver 19:362
Judith Johnson Sherwin 15:480

**Dempsey, David**
Patrick Boyle 19:67
Martha Gellhorn 14:195
Willard Motley 18:357
Terry Southern 7:454

**Dempsey, Michael**
Robert Altman 16:20
Lindsay Anderson 20:14
Francis Ford Coppola 16:248
John Huston 20:171
Richard Lester 20:226
George Lucas 16:408
Ken Russell 16:546

**Denby, David**
Woody Allen 16:2
John Cassavetes 20:55
Francis Ford Coppola 16:237, 241, 245
Brian De Palma 20:81
Bob Fosse 20:126
Werner Herzog 16:334
Richard Lester 20:232
Martin Scorsese 20:325
Joan Micklin Silver 20:345
Steven Spielberg 20:366, 367
Andy Warhol 20:419

**Deneau, Daniel P.**
Hermann Hesse 3:249
Jakov Lind 1:178
Alain Robbe-Grillet 4:449

**Denham, Paul**
Louis Dudek 11:159

**Denne, Constance Ayers**
Joyce Carol Oates 6:372

**Denney, Reuel**
Conrad Aiken 1:3

**Dennis, Sr. M., R.S.M.**
E. M. Almedingen 12:1

**Dennis, Nigel**
Louis-Ferdinand Céline 1:57
William Golding 17:167
Günter Grass 11:253
Robert Pinget 7:305
E. B. White 10:531

**Dennis, Patrick**
Françoise Sagan 17:422

**Dennison, George**
Paul Goodman 4:197

**DeRamus, Betty**
Joyce Carol Oates 3:364

**Deredita, John**
Pablo Neruda 7:257
Juan Carlos Onetti 7:278

**Deren, Maya**
Maya Deren 16:252

**Der Hovanessian, Diana**
David Kherdian 6:280

**Derman, Lisa**
Ken Follett 18:156

**De Santana, Hubert**
Brian Moore 19:332

**Desilets, E. Michael**
Frederick Wiseman 20:471

**Desmond, Harold F., Jr.**
Melvin Berger 12:38

**Des Pres, Terrence**
Peter Matthiessen 11:360

**Dessner, Lawrence Jay**
Mario Puzo 6:429

**De Teresa, Mary**
Laura Nyro 17:318

**Detweiler, Robert**
John Updike 2:442

**Deutsch, Babette**
W. H. Auden 2:21
Louise Bogan 4:68
E. E. Cummings 3:116
Richard Eberhart 11:176
T. S. Eliot 2:125
William Empson 8:201
Robert Frost 3:171
Jean Garrigue 8:239
H. D. 3:217
Robinson Jeffers 15:300
Stanley Kunitz 11:319
Marianne Moore 2:290
St.-John Perse 4:398
Ezra Pound 2:339
Kathleen Raine 7:351
John Crowe Ransom 2:361
Theodore Roethke 3:432
Carl Sandburg 4:463
Edith Sitwell 2:402
Stephen Spender 2:419
Allen Tate 2:427
Richard Wilbur 9:568
William Carlos Williams 2:466
Marya Zaturenska 11:579

**DeVault, Joseph J.**
Mark Van Doren 6:541

**Dever, Joe**
Edna Ferber 18:151

**Devert, Krystyna**
Hermann Hesse 2:189

**DeVitis, A. A.**
Graham Greene 1:133

**Devlin, John**
Ramón Sender 8:478

**De Vries, Daniel**
Stanley Kubrick 16:387

**De Vries, Peter**
James Thurber 5:429

**Devrnja, Zora**
Charles Olson 9:412
Charles Simic 9:478

**Dewsnap, Terence**
Christopher Isherwood 1:156

**Dey, Susnigdha**
Octavio Paz 19:368

**Dial, John E.**
José María Gironella 11:237

**Díaz, Janet Winecoff**
Fernando Arrabal 18:17
Miguel Delibes 18:111
Ana María Matute 11:363

**Dick, Bernard F.**
Michelangelo Antonioni 20:41
William Golding 1:120
John Hersey 2:188
Iris Murdoch 6:342
Mary Renault 3:426

I. A. Richards 14:454
Stevie Smith 8:492
Gore Vidal 4:558

**Dick, Kay**
Simone de Beauvoir 4:48

**Dickens, Monica**
Colin Thiele 17:495

**Dickey, Chris**
Kurt Vonnegut, Jr. 5:470

**Dickey, James**
Conrad Aiken 1:3
John Ashbery 2:16
John Berryman 1:33
Kenneth Burke 2:87
Stanley Burnshaw 3:91
Hayden Carruth 4:93
E. E. Cummings 1:68
J. V. Cunningham 3:120
Robert Duncan 1:82
Richard Eberhart 3:133
William Everson 1:96
Robert Frost 1:111
Allen Ginsberg 1:118
David Ignatow 4:247
Robinson Jeffers 2:214
Galway Kinnell 1:167
James Kirkup 1:169
John Logan 5:252
Louis MacNeice 1:186
William Meredith 4:347
James Merrill 2:272
W. S. Merwin 1:211
Josephine Miles 1:215
Marianne Moore 1:226
Howard Nemerov 2:305
Mary Oliver 19:361
Charles Olson 1:262; 2:327
Kenneth Patchen 1:265
Sylvia Plath 2:337
Herbert Read 4:439
I. A. Richards 14:452
Theodore Roethke 1:290
May Sarton 4:470
Frederick Seidel 18:474
Anne Sexton 2:390
Louis Simpson 4:497
William Jay Smith 6:512
William Stafford 4:519
Allen Tate 6:527
Derek Walcott 14:548
Robert Penn Warren 1:352; 18:538
Theodore Weiss 3:515
John Hall Wheelock 14:571
Reed Whittemore 4:588
Richard Wilbur 3:531
William Carlos Williams 1:370
Yvor Winters 4:590

**Dickey, R. P.**
Lawrence Ferlinghetti 6:183
Robert Lowell 5:258

**Dickey, William**
Daniel J. Berrigan 4:56
John Berryman 13:75
Hayden Carruth 7:40
James Dickey 2:115
William Everson 5:121
W. S. Merwin 2:277
George Oppen 7:281

CRITIC INDEX

Richard Wilbur 14:577

**Dickins, Anthony**
Vladimir Nabokov 2:304

**Dickinson, Hugh**
Eugène Ionesco 6:250

**Dickinson-Brown, R.**
Barry Spacks 14:510
Lewis Turco 11:551

**Dickstein, Lore**
Gail Godwin 8:247
Judith Guest 8:254
Sue Kaufman 3:263
Judith Rossner 6:469
Isaac Bashevis Singer 3:456

**Dickstein, Morris**
John Barth 7:24
Donald Barthelme 6:29
R. P. Blackmur 2:61
John Cassavetes 20:55
Daniel Fuchs 8:220
John Gardner 3:184
Günter Grass 11:252
Philip Roth 4:454
Hunter S. Thompson 17:509
Rudolph Wurlitzer 2:484

**Didion, Joan**
Woody Allen 16:13
John Cheever 8:137
Elizabeth Hardwick 13:265
Doris Lessing 2:240
Norman Mailer 14:352
V. S. Naipaul 18:365
J. D. Salinger 12:511

**Dienstag, Eleanor**
Sylvia Ashton-Warner 19:22
Lee Kingman 17:246

**Diez, Luys A.**
Juan Carlos Onetti 7:280

**Dillard, Annie**
Evan S. Connell, Jr. 4:109

**Dillard, R.H.W.**
W. S. Merwin 8:389
Wright Morris 18:351
Vladimir Nabokov 2:304
Colin Wilson 3:537

**Diller, Edward**
Friedrich Dürrenmatt 11:171

**Dillingham, Thomas**
Susan Fromberg Schaeffer 6:488

**Dillon, David**
William Goyen 14:211
John Hawkes 4:218
Edwin O'Connor 14:393
Tillie Olsen 13:433
Wallace Stegner 9:509

**Dillon, Michael**
Thornton Wilder 6:571

**Dimeo, Steven**
Ray Bradbury 3:85

**Di Napoli, Thomas**
Günter Grass 11:247

**Dinnage, Rosemary**
A. S. Byatt 19:77
Isak Dinesen 10:152
Elizabeth Hardwick 13:264
Doris Lessing 6:303
Fay Weldon 19:468

**Dinoto, Andrea**
Walter Farley 17:118

**Di Piero, W. S.**
John Ashbery 4:22
John Hawkes 9:269
Philip Levine 14:321
Sam Peckinpah 20:282

**Dirda, Michael**
James Dickey 15:177
Henry Green 13:251
John Knowles 10:303
Gilbert Sorrentino 14:500
Alice Walker 19:452

**Disch, Thomas M.**
Arthur C. Clarke 18:106
Philip José Farmer 19:168
Anne Tyler 18:529

**Ditlea, Steve**
Willie Nelson 17:302

**Ditsky, John**
Richard Brautigan 12:69
John Hawkes 2:186
Erica Jong 8:313
Joyce Carol Oates 2:316

**Dix, Carol**
Martin Amis 4:20

**Dixon, Bob**
Alan Garner 17:149

**Dixon, John W., Jr.**
Elie Wiesel 3:527

**DiZazzo, Raymond**
Robert L. Peters 7:303

**Djilas, Milovan**
Aleksandr I. Solzhenitsyn 2:408

**Djwa, Sandra**
Margaret Laurence 13:341
E. J. Pratt 19:381

**Dobbs, Kildare**
Margaret Laurence 3:278
Alice Munro 6:341

**Dobie, Ann B.**
Muriel Spark 2:416

**Dobrez, L.A.C.**
Jean Genet 14:205

**Doctorow, E. L.**
E. L. Doctorow 15:179
Mary Lee Settle 19:411

**Dodd, Wayne**
Madeleine L'Engle 12:350

**Dodsworth, Martin**
Robert Bly 2:65
Donald Davie 8:163
James Dickey 2:115
Marianne Moore 2:291

**Doerksen, Daniel W.**
Margaret Avison 4:36

**Doerner, William R.**
James Herriot 12:282

**Doherty, Andy**
Frank Zappa 17:592

**Dohmann, Barbara**
Jorge Luis Borges 2:69
Julio Cortázar 2:101
Gabriel García Márquez 2:147
Juan Carlos Onetti 7:276
Juan Rulfo 8:461
Mario Vargas Llosa 3:493

**Dollen, Charles**
William Peter Blatty 2:64
Paul Gallico 2:147
N. Scott Momaday 2:289

**Dombroski, Robert S.**
Carlo Emilio Gadda 11:208

**Domowitz, Janet**
Alice Adams 13:3

**Donadio, Stephen**
John Ashbery 2:19
James Baldwin 17:33
Richard Fariña 9:195
Sandra Hochman 3:250

**Donaghue, Denis**
Barthelme, Donald 13:62

**Donahue, Francis**
Antonio Buero Vallejo 15:96
Camilo José Cela 4:97; 13:147

**Donahue, Walter**
Sam Shepard 4:491

**Donahugh, Robert H.**
Allan W. Eckert 17:104

**Donald, David Herbert**
Alex Haley 12:246

**Donaldson, Scott**
Ernest Hemingway 13:276
Philip Roth 1:293

**Donnard, Jean-Hervé**
Eugène Ionesco 6:249

**Donnelly, Dorothy**
Marge Piercy 3:384

**Donner, Jorn**
Ingmar Bergman 16:52

**Donoghue, Denis**
A. R. Ammons 9:27
John Ashbery 15:34
W. H. Auden 3:24
Saul Bellow 2:51
Elizabeth Bishop 13:95
Marie-Claire Blais 2:63
Kenneth Burke 2:88
Austin Clarke 9:167
C. Day Lewis 6:129
Richard Eberhart 11:175
T. S. Eliot 2:126
John Fowles 10:188
William H. Gass 11:225
William Golding 3:196
Shirley Ann Grau 4:209
Graham Greene 9:250
Seamus Heaney 14:245
Anthony Hecht 8:269
Paul Horgan 9:278

Randall Jarrell 1:160
Robert Lowell 4:295
James Merrill 2:274; 18:331
W. S. Merwin 2:277
Marianne Moore 2:291
Robert Pinsky 19:370
Ezra Pound 2:340
Philip Roth 6:476
Frederick Seidel 18:475
Christina Stead 2:422
Mark Strand 18:515
Allen Tate 6:527; 9:521; 11:526
Charles Tomlinson 2:437
Lionel Trilling 9:530; 11:543
Derek Walcott 2:460
Anne Waldman 7:507
Robert Penn Warren 4:579; 13:581
Rebecca West 7:525
William Carlos Williams 2:467

**Donoghue, Susan**
Joni Mitchell 12:435, 436

**Donohue, Agnes McNeill**
Jessamyn West 17:553

**Donohue, John W.**
Earl Hamner 12:259

**Donovan, Josephine**
Sylvia Plath 3:390

**Dooley, D. J.**
Earle Birney 6:71

**Dooley, Dennis M.**
Robert Penn Warren 10:517

**Dorfman, Ariel**
Miguel Ángel Asturias 13:39

**Dorian, Marguerite**
Mircea Eliade 19:147

**Dorsey, David**
Alex La Guma 19:277

**Dorsey, Margaret A.**
Babbis Friis-Baastad 12:214
Larry Kettelkamp 12:305
Andre Norton 12:458, 459

**Dos Passos, John**
E. E. Cummings 12:139

**Doubrovsky, J. S.**
Eugène Ionesco 6:247

**Doubrovsky, Serge**
Albert Camus 11:93

**Doughtie, Edward**
James Dickey 15:176

**Douglas, Ann**
James T. Farrell 11:196

**Douglas, Ellen**
Flannery O'Connor 6:381
May Sarton 4:471

**Douglas, George H.**
Edmund Wilson 2:477

**Dowd, Nancy Ellen**
Frederick Wiseman 20:468

**Dowie, William**
Sylvia Plath 17:364

CRITIC INDEX

**Dowling, Gordon Graham**
Yukio Mishima 6:337

**Downer, Alan S.**
Thornton Wilder 5:495

**Downing, Robert**
Orson Welles 20:433

**Doxey, William S.**
Ken Kesey 3:267
Flannery O'Connor 3:368

**Doyle, Charles**
James K. Baxter 14:60
See also Doyle, Mike

**Doyle, Jacqueline**
Sean O'Casey 15:406

**Doyle, Mike**
Irving Layton 2:236
A. W. Purdy 6:428
Raymond Souster 5:395, 396
See also Doyle, Charles

**Doyle, Paul A.**
Pearl S. Buck 11:71
Paul Vincent Carroll 10:96
James T. Farrell 8:205
MacKinlay Kantor 7:195
Seán O'Faoláin 1:259; 7:273
Evelyn Waugh 1:359

**Drabble, Margaret**
Michael Frayn 3:164
John Irving 13:295
Philip Larkin 8:333; 9:323
Iris Murdoch 4:367
Muriel Spark 8:494
John Updike 15:544

**Dragonwagon, C.**
Stevie Wonder 12:663

**Drake, Robert**
Carson McCullers 12:426
Reynolds Price 3:405
Eudora Welty 5:478

**Draper, Charlotte W.**
Andre Norton 12:471

**Draudt, Manfred**
Joe Orton 13:436

**Draya, Ren**
Tennessee Williams 15:579

**Drew, Fraser**
John Masefield 11:356

**Drexler, Rosalyn**
Anaïs Nin 14:387

**Dries, Linda R.**
Allan W. Eckert 17:105

**Driver, Christopher**
Yukio Mishima 4:357

**Driver, Sam N.**
Anna Akhmatova 11:6

**Driver, Tom F.**
Jean Genet 1:115
Lorraine Hansberry 17:182
Arthur Miller 1:215; 2:279

**Druska, John**
John Beecher 6:49

**Dryden, Edgar A.**
John Barth 5:52

**Duberman, Martin**
Ed Bullins 1:47
Laura Z. Hobson 7:163
David Mamet 15:355

**Duberstein, Larry**
Joel Lieber 6:312

**Dubois, Larry**
William F. Buckley, Jr. 7:34
Walker Percy 8:445

**Du Bois, W.E.B.**
Arna Bontemps 18:62

**Dubro, Alec**
Jim Morrison 17:288
Laura Nyro 17:313

**Duchêne, Anne**
Alberto Moravia 18:347

**Duddy, Thomas A.**
Louis Zukofsky 11:581

**Dudek, Louis**
Daryl Hine 15:281
Irving Layton 15:320
Alden Nowlan 15:399
James Reaney 13:474
Raymond Souster 14:501

**Duffey, Bernard**
W. H. Auden 4:3
Jack Kerouac 1:66

**Duffy, Dennis**
Philip Child 19:102
Matt Cohen 19:111

**Duffy, Martha**
James Baldwin 4:41
Jean Cocteau 1:59
Joan Didion 1:75
Nikki Giovanni 2:164
Lillian Hellman 4:221
D. Keith Mano 10:328
Tom McHale 5:281
Grace Paley 4:393
Walker Percy 2:334
Sylvia Plath 2:336
Judith Rossner 6:470
Bernice Rubens 19:404
Patrick White 3:523

**Duhamel, P. Albert**
Flannery O'Connor 1:253
Paul Scott 9:477

**Dukes, Ashley**
Emlyn Williams 15:577

**Dullea, Gerard J.**
Gregory Corso 11:123

**Dumas, Bethany K.**
E. E. Cummings 12:159

**Dunbar, Ernest**
Jules Archer 12:21

**Duncan, Erika**
William Goyen 8:251
Anaïs Nin 8:425

**Duncan, Robert**
John Wieners 7:536
Frank Zappa 17:591

**Dunlop, John B.**
Vladimir Voinovich 10:509

**Dunn, Douglas**
Giorgio Bassani 9:77
John Berryman 4:62
George Mackay Brown 5:78
Donald Davie 5:115
Lawrence Durrell 4:147
D. J. Enright 4:156; 8:203
Gavin Ewart 13:209
Geoffrey Grigson 7:136
John Hawkes 7:141
Seamus Heaney 7:150
Dan Jacobson 14:290
Erica Jong 6:268
Christopher Middleton 13:388
Leslie Norris 14:387
Sylvia Plath 5:339
William Plomer 4:407
Peter Porter 13:452
Peter Redgrove 6:446
Kenneth Rexroth 11:473
Jon Silkin 6:499
Anne Stevenson 7:463
Charles Tomlinson 6:534
Andrew Young 5:25

**Dunson, Josh**
Phil Ochs 17:330, 333

**Dupee, F. W.**
Kenneth Koch 5:218
Robert Lowell 3:299
Norman Mailer 11:339
Bernard Malamud 3:321
W. S. Merwin 3:338
John Osborne 5:330
J. F. Powers 4:418

**DuPlessis, Rachel Blau**
Edward Albee 13:6
H. D. 14:229

**Dupree, Robert S.**
Caroline Gordon 13:245
Allen Tate 6:525

**Durbin, Karen**
Eleanor Clark 5:107

**Duree, Barbara Joyce**
Lenora Mattingly Weber 12:633

**Durgnat, Raymond**
Robert Bresson 16:110
Tod Browning 16:122
Luis Buñuel 16:142, 150
John Cassavetes 20:44, 45
Claude Chabrol 16:168
René Clair 20:66
Shirley Clarke 16:216
Rainer Werner Fassbinder
20:119
Federico Fellini 16:273
Jean-Luc Godard 20:129
John Huston 20:168
Kon Ichikawa 20:177
Richard Lester 20:219
Roman Polanski 16:163, 468
Ann Quin 6:442
Jean Renoir 20:291, 304
François Truffaut 20:382
Lina Wertmüller 16:587

**Durham, Frank**
Elmer Rice 7:363

**Durham, Philip**
Dashiell Hammett 3:218;
19:194

**Durrant, Digby**
Caroline Blackwood 6:80
Penelope Fitzgerald 19:174
Julia O'Faolain 6:383

**Durrell, Gerald**
Joy Adamson 17:2

**Durrell, Lawrence**
Odysseus Elytis 15:219
George Seferis 5:385

**Dust, Harvey**
Jules Archer 12:17

**Duvall, E. S.**
Ann Beattie 13:66

**Du Verlie, Claude**
Claude Simon 4:497

**Dwyer, David J.**
Mary Renault 3:426

**Dyck, J. W.**
Boris Pasternak 18:381

**Dyer, Peter John**
René Clair 20:64
Jean Cocteau 16:227
Pier Paolo Pasolini 20:260
Jean Renoir 20:291
Luchino Visconti 16:563
Billy Wilder 20:459

**Dyson, A. E.**
Jorge Luis Borges 19:50
Ted Hughes 14:269
Sylvia Plath 11:446

**Dyson, William**
Ezra Pound 1:276

**Dzwonkoski, F. Peter, Jr.**
T. S. Eliot 6:163

**Eagle, Herbert**
Aleksandr I. Solzhenitsyn 9:504
Ludvík Vaculík 7:495

**Eagle, Robert**
Thomas Hinde 11:274
Alberto Moravia 7:244
Flann O'Brien 4:385

**Eagleton, Terry**
George Barker 8:45
John Berger 19:39
Donald Davie 8:162
Thom Gunn 6:221
Seamus Heaney 7:150
Hermann Hesse 11:272
Elizabeth Jennings 14:293
William Plomer 8:447
Stevie Smith 8:491
Maura Stanton 9:508
Charles Tomlinson 6:535
John Wain 11:561
Andrew Young 5:525

**Eakin, Mary K.**
Mary Stolz 12:553

**Earl, Pauline J.**
Frank B. Gilbreth, Jr. and
Ernestine Gilbreth Carey
17:156

**CRITIC INDEX**

**Early, Len**
Bill Bissett 18:59

**Eastman, Fred**
Marc Connelly 7:55

**Eaton, Anne T.**
Sally Benson 17:47
John R. Tunis 12:593

**Eaton, Charles Edward**
Robert Frost 9:225

**Eberhart, Richard**
Djuna Barnes 8:48
William Empson 19:152
Robert Frost 13:227
Allen Ginsberg 13:239
Archibald MacLeish 3:310
Ezra Pound 7:324
Kenneth Rexroth 2:370

**Ebert, Roger**
Charles Chaplin 16:199

**Echevarría, Roberto González**
Alejo Carpentier 11:101
Julio Cortázar 10:114; 13:158
Carlos Fuentes 10:209
Severo Sarduy 6:486

**Eckley, Grace**
Edna O'Brien 5:312

**Eckley, Wilton**
Harriette Arnow 18:10

**Eckman, Martha**
Colin Wilson 14:583

**Eddins, Dwight**
John Fowles 10:183

**Eddy, Elizabeth M.**
Jonathan Kozol 17:250

**Edel, Leon**
Lawrence Durrell 1:85
William Faulkner 1:100
Ernest Hemingway 10:265
Alain Robbe-Grillet 1:286
Nathalie Sarraute 1:303

**Edelberg, Cynthia Dubin**
Robert Creeley 15:151

**Edelheit, S. J.**
Anthony Burgess 13:126

**Edelman, Sarah Prewitt**
Robert Lowell 15:344

**Edelstein, Arthur**
William Faulkner 1:102
Janet Frame 6:190
Jean Stafford 7:458
Angus Wilson 2:472

**Edelstein, J. M.**
Patricia Highsmith 2:193

**Edelstein, Mark G.**
Flannery O'Connor 6:381

**Edenbaum, Robert I.**
Dashiell Hammett 3:219
John Hawkes 2:185

**Eder, Richard**
Athol Fugard 14:191
Hugh Leonard 19:283
Edna O'Brien 8:430
Bernard Pomerance 13:445
Gerome Ragni and James Rado 17:388
Lanford Wilson 14:590

**Edinborough, Arnold**
Earle Birney 6:70
Jay Macpherson 14:345

**Edmiston, Susan**
Maeve Brennan 5:72

**Edmonds, Walter D.**
Esther Forbes 12:204

**Edwards, C. Hines, Jr.**
James Dickey 4:121

**Edwards, Henry**
David Bowie 17:60
Bruce Springsteen 17:479

**Edwards, K. Anthony**
Henry Gregor Felsen 17:125

**Edwards, Margaret A.**
Betty Cavanna 12:99
Maureen Daly 17:89
Mary Stolz 12:546

**Edwards, Mary Jane**
Paulette Jiles 13:304
Susan Musgrave 13:401

**Edwards, Michael**
René Char 14:130
Donald Davie 5:114
Charles Tomlinson 4:547

**Edwards, Paul**
Amos Tutuola 14:540

**Edwards, Sharon**
Jessamyn West 7:522

**Edwards, Thomas R.**
Lisa Alther 7:14
Kingsley Amis 8:12
James Baldwin 4:41
Donald Barthelme 8:49
Thomas Berger 18:56
Richard Brautigan 12:73
Frederick Buechner 2:83
Charles Bukowski 2:84
Anthony Burgess 5:88
John Cheever 7:48
Evan S. Connell, Jr. 4:108
Stanley Elkin 4:153
Leslie A. Fiedler 4:161
Paula Fox 2:140
John Gardner 2:151; 5:133
Gail Godwin 8:248
Herbert Gold 4:193
James Hanley 8:266
Diane Johnson 13:306
James Jones 10:293
Yoram Kaniuk 19:239
Jerzy Kosinski 2:233
George Lamming 2:235
Norman Mailer 2:264
Harry Mathews 6:616
Peter Matthiessen 7:211
Mary McCarthy 14:363
Thomas McGuane 3:330

Leonard Michaels 6:324
Brian Moore 7:237
Alice Munro 19:347
Tim O'Brien 19:358
Ishmael Reed 2:368
Mordecai Richler 18:454
Philip Roth 3:437
André Schwarz-Bart 2:389
Hubert Selby, Jr. 2:390
Wilfrid Sheed 4:488
Gilbert Sorrentino 14:500
John Updike 5:460
Derek Walcott 4:576
Tom Wolfe 1:375

**Edwards, William D.**
Jules Archer 12:18

**Eggenschwiler, David**
Flannery O'Connor 6:378
William Styron 5:419

**Egoff, Sheila**
Julia W. Cunningham 12:165
Leon Garfield 12:218
Christie Harris 12:265

**Egremont, Max**
Anna Kavan 13:317
Seán O'Faoláin 7:276
Anthony Powell 7:341; 9:438
Gillian Tindall 7:474
Ludvík Vaculík 7:496

**Ehre, Milton**
Aleksandr I. Solzhenitsyn 2:412

**Ehrenpreis, Irvin**
John Ashbery 6:13
W. H. Auden 9:58
T. S. Eliot 13:200
Donald Hall 13:260
Anthony Hecht 13:269
Geoffrey Hill 8:293
Donald Justice 6:272
Robert Lowell 1:180; 8:353
George Oppen 7:285
John Updike 5:455
Robert Penn Warren 18:537

**Eiseley, Loren**
J.R.R. Tolkien 12:566

**Eiseman, Alberta**
Betty Cavanna 12:100
Maureen Daly 17:89
William Mayne 12:390
Lenora Mattingly Weber 12:633

**Eisen, Dulcie**
Ronald Tavel 6:529

**Eisenberg, J. A.**
Isaac Bashevis Singer 1:310

**Eisinger, Chester E.**
Carson McCullers 12:421
Arthur Miller 6:331

**Eisinger, Erica M.**
Marguerite Duras 11:165
Georges Simenon 18:484

**Eisner, Lotte H.**
René Clair 20:64
Fritz Lang 20:210, 213

**Eliade, Mircea**
Mircea Eliade 19:146

**Elias, Robert H.**
James Thurber 5:431

**Eliot, T. S.**
Marianne Moore 13:392; 19:336

**Elizondo, Salvador**
Octavio Paz 3:376

**Elkin, Stanley**
Frederick Forsyth 2:136

**Elleman, Barbara**
Melvin Berger 12:42
Barbara Corcoran 17:77
Madeleine L'Engle 12:351
Sonia Levitin 17:265
Anne McCaffrey 17:282, 284
Katherine Paterson 12:485
Zilpha Keatley Snyder 17:475

**Ellestad, Everett M.**
Pär Lagerkvist 13:333

**Elley, Derek**
Mel Brooks 12:79
Werner Herzog 16:324
Yasujiro Ozu 16:455
Pier Paolo Pasolini 20:266, 269
Ken Russell 16:549
Carlos Saura 20:315
François Truffaut 20:404

**Ellin, Stanley**
Robert Cormier 12:138
Richard Elman 19:151

**Elliott, David**
Roman Polanski 16:470

**Elliott, George P.**
Jean Giono 4:187
Robert Graves 2:176
Norman Mailer 3:317
Susan Sontag 10:485
David Wagoner 3:507

**Elliott, Janice**
Patricia Highsmith 2:193
Aleksandr I. Solzhenitsyn 1:321

**Elliott, Robert C.**
Ursula K. LeGuin 8:341

**Elliott, William I.**
Shusaku Endo 7:95

**Ellis, James**
John Knowles 1:169

**Ellison, Harlan**
Barry N. Malzberg 7:208
Roman Polanski 16:464

**Ellison, Ralph**
Richard Wright 9:583

**Ellmann, Mary**
John Barth 2:39
Vladimir Nabokov 1:244
Joyce Carol Oates 3:364
Sylvia Plath 17:350
Richard Price 12:490
Aleksandr I. Solzhenitsyn 1:321
J.R.R. Tolkien 12:571
Michel Tournier 6:538
Rebecca West 7:526
Vassily S. Yanovsky 2:485

CRITIC INDEX

**Ellmann, Richard**
W. H. Auden 9:55
Giorgio Bassani 9:76
Samuel Beckett 2:47
Elizabeth Daryush 19:119

**Elman, Richard**
William Bronk 10:73
Frederick Busch 10:91
Thomas McGuane 18:323
Richard Price 12:490
Françoise Sagan 17:426
Zilpha Keatley Snyder 17:471

**Elman, Richard M.**
Charles Bukowski 9:137
Hannah Green 3:202
Jack Spicer 8:497
Hunter S. Thompson 9:526
Rudolf Wurlitzer 2:482

**Elon, Amos**
Yehuda Amichai 9:22

**Elsaesser, Thomas**
Rainer Werner Fassbinder
20:110

**Elsom, John**
Alan Ayckbourn 5:35
Samuel Beckett 6:43
Edward Bond 6:85
Michael Frayn 7:108
Arthur Miller 15:376
David Rudkin 14:470
Sam Shepard 6:496
Tom Stoppard 5:412
E. A. Whitehead 5:488

**Elstob, Peter**
Len Deighton 4:119

**Emanuel, James A.**
Langston Hughes 1:147

**Emblidge, David**
E. L. Doctorow 11:143

**Emerson, Donald**
Carson McCullers 12:420

**Emerson, Gloria**
Michael Cimino 16:213

**Emerson, Ken**
David Bowie 17:61
Bruce Springsteen 17:477
Stevie Wonder 12:657

**Emerson, O. B.**
Marion Montgomery 7:232

**Emerson, Sally**
William Mayne 12:404

**Emerson, Stephen**
Gilbert Sorrentino 7:450

**Emmons, Winfred S.**
Katherine Anne Porter 1:273

**Endres, Robin**
Milton Acorn 15:10

**Engel, Bernard F.**
Marianne Moore 1:227

**Engel, Eva J.**
Hermann Hesse 17:202

**Engel, Howard**
Morley Callaghan 14:102

**Engel, Marian**
Penelope Gilliatt 2:160
Margaret Laurence 3:278
Françoise Mallet-Joris 11:356
Joyce Carol Oates 6:372
Françoise Sagan 6:481
Michel Tournier 6:537

**England, David A.**
Garry Marshall 17:278

**Engle, Gary**
Robert Altman 16:22

**Engle, Paul**
Charles M. Schulz 12:531

**English, Raymond**
Carl Zuckmayer 18:553

**Enright, D. J.**
John Ashbery 9:49
Simone de Beauvoir 14:66
Heinrich Böll 3:74; 11:52
Anthony Burgess 4:80; 15:103
Stanley Burnshaw 3:90
James Clavell 6:114
Lawrence Durrell 6:151
Witold Gombrowicz 4:195
Günter Grass 2:271; 4:202
Robert Graves 2:175
Hermann Hesse 3:243
Randall Jarrell 9:296
Yasunari Kawabata 5:206;
9:316
Thomas Keneally 14:302
Carolyn Kizer 15:308
Milan Kundera 9:321
Philip Larkin 3:276
Doris Lessing 3:282
Czesław Miłosz 5:291
Yukio Mishima 4:353
Vladimir Nabokov 3:352
V. S. Naipaul 4:371
Ezra Pound 3:395
Stevie Smith 3:460
C. P. Snow 9:496
Muriel Spark 3:463
John Updike 2:439

**Enslin, Theodore**
George Oppen 7:281

**Eoff, Sherman H.**
Jean-Paul Sartre 1:303
Ramón Sender 8:477

**Ephron, Nora**
Erich Segal 3:447
Garry Trudeau 12:589

**Epps, Garrett**
Thomas Berger 11:47
Nicholas Delbanco 13:174
John Salyes 14:483
Alan Sillitoe 19:421

**Epstein, Joseph**
E. M. Forster 4:165
Nadine Gordimer 18:188
Mark Harris 19:205
Joseph Heller 5:174
Alan Lelchuk 5:241
Aleksandr I. Solzhenitsyn 2:409

Stephen Spender 5:402
Edmund Wilson 2:477; 8:551

**Epstein, Lawrence J.**
Elie Wiesel 5:493

**Epstein, Seymour**
Saul Bellow 13:72
Jerome Charyn 18:99

**Erickson, Peter**
Alice Walker 19:451

**Ericson, Edward, Jr.**
Thornton Wilder 10:533

**Ericson, Edward E., Jr.**
C. S. Lewis 6:310
Aleksandr I. Solzhenitsyn 4:509

**Erlich, Richard**
Harlan Ellison 13:203

**Erlich, Victor**
Joseph Brodsky 6:96

**Ermolaev, Herman**
Mikhail Sholokhov 15:481

**Ernst, Margaret**
Andre Norton 12:455

**Eron, Carol**
John Hawkes 4:218

**Eskin, Stanley G.**
Nicholas Delbanco 6:130

**Esmonde, Margaret P.**
Zilpha Keatley Snyder 17:474

**Esslin, Martin**
Arthur Adamov 4:5
Edward Albee 2:4; 9:10
John Arden 6:5
Samuel Beckett 1:24; 4:52;
6:33, 44
Edward Bond 13:98
Friedrich Dürrenmatt 4:139
Max Frisch 3:167
Jack Gelber 1:114
Jean Genet 1:117
Günter Grass 4:201
Graham Greene 9:250
Rolf Hochhuth 4:231
Eugène Ionesco 1:154; 4:252
Arthur Kopit 1:170
Sławomir Mrożek 3:344
Robert Pinget 7:306
Harold Pinter 1:268; 6:407, 414
Peter Shaffer 18:477
Neil Simon 6:506
Wole Soyinka 14:505
Peter Weiss 3:515

**Estess, Sybil**
Elizabeth Bishop 9:95

**Estess, Ted L.**
Samuel Beckett 11:41

**Estrin, Barbara L.**
Adrienne Rich 18:450

**Esty, William**
James Baldwin 17:21

**Ettin, Andrew V.**
James Merrill 2:273

**Evanier, David**
John Updike 15:547

**Evans, Ann**
Judy Blume 12:46

**Evans, Don**
Ed Bullins 5:82

**Evans, Donald T.**
Alice Childress 12:105

**Evans, Eli N.**
James Dickey 7:86

**Evans, Ernestine**
Jessamyn West 17:544
Jade Snow Wong 17:565

**Evans, Fallon**
J. F. Powers 1:279

**Evans, Garet Lloyd**
Harold Pinter 11:444

**Evans, Gwyneth F.**
Christie Harris 12:267

**Evans, Oliver**
Paul Bowles 1:41
Babette Deutsch 18:119
Carson McCullers 12:425

**Evans, Robley**
J.R.R. Tolkien 3:478

**Evans, Timothy**
Isaac Bashevis Singer 11:499

**Evarts, Prescott, Jr.**
John Fowles 2:138

**Everson, Edith A.**
E. E. Cummings 15:157

**Evett, Robert**
Terrence McNally 7:219
Lanford Wilson 7:548

**Ewart, Gavin**
William Sansom 2:383
Sylvia Townsend Warner
19:461

**Ewen, David**
Gerome Ragni and James Rado
17:385

**Ewers, John C.**
Jamake Highwater 12:286

**Ewing, Dorothy**
Miguel Delibes 18:110

**Eyles, Allen**
Francis Ford Coppola 16:231
John Huston 20:169
Ken Russell 16:541

**Eyre, Frank**
Peter Dickinson 12:170
Eilís Dillon 17:98
Leon Garfield 12:223
Alan Garner 17:142
William Mayne 12:396
Colin Thiele 17:494

**Eyster, Warren**
James Dickey 1:74

**Faber, Nancy W.**
Frank Bonham 12:50

CRITIC INDEX

**Faber, Roderick Mason**
Tennessee Williams **19**:474

**Fabio, Sarah Webster**
Nikki Giovanni **19**:190

**Fabre, Michel**
James Baldwin **3**:31
Chester Himes **2**:195

**Fadiman, Anne**
Fran Lebowitz **11**:322

**Fadiman, Clifton**
Carson McCullers **12**:409

**Fadiman, Edwin**
Laura Z. Hobson **7**:163

**Faery, Rebecca B.**
Richard Wilbur **9**:570

**Fager, Charles E.**
Bob Dylan **12**:185

**Fahey, James**
Evan S. Connell, Jr. **4**:109

**Fairchild, B. H., Jr.**
Steven Spielberg **20**:364

**Faith, Rosamond**
Rosemary Wells **12**:638

**Falck, Colin**
A. Alvarez **5**:16
John Berryman **2**:55
William Empson **3**:147
Geoffrey Grigson **7**:136
Thom Gunn **6**:220
Seamus Heaney **7**:149
Ted Hughes **9**:280
Philip Larkin **3**:275, 276
Robert Lowell **2**:245; **5**:256
George MacBeth **9**:340
Anne Sexton **8**:483
Charles Tomlinson **2**:436

**Falk, Doris V.**
Lillian Hellman **14**:258

**Falk, Signi**
Tennessee Williams **1**:367

**Falke, Wayne**
Kenzaburō Oe **10**:372
Jun'ichiro Tanizaki **14**:525
John Updike **5**:453

**Falkenberg, Betty**
Beryl Bainbridge **18**:34
Marge Piercy **18**:408
Patrick White **18**:549

**Fallis, Laurence S.**
Ruth Prawer Jhabvala **4**:259

**Fallowell, Duncan**
Giorgio Bassani **9**:77
John Berger **2**:54
William Peter Blatty **2**:64
Richard Brautigan **12**:72
Robert Coover **3**:114
Mark Helprin **7**:152
Ruth Prawer Jhabvala **8**:312
Anna Kavan **13**:316
Jerzy Kosinski **3**:274
Iris Murdoch **4**:368
Tim O'Brien **7**:272
Seán O'Faoláin **7**:274

Mervyn Peake **7**:303
David Plante **7**:308
Françoise Sagan **9**:468
James Salter **7**:388
Hubert Selby, Jr. **2**:390
Terry Southern **7**:454
Muriel Spark **3**:465; **8**:493
Auberon Waugh **7**:514

**Fallows, James**
George V. Higgins **18**:233

**Fandel, John**
E. E. Cummings **3**:120

**Fandray, David F.**
David Bowie **17**:62

**Fanger, Donald**
Aleksandr I. Solzhenitsyn **1**:319

**Fanning, Peter**
Alan Garner **17**:149

**Fantoni, Barry**
S. J. Perelman **15**:418
Brian Wilson **12**:60

**Farber, Manny**
Maya Deren **16**:251
John Ford **16**:305
Alfred Hitchcock **16**:338, 339
John Huston **20**:159
Akira Kurosawa **16**:394

**Farber, Stephen**
Lindsay Anderson **20**:15
Francis Ford Coppola **16**:231, 232, 235
Richard Lester **20**:225
Sam Peckinpah **20**:274
Ken Russell **16**:548
Martin Scorsese **20**:327
Steven Spielberg **20**:358
François Truffaut **20**:396
Luchino Visconti **16**:569
Orson Welles **20**:446
Billy Wilder **20**:461, 464, 465

**Farmer, Betty Catherine Dobson**
Donald Barthelme **13**:58

**Farmer, Penelope**
Alan Garner **17**:147
William Mayne **12**:401

**Farmiloe, Dorothy**
Hugh MacLennan **14**:341

**Farnsworth, Emily C.**
Robert Newton Peck **17**:343

**Farrell, Diane**
Andre Norton **12**:459

**Farrell, James T.**
James M. Cain **11**:84
Ben Hecht **8**:269
Frank O'Connor **14**:395

**Farrell, John P.**
Richard Wilbur **3**:532

**Farrison, W. Edward**
Lorraine Hansberry **17**:191

**Farwell, Harold**
John Barth **5**:50

**Farwell, Ruth**
George Mackay Brown **5**:77

**Farzan, Massud**
Ahmad Shamlu **10**:469

**Fassbinder, Rainer Werner**
Claude Chabrol **16**:181

**Faulks, Sebastian**
Yasunari Kawabata **9**:316

**Fawcett, Graham**
Anthony Burgess **8**:111

**Fay, Eliot G.**
Jacques Prévert **15**:437

**Fearing, Kenneth**
George Tabori **19**:435

**Featherstone, Joseph**
Katherine Anne Porter **3**:392
Frederick Wiseman **20**:468

**Feaver, Vicki**
Sylvia Townsend Warner **19**:460

**Feaver, William**
Michael Ayrton **7**:19

**Feder, Lillian**
Conrad Aiken **5**:8
W. H. Auden **4**:33, 34, 35
George Barker **8**:43
Samuel Beckett **6**:37
T. S. Eliot **6**:160
Robert Graves **6**:210
Ted Hughes **9**:281
Robert Lowell **4**:301
Ezra Pound **3**:396; **4**:414

**Federman, Raymond**
Samuel Beckett **9**:79

**Feeney, Joseph J., S.J.**
Jessie Redmon Fauset **19**:171

**Feied, Frederick**
John Dos Passos **1**:80
Jack Kerouac **1**:166

**Feifer, George**
Aleksandr I. Solzhenitsyn **7**:444

**Feiffer, Jules**
Richard Lester **20**:223

**Fein, Richard J.**
Robert Lowell **3**:304

**Feingold, Michael**
Dannie Abse **7**:2
E. L. Doctorow **15**:179
Athol Fugard **9**:235
John Guare **8**:252,253
Peter Handke **8**:263
John Hopkins **4**:234
Jim Jacobs and Warren Casey **12**:294
Ira Levin **3**:294
Miguel Piñero **4**:401
Sam Shepard **17**:444, 445, 447
Elizabeth Swados **12**:557, 561
Tennessee Williams **7**:544

**Feinstein, Elaine**
Gail Godwin **8**:247
William Golding **2**:169
Nadine Gordimer **3**:202
George MacBeth **5**:265
Olivia Manning **19**:301

Mary McCarthy **3**:329
Grace Paley **6**:339
Christina Stead **5**:403

**Feirstein, Frederick**
Robert Graves **2**:177

**Feld, Michael**
Richard Brautigan **12**:63
John Updike **2**:445

**Feld, Rose**
Sally Benson **17**:47
Agatha Christie **12**:114
Madeleine L'Engle **12**:345
Mary Renault **17**:389
Françoise Sagan **17**:420
Jack Spicer **8**:497

**Feld, Ross**
Paul Blackburn **9**:98
Laurie Colwin **13**:156
William H. Gass **11**:225
Eudora Welty **14**:566
Tom Wolfe **9**:578

**Feldman, Anita**
Irwin Shaw **7**:412

**Feldman, Hans**
Stanley Kubrick **16**:391

**Feldman, Irma P.**
Helen Yglesia **7**:558

**Feldman, Morton**
Frank O'Hara **2**:322

**Felheim, Marvin**
Ben Hecht **8**:272
Lillian Hellman **14**:255
Carson McCullers **1**:208
Eudora Welty **1**:361

**Fell, John L.**
Rainer Werner Fassbinder **20**:117

**Fellows, Jo-Ann**
Mazo de la Roche **14**:150

**Felsen, Henry Gregor**
Henry Gregor Felsen **17**:123

**Felstiner, John**
Pablo Neruda **1**:247; **2**:309; **5**:302

**Felton, David**
Lily Tomlin **17**:519

**Fender, Stephen**
Jacob Epstein **19**:162
Richard Price **12**:491
John Sayles **10**:462

**Fenin, George N.**
Vittorio De Sica **20**:86
Billy Wilder **20**:457, 458

**Fenton, James**
W. H. Auden **6**:18
Giorgio Bassani **9**:76
Douglas Dunn **6**:148
Gavin Ewart **13**:210
Josephine Poole **17**:372
Charles Tomlinson **6**:534

**Ferguson, Alan**
Ivo Andrić **8**:20

CRITIC INDEX

**Ferguson, Frances**
Randall Jarrell 13:301
Robert Lowell 4:302

**Ferguson, Otis C.**
Frank Capra 16:154, 155, 156
Charles Chaplin 16:190, 192
John Ford 16:303, 304
Alfred Hitchcock 16:337
Rouben Mamoulian 16:420
Orson Welles 20:432

**Ferguson, Suzanne**
Djuna Barnes 3:36
Randall Jarrell 2:209

**Fergusson, Francis**
René Clair 20:59

**Fernandez, Jaime**
Jun'ichirō Tanizaki 8:511

**Ferrari, Margaret**
Marge Piercy 6:402
Hilma Wolitzer 17:561

**Ferrer, José M.**
Garry Marshall 17:274

**Ferrer, Olga Prjevalinskaya**
Eugène Ionesco 6:256

**Ferretti, Fred**
Norman Lear 12:326

**Ferrier, Carole**
Sylvia Plath 17:369
Diane Wakoski 7:505

**Ferris, Ina**
Rudy Wiebe 11:567

**Ferris, William H.**
W.E.B. Du Bois 13:180

**Ferry, David**
Theodore Roethke 1:291

**Fetherling, Doug**
Hugh Garner 13:235,236
A. W. Purdy 14:435
Mordecai Richler 3:431
Robin Skelton 13:506

**Feuer, Kathryn B.**
Aleksandr I. Solzhenitsyn 7:445

**Feuser, Willfried F.**
Chinua Achebe 7:6

**Fialkowski, Barbara**
Maxine Kumin 13:326

**Fiamengo, Marya**
Susan Musgrave 13:400

**Fickert, Kurt J.**
Friedrich Dürrenmatt 4:139
Hermann Hesse 17:201

**Fiedler, Leslie A.**
John Barth 3:38
Saul Bellow 1:27, 31; 3:48
Truman Capote 19:79
Leonard Cohen 3:109
Bob Dylan 3:130
Philip José Farmer 19:164
William Faulkner 1:101; 3:149
Allen Ginsberg 2:162; 3:193
John Hawkes 3:221

Ernest Hemingway 1:143;
3:232, 33
John Hersey 7:153
Randall Jarrell 1:160
Robert Lowell 2:246
Norman Mailer 3:311
Bernard Malamud 9:341, 351
Henry Miller 2:282
Alberto Moravia 2:293
Wright Morris 1:232
Vladimir Nabokov 1:239
Ezra Pound 7:329
John Crowe Ransom 2:363
Mordecai Richler 5:375
Henry Roth 6:470
J. D. Salinger 12:512
Kurt Vonnegut, Jr. 12:603
Robert Penn Warren 4:579
Richard Wilbur 3:530
Herman Wouk 1:376

**Field, Andrew**
Vladimir Nabokov 1:242
Yevgeny Yevtushenko 1:382

**Field, Colin**
Eilís Dillon 17:98
William Mayne 12:392

**Field, George Wallis**
Hermann Hesse 1:147

**Field, Joyce**
Bernard Malamud 9:348

**Field, Leslie**
Bernard Malamud 9:348

**Field, Louise Maunsell**
Edna Ferber 18:150

**Field, Trevor**
Julien Green 11:261

**Fields, Beverly**
Anne Sexton 2:391

**Fields, Kenneth**
J. V. Cunningham 3:121
Robert Lowell 4:299
N. Scott Momaday 2:290
Marya Zaturenska 6:585

**Fifer, Elizabeth**
Maxine Hong Kingston 12:314

**Filer, Malva E.**
Julio Cortázar 10:117

**Finch, John**
E. E. Cummings 12:144

**Fincke, Gary**
Ben Hecht 8:271

**Finc, Dennis**
Neil Young 17:573

**Finel-Honigman, Irène**
Albert Camus 11:96

**Finger, Louis**
John Le Carré 9:326

**Finholt, Richard**
James Dickey 10:142
Ralph Ellison 11:184

**Finkle, David**
John Fowles 9:215
Mordecai Richler 18:459

**Finlay, John**
Elizabeth Daryush 19:122

**Finlayson, Iain**
Peter Rushforth 19:405

**Finley, M. I.**
Michael Ayrton 7:17

**Finn, James**
James Baldwin 17:23, 24
François Mauriac 4:339
P. G. Wodehouse 2:480

**Firchow, Peter**
Aldous Huxley 8:305

**Firchow, Peter E.**
W. H. Auden 11:17
Aldous Huxley 18:266

**Fireside, Harvey**
Andrei Sinyavsky 8:489, 490

**Firestone, Bruce M.**
Anthony Burgess 10:89

**Firmat, Gustavo Pérez**
Dámaso Alonso 14:24

**First, Elsa**
Carlos Castaneda 12:91

**Fisch, Harold**
Aharon Megged 9:374

**Fischer, John Irwin**
Catharine Savage Brosman
9:135

**Fischer, Lucy**
René Clair 20:67

**Fischer, Marjorie**
Margot Benary-Isbert 12:30
Joseph Krumgold 12:317

**Fischler, Alexander**
Eugène Ionesco 15:297

**Fisher, Elizabeth**
Jessamyn West 17:553

**Fisher, Emma**
Beryl Bainbridge 18:32
John Berryman 10:47
Anaïs Nin 14:386
Peter Porter 13:452
R. S. Thomas 13:544

**Fisher, Margery**
E. M. Almedingen 12:6
Ruth M. Arthur 12:25, 26
Honor Arundel 17:14, 16
Judy Blume 12:47
Mavis Thorpe Clark 12:130,
131, 132
Robert Cormier 12:135, 137
Julia W. Cunningham 12:164,
165
Maureen Daly 17:91
Peter Dickinson 12:169, 174,
177
Eilís Dillon 17:95, 96, 97
Walter Farley 17:118
Esther Forbes 12:211
Leon Garfield 12:216, 217,
218, 223, 227, 231, 233,
234
Alan Garner 17:135, 136, 148

William Mayne 12:389, 405
Emily Cheney Neville 12:450
Andre Norton 12:469, 470
Katherine Paterson 12:485
Josephine Poole 17:373
Otfried Preussler 17:375, 376
Zilpha Keatley Snyder 17:474
Colin Thiele 17:493, 494, 495,
496
J.R.R. Tolkien 12:586
Rosemary Wells 12:638
Robert Westall 17:555, 556,
559

**Fisher, William J.**
William Saroyan 8:466

**Fiske, Minnie Maddern**
Charles Chaplin 16:187

**Fisketjon, Gary L.**
Thomas McGuane 18:323

**Fison, Peter**
C. P. Snow 13:511

**Fitts, Dudley**
Mary Renault 17:394, 398

**Fitzgerald, Edward J.**
Mark Harris 19:200

**Fitzgerald, Penelope**
Barbara Pym 19:388

**Fitzgerald, Robert**
Seamus Heaney 7:151
Robert Lowell 11:325; 15:345
Flannery O'Connor 15:409

**Fitzlyon, Kyril**
Aleksandr I. Solzhenitsyn 1:321

**Fitzsimmons, Thomas**
Elizabeth Hardwick 13:264

**Fiut, Aleksander**
Czesław Miłosz 11:379

**Fixler, Michael**
Isaac Bashevis Singer 1:311

**Flagg, Nancy**
Jorge Amado 13:11

**Flaherty, Joe**
Richard Brautigan 9:124
Edwin Newman 14:379

**Flamm, Dudley**
Robert M. Pirsig 4:404

**Flanagan, John T.**
Jessamyn West 17:551, 552

**Flanders, Jane**
James Dickey 15:177
Katherine Anne Porter 10:396

**Flanner, Janet**
André Malraux 4:326

**Flatto, Eric**
Stanley Kubrick 16:382

**Flaxman, Seymour L.**
Hermann Hesse 17:196

**Fleckenstein, Joan S.**
Edward Albee 11:13

CRITIC INDEX

**Fleischer, Leonard**
Woody Allen 16:6
John A. Williams 5:496

**Fleischer, Leonore**
Nora Ephron 17:110

**Fleishman, Avrom**
John Fowles 9:210

**Fleming, Alice**
Zilpha Keatley Snyder 17:471

**Fleming, Robert E.**
Ronald L. Fair 18:140
John A. Williams 5:496

**Fleming, Thomas J.**
Ira Levin 6:305
Emily Cheney Neville 12:450

**Fleshman, Bob**
David Madden 15:350

**Fletcher, John**
Uwe Johnson 5:201
Kamala Markandaya 8:377
Jean-Paul Sartre 7:398

**Fletcher, Peggy**
Joe Rosenblatt 15:447

**Flexner, James Thomas**
Esther Forbes 12:209

**Flint, R. W.**
A. R. Ammons 8:15; 9:29
Irving Feldman 7:102
Anthony Hecht 8:267
Randall Jarrell 1:159
Karl Shapiro 8:486
Charles Tomlinson 13:550

**Flippo, Chet**
Willie Nelson 17:302, 303,
304, 305
Sam Shepard 17:445

**Floan, Howard R.**
William Saroyan 1:301

**Flood, Jeanne**
Brian Moore 5:294

**Flora, Joseph M.**
Vardis Fisher 7:103
Günter Grass 6:209
J. E. Wideman 5:490
Nancy Willard 7:539

**Flower, Dean**
Dan Jacobson 14:291
Vladimir Nabokov 15:393
Marge Piercy 14:421
Frederic Raphael 14:438
Hubert Selby, Jr. 8:477
Helen Yglesias 7:559
Al Young 19:479

**Flowers, Ann A.**
Barbara Corcoran 17:78
Leon Garfield 12:239
Katherine Paterson 12:486

**Flowers, Betty**
Donald Barthelme 5:56

**Fludas, John**
Rita Mae Brown 18:73
Richard Price 12:491

**Folejewski, Zbigniew**
Maria Dąbrowska 15:165, 167

**Foley, Barbara**
E. L. Doctorow 18:121

**Folsom, L. Edwin**
W. S. Merwin 13:384

**Fong, Monique**
Vittorio De Sica 20:95

**Fontenla, Cesar Santos**
Carlos Saura 20:320

**Fontenot, Chester J.**
Alex Haley 8:260
Alice Walker 19:450

**Foose, Thomas T.**
Jean Renoir 20:287

**Foote, Audrey C.**
Anthony Burgess 4:81
Nathalie Sarraute 2:386
Christina Stead 5:404
Mary Stewart 7:468

**Foote, Jennifer**
Richard O'Brien 17:325

**Foote, Timothy**
W. H. Auden 3:26; 6:24
Anthony Burgess 5:89
Peter De Vries 2:114
John Gardner 3:187
John le Carré 5:232
V. S. Pritchett 5:352
Aleksandr I. Solzhenitsyn 4:516
Tom Stoppard 4:525
Tom Wolfe 2:481

**Forbes, Alastair**
Lawrence Durrell 13:189

**Forbes, Jill**
René Clair 20:66
Rainer Werner Fassbinder
20:116
Joan Micklin Silver 20:341

**Forche, Carolyn**
Ai 14:8

**Ford, Nick Aaron**
Harper Lee 12:341
Willard Motley 18:356

**Ford, Richard J.**
Hermann Hesse 2:189

**Forman, Jack**
Jules Archer 12:18, 20
Frank Bonham 12:51
Katherine Paterson 12:485, 486

**Fornatale, Peter**
Laura Nyro 17:314
Brian Wilson 12:646

**Forrest, Alan**
W. H. Auden 3:27
Mario Puzo 2:352

**Forrey, Robert**
Ken Kesey 11:316
Andrew Sinclair 14:488

**Forster, Leonard**
Günter Grass 15:262

**Fortin, René E.**
Boris Pasternak 7:296

**Foster, David W.**
Camilo José Cela 4:96

**Foster, David William**
Jorge Luis Borges 3:78; 6:89
Julio Cortázar 10:118
Ernesto Sábato 10:445

**Foster, Isabel**
Robert Francis 15:234

**Foster, John Wilson**
Seamus Heaney 5:170
Brian Moore 1:225

**Foster, Richard**
Norman Mailer 1:190; 8:365

**Foster, Roy**
Brian Moore 19:333

**Foster, Ruel E.**
Jesse Stuart 1:328

**Fotheringham, Hamish**
William Mayne 12:388

**Fowler, Alastair**
Charles M. Schulz 12:532

**Fowler, Douglas**
Thomas Pynchon 18:438

**Fowler, F. M.**
Günter Eich 15:203

**Fowlie, Wallace**
Michel Butor 8:119
René Char 9:158
Jean Cocteau 15:133
Jean Genet 5:135
Julien Green 11:258
Henri Michaux 8:392
Anaïs Nin 4:378; 11:398
Jules Romains 7:379

**Fox, Charles**
Akira Kurosawa 16:396

**Fox, Gail**
Phyllis Webb 18:542

**Fox, Hugh**
William Carlos Williams 5:509

**Fox, Terry Curtis**
Rita Mae Brown 18:73
Marguerite Duras 20:103
Max Frisch 18:162
Athol Fugard 14:192
Jean-Luc Godard 20:152
Simon Gray 14:215
John Guare 14:221
George V. Higgins 18:235
George Lucas 16:415
Harold Pinter 15:425
Martin Scorsese 20:333

**Fox-Genovese, Elizabeth**
Susan Cheever 18:102
William Gaddis 8:226

**Fraenkel, Heinrich**
Leni Riefenstahl 16:521

**Frakes, James R.**
Nelson Algren 4:17
Wendell Berry 4:59
E. M. Broner 19:70
Bruce Jay Friedman 5:127
Patricia Highsmith 2:194
Stanley Hoffman 5:185
Julius Horwitz 14:266
Evan Hunter 11:280
Diane Johnson 5:198
Michael Mewshaw 9:376
Muriel Spark 2:418
Richard G. Stern 4:522

**France, Arthur**
Lorraine Hansberry 17:185

**France, Peter**
Anne Hébert 13.267

**Francescato, Martha Paley**
Julio Cortázar 10:116

**Francis, Wynne**
Louis Dudek 19:137

**Frank, Armin Paul**
Kenneth Burke 2:89

**Frank, Joseph**
Djuna Barnes 8:47
Yves Bonnefoy 15:74
André Malraux 4:327
Aleksandr I. Solzhenitsyn 7:443

**Frank, Mike**
Joseph Heller 11:266

**Frank, Sheldon**
T. Alan Broughton 19:72
Margaret Laurence 6:289
Hans Erich Nossack 6:365
Al Young 19:480

**Frankel, Bernice**
Mary Stolz 12:547

**Frankel, Haskel**
Bruce Jay Friedman 3:165
Muriel Spark 2:417
Peter Ustinov 1:346
Charles Webb 7:514

**Frankenberg, Lloyd**
Marianne Moore 19:337

**Franklin, Allan**
Jorg Luis Borges 9:116

**Franklin, H. Bruce**
J. G. Ballard 3:32

**Fraser, G. S.**
Basil Bunting 10:86
Robert Creeley 1:67
C. Day Lewis 6:127
Nigel Dennis 8:172
Lawrence Durrell 4:145; 13:184
Jean Garrigue 2:153
Randall Jarrell 9:296
Robert Lowell 2:249; 11:325
Hugh MacDiarmid 11:337
W. S. Merwin 1:214
C. P. Snow 4:502
Gary Snyder 1:318
Andrei Voznesensky 15:552
Louis Zukofsky 1:385

**Fraser, John**
Louis-Ferdinand Céline 1:56;
4:102
Yvor Winters 4:592; 8:552

**Fraser, Kathleen**
Adrienne Rich 3:429

**Fraser, Keath**
Alden Nowlan 15:398
Sinclair Ross 13:492

**Fraser, Russell**
Eugenio Montale 18:341

**Frayne, John P.**
John Ford 16:320

**Frazer, Frances M.**
Christie Harris 12:268

**Frazer, Mary**
Frederick Wiseman 20:477

**Fredeman, W. E.**
Earle Birney 6:72

**Fredrick, E. Coston**
Barbara Corcoran 17:75

**Free, William J.**
Federico Fellini 16:284
Tennessee Williams 15:581

**Freedberger, Peter**
Stan Lee 17:261

**Freedman, Morris**
Sylvia Ashton-Warner 19:23

**Freedman, Ralph**
Saul Bellow 1:29
Hermann Hesse 1:146; 17:203

**Freedman, Richard**
A. Alvarez 13:10
Hortense Calisher 2:96
Dick Francis 2:142
Lois Gould 4:199
Tim O'Brien 19:356
S. J. Perelman 9:416
P. G. Wodehouse 5:517

**Freedman, William**
Henry Roth 11:487

**Freeman, Anne Hobson**
Reynolds Price 13:463

**Freeman, Gillian**
Robert Nye 13:412

**Fremantle, Anne**
W. H. Auden 1:10
Auberon Waugh 7:513
Vassily S. Yanovsky 18:551

**Fremont-Smith, Eliot**
Richard Adams 4:6
Martin Amis 4:20
Max Apple 9:33
Louis Auchincloss 4:31
Laurie Colwin 13:156
E. L. Doctorow 6:132
Lawrence Durrell 6:152
Gael Greene 8:252
Joseph Heller 5:173; 11:268
Lillian Hellman 4:221
John Irving 13:294
Marjorie Kellogg 2:223
Jascha Kessler 4:269

Arthur Koestler 3:271
Jerzy Kosinski 1:172
John le Carré 9:327
Alan Lelchuk 5:243
Norman Mailer 4:322
James A. Michener 5:289
Richard Price 6:426; 12:490
Philip Roth 4:453, 455
Alix Kates Shulman 10:476
Gore Vidal 6:54
Irving Wallace 7:510
Patrick White 3:524

**French, Allen**
Esther Forbes 12:206

**French, Janet**
Otfried Preussler 17:375

**French, Marilyn**
Margaret Atwood 15:39

**French, Ned**
William H. Gass 15:255

**French, Philip**
Bernardo Bertolucci 16:101
Jorge Luis Borges 4:75
Truman Capote 8:132
Eleanor Clark 19:107
Graham Greene 3:212; 6:220
Richard Lester 20:219

**French, Robert W.**
Joyce Carol Oates 1:251

**French, Warren**
William Goldman 1:123
R. K. Narayan 7:254
James Purdy 2:349
J. D. Salinger 1:297; 12:514
John Steinbeck 1:324; 5:406
Thornton Wilder 1:366

**Fretz, Sada**
Julia W. Cunningham 12:165
John Neufeld 17:308

**Friar, Kimon**
Margaríta Karapánou 13:314
Yannis Ritsos 6:463
Vassilis Vassilikos 8:524

**Fricke, David**
Mick Jagger and Keith Richard
17:242
Frank Zappa 17:592

**Fried, Lewis**
James T. Farrell 11:191

**Friedberg, Maurice**
Aleksandr I. Solzhenitsyn
1:319; 7:435

**Friedenberg, Edgar Z.**
James Baldwin 17:24
Mark Harris 19:201
Hermann Hesse 2:190
Frederick Wiseman 20:472

**Friedman, Alan**
William S. Burroughs 5:93
John Gardner 7:112
Erica Jong 18:279
Yukio Mishima 4:357
Amos Oz 8:435
John Rechy 18:442
Ishmael Reed 2:367

André Schwarz-Bart 2:389
John Kennedy Toole 19:443
Elie Wiesel 3:528

**Friedman, Alan J.**
Thomas Pynchon 6:434

**Friedman, Alan Warren**
Saul Bellow 8:69
Lawrence Durrell 1:87
Bernard Malamud 8:375

**Friedman, Jack**
Wendell Berry 4:59
José Lezama Lima 4:290

**Friedman, John**
William Eastlake 8:200

**Friedman, Melvin J.**
Bruce Jay Friedman 5:127
Eugène Ionesco 6:256
André Malraux 4:333
R. K. Narayan 7:255
Flannery O'Connor 1:253
Isaac Bashevis Singer 1:313

**Friedman, Norman**
E. E. Cummings 1:69; 12:149;
15:153
David Ignatow 7:174

**Friedrichsmeyer, Erhard**
Uwe Johnson 15:302

**Frieling, Kenneth**
Flannery O'Connor 13:416

**Friesem, Roberta Ricky**
Lenora Mattingly Weber 12:635

**Friesen, Gordon**
Phil Ochs 17:329, 330

**Frith, Simon**
Mick Jagger and Keith Richard
17:240
Bob Marley 17:272
Patti Smith 12:543
Peter Townshend 17:538
Neil Young 17:580

**Fritz, Jean**
Ruth M. Arthur 12:24
Barbara Corcoran 17:73
Joseph Krumgold 12:318
Zilpha Keatley Snyder 17:472
Mary Stolz 12:553

**Frohock, W. M.**
James M. Cain 11:84
Erskine Caldwell 1:51
James Gould Cozzens 4:113
John Dos Passos 1:77
James T. Farrell 1:97
William Faulkner 1:99
Ernest Hemingway 1:141
André Malraux 4:324; 13:366
John Steinbeck 1:323
Robert Penn Warren 1:351

**Frost, Lucy**
John Hawkes 3:223

**Fruchtbaum, Harold**
Loren Eiseley 7:90

**Frye, Northrop**
Charles Chaplin 16:192
Louis Dudek 11:158; 19:136,
137
Daryl Hine 15:280
Dorothy Livesay 15:339
E. J. Pratt 19:376, 379
A.J.M. Smith 15:516

**Fryer, Jonathan H.**
Christopher Isherwood 9:292

**Fuchs, Daniel**
Saul Bellow 3:62

**Fuchs, Vivian**
Thomas Keneally 10:299

**Fuchs, Wolfgang**
Charles M. Schulz 12:528

**Fuentes, Carlos**
Luis Buñuel 16:137

**Fugard, Athol**
Athol Fugard 14:189

**Fulford, Robert**
George Bowering 15:81
Michael Cimino 16:214
Mavis Gallant 18:172
Brian Moore 3:340
Mordecai Richler 3:429
Philip Roth 3:435
Raymond Souster 14:504

**Fuller, Edmund**
Paul Bowles 1:41
Frederick Buechner 4:80
James Gould Cozzens 1:65
Jan de Hartog 19:130
James Jones 1:161
Thomas Keneally 19:248
Jack Kerouac 1:165
Alan Paton 4:395
Mary Renault 17:392
Mary Lee Settle 19:408
J.R.R. Tolkien 1:335
Herman Wouk 1:375

**Fuller, Elizabeth Ely**
Isak Dinesen 10:150

**Fuller, John**
Anna Akhmatova 11:9
Thom Gunn 3:215
Michael Hamburger 14:234
Randall Jarrell 2:208
Leslie Norris 14:387
Robert Pinsky 19:370
William Plomer 4:406
Ann Quin 6:441
Kathleen Raine 7:353
Jon Silkin 6:499
Andrew Young 5:523

**Fuller, Roy**
W. H. Auden 3:25
Aldous Huxley 5:192
A.J.M. Smith 15:513
C. P. Snow 19:427
Stephen Spender 2:420
Allen Tate 14:532
Lionel Trilling 9:530

**Fulton, Robin**
Pär Lagerkvist 10:313

**Furbank, P. N.**
E. M. Forster **4**:165, 168
William Golding **17**:176
Elizabeth Jennings **14**:291
Uwe Johnson **10**:284
Gore Vidal **4**:556

**Furlong, Vivienne**
Honor Arundel **17**:18

**Fussell, B. H.**
Peter Taylor **4**:543

**Fussell, Edwin**
Wendell Berry **6**:61
Hayden Carruth **7**:40

**Fussell, Paul**
Thomas Keneally **8**:318
Paul Theroux **15**:533

**Fussell, Paul, Jr.**
Karl Shapiro **4**:486

**Fytton, Francis**
Paul Bowles **2**:78

**Fyvel, T. R.**
Ilya Ehrenburg **18**:133

**Gabbard, Krin**
Tess Gallagher **18**:170

**Gabree, John**
Mick Jagger and Keith Richard
**17**:223
John Lennon and Paul
McCartney **12**:364

**Gadney, Reg**
George V. Higgins **7**:158
Patricia Highsmith **2**:194
Ross Macdonald **2**:257
Alistair MacLean **3**:309

**Gagné, Sarah**
Melvin Berger **12**:42
Larry Kettelkamp **12**:307
Alvin Silverstein and Virginia
B. Silverstein **17**:456

**Gaillard, Frye**
Willie Nelson **17**:304

**Gaines, Richard H.**
Chester Himes **2**:196

**Gaiser, Carolyn**
Gregory Corso **1**:63

**Gaither, Frances**
Esther Forbes **12**:210

**Galassi, Jonathan**
John Berryman **6**:63
Robert Duncan **2**:123
Robert Graves **6**:212
Seamus Heaney **7**:147
Randall Jarrell **9**:297
Eugenio Montale **7**:231
Howard Nemerov **9**:396
George Oppen **13**:434

**Galbraith, John Kenneth**
Edwin O'Connor **14**:389
William Safire **10**:446

**Gall, Sally M.**
Kenneth O. Hanson **13**:263
Eleanor Lerman **9**:329
Charles Wright **6**:580

**Gallagher, D. P.**
Adolfo Bioy Casares **8**:94;
**13**:83
Jorge Luis Borges **6**:88
G. Cabrera Infante **5**:96
Gabriel García Márquez **8**:230
Pablo Neruda **7**:257
Octavio Paz **6**:394
Manuel Puig **10**:420
Mario Vargas Llosa **6**:543

**Gallagher, David**
G. Cabrera Infante **5**:95
Manuel Puig **3**:407

**Gallagher, Michael**
Shusaku Endo **7**:95

**Gallant, Mavis**
Simone de Beauvoir **4**:48
Louis-Ferdinand Céline **7**:46
Günter Grass **4**:205
Vladimir Nabokov **2**:303

**Galler, David**
Ted Hughes **2**:198
Howard Nemerov **2**:307

**Galligan, Edward L.**
Georges Simenon **1**:309

**Galloway, David D.**
Saul Bellow **3**:51, 55
Stanley Elkin **4**:152
Dan Jacobson **4**:253
J. D. Salinger **3**:445
William Styron **3**:473
John Updike **3**:486

**Gannon, Edward, S.J.**
André Malraux **4**:326

**Gant, Lisbeth**
Ed Bullins **5**:82

**Ganz, Arthur**
Harold Pinter **6**:416

**Ganz, Earl**
John Hawkes **1**:139
Flannery O'Connor **2**:318

**Garcia, Irma**
Nicholosa Mohr **12**:447

**Gard, Roger**
Shirley Hazzard **18**:214

**Gardiner, Harold C.**
Robert Cormier **12**:134

**Gardner, Averil**
William Empson **19**:156

**Gardner, Erle Stanley**
Meyer Levin **7**:203

**Gardner, Harvey**
Jimmy Breslin **4**:76

**Gardner, John**
Saul Bellow **10**:44
Anthony Burgess **2**:84
Italo Calvino **8**:129
E. L. Doctorow **15**:178
John Fowles **9**:215
William H. Gass **1**:114
John Knowles **4**:271
Brian Moore **8**:395
Charles Newman **8**:419

Joyce Carol Oates **19**:354
Walker Percy **8**:442
Philip Roth **2**:379
William Styron **15**:525
J.R.R. Tolkien **12**:585
Patrick White **9**:567
Thomas Williams **14**:582
Larry Woiwode **6**:578

**Gardner, Marilyn**
Barbara Corcoran **17**:69
Mary Stolz **12**:554

**Gardner, Peter**
Allan W. Eckert **17**:108
John Hersey **9**:277

**Gardner, Philip**
Willim Empson **19**:156
D. J. Enright **4**:155
Philip Larkin **5**:230; **18**:293

**Gardner, R. H.**
William Inge **19**:228

**Garebian, Keith**
Patrick White **9**:563

**Garfield,Evelyn Picon**
Julio Cortázar **13**:163

**Garfield, Leon**
William Mayne **12**:395

**Garfitt, Roger**
George Barker **8**:46
James K. Baxter **14**:60
Martin Booth **13**:103
Joseph Brodsky **6**:96
Robert Creeley **4**:118
Eilís Dillon **17**:99
Douglas Dunn **6**:148
Geoffrey Grigson **7**:136
Donald Hall **13**:259
Anthony Hecht **19**:209
Anna Kavan **5**:206
Reiner Kunze **10**:310
Philip Larkin **8**:332
George MacBeth **5**:263
László Nagy **7**:251
Leslie Norris **14**:388
Julia O'Faolain **6**:383
Vasko Popa **19**:375
Peter Porter **5**:346
Thomas Pynchon **3**:418
Peter Redgrove **6**:445
Bernice Rubens **19**:403
Ward Ruyslinck **14**:471
C. H. Sisson **8**:490
Anne Stevenson **7**:462
Derek Walcott **4**:575

**Garis, Leslie**
Doris Lessing **6**:302

**Garis, Robert**
Herbert Gold **4**:191
Anthony Powell **3**:400

**Garner, Alan**
Leon Garfield **12**:219

**Garnet, Eldon**
B. P. Nichol **18**:367

**Garnick, Vivian**
Toni Morrison **10**:355

**Garrard, J. G.**
Aleksandr I. Solzhenitsyn
**2**:411; **9**:503

**Garrett, George**
John Cheever **3**:107
Babette Deutsch **18**:119
Sue Kaufman **8**:317
Wright Morris **3**:342; **18**:351

**Garrigue, Jean**
Mary McCarthy **14**:357
Marianne Moore **1**:228

**Garson, Helen S.**
Truman Capote **19**:85
John Hawkes **9**:268

**Garvin, Larry**
Piri Thomas **17**:501

**Gasque, Thomas J.**
J.R.R. Tolkien **1**:337

**Gass, William H.**
Donald Barthelme **3**:43
Jorge Luis Borges **3**:76
Robert Coover **3**:113
William H. Gass **15**:257
Vladimir Nabokov **3**:351
J. F. Powers **1**:281
Philip Roth **3**:437
Isaac Bashevis Singer **3**:454
Susan Sontag **10**:484

**Gassner, John**
Edward Albee **3**:6, 7
Jean Anouilh **3**:11, 12
Samuel Beckett **3**:44, 45
Brendan Behan **8**:63
Lillian Hellman **4**:220
William Inge **8**:307
Eugène Ionesco **4**:250
Archibald MacLeish **3**:310
Arthur Miller **6**:330
John Osborne **5**:330
Harold Pinter **3**:386
Thornton Wilder **5**:495
Tennessee Williams **5**:498, 500

**Gates, David**
Samuel Beckett **9**:83

**Gathercole, Patricia M.**
Tommaso Landolfi **11**:321

**Gathorne-Hardy, J.**
Vladimir Nabokov **3**:354

**Gatt-Rutter, John**
Italo Calvino **11**:89

**Gauch, Patricia Lee**
Robert Newton Peck **17**:343

**Gaudon, Sheila**
Julien Gracq **11**:245

**Gaull, Marilyn**
E. E. Cumming **12**:156

**Gaurilović, Zoran**
Dobrica Ćosić **14**:132

**Gavin, Willam**
Auberon Waugh **7**:514

**Gayle, Addison, Jr.**
Gwendolyn Brooks **1**:46
Ernest J. Gaines **18**:167

**Gealy, Marcia B.**
Bernard Malamud **18**:317

**Gearing, Nigel**
Pier Paolo Pasolini **20**:266

**Geary, Joyce**
Jade Snow Wong **17**:566

**Gebhard, Ann**
Barbara Corcoran **17**:75

**Geddes, Gary**
Raymond Souster **5**:395

**Geduld, Harry M.**
Woody Allen **16**:8

**Geering, R. G.**
Shirley Hazzard **18**:216
Christina Stead **2**:42

**Geherin, David J.**
Joan Didion **8**:173

**Geis, Richard E.**
Peter Dickinson **12**:172

**Geismar, Maxwell**
Nelson Algren **4**:16
John Beecher **6**:48
Saul Bellow **1**:27
Camilo José Cela **13**:145
James Gould Cozzens **1**:66
John Dos Passos **1**:77
William Faulkner **1**:100
William Gaddis **19**:185
Nadine Gordimer **5**:146
Ernest Hemingway **1**:142
John Hersey **1**:144
Norman Mailer **1**:187
Henry Miller **4**:350
Henry Roth **6**:471
J. D. Salinger **1**:295
William Styron **1**:329
Leon Uris **7**:490
Herman Wouk **1**:376

**Gelb, Arthur**
Alice Childress **12**:104

**Geldzahler, Henry**
Andy Warhol **20**:414

**Gelfant, Blanche H.**
Yasunari Kawabata **9**:316
Jack Kerouac **5**:213
Jean Stafford **7**:459
James Welch **14**:558

**Gellatly, Peter**
C. Day Lewis **6**:128

**Gelpi, Albert**
William Everson **14**:164
Adrienne Rich **6**:457

**Geltman, Max**
Arthur Koestler **8**:325
Ezra Pound **5**:349; **7**:338

**Genêt**
Françoise Sagan **17**:422, 423

**Geng, Veronica**
Francis Ford Coppola **16**:246
Nadine Gordimer **5**:148

**George, Diana L.**
Lionel Trilling **9**:532

**George, Michael**
J. B. Priestley **5**:350

**Gerald, John Bart**
Robert Lowell **3**:302
Robert Stone **5**:11

**Gerhardt, Lillian N.**
Betty Cavanna **12**:101

**Geringer, Laura**
Toni Cade Bambara **19**:34

**Gerlach, John**
Robert Bresson **16**:118

**German, Howard**
Iris Murdoch **15**:383

**Gerould, Daniel C.**
Tadeusz Różewicz **9**:463

**Gerrard, Charlotte F.**
Eugène Ionesco **9**:286

**Gerrold, David**
Gene Roddenberry **17**:403

**Gerson, Ben**
David Bowie **17**:59
John Lennon and Paul
    McCartney **12**:366, 377

**Gerson, Villiers**
John Wyndham **19**:474

**Gersoni-Stavn, Diane**
See Stavn, Diane Gersoni

**Gerstein, Evelyn**
Fritz Lang **20**:201

**Gerstenberger, Donna**
Iris Murdoch **6**:348

**Gertel, Zunilda**
José Donoso **4**:128
Juan Carlos Onetti **7**:278

**Gervais, Marc**
Pier Paolo Pasolini **20**:260

**Getz, Thomas H.**
Geoffrey Hill **18**:241

**Giacoman, Helmy F.**
Alejo Carpentier **11**:97

**Gianakaris, C. J.**
Arthur Miller **15**:376

**Giannaris, George**
Vassilis Vassilikos **8**:524

**Giannetti, Louis D.**
Federico Fellini **16**:295

**Giannone, Richard**
Kurt Vonnegut, Jr **12**:620

**Giard, Robert**
Claude Chabrol **16**:169, 175

**Gibbons, Boyd**
James A. Michener **11**:374

**Gibbons, Reginald**
Robert Hayden **14**:241
Theodore Weiss **14**:553

**Gibbs, Beverly J.**
Juan Carlos Onetti **10**:374

**Gibbs, Robert**
Margaret Avison **2**:29

**Gibbs, Wolcott**
Sally Benson **17**:50
Emlyn Williams **15**:576

**Gibian, George**
Varlam Shalamov **18**:478
Aleksandr I. Solzhenitsyn **7**:447

**Gibson, Arthur**
Ingmar Bergman **16**:62

**Gibson, Donald B.**
James Baldwin **3**:32
Imamu Amiri Baraka **5**:46
Ralph Ellison **3**:143
Langston Hughes **5**:19
Jean Toomer **13**:551

**Gibson, Kenneth**
Roch Carrier **13**:143

**Gibson, Margaret**
Judith Wright **11**:578

**Giddings, Paula**
Nikki Giovanni **19**:191
Margaret Walker **1**:351

**Gide, André**
Hermann Hesse **11**:270
Pär Lagerkvist **7**:199

**Gidley, Mick**
William Faulkner **3**:156

**Gies, Judith**
Frederick Busch **18**:86

**Gifford, Henry**
Joseph Brodsky **13**:117
Marianne Moore **4**:361

**Gilbert, Sandra M.**
Maya Angelou **12**:13
Jean Garrigue **8**:239
Sandra Hochman **8**:297
Diane Johnson **5**:200
Kenneth Koch **8**:323
Eleanor Lerman **9**:329
Audre Lorde **18**:308
Sylvia Plath **17**:361
Anne Sexton **4**:484
Kathleen Spivack **6**:521
Diane Wakoski **9**:554

**Gilbert, W. Stephen**
Peter Handke **5**:163
Richard O'Brien **17**:322, 324
J. B. Priestley **5**:350
David Storey **5**:416

**Gilbert, Zack**
Leon Forrest **4**:164

**Gilder, Joshua**
Dee Brown **18**:71
Jerzy Kosinski **15**:316

**Giles, Dennis**
Jean-Luc Godard **20**:151

**Giles, Mary E.**
Juan Goytisolo **10**:243

**Gill, Brendan**
Edward Albee **5**:12
Alan Ayckbourn **5**:36; **8**:34;
    **18**:29
John Bishop **10**:54
Anne Burr **6**:104
D. L. Coburn **10**:107
Noel Coward **9**:172, 173
James Gould Cozzens **11**:126
Charles Gordone **1**:125
John Guare **14**:221
Bill Gunn **5**:152
Lorraine Hansberry **17**:189
Lillian Hellman **18**:227
John Hopkins **4**:233
Preston Jones **10**:296
James Kirkwood **9**:319
Pavel Kohout **13**:323
Ira Levin **6**:306
David Mamet **9**:360
Terrence McNally **7**:219
Arthur Miller **6**:334
Peter Nichols **5**:307
Clifford Odets **2**:319
John O'Hara **6**:385
Dorothy Parker **15**:414
Harold Pinter **15**:425
Roman Polanski **16**:464
Gerome Ragni and James Rado
    **17**:388
Ronald Ribman **7**:358
William Saroyan **8**:468
Murray Schisgal **6**:490
Peter Shaffer **5**:386
Sam Shepard **17**:437
Martin Sherman **19**:416
Neil Simon **6**:505; **11**:495
Isaac Bashevis Singer **15**:509
John Steinbeck **5**:408
Tom Stoppard **4**:526; **5**:413;
    **8**:504; **15**:521
David Storey **2**:424
Lily Tomlin **17**:518
Gore Vidal **2**:449
Andy Warhol **20**:419
Tennessee Williams **5**:503;
    **8**:548
Lanford Wilson **7**:547
Robert Wilson **7**:550

**Gillen, Francis**
Donald Barthelme **2**:40

**Gillespie, Beryl C.**
Barbara Corcoran **17**:78

**Gillespie, John T.**
Frank Bonham **12**:51, 55
Alice Childress **12**:107

**Gillespie, Robert**
Eric Ambler **6**:2
Jorge Luis Borges **6**:91
John le Carré **9**:326

**Gillett, John**
Kon Ichikawa **20**:178, 180
Fritz Lang **20**:209
Yasujiro Ozu **16**:446
Satyajit Ray **16**:477
Josef von Sternberg **20**:374
Billy Wilder **20**:458

**CRITIC INDEX**

**Gilliatt, Penelope**
Woody Allen **16**:2, 7
Robert Altman **16**:30
Samuel Beckett **4**:49
Claude Chabrol **16**:179
Shirley Clarke **16**:216
Noel Coward **9**:172
Brian De Palma **20**:76
Rainer Werner Fassbinder
   **20**:108, 112, 114, 115
Jean-Luc Godard **20**:141
Werner Herzog **16**:326
John Huston **20**:173
Buster Keaton **20**:195
Richard Lester **20**:230
Joe Orton **4**:387
Roman Polanski **16**:472
Satyajit Ray **16**:487
Ken Russell **16**:550
Carlos Saura **20**:317
Melvin Van Peebles **20**:409,
   412
Lina Wertmüller **16**:589, 595
Vassily S. Yanovsky **18**:550

**Gillis, William**
Friedrich Dürrenmatt **11**:170

**Gilman, Harvey**
Howard Nemerov **6**:362

**Gilman, Richard**
Richard Adams **4**:7
Edward Albee **5**:10
John Arden **6**:6
James Baldwin **15**:41; **17**:35,
   44
Imamu Amiri Baraka **5**:44
Donald Barthelme **2**:40
Saul Bellow **6**:49
J. P. Donleavy **6**:140
Bruce Jay Friedman **5**:126
William H. Gass **2**:154
Jack Gelber **1**:114; **6**:196
Graham Greene **6**:214
Rolf Hochhuth **11**:274
Eugène Ionesco **6**:249
Kenneth Koch **5**:218
Norman Mailer **2**:260; **8**:367
Bernard Malamud **18**:320
William Maxwell **19**:307
Michael McClure **10**:331
Arthur Miller **6**:326, 327
Sean O'Casey **5**:319
Walker Percy **18**:399
Harold Pinter **6**:405, 406, 410
Reynolds Price **6**:424
John Rechy **7**:356
Philip Roth **3**:438
Howard Sackler **14**:478
Robert Shaw **5**:390
Neil Simon **6**:502
John Updike **2**:440
Tennessee Williams **5**:499

**Gilmore, Mikal**
Bob Marley **17**:269, 270
Bruce Springsteen **17**:486
Stevie Wonder **12**:660

**Gilroy, Harry**
Frank B. Gilbreth, Jr. and
   Ernestine Gilbreth Carey
   **17**:153

**Gilsdorf, Jeanette**
Robert Creeley **4**:118

**Gindin, James**
Kingsley Amis **2**:4
Saul Bellow **3**:54
Truman Capote **3**:100
Margaret Drabble **10**:165
E. M. Forster **3**:160
John Fowles **10**:189
William Golding **2**:165; **3**:198
Rosamond Lehmann **5**:238
Doris Lessing **2**:238
Iris Murdoch **2**:295; **3**:347
John Osborne **2**:327
Philip Roth **3**:436
Alan Sillitoe **3**:447, 448
David Storey **2**:423; **4**:528
John Wain **2**:457
Angus Wilson **2**:470; **3**:534

**Gingher, Robert S.**
John Updike **5**:454

**Gingrich, Arnold**
Chester Himes **2**:196

**Ginsberg, Allen**
Gregory Corso **11**:123
Jack Kerouac **2**:228; **14**:306
Ezra Pound **18**:420

**Giovanni, Nikki**
Alice Walker **5**:476

**Gipson, Carolyn**
W.E.B. Du Bois **2**:120

**Girson, Rochelle**
Peter S. Beagle **7**:25

**Gitlin, Todd**
James Baldwin **2**:32
Robert Bly **2**:66
Bob Dylan **4**:150
Paul Goodman **7**:130
Denise Levertov **2**:243
Marge Piercy **3**:383

**Gitzen, Julian**
Robert Bly **10**:56
Seamus Heaney **5**:172
Ted Hughes **4**:237
Denise Levertov **5**:250
Peter Redgrove **6**:446
R. S. Thomas **6**:531
Charles Tomlinson **2**:437; **4**:548
Ted Walker **13**:566

**Giuliano, William**
Antonio Buero Vallejo **15**:98

**Givner, Joan**
Katherine Anne Porter **7**:319;
   **10**:398; **13**:450; **15**:432
Eudora Welty **5**:479

**Glaessner, Verina**
François Truffaut **20**:404

**Glasser, William**
J. D. Salinger **8**:464

**Glassman, Peter**
Shirley Ann Grau **9**:240

**Glatstein, Jacob**
Marianne Moore **4**:358

**Glauber, Robert H.**
Mary Oliver **19**:361

**Gleason, George**
Sonia Levitin **17**:266
Robert Newton Peck **17**:342

**Gleason, Judith**
Aimé Césaire **19**:95

**Gleason, Judith Illsley**
Chinua Achebe **7**:3

**Gleason, Ralph J.**
Nelson Algren **10**:7
Bob Dylan **6**:156; **12**:181
Martin Mull **17**:299
Paul Simon **17**:459

**Gleicher, David**
Margaret Atwood **3**:19

**Glen, Duncan**
Hugh MacDiarmid **4**:311

**Glendinning, Victoria**
Margaret Atwood **15**:38
Melvyn Bragg **10**:72
Anthony Burgess **5**:87
Angela Carter **5**:101
Roald Dahl **6**:122
Anita Desai **19**:134
Penelope Fitzgerald **19**:173
Doris Grumbach **13**:258
James Hanley **13**:262
Chester Himes **7**:159
Russell C. Hoban **7**:160
Ursula Holden **18**:258
Elizabeth Jane Howard **7**:164
Alison Lurie **18**:310
Olivia Manning **19**:303
Joyce Carol Oates **11**:404
Edna O'Brien **13**:416
Barbara Pym **13**:471
Françoise Sagan **9**:468
Alan Sillitoe **6**:500
J.I.M. Stewart **7**:466
Fay Weldon **11**:565
Eudora Welty **14**:565

**Glenn, Jerry**
Paul Celan **10**:102, 104; **19**:89

**Glenn, Jules**
Anthony Shaffer **19**:414

**Glick, William**
Walter Farley **17**:115

**Glicksberg, Charles I.**
Arthur Adamov **4**:6
Albert Camus **1**:52
Jean Genet **5**:136
Hermann Hesse **3**:244
Aldous Huxley **3**:254
Eugène Ionesco **9**:288; **11**:290
Robinson Jeffers **3**:260
André Malraux **1**:201
Kenneth Patchen **18**:392

**Glimm, James York**
Thomas Merton **3**:337; **11**:372

**Gloster, Hugh M.**
Arna Bontemps **18**:63
Jessie Redmon Fauset **19**:170

**Glover, Al**
Michael McClure **6**:320

**Glover, Elaine**
John Fowles **6**:188
Nadine Gordimer **7**:131
Joseph Heller **8**:279
Tim O'Brien **7**:271

**Glover, Tony**
Chuck Berry **17**:53
Patti Smith **12**:534

**Glover, Willis B.**
J.R.R. Tolkien **1**:340

**Goatley, James L.**
Roy A. Gallant **17**:132

**Godard, B.**
Audrey Thomas **13**:540

**Goddard, Donald**
Lothar-Günther Buchheim
   **6**:102

**Godden, Rumer**
Carson McCullers **12**:418

**Godfrey, Dave**
Joan Barfoot **18**:35
Hugh MacLennan **14**:343

**Godshalk, William L.**
Kurt Vonnegut, Jr. **3**:500

**Godwin, Gail**
Beryl Bainbridge **5**:39
Ann Beattie **13**:64
Julien Green **3**:205
Doris Grumbach **13**:258
Shirley Hazzard **18**:220
Vassily S. Yanovsky **18**:552

**Goitein, Denise**
Nathalie Sarraute **10**:457

**Gold, Herbert**
Mel Brooks **12**:78
Richard Condon **10**:111
John Dos Passos **4**:136
Alistair MacLean **13**:364
Aleksandr I. Solzhenitsyn **2**:409
Terry Southern **7**:454
Gore Vidal **6**:550

**Gold, Ivan**
Shusaku Endo **14**:162
George V. Higgins **10**:273
Paul Horgan **9**:279
Jerzy Kosinski **15**:316
Frederic Raphael **14**:437
John Updike **2**:440
John A. Williams **13**:599
Helen Yglesias **7**:558

**Gold, Peter**
José María Arguedas **18**:5

**Goldberg, Steven**
Bob Dylan **6**:154

**Goldberg, Vicki**
Paul Theroux **11**:530

**Golden, Robert E.**
Thomas Pynchon **3**:409

**Goldensohn, Lorrie**
Ira Sadoff **9**:466
Maura Stanton **9**:508

**Goldfarb, Clare R.**
Aleksandr I. Solzhenitsyn **7**:443

**Goldknopf, David**
 Kurt Vonnegut, Jr. **12**:600

**Goldman, Albert**
 Bob Dylan **3**:130; **12**:186
 John Lennon and Paul
  McCartney **12**:367

**Goldman, Eric F.**
 Dalton Trumbo **19**:445

**Goldman, Mark**
 Bernard Malamud **1**:197

**Goldman, Merle**
 Jules Archer **12**:19

**Goldman, Michael**
 Joyce Carol Oates **3**:361

**Goldman, William**
 Ross Macdonald **1**:185

**Goldmann, Lucien**
 Witold Gombrowicz **11**:239

**Goldsmith, Arnold L.**
 John Steinbeck **9**:515

**Goldsmith, Claire K.**
 Alvin Silverstein and Virginia
  B. Silverstein **17**:455

**Goldsmith, David H.**
 Kurt Vonnegut, Jr. **4**:562

**Goldstein, Eric**
 Susan Cheever **18**:102

**Goldstein, Laurence**
 Robert Frost **13**:230
 David Ignatow **4**:248
 Adrienne Rich **7**:372
 James Wright **3**:541

**Goldstein, Malcolm**
 Thornton Wilder **1**:365

**Goldstein, Richard**
 Bob Dylan **3**:130; **12**:182
 John Lennon and Paul
  McCartney **12**:357

**Goldstein, Toby**
 Jonathan Kozol **17**:252
 Jim Morrison **17**:294

**Goldstone, Richard H.**
 Thornton Wilder **6**:574

**Golffing, Francis**
 Salvatore Quasimodo **10**:429

**Gomez, Joseph A.**
 Ken Russell **16**:550

**Gömöri, George**
 László Nagy **7**:251

**Goodfriend, James**
 Laura Nyro **17**:314

**Goodheart, Eugene**
 Cynthia Ozick **3**:372
 Theodore Roethke **1**:292
 John Seelye **7**:405
 William Carlos Williams **5**:510

**Goodman, Charlotte**
 Joyce Carol Oates **15**:400

**Goodman, Ellen**
 Maureen Daly **17**:91

**Goodman, Henry**
 Elia Kazan **16**:367

**Goodman, James**
 George Seferis **5**:385

**Goodman, Paul**
 James Baldwin **17**:23
 Ernest Hemingway **1**:144

**Goodman, Robert L.**
 David Kherdian **6**:280

**Goodman, Walter**
 Thomas Berger **8**:83

**Goodrich, Norma L.**
 Jean Giono **4**:187; **11**:230

**Goodrick, Susan**
 Robert Crumb **17**:86

**Goodsell, James Nelson**
 Jules Archer **12**:18
 Allan W. Eckert **17**:106, 107
 Piri Thomas **17**:498

**Goodstein, Jack**
 Alain Robbe-Grillet **2**:376

**Goodwin, Michael**
 Chuck Berry **17**:51
 John Brunner **10**:80
 Samuel R. Delany **14**:143
 Joanna Russ **15**:461
 Andy Warhol **20**:420

**Goodwin, Polly**
 Honor Arundel **17**:12
 Eilís Dillon **17**:94
 Lee Kingman **17**:245
 Emily Cheney Neville **12**:450

**Goodwin, Stephen**
 Eleanor Clark **19**:108
 Ella Leffland **19**:280
 Walker Percy **2**:335
 Peter Taylor **1**:334
 John Kennedy Toole **19**:442

**Gordimer, Nadine**
 Chinua Achebe **3**:2
 Simone de Beauvoir **14**:67
 V. S. Naipaul **4**:372
 James Ngugi **3**:358

**Gordon, Andrew**
 Ishmael Reed **2**:368

**Gordon, Caroline**
 Flannery O'Connor **15**:411

**Gordon, Cecelia**
 Ruth M. Arthur **12**:27

**Gordon, David J.**
 Herbert Gold **4**:192
 William Golding **1**:122
 Uwe Johnson **5**:200
 Brian Moore **1**:225
 Vladimir Nabokov **1**:245
 Tom Stoppard **1**:328

**Gordon, Jan B.**
 Richard Adams **5**:4
 John Braine **3**:86
 Doris Lessing **6**:292
 Iris Murdoch **3**:349

**Gordon, Mary**
 Diane Johnson **13**:306
 Maxine Hong Kingston **19**:249
 Mary McCarthy **14**:359
 Edna O'Brien **13**:416
 Walker Percy **18**:401

**Gornick, Vivian**
 Paula Fox **2**:140
 Nadine Gordimer **18**:190
 Lillian Hellman **8**:282; **18**:227
 Jonathan Kozol **17**:253
 Alberto Moravia **18**:347
 Grace Paley **4**:391
 Marge Piercy **18**:407

**Gose, Elliot**
 Marie-Claire Blais **13**:96
 Gwendolyn MacEwan **13**:357

**Gossett, Louise Y.**
 William Goyen **14**:209
 Flannery O'Connor **1**:256

**Gossman, Ann**
 Lawrence Durrell **1**:87
 Iris Murdoch **15**:387

**Gostnell, David**
 Alvin Silverstein and Virginia
  B. Silverstein **17**:456

**Gott, Richard**
 Carlos Castaneda **12**:86

**Gottfried, Martin**
 John Guare **14**:222
 Lorraine Hansberry **17**:189
 Bernard Pomerance **13**:445
 Howard Sackler **14**:479
 Sam Shepard **17**:436
 George Tabori **19**:438
 Lanford Wilson **7**:547

**Gottlieb, Annie**
 Maya Angelou **12**:11
 Henry Bromell **5**:74
 Louis-Ferdinand Céline **4**:104
 Lois Gould **10**:241
 Charles Johnson **7**:183
 Tillie Olsen **4**:386

**Gottlieb, Elaine**
 Isaac Bashevis Singer **6**:507

**Gottlieb, Gerald**
 John R. Tunis **12**:599

**Gottschalk, Jane**
 Ralph Ellison **11**:181

**Gould, Gerald**
 Edna Ferber **18**:150

**Gould, Jack**
 John Lennon and Paul
  McCartney **12**:354

**Gould, Jean**
 Elmer Rice **7**:363

**Goulianos, Joan Rodman**
 Lawrence Durrell **8**:193

**Gow, Gordon**
 Lindsay Anderson **20**:18
 Michelangelo Antonioni **20**:40
 John Cassavetes **20**:45
 Claude Chabrol **16**:170
 René Clair **20**:66

 Vittorio De Sica **20**:88, 91
 Bob Fosse **20**:125
 Alfred Hitchcock **16**:353
 John Huston **20**:168
 Elia Kazan **16**:374
 Nagisa Oshima **20**:246
 Satyajit Ray **16**:479
 Alain Resnais **16**:510
 Ken Russell **16**:542, 543
 Jerzy Skolimowski **20**:352
 Steven Spielberg **20**:359
 Agnès Varda **16**:555
 Peter Weir **20**:428
 Orson Welles **20**:439, 452

**Gower, Herschel**
 Peter Taylor **18**:525

**Goyen, William**
 Truman Capote **19**:81
 Anaïs Nin **4**:379

**Goytisolo, Juan**
 Carlos Fuentes **10**:204

**Grady, Wayne**
 Matt Cohen **19**:116

**Graff, Gerald**
 Donald Barthelme **6**:30
 Saul Bellow **6**:54
 Stanley Elkin **6**:169
 Norman Mailer **8**:372

**Graham, Desmond**
 Jorge Luis Borges **8**:103
 James Hanley **13**:262
 Anthony Hecht **13**:269
 Philip Larkin **5**:229
 Robert Lowell **11**:329
 John Montague **13**:392
 Eugenio Montale **9**:388
 Peter Porter **13**:453

**Graham, John**
 John Hawkes **3**:221
 Ernest Hemingway **3**:236
 Gibbons Ruark **3**:441

**Graham, Kenneth**
 Richard Adams **5**:5
 Laurens Van der Post **5**:463

**Graham-Yooll, Andrew**
 Gabriel García Márquez
  **15**:253

**Grahn, Judy**
 Alta **19**:19

**Grande, Brother Luke M., F.S.C.**
 Marion Montgomery **7**:232

**Granetz, Marc**
 Donald Barthelme **13**:61
 John Gardner **18**:183

**Grange, Joseph**
 Carlos Castaneda **12**:86

**Grant, Annette**
 Shirley Ann Grau **4**:209

**Grant, Damian**
 W. H. Auden **6**:17
 Seamus Heaney **5**:172
 Sylvia Plath **2**:337
 Peter Porter **5**:347

**CRITIC INDEX**

**Grant, Judith Skelton**
Robertson Davies 13:173

**Grant, Patrick**
Robert Graves 11:257

**Grau, Shirley Ann**
William Goyen 8:250
Marion Montgomery 7:233

**Graver, Lawrence**
Samuel Beckett 6:40
Doris Lessing 2:242
Carson McCullers 1:209
Iris Murdoch 3:347
Muriel Spark 2:417
Paul Theroux 8:513
William Trevor 7:475

**Graves, Elizabeth Minot**
Lee Kingman 17:246
Sonia Levitin 17:263
Zilpha Keatley Snyder 17:471

**Graves, Peter**
Jurek Becker 19:36
Christa Wolf 14:595

**Graves, Peter J.**
Friedrich Dürrenmatt 15:196

**Graves, Robert**
Yevgeny Yevtushenko 1:382

**Gray, Francine du Plessix**
Oriana Fallaci 11:190
Max Frisch 14:184

**Gray, Mrs. Hildagarde**
Katherine Paterson 12:485

**Gray, James**
Pearl S. Buck 7:32
Jules Roains 7:381

**Gray, John**
Paul Bowles 2:79

**Gray, Mrs. John G.**
Jules Archer 12:20
M. E. Kerr 12:298

**Gray, Paul**
Lisa Alther 7:12
Samuel Beckett 6:44
Adolfo Bioy Casares 8:94
Vance Bourjaily 8:104
Jimmy Breslin 4:76
William F. Buckley, Jr. 7:35
Alex Comfort 7:54
Evan S. Connell, Jr. 6:116
Peter De Vries 7:78
Thomas M. Disch 7:86
John Gardner 5:132
William H. Gass 8:246
Russell C. Hoban 7:160
Maureen Howard 5:189
Elia Kazan 6:274
Maxine Hong Kingston 12:312
Peter Matthiessen 5:274
V. S. Naipaul 7:253
Seán O'Faoláin 7:274
Cynthia Ozick 7:288
Reynolds Price 6:425
Robert Stone 5:409
John Updike 5:457
Sylvia Townsend Warner
19:459

James Welch 6:561
Fay Weldon 6:562

**Gray, Paul Edward**
Eleanor Clark 19:106
John Fowles 1:109
Iris Murdoch 1:236
Joyce Carol Oates 1:251
Eudora Welty 1:363

**Gray, Richard**
Erskine Caldwell 14:96
Donald Davidson 19:124
William Faulkner 11:202
Carson McCullers 12:430
John Crowe Ransom 11:469
William Styron 11:520
Tennessee Williams 11:577

**Gray, Ronald**
Heinrich Böll 9:112

**Greacen, Robert**
W. H. Auden 3:25
Samuel Beckett 4:50
Margaret Drabble 2:117
Bernard Kops 4:274
Doris Lessing 3:287
Harold Robbins 5:378
Isaac Bashevis Singer 3:457
Vassilis Vassilikos 4:551

**Grealish, Gerald**
Gilbert Sorrentino 14:498

**Grebanier, Bernard**
Thornton Wilder 1:365

**Grebstein, Sheldon Norman**
Ernest Hemingway 3:235
Bernard Malamud 11:348
John O'Hara 1:261

**Greeley, Andrew M.**
Richard Bach 14:36

**Green, Alan**
Peter De Vries 3:126
Michael Frayn 3:164

**Green, Benny**
John Fowles 6:186
Compton Mackenzie 18:316
Brian Moore 7:238
V. S. Naipaul 18:359
John O'Hara 6:383
S. J. Perelman 15:417
Charles M. Schulz 12:533

**Green, Calvin**
Pier Paolo Pasolini 20:264
Eric Rohmer 16:529

**Green, Gerald**
Thomas Berger 3:63

**Green, Harris**
Jim Jacobs and Warren Casey
12:293

**Green, James L.**
John Hawkes 14:237

**Green, Kate**
Anne Sexton 15:473

**Green, Laurence**
Joan Micklin Silver 20:342

**Green, Marc**
Robert Altman 16:43

**Green, Martin**
E. L. Doctorow 6:138
B. S. Johnson 6:263
Doris Lessing 15:333
Philip Roth 15:449
J. D. Salinger 1:298

**Green, Peter**
William Golding 17:162

**Green, Philip**
E. E. Cummings 12:147

**Green, Randall**
John Hawkes 4:217
Aleksandr I. Solzhenitsyn 4:512

**Green, Robert J.**
Roch Carrier 13:141
Athol Fugard 9:233

**Green, Robin**
Stan Lee 17:257

**Green, Roger Lancelyn**
Alan Garner 17:135

**Green, Timothy**
W. H. Auden 14:27

**Greenberg, Judith L.**
Patrick Modiano 18:338

**Greenberg, Martin**
Reiner Kunze 10:310

**Greenblatt, Stephen Jay**
Evelyn Waugh 13:585

**Greene, Daniel**
Don L. Lee 2:237

**Greene, George**
Paul West 7:522

**Greene, Graham**
Sally Benson 17:47
Frank Capra 16:154, 155

**Greene, James**
Eugenio Montale 9:388

**Greene, Robert W.**
René Char 14:124
Francis Ponge 18:417
Raymond Queneau 10:430

**Greenfeld, Josh**
Emily Cheney Neville 12:451
Philip Roth 2:378
Paul Zindel 6:586

**Greenfield, Jeff**
Jonathan Kozol 17:255
John Lennon and Paul
McCartney 12:378
Dan Wakefield 7:503

**Greenman, Myron**
Donald Barthelme 6:29

**Greenspan, Miriam**
Maxine Hong Kingston 12:313

**Greenspun, Roger**
Bernardo Bertolucci 16:94
Brian De Palma 20:74
Marguerite Duras 20:98
Federico Fellini 16:283
Bob Fosse 20:122
Alfred Hitchcock 16:354

Akira Kurosawa 16:404
Fritz Lang 20:211
Jean Renoir 20:303
Carlos Saura 20:314, 315
Jerzy Skolimowski 20:349, 353
Melvin Van Peebles 20:411

**Greenstein, Michael**
Dorothy Livesay 15:342

**Greenway, John**
Norman Mailer 2:262
Joseph Wambaugh 18:532

**Greenya, John R.**
Ronald L. Fair 18:139
Budd Schulberg 7:403

**Greggs, R.**
Robert Westall 17:559

**Gregor, Ian**
Graham Greene 6:214

**Gregor, Ulrich**
Leni Riefenstahl 16:521

**Gregory, Charles**
Robert Altman 16:27

**Gregory, Helen**
Betty Cavanna 12:103

**Gregory, Hilda**
Joyce Carol Oates 1:251; 2:315
Mark Strand 6:522
Nancy Willard 7:540

**Gregory, Horace**
Morley Callaghan 14:99
Laura Riding 7:373

**Greider, William**
William Safire 10:447

**Greiner, Donald J.**
Djuna Barnes 8:48
Frederick Busch 10:91
John Hawkes 1:138; 4:213;
7:145
Kurt Vonnegut, Jr. 3:499

**Grella, George**
Ian Fleming 3:158
Dashiell Hammett 19:197

**Grenier, Cynthia**
Satyajit Ray 16:476

**Grier, Edward F.**
Jonathan Williams 13:600

**Griffin, Bryan**
John Irving 13:27

**Griffin, Robert J.**
Cid Corman 9:169

**Griffith, Albert J.**
Carson McCullers 1:209
Peter Taylor 1:334; 4:542;
18:526
John Updike 5:455

**Grigsby, Gordon K.**
Kenneth Rexroth 1:284

**Grigson, Geoffrey**
Yasunari Kawabata 18:280
Robert Lowell 3:302
Kathleen Raine 7:351

**Grimwood, Michael**
William Faulkner 14:174

**Griswold, Jerry**
Kcn Kesey 3:268

**Groberg, Nancy**
Mark Harris 19:199

**Groden, Michael**
William Faulkner 9:198

**Gropper, Esther C.**
Hermann Hesse 2:189; 3:244

**Grosholz, Emily**
Richard F. Hugo 18:264
Mary Oliver 19:363

**Gross, Amy**
Lily Tomlin 17:516

**Gross, Barry**
Arthur Miller 10:344

**Gross, Beverly**
John Barth 14:49
Jonathan Baumbach 6:32
Saul Bellow 2:52
B. H. Friedman 7:109
Peter Spielberg 6:514

**Gross, Harvey**
T. S. Eliot 6:161
André Malraux 4:335
Ezra Pound 4:414

**Gross, John**
V. S. Pritchett 15:441

**Gross, Michael**
David Bowie 17:62

**Gross, Theodore L.**
J. D. Salinger 1:300

**Grosskurth, Phyllis**
Margaret Atwood 2:20
Gabrielle Roy 14:463

**Grossman, Edward**
Simone de Beauvoir 2:44
Saul Bellow 8:80
Thomas Berger 3:63
Heinrich Böll 3:75
Joseph Heller 5:181
Doris Lcssing 3:287
Vladimir Nabokov 3:355
Kurt Vonnegut, Jr. 5:466

**Grossman, Joel**
Philip Roth 9:459

**Grossman, Loyd**
Peter Townshend 17:536

**Grossvogel, David I.**
Agatha Christie 12:127
Julio Cortázar 10:112
Jean Genet 14:196

**Groth, Janet**
John Cheever 8:136

**Groves, Margaret**
Nathalie Sarraute 4:470

**Grumbach, Doris**
Maya Angelou 12:12
Simone de Beauvoir 4:49
Kay Boyle 5:66
Frederick Busch 18:85
Hortense Calisher 8:124

Arthur A. Cohen 7:50
Joan Didion 8:175
E. L. Doctorow 6:131
Daphne du Maurier 11:164
Stanley Elkin 4:154; 14:158
Leslie A. Fiedler 13:214
Nadine Gordimer 18:188
Susan B. Hill 4:288
Maureen Howard 5:188
Alison Lurie 4:307
Cormac McCarthy 4:342
Mary McCarthy 5:276
A. G. Mojtabai 9:385
Brian Moore 5:297
Penelope Mortimer 5:299
Tim O'Brien 19:357
Julia O'Faolain 6:383
Aldo Palazzeschi 11:431
Jayne Anne Phillips 15:421
Judith Rossner 9:457
J. R. Salamanca 4:461
May Sarton 4:471; 14:480
Clancy Sigal 7:425
Anne Tyler 7:479
John Updike 15:546
Nancy Willard 7:538, 539
Hilma Wolitzer 17:561, 564
Sol Yurick 6:584

**Grunfeld, Frederick V.**
John Lennon and Paul
    McCartney 12:361

**Grunwald, Beverly**
Maureen Daly 17:90

**Gubar, Susan**
H. D. 14:225

**Gubbins, Bill**
Brian Wilson 12:648

**Guerard, Albert J.**
Donald Barthelme 5:53
Jerome Charyn 5:103
John Hawkes 2:183; 3:222;
    15:278

**Guereschi, Edward**
Joyce Carol Oates 15:403

**Guernsey, Otis L., Jr.**
Sally Benson 17:49

**Guerrard, Philip**
Mervyn Peake 7:301

**Guggenheim, Michel**
Françoise Sagan 17:421

**Guicharnaud, Jacques**
Fernando Arrabal 18:16
Michel de Ghelderode 11:226
Eugène Ionesco 6:254
Henri de Montherlant 19:326
Jean-Paul Sartre 1:304
Claude Simon 15:485

**Guicharnaud, June**
Michel de Ghelderode 11:226

**Guild, Nicholas**
Paul Theroux 11:530

**Guimond, James**
Gilbert Sorrentino 3:461

**Guiton, Margaret Otis**
Louis Aragon 3:12
Marcel Aymé 11:21
Albert Camus 1:54
Louis-Ferdinand Céline 1:57
Jean Cocteau 1:59
Georges Duhamel 8:186
Jean Giono 4:183
Julien Green 3:203
André Malraux 1:202
François Mauriac 4:337
Raymond Queneau 2:359
Jules Romains 7:381
Jean-Paul Sartre 1:306

**Gullason, Thomas A.**
Carson McCullers 4:344
Flannery O'Connor 1:259

**Gullette, David**
Mark Strand 18:518

**Gullon, Agnes**
Pablo Neruda 7:260

**Gunn, Edward**
Djuna Barnes 4:44

**Gunn, James**
Isaac Asimov 19:29

**Gunn, Thom**
Barbara Howes 15:289
David Ignatow 7:173
Donald Justice 19:232
W. S. Merwin 13:383
Christopher Middleton 13:387
Howard Nemerov 9:393
Charles Olson 11:414
Louis Simpson 7:426, 427

**Gunston, David**
Leni Riefenstahl 16:520

**Guralnick, Peter**
Willie Nelson 17:304

**Gurewitsch, M. Anatole**
William Gaddis 6:195

**Gurian, Jay**
Thomas Berger 18:55

**Gurko, Leo**
Ernest Hemingway 6:226
John P. Marquand 10:331
Edward Lewis Wallant 5:477

**Gussow, Mel**
Ed Bullins 1:47
Charles Gordone 1:125
Howard Sackler 14:480
Sam Shepard 17:438
Elizabeth Swados 12:558

**Gustafson, Richard**
Reg Saner 9:469

**Gustainis, J. Justin**
Stephen King 12:311
Amos Oz 11:429

**Gutowski, John A.**
Joan Micklin Silver 20:345

**Guttenplan, Don David**
Arna Bontemps 18:65

**Gwynn, Frederick L.**
J. D. Salinger 1:295

**Gysin, Fritz**
Jean Toomer 13:552

**Gyurko, Lanin A.**
Julio Cortázar 5:108; 10:112;
    13:159

**Haas, Diane**
Judy Blume 12:46

**Haas, Joseph**
Bob Dylan 12:180
Jerome Weidman 7:517

**Haberl, Franz P.**
Max Frisch 9:218; 14:184
Peter Weiss 15:565

**Hack, Richard**
Kenneth Patchen 2:332
Colin Wilson 3:537

**Hackett, C. A.**
Henri Michaux 19:311

**Hackney, Louise Wallace**
John Ford 16:303

**Hadas, Moses**
Mary Renault 17:392
Marguerite Yourcenar 19:481

**Hadas, Pamela White**
Marianne Moore 10:348

**Hadas, Rachel**
Yannis Ritsos 13:487
Robert Penn Warren 18:534

**Haenicke, Diether H.**
Heinrich Böll 6:83
Paul Celan 10:101
Friedrich Dürrenmatt 8:194
Günter Eich 15:204
Max Frisch 9:217
Günter Grass 6:207
Uwe Johnson 5:201
Reiner Kunze 10:310
Anna Seghers 7:408
Carl Zuckmayer 18:553

**Haffenden, John**
John Berryman 10:45
Robert Lowell 11:330

**Haft, Cynthia**
Aleksandr I. Solzhenitsyn 7:435

**Hagan, Candace**
Philip Roth 15:453

**Hagan, Patti**
Barbara Corcoran 17:73

**Haglin, Donna**
Henry Gregor Felsen 17:123

**Hagopian, John V.**
James Baldwin 1:15
William Faulkner 3:157
J. F. Powers 1:282

**Hague, René**
David Jones 7:189

**Hahn, Claire**
William Everson 5:122
Jean Garrigue 8:239
Audre Lorde 18:309

**Hahn, Emily**
Martha Gellhorn 14:196

**CRITIC INDEX**

**Hainsworth, J. D.**
John Arden 13:24

**Hájek, Igor**
Bohumil Hrabal 13:291

**Halderman, Marjorie**
Larry Kettelkamp 12:304

**Hale, Nancy**
Jessamyn West 7:522; 17:552, 554

**Hale, Thomas A.**
Aimé Césaire 19:97

**Hales, David**
Berry Morgan 6:340

**Halio, Jay L.**
William Gaddis 10:212
John Gardner 10:220
Ernest Hemingway 6:230
Mary McCarthy 5:276
Reynolds Price 13:464
Isaac Bashevis Singer 1:314; 6:509
C. P. Snow 6:517
Aleksandr I. Solzhenitsyn 7:434
Alice Walker 5:476
Paul West 14:569

**Hall, Donald**
Russell Edson 13:191
Allen Ginsberg 3:195
Thom Gunn 18:202
Mark Harris 19:205
Seamus Heaney 14:242, 245
Geoffrey Hill 18:241
Richard F. Hugo 18:263
Robert Lowell 15:344
Peter Matthiessen 11:361
Rod McKuen 3:333
Marianne Moore 4:362
David Wagoner 15:559
Thomas Williams 14:583

**Hall, Elizabeth**
Frank Herbert 12:275
Stephen King 12:309

**Hall, James**
Saul Bellow 3:50
Elizabeth Bowen 3:82
William Faulkner 3:152
Graham Greene 3:207
Iris Murdoch 2:296
J. D. Salinger 3:444
Robert Penn Warren 4:577

**Hall, James B.**
Mario Puzo 1:282

**Hall, Joan Joffe**
Wendell Berry 4:59
Marie-Claire Blais 6:81
Shirley Ann Grau 4:210
Ursula K. LeGuin 8:342
Robert Stone 5:410
John Updike 5:458
Jessamyn West 17:550

**Hall, John**
Gary Snyder 1:318

**Hall, Linda B.**
Carlos Fuentes 8:222
Gabriel García Márquez 10:214
Maxine Hong Kingston 12:314

**Hall, Mordaunt**
Tod Browning 16:121
Frank Capra 16:153

**Hall, Richard W.**
Ezra Pound 5:348

**Hall, Stephen**
R. H. W. Dillard 5:116

**Hall, Wade**
Jesse Stuart 11:511

**Halle, Louis J.**
William Golding 17:157

**Haller, Robert S.**
Martin Booth 13:104
Alan Sillitoe 6:500

**Halliday, Mark**
Eleanor Lerman 9:329

**Halman, Talat Sait**
Yashar Kemal 14:299, 300, 301

**Halpern, Daniel**
David Wagoner 5:475

**Halsey, Martha T.**
Antonio Buero Vallejo 15:99

**Hamalian, Leo**
Jean-Luc Godard 20:141

**Hamburger, Michael**
Paul Celan 19:93
Robert Pinsky 19:370

**Hamill, Pete**
Seán O'Faoláin 7:272
Leon Uris 7:492

**Hamill, Sam**
Greg Kuzma 7:197

**Hamilton, Alice**
Samuel Beckett 10:31
John Updike 2:443; 5:449

**Hamilton, Daphne Ann**
Melvin Berger 12:41, 42
Roy A. Gallant 17:132

**Hamilton, Ian**
Kingsley Amis 2:6
Robert Lowell 2:246; 4:303
Louis MacNeice 4:317
Christopher Middleton 13:387

**Hamilton, James Shelley**
René Clair 20:58, 61
John Ford 16:303
Rouben Mamoulian 16:420
Jean Renoir 20:286

**Hamilton, Kenneth**
Samuel Beckett 10:31
John Updike 2:443; 5:449

**Hamilton, Mary**
Paul Vincent Carroll 10:98

**Hamilton, William**
Albert Camus 1:52
Paul Goodman 7:128

**Hamilton-Paterson, James**
Anne McCaffrey 17:281

**Hammond, John G.**
Robert Creeley 8:151

**Hammond, Jonathan**
Athol Fugard 9:229

**Hamner, Robert D.**
V. S. Naipaul 13:402

**Hampshire, Stuart**
Christopher Isherwood 11:296

**Handa, Carolyn**
Conrad Aiken 10:1

**Handlin, Oscar**
Yuri Krotkov 19:264
Hunter S. Thompson 17:503

**Handzo, Stephen**
Michelangelo Antonioni 20:36
Frank Capra 16:160

**Hanna, Thomas L.**
Albert Camus 9:143

**Hannabuss, C. Stuart**
Leon Garfield 12:230, 234
Andre Norton 12:463
Josephine Poole 17:372
J.R.R. Tolkien 12:575

**Hannah, Barry**
William Eastlake 8:200

**Hanne, Michael**
Elio Vittorini 9:551

**Hansen, Arlen J.**
Richard Brautigan 3:90

**Hansen, Arthur G.**
Richard Bach 14:35

**Hansen, Olaf**
Peter Handke 10:259

**Harada, Violet H.**
Barbara Corcoran 17:77

**Harcourt, Joan**
Roch Carrier 13:141

**Harcourt, Peter**
Ingmar Bergman 16:50, 72
Luis Buñuel 16:141
Federico Fellini 16:290
Jean-Luc Godard 20:143
Richard Lester 20:221
Jean Renoir 20:292, 305
Alain Resnais 16:511

**Hardee, Ethel R.**
Robert Newton Peck 17:337

**Harder, Worth T.**
Herbert Read 4:443

**Hardie, Alec M.**
Edmund Blunden 2:65

**Hardin, Nancy Shields**
Margaret Drabble 3:129
Doris Lessing 6:297

**Harding, D. W.**
Roy Fuller 4:178

**Hardison, O. B., Jr.**
Paul Bowles 19:59
Larry McMurtry 7:215

**Hardwick, Elizabeth**
Renata Adler 8:6
Lillian Hellman 14:257
Doris Lessing 3:285
Flannery O'Connor 15:408
Marge Piercy 3:383
Sylvia Plath 17:355
Alexsandr I. Solzhenitsyn 10:480

**Hardwick, Mollie**
Roald Dahl 18:108
Penelope Fitzgerald 19:174

**Hardy, Barbara**
A. Alvarez 5:18

**Hardy, John Edward**
Katherine Anne Porter 15:428

**Hardy, Melody**
Arthur C. Clarke 4:105

**Hare, David**
Ngaio Marsh 7:209

**Hargrove, Nancy D.**
T. S. Eliot 6:165

**Harker, Jonathan**
Roman Polanski 16:462
Satyajit Ray 16:475

**Harker, Ronald**
Mary Renault 17:401

**Harmon, Elva**
Eilís Dillon 17:96
William Mayne 12:392

**Harmon, William**
Louis Zukofsky 18:560

**Haro, Robert P.**
Piri Thomas 17:498

**Harold, Brent**
William Faulkner 11:199
Vladimir Nabokov 6:356

**Harper, Howard M., Jr.**
John Barth 1:18
Saul Bellow 1:33
Jerzy Kosinski 1:172
Vladimir Nabokov 1:245
Philip Roth 1:293

**Harper, Michael S.**
Robert Hayden 9:269; 14:241

**Harper, Ralph**
Eric Ambler 4:18

**Harper, Robert D.**
Wright Morris 18:349

**Harper, Roy**
Jimmy Page and Robert Plant 12:481

**Harrington, Curtis**
Josef von Sternberg 20:371

**Harrington, Michael**
Theodore Roethke 3:433

**Harrington, Stephanie**
Norman Lear 12:327, 334

**Harris, Bertha**
Rita Mae Brown 18:72

**Harris, Bruce**
John Lennon and Paul
McCartney **12**:371
Jimmy Page and Robert Plant
**12**:475
Neil Young **17**:569

**Harris, Helen**
Penelope Gilliatt **13**:239
Ian McEwan **13**:371

**Harris, Jane Gary**
Boris Pasternak **10**:382

**Harris, Janet**
June Jordan **11**:312

**Harris, Karen**
Barbara Corcoran **17**:78

**Harris, Leo**
Ngaio Marsh **7**:209
Julian Symons **2**:426

**Harris, Lis**
Truman Capote **3**:100
Amos Oz **11**:429
Grace Paley **4**:392
Georges Simenon **18**:486

**Harris, Marie**
Marge Piercy **6**:403

**Harris, Mark**
E. L. Doctorow **18**:125
Mordecai Richler **18**:455

**Harris, Michael**
Thomas Berger **5**:60
Andre Dubus **13**:183
John Gardner **5**:133

**Harris, Robert R.**
William Wharton **18**:542

**Harris, Wilson**
George Lamming **4**:279
V. S. Naipaul **4**:374

**Harrison, Barbara Grizzuti**
Joan Didion **14**:153
Ruth Prawer Jhabvala **4**:257
Iris Murdoch **6**:343
Adrienne Rich **18**:448

**Harrison, Bernard**
Muriel Spark **18**:502

**Harrison, Jim**
Peter Matthiessen **11**:360
Larry McMurtry **2**:272

**Harrison, Joseph G.**
Mary Renault **17**:395

**Harrison, Keith**
Margot Benary-Isbert **12**:34
John Berryman **3**:69
Marge Piercy **14**:422

**Harrison, Tony**
Lorine Niedecker **10**:360

**Harron, Mary**
Joan Armatrading **17**:10

**Harsent, David**
Joe Orton **13**:437

**Harss, Luis**
Jorge Luis Borges **2**:69
Julio Cortázar **2**:101
Gabriel García Márquez **2**:147
Juan Carlos Onetti **7**:276
Juan Rulfo **8**:461
Mario Vargas Llosa **3**:493

**Hart, Henry**
Carlos Saura **20**:314
Billy Wilder **20**:457, 458, 459

**Hart, Jane**
Carson McCullers **12**:416

**Hart, Jeffrey**
E. L. Doctorow **6**:136
Robert Frost **15**:243
Auberon Waugh **7**:514

**Hart, John E.**
Jack Kerouac **3**:264

**Hart, Johnny**
Charles M. Schulz **12**:527

**Hart-Davis, Rupert**
Agatha Christie **12**:114

**Harte, Barbara**
Janet Frame **3**:164

**Harth, Erica**
Simone de Beauvoir **14**:68

**Hartley, George**
Philip Larkin **5**:230

**Hartley, Lodwick**
Katherine Anne Porter **13**:446

**Hartman, Charles**
Shirley Clarke **16**:218

**Hartman, Geoffrey**
Ross Macdonald **2**:257

**Hartman, Geoffrey H.**
A. R. Ammons **2**:13
André Malraux **9**:358

**Hartt, Julian N.**
Mary Renault **3**:426

**Hartung, Philip T.**
John Ford **16**:304
Laurence Olivier **20**:238
Gordon Parks **16**:458
Budd Schulberg **7**:402

**Harvey, David D.**
Herbert Read **4**:440

**Harvey, G. M.**
John Betjeman **10**:52

**Harvey, John**
V. S. Pritchett **15**:442

**Harvey, Lawrence E.**
Samuel Beckett **9**:80

**Harvey, Robert D.**
Howard Nemerov **2**:306

**Haskell, Molly**
Woody Allen **16**:6
Marguerite Duras **20**:100
Elaine May **16**:434, 436
François Truffaut **20**:397

**Hasley, Louis**
Peter De Vries **1**:72
Joseph Heller **5**:173
S. J. Perelman **3**:381
James Thurber **11**:532
E. B. White **10**:526

**Hass, Robert**
Robert Lowell **9**:336

**Hassan, Ihab**
John Barth **2**:36
Samuel Beckett **1**:23
Saul Bellow **1**:29
Thomas Berger **18**:53
André Breton **2**:81
Frederick Buechner **4**:79
William S. Burroughs **2**:91
Truman Capote **1**:55
J. P. Donleavy **1**:75
Ralph Ellison **1**:94
Jean Genet **2**:159
Allen Ginsberg **2**:164
Herbert Gold **4**:190
Ernest Hemingway **3**:237
Norman Mailer **1**:188, 189;
**4**:319
Bernard Malamud **1**:195, 196
Carson McCullers **1**:207, 208
Henry Miller **1**:222
Vladimir Nabokov **1**:239
Alain Robbe-Grillet **2**:375
J. D. Salinger **1**:296; **3**:446
Nathalie Sarraute **2**:385
Jean Stafford **7**:455
William Styron **1**:330; **11**:514
Kurt Vonnegut, Jr. **12**:610

**Hassett, John J.**
José Donoso **4**:129

**Hatch, James V.**
Alice Childress **12**:106

**Hatch, Robert**
Anne Burr **6**:104
Francis Ford Coppola **16**:234
Rainer Werner Fassbinder
**20**:115, 119
Federico Fellini **16**:300
Werner Herzog **16**:326
Alfred Hitchcock **16**:340
Fletcher Knebel **14**:307
George Lucas **16**:412
Nagisa Oshima **20**:257
Carlos Saura **20**:317
François Truffaut **20**:408
Orson Welles **20**:439
Lina Wertmüller **16**:597
Frederick Wiseman **20**:467

**Hatfield, H. C.**
George Tabori **19**:435

**Hatfield, Henry**
Günter Grass **2**:173

**Hauck, Richard Boyd**
Kurt Vonnegut, Jr. **5**:465

**Haugaard, Kay**
Betty Cavanna **12**:102

**Haugh, Robert**
John Updike **7**:489

**Haugh, Robert F.**
Nadine Gordimer **18**:184

**Hauptman, Ira**
John Buell **10**:81

**Hausermann, H. W.**
Herbert Read **4**:438, 439

**Havard, Robert G.**
Jorge Guillén **11**:262

**Haverstick, S. Alexander**
John Knowles **4**:271

**Havighurst, Walter**
Allan W. Eckert **17**:105
Edna Ferber **18**:152
Betty Smith **19**:423

**Haviland, Virginia**
E. M. Almedingen **12**:5
Ruth M. Arthur **12**:25
Margot Benary-Isbert **12**:30
Betty Cavanna **12**:100
Mavis Thorpe Clark **12**:130,
131
Barbara Corcoran **17**:70
Julia W. Cunningham **12**:165
Eilís Dillon **17**:93
Leon Garfield **12**:218
Christie Harris **12**:264
Jamake Highwater **12**:287
Larry Kettelkamp **12**:304
Joseph Krumgold **12**:317
Jean Lee Latham **12**:323
John Neufeld **17**:307
Andre Norton **12**:456, 466
Josephine Poole **17**:372
Mary Rodgers **12**:494
Zilpha Keatley Snyder **17**:472
Mary Stolz **12**:546, 550, 555
Colin Thiele **17**:494

**Hawk**
Richard O'Brien **17**:324

**Hawkes, John**
John Barth **10**:21
John Hawkes **15**:277
Flannery O'Connor **1**:254

**Hawkins, Robert F.**
Vittorio De Sica **20**:85

**Haworth, David**
Bernice Rubens **19**:402
Morris L. West **6**:563

**Hay, John**
Eleanor Clark **19**:104

**Hay, Samuel A.**
Ed Bullins **5**:83

**Hayakawa, S. I.**
E. E. Cummings **12**:144

**Haycraft, Howard**
Agatha Chistie **12**:118

**Hayden, Brad**
Richard Brautigan **12**:72

**Hayes, Brian P.**
Joyce Carol Oates **1**:252

**Hayes, E. Nelson**
J. R. Salamanca **4**:461

**Hayes, Harold**
Joy Adamson **17**:6

**Hayes, Noreen**
J.R.R. Tolkien **1**:336

**Hayes, Richard**
Sally Benson **17**:50
Paul Bowles **19**:57
Truman Capote **19**:80

**Hayman, David**
Samuel Beckett **11**:34
Louis-Ferdinand Céline **7**:42

**Hayman, Ronald**
Robert Duncan **7**:88
Robert Frost **4**:174
Allen Ginsberg **6**:198
Arthur Miller **6**:331
Charles Olson **5**:327
Anne Sexton **4**:482
Peter Shaffer **14**:485
David Storey **5**:414
Charles Tomlinson **4**:544
Tom Wolfe **15**:586

**Haynes, Elizabeth**
Andre Norton **12**:459

**Haynes, Muriel**
Shirley Ann Grau **4**:208
Lillian Hellman **4**:222
Thomas Keneally **5**:210

**Hays, Peter L.**
Henry Miller **9**:379

**Hayward, Max**
Andrei Voznesensky **1**:349

**Hazo, Samuel**
John Berryman **2**:57

**Hazzard, Shirley**
Jean Rhys **2**:371
Patrick White **3**:522

**Headings, Philip R.**
T. S. Eliot **1**:91

**Heald, Tim**
Brian Moore **19**:333

**Healey, James**
Catharine Savage Brosman **9**:135
Michael Casey **2**:100
Leonard Cohen **3**:110

**Heaney, Seamus**
David Jones **7**:187

**Hearron, Thomas**
Richard Brautigan **5**:68

**Heath, Jeffrey M.**
Evelyn Waugh **8**:543

**Heath, Stephen**
Nagisa Oshima **20**:251, 252

**Heath, Susan**
Martin Amis **9**:25
John Hersey **7**:154
Yasunari Kawabata **5**:208
John Knowles **4**:272
Yukio Mishima **6**:337
Anaïs Nin **4**:379
Richard Price **12**:489
V. S. Pritchett **5**:353
Kurt Vonnegut, Jr. **3**:503

**Heath, William**
Paul Blackburn **9**:100

**Hecht, Anthony**
W. H. Auden **2**:22
Ted Hughes **2**:198
James Merrill **2**:273
Marianne Moore **2**:291
Howard Nemerov **2**:306
L. E. Sissman **9**:489
Richard Wilbur **9**:570

**Heck, Francis S.**
Marguerite Duras **11**:166

**Heckard, Margaret**
William H. Gass **8**:244

**Heckman, Don**
John Lennon and Paul McCartney **12**:358

**Hector, Mary Louise**
Margot Benary-Isbert **12**:32, 33
Mary Stolz **12**:552

**Heffernan, Michael**
Albert Goldbarth **5**:143
Gibbons Ruark **3**:441

**Heffernan, Thomas Farel**
Robert Newton Peck **17**:339

**Heidenry, John**
Agatha Christie **6**:110
Robert M. Pirsig **4**:405

**Heifetz, Henry**
Bernardo Bertolucci **16**:84

**Heilbrun, Carolyn G.**
Christopher Isherwood **14**:279
C. P. Snow **19**:428

**Heilbut, Anthony**
Stanley Elkin **9**:191

**Heilman, Robert B.**
Edward Albee **5**:11
Max Frisch **3**:168
Harold Pinter **3**:386
Katherine Anne Porter **15**:426

**Heimberg, Martha**
Shirley Hazzard **18**:220
John Updike **15**:547
Tom Wolfe **15**:586

**Heims, Neil**
Paul Goodman **4**:198

**Heineman, Alan**
Frank Zappa **17**:586

**Heiney, Donald**
Jean Anouilh **8**:22
Natalia Ginzburg **11**:227
Alberto Moravia **2**:294
Elio Vittorini **9**:546, 548

**Heins, Ethel L.**
Ruth M. Arthur **12**:24
Barbara Corcoran **17**:70
Julia W. Cunningham **12**:166
Peter Dickinson **12**:177
Eilís Dillon **17**:97
Leon Garfield **12**:231
Lee Kingman **17**:246, 247
Joseph Krumgold **12**:318
Emily Cheney Neville **12**:451

Katherine Paterson **12**:487
Zilpha Keatley Snyder **17**:469, 471

**Heins, Paul**
Frank Bonham **12**:50
Robert Cormier **12**:136
Julia W. Cunningham **12**:164, 166
Peter Dickinson **12**:171
Alan Garner **17**:142
Madeleine L'Engle **12**:347
William Mayne **12**:398, 402
Nicholasa Mohr **12**:446
Zilpha Keatley Snyder **17**:471
Colin Thiele **17**:496

**Heiserman, Arthur**
J. D. Salinger **12**:496

**Heller, Amanda**
Max Apple **9**:32
John Cheever **8**:138
Don DeLillo **8**:171
Joan Didion **8**:175
William Gaddis **6**:194
Mary Gordon **13**:249
Mark Helprin **7**:152
Leonard Michaels **6**:325
Fay Weldon **11**:566
Larry Woiwode **6**:579

**Heller, Michael**
William Bronk **10**:75
Cid Corman **9**:170
George Oppen **7**:284; **13**:434
Charles Reznikoff **9**:449

**Hellmann, John**
Mick Jagger and Keith Richard **17**:226
Hunter S. Thompson **17**:511

**Helms, Alan**
John Ashbery **2**:18
Robert Bly **10**:61
Richard F. Hugo **18**:261
Galway Kinnell **13**:321
Philip Levine **4**:287
William Meredith **13**:373

**Helms, Randel**
J.R.R. Tolkien **12**:578

**Hemenway, Leone R.**
Melvin Berger **12**:39

**Hemenway, Robert**
Zora Neale Hurston **7**:170

**Hemmings, F.W.J.**
Mary Stewart **7**:467

**Henault, Marie**
Peter Viereck **4**:559

**Henderson, Tony**
Patricia Highsmith **4**:226

**Hendin, Josephine**
John Barth **3**:42
Donald Barthelme **6**:28
Richard Brautigan **1**:45
William S. Burroughs **5**:92
Janet Frame **2**:142
John Hawkes **15**:276
John Hersey **2**:188
Marjorie Kellogg **2**:224

Robet Kotlowitz **4**:275
Doris Lessing **3**:286
Michael McClure **6**:316
Joyce Carol Oates **6**:371; **9**:404
Flannery O'Connor **6**:375; **13**:421
Thomas Pynchon **6**:436
Hubert Selby, Jr. **1**:307; **4**:482
Paul Theroux **5**:427
John Updike **9**:536
Kurt Vonnegut, Jr. **4**:569

**Hendrick, George**
Mazo de la Roche **14**:148
Jack Kerouac **2**:227
Katherine Anne Porter **1**:273

**Hendricks, Flora**
Jessamyn West **17**:544

**Hendricks, Sharon**
Melvin Berger **12**:42

**Henighan, T. J.**
Richard Hughes **1**:149

**Henkel, Wayne J.**
John Knowles **4**:272

**Henkels, Robert M., Jr.**
Robert Pinget **13**:443, 444
Raymond Queneau **10**:430

**Henkin, Bill**
Richard O'Brien **17**:325

**Henniger, Gerd**
Francis Ponge **18**:416

**Henninger, Francis J.**
Albert Camus **4**:93

**Henry, Avril**
William Golding **10**:237

**Henry, Gerrit**
Russell Edson **13**:190
W. S. Merwin **5**:287

**Hentoff, Margaret**
Paul Zindel **6**:586

**Hentoff, Margot**
Joan Didion **8**:174

**Hentoff, Nat**
Bob Dylan **12**:180
Paul Goodman **4**:197
Alex Haley **12**:243
Jonathan Kozol **17**:250
Colin MacInnes **4**:314

**Henze, Shelly Temchin**
Rita Mae Brown **18**:74

**Hepburn, Neil**
Rayner Heppenstall **10**:273
Patricia Highsmith **14**:260
Mary Hocking **13**:285
Ursula Holden **18**:257
Thomas Keneally **5**:211; **10**:299
Tim O'Brien **7**:272
David Plante **7**:308
Frederic Raphael **14**:437
William Sansom **6**:484
William Trevor **7**:477
John Updike **7**:489
Elio Vittorini **14**:547
Fay Weldon **9**:559

**Hepner, Arthur**
John R. Tunis **12**:594

**Herbert, Cynthia**
Hilma Wolitzer **17**:562

**Herbert, Kevin**
Mary Renault **17**:394

**Herbold, Tony**
Dannie Abse **7**:2
Michael Hamburger **5**:159

**Herman, Gary**
Peter Townshend **17**:528

**Hermann, John**
J. D. Salinger **12**:510

**Hern, Nicholas**
Peter Handke **15**:265

**Hernández, Ana María**
Julio Cortázar **13**:162

**Hernlund, Patricia**
Richard Brautigan **5**:67

**Herr, Marian**
Otfried Preussler **17**:374

**Herr, Paul**
James Purdy **2**:347

**Herrera, Philip**
Daphne du Maurier **6**:147

**Herron, Ima Honaker**
William Inge **19**:228

**Hertz, Peter D.**
Hermann Hesse **17**:212

**Hertzel, Leo J.**
J. F. Powers **1**:281

**Heseltine, Harry**
Frank Dalby Davison **15**:170

**Hesse, Eva**
Ezra Pound **7**:329

**Hesseltine, William B.**
MacKinlay Kantor **7**:194

**Hewes, Henry**
Edward Albee **2**:2; **13**:3
Robert Bolt **14**:91
Ed Bullins **5**:84
Truman Capote **19**:81
Günter Grass **2**:173
Jim Jacobs and Warren Casey
**12**:293
Terrence McNally **7**:216
David Rabe **4**:425
Gerome Ragni and James Rado
**17**:379
Anthony Shaffer **19**:413
Peter Shaffer **5**:388
Tom Stoppard **4**:524
Melvin Van Peebles **2**:447
Gore Vidal **2**:450
Joseph A. Walker **19**:454
Tennessee Williams **2**:465

**Hewitt, Nicholas**
Louis-Ferdinand Céline **15**:125

**Heyen, William**
Robert Bly **5**:61
Louise Bogan **4**:68
John Cheever **3**:106
E. E. Cummings **3**:118
James Dickey **2**:117

Richmond Lattimore **3**:278
Denise Levertov **1**:177
Hugh MacDiarmid **2**:253
Arthur Miller **6**:336
Theodore Roethke **3**:433
Anne Sexton **6**:491
W. D. Snodgrass **6**:513
William Stafford **4**:520
Lewis Turco **11**:550
John Updike **3**:485
Richard Wilbur **3**:533
William Carlos Wiliams **2**:468

**Heymann, Hans G.**
Horst Bienek **7**:29

**Heywood, Christopher**
Peter Abrahams **4**:1

**Hibberd, Dominic**
William Mayne **12**:406

**Hichens, Gordon**
Shirley Clarke **16**:217

**Hickey, Dave**
B. H. Friedman **7**:108

**Hicks, Granville**
Louis Auchincloss **4**:28, 30;
**9**:52, 53; **18**:24
James Baldwin **2**:31
Peter S. Beagle **7**:25
Truman Capote **19**:80
James Gould Cozzens **1**:66
Herbert Gold **4**:189
Shirley Ann Grau **4**:207
Mark Harris **19**:200
Dan Jacobson **14**:290
Elia Kazan **6**:273
Ken Kesey **6**:277
Jonathan Kozol **17**:248
Meyer Levin **7**:204
Bernard Malamud **1**:200;
**11**:345
Harry Mathews **6**:314
Flannery O'Connor **1**:258
Katherine Anne Porter **7**:312
Reynolds Price **3**:404, 405
Ann Quin **6**:442
Mary Renault **17**:397
J. D. Salinger **12**:502
Upton Sinclair **15**:499
Kurt Vonnegut, Jr. **2**:451;
**12**:602
Auberon Waugh **7**:514
Eudora Welty **14**:561
Glenway Wescott **13**:590
Herman Wouk **1**:376

**Hieatt, Constance B.**
John Fowles **15**:231

**Hiesberger, Jean Marie**
Charles M. Schulz **12**:533

**Higgins, Bertram**
Fritz Lang **20**:200

**Higgins, James**
Jonathan Kozol **17**:255

**Higham, Charles**
Alfred Hitchcock **16**:342
Andrzej Wajda **16**:578
Orson Welles **20**:443

**Highet, Gilbert**
Henry Miller **1**:224
Ezra Pound **1**:276

**Highsmith, Patricia**
Georges Simenon **2**:398

**Highwater, Jamake Mamake**
Joan Armatrading **17**:7

**Hilburn, Robert**
Chuck Berry **17**:54

**Hildick, Wallace**
William Mayne **12**:390

**Hill, Donald L.**
Richard Wilbur **3**:530

**Hill, Douglas**
Joan Barfoot **18**:35

**Hill, Helen G.**
Norman Mailer **4**:321

**Hill, Susan**
Daphne du Maurier **6**:146
Bruce Springsteen **17**:486

**Hill, William B.**
Peter De Vries **10**:137

**Hill, William B., S.J.**
Robert Cormier **12**:133
Paul Gallico **2**:147
Bernard Malamud **5**:269
Anthony Powell **10**:417
Muriel Spark **2**:418

**Hilliard, Stephen S.**
Philip Larkin **9**:323

**Hilton, James**
Jan de Hartog **19**:130

**Hilton, Robert M.**
Henry Gregor Felsen **17**:124

**Hilty, Hans Rudolf**
Odysseus, Elytis **15**:218

**Himmelblau, Jack**
Miguel Ángel Asturias **8**:25

**Hinchcliffe, P. M.**
Ethel Davis Wilson **13**:610

**Hinchliffe, Arnold P.**
John Arden **13**:28
Edward Bond **6**:86
T. S. Eliot **13**:195
Harold Pinter **1**:267

**Hinden, Michael**
John Barth **3**:41

**Hindus, Milton**
Louis-Ferdinand Céline **1**:56;
**15**:122

**Hingley, Ronald**
Aleksandr I. Solzhenitsyn
**1**:319; **4**:515; **7**:445
Andrei Voznesensky **1**:349

**Hinton, David B.**
Leni Riefenstahl **16**:525

**Hinz, Evelyn J.**
Doris Lessing **6**:293
Anaïs Nin **1**:248; **4**:377

**Hipkiss, Robert A.**
Ernest Hemingway **3**:242

**Hippisley, Anthony**
Yuri Olesha **8**:433

**Hirsch, Edward**
Geoffrey Hill **8**:296
Isaac Bashevis Singer **11**:499
Charles Tomlinson **13**:546

**Hirsch, Foster**
Federico Fellini **16**:295
Ernest Hemingway **1**:144
Mary McCarthy **3**:328
Laurence Olivier **20**:242
Tennessee Williams **5**:505;
**19**:471

**Hirt, Andrew J.**
Rod McKuen **3**:332

**Hislop, Alan**
Richard Elman **19**:150
Jerzy Kosinski **2**:233
Wright Morris **3**:344
Frederic Prokosch **4**:422

**Hiss, Tony**
Patti Smith **12**:536

**Hitchcock, George**
Diane Wakoski **7**:503

**Hitchens, Gordon**
Vittorio De Sica **20**:91
Orson Welles **20**:437

**Hitrec, Joseph**
Ivo Andrić **8**:19

**Hjortsberg, William**
Angela Carter **5**:101
Rosalyn Drexler **2**:120

**Hoag, David G.**
Melvin Berger **12**:40
Roy A. Gallant **17**:132

**Hoagland, Edward**
Erskine Caldwell **8**:123
Peter Matthiessen **11**:359
William Saroyan **8**:468; **10**:454

**Hoban, Russell**
Leon Garfield **12**:232
William Mayne **12**:403

**Hobbs, Glenda**
Harriette Arnow **18**:14, 16

**Hobbs, John**
Galway Kinnell **13**:318

**Hoberman, J.**
Jean-Luc Godard **20**:155
Nagisa Oshima **20**:256
Pier Paolo Pasolini **20**:270
Satyajit Ray **16**:495
Martin Scorsese **20**:333

**Hobsbaum, Philip**
Sylvia Plath **17**:353

**Hobson, Harold**
Christopher Fry **14**:188
Simon Gray **14**:215

**Hobson, Laura Z.**
Norman Lear **12**:327

**Hochman, Baruch**
S. Y. Agnon **4**:12
Isaac Bashevis Singer **1**:312

**Hodgart, Matthew**
Kingsley Amis **5**:23
V. S. Pritchett **5**:353
J.R.R. Tolkien **12**:568

**Hodgart, Patricia**
Paul Bowles **2**:78

**Hodgson, Maria**
Dirk Bogarde **19**:42

**Hoeksema, Thomas**
Ishmael Reed **3**:424

**Hoellering, Franz**
Alfred Hitchcock **16**:338

**Hoerchner, Susan**
Denise Levertov **5**:247

**Hoffa, William Walter**
Ezra Pound **2**:343

**Hoffman, Barbara**
Nora Ephron **17**:112

**Hoffman, Daniel**
A. R. Ammons **2**:11
W. H. Auden **2**:25
Richard Eberhart **3**:133, 134
Ted Hughes **2**:198
Robert Lowell **2**:247
Carl Sandburg **15**:468
Robin Skelton **13**:507

**Hoffman, Eva**
Anne Tyler **18**:529

**Hoffman, Frederick J.**
Conrad Aiken **1**:2
James Baldwin **1**:15
Samuel Beckett **1**:21
Saul Bellow **1**:30
John Dos Passos **1**:79
Jaes T. Farrell **4**:157
William Faulkner **1**:100
John Hawkes **4**:212
Ernest Hemingway **1**:142
Aldous Huxley **11**:281
Flannery O'Connor **15**:410
Katherine Anne Porter **1**:272
Theodore Roethke **3**:434
Philip Roth **4**:451
John Steinbeck **1**:325
William Styron **15**:524
Robert Penn Warren **1**:353

**Hoffman, Michael J.**
Henry Miller **1**:224

**Hoffman, Nancy Y.**
Anaïs Nin **4**:380
Flannery O'Connor **3**:369

**Hoffman, Stanton**
John Rechy **14**:443

**Hofstadter, Marc**
Yves Bonnefoy **15**:73

**Hogan, Randolph**
Larry Kettelkamp **12**:305

**Hogan, Robert**
Paul Vincent Carroll **10**:97
Hugh Leonard **19**:280
Arthur Miller **1**:216
Elmer Rice **7**:361

**Hogan, William**
Jessamyn West **17**:548

**Hoggart, Richard**
W. H. Auden **1**:9
Graham Greene **6**:217

**Hokenson, Jan**
Louis-Ferdinand Céline **9**:152

**Holahan, Susan**
Frank O'Hara **5**:324

**Holbert, Cornelia**
Kenzaburō Ōe **10**:373

**Holberton, Paul**
Mary Renault **17**:401

**Holden, Anthony**
Rayner Heppenstall **10**:272
Daniel Hoffman **13**:286

**Holden, David**
Piers Paul Read **4**:445

**Holden, Jonathan**
John Ashbery **15**:30
Nancy Willard **7**:540

**Holden, Stephen**
Bob Dylan **12**:191
John Lennon and Paul
   McCartney **12**:372
Joni Mitchell **12**:438
Martin Mull **17**:298
Laura Nyro **17**:319
Buffy Sainte-Marie **17**:431
Paul Simon **17**:463, 464, 467
Patti Smith **12**:535
Elizabeth Swados **12**:561
Lily Tomlin **17**:522
Neil Young **17**:572

**Holder, Alan**
Robert Lowell **5**:256

**Holder, Stephen C.**
John Brunner **8**:107

**Holditch, W. Kenneth**
Tennessee Williams **19**:471

**Holland, Bette**
Eleanor Clark **5**:106

**Holland, Laurence B.**
Wright Morris **18**:353

**Holland, Norman N.**
Federico Fellini **16**:272
Stanley Kubrick **16**:377
Alain Resnais **16**:497

**Holland, Philip**
Leon Garfield **12**:236

**Holland, Robert**
Elizabeth Bishop **13**:95
Marilyn Hacker **9**:258
Richard F. Hugo **18**:263
Cynthia Macdonald **13**:356
David Slavitt **14**:491
James Welch **14**:559

**Hollander, John**
A. R. Ammons **2**:12
Howard Moss **7**:247
S. J. Perelman **15**:419

**Hollinghurst, Alan**
Donald Justice **19**:236

**Hollington, Michael**
Günter Grass **11**:250

**Hollingworth, Roy**
Jim Jacobs and Warren Casey
   **12**:295

**Hollis, Christopher**
Evelyn Waugh **19**:461

**Hollis, James R.**
Harold Pinter **11**:439

**Hollowell, John**
Truman Capote **19**:82

**Holman, C. Hugh**
John P. Marquand **10**:328
Robert Penn Warren **4**:576

**Holmes, Carol**
Joseph McElroy **5**:279

**Holmes, Charles M.**
Aldous Huxley **11**:283

**Holmes, Charles S.**
James Thurber **5**:439, 441

**Holmes, H. H.**
Roy A. Gallant **17**:126
Andre Norton **12**:456
John Wyndham **19**:474

**Holmes, John Clellon**
Jack Kerouac **2**:227

**Holmes, Kay**
Emma Lathen **2**:236

**Holroyd, Michael**
William Gerhardie **5**:139

**Holsaert, Eunice**
Madeleine L'Engle **12**:344

**Holt, John**
Jonathan Kozol **17**:249

**Holtze, Sally Holmes**
Sonia Levitin **17**:266

**Holzinger, Walter**
Pablo Neruda **9**:396

**Hood, Robert**
Emily Cheney Neville **12**:449

**Hood, Stuart**
Josef Škvorecký **15**:510
Aleksandr I. Solzhenitsyn **1**:319

**Hoops, Jonathan**
Ingmar Bergman **16**:58
Agnès Varda **16**:558

**Hope, Christopher**
Nadine Gordimer **5**:147; **18**:187
V. S. Naipaul **18**:361
Louis Simpson **9**:486
Derek Walcott **9**:556

**Hope, Francis**
Sylvia Plath **17**:345

**Hope, Mary**
Richard Brautigan **12**:74
Brigid Brophy **11**:68
Eilís Dillon **17**:100
Martha Gellhorn **14**:195
James Hanley **13**:261

Fay Weldon **11**:566

**Hope-Wallace, Philip**
Orson Welles **20**:433

**Hopkins, Crale D.**
Lawrence Ferlinghetti **10**:174

**Hopkins, J.G.E.**
Maureen Daly **17**:87

**Hopkins, Jerry**
Jim Morrison **17**:288

**Hopkinson, Shirley L.**
E. M. Almedingen **12**:3

**Horak, Jan-Christopher**
Werner Herzog **16**:330

**Horchler, Richard**
John Neufeld **17**:307

**Horia, Vintila**
Mircea Eliade **19**:144

**Horn, Carole**
Caroline Blackwood **6**:80

**Horn, Richard**
Henry Green **13**:253

**Hornak, Paul T.**
Colin Wilson **14**:585

**Horner, Patrick J.**
Randall Jarrell **13**:303

**Horovitz, Carolyn**
Esther Forbes **12**:210
Joseph Krumgold **12**:318
Madeleine L'Engle **12**:347

**Horowitz, Michael**
Jack Kerouac **5**:214

**Horowitz, Susan**
Ann Beattie **8**:54

**Horton, Andrew**
James Welch **14**:560

**Horton, Andrew S.**
Ken Kesey **6**:278
John Updike **7**:487

**Horvath, Violet M.**
André Malraux **4**:332

**Horwood, Harold**
E. J. Pratt **19**:377

**Hosking, Geoffrey**
Aleksandr I. Solzhenitsyn
   **18**:499
Vladimir Voinovich **10**:507
Alexander Zinoviev **19**:488

**Houston, Beverle**
Bernardo Bertolucci **16**:92
John Cassavetes **20**:50
Roman Polanski **16**:466

**Houston, Penelope**
Michelangelo Antonioni **20**:23,
   29
Charles Chaplin **16**:197
John Ford **16**:308
Alfred Hitchcock **16**:341, 342,
   344
Elia Kazan **16**:362
Buster Keaton **20**:189, 193

Richard Lester 20:223
Laurence Olivier 20:239
Satyajit Ray 16:480
Alain Resnais 16:498
Eric Rohmer 16:528
Orson Welles 20:434, 435
Billy Wilder 20:456

**Houston, Robert**
Mary Lee Settle 19:411

**Houston, Stan**
Isaac Bashevis Singer 15:509

**Howard, Ben**
Michael Benedikt 14:81
Ed Dorn 18:129
Loren Eiseley 7:92
Marilyn Hacker 5:155
Anne Sexton 6:494
John Wain 15:560

**Howard, Jane**
Maxine Kumin 5:222

**Howard, Lawrence A.**
Robert Newton Peck 17:340

**Howard, Leon**
Wright Morris 1:232

**Howard, Maureen**
Donald Barthelme 8:50
Samuel Beckett 11:43
Jorge Luis Borges 1:38
Paul Bowles 2:79
Isak Dinesen 10:150
Margaret Drabble 2:117;
  10:163, 165
Mary Gordon 13:249
Peter Handke 8:261
Lillian Hellman 8:281
P. D. James 18:275
Doris Lessing 6:301
Toni Morrison 10:356
Joyce Carol Oates 15:402
Philip Roth 1:292
Isaac Bashevis Singer 11:502
Paul Theroux 15:533
John Updike 9:537
Kurt Vonnegut, Jr. 1:347
Tennessee Williams 1:369

**Howard, Richard**
A. R. Ammons 2:12; 5:24
John Ashbery 2:17, 18; 13:30
W. H. Auden 2:26; 3:23
Imamu Amiri Baraka 10:18
Donald Barthelme 13:61
Marvin Bell 8:67
Robert Bly 5:61
Millen Brand 7:29
Gregory Corso 1:63
Robert Creeley 15:150
James Dickey 7:79
Irving Feldman 7:102
Paul Goodman 7:128
Daryl Hine 15:281
Daniel Hoffman 6:244
John Hollander 5:185
Uwe Johnson 5:201
Galway Kinnell 5:215
Kenneth Koch 5:219
Denise Levertov 5:245
Philip Levine 5:251
John Logan 5:252, 254

William Meredith 4:348; 13:372
James Merrill 2:274
W. S. Merwin 2:277; 5:284
Howard Moss 7:249
Frank O'Hara 5:323
Sylvia Plath 5:338
Adrienne Rich 3:428
Raphael Rudnik 7:384
Gary Snyder 5:393
William Stafford 7:460
Mark Strand 18:515
Allen Tate 4:538
Peter Taylor 18:523, 524
Mona Van Duyn 3:491
David Wagoner 5:473
Robert Penn Warren 6:557
Theodore Weiss 3:516
James Wright 5:518; 10:547
Vassily S. Yanovsky 2:485

**Howard, Thomas**
Frederick Buechner 2:82

**Howarth, David**
Gavin Ewart 13:209

**Howarth, R. G.**
Frank Dalby Davison 15:170

**Howe, Fanny**
Clarence Major 19:299

**Howe, Irving**
James Baldwin 3:31; 17:21
Jurek Becker 19:36
Saul Bellow 3:49, 60; 8:79
Louis-Ferdinand Céline 3:101
James Gould Cozzens 4:111
Ralph Ellison 3:141
William Faulkner 3:151
Paula Fox 2:139
Robert Frost 3:170
Daniel Fuchs 8:221
Henry Green 13:252
James Hanley 8:265
Ernest Hemingway 3:232
Arthur Koestler 15:312
György Konrád 4:273
Jerzy Kosinski 1:171
Norman Mailer 3:311
Bernard Malamud 8:376
Octavio Paz 3:377
Sylvia Plath 1:270; 3:391
Ezra Pound 2:344
V. S. Pritchett 13:467
Ishmael Reed 13:477
Philip Roth 2:380; 3:440
Delmore Schwartz 10:466
Varlam Shalamov 18:479
Ignazio Silone 4:492, 494
Isaac Bashevis Singer 1:311
Lionel Trilling 9:533
Edmund Wilson 3:538
Richard Wright 3:545; 9:585

**Howe, Parkman**
Jim Harrison 14:235

**Howe, Russell Warren**
Alex Haley 12:247

**Howell, Christopher**
Harry Martinson 14:356

**Howell, Elmo**
Flannery O'Connor 3:369

**Howes, Victor**
Robert Francis 15:236
Muriel Rukeyser 15:457
May Swenson 14:521

**Howlett, Ivan**
John Osborne 5:333

**Howley, Edith C.**
Robert Newton Peck 17:338

**Howley, Veronica**
Barbara Corcoran 17:76

**Hoyem, Andrew**
Larry Eigner 9:180

**Hoyenga, Betty**
Kay Boyle 1:42

**Hoyt, Charles Alva**
Bernard Malamud 1:196
Muriel Spark 2:414
Edward Lewis Wallant 5:477

**Hubbard, Henry W.**
Roy A. Gallant 17:128

**Hubbell, Jay B.**
John Hall Wheelock 14:570

**Hubert, Renée Riese**
André Breton 2:80
Alain Robbe-Grillet 4:449
Nathalie Sarraute 4:470

**Hubin, Allen J.**
Michael Crichton 6:119
Peter Dickinson 12:168, 169
Harry Kemelman 2:225
Julian Symons 14:523

**Huck, Charlotte S.**
Julia W. Cunningham 12:164
Joseph Krumgold 12:320

**Huddy, Mrs. D.**
Eilís Dillon 17:98

**Hudson, Christopher**
John Montague 13:390

**Hudson, Liam**
William H. Gass 15:256

**Hudson, Peggy**
Earl Hamner, Jr. 12:259
Norman Lear 12:330

**Hudson, Theodore R.**
Imamu Amiri Baraka 14:44

**Huebner, Theodore**
Anna Seghers 7:408

**Huff, Theodore**
Charles Chaplin 16:194

**Huggins, Nathan Irvin**
Arna Bontemps 18:65

**Hughes, Carl Milton**
Chester Himes 4:229
Willard Motley 18:355
Ann Petry 1:266
Richard Wright 1:377
Frank G. Yerby 1:381

**Hughes, Catharine**
Edward Albee 2:3; 9:6
Samuel Beckett 2:47
Daniel J. Berrigan 4:57
Ed Bullins 5:82
D. L. Coburn 10:108

Allen Ginsberg 2:164
Charles Gordone 4:199
Rolf Hochhuth 4:232
James Kirkwood 9:320
Carson McCullers 12:419
Mark Medoff 6:323
David Rabe 4:427
Robert Shaw 5:391
Sam Shepard 17:438
Neil Simon 11:496
Megan Terry 19:439
Michael Weller 10:526
Tennessee Williams 2:466;
  5:502
Lanford Wilson 14:590

**Hughes, Catharine R.**
Anthony Shaffer 19:413
Megan Terry 19:440
Douglas Turner Ward 19:457

**Hughes, Daniel**
John Berryman 3:70

**Hughes, Dorothy B.**
Donald E. Westlake 7:528

**Hughes, Douglas A.**
Elizabeth Bowen 15:77

**Hughes, James**
Louis Auchincloss 9:53

**Hughes, John W.**
Dannie Abse 7:1
Joy Adamson 17:4
John Ashbery 2:17
W. H. Auden 2:26
John Ciardi 10:106

**Hughes, Langston**
James Baldwin 17:21

**Hughes, Olga R.**
Boris Pasternak 7:297

**Hughes, R. E.**
Graham Greene 1:131

**Hughes, Riley**
Robert Cormier 12:133

**Hughes, Robert**
Elia Kazan 16:363

**Hughes, Ted**
Joy Adamson 17:3
Leon Garfield 12:219
Sylvia Plath 1:270
Clancy Sigal 7:423
Isaac Bashevis Singer 15:503

**Hughes-Hallett, Lucy**
Thomas Keneally 14:302
Bernard Slade 11:508

**Hughson, Lois**
John Dos Passos 4:136

**Hugo, Richard**
Theodore Roethke 8:458

**Hulbert, Ann**
Ann Beattie 13:65
Eleanor Clark 19:107
Joan Didion 14:152
Mavis Gallant 18:172
Patrick White 18:548

**Hulbert, Debra**
Diane Wakoski 4:572

CRITIC INDEX

**Hulcoop, John**
Phyllis Webb **18**:540

**Hull, Elizabeth Anne**
Robert Heinlein **14**:254

**Hume, Kathryn**
C. S. Lewis **6**:308

**Humes, Walter M.**
Robert Cormier **12**:137

**Humphrey, Robert**
William Faulkner **1**:98

**Humphreys, Hubert**
Jules Archer **12**:19

**Hungerford, Alice N.**
Henry Gregor Felsen **17**:122, 123

**Hunt, Albert**
John Arden **6**:5

**Hunt, David**
Lillian Hellman **14**:257

**Hunt, George W., S. J.**
John Updike **15**:543

**Hunt, Peter**
Peter Dickinson **12**:176
Leon Garfield **12**:233
William Mayne **12**:406

**Hunter, Evan**
George V. Higgins **18**:234

**Hunter, Jim**
Anne Tyler **11**:552

**Hunter, Kristin**
Ann Beattie **8**:55

**Hunter, Tim**
Stanley Kubrick **16**:382

**Hunter, William**
Charles Chaplin **16**:189
Fritz Lang **20**:202

**Huntington, John**
Arthur C. Clarke **18**:105

**Hurren, Kenneth**
Samuel Beckett **6**:43
Christopher Fry **2**:144
John Hopkins **4**:234
Peter Nichols **5**:306
Harold Pinter **6**:418
Peter Shaffer **5**:388
Neil Simon **6**:505
Tom Stoppard **4**:527
David Storey **5**:415
James Thurber **11**:534

**Hush, Michele**
Brian Wilson **12**:645

**Huss, Roy**
Michelangelo Antonioni **20**:37

**Hussain, Riaz**
Philip K. Dick **10**:138

**Hutchens, John**
Carl Theodor Dreyer **16**:256

**Hutchens, John K.**
Jessamyn West **17**:546
P. G. Wodehouse **2**:481

**Hutchings, W.**
Kingsley Amis **13**:12

**Hutchinson, Joanne**
Ivy Compton-Burnett **15**:139

**Hutchison, Alexander**
Luchino Visconti **16**:571

**Hutchison, David**
Robert Altman **16**:20

**Hutchison, Joanna**
Peter Dickinson **12**:172

**Huth, Angela**
John Irving **13**:297

**Hutman, Norma L.**
John Gardner **18**:173

**Hux, Samuel**
John Dos Passos **8**:182

**Huxley, Elspeth**
Joy Adamson **17**:5

**Huxley, Julian**
Joy Adamson **17**:4
Aldous Huxley **3**:253

**Hyde, Austin T., Jr.**
Alvin Silverstein and Virginia
B. Silverstein **17**:456

**Hyde, Lewis**
Vicente Aleixandre **9**:18

**Hyde, Virginia M.**
W. H. Auden **3**:23

**Hyman, Stanley Edgar**
W. H. Auden **2**:22
James Baldwin **2**:32
Djuna Barnes **3**:36
John Barth **2**:35
Truman Capote **3**:99
James Gould Cozzens **11**:124
E. E. Cummings **3**:117
T. S. Eliot **6**:159
William Faulkner **3**:152
Janet Frame **2**:141
Bruce Jay Friedman **3**:165
William Golding **2**:168
Ernest Hemingway **3**:234
Norman Mailer **2**:258
Bernard Malamud **2**:265
Wallace Markfield **8**:378
Henry Miller **2**:283
Marianne Moore **2**:291
Vladimir Nabokov **2**:299
Flannery O'Connor **1**:257
Seán O'Faoláin **7**:273
J. F. Powers **4**:419
James Purdy **2**:348
Thomas Pynchon **2**:353
John Crowe Ransom **2**:363
Alain Robbe-Grillet **2**:374
J. D. Salinger **3**:444
Isaac Bashevis Singer **3**:452
John Steinbeck **5**:405
Jun'ichiro Tanizaki **8**:510
John Updike **2**:440
Yvor Winters **4**:589
Herman Wouk **9**:579

**Hyman, Timothy**
Federico Fellini **16**:288

**Hynes, Joseph**
Graham Greene **9**:244
Evelyn Waugh **3**:511

**Hynes, Samuel**
W. H. Auden **1**:11; **3**:24
C. Day Lewis **10**:130, 131
T. S. Eliot **10**:172
E. M. Forster **3**:161
William Golding **1**:122
Graham Greene **6**:219
Louis MacNeice **4**:317; **10**:326
Jean Rhys **19**:393
Stephen Spender **5**:401; **10**:488
J.I.M. Stewart **7**:464
Vassily S. Yanovsky **18**:550

**Ianni, L. A.**
Lawrence Ferlinghetti **2**:133

**Idol, John**
Flannery O'Connor **3**:366

**Ignatow, David**
Denise Levertov **8**:347
George Oppen **7**:282
Diane Wakoski **7**:506

**Inge, M. Thomas**
Donald Davidson **13**:168

**Ingram, Phyllis**
Betty Cavanna **12**:102

**Innis, Doris**
Jesse Jackson **12**:289

**Irby, James E.**
Julio Cortázar **15**:146

**Irele, Abiola**
Chinua Achebe **7**:3

**Irving, John**
John Cheever **11**:121
Jayne Anne Phillips **15**:420

**Irwin, Colin**
Paul Simon **17**:466

**Irwin, John T.**
George P. Elliott **2**:131
William Faulkner **14**:168
William Heyen **13**:281
David Ignatow **7**:177
Louis MacNeice **1**:187
Thomas Merton **3**:336
William Jay Smith **6**:512
David Wagoner **3**:508
Theodore Weiss **3**:517

**Irwin, Michael**
A. S. Byatt **19**:76
Isak Dinesen **10**:149
V. S. Pritchett **13**:467
Paul Theroux **11**:528
John Updike **9**:539

**Isaac, Dan**
Rainer Werner Fassbinder
20:119
Isaac Bashevis Singer **3**:453
Elie Wiesel **5**:493

**Isaacs, Harold R.**
Lorraine Hansberry **17**:183

**Isaacs, Hermine Rich**
Orson Welles **20**:431

**Isbell, Harold**
John Logan **5**:253

**Isherwood, Christopher**
Katherine Anne Porter **13**:446

**Ishiguro, Hidé**
Yukio Mishima **9**:384

**Isler, Scott**
Jim Morrison **17**:294

**Isola, Carolanne**
Anne McCaffrey **17**:283

**Italia, Paul G.**
James Dickey **10**:139

**Itzin, Catherine**
Jack Gelber **6**:197

**Iverson, Lucille**
Judith Leet **11**:323

**Ives, John**
Sonia Levitin **17**:265
Josephine Poole **17**:372

**Iwamoto, Yoshio**
Yasunari Kawabata **18**:281
Yukio Mishima **9**:381

**Iwasaki, Akira**
Akira Kurosawa **16**:397

**Izard, Anne**
Babbis Friis-Baastad **12**:213
John R. Tunis **12**:597

**Jackel, David**
Matt Cohen **19**:112
James Reaney **13**:476
Robin Skelton **13**:508
Raymond Souster **14**:505

**Jackson, Al**
Andre Norton **12**:463

**Jackson, Angela**
Lucille Clifton **19**:109
Henry Dumas **6**:145

**Jackson, Blyden**
Gwendolyn Brooks **5**:75
Robert Hayden **5**:169
Langston Hughes **5**:191
Margaret Walker **6**:554

**Jackson, Esther Merle**
Tennessee Williams **7**:540

**Jackson, Joseph Henry**
Irving Stone **7**:468

**Jackson, Paul R.**
Henry Miller **14**:370, 374

**Jackson, Richard**
Robert Pack **13**:439
Robert Penn Warren **13**:578
Charles Wright **13**:614

**Jackson, Richard L.**
Ramón Gómez de la Serna
9:239

**Jackson, Robert Louis**
Aleksandr I. Solzhenitsyn **7**:446

**Jackson, Seán Wyse**
Dirk Bogarde **19**:43

**Jacob, Gilles**
Robert Bresson **16**:110
François Truffaut **20**:383

**Jacob, John**
Jonathan Williams **13**:601

**Jacobs, Diane**
Claude Chabrol **16**:178
Lina Wertmüller **16**:592

**Jacobs, Lewis**
Charles Chaplin **16**:191
Rouben Mamoulian **16**:422

**Jacobs, Nicolas**
David Jones **4**:261

**Jacobs, Rita D.**
Saul Bellow **10**:42

**Jacobs, Ronald M.**
Samuel R. Delany **8**:168

**Jacobs, William Jay**
John R. Tunis **12**:598

**Jacobsen, Josephine**
Arthur Gregor **9**:256
Daniel Hoffman **6**:242
David Ignatow **4**:249
Denise Levertov **3**:293
Howard Moss **14**:375
James Schevill **7**:401
Mona Van Duyn **7**:498

**Jacobson, Dan**
S. Y. Agnon **14**:1
James Baldwin **17**:22
D. J. Enright **4**:155
Andrei Sinyavsky **8**:490

**Jacobson, Irving**
Arthur Miller **6**:333; **10**:345

**Jacobus, John**
Charles M. Schulz **12**:531

**Jacobus, Lee A.**
Imamu Amiri Baraka **5**:46

**Jacoby, Tamar**
Maxine Hong Kingston **19**:250

**Jaehne, Karen**
Werner Herzog **16**:329

**Jaffe, Dan**
A. R. Ammons **2**:12
John Berryman **2**:57
Sylvia Plath **17**:346
Gary Snyder **2**:406
Hollis Summers **10**:493

**Jaffe, Harold**
Peter S. Beagle **7**:26
Kenneth Rexroth **2**:369

**Jaffee, Cyrisse**
Betty Cavanna **12**:102
Stan Lee **17**:261
Hilma Wolitzer **17**:563

**Jahiel, Edwin**
Marguerite Duras **6**:150
Antonis Samarakis **5**:381
Vassilis Vassilikos **4**:552

**Jahn, Janheing**
Camara Laye **4**:282

**Jahn, Mike**
Chuck Berry **17**:53
Mick Jagger and Keith Richard **17**:229
Jim Morrison **17**:291
Paul Simon **17**:464

**Jamal, Zahir**
Olivia Manning **19**:302
Alberto Moravia **11**:384
William Trevor **14**:535
John Wain **15**:561

**James, Clive**
W. H. Auden **3**:28
John Betjeman **6**:66
Lillian Hellman **8**:280
Philip Larkin **5**:225, 229
John le Carré **9**:327
Norman Mailer **3**:317
Aleksandr I. Solzhenitsyn **7**:436
Evelyn Waugh **19**:465
Yvor Winters **8**:553
Alexander Zinoviev **19**:490

**James, Kathryn C.**
Christie Harris **12**:263

**James, Louis**
Jean Rhys **14**:447

**James, Stuart**
James A. Michener **5**:290

**Jameson, Fredric**
Larry Niven **8**:426

**Janeway, Elizabeth**
Sylvia Ashton-Warner **19**:22
Pamela Hansford Johnson **7**:184
Françoise Sagan **17**:417, 420
Jessamyn West **7**:519

**Janeway, Michael**
Anne Tyler **7**:479
Tom Wicker **7**:533

**Janiera, Armando Martins**
Kōbō Abe **8**:1
Jun'ichirō Tanizaki **8**:510

**Jannone, Claudia**
Philip José Farmer **19**:166

**Janson, Michael**
Alta **19**:19

**Jarrell, Randall**
Conrad Aiken **3**:3
W. H. Auden **2**:21
John Berryman **13**:75
Elizabeth Bishop **1**:34; **4**:65
R. P. Blackmur **2**:61
Alex Comfort **7**:54
E. E. Cummings **3**:116
Robert Frost **1**:109; **3**:169
Robert Graves **1**:126; **2**:174
David Ignatow **7**:173
Robinson Jeffers **2**:213
Robert Lowell **1**:178; **2**:246
Josephine Miles **1**:215
Marianne Moore **1**:226; **2**:290; **19**:338
Ezra Pound **2**:340
John Crowe Ransom **2**:361
Theodore Roethke **3**:432
Muriel Rukeyser **6**:478
Carl Sandburg **4**:462

Karl Shapiro **4**:485
Christina Stead **2**:420
Richard Wilbur **3**:530
William Carlos Williams **1**:369; **2**:467

**Jaszi, Peter**
Stanley Kubrick **16**:382

**Jeanneret, F.**
Adolfo Bioy Casares **13**:87

**Jebb, Julian**
Bernardo Bertolucci **16**:91
Alison Lurie **5**:259
François Truffaut **20**:406

**Jefferson, Margo**
Beryl Bainbridge **5**:39
James Baldwin **17**:43
Rosalyn Drexler **6**:142
Nadine Gordimer **7**:133
Jack Heifner **11**:264
Elizabeth Jane Howard **7**:164
Gayl Jones **6**:265
V. S. Naipaul **7**:253
Juan Carlos Onetti **7**:280

**Jeffords, Ed**
Jim Morrison **17**:289

**Jelenski, K. A.**
Witold Gombrowicz **7**:123

**Jellinck, Frank**
Rex Stout **3**:472

**Jenkins, Cecil**
André Malraux **4**:336

**Jenkins, David**
A. R. Ammons **5**:28
Patrick Boyle **19**:68

**Jenkins, J. S.**
Eilís Dillon **17**:97

**Jenkins, Peter**
Simon Gray **14**:215

**Jennings, Elizabeth**
Robert Frost **3**:171

**Jervis, Steven A.**
Evelyn Waugh **1**:359

**Jochmans, Betty**
Agatha Christie **8**:142

**Joe, Radcliffe**
Gerome Ragni and James Rado **17**:388

**John, Roland**
Stanley J. Kunitz **6**:287

**Johnson, Abby Ann Arthur**
Penelope Gilliatt **10**:229

**Johnson, Albert**
Lindsay Anderson **20**:14
John Cassavetes **20**:44, 45
Shirley Clarke **16**:217

**Johnson, Alexandra**
Isaac Bashevis Singer **15**:507

**Johnson, Ann S.**
David Garnett **3**:188

**Johnson, Carolyn**
Hilma Wolitzer **17**:562

**Johnson, Colton**
Anthony Kerrigan **6**:276

**Johnson, Curtis**
Guy Davenport, Jr. **6**:125

**Johnson, Diane**
Beryl Bainbridge **14**:37
Don Barthelme **13**:59
Don DeLillo **8**:172
Joan Didion **8**:176
Nadine Gordimer **5**:147
Erica Jong **8**:315
Maxine Hong Kingston **12**:313
Doris Lessing **3**:286; **10**:316
Norman Mailer **14**:354
James Alan McPherson **19**:310
Toni Morrison **10**:355
Joyce Carol Oates **3**:361
Jean Rhys **6**:453
Muriel Spark **3**:465
Gore Vidal **10**:502
Paul West **7**:524

**Johnson, Douglas**
Louis-Ferdinand Céline **7**:45
Claude Mauriac **9**:367

**Johnson, Ernest A., Jr.**
Miguel Delibes **18**:109

**Johnson, Greg**
Joyce Carol Oates **15**:401
John Updike **9**:538

**Johnson, Halvard**
Gary Snyder **1**:318

**Johnson, Helen Armstead**
Joseph A. Walker **19**:454

**Johnson, Ira D.**
Glenway Wescott **13**:592

**Johnson, James William**
Katherine Anne Porter **7**:311

**Johnson, Kenneth**
Richard Wilbur **6**:570

**Johnson, Lee R.**
Eilís Dillon **17**:99

**Johnson, Manly**
David Ignatow **14**:277

**Johnson, Marigold**
Bernard Malamud **3**:324

**Johnson, Nora**
Darcy O'Brien **11**:405

**Johnson, Pamela Hansford**
Olivia Manning **19**:302
Françoise Sagan **17**:419

**Johnson, Richard**
W. H. Auden **2**:26

**Johnson, Richard A.**
Turner Cassity **6**:107
Anthony Hecht **8**:268
Delmore Schwartz **2**:387

**Johnson, Robert K.**
Francis Ford Coppola **16**:244

**Johnson, Rosemary**
John Ashbery **13**:35
May Swenson **14**:520

**CRITIC INDEX**

**Johnson, Sidney M.**
Hermann Hesse **17**:197

**Johnson, Thomas S.**
Bob Dylan **12**:194

**Johnson, Tom**
Archibald Macleish **14**:338

**Johnson, Wayne L.**
Ray Bradbury **15**:85

**Johnson, William**
Robert Altman **16**:20
Kon Ichikawa **20**:179, 184
Eric Rohmer **16**:532
Martin Scorsese **20**:326
Jerzy Skolimowski **20**:354
Orson Welles **20**:439, 442

**Johnston, Albert H.**
Nora Ephron **17**:110
Patti Smith **12**:541

**Johnston, Arnold**
William Golding **3**:198

**Johnston, Clarie**
Nagisa Oshima **20**:250

**Johnston, Dillon**
Austin Clarke **6**:111
Albert Goldbarth **5**:143
Seamus Heaney **7**:147

**Johnston, Kenneth G.**
William Faulkner **11**:199

**Johnstone, J. K.**
E. M. Forster **3**:160

**Joly, Jacques**
Jean Renoir **20**:294

**Jonas, George**
Margaret Atwood **3**:19
Gwendolyn MacEwan **13**:357
Raymond Souster **14**:504

**Jonas, Gerald**
Poul Anderson **15**:14
Isaac Asimov **9**:49; **19**:27
Arthur C. Clarke **13**:155
Samuel R. Delany **8**:168, 169;
  **14**:148
Harlan Ellison **13**:203
Frank Herbert **12**:278, 279
Ursula K. LeGuin **8**:343
Stanislaw Lem **15**:330
Barry N. Malzberg **7**:209
Vonda N. McIntyre **18**:326
Larry Niven **8**:426
Andre Norton **12**:470
Frederik Pohl **18**:412
Keith Roberts **14**:464
Joanna Russ **15**:461, 462
Kate Wilhelm **7**:538

**Jones, A. R.**
James Baldwin **17**:27
Sylvia Plath **9**:430

**Jones, Allan**
David Bowie **17**:63, 65
Mick Jagger and Keith Richard
  **17**:235
Laura Nyro **17**:315, 317, 319
Richard O'Brien **17**:324
Neil Young **17**:576, 577, 580

**Jones, Alun R.**
Philip Larkin **13**:335
Eudora Welty **1**:362; **2**:460

**Jones, Bedwyr Lewis**
Kate Roberts **15**:445

**Jones, Bernard**
John Cowper Powys **9**:441

**Jones, Brian**
Howard Nemerov **2**:306

**Jones, D. A. N.**
Dirk Bogarde **19**:41
Ed Bullins **1**:47
John Fowles **6**:184
Julius Horwitz **14**:266
Mervyn Jones **10**:295
Yoram Kaniuk **19**:239
Milan Kundera **19**:267
John Wain **11**:564
Fay Weldon **11**:565
Vassily S. Yanovsky **18**:551

**Jones, D. Allan**
John Barth **5**:52

**Jones, D. G.**
Earle Birney **6**:76; **11**:49
Philip Child **19**:102
Phyllis Gotlieb **18**:192
Anne Hébert **4**:219
Irving Layton **2**:237

**Jones, David R.**
Saul Bellow **13**:69

**Jones, Du Pre**
Sam Peckinpah **20**:272

**Jones, Edward T.**
John Updike **3**:487

**Jones, Ernest**
William Maxwell **19**:306
Aldo Palazzeschi **11**:431
Budd Schulberg **7**:403

**Jones, Granville H.**
Jack Kerouac **2**:226

**Jones, Howard Mumford**
Olivia Manning **19**:299

**Jones, John Bush**
Harold Pinter **9**:418

**Jones, John M.**
Kate Roberts **15**:445

**Jones, LeRoi**
Robert Creeley **15**:149

**Jones, Louisa E.**
Raymond Queneau **10**:431

**Jones, Margaret E. W.**
Ana María Matute **11**:362, 365

**Jones, Rhodri**
Leon Garfield **12**:227, 235

**Jones, Richard**
Graham Greene **14**:218
L. P. Hartley **2**:182
Anthony Powell **7**:346

**Jones, Robert F.**
James Jones **3**:262

**Jones, Roger**
Saul Bellow **10**:39

**Jones, Sumie**
Jun'ichiro Tanizaki **14**:527

**Jong, Erica**
Sara Davidson **9**:174
Doris Lessing **3**:287
Anne Sexton **4**:483; **8**:484
Eleanor Ross Taylor **5**:425

**Joost, Nicholas**
T. S. Eliot **9**:190
Ernest Hemingway **19**:217

**Jordan, Alice M.**
Henry Gregor Felsen **17**:120
Esther Forbes **12**:207
Lee Kingman **17**:243
Andre Norton **12**:455
John R. Tunis **12**:593

**Jordan, Clive**
Martin Amis **4**:19
Dan Jacobson **4**:253
G. Josipovici **6**:271
Milan Kundera **19**:266
Yukio Mishima **4**:356
Thomas Pynchon **6**:432
Gillian Tindall **7**:473
Ludvík Vaculík **7**:494
Kurt Vonnegut, Jr. **4**:567

**Jordan, Francis X.**
Gore Vidal **10**:51

**Jordan, June**
Maya Angelou **12**:13
Millen Brand **7**:30
Nikki Giovanni **2**:165
Zora Neale Hurston **7**:171
Gayl Jones **9**:306
Marge Piercy **6**:402
Richard Wright **14**:595

**Jose, Nicholas**
Noel Hilliard **15**:280

**Joseph, Gerhard**
John Barth **1**:17

**Joseph, Michael**
Margery Allingham **19**:12
John Wyndham **19**:475

**Josipovici, Gabriel**
Saul Bellow **3**:54
Vladimir Nabokov **3**:353

**Joye, Barbara**
Ishmael Reed **13**:476
John A. Williams **13**:598

**Judson, Jerome**
John Ciardi **10**:105

**Juhasz, Suzanne**
Alta **19**:18

**Jumper, Will C.**
Robert Lowell **1**:178

**Jürma, Mall**
Ivar Ivask **14**:287

**Justus, James H.**
John Berryman **4**:60
John Crowe Ransom **4**:431
Karl Shapiro **4**:487
Robert Penn Warren **4**:578, 582

**Kabakoff, Jacob**
Aharon Megged **9**:375

**Kabatchnik, Amnon**
William F. Buckley, Jr. **7**:36

**Kadish, Doris Y.**
Jean Genet **14**:203

**Kael, Pauline**
Woody Allen **16**:4
Robert Altman **16**:23, 28
Michelangelo Antonioni **20**:30,
  38
Ingmar Bergman **16**:70
Bernardo Bertolucci **16**:89
Mel Brooks **12**:76
Luis Buñuel **16**:137
John Cassavetes **20**:46, 48
Francis Ford Coppola **16**:233,
  240
Brian De Palma **20**:75, 77, 79,
  81, 83
Marguerite Duras **20**:102
Federico Fellini **16**:280, 282
Bob Fosse **20**:122
Jean-Luc Godard **20**:137, 138,
  154
Werner Herzog **16**:325
John Huston **20**:170, 173
Elia Kazan **16**:364, 373
Stanley Kubrick **16**:378, 393
Richard Lester **20**:226, 229
George Lucas **16**:409
Norman Mailer **3**:315
Elaine May **16**:432
Sam Peckinpah **20**:281
Satyajit Ray **16**:485, 488
Jean Renoir **20**:296
Erich Rohmer **16**:537
Ken Russell **16**:543
Martin Scorsese **20**:335
Steven Spielberg **20**:357, 360,
  366
François Truffaut **20**:383, 384,
  385, 392, 404
Agnès Varda **16**:559
Luchino Visconti **16**:570, 575
Peter Weir **20**:429
Lina Wertmüller **16**:591
Frederick Wiseman **20**:469

**Kagan, Norman**
Stanley Kubrick **16**:385

**Kagan, Shel**
Frank Zappa **17**:593

**Kahn, Lothar**
Arthur Koestler **3**:271
Jakov Lind **4**:293
André Schwarz-Bart **4**:479
Peter Weiss **3**:515
Elie Wiesel **3**:527

**Kaiser, Walter**
George Seferis **11**:493

**Kakish, William**
Peter Hundke **10**:260

**Kalem, T. E.**
Edward Albee **2**:2; **5**:12
Kingsley Amis **3**:8
Samuel Beckett **2**:47
Ed Bullins **5**:84
Anne Burr **6**:104

Friedrich Dürrenmatt 4:141
Jules Feiffer 8:216
Robert Graves 2:177
Bill Gunn 5:152
John Hopkins 4:234
Ira Levin 3:294
Terrence McNally 7:217
Jason Miller 2:284
Peter Nichols 5:307
Sean O'Casey 5:319
Murray Schisgal 6:490
Neil Simon 6:506
Isaac Bashevis Singer 6:511
Aleksandr I. Solzhenitsyn 1:321
Tom Stoppard 4:526
David Storey 2:424, 425; 4:530
Thornton Wilder 6:572
Tennessee Williams 7:545
Robert Wilson 7:550

**Kalstone, David**
A. R. Ammons 2:12
John Ashbery 2:17; 13:31
John Berryman 3:69
Elizabeth Bishop 13:95
A. D. Hope 3:250
Philip Levine 5:250
Robert Lowell 11:326
James Merrill 2:273, 275;
  13:378
Robert Pinsky 19:371
Adrienne Rich 11:475
James Schuyler 5:383

**Kameen, Paul**
Daniel J. Berrigan 4:57
Robert Lowell 3:303

**Kamin, Ira**
Charles Bukowski 9:137

**Kaminsky, Stuart M.**
Elaine May 16:435

**Kane, B. M.**
Christa Wolf 14:594

**Kane, Patricia**
Chester Himes 7:159

**Kanfer, Stefan**
Truman Capote 19:85
Jerzy Kosinski 6:285
Terrence McNally 7:218
Brian Moore 7:237
Paul Simon 17:458
Isaac Bashevis Singer 3:453;
  6:510
John Steinbeck 5:408
Dalton Trumbo 19:447

**Kanon, Joseph**
Robert Altman 16:29
Louis Auchincloss 4:29
Carlos Castaneda 12:88
Daphne du Maurier 6:147
Penelope Gilliatt 2:160
Jacqueline Susann 3:475
Hunter S. Thompson 17:505
John Updike 2:444

**Kantra, Robert A.**
Samuel Beckett 3:46

**Kaplan, Abraham**
John Ford 16:306

**Kaplan, Fred**
Francis Ford Coppola 16:239
Bob Fosse 20:125
Roman Polanski 16:470
François Truffaut 20:381

**Kaplan, George**
Alfred Hitchcock 16:349

**Kaplan, Johanna**
Dan Jacobson 4:254
Cynthia Ozick 7:287

**Kaplan, Samuel**
John Neufeld 17:311

**Kaplan, Stephen**
Stanley Kubrick 16:382

**Kaplan, Sydney Janet**
Doris Lessing 6:296

**Kapp, Isa**
Thomas Berger 18:57
John Cheever 11:120
Oriana Fallaci 11:189
Jascha Kessler 4:269
Grace Paley 4:394
Philip Roth 4:459

**Kappel, Lawrence**
Thomas Pynchon 18:439

**Karanikas, Alexander**
Donald Davidson 19:123

**Kardokas, Christine**
Zilpha Keatley Snyder 17:475

**Kareda, Urjo**
Alice Munro 19:345

**Karimi-Hakkak, Ahmad**
Ahmad Shamlu 10:470

**Karl, Frederick R.**
Samuel Beckett 1:20
Elizabeth Bowen 1:40
John Braine 1:43
Ivy Compton-Burnett 1:60
Lawrence Durrell 1:83
E. M. Forster 1:103
William Golding 1:119
Henry Green 2:178
Graham Greene 1:132
L. P. Hartley 2:181
Joseph Heller 1:140
Aldous Huxley 1:150
Christopher Isherwood 1:155
Pamela Hansford Johnson 1:160
Doris Lessing 1:173, 175
Iris Murdoch 1:233
P. H. Newby 2:310
Anthony Powell 1:277
William Sansom 2:383
C. P. Snow 1:314, 315, 316
Muriel Spark 2:414
Evelyn Waugh 1:357
Angus Wilson 2:471

**Karlen, Arno**
Edward Dahlberg 7:62

**Karlinsky, Simon**
Vladimir Nabokov 1:241; 2:305
John Rechy 7:357
Aleksandr I. Solzhenitsyn 2:408
Yevgeny Yevtushenko 1:382

**Karp, David**
James Baldwin 17:21
Meyer Levin 7:203

**Kasack, Wolfgang**
Aleksandr I. Solzhenitsyn 7:434

**Kasindorf, Martin**
Christopher Hampton 4:212
Norman Lear 12:335

**Kass, Judith M.**
Robert Altman 16:38, 40

**Katope, Christopher G.**
Jessamyn West 17:548

**Kattan, Naim**
Mordecai Richler 5:373

**Katz, Claire**
Flannery O'Connor 6:379, 380

**Katz, Donald R.**
Thomas McGuane 18:325

**Katz, Jonathan**
Albert Goldbarth 5:144

**Kauffmann, Stanley**
Edward Albee 2:3; 5:11, 14
Robert Altman 16:29, 44
Lindsay Anderson 20:16
Fernando Arrabal 2:15; 9:41
Alan Ayckbourn 5:37
Ingmar Bergman 16:57
John Berryman 3:69
Bernardo Bertolucci 16:90, 94,
  100
Mel Brooks 12:80
Ed Bullins 7:36
Luis Buñuel 16:135
Anthony Burgess 2:86
John Cassavetes 20:47, 49
Charles Chaplin 16:203, 206
Michael Cimino 16:213
D. L. Coburn 10:108
Francis Ford Coppola 16:234
Vittorio De Sica 20:95, 96
E. L. Doctorow 6:133
Carl Theodor Dreyer 16:262
Rainer Werner Fassbinder
  20:109, 113
Federico Fellini 16:279, 281,
  283
Bob Fosse 20:122, 124, 127
Athol Fugard 5:130; 9:230
Jean-Luc Godard 20:139, 140
John Guare 14:220
Peter Handke 5:164
Lorraine Hansberry 17:184
James Leo Herlihy 6:234
Werner Herzog 16:327, 334
John Huston 20:175
Buster Keaton 20:194
James Kirkwood 9:319
Jerzy Kosinski 1:171; 2:233
Stanley Kubrick 16:382, 383,
  390
Richard Lester 20:224, 228,
  231
George Lucas 16:407, 408, 411
Elaine May 16:435
Albert Maysles and David
  Maysles 16:439
Arthur Miller 2:280
Henry Miller 4:350

Henri de Montherlant 19:326
Peter Nichols 5:307
Hugh Nissenson 9:399
Edna O'Brien 3:365
John O'Hara 2:325
Nagisa Oshima 20:255
Yasujiro Ozu 16:448
Pier Paolo Pasolini 20:260
Miguel Piñero 4:402
Harold Pinter 3:386, 387;
  6:417; 15:421
Roman Polanski 16:464
Bernard Pomerance 13:446
David Rabe 4:425, 426; 8:450
Terence Rattigan 7:356
Satyajit Ray 16:486
Jean Renoir 20:300, 302
Eric Rohmer 16:531, 537
Ken Russell 16:543, 547
Françoise Sagan 17:424
James Salter 7:387
Carlos Saura 20:317
André Schwarz-Bart 2:388
Martin Scorsese 20:325, 335
Irwin Shaw 7:412
Sam Shepard 17:434, 446
Joan Micklin Silver 20:341
Steven Spielberg 20:360, 367
John Steinbeck 5:408
Tom Stoppard 4:527; 15:524
Elizabeth Swados 12:560
François Truffaut 20:386, 389
Melvin Van Peebles 20:410
Gore Vidal 2:450
Luchino Visconti 16:567, 570
Kurt Vonnegut, Jr. 2:452
Andrzej Wajda 16:584
Joseph A. Walker 19:455
Orson Welles 16:453
Lina Wertmüller 16:587, 591,
  598
Billy Wilder 20:465
Tennessee Williams 5:504;
  7:545
Lanford Wilson 14:593
Robert Wilson 9:576

**Kaufman, Donald L.**
Norman Mailer 2:263

**Kaufman, Marjorie**
Thomas Pynchon 18:432

**Kavanaugh, Patrick**
Frank O'Connor 14:400

**Kaveney, Roz**
Doris Lessing 15:332
Frederik Pohl 18:412

**Kay, George**
Eugenio Montale 18:340

**Kaye, Howard**
Yvor Winters 4:593

**Kaye, Lenny**
Mick Jagger and Keith Richard
  17:224, 239
Jim Morrison 17:292
Jimmy Page and Robert Plant
  12:475
Paul Simon 17:446
Peter Townshend 17:532
Stevie Wonder 12:656

**CRITIC INDEX**

**Kaysen, Xana**
Jerzy Kosinski **10**:309

**Kazin, Alfred**
Renata Adler **8**:7
James Baldwin **1**:13; **13**:52
Donald Barthelme **13**:54
Brendan Behan **1**:25
Saul Bellow **1**:28; **3**:61
Jane Bowles **3**:84
Paul Bowles **1**:41
William S. Burroughs **5**:91
Albert Camus **2**:97
Louis-Ferdinand Céline **9**:158
John Cheever **3**:108
James Gould Cozzens **4**:116
E. E. Cummings **8**:155
Joan Didion **3**:127
Lawrence Durrell **1**:83
Ralph Ellison **1**:93; **3**:146
Frederick Exley **6**:170
Gabriel García Márquez **2**:149
William H. Gass **8**:240
Paul Goodman **4**:195
Graham Greene **1**:131
Joseph Heller **11**:265
Ernest Hemingway **3**:242
Maureen Howard **14**:268
David Ignatow **4**:249
Jack Kerouac **1**:165
Alan Lelchuk **5**:241
Robert Lowell **1**:179
Norman Mailer **1**:187
Bernard Malamud **1**:194; **3**:326
Wallace Markfield **8**:379
John P. Marquand **2**:271
Mary McCarthy **3**:329
Carson McCullers **4**:345
Vladimir Nabokov **3**:356; **8**:418
V. S. Naipaul **4**:373; **9**:393
Joyce Carol Oates **2**:313; **3**:363
Flannery O'Connor **1**:259;
  **3**:370
Julia O'Faolain **19**:359
John O'Hara **1**:260; **3**:371
Walker Percy **2**:334
Ann Petry **1**:266
Thomas Pynchon **3**:419
Kenneth Rexroth **1**:284
Philip Roth **1**:292
J. D. Salinger **1**:295, 296;
  **3**:446, 458
Karl Shapiro **4**:484
Isaac Bashevis Singer **1**:310;
  **3**:457; **9**:487
C. P. Snow **1**:314
Aleksandr I. Solzhenitsyn
  **2**:410; **4**:515
Susan Sontag **13**:515
John Steinbeck **13**:530
Peter Taylor **4**:543
Paul Theroux **8**:514
John Updike **3**:488; **9**:538
Kurt Vonnegut, Jr. **3**:505
Robert Penn Warren **1**:352;
  **4**:582
Edmund Wilson **2**:475
Abraham B. Yehoshua **13**:618

**Keane, Patrick**
Galway Kinnell **5**:216

**Kearns, Edward**
Richard Wright **1**:379

**Kearns, Lionel**
Earle Birney **6**:77

**Keates, Jonathan**
Dirk Bogarde **19**:42
Jorge Luis Borges **6**:94
John Fowles **10**:187
Anthony Hecht **19**:208
John Hersey **7**:155
Ursula Holden **18**:257

**Keating, Peter**
Erica Jong **8**:315

**Kee, Robert**
Agatha Christie **12**:115

**Keefe, Joan**
Flann O'Brien **10**:362

**Keeley, Edmund**
Odysseus Elytis **15**:221
George Seferis **11**:492

**Keen, Sam**
Carlos Castaneda **12**:93

**Keenan, Hugh T.**
J.R.R. Tolkien **1**:336

**Keene, Donald**
Yukio Mishima **2**:287; **4**:354
Jun'ichirō Tanizaki **8**:509

**Keene, Frances**
Françoise Sagan **17**:417

**Keeney, Willard**
Eudora Welty **1**:361

**Keffer, Charles J.**
Robin Cook **14**:131

**Keils, R. M.**
Vladimir Nabokov **11**:391

**Keith, Philip**
J. E. Wideman **5**:489

**Keith, W. J.**
Louis Dudek **19**:138
Rudy Wiebe **14**:573

**Kelleher, Ed**
David Bowie **17**:58

**Kelleher, Victor**
Muriel Spark **13**:523

**Kellen, Konrad**
Lina Wertmüller **16**:596

**Keller, Jane Carter**
Flannery O'Connor **3**:365

**Keller, Marcia**
Agatha Christie **12**:117

**Kellman, Steven**
Max Frisch **14**:184

**Kellman, Steven G.**
Aharon Megged **9**:374
Iris Murdoch **15**:385
Robert Pinget **13**:442

**Kellogg, Gene**
Graham Greene **3**:208
François Mauriac **4**:339
Flannery O'Connor **3**:365
J. F. Powers **4**:419
Evelyn Waugh **3**:511

**Kelly, Ernece B.**
Maya Angelou **12**:9

**Kelly, Frank**
David Madden **15**:350

**Kelly, James**
Irwin Shaw **7**:411

**Kelman, Ken**
Carl Theodor Dreyer **16**:259
Leni Riefenstahl **16**:522

**Kemball-Cook, Jessica**
Andre Norton **12**:465

**Kemme, Tom**
Shusaku Endo **19**:161

**Kemp, Barbara**
Françoise Sagan **17**:427

**Kemp, John C.**
Robert Frost **15**:245

**Kemp, Peter**
Frederick Busch **18**:84
Roald Dahl **18**:108
Lawrence Durrell **13**:189
Buchi Emecheta **14**:160
Barbara Pym **19**:387
Fay Weldon **19**:468

**Kempton, Murray**
Gore Vidal **4**:554

**Kendle, Burton**
John Cheever **15**:128

**Kendle, Judith**
Morley Callaghan **14**:102

**Keneas, Alex**
Ira Levin **6**:305

**Kenefick, Madeleine**
Gayl Jones **6**:265
Cynthia Ozick **7**:290

**Kennard, Jean E.**
Anthony Burgess **10**:86
William Golding **10**:233
Joseph Heller **8**:275
James Purdy **10**:421
Kurt Vonnegut, Jr. **12**:611

**Kennaway, James**
Simon Raven **14**:439

**Kennebeck, Edwin**
Terry Southern **7**:453
Marguerite Yourcenar **19**:482

**Kennedy, Andrew K.**
John Arden **6**:10
Samuel Beckett **6**:46
T. S. Eliot **6**:166
John Osborne **11**:422
Harold Pinter **6**:419

**Kennedy, Dorothy Mintzlaff**
Raymond Federman **6**:181
Howard Nemerov **6**:363

**Kennedy, Eileen**
Penelope Gilliatt **10**:230

**Kennedy, Harlan**
Michelangelo Antonioni **20**:42
Federico Fellini **16**:300
Werner Herzog **16**:330

**Kennedy, John S.**
John Steinbeck **1**:323; **13**:532

**Kennedy, Ray**
Joseph Wambaugh **3**:509

**Kennedy, Susan**
Rita Mae Brown **18**:75
Susan Cheever **18**:101
J.I.M. Stewart **14**:512

**Kennedy, William**
Jorge Amado **13**:11
Thomas Bernhard **3**:64
Carlos Castaneda **12**:92
Robertson Davies **2**:113
Don DeLillo **10**:134
Gabriel García Márquez **8**:232
John Gardner **7**:111
Joseph Heller **5**:179
Elia Kazan **6**:273
Jerzy Kosinski **15**:316
William Kotzwinkle **5**:219
Peter Matthiessen **7**:211
Mordecai Richler **5**:378
Piri Thomas **17**:500

**Kennedy, X. J.**
A. R. Ammons **2**:13
Edward Dahlberg **7**:62
Eleanor Lerman **9**:328
James Merrill **2**:275
Robert Pack **13**:438
David Wagoner **15**:558

**Kennelly, Patricia**
Jim Morrison **17**:288, 289

**Kenner, Hugh**
W. H. Auden **2**:29
Samuel Beckett **11**:43
Robert Bly **10**:62
Guy Davenport, Jr. **14**:142
John Dos Passos **8**:182
Ernest Hemingway **8**:285
Irving Layton **15**:319
Marianne Moore **4**:360; **13**:397;
  **19**:340
Vladimir Nabokov **6**:357
George Oppen **7**:283, 285
Sylvia Plath **17**:366
Ezra Pound **2**:345; **4**:412; **7**:325
Mary Renault **11**:472
W. D. Snodgrass **18**:492
Richard G. Stern **4**:522
William Carlos Williams **2**:469;
  **13**:605
James Wright **10**:546
Louis Zukofsky **7**:561, 562

**Kenney, Edwin J., Jr.**
Elizabeth Bowen **11**:61
Iris Murdoch **6**:345

**Kent, Cerrulia**
Laura Z. Hobson **7**:164

**Kent, George E.**
James Baldwin **1**:15
Gwendolyn Brooks **1**:46; **15**:94
Nikki Giovanni **19**:192
Chester Himes **4**:229
Ishmael Reed **13**:477

**Kerans, James**
Jean Renoir **20**:289

**Kermode, Frank**
W. H. Auden 2:25; 14:33
Beryl Bainbridge 8:37
Samuel Beckett 2:46
T. S. Eliot 2:126, 128
E. M. Forster 10:178
William Golding 2:167, 169;
17:161, 167
Nadine Gordimer 10:240
Graham Greene 6:215
Peter Handke 5:165
Christopher Isherwood 11:296
Stanley Kunitz 14:312
Henry Miller 2:282
Iris Murdoch 2:298
I. A. Richards 14:453
Philip Roth 3:440
J. D. Salinger 12:497
Muriel Spark 2:414, 415, 418;
18:500
Marguerite Yourcenar 19:483

**Kern, Anita**
Buchi Emecheta 14:159

**Kern, Edith**
Samuel Beckett 2:47; 14:70

**Kern, Robert**
Richard Brautigan 12:71
Gary Snyder 9:500

**Kernan, Alvin B.**
Philip Roth 4:453
Evelyn Waugh 1:358

**Kernan, Margot S.**
Claude Chabrol 16:172

**Kerr, Baine**
N. Scott Momaday 19:318

**Kerr, Elizabeth M.**
William Faulkner 14:178

**Kerr, John Austin, Jr.**
José Rodrigues Miguéis
10:341

**Kerr, Walter**
Sally Benson 17:50
Alice Childress 12:106
Jan de Hartog 19:130
Charles Gordone 1:124
Lorraine Hansberry 17:184, 190
Jim Jacobs and Warren Casey
12:292
Harold Pinter 1:267
Gerome Ragni and James Rado
17:386, 387
Martin Sherman 19:415
Neil Simon 6:503
Megan Terry 19:440
Kurt Vonnegut, Jr. 12:605
Douglas Turner Ward 19:458
Michael Weller 10:526
Tennessee Williams 19:473

**Kerrane, Kevin**
Robert Coover 7:59

**Kerrigan, Anthony**
Jorge Luis Borges 4:74; 9:115;
13:109
Camilo José Cela 13:145

**Kerr-Jarrett, Peter**
Octavio Paz 6:397

**Kertzer, Jon**
Matt Cohen 19:114

**Kessler, Edward**
Daniel Hoffman 6:242
Charles Wright 6:580

**Kessler, Jascha**
A. R. Ammons 5:28
Imamu Amiri Baraka 2:34
Charles Bukowski 5:79
James Dickey 7:79
Loren Eiseley 7:91
Irving Feldman 7:101
Lawrence Ferlinghetti 10:174
Robert Graves 2:176
Sandra Hochman 8:297
Ted Hughes 2:201
June Jordan 5:203
Yoram Kaniuk 19:241
Anthony Kerrigan 4:269
György Konrád 10:304
Don L. Lee 2:238
Thomas Merton 3:335
Robert Pack 13:438
Kenneth Patchen 18:394
Octavio Paz 10:388
John Crowe Ransom 11:467
Muriel Rukeyser 15:460
Karl Shapiro 8:485; 15:478
Muriel Spark 8:492
May Swenson 14:521
John Wain 11:561, 563
Robert Penn Warren 4:578
Louis Zukofsky 7:560

**Kettle, Arnold**
John Berger 2:55
Ivy Compton-Burnett 3:111
E. M. Forster 3:159
Graham Greene 3:206
Aldous Huxley 3:252

**Keyes, Mary**
Phyllis Gotlieb 18:192

**Keyser, Barbara Y.**
Muriel Spark 8:494

**Keyser, Lester J.**
Federico Fellini 16:294

**Kherdian, David**
Philip Whalen 6:565

**Kibera, Leonard**
Alex La Guma 19:275

**Kibler, Louis**
Alberto Moravia 11:382; 18:344

**Kidder, Rushworth M.**
E. E. Cummings 8:161; 15:155,
158

**Kidel, Mark**
Bob Dylan 12:198

**Kieffer, Eduardo Gudiño**
Jorge Luis Borges 9:117

**Kieley, Benedict**
Brendan Behan 11:44
John Montague 13:391

**Kiely, Robert**
Richard Adams 18:2
Louis Auchincloss 18:26
Maeve Brennan 5:73
Frederick Busch 18:85
Hortense Calisher 2:96

Susan Cheever 18:101
Michael Frayn 7:106
Gabriel García Márquez 2:148
William H. Gass 2:155
Bernard Malamud 3:323
Joyce Carol Oates 19:356

**Kieran, Margaret Ford**
Walter Farley 17:117
Mary Stolz 12:547

**Kiernan, Robert F.**
John Barth 3:42

**Killam, G. D.**
Chinua Achebe 1:1

**Killinger, John**
Fernando Arrabal 9:37

**Kilroy, Thomas**
Samuel Beckett 3:45

**Kimball, Arthur G.**
Yasunari Kawabata 9:309
Jun'ichirō Tanizaki 14:526

**Kimmel, Eric A.**
Emily Cheney Neville 12:452

**Kimzey, Ardis**
Leslie Norris 14:388

**Kinder, Marsha**
Michelangelo Antonioni 20:31
Ingmar Bergman 16:75
Bernardo Bertolucci 16:92
Luis Buñuel 16:144
John Cassavetes 20:50, 52
Richard Lester 20:223
Roman Polanski 16:466
Carlos Saura 20:320
Peter Weir 20:429

**Kindilien, Glenn A.**
Saul Bellow 10:44

**King, Bruce**
Nadine Gordimer 10:240
Ruth Prawer Jhabvala 8:312
V. S. Naipaul 9:392

**King, Charles L.**
Ramón Sender 8:479

**King, Edmund L.**
Jorge Guillén 11:263

**King, Francis**
Louis Auchincloss 18:26
Shusaku Endo 14:161
Herbert Gold 14:208
Graham Greene 18:195
Aldous Huxley 5:193
Iris Murdoch 11:388
Barbara Pym 19:388
Muriel Spark 13:525
Fay Weldon 19:469

**King, Larry L.**
Kurt Vonnegut, Jr. 12:602

**King, Thomas M.**
Jean-Paul Sartre 7:394

**Kingsbury, Mary**
M. E. Kerr 12:298

**Kingston, Carolyn T.**
Margot Benary-Isbert 12:35
Emily Cheney Neville 12:453

**Kinkead, Gwen**
Penelope Gilliatt 2:161

**Kinnamon, Keneth**
James Baldwin 13:52

**Kinney, Arthur F.**
Dorothy Parker 15:415

**Kinney, Jeanne**
Carson McCullers 4:344;
12:427

**Kinsella, Anna M.**
Alberto Moravia 7:242

**Kinsella, Thomas**
Austin Clarke 6:111

**Kinsey, Helen E.**
Margot Benary-Isbert 12:33

**Kinzie, Mary**
Jorge Luis Borges 2:73
Ted Hughes 14:271

**Kirby, Emma**
Lenora Mattingly Weber 12:633

**Kirby, Martin**
Walker Percy 8:440

**Kirby-Smith, H. T., Jr.**
Elizabeth Bishop 4:66
Arthur Gregor 9:254

**Kirk, Elizabeth D.**
J.R.R. Tolkien 1:341

**Kirk, John M.**
Mario Vargas Llosa 15:549

**Kirk, Russell**
Ray Bradbury 10:68

**Kirkham, Michael**
Charles Tomlinson 4:543

**Kirsch, Robert**
Jascha Kessler 4:270

**Kish, Anne V.**
Jim Harrison 14:237

**Kisner, Sister Madeleine**
T. S. Eliot 15:216

**Kissel, Susan**
Robert Coover 15:145

**Kitchin, Laurence**
John Arden 13:24
Arnold Wesker 5:481

**Kitching, Jessie B.**
E. M. Almedingen 12:3

**Kitman, Marvin**
Garry Marshall 17:277

**Kitses, Jim**
Elia Kazan 16:369

**Kittrel, William**
Edna Ferber 18:151

**Kizer, Carolyn**
Ted Hughes 2:201

**Klaidman, Stephen**
Juan Goytisolo 5:150

**Klappert, Peter**
Daniel Mark Epstein 7:97
Kathleen Spivack 6:520

**Klarmann, Adolf D.**
Friedrich Dürrenmatt **11**:168

**Klein, A. M.**
A.J.M. Smith **15**:512

**Klein, Gillian Parker**
François Truffaut **20**:398

**Klein, Julia M.**
Marilyn French **18**:159
Erica Jong **18**:279

**Klein, Marcus**
Saul Bellow **1**:29
Ralph Ellison **1**:94

**Klein, Theodore**
Albert Camus **11**:95

**Kleinberg, Seymour**
Isaac Bashevis Singer **3**:458

**Klemtner, Susan Strehle**
John Fowles **15**:232
William Gaddis **10**:212

**Kliman, Bernice W.**
Philip Roth **3**:438

**Klin, George**
Yoram Kaniuk **19**:240

**Kline, T. Jefferson**
André Malraux **15**:353

**Kling, Vincent**
Rainer Werner Fassbinder
**20**:111

**Klinkowitz, Jerome**
Imamu Amiri Baraka **5**:45
Donald Barthelme **3**:43; **5**:52;
  **6**:29; **13**:60
Jonathan Baumbach **6**:32
Erica Jong **6**:269
Jerzy Kosinski **3**:272
Clarence Major **19**:294, 295
Flann O'Brien **7**:269
Gilbert Sorrentino **3**:462
Steven Spielberg **20**:365
Ronald Sukenick **3**:475; **4**:530
Hunter S. Thompson **17**:510
Kurt Vonnegut, Jr. **1**:348;
  **3**:500; **4**:563
Thomas Williams **14**:583

**Klockner Karen M.**
Madeleine L'Engle **12**:352

**Kloman, William**
Laura Nyro **17**:312
Gerome Ragni and James Rado
**17**:380

**Klotman, Phyllis R.**
Ronald L. Fair **18**:142
Langston Hughes **15**:292

**Klug, M. A.**
Saul Bellow **15**:50

**Kmetz, Gail Kessler**
Muriel Spark **8**:493

**Knapp, Bettina Liebowitz**
Jean Anouilh **8**:24
Jean Cocteau **8**:145
Georges Duhamel **8**:187
Marguerite Duras **6**:151
Jean Genet **1**:116

**Anna Kavan 13:317**
Robert Pinget **7**:305
Nathalie Sarraute **8**:469

**Knapp, James F.**
T. S. Eliot **6**:163
Ken Kesey **11**:317
Delmore Schwartz **2**:387

**Knapp, John V.**
John Hawkes **7**:145

**Knelman, Martin**
W. Somerset Maugham **11**:370
Harold Pinter **9**:421
Mordecai Richler **5**:377

**Knickerbocker, Brad**
Allan W. Eckert **17**:108

**Knieger, Bernard**
S. Y. Agnon **8**:8

**Knight, Arthur**
Woody Allen **16**:1
Gordon Parks **16**:457

**Knight, Damon**
Brian Aldiss **14**:10
Isaac Asimov **3**:16
Ray Bradbury **3**:84
Robert A. Heinlein **3**:224

**Knight, G. Wilson**
Sean O'Casey **11**:406
John Cowper Powys **7**:347

**Knight, Karl F.**
John Crowe Ransom **4**:428

**Knight, Susan**
Frederick Busch **7**:38
John Gardner **3**:186
József Lengyel **7**:202

**Knittel, Robert**
Riccardo Bacchelli **19**:31

**Knobler, Peter**
Bob Dylan **12**:189
Phil Ochs **17**:333
Bruce Springsteen **17**:476, 484

**Knoll, Robert E.**
Kay Boyle **19**:64
Wright Morris **18**:351, 355
Ezra Pound **3**:398

**Knoll, Robert F.**
Ken Russell **16**:542

**Knopp, Josephine**
Elie Wiesel **5**:491

**Knorr, Walter L.**
E. L. Doctorow **11**:142

**Knowles, A. Sidney, Jr.**
Marie-Claire Blais **2**:63
Frederic Prokosch **4**:421

**Knowles, Dorothy**
Eugène Ionesco **11**:290

**Knowles, George W.**
Marie-Claire Blais **13**:96

**Knowles, John**
Françoise Sagan **17**:423

**Knudsen, Erika**
Elisaveta Bagryana **10**:11

**Kobler, Turner S.**
Rebecca West **7**:526

**Koch, Christopher**
Richard Elman **19**:149

**Koch, Kenneth**
Frank O'Hara **2**:322

**Koch, Stephen**
Hermann Hesse **3**:243
Reynolds Price **6**:425
Nathalie Sarraute **8**:472
Christina Stead **5**:404
Gore Vidal **4**:554
Andy Warhol **20**:420

**Kodjak, Andrej**
Aleksandr I. Solzhenitsyn
**18**:495

**Koenig, Peter William**
William Gaddis **10**:209

**Koenig, Rhoda**
Roald Dahl **18**:108
Paul Theroux **15**:535

**Koester, Rudolf**
Hermann Hesse **17**:205

**Koethe, John**
John Ashbery **2**:17; **3**:15
Sandra Hochman **3**:250
Theodore Weiss **3**:517

**Kofsky, Frank**
Mick Jagger and Keith Richard
**17**:220

**Kogan, Rick**
Richard Price **12**:489

**Kohler, Dayton**
Carson McCullers **12**:413
Jesse Stuart **14**:513

**Kohn, Hans**
E. M. Almedingen **12**:2

**Kolb, Muriel**
Alvin Silverstein and Virginia
  B. Silverstein **17**:451

**Kolker, Robert Phillip**
Robert Altman **16**:30
Ken Russell **16**:545
Martin Scorsese **20**:336

**Kolodin, Irving**
Buffy Sainte-Marie **17**:430

**Kolodny, Annette**
Thomas Pynchon **3**:412

**Kolonosky, Walter F.**
Vladimir Voinovich **10**:508

**Koltz, Newton**
Wright Morris **3**:343
Patrick White **3**:524

**Koniczek, Ryszard**
Andrzej Wajda **16**:584

**Koning, Hans**
Jerzy Kosinski **15**:315
Aleksandr I. Solzhenitsyn
**18**:498

**Koningsberger, Hans**
John Huston **20**:171

**Korg, Jacob**
Bernard Malamud **2**:269

**Korges, James**
Erskine Caldwell **1**:51

**Korn, Eric**
Philip K. Dick **10**:138
Harlan Ellison **13**:203
Rayner Heppenstall **10**:272
Jack Kerouac **14**:307
Richard O'Brien **17**:323
Judith Rossner **9**:457
Claude Simon **9**:482
Gore Vidal **10**:502
Fay Weldon **11**:566
William Wharton **18**:543
Tom Wolfe **15**:587

**Kornfeld, Matilda**
Zilpha Keatley Snyder **17**:473

**Kornfeld, Melvin**
Jurek Becker **7**:27

**Kosek, Steven**
Kurt Vonnegut, Jr. **4**:569

**Kostach, Myrna**
Rudy Wiebe **6**:566

**Kostelanetz, Richard**
R. P. Blackmur **2**:61
Ralph Ellison **3**:141
Ezra Pound **2**:344

**Kostis, Nicholas**
Julien Green **11**:259

**Kostolefsky, Joseph**
Frank Capra **16**:156

**Kotin, Armine**
Jean Arp **5**:33

**Kotlowitz, Robert**
Gerome Ragni and James Rado
**17**:382
Howard Sackler **14**:479

**Kott, Jan**
Andrei Sinyavsky **8**:488

**Kountz, Peter**
Thomas Merton **11**:372
Frank Zappa **17**:589

**Kovács, Katherine Singer**
Jorge Luis Borges **19**:49

**Kovar, Helen M.**
Christie Harris **12**:261

**Kozak, Ellen M.**
Gene Roddenberry **17**:413

**Kozloff, Max**
Agnès Varda **16**:557

**Kozol, Jonathan**
Marjorie Kellogg **2**:223

**Kracauer, Siegfried**
Fritz Lang **20**:202
Leni Riefenstahl **16**:519
Josef von Sternberg **20**:370

**Kraemer, Chuck**
Frederick Wiseman **20**:475

**Kramer, Aaron**
Stanley J. Kunitz **6**:287

**Kramer, Hilton**
Donald Barthelme 8:50
E. L. Doctorow 6:137
Robert Lowell 8:357
Archibald MacLeish 8:362
Mary McCarthy 5:276
Marianne Moore 19:342
L. E. Sissman 9:492
Allen Tate 11:527; 14:530
Robert Penn Warren 8:538

**Kramer, Jane**
Maxine Hong Kingston 12:312
V. S. Naipaul 18:363

**Kramer, Nora**
Betty Cavanna 12:99

**Kramer, Peter G.**
William Goyen 5:149

**Krance, Charles**
Louis-Ferdinand Céline 9:153

**Kraus, Elisabeth**
John Hawkes 7:146

**Kreidl, John Francis**
Alain Resnais 16:514

**Kreitzman, Ruth**
Bernardo Bertolucci 16:86

**Krensky, Stephen**
Frank Bonham 12:55

**Krickel, Edward**
James Gould Cozzens 1:67
William Saroyan 1:302

**Kridl, Manfred**
Maria Dąbrowska 15:165

**Kriegel, Harriet**
Nora Ephron 17:112

**Kriegel, Leonard**
T. S. Eliot 6:166
James T. Farrell 11:193
Günter Grass 2:172
James Jones 10:293
Iris Murdoch 1:234
Ezra Pound 7:333
Harvey Swados 5:423
Edmund Wilson 2:475

**Krim**
James Jones 10:290

**Krim, Seymour**
Ernest Hemingway 19:219
Jack Kerouac 14:303

**Krispyn, Egbert**
Günter Eich 15:202

**Kroll, Ernest**
Peter Viereck 4:559

**Kroll, Jack**
Edward Albee 2:1
Jean Anouilh 3:12
W. H. Auden 3:27
Alan Ayckbourn 5:36
Saul Bellow 6:55
Mel Brooks 12:80
Ed Bullins 1:47
Anne Burr 6:103, 104
Rosalyn Drexler 2:119
Frederick Exley 6:171

Jules Feiffer 8:216
Jean Genet 2:158
John Guare 8:253
Bill Gunn 5:152
Ted Hughes 2:200
Stanley J. Kunitz 6:286
Ira Levin 6:306
David Mamet 9:360
Terrence McNally 7:218
Mark Medoff 6:322
Arthur Miller 2:280; 6:334
Jason Miller 2:284
Rochelle Owens 8:434
Miguel Piñero 4:402
Terence Rattigan 7:355
Jonathan Reynolds 6:451
Ronald Ribman 7:358
Murray Schisgal 6:490
Neil Simon 6:504
Tom Stoppard 5:414
David Storey 2:424, 426
Elizabeth Swados 12:559
Lily Tomlin 17:518
Kurt Vonnegut, Jr. 2:452
Lanford Wilson 7:548

**Kroll, Judith**
Sylvia Plath 17:359

**Kroll, Steven**
Irvin Faust 8:215
Thomas McGuane 3:330
Dan Wakefield 7:503
Irving Wallace 7:510

**Kronenberger, Louis**
Babette Deutsch 18:118
Edna Ferber 18:150
Henri de Montherlant 19:322

**Krouse, Agate Nesaule**
Agatha Christie 12:119
J.I.M. Stewart 14:512
Fay Weldon 19:466

**Krumgold, Joseph**
Joseph Krumgold 12:319

**Krupka, Mary Lee**
Margot Benary-Isbert 12:33, 34

**Krutch, Joseph Wood**
Brigid Brophy 11:67
Erskine Caldwell 8:122
Elmer Rice 7:360
Emlyn Williams 15:576, 577

**Krzyzanowski, Jerzy R.**
Tadeusz Konwicki 8:325

**Kuczkowski, Richard**
Anthony Burgess 13:125
Don DeLillo 13:179
Susan Sontag 10:485

**Kuehl, Linda**
Doris Lessing 3:282
Iris Murdoch 3:345; 15:381
Marge Piercy 3:384
Muriel Spark 2:417
Eudora Welty 5:479
Thomas Williams 14:582

**Kuehn, Robert E.**
Aldous Huxley 11:284

**Kuhn, Doris Young**
Julia W. Cunningham 12:164
Joseph Krumgold 12:320

**Kuhn, Ira**
Uwe Johnson 15:304

**Kuhn, Reinhard**
Henri Michaux 19:312, 313

**Kuncewicz, Maria**
Maria Dąbrowska 15:166

**Kunitz, Isadora**
Alvin Silverstein and Virginia
B. Silverstein 17:454

**Kunitz, Stanley**
John Berryman 8:86
Robert Creeley 8:152
Robert Frost 9:223
Jean Garrigue 8:240
H. D. 8:255
Robert Lowell 9:334
Marianne Moore 8:397; 10:346
John Crowe Ransom 11:467
Theodore Roethke 8:458

**Kunz, Don**
James Welch 14:559

**Kunzle, David**
Stan Lee 17:258

**Kupferberg, Herbert**
Yoram Kaniuk 19:238

**Kustow, Michael**
Jean-Luc Godard 20:130
Arnold Wesker 3:519

**Kuzma, Greg**
Barry Spacks 14:510

**Kyle, Carol A.**
John Barth 9:65

**LaBarre, Weston**
Carlos Castaneda 12:88

**Laber, Jeri**
Ilya Ehrenburg 18:132
Aleksandr I. Solzhenitsyn
2:411; 4:514

**Labrie, Ross**
Thomas Merton 11:373

**La Charité, Virginia**
René Char 9:167; 11:113;
14:128
Henri Michaux 19:314

**Lacy, Allen**
Gilbert Sorrentino 14:501

**La Farge, Oliver**
Robert Lewis Taylor 14:534

**Lafore, Laurence**
Shirley Hazzard 18:214
William Maxwell 19:307
James Alan McPherson 19:309
Irving Wallace 7:509
Jessamyn West 17:550

**LaFrance, Marston**
Evelyn Waugh 1:358

**Lahr, John**
Edward Bond 13:103
Arthur Kopit 1:171
Darcy O'Brien 11:405
Joe Orton 4:388; 13:435, 436
John Osborne 11:422

Harold Pinter 6:411
Richard Price 12:489
Mordecai Richler 18:454
Sam Shepard 4:491; 17:447

**Laidlaw, Marc**
Stephen King 12:311

**Laing, Alexander**
Esther Forbes 12:208

**Laitinen, Kai**
Paavo Haavikko 18:205
Hannu Salama 18:460

**Lake, Steve**
Phil Ochs 17:332
Patti Smith 12:536

**Lally, Michael**
Charles Bukowski 9:138
Larry Eigner 9:182
Kenneth Koch 8:323
Howard Moss 7:249
Anne Sexton 6:493

**Lambert, Gavin**
Lindsay Anderson 20:11
Robert Bresson 16:102
Luis Buñuel 16:129
Charles Chaplin 16:195
Agatha Christie 8:142
René Clair 20:63, 64
John Huston 20:160, 161, 162
Stanley Kubrick 16:376, 377
Fritz Lang 20:205
John O'Hara 6:384
Jean Renoir 20:288

**Lambert, J. W.**
Edward Albee 2:4
Alan Ayckbourn 5:35
Peter Barnes 5:50
Edward Bond 4:70; 6:84
A. E. Ellis 7:95
Michael Frayn 7:108
Athol Fugard 5:130
Trevor Griffiths 13:256
John Osborne 2:328
Sam Shepard 6:496
Bernard Slade 11:508
Tom Stoppard 3:470; 5:413
David Storey 2:425; 4:530
Arnold Wesker 3:518

**Lamie, Edward L.**
John Brunner 8:110

**Lamming, George**
Ishmael Reed 3:424
Derek Walcott 4:574

**Lamont, Rosette C.**
Fernando Arrabal 9:35
Eugène Ionesco 1:155; 6:252,
256; 9:287
Boris Pasternak 18:387

**Lamport, Felicia**
S. J. Perelman 5:337

**Landau, Jon**
Bob Dylan 12:190
Mick Jagger and Keith Richard
17:221, 224, 233
John Lennon and Paul
McCartney 12:377
Joni Mitchell 12:438
Jimmy Page and Robert Plant
12:475

CRITIC INDEX

Sam Peckinpah **20**:278
Martin Scorsese **20**:324
Paul Simon **17**:461
Bruce Springsteen **17**:478
Stevie Wonder **12**:655, 657

**Landess, Thomas**
Thomas Merton **1**:211

**Landess, Thomas H.**
John Berryman **2**:60
Caroline Gordon **6**:205; **13**:247
William Meredith **4**:349
Marion Montgomery **7**:234
William Jay Smith **6**:512
Allen Tate **4**:540
Mona Van Duyn **3**:491
Eudora Welty **1**:363
James Wright **3**:541

**Landy, Francis**
A. Alvarez **13**:9

**Lane, James B.**
Harold Robbins **5**:379
Piri Thomas **17**:499

**Lane, John Francis**
Michelangelo Antonioni **20**:38
Vittorio De Sica **20**:90

**Lane, Patrick**
Andrew Suknaski **19**:433

**Lanes, Selma G.**
Richard Adams **4**:9

**Lang, Doug**
Donald Justice **19**:233
Cynthia MacDonald **19**:291

**Lang, Olga**
Pa Chin **18**:371

**Langbaum, Robert**
Samuel Beckett **9**:85
E. M. Forster **1**:107
Galway Kinnell **13**:321

**Langer, Elinor**
Marge Piercy **18**:408

**Langer, Lawrence L.**
Paul Celan **19**:91

**Langford, Paul**
Leon Garfield **12**:233

**Langlois, Walter**
Pearl S. Buck **18**:77
André Malraux **9**:355

**Langton, Jane**
William Mayne **12**:402
Mary Rodgers **12**:493
Zilpha Keatley Snyder **17**:472, 473, 474
Rosemary Wells **12**:637

**Lant, Jeffrey**
Jonathan Kozol **17**:253

**Lardner, David**
Alfred Hitchcock **16**:339

**Lardner, John**
Irwin Shaw **7**:409

**Lardner, Susan**
Toni Cade Bambara **19**:34
György Konrád **10**:305
Thomas McGuane **18**:324
Joyce Carol Oates **9**:404
Wilfrid Sheed **2**:393

**Larkin, Joan**
Rita Mae Brown **18**:73
Hortense Calisher **4**:88
Audre Lorde **18**:307

**Larkin, Philip**
Barbara Pym **19**:386

**LaRocque, Geraldine E.**
Madeleine L'Engle **12**:348

**Larrabee, Eric**
Cornelius Ryan **7**:385

**Larrieu, Kay**
Larry Woiwode **10**:542

**Larsen, Anne**
Lisa Alther **7**:11
William Kotzwinkle **14**:310
Leonard Michaels **6**:325

**Larsen, Eric**
Charles Newman **8**:419

**Larsen, Ernest**
Jerome Charyn **18**:100
Gilbert Sorrentino **14**:499

**Larson, Charles**
Hyemeyohsts Storm **3**:470

**Larson, Charles R.**
Peter Abrahams **4**:2
Chinua Achebe **5**:1
Ayi Kwei Armah **5**:31
Leslie A. Fiedler **4**:163; **13**:211
Camara Laye **4**:284
Kamala Markandaya **8**:377
Peter Matthiessen **7**:210
V. S. Naipaul **7**:253; **18**:359
R. K. Narayan **7**:255
James Ngugi **7**:263
Simone Schwarz-Bart **7**:404
Raymond Sokolov **7**:430
Wole Soyinka **5**:396
Jean Toomer **13**:556
Amos Tutuola **5**:445
Ngugi Wa Thiong'o **13**:583, 584
James Welch **6**:561

**Lasagna, Louis, M.D.**
Michael Crichton **2**:108

**LaSalle, Peter**
J. F. Powers **8**:448

**Lask, I. M.**
S. Y. Agnon **4**:10

**Lask, Thomas**
Richard Brautigan **12**:60
Kenneth O. Hanson **13**:263
Bohumil Hrabal **13**:291
David Ignatow **7**:177
P. D. James **18**:273
Ross Macdonald **1**:185
Clarence Major **19**:294
John Sayles **14**:484
Georges Simenon **8**:486
Josef Škvorecký **15**:510

W. D. Snodgrass **2**:405
Piri Thomas **17**:502

**Laska, P. J.**
Imamu Amiri Baraka **10**:21

**Laski, Marghanita**
Patricia Highsmith **14**:260

**Lassell, Michael**
Tennessee Williams **11**:573

**Lasson, Robert**
Mario Puzo **2**:352

**Latham, Aaron**
Jack Kerouac **2**:228

**Lathen, Emma**
Agatha Christie **12**:123

**Latiak, Dorothy S.**
Jules Archer **12**:17

**Latimer, Jonathan P.**
Francis Ford Coppola **16**:236

**Latrell, Craig**
Harold Pinter **9**:421

**Latshaw, Jessica**
Christie Harris **12**:268

**Lattimore, Richmond**
John Berryman **2**:59
Jorge Luis Borges **2**:73
Edgar Bowers **9**:121
Joseph Brodsky **6**:97
Michael Casey **2**:100
Alan Dugan **6**:144
Daniel Hoffman **6**:243
John Hollander **14**:265
Galway Kinnell **13**:318
Vladimir Nabokov **8**:407
Adrienne Rich **7**:364
I. A. Richards **14**:453
L. E. Sissman **9**:491
Andrei Voznesensky **15**:557

**Lattin, Vernon E.**
N. Scott Momaday **19**:320

**Lauder, Rev. Robert E.**
Ingmar Bergman **16**:77
John Cassavetes **20**:52, 328

**Laughlin, Rosemary M.**
John Fowles **2**:138

**Laurence, Margaret**
Chinua Achebe **7**:3
Wole Soyinka **14**:507
Amos Tutuola **14**:538

**Laut, Stephen J., S.J.**
John Gardner **10**:220

**Lavender, Ralph**
Alan Garner **17**:150
Otfried Preussler **17**:375
Robert Westall **17**:557

**Lavers, Annette**
Sylvia Plath **9**:425

**Lavers, Norman**
John Hawkes **2**:186

**Lavine, Stephen David**
Philip Larkin **8**:336

**Law, Richard**
Robert Penn Warren **13**:570

**Lawall, Sarah N.**
Yves Bonnefoy **9**:113; **15**:72
Francis Ponge **18**:413

**Lawler, Daniel F., S.J.**
Eleanor Hibbert **7**:156

**Lawler, James R.**
René Char **11**:117

**Lawless, Ken**
J. P. Donleavy **10**:155

**Lawrence, D. H.**
Edward Dahlberg **7**:61
Ernest Hemingway **10**:263

**Lawrence, Isabelle**
Lee Kingman **17**:244

**Lawrence, Peter C.**
Jean Lee Latham **12**:324

**Laws, Frederick**
Sally Benson **17**:47

**Laws, Page R.**
Uwe Johnson **15**:307

**Lawson, Lewis A.**
William Faulkner **3**:153
Flannery O'Connor **1**:255
Eudora Welty **14**:567

**Lawton, A.**
Yevgeny Yevtushenko **13**:620

**Lazarus, H. P.**
Budd Schulberg **7**:401

**Lazere, Donald**
Albert Camus **14**:107

**Lea, Sydney**
Philip Levine **14**:319

**Leach, Edmund**
Carlos Castaneda **12**:85

**Leaf, David**
Brian Wilson **12**:652

**Leahy, Jack**
David Wagoner **5**:474

**Leak, Thomas**
Michael Shaara **15**:474

**Leal, Luis**
Juan Rulfo **8**:462

**Leaming, Barbara**
Rainer Werner Fassbinder **20**:114

**Lear, Norman**
Norman Lear **12**:328

**Learmont, Lavinia Marina**
Hermann Hesse **2**:191

**Leary, Lewis**
Lionel Trilling **9**:534

**Leary, Timothy**
Bob Dylan **12**:193

**Leavell, Frank H.**
Jesse Stuart **14**:514

**Leavis, F. R.**
John Dos Passos **11**:152
C. P. Snow **13**:512

**Leavitt, Harvey**
Richard Brautigan **5**:67

**Lebel, J.-P.**
Buster Keaton **20**:190

**Lebowitz, Alan**
Ernest Hemingway **1**:144

**Lebowitz, Naomi**
Stanley Elkin **4**:152
E. M. Forster **4**:166
J. F. Powers **1**:279

**Lecker, Robert**
Hugh Hood **15**:286

**LeClair, Thomas**
John Barth **7**:23
Saul Bellow **6**:53
Anthony Burgess **1**:48
Carlos Castaneda **12**:95
Jerome Charyn **5**:103; **8**:135
Don DeLillo **10**:135; **13**:179
J. P. Donleavy **1**:76; **4**:124;
**6**:141; **10**:154
Stanley Elkin **6**:170; **9**:190
John Gardner **8**:236; **18**:179,
183
John Hawkes **7**:141, 144
Joseph Heller **8**:278
Flannery O'Connor **13**:420
Walker Percy **6**:400; **14**:412
David Plante **7**:307
Thomas Pynchon **6**:435
Tom Robbins **9**:454
Michael Shaara **15**:474
Ronald Sukenick **6**:523
Harvey Swados **5**:420

**LeClercq, Diane**
Patricia Highsmith **2**:194
Susan B. Hill **4**:226
William Sansom **6**:483

**Ledbetter, J. T.**
Galway Kinnell **13**:320
Mark Van Doren **6**:542

**Lee, A. Robert**
Chester Himes **18**:249

**Lee, Alvin**
James Reaney **13**:472

**Lee, Brian**
James Baldwin **17**:35

**Lee, Charles**
Earl Hamner, Jr. **12**:257
Mary Renault **17**:391

**Lee, Dennis**
Paulette Giles **13**:304
A. W. Purdy **6**:428

**Lee, Don L.**
Nikki Giovanni **4**:189
Conrad Kent Rivers **1**:285

**Lee, Dorothy**
Joseph A. Walker **19**:455

**Lee, Dorothy H.**
Harriette Arnow **18**:13

**Lee, Hermione**
J. G. Ballard **14**:40
Jurek Becker **19**:36
Elizabeth Bowen **11**:65
Penelope Fitzgerald **19**:173
Nadine Gordimer **18**:189
Thomas Keneally **14**:302
Flannery O'Connor **15**:413
Julia O'Faolain **19**:360
Andrew Sinclair **14**:490
J.I.M. Stewart **14**:513

**Lee, James W.**
John Braine **1**:43

**Lee, L. L.**
Thomas Berger **18**:54

**Lee, Lance**
Thom Gunn **18**:201

**Lee, Robert A.**
Alistair MacLean **13**:359

**Lee, Stan**
Stan Lee **17**:261

**Leech, Margaret**
Esther Forbes **12**:206

**Leeds, Barry H.**
Ken Kesey **6**:278
Norman Mailer **1**:191
D. Keith Mano **2**:270

**Leeming, Glenda**
John Arden **6**:9

**Leer, Norman**
Bernard Malamud **8**:374

**Lees, Gene**
John Lennon and Paul
McCartney **12**:358
Gerome Ragni and James Rado
**17**:383

**Leet, Herbert L.**
Frank B. Gilbreth and
Ernestine Gilbreth Carey
**17**:155

**Leet, Judith**
May Sarton **14**:482

**Leffland, Ella**
Lois Gould **10**:242

**Legates, Charlotte**
Aldous Huxley **11**:287

**LeGuin, Ursula K.**
John Gardner **18**:181
Doris Lessing **15**:334

**Lehan, Richard**
Walker Percy **2**:332
Wilfrid Sheed **2**:392
Susan Sontag **1**:322

**Lehman, David**
W. H. Auden **11**:20
David Ignatow **7**:182
Charles Reznikoff **9**:449
Ira Sadoff **9**:466

**Lehmann, John**
W. Somerset Maugham **11**:370
Edith Sitwell **2**:403

**Lehmann, Rosamond**
Mary Renault **17**:390

**Lehmann-Haupt, Christopher**
Louis Auchincloss **18**:25
Thomas Berger **18**:56
Truman Capote **19**:85
Jerome Charyn **18**:99
Susan Cheever **18**:100
Michael Crichton **2**:109
Robert Crumb **17**:82
Rosalyn Drexler **2**:119
Stanley Elkin **14**:157
Marilyn French **18**:159
John Gardner **18**:180
Pete Hamill **10**:251
George V. Higgins **18**:234
P. D. James **18**:276
Ella Leffland **19**:277, 278
Hugh Leonard **19**:282
Clarence Major **19**:291
Charles Newman **2**:311
Robert Newton Peck **17**:336
Richard Price **12**:488
Mordecai Richler **18**:452
Peter Rushforth **19**:406
Hunter S. Thompson **17**:504
Al Young **19**:479

**Leib, Mark**
Sylvia Plath **3**:389

**Leibowitz, Herbert**
Elizabeth Bishop **13**:91
Robert Bly **2**:66
Edward Dahlberg **14**:136
Jean Garrigue **2**:153
Philip Levine **14**:320
Robert Lowell **4**:297
Josephine Miles **2**:278
Kenneth Rexroth **6**:451
Theodore Roethke **3**:434
Delmore Schwartz **2**:388
Judith Johnson Sherwin **15**:479
Isaac Bashevis Singer **3**:453
W. D. Snodgrass **2**:405
Gary Snyder **5**:395
Mona Van Duyn **3**:492
Jonathan Williams **13**:600
William Carlos Williams **9**:574
Edmund Wilson **3**:540

**Leibowitz, Herbert A.**
Frank O'Hara **2**:321

**Leigh, David J., S.J.**
Ernest Hemingway **6**:233

**Leiter, Robert**
Janet Frame **6**:190
Nadine Gordimer **7**:132
Cormac McCarthy **4**:342
Jean Rhys **6**:453
Clancy Sigal **7**:424
Larry Woiwode **10**:541

**Leiter, Robert A.**
William Maxwell **19**:308

**Leith, Linda**
Hubert Aquin **15**:17
Matt Cohen **19**:112

**Leithauser, Brad**
Marianne Moore **19**:340
Jean Stafford **19**:431
Evelyn Waugh **19**:465

**Lejeune, Anthony**
Agatha Christie **12**:117
Paul Gallico **2**:147
Anthony Powell **7**:345
P. G. Wodehouse **2**:480

**Lejeune, C. A.**
René Clair **20**:59
Jean Cocteau **16**:224
Elia Kazan **16**:360

**Lekachman, Robert**
William F. Buckley, Jr. **18**:83
Richard Elman **19**:151
Ken Follett **18**:156

**Lelchuk, Alan**
Isaac Bashevis Singer **11**:500

**Lellis, George**
Rainer Werner Fassbinder
**20**:107
Martin Scorsese **20**:324

**Lelyveld, Joseph**
Buchi Emecheta **14**:160

**LeMaster, J. R.**
Jesse Stuart **8**:507; **11**:509

**Lemay, Harding**
J. R. Salamanca **4**:461

**Lemmons, Philip**
Brian Moore **8**:396
William Trevor **7**:478

**Lemon, Lee T.**
Kenneth Burke **2**:87, 89
Louis-Ferdinand Céline **3**:105
Guy Davenport, Jr. **6**:124
Judith Guest **8**:254
Jack Kerouac **5**:213
Jerzy Kosinski **10**:306
Joyce Carol Oates **6**:369
John Rechy **1**:283
Andrew Sinclair **14**:488
C. P. Snow **4**:503
Patrick White **5**:485
Yvor Winters **4**:591

**Lenardon, Robert J.**
Mary Renault **17**:401

**L'Engle, Madeleine**
Mary Stolz **12**:552

**Lennox, John Watt**
Anne Hébert **13**:266

**Lensing, George**
James Dickey **4**:120
Robert Lowell **1**:183
Louis Simpson **4**:498
Louis Zukofsky **1**:385

**Lenski, Branko**
Miroslav Krleža **8**:329

**Lent, Henry B.**
John R. Tunis **12**:596

**Lentfoehr, Sister Therese**
David Kherdian **6**:281

**Leonard, John**
Lisa Alther **7**:12
Louis Auchincloss **18**:25
Saul Bellow **6**:56
John Berger **19**:41
E. M. Broner **19**:71

CRITIC INDEX

T. Alan Broughton **19**:73
Jerome Charyn **18**:98
John Cheever **3**:107; **8**:139
Anita Desai **19**:135
Joan Didion **1**:74; **14**:151
Nora Ephron **17**:113
Max Frisch **18**:162
Shirley Hazzard **18**:218
Maxine Hong Kingston **19**:249
Doris Lessing **3**:285
Alison Lurie **4**:306
Larry McMurtry **2**:271
V. S. Naipaul **18**:361
Joyce Carol Oates **19**:355
Thomas Pynchon **3**:414
Wilfrid Sheed **2**:393
Gilbert Sorrentino **14**:499
Anne Tyler **18**:529
Joseph Wambaugh **18**:532
Alexander Zinoviev **19**:486

**Leonard, William J.**
Hugh Leonard **19**:283

**LePellec, Yves**
John Updike **15**:540

**Le Pelley, Guernsey**
William F. Buckley, Jr. **18**:82

**Lerman, Sue**
Agnès Varda **16**:559

**Lernoux, Penny**
Mario Vargas Llosa **9**:544

**LeSage, Laurent**
Robert Pinget **7**:305
Françoise Sagan **17**:423

**Leslie, Omolara**
Chinua Achebe **3**:2

**Lesser, Rika**
Paul Celan **19**:94

**Lessing, Doris**
Kurt Vonnegut, Jr. **2**:456

**Lester, Julius**
Henry Dumas **6**:146
Lorraine Hansberry **17**:192

**Lester, Margot**
Dan Jacobson **4**:256
Hugh Nissenson **9**:400

**Le Stourgeon, Diana E.**
Rosamond Lehmann **5**:235

**Letson, Russell**
Philip José Farmer **19**:167

**Levensohn, Alan**
Christina Stead **2**:422

**Levenson, J. C.**
Saul Bellow **1**:29

**Levenson, Michael**
Herbert Gold **7**:121
Tom McHale **5**:282
John Updike **5**:460

**Leventhal, A. J.**
Samuel Beckett **11**:32

**Lever, Karen M.**
John Fowles **15**:234

**Leverence, John**
Irving Wallace **13**:567

**Levertov, Denise**
Imamu Amiri Baraka **14**:42
Russell Edson **13**:190
H. D. **14**:223
David Ignatow **7**:173
John Wieners **7**:535

**Levey, Michael**
William Faulkner **1**:102
W. Somerset Maugham **1**:204

**Levi, Peter**
David Jones **4**:261; **13**:307
George Seferis **5**:384
Yevgeny Yevtushenko **1**:381

**Leviant, Curt**
S. Y. Agnon **4**:12
Jakov Lind **4**:292
Isaac Bashevis Singer **3**:453
Elie Wiesel **3**:530

**Levin, Bernard**
Aleksandr I. Solzhenitsyn **7**:436

**Levin, Dan**
Yasunari Kawabata **2**:223

**Levin, David**
James Baldwin **17**:26

**Levin, Elena**
Yevgeny Yevtushenko **1**:382

**Levin, Irene S.**
Elizabeth Swados **12**:558

**Levin, Martin**
Brian Aldiss **5**:14
J. G. Ballard **14**:39
Patrick Boyle **19**:67
A. S. Byatt **19**:75
Taylor Caldwell **2**:95
Austin C. Clarke **8**:143
Robert Cormier **12**:134
Margaret Craven **17**:79
Allan W. Eckert **17**:107
George MacDonald Fraser
    **7**:106
Paul Gallico **2**:147
Natalia Ginzburg **5**:141
Earl Hamner, Jr. **12**:258
Fletcher Knebel **14**:309
William Kotzwinkle **5**:220
Richard Llewellyn **7**:207
John McGahern **5**:280
Alice Munro **6**:341
Leslie Norris **14**:388
Craig Nova **7**:267
J. B. Priestley **2**:347
Ann Quin **6**:441
Frederic Raphael **14**:437
Jean Rhys **2**:371
Judith Rossner **6**:468
David Slavitt **14**:491
Terry Southern **7**:452
David Storey **4**:530
Jesse Stuart **8**:507
Hollis Summers **10**:493
Elizabeth Taylor **4**:541
Fredrica Wagman **7**:500
David Harry Walker **14**:552
Thomas Williams **14**:581
P. G. Wodehouse **2**:479; **5**:516

Hilma Wolitzer **17**:561
John Wyndham **19**:475
Louis Zukofsky **2**:487

**Levin, Meyer**
Elmer Rice **7**:358
Henry Roth **6**:472

**Levin, Milton**
Noel Coward **1**:64

**Levine, George**
John Gardner **7**:113
Paul Goodman **2**:171
Juan Carlos Onetti **7**:279
Thomas Pynchon **3**:414

**Levine, June Perry**
Vladimir Nabokov **6**:352;
    **11**:396

**Levine, Paul**
Truman Capote **1**:55; **3**:99
J. D. Salinger **12**:498

**Levine, Suzanne Jill**
Severo Sarduy **6**:486
Mario Vargas Llosa **6**:547

**Levitas, Gloria**
Frank Bonham **12**:54
Sonia Levitin **17**:263

**Levitin, Alexis**
J.R.R. Tolkien **12**:574

**Levitin, Sonia**
Sonia Levitin **17**:264

**Levitt, Morton P.**
Michel Butor **3**:92
Claude Simon **4**:495

**Levitt, Paul M.**
Brendan Behan **11**:45
Jorge Luis Borges **9**:116
Michel de Ghelderode **11**:226

**Levitzky, Sergei**
Aleksandr I. Solzhenitsyn **4**:507

**Levy, Eric P.**
Samuel Beckett **18**:49

**Levy, Francis**
Thomas Berger **3**:64
Ruth Prawer Jhabvala **4**:257
Megan Terry **19**:441

**Levy, Frank**
Norman Lear **12**:330

**Levy, Jacques**
Sam Shepard **17**:435

**Levy, Paul**
Kingsley Amis **13**:14
James Baldwin **15**:41
A. S. Byatt **19**:77
Roald Dahl **6**:122
E. L. Doctorow **11**:141
Doris Lessing **6**:301
William Styron **15**:529

**Lewald, H. Ernest**
Ernesto Sábato **10**:446

**Lewis, Alan**
David Bowie **17**:59
William Inge **19**:227
Neil Young **17**:569, 570, 571

**Lewis, C. S.**
J.R.R. Tolkien **1**:336; **12**:563

**Lewis, Caroline**
Bob Fosse **20**:124

**Lewis, Constance**
Ivy Compton-Burnett **15**:141

**Lewis, Janet**
Caroline Gordon **6**:206

**Lewis, Marshall**
Leni Riefenstahl **16**:520

**Lewis, Naomi**
Leon Garfield **12**:217
Alan Garner **17**:134

**Lewis, Paula Gilbert**
Gabrielle Roy **10**:440

**Lewis, Peter**
Horst Bienek **11**:48

**Lewis, Peter Elfed**
Marvin Bell **8**:65
Ruth Prawer Jhabvala **8**:313

**Lewis, R.W.B.**
Graham Greene **1**:131
André Malraux **4**:328
John Steinbeck **9**:512

**Lewis, Robert W.**
Edward Lewis Wallant **10**:516

**Lewis, Robert W., Jr.**
Ernest Hemingway **1**:142

**Lewis, Stuart**
Bruce Jay Friedman **3**:166

**Lewis, Theophilus**
Gerome Ragni and James Rado
    **17**:382
Neil Simon **6**:502, 503
Douglas Turner Ward **19**:457

**Lewis, Tom J.**
Stanislaw Lem **8**:344

**Lewis, Wyndham**
Ezra Pound **7**:322

**Ley, Charles David**
Vicente Aleixandre **9**:10

**Leyda, Jay**
Akira Kurosawa **16**:395

**Lhamon, W. T., Jr.**
Anthony Burgess **5**:89
Bob Dylan **6**:158; **12**:192
John Gardner **3**:187
William Kennedy **6**:275
Joseph McElroy **5**:280
Robert M. Pirsig **4**:405
Thomas Pynchon **3**:412; **18**:430
Kurt Vonnegut, Jr. **4**:568

**Libby, Anthony**
Robert Bly **15**:62
Theodore Roethke **11**:484
William Carlos Williams **2**:470

**Libby, Margaret Sherwood**
Margot Benary-Isbert **12**:33
Betty Cavanna **12**:100
Maureen Daly **17**:90
Eilís Dillon **17**:93
Leon Garfield **12**:215

Christie Harris 12:261
Jean Lee Latham 12:323

**Libby, Marion Vlastos**
Margaret Drabble 5:117

**Liberman, M. M.**
Katherine Anne Porter 1:274;
7:318
Jean Stafford 4:517

**Libhart, Byron R.**
Julien Green 11:260

**Librach, Ronald S.**
Ingmar Bergman 16:81

**Lichtenberg, Jacqueline**
Gene Roddenberry 17:407

**Liddell, Robert**
Ivy Compton-Burnett 15:135

**Lieber, Joel**
Richard Elman 19:150
Lois Gould 4:199

**Lieber, Todd M.**
Ralph Ellison 3:144
Robert Frost 9:221
John Steinbeck 5:406

**Lieberman, Laurence**
Rafael Alberti 7:10
A. R. Ammons 2:11
John Ashbery 9:44
W. H. Auden 2:28
John Berryman 1:33
Edward Brathwaite 11:67
James Dickey 1:73; 2:115
Arthur Gregor 9:252
Anthony Hecht 8:268
Zbigniew Herbert 9:271
Richard Howard 7:165
Richard F. Hugo 18:259
Galway Kinnell 1:168
Stanley J. Kunitz 6:286
W. S. Merwin 1:212; 3:338
Howard Moss 7:248
Howard Nemerov 2:307
Kenneth Patchen 18:394
John Peck 3:378
Kenneth Rexroth 2:371
W. D. Snodgrass 2:405
William Stafford 4:520, 521
Mark Strand 6:521
Ted Walker 13:565
Theodore Weiss 3:517
Reed Whittemore 4:588

**Lifton, Robert Jay**
Albert Camus 2:99
Kurt Vonnegut, Jr. 2:455

**Light, Carolyn M.**
Madeleine L'Engle 12:347

**Lima, Robert**
Jorge Luis Borges 6:88
Ira Levin 6:306
Colin Wilson 3:538

**Lindberg-Seyersted, Brita**
Bernard Malamud 9:343

**Lindborg, Henry J.**
Doris Lessing 6:299

**Lindeman, Jack**
Robert Francis 15:235

**Lindfors, Bernth**
Chinua Achebe 7:4

**Lindner, Carl M.**
Robert Frost 3:175
James Thurber 5:440

**Lindop, Grevel**
John Berryman 3:66
Bob Dylan 4:148

**Lindquist, Jennie D.**
Margot Benary-Isbert 12:32
Walter Farley 17:116
Lee Kingman 17:244
William Mayne 12:387
Mary Stolz 12:546, 550
Lenora Mattingly Weber 12:633

**Lindsey, Byron**
Joseph Brodsky 13:116

**Lindsey, David A.**
Jules Archer 12:22

**Lindstrom, Naomi**
Bob Dylan 12:191

**Linehan, Eugene J., S.J.**
Taylor Caldwell 2:95
James Herriot 12:283
Irving Wallace 7:509

**Lingeman, Richard R.**
Richard Bach 14:36
James Herriot 12:283
Mary McCarthy 14:362
Charles M. Schulz 12:531
Erich Segal 10:466
Garry Trudeau 12:590

**Lipsius, Frank**
Herbert Gold 7:121
Bernard Malamud 2:268
Henry Miller 2:283
Thomas Pynchon 6:434

**Lipton, Eden Ross**
Robert Newton Peck 17:339

**Listri, Pier Francesco**
Allen Tate 6:525

**Litsinger, Kathryn A.**
Andre Norton 12:465

**Littell, Robert**
Robert Frost 15:240
Jean Toomer 13:550

**Little, Roger**
St.-John Perse 4:400; 11:433,
436

**Littlejohn, David**
James Baldwin 5:40
Imamu Amiri Baraka 5:44
Samuel Beckett 2:45
Jorge Luis Borges 2:68
Gwendolyn Brooks 5:75
Lawrence Durrell 4:144
Ralph Ellison 11:179
Jean Genet 2:157
John Hawkes 2:183
Robert Hayden 5:168
Joseph Heller 3:229
Chester Himes 7:159
Langston Hughes 5:190
Robinson Jeffers 2:214

John Oliver Killens 10:300
Henry Miller 2:281, 283
Ann Petry 7:304
Jean Toomer 13:551
J. E. Wideman 5:489
Richard Wright 9:583

**Littler, Frank**
Nigel Dennis 8:173

**Litwak, Leo E.**
Hunter S. Thompson 17:503

**Liv, Gwen**
Barbara Corcoran 17:70

**Lively, Penelope**
Penelope Fitzgerald 19:175

**Livesay, Dorothy**
Milton Acorn 15:8
Louis Dudek 11:159
E. J. Pratt 19:378

**Livingstone, Leon**
Azorín 11:25

**Llorens, David**
Nikki Giovanni 19:190

**Llosa, Mario Vargas**
José María Arguedas 18:9

**Lloyd, Peter**
Leonardo Sciascia 9:476

**Locke, Richard**
Donald Barthelme 8:52
Ann Beattie 18:37
Thomas Berger 8:83
Heinrich Böll 3:73
John Cheever 8:139
Joan Didion 8:175
Joseph Heller 11:268
John le Carré 5:233
Vladimir Nabokov 2:303; 8:418
Thomas Pynchon 2:356
John Updike 1:345; 9:540

**Lockerbie, D. Bruce**
C. S. Lewis 1:177

**Locklin, Gerald**
Richard Brautigan 12:67

**Lockwood, William J.**
Ed Dorn 10:159

**Lodge, David**
Kingsley Amis 2:10
William S. Burroughs 2:92
Mary Gordon 13:250
Graham Greene 1:134; 3:206
Ted Hughes 2:199
Doris Lessing 15:332
Norman Mailer 4:321
Alain Robbe-Grillet 4:447
Wilfrid Sheed 2:394
Muriel Spark 13:525

**Loewinsohn, Ron**
Richard Brautigan 12:59

**Logan, John**
E. E. Cummings 3:117

**Logan, William**
Gabriel García Márquez
15:253
Robert Hayden 14:240
Michael Ondaatje 14:410
Derek Walcott 14:548

**Lomas, Herbert**
Roy Fuller 4:179
John Gardner 7:115
Paul Goodman 4:196
John Hawkes 7:143
Robert M. Pirsig 6:421
Ezra Pound 3:398

**Long, Margo Alexander**
John Neufeld 17:311

**Long, Robert Emmet**
Ernest Hemingway 3:237
Edmund Wilson 8:550

**Longley, Edna**
Douglas Dunn 6:147
Seamus Heaney 5:170
Thomas Kinsella 19:256
Marge Piercy 18:409

**Longley, John Lewis, Jr.**
Robert Penn Warren 1:355

**Longstreth, T. Morris**
Frank B. Gilbreth and
Ernestine Gilbreth Carey
17:154
Jean Lee Latham 12:322

**Longsworth, Polly**
Madeleine L'Engle 12:349

**Lopez, Daniel**
Bernardo Bertolucci 16:97

**Loprete, Nicholas J.**
William Saroyan 10:457

**Lorch, Thomas M.**
Edward Lewis Wallant 10:512

**Lorich, Bruce**
Samuel Beckett 6:34

**Losinski, Julie**
Christie Harris 12:263

**Lothian, Helen M.**
Christie Harris 12:262

**Loubère, J.A.E.**
Claude Simon 15:490

**Lourie, Richard**
Joseph Brodsky 13:114

**Loveman, Amy**
William Maxwell 19:305

**Lowell, Amy**
Robert Frost 13:222

**Lowell, Robert**
W. H. Auden 1:9
John Berryman 2:57
Randall Jarrell 2:207; 13:298
Stanley J. Kunitz 6:285
Sylvia Plath 17:347
I. A. Richards 14:452
Allen Tate 4:535

**Lowenkron, David Henry**
Samuel Beckett 6:40

**Lowenthal, Lawrence D.**
Arthur Miller 15:374

**Lowrie, Rebecca**
Maureen Daly 17:88

CRITIC INDEX

**Lubbers, Klaus**
Carson McCullers **12**:423

**Lubow, Arthur**
Michael Cimino **16**:211
George Lucas **16**:414

**Lucas, John**
Ezra Pound **7**:332

**Lucey, Beatus T., O.S.B.**
Daphne du Maurier **6**:146

**Luchting, Wolfgang A.**
José María Arguedas **10**:9
José Donoso **4**:126, 127
Gabriel García Márquez **2**:150
Alain Resnais **16**:499
Mario Vargas Llosa **10**:496

**Lucid, Luellen**
Aleksandr I. Solzhenitsyn
**10**:480

**Lucid, Robert F.**
Ernest Hemingway **6**:232
Norman Mailer **4**:323

**Lucie-Smith, Edward**
Sylvia Plath **9**:424

**Luckett, Richard**
Anthony Powell **7**:339
Robert Penn Warren **6**:555
Edmund Wilson **3**:540

**Luckey, Eleanore Braun**
Honor Arundel **17**:19

**Ludlow, Colin**
David Mamet **15**:356
Tom Stoppard **15**:520

**Ludwig, Jack**
Bernard Malamud **2**:269
Mordecai Richler **18**:452

**Ludwig, Linda**
Doris Lessing **6**:301

**Lueders, Edward**
Jorge Luis Borges **2**:72
George MacBeth **2**:252

**Lugg, Andrew M.**
Andy Warhol **20**:417

**Lukacs, John**
Aleksandr I. Solzhenitsyn **7**:438

**Lukacs, Paul**
Anthony Burgess **13**:125

**Lukens, Rebecca J.**
Mavis Thorpe Clark **12**:132
Madeleine L'Engle **12**:351

**Lumley, Frederick**
Terence Rattigan **7**:354

**Lumport, Felicia**
Jessamyn West **7**:520

**Lundquist, James**
J. D. Salinger **12**:518
Kurt Vonnegut, Jr. **12**:615

**Lupack, Alan C.**
Gwendolyn Brooks **15**:95

**Lupoff, Richard**
Kurt Vonnegut, Jr. **12**:629

**Lurie, Alison**
Richard Adams **5**:7
Iris Murdoch **3**:348

**Luschei, Martin**
Walker Percy **3**:378

**Lustig, Irma S.**
Sean O'Casey **9**:411

**Luttwak, Edward**
Bernard Malamud **3**:325

**Lydenberg, Robin**
Jorge Luis Borges **13**:111, 113

**Lydon, Michael**
Chuck Berry **17**:52

**Lydon, Susan**
John Lennon and Paul
McCartney **12**:362

**Lye, John**
A. W. Purdy **14**:433

**Lyell, Frank H.**
Harper Lee **12**:340

**Lyles, Jean Caffey**
Richard Bach **14**:35

**Lyles, W. H.**
Stephen King **12**:310

**Lynch, Dennis Daley**
William Stafford **7**:462

**Lynch, Michael**
Richard Howard **7**:168
Michael McClure **10**:332

**Lyne, Oliver**
Ted Hughes **9**:282

**Lynen, John F.**
Robert Frost **1**:110

**Lyon, George W., Jr.**
Allen Ginsberg **3**:194

**Lyon, James K.**
Paul Celan **19**:87

**Lyon, Laurence Gill**
Jean-Paul Sartre **18**:463

**Lyon, Melvin**
Edward Dahlberg **1**:72

**Lyons, Bonnie**
Margaret Atwood **8**:33
Henry Roth **2**:378; **6**:473
Delmore Schwartz **10**:463

**Lyons, Donald**
Luchino Visconti **16**:574

**Lyons, Eugene**
Walker Percy **6**:399
John Updike **3**:486

**Lyons, Gene**
Peter Benchley **8**:82
Len Deighton **7**:75
John Hersey **9**:277
Elia Kazan **6**:274
George MacBeth **9**:340
Hunter S. Thompson **17**:515
John Updike **13**:562
Irving Wallace **7**:510
Robert Penn Warren **8**:540

Richard Yates **7**:555

**Lyons, John O.**
Vladimir Nabokov **1**:241

**Lytle, Andrew**
Allen Tate **4**:535

**MacAdam, Alfred**
Thomas Pynchon **11**:455

**MacAndrew, Andrew R.**
Yuri Olesha **8**:430

**Macaulay, Jeannette**
Camara Laye **4**:285

**Macauley, Robie**
Toni Cade Bambara **19**:33
R. P. Blackmur **2**:61
Shirley Hazzard **18**:214
James Alan McPherson **19**:310
Jean Rhys **14**:446
Patrick White **9**:566

**MacBeth, George**
Robert Nye **13**:412

**MacBride, James**
Jessamyn West **17**:544

**MacBrudnoy, David**
George MacDonald Fraser
**7**:106

**MacCabe, Colin**
Jean-Luc Godard **20**:146

**Maccoby, Hyam**
Ezra Pound **18**:420

**MacDiarmid, Hugh**
Ezra Pound **4**:413

**Macdonald, Dwight**
Charles Chaplin **16**:199
James Gould Cozzens **4**:111
Federico Fellini **16**:274
Rouben Mamoulian **16**:424
Philip Roth **1**:293

**MacDonald, John D.**
James M. Cain **11**:87

**Macdonald, Rae McCarthy**
Alice Munro **10**:357

**Macdonald, Ross**
Nelson Algren **10**:8
Dashiell Hammett **5**:160

**MacDonald, S. Yvonne**
Christie Harris **12**:266

**MacDonald, Scott**
Erskine Caldwell **14**:96

**Macdonald, Susan**
Pier Paolo Pasolini **20**:262

**MacFadden, Patrick**
Albert Maysles and David
Maysles **16**:438, 440
Pier Paolo Pasolini **20**:260

**MacInnes, Colin**
James Baldwin **1**:14; **17**:25
Brendan Behan **15**:44
Alex Haley **12**:244

**MacIntyre, Alasdair**
Arthur Koestler **1**:170

**MacIntyre, Jean**
Barbara Corcoran **17**:77

**Maciuszko, George J.**
Czesław Miłosz **5**:292

**Mackay, Barbara**
Imamu Amiri Baraka **10**:19
Ed Bullins **7**:37
James Kirkwood **9**:319

**MacKay, L. A.**
Robert Finch **18**:154

**MacKenzie, Nancy K.**
Babette Deutsch **18**:120

**MacKenzie, Robert**
Norman Lear **12**:337

**MacKinnon, Alex**
Earle Birney **6**:79

**Macklin, F. Anthony**
Robert Altman **16**:34
Stanley Kubrick **16**:381
Gore Vidal **2**:449

**MacLaren, I. S.**
A.J.M. Smith **15**:517

**Maclean, Alasdair**
Elizabeth Jennings **14**:292
D. M. Thomas **13**:541

**MacLean, Kenneth**
William Heyen **18**:229

**MacLeish, Archibald**
Ezra Pound **3**:399

**MacLeish, Roderick**
Eric Ambler **6**:3
Richard Condon **8**:150
Len Deighton **7**:74
Ken Follett **18**:155
George V. Higgins **4**:224

**MacManus, Patricia**
Shirley Hazzard **18**:214
Françoise Sagan **17**:424

**Mac Namara, Desmond**
Jessamyn West **17**:550

**Macnaughton, W. R.**
Ernest Hemingway **8**:286

**MacPike, Loralee**
Fay Weldon **19**:470

**MacQuown, Vivian J.**
Mary Stolz **12**:552

**MacShane, Frank**
Jorge Luis Borges **2**:76
Edward Dahlberg **1**:71; **14**:138
Barbara Howes **15**:290
Clarence Major **19**:292
W. S. Merwin **1**:212
Alberto Moravia **18**:348
Pablo Neruda **9**:399

**MacSween, R. J.**
Ivy Compton-Burnett **10**:110
Evelyn Waugh **19**:462

**Madden, David**
James M. Cain **3**:96; **11**:86
William Gaddis **1**:113
Wright Morris **1**:230; **3**:343
Sam Shepard **17**:434

**Maddocks, Melvin**
Richard Adams **4**:7
Kingsley Amis **2**:7, 8
John Beecher **6**:48
Heinrich Böll **3**:75
Paul Bowles **2**:78
J. P. Donleavy **6**:142
Ernest J. Gaines **3**:179
John Gardner **2**:152
Mark Harris **19**:201
Joseph Heller **5**:176
Thomas Keneally **5**:209, 212
Doris Lessing **2**:239 **6**:298, 303
Bernard Malamud **2**:267
Thomas Pynchon **2**:354
Piers Paul Read **4**:444
Philip Roth **4**:456
Cornelius Ryan **7**:385
Angus Wilson **3**:536

**Madsen, Alan**
Andre Norton **12**:457

**Madsen, Axel**
Jerzy Skolimowski **20**:347

**Madsen, Børge Gedsø**
Kjeld Abell **15**:1

**Magalaner, Marvin**
E. M. Forster **1**:103
Aldous Huxley **1**:150

**Magee, William H.**
Philip Child **19**:100

**Magid, Nora L.**
Mordecai Richler **9**:450; **18**:456
Françoise Sagan **17**:416

**Magliola, Robert**
Jorge Luis Borges **10**:68

**Magner, James E., Jr.**
John Crowe Ransom **4**:431

**Magny, Claude-Edmonde**
John Dos Passos **15**:182
William Faulkner **18**:143
André Malraux **15**:351

**Mahlendorf, Ursula**
Horst Bienek **7**:28

**Mahon, Derek**
Patrick Boyle **19**:68
Austin Clarke **9**:168
Donald Davie **10**:125
Frederick Exley **11**:186
John le Carré **5**:233
József Lengyel **7**:202
Hugh MacDiarmid **19**:289
John Montague **13**:390
Brian Moore **8**:394
Edna O'Brien **8**:429

**Mahon, Vincent**
Marilyn French **18**:157

**Maida, Patricia D.**
Flannery O'Connor **10**:364

**Mailer, Norman**
Bernardo Bertolucci **16**:92

**Mairowitz, David Zane**
Edward Bond **6**:86

**Maitland, Jeffrey**
William H. Gass **11**:224

**Maitland, Sara**
Flann O'Brien **5**:314

**Majdiak, Daniel**
John Barth **1**:17

**Majeski, Jane**
Arthur Koestler **8**:324

**Majkut, Denise R.**
Bob Dylan **4**:148

**Major, Clarence**
Ralph Ellison **3**:146
Rudolph Wurlitzer **15**:588

**Malamut, Bruce**
Peter Townshend **17**:536

**Malanga, Gerard**
Anne Waldman **7**:508

**Malcolm, Donald**
James Baldwin **17**:22
Mark Harris **19**:200

**Malin, Irving**
Saul Bellow **13**:70
Paul Bowles **19**:61
Frederick Busch **7**:39
Hortense Calisher **4**:87
Jerome Charyn **18**:98
Eleanor Clark **5**:105
B. H. Friedman **7**:109
John Hawkes **4**:217
Joseph Heller **5**:182
Ken Kesey **6**:278
Carson McCullers **4**:344
Flannery O'Connor **2**:317
Walker Percy **8**:445
James Purdy **2**:347
Philip Roth **15**:449
Muriel Spark **5**:398; **8**:496
Peter Spielberg **6**:519
Harvey Swados **5**:421
Elie Wiesel **5**:490

**Malkin, Lawrence**
Harold Pinter **6**:418

**Malko, George**
Frederick Buechner **4**:80

**Malkoff, Karl**
Robert Duncan **15**:189
Kenneth Rexroth **1**:284
Theodore Roethke **1**:291
May Swenson **4**:533

**Mallalieu, H. B.**
John Gardner **7**:116
Pablo Neruda **7**:261
David Pownall **10**:419

**Mallerman, Tony**
Satyajit Ray **16**:479

**Mallet, Gina**
Iris Murdoch **1**:237
Tennessee Williams **7**:545

**Malley, Terrence**
Richard Brautigan **3**:88

**Malmfelt, A. D.**
Brian De Palma **20**:73

**Malmström, Gunnel**
Pär Lagerkvist **13**:330

**Maloff, Saul**
Nelson Algren **4**:18
Louis Auchincloss **4**:30
James Baldwin **17**:23
Heinrich Böll **9**:110
Frederick Busch **7**:38
Edward Dahlberg **7**:68
Ernest Hemingway **3**:236
Milan Kundera **9**:321
Norman Mailer **2**:264
Vladimir Nabokov **6**:356
Flannery O'Connor **3**:365
Clifford Odets **2**:319
Sylvia Plath **2**:336; **17**:358
Philip Roth **3**:435; **4**:455
Alan Sillitoe **1**:307
Josef Škvorecký **15**:512
Calder Willingham **5**:512

**Malone, Michael**
Thomas Berger **18**:57

**Maloney, Douglas J.**
Frederick Exley **6**:171

**Maltin, Leonard**
Woody Allen **16**:5

**Malzberg, Barry N.**
Ursula K. LeGuin **13**:349

**Mamber, Stephen**
Albert Maysles and David
Maysles **16**:441, 442
Frederick Wiseman **20**:470,
473, 476

**Mandel, Eli**
Andrew Suknaki **19**:432

**Mandel, Siegfried**
Uwe Johnson **5**:200
Mary Renault **17**:393

**Mandelbaum, Allen**
Giuseppe Ungaretti **7**:481

**Mandelbaum, Bernard**
Elie Wiesel **11**:570

**Mander, Gertrud**
Peter Weiss **15**:566

**Mander, John**
Günter Grass **6**:208

**Manfred, Freya**
Erica Jong **18**:277

**Mangelsdorff, Rich**
Michael McClure **6**:318

**Mangione, Jerry**
Andrea Giovene **7**:116

**Mankiewicz, Don**
Jessamyn West **17**:546

**Manlove, C. N.**
J.R.R. Tolkien **12**:580

**Mann, Charles W., Jr.**
Jonathan Kozol **17**:248

**Mann, Elizabeth C.**
Mary Stolz **12**:551

**Mann, Golo**
W. H. Auden **3**:29

**Mann, Jeanette W.**
Jean Stafford **7**:458

**Mann, Thomas**
Hermann Hesse **11**:270

**Mannes, Marya**
Françoise Sagan **17**:422

**Manning, Olivia**
Beryl Bainbridge **14**:36
Sylvia Townend Warner **7**:511

**Mano, D. Keith**
Richard Adams **4**:9
J. G. Ballard **3**:34
Thomas Berger **5**:60
Daniel J. Berrigan **4**:58
Jorge Luis Borges **2**:71
John Cheever **3**:108
Evan S. Connell, Jr. **6**:117
Peter DeVries **10**:136
J. P. Donleavy **4**:125
Richard Elman **19**:151
Irvin Faust **8**:214
William Gerhardie **5**:140
James Hanley **3**:221
Joseph Heller **5**:180
George V. Higgins **4**:224
B. S. Johnson **6**:263, 264
Erica Jong **8**:315
Yuri Krotkov **19**:264
James A. Michener **11**:376
Vladimir Nabokov **2**:301
Hugh Nissenson **9**:400
Richard O'Brien **17**:325
John O'Hara **2**:325
Philip Roth **4**:458
William Saroyan **10**:456
Alexander Theroux **2**:433
John Updike **2**:444; **5**:456
Patrick White **3**:525
Tennessee Williams **7**:546

**Mansbridge, Francis**
Rudy Wiebe **14**:573

**Mansell, Mark**
Harlan Ellison **13**:208

**Manso, Susan**
Anaïs Nin **8**:424

**Manthorne, Jane**
Frank Bonham **12**:50, 51
Mavis Thorpe Clark **12**:130
Allan W. Eckert **17**:106
James Herriot **12**:283
Andre Norton **12**:457

**Manvell, Roger**
René Clair **20**:63
Fritz Lang **20**:204
Jean Cocteau **16**:227
Leni Riefenstahl **16**:521
Agnès Varda **16**:554
Andrzej Wajda **16**:577
Orson Welles **20**:433, 447

**Mao, Nathan K.**
Pa Chin **18**:373

**Maples, Houston L.**
Joseph Krumgold **12**:318
William Mayne **12**:392

**Marafino, Elizabeth A.**
Sonia Levitin **17**:265

**Marcello, J. J. Armas**
Mario Vargas Llosa **10**:499

**Marciniak, Ed**
Frank Bonham **12**:50

**Marcorelles, Louis**
René Clair **20**:65
Elia Kazan **16**:373
Eric Rohmer **16**:528

**Marcotte, Edward**
Alain Robbe-Grillet **6**:467

**Marcus, Adrianne**
Anna Kavan **13**:316
Jon Silkin **2**:395
William Stafford **4**:520

**Marcus, Greil**
Wendell Berry **8**:85
E. L. Doctorow **6**:134
Bob Dylan **12**:197
John Irving **13**:294, 295, 296
John Lennon and Paul
   McCartney **12**:382
Richard Price **12**:490
John Sayles **10**:460
Patti Smith **12**:535
Raymond Sokolov **7**:431
Robert Wilson **9**:576

**Marcus, Mordecai**
William Everson **1**:96
Robert Frost **9**:224
Ted Hughes **2**:203
Bernard Malamud **1**:199

**Marcus, Steven**
William Golding **2**:165
Dashiell Hammett **10**:252
Bernard Malamud **2**:265
Irving Stone **7**:470

**Maremaa, Thomas**
Robert Crumb **17**:84

**Margolies, Edward**
Chester Himes **18**:244

**Marguerite, Sister M., R.S.M.**
Eleanor Hibbert **7**:155

**Mariani, John**
Aleksandr I. Solzhenitsyn **7**:440

**Mariani, Paul**
Robert Penn Warren **8**:536
William Carlos Williams **9**:572

**Marill-Albérès, René**
Jean-Paul Sartre **1**:304

**Marinucci, Ron**
Isaac Asimov **19**:29

**Marius, Richard**
Frederick Buechner **4**:79

**Mark, M.**
Bruce Springsteen **17**:483

**Mark, Rachel**
Tom Wolfe **15**:587

**Marken, Jack W.**
N. Scott Momaday **19**:320

**Marker, Frederick J.**
Kjeld Abell **15**:3

**Markmann, Charles Lam**
Julien Green **3**:205
Joyce Carol Oates **2**:313

**Markos, Donald**
Hannah Green **3**:202

**Markos, Donald W.**
James Dickey **1**:74

**Markow, Alice Bradley**
Doris Lessing **6**:297

**Marks, Mitchell**
Frederick Busch **7**:38

**Marnham, Patrick**
Paul Theroux **15**:535

**Marowitz, Charles**
John Arden **13**:23
Ed Bullins **1**:47
John Osborne **5**:331
Tom Stoppard **1**:327
Tennessee Williams **11**:576

**Marquad, Jean**
André Brink **18**:69

**Marranca, Bonnie**
Peter Handke **8**:261; **10**:256

**Marsh, Dave**
Bob Dylan **12**:192
Jimmy Page and Robert Plant
   **12**:480
Patti Smith **12**:539
Bruce Springsteen **17**:486
Peter Townshend **17**:527, 531,
   533, 535, 541
Brian Wilson **12**:654
Neil Young **17**:574

**Marsh, Fred T.**
Carson McCullers **12**:409

**Marsh, Irving T.**
Jean Lee Latham **12**:323

**Marsh, Pamela**
Agatha Christie **1**:58
Jan de Hartog **19**:131
Ronald L. Fair **18**:140
Joseph Krumgold **12**:317
Robert Newton Peck **17**:336
Josephine Poole **17**:372
Mary Stolz **12**:552

**Marshak, Sondra**
Gene Roddenberry **17**:407

**Marshall, Donald**
Stanislaw Lem **8**:343

**Marshall, Margaret**
René Clair **20**:60
Josef von Sternberg **20**:370

**Marshall, Megan**
Thornton Wilder **15**:575

**Marshall, Tom**
Margaret Atwood **8**:29
William Heyen **13**:282
Gwendolyn MacEwen **13**:358
P. K. Page **7**:292

**Marten, Harry**
Paul Bowles **19**:60
Stanley Kunitz **14**:313
Denise Levertov **15**:338
Muriel Rukeyser **15**:457

**Martin, Allie Beth**
Walter Farley **17**:118

**Martin, Brian**
Alan Sillitoe **19**:422

**Martin, Bruce K.**
Philip Larkin **13**:338

**Martin, Gerald**
Miguel Angel Asturias **13**:37

**Martin, Graham**
Roy Fuller **4**:177
Robert Pinget **13**:444

**Martin, James**
May Sarton **14**:480

**Martin, Jay**
Robert Lowell **1**:181

**Martin, Judith**
Erica Jong **18**:278

**Martin, Robert A.**
Arthur Miller **10**:346

**Martin, Robert K.**
Richard Howard **10**:274

**Martin, Sandra**
Hugh Garner **13**:237

**Martin, Terence**
Ken Kesey **11**:314

**Martin, Wallace**
D. J. Enright **8**:204

**Martineau, Stephen**
Susan Musgrave **13**:401
James Reaney **13**:475

**Martinez, Z. Nelly**
José Donoso **8**:178

**Martins, Wilson**
Carlos Drummond de Andrade
   **18**:5

**Martinson, Steven D.**
Günter Eich **15**:205

**Martz, Louis L.**
Robert Creeley **1**:67
Phyllis Gotlieb **18**:192
John Hollander **14**:261
X. J. Kennedy **8**:320
Robert Lowell **1**:181
Lisel Mueller **13**:400
Joyce Carol Oates **9**:403
Robert Pinsky **9**:417
Ezra Pound **1**:276
Reg Saner **9**:469
Jon Silkin **2**:396
William Stafford **4**:521
Mark Strand **18**:515
John Wain **2**:458
Al Young **19**:477

**Martz, William J.**
John Berryman **1**:34

**Marwell, Patricia McCue**
Jules Archer **12**:22

**Masing-Delic, Irene**
Boris Pasternak **18**:389

**Masinton, Charles G.**
J. P. Donleavy **10**:153

**Maskell, Duke**
E. M. Forster **1**:108; **9**:203

**Maslin, Janet**
Marguerite Duras **20**:103
Rainer Werner Fassbinder
   **20**:114
Alex Haley **12**:254
Werner Herzog **16**:328
Joni Mitchell **12**:440, 443
Laura Nyro **17**:318
Mary Rodgers **12**:495
Buffy Sainte-Marie **17**:431
Paul Simon **17**:466
Bruce Springsteen **17**:480
Lina Wertmüller **16**:589
Neil Young **17**:573

**Mason, Ann L.**
Günter Grass **4**:204; **11**:247

**Mason, Michael**
Donald Barthelme **8**:53
John Cheever **15**:131
Robert Coover **15**:143
George V. Higgins **10**:273

**Massie, Allan**
David Harry Walker **14**:552

**Massingham, Harld**
George Mackay Brown **5**:76

**Mast, Gerald**
Buster Keaton **20**:194

**Masterman, Len**
Roman Polanski **16**:468

**Masters, Anthony**
David Rudkin **14**:470

**Mathews, F. X.**
P. H. Newby **13**:408, 410

**Mathews, Laura**
James Hanley **13**:261
Richard Price **12**:491

**Mathews, Richard**
Brian Aldiss **14**:10

**Mathewson, Joseph**
J.R.R. Tolkien **12**:566

**Mathewson, Rufus W., Jr.**
Boris Pasternak **7**:299
Mikhail Sholokhov **7**:421
Aleksandr I. Solzhenitsyn **7**:441

**Mathewson, Ruth**
Alejo Carpentier **8**:134
Joan Didion **8**:176
J. P. Donleavy **10**:154
Margaret Drabble **8**:184
Paula Fox **8**:219
James Hanley **13**:260
Christina Stead **8**:500
Robert Penn Warren **8**:540

**Matlaw, Myron**
Alan Paton **10**:387

**Matson, Marshall**
Margaret Atwood **15**:36

**Matthews, Charles**
John Hawkes **2**:183

**Matthews, Dorothy**
J.R.R. Tolkien **12**:583

**Matthews, J. H.**
André Breton **2**:80

**Matthews, James H.**
Frank O'Connor **14**:396

**Matthews, Robin**
Robin Skelton **13**:507

**Matthews, T. S.**
Edmund Wilson **8**:551

**Matthews, Virginia H.**
Betty Cavanna **12**:98

**Matthias, John**
Elizabeth Daryush **6**:123
Michael Hamburger **5**:158
Elizabeth Jennings **14**:293
David Jones **7**:189
Anne Stevenson **7**:463
D. M. Thomas **13**:542
R. S. Thomas **6**:530

**Maunder, Gabrielle**
Ruth M. Arthur **12**:27
Alvin Silverstein and Virginia
B. Silverstein **17**:450

**Maurer, Robert**
A. Alvarez **5**:17
Robertson Davies **7**:73
José Donoso **8**:180
MacDonald Harris **9**:258
Pablo Neruda **9**:398
Clancy Sigal **7**:425

**Maurer, Robert E.**
E. E. Cummings **8**:155

**Mauriac, Claude**
Samuel Beckett **2**:44
Albert Camus **2**:97
Henry Miller **2**:281
Alain Robbe-Grillet **2**:373
Nathalie Sarraute **2**:383
Georges Simenon **2**:396

**Maurois, André**
Aldous Huxley **3**:253
Jules Romains **7**:381

**Maury, Lucien**
Pär Lagerkvist **7**:198

**Maxwell, D. E. S.**
Brian Friel **5**:128

**May, Charles Paul**
Joy Adamson **17**:1

**May, Derwent**
Nadine Gordimer **5**:145
Alfred Hitchcock **16**:340
Ted Hughes **14**:270
Alison Lurie **4**:305
Tadeusz Różewicz **9**:463
Louis Simpson **9**:485

**May, Jill P.**
Robert Newton Peck **17**:341

**May, John R.**
Kurt Vonnegut, Jr. **2**:455

**May, Keith M.**
Aldous Huxley **4**:242

**May, Yolanta**
Emma Tennant **13**:536

**Mayer, David**
Thornton Wilder **15**:574

**Mayer, Hans**
Friedrich Dürrenmatt **4**:140
Witold Gombrowicz **4**:193
Günter Grass **4**:202
Jean-Paul Sartre **4**:473

**Mayer, Thomas**
Maya Deren **16**:253

**Mayhew, Alice**
Graham Greene **1**:134
Claude Mauriac **9**:363

**Maynard, Robert C.**
Alex Haley **8**:259
Garry Trudeau **12**:588

**Mayne, Richard**
Saul Bellow **8**:70
J.I.M. Stewart **7**:465

**Mayne, William**
Eilís Dillon **17**:95

**Mayo, Clark**
Kurt Vonnegut, Jr. **12**:617

**Mayoux, Jean-Jacques**
Samuel Beckett **18**:41

**Mazrui, Ali A.**
Alex Haley **12**:249

**Mazzaro, Jerome**
Elizabeth Bishop **9**:88
David Ignatow **7**:175, 178
Randall Jarrell **8**:259
Robert Lowell **4**:295, 298
Cynthia Macdonald **19**:291
Joyce Carol Oates **3**:359
Ezra Pound **4**:417
John Crowe Ransom **2**:366
W. D. Snodgrass **6**:514
William Carlos Williams **5**:508

**Mazzocco, Robert**
John Ashbery **3**:15
Chester Kallman **2**:221
Philip Levine **5**:251
Mario Luzi **13**:354
William Meredith **4**:348
Anne Sexton **6**:492
Eleanor Ross Taylor **5**:426
Gore Vidal **6**:548
Derek Walcott **14**:551

**McAleer, John J.**
MacKinlay Kantor **7**:195
Alain Robbe-Grillet **10**:438

**McAllister, H. S.**
Carlos Castaneda **12**:92

**McAllister, Mick**
Michael McClure **6**:319

**McArthur, Colin**
Roman Polanski **16**:464
Andrzej Wajda **16**:579

**McAuley, Gay**
Jean Genet **10**:225
Peter Handke **10**:254

**McBride, James**
Frank Bonham **12**:49

**McBride, Joseph**
John Ford **16**:310, 314
Alfred Hitchcock **16**:348
Orson Welles **20**:447, 450
Billy Wilder **20**:462, 463, 464

**McCabe, Bernard**
Wilfrid Sheed **10**:474

**McCaffery, Larry**
Donald Barthelme **5**:55
William H. Gass **8**:242

**McCahill, Alice**
Elizabeth Taylor **2**:432

**McCall, Dorothy**
Jean-Paul Sartre **7**:388; **13**:498

**McCalla, Nelle**
Maureen Daly **17**:89

**McCandlish, George**
Jan de Hartog **19**:132

**McCann, Sean**
Brendan Behan **15**:46

**McCarten, John**
Robert Bolt **14**:88
Alfred Hitchcock **16**:339
Douglas Turner Ward **19**:456

**McCarthy, Abigail**
John Updike **15**:546

**McCarthy, Colman**
P. G. Wodehouse **5**:516

**McCarthy, Dermot**
Bill Bissett **18**:62

**McCarthy, Harold T.**
Henry Miller **9**:377
Richard Wright **3**:545

**McCarthy, Mary**
William S. Burroughs **2**:90
Ivy Compton-Burnett **3**:112
Mary McCarthy **14**:361
Vladimir Nabokov **2**:301
J. D. Salinger **3**:444
Nathalie Sarraute **2**:384

**McCarty, John Alan**
Roman Polanski **16**:467

**McCawley, Dwight L.**
Theodore Roethke **19**:401

**McClain, Ruth Rambo**
Toni Morrison **4**:365

**McClanahan, Ed**
Richard Bautigan **12**:64

**McClatchy, J. D.**
A. R. Ammons **5**:31
Louise Glück **7**:119
Anthony Hecht **19**:210
Richard Howard **7**:167
Donald Justice **19**:237
Robert Lowell **8**:355
James Merrill **6**:324
Howard Moss **14**:376
Robert Pinsky **9**:417
Sylvia Plath **5**:346
Ira Sadoff **9**:466
Anne Sexton **15**:471
W. D. Snodgrass **18**:490
Maura Stanton **9**:507
Diane Wakoski **7**:504
Robert Penn Warren **6**:557
Theodore Weiss **8**:546
Charles Wright **6**:581

**McCleary, Dorothy**
Eilís Dillon **17**:94

**McClellan, Edwin**
Yukio Mishima **6**:338

**McClelland, David**
Flann O'Brien **5**:315
Patti Smith **12**:536

**McCloskey, Mark**
Robert Francis **15**:235

**McClure, Michael**
Sam Shepard **17**:441

**McCluskey, John**
James Baldwin **17**:39

**McComas, J. Frances**
Frank Herbert **12**:270

**McConnell, Frank**
John Barth **7**:25; **14**:57
Saul Bellow **6**:54
John Gardner **7**:115
Graham Greene **14**:217; **18**:198
Norman Mailer **14**:353

**McConnell-Mammarella, Joan**
Carlo Emilio Gadda **11**:210

**McConville, Edward**
John Sayles **10**:461

**McCormick, E. H.**
James K. Baxter **14**:59

**McCormick, Lynde**
Bruce Springsteen **17**:479

**McCormick, Ruth**
Nagisa Oshima **20**:249, 252

**McCourt, James**
Eric Rohmer **16**:538

**McCue, Michael**
Margaret Craven **17**:80
Anne McCaffrey **17**:283
John Neufeld **17**:310

**McCullers, Carson**
Carson McCullers **12**:417

**McCullough, Frank**
George Garrett **3**:189

**McCutcheon, R. S.**
Alvin Silverstein and Virginia
B. Silverstein **17**:455

**McDaniel, Richard Bryan**
Chinua Achebe **7**:6

**McDiarmid, Matthew P.**
Hugh MacDiarmid **11**:334

**McDonald, Edward R.**
Friedrich Dürrenmatt **15**:199

**McDonald, James L.**
John Barth **2**:38

**McDonald, Susan S.**
Harriet Waugh **6**:560

**McDonnell, Christine**
Roy A. Gallant **17**:133

**McDonnell, Jane Taylor**
Galway Kinnell **2**:230

CRITIC INDEX

**McDowell, Frederick P. W.**
John Braine 1:43
Lawrnce Durrell 1:87
E. M. Forster 1:107; 10:181
Doris Lessing 1:175
Iris Murdoch 1:236
Frederic Raphael 2:366
Muriel Spark 2:416

**McDowell, Myles**
Leon Garfield 12:228
William Mayne 12:404

**McDowell, Robert**
Thomas Merton 11:374

**McDowell, Robert E.**
Thomas Keneally 10:298

**McElroy, Joseph**
Samuel Beckett 2:48
Italo Calvino 5:99
Vladimir Nabokov 2:304

**McElroy, Wendy**
Gabriel García Márquez
10:217

**McEvilly, Wayne**
Anaïs Nin 1:248

**McEvoy, Ruth M.**
Henry Gregory Felsen 17:121

**McFadden, George**
Robert Lowell 9:333

**McFee, William**
Edna Ferber 18:151

**McFerran, Douglas**
Carlos Castaneda 12:93

**McGann, Jerome**
Robert Creeley 2:106; 8:151
David Jones 7:188
X. J. Kennedy 8:320
Eleanor Lerman 9:331

**McGann, Jerome J.**
Michael Benedikt 14:81
Turner Cassity 6:107
Daniel Mark Epstein 7:97
A. D. Hope 3:251
Donald Justice 6:272
Galway Kinnell 13:320
Muriel Rukeyser 6:479
Judith Johnson Sherwin 7:415

**McGee, David**
Bruce Springsteen 17:479

**McGeehin, R.**
Mary Renault 17:402

**McGerr, Celia**
René Clair 20:69

**McGhan, Barry**
Andre Norton 12:459

**McGilchrist, Iain**
W. H. Auden 9:57

**McGinley, Phyllis**
Margery Allingham 19:13

**McGinnis, Wayne D.**
Roman Polanski 16:471
Kurt Vonnegut, Jr. 8:529

**McGinniss, Joe**
Nora Ephron 17:113
George V. Higgins 4:222

**McGovern, Hugh**
George Tabori 19:436

**McGrath, Joan**
Gwendolyn MacEwen 13:358

**McGregor, Craig**
Bob Dylan 4:148

**McGuane, Thomas**
Richard Brautigan 1:44
John Hawkes 2:185

**McGuinness, Arthur E.**
Seamus Heaney 14:242

**McGuinness, Frank**
Kingsley Amis 1:6
Andrew Sinclair 2:400

**McGuire, Alice Brooks**
Betty Cavanna 12:98
Jean Lee Latham 12:322

**McHale, Tom**
Diane Johnson 5:198
D. Keith Mano 2:270
J. F. Powers 8:447

**McHargue, Georgess**
Barbara Corcoran 17:71, 74
Nicholasa Mohr 12:447
John Neufeld 17:308
Zilpha Keatley Snyder 17:473

**McInerney, John**
John Knowles 10:303

**McInerny, Ralph**
Anthony Burgess 4:80

**McKegney, Michael**
Claude Chabrol 16:171

**McKenna, Andrew J.**
Patrick Modiano 18:338

**McKenzie, Alan T.**
John Updike 5:452

**McKinley, Hugh**
Anthony Kerrigan 6:275

**McKinnon, William T.**
Louis MacNeice 10:324

**McLane, Daisann**
Laura Nyro 17:320
Neil Young 17:579

**McLaughlin, Pat**
Charles M. Schulz 12:533

**McLay, C. M.**
Margaret Laurence 3:278
Ethel Davis Wilson 13:609

**McLean, David G.**
Lewis Turco 11:551

**McLellan, Joseph**
Richard Adams 18:1
Richard Bach 14:36
Donald Barthelme 8:52
John Berryman 8:90
Dee Brown 18:70
Max Frisch 18:163
Arthur Hailey 5:156

Robert Heinlein 8:275
George V. Higgins 10:274
John le Carré 15:324
John Sayles 7:399
J.R.R. Tolkien 8:515

**McLennan, Winona**
Alvin Silverstein and Virginia
B. Silverstein 17:453

**McLeod, A. L.**
Thomas Keneally 19:248
Patrick White 7:531

**McLeod, Alan L.**
Thomas Keneally 19:243

**McLuhan, Herbert Marshall**
John Dos Passos 11:154

**McMahon, Joseph H.**
Jean-Paul Sartre 7:389

**McMahon, Patricia**
Alan Garner 17:151

**McMahon-Hill, Gillian**
Russell C. Hoban 7:161

**McMichael, James**
May Sarton 4:471

**McMullen, Roy**
Nathalie Sarraute 2:385

**McMurtry, Larry**
Vardis Fisher 7:103
Ernest J. Gaines 11:217
Ward Just 4:265
Wright Morris 18:353

**McNally, John**
Carson McCullers 12:429

**McNeil, Helen**
Olivia Manning 19:304
Jean Rhys 19:392
Philip Roth 15:454
Colin Wilson 14:584

**McNeil, Nicholas J., S.J.**
Eleanor Hibbert 7:156

**McNeill, William H.**
Charles M. Schulz 12:524

**McNelly, Willis E.**
Ray Bradbury 10:70
Robert Heinlein 8:274
Frank Herbert 12:277
Kurt Vonnegut, Jr. 2:452

**McNevin, Tom**
George V. Higgins 18:235

**McPheeters, D. W.**
Camilo José Cela 4:98

**McPheron, Judith**
Jamake Highwater 12:287

**McPherson, Hugo**
Morley Callaghan 14:99
Mordecai Richler 5:374
Gabrielle Roy 14:465

**McPherson, Sandra**
William Heyen 13:283

**McPherson, William**
Margaret Atwood 8:30
Paula Fox 8:218
John Gardner 8:235
Günter Grass 11:252
Maxine Hong Kingston 12:312
Maxine Kumin 5:222
Ross Macdonald 14:328
John Updike 5:457; 13:563

**McRobbie, Kenneth**
Seamus Heaney 14:242

**McSweeney, Kerry**
Brian Moore 19:330
V. S. Naipaul 9:391
Anthony Powell 9:435
Simon Raven 14:439

**McVay, Douglas**
Claude Chabrol 16:182
Vittorio De Sica 20:91
Satyajit Ray 16:475

**McWilliams, Dean**
Michel Butor 3:94; 15:115
Marguerite Duras 3:129; 20:100

**McWilliams, Donald E.**
Frederick Wiseman 20:471

**McWilliams, Nancy R.**
John Steinbeck 5:405

**McWilliams, W. C.**
Mary Renault 11:472

**McWilliams, Wilson C.**
John Steinbeck 5:405

**Meades, Jonathan**
Simone de Beauvoir 2:43
Jorge Luis Borges 1:39; 3:77;
4:74
Louis-Ferdinand Céline 3:105
Iris Murdoch 2:297
Vladimir Nabokov 2:302; :354
Alain Robbe-Grillet 1:289;
2:376; 4:448
Keith Roberts 14:463
Kurt Vonnegut, Jr. 2:455

**Meckier, Jerome**
Aldous Huxley 11:285; 18:267
Evelyn Waugh 3:512; 19:462

**Medawar, Peter**
Arthur Koestler 6:281; 8:324

**Mednick, Liz**
Rita Mae Brown 18:73
Susan Sontag 13:518

**Medvedev, R. A.**
Mikhail Sholokhov 15:483

**Meehan, Thomas**
Bob Dylan 12:180

**Meek, Margaret**
Peter Dickinson 12:175
Alan Garner 17:138, 148, 149,
150
William Mayne 12:391, 394,
399, 405
Robert Westall 17:559

**Meeter, Glenn**
Kurt Vonnegut, Jr. 4:566

**Megaw, Moira**
W. H. Auden 6:24

**Megged, Aharon**
S. Y. Agnon 4:14

**Meiners, R. K.**
James Dickey 7:81
Robert Lowell 1:182
Delmore Schwartz 2:387
Allen Tate 4:536

**Meinke, Peter**
W. H. Auden 6:20
John Beecher 6:48
John Dos Passos 4:136
H. D. 8:256
Marilyn Hacker 5:155
Ted Hughes 4:236
Philip Levine 5:250
William Meredith 13:372
Howard Nemerov 2:307
Muriel Rukeyser 6:478
Anne Sexton 4:483
Diane Wakoski 7:504
Robert Penn Warren 6:555
Charles Wright 6:579

**Meisel, Perry**
Joni Mitchell 12:440

**Mekas, Jonas**
Andy Warhol 20:415

**Melanson, Jim**
Richard O'Brien 17:322

**Mellard, James M.**
Bernard Malamud 1:198
François Mauriac 9:367
Kurt Vonnegut, Jr. 3:504;
4:565

**Mellen, Joan**
Ingmar Bergman 16:71
Luis Buñuel 16:135
Jean-Luc Godard 20:142
Kon Ichikawa 20:185
Akira Kurosawa 16:403
Elaine May 16:434
Nagisa Oshima 20:253, 255
Eric Rohmer 16:533
Carlos Saura 20:314

**Mellers, Wilfrid**
Bob Dylan 12:187
John Lennon and Paul
McCartney 12:374

**Mellor, Isha**
Sol Yurick 6:583

**Mellors, John**
Martin Amis 4:20
Louis Auchincloss 6:15
Beryl Bainbridge 10:17
Thomas Berger 5:60
Caroline Blackwood 9:101
Dirk Bogarde 19:43
Melvyn Bragg 10:72
Angela Carter 5:102
Peter De Vries 7:77
Shusaku Endo 7:96; 14:160
Penelope Fitzgerald 19:173
John Fowles 6:188
Herbert Gold 14:208
John Hawkes 7:141

Mark Helprin 10:260
Rolf Hochhuth 18:256
Ursula Holden 18:258
Dan Jacobson 4:253
Ruth Prawer Jhabvala 8:312
G. Josipovici 6:270
Bernard Malamud 5:269
Olivia Manning 19:303
Ian McEwan 13:370
Stanley Middleton 7:219
Yukio Mishima 4:357
Brian Moore 19:334
Alberto Moravia 7:244
Iris Murdoch 4:369
Julia O'Faolain 6:382; 19:360
Sean O'Faoláin 14:407
V. S. Pritchett 5:353
Frederic Raphael 14:438
Piers Paul Read 4:444; 10:435
J. R. Salamanca 15:464
William Sansom 6:484
Nathalie Sarraute 10:460
Penelope Shuttle 7:422
Alan Sillitoe 6:499; 19:420
Wole Soyinka 5:398
Richard G. Stern 4:523
David Storey 8:504
Ludvík Vaculík 7:495
John Wain 15:561
Charles Webb 7:516
Patrick White 5:48

**Mellown, Elgin W.**
Jean Rhys 2:373
John Wain 2:458

**Melly, George**
Jean Arp 5:33

**Melnyk, George**
Andrew Suknaski 19:432

**Meltzer, R.**
John Lennon and Paul
McCartney 12:382
Jim Morrison 17:290
Patti Smith 12:538

**Melville, Robert**
Herbert Read 4:438
Susan Sontag 13:515

**Mendelsohn, John Ned**
David Bowie 17:57, 58
Jimmy Page and Robert Plant
12:473, 474
Peter Townshend 17:527
Neil Young 17:570

**Mendelson, David**
Eugène Ionesco 6:255

**Mendelson, Edward**
John Berryman 4:61
Thomas Pynchon 3:415; 6:439

**Mengeling, Marvin E.**
Ray Bradbury 1:42

**Mephisto**
Maya Deren 16:252

**Mercer, Peter**
John Barth 9:61

**Merchant, W. Moelwyn**
R. S. Thomas 13:542

**Mercier, Jean F.**
Ruth M. Arthur 12:27
Melvin Berger 12:42
Betty Cavanna 12:103
Jamake Highwater 12:288
M. E. Kerr 12:300
Madeleine L'Engle 12:352
Katherine Paterson 12:484, 486
Rosemary Wells 12:637

**Mercier, Vivian**
Samuel Beckett 6:38; 14:79
Michel Butor 11:78
Harry Crews 6:118
J. P. Donleavy 4:125
E. M. Forster 2:135
George V. Higgins 4:222
Aldous Huxley 5:193
Iris Murdoch 4:368
Raymond Queneau 5:360
Alain Robbe-Grillet 6:465
Nathalie Sarraute 4:466
Claude Simon 4:496

**Meredith, William**
John Berryman 2:59; 3:68
Anthony Hecht 8:268
Robert Lowell 2:248
Muriel Rukeyser 10:442

**Merideth, Robert**
Norman Mailer 1:192

**Meritt, Carole**
Alex Haley 12:250

**Merivale, Patricia**
Vladimir Nabokov 1:242

**Merkin, Daphne**
Ann Beattie 13:65
André Brink 18:68
Michael Brodsky 19:69
A. S. Byatt 19:77
Vincent Canby 13:132
Joan Didion 14:152
Jacob Epstein 19:162
Penelope Gilliatt 13:239
Thomas Keneally 14:302
Ella Leffland 19:278
A. G. Mojtabai 15:378
Jayne Anne Phillips 15:421
Chaim Potok 7:321
V. S. Pritchett 15:443
Philip Roth 15:452
John Updike 13:559; 15:546

**Mermier, Guy**
Françoise Sagan 17:424

**Merriam, Eve**
Jacques Prévert 15:440

**Merrick, Gordon**
Truman Capote 19:82

**Merrill, James**
Francis Ponge 18:415

**Merrill, Reed B.**
William H. Gass 8:245

**Merrill, Robert**
Vladimir Nabokov 15:396
Kurt Vonnegut, Jr. 8:534

**Merrill, Thomas F.**
Allen Ginsberg 1:118
Charles Olson 11:417

**Merry, Bruce**
Mario Luzi 13:352
Elio Vittorini 14:544

**Mersand, Joseph**
Elmer Rice 7:359

**Mersmann, James F.**
Robert Bly 5:62
Robert Duncan 4:142
Allen Ginsberg 4:182
Denise Levertov 5:247
Diane Wakoski 7:507

**Merton, Thomas**
Albert Camus 1:52
J. F. Powers 1:281

**Meserve, Walter**
James Baldwin 17:36

**Mesher, David R.**
Bernard Malamud 9:346;
11:353

**Mesic, Michael**
James Dickey 4:121
Chester Kallman 2:221

**Mesnet, Marie-Béatrice**
Graham Greene 3:210

**Messer, Bill**
Peter Dickinson 12:171

**Metcalf, Paul**
Charles Olson 9:413

**Metzger, C. R.**
Lawrence Ferlinghetti 10:176

**Mews, Siegfried**
Carl Zuckmayer 18:553, 557

**Mewshaw, Michael**
Jonathan Baumbach 6:31
Doris Betts 3:73
Robertson Davies 7:74
William Eastlake 8:200
B. H. Friedman 7:108
Graham Greene 18:195
Robert F. Jones 7:192
Stephen King 12:310
David Slavitt 5:391
Raymond Sokolov 7:430
Peter Spielberg 6:519
Robert Lewis Taylor 14:534
Paul Theroux 5:427

**Meyer, Ellen Hope**
Erica Jong 4:264
Joyce Carol Oates 2:315

**Meyer, Karl E.**
Garry Marshall 17:278
Frederick Wiseman 20:475

**Meyer, Marianne**
Joan Armatrading 17:10

**Meyer, Michael**
Harry Martinson 14:356

**Meyer, Thomas**
Lorine Niedecker 10:360

**Meyers, Jeffrey**
E. M. Forster 3:162; 4:169
Doris Lessing 2:241
André Malraux 4:333

**Meyers, Robert B.**
Robert Altman 16:26

**Mezan, Peter**
Ken Russell 16:544

**Mezey, Robert**
Jerome Rothenberg 6:478
Gary Snyder 9:498

**Michaels, Leonard**
John Barth 2:37
Samuel Beckett 11:43
Thomas Berger 11:46
Jorge Luis Borges 2:77
Dashiell Hammett 5:160
Peter Handke 8:264
Joseph Heller 11:269
Erica Jong 8:314
Bernard Malamud 3:324
Peter Matthiessen 11:361
Vladimir Nabokov 8:417

**Michaels, Robert G.**
Woody Allen 16:3

**Michalczyk, John J.**
Fernando Arrabal 18:23

**Michałek, Bolesław**
Andrzej Wajda 16:581

**Michel, Sonya**
Joan Micklin Silver 20:342

**Michelson, Aaron I.**
Martha Gellhorn 14:196

**Michelson, Bruce**
Richard Wilbur 14:579

**Michener, Charles**
Albert Maysles and David
Maysles 16:444

**Michener, Charles T.**
Anthony Powell 3:402; 7:343

**Middlebrook, Diane**
Allen Ginsberg 6:199

**Miesel, Sandra**
Poul Anderson 15:11

**Mihailovich, Vasa D.**
Miroslav Krleža 8:330
Vasko Popa 19:373, 375

**Miklitsch, Robert**
Robert Hass 18:211

**Milano, Paolo**
Riccardo Bacchelli 19:32

**Milch, Robert J.**
Chaim Potok 2:338

**Milder, Robert**
Flannery O'Connor 13:417

**Mileck, Joseph**
Hermann Hesse 17:198

**Miles, G. E.**
Betty Smith 19:423

**Miles, Keith**
Günter Grass 15:259

**Miles, William**
Langston Hughes 1:148

**Milford, Nancy**
Louise Bogan 4:69

**Millar, Daniel**
Jean Renoir 20:297

**Millar, Gavin**
Robert Altman 16:42
Lindsay Anderson 20:13
Ingmar Bergman 16:80
Claude Chabrol 16:172, 184
Michael Cimino 16:210

**Millar, Margaret**
Daphne du Maurier 6:146

**Millar, Neil**
David Harry Walker 14:552

**Millar, Sylvia**
Erskine Caldwell 14:95
Carlos Saura 20:315

**Miller, Adam David**
Alex Haley 12:249

**Miller, Alice**
Rosemary Wells 12:637

**Miller, Baxter**
Langston Hughes 10:282

**Miller, Charles L.**
Joy Adamson 17:4

**Miller, David**
Michael Hamburger 5:158

**Miller, Gabriel**
Alfred Hitchcock 16:353

**Miller, Henry**
Luis Buñuel 16:127
Blaise Cendrars 18:91
Anaïs Nin 14:379

**Miller, James E., Jr.**
William Faulkner 6:180
J. D. Salinger 1:298; 12:496

**Miller, Jane**
Ursula Holden 18:257
Julius Horwitz 14:267
Alain Robbe-Grillet 14:462
Simone Schwarz-Bart 7:404

**Miller, Jeanne-Marie A.**
Imamu Amiri Baraka 2:35
Gwendolyn Brooks 1:46; 4:78
Charles Gordone 4:198

**Miller, Jim**
Jimmy Page and Robert Plant
12:477
Bruce Springsteen 17:482, 485
Brian Wilson 12:644, 648
Neil Young 17:571

**Miller, Jim Wayne**
Jesse Stuart 11:513

**Miller, Jordan Y.**
Lorraine Hansberry 17:188

**Miller, Karl**
Kingsley Amis 13:14
Martin Amis 4:21
James Baldwin 17:28
John Berger 19:38
Paula Fox 8:218
Ted Hughes 4:236

Dan Jacobson 4:256
Hugh MacDiarmid 2:254
Flann O'Brien 5:316
Barbara Pym 13:470
Anne Roiphe 9:456
Emma Tennant 13:537
Paul Theroux 11:530
Michel Tournier 6:538

**Miller, Mark**
Sam Peckinpah 20:279

**Miller, Neil**
Julio Cortázar 2:103

**Miller, Nolan**
Henry Bromell 5:73
Tillie Olsen 13:433

**Miller, R. Baxter**
Langston Hughes 15:293

**Miller, Sara**
Anne McCaffrey 17:283

**Miller, Stephen**
Zbigniew Herbert 9:272

**Miller, Tom P.**
William Stafford 4:521

**Miller, Vincent**
T. S. Eliot 9:182
Ezra Pound 13:462

**Millgate, Michael**
James Gould Cozzens 4:114
John Dos Passos 4:133

**Millichap, Joseph R.**
Carson McCullers 12:428

**Milliken, Stephen F.**
Chester Himes 18:247

**Mills, James**
George V. Higgins 4:222

**Mills, John**
John Arden 13:26

**Mills, Nicolaus**
Joan Micklin Silver 20:344

**Mills, Ralph J., Jr.**
Yves Bonnefoy 9:112
René Char 9:160
Lucille Clifton 19:109
Richard Eberhart 3:134, 135
David Ignatow 7:174, 179
Maxine Kumin 5:222
Denise Levertov 2:243; 3:293
Philip Levine 4:287
Kathleen Raine 7:351
Theodore Roethke 1:291
Anne Stevenson 7:462
Jonathan Williams 13:600

**Millstein, Gilbert**
Irvin Faust 8:215
John R. Tunis 12:598

**Milne, Tom**
Robert Altman 16:42
Ingmar Bergman 16:54, 55
Robert Bresson 16:112, 119
Mel Brooks 12:79
Claude Chabrol 16:175, 178
René Clair 20:68
Francis Ford Coppola 16:232

Vittorio De Sica 20:97
Bob Fosse 20:121
Jean-Luc Godard 20:129, 131
Kon Ichikawa 20:179, 181, 183
Stanley Kubrick 16:379
Akira Kurosawa 16:404
Rouben Mamoulian 16:424
John Osborne 5:330
Yasujiro Ozu 16:447
Gordon Parks 16:459
Sam Peckinpah 20:273
Roman Polanski 16:463
Satyajit Ray 16:483, 487, 488,
495
Jean Renoir 20:292, 293
Martin Scorsese 20:330, 331
Steven Spielberg 20:357, 358
Josef von Sternberg 20:377
Andrzej Wajda 16:578
Peter Weir 20:425
Orson Welles 20:442

**Milne, W. Gordon**
John Dos Passos 4:134

**Milner-Gulland, Robin**
Andrei Voznesensky 1:349
Yevgeny Yevtushenko 1:381

**Milosh, Joseph**
John Gardner 10:220

**Milton, Edith**
Beryl Bainbridge 10:17
Frederick Buechner 9:136
Nadine Gordimer 18:190
Alison Lurie 18:311
Olivia Manning 19:303
V. S. Naipaul 18:361
Alan Sillitoe 10:477
William Styron 15:528

**Milton, John R.**
Vardis Fisher 7:105
N. Scott Momaday 2:290
James Welch 14:558

**Milton, Joyce**
Jules Feiffer 8:217

**Milun, Richard A.**
William Faulkner 6:177

**Milward, John**
David Bowie 17:65

**Mindlin, M.**
Yehuda Amichai 9:22

**Miner, Robert G., Jr.**
Charles M. Schulz 12:529

**Minogue, Valerie**
Michel Butor 11:82
Alain Robbe-Grillet 10:437
Nathalie Sarraute 10:458

**Mintz, Alan**
Yoram Kaniuk 19:240

**Miroff, Bruce**
Neil Young 17:569

**Mirsky, Mark J.**
John Hawkes 7:145

**Mirsky, Mark Jay**
Samuel Beckett **6**:38
Anthony Burgess **4**:83
Günter Grass **4**:205
Flann O'Brien **5**:314
Manuel Puig **3**:407

**Mishima, Yukio**
Yasunari Kawabata **18**:280

**Mitchell, A.C.W.**
Kenneth Slessor **14**:497

**Mitchell, Gregg**
Paul Simon **17**:460
Bruce Springsteen **17**:476, 478

**Mitchell, Julian**
Ivy Compton-Burnett **10**:110

**Mitchell, Juliet**
Norman Mailer **1**:192

**Mitchell, Loften**
Alice Childress **12**:104

**Mitchell, Marilyn L.**
John Steinbeck **9**:516

**Mitchell, Penelope M.**
Roy A. Gallant **17**:128, 130
Christie Harris **12**:263

**Mitchell, W.J.T.**
Hubert Selby, Jr. **4**:481

**Mitchison, Naomi**
W. H. Auden **9**:57

**Mitgang, Herbert**
Giorgio Bassani **9**:75
Michael Mott **15**:379
Carl Sandburg **15**:468
Leonardo Sciascia **9**:475

**Mittleman, Leslie B.**
Kingsley Amis **8**:11

**Mitton, Pat**
Christie Harris **12**:265

**Miyoshi, Masao**
Yasunari Kawabata **9**:311

**Mizejewski, Linda**
James Dickey **15**:174

**Mizener, Arthur**
James Gould Cozzens **4**:115
John Dos Passos **4**:133
Anthony Hecht **8**:266
Anthony Powell **10**:408
J. D. Salinger **12**:501
James Thurber **5**:439
Edmund Wilson **2**:475

**Mo, Timothy**
Jennifer Johnston **7**:186
John le Carré **5**:234
Colin MacInnes **4**:35
Wilfrid Sheed **4**:489
Harriet Waugh **6**:559

**Moeller, Hans-Bernhard**
Peter Weiss **15**:563

**Moers, Ellen**
Lillian Hellman **2**:187
Adrienne Rich **18**:447

**Moffett, Judith**
Daniel Hoffman **13**:287
James Merrill **13**:376; **18**:329

**Mojtabai, A. G.**
Yasunari Kawabata **5**:208
Thomas Keneally **5**:211
Joyce Carol Oates **15**:402
Anne Tyler **18**:530
Richard Yates **8**:555

**Mok, Michael**
Aleksandr I. Solzhenitsyn **2**:409

**Mole, John**
Ted Hughes **14**:271
Louis Simpson **7**:428
R. S. Thomas **6**:530; **13**:545
Theodore Weiss **14**:555

**Molesworth, Charles**
John Ashbery **15**:26
John Berryman **2**:56; **8**:89
Robert Bly **15**:64
Hayden Carruth **18**:89
Robert Hass **18**:210
Ted Hughes **4**:236
Erica Jong **18**:278
Donald Justice **19**:233
Galway Kinnell **3**:269
Leslie Norris **14**:387
Michael Ondaatje **14**:410
Marge Piercy **14**:421
Robert Pinsky **19**:369
Anne Sexton **8**:483
Charles Tomlinson **4**:548

**Molina, Ida**
Antonio Buero Vallejo **15**:103

**Molloy, F. C.**
John McGahern **9**:370

**Molnar, Thomas**
Françoise Sagan **17**:419

**Moloney, Michael F.**
François Mauriac **4**:337

**Momaday, N. Scott**
Dee Brown **18**:70
Jamake Highwater **12**:288

**Momberger, Philip**
William Faulkner **6**:179

**Monaco, James**
Woody Allen **16**:15
John Cassavetes **20**:54
Claude Chabrol **16**:182
Francis Ford Coppola **16**:248
Jean-Luc Godard **20**:148
Richard Lester **20**:228
Gordon Parks **16**:460
Alain Resnais **16**:511
Martin Scorsese **20**:333
Andrew Sinclair **14**:489
Steven Spielberg **20**:359, 365
François Truffaut **20**:399
Melvin Van Peebles **20**:412

**Monagan, John S.**
Anthony Powell **7**:342

**Monas, Sidney**
Ilya Ehrenburg **18**:134
Aleksandr I. Solzhenitsyn **4**:511
Andrei Voznesensky **15**:552

**Mondello, Salvatore**
Stan Lee **17**:259

**Monegal, Emir Rodríguez-**
See Rodríguez-Monegal, Emir

**Monet, Christina**
Mark Medoff **6**:323

**Monguió, Luis**
Rafael Alberti **7**:8

**Monheit, Albert**
Roy A. Gallant **17**:126

**Monley, Keith**
Frederick Busch **18**:86
Ella Leffland **19**:279

**Monogue, Valerie**
Harold Pinter **6**:404

**Monroe, Harriet**
Marianne Moore **19**:335

**Monsman, Gerald**
J.R.R. Tolkien **1**:339

**Montagnes, Anne**
Phyllis Gotlieb **18**:192
Brian Moore **5**:297
Audrey Thomas **13**:538

**Montague, John**
Thomas Kinsella **19**:251
Hugh MacDiarmid **11**:333

**Monteiro, George**
Bob Dylan **4**:149
Robert Frost **4**:174; **10**:199
Ernest Hemingway **6**:231

**Montgomery, Marion**
T. S. Eliot **6**:163
Robert Frost **10**:195
Flannery O'Connor **1**:258

**Montgomery, Niall**
Flann O'Brien **7**:269

**Moody, Michael**
Mario Vargas Llosa **9**:544

**Moody, Richard**
Lillian Hellman **18**:221

**Moon, Eric**
Frederic Raphael **14**:436

**Mooney, Philip**
Albert Camus **14**:115

**Mooney, Stephen**
Josephine Miles **14**:368

**Moorcock, Michael**
Angus Wilson **3**:535

**Moore, Anne Carroll**
Margot Benary-Isbert **12**:30

**Moore, Brian**
Robertson Davies **2**:113

**Moore, D. B.**
Louis MacNeice **4**:316

**Moore, Gerald**
Chinua Achebe **11**:1

**Moore, Harry T.**
Arthur Adamov **4**:5
Kay Boyle **5**:65
John Dos Passos **4**:132
E. M. Forster **1**:106
Herbert Gold **4**:190
Rolf Hochhuth **18**:250
Eugène Ionesco **4**:252

James Jones **3**:262
Meyer Levin **7**:204
Henry Miller **4**:350
Alain Robbe-Grillet **2**:374
Nathalie Sarraute **2**:384
Georges Simenon **2**:397
Claude Simon **4**:494
John Steinbeck **5**:405

**Moore, Honor**
Marilyn Hacker **5**:156
June Jordan **5**:203

**Moore, Hugo**
Hugh MacDiarmid **4**:311

**Moore, Jack B.**
Carson McCullers **12**:425
Frank Yerby **7**:556

**Moore, John Rees**
James Baldwin **2**:31
Samuel Beckett **10**:29
J. P. Donleavy **1**:76; **4**:124
Robert Penn Warren **6**:558

**Moore, Marianne**
E. E. Cummings **12**:141
Ezra Pound **7**:322
Edith Sitwell **9**:493
William Carlos Williams **13**:601

**Moore, Maxine**
Isaac Asimov **9**:49

**Moore, Michael**
William Wharton **18**:543

**Moore, Richard**
George Garrett **3**:192

**Moore, Stephen C.**
John Cheever **7**:49
Robert Lowell **3**:301

**Moore, T. Inglis**
Kenneth Slessor **14**:495

**Moorman, Charles**
C. S. Lewis **14**:323
J.R.R. Tolkien **1**:337

**Moramarco, Fred**
John Ashbery **4**:22; **9**:42
Robert Creeley **1**:67
David Ignatow **7**:181
Galway Kinnell **2**:229
W. S. Merwin **1**:213
Frank O'Hara **13**:424
Ezra Pound **18**:425
James Schevill **7**:401

**Moran, Ronald**
Wendell Berry **4**:59
Robert Creeley **4**:117
David Ignatow **4**:248
Marge Piercy **6**:402
Louis Simpson **4**:498
James Tate **6**:528

**Moravia, Alberto**
Truman Capote **13**:132

**Mordas, Phyllis G.**
Melvin Berger **12**:40

**Morel, Jean-Pierre**
André Breton **15**:88

**Morello-Frosch, Marta**
Julio Cortázar 2:104
Gabriel García Márquez 3:183

**Morgan, Edwin**
John Berryman 10:47
James Blish 14:83
Anthony Burgess 15:104
Ilya Ehrenburg 18:137
Hugh MacDiarmid 11:338
Eugenio Montale 9:387
Rudolph Wurlitzer 15:587

**Morgan, Ellen**
Doris Lessing 3:288

**Morgan, John**
Günter Grass 6:209

**Morgan, Robert**
Geoffrey Hill 8:294

**Morgan, Speer**
Dan Jacobson 4:256

**Morgan, Ted**
Norman Mailer 14:354
Alice Munro 19:346

**Morgenstern, Dan**
Frank Zappa 17:587

**Morgenstern, Joseph**
Gordon Parks 16:458
Melvin Van Peebles 20:410

**Moritz, A. F.**
Andrew Suknaski 19:433

**Morley, Patricia A.**
Margaret Atwood 13:41
Patrick White 7:529

**Morley, Sheridan**
Terence Rattigan 7:354

**Morrell, A. C.**
Jean Rhys 19:390

**Morris, Alice**
Christina Stead 2:422

**Morris, C. B.**
Rafael Alberti 7:9
Vicente Aleixandre 9:12

**Morris, Christopher D.**
John Barth 7:23

**Morris, George**
Brian De Palma 20:82
Eric Rohmer 16:539
Martin Scorsese 20:329
Billy Wilder 20:466

**Morris, H. H.**
Dashiell Hammett 10:253

**Morris, Harry**
Louise Bogan 4:68
James Dickey 1:73
Jean Garrigue 2:154
John Hollander 2:197
George MacBeth 2:251
Louis Simpson 4:498

**Morris, Ivan**
Yasunari Kawabata 2:222

**Morris, Jan**
Laurens van der Post 5:464

**Morris, Jeff**
Robert Francis 15:238

**Morris, John N.**
Ai 14:7
Kenneth O. Hanson 13:263
Donald Justice 6:271
Adrienne Rich 7:370
Mark Strand 6:521
Nancy Willard 7:539
Charles Wright 6:580; 13:612

**Morris, Robert K.**
Anthony Burgess 4:81; 5:86
Lawrence Durrell 4:146
John Fowles 6:189
James Hanley 5:167
Doris Lessing 6:290
Olivia Manning 5:271
Anthony Powell 1:278; 3:404;
7:345
V. S. Pritchett 5:354
C. P. Snow 6:515
Thornton Wilder 6:578

**Morris, Wesley**
John Crowe Ransom 4:433

**Morris, Wright**
Ernest Hemingway 1:141

**Morrison, Blake**
Beryl Bainbridge 14:37
André Brink 18:69
Donald Davie 10:124
Jacob Epstein 19:162
Gabriel García Márquez
15:252
Patricia Highsmith 14:261
Thomas Keneally 14:301
Eugenio Montale 18:343
Anaïs Nin 14:386
Robert Pinsky 19:370
Frederic Raphael 14:438
Andrew Sinclair 14:489
Yevgeny Yevtushenko 13:620

**Morrison, Harriet**
Frank Bonham 12:53

**Morrison, J. Allan**
Leon Garfield 12:226, 234

**Morrison, J. M.**
Hugh MacDiarmid 2:254

**Morrison, John W.**
Jun'ichirō Tanizaki 8:509

**Morrison, Lillian**
Eilís Dillon 17:93
Mary Stolz 12:549, 551

**Morrison, Philip**
Roy A. Gallant 17:129
Christie Harris 12:262
Larry Kettelkamp 12:304

**Morrison, Phylis**
Roy A. Gallant 17:129
Christie Harris 12:262
Larry Kettelkamp 12:304

**Morrison, Theodore**
Robert Frost 1:111

**Morrissette, Bruce**
Alain Robbe-Grillet 1:27;
14:455

**Morrissey, Daniel**
John Updike 7:488

**Morrow, Lance**
John Fowles 6:187
Erica Jong 8:314
Yasunari Kawabata 5:208
James A. Michener 5:290
Yukio Mishima 4:356, 358

**Morse, J. Mitchell**
Kingsley Amis 2:6
James Baldwin 2:32
Richard Elman 19:150
Bruce Jay Friedman 3:165
Joanne Greenberg 7:134
Jakov Lind 2:245
Mary McCarthy 1:207
Vladimir Nabokov 2:299
Peter Weiss 3:514

**Morse, Jonathan**
John Dos Passos 11:156

**Morse, Samuel French**
W. H. Auden 6:18
Margaret Avison 2:29
John Berryman 3:65
Robert Lowell 3:301
Louis Zukofsky 1:385

**Morthland, John**
Bob Marley 17:269

**Mortifoglio, Richard**
Laura Nyro 17:320

**Mortimer, John**
James Thurber 5:433

**Mortimer, Penelope**
Elizabeth Bishop 9:89
Nadine Gordimer 7:132
Fay Weldon 6:562
Tom Wolfe 15:586

**Mortimore, Roger**
Carlos Saura 20:315

**Morton, Donald E.**
Vladimir Nabokov 15:390

**Morton, Frederic**
Richard Elman 19:149

**Moscoso-Gongora, Peter**
José Lezama Lima 10:319

**Moser, Gerald M.**
José Rodrigues Miguéis
10:340

**Moses, Carole**
Ernest Hemingway 19:220

**Moses, Edwin**
Albert Camus 9:148

**Moses, Joseph**
E. L. Doctorow 11:140

**Moses, Robbie Odom**
Edward Albee 11:12

**Moses, Wilson J.**
W.E.B. DuBois 13:182

**Mosher, Harold F., Jr.**
Paul Simon 17:462

**Mosher, John**
Alfred Hitchcock 16:338

**Moskowitz, Moshe**
Chaim Grade 10:248

**Moskowitz, Sam**
John Wyndham 19:474

**Mosley, Nicholas**
J. P. Donleavy 10:155

**Moss, Elaine**
Margaret Craven 17:80
Madeleine L'Engle 12:347

**Moss, Howard**
W. H. Auden 6:20
Elizabeth Bishop 1:35; 9:91
Elizabeth Bowen 1:41; 3:84
Graham Greene 6:217
Flann O'Brien 1:252
Katherine Anne Porter 1:272
Jean Rhys 6:454
Nathalie Sarraute 1:302
Eudora Welty 2:463

**Moss, Leonard**
Arthur Miller 1:217

**Moss, Robert F.**
John Berryman 13:76
Lawrence Durrell 6:153
John O'Hara 6:384
Richard Wright 14:596

**Moss, Stanley**
Stanley J. Kunitz 6:286

**Mossman, Elliott**
Boris Pasternak 10:382

**Motion, Andrew**
Buchi Emecheta 14:159
John Hollander 14:265
Thomas Keneally 19:247
Seán O'Faoláin 14:407

**Motley, Joel**
Leon Forrest 4:164

**Mott, Michael**
A. R. Ammons 8:15
Geoffrey Grigson 7:135
Elizabeth Jennings 14:292
David Jones 7:186
D. M. Thomas 13:541
Charles Tomlinson 13:545

**Mottram, Eric**
Fielding Dawson 6:126
Carolyn Kizer 15:309
Michael McClure 6:317
Arthur Miller 1:218
Gilbert Sorrentino 7:449
Diane Wakoski 4:572
Jonathan Williams 13:601

**Moulton, Priscilla L.**
E. M. Almedingen 12:1
Christie Harris 12:262
Lee Kingman 17:245
Mary Renault 17:397

**Mount, Ferdinand**
Peter Handke 10:257
Bernice Rubens 19:403

**Movius, Geoffrey H.**
William Carlos Williams 9:575

**Moyer, Charles R.**
Jonathan Kozol 17:250

**Moyer, Kermit**
Robert Altman **16**:34

**Moynahan, Julian**
Louis Auchincloss **9**:54
Frederick Buechner **9**:137
Anthony Burgess **8**:113
J. P. Donleavy **4**:126
Ernest J. Gaines **11**:218
John Irving **13**:293
Jack Kerouac **2**:228
Ken Kesey **6**:277
John le Carré **15**:326
Tom McHale **3**:331
A. G. Mojtabai **15**:378
Brian Moore **3**:341; **8**:394
Seán O'Faoláin **7**:274; **14**:404
Anne Roiphe **9**:455
Karl Shapiro **15**:477
Wilfrid Sheed **10**:472
James Tate **2**:431
John Wain **15**:562
William Wharton **18**:542

**Moynihan, Julian**
Alan Sillitoe **19**:421
C. P. Snow **19**:428
James Thurber **11**:532

**Możejko, Edward**
Elisaveta Bagryana **10**:13

**Muchnic, Helen**
Ilya Ehrenburg **18**:137
Mikhail Sholokhov **7**:418, 421
Aleksandr I. Solzhenitsyn **9**:507

**Mudrick, Marvin**
Donald Barthelme **2**:39
William S. Burroughs **2**:90
E. M. Forster **2**:135
John Fowles **2**:137
Jerzy Kosinski **2**:231
Doris Lessing **2**:239
Norman Mailer **1**:192
Bernard Malamud **1**:200
Vladimir Nabokov **3**:355
Joyce Carol Oates **2**:314
Nathalie Sarraute **2**:384; **4**:468
David Wagoner **3**:508

**Mudrovic, Mike**
Claudio Rodríguez **10**:440

**Mueller, Lisel**
Robert Bly **1**:37
Louise Glück **7**:118
Michael S. Harper **7**:138
Jim Harrison **6**:223
Anthony Hecht **8**:268
W. S. Merwin **1**:212
Marge Piercy **6**:401
Peter Viereck **4**:559
Alice Walker **6**:553
Reed Whittemore **4**:588

**Muggeridge, Malcolm**
Paul Scott **9**:478

**Mulhallen, Karen**
Audrey Thomas **13**:538

**Mullen, Patrick B.**
E. E. Cummings **12**:157

**Mullen, Richard D.**
James Blish **14**:82

**Muller, Gilbert H.**
William Faulkner **8**:212

**Müller-Bergh, Klaus**
José Lezama Lima **4**:288

**Mullin, Michael**
Orson Welles **20**:451

**Mumford, Olive**
Larry Kettelkamp **12**:304

**Munk, Erika**
Martin Duberman **8**:185
Peter Handke **15**:268
David Rudkin **14**:471
Elizabeth Swados **12**:560, 561
Lanford Wilson **14**:591

**Murch, Anne C.**
Arthur Kopit **18**:287

**Murchison, John C.**
Jorge Luis Borges **2**:71, 75

**Murchison, W., Jr.**
John Dickson Carr **3**:101

**Murchland, Bernard**
Albert Camus **2**:97
Jean-Paul Sartre **7**:396

**Murdoch, Brian**
Heinrich Böll **15**:68

**Murdoch, Charles**
John Glassco **9**:236

**Murdoch, Iris**
A. S. Byatt **19**:76

**Murdock, Kenneth B.**
Esther Forbes **12**:203

**Murillo, L. A.**
Jorge Luis Borges **4**:70

**Murphy, Brian**
Luis Buñuel **16**:134
Eric Rohmer **16**:529

**Murphy, Catherine A.**
Mary Lavin **18**:306

**Murphy, Mrs. J. M.**
Honor Arundel **17**:14

**Murphy, Reverend James M.**
Carlos Fuentes **13**:232

**Murphy, Joan**
Colin Thiele **17**:495

**Murphy, Richard**
Thom Gunn **18**:203
Philip Larkin **5**:231

**Murphy, Robert**
Allan W. Eckert **17**:104

**Murr, Judy Smith**
John Gardner **10**:219

**Murra, John V.**
Amos Tutuola **14**:537

**Murray, Atholl C.C.**
David Jones **7**:188

**Murray, Charles Shaar**
Peter Townshend **17**:533

**Murray, Donald C.**
James Baldwin **13**:53

**Murray, Edward**
Samuel Beckett **6**:35
William Faulkner **6**:176
Ernest Hemingway **6**:229
Eugène Ionesco **6**:251
Arthur Miller **6**:327, 332
Alain Robbe-Grillet **6**:466
Tennessee Williams **5**:501

**Murray, G. E.**
Ai **14**:9
Anthony Hecht **13**:269
Howard Moss **14**:376
Michael Ondaatje **14**:410
Robert Pack **13**:439
Derek Walcott **14**:550

**Murray, Jack**
Alain Robbe-Grillet **1**:287

**Murray, John J.**
Robert Penn Warren **4**:579

**Murray, Michael**
Edward Albee **2**:3

**Murray, Michele**
Robert Cormier **12**:134
Paula Fox **2**:140
Susan B. Hill **4**:227
Robert Kotlowitz **4**:275
Pär Lagerkvist **7**:200
Mary Lavin **4**:282
William Mayne **12**:399
Grace Paley **4**:392

**Murray, Philip**
Aldous Huxley **3**:256

**Murray, Thomas J.**
Mary Lavin **18**:302

**Murray, William J.**
Melvin Berger **12**:38

**Murtaugh, Daniel M.**
Marie-Claire Blais **4**:67
Eilís Dillon **17**:100
Wilfrid Sheed **2**:393

**Mus, David**
T. S. Eliot **2**:129

**Musher, Andrea**
Diane Wakoski **7**:505

**Muske, Carol**
Jon Anderson **9**:31
Lucille Clifton **19**:110
Adrienne Rich **18**:448
Charles Wright **13**:613

**Mutiso, Gideon-Cyrus M.**
Alex La Guma **19**:272

**Myers, Andrew B.**
Alan Garner **17**:137

**Myers, Robert J.**
Lothar-Günther Buchheim **6**:100

**Myers, Tim**
Arthur C. Clarke **18**:107
Nicholas Delbanco **13**:175

**Myles, Lynda**
George Lucas **16**:416

**Myrsiades, Kostas**
Yannis Ritsos **6**:463; **13**:487, 488

**Nadeau, Maurice**
Louis Aragon **3**:13
Simone de Beauvoir **1**:19
Samuel Beckett **1**:22
Michel Butor **1**:49
Albert Camus **1**:54
Louis-Ferdinand Céline **1**:56
Jean Genet **1**:115
Jean Giono **4**:185
Raymond Queneau **2**:359
Alain Robbe-Grillet **1**:288
Françoise Sagan **3**:444
Nathalie Sarraute **1**:303
Jean-Paul Sartre **1**:305
Claude Simon **4**:495

**Nadeau, Robert L.**
Djuna Barnes **11**:29

**Naiden, James**
Lorine Niedecker **10**:360

**Naipaul, Shiva**
Miguel Ángel Asturias **8**:27
José Donoso **4**:130

**Naipaul, V. S.**
Jorge Luis Borges **2**:77
P. H. Newby **13**:407
Jean Rhys **2**:372
Françoise Sagan **17**:422

**Nalley, Richard**
Donald Hall **13**:259

**Namjoshi, Suniti**
Jay Macpherson **14**:347
P. K. Page **18**:377

**Nance, William L.**
Truman Capote **13**:133

**Nance, William L., S.M.**
Katherine Anne Porter **7**:314

**Napolin, Leah**
E. M. Broner **19**:71

**Nardi, Marcia**
Babette Deutsch **18**:118

**Nardin, Jane**
Evelyn Waugh **8**:544

**Nardo, A. K.**
C. S. Lewis **14**:325

**Naremore, James**
John Huston **20**:172
Philip Larkin **5**:226

**Nassar, Eugene Paul**
Ezra Pound **7**:335

**Nathan, George Jean**
Noel Coward **9**:171
Lillian Hellman **18**:220
Terence Rattigan **7**:353
Elmer Rice **7**:359
George Tabori **19**:437

**Natov, Roni**
Leon Garfield **12**:239

**Naughton, John**
A. Alvarez **13**:9
Beryl Bainbridge **18**:33
John Berger **19**:38
Ursula Holden **18**:258

**Navarro, Carlos**
Jorge Luis Borges **3**:79

**Navasky, Victor S.**
Jules Archer **12**:21
Meyer Levin **7**:204

**Navone, John J.**
Federico Fellini **16**:273

**Nazareth, Peter**
James Ngugi **7**:266

**Nebecker, Helen E.**
Shirley Jackson **11**:302

**Necker, Walter**
Joy Adamson **17**:2

**Needleman, Ruth**
Octavio Paz **3**:375

**Neil, J. Meredith**
Jack Kerouac **14**:306

**Neimark, Paul G.**
Agatha Christie **1**:58

**Neiswender, Rosemary**
E. M. Almedingen **12**:4

**Nekrich, Alexsandr**
Alexander Zinoviev **19**:485

**Nelson, Alix**
Nora Ephron **17**:111
Mary Rodgers **12**:494

**Nelson, Anne**
Jonathan Kozol **17**:254

**Nelson, Dorothy H.**
Esther Forbes **12**:211

**Nelson, Howard**
Robert Bly **10**:54
Robert Francis **15**:237

**Nelson, Hugh**
Harold Pinter **6**:413

**Nelson, Joyce**
Frank Capra **16**:161
Kurt Vonnegut, Jr. **4**:562

**Nelson, Paul**
David Bowie **17**:64
John Lennon and Paul
McCartney **12**:378
Willie Nelson **17**:303
Paul Simon **17**:465
Patti Smith **12**:538
Bruce Springsteen **17**:484
Neil Young **17**:576, 581

**Nelson, Raymond**
Chester Himes :196

**Nemerov, Howard**
Conrad Aiken **3**:4
Kingsley Amis **2**:5
Djuna Barnes **3**:36
Kenneth Burke **2**:89
James Dickey **4**:120
Daniel Hoffman **13**:286
Harry Mathews **6**:315
Marianne Moore **4**:359
Howard Moss **7**:247
Kathleen Raine **7**:353

**Nesbitt, Bruce**
Earle Birney **11**:49

**Ness, David E.**
Lorraine Hansberry **17**:191

**Nettelbeck, Colin W.**
Louis-Ferdinand Céline **3**:103

**Neufeldt, Leonard**
David Wagoner **15**:560

**Neumark, Victoria**
Carlos Fuentes **13**:232

**Nevins, Francis M., Jr.**
Ellery Queen **3**:421; **11**:458
Rex Stout **3**:471

**Nevius, Blake**
Ivy Compton-Burnett **1**:62

**New, W. H.**
Ethel Davis Wilson **13**:608

**New, William H.**
Margaret Avison **4**:36
Robertson Davies **7**:73
Simon Gray **9**:241
Hugh Hood **15**:286
Alden Nowlan **15**:399

**Newberry, Wilma**
Ramón Gómez de la Serna
**9**:237

**Newby, P. H.**
Penelope Fitzgerald **19**:174

**Newfield, Jack**
Bob Dylan **12**:183

**Newlin, Margaret**
H. D. **14**:225
Sylvia Plath **3**:389

**Newlove, Donald**
Peter Benchley **4**:53
Joseph Brodsky **4**:78
Thomas Kinsella **4**:271
W. S. Merwin **5**:287
J. D. Salinger **8**:463

**Newman, Anne R.**
Elizabeth Bishop **15**:59

**Newman, Barbara**
Jamake Highwater **12**:288

**Newman, Charles**
James Baldwin **13**:48
Saul Bellow **6**:59
Sylvia Plath **9**:421
Philip Roth **4**:457

**Newman, Christina**
Brian Moore **8**:395

**Newman, Michael**
W. H. Auden **6**:25

**Newton, David E.**
Roy A. Gallant **17**:130, 133

**Newton, Francis**
John Lennon and Paul
McCartney **12**:353

**Neyman, Mark**
Allan W. Eckert **17**:108

**Nichol, B. P.**
Earle Birney **6**:76

**Nicholas, Brian**
Graham Greene **6**:214

**Nicholas, Charles A.**
N. Scott Momaday **19**:317

**Nicholas, Robert L.**
Antonio Buero Vallejo **15**:97

**Nichols, Bill**
Bernardo Bertolucci **16**:85

**Nichols, Kathleen L.**
Ernest Hemingway **19**:221

**Nichols, Stephen G., Jr.**
John Hawkes **3**:221

**Nicholson, C. E.**
Theodore Roethke **11**:486

**Nicholson, Kris**
Neil Young **17**:575

**Nickerson, Edward A.**
Robinson Jeffers **15**:301

**Nickerson, Susan L.**
Anne McCaffrey **17**:282, 283,
284

**Nicol, Charles**
Kingsley Amis **5**:22
Brigid Brophy **6**:100
Anthony Burgess **5**:90
John Cheever **11**:121
Peter De Vries **7**:77
Dashiell Hammett **5**:162
John Hawkes **4**:218; **7**:144
John Irving **13**:293
Milan Kundera **9**:320; **19**:268
Norman Mailer **4**:323
Vladimir Nabokov **1**:244
Kurt Vonnegut, Jr. **3**:504;
**8**:534; **12**:602

**Niemeyer, Gerhart**
Aleksandr I. Solzhenitsyn **7**:439

**Niester, Alan**
Frank Zappa **17**:590

**Nightingale, Benedict**
Alan Ayckbourn **5**:35; **18**:30
Edward Bond **4**:70
A. E. Ellis **7**:93
Michael Frayn **7**:107
John Hopkins **4**:234
David Mercer **5**:284
Sławomir Mrożek **13**:399
Peter Nichols **5**:305, 306
Joe Orton **13**:435
John Osborne **5**:333
J. B. Priestley **5**:350
Gerome Ragni and James Rado
**17**:382
Anthony Shaffer **19**:415
Neil Simon **6**:504
Tom Stoppard **5**:412
David Storey **5**:415
E. A. Whitehead **5**:488

**Nilsen, Alleen Pace**
Maya Angelou **12**:14
Judy Blume **12**:44
M. E. Kerr **12**:300
Nicholosa Mohr **12**:447
John R. Tunis **12**:599

**Nimmo, Dorothy**
Judy Blume **12**:45

**Nissenson, Hugh**
Chaim Potok **2**:338; **7**:321

**Nist, John**
Carlos Drummond de Andrade
**18**:3, 4

**Nitchie, George W.**
Robert Lowell **8**:350
George MacBeth **2**:251
Marianne Moore **8**:397

**Nkosi, Lewis**
André Brink **18**:68
Alex La Guma **19**:272

**Noble, David W.**
James Baldwin **4**:40

**Nokes, David**
Michael Mewshaw **9**:377

**Nolan, Paul T.**
Marc Connelly **7**:55

**Noland, W. Richard**
Elliott Baker **8**:38

**Nomad, Max**
Ignazio Silone **4**:493

**Noonan, Tom**
Rainer Werner Fassbinder
**20**:118

**Nordberg, Robert B.**
Jonathan Kozol **17**:252

**Nordell, Roderick**
William Golding **17**:172
Mark Harris **19**:201

**Nordyke, Lewis**
Robert Lewis Taylor **14**:533

**Norman, Albert H.**
Richard Brautigan **12**:58

**Norman, Doreen**
Otfried Preussler **17**:375

**Norman, Gurney**
Richard Brautigan **12**:64

**Norman, Mary Anne**
Dee Brown **18**:71

**Norris, Ken**
George Bowering **15**:81

**Norris, Leslie**
Andrew Young **5**:525

**Norrish, P. J.**
Henri de Montherlant **19**:329

**Norsworthy, James A.**
Jamake Highwater **12**:286
Zilpha Keatley Snyder **17**:474

**North, R. J.**
Andre Malraux **13**:367

**Northey, Margot**
Matt Cohen **19**:115
Mordecai Richler **18**:451

**Norton, Dale**
Alex Haley **12**:248

**Norton, Elliot**
Lily Tomlin **17**:517

**Norwood, Gilbert**
Agatha Christie **12**:113

**Norwood, W. D., Jr.**
C. S. Lewis **1**:177

**Noth, Dominique Paul**
Garry Trudeau **12**:589

**Nott, Kathleen**
Graham Greene **14**:217

**Novak, Michael**
Norman Lear **12**:338

**Novak, Michael Paul**
Robert Hayden **5**:169

**Novak, William**
Grace Paley **6**:391
Susan Fromberg Schaeffer
**6**:488

**Novick, Julius**
Edward Albee **9**:10
John Bishop **10**:54
Simon Gray **9**:242
Hugh Leonard **19**:284
David Mamet **9**:360
Sean O'Casey **11**:411
David Rabe **4**:425
Howard Sackler **14**:478
Neil Simon **11**:496
Isaac Bashevis Singer **15**:509
Tom Stoppard **4**:525; **8**:504
David Storey **8**:505
Tennessee Williams **8**:548
Lanford Wilson **14**:592

**Nowell-Smith, Geoffrey**
Michelangelo Antonioni **20**:27
Bernardo Bertolucci **16**:100
Luis Buñuel **16**:131
Richard Lester **20**:218
Pier Paolo Pasolini **20**:259
Luchino Visconti **16**:573

**Nowlan, Alden**
Hugh Hood **15**:283

**Nugent, Frank S.**
Tod Browning **16**:121
John Ford **16**:304
Jean Renoir **20**:287

**Nugent, Robert**
René Char **11**:111

**Nyabongo, V. S.**
Alice Walker **6**:554

**Nye, Robert**
Brigid Brophy **6**:98
E. M. Forster **3**:162
David Garnett **3**:189
Graham Greene **3**:214
Hermann Hesse **17**:218
Bernard Malamud **5**:269
Anthony Powell **3**:402
John Cowper Powys **7**:349
William Sansom **6**:483
Penelope Shuttle **7**:422

**Nye, Russel**
John Lennon and Paul
McCartney **12**:366

**Nygaard, Anita**
Joy Adamson **17**:5

**Nyren, D.**
Marie-Claire Blais **13**:97

**Nyren, Dorothy**
Russell Edson **13**:190

**Oakley, Helen**
Lenora Mattingly Weber **12**:633

**Oates, Joyce Carol**
Harriette Arnow **2**:14
James Baldwin **5**:42
Paul Bowles **19**:60
Frederick Busch **7**:38
James M. Cain **3**:95
Carlos Castaneda **12**:88
John Cheever **11**:120
Robert Coover **7**:58
Robert Creeley **8**:152
Roald Dahl **1**:177
James Dickey **7**:83
Joan Didion **8**:175
Margaret Drabble **2**:118; **5**:117
Andre Dubus **13**:183
James T. Farrell **4**:158
Janet Frame **2**:141
Tess Gallagher **18**:170
Gail Godwin **5**:142
William Golding **17**:180
William Goyen **8**:250
Jim Harrison **6**:224
Anne Hébert **13**:268
David Ignatow **14**:276
Maxine Kumin **5**:222
Philip Larkin **8**:337
Mary Lavin **4**:282
Stanislaw Lem **15**:328
Doris Lessing **2**:241
Philip Levine **4**:286, 288
Alison Lurie **18**:310
Norman Mailer **11**:341
Bernard Malamud **3**:323
Berry Morgan **6**:339
Alice Munro **6**:342; **19**:346
Iris Murdoch **1**:237; **11**:389
Vladimir Nabokov **2**:304
Charles Newman **2**:312; **8**:419
Flannery O'Connor **1**:258
Mary Oliver **19**:362
Sylvia Plath **2**:338; **5**:340
Gilbert Rogin **18**:458
Philip Roth **4**:454
J. R. Salamanca **15**:463
Anne Sexton **6**:492
Jean Stafford **19**:430
Elizabeth Taylor **2**:433
Peter Taylor **1**:335
Paul Theroux **8**:512
William Trevor **9**:529
John Updike **2**:441; **13**:561
Kurt Vonnegut, Jr. **12**:603
Fay Weldon **9**:559
Eudora Welty **1**:363
Richard Yates **7**:554

**Oberbeck, S. K.**
Kingsley Amis **2**:7
Frederick Forsyth **5**:125
John Hawkes **1**:137
John Hersey **7**:154
John Irving **13**:293
Norman Mailer **2**:264

Joyce Carol Oates **2**:315
Georges Simenon **2**:398
Kurt Vonnegut, Jr. **3**:502
Stevie Wonder **12**:655

**Oberg, Arthur**
John Berryman **4**:66
Galway Kinnell **3**:270
Greg Kuzma **7**:197
Philip Levine **2**:244
John Matthias **9**:362
Josephine Miles **14**:369
Joyce Carol Oates **6**:367
Robert Pack **13**:438
Sylvia Plath **14**:422; **17**:349
Anne Sexton **4**:482
Mona Van Duyn **7**:498
Derek Walcott **9**:556

**Oberhelman, Harley D.**
José Donoso **11**:146

**O'Brien, Conor Cruise**
Jimmy Breslin **4**:76
Graham Greene **3**:214
Seamus Heaney **7**:149

**O'Brien, Edna**
Françoise Sagan **17**:428

**O'Brien, James H.**
Liam O'Flaherty **5**:321

**O'Brien, John**
Clarence Major **19**:293
Gilbert Sorrentino **7**:450

**O'Brien, Kate**
Elias Canetti **14**:118

**Obuchowski, Chester W.**
Pierre Gascar **11**:220

**Obuchowski, Mary Dejong**
Yasunari Kawabata **9**:316

**Occhiogrosso, Frank**
Georges Simenon **18**:481

**O'Connell, Shaun**
Marjorie Kellogg **2**:224
Gilbert Sorrentino **7**:447

**O'Connor, Garry**
Jean Anouilh **8**:24

**O'Connor, Gerald**
J.R.R. Tolkien **12**:576

**O'Connor, John J.**
Earl Hamner, Jr. **12**:258
Norman Lear **12**:333, 334, 337
Garry Marshall **17**:275, 276
Lanford Wilson **7**:547

**O'Connor, Mary**
Caroline Gordon **6**:203

**O'Connor, William Van**
Kingsley Amis **1**:5
Donald Davie **5**:113
D. J. Enright **4**:154
Elizabeth Jennings **5**:197
Philip Larkin **3**:275
Iris Murdoch **1**:234
Ezra Pound **1**:275
John Wain **2**:458

**O'Daniel, Therman B.**
Ralph Ellison **1**:95

**Odell, Brian Neal**
Arna Bontemps **18**:64

**O'Doherty, Brian**
Flann O'Brien **5**:314

**O'Donnell, Donat**
Sean O'Faoláin **14**:402

**O'Donnell, Thomas D.**
Michel Butor **11**:81
Claude Simon **15**:495

**O'Faoláin, Julia**
Beryl Bainbridge **10**:15; **18**:33
Mark Helprin **10**:260
Alice Munro **19**:346
Edna O'Brien **5**:311
Isaac Bashevis Singer **9**:489

**O'Faoláin, Seán**
Daphne du Maurier **11**:162
Ernest Hemingway **13**:272

**Oglesby, Leora**
Frank Bonham **12**:50

**Ogunyemi, Chikwenye Okonjo**
Toni Morrison **10**:354
Amos Tutuola **14**:542

**O'Hara, J. D.**
Kingsley Amis **8**:11
Donald Barthelme **5**:54
Ann Beattie **8**:54
Samuel Beckett **6**:39; **14**:73
Jorge Luis Borges **2**:77
Kay Boyle **5**:66
Richard Brautigan **12**:58
Anthony Burgess **5**:86, 88
Louis-Ferdinand Céline **4**:103
John Cheever **15**:129
Laurie Colwin **13**:156
Robert Crumb **17**:82
Roald Dahl **6**:121
Edward Dahlberg **7**:71
Don DeLillo **13**:178
William Gaddis **19**:186
Lawrence Durrell **6**:152
William Golding **17**:170
Peter Handke **15**:268
George V. Higgins **4**:223
José Lezama Lima **4**:288
Vladimir Nabokov **1**:246
Judith Rossner **6**:469
C. P. Snow **9**:498
Kurt Vonnegut, Jr. **12**:608
Paul West **14**:569

**O'Hara, T.**
Derek Walcott **4**:575

**O'Hara, Tim**
Ronald Sukenick **4**:531

**Ohmann, Carol B.**
Alex Haley **12**:244
J. D. Salinger **12**:516
Muriel Spark **2**:414

**Ohmann, Richard M.**
Pär Lagerkvist **7**:199
J. D. Salinger **12**:516

**Okam, Hilary**
Aimé Césaire **19**:98

**O'Keeffe, Timothy**
Patrick White **3**:521

**Okri, Ben**
Anita Desai **19**:134

**Okun, Milton**
Phil Ochs **17**:330
Buffy Sainte-Marie **17**:430

**Olderman, Raymond M.**
John Barth **3**:40
Peter S. Beagle **7**:26
Stanley Elkin **4**:153
John Hawkes **3**:222
Joseph Heller **3**:229
Ken Kesey **3**:266
Thomas Pynchon **3**:411
Kurt Vonnegut, Jr. **3**:505

**Oldfield, Michael**
Jim Morrison **17**:291
Jimmy Page and Robert Plant **12**:477

**Oldham, Andrew**
Brian Wilson **12**:640

**Oldsey, Bernard S.**
William Golding **2**:167

**Oliphant, Dave**
Albert Goldbarth **5**:143

**Oliver, Edith**
Ed Bullins **5**:83; **7**:36
Anne Burr **6**:103
Alice Childress **12**:105
Athol Fugard **14**:191
Jack Gelber **14**:193
Simon Gray **14**:214, 215
John Guare **8**:253; **14**:220, 221
Christopher Hampton **4**:211
Jim Jacobs and Warren Casey **12**:292
Arthur Kopit **18**:286
David Mamet **15**:355, 358
Mark Medoff **6**:322
Rochelle Owens **8**:434
Gerome Ragni and James Rado **17**:379
Terence Rattigan **7**:355
Jonathan Reynolds **6**:451
Sam Shepard **6**:497; **17**:435, 442
Tom Stoppard **3**:470; **4**:525
Elizabeth Swados **12**:557, 559
George Tabori **19**:437
Megan Terry **19**:440
Kurt Vonnegut, Jr. **12**:605
Derek Walcott **2**:460; **14**:551
Joseph A. Walker **19**:455
Douglas Turner Ward **19**:457,458
Richard Wesley **7**:518
Lanford Wilson **14**:591

**Oliver, Raymond**
Arthur Gregor **9**:255

**Oliver, Roy**
Arthur A. Cohen **7**:51

**Olivier, Edith**
Esther Forbes **12**:203

**Olmert, Michael**
Philip Roth **4**:452

**Olney, James**
Chinua Achebe **1**:2
Loren Eiseley **7**:92

**Olsen, Gary R.**
Hermann Hesse **6**:238

**Olshen, Barry N.**
John Fowles **9**:210

**Olson, Carol Booth**
A. G. Mojtabai **15**:377

**Olson, David B.**
Robert Penn Warren **10**:518

**Olson, Lawrence**
Yukio Mishima **2**:288

**Olson, Toby**
Diane Wakoski **7**:505

**O'Meally, Robert G.**
Robert Hayden **14**:240

**O'Neill, Kathleen**
Michel Butor **11**:80

**O'Neill, Tom**
Giuseppe Ungaretti **11**:557; **15**:537

**Onley, Gloria**
Margaret Atwood **4**:25; **13**:42

**Onyeama, Dillibe**
Alex Haley **12**:252

**Opdahl, Keith**
Saul Bellow **3**:51; **15**:55
Jim Harrison **14**:236

**Oppenheim, Shulamith**
Leon Garfield **12**:230

**Oppenheimer, Joel**
Robert Creeley **15**:153
Anthony Hecht **19**:208
Philip Roth **4**:457
William Saroyan **10**:456
L. E. Sissman **18**:489
Andrei Voznesensky **15**:557

**Ordóñez, Elizabeth**
Ana María Matute **11**:366

**O'Reilly, Timothy**
Frank Herbert **12**:279

**Orenstein, Gloria Feman**
Fernando Arrabal **18**:20

**Orgel, Doris**
Emily Cheney Neville **12**:453

**Oriard, Michael**
Don DeLillo **13**:175

**Orme, John**
Bob Marley **17**:273

**Ormerod, Beverley**
Édouard Glissant **10**:230

**Ormerod, David**
V. S. Naipaul **4**:371

**Ornstein, Jacob**
Camilo José Cela **4**:95

**O'Rourke, William**
Rosalyn Drexler **2**:120
Craig Nova **7**:267

**Orr, Leonard**
Richard Condon **4**:107

**Orr, Nancy Young**
Barbara Corcoran **17**:69

**Ortega, Julio**
José María Arguedas **18**:7, 8

**Orth, Maureen**
Bob Dylan **3**:130
Stevie Wonder **12**:657

**Ortiz, Gloria M.**
Pablo Neruda **7**:260

**Ortiz, Miguel A.**
Alice Childress **12**:108
Nicholosa Mohr **12**:448

**Ortmayer, Roger**
Federico Fellini **16**:286

**Orton, Gavin**
Eyvind Johnson **14**:294

**Orwell, George**
Alex Comfort **7**:52
Graham Greene **6**:216

**Osborn, John Jay, Jr.**
George V. Higgins **18**:234

**Osborn, Neal J.**
Kenneth Burke **2**:87

**Osborne, Charles**
William Faulkner **1**:102
W. Somerset Maugham **1**:204

**Osborne, David**
Albert Camus **2**:99

**Osborne, Linda B.**
Sylvia Ashton-Warner **19**:24
Ella Leffland **19**:278

**Osborne, Trudie**
Madeleine L'Engle **12**:345

**Osgood, Eugenia V.**
Julien Gracq **11**:244

**Ostriker, Alicia**
Ai **4**:16
Cid Corman **9**:170
Alan Dugan **2**:121
Paul Goodman **7**:131
John Hollander **14**:262
Sylvia Plath **17**:348
May Swenson **14**:518
Anne Waldman **7**:508

**Ostroff, Anthony**
Donald Justice **6**:271
Kathleen Spivack **6**:520
Mark Van Doren **6**:542

**Ostrom, Alan**
William Carlos Williams **1**:370

**Ostrovsky, Erika**
Louis-Ferdinand Céline **4**:98

**O'Toole, Lawrence**
Werner Herzog **16**:335

**Otten, Anna**
Heinrich Böll **2**:66
Michel Butor **8**:120; **15**:120
Alain Robbe-Grillet **6**:467; **8**:453
Nathalie Sarraute **2**:386
Claude Simon **4**:497

**Ottenberg, Eve**
Erskine Caldwell **14**:95
Vonda N. McIntyre **18**:327

**Overbey, David L.**
Luis Buñuel **16**:151
Claude Chabrol **16**:178
Werner Herzog **16**:324, 333
Fritz Lang **20**:212
Richard Lester **20**:227

**Överland, Orm**
Arthur Miller **15**:371

**Oviedo, José Miguel**
Mario Vargas Llosa **10**:497, 500

**Owen, Carys T.**
Louis-Ferdinand Céline **9**:155

**Owen, I. M.**
Robertson Davies **7**:72
Mavis Gallant **18**:173

**Owen, Ivon**
Robertson Davies **13**:171

**Owens, Brad**
Mark Harris **19**:205
John Kennedy Toole **19**:442

**Owens, Iris**
Lois Gould **4**:200

**Owens, Rochelle**
Diane Wakoski **7**:505

**Owens, Tony J.**
William Faulkner **18**:145

**Ower, John**
Frank Herbert **12**:273
Mordecai Richler **9**:451
Edith Sitwell **9**:494

**Ower, John B.**
Edith Sitwell **2**:404

**Ownbey, Steve**
George V. Higgins **10**:273
Georges Simenon **8**:486

**Owomoyela, Oyekan**
Chester Himes **7**:159

**Oxenhandler, Neal**
Jean Cocteau **16**:225
Jean Genet **14**:203

**Oxley, Brian**
Geoffrey Hill **18**:240

**Ozick, Cynthia**
Saul Bellow **10**:43
Frederick Buechner **2**:83
Mark Harris **19**:202
Bernard Malamud **11**:346
Hugh Nissenson **4**:380

**Pa Chin**
Pa Chin **18**:371

**Pace, Eric**
Joseph Wambaugh **3**:508

**Pacernick, Gary**
Millen Brand **7**:30

**Pachter, Henry**
Paul Goodman **7**:129

**Pachter, Henry M.**
Hermann Hesse **6**:236

**Pacifici, Sergio J.**
Elio Vittorini **14**:543

**Pack, Robert**
James Schevill **7**:400
Mark Strand **18**:514

**Packard, Nancy H.**
Grace Paley **6**:393

**Packard, William**
Kenneth Patchen **18**:394

**Paddock, Lisa**
William Faulkner **18**:147

**Page, James A.**
James Baldwin **3**:32
Ralph Ellison **3**:145
Richard Wright **3**:546

**Page, Malcolm**
John Arden **13**:25

**Pagès, Irène M.**
Simone de Beauvoir **14**:68

**Palevsky, Joan**
Isak Dinesen **10**:148

**Paley, Maggie**
Laura Nyro **17**:313

**Palley, Julian**
Azorín **11**:25

**Palmer, Eustace**
Chinua Achebe **7**:5
James Ngugi **7**:265

**Palmer, James W.**
Francis Ford Coppola **16**:242

**Palmer, Penelope**
Charles Tomlinson **6**:536

**Palmer, R. Roderick**
Haki R. Madhubuti **6**:313
Sonia Sanchez **5**:382

**Palmer, Robert**
Sam Shepard **17**:445

**Palmer, Tony**
Bob Dylan **12**:196
Jimmy Page and Robert Plant **12**:481

**Pancella, John R.**
Robert Newton Peck **17**:340

**Paniagua, Lita**
Luis Buñuel **16**:134

**Panshin, Alexei**
Robert A. Heinlein **3**:224

**Panter-Downes, Mollie**
Robert Bolt **14**:91
John Le Carré **9**:327

**Paolucci, Anne**
Federico Fellini **16**:278

**Papatzonis, Takis**
Giuseppe Ungaretti **11**:557

**Parachini, Allan**
Garry Trudeau **12**:589

**Parameswaran, Uma**
Derek Walcott **9**:557

**Pareles, Jon**
Joan Armatrading **17**:9
Bob Dylan **12**:197
Mick Jagger and Keith Richard **17**:240
Joni Mitchell **12**:443
Frank Zappa **17**:593, 594

**Parente, Diane A.**
James Dickey **10**:142

**Parente, William J.**
Alexsandr I. Solzhenitsyn **10**:479

**Parham, Sidney F.**
Peter Weiss **15**:568

**Parini, Jay**
Daniel Halpern **14**:232
Christopher Middleton **13**:388

**Parisi, Joseph**
X. J. Kennedy **8**:320
Susan Fromberg Schaeffer **11**:491
Mark Van Doren **6**:543
Robert Penn Warren **18**:536

**Park, Clara Claiborne**
Brigid Brophy **6**:99
James Merrill **13**:377; **18**:330
Richard Wilbur **9**:568

**Park, John G.**
Shirley Jackson **11**:302

**Park, Sue Simpson**
Gwendolyn Brooks **15**:94
Joyce Carol Oates **11**:400

**Parke, Andrea**
Mary Stolz **12**:548

**Parkhill-Rathbone, James**
C. P. Snow **1**:317; **6**:518

**Parkinson, Robert C.**
Frank Herbert **12**:271

**Parkinson, Thomas**
Robert Lowell **1**:179, 180
Gary Snyder **1**:317

**Parr, J. L.**
Calder Willingham **5**:510

**Parrinder, Patrick**
Philip K. Dick **10**:138
B. S. Johnson **9**:302
V. S. Naipaul **18**:360
Frederik Pohl **18**:411

**Parris, Robert**
Françoise Sagan **17**:418

**Parrish, Anne**
Esther Forbes **12**:202

**Parrish, Paul A.**
Elizabeth Bowen **11**:59

**Parsons, Ann**
William Carlos Williams **2**:469

**Parsons, Gordon**
Ruth M. Arthur **12**:27
Leon Garfield **12**:231, 241

**Parsons, I. M.**
Agatha Christie **12**:112

**Parsons, Thornton H.**
John Crowe Ransom **2**:364

**Partridge, Marianne**
Patti Smith **12**:538

**Partridge, Ralph**
Agatha Christie **12**:113, 114

**Partridge, Robert**
Willie Nelson **17**:304

**Paschall, Douglas**
Theodore Roethke **3**:434

**Pasinetti, P. M.**
Eleanor Clark **19**:105

**Pasolli, Robert**
Sam Shepard **17**:434

**Paterson, Katherine**
Anita Desai **19**:135
Rosemary Wells **12**:639

**Patrouch, Joseph F., Jr.**
Isaac Asimov **19**:24

**Patten, Brian**
Isaac Asimov **3**:17
Kurt Vonnegut, Jr. **3**:504

**Patten, Frederick**
Stephen King **12**:310
Andre Norton **12**:471

**Patten, Karl**
Graham Greene **1**:131

**Patterson, Rob**
Martin Mull **17**:300

**Pattison, Barrie**
Brian De Palma **20**:77

**Pattow, Donald J.**
Dashiell Hammett **19**:198

**Paul, Jay S.**
William Goyen **14**:211, 212

**Paul, Sherman**
Paul Goodman **1**:123
Charles Olson **11**:420
Boris Pasternak **7**:295
Edmund Wilson **1**:373

**Paulin, Tom**
Kingsley Amis **13**:15
Robin Cook **14**:131
Robert Coover **15**:145
John Fowles **10**:189
Patricia Highsmith **14**:261
Dan Jacobson **14**:290
Jerzy Kosinski **10**:308
Sean O'Faoláin **14**:406
William Trevor **14**:536
Ian McEwan **13**:370
Barbara Pym **13**:469

**Pauly, Rebecca M.**
Kurt Vonnegut, Jr. **12**:609

**Pauly, Thomas H.**
John Ford **16**:313

**Pavletich, Aida**
Joan Armatrading **17**:11
Laura Nyro **17**:321
Buffy Sainte-Marie **17**:431

**Pawel, Ernst**
Heinrich Böll **2**:67; **9**:109
Hermann Hesse **2**:192
Jakov Lind **2**:245

**Payne, James Robert**
Imamu Amiri Baraka **14**:48

**Payne, Jocelyn**
David Slavitt **14**:491

**Payne, Robert**
Yuri Olesha **8**:432
Boris Pasternak **7**:292
Mary Renault **17**:397

**Paz, Octavio**
Elizabeth Bishop **9**:89
André Breton **9**:129
Alexsandr I. Solzhenitsyn **10**:478
William Carlos Williams **5**:508

**Peacock, Allen**
Frederick Busch **18**:86

**Pearce, Philippa**
Alan Garner **17**:136

**Pearce, Richard**
Saul Bellow **8**:72
John Dos Passos **8**:181
John Hawkes **9**:266
Henry Roth **6**:473
William Styron **11**:515

**Pearlman, Sandy**
Jim Morrison **17**:287

**Pearson, Alan**
Joe Rosenblatt **15**:447

**Pearson, Carol**
Joseph Heller **11**:265

**Pearson, Gabriel**
John Berryman **2**:55
T. S. Eliot **13**:192

**Pearson, Norman Holmes**
Ezra Pound **2**:340

**Pease, Howard**
Henry Gregor Felsen **17**:121
John R. Tunis **12**:596

**Peavy, Charles D.**
Hubert Selby, Jr. **1**:306
Melvin Van Peebles **20**:410

**Pechter, William S.**
Lindsay Anderson **20**:16
Ingmar Bergman **16**:48
Frank Capra **16**:158
John Cassavetes **20**:49
Francis Ford Coppola **16**:234, 238
Federico Fellini **16**:282
Elaine May **16**:432
Satyajit Ray **16**:482, 494
Jean Renoir **20**:298
Orson Welles **20**:448
Lina Wertmüller **16**:589

**Peck, Richard**
Robert Cormier **12**:135
Katherine Paterson **12**:485

CRITIC INDEX

**Peden, William**
James Baldwin **8**:40
Doris Betts **6**:70
Paul Bowles **19**:58
Ed Bullins **7**:37
John Cheever **7**:49
Laurie Colwin **5**:108
James T. Farrell **8**:205
Ernest J. Gaines **11**:217
Mavis Gallant **18**:170
Shirley Ann Grau **9**:240
Chester Himes **7**:159
Langston Hughes **10**:281
Grace Paley **6**:392
Ann Petry **7**:305
William Saroyan **8**:468
Mary Lee Settle **19**:409
Irwin Shaw **7**:411
Isaac Bashevis Singer **6**:509
Jesse Stuart **8**:507
Peter Taylor **18**:523
Tennessee Williams **5**:502
Richard Wright **14**:596

**Peel, Marie**
John Osborne **2**:329
Peter Redgrove **6**:445, 446
Penelope Shuttle **7**:423
Alan Sillitoe **3**:448
David Storey **2**:425
R. S. Thomas **6**:531

**Pekar, Harvey**
Robert Crumb **17**:82
Frank Zappa **17**:585

**Pelli, Moshe**
S. Y. Agnn **8**:8

**Pelorus**
Judy Blume **12**:45
Robert Cormier **12**:135
Alan Garner **17**:147

**Peltier, Ed**
Peter Weir **20**:424

**Pemberton, Clive**
Leon Garfield **12**:219

**Pendergast, Constance**
Mavis Gallant **18**:171

**Penner, Allen R.**
Alan Sillitoe **1**:308

**Penner, Dick**
Vladimir Nabokov **15**:395

**Penner, Jonathan**
Graham Greene **18**:196
V. S. Pritchett **15**:443
Philip Roth **15**:450

**Pennington, Lee**
Jesse Stuart **11**:508

**Peppard, Murray B.**
Friedrich Dürrenmatt **1**:81

**Pepper, Nancy**
Anaïs Nin **11**:399

**Perazzini, Randolph**
Robert Frost **13**:229

**Percy, Walker**
Walter M. Miller, Jr. **4**:352
Marion Montgomery **7**:232
Jean-Paul Sartre **13**:506
John Kennedy Toole **19**:441
Eudora Welty **1**:362

**Percy, William**
Joy Adamson **17**:2

**Perebinossoff, Phillipe R.**
Jean Renoir **20**:308

**Perera, Victor**
Miguel Ángel Asturias **3**:18

**Perez, Gilberto**
Beryl Bainbridge **10**:16
Ingmar Bergman **16**:81
Werner Herzog **16**:335
Yuri Krotkov **19**:266
Alan Sillitoe **10**:477
Anne Tyler **11**:553

**Pérez Firmat, Gustavo**
José Lezama Lima **10**:319

**Perkins, David**
W. H. Auden **11**:19
Richard Eberhart **11**:179
Ezra Pound **3**:397
Carl Sandburg **10**:449

**Perkins, Huel D.**
John A. Williams **13**:599

**Perlberg, Mark**
Larry Eigner **9**:181
Michael S. Harper **7**:138
George Oppen **7**:285

**Perloff, Marjorie G.**
John Berryman **2**:59
Ed Dorn **10**:156
Clayton Eshleman **7**:99
Thom Gunn **3**:216
Ted Hughes **2**:204; **4**:235
Richard F. Hugo **6**:244
Erica Jong **6**:270
Galway Kinnell **2**:230
Denise Levertov **2**:243
Robert Lowell **1**:181
Frank O'Hara **2**:322; **5**:325;
   **13**:425
Charles Olson **11**:415
Sylvia Plath **9**:432; **17**:368
Ezra Pound **10**:400
Adrienne Rich **7**:369
Françoise Sagan **6**:482
May Sarton **14**:481
Mark Van Doren **10**:496
Mona Van Duyn **3**:492
Diane Wakoski **7**:504
John Wieners **7**:537
James Wright **3**:542, 544

**Perrick, Eve**
Ira Levin **3**:294

**Perrin, Noel**
James Gould Cozzens **11**:132

**Perrine, Laurence**
John Ciardi **10**:105

**Perry, R. C.**
Rolf Hochhuth **11**:276

**Perry, Ruth**
Doris Lessing **15**:330

**Peter, John**
Edward Bond **13**:102
William Golding **17**:158

**Peterkiewicz, Jerzy**
Witold Gombrowicz **4**:195
Alain Robbe-Grillet **4**:447

**Peters, Daniel James**
Thomas Pynchon **3**:412

**Peters, Margot**
Agatha Christie **12**:119
J.I.M. Stewart **14**:512

**Peters, Robert**
Charles Bukowski **5**:80
Clayton Eshleman **7**:99
Michael McClure **6**:316
W. D. Snodgrass **18**:492
Anne Waldman **7**:508

**Peters, Robert L.**
Hollis Summers **10**:493

**Petersen, Carol**
Max Frisch **18**:160

**Petersen, Clarence**
Nora Ephron **17**:110
Charles M. Schulz **12**:527
Wilfrid Sheed **2**:392

**Peterson, Mary**
Jayne Anne Phillips **15**:419

**Peterson, Richard F.**
Mary Lavin **18**:303

**Peterson, Virgilia**
Sylvia Ashton-Warner **19**:22
Jan de Hartog **19**:131
Betty Smith **19**:424
George Tabori **19**:436
Jessamyn West **17**:548

**Petit, Christopher**
Peter Townshend **17**:539

**Petric, Vlada**
Carl Theodor Dreyer **16**:266

**Petrie, Graham**
Jean Renoir **20**:302
Eric Rohmer **16**:529
François Truffaut **20**:386

**Petrie, Paul**
A. Alvarez **5**:16

**Petroski, Catherine**
Penelope Gilliatt **13**:237

**Petrović, Njegoš M.**
Dobrica Cosić **14**:132

**Petticoffer, Dennis**
Richard Brautigan **12**:73

**Pettingell, Phoebe**
Donald Hall **1**:137
Anthony Hecht **19**:207
John Hollander **14**:266
Barbara Howes **15**:289
Philip Levine **9**:332; **14**:320
Robert Lowell **8**:353
James Merrill **13**:382
John Wain **11**:563

**Pettit, Arthur G.**
Sam Peckinpah **20**:280

**Pettit, Michael**
Paul Bowles **19**:59

**Pettit, Philip**
J.R.R. Tolkien **3**:483

**Pevear, Richard**
A. R. Ammons **3**:10
Charles Causley **7**:42
Guy Davenport, Jr. **14**:139
Richmond Lattimore **3**:277
Denise Levertov **3**:292
Hugh MacDiarmid **4**:313
James Merrill **3**:334
Pablo Neruda **5**:301
George Oppen **7**:286
Peter Porter **13**:452
Ezra Pound **2**:343
Louis Zukofsky **7**:563

**Peyre, Henri**
Marcel Aymé **11**:21
Simone de Beauvoir **1**:19
Albert Camus **1**:53; **14**:106
Louis-Ferdinand Céline **1**:57
René Char **9**:162
Georges Duhamel **8**:186
Jean Giono **4**:185
Julien Green **3**:203
André Malraux **1**:201
François Mauriac **4**:338
Henri de Montherlant **19**:324
Raymond Queneau **5**:358
Alain Robbe-Grillet **4**:446
Jules Romains **7**:383
Nathalie Sarraute **4**:464
Jean-Paul Sartre **1**:305
Claude Simon **4**:494

**Pfeffercorn, Eli**
Abraham B. Yehoshua **13**:616

**Pfeiffer, John R.**
John Brunner **8**:105

**Pfeil, Fred**
John Berger **19**:40

**Phelps, Donald**
Fielding Dawson **6**:125
Gilbert Sorrentino **7**:451

**Phelps, Robert**
Dan Wakefield **7**:502

**Phillips, Allen W.**
Octavio Paz **3**:376

**Phillips, Delbert**
Yevgeny Yevtushenko **3**:547

**Phillips, Frank Lamont**
Maya Angelou **12**:12

**Phillips, Gene D.**
Ken Russell **16**:551

**Phillips, James E.**
Laurence Olivier **20**:237

**Phillips, Klaus**
Jurek Becker **19**:35

**Phillips, Norma**
Alan Sillitoe **6**:501

**Phillips, Robert**
Hortense Calisher **8**:125
Arthur A. Cohen **7**:52
James T. Farrell **4**:158
Allen Ginsberg **6**:199
William Goyen **5**:148, 149;
 **14**:213
William Heyen **18**:231
Richard Howard **10**:275
Robert Lowell **4**:303
Bernard Malamud **3**:325
Carson McCullers **4**:345;
 **12**:432
James Alan McPherson **19**:310
Brian Moore **7**:239
Joyce Carol Oates **11**:404
Anne Sexton **15**:470
Patrick White **4**:586
Marya Zaturenska **11**:579

**Phillips, Steven R.**
Ernest Hemingway **3**:241

**Piazza, Paul**
Christopher Isherwood **14**:281

**Piccoli, Raffaello**
Riccardo Bacchelli **19**:30

**Pichaske, David R.**
John Lennon and Paul
 McCartney **12**:373

**Pick, Robert**
Frank Yerby **7**:556

**Pickar, Gertrud B.**
Max Frisch **14**:181

**Pickering, James S.**
Alvin Silverstein and Virginia
 B. Silverstein **17**:450

**Pickering, Sam, Jr.**
Anthony Powell **7**:338
P. G. Wodehouse **5**:517

**Pickering, Samuel**
Alan Garner **17**:151

**Pickering, Samuel F., Jr.**
Joyce Carol Oates **6**:369

**Pickrel, Paul**
Aldo Palazzeschi **11**:431
Sylvia Townsend Warner **7**:511

**Picon, Gaëtan**
Jean Anouilh **13**:21
Michel Butor **8**:119
Albert Camus **9**:144
Henri Michaux **8**:392

**Piercy, Marge**
Alta **19**:18
Margaret Atwood **3**:20
Margaret Laurence **6**:289
Joanna Russ **15**:461
Alice Walker **9**:557

**Pigaga, Thom**
John Hollander **2**:197

**Piggott, Stuart**
David Jones **4**:261

**Pike, B. A.**
Margery Allingham **19**:13, 14,
 15, 16, 17, 18

**Pilger, John**
Michael Cimino **16**:211

**Pinchin, Jane Lagoudis**
Lawrence Durrell **13**:186
E. M. Forster **13**:220

**Pinckney, Darryl**
James Baldwin **17**:44
Imamu Amiri Baraka **14**:48
Jacob Epstein **19**:163
Gayl Jones **9**:307
John Rechy **18**:442
Richard Wright **9**:585

**Pinkerton, Jan**
Peter Taylor **1**:333

**Pinsker, Sanford**
Bernard Malamud **3**:322;
 **18**:321
Joyce Carol Oates **11**:402
Isaac Bashevis Singer **3**:454
John Updike **7**:489

**Pinsky, Robert**
John Berryman **8**:93
Elizabeth Bishop **15**:61
Ted Hughes **9**:282
Philip Levine **9**:332
Cynthia MacDonald **13**:355
Theodore Roethke **8**:461
Raphael Rudnik **7**:384
Mark Strand **18**:517

**Pippett, Aileen**
Julia W. Cunningham **12**:163

**Pit**
Richard O'Brien **17**:323

**Pitou, Spire**
Jean Cayrol **11**:110

**Pittock, Malcolm**
Ivy Compton-Burnett **10**:108

**Planchart, Alejandro Enrique**
John Lennon and Paul
 McCartney **12**:359

**Plant, Richard**
Eleanor Clark **19**:105

**Plater, William M.**
Thomas Pynchon **18**:433

**Plumb, Robert K.**
Roy A. Gallant **17**:126

**Plumly, Stanley**
Lisel Mueller **13**:399

**Plummer, William**
Jerome Charyn **18**:99
Stanley Elkin **14**:157
Jerzy Kosinski **10**:306

**Poague, Leland A.**
Frank Capra **16**:162
Bob Dylan **6**:156

**Pochoda, Elizabeth**
Djuna Barnes **11**:30
Milan Kundera **19**:268
Tim O'Brien **19**:357

**Pochoda, Elizabeth Turner**
Anna Kavan **13**:316
Tadeusz Konwicki **8**:327
Alan Lelchuk **5**:245
Joyce Carol Oates **6**:373

**Podhoretz, Norman**
James Baldwin **1**:13, 14
Saul Bellow **1**:28
Albert Camus **1**:52
J. P. Donleavy **1**:75
George P. Elliott **2**:130
William Faulkner **1**:98
William Golding **17**:160
Paul Goodman **1**:123
Joseph Heller **1**:139
Thomas Hinde **6**:239
Jack Kerouac **1**:165
Norman Mailer **1**:188
Bernard Malamud **1**:194
Mary McCarthy **1**:205
John O'Hara **1**:260
Philip Roth **1**:292
Nathalie Sarraute **1**:302
John Updike **1**:343
Edmund Wilson **1**:372, 373

**Poger, Sidney**
T. S. Eliot **15**:212

**Poggi, Gianfranco**
Luchino Visconti **16**:563

**Poggioli, Renato**
Eugenio Montale **7**:221

**Poirier, Richard**
John Barth **3**:40
Saul Bellow **8**:74
Jorge Luis Borges **3**:77
T. S. Eliot **3**:140
Robert Frost **4**:176; **9**:226
Lillian Hellman **4**:221
John Hollander **14**:264
Jonathan Kozol **17**:251
John Lennon and Paul
 McCartney **12**:368
Norman Mailer **2**:263, 265;
 **3**:314; **4**:322; **14**:349
Vladimir Nabokov **6**:354
Thomas Pynchon **2**:355; **3**:409;
 **18**:429
William Styron **3**:474
Gore Vidal **4**:553
Rudolph Wurlitzer **2**:482; **4**:597

**Polacheck, Janet G.**
Jules Archer **12**:18

**Poland, Nancy**
Margaret Drabble **5**:118

**Polar, Antonio Cornejo**
José María Arguedas **18**:7

**Polishook, Irwin**
Allan W. Eckert **17**:107

**Pollak, Richard**
Jan de Hartog **19**:132

**Pollitt, Katha**
Alice Adams **13**:1, 2
Margaret Atwood **8**:30
Anita Desai **19**:133
Sandra Hochman **8**:298
Maureen Howard **14**:268
Dan Jacobson **14**:291
Yashar Kemal **14**:300
Ella Leffland **19**:279
James Purdy **10**:425
Françoise Sagan **17**:428
Anne Tyler **7**:479

William Wharton **18**:542

**Pollock, Bruce**
Mick Jagger and Keith Richard
 **17**:235
Paul Simon **17**:465

**Pollock, Zailig**
A. M. Klein **19**:262

**Polt, Harriet**
Bernard Malamud **18**:322

**Polt, Harriet R.**
René Clair **20**:66

**Ponnuthurai, Charles Sarvan**
Chinua Achebe **5**:3

**Pontac, Perry**
Miguel Piñero **4**:401

**Pool, Gail**
Anne Sexton **10**:468

**Poore, Charles**
Wilfrid Sheed **2**:392
Jessamyn West **17**:549

**Popkin, Henry**
Albert Camus **9**:145

**Portch, Stephen R.**
Flannery O'Connor **15**:412

**Porter, Carolyn**
Lina Wertmüller **16**:593

**Porter, Katherine Anne**
Kay Boyle **19**:61
Ezra Pound **7**:325

**Porter, M. Gilbert**
Saul Bellow **2**:54; **8**:72

**Porter, Michael**
Horst Bienek **11**:48

**Porter, Peter**
W. H. Auden **14**:31
Gavin Ewart **13**:208
Seamus Heaney **14**:244
Ted Hughes **14**:273
Sylvia Plath **17**:352
Stevie Smith **3**:460
Judith Wright **11**:578

**Porter, Raymond J.**
Brendan Behan **8**:64

**Porter, Robert**
Milan Kundera **4**:276

**Porterfield, Christopher**
Kingsley Amis **2**:8
Christopher Fry **2**:143
Ted Hughes **2**:199
Donald E. Westlake **7**:528

**Poss, Stanley**
John Hollander **8**:301
Philip Larkin **13**:337
Cynthia Macdonald **13**:355
P. H. Newby **2**:310
Adrienne Rich **7**:370
Theodore Roethke **8**:460
Nancy Willard **7**:539

**Postell, Frances**
Christie Harris **12**:263

**Postlewait, Thomas**
Samuel Beckett **18**:46

**Potamkin, Harry Allan**
Carl Theodor Dreyer **16**:255

**Potok, Chaim**
Paul West **7**:523

**Potoker, Edward Martin**
Michael Mott **15**:379
Judith Rossner **9**:456
Ronald Sukenick **6**:524

**Potts, Paul**
George Barker **8**:43

**Potts, Stephen W.**
Stanislaw Lem **15**:330

**Pouillon, Jean**
William Faulkner **8**:208

**Pound, Ezra**
Robert Frost **15**:239
Marianne Moore **19**:335
William Carlos Williams
**13**:602

**Povey, John F.**
Chinua Achebe **1**:1; **7**:6
Cyprian Ekwensi **4**:151
Wole Soyinka **14**:506

**Powell, Anthony**
Evelyn Waugh **3**:513

**Powell, Bertie J.**
Lorraine Hansberry **17**:193

**Powell, Dilys**
Elia Kazan **16**:361

**Powell, Meghan**
Stan Lee **17**:262

**Powell, Michael**
Martin Scorsese **20**:340

**Powell, Neil**
Thom Gunn **3**:216

**Power, K. C.**
Michael McClure **6**:321

**Power, Victor**
Hugh Leonard **19**:281

**Powers, Thomas**
Tom Wolfe **15**:583

**Pratt, Annis**
Doris Lessing **3**:288; **6**:292

**Pratt, John Clark**
John Steinbeck **1**:326

**Pratt, Linda Ray**
Sylvia Plath **3**:390

**Pratt, Sarah**
V. S. Pritchett **13**:468

**Pratt, William**
John Berryman **10**:45
Joseph Brodsky **6**:97
Daniel Halpern **14**:232
Ezra Pound **18**:427
Andrei Voznesensky **15**:554

**Prendowska, Krystyna**
Jerzy Kosinski **15**:313

**Prescott, Orville**
Michael Ayrton **7**:17
Earl Hamner, Jr. **12**:257
Betty Smith **19**:422
J.I.M. Stewart **7**:466
Robert Penn Warren **8**:543

**Prescott, Peter S.**
Alice Adams **6**:1
Richard Adams **4**:7
Eric Ambler **6**:3
Kingsley Amis **3**:8
Martin Amis **4**:20
Donald Barthelme **5**:54
William Peter Blatty **2**:64
Vance Bourjaily **8**:104
Kay Boyle **5**:65
Richard Brautigan **5**:71
Lothar-Gunther Buchheim
**6**:101
Anthony Burgess **5**:85
Agatha Christie **12**:120
Michael Crichton **6**:119
Robertson Davies **7**:73
Len Deighton **7**:75
Don DeLillo **8**:171
Peter De Vries **7**:78
John Dos Passos **4**:137
Lawrence Durrell **6**:151
Leslie A. Fiedler **4**:161
John Fowles **6**:186
Michael Frayn **3**:165
Nadine Gordimer **5**:146
Graham Greene **3**:213
Lillian Hellman **4**:221
George V. Higgins **4**:223
Russell C. Hoban **7**:161
Geoffrey Household **11**:277
Dan Jacobson **4**:254
Diane Johnson **5**:198
Robert F. Jones **7**:193
Thomas Keneally **8**:318
William Kennedy **6**:275
Jerzy Kosinski **6**:285
John Le Carré **5**:232, 234
Doris Lessing **2**:241
Peter Matthiessen **5**:274
Cormac McCarthy **4**:341
John McGahern **5**:280
A. G. Mojtabai **9**:385
Brian Moore **7**:236
Toni Morrison **4**:365
Penelope Mortimer **5**:299
Joyce Carol Oates **6**:374
Flann O'Brien **5**:314
Reynolds Price **6**:425
Philip Roth **2**:378; **4**:455; **6**:475
Isaac Bashevis Singer **3**:458
Aleksandr I. Solzhenitsyn **4**:516
Muriel Spark **5**:399
Robert Stone **5**:409
Harvey Swados **5**:422
Paul Theroux **5**:428
Michel Tournier **6**:537
William Trevor **7**:478
John Updike **5**:455, 458
Gore Vidal **4**:554
Jessamyn West **7**:521
Patrick White **3**:524
P. G. Wodehouse **5**:515
Larry Woiwode **6**:579
Richard Yates **7**:555

**Presley, Delma Eugene**
John Fowles **3**:163
Carson McCullers **4**:346

**Press, John**
John Betjeman **6**:67
Philip Larkin **8**:339
Louis MacNeice **4**:316

**Price, Derek de Solla**
John Brunner **10**:80
Ursula K. LeGuin **8**:343

**Price, James**
Martin Amis **9**:26
Beryl Bainbridge **8**:37
Caroline Blackwood **9**:101
Frank Capra **16**:157
Margaret Drabble **8**:184

**Price, John D.**
St.-John Perse **11**:434

**Price, L. Brian**
Jean Genet **14**:203

**Price, Martin**
Robert Bolt **14**:87
Mavis Gallant **18**:171
Marjorie Kellogg **2**:224
Iris Murdoch **1**:236; **3**:349
Joyce Carol Oates **1**:251
Nathalie Sarraute **4**:469
C. P. Snow **1**:317
David Storey **4**:530
Angus Wilson **5**:514

**Price, R.G.G.**
Kingsley Amis **2**:7
Paul Bowles **2**:78
L. P. Hartley **2**:182
Josephine Poole **17**:371
Elizabeth Taylor **2**:432

**Price, Reynolds**
Lucille Clifton **19**:110
William Faulkner **1**:102; **3**:151
Graham Greene **3**:212
Toni Morrison **10**:355
Walker Percy **8**:442
James Welch **6**:560
Eudora Welty **2**:463

**Priebe, Richard**
Wole Soyinka **3**:463

**Priestley, J. B.**
T. S. Eliot **3**:135
William Faulkner **3**:150
Ernest Hemingway **3**:232
Ezra Pound **3**:394

**Prigozy, Ruth**
Larry McMurtry **3**:333

**Primeau, Ronald**
John Brunner **8**:109

**Prince, Peter**
Martin Amis **4**:19
Charles Bukowski **5**:80
Anthony Burgess **4**:84
John Fowles **6**:184
Thomas Hinde **11**:273
Yashar Kemal **14**:299
Thomas Keneally **5**:210
Patrick Modiano **18**:338
Alice Munro **6**:341

David Pownall **10**:419
Piers Paul Read **4**:444
Philip Roth **3**:439

**Pringle, David**
J. G. Ballard **14**:40

**Pringle, John Douglas**
Hugh MacDiarmid **4**:312

**Pritchard, William H.**
Dannie Abse **7**:1
Margaret Atwood **3**:19
Wendell Berry **8**:85
John Berryman **3**:72; **8**:90
Henry Bromell **5**:74
Anthony Burgess **1**:48; **4**:84
Jerome Charyn **18**:99
Donald Davie **8**:162, 163
John Fowles **9**:214; **10**:189
Allen Ginsberg **3**:195
Robert Graves **2**:177
Marilyn Hacker **9**:257
Seamus Heaney **14**:242
John Hollander **5**:187
Ted Hughes **9**:281
Richard F. Hugo **6**:244; **18**:260
Alan Lelchuk **5**:245
Denise Levertov **2**:242; **15**:338
Philip Levine **2**:244
Robert Lowell **1**:184
Louis MacNeice **4**:316
Wright Morris **18**:354
Iris Murdoch **8**:406
Vladimir Nabokov **3**:353
Howard Nemerov **6**:363
Anthony Powell **7**:339
Thomas Pynchon **3**:418
Kenneth Rexroth **2**:369
Adrienne Rich **3**:427; **6**:459
Susan Fromberg Schaeffer
**6**:489
Anne Sexton **15**:473
L. E. Sissman **18**:488
Aleksandr I. Solzhenitsyn **4**:510
Kathleen Spivack **6**:520
Richard G. Stern **4**:523
Robert Stone **5**:410
May Swenson **4**:532
Elizabeth Taylor **2**:433
Paul Theroux **11**:531
John Updike **3**:487
Richard Wilbur **6**:571
James Wright **3**:544
Rudolph Wurlitzer **4**:597
Richard Yates **7**:556

**Pritchett, V. S.**
Kingsley Amis **13**:15
Simone de Beauvoir **4**:48; **14**:67
Samuel Beckett **4**:50
Max Frisch **14**:183
William Golding **2**:168; **17**:160, 166
Juan Goytisolo **5**:151; **10**:245
Arthur Koestler **15**:309
Mary Lavin **18**:301
John le Carré **15**:326
Compton Mackenzie **18**:313
Norman Mailer **2**:262
Carson McCullers **12**:415
William Maxwell **19**:305
Vladimir Nabokov **6**:356
Flann O'Brien **10**:364

Frank O'Connor **14**:395
John Cowper Powys **15**:435
Aleksandr I. Solzhenitsyn **1**:320
Paul Theroux **8**:513
James Thurber **5**:433
William Trevor **14**:536
Gore Vidal **8**:529

**Procopiow, Norma**
Marilyn Hacker **5**:155
Eleanor Lerman **9**:329
Anne Sexton **4**:483

**Proffer, Carl R.**
Aleksandr I. Solzhenitsyn **9**:506

**Pronko, Leonard Cabell**
Jean Anouilh **13**:16
Jean Genet **14**:201
Eugène Ionesco **1**:154

**Proteus**
Agatha Christie **12**:112
Edna Ferber **18**:151

**Prothro, Laurie**
May Sarton **14**:482

**Prouse, Derek**
Elia Kazan **16**:364
Laurence Olivier **20**:237

**Pryce-Jones, Alan**
Michael Ayrton **7**:16
John Betjeman **6**:69
Italo Calvino **5**:98
Vladimir Nabokov **1**:246

**Pryor, Thomas M.**
Sally Benson **17**:49

**Pryse, Marjorie**
Helen Yglesias **7**:558

**Puckett, Harry**
T. S. Eliot **10**:167

**Puetz, Manfred**
John Barth **9**:72
Thomas Pynchon **6**:434

**Pugh, Anthony R.**
Alain Robbe-Grillet **4**:450

**Pulleine, Tim**
Woody Allen **16**:9
Claude Chabrol **16**:184
Carlos Saura **20**:319
Peter Weir **20**:428

**Punnett, Spencer**
Edwin Newman **14**:378

**Purcell, H. D.**
George MacDonald Fraser **7**:106

**Purdy, A. W.**
Earle Birney **6**:73

**Purdy, Al**
Bill Bissett **18**:59

**Purdy, Strother**
Luis Buñuel **16**:133

**Purdy, Theodore, Jr.**
William Maxwell **19**:304

**Purtill, Richard**
J.R.R. Tolkien **12**:577

**Putney, Michael**
Hunter S. Thompson **17**:504

**Puzo, Mario**
James Baldwin **17**:34

**Pye, Michael**
George Lucas **16**:416

**Pym, Christopher**
Julian Symons **14**:522

**Pym, John**
René Clair **20**:69

**Pyros, J.**
Michael McClure **6**:320

**Quacinella, Lucy**
Lina Wertmüller **16**:596

**Quance, Robert A.**
Miguel Delibes **18**:115

**Quant, Leonard**
Robert Altman **16**:35

**Quennell, Peter**
Robert Graves **6**:210

**Quigly, Isabel**
Robert Bresson **16**:104
Frank Capra **16**:157
Claude Chabrol **16**:168
Natalia Ginzburg **11**:230
Jean-Luc Godard **20**:130
Pamela Hansford Johnson **1**:160
Elio Vittorini **14**:547

**Quinn, Sister Bernetta, O.S.F.**
Alan Dugan **2**:121
David Jones **4**:259
Ezra Pound **4**:416; **7**:326
William Stafford **7**:460
Allen Tate **4**:539
Derek Walcott **2**:460
See also Bernetta (Quinn), Sister Mary, O.S.F.

**Quinn, James P.**
Edward Albee **5**:11

**Quinn, Michael**
William Golding **17**:164

**Quinn, Vincent**
H. D. **14**:224

**R**
David Jones **4**:259
Arthur Koestler **6**:281
Aleksandr I. Solzhenitsyn **4**:506

**Raban, Jonathan**
A. Alvarez **5**:18
Kingsley Amis **8**:11
Beryl Bainbridge **5**:40
John Barth **1**:17
Saul Bellow **1**:32
E. L. Doctorow **11**:141
Stanley Elkin **6**:169
Nadine Gordimer **5**:145
Erica Jong **4**:265
Mary McCarthy **1**:207
Ian McEwan **13**:369
John McGahern **9**:369
Stanley Middleton **7**:220
Brian Moore **1**:225
Iris Murdoch **4**:369
Vladimir Nabokov **6**:359

Jean Rhys **6**:456
Richard G. Stern **4**:523
Hunter S. Thompson **17**:505
William Trevor **7**:476

**Rabassa, Gregory**
Alejo Carpentier **11**:99
Julio Cortázar **15**:147
Gabriel García Márquez **3**:180
Mario Vargas Llosa **15**:551

**Rabinovitz, Rubin**
Kingsley Amis **5**:20
Samuel Beckett **6**:40, 41
Norman Mailer **5**:267
Iris Murdoch **1**:235; **2**:297
C. P. Snow **4**:500
Angus Wilson **5**:512

**Rabinowitz, Dorothy**
Beryl Bainbridge **8**:36
Elliott Baker **8**:40
Giorgio Bassani **9**:77
Maeve Brennan **5**:72
Anthony Burgess **5**:88
Hortense Calisher **4**:87; **8**:124
John Cheever **3**:107
Lois Gould **4**:201
Peter Handke **5**:165
Mark Helprin **7**:152
Dan Jacobson **4**:254
Ruth Prawer Jhabvala **4**:256, 257; **8**:311
Robert Kotlowitz **4**:275
Mary Lavin **4**:281
Doris Lessing **2**:241
Meyer Levin **7**:205
Larry McMurtry **11**:371
Brian Moore **7**:237
Wright Morris **3**:344
Edna O'Brien **5**:312
John O'Hara **6**:384
Grace Paley **4**:392
S. J. Perelman **5**:337
Philip Roth **3**:437
Anne Sexton **10**:468
John Updike **2**:445
Gore Vidal **4**:553
Dan Wakefield **7**:503
Joseph Wambaugh **3**:509
Harriet Waugh **6**:560
Arnold Wesker **5**:482

**Rabkin, David**
Alex La Guma **19**:273

**Rabkin, Eric S.**
Donald Barthelme **13**:58
Frederik Pohl **18**:410

**Rabkin, Gerald**
Derek Walcott **9**:556

**Rachewiltz, Boris de**
Ezra Pound **7**:331

**Rachleff, Owen S.**
Woody Allen **16**:9

**Rachlis, Kit**
Neil Young **17**:582

**Rackham, Jeff**
John Fowles **2**:138

**Radcliff-Umstead, Douglas**
Alberto Moravia **11**:381

**Rader, Dotson**
Hubert Selby, Jr. **4**:481
Yevgeny Yevtushenko **3**:547

**Radford, C. B.**
Simone de Beauvoir **4**:45, 46

**Radin, Victoria**
Sara Davidson **9**:175

**Radke, Judith J.**
Pierre Gascar **11**:221

**Radley, Philippe**
Andrei Voznesensky **15**:554

**Radner, Rebecca**
Lenora Mattingly Weber **12**:635

**Radu, Kenneth**
Christie Harris **12**:264

**Rae, Bruce**
John R. Tunis **12**:593

**Raeburn, John**
Frank Capra **16**:163

**Rafalko, Robert**
Eric Ambler **9**:22

**Rafalko, Robert J.**
Philip K. Dick **10**:138

**Raff, Emanuel**
Henry Gregor Felsen **17**:124

**Raffel, Burton**
J.R.R. Tolkien **1**:337
Louis Zukofsky **11**:580

**Ragusa, Olga**
Alberto Moravia **2**:292

**Rahv, Betty T.**
Albert Camus **9**:148
Alain Robbe-Grillet **8**:451
Nathalie Sarraute **8**:469
Jean-Paul Sartre **7**:395

**Rahv, Philip**
Saul Bellow **2**:50
Richard Brautigan **12**:57
T. S. Eliot **2**:126
Ernest Hemingway **3**:231
Arthur Miller **2**:278
Delmore Schwartz **10**:462
Aleksandr I. Solzhenitsyn **2**:411

**Raidy, William A.**
Sam Shepard **17**:449

**Raine, Craig**
Geoffrey Hill **18**:237
Ted Hughes **14**:272
Harold Pinter **6**:419
Ted Walker **13**:566

**Raine, Kathleen**
David Jones **2**:216; **7**:191
St.-John Perse **4**:399
Herbert Read **4**:440

**Rainer, Dachine**
Rebecca West **7**:525

**Rama Rau, Santha**
Khushwant Singh **11**:504

**Rampersad, Arnold**
Alex Haley **12**:247

**Ramras-Rauch, Gila**
S. Y. Agnon **4**:14
Yoram Kaniuk **19**:241

**Ramsey, Paul**
Robert Bly **5**:62
Edgar Bowers **9**:121
Hayden Carruth **10**:100
Larry Eigner **9**:181
John Hollander **14**:265
Eleanor Lerman **9**:328
W. S. Merwin **5**:286
N. Scott Momaday **19**:318
Michael Mott **15**:380
Howard Nemerov **9**:394
Richard Wilbur **14**:577

**Ramsey, Roger**
Friedrich Dürrenmatt **4**:140
Pär Lagerkvist **10**:311

**Ranbom, Sheppard J.**
Philip Roth **15**:453

**Rand, Richard A.**
John Hollander **5**:187

**Randall, Dudley**
Robert Hayden **5**:168
Audre Lorde **18**:307
Margaret Walker **6**:554

**Randall, Julia**
Howard Nemerov **2**:308
Gabrielle Roy **10**:441

**Randall, Margaret**
Judith Johnson Sherwin **15**:479

**Ranjbaran, Esmaeel**
Ahmad Shamlu **10**:469

**Rank, Hugh**
Edwin O'Connor **14**:390

**Ranly, Ernest W.**
Kurt Vonnegut, Jr. **2**:453

**Ransom, John Crowe**
Donald Davidson **13**:167
Randall Jarrell **1**:159
Marianne Moore **19**:337
Allen Tate **4**:535

**Ransom, W. M.**
Galway Kinnell **3**:268

**Raphael, Frederic**
James Baldwin **17**:41
Michael Frayn **7**:107
Jakov Lind **4**:293

**Rascoe, Judith**
Laurie Colwin **5**:107

**Rasi, Humberto M.**
Jorge Luis Borges **2**:74

**Rasso, Pamela S.**
William Heyen **13**:284

**Ratcliff, Michael**
Thomas Keneally **14**:303

**Rathburn, Norma**
Margot Benary-Isbert **12**:32

**Ratner, Marc L.**
John Hawkes **14**:237
William Styron **5**:418

**Ratner, Rochelle**
Clayton Eshleman **7**:100
Patti Smith **12**:541

**Rave, Eugene S.**
Barbara Corcoran **17**:78

**Raven, Simon**
Dan Jacobson **14**:289

**Ravenscroft, Arthur**
Chinua Achebe **11**:1

**Rawley, James**
James Baldwin **15**:43
Donald Barthelme **13**:63

**Ray, David**
E. E. Cummings **12**:151

**Ray, Robert**
James Baldwin **2**:34
J.I.M. Stewart **7**:466

**Ray, Sheila G.**
E. M. Almedingen **12**:7

**Rayme, Anne C.**
Larry Kettelkamp **12**:307

**Raymond, John**
Daphne du Maurier **11**:163
Françoise Sagan **17**:417
Georges Simenon **3**:449

**Raynor, Henry**
Laurence Olivier **20**:236

**Raynor, Vivien**
Evan S. Connell, Jr. **6**:115
Iris Murdoch **3**:348
Edna O'Brien **3**:364

**Rayns, Tony**
Shirley Clarke **16**:219
Maya Deren **16**:253
Rainer Werner Fassbinder
   **20**:107, 108
Werner Herzog **16**:321, 322
Richard O'Brien **17**:323
Nagisa Oshima **20**:251

**Rea, Dorothy**
Auberon Waugh **7**:514

**Read, Esther H.**
Melvin Berger **12**:40

**Read, Forrest, Jr.**
Ezra Pound **7**:327

**Read, Herbert**
Allen Tate **4**:535

**Read, S. E.**
Robertson Davies **13**:172

**Real, Jere**
Peter Shaffer **5**:388

**Reaney, James**
Jay Macpherson **14**:345

**Reardon, Betty S.**
Jessamyn West **17**:554

**Rebay, Luciano**
Alberto Moravia **7**:239

**Rechnitz, Robert M.**
Carson McCullers **1**:209

**Reck, Rima Drell**
Louis-Ferdinand Céline **7**:44
Françoise Mallet-Joris **11**:355

**Redding, Saunders**
Shirley Ann Grau **4**:208
Richard Wright **1**:377

**Redfern, W. D.**
Jean Giono **4**:186

**Redman, Ben Ray**
Dalton Trumbo **19**:444
Marguerite Yourcenar **19**:482

**Redman, Eric**
André Brink **18**:69

**Redmon, Anne**
Judy Blume **12**:45

**Redmond, Eugene B.**
Clarence Major **19**:293

**Reed, Bill**
Frank Zappa **17**:586

**Reed, Diana**
J. G. Ballard **6**:28
John Wyndham **19**:476

**Reed, Henry**
Mary Renault **17**:391

**Reed, Ishmael**
Chester Himes **2**:195

**Reed, John**
Arthur Hailey **5**:156
Ngugi Wa Thiong'o **13**:583

**Reed, John R.**
William Dickey **3**:127
D. J. Enright **4**:155
William Heyen **18**:233
Daniel Hoffman **6**:243
John Hollander **8**:302
Richard Howard **7**:169; **10**:276
Judith Leet **11**:323
James Merrill **8**:388
Charles Reznikoff **9**:450
David Wagoner **3**:508
Philip Whalen **6**:566

**Reed, Peter J.**
Kurt Vonnegut, Jr. **3**:495;
   **12**:626

**Reed, Rex**
Laura Nyro **17**:313
Gordon Parks **16**:460
Tennessee Williams **2**:464

**Reedy, Gerard**
C. S. Lewis **6**:308
Walker Percy **18**:402

**Reedy, Gerard C.**
Richard Price **12**:490

**Rees, David L.**
Otfried Preussler **17**:375
Colin Thiele **17**:494

**Rees, Goronwy**
Richard Hughes **11**:278

**Rees, Samuel**
David Jones **13**:309

**Reeve, Benjamin**
Grace Paley **4**:393

**Reeve, F. D.**
Joseph Brodsky **6**:98
Aleksandr I. Solzhenitsyn **1**:319
Alexander Zinoviev **19**:489

**Regan, Robert Alton**
John Updike **5**:454

**Regier, W. G.**
W. H. Auden **3**:22
Michael Benedikt **4**:54
Kenneth O. Hanson **13**:263
Howard Moss **14**:375
Howard Nemerov **9**:395
Pablo Neruda **5**:305
Francis Ponge **6**:423

**Reibetanz, John**
Philip Larkin **8**:334

**Reichek, Morton A.**
Chaim Grade **10**:249

**Reid, Alastair**
Jorge Luis Borges **2**:73
Hayden Carruth **18**:89
Pablo Neruda **5**:302
John Updike **13**:561

**Reid, Alfred S.**
Karl Shapiro **15**:476

**Reid, B. L.**
V. S. Pritchett **13**:465

**Reid, Beryl**
Barbara Corcoran **17**:74
Lee Kingman **17**:246
Sonia Levitin **17**:264

**Reid, Christopher**
Ted Hughes **14**:272

**Reigo, Ants**
A. W. Purdy **14**:434

**Reilly, John M.**
Chester Himes **18**:245
B. Traven **11**:538

**Reilly, Peter**
Joan Armatrading **17**:10
Joni Mitchell **12**:436
Paul Simon **17**:460
Frank Zappa **17**:592

**Reilly, Robert J.**
C. S. Lewis **3**:298
J.R.R. Tolkien **1**:337; **3**:477

**Reinhardt, Max**
Charles Chaplin **16**:187

**Reisz, Karel**
Vittorio De Sica **20**:86
Elia Kazan **16**:361

**Reitberger, Reinhold**
Chares M. Schulz **12**:528

**Reiter, Seymour**
Sean O'Casey **5**:319

**Reitman, David**
Frank Zappa **17**:588

**Remini, Robert V.**
Gore Vidal **8**:526

**Renault, Mary**
William Golding **17**:161

**Rendle, Adrian**
Sam Shepard **17**:433
Tom Stoppard **3**:470

**Renek, Morris**
Erskine Caldwell **8**:123

**Rennie, Neil**
Robin Skelton **13**:507

**Renoir, Jean**
Charles Chaplin **16**:194

**Renshaw, Robert**
J.R.R. Tolkien **1**:336

**Resnik, Henry S.**
Nora Ephron **17**:110
Richard Fariña **9**:195
John Irving **13**:292
Wilfrid Sheed **2**:392
J.R.R. Tolkien **12**:566

**Rexine, John E.**
Vassilis Vassilikos **4**:552

**Rexroth, Kenneth**
Robert Creeley **4**:116
Robert Duncan **1**:82; **2**:123
T. S. Eliot **2**:127
William Everson **1**:96; **14**:162
Allen Ginsberg **2**:164; **3**:193, 194
William Golding **3**:196
Paul Goodman **2**:169
Robinson Jeffers **2**:211
Pär Lagerkvist **13**:334
Denise Levertov **1**:175; **2**:243; **3**:292
W. S. Merwin **2**:278; **3**:338
Henry Miller **1**:219
Marianne Moore **2**:292
Kenneth Patchen **2**:332
Laura Riding **3**:432
Muriel Rukeyser **6**:478
Carl Sandburg **1**:300; **4**:463
Isaac Bashevis Singer **3**:452
Edith Sitwell **2**:403
Gary Snyder **2**:407
Jean Toomer **4**:548
Philip Whalen **6**:565
William Carlos Williams **1**:371; **2**:469
Yvor Winters **4**:594

**Reynal, Eugene**
Margery Allingham **19**:11

**Reynolds, Gary K.**
Anne McCaffrey **17**:284

**Reynolds, Horace**
Olivia Manning **19**:299

**Reynolds, R. C.**
Larry McMurtry **7**:215

**Reynolds, Stanley**
Frederick Exley **11**:186
Anna Kavan **5**:205
Robert Penn Warren **4**:582

**Rheuban, Joyce**
Josef von Sternberg **20**:375

**Rhoads, Kenneth W.**
William Saroyan **10**:455

**Rhode, Eric**
James Baldwin **17**:40
Robert Bresson **16**:105, 113
Vittorio De Sica **20**:89
Satyajit Ray **16**:477, 479
François Truffaut **20**:381

**Rhodes, Joseph, Jr.**
W.E.B. Du Bois **2**:120

**Rhodes, Richard**
Chester Himes **2**:194
MacKinlay Kantor **7**:196
Michael Shaara **15**:474
Wilfrid Sheed **2**:394

**Ribalow, Harold U.**
Meyer Levin **7**:205
Henry Roth **6**:471
Arnold Wesker **3**:518

**Ribalow, Menachem**
S. Y. Agnon **4**:10

**Rice, Edward**
Thomas Merton **3**:337

**Rice, Julian C.**
Ingmar Bergman **16**:76
LeRoi Jones **1**:163
Martin Scorsese **20**:327

**Rice, Susan**
Gordon Parks **16**:457

**Rich, Adrienne**
Hayden Carruth **18**:87
Jean Garrigue **8**:239
Paul Goodman **2**:170
Robert Lowell **3**:304
Robin Morgan **2**:294
Eleanor Ross Taylor **5**:425

**Rich, Alan**
Alan Ayckbourn **8**:34
Jules Feiffer **8**:216
Jack Gelber **14**:194
Simon Gray **9**:241
John Guare **8**:253
Preston Jones **10**:297
Tom Stoppard **8**:501, 503
Elizabeth Swados **12**:558
Tennessee Williams **7**:545
Lanford Wilson **7**:549

**Rich, Frank**
Garry Marshall **17**:276, 278
Hugh Leonard **19**:284

**Rich, Nancy B.**
Carson McCullers **10**:336

**Richards, I. A.**
E. M. Forster **13**:215

**Richards, Jeffrey**
Frank Capra **16**:160

**Richards, Lewis A.**
William Faulkner **3**:153

**Richardson, D. E.**
Catharine Savage Brosman **9**:135

**Richardson, Jack**
John Barth **3**:39
Saul Bellow **8**:71
T. S. Eliot **9**:182
Trevor Griffiths **13**:257
Jack Kerouac **2**:227

Arthur Miller **2**:280
Vladimir Nabokov **2**:300
Peter Shaffer **5**:389
Tom Stoppard **4**:527
Megan Terry **19**:438

**Richardson, Maurice**
J.R.R. Tolkien **12**:565

**Richardson, Tony**
Luis Buñuel **16**:128
John Huston **20**:163
Akira Kurosawa **16**:395
Jean Renoir **20**:288
Josef von Sternberg **20**:373
Orson Welles **20**:433

**Richart, Bette**
Phyllis McGinley **14**:364

**Richie, Donald**
Kon Ichikawa **20**:177
Akira Kurosawa **16**:396, 398
Yukio Mishima **2**:288; **4**:357
Nagisa Oshima **20**:246
Yasujiro Ozu **16**:450

**Richie, Mary**
Penelope Mortimer **5**:300

**Richler, Mordecai**
Ken Kesey **3**:267
Bernard Malamud **2**:267
Mordecai Richler **18**:458
Isaac Bashevis Singer **15**:508
Alexander Theroux **2**:433

**Richman, Robert**
John Gardner **18**:180

**Richman, Sidney**
Bernard Malamud **1**:198

**Richmond, Jane**
E. L. Doctorow **6**:131
Thomas McGuane **3**:329

**Richmond, Velma Bourgeois**
Muriel Spark **3**:464

**Richter, David H.**
Jerzy Kosinski **6**:283

**Richter, Frederick**
Kenzaburō Oe **10**:373

**Ricks, Christopher**
Giorgio Bassani **9**:75
Samuel Beckett **2**:48
Charles Causley **7**:41
Robert Creeley **2**:108
William Golding **17**:169
Nadine Gordimer **7**:131
Marilyn Hacker **5**:155
Anthony Hecht **19**:207
Geoffrey Hill **8**:293
Richard Howard **7**:167
Galway Kinnell **5**:217
Robert Lowell **1**:181; **9**:335
Louis MacNeice **1**:186
Reynolds Price **6**:423
Christina Stead **8**:499
Peter Taylor **18**:524
John Updike **1**:346
Robert Penn Warren **6**:556
Patrick White **4**:586

**Ricou, Laurie**
Andrew Suknaski **19**:434

**Riddel, Joseph N.**
C. Day Lewis **10**:125
T. S. Eliot **13**:195

**Rideout, Walter B.**
John Dos Passos **4**:131
Randall Jarrell **2**:207
Norman Mailer **4**:318
Henry Roth **2**:377
Upton Sinclair **11**:497

**Ridley, Clifford A.**
Julian Symons **2**:426

**Riefenstahl, Leni**
Leni Riefenstahl **16**:521

**Rieff, David**
Anthony Burgess **13**:124
Ilya Ehrenburg **18**:138

**Riemer, Jack**
Chaim Potok **14**:430
Elie Wiesel **11**:570

**Riera, Emilio G.**
Luis Buñuel **16**:130

**Ries, Frank W. D.**
Jean Cocteau **15**:134

**Ries, Lawrence R.**
William Golding **10**:239
Ted Hughes **9**:283
John Osborne **11**:424
Anthony Powell **9**:439
Alan Sillitoe **10**:476
John Wain **11**:561

**Riesman, Paul**
Carlos Castaneda **12**:87

**Righter, William**
André Malraux **4**:329

**Riley, Brooks**
Lina Wertmüller **16**:593

**Riley, Clayton**
Charles Gordone **1**:124
Melvin Van Peebles **20**:412

**Riley, Peter**
Jack Spicer **18**:512

**Rimanelli, Giose**
Alberto Moravia **18**:343

**Rimer, J. Thomas**
Shusaku Endo **19**:160
Yasunari Kawabata **18**:283

**Rimmon-Kenan, Shlomith**
Jorge Luis Borges **19**:54

**Rinear, David L.**
Arthur Kopit **18**:289

**Ringel, Harry**
Alfred Hitchcock **16**:352

**Rinzler, Alan**
Bob Dylan **12**:198

**Rinzler, Carol Eisen**
Judith Rossner **6**:469

**Ripley, Josephine**
Frank B. Gilbreth, Jr. and Ernestine Gilbreth Carey **17**:155

CRITIC INDEX

**Risdon, Ann**
T. S. Eliot **9**:190

**Ritholz, Robert E.A.P.**
Martin Mull **17**:299

**Ritter, Jess**
Kurt Vonnegut, Jr. **4**:563

**Ritter, Karen**
Lee Kingman **17**:247

**Ritterman, Pamela**
Richard Brautigan **12**:57

**Riva, Raymond T.**
Samuel Beckett **1**:25

**Rivera, Francisco**
José Donoso **4**:129

**Rivers, Cheryl**
Susan Cheever **18**:102

**Rizza, Peggy**
Elizabeth Bishop **4**:66

**Rizzardi, Alfredo**
Allen Tate **4**:538

**Robbe-Grillet, Alain**
Samuel Beckett **10**:25

**Robbins, Henry**
Stanley Elkin **14**:158

**Robbins, Ira A.**
David Bowie **17**:66

**Robbins, Jack Alan**
Louis Auchincloss **4**:28
Herbert Gold **4**:189
Bernard Malamud **1**:200
Flannery O'Connor **1**:258

**Roberts, Cecil**
W. Somerset Maugham **11**:370

**Roberts, David**
R. V. Cassill **4**:94

**Roberts, Thomas J.**
Italo Calvino **8**:129

**Robertson, P.**
Otfried Preussler **17**:375

**Robins, Wayne**
Joni Mitchell **12**:438
Neil Young **17**:574

**Robinson, Beryl**
Andre Norton **12**:462
Robert Newton Peck **17**:337, 340
Mary Rodgers **12**:494

**Robinson, Christopher**
Odysseus Elytis **15**:219

**Robinson, David**
Robert Altman **16**:19
Luis Buñuel **16**:130
Orson Welles **20**:434

**Robinson, Debbie**
Roy A. Gallant **17**:130

**Robinson, Hubbell**
Gordon Parks **16**:459

**Robinson, James K.**
Robert Francis **15**:239
John Hollander **14**:263
David Ignatow **14**:275
Archibald MacLeish **14**:338
Josephine Miles **14**:370
David Wagoner **15**:559

**Robinson, Jill**
Alice Adams **6**:2
Anna Kavan **5**:206
Fran Lebowitz **11**:322
Larry McMurtry **11**:371

**Robinson, Louie**
Norman Lear **12**:332

**Robinson, Robert**
Saul Bellow **6**:54

**Robinson, Spider**
Frederik Pohl **18**:413

**Robinson, W. R.**
George Garrett **3**:190

**Robson, Jeremy**
W. H. Auden **4**:33
Leonard Cohen **3**:110

**Rockett, W. H.**
George Ryga **14**:473

**Rockwell, John**
Peter Handke **5**:164
Gerome Ragni and James Rado **17**:384
Patti Smith **12**:537
Bruce Springsteen **17**:478
Stevie Wonder **12**:661

**Rodgers, Audrey T.**
T. S. Eliot **6**:162, 166

**Rodman, Selden**
Carlos Fuentes **10**:207
Derek Walcott **14**:551

**Rodrigues, Eusebio L.**
Saul Bellow **3**:56; **6**:52

**Rodríguez-Monegal, Emir**
Adolfo Bioy Casares **13**:84
Jorge Luis Borges **2**:72; **3**:80
Gabriel García Márquez **3**:183
Juan Carlos Onetti **7**:276, 279

**Rodriguez-Peralta, Phyllis**
José María Arguedas **10**:8

**Rodway, Allan**
Samuel Beckett **4**:51
Tom Stoppard **8**:502

**Roe, Shirley**
Roy A. Gallant **17**:131

**Rogan, Helen**
Maeve Brennan **5**:73
John Gardner **5**:134
Jennifer Johnston **7**:186
Irving Wallace **7**:510

**Rogers, D.**
I. A. Richards **14**:455

**Rogers, Deborah C.**
J.R.R. Tolkien **12**:584

**Rogers, Del Marie**
Reynolds Price **6**:423

**Rogers, Ivor A.**
Robert Heinlein **14**:251

**Rogers, Linda**
Margaret Atwood **4**:27
Paulette Jiles **13**:304
Susan Musgrave **13**:400
Angus Wilson **5**:515

**Rogers, Michael**
Peter Benchley **4**:54
Richard Brautigan **12**:70
Bob Dylan **12**:187
John Gardner **3**:188
Richard Price **12**:489
Piers Paul Read **4**:445

**Rogers, Norma**
Alice Childress **12**:106

**Rogers, Pat**
Daphne du Maurier **11**:163

**Rogers, Philip**
Chinua Achebe **11**:3

**Rogers, Thomas**
Vladimir Nabokov **6**:358
Tom Stoppard **1**:328

**Rogers, Timothy**
Alan Garner **17**:135

**Rogers, W. G.**
Pearl S. Buck **7**:33
Joanne Greenberg **7**:134

**Roginski, Ed**
Peter Weir **20**:426

**Rogoff, Gordon**
David Mamet **9**:361

**Rohlehr, Gordon**
V. S. Naipaul **4**:372

**Rohmer, Eric**
Ingmar Bergman **16**:45
Alfred Hitchcock **16**:357

**Rohter, Larry**
Carlos Fuentes **8**:223
Yashar Kemal **14**:300

**Roiphe, Anne**
Earl Hamner, Jr. **12**:259

**Rollins, Ronald G.**
Sean O'Casey **9**:409

**Rolo, Charles J.**
Marcel Aymé **11**:21
William Gaddis **19**:185
Martha Gellhorn **14**:195
Pär Lagerkvist **7**:198
Françoise Sagan **17**:420
Irwin Shaw **7**:411

**Roman, Diane**
Paul Vincent Carroll **10**:98

**Romano, John**
James Baldwin **17**:42
Ann Beattie **8**:56
Thomas Berger **11**:47
Frederick Busch **10**:92
Laurie Colwin **13**:156
John Gardner **18**:182
Graham Greene **18**:196
Ella Leffland **19**:279
Joyce Carol Oates **9**:406

**Walker Percy **18**:398
Sylvia Plath **5**:342
John Updike **15**:544
Gore Vidal **10**:501

**Rome, Florence**
Muriel Spark **3**:465

**Rompers, Terry**
Jim Morrison **17**:294

**Ronge, Peter**
Eugène Ionesco **6**:249

**Rooke, Constance**
P. K. Page **18**:380
Katherine Anne Porter **15**:430

**Roosevelt, Karyl**
Diane Johnson **13**:304

**Root, William Pitt**
Sonia Sanchez **5**:382
Anne Sexton **4**:483
Peter Wild **14**:580

**Rorabacher, Louise E.**
Frank Dalby Davison **15**:171

**Rorem, Ned**
Paul Bowles **2**:79
Tennessee Williams **5**:502

**Rose, Ellen Cronan**
Doris Lessing **6**:300

**Rose, Ernst**
Hermann Hesse **1**:145

**Rose, Frank**
Peter Townshend **17**:540

**Rose, Kate**
Richard Brautigan **12**:59

**Rose, Lois**
J. G. Ballard **3**:33
Arthur C. Clarke **4**:104
Robert A. Heinlein **3**:226
C. S. Lewis **3**:297
Walter M. Miller, Jr. **4**:352

**Rose, Marilyn**
Julien Green **3**:204

**Rose, Marilyn Gaddis**
Robert Pinget **13**:441

**Rose, Phyllis**
Jean Rhys **19**:394

**Rose, Stephen**
J. G. Ballard **3**:33
Arthur C. Clarke **4**:104
Robert A. Heinlein **3**:226
C. S. Lewis **3**:297
Walter M. Miller, Jr. **4**:352

**Rose, Willie Lee**
Alex Haley **8**:260

**Rosen, Carol**
Sam Shepard **17**:448

**Rosen, Marjorie**
Elaine May **16**:433
Albert Maysles and David Maysles **16**:444

**Rosen, Norma**
Paula Fox **8**:218
Françoise Sagan **17**:425

**Rosen, R. D.**
James Tate 6:528

**Rosenbaum, Jean**
Marge Piercy 18:404

**Rosenbaum, Jonathan**
Robert Altman 16:31, 39
Robert Bresson 16:118
John Cassavetes 20:50
Carl Theodor Dreyer 16:268
Rainer Werner Fassbinder
20:108
Yasujiro Ozu 16:454
Roman Polanski 16:472
Jean Renoir 20:304

**Rosenbaum, Olga**
Bernice Rubens 19:404

**Rosenbaum, Ron**
Richard Condon 4:106

**Rosenberg, Harold**
Stanley Kubrick 16:390
André Malraux 4:334
Anna Seghers 7:407

**Rosenberg, Ross**
Philip José Farmer 19:168

**Rosenberger, Coleman**
Carson McCullers 12:412

**Rosenblatt, Jon**
Sylvia Plath 17:364

**Rosenblatt, Roger**
Renata Adler 8:5
Norman Lear 12:332
Ludvík Vaculík 7:496
Thornton Wilder 6:572

**Rosenblum, Michael**
Vladimir Nabokov 15:394

**Rosenfeld, Alvin H.**
Saul Bellow 15:52
Herbert Gold 7:122
Jakov Lind 4:293
Nelly Sachs 14:476
William Styron 15:529

**Rosenfeld, Paul**
Ernest Hemingway 19:210

**Rosenfeld, Sidney**
Elias Canetti 14:124

**Rosengarten, Herbert**
Margaret Atwood 8:33

**Rosenman, John B.**
Ray Bradbury 15:84

**Rosenstone, Robert A.**
Frank Zappa 17:585

**Rosenthal, David H.**
Louis-Ferdinand Céline 7:45
Austin C. Clarke 8:143
Nicanor Parra 2:331

**Rosenthal, Lucy**
Hortense Calisher 2:96
Richard Llewellyn 7:207
Sylvia Plath 2:336
Alix Kates Shulman 2:395

**Rosenthal, M. L.**
Yehuda Amichai 9:25
A. R. Ammons 2:13
Imamu Amiri Baraka 2:34;
10:19
John Berryman 2:56
John Betjeman 2:60
Kay Boyle 1:42
John Ciardi 10:105
Austin Clarke 6:110
Robert Creeley 2:105
E. E. Cummings 1:68
James Dickey 2:115; 7:81
Robert Duncan 2:122
Richard Eberhart 11:178
T. S. Eliot 2:125
D. J. Enright 4:155
Robert Frost 1:110
Allen Ginsberg 1:118; 2:162
Paul Goodman 1:124; 4:196
Thom Gunn 18:203
Michael Hamburger 14:234
Jim Harrison 6:223
Ted Hughes 2:197; 9:280
Randall Jarrell 13:299
X. J. Kennedy 8:320
Galway Kinnell 1:168
Thomas Kinsella 4:270; 19:254
Philip Larkin 3:275, 277
Denise Levertov 2:242
Robert Lowell 1:179; 2:247
George MacBeth 2:251
Hugh MacDiarmid 2:253
W. S. Merwin 1:211
Marianne Moore 1:226
Charles Olson 2:326
Robert L. Peters 7:304
Sylvia Plath 2:335
Ezra Pound 1:274; 7:332
Kenneth Rexroth 1:283
Theodore Roethke 3:432
Delmore Schwartz 2:387
Anne Sexton 2:391
Karl Shapiro 4:484
Charles Tomlinson 2:436
Reed Whittemore 4:588
Richard Wilbur 14:577
William Carlos Williams 1:370

**Rosenthal, R.**
Paula Fox 2:139

**Rosenthal, Raymond**
Edward Dahlberg 7:66
Tennessee Williams 8:547

**Rosenthal, Stuart**
Tod Browning 16:123

**Rosenthal, T. G.**
Michael Ayrton 7:20

**Rosenzweig, A. L.**
Peter Dickinson 12:169

**Rosenzweig, Paul**
William Faulkner 14:176

**Roshwald, Miriam**
S. Y. Agnon 8:9

**Ross, Alan**
Kingsley Amis 2:7
Alberto Moravia 7:244
Satyajit Ray 16:486

**Ross, Alec**
David Bowie 17:66, 67

**Ross, Catherine Sheldrick**
Hugh MacLennan 14:344

**Ross, Gary**
Margaret Atwood 4:27

**Ross, James**
Reynolds Price 6:426

**Ross, Mary**
Madeleine L'Engle 12:344

**Ross, Morton L.**
Norman Mailer 1:192

**Ross, Nancy Wilson**
Sylvia Ashton-Warner 19:20

**Ross, Robert**
Tess Gallagher 18:168, 169

**Rossi, Louis R.**
Salvatore Quasimodo 10:427

**Rosten, Norman**
Lucille Clifton 19:109
James Tate 2:431

**Roston, Murray**
Aldous Huxley 18:270

**Roszak, Theodore**
Paul Goodman 2:170

**Roth, Philip**
Edward Albee 9:1
James Baldwin 17:27
Saul Bellow 6:52
Norman Mailer 5:268
Bernard Malamud 5:269; 8:376
J. D. Salinger 8:464
Fredrica Wagman 7:500

**Rotha, Paul**
Buster Keaton 20:189

**Rothberg, Abraham**
Graham Greene 3:211
Gary Snyder 9:499
Aleksandr I. Solzhenitsyn
4:507; 7:437

**Rothchild, Paul**
Jim Morrison 17:285

**Rothenbuecher, Bea**
Roman Polanski 16:469

**Rother, James**
Vladimir Nabokov 11:391
Thomas Pynchon 11:453

**Rothery, Agnes**
Frans Eemil Sillanpää 19:418

**Rothman, Nathan L.**
Kay Boyle 19:63
Jessamyn West 17:543
Frank Yerby 7:556

**Rothschild, Elaine**
Elaine May 16:431

**Rothstein, Edward**
Agatha Christie 8:141

**Rottensteiner, Franz**
Philip José Farmer 19:165

**Roud, Richard**
Michelangelo Antonioni 20:19
Bernardo Bertolucci 16:86
Marguerite Duras 20:101
Jean-Luc Godard 20:132
François Truffaut 20:382, 405
Luchino Visconti 16:566

**Roudiez, Leon S.**
Michel Butor 8:114
Jean Cocteau 15:132
Claude Mauriac 9:363

**Rout, Kathleen**
Flannery O'Connor 15:412

**Routh, Michael**
Graham Greene 9:246

**Rovit, Earl H.**
Saul Bellow 1:31; 8:71; 13:71
Kay Boyle 19:66
Ralph Ellison 1:93
John Hawkes 2:184
Norman Mailer 8:372
Bernard Malamud 1:195

**Rowan, Diana**
Heinrich Böll 11:58

**Rowan, Louis**
Diane Wakoski 7:506

**Rowan, Thomas**
J. F. Powers 1:281

**Rowland, Richard**
Carl Theodor Dreyer 16:257

**Rowley, Peter**
Paula Fox 2:139
John Knowles 4:272

**Rowse, A. L.**
Flannery O'Connor 2:318
Barbara Pym 13:469

**Roy, Emil**
John Arden 15:18
Sean O'Casey 15:403

**Roy, Joy K.**
James Herriot 12:284

**Ruark, Gibbons**
Andrei Voznesensky 1:349

**Ruben, Elaine**
Maureen Howard 5:189

**Rubenstein, Roberta**
Robert Altman 16:21
Margaret Atwood 8:31
Doris Lessing 6:303; 10:316

**Rubin, Louis D., Jr.**
Donald Davidson 19:126
William Faulkner 1:101
Carson McCullers 10:338
John Crowe Ransom 4:428;
5:365
Carl Sandburg 10:450
Susan Sontag 10:484
William Styron 3:473
Allen Tate 9:523; 14:533
Robert Penn Warren 1:353;
4:577
Eudora Welty 1:361

**Rubins, Josh**
Brigid Brophy 11:69
Agatha Christie 6:108
Jacob Epstein 19:162
William Trevor 14:537

**Rubinstein, E.**
Buster Keaton 20:195

**Ruby, Michael**
Charles M. Schulz 12:528

**Rudin, Ellen**
Emily Cheney Neville 12:449

**Rueckert, William**
Wright Morris 7:245

**Ruffin, Carolyn F.**
Sylvia Ashton-Warner 19:23
Vonda N. McIntyre 18:327

**Rukeyser, Muriel**
John Crowe Ransom 11:466

**Rule, Jane**
Rita Mae Brown 18:72

**Rupp, Richard H.**
John Updike 1:343

**Ruppert, Peter**
Max Frisch 18:161

**Rushing, Andrea Benton**
Audre Lorde 18:309

**Ruskamp, Judith S.**
Henri Michaux 8:392

**Russ, Joanna**
Poul Anderson 15:15
Isaac Asimov 19:28
Adrienne Rich 18:447
Robert Silverberg 7:425
Kate Wilhelm 7:537

**Russ, Lavinia**
Ruth M. Arthur 12:25
Judy Blume 12:44
M. E. Kerr 12:298

**Russell, Charles**
John Barth 7:22
Richard Brautigan 9:123
Jerzy Kosinski 6:284
Vladimir Nabokov 6:353
Ronald Sukenick 6:523

**Russell, J.**
Honor Arundel 17:18

**Russell, John**
André Malraux 9:357
Anthony Powell 3:402

**Russell, Julia G.**
Honor Arundel 17:15

**Ryan, Frank L.**
Daniel J. Berrigan 4:56
Anne Hébert 4:220
Françoise Sagan 17:426

**Ryan, Marjorie**
Diane Johnson 5:198

**Ryan, Richard W.**
Anne McCaffrey 17:281

**Ryf, Robert S.**
Henry Green 2:179
B. S. Johnson 9:299
Doris Lessing 10:313
Vladimir Nabokov 6:353
Flann O'Brien 7:268

**Ryle, John**
John Berger 19:40
Penelope Fitzgerald 19:173
Mark Helprin 10:261

**Rysten, Felix**
Jean Giono 11:232

**Saal, Hubert**
Mary Renault 17:393
Irwin Shaw 7:411

**Sabin, Edwin L.**
Lenora Mattingly Weber 12:631

**Sabiston, Elizabeth**
Philip Roth 6:475
Ludvík Vaculík 7:497

**Sabri, M. Arjamand**
Thomas Pynchon 3:417

**Sacharoff, Mark**
Elias Canetti 3:98

**Sachner, Mark J.**
Samuel Beckett 14:71

**Sachs, Marilyn**
Nicholasa Mohr 12:445, 446
Robert Newton Peck 17:338

**Sackville-West, Edward**
Ivy Compton-Burnett 15:137

**Sadler, Frank**
Jack Spicer 18:508

**Sadoff, Dianne F.**
Gail Godwin 8:247

**Sadoff, Ira**
Tess Gallagher 18:168
Robert Hass 18:210
Philip Levine 14:315

**Säez, Richard**
James Merrill 6:323

**Sagan, Carl**
Paul West 14:568

**Sagar, Keith**
Ted Hughes 2:203

**Sage, Lorna**
Brian Aldiss 14:14
Olga Broumas 10:76
Patricia Highsmith 14:261
Erica Jong 6:267
Iris Murdoch 11:384
Vladimir Nabokov 8:412
Sylvia Plath 11:450
Philip Roth 15:455
Françoise Sagan 17:429

**Sage, Victor**
David Storey 8:505

**Said, Edward W.**
R. P. Blackmur 2:61
Paul Goodman 2:169
V. S. Naipaul 18:364

**Sainer, Arthur**
Martin Duberman 8:185
Max Frisch 18:163
Jack Gelber 14:194
Simon Gray 9:242
Michael McClure 6:317
Miguel Piñero 4:401

**St. John-Stevas, Norman**
C. S. Lewis 6:308

**St. Martin, Hardie**
Blas de Otero 11:424

**Sakurai, Emiko**
Kenzaburō Oe 10:374
Kenneth Rexroth 11:474

**Salamon, Lynda B.**
Sylvia Plath 17:350

**Sale, Roger**
Richard Adams 18:2
E. M. Almedingen 12:3
A. Alvarez 13:10
Kingsley Amis 5:22
Saul Bellow 6:61
Thomas Berger 8:84
Richard Brautigan 12:70
Frederick Buechner 2:83; 6:103
Anthony Burgess 5:87
Frederick Busch 10:94
Agatha Christie 8:141
Richard Condon 8:150
Robertson Davies 7:72
E. L. Doctorow 6:135
Margaret Drabble 2:118, 119;
   8:183
George P. Elliott 2:131
Frederick Exley 6:172
Leslie A. Fiedler 4:162
B. H. Friedman 7:109
Paula Fox 2:141
Herbert Gold 7:121
Witold Gombrowicz 7:122
Dashiell Hammett 5:161
John Hawkes 4:214
Mark Helprin 10:261
Maureen Howard 5:188; 14:267
Ken Kesey 6:278
John Le Carré 5:234
Alan Lelchuk 5:240
Doris Lessing 2:239, 242;
   6:299, 304
Alison Lurie 4:306
Ross Macdonald 2:255
David Madden 5:266
Norman Mailer 2:261; 4:319
Peter Matthiessen 7:212
Iris Murdoch 8:404
Tim O'Brien 7:271
Grace Paley 6:392
J. F. Powers 8:447
Richard Price 6:427
Judith Rossner 6:470
Philip Roth 2:381; 6:476
Andrew Sinclair 2:400
Isaac Bashevis Singer 9:487
Robert Stone 5:410
Paul Theroux 5:428
J.R.R. Tolkien 1:338
Anne Tyler 11:553
Mario Vargas Llosa 6:547
Kurt Vonnegut, Jr. 8:532
David Wagoner 5:475

James Welch 14:558
Larry Woiwode 10:541

**Salemi, Joseph S.**
William Gaddis 19:187

**Salisbury, Harrison E.**
Aleksandr I. Solzhenitsyn 4:511

**Salkey, Andrew**
Ngugi Wa Thiong'o 13:584

**Salmon, Sheila**
Barbara Corcoran 17:77

**Salomon, I. L.**
Robert Duncan 4:142

**Salomon, Louis B.**
Carson McCullers 12:408

**Salter, D.P.M.**
Saul Bellow 2:53

**Salway, Lance**
Robert Cormier 12:136
Peter Dickinson 12:168
Alan Garner 17:147
Robert Westall 17:556

**Salzman, Eric**
Frank Zappa 17:591

**Salzman, Jack**
John Dos Passos 4:138
Jack Kerouac 2:229
Tillie Olsen 4:386

**Samet, Tom**
Henry Roth 11:488

**Sammons, Jeffrey L.**
Hermann Hesse 11:271

**Sampley, Arthur M.**
Robert Frost 1:112

**Sampson, Edward C.**
E. B. White 10:529

**Samuels, Charles Thomas**
Richard Adams 4:7
Michelangelo Antonioni 20:33
Donald Barthelme 3:43
Robert Bresson 16:115
Lillian Hellman 2:187
Alfred Hitchcock 16:348
Stanley Kubrick 16:384
Christina Stead 2:421
John Updike 1:344; 2:442
Kurt Vonnegut, Jr. 2:454

**Samuelson, David N.**
Arthur C. Clarke 18:103

**Sanborn, Sara**
Anthony Burgess 4:84
Rosalyn Drexler 6:143
Alison Lurie 4:305
Joyce Carol Oates 3:363

**Sandars, N. K.**
David Jones 4:260

**Sandeen, Ernest**
R. P. Blackmur 2:62

**Sander, Ellen**
Mick Jagger and Keith Richard
17:223
John Lennon and Paul
McCartney 12:364
Joni Mitchell 12:435
Paul Simon 17:459
Neil Young 17:569
Frank Zappa 17:585

**Sanders, Charles**
Theodore Roethke 19:402

**Sanders, Charles L.**
Norman Lear 12:330

**Sanders, David**
John Hersey 1:144; 7:153

**Sanders, Ed**
Allen Ginsberg 4:181

**Sanders, Frederick L.**
Conrad Aiken 3:5

**Sanders, Ivan**
Dobrica Ćosić 14:132
György Konrád 4:273; 10:304
Milan Kundera 4:278
József Lengyel 7:202
Amos Oz 8:436

**Sanders, Peter L.**
Robert Graves 2:176

**Sanderson, Stewart F.**
Compton Mackenzie 18:315

**Sandler, Linda**
Margaret Atwood 8:29, 30
Ernest Buckler 13:123

**Sandoe, James**
Margery Allingham 19:13

**Sandrof, Ivan**
Jean Lee Latham 12:324

**Sandwell, B. K.**
Mazo de la Roche 14:148

**Sanfield, Steve**
Michael McClure 6:320

**Sargeant, Winthrop**
Vittorio De Sica 20:87
Robert Lewis Taylor 14:534

**Sargent, David**
Robert Wilson 9:576

**Sargo, Tina Mendes**
Luchino Visconti 16:566

**Sarland, Charles**
William Mayne 12:402

**Sarlin, Bob**
Chuck Berry 17:54
Mick Jagger and Keith Richard
17:229
Laura Nyro 17:316
Neil Young 17:572

**Sarotte, Georges-Michel**
William Inge 19:229
John Rechy 18:442

**Saroyan, Aram**
Kenneth Koch 8:323
Frank O'Hara 13:424
Anne Waldman 7:508

**Saroyan, William**
Flann O'Brien 10:362

**Sarris, Andrew George**
Woody Allen 16:7, 11
Robert Altman 16:36, 38, 43
Mel Brooks 12:75
Michael Cimino 16:209
Francis Ford Coppola 16:245
Brian De Palma 20:80
Rainer Werner Fassbinder
20:115
Federico Fellini 16:271, 297
John Ford 16:308
Bob Fosse 20:127
Jean-Luc Godard 20:137, 153
Werner Herzog 16:333
Alfred Hitchcock 16:341, 357
John Huston 20:174
Elia Kazan 16:364, 366
Buster Keaton 20:196
Stanley Kubrick 16:380
Akira Kurosawa 16:406
Richard Lester 20:231, 232
Norman Mailer 3:315
Sam Peckinpah 20:282
Roman Polanski 16:473
Jean Renoir 20:308
Alain Resnais 16:504, 518
Carlos Saura 20:318
Wilfrid Sheed 4:487
Joan Micklin Silver 20:344
Jerzy Skolimowski 20:354
François Truffaut 20:383, 404,
406, 407
Lina Wertmüller 16:599
Billy Wilder 20:461, 466

**Sartre, Jean-Paul**
Albert Camus 14:104
John Dos Passos 11:153
William Faulkner 9:197
Jean Genet 2:155

**Saunders, Charles**
May Swenson 14:522

**Sauzey, François**
Jean-Paul Sartre 18:473

**Savage, D. S.**
E. M. Forster 13:216
Christopher Isherwood 14:286
Mary Renault 17:391

**Savvas, Minas**
Yannis Ritsos 13:487

**Sayre, Henry M.**
John Ashbery 15:31

**Sayre, Nora**
Marguerite Duras 20:99
Iris Murdoch 1:236
Richard O'Brien 17:325
Anne Roiphe 3:434
Elizabeth Taylor 2:432
Kurt Vonnegut, Jr. 3:502

**Sayre, Robert F.**
James Baldwin 1:15

**Scaduto, Anthony**
Bob Dylan 4:148

**Scammell, William**
John Berger 19:40
Patrick White 18:547

**Scanlan, Margaret**
Iris Murdoch 15:387

**Scannell, Vernon**
Martin Booth 13:103
Randall Jarrell 9:298
George MacBeth 9:341

**Scarbrough, George**
Babette Deutsch 18:119
James Schevill 7:400

**Scarf, Maggie**
Lillian Hellman 18:228
Susan Sontag 10:487

**Schaap, Dick**
Mario Puzo 2:351

**Schaefer, J. O'Brien**
Margaret Drabble 5:119

**Schafer, William J.**
Mark Harris 19:202
David Wagoner 3:507

**Schaffner, Nicholas**
John Lennon and Paul
McCartney 12:385

**Schapiro, Leonard**
Aleksandr I. Solzhenitsyn 7:440

**Schatt, Stanley**
Langston Hughes 10:279
Isaac Bashevis Singer 3:459
Kurt Vonnegut, Jr. 1:348;
4:560; 12:614

**Schaub, Thomas Hill**
Thomas Pynchon 18:430

**Schechner, Mark**
Lionel Trilling 11:540

**Schechner, Richard**
Edward Albee 11:10
Eugène Ionesco 6:253

**Scheerer, Constance**
Sylvia Plath 9:432

**Schein, Harry**
Carl Theodor Dreyer 16:258

**Schevill, James**
Kenneth Patchen 18:395

**Schickel, Richard**
Woody Allen 16:3
Robert Altman 16:24
Michelangelo Antonioni 20:30
Louis Auchincloss 9:54
Ingmar Bergman 16:58, 63
John Cassavetes 20:47
Charles Chaplin 16:202
Francis Ford Coppola 16:236
Joan Didion 1:75
Jean-Luc Godard 20:143
Norman Lear 12:333
Alan Lelchuk 5:242
Richard Lester 20:227
Ross Macdonald 1:185
Garry Marshall 17:276
Thomas Pynchon 2:358
Satyajit Ray 16:481
Alain Resnais 16:504
Eric Rohmer 16:530
Carlos Saura 20:318
Peter Shaffer 5:387

Luchino Visconti 16:567
Andy Warhol 20:420
Frederick Wiseman 20:470, 475

**Schickele, Peter**
John Lennon and Paul
McCartney 12:355

**Schier, Donald**
André Breton 2:81

**Schiff, Jeff**
Mary Oliver 19:362

**Schillaci, Peter P.**
Luis Buñuel 16:140

**Schiller, Barbara**
Brigid Brophy 11:68

**Schjeldahl, Peter**
Paul Blackburn 9:100
André Breton 2:80; 9:129
Russell Edson 13:191
Gerome Ragni and James Rado
17:384
James Schevill 7:400
Diane Wakoski 11:564

**Schlant, Ernestine**
Christa Wolf 14:593

**Schlesinger, Arthur, Jr.**
Woody Allen 16:11
Michael Cimino 16:209
Bob Fosse 20:127

**Schlueter, June**
Samuel Beckett 18:43
Peter Handke 15:269
Arthur Miller 10:346
Tom Stoppard 15:522

**Schlueter, Paul**
Pär Lagerkvist 7:201
Doris Lessing 1:174; 3:283
Mary McCarthy 1:205
Gabrielle Roy 14:469
Robert Lewis Taylor 14:535

**Schmering, Chris**
Satyajit Ray 16:494

**Schmerl, Rudolf B.**
Aldous Huxley 3:255

**Schmidt, Arthur**
Joni Mitchell 12:437
Brian Wilson 12:641, 645
Frank Zappa 17:589

**Schmidt, Elizabeth**
Margaret Craven 17:80

**Schmidt, Michael**
Donald Davie 8:165
Philip Larkin 18:300
George MacBeth 2:252
Jon Silkin 2:396
Charles Tomlinson 13:548

**Schmidt, Pilar**
Lenora Mattingly Weber 12:634

**Schmitz, Neil**
Donald Barthelme 1:19
Richard Brautigan 3:90
Robert Coover 3:113; 7:58
Thomas Pynchon 6:435
Ishmael Reed 5:368; 6:448

**CRITIC INDEX**

Al Young 19:478

**Schneck, Stephen**
Richard Brautigan 1:44
LeRoi Jones 1:162

**Schneckloth, Tim**
Frank Zappa 17:592

**Schneidau, Herbert N.**
Ezra Pound 4:408

**Schneider, Alan**
Edward Albee 11:10

**Schneider, Duane**
Anaïs Nin 1:248; 11:396

**Schneider, Elisabeth**
T. S. Eliot 3:140

**Schneider, Harold W.**
Muriel Spark 13:519

**Schneider, Mary W.**
Muriel Spark 18:504

**Schneider, Richard J.**
William H. Gass 8:240

**Schoenbrun, David**
Cornelius Ryan 7:385

**Schoenstein, Ralph**
Garry Trudeau 12:590

**Scholes, Robert**
Jorge Luis Borges 10:63
Lawrence Durrell 8:190
John Hawkes 9:262; 15:273
Frank Herbert 12:276
Sylvia Plath 17:351
Frederik Pohl 18:410
Ishmael Reed 5:370
Kurt Vonnegut, Jr. 2:451;
   4:561

**Schorer, Mark**
Truman Capote 3:98
Martha Gellhorn 14:195
Lillian Hellman 4:221
Carson McCullers 4:344
Katherine Anne Porter 7:312

**Schott, Webster**
Richard Adams 5:6
Louis Auchincloss 4:31
W. H. Auden 2:25
Donald Barthelme 2:41
Saul Bellow 8:69
William Peter Blatty 2:63
Vance Bourjaily 8:103
Vincent Canby 13:131
James Clavell 6:113
Robert Coover 7:57
Michael Crichton 2:108
John Gardner 10:223
Shirley Hazzard 18:219
Ira Levin 6:305
David Madden 15:350
Larry McMurtry 2:272
Sylvia Plath 2:338
Raymond Queneau 10:432
Philip Roth 3:436
Susan Fromberg Schaeffer
   11:492
Georges Simenon 2:398
Harvey Swados 5:421
Thomas Tryon 11:548

Elio Vittorini 6:551
Jessamyn West 7:520
Patrick White 18:549
Tennessee Williams 5:506

**Schow, H. Wayne**
Günter Grass 11:248

**Schrader, George Alfred**
Norman Mailer 14:348

**Schrader, Paul**
Robert Bresson 16:115
Brian De Palma 20:72
Carl Theodor Dreyer 16:263
Albert Maysles and David
   Maysles 16:440
Yasujiro Ozu 16:449
Sam Peckinpah 20:273

**Schraepen, Edmond**
William Carlos Williams 9:575

**Schramm, Richard**
Philip Levine 2:244
Howard Moss 7:248

**Schrank, Bernice**
Sean O'Casey 11:411

**Schreiber, Jan**
Elizabeth Daryush 6:122

**Schreiber, LeAnne**
Jerome Charyn 8:135

**Schroeder, Andreas**
Michael Ondaatje 14:408

**Schroth, Raymond A.**
Norman Mailer 2:261; 3:312

**Schruers, Fred**
Joan Armatrading 17:9
Neil Young 17:576

**Schulder, Diane**
Marge Piercy 3:385

**Schuler, Barbara**
Peter Taylor 1:333

**Schulman, Grace**
Jorge Luis Borges 13:110
Richard Eberhart 3:134
Pablo Neruda 5:302
Octavio Paz 6:395
Adrienne Rich 3:427
Mark Van Doren 6:541
Richard Wilbur 9:569

**Schulps, Dave**
Peter Townshend 17:537

**Schulz, Charles M.**
Charles M. Schulz 12:527

**Schulz, Max F.**
John Barth 9:68
Norman Mailer 1:190
Bernard Malamud 1:199
Kurt Vonnegut, Jr. 1:347

**Schusler, Kris**
Robert Lewis Taylor 14:534

**Schuster, Arian**
Richard Brautigan 12:74

**Schuster, Edgar H.**
Harper Lee 12:341

**Schwaber, Paul**
Robert Lowell 1:184

**Schwartz, Barry N.**
Eugène Ionesco 15:296

**Schwartz, Delmore**
John Dos Passos 15:180
Randall Jarrell 1:159
Robinson Jeffers 11:304

**Schwartz, Edward**
Katherine Anne Porter 7:309

**Schwartz, Howard**
David Ignatow 7:178

**Schwartz, Julius**
Roy A. Gallant 17:127

**Schwartz, Kessel**
Vicente Aleixandre 9:15
Adolfo Bioy Casares 8:94
Antonio Buero Vallejo 15:96
Gabriel García Márquez
   10:215
Juan Rulfo 8:462

**Schwartz, Lloyd**
Elizabeth Bishop 9:93, 97

**Schwartz, Lynne Sharon**
Beryl Bainbridge 5:40
Eleanor Clark 19:107
Natalia Ginzburg 5:141
Susan Fromberg Schaeffer
   11:491
Alix Kates Shulman 10:475
Anne Tyler 11:552
Fay Weldon 9:560

**Schwartz, Nancy Lynn**
E. M. Broner 19:72
Jill Robinson 10:438

**Schwartz, Paul J.**
Samuel Beckett 6:41
Alain Robbe-Grillet 8:453

**Schwartz, Ronald**
Miguel Delibes 8:169
José María Gironella 11:234

**Schwartz, Sheila**
E. M. Broner 19:72

**Schwarz, Alfred**
Jean-Paul Sartre 18:469

**Schwarz, Egon**
Hermann Hesse 17:211

**Schwarzbach, F. S.**
Thomas Pynchon 9:443

**Schwarzchild, Bettina**
James Purdy 2:349

**Schwerer, Armand**
Diane Wakoski 7:506

**Scobbie, Irene**
Pär Lagerkvist 10:312

**Scobie, Stephen**
Bill Bissett 18:59
John Glassco 9:237
John Newlove 14:377
B. P. Nichol 18:366, 368
Michael Ondaatje 14:408

**Scobie, W. I.**
Melvin Van Peebles 2:448
Derek Walcott 2:459

**Scofield, Martin**
T. S. Eliot 9:186

**Scoggin, Margaret C.**
Walter Farley 17:116
Henry Gregor Felsen 17:120
Mary Stolz 12:547, 549, 550,
   552
John R. Tunis 12:594

**Scoppa, Bud**
Mick Jagger and Keith Richard
   17:228
John Lennon and Paul
   McCartney 12:366
Jimmy Page and Robert Plant
   12:479
Neil Young 17:572, 575

**Scott, Alexander**
Hugh MacDiarmid 4:310

**Scott, Carolyn D.**
Graham Greene 1:130

**Scott, Helen G.**
Alfred Hitchcock 16:346

**Scott, J. D.**
Andrew Sinclair 2:400

**Scott, Lael**
Mary Stolz 12:554

**Scott, Malcolm**
Jean Giono 11:232

**Scott, Nathan A., Jr.**
Charles M. Schulz 12:522
Richard Wright 1:378

**Scott, Peter Dale**
John Newlove 14:377
Mordecai Richler 5:372

**Scott, Tom**
Hugh MacDiarmid 4:309
Ezra Pound 4:413

**Scott, Winfield Townley**
David Ignatow 7:173
Louis Simpson 7:426

**Scott-James, R. A.**
Edith Sitwell 9:493

**Scouffas, George**
J. F. Powers 1:280

**Scruggs, Charles W.**
Jean Toomer 4:549

**Scruton, Roger**
Sylvia Plath 5:340

**Sculatti, Gene**
Brian Wilson 12:642

**Scupham, Peter**
W. H. Auden 6:16
Elizabeth Daryush 19:121
Robert Graves 6:211
H. D. 8:257
Elizabeth Jennings 14:293
David Jones 4:262
D. M. Thomas 13:542

CRITIC INDEX

**Searle, Leroy**
Dannie Abse 7:2
Erica Jong 4:264

**Searles, Baird**
Anna Kavan 5:205
Andre Norton 12:459

**Searles, George J.**
Joseph Heller 8:279

**Seaver, Richard**
Louis-Ferdinand Céline 1:57

**Seay, James**
James Wright 3:543

**Sedgwick, Ellery**
Esther Forbes 12:208

**Seebohm, Caroline**
Isaac Asimov 19:29
Dirk Bogarde 19:42
Kamala Markandaya 8:377

**Seed, David**
Isaac Bashevis Singer 9:487

**Seelye, John**
Donald Barthelme 2:41
Richard Lester 20:218, 219
Norman Mailer 3:316
Marge Piercy 3:383
Charles M. Schulz 12:531
James Thurber 5:439
David Wagoner 5:474

**Segal, Erich**
Robert Lowell 15:348

**Segal, Lore**
Joan Didion 1:75

**Segovia, Tomás**
Octavio Paz 3:376

**Seib, Kenneth**
Richard Brautigan 1:44

**Seibles, Timothy S.**
James Baldwin 15:43

**Seiden, Melvin**
Vladimir Nabokov 2:302

**Seidlin, Oskar**
Hermann Hesse 17:216

**Seidman, Hugh**
Denise Levertov 15:338
Mary Oliver 19:362

**Seidman, Robert**
John Berger 19:39

**Seitz, Michael**
Luchino Visconti 16:574

**Selby, Herbert, Jr.**
Richard Price 6:427

**Seldes, Gilbert**
Charles Chaplin 16:188

**Seligson, Tom**
Piri Thomas 17:500
Hunter S. Thompson 9:527

**Sellick, Robert**
Shirley Hazzard 18:218

**Sellin, Eric**
Samuel Beckett 2:47

**Selzer, David**
Peter Porter 5:346

**Semkow, Julie**
Joan Micklin Silver 20:341

**Sena, Vinad**
T. S. Eliot 6:159

**Sennwald, Andre**
Rouben Mamoulian 16:421

**Servodidio, Mirella D'Ambrosio**
Azorín 11:24

**Sesonske, Alexander**
Jean Renoir 20:309

**Seton, Cynthia Propper**
Marilyn French 18:158
Barbara Pym 19:387
Muriel Spark 18:505

**Sewell, Elizabeth**
Muriel Rukeyser 15:458

**Seybolt, Cynthia T.**
Jules Archer 12:21, 22

**Seydor, Paul**
Sam Peckinpah 20:283

**Seymour-Smith, Martin**
Robert Graves 1:128

**Sgammato, Joseph**
Alfred Hitchcock 16:351

**Shadoian, Jack**
Donald Barthelme 1:18

**Shaffer, Dallas Y.**
Jules Archer 12:16
Frank Bonham 12:53

**Shah, Diane K.**
Richard O'Brien 17:325

**Shahane, Vasant Anant**
Khushwant Singh 11:504

**Shands, Annette Oliver**
Gwendolyn Brooks 4:78, 79
Don L. Lee 2:238

**Shannon, James P.**
J. F. Powers 1:279

**Shapcott, Thomas**
Frank O'Hara 2:323
W. R. Rodgers 7:377

**Shapiro, Charles**
Meyer Levin 7:203
David Madden 5:265
Joyce Carol Oates 3:363
Anthony Powell 1:277
Harvey Swados 5:420
Jerome Weidman 7:517

**Shapiro, David**
Elizabeth Bishop 15:60
Hayden Carruth 10:100
X. J. Kennedy 8:320
Josephine Miles 14:370
Eric Rohmer 16:539

**Shapiro, Jane**
Rosalyn Drexler 6:143

**Shapiro, Karl**
W. H. Auden 1:8; 3:21
T. S. Eliot 3:136
Rod McKuen 1:210
Henry Miller 4:349
Ezra Pound 3:394
William Carlos Williams 5:506

**Shapiro, Laura**
Elizabeth Swados 12:560

**Shapiro, Marianne**
Elio Vittorini 14:546

**Shapiro, Paula Meinetz**
Alice Walker 6:553

**Shapiro, Susin**
Joan Armatrading 17:7

**Sharma, P. P.**
Arthur Miller 15:370

**Sharp, Sister Corona**
Friedrich Dürrenmatt 15:201
Eugène Ionesco 15:297

**Sharpe, Patricia**
Margaret Drabble 10:162

**Shattan, Joseph**
Saul Bellow 8:80

**Shattuck, Roger**
Jean Arp 5:32
Saul Bellow 6:57
Alain Robbe-Grillet 2:376
Octavio Paz 19:365

**Shaughnessy, Mary Rose**
Edna Ferber 18:152

**Shaw, Arnold**
Chuck Berry 17:53

**Shaw, Evelyn**
Melvin Berger 12:37

**Shaw, Greg**
Brian Wilson 12:647

**Shaw, Irwin**
James Jones 10:290

**Shaw, Peter**
Robert Lowell 8:351
Hugh Nissenson 9:400
Ezra Pound 18:422

**Shaw, Robert B.**
A. R. Ammons 3:11
W. H. Auden 2:26
Wendell Berry 8:85
Stanley Burnshaw 3:91
Babette Deutsch 18:120
James Dickey 2:117
Robert Duncan 7:88
Robert Francis 15:238
Allen Ginsberg 6:201
John Glassco 9:236
Richard Howard 7:166
Barbara Howes 15:289
David Ignatow 4:248
Stanley Kunitz 14:313
Philip Larkin 8:338
William Meredith 4:348
Adrienne Rich 6:457
Raphael Rudnik 7:384
Charles Simic 6:501; 9:479
Allen Tate 2:430

Mark Van Doren 6:541
Eudora Welty 14:566
Marya Zaturenska 6:585

**Shayon, Robert Lewis**
Norman Lear 12:329
Gene Roddenberry 17:403

**Shea, Robert J.**
Budd Schulberg 7:403

**Shear, Walter**
Bernard Malamud 1:197

**Shechner, Mark**
Tadeusz Konwicki 8:328
Mordecai Richler 18:453
Philip Roth 15:451
Isaac Bashevis Singer 15:508

**Shedlin, Michael**
Woody Allen 16:2

**Sheed, Wilfrid**
Edward Albee 1:4
James Baldwin 1:16; 8:42
Robert Coover 7:58
Robert Frost 1:110
William Golding 1:121
Joseph Heller 5:182
James Jones 1:162
Norman Mailer 1:193; 4:320
Terrence McNally 7:216
Arthur Miller 1:217
Alberto Moravia 2:292
Iris Murdoch 1:236
P. H. Newby 13:409
John Osborne 1:263
Walker Percy 2:332
Neil Simon 6:503
William Styron 1:330
John Updike 1:343
Kurt Vonnegut, Jr. 1:347
Douglas Turner Ward 19:456
Evelyn Waugh 3:512
Arnold Wesker 3:518
Tennessee Williams 1:369
Tom Wolfe 2:481

**Sheehan, Donald**
John Berryman 1:34
Richard Howard 7:166
Robert Lowell 1:181

**Sheehan, Edward R. F.**
Edwin O'Connor 14:392

**Sheehan, Ethna**
E. M. Almedingen 12:1
Christie Harris 12:261

**Shelton, Austin J.**
Chinua Achebe 7:4

**Shelton, Frank W.**
Robert Coover 7:60
Ernest Hemingway 10:269

**Shelton, Robert**
Joan Armatrading 17:10
Bob Dylan 12:179

**Shepard, Paul**
Peter Matthiessen 5:273

**Shepard, Ray Anthony**
Alice Childress 12:107
Nicholasa Mohr 12:446

CRITIC INDEX

**Shepard, Richard F.**
Sam Shepard **17**:433

**Shepherd, Allen**
Reynolds Price **3**:405, 406
Robert Penn Warren **1**:355

**Shepherd, Naomi**
S. Y. Agnon **14**:1

**Sheppard, R. Z.**
Louis Auchincloss **4**:30
Saul Bellow **6**:55
William Peter Blatty **2**:64
Lothar-Günther Buchheim
**6**:101
Anthony Burgess **5**:85
Peter De Vries **2**:114
E. L. Doctorow **6**:133
Nora Ephron **17**:113
Alex Haley **8**:260
Frank Herbert **12**:270
James Leo Herlihy **6**:235
Dan Jacobson **4**:254
Bernard Malamud **2**:266
S. J. Perelman **5**:338
Ishmael Reed **5**:370
Harvey Swados **5**:422
Michel Tournier **6**:537
Mario Vargas Llosa **6**:545
Gore Vidal **6**:548
Paul West **7**:523
Hilma Wolitzer **17**:561

**Sheps, G. David**
Mordecai Richler **13**:481

**Sheridan, Robert N.**
Henry Gregor Felsen **17**:124

**Sherman, Beatrice**
Margery Allingham **19**:13
Sally Benson **17**:48
Dalton Trumbo **19**:445

**Sherrard-Smith, Barbara**
Zilpha Keatley Snyder **17**:472

**Sherry, Vincent B., Jr.**
W. S. Merwin **18**:335

**Sherwood, R. E.**
Buster Keaton **20**:188

**Sherwood, Terry G.**
Ken Kesey **1**:167

**Shewey, Don**
Joan Armatrading **17**:11
Frank Zappa **17**:594

**Shifreen, Lawrence J.**
Henry Miller **14**:372

**Shinn, Thelma J.**
Flannery O'Connor **6**:375
Ann Petry **7**:304
William Saroyan **10**:452

**Shipp, Randy**
Robert Lewis Taylor **14**:535

**Shippey, T. A.**
Samuel R. Delany **14**:147
Robert Nye **13**:414
Frederik Pohl **18**:410
Mary Lee Settle **19**:410
John Steinbeck **13**:535

**Shippey, Thomas**
Lothar-Günther Buchheim
**6**:100

**Shivers, Alfred S.**
Jessamyn West **7**:520

**Shoemaker, Alice**
William Faulkner **14**:175

**Shore, Rima**
Yevgeny Yevtushenko **13**:619

**Shorris, Earl**
Donald Barthelme **2**:42
John Gardner **3**:184
William H. Gass **2**:155
Thomas Pynchon **3**:414

**Short, Robert L.**
Charles M. Schulz **12**:522, 525

**Shorter, Eric**
Alan Ayckbourn **5**:36; **18**:29
Agatha Christie **12**:118
Hugh Leonard **19**:282
Thornton Wilder **15**:574

**Shoukri, Doris Enright-Clark**
Marguerite Duras **3**:129

**Showalter, Dennis E.**
Robert Heinlein **14**:246

**Showalter, Elaine**
Mary McCarthy **3**:329

**Showers, Paul**
Peter De Vries **2**:114
James Herriot **12**:283
John Seelye **7**:407
Alvin Silverstein and Virginia
B. Silverstein **17**:454

**Shrapnel, Norman**
Marge Piercy **18**:406

**Shrimpton, Nicholas**
Bernice Rubens **19**:405
C. P. Snow **19**:428

**Shuman, R. Baird**
William Inge **1**:153
Clifford Odets **2**:318, 320

**Shuttleworth, Martin**
Christina Stead **2**:421

**Shuttleworth, Paul**
Leon Uris **7**:492

**Siaulys, Tony**
Sonia Levitin **17**:266

**Sibbald, K. M.**
Jorge Guillén **11**:263

**Sicherman, Carol M.**
Saul Bellow **10**:37

**Siconolfi, Michael T., S.J.**
Audre Lorde **18**:309

**Siebert, Sara L.**
Maureen Daly **17**:89

**Siegal, R. A.**
Judy Blume **12**:47

**Siegel, Ben**
Saul Bellow **8**:78
Bernard Malamud **1**:195
Isaac Bashevis Singer **1**:313

**Siegel, Joel E.**
Robert Altman **16**:33
Albert Maysles and David
Maysles **16**:445

**Siegel, Paul N.**
Norman Mailer **5**:266

**Siegel, Robert**
Al Young **19**:480

**Siemens, William L.**
Julio Cortázar **5**:110

**Sigal, Clancy**
Kingsley Amis **3**:9; **5**:22
Patrick Boyle **19**:67
Melvyn Bragg **10**:72
E. L. Doctorow **18**:127
Alan Sillitoe **3**:448

**Sigerson, Davitt**
Brian Wilson **12**:653

**Siggins, Clara M.**
Taylor Caldwell **2**:95
Alan Garner **17**:146
Lillian Hellman **4**:221
Saul Maloff **5**:270

**Silbajoris, Rimvydas**
Boris Pasternak **10**:387

**Silber, Irwin**
Bob Dylan **12**:181

**Silenieks, Juris**
Édouard Glissant **10**:231

**Silet, Charles L. P.**
David Kherdian **9**:317, 318

**Silkin, Jon**
Geoffrey Hill **5**:183

**Silko, Leslie Marmon**
Dee Brown **18**:71

**Silver, Adele Z.**
E. M. Broner **19**:70

**Silver, Charles**
Orson Welles **20**:446

**Silver, David**
Peter Townshend **17**:527

**Silver, George A.**
John Berger **19**:37

**Silver, Philip**
Dámaso Alonso **14**:22

**Silverman, Hugh J.**
Jean-Paul Sartre **18**:472

**Silverman, Malcolm**
Jorge Amado **13**:11

**Silverman, Michael**
Nagisa Oshima **20**:253

**Silverstein, Norman**
James Dickey **7**:81
Buster Keaton **20**:195

**Silvert, Conrad**
Peter Matthiessen **7**:210

**Silvey, Anita**
Otfried Preussler **17**:377

**Simels, Steve**
Martin Mull **17**:300
Jimmy Page and Robert Plant
**12**:476
Gene Roddenberry **17**:414
Patti Smith **12**:537
Bruce Springsteen **17**:485
Peter Townshend **17**:535
Brian Wilson **12**:651
Neil Young **17**:579

**Simenon, Georges**
Georges Simenon **3**:451

**Simic, Charles**
Vasko Popa **19**:374

**Simmons, Ernest J.**
Mikhail Sholokhov **7**:416, 420

**Simmons, Ruth J. S.**
Aimé Césaire **19**:97

**Simmons, Tom**
Richard F. Hugo **18**:263

**Simon, John**
Edward Albee **2**:1; **5**:13; **11**:11;
**13**:3, 4
Woody Allen **16**:7, 13
Robert Altman **16**:33, 36
Lindsay Anderson **20**:14
Jean Anouilh **13**:22
Michelangelo Antonioni **20**:40
Alan Ayckbourn **8**:34; **18**:29
James Baldwin **17**:40
Peter Barnes **5**:49
Samuel Beckett **3**:47
Ingmar Bergman **16**:77
Bernardo Bertolucci **16**:100
Robert Bolt **14**:88
Mel Brooks **12**:80
Ed Bullins **5**:84; **7**:36
Anne Burr **6**:104
John Cassavetes **20**:51
Claude Chabrol **16**:179
Francis Ford Coppola **16**:240
Brian De Palma **20**:74, 76
Martin Duberman **8**:185
Marguerite Duras **20**:98
Rainer Werner Fassbinder
**20**:112
Jules Feiffer **2**:133
Federico Fellini **16**:289, 297,
300
Lawrence Ferlinghetti **2**:134
Bob Fosse **20**:124
Athol Fugard **9**:230; **14**:191
Frank D. Gilroy **2**:161
Jean-Luc Godard **20**:135
Charles Gordone **1**:124
Günter Grass **11**:252
Simon Gray **14**:215
John Guare **14**:222
Bill Gunn **5**:153
Christopher Hampton **4**:211
Joseph Heller **11**:265
Lillian Hellman **8**:281; **18**:226
Alfred Hitchcock **16**:353
Rolf Hochhuth **11**:275
Bohumil Hrabal **13**:290
William Inge **8**:308
Pavel Kohout **13**:323
Arthur Kopit **1**:171; **18**:291
Stanley Kubrick **16**:390

Richard Lester **20**:230, 231
Denise Levertov **15**:336
Ira Levin **3**:294
Robert Lowell **4**:299; **11**:324
Norman Mailer **2**:259; **3**:316
David Mamet **15**:356, 358
Elaine May **16**:436
Albert Maysles and David
　Maysles **16**:444
Terrence McNally **4**:347;
　**7**:217, 218, 219
Mark Medoff **6**:321, 322
Christopher Middleton **13**:387
Arthur Miller **2**:279, 280; **6**:335
Jason Miller **2**:284, 285
Joyce Carol Oates **11**:400
Joe Orton **4**:387
John Osborne **2**:328; **11**:421
Nagisa Oshima **20**:245, 256
Rochelle Owens **8**:434
Gordon Parks **16**:460
Pier Paolo Pasolini **20**:262
Sam Peckinpah **20**:274
S. J. Perelman **5**:337
Harold Pinter **3**:386, 387;
　**11**:443; **15**:425
Sylvia Plath **17**:345
Roman Polanski **16**:471
Bernard Pomerance **13**:446
David Rabe **8**:449, 451
Gerome Ragni and James Rado
　**17**:381, 388
Satyajit Ray **16**:489
Jean Renoir **20**:307
Jonathan Reynolds **6**:452
Eric Rohmer **16**:538
Howard Sackler **14**:478
Carlos Saura **20**:318
Murray Schisgal **6**:490
Peter Shaffer **5**:387, 389
Ntozake Shange **8**:484
Sam Shepard **6**:497; **17**:435,
　449
Martin Sherman **19**:415
Joan Micklin Silver **20**:343
Neil Simon **6**:506; **11**:495, 496
Isaac Bashevis Singer **15**:509
Bernard Slade **11**:507
Steven Spielberg **20**:361
John Steinbeck **5**:408
Tom Stoppard **3**:470; **4**:525,
　526; **5**:412; **8**:504
David Storey **4**:528; **5**:415, 417
Elizabeth Swados **12**:559, 562
Ronald Tavel **6**:529
François Truffaut **20**:385, 405
Melvin Van Peebles **2**:448
Gore Vidal **2**:450; **4**:554;
　**10**:503
Andrzej Wajda **16**:578
Derek Walcott **2**:460; **14**:550
Peter Weiss **3**:513
Michael Weller **10**:526
Lina Wertmüller **16**:590, 598
Billy Wilder **20**:460
Thornton Wilder **10**:535
Tennessee Williams **2**:464;
　**5**:501; **7**:544; **8**:549; **11**:571
Lanford Wilson **14**:591, 592
Robert Wilson **7**:550, 551

**Simon, John K.**
Michel Butor **15**:112

**Simonds, C. H.**
Joan Didion **1**:74

**Simonds, Katharine**
Sally Benson **17**:47

**Simpson, Allen**
Albert Camus **11**:96

**Simpson, Clinton**
Ilya Ehrenburg **18**:130

**Simpson, Elaine**
Andre Norton **12**:456

**Simpson, Louis**
Robert Bly **2**:65
Allen Ginsberg **13**:241
James Merrill **8**:380
Kenneth Rexroth **2**:370
W. D. Snodgrass **2**:405

**Sinclair, Dorothy**
Erich Segal **10**:467
David Slavitt **14**:491

**Sinclair, Karen**
Ursula K. LeGuin **13**:350

**Singer, Alexander**
René Clair **20**:63

**Singer, Isaac B.**
Otfried Preussler **17**:376

**Singer, Marilyn**
Frank Bonham **12**:54

**Singh, G.**
Eugenio Montale **7**:223, 226
Ezra Pound **2**:342, 344; **7**:334

**Sinyavsky, Andrei**
Robert Frost **4**:174

**Sire, James W.**
C. S. Lewis **1**:177

**Sisco, Ellen**
Jamake Highwater **12**:286

**Sisk, John P.**
Mark Harris **19**:200
J. F. Powers **1**:280

**Sissman, L. E.**
Kingsley Amis **2**:7; **5**:22
Martin Amis **4**:21
Jimmy Breslin **4**:76
Michael Crichton **6**:119
J. P. Donleavy **4**:126
J. G. Farrell **6**:174
Natalia Ginzburg **5**:141
Joseph Heller **8**:278
Dan Jacobson **4**:255
Thomas McGuane **3**:329
Tom McHale **3**:332; **5**:282
Brian Moore **7**:237
Gilbert Rogin **18**:458
Anne Roiphe **3**:434
John Updike **2**:441
Evelyn Waugh **3**:513
Fay Weldon **6**:563
Emlyn Williams **15**:578
Edmund Wilson **2**:478
Al Young **19**:477

**Sisson, C. H.**
H. D. **8**:257

**Sitterly, Bancroft W.**
Roy A. Gallant **17**:127

**Sjöberg, Leif**
Eyvind Johnson **14**:296, 297
Harry Martinson **14**:355, 356

**Skau, Michael**
Lawrence Ferlinghetti **10**:177

**Skelton, Robin**
Anthony Kerrigan **6**:276
Dorothy Livesay **4**:294
John Newlove **14**:378

**Skerrett, Joseph T., Jr.**
Ralph Ellison **11**:182

**Sklar, Robert**
J.R.R. Tolkien **12**:568

**Skloot, Floyd**
Thomas Kinsella **19**:255

**Skodnick, Roy**
Gilbert Sorrentino **7**:448

**Skoller, Don**
Carl Theodor Dreyer **16**:262

**Skow, Jack**
John Gardner **5**:132
Robert Graves **2**:176

**Skow, John**
Richard Adams **5**:5
Richard Brautigan **3**:86
Arthur A. Cohen **7**:52
Richard Condon **4**:107; **6**:115
Julio Cortázar **5**:109
Robertson Davies **2**:113
Lawrence Durrell **6**:152
Charles Johnson **7**:183
Robert F. Jones **7**:193
Sue Kaufman **3**:263
Yasunari Kawabata **5**:208
Milan Kundera **4**:277
John D. MacDonald **3**:307
Iris Murdoch **4**:370
Vladimir Nabokov **6**:354
Harold Robbins **5**:379
Susan Fromberg Schaeffer
　**6**:488
Irving Stone **7**:471
Kurt Vonnegut, Jr. **4**:568
Morris L. West **6**:564
Patrick White **3**:525

**Škvorecký, Josef**
Pavel Kohout **13**:325

**Slade, Joseph W.**
James T. Farrell **11**:192

**Slansky, Paul**
Martin Mull **17**:300

**Slater, Candace**
Elizabeth Bishop **13**:88
Salvatore Espriu **9**:193

**Slater, Jack**
Stevie Wonder **12**:662

**Slater, Joseph**
Nelly Sachs **14**:475

**Slaughter, Frank G.**
Millen Brand **7**:29

**Slavitt, David R.**
George Garrett **11**:220
Maureen Howard **14**:267
Ann Quin **6**:441

**Slethaug, Gordon E.**
John Barth **2**:38

**Sloan, James Park**
Alice Childress **15**:131
David Madden **15**:350

**Slonim, Marc**
Ilya Ehrenburg **18**:133
Mikhail Sholokhov **7**:415, 418
Aleksandr I. Solzhenitsyn **1**:320
Marguerite Yourcenar **19**:482

**Sloss, Henry**
Richard Howard **10**:276
James Merrill **8**:381, 384
Reynolds Price **3**:406
Philip Roth **1**:293

**Slung, Michele**
P. D. James **18**:273

**Slusser, George Edgar**
Arthur C. Clarke **13**:151
Samuel R. Delany **14**:143
Harlan Ellison **13**:204
Robert Heinlein **14**:246
Ursula K. LeGuin **13**:345

**Smeltzer, Sister Mary Etheldra**
Larry Kettelkamp **12**:306

**Smith, A.J.M.**
Earle Birney **6**:74
Stanley Kunitz **14**:312
Irving Layton **15**:318
P. K. Page **7**:291
A.J.M. Smith **15**:515

**Smith, Barbara**
Ishmael Reed **6**:447
Alice Walker **6**:553

**Smith, C.E.J.**
Mavis Thorpe Clark **12**:130
Leon Garfield **12**:231

**Smith, Dave**
Harry Crews **6**:118
Albert Goldbarth **5**:144
Daniel Halpern **14**:232
William Heyen **18**:232
Cynthia Macdonald **19**:290
Louis Simpson **7**:429
Barry Spacks **14**:511
Robert Penn Warren **13**:581

**Smith, David E.**
E. E. Cummings **8**:158

**Smith, Eleanor T.**
Jessamyn West **17**:547

**Smith, F. C.**
Henry Gregor Felsen **17**:121

**Smith, Grover**
T. S. Eliot **15**:206
Archibald MacLeish **8**:359

**Smith, H. Allen**
Jacqueline Susann **3**:476

**Smith, Harrison**
Ilya Ehrenburg **18**:132
Madeleine L'Engle **12**:345
Mary Renault **17**:392
Jessamyn West **17**:546

**Smith, Iain Crichton**
Hugh MacDiarmid **11**:336

**Smith, Jack**
Josef von Sternberg **20**:373

**Smith, Janet Adam**
Richard Adams **4**:8
J.R.R. Tolkien **2**:435

**Smith, Jennifer Farley**
Margaret Craven **17**:79
Allan W. Eckert **17**:108

**Smith, Joan**
Piri Thomas **17**:502

**Smith, Liz**
Truman Capote **8**:133

**Smith, Mason**
Richard Brautigan **12**:60

**Smith, Maxwell A.**
Jean Giono **4**:184
François Mauriac **4**:340

**Smith, Michael**
Rosalyn Drexler **2**:119
Anthony Kerrigan **6**:275
Tom Stoppard **1**:327
Robert Wilson **7**:549

**Smith, Phillip E., II**
Charles Olson **11**:420

**Smith, Raymond J.**
James Dickey **10**:141

**Smith, Robert**
Jimmy Page and Robert Plant
**12**:481

**Smith, Robert W.**
Varlam Shalamov **18**:479

**Smith, Roger H.**
John D. MacDonald **3**:307

**Smith, Sherwin D.**
Charles M. Schulz **12**:530

**Smith, Sidonie Ann**
Maya Angelou **12**:10

**Smith, Stan**
Sylvia Plath **17**:357

**Smith, Stevie**
Edna Ferber **18**:152

**Smith, William James**
Kurt Vonnegut, Jr. **12**:601

**Smith, William Jay**
Elizabeth Bishop **13**:89
Louis MacNeice **4**:315
Frederick Seidel **18**:474
Sylvia Townsend Warner
**19**:459

**Smyth, Pat**
William Mayne **12**:395

**Smyth, Paul**
Derek Walcott **4**:575

**Sniderman, Stephen L.**
Joseph Heller **3**:230

**Snodgrass, W. D.**
Theodore Roethke **8**:455

**Snow, C. P.**
Norman Mailer **4**:322

**Snow, George E.**
Aleksandr I. Solzhenitsyn **4**:507

**Snow, Helen F.**
Pearl S. Buck **7**:33

**Snowden, J. A.**
Sean O'Casey **9**:406

**Snyder, Stephen**
Pier Paolo Pasolini **20**:271

**Snyder-Scumpy, Patrick**
Martin Mull **17**:297, 298

**Sobejano, Gonzalo**
Dámaso Alonso **14**:20

**Sobran, M. J., Jr.**
Norman Lear **12**:338

**Socken, Paul G.**
Anne Hébert **13**:268
Gabrielle Roy **14**:469

**Soderbergh, Peter A.**
Upton Sinclair **11**:497

**Sodowsky, Alice**
George Lucas **16**:409

**Sodowsky, Roland**
George Lucas **16**:409

**Soile, Sola**
Chinua Achebe **11**:4

**Sokel, Walter Herbert**
Heinrich Böll **9**:102

**Sokolov, Raymond A.**
André Brink **18**:67
E. L. Doctorow **6**:132
Julius Horwitz **14**:267
Dan Jacobson **4**:254
Gayl Jones **6**:265
Thomas Keneally **8**:319
József Lengyel **7**:202
John Sayles **7**:400
Hilma Wolitzer **17**:563

**Solecki, Sam**
Earle Birney **11**:50

**Solnick, Bruce B.**
George Garrett **11**:220

**Solomon, Barbara Probst**
Juan Goytisolo **5**:151
João Ubaldo Ribeiro **10**:436
Mario Vargas Llosa **10**:500

**Solomon, Linda**
David Bowie **17**:61

**Solomon, Norman**
Jonathan Kozol **17**:253

**Solomon, Philip H.**
Louis-Ferdinand Céline **15**:123

**Solomon, Stanley J.**
Francis Ford Coppola **16**:244

**Solotaroff, Theodore**
Saul Bellow **1**:33
Paul Bowles **1**:41
Anthony Burgess **1**:48
William S. Burroughs **1**:48
Albert Camus **9**:146
Alex Comfort **7**:54
George P. Elliott **2**:130
John Fowles **6**:185
Herbert Gold **7**:120
Paul Goodman **1**:123
Günter Grass **1**:125
Stanislaw Lem **8**:344
Bernard Malamud **1**:196, 200
Henry Miller **1**:219
Flannery O'Connor **1**:256
Katherine Anne Porter **1**:271
V. S. Pritchett **5**:352
James Purdy **2**:348
Philip Roth **4**:451
Jean-Paul Sartre **1**:304
Hubert Selby, Jr. **8**:474
Susan Sontag **1**:322
Vladimir Voinovich **10**:508
Richard Wright **1**:377
Richard Yates **7**:553

**Solzhenitsyn, Alexander**
Mikhail Sholokhov **15**:480

**Somer, John**
Kurt Vonnegut, Jr. **4**:566

**Somers, Paul P., Jr.**
Ernest Hemingway **8**:283

**Sommer, Sally R.**
Alice Childress **12**:108

**Sommers, Joseph**
Miguel Ángel Asturias **13**:39

**Sonkiss, Lois**
Jamake Highwater **12**:286

**Sonnenfeld, Albert**
Heinrich Böll **9**:107

**Sonntag, Jacob**
Amos Oz **8**:435
Isaac Bashevis Singer **3**:456
Arnold Wesker **3**:519

**Sontag, Susan**
James Baldwin **4**:40
Ingmar Bergman **16**:56
Robert Bresson **16**:106
Albert Camus **4**:88
Paul Goodman **2**:170
Rolf Hochhuth **4**:230
Eugène Ionesco **4**:251
Alain Resnais **16**:501
Nathalie Sarraute **4**:465
Jean-Paul Sartre **4**:475
Peter Weiss **15**:564

**Sonthoff, Helen W.**
Phyllis Webb **18**:540
Ethel Davis Wilson **13**:606

**Sorban, M. J., Jr.**
Woody Allen **16**:8

**Sorenson, Marian**
Allan W. Eckert **17**:103
Lee Kingman **17**:245

**Sorrentino, Gilbert**
Paul Blackburn **9**:99
Richard Brautigan **12**:57
Robert Creeley **2**:106
Robert Duncan **2**:122
William Gaddis **8**:227
Charles Olson **2**:327
John Wieners **7**:535, 536
Louis Zukofsky **7**:563

**Soskin, William**
Esther Forbes **12**:204

**Sotiron, Michael**
Hugh Garner **13**:237

**Soule, Stephen W.**
Anthony Burgess **5**:90

**Soupault, Philippe**
René Clair **20**:60

**Sourian, Peter**
Albert Camus **2**:98
Eleanor Clark **5**:105
Jack Kerouac **2**:227
Norman Lear **12**:336
Eric Rohmer **16**:535
William Saroyan **8**:468
Vassilis Vassilikos **4**:552

**Southerland, Ellease**
Zora Neale Hurston **7**:171

**Southern, David**
Michael McClure **6**:320

**Southern, Terry**
William Golding **17**:165
John Rechy **1**:283
Kurt Vonnegut, Jr. **12**:601

**Southworth, James G.**
E. E. Cummings **3**:115
Robert Frost **3**:168
Robinson Jeffers **3**:257
Archibald MacLeish **3**:309
Laura Riding **7**:373

**Souza, Raymond D.**
Octavio Paz **10**:392
Ernesto Sábato **10**:444

**Spacks, Patricia Meyer**
Kingsley Amis **5**:24
Nicholas Delbanco **6**:130
Hannah Green **3**:202
Joseph Heller **5**:183
Jennifer Johnston **7**:186
D. Keith Mano **10**:328
Alberto Moravia **2**:294
Iris Murdoch **6**:347
J. R. Salamanca **15**:463
Anne Sexton **8**:483
Andrew Sinclair **2**:402
Muriel Spark **2**:419; **5**:400
Peter Spielberg **6**:520
J.R.R. Tolkien **1**:336
Elio Vittorini **6**:551
Eudora Welty **2**:464
Paul West **7**:524
Patrick White **4**:587

**Spain, Francis Lander**
Margot Benary-Isbert **12**:31

**Spann, Marcella**
Ezra Pound **4**:413

**Spanos, William V.**
Yannis Ritsos 6:460
Jean-Paul Sartre 18:466

**Spaulding, Martha**
Laurie Colwin 13:156
Kamala Markandaya 8:377
J.R.R. Tolkien 8:516

**Spears, Monroe K.**
W. H. Auden 2:22
John Berryman 2:57
James Dickey 2:116
T. S. Eliot 2:127
Robert Graves 11:254
Ted Hughes 2:199
David Jones 2:217
Madison Jones 4:263
Robert Lowell 2:248
Ezra Pound 2:342
John Crowe Ransom 2:366
Karl Shapiro 4:487
Allen Tate 2:430
John Kennedy Toole 19:443
Robert Penn Warren 1:355;
    4:579; 18:539

**Spector, Ivar**
Mikhail Sholokhov 7:420

**Spector, Robert D.**
William Bronk 10:73
Robert Duncan 7:87
D. J. Enright 4:156
David Ignatow 7:174
Carolyn Kizer 15:308
Kenneth Rexroth 2:371

**Speer, Diane Parkin**
Robert Heinlein 8:275

**Spence, Jon**
Katherine Anne Porter 7:320

**Spencer, Benjamin T.**
Edward Dahlberg 7:70

**Spencer, Jack**
André Schwarz-Bart 2:388

**Spencer, Sharon**
Djuna Barnes 3:38
Jorge Luis Borges 3:77
Julio Cortázar 3:114
Carlos Fuentes 3:175
Anaïs Nin 4:376; 14:381
Alain Robbe-Grillet 4:448

**Spendal, R. J.**
James Wright 10:546

**Spender, Stephen**
A. R. Ammons 2:12
W. H. Auden 3:25, 27
James Baldwin 17:25
Robert Graves 2:177
Thom Gunn 3:216
Ted Hughes 2:200
Aldous Huxley 3:253; 5:192;
    8:304
David Jones 13:312
Arthur Koestler 15:311
Philip Levine 4:287
James Merrill 3:335
W. S. Merwin 3:340
Eugenio Montale 7:225
Elsa Morante 8:403

Sylvia Plath 9:429
William Plomer 4:406
Nelly Sachs 14:475
James Schuyler 5:383
Gore Vidal 2:450; 8:527
James Wright 3:541

**Spicer, Edward H.**
Carlos Castaneda 12:85

**Spiegel, Alan**
Stanley Kubrick 16:392
Jean-Paul Sartre 7:398

**Spiegelman, Willard**
John Betjeman 10:53
Richard Howard 7:169
James Merrill 8:384
Adrienne Rich 7:370

**Spieler, F. Joseph**
Robert Wilson 9:577

**Spilka, Mark**
Ernest Hemingway 10:263
Doris Lessing 6:300
Erich Segal 3:446

**Spina, James**
Jimmy Page and Robert Plant
    12:482

**Spitz, David**
William Golding 17:172

**Spitz, Robert Stephen**
Pete Hamill 10:251

**Spivack, Kathleen**
Robert Lowell 2:248

**Spivey, Herman E.**
William Faulkner 6:176

**Spivey, Ted R.**
Conrad Aiken 5:9
Flannery O'Connor 1:255

**Sprague, Rosemary**
Marianne Moore 4:362

**Sprague, Susan**
Mavis Thorpe Clark 12:132
Barbara Corcoran 17:77

**Springer, Cole**
Frank Zappa 17:593

**Spurling, Hilary**
Anthony Powell 10:417

**Spurling, John**
Peter Barnes 5:50
Samuel Beckett 6:42
Peter Benchley 4:54
Anna Kavan 13:315
Francis King 8:322
David Mercer 5:284
Yukio Mishima 9:384
Peter Nichols 5:308
David Plante 7:307
Peter Shaffer 5:388
Elie Wiesel 5:491

**Squires, Radcliffe**
Caroline Gordon 6:204
Randall Jarrell 6:260
Robinson Jeffers 11:305
Mario Luzi 13:353
Frederic Prokosh 4:420

Allen Tate 2:429; 4:540; 11:524
Robert Penn Warren 18:537

**Sragow, Michael**
Brian De Palma 20:83

**Srivastava, Narsingh**
W. H. Auden 14:26

**Stabb, Martin S.**
Jorge Luis Borges 19:44
José Donoso 11:149

**Stableford, Brian M.**
James Blish 14:84

**Stade, George**
Kingsley Amis 8:10
E. E. Cummings 3:119
Guy Davenport, Jr. 14:142
E. L. Doctorow 6:132; 18:126
Max Frisch 18:163
John Gardner 3:186
Robert Graves 1:129
Jerzy Kosinski 3:272
Alan Lelchuk 5:243
Doris Lessing 15:331
Joseph McElroy 5:279
Henry Miller 14:371
Jean Rhys 6:452
Wilfrid Sheed 4:488
Muriel Spark 2:416
John Updike 5:458
Kurt Vonnegut, Jr. 3:501

**Stafford, I. Elizabeth**
Lee Kingman 17:244

**Stafford, Jean**
M. E. Kerr 12:296, 298
James A. Michener 5:289
Jessamyn West 17:552
Paul West 7:523

**Stafford, William**
Millen Brand 7:29
Richard Eberhart 19:142
Loren Eiseley 7:93
Barbara Howes 15:289
David Kherdian 6:280
Kenneth Rexroth 2:370
Louis Simpson 7:427
May Swenson 14:518
Theodore Weiss 8:546

**Stallknecht, Newton P.**
Amos Tutuola 5:445

**Stallman, Robert W.**
Ernest Hemingway 13:271;
    19:212

**Stambolian, George**
Sam Shepard 4:490

**Stamelman, Richard**
Yves Bonnefoy 15:75
Francis Ponge 18:415

**Stampfer, Judah**
Saul Bellow 6:60
Philip Roth 6:476

**Staneck, Lou Willet**
John Neufeld 17:310

**Stanford, Ann**
May Swenson 4:533

**Stanford, Derek**
A. Alvarez 13:9
Earle Birney 4:64
Robert Creeley 2:106
C. Day Lewis 1:72
Lawrence Durrell 4:147
Geoffrey Hill 18:238
Aldous Huxley 5:192
Elizabeth Jennings 5:197
Hugh MacDiarmid 4:313
Louis MacNeice 1:187
Robert Nye 13:413
William Plomer 4:406
Carl Sandburg 15:470
Stephen Spender 1:322; 2:419
Yevgeny Yevtushenko 3:547

**Stanford, Donald E.**
Elizabeth Daryush 19:122
Caroline Gordon 6:202
Marianne Moore 4:364
Ezra Pound 10:407
Allen Tate 2:430
Yvor Winters 4:591

**Stange, Maren**
Susan Sontag 10:486

**Stankiewicz, Marketa Goetz**
Pavel Kohout 13:323
Sławomir Mrożek 3:345

**Stanleigh, Bertram**
Frank Zappa 17:584

**Stanlis, Peter L.**
Robert Frost 3:174

**Stannard, Martin**
Evelyn Waugh 13:588

**Staples, Hugh B.**
Randall Jarrell 6:261
Robert Lowell 2:246

**Stark, Freya**
Paul Bowles 19:58

**Stark, John O.**
John Barth 7:22
Jorge Luis Borges 8:94
E. L. Doctorow 6:131
William Gaddis 8:228
Vladimir Nabokov 8:407

**Stark, Myra**
Adrienne Rich 11:477

**Starr, Carol**
John Neufeld 17:310

**Starr, Kevin**
E. L. Doctorow 6:136
John Dos Passos 8:181

**Starr, Roger**
Anthony Powell 3:403

**Stasio, Marilyn**
Anne Burr 6:105
John Hopkins 4:234
Terrence McNally 4:346, 347
Jason Miller 2:284
David Rabe 4:426
Murray Schisgal 6:491
Melvin Van Peebles 2:448

**States, Bert O.**
Harold Pinter 6:412

CRITIC INDEX

**Stathis, James J.**
William Gaddis **19**:186

**Stavin, Robert H.**
Alvin Silverstein and Virginia
B. Silverstein **17**:450

**Stavn, Diane Gersoni**
Frank Bonham **12**:51
Barbara Corcoran **17**:72
M. E. Kerr **12**:297
Joseph Krumgold **12**:320
Emily Cheney Neville **12**:451

**Stavrou, C. N.**
Edward Albee **5**:12

**Steck, Henry J.**
Jules Archer **12**:20

**Steck, John A.**
Al Young **19**:480

**Steegmuller, Francis**
Patrick Modiano **18**:338

**Steel, Ronald**
Pavel Kohout **13**:323

**Steele, Timothy**
W. S. Merwin **18**:336

**Steene, Birgitta**
Ingmar Bergman **16**:54, 59, 64

**Stefanile, Felix**
William Bronk **10**:73
Lewis Turco **11**:552

**Stegner, Page**
Vladimir Nabokov **1**:239

**Stegner, Wallace**
N. Scott Momaday **19**:318

**Stein, Benjamin**
Joan Didion **8**:177

**Stein, Charles**
Jerome Rothenberg **6**:477

**Stein, Elliott**
Andrzej Wajda **16**:584

**Stein, Howard F.**
Alex Haley **12**:251

**Stein, Robert A.**
J. V. Cunningham **3**:122

**Stein, Ruth M.**
Jamake Highwater **12**:287
Anne McCaffrey **17**:283, 284
Robert Newton Peck **17**:342

**Steinberg, Karen Matlaw**
Yuri Krotkov **19**:265

**Steinberg, M. W.**
John Arden **15**:23
Robertson Davies **7**:72
A. M. Klein **19**:258, 261
Arthur Miller **1**:215

**Steiner, Carlo**
Giuseppe Ungaretti **7**:483

**Steiner, George**
Jorge Luis Borges **2**:70
C. Day Lewis **6**:126
Lawrence Durrell **4**:144
Paul Goodman **7**:127
Graham Greene **6**:220

Aldous Huxley **5**:194
Thomas Keneally **8**:318; **10**:298
Robert M. Pirsig **4**:403
Sylvia Plath **11**:445
Jean-Paul Sartre **7**:397
Aleksandr I. Solzhenitsyn **4**:516
John Updike **5**:459
Patrick White **4**:583

**Stengel, Richard**
Brian Moore **19**:333

**Stepanchev, Stephen**
John Ashbery **2**:16
Imamu Amiri Baraka **2**:34
Elizabeth Bishop **4**:65
Robert Bly **2**:65
Robert Creeley **2**:105
James Dickey **2**:115
Alan Dugan **2**:121
Robert Duncan **2**:122
Jean Garrigue **2**:153
Allen Ginsberg **2**:162
Randall Jarrell **2**:208
Robert Lowell **2**:247
W. S. Merwin **2**:276
Charles Olson **2**:325
Kenneth Rexroth **2**:369
Karl Shapiro **4**:485
Louis Simpson **4**:498
William Stafford **4**:519
May Swenson **4**:532
Richard Wilbur **6**:568

**Stephen, Sidney J.**
A. M. Klein **19**:260

**Stephens, Donald**
Dorothy Livesay **4**:294
Sinclair Ross **13**:490
Rudy Wiebe **6**:567

**Stephens, Martha**
Richard Wright **1**:379

**Stephens, Robert O.**
Ernest Hemingway **3**:239

**Stephenson, Edward R.**
John Hawkes **15**:277

**Stephenson, William**
James Dickey **4**:122

**Stepto, Robert B.**
Michael S. Harper **7**:139

**Stern, Daniel**
James Baldwin **17**:33
Paul Bowles **2**:79
Joanne Greenberg **7**:134
Marjorie Kellogg **2**:223
Jakov Lind **4**:292
Bernard Malamud **3**:324
Chaim Potok **2**:339
Ann Quin **6**:441
Piri Thomas **17**:497
Paul West **7**:523
Elie Wiesel **3**:529

**Stern, David**
Robert Kotlowitz **4**:275
Amos Oz **5**:334

**Stern, J. P.**
Eric Rohmer **16**:537

**Stern, James**
William Golding **17**:158

**Sterne, Richard C.**
Octavio Paz **10**:391

**Sterne, Richard Clark**
Jerome Weidman **7**:517

**Stetler, Charles**
Richard Brautigan **12**:67
James Purdy **4**:423

**Stevens, Peter**
A. R. Ammons **8**:14
Margaret Atwood **4**:24
Dorothy Livesay **15**:339
A. W. Purdy **3**:408

**Stevens, Shane**
Ronald L. Fair **18**:139
John Rechy **7**:356

**Stevens, Wallace**
Marianne Moore **10**:347

**Stevenson, Anne**
Elizabeth Bishop **1**:35
Michael Hamburger **14**:235
Barbara Howes **15**:290
Elizabeth Jennings **14**:292, 293
Peter Porter **13**:453
Muriel Rukeyser **15**:457
May Swenson **14**:521
R. S. Thomas **13**:544
Charles Tomlinson **13**:548

**Stevenson, David L.**
James Jones **3**:260
Jack Kerouac **2**:226
William Styron **1**:329

**Stevenson, Patrick**
W. R. Rodgers **7**:377

**Stevenson, Warren**
Hugh MacLennan **14**:343

**Stevick, Philip**
John Barth **14**:57
Donald Barthelme **8**:53
William S. Burroughs **5**:93
William H. Gass **8**:247
Jerzy Kosinski **6**:283
Jan Stafford **4**:518
Kurt Vonnegut, Jr. **5**:465

**Stewart, Alastair**
Kon Ichikawa **20**:176

**Stewart, Corbet**
Paul Celan **10**:102

**Stewart Douglas**
Robert D. FitzGerald **19**:175

**Stewart, Garrett**
Buster Keaton **20**:197
Steven Spielberg **20**:361

**Stewart, Harry E.**
Jean Genet **10**:225; **14**:201

**Stewart, Ian**
Françoise Sagan **17**:428

**Stewart, J.I.M.**
Compton Mackenzie **18**:316

**Stewart, John L.**
John Crowe Ransom **2**:362

**Stewart, Robert Sussman**
Heinrich Böll **2**:67

**Stewart, Ruth Weeden**
William Mayne **12**:387

**Stiller, Nikki**
Louis Simpson **9**:486

**Stilwell, Robert L.**
A. R. Ammons **3**:10
Sylvia Plath **1**:269
Jon Silkin **2**:395
James Wright **3**:540

**Stimpson, Catharine R.**
Thom Gunn **18**:199
Tillie Olsen **13**:432
Marge Piercy **6**:403
J.R.R. Tolkien **1**:338

**Stineback, David C.**
Allen Tate **9**:525

**Stinnett, Caskie**
S. J. Perelman **15**:419

**Stinson, John J.**
Anthony Burgess **4**:82

**Stitt, Peter A.**
John Ashberry **13**:34
John Berryman **10**:46
Daniel Halpern **14**:232
William Heyen **13**:282; **18**:232
David Ignatow **14**:277
James Merrill **18**:330
Louis Simpson **7**:429
Mark Strand **18**:521
Robert Penn Warren **10**:519
Charles Wright **13**:614
James Wright **10**:542

**Stock, Irvin**
Saul Bellow **2**:50
Mary McCarthy **1**:206

**Stock, Robert**
Theodore Weiss **14**:555

**Stocking, Marion Kingston**
Galway Kinnell **1**:168
Gary Snyder **1**:318

**Stoelting, Winifred L.**
Ernest J. Gaines **18**:165

**Stokes, Eric**
Kamala Markandaya **8**:378

**Stokes, Geoffrey**
Stanley Elkin **14**:158
John le Carré **15**:325
Phil Ochs **17**:335

**Stoltzfus, Ben F.**
Ernest Hemingway **13**:279
Alain Robbe-Grillet **1**:285;
**14**:456

**Stolz, Herbert J.**
Larry Kettelkamp **12**:307

**Stone, Chuck**
Garry Trudeau **12**:590

**Stone, Elizabeth**
John Fowles **9**:213
John Gardner **8**:234
Cynthia Macdonald **13**:355;
**19**:290
Joan Micklin Silver **20**:344
Lily Tomlin **17**:520

**Stone, Laurie**
Margaret Atwood **15**:38
Max Frisch **9**:217
Elizabeth Hardwick **13**:266
Shirley Hazzard **18**:219
Anaïs Nin **8**:423
Anne Roiphe **9**:455
Dalton Trumbo **19**:447
Tom Wolfe **15**:584

**Stone, Robert**
William Kotzwinkle **14**:309
Peter Matthiessen **5**:274

**Stone, Wilfred**
E. M. Forster **15**:229

**Stone, William B.**
Alice Munro **19**:347

**Stoneback, H. R.**
William Faulkner **8**:213

**Stonier, G. W.**
Charles Chaplin **16**:187

**Storch, R. F.**
Harold Pinter **6**:409

**Storey, Robert**
David Mamet **15**:357

**Storr, Catherine**
Eilís Dillon **17**:98
Leon Garfield **12**:221

**Story, Jack Trevor**
C. P. Snow **6**:517

**Stothard, Peter**
Lawrence Durrell **13**:188

**Stouck, David**
Marie-Claire Blais **2**:63
Hugh MacLennan **2**:257

**Stover, Leon E.**
Frank Herbert **12**:276

**Stowers, Bonnie**
Hortense Calisher **4**:88
Saul Maloff **5**:271

**Strachan, W. J.**
Sylvia Townsend Warner **19**:460

**Strandberg, Victor H.**
John Updike **13**:557
Robert Penn Warren **13**:573

**Stratford, Philip**
Graham Greene **6**:212

**Straub, Peter**
Michael Ayrton **7**:19
Beryl Bainbridge **8**:36
James Baldwin **4**:43
J. G. Ballard **3**:35
Donald Barthelme **3**:44
Brian Glanville **6**:202
Hermann Hesse **6**:237
Julius Horwitz **14**:266
Jack Kerouac **3**:266
Francis King **8**:321
Margaret Laurence **6**:290
Olivia Manning **5**:273
Thomas McGuane **7**:213
Michael Mewshaw **9**:376
James A. Michener **5**:291

Anaïs Nin **8**:419
Joyce Carol Oates **9**:402
Flann O'Brien **4**:385
Simon Raven **14**:442
Simone Schwarz-Bart **7**:404
Isaac Bashevis Singer **6**:509
Richard G. Stern **4**:523
John Updike **5**:457
Morris L. West **6**:563

**Strauch, Carl F.**
J. D. Salinger **12**:505

**Strauss, Harold**
Dalton Trumbo **19**:44

**Strauss, Theodore**
Rouben Mamoulian **16**:424

**Strebel, Elizabeth Grottle**
Jean Renoir **20**:309

**Street, Douglas O.**
Lawrence Ferlinghetti **6**:183

**Strehle, Susan**
John Gardner **10**:218

**Stresau, Hermann**
Thornton Wilder **15**:571

**Strick, Philip**
Ingmar Bergman **16**:80
Werner Herzog **16**:330
Kon Ichikawa **20**:182
Nagisa Oshima **20**:246
Pier Paolo Pasolini **20**:264
Jerzy Skolimowski **20**:348
Andrzej Wajda **16**:580
Peter Weir **20**:424

**Strong, L.A.G.**
John Masefield **11**:356

**Stroupe, John H.**
Jean Anouilh **13**:22

**Strouse, Jean**
Bob Dylan **12**:185

**Strout, Cushing**
William Styron **5**:420

**Strozier, Robert M.**
Peter De Vries **7**:78
S. J. Perelman **5**:337
P. G. Wodehouse **5**:517

**Struve, Gleb**
Ilya Ehrenburg **18**:131
Vladimir Nabokov **1**:241

**Struve, Nikita**
Aleksandr I. Solzhenitsyn **7**:433

**Stuart, Alexander**
Richard O'Brien **17**:323
Pier Paolo Pasolini **20**:266

**Stuart, Dabney**
Ted Hughes **2**:201

**Stubblefield, Charles**
Sylvia Plath **1**:270

**Stubbs, Harry C.**
Melvin Berger **12**:38
Roy A. Gallant **17**:129, 131, 132
Alvin Silverstein and Virginia B. Silverstein **17**:451, 454

**Stubbs, Helen**
William Mayne **12**:399

**Stubbs, Jean**
Julio Cortázar **2**:102
Daphne du Maurier **6**:147
George Garrett **3**:193
Elizabeth Hardwick **13**:265
Eleanor Hibbert **7**:155
Anaïs Nin **8**:421

**Stubbs, John C.**
John Hawkes **1**:138

**Stubbs, Patricia**
Muriel Spark **3**:466

**Stuckey, W. J.**
Pearl S. Buck **18**:76

**Stuewe, Paul**
Joan Barfoot **18**:35

**Stull, William L.**
William S. Burroughs **15**:111

**Stumpf, Thomas**
Hayden Carruth **7**:41
Daniel Mark Epstein **7**:97
Ishmael Reed **5**:368
Muriel Rukeyser **6**:479

**Stupple, A. James**
Ray Bradbury **10**:69

**Sturgeon, Ray**
Joni Mitchell **12**:443

**Sturgeon, Theodore**
Poul Anderson **15**:10
Isaac Asimov **3**:16
Michael Crichton **2**:108
Harlan Ellison **13**:202
Frank Herbert **12**:276
Barry N. Malzberg **7**:208

**Sturm, T. L.**
Robert D. FitzGerald **19**:180

**Sturrock, John**
Jorge Amado **13**:12
Jorge Luis Borges **13**:105
Peter De Vries **3**:125
Gabriel García Márquez **8**:233; **10**:217
Alain Robbe-Grillet **8**:454
Claude Simon **15**:486

**Styron, William**
Terry Southern **7**:453

**Subramani**
W. Somerset Maugham **15**:368

**Suczek, Barbara**
John Lennon and Paul McCartney **12**:369

**Suderman, Elmer F.**
John Updike **2**:443; **3**:488

**Sugg, Alfred R.**
Richard Lester **20**:222

**Sugrue, Thomas**
Riccardo Bacchelli **19**:31
Mary Renault **17**:390

**Sukenick, Lynn**
Maya Angelou **12**:12
Doris Lessing **3**:288
Anaïs Nin **8**:421
Robert L. Peters **7**:303

**Sukenick, Ronald**
Carlos Castaneda **12**:89
Rudolph Wurlitzer **2**:483

**Sullivan, Anita T.**
Ray Bradbury **3**:85

**Sullivan, Jack**
Richard Condon **8**:150
Robin Cook **14**:131
Guy Davenport, Jr. **14**:142
Paul Horgan **9**:279
Stephen King **12**:309
Wright Morris **18**:354
J. B. Priestley **9**:442
Julian Symons **14**:524

**Sullivan, Kevin**
Thomas Kinsella **19**:251
Flann O'Brien **5**:316
Sean O'Casey **5**:320

**Sullivan, Mary**
B. S. Johnson **6**:262
William Sansom **6**:483
Fay Weldon **6**:562

**Sullivan, Nancy**
May Swenson **4**:534

**Sullivan, Patrick**
Frederick Wiseman **20**:473

**Sullivan, Peggy**
Barbara Corcoran **17**:72
Lee Kingman **17**:244

**Sullivan, Richard**
Harper Lee **12**:340
William Maxwell **19**:306
Betty Smith **19**:423
Mary Stolz **12**:547

**Sullivan, Rosemary**
Marie-Claire Blais **6**:81
P. K. Page **18**:378
Theodore Roethke **19**:398

**Sullivan, Ruth**
Ken Kesey **6**:278

**Sullivan, Tom R.**
William Golding **8**:249
Michel Tournier **6**:538

**Sullivan, Victoria**
Saul Bellow **8**:76

**Sullivan, Walter**
Donald Barthelme **1**:19
Saul Bellow **8**:81
Elizabeth Bowen **11**:64
Eleanor Clark **19**:106
Guy Davenport, Jr. **6**:124
Margaret Drabble **8**:184
Andre Dubus **13**:182
George Garnett **11**:219
William Golding **2**:166, 168
Graham Greene **6**:219
Richard Hughes **11**:278
Bernard Malamud **1**:200
William Maxwell **19**:309
Joyce Carol Oates **6**:368; **9**:405

CRITIC INDEX

Flannery O'Connor 2:317
John O'Hara 6:385
Reynolds Price 13:464
V. S. Pritchett 13:465
Jean Rhys 6:456
Alan Sillitoe 6:501
William Trevor 14:535
Anne Tyler 11:553

Sullivan, Wilson
Irving Stone 7:470

Sullivan, Zohreh Tawakuli
Iris Murdoch 6:346; 11:386

Sullivan-Daly, Tess
Michael Mott 15:380

Sultan, Stanley
Ezra Pound 7:331

Sultanik, Aaron
E. L. Doctorow 18:120
Lina Wertmüller 16:595

Suplee, Curt
Thomas Berger 11:46

Surette, Leon
George Bowering 15:84

Sussex, Elizabeth
Lindsay Anderson 20:15
Satyajit Ray 16:482
Agnès Varda 16:555
Lina Wertmüller 16:586
Billy Wilder 20:460

Suter, Anthony
Basil Bunting 10:83, 84

Suther, Judith D.
Eugène Ionesco 11:292

Sutherland, Donald
Rafael Alberti 7:10
Octavio Paz 10:389
St.-John Perse 4:399
Francis Ponge 6:422

Sutherland, J. A.
Philip José Farmer 19:168

Sutherland, John
Robert Finch 18:153
P. K. Page 18:376

Sutherland, Ronald
Roch Carrier 13:140
Hugh MacLennan 14:342

Sutherland, Stuart
A. Alvarez 13:8
Peter De Vries 10:137

Sutherland, Zena
E. M. Almedingen 12:3, 4, 7
Honor Arundel 17:13
Melvin Berger 12:39, 40, 41
Judy Blume 12:44
Frank Bonham 12:49, 50, 51,
  52, 53, 54, 55
Betty Cavanna 12:102
Alice Childress 12:107
Mavis Thorpe Clark 12:132
Barbara Corcoran 17:74, 76, 78
Babbis Friis-Baastad 12:214
Roy A. Gallant 17:132
Jesse Jackson 12:290, 291
M. E. Kerr 12:298

Larry Kettelkamp 12:305, 306,
  307
Lee Kingman 17:247
Joseph Krumgold 12:318, 321
Madeleine L'Engle 12:350
Sonia Levitin 17:264, 265
Anne McCaffrey 17:282, 284
Nicholosa Mohr 12:447
John Neufeld 17:308, 310
Emily Cheney Neville 12:450,
  451, 452
Katherine Paterson 12:484, 486
Robert Newton Peck 17:338,
  339, 340, 342
Josephine Poole 17:373
Alvin Silverstein and Virginia
  B. Silverstein 17:451, 454,
  455
Zilpha Keatley Snyder 17:470,
  473, 475
Mary Stolz 12:551, 553, 554,
  555
Colin Thiele 17:495, 496
John R. Tunis 12:599
Lenora Mattingly Weber 12:634
Rosemary Wells 12:639
Jessamyn West 17:552
Hilma Wolitzer 17:563

Sutton, Graham
W. Somerset Maugham 11:367

Sutton, Martyn
Joan Armatrading 17:10

Sutton, Walter
Allen Ginsberg 4:181
Robert Lowell 4:303
Thomas Merton 3:336
Marianne Moore 4:364
Ezra Pound 3:395

Swados, Harvey
David Ignatow 4:249

Swann, Brian
Theodore Roethke 19:396

Swartley, Ariel
Joan Armatrading 17:8
Joni Mitchell 12:442
Bruce Springsteen 17:490

Swartney, Joyce
Charles M. Schulz 12:533

Sweeney, Patricia Runk
M. E. Kerr 12:301

Sweet, Louise
Frederick Wiseman 20:477

Swenson, John
Willie Nelson 17:303
Peter Townshend 17:533, 540
Frank Zappa 17:591

Swenson, May
Robin Morgan 2:294
Anne Sexton 2:392
W. D. Snodgrass 2:406

Swift, John N.
John Cheever 15:129

Swift, Jonathan
Gerome Ragni and James Rado
  17:385

Swift, Pat
George Barker 8:44

Swigg, Richard
E. M. Forster 9:209
Philip Larkin 9:324

Swigger, Ronald T.
Raymond Queneau 2:359

Swinden, Patrick
C. P. Snow 4:503

Swing, Raymond
John R. Tunis 12:596

Swink, Helen
William Faulkner 3:154

Swiss, Thomas
Donald Justice 19:234

Sykes, Christopher
Aldous Huxley 4:244; 8:303

Sykes, Gerald
Jessie Redmon Fauset 19:169

Sykes, S. W.
Claude Simon 9:483

Sylvester, R. D.
Joseph Brodsky 13:114

Symons, Julian
Eric Ambler 4:18
W. H. Auden 2:28
Beryl Bainbridge 18:34
John Berryman 2:59
Edward Brathwaite 11:66
John Dickson Carr 3:101
John Cheever 8:140
Agatha Christie 6:107; 8:140;
  12:121, 126
John Creasey 11:134
C. Day Lewis 6:129
Len Deighton 4:119
Friedrich Dürrenmatt 4:141
Ian Fleming 3:159
Roy Fuller 4:178
Dashiell Hammett 3:219
Lillian Hellman 4:222
Patricia Highsmith 2:193; 4:225
Chester Himes 4:229
Evan Hunter 11:279
P. D. James 18:276
Eliabeth Jennings 14:292
John le Carré 3:282
John D. MacDonald 3:307
Ross Macdonald 3:307
Mary McCarthy 3:326
Henry Miller 2:281
Ellery Queen 3:421
Simon Raven 14:442
Kenneth Rexroth 11:473
Laura Riding 3:431
Georges Simenon 3:451; 8:487;
  18:485
Louis Simpson 4:498
Maj Sjöwall 7:501
C. P. Snow 4:500
Mickey Spillane 3:469
J.I.M. Stewart 14:511
Rex Stout 3:471
William Styron 15:528
Per Wahlöö 7:501
Robert Penn Warren 4:577

Patrick White 3:523
Angus Wilson 3:536

Syrkin, Marie
Henry Roth 6:472

Szanto, George H.
Alain Robbe-Grillet 1:288

Szogyi, Alex
Lillian Hellman 2:187
Isaac Bashevis Singer 11:501

Szporluk, Mary Ann
Vladimir Voinovich 10:504

Tabachnick, Stephen E.
Conrad Aiken 5:9

Taëni, Rainer
Rolf Hochhuth 18:252

Tait, Michael
James Reaney 13:472

Takiff, Jonathan
Lily Tomlin 17:521

Talbot, Emile J.
Roch Carrier 13:144

Talbott, Strobe
Aleksandr I. Solzhenitsyn 4:516

Taliaferro, Frances
Frederick Busch 18:85
Laurie Colwin 13:157
Andre Dubus 13:184
Nadine Gordimer 5:147
Maureen Howard 14:268
Tom McHale 5:283

Tallenay, J. L.
Charles Chaplin 16:195

Tallman, Warren
Earle Birney 11:50
Ernest Buckler 13:118
Robert Creeley 11:135
Robert Duncan 15:187
Jack Kerouac 14:304
John Rechy 14:445
Mordecai Richler 3:430
Sinclair Ross 13:490

Tambling, Jeremy
Brian Aldiss 14:15
J.I.M. Stewart 14:513

Tamkin, Linda
Anaïs Nin 14:387

Tanner, Alain
Luchino Visconti 16:561

Tanner, Stephen L.
Ernest Hemingway 8:288

Tanner, Tony
John Barth 1:17; 2:37; 14:55
Donald Barthelme 2:40
Richard Brautigan 12:66
William S. Burroughs 2:92
William Gaddis 3:177
John Gardner 2:152
John Hawkes 2:185; 7:143
Ernest Hemingway 10:266
Norman Mailer 1:189
Bernard Malamud 2:267
James Purdy 2:351; 4:422
Thomas Pynchon 6:430, 432

CRITIC INDEX

Susan Sontag 1:322
John Updike 2:445
Kurt Vonnegut, Jr. 12:606

**Tapply, Robert S.**
Roy A. Gallant 17:128

**Tapscott, Stephen**
Friedrich Dürrenmatt 11:173
Hugh MacDiarmid 19:288

**Tarantino, Michael**
Marguerite Duras 20:100, 101
Elaine May 16:437

**Tarkka, Pekka**
Hannu Salama 18:461

**Tarn, Nathaniel**
William H. Gass 1:114

**Tarratt, Margaret**
Nagisa Oshima 20:246
Gordon Parks 16:459
Luchino Visconti 16:568
Frederick Wiseman 20:474

**Tarshis, Jerome**
J. G. Ballard 3:34

**Tate, Allen**
Edward Dahlberg 14:134
Donald Davidson 13:167
John Crowe Ransom 2:363;
5:364
Eudora Welty 1:362

**Tate, J. O.**
Flannery O'Connor 13:421

**Tate, Robert S., Jr.**
Albert Camus 1:54

**Tatham, Campbell**
John Barth 1:18
Raymond Federman 6:181
Thomas Pynchon 2:354

**Tatum, Charles M.**
José Donoso 11:146

**Taubman, Howard**
James Baldwin 17:27, 31
Arthur Kopit 18:286
Gerome Ragni and James Rado
17:379

**Taubman, Robert**
Patrick Boyle 19:67
Cynthia Ozick 7:287
Sylvia Plath 17:345

**Taus, Roger**
William Everson 14:167

**Tavris, Carol**
Kate Wilhelm 7:538

**Taylor, Clyde**
Imamu Amiri Baraka 5:47

**Taylor, D. W.**
Eilís Dillon 17:99

**Taylor, David**
John Rechy 18:443

**Taylor, Eleanor Ross**
Elizabeth Bishop 15:59
Sylvia Plath 17:347

**Taylor, F. H. Griffin**
George Garrett 3:192; 11:219
Robert Lowell 1:181
Theodore Weiss 3:516

**Taylor, Gordon O.**
Mary McCarthy 14:358

**Taylor, Harry H.**
William Golding 17:170

**Taylor, Henry**
Marvin Bell 8:64
Irving Feldman 7:103
X. J. Kennedy 8:319
William Meredith 13:373
Howard Nemerov 6:363
Flannery O'Connor 1:258
John Hall Wheelock 14:570
James Wright 5:521

**Taylor, Jane**
Galway Kinnell 1:168

**Taylor, John Russell**
Lindsay Anderson 20:17
Michelangelo Antonioni 20:28
John Arden 6:4
Alan Ayckbourn 5:34
Brendan Behan 11:44
Ingmar Bergman 16:50
Edward Bond 4:69
Robert Bresson 16:108
Mel Brooks 12:78
Luis Buñuel 16:132
Claude Chabrol 16:180
Vittorio De Sica 20:90
Marguerite Duras 20:99
Federico Fellini 16:274, 281,
288
Alfred Hitchcock 16:344
John Huston 20:170, 171
Stanley Kubrick 16:388
Fritz Lang 20:208
Hugh Leonard 19:282
David Mercer 5:283
Peter Nichols 5:305
Joe Orton 4:388
Pier Paolo Pasolini 20:266
Harold Pinter 11:436
Terence Rattigan 7:354
Satyajit Ray 16:490
Alain Resnais 16:502
Peter Shaffer 14:484, 485;
18:477
Robert Shaw 5:390
Tom Stoppard 4:524
David Storey 4:528
Andy Warhol 20:423
E. A. Whitehead 5:488
Billy Wilder 20:461

**Taylor, Katharine**
Sylvia Ashton-Warner 19:21

**Taylor, Lewis Jerome, Jr.**
Walker Percy 6:399

**Taylor, Mark**
W. H. Auden 3:27
John Berryman 3:72
Tom McHale 5:282
Walker Percy 3:378
Earl Rovit 7:383
Edmund Wilson 8:550
Richard Yates 8:555

**Taylor, Michael**
Gillian Tindall 7:474

**Taylor, Stephen**
John Huston 20:169

**Taylor, William L.**
J.R.R. Tolkien 12:569

**Tebbel, John**
Charles M. Schulz 12:527

**Téchiné, André**
Carl Theodor Dreyer 16:268

**Teich, Nathaniel**
Pier Paolo Pasolini 20:267

**Temple, Joanne**
John Berryman 3:72

**Temple, Ruth Z.**
C. S. Lewis 14:321
Nathalie Sarraute 1:303; 2:386

**Templeton, Joan**
Sean O'Casey 11:406

**Tenenbaum, Louis**
Italo Calvino 5:97

**Tennant, Emma**
J. G. Ballard 6:28
Italo Calvino 5:100
Thomas Hinde 6:242
Penelope Mortimer 5:298

**Teo, Elizabeth A.**
Jade Snow Wong 17:567

**Terbille, Charles I.**
Saul Bellow 6:52
Joyce Carol Oates 6:371

**Teresa, Vincent**
Mario Puzo 2:352

**Terrien, Samuel**
Fernando Arrabal 2:15

**Terris, Susan**
Rosemary Wells 12:639

**Terry, Arthur**
Vicente Aleixandre 9:17
Salvador Espriu 9:192
Octavio Paz 10:393

**Terry, C. V.**
Frank B. Gilbreth, Jr. and
Ernestine Gilbreth Carey
17:154

**Tessitore, John**
Francis Ford Coppola 16:247

**Testa, Bart**
Frank Zappa 17:591

**Teunissen, John T.**
Doris Lessing 6:293

**Thale, Jerome**
C. P. Snow 19:425

**Thelwell, Mike**
James Baldwin 17:36

**Therese, Sister M.**
Marianne Moore 1:229

**Theroux, Paul**
Frederick Buechner 2:83
Anthony Burgess 5:89
John Cheever 7:48
Peter De Vries 3:126; 7:76
Lawrence Durrell 6:151
George MacDonald Fraser
7:106
Nadine Gordimer 5:147
Shirley Ann Grau 4:209
Graham Greene 3:213
Ernest Hemingway 6:229
Susan B. Hill 4:226
Erica Jong 4:264
Yashar Kemal 14:299
John Knowles 4:272
Milan Kundera 4:276
Mary McCarthy 5:277
Yukio Mishima 4:356
Brian Moore 3:341; 7:236
V. S. Naipaul 4:373, 374;
7:252
Cynthia Ozick 7:288
S. J. Perelman 9:415
Jean Rhys 2:372
Georges Simenon 18:487
David Storey 4:529
Peter Taylor 4:542
John Updike 13:563
Kurt Vonnegut, Jr. 5:470

**Thesen, Sharon Fawcett**
Gilbert Sorrentino 14:498

**Thiher, Allen**
Fernando Arrabal 9:33
Luis Buñuel 16:149
Louis-Ferdinand Céline 4:101
Henri de Montherlant 19:328
François Truffaut 20:402

**Thody, Philip**
Albert Camus 4:91; 14:116
Jean-Paul Sartre 4:476

**Thomas, Carolyn**
David Jones 7:191

**Thomas, Clara**
Margaret Laurence 3:281;
13:342

**Thomas, D. M.**
Martin Booth 13:103
Yuri Krotkov 19:265
John Matthias 9:362

**Thomas, David**
James Baldwin 5:43

**Thomas, David P.**
Christopher Isherwood 1:157

**Thomas, John**
Bernardo Bertolucci 16:84
Tod Browning 16:122
Jean-Luc Godard 20:134

**Thomas, John Alfred**
Josef von Sternberg 20:369

**Thomas, M. Wynn**
Katherine Anne Porter 10:394

**Thomas, Paul**
Rainer Werner Fassbinder
20:109
Lina Wertmüller 16:593

**Thomas, Peter**
John Betjeman 6:65
Robert Kroetsch 5:220

**Thomas, Ross**
Herbert Gold 14:209

**Thomas, S. L.**
John R. Tunis 12:592

**Thompson, Dody Weston**
Pearl S. Buck 18:78

**Thompson, Eric**
Matt Cohen 19:112
T. S. Eliot 2:125

**Thompson, Howard**
Robert Altman 16:19
Brian De Palma 20:73
Garry Marshall 17:274
Martin Scorsese 20:324
Jerzy Skolimowski 20:347
Andy Warhol 20:417

**Thompson, John**
James Baldwin 17:34
John Berryman 3:71
Irving Feldman 7:102
Natalia Ginzburg 5:141
Nadine Gordimer 18:191
Joseph Heller 5:176
Robert Lowell 9:338
Amos Oz 5:335
John Updike 13:560

**Thompson, Kent**
Hugh Hood 15:284

**Thompson, Lawrence**
Robert Frost 13:224

**Thompson, Leslie M.**
Stephen Spender 10:487

**Thompson, R. J.**
John Hawkes 4:214
Mary Lavin 4:282

**Thompson, Robert B.**
Robert Frost 13:230

**Thompson, Toby**
Bruce Jay Friedman 5:126

**Thomsen, Christian Braad**
Rainer Werner Fassbinder
20:105

**Thomson, David**
Fritz Lang 20:213

**Thomson, George H.**
J.R.R. Tolkien 1:335

**Thomson, Jean C.**
Barbara Corcoran 17:72
Eilís Dillon 17:97
Leon Garfield 12:216
Madeleine L'Engle 12:347
John Neufeld 17:307, 308

**Thomson, Peter**
Harold Pinter 15:422

**Thomson, R.D.B.**
Andrei Voznesensky 15:554

**Thorburn, David**
Renata Adler 8:7
Ann Beattie 8:57
Judith Guest 8:254
Norman Mailer 3:315
Thomas Pynchon 3:416

**Thorp, Willard**
W. D. Snodgrass 2:404

**Thorpe, Michael**
Doris Lessing 3:291

**Thurman, Judith**
Joyce Carol Oates 6:374
Jean Rhys 6:456
Laura Riding 7:374
Agnès Varda 16:560

**Thwaite, Ann**
E. M. Almedingen 12:5

**Thwaite, Anthony**
W. H. Auden 6:24
Charles Causley 7:41
Douglas Dunn 6:148
Shusaku Endo 19:160
Geoffrey Grigson 7:136
Seamus Heaney 7:147
David Jones 7:187
Yashar Kemal 14:301
Thomas Keneally 19:242
Philip Larkin 13:335
R. K. Narayan 7:256
Darcy O'Brien 11:405
Sylvia Plath 14:426
C. P. Snow 4:503

**Tibbetts, John**
Frank Capra 16:165
Josef von Sternberg 20:377

**Tickell, Paul**
Frank Zappa 17:595

**Tiessen, Hildegard E.**
Rudy Wiebe 14:572

**Tiffin, Chris**
Thomas Keneally 19:243

**Tillinghast, Richard**
James Merrill 2:274
Adrienne Rich 3:427

**Tilton, John W.**
Anthony Burgess 15:104
Kurt Vonnegut, Jr. 12:614

**Timmerman, John H.**
C. S. Lewis 14:324

**Timms, David**
Philip Larkin 5:223

**Timpe, Eugene F.**
Hermann Hesse 17:210

**Tindal, Gillian**
Louis-Ferdinand Céline 7:45
Leon Garfield 12:227

**Tindall, William York**
Samuel Beckett 1:22

**Tinkle, Lon**
Jean Lee Latham 12:324
Hollis Summers 10:493

**Tintner, Adeline R.**
François Truffaut 20:406

**Tisdale, Bob**
John Hawkes 4:215

**Tobias, Richard**
Thomas Kinsella 19:256

**Tobias, Richard C.**
James Thurber 5:435

**Tobin, Patricia**
William Faulkner 3:155

**Tobin, Richard L.**
Lothar-Günther Buchheim
6:101

**Todd, Richard**
Renata Adler 8:4
Louis Auchincloss 9:54
Donald Barthelme 8:49
Saul Bellow 6:55, 61
Thomas Berger 3:64
Eleanor Bergstein 4:55
Vance Bourjaily 8:104
E. L. Doctorow 6:138
Andre Dubus 13:183
Bruce Jay Friedman 5:126
John Hawkes 4:216
Sue Kaufman 8:317
William Kotzwinkle 5:220
Cormac McCarthy 4:343
Robert Newton Peck 17:337
Walker Percy 8:443
Marge Piercy 6:402
Robert M. Pirsig 6:420
Judith Rossner 6:470
John Updike 7:489
Kurt Vonnegut, Jr. 3:501
Richard Yates 7:555

**Toeplitz, Krzysztof-Teodor**
Jerzy Skolimowski 20:348
Andrzej Wajda 16:579

**Toliver, Harold E.**
Robert Frost 4:175

**Tomalin, Claire**
Beryl Bainbridge 10:15
Charles Newman 2:311
Paul Theroux 5:427

**Tonks, Rosemary**
Adrienne Rich 3:428

**Toolan, David S.**
Tom Wicker 7:535

**Torchiana, Donald T.**
W. D. Snodgrass 2:404

**Tosches, Nick**
Mick Jagger and Keith Richard
17:240
Jim Morrison 17:293

**Totton, Nick**
Beryl Bainbridge 8:37
J. G. Ballard 14:39
Heinrich Böll 9:111
Patrick Boyle 19:68
André Brink 18:67
Gail Godwin 8:249
James Hanley 8:265
Mary Hocking 13:285
Francis King 8:322
Alistair MacLean 13:364
Iris Murdoch 8:405

**Vladimir Nabokov 8:417**
David Pownall 10:419
Frederic Raphael 14:437
Piers Paul Read 10:434

**Tovey, Roberta**
William Kotzwinkle 14:311

**Towers, Robert**
Renata Adler 8:4
Donald Barthelme 13:59
Ann Beattie 18:38
Michael Brodsky 19:69
John Cheever 8:138; 11:122
E. L. Doctorow 18:127
Stanley Elkin 9:191
John Gardner 8:233
Graham Greene 18:197
Lillian Hellman 18.228
Diane Johnson 13:305
Doris Lessing 15:335
Bernard Malamud 18:319
Ian McEwan 13:371
Larry McMurtry 7:214
Flannery O'Connor 13:422
Walker Percy 8:444; 18:401
Anthony Powell 9:435
V. S. Pritchett 15:444
Philip Roth 9:461; 15:451
James Salter 7:387
Wilfrid Sheed 10:473
Paul Theroux 8:512
John Updike 13:559
Kurt Vonnegut, Jr. 8:533
Rebecca West 9:562
William Wharton 18:543

**Towns, Saundra**
Gwendolyn Brooks 15:93

**Townsend, John Rowe**
Honor Arundel 17:18
Peter Dickinson 12:172
Esther Forbes 12:211
Leon Garfield 12:222, 224
Alan Garner 17:143
Jesse Jackson 12:291
Madeleine L'Engle 12:350
William Mayne 12:397
Andre Norton 12:460

**Townsend, R. C.**
William Golding 17:168

**Townshend, Peter**
Peter Townshend 17:534

**Toynbee, Philip**
Arthur Koestler 1:170
Mary Renault 17:399
Mordecai Richler 5:375

**Trachtenberg, Alan**
Henry Miller 4:351
Tom Wolfe 9:578

**Tracy, Honor**
Graham Greene 3:206

**Tracy, Phil**
Kingsley Amis 3:9

**Traschen, Isadore**
William Faulkner 9:201

**Traubitz, Nancy Baker**
Tennessee Williams 15:578

**Trease, Geoffrey**
Leon Garfield **12**:216, 217
William Mayne **12**:390

**Treece, Henry**
Herbert Read **4**:437

**Treglown, Jeremy**
Brian Aldiss **14**:14
Brigid Brophy **11**:68
Parel Kohout **13**:325
Olivia Manning **19**:302
Joyce Carol Oates **11**:403
Barbara Pym **13**:470
Tom Robbins **9**:454
J.I.M. Stewart **14**:512

**Trewin, J. C.**
Robert Bolt **14**:89
Agatha Christie **12**:125

**Trickett, Rachel**
Olivia Manning **19**:302
James Purdy **2**:349
Andrew Sinclair **2**:401
Wallace Stegner **9**:508
Angus Wilson **2**:473

**Trilling, Diana**
Margery Allingham **19**:12
Ilya Ehrenburg **18**:131
Esther Forbes **12**:209
Martha Gellhorn **14**:194
Aldous Huxley **8**:304
Frank O'Connor **14**:395
Jean Rhys **19**:392
Irwin Shaw **7**:410
Betty Smith **19**:422

**Trilling, Lionel**
E. M. Forster **1**:104
Robert Graves **2**:174

**Trilling, Roger**
Bob Marley **17**:270

**Trimpi, Helen P.**
Edgar Bowers **9**:121, 122

**Trodd, Kenith**
Andrew Sinclair **2**:400

**Trotsky, Leon**
André Malraux **13**:364

**Trotter, Stewart**
Jean Genet **5**:137
Graham Greene **6**:220

**Trowbridge, Clinton**
John Updike **2**:442

**Troy, William**
Carl Theodor Dreyer **16**:256
Fritz Lang **20**:202
Josef von Sternberg **20**:370

**True, Michael**
Daniel J. Berrigan **4**:58
Robert Francis **15**:236
Paul Goodman **2**:169
Flannery O'Connor **13**:422
Karl Shapiro **15**:477

**Trueblood, Valerie**
Margaret Atwood **13**:43
Tess Gallagher **18**:168
Gilbert Sorrentino **14**:499
Derek Walcott **14**:548

**Truffaut, François**
Ingmar Bergman **16**:70
Luis Buñuel **16**:136
Frank Capra **16**:161
Charles Chaplin **16**:198
John Ford **16**:314
Alfred Hitchcock **16**:341, 346
Elia Kazan **16**:366
Fritz Lang **20**:208
Agnès Varda **16**:553
Billy Wilder **20**:457

**Truscott, Lucian K.**
Bob Dylan **3**:131

**Trussler, Simon**
John Arden **15**:19

**Tsuruta, Kinya**
Shusaku Endo **7**:96

**Tsvetaeva, Marina**
Boris Pasternak **18**:386

**Tuch, Ronald**
Charles Chaplin **16**:204

**Tucker, Carll**
Imamu Amiri Baraka **10**:19
Ed Bullins **7**:37
Jules Feiffer **8**:216
Richard Howard **7**:169
Robert Lowell **9**:338
Archibald MacLeish **8**:363

**Tucker, James**
Anthony Powell **7**:338; **10**:409

**Tucker, Ken**
Joan Armatrading **17**:9
Patti Smith **12**:543
Neil Young **17**:576, 580

**Tucker, Martin**
Chinua Achebe **3**:1
André Brink **18**:67
Cyprian Ekwensi **4**:152
Nadine Gordimer **3**:201
Jan de Hartog **19**:131, 132
Ernest Hemingway **3**:234
Jerzy Kosinski **1**:172
Bernard Malamud **3**:322
James Ngugi **3**:357
Cynthia Ozick **7**:287
Alan Paton **4**:395
William Plomer **4**:406
Ishmael Reed **13**:477
Wole Soyinka **3**:462
Amos Tutuola **5**:443
Laurens van der Post **5**:463

**Tucker, Nicholas**
Honor Arundel **17**:16
Judy Blume **12**:45

**Tunney, Gene**
Budd Schulberg **7**:402

**Tuohy, Frank**
Nadine Gordimer **18**:188
Sean O'Faoláin **14**:405

**Turan, Kenneth**
Gene Roddenberry **17**:414
Elie Wiesel **11**:570

**Turco, Lewis**
Edward Brathwaite **11**:67
Robert Hayden **9**:270
Donald Justice **19**:232

**Turin, Michele**
Alix Kates Shulman **10**:476

**Turnbull, Colin M.**
Christie Harris **12**:262

**Turnbull, Martin**
François Mauriac **4**:340

**Turnell, Martin**
Graham Greene **1**:134

**Turner, Alice K.**
Jamake Highwater **12**:285

**Turner, Darwin**
Ishmael Reed **13**:477
Alice Walker **9**:558

**Turner, E. S.**
Mircea Eliade **19**:148
Daphne du Maurier **11**:164

**Turner, Gil**
Bob Dylan **12**:179

**Turner, R. H.**
Claude Chabrol **16**:167

**Turner, Steve**
Peter Townshend **17**:537

**Tuttleton, James W.**
Louis Auchincloss **4**:29

**Tyler, Anne**
Richard Adams **18**:2
Toni Cade Bambara **19**:33
John Cheever **11**:121
Anita Desai **19**:134
Joan Didion **14**:151
Jacob Epstein **19**:162
Marilyn French **10**:191
Mavis Gallant **18**:172
Penelope Gilliatt **13**:238
Lois Gould **10**:241
Sue Kaufman **8**:317
Thomas Keneally **10**:299
Maxine Hong Kingston **19**:250
Ian McEwan **13**:370
Bernice Rubens **19**:404
Mary Lee Settle **19**:410
Alix Kates Shulman **10**:475
Susan Sontag **13**:516
Paul Theroux **11**:529
William Trevor **7**:478

**Tyler, Parker**
Charles Chaplin **16**:196
Laurence Olivier **20**:235
Agnès Varda **16**:554
Andy Warhol **20**:416
Orson Welles **20**:438

**Tyler, Ralph**
Richard Adams **5**:5
Agatha Christie **6**:109
S. J. Perelman **9**:416
Jean Rhys **6**:455

**Tyler, Tony**
John Lennon and Paul
McCartney **12**:379

**Tyms, James D.**
Langston Hughes **5**:191

**Tynan, Kenneth**
Roman Polanski **16**:463
Tom Stoppard **15**:518

**Tyrmand, Leopold**
Witold Gombrowicz **7**:124

**Tyrrell, William Blake**
Gene Roddenberry **17**:407

**Tytell, John**
Jack Kerouac **3**:264

**Uglow, Jennifer**
Marge Piercy **18**:408

**Uhelski, Jaan**
Jimmy Page and Robert Plant
**12**:478

**Uibopuu, Valev**
Ivar Ivask **14**:287

**Ulam, Adam**
Agatha Christie **12**:120

**Ulfers, Friedrich**
Paul Celan **19**:92

**Ullman, Montague**
Melvin Berger **12**:42
Larry Kettelkamp **12**:308

**Unger, Arthur**
Alex Haley **12**:253

**Unger, Leonard**
T. S. Eliot **1**:90

**Unsworth, Robert**
Mavis Thorpe Clark **12**:131
Sonia Levitin **17**:265

**Unterecker, John**
Lawrence Durrell **1**:84
Ezra Pound **4**:415
Kenneth Rexroth **2**:370

**Untermeyer, Louis**
Robert Francis **15**:235
Robert Frost **13**:223; **15**:239

**Updike, John**
Michael Ayrton **7**:20
Ann Beattie **8**:55
Samuel Beckett **6**:45
Saul Bellow **6**:56
Jorge Luis Borges **8**:100
Italo Calvino **5**:101; **8**:130
Albert Camus **9**:149
John Cheever **7**:50
Julio Cortázar **5**:109
Don DeLillo **10**:135
Margaret Drabble **8**:183
Shusaku Endo **19**:160, 161
Daniel Fuchs **8**:221
Witold Gombrowicz **7**:124
Günter Grass **2**:172; **4**:206
Ernest Hemingway **8**:285
Ruth Prawer Jhabvala **8**:312
Gayl Jones **6**:266; **9**:307
Erica Jong **4**:263
Jerzy Kosinski **6**:282
Milan Kundera **19**:269
Alex La Guma **19**:275
Stanislaw Lem **15**:329
Alberto Moravia **7**:243
Wright Morris **7**:245
Iris Murdoch **6**:344
Vladimir Nabokov **2**:301;
**3**:351; **6**:355; **8**:414, 415,
416, 417; **11**:395
V. S. Naipaul **13**:407

**CRITIC INDEX**

R. K. Narayan 7:256
Flann O'Brien 7:269, 270
Tim O'Brien 19:358
John O'Hara 11:414
Robert Pinget 7:306
Harold Pinter 15:423
Raymond Queneau 5:359, 362
Jean Rhys 19:395
Alain Robbe-Grillet 8:452
Françoise Sagan 6:481
J. D. Salinger 12:513
Simone Schwarz-Bart 7:405
L. E. Sissman 18:487
Wole Soyinka 14:509
Muriel Spark 5:400
Christina Stead 8:499, 500
James Thurber 5:433
Anne Tyler 7:479; 18:530
Sylvia Townsend Warner
7:512; 19:460
Edmund Wilson 8:551

**Uphaus, Robert W.**
Kurt Vonnegut, Jr. 5:469

**Urang, Gunnar**
C. S. Lewis 3:298
J.R.R. Tolkien 2:434

**Urbanski, Marie Mitchell Oleson**
Joyce Carol Oates 11:402

**Urbas, Jeannette**
Gabrielle Roy 14:468

**Uroff, Margaret D.**
Sylvia Plath 3:391; 17:354

**Ury, Claude**
Jules Archer 12:17

**Usborne, Richard**
MacDonald Harris 9:261

**Uscatescu, George**
Mircea Eliade 19:145

**Usmiani, Renate**
Friedrich Dürrenmatt 8:194

**Vaizey, John**
Kingsley Amis 5:22

**Valdéz, Jorge H.**
Julio Cortázar 13:165

**Valgemae, Mardi**
Sławomir Mrożek 13:398
Jean-Claude Van Itallie 3:493

**Valley, John A.**
Alberto Moravia 7:243

**Vallis, Val**
Judith Wright 11:578

**Van Brunt, H. L.**
Jim Harrison 6:224

**Van Buren, Alice**
Janet Frame 2:142

**Vance, Joel**
Chuck Berry 17:56
David Bowie 17:63
Bob Marley 17:268
Paul Simon 17:467

**Vande Kieft, Ruth M.**
Flannery O'Connor 1:258
Eudora Welty 1:360

**Vandenbroucke, Russell**
Athol Fugard 9:230

**Van den Haag, Ernest**
William F. Buckley, Jr. 7:34

**Van den Heuvel, Cor**
James Wright 10:545

**Vanderbilt, Kermit**
Norman Mailer 3:319
William Styron 3:474

**Vanderwerken, David L.**
Richard Brautigan 5:69

**Van Doren, Carl**
Esther Forbes 12:205, 208

**Van Doren, Mark**
René Clair 20:62
E. E. Cummings 12:139
Robert Frost 13:223; 15:241
Robinson Jeffers 11:304
John Cowper Powys 7:346

**Van Duyn, Mona**
Margaret Atwood 2:19
Adrienne Rich 3:427
Anne Sexton 2:391

**Van Dyne, Susan R.**
Adrienne Rich 18:445

**Van Gelder, Lawrence**
Nagisa Oshima 20:250

**Vanjak, Gloria**
Jim Morrison 17:290

**Van Matre, Lynn**
Lily Tomlin 17:517

**Vanocur, Sander**
Fletcher Knebel 14:307

**Vansittart, Peter**
Lawrence Durrell 13:189
Piers Paul Read 10:436

**Van Wert, William F.**
Marguerite Duras 20:103
Alain Resnais 16:516

**Vardi, Dov**
Abraham B. Yehoshua 13:617

**Vargas Llosa, Mario**
Gabriel García Márquez 3:181

**Vargo, Edward P.**
John Updike 7:486

**Vas, Robert**
Lindsay Anderson 20:12
Robert Bresson 16:105

**Vásquez Amaral, José**
Julio Cortázar 13:157

**Vassal, Jacques**
Phil Ochs 17:331
Buffy Sainte-Marie 17:431

**Vaughan, Dai**
Carl Theodor Dreyer 16:265

**Vaughan, Stephen**
Thomas Keneally 14:302

**Veidemanis, Gladys**
William Golding 17:169

**Velie, Alan R.**
James Welch 14:561

**Venable, Gene**
Fletcher Knebel 14:309

**Venclova, Tomas**
Aleksandr I. Solzhenitsyn
18:497

**Vendler, Helen**
A. R. Ammons 2:14
Margaret Atwood 8:29
John Berryman 3:68; 10:46
Elizabeth Bishop 9:90
Olga Broumas 10:77
Hayden Carruth 7:41
Lucille Clifton 19:109
E. E. Cummings 3:119
D. J. Enright 8:203
Allen Ginsberg 2:163; 3:195
Louise Glück 7:118
Seamus Heaney 7:152
John Hollander 5:187
Richard F. Hugo 6:245
Randall Jarrell 9:295
Erica Jong 4:263
Maxine Kumin 13:326
Audre Lorde 18:308
Haki R. Madhubuti 6:313
Mary McCarthy 3:328
James Merrill 2:275; 18:328
W. S. Merwin 18:332
Josephine Miles 14:369
Marianne Moore 19:341
Howard Moss 7:250
Joyce Carol Oates 3:361
Frank O'Hara 5:323
Octavio Paz 4:397
Sylvia Plath 17:353
Adrienne Rich 7:367; 18:444
I. A. Richards 14:454
Irwin Shaw 7:414
David Slavitt 14:490
Allen Tate 2:429
Charles Tomlinson 6:535
Diane Wakoski 7:504
Robert Penn Warren 10:525;
18:533
Charles Wright 6:581

**Venturi, Lauro**
Jean Renoir 20:288

**Verani, Hugo J.**
Juan Carlos Onetti 7:277

**Vernon, John**
Michael Benedikt 4:54
William S. Burroughs 15:108
James Dickey 7:82
Richard F. Hugo 18:264
David Ignatow 4:247
James Merrill 3:334
W. S. Merwin 1:213
Thomas Pynchon 11:452

**Verschoyle, Derek**
Rayner Heppenstall 10:271

**Vesselo, Arthur**
Laurence Olivier 20:235

**Vickery, John B.**
John Updike 5:451

**Vickery, Olga W.**
John Hawkes 4:213

**Vickery, R. C.**
Jules Archer 12:23

**Vidal, Gore**
Louis Auchincloss 4:31
John Barth 14:51
Italo Calvino 5:98
John Dos Passos 4:132
William H. Gass 11:224
E. Howard Hunt 3:251
Doris Lessing 15:333
Norman Mailer 2:265
Carson McCullers 12:418
Henry Miller 2:282
Yukio Mishima 2:287
Anaïs Nin 4:376
John O'Hara 2:323
Thomas Pynchon 11:452
Alain Robbe-Grillet 2:375
Aleksandr I. Solzhenitsyn 4:510
Susan Sontag 2:414
Tennessee Williams 7:546

**Vidal-Hall, Judith**
Leon Garfield 12:230

**Viguers, Ruth Hill**
E. M. Almedingen 12:2
Ruth M. Arthur 12:24
Margot Benary-Isbert 12:33
Betty Cavanna 12:100
Eilís Dillon 17:95
Leon Garfield 12:218
Christie Harris 12:261, 262
Lee Kingman 17:244, 245
Joseph Krumgold 12:320
Madeleine L'Engle 12:345, 346
William Mayne 12:393
Emily Cheney Neville 12:450,
451
Josephine Poole 17:370
Zilpha Keatley Snyder 17:469,
470
Mary Stolz 12:553
Lenora Mattingly Weber 12:632

**Vilhjalmsson, Thor**
Gabriel García Márquez 2:150

**Viljanen, Lauri**
Frans Eemil Sillanpää 19:417

**Vine, Richard**
Stanley Kunitz 11:319

**Vintcent, Brian**
Marie-Claire Blais 4:67
Roch Carrier 13:143
Anne Hébert 4:220

**Viorst, Judith**
Lois Gould 10:243

**Vogel, Dan**
William Faulkner 6:177, 178
Arthur Miller 6:333
Robert Penn Warren 6:556
Tennessee Williams 5:504

**Volpe, Edmond L.**
James Jones 1:162

**Vonalt, Larry P.**
John Berryman 3:66; 4:60
Marianne Moore 1:230

**Von Hallberg, Robert**
Charles Olson 6:386
W. D. Snodgrass 18:495

**Vonnegut, Kurt, Jr.**
Robert Altman 16:32
Joseph Heller 5:175
Hermann Hesse 17:219
Stanislaw Lem 15:328
Hunter S. Thompson 17:506

**Von Tersch, Gary**
Buffy Sainte-Marie 17:431

**Voorhees, Richard J.**
P. G. Wodehouse 1:374

**Vopat, Carole Gottlieb**
Jack Kerouac 3:265

**Voss, Arthur**
James T. Farrell 11:191
John O'Hara 11:413
Dorothy Parker 15:414
Jean Stafford 19:430

**Wachtel, Nili**
Isaac Bashevis Singer 15:504

**Waddington, Miriam**
Joan Barfoot 18:35
Hugh Garner 13:234
A. M. Klein 19:258

**Wade, David**
J.R.R. Tolkien 2:434

**Wade, Michael**
Peter Abrahams 4:2

**Waelti-Walters, Jennifer R.**
Michel Butor 15:113

**Wagenaar, Dick**
Yasunari Kawabata 18:281

**Waggoner, Diana**
William Mayne 12:406

**Waggoner, Hyatt H.**
E. E. Cummings 3:117
Robert Duncan 2:122
T. S. Eliot 2:127
Robert Frost 3:173
H. D. 3:217
Robinson Jeffers 2:214
Robert Lowell 3:300
Archibald MacLeish 3:310
Marianne Moore 2:292
Ezra Pound 2:341
John Crowe Ransom 2:363
Theodore Roethke 3:432
Carl Sandburg 4:463
Karl Shapiro 4:485
Lewis Turco 11:549
Richard Wilbur 3:532
William Carlos Williams 2:468

**Wagner, Dave**
Robert L. Peters 7:303

**Wagner, Dick**
Yukio Mishima 9:381

**Wagner, Geoffrey**
R. P. Blackmur 2:61
Josef von Sternberg 20:372

**Wagner, Linda Welshimer**
William Faulkner 1:103
Robert Hass 18:208
Ernest Hemingway 6:231;
19:215
Denise Levertov 1:176; 5:247
Philip Levine 9:332

Phyllis McGinley 14:365
W. S. Merwin 13:383
Joyce Carol Oates 19:349
Diane Wakoski 9:554, 555

**Waidson, H. M.**
Heinrich Böll 11:55

**Wain, John**
Sylvia Ashton-Warner 19:20
William S. Burroughs 5:91
Eleanor Clark 19:105
Edward Dahlberg 7:66
C. Day Lewis 6:127
Günter Grass 2:173; 4:202
Michael Hamburger 5:158
Ben Hecht 8:270
Ernest Hemingway 3:233
Aldous Huxley 5:192
Archibald MacLeish 14:336
Flann O'Brien 4:383
Sylvia Plath 17:345
C. P. Snow 4:500

**Wainwright, Andy**
Earle Birney 6:77

**Wainwright, Jeffrey**
Ezra Pound 7:332

**Wakefield, Dan**
J. D. Salinger 12:500
Harvey Swados 5:422
John R. Tunis 12:597
Leon Uris 7:490

**Wakoski, Diane**
Clayton Eshleman 7:98
David Ignatow 4:248
John Logan 5:255
Robert Lowell 4:304
Anaïs Nin 4:377
Jerome Rothenberg 6:477

**Walcott, Ronald**
Hal Bennett 5:57, 59
Charles Gordone 4:199

**Walcutt, Charles Child**
James Gould Cozzens 4:114
John O'Hara 1:262

**Waldemar, Carla**
Anaïs Nin 11:399

**Waldmeir, Joseph**
John Updike 5:450

**Waldron, Edward E.**
Langston Hughes 15:291

**Waldron, Randall H.**
Norman Mailer 3:314

**Waldrop, Rosemary**
Hans Erich Nossack 6:365

**Walkarput, W.**
Vladimir Nabokov 11:392

**Walker, Alice**
Ai 4:16
Alice Childress 15:132
Buchi Emecheta 14:159
Flannery O'Connor 6:381
Derek Walcott 4:576

**Walker, Carolyn**
Joyce Carol Oates 3:360

**Walker, Cheryl**
Richard Brautigan 12:68
Adrienne Rich 3:428
Robert Penn Warren 6:558

**Walker, David**
Anne Hébert 13:268

**Walker, Greta**
Babbis Friis-Baastad 12:214

**Walker, Jim**
Clarence Major 19:292

**Walker, Keith**
John Rechy 14:445

**Walker, Michael**
Claude Chabrol 16:173
Jerzy Skolimowski 20:350

**Walker, Robert G.**
Ernest Hemingway 8:287

**Walker, Ted**
Andrew Young 5:523

**Wall, Richard**
Behan, Brendan 15:46

**Wall, Stephen**
P. H. Newby 13:408

**Wallace, Herbert W.**
Alvin Silverstein and Virginia
B. Silverstein 17:455

**Wallace, Irving**
Irving Wallace 13:568

**Wallace, Margaret**
Dee Brown 18:70

**Wallace, Michele**
Ntozake Shange 8:485

**Wallace, Ronald**
John Hawkes 15:274

**Wallace, Willard M.**
Robert Newton Peck 17:340

**Wallace-Crabbe, Chris**
Kenneth Slessor 14:492

**Wallenstein, Barry**
James T. Farrell 11:195
Ted Hughes 2:200

**Waller, Claudia Joan**
José Lezama Lima 10:317

**Waller, G. F.**
Joyce Carol Oates 19:350
Paul Theroux 8:514

**Waller, Gary F.**
T. Alan Broughton 19:74
William Maxwell 19:309

**Walley, David G.**
Peter Townshend 17:526
Frank Zappa 17:585, 588

**Wallis, Bruce**
Katherine Anne Porter 15:430

**Wallis, C. G.**
Jean Cocteau 16:220

**Walsh, Chad**
Robert Bly 2:66
Stanley Burnshaw 13:129
Robert Graves 6:212
Ted Hughes 2:197
Fletcher Knebel 14:308
Philip Larkin 5:228
Cynthia Macdonald 13:355
Archibald MacLeish 3:311
Howard Nemerov 2:306
Jerome Weidman 7:517

**Walsh, Moira**
Gordon Parks 16:458

**Walsh, Nina M.**
Alvin Silverstein and Virginia
B. Silverstein 17:452

**Walsh, Thomas F.**
Katherine Anne Porter 13:449

**Walsh, William**
Earle Birney 6:78
Robert Finch 18:155
A. M. Klein 19:261
R. K. Narayan 7:254
Thomas Tryon 11:548
Patrick White 3:521; 4:583,
584; 7:532; 9:567; 18:546

**Walsten, David M.**
Yukio Mishima 2:286

**Walt, James**
Jean Cayrol 11:110
Ward Just 4:266
John O'Hara 6:385
J. R. Salamanca 4:462

**Walter, James F.**
John Barth 10:22

**Walter, Sydney Schubert**
Sam Shepard 17:435

**Walters, Jennifer R.**
Michel Butor 3:93

**Walters, Margaret**
Brigid Brophy 6:99

**Walton, Alan Hull**
Colin Wilson 3:537; 14:585

**Walton, Edith H.**
Sally Benson 17:46, 48
Maureen Daly 17:87
Esther Forbes 12:204
Mary Renault 17:390

**Walton, Richard J.**
Jules Archer 12:20

**Walzer, Judith B.**
Marge Piercy 18:407

**Walzer, Michael**
J. D. Salinger 12:503

**Wanamaker, John**
Joy Adamson 17:6

**Wand, David Hsin-Fu**
Marianne Moore 13:396

**Ward, A. C.**
W. H. Auden 1:8
Samuel Beckett 1:21
Edmund Blunden 2:65
Ivy Compton-Burnett 1:62
Noel Coward 1:64

T. S. Eliot **1**:90
E. M. Forster **1**:104
Christopher Fry **2**:143
Robert Graves **1**:128
Graham Greene **1**:132
Aldous Huxley **1**:150
W. Somerset Maugham **1**:204
Iris Murdoch **1**:234
J. B. Priestley **2**:346
Edith Sitwell **2**:403
C. P. Snow **1**:316
Evelyn Waugh **1**:358
Arnold Wesker **3**:518
P. G. Wodehouse **1**:374

**Ward, Andrew**
Bob Dylan **12**:197

**Ward, David E.**
Ezra Pound **1**:275

**Ward, Ed**
Bob Marley **17**:268

**Ward, J. A.**
S. J. Perelman **9**:414

**Ward, Leo**
Harper Lee **12**:341

**Ward, Margaret Joan**
Morley Callahan **3**:97

**Ward, P.**
N. Scott Momaday **19**:318

**Ward, Robert**
Bruce Springsteen **17**:479
Lily Tomlin **17**:523

**Wardle, Irving**
Hugh Leonard **19**:282
Richard O'Brien **17**:324

**Warkentin, Germaine**
A. W. Purdy **3**:408

**Warme, Lars G.**
Eyvind Johnson **14**:297

**Warner, Alan**
Ken Russell **16**:543

**Warner, Edwin**
Jorge Luis Borges **2**:71

**Warner, John M.**
John Hawkes **3**:223

**Warner, Jon M.**
George MacBeth **5**:263

**Warner, Rex**
E. M. Forster **1**:105

**Warnke, Frank J.**
William Golding **17**:166
Richard Yates **7**:553

**Warnock, Mary**
Brigid Brophy **6**:98
Iris Murdoch **8**:404

**Warren, Austin**
E. M. Forster **15**:223

**Warren, Robert Penn**
James Dickey **10**:140
Alex Haley **12**:243
Katherine Anne Porter **13**:447
Eudora Welty **1**:362; **14**:562

**Warsh, Lewis**
Richard Brautigan **3**:86
B. P. Nichol **18**:366

**Warshow, Paul**
Buster Keaton **20**:197

**Warshow, Robert**
Arthur Miller **1**:215

**Washburn, Martin**
Richard Adams **4**:7
Anthony Burgess **4**:84
Nicholas Delbanco **6**:129
John Gardner **3**:187
Lois Gould **4**:200
Juan Goytisolo **5**:150
Günter Grass **4**:206
Dan Jacobson **4**:255
György Konrád **4**:273
Denise Levertov **3**:293
Alison Lurie **4**:306

**Washington, Mary Helen**
Arna Bontemps **18**:66
Alice Walker **6**:554; **19**:452

**Washington, Peter**
Seamus Heaney **7**:149
Peter Porter **13**:451
Stevie Smith **8**:491
R. S. Thomas **13**:544

**Wasilewski, W. H.**
Theodore Roethke **11**:486

**Wasserman, Debbi**
Murray Schisgal **6**:490
Sam Shepard **4**:489
Tom Stoppard **4**:525
Richard Wesley **7**:519

**Waterhouse, Keith**
Harper Lee **12**:341

**Waterman, Andrew**
Daniel Hoffman **13**:286
John Matthias **9**:361

**Waterman, Arthur**
Conrad Aiken **3**:5

**Waters, Chris**
Tim O'Brien **7**:271

**Waters, Harry F.**
Norman Lear **12**:335, 338
Garry Marshall **17**:276

**Waters, Michael**
Robert Hass **18**:209

**Waterston, Elizabeth**
Irving Layton **2**:236

**Watkins, Floyd C.**
Robert Frost **9**:219
Ernest Hemingway **3**:239

**Watkins, Mel**
James Baldwin **2**:33
Ernest J. Gaines **11**:218
Simone Schwarz-Bart **7**:404
Alice Walker **5**:476
Al Young **19**:479

**Watkins, Tony**
Alan Garner **17**:141, 150

**Watson, Edward A.**
James Baldwin **17**:31

**Watson, Ian**
Elias Canetti **14**:119

**Watson, J. P.**
J.R.R. Tolkien **2**:434

**Watt, Donald J.**
Aldous Huxley **18**:266

**Watt, F. W.**
A. M. Klein **19**:260
Raymond Souster **14**:504

**Watt, Ian**
John Fowles **2**:137

**Watt, Roderick H.**
Uwe Johnson **15**:305

**Watts, Harold H.**
Robert Frost **15**:241
Aldous Huxley **1**:151
Gabriel Marcel **15**:359
Ezra Pound **7**:323

**Watts, Michael**
David Bowie **17**:60
Mick Jagger and Keith Richard **17**:230, 242
Jim Morrison **17**:290
Martin Mull **17**:299
Paul Simon **17**:460
Bruce Springsteen **17**:478
Neil Young **17**:571, 575

**Watts, Richard**
Lanford Wilson **7**:548

**Waugh, Auberon**
Michael Ayrton **7**:18
James Leo Herlihy **6**:235
Elizabeth Jane Howard **7**:164
Tom Robbins **9**:453
Gillian Tindall **7**:474
William Trevor **7**:476
P. G. Wodehouse **5**:516

**Waugh, Evelyn**
Graham Greene **14**:216
Aldous Huxley **11**:281
Christopher Isherwood **14**:278

**Waugh, Harriet**
Emma Tennant **13**:536

**Way, Brian**
Edward Albee **9**:2

**Weales, Gerald**
Edward Albee **9**:4
Beryl Bainbridge **4**:39
Elizabeth Bowen **6**:95
Ivy Compton-Burnett **1**:63
J. P. Donleavy **4**:123
Lorraine Hansberry **17**:183, 187
John Hawkes **1**:139; **4**:213
John Huston **20**:168
William Inge **19**:226
Robert Lowell **4**:299
Norman Mailer **3**:319; **4**:319
Bernard Malamud **1**:201
Mark Medoff **6**:322
Arthur Miller **1**:218
Harold Pinter **9**:420
James Purdy **2**:348; **4**:422
David Rabe **4**:427
Gerome Ragni and James Rado **17**:380

Ronald Ribman **7**:357
Peter Shaffer **5**:390
Sam Shepard **4**:489; **17**:436
Wole Soyinka **3**:463
Tom Stoppard **1**:327; **8**:502
David Storey **2**:424
James Thurber **5**:430
Douglas Turner Ward **19**:456
Robert Penn Warren **1**:356
Thornton Wilder **10**:536
Tennessee Williams **1**:368; **2**:466; **19**:470

**Weatherhead, A. Kingsley**
Robert Duncan **1**:82; **7**:88
Marianne Moore **4**:360
Charles Olson **1**:263
Stephen Spender **1**:323
William Carlos Williams **1**:371

**Weathers, Winston**
Par Lägerkvist **7**:200

**Weaver, Mike**
William Carlos Williams **13**:603

**Webb, Phyllis**
D. G. Jones **10**:285

**Weber, Brom**
Thomas Berger **5**:60
Edward Dahlberg **7**:69
Bernard Kops **4**:274
C. P. Snow **4**:503
John Updike **2**:442

**Weber, Robert C.**
Robert Duncan **15**:189

**Weber, Ronald**
Saul Bellow **1**:32

**Webster, Grant**
Allen Tate **2**:427

**Webster, Harvey Curtis**
James Baldwin **17**:20
Maxine Kumin **13**:329
Bernice Rubens **19**:404
C. P. Snow **13**:514

**Webster, Ivan**
James Baldwin **4**:43
Gayl Jones **6**:266

**Weeks, Brigitte**
Judy Blume **12**:46
Marilyn French **10**:191
M. E. Kerr **12**:301
Iris Murdoch **8**:405

**Weeks, Edward**
Margaret Atwood **4**:25
Jorge Luis Borges **1**:39
Lothar-Günther Buchheim **6**:102
Pearl S. Buck **7**:33
Daphne du Maurier **6**:147; **11**:163
Loren Eiseley **7**:91
Edna Ferber **18**:152
Esther Forbes **12**:208
Frank B. Gilbreth, Jr. and Ernestine Gilbreth Carey **17**:153
James Herriot **12**:283
Yasunari Kawabata **5**:208

Madeleine L'Engle 12:344
Peter Matthiessen 5:273, 275
Iris Murdoch 6:344
Vladimir Nabokov 6:357
May Sarton 14:480
André Schwarz-Bart 4:480
Michael Shaara 15:474
Irwin Shaw 7:413
Mikhail Sholokhov 7:418
Joseph Wambaugh 3:509
Jessamyn West 7:519; 17:545
Herman Wouk 1:377

**Weeks, Ramona**
Lucille Clifton 19:108

**Weeks, Robert P.**
Ernest Hemingway 19:214

**Weesner, Theodore**
Robert Cormier 12:134

**Wegner, Robert E.**
E. E. Cummings 12:153

**Weibel, Kay**
Mickey Spillane 13:525

**Weigel, John A.**
Lawrence Durrell 1:86

**Weightman, John**
Alan Ayckbourn 5:37
Simone de Beauvoir 4:49
Albert Camus 2:98
Louis-Ferdinand Céline 4:100
Marguerite Duras 6:149
A. E. Ellis 7:94
Jean Genet 5:136, 139
Jean-Luc Godard 20:140
André Malraux 9:359
Peter Nichols 5:308
Francis Ponge 6:422
Gerome Ragni and James Rado 17:382
Alain Robbe-Grillet 2:377
Nathalie Sarraute 4:468, 469
Jean-Paul Sartre 9:473
Tom Stoppard 5:412
David Storey 5:416
Gore Vidal 4:555

**Weil, Dorothy**
Arna Bontemps 18:63

**Weiler, A. H.**
Jean Cocteau 16:223
Werner Herzog 16:321
Elia Kazan 16:362
Alain Resnais 16:496

**Weinberg, Helen**
Saul Bellow 2:53
Ralph Ellison 11:180
Herbert Gold 4:192
Norman Mailer 2:261
Philip Roth 4:452

**Weinberg, Herman G.**
Josef von Sternberg 20:374

**Weinberger, Deborah**
Adolfo Bioy Casares 13:86

**Weinberger, Eliot**
Robert Bly 15:63

**Weinberger, G. J.**
E. E. Cummings 8:160

**Weinfield, Henry**
Gilbert Sorrentino 7:448, 449

**Weintraub, Stanley**
William Golding 2:167
C. P. Snow 9:497, 498

**Weisberg, Robert**
Stanley Burnshaw 3:92
Randall Jarrell 2:211
Richmond Lattimore 3:277

**Weisman, Kathryn**
Larry Kettelkamp 12:308

**Weiss, Jonathan M.**
Gabrielle Roy 14:470

**Weiss, Paulette**
Jim Morrison 17:294

**Weiss, Peter**
Peter Weiss 15:563

**Weiss, Theodore**
Donald Davie 5:115
Ezra Pound 10:405

**Weiss, Victoria L.**
Marguerite Duras 6:150

**Weissenberger, Klaus**
Paul Celan 19:93

**Weixlmann, Joe**
John Barth 14:54
Ronald L. Fair 18:142

**Weixlmann, Sher**
John Barth 14:54

**Welburn, Ron**
Imamu Amiri Baraka 2:35
Don L. Lee 2:237
Clarence Major 19:291
Dudley Randall 1:283

**Welch, Chris**
David Bowie 17:64
Jimmy Page and Robert Plant 12:476, 478
Peter Townshend 17:524, 538

**Welch, Elizabeth H.**
Jules Archer 12:19

**Welcome, John**
P. D. James 18:272

**Welding, Pete**
Chuck Berry 17:52

**Wellek, Rene**
R. P. Blackmur 2:62
Kenneth Burke 2:89

**Weller, Sheila**
Ann Beattie 8:55
Gael Greene 8:252
Diane Wakoski 7:507

**Wells, John**
Bob Dylan 12:200

**Wellwarth, George**
Arthur Adamov 4:5
Edward Albee 2:1
John Arden 6:8
Samuel Beckett 2:46
Brendan Behan 8:63
Friedrich Dürrenmatt 4:138

Max Frisch 3:166
Jean Genet 2:157
Michel de Ghelderode 6:197
Eugène Ionesco 4:251
Arthur Kopit 18:287
Bernard Kops 4:274
John Osborne 2:327
Harold Pinter 3:385
Arnold Wesker 3:518

**Welty, Eudora**
Margery Allingham 19:12
Elizabeth Bowen 6:94
Annie Dillard 9:175
E. M. Forster 3:161
Ross Macdonald 2:255
V. S. Pritchett 13:467
Jessamyn West 17:544
Patrick White 5:485

**Welz, Becky**
Betty Cavanna 12:101

**Wendell, Carolyn**
Vonda N. McIntyre 18:326

**Werner, Alfred**
Hermann Hesse 17:195

**Werner, Craig**
Tom Stoppard 15:520

**Wernick, Robert**
Wright Morris 3:343

**Wersba, Barbara**
Julia W. Cunningham 12:164, 165, 166
Leon Garfield 12:222

**Wertime, Richard A.**
Guy Davenport, Jr. 14:139
Hubert Selby, Jr. 8:475

**Weschler, Lawrence**
Mel Brooks 12:82

**Wescott, Glenway**
Katherine Anne Porter 7:313

**Wesker, Arnold**
William Styron 15:531

**Wesling, Donald**
Ed Dorn 10:157

**Wesolek, George**
E. E. Cummings 12:152

**West, Anthony**
Jorge Amado 13:11
Yehuda Amichai 9:22
James Baldwin 17:20
Paul Bowles 19:58
Edwin O'Connor 14:389
Leonardo Sciascia 9:474
Sylvia Townsend Warner 7:512

**West, Paul**
Miguel Ángel Asturias 3:18
Michael Ayrton 7:18
Samuel Beckett 2:48
Earle Birney 6:72
Heinrich Böll 3:74
Michel Butor 8:113
Alejo Carpentier 11:99
Camilo José Cela 13:146
Louis-Ferdinand Céline 1:57
Jean Cocteau 15:132

Evan S. Connell, Jr. 4:108
Julio Cortázar 2:103
Guy Davenport, Jr. 6:123
José Donoso 4:127
Richard Elman 19:151
Gabriel García Márquez 10:215
John Gardner 2:150
William H. Gass 11:224
William Golding 1:122
Peter Handke 5:166
MacDonald Harris 9:261
Uwe Johnson 5:202
Jakov Lind 2:245
Charles Newman 2:311
Robert Nye 13:413
Sylvia Plath 1:271
André Schwarz-Bart 2:389
Allen Tate 11:526
Robert Penn Warren 1:353

**West, Ray B.**
Katherine Ann Porter 1:272

**West, Richard**
Michael Cimino 16:211

**Westall, Robert**
Robert Westall 17:557

**Westbrook, Max**
Saul Bellow 1:30
William Faulkner 1:101
Ernest Hemingway 1:143
J. D. Salinger 1:299
John Steinbeck 1:326
Robert Penn Warren 1:355

**Westbrook, Perry D.**
Mary Ellen Chase 2:100

**Westbrook, Wayne W.**
Louis Auchincloss 4:30

**Westburg, Faith**
Adolfo Bioy Casares 4:64
Jerzy Kosinski 3:274

**Westerbeck, Colin L., Jr.**
Robert Altman 16:42
Lindsay Anderson 20:17
Mel Brooks 12:76, 77
Charles Chaplin 16:204
Vittorio De Sica 20:96
Bob Fosse 20:123
Werner Herzog 16:327, 336
Steven Spielberg 20:359
Lina Wertmüller 16:587

**Westervelt, Linda A.**
John Barth 14:52

**Westfall, Jeff**
Theodore Roethke 19:401

**Westhuis, Mary G.**
Robert Newton Peck 17:342

**Westlake, Donald E.**
Gael Greene 8:252

**Weston, John**
Paul Zindel 6:586

**Weston, John C.**
Hugh MacDiarmid 11:335

**Wetzsteon, Ross**
Charles Gordone 1:124
May Sarton 4:472
Lily Tomlin 17:518

**Whedon, Julia**
Judy Blume **12**:46
Penelope Gilliatt **2**:160

**Wheeler, Charles**
William Safire **10**:447

**Wheelock, Carter**
Jorge Luis Borges **2**:76; **3**:81;
**4**:72; **6**:90; **13**:104
Julio Cortázar **5**:109

**Wheelock, John Hall**
Allen Tate **4**:536

**Whelan, Gloria**
Margaret Laurence **13**:342

**Whelton, Clark**
Joan Micklin Silver **20**:343

**Whichard, Nancy Winegardner**
Patrick White **4**:583

**Whicher, Stephen E.**
E. E. Cummings **3**:116

**Whipple, T. K.**
Erskine Caldwell **14**:93

**Whissen, Thomas R.**
Isak Dinesen **10**:144, 149

**Whitaker, Jennifer Seymour**
Alberto Moravia **7**:243

**Whitaker, Thomas R.**
Conrad Aiken **3**:3

**White, Charles, S. J.**
Mircea Eliade **19**:147

**White, E. B.**
James Thurber **5**:432

**White, Edmund**
John Ashbery **6**:11; **15**:33
James Baldwin **17**:41
Edward Dahlberg **7**:65
Thomas M. Disch **7**:87
Lawrence Durrell **6**:153
Jean Genet **5**:138
Russell C. Hoban **7**:161
Eugène Ionesco **11**:290
Yasunari Kawabata **5**:207
Marjorie Kellogg **2**:224
Fran Lebowitz **11**:322
José Lezama Lima **4**:290
Harry Mathews **6**:315
William Maxwell **19**:308
James Merrill **18**:328
Yukio Mishima **4**:355
Howard Moss **7**:248
Vladimir Nabokov **2**:304
James Schuyler **5**:383
Muriel Spark **18**:505
Gore Vidal **8**:527
Paul West **14**:569
Tennessee Williams **5**:503

**White, Gertrude M.**
W. D. Snodgrass **10**:477;
**18**:494

**White, Jean M.**
Dick Francis **2**:143
P. D. James **18**:272
Ross Macdonald **3**:308
George Simenon **2**:398
Maj Sjöwall **7**:502

Per Wahlöö **7**:502
Donald E. Westlake **7**:529

**White, John**
Michael Ayrton **7**:18

**White, John J.**
MacDonald Harris **9**:259

**White, Patricia O.**
Samuel Beckett **1**:25

**White, Ray Lewis**
Gore Vidal **2**:448

**White, Robert J.**
Pier Paolo Pasolini **20**:269

**White, Timothy**
Bob Marley **17**:268, 269, 271,
272

**White, Victor**
Thornton Wilder **10**:536

**White, William Luther**
C. S. Lewis **3**:295

**Whitebait, William**
Jean Cocteau **16**:226

**Whitehall, Richard**
John Huston **20**:168
Jean Renoir **20**:291

**Whitehead, James**
Jim Harrison **6**:224
Stanley J. Kunitz **6**:287
Adrienne Rich **3**:427
Gibbons Ruark **3**:441

**Whitehead, John**
Louis MacNeice **1**:186

**Whitehead, Peter**
Pier Paolo Pasolini **20**:263

**Whitehead, Ralph, Jr.**
Hunter S. Thompson **17**:514

**Whitehead, Ted**
Woody Allen **16**:9
Michael Cimino **16**:210
Peter Townshend **17**:539

**Whitehead, Winifred**
Eilís Dillon **17**:100

**Whitlock, Pamela**
Eilís Dillon **17**:93

**Whitman, Alden**
Norman Mailer **14**:353

**Whitman, Ruth**
Adrienne Rich **6**:459
Anne Sexton **6**:494

**Whitney, Phyllis A.**
Mary Stolz **12**:551

**Whittemore, Bernice**
Ilya Ehrenburg **18**:130

**Whittemore, Reed**
Allen Ginsberg **2**:163
James Kirkwood **9**:320
Charles Olson **2**:326
Tom Robbins **9**:453

**Whittington-Egan, Richard**
Truman Capote **8**:133
Rayner Heppenstall **10**:272

**Whitton, Kenneth S.**
Friedrich Dürrenmatt **15**:198

**Whitty, John**
Tennessee Williams **11**:575

**Wickenden, Dan**
Brigid Brophy **11**:68
Jessamyn West **17**:545

**Wickenden, Dorothy**
Ella Leffland **19**:280

**Wickes, George**
Henry Miller **1**:221
Anaïs Nin **1**:247

**Wideman, John**
Toni Cade Bambara **19**:34
Richard Wright **14**:596

**Widmer, Kingsley**
John Dos Passos **4**:133
Leslie A. Fiedler **4**:160
Allen Ginsberg **13**:239
Herbert Gold **4**:191
Jack Kerouac **14**:305
Henry Miller **1**:220

**Wiegand, William**
J. D. Salinger **1**:295
Jerome Weidman **7**:516

**Wiegner, Kathleen**
Michael Benedikt **14**:82
Judith Leet **11**:323
Diane Wakoski **9**:555

**Wiersma, Stanley M.**
Christopher Fry **2**:144; **10**:202

**Wiesel, Elie**
Richard Elman **19**:148
Chaim Grade **10**:246

**Wieseltier, Leon**
Yehuda Amichai **9**:24
Isaac Bashevis Singer **11**:502
Elie Wiesel **3**:529

**Wiggins, William H., Jr.**
John Oliver Killens **10**:300

**Wilbur, Richard**
Barbara Howes **15**:288

**Wilce, Gillian**
Beryl Bainbridge **18**:32

**Wilcher, Robert**
Samuel Beckett **11**:35

**Wilcox, Thomas W.**
Anthony Powell **7**:341

**Wilde, Alan**
Donald Barthelme **13**:55
Christopher Isherwood **1**:156;
**9**:290

**Wilder, Virginia**
M. E. Kerr **12**:301

**Wildgen, Kathryn E.**
François Mauriac **9**:368

**Wilding, Michael**
L. P. Hartley **2**:182
Jack Kerouac **5**:215
Christina Stead **2**:422, 423

**Wildman, John Hazard**
Mary Lavin **4**:281
Joyce Carol Oates **6**:367
Reynolds Price **6**:423
Muriel Spark **13**:520

**Wilentz, Amy**
Frederick Busch **18**:85

**Wilhelm, James J.**
Ezra Pound **4**:418

**Wilkes, G. A.**
Robert D. FitzGerald **19**:178

**Wilkes, Paul**
Shusaku Endo **14**:162

**Wilkinson, Doris Y.**
Chester Himes **7**:159

**Willard, Nancy**
Pierre Gascar **11**:222
Pablo Neruda **1**:246
J.R.R. Tolkien **8**:515

**Willett, Ralph**
Clifford Odets **2**:319

**Williams, Anne**
Richard Wilbur **14**:578

**Williams, David**
Kon Ichikawa **20**:183
Christina Stead **2**:423
John Wyndham **19**:476

**Williams, Forrest**
Federico Fellini **16**:279

**Williams, Gladys**
Leon Garfield **12**:226

**Williams, Hugo**
Horst Bienek **7**:29
Richard Brautigan **12**:60
William S. Burroughs **5**:92

**Williams, John**
Henry Miller **1**:223

**Williams, Jonathan**
Richard Brautigan **3**:87
Rod McKuen **3**:333
Anne Sexton **4**:482

**Williams, Linda L.**
Bernardo Bertolucci **16**:99

**Williams, Lloyd**
James Ngugi **7**:262

**Williams, Miller**
Donald Davidson **2**:111
John Crowe Ransom **4**:434
Hollis Summers **10**:493
Andrei Voznesensky **1**:349

**Williams, Paul**
Mick Jagger and Keith Richard
**17**:231
Jim Morrison **17**:285
Bruce Springsteen **17**:482
Brian Wilson **12**:641
Neil Young **17**:568, 577

**Williams, Raymond**
Aleksandr I. Solzhenitsyn **2**:407

CRITIC INDEX

**Williams, Richard**
Joan Armatrading 17:7
Chuck Berry 17:52
Allen Ginsberg 6:201
Laura Nyro 17:313
Paul Simon 17:461
Bruce Springsteen 17:477
Richard Wilbur 6:568
Brian Wilson 12:644, 646, 650
Neil Young 17:569

**Williams, Sherley Anne**
James Baldwin 3:32
Imamu Amiri Baraka 3:35;
10:20
Ralph Ellison 3:144
Haki R. Madhubuti 6:313

**Williams, Tennessee**
Paul Bowles 19:56
William Inge 8:307
Carson McCullers 12:412

**Williams, William Carlos**
David Ignatow 14:274
Marianne Moore 10:348
Kenneth Patchen 18:391
Carl Sandburg 15:466

**Williamson, Alan**
Jon Anderson 9:31
Robert Bly 5:65; 15:68
Robert Creeley 15:153
Galway Kinnell 5:216
Robert Lowell 4:304
L. E. Sissman 18:489
Gary Snyder 5:394
Barry Spacks 14:510
Allen Tate 14:528
James Wright 3:541; 5:519, 521

**Williamson, Chilton, Jr.**
Norman Lear 12:331

**Willis, Don**
Fritz Lang 20:215
Josef von Sternberg 20:378

**Willis, Donald C.**
Luis Buñuel 16:151
Frank Capra 16:161
Yasojiro Ozu 16:455

**Willis, Ellen**
David Bowie 17:59
Bob Dylan 3:131; 12:183, 186
Paul Simon 17:459
Stevie Wonder 12:658

**Willis, J. H., Jr.**
William Empson 3:147

**Wills, Garry**
James Baldwin 17:25
Thomas Keneally 5:210
James A. Michener 11:375
Vladimir Nabokov 3:356
Hunter S. Thompson 17:514

**Wilmington, Michael**
John Ford 16:310, 314
Billy Wilder 20:462, 463

**Wilms, Denise Murko**
Jules Archer 12:23
Frank Bonham 12:55
Betty Cavanna 12:103
Barbara Corcoran 17:78
Roy A. Gallant 17:133

Larry Kettelkamp 12:306
Sonia Levitin 17:266
Piri Thomas 17:502

**Wilner, Eleanor**
Adrienne Rich 7:369

**Wilson, A. N.**
Barbara Pym 19:388

**Wilson, Angus**
Kingsley Amis 3:9
L. P. Hartley 2:181
Christopher Isherwood 11:294
John Cowper Powys 15:433

**Wilson, Bryan**
Kenneth Rexroth 11:473

**Wilson, Colin**
Jorge Luis Borges 3:78
Christopher Isherwood 11:297

**Wilson, David**
Dirk Bogarde 19:43
Nagisa Oshima 20:248
Ken Russell 16:547
François Truffaut 20:389
Joseph Wambaugh 18:533

**Wilson, Douglas**
Ernest Hemingway 3:241

**Wilson, Edmund**
W. H. Auden 2:21; 4:33
Marie-Claire Blais 2:62; 4:66
Kay Boyle 19:62
Morley Callaghan 3:97
Agatha Christie 12:114
John Dos Passos 4:130
Anne Hébert 4:219
Hugh MacLennan 2:257
André Malraux 13:365
William Maxwell 19:305
Carson McCullers 12:410
Katherine Anne Porter 7:309
Aleksandr I. Solzhenitsyn 2:407
John Steinbeck 13:529
J.R.R. Tolkien 2:433
Evelyn Waugh 13:584
Angus Wilson 2:470

**Wilson, Evie**
Margaret Craven 17:80
Anne McCaffrey 17:283
John Neufeld 17:310

**Wilson, Frank**
Françoise Sagan 17:427
Susan Sontag 13:519

**Wilson, George**
Fritz Lang 20:213

**Wilson, J. C.**
Wright Morris 7:246

**Wilson, Jane**
Andrew Sinclair 2:401

**Wilson, Jason**
Octavio Paz 19:365

**Wilson, Jay**
Andy Warhol 20:416

**Wilson, Keith**
David Kherdian 6:280

**Wilson, Milton**
Milton Acorn 15:8
Earl Birney 6:74, 75
A.J.M. Smith 15:514

**Wilson, Raymond J.**
Isaac Asimov 19:26

**Wilson, Reuel K.**
Tadeusz Konwicki 8:328
Stanislaw Lem 15:326

**Wilson, Robert**
Mark Harris 19:206

**Wilson, Robley, Jr.**
Daniel J. Berrigan 4:56
Richard Howard 7:165
Philip Levine 4:285

**Wilson, William E.**
Jessamyn West 17:545

**Wimble, Barton**
Allan W. Eckert 17:108

**Wimsatt, Margaret**
Margaret Atwood 3:19
Robertson Davies 13:173
Graham Greene 3:208

**Winch, Terence**
Ann Beattie 13:64
W. S. Merwin 8:388, 390
Flann O'Brien 10:363

**Winchell, Mark Royden**
Robert Penn Warren 13:579

**Windsor, Philip**
Josef Skvorecký 15:511
Aleksandr I. Solzhenitsyn 7:441

**Winegarten, Renee**
Ruth Prawer Jhabvala 4:258
Bernard Malamud 3:324; 8:375
André Malraux 1:203
Grace Paley 6:392

**Winehouse, Bernard**
Conrad Aiken 10:2

**Wing, George Gordon**
Octavio Paz 3:376

**Winks, Robin W.**
William F. Buckley, Jr. 18:82
Len Deighton 7:75
P. D. James 18:273
David Harry Walker 14:552

**Winnington, Richard**
Vittorio De Sica 20:85
Alfred Hitchcock 16:340

**Winston, Joan**
Gene Roddenberry 17:407

**Winston, Richard**
Mary Renault 17:393, 399

**Winter, Thomas**
Anthony Burgess 4:81

**Winterich, John T.**
Frank B. Gilbreth, Jr. and
Ernestine Gilbreth Carey
17:152, 154

**Winters, Yvor**
Elizabeth Daryush 19:119
Robert Frost 10:192

**Wintz, Cary D.**
Langston Hughes 10:279

**Wirth-Nesher, Hana**
Amos Oz 11:427

**Wisse, Ruth R.**
Saul Bellow 8:68
Chaim Grade 10:246
Cynthia Ozick 7:289

**Wistrich, Robert**
A. E. Ellis 7:93

**Witcover, Jules**
Hunter S. Thompson 17:507

**Witemeyer, Hugh**
Guy Davenport, Jr. 14:141

**Witherington, Paul**
Bernard Malamud 11:352

**Witt, Harold**
Conrad Aiken 1:4

**Witte, Stephen**
George Lucas 16:409

**Wixson, Douglas Charles, Jr.**
Thornton Wilder 10:531

**Wohlers, H. C.**
Melvin Berger 12:40

**Woiwode, L.**
John Cheever 3:107

**Wolcott, James**
William F. Buckley, Jr. 7:35
Alex Haley 12:253
Peter Handke 10:255
Norman Lear 12:333, 337, 338
Norman Mailer 14:351
Laura Nyro 17:319
Jimmy Page and Robert Plant
12:480
Mordecai Richler 18:456
Wilfrid Sheed 10:472
Lily Tomlin 17:516
Anne Tyler 18:530
Gore Vidal 8:528
Frederick Wiseman 20:476

**Wolf, Barbara**
Yukio Mishima 2:288; 6:338

**Wolf, Manfred**
Brigid Brophy 11:68

**Wolf, William**
Gordon Parks 1:265

**Wolfe, Don M.**
Shirley Hazzard 18:213

**Wolfe, G. K.**
Kurt Vonnegut, Jr. 3:495

**Wolfe, George H.**
William Faulkner 9:203

**Wolfe, H. Leslie**
Laurence Lieberman 4:291

**Wolfe, Morris**
Matt Cohen 19:111

**Wolfe, Peter**
Richard Adams 5:6
A. Alvarez 5:20
Maeve Brennan 5:72
Laurie Colwin 5:108
Dashiell Hammett 19:199

**Jakov Lind 1**:177
Ross Macdonald **14**:329
Walker Percy **2**:333
Mary Renault **3**:425
Georges Simenon **18**:487
Charles Webb **7**:515
Patrick White **3**:522

**Wolfe, Tom**
John Lennon and Paul
   McCartney **12**:355, 363

**Wolff, Geoffrey**
John Barth **14**:56
Frederick Buechner **2**:83
Arthur A. Cohen **7**:52
Julio Cortázar **3**:115
J. P. Donleavy **6**:140
George P. Elliott **2**:131
Paula Fox **8**:217
John Gardner **2**:152
James Jones **3**:261
Jerzy Kosinski **1**:171; **3**:272;
   **6**:282
D. Keith Mano **2**:270
Peter Matthiessen **5**:273
Wright Morris **7**:247
Donald Newlove **6**:363
Ezra Pound **2**:342
Thomas Pynchon **2**:356
Isaac Bashevis Singer **3**:456

**Wolfley, Lawrence C.**
Thomas Pynchon **9**:444

**Wolitzer, Hilma**
Richard Yates **8**:556

**Wolkenfeld, J. S.**
Isaac Bashevis Singer **1**:311

**Wolkoff, Lewis H.**
Anne McCaffrey **17**:281

**Woll, Josephine**
Varlam Shalamov **18**:480

**Wollen, Peter**
John Ford **16**:310

**Wollheim, Donald A.**
Isaac Asimov **1**:8
Ray Bradbury **1**:42
Arthur C. Clarke **1**:59
Harlan Ellison **1**:93
Philip Jose Farmer **1**:97
Edmond Hamilton **1**:137
Robert A. Heinlein **1**:139
Andre Norton **12**:466
Clifford D. Simak **1**:309
A. E. Van Vogt **1**:347
Kurt Vonnegut, Jr. **1**:348

**Wong, Jade Snow**
Jade Snow Wong **17**:566

**Wood, Adolf**
Louis Auchincloss **18**:25

**Wood, Anne**
Leon Garfield **12**:232

**Wood, Charles**
Kurt Vonnegut, Jr. **4**:565

**Wood, Gayle**
Margaret Atwood **15**:37

**Wood, Karen**
Kurt Vonnegut, Jr. **4**:565

**Wood, Michael**
Miguel Ángel Asturias **3**:18
J. G. Ballard **14**:39
John Barth **2**:37
Donald Barthelme **2**:41
John Betjeman **6**:66
Adolfo Bioy Casares **4**:63
Elizabeth Bishop **9**:95
Jorge Luis Borges **2**:72
Anthony Burgess **8**:112
Italo Calvino **8**:131
Alejo Carpentier **11**:101
Evan S. Connell, Jr. **6**:116
Francis Ford Coppola **16**:246
Julio Cortázar **2**:105
Lawrence Durrell **6**:153
T. S. Eliot **10**:169
Stanley Elkin **4**:154
William Empson **8**:201
Ken Follett **18**:156
Carlos Fuentes **8**:225
Gabriel García Márquez
   **15**:254
John Gardner **5**:131; **8**:235
Juan Goytisolo **5**:150
Judith Guest **8**:253
John Hawkes **4**:219
Seamus Heaney **7**:147
John Hollander **14**:263
Erica Jong **4**:264
John le Carré **15**:324
Stanislaw Lem **8**:345
John Lennon and Paul
   McCartney **12**:365
José Lezama Lima **4**:289
Ross Macdonald **14**:328
Norman Mailer **3**:316
Thomas McGuane **3**:330
A. G. Mojtabai **9**:385
Brian Moore **8**:395
Berry Morgan **6**:340
Vladimir Nabokov **2**:303
Pablo Neruda **5**:303
Hans Erich Nossack **6**:365
Robert Nye **13**:413
Joyce Carol Oates **2**:316
Grace Paley **4**:392
Octavio Paz **4**:396
Peter Porter **13**:451
Ezra Pound **2**:345
Anthony Powell **3**:403
Manuel Puig **3**:407
Thomas Pynchon **2**:357
Raymond Queneau **10**:432
Jean Rhys **14**:446
Philip Roth **4**:456
Severo Sarduy **6**:487
Isaac Bashevis Singer **3**:459
Susan Sontag **13**:517
Muriel Spark **5**:399; **8**:495
J.R.R. Tolkien **12**:570
Charles Tomlinson **6**:534
John Updike **2**:445
Mario Vargas Llosa **6**:546
Gore Vidal **8**:525
Kurt Vonnegut, Jr. **3**:503
Eudora Welty **2**:463
Angus Wilson **3**:535
Rudolph Wurlitzer **2**:483

**Wood, Peter**
Peter De Vries **2**:114
Alberto Moravia **2**:293

**Wood, Robin**
Robert Altman **16**:31
Michelangelo Antonioni **20**:34
Ingmar Bergman **16**:60
Frank Capra **16**:164
Claude Chabrol **16**:173
Carl Theodor Dreyer **16**:264
John Ford **16**:311
Alfred Hitchcock **16**:354
Rouben Mamoulian **16**:428
Pier Paolo Pasolini **20**:268
Satyajit Ray **16**:483

**Wood, Susan**
Alice Adams **13**:2
Margaret Atwood **15**:36
T. Alan Broughton **19**:74
Penelope Gilliatt **10**:230
Robert Hass **18**:210
John Wain **11**:564

**Wood, William C.**
Wallace Markfield **8**:380

**Woodbery, W. Potter**
John Crowe Ransom **11**:467

**Woodcock, George**
Earle Birney **6**:71, 75; **11**:51
Camilo José Cela **13**:145
Louis-Ferdinand Céline **9**:158
Matt Cohen **19**:113
Robert Finch **18**:154
Hugh Garner **13**:236
Jean Genet **5**:138
Irving Layton **15**:321
Denise Levertov **5**:246
Hugh MacDiarmid **2**:255
Hugh MacLennan **14**:339
Brian Moore **1**:225; **3**:341
Alden Nowlan **15**:399
A. W. Purdy **14**:431
Herbert Read **4**:441
Kenneth Rexroth **2**:70, 371
Mordecai Richler **5**:375
Gabrielle Roy **14**:469
A.J.M. Smith **15**:515
Andrew Suknaski **19**:432
Rudy Wiebe **11**:569

**Woodfield, James**
Christopher Fry **10**:200; **14**:187

**Woodruff, Stuart C.**
Shirley Jackson **11**:301

**Woods, Crawford**
Ross Macdonald **3**:308
Isaac Bashevis Singer **3**:457
Hunter S. Thompson **9**:526

**Woods, William C.**
Lisa Alther **7**:13
Leon Uris **7**:492

**Woods, William Crawford**
Jim Harrison **6**:225

**Woodward, C. Vann**
William Styron **3**:473

**Woodward, Helen Beal**
Frank B. Gilbreth, Jr. and
   Ernestine Gilbreth Carey
   **17**:155

**Woolf, Virginia**
E. M. Forster **15**:222
Ernest Hemingway **19**:211

**Woollcott, Alexander**
Dorothy Parker **15**:414

**Wooten, Anna**
Louise Glück **7**:119

**Worsley, T. C.**
Stephen Spender **10**:488

**Worth, Katharine J.**
Edward Bond **13**:99

**Worton, Michael J.**
René Char **11**:115

**Wrenn, John H.**
John Dos Passos **1**:77

**Wright, Basil**
Luis Buñuel **16**:129
Charles Chaplin **16**:192

**Wright, Cuthbert**
Compton MacKenzie **18**:313

**Wright, David**
C. Day Lewis **6**:126
Hugh MacDiarmid **19**:289

**Wright, Elsa Gress**
Carl Theodor Dreyer **16**:262

**Wright, George T.**
W. H. Auden **1**:10
T. S. Eliot **3**:137

**Wright, James**
Richard F. Hugo **6**:244

**Wright, Judith**
Robert D. FitzGerald **19**:176
Kenneth Slessor **14**:493

**Wright, Richard**
Arna Bontemps **18**:63
Carson McCullers **12**:408

**Wunderlich, Lawrence**
Fernando Arrabal **2**:16

**Wyatt, David M.**
Ernest Hemingway **8**:288;
   **19**:223
Robert Penn Warren **8**:541

**Wyatt, E.V.R.**
Jade Snow Wong **17**:566

**Wylder, Delbert E.**
William Eastlake **8**:198

**Wylie, Andrew**
Giuseppe Ungaretti **11**:556

**Wylie, John Cook**
Earl Hamner, Jr. **12**:257

**Wylie, Philip**
Sally Benson **17**:49

**Wymard, Eleanor B.**
Annie Dillard **9**:177

**Wyndham, Francis**
Caroline Blackwood **6**:79
Elizabeth Bowen **15**:78
Agatha Christie **12**:120
Aldous Huxley **18**:265

**Yacowar, Maurice**
Woody Allen **16**:16
Alfred Hitchcock **16**:351

CRITIC INDEX

**Yagoda, Ben**
Margaret Drabble 10:164
Henry Green 13:254
Tom Wolfe 15:585

**Yakir, Dan**
Peter Weir 20:428

**Yamanouchi, Hisaaki**
Yasunari Kawabata 18:285

**Yamashita, Sumi**
Agatha Christie 12:117

**Yannella, Philip R.**
Pablo Neruda 5:301
Louis Zukofsky 18:557

**Yardley, Jonathan**
Chinua Achebe 3:2
Kingsley Amis 2:8
Hal Bennett 5:59
Wendell Berry 4:59; 6:62
Doris Betts 3:73
Frederick Buechner 6:102
Harry Crews 6:117, 118
Peter De Vries 7:77
James Dickey 2:116
Frederick Exley 6:171
William Faulkner 3:158
Leslie A. Fiedler 13:213
Brian Glanville 6:202
James Hanley 5:167, 168
Jim Harrison 6:224
John Hersey 9:277
George V. Higgins 7:157
Diane Johnson 5:199
Madison Jones 4:263
Ward Just 4:266
Thomas Keneally 8:319; 10:299
John Knowles 4:271; 10:303
Benard Malamud 2:267
Saul Maloff 5:271
Cormac McCarthy 4:342
James A. Michener 11:375
A. G. Mojtabai 5:293
Toni Morrison 4:365
Robert Newton Peck 17:337
Walker Percy 3:381
Piers Paul Read 4:444
J. R. Salamanca 4:462
John Seelye 7:406
Wilfrid Sheed 2:394; 4:488
Thomas Tryon 3:483
Jerome Weidman 7:518
Eudora Welty 2:462
Tom Wicker 7:533
Calder Willingham 5:511, 512

**Ya Salaam, Kalumu**
Nikki Giovanni 4:189

**Yates, Donald A.**
Jorge Amado 13:11
John Dickson Carr 3:100
Carlos Fuentes 13:232

**Yates, John**
Francis Ford Coppola 16:241

**Yates, Norris W.**
Günter Grass 4:203
James Thurber 5:433

**Yenser, Stephen**
Ai 14:9
Philip Levine 14:315
Robert Lowell 3:305
James Merrill 3:335
Robert Pinsky 19:372
Adrienne Rich 11:479
W. D. Snodgrass 18:493
Robert Penn Warren 8:537, 540

**Yglesias, Helen**
Ludvík Vaculík 7:494

**Yglesias, Jose**
Christina Stead 2:421
Mario Vargas Llosa 6:547

**Yglesias, Luis E.**
Pablo Neruda 7:262; 9:398

**Yoder, Edwin M.**
MacKinlay Kantor 7:195

**Yoder, Jon A.**
Upton Sinclair 15:501

**Yohalem, John**
Richard Brautigan 5:70
James McCourt 5:277
Charles Webb 7:516

**Yolen, Jane**
Jamake Highwater 12:287
Zilpha Keatley Snyder 17:470

**Young, Alan**
Donald Justice 19:236
Christopher Middleton 13:389

**Young, Alan R.**
Ernest Buckler 13:118, 119

**Young, Charles M.**
Mel Brooks 12:83
Patti Smith 12:543

**Young, Colin**
Kon Ichikawa 20:177

**Young, David**
Robert Francis 15:236

**Young, Dora Jean**
Katherine Paterson 12:484

**Young, Dudley**
Carlos Castaneda 12:84

**Young, Israel G.**
Bob Dylan 12:180

**Young, James O.**
Jessie Redmon Fauset 19:170

**Young, Jon**
Joan Armatrading 17:10
Chuck Berry 17:55

**Young, Kenneth**
Compton Mackenzie 18:314

**Young, Marguerite**
Carson McCullers 12:411
Mark Van Doren 10:495

**Young, Peter**
Andrei Voznesensky 1:348

**Young, Philip**
Ernest Hemingway 13:273

**Young, Stark**
Emlyn Williams 15:576

**Young, Thomas Daniel**
Donald Davidson 13:168
John Crowe Ransom 4:433, 436

**Young, Tracy**
Lily Tomlin 17:520

**Young, Vernon**
Woody Allen 16:10
W. H. Auden 2:28
Ingmar Bergman 16:66
George Mackay Brown 5:77
Charles Chaplin 16:197
J. V. Cunningham 3:121
Vittorio De Sica 20:86, 90
William Dickey 3:126
Odysscus Elytis 15:220
Lawrence Ferlinghetti 6:183
William Heyen 18:231
John Hollander 2:197
Richard F. Hugo 6:245
John Huston 20:172
Donald Justice 19:232
Galway Kinnell 13:320
Akira Kurosawa 16:397
Laurence Lieberman 4:291
Robert Lowell 5:258
Cynthia Macdonald 19:291
W. S. Merwin 13:384
Josephine Miles 14:369
Michael Mott 15:380
Pablo Neruda 1:247
Robert Pack 13:439
Nicanor Parr 2:331
Roman Polanski 16:469
Yannis Ritsos 6:464
Carlos Saura 20:319
Martin Scorsese 20:329
Frederick Seidel 18:475
Jon Silkin 2:396
David Slavitt 14:490
Maura Stanton 9:508
James Tate 2:432
Diane Wakoski 2:459; 4:573
Ted Walker 13:566
Peter Weir 20:429

**Youngblood, Gene**
Stanley Kubrick 16:391

**Younge, Shelia F.**
Joan Armatrading 17:8

**Youree, Beverly B.**
Melvin Berger 12:41

**Yourgrau, Barry**
Mordecai Richler 18:452
Peter Rushforth 19:406

**Yuill, W. E.**
Heinrich Böll 11:52

**Zabel, Morton Dauwen**
Glenway Wescott 13:591

**Zacharias, Lee**
Truman Capote 13:139

**Zak, Michele Wender**
Doris Lessing 6:294

**Zaller, Robert**
Bernardo Bertolucci 16:94
Anaïs Nin 4:377

**Zarookian, Cherie**
Barbara Corcoran 17:71

**Zatlin, Linda G.**
Isaac Bashevis Singer 1:312

**Zaturenska, Marya**
Laura Riding 7:373

**Zavatsky, Bill**
Ed Dorn 10:157

**Zehender, Ted**
Tod Browning 16:123

**Zehr, David E.**
Ernest Hemingway 8:286

**Zeik, Michael**
Thomas Merton 3:337

**Zelenko, Barbara**
Nora Ephron 17:111

**Zeller, Bernhard**
Hermann Hesse 2:190

**Zeman, Marvin**
Jean Renoir 20:300

**Zetterberg, Bettijane**
Hilma Wolitzer 17:562

**Zeugner, John F.**
Gabriel Marcel 15:364
Walker Percy 18:396

**Zibart, Eve**
Penelope Gilliatt 13:238

**Zilkha, Michael**
Mark Medoff 6:323

**Zimbardo, Rose A.**
Edward Albee 13:3

**Zimmerman, Eugenia N.**
Jean-Paul Sartre 9:472

**Zimmerman, Paul**
R. K. Narayan 7:256

**Zimmerman, Paul D.**
E. M. Forster 2:135
Lois Gould 4:199
Stanley Kubrick 16:383
Leni Riefenstahl 16:524
Melvin Van Peebles 20:412

**Zimmerman, Ulf**
Rolf Hochhuth 18:255

**Ziner, Feenie**
Frank Bonham 12:53

**Zinnes, Harriet**
Robert Bly 1:37
Robert Duncan 1:83
Anaïs Nin 4:379; 8:425
Ezra Pound 3:399
May Swenson 4:533, 534
Mona Van Duyn 7:499

**Ziolkowski, Theodore**
Heinrich Böll 2:67; 6:83
Hermann Hesse 1:145, 146; 3:248; 17:209
Hans Erich Nossack 6:364

**Zipes, Jack D.**
Christa Wolf 14:593

**CRITIC INDEX**

**Zivanovic, Judith**
Jean-Paul Sartre 9:470

**Zivkovic, Peter D.**
W. H. Auden 3:23

**Zivley, Sherry Lutz**
Sylvia Plath 9:431

**Zolf, Larry**
Mordecai Richler 5:376

**Zorach, Cecile Cazort**
Heinrich Böll 15:70

**Zoss, Betty**
Jesse Jackson 12:290

**Zucker, David**
Delmore Schwartz 10:464

**Zuckerman, Albert J.**
Vassilis Vassilikos 4:551

**Zuger, David**
Adrienne Rich 7:372

**Zukofsky, Louis**
Charles Chaplin 16:190

**Zunser, Jesse**
Akira Kurosawa 16:394

**Zweig, Paul**
Richard Adams 5:6
A. R. Ammons 5:29
John Ashbery 2:18
James Dickey 15:178
William Dickey 3:126
Clayton Eshleman 7:100
Allen Ginsberg 13:240
Günter Grass 11:254
John Hollander 5:186
David Ignatow 7:181
Kenneth Koch 8:322
Philip Levine 4:286
Peter Matthiessen 11:358
Leonard Michaels 6:325
Czesław Miłosz 5:292
Vladimir Nabokov 3:354
Pablo Neruda 5:303
Joyce Carol Oates 15:402
Frank O'Hara 13:424
George Oppen 7:284
Charles Simic 6:502
William Stafford 7:461
Diane Wakoski 4:571
James Wright 3:542

CRITIC INDEX